# Hints of a *Perfect Splendour*

# AELFRIDA TILLYARD

# Hints of a *Perfect Splendour*

## A NOVEL BIOGRAPHY

I followed ever, where by land and sea
Vanishing lovely shapes have haunted me,
Swift touches, sounds, and gleams–
Hints of a perfect splendour...

*FW Stokoe*

*To Rosemary from the author — Sheila*

**SHEILA MANN**

Published by Wayment Print & Publishing Solutions Ltd

© Sheila Mann, 2013

Designed by Paul Barrett Book Production, Cambridge. www.pbbp.co.uk
Print production by Wayment Print & Publishing Solutions Ltd, www.waymentprintandpublishing.co.uk

ISBN 978-0-9926034-0-3

A CIP catalogue record for this book is available from the British Library

Printed and bound in Great Britain, by 4edge Ltd, Hockley, Essex.

# Contents

# Preface

I first encountered Aelfrida Tillyard on a freezing January day in 2003 in the Old Library of Jesus College, Cambridge. I wasn't looking for her (it was only later that I realised the significance of her omission from the memoirs I was studying, memoirs which I did not then know were those of her younger brother) nor was I aware of her existence: a shadowy 'Mrs Graham' had made a brief and tantalising appearance in material pertaining to another research project but I had as yet no reason to connect her with the woman who was to take over my life for a decade. Engrossed in Eustace Tillyard's reminiscences, I paid scant attention when archivist Frances Willmoth handed me a copy of a 1913 anthology compiled by one Aelfrida Tillyard with the diffident comment 'I don't know if this is relevant' but knowing that Eustace Tillyard's father's given name was Alfred, I scribbled a reminder to myself ('Aelfrida Tillyard ?his daughter') notable for the incongruity of its situation among data on past and present Cambridge nursing homes. Its relevance, however, soon became apparent. Googling 'Aelfrida Tillyard' brought up brief but intriguing references; Aelfrida, it seemed, was a forgotten 20th century writer who had been briefly but significantly associated with a notorious occultist.

Armed with this information I returned hotfoot to Jesus College and to *Cambridge Poets 1900–1913* to make some serendipitous discoveries. One led me to three of Aelfrida's surviving relatives by blood or marriage, the other to Girton College from whose archivist Kate Perry I elicited the exciting information that the college possessed not only an extensive collection of Aelfrida's published and unpublished literary remains but 75 volumes of her diary also. To my chagrin and frustration, however, I discovered that material held at Girton was embargoed (at Aelfrida's request) until 2005.

Pending access and with the help of Aelfrida's collateral family members (she left no direct descendants) and of enterprising bookfinders, I began to compose an account of what already seemed an unusual personality and an unusual life. Visits to the British Library and to Cambridge University Library uncovered more but as yet incomprehensible material and by dint of following every lead, however short or improbable, I uncovered further traces of my elusive subject. (Cambridge nursing homes were relegated to 'unfinished business' though intriguing correspondences between them and Aelfrida herself were beginning to emerge.) The Girton College archive opened its welcoming doors and Aelfrida's literary remains to me on 1 May 2005 and I was able to view my primary material at last, material unavailable to a researcher since final depositions were made shortly before and after Aelfrida's death in December 1959.

In his introduction to *The Worlock Archive* Clifford Longley describes how, beginning his research, he uncovered "the whole of a man's life reduced to cardboard boxes" and notes that the process of bringing his material to light and life involved "a long and complicated detective investigation" and that although a single glance at each item in the boxes might reveal nothing, "two glances ... begin to reveal a hidden drama". He notes too – and in the context of my own research, perspicaciously – that, given that there had been a writer, "is there not somewhere else an intended reader?" for had the writer not wished the contents of the boxes to be read, he would have destroyed them. This being so, a biographer's task is to open the boxes and reveal the "secrets" contained therein, secrets which might pertain both to the subject of a proposed biography and to other people such as "we may not have known before". And so it is with Aelfrida and her family.

But though agreeing with Owen Chadwick's comment in *The Spirit of the Oxford Movement* that "reserve is not the best virtue for a biographer" and that a biographer must "eschew the scruples of delicacy", I also believe that family reticences must be respected when it is possible to provide a vivid sense of one's subject in other ways and that material which already embraces actual and attempted suicide, euthanasia, marital rape, real or implied adulteries, emotional, physical and substance abuse, and a closer than normal relationship between two people too closely related to marry contains sufficient excitement of its own. To pry further is prurience; what I have written is therefore as truthful and as fair as I can make it and when I have perforce resorted to supposition I have made it clear that my version is the truth as I see it but not necessarily the whole truth. As Robert Skidelsky notes in his magisterial biography of John Maynard Keynes (a man known to Aelfrida from childhood – and no more beloved for that) "the biographer has a choice ... to tell the whole truth as he sees it or to tell as much of the truth as is compatible with doing good"; he also defines biography as "fiction constrained by fact" and as "voyeurism embellished with footnotes", statements which in Aelfrida's case are absolutely true for she, like Keynes, is one of those "marvellous subjects" who have led "interesting lives [and] whose lives make a good story ... because crammed with events and emotions with which people can identify even though their 'achievements' – except in the art of living – were mediocre". In Aelfrida's case, the 'achievement' for which she hoped to be remembered was ineluctably 'mediocre' and disaster, not mediocrity, characterised her 'art of living'.

But whereas it is easy to be kind by omission to Aelfrida and to those whose lives crossed hers, what sins of commission may one commit by telling the truth *as one sees it*? Perhaps like Emily Dickinson (and Aelfrida herself) it is best to "tell all the truth but tell it slant", leaving readers to make their own deductions (which may or may not be correct), to be dazzled "gradually" as more and more is revealed or reveals itself, and to realise with regard to Aelfrida's biography that "success in circuit lies".

But if success lies in circuit, what circuitous routes must one take in order to decipher what may (or may not be) 'true' or 'the truth' with regard to a woman of whom it may be said, as Churchill said of Russia, that she is a riddle wrapped in a mystery inside an enigma? (Her husband called her a 'cypher'.) A riddle, a mystery, and an enigma within which she firmly intends to remain: as she herself wrote in March 1940 apropos the only woman in whom she met her match 'she is the most inscrutable person I have ever met and the more one knows her, the more does one have to adjust one's impression'. And writing to her elder brother apropos Henry James' novel *The Golden Bowl*, she noted that James had composed a book in which 'no single individual sentence will be ... intelligible and the meaning ... as a whole will not flash on you ... until the very last page'. Or perhaps in her own case, not even then: *my* last pages are conjecture.

The conundrums with which Aelfrida presents us are legion – and deliberate. Documents preserved by her (she destroyed myriads) are presented *as if* they provide a comprehensive and authentic account of her life but as one tracks her through the paper labyrinth of her written remains, two things become apparent. First, diaries, even when written in virtually real time, are written with a view to publication (by herself or another) and are therefore 'copy' preserved by a conscientious but not dispassionate observer for future use, and entries elide or conceal or are conspicuous by their absence. Second, it is frequently because of inspired guesses or because she herself hints elsewhere (chiefly, but not exclusively, in her novels and poetry) at what really happened or following comparative collation of diary with other material and

with crucial secondary sources that it becomes possible to gain a glimpse of what (may have) happened.

What Aelfrida presents to us is more than merely the quotidian life of a forgotten 20th century woman writer whose literary output encompasses articles in journals and newspapers, novels (*romans à clef*, rather), poetry, biography, studies of Comparative Religion, and homiletic works in *devotio moderna* tradition, all offering, as the dust jacket to one of the latter proclaims, "inexhaustible material for ... study". Her diaries, too, begun in 1896 in Queen Victoria's reign and ending in 1959 in that of Victoria's great-great grand-daughter, are fascinating social documents and extraordinarily vivid accounts capable of moving a reader to horror, to anger, to exasperation, to tears, to laughter, and even to reluctant sympathy as one follows the struggles of an inherently disordered mind as it confronts forces which continually threaten (and sometimes more than threaten) to overwhelm it. Diaries of which quoted excerpts provide only hints of Aelfrida's interactions with people (some famous: unwittingly but not, one suspects, unwillingly, she contrives to insert herself into 20th century history) and which recount a story so seemingly improbable in its twists and turns, reverses and coincidences, that were it a novel one would criticise it as implausible.

Just as Aelfrida's own books contain stories within stories whose plots must be unravelled because of what seeming fiction reveals of her life and whose references must be followed up because all resonate with significance, so one must be aware that the material she preserved is presented in fictionalised accounts of multi-layered complexity written by a woman with agendas of her own who is as likely to censor as to reveal in her efforts to create (as she said in 1929 of John Middleton Murry's *God: the Science of Metabiology*) "a more gracious superstructure" on foundations of "bleakest and barest" psychopathology.

For these and for other reasons (should one, for example, reveal early on the childhood hurt which turned adult Aelfrida into a monster in thought, word, and deed or risk incomprehensibility by revealing it later?), I have chosen to frame her life as 'metabiography', my justification being that because she herself wrote her life as fiction, so I too may 'fictionalise' it. Hence although I have followed biographical convention by describing it chronologically, I have taken the liberty of pursuing some issues thematically and of revisiting both issues and themes at different times and from different perspectives as further evidence corroborates or undermines the 'truth' of my narrative. To do so requires the use of literary devices such as back stories, recapitulations, and anticipations, the speeding up or slowing down of my narrative, and inclusion of material of seemingly minor relevance at the (temporary) expense of vital information: if such syncopation gives rise to confusion, I ask readers to bear with me: interruptions to flow and intelligibility provide an idea of the difficulty inherent in deciphering Aelfrida's version of her life and enable such as persevere to win through to some sort of ending and solution.

But where to stop? With her death? No; aspects of her life remain perforce unwritten. (A niece's comment that there can be nothing 'publishable' about 'that terrible aunt' is far from true.) As Bart Schultz said of his biography of Henry Sidgwick, Aelfrida's story is one which takes its writer "on a very long, very strange trip which could well go on forever"; its retrieval from the cardboard boxes in which it lay sequestered for over half a century is therefore not the end but the beginning of another journey.

# Acknowledgements

A book which has taken a decade to research and write and which, while it concentrates on one woman's life, includes personal histories ranging from the 18th to the 21st centuries, must necessarily owe much to many people. May I therefore express my gratitude to the following: Ace Taxis (Monmouth), Aileen Adams, John Alban (Norfolk Record Office), Sue Andrews, Mary Archer; Stephen Beaumont, Clive Bellino, the staff of the British Library, Mollie Burns (St John's Home); the staff of Cambridgeshire Archives and of the Cambridgeshire Collection, Sheila Caws (Isle of Wight Heritage), Barrie Clark, M. Clewlow, James Cox (Gonville & Caius Archive); Martin Daunton, Sister Mary David OSB, Heather Dixon, Margaret Driver; Kim Field, Michael French, Caroline Friend; David Gill, Malcolm and Margaret Guite, Pauline Guy (Cambridge City Council Dept. of Environment and Planning); Angela Haines, Bill Heidrick (OTO), John and Nicholas Heffer, Margaret Hepher, John Hibbs, Meryl Hirons, Sue Holgate, Geoffrey Houghton, John and Catherine Hubbard, Father Peter Huckle SSJE, Julia Hudson (Society of Friends); Tess Jessup (Ventnor Public Library), Bobbie Judd (St Andrew's Hospital, Northampton); Richard Kaczynski, Helen Lessels (University of Edinburgh Alumni), Julius Lippner, Julian Lock (Regents Park College Oxford Archive); Margaret Macley, John Maiden, Ged Martin, Louise Milbourn (Lolworth History Group), David Minns (HM Coroner Cambridge), S. Mounsey (Hampshire Libraries and Information Service); Elspeth Naylor, Adrian Newman (Photography), Norfolk Museums and Archaeology Service; Oxford Crematorium; Rosemary Peacocke, Mike Petty, DJ Piper, Rosalind Pulvermacher (Foreign Office Historians); Elspeth Raynar, Hilary Ritchie (Addenbrooke's Hospital Archive), Jennie Roffman; Barbara Scruby (Coroner's Office Cambridge), Joan Slonczewski, Scotland's People (Records Enterprise Edinburgh); Margaret Thompson (Westminster College Cambridge); Malcolm Underwood (St John's College Cambridge Archive), the University Library Cambridge (especially Rare Books); David Verey; Stuart Warren, Margaret Wenham, West Norfolk Tourist Information Centre Hunstanton, Elizabeth Wigmore (Suffolk County Council Libraries and Heritage), Emma Willson (ICE), Tamsin Wimhurst, David Woodruff (Strict Baptist Historical Society); Michael Yelton, Philip Young (Yorke Collection, Warburg Institute, London). The Master and Fellows of Jesus College Cambridge and of King's College Cambridge and the Warden and Fellows of Nuffield College Oxford for their kind permission to reproduce material in their respective collections.

Those to whom I owe a particular debt of gratitude include: the Mistress and Fellows of Girton College, Cambridge who granted me access to material held in the college's library and archive; Frances Gandy, Jenny Blackhurst, and Hannah Weston of the college library and archive; Kate Perry, college archivist emerita, whose helpfulness and encouragement cannot be overstated; Joan Bullock-Anderson's cataloguing of extant and acquired material made researching easier. I also owe enormous gratitude to Angela Yaffey nee Tillyard and to the late Stephen and Margot Tillyard for providing access to invaluable literary and photographic material and to their children Ruth, Virginia, Stella and Jason and to Veronica Sankaran and Walter Tillyard for allowing me to quote material designated (by me) the Margot Tillyard Collection. The Society of the Sacred Cross in Monmouthshire afforded me hospitality as I researched what Mother Superior Mary Jean rightly called 'this terrible story' and provided me with valuable insights into Aelfrida's life there as a resident tertiary and into the Religious Life. The late Nicholas Bishop-Culpeper helped me with material pertaining to Aleister Crowley, saved me from one egregious error and, knowing he was dying, gave me several important documents. I am also grateful to William Breeze (Frater Hymenaeus Beta), executive director of the Ordo Templi Orientis, for granting me formal permission to quote published and unpublished material pertaining to Aleister Crowley whose copyright the OTO owns. Quotations from letters from CR & SSJE Fathers are used with permission. Roger and Lorna Finlay of Barlow Moor Books have gone beyond the call of duty in the interest of furthering my research. Paul Barrett of Paul Barrett Book Production has worked wonders with text and illustrations and Richard Hall with copy.

Lastly, I would like to pay tribute to my husband, George Mann, without whose moral and practical support, common sense, IT skills, medical knowledge, and ability to decipher handwriting of palimpsestic opacity, this book might never have seen the light of day.

Considerable efforts have been made to trace copyright owners of certain private papers quoted; the author apologises for any inadvertent infringements.

# Picture acknowledgements

The Mistress & Fellows of Girton College, The Society of the Sacred Cross, The Community of St Mary's Abbey (Malling), the Ordo Templi Orientalis, Baedeker *Paris* (1896), Bridgeman Art Library, the Cambridgeshire Collection, The Leys School, Cambridge, Jennie Roffmann, David Verey, the late Margot Tillyard, Sheila Mann. There are a few photographs which cannot now be attributed; to the photographers, I offer my apologies.

# Abbreviations

| | |
|---|---|
| BNF | British National Formulary |
| CDN | Cambridge Daily News |
| CIP | Cambridge Independent Press |
| CN | Cambridge News |
| ENCYC.BRIT | Encyclopaedia Britannica |
| GC | Girton College |
| GCAC | Girton College Academic |
| GCPPG A1 | Girton College Personal Papers Graham (Alethea) |
| GCPPG A1 | Girton College Personal Papers Graham (Agatha) |
| GCPPT | Girton College Personal Papers Tillyard (Aelfrida) |
| JC | Jesus College |
| JCOL | Jesus College Archive |
| KC | King's College |
| KCA | King's College Archive |
| KJV | King James Version (*The Bible*) |
| MCJ | Military and Civil Journal |
| MTC | Margot Tillyard Collection |
| NCR | Newnham College Register |
| NCO | Nuffield College Oxford |
| ODNB | Oxford Dictionary of National Biography |
| PAM | Pamphlet Box (Tymawr Library) |
| SSC | Society of the Sacred Cross |
| WCA | Westminster College Archive |

# A Record ... of my Children

Sitting at her bureau in the drawing room of St Mary's Villa, her new house on the fashionable road leading to Cambridge railway station, sometime in the autumn of 1881, Catharine Sarah Tillyard née Wetenhall headed up a small hard-backed notebook *A record of the being, doing and saying of my children*. The only child of prosperous hop merchant Henry Joseph Wetenhall and his wife Emma née Barrett, Catharine was then twenty-nine, a slim petite woman whose glorious hair "chestnut and gold, bright bronze and auburn rare", though plaited into the demure coronet befitting a married woman, had once enmeshed many besotted young men in its "amorous strands and curls"[1], two of whom would figure in the story of her only daughter and herself. To show off her hair to best advantage Catharine chose autumnal colours for her clothes, colours appropriate also to her September birthday. But it was not only Catharine's appearance which caused young men to cluster round her like bees round a honeypot; it was also her "sweet uniqueness", for Catharine was one of "the most fascinating young ladies" with an animated expression, a ready wit ("now Miss Wetenhall", young men would beg her, "*talk*")[2] and an ability to flirt deliciously. (Even at fifty, wrote her daughter, 'you should have seen her make eyes at a man!')[3] She was also "impetuous ... ardent, enthusiastic, full of violent likes and dislikes"[4] and possessed "as much variety as Cleopatra" because her "April nature" meant that "sunshine and tears were never far from each other".[5] She also possessed a full measure of "that most difficult thing to convey", namely charm – and charming she continued to be until she was "eighty and making ready to join her beloved dead".[6] And every trait save her auburn hair was inherited by her daughter.

One of the coterie of young men who found Catharine Wetenhall "sparklingly irresistible"[7] was Alfred Isaac Tillyard, born in Norwich on 3 April 1852. Alfred, eldest son of deceased Isaac Tillyard, was reading for the classical tripos at St John's College, he, his mother, and four of his surviving siblings[8] having moved from Norwich to Cambridge at the time of his matriculation in 1871; their having done so became the cause of Alfred's earliest meeting with the twenty-one-year-old woman who nine years later was to become his wife.

**Catharine Tillyard with Conrad Francis c1888**

Arriving in Cambridge in 1871, Alfred's mother, Mary Tillyard, together with her daughters Fanny, Anna, and Alice and six-year-old son Frank, established herself in a house in Fitzwilliam Road, coincidentally close to Fordfield, the Wetenhalls' newly-built house on a road known as The Avenue. Hearing of the Tillyards' arrival in the neighbourhood, Emma Wetenhall paid a social call and, impressed by Mary Tillyard's spirituality and "great dignity and keen intellectual powers", introduced her not only to her own and her husband's circle of friends, "serious-minded, intellectual people [who] studied Theology and Literature and had opinions on Politics, Ethics and Things that mattered"[9], but also to her daughter. Alice, Fanny, Anna, and Alfred Tillyard soon became great friends with singleton Catharine Wetenhall, attending public lectures and indulging in private amateur theatricals together.

There was, however, more to Catharine Wetenhall than a love of skating, tennis, croquet, and bowls, attending her father's "frequent and amusing" parties, dancing, and travel. (Henry Joseph considered the Cambridge climate 'relaxing', i.e. enervating, and believed three holidays a year absolutely "necessary to health".) Although she enjoyed "being charming" (she received her first proposal at fourteen and only a few years later "three offers of marriage in the same week"), Catharine "also wished to be well informed". Informed she already was, having been educated by governesses and at a small local private school, then for two years at a girls' boarding school in Surrey held by her in the greatest contempt because of its insistence on rote learning, finally, chaperoned by a slightly older ward of her father's (a "budding governess"), for several months in Paris at a "finishing school for young ladies"[10], but for intelligent Catharine Wetenhall this was not enough. Encouraged, therefore, by her mother and more particularly by Mary Tillyard but not her father who, though proud of his heiress daughter's intellect, did not wish to see her become a bluestocking, Catharine began (without her father's knowledge) a course of study for the Cambridge Higher Local Certificate[11] with classical scholar Alfred Tillyard to coach her in Latin, her weakest subject. She subsequently gained a first class pass, some of her papers,

according to an examiner, being '*brilliant*'[12]; inspired by her success she then gained an LLA from St Andrew's University, at which point even her father, apprised of necessity of her subterfuge, expressed pride in his daughter's accomplishment. At this point, too, it seems both Mary Tillyard and her son began to think that a modest, wealthy, healthy girl like Catharine Wetenhall with her wide-ranging interest in politics, education, literature, history, and languages would make an excellent wife for a young graduate newly embarked on a teaching career at the Leys School in Trumpington Road[13] and "intelligent and virtuous" Alfred set out to win her heart.[14]

Alfred, however, had a rival: James Rendel Harris, "the handsomest, most brilliant [and] most whimsical" of the "specially assiduous"[15] young men who clustered round Miss Wetenhall. He also had a problem: Catharine had already given her heart to Rendel Harris and it looked likely that he and not Alfred Tillyard would win her hand also.

James Rendel Harris[16], born, like his rival and his inamorata, in 1852, had two advantages over the former: he had come higher in the mathematical tripos than Alfred Tillyard in the classical tripos and he had been elected (or was about to be, exact dating of Wetenhall/Tillyard history is often difficult) fellow of Clare College. (Alfred Tillyard, conversely, was not offered a St John's

Fordfield c1869

fellowship; in 1875 he had offered himself for a fellowship at Hertford College, Oxford as a test case – the fellowship for which he applied was restricted to members of the Church of England and Alfred was then a Baptist – but having been refused, took legal action. He lost his case and remained a schoolmaster.)[17] But a later reference to the 'pious lovemaking'[18] conducted by Rendel Harris showed that all was not well: inspired by the 1873-1875 tour of England by American evangelists Dwight Moody and Ira Sankey and by 'Holiness Conventions' (*sic*) convened by Quakers Robert Pearsall and Hannah Smith, Rendel Harris announced that he had undergone an "experience of sanctification"[19] and became a 'religious idealist, almost a fanatic'.[20] Nonconformist Catharine found his pretensions to perfection 'conceited' (he expressed a hope of becoming a second St Francis with Catharine, whom he called 'Clare', as his helpmeet in terms of a 'spiritual affinity'), his 'sermonettes instead of manly straightforward love-making' insufferable, and his hopes that Catharine too 'would barter earthly joys for heavenly' impossible, and when Rendel Harris announced that he loved her too much to marry her and was giving her up 'as a first step in detachment'[21] – but, adding insult to injury, would continue to take out books for her from the university library – Catharine lost her temper; she was, in fact, so furious "that she felt as though darts of red flame leapt out of her eyes at him and … realised that if a look could have been an act, she would have been a murderess".[22] She then told him to "go! and never let me see you again".[23] (In fact, she did; Rendel Harris left Cambridge in 1882 but returning ten years later, joined Catharine and her husband on the platform at a public debate on the position of women with regard to the latest Education Bill, there to be described by Catharine's daughter – she found the situation rather piquant – as 'witty and rather mad').[24] But of Catharine Wetenhall it was said that Rendel Harris' defection 'broke [her] heart and did [her] no good'.[25]

Seizing his opportunity, Alfred Tillyard began a lengthy and assiduous courtship. He finally plucked up courage to propose as he and Catharine walked home from chapel and on 3 August 1880 Catharine Wetenhall, Lady Literate in Arts, and "only child of Henry Joseph and Emma Wetenhall [of] Fordfield, Cambridge" married "Alfred Tillyard MA of St John's College" at the St Andrew's Street Baptist Chapel. The officiating minister was assisted by the Rev Athol Cliff, "brother-in-law of the bridegroom", Athol having married Alfred's sister Alice; no further mention of the groom's parentage or family appeared in the announcement.[26] The same year and adding injury to his earlier insult, James Rendel Harris married a Quakeress ten years older than himself

(she was, wrote Catharine's partisan daughter, one of the most unattractive women she had ever met)[27]; there were no children of the marriage.

Following their wedding, untravelled Alfred and seasoned traveller Catharine Tillyard departed on an extended honeymoon abroad. They returned to Cambridge in 1881, Alfred to resume his assistant master's post at The Leys School, pregnant Catharine to await birth of her first child and to head up her *Record*.

The first child of whom Catharine's *Record* recorded the 'being' was born on 18 November 1881 at St Mary's Villa; a boy, he was christened Henry after his paternal grandfather, Julius (a nod, perhaps to his classicist father and the name by which he was usually known) Wetenhall Tillyard. Julius, sad to relate, was such a 'poor little baby covered with eczema [and] always wailing' that his paternal grandmother hoped, not entirely as a joke, that 'God would take him back again'. (His maternal grandfather, conversely, felt more kindly disposed towards the "poor miserable little object", proudly asking visitors if they would inspect "Our Baby".)[28] Nor as he grew up, was Julius a happy toddler, being given to fits of "peevishness and bad temper"[29] from which the only person who could divert him was his young cousin May, daughter of Alice and Athol Cliff. His childhood unhappiness and adult "tendency to pessimism"[30] were variously attributed to his "delicate infancy"[31] and to his mother having been still 'under the influence of Rendel Harris' cruel treatment at the time of his conception'[32] but the truth may lie elsewhere: Catharine had not, it seems, married Alfred Tillyard because she had transferred her affections to her new suitor; indeed, she had expressed doubts with regard to their relationship and may have only agreed to marry him – and then reluctantly – when confronted in her late twenties with the prospect of perpetual spinsterhood. She may even, judging by the tone of entries in her record of Julius' early life, have taken against her first-born son because he resembled neither the man she loved nor her auburn-haired mother nor her fair-haired and blue-eyed father but the black-haired and sombre-featured man she had married.

In January 1883 Catharine became pregnant for the second time. Henry Joseph Wetenhall did not, however, live to see the birth of his second grandchild; he died, after a prolonged and distressing illness one of whose symptoms was a conviction that he had lost all his money and would be obliged to leave his beloved Fordfield, on 20 August 1882 and was buried in the family vault in Cambridge's Histon Road Cemetery, a tomb shared with his Barrett in-laws and his wife's brother. Sometime prior to his death (he was latterly bed-ridden) Alfred and Catharine moved into Fordfield; Emma Wetenhall's health too had not been good for some years and although Catharine hated sick-rooms, she deemed it appropriate that she and her husband and little Julius leave St Mary's Villa and return to Fordfield in order that she, a daughter who "could not have been more dutiful or more devoted"[33], could care for and comfort her parents. It was therefore in mourning for her father, married to a man whom she respected but did not love, living in a house of which she was not the mistress, burdened by "poor sickly little Julius"[34], and with the care of a sickly, elderly, widowed mother laid on her unwilling shoulders, that Catharine Tillyard awaited the birth of her second child.

She waited without her husband. On 11 January 1883 Alfred Tillyard was admitted a student of the Middle Temple, London, to read for the bar. (He later migrated to Gray's Inn, being admitted there on 20 December 1887. He was called to the bar on 26 January 1888[35] but never practised; in later years he both coached and examined in Law.) Family history does not relate why Alfred Tillyard undertook this complete change of career at the age of thirty – possibly school-teaching had begun to bore him, possibly he was inspired by his earlier experience of academic litigation – but either way he must have spent a good deal of time between 1883 and 1888 away from the house of which he was not the master: Emma Wetenhall, though frequently confined to bed, continued as head of household and held the purse-strings.

When at home, Alfred Tillyard must have been sober company. Visitors found Catharine's tall, dark, bearded husband rather formidable because "he had no small talk though he could be extremely witty"[36] and because he tended to expound at length, though always interestingly, on serious topics. (He and Catharine as two educated and intelligent people with "a tremendous zest for learning"[37] and a taste for its delights must have much in common in this respect, if no other.) Alfred's sobriety as a young man may have resulted from his becoming male head of the Tillyard household at eighteen with a delicate mother, three immature and unsophisticated younger sisters, and Frank, a "very clever active small boy"[38], to his charge, for as a youngster he had been high spirited and full of fun. He was also extremely bright, reading fluently from an early age and winning numerous prizes in classics and history at a school where he was not only "the cleverest boy [but also] the first to win a scholarship to Cambridge".[39] Although taught to look on the Church of England in general and Norwich "Church people" in particular as a "hotbed of prejudice and superstition" (a prejudice confirmed by his winning the school prize for Divinity but having it withheld on the grounds "that no Dissenter could really understand the truth of the Christian religion"; ironically, the Tillyards had once

been members of the Church of England but by Alfred's time were "wholeheartedly and enthusiastically chapel", young Alfred being so prone to defend Nonconformity "with fiery eloquence" that he was known at school as "The Ranter"), Alfred's enthusiasm for "religious freedom [in general] and for good causes"[40] in particular was as marked as his love of sport and of "long country walks at a tremendous pace"[41], and in general he exhibited "a thoroughness, a reasonableness, a broad understanding of Christian principles and … behaviour, [all] combined with warm … piety".[42] His college days, despite the weight of family responsibility he bore, were therefore extremely happy, "wide ranging discussions with friends"[43] relieving the pressure of academic study. Once graduated, however, Alfred evinced no desire to enter the family business but, thwarted of an academic career by his unsuccessful challenge to Hertford College and being, as his future wife discovered, both even-tempered and a "born teacher and an enthusiast for Education"[44], became perhaps by default a schoolmaster. At some point too, he departed from his natal Baptist affiliation to join the newly-established Cambridge Presbytery with its strong Scottish Presbyterian element, Catharine joining him there. And Alfred's daughter inherited many of his traits.

Fordfield, the house from which Catharine married and to which she and her husband reluctantly returned, using as their quarters the west-facing bedroom and dressing room occupied until her marriage by Catharine herself, was, externally at least, a splendid and imposing edifice. (Internally it was a monument to mid-Victorian bad taste, crammed with ornate fireplaces, stained glass, heavy over-ornamented furniture in dark woods, and bric-à-brac.) Designed in the Italianate style fashionable in the 1860s – it was erected specifically for the client who "approved [his architect's] design"[45] – the walls were of cream Cambridge brick enlivened by friezes in bands of red and blue brick and by terracotta plaques. Roughly rectangular in shape with bay windows protruding on three sides, the house stood four storeys high, its cellars and semi-basement kitchen being mostly concealed by the mound on which it was raised. Steps led down from the house's south and west façades to a formal 'Italian' or 'panel' garden, fully replanted twice a year, and to extensive lawns shaded by specimen "forest trees"[46] planted before the house was completed so that they might be well established before the owner and his family moved in. A shrubbery of evergreens, together with a fernery and a small group of flowering trees provided shady spots for afternoon tea and shielded the house from The Avenue, a gated tree-lined road little more than a country lane open only to pedestrians and cyclists but soon to become busier as more houses were built along its length under the auspices of the National Freehold Land Society.[47]

Entry to house and garden was effected by a gate at the plot's south east corner from whence an oval carriage drive led past the front door to a group of outbuildings incorporating the gardener's house (Fordfield Cottage), all or in part overseen by Emma Wetenhall from her south-facing bedroom with its triple-aspected window. A path, concealed by a laurel hedge, led from the terrace and veranda fronting the house's western façade to a kitchen garden (the 'garden-at-the-back') held under lease from the University Botanic Garden which then occupied only half its potential acreage. To Fordfield's immediate east lay the Royal Albert Almshouses of 1859 whose polychromatic façades complemented Fordfield's own and beyond them Hills Road on which there were then few buildings though the proximity of the railway station promised more; to its west and south stood other large private houses.

Though sizeable too, Fordfield contained surprisingly few rooms. On the ground floor, apart from a Doulton-tiled hall and a grandiose staircase lit by a large stained glass window (there was a secondary staircase for servants' use), there was a drawing room opening through French windows to the veranda, a dining room, a study, and a snug, and on the first floor a bathroom but only three bedrooms named the West, East, and South Rooms respectively. The attic floor, conversely, was surprisingly spacious, containing a nursery suite and rooms for resident staff. Stained glass panels in a ground floor door bore two sets of initials: 'HJW' for Henry Joseph Wetenhall, the house's proud commissioner but said to be "a little too fond"[48] of it, and 'CSW' for the beautiful daughter for whom the house was designed to be a setting. It was also, of course, designed as a pretentious symbol ("all invited admiration, with a self-conscious air")[49] of 'HJW's' status as self-made Cambridge merchant and insurance agent and as a Liberal Party supporter prominent in local civic life as Alderman Wetenhall. (Though most of his money was earned by canny dealing, some funding for his nouveau riche house must have derived from the sale to the expanding city of his hop fields in the Romsey area of Cambridge; the town, shortly to enjoy a building boom, was hoping to expand eastwards.) Emma Wetenhall's initials did not appear but she may be emblematically represented in the coloured glass adorning the landing window whose depiction of flowers (and of hops, a motif visible in Henry's and Catharine's panels too) show clumps of leaves and flowers 'from nature' as recommended by an influential contemporary publication, Owen Jones' *Grammar of Ornament*, a tribute perhaps to her new house's rural origins on the Ford Field,

one of Cambridge's large medieval 'fields', to its flower gardens being under her special care, and to her childhood penchant for gardening: the central Cambridge house in which Emma grew up had no garden so she and her older sister laid out a small one between two buttresses of King's College Chapel, the plot, to the little girls' joy, being left unmolested by undergraduates, dons, and college porters alike. 1869, the year of Fordfield's completion and of Henry Joseph, Emma, and Catharine taking possession of it was carved on an ornamental stone plaque inserted in one of its walls.

It was therefore from Fordfield that Catharine Tillyard sent toddler Julius, accompanied by his nurse Louisa Hoye, to spend a few days being petted up by aunties 'full of fun', by his young uncle, and by his paternal grandmother[50], recently removed to Harston, a small village to the south of Cambridge (with Alice married, Anna and Fanny now working or training as nurses in London, and Frank about to matriculate at Oxford to read mathematics[51], Mary Tillyard had no further need of her large Cambridge house), pending the arrival of her second child.[52]

Catharine and Alfred Tillyard's first and only daughter was born at Fordfield at 8.20 am on 5 October 1883. (Informed of the baby's sex, Catharine is said to have cried "all that trouble for a *girl*!"[53]; little Julius, hearing of the arrival of a sister, commented solemnly that she was "to play with, not to eat"[54]; Alfred Tillyard's comment on the daughter who was to bear a feminised version of his own name went unrecorded.) Weighing only five pounds at birth, the tiny girl, dressed in an heirloom robe made by her maternal great-great-grandmother, was christened Aelfrida Catharine Wetenhall (Catharine insisted that all her and Alfred's children include her family name among their given ones) and a record of her 'being, doing and saying' duly instituted in her mother's book.

Little Frida, as she was known, though dark-haired and brown-eyed like her brother, was quite different in behaviour and personality. Whereas Julius, with his "affection of the skin", developmental delays, and "odd fears" (he was terrified by a harp brought to one of his mother's At Homes by Marie Feyler, doctor friend of his Tillyard aunts) was generally "a great trial to … his parents", healthy, "remarkably friendly", and "wonderfully fearless" Frida was "splendid from the first" – a good sleeper, placid (Catharine nicknamed her "little Griselda" for being so "good and sweet and patient"), "not at all shy", passed all her developmental milestones in good time, and "*charmed*"[55] the grandmother who felt no need to ask God to take her back.

Having weaned Frida in May 1884, Catharine and Alfred departed for Canada and the United States to visit one of her paternal aunts and to attend Temperance

Association meetings. (Henry Julius had kept a good cellar but Catharine, influenced by her future husband, had become an abstainer; she had also made it a condition of marrying Alfred that she be allowed to visit her father's Canadian and American relatives whenever she wished.) Returning in September, her parents found Frida contented and recognisant of them (she had remained at Fordfield with Louisa, now her nurse, and Emma Wetenhall, Julius being sent to Harston under the care of Mary Tillyard) and soon to show signs of being "well forward" in walking, talking, imaginative play, and musical appreciation. After that there was no holding her: she was soon walking "capitally" and had become a chatterbox, soliloquising at length over whatever she was doing. (Julius, on the other hand, was "solemn and reflective like his father".) She also invented epithets for herself and amusing names for unfamiliar objects or places and though "very decided with her negatives" and "self-willed and disobedient" and liable to hit out if annoyed or thwarted[56] – it must have been of little Frida that Alfred Tillyard later wrote that small children with a well-developed sense of self were quick to use the personal pronoun[57] – was capable of behaving well at children's parties held for herself and her brother and even, when allowed to attend a Liberal garden party at Fordfield, of appearing in her best frock to make a brief but appropriate speech ("YOU MUST ALL VOTE FOR MR GLADSTONE") and of responding gracefully to the cheers and applause which greeted it.[58] And in all this she proclaimed her adult self.

Julius' reaction to his sister was typical. Initially attracted to her, the nervous little boy was so terrified by hearing her cry that he would not come near her for some days. He also showed signs of jealousy of the sibling whom everyone praised and admired and either ignored her presence or, as she grew older, teased her. But touched, perhaps, by his small sister's response (she bore his teasing with patience and even seemed to love him all the better for paying attention to her) and her obvious admiration for her sad and solemn brother (she regarded everything he did as "wonderful and interesting" and wished to play with him at every opportunity), he grew fonder of her, remembering late in life that they had been a "happy pair"[59] even when squabbling. (It must have been on one of those occasions that Julius said sadly that he did *try* to love his sister but it was "such hard work" because she was so "interfering" and that he sometimes wished someone would buy her.)[60] Their mother phrased it more strongly; Julius and Frida, she wrote, were "growing very fond of each other".[61]

Toddlerhood, however, did not improve Frida's tendency to be self-willed and disobedient; it rather

enhanced it, Catharine noting in late 1885 that her daughter had become "very insubordinate", in October 1886 that though it was sometimes possible to reason with her, in general she was "fearfully cheeky and disobedient" and "quite unrepentant when naughty [saying] 'what fun! I like to make jokes of everything'", and in July 1887 that she was "the embodiment of contrariness [whom one had] only to tell her to do something for her to do the exact opposite". (Writing later of such episodes, insouciant Aelfrida noted that "the punishments [she] received for … childish faults were barely sufficient to satisfy [her] sense of justice and certainly never made [her] afraid of those who inflicted them".)[62] More positively she was "very pretty and winsome", keen to participate in nursery "dramatic performances" of Biblical or classical stories and to pick up words and phrases from Florentine Neron, the French nursemaid who replaced Louisa in 1887, happy to listen in to Julius' home lessons, and amusingly inclined to behave in a rather "fascinating" manner to strangers, particularly gentlemen towards whom she acted "very coquettish".[63] She also evinced signs of being very observant and of possessing an excellent memory, her earliest memory of all being datable to her being less than eighteen months old and still sleeping in her parents' bedroom ("suddenly a head appears over the side of my cot. It has short black hair, a curly beard and very kind eyes. It is Papa's … I was expecting Mamma's, with her long chestnut curls and lovely smile …"), the second to being roused from sleep as a toddler to see the aurora borealis flame rose-gold "behind the black boughs of leafless trees" to the north-northwest of Fordfield, the third to her being old enough to walk the mile to Presbyterian services and sufficiently precocious to enjoy the lengthy sermons because in the course of them she could "learn new words".[64]

A possible reason for the regression in Frida's behaviour as a toddler was the arrival the day after her third birthday of the Tillyards' second son, Conrad Francis Wetenhall, born 6 October 1885. Conrad, to his mother's joy, was "not at all sickly" as "wretched … Julius" had been nor, being a "sunny child" of equable temperament, did he share his elder brother's nervousness, "unchildlike tendency to pessimism", and "sudden fits … of despair [during which] he used to cast himself on the floor and refuse to be comforted". Nor, however, did he share his sister's extroversion, being "rather grave in repose", a gravity not morbid like Julius' but "lit up … as if [by] an inner joy"; nor, fortunately, though possessing "tastes and opinions of his own", did he share her tendency to self-centredness and self-will.[65] Julius, displaced from his mother's cool affection yet again, displayed notwithstanding much devotion to the baby, expressing the twin hopes that the child would soon call him by name and that the family would be able to "keep him always".[66] Frida, less keen on relegation, nevertheless accepted her new brother and as soon as he was old enough, found a place for him in the games and pursuits she already enjoyed with Julius, known to her as 'Dudu'.

Conrad was also very beautiful (" 'e ought to 'ave been a gal" was a common comment)[67], his fine golden hair, delicate features, blue eyes, and rosy cheeks in marked contrast to his sister's and brother's dark colouring, heavy features, and pallor.[68] (Frida, regarding herself in a mirror, thought "how plain she was, with short hair like a boy's and cut in a fringe too".)[69] His smile was "exquisitely tender" and his laugh "most musical", he never drew attention to himself, was '*never*' naughty or sulky or bad tempered, and if hurt "did not cry out but … smiled through his tears". (Whether he was truly the 'angel-child' of his sister's later description is open to doubt, but corroboration appears in others' descriptions too, one calling him "a little *love*"[70], the other, "too good to live".)[71] No wonder, then, that for these reasons and for his resemblance to her father that Conrad rapidly became his mother's favourite; indeed, from "the expression of happiness on her face" one could easily deduce that her third child, though an added burden on a woman in constant attendance on an invalid mother and with nervous Julius and tempestuous Frida to care for, was "an unusually happy and precious one".[72] Neither Julius nor Frida, it seems, resented Catharine's overt favouritism, Julius perhaps because he already knew he was not and never could be his mother's favourite and Frida because she did not care, but a 'memory picture' drawn many years later speaks volumes: "picture the nursery at Fordfield, the gas not yet lit, firelight; and the big crimson-covered armchair that was once in Papa's rooms at St John's college … Mama … comes in quietly … all warm and cuddly in a soft brown dress [to read] to us after tea … There is room for one child on her knees and one on each of the chair's big arms" – and neither Julius nor Frida, so the writer says, resented Conrad being in the place of honour on his mother's lap.[73]

Conrad, though good (a hagiographic account is all we have, Julius and Catharine Tillyard having agendas of their own for sentimentalising their remembrance of him and Frida on her own admission being too young to remember details and having to rely for much of her account on those of her mother and elder brother), never refused to enter into his older siblings' games. On wet days these took place in the nursery but on fine days in the garden, each child wearing a red coat so as to be visible at all times. Nor was Conrad above behaving badly, joining his siblings in behaviour to which the compound

**Alfred Tillyard (centre, with beard) c 1880**

family adjective "Naughty-Bad-Wicked-Sinful" might apply.[74]

On only two occasions, however, was Conrad deliberately excluded on the grounds that he was too young, something he did not seem to mind for he was prone to "going off alone" to contentedly contemplate a flower or the summer sky, wordless meditations uninterrupted by his brother or sister.[75] The first occasion was Sunday "dining room tea", a sumptuous and formal occasion preceded by grace, eaten at table, and usually attended by visitors or by adult members of the children's extended family and on one momentous occasion by a Tamil law student of Alfred Tillyard's of whom little Frida innocently enquired if he was "a man or a monkey" "and nobody guessed that I would much rather he *had* been a monkey".[76] (Tea over, Conrad was allowed to join the family in the drawing room to illustrate Bible texts written out for them by their mother – Frida's was LEAD ME IN THY TRUTH AND TEACH ME – after which hymns were sung round the piano, Julius and Frida preferring *Jerusalem the Golden* "because it came from the Latin, and Latin, we believed, was the language of heaven" and peaceable Conrad *Onward Christian Soldiers*.)[77] The second occasion – or, rather, series of occasions – was during the playing of a game taken extremely seriously by Julius and Frida: "Gods and Goddesses".

The kitchen garden contained a rockery built from "large stones, brickbats and remains of drain pipes, part of the Victorian *mise-en-scène*" remaining from the erection of Fordfield fifteen years earlier. The rockery, decorated by the gardener with lobelias and geraniums, was named by Dudu and Frida "Mount Olympus" after the "real Mount Olympus … in Greece", home in Greek mythology of the classical gods and goddesses of which their father told them stories, and so vividly did they imagine themselves to be 'Poseidon' and 'Athene' (Frida chose Athene because the goddess was known for her wisdom but seldom spoke, qualities the child hoped she could assimilate by imitation) and so solemnly did they tend their "sanctuary" and make offerings of fruit that "a rich numinous atmosphere" overhung what was essentially a heap of flowery rubble. The "rituals" played out in by 'Poseidon' and 'Athene' were also very private and only on rare and rather unsatisfactory occasions were neighbouring children invited to join them[78]; they were also enacted for five or six years, an unusually lengthy period of time for a childhood game involving assumed characters and an imaginary place and played by children not otherwise given to fantasies (they never, for example, believed in Santa Claus), but by the early 1890s it seems that 'Gods and Goddesses' was no longer part of Julius and Frida's repertoire. Perhaps they grew tired of the game but, as we shall see, there may have been an altogether sadder reason for abandoning it.

In 1888 Julius was six, Frida, four, and Conrad, two, rising three. All three began their education in the Fordfield garden, 'pointings-out of birds and butterflies and beetles'[79] taking place as the children trotted round after Emma Wetenhall and the gardener as they chose the position for the hundred rose bushes newly imported from France.[80] (In later life her grand-daughter remembered "roses, roses [everywhere] … over the summer house, on poles, against walls, up trees"[81] and her son-in-law a small child, almost certainly Frida, who, even at an early age was given to quizzical questioning – "if I wrapped a farthing up in silver paper to make it look like sixpence and spent it in a shop, would that be High Treason?"[82] being one – enquiring, on being told by her mother to "look at those pretty flowers", "why are flowers pretty?")[83] They also walked with their parents in the shady shrubbery of "holly and laurel, box and myrtle, yew and bay"[84] to inspect Catharine's dolls' houses built, like 'Mount Olympus', from pieces of stone left over from the building of the house. (An odd pursuit for a young lady of

seventeen.) Formal and herbaceous flower beds too contained fascinating wild life at different times of year for money was no object when spent on the garden (horses and carriages had been given up on Henry Joseph's death but few other economies practised) and different insects and birds could be studied as the seasons passed. Formal lessons came later and included the rudiments of reading and writing, some history and geography, and Bible stories.[85] They were conducted by Catharine Tillyard who not only made learning fun with tales of "Alfred-and-the-Cake, Moses-in-the-Bulrushes, and Daniel-in-the-Lions'-Den"[86] but also augmented the older children's home instruction with visits to Cambridge's many museums. Alfred Tillyard gave Julius his first lessons in Latin, Latin for the boy's classicist father having "a special dignity and importance"[87] because of what it imparted of an important period of British history, because it was an excellent mental exercise, and because it opened doors to future studies in other disciplines. But in 1888 one child's illness was to change the family's lives for ever.

Even as an old lady, Frida still remembered the event vividly: "in the summer of 1888 there was an outbreak of diphtheria in Cambridge. Julius and Conrad were taken ill [and] I was hurried away into the country to stay with … our paternal grandmother"[88], a bald account which entirely fails to impart the drama and trauma of the situation. Reconstructing what happened from later factual, fictional, and fictionalised accounts of June 1888, we discover Julius asleep "in a pose of extreme lassitude, [the] shadows round his features … grey and unhealthy, his lips pale, his hair damp with sweat"[89] and, when awake, feeling "all around [him] black darkness … shutting [his] eyes and mouth", a darkness into which he kept "slipping back down"[90] until aroused by Florentine Neron who had been delegated to nurse him. Conrad, cared for by his mother and too young to describe his symptoms or to feel fear, "never complained or showed any impatience but accepted her ministrations with little smiles and signs of affection"[91] but in spite of throat sprays and inhalations of iodine vapour became more and more ill as the diphtheria bacillus obstructed his throat with its morbid membranes. A "tracheotorny" (*sic*; actually tracheotomy, an incision made below the larynx to bypass a higher obstruction to breathing) was considered but Conrad was believed to be too weak to undergo the operation[92] and Catharine faced the inevitable death from suffocation and general toxicity of the adorable small boy whose party trick was blowing "on the back of your watch to make it open".[93]

But what of Frida? What happened to the little girl was so terrible that she could never bring herself to describe it directly; she put it instead in a novel as something which happened to a small refugee whom she called 'Mara' and it is from *The Centaur* written over fifty years after the event and from other documents to be quoted in due course that following account is taken:

Julius and Conrad begin to show symptoms of diphtheria after the three children have been put to bed in the night nursery. The doctor visits, confirms the dreaded diagnosis and prescribes sprays and inhalations which fill the room with strong-smelling vapour. Symptom-free Frida is lifted from her bed and carried downstairs to her parents' room. Placed in her mother's bed, she falls asleep again only to be woken sometime later and dressed hurriedly "in some other child's clothes"[94] borrowed, it may be, from the Creightons next door for fear of infection being transmitted on Frida's own. Frightened, she hides in the darkness beneath the bed but a "dark evil [face] … with long hair-like waves moving darker against the dark" (her father, though she is too terrified to recognise him) espies her and she is dragged protesting into the light, light over which a remnant of darkness (a trailing drapery, perhaps) "hangs like a great curved wave about to break".[95] Blandishments and cajolings fail to calm her and the child's natural questionings (she "did not even know that [her] brothers were sick")[96], usually answered so patiently, are countered by threats of a whipping. ("*Why* will you whip me?")[97] Struggling desperately in her father's arms, she is carried downstairs and placed in a straw-lined cart which she fails to recognise as belonging to one of the two carriers who ply regularly or as occasion demands between Cambridge and the "cottage in the country" where, although she does not know it, she is to live "for months".[98] (Or for what seems like months to a small child.) Alfred Tillyard cycles on ahead to apprise his mother of the emergency. The little girl is set down at the carrier's usual stop in Harston, a pub called The Old English Gentleman, whence she is collected and hurried across the road to her grandmother's house. Her father, throwing "a leg over … his tall bicycle … [rides] off down the drive"[99] without telling his abandoned daughter where he is going or when – or if – he will return. Separated from home, parents, and brothers, Frida weeps inconsolably, "wailing and sobbing and calling for [Mama]"[100] and nothing Mary Tillyard can do will comfort her. Eventually she is put to bed alone in a room so dark that she cannot see its familiar features and seeming all the darker for its lack of night-light. (She is unable to sleep in a dark room thereafter.) Desperate to return home, she subsequently "wanders off towards Cambridge", making her first stop at the place from which the carrier's cart will return her – as she hopes – to Fordfield but, still so upset that she cannot even remember her surname, she is found and brought back

to her grandmother's by a visiting auntie, an aunt not as 'full of fun' as on previous visits but anxious and cross. Mary Tillyard, however, gently explains that little girls must not wander off alone; she also, it seems, offers some explanation for Frida having been suddenly sent away from home, the little girl then experiencing "intense gratitude … at having things made clear to [her]".[101]

Mary Tillyard may have 'made clear' to little Frida the nature and severity of her brothers' illness but she did not tell her everything. At seven pm on 24 June 1888 Conrad, the "angel-child" who had "spent [only] a few years [on] this earth", was "called home".[102] His bereft mother later described to the daughter who survived him how he looked on his death bed: the "dead child lay with his arms above his head as he put them so often in sleep. His head was slightly to one side on the pillow, his long lashes touched his cheeks, his lips just parted … The thought came that the child was like a flower … a flower that was white and stiff and beautiful … like … the orange blossom that had crowned [her] head on her wedding day … [She] felt as if … not only [Conrad] the baby had died but with him had died the jolly little chap learning to walk, the schoolboy, the youth, the man. [It was] as if a great stretch of the future, a whole shining track of happy life, had been taken right away and cast into an abyss of nothingness".[103] And Catharine, whose neatly penned record of the being, doing, and saying of her children began with the birth of her first son, concluded it with lines written in desperate pencil on the death of her second: "our beautiful Conrad – so sturdy, strong, healthy, lovely was seized with fatal diphtheria and was gone from us almost before we realised the danger … My circle is broken – and half the joy of life is fled … May God have mercy upon me".[104]

In one emotionless line she noted that Julius survived.

## Notes

1 Tillyard, Ae. *My mother's hair*, written at Le Vésinet on 27 October 1913. (*The Garden and the Fire* p 46).

2 GCPPT 2|27|2(2).

3 GCPPT 1|1|10 5 June 1903.

4 GCPPT 2|27|2.

5 GCPPT 1|1|72 11 September 1955.

6 GCPPT 2|23.

7 GCPPT 2|27|2.

8 Isaac Tillyard (b 1821) died of tuberculosis c 1866; one son and two daughters predeceased him, dying of the same disease. A third daughter died very young of unknown cause.

9 GCPPT 2|27|1(10).

10 GCPPT 2|25|3 *Aunt Laura*.

11 The Cambridge Higher Local Examination was inaugurated in 1869. Open to both men and women, a pass was regarded as equivalent to a university entry level examination. For further details see Robinson, J. pp 42–43.

12  GCPPT 1|1|51 23 August 1936.

13  The Leys School, a Methodist foundation opened on 16 February 1853, its first headmaster and Alfred Tillyard's first and only employer, being William Moulton. For further details see Houghton, G. and Houghton, P. *Well Regulated Minds and Improper Moments.*

14  GCPPT 2|27|2(2).

15  GCPPT 2|27|1(2).

16  For further details of the life of James Rendel Harris, mathematician, biblical scholar and luminary of the Society of Friends, see Falcetta, A. *James Rendel Harris* and Soskice, J. *Sisters of Sinai.*

17  Brock, M. and Curthoys, M. Vol. vii pt 2 p 118.

18  GCPPT 1|1|59 27 September 1941.

19  Falcetta, A. pp 1–15. The Perfectionist Movement, a revivalist movement whose members were encouraged to seek Christian perfection in terms of a strict code of personal morality including abstinence from worldly pleasures and amusements, was imported from the United States. In England it spread under the name of the Keswick Movement (begun 1875) being particularly associated with Nonconformism. (Rendel Harris was then a Congregationalist.) For further details see httpp:||mb-soft.com|believe|next|holiness.htm

20  GCPPT 2|27|2 (2).
    GCPPT 2|25|2 (6).

21  GCPPT 2|25|2(6).
    GCPPT 1|1|66 20 March 1949.

22  Tillyard, Ae. *The Closer Walk with God* p 128.

23  GCPPT 2|27|2 (12).

24  GCPPT 1|1|9 30 October 1902.

25  GCPPT 2|27|2 (2).

26  *Cambridge Chronicle* 7 August 1880.

27  GCPPT 2|27|2.

28  GCPPT 1|1|69 18 November 1951.
    GCPPT 2|27|1 (1).

29  Tillyard, HJW. Introduction to *The Letters of ACW Tillyard* (MTC)

30  GCPPT 2|26|3. *Nadja Laptchinski.*

31  ibid.

32  GCPPT 1|1|18 9 August 1911.

33  GCPPT 2|27|2(2).

34  GCPPT 2|27|2 (6).

35  *The Times* 10 October 1929. Obituary of A I Tillyard.

36  GCPPT 2|24|2 (12).

37  GCPPT 2|25|2 (6).

38  ibid.

39  ibid.

40  ibid.

41  GCPPT 2|24|2 (12).

42  GCPPT 2|25|2 (6).

43  ibid.

44  ibid.

45  GCPPT 2|27|1 (1).

46  GCPPT 2|27|2 (3).

47  The NFLS, founded in 1852, was a Liberal organisation whose object was extension of the franchise by allowing subscribing members to accumulate by purchase strips of land to a total rental value of forty shillings at which point they were deemed landowners eligible to vote. The Fordfield plot and those immediately to its west were not, however, included in the scheme though Mary Tillyard's house certainly was. The Fordfield plot was also the largest in the area. For further details see Mann, S. *The Hope Nursing Home* and the Morland, Wilkinson Agreement 1 December 1852 (National Freehold Land Society).

48  GCPPT 2|27|1(2).

49  Tillyard, Ae. *The Glory of the West* p 103 (GCPPT 2|16|3).

50  GCPPT 1|1|66 9 September 1949.

51  For a synopsis of the life of Frank (later Sir Frank) Tillyard CBE (1865–1961) as mathematician, social worker, lawyer (he was called to the bar in 1890) and academic see *Who Was Who* Vol. VI.

52  GCPPT 1|1|66 9 September 1949.

53  Tillyard, HJW. Introduction to *The Letters of ACW Tillyard* (MTC).

54  Tillyard, C. *A record of the being, doing, and saying of my children* (MTC).

55  ibid. Grisilda (more properly 'Griselda') was the eleventh century heroine of many romances. Married to a husband who maltreated her, her patient acceptance of his slights eventually effected a change of heart.

56  ibid.

57  Tillyard, A I. *Stones of Stumbling* p 137.

58  GCPPT 2|25|3 (1:2)

59  Tillyard, HJW. Introduction to *The Letters of ACW Tillyard* (MTC).

60  Tillyard, C. *A record of the being, doing and saying of my children* (MTC).

61  ibid.

62  Tillyard, Ae. *The Approaching Storm* p 137.

63  Tillyard, C. *A record of the being, doing and saying of my children* (MTC).

64  GCPPT 2|23 *The Watchword* December 1953.

65  GCPPT 2|25|2 (5).

66  Tillyard, C. *A record of the being, doing and saying of my children* (MTC).

67  Tillyard, HJW. Introduction to *The Letters of ACW Tillyard* (MTC).

68  GCPPT 2|23. *The Watchword* March 1954.

69  GCPPT 1|25|1 (1).

70  GCPPT 2|23 *The Watchword* March 1954.

71  Tillyard, HJW. Introduction to *The Letters of ACW Tillyard* (MTC).

72  GCPPT 2|25|2 (5).

73  GCPPT 2|23. *The Watchword* June 1958.

74  GCPPT 2|23. *The Watchword.* December 1955.
    GCPPT 2|23 *The Watchword* March 1954.

75  GCPPT 2|23 *The Watchword* March 1954.

76  GCPPT 2|23 *The Watchword* December 1955.
    See also Tillyard, Ae *Concrete* pp 169–170 in which the story appears in fictionalised form.

77  GCPPT 2|26|4 (8).

78  GCPPT 2|26|4 (9).
    GCPPT 2|26|4 (10)

79  Tillyard, Ae. The *Way We Grow Up* pp 193–194.

80  GCPPT 2|23 *The Watchword* June 1955.

81  Tillyard, Ae. *The Way We Grow Up* p 39.

82  GCPPT 1|1|47 21 May 1935.

83  Tillyard, A I. *Stones of Stumbling* p 36.

84  Tillyard, Ae. *The Approaching Storm* p 44.

85  Tillyard, Ae. *The Approaching Storm* pp 73–74.

86  ibid. p 56.

87  Tillyard, HJW. Introduction to *The Letters of ACW Tillyard* (MTC).

88  GCPPT 2|23 *The Watchword* March 1954.

89  Tillyard, Ae. *The Way We Grow Up.* p 51.

90  Tillyard, Ae. *The Making of a Mystic* p 18.

91  GCPPT 2|23 *The Watchword* March 1954.

92  Tillyard, HJW. Introduction to *The Letters of ACW Tillyard* (MTC).

93  Tillyard, Ae. *The Way We Grow Up* p 154.

94  Tillyard, Ae. *The Centaur* p70. (GCPPT 2|21|1).

95  GCPPT 1|1|73 1 September 1956.

96  GCPPT 2|25|2(5).

97  GCPPT 1|1|46 18 January 1935.

98  Tillyard, Ae. *The Centaur* p 70.

99  ibid. p 30.

100 ibid. p 44.

101 GCPPT 2|23 *The Watchword* March 1955.

102 GCPPT 2|23 *The Watchword* March 1954.

103 Tillyard, Ae. *The Way We Grow Up.* pp 193–194.

104 Tillyard, C. *A record of the being, doing and saying of my children* (MTC).

# The Children in the Garden

"When I returned to Fordfield", Frida remembered, "there was a look of sadness in my mother's eyes which she never entirely lost. Julius was pale and ... much taller".[1] (He had survived "with a worse temper and [a] twitching face", the latter attributed to St Vitus Dance, usually associated with rheumatic fever but probably a nervous tic; either way, it and perpetual minor illnesses rendered him unfit for formal schooling until he was nearly ten.) Brother and sister enjoyed a "glad reunion" after which they never again "had a big quarrel".[2] But where was Conrad?

Conrad, it seemed, had vanished without trace: no-one spoke of him and Frida did not dare to ask. Eventually the cook took pity on the bewildered child and "informed [her] solemnly that [Conrad] had gone to Jesus". "Knowing nothing of death", Frida found it "quite reasonable that Conrad, who was so good, should have gone to Jesus" and enquired when she and Julius were to join him. The answer was unequivocal: "not for a long time yet", an answer the child, knowing herself no paragon, found reasonable too. She was also comforted by the fact that Julius, though "a very good little boy ... was left to play with [her]".[3] Neither of her parents, it seems, could bring themselves to enlighten her; the nearest Catharine came to an explanation was by reading the chapter in *The Water Babies* in which 'Tom', the former child chimney sweep, is forced to part company with 'Ellie' the "little white lady" whom he has loved ever since he erupted from a sooty chimney into her bedroom and, frightened at the prospect of hearing her voice "calling him and growing fainter and fainter till all was silent", searches frantically through "halls and chambers" but cannot find her. What must, however, have confused Catharine's young listener is knowing that 'Tom' *does* see 'Ellie' again, in the first instance soon after her initial disappearance, in the second, after many years when both are grown up. Even more confusing is that 'Tom', who had sometimes been "naughty" to and cross with 'Ellie' before their separation, convinces himself that her disappearance is due to his having somehow "killed"[4] her and that his earlier determination to be "clean" because 'Ellie' finds him "so dirty"[5] has contributed to her death, a confusion indeed given that later in life Frida included author Charles Kingsley in her

**Aelfrida Tillyard c1893**

personal list of "pedagogues [who] lead souls to Christ"[6] and that Kingsley himself dedicated the book to "good little [children]" as a "riddle" only they could read and if they could not, no "grown up folk" would be able to decipher it for them.

Within weeks of Frida's return home (we may deduce that it took place sometime prior to Julius' November birthday because their maternal grandmother had arranged presents for both children; to celebrate Frida's fifth birthday the day before what would have been Conrad's third would have been too poignant) she and her brother were both sent away; indeed, as happens to 'Mara', for the next few months they were "moved hastily from one place to another"[7] without explanation.

Their first major move took place in December 1888 when their maternal grandmother took seven year old Julius and five year old Frida to London, to the "square grey house" in Finchley to which their paternal grandmother had moved shortly after Frida's return home.[8] (Mary Tillyard's move may have been so as to enable her daughters to return home more easily on their days off but given that Mary herself, a sufferer since adolescence from curvature of the spine, was now severely crippled, it may be that her daughters wished to have her nearer to themselves.) Neither child enjoyed itself in spite of attempts to make their first Christmas without their parents a happy one. Julius (then, or on another occasion; his recollections are unclear) was subjected to moral pressure by Aunt Fanny ("does Julius want a fairy story for Christm[as] or shall I buy a poor slum boy an overcoat?")[9] and found the whole situation "strange"; in fact, he bore a grudge against his parents for the rest of his life, telling his sister when both were in their seventies that Christmas Day was first and foremost a children's "day of days" and "the starting point of their religious life" and that for neither reason should they be made to entertain "regrets or bitter-sweet recollections" just because their parents were in mourning.[10] Frida was "very unhappy" and was glad when she and Julius were taken home.[11]

Further absences from Fordfield appear to have preceded and followed this one – prior to Mary Tillyard's move to Finchley, both children seem to have stayed briefly in Harston, an insensitive act, given that the place had unpleasant associations for one of them and that Julius recalled his parents visiting on a Sunday and his mother sobbing on his shoulder at the suggestion that they sing Conrad's favourite hymn, and sometime early in 1889 their father seems to have taken them to a Norfolk seaside resort "and found it a great strain"[12] – but by mid-1889 they appear to have been settled once again in Cambridge, there to enjoy the company of "perfect darling" Mademoiselle Marie Aubriet, familiarly known as 'Zelle'.

Zelle was a twenty-five-year-old Frenchwoman engaged to teach the children her native tongue in the pleasantest possible way: learning "gay little French songs" and the French names for children's toy animals, recitation of Aesop's *Fables* with much "dramatic emphasis" and of French verbs while marching round the nursery. Zelle also played with them in the garden, taught them French games, and was even allowed to take them to a First Communion and a Christmas Crib at what was then a "little Roman Catholic Church", the forerunner of what was soon to be a towering edifice on the corner of Cambridge's Lensfield and Hills Roads.[13] In short she became and was treated as family and her healing influence on the disturbed lives of Julius and the "*petite Frida*" who frequently referred to her as 'golden-hearted' ('Zelle *au coeur d'or*')[14] cannot be underestimated.

They needed healing on three counts. First, because of the events through which they had just lived, second, because of their parents' reaction to the events and actions with regard to their surviving children, third, because, as they were about to discover, they had been supplanted in their mother's affections yet again: within two months of Conrad's death, Catharine Tillyard was pregnant. We do not know whether this was by accident or design – given her extreme grief-reaction it may have been the latter, a replacement for her dead son being thought to be the best means of alleviating her sorrow – but certainly she was given very little time in which to grieve and it may have been for this reason and because grief exacerbated unpleasant symptoms of early pregnancy (and because, dreadful thought, she resented the presence of her two surviving children) that Julius and Frida spent so much time away from Fordfield in late 1888 and early 1889. Be this as it may, Julius' comment that he "had been sure that God would send us a babe to take Conrad's place"[15] tells us as much about his disillusioned view of his mother's affections as Frida's puzzled statement that she "did just wonder whether Conrad was coming back" when she saw preparations being made for a new arrival.[16] Common sense persuaded her that this was unlikely given that if Conrad was "with Jesus", he would be unlikely to *want* to return and the arrival on 19 May 1889 of a "crumpled red-faced little mite with hair exactly the colour of carrots"[17] convinced her.

The mite's elder and only sister expressed herself greatly disappointed with him: he was unable to play with her immediately and she "had expected him to be fair-haired and blue-eyed" but "this wee mite … was nothing like Conrad". He was to be called Eustace Mandeville Wetenhall Tillyard, the name, she thought, more impressive than the child.[18]

The new baby's second name was given in memory of a Fenian martyr, Alfred and Catharine Tillyard as ardent Liberal supporters of Home Rule for Ireland having met the martyr's widow on a visit to Ireland while Conrad was still alive; his first, Eustace, meaning 'blooming', 'fruitful', or 'good harvest', was appropriate given the circumstances preceding his birth, and within a short time he was nicknamed 'Little Blessing'[19] and the whole family professed itself glad to have him. The name by which he was generally known, however, was 'Quicky'[20] (the Tillyards were keen on nicknames: Catharine was successively 'Mama or Wutch or Chiara or Cara'[21]; Alfred successively 'Papa', 'Sweeter' because of his even temper, or 'Oracle' after Julius began school and learned about

"Greek and Roman oracles"[22]; Aelfrida was 'Frida' or 'Tit', Julius invariably 'Dudu') but once old enough to be dressed in the sailor suits fashionable for little boys, Eustace became 'Swab' or 'Easy'[23], the latter easily the most appropriate epithet for Eustace was an easy-going child happy to amuse himself alone in the garden or with small playmate Kathleen Haddon, daughter of the anthropologist. (In later life Aelfrida wondered if Eustace had enjoyed his early childhood as much as she and Julius had enjoyed theirs but as a child of equable temperament born after the traumatic events surrounding his predecessor's death, it is likely that in his own quiet way he did.) He was also "remarkably sweet-natured" and though never an "angel-child" like Conrad, was pious enough to please his doting grandmother (Frida later recounted the story of Eustace conducting a nursery service at which he gave the briefest of sermons – "dear people, it is better to be good than to be bad" – and when urged by his grandmother and sister to continue, saying "there isn't any more. I have said what I wanted to say and now I shall stop")[24] and possessed of sufficient abundance of "charm of manner" and of "glorious auburn curls"[25] to endear him to his mother.

As a baby, Eustace had his own nurse, Rose Prior, known as 'Bosey'. Bosey, a girl not unlike Catharine Tillyard in appearance, immediately became Frida's "first object of *conscious* devotion"[26], the child turning to her as in other circumstances she might have turned to her mother. ("I adored her", she later wrote, "as I have never adored another woman"[27]; she also suffered sleepless nights after Bosie left.) Loving Bosie with a romantic love quite different from the cooler devotion accorded to God and her parents, a love the child could not conceive would be other than lifelong, little Frida also received her first remembered disillusion: learning from *Horner's Penny Stories*, subtitled *Life from the Religious Point of View*, that "theatregoing was wicked because if Our Lord came at his second Advent and found us in such worldly surroundings, we should not dare to meet Him", Bosie and Frida decided to abjure the dangerous practice forthwith and for ever; Bosie, however, sneaked out to see *East Lynne*, leaving Frida to weep secret tears at the discovery of her idol's fallibility. But the impression made by Horner's threat convinced her that attendance at the theatre would send her straight to Hell and later made her notorious for refusing to attend formal theatrical performances and to suffer pangs of conscience if forced to do so.[28] (Charity and educational performances were exempt, nor did she object to acting on the public stage herself provided the play was put on in support of a good cause.) From this time on, an unusual trait in a child reared to be questioning but one which demonstrates

Bosie's emotional hold over her, we find child and adult Aelfrida liable to believe implicitly everything she read even if what she read did not tally with what common sense told her was correct belief or caused her embarrassment when she acted on its precepts. Also of interest are Frida's attempts 'to make a lady' of Bosie by, *inter alia,* instructing her in algebra and history (Bosie remained obstinately unladyfied and a simple, loving Fenland girl) and Bosie's reaction to Frida: though said to be rather 'heavy-handed' with Eustace (he resented it and in later life willingly paid her a pension), she seems to have discerned his sister's recent (and as we shall see, continuing) distress and distresses and to have been 'always gentle'[29] with her as a result.

Frida's unhappiness was, however, due to more than being moved around without warning or explanation at a time when "places and persons which seemed trustworthy disappeared [and] world after world failed [her]"[30]; it was also due to changes in Catharine's and Alfred's personalities as a result of the traumas both had recently undergone and of events in their earlier lives which predisposed them to react as they did to the sad but in Victorian times sadly common death of a small child.

Although Frida's mother had hitherto appeared serene, the fact that Catharine was also described as a woman of volatile temperament suggests that her reaction to Conrad's death revealed aspects of her personality hitherto kept under firm control and for which further explanation must be sought for with the child on whom she had invested all her love and her emotional hopes for the future gone from her life forever, Catharine, it seems, exhibited such extreme grief that she became temporarily deranged. "Out of her mind [and] living in a world of her own", reacted inconsistently and with emotional violence towards her surviving son, now barely convalescent, alternately rejecting and weeping remorsefully over the bewildered boy. Eventually – and possibly only after medical intervention – she recovered, so that by the time of Frida's return to Fordfield (a return delayed, perhaps, by her mother's illness) she was "almost herself but not quite"[31], further recovery taking place only after the birth of the baby who was indeed a 'good harvest' and 'little blessing'. But the look of sadness which returning Frida discerned in her mother's eyes was due not only to the death of an adored child; it may have been also due to the fact that Conrad's death, a kind of rejection of her love for him, reminded her of an earlier rejection inflicted by a man whom Conrad closely resembled and whom she herself had adored: her father.

Henry Joseph Wetenhall, for all his "elegance ... grace [and] goodwill" ("his blue eyes shine benevolently, his neat mutton–chop whiskers set off his strong manly features [and] nothing but loving or edifying or – to men – business–like or authoritative words ever flow from his well-shaped mouth"), his sociability, his business probity (his customers, it was said, "knew good merchandise when it [was] offered to them")[32], his piety, and his benevolence towards family and friends and their orphaned or fatherless children, was an unhappy man whose bonhomie disguised and compensated for childhood abandonments.

Born on 21 March 1816 in his mother's native Suffolk village, Henry Joseph was the second child and first son of Henry Wetenhall and his wife Sarah, née Fulcher.[33] In 1821 or 22 and accompanied by their four children (five more were born later, not all of whom survived childhood) Henry and Sarah moved to the Barnwell area of Cambridge, the town in which Henry's father, Samuel Joseph Wetenhall, had settled in the middle of the preceding century, his present and prosperous business being the surveillance and care of the fabric of Cambridge colleges. Whether Samuel Wetenhall appreciated Henry's return to Cambridge may be doubted, for prior to his marriage to Sarah Fulcher and departure for rural Suffolk, Henry had been a rake and a wastrel and it seems it was only a sudden conversion which led to a sober mode of life. Membership of an exclusive Nonconformist sect, the Strict and Particular Baptists[34], saved him from his dissolute former life, baptism by immersion being a very public way to declare his allegiance (he had been raised in the Church of England) and his abhorrence of reprobate behaviour. It was therefore unfortunate that Henry's adherence to what was regarded by his Cambridge family and Cambridge society as a strange and joyless sect did nothing to advance his career: a small private school which he ran failed to thrive, and it was only by working as a plumber, glazier, and painter and decorator that he was able to support his rapidly enlarging family. To help him out and also perhaps to reduce family tensions in another way, for the child, though angelic in appearance, had a violent temper and had recently attacked a younger brother with a knife, Samuel Wetenhall took Henry and Sarah's eldest son, Henry Joseph, then aged about ten, into his own household, an unhappy experience for a young boy who had been led by his mother to believe that he was a miserable and possibly unredeemable sinner worthy of being sent away from home in consequence of a childish fit of temper and who now found himself living with an elderly, ill-tempered, and uneducated step-grandmother inferior in every way to Samuel's first wife, Ann Addison, a charming and well-educated young woman related to the poet. It also seems that within a few years

of Henry Joseph coming to live with his grandfather, Samuel Wetenhall died, leaving his grandson to the termagant care of a woman unfit for and unpractised in the care of children. Probably underfed and certainly under-educated, young Henry Joseph was then permanently abandoned by his supposedly loving but certainly negligent parents, their only excuse (or only recorded excuse) being increasing impecuniosity.

Impecuniosity occasioned further changes in Henry Joseph's already sad life. In 1833 Henry and Sarah's eldest daughter Harriette, Henry Joseph's senior by two years, was married off to ardent Wesleyan John Warren, a man she did not love and, rather oddly given his religious beliefs, a wine and spirits merchant. On 5 July 1837, Henry and Sarah Wetenhall and five of their surviving children left England for America. The ship was diverted to Montreal in Canada whence Henry and Sarah and some of their children moved to New York where both died without seeing their elder children again, Harriette having been left behind with her husband and Henry Joseph because it seems not to have occurred to his parents to take a handsome and hardworking son of twenty-one with them.

Fortunately for Henry Joseph, his step-grandmother's death shortly after his parents' departure freed him from her negligent care; he and she had already moved in with the Warrens, so Henry Joseph had not only a roof over his head and his sister's growing brood of children to cheer him, but also an occupation. As John Warren's salesman, he travelled to hotels and inns in and around Cambridge, nights away from home being used as opportunities to remedy his defective education. He was also fortunate in meeting and on 13 March 1848, marrying Emma Barrett, the twenty-five-year-old, chestnut-ringletted daughter of George and Catharine Mary Barrett, George and his brother Robert being joint proprietors of their late father's business as a china, glass, and earthenware dealer on Cambridge's Market Hill, and Catharine the daughter of a gentleman, Thomas Castle. Thomas Castle's death having left his daughter penniless, the young woman was forced to open a millinery shop in London's Gower Street and it was from the prospect of penurious spinsterhood that Catharine was rescued at the age of nearly thirty by well-to-do George Barrett.

In several respects, therefore, Henry Joseph's life might be said to have taken a turn for the better. His improving business and social prospects (easily traceable in contemporary street directories) are witnesses by his becoming a hop merchant with his own hop field east of the town and by 1864 an agent for two life insurance companies, and by his first marital home being situated on gentrified Maid's Causeway and his second, following a brief sojourn on Hills Road pending the building of his new house, Fordfield in The Avenue. He also became councillor for East Barnwell ward and in 1867 Alderman Wetenhall, and was an active member of several town council committees. He was also the husband of an attractive and well-educated wife whose deportment, diction, and facility in French and Italian had been drilled into her at Llandaff House, a fashionable private school on Cambridge's Regent Street patronised by local gentry at which friendships with their daughters, together with her mother's gentility, allowed Emma Barrett to rise above the circumstances of her birth above her family's shop.

It seems, however, that ideally matched as Henry Wetenhall and Emma appeared to be, circumstances surrounding their marriage provided an inauspicious omen for their life together. Emma, a timid and reserved child, had been particularly devoted to and always reluctant to leave her mother, and Catharine's death on Christmas Day 1845 deprived her of her chief comforter. The premature death on 25 November 1847 of her beloved elder brother George, meant Emma's attendance at her wedding in dove-grey half-mourning and her resumption of full mourning before departing for her honeymoon and this, together with the experience of being nearly crushed to death in a London crowd surging over Westminster Bridge, seems to have created associations in Emma's mind between marriage and mortality and the way in which bonds of affection could be shattered by unforeseen events.

It may be, too, that Emma's reticence was a manifestation of prudishness taken to extremes (she never, for example, allowed Henry Joseph to see her naked)[35], for she and her husband, both members of notably fecund families, had only one child and that born after four years of marriage. It may also be that the onset of Emma Wetenhall's chronic ill-health in 1869 was welcomed by her as a means of evading her husband's unwelcome attentions, for although much was genuine (she suffered from a recurrent neuralgia requiring three surgical interventions[36] and later from attacks of 'peritonitis', probably diverticular disease), it is possible to deduce that ill-health did not prevent her from doing what she wanted to do and that the decline in her health at the time of her daughter's departure for school and finishing school owed as much to hypochondria as it did to disabling symptomatology.

It is also possible that Emma's valetudinarianism was a form of attention-seeking due in part to jealousy of the extremely close bond between her dashing extrovert husband and her beautiful cultivated daughter and in part to events of more sinister import. On the back page of the volume of a diary written while adult Aelfrida was compiling an informal history of her family, we find a brief reminder to herself of topics for possible inclusion; two concerning her mother ('CST') are included but two are not, the first a reference to someone having had a 'fright in the attic at Hills Road', the second to someone being a 'wife-beater'.[37] The evidence is, of course, circumstantial, but can it be that Catharine Wetenhall surprised her father intimately entwined with a maid in the attic of their temporary home and that her discovery that the man she had "thought … quite perfect, everything a man should be"[38] gave rise to her subsequent 'fundamental and profound distrust of human nature'[39]? And can it also be that this was the reason for Emma Wetenhall's apparently "grudging attitude" to her generous and sociable husband and for her "always watching over him as though he was going to do something wrong", an attitude eminently understandable given that evidence suggests that Henry Joseph may have been a philanderer from the early days of their marriage (he may even have fathered an illegitimate child) and that Catharine's own birth resulted from the couple's reunion following a particularly flagrant episode, Catharine herself being apprised of this by her mother following her father's death?[40] (Another reason, it may be, for her unhappiness during and immediately after her second pregnancy; as 'Blanche', the character in Catharine's daughter's novel which appears to describe the above events says, "I cannot tell you how unhappy I was when I heard about my father. I had not only lost him but all love for him [and] was ashamed that I had ever been his companion … Something died in me after his death [and] after that I never cared to be intimate with anyone".)[41] As to Henry Joseph being a 'wife-beater': can it be that when his wife heaped reproaches on his head, he, possessor of a violent temper, assaulted her, and that it was this as much as anything which was responsible for her strategic withdrawal into ill-health?

There was, however, a further reason for Catharine Tillyard's fundamental and profound distrust of human nature, a reason which stems from her father's behaviour towards herself as she grew into an attractive adolescent. Although Catharine, as the only child and daughter of two parents whose own affectional bonds had been broken in childhood or young adulthood, was a "uniquely-precious baby" designed, it may be, to heal or renew bonds more recently ruptured, she was not spoilt, her imperious demand "'*I want it*', whatever 'it' may have been" being answered by Henry Joseph with the words "*but is that any reason* why you should have it?' But although childhood punishment was inflicted by both parents becoming "cold and distant" and expressing unlove for their daughter's "naughty ways"[42], Henry Joseph's later behaviour towards Catharine verged on the vindictive. Aged fourteen, Catharine suffered a serious illness whose chief symptom was that her throat "pained [her] excessively"; indeed, so severe was her illness that "from the anxious faces around [her she] understood that [she] was expected to die".[43] She did not, and during her lengthy convalescence her hair was allowed to grow until it reached below her waist. Walking in town with his daughter one day, Henry Joseph overheard one undergraduate say to another "what wonderful hair", whereupon "he took her straight to a hairdresser and had it all cut off".[44] Her hair regrown and Catharine having recently received several proposals, her parents "woke up to the fact that [she was] extremely attractive – and sent [her] away to boarding school".[45] Emma, it seems, colluded with her husband in this particularly cruel piece of behaviour – Catharine had never been separated from her parents and can hardly have understood why an innocent admission to her mother of offers of marriage occasioned such extreme punishment – for a letter written to "my own darling mamma" by her tearful and very loving and lonely little daughter Katie Wetenhall from Norbury House School in Reigate expressed such abject misery at being sent away[46] that one wonders why her parents did not immediately relent and bring her home. (The letter being sent to the Wetenhalls' Hills Road address may be no more than coincidental but, given the memorandum in Aelfrida's diary and her subsequent disclosures of Henry Joseph's behaviour, it may not; Katie, it may be, had been sent away from home because a scandal was about to break.) When Catharine returned from school two years later she may have been "a grown up young lady"[47] but she was certainly a profoundly damaged one. Not only had she had to come to terms with loss of her dominant father's approval and (seemingly) unconditional love (and also, it may be, with disillusionment regarding his moral probity) and with what must have seemed like her beloved mother's betrayal in siding with a man whose behaviour she appeared to condone by encouraging that man's unkind actions towards her daughter (actions explicable but not excusable because Emma herself had been sent to finishing school when she reached an age when undergraduates complimented her as they walked past her father's shop), but she had also found herself the blameless victim of her grandfather's and even great-grandfather's actions vis-à-vis her father. Little wonder, then, that she grew up distrustful and 'for all her saintliness', an 'untamed rebel'[48] who raged silently against life's injustices, abhorred sexualised behaviour even if appropriately enacted ("I felt such contempt [for] every man I met [and] as for letting a man touch my hand, kiss me...") and called women who allowed themselves to be hoodwinked by men who professed to love them "dupes".[49]

Her experiences as an impressionable adolescent left Catharine vulnerable, "defenceless if anyone was, even by accident, unkind to her", and with "something pathetic" about her (Alfred Tillyard attributed this "to her having been too severely disciplined by her parents"; Catharine, for reasons of her own, denied the imputation), pathos later becoming "part of her charm, evoking chivalry in men and a desire to mother her in women".[50] She was also so emotionally insecure that she was unable to separate herself from parents who had behaved (and in widowed Emma Wetenhall's case continued to behave) in a controlling fashion. Marriage brought her a degree of independence but she soon felt compelled to move back to her childhood home and to seek approval in other ways as if by doing so she could restore the *status quo ante* of her idyllic childhood and compensate for (imagined) inadequacies in her own personality which might have caused her parents to act towards her as they did.

Her daughter's later references to Catharine's 'saintliness' and to her possessing 'as much goodness as Elizabeth Fry'[51], were not, therefore, traits based on innate goodness of character or on possession of a genuine social conscience, or even, as was the case with many middle-class Cambridge wives, a need to fill lives rendered empty by their husbands' work ethic or, as with many academics' wives, because their husbands used their college as their chief form of social life, returning home only to sleep. They were based on a deeply-felt need to be needed, on a desire to disguise painful feelings of unworthiness, and on a wish to overcome this by expending enormous amounts of energy in helping other people: 'how much inner turmoil', Catharine's daughter perceptively noted, 'went to the making of her life of devotion'.[52]

Catharine's life of devotion began in her early teens during which she spent several hours on Sunday mornings and afternoons as a Sunday School teacher at the St Andrew's Street Baptist Church of which her father was superintendent. It continued after her return from her Parisian finishing school and, following her marriage but before completion of her family in 1889, with increasing involvement in formal and informal philanthropic endeavours pertaining to the education of and opening of various professions to girls, Temperance, Women's Suffrage (of which she was an ardent but never a fanatical supporter), and local Liberal politics, and with her acting as a model landlord to tenants of properties bequeathed to her by her father and mother; indeed, devotion to good works resulted in her serving on more than twenty committees. Lists of her achievements which appear in obituary notices and appreciations retained in papers belonging to and in at least one instance composed by her descendants, show how busy she was; they also show how a woman who 'torment[ed] herself by trying to be unselfish twenty-five hours out of twenty-four' and was prepared to run the risk of physical and emotional exhaustion rather than allow herself to be 'charmed away' from meetings and worries[53], so great was her need 'to devote herself and to be appreciated'.[54] One thing, however, married Catharine Tillyard would never do: she refused to participate in "any definitely Christian work … on her own account", an odd refusal given that she also believed that everything she performed "should be and could be permeated with the spirit of Christ". Can it be that the woman who publicly proclaimed herself so unworthy because she "knew so little of spiritual things" that she refused to take the Sunday School infant class except in an emergency[55] was prepared to martyr herself in support of 'too-numerous committees'[56] concerned with women's rights, Temperance, education and politics but, recalling her father's hypocrisy in matters of religion, shied away from an endeavour which particularly reminded her of it?

Two people, it seems, understood Catharine Tillyard's compulsion: her husband, a man "who could take hard knocks" but who was "always gentle" to his wife[57], and her first cousin Ancifera Gregory.

Ancifera, otherwise known as 'Annie' or 'Ancie', was the daughter of the only member of his émigré siblings ever seen again by Henry Joseph Wetenhall, his younger sister Eliza, born in 1820. Sometime between 1837 and Ancifera's birth in 1849, Eliza married fellow immigrant George Gregory. Following her husband's early death, Eliza remarried but discovering her second husband, though religious, to be a bully, she left him and fled to England with the help of money forwarded by Henry Joseph. Overjoyed at seeing his sister again, Henry Joseph suggested that she live with him and his wife but Eliza, being of an independent nature, preferred to support herself and moved to London to do so. She agreed, however, to leave her daughter in the care of "Uncle Wetenhall" to be raised by him as companion to little Katie Wetenhall and to be educated as befitted the governess and school teacher she was to become.[58]

Though romantic by nature, Ancifera never married. A frequent visitor to Fordfield in later life, she loved Catharine 'more than anyone in the world'[59], Catharine being 'her heroine and her child as well as her "sister" and companion' and the person round whom Ancifera's interests centred even after the courses of the two women's lives parted.[60] She was also Catharine's protector and partisan, on one occasion turning Rendel Harris

**Emma Wetenhall née Barrett c1882**

out of the room[61] and on another criticising Henry Joseph Wetenhall "quite severely".[62] We are not told why but given what we know of his behaviour towards his daughter and suspect of his behaviour towards his wife, it may be guessed at. It is also worth noting that Ancifera, with her intimate knowledge of life at Fordfield, may have been the compiler of the family record mentioned in a footnote to this chapter, for its introduction not only refers to its being written "for the few who loved 'Chiara' and … who care to follow how she came to be what she was" but also to the fact that every family, regardless of social status, possesses "skeletons in cupboards" which "deserve" (*sic*) to be put on record if only to prevent "any precious bit of human history from perishing".[63]

What then of Alfred Tillyard, a 'Tillyard who could take hard knocks' but who had had to adopt a more supportive role than usual vis-à-vis a wife devastated by grief at the same time as he engineered a return to normality for a son and daughter whose stable world had been severely shaken? What were the 'skeletons in cupboards' in *his* past which might influence his present reactions and future behaviour?

Alfred Tillyard's briefly held nickname 'Sweeter'[64] may have denoted an equable temperament but from comments made later in life by his daughter (she describes her father as being 'near' but invariably 'aloof and distant'[65] and herself as being surprised when he '*actually* hugged'[66] her following her return from a lengthy absence abroad, and records instances of cheerfulness or amusement – or of demonstrated sorrow – as if they were rare events) it may be that what had first appeared as *gravitas* self-imposed on an adolescent boy recently become head of his death-diminished family was the beginning of a life-long tendency to depression exacerbated by recent events and later by physical ill-health and distressing family circumstances, of which flatness of affect was one of the symptoms. His tendency to take long walks alone and his apparent need to escape the demands made on him by his wife and family by spending holidays with Frank Tillyard following his mother's death and Frank's marriage to Katharine Ridley (worth noting in passing is that Catharine Tillyard did the same, holidaying for several weeks at a time with Ancifera or other female friends, an unconventional gesture for the time) also suggests a man not always at ease with himself or his wife.

Alfred Tillyard, however, and to a greater extent than his wife, had a profound religious faith to sustain him, a faith inherited from a mother who accepted the deaths of her husband and four of her nine children before they were twelve with Christian resignation. Frida's first intimation of this created a life-long impression: aged about six and sobbing with pain from a finger crushed in the nursery door, she ran down to her parents' bedroom where, so urgent was her need for comfort that she entered without knocking, she encountered her father, eyes shut, on his knees beside his bed and "understood in a flash that Papa like Moses was speaking with God".[67] (Her parents' reaction to the sudden intrusion of an injured child speaks volumes: Catharine, who might have been expected to rush to comfort her sobbing daughter, made hushing signals, but Alfred, whose traits might lead us to expect a sterner reaction, sprang up to investigate and condole, mixed signals indeed to a child already confused by events.) But though religious, Alfred Tillyard was also a good hater, hating not only "hypocrisy, flattery, time-serving, self-seeking … idleness, pretensions, love of money [and] greediness" and "drunkenness, gambling and betting", all admirable hates, but also, it seems, qualities or circumstances which he deemed "sins" but others did not, a characteristic which rendered him liable to be called "austere"[68] at best and possibly something ruder at worst. (His 1902 description of the Church of England as 'an organised injustice'[69] also shows his ability to bear

a grudge: although the repeal in 1871 of the Test Act of 1667 which enforced attendance of Nonconformist university students at college chapel services and debarred them from divinity degrees and from university or college posts barely affected one who matriculated that year, the injustice of his debarment from the Hertford College fellowship continued to rankle.) His austerity also smacked of deeper hatreds: although publicly inclined to speak and act charitably towards others, Alfred Tillyard was liable to behave uncharitably towards members of his own family, particularly if they were female and did not comply (or appear to comply) with mores and sanctions upheld or imposed by himself. His tendency to act in this way was not, however, his alone: his mother, also a professor of Christian charity, had broken the heart of her then nineteen-year-old daughter Alice (interestingly, too, 'the most reserved of all the Tillyards'[70]; was a tendency to depression a family trait?) by not only preventing her from marrying the man she loved – perhaps no bad thing, given that her mother disapproved of his behaviour – but also by marrying her off to a man not of Alice's choosing, the Rev Athol Cliff, twenty years older than herself, Alice thereafter being emotionally 'frozen', and an uncle, Robert Tillyard, had dealt so unkindly with a daughter hoping to marry a man she loved that the girl suffered a mental breakdown and lived thereafter in walled seclusion with a female keeper.

There were, however, other Tillyard family traits inherited by Alfred Tillyard or vehemently reacted to by him in early or later life. His hatred of drunkenness stemmed from a male relative having been "the black sheep of an eminently white family" as a young man because he drank (he later underwent sudden conversion, married a "suitable young lady", and became deacon of his local chapel) and from another being so addicted to alcohol that he died of chronic alcohol poisoning[71], but to his teetotalism Alfred added a twist all his own: he insisted in imposing his views on other people with an obstinacy (another family trait) detrimental to social or business relationships.

Talking in 1912 to Alfred's Aunt Rachel, one of Isaac Tillyard's spinster sisters, Aelfrida obtained 'a very clear idea' of other Tillyard characteristics inherited by her father. Writing of her paternal ancestors that 'they are not a handsome race nor particularly loveable but stern, honest, intellectual … [and] have talents for languages and public speaking', she went on to say that they were 'religious almost to fanaticism', 'mystical and always seem[ed] to live very near to the unseen', 'peculiarly sensitive to telepathic messages' and, deep down, 'exceedingly emotional and full of passion'. Noting too that Rachel had also told her 'love-stories … too long and complicated to put down here', Aelfrida expressed pleasure in being a member 'of such a family'[72]; had she suspected, however, the dominant position religious intolerance amounting almost to fanaticism would play in her own and her father's life and religiosity amounting almost to addiction in her own, she might not have expressed her joy in her heredity in a poem dedicated to her father in which she praises "sires and dames long dead".[73]

1888 was a year of change in Alfred Tillyard's life in ways other than those induced by the tragic death of a small son and his being called to the Bar, for then or shortly thereafter he became editor and proprietor of a local Liberal weekly newspaper, the *Cambridge Independent Press and University Herald*.[74]

As one of Miss Wetenhall's undergraduate admirers, Alfred Tillyard had written in her 'Confession Album' confessions of his own: his idea of happiness was "seeing himself in print", of misery, "being in debt".[75] As editor of and contributor to a prestigious local newspaper of higher intellectual tone than other Cambridgeshire papers and as the future author of three lengthy books (a history of university reform and two on religious topics), Alfred Tillyard was justified in describing himself on his youngest son's marriage certificate as a 'writer'. Judging, however, by his *CIP* obituary he was also extremely active in public life, being "a keen devotee of local government work … in borough and county spheres", "closely identified with municipal matters" and propounding conspicuously "progressive" policies, and an "ardent educationalist".[76]

Though not impelled by the same motives as his wife, Alfred Tillyard's life was filled with as many preoccupations as hers[77]; more, in fact, for his public life began earlier and was not interrupted by child-bearing. Bearing in mind his editorship of the *CIP* and other interests – he was also founder/director of the Cambridge Steam Laundry, a model laundry on rural Cherry Hinton Road, on the board of the Barnwell Coffee Palace Co., a temperance boarding house on Newmarket Road, a governor of Cambridge's School of Arts and Crafts, involved in the establishment of Homerton College, a non-sectarian teachers' training college opened in 1884, and the benevolent owner/ landlord of properties in Cambridge's newly-extended area of artisanal housing – it is surprising he found time to educate Julius prior to the latter being well enough to attend school. His close involvement with municipal duties saw him serving on numerous city and county council committees, his interest in education on the governing bodies of two local schools for boys, the long-established Perse and the recently-founded Cambridge and County School for Boys (his wife sat on the boards of the corresponding schools for girls),

and his interest in national politics as chairman of the Cambridge Liberal Club. Somewhat later he was also a magistrate for the county and from 1904-1919, an alderman. As a recent convert to Presbyterianism, he was also closely associated with the establishment of St Columba's Presbyterian Church and Sunday School on Cambridge's Downing Street in 1891, and in 1899 was invited to join its governing body (was he, one wonders, among those whose "conscientious scruples" were responsible for the church's 1898 decision to use unfermented wine at Communion?)[78], an Elder versed in law and possessing extensive knowledge of town affairs (the majority of the Elders were 'gown' i.e. on the other side of the divide separating the urban population of Cambridge from its university and collegiate one) being extremely useful to the fledgling Presbyterian establishment. Worth noting, however, is that even if only a moiety of adult Aelfrida's account of her 1912 conversation with Rachel Tillyard is true (she had reasons of her own for presenting it in the way she did), more may have lain beneath Alfred Tillyard's urbane and philanthropic exterior than anyone acquainted with his public life suspected.

What then of Alfred and Catharine's children in the years immediately following the events of 1888/89, the 'children in the garden'[79] on whom adult Aelfrida looked back in memory half a century later, whose world after world had failed, worlds peopled by persons who had seemed trustworthy but whose present purpose in life was, so it seemed, to lead them deeper and deeper into "childhood's troubled maze"?[80]

Reunited after their separation at the time of Conrad's death, Dudu and Frida ran into each other's arms – and metaphorically speaking, never left them again.[81] (It is surely no coincidence that twins recur in adult Aelfrida's novels as boy and girl twins whose chief characteristic is "togetherness" and whom threats of separation cause to "burst into tears at once" and to beg "please, *please* PLEASE *don't separate us*"[82]; as twins born to reconciled parents, one "absurdly … like his father", the other named after her maternal grandmother[83]; as twins whose fictional mothers are respectively 'Alice' who is Aelfrida herself and 'Blanche' who is both Aelfrida and her own mother; and, more sinisterly, as Nigerian twins doomed to being pounded to death in jars "because a devil is the father of one of them … and it is safer to make away with both".)[84] Their inability ever to leave each other's arms was far more than the natural tendency of two children close in age "to do everything together" and of the elder to adopt a protective and educational – almost one might say, a quasi-paternal – role with regard to the younger (Julius, wrote adult Aelfrida, "was always helping me, encouraging me, making everything delightful …

when I was silly he did not scold me [but] just looked grave") and the younger an adoring one ("I used to long to be good and as clever as he thought I was") vis-à-vis her "big brother"[85]; it was the beginning of life-long co-dependency during which the siblings clung to each other as if, apart, they were only half a person, Julius being ultimately unable to love anyone but the sister he loved 'better than he [did] anyone else in the world' and Aelfrida (though less overtly) anyone but 'my own Dudu'.[86]

Writing in later life of two fictional brothers (not, in this instance, twins) Aelfrida describes the elder 'George Harvey' as being "so drilled and bullied by his mother that he became a model of chill, stiff deportment". ('Will Harvey', his junior by four years and "a handsome lad with brown ... curls", she describes as able to evade his mother's discipline and retain his good humour and spontaneity.)[87] This literary indictment of Catharine Tillyard's behaviour towards a son unloved since birth rings true in view of her almost-canonisation of Conrad and of the way in which her behaviour affected her eldest son, for Julius, already prone to gloominess, a trait he may have inherited from his father, to behaving distantly and undemonstratively (defensive traits but possibly in imitation of his father too), and to uncontrollable rages, now began to show other symptoms of personality disorder: having "no idea that such a thing as friendship existed"[88]; difficulty in relating to women or, in the case of Catharine Tillyard, an inability 'to go against [his mother's] wishes'[89] even if this resulted in unhappiness for himself, a disability attributed by his sister to Catharine having been 'under the influence of Rendel Harris' cruel treatment at the time of [his] conception' and Harris' 'physical (*sic*) inability' to relate to women having been 'handed down to Dudu as something temperamental'.[90] He also tended to anticipate failure rather than success, a trait wrongly attributed by his sister to 'modesty'[91]; exhibited an 'almost morbid fear of responsibility'[92] stemming, perhaps, from fears that he had in some way contributed to Conrad's death (we are never told which brother caught the infection first) and a wish never to place himself again in an analogous situation; manifested escapist tendencies by being 'more fond of books and less of life'[93]; and experienced impulses toward self-destruction. The symptoms became more marked as he grew older until even his sister's optimistic hopes that Julius would be able 'to turn abnormal to normal ... and have his chance of human happiness like the rest of us'[94] turned to pessimism for his future: 'I pray every day for Dudu's happiness but God does not agree with me evidently'.[95] Yet given that Julius himself wrote of childhood that it was "an overrated time"[96] and that he was much

happier once he had left home, and that the unhappy boy was admonished by his mother and grandmother that it was his *duty* to be "sweet-tempered, serene [and] content" as a sign of gratitude for everything his parents did and had done for him and that performance of his "duty of happiness" would help him with "grown-up cares"[97], how could he not regard it with bitterness? But how is it that in later life he was emotionally unable to leave Fordfield, the place of his greatest unhappiness? Was it a need to make up to his mother for the loss of Conrad? Or was it because the house was redolent even in her absence of the sister he loved more than anyone else in the world or, she being present, the only place where he could find unconditional love and security?

Frida's attachment to Fordfield was less, it seems, to the people who lived there than to the house itself, the only place in the world where, irrespective of Julius' presence or absence, she felt 'at home and safe'.[98] It was, it also seems, a need to reassure herself that the home from which she had been unceremoniously ejected was still there that she returned to it again in fact or in spirit, a home which, in spirit if not in fact, she never really left. (One of the 'stock nightmares' from which she suffered all her life was of 'going back to Fordfield ... and finding the house all different ... and no place for me'.)[99] But whereas Julius reacted to the event and sequelae of Conrad's death by developing coping mechanisms which accorded with his particular temperament and which rendered him apparently compliant and seemingly attentive, his sister's reaction, though mediated by the same event and sequelae, developed in accordance with her own particular temperament and rendered her as angry and as untamed a rebel as her mother.

Manifestations of the degree of disturbance from which little Frida suffered appeared soon after the events of 1888/89. She began to see (or to imagine that she saw) a ghost, not, as one might expect, of the dead baby brother she barely remembered but of Henry Joseph, the 'Deargrandpapa' whom she had never seen. (Her description of the ghost as a "figure with grey-white hair and side whiskers that used to haunt the terrace ... or [gaze] out over trim lawns and [the] panel garden brilliant with flowers"[100] could equally apply to Fordfield's then gardener, Hubbard, but to an impressionable and overwrought child a gardener could easily become a ghost.) She developed a 'great repulsion from hairy things'[101] and became, in marked contrast to her earlier confident approach to 'gentlemen', scared of all men and of her father in particular. ("The more I thought the more terrified I felt", she later wrote, the best thing being "to keep out of his way as much as possible"; she even crawled into the cupboard under the stairs when he returned home unexpectedly.)[102] She also developed "a horror of great darkness" and of "storms" and "high explosive"[103] (metaphorically, of storms of explosive anger such as her father had evinced prior to removing her from Fordfield) but managed to conceal and dominate it because "too proud ... to confess her weakness"[104] and to attribute her fear of the dark and of confined spaces to 'having been brought up on ... stories of Persephone, Polyphemus, ... the Styx, Acheron and Lethe'.[105]

She also, it seems, began to suffer from bad dreams: children (not herself) became 'lost' and could not be found[106]; of children dying ("does it hurt very, very badly to die? Times ... I wake up, nights, all suffocated and ... I can't breathe and I think I am dead, only I'm not")[107], the latter a theme in three later novels in which children die of pneumonia or from trauma or are expected to die of an unnamed disease whose chief symptom is headaches or, in a poem, will themselves to die: "we'll sleep, never wake again"[108]; of "a horrible devil ... waiting by the washstand ... to carry [her] away".[109] And with dreams or waking dreams like these to torment her and with Conrad's deathbed continually ruminated upon by the mother in whose affections Conrad had replaced Frida herself, how could the child do other than long for death, death which would relieve her from "the hideousness of ... dreams" from which she woke "in a cold sweat of terror" and to forestall which she "would lie awake with eyes wide open, trembling with fear" lest sleep prevail and they arrive. And death's preliminary, dying, would restore her mother to her when her little daughter became "very ill and near to death".[110]

It was not only morbid dreams which wracked the child, however, but also guilt: "her sick imaginings, her remorse, seemed like so many devils waiting to carry her soul to Hell ... She sprang out of bed, fell on her knees, prayed wildly for mercy".[111] But what had happened to provoke it? Was it that she had survived and Conrad had not? Or that, like 'Tom', she had been 'dirty' in some way and Conrad had died to make her 'clean', a belief underlined by the fact that rather than physically chastise or use harsh words to a child of whom her horrified parents had become aware of the damage they had unthinkingly inflicted by removing her suddenly and without explanation from danger to safety (or in her eyes, from a place of safety to one of darkness, desertion, and deprivation), Alfred and Catharine Tillyard decided to punish misbehaviour by subjecting her to moral pressure of the kind used by Henry Julius on Little Katie rather than add to her distress by infliction of corporal punishment or show of anger? Either is possible, but the effect was the opposite of that intended, for guilt-inducing moral pressure out of all proportion to the childish crime committed (a

fortnight's banishment from 'Mount Olympus' for picking two strawberries without permission[112], for example) could be equated with punishment for some never-explained 'sin', and being sent to bed for refusing to apologise for a misdemeanour with rejection by both parents and even by *God* withdrawing his love so that He too became not, as before, a Presence "walking in the garden" with the children or "permeating the soft darkness of the night nursery with His love" but akin to a "giant with a big stick" (Julius' expression, for he too suffered in this way)[113] or someone whose absence from the night nursery left it no longer "alive with ... gracious presence"[114] but suddenly and bewilderingly 'dark'. And to the child lying sleepless there and knowing herself to be "hardly ever good and not pleasing to Him at all", the nursery became a place where it was "dreadful, dreadful" to be – and "to be left out".[115]

There was too the "invasion" of Frida's dreams and terrors by a picture common in Victorian homes (she could never remember later where she had seen it but the vividness of the impression remained) of "a great eye ... accompanied by the text *'Thou God seest me'*. The eye, "gigantic, lidless [and] horrible", was, she had been told, "the eye of God which followed Cain wherever he tried to hide his guilt"; to a child now suffering from a sense of guilt so global, amorphous, and inexplicable as to be beyond her small comprehension, invasion of sleep and half-waking states by this symbol of "God's wrath" (wrath not hot and bright, but of an "icy darkness") served to worsen her "sick imaginings".[116] Compared to this, a smack or a scolding whose direct connection to a childish crime was obvious would have made more sense and been infinitely preferable.

To the frightened anxious child two behavioural options were available: to placate the angry Deity and to compartmentalise her life. She opted for both, the first by always "putting her[self] in the wrong" and by pleading, if accused of any real or imagined misdemeanour, "to faults of manner but ... none of intention"[117] and by tolerating unkind behaviour if this resulted in approval and recognition, the second, by developing the protective faculty of mentally dissociating herself from unpleasant happenings, thoughts, or recollections but a faculty which resulted in her becoming unable to learn by experience or to discriminate between good and bad actions on her part vis-à-vis those whose lives coincided with or impinged on her own and which was manifest in her ability to pass without missing a beat from a situation of high positive or negative emotional charge to one of no import at all, to bestow on each situation the same emotional importance, and to disregard the consequences of both entirely. As survival mechanisms go, both were admirably successful in childhood and adolescence but once she reached adulthood she became vulnerable: so globally and inexplicably guilty did she feel, no action of hers would suffice to atone for real or imagined sins or propitiate an angry Deity and never having properly come to terms with the events surrounding Conrad's death, she became unable deal with events which replicated them or aspects of them except by disassociating herself from them.

A contributory factor is that the events were never discussed except in terms of sentimentalisation so profound and so actuality-altering that it was only later in life and through the distorting medium of fiction that Aelfrida was able to come to terms with what really happened – and then only in part. Hence although she liked to think that her feet were "carefully ... led" through "childhood's troubled maze"[118], in one vital respect they were not led at all: because the events surrounding Conrad's death were never discussed, no information was provided which might have explained to little Frida why her parents behaved as they did then or later (as adult Aelfrida wrote of the aftermath of another traumatic event, "we all pretended everything was all right")[119] and Julius' and her own dysfunctionality was disguised by attributing it "to some other cause"[120] more socially acceptable to outsiders and domestically to the family itself. (The pretence that 'everything at Fordfield was all right' was, in fact, so persuasive and pervasive that there were said to be no crises or dramatic moments at all[121], something which evidence proves untrue.) Worse still, natural emotions, particularly negative ones, were repressed ('at Fordfield nobody lost their tempers'[122], a statement true only up to a point), a learnt pattern of behaviour particularly noticeable in and used to particular effect by adult Julius and Aelfrida. Repression of emotion was compensated for (and its symptoms treated by) employment of other means of release, in Julius' case by losing himself in intensive research and by living and working abroad, in Aelfrida's through behaviour of a compulsive or even an addictive nature. And so strongly imprinted was Alfred and Catharine Tillyard's tendency to secrecy and suppression and propagandistic transformation that in later life Frida found it impossible to approach the truth in any other way.

Three other traits also began to manifest themselves at this period of Frida's life: a tendency to risky behaviour, emotional neediness, and a need to be firmly in control of her own and other's lives.

Already described as fearless, Frida's conduct following Conrad's death became behaviour in which she actively sought out and enjoyed situations which placed her in actual or metaphorical danger. Quite why she felt impelled to act in this way – and indeed, sometimes signally failed to act in a way which accorded with the realities of the situation in which she found herself – is hard to tell; possibly the permanent state of emotional arousal in which she now lived impelled her to do so; possibly she found such behaviour rewarding insofar as it attracted her parents' attention, a pleasurable response even if it resulted in a scolding or their begging her to 'maintain a sense of proportion', adolescent Frida noting with more insight than she usually displayed that a sense of proportion was exactly what she lacked.[123] Possibly she had become conditioned to act and react in this way to events which inspired mixed frissons of fear and reward i.e. removal from home and bestowal of presents on her return; possibly her pervasive sense of guilt required exposure to potential punishment. Whatever the reason, it seems that a child who had earlier taken delight in doing what she should not now behaved as if her life was devoid of boundaries and this in a manner which easily surpassed the testing of boundaries normal in growing children and adolescents. It seems, therefore, that Frida could not help but indulge in certain modes of behaviour, that she behaved without caution, and that she behaved (on other people's terms if not her own) bizarrely or irrationally and without appearing to be in control of her actions or to weigh up their possible consequences, be these physical (e.g. insisting on riding a horse too large and powerful for a girl who had hitherto ridden only ponies so that when it fell or bolted or she attempted a manoeuvre beyond her capabilities, she risked injury and worse, her only comment being that she was 'not in the least scared')[124] or societal: conducting 'flirtations' with married men older than herself, one in a family setting (a picnic at Hunstanton) resulting in uncle Athol Cliff saying 'some rather nasty things'[125] to her concerning her attitude towards local architect Herbert Ibberson, one so public and brazen that her hostess sent her home early in disgrace, Frida's insouciant comment being that though her behaviour *had* been shocking, it did not much matter 'because I shall probably never see [the man] again'.[126]

Although adult Aelfrida liked to regard herself – and to have others regard her – as a coolly detached observer of life, it was in fact her tendency to live her life as if it was a play of which she was simultaneously author, stage manager, and leading lady which spoke volumes of two other aspects of her personality: her emotional neediness and her need to control other people.

Rejected, as she thought, by formerly loving parents, Frida grew up both needy for affection and greedy of it. Her craving took many forms but however much affection was bestowed on her, neither the craving nor her appetite could be filled and people or institutions to whom or to which she attached herself were invariably and sooner or later found wanting because none could bestow on her the volume of affection she craved and all save one (and Julius was not that one) were eventually cast aside – though not before they had been pitilessly exploited. But so needy was adult Aelfrida for affection that she was unable to appreciate until it was too late the damaging effect on those onto whom she latched or of her manipulation of them in order to comply with her emotional demands or of the harm done them when, found wanting, they were cast out of her emotional life even if or although they remained physically within her orbit or were toyed with by being alternately embraced and rejected according to whether or not her emotional demands were met or unmet. Worse still, she invariably convinced herself that *she* was the victim of *others'* inability to love her to the required extent and if and when they managed to free themselves, victim of a 'crime' committed against her blameless self.

In pursuit of her emotional ends adult Aelfrida was also prepared to act as if it was not she but others who were needy and to take advantage of any real or imagined weakness to achieve her ends. She was also prepared to act the part of victim if by such means she could attract or retain an admirer, and although normally uncaring of other people's feelings, was prepared to tailor her behaviour to embrace them for her own ends; alternatively she would attract potential victims by appearing as a supremely confident and utterly charming person whose engagement with them could only be regarded as flattering while at the same time giving away as little of herself as possible. (And if she failed to engage, a negative relationship or outright rejection sufficed because in it she was able to discern features which could then be exploited in relation to someone else.) Her need to engage was also fed by personality traits directly associated with the traumatic events of June 1888: a belief that childhood maltreatment entitled her to favourable treatment (particularly by those who had maltreated her) as an adult; a tendency to exaggerate her abilities in whichever field of endeavour she was currently interested; a sense of enormous self-importance which led to arrogance and to a belief that only certain people were worthy of her attention or of association with her; a preoccupation with attainable (as she thought, but actually unattainable) goals (a perfect love, relationship, or splendour), goals by their very nature suitable for a superior person like herself and manifest in a manner worthy of themselves and her. And if in order to achieve her goals it was necessary to exercise – even over-exercise – her already vivid imagination, then this she would do even to the extent

Henry Joseph Wetenhall c1856

of moving herself away from objective reality; conversely, if it was necessary to physically remove herself from a situation she found intolerable because it failed to accord with her fantastic version, this she would also do even at the expense of common sense or common decency.

If a need for affection formed the obverse of Aelfrida's adult personality, a need to take control formed its reverse, a single episode of extreme childish fear engendering a desire to ensure her future safety by rigorously controlling her environment and the lives of people with whom she came in contact. She controlled them in different ways, each appropriate to their position in her life and their status in her eyes: by ensconcing herself uncompromisingly where she wished to be, by bullying, by affecting compliance to the point of cringing, by acting in such a way as to attract attention, by attempting to engender pity, by seeming to distance herself, by smothering with what she called love, even by staring. (But rarely by showing anger and even more rarely by confrontation or by weeping – though it is interesting to note that she taught herself to weep in a dramatically un-childlike and controlling fashion: 'I have learnt to cry like the heroines of novels. My eyes just get full of tears which afterwards roll down my cheeks'.)[127] And if people or environments refused to be controlled or escaped her control, she revenged herself, usually privately but sometimes very publicly. She also sought control by associating herself with exclusive and possibly authoritarian organisations, this not only increasing her status in other people's eyes (and, of course, her own) but also fulfilling a hope and need that she might gain control by the very act of entering them. And if entry to such organisations did not permit the degree of control she needed or impinged too much on the "compulsive self-reliance"[128] practised since 1888 (it being, it seemed, only herself on whom she could ultimately rely), she left them, using as her excuse that a force greater than herself impelled her to act in this way.

Frida's life between the ages of five and ten, though not devoid of incident, is a time for which we have comparatively little information. Whether this omission was deliberate or accidental, it is impossible to tell, but such information as we have speaks volumes. We know, for example, that she was "small for her age".[129] (Childhood growth retardation may be a symptom of stress.) That in 1891 she was, together with her cousin May Cliff, a reluctant and 'very solemn' bridesmaid at the wedding of 'Uncle Frank' Tillyard. (Perhaps it was her flame-coloured velvet dress which solemnised her; May, aged eleven, wore white and was 'sweetly pretty … with … a smile!')[130] That Mary Tillyard (now known as 'Other Dear', Emma Wetenhall being 'Dear'), too ill to attend the wedding, died a few weeks later without being seen again by a granddaughter who took herself off to read the Burial Service privately and to think "how happy Other Dear must be with a new body instead of her poor crooked one".[131] That, also in 1891 and inspired by Queen Victoria's *More Leaves from a Journal of our Life in the Highlands* of 1885, she began to keep a diary but "reading through the notebooks a year or so later … was mortified to find that [she] had put on record [her] thoughts and impressions, … thought what a little fool [she] was and destroyed the volumes".[132] That "though not vain of her looks", she developed under Zelle's care "a taste for clothes" and a Frenchified air.[133] We also know that she and Julius began to attend school.

Julius, aged ten, was sent to a recently-founded preparatory school, St Faith's known familiarly as 'Goody's' after its headmaster Ralph Goodchild; Frida, then eight, to the Perse School for Girls, a short walk from her home. Ill-health was, of course, the Tillyards' excuse for Julius' delayed arrival at school; Aelfrida's similarly delayed arrival (the Education Act of 1870 had made formal education compulsory for all children from age five) is unexplained but given that she describes school as presented to her as "the way to the grand country of … being grown up"[134], we may guess that more benign tactics were employed by her parents those employed three years.

The Perse School for Girls was not held in high esteem, in part because influential Cambridge ladies thought "day schools for girls were Bad"[135], in part because its teaching methods were old-fashioned. (Frida was put off history for life, regarding it as nothing but lists of "battles and dates and kings"[136] and stories of people who were '*dead*', a 'lifeless Past' whose weight 'spread itself like a pall over [her] natural curiosity'.)[137] It also reeked of snobbery, the daughters of Cambridge crème-de-la-crème families ("Butlers, Jebbs, Darwins … Masters of Colleges") who deigned to send their female offspring there ranking highest (they were "IT"), those of business men above those of dissenting ministers, elementary teachers, and dentists, and they above those of "common townees"[138], but it was none of these factors which occasioned Frida's early departure: it was school phobia.

Departure from the Perse after only three terms was later attributed by her to reasons quite other than the traumatic events of three years earlier: victimisation by her peers (she was sent to Coventry, an incident which though she later claimed to have enjoyed it because it allowed her greater privacy – and also, it may be, to taste the joys of martyrdom and to be able to negotiate from a position of superior strength by seeing it through silently and composedly; perhaps it reminded her of an earlier 'banishment')[139] being attributed to expressing Liberal convictions too forcefully in an essentially Tory school and unpopularity with the teachers to her public correction of a student teacher's French. (Advanced in some subjects as she was, it was soon thought expedient to place her in a class "where the teacher knew more French than I thought I did"[140] and with girls two classes ahead of her in Latin.) Other and more likely reasons are also hinted at: an inability to relate to other girls ("I left school without having … made a bosom friend"[141] because "I don't feel I am or ever can be one of them")[142], ostensibly because she felt no desire "to establish emotional relationships [with] people"[143] or to behave (as Julius put it) *more puellarum*[144] ("I had no G.P. on a mistress" i.e. a "Grand Pash" or 'crush'), Frida considering "fashions and crazes"[145] indulged in by her peers as unattractive and incomprehensible. She also showed a tendency to behave towards her classmates in a manner which might discourage overtures of friendship, having brought to school what she called "a number of principles and convictions on religion, politics and manners"[146] which she was unable to relinquish because they provided security in an unfamiliar world in which she felt "bewildered"[147] and because they made her feel priggishly superior to girls who did not share them. And having been kept at home for eight years, she was unused to meeting other girls en masse except at parties. (She had no such problems with boys, regarding, them, it seems, as versions of Julius, boys in return regarding her as "always a favourite"[148] with themselves.) Lastly, the regimented school day and necessity of wearing particular clothes – there was no uniform as such but dark dresses and straw or felt hats were de rigueur – irked her because they symbolised conflicts engendered between how she would like to behave and how she was expected to behave, and the "hubbub of eager conversation" in cloakroom and playground[149] was distressingly noisy to a child whose preference was for "wondering and dreaming" alone or with Julius in Fordfield garden. Hence in spite of being prepared to "take the rough with the smooth" with regard to school and although endowed "with an all-embracing curiosity and ... quite ready to learn anything and everything" and to look on "each new acquaintance as a country waiting to be explored", Frida found herself "beginning to flag" long before she completed her first school year.[150] But it was a single specific event which made school "definitely too much"[151] for her to bear: the closing of a door.

Promotion to a senior class for Latin meant taking herself from one end of the school to the other in a short time. Passing an external door one day, curiosity impelled her to open it and to step out into the street. A gust of wind slammed the door behind her and she was (temporarily) unable to return. Though the panic which seized her had much to do with this being a "bit of naughtiness", it is obvious that the "terrible fear" which stabbed her stemmed less from 'naughtiness' and more from the thought which flashed into her mind "what if she should be excluded for ever?" (Excluded, that is to say, as she been from Fordfield, excluded, as it now seemed increasingly likely, from Julius' life, excluded too, from Zelle's, for it appears that Zelle departed contemporaneously with the start of Julius' and Frida's formal education.) The Biblical phrase "and the door was shut" which appears in the parable of the wise and foolish virgins promoted "a thrill of horror" in Frida's mind thereafter [152] and her use of the loaded word 'banished' to describe what any other child would have regarded as misadventure is doubly significant; not only did the event remind her of an earlier exclusion but "the locked door and herself standing outside" also became another thought-form into which recurrent dreams arranged

themselves.[153] Fear of reprimand (she had already suffered a telling-off by her father for criticising a teacher, he having chosen not to enquire why his bright daughter had achieved very low marks for arithmetic[154]; her mother, victim of an intentionally spiteful episode as a child, might have been more sympathetic had she cared to ask) seems to have prevented her from discussing the matter with her parents, with dire results: an episode of childish naughtiness was subsumed into and enhanced her already overwhelming sense of guilt, leaving her, as she thought, numbered among the "ungodly".[155] It also created in her mind the fearful belief that Hell could be nothing but "self-merited exclusion" from God's presence. For Aelfrida to say later in life when preparing the incident for publication that as an adult her "whole spiritual life" – indeed, her whole life – "received its structure from a gust of wind and a slammed door" may be an exaggeration, but given that finding herself outside the door in an empty street her first thought was that she might have entered a "City of the Dead"[156], an exaggeration which contained so much truth that it was hardly an exaggeration at all.

Frida's difficulty in being sent away from home even to a school a short distance from Fordfield was enhanced by arriving in the third term of the school year when that year's syllabus was two thirds completed (her use of the words 'unfamiliar' and 'mystified' show her confusion but she dared not reveal her ignorance by asking for explanations) and friendships among her peers already forged, but the anxiety of being compelled to regularly leave a home and a family who might not be there on her return or allow her in when she returned provoked a recurrence of distressing symptoms first manifest three years earlier: "screaming fits in the night"[157] (attributed by adult Aelfrida to "too much homework" preying on the mind of a "nervous" child), to a feeling of "continual oppression as if [she] were doing wrong", and to nightmares. New symptoms also manifested themselves: anxiety made her forgetful, she began to suffer from headaches, and she became "disinclined to eat [her] meals".[158]

Physical symptoms made Alfred and Catharine Tillyard take notice but rather than blame themselves, they tried a physical remedy: "my parents thought Callisthenics might be good for me"[159], a hint that it may have been in an attempt to 'brace-up' (as the expression went) their 'nervous' daughter that Frida was sent to school in the first place. Gymnastics designed to promote bodily fitness proved ineffectual so they sought medical advice. There being, as adult Aelfrida later noted, "no psychologists ... in those days ... to know about our inmost motives"[160], Frida was subjected instead to "a sedative and a good talking-to", her headaches deemed "probably psychological" (the doctor, it seems, did not go so far as to say that school *caused* her headaches but intimated that attendance caused her to *imagine* that she had headaches; her parents agreed)[161], and removal from school at the end of her fourth term advised.

It must have been difficult for two such ardent believers in female education as Alfred and Catharine Tillyard to remove a daughter who might, had they not damaged by their unfeeling and unthinking behaviour and by their present demeanour, the one aloof, the other a suppressed hysteric and compulsive care-giver to people not her daughter, have become a bright star in Cambridge's educational firmament, but when Frida became noticeably disabled by her symptoms (food-refusal seems to have worried her mother most for she was watchful of her daughter's eating habits thereafter), a more socially and personally acceptable explanation of them was promulgated, namely that she was in danger of developing "lateral curvature" of the spine "from carrying a satchel full of heavy books" and that her headaches and loss of appetite "suggested that [she] was doing too much"[162] for a nervous undersized nine year old. She was therefore allowed to leave the "kind of Dark Ages"[163] embodied by the Perse and to study 'Greek and Italian and so forth'[164] at her own pace by herself in her own home.

The Tillyards naturally blamed their daughter, calling her 'temperamental' and 'tiresome'[165] and criticising her for being unable to control herself or to listen to reason. (There were also suggestions from outsiders who did not suspect the literal truth of their remarks that Frida had been "spoilt"[166], not least by being allowed to remain at home so long after she should have gone to school.) Time spent on her own free from external pressures seems, however, to have been exactly what she needed and when a solution to her educational problems presented itself in the shape of "a lady [inviting her] to join a class consisting of her daughter and one other girl for three mornings a week"[167], she jumped at the chance. Her parents accepted the offer with unfeigned gratitude, for living as they did "in surroundings where intellectual gifts were supremely valued"[168], what value could they place on a daughter who appeared incapable of making the most of hers? The move was a success, Frida receiving instruction "as good as real university coaching [while] still a child".[169] From Frida's point of view, too, it seemed that happier times were about to begin.

The new era, however, was to bring problems of its own, for nine- or ten-year-old Frida (we never learn the duration of her period of solo study) would never be 'normal'. Although she herself realised early on that she was somehow different from other people, it was not until much later in life that she grasped the extent of the

damage, noting perceptively that she 'supposed' that "in some ways [her upbringing] was a good one"[170] because it encompassed existence in "a normal middle-class home and in a comfortable well-ordered, well-disciplined Christian household". (But who, she asked, "shall say now what kind of home is normal and what is not?")[171] She also noted that "of course, a broken home gives a child a bad start"[172] and that those "brought up in security ... can hardly imagine what such a childhood involves".[173] Such an upbringing, she added, would tend to sow "seeds of mental trouble" which would "germinate in the years to come" in the minds of "boys and girls" subjected to "separations [and] bereavements", seeds whose fruits would be manifest as "terrified, rebellious, even despairing thoughts"[174] and as destructive emotions like "jealousy and hatred" and "ignorance of gratitude".[175] Let us hope, she concludes, that "the damage has not been irreparable".[176] But as everything written by or about Aelfrida so far has shown, it was.

## Notes

1  References to The Children in the Garden GCPPT 2|25|2(5).

2  Tillyard, HJW. Introduction to *The Letters of ACW Tillyard* (MTC).

3  GCPPT 2|25|2(5).

4  Kingsley, C. *The Water Babies* ch 6 "the very saddest part of [the] story".

5  ibid. ch 2.

6  Tillyard, Ae. *Christian Old Age* p 91 (GCPPT 2|17).

7  Tillyard, Ae. *The Centaur* p 70 (GCPPT 2|21|1).

8  Tillyard, Ae. GCPPT 2|23 *The Watchword* March 1955.

9  GCPPT 1|1|72a Tillyard, HJW. Notes for a '*Family Chronicle*' 1954/55.

10  GCPPT 1|1|73a Letter from Julius Tillyard to Aelfrida dated 'Christmas 1956'.

11  GCPPT 2|3 *The Watchword* March 1955.

12  GCPPT 1|1|72a Tillyard, HJW. Notes for a '*Family Chronicle*' 1954/55.

13  GCPPT 2|23 *The Watchword* December 1954.

14  GCPPT 1|1|73 15 March 1956.

15  Tillyard, HJW. Introduction to *The Letters of ACW Tillyard* (MTC).

16  GCPPT 2|25|2 (5).

17  GCPPT 2|26|2(3). An envelope inscribed "[Eustace's] little curls cut off ... when he was 2 years and 10 months old. March 12th 1892" (MTC) confirms his sister's description.

18  GCPPT 2|23 *The Watchword* December 1956. Eustace himself endured so much teasing as a child because of his given names (the gardener's wife, mishearing, cried out that he was a "fine boy and no mistake but they might have called him something better than useless"), that he resolved that *his* children would have only one name each and that a sensible one.

19  GCPPT 1|1|72a Letter from Aelfrida (Tit) to Alfred Tillyard (Oracle) of 21 December 1904.

20  The name 'Quicky' was derived from 'Quicksilver' a common name for mercury, not because Eustace had a mercurial temperament but because his elder siblings in their roles of 'Poseidon' and 'Athena' decided that the new baby would be 'Mercury', messenger of the gods. The name Mercury was transliterated by Nathaniel Hawthorne in *The Wonder Book* (1852) as Quicksilver and "further debased for everyday use to Quicky" by the Tillyards. (GCPPT 2|24 and 2|25 *Quicky and God – and Gods and Goddesses*). Ironically by the time Eustace was old

enough to join his elder siblings' games they no longer played 'gods and goddesses' but the name stuck.

21 GCPPT 1|1|72 11 September 1955.

22 GCPPT 2|23 *The Watchword* June 1957.

23 The names probably derive from Frederick Marryat's 1836 naval adventure story *Mr Midshipman Easy* and from the nautical nickname for midshipmen and other officers.

24 GCPPT 2|26|2 (3)23 .

GCPPT 2|23 *The Watchword* December 1956. A similar story is told of Charles Kingsley as a child (Chitty, S. p 28) which may have coloured Aelfrida's recollections of Eustace's behaviour. The version of Kingsley's life with which the Tillyards would have been familiar was the hagiographic account published by his widow in 1877; Chitty's 1974 biography *The Beast and the Monk* reveals more of the truth.

25 GCPPT 2|23 *The Watchword* December 1956.

26 GCPPT 1|1|60 3 November 1942.

27 GCPPT 1|1|21 16 February 1917.

28 GCPPT 1|1|60 3 December 1942.

GCPPT 2|27|2(4)

29 GCPPT 2|27|2(4).

30 Tillyard, Ae. *The Centaur* p 155.

31 ibid. pp 49 and 96.

32 GCPPT 2|27|1(1).

33 Data forming the basis of this and subsequent paragraphs is taken from an anonymous history of the Wetenhall, Barrett, and Warren families written (by context) sometime in 1933 (MTC). Dating and statements of fact are sometimes at variance but a reasonably accurate account can be compiled with the help of evidence provided elsewhere in the family papers, from gravestones and from nineteenth century Cambridge street directories and other historical documents.

34 The Strict Baptist chapel in Rattlesden was founded in 1813 but history does not relate if Sara Fulcher (a very religious young lady) was already a member and influenced her husband's conversion or if Henry joined first and his wife later. The sect was a separatist Calvinist movement established early in the nineteenth century as a counterblast to what its members regarded as the increasing laxity and inclusive nature of contemporary established religion; its chief tenet was that of 'particular' or 'limited' atonement ie that Christ died for those predestined by God for redemption, among whom members of its 'strict' or 'closed' communion counted themselves. For further details see Dix, K *Strict and Particular* and Breed, G. *Particular Baptists in Victorian England*.

35 GCPPT 2|27|1(1).

36 Tillyard, HJW. Introduction to *The Letters of ACW Tillyard* (MTC).

37 GCPPT 1|1|72 Note on last page of volume.

38 Tillyard, Ae. *The Way We Grow Up* p 150.

39 GCPPT 1|1|36 14 April 1929.

40 Tillyard, Ae. *The Way We Grow Up* pp 150–151.

41 ibid. pp 151–152.

42 GCPPT 2|23 *The Watchword* June 1958.

43 GCPPT 2|27|2(2).

44 GCPPT 2|23 *The Watchword* June 1958.

45 GCPPT 2|27|2(2).

46 GCPPT 1|1|74a Letter from Catharine Wetenhall to Emma Wetenhall of 7 February [18]68.

47 GCPPT 2|27|2(2).

48 GCPPT 1|1|36 14 April 1929.

49 Tillyard, Ae. *The Way We Grow Up* p 152.

50 GCPPT 2|23 *The Watchword* June 1958.

51 GCPPT 1|1|72 11 September 1955. Elizabeth Fry (1780–1845) was a Quaker prison reformer.

52 GCPPT 1|1|32 21 August 1926.

53 GCPPT 1|1|13 6 February, 19 March and 5 May 1906.

54 GCPPT 1|1|16 13 August 1908.

55 Tillyard, Ae. *The Glory of the West* p 153 (GCPPT 2|16|3).

56 GCPPT 1|1|18 5 July 1912.

57 GCPPT 2|23 *The Watchword* June 1958.

58 For further details of Eliza and George Gregory and of Ancifera Gregory, see GCPPT 2|2|1(5&6) and 2|25|3(8).

59 GCPPT 1|1|48 30 May 1935.

60 GCPPT 1|1|43 17 February 1933.

61 GCPPT 2|25|3(8).

62 GCPPT 2|27|(2).

63 Introduction and pp1–2 of an otherwise unpaginated account. The three handwritten pages of the account (the remainder are typed by an inexperienced typist) are not in the handwriting of any of Catharine Tillyard's immediate descendants but we know that during a visit paid to Fordfield two months after Catharine Tillyard's death, Ancifera Gregory and Aelfrida went through Catharine's effects including diaries and photographs and spent much time in reminiscence (GCPPT 1|1|43 17 February 1933) and it may have been this which inspired Ancifera (if the complier was indeed she) to begin it.

64 GCPPT 1|1|14 18 April 1898.

65 GCPPT 1|1|37 25 December 1929.

66 GCPPT 1|1|15 14 December 1907.

67 GCPPT 2|23 *The Watchword* June 1957.

68 ibid.

69 GCPPT 1|1|9 21 September 1902.

70 GCPPT 1|1|47 28 March 1935.

71 GCPPT 2|27|1(9) There also seems to have been 'a Tillyard in Holy Orders' who went out with the Society for the Propagation of the Gospel to Virginia, a fact of which the family was very proud until they discovered him to have been a '*disreputable* drunkard' (GCPPT 1|1|75 22 August 1958).

72 GCPPT 1|1|18 4 August 1912.

73 Tillyard, Ae. *Heredity* (*The Garden and the Fire* p 54) The poem was written in Cambridge on 12 August 1912.

74 The *CIP*'s university connection was important to Alfred Tillyard's later career as an author for discussions on university reforms which took place in 1907 and which formed the basis of three articles (*The Reform of Cambridge University*) published in the *CIP* on 11, 18 and 25 October that year (the articles are unsigned but are discernibly by Tillyard himself because passages from them were incorporated verbatim and without acknowledgement in his first book) inspired his *A History of University Reform*. The work contains an exposition of reforms which had already occurred at Oxford and Cambridge, a summary of what remained to be done and suggestions as to how future reforms should be carried out and was subsequently referred to by the Royal Commission on Universities meeting at the time of its publication, a fact which gratified an author who, as he pointed out in its preface, had held no university position since his graduation thirty years earlier.

75 GCPPT 2|27|2(2).

76 *CIP* (obituary) 11 November 1929.

77 *The Times* (obituary) 10 October 1929.

78 Knox, R.B. pp 17–18 and 36.

79 GCPPT 1|1|45 1 August 1934.

80 Tillyard, Ae. *Heredity* (*The Garden and the Fire* p 54).

81 For a formal exploration of what follows see Bowlby, J. *The Making and Breaking of Affectional Bonds* and *Loss, Sadness and Depression*.

82 Tillyard, Ae. *Just Alice* pp 270 and 275. (GCPPT 2|19).

83 Tillyard, Ae. *The Way We Grow Up* pp 276–277.

84 ibid. p 257.

85 Tillyard, Ae. *Messages* pp 54–58.

86 GCPPT 1|1|13 20 and 25 June 1905.

87 Tillyard, Ae. *Just Alice* p 9.

88 Tillyard, Ae. *Naomi da Costa* pp 102–103 (GCPPT 2|22).

89 GCPPT 1|1|26 17 October 1921.

90 GCPPT 1|1|18 9 August 1911.
91 GCPPT 1|1|13 25 June 1905.
92 GCPPT 11|26 30 January 1922.
93 GCPPT 1|1|13 25 June 1905.
94 GCPPT 1|1|18 8 January 1913.
95 GCPPT 1|1|14 14 January 1907.
96 GCPPT 1|1|72a Tillyard, HJW. Notes for a 'Family Chronicle' 1954/55.
97 Tillyard, Ae. *Messages* pp 21–27.
98 GCPPT 1|1|53 9 July 1937.
99 GCPPT 1|1|70 2 March 1953.
100 GCPPT 2|27|2 (6).
101 GCPPT 1|1|55 31 July 1938.
102 Tillyard, Ae. *Naomi da Costa* pp 12–13.
103 Tillyard, Ae. *The Centaur* pp 24–25. (GCPPT 2|21|1)
104 Tillyard, Ae. *The Way We Grow Up* p 237.
105 GCPPT 1|1|69 9 April 1952.
106 GCPPT 1|1|70 2 March 1953.
107 Tillyard, Ae. *The Way We Grow Up* p 52.
108 Tillyard, Ae. *An incident in the flight from Poland* (*The Garden and the Fire* p 12), written in Cambridge on 26 August 1916.
109 Tillyard, Ae. *The Way We Grow Up* p 52.
110 ibid. p 236. In Catharine Tillyard's dedicated copy of this novel the paragraphs containing the passages quoted here are marked; the markings may not, of course, have been made by Catharine or Aelfrida but how poignant if they were.
111 ibid.
112 GCPPT 2|23 *The Watchword* March 1957.
113 Tillyard, Ae. *Can I be a Mystic?* pp 28–29.
114 Tillyard, Ae. *The Fruits of Silence* pp14–17.
115 Tillyard, Ae. *The Closer Walk with God* p114.
116 Tillyard, Ae. *The Way We Grow Up* p 236.
117 GCPPT 1|1|22 30 November 1917 and 18 February 1918.
118 Tillyard, Ae. *Heredity* (*The Garden and the Fire* p 54).
119 GCPPT 1|1|20 5 October 1914.
120 Bowlby, J. *The Making and Breaking of Affectional Bonds.* p 170.
121 Tillyard, Ae. *Naomi da Costa* pp 102–103.
122 GCPPT 1|1|75 19 March 1959.
123 GCPPT 1|1|6 1 February 1901.
124 GCPPT 1|1|7 14 May 1901.
125 GCPPT 1|1|9 25 August 1902.
126 GCPPT 1|1|5 8 August 1900.
    GCPPT 1|1|9 8 July 1902.
127 GCPPT 1|1|7 26 April 1901.
128 Bowlby, J. *Loss* p 171 and *The Making and Breaking of Affectional Bonds* p 170.
129 GCPPT 2|24|2 *Little Frida Goes to School.*
130 GCPPT 1|1|71 23 March 1954.
131 GCPPT 2|23 *The Watchword* March 1955.
132 GCPPT 1|1|65a Envelope headed 'to go with my diaries. 26 September 1935'.

133 Tillyard, HJW. Introduction to *The Letters of ACW Tillyard* (MTC).
134 GCPPT 2|24|2 *Little Frida goes to School.*
135 Raverat, G. p 61.
136 Tillyard, Ae. *Messages* pp 4–9.
137 Tillyard, Ae. *The Glory of the West* p 371. (GCPPT 2|16|1 Pt 2.)
138 Tillyard, HJW. Introduction to *The Letters of ACW Tillyard* (MTC).
139 GCPPT 2|24|1 *Little Frida Leaves School.*
    GCPPT 1|1|62a Letter from Aelfrida to Mother Guenvrede SSC of 29 July 1944.
140 GCPPT 2|24|1 *Little Frida Leaves School.*
141 ibid. This was not quite true; Aelfrida subsequently describes a friendship with a girl two years older than herself who, she said, used to 'worship' the younger girl. (GCPPT 1|1|9 30 May 1905). To Aelfrida's chagrin the friendship was not maintained after she left the Perse.
142 Tillyard, Ae. *Naomi da Costa* p 62.
143 Tillyard, Ae. *Just Alice* pp 53–60.
144 Tillyard, HJW. Introduction to *The Letters of ACW Tillyard* (MTC).
145 GCPPT 2|24|1 *Little Frida Leaves School.*
    Tillyard, Ae. *Just Alice* pp 53 – 60 and 212.
146 GCPPT 2|24|1 *Little Frida Leaves School.*
147 Tillyard, Ae. *Naomi da Costa* p 62.
148 Tillyard, HJW. Introduction to *The Letters of ACW Tillyard* (MTC).
149 GCPPT 2|24|2 *Little Frida goes to School.*
150 GCPPT 2|24|1 *Little Frida leaves School.*
    GCPPT 2|24|2 *Little Frida goes to School.*
151 GCPPT 2|24|1 *Little Frida leaves School*
152 Tillyard, Ae. *Christian Old Age* pp 7–8.
153 GCPPT 2|24|1 *Little Frida Leaves School.*
    Tillyard, Ae. *Christian Old Age* pp 7–8.
154 GCPPT 2|23 *The Watchword* June 1957.
155 GCPPT 2|24|1 *Little Frida leaves School.*
156 Tillyard, Ae. *Christian Old Age.* pp 7–8.
157 Tillyard, Ae. *Naomi da Costa* pp 78–79.
158 GCPPT 1|1|57 6 March 1940.
159 GCPPT 2|24|1(1) *Little Frida leaves School.*
160 GCPPT 2|27|1(1).
161 Tillyard, Ae. *Just Alice* pp 169–170.
162 GCPPT 2|24|1 *Little Frida leaves School.*
163 Tillyard, Ae. *Just Alice* pp 169–170.
164 GCPPT 1|1|57 8 March 1940.
165 ibid.
166 Tillyard, Ae. *Naomi da Costa* p 62.
167 GCPPT 2|24|1 *Little Frida leaves School.*
168 Tillyard, Ae. *The Closer Walk with God* p 61.
169 Tillyard, HJW. Introduction to *The Letters of ACW Tillyard* (MTC).
170 Tillyard, Ae. *Naomi da Costa.* pp 102–103.
171 Tillyard, Ae. *The Centaur* pp 89–90. (GCPPT 2|21|3).
172 Tillyard, Ae. *The Centaur* p303 (GCPPT 2|21|1).
173 ibid. p 70.
174 Tillyard, Ae. *The Centaur* pp 89–90 (GCPPT 2|21|3).
175 ibid. p303 (GCPPT 2|21|1).
176 ibid. p 70 (GCPPT 2|21|1).

# The Way We Grow Up

The lady whose class young Frida joined following her ignominious departure from the Perse was Margaret Verrall, wife of Arthur Verrall of Trinity College, a couple jokingly described by adult Aelfrida as "very cultured, in fact … as cultured as it is possible for anyone to be". Margaret Verrall, no mean scholar herself (she was a graduate of and former lecturer at Newnham College) was a strict teacher of whom adult Aelfrida recalled being "terrified" because Mrs Verrall expected her new pupil to be as "industrious and accurate" as her own daughter Helen, "a sweet-natured, normal little girl trying desperately hard to be and do everything that earnest and distinguished parents expected of her", and to concentrate on *Bayfield's Latin Prose* instead of Frida's own "idea of learning": "Exploration and Discovery".[1] Lessons took place in a dedicated schoolroom at the top of the Verralls' house in Selwyn Gardens and though they took place only three mornings a week, were no sinecure, consisting as they did of Latin with Mrs Verrall and mathematics with Newnham don Mary Rickett; on days when no lessons took place and during the very short holidays allowed and unless she was absent from Cambridge, Frida was expected to study for two hours by herself. On weekday afternoons she attended German classes conducted by the Haddons' Swiss-German governess and as she grew more proficient, at Llandaff House. History and geography lessons from her mother were crammed in as space and time allowed in the latter's busy schedule. In French, of course, she was already proficient (she was also able to speak it at home, there being always "some French woman or other"[2] around the nursery, the latest being Bosie's successor, Jeanne Guy), but as 'a little severe mind-discipline'[3] she nightly practised mental arithmetic in that language; she also, when Eustace was old enough to begin home tuition with his father (he too did not attend school until he was eight), sat in on Greek lessons though she never became as fluent in that language as her brothers. English literature, other than children's classics, Shakespeare, and Dickens does not seem to have figured largely in her education (Eustace later described his family as "cultivated but not exactly literary")[4] nor any art or science. (Julius' account of his sister's education includes physics but she herself makes no reference to this and judging by her adult self's scandalised remarks

**Aelfrida, Julius, and Eustace Wetenhall with a friend c1895**

on the subject, biology was not included either.) Hence although Frida was provided with instruction 'as good as university coaching' in some subjects, of others she remained woefully ignorant and it may be for this reason that in November 1898 she obtained only a third class pass in the junior section of the same Local Examination taken by her mother in which mathematics were tested but languages and classics were not.

Of the other two girls seated round the schoolroom table (more joined them later but Aelfrida preferred to portray her classmates as an exclusive group) one was Helen Verrall, burdened like Frida herself with family surnames for middle names "which certainly gives a child something live up to"[5], a conventional little girl content to let Frida take the lead in games they played. (She was also disparagingly referred to by the latter as 'the virtuous Helen'[6] because stolid as she was, Helen could never be anything *but* virtuous; nor could she ever be as beautiful as her namesake, Helen of Troy, worship though her parents might — they were not, to Frida's dismay, churchgoers — "the Good, the Beautiful and the

True at some unseen Hellenic shrine".)[7] The other girl attracted Frida immediately because her dark, vivid, and unconventional brilliance echoed her own and she and Silvia soon became friends and – but only in fun ('*pour rire*') – enemies[8], Silvia being later to refer enviously to her fellow pupil's 'damn good brains'.[9]

Silvia had other attractions too: she had two brothers, one (Leo) as darkly brilliant as herself, she owned a pony on which Frida learnt to ride, she had a 'beautiful and fashionable' mother whose 'worldliness and showiness'[10] contrasted with Catharine Tillyard's unshowy (though not unworldly) demeanour, and her father, Frederic Myers, "school inspector, poet and spooker"[11], was a founder member of the Society for Psychical Research with which Margaret Verrall was also associated. Two further aspects of this glamorous Cambridge family drew Frida to it: its being mysteriously similar to her own in being "not hand in glove with the university set nor out of it but in some puzzling way above it", and, something particularly fascinating to a girl who saw ghosts, "there was always a chance of meeting [a medium] when you went to Leckhampton House"[12], the large house off Grange Road built by Myers for his family in 1881, the year prior to the founding of the SPR, and by the time of Frida's association with it an active centre of psychical research where "séances … produced most astonishing manifestations".[13]

It was in the garden of Leckhampton House that twelve-year-old Frida met one of the mediums in whom Frederic Myers was particularly interested, Eusepia Palladino, the Italian psychic brought to England by Myers and his associates in the summer of 1895 in order to ascertain if Eusapia was (as some suspected) a fraud or if she possessed truly mediumistic powers.[14] Aelfrida's later account of her meeting with Eusapia Palladino is intensely dramatic: arriving one day "merely intending to canter about the [paddock] on … the Welsh pony … Mr Myers called me [to meet] a foreign-looking lady [wearing] an untidy white silk wrapper … Looking at me intently [Eusapia] … caught both my hands in hers and cried 'you are a medium!'"

Frida, so she said, had not "the slightest idea what a medium was". (This may be so, but in Frida's hearing her father had already expressed shocked concern that "the Verralls were dabbling in Psychical Research" – Arthur Verrall, in fact, was not – and approached Mrs Verrall who assured him that she never discussed the subject with her pupils, and Frida herself had read enough SPR literature to be able to provide accurate spoofs thereof in Tillyard family magazines. She was also sufficiently aware of the medium's name to call one of Julius' bantams 'Ussapia'.) She was therefore somewhat put out to find herself hailed as one by someone who "knew nothing

about what I was or was not"[15] but Frederic Myers was sufficiently impressed by Eusapia's pronouncement to promise to "initiate" Frida when she was seventeen. ('I wonder – into what?'[16] wrote adult Aelfrida, being by then aware of Cambridge gossip with regard Myers' odd reputation with regard to male and female sexuality[17]; circumstances intervened and Myers was unable to initiate her, though had the prospect of his doing so been likely her parents would certainly have forbidden it.) Having herself "no desire to investigate the land of the shades"[18] at that point, Frida began to distance herself from a man whose tendency to "draw [her] down beside him on a garden seat" and to put his arm round her very demonstratively while he quoted poetry to her or talked 'vaguely [and] grandiloquently … of Higher Things' she found disconcerting: "when he did this I remembered it was time for me to go home". (Myers also sported a beard, something which may have awakened uneasy memories even as she was flattered by attention from a man she thought might in other circumstances have become 'a great mystic'.)[19] Julius, however, threw a different light on the subject when he noted (probably after his sister's death and as we shall see, definitely incorrectly) that "it was surely by the grace of God" that Frida never became what was then derisorily termed a 'spookist' or was tempted into "necromantic experiments"[20] by a man whose *Human Personality and its Survival after Bodily Death* was posthumously published in 1903.

Attendance at the socially stratified and snobbish Perse and association with a family who were neither hand in glove with the university nor out of it and with a Cambridge family who were so much part of a "small and exclusive" academic world in which "town did not count at all"[21] that they lived, socio-academically speaking, in the "best part of Cambridge" in "precincts" where no "nips or oiks or even townees"[22] would dare to live, seems to have awakened Frida to her own family's anomalous position as one "*in Cambridge but not of it*" and as one which could with justification be termed '*townee*'[23] in spite of her father having graduated from St John's College. (On her mother's side she had a longer Cambridge pedigree than most academics but it was, of course, a 'townee' not a university pedigree.) Her growing realisation had one immediate and two delayed effects: social insecurity became superimposed on and another symptom of wider and deeper insecurities with regard to her position and permanence within the family circle and not until much later in life could she bring herself to describe her 'townee' origins. (Her usual description of her family emphasised the scholarly, legal, medical, literary, or scientific qualifications of her father's and her own generations, not the achievements of past generations.) She also became an egregious snob.

Worse, however, than being a 'townee' was being 'in trade' (as the contemporary expression had it) and her 'trade' background was something with which Frida found it difficult to come to terms, so difficult, indeed, that it was not until long after it had ceased to matter (except to her and possibly also to Julius and Eustace, one of whom would disapprove of a son-in-law's livelihood, the other omit the word 'hop' from his description of his 'merchant' grandfather)[24] that she spoke or wrote of it.

Mary Tillyard's departure from Cambridge to London removed one source of shame though the existence in Norwich of boot and shoe manufacturers Tillyard and Howlett may have caused Frida to remember with dismay that her Norwich relatives were listed in nineteenth century trade and street directories and census returns as leather merchants, curriers (dressers and dyers of tanned leather), shoemakers, and proprietresses of small shoe shops, and that the Tillyards' Yarmouth origins suggested connections with the fishing industry or coastal trade.[25]

On her mother's side it was worse. Not only had hop merchant Henry Joseph Wetenhall (he was still listed in the 'trade' rather than the 'gentry' section of local street directories even after his apotheosis as owner/builder of his statement house on its mound in The Avenue) died within living memory, but those with longer memories might have known of Wetenhalls in humbler circumstances: the building and associated trades, breeches makers, soldiers, sailors, small school teachers, and so on. His death without leaving descendants with that name (save as a third given name) was also unlikely to promote premature forgetfulness, for his widow Emma Wetenhall still lived at Fordfield. Hence try as Henry Joseph Wetenhall's daughter might to claim illustrious ancestors by asserting a relationship to one Sir Henry Whetenhall (or Wettenhall or Wettinghall, the name was one of infinite variety even in Cambridge street directories) of Wellingborough in Lincolnshire, a connection initially claimed by Henry Joseph who placed a stag's head, said to be the family's emblem, in the stained glass window of Fordfield's entrance hall, Emma's married surname continued redolent of 'trade'.

As also, of course, did Emma's maiden name whose connections with the china and glass trade could hardly be denied: Barrett's china shop, once situated on the ground floor of a modest red brick building dwarfed by Great St Mary's Church, was now a sizeable emporium housed in a prominent turreted and bracketed Victorian building and an unmistakeable feature of Cambridge market place. Worse still, it seems, was the Barretts' pride in their ancestry. In 1782 Samuel Barrett, foreman of Josiah Wedgwood's Staffordshire pottery company, had migrated to Cambridge, a town already famous for crockery displayed at its annual Midsummer Fair (sometimes styled 'Pot Fair' because of this) as Wedgwood's local agent so that the company could "push the sale of fine china" to Cambridgeshire gentry inhabiting "the Halls and Great Houses of the county"[26] and to Cambridge colleges. From small beginnings in Jesus Lane, the business had increased to two shops, a depot, and a tenement for its workers in a Barnwell street named Staffordshire Street. Hence try as adult Aelfrida might to distance herself from people she referred as her 'remote Barrett cousin[s]'[27], the presence in Cambridge of living Barrett relations, of commercial properties emblazoned with the Barrett name, of Barrett tombs in Histon Road cemetery, and of daguerreotypes of Barrett family members and of the Barrett family Bible complete with family tree at Fordfield itself, can have done nothing to allow her to forget.

There was also the rather embarrassing tendency of Frida's extended family to marry into 'trade', Crundwells being descended from tanners and hop growers (or as a family record preferred to put it, well-to-do farmers), Boyles from a partner in the Minton pottery, rival in Staffordshire to the Wedgwoods, and Warrens from a wine and spirit merchant and from coal merchants (to see one of their wagons in a Cambridge street was agony to Frida; there were also several Warren tombs in the group of family graves surrounding Henry Joseph Wetenhall's) who had themselves married into families associated with milling, farming and – what was worse, for their department store was well known in Cambridge – merchandising, 'trade' in the purest sense.

Frida's social insecurities may have been heightened by her mother's tendency – a tendency marked, it may be, by her own insecurities with regard to where "the foot of her [societal] ladder was planted" – to regard her husband's position in Cambridge as less elevated than it should have been. Not only could journalism be regarded as a trade but there was also a degree of social opprobrium attached to it insofar as what started out as investigative journalism could easily degenerate into scandal-mongering and what was printed liable to bias insofar as a newspaper proprietor's personal views inevitably influenced his paper's content; furthermore, the sale of any newspaper depends on providing its readers with what they want to read. (It is worth remembering that the respectable *CIP* was not – or, rather, had not been until recently – above retailing gossip, that Alfred Tillyard was a fanatical Liberal, and that it was because its proprietor/editor's views diverged too widely from those of his readers that he was later forced to resign.) In all respects, therefore, Catharine Tillyard, anxious to see her daughter removed from the inherited taint of 'trade' in order to marry well, saw no shame in acting the part of a "social climber".[28]

Catharine's social climbing seems to have begun soon after Conrad's birth marked (as she thought) the completion of her family; prior to that she was chiefly engaged in local Liberal politics and in supporting Alfred Tillyard's campaigns for Teetotalism. Hence although Conrad's death may have been responsible for propelling her into the "very very busy" life of "committees and case-papers" with which she filled hours otherwise given to melancholic broodings over her dead child, it was also, it seems, a desire to rise in society which propelled her onto committees on which she met "all sorts of aristocratic ladies"[29] and the wives of eminent Cambridge academics, of whom Florence Keynes, wife of John Neville Keynes, lecturer in moral sciences at Pembroke College, was paradigmatically one.[30]

Florence Keynes, born in 1861, was herself already active in social work endeavour (Aelfrida was later to describe her as "the blessing and the terror of the Cambridge poor")[31] and it may have been under the younger woman's care and guidance that distraught Catharine Tillyard was induced to undertake activities which would allow her to focus her attention on needy others instead of her needy self. Florence, furthermore, had three children (her eldest son, John Maynard Keynes, was only four months older than Frida) and was well placed to commiserate with a woman who had recently lost a child of much the same age as her own, to rejoice when Eustace was old enough to join his sister in games with Maynard and his younger siblings Margaret and Geoffrey (Julius and Maynard were later contemporaries at St Faith's; unlike his sister who chose to remember young Maynard as a spoilt mummy's boy, Julius made no later comments regarding the Keynes children) and to support Catharine Tillyard through family trials in times to come.

Catharine Tillyard's campaign as 'social climber' was carefully orchestrated, so carefully in fact that although her daughter was later to write rather disparagingly of it, she herself had no hesitation in emulating her mother when occasion demanded. Catharine began by employing her contacts with philanthropic "dons' wives" as an excuse for weekly At Homes to which those ladies were invited and for providing at them the splendiferous teas for which Fordfield became renowned, and for inviting wives and husbands (the latter being the real reason for her acting as she did: "if only she could gather dons around her...") to "recherché ... 'little' dinners and 'little' lunches"[32] at which she proclaimed herself an ardent admirer of Cambridge's "Aristocracy of Intellect". Realising, however, that entrée to this 'aristocracy' demanded more of her than her cook's culinary skills and that if she was to become (as once before) the initiator of "a buzz of highbrow conversation" and

"the centre of intellectual discussion" she would have to qualify herself for entry first, Catharine began to read *The Times* assiduously from leading article to "last-leader humour".[33] It seems she was successful: her children became the playmates of children of the first generation of university dons permitted by statute to marry without relinquishing their college place and Fordfield became once more (but not completely: the Tillyards never wholly overcame their 'trade' and 'townee' taints) a but not *the* place of resort for Cambridge's academic intelligentsia. Academia reciprocated, the Tillyards and, when they were old enough, their children, being invited to parties in college Masters' Lodges and to the private houses of married dons – but here again, and for a different but associated reason, those with whom the Tillyards chiefly mixed, though no less part of Cambridge's 'aristocracy of intellect', were of Nonconformist rather than Anglican persuasion, the majority of their academic friends being drawn from the largely university-based congregation of St Columba's Church. This, together with their Liberal politics (the Liberal party attracted Nonconformists and businessmen) and teetotal principles may have been another reason for their de facto if not *de jure* marginalisation by Cambridge society's crème de la crème: "Tillyards", as adult Aelfrida noted, "are used to being in a minority".[34]

Minority or not, Frida's later childhood and early adolescence was probably a happy and privileged time during which, or so it must have seemed to her relieved parents, the storms and stresses of earlier years cleared away. Materially the Tillyard children wanted for nothing, though life at Fordfield was comfortable rather than luxurious, frugality encouraged, and waste of any kind decried. The Christian religion in general and Presbyterianism in particular were pervasive but not portentous influences in their lives, the tenor of their religious beliefs and practices being chiefly coloured by the way in which "grown up people's voices [adopted] a specially ... reverent intonation when they read what Jesus did and particularly when they read His words aloud" (the children instinctively avoided New Testament stories when acting out Biblical stories in the nursery lest their behaviour seem disrespectful to "His holy deeds and words") and by being taught that God was "the real master of Fordfield" even though it belonged to 'Dear'. Of this master it was also said that His every bidding was to be performed cheerfully and willingly in terms of "an intense unquestioned belief" that "Christianity was wholly true and God and Jesus altogether to be worshipped", that the Bible was a book "entirely in a class by itself", and that doubts which might creep into one's mind on the subject of belief were "rather silly" and "only fit for undergraduates in their second year".[35] (Interestingly, in view of their parents' insistence on their particular brand of 'True Religion'[36], neither Julius nor Frida experienced any difficulty in reconciling their "Christian prayers [of] every evening and on Sundays [worshipping] … the Christian God" with their pagan weekday games of 'Gods and Goddesses' in the kitchen garden during which they "placated" – a powerful word, given that Frida was not, so she said, afraid of deities, pagan or otherwise – the Greek pantheon "by impersonating them".)[37] Furthermore, inclusion in religious ceremonies was regarded as a *privilege* insofar as "small people were admitted to occupations which grownups prized" i.e. to Sunday attendance at church because "Sunday was … the best day of the week". ("It was so superior … that it even had hymns addressed to it".) An even greater privilege was being allowed to stay for the "forty minutes of Presbyterian intellectualism"[38] which comprised the sermon – but relegated to a side-aisle pew in case misbehaviour brought on by boredom and discomfort (as had once happened) occurred.

Though discipline was enforced, Catharine and Alfred Tillyard's child-rearing regime was ahead of its time insofar as the children generally and vocal Frida in particular were expected to be seen *and* heard: indeed, as Alfred Tillyard firmly informed Florence Boyle, a cousin of his wife's who complained that at table Frida was encouraged "to air her opinions which are, of course, completely valueless", it was important to him to hear his children's voiced thoughts, that Frida's opinions, far from being valueless, possessed intrinsic merit "as the opinions of a child", and that development of the art of 'suitable' conversation was a *duty* owed by a child to its family and society.[39] Florence's second criticism, namely that 'the children [were] dragged in everywhere'[40], was more justified, for Julius (when not at school), Frida (whose hours of formal schooling were shorter) and even Eustace frequently accompanied their parents to events they might have been expected to attend alone but which they decided would benefit their children morally or educationally. In May 1897, for example, Frida and Eustace singly or together accompanied their parents on two important occasions: to the University Senate House to hear the result of voting for or against the awarding of degrees to women students (the Tillyards were 'of course … in favour of women having degrees' and, caught up in the crowd, forced witnesses of rowdy undergraduates' unpleasant behaviour towards those who voted in favour) and to the laying of the foundation stone of Westminster Theological College, a Nonconformist establishment occupying a prominent position on the corner of Cambridge's Queens and Madingley Roads.[41]

And although inclusion in 'grown-up' activities such as these was interspersed with childish sociability – birthday parties at the Haddons, tea parties with Helen Verrall or with children of members of St Columba's – it is obvious that many were undertaken with the specific aim of acquainting Frida with the social mores and responsibilities of young ladies in her position and, young as she was, of making her known to mothers of potential suitors, an activity known as 'aunting' (the inclusion of aunts expanded marital networking's potential exponentially) when applied by female relatives to eligible girls who had 'come out' into society at the age of seventeen or eighteen and to young men deemed suitable by a mama for engineering into an alliance with her daughter: attendance at an At Home party (a major summer social event not to be confused with modest weekly 'At Homes' held for women friends) or at a 'Cambridge Place Mothers'[42] party held annually at Fordfield for working-class woman members of a mission opened in a disadvantaged area of the town as part of St Columba's pastoral work among the local poor; a chaperoned visit to a male cousin's college rooms or a tea party at Newnham with Presbyterian female students attending St Columba's; a visit to an infant school maintained by the local board of education to inspect modern teaching methods or to Girton to watch an 'entertainment'[43] put on by local schoolchildren; a 'trip' to Babraham Hall, home of local gentry, to arrange a Sunday School picnic in the grounds. (Frida did not herself attend Sunday School – that was for poor 'townee' children – but was happy to participate in cricket matches with teams of boys and girls from it.) With her father, Frida also attended 'an awfully grand affair', a garden party in Trinity College fellows' garden hosted by the then mayor of Cambridge, Horace Darwin.[44]

In one respect, however, Frida seems to have differed from her peers: for a young person of her sex and era she was allowed a considerable amount of freedom and though frequently accompanied on local expeditions, it was not unknown for her to undertake journeys away from or back to Cambridge alone, experiences which fostered confidence and independence in one devoid by circumstance of both and enabled her to deal pragmatically with problems encountered en route: cheeky 'oiks' (quelled by force of personality), not being met at her destination (she transported her own belongings and organised her own arrival), runaway donkeys (a story not related to her parents), and mechanical breakdowns.

Mechanical breakdowns, chiefly punctures, necessitating a long walk home or causing a "sudden spill" when a sharp object caught under the single hand-brake of a bicycle with pneumatic tyres but no inner tube made "a long slit … along the tyre"[45], were a problem frequently encountered and composedly dealt with by "the earliest girl cyclist in Cambridge"[46] in her "hideous brown alpaca bicycling dress, [its] brown knickers scarcely hidden by a short skirt attached to a plain bodice with a sailor collar"[47], an outfit deemed scandalously revealing even for a girl of ten by conservative Warren relations. But it was not only Frida who bicycled – the newly fashionable pursuit was adopted enthusiastically by Cambridge ladies because of the freedom of movement it allowed (it was deemed too frivolous to be indulged in on Sundays[48] and masculine worries were expressed regarding the indecency of exposed ankles and the sexual satisfaction to be derived from bicycle saddles) and by the whole Tillyard family save Julius. Rides of up to twenty miles were undertaken (nine-year-old Eustace's first ride was a return trip of eight miles, his second ten; aunts Anna and Fanny thought nothing of cycling in full Victorian dress from London to Cambridge; and a solo visit to young friends living in Odsey near Royston – their father, George Fordham, was a gentleman farmer, JP, and 'notable expert' in cartography[49] – involved Frida in a lengthy ride there and another back of which she wrote nonchalantly that 'the seventeen miles seemed like five')[50], with rain the only excuse for cancelling or abandoning an outing: returning from a visit to Warren relatives in St Ives (a twenty-two-mile round trip, abandoned after four miles two days earlier because a storm threatened) Frida and her mother got very wet but 'we changed our clothes and ... think we shall be none the worse'.[51]

Other fashionable modern hobbies practised by the Tillyards encompassed lawn tennis played on their own or other families' courts (the children also played squash and, later, 'ping pong' as table tennis was then called), and stamp collecting, the latter an enthusiasm on which considerable sums were expended and considerable expertise shown by Frida who not only possessed an album of her own but was also allowed to undertake 'the great work' of sorting '15,000 imperforate red penny English according to their characteristics', these then to form the basis of the family's 'English specialism'.[52] Julius was also a keen photographer who made his own cameras and simpler ones for his brother and sister and developed his own films (he was not, so his sister later wrote, "one of those amateurs who call themselves photographers, [but] worked with a half-plate stand camera and produced beautiful pictures")[53] and allowed Frida to use his equipment; indeed, it is largely due to Julius' and Frida's interest in photography that so many family photographs exist.

Garden pursuits continued though those of earlier childhood were now abandoned in favour of building a hut (ever-pessimistic Julius was 'sure it won't be a success')[54] and keeping chickens, though not gardening as

such – that was the gardener's preserve – except insofar as Frida noted the theological affinities of one particular incumbent (Hubbard, she said, "looked like an apostle ... and by ... indefinable silent intimation ... walked with God")[55] and wondered if she might later follow his example as a 'lady-gardener'. Literary pursuits played an increasingly important role: Julius, now so fluent in Latin that he could converse and keep his diary in it, being so appreciative that he was moved to copy out Latin hymns for the sheer beauty of their language[56], Frida discovering the joys of reading: "curled up in an armchair in [her] father's study with an apple for refreshment", she poured over books some might think incongruous reading for a girl barely in her teens: Bunyan's *Pilgrim's Progress* whose "vivid illustrations haunted [her] imagination for days afterwards", Milton's *Paradise Lost,* John Wesley's *Journal,* John Greenleaf Whittier's hymn-like poems, *The Christian Year,* "some old volume of the legends of the saints", and *Quo Vadis,* a newly published and translated novel by Polish writer Henryk Sienkiewiecz[57], whose religious overtones seemed unlikely to appeal to a girl who "found simple Low Church Christianity extremely satisfying"[58] and whose church attendance, 'privileged' though it was, was enjoyed chiefly for the feeling of importance it engendered, as a social occasion, and for the superb Sunday lunch which followed it. All, however, were books devoured for what they suggested of "further adventures when one should be grown up".[59]

Literary pursuits were not, however, confined to reading. Between 1890 and 1892 and possibly later still, Julius and Frida collaborated in the production of home-made magazines, small stitched booklets with an illustrated cover and containing illustrations within the text also: *The Monthly Pets, The Monthly Illustrated,* and *Blue and Green,* the latter notable for being 'edited by Miss F Tillyard'.[60] Entries probably written by Frida refer to seaside holidays, to Eustace's propensity for playing up after being put to bed 'because he is afraid of the dark'[61], and to nursery tea, an illustrated dialogue between a small girl and her nurse being followed by little Lily's descent to the drawing room where her mother reads aloud to her; a watercolour cartoon of Mercury with his caduceus entitled "I've seen Appolo (*sic*) Quicky. Oh! let's go"[62] is possibly also by her. (Eustace himself was probably too young to contribute though he appears as the "little boy in breeches" who rules the household and who plays practical jokes on his sister and ruins his brother's hat by using it as a football; a fragmentary story about a midshipman who takes charge in a fight with pirates on a voyage to Jamaica may have been written specially for him.) Julius' probable contributions include comic poems and a serial entitled *My Adventures in the Arctic Region.* (Frank

Tillyard's serial, *Arthur Foster,* was a school story whose hero 'Henry Drews' bore Henry Julius' childish name for himself.) More interesting, perhaps, than the content of the siblings' literary productions – though this in itself is interesting for what it reveals of their lives and unspoken nuances thereof – is what the productions reveal of Frida's already well-developed literary capacity in which creativity, wit, an ear for dialogue, and an ability to invent and sustain a plot is manifest.

References to military musicians and an illustration of a four-man band suggest that the young Tillyards' practical creativity was not confined to the making of craft items for bazaars, to the building of huts, and to the creation of house magazines: the increasingly militarised political manoeuvring in South Africa which preceded the Boer War of 1899–1902 inspired them to form 'the Fordfield company of the Cambridge Volunteers' with Julius ('Lieutenant', then 'Captain' Tillyard) as its commanding officer, Frida ('Lieutenant Wetenhall') as second in command, Eustace as 'Corporal Mandeville', and co-opted visitors and nursemaids as lance corporals and privates.[63] Each child played an instrument in the company band and at Frida's instigation ('a brilliant idea … confided to Julius')[64] put on concerts for their parents, 'Dear', and visitors and, on one memorable occasion, for Zelle (co-opted into the company as 'Lance Corporal Aubriet') when she paid a pre-marriage visit to her former pupils.

Although it is hard to discern at this distance and from accounts written much later by adult Aelfrida whether Alfred and Catharine Tillyard's unusually liberal upbringing of their surviving children was advanced for the Victorian era because of their interest in modern educational methods (although much of Julius', Frida's and Eustace's lives were based in and around the second floor nursery suite, they were by no means sequestered there nor was their play confined to the enactment of religious stories or the reading of 'improving' books and though Sunday was kept as a special day, 'Dear's' attempts to impose a Sabbatarian regime were overridden by her son-in-law's insistence on outdoor activities), or an attempt to repair the damage inflicted on their two older children in 1888/89, or a mixture of the two of which Eustace was a double beneficiary, all three children benefited enormously. Headstrong, impetuous, and self-centred Frida probably benefited most (Julius, depressed and repressed, benefited too, but in other ways, liberation from his mother's tyranny being possibly the greatest), absorbing positive lessons concerning collaboration and cooperation, stoic endurance of difficult situations, perseverance with formidable tasks (every volume of every magazine 'edited by Miss Frida Tillyard' was issued in several identical copies, each of which had to be copied out and its

illustrations redrawn), and the importance of self-education and solo study and of productive pastimes. (Trivial or time-wasting pastimes were forbidden in any case and specifically girlish pursuits seem to have played little part in Frida's life.) The part to be played in a Christian life by sensitivity to the needs of disadvantaged or weaker members of society was also emphasised, the Cambridge Place Mothers' tea-party being a case in point, for not only was an abundance of nourishing food provided but hymns were also sung and prayers said. But although Frida absorbed the lessons and was later keen to criticise their non-observance in others, she either failed to see their relevance to herself or honoured them more in the breach than in the observance and this, together with certain negative lessons unconsciously absorbed during the impressionable years of early childhood, were to manifest themselves as unendearing character traits which soured relationships with those not privy or unsympathetic to formative influences and events in her earlier life.

Among the negative lessons was the advantage accruing to one noted by her grand-daughter to be 'quite an invalid'.[65] At the time of writing (the latter months of 1897) this was true but as late as mid-July 1897 Emma Wetenhall's health had so far improved that she was able to leave her bedroom ('Dear … came downstairs today')[66] and even to pay rare visits to church ('it must be years since she last went')[67] or, her Bath chair pushed by members of the family, to pay social calls; she was also well enough to accompany Catharine Tillyard, Eustace, and Frida on an extended summer holiday in Bedfordshire. Her death on 30 November that same year therefore seems to have taken the family by surprise because she had been "so often at the point of death that [her] last moment was unexpected when it did come"[68], sudden worsening of her health in the autumn seeming to presage another crisis (they were frequent) rather than terminal illness. The engagement of a "nurse-attendant"[69] to lighten Catharine Tillyard's already heavy nursing load (she attended to her bedridden mother's needs for two to three hours every morning) announced the beginning of the end and Aunt Fanny, now a qualified nurse, was summoned from London to oversee 'Dear's' final hours. Frida, for her part, found her first sight of a corpse solemnising and her experience of a Victorian funeral 'dreadful' because she did not 'seem to be any use'[70] and because her mother rejected offers of help. Her reaction, however, was not grief but disengagement: 'I seem like a person in a story'.[71]

More relevant to Frida's future conduct were unconscious lessons absorbed from 'Dear's' comportment in general and from the advantages accruing to one deemed 'quite an invalid' even when comparatively well: regular daughterly attendance; tender nursing care; expressions of surprise and delight when one was sufficiently recovered to re-enter the family circle; special transport arrangements guaranteed to draw sympathetic glances; a bedroom somewhat removed from the bustle of family life but a place where "all the movement of the house centred in her" nevertheless, a room entered only by invitation and where there was "only quietness"[72] and to which an invalid could retreat at any time and where objects of special interest were displayed on Sundays; subjection only to occupations thought suitable for one of impaired strength; provision of "special delicacies"[73] in order that one might maintain such strength as one had; having one's welfare considered before anyone else's; the importance of wearing distinctive even if rather old-fashioned items of dress (in 'Dear's' case, a black silk dress and an impressive tulle cap) which singled one out as worthy of notice and respect; the advantage – as if the above were insufficient – of being regarded as "not an ordinary person … but not yet an angel" because one keeps one's Bible and Prayer Book always to hand and because one is regarded as something of a "*moritura*"[74], literally someone about to die but for practical purposes someone waiting with Christian patience and submission until God wills death. Finally, an edifying deathbed to which absent members of the family are 'sent for'.[75]

It was not only in matters of health that Frida's maternal grandmother set standards of behaviour which her granddaughter thought worthy of emulation. (Emma Wetenhall's conduct was not untypical: Frida's Cambridge contemporary Gwen Raverat noted that in her grandparents' house an unwholesome attitude to sickness prevailed, that ill-health was considered the norm, that it was generally regarded as "a distinction and a mournful pleasure to be ill", that far too much attention was paid to minor illnesses, and that children tended to imitate the invalidish habits of adults to whom they were particularly attached.)[76] For one thing, observant Frida noted the way in which Emma Wetenhall wielded authority as the 'master' of Fordfield but concealed her iron fist in a pious glove; for another, how easy it was to be rewarded for behaviour which in another person or context might be regarded as selfish by behaving in a meek but manipulative manner e.g. by "never grumbl[ing] or expect[ing] any [one] to sympathise … over anything". She also noted how pleasant it was to accept favours even as one proclaimed oneself "far too sensitive"[77] to ask them and how beneficial it was to one's self-esteem and to the esteem in which one was held by others to be seen to perform 'good works' such as visiting a "queer-looking old pauper" bedridden with dropsy to bestow on her flowers and gifts and to discuss God with her in a frank manner *never* adopted at home.[78]

Other lessons to be learnt resulted from Frida's observations of the family's relationship with its servants, specifically with employee Ellen Ison. Ellen, one of eight children of an agricultural labourer in a Cambridgeshire village, came to Fordfield sometime during Julius' and Frida's childhood. Originally employed as a housemaid, she arrived on a week's trial but was still there thirty years later, her attributes of being "always happy, always ready to help, full of fun in the kitchen, delighted if she were called on to give extra care [and] a perfect nurse if anyone were ill"[79] endearing her to the whole family and ensuring promotion from maid to cook before she and the Tillyards parted company in 1919. Well treated as were all the Fordfield servants (neither Emma Wetenhall nor Catharine Tillyard had difficulty in finding or keeping staff: departing servants replaced themselves "by a sister, a cousin or a friend")[80], Ellen reciprocated by adopting the family as her own, sharing its joys and sorrows and by her happiness and with her "bright eyes and broad smile"[81] bringing cheer to what must have been a rather cheerless house; indeed, she became so much a part of the family that she accompanied members on holiday to look after the children or to assist 'Dear'. The family became even more reliant on Ellen following Emma Wetenhall's death, Catharine Tillyard in particular regarding Ellen as a friend and acting as if 'the foundations of her world'[82] rested on her diminutive servant's shoulders.

The lessons Frida learnt from Ellen Ison's relationship with her mother and grandmother were mixed: that if one served with dog-like devotion, one was treated well and though only a servant was rewarded by inclusion in one's employer's pleasures; that regardless of being treated as a family friend, one must never forget one's place in the social hierarchy for if one did, one would be liable to be dismissed from one's post; that servants by their very nature were there to *serve* and could be exploited with impunity. Only much later did adult Aelfrida remember with regret days in bed taken 'without remorse'[83] with Ellen to wait on her, she herself retiring to bad merely for a little peace and quiet or because she had an indisposition so minor that without Ellen she would have soldiered on. And only much later still did she note that by expecting Ellen to give up her own holiday to attend to 'Dear' on hers, the Tillyards were imposing on her good nature and exploiting her need for money to support a widowed mother who 'managed' her family only by undertaking menial tasks by day and, sometimes, by night.

Frida's attraction to boys of her own age continued throughout her later childhood. Boys seem to have regarded, the sparky, inventive, talkative young girl with her enjoyment of boyish pursuits as one of themselves though there was often a romantic element involved too:

she names more than one "little sweetheart" encountered by the age of ten, among them Oswin Creighton ("I could never marry anyone with red hair … worse still, he called me F'ida and a 'feeder' was a bib such as we had to wear at meals")[84], Willie Lindsay a 'gentle fair-haired little boy … who proposed to me one morning in the rain … I disliked [him] intensely'[85], and Ernest Haddon, a 'subdued … heavy, informative and wonderfully friendly'[86] boy for whom Frida herself felt an 'abortive passion'.[87] (Other 'passions' included the Fordfield boot-boy and a local curate.) She also enumerates presents presented by young admirers such as sweets and a mole. (Hubbard exhibited a 'small rage' with regard to the latter.) But it was to Julius that her affections were chiefly given. Writing at the age of thirteen 'and ¾', Frida noted how she and her brother had 'always been companions'[88] and "used to do everything together"[89] and that although they had now abandoned childish pursuits 'played together', their relationship had developed into one of mutual admiration and exchanged confidences, Julius confiding his plans to a sister towards whom he was invariably helpful and uncensorious, whom he never scolded when she was silly but "just looked grave", and on whom he 'never looked down [as] some boys do to their sister', Frida listening avidly to what 'Dudu' had to say and longing to be "as good and clever" as he believed her to be.[90]

But Julius, two years older than his beloved sister, was now adolescent. In September 1895, parting company with his preparatory school acquaintance 'Maynardus' Keynes (at a lunch party held in 1931 'Maynardus' reminisced to Dudu and Frida about their 'childhood together'; sadly, adult Aelfrida did not record what he said)[91], he departed aged nearly fourteen and at 'Dear's' command because it was something of a Barrett tradition, and also, it may be, because it was thought judicious to separate him from the sister to whom he was emotionally attached, for a boarding establishment "which could *just* claim to be a Public School"[92], Tonbridge School in Kent.

He hated it. Separated from the "*summa … concordia*" of Fordfield (an unwitting irony, surely, given how little harmony had once reigned there, though he retained – and missed – the friendship extended to him by his beloved '*soror*') and prone to despise his fellow scholars as cowardly, crude, stupid, lying, blasphemous and sodomitical[93], Julius decided that in order to be "*let alone*" and to prevent other boys from thinking him "different" to themselves, he would "conform outwardly … while remaining inwardly aloof from [his] companions".[94] He therefore feigned an interest in sport, clubs, fads and even in the Public School Volunteers with whom he, the most pacific of people, attended camp. (Hence references by his sister to Julius 'drilling' his younger '*soror*' and '*frater*' when home on holiday and to their enjoying it 'awfully'[95], to the siblings' Fordfield 'Company', and in his own short stories to the impedimenta of a quasi-military camp.) Being, as his sister noted, 'very clever' and "keen on work"[96], Julius flourished academically, winning two scholarships and combining his existing interest in classical languages and music with a new love of mathematics in a manner which augured well for a later lifelong interest; he also made a lifelong friend in one James Stark whose life as boy and man was to be curiously intertwined with that of Julius' sister but both at Tonbridge and later had otherwise very few. His departures for school at the beginning of each term were greeted with downcast demeanour and by Frida with dismay, her wishing 'Dudu had been with us'[97] on social occasions demonstrating how much she missed him and her worrying that, when at home, Julius found her company boring and herself 'stupid' in comparison to his intellectual pursuits[98] that she feared that his and her former closeness might be lessening.

This was not the case – brother and sister closeness was to be lifelong – though Frida's irrational but explicable worries on that score may have contributed to the tenacity with which she adhered to a friendship begun in the summer of 1892 with a girl a few months younger than herself and ever after regarded as her 'Dearest and Best Friend'.[99]

Lucy Alice Longstaffe, born in May 1884, was the daughter of barrister, later County Court judge, Amyas Longstaffe, whose family the Tillyards met on a seaside holiday in Littlehampton, then one of the fashionable resorts (Bexhill, Bournemouth, and Hunstanton were others) to which they moved for an extended period in the summer when Julius, Eustace, and Frida were small, together with Ellen, 'Bosey', and "mountains of luggage". (With his family settled in rented accommodation, Alfred Tillyard "used to go off to Cambridge now and then to write letters and see that Fordfield was all right".) Having singled out Lucy from a group of holidaying children to be her 'Best Friend' and both sets of parents having ascertained that the girls' friendship was more than a holiday affair, it was arranged that Lucy pay an annual visit to Cambridge and that Frida accompany Lucy on summer holidays and pay shorter visits to the Longstaffes' London residence, the latter in particular a plan with which Frida readily concurred ("the idea of going to stay with my dear little [friend] was almost overwhelmingly sweet")[100] even if this meant temporary separation from her beloved Julius. (That Julius may have felt somewhat put out by his sister's sudden intimacy with and affection for a child other than himself may be deduced from his description of Lucy as a "pale, quiet, rather simple-minded girl"[101] whose admiration for his sister was limited only by her disapproval of Frida's pranks. Catharine Tillyard, conversely, described her as "a sweet girl … better looking than Frida but not nearly as fetching'".[102] Adult Aelfrida remembered Lucy as a perfect little lady whose opinions, if she had them, were, unlike Frida's own, kept to herself.)[103] Reciprocal visits duly took place, Frida discovering on Lucy's to Fordfield that she loved Lucy more and more each time "though not, of course, as much as Julius"[104] and that on Lucy's departure she felt 'so lonely without her' and wished Lucy could live at Fordfield 'always'.[105]

Want of a local girlish playmate and confidante – it is surely significant that Frida fastened onto Lucy at just the time when she found herself friendless at the Perse and separated from Julius by his beginning formal schooling at St Faith's – seems to have enabled her to overcome her fear of leaving home. ("Few experiences in life are more thrilling to the inexperienced than going all alone into a different home where not only the house and furniture are different but the family look at everything from a different point of view"[106] would have been an unlikely statement for her to have made at this point in her life had she not been about to visit her 'Dearest and Best Friend' in London, Hampshire, or the Home Counties.) Such visits were also instrumental in introducing her to a normal happy family whose contrast to her own may have caused the perceptive girl to realise just how 'different' hers was (and why) and to decide as a result never to reveal its strangeness.

Mrs Longstaffe, though dismissed by Julius as a 'social climber' (this may have been sour grapes; the Longstaffes, as Frida's later descriptions of a "diner-de-family" which was very much "the Real Thing, with men-servants in livery behind our chairs" and visits to the Hampstead mansion of "Sir Spencer Wells, the great doctor [who] might have come straight from tending Queen Victoria"[107], or to parties held in Park Lane show, the Longstaffes moved in social circles higher than the Tillyards, a fact which doubtless endeared them to Catharine Tillyard and encouraged her to do everything possible to maintain her growing daughter's friendship with theirs) seems to have been 'warm-hearted and welcoming' and 'always very sweet' to Frida, teasing her as she grew up about the 'bed curtains' of long hair replacing her fringe and bob and nicknaming her 'Friday'[108] to emphasise how helpful the latter was to her husband in copying out legal drafts in her neat hand. (Frida's own mother, though 'so sweet that it [was] no use trying to describe her'[109], devoted more time to good works and to her own mother than to her daughter.) With clean-shaven Amyas Longstaffe Frida was so much at ease that she called him 'Dad' (of her own father she wrote 'we … love him very much

and are not a bit afraid of him'[110] as if to convince herself that it was so; with Oswin Creighton's heavily-bearded father, on the other hand, she had felt sufficiently at ease prior to Conrad's death to sit on his knee 'munching ice and cinnamon [while] listening to his wonderful stories')[111] and indulged in "great arguments" in the course of which he and she "thrashed out" topics (Temperance and theatres)[112] concerning which Frida had already expressed worries undisclosed to her parents ("those who went to the theatre went to Hell")[113] or with regard to which she was being indoctrinated (of a claret cup offered at a Longstaffe party she wrote "it reeked of the Devil")[114] or to which she had already closed her mind to there being any other point of view, namely religion.

But perhaps the most significant event of the five years (1891–96) during which Frida passed from childhood to adolescence happened on 23 December 1896: she recommenced her diary.

## Notes

1 GCPPT 2|25|1(2).
2 JCA Mss R32 *Reminiscences /EMW Tillyard.*
3 GCPPT 1|1|1 9 March 1897.
4 JCA Mss R32 *Reminiscences /EMW Tillyard.*
5 GCPPT 2|25|1(2).
6 GCPPT 1|1|27 6 September 1923.
7 GCPPT 2|25|1(2).
8 GCPPT 1|1|27 29 June 1923.
9 GCPPT 1|1|21 4 November 1916.
10 GCPPT 1|1|60 18 January 1943.
11 Tillyard, HJW. Introduction to *The Letters of ACW Tillyard* (MCT). Information on the SPR is widely available but three books on which I have chiefly relied in what follows are Blum, D. *Ghost Hunters*, Katz, D. *The Occult Tradition*, and Schultz, B. *Henry Sidgwick.*
12 GCPPT 2|25|1(2).
13 Tillyard, Ae. *Just Alice* p 131 (GCPPT 2|19).
14 Blum, D. p 201.
   Katz, D. p 128.
15 GCPPT 2|25|1(2).
16 GCPPT 1|1|60 18 January 1943.
17 Schultz, B. pp 93–94 and 238–284.
18 GCPPT 2|25|1(2).
19 GCPPT 2|25|1(2).
   GCPPT 1|1|60 18 January 1943.
20 Tillyard, HJW. Introduction to *The Letters of ACW Tillyard* (MTC).
21 Raverat, G. p 47.
22 GCPPT 2|25|1(2). An 'oik' was a person (usually but not invariably from a lower social class than oneself) who behaved in an uncouth or obnoxious manner and a 'nip' a lower class minor criminal. Lower class people with whom one came in contact in a business or service capacity were 'persons'; all or none might be 'townees', some might be 'in trade'.
23 GCPPT 1|1|71 10 February 1954. The phrase is repeated verbatim in *Just Alice* p 2.
24 JCA R32 *Reminiscences /EMW Tillyard.*
25 It is possible that the Tillyard connection with the manufacture of leather goods stemmed from the seventeenth century marriage of a Yarmouth Tillyard with a Norwich girl of Huguenot descent; Huguenots were often experienced leather workers especially with regard to leather required for luxury products.

26 GCPPT 2|27|1(1).
27 GCPPT 1|1|44 22 May 1933.
28 Tillyard, Ae. *Naomi da Costa* p 133 (GCPPT 2|22).
29 ibid. p 16.
30 For the background to what follows I am indebted to Robert Skidelsky's magisterial *John Maynard Keynes* (1992).
31 Tillyard, Ae. *Marrying a Stranger* pp 25–26 (GCPPT 2|6).
32 Tillyard, Ae, *Naomi da Costa* p 133.
33 Tillyard, Ae. *Naomi da Costa*. p 133.
34 GCPPT 2|24|1 *Little Frida leaves School*.
35 GCPPT 2|26|4(9)
   Tillyard, Ae. *Marrying a Stranger* pp 61–63.
36 GCPPT 2|26|4(9).
37 GCPPT 2|26|4(2).
38 Tillyard, Ae. *Christian Old Age* pp 9–10 (GCPPT 2|17).
39 GCPPT 2|23 *The Watchword* June 1957.
   GCPPT 1|1|62 30 April 1944. Florence Boyle ('Aunt Florence') was one of the two daughters of Emma Wetenhall's sister Susanna. She was known for her plain speaking and her tendency to criticise aspects of life at Fordfield. She never married. For details of her life see GCPPT 2|27|2(4).
40 GCPPT 1|1|2 15 July 1897.
41 GCPPT 1|1|1 21 and 25 May 1897.
42 GCPPT 2|23 *The Watchword* June 1956.
43 GCPPT 1|1|1 20 March 1897.
44 GCPPT 1|1|2 17 June 1897.
45 Tillyard, Ae. *Just Alice* p 105.
46 Tillyard, HJW. Introduction to *The Letters of ACW Tillyard* (MTC).
47 GCPPT 2|27|1(6).
48 For the early history of bicycling in Cambridge see Keynes, F. *Gathering up the Threads* and Keynes, M. *A House by the River*.
49 GCPPT 2|25|3(10).
50 GCPPT 1|1|2 3 August 1897.
51 ibid. 13 August 1897. A pencil sketch of herself and her mother cycling in pouring rain has 'rain' written underneath.
52 GCPPT 1|1|2 19 July and 9 August 1897.
53 Tillyard, Ae. *The Way We Grow Up* p 45.
54 GCPPT 1|1|1 17 April 1897.
55 GCPPT 2|27|2 (3).
56 Tillyard, Ae. *Messages* pp 9–15.
57 *Quo Vadis*, first published in 1895 and in English in 1896, tells the story of the love of a Roman patrician living in the reign of Nero for a young Christian woman. The novel is notable both for its accurate historical details and for the appearance in it of real people, including Nero himself and Saints Peter and Paul. Henryk Sienkiewicz (1846–1916) was a prolific popular novelist and was awarded the Nobel Prize for Literature in 1905.
58 Tillyard, Ae. *Marrying a Stranger* pp 61–63.
59 Tillyard, Ae. *Christian Old Age* pp 6–7.
60 Copies of the magazines are preserved in Tillyard family papers.
61 GCPPT 1|1|2 7 July 1897.
62 *The Monthly Pets* 1891 (MTC).
63 GCPPT 1|1|2 30 July 1897.
64 GCPPT 1|1|2 31 July 1897.
65 GCPPT 1|1|4 Undated addendum to this volume written (by context) between late August and early November 1897
66 GCPPT 1|1|1 13 April 1897.
67 GCPPT 1|1|2 6 June 1897.
68 Tillyard, Ae. *The Glory of the West* pp 95–101 (GCPPT 2|16|3).
69 GCPPT 2|23 *The Watchword* June 1955.
70 GCPPT 1|1|4 8 December 1897.
71 ibid. 1 December 1897.
72 Tillyard, Ae. *The Glory of the West* pp 95–101.
73 Tillyard, Ae. *Christian Old Age* p 55.
74 Tillyard, Ae. *The Glory of the West* pp 95–101.
75 GCPPT 1|1|4 1 December 1897.
76 Raverat, G. p 121.
77 Tillyard, Ae. *Christian Old Age* pp 55–56.
78 Tillyard, Ae. *The Glory of the West* pp 95–101.
   GCPPT 2|24|1 *A Visit to Mrs Law*.
79 GCPPT 2|23 *The Watchword* June 1954.
80 GCPPT 2|25|2 *The Strawberry Eater*.
81 GCPPT 2|27|1(11).
82 GCPPT 1|1|25 17 May 1920.
83 GCPPT 1|1|67 11 March 1950.
84 GCPPT 2|26|4(10). Oswin Creighton later acted as chaplain to British forces fighting in the Dardanelles during the Great War. He died aged 35 in 1918.
85 GCPPT 1|1|9 22 June 1902.
   GCPPT 1|1|25 1 July1921. William Lindsay, having always preferred the violin to cricket, later became Professor of Music at the University of Minnesota.
86 Ernest Haddon, born in 1882, graduated from Cambridge in 1904. In April 1905 he took up a local government post in Uganda, a country to which he devoted much of the rest of his working life. He and Aelfrida met at intervals during their adult lives, he a life-long bachelor, 'grumpy and cold, longing to be back in Uganda' (GCPPT 1|1|20 1 August 1914) or 'fat and … rather depressing' and prone to discourse at length on 'elephants and jungle' GCPPT 1|1|28 3 November 1924), she relieved at not having married him.
87 GCPPT 1|1|9 26 September 1902.
88 GCPPT 1|1|4 Undated addendum.
89 Tillyard, Ae. *Messages* pp 54–58, chapter entitled 'Brothers and Sisters'.
90 Tillyard, Ae. *Messages* pp 54–58.
   GCPPT 1|1|4 Undated addendum.
91 GCPPT 1|1|40 29 November 1931.
92 Tillyard, Ae. *The Centaur* p 55 (GCPPT 2|21|1).
93 Tillyard, HJW, *Synopsis of Diaries* (MTC).
94 Tillyard, Ae. *The Centaur* pp 53 and 303 (GCPPT 2|21|1).
95 GCPPT 1|1|1 28 April 1897.
96 GCPPT 1|1|4 Undated addendum.
   Tillyard, Ae. *Naomi da Costa* p 102.
97 GCPPT 1|1|1 5 May 1897.
98 ibid. 13 April 1897.
99 GCPPT 1|1|3 Dedicatory inscription to volume.
100 GCPPT 2|25|3(6).
101 Tillyard, HJW. Introduction to *The Letters of ACW Tillyard* (MTC).
102 Tillyard HJW. *The Letters of ACW Tillyard* (MTC). Undated (by context 1902) letter from Catharine Tillyard to Ancifera ('Annie') Gregory.
103 GCPPT 2|25|3(6).
104 GCPPT 2|25|3(6a).
105 GCPPT 1|1|1 1 May 1897.
106 GCPPT 2|25|3(6a).
107 ibid.
108 GCPPT 1|1|52 24 June 1937. The nickname probably derives from 'Man Friday', Robinson Crusoe's resourceful servant in Daniel Defoe's *Robinson Crusoe*, a book not originally intended for children but by the 1880s a firm favourite with them.
109 GCPPT 1|1|4 Undated addendum.
110 ibid.
111 GCPPT 1|1|6 26 January 1901. In her introduction to published excerpts from her father's letters (*Counsel for the Young* p xi) Louise Creighton writes of his great love of children and of his "unfailing capacity for romping and telling … stories", a capacity perhaps unexpected in Cambridge's Professor of Ecclesiastical History 1885–1891.
112 Tillyard, HJW *The Letters of ACW Tillyard* (MTC). Letter from Aelfrida to Julius Tillyard of 8 July 1902.
113 GCPPT 2|23 *The Watchword* December 1956.
114 GCPPT 2|5|3(6a).

# Estimable Autobiography

Writing in 1945 to a woman to whom she was about to confide certain volumes of her diary for safekeeping, Aelfrida provided a reason for conserving them ("when I was about nine-years-old I formed an opinion that if any person, dull or stupid, living in whatever circumstances were to keep a diary steadily that diary would be of value to the world in general [and because] I had an idea that everybody ought to give an account of their lives for their own future edification and for the benefits of students of human nature [though] I never so far as I know kept a diary because I considered myself in any way exceptional … I began with a solemn sense of duty") and an excuse for having discarded one after a comparatively short time: "a tiresome little friend of mine somehow peeped at the book and rehearsed some of my private remarks at a tea party … I then destroyed everything I had written".[1]

The 'tiresome little friend' who displayed Frida's diary at her mother's At Home was Ruth Schechter, daughter of Solomon Schechter, Reader in Rabbinic Law at Cambridge University, "a great scholar who thinks and writes and dreams and speaks in the purest Hebrew".[2] Ruth, a few years younger than Frida, was first encountered some time after the Schechter family arrived in Cambridge in 1890; thereafter the girls met frequently at their respective houses, Ruth spending whole days at Fordfield (she adhered to Jewish dietary laws, the gentile Presbyterian Tillyards respecting both these and other aspects of Ruth's religion) and Frida enjoying the Schechters' Sabbath prayers, these making her wish that her own family held family prayers rather than merely reciting grace before the main meal of the day and singing hymns on a Sunday evening. (Frida's appreciation of what she was later to describe as "the sacred company of the Hebrews"[3] did not, however, prevent her from making derogatory remarks about 'rich Jews' or 'Jew-boys' or from writing in 1924 that Christianity was "an improvement on Judaism"[4], but neither did she distinguish between the general and the particular in any other respects.) Frida was delighted to have another girl as a friend, describing Ruth as "the pearl of all the Schechters" and as "lovely to look at", and was entranced when Ruth, dressed "in all the brightest coloured garments Fordfield could produce", acted out "scene after

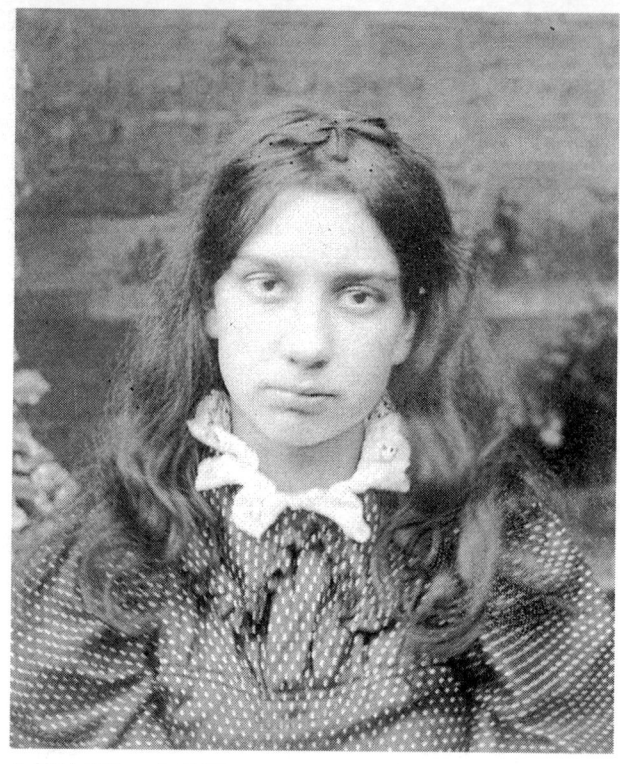

**Aelfrida Tillyard c1895**

scene from Jewish history"[5] or chanted Hebrew songs and recited the Old Testament. Ruth's betrayal of the friendship by abstracting Frida's diary and reading it aloud to Mrs Schechter's guests upset the latter on two counts: it was her own fault for leaving it lying around in the nursery (keep your diary "carefully under lock and key"[6], was her advice and, later, practice) and she had "put idiotic thoughts down on paper". "Deeply wounded and ashamed", she tore out the offending pages and decided "never to give [her]self away again", a vow honoured, unlike so many of adult Aelfrida's, more in the observance than the breach.

Of what nine and ten-year-old Frida's 'private remarks' consisted she does not say but betrayal of her confidences and destruction of everything written so far when she was about eleven (she is infuriatingly vague on dates with reference to this episode and her accounts of it vary) was followed by a period of diary silence. Then she "began again but very cautiously, writing of places and events rather than of people and emotions" and it is at this point – 23 December 1896 – that we encounter the first of seventy-five volumes spanning sixty-three years, volumes which certainly possess "historic value" and in which adolescent Frida gradually "launched out a bit and … became less formal". And within a short time they made – and continued to make until the end of the last volume – "very lively reading indeed".[7]

The first two volumes apart (volume one is a small pocketbook, the second a notebook 'swapped … from Quicky for a bow and a savings bank. Which accounts for the various scribbles')[8], youthful Frida's and adult Aelfrida's diaries were written in lined exercise books with stiff or semi-stiff covers; a few have marbleised end papers ('isn't this a beautiful book?')[9] but most have plain ones employed by the diarist as a title and date page, as a jotter, as somewhere to write nature notes or insert photographs or cuttings or to add overflow entries and later comments. She bought most volumes herself but her family must have known her preferred format, at least one being bought by Catharine Tillyard ('[she] remarks on handing me this diary "Lord Rosebury would have written across it EFFICIENCY"; 'dear me', commented its recipient, 'are we reduced to being efficient!')[10] and one, a birthday present, by Julius who inscribed it 'Aelfrida C W Tillyard d. d. HJWT Die Nativitatis 1906'.[11] Some volumes contain small sketches to illustrate the text or to clarify a description, many contain inserted letters or newspaper cuttings or other people's drawings; pressed flowers form particularly poignant memorabilia. In the course of the seventy-five volumes her handwriting develops from a careful childish fist through the firm upright script constituting the majority of the entries to the few shaky passages written in old age and ill health and although when unwell or *emotionée* (her word) she may omit or substitute words (e.g. 'committee' for 'committed') or ramble, in general her text is lucid and legible in spite of her rarely rereading entries once written unless to add a postscript or a marginal comment days or even years later in a retrospective attempt to explain or justify events or behaviour described earlier, an omission which allows impressions and descriptions, monologues and dialogues, to stand in all their spontaneity and immediacy, their humour and pathos, and their different languages: French, Italian, Latin, Greek, German, English dialect, even Catalan.

Entries vary in length: although she usually felt 'that half a page is enough each day unless something extraordinary happens', she might 'as a luxury' permit herself a whole page[12] because 'she who keeps a diary must keep it well'[13] or under pressure of events or hectic thoughts fill several; if hardly able to bear to write, there may be little more than a single line. Entries, made almost every day as an adult ('how do you do, my poor neglected diary!'[14] is an unusual comment) are less frequent in childhood and adolescence ('I have not written … for ever so long')[15] and in later life when fatigue and infirmity made writing difficult; usually written in the evening, they might be postponed to the following day if night brought no conclusion or if circumstances precluded composition but on particularly dramatic occasions they are composed in real time. Variable entry length and frequency or infrequency of writing means that volumes last for longer or shorter periods of time: several years is not unusual but nor is a few months if she has much angst to express or many extraordinary happenings to describe; then, too, though she tried to begin a new volume with a description of 'something important'[16] or even 'epoch-making'[17] (and sometimes to end it on a note of suspense), she realised that 'one can't expect a new epoch every year or so'[18] or noted why she was beginning a new volume 'without explanation or apology'.[19] (Several volumes begin with a summary of recent events and at least one with a *mea culpa*; one asks in a moment of disillusion 'why begin a new volume … with anything in particular?')[20] Mostly, however, she began with a 'pleasant little thrill'[21] of anticipation and with a resolution: 'to write a trifle better!'[22]

In a short passage written thirty years after recommencing her diary, Aelfrida described the value to the diarist of keeping one: it provides a "dumping ground for undesirable remarks" which, if blurted out, might provoke animosity in others; "clever, cutting remarks about your friends and acquaintances" (an Aelfrida speciality) "are better in [its] pages than on your lips"; "reading over an old diary is a salutary experience and an infallible source of blushes" when one realises what a complacent fool one has been and how one has ignored even one's most salient faults; one can see how (if not always why) God failed to grant certain prayers and placed barriers across "flower-strewn lanes" which seemed tempting at the time, yet when "sad and depressed" one can find consolation in looking back on "times of pleasant joy and wonder" when He seemed "very near". More importantly, keeping a diary adds to the "pleasure of every day" and to the "interest of life" in general because not only can one extract "a double pleasure from a joy by writing an account of it" but "even an unpleasant event [can] be … gratefully received as 'good copy'". (And what 'copy' she was later to make of them!) Most importantly, "to write about anything is part of the important process of making it [one's] own, of gathering it into one's soul forever".[23] And for a diarist who will become (if not one already because of the harsh messages life has taught her) a consummate egoist ('you see, I do find myself so interesting [that] I never have a dull moment!')[24], how else can one look upon one's diary but as "one of [one's] best friends"[25], a friend to whom one can grumble in private 'to relieve feelings' ('I *only* do to *you*')[26] or praise as one would a beloved intimate ('Oh diary, do you know. I've been writing such a sweet bit in defence of diaries … I thought of you and it inspired me')[27] or employ as a means of chiding oneself for split infinitives or for bad taste in music or for not writing 'a trifle better' ('where are the high and noble thoughts that ought to adorn the pages of this diary?' a question posed in June 1900 and answered in 1904 with 'ought they? Where, indeed? ACWT')[28] or for wishing that a dentist's inconveniently-timed bill need not be given grudging priority over 'the new dresses and hat I hoped to buy at the summer sales'.[29] A friend, too, who might also address one very sternly (apropos the summer sales, 'Aelfrida, you ought to be ashamed of yourself!' and receive the meek reply 'Please ma'am, I am!') or in a more anguished moment proffer good advice ('Oh *pray,* Aelfrida, pray as you have never prayed before')[30] or remind you that you are a 'fool, Aelfrida, fool, fool, fool!"[31]

Discussing with a (human) friend in November 1925 'journals and diaries as works of art', Aelfrida was moved to ask herself what 'form of art' her own diary would be. It was, she decided, 'to be a tragedy', a literary composition, that is to say, in which is depicted a series of sorrowful or otherwise unfortunate events culminating in catastrophe or a dramatic rendering in which the chief character is brought to disaster through uncontrolled passion or because of an unaddressed personality defect, the reader or observer experiencing in both cases a cleansing kind of terror as a result of their participation in what they regard either as a depiction of fatalistic forces beyond human control or the working-through of complex personal problems by one who suffers them. And tragedy being, for Aelfrida, 'the highest form of Art'[32], perhaps this was no bad thing for insofar as her particular 'tragedy' would reveal '"An Englishwoman's Life Story" in all its [tragic] details'.[33]

Adolescent Frida does not tell us why she restarted her diary at age thirteen but we may hazard some guesses: Lucy, her only female confidante, was seen at irregular intervals; she was now separated from Julius for much of the year and though brother and sister corresponded regularly, letters were poor substitutes for personal contact and might be read by those for whom they were not intended; we know that Julius kept a diary prior to 1892 and it may be in emulation of her 'big brother' that Frida wrote one too; beginning to experience the storms and stresses of puberty and finding it difficult to confide in her parents but recalling her relief at being able to confide 'idiotic thoughts' to paper, she began to do so again.

For her own part, Frida turned to her diary as 'an imaginary person'[34] to whom she could reveal her private and intimate thoughts, confess her sins, describe her response to events and to other people, and in whose company she could escape from the pressures of life by writing 'nonsense' ('but as I write for myself and not for anyone else it really doesn't matter')[35] or 'petty trivialities'[36] or 'trivial events'.[37] But even as she scolded herself for recording trivia ('I fill my diary with useless little accounts of silly petty events … I suppose I am self-centred [but] I don't see how in a diary one can be otherwise … next year I want to keep a different sort of diary and see if I can't progress a little. Yours penitently…')[38], she realised the importance of what was to become a private confessional: 'the fact is, nothing important happens or if it does I don't realise that it is important until long after … so I … make notes of everything and anything'[39] but the minutiae of everyday life were 'worth writing about because they help to make up my life'[40] and however ridiculous her response to the world might seem to an observer, her feelings 'were real to me'.[41] Perhaps most important of all to an insecure adolescent whose need to be loved and to be in control motivated everything she did, 'I hope no one will read this diary because here I put down my inmost thoughts and I would rather people liked me, thinking I was nicer than I really am than that they should know me and dislike me'.[42]

But it was not only as a confidant and confessional that Frida recommended her diary in 1896; it was also because having suddenly becoming conscious of an "inner life", she, like another of her diarist exemplars, Frédéric Amiel, sought "a safe shelter wherein [her] questionings of fate and the future" might be concealed and a receptacle wherein "the voice of grief" arising from her "soul's cry for inward peace" might be "freely heard"[43] by the sympathetic ear of the Deity to whom she was already accustomed to address her prayers. More even than this – and given that her diary was a tragedy, one of the aims of which was to promote catharsis in its readers or auditors – was her need as a seriously disturbed girl on the verge of puberty to try to purge herself of the feelings of guilt which had oppressed her since Conrad's death, feelings forgotten when safely liberated from the Perse but which for unknown reasons returned to haunt her now, feelings whose painfulness can be gauged from her own despairing explanations: 'this notebook is my rubbish heap'[44]; 'this diary is my safety valve'[45]; 'I have written a lot of nonsense but I must write it … or I should go mad'.[46]

It was for this if no other reason that Frida never thereafter save once involuntarily separated herself from the current volume of her diary, noting retrospectively of that occasion that 'it is really a mistake to go away and leave one's diary behind'[47] because she had felt 'so "*congested*"'[48] when deprived of it. And if she deliberately left it behind – a volume might be 'too full of indiscretions'[49] to be taken where locks and keys were unavailable or she was in a situation in which she might be 'betrayed into tedious raptures'[50] were she to have her diary to hand – she sometimes bought an equivalent volume in order to relieve the 'congestion' she experienced when deprived of it.

Tragedy may be the highest form of art but like all forms of art requires an audience if it is not to languish unread, unseen, or unheard. In spite, therefore, of Frida's hopes that no-one would read her diary because it contained her inmost thoughts (and because it contained 'humiliations' as well as 'consolations' but because 'one should be honest in a diary, however humiliating this may be'[51], she included humiliations in it), the growing feeling that she certainly 'had something to write about' even if that 'something' encompassed only 'holidays and walks'[52] impelled her as she reached marriageable age in 1900/01 to write for 'posterity' in the shape of her 'descendants'.[53] ('I am getting quite virtuous. I wrote in my diary yesterday and I am doing so today. How grateful posterity ought to be!')[54] She therefore ensured that completed volumes were 'put away in a safe place for posterity ... or for the w.p.b.!'[55] should 'posterity' not deem them worthy of reading and retaining and discard them in an appropriate receptacle. She also began to, as she put it, launch out a bit and to cease to confine herself to 'places and events'.[56]

The *journal intime* read at age fifteen whose author directs his literary executors to "publish those parts of the journal which might seem to him to possess either interest as thought or value as experience"[57] seems to have inspired Aelfrida to write her diary 'with the ... idea that it may one day be published'.[58] (That she might be paid 'two guineas a page!'[59] were the diary to be published in her lifetime was an even greater impetus.) From this point, therefore, her diary was written not only with an eye to a future editor (e.g. people mentioned earlier without explanation, as they would be in a purely private diary or a diary written solely for family members, are provided with brief biographies or a reminder as to who they are, and reference is made to the need to check another volume 'for news to fill the gap'[60] if more than one volume covers an event; an editor is even advised to look for relevant material in 'notebooks'[61] other than those in which her diary was composed) but also with

**Letter from Aelfrida Graham née Tillyard to Miss KT Butler of Girton College 6 March 1945**

thoughts of a future biographer: 'you know how matters stand'[62] being addressed to one presumably so familiar with her life to date that no explanation is needed on her beginning a new volume of her diary; 'you shall read it. I have it upstairs'[63], written with regard to an important letter; 'I may, perhaps, copy it out for you'[64], written of a prayer to be included in a lecture she was to give; 'I may have told you this before'[65], written in a moment of forgetfulness; a threat or promise that 'if you want to know ... what I am doing you need only refer to back numbers of this estimable autobiography of yours truly and there you will find what you want and perhaps a little more too'.[66]

Such frequent and intimate references by the writer of the diary to the 'you' for whom she is now writing provide a biographer with two immediate benefits: first, they help to overcome an uncomfortable feeling of intruding on a private, personal and revealing record, a feeling which knowledge that the record was carefully preserved for future perusal by someone who might be – indeed, under the circumstances almost certainly would be – a complete stranger, does not always mitigate; second, they

**First page of Aelfrida's diary 24 March 1897**

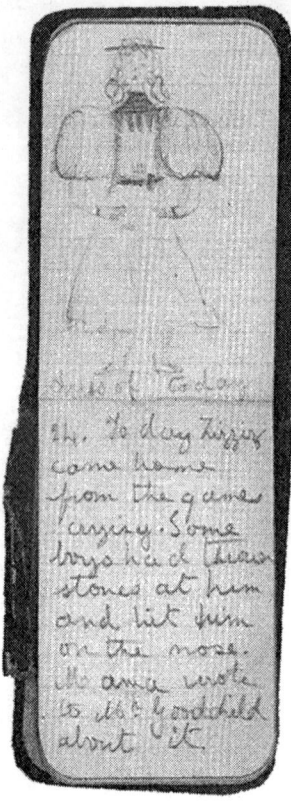

connection it is interesting to discover that within a few years of restarting her diary, Aelfrida conceived its keeping as a '*duty*', not only to herself but to 'the world' also.[69]

It is important to note, however, that being always aware of the single or collective 'you' for whom she wrote, Aelfrida's legacy 'to the world', though certainly an 'Englishwoman's life story', was by no means replete with (as she originally promised) 'all its details'[70], that her statement 'one should be honest in a diary'[71] was predicated on the conditional not the imperative, and that her promise that, reading her diary, we will discover that it contains 'things I *don't* talk about elsewhere'[72] was broken as soon as made.

Her reasons were various: to maintain a modicum of privacy because 'if I wrote or had ever written a true and full account of what passes … you would have the most wonderful book ever written. But I neither can tell you nor wish'[73]; fear of writing an account so intrinsically and unavoidably subjective ('a diary *should* be about the writer thereof')[74] that she would realise 'with horrible clearness' that she had provided 'an utterly wrong impression of personalities and events', an impression *so* wrong that she would have done better to have 'lied from the beginning'[75]; realisation that writing for an audience inevitably involved omission of material referring to herself or others which ought never to be made public and this even though omission would devalue her diary as a 'psychological document' and mean that almost 'everything that counts'[76] had to be left out. Little wonder, then, she warns us that because she is forced to use words to express herself, she also uses them 'but to conceal [her]self' and that words are both the 'dress' and the disguise of her thoughts[77], not the revelation of them. In this sense in particular, her diary is certainly a 'form of art', a cleverly contrived device or artefact whose complexity of construction and content is equal to a piece of music whose themes and variations reveal themselves only gradually to the listener or a painting beneath whose thick impasto lie layer upon layer of barely revealed *pentimenti*: 'how elusive', as elderly Aelfrida wrote ostensibly apropos a quarrelling group of old ladies, each with her own version of the argument but even more appropriately with regard to her own 'Life Story', 'how elusive is the truth in contemporary History!!'[78]

Elusive indeed, for not only does the very first volume of her diary fail to disclose a matter which has been weighing heavily on her mind for a year ('this diary', as she later warns us, 'does not represent more than small part of my interests'[79]; the matter and her reasons for non-disclosure will be revealed later) but as supplementary evidence sooner or later reveals, she also omits matters which are of more import in the context of her life

add enormously to the intimacy of the experience, for the diaries are indeed 'very lively', their contents make absorbing, even compulsive, reading, and their personal style makes it seem as if the 'you' Aelfrida addresses is present as she writes and that she is narrating the story as she composes it or is so close to her in thought that 'you' are living her life as she lives and describes it. And a chance remark ('no-one reads this book', apropos a period of intensely intrusive thoughts on a very private subject)[67] pulls 'you' up short: are 'you' are no more than the 'imaginary friend' to whom she, 'as all girls and women are supposed to do'[68], addresses her thoughts because it helps her overcome the impersonality of the blank page? But as her 'you', you also exist because she, the protagonist in her particular tragedy, requires an audience before whom to play out her scenes in all their pathos (and humour) before she can truly feel that she has achieved catharsis – or catharsis by proxy. Not only this: publication will ensure that her particular personal 'tragedy' will reach a wider audience still, a plural 'you' who as a result of their collective participation will themselves achieve a kind of catharsis because so much of what she writes will resonate in sympathy with their own 'tragic' experiences and in so resonating will allow them to move from the particular to the universal and to move on – in which as a whole than those she reveals. (And if certain omissions can be proved, how many more remain undisclosed through lack of evidence?) Or she may slant entries so that the evidence she provides is in a form approved by her or describe an event days, months, or even years after it occurs, in which case we are justified in asking to what extent the passage of time and altered recall operate upon it. Or she may report it in such fragmentary form that only after reading many volumes does one achieve a complete picture (or as complete a picture as she chooses to provide) or she may omit it altogether from her diary only to produce or reproduce it elsewhere. Or she may make it known that she has written it – and then destroy it. (And tell us she destroyed it.) Or she may refer 'readers of this diary'[80] seeking further information about her to a person in whom she has confided while ensuring that by the time they know whom to ask, her confidants will be safely dead. Or she appears so openly confiding that her readers delude themselves into thinking that they can dispense with the circumstantial evidence, guesswork, intuition and serendipitous discoveries on which they have hitherto relied and which may have caused them to believe (as Aelfrida herself said of a distant cousin) that they 'can read her like a book *now that [they] know the language*'[81], only to find the 'book' they open riddled, metaphorically speaking, with bookworm holes and with pages uncut or torn out or palimpsested to the point of illegibility.

Finally it is important to remember that in terms of *diaristic* autobiography the difficulties of interpretation imposed on a reader by Aelfrida being simultaneously the subject who records and the object of her recordings, the case in any autobiography but worsened in this instance insofar as her need to shape her 'History' into a coherent narrative (coherent on her terms, that is to say) may be at variance with events themselves as they happen simultaneously or successively at the place and time of writing or separated from one or both by time or geography, causes her to write in real time an account of her life more usually written retrospectively, at a single point in time, and with a particular end in view. It is also important to remember that young Frida and adult Aelfrida frequently find themselves (or are found to be by a reader of their diaries) on the verge of or mired deep in a period of mental disequilibrium, something which raises in the reader's mind questions regarding the veracity or otherwise of reportage which is already a 'form of art' voided of 'everything that counts'.

On the first page of the 'estimable autobiography' begun on 23 December 1896 thirteen-year-old Frida sets her scene – 'Fordfield, The Avenue, Cambridge' – and provides a list of characters in her 'tragedy':

Mama ('43'; in fact, forty-four).
Papa ('45'; in fact, the same).
Dear ('75'; in fact, seventy-six).
Julius 15.
Frida 13.
Eustace 7.
Lizzie, the cook.
Ellen (Ison) the housemaid.
Jeanne (Guy) the nursemaid.
Hubbard, the gardener.
Edward, the 'boy'.
Romulus the (house) cat.
Chanticleer, the cock.
Pertilote and 'Ussapia' (*sic*), Julius' bantams.
Bobby, the (outdoor) cat.
And 'about 20 hens (not bants)'.[82]

A reader aware of the vast number of Barretts, Tillyards, Warrens, Boyles, Crundwells, and Wetenhalls of which Frida's extended family was composed might be surprised by her next statement – 'we have very few relations indeed' – until they read her third – 'we have only two first cousins and only 3 real aunts'– and realise that it is her *immediate* family of which she writes. (The two first cousins were May Cliff, daughter of Athol and Alice Cliff, and Frank Tillyard's first child Margaret, born in 1895; the three 'real' aunts were Alfred and Frank Tillyard's sisters, married Alice and unmarried Fanny and Anna. Frank's wife, being only an aunt by marriage, did not count.) A short but revealing description of the Tillyard children follows ('Eustace does not go to school. I go to lessons at Mrs Verrall's and Julius goes to Tonbridge. We do not know many children. My greatest friend is Lucy Longstaffe and Eustace's is Kathleen Haddon, but I don't think Julius has one'.)[83] Not until volume four do Alfred and Catharine Tillyard reappear: 'Papa is Editor of the *Cambridge Independent Press* founded in 1809 (I think) … Mama is so sweet that it is no use trying to describe her. She rides a bicycle'.[84]

Although adult Aelfrida later apologised for the "dulness"[85] (*sic*) of her early diaries and for their being "dull of set purpose"[86] because of Ruth Schechter's betrayal of the contents of preceding volumes, the first volume, besides introducing some 'very interesting people'[87] who will sooner or later play a part in her life, includes descriptions of contemporary Cambridge events written so vividly that it is already apparent that one of Frida's gifts (others being a linguistic ability and a quick eye for detail) is that of being able to express herself on paper. The second volume, though it covers only a short period (March – August 1897) is remarkable for its flashes of humour (apropos a herd of zebra, 'we got quite close but did not touch them because we remembered that they had hind legs')[88] and irony (Eustace's behaviour in a sandpit being 'not quite as irreproachable as usual')[89] and for the diarist's ability to sustain a narrative: a reference at the end of the preceding volume to Fordfield being 'shut up' 'and now my diary is finished. Goodbye diary'[90] heralds a vivid and flowing description in the next volume of a June holiday at Woburn Sands in Bedfordshire, complete with visits to farms, churches, 'Bobrick Hill' woods ('*not* Bobrick Hill. "Bow Brickhill"', she scolds herself)[91] and a stately home. And as if to prove that it was not *quite* true that she thought 'of nothing but myself and my own affairs'[92], she also refers to 'contemporary History', writing on 29 June 1897 that 'this is a day to be remembered … Our Gracious Queen Victoria has reigned 60 years', a patriotic statement followed by a royal cricket score ('George III c. Death, b. Time 59; Victoria not out 60')[93] whose sophistication suggests plagiarism.

But elderly Aelfrida's statement that it was not until she received her first offer of marriage 'at 15' that she 'launched out a bit'[94] with regard to the emotional content of her diary is not quite true: volume 2 shows that at 13¾ 'ACWT' is entering puberty ('Mamma bought me my first coat and skirt. It makes me look and feel so very grown up'[95]; a week earlier she, who never faints, fainted in church), and volume 3, a present from her 'Dearest and Best Friend Lucy Longstaffe', begins with a cry from the heart far removed from the voice she later liked to think expressed the 'gay brave air'[96] of her girlhood: '16 August. Mama has told me today that she and Sweeter are going with Julius to France and Quicky and I are to be left at home … I have always adored Julius and I had so looked forward to spending our holidays together. Oh! Why do they take him away? I do want him so much'.[97] (Julius' account is less revealing: "*Aestate cum parentibus in Gallium loco Berneval*".)[98] Though the entry (significantly, perhaps, the only one in this volume) is notable for other things too – a typical teenage strop ('it is unfair') though one, atypically for a teenager but typically for 'ACWT', voiced only to her diary; a typical Frida refusal to reveal her true feelings ('I pretend I don't mind. I would not let Mama know … for anything'); the earliest manifestation of an ability to compartmentalise her feelings: after 'so much' the entry continues without a break 'This evening Julius, Quicky and I gave a grand military and civil concert' and describes its programme in humorous detail.

Frida's parents, knowing that she would resent being separated from Julius but perhaps anxious to separate pubertal sister from maturing brother, did not announce their Berneval holiday until ten days prior to departure; the gift to Frida on their day of departure of a "dear cross-grained" Ayrshire terrier Dick (actually 'Dic'; he

was named after Skeat's *Anglo-Saxon Dictionary*) who loved his new mistress 'better than anyone else'[99] but (a curious omission) not noted in her diary until October. Her diary is also notable as much for what it contains (the composition of Frida's first short story, entered for a competition in a magazine edited by family friends; her reading on 9 September of a book entitled *A Broken Vow*) as for what it omits: Julius and his parents did not return until 16 September but neither their holiday communications nor their return were recorded. Furthermore, two long gaps in the next volume of her diary are broken by two telling comments ('I have not written in you for ever so long, have I, little diary?' and 'tomorrow is my 14th birthday. I am getting quite grown up. Ugh')[100], both revealing in their own way: not everything about which she feels deeply is recorded and growing up suggests that further separations from Julius are on the cards.

## Notes

1  GCAC 9|6|33. Letter from Aelfrida C W Graham to Miss K. Butler of 6 March 1945.
2  GCPPT 2|26|3 *The Schechters*. For more on Solomon Schechter's life in Cambridge, see Soskice, J. pp 105–106 and 278–279.
3  GCPPT 2|26|3. *The Schechters*.
4  Tillyard, Ae. *Messages* pp 82–87.
5  GCPPT 2|26|3. *The Schechters*.
6  Tillyard, Ae. *Messages* pp 122–125.
7  GCAC 7|6|3|3 Letter from Aelfrida C W Graham to Miss K Butler of 6 March 1945.
8  The second volume (GCPPT 1|1|2) may have been an 1896 birthday present to 'Eustace Mandeville Wetenhall Tillyard age 7' for it contains a boyish doodle of a man in a hat smoking a pipe below the heading 'TILLYARD VOL 1'. According to adult Aelfrida its only entry ran as follows "on Friday we were going to church. I sliped (*sic*) into a brok (*sic*). It was very cold" (Tillyard, Ae. *Messages* pp 122–125).
9  GCPPT 1|1|10 22 November 1902.
10  GCPPT 1|1|14 17 September 1906.
11  GCPPT 1|1|15 [5 October] 1906.
12  GCPPT 1|1|11 19 April 1904.
13  ibid. 30 May 1904.
14  GCPPT 1|1|21 14 July 1916.
15  GCPPT 1|1|4 4 October 1897.
16  GCPPT 1|1|21 14 July 1916.
17  GCPPT 1|1|28 20 February 1924.
18  ibid.
19  GCPPT 1|1|34 30 November 1926.
20  GCPPT 1|1|15 10 May 1907.
21  GCPPT 1|1|25 10 August 1919.
22  GCPPT 1|1|34 30 November 1926.
23  Tillyard, Ae. *Messages* pp 122–125.
24  GCPPT 1|1|40 23 June 1931.
25  Tillyard, Ae. *Messages* pp 122–125.
26  GCPPT 1|1|25 6 June 1921.
    GCPPT 1|1|37 28 January 1930.
27  GCPPT 1|1|9 28 August 1902. The 'sweet bit' to which Aelfrida refers is a brief reference in the women's column of her father's newspaper (*C.I.P.* 22 August 1902) on the fascination of writing books, novels, stories, letters "and possibly diaries".

28  GCPPT 1|1|5 2 June 1900.
29  GCPPT 1|1|26 29 June 1922.
30  GCPPT 1|1|25 10 August 1919.
31  GCPPT 1|1|52 17 November 1936.
32  GCPPT 1|1|30 13 November 1935.
33  GCPPT 1|1|9 27 November 1901.
34  GCPPT 1|1|33 26 July 1926.
35  GCPPT 1|1|5 28 August 1900.
36  GCPPT 1|1|28 13 December 1924.
37  GCPPT 1|1|6 4 September 1900.
38  GCPPT 1|1|6 14 February 1901.
     GCPPT 1|1|28 13 December 1924.
39  GCPPT 1|1|9 27 November 1901.
40  GCPPT 1|1|6 4 September 1900.
41  GCPPT 1|1|5 2 September 1900.
42  ibid.
43  Amiel, F. Introduction p viii. Henri-Frederic Amiel (1821–1874) was successively Professor of Aesthetics and French Literature (1849) and Moral Philosophy (1854) in Geneva, the town of his birth. His *Journal Intime,* translated and introduced by Mary Ward (Mrs Humphrey Ward) in 1898, covers a period of more than thirty years and acted as "the confidant of his most private and intimate thoughts; a means whereby [he] became conscious of his own inner life; a safe shelter wherein his questionings of fate and the future, the voice of self-examination and confession, the soul's cry for inward peace, might make themselves freely heard" and as an outlet for one for whom "the things of the Soul were the sovereign realities of existence" (Introduction pvii).
44  GCPPT 1|1|60 23 July 1940.
45  GCPPT 1|1|43 27 November 1932.
46  GCPPT 1|1|5 2 September 1900.
47  GCPPT 1|1|18 15 December 1912.
48  GCPPT 1|1|42 27 August 1932.
49  GCPPT 1|1|28 28 July 1924.
50  GCPPT 1|1|42 27 August 1932.
51  GCPPT 1|1|27 16 March 1923.
     GCPPT 1|1|32 2 March 1926.
52  GCPPT 1|1|65a 26 September 1935. Envelope headed 'to go with my diaries'.
53  GCPPT 1|1|6 1 February 1901.
54  GCPPT 1|1|6 2 November 1900.
55  GCPPT 1|1|7 5 April 1901.
56  GCAC 4|6|3|3. Letter from Aelfrida CW Graham to Miss K. Butler of 6 March 1945.
57  Amiel, F. Introduction p vii.
58  GCPPT 1|1|12 17 May 1905.
59  GCPPT 1|1|13 21 June 1906.
60  GCPPT 1|1|28 28 July 1924.
61  GCPPT 1|1|20 11 June 1914.
62  GCPPT 1|1|25 10 August 1919.
63  GCPPT 1|1|11 14 July 1904.
64  GCPPT 1|1|21 4 March 1917.
65  GCPPT 1|1|10 6 September 1903.
66  GCPPT 1|1|7 5 April 1901.
67  GCPPT 1|1|26 5 February 1922.
68  GCPPT 1|1|33 Undated entry but by context c. 26 July 1926.
69  GCPPT 1|1|20 1 August 1914.
70  GCPPT 1|1|9 27 November 1901.
71  GCPPT 1|1|32 2 March 1926.
72  GCPPT 1|1|43 27 November 1932.
73  GCPPT 1|1|12 9 May 1905.
74  GCPPT 1|1|22 16 July 1918.
75  GCPPT 1|1|12 9 May 1905.
76  ibid. 17 May 1905.
77  GCPPT 1|1|14 3 October 1906.
78  GCPPT 1|1|74 29 March 1957.
79  GCPPT 1|1|43 27 November 1932.
80  GCPPT 1|1|6 1 February 1901.
81  GCPPT 1|1|13 29 August 1906.
82  GCPPT 1|1|1 23 December 1896. Chanticleer and Pertilote are the cock and hen who figure in *The Nun's Priest's Tale* in Chaucer's *Canterbury Tales*. Pertilote (usually misspelt by her daughter) was also the pen-name used by Catharine Tillyard when writing the women's column for her husband's newspaper.
83  GCPPT 1|1|1 23 December 1896.
84  GCPPT 1|1|4 Undated addendum. The *CIP* was actually founded in 1839.
85  GCPPT 2|26|3 *The Schechters*.
86  GCPPT 1|1|65a 26 September 1935. Envelope headed 'to go with my diaries'.
87  GCPPT 1|1|1 26 March 1897.
88  GCPPT 1|1|2 19 June 1897.
89  GCPPT 1|1|2 21 June 1897.
90  GCPPT 1|1|2 27 May 1897.
91  GCPPT 1|1|1 5 and 18 June 1897.
92  GCPPT 1|1|22 16 July 1918.
93  GCPPT 1|1|2 20 June 1897.
94  GCAC 4|6|3|3 Letter from Aelfrida CW Graham to Miss K. Butler of 6 March 1945.
95  GCPPT 1|1|2 5 July 1897.
96  GCPPT 1|1|23 21 September 1918.
97  GCPPT 1|1|3 16 August [1897].
98  Tillyard, HJW. *Summary of Diaries* (MTC).
99  GCPPT 1|1|4 4 October 1897; a sketch of 'Dick (after James Stark)' is pasted in the back of this volume.
     Tillyard, Ae. *Messages* pp 106–109.
100 GCPPT 1|1|4 4 October 1897.

# Especially to Gentlemen

R e-reading 'an early diary … written when I was thirteen', Aelfrida wrote critically that not only was there 'hardly a glimmer of intelligence' in it but also that the diary's content demonstrated 'only the same inexplicable need that I still … have of chronicling entirely unimportant external events'.[1] She was wrong on most counts: even her earliest volumes demonstrate a vivid intelligence (a superior young man with whom Frida had just discussed 'comics, Trig, Latin and Greek' was stunned when she carried on a conversation in fluent French with the family governess and was moved to ask in awed tones if there was *nothing* that she did not know)[2], her need to chronicle was not inexplicable, and the events she chronicled were not entirely unimportant. They were, however, and in the main external.

True, high intelligence did not even then go hand in hand with common sense, in part because perspicacity was often expended on an absorbing interest deliberately fenced off from daily life and even at times from her diary, in part because of other people's unfavourable reactions when it obtruded, and in part because she thought it too important to be included among the 'unimportant external events' she chronicled. Her 'need' to chronicle and the reason for it being a need have been already noted and explained by her slightly older self but her reference to the 'entirely unimportant' and 'external' events she 'needs' to chronicle is curious insofar as she herself has already informed us of her reason for doing so: because they are aspects of her life. There are, however, two other reasons more obliquely hinted at: they

**Aelfrida Tillyard (2nd left) at Holkham 25 August 1902**

are aspects not only of her quotidian but also of her nascent inner life and they are a means of disguising her thoughts and feelings insofar as anyone reading her diary surreptitiously in the present or by design in the future will be beguiled into thinking that 'entirely unimportant external events' are all that concern her. With this in mind we now turn to two 'events' which will preoccupy adolescent Frida and adult Aelfrida for the rest of her life: literary composition and men.

Christmas 1897 saw fourteen-year-old Frida tête-à-tête with her father: 'Papa has been talking to me as if I were grown up. Some of the things I will not put down but I will mention one thing. He has been encouraging me to write'.[3] (She also fails to put down *why* her father decided to encourage her to write at this point; possibly he did not tell her.) An account written in 1943 expands this brief description of what was to become a consuming passion: she had, so she said, decided to follow the example of Annie Steel[4] and become a 'lady gardener' but on her father showing her an article describing Mrs Steel as one who 'gardened in a lady-like way in the intervals of authorship' and because Frida herself 'had a profound respect' for his judgement, she changed her mind and began to write 'seriously'.[5] ('Seriously', it seems, meant 'for print', not, as before, for her own amusement 'or to get pennies out of my elders'.)[6] A fortnight later she noted not only that she had 'quite made up [her] mind' to write, but also and more ambitiously, that she had decided to write a book of which she had already planned 'the plot and some of the principal scenes'. (She had not, she added, thought of a title 'but there is plenty of time for that'.)[7] Of the book we hear nothing more – it was to be two years before she embarked on 'a long novel to be called possibly *Love and Mathematics*'[8] – but as an aid to composition she gained 'a new accomplishment! I have learned ... to use a typewriter'.[9] Diary descriptions too become consciously 'literary' ('not without reason has Surrey been called the garden of England'[10], written of a visit to Crundwell relations in Farnham; 'we partook of a delightful cup of *café au lait*'[11], written of her first trip abroad, a visit to Dieppe with Ancifera Gregory) until realisation that she was writing as she 'thought [she] *ought* to write and not as [she] felt' restored a more '*genuine*' tone.[12]

As a serious 'author' and the daughter of a newspaper editor and proprietor, Frida was always on the lookout for 'copy': of a coastguard met on a visit to otherwise 'stupid little' Seaford, she noted 'I would like to cultivate that man and make him tell me stories'.[13] She was open to criticism – showing May Cliff stories already composed, she commented 'I wish ... to do good by my stories but ... they are so bad'[14] – and to discussion,

asking of the same cousin 'whether it is necessary to have one's heart broken before one can write a really great ... book'. (Her conclusion was that she knew 'it [was] necessary to *love*' but was unsure about the heartbreak.)[15] But her 'wild wish!' to be 'a celebrated authoress'[16] may have impelled her to destroy stories she thought 'so bad', leaving us only a list of titles.

Criticism was also extended to stories (all subsequently destroyed) written when the as-yet-be-celebrated authoress was sixteen: *An Artist's Model* had 'a good plot ... very badly worked out'[17], *Was He a Hero?* (2,250 carefully counted words) was 'the best thing I have written' ('it was absurdly bad. ACWT 1904')[18], a dialogue (*A Verbal Difficulty*) had a 'slight' plot but was 'rather amusing'[19], and *Army and Navy* ('the most humorous one I have written ... Papa laughed like anything')[20] was an early example of arch but clever wit first demonstrated in a family magazine, *The Military and Civil Journal*, begun in February 1900.

The journal, familiarly known as the '*MCJ*', (the Tillyard children had already held 'military and civil' concerts but with the Boer War, otherwise known as the South African War, in full swing and widely reported in Alfred Tillyard's newspaper, a 'military and civil' title was suitable for a magazine whose reportage covered both military and civil news) was produced under ten-year-old Eustace's direction, he (as 'EMWT', 'Ed', or 'Lieutenant Mandeville') and Frida (variously 'Lieutenant Wetenhall DSO', 'ACWT', or 'FT') writing the greater part of it with contributions from Julius ('Captain Tillyard' or 'HJWT') in English, German, and Latin and from selected outsiders of whom James Stark ('Sergeant Stark') was one. Frida's contributions ranged from poetry (chiefly doggerel and parody, sometimes in French) through serialised plays and stories to interviews (*Interview with Hubbard* refers to his favourite flowers and quotes him as telling a small nephew who wanted to run about the garden on a Sunday to "steal away to some quiet nook and count up your mercies"[21], a saying later appropriated and adapted by adult Aelfrida to refer to herself: "steal away, Miss Frida, to some quiet nook and read your bible")[22], witticisms ("*Answers to Correspondents.* No. Kid gloves are not made out of the skins of babies")[23], and pen and ink illustrations, some water-coloured, by "one of the most eminent artists of the day".[24] (Worth bearing in mind when enjoying Frida's whimsical and witty contributions is that they were written by an adolescent who has recently admitted that she *has* to write or 'go mad' and that who employed wit and whimsy at unhappy periods of her life for their cathartic effect and as a means of disguising her true feelings.) And it may have been that, inspired by the success of her comic poems in the magazine for the "priv'ledge of reading" which she and the editor charged "only a single penny"[25], she sent one to the *Boys' Own Paper* under her initials ACWT. To her surprise and delight it was published, without authorial acknowledgement, it is true ('the ways of editors are strange'), and without payment, but it nevertheless was her first work to appear in print. Sweeter even than this was to have a young man remark 'in his most scholastic manner' that the poem was good and that she possessed 'the gift'.[26]

The young man whose praise for her literary 'gift' so overwhelmed teenage Frida that she became positively 'madcap' (*étourdie*) over a game of cards with him (she blamed it on the whist)[27] was one of two who chiefly claimed her attention at this time. Both were distantly related to her, one died tragically young, the other provided seriocomic amusement for years. Both figure in her diary but only one in the *MCJ*.

The young man who figured in and who was most unkindly spoofed in the *MCJ* (an advertisement for "Dr Emptyhead's Educational Establishment"[28] was one of the kinder entries) was Percival Stanley, son of Jacob and Harriette Stanley. Harriette née Warren was the daughter of Henry Joseph Wetenhall's sister of the same name; her children, of which she had six, all much older than the Tillyard children, were therefore related in distant cousinage. Jacob (Jake) Stanley came from a family of mine owners and steel magnates but had abandoned industry for art and he and Harriette lived in a chaotically artistic household in London. Visiting sometime prior to recommencing her diary in December 1896, Frida was shocked by a Bohemian lifestyle so different from the Tillyards' ('all in their house is so shabby, so untidy … it is a sweet place to visit but rather an uncomfortable one to stay at'[29]; she was later to write a short story about the Stanleys and to put them in a novel)[30] but found herself attracted to relations whose 'guileless and childlike'[31] joy in family life and each other contrasted markedly with the tense and sometimes rather gloomy atmosphere prevailing at Fordfield. At a family dance she danced several times with a young man she called 'cousin Percy'; this was not, however, Frida's first meeting with him and his booking several dances with her was not mere cousinly politeness, for Percy, twelve years her senior, had already encountered her in Cambridge, he having matriculated there in October 1896.

Sometime between that date and December 1896 Eustace caught chicken pox. Lest Frida also catch it (Julius was away at school) she was bundled off to the Verralls, a visit she did not altogether enjoy because although the Verralls' house was considered "very tasteful" and Dr Verrall "egged [her] on" conversationally at meals at which she made the acquaintance of Newnham luminaries like classicist Jane Harrison, "given the choice between staying at Fordfield and catching chicken pox or spending a fortnight with the Verralls I should have unhesitatingly chosen home". ("I was not asked", she adds; two years later she caught measles from Eustace, stayed at home, and was ill for a month.) To help her endure her stay, choral scholar and potential ordinand Percy Stanley was asked to escort her on "authorised cycle rides"[32] several times a week.

Between 1896 and 1898 Percy (his 'guileless and childlike nature' also prevented him from passing examinations; he did not graduate until 1903 and not until 1904 did Frida note with a 'coo!!!!'[33] that he was qualified to begin his clerical career) visited Fordfield regularly to swap stamps, to argue theology, and to chaperone his adolescent girl cousin on further cycle rides. At some point during the two years during which Frida seems to have thought of him as no more than another elder brother, Percy, "always very kind" to her, also fell in love with her and while fifteen year old Frida was seeing him out one evening, tried to kiss her. Thinking it her "duty to be indignant", she rebuffed him. Percy informed her that he loved her "more than [his] life", that he hoped that she would be his wife, and departed. Frida ran upstairs and "in a transport of vicarious (*sic*) excitement" thanked God "Who had made her a woman". (She had, so she said, "no thought of returning [Percy's] love. It was the glory of receiving it that overwhelmed [her]".) Poor Percy; not only did adult Aelfrida write snubbingly of the diary entry recording the event ('*Friday August 18th 1899 8 am* I have just had my first real proposal. It's Cousin Percy of Nightingale Lane') that it was 'naïve! ACWT 1904' but on that same Friday August 18th (a date marked with a big X and subsequently described as the day her diary really began to be '*genuine*'), 'told Mama and she was very angry'.[34]

What Frida later described as 'the matter with Percy' was settled by Catharine Tillyard having a 'talk' with him, after which Percy expressed penitence and the Tillyard females decided to act as if nothing had happened. Percy confided his woes to a novel ('I suppose I am the heroine. I have been writing some stories too but he is certainly not my hero!')[35] and Frida her thoughts to her diary. But the matter was far from 'settled'; Percy continued so 'attentive'[36] that by mid-May 1900 Frida found him 'quite a nuisance with his amorous speeches and tender glances'. She also found it 'boring … to be thought such a lot of'[37] and although she expressed sympathy for Percy's plight, discouraged her swain as much as possible. Matters continued thus throughout the summer, Percy pressing his suit with 'a sweet little

Tennyson' with significant lines of *Maud* marked 'and – actually – a forget-me-not' marking another place[38] and sentimental songs sung at the Fordfield piano and demonstrated 'extreme sentimentalism' by abstracting one of Frida's gloves as an amatory souvenir: 'he actually said that he spent all last night kissing it … I really think Percy is a little mad'. ('I really did! ACWT 1904'.)[39] Frida alternately encouraged him ('out of sheer perverseness [I] tossed him the pretty rosebud I had been wearing')[40] or flirted with other young men – of whom there was no shortage in her life – or, when Percy's behaviour became too importunate (diary entries suggest that he was virtually stalking her), reported 'the inevitable Percy' ('I am quite sorry that I have such a specimen *for a cousin*')[41] to her mother.

Catharine Tillyard's earlier interventions notwithstanding, Percy continued to pester (reporting one of his particularly poignant pleas verbatim, Frida concluded that 'lovers' were 'a most abominable nuisance' and that she would prefer to be left in peace)[42], to haunt Fordfield, and even to inveigle her into situations where she could not help but be alone with him. Catharine Tillyard then wrote one of her rare severe letters, reminding him that he was 'rather overstepping the bound of cousinly relations'.[43] Grumbling that he was ill-used and that there was a 'conspiracy' against him, Percy desisted, though not without threatening 'to *make* [Frida] like him'[44] (she never did, though she retained an amused affection for him) and even, on hearing that she had been – on her own admission – 'Flirting' while staying with Lucy, to murder her. (She 'had better look to [herself]', he informed his cousin, 'for [she] had a dangerous man – no, a devil – to deal with … and it was only his better self that made him warn [her] etc. etc.'; Frida, so she said, 'laughed in his face and asked him what low theatre he had been frequenting that he had become so melodramatic'.)[45] He was the first but not the last man to threaten to do so.

In June 1905, Percy, now a curate and 'fatter … sentimental, fatuous [and] deficient still in sense of humour', met his inamorata for not quite the last time. In what heartless Aelfrida described as a '*scène de comédie*' (Percy was still 'very miserable' concerning her, his misery deepened by discovery that Aelfrida, now twenty-one, was engaged to another man, and manifest by his actually weeping at the piano as he sang to her), the man to whom she was engaged laughingly informed her that 'poor Percy' was under the mistaken impression that she preferred himself 'and merely held to the engagement through some perverted sense of honour'. Made suddenly aware of Percy's decade-long devotion during which he had generally behaved towards her in a 'very loving and tender' manner[46] that he was now 'more serious [and] improved by hard work', Aelfrida was smitten with remorse ('Oh Percy!') and behaved kindly and sympathetically to her forlorn admirer[47]; this did not, however, prevent her from noting waspishly in 1914 that Percy, now forty-three to her thirty, was engaged to 'a spinster of 35 … said to be rather common'[48], waspishness explicable, perhaps, in the light of what had transpired since their last meeting, for recent events might have almost persuaded her that she would have done better to marry the man who had hoped that teenage Frida would marry him 'some day' when she was older and he had 'made a position'[49] for himself than the fiancé married in 1907.

Prior to Aelfrida's engagement, 'poor Percy' suffered two rivals, one the young man who was soon to die tragically young, the other an older man who would die as the result of a tragic accident in 1916.

Noting in November 1898 that she had been 'so busy' that she had had no time to write in her diary (a gap between 5 September and 27 November may attest to this but may also attest to Frida's reluctance to confide certain matters to it) and that 'besides, little of any importance had happened' (an absolutely untrue statement), Frida consoled herself that two international events had made newspapers exciting reading, 'the Dreyfus Drama' being one, 'the Egyptian War' the other.[50] Of greater personal relevance than anti-Semitic injustice inflicted on a Franco-Jewish captain, however, was the campaign conducted by Horatio Herbert Kitchener CB KCMG, "the greatest of British Generals", against "the Dervishes at Omdurman" which resulted in "a decisive victory … and the entry of British and Egyptian forces into Khartoum"[51], and it was the occasion of a visit paid to Cambridge by the campaign's 'splendid commander' which 'induced' Frida to bring her diary up to date: 'Lord Kitchener has been to Cambridge to receive an honorary degree and the freedom of this ancient city. As Papa is a councillor, we had tickets [for] the town hall. As Lord Kitchener came in everyone stood up and *howled*. He looked very grave and dignified and handsome and stern'.[52]

Later the same day Lord Kitchener, Frida, and Councillor Tillyard (Papa was "robed for the occasion"; Lord Kitchener had changed from the "ordinary morning attire" worn for the civic ceremony into "the … full dress uniform of his rank" for the university one and looked "every inch the great soldier of the Queen that he is") repaired, together with invited dignitaries, to the Senate House where "the Vice-Chancellor amid raging cheers conferred upon Lord Kitchener the degree of LLD".[53] The presence of numerous undergraduates made the ceremony a noisy one and Frida's lively reporting brings it vividly to life: 'the undergraduate is possessed of good lungs and high spirits and when he means to make a row he jolly well knows how to [and when] the impossibles in the gallery [let down from the ceiling the effigy of] a Huge Dervish, the Sirdar began to laugh. He does laugh nicely'[54] – at which point 'ACWT' found herself "wildly gone"[55] on a man old enough to be her father and a year older than her own.

Herbert Kitchener was then a slim, blue-eyed, suntanned and very tall bachelor of forty-seven of rather more benign though no less heroic aspect than the poster Kitchener exhorting young men in 1914 that their country needed them; in this and as a professional soldier he was also as far removed from cousin Percy as he could possibly be. Cambridge ladies, Florence Keynes among them, were not immune to his charms and teenage Frida developed what she later described as "a Grand Pash ... Mush or Crush"[56] on him. Her (later and somewhat rationalised) reason for doing so is interesting. True, she was already predisposed to find men in uniform and positions of authority handsome: Julius in his Tonbridge School Volunteers outfit cut a surprisingly dashing figure and a glimpse of a soldier at Aldershot had occasioned rapture ('the most handsome man [I] had ever seen and his figure was perfect'. 'I'm shocked. ACWT 1904')[57], but her 'g.p.' on Lord Kitchener arose for other reasons. In Julius' absence at school she needed someone to admire and fastened her temporarily unfocused adoration on a man who appeared in Cambridge at precisely the right moment, and unlike Julius or Percy or other young men now paying her attention, Kitchener was unattainable: of what she later described as "a genuine piece of hero-worship", she wrote of how she was happy to adore him from "a psychological distance" as a man "above ordinary human pettiness [and] supremely devoted to his God and his country", that she never expected to meet him because they moved in different social circles, and – interestingly – that at that point in her life "almost anyone ... would have done".[58]

A 'Mush or Crush' it certainly was (Julius described it as a "brief infatuation"[59] but it endured for seven years) and after obtaining the great man's autograph ('Kitchener of Khartoum', inscribed on the back of a letter requesting it)[60], Frida settled down to hero worship and to make Kitchener the hero of her first novel, *The Ending of the Way*, described by Julius as "rather schoolgirlish"[61] but by a kinder critic (Swiss doctor Marie Feyler) as being, in spite of certain '*gaucheries*' and some decidedly weak points (a smallpox scene, for example, was 'a ludicrous hash, medically speaking') much better in terms of wit, characterisation, vocabulary, dialogue, and style than one would expect of a novice novelist. Frida therefore 'wriggled in [her] chair with joy' when Marie assured her that

there was no reason why she should not become a 'celebrated authoress' because she had the requisite gifts, for Marie, a professional single woman and something of a medical pioneer, was someone whose literary opinion she valued. (The novel was dedicated to Marie "in recognition of the generous amounts of jam with which she surrounded the pill of ... wholesome and nasty home truths"; Marie, it seems, also asked Frida probing questions about herself after reading the novel and had 'dissected' some of Frida's 'thoughts and inmost sentiments' as a result.) To her diary, however, she confided thoughts and sentiments undisclosed to the doctor/critic: handing over her typescript to Marie made her feel 'like a woman whose son had left her for the first time' (she was later to describe many of her books as her babies and to feel bereft when she gave birth to them) and although she had succeeded in portraying herself as the novel's heroine 'Ruby Latimer' ('Ruby is me, of course'), her hero 'Lord de Mountfort' (otherwise Lord Kitchener) was anything but the 'sublime!' personage she intended, being 'feeble, vague, unconvincing [and] indefinite'. The failure of this latter portrayal hurt Frida deeply because 'if he failed, the book has failed', but it was not her having failed in literary terms which upset her most: 'perhaps', she wrote, 'this is an omen – my life will be a success but I shall never get what I care for above all?'[62] The two-volume novel, the first of several *romans à clef*, over which she lavished so much time and attention – too much attention, perhaps, for Alfred Tillyard felt obliged to forbid her to write because the excitement of composition gave her insomnia, subjecting her instead to a regimen of domestic tasks and long bicycle rides; Frida, aware there was some truth in what he said, submitted even as she admitted that she would much rather be 'persuaing' (*sic*) the fortunes of her 'charming heroine'[63] – was later destroyed.

There the matter might have rested had it not been for the outbreak of the Boer War in 1899. Frida was unsure which side to support, 'the pious Boers who put their trust in [God]' or the British with Lord Kitchener as their Chief of Staff, but given that the war would allow 'Lord de Mountfort' to 'add another wreath to his crown of laurels'[64], plumped for the latter. News from the front, particularly of the successive reliefs of Kimberley, Ladysmith and Mafeking, added fuel to the flames of her 'Mush or Crush': 'sometimes I wonder how I can *live* while ... never, *never* looking on his face ... Is it *love*, I wonder, that I feel for him? It hurts – sometimes I can hardly bear it – and yet I would not have it cease ... Is 16 young to feel that I have wanted – and still want – *one* thing and that has been denied me and, after that, nothing matters?'[65] And so on – and on: 'it is bad enough to long for him with all my heart and being ...I can hardly believe that I once swore … never [to] give a thought to any man who did not on his bended knee beg me to so [but] now − now − I think of him hourly − he is never out of my thoughts … But … I am proud, *proud* of loving him and I will do so for ever because − because I must'.[66]

In spite of her ability to disguise anguish in humour as numerous articles by 'Lieutenant Wetenhall' in contemporary editions of the *MCJ* attest or to confide it solely to the pages of her diary or to her novel ('it is so lonely to write … I know the meaning though no one else does')[67] or to become so unwontedly silent that her father commented on it, Frida's 'Grand Passion' soon became evident to members of her family, Eustace, '*l'enfant terrible*', teasing her unmercifully and her parents laughing at her. May Cliff, when confided in, was gently sympathetic but Lucy, the only person to whom Frida revealed the depths of her passion because 'I *must* have her sympathy', reacted rather frivolously (she called Lord Kitchener 'dear Herbert K') and behaved so heartlessly that Frida wailed to her diary 'does not my own Lucy care? Does she not mind wounding my feelings?' and wondered if she had been wrong in thinking that 'other people will take me as seriously as I take myself'.[68]

Four people did. Two were her parents who, though they laughed over 'Tit's' infatuation were worried by a particular manifestation of it: sometime in June 1900 a 'rather strange thing' happened to their adolescent daughter, a 'thing' un-confided (at the time) to her diary and only confided to Silvia Myers because, being her father's daughter, she would be 'interested in such apparitions'. She was. She also assured Frida that it was of the 'utmost importance' that she record it. So aged '16¾', she did.

In bed late one night early in June 1900, her eyes closed but unable to sleep, something moved her to open them; what she saw was a 'curious sight' of such vividness that on waking next morning the impression was still clear: her room, she wrote, seemed to have expanded and at the other end of it she saw a bed identical to her own on which lay 'the figure of a strong man … either dead or dying'. Sitting by the bed was a girl dressed in a flowing white garment, her head bowed with grief and her attitude one of 'absolute despair'. Getting out of bed, Frida approached the girl − only to discover she was '*myself*'! Looking beyond the girl to the dead or dying man she *thought* she recognised him as Lord Kitchener, chiefly because all her thoughts were then of him. (Rumours had arrived in England that Kitchener had been killed and Frida's poetic reaction to them − a poem entitled *Vision of Sorrow* whose first line runs "They told me that my love was dead" − antedated and

almost certainly inspired what she 'saw'; four years later, however, and in spite of recalling the scene 'with absolute clearness', she noted 'I do not really know who it was. ACWT 1904'.) At that point the 'vision' (her word) was interrupted by a voice saying 'coldly and impassively "this is your future life. This is your *fate*!"' and terminated by a flash of lightning. Frida returned to bed and fell asleep. The next day she described her experience Catharine Tillyard and cousin Percy, making light of it so as not to alarm her mother but noting that both she and Percy were 'wonderfully impressed'. She subsequently and reluctantly disclosed the man's name to her mother and Catharine, presumably, to her husband for it was shortly after this that Alfred Tillyard forbade her to write until her mind was more settled; Frida herself wondered if the 'vision' (or dream or somnambulant experience or 'warning from the spirit world'; more correctly, a hypnopompic hallucination) would come true (she would, she wrote, love to weep by Lord Kitchener's bedside 'but not if it did him harm!') but was in two minds as to 'whether or not to attach any importance to what [she] saw'.[69] Later, it seems, she did, for the 'vision' she saw that night was not her first but − as she chooses to tell us only many years later − her second, third or even fourth and, regardless of its actual numerical order, one among many more.

Cousin Percy, a man whose theological training and personal affection for her would incline him to deal lovingly and kindly with a girl 'dreaming 'of supernatural and possibly prophetic events, was more understanding. A month after Frida retailed her 'vision' to himself and her mother, Percy, together with another undergraduate, took Frida, her mother, and Eustace upriver to Granchester in 'two charming Canaders' (i.e. canoes.) All went well until a thunderstorm frightened nine year old Eustace so much that he insisted on returning with his mother and the other man, leaving Percy and Frida alone together in the second canoe. (The latter later wondered if their being put together was engineered; given Catharine and Alfred Tillyard's reaction to their daughter's 'vision', this may be so.) 'What happened on the way home', wrote Frida of the journey back to Cambridge, 'can best be told by a sort of story that I wrote about it … it occurred nearly exactly as I have written it … and a lot more besides'.[70]

The story, entitled *Lightning and Lilliard*, featured herself as 'Lilliard' and Percy as 'Travers' and the dialogue which took place between the distant cousins as they paddled damply downstream recapitulated much of a previous conversation between Percy and Frida on the possibility or impossibility of marriage between themselves. Of more relevance to recent events was 'Travers' taxing 'Lilliard' with being fonder of a man known to himself and 'Lilliard' (and from previous conversations as Percy and Frida) as the 'Duke'. (The 'Duke' was 'Lord de Mountfort' and it was as 'the' or 'my' 'Duke' that Frida referred to Lord Kitchener when teased about him by her family or confronted concerning him by lovelorn Percy Stanley, he asking if at some time she might "give up the idea of your Duke" and entertain thoughts of himself, she replying that she was "really so attached to [her] Duke", a 'charming' man with a 'long pedigree' about whom she was shortly to begin the second volume of the novel whose 'meaning' she knew 'though no-one else will'[71], that thoughts of Percy were impossible.) The dialogue between 'Lilliard' and 'Travers' is more allusive but it seems 'Travers' reminded 'Lilliard' of his disappointed hopes and that 'Lilliard' responded by admitting something of the depths of *her* unrequited love and that she disguised her heartbreak with "amusing and sometimes even witty … cynicism". ("I am a good actress, am I not?") 'Travers' then expressed sympathy for "poor little" 'Lilliard' – he and she were metaphorically as well as literally in the same boat – and the story ends with 'Travers' and 'Lilliard' rejoining the rest of the party at a landing stage upstream of the bathing stations at Sheep's Green and Coe Fen where men and boys swam naked. Of what the 'lot more besides' consisted, Frida does not say except to hint that Percy 'was a good deal sillier than 'Travers', that what he said was 'unimportant' and that she herself might have behaved in a rather 'unmaidenly' fashion by revealing her naked emotions, a revelation she blamed on residual 'electricity' present in the air.[72]

The other person who took her infatuation seriously was Julius. Julius was not immediately privy his sister's love for 'the Duke'; indeed, it seems Frida concealed the fact that she had 'loved someone a thousand times better than my own dearest brother' for the best part of two years lest she hurt his feelings. A letter of November 1900 expressing his devotion moved her to confide in him but having posted her reply, she regretted having done so, not because she might have hurt his feelings but because Julius was 'such a child' in matters of the heart.[73] (In 1904 a revealing addendum noted 'I suppose that must be true since I have said it but *now* I am never sorry for what I have done! ACWT'.)[74] Julius' reply was maturely sympathetic: "My dear Tit, you ask me not to pity you and indeed I will not, not because I cannot … realise your situation, indeed it is not likely that I could. But … I share the great privilege of sharing your confidence … Thank you for your trust". He then assures her that revealing her secret even to "unimaginative" Lucy or to someone like himself "who can try to sympathise but cannot understand" is better than "nursing a hidden flame" and offers practical advice: "if ever you feel bad,

write verses … next morning read them over and *livrez aux flammes*. It's a capital idea as I know full well".[75]

The letter itself is revealing; more revealing still is the entry in Frida's diary in which she quotes it. It is obvious that she has not revealed 'the Duke's' identity to her brother but has left Julius to assume he is an older man of her acquaintance whose failure to respond is "simply because he thinks you are still a little girl" and she glosses Julius' sober and sensitive reply with frivolous comments ('very consoling this!'; 'this is rather sarcastic. I'm afraid!'; 'that is rather pretty'), something which suggests that Julius may not have been altogether wrong in regarding her as a "silly schoolgirl" not to be taken as seriously as she herself would like to be taken. Or was it in her role as a 'good actress' that the entry ends with the dismissive comment that 'the whole affair is so supremely ridiculous … let's make fun of it'?[76] More to the point, perhaps, she does not consign Julius' letter to the flames and one and three week gaps between this and following diary entries may indicate periods of thoughtfulness; indeed, her entry for 12 December 1900 quotes a poem whose author suggests that winter should not be a season for brooding on past affections (*souvenirs défunts*) so much as a time for renouncing the pursuit of impossible happinesses in favour of a primaveral rebirth of new loves and new interests.[77]

A fifth person – someone in whom Frida had not confided – seemed uncannily aware of feelings Frida herself had hoped were dying down but if her reaction to family gossip concerning Lord Kitchener was anything to go by ('Good God! How it hurt … I hoped I had forgotten [but] it is worse than ever'), had not. The person was Ruth Schechter, now twelve and, so she said, in love with and even engaged to a young man of twenty and apt to wonder, to Frida's discomfiture, why novelists needed to draw on their imaginations when writing romances when they could use her own and Frida's lives as plots. Asking herself how Ruth could *possibly* know about Lord Kitchener, Frida agreed to allow Ruth to tell her fortune. The experience was not a comfortable one, for Ruth, speaking in a 'low tense voice' and gazing at Frida with eyes which 'seemed to see through [her] and away into time', seemed to know 'the whole miserable story [and] all … [her] ridiculous, extravagant feelings', her future ("your love has brought you sorrow and … will bring you more. He will never care"), and her character: "you go to extremes too much and you are too desperately gay and too gaily desperate".[78] Thanking Ruth with a kiss and some chocolate cake, Frida stole chastened away.

What remains of Frida's 'Grand Passion' is soon told. By the summer of 1901 she thought of Lord Kitchener only in flashes though she reassured herself 'I love him still and …always shall'[79]; two years later she deemed 'the whole affair … absurd' (she also admitted that she *had* cared 'a great deal' for him in a real though rather ridiculous way)[80] and even wrote a spoof account for the *MCJ* of *How the Duke came to Fordfield* as part of a supposed study of 'the Housing of the Middle Classes'.[81] November 1904 saw a rapid change of heart: apropos Lord Kitchener 'whom only a month ago I thought I still loved', she wrote 'what has happened to my feelings about him[?] … it is as though a black curtain had fallen … and hidden him from my sight … it is all gone, I can remember nothing'.[82] Kitchener's death in 1916 left her unmoved and in 1950, reading over old diaries with the brother to whom she had confided her love for 'the Duke', now revealed as Kitchener of Khartoum, she noted 'why did I say I was "in love" with Lord Kitchener? … Never in my day-dreams did I ever imagine myself entering my hero's life … I had no idea what "in love" meant … it was [only] adolescent hero-worship [and] I merely wanted to admire what seemed to be admirable'.[83]

That may be so but adolescent Frida's 'Mush or Crush' on Herbert Kitchener was symptomatic of two things. First, that in spite of protestations that if any forward young men dared launch "Cupid's darts" in her direction she would arm herself with metaphorical "wet blankets and buckets of water"[84] to quench their ardour, she now found herself unable to live without being interested in to the point of preoccupation with 'first [one] man and then another', a trait she described as 'so *silly*'[85] but of which she was unable to cure herself and which caused her to create round the man in question an intense glamour which ceased as abruptly as it had arisen and which, once gone, was never rekindled. Second, and although her 'Grand Passion' died, it had the unfortunate effect of making her believe for longer than was wise that she was "incapable of another kind of affection for a man" and that were she to wish to have children, she "must needs" marry solely for procreation, a husband being in this respect "a necessary evil".[86]

Percy's other young male rival for adolescent Frida's affections was a 'very distant cousin' of whom she was sure she might soon become 'very fond'.[87] Archibald (Archie) Stent was indeed a 'distant' cousin, being related to Frida only insofar as his father came from the same West Country family as Ancifera Gregory; an alumnus of Kings, he was also the newly appointed mathematics master at King's College Choir School. Frida and Archie met for the first time on 9 May 1900 at a dance at which sixteen-year-old Frida was the belle of the ball in a white muslin dress and 'was actually asked to dance by every dancing gentleman there'. (The 'dancing gentlemen' also included two closer cousins, one being Percy, the

Lord Kitchener's visit to Cambridge 24 November 1898

other Howard Warren, scion of another branch of her extended family and in later life a solicitor and one of her trustees.) She appointed two dances to Percy, two to Howard, and four to Archie who was immediately 'astonishingly friendly' (he called her 'Frida' instead of 'Miss Tillyard'!) but who in spite of this breach of etiquette 'contributed greatly to [her] enjoyment'.[88]

To Percy's dismay and in spite of her passion for Lord Kitchener, Archie and Frida become fast friends, she regarding him as 'very jolly indeed'[89] and even though he made her 'abominably wild'[90] with his teasing, found his attentions more acceptable than Percy's. (She particularly enjoyed a chaperoned trip on the Cam in 'the most charming Canader imaginable … the evening was glorious and "Paradise" was at its best'.)[91] Within two months of their meeting, their relationship had passed beyond mere friendship, Archie suggesting to Frida that she call him 'Uncle Archibald' because 'he wished to know how it felt to stand to [her] "in an avuncular capacity"' and Frida responding flirtatiously and with 'a warm handclasp' and even, following a tête-à-tête in the kitchen garden and though she was aware that her behaviour might exceed the limits of propriety, by suggesting that as 'uncle' and 'niece' and because 'I have to throw myself into a part thoroughly', she ought to be allowed to kiss him on the cheek. Archie did not accept her suggestion but later, knowing that term was about to end and that he would not see her for some time, exchanged sprigs of lavender with her as symbols of their new relationship and blew her a kiss as he walked away.[92]

Frida, however, had a rival for Archie's affections, a young lady called Kate to whom he was not engaged but to whom he wrote every day. A 'long excursus on the *absolute impossibility* of a platonic friendship between and a woman' delivered by Archie in June 1900 puzzled Frida so much (she had no idea what he was talking about) that she decided to regard him as an 'interesting psycological (*sic*) study' and, when she understood him better, to put him in a novel.[93] (She did; Archie duly appeared as 'Doctor Berisford' in *The Ending of the Way* with the comment that the character was drawn 'really well'; Marie Feyler, noting astutely that Frida portrayed more than one beloved in her *roman-à-clef*, taxed its author with her '*passion*'.)[94] In spite, however, of discovering that Archie's attachment to Kate was not an engagement (Kate was the wife of the headmaster at the school at which Archie had previously taught; her husband was a drunkard and she had turned to Archie for protection and support, but he, though 'very intimate with her', had insisted on a platonic relationship only – 'he would never have married her', as adult Aelfrida euphemistically put it – and left the school hurriedly before their intimacy became a scandal)[95], Frida, it seems, had 'fallen as deeply in love with him as is possible for a girl of … 16'[96], though with unattainable Lord Kitchener occupying her thoughts, pretended she had not ('he means nothing') and to be relieved that the end of term meant she would not see Archie for some months.[97]

She and Archie never met again. Her feeling that Archie had something inexplicably 'pathetic'[98] about him portended more than she realised: whether it was the strain of his 'pure love' for Kate or 'overwork' in Cambridge (he was working for a higher degree in the intervals of teaching) or for some other reason, early in 1901 Frida, then abroad, received 'news from home … tinged with melancholy … Archie is paralysed and dying'.[99] His illness ran a rapid course; a single line entry occupying two facing pages of her diary and the insertion of a pasted-in cutting from a newspaper shows the depth of her heartbreak for a man she had almost persuaded herself she did not love:

'I have just heard that Archie is dead'.
"STENT – April 29th [1901] at Whitchurch Canonicorum Vicarage, William Archibald Herbert Stent … late Mathematical Master of King's College Choir School, aged 27".[100]

Trying to distract herself with physical activity in the hope that exercise would 'blow away … thoughts I wished to put out of my mind', Frida found herself brooding instead over 'the conversations we had together … his looks and his gestures'[101], over the afternoon when she stood in Fordfield garden watching with tears in her eyes her 'nicest cousin walk down the Avenue throwing kisses on the way', over the 'tiny sprig of lavender' that was her only physical reminder of him.[102] (Wandering round the garden three years later, she 'set up imaginary monuments' to show where particularly poignant things had happened; one 'monument' was the lavender bush from which Archie's sprig was picked.)[103] She also found herself comparing '*intensely human*' Archie with the god-like 'statue on the pedestal' and unhearing 'idol' who was 'you know who' and hoping that Lord Kitchener (if 'you know who' was he; she makes enigmatic reference to someone else) would not be hurt if she allotted Archie 'a *special* place' in her heart or placed him in one of the 'unfilled … nitches' (*sic*) surrounding her 'idol'. She also tried to persuade herself that although she *did* 'care for' Archie, it was not in a 'being-in-love sort of way'. (Or even in a 'cousinly' or 'sisterly' way, so 'mixed' were her emotions and so undecided his place in her affections.)[104] Worse was to follow: her mother, she discovered, had known of Kate's existence before Archie came to Cambridge and had deliberately allowed her daughter to believe that Archie and Kate were engaged lest Frida became too fond of him, and Kate, her husband now in a 'lunatic asylum', had tended Archie throughout his last illness.[105] 'Things might have been worse', Frida concluded on learning this, for she too 'might have been in love with Archie' and, nonsensical as it seemed when written down, he might have loved her had neither loved someone else.[106] But what we do not learn until much later though with hints thrown out might have guessed earlier, is that the 'someone else' whom Frida *truly* loved was neither Herbert Kitchener nor the unnamed man 'on the tall black horse'[107] to whom she enigmatically alludes when comparing Archie and 'the Duke'. But nor was he any of the other men with whom she played at 'Flirting' of whom between 1898 and 1900 there were many.

The young men (they included yet another distant cousin: 'Harry Shipway from America [who] is "doing" Europe in about a month in true Yankee fashion'; he brought her 'candy'[108] from Henry Joseph's brother Samuel) were chiefly but not exclusively Nonconformist undergraduates invited to Sunday tea by Alfred and Catharine Tillyard. They also included Julius' school friend, James Stark nervously supposing that Frida was doing her best to 'catch' him and 'carefully on his guard against … sentimentality'[109] and Francis (Frank) Fulford, of whom Frida says surprisingly little though she rated the future Cambridge vicar highly, those introduced (reluctantly) by Percy or by young men who had already gained entrée to Fordfield (of the Bull brothers Charlie and Harry, Frida preferred the latter, Charlie being merely 'a jolly little boy' but Harry rather 'mad', the latter trait appealing to the reckless side of her own nature and adding spice to the 'lovely talk[s]' she enjoyed with him under the jealous eye of cousin Percy who timed their duration)[110], those met at dances, garden parties, and picnics such as 'handsome and haughty'[111] Leo Myers, and those connected by marriage to her Hunstanton relatives, in particular 'charming' Roy Page to whom Frida felt attracted until she discovered that his managing mother was 'aunting' for a son who had recently suffered a 'complete breakdown' due to overwork. To Frida's relief, Roy was packed off to Australia to recover, there to marry an older woman and to die in 1917.[112]

It was not only in Cambridge that Frida flirted with young men to Percy's chagrin and 'to [her] heart's content'[113] under Catharine's amused but watchful eyes or those of chaperoning hostesses; it was also when away from home and with older men of whom she knew nothing. Whether it was their age or their personalities or because temporarily freed from Fordfield rules of conduct, she mistook liberty for licence, it is hard to say but one occasion in particular typifies behaviour which was at best risky and at worst *risqué*.

Staying in Hampshire with Lucy Longstaffe in July 1900 soon after saying goodbye to Archie Stent, Frida found her sixteen-year-old 'dearest and best friend' in the throes of a flirtation with 'young gentleman cadet' Robin Smart, a flirtation contrived by Mrs Longstaffe to see if her daughter and Robin were as compatible as her hopes for a match between them were high. (They were not: Lucy, after a brief engagement to James Stark, married someone else; Robin Smart fell heavily for Frida whom he initially disliked and was killed in the Great War several years after she repulsed him.) Contrasting her own feelings for her 'big solder' with Lucy's tepid ones for Robin and noting how much she wanted Lord Kitchener to gaze at her as Robin at Lucy, she commented pointedly that 'anyone with a sense of humour' would be amused by the way Robin and Lucy 'made love to each other in cold blood … to see how they would like it if they did it in hot'.[114] Whether in emulation of her friend or fired by the positive results of her brief relationship with Archie Stent or possessed by a need to prove that she was *not* powerless where men (especially older men) were concerned or by a need (she called it an 'instinct') 'to try and touch and awaken every man I meet'[115], Frida, a true coquette or a damaged personality according to one's point of view, embarked on a brief relationship ('it was to be a flirtation and by Jove it was! … the fastest bit of flirting I have ever done', a fine ambiguity given that 'fast' in this context could mean that she flirted speedily or recklessly; to call a woman 'fast' was not to pay her a compliment) with a fellow

guest, one Dumville Smythe, a single man of 'about 28, handsome [with] a keen sense of humour [who] knows the rules of flirtation'.[116]

The 'flirtation' succeeded beyond her hopes. She began by confusing her prey by dressing and behaving at one moment as if she were 'out', at the next as if she were not. She then obtained Mr Smythe's address and proposed that they correspond, behaviour which so shocked Robin Smart that he begged Lucy to rescue her friend from the clutches of a 'blasé roué'. Roué or not, Dumville Smythe seems to have abided by the rules of flirtation until shortly after Frida's arrival home; a letter from him to her was pounced upon by Catharine Tillyard who seemed disposed to consider Mr Smythe 'an eligible "*parti*"' (she asked for details of his 'appearance, morals and income')[117] but who on further investigation forbade further correspondence or at most 'a curt p.c.' (She also opened more of Mr Smythe's letters before passing them on to her daughter.)[118] Frida did not know whether to be more amused at her mother's reaction to 'some designing wretch who wishes to make love to her daughter'[119] or at her own success in attracting 'an inveterate flirt' whom she would probably never see again (a fact which somehow made her behaviour in Hampshire less 'shocking')[120], for whom she did not care in the least, and with whom she had had 'some fun' even if (in retrospect) she had been rather 'silly'.[121]

The story, however, does not end there. Dumville Smythe and Frida, or rather Aelfrida, for she had by then 'come out', met once more. In July 1901 while staying with the Longstaffes in London, Aelfrida attended their 'squash', the current term for a crowded social function. Believing herself to be 'someone quite different'[122] to the fast-flirting teenager of the year before, she proved herself 'fast' in the worst possible sense by flirting heavily with Mr Smythe, one of the two men forming "an oasis … in the desert of all the fashionably dressed ladies", in front of his new wife. Her sober letter to Julius describing the event fails to describe Lucy's mother's wrath or her own abrupt dismissal, a dismissal so abrupt ("one of the men was married … I shall be gone soon")[123] that, passing across London to Kings Cross, she was unable to catch a glimpse of Lord Kitchener on a triumphal visit to England to celebrate the end of the Boer War.

In a later novel adult Aelfrida has a female character grade men of her acquaintance as "impossible", "possible" and "promising" and add comments on their "characters and absurdities"[124] to each category. She herself placed them in 'classes'. Class 1 (it contained only four names: Archie Stent, Dumville Smythe, one of the Bull brothers, probably Harry, and a 'Mr Letham') was at the top. Class 2 contained six names including James Stark,

Frank Fulford, Roy Page (he only just missed Class 1), and three others, one to be described in due course, one a 'Mr Whittaker', and one Russell Fordham, eldest son of the Fordham family of Odsey, formerly 'rude and disagreeable [but] now handsome and usually …attentive'.[125] The third class was too 'huge' to list individual names; a fourth existed but was not enlarged upon.[126]

Messrs Letham (actually, Leatham) and Whittaker were young dons, both mathematicians, James Leatham, aged thirty, being Frida's favourite because of his sense of humour, his 'fetching [Irish] brogue' and his ability to pay compliments[127], her mother's Presbyterian Edmund Whittaker, aged twenty-seven, but in Frida's eyes 'quite oppressively good … and you would trust him to any extent but he is a little dull'.[128] Her comments are relevant, for with her daughter now officially 'out' Catharine Tillyard was 'aunting' for possible husbands and, having noted Frida's preference for older men and her own for a man whose *gravitas* and maturity would act as a brake on a young woman whose behaviour was verging on the unconventional and the improper, was taking steps to find one – and who more suitable than Cambridge dons ten years older than Frida herself, settled in their academic careers but young enough to appreciate a wife whose own education was nearing completion (Frida, together with Helen Verrall, was currently coached by recent graduates) and included 'Latin, Greek, Philosophy, Italian, Literature, History (Roman) and piccolo playing'[129], and who came from a respected local family, wrong side of the 'town–gown' divide though it might be. Neither gentleman, however, evinced any interest in Frida as a possible '*parti*': included in the news 'tinged with melancholy' received in 1901, was Edmund Whittaker's engagement to a Mary Boyd – 'Mama's little plan knocked down' – and John Leatham's to a 'Belfast girl' – 'my little ditto dittoed'.[130] But all was not lost: girls had brothers and brothers had their uses.

The spring of 1900 saw Frida suddenly engaged in relationships of a different kind: 'all the girls I know have taken to putting their arms round me and being very affectionate!'[131] Although she professed ignorance of the cause of this unusual phenomenon – other than Lucy Longstaffe and Silvia Myers, she was not disposed to female friendships – two possible reasons present themselves. The first is that Frida's vivacious personality had begun to prove as attractive to girls of her own age as to young and slightly older men; the second, that Frida had an older brother due to matriculate at a Cambridge college in October ('hurrah! Julius has got a scholarship … at Caius. Hurrah! … I am so happy, so blissfully radiant … I cannot thank God enough')[132] who during school holidays and exeats brought male acquaintances home to Fordfield for tea and tennis. Hence girls who had been only names or, like Dorothea Conybeare, Perse contemporaries during Frida's unhappy stay, suddenly showed an interest in becoming bosom friends with a girl in whom they had previously shown little or none. It was, however, with only one of these that Frida engaged in reciprocal friendship (her more usual view of Cambridge contemporaries was as rivals or inferiors in 'Flirting' terms) though less because of the charms of Dorothea's handsome brother James, ordained in 1891, on whom she cast a covetous but unrequited eye, than because she was 'aunting' in a small way for Julius and regarded Dorothea as a potential wife. (Dorothea was also distantly related to Lord Kitchener 'and the thought that I should be … a little nearer to my hero' threw Frida into a 'state of agitation'.)[133] But Julius had eyes only for his sister and neither Dorothea nor Lucy (also 'aunted for' by a sister who enjoyed marrying off Julius in her mind to girls of her own choosing) became Mrs HJW Tillyard, though in Dorothea's case not for lack of trying. But none of the young men Julius brought home married his sister – or any of her female friends.

Packed with incident though the years 1898–1900 had been – and what has been described here is only an abbreviated version of Frida's 'passions', large and small, her holidays and visits, her education, her flirtations, her earliest literary efforts, and her home and social life, particularly the latter to which she makes frequent excited references to 'heaps of parties'[134], to 'lovely new dress[es]' ('people may say that dress makes no difference to one's happiness but … I can never enjoy myself unless I feel *suitably* clothed')[135] and to being 'young' and life being 'fun'[136] and with the prospect of more 'fun' in store – to judge by contemporary diary entries she was often desperately gay or gaily desperate rather than truly happy. References to her lack of happiness even in matters concerning which she might expect to be happy are both cryptic ('I am unhappy yet my unhappiness is the greatest joy of my life … and for all God's other gifts may I be truly thankful'[137]; 'Heaven knows, I feel sad enough sometimes … when – but *no*! I said I wouldn't and I shan't'[138]; 'I suppose I am happy … and yet and yet – what a *fool* I am!')[139] and sufficiently frequent and anguished and adorned with punctuation marks and underlinings ('What is fun but a … narcotic? … Frida Tillyard, you are a little *fool*!'[140]; 'sometimes when I can't sleep, I wonder if I am mad', albeit 'I am too commonplace … to even aspire to the dignity of mental aberration'. 'Oh!!! ACWT 1904')[141] to suggest that for all her apparent gaiety, Frida and sorrow were well acquainted and that the "despair" which "laid cold hands on [her] heart"[142] was an omnipresent phenomenon.

But what other than unrequited love and the pressure of what Julius punningly called Percy's "persecution"[143] (Frida's father played no part in admonishing Percy and Percy might not have been so pressing had Julius been in Cambridge to provide brotherly protection) could have caused adolescent Frida at 'silly, silly sixteen'[144] to feel so globally unhappy? True, she has confided more to her diary than to any human being, unmasking there her 'follies … thoughts [and] very heart' (she also urges her diary to 'keep [her] secrets well'[145]; it does, and not until much later does it divulge them with the help of an inconspicuous notebook) but those unconfided may be guessed: the prospect of being prepared by her mother for the marriage market, with all that that implied of being released from the constraints of childhood only to find herself handed over to the authority of that necessary evil, a husband; Julius' impending return to Cambridge, for a brother who adored her might be both hurt and annoyed by her 'Flirting' and expect her to pay more attention to himself than to other men; her being expected to pay duty calls as if married already (At Homes were boring and if there was 'a little music'[146], worse than boring; at a garden party at Homerton Teachers Training College, the ices were 'poisonous'[147] and the lady trainees common) and to play an active part in the social services provided by the congregation of St Columba's Church which, prosperous itself, dispensed charity to the local poor.

Frida's baptism and first Communion took place sometime early in 1899 (she was too busy, she said, to record them at the time), qualifying her to act as relief instructor at St Columba's Sunday School. Her class consisted of ten 'townee' boys aged eleven to thirteen but unfazed by taking on what others might consider a difficult undertaking (she was not much older than the older boys but lacked neither self-importance nor self-confidence and had been bossing Eustace for years), she soon had her class in hand ('the cheeky ones [are] quiet and orderly and the shy ones have begun to answer well') and began to enjoy herself. Sunday School teachers were also expected to visit the homes of their pupils, to accompany them on school trips, and to take an interest in the lives and future prospects of individual boys, so she did. The boys reciprocated, crowding round 'teacher's' chair to tell her 'how many runs they made at cricket or how their brothers in Africa are getting on or some bit of praise they had from their employers'. 'They seem', wrote flattered but exhausted Frida, 'to think I know everything … for they ask me dreadful questions about everything under the sun', itself a testimonial to Frida's ability to draw them out – and to instruct, for it was in the boys' class that she first became aware of her potential as an

educator. (And also, one might add, of the gratification of 'getting a hold on' other people's minds and lives.) The boys' fondness for and admiration of her had an unforeseen consequence: for the first time in her life, Frida realised that she was both 'selfish, idle [and] hypocritical'[148] and unworthy of respect and awoke to the baser aspects of her nature. This, and a minor 'pash' on the then Minister of St Columba's, caused her to take religion more seriously than before and to derive consolation from it – as witness increased references to Deity in her diary and to the appearance there of pious quotations. ("*Foi en tout*"; "what is the chief end of man? To glorify God and to enjoy Him for ever"[149], and so on.) But contemporary accusations from Silvia Myers that she was becoming very 'pi'[150] (i.e. pious in a sanctimonious way) also manifest the beginnings of what would become one of her less endearing traits.

Further worries occurred in November 1899 when Frida was otherwise engaged with official occasions (the opening of Westminster College), with mixed metaphorical jubilations regarding Julius' Cambridge scholarship ('he licked 70 candidates into a top hat!'), and with 'the matter with Percy'. Recorded in the same entry as the above is that 'Sweeter' had been elected mayor of Cambridge.

Alfred Tillyard was elected on 9 November 1899; his daughter's prognostications that his year's mayoralty would be 'fun' did and did not come true. True, she enjoyed 'Papa's big party'[151] at the Town Hall on 10 May 1900, otherwise memorable for her first meeting with Archie Stent) and attended a council meeting 'to see Papa preside' (it was 'very interesting' but gave her 'an awful headache')[152] from which she collected 'copy' (a lengthy description of Cambridge local government appears in her 1924 book *Messages*) and the status afforded 'the Mayor's daughter' when she acted as bridesmaid to a former Fordfield cook. (The same cook who had informed her that Conrad had gone to Heaven.) She also made fun of her parents in the *MCJ*: "the Lady Mayoress is, we regret to say, suffering from a severe attack of influenza but would be well enough by 9 May to give a brilliant and recherché party"; a sketch of "Councillor AI Tillyard MA Mayor of Cambridge" on his tricycle.[153] But there was a darker side too to being in the public eye and although the mayor's daughter found certain events rather thrilling, she also gained an unusually early experience of the power of the mob, of the press, and of public opinion.

As mayor and mayoress, Alfred and Catharine Tillyard expected their children (even eleven-year-old Eustace, described by his sister as 'Worthless') to support them in the course of their civic duties, be those a lunch with 'worthy farmers … in the fens' or a breakfast given for Cambridge Volunteers bound for the South African War.[154] But as events which erupted in Cambridge as a result of British victories in that war were to prove, Alfred Tillyard's tenure of the joint positions of mayor and magistrate was not without danger to his family.

News of the relief of besieged Kimberley evoked only quiet rejoicing in a town whence so many young men had gone as Volunteers but the relief of Ladysmith on 29 February 1900 was the occasion for 'a "rag à la Sirdar" …on Market Hill' in the course of which 'bonfires were made [with] fuel supplied from … shutters, ladders [and] the bandstand on Christ's Pieces'.[155] Presiding at next day's Sessions, Alfred Tillyard dispensed severe justice to an undergraduate and a 'townee'. (The 'townee' had wounded a policeman and was a regular offender but magistrate Tillyard was harder on the student because he was president of the Cambridge Junior Christian Union and had a Bible in his pocket when arrested; graduate members of the university and two other townsmen were also convicted.) Convictions of felony when applied to regular 'townee' offenders were one thing but when applied to "young men of education" described by Alfred Tillyard as no better in the current context than "cads" living in the rough Barnwell area of town[156] quite another, and to Frida's delight ('what a lark!') and her mother and Eustace's alarm, a mob of 'roughs'[157] composed chiefly of 'varsity men' but with 'townees' among them besieged Fordfield for several nights between 2 and 10 March. Although the 3 March copy of the *MCJ* provided a mock-heroic account ("in consequence of the Mayor … sending a man to prison for 3 months … a huge gang … were coming to set fire to and to wreck this noble mansion … [but] there was no loss of life") and that of 8 March light-hearted advice on *What to do if attacked by rioters* ("have plenty of water in case you faint")[158], the incident was ugly and it was only due to a police presence day and night that nobody and nothing was hurt or damaged.

What Frida might have but unfortunately did not learn from an affair which was less a 'lark' as an occasion on which the actions of a single member of the Tillyard family resulted in unpleasant consequences for all, was that not only did actions, even seemingly right or justified ones, have consequences, but also that the consequences might be both unforeseen and damaging – to reputations, if not to property and persons. Not only this, but to calm the situation Alfred Tillyard was forced to retract his statement concerning 'oafs' (something reported at gloating length by a rival local newspaper) and was subjected to the indignity of having his sentences overturned by the Home Secretary as a result of

a "signed petition from Cambridge for a grant of Free Pardon to the defendants"[159] stating that charges of theft did not warrant convictions for felony. The event was summarised by Alfred's daughter as a 'slap in the face for justice, law and order' and her father.[160]

An *MCJ* report by 'Lieutenant Mandeville' reporting "the greatly longed for news" of the relief of Mafeking on 17 May 1900 and an imaginary interview, by-lined "Mafeking May 19th", conducted with Colonel Baden-Powell, in which the colonel, addressing 'Lieutenant Mandeville', noted that the latter came from Cambridge, played cricket, collected stamps, enjoyed "fighting" and had lately "been sticking a lot of Boers with a bayonet", also included references to "a big bonfire [being] by the Mayoress lit" and to the mayor thinking it "wise to fly"[161] the event. The bonfire in question ('as big as this house and enclosed by iron railings') was lit by Catharine Tillyard but when undergraduates remarked on unpopular Alfred Tillyard's presence as mayor, the family was advised by plain clothes policemen in attendance on them that there would be a 'row' if he stayed. The group was therefore obliged to 'ignominiously slink home by side alleys'.[162] What Frida again failed to note was that personal unpopularity arising as a result of seemingly righteous actions might continue long after the actions themselves were history.

With her home threatened by a hostile mob ('the undergrads generally use rockets to break windows … last night [they] brought tar barrels to set the house on fire'; with only forty policemen against four hundred rioters, the affair might have meant the ending of Frida's 'lovely adventure'[163] in mayhem at best and tragedy at worst), her personal space invaded by Percy Stanley, her passion for Lord Kitchener causing her to become 'hysterical'[164] (her mother's word) at the mere mention of his name, her father piling on pressures of an educational nature (she was still expected to do several hours study a day even in the holidays), the frenetic gaiety of her flirtations masking deeper unhappinesses, the unappealing prospect of the marriage market before her, and present realisation before her that given the life she led, she was in danger of becoming 'horrid, worldly and selfish'[165], Frida was glad to be 'going away' even if 'going away' meant to a household 'composed of one old maid', for although this life would present 'a very wide horizon for [her] to study' it would also be 'a quieter corner of the world'.[166] But where Frida is and Aelfrida will be, no corner of the world could or would be quiet and it was and will be as much from internal as from external storms and stresses that Frida and Aelfrida will find themselves running away in a pattern of escapes which are no escapes because the emotional burdens they carry go with them.

And where Frida is going in October 1900 will become notorious not only for the contrast between what she does or intends to do and what her parents intend her to do, but also for being the place where her sentimental education – her education, that is to say, in how and how not to conduct herself towards men in matters of the heart – really begins.

A diary entry made a few weeks prior to departure sums up where she, her family, and her best friend stand at this crossroads in her life:

'Papa is Mayor'.

'Mama is – isn't it strange? Mayoress'.

Julius 'has left Tonbridge where he won more honours than any boy had ever won' and is spending his holiday 'basket-making and writing a long school story'.

'Swab' is now at 'Mr Goodchild's' and will probably remain there two more years.

Lucy Longstaffe is loved 'much more than I could ever love a sister'.

Frida herself is not altogether sorry that lessons have finally come to an end 'for I am going to Lausanne and I am looking forward to seeing something of the world'.[167]

# Notes

1 GCPPT 1|1|45 27 November 1933.
2 GCPPT 1|1|4 18 January 1900.
3 ibid. 21 December 1897.
4 Flora Annie Steel (1847–1929) was the school inspector wife of an official in the Indian Civil Service, a proponent of women's education and author of numerous short stories, novels and children's books on the subject of Anglo–Indian life in the Punjab. She was also a keen gardener. Aelfrida names her incorrectly as 'Florence Annie Steele'.
5 GCPPT 1|1|61 13 March 1943.
   GCPPT 1|1|4 21 December 1897.
6 GCPPT 1|1|61 13 March 1943.
7 GCPPT 1|1|4 6 January 1898.
8 ibid. 24 February 1900.
9 ibid. 31 March 1898.
10 ibid. 30 March 1898.
11 ibid. 3 September 1898.
12 ibid. 5 September 1898.
13 ibid. 25 and 29 August 1898.
14 ibid. 9 January 1900.
15 ibid. 18 January 1900.
16 ibid. 9 January 1900.
17 ibid. 24 February 1900.
18 ibid.
19 ibid. 'St Patrick's Day' (17 March ) 1900.
20 ibid. 17 April 1900.
21 GCPPT 2|2a Vol. 1 No. 3. 3 March 1900.
22 GCPPT 2|27|2(3).
23 GCPPT 2|2a Vol. 1 No. 3. 3 March 1900.
24 GCPPT 2|2a Vol. 1 No. 1. 7 February 1900.
25 GCPPT 2|2a Vol. 1 No. 6. (Undated).
26 GCPPT 1|1|5 25 June 1900.
27 ibid.
28 GCPPT 2|2a Vol. 2 No. 2 September 1903.
29 GCPPT 1|1|9 30 March 1902.
30 For Aelfrida's later description of the Stanleys see GCPPT 2|26|2(2) *The Stanleys* and *The Way We Grow Up* where the Stanleys appear as the 'Cardons'.
31 GCPPT 1|1|71 19 October 1953.
32 GCPPT 2|26|4(2).
33 GCPPT 1|1|11 13 May 1904.
34 GCPPT 1|1|4 18 August 1899.
   Tillyard, Ae. *O Passionate World* pp 197–198 (GCPPT 2|11).
35 GCPPT 1|1|4 10 November 1899.
36 ibid. 1 May 1900.
37 ibid. 17 May 1900.
38 ibid. 20 May 1900.
39 GCPPT 1|1|5 12 June 1900.
40 ibid. 13 June 1900.
41 ibid. 12 June 1900.
42 ibid. 3 June 1900.
43 ibid. 17 July 1900.
44 ibid. 18 July 1900.
45 ibid. 11 August 1900.
46 GCPPT 1|1|4 10 May 1900.
47 GCPPT 1|1|12 9 June 1905.
48 GCPPT 1|1|20 17 April 1914.
49 GCPPT 1|1|5 3 June 1900.
50 GCPPT 1|1|4 27 November 1898.
51 *Cambridge Daily News* 24 November 1998. For details of Herbert Kitchener's life and military career, see *ODNB* 33 pp 829–236.
52 GCPPT 1|1|4 27 November 1898.
53 *CDN* 24 November 1898.
54 GCPPT 1|1|4 27 November 1898. 'Sirdar' was the local title awarded Lord Kitchener as Commander-in-Chief of the Anglo-Egyptian army.
55 GCPPG.A1.1. 27 April 1924.
56 GCPPT 2|26|3 *The Schechters.*
57 GCPPT 1|1|4 31 March 1898.
58 GCPPT 2|26|3 *The Schechters.*
59 Tillyard, HJW. Introduction to *The Letters of ACW Tillyard* (MTC).
60 GCPPT 1|1|4 12 December 1898. Kitchener was created Baron Kitchener of Khartoum in 1898.
61 Tillyard HJW. Introduction to *The Letters of ACW Tillyard* (MTC). We do not know whence Frida derived the novel's title; the phrase was commonly used to describe a life drawing to its close.
62 GCPPT 1|1|7 7 June 1901.
63 GCPPT 1|1|5 14 July 1900.
64 GCPPT 1|1|4 25 December 1899.
65 ibid. 13 May 1900.
66 GCPPT 1|1|5 29 June 1900.
67 ibid. 4 June 1900.
68 ibid. 11 June 1900.
69 ibid. 14 June 1900.
70 ibid. 20 July 1900.
71 ibid. 3 and 4 June 1900.
72 ibid. 20 July 1900.
73 GCPPT 1|1|6 1 November 1900.
74 ibid. 14 November 1900.
75 ibid.
76 ibid.
77 ibid. 12 December 1900.
78 GCPPT 1|1|6 20 September 1900.
79 GCPPT 1|1|8 18 August 1901.
80 GCPPT 1|1|12 21 August 1903.
81 GCPPT 2|2a Vol. 2 No. 2. September 1903.
82 GCPPT 1|1|12 11 November 1904.

83  GCPPT 1|1|67 2 September 1950.
84  GCPPT 2|26|2(2).
85  GCPPT 1|1|30 15 February 1925.
86  GCPPT 2|26|3 *The Schechters*.
87  GCPPT 1|1|4 10 and 13 May 1900.
88  ibid.10 May 1900.
89  ibid. 13 May 1900.
90  GCPPT 1|1|5 10 June 1900.
91  ibid. 23 June 1900. 'Paradise' was not in this instance the Garden of Eden but the local name for a small riverside wood between Coe Fen and Grantchester.
92  ibid. 4 and 22 July 1900.
93  ibid. 10 June 1900.
94  GCPPT 1|1|7 31 May and 1 June 1901.
95  GCPPT 1|1|8 28 July 1901.
    GCPPT 1|1|13 1 August 1906.
96  GCPPT 1|1|73 26 May 1956.
97  GCPPT 1|1|5 22 July 1900.
98  GCPPT 1|1|4 20 May 1900.
99  GCPPT 1|1|6 22 March 1901.
100  GCPPT 1|1|7 11 May 1901.
101  ibid. 2 May 1901.
102  GCPPT 1|1|6 2 March 1901.
103  GCPPT 1|1|11 22 May 1904.
104  GCPPT 1|1|7 2 May 1901.
105  GCPPT 1|1|6 22 March 1901.
    GCPPT 1|1|8 28 July 1901.
106  GCPPT 1|1|6 22 March 1901
    GCPPT 1|1|8 26 July 1901.
107  GCPPT 1|1|7 2 May 1901.
108  GCPPT 1|1|4 11 August 1898. Harry Shipway was the son of Harry Joseph Wetenhall's sister Sarah who married a George Shipway sometime after Henry and Sarah Wetenhall's arrival in America.
109  ibid. 15 April 1900.
110  GCPPT 1|1|4 21 May 1900.
    GCPPT 1|1|5 9 June and 16 and 20 July 1900. Charles Bull later took Holy Orders; Harry Bull preferred the Indian Civil Service to early death and was last heard of in Bombay.
111  GCPPT 1|1|5 30 June 1900.
112  GCPPT 1|1|5 27 June 1900.
    GCPPT 1|1|10 6 September 1903.
113  GCPPT 1|1|5 18 July 1900.
114  ibid. 8 August 1900.
115  GCPPT 1|1|32 7 March 1926.
116  GCPPT 1|1|5 8 August 1900.
117  ibid. 26 August 1900.
118  GCPPT 1|1|5 26 and 30 August 1900.
    GCPPT 1|1|6 23 October 1900.
119  GCPPT 1|1|6 23 October 1900.
120  GCPPT 1|1|5 8 and 26 August 1900.
121  ibid. 30 August 1900.
122  ibid. 8 August 1900.
123  Tillyard, HJW. *The Letters of ACW Tillyard*. (MTC). Letter from Aelfrida to Julius Tillyard of 8 July 1902.
124  Tillyard, Ae. *Marrying a Stranger* p 168 (GCPPT 2|6).

125  GCPPT 1|1|5 26 August 1900.
126  ibid. 2 September 1900.
127  ibid. 2 June 1900. For details of John Leatham's academic career, see Venn, J. Part 2 Vol. 4.
128  ibid. 28 August 1900. For details of Edmund Whittaker's illustrious career, see Venn, J. Part 2 Vol. 6.
129  ibid. 19 June 1900.
130  GCPPT 1|1|6 22 March 1901. Messrs Whittaker and Leatham's defection did not pass without scurrilous comment; the *MCJ* of 15 January 1903 (Vol. 2 No 1) contains a description of an aunt 'aunting' for three orphaned nieces in her charge: "Oct 12th. The men are up. I have selected one or two. [Mr Whittaker is] in a remarkably good position and *so* talented … Could dear Elsie fancy Mr Le[a]tham? … May 14th. That horrid Mr Le[a]tham has been engaged to some nasty Irish girl all along. I think it wicked to trifle with girls' affections …" (GCPPT 2|2a).
131  GCPPT 1|1|5 29 May 1900.
132  GCPPT 1|1|4 17 November 1899.
133  GCPPT 1|1|7 26 May 1901.
134  GCPPT 1|1|4 9 January 1900.
135  GCPPT 1|1|5 28 May 1900.
136  ibid. 2 June 1900.
137  GCPPT 1|1|4 21 May 1900.
138  GCPPT 1|1|5 2 June 1900.
139  ibid. 5 June 1900.
140  ibid. 10 June 1900.
141  ibid. 2 September 1900.
142  ibid. Poem entitled *Vision of Sorrow* inscribed in back of volume.
143  GCPPT 1|1|6 14 November 1900.
144  GCPPT 1|1|5 10 June 1900.
145  GCPPT 1|1|4 23 May 1900.
146  GCPPT 1|1|5 29 May 1900.
147  ibid. 23 June 1900.
148  ibid. 2 September 1900.
149  GCPPT 1|1|9 Inscriptions on first page and inside end cover.
150  GCPPT 1|1|4 5 May 1900.
151  ibid. 10 May 1900.
152  GCPPT 1|1|6 20 September 1900.
153  GCPPT 2|2a. Vol. 1 No. 2 16 February 1900; Vol. 1 No. 6 (undated).
154  GCPPT 1|1|5 2 September 1900.
155  GCPPT 1|1|4 2 March 1900.
156  *CDN* 1,2,3,5 March and 2 and 19 May 1900.
157  GCPPT 1|1|4 2 March 1900.
158  GCPPT 2|2a Vol. 1 No. 3 3 March 1900; Vol. 1 No. 4. 8 March 1901.
159  Letter from the Under-Secretary of State to Alfred Tillyard of 17 March 1900 (MTC).
160  GCPPT 1|1|4 20 March 1900.
161  GCPPT 2|2a Vol. 1 No. 8 Undated but by context 19 or 20 May 1900.
162  GCPPT 1|1|4 20 May 1900.
163  ibid. 6 and 7 March 1900.
164  ibid. 3 March 1900.
165  GCPPT 1|1|5 14 August 1900.
166  GCPPT 1|1|6 4 and 20 September 1900.
167  ibid. 4 September 1900.

# Avenue des Alpes

The Lausanne in which sixteen-year-old Frida found herself on 29 September 1900 was a town only just breaking free from the mediaeval walls which had hitherto confined it to the hilltop on which perched its castle and cathedral; beyond the valley through which ran the railway connecting Lausanne with the rest of Europe, the gently-sloping Lake Leman littoral with its small lakeside ports remained essentially rural. The town also contained a thriving British expatriate community drawn to the Vaud canton by its being an island of Protestantism in a Catholic sea and a centre of advanced and outward-looking culture and commerce in contrast, the rest of Switzerland being considered (by the Vaudois at least) to be stuffy and backward-looking. The British colony had its own churches, boarding schools, and library, and included Presbyterians with family connections to the congregation of St Columba's, and this and Vaud being a French-speaking canton persuaded Alfred and Catharine Tillyard that Lausanne would provide a suitable environment in which an adolescent daughter could further her linguistic and social education in a milieu where she would be in the care and company of kindred souls.

No 3 Avenue des Alpes where Frida lodged under the strict chaperonage of 'old maid' Mlle Dumur had been vouched for by others but not personally inspected by her parents. (Catharine Tillyard accompanied Frida as far as Paris but left her to make the rest of the journey attached to a guided tour.) The apartment block stood on a rise above the station in what must then have been a garden suburb, a tall building in restrained Belle Epoque style with glimpses of 'the real genuine Alps in all their grandeur and solemnity'[1] on one side and on the other "a superb view of the lake" and the mountains bordering it to the south. Lacking the spaciousness of Fordfield (and its chilly, introspective Victorian gloom), Mlle Dumur's apartment nevertheless possessed alluring compensations. In summer "wide-flung casement windows and glass doors" were opened to sunshine and breezes; in winter, expanses of shining parquet floors were covered with carpets, double windows installed, and an immense stove in the hall provided so much heat that Frida only had to keep her bedroom door open "to be warmer than you would be by the warmest English fireside".[2]

Avenue des Alpes, Lausanne

Within two months of her arrival, seventeen-year-old Frida flattered herself that she was 'getting to know everyone worth knowing and a good many who aren't'. (She was less pleased at having to swear 'eternal friendship with three girls I don't in the least care for'[3] but her description of her impact on them as "quite a *veni, vidi, vici* sort of thing, a *coup de main*, a look-and-die affair"[4] shows that her wit, vivacity, and charm carried as much clout among European *jeunes filles* as it did among Cambridge misses and undergraduates.) When not engaged with British colony (or more specifically, Presbyterian colony) activities, Mlle Dumur introduced her lodger to her own social circle (Frida's description of a *thé-de-dames* at which local ladies met to eat sticky or creamy cakes, to do 'fancy work', and to exchange gossip is both amusing and acutely observed) and to members of her own family who then included their foreign visitor in Christmas, Easter, and other activities and showed her something of the local countryside. ('Swiss trains are sweet. They have overhanging eaves like chalets'.)[5] Swiss mountain scenery with its 'purple gentians, Canterbury bells, dog daisies, wild pinks' and masses of narcissi whose scent 'almost intoxicated'[6] her and its peasant ceremonies ("I remember … going up the mountain path between trees of rhododendron in flower … to the high pastures to see the priest bless the cows and meadows")[7] enchanted her, though it has to be said that the style of her enthused descriptions owes much to her Baedeker guide and even more to Mary Annette Russell's novel *Elizabeth and her German Garden* in which luscious descriptions of wild and garden flowers abound.

Lessons took up much time because they required 'preparation and a good deal of solid reading at home'[8] and because they took place every weekday. In fact, Frida attended two local secondary schools (*gymnase*) at one of which she studied French composition, dictation and literature ('Verlaine … and all the rest of the worthless moderns')[9] in a *classe d'étrangères* and at the other, Italian and the history of art. As a budding writer she excelled in composition, one essay, 'a rather highly spiced' description of a Cambridge college rag, thought by Frida to demonstrate a little too much of her 'affection for undergrads!' being described by her teacher as both very clever ('quite true') and as demonstrating '*beaucoup d'ésprit*'[10], others (in which, as her teacher noted, she invariably described a husband, a lover, or some man or another; Frida's insouciant reply was that was the way life was) bringing about promotion to the top class for Swiss natives, 'the highest honour' for a foreigner, because of the fluency of her French, the purity of her style, and the originality of her thought.[11]

It was not, however, Verlaine who opened Frida's eyes to "many things not discussed at Fordfield"[12], it was Mlle Dumur. Funny old spinster though she may have been, Mlle Dumur collected modern novels and it was reading novels by Marie Louise Ramé (Ouida), Pierre Loti's *Pêcheur d'Islande*, and Oscar Wilde's *The Picture of Dorian Grey* (and Victor Hugo's tragedy *Le Roi s'amuse*, though this may have been a set text)[13] which encouraged Frida to take the next step in her sentimental education. Horses provided another reason.

Instead of her usual long walks and bicycle rides, Frida took riding lessons at an equestrian establishment at nearby Bellerive, the Manège Dufour, run by a professional instructor and his wife. By November 1900 she was practising quite advanced manoeuvres and taking small jumps and was able to mount and dismount at a trot (she rode astride wearing culottes) and to ride without using stirrups or reins. Lessons, group and solo, took place on Monday mornings and Thursday afternoons and were enjoyable not only because during them she was free from Mlle Dumur's chaperonage but also because she rapidly developed a 'crush' on the dashing owner of the *manège* from whose wife she inveigled a photograph of Jules Dufour himself 'in a smart light suit, leaning against a post smoking a cigarette'[14], a photograph which, together with one of Madame Dufour (a subterfuge: Frida did not want one of his wife but to ask for both was the only method of obtaining it) she stuck in the back of the current volume of her diary.

Details of riding lessons and horses ridden occupied many pages of her journal thereafter. She preferred 'difficult' horses because they offered more of a challenge – one wonders at M Dufour allowing a novice to ride them but she may have pretended to be more experienced than she was – and because they allowed her to behave recklessly, something she needed to do in order to put sad thoughts of Archie Stent out of her mind (it was in Lausanne that she heard the news of his fatal illness, of his being in 'a dreadful state', and that his mother was praying for death to end it)[15], and it may be, to court death herself: apropos a potentially fatal fall into the lake in the course of which her horse nearly rolled on her then, restored to its feet, bolted, she gloated in macabre fashion over the prospect of being 'reduced … to a pulp'[16] as if the prospect was not unwelcome.

There was also the likelihood that her bravery (in truth, bravado) would endear her to M Dufour and that some of her recklessness was engendered by a desire to show off to an older man who had already said of her "Miss Tillyard is quite charming", that he would like to know her better were it not that her being 'so haughty' discouraged him[17], and that she had the makings of a 'first-class *amazone*'.[18] (One of the many ironies in Aelfrida's later life was that, one notable occasion apart, the '*amazone*' thereafter rode only bicycles.) In public, Frida excused her haughtiness as a manifestation of English reserve but in the privacy of her diary noted that she 'would have liked to bestow a very intimate salute on such a handsome gent as her riding master' but lacking the courage to do so, would amend her haughtiness '*gradually*' so that M Dufour would not guess that the melting of her supposed reserve 'was not – well, not spontaneous'[19], a nicely calculated and calculating piece of behaviour in one already practised at dissimulation.

It seems, however, that she did not dissimulate as well as she thought; in late March 1901 Mlle Dumur lectured her 'on the wickedness of being in love with a married man'.[20] Perhaps she was: in the next volume but one of her diary she inserted a cut-out picture of a horseman on the reverse of which is an advertisement for a '*soirée equestrienne*' and in the current volume she notes in connection with two other men for whom she nursed secret passions (Archie Stent and Herbert Kitchener) that a third was the rider of 'a tall black horse'[21], namely (she does not name him) Dufour, who habitually rode Vasca, otherwise '*le grand noir*'. And with the habit already ingrained of expressing pent-up emotions in fictional form, one who not long before had noted that apart from having very little time in which to write novels, stories, or essays in *English,* she was also so bombarded with new impressions that she could not 'sop up and squeeze out at the same time' (this did not mean, she added, that she had relinquished 'all idea of being an authoress')[22], wrote two perfect short stories, preserved only because written in her diary and featuring Jules Dufour. The first, *A Bread and Butter Miss,* describes a younger single Dufour being "chucked" by a schoolgirl from a local *pensionnat* to whom he has become engaged[23], the other, entitled *Wednesday and Saturday from 2–4,* the relationship between shortly-to-be-married Dufour and a "Mlle Bloomer" who attends his *manège* ("*spécialité: leçons pour dames*") and insists on riding the most difficult horses at the times and on the days specified in the title, days in and times at which she only comes fully alive because she has fallen in love with her riding master.[24] How much of either story is embellished gossip, how much wishful thinking (in 1904, Aelfrida added a tart comment to the second story '*très sentimental!* ACWT'), how much autobiography, and how much a young writer inspired by 'copy' at hand, is hard to say, but briefly in love with Jules Dufour she obviously was. It is also obvious that what she experienced was a conventional 'crush' of which its object may have been aware but did nothing to encourage and which died a natural death when she left Lausanne: indeed, revisiting Lausanne in April 1903 when she, accompanied by Lucy Longstaffe, delivered fourteen-year-old Eustace into Mlle Dumur's hands when he too was about to become a '*collégien*', Aelfrida found herself unmoved by Jules Dufour's charms and was so delighted at having to return home early (Lucy was to be presented at court and was not allowed to travel alone) that she could barely act in a 'suitably melancholy'[25] manner on the day of departure.

In 1900, however, as later in 1903, Frida found herself suffering both 'from an excess of female society' and from a dearth of 'gentlemen friends'[26] and glut and dearth made life in Lausanne less exciting than she anticipated. She had also hoped that as an objective observer of life in Switzerland and as a 'pietist', a word on which she does not enlarge at this point, she was 'above the usual weakness of [her] sex' with regard to men ('oh you little humbug! What a pose! ACWT 1904') but being 'deprived altogether of the society of ... "pet undergrads"' ('the inevitable vulgarity of the young. ACWT 1904')[27] caused her to discover that she had deceived herself as to the purity of her intentions and that the colourful customs of local students notwithstanding, Swiss *étudiants* in no way measured up in charm or high spirits to Cambridge undergraduates.[28] Rather, therefore, than submit herself to the 'disagreeable necessity' of purely female friendships, she cast about for masculine company.

She found little; the few available men were either unsuitable or encountered under the watchful eye of Mlle Dumur. At a ball held early in 1901 (quitted just before midnight so as not 'to go on dancing into Sunday'; she admitted that her behaviour 'did look rather like cant'), she made a 'real conquest' of a 'large ... fair haired and sentimental German' with whom she danced eight dances and sat out two. The German, she wrote, 'made love [so] *hard* all the time', asking her 'age ... fortune, etc.', that 'the only wonder was that he did not ask for [her] hand then and there'.[29] (He may have believed Aelfrida older than she was, for she now wore long skirts and would have dressed her hair for the occasion and this, together with her assured attitude, slender carriage, and height – she was no longer small for her age – may have made her appear as 'grown up'[30] as she believed herself to be.) Her lack of years and fortune discouraged her potential suitor for thereafter he only bowed on meeting but Frida found her 'tall and huge'[31] suitor overwhelming and though glad of an opportunity for 'Flirting', did not encourage his attentions. Her subsequent discovery that von Wegel was both 'rich and a baron'[32] might have caused her to behave more encouragingly but thereafter she turned her attentions to safely married men of whom Jules Dufour was one and a Charles Cornay another.

Charles Cornay was the wine merchant husband of Mlle Dumur's niece Hélène. Noting on first hearing of Hélène that as a young girl she had been a bright opinionated child who *would* speak the truth in spite of her aunt's warning that "in the world one never says what one thinks" and that there was material for 'half a hundred novels ... stories and romances' even in staid Lausanne, Frida convinced herself that the change in Hélène's attitude to life on marrying Charles Cornay (she had given up visiting the poor and going to church and had become frivolous and worldly) was due to her husband, a man who considered marriage to be 'a treaty between two parties for their mutual advantage', having 'broken ... in' his wife to his own way of thinking. Meeting the villain himself shortly afterwards, Frida admitted that in spite of considering religion to be 'tomfoolery' and preferring women who were 'amenable, pretty and not too intelligent', Cornay was as 'good and kind' as any man who was not a Christian could be[33] – as witness his rescuing her from embarrassment during Christmas festivities (festivities all the more festive because they celebrated the arrival of the 20th century) by informing the company that many people in England were '*tempirant*' and that Frida's teetotal convictions should not be disparaged.[34] But having begun the new century on her knees asking God's help 'to spend all of it ... as I ought to do', Frida was mortified to find herself on the new century's second day being 'very nice indeed' to Charles Cornay and wishing for opportunities 'of being nicer still'. A brisk reminder to herself that 'being silly' with a man who was 'young, handsome and *married*' hardly accorded with her request (it came, rather, under the heading of 'wickedness') was less effective than a visit paid on 2 January to inspect a dress to be worn by Hélène Cornay at a 'swell' ball to which Frida herself did not intend to go because, together with the rest of the English colony, she was mourning the death of Queen Victoria and thought it unseemly to 'gad about'.[35]

Her visit to Mme Cornay's boudoir was educational on two counts. First, because she realised that the 'excessive amiability' shown her by Hélène's husband was humbug and that he would behave in this way to *any* woman provided she was pretty and responsive ('he always had more passion than principle'[36], she wrote a few years later on hearing of the Cornays' divorce), second, that a young married couple's bedroom exuded an air of erotic intimacy uncomfortably enhanced by the fact of Mme Cornay's dress or, rather, the 'want of it', revealing so much of her 'pretty breast' that it was 'positively indecent'.[37] (A sketch illustrates her point; Mme Cornay's voluptuous bosom was due to her being six months pregnant.) The bedroom with its aura of masculine sexuality and feminine fecundity and its contrast with her own parents' chaste and chilly one filled Frida with fascinated revulsion and it may have been with memories of the Cornays that during her 1903 visit to Lausanne she enquired of Marie Feyler what in the latter's opinion made for marital happiness. Marie's reply ('physical compatibility') both shocked her questioner ('what a bore "all that sort of thing" is') and made her decide that should she herself ever marry, she would love her husband only 'as a sister' and conceive by means of 'pills or patent medicines' ('children producers'), sentiments which did not augur well for any marriage into which she chose to enter and even less well for the man to whom she was currently engaged.

Marie's views, though negatively influential in one respect, provided positive reinforcement in others. First and foremost, '*Mlle le Docteur* Feyler' was a single woman who did not appear to need or want a 'necessary evil' (i.e. a husband) in order to make a success of her life. (She may also have provided a role model lacking in Cambridge where all the women Frida knew save the 'Aunties' were or had been married; Perse school teachers never provided one, for of them she was either scared – an unhappy memory resurfaced on her being asked by a Swiss teacher to see her after school of 'letters written by the "head" to one's Papa' and the 'terror' such letters induced[38] – or contemptuous.) Second, as someone who had known Frida all the latter's life (it was almost seventeen years since Marie and Frida had first met), Marie

was disconcertingly familiar with details of it ('there are *some* things I really shouldn't like known', noted Frida apprehensively)[39] and was better placed personally and professionally than other outsiders to advise her on the problems which currently beset her. Third, she was one of the few people for whom Frida actually *cared*, calling Marie a 'perfect darling'.[40] (Years later she was to admit to a 'g.p' on Marie but also to knowing that Marie was too 'intellectual' to care for her in return[41]; possibly it was Marie's impersonal professionalism which attracted a girl in need of someone with whom to discuss her current preoccupations.) Fourth, Marie seemed trustworthy, Frida confiding her worries on sexual and religious matters and allowing Marie to read *The Ending of the Way* because she wished her 'to know me, all of me'.[42] Lastly, it was Marie provided her with an experience of sick babies ('poor little wretches ... it was too sad')[43] in the course of a visit to the big cantonal hospital where she was now assistant paediatrician, a visit which may have helped Frida come to terms with the fact that sick children could and did die and that nothing she or a doctor could do could prevent it.

It was also in Lausanne, however, that Frida found herself the object of adoration of a small girl. Mlle Dumur's close family included her married sister Suzanne and Suzanne's two children aged about four and five and it was to little France Bocion that Frida became particularly attached because of the child's sweetness and cleverness and because France, like her brother Pierre and their small friends, reciprocated by calling her '*petite soeur*' or '*chère miss*' and by following her around; indeed, it seems that much of Frida's spare time was spent reading and singing to France in English and French and, on walks, alleviating her fatigue with stories. (Photographs of France adorn her diary.) Hoping that her own future children would be as 'clever and as sweet'[44] as France (and possibly girls like her too), Frida came to the conclusion that 'the love of children [was] better worth having than anyone else's'[45] – she had, of course, already experienced the affection of the slightly older boys of her Sunday School class but they were both boys and her social inferiors and though she felt deeply for some of them, they did not move her in the same way – and that her future lay in "marriage and motherhood" rather than a career.[46] And this even if the first was an unpleasant prerequisite for the second in the social circles in which she moved.

By late April 1901, however, Frida was beginning to count the weeks until departure. Much had happened to her in Lausanne – more, perhaps, than she with her hopes of a smaller world and a quieter life had banked upon – and much, it seems, was expected of her back in Cambridge: "I am to return home with a good deal of 'polish'".[47] Though sorry to leave Lausanne – 'not the people, for besides Marie Feyler and France there was not a soul here I care tuppence about but the view from my window [of] the Jura and the glorious Alps and the life and the talking French and more than all, the horses'[48] – a place where she had 'thoroughly enjoyed' her studies, met people from 'so many nationalities', and unexpectedly excited at the prospect of her 'really last'[49] day at school, Frida entertained mixed feelings at this important juncture: 'I have learnt a great deal from my stay … and I have learnt too what a lot I still have to learn'.[50] She had.

Conscious as never before of years and volumes of her diary passing, she noted of both that she hoped 'time spent [was] not … so much time lost' ('no, my dear, it wasn't … AT 1924')[51] and that although 'a short chapter … but very interesting'[52] of her life was closing, another was about to open. But a hope hoped in the volume preceding her visit to Lausanne remained unfulfilled: noting the difference between her own home life and the Longstaffes' ('they drink and they swear and they smoke and they make fun of things that I hardly like to hear mentioned freely at all'), Frida had prayed not to 'deteriorate' into a worldly selfish person while in Switzerland, adding that whether she improved or '[did] the other thing', of one thing she could be sure: 'I shan't stand still'.[53] She did not – and it was because her stay was not yet over that she did not.

Her round of farewell visits completed, Frida looked forward to the arrival in Lausanne of her parents and brothers en route for an extended Alpine holiday. That she had been homesick on her first solo trip abroad is obvious from her enthusiastic reception of letters from home ('Silvia and Lucy are very constant'; letters from her mother were eagerly awaited and treasured when they came)[54] but the hysterical joy ('I am almost too happy! … What have I done that I should be so happy?') with which she welcomed them was so excessive that Marie Feyler hastened to calm her. She was particularly excited by re-encountering 'taller and much more stylish' Julius for the first time in nine months.[55] (Her father, she noted, was unchanged, her mother 'paler and greyer', and twelve-year-old Eustace '*huge*' with phenomenally big feet; her family thought her improved and 'not a bit fat'.) Of the content of Lucy's letters we know nothing and of Silvia Myer's only that her father died in Rome after a brief illness (Frida took careful note of the contrast between assertions in two of Silvia's communications, one that death was 'the end', the second, as befitted the daughter of a proponent of post-mortem existence, that Silvia would 'see' her father again)[56] but of those exchanged between herself and Julius, Frida tells us only

M. Dufour, Lausanne 1900

as much as she wishes us to know: that Julius was enjoying 'his new life at Caius'; that his letters were 'clever [and] amusing' (*sic*: not a word one readily associates with gloomy Julius but with his sister he relaxed into ponderous wit) and that they contained 'tendernesses' (he called them "utter bilge" but sent the letter containing them anyway); that no other girls, however delightful, appealed to him as much as the 'dearest Tit' to whom he sent 'oceans of love'.[57]

Her excitement at being reunited with Julius ('how nice it is to be happy!'[58] is the curious expression she uses) having been tempered by events (a heavy fall from a horse as a result of attempting a jump beyond her capabilities when showing off her equestrian skills to her parents left her mildly concussed; an attack of German measles) and by Dr Feyler's intervention (it may be that Frida was sent to Lausanne specifically because Marie was there to keep a watchful eye on a girl whose recent behaviour had caused parental anxiety), Frida prepared to embark on the next stage of her sentimental education.

Finhaut, the small Alpine town in which the Tillyards were to spend an eventful two months before moving to Argentières and thence back to Lausanne and to Cambridge after a four month absence, though described by Frida as "a somewhat primitive mountain resort"[59], was actually a thriving tourist centre with eleven hotels and spectacular views of Mont Blanc and the holiday involved long walks and guided crossings of glaciers. ('Mountaineering', as the family called their activities, was dismissed by Aelfrida as "only a superior kind of picnic in those days".)[60] But Finhaut's reputation and its accessibility by train attracted more than family groups, and soon after the Tillyards' arrival, Frida, to her parents' alarm and dismay, began 'Flirting' heavily with young men holidaying there and became emotionally embroiled with two.

With the first, Anton Weiss, she might not have gone as far as she did had 'darling Dudu'[61] been there to intervene, but Julius, obliged to return to Cambridge early in July for the long vacation term, did not return until late August by which time this particular – and as it turned out, rather dangerous – bit of 'Flirting' was over. Though Anton Weiss, first violin of the Vienna Opera, Austrian by nationality and Jewish by religion, was in Frida's eyes 'an atheist of the worst type' because now an unbeliever (she would have liked to convert him to Christianity but thought it too difficult even for one as persuasive as herself) and was either way a 'nip' to whom she objected 'very strongly', it seems she had no objection to flirting with him 'outrageously'. By mid-July, however, her 'nasty Austrian' had begun to treat her 'with a sort of proprietorship' (he had rivals; two young engineers had recently arrived at the Hotel du Perron) and to hint at marriage but she, though bemused by the rapidity of his approach ('these foreigners are so queer, you never know where you have them')[62], was both flattered and unsurprised when Weiss formally asked for her hand in marriage. Declining his offer – Weiss accused her of breaking his heart and of encouraging him only insofar as she wanted to add him to her 'collection of unfortunate victims etc. etc.'[63] – because no Tillyard could possibly marry an atheistic, proprietorial 'nip' (there is no mention of love or even affection in all this), Frida noted nevertheless that she liked 'Tony' better than the first man (Percy Stanley) who had proposed to her and that she hoped future suitors ('*prétendants*') would continue the 'arithmetical progression to attractiveness!' begun by them. ('They have – more or less! ACWT 1904'.)[64]

Her flip dismissal, though it spoke volumes of her attitude to people in general, failed to warn her of what was to come: Anton Weiss, 'encouraged I suppose by my amiability, dared to suggest that as I could not be his wife, I might be his "*maitresse*" … [and] even went so far as to ask me to appoint a time and a place for —'.[65] Horrified by Weiss' attempted seduction (she was even more horrified when she discovered that Weiss had been 'misbehaving' with a female post office clerk while supposedly

courting herself) but having herself acted either from *naïveté* or as deliberately as he ("I thought he only meant it for a rather continental i.e. [a] … rather fast flirtation and lent myself to it with all the grace in the world)"[66] 'Humiliated [and] lowered' and 'disgusted' with both Weiss and herself (Weiss she called a 'little worm!', herself she castigated for not having stopped him earlier), Frida justified her behaviour (to herself; she told no-one of the escapade save Julius) by placing the blame on Weiss' shoulders ('the look in his eye made me see what he was driving at') rather than her own: 'I … treated him as I should an English gentleman!'[67] But she missed Weiss 'very much'[68] because he had provided a welcome opportunity of spicing up what had so far promised to be a dully domestic holiday and, grossly insulted though she was, immediately looked to the charming young engineers for entertainment and excitement.

Of the young engineers – they were working on the Jungfrau railway – Frida initially preferred the Frenchman because he was handsome and laughed at her witty remarks, but it was to the quieter of the two, twenty-five-year-old Swiss-German Hans Heinrich Peter that she "gave an undecided yes"[69] ('I think I *will* be his wife')[70] when he asked her to marry him within six weeks of their first meeting.

Her parents were displeased when she broke the news but neither they nor puzzled and miserable Julius had it explained to them how Frida could contemplate 'marrying one man while [in] love [with] another', namely Lord Kitchener. To them, as to Hans Peter, Frida merely stated her terms: a year's abstinence for him – the Tillyards thought he drank too much though he probably drank no more than any young man on a short break from an arduous job and never appeared inebriated – and a year's separation for both before she finally consented; if her betrothed failed to agree to either condition she would 'pretend I really didn't dream of accepting him … the proper deceitful course for a young lady to take'. Her reason as told to her diary was simple: 'I wish to be at rest. I want to have done with longing for what I can't and mustn't have'.[71]

This very odd statement (and it is only years later that its import and importance become clear: what was it, for example, that seventeen-year-old Frida 'mustn't' have and why must she pursue a 'deceitful' course?) explains something but not all of her present unhappiness. She is still emotionally in thrall to Lord Kitchener whom she still loves and 'always shall'[72] but there is something else: she cannot help acting towards men in such a way that they, believing her to be attracted to them, find themselves willy-nilly attracted to her; as Hans Peter himself informed Frida early in their relationship, she could 'make any man under the sun fall in love with [her], even himself', he being 'difficult game', 'if she would only go about it in a more methodical way'.[73] (She herself did not, indeed, could not see or understand what motivated her to behave in this way; on being asked by an English acquaintance in Lausanne 'how it was that all the men liked [her] so', she could only reply that she 'didn't think [she] did anything in particular', but it is obvious from what was said next that she had already honed her ensnaring technique and went about it methodically: without revealing anything of herself she attracted men by talking to them chiefly 'about themselves'.)[74] But something – her love for Lord Kitchener, perhaps, or the new piety at which she hints when discussing religion with Marie Feyler or when visiting the (Catholic) church in Finhaut to pray because 'it is so quiet there – but...'[75] (a 'but' which begs the question: 'but what?') prevents her from allowing herself to fall in love with a flesh and blood young man lest, possibly, he displace her 'hero' from her affections. But what better way of remaining true to him and to achieve 'rest' (a girl who is engaged will not be pestered by other men) than by engaging to a man she has no intention of marrying, with whom she is not in love (Switzerland, she wrote later, 'gave me two people to love'[76] neither of whom was Hans Peter) and who, because of his occupation, is unlikely to pursue her to England.

Poor Hans Peter, a man so 'dignified, humble and good' that unlike Anton Weiss or Percy Stanley he does not 'fuss'[77] the girl with whom he has fallen in love but whom, his brief vacation over, he arranges to visit wherever she is staying, agrees to drink less if that is one of her conditions ("you only have to command and I will obey"; 'so if I do marry him, at least I can be proud of my husband', diarises Frida on hearing this), who will write every day when they are apart (Frida too writes every day but does not send every letter), a man of whom Frida notes shortly after their first separation (at which she 'just shook hands' with him on saying goodbye but 'looked into his eyes rather differently'[78]), that she feels 'perfectly cool' about him, asks herself 'why should [she] bother to ... think about him?', states that if she were 'in love' or if it was her first proposal, things might be different, and adds jokingly that she 'supposes' she won't 'keep it up for long!'[79] Poor Hans Peter for other reasons too, for in spite of the Tillyards' snobbery (they thought his table manners 'rough'; he promised amendment) and teetotal principles (even Catharine Tillyard stated that her daughter's determination to turn her fiancé into a total abstainer was asking too much of him), the young engineer was perfect husband material: a few years older than Frida herself, well educated, from a wealthy background but keen to make his own way in the world by working hard at 'making railways and tunnels and things', 'already celebrated' as a linguist and an inventor (his 'extraordinary mathematical genius' had resulted in creation of a 'logarithm instrument', a slide rule specially adapted for his particular discipline), a Protestant ('we shall be able to serve God together'), a 'manly man and … good and true'. (The otherwise paragon could not waltz but Frida was prepared to overlook 'slight failings' of this nature.) And with this her parents, with whom Frida had not come to an agreement regarding her future husband but 'we agree-ish!'[80], had to be content though Lucy, informed by Frida of her conquest, was 'disgusted' and, begging her friend 'by all that is holy' to give up Hans Peter, asked her 'never to flirt (*sic!*) again'.[81]

The Tillyards' holiday and Hans Peter's courtship proceeded in tandem. Enrico (Frida's name for her fiancé; Hans Heinrich was insufficiently euphonious) visited regularly by appointment but only once and to Frida's displeasure (she was 'hot and dusty and messy' following a scramble across the Mer de Glace)[82] unannounced. Deprived of both parents at age eleven, he was prepared not only to bestow his affection (he described as his love as 'his whole life', adding that he would love her until his death; it is 'nice to be loved so much' was Frida's lukewarm response)[83] but even to venerate 'a small child of 17'[84], a deliberately infantilising description on Frida's part aimed at absolving herself of culpability. (She 'looked at least 21 and might be older', said another girl of her.)[85] He also accepted Frida's maidenly reticence concerning expressions of affection: holding hands ('I felt my touch thrill him'[86]; Frida, it seems, was already writing her next novel in her head with Enrico as 'copy'[87]; as 'Max von Thiele', an Emden engineer, he appears in *Marrying a Stranger*); passionate gazes ('I was a little frightened, men … can't take things calmly')[88]; a kiss on the cheek ('he was not *dis*satisfied with it but he was *un*satisfied')[89]; finally, four or five 'burning kisses on [her] lips' as he held her in his arms.[90]

Although Frida dismissed her first mouth kisses flippantly ('we behaved like 'Arry and 'Arriette on 'Ampstead 'Eath' ), her emotions on receiving them were very dark ('I felt I had surrendered, that I was no longer quite my own … I got frightened and ran away … trembling all over') and it was not until Enrico desisted and apologised that she, by dint of playing at being 'haughty and self-possessed', recovered sufficiently to pretend to herself that she had not 'yielded' or lost control of herself and the situation.[91] (In a much later novel – not *Marrying a Stranger* – the heroine describes a similar occasion as leaving her feeling fouled and soiled until she has a bath and washes her hair, after which she

**Julius Tillyard as a young man**

"felt all right again".)[92] Darkness is obvious too from her refusing an engagement ring (material and public evidence of having 'yielded'), from discussions with Enrico as to what he and she would have to learn or unlearn when or if they married (descriptions are all in the conditional tense), from her edgy refusal to answer Enrico's question "do you love me or do you not?", and from her noting that she did *not* consider herself 'bound to' Enrico in any way and that should her mother 'try and make [her] marry some other man' she would dismiss Enrico without a qualm.

By this time Catharine Tillyard was beside herself with worry. (We hear less of Alfred; perhaps he deputed his wife to deal with their wayward daughter.) Not only had Frida, whose devil-may-care air may not have deceived her parents as much as she thought, informed her mother that though she was 'not "in love" with [Herr] Peter', she intended to marry him in spite of this (Catharine's opinion that Frida was doing 'a very wicked thing' in marrying Enrico when she was in love with someone else was not, perhaps, valued highly by her daughter, given that Catharine had behaved in the same way to Frida's father) and that she was sure she was 'doing right'[93], but

she had also given her mother *The Ending of the Way* ('it seemed … an irony of fate that I should be acquiescing in the love of one man while Wutch was reading … the story of my love for another')[94], an irony even more ironic had Frida stopped to consider that her mother was perhaps not as 'unconscious' as the former believed of the autobiographical nature of the novel and was as perturbed as Marie Feyler at what the story revealed of adolescent unhappiness verging on melancholia (a word used by Frida herself to describe her feelings on reading a poem which advised her to relinquish the pursuit of "*bonheur impossible*")[95] and of feelings of almost pathological intensity for an unattainable ideal. And what of the physical side of marriage, a subject not yet discussed? Would a 'serious talk' remind obstinate Frida that 'one spends with one's husband not only *days* but *nights*'[96] and prove sufficient to discourage her?

It would not; indeed, diary entries suggest that it may even have strengthened Frida's resolve to marry her 'future husband'[97], to force him to conform to her social mores and to apply moral pressure ('what right have you to ask me to be unhappy? … you care more about your success than … my happiness', apropos Enrico's drinking habits)[98] when Enrico seemed unwilling to submit or even compromise. But she seems to have tried to open Enrico's eyes to her true feelings by allowing him to read *The Ending of the Way* (what he thought of it went unrecorded) and by openly discussing with him, 'though it is not considered proper to talk about such things'[99], the upbringing of any children they might have. (She pretended to be in earnest by ordering a coat, skirt, and blouse in Enrico's favourite colours. The outfit was deemed 'an error of taste. ACWT 1904'[100] and barely worn after her return to England.) She also found herself unable to return her 'husband's' love 'measure for measure'[101] or even, as they parted at Lausanne station for the stipulated year, to tell him that she loved him: 'I would have given anything … to tell him that I did but could not. So he has gone …!'[102] And with that Frida said goodbye to the *manège* horses she loved more than Hans Peter and she and her family departed for England.

Returning to Cambridge within days of her eighteenth birthday, Frida noted on that important occasion that although unable to write Lord Kitchener's name or daring to look at his picture without emotion, her feelings for Enrico were of 'calm affection' ('which curiously enough, I still feel. ACWT 1904'), an affection she tried to put into words in an 'amicable letter'[103] to the man to whom she considered herself 'engaged – or at least partly so' but from whom she accurately described herself as 'semi-detached'.[104] She seems, however, to have taken (or pretended to others to have taken) her semi-engagement sufficiently seriously to engage a Fräulein Kluger with whom to talk 'much German'[105] so that she and Enrico could converse more easily (they had used Italian as a common language) and to ask the opinion of Cambridge mathematicians on Enrico's '*règle à calculs*'. (One of them described it as a 'work of genius' and made helpful suggestions[106]; the other, Edmund Whittaker, now gloomily married to an invalid, Frida's snide comment on the relationship being if this was 'married bliss', she wanted none of it, was only 'feebly interested'.)[107] She also hinted blushingly to an engineering student that all the nicest men she knew were engineers and informed cousin May Cliff that she had 'engaged herself to a man'.[108] (May, though 'wildly excited' at the news, was also 'very much shocked': not only had Frida told her that she did not love Enrico – but *not* that she loved someone else – but the previous day she had flirted with Herbert Ibberson, the Hunstanton 'New Art' architect who had 'raved about' her on their first meeting, and in the course of the picnic at Holkham which his wife did not attend, had behaved so outrageously that May's father said 'some rather nasty things' to his niece afterwards; Frida's own reaction to Athol and May Cliff's strictures was that from *their* point of view her behaviour '*was* wrong'[109] but from her own not, possibly because the agreed year was by then almost up and in spite of having decided to marry Enrico at St Columba's, she had no intention of marrying him anywhere at all.) She also expressed dismay when communications from Enrico failed to arrive (she was, she wrote, grateful for his goodness to her 'at a rather difficult time' and required confirmation that *he* still loved *her*)[110] and was sure that it was God's will that she marry 'a man I do not care about', God Himself having arranged the matter '*so* plainly'[111] in the course of a Finhaut night unrecorded in her diary.

The chief end of man being to glorify God and – in Frida's diary – 'to conceal his deeper feelings', she pretended to her anxious mother that her duty was 'wonderfully clear', that she was 'in love with [her] future husband', and that she had forgotten 'the other' ('if, indeed, I ever cared for him!'), namely Lord Kitchener[112], a pretence made easier by Enrico bombarding her with information about and pictures of the Jungfrau railway and his work thereon and who, in spite of her writing to him in March 1902 to ask if he was 'tired' of her[113] (she was, it seems, becoming bored with the silly charade and there were new men on the horizon), replied with a 'beautiful' love letter ('you must read [it]. I have it upstairs')[114] in which he stated that he had no intention of giving her up.

This was not at all what Frida intended; indeed, she went so far as to write Enrico "a very silly letter about all [her] flirtations with other men" to see if that would provide sufficient discouragement. It seems it did not – or not immediately – for Enrico replied in his usual friendly fashion and showed no hint of allowing her to achieve her aim of forcing him to jilt her. He must, however have realised that there was no hope of marrying her – Julius described the rupture as the couple having "drifted apart"[115] but the rupture was more decisive than this – for Frida's hopes of meeting Enrico in Switzerland in 1903 (he responded to her news with 'a very passionate letter imploring to be allowed to see [her]')[116] in order to conduct a 'lovely interview' (she even propounded a dramatic scene in which Enrico either poignarded her or drowned her in Lake Leman) in which she would icily reject him by saying that he had not 'proved himself' to her satisfaction and had 'presumed' on her good nature, were dashed when she received a telegram saying that pressure of work prevented him from coming to Lausanne and which from his use of the formal '*vous*' made even Frida realise that all was over.[117]

Having achieved her aim ('The Lord has given and the Lord has taken away. Blessed be the name of the Lord!') but much to her parents' relief that the engagement had died a natural death without "scenes" or something "dreadful and dramatic"[118] happening, Frida realised with horror not that she had deliberately driven away a good man who truly loved her, but that having driven him away, she had laid herself open to offers from other men, offers she would be hard put to refuse unless the man was wildly unsuitable in either her parents' eyes (she was still a minor) or her own.

But having once having used unattainable Lord Kitchener as an excuse for not marrying she now had to justify both her engagement (such as it was) and her breaking it off to the world and to herself. To Julius, still puzzled as to his sister's motives for becoming engaged to a man she did not love, she tried to explain that it was

**An early Swiss railway engine**

not, in her view, "unbearable to marry one man while you love another": "an ordinary man", she wrote, "can give you some of the things the fairy prince would have done – devotion, a home, perhaps intelligent companionship, anyway friendship and children" – and besides who would be so foolish as to allow themselves to be "*starved*" of such things when they were readily available?[119] In her diary, however, she recorded something closer to the truth: 'I [could] never marry Enrico [because] … I could never *trust* him'[120], but as she fails to disclose the cause of her mistrust, she leaves us little closer to knowing which aspect of the '*quiet* happiness'[121] she longed for would have been compromised. Publicly, she preferred to have people regard her as 'a martyr to [her] principles', it being because Enrico would not give up beer that he gave her up instead[122], but this, though a valid excuse for a young woman from a staunchly tee-total family, was a cover story: for reasons disclosed only much later, she intended to remain 'a spinster'; she had no intention of submitting to an older man's authority, preferring to marry, if she had to marry, 'some meek little boy of [her] own age' who would do as he was told; she preferred change and excitement to quiet domesticity and if quiet domesticity threatened, would act in such a way as to create unquiet excitement (it provided better 'copy'); her emotional neediness was such that one man's love was inadequate; Enrico's charms were insufficiently 'strong' to make her forget Lord Kitchener. ('I can't help loving Lord Kitchener …so I had better be free to love him'.)[123] Lastly, Enrico was now 'elephantine *and hirsute*' (hairy men, though Frida no longer remembered why, had unpleasant associations for her), a photograph taken in one of the Jungfrau railway tunnels which showed that 'oh, horror of horrors!'[124], he had grown a beard, being enough to turn Frida decisively against him.

In spite of Ancifera Gregory's prediction that Enrico would one day 'turn up' to 'claim' her younger relative[125] and his own protestations of undying love, Enrico did not remain one of Frida's 'unfortunate victims': in March 1905 a letter addressed to herself but opened in her absence by her mother informed both ladies that he was engaged to 'a Fraulein Emmy something of Zurich'. 'Very suitable I am sure … but what difference does it make to *me*?'[126] was Frida's snide comment, but though she now regarded Enrico's defection as providential, she *did* mind and fifty years later still bore something of a grudge: Enrico, she wrote, had been 'vulgar and repulsive', a man who 'would never be at home in [her] milieu', someone to whom she had been attracted merely by his intellect, because she hoped to convert him to her way of thinking, and because she was moved by his unhappy childhood, and someone she gave up because 'drawn away by

the silent influence of [her] parents'. What this said of her lack of judgement or her inability to love or even relate to a man who possessed an 'outstanding personality and great will power'[127], she did not say.

Enrico, later distinguished Swiss engineer Heinrich Peter, had his revenge: at Christmas 1906 Frida received a card from "Herr Peter *und Frau*" and, being herself engaged to a young man so penniless that she was supporting him with her own savings, wrote wittily to Julius to say that the Peters "live in a *schloss* at Zurich" and "think what I have missed!".[128] Early the following year and about to marry a 'little boy' of her own age, she received a prospectus announcing that Herr Peter was setting up 'a kind of school of engineering' and this further reminder of what might have been inspired her to record her wonder that she had ever had the courage to consider marriage to her 'ex-fiancé'[129] and that even now the mere thought of marriage to anyone at all made her 'tremble'.[130]

## Notes

1  GCPPT 1|1|6 29 September 1900.
2  Tillyard, Ae. *Just Alice* p 204. (GCPPT 2|19).
3  GCPPT 1|1|6 10 November 1900.
4  Tillyard, HJW. *The Letters of ACW Tillyard* (MTC). Letter from Aelfrida to Julius Tillyard of 5 April 1901.
5  GCPPT 1|1|7 19 May 1901.
6  ibid. 24 May and 12 June 1901.
7  Tillyard, Ae. *Messages* p 40.
8  GCPPT 1|1|6 26 January 1901.
9  GCPPT 1|1|7 16 May 1901.
10  GCPPT 1|1|6 23 February 1901.
11  GCPPT 1|1|7 9 May 1901.
12  Tillyard, HJW. Introduction to *The Letters of ACW Tillyard* (MTC).
13  Marie Louise Ramé (1839–1908), daughter of a French father and an English mother, was the author of highly wrought and (for the time) rather scandalous novels; Oscar Wilde, Pierre Loti and Victor Hugo led unconventional lives. Readings of any of these authors would have been discouraged at Fordfield.
14  GCPPT 1|1|7 5 June 1901.
15  ibid. 2 May 1901.
16  ibid. 14 May 1901.
17  ibid. 13 February 1901.
18  ibid. 4 June 1901.
19  GCPPT 1|1|6 13 February 1901.
20  ibid. 22 March 1901.
21  GCPPT 1|1|7 2 May 1901.
22  GCPPT 1|1|6 23 February 1901.
23  GCPPT 1|1|7 9 May 1901.
24  ibid. 5 April 1901.
25  GCPPT 1|1|10 1 May 1903.
26  ibid. 4 April and 4 May 1903.
27  GCPPT 1|1|6 12 December 1900.
28  ibid. 10 November 1900.
29  ibid. 11 January 1901.
30  GCPPT 1|1|7 12 June 1901.
31  ibid. 16 April 1901.

32 GCPPT 1|1|6 13 February 1901.
33 ibid. 12 December 1900.
34 ibid. 2 January 1901.
35 ibid. 26 January 1901.
36 GCPPT 1|1|21 24 April 1916.
37 GCPPT 1|1|6 26 January 1901.
38 GCPPT 1|1|7 9 May 1901.
39 GCPPT 1|1|6 5 October 1900.
   GCPPT 1|1|7 31 May 1901.
40 GCPPT 1|1|6 5 October 1900.
41 GCPPT 1|1|28 28 July 1924.
42 GCPPT 1|1|7 31 May 1901.
43 ibid. 31 May 1901.
44 ibid. 27 April 1901.
45 GCPPT 1|1|6 23 February 1901.
46 Tillyard, HJW. Introduction to *The Letters of ACW Tillyard* (MTC).
47 ibid. Letter from Aelfrida to Julius Tillyard of 6 November 1900.
48 GCPPT 1|1|7 30 May 1901.
49 ibid. 12 June 1901.
50 ibid. 15 June 1901.
51 GCPPT 1|1|6 5 April 1901.
52 GCPPT 1|1|7 15 June 1901.
53 GCPPT 1|1|5 14 August 1900.
54 GCPPT 1|1|6 1 November 1900.
55 GCPPT 1|1|7 15 June 1901.
56 GCPPT 1|1|6 26 January 1901.
57 ibid. 1 November 1900.
58 GCPPT 1|1|7 15 June 1901.
59 GCPPT 2|25|3(10).
60 ibid.
61 GCPPT 1|1|8 21 August 1901. The 'sic' is Aelfrida's.
62 ibid. 12, 16 and 17 July 1901.
63 ibid. 29 July 1901.
64 ibid. 21 July 1901.
65 ibid. 25 July 1901.
66 Tillyard, HJW. *Letters of ACW Tillyard* (MTC). Letter from Aelfrida to Julius Tillyard of 30 [July] 1901.
67 GCPPT 1|1|8 25 July 1901.
68 ibid. 9 August 1901.
69 Tillyard, HJW. Introduction to *The Letters of ACW Tillyard*. (MTC).
70 GCPPT 1|1|8 23 August 1901.
71 ibid. 1 September 1901.
72 ibid. 18 August 1901.
73 ibid. 21 August 1901.
74 ibid. 17 September 1901.
75 ibid. 16 July 1901.
76 GCPPT 1|1|12 16 April 1905.
77 GCPPT 1|1|8 23 August 1901.
78 ibid. 27 August 1901.
79 ibid. 28 August 1901.
80 ibid. 11 and 16 August and 2 September 1901.
81 ibid. 14 September 1901.
82 ibid. 7 September 1901.
83 ibid. 2 and 6 September 1901.
84 ibid. 6 September 1901.
85 ibid. 17 September 1901.
86 ibid. 2 September 1901.
87 ibid. 21 August 1901.
88 ibid. 2 September 1901.
89 ibid. 23 September 1901.
90 ibid. 16 September 1901.
91 ibid.
92 Tillyard, Ae. *Naomi da Costa* p124 (GCPPT 2|22).
93 ibid. 6 September 1901.
94 ibid. 23 September 1901.
95 GCPPT 1|1|6 14 November 1900.
96 GCPPT 1|1|8 16 September 1901.
97 ibid. 6 September 1901.
98 ibid. 16 September 1901.
99 ibid. 23 September 1901.
100 ibid. 17 September 1901.
101 ibid. 6 September 1901.
102 ibid. 23 September 1901.
103 ibid. 5 October 1901.
104 ibid. 8 October 1901.
105 GCPPT 1|1|9 19 December 1901.
106 GCPPT 1|1|8 8 October 1901.
107 ibid. 11 October 1901.
108 GCPPT 1|1|9 26 August 1902.
109 ibid. 23 and 25 August 1901.
110 GCPPT 1|1|8 6 and 7 November 1901.
111 GCPPT 1|1|9 30 December 1901.
112 ibid.
113 ibid. 8 March 1902.
114 GCPPT 1|1|10 7 January 1903.
115 Tillyard, HJW. *The Letters of ACW Tillyard* (MTC). Letter from Aelfrida to Julius Tillyard of 2 August 1903, footnoted with this comment by Julius himself.
116 GCPPT 1|1|10 31 March 1903.
117 ibid. 31 March and 3 and 25 April 1903.
118 Tillyard, Ae. *Marrying a Stranger* p 25 (GCPPT 2|6).
119 Tillyard, HJW. *The Letters of ACW Tillyard* (MTC). Letter from Aelfrida to Julius Tillyard of [ ] September 1902.
120 GCPPT 1|1|9 6 October 1902.
121 GCPPT 1|1|8 23 September 1901.
122 ibid. 9 May 1902.
123 GCPPT 1|1|10 7 January 1903.
124 GCPPT 1|1|10 13 November 1903.
125 GCPPT 1|1|9 29 July 1902.
126 GCPPT 1|1|11 5 and 6 March 1905.
127 GCPPT 1|1|67 2 September 1950.
128 Tillyard, HJW. *The Letters of ACW Tillyard* (MTC). Letter from Aelfrida to Julius Tillyard of 23 April 1907.
129 GCPPT 1|1|10 18 January 1903.
130 GCPPT 1|1 14 2 January 1907.

# A 'finished' young lady

Describing his sister's triumphant return to Cambridge in late September 1901 (she received 'quite an ovation' from the staid congregation of St Columba's, was congratulated on the un-English stylishness of her appearance, and was amused at how 'proud and happy' her parents were at her enthusiastic reception)[1], Julius noted that "Frida had come back ... definitely 'out'" and with the intention of being "charming, approachable and sympathetic" even while standing "no nonsense from any young ass"[2] who presumed on acquaintance. Frida herself (or Aelfrida as we must now call the '"finished" young lady' replacing the 'little girl' who departed Cambridge a year earlier) noted that she looked 'grown up and perhaps a little formidable'[3] (besides being taller than average she dressed herself and her hair in a manner too advanced for her mother's friends who criticised her '*tout ensemble*')[4] had also 'grown older' because matured by 'many new experiences' recently undergone.[5]

Maturity had unforeseen consequences, one positive, one negative. On the one hand, 'I can now take myself seriously and know that my feelings are genuine [and] I need no longer laugh at myself ... [and] may consider myself ... a reasonable being', a remark made on her eighteenth birthday; she could also rejoice in being 'grown up [and] a woman'[6] free to "take [her] place in the world ... [and] to have a lot of liberty".[7] On the other, she seemed to have outgrown her Cambridge school-friends, both Helen Verrall and Silvia Myers (the former 'out' but 'stupider and lumpier than ever' and looking as if 'she didn't know whether she was "out" or not', the latter, in spite of her 'matronly figure', not yet 'out' but soon to be so, to employ cosmetics, and to prefer 'motor cars and dresses from Worth' to 'pi' discussions of religion) kissing her effusively but seeming 'horribly afraid'[8] of her. With a sudden sense of personal if not social superiority, Aelfrida proceeded to 'mash'[9] (i.e. lord it over) them.

Returning to Cambridge with 'a good deal of polish' and 'with a great facility [of] saying polite lies as if I meant them and talking when I have nothing to say'[10] (a facility which never left her and which she employed to great effect), Aelfrida found herself a fully-fledged member of interlocking social circles: her mother's At

**Castlebrae**

Homes and dinner parties at which she was expected to make conversation appropriate to the occasion (she also used them as 'copy', writing of one lady visitor that only her position as the wife of the Master of a college "saved her from being vulgar")[11] and her first formal dinner party hosted by redoubtable Scottish widowed sisters Mesdames Lewis and Gibson, soon to depart for Sinai for the second time.

The 'Learned Twins', as Aelfrida called Agnes Lewis and Margaret Gibson, "were not like other learned ladies you have ever known ... they were like each other and like no-one else". Eccentrically dressed "in silks and satins trimmed or veiled in lace and wearing an assortment of ornaments from Egyptian tomb-beads to Scotch Cairngorms ... their stuffy figures [and] bunchy garments ... never made them look smart" but they possessed dignity, charm, and lively minds (at an At Home they displayed a lump of radium and proudly informed Aelfrida that "*a woman* had discovered radium and it was epoch-making") and extended as much generosity to newly 'finished' Aelfrida at Castlebrae, their Scotch baronial house at the foot of Castle Hill, as they did to the "Greek Orthodox archimandrites … Waldensians, missionaries from China … ordinands from Athens", Cambridge and foreign academics, and other "strange people" whom she was likely to meet there. Not only did the two ladies look and dress alike (Aelfrida had difficulty in distinguishing one from the other but generally decided that "one is Mrs Lewis and the other – isn't") but it was also their custom "to speak … both at the same time, pausing every now and then to contradict each other" ("I was giving a lecture on Mount Sinai – ", "No Maggie dear, it was the palimpsest – " , "Agnes, it was the night of the awful storm at the monastery when the dragoman spilt the soup")[12] and it was the charming confusion of their conversation as much as anything (there were other reasons too, not least the sisters' potential as 'copy') which attracted Aelfrida to their house though her interests lay elsewhere than in Syriac gospels, the twins' fascinating stories of their research in Egypt and elsewhere evoking little more than gentle mockery and a glimmer of appreciation of their great intellects and promotion of scientific biblical studies.

Aelfrida's 'first grown up ball' (a much more exciting topic than codices Lewis or Sinaiticus) took place at the Cambridge home of distant 'townee' relatives, the Eaden Lilleys being proprietors of one of the town's department stores. (She records no contemporary 'coming out' celebrations of her own; the ball was merely an occasion at which she coincidentally made her first official appearance as a 'finished' young lady, a curious omission given her mother's propensity for social climbing but perhaps the Tillyards felt it inappropriate to advertise their daughter's eligibility while the latter was unofficially engaged to Enrico; once the so-called engagement was called off, they held a dance at Fordfield.) Clad in a white silk dress ornamented with 'pretty carnations', Aelfrida was 'the only girl who danced more than once with the same man!'[13], a mark of popularity but also rather 'fast' behaviour. Other balls followed ('I got plenty of partners and two ices'[14], she reports of one and of another that she had discovered the joys of 'sitting out'[15] selected dances with partners with whom she preferred to flirt than dance) but always with Julius as escort ('it is lovely to have him up at Cambridge!'[16] wrote his sister, and it may have been as much for his use as protector as from affection that she appreciated him) but so strict were contemporary rules of chaperonage that her mother or

younger brother accompanied her even to 'tea in Dudu's rooms at Caius', an unchaperoned visit to a man's rooms in a men's college (be that man a brother or not) being an enormity.[17] Hence although 'grown up' Aelfrida had anticipated 'a lot of liberty', she had less real liberty than before. Furthermore, it seemed as if her 'really last' lessons in Lausanne were far from last for she was now expected to become both accomplished ('I believe I am to have a nice voice', she wrote of singing lessons begun within a few days of arriving home but 'I still can't sing in tune', added 'ACWT' in 1904)[18] and a linguist, Italian lessons with Miss Marion Harrison of Newnham in that lady's private house near the college being added to German lessons undertaken on Enrico's behalf.

Although Aelfrida was shortly to complain that she had 'sweated [Italian] all morning', she had acquired a degree of fluency in the course of conversations with Enrico, a secret she failed to impart to 'meek … middle aged' Miss Harrison when the don expressing herself 'very much astonished' that Miss Tillyard had learnt so much of the language in so short a time.[19] The Italian over which she 'sweated' was Dante, in whom she was soon 'revelling' and of whose *Divine Comedy* she was soon to own a copy, a Christmas present from Julius. She found Dante's description of doomed lovers Paolo and Francesca particularly poignant ('it is beautiful … yet wrong, I know. Dante, Dante, why dost thou make wickedness so beguiling. Thou hast placed them in Inferno but thou has placed them *together*')[20] and it was with the intention of reading more of this entrancing author in his native tongue that she studied Italian assiduously for two years.

It seems, however, that her parents' motives for further educating their daughter were other than her own – they had not been apprised of her having opted for 'marriage and motherhood' should spinsterhood prove impossible, though her 'perfect pleasure' on the rare occasions when she was able to play with 'charming mite[s]'[21] should have suggested as much – for with both enthusiastically supportive of higher education for women, it seems they envisaged a teaching career (or, rather, a career in teaching until such time as she married), as a preliminary to which a degree in modern languages at Girton or Newnham would be advisable. To this end and to the end of finding a suitable husband as a result of academic qualifications gained at one of Cambridge's two women's colleges (there was, it seems, no question her becoming a 'common … Homertonian'[22], Homerton being an establishment attended by those for whom the expense of a university education was beyond their means), Alfred Tillyard went so far as to exclaim "Tit … you ought to marry a great man" and to suggest Lord Kitchener and that he himself would arrange an introduction, on hearing Aelfrida expatiate on 'Education with a capital E'.[23] The Tillyards therefore undertook the expense of private lessons, brought their daughter to the notice of Constance Jones, the then Mistress of Girton, and encouraged Aelfrida to attend formal and informal college events at Newnham. (Having already decided that she had no desire to emulate Helen Verrall and become 'a Newnhamite', Aelfrida used the occasions to poke fun at students who, had they 'dressed more and worked less', discussed matters other than academic 'shop', been less interested in cocoa parties and more in men, and not knitted and crocheted during serious debates, would have been of greater interest to a 'frivolous outsider' like herself; she also collated her impressions of college life and of 'badly mannered and badly combed' but 'very clever' young ladies[24] for future 'copy'.) They also arranged for her to stay with a family in Italy in order to perfect her colloquial Italian but the trip was cancelled on Alfred Tillyard discovering that he had "a good deal to worry him"[25], worries which came to a very public head in August 1903 when he was hauled before his fellow magistrates 'for refusal to pay the Education Rate'.[26]

To further their end of pushing their daughter towards a career in education, the Tillyards also encouraged her to undertake "a little part time teaching"[27], Aelfrida herself having expressed enthusiasm after watching specimen lessons at the Perse School for Boys, shortly to be attended by Eustace, in which French and Latin were conducted 'on the conversational system' and been inspired by the excellence of the results and by an open day at the girls' County School to declare that she had a 'mission'[28] to teach French in that way. (Later comments that she was only 'playing' at being 'a school marm'[29] and that she was easily bored by 'maidens of the lower middle class'[30] suggest that she herself had no serious intention of making teaching her career.) Unhappy memories of her own school days also made her determined not to inflict the stultifying teaching methods of the Perse School for Girls on her new pupils and shortly after taking up 'part time teaching' at the County School for Girls in September 1903, nineteen-year-old Frida was working to a method 'of [her] own invention' and finding it 'very successful'[31] in attracting and retaining her pupils interest, so successful, in fact, that the headmistress, sitting in on one of the lessons, described her 'method' as "marvellous, astonishing etc., etc.", herself as amazed (*épatée*) by the girls' progress[32], and increased Miss Tillyard's two classes to three.

'Grown up' Aelfrida soon had little time to dream; indeed, as she complained shortly after her return from Switzerland, she had no time to write her diary (judging by lengthy and frequent entries, she found some) or to write 'anything'[33] else, 'anything' consisting of contributions to the *MCJ*, of short stories based on people she knew (one unfortunate heroine was abandoned "in the middle of a proposal"[34] while she wrote to Julius, then abroad), of "bad"[35] poetry, and of at least one unnamed novel (novel-writing was her chief aim in life after "marriage and motherhood"[36]), all of which save for *MCJ* contributions were later destroyed. Her time was otherwise filled by instruction in domestic duties usually carried out by the servants whom as a married woman she would have to supervise, and though these (cookery lessons with the Fordfield cook, plain sewing, 'turning out', i.e. thoroughly cleaning, a room by 'sweeping, scrubbing, dusting – everything!')[37] were approached light-heartedly ('I looked sweet in a cap and apron') in the belief that she was unlikely to practice them on a permanent basis herself, they were dismissed as 'tiring'[38] (physically exhausting and intellectually stultifying) occupations to be avoided if possible – even in a supervisory capacity – in the future.

As another unforeseen consequence of growing up, Aelfrida found herself included willy-nilly in Cambridge 'good works': 'evidently', she diarised wryly, 'I am not to be allowed to be idle!'[39] Although she was later to describe her life of service as 'getting into harness … again'[40], such works as she had performed prior to leaving for Switzerland paled in quantity and significance beside those she was expected to perform on her return, works, it must be noted, inspired less by Catharine Tillyard's 'life of devotion' and more as a result of pressure exerted by the 'Learned Twins', Mrs Lewis and Mrs Gibson possessing not only sufficient wealth to enable them to underwrite a local mission (the York Street Mission, opened in 1905) a church (St Columba's, in 1891) and even a college (Westminster, in 1899) but a strong social conscience and a Presbyterian work ethic also. When, therefore, these ladies 'asked' Aelfrida within days of her return to engage in projects of "religious mission and social improvement"[41], she was unable to resist.

Her life of mission and improvement began with a Sunday School 'infant class'[42] consisting of much the same small boys with whom she had already created such rapport prior to leaving for Lausanne but whose delight in her return was tempered by the class being divided into two when the rowdier element misbehaved during her absence on holiday (with her they were so 'angelically good' that she was 'afraid they won't live long!!')[43] and allocated a male teacher. Nor were her 'cherubs' as young as the term 'infant' suggests: some were already at work and all were old enough to be able to read and write, to act in plays she wrote for them (a prompt copy was 'all over blood' from having been conned at the local abattoir)[44], to visit Fordfield for sumptuous teas and to be taught 'to be *gentlemen*'[45], and to accompany her to the Fitzwilliam Museum. And as was expected of her and in her plainest clothes (one dressed simply 'when … visiting the poor' so as not to make them feel inferior)[46], she went 'district visiting' her 'cherubs'' mothers, 'all such nice women, so hard-working and uncomplaining', with whom she had 'lovely chats' in the 'wilds of Romsey Town'.[47] She also made an effort to know the boys themselves, listing their names in her diary, noting particular aptitudes in case provision could be made to further them, and expending so much time, energy, and affection on them that the boys, meeting her when she visited one of their 'shockingly over-crowded' schools[48] or accompanied them on a Sunday School 'treat', demonstrated their delight by cheering and mobbing her. Such, however, was her ability to stand no nonsense from any 'young ass', be this a Viennese violinist, a Cambridge undergraduate, or one of the older and "very rough"[49] 'Hooligans' whose Sunday School class had the reputation of being 'unmanageable'[50], that Aelfrida's initial engagement with teenage tearaways in 1901 had become a 'permanent engagement' by 1905, she 'most triumphantly' taking them on and they, 'quite charmed'[51], begging her to continue as their teacher.

Her interest in 'cherubs' and 'cherub-mammas'[52] went beyond the call of duty. On one boy, a fourteen-year-old dying of rheumatic heart disease, she lavished nourishing food ("sparrowgrass", said Hubbard sourly when she begged asparagus for her 'sick cherub', "is for the gentry")[53] and expended so much money on nursing equipment that she had none left and had to beg and borrow from friends, on another, Joe Billings (a 'cherub' later immortalised in a novel as 'Jim Bowles' the heroine's "beloved bad boy"[54], the more beloved, it seems, because Jim/Joe was perpetually 'in a fair way of going to be bad' and his continual flouting of convention appealed to one who continued to do likewise), career advice and informed talks (she 'dare not preach', she wrote, lest she antagonise him) and by doing so kept him more or less 'straight' as he progressed from milkman's boy to army private, something both he and his worried mother seem to have appreciated.[55] But what Joe chiefly appreciated (he, like other 'cherubs', was 'hugely bucked' at being asked) was being asked to inscribe his name in what Aelfrida called 'an old birthday book'[56] but later described as an 'intercession book' given to her by the bishop at her confirmation in which she wrote the names of persons or institutions to be prayed for.

Gratifying though it was to 'devote herself and to be appreciated'[57]– and in behaving in this way she was

certainly modelling herself on her mother and for much the same reasons – Aelfrida realised that good as it made her feel because it fulfilled her need to be needed and to know that God and His 'recording angel'[58] would recognise the pious behaviour of a 'good girl' performing 'good works' and rate her highly as a result[59], playing Lady Bountiful to 'cherubs' and 'Hooligans' had its drawbacks. For one thing it took up a lot of time which might have been devoted to pleasanter pursuits such as 'Flirting' or writing novels, for during the holidays she ran a 'holiday school' for her Sunday School pupils at which she applied a 'carefully thought-out system' of education (talks on Municipal Government, reading *The Water Babies*)[60] which required a good deal of preparation. For another, dragging herself round the wilds of Romsey Town in clothing of subdued colour and cut lost its charms when 'dressing simply' resulted in being mistaken for an errand-running housemaid. Then, too, nagging doubts arose: would the boys on whom she lavished so much time and energy forget her as soon as she and they parted company and did 'missions of religious and social improvement' *really* do any good in the long term[61], given that opportunities of the kind she offered were "irrelevant to … needs"[62] and that the hold of missions with a religious bias over Cambridge's urban poor was tenuous to say the least.

A prime example, in Aelfrida's eyes, was the St Columba's Band of Hope with which, at Mesdames Lewis and Gibson's request, she was also associated. (Neither the Learned Twins nor Aelfrida herself questioned their moral right to impose their own mores and beliefs on the inhabitants of Romsey Town because they assumed that their position in local society and the biddings of Presbyterianism entitled them to do so, but the fact that the Band of Hope, a temperance organisation aimed at instilling a horror of 'demon drink' and a desire to sign a pledge of total abstinence into working-class children, was plagued with poor attendance – most children attended only for the free food and drink provided at meetings – and was soon wound up, says much for the determination of the Cambridge working class not to be improved.) The addition of Band of Hope activities to her schedule impinged further still on Aelfrida's 'liberty' for in addition to her Sunday School classes, Italian lessons on Wednesday, Bible lectures on Tuesdays, and French lessons given thrice weekly for five hours a week at £5 a term to a Dorothy Smith whose education had been 'scrappy'[63], she now added the St Columba's Band of Hope meetings on Thursday evenings and paid visits to Fenland villages to inspire existing Bands with fervour for 'the Temperance cause'.[64] It was not long, however, before she found Band of Hope activities 'odiously dull' in spite of her efforts to improve them, to regard meetings held for young abstainers as 'rot'[65], and to cut sessions if something better offered.

Discoveries made in the course of meetings, however, provided further ammunition for her newly-empowered self. Early in 1902 she found herself expected to provide an address and this, her first attempt at public speaking, was something of a success. Unfazed by the impromptu nature of her speech, she spoke for twenty minutes in the present tense on an imaginary journey she and the children were taking from Paris to Switzerland and on 'the temperance lessons …found on our way'[66]; indeed, she was so carried away by her story that she found it hard to stop. A meeting later the same year provided an even better example of her newfound ability to preach and teach, to improvise and dramatize, and of her powers of persuasion: the children she merely congratulated on 'having begun their temperance work so early' and, paraphrasing a poem quoted by a Lausanne missionary, reminded them that 'at the ending of the way' Christ Himself would reward their endeavours as exemplars of abstinence. To the adults, however, she spoke in the manner of a revivalist preacher confronted with sinners who '*must* be helped': 'I am in the pulpit, you know, so I lean on the big Bible and plead'. Discovering that she could make them laugh and cry, she briefly experienced 'an intoxicating sense of power' ('it may be only a little meeting but I can do what I want with it. Hurrah!') and on returning home declared she would be either 'a famous writer or a famous speaker'[67] before retiring to bed to plan her future. (A decade later she employed the experience as 'copy', including her subsequent realisation that her behaviour had been rather 'ludicrous' and that she might have made "a damned ass of [her]self".)[68] Within a few months of her return from Switzerland, therefore, Aelfrida, now introduced as one 'whose heart [was] in the temperance cause'[69] (it was not, as one who numbered herself among 'good people – or people who pretend to be'[70], knew full well), had been elected secretary of the Cambridge and Huntingdon branch of the British Women's Temperance Association of which her mother was already a member and had encountered one of the leading lights in the movement: Agnes Slack.

According to her hagiographic biography of formidable Miss Slack, Aelfrida first met the lady she called successively 'Aunt Agnes' and 'Agnes' in 1896; her first mention of her, however, appears in March 1902 when Agnes arrived at Fordfield to find her courtesy niece 'addressing Temperance circulars and talking BoH and BWTA' in a '*mise-en-scène*' which could hardly have been improved upon[71] had it been pre-arranged. (Perhaps it had.) Agnes Slack being a lady whose "vigorous propaganda"[72] was

hard to resist, Aelfrida consented to wear the white ribbon denoting one never to drink alcohol and thereafter sported it in her lapel for some time – though not, as originally promised, 'till I die'.[73]

Miss Slack, though capable of "evoking enthusiastic admiration from women"[74], was not as successful in recruiting Aelfrida's affections as her mother's; indeed, and in marked contrast to her anodyne biography (a biography commissioned by the lady herself with enthusiastic support from her female admirers), Aelfrida's diarised descriptions of the 'exacting, dictatorial, argumentative' lady who 'would hold forth … as if she were addressing a [public meeting]', who though said to be soft hearted, bullied Catharine Tillyard and utterly silenced her husband, and whose monstrous snobbishness, catch-phrases, 'autocratic pronouncements', and endlessly-proclaimed views grated on the ear[75], together with her lampoonings of Agnes in contemporary editions of the *MCJ*[76], demonstrate both the similarities between 'aunt's' and 'niece's' characters and the difficulty experienced by the latter in living under the same roof as the former. As a public figure and a private person Agnes nevertheless made an enormous impression on adolescent Aelfrida, the latter consciously modelling herself on the former ostensibly because both ladies cared 'more about temperance [than] any other question' (at the risk of becoming 'a martyr to my principles', Aelfrida declared herself ready 'to give my life to the cause of temperance … insofar as I can')[77] but actually because the enormous power wielded by Agnes over men and women underlined her recent discovery that she could wield the same.

But Aelfrida's subsequent move from holder of private convictions to publicly proclaimed idealist (she refused to help at a Coronation dinner held by the then Mayor of Cambridge for the town's working-class elderly because beer was to be served and wilfully misunderstood St Columba's current incumbent when he reminded her that moral principles were 'reins, not fetters')[78] was not without contradictions and problems. On the one hand, she never thought it odd that a family devoted to 'the cause of temperance' should own, edit, and write for a newspaper which carried advertisements for alcoholic beverages. On the other, the glory of being a "temperance advocate"[79] was rapidly dimmed by association with 'delegates … frowsty, frumpy and fanatical' , by a feeling that promises of 'giving oneself to the cause' and hopes of being 'early established in grace' as a result were 'such … humbug' when applied to herself ('if only some of these good people could read my diary'), that 'talking temperance' was boring compared to 'Flirting', that handing out Temperance tracts to unwilling recipients ('I … loathe Tracts')[80] was a waste of time, as also was having to read aloud 'pages of enthusiasm' at meetings whose minutes, drafts, and resolutions was hardly inspiring to a '*dear* young secretary'[81] who would rather be composing novels. There also were the 'churlish'[82] reactions of stolid 'lower middle class' Fenlanders to a Cambridge 'townee' too snobbish to take her diary with her ('it is not meant for the lower middle classes') when with a white ribbon on her coat and her elder brother (also a teetotaller) as escort, she arrived in their village to 'study' them and to revive their vanished enthusiasm for a cause she herself was later to describe as 'temperance – ugh!'[83] (And to support for the rest of her life, save for two notable occasions.) And public proclamation of 'Abstinence' and private conviction that anyone hoping to become closely associated with her should embrace Temperance too had already caused problems and were soon to pose more.

It was however, two of her real aunts whose decision to open their niece's eyes to social problems far worse than Cambridge's and if possible to change her from a "rather selfish young woman too much interested in [her] own experience of life"[84] into a worthier Tillyard which effected an even greater change in Aelfrida's views on philanthropy.

Aunts Fanny and Anna Tillyard were far from being strangers to their niece for, following their mother's death, they passed longer or shorter holidays at Fordfield to recover from the rigours of nursing London's East Enders; they also invited their niece to accompany them on a week's holiday at Walberswick in Suffolk in August 1899. At Walberswick they lodged at 'The Noted Bun Shop' whose 'mad landlady' was nothing like a 'neat-handed Phyllis' trained by Catharine Tillyard, rode bicycles 'in paths of sand wherein one sinks even to the depth of 6 inches', 'did' 'two churches each day'[85], and enjoyed a happy and relaxing visit. With her aunts' example before her eyes, Aunt Anna with her "adventurous disposition" and her ability to be "a person you always noticed, even in a room full of people", Aunt Fanny who, though "not handsome", was endowed with the "loving smile and low voice that guardian angels reserve for the rather plain" and the ability to see people 'not as they are but as by the grace of God they may become', and both aunts 'wonderfully cheerful' and living life as it ought to be lived ('it is nothing but being good')[86], impressionable Aelfrida found herself 'registering a vow [to] work with "the Aunties" for a little while'.[87]

Two and a half years later her vow was fulfilled when 'the Aunties' invited her to spend her Christmas vacation at the small Medical Mission hospital in Canning Town of which Anna Tillyard was foundress–matron and Fanny Tillyard dispenser and "head of the hostel for nurses and midwives over a hopelessly vast district".[88] Aelfrida's

---

Auntie Anna was a very good woman, and Auntie Fanny was a saint. Aunt Anna was good looking, with black hair and fine black eyes, and she was a person you always noticed, even in a room full of people. There was not much scope, in those days, for a young woman with an adventurous disposition, and a good many of Other Dear's friends were shocked when Anna Tillyard entered the London Hospital as a probationer. As ward-maids had not been thought of, the probationers scrubbed the floors and did all the heavy work during a 12-hour day. When a nurse was on night duty, two cold sausages on a plate were left ready for her dinner.

Nothing discouraged Auntie Anna, and presently she became Sister George of George Ward.

After Other Dear died, Auntie Fanny joined Auntie Anna at the London. She was small and frail, not handsome, but endowed with the specially loving smile and low voice that guardian angels reserve for the rather plain. Auntie Fanny survived her nurse's training and 'did her Middie' as well. Both the Aunties were often at Fordfield, recovering from 'flu, or resting, and Julius and I considered them as part of the family.

*The Aunties*

first encounter with 'indescribable slums where unemployment, sweated labour, drink and crime held sway'[89], where there were few women in the streets because "they had no money so they could not shop" (but neither could they "be busy over housework or cooking for most of the household belongings had gone to the pawnbrokers and they had no fire and nothing to cook") shocked her to the core: "it was like coming to a different world". It was, for she was not there as an observer but as one "deputising for a nurse who away ill"[90] and as such was expected to live in the nurses' hostel, to get up at 6.30 am every day, to sweep and dust her room before breakfast, and to work short shifts on the wards "taking temperatures, pulses and respirations", filling in charts, giving out meals, carrying out basic nursing care, and helping with the dressing of wounds and lancing of abscesses. She was also expected to work through a list of assigned 'cases' in the local community on which she had to gather information and report back to Aunt Fanny ("don't touch anyone or anything", she was warned, "and be sure you don't sit down anywhere or you'll bring home more than you bargained for"; she was also forbidden "to give any money or make any promises")[91], a task she found more tiring and depressing – Canning Town, she discovered, was "all noise and dirt and people dying on rags behind damp walls full of bugs"[92] – than anything previously encountered.

Fortunately, "not all the days were so heart-breaking". On the wards she was able to chat up the doctors, to achieve a degree of rapport with the "real Canning Townees" she nursed, and to foster friendships with the nurses, and at Christmas Canning Town proved not to be "the manless desert" she had imagined: "one night …

we had a gay evening and a brief dance at Mansfield House".[93]

Mansfield House was one of the settlement houses "bought to provide socially-conscious university students with opportunities to live and work in working class neighbourhoods" and "inspiration ... as well as practical support ... through working with youth clubs"[94] and vocational training for local men and boys. Aelfrida had been introduced to the idea of university settlements earlier in 1902 at a meeting less memorable for its content (settlements seemed to attract 'plain, serious, thoughtful' – and probably vegetarian – undergraduates or "ranting socialist[s] in collarless flannel shirts and red neckerchiefs") than for the attractions of the 'amiable – possibly even more than amiable' undergraduate sitting at her feet[95] and had evinced an interest in institutions whose aims were to break down interclass barriers, to help the disadvantaged by providing them with free legal aid and secondary education, to ameliorate the dreadful conditions in which most of them lived, to prevent young people from being drawn into crime and, incidentally, to evangelise the urban poor more effectively than any clergyman. She seems, however, to have treated her visit to Mansfield House more as light relief from having 'never had ... to do so much in my life before'[96] than as an opportunity to come into contact "with some of the best and noblest souls the world contains"[97] and apart from a visit to 'The Wave Doss-House' (actually a Temperance lodging house for dockers and sailors) at which she served supper but from which she was spirited away before after-dinner entertainments became too rowdy, and two services at a local mission hall at which she addressed a female audience who, so she said, 'listened thirstily' to what she had to say, evinced less interest in outreach programmes than in the benefits accruing to herself by having attended them: 'the men all buzzed round me' (written of the dance) and 'I feel stronger than I did to go on with life and to do my duty', written of the Mission Hall.[98]

Nor did she return home imbued with "increased fervour in philanthropic work"; indeed, it seems that though "rich in experience" of "the homes of the poor" and in ways of dealing with "the ... outcast, the degraded [and] the sick"[99] and feeling in consequence 'as if she had just come out of church [having] washed away a few of the stains of worldliness that [she bore] upon [her] white robe of purity'[100], Aelfrida was more revolted and disillusioned than uplifted and inspired by her visit. For one thing, noting Mansfield House's 'artistic' rooms ('much like the don's rooms at Cambridge', as she wrote of the one in which Julius was then ensconced, he working at Mansfield House while she was at the Mission) and the

'college combination room' appearance of communal areas, she wondered if 'working among the poor were [not] a fashionable fad and little more'[101]; for another, realisation that some of her own family's income derived from its inheritance or acquisition of "slum property"[102] (as Staffordshire Street now was) whose rents helped to pay for satin dresses and pretty hats may have reminded her of something she preferred to ignore. More revealing still were comments made some years later but put into a fictional woman's mouth: discussing "slumming" with a cousin, 'Marjorie Lane' admits that "the poor in the mass ... street after street, mile after mile of them, all drunken and all dirty and all starving" do not attract her in the least; that whereas she could cope with "one or two men out of work and five or six drunken women and a couple of dozen starving children"[103], she was revolted by the thought of tending "the unsightly, the repulsive [and] the perverse"[104] en masse; that the good women with whom she associated at "St Monica's Settlement" were not, as they liked people to think, "far too good to be true" but "sugar on the top and ... cattiness underneath" (and they fussed over "pet priests" to boot); finally that what she required of *any* vocation was that it take her "among beautiful surroundings" and allow her to wear her "best clothes".[105]

Having therefore decided that 'slumming' was not the form her personal philanthropy would take, that sustained hard physical work was not her *métier,* that she had no desire to emulate her saintly aunts by working for others 'to the Glory of God'[106], that it was quite beyond her capacity for self-denial to deny a wish for recognition, comfort or power[107], and that it was a waste of time, energy, and money to expend them on semi-criminal elements whose intemperate habits and casual attitude to life and work had contributed to their misfortunes ("we support them when they won't work, we deluge them with luxuries when they are ill and teach them morris dancing when they are well. No wonder the papers [describe] The Crushing Burden of the Middle Classes"; only much later did she note that she had "consciously" failed to understand both the social problems of "the East End of London ... in the middle of the blackest period of unemployment" and her aunts' Christian response to it)[108], the self-styled "crude young thing in [her] teens"[109] confined herself to advocating good works but ensuring that they were carried out by others, to consecrating herself to God in sedentary fashion, to never denying her wish for recognition, comfort, and power, and to diverting her charitable efforts to those she deemed the *deserving* poor. More positively and though they thought her selfish and "useless to anyone but [herself]"[110], the Aunties had taken a personal interest in a young woman whose life increasingly appeared aimless and reactive rather than full of "sustained well-directed [and] fruitful action" like theirs and it was not their fault that their plans to give her life direction had spectacularly misfired and that had she been able to respond appropriately, her life too might have been one in which humility, altruism, right affection, and carefree joy played a greater part than pride, ego-centricity, "ill-directed" affection, "uncertain" detach-ment, "worries and solicitudes", and suffering.[111] But it was with appreciation which came only with increasing insight into her own personality defects that Aelfrida later used Aunts Anna ("a very good woman") and Fanny ("a saint")[112] as 'copy' – but 'copy' which did not appear in the profane setting of a novel (as with the Learned Twins) but in a homiletic book and a moralising article.

A more congenial (but still 'tiring') activity was one for which credentials acquired in the pursuit of 'cases' in London's East End and at meetings of the women's Liberal Federation (Aelfrida, the 'youngest speaker they have ever had', had suggested that factories should be moved out of cities to rural sites, citing the Chivers, a local jam-making family, as an example of what could be done in this respect, and that "large numbers [of people] should move out of towns into the country … a scheme … [already] taken up by the admirable 'Garden City Association'") could be put to practical use in local vil-lages without the need for too much hard work or waste of writing time. By now accustomed to public speaking ('I stalked off without the slightest hesitation', she noted on being called to a platform, 'made my point briefly and left … pleasantly conscious of hearing Agnes [Slack] say "very good indeed"')[113] and to researching into 'social questions', Aelfrida was delighted to be co-opted into investigations in support of a concern regularly aired in her father's newspaper: the provision of suitable housing in rural Cambridgeshire.

The problems caused by Cambridge's sudden and extensive 19th century expansion gave rise to "grave evils" in what was effectively a "new town" to the east of the town's historic core. (There was, for example, a public house every thirty-six yards along East Road off which Staffordshire Street opened.)[114] These were publicised in 1906 in Eglantyne Jebb's *Cambridge. A Brief Study in Social Questions*[115] (academic Cambridge's "complete detach-ment from the … squalor, poverty and misery … at [its] gates", wrote Miss Jebb, was underlined by the efforts of "a handful of earnest people"[116], often those same aca-demics' female relatives – to alleviate it), but it was an associated investigation into the 'Housing Question'[117] on which Aelfrida found herself engaged in summer 1903. (Later that year she records that 'Miss Eglantine (*sic*) Jebb' called 'on business'[118] but her not being involved

in Miss Jebb's investigation of Cambridge's particular 'housing question' suggests either that Aelfrida refused to go 'slumming' again or was forbidden to do so lest she bring infection home: smallpox, scarlet fever, and diph-theria were endemic in the Barnwell area of town where the Tillyards' properties were situated and on returning from village investigations she had a bath and a com-plete change of clothing before rejoining the family.)[119] Insanitary and barely habitable cottages were found in local villages too and it was to one of these that Aelfrida cycled in late August and early September 1903 for the purpose of 'collecting statistics' on the rents, water sup-plies ('very defective') number of inhabitants ('some bad cases of overcrowding') and state of repair ('picturesque, tumbledown, inconvenient dwellings' abounded) of Comberton properties. Though the visits were arranged by the local 'housing lady', Aelfrida had no compunction in using her father's name ("Mr Tillyard said he thought you would not mind showing me your cottage") to gain entry nor did she scruple to lunch at the local pub (the quiet back parlours of country public houses often lodged teetotallers drinking tea or lemonade) and was, rather to her surprise, made welcome by villagers eager to show her round. Whether this was because they hoped 'statistics' might lead to improved housing conditions or because Aelfrida having, as she said, lived in a 'democratic country' (i.e. Switzerland) found herself better able 'to treat all men as equals and not to patronise anyone'[120] (*sic*), she does not say, but her summer holiday tasks – besides 'Blue Books' (lists of properties and residents germane to her investigation), she was also busy with Italian lessons and a 'new story'[121] – were more to her taste than that of the previous December. Comberton's 'housing question' also provided 'copy': 'Roy Hadstock', inspecting his new wife's Cambridgeshire estate, listens to her tenants' grievances and draws up lists of the "leaky roofs, cracked boilers and polluted wells" to which atten-tion ought to be paid but is not[122], an echo perhaps, of Aelfrida's own views on the futility of surveys such as hers in which greater emphasis was placed on collecting statistics than on improving the cottagers' lot.

The problem with Aelfrida's 'vocations', be these abstinence, philanthropy, teaching, or novel-writing, was that none save the last and that only approximately called out 'the best in [her]' or made her 'feel it in [her] heart'[123] as something to which she could justifiably devote her life; indeed, within a year or two of praising the joys of being 'finished', it began to seem as if her life was becoming a 'tragedy' in this if no other respect.

A party attended in May 1903 at which palmis-try was practised and fortunes told from playing cards proved both informative and uncannily correct. From her client's 'most interesting hand' the palmist discerned 'great abilities [and] boundless imagination', predicted that she would be 'a writer of fiction', and advised her to forget about flirting 'and go in for literature' instead for 'you are bound to succeed'. The cards agreed ('you have remarkable abilities … you will certainly succeed in literature if you do not allow your energies to be taken up by other things') but warned of unfortunate character traits ('your temperament is rather too extreme, sometimes you are elated and at other times have corresponding fits of depression') and that 'with regard to your past life you have already been deceived by a man whom you trusted absolutely'. 'We shall see', wrote Aelfrida after transcribing the predictions, 'how much will come true'.[124] Much did.

Boredom played a part in the current act of her 'tragedy'. Once home from Switzerland, Aelfrida realised that what she was living was not 'life'[125] but a kind of half-life filled with 'vocations' to which she was not called and with trivialities which did little to break the monotony ('I have kept a gospel service … I have been to the dentist, I have peppered the biscuits I didn't eat at the Albany Café … I have seen Mrs Haslam and I have not seen Mrs Venn')[126] and that what stretched before her was not 'liberty' but an 'arid desert of years'[127] to be escaped only temporarily (a visit to 'Buffalo Bill's *Wild West*!!' aroused 'elemental passions' in her supposedly 'calm and dignified self'[128] but a river trip with a hundred girls from the County School quenched them) or endured until the marriage predicted by the palmist ('you *will* get married, in two or three years' time')[129] released her into what might not be quiet happiness but ennui of another kind.

Failing 'vocation', marriage seemed increasingly inevitable to one who stated that '*no* man [was] preferable to a *bad* man' and a 'fairly average husband … better than none at all'.[130] (And *much* better than 'a Cambridge tradesman', the worst fate imaginable.)[131] True, her 'vocation' was tending more to motherhood than to marriage ('Italian and … gardening and tennis can't fill my life. If [only] I had a baby – . Do you see? Something of my own to love') but to motherhood less for the sake of children per se than in order to assuage an inner emptiness so acute and so overwhelming ('I am so lonely, so terribly terribly lonely … God grant that some day I may be able to fill the pages of my diary with the doings of little children who will call me "mother"')[132] that the pesterings of lower middle class schoolgirls on a school trip ('I have been mauled, adored, caressed [and] petted until I am quite bewildered [but] I love to be loved by my girls') could do no more than temporarily assuage it.

Maternity, however, presupposed marriage to a man her children would call 'father' and this reason alone caused Aelfrida to burst out 'I want to get married. I do really'[133] shortly before attendance at the wedding of the family solicitor's daughter elicited the darkly prophetic comment 'I loathe other people's weddings. I wonder if I shall loathe my own!'[134] And if this were to be the case, what comfort could she find in biblical texts advising her to "take no thought of whom ye shall wed or with what man ye shall be mated for the Lord knoweth ye have need of this thing".[135]

In spite of frequent attendance at "mating-dance[s]", she had not yet found a suitable man with whom to 'mate' – her "mating-engagement" to Hans Peter was a sham – and looking to marriage to drive away "the mist of futility which … hung over everything" (but would marriage be only "futility à deux"?)[136] was thwarted by the knowledge that Herbert Kitchener, 'the man I love … the one earthly thing I desire above all others', the one man for whom she was 'just mad with longing' ('I could throw myself at his feet and implore him to let me love him') was unattainable ('I am like the sunflower turning ever towards the light it loves without … hope of reaching it')[137] and that Archie Stent, her 'true friend' with whom 'Platonic friendship' was such a 'success'[138] that it might have ripened into love, was dead. In fact, as she informed Newnhamite friend Pattie Craske, it seemed better 'not to marry the man one loved'[139] but to accept a man about whom one was *not* passionate because, though not in any way a soul-mate, he could provide the children for whom one longed.

That Aelfrida was indeed deeply unhappy (her tears, she tells us firmly, were not 'of maudlin sentimentality and foolish … repinings' nor was she feigning 'love-sickness for … want of something better to do')[140] is obvious from contemporary diary entries in which she writes that she *has* to laugh at everything (*de rire de tout*) in order to stop herself weeping over it (*pour ne pas en pleurer*)[141] and describes her belief that 'earthly happiness' is an impossibility ('we were never meant to seek it', a belief supported by biblical texts chosen for their appositeness), and from behaviour which would ensure that if anyone asked her "are you happy?" she would 'be able to reply with a calm smile and without the necessity of lying "well, I really haven't had time to think!"'[142]

Nor did she allow herself time to think. The beginning of each new academic year was not only the moment at which Aelfrida made her new year resolutions[143] but also the signal for her mother to send At Home cards to newly-matriculated Nonconformist undergraduates ('Presbyterian freshers')[144] attending St Columba's (Westminster College students were invited to Castlebrae, the home of their benefactress twins, to which Aelfrida and Catharine Tillyard were also invited; other wives, 'town' and 'gown', also invited 'freshers' to 'squashes' and At Homes, thus exposing 'finished' young ladies like Miss Tillyard to even greater numbers of potential 'mates') and it was not long before 'freshers' duly began to call and Aelfrida to 'approve distinctly' of two: Clive Carey, organ scholar of Clare, with his 'sweet dimple'[145] and other attributes (good looks, cleverness, beautiful voice, and an ability to dance and play tennis) and Geoffrey Hatten, an old Tonbridgian now at Caius (the men's colleges are always carefully noted in Aelfrida's diary and only undergraduates from the more fashionable ones – or her brother's college – encouraged) and 'tall, dark and clean … [and] very "manly" looking' (necessary attributes these) whose 'soulful eyes, musical genius and … great admiration' for herself (admiration so great that on leaving Cambridge three years later 'his eyes filled with tears' as he said goodbye to one on whom he was, as the expression was, 'gone'), caused her both to dream about him and to give some serious consideration to his 'hopeful … lovemaking'. ('I could get very fond of Geoffrey Hatten'.)[146] But 'freshers', though fun, had to "[cram] … for stiff exams"[147] and were 'foemen not worthy of [her] steel'[148] for a "grown-up child"[149] who preferred admirers 'older 6 or 7 years at least'[150] than herself or older still: 'a nice MA of about 30' with whom she flirted 'shockingly'[151], or a postgraduate 'blood' who 'completely lost his head [and] put his arms round me'[152] and from whom she had to be rescued by a younger admirer. Of whom she had so many that to list and describe them all would require not just a separate chapter but another volume, for within a short time of her return from Switzerland and while still nominally engaged to 'Enrico', Aelfrida had cast her spell over a myriad young men, referred to those most heavily smitten as her 'slain', and worried amusedly lest one victim's jealously impel him to convert two others 'into real "slain"'.[153]

Some 'slain' were long-standing fatalities: Percy Stanley ('still available … if I *badly* want a husband')[154] and Ernest Haddon ('you remember, I *have* been engaged to Ernest and … have [even] kissed him … sitting on his knee in their summer house' at the age of 'eleven or so', Ernest being then a 'little boy' of twelve; 'Mamma', she adds, was 'pleased that I had made … *one* conquest – or rather, confirmed an old one!')[155], the latter going so far as to produce a razor during a tea party in Julius' rooms and to threaten with the utmost seriousness "you will drive me to [suicide] one day Frida. I only hope I may not be obliged to kill you first".[156] Others fell hard and immediately during their Cambridge years (there were very few of whom Aelfrida noted 'I do not affect them at all')[157] but moved on literally and emotionally later. Of these, five are worth describing in more detail because to do

so demonstrates the effect Aelfrida had on them and her technique for attracting men.

Two were brothers. Garden Blaikie, 'just ordained at Westminster and going out as a "mish" to Amoy', was met (on his part, at least) just too late. Inviting her after one day's acquaintance to his farewell dinner at Castlebrae, Garden waxed sentimental, hoping that Aelfrida would 'still be here in 7 years' on the occasion of his first leave but on taking her hand to say goodbye said sadly "I shall not see you again"; he did, but only once and briefly when in 1908 as a dull 'Chinese missionary' with an 'admirable but plain' older wife, he was briefly sparked into life by the now-married lady who had once declared 'I do *not* love … Garden' but had nevertheless inserted a picture of him in her diary. ('I don't know where it is', she confessed in 1904, adding that she had given 'a very colourless account of the Blaikie episode', Garden having by his brother's account become 'awfully fond' of her after very short acquaintance.)[158] Cuthbert, 'brother of the celebrated Garden', known to Aelfrida as 'Baby Blaikie' to distinguish him from his elder brother and because he was a year younger than herself, was an altogether different proposition: 'an arrant flirt for his age', he pretended to be engaged to her as an excuse for calling her 'Frida' and said things 'that would show well in a breach of promise case'. Far from being shocked (Cuthbert, though a 'naughty little … boy', was so 'amusing' that he was both forgiven and used as a stimulant to wilder behaviour on his 'fiancée's' part), she 'flirted outrageously' with him on several occasions but having 'got all the personal fun needed out of him', handed him on to Pattie Craske.[159]

The course of Aelfrida's relationship with "Mr Barkway of Westminster"[160] ran rather differently to her brief one with Garden Blaikie or that with his brother which lasted from 1903 to 1906, for James Barkway, 'otherwise known as "the Nose" or "Nosey"' because his 'unfortunate proboscis' made him look like a 'melancholy eagle'[161] and caused him to walk with head bent as if by doing so he could conceal his prominent facial feature, was a postgraduate student five years older than Aelfrida herself. First met in May 1900, his reputation for being 'precious' and his being a candidate for the priesthood discouraged closer acquaintance, but realisation that Barkway was 'really quite a wit in [a] funny canny Scotch way' (on her return from Lausanne he asked "have you come home … with the intention of being very 'demure?'" when it was obvious that far from being 'very demure', she intended to be a flirt) made her decide, to her mother's delight, to cultivate the 'decidedly amusing' theologian's acquaintance.[162]

An 'amusing' friendship ensued – it was, they decided, to be only 'Platonic … i.e. an excuse for a

```
                  And I loved grey-green days
  and whispy white mists, and winter sunsets behind bare  trees
  and still, starlit evenings - but garden parties need sun,
  and at Cambridge sunshine was always provided, along with the
  ices in little glass plates and the sandwiches (to be avoided
  if possible) and the petits fours, and the band (if possible
  in the distance) and the smiling chattering ladies, and the
  parvdes and the huge hats and the pretty dresses and the
  green grass and little seats , and flowers smiling and opening
                         mown
  wide,wide, and the winding paths ,and the bushes that suggested
  hide-and-seek or Secrets, and the grave tall trees that
  looked down so benevolently.  How soon a garden party was
  over !  You came, you greeted your hostess, you flirted
  from one charming  acquaintance to another, you accepted
  refreshments, you took a last look round to see if you had
  missed a friend, and then there was the hostess saying good-
  bye, and maybe the host too, dragged from his lab. or his coll-
  ege rooms to do the polite, and everything is over, the waiters
  and the waitresses are clearing away cups and saucers and ice-
  plates, and folding tables, and perhaps the son of the house
  is cramming chocolate biscuits into his mouth because he
  thinks no one is looking, and the cat is drinking up super-
  fluous milk more than it ever had in its life before, and the
  sun is going down and trees sending out lengthening shadows to
  claim the garden as their own, and the garden-party is over !
```

*Garden Parties*

good flirtation'[163], Barkway suggesting that Aelfrida start a salon at which she 'was to stand on the hearthrug and hold forth for hours to an adoring circle of men' (plain mousy girls were also to be admitted but only 'in small quantities') and that if there were a vacancy in her first class he would like to be admitted ('No, Mr Barkway', wrote Aelfrida, remembering the disastrous consequences for men admitted to it, 'no more first classes for me')[164] and Aelfrida alternately ignoring him or bowing coldly in reply to a 'sweet smile'[165] or, carefully posed on a Fordfield sofa 'so as not to show each other our respective profiles!', luring him on with witty talk and meaningful glances.[166] But Aelfrida's hope that Barkway (now styled 'The Anteater') was *not* going to fall in love with her came true, for in spite of his tendency to pay 'elaborate attention' to her ('if any other man had said … the things he said … I should have called it making love')[167], his engagement to Mary Dykes, daughter of the Principal of Westminster College ('what a good thing it is that almost all men can find some girl to have them!'[168] wrote Aelfrida waspishly on receiving the news in December 1902) caused her to wonder whether James' attentions had not been 'merely Platonic friendliness'[169] after all or if she had made a fool of herself in mistaking quiet amusement at her social antics (e.g. her tending to monopolise the conversation at any gathering of which she was part) for 'trembling admiration'[170] and a canny 'Scotch' gaze for a sentimental look. At later meetings, however, she was less sure, for Barkway, though now in 'priestly garb' and 'older and … grave

and parsonic' – and from 1906, married – still showed a tendency to be 'more amiable than he meant'[171] and there *had* been an incident in May 1902 when, showing her over Westminster College (a college previously visited with besotted Garden Blaikie) he had taken her up the tower (now known to her as 'Blaikie tower'), quoted poetry to her, and been disinclined to descend, but come November 1906 she dismissed him as 'bloodless' and as worthy only of contemplating his "precious profile in stained glass windows".[172] Sadly, however, we shall never read Aelfrida's delineation of James Barkway in her current novel in which she made him speak the exact words he said to her the following day ('it was quite uncanny [and] really quite creepy')[173], for it was later destroyed.

Barkway was not, however, Aelfrida's only ecclesiastical admirer. Attending a Waldensian Mission meeting at Castlebrae in May 1902, she met 'a lovely-looking boy' of twenty-seven 'with a pale face, flashing black eyes and dark wavy hair', Paolo Coïsson. Realising that he was Italian, she seized the opportunity to find out more about 'this most charming of pastors' with 'courtly manners' by showing him round some Cambridge colleges.[174] Replying a few days later to a letter of thanks, Aelfrida found herself showered with letters in return, some merely 'very sweet', others showing by their length, incoherence, and effusiveness that Signor Coïsson had joined the 'slain'. Presents followed, including books with 'some of the tender passages … marked' ('I am glad that Mamma does not understand Italian')[175], together with requests that she think about him sometimes and that she send him her photograph. (She refused; to do so would have implied a deeper intimacy than she cared to provoke.) Time and geography separated the smitten pastor from his *signorina* ("our friendship is not what it used to be", he wrote sadly two years later)[176] and in spite of hints that they meet on his visit to England in 1913, it was not until February 1918 after a sixteen year correspondence that Paolo and Aelfrida met in Cambridge and by chance. Recognising him immediately – though he was in army uniform, his 'big gentle blue eyes and white idealistic forehead' were just as she remembered – Aelfrida invited him to Fordfield where they talked late into the evening of 'how he had thought of marriage once, *had hoped* – a long reproachful pause – and now never, never'. Aelfrida, now married herself, 'pointed out the advantages of the married state' (ironically, she had just discovered her husband's infidelity) but felt 'no sentiment to match his'.[177] Learning a decade later that Coïsson remained unwed ('I should be sorry and yet touched', she wrote, if it was because of his love for herself)[178], she last beheld fifty-six- year-old Coïsson, 'shorter and fatter and browner and very bald but immensely friendly', honeymooning in England in 1934 with a wife twenty years his junior and hoped he would be 'very happy'.[179]

The last of Aelfrida's 'slain' to be considered in detail was a young man first met in August 1902. Archibald Venn was as vulnerable in his way as Garden Blaikie (about to leave England alone to take up his first post in a foreign country on the other side of the world) and Paolo Coïsson (a lonely foreigner and member of a minority religious sect) in theirs. Nineteen-year-old Archie, described by Aelfrida as 'plain and delicate' and as possessing 'the charm of a boy who has been a great deal with [older] people'[180] (he was the only child of elderly parents, his father being John Venn FRS[181] and his mother Susanna, née Edmonstone, a novelist) was, 'judging by the celerity with which he has got fond of me'[182], immediately smitten and over games of tennis and 'ping-pong' and at dances made it clear that he considered himself a swain entitled to murmur 'loverlike … sweet things'[183] in her ear.

Although she felt sorry for a child whose mother had borne no living children until she was forty, who would have been happier if her sole surviving child had been a girl, whose life was 'one long fight against pain', and whose mental health was precarious[184], and although , as Alfred Tillyard informed her, 'Venn will be very rich'[185] (a point worth noting by a young woman chagrined by the thought that her family's modest middle class means might be a reason for men being reluctant to marry – as opposed to flirt with – her: 'it is only that I have not five hundred a year that I have not babies of my own')[186], she hoped Archie would 'gradually get tired of [her]'[187] because he was 'so undistinguished'[188], because he was spotty, red haired, and served at tennis with his mouth open, because after Archie Stent she could never fall in love with another Archibald, and because she was, for reasons still undisclosed, less interested in Archie than in his 'eccentric old mother' and her 'strange and prophetic' (and therefore 'interesting') moods.[189]

It was not only Archie who was, as teenage Eustace crudely put it, "on the job"[190] with regard to his sister, it was Susanna Venn as well and within months of Aelfrida's first meeting with her son Susanna was 'aunting' hard on Archie's behalf. "If only I had a daughter like Aelfrida"[191], she told Catharine Tillyard, a wish which might have been taken at face value had it not been for Mrs Venn's subsequent palmistry-prophecy that Aelfrida would marry twice, the first time to a 'delicate' boy of her own age, the second to a widower with four children. Aelfrida graciously invited Mrs Venn 'to *both* [her] weddings'[192] but was not then aware that the first part of that lady's prophecy was soon to be fulfilled; but nor was Mrs Venn aware that within months Archie, deemed 'too young

and too fickle for so serious a matter as an engagement' when the girl in question was not Aelfrida, would engage himself to and subsequently marry a childhood friend. 'Two silly little children', stated one who said she "wouldn't have married [Archie] if he had been the last man on earth"[193] but who would have liked the chance to refuse him.

Writing of one of her 'most respectful' but unprepossessing adorers, Aelfrida, not herself endowed with conventional prettiness, wondered why she was 'so attractive to unattractive men'.[194] The reason was not hard to find: she treated all men alike so that those already attractive believed themselves more so and those unattractive, attractive to such an extent that when dismissed by Aelfrida they found no difficulty in attracting another girl. But what was it that made Aelfrida so 'fascinating' to gentlemen? An inherited ability to charm and to be charming? Emulation of Ruth Schechter's ability to become the centre of attention? (It was only recently that she and Aelfrida had parted company.) Perhaps both, but it was with more than gestures (choosing Archie Venn's favourite cakes for a tennis party, for example) that she attracted men to her; it was her seductive ability to put men at their ease, particularly young men unsure of themselves in unfamiliar surroundings ('I soon drew him out'[195], she reports of one), to create a feeling of intimacy with each one even when surrounded by 'half a dozen men at once'[196], to enliven a humdrum social gathering with her presence ("I … needed no stimulus to produce exhilaration at parties")[197], to show an interest in even the dullest person ('I have been interested in so many ordinary things … that when anyone attacks me on any of them … I glow in response [and] it seems as if my whole life must have been given up to that particular [man]')[198], to flatter ('being nice to people')[199], to initiate and maintain eye contact ('I … had the satisfaction of seeing in his eyes that look … of admiration that I see in most men's eyes')[200], to make men laugh at her 'epigrams', to assure them that they danced 'almost as well as they sat out'[201], to imply that she 'wanted to say things [she] did not dare to'[202], to carry men off in turn to the kitchen garden 'to eat gooseberries and … pay me a compliment'.[203] ("I like to be made love to in the garden not indoors. Indoors … all the furniture seems to look on".)[204] No wonder, then, that so many men were 'slain' and had 'a rare time'[205] in her company.

And Aelfrida in theirs. As a true coquette possessing 'the instinct to try and … awaken the admiration of every man I meet'[206], who 'usually approved of flirting'[207] (Band of Hope meetings run by Westminster College undergraduates were an exception), and whose motto at this time was 'fascinate every *possible* man you meet!'[208] ("at it again!"[209] Ernest Haddon's father used to say and "I knew you wanted your little flirt"[210] her own as he watched her escort a young man into a private corner of the Fordfield garden; her mother, "similarly admired in the 1870s"[211], was amused at and seldom displeased by her daughter's behaviour), Aelfrida found herself in the springtime of a life not hitherto renowned for its brightness feeling "that life ... might prove amusing after all" and that she was more alive than "in those long grey days"[212] of childhood. She also and perhaps for the first time in her life felt both young ('I am not yet very old, am I?')[213] and young at heart ('*diable,* go it while you are young!' ran a diary entry in which she chided herself for 'silliness')[214] and this in spite of fears that at age thirty she might have to 'give up thinking and writing about men' ('Query. Will my diary be less interesting?') [215] and settle down: 'perhaps you think I give too much prominence in these pages ... to the everlasting young man. Never mind. Time enough when I am older to ... be solemn and proper. The men won't admire me for ever. Someday I shall be middle-aged and serious through and through, not half merry and half sad. I shall be *drab* one day, just like all the rest'.[216]

Half merry and half sad: how accurate a picture of herself Aelfrida painted at age nineteen. On the one hand, a young woman who could flirt 'and enjoy it thoroughly' (but given her new religiosity, hope she was not 'wicked' to do so)[217], on the other, a damaged child whose intrinsic and all-pervading sadness overshadowed her entire being, manifesting itself paradoxically in 'challenging gaiety' rather than in the 'radiant dignity' of a normal young woman'.[218]

Manifestations of Aelfrida's disordered personality have been touched upon already in the context of her childhood and adolescence. What we see now is their persistence into young adulthood and into a period of her life where adult relationships had to be entered into, adult decisions made, and adult responsibilities assumed.

A 1904 addition to a 1901 diary entry ('I have learnt much but I have changed little. The chief difference is that I feel more powerful')[219] and a diary entry made in 1902 (after discussing 'many things, chiefly flirting and how to be happy', with Silvia Myers, Aelfrida noted that though she publically scorned Silvia's 'commonplace' wish to find happiness through humble submission to a man she loved, her own unstated desire was the same: 'to be [his] slave')[220] show her extending her need to be in control and her emotional neediness onto men as potential 'mates' and potential fathers of potential children. Neediness showed itself in sequence ('one man and then another')[221] quantity ('I have [no] ... young men ... to spare, not even the humblest')[222] and in unhappiness if unable to 'kindle [a] fire ... and leave it to smoulder'[223]

in a man's heart because this implied rejection. (A man's qualities were less important than his response and the thrill of the chase, not the feelings he aroused.) But having attracted a man, she behaved badly towards him, manifesting her power by subjecting even those who behaved most lovingly towards her to a regime which ranged from negligence to neglect and from coolness ('cutting' someone in the street) to emotional cruelty (in the course of a game of tennis in which a serious suitor was playing, she 'amused [her]self by taking all the young men in turn into the kitchen garden and making them each pay [her] a compliment as [they] passed [him]')[224], the man concerned never knowing what her response would be. Worse still, she had no idea of how to be friends with a man (i.e. to enter into a relationship of equals) because to be friends was to admit him to an intimacy she did not feel and could not entertain. Indeed, so distorted was her sense of self-worth (a child sent away without explanation could not be valuable in her parents' eyes; no-one ever told her that it was *because* she was valuable she had been sent away) and so powerful her need to punish herself for the unknown 'sin' for which she had been sent away – and continued to send herself away as soon as a man seemed about to break down her defences – that her comment regarding to her behaviour (her 'being nice to people' was merely a means of ensnaring another 'victim', 'flirting', the bait) speaks volumes: 'so', she wrote, 'do I unwittingly deceive many'.[225]

'Flirting', though it temporarily fulfilled a need, was a dangerous pursuit insofar as a besotted 'victim' might misinterpret her behaviour and make her an offer of marriage, something she 'must not let'[226] happen because of what acceptance implied of surrender. But how to stop men becoming sufficiently close or serious enough to propose? An answer, she discovered, having practised on 'little Blaikie', was to '[play] the ingénue', a technique so successful that she 'was inspired to try it again – on someone else'[227] and, finding that it worked, employed it again and again as if reversion to a childhood state of ingenuous innocence could protect her from long grey days of marriage in the future.

As befitted a well-brought-up Victorian girl Aelfrida was inevitably subjected to an enforced innocence from which hints of sexuality were ruthlessly expunged. Seen in this light, 'ingénue' behaviour could be regarded as *naïveté* and feared powerlessness in the face of masculine domination no more than realisation that as a female minor she was indeed powerless in many social and legal respects, were it not for her deliberate adoption of the pose. Hence although her later admission that she 'never thought about sex'[228] until marriage forced her to do so is probably true, her having only the 'vaguest notion of what "falling in love" meant'[229] or having 'no idea what love between man and woman was'[230] is evidence of a disordered personality unwilling *and unable* to love or let herself love because of the dangers implicit in surrender (however loving) of self to other.

Being unfortunately blind to the problems inherent in as well as to the motives for her behaviour (or having deliberately blinded herself), Aelfrida's propensity to regard 'Flirting' as a 'game'[231] and a means to an end rather than a device by means of which she could attract and commit herself to a single 'mate', laid her open to desertion, danger, and social stricture; indeed, it does not seem to have occurred to her that the reason for men's desertion of her for another woman lay within herself or that men deeply in love with her were repulsed by supposedly flirtatious but actually pathological behaviour during which what had seemed like warm interest in themselves as individuals became inexplicably transformed into unpleasantly capricious teasing, then into dismissive arrogance bordering on the vengeful – as witness James Barkway who may indeed have loved her more than platonically for a time[232] but who, his eyes opened by her behaviour towards him, announced at a Fordfield 'squash' that "time passes and so do opportunities"[233] and engaged himself to someone else.

The danger inherent in driving men away by demanding and capricious behaviour was not apparent to a young woman who would go to almost any lengths to attract them:

> "The Flapper is a grown-up child
> (Or bird of prey some people class her)
> In colours gay no flowers surpass her
> And, like the flowers, she's sometimes wild"[234],

but her obsessive need to be the centre of every man's attention and the intensity with which she attracted men by her apparent lust for living life to the full (*her* life, not theirs) had two unforeseen consequences, one with regard to herself, one with regard to the men aroused by her attention-seeking and – though she professed not to realise it – sexualised behaviour. (When Julius, the true object of her affection and therefore 'nicer than all the other men put together'[235], graduated in summer 1904, was much out of England during the following year and in autumn 1905 left for the British School at Athens where he was to remain for three, vacations excepted, his sister's attention-seeking behaviour, lacking its true focus, became less inhibited still and led to her committing two major errors with regard to men.) The first was her inevitable inclusion among 'young people' deemed 'fast', by whose 'abandonment and devilry' she pretended to be 'shocked and ruffled' (perhaps in a sense she was, because

of its contrast with the 'simple goodness' of a man like Geoffrey Hatten), but in whose madcap behaviour "that little Tillyard girl" joined 'with the best of them'[236], the second, her censoriousness regarding the result of "deliberately attempting to rouse [men's] desires"[237]: hearing that the daughter of an impoverished 'townee' family had turned to prostitution to supplement the family income, Aelfrida saw no connection between her own titillating behaviour and the need of the men she titillated to turn to local girls to alleviate their frustration[238], castigating the girl but never associating the latter's actual neediness with her own emotional one.

Perhaps, in truth, she did not understand the connection between the "flash of passion" in a man's eyes and what this signified of his "getting warm"; perhaps she *was* "really only beautifully innocent" (but if that was true, what was Catharine Tillyard doing, given that so much of her daughter's 'Flirting' occurred at home or in her mother's presence?) – but perhaps she did, and was not. "The matter [was] made plain to her" in 1903 by Robin Smart, he, now a 'broad, splendidly male [and] intensely aristocratic looking' young soldier with whom in spite of protestations to the contrary Aelfrida seems to have flirted, enquiring if she were not afraid of burning her fingers when she played with fire and on her answering "oh, *dear* no!", informing her "well, you will some day"[239], and in 1904 by her fiancé when, watching her making-up to another man, he explained 'what that sort of "flirting" meant'. (She professed herself "shocked and insulted" by his remark and 'humiliated' by discovering how her behaviour appeared to others.) But in spite of diarised assurances that 'never again!' would she behave like that, her protestations were immediately countered by assurances she was '*not*' in danger of becoming 'a "nice sensible modest girl"'[240] and the young man who issued her second warning joined her 'collection of unfortunate victims' precisely because her behaviour was incapable of amendment.

## Notes

1   GCPPT 1|1|8 29 September 1901.
2   Tillyard, HJW. Introduction to *The Letters of ACW Tillyard* (MTC).
3   GCPPT 1|1|8 29 September 1901.
4   ibid. 14 October 1901.
5   ibid. 29 September 1901.
6   ibid. 5 October 1901.
7   Tillyard, HJW. *The Letters of ACW Tillyard* (MTC). Letter from Aelfrida to Wilhelmina (Mina) Kaufmann of 6 December 1902.
8   GCPPT 1|1|6 8 September 1900
    GCPPT 1|1|8 29 September 1901.
9   GCPPT 1|1|8 3 October 1901.
10  Tillyard, HJW. *The Letters of ACW Tillyard* (MTC). Letter from Aelfrida to Julius Tillyard of 9 November 1900.

11 Tillyard, Ae. *Marrying a Stranger* pp 25–26. (GCPPT 2|6).

12 GCPPT 2|25|2 *Mrs Lewis and Mrs Gibson*.
GCPPT 2|2a Vol. 2 No 1 15 January 1903.
For fuller and more formal accounts of the 'Learned Twins' see Whigham Price, A. *The Ladies of Castlebrae* and Soskice, J. *Sisters of Sinai*.

13 GCPPT 1|1|8 16 November ('October' in error) 1901.

14 GCPPT 1|1|9 13 January 1901.

15 ibid. 17 January 1902.

16 GCPPT 1|1|8 12 October 1901.

17 GCPPT 1|1|8 12 October 1901.
GCPPT 1|1|9 20 January 1902

18 GCPPT 1|1|8 3 October 1901.

19 ibid. 15 and 16 October 1901.

20 ibid. 23 October 1901. The story of Francesca da Rimini and her adulterous love for Paolo da Verruchio, her husband's brother, appears in Dante's *Divine Comedy*: Hell V: 88-138.

21 GCPPT 1|1|10 3 July 1903.

22 GCPPT 1|1|9 25 October 1902.

23 ibid. 27 June 1902.

24 GCPPT 1|1|8 12 November 1901.
GCPPT 1|1|9 18 November 1902.
Tillyard, HJW. *The Letters of ACW Tillyard* (MTC). Letter from Aelfrida to Julius Tillyard of 2 August 1902
GCPPT 2|2a Vol. 2 September 1903.

25 GCPPT 1|1|10 15 July 1903.

26 ibid. 25 August 1903. Alfred Tillyard was deeply concerned by certain issues in the field of education particularly those arising after the passing of the Education Act (otherwise known as the Balfour Act after the Prime Minister who sponsored it) of 1902. The Balfour Act resulted in reorganisation of the administration of elementary and secondary schools, county councils replacing parochial boards as the overall authority in each district. To the notion of a rationalised national system Alfred Tillyard gave his full support but his support for a system relying on public rather than parochial control placed him in a difficult personal position as a Nonconformist and as a public figure caused him some embarrassment, and his refusal to pay the Education Rate on grounds of conscience was an indication of conflict of interest. Passive Dissent (as such a refusal was known) was a burning issue in Cambridge and Alfred Tillyard was fortunate not to have goods distrained in lieu of payment as happened to other local dissenters. (Aelfrida's satirical comment on the affair – of her father she wrote that "he *likes* to pose as a martyr / Refusing conscience rights to barter" – appears in the *MCJ* of October 1903. GCPPT 2|2a Vol. 2 no 3.) The government circumvented the problem posed by Nonconformist schools by passing the Local Educational (Local Authority Default) Act in 1904.

27 Tillyard, HJW. Introduction to *The Letters of ACW Tillyard* (MTC).

28 GCPPT 1|1|10 29 June and 1 July ('June' in error) 1903.

29 ibid. 29 September 1903.

30 GCPPT 1|1|11 2 July 1904.

31 GCPPT 1|1|10 22 September 1903.

32 ibid. 14 October 1903.

33 GCPPT 1|1|8 30 September 1901.

34 Tillyard, HJW. *The Letters of ACW Tillyard* (MTC). Letter from Aelfrida to Julius Tillyard of 15 September 1902.

35 ibid. Letter from Aelfrida to Julius Tillyard of [ ] September 1902.

36 ibid. Introduction.

37 GCPPT 1|1|9 2 May 1902.

38 ibid. 2 May 1902.

39 GCPPT 1|1|8 30 September 1901.

40 GCPPT 1|1|10 5 May 1903.

41 Meacham, S. p 368.

42 GCPPT 1|1|8 30 September 1901.

43 GCPPT 1|1|9 20 April and 8 June 1901.

44 ibid. 3 January 1902.

45 ibid. 20 April 1902.

46 ibid. 19 April 1902.

47 GCPPT 1|1|9 19 April and 26 June 1902.
GCPPT 1|1|10 9 July 1903.

48 GCPPT 1|1|10 29 October 1903.

49 Tillyard, HJW. Introduction to *The Letters of ACW Tillyard* (MTC).

50 GCPPT 1|1|9 22 December 1901.

51 GCPPT 1|1|12 16 April 1905.
GCPPT 1|1|13 15 January 1906.

52 GCPPT 1|1|13 14 July 1905.

53 GCPPT 2|27|2(3).

54 Tillyard, Ae. *Marrying a Stranger* p 20 (GCPPT 2|6).

55 GCPPT 1|1|9 8 January 1902.
GCPPT 1|1|10 13 November 1903.
GCPPT 1|1|11 8 June 1904.

56 GCPPT 1|1|9 13 April 1902.

57 GCPPT 2|23 *The Watchword* September 1959.

58 GCPPT 1|1|16 13 August 1908.

59 GCPPT 1|1|10 15 October 1903.

60 GCPPT 1|1|11 1 August 1904.

61 GCPPT 1|1|10 13 October 1903.
GCPPT 1|1|13 5 April 1906 (1905' in error).

62 Meacham, S. pp 359 and 363.

63 GCPPT 1|1|9 29 August 1902.

64 ibid. 22 April 1902. The Temperance Movement was at its height between 1870 and 1914.

65 ibid. 30 November 1901 and 30 January 1902.

66 ibid. 10 January 1902.

67 ibid. 22 April 1902.

68 GCPPT 1|1|9 22 April 1902.
Tillyard, Ae. *Marrying a Stranger* pp 104–110.

69 GCPPT 1|1|9 22 April 1902.

70 ibid. 11 February 1902.

71 ibid. 5 March 1902.

72 Tillyard, HJW. Introduction to *The Letters of ACW Tillyard* (MTC).

73 GCPPT 1|1|9 10 March 1902.

74 Tillyard Ae. *Agnes E. Slack*. p xii.

75 GCPPT 1|1|11 16 February 1904.
GCPPT 1|1|13 26 January 1906.
GCPPT 1|1|27 26 August and 1 September 1922.

76 GCPPT 2|2a Vol. 2 [unnumbered] November 1904 ("Opinions of Celebrities") and Vol. 2 [unnumbered] November 1906 ("Books not to read: *Katie Dear*, a book of maxims by Agnes S.").

77 GCPPT 1|1|9 9 May 1902.

78 ibid. 23 June 1902.

79 Tillyard, HJW. The *Letters of ACW Tillyard* (MTC). Letter from Aelfrida to Wilhelmina (Mina) Kaufmann of 8 May 1911.

80 GCPPT 1|1|9 17 June 1902.

81 GCPPT 1|1|9 22 October 1902.
GCPPT 1|1|10 3 March 1903.

82 GCPPT 1|1|11 5 April 1904.

83 GCPPT 1|1|13 23 January 1906.

84 GCPPT 2|23 *The Watchword* December 1957.

85 GCPPT 1|1|4 19-24 August 1899.
GCPPT 1|1|73 25 January 1957.

86 GCPPT 1|1|4 24 December 1906.
GCPPT 1|1|44 18 May 1933.
GCPPT 2|23 *The Watchword* December 1957.

87 GCPPT 1|1|4 17 May 1900.

88 GCPPT 2|23 *The Watchword* December 1957.

89 GCPPT 1|1|62 15 December 1944.

90 GCPPT 2|23 *The Watchword* December 1957.

91  GCPPT 2|23 *The Watchword* December 1957.
Tillyard, Ae. *Just Alice* p 116-118 (GCPPT 2|19).

92  Tillyard, Ae. *Marrying a Stranger* p 260.

93  GCPPT 2|23 *The Watchword* December 1957.

94  Mulley, C. p 46.

95  GCPPT 1|1|9 5 May 1902.
GCPPT 1|1|10 6 January 1903.

96  GCPPT 1|1|10 26 November 1902.

97  *CIP* 23 August 1901, Women's Column, by-lined 'Pertilote', describing "London Settlements".

98  GCPPT 2|23 *The Watchword* December 1957.
GCPPT 1|1|10 6 January 1903 (retrospective account).

99  *CIP* 23 August 1901 (Women's Column).

100  GCPPT 1|1|10 6 January 1903.

101  ibid. 26 December 1902.

102  Tillyard, Ae. *Just Alice* p 120.

103  Tillyard, Ae. *Marrying a Stranger* p 161.

104  Tillyard, Ae. *A Little Road-Book for Mystics* p 133.

105  Tillyard, Ae. *Marrying a Stranger* p 161.

106  GCPPT 1|1|62 15 December 1949.

107  Tillyard, Ae. *A Little Road-Book for Mystics* p 132.

108  Tillyard, Ae. *Marrying a Stranger* pp 171-178.
Tillyard, Ae. *A Little Road-Book for Mystics* pp 132-133.
GCPPT 2|23 *The Watchword* December 1957.

109  Tillyard, Ae. *A Little Road-Book for Mystics* p 132.

110  ibid. p 133.

111  ibid.

112  GCPPT 2|23 *The Watchword* December 1957.

113  GCPPT 1|1|9 9 May 1902. Aelfrida's speech to the WLF was reported in the *Daily News* ('the big London paper') and 'Miss Tillyard's' comments as quoted by it were noted in her diary, underlined in red ink with the added comment 'what price fame! Snub me … someone, *please!*' Her reference to 'the admirable "Garden City Association"' is to the association inaugurated in 1902 with the aim of promoting Ebenezer Howard's notion of garden cities ringed by factories, warehouses and a railway. The first 'garden city', Letchworth in Hertfordshire, was opened in 1903; an exhibition of 'Cheap Cottages' held there in 1907 was caricatured by Aelfrida in the *MCJ* of September 1907 in *Sorority*, a play supposedly by John Galsworthy. Aunt Anna, a proponent of garden cities, moved to Letchworth on retirement together with Aunt Fanny (they were later joined by widowed Aunt Alice Cliff), rating her faith in schemes such as this higher than the opprobrium gained by living in such a 'cranky place' (GCPPT 1|1|62 15 December 1944).

114  Jebb, E. pp 26 and 98-99.

115  For more on Eglantyne Jebb (1876-1928) and her work in Cambridge see Wilson, F. *Rebel Daughter of a Country House*, Symonds, R. *Far above Rubies* (pp 69-91), and Mulley, C. *The Woman Who Saved the Children*.

116  Wilson, F. pp 102-105.

117  GCPPT 1|1|10 28 August 1903.

118  ibid. 26 October 1903.

119  GCPPT 1|1|10 28 August 1903.

120  GCPPT 1|1|8 10 October 1901.

121  GCPPT 1|1|10 28 August and 2, 7 and 10 September 1903.

122  Tillyard, Ae. *The Way We Grow Up* pp 152-153.

123  Tillyard, Ae. *Marrying a Stranger* p 161.

124  GCPPT 1|1|10 29 May 1903.

125  GCPPT 1|1|11 13 August 1904.

126  ibid. 31 March and 19 April 1904.

127  ibid. 30 June 1904.

128  ibid. 24 June 1904, the day WF Cody's show visited Cambridge.

129  GCPPT 1|1|10 29 May 1903.

130  GCPPT 1|1|9 23 June 1902.

131  ibid. 23 July 1902.

132  ibid. 6 September and 11 and 20 November 1902.

133  GCPPT 1|1|9 6 September 1902.

134  ibid. 11 September 1902.

135  GCPPT 1|1|10 5 March 1903.

136  Tillyard, Ae. *Concrete* pp 13, 18 and 62.

137  GCPPT 1|1|9 6 September and 11 November 1902.

138  ibid. 12 April and 30 September 1902.

139  GCPPT 1|1|10 22 October 1903.

140  GCPPT 1|1|9 6 September 1902.

141  ibid. 20 November 1902.

142  GCPPT 1|1|10 8 December 1902. The texts are inscribed on the inside front cover of this volume.

143  GCPPT 1|1|11 1 January 1904.

144  GCPPT 1|1|8 11 November 1901.

145  GCPPT 1|1|8 25 November 1901. For further details of the life of Thomas Clive Savil Carey (1883-1968) composer, director, singer, and teacher, see the *ODNB* Vol. 10 pp 69-70.

146  GCPPT 1|1|9 15 November 1902.
GCPPT 1|1|10 23 February 1903.
GCPPT 1|1|11 27 and 29 April and 18 July 1904.
GCPPT 1|1|12 29 May 1905.
Geoffrey Hatten, though an organ scholar, later became a solicitor.

147  GCPPT 2|2a Vol. 2 undated but by context early 1904. *Tails with a Twist. The Flapper.*

148  GCPPT 1|1|9 30 November 1901.

149  GCPPT 2|2a Vol. 2. Undated but by context early 1904. *Tails with a Twist. The Flapper.*

150  GCPPT 1|1|11 2 May 1904.

151  GCPPT 1|1|9 15 July 1902.

152  GCPPT 1|1|9 4 November 1902.
GCPPT 1|1|10 16 August 1903.

153  GCPPT 1|1|10 22 December 1902. Aelfrida's epithet may be taken from *Brahma*, a poem by Ralph Waldo Emerson: "… if the slain think he is slain / They know not well the subtle ways / I keep, and pass, and turn again". In a later novel a young woman with many male admirers terms them "The Smitten". (*Just Alice* p 126).

154  GCPPT 1|1|9 30 March 1902.

155  GCPPT 1|1|8 11 November 1901.
GCPPT 1|1|9 7 January 1902.

156  GCPPT 1|1|10 4 December 1902.

157  GCPPT 1|1|13 13 August 1906.

158  GCPPT 1|1|8 30 and 31 October and 3 November 1901 (Aelfrida's 1904 comment is appended to the latter date).
GCPPT 1|1|11 8 August 1904.
GCPPT 1|1|15 20 January 1908. Garden Blaikie, missionary to the English Presbyterian Church in China, died of appendicitis while on leave in England in May 1908 aged 31.

159  GCPPT 1|1|11 4 March, 31 July and 8 August 1904. Cuthbert James Blaikie (1884-1967) became a colonel in the Royal Army Medical Corps during the Great War and married a nurse. A breach of promise case could be brought by a jilted woman (or her family acting on her behalf) against a man who had reneged on a promise to marry her; Aelfrida, knowing better 'than to take the words of a freshman seriously' (GCPPT 1|1|11 8 August 1904), refrained from doing so.

160  GCPPT 2|2a Vol. 2 No 1. 15 January 1903. *Interview with Mrs Lewis and Mrs Gibson.*

161  GCPPT 1|1|5 28 May 1900.
GCPPT 1|1|8 21 October 1901.

162  GCPPT 1|1|5 28 May 1900.
GCPPT 1|1|8 14 October 1901.

163  GCPPT 1|1|9 4 December 1901.

164  GCPPT 1|1|8 23 October 1901.

165  GCPPT 1|1|9 1 December 1901.

166 GCPPT 1|1|8 14 November 1901.
167 GCPPT 1|1|9 3 March 1902.
    GCPPT 1|1|10 10 February 1903.
168 GCPPT 1|1|10 8 December 1902.
169 GCPPT 1|1|9 3 March 1902.
170 GCPPT 1|1|14 22 November 1906.
171 GCPPT 1|1|10 8 December 1902.
    GCPPT 1|1|14 22 November 1906.
    GCPPT 1|1|20 7 August 1914.
172 GCPPT 1|1|14 22 November 1906.
    GCPPT 2|2a Vol. 2. Unnumbered and undated copy but by context
    December 1903, article entitled *How I should like to spend Christmas*.
    For the career of 20th century Bishop James Lumsden Barkway
    (1878-1968) see *Who Was Who* Vol. VI.
173 GCPPT 1|1|9 4 December 1901.
174 GCPPT 1|1|9 10 May 1902. The Waldensian Church, a dissent-
    ing and eventually excluded branch of Roman Catholicism, was
    founded c1770. Persecuted throughout Europe as heretical, it even-
    tually established itself as a reformist evangelical Protestant sect in the
    Piedmont region of Italy. Its insistence on high moral standards and
    its upholding of scriptural as opposed to sacerdotal authority would
    have appealed to the staunchly Presbyterian ladies of Castlebrae. For
    further details, see Frasetto, M. ch4 pp 56–76.
175 GCPPT 1|1|9 12, 13, and 15 May and 6 June 1902.
176 GCPPT 1|1|11 27 April 1904.
177 GCPPT 1|1|22 24 February 1918.
178 GCPPT 1|1|34 18 May 1927.
179 GCPPT 1|1|40 29 July 1931.
180 GCPPT 1|1|9 19 August 1902.
181 For the life and academic pedigree of John Venn (1834–1923) see
    Annan, N. pp 332–338 and the *ODNB* Vol. 56 pp 259-260.
182 GCPPT 1|1|9 1 September 1902.
183 GCPPT 1|1|10 1 December 1903.
184 GCPPT 1|1|10 8 January 1903.
    GCPPT 1|1|17 3 June 1910.
185 GCPPT 1|1|9 9 September 1902.
186 GCPPT 1|1|12 26 October 1904.
187 GCPPT 1|1|10 8 January 1903.
188 GCPPT 1|1|41 14 March 1932.
189 GCPPT 1|1|17 3 June 1910.
    GCPPT 1|1|74 20 March 1958.
190 GCPPT 1|1|10 13 November 1903.
191 ibid. 21 January 1903.
192 GCPPT 1|1|11 13 March 1904.
193 GCPPT 2|25|2 (4).
194 GCPPT 1|1|8 26 June and 17 July 1901.
195 GCPPT 1|1|9 7 February 1902.
196 Ibid. 30 January 1902.
197 GCPPT 2|25|2 *Mrs Lewis and Mrs Gibson.*
198 GCPPT 1|1|15 20 December 1907.
199 ibid.
200 GCPPT 1|1|9 7 February 1902.
201 GCPPT 1|1|11 20 January 1904.
202 GCPPT 1|1|9 4 February 1902.
203 ibid. 21 July 1902.
204 Tillyard, Ae. *Marrying a Stranger* p 13.
205 GCPPT 1|1|9 30 January 1902.
206 GCPPT 1|1|32 7 March 1926.
207 GCPPT 1|1|8 30 October 1901.
208 GCPPT 1|1|11 20 September 1904.
209 GCPPT 1|1|30 19 January 1925.
210 GCPPT 1|1|9 30 June 1902.
211 Tillyard, HJW. Introduction to *The Letters of ACW Tillyard* (MTC).
212 Tillyard, Ae. *Marrying a Stranger* p 125.
213 GCPPT 1|1|11 19 April 1904.
214 GCPPT 1|1|9 4 December 1901.
215 GCPPT 1|1|11 19 April 1904.
216 GCPPT 1|1|9 20 November 1902.
217 ibid.
218 GCPPT 1|1|9 29 July 1904.
219 GCPPT 1|1|8 26 November 1901.
220 GCPPT 1|1|9 12 August 1902.
221 GCPPT 1|1|30 15 February 1925.
222 GCPPT 1|1|10 22 December 1902.
223 GCPPT 1|1|9 7 February 1902.
224 ibid. 21 July 1902.
225 GCPPT 1|1|15 20 December 1907.
226 GCPPT 1|1|11 27 July 1904.
227 ibid. 31 July 1904.
228 GCPPT 1|1|18 17 September 1912.
229 GCPPT 1|1|28 3 March 1924.
230 GCPPT 1|1|72 7 July 1954.
231 Tillyard, Ae. *Marrying a Stranger* p 125.
232 GCPPT 1|1|72 7 July 1954.
233 GCPPT 1|1|9 30 January 1902.
234 GCPPT 2|2a Vol. 2. Undated, probably early 1904. *Tails with a Twist.
    The Flapper.*
235 GCPPT 1|1|8 25 November 1901.
236 GCPPT 1|1|1 1 May 1904.
237 Tillyard, Ae. *Marrying a Stranger* p 170.
238 It should be noted in Aelfrida's defence that working-class 'townee'
    girls regarded paid sexual intercourse with undergraduates as an
    excellent source of income, such personable, clean, polite, and pecu-
    nious young men being infinitely preferable to the Barnwell 'oafs'
    with whom magistrate Alfred Tillyard once memorably compared
    them. The unfortunate corollary of this was that some undergraduates
    regarded 'townee' girls in general as 'fair game' and it may have been
    in order to keep their adolescent daughters out of harm's way that
    Henry Joseph Wetenhall and (with more reason, given his city centre
    house and shop) George Barrett sent their adolescent daughters to
    boarding school.
239 GCPPT 1|1|10 16 August 1903.
240 Tillyard, Ae. *Marrying a Stranger* p 170.

# Vadius and Little Friend

In June 1913 Aelfrida found an old family 'confession album'. Entries made in 1902 made revealing reading, Catharine Tillyard's being 'pure and aspiring and unhumorous', Alfred Tillyard's 'grave, with a little clumsy humour'. In the section embracing 'current state of mind', Julius's was one of 'general uncertainty', Eustace's 'placid contentment', Aelfrida's 'enquiring'. The latter's fuller confession, however, sums her up exactly: her 'chief characteristic' was 'real – and sometimes apparent – cleverness', her 'idea of happiness', 'enjoying conscious superiority', and her greatest tolerance for '[her] own faults'. Apropos men, what she 'admired most' was their 'power of admiring the fair sex (if not myself)' and in answer to the question what she would most like to be, replied succinctly: 'my own husband'. ('I haven't changed much have I!!')[1] And it is to the question of Aelfrida's 'own husband' we now turn.

1902 was an eventful year for the Tillyards in several ways. In June, Julius ('Hurrah! Hurrah!! Hurrah!!!')[2] gained a first class pass in part one of the Classics tripos. In August, Alfred Tillyard 'chucked his town council work'.[3] We are not told why or if his decision was a sudden one: two years had passed since his public shaming following the relief of Mafeking, his arraignment before his fellow magistrates was a year in the future, and his being 'made an Alderman of the county'[4] suggests that he was highly regarded, but his fiftieth birthday and election as President of the Cambridge Free Church Federation may have persuaded him to reduce his workload in one area in order to devote more time to his work in others. And Eustace, normally 'a huge strong lad'[5], caught diphtheria while staying with relatives in Farnham and was admitted to an isolation hospital.

He did not die. His age (thirteen) and stamina and administration of antitoxin to "destroy diphtheritic [disease]"[6] ensured his recovery though he did not leave hospital for three weeks, was quarantined from his sister for eight, and returned to Cambridge, "a little thin" but no longer an invalid[7], following a period of convalescence at Worthing accompanied by his relieved parents (Catharine Tillyard had been distraught) and his curiously unemotional sister who even in the acute phase of his illness records a 'boisterous' river picnic[8], her first meeting with Archie Venn, cycle rides with her father

```
/ - I -

          PARTIES .  I.  TRINITY .

        The rain is pouring down pitilessly as we drive up to the
great gate.  It seems to gurgle and splash and ripple on all
sides - above heads, under feet, between us and the distant
door of the Master's Lodge, filling the court with falling
drops and gold-gleaming puddles.  The chapel is a dark wall
but light shines dimly from many windows, and blazes from the
wide open Lodge door.
        A courteous porter approaches us.  Would we like to
wait for The Chair ?  Far away across the court a tiny vehicle
drawn by two men advances towards us.  Two ladies, however, are
already waiting for it, so we retreat into the porter's lodge
and warm the tips of our satin slippers by his fire, until The
Chair has dropped its freight and come back through the streaming
rain for us.  We get in.  The Chair is rather like Cinderella's
Coach, upholstered in flowery calendared chintz, and making us
feel that we ought to be wearing wigs and panniers, if we
cannot manage glass shoes.
        The hall is crowded.  Don's wives may look dowdy by
day but not at an evening party in Trinity Lodge.  The Master,
Dr. Butler, and his wife( his second wife by the way ) are
standing near the head of the stairs.  No one could look more
dignified than the old Master with his full white beard and
benevolent expression.  He wears court dress, complete with
silver buckles on his shoes, and he towers above his wife who is
small, wiry and rather nervous-looking.  She is the famous
Agneta Ramsay, whose distinction in the Classical Tripos
inspired Punch's famous cartoon in which Mr. Punch is seen
opening the door of a first class railway carriage, marked on
the window LADIES ONLY .
```

**Parties at Trinity**

(her mother was at Eustace's bedside), and that when finally allowed to meet her younger brother, supposed he *had* been ill but that she found it hard to believe given "the picture of health"[9] he now was.

True, she had singlehandedly prepared an *MCJ* to cheer the 'Lieutenant Mandeville' who had "succumbed to Diphtheria, a disease nasty to spell and still nastier to have"[10] but her chief worry at this worrying time was Julius who, "in Germany grappling with the barbarous language of the country and amazing the natives by the ability with which he wields a ... racquet"[11], wrote to inform his sister (he said nothing to his parents) that he was 'afraid' he was falling in love with his sixteen-year-old tennis partner, 'a *mädle (sic)* called Minnchen'.[12] Her heart sinking on several scores on her own account and on her brother's and with Julius abroad and herself in Worthing,

Aelfrida could do no more than beg him not to act rashly – and to hint that she too, though still "in love" with Lord Kitchener, had met "several men with whom [she] would be perfectly prepared to spend her whole life".[13] And that one of those 'several men' was showing every intention of passing *his* 'whole life' with *her*.

Alfred and Catharine Tillyard's ambivalent feelings regarding their only daughter, already evident in encouraging her to engage with members of society less well-off spiritually, educationally, or materially than herself while describing as her 'greatest fault' her attempts 'to be "Little Providence" to people'[14], are particularly evident in the period following her return from Switzerland and in connection with a possible marriage. True, they had suffered something of a shock concerning her sudden decision to become engaged to "a kind of a Jack–in–the–box, leaping … out of a horrid box made in Germany"[15] but their tendency to '[rake] it all up again!'[16] when she received letters from Hans Peter seems at odds with their earlier disapproval. (Perhaps the prospect of a Swiss-German engineer as a son-in-law seemed less terrible as Hans Peter's fame and prosperity increased.) Then again, given that Archie Venn was the only child of eminent 'gown' and wealthy parents living in a fine house on one of Cambridge's most fashionable roads, it seems odd that they advised Aelfrida not to accept him as a suitor (perhaps reports of Susanna Venn's mental instability put them off) but urged that he '*must not* be refused'[17] while simultaneously forbidding her to throw herself away on a young don of impeccable academic and Presbyterian pedigree simply because the man in question was not rich though his prospects were good. Then too, and forgetting that they themselves had not married till both were nearly thirty, their expressed concern on their daughter's twentieth birthday that she was 'so old'[18] and still unmarried seems at odds with a declaration made shortly before her twenty-first that they "[did] not want to get rid of [their] little girl"[19] and, given their insistence that Aelfrida undertake occupations aimed at strengthening and stretching her mind, their reaction to her announcement one evening that she proposed 'to give up flirting and begin a life of consistent seriousness' (she announced her intention in her 'most flippant tone' but her intent was earnest) was odd indeed: Catharine 'proposed to retire to a lunatic asylum', Alfred 'looked many things', and both implored her 'to go on being lively and to flirt' and to "lead a butterfly existence".[20]

The timing of the conversation and the adult Tillyards' startled – and startling – reaction was not fortuitous: ten days earlier Aelfrida's plans to spend two months in Italy with the family of a Cambridge governess from whom she had been receiving instruction in colloquial Italian

were annulled by their statement that they '[could] not stand the extra worry of [her] being away'. But why 'worry'? And why (other than the possibility that she might engage herself to another unsuitable young man; they appear to have had no reservations concerning the governess) should their daughter's absence occasion them 'extra worry'? And what, other than his impending court case, occasioned Alfred Tillyard such a 'great deal'[21] of worry that he refused his consent?

From hints in Aelfrida's diary we may infer that both Tillyards were worried about her, that their worries were not unfounded, and that worries regarding her apparent disinclination to do more than flirt with potential suitors were in fact the least of their worries.

What worries, then, did they have apart from the obvious one that something had happened during their daughter's adolescence to change her from the seemingly normal girl she had become on leaving the Perse (normal, that is apart from her too-close relationship with her elder brother) into a young woman who admitted she was "a child who had failed to grow up", whose actions were both "ill-directed and uncertain in their effects" and, "something rather queer", an "eccentric being … useless to anyone but [her]self"?[22]

Eccentricity manifested itself in several ways. In the contrast between social graces ('the number of people I successfully introduced to each other is simply appalling', written jocularly of a Fordfield garden party)[23] and awareness of social position (of a reception at Trinity College, she wrote only half-jokingly of her snobbish delight in being marked with "with the mysterious mark of being 'In it'"!)[24] in one gratified by being asked to act appropriately by the minister of St Columba's (on hearing of the importance of social intercourse between members of the congregation, Aelfrida 'chuckled at being told to make [my] delight my duty')[25] but whose 'unfortunate conscience'[26] prevented her from attending the theatre and whose need for "solitude" made her "stand [so] aloof"[27] that she asked to move from the first floor bedroom to which as sole daughter of the house she was entitled to a former nursery on the attic storey, a room over which she expressed herself 'wild with delight' because of its isolated position.[28] In the contrast between her former robust health and a kind of creeping invalidism in which childhood headaches recurred and minor infections were less easily thrown off. In the contrast between an interest in 'clothes and personal adornment' natural in a young woman compensating for lack of conventional beauty by wearing the latest fashions and an asceticism manifest in fasting 'more or less' in Lent (less rather than more: she continued to eat chocolates), in keenness to see if she could accomplish more 'out of curiosity'[29], and in her 'getting thin', a problem she attributed to having behaved 'like a perfect idiot' over a man she 'was not one least little bit in love with!'[30] but actually of at least a year's standing, as demonstrated by a suggestion made in May 1903 by a young doctor met – and flirted with – in March 1902 that she "ought to be made to eat more".[31] In the contrast between behaviour which was almost manic in its gaiety ('flying', her mother called it as she tried to bring her daughter 'down')[32] with 'Flirting' used – or abused – like a drug ('flirtations are like chocolate creams, you like them and you want more and you have more …') but revolting her when indulged in to excess ('…and then they make your tongue sore and you wish you hadn't')[33] and worries which came 'flood[ing]' in on [her] again'[34] the moment she desisted. For gloomy ruminations on the pointlessness of existence, however, there seemed a remedy: 'religious emotions'[35], but the contrast between quiet acceptance of the consolations of religion and religious emotions running so high that they could no longer be confined to private life was something her parents found hard to dismiss as a phase gone through by many adolescents.

From hints thrown out during both visits to Lausanne, it appears that Aelfrida, freed from the confines of Cambridge Presbyterianism, was developing an interest in forms of religion which laid emphasis on *personal* religious experience, on *individual experience* independent of formal worship, and on emotive expressions of or reveries upon particular aspects of New Testament history and interpretation. On neither visit does she enlarge on her subject but her mentioning during her second visit that she had discussed aspects of one of these forms with Marie Feyler, a doctor of whom she was keen that the latter knew 'all' of her, suggests that her new interest was suspected by her parents and that they, already concerned by their daughter's increasing religiosity, had become more concerned still in 1902, the year in which Aelfrida's sense of social and religious propriety seemed to have deserted her. (Her flirtations with married Messrs Ibberson and Smythe and her interest in Waldensian Paolo Coïsson took place during that time and all were known or made known to Catharine and Alfred Tillyard.) Indeed, though Aelfrida continued to pay lip service to Presbyterianism, she appeared to be framing a creed for herself whose esotericism (its adoption of a set of beliefs garnered from mediaeval theologians, 19th century Tractarians, and eastern mystics), subjectivity (material studied was assimilated without reference to wider interpretation or discussion and its devotional forms could only be deduced from their public manifestations), secrecy (she discussed it with no-one but Julius and he does not seem to have divulged

their conversations to his parents), and tendency to cause withdrawal into ideological and even physical isolation, would be likely to deter potential husbands unless of a particularly understanding nature: few men would have patience with a wife who called Christmas merriment 'a sad affair' and who preferred to 'meditate piously'[36] for the duration of the festivities.

And how to deal with a daughter whose religiosity was evident even in her holiday reading: "my selection of holiday books always includes Thomas à Kempis [and] Omar Khayyám"[37]? Though 'holiday books' also included Walter Scott and Jane Austen, *Quo Vadis* ('an improving book')[38], *Undine,* the story of a water nymph without a soul but gaining one – and with it the innate pain of human existence – by marrying a human and bearing him a child[39], and *Robert Elsmere,* with its description of the havoc wreaked on his family by a young clergyman forced to resign his living because he no longer believes what he is expected to preach[40], could hardly be described as light reading. ("My taste", Aelfrida admitted, "may be peculiar"[41], and a seemingly innocuous book, Robert Buchanan's *Idylls and Legends of Inverburn,* resonated with untold secrets.)[42] Books pressed on others gain significance too: Thomas à Kempis' *Imitation of Christ* on Silvia Myers (whose mother may have told Catharine Tillyard) and on Hans Peter ('a nice cool present' which might encourage him to 'declare for celibacy' thereby freeing her 'to angle for someone else')[43], and Marie Bashkirtseff's journal, or, rather, 'the name of the book [she] wrote about herself and other people'[44], on Dumville Smythe.

Public declarations of her new creed though presents of this nature undoubtedly were (and, possibly, cries for help which, because so obliquely uttered, fell on deaf ears; Marie Bashkirtseff's glorying in being 'passionate' about aspects of her spiritual life, her imaginary 'duke' – her parentage was known but she pretended her father was a Russian aristocrat – and the fact that she both 'puzzled [and] frightened'[45] herself being perhaps intended by Aelfrida as warnings to those who saw her reading the dead girl's diaries that perhaps all was not well with her own mind and that, given her recent inability to shake off chest infections, she too might die young of tuberculosis), an outburst inspired by reading John Wesley's journal which caused her to declare at Sunday prayers "what a farce it seems to sing such words!" on realising the contrast between her own life and "the life of toil, the mean abode" propounded in the hymn[46], and a tendency at parties to replace 'Flirting' with theological discussions, were liable to be construed as unfortunate traits by the parents of one supposedly looking for a husband. They were also reasons for them both wanting and not wanting Aelfrida to marry: though a husband and children might divert her mind from present preoccupations, marriage might expose her 'peculiar' state of mind to others besides her immediate family. And from indirect but reliable evidence provided by a writer friend in whom Aelfrida later confided, we may deduce that Alfred and Catharine Tillyard consulted the family doctor and that he advised marriage as a cure for the 'nervous troubles'[47] from which their daughter manifestly suffered.

On 24 February 1902 a young Caius don attended one of Catharine Tillyard's At Homes. He and Aelfrida 'discovered a common enthusiasm for the bagpipes and George Eliot' (neither recorded as enthusiasms heretofore) and arranged to meet again 'to teach each other things' (*sic*). Catharine Tillyard thought him 'something of a *parti*'[48] and promptly issued further invitations.

John Forbes Cameron[49] was indeed a possible match: he was twenty-eight, had come to Cambridge in 1895 after graduating with first class honours from Edinburgh University', and was now a fellow of Caius and Lecturer in Mathematics. He was, moreover, of impeccable Presbyterian lineage and the son of a Perthshire schoolmaster of whose six other children some were at university and one studying for the Bar, all, as Aelfrida noted ironically, 'fairly respectable' occupations.[50] Two things, however, told against him; though rather handsome with periwinkle blue eyes and well-shaped hands, John Forbes' hair was of the 'strangest red-gold colour'[51] (and Aelfrida, of course, could never marry a man with red hair) and, 'lament[ing] his poverty' (poverty she thought 'comparative rather than actual'), he was reluctant to marry while four fifths of his salary went to support his family[52], this moving Catharine Tillyard to exclaim "Frida … you are *not* to throw yourself away on Mr Cameron!"[53] Her mother's warning notwithstanding, Aelfrida expressed herself pleased with a man of her preferred age who was neither a 'fresher' nor a 'townee', wrote to Hans Peter suggesting they part as '*quondam bons amis*'[54], and set out to enchant her new 'slain' by taking him off (to James Barkway's dismay) to the kitchen garden where John Forbes, asking if she did not prefer himself to mere undergraduates and declaring himself an ardent admirer, joined the ranks of her unfortunate victims after a two month acquaintance; indeed, by mid May 1902 his devotion was so publicly apparent that Paolo Coïsson enquired if Cameron was Aelfrida's 'brother or … husband!!!'[55] He also begged the pleasure of taking her to his college's May Ball.

The Caius May Ball took place, as Cambridge 'May' Balls traditionally do, in June and to it Aelfrida, chaperoned by her mother and accompanied by Lucy Longstaffe, duly went, wearing her white dress and looking 'quite [her] best'. Describing the ball at length and

her tête-à-têtes with John Forbes Cameron apparently verbatim ("by Jove, Miss Tillyard, you do look handsome"; they 'sat out' sixteen dances altogether though both danced 'duty dances' with others), Aelfrida also noted (gleefully) that Cameron had 'behaved in the *most* scandalous way' towards herself. Indeed he had, placing his arm round her waist, holding her 'very tight' as they posed for the traditional survivors' photograph at 6am, and even attempting to kiss her – but so had she, confounding a college servant's description of her as 'a good young lady' by going unchaperoned (her mother, by accident or design, was at supper) to Cameron's rooms.

This compromising bit of behaviour which neither should have undertaken could not have been undertaken secretly – Caius is a small college, Tree Court where they had 'sat out' so many dances was that through which guests entered and left and Caius Court, onto which John Forbes' rooms opened, led to the hall where dancing took place – and Aelfrida, usually so particular about being chaperoned, could hardly have been unaware of the risk to her reputation (and to Cameron's as a don and as an older man who should have known better) in going alone to or possibly being found in 'bachelor chambers'. Perhaps she did not care, perhaps it was all a 'game', perhaps she wished to trap John Forbes into marriage; she does not say, though she intimates that nothing unseemly took place. But if even college servants knew she was 'Mr Tillyard's … sister'[56], how many other people present also knew and could have reported her behaviour to Julius (present at the ball) or to her parents?

Perhaps they did. Cameron, it seems, was so embarrassed by what had taken place ('*il se repent déjà*', was Aelfrida's scornful comment) that he 'turned crimson to the roots of his hair'[57] at their next meeting. Ancifera Gregory, holidaying at Fordfield in July, was told by Catharine Tillyard 'with a queer smile' that the man on whom she had advised her daughter not to throw herself away had suddenly become '*very* … eligible'. ('I see', noted her daughter, that 'she would [now] *love* me to marry a fellow of a college'; Catharine subsequently urged her to 'court' John Forbes, ostensibly because he himself, though in love, was too shy to say so[58] but possibly because a serious and suitable suitor having presented himself, it would not do to turn him down.) Mutual friends began to hint archly that a husband by the name of John could be known familiarly as 'Jock' if he were Scots, a remark to which Aelfrida replied in John Forbes Cameron's hearing that she would never marry a man called John because she disliked the name.[59]

She had good reason to do so. First, as she informed Julius, Cameron, fond of her as he was, was not her favourite suitor though she would "probably" accept him if her parents wished it; second, she was certain that he did "*not* mean to propose" and that as matters stood it seemed "a little ludicrous" to say she would accept Cameron he ventured to "name the day".[60] But why, given his obvious enthusiasm for herself and his anxiously asking for an assurance that "there was no man in the Varsity"[61] for whom Aelfrida already cared, was John Forbes already repenting his behaviour at the Caius ball and unlikely to propose? The truth was that Aelfrida had – and knew she had – a 'rival!!!'[62] in the form of a 'pretty and amiable … and altogether rather girlish and sweet'[63] young woman of Cameron's own age, regarding whom Aelfrida was later able to 'forgive … everything'[64] *except* her name: Elfrida.

Aelfrida had known before the Caius ball that John Forbes Cameron was being 'angled for' by Jane Sturge, a 'plump Quakeress with two eligible daughters', as a husband for her younger daughter (her elder daughter's engagement was announced shortly after the ball, Aelfrida predicting that 'Mrs "Campaigner" Sturge' only needed to hook John Forbes in order to 'die happy')[65] and it may be that her risqué behaviour at the ball was a deliberate attempt to replace Elfrida with herself. (It is hard to ascertain the truth because throughout her relationship with Cameron, Aelfrida consistently casts herself as an innocent victim.) Already disadvantaged because Miss Sturge was 'pretty and amiable' and rich[66], Aelfrida was soon to hear rumours of John Forbes and Elfrida's impending engagement, but on taxing the former directly ("answer me one thing … are you engaged?") and receiving a negative reply, decided to persevere with whatever campaign she was pursuing ('I still prefer Dick … my dog … to John Forbes Cameron')[67] and to pursue 'stupid John Forbes Cameron'[68] whom she knew was in love with her but would never propose.

She did not, of course, want him to, but that was not the point. Her pride was hurt and to punish him (and perhaps to provoke him into proposing) she behaved badly: John Forbes was the man she teased by parading compliment-paying undergraduates past him as he played tennis, towards whom she displayed 'haughty' behaviour (behaviour justified under the circumstances, one might think, but censured by her father as likely to rob her of Cameron or any 'lovers')[69] when he gazed at her in a 'puzzled, adoring, pleading, *doggy*'[70] manner, and to whom she hinted 'with a provoking blush' that there *was* another man in her life (Hans Peter, shortly to be designated her 'ex-fiancé') that she would like John Forbes 'to look for Enrico'[71] while holidaying in Switzerland. (But what, she wrote in November 1902, 'do I care about … Cameron and Enrico …? They are nothing to me – compared to my one hero … Lord

Kitchener'.)[72] But rumours of 'the engagement with Miss Sturge'[73] pursued her. Passing along Silver Street in December 1902, Aelfrida spotted Cameron approaching the house belonging to George and Maud Darwin with whom Mrs Sturge was currently staying; suspecting that 'the engagement between him and Miss Frida [was] at last a fait accompli', she pretended not to see him and walked away feeling unutterably lonely and as if the only thing to do was to 'withdraw [her] remit from all earthly affections'.[74]

But Aelfrida being Aelfrida and unable to cease tormenting a 'victim' and John Forbes being yet another man over whom she had, he said. "so much influence that he [had] no will left" (she replied that she always consulted her victims' 'convenience')[75], the Silver Street incident was by no means the last of Cameron.[76] A January 1903 letter from Aelfrida asking why Cameron was "so cross?" elicited the response that there were "some things" he could not possibly explain and that when they next met, it would be best "if they were not referred to". (His writing, Aelfrida noted, was 'agitated'.)[77] But a belated coming-out dance at Fordfield on 20 February at which she danced seven dances with Cameron (most men got one, some were 'cut') and during which he took her out on the terrace and declared (among other things, reported verbatim) that she was "the only woman in the world" for him[78], set tongues wagging, 'all Caius' being so sure that Cameron was about to propose that they asked if congratulations were in order and the Master 'so much interested' that he hinted at financial help to enable his young don to marry.[79]

All seemed to be going well: John Forbes continued to treat Aelfrida gently (unlike Enrico, he did not press physical attentions on her or attempt to kiss her again), to ask questions implying thoughts of married life together ("should you want me to give up smoking too?")[80], and to say 'very tender and lovely things'[81] to her in private, and Aelfrida, though she chided herself for not having withdrawn her heart from 'earthly affections' and for acting like a 'beastly little flirt'[82], found herself behaving towards Cameron in an unexpectedly tender fashion. ('Our hands touched', she reports as she gives him violets from the garden.)[83] She even, though she denied it ('don't mistake, my friends. I don't love him. I have never… and shall never love but one man – Lord Kitchener')[84], admitted to falling if not in love, at least in '*liking*' with a man whom she now wished she liked 'a little more or a little less'.[85]

Discovering that Cameron's 'non-proposals' were upsetting her health and that she was 'behaving like a perfect idiot, losing my sleep and getting thin over a man I am not one least bit in love with … I don't know

**Aelfrida Tillyard (centre) as 'Bélise'**

of opium large enough to render her somnolent but small enough to enable her to complete the current and sixty-five further volumes of her diary.

Cameron's reply was chastening. She refused to copy it into her diary but it seems that he accused her of behaving badly towards him – which was true – and of being still in love with Hans Peter – which, as Aelfrida had earlier assured him, was untrue though she continued to fear Hans' 'influence'[91], an odd word whose import she failed to explain – and that she herself realised too late that in John Forbes Cameron she had had a 'great gift bestowed on [her] and had wantonly cast it aside'.[92] Worse followed, for John Forbes and Aelfrida continued to meet, he to woo and she to declare that though not offended by his letter, she now chose not to respond to or even to believe his passionate words. Close to breaking point ('I do not think I can stand … all this … much longer'[93], wrote the young woman who regularly subjected her own 'victims' to the same treatment), she decided to force Cameron's hand by arranging a formal talk during which she would 'ask him gently and kindly the why and wherefore of it all', not as a flirt but as the friend she would like (and prefer) to be 'if only one could'.[94]

The momentous meeting between Aelfrida and the man dwindling by default into a 'little friend'[95] took place on 14 December 1903. Her account of the confrontation occupies several pages of her diary and forms one of the marvellous set pieces which must have been written with an eye to future 'copy'. Not all do; this one does, but in a less staged (and stagey) form which may (or may not) correspond more truthfully to what actually took place than the version transcribed: 'To send for a man you don't care for, to propose to him, to get refused and to feel distinctly pleased with oneself hardly sounds sane but that is what I did yesterday and [today] I am sane as ever I was. I don't know why I did it, whether it was from curiosity or a literary sense or what but I did it and did it well. It was a consummate piece of acting … [because] I had arranged it all beforehand, my words, my tone, my pose, everything … it was most artistically done … I sent for John Forbes Cameron [and] this is more or less what happened …'[96] What happened in synopsis and in the novel was as follows:

> Marjorie: "Are you going to ask me to marry you?"
> Victor:   "Since you ask me, no. I did not intend to".
> Marjorie: "Why not?"[97]

What 'more or less' happened at Fordfield – Aelfrida, so she said, 'said a good deal … which I cannot here repeat'[98]; possibly it included the immortal lines:

what is the matter with me [and wish] I had never been born'[86], Aelfrida was further dismayed when she sampled the latest grist to the Cambridge rumour-mill, namely that she and Cameron 'were *not* going to make a match of it'. (Susanna Venn, hearing the news, began to 'aunt' vigorously for Archie again; Julius, who perhaps knew more than his sister of John Forbes' affairs of the heart and who had more than once adopted the attitude of 'the Dragon guarding the Princess' in the course of Cameron's visits to Fordfield[87], called him a 'rotter'.)[88] The summer vacation intervened; Cameron departed "to get cured of his love sickness" and Aelfrida, hearing from a visitor that there was 'an appalling amount of insanity among dons' and deciding that it was Cameron's own 'touch' of madness which accounted for his 'intense melancholy' and his reluctance to marry her, wrote to ask him to inform her 'frankly and candidly' if she should resign herself to '*la vie sans Cameron*'[89] and took 'by mistake'[90] an overdose

Marjorie:   "Unhappiness … takes you over and bends you across its knee and … snap! you are broken for ever".

Victor:   "You ought not to allow yourself to be so morbid"[99] –

was that Aelfrida seized the opportunity to relieve long pent-up feelings by saying to Cameron 'all … the things that I long to say to Lord Kitchener and never shall'. Catharsis, however, was temporarily overridden by terror when, on finishing her confession, she 'feared for one moment that Cameron would tell me he was prepared to overcome the obstacle that divides us and have me at any price. And I did not want to become engaged to Cameron'. But though 'relief mingled with pique' when she discovered what the 'obstacle' was, she was safe: the 'obstacle' (surprise, surprise) 'was Elfrida Sturge', to whom John Forbes had proposed long before he knew Aelfrida Tillyard. Elfrida Sturge, however, had been so long making up her mind that John Forbes issued an ultimatum: "this is [your] last chance … I shall not ask you again". Eternally grateful that she 'could see that deep down in his … staunch Scottish heart, he meant to be true to the other girl', Aelfrida seized the opportunity ('I was *very* noble!') to press her rival's claim and to free herself from Cameron's matrimonial clutches.[100]

Explanations followed. Cameron, realising that he had 'been just a little mean'[101], pleaded that 'madness [came] upon him' with regard to Aelfrida, and Aelfrida played the martyr ('poor, wounded, bruised little me!') and let her voice 'quiver pathetically' as she spoke of being unable to bear her 'pain' any longer and being forced into speaking ('oh, it was artistic!') before they parted very good friends[102] who would undoubtedly meet again in parallel rather than converging universes.

They did, she bowing coldly but with 'a wicked little joy in [her] heart'[103] while maintaining a pose of 'dignified sorrow'[104] when they met, which was seldom. (And flirting madly with other gentlemen friends in the meantime, for though she pretended that Cameron's presence '[drove] away all [her] lovers!'[105], it was only James Barkway who actually 'thought it was no go'[106] – and went.) But it was not until 1 May that John Forbes, prodded by 'Learned Twin' Agnes Lewis, finally proposed to Elfrida Sturge and not until 16 May 1904 that Aelfrida Tillyard, receiving the news, wrote scornfully 'I hope Little Friend will be happier than such a meek-minded man deserves to be'.[107]

Her thoughts a 'strange tangle'[108] of men she loved or had professed to love or had pretended to love, Aelfrida worried on two scores: first, why she had proposed to John Forbes 'whom [she] did not in the least care for'[109] (she may have guessed why for no interrogation point follows her question; she blamed it on being over-endowed with Bergsonian *élan vital*), second, though endowed with life-force sufficient to make men 'lose their senses' in her presence, that she was 'incapable of inspiring … deep lasting affection' and ought to 'give up [her] admirers on the chance of getting one solemn, old-fashioned husband'.[110] Leaving her questions unanswered except by 'h'm', she made two resolutions, the first, 'to be as good as I can'[111], after which she drew a line beneath that particular entry, the second (the first entry in a new volume), to 'be fairly brief in my entries for a while … after the amazing indiscretions of the last volume'.[112] She broke both, the second within two pages, the first, and more important, within five weeks. On 22 January 1904 she met 'Mr Michaelides of King's'[113]; on 13 February she 'flirted gloriously with Mr Michaelides'[114]; on 22 February 'Mr Michaelides called at the earliest possible opportunity'[115]; on 16 May, John Forbes Cameron announced his engagement; on 31 May Aelfrida informed her diary 'I am engaged to Mr Michaelides'[116]; on 3 June she attended a Castlebrae garden party: 'Cameron was there with Frida Sturge', she 'radiant', he casting 'long keen looks' on herself ('he *did* love me. I met him the other day – and he still looks at me in the same way. ACWT 1919'), whereupon she turned her back on him and 'flirted outrageously with Baby Blaikie'.[117]

Revenge or rebound or yet another manifestation of Aelfrida's need to attach herself to one man after another? All are possible. She had, after all, been jilted by, as Julius put it (Julius, to whom Aelfrida wrote in August 1902 that she would do "*nothing*" with regard to John Forbes Cameron, not even obey her father's injunction to "kindly encourage him a little" without her elder brother's "signed sanction"[118]; we do not know if she received it), "a young don …who pursued [her] with obvious admiration but who was half-engaged to another girl"[119], a hurtful thing to happen to any woman (and in Aelfrida's case to a young woman who had now had *two* potential husbands 'break with' her at a point when marriage seemed possible if not probable)[120] but particularly to one whose ability to form healthy relationships with men had been damaged since childhood. But of two things we may be sure: 'quiet happiness' has eluded her again and, one 'victim' having escaped her clutches, she is about to add another to her collection of unfortunates.

Aelfrida's first meeting with 'Mr Michaelides of King's' took place during rehearsals for a Molière play, *Les Femmes Savantes,* to be put on as a fund-raising measure on behalf of the Perse School at which Eustace was now a pupil. She had been invited to take part by Lilly Frazer[121], wife of anthropologist James Frazer of Trinity College, friend of Alfred and Catharine Tillyard. By an earlier marriage to master mariner Charles Grove, Mrs Frazer had two children, one of whom (Granville) briefly found himself in Frida's 'class 2', the other (also Lilly, known to Aelfrida as the 'Minor Grove' to distinguish her from her mother) had introduced Aelfrida to public lectures given by eminent academics, this inspiring her to add 18th century German philosophy to her current reading list. It was, however, the 'Minor Grove's' mother, nicknamed the 'Strawberry Eater'[122] by the Tillyards, who was instrumental in introducing Aelfrida to her future husband by asking her shortly after the latter's revelatory conversation with John Forbes Cameron if she would act Bélise in *Les Femmes Savantes*.

Unwell and despondent – she had been ill with 'bronchitis' since the day following John Forbes 'explanation' and in spite of declaring herself not at all 'melancholy' at the ending of her 'understanding' with him, was not looking forward to Christmas, 'a sad affair … when one's girlhood is past'[123] – Aelfrida jumped at the prospect: 'it was I who first suggested that we should produce that piece and I have always wanted to act "Bélise"'.[124] She also, a Tillyard acronym 'NMRCS' standing for "never mind, revenge comes soon"[125], decided to invite John Forbes Cameron to watch her perform and within days was word-perfect in her part.

The 'we' to whom Aelfrida referred was Mrs Frazer's Company of French Actors and that she was allowed to join says much for the perfection of her French (she was scornful of the 'Strawberry Eater's' fulsome praise: 'any girl … who had been taught by Zelle would have spoken French as well as I did') and for her acting ability (the 'Strawberry Eater' 'might flatter her way into professors' households but she chose her actors and actresses for merit alone')[126], particularly as Mrs Frazer was a native French speaker and another member of the company a former actor at the Comédie Française. *Les Femmes Savantes* was not, however, Aelfrida's first encounter with the Company; she had acted with them since her late teens following promotion from roles in the short French plays Mrs Frazer wrote for children ("in Frida", wrote Julius, "she found a talented actress [but] I had gone to boarding school and missed the fun"; Eustace was "roped in for minor parts"[127], one of which was about to be the notary in *Les Femmes Savantes* but his sister omitted him from her cast list) and staged in the 'big iron gymnasium at Miss Hughes' training college'[128] as demonstrations of the "new ideas" on the teaching of languages to children with which Cambridge had been "humming" since the introduction and enthusiastic endorsement of a new

form of "language-teaching"[129] by the training college's founder-principal Elizabeth Hughes[130] and by Dr Rouse, headmaster of the Perse School for Boys.[131]

Aelfrida herself had been "in the thick of the movement"[132] supporting the 'Direct Method' of teaching children modern languages. (And in the case of Dr Rouse, Latin and Greek also.) The 'Method', though not absolutely abandoning the learning of grammar and vocabulary, concentrated on teaching a language as it would be learnt by a native speaker through the medium of conversation, plays, and games, textbooks being used only as adjuncts to oral exercises. The 'Method', of course, had been practised, albeit informally, on all three Tillyard children already thanks to their parents' advanced educational views but Frida herself (under protest; she hated cooking and her French was already fluent) had also been subjected to cookery classes conducted in French by Miss Hughes' students in Mrs Frazer's own house as practical demonstrations of what could be achieved using it. It was, however, her visit to the Perse prior to the start of her own brief teaching career which inspired her to use a combination of Zelle's and Miss Hughes' methods on her own classes to great effect.

The six performances of *Les Femmes Savantes* were significant because they marked the apogee and end of Aelfrida's stage career ('I don't think I shall ever act [in] anything again. Not that I do it badly – I did it extremely well – but I honestly think … all the admiration … is not good for me')[133] and because she 'flirted gloriously with Mr Michaelides whenever [she] was not on stage'.[134] Mr Michaelides' reaction (he 'fell down and worshipped')[135] was balm to the soul of one already reassured that her ability to attract men had not deserted her by the other men in the cast informing her she was 'perfect' in her role (a back-handed compliment, as we shall see), by a sumptuous costume of 'rich cream satin with a panel of real French pink and gold rose pattern brocade and … a bertha of rare old lace belonging to my great-great-grandmother' which made her look 'far too handsome'[136], and by Julius describing her impersonation of the coquettish old maid as "fairly [bringing] the house down".[137]

Although it was unusual for Aelfrida to agree to or to suggest that she take the part of a minor character – in art, as in life, she preferred centre-stage – Mrs Frazer showed considerable astuteness in allotting her the role of Bélise and events preceding and which were to follow *Les Femmes Savantes* bear witness to appropriate casting. True, Mrs Frazer accused her of insufficiently accentuating her character's maturity, but other features of the role are apposite to the point of being uncannily accurate: Bélise is an eccentric spinster of a certain age so blinded by self-love that she believes a man has only to set eyes on her to become uncontrollably smitten. Her narcissistic illusions give rise to unintentionally comic attempts to live out the fictions ('*visions*' or '*chimères*') created as she throws herself at one man after another.[138] Unlike Bélise, however, Aelfrida does have real romantic passages with a variety of young and not so young men; indeed, one of these is about to happen and is brought about by the very play in which she plays such an appropriate part.

Even more appropriately, Bélise has pretensions to the kind of knowledge satirised by Molière as conducive less to learning than to domestic disquiet because acquisition of undomestic skills result in bluestockings like herself laying affected and pretentious claims to knowledge which is of no earthly use to a woman whose proper sphere is in the home; it is, he implies, only perversity which causes Bélise and other *femmes savantes* to acquire knowledge which has no functional purpose merely for the sake of acquiring it. To the question of the personal value of their activities must also be added questions of the masculine domestic tyranny which tries to prevent them, as dependent relatives, either from acquiring such dangerous skills in the first place or, if gained in spite of this, from using them inside or outside their proper role as wife, mother, and upholder of the domestic status quo.

In Bélise's case it is the books she *reads* and her desire to escape from the traditional female pursuits of church, cradle, and cookery into a world where learning is pursued for its own sake not as just one of several vagaries of behaviour ('*étranges de conduite*') which make her appear deranged (*folle*) in the eyes of Chrysale, the brother in whose house she lives. In Aelfrida's case, however, it will be the books she *writes* which offend because they reveal stormy or stressful relationships her family would rather remained undisclosed, or because they deal with a spiritual state whose disclosure will cause her experiences to appear as manifestations of a disordered mind and those to whom she turns for spiritual guidance as mystagogues at best and at worst, charlatans.

The part of Vadius, played by 'Mr Michaelides', was as aptly cast as that of Bélise. Vadius too is a farcical character whose role as an admirer of the learned ladies of Chrysale's household (he is introduced by another character as "*l'homme qui meurt du désire de vous voir*") is a minor one ('it is sad', wrote Aelfrida, 'that … charming … Mr Michaelides … comes to so few rehearsals')[139] but like that of Bélise herself, is pivotal to the *real* romantic interest, the wooing of Henriette by Clitandre. And both roles contribute to the comic atmosphere which acts as a foil to the potentially tragic outcome of the young lovers' wooing: Mr Michaelides' acting, wrote Julius, "now graceful and courtly but soon extravagantly comical [was] the outstanding feature of a memorable

performance".[140] Even more to the point, Vadius, a smug pedant, evokes the fashionable seventeenth century French interest in all things Greek; as the three bluestockings, Chrysale's wife, sister, and daughter, rhapsodise, he even speaks the language:

Philamente:  "*Du Grec, ô ciel! Il sait du Grec, ma soeur!*"
Bélise:  "*Ah! ma nièce, du Grec!*"
Armande:  "*Du Grec! Quel bonheur!*"
Philamente:  "*Quoi, monsieur sait du Grec? Ah, permettez, de grâce,*
  *Que pour l'amour du Grec, Monsieur, on vous embrasse*".[141]

Mr Michaelides did indeed 'know Greek' (he had other attributes too: he spoke fluent French and was neither red-haired nor hirsute), not because he was reading classics – his subject was history, though he had originally intended to read classics with a view to entering the Indian Civil Service – but because he was half Greek, his mother being "a widely travelled American and his father a Greek merchant and a fine scholar"[142] who, marrying in 1881, now had three children: Constantine Cleanthes, born 29 December 1882, so twenty one to Aelfrida's twenty; Helen, aged twenty, and Irene, thirteen.

Although Aelfrida's parents asked nervously "who are his people? … These things count for so much"[143] and Julius persistently believed there was some mystery about the Michaelides' marriage[144], the truth was not hard to discover.

Constantine's father was certainly a 'Greek merchant' – he occupied a position in the English branch of Ralli Bros, one of the great Greek banking and mercantile families –, his family hailing from Molinos on the island of Lesbos where relatives, including Constantine's grandmother, still lived. Lesbos was then under Ottoman rule but, like the Greek mainland and other Greek islands, remained fiercely proud of its Hellenic patrimony, and Molinos in particular was a source of inspiration for writers and poets owing to the beauty of its situation and the attractive appearance of its houses. As 'Argyris Ephtaliotes', Cleanthes Michaelides was indeed a 'fine scholar', composing poetry and prose in honour of the place he still called 'my island' after many years' absence.[145]

Micky, as his undergraduate friends called Constantine, was very much his father's son in his taste for languages and literature. He was also "an eager, friendly talker, and those who knew him best during his first two years [at Cambridge] remember him enthusiastically … though not always lucidly, discoursing on such themes as music and the style of Meredith and Henry James. He founded a society for the reading of Balzac's novels aloud in French and in his third year … mystified Lowes Dickinson's

Discussion Society with a paper on D'Annunzio".[146] An enthusiastic admirer of Constantine's gifts and promise was Oscar Browning, always known as 'OB'[147], under whose tutelage and possibly under whose influence also[148] Constantine had chosen to read history. "At King's, OB's love for Michaelides was soon the funniest joke of the term. Nathaniel Wedd, one of his colleagues, wrote about it in his private diary ... 'Sometimes ... OB's power of idealisation did lead to ridiculous results. This was notably the case with a certain Constantine Michaelides ... [who] had a wonderful gift of phrasemaking and a certain intellectual audacity that completely captivated OB. One of OB's favourite remarks to scholars who thought well of themselves was 'well, you seem an awful swell in your own eyes ... but I tell you this: in your old age you will have only one thing to boast of. You will talk of the days "when I was at King's with Michaelides". This remark, often made in the presence of the hero himself, seemed to many people injudicious'".[149]

Injudicious or not, OB's friendship was of great benefit to a young man matriculating at Cambridge in 1901 on a scholarship from a provincial grammar school, of foreign parentage, and whose relationship with his father was distant. The friendship was reciprocated, Constantine writing to OB at the end of his first term to thank him for his support and adding "perhaps it may be better ... to let you imagine it as intensely as you can, how much ... I owe to you and the affection which I have towards you".[150] The correspondence continued during OB's visit to Lord Curzon in 1901–1902 during which he stayed with one of his earliest loves while corresponding with one of his last ("you say you are drifting towards India but you can never drift away from ... the affection of Constantine C. Michaelides")[151]; Constantine, meanwhile, assured his mentor that "my work is getting straight and the interstices are being filled with music and literature and people".[152] When OB returned (he had hoped Constantine could meet him in Venice but this proved impossible), he stayed with the Michaelides family in the Merseyside town of Blundellsands where they then lived though they were shortly to move to Hessle in East Yorkshire. OB had therefore made the acquaintance of both Constantine and Aelfrida and their respective parents before 'Vadius' and 'Bélise' met, he, like Alfred and Catharine Tillyard, being active in Liberal politics and if he accepted Catharine's invitations as her daughter hints, an attender at the latter's Liberal garden parties at Fordfield.

The friendship did not endure beyond Constantine's triumph in the first part of his tripos and his subsequent switch to Moral Sciences. His passion for Aelfrida removed him from OB's orbit and in spite of OB

reminding Constantine of his affection shortly before the latter's graduation ceremony[153], of his enthusiastic shouts of 'Micky! Micky!' at the ceremony itself, of his gracing the post-ceremony tea in Constantine's rooms (he arrived with the typical OB remark "I come straight from the Duchess of Albany")[154], and of his joy at Constantine looking so much happier since his engagement, the close relationship between mentor and pupil was essentially over. Eight months later Constantine, hard up and wanting to treat Aelfrida, had so far abandoned OB as to sell two books given to him by his former tutor, confiding to Aelfrida that whenever he now encountered OB he felt 'as though a slug had crawled across his soul and left a slimy track'[155], a remark which had repercussions a few months later when, OB having sent Constantine a valedictory sonnet on the occasion of the former's impending retirement, its receipt was acknowledged by Aelfrida (an episode *not* noted in her diary) in a letter which pulverised the poem's grammar, metre, language (it was written in Italian) and imagery.[156] Poor OB. Constantine's few subsequent letters are business-like and speak of 'a long neglect'.[157]

'Flying' once again – not only had she found herself 'quite the lioness of the evening'[158] at a 'squash' at Trinity where she was congratulated on her acting and had mentally compared other young men "with Vadius who was, though [she] did not know it then, to be [her] husband"[159] and found them wanting, Aelfrida had also had the pleasure of acknowledging 'little friend' as she passed John Forbes in the street while chatting up Louis von Glehn, fellow actor and Perse teacher[160] with whom she had flirted until the arrival on the scene of 'Mr Michaelides' – but she had also broken every good resolution to behave, had 'flirted gloriously', and had wondered why it was so easy 'to yield to temptation'.[161]

With 'Mr Michaelides' it was not difficult to do so for, following another 'long flirt' with a man she had decided was 'either very *naïf* or very much accomplished'[162], he paid his first visit to Fordfield: 'I was glad', she wrote, 'that Mr Michaelides called at the earliest possible opportunity [and] that he talked to me all the time'.[163] ("He talked to Frida for two hours and made love glibly", was Julius' later version of their meeting; his contemporary diary account called Mr Michaelides "charming".)[164] After that there was no holding her:

> 27 February 1904. 'Vadius took my hand ... and said "*adorable Bélise*" ... he says he is hoping to be a literary man and couldn't we write a novel together'.[165] (They began it – it was to be called *Robert Renshaw* – but Aelfrida's co-author soon admitted that its composition was a pretext to enable him to contact

her on a regular basis and the enterprise foundered, though not before Aelfrida made a bonfire of 'a great many of [her own] manuscripts' so as to disburden herself of 'all that trash'[166] before facing her new admirer.)

9 March: 'His name is Constantine !!!'[167]

10 March: 'I did not enjoy tea at Vadius' chaste, elegant rooms ... as much as I ought to have done for I was troubled by my first attack of shyness ... most of the conversation was addressed to [Mama] but he looked at me with such honest boyish admiration that I was inclined to say "Don't! You are a genius and I am only *me*"'. (Bashfulness did not, however, prevent her from noticing that 'remarkable' as Constantine was – he was, as he demonstrated, an accomplished pianist – his rooms did not 'show signs of their owner being very rich'.)[168]

29 April 'Vadius says I am the cleverest, most brilliant, most fascinating and most wonderful woman he has ever met and that he has put me on a pedestal and worships me. I call that admiration [but] is it also love? ... The question of whether he is a genius or a mountebank is still unsolved'.[169]

3 May: 'The fact is he is pleased to pose as most passionately in love with me, as swept off his feet by overmastering emotion etc., etc.' (He was, said Ancifera Gregory acutely, "in love with Love" not with Aelfrida; Aelfrida dismissed the remark as another of Ancifera's snubs.) 'And the pose may last a fortnight or even ... with luck ... a month'.[170]

But Constantine's persistence, brilliance ('I reverence genius', she wrote of the man she now called 'my poet') and academic ability (he had obtained a first class in the History tripos and so must be 'extremely clever' as well as 'brilliant')[171] had begun to impress even a hardened flirt. Or was she merely in thrall to the charms of a charlatan, Constantine himself having already admitted to 'posing'?[172] Catharine Tillyard did not take her daughter's new admirer "seriously"[173] and even Aelfrida professed herself 'clear-sighted' about him – though not, it has to be said, until fifteen years later.[174]

9 May: 'He said to me ... "perhaps I am *the one*". It might be ...'[175]

12 May: 'If I tell you that my life must always be richer and fuller because I have met Constantine Michaelides, you will tell me not to talk sentiment'.[176]

22 May: '"I am never bored", said Vadius, "when I am with someone I love"'. It is the emphasis on *love* that I want to remember ...'[177]

13 May: 'The day after seeing my poet, I always want to dream ...'[178]

14 May: 'I said to him that if I were his mother, I would ... put him in a Greek temple to keep off all tourists'.[179]

17 May: 'He adores me, he wishes to *marry me*'.[180]

14 May: 'What did he say? What has he not said? But to marry that brilliant boy, to make him settle down, to ask him for money to pay the baker, to make him interview the plummer (*sic*) and put silver in the plate for the privelege (*sic*) of being good ... it would be a crime!' ('Yes, dear and only love, has it been a crime? I ask thy pardon'. Marginal note 1919.)[181]

23 May: 'What touched me most ... was my poet saying "another thing that you and I have in common is – you will understand – the maternal instinct". He [longs] to take a little boy in his arms ...'[182]

7 May: 'You may think what you like of me but I would be a good mother. Oh God, is it too much to ask, that I may have children!'[183]

28 May 6.30 pm: 'The supreme letter came from Vadius at 10.30 this morning. Prosaically ... I was darning stockings. He is coming to see me tomorrow. I feel intensely serious, humble and grateful. I hold my head higher because Constantine Michaelides loves me'.[184]

29 May: 'I cannot tell you the subtileties (*sic*) of our discourse ... we simply talked out the matter of our relationship as if we [were] each other's grandmothers'.[185]

30 May: 'I had a real love letter from him this morning'.[186]

31 May: 'I am engaged to be married to Constantine Michaelides'.[187]

Thirteen years later she recalled the day: 'the garden looks much as it did then – all the lilac and laburnum and chestnut full of blossom and the sun as golden as ever ... [I remember] Constantine coming ... to meet me, the breeze stirring his long hair, his eyes full of love ... [I remember] Constantine walking by my side a little self-conscious and very ardent and beautiful ... [and] so *sure* of happiness, so certain ... that our marriage would be more beautiful than any other had ever been ...'[188]

The only problem – or, rather, not the *only* problem, Constantine having confessed "with pain and humility that he is far too poor to think of marriage at present" (the Tillyards admitted to being "relieved that he has no immediate prospects"), was that Aelfrida did not reciprocate his affection. "The young lady", wrote her mother, "is interested, flattered and amused but not yet in love!"[189]

Was it therefore *only* revenge which caused Aelfrida to accept Constantine's proposal within two weeks of the announcement of John Forbes Cameron's to Elfrida Sturge or was it anxiety ("we are not so silly as to refuse dinner because there is not any turtle soup. We don't want to be *starved*"[190], as she informed Julius apropos Hans Peter and Lord Kitchener, a man whom she still adored even while marvelling that her love 'should be proof against'[191] her engagement to Constantine) or was she was so desperate for "devotion and children"[192] that she considered marrying a man she did not love without 'a moment's hesitation'[193] in order to obtain them? All three perhaps, though she had the grace to intimate that she 'could not love … could not love' a future husband who, knowing that she was not as in love with him as he with her, promised 'to show himself so brilliant that [her] *grande passion* should be for him'[194] alone ("he seems", wrote Catharine Tillyard, "to have immense faith in his powers and perseverance"[195]; to Aelfrida, however, Constantine confided that though he knew how to win her, he did not feel 'big enough for the job') by warning him that she was and would likely remain 'cold … as ice towards his beauty, his passion, his genius', that she did *not* 'care for him' but that she wished he would or could try to 'make her care'[196] ("I will make you love me", was his response) and that, 'dispassionate' as she was, she would marry him whenever he asked her to do so.[197] But she also asked him what he would do if, later on, he found 'someone [else]' who would engage with him more 'smoothly' than herself and informed him that if ever he found himself 'bored' by her he was to 'stay away'. ("Spare me!" was Constantine's anguished reply.)[198] To her diary, however, she asked if she could be sufficiently 'great' to hope that, 'later on', he would 'go away of his own accord'.[199]

Abandonment of their joint literary endeavour and Aelfrida's holocaust of 'a great many of [her] manuscripts'[200] meant that neither she nor Constantine was currently *writing* a novel; that did not prevent them from *living* one. Unfortunately, and though the effect on both was "pretty and romantic"[201], it was not the same novel.

For Constantine, the novelist par excellence was Gabriele D'Annunzio[202] whose overwrought plots and orotund phraseology influenced his declarations to Aelfrida ("how magnificent of you to exist! You have made the whole world anew for me … I wish I could put my soul into a cup … and give it to you to drink")[203] and echoed throughout the 'pagan poem' (probably the essay with which he confounded Lowes Dickinson) read aloud to Aelfrida and her mother in May 1904, the younger woman finding herself 'intoxicated' by 'the passages that spoke of love' and 'the bits that spoke of passion'

and marvelling that it was *she* who had inspired him to write it. (In a marginal note of 1919, she added that the essay was 'outspokenly sensual' and that she had utterly failed to register the fact at the time.)[204] For Aelfrida, it was Maurice Maeterlinck[205] and Henry James. She had been reading Maeterlinck's poetry during her abortive affair with John Forbes Cameron[206]; now she imitated his dialogues with Cameron's successor on paper and in real life (her diary entry for 14 June 1904 headed *Ecoutez l'adieu de Constantin'* – they were to be separated for two weeks – is Maeterlinck to a T[207]; a month earlier she had written a short story, *Les Enfants de la Terre,* describing it as 'a flagrant imitation … bathetic, wierd (*sic*) and beautiful' and noting that it was 'so much easier to write in French') and in July stated that she and her fiancé had been 'burlesquing Maeterlinck' in the privacy of the kitchen garden. Henry James'[208] new novel, *The Wings of the Dove,* was read with her mother's consent (it was a present from Constantine) and, it seems, lived, for diary entries ('I cannot tell you the endless subtleties (*sic*) of our discourse [but] … we have been discussing the psycological (*sic*) aspect of our situation')[209] and conversations with Constantine regarding the psychological subtleties of their situation are reminiscent of Jamesian characters whose vision of life is so artificial as to make one think that the self-centred and complex world they inhabit is an artefact created by themselves for their own amusement.

Was there, in fact, any distinction in Aelfrida's mind at this point between fiction and reality or was she living out another novel (she had, after all completed one and begun at least one other) with the intention of turning life into art with an eye to future publication à la Bashkirtseff, she herself being the 'most interesting book of all'? If so, was she merely using Constantine as 'copy'? And how much of the dialogue she reports apparently verbatim and certainly at length in English and French was fictive or imaginatively transformed – or even plagiarised, for resemblances between it and that spoken in Volume 1 of Susanna Venn's 1893 novel *Some Married Fellows* is startling, in particular the episode in which 'Randall Keltridge' explains to fiancée 'Helen Applewood' why he cannot marry her and she replies encouragingly that their marriage "shall … go on as we intended"? [210] And how much was she influenced by Constantine himself, his tendency to address her as 'Bélise' and sign himself 'Vadius' suggesting that perhaps Molière may have played as great a role in his wooing than D'Annunzio and that as a hopeful *littérateur* (his chief ambition; to gain a college fellowship was his second) he too may have been seeking 'copy'? All are possible. But there is more: rereading in 1919 those pages of her diary in which she detailed the early days of her relationship with Constantine, Aelfrida noted that she was 'filled with an immense pity' because 'Constantine and Aelfrida move blindly, like figures in a Greek tragedy impelled by some overmastering fate. On the whole I prefer Constantine to Aelfrida – he is wonderfully beautiful, radiant – but he has lived too much in the atmosphere of French novels, and though he watches himself, he does not see how absurd he is. As for Aelfrida, I admire her high spirits and her enthusiasms … Her vanity, however, revolts me, and her blindness to her own faults. She, too, is always watching herself act and yet she never sees what she is like. I suppose she is myself and I can remember exactly what she felt … but she seems more alien from myself than do the dear ones around me now'.[211] Of Aelfrida's 'fate' we are beginning to be aware: Constantine's has been hinted at and will be revealed later.

Dramatic (or dramatized) events continued throughout June and July. Constantine spent a considerable part of every day at Fordfield and continued to press his suit with romantic gestures and 'his whole body quivering with passion'.[212] Aelfrida, though moved by his ardour, encouraged him ('"kiss me … where Vadius kissed Bélise" … and I showed him the place just where my breast is round and white and alive')[213], her earlier decision not to let him touch even her hand having been forgotten following their first kiss on 9 June, an occasion on which Constantine took the initiative 'reverently not grossly': 'putting his hands on my shoulders, [he] stooped and kissed me passionately' or fending him off as occasion demanded: with memories of Hans Peter's grossness, she begged him to spare her lips, offering her forehead or cheek.[214] Eventually, she 'kissed Constantine of [her] own accord'[215], decided that she liked him to touch her[216], and became 'wild with delight' when he did; next, she informed him coolly that he and she were 'engaged in the only way that it is possible for two people of our temperament to be engaged'.[217] Her diary records her ambivalence: 'Let suffering come if it will, nothing can wrench from me these glorious days when I am young and beautiful and Constantine loves me … I am pledged to Constantine Michaelides[218]… I do not suppose, entre nous, that I *shall* marry Constantine, though, of course, I will if he wants me to …[219] Constantine is so completely apart from all my life. I *cannot* join him on'. (Marginal note 1919: 'this is one of the wisest remarks in the book'.)[220] Not only this, but following an episode during which Constantine, weeping with emotion, called her his wife, she admitted that 'since [she was] telling the truth', his passionate embraces 'suffocated' and bored her[221] and, after noting that she wrote to him daily when they were apart ('diary, judge me not harshly. I no longer

**Constantine Michaelides (extreme left) as 'Vadius'**

give my best to you'), that her letters were 'more than half "pose"'.[222]

An unexpected episode almost persuaded her that Constantine was indeed 'the man whom I have chosen for my husband'.[223] On 14 July she was lying on the sofa recovering from a headache, Constantine at the piano playing Beethoven. Suddenly she was aware of two other people in the room – a beautiful adolescent boy and a girl (brother and sister, she thought, she possessing 'wonderful strength of character', he an 'abnormal sensitiveness') whom she saw and heard clearly; both, she believed, had a look of Constantine about them. (There was also a 'wee thing of four who died' whose presence Aelfrida sensed but could not see.) Later the same day she 'saw' the boy and girl again, in an unfamiliar room whose features she describes in detail. She and Constantine were present once again, he 'altered and his character grown', she 'matronly, serene … but I could see that I had suffered'. The girl played to them music she composed herself while her brother looked on with infinite tenderness. Dazed by the experience, Aelfrida struggled to describe 'the strangeness of it' to Constantine. (She did not try to interpret what she had seen, although the association of the boy and girl and the dead 'wee one' must have reminded her of the relationship between Conrad, Julius, and herself.) Constantine, fortunately, regarded his fiancée's visionary experience as a positive omen, reassuring her 'now you are indeed my wife'. The following day she wrote: 'since last night, everything is changed. Constantine … is my husband, I his wife. We have begun our life together'. And suddenly she realised with dismay that she stood 'face to face with the inevitable'.[224]

Before 'life together' could begin, certain practical problems had to be solved. The first, presenting as early as 2 June, was the Oracle declaring 'most emphatically' that he would never consent to his daughter's formal engagement to a 'penniless undergraduate'. As neither Constantine nor Aelfrida had money of their own and as Aelfrida had not yet reached her majority, lack of funds presented a major obstacle to matrimony and Constantine's wishing that Aelfrida was already twenty-one so he could marry her 'right away … and hang the consequences' filled her with apprehension that on 5 October 1904 'he will … be mad enough to ask me to do so'.[225] Constantine was, however, allowed to make formal representation to Alfred Tillyard to be considered his daughter's official suitor. The interview did not run on conventional lines, for Constantine did not actually ask for Aelfrida's hand: '"Sir", said Constantine, "I want your permission to make your daughter love me". "They all have that", replied the Oracle with a smile'. Constantine then informed Alfred Tillyard, somewhat to the latter's surprise, that although he considered himself 'absolutely bound to Aelfrida', Aelfrida was not to consider herself bound to him because Constantine did not know if he himself was 'capable of always loving one woman'. Her father, Aelfrida concluded, respected Constantine for his frankness but could not help feeling that such sentiments from a lover were 'unusual, to say the least'.[226]

Following his interview with Constantine, Alfred Tillyard called Aelfrida into his study. Knowing her propensity to be 'charming … especially to gentlemen', he told her: "now Frida, you have an authorised lover. Remember to behave to other men as though this were the case". Having earlier explained to her mother 'what with her permission my position is with regard to my poet', Aelfrida pouted in reply: "I see. I am to behave to other men as though I were engaged, and to Constantine

as though I were *not*" – and departed for a college concert at which she deliberately singled out an admirer with whom to flirt and forgot all about Constantine, the man whom she had just kissed for the first time of her own accord and whose 'wife' she now considered herself to be. Although she later confessed (to her diary) that she was 'a very naughty girl'[227], her behaviour that evening and on other occasions during her relationship with Constantine was monstrously indiscreet: shortly after Constantine's departure from Cambridge for the Long Vacation she deliberately flirted and 'played the ingénue' with several of her admirers, almost provoking one into a declaration of marriage while pretending to be engaged to a second in order to discourage a third. Admittedly neither she nor Constantine had formally announced their engagement (if engagement it was) but to have occupied herself with amorous intrigues with men known to each other and to Constantine (or if not, moving in the same academic circles as himself) was risky behaviour when she was concurrently and without irony recording that 'Constantine is in every way exquisite … I want to be good, really good to be his wife'.[228]

The second problem was Constantine's mother. That the relationship between Constantine and Anatolia Michaelides was of a stronger nature than that usual between mothers and only sons is evident from letters written by her to Oscar Browning between 1901 and 1904 in which she fulsomely thanks the latter for his help to and encouragement of her son. The most revealing, with far-reaching consequences for Constantine's relationship with Aelfrida, was written on 24 October 1901 shortly after her son's arrival in Cambridge: "Constantine is more to me than son … he is dearest friend and companion … we have loved the same things in the same way, and I have always found him a great help and inspiration [with] his quick grasp and clear vision and comprehension of things – he has never had any other companion but me … and it has left him very unspoilt and his heart and thoughts clean and elevated".[229]

Knowing that Constantine reciprocated his mother's overwrought affection, his 'wife' realised the importance of winning over Mrs Michaelides as soon as possible. The opportunity presented itself during a visit to Cambridge by '*la famille* Michaelides' (Anatolia and her daughters) early in June 1904. The first meeting, attended by Aelfrida and her mother, took place in Constantine's rooms. (Catherine Tillyard, aware that two days earlier her husband had forbidden Aelfrida to become engaged to a 'penniless undergraduate' and to visit his family home, prevented the 'occasion from becoming a "situation"' by treating 'anything meaningful as quite ordinary and ignor[ing] anything important' and by behaving 'in the most persistent and courageous way'.)[230] Knowing too that Anatolia and her daughters 'were all their (*sic*) to look at me', Aelfrida behaved as though perfectly at ease; she also stated 'I noticed that I impressed her as a woman who "counts for something". She … thought me stylish and distinguished-looking from the first. Then a touch of humility, an attitude of deference to her and a readiness to love her warmed her heart towards me, and I saw that she wanted me for a daughter'. (Marginal note 1919: 'I was *absolutely* wrong about Anatolia – I simply wrote down what Constantine told me and never looked for myself'.) On leaving, Mrs Michaelides drew her arm through Aelfrida's, the latter thanking Anatolia for her goodness and hoping for forgiveness for being about to remove her son from her orbit. Concluding her account with a description of Anatolia herself ('obviously American, handsome, keen, with a rather exaggerated figure, a sharp voice and most intelligent black eyes … I picture her as uncompromisingly moral, intensely critical in the kindest possible way, and having a background of romance somewhere *au fond de son coeur*'), Aelfrida decided she could become 'very fond of Constantine's mother' and that she had been 'accepted' by Mrs Michaelides. Adding poignancy to the episode, Anatolia treated Aelfrida 'as though I [too] adored her boy'.[231]

But 'l'Américaine' was already making trouble, asking Constantine to pass on to Aelfrida the warning that he was 'very changeable' because his 'heart and thoughts' had been bestowed on others, notably on a younger and an older woman. ('Juanita', as the latter liked to be called, had once suggested that she and Constantine indulge in an adulterous affair and still wrote 'sickly sensual' letters to him.)[232] She also warned Constantine that he would forget Aelfrida. (Had she, Aelfrida asks herself at this point, 'invented' her 'brother and sister' vision because earlier that day Constantine had been weeping over his mother's 'cruel prophecy' and because she felt the need 'of saying something stronger' to combat it or had she 'really seen a vision?' She does not say, but in a marginal note of 1919 admits – ambiguously – that something about the episode was 'all wrong'.)[233] Anatolia's cautions, a foretaste of the mischief she would delight in causing in the future, merely strengthened Constantine's desire: 'he often tells of what we shall do when we are married'. Aelfrida regarded the matter more realistically, telling Constantine 'you may have been in love before, but I am sure you have never been in love with anyone like me. It is on *that* fact, far more than your own constancy, that I rest my belief that you will not forget me'.[234]

Anatolia's ambivalent feelings with regard to the relationship between her son and his (unofficial) fiancée found an echo in those of the latter's parents. (Julius,

though he liked Constantine – but was it he or Aelfrida who mockingly included a "Greekling" in a contemporary *MCJ*[235] – 'saw through' Anatolia and noted that she and her son associated with a raffish set of "Franco–Slavo–American[s]"[236] in the course of frequent visits to Paris.) Although later descriptions of Constantine's arrival at Fordfield in 1904 suggest he took more Tillyards than Aelfrida "by storm"[237] – Alfred Tillyard described him as 'rare and brilliant'[238] (or was this a hint of sarcasm?) and he endeared himself to Catharine Tillyard by playing the piano and by his attentiveness to herself and to Dick the dog – her parents' behaviour was more than usually ambiguous: though they looked on indulgently while the young lovers wandered together in the garden, they complained that Constantine and Aelfrida 'made a faction' from which they themselves excluded and only grudgingly agreed that the 'faction' should 'stand first in intimacy' with each other.[239] And why did Constantine and Aelfrida feel obliged to exchange confidences in the kitchen garden 'as a fairly safe place'?[240] And why should Aelfrida confide to her diary that she had told no-one of her engagement ('and they will not guess') because she felt it 'not right that [she] should'? Was it solely because her father 'might not call [it] an engagement'?[241] But as she appears to have paraded the event when John Forbes' sister visited Fordfield in the hopes that Isabella Cameron would 'tell Little Friend' and admits to telling Lilly Grove in an attempt to warn her off (Lilly had fallen in love with Constantine 'at the time of the acting'; she played Armande)[242] and did not seem to mind if two relevant people informed others, she should not have been surprised that the news had entered the public domain by early August.

There was, however, another reason why Aelfrida might wish to keep her engagement secret: her religiosity. Following an amatory episode during which Constantine covered her in hot kisses ('*baisers chauds*'; the episode was largely recorded in Maeterlinckian French) and declared "we will sleep like this" as he rested his head on her breast and she 'caressed his cool soft hair with [her] cheek', Aelfrida 'lay awake all night suffering … as I have never suffered before' because she could not bring herself to love her fiancé and because, as she later admitted on her knees in church while 'praying, weeping [and] praising God', she believed that 'supreme moments of passion' were wrong and should not be repeated.[243] They were – on several occasions – but one in particular seemed to indicate that there might be more to marriage than exchange of literary 'epigrams', play-acting, opportunities to travel, and 'perfectly charming' episodes of domesticity[244]: lying with Aelfrida in a remote corner of Fordfield garden, Constantine suddenly flung away the copy of Swinburne's *Tristan and Iseult* he was reading aloud and began to kiss her so passionately that she almost swooned with delight and he himself appears to have reached orgasm. Torn between a desire to discover if there was indeed 'even more than this' to the physical side of marriage and a wish to disassociate herself from the 'jewelled love' of a sexually-aroused young man in favour of placing herself under 'the care of God'[245], Aelfrida informed Constantine that he and she must never behave with such abandon again. (A resolve later broken but with important implications for their married life.) She then tried to persuade herself (she was assisted by a conveniently-timed 'vision' during a Communion at which she offered 'Constantine's love before God's table' and during which she was rewarded with a 'vision' of Christ crucified, seen 'with these mortal eyes')[246] that Deity Himself was in favour of her uniting herself with a man to whom she had already said (in thought) while standing with him in Caius College chapel 'I Aelfrida take thee, Constantine ...' and of whom she had written 'this is the man whom I have chosen for my husband'.[247] And how fortunate under the circumstances that her transformation of a normal physiological reaction to sexual stimulation into a quasi-mystical union of souls sanctified by God should be supported by a belief that she had come to 'know God better because I know Constantine'[248] and by Constantine's sudden rediscovery of religion: 'he wishes me to teach him to be a Christian ... [and] prays every day, as I wished him [to] "O Lord, make me and Aelfrida good"'.[249]

But why, other than being 'changeable', should besotted Constantine 'forget' Aelfrida? The answer lies in his fiancée's diary entry for 5 July: 'now listen. All is decided for my spending next winter in Florence'.[250] Announced without preamble – the decision appears to have been taken by Alfred and Catharine Tillyard without consulting her – Aelfrida nevertheless pronounced herself 'delighted beyond words' and 'wildly excited'[251] at the prospect. Teaching 'maidens of the lower middle class'[252] had begun to bore her though she enjoyed the effect on her observing parents, fiancé, and elder brother of the 'pretty pose' she adopted as the 'maidens' crowded round her following a performance of a play she had written for them to kiss her goodbye and to give her a present[253], but why should she express such extreme delight at parting from a fiancé whom she was about to introduce to the Olympian gods of her childhood as another 'young god' (*un jeune dieu*) and describe as someone with whom she had 'discovered or even invented happiness'?[254] (A deity, too, who wept in her lap at the prospect of parting.) Was it because Constantine's physical passion *and* his cloying devotion 'bored ... and half suffocat[ed]' her?[255] Why

should his wish to marry her as soon as possible make her 'tremble and shrink' and even ask if she was 'made to be married'?[256] Was it a desire for emotional *Lebensraum* as well as for new places and sensations which made her keen to go?

But although a season in Italy might have provided Aelfrida with time and emotional space in which to consider the problems inherent in her relationship more objectively and to decide to break with Constantine while she could, preoccupation with other issues so filled her mind that she was unable to achieve clarity of vision and lost the power to act decisively. The feeling that she was already trapped in a marriage she only partly desired seems to have paralysed her will to such an extent that it even influenced her farewell to Constantine: 'I ... nerved myself to it. I gave him my hand and said in a very low voice "Goodbye, my husband". His eyes flamed and I broke away and left the room. *Now* I feel untamed, free – and yet I suppose I want to, I must, I ought to marry'.[257]

On 30 September 1904 ('No time to write. Goodbye diary')[258], she left Cambridge for Italy.

## Notes

1  GCPPT 1|1|19 30 June 1913.
2  GCPPT 11|9 14 June 1902. The entry is written in red ink.
3  ibid. 6 August 1902.
4  GCPPT 1|1|11 21 March 1904.
5  GCPPT 1|1|10 12 September 1903.
6  GCPPT 2|2a Extra Number September 1902. Poem entitled *Our Wastepaper Basket*.
7  Tillyard, HJW. *The Letters of ACW Tillyard* (MTC). Letter from Aelfrida to Julius Tillyard of 15 September 1902.
8  GCPPT 1|1|9 19 August 1902.
9  Tillyard, HJW. *The Letters of ACW Tillyard* (MTC). Letter from Aelfrida to Julius Tillyard of 12 September 1902.
10  GCPPT 2|2a. Vol. 1 Extra Number September 1902. Editor's introduction.
11  ibid.
12  GCPPT 1|1|9 24 September 1902.
13  ibid. Letter from Aelfrida to Julius Tillyard of 15 September 1902.
14  GCPPT 1|1|69 25 October 1951.
15  Tillyard, Ae. *Marrying a Stranger* p 25 (GCPPT 2|6).
16  GCPPT 1|1|9 6 October 1902.
17  GCPPT 1|1|10 8 January 1903.
18  ibid. 5 October 1903.
19  Tillyard, HJW. *The Letters of ACW Tillyard (MTC)*. Letter from Catharine Tillyard to Ancifera (Annie) Gregory of 31 May 1904.
20  GCPPT 1|1|10 26 July 1903.
21  ibid. 15 July 1903.
22  Tillyard, HJW. *The Letters of ACW Tillyard* (MTC). Letter from Aelfrida to Mina Kaufmann of 8 May 1911.
    Tillyard, Ae. *A Little Road-Book for Mystics* pp 133–134.
23  GCPPT 1|1|9 21 July 1902.
24  GCPPT 2|25|3(1.1)
25  GCPPT 1|1|9 20 October 1902.
26  GCPPT 1|1|10 27 November 1903.
27  Tillyard, Ae. *A Little Road-Book for Mystics* pp 133–134.
28  GCPPT 1|1|9 3 April 1902.

29 GCPPT 1|1|10 25 February and 14 March 1903.
30 ibid. 14 June 1903.
31 ibid. 25 May 1903.
32 GCPPT 1|1|9 19 February 1902.
33 ibid. 22 October 1902.
34 GCPPT 1|1|11 16 April 1904.
35 GCPPT 1|1|10 25 February 1903.
36 GCPPT 1|1|11 25 December 1903.
37 *CIP* Women's column of 15 August 1902.
38 GCPPT 1|1|8 3 October 1901.
39 *Undine* (1811) by Romantic writer Friedrich de la Motte Fouqué (1777–1843) was a novel much read around this time and though not translated into English until 1909, could have been read by Aelfrida in French or German in 1901.
40 *Robert Elsmere*, published in 1888, was written by Mary (Mrs Humphrey) Ward (1851–1920), an author familiar to Aelfrida from discussions with her father and because Dorothea Conybeare's mother was said to have been the model for 'Catherine Leyburn' (GCPPT 1|1|5 2 June and 14 July 1900).
41 *CIP* Women's column of 15 August 1902.
42 Robert Buchanan (1841–1901) was a poet, novelist and dramatist who in 1870 published a study of Mysticism, *The Book of Orm*.
43 GCPPT 1|1|9 25 December 1901.
44 GCPPT 1|1|5 8 August 1900. Marie Bashkirtseff (1858–1884) Ukrainian painter, sculptor and diarist, kept a journal from age 13. Excerpts from the journal's 106 volumes were published in Paris in 1889 as *I am the most interesting book of all*.
45 GCPPT 1|1|11 5 April 1904.
46 ibid. 1|1|11 7 March 1904.
47 Erlande, A. *Edmée Combres* pp 111–112.
48 GCPPT 1|1|9 24 February 1902.
49 Details of John Forbes Cameron's life have been taken from his *Times* obituary (preserved in GCPPT 1|1|69a) and Aelfrida's associated comment of 24 March 1952 (GCPPT 1|1|69).
50 GCPPT 1|1|10 3 March 1903.
51 GCPPT 1|1|9 3 May 1902.
52 GCPPT 1|1|10 24 January and 21 February 1903.
53 GCPPT 1|1|9 8 and 10 May 1902.
54 GCPPT 1|1|1 1 30 December 1903.
55 GCPPT 1|1|9 10 May 1902.
56 ibid. 11 June 1902.
57 ibid. 13 June and 3 July 1902.
58 ibid. 28 July, 3 and 26 August 1902.
59 ibid. 18 October 1902.
60 Tillyard, HJW. *The Letters of ACW Tillyard (MTC)*. Letter from Aelfrida to Julius Tillyard of 2 August 1902.
   GCPPT 1|1|9 26 August 1902.
61 GCPPT 1|1|9 4 August 1902.
62 ibid. 18 October 1902.
63 GCPPT 1|1|13 7 July 1905.
64 GCPPT 1|1|12 14 August 1905.
65 GCPPT 1|1|9 10 May, 8 and 23 June 1902.
66 At the time of Elfrida's birth her father, John Edward Sturge, was a wealthy business man with interests in Birmingham and the Caribbean. Widowed early, Mrs Sturge thereafter lived entirely in England and having friends in Cambridge, visited that town regularly. Joseph Sturge (1793–1851), the well-known anti-slavery campaigner, was a collateral relation.
67 GCPPT 1|1|9 18 and 20 October 1902.
68 ibid. 27 October 1902.
69 ibid.
70 ibid. 18 October 1902.
71 ibid. 4 August and 18 October 1902.
72 ibid. 11 November 1902.
73 GCPPT 1|1|10 19 January 1903.
74 ibid. 2 February 1903.
75 GCPPT 1|1|9 18 November 1902.
76 GCPPT 1|1|10 24 January 1903.
77 ibid.
78 ibid 21 February 1903.
79 ibid. 7 March 1903.
80 ibid. 19 March 1903.
81 ibid. 22 May 1903.
82 ibid. 14 and 22 May 1903.
83 ibid. 19 March 1903. Faded violets are pressed between the diary pages in which this entry appears.
84 ibid. 20 March 1903.
85 ibid. 14 May 1903.
86 ibid. 22 May and 14 June 1903.
87 ibid. 19 March 1903.
88 ibid. 23 June 1903. The *MCJ* of June 1910 (GCPPT 2|2a) lists among "*Books not to read*" a volume entitled *The Complete Rotter by John Forbes*. It is accompanied by a spoof revue from a student magazine describing it as an "*Exhaustive Treatise*".
89 GCPPT 1|1|10 3, 4, 8 and 11 July 1903.
90 ibid. 25 September. 1903.
91 ibid. 21 February 1903.
92 ibid. 3 October 1903.
93 ibid. 6 November 1903.
94 ibid. 15 November 1903.
95 ibid. 19 November 1903.
96 ibid. 15 December 1903.
97 Tillyard, Ae. *Marrying a Stranger* pp 195–197.
98 GCPPT 1|1|10 15 December 1903.
99 Tillyard, Ae. *Marrying a Stranger* p 191.
100 GCPPT 1|1|10 15 December 1903.
101 ibid. 24 January 1903.
102 ibid. 15 December 1903.
103 GCPPT 1|1|11 20 February 1904.
104 ibid. 27 April 1904.
105 GCPPT 1|1|10 5 June 1903.
106 GCPPT 1|1|9 10 October 1902.
107 GCPPT 1|1|11 16 May 1904. An *MCJ* of early 1904 (GCPPT 2|2a) has "Little Friend" answer the question "How I should like to spend Christmas' with the words "I am sure you will understand that there are some questions which cannot be answered and it were better if they were not referred to".
108 GCPPT 1|1|11 22 September 1904.
109 1|1|14 12 January 1907.
110 GCPPT 1|1|10 15 December 1903.
111 ibid.
112 GCPPT 1|1|11 15 December 1903.
113 ibid. 22 January 1904.
114 ibid. 13 February 1904.
115 ibid. 22 February 1904.
116 ibid. 31 May 1904.
117 ibid. 3 June 1904.
118 Tillyard, HJW. *The Letters of ACW Tillyard (MTC)*. Letter from Aelfrida to Julius Tillyard of 2 August 1902.
119 ibid. Introduction.
120 Erlande, A. *Edmée Combres* pp 111–112.
121 For details of the lives of Elizabeth (Lilly) Fraser (1854/5–1941) and James Frazer (1854–1941) see the *ODNB* Vol. 20 pp 894–895 and pp 892–893 respectively.
122 GCPPT 2|25|2 *The Strawberry Eater*. Aelfrida's description of Mrs Frazer's life is basically accurate though even into old age she persisted in regarding the latter as a woman with a mysterious past chiefly because of her own lack of knowledge of events therein. Mrs Frazer's

'Strawberry Eater' soubriquet arose as a result of her having gained entry to Cambridge 'gown' society through her second marriage, a 'Strawberry Eater' in Fordfield parlance being someone to whom good fortune occurred serendipitously. The name stuck, Aelfrida referring to Mrs Frazer (though never to her face) by that name long after the latter became Lady Frazer when her husband was knighted in 1912. Mrs Frazer's good fortune and pretensions (the Tillyards regarded her as an adventuress) were mercilessly mocked in several numbers of the *MCJ*.

123  GCPPT 1|1|11 25 December 1903.
124  ibid. 20 December 1903.
125  Tillyard, Ae. *Marrying a Stranger* p75.
126  GCPPT 2|25|2 *The Strawberry Eater.*
127  Tillyard, HJW. Introduction to *The Letters of ACW Tillyard* (MTC).
128  GCPPT 1|1|4 18 April and 20 May 1898. The 'big iron gymnasium' was the "iron room or 'tin tabernacle'" (Hirsch, P. & McBeth, M. Pt2 p10) in which college lectures took place. It was erected in the grounds of successive college buildings.
129  Tillyard, HJW. Introduction to *The Letters of ACW Tillyard* (MTC).
130  For details of Elizabeth Hughes and the Cambridge Training College for Post Graduate Women, see the *ODNB* Vol. 28 pp 644–645 and Hughes, M. pp 119–145 for the history of its early days.
131  For details of pioneering British teacher HD Rouse (1863–1956) and his method of 'Language-teaching', see Mitchell, S. pp 133–139. Dr Rouse was headmaster of the Perse from 1902–1928.
132  Tillyard, HJW. Introduction to *The Letters of ACW Tillyard* (MTC). Both Margaret Verrall and Kate Street, headmistress of the Perse School for Girls during Frida's brief stay, were keen supporters of the 'Direct Method'. Aelfrida notes the presence of Miss Hughes' students at the Perse and Lady Frazer's house but not in Selwyn Road; perhaps she was too old by then to be taught by them there. For further details, see Martin. G. pp33–34 and Hirsch, P. & McBeth, M. Pt2 p149.
133  GCPPT 1|1|11 10 February 1904.
134  ibid. 13 February 1904.
135  ibid. 12 February 1904.
136  ibid. 1, 8, and 12 February 1904.
137  Tillyard, HJW. Introduction to *The Letters of ACW Tillyard* (MTC).
138  For this synopsis of Bélise's character and other comments on Molière's learned ladies, I am indebted to H. Gaston Hall's introduction to *Les Femmes Savantes.*
139  GCPPT 1|1|11 31 January 1904.
140  Tillyard, HJW. Introduction to *The Letters of ACW Tillyard* (MTC).
141  Molière. *Les Femmes Savantes* Act 3 scene iii.
142  KC *Annual Report* 17 November 1934.
143  Tillyard, Ae. *Marrying a Stranger* p 7.
144  Tillyard, HJW. Introduction to *The Letters of ACW Tillyard* (MTC).
145  Although not alone in reviving interest in the traditions of Greek peasant life currently overshadowed by Ottoman authoritarianism and by Western European scholastic emphasis on classical Greek studies, Argyris Ephtaliotes (1849–1923) was an important influence in the late nineteenth century renaissance of modern Greek (demotic) literature and in the interest in peasant and pastoral life which formed its subject matter. Of particular significance in the present context is that his *Tales from the Isles of Greece* was translated into English in 1897 by the same Dr Rouse whose methods of teaching languages in Cambridge were to attract attention from forward-thinking educationalists. Argyris sent Aelfrida a copy of Rouse's translation on 25 May 1905, she reciprocating by translating one of his poems, *The River of Life,* on 4 August 1911 while staying in Hessle and by later publishing it with an acknowledgment in an anthology of her own verse, *The Garden and the Fire* p23, section entitled 'poems about love'.
146  KC *Annual Report* 17 November 1934.
147  For more on Oscar Browning see Anstruther, I. *Oscar Browning* and Annan, N. pp 100–106.
148  KCA OB i/A Graham CC. A letter dated 18 December 1900 from Constantine Michaelides (still a schoolboy) to Oscar Browning suggests that this could be the case; on 27 May 1901 a list of the positions of Cambridge colleges in the different Triposes sent by OB to Constantine demonstrated to the latter the 'undisputed supremacy of King's in History'.
149  Anstruther, I. pp 173–174.
150  KCA OBi/A: Graham CC. Letter from Constantine Michaelides to Oscar Browning of 11 December 1901.
151  ibid. Letter from Constantine Michaelides to Oscar Browning of 19 December 1901.
152  ibid. Letter from Constantine Michaelides to Oscar Browning of 4 January 1902.
153  GCPPT 1|1|12 10 June 1905.
154  GCPPT 1|1|13 20 June 1905. The undated *MCJ* of early 1904 containing the article *How I should like to spend Christmas* has 'OB' declare "with 4 or 5 kings or emperors".
155  GCPPT 1|1|13 26 February 1906.
156  KCA OB 1/1644 Tillyard. Letter from Aelfrida to Oscar Browning of 11 May 1906.
157  ibid. OB i/A: Graham CC. Undated letter (by context 1908) from Constantine Michaelides to Oscar Browning.
158  GCPPT 1|1|11 17 February 1904.
159  GCPPT 2|25|3 (1).
160  GCPPT 1|1|11 20 February 1904. Louis von Glehn ('de Glehn' from 1914 to disguise his Alsatian descent), a man about twenty years older than Aelfrida, had harboured sentimental feelings for her for some time as several diary references show.
161  ibid. 13 February 1904.
162  ibid. 20 February 1904.
163  ibid. 22 February 1904.
164  Tillyard, HJW. Introduction to *The Letters of ACW Tillyard* (MTC).
165  GCPPT 1|1|11 27 February 1904. An undated *MCJ* of around this date contains an article entitled *Les Fashions*; it includes an illustration of a "*Femme Savante* – the irresistible Bélise" and the added comment "she looks it too!"
166  ibid. 14, 22, and 26 May 1904.
167  ibid. 9 March 1904.
168  Ibid. 10 March 1904.
169  Ibid. 29 April 1904.
170  GCPPT 1|1|11 3 May 1904.
     GCPPT 2|25|3 (8).
171  GCPPT 1|1|11 9 and 11 May 1904.
172  Ibid. 22 February 1904.
173  Tillyard, HJW. Introduction to *The Letters of ACW Tillyard* (MTC).
174  GCPPT 1|1|11 11 May 1904. Marginal note (1919 but otherwise undated) to this entry.
175  ibid. 9 May 1904.
176  ibid. 12 May 1904.
177  ibid. 19 May 1904.
178  ibid. 13 May 1904.
179  ibid. 14 May 1904.
180  ibid. 17 May 1904.
181  ibid. 14 May 1904.
182  ibid. 23 May 1904.
183  ibid. 7 May 1904.
184  ibid. 28 May 1904.
185  ibid. 29 May 1904.
186  ibid. 30 May 1904.
187  ibid. 31 May 1904. The date of this entry is underlined twice.
188  GCPPT 1|1|22 31 May 1917.
     GCPPT 1|1|67 31 May 1950.
189  Tillyard, HJW. *The Letters of ACW Tillyard* (MTC). Letter from Catharine Tillyard to Ancifera (Annie) Gregory of 31 May 1904.

190 Tillyard, HJW. *The Letters of ACW Tillyard* (MTC). Letter from Aelfrida to Julius Tillyard of [ ] September 1902.

191 GCPPT 1|1|11 1 June 1904.

192 Tillyard, HJW. *The Letters of ACW Tillyard* (MTC). Letter from Aelfrida to Julius Tillyard of [ ] September 1902.

193 GCPPT 1|1|11 28 May 1904.

194 Ibid. 22 May 1904.

195 Tillyard, HJW. *The Letters of ACW Tillyard* (MTC). Letter from Catharine Tillyard to Ancifera (Annie) Gregory of 31 May 1904. GCPPT 1|1|11 26 May 1904.

196 GCPPT 1|1|11 26 and 29 May 1904.

197 Ibid. 31 May 1904. A marginal note added in May 1919 emphasises Aelfrida's emotional confusion of 1904: 'All this puzzles me now! What *did* I feel?'

198 ibid. 14 and 17 May 1904.

199 Ibid. 14 May 1904.

200 Ibid. 12 May 1904.

201 Tillyard, HJW. *The Letters of ACW Tillyard* (MTC). Letter from Catharine Tillyard to Ancifera (Annie) Gregory of 31 May 1904.

202 Gabriele D'Annunzio (1863–1938) was an Italian poet, playwright, journalist, political activist, and lover whose work was much – and often uncritically – admired and imitated by the younger generation.

203 GCPPT 1|1|11 26 July 1904.

204 ibid. 14 and 15 May 1904.

205 Maurice Maeterlinck (1862–1949), Belgian by birth, composed his plays, poems and essays in French. His themes, often couched in symbolist language and imagery, with their emphasis on death and on the meaning (or meaninglessness) of life would have appealed to Aelfrida at this point in her own; his wish to have his plays performed by impersonal marionettes rather than human actors may also have appealed to one who increasingly found herself pressured into relationships by men when her wish was to remain emotionally disassociated from them. Maeterlinck was also a noted plagiarist, a point which may have some bearing on Aelfrida's later novels.

206 GCPPT 2|2a A poem entitled *Amour et Destinée* by "Maeter Mauricelink" appears in the *MCJ* Vol. 2 No 3 October 1903.

207 GCPPT 1|1|11 8 May, 14 June and 19 July 1904.

208 Henry James (1843–1916), American by birth, lived most of his life in England and became a naturalised English subject in 1915. His novels, describing the impact on visiting Americans of European life and manners and including lengthy interior monologues, sudden revelations and the narrations of unreliable witnesses, must have resonated in the mind of one whose diary and later novels were often extremely Jamesian and whose Cambridge life was currently impacted upon by a Graeco-American.

209 GCPPT 1|1|11 29 May 1904.

210 Venn, S. *Some Married Fellows* Vol. 1 pp 259–260. Aelfrida read the novel at age fifteen. Her later self, realising how much of her own marriage both volumes portrayed, noted that it was "a heartrending book but terribly true of one aspect of Cambridge life" (GCPPT 2|25|3 (4)).

211 GCPPT 1|1|11 23 July 1904. Postscript dated 21 January 1919.

212 ibid. 7 June 1904.

213 ibid. 11 June 1904.

214 ibid. 9 June 1904.

215 ibid. 11 June 1904.

216 ibid. 7 and 9 June 1904.

217 ibid. 2 June 1904.

218 ibid. 5 and 12 June 1904.

219 ibid. 7 June 1904.

220 ibid. 15 July 1904.

221 ibid. 26 July 1904.

222 ibid. 5 July and 31 August 1904.

223 ibid. 21 June 1904.

224 ibid. 24 and 25 July 1904.

225 ibid. 1 June 1904.

226 ibid. 11 June 1904.

227 ibid. 7 June 1904.

228 ibid. 10 June 1904.

229 KCA OBi/A: Michaelides, L. Letter from Anatolia (Lila) Michaelides to Oscar Browning of 24 October 1901.

230 GCPPT 1|1|11 5 June 1904.

231 ibid. 4 June 1904.

232 ibid 19 May and 22 July 1904.

233 ibid. 24 July 1904.

234 ibid. 20 July 1904.

235 GCPPT 2|2a August 1904 *"Our Silly Season topic: my idea of a perfect holiday"*.

236 GCPPT 1|1|24 16 June 1919.
Tillyard, HJW. Introduction to *The Letters of ACW Tillyard* (MTC).

237 Tillyard, HJW. *Introduction to The Letters of ACW Tillyard* (MTC).

238 GCPPT 1|1|11 7 May 1904.

239 ibid. 13 and 15 July 1904.

240 ibid. 13 July 1904.

241 ibid. 1 June 1904.

242 ibid. 22 July and 12 and 20 September 1904.

243 ibid. 14 June 1904.

244 ibid. 16 July and 16 September 1904.

245 ibid. 16 July 1904.

246 ibid. 26 June 1904.

247 ibid. 10 and 21 June 1904.

248 ibid. 12 June 1904.

249 ibid. 12 June and 13 July 1904.

250 ibid. 5 July 1904.

251 ibid. 5 July and 2 September 1904.

252 ibid. 2 July 1904.

253 ibid. 14 July 1904.

254 ibid. 19 July 1904.

255 ibid. 26 July 1904.

256 ibid. 22 and 27 September 1904.

257 GCPPT 1|1|12 2 October 1904.

258 GCPPT 1|1|11 29 September 1904.

# Florence and Young Italy

Aelfrida arrived in Florence on 3 October 1904 with the intention of attending university lectures as an '*auditrice*' or informal student. Two days later she celebrated her twenty-first birthday, exploring the city with Florence Boyle who happened to be staying there at the time of her niece's arrival and noting that her 'birthday party' consisted of a visit to the Ponte Vecchio and her 'guests' the spirits of Constantine and all the other 'great men' (*sic*) who had ever crossed it.[1]

Her departure for Italy shortly before a birthday usually honoured as a special event – contrast Aelfrida's sad little celebrations in Florence (the following year she wrote that in spite of being ill, her twenty-second birthday was *much* nicer than her twenty-first) with the two-day festivities surrounding Julius' twenty-first birthday in Cambridge in November 1902 – seems odd and rather punitive, given that the Florentine academic year was to start a month late because of the impending General Election[2] and something which could have been ascertained before she left England. Her going abroad shortly before the day on which she gained her majority *may* have been coincidental but might also be attributed to her parents' desire to detach her from the *second* young man of foreign extraction to whom she had spontaneously engaged herself within three years or to prevent premature marriage to an impecunious young man who had declared his intention of marrying their daughter as soon as she was old enough to marry without parental consent. It may have been intended to remove a distracting influence during Constantine's final year at university (this suggests collusion between the Tillyards and Anatolia Michaelides of which neither Constantine nor Aelfrida were aware), the older generation rightly believing that anguished conversations in Maeterlinckian French ("*Tu m'aimes pas, avoue le.*" "*Je ne t'aime pas*")[3] were unconducive to academic study, for though he waxed eloquent "about the stimulus his love [was] to his work"[4], Constantine was unusual in openly conducting (and being allowed to conduct) a relationship with a girl of his own class during term-time (the authorities turned a blind eye to clandestine affairs with girls of a lower class) and in the amount of time he devoted to his (as yet unofficial) fiancée, to reading French novels with her, and playing music to her to the detriment of Moral

**Giovanni Papini (Gian Falco) c1920**

Sciences, and though his joy in the relationship was obvious (Aelfrida, meeting him in the street three days after agreeing to marry him, noted that he was 'blithe as a song of spring'[5] and his university contemporaries his ebullience as he bounced through college courts "as though on india-rubber")[6], it is also obvious that his mind was on his fiancée, not his work. Or was it merely to add to Aelfrida's credentials as a language teacher, teaching – for which she had already displayed an aptitude – being the career planned for her by her parents, or to provide her with a taste of the university life she seemed strangely reluctant to consider as a preliminary to teaching or as a career in itself? (Had her intelligent and enquiring mind been properly occupied and trained in a rigorous academic environment, some, if not all, of her future problems might have been prevented.) There may be elements of the truth in all the above reasons but her own comment 'I feel as though I were once more seventeen and had been sent away from home to get over the awkward age'[7], speaks volumes.

With an empty month before the beginning of term, Aelfrida occupied herself with exploring Florence, including parts not normally visited by Baedeker-toting tourists, with improving her spoken Italian while staying at a pension run by the Protestant widow of a university professor, with visiting nursery and elementary schools in order to be able to report back on these to her father, and with voluntary work (possibly at Signor Coïsson's suggestion) at the dispensary at the Waldensian Missione Medica. She also discovered the beauties of Florentine Renaissance art, regularly visiting churches and museums and returning again and again to her favourite paintings. (The Tillyards, as Eustace later noted, were 'not strong on visual arts'[8] and this was Aelfrida's first exposure to them; she described her favourite picture, Andrea del Sarto's *Madonna delle Arpie*, as 'the most beautiful picture in the world'[9], placing a copy in a kind of shrine in her room and sending one to Constantine.) In spite of this, activity during the early part of her stay in Florence seems to have been rather solitary. True, she had introductions to English visitors and residents (she was under the nominal care of a Mrs Cox, wife of a Cambridge professor, who was wintering in Florence with her daughters) but found them insular and less keen than herself to live the life of a Florentine. They therefore remained on the level of acquaintances only; indeed, her only potential friendship, quickly curtailed by her moving to another pension on the grounds of incompatibility with guests at the first, was with Giovanni Brentano, son of Franz Brentano the philosopher.[10]

Aelfrida's reluctance to join the activities of English expatriates can also be ascribed to an enthusiasm they did not share. Visits to Florence's numerous churches were not made solely for reasons of aesthetic appreciation: full of her 'new thirst'[11] for a very personal and very spiritual religion, she went to pray.

Her reference to her 'new' thirst comes as something of a surprise, for apart from pious attempts to convert essentially agnostic Constantine to Christianity (he was raised in the Greek Orthodox faith but appears to have lost any religious convictions he may have had; his response to Aelfrida's proselytising reads more like another attempt to capture and retain her affections than a genuine conversion), it is obvious that what her older self described as a 'scarlet thread' of religion already guided her through the labyrinth of her life[12] and that religious enthusiasms increasingly occupied her thoughts. But if one of her parents' aims in sending her to Italy was to divert her

from preoccupation with her personal and particular brand of religiosity by means of attendance at a rigorous course of university lectures in a foreign language, postponement of the start of the university term and Aelfrida having to ask herself 'what am I to do with myself without lectures?'[13], spoiled their aim and her answer came pat: 'I had not asked myself what God would have of me here … At present I am to be given more time to think of Him and to cultivate the devotional spirit'.[14]

Thirty years later she explained why she behaved as she did: "I remember when I was twenty-one, spending the winter in Florence in order to study psychology and literature at the University. When I arrived … I found that, owing to the elections, the University would be closed for a month. I therefore determined that I would make the time a 'holy month'. (I was a Presbyterian then, but I must have had an instinctive appreciation of Catholic practices.) I decided to hear Mass every day in the Cathedral, visit all the city's churches in turn, and spend as much of my time as possible in meditation. I bought … a book of devotion, partly in Latin and partly in Italian, called *La Filotea*" (elsewhere she calls it a 'quaint and naïve devotional book which I have been reading with delight') "and moved by a great impulse towards God, I began my retreat".[15]

Her 'appreciation of Catholic practices' began by being emotionally overwhelmed by Mass at the Duomo: 'it was wonderful but absolutely sensual, an indulgence only to be allowed to one's self sometimes'. (In fact, she went there regularly, noting of the dearth of distracting sightseers on 1 November as tourists departed for the winter 'nothing but the Florentines … and, I think, God'.)[16] What she omits to tell us is that her appreciation of 'such practices' had begun even before she left Cambridge. Diary references to 'praying, weeping and praising God' and to offering Constantine's love for her at 'God's table during Communion' suggest that practices of this nature did not take place at St Columba's where the Communion ritual was different and where weeping and praying might be noticed by officious Presbyterian wives and reported to her parents, but in another church altogether. But where in Cambridge could Aelfrida find a small secluded church where she was unknown and to which her parents and their friends were unlikely to penetrate? Though the answer she provides ('St Mary's') is ambiguous insofar as it does not absolutely identify the church, one can deduce that it was not the Anglican church known as 'Great St Mary's' on the Market Square but Anglo-Catholic St Mary the Less (familiarly known as 'Little St Mary's') whose door, opening off a narrow lane leading from Trumpington Street to the river, was concealed from the inquisitive gaze of passers-by.[17] In

Florence, however, her craving for spiritual satisfaction led her to attend services or preaching sessions in progress at whichever church she happened to visit – of a sightseeing trip to San Miniato, for example, she wrote that she stayed for Mass 'for I could not help it … I found it indescribably beautiful … I felt a passion of devotion and joy';[18] she also made a point of visiting empty churches in order to be able meditate in beautiful, tranquil, and private surroundings. Localised political unrest then ensured that university lectures did not begin until 5 December and her 'holy month' extended to two. The unexpected extension provided her with ample opportunities to assuage her 'thirst', for apart from the Waldensian Mission and one or two teaching sessions in Sunday Schools attended by both adults and children, she had nothing to do save assuage it in various Roman Catholic churches whose lovely and uplifting services 'quieted [her] feelings'[19] and made her increasingly unsatisfied with Protestant ritual.

Wishing to share her new enthusiasm and modifying her earlier decision to 'cultivate her devotional spirit' instead of performing 'any active work'[20] for God (perhaps because Waldensians at the Medical Mission had reminded her that *all* Christians must proselytise), she read an Italian bible to fellow-lodgers at the Pensione Rigutini: 'oh it was hard … I meekly asked them if they would listen'; her embarrassment was lessened not only by their agreeing but also because 'I had done my hair *à l'espagnole* with a high comb, a floating black thing behind, and a scarlet flower in it, and felt that I looked handsome'.[21] Proselytising gave rise to so much unpleasantness between herself and a vociferous German fellow-lodger that she braved her mother's wrath and moved to the Pensione Corsi on the Via del Prato.

Once settled, she also wrote to and received letters from Constantine who missed her so much that he tried (unsuccessfully) to obtain a tutorship in Florence for the Christmas vacation: 'is it not a dear boy and am I not blessed far, far beyond my deserts?'[22] (Anatolia wrote too in reply to a letter of Aelfrida's in which the latter asked 'if I might sometimes tell her what I am doing, for I wished her to know me'; the letter, she added, 'was perhaps the most sincere I have ever written'. Believing from Anatolia's response that 'she ranks me among the people who understand', an addendum fifteen years later speaks volumes: 'poor mistaken Aelfrida!')[23] Absence from Constantine also made her heart grow fonder. On 11 November she received a letter 'and all in a moment … I knew that I loved him … I love him with the whole strength of my being, with a love equal to his own. At first I was frightened, for it is a very terrible thing to love one's husband passionately … Oh, let us marry soon,

Constantine, and then I can tell you the truth'. (It was in this entry, too, that she noted a startling discovery, namely that she had fallen out of love with Lord Kitchener: 'what has happened to my feelings about him I do not know … it is as though a black curtain had fallen over him and hidden him from my sight'.)[24] Two weeks later she wrote 'I long to tell [Constantine] that I love him … I do not think now that I am afraid of his knowing', adding that 'I must be married to him soon – to bear his name, to make him the father of my children. Lord, that this may be Thy will!'[25] At the same time, however, she made the curious comment that 'it seems wrong to withhold such knowledge from him, and yet it must not be written'. But why should it 'not be written'? And what was the 'knowledge' she could not disclose? Was there a parental prohibition in force to that effect – Constantine, indeed, complained that he found her letters from Florence 'cold' and Aelfrida herself admitted that she was worried about falling back into 'coldness' if parted from him again[26] – or was it because she herself felt that secrecy was necessary? And if so, why, and concerning what?

Reluctance to inform Constantine that she now loved him cannot be attributed merely to contemporary considerations of what was right and proper. It hints, indeed, it more than hints, at realisation that au fond she did not love Constantine and considered that joining her life to his was a mistake, her continuing ambivalence being demonstrated by her admission on 11 November that 'my love has been created by his' (i.e. was not willed or spontaneous) and by her franker admission of 13 December 'I believe I do not love him. Under great stress of feeling I imagined that I did, but I do not believe it to be true. I confess it with shame. I am in love with no one'.[27]

The need to solve her amatory and religious dilemmas was postponed by being able to plunge at last into the student life she might have enjoyed so much at Girton or Newnham but which in the event she explored only vicariously or peripherally. Unlike Cambridge, where female students existed but were not considered part of the university proper, Florence had no such inhibitions, and Aelfrida felt immediately at home at the Royal Institute of Superior Studies. (An English lady attending a public lecture there told a friend "there are women-students too. There is one of them". The friend stared at Aelfrida before announcing "Yes, she is quite the Italian type, isn't she?" 'Delight of Aelfrida!')[28] Her lecture schedule was heavy – three days a week she attended lectures on Philosophy from Francesco de Sarlo, an important twentieth century philosopher and experimental psychologist (after attending his lecture on the relationship between thought and the nature of the human body, she wrote 'it was the throwing open of gates of a new paradise of learning')[29]; on a further three she attended lectures on the History of Philosophy and, by special permission, 'students only' lectures on Greek Philosophers. Three days a week, including Saturday mornings, she attended lectures on Italian literature given by Guido Mazzoni, the well-known writer, translator, and literary critic. And as if coping with university-standard lectures in a foreign language was not enough, on Monday and Friday evenings she gave English lessons to two young men of her acquaintance. 'Hard work, my friends – for me!' she wrote of her life during December and January, though she added 'oh, I want to learn everything and see everything and know everything … *La tête me tourne quand je pense aux richesses de la vie*!'[30]

One of the young men to whom Aelfrida gave English lessons was Giunio Corsi, son of the proprietress of the *pensione* to which she moved on 2 December. Aelfrida found Giunio 'most attentive' and 'most attractive' and soon began flirting ('I don't want to fascinate [him], it bores me' yet 'I feel as if I must!!')[31] but though her acquaintance was brief, Giunio provided the key to her next adventure – her discovery of '*Giovane Italia*'.

The Young Italy Movement derived from a nationalist movement founded by Giuseppi Mazzini in 1832 while exiled in France because of his association with the revolutionary society known as the Carbonari. Attempted uprisings in Italy in 1834 and 1844 having failed, the Carbonari were superseded by the Risorgimento led by Cavour and Garibaldi. The Risorgimento's aims of Italian unification and independence were achieved in the 1860s and 70s and it would seem that by the time of Aelfrida's arrival in Florence in 1905 there was nothing left to fight for. But the Italy which came into being in the late nineteenth century was regarded by early twentieth century intellectuals in general and by a group of thinkers living in Florence in particular as having sold out to "the modest, myopic ruling class", Italy and Italians being only "pale shadows of the nation that had been envisaged and of the heroes that had created it." Italy was now "*Italietta*" (Small Italy) or "*Italia Vile*" (Vile Italy), a product of the "triumphant vulgarity of Italy's new masters, the lower middle classes and their new-found commercial prosperity based on hard work, sacrifice, and thrift" and a society "very different from the great nation that the Risorgimento had seemed to promise".[32] The Florentine intellectuals whom Aelfrida was shortly to meet through the unlikely medium of one "whose favourite conversation is about picture postcards"[33], were known as the *Vociani* from the title of their influential review *La Voce*. Seeing themselves as "a revolutionary vanguard, an enlightened elite that rejected all the meditations of bourgeois political life and

parliamentary democracy", the *Vociani* turned to philosopher and leading Italian intellectual Bernadetto Croce as one on whom to model their "assault on the constricting categories of thought and action" in which they found themselves confined but Croce became impatient with the *Vociani's* drift "into a mystical world that bore little relation to reality" and disassociated himself from them. They then looked to Gabriele D'Annunzio as the "poet-seer who would re-create Italy's Golden Age"[34] although, Aelfrida noted, 'his fatalism and his immorality are not generally approved of'.[35] And as one whose head was already spinning because of the sudden widening of her spiritual and intellectual horizons, she found herself unable to resist the spiritual and intellectual charms of *Giovane Italia* and of the young Italians who led it.

Her account of how she discovered 'Young Italy' through the unlikely person of Giunio Corsi is almost identical to an account written to her father on 21 December 1904: "Dear Oracle … I came here, as you know, longing to find the brilliant men and women who are going to make Italy a great nation again, the …'*Giovane Italia*', the '*dannunziani*', in fact the force and power of the country. And how was I to guess that Giunio Corsi who has been a clerk in a bank … had anything to do with '*Giovane Italia*'? Sometimes, it is true, he would make remarks that made me open my eyes" (she failed to say that Giunio had presented her with a bullet from his revolver as a keepsake three days prior to student demonstrations on 9 December) "and he gave me some of the books that represent modern Italian thought" (one was *La Vita Intima* by 'Giuliano il Sofista', pen-name of Giuseppe Prezzolini whom she was shortly to meet) "but I took that as showing deference to my tastes rather than any definite tastes of his own. When he told me that he was a great friend of all this circle of men, I simply did not believe him".[36]

An introduction to the salon at which the Young Italians met persuaded Aelfrida that Giunio Corsi was not only speaking the truth but was also 'the person par excellence to show me what I wanted to see'. It also persuaded her that she did indeed possess entrée into the circle and that (in a diary entry not transcribed to her father) she should give up flirting with Giunio and 'reserve him for higher things, to be the key to Modern Italy!'[37]

As her 'key' was shortly to depart for Egypt, Giunio handed over Aelfrida to young barrister Alfredo Bona, Alfredo offering to provide her with any books or introductions she required. (She was later warned that Bona was 'a follower of D'Annunzio not only in politics and literature but also in morals', a reason, maybe, for her keeping a long hatpin beside her bed "for fear of trouble".)[38] She also met, and formed a real friendship with, Robert Assagioli, the young medical student providing her with literature about the movement including copies of the periodical *Leonardo* (to which he contributed articles) and with tickets for a lecture *Quale è il valore della scienza?* to be given by Giovanni Papini (otherwise known as 'Gian Falco') at the *Circolo Filologico* where she would be 'introduced and received as one of them!'

Aelfrida's visit to the *Circolo Filologico* on the evening of 16 January 1905 (she was chaperoned by Mrs Cox) was the highlight of her stay in Florence: 'Papini … took out his notes and solemnly, impassively, sublimely made fun of all the serious people present, of his subject, and … of the grave and weighty traditions of the *Circolo Filologico*. It was the wittiest thing I have ever heard, … rage for some of the professors, perplexing for most of the ladies … and for the *Leonardisti* and for me pure, undiluted, exquisite enjoyment'.[39] After the lecture she was introduced by Dotti, a Young Italian friend of Giunio Corsi's, to the most important members of the group, Giovanni Papini and Giuseppe Prezzolini.[40] Of the two "Young Futurists"[41] (the ages of the group to which Papini and Prezzolini belonged ranged from sixteen to twenty-four), Aelfrida felt more immediate rapport with Prezzolini whom she described as a 'mystic' ("Gian Falco uses him as a telescope when he wishes to look at the stars")[42] but it was with the pushier and 'interesting but too supercilious' Papini, "a man whose instinct forced him to dominate and [who] only cares for thought as a whip that will make him master of his fellows"[43], that she was to carry on a sustained friendship and correspondence. Prezzolini and Papini having been formally introduced, she spoke primarily to the latter, congratulating him on the way he had treated his contentious topic. 'Then followed', she wrote, 'such a time as comes to a girl only twice or thrice in … her life – Papini and I fought a duel of absurdity and paradox … while the twenty or thirty young men who had not been introduced murmured applause at anything particularly brilliant'. Presently, however, 'I became aware that a young lady holding a salon in one of the most serious rooms in Florence was creating some sensation … so very, very reluctantly I bowed to Young Italy and swept away'.[44]

Unchaperoned meetings with members of the movement took place over the next fortnight. Though unsure if Papini's lecture marked the beginning or the climax of her involvement with Young Italy, Aelfrida 'paid [her] price of admission' by taking out a subscription to *Leonardo*[45] and was thereafter gratified to receive articles, books, and letters. Towards the end of January, however, she had an unpleasant surprise, Dotti informing her that Young Italy in the shape of its more plebeian

members (Dotti was a pawnbroker's clerk) 'had come to the conclusion that I must marry one of them and live in Florence, and would I please make up my mind which'. (He also suggested that if one married her, the others could 'have a go at her'.) Realising what Dotti's suggestion implied – the young man supposed her to have money and regarded it as an affront to Florentine manhood if neither he nor one of his friends succeeded in bedding her – Aelfrida suddenly understood: 'what they appreciate in me is [only] my figure and my unused capacity for passionate emotion. I suppose that is what D'Annunzio taught them'. (As if to emphasise the D'Annunzian aspects of the affair, Constantine had recently sent her that author's *L'Innocente* and she had been asking herself if his choice of book was not indicative that 'all his love for me was nothing but desire and even to him the only gift I give him in marriage is my poor body'; a note added in 1919 lamented 'Alas, alas, it was more than half true'.) Fleeing to the Duomo for comfort, she found herself praying 'for purity, for safety, for strength … to the Mother of God'.[46] She then went shopping for cakes because Gian Falco and Roberto Assagioli were coming to see her that evening.

The evening was not a success. In spite of Gian Falco offering to undertake her further education in the manners and customs of Young Italy and urging that she write for *Leonardo* and of Assagioli's gentle adoration (Aelfrida had earlier decided that in spite of being charming and much in love with her, he was also too young – he was only a year older than Eustace – to flirt with), both of which did much to assuage her lacerated feelings, she was beginning to feel extremely unwell. The nightmare day, its horrors compounded by receiving a letter from Corsi warning her against his friends and by Falco asking her how she, '*che ha le passione forti*', dared to go alone among the young men of *Giovane Italia*, ended with her retiring to bed feeling feverish and shivery.[47] A three-week gap in her diary entries (25 January to 14 February 1905) reveals the cause: 'I have been ill with influenza, jaundice, and then a mild attack of bronchitis', or, as a note added in 1919 stated, 'it was really malaria and blackwater fever and I nearly died'.[48]

Apart from a septic finger and a brief illness in November 1904 which Aelfrida ascribed to food poisoning but which, with its associated shivering fits, fever, and 'delirium'[49], may have been the onset of what was to prove a recurrent problem, Aelfrida's health was good during the earlier part of her stay in Florence. (Her diary, however, fails to mention the "palpitations" noted by her mother[50], precursors, it may be, of the panic attacks from which she later suffered.) Her medicine chest contained quinine but she does not say if she actually took it prophylactically in what was then a malarial area and she certainly gave her supply to Giunio Corsi when he left for Egypt, and if she is correct in saying that her malarial infection was indeed 'blackwater fever', she was fortunate to survive. (Family accounts of her illness paint a different picture, her mother describing it as "Influenza, Jaundice, Bronchitis [and] Congestion of the Lungs" and Julius as "a fever which was taken for malaria"[51], but as Aelfrida herself was later to suffer debilitating attacks of what sounds very like malaria, we may assume her diagnosis, if not its dramatic reference to a malignant form of the disease, was correct.) She was nursed at the Pensione Corsi by Mrs Cox, moving as soon as she was well enough to travel to convalesce at the convent of the Little Sisters of Mary at Fiesole.[52] Even the prospect of going there made her feel better: 'I am in the highest spirits about it. A new and unexpected experience!'[53]

After the hectic excitement of her 'new thirst', of university life, of *Giovane Italia,* and of her recent illness, Aelfrida revelled in Fiesolean peace: 'it is so restful here. I feel quieter and stronger already ... The convent is very still. There are [sacred] pictures everywhere ... and ... a holy water stoup in my room'.[54] Her room overlooked the garden 'where bamboos and palm trees grow, with hyacinths already in flower ... and a statue of Our Lady guarding the place with outstretched hands. Beyond are olive groves ... where you look up through silver leaves at the sky as blue as a kingfisher's wing ... and ... in the distance is Florence and the silver river. It seems as though the beauty of it must make me well ... And somehow all of it seems to be holy ground'.[55]

The convent may have been ideal from the point of view of Aelfrida's physical recovery ('the nuns are so peaceful and cheery and oh, so very, very kind'; they were, her mother noted tartly, "paid – and handsomely – to be kind!")[56] but was the worst possible place from the point of view of her spiritual and emotional well-being. A quiet retreat in a tranquil Catholic convent with English-speaking nuns who, wrote Aelfrida, made no attempt to convert their only Protestant patient (according to Julius, the nuns did their best to convert her, the Tillyards not realising at that point "how near they came")[57] but were happy to answer questions regarding 'Catholic practices' to which she felt drawn (she was there over Lent and Easter and recounts in detail the services she attended) might have seemed an excellent opportunity for Aelfrida to disburden herself of some of the religious doubts which beset her during her 'holy month', for her 'new thirst' had by no means been assuaged by regular attendance at Mass. But growing familiarity with Catholic ritual posed more questions than it answered: "now and then, it is true, I was happy and at peace; but more often

it was with me as with John Bunyan. No sooner did the Devil see me on my knees than he would ... suggest that I should quit my prayers and have done. The words he poured into my ears were words of doubt. Not the kind of doubt that finds its way into the heart and paralyses the affections" (a reference to the ambivalence of her feelings for Constantine, though she also worried lest religious feelings too were no more than 'emotional pose' and that, as with men's affections, she was someone who only 'played' with religion), but "the doubt that torments the intellect".[58]

It was not, however, to the nuns that Aelfrida turned for help (she found the Sisters 'too placid to be instructive' though a book lent by one of them explained 'the Mystery of Benediction', a service she attended every day)[59], it was to others temporarily resident at the convent. Although her initial impression was that 'the other patients look most uninteresting'[60], she soon found them to be intelligent men and women, Anglican converts or seminarists or priests seconded for rest and recuperation from the Irish College in Rome, with whom she could discuss matters of doctrine on a sympathetically intellectual level. The discussions and her readings in the books they lent her did little to calm her feverish questioning ('I had first enquired half-frivolously about the Catholic Church. Now I ... am sincere ... Did Jesus found a Society, a Church for the help and guidance of His people? ... if He founded a Church is it the Catholic Church?')[61]; indeed, they brought her close to breaking point. Years later she explained why: "I could see no way to God but *the way of correct belief.* It seemed to me that, until my mind had grasped all the intricacies of Theology, I could not adore God ... True, I was in my place at church ... but theological difficulties seemed to make any personal apprehension of the Deity impossible. At one time my anguish was so great that I feared I must lose ... my reason. I was certain that my mind must be clear on all points of dogma or I should be lost everlastingly; and reach dogmatic certainty I could not".[62]

Recurrence of fever brought respite ('I had peace again for the few days I was too tired to think')[63] but once recovered, she brooded again 'on the different concepts of the Christian life. Studying my Bible, I find confirmation of almost anyone's conception. This is very puzzling'.[64] Following 'another feverish attack and more misery' during which insomnia caused her to 'think and think and think' obsessively on the 'theological difficulties' she perceived as implicit in what she wished to believe and which were at odds with the Presbyterianism in which she had been brought up she wrote 'it must, I suppose, do one good to battle, but oh, how it hurts!' Obsessive questioning ("'Church or no Church?"

"Fallible or Infallible?" "Trans-substantiation or a mere sign?" "Individualism or Authority?"') continued until she became 'perfectly sick and dazed'. She also worried about what it would mean to her father, an Elder of the Free Church, if she became a Catholic but finally found a sort of peace in deciding to press on with her enquiries 'guided by God himself' and in concluding that if conversion was not to be, she had at least learned to love and reverence Catholicism.[65]

Thoughts of religion reminded Aelfrida of home. 'You see, I have to be very well informed and my faith, if possible, very very clear, because of Constantine. He used to be an atheist but God's Grace allowed me to help him and he believes. But – did I tell you? He wrote to me not long ago that he loved me better than God. It is terrible … When I get home, there will be many, many things to discuss about religion'.[66] Her making a sudden connection between her putative fiancé and her faith may have been stimulated by another patient, a former Anglican now a tertiary in the Third Order of St Francis[67], exhibiting a fragment of what she said was St Francis' tunic for shortly afterwards Aelfrida had a dream-vision in which she seemed to pass 'all the hours in familiar and sweet conversation with San Francesco and Santa Chiara'.[68] The dream, though comforting, had important implications: although Aelfrida merely remarked at the time that she found it edifying, her statement that were she Catholic, she would rate it rather higher than a dream suggests that she also noted the relationship between the two saints, a man and a woman who, though they loved each other passionately, sublimated their passion through their ministry, their deep *spiritual* companionship being one she would prefer to exist between herself and Constantine. Yet she continued to protest that she was prepared to marry Constantine and bear his children and had written on Christmas Day 1904 that 'the day of the gratification of motherhood no longer reminds me of joys in which I will have no part. Now there is Constantine my husband. And there will be, if God wills, some day, children'.[69]

Early in March 1905 came the diary entry 'Prepare for a shock! I am going to leave Italy on Friday'[70] (she had already sent a telegram requesting "journey money")[71], Mrs Cox having deemed it advisable for her to return to Fordfield as soon as her health allowed. Her family too had been 'really unhappy about [her]'.[72] Catharine Tillyard chiefly wished to free her from the clutches of Young Italy (she had offered to come to Florence to nurse her daughter but Aelfrida refused her care), Alfred Tillyard was beside himself with worry about her health, and Constantine was concerned about her enthusiasm for Catholicism and her involvement with less reputable members of *Giovane Italia*, all three agreeing that it would be better for the daughter and fiancée who, in the course of a five month stay in Italy had got herself "into all kinds of muddles and nearly [died]" to "return ignominiously to England, long before [her] year's studies at the University [were] at an end".[73]

To her surprise, Aelfrida realised she was glad to go. True, she been seriously ill but she had also been lonely; apart from Giunio Corsi (who had gone to Egypt 'and had no further use for [her]')[74], she had made no real friends and in the convent had found that 'what with being ill and being so much alone', she was 'forgetting how to laugh'[75] and struggles with Catholic dogma and disillusion with Young Italy compounded her unhappiness. Reviewing what had happened during the past six months in order to 'prove … the extreme sourness of the Florentine grape', she asked herself 'What am I sorry to leave?' Acquaintances at the Pensione Corsi, her English friends, and her fellow-students at the *Instituto Superiore*? 'No – I don't care a bit about anyone I met in Florence'.[76] Lectures? No: 'I have missed so much that I fear I should understand but little were I to go back. Besides I shall never be a philosopher'. Young Italy? 'Possibly. I am, however, being delivered from temptation – the theory I can pick up from the *Leonardo*. Besides I have been having a most interesting half-intellectual, half-humorous correspondence with Gian Falco'.[77] (On 27 February she had written with a rare flash of humour that 'too much lives of the Saints' made a return to secular matters imperative and that she had 'written to Gian Falco – and [her] note was not quite as stiff as it was meant to be', asking for the January edition of *Leonardo*. His reply, addressed to '*mia cara alumna*', advised her that he was at her disposal as far as her education 'in things Leonardesque' was concerned. His letter cheered her enormously.)[78] The sights of Florence? 'Seen 'em'. The convent? 'Yes, indeed … It has been good to be here … The best bit of it all … *the time spent nearest to God*'. (Note added in 1919: 'that was always the best'.) She then asked herself 'shall I moralise on what I have seen and learnt in Italy? Shall I ask myself if I am more capable, more interesting, more loveable, better for all my experiences? It has been a wonderful, a glorious time. But I have suffered – and others too'.[79]

What *did* Aelfrida gain from her stay in Florence? She herself chiefly remembered the 'loveliness and ecstasy of beauty and devotion', her 'intellect [being] on fire with problems [and] adventure', and 'quick glowing contacts with people and things'.[80] What she failed to list encompassed confidence in her ability to stand on her own feet in a foreign country and in crisis situations; an ability to speak a foreign language like a native and to so immerse herself in the life of a country that she was accepted *as* a native; acceptance as an intellectual by members of the Florentine intelligentsia who took her on her own merits as someone with a good mind and the ability to apply it; the opening of that mind to new disciplines such as Experimental Psychology, a subject on which she had not yet touched; being accepted *for herself*, not for who she was in relation to other people (Alderman and Mrs Tillyard's only daughter Frida; Julius' witty younger sister Tit; Eustace's glamorous older sister; Constantine's flirtatious but rather intense sweetheart who was allowed to spend hours with him alone in the Fordfield garden but was forbidden to accompany him to a concert unchaperoned.) In Florence she was Signorina Tillyard, an independent young woman – a 'New Woman' almost – who explored the city alone and made friends with the Italians who lived and worked there and who informed her mother how much she loved being there and that it grieved her "to see the days slip by".[81]

She broke her journey home in Paris where she was met by her mother, '*très émotionée*' at the sight of her too-thin and still-unwell daughter. (Florence, Catharine wrote to Julius, "cannot have suited her from the beginning".)[82] Anatolia was there too, giving her violets and 'quite ready to adore [her]'. (Undated note: 'No, Aelfrida! No! She didn't!') Ominously, she was accompanied by a girl 'tall, slender and pretty in a delicate youthful way' whom she and Constantine had known for two years. Aelfrida herself 'had been feeling so much that [she] had become quite numb'[83] but of three things she was quite sure: that 'the Catholic Church' was the one to which she must adhere; that God would 'guide [her] right', albeit with the proviso that He would only do so were she 'in earnest' (God, she noted, 'does not guide those who play with religion and whose deepest feelings are but emotional pose' and she would be miserable did she not believe that God would guide not only herself but '[her] husband and the children he [would] give [her]' too)[84]; and that she 'must' and 'ought to' marry Constantine Michaelides, the man whom she had persuaded herself that she loved 'with the whole strength of [her] being [and] with a love equal to his own'.[85] And of whom she had once noted that at the bottom of her heart she did not take him 'seriously'[86] and he of her that he had once thought her ('forgive me') 'unscrupulous'.[87]

'The question now is', Aelfrida asked herself the day before leaving Italy, 'will Constantine love me when he sees me? With all my conceit and undaunted admiration of myself, I always think "Who am I that *he* should love me? How can *he* love me?" I long to see him …' They met the day after her return: 'I waited for him trembling and I know I turned white when I heard his step on the

terrace. He came straight in, put his arms round me, his head on my shoulder and burst into tears … As soon as he touched me I knew that I should never be afraid again and that everything was henceforth to be more beautiful than ever'.[88] She was mistaken.

## Notes

1   GCPPT 1|1|12 5 October 1904.
2   Following a series of industrial and agrarian strikes the previous year, September 1904 saw a general strike in Italy. Riots broke out in several places, including Florence, fomented by professional agitators who hoped to transform very real working class grievances into frankly revolutionary activities (*Encyc. Brit.* Vol. 15 p 81). Delaying the start of the University term until after the General Election in October 1904 was a matter of political expediency because it lessened the chance of student riots. Aelfrida reports an anticlerical student demonstration held not long after lectures began on 6 December; it was broken up by sailors from the barracks on the Borgo Ognissanti, their commanding officer threatening to fire on the crowd unless it dispersed.
3   GCPPT 1|1|11 14 June 1904.
4   Tillyard, HJW. *The Letters of ACW Tillyard* (MTC) Letter from Catharine Tillyard to Ancifera (Annie) Gregory of 31 May 1904.
5   GCPPT 1|1|11 3 June 1904.
6   KC *Annual Report* 17 November 1934.
7   GCPPT 1|1|12 October 1904.
8   JCA MSS R.2.32. Tillyard, EMW. *Reminiscences.*
9   GCPPT 1|1|12 18 December 1904.
10  ibid. 16 October and 11 November 1904.
11  ibid. 17 October 1904.
12  GCPPT 1|1|11 Postscript 21 January 1919.
13  GCPPT 1|1|12 20 October 1904.
14  ibid. 16 October 1904.
15  GCPPT 1|1|12 17 October 1904.
    Tillyard, Ae. *The Closer Walk with God* pp 48–9. The book was most likely an Italian translation of St François de Sales' *Introduction à la vie dévote* of 1619 in which the lady for whom it was originally written is addressed as '*Philothée*'. De Sales' final admonition to '*Philothée*' to "*Vive Jésus*" ("Live Jesus") would have had great appeal for Aelfrida at this point in her life.
16  GCPPT 1|1|12 8 October and 1 November 1904.
17  GCPPT 1|1|11 4 June 1904.
18  GCPPT 1|1|12 25 October 1904.
19  ibid. 22 October 1904.
20  ibid. 16 October 1904.
21  ibid. 24 October 1904.
22  ibid. 25 October 1904.
23  ibid. 19 October 1904.
24  ibid. 11 November 1904.
25  ibid. 26 and 28 November 1904.
26  ibid. 4 and 8 April 1905.
27  ibid. 11 November and 13 December 1904.
28  ibid. 14 December 1904.
29  ibid. 12 January 1905. De Sarlo founded the Experimental Psychology Laboratory in 1903; it was considered one of the most important Italian centres of experimental research and was equipped with some of the most advanced equipment of the time. Aelfrida, writing in January 1905, hoped that she would know the laboratory 'intimately' but the strain of following 'the explanation of weird psychological machines' reduced her to a day in bed (GCPPT 1|1|12 20 January 1905).
30  GCPPT 1|1|12 12 December 1904 and 12 January 1905.

31 ibid. 2 and 4 December 1904.
32 Baranski, Z. and West, R. pp 83–84.
33 GCPPT 1|1|72a Letter from Aelfrida to Alfred Tillyard of 21 December 1904.
34 Baranski, Z. and West, R. pp 83–84. Constantine sent Aelfrida several of D'Annunzio's books while she was in Florence, her only comment on *La Gioconda* being that it seemed curiously far from her current religious preoccupations (GCPPT 1|1|12 18 October 1904).
35 GCPPT 1|1|12 11 January 1905.
36 GCPPT 1|1|72a Letter from Aelfrida to Alfred Tillyard of 21 December 1904.
37 GCPPT 1|1|12 9, 20 and 28 December 1904.
38 GCPPT 1|1|12 4 and 15 January 1905.
    Tillyard, HJW. Introduction to *The Letters of ACW Tillyard* (MTC).
39 GCPPT 1|1|12 11,13 and 17 January 1905.
40 Giovanni Papini (1881–1956) was a Florentine poet, editor, and essayist. His "formal education was relatively limited … but through his assiduous reading and attendance at university lectures as an auditor, he acquired an impressive culture and knowledge of literature and philosophy". In 1903, in association with Prezzolini, a school friend, Papini founded *Leonardo*; after *Leonardo* ceased publication in 1907, Papini was associated with Prezzolini's periodical *La Voce* founded in 1913. Papini's first important book *Il Crepuscolo dei Filosofi* of 1906 represented "a precocious reassessment of the ideas of major nineteenth century thinkers" and concluded "by rejecting their oppressive influence on contemporary thought because of their lack of philosophical certainty". (If the lecture attended by Aelfrida in Florence in January 1905 was a preliminary study for Papini's book it is not surprising that 'it was rage for some of the professors' who, as Aelfrida put it in her letter to her father, were largely 'conservative [and] stick-in-the-mud'). Giuseppe Prezzolini, (1882–1982) was a self-taught critic, essayist, journalist and teacher who after serving in the army in the Great War and a career in teaching and the cultural service of the League of Nations, devoted his time to "assembling a historical record of his early friendships and correspondence", notably the two volume edition of his correspondence with Papini between 1900 and 1956, *Storia di un'Amicizia* (1966–68). Although Aelfrida is not mentioned in *Storia*, a photograph which forms its frontispiece shows the two men at the time of their acquaintance with her (Bondanella, P. and Bondanella, J. pp 422–423 and pp 472–473).
41 Tillyard, Ae. *Christian Old Age* pp 15–16 (GCPPT 2|17).
42 Tillyard, Ae. *The Florentine Movement* in *The Independent Review Vol. 9 No 31*. April–June 1906 pp 71–79.
43 GCPPT 1|1|12 17 January 1905.
    Tillyard, Ae. *The Florentine Movement* (ibid).
44 GCPPT 1|1|12 17 January 1905.
45 ibid. 18 January 1905.
46 ibid. 14 February 1905.
47 ibid.
48 ibid.
49 ibid. 12 November 1904.
50 Tillyard, HJW. *The Letters of ACW Tillyard* (MTC). Letter from Catharine Tillyard to Julius Tillyard of 21 March 1905.
51 ibid. and Introduction.
52 The convent – the sisters were sometimes known as the 'Blue Nuns' from the colour of their habit – belonged to an Irish Catholic nursing order; its probable position was the former Villa Girolama, via Vecchia Fiesolana, above the Badia and below the Ospedale.
53 GCPPT 1|1|12 17 February 1905.
54 ibid. 18 February. 1905.
55 ibid. 18 February 1905.
    Tillyard, Ae. *Messages* p 67.
56 GCPPT 1|1|12 18 February 1905.
    Tillyard, HJW. *The Letters of ACW Tillyard* (MTC). Letter from Catharine Tillyard to Julius Tillyard of 21 March 1905.
57 Tillyard, HJW. Introduction to *The Letters of ACW Tillyard* (MTC).
58 Tillyard, Ae. *The Closer Walk with God*. p 49.
59 GCPPT 1|1|12 27 February and 5 March 1905. Benediction of the Blessed Sacrament is an optional extra-liturgical ceremony sometimes subsumed into the evening office of Compline. An intensely dramatic and recently revived English Catholic rite (the conducting priest incenses the Sacrament which, removed from the tabernacle, has been placed in an enthroned monstrance and makes the sign of the cross over the congregation with the monstrance) the ceremony is accompanied by prayers and singing of a hymn or other holy song. (Heimann, M. pp 46–51 and 91) The ceremony's impressive ritual with its curative and protective associations appealed deeply to Aelfrida at this vulnerable period of her life (GCPPT 1|1|12 19 February 1905).
60 GCPPT 1|1|12 18 February 1905.
61 ibid. 28 February and 9 March 1905.
62 Tillyard, Ae. *The Closer Walk with God* pp 49–50.
63 GCPPT 1|1|12 5 March 1905.
64 ibid. 25 February 1905.
65 ibid. 28 February and 14 March 1905.
66 ibid. 27 February 1905.
67 The Third Order of St Francis, founded in 1865, was a Catholic institution aimed at enabling lay people of either sex "to partake as nearly in the Franciscan tradition as was compatible with life in the world". (Heimann, M. pp 131–132). The Order's Rule prescribed poverty and chastity (vows were not strictly binding and were renewable yearly), grace before and after meals and moderation in all things. Biographies of members of the Order suggest a connection between membership and the experiencing of psychophysiological phenomena (ibid p129) particularly in women, a point of particular relevance with regard to Aelfrida, who, though never a member herself, was both suggestible and (much later) a tertiary.
68 GCPPT 1|1|12 25 February 1905.
69 ibid. 25 December 1904.
70 ibid. 11 March 1905.
71 Tillyard, HJW. *The Letters of ACW Tillyard* (MTC). Letter from Catharine Tillyard to Julius Tillyard of [ ] March 1905.
72 GCPPT 1|1|12 11 March 1905.
73 GCPPT 2|27|2(4).
74 GCPPT 1|1|12 16 March 1905.
75 ibid 28 February 1905.
76 ibid. 16 March 1905.
77 ibid. 11 March 1905.
78 ibid. 27 February 1905. The 'lives of the Saints' referred to by Aelfrida may have been *Lives of the English Saints* of 1901 (ed Barrow, J. et al) or Alban Butler's earlier 5 volume work encompassing 'Fathers, Martyrs and principal Saints', of which numerous editions had appeared since 1759.
79 ibid. 11 March 1905.
80 GCPPT 1|1|38 2 August 1930.
81 GCPPT 1|1|72a. Letter from Aelfrida to Catharine Tillyard of 7 November 1904.
82 Tillyard, HJW. *The Letters of ACW Tillyard* (MTC). Letter from Catharine Tillyard to Julius Tillyard of 21 March 1905.
83 GCPPT 1|1|12 23 March 1905.
84 ibid. 9 and 11 March 1905.
85 ibid. 11 November 1904.
86 GCPPT 1|1|11 28 May 1904.
87 ibid. 23 July 1904.
88 GCPPT 1|1|12 16 and 24 March 1905.

# Malise

To her surprise and annoyance, Aelfrida's homecoming was not greeted with the acclaim which followed her return from Switzerland ('no one cares to hear a word of what I did in Italy … they all seem to wish to forget the whole episode')[1] and Catharine Tillyard seemed remarkably informed regarding her daughter's antics in Florence; possibly Mrs Cox, privy to some of Aelfrida's dealings with *Giovane Italia* and to all her illnesses, been more aware than the latter knew and had reported back. Another cause of surprise and annoyance was her discovery that Constantine had become so firmly entrenched at Fordfield during her absence as to have become 'one of us' (he had even adopted the family habit of signing off letters 'Big Love'), acceptance underlined by the recruitment of "Major Michaelides" to the staff of the *MCJ*, an event marked by a Latin editorial by Julius describing "*considerabili jubilatione*" and by an article and poem from the 'Major' himself.[2] He also appeared to revel in his first taste of proper family life since boyhood: as a small child he had tried to block out his parents' quarrels by putting his fingers in his ears, his mother frequently left home or, if living at home, left the children alone while she socialised in 'an atmosphere of intrigue and passion, love of money and glamour of sex', and, wherever the family lived and to Argyris' annoyance, filled the house with 'odd people'.[3] An only son, he enjoyed the brotherly presence of Eustace, now an irreverent adolescent (of a grandiose story recounted by Constantine, Aelfrida remarked that it was 'like the Book of Revelations … but Swab made rude remarks'; a note of 1919 adds 'Swab was right, I fear')[4] and with Catharine Tillyard in particular had achieved a loving friendship, nicknaming her 'Chiara' (the name by which she will henceforth be known) and chatting to her by the fireside for hours. She in turn relished the company of a young man whose similarity to dead Conrad was striking (had Conrad lived he would have been sixteen); indeed, his physical beauty caused even the Oracle, less moved than the rest of his family by his prospective son-in-law's charms, to note 'the strange unearthly radiance' which seemed to stream from Constantine's face and hair.[5] (Chiara nicknamed him "the marble Faun" because she sensed something "unhuman" about him[6] and both Julius and a child visitor described him as or asked him

**Anatolia Michaelides (centre) with Irene (left) and Helen (right) Michaelides**

if he were "young … Phoebus Apollo".[7] In 1905 too he was still very slightly built and ate 'as though from courtesy to mortals and not as if he needed food')[8]. And if he was sometimes high-handed as when he read "before [her] eyes" a letter from Julius to Aelfrida which, Chiara noted, she herself was forbidden to see[9] or extravagantly emotional (he had made as if to kiss his future mother-in-law in public), he was always ready to go down on his knees to apologise and one could easily forgive a young man who had become "simpler, better and more loveable" and "so much less fond of D'Annunzio" as a result of "coming to Fordfield"[10], who throughout his fiancée's absence in Florence and his mother's opposition to his marriage had behaved "very finely [and with] extraordinary self-control, dignity and determination"[11], who was devotedly in love with Frida, and who because of his family circumstances 'did so need to be loved'.[12]

Was it therefore his wife's affection for this re-incarnation of Conrad which persuaded Alfred Tillyard to give his approval to Constantine and Aelfrida becoming officially engaged soon after her return from Florence? Constantine was still a 'penniless undergraduate' but his prospects had improved insofar as he was confidently expected to get a First and after that a college fellowship, and this too may have swayed Aelfrida's father in favour of the marriage. His devotion to Aelfrida during their six-month separation and her own comment shortly after her return that it was because Constantine was not with her in Italy 'that [she] could not get well' and that even in Cambridge she felt 'cold and listless' if he was absent[13] (that the latter feeling was 'against her will' was one she shared only with her diary) may also have influenced the Oracle's decision.

That her father's permission was not altogether agreeable can be seen from events leading up to Aelfrida's formal betrothal; indeed, it seems she bowed reluctantly to pressure from parents who misinterpreted her true wishes. Prior to Constantine paying a flying visit to Hessle (the Oracle and Chiara insisted on "signed sanction" from his parents before "publishing the engagement")[14] where he 'routed his father out of bed in the small hours … got a sermon and consent to his engagement' and to Anatolia writing a gushing letter to Chiara giving *her* agreement (but at the same time writing to her son to dissuade him)[15], Aelfrida had confessed that the emotional numbness experienced on leaving Florence had not left her. She blamed it on the 'crush' on Lord Kitchener which 'had filled [her] life for many years and now it had gone all of a sudden, but … it [had] left [her] tired out and perhaps without the power of caring again'[16] but to her diary confessed that she felt 'unhappy at being "settled", angry at [her]self for being so'.[17]

Dislike of being 'settled' was rapidly outweighed by discovering that she had a rival for Constantine's affections in the shape of Valentine Crocius, the 'tall, slender and pretty' girl met at Anatolia's flat in Paris. Aelfrida's naming her as 'Vally Crocius, of course'[18] shows Vally's existence came as no surprise; failing to obtain a tutor's post in Florence for the Christmas vacation, Constantine had spent the holiday in Paris with his mother and 'half desperate' because of Aelfrida's 'cold and selfish' letters from Italy and despairing of ever making her care for him, had let the Luxembourgeoise music student 'pet him'.[19]

Vally Crocius, was, in fact, Anatolia's preferred candidate for her son's future wife, something which became evident during a visit to Cambridge on which Anatolia was accompanied by Vally herself. In the course of the visit she informed Chiara (who immediately informed her daughter) that not only had she tried to dissuade Constantine from marrying Aelfrida but that 'all along she [had] … been deliberately working to get him away … using all her influence' and using besotted Vally as bait.[20] A pair of determined ladies thwarted her: Lady Frazer and Aelfrida herself. The Strawberry Eater had

always looked benevolently on "the love between the two stars of *Les Femmes Savantes*"[21] and, casting an unfavouring eye on Anatolia's latest attempt to separate 'Vadius' from 'Bélise', removed Valentine firmly from the Tillyard orbit on the pretext of showing her the gaieties of Cambridge's May Week. Aelfrida herself, aware that she had recently lost a prospective husband to Elfrida Sturge, decided to carry out her threat to place her fiancé 'in a … temple with a high wall all round to keep off tourists'[22] such as Vally and, realising at last that blowing hot and cold on Constantine's affections was likely to drive him away ('he says his love has been in vain and that he must go [back] to Paris "where they cared for him"')[23], took the step she was reluctant to take. Following an emotional episode (not a quarrel, she assures us) during which it seemed she might lose Constantine for ever, she made the momentous decision: '*il s'agissait de mentir*'. If keeping Constantine was a matter of lying, she would lie and in a D'Annunzian scene, she did: 'I knew what he was waiting for. It was my duty to say it … "sometimes I have thought I loved you and then again I was cold and indifferent … let me think". I struggled with myself. He waited with clenched fists and bent head. Then I came and put both my hands in his. "Absolute surrender," I said. His joy was almost more than I could bear. I too was utterly exhausted with my emotions … I had to say "*je t'aime*" three times before he left me'.[24]

A further dimension, however, is added to this touching and climactic scene when we consider where it took place, Aelfrida's diarised comments thereon, and other documentation touching on her relationship with Constantine. As to place: the scene occurred early in April, the day being perhaps being too cold or too wet to be enacted in the garden. From written and pictorial evidence provided by Aelfrida herself we may deduce that Fordfield's dining room and drawing room both contained mirrors, the former two, the latter one. If the scene took place in the dining room (the only really private place on the ground floor because used only at meal times) it would have been reflected twice, once in the overmantel mirror, once in the mirror opposite, and thereafter to infinity in a series of endless vistas of diminishing Constantines and Aelfridas, if in the drawing room once but if in that room and in front of the elaborate mirror later bequeathed to Girton College, as if the 'celebrated Bélise' was taking part in a play whose *coup de théâtre* took place beneath a proscenium arch from whose summit a gilded head looked down at the drama unfolding below. But in Aelfrida's stage-managed scene no mirror reflected the truth, none of the vistas led "on and on into enchanted distances"[25], and the denouement was tragic: she may have been 'utterly exhausted' by her emotions but she added 'don't laugh!' (*ne riez pas!*) to remind a biographer that she was acting. Remarks made as she (metaphorically) removed her make-up ('so you see it is said. Is it true. Do I love him'[26]; note the lack of question marks) suggest that a letter to Julius written five days later was lying or deluded. Of Constantine she wrote that she now loved him "wholeheartedly", belonged to him "absolutely", and that that feeling made her extremely happy – elsewhere she noted that when she began to love him 'it was like letting loose a mighty river' – but also that she had told no one save Julius of this and that her mother continued to praise the "moderation" of her feelings and the "coolness" of her – professed – emotions[27], and a note added in 1919 apropos her 'absolute surrender' entry of 8 April 1905 (with consummate irony, the note follows immediately after an entry in which she records that 'this volume of my diary ends while Constantine is writing by my side and I am loving him with my whole being')[28] asks querulously how could she have known that a year or two later Constantine would be 'growling over his dinner and over my religion and over all our life together'.[29]

Aelfrida's acting ability was enhanced by her ability to compartmentalise her life according to the part or the play she currently enacted and with it the emotion appropriate to the act or scene in which she currently appeared; she also possessed an actress's ability to turn her emotions on and off at will. (A striking example is provided by her behaviour immediately following the dramatic scene in July 1904 during which Constantine, weeping in her lap, called her his 'wife': she took part in a 'Floral Fête' at which she flirted with Geoffrey Hatten knowing that her pretty butter muslin dress '*à la Grecque*' was wasted –'a tragedy, *mes amis*, a tragedy'[30] – on the man with whom she was flirting because she was pledged to Constantine.) The demonstration of abilities such as these gives a curiously disjointed effect to her account of what must have been a time when her emotions were fully engaged on an daily basis; only on very rare occasions does her emotional train of thought carry over to the following day and even if rendered sleepless by what transpired the previous day, she appears to forget or disregard it immediately on waking. But though her ability to compartmentalise and control her emotions was effective in terms of performance art – the scene ended, the curtain fell, the play was over for the day – it was liable to leave her emotionally vulnerable when she found herself involved in events which could not be concluded so neatly because they involved people or events unamenable to compartmentalisation or stage management, marriage being one and Constantine another.

Three further problems manifest themselves at this point. They concern Aelfrida's perception of her fiancé, her recording of current events, and her religious convictions, the latter in particular contributing to what was indeed a 'very emotional time'.[31]

As part of the scene of high drama staged between Constantine and herself on 8 April 1905 (did she don an appropriate costume: of a confrontation with Anatolia she wrote that she had not only 'prepared [herself] for a … scene of melodrama' but had also ensured that she looked 'handsome and well dressed' – had she also rehearsed it, as with John Forbes Cameron? – and on a later occasion noted that, appropriately clad, she had gone through a ceremony "with the rather sad dignity"[32] befitting her interpretation of it), she had noted apropos her non-questions regarding love and the truth that she did not love Constantine as one 'should love a man' but as one 'would love a beautiful creature that is half a god'. (Her demi-god, she added, could 'read the secrets of men's hearts', loved her in a fashion 'not like the earthly loves of men', and was almost 'too fair' to be anyone but an Immortal.)[33] Unfortunately for all concerned but particularly for her most recent 'victim', confusion of an ordinary, if rather pretentious, young man with a normal young man's interests and appetites with the 'gods' of childhood games surpassed the normal idealisation expected of a fiancée who had recently stated that 'at last' ('it seems') she loved him[34], became the delusional creation of an 'ideal' to be worshipped as one might worship a god – or God.

The second problem concerns interpretation of Aelfrida's contemporary diary entries in view of her new reluctance to confide in it. This is rather more than merely 'the fault of Constantine that my diary does not get written'[35] for she had always found or made time before, particularly when her life was especially interesting, as now. Recurrence of malaria provides a genuine excuse ('Oh diary, have you been neglected!')[36] as does reticence regarding sexual experimentation between herself and Constantine ('I can never tell you what Constantine and I do', after he has been submitting her 'to all kinds of sensual caresses')[37], as does inability to recall or transcribe the brilliances of Constantine's repartee ('Oh swine of a diary, before whom I cast none of the pearls of Constantine's conversation!')[38] or a wish not to transcribe some of the more intimate things he said or wrote to her because 'some things are too sacred to be told'.[39] There is more to her omissions than this: on 17 May 1905 she notes that 'almost everything that counts is left out'.[40] While this may also be attributable to a wish not to disclose the intimacies of her relationship with Constantine, placing the entry in context produces some surprises – not only had she recently recorded a very intimate moment ('in the evening as I lay in his arms and he in mine – that is our way of saying good-night – I felt and he felt the supreme happiness of loving each other perfectly and purely with our souls, with our minds and with our bodies. When he wants to kiss me he says *"baiser tes lèvres"*')[41] but she had also described a friend who 'could hardly attend to anything I said but gazed at Constantine in a sombre despairing way'[42] and written of a ball that 'a dance when one is engaged to be married is very different when one is *not*' – and we discover a major cause of current chagrin: 'Aelfrida, your flirting days ARE over'.[43]

The deleterious effect of impending matrimony on 'Flirting' may be one reason for describing her diary as declining in value as a 'psychological document' but there was, it seems, another: her first and only meeting with Ralph Paget and her introduction to Constantine's best friend and future best man, Eric Silvanus.

To Ralph Paget Aelfrida took an instant dislike, less, it seems, because of his 'oddly sensual face and glittering eyes' or because, though 'intelligent and cultured', he had a tendency to 'melodrama' and more because he was a 'beast' who had fallen 'madly in love with "Tino" in Rome four years ago'.[44] This unwelcome reminder that there was something unwholesome about Constantine's friendships with men (or women; 'Juanita' was always at the back of her mind) was underlined on 1 May 1905, the day on which she first met 'the man Constantine loves best – Eric Silvanus, [a] young schoolmaster ... described by Constantine himself as 'one of "our sort"'[45] and as someone with whom he regularly corresponded. Eric, twenty-four to Constantine's twenty-two and Aelfrida's twenty-one, was described by the latter as possessing 'a noble face and ... beautiful ... dreamy eyes' (but also as if he did not look as if he had 'lived'), as watching over Constantine 'in a way that is lovely to see', and as someone whose 'great powers of self-restraint and intense moral convictions' must be influential on a young man over whose developing moral character he rejoiced 'unfeignedly'. In spite of fears that there might exist between Eric and Constantine a love that dare not speak its name (Aelfrida professed ignorance regarding homosexual love but Constantine's friendship with Oscar Browning and her own references to "mysogyny" (*sic*) at King's[46] suggest awareness that not all sexual preferences were heterosexual), Aelfrida treated Eric 'as though we had always been friends' and Eric, it seems, reciprocated by accepting her 'as a fit mate for Constantine': 'we can be friends without fear', she noted happily.[47] But there was more, for Eric's and Constantine's names were associated a few months later with regard to a Christmas visit engineered

by Anatolia without informing her son, a visit concerning which Aelfrida informed her diary that such matters were 'among the many things' she no longer confided to it.[48] But what in terms of this or any other aspects of her relationship with her fiancé are we to make of two statements also made by her about this time? The first, written only a few months before her marriage, notes that although she fears her diary is not as 'clever' as it used to be, this was important because she was 'cleverest ... when most vacuous' and because neither cleverness nor vacuity mattered 'except from the point of view of my future readers'.[49] The second, written within days of her formal engagement, runs as follows: 'if I wrote or had even written a true and full account of what passes between Constantine and me, you would have the most wonderful book ever written. But I neither can tell you, nor wish. And when I do try, I see with horrible clearness what an utterly wrong impression I have given and how I had better have lied from the beginning'.[50]

As the official fiancée of one of King's most popular undergraduates, Aelfrida was able to enter more fully into collegiate and intercollegiate social life than as Julius' younger sister, enjoying intellectual sparring matches with philosopher John McTaggart, the Trinity lecturer on Moral Sciences noted for his ability, unusual in many of his contemporaries, to get on well with the wives and girl-friends of his students and colleagues, though she had begun to feel that he had become so 'purely mystic' as to have forgotten all the arguments that led him to his present philosophy.[51] She also met 'earnest and would-be remarkable' Goldsworthy Lowes Dickinson (another protégé of OB's) who, despite trying 'to bear the world's burdens on his shoulders and ask[ing] questions which neither intellect nor his heart can solve'[52], was supportive to Constantine when the latter abandoned History for Moral Sciences: questions of ethics and political thought did not come easily to one whose interests were musical and literary.

Other luminaries entered her orbit during Constantine's last term at Cambridge and the months which followed: philosopher GE Moore whose *Principia Ethica* of 1903 was on Constantine's reading list; Lytton Strachey, then a sixth year student at Trinity, and Bertrand Russell who had left Trinity almost a decade earlier. Her pen-portraits of Strachey and Russell are pin-sharp: at a tea party in Constantine's rooms 'there was present one Strachey, a curiously long and bony creature with a ... little squeaky voice that reminds you of the top notes of a clarinet when the instrument gets beyond the player's control. He dressed in brown and green as though he were trying to look like a lean, bony tree just bursting into leaf ...[and] revealed himself as a man of some taste and wit'[53] and, on a more formal occasion, 'when I had seen an ungainly man with a plain but vaguely aristocratic face come in and be introduced as Russell I looked at Constantine to ask "Is this the Honourable Bertrand, the mathematician, the philosopher, the *dialectician,* the man who  is as clever as he can be without being a genius?"'[54] It was, so she decided to draw him out, asking him (apropos M[c]Taggart) to define and discuss the meaning of the word 'mystic'. And a future economist whom she already knew and had disliked since childhood she described as 'the great Maynard Keynes whose … pose in college is rather atheistic and obscene, at home or to me, puritanical and shocked. He is brilliant, superficially, anywhere', even, it seemed, on a visit to Fordfield during which Maynard greeted Constantine, his contemporary at King's, as 'the one intellectual oasis in the desert of Nonconformist conscience here' but condescended sufficiently to show interest in her own remarks.[55] But Constantine, intellectual oasis or not, was currently smarting under the humiliation of finding himself at his graduation ceremony 'in a crowd of third and second class men' and not 'the loudest, certainly the most sympathetic cheer' Aelfrida had ever heard a graduand receive or OB's love (he had visited Constantine's rooms to assure him of his continuing affection and had 'poured out praises' of 'Mickey's' genius) or the sympathy of friends who blamed his 'peculiar English' or 'that damned idiot' his examiner for his misfortune [56] could console Constantine for failing to secure a First.

That Constantine had had premonitions of failure is shown by entries in Aelfrida's diary: his being 'absurdly sensitive' about his impending examinations; that if she 'had not been a perfect angel we should have *possibly* quarrelled'; her taking him for long walks in an attempt to 'slacken the bent bow of his mind'.[57] Overnight the histrionics of the previous months disappeared; now she offered solid loving support. But was this qualms of conscience: she had neither dissuaded Constantine from spending almost every afternoon and evening at Fordfield (he arrived after morning lectures and left at 10pm) nor pressed him to devote more time to study and to revision. But failure to gain a First was his own fault too: it seems he believed Aelfrida's and OB's assertions that he was a genius with such a good mind that a First Class degree was virtually assured. (His achievement of a First Class in Part 1 of his examinations would have encouraged this supposition.) And had he continued with History, support from OB (the 'pastoral don' par excellence)[58] might have ensured the First he coveted and expected.

As it was, 'it is all over at last. Constantine has got a Second Class. It is a nightmare'. (Note added 1919 'How absurd to feel that the world had ended because of the second class!')[59] His parents were furious. Anatolia called him selfish and lazy. Argyris accused him of ingratitude. Constantine vowed never to return home until earning his own living. Aelfrida's comment was 'much melodrama' but it is obvious that her distracting presence in Constantine's life at this crucial time had been noted, particularly by his mother.[60] She therefore decided to make the best of a bad job and in an act of splendid rationalisation stated that 'to feel convinced … that a second class was the best thing in the world for Constantine is more than philosophical, it is sublime!'[61] Constantine then decided to apply for a prolongation of his existing scholarship in order to work for a fellowship (he had been so sure of gaining a First that Aelfrida had helped him choose a topic for his dissertation), though less because he thought he deserved one than because a fellowship would 'give him time to do something in literature'.[62] He was supported in this by his mother: Aelfrida, seeing 'the guiding hand of Providence' in a second class degree, wished Constantine 'to have courage and simply to go in for literature'. Leaving it to James Frazer and others to effect introductions to further her fiancé's literary career, she decided her own contribution would be provision of financial support (she immediately gave him £50, all she had, and prayed 'oh, money, roll in fast!')[63], for at this point Argyris withdrew funding, Constantine being told 'to make a career for himself or starve'.[64]

To her delight the newly-opened County School for Boys appointed her teacher of French (she was 'through experience, a most excellent teacher' and soon got the boys talking French)[65] at a salary of £40 a year. She was therefore assured of a steady income and a job which, though it occupied four mornings a week, allowed her plenty of time for other paying pursuits: private French and Italian lessons given to friends and undergraduates, two series of subscription lectures on Italian literature and history, and 'a little book of French games for schools' composed with a view to publication.[66]

To say that Aelfrida's literary career was initiated by her fiancé's academic failure and that serious thoughts of earning a living by her pen began now is inexact: she had been producing novels, short stories, and dialogues since 1897 with the hope of becoming a 'celebrated authoress'. But though inspired by Constantine's efforts at producing articles suitable for publication (the contrast between his *Swinburne and the Sea* of 1905 and 'his D'Annunzio phase' of the previous year was 'so striking as to be funny')[67], she believed she herself lacked his 'spark of the divine fire', noting that although she would make 'a better schoolmaster … cook, sanitary inspector, journalist, soldier, parson, lawyer, doctor, actor, flower girl, or clerk' than he, she lacked literary 'genius'. Constantine, blind to the limitations of his own genius, agreed, but told her that her work would need to be as good as Jane Austen's, George Eliot's, or Charlotte Brontë's if it was to be published; Aelfrida responded that if her books made as much money as those of best-selling authoress Marie Corelli she would be satisfied[68], but encouraged by his belief in her, worked on steadily. But whereas Constantine was the first to earn money – an article by him appeared in the January 1906 *Independent Review* founded by Lowes Dickinson to encourage young writers – his literary career never took off. Aelfrida, on the other hand, though discouraged when some short stories were rejected by an unnamed publisher in December 1905 ('I feel as though I had been given a penny and told to go away!')[69] not only pursued a literary career but was also the first to publish a book, something Constantine never achieved in spite of prodigious plans mooted early in 1906 'of writing novels made of the life of the whole world as Balzac's were made of the life of one nation'.[70] (Balzac was the subject of his dissertation.) As it was, his hopes of a fellowship and of a literary career foundered together and it was Aelfrida whose powers of observation, capacity for hard work, and tenacity regarding uncooperative publishers was to provide them with an income until they married and who was later to live (to some extent at least) by her pen.

Her career proper began with a 'little book of French games' *Le Livre des Jeux* (it actually consists of twelve games and seven songs) published by Blackie on 23 March 1906 and looking like 'a new born child … small and red' because of its crimson cover.[71] The games, though using fairly advanced conversational French, would be familiar to English pupils, for they included charades, 'I love my love with an A', and recall in correct order of ever-lengthening lists of items; the songs have easy tunes (musical notation is provided) and mostly consist of well-known compositions for French children e.g. *Sur le pont d'Avignon, Savez-vous planter les choux,* and *Il était une bergère.* But where one would expect to find *Alouette, Au clair de la Lune,* or *Frère Jacques,* one finds three songs whose sinister or sexual undertones make them unsuitable for Edwardian *jeunes filles* aged nine to thirteen: *Chanson de la Mariée* reminds a new bride of the less pleasant aspects of marriage and *La Pêche des Moules* has a young girl inform her mother that she will not go collecting mussels again because she is molested by village boys. *La Maison Blanche* is the oddest of the three with its description of people living '*intimes/Unis et joyeux*' in a white house built by themselves who become victims of "*méchants envieux*" who first invade, then break up, the "*noeud fraternel*" and pour scorn on the harmony which formerly prevailed there.

The theme of *Chanson de la Mariée* is a traditional one insofar as it describes the downside of marriage (no more 'Flirting', submission to a master–husband, domestic drudgery); indeed, Aelfrida addressed it again in a later poem (as also did Mary Coleridge, with whose poetry Aelfrida was familiar, in her poem *Marriage*)[72] and if the poem is not wholly Aelfrida's own, was probably adapted from a French source, a contention supported by a verse referring to the care to be lavished by Breton peasants on their flocks and herds. The case with *La Pêche des Moules,* also a traditional song, is slightly different insofar as '*moules*' is an obscene term for the female genitalia, something which Aelfrida could have learnt from Constantine of whom she concurrently records that on long unchaperoned walks in the Cambridgeshire countryside they were wont to 'play with' each other and by whom a suggestive poem (*A little Piece about a French Pussy*) appeared in a contemporary *MCJ*.[73] *La Maison Blanche*, on the other hand, was a song heard by Aelfrida in Lausanne as she watched a procession celebrating cantonal freedom from domination and although her inclusion of what is essentially propaganda in a book of children's songs seems odd, it is not: of the three poems described, it comes closest to reflecting her state of mind while composing *Le Livre des Jeux*. While the *Chanson* may reflect her reluctance to marry and to become 'settled' and *La Pêche* her ambiguous distaste for and attraction to sexually-charged 'games' ("*caresses*") played (as of necessity they had to be, given that social mores enforced premarital chastity) between herself and her fiancé during their long engagement, *La Maison Blanche,* with its intimations of lives formerly lived in happy fraternal intimacy but now rent asunder by envious outsiders who deride what was once a flourishing and God-given relationship[74] hints at something more. It may also provide another reason for Julius' sister's reluctance to marry: her beloved brother had been physically if not emotionally supplanted by another man.

Improbable as this interpretation seems, it can be supported by reference to what is already known – and to what will soon become evident – concerning Aelfrida's propensity for presenting events or emotions from her own life in a literary disguise whose esoteric meaning is difficult to decipher unless or until one knows what was going on in her life at the time she wrote; indeed, a comparison of *Le Livre des Jeux* with two books of poetry for children written by her some years later (*Bammie's Book* of 1915 and *Verses for Alethea* of 1920) confirms how much of her contemporary emotional state is evoked and again reveals that some sentiments expressed are inappropriate for children of the ages for whom the poems were written. Other anthologies expressive of her current state of mind will be discussed in due course with reference to her life at the time but worth noting here is that all serve the same function of acting as a safety valve for opinions and emotions it was unwise to express, even in her diary.

Subterfuge or not, Aelfrida was proud of her first book, gratified at the sum (10 guineas) received from her publishers, and pleased that her teaching activities had raised £30 ('ground off the grindstone, that money, Aelfrida') which she hastened to invest in order to augment it.[75]

Subscription lectures on Italian literature took place in 1905 and 1906 at Fordfield; following the lecture, Italian conversation and an informal discussion of Aelfrida's chosen topic took place around the tea-table. The first series began on 14 October 1905, the second on 23 October 1906, subjects ranging from Gabriele D'Annunzio and Giovanni Verga (Verga's books echo those of Argyris Ephtaliotes in their depiction of lower class and peasant life and regional affiliation)[76], to Benedetto Croce[77] and to Giovanni Papini and *Giovane Italia*.

A lively correspondence with Gian Falco had continued since Aelfrida's enforced return from Florence, her '*caro maestro*' being 'most useful and most kind'[78] with regard to preparation of her lectures. A month before her lecture on Young Italy he supplied background material and further information (Aelfrida's comment on the lecture was that 'it *was* good', being 'clear and interesting and imaginative'[79]; given her enthusiasm for the cause and her having received advice from one of its leading proponents when preparing it, it could hardly have been otherwise) and asked if she would allow him to send her 'presents'. (His circumspection was due to the fact that a postcard he had sent her quoting Marlowe's line "come live with me and be my love" had been answered by Aelfrida with Constantine's copy of *Principia Ethica* and a letter informing her wooer that she was engaged; Gian Franco replied asking her to disregard his message.)[80] He subsequently sent journals and books, his own *Il Crepuscolo dei Filosophi* among them, and warned her that he might even come to England to see her. ('There is no mistaking what he means', Aelfrida noted, adding 'he is useful to me, but...')[81] By May 1906 his letters had become even 'more frequent and more – friendly' and he had sent her a photograph of himself for her 'private use'. (His still plying her with books, letters, and journals as late as November 1906 caused Constantine to declare that Falco had not only been in love with her but was still.)[82] He also begged her to translate his book *Il Tragico Quotidiano* into English[83], a labour of love on her part and one which might bring financial rewards in its train.

The translation, completed in July 1906, was submitted to Fisher Unwin, together with 'Italian essays' (possibly transcriptions of her lectures) written during the previous year. Fisher Unwin's initial interest (she was commissioned to write sufficient essays to fill a book and to translate two of Gian Falco's books to be published in one volume) was not, however, sustained mainly because, prominent as Gian Falco was in Florence, the Young Italy movement was thought to be of little interest to English readers; publication was therefore regarded as an uncommercial proposition and the project abandoned. This was doubly unfortunate insofar as it affected Aelfrida financially (she had hoped for £25 for *Il Tragico Quotidiano* and for a smaller sum for her essays) and wasted her hard work of the previous months. (It was not till some years later that Gian Falco's writings were published in translation in England but not in translation by her.) There was, however, the consolation of being thought capable by an Italian writer of translating his works, a compliment indeed to one whose mastery of the Italian language was of comparatively recent date. But inspired by her correspondence, her translations, her lectures, and her own writing on matters Italian, Aelfrida began a novel with an Italian theme; sadly she and it soon 'became too D'Annunzian'[84] and it was not until March 1907 that she began *Our Lady of the Grove* 'all about modern Italy'.[85] A further novel, provisionally entitled *The Love of Money*, begun in January 1906 and described as 'a very serious novel about the lower middle classes in Cambridge'[86] for which she had plenty of 'copy' from her own experience of those forced by circumstances to live frugally or in degrees of poverty, was, however, accepted by Fisher Unwin to be included in their First Novel series.

Amusing letters arrived to cheer her before and after Christmas 1906. Earlier that year Gian Falco had travelled to Paris where he was introduced by his latest mentor, Henri Bergson, to important artistic and literary figures; he also met two people who would have liked to be numbered among them: Constantine and Anatolia Michaelides. The meeting between Constantine and Gian Falco was cordial, her '*maestro*' writing to Aelfrida that he had fallen as much in love with her fiancé as with herself ('*proprio come con Lei*') and Aelfrida recording her delight: 'of course [Constantine] always charms women but it is an excitement when men succumb too'.[87] Of Gian Falco's subsequent comment on Constantine's mother, namely that he liked her in "spite of her love of humanity", Aelfrida commented dryly 'he has insight'.[88]

'Love of humanity' notwithstanding, Anatolia's behaviour towards her prospective daughter-in-law continued '*très exigeante*'.[89] Her deliberate trouble-making had already roused the Oracle to unusual anger; it had also made Aelfrida determined to 'deal with' Anatolia once and for all ('I am stronger than she is') and to make

Anatolia love her by force.[90] Confronting Anatolia at the time of Constantine's graduation (the occasion on which, despite Aelfrida's belief that exacting Anatolia was 'adapting herself wonderfully' to the engagement and would soon learn to love her son's fiancée, Mrs Michaelides confided to Chiara that she was trying to separate Constantine and Aelfrida but, disconcertingly, that she believed Constantine was right in his choice of wife and that Chiara's daughter was the one woman in the world for him)[91], Aelfrida told her that she saw through her machinations but loved her in spite of this. Recording that Anatolia was 'grateful and humble' and had been 'dealt with' to such an extent that the battle of wills between them, though 'not altogether won', would soon be over, she was dismayed to discover that Anatolia had gone straight to Constantine and been 'very brutal'.[92] Regarding the mother-son conflict as 'perhaps a necessary stage before *he* takes the upper hand', she played a devious game, 'just for future reference' releasing Constantine from his engagement and telling him he should not break with his family because of her; she also sent him to talk to Anatolia and to tell her that although the intimacy between him and his mother could never be the same ('he will never be ruled by Anatolia as he used to be', was her private thought), the 'more-than-son' friendship between them would not be broken. To Anatolia she said that Constantine's love for his mother was so beautiful that rather than spoil it she had offered to break off the engagement. Anatolia, in reply, took Aelfrida in her arms 'and I knew the battle was won, once and for all'.[93] And having decided that Anatolia had now come to terms with the fact that she could not dominate Aelfrida but must adore her instead, the latter, believing that everything was now arranged perfectly (note of 1922 'I was a proud and vain young thing but … ought I to have failed so hopelessly?')[94], accepted an invitation to Hessle.

Though aware of the dissention between Constantine's parents ('they generally differ'[95]; in fact, they lived largely apart, Anatolia in Paris with Irene, and Argyris in Hessle with Helen), Aelfrida found it difficult to come to deal with the Michaelides' troubled relationship and with the effect this had on their son. Constantine sided with his mother, even to the extent of maintaining 'a kind of Anatolia-cult' in which he hoped his fiancée would join him as 'a kind of priestess' but it was not until she saw mother and son together that she realised the closeness of their relationship was and became 'a little disgusted at the … physical familiarity that existed between [them]': Anatolia undressed in her son's presence, wandered about in her night gown, kissed him on the lips, and sat on his knee. She also believed this excessive closeness to be the basis of Constantine's 'unjustifiable and irrational

hostility'[96] to Argyris, a finer character but 'for all his … passionate southern nature, his exquisite artistic sense, and his understanding of life', so weak that he could not or would not stand up to his dictatorial wife.[97]

With Argyris, 'dark, thin, adoring his cold wife, infinitely sad, and homesick for his Greek island', Aelfrida immediately became friends: 'he worships me … you should see how he follows me about with his wonderful eyes, how he gives me flowers and trembles with joy when I kiss him'. She had not understood why Constantine and his father had been strangers to each other but now saw that this was Anatolia's doing; she also realised that although Anatolia tried to impress her by reading aloud sentimental passages from a diary kept during Argyris' courtship and the early years of their marriage, she was now almost completely estranged from him, manifesting her dislike by being 'very nasty' to him and by alienating his only son from him. She was, however, 'fascinating' towards Aelfrida, 'trying to make [her] her slave by being quite adorable' but in a desperate attempt to dissuade the latter from marrying her son, discussed the folly of loving only one man and the miseries of married life and hinted that Aelfrida's own married life might also be less than satisfactory. Argyris too confided details of the tangled relationship between himself, his wife, and his son, not in an attempt to effect a breach between Aelfrida and Constantine but because he believed his son unworthy of her.[98]

Hoping she had effected a reconciliation between Constantine and Argyris ('Argyris, because of me, believes in his son and wishes to know him, while Constantine loves him and almost for the first time kissed him as he was leaving')[99] and between Anatolia and her husband, Aelfrida was soon disillusioned: her attempts at intercession had made matters worse. Anatolia began by writing 'very cruel' letters to her son in which she attacked his fiancée and tried to alienate Constantine from her. Constantine swore his mother's influence was so deadly that he would prefer not to see her for two or three years (in fact, he was to spend Christmas in Paris with her) while protesting that his devotion to her was greater than before.[100] (Commenting on this in 1924, Aelfrida noted perceptively that when Constantine's affection for herself was at its height, 'he was bitter against his mother – the slave hating his chains – but he could never free his unconscious from her influence'.)[101] Argyris, on the other hand, continued to be kindly disposed towards his son and affectionate towards Aelfrida, sending her presents of books inscribed 'to dear Aelfrida' and enjoying her company on a second visit to Ephtalon made in his wife's absence: 'he approves of me thoroughly … I have made mistakes with Anatolia but I shall not with him'.[102]

As daughter and sister of classical scholars Aelfrida should have known to fear Greeks bearing gifts. First there was Constantine with his gift of books, chiefly the D'Annunzios which she read with a mixture of fascination and loathing and who kissed her for the first time after presenting her with one. (Dick, the dog, who obviously knew a thing or two about Greeks and gifts, 'got up from the hearthrug and flew at him'.)[103] Now there was Argyris with his *Tales from the Isles of Greece,* but as Aelfrida was about to learn, Argyris' consent to her marriage with his son was not given unconditionally: long before Constantine asked for formal consent to marry Aelfrida, he had informed her that he could not afford to marry at once because he had no money of his own and that his father expected him to support his mother and two sisters in the event of his (Argyris') death.[104] As Argyris was then only fifty-five, the likelihood of his dying before Constantine was earning enough to support himself, a wife, and three other female dependents seemed remote but the possibility had to be faced and financial provision made.

What Aelfrida did *not* know and did not discover until a year after her engagement became official, was that when Argyris gave his consent in April 1905 he had made his son promise in writing that he would not marry until Helen and Irene were provided for by 'marriage or income'.[105] The promise came to light during Aelfrida's second visit to Hessle in April 1906 when she confided to Helen that she and Constantine hoped to marry sooner rather than later and Helen immediately informed her father. Aelfrida's prediction that 'in the very near future there may be trouble with Argyris' and that 'the matter may be serious'[106] was fulfilled, the 'Argyris business' being settled only after negotiations between herself, her fiancé, and his father during which Argyris released his son from his promise but only if Aelfrida and Constantine did not marry for five years. They disagreed, and when, in spite of further negotiations, Argyris continued recalcitrant, Aelfrida 'put the whole matter in the Oracle's hands'.[107] The two fathers appear to have reached an agreement but Aelfrida, it seems, was forced to repay money advanced to Constantine for current maintenance from her own earnings. She makes no further comment with regard to the matter or to her accidental discovery that the latter had been less than honest with her in concealing the matter for a year; she did, however, express her annoyance by smacking Constantine's face ('I must have hurt him … He took it sublimely'), rationalising her behaviour as an attempt to help Constantine by 'cut[ting] away all his worries' (*sic*), he having been concerned that he and Aelfrida had been 'wrongly exciting' their

love if their marriage had to be postponed until Helen and Irene were married or dowered.[108]

That Anatolia may have had a hand in the matter may be deduced from her arrival at Fordfield the following month with the intention, said the Oracle, of discovering if the 'Argyris business' had caused the hoped-for rift between her son and his fiancée.[109] If so, she was disappointed, the relationship being 'more wonderful than ever'.[110] But why did Aelfrida herself not use the 'Argyris business' as a legitimate device for breaking her engagement to Constantine, an engagement undertaken with so much initial reluctance on her part? Was it pride that stopped her or a desire to prevail over Anatolia? Or was it, as she continued to persuade herself, her love for Constantine? But it was another matter altogether which nearly occasioned the rift desired by her future mother-in-law: the church she now believed to be hers 'more than any other'.[111]

Shortly after returning from Florence in March 1905 Aelfrida experienced an upsurge in her desire for closer adherence to the doctrines of Roman Catholicism. Constantine was not at first sympathetic, saying that 'religious she would always be but a Christian, no' and accusing her of not believing everything she thought she did, and on her informing him that man's first duty was to save his soul 'no matter at what cost − even at the cost of … one's earthly happiness', saying she was 'the most utterly heartless and coldly selfish' person and that Christ Himself would be the first to condemn her if she continued in her belief. (Note of 1919: 'alas, was he jealous even then − or did my love of God leave my inmost heart cold to man?')[112] A year later, however, and having himself studied Catholic theology in the interim, he was accompanying her to 'that place that I have chosen mine'[113], the Catholic church of Our Lady and the English Martyrs which stood "steadfast [and] challenging, at the four cross-roads"[114] of one of Cambridge's traffic hubs, they praying together there ('sometimes I can pray *only* there')[115] and even attending services, especially Benediction because of 'the dear convent at Fiesole'.[116]

But problems of a religious nature continued to arise whenever Constantine and Aelfrida 'talked over' Catholicism, their talks hurting her 'so awfully that [she] felt ill from the pain'. (Irritatingly, given the importance of the subject, she had 'no time to explain [it] to you, diary'.)[117] The problems were unwittingly worsened by Gian Falco sending her a new novel by Antonio Fogazzaro, *Il Santo*. (The volume, part of a trilogy, depicts the conflict experienced by the hero, a religious ascetic, between his religious beliefs and his love for a woman who first tries to turn him away from his vocation but is later won over by his sincerity and ministers chastely to him until his death.)[118] That the novel appealed to Aelfrida is evident from her own attempts during 1905 and 1906 to combine sacred and profane love ('I cannot dissociate my love of Constantine and my love of God')[119] even at the risk of her relationship with the former becoming as chastely spiritual as that of Fogazzaro's characters or of St Francis and St Clare – or even ending altogether, for Constantine continued 'rather cruel' about her obsession. He did, however, investigate the possibility of her converting to the Greek Orthodox faith or of both becoming Catholics in order to reconcile their religious differences but in the event did nothing, saying that their hearts 'might indeed have been satisfied but not their heads'.[120]

Constantine's chief objection to Roman Catholicism was that the secrecy of the confessional undermined the absolute openness and trust which should exist between husband and wife[121], an ironic belief given Aelfrida's discovery of his secret contract with Argyris. He also feared lest continuing attendance at Our Lady and the English Martyrs (following increasingly acrimonious discussions she now attended alone, kneeling 'before each of the Stations of the Cross and pray[ing] that God might make the truth plain to [her]')[122] would cause her unilateral conversion to the Catholic faith.

Constantine' worries coincided with those of Aelfrida's parents, Chiara chiding her gently and the Oracle as was his wont making no comment but speaking volumes by his behaviour. Although theirs may have begun as concern that it was hardly proper for a baptised Presbyterian and the daughter of well-known pillars of the Free Church to be seen on her knees and sometimes in tears in a Catholic church, the Tillyards soon became so worried about Aelfrida's mental state (they did not go as far as Constantine, shortly to inform his fiancée that rather than let her sacrifice herself to 'wishes and delusions', he would prefer to kill her)[123] that they asked the family doctor to talk her. Dr Weston, according to Aelfrida, told her that she was 'burning herself up with too much thinking', banned her from 'serious reading or writing', and said she was 'not to think about *problems* of any kind'. Though agreeing with the accuracy of his diagnosis concerning the fragility of her mental state, she found it difficult to live the quiet life he recommended – 'he tells me I *must* waste my time' – because wasting time was so boring and because filling pages of her diary with trivia ('7.30 Awoke. 8.00 received a visit from my father who very civilly [enquired] about my health') was unlikely to endear her to future readers.[124] And when even a chance remark by her mother was enough to set her ruminating on Roman Catholicism, 'it was only because [Constantine] helped that [she] was able to be *sane*'.[125]

It was not, however, her obsession with Roman Catholicism per se that caused doubts to be cast on Aelfrida's sanity, it was also the recurrence of doctrinal and dogmatic problems which beset her in Fiesole. One of the priests resting at the convent had been a Father Orozy, an English convert (from Presbyterianism, as it happened) whose personality embodied 'the modern liberal Catholic character at its best'[126] and whose rigorously intellectual exposition of New Catholicism and loans of books on the subject both inspired her interest in and exacerbated her indecision on matters doctrinal: 'on the one hand the infallibility of the Catholic Church, on the other "Thou, oh Christ, art all I want"... It must, I suppose, do one good to battle, but oh, how it hurts!'[127] The amalgamation of Father Orozy's liberalised intellectualism and Fogazzaro's ascetic hero emotively urging the Pope to reform the Catholic Church by purging it of falsehood, greed, conservatism, and excessive clericalism[128] caused Aelfrida's intellectual interest in New Catholicism to collide with emotions aflame with love of the Church itself. (Her interpretations of the teachings of Roman Catholicism in general were sometimes 'so grossly wrong', however, that she felt she ought to apologise to every priest she met.)[129] At the same time, therefore, as she sympathised with the aims of those who wished to create a church freed from the trammels of stylised ritual, of devotional writings of a conventional and unthinking piety, and of a narrow-minded theology unable to come to terms with modern scientific discoveries and methodologies, she desperately desired the comforts of the prescribed rites of Mass and Benediction, for only they, it seemed, could provide stability, meaning, and order in her unstable, meaningless, and disordered world.

Asking herself how she could resolve her 'torments – for torments they have indeed been', Aelfrida decided that the best thing for herself and Constantine was to become Liberal Catholics in the modern mould, allying themselves with those who believed in the 'new church' which would shortly arise 'out of the ruin of Infallibility and Ecclesiasticism and Clericalism' but at the same time maintaining their freedom of thought with regard to matters in which New Catholicism seemed out of step with their personal views on religion. Informing Constantine of her decision on a country walk over the Gog Magog hills to the south of Cambridge, she was dismayed to discover that although he agreed with her ideas on New Catholicism, he believed it to be 'treacherous and foolhardy' to convert on her terms. He also reminded her of a promise made earlier never to take an important step such as this without his concurrence and company. Realising that they had reached a crisis in their relationship (only a few days earlier she had announced that if Catholicism were as true as she believed it to be, she would prefer Constantine to become a priest rather than marry her), Aelfrida came to a desperate decision. Returning home she 'prayed as I have never prayed before and then got the Bible and took the first oath I have ever taken in my life: "In the name of Almighty God – I promise never to join the Roman Catholic Church unless my husband asks it of me. Meanwhile I will do nothing to persuade him to take such a step but I will rather resist the influence of the Church, believing as I do that it is a wrong and harmful one"'. She later described the oath as 'dramatic, but … nonetheless in deadly earnest', adding that to take it was not only 'right' but also that 'only I know what it means'.[130] What it meant, of course, was putting her 'whole soul and body'[131] in Constantine's power as expressed in her promise of 'absolute surrender'.

Her oath by no means concluded the affair. Realising that she could no longer safely express religious preoccupations *en clair* even in her diary, Aelfrida made the conscious decision to codify what she dare not write or speak. With the exception of *Epping Forest*, the first nine poems in the section headed 'Early Sonnets' in her first book of poetry, published in 1910, read like disguised diary entries for the period April–December 1906; furthermore, because they are dated they can be correlated with diary entries revealing aspects of her life when the poems were written. She does not say why she subsequently decided to publish such extremely personal poems or why she was prepared to run the risk of embarrassing Constantine, Chiara, and the Oracle to whom the significance of the poems would be abundantly clear. Was there, perhaps, an element of revenge in what she did? Or was she desperate to reveal her privy thoughts to future readers of her diaries or diary-substitutes because of the important messages which would be transmitted to those whose more complete and possibly more sympathetic understanding of her religious and emotional dilemmas would vindicate her not very 'sane' behaviour of 1905 and 1906? If the latter, the 'Early Sonnets' section of *To Malise* can be ranked among her earliest published expressions of the *Apologia pro vita sua* to which all but one of her subsequent published and unpublished works contribute.

A significant 'explanation' appears in a sonnet of 1906, D'Annunzio's *Il Piacere, The Child of Pleasure* being a novel of which she later noted 'I hated *Il Piacere* and wished Constantine had not given it to me'.[132] She was reading it during the visit paid to Argyris and Helen Michaelides in April 1906 three months after swearing her oath to the former's son and latter's brother that she would not convert to Catholicism without Constantine's consent. Discussions between Aelfrida and Constantine preceding that crucial event had occurred a week earlier on the day in which Aelfrida's hurtfully expressed wish that her fiancé become a Catholic priest 'and many other similar bits of blasphemy against our marriage' were juxtaposed with overtly sexual behaviour, the snug at the public house where they had tea seeing 'much that even inn rooms might conceivably be shocked at'.[133] Her behaviour during the visit to Hessle is strikingly coincident, combining as it does the sensuality of *Il Piacere* and religious fervour re-ignited (if the oath can be said to have extinguished it) by a visit to a convent. The convent, an Augustinian teaching order of French nuns, was already known to the Michaelides family and it was Helen's suggestion that she and Aelfrida visit it. Aelfrida entered trembling, for the experience brought her devotion to the Fiesolean convent and to Roman Catholicism flooding back; she became even more distressed when the Mother Superior, assuming from their conversation that she was a Catholic, invited her to partake in Benediction. She declined, but knelt instead before the Holy Sacrament with 'anguish re-aroused in [her] heart' to pray that God would help her keep her promise to Constantine. That evening, the elevated mood inspired by her conventual experience coincided with her reading of D'Annunzio's novel of 'morbid sensuality and spiritual rapture' to such an extent that she felt moved to embrace Helen 'as if I had been a man … I put my arms round her neck and drew her whole body against mine and when she let her head fall back I kissed her full on the lips and felt her quiver all over'. She then went to bed filled with 'a strange feeling of physical triumph' at having made Helen hers – and, it may be, at having circumvented Constantine's interdict to the extent of visiting and praying in a convent to which she went at the instigation of his sister on whom (in default of her brother) she had revenged herself by imposing on her the controlling side of her own nature. Her poem, therefore, does indeed merit the 'deep psychological interest' she bestowed on the whole strange episode.[134]

She later repented her actions, writing that the diary entry distressed her and asking 'was I mentally a little unwell after too much emotional strain and physical overwork or was it the Devil urging me?'[135], the former a distinct possibility given that eight days later and with no intervening entry (an unusual occurrence) she began to describe the convent visit again, only to break off with a 'dear me! I see I have written about this before'. ('But let it stand', she adds, 'just to show whether I distort the truth when I look at it through the medium of a week and a diary'.)[136] Evidence of unintentional amnesia rare elsewhere in her diaries (intentional amnesia is not uncommon) arouses almost as much 'psychological interest' in her reader as the episode did in herself for it shows just how emotionally 'unwell' she was. Even more interesting is that on 22 April, i.e. during her eight days of diary silence, Aelfrida wrote two sonnets. The first was entitled *A Convert to the Catholic Church*, the second, *Il Bacio*, most probably from content and title – *The Kiss* – the sonnet subsequently published as *D'Annunzio's Il Piacere*. She later showed both sonnets to Constantine who was (understandably) 'passionately unreasonable'.[137] (He had every right to be. The latter poem asserts that although Aelfrida wishes to mingle Constantine's soul with hers, his sensuality, "burning with lust", prevents her from doing so; in the first poem she proposes to surrender herself to the Catholic church and to sacrifice all she holds dear in order to be able to fall "at peace ... before [its] altars.) Was this revenge for having discovered her fiancé's compact with Argyris during the same visit to Hessle or for his having forced her to renounce Roman Catholicism? Or a cry for help disguised as a sonnet? She does not say; both are possible. But the episode with Helen also demonstrates another aspect of Aelfrida's emotional exhaustion, namely her lack of concern, amounting to *belle indifférence*, to the risks she ran vis-à-vis Constantine regarding her unscheduled visit to a Catholic convent (Helen, impressed with the atmosphere of purity, love, and holy thoughts, almost decided to convert to Catholicism, Aelfrida encouraging her 'with words made bitter by all that I had suffered ... that if she was seeking the truth neither I nor anyone else had a right to keep her from looking there')[138] and quasi-lesbian advances to his sister; indeed, it is almost as if she was trying to provoke him into breaking off their engagement. It was not, however, until 1930 that she marshalled her thoughts sufficiently to be able to put the matter in perspective by attempting to reconcile her confusion of 'sacred' and 'profane' love of a quarter of a century earlier with her now greater knowledge of human nature in terms of there being 'some definite psychological connection between religion and sex'. "Our most fundamental needs", she writes, "are, it has been said, the hunger for bread, the hunger for sex, and the hunger for the Infinite. These three lie at the very base of our nature, and are inescapable. When we stir up and stimulate the last and most important of the three, we very likely also rouse the second".[139] At the time, however, she consoled herself with the thought that earthly marriage was a sacramental symbol "of the union of Christ and the church"[140] and by persuading Constantine that less torrid physical behaviour would enhance the spiritual side of their relationship.

The breakdown in Aelfrida's mental and emotional health of 1905/6 was mirrored by a coincident breakdown in her physical health. This was due to more than mere physical strain though when one considers her need to earn money to support herself and her future husband and the punishing schedule she set herself, physical fatigue alone could account for her existing so 'healthlessly'.[141] To her already heavy work load of County School teaching (the Direct Method was harder than teaching by rote), extra-curricular activities, and taking Sunday School classes every Sunday afternoon (instead of 'cherubing', she now taught the difficult 'Hooligans' exclusively), of working on her novels and on her book of essays for Fisher Unwin, of translating Gian Falco's books, of preparing her Italian lectures (Verga, for example, she researched in the British Museum library, though Julius, visiting Rome, also sent copies of Verga's works, notably "a supposed collection of letters written by a girl destined for a convent life to her best friend")[142], of giving French and Italian lessons, and of writing and publishing *Le Livre des Jeux*, she now added the transcription, first by hand, then by typewriter, of Constantine's dissertation, noting in November 1905 that this took up 'all [her] spare time and more than all [her] energies'.[143] She also acted as Constantine's research assistant, copying out relevant passages of Balzac for up to four hours a day and even wrote sections herself. At weekends she and Constantine went for lengthy walks – ten to fifteen miles was not uncommon – to clear their heads of the 'thousand pages of foolscap' which comprised the dissertation.[144]

Beginning in October 1905 but with the bulk of her ill-health occurring throughout 1906, Aelfrida's diary records at least six episodes of malaria, five chest infections (one prolonged) and an unspecified illness in November 1906 which kept her in bed for a week. Gaps in entries testify to the enervating effects of her various ailments, as does her having to relinquish her classes at the County School for Boys on Dr Weston's advice, something she 'minded bitterly'[145] because teaching had been her major source of income.

Dr Weston was, in fact, far more worried about the state of her chest than he was about recurrent attacks of 'Florentine fever' during which she did nothing but 'burn and shiver'[146] especially when, as sometimes happened, congestion of the lungs and pleural pain followed a bout of malaria. His chief worry was that Aelfrida's pulmonary symptoms presaged tuberculosis ('consumption') then an incurable disease with a predilection for young people and of which frenetic ruminations on religious matters and physical and mental hyperactivity could have been a symptom. Though she found it difficult, if not impossible, to adhere to Dr Weston's prescription of physical and mental repose because her 'chiefest' means of amusing herself seemed to be 'overwork', further attacks of illness and an inability to get well however hard she tried ('I have been in bed most of the time … when I talk or do anything I get ill again')[147], coupled with the dread of tying a healthy young fiancé to a phthisic invalid or of having to relinquish him altogether in the event of chronic disability or death, persuaded her to live a life so quiet as to be hardly worth recording in her diary. (Perceptive Dr Weston, noting that "her general vitality was low" and that she "used her brain too much", suggested she "find some occupation which … would employ her hands [but] not be too stimulating to her brain"[148]; piano playing was chosen but only listlessly practised.) Enforced rest, however, allowed her time to brood on religion and, not surprisingly, on death (a welcoming thought to one so ill and so miserable), the latter theme becoming, as evidenced by her poetry and diaries, another obsession. But not even to Julius did Aelfrida disclose this, her only comment on or explanation for her physical and mental collapse being that for the past year or so she had been debating "whether or not [she] ought to become an RC" but had finally decided that she "never could", the strain of earlier indecision and final decision not becoming manifest until afterwards and it was that "and overwork" which was preventing her from "getting quite well".[149]

Away from Cambridge, unhappiness beset her still. A visit in August 1906 to Archie Stent's family in Whitchurch Canonicorum found her 'seeing' dead Archie 'everywhere'[150] and life in a parish whose incumbent had converted from Nonconformism to Anglicanism reawakening her desire to convert from Nonconformism to Catholicism in spite swearing not to do so. Then, too, Anatolia had been 'cruel to' and 'worrying' Constantine, and Aelfrida, immured in Dorset[151], again experienced the disquieting symptoms first experienced in Florence: 'I have strained my heart [which] flaps about … like an imprisoned songbird'.[152] But the arrival of her fiancé for a short holiday, the onset of perfect weather, and long walks through Dorset countryside cheered her up: 'we have let the sleeping dogs of Realism and Idealism lie and have devoted ourselves to love-making!'[153]

Among 'sleeping dogs' to be let lie were mementoes of past loves. Having already burnt letters from male admirers, Aelfrida suddenly remembered Hans Peter's. After reading some aloud to Constantine and being asked by him if she would like him to keep them for her, she replied she would rather they were destroyed; 'Enrico's' letters therefore joined the flames. Love letters to Constantine provoked amusement (Aelfrida, reading a timidly affectionate letter and turning to the signature,

"Who is Mabel?" Constantine: "Mabel? … Which Mabel is that? Let me look. Oh yes, of course, I remember now. There were several just then")[154] but also anxiety, for 'Juanita' remained on the periphery of Constantine's life and mutual attraction existed in spite of protestations that he had spurned her for ever. ('Juanita's' letters too joined the holocaust.) Whether letters from Ralph Paget such 'as a man could … only have written to a woman'[155] were also burnt went unrecorded.

Eric Silvanus, however, proved harder to shake off than Ralph. To Aelfrida's dismay he had begun to show signs of transferring his affection from Constantine to herself, seeking emotional contact and writing letters ending "You see, I love you very much". ('How very convenient to be the sort of person who *can* say that kind of thing', was her acid response.)[156] He even proposed joining them wherever Constantine's future career might take them, this causing the latter to write 'the most proper letter, telling him that he must bide at home' and that a family did not consist of "a husband, a wife, and a young man", a sentiment to which Aelfrida added 'True, O Constantine! Most true'.[157] (Of Gian Falco jokingly threatening to do the same, Aelfrida commented: 'he and Eric might start housekeeping together'.)[158] And as if matters were not already complicated enough, Aelfrida now discovered that Eric was also 'very fond' of Anatolia, so fond, indeed, that he was 'as nearly in love as he could be without being wicked'[159] – or possibly he had been 'wicked', Constantine fearing that Eric had actually made love to her.

Constantine's career, it now transpired, did not lie in Academe or Literature but (and rather ironically in view of his earlier intention of entering the Indian Civil Service) in the Consular Service where his "manifest talents and charm" and "his taste for languages, his varied interests and his natural sociability found free scope and he did good work and made many friends".[160]

Earliest intimations appear shortly after his graduation as a consequence of his parents' angry reaction to his second class degree when Aelfrida recorded that her fiancé was 'thinking of the Consular Service[161], but it was not until 16 March 1906 that his thoughts crystallized and his career began in earnest: he failed to obtain fellowship. A college fellowship, said Aelfrida, would have 'spoiled' him; 'as a remittance man in the colonies, he [would] have to fight'. This, she added, would be 'better' for him and 'he [would] only suffer a very little, for Anatolia's sake'.[162]

To describe one's future husband as a 'remittance man' seems harsh for two reasons. First, and although Anatolia had called Constantine 'selfish, lazy, ungrateful [and] a cur etc., etc.'[163] on hearing of his second class degree,

Aelfrida's 1905/06 description of him as 'a young genius trying to do his best' under difficult circumstances (in 1904 he had been merely a '*poseur exalté*') was closer to the mark. Second, the term was more appropriate to a man of bad character paid by his family to stay out of England than to a twenty-three-year-old who had spent months labouring over a dissertation and who was about to embark on a short but intensive course of study for competitive examinations regarded as being of university standard and very hard work. Perhaps it was only the thought that serious work in a foreign country would help to 'form aright' (with his wife's help, of course) the erstwhile *poseur's* character[164] that made her describe Constantine as a remittance man (what this said of herself as a remittance man's wife, she did not say), for she could not then have known that Constantine, in disgrace, would be paid to stay out of England (though not in the colonies) and that she herself would exist on remittances for nearly fifteen years. Perhaps she only intended to hint that positions in the Consular Service were commonly taken up by Oxford and Cambridge graduates awarded degrees which fell short of expected levels of academic achievement. Be this as it may, it was through Chiara's good offices that Constantine got into the Consular Service, she having met a "Liberal lady" who knew the Foreign Minister's secretary and, as Julius noted, "influence … can do so much".[165]

Constantine's studies required him to live in London during the week until his examinations in July 1906. Aelfrida wrote to OB to inform him that "Mr Michaelides is still in town, learning arithmetic"[166] and to Constantine to keep up his spirits. (Her *Chinese Poem – Love* with its hint that separation from herself and from Fordfield's home comforts were necessary if he was "to make [himself] a mandarin / By simple force of cram" later appeared in *To Malise* in the section entitled 'poems not to be taken so seriously' but her anxiety regarding the result of the examination was natural seeing that the date and even the possibility of her marriage depended on it.)[167] It was fortunate, therefore, that Constantine passed his examinations on 13 September 1906 and that Aelfrida's concerns about shortages of vacant posts were calmed following assignation of vice-consular positions to all qualifying candidates provided they passed a medical examination: '*their* doctor, *his* expense'.[168] Constantine was lucky; Maynard Keynes, also sat the Civil Service examination in 1906 but having obtained his lowest mark in Economics, was obliged to enter the India Office instead of the Treasury.[169] Constantine, forbearing to gloat, wrote him a brief note: "Dear Keynes, heartiest congratulations. This is a triumph. Beware the subduing effects of a frock coat and top hat. I shall also

soon be tottering under the weight of office. Ever yours, Constantine Graham (Michaelides that was)".[170]

Constantine's decision to change his surname on joining the Consular Service was prompted by a desire to anglicise it and himself, for prejudice against foreign entrants was rife. (His new name was unintentionally symbolic of his symbiotic relationship with his mother, Graham being Anatolia's maiden name, and had distanced him further from the father whose surname he no longer bore.[171] His having a different surname from his father also gave rise to an amusing incident, a visitor believing 'Constantine Graham [to be] the result of an early indiscretion on the part of Mrs Michaelides'; coincidentally, Alfred Tillyard had recently banned Anatolia from Fordfield because what he now knew about her showed her not to be 'respectable'.)[172] A newspaper cutting pasted into Aelfrida's diary following the entry for 22 September 1906 announced that Constantine had "formally and absolutely RENOUNCED, relinquished and abandoned the … said SURNAME of MICHAELIDES", her own comment being 'There! You see it is done. Does it not look irrevocable?'[173] She did not mind: 'I have sent my first letter off to Constantine Graham Esq. Dear me, how very quickly I have transferred my affections from Mr Michaelides to Mr Graham'. She was also amused to find her fiancé reverting to his old name and ways as occasion demanded: 'Constantine has psychologically become Michaelides again! It is most exciting. For the last two weeks he has been awfully Graham … interested in [Foreign Office] business and practical life … I was almost alarmed…'[174] The change of name would, of course, affect her too: 'I am to be called Aelfrida Graham – and to be Scotch after all'.[175]

Helped by a Scots neighbour, Constantine and Aelfrida explored the origins of their new surname; the result rendered them both 'very Scottish' immediately. (Aelfrida was later to boast that 'we, I say "we" advisedly', were descended from the Grahams of Claverhouse, Anatolia's Graham ancestors having emigrated early in the 1800s from Scotland to the USA.) Their entitlement to the Graham tartan ('for whose unobtrusiveness let us be devoutly thankful') was celebrated by the purchase of a travelling rug in that pattern[176] and to the surname by Aelfrida calling her first published book of poetry *To Malise*, Malise being a Christian name borne by male Grahams. As might be expected, Constantine's change of name was the occasion for much mirth in the *MCJ*, Julius in the guise of 'Michael the Macharite' composing a ballad (*A Michaelides Legend*) telling of one 'Tam Graham' thrown out by his father for being an 'aesthete' and of 'Tam's' picaresque adventures in "fair Byzance" with a disguised and orphaned Auvergnat princess.[177]

With Constantine '– *Graham*, if you please – safely inside the Consular Service', Aelfrida hoped for 'a quiet and uneventful time' of not less than three months or more than six before becoming Mrs Constantine Graham.[178] The date of her wedding depended on the Consular Service's decision regarding the timing of Constantine's first posting and it was not until November that she was able to arrange one: 26 January 1907.[179] Further uncertainty arose with regard to placement ('Rio was practically a certainty … then the news was all reversed and everything is as undecided as ever')[180] and it was only four days before the actual date of the ceremony that they heard, in the first of several Foreign Office diktats to affect their personal circumstances and married life, that they were being posted to Russia in February.[181] This left them only a short time to acquire visas and buy suitable clothing ('sealskin and mink for Constantine and musquash for me')[182]and weapons: a pistol for Constantine and a dagger for Aelfrida. They also took lessons in Russian and talked 'polite platitudes' to all and sundry about the Black Sea coast.[183] A round of farewells and they were off: 'Diary, we meet [again] at Odessa'.[184]

But first, 'I suppose I want, I must, I ought to marry — '.

## Notes

1  Tillyard, HJW. *The Letters of ACW Tillyard* (MTC). Letter from Aelfrida to Julius Tillyard of 26 March 1905.
2  ibid and letter from Catharine Tillyard to an unstated recipient (undated but annotated "perhaps 1905"). GCPPT 2|2a September 1905.
3  GCPPT 1|1|24  12 July 1919.
4  GCPPT 1|1|12  26 March 1905.
5  ibid. 8 April 1905.
6  Tillyard, HJW. *The Letters of ACW Tillyard* (MTC). Undated letter ("perhaps 1905") from Catharine Tillyard to an unstated recipient.
7  ibid and note in Introduction.
8  GCPPT 1|1|12  8 April 1905.
9  Tillyard, HJW. *The Letters of ACW Tillyard* (MTC). Letter from Catharine Tillyard to Julius Tillyard of [  ] January 1906.
10  ibid. Letter from Aelfrida to Julius Tillyard of 26 March 1905.
11  ibid. Undated letter from Catharine Tillyard to an unstated recipient of 1904.
12  GCPPT 1|1|12  6 April 1905.
13  ibid. 9 April 1905.
14  Tillyard, HJW. *The Letters of ACW Tillyard* (MTC). Letter from Catharine Tillyard to Julius Tillyard of 4 April 1905.
15  GCPPT 1|1|12  1 and 13 April 1905.
16  ibid. 13 April 1905.
17  ibid. 1 April 1905.
18  ibid. 23 March 1905.
19  ibid. 6 April 1905.
20  ibid. 15 June 1905.
21  Tillyard, HJW. Introduction to *The Letters of ACW Tillyard* (MTC).
22  GCPPT 1|1|11  11 May 1904.
23  GCPPT 1|1|12  8 April 1905
24  ibid.

25  2|26|4(8). Illustration to *The Monthly Illustrated* April 1891 (MTC).
26  GCPPT 1|1|12  8 April 1905.
27  Tillyard, HJW. *The Letters of ACW Tillyard* (MTC). Letter from Aelfrida to Julius Tillyard of 13 April 1905. GCPPT 1|1|12  25 April 1905.
28  GCPPT 1|1|12  11 June 1905.
29  ibid. Note added on last page 1919.
30  GCPPT 1|1|11  26 and 27 July 1904.
31  GCPPT 1|1|74  5 July 1954.
32  GCPPT 1|1|13  20 June 1905. Tillyard, Ae. *The Centaur* p 317 (GCPPT 2|21|1).
33  GCPPT 1|1|12  8 April 1905.
34  ibid. 18 April 1905.
35  ibid. 1 April 1905.
36  GCPPT 1|1|13  10 October 1905.
37  ibid. 21 November 1905 and 12 March 1906.
38  ibid. 4 September 1904.
39  GCPPT 1|1|12  24 March 1905.
40  ibid. 17 May 1905.
41  ibid. 14 May 1905.
42  ibid. 15 May 1905.
43  ibid. 2 May 1905.
44  ibid. 29 April 1905.
45  GCPPT 1|1|11  22 July 1904. For details of the parentage and Cambridge and post-Cambridge career of Eric Miles Silvanus, see Venn, J. Part 2 Vol. 5. Further details as they touch on Aelfrida's own life will be disclosed when relevant.
46  GCPPT 2|2a June 1910. *College News. King's*.
47  GCPPT 1|1|12  1 May 1905.
48  GCPPT 1|1|13  26 November 1905.
49  ibid. 7 September 1906.
50  GCPPT 1|1|12  9 May 1905.
51  ibid. 8 May 1905.
52  GCPPT 1|1|14  25 and 31 January 1907.
53  ibid. 5 May 1905.
54  ibid. 8 May 1905.
55  ibid. 11 June and 4 September 1905.
56  ibid. 11 and 20 June 1905.
57  ibid. 24, 25, and 26 May 1905.
58  Annan, N. Heading to ch. 6.
59  GCPPT 1|1|12  10 June 1905
60  GCPPT 1|1|13  9 June 1905.
61  GCPPT 1|1|12  11 June 1905.
62  GCPPT 1|1|13  22 and 23 June 1905.
63  GCPPT 1|1|12  10 June 1905. GCPPT 1|1|13  21 June 1905.
64  GCPPT 1|1|18  20 November 1911.
65  GCPPT 1|1|13  21 September 1905 and added note 1922.
66  GCPPT 1|1|13  21 June 1905.
67  ibid. 18 August 1905. A sample of Constantine's 'D'Annunzian phase' can be found in the *MCJ* of July 1906 (GCPPT 2|2a) in which appeared the first part (it covered several volumes) of *The Wine of the Forbidden Fruit*, accurately described in an editorial note as an "*historia … sensationalis et melodramatica*".
68  GCPPT 1|1|12  10 August 1905.
69  GCPPT 1|1|13  23 December 1905.
70  GCPPT 1|1|12  1 January 1906.
71  *Le Livre des Jeux* formed part of Blackie's Modern Language series which included French and German texts designed to attract and hold the attention of children just starting to learn a foreign language. The book, wrote Aelfrida in her preface, arose from her own experience of teaching French conversation to classes of girls aged nine to thirteen years; games, she found, were more useful than anything else in instilling into

the Gladyses and Ediths of her unnamed school (by context, the County School for Girls) the "wish and the power to speak French". The book, however, was not designed to be used in class but by children and their teachers as preparation for classes and as a source of inspiration for further games and songs; in this way, French would be learnt, "with spirit," away from the drudgery of textbooks and blackboards. The introduction was by Miss Hughes of the 'Direct Method' herself: "English children of today are starting with pleasure and zeal the conquest of modern languages by means of conversational lessons full of interest" , their teachers, inspired by educational theorists like Maria Montessori who tried to fit educational methods to the interests and the needs of the child (rather than, as was formerly the case, the child to the educational method), making use of their pupil's love of games "for the purpose of overcoming the first difficulties of learning French". Aelfrida's compilation of French games and songs may have been inspired by memories of those taught by Zelle but it also owes something to, though does not exactly duplicate, Louis A. Barbe's *French Songs and Music* (1905) and, apart from *Malbrouk,* has a feminine flavour more appropriate to 9–13 year-old girls. She may also have turned to the Strawberry Eater for help, as witness her asking the latter's permission to dedicate *Le Livre des Jeux* to her (GCPPT 1|1|13 27 September 1905); in the event she did not actually do so. Proofs of the book were corrected by Louis de Glehn.

72  Tillyard, Ae. *Dirge for Tatyana's Bridal Day* (*The Garden and the Fire* p 26. Section entitled 'poems about love'). The poem was written in Cambridge on 6 November 1914.
Coleridge, M. *Marriage. Collected Poems* p 215.

73  GCPPT 1|1|13 27 July 1906.
GCPPT 2|2a September 1905. The poem, bylined "Major Michaelides", is written in French but is tagged in Latin as being written for the instruction of children "*per directum methodum*".

74  GCPPT 1|1|10 16 April 1903.
Tillyard Ae. *La Maison Blanche* (*Le Livre des Jeux* p 62).

75  GCPPT 1|1|13 9 January 1906.

76  For details of Giovanni Verga see http://www.initaly.com/regions/sicily/910verga.htm

77  Croce heard about Aelfrida from Gian Falco and sent six copies of his new journal *La Critica* to provide material for her lectures. (GCPPT 1|1|13 28 October 1915).

78  GCPPT 1|1|13 10 August 1905.

79  ibid. 15 December 1905.

80  ibid. 10 and 18 August 1905.

81  ibid. 18 November 1905.

82  GCPPT 1|1|13 29 May and 23 October 1905.
GCPPT 1|1|14 29 November 1906.
Prezzolini, not to be outdone by one who had pushed him aside at the *Circolo Filologico* in order to monopolise Aelfrida, also sent two of his own books. (GCPPT 1|1|14 11 December 1906).

83  GCPPT 1|1|13 8 May 1906. *The Tragedy of Everyday,* he explained to Aelfrida, had as its central idea "the discovery of the extraordinary in the ordinary, of the terrible and the awful (*del terribile e del pauroso*) in the habitual and the common". (Letter from Gian Falco quoted in her article in The *Florentine Movement* in the *Independent Review* No 31 Vol. 9 April – June 1906 pp 71–79). Of her article being accepted by the *Review,* Aelfrida wrote 'Gian Falco will be glad!' (GCPPT 1|1|13 16 March 1906).

84  GCPPT 1|1|13 6 January 1906.

85  GCPPT 1|1|14 28 March 1907.

86  GCPPT 1|1|13 6 January 1906.

87  GCPPT 1|1|14 28 December 1906. Aelfrida's correspondence with Gian Falco had a belated sequel. Tucked into the volume of her diary which covers her visit to Italy (GCPPT 1|1|12a) is a letter from Florence dated 2 December 1926. Having discovered from Cambridge acquaintances who were ardent Fascists that Prezzolini had been banished to Paris and that Papini was probably in prison, something

that seemed strange given both men's support for Mussolini, Aelfrida had written to Papini to discover the truth; she also informed him that she had two adolescent daughters who were learning Italian. Gian Falco, whose letter, rather guarded in tone, began formally '*Cara Signora*' and was signed even more formally 'G. Papini', informed Aelfrida that he too had two adolescent daughters and that they were studying English but goes little further than this. Rather touchingly, she did not destroy the letter when she later disposed of so many personal papers. Of another letter received on 3 January 1927 Aelfrida noted 'I was pleased to get a letter after a long silence from my old friend Papini … Gian Falco's letters are not as lively as they used to be; there is something ponderous, middle aged and successful about them. However, he also sent me his photograph – he is uglier than ever!' The photograph, tucked into the volume of her diary which covers this later correspondence (GCPPT 1|1|34), is inscribed on the back "To Mrs Aelfrida Graham /*Il vecchio amico*/Giovanni Papini /Firenze Dicembre 1926".

88  GCPPT 1|1|14 20 December 1906.

89  GCPPT 1|1|13 17 June 1905.

90  ibid. 16 and 18 June 1905.

91  ibid. 15 June 1905.

92  ibid. 19 June 1905.

93  ibid. 19 and 20 June 1905.

94  ibid. 21 and 23 June 1905.

95  ibid. 19 June 1905.

96  GCPPT 1|1|28 14 July 1924.

97  GCPPT 1|1|13 18 June 1905.

98  ibid. 19 June 1905.

99  ibid. 12 July 1905.

100  ibid. 28 July 1905.

101  GCPPT 1|1|28 14 July 1924.

102  GCPPT 1|1|13 10 October 1905 and 16 April 1906.

103  GCPPT 1|1|11 9 June 1904.

104  ibid. 29 May 1904.

105  ibid. 13 1 May 1906.

106  ibid. 26 April and 1 May 1906.

107  ibid. 1 May 1906.

108  GCPPT 1|1|13 14 May 1906.

109  ibid. 28 June 1906.

110  ibid. 14 May 1906.

111  ibid. 18 August 1905.

112  GCPPT 1|1|12 4 April 1904 and note at end of this volume.

113  GCPPT 1|1|13 26 August 1905.

114  Tillyard, Ae. *The Church of Our Lady and the English Martyrs. Cambridge.* (*The Garden and the Fire* p 66. Section entitled 'borderland poems'). The poem was written in Cambridge on 'Easter Day' 1913.

115  GCPPT 1|1|13 29 October 1905.

116  ibid. 5 September 1905.

117  ibid. 6 December 1905.

118  Bondanella, P. and Bondanella, J. ed. p 221. The theme of *Il Santo* made such an impression on Aelfrida that she later wove a version of the story into an unpublished novel (*Marrying a Stranger*) describing a female character ('Frauke') as the woman destined for the hero's helpmeet "to tend him and serve him and who shall unite in herself perfect humility and self-effacement". (To ensure the impossibility of a sexual relationship between 'Frauke' and the hero, here called 'Max', Aelfrida makes them half-siblings). 'Max's' religion is not, however Catholicism, but Socialism, albeit as a student he had briefly believed himself "lost for ever if he could not believe in the Immaculate Conception" (GCPPT 2|6 pp 96–7 and 123).

119  GCPPT 1|1|13 15 November 1905.

120  GCPPT 1|1|74 5 July 1957.

121  Constantine's doubts were shared by the future husband of Christian mystic Evelyn Underhill when that lady came under the influence

of Catholic convert RH Benson shortly before her marriage in 1907. Father Benson, coincidentally, was curate at Our Lady and the English Martyrs from 1905 to 1908 but Aelfrida does not record if she met him.

122 GCPPT 1|1|13  11 January 1906.

123 ibid. 22 January 1906. Constantine did not, perhaps, act as badly as Aelfrida suggests – or perhaps he later repented of his harshness – for six months later she records that he bought her a 1701 book of devotion containing 'the vulgate psalms, a Latin ordinary of the Mass and the psalms … in French and Latin' (ibid. 9 July 1906).

124 ibid. 1 February and 21 June 1906.

125 ibid. 2 April 1906.

126 GCPPT 1|1|12  6, 7, and 9 March 1905.

127 ibid. 28 February 1905.

128 Bondanella, P. and Bondanella, J. p 221. *Il Santo* was condemned by the Catholic Church and placed on the Index of Prohibited Books.

129 Tillyard, HJW. *The Letters of ACW Tillyard* (MTC). Letter from Aelfrida to Julius Tillyard of 13 April 1905.

130 ibid. 15 and 22 January 1906.

131 ibid. 2 April 1906.

132 ibid. Note of July 1957 to entry for 18 April 1906. *The Child of Pleasure* was, in fact, the author's earliest novel and depicted "a decadent aristocracy that [lived] according to the dictates of the Nietzschean Superman, [loved] with a passion oscillating between a morbid sensuality and spiritual rapture, and [spoke] and [wrote] in phrases that have the vacuous grace of *Art Nouveau* ironwork" (Bondanella, P. and Bondanella, J. p 150), a description echoed in Aelfrida's sonnet.

133 GCPPT 1|1|13  15 January 1906.

134 ibid. 18 April 1906.

135 ibid. Note of 7 July to entry for 18 April 1906. The note ends with the words 'Anyhow I repent me now'.

136 ibid. 26 April 1906.

137 ibid. The poems were written in Cambridge in April 1906, *Il Piacere* on an unnamed date, *A Convert* on the 22nd; both appear in *To Malise*, pages 26 and 27 respectively. Five other poems, two (*King Midas* and *Saint Midas*) written in Cambridge in July 1902 and three (*Whitchurch Vale, Ecclesia Prohibitet* and *Written on the Beach*) composed in Dorset in August 1906 (Aelfrida's dating of *Whitchurch Vale* may be inaccurate, this in itself providing further evidence of her disordered mental state at this time) manifest the same anguish; they are also crammed with images of sickness, physical, emotional, and spiritual. The five poems also appear in *To Malise* pp 28–32.

138 GCPPT 1|1|13  18 April 1906.

139 Tillyard, Ae. *Can I be a Mystic?* pp 67–68.

140 Tillyard, HJW. *The Letters of ACW Tillyard* (MTC) Letter from Aelfrida to Julius Tillyard of 13 April 1905.

141 GCPPT 1|1|13  12 July 1906.

142 Tillyard, HJW. *The Letters of ACW Tillyard* (MTC) Letter from Aelfrida to Julius Tillyard of 3 January 1906.

143 GCPPT 1|1|13  23 November 1905.

144 ibid. 13 December 1905.

145 ibid. 19 June 1906.

146 ibid. 6 June 1906.

147 ibid. 2 March and 3 July ('June' in diary) 1906.

148 Tillyard, HJW. *The Letters of ACW Tillyard* (MTC) Letter from Catharine Tillyard to an unnamed correspondent of 31 January 1906.

149 ibid. Letter from Aelfrida to Julius Tillyard of 20 February 1906.

150 GCPPT 1|1|13  1 August 1906.

151 ibid. 9 and 20 August 1906.

152 ibid. 7 September 1906.

153 ibid. 25 August 1906.

154 ibid. 28 and 29 August 1905.

155 GCPPT 1|1|11  22 July 1904.

156 GCPPT 1|1|13  7 September 1906.

157 GCPPT 1|1|14  17 September 1906.

158 ibid. 28 December 1906.

159 GCPPT 1|1|13  1 May 1906.

160 Anstruther, I. p174.
KC *Annual Report* 17 November 1934.

161 GCPPT 1|1|13  21 August 1905.

162 ibid. 16 March 1906.

163 ibid. 19 June 1905.

164 ibid. 18 August 1905.

165 Tillyard, HJW. Introduction to *The Letters of ACW Tillyard* (MTC).

166 KCA OB i/A: Graham CC. Letter from Aelfrida to Oscar Browning dated 11 May 1906. Her cold message was the sting in the tail of the letter in which she criticised OB's sonnet so mercilessly.

167 GCPPT 1|1|13  27 July 1906.

168 ibid. 15, 30 and 31 August 1906.

169 Annan, N. p 77.

170 KCA JMK PP/45/124 Undated letter from Constantine Graham to Maynard Keynes.

171 In contrast to most other entries, Constantine's parents are unnamed in his entry in *Who Was Who* (Vol. 3 1929–1940).

172 GCPPT 1|1|16  16 September and 21 November 1908.

173 GCPPT 1|1|14  22 and 26 September 1906.

174 GCPPT 1|1|13  31 August and 18 December 1906.

175 ibid. 30 August 1906. The next volume of the diary (GCPPT 1|1|14) is inscribed on the first page as usual with her name Aelfrida CW Tillyard. Above the Tillyard she later wrote 'Graham Jne' (i.e. *jeune*); in Constantine's writing is added a Tillyard catch phrase: 'Better so'.

176 GCPPT 1|1|14  19 September 1906.
GCAC 4|6|3|3 Letter from Aelfrida to Helen McMorran of November 5 November 1958.

177 GCPPT 2|2a November 1906, January and September 1907.

178 GCPPT 1|1|14  17 September 1906.

179 ibid. 22 November 1906.

180 ibid. 8 January 1907.

181 ibid. 16 January 1907.

182 ibid. 25 January 1907.

183 ibid. 28 January 1907.

184 ibid. 31 January 1907.

# The Marriage of Miss Tillyard

The announcement of the wedding published in Alfred Tillyard's *Cambridge Independent Press* is so idiosyncratic that it could only have been written by the bride herself and should be construed, like one of her poems, as a device which conceals as much as it reveals:

> "There was celebrated at St Columba's Presbyterian Church, Cambridge, on Saturday afternoon at two o'clock the wedding of Miss Aelfrida Catharine Tillyard, only daughter of Mr and Mrs AI Tillyard of 'Fordfield', ... Cambridge, and Mr Constantine Graham, of King's College, Cambridge, only son of Mr CC Michaelides of Hessle, Yorkshire, formerly of Mytilene, known in modern Greek literature as 'Argyris Ephtaliotes'. The bridegroom was placed first class in the first part of the Historical Tripos of 1903, and second class in the second part of the Moral Science Tripos in 1905".

After describing the bride's dress and flowers, the announcement continues:

> "Her bridesmaids were Miss Verrall, of Cambridge, and Miss Longstaffe, of Kensington … Mr Eric Silvanus, of King's College, was the best man … Following the ceremony a reception was held at Fordfield".[1]

To omit the date of the wedding from the announcement is unusual as is inclusion of the father–in–law's *nom-de-plume* (and why this but not her father's aldermanic title?), the husband's second class degree, and a description of groom and best man as 'of King's College' when neither were presently associated with that institution. To exclude all mention of the groom's mother is strange indeed. And why was not one of Constantine's sisters bridesmaid in place of Helen Verrall of whom Aelfrida always wrote disparagingly and whom she did not particularly like? And why no mention of a honeymoon? For some of the answers and for other information relevant to the ceremony we must turn to the bride's diaries and to other documents written around this time of which perhaps the most ironic is a letter written by the bride to a girl she had met only recently but with whose life her own was eventually to be bound up: "I am sorry you did not like my wedding notice in the paper. It was so much simpler than most".[2]

**Constantine Graham né Michaelides and Aelfrida Tillyard 1906**

Doubly ironic under the circumstances was Aelfrida's slightly earlier comment to the effect that a reader of her diary should not be surprised that she wrote so little about her 'own nearest ones'; it was, she intimated, not necessarily for her to do so because any reader of that document would instinctively '*feel*' how 'perfectly united we all are'.[3] Perhaps she and they pretended that it was so but contemporary evidence suggests otherwise. Nor was her 'wedding notice' as simple as she said.

Between Anatolia and Argyris dissention was to be expected, the imminence of their silver wedding anniversary only serving to underline the almost complete breach between them, she rarely returning to Hessle, he embittered and lonely because alone and yet unfree. The breach, it seemed, was widened by Argyris' 'gleeful'[4] and manifest pleasure at his son's marriage to a girl with whom he enjoyed a mutually affectionate relationship and by

Anatolia's disapproval of it, disapproval now so absolute that she had decided to stand 'aloof' not only from her son and his fiancée but also from the ceremony. ('I wish', wrote her future daughter-in-law, 'she could have taken her rightful place [though] for her sake … more than mine'.)[5] Ancifera Gregory had, of course, already had her say; it was now for perceptive Aunts Anna and Fanny to add theirs, the former believing it "rather a triumph for *any* man to have won Frida", the latter that it would do Frida good to fall in love because "it might make her less selfish".[6] (Anna was right, Fanny wrong.) Clear-sighted Eustace, now described by Aelfrida as "a person of youthful enthusiasms yet middle-aged judgement"[7], wrote wittily in the *MCJ* of bookbinding (his hobby) as a metaphor for marriage and of lovemaking, the latter, like dancing, being a being a "foolish but necessary art"[8], but otherwise emulated Anatolia in remaining aloof, it never seeming to occur to him to be on "anything but the best of distant terms" with an elder sister who on her own admission had "teased him too much when he was little".[9] (He said, 'bullied'.) As to the Oracle and Chiara the former, it seems, was so determined to get his daughter off his hands that he accompanied her to the register office to obtain the marriage licence ('I felt very small and meek', wrote Aelfrida, 'as I … trailed in [his] wake'; was this, she wondered, a 'a curious foretaste' of how she would feel as he led her up the aisle on her wedding day?)[10] and the latter, though 'simply perfect … as always'[11] in her behaviour towards a daughter whose physical and mental health alike continued fragile and her abnormally strong affection for her elder brother no less diminished by his absence in Greece, so keen to see Frida wed that trunks bearing the bride's new initials (ACWG) were ordered well in advance and a lavish trousseau prepared. But as to them too – and her comment speaks volumes – Aelfrida, as she noted in a letter to Julius[12], watched their behaviour without trying to share their thoughts, thoughts to which she was indifferent either because she did not care or because she had so many of her own as to be unable to encompass anyone else's. Or perhaps because she did not want to know.

Relationships between Julius and Aelfrida and between Julius and Constantine were also problematical. Julius' reaction ('he said "oh!" as though he were shocked')[13] to his sister's informing him on his return to England in November 1906 for the Christmas holidays (and presumably, to attend her wedding though her account fails to mention him; as he was still in England after it, we may guess that he did so) that it was time she was married (a curious expression in itself) was only to be expected given that "the person he loved most in all the world was his sister".[14]

Deeply hurt, it seems, when she became engaged to Constantine, Julius had taken some time to become 'intimate'[15] with him (perhaps he had hoped that the engagement would fizzle out like that to Hans Peter) but judging by the future brothers-in-law's teasing of each other in the *MCJ*[16], intimacy of a kind had been achieved (at Aelfrida's urging, it has to be said), Julius having come to better understand and even to respect a young man who now knew "the worth of other feelings besides those gloated over by D'Annunzio"[17] and Constantine having achieved a degree of fraternal feeling (in a letter of September 1907 he even signs himself "ever most lovingly")[18] for his rival. But for Aelfrida to feel obliged to 'pray every day for Dudu's happiness'[19] and for Julius to feel the need to express his feelings in lachrymose Latin verse ("*in oculis stant lachrimae / Et semper cogito de te*")[20] suggests that God, as his sister feared, 'evidently … does not agree with me'.[21]

Julius did not agree with Aelfrida for another reason too: the arrival in Cambridge of Wilhelmina Kaufmann, now aged eighteen, the 'very maternal, deeply religious … ethical and romantic' German girl whom, it seemed, he intended to marry. Met by Aelfrida for the first time in May 1906 when Mina visited Fordfield, the former commented without much enthusiasm that she would 'like [Mina] for a sister-in-law' and with glee that Julius *still* loved herself 'better than Minnchen'.[22]

Mina's arrival in England to meet Julius' family and to perfect her English provoked something of a crisis: 1906 was the year in which Aelfrida's physical and mental health gave rise to increasing parental concern (she continued to have 'a good deal of pain in [her] lungs'[23] until shortly before her wedding and was beginning to wonder if 'life' was not after all going to be too much for her[24] and that death, even though it meant parting from Constantine, might be preferable; she had also been informed by Dr Weston that she was "too intellectual" for her own good)[25] and twenty-five-year-old Julius' lack of academic and hence of financial success – he had been turned down for a fellowship at Caius – and 'uncertainty about [his] future with Mina and wage-earning'[26] were worrying his parents on several counts. But only Aelfrida knew at this point that Mina herself had a rival, Julius having been 'flirted with' and admired by 'a lively Russian'[27] in the course of his lengthy and much interrupted wooing of Fräulein Kaufmann.

If Aelfrida's description of her own family as 'perfectly united' fell somewhat short of the truth – her diary entry does not read ironically but she may have been trying to persuade herself that unity was the order of the day – how much shorter did it fall with regard to the relationship which existed between herself and her fiancé as months and then days went by 'with a kind of grinning irrevocability almost appalling'. 'Irrevocability' was to be borne with 'heroic joy'[28] because of her love for Constantine (but was it only to relieve her feelings that she flirted so hard with a former admirer that she reduced him 'to a state of trembling admiration' for which, so she said, she was 'sorry afterwards', not on her own account but because James Barkway was now a married man and she had conveniently forgotten and so had 'remembered all the wrong things'?)[29] but also with a 'great deal'[30] of fear as the nearness of the step she was about to take became borne upon her.

Her emotions in the months preceding her wedding were confused. On the one hand and if the evidence of her sonnet *One of the Musings of a Pious Girl* is to be believed, "restlessness" in matters of religion remained unabated: should she, for example, accept and take joy in the imperfect and sometimes conflicting conditions of life on earth or should she wait unhappily in "ceaseless hope" that after death she would find "heavenly peace"?[31] Would her adoption of Constantine's religion result in 'anguish and self-questioning' or in peace for herself but alienation from Constantine insofar as expressed wishes for 'peace' by whatever means appeared to dull *his* perception of God? (Constantine, it seemed, continued to veer between being 'almost brutally passionate and sensual' and 'rather cruel, especially over Christianity', the latter something she did not always confide to her diary lest she find it harder than ever to persuade herself that her fiancé was 'perfect as always' and that their mutual love did not 'at any moment … cease growing stronger'.)[32] Constantine too suffered strain as his wedding approached: having been accepted for the Consular Service he was now (as predicted to Maynard Keynes) wearing a frock coat and 'tottering under the weight of office' as he shuttled between Foreign Office and Board of Trade to learn his trade, the strain manifesting itself chiefly in accusations that Aelfrida was being 'flippant' when he expressed 'dreadfully serious'[33] concerns concerning the unfortunate coincidence of new career and impending matrimony and she tried to cheer him up by treating both matters light-heartedly. More positively, however, he professed himself 'most beautifully in a hurry to get the wedding licence and in every way to prove himself a *parti sérieux*'[34] towards a fiancée (and a family) with whom he must perforce unite himself because he now had no-one else to whom to turn.

As the day of her marriage drew closer, Aelfrida, who had formerly merely tolerated the company of women and who had, Lucy Longstaffe excepted, very few female friends, began to withdraw little by little from the masculine company she once sought so eagerly. (She nevertheless allowed herself her first ride in a motor car and a very brief flirtation with its driver, the son of one of her lady pupils.) Instead, and almost as if unconsciously seeking protection, she moved more and more in a feminine milieu even to the extent of actively seeking out the company of members of her own sex. Although this might be seen as a normal part of preparation for her wedding, for someone who usually took great interest in clothes Aelfrida was surprisingly unmoved by the excitements of trousseau and wedding dress – Lucy, she recorded, was 'taking much more interest in the … arrangements than I do'.[35] (Apart from a brief mention of her engagement ring – "a very chaste ring with one large diamond in it", chosen by Constantine with Eric Silvanus' help[36] – and slightly lengthier ones about a wedding ring to be made out of three generations of grandmothers' rings, a wedding dress trimmed with 'masses' of Limerick lace[37], and a reference to wedding presents 'tumbling in'[38] – Lucy gave her a coral necklace, the Learned Twins "a kind of bolero of magnificent Spanish lace"[39], and Oscar Browning, whom she thanked in a much more gracious letter then her previous one, 'some pretty things for the table'[40] – Aelfrida provides almost no information: what excited her more was an offer from Fisher Unwin to publish *The Love of Money*.) Nor was it solely a desire to say goodbye to acquaintances from whom she would shortly be parted for longer or shorter periods as the exigencies of Constantine's career demanded for entries in her diary show that there was more to her sudden switch of allegiance than this; once so fearless, she was now afraid. Absolute surrender, she realised with horror, meant more than merely agreeing to love her future husband; it also meant loss of her virgin state and diminution of her personal liberty, and marriage much more than just 'wedding arrangements and … clothes'.[41]

She had already worked out a means of avoiding loss of physical autonomy by proposing to Constantine that he and she abstain from intercourse until they had put aside enough money to comply with Argyris' desire to see his daughters dowered before his death; this way they would run no risk of her becoming pregnant until Helen and Irene's financial security was assured. Her suggestion that she and Constantine 'live together as brother and sister' whatever the cost to their personal happiness sounds altruistic but was not: 'I am going to tell you something frankly, almost crudely … *I* knew how one could avoid begetting children but thought it wrong to take pleasure without its consequences'. (Note added in 1921: 'This did not mean the use of contraceptives which would have filled me with horror – only not coming together except at special times when conception is less likely'.)[42] A 'brother and sister' relationship, too, would delay the physical consummation she dreaded, not because it might result in pregnancy (she ardently wanted children) but because it would detract from her bodily and hence her spiritual purity. (Forty years later she was to write of how often women in possession of "virgin-natures" were "very unhappy when they married because such women not only required psychological solitude in which to reach [spiritual] maturity" but also needed to remain bodily chaste also if they were not to feel as overwhelmed "by the pressure of a man's personality on their own" as they did by the pressure of his body on theirs.)[43] It seems too she also hoped that the moral potency ascribed by Christian thought to those of 'virgin mind' would apply to Constantine as well as to herself, writing on the eve of their wedding 'our last night of virginity, Constantine, may thy purity ever be sustained!'[44] and that she hoped to establish with her erstwhile Vadius a love "pure as the morning star"[45], as Bélise put it, from which the profane and carnal would be banished and only the sacred and spiritual remain.

Chiara, however, gave the game away, forcing her daughter to take the step of making a proposal which pleased her Vadius better than one of marital chastity. Shortly before the marriage, Constantine, with whom Catharine Tillyard had already discussed his responsibility with regard to children, had 'the talk' (as Aelfrida put it), with his future mother-in-law and discovered what his fiancée knew already but had refrained from telling him, namely that sexual intercourse was less likely to result in conception if indulged in only during the 'safe period' of a woman's menstrual cycle. Encouraged by Chiara urging that 'only that way could there be perfect harmony … between husband and wife', Constantine was emboldened to ask Aelfrida if she would permit sexual intercourse from the beginning of their marriage. Left with little choice in the matter, she reluctantly agreed ('all my independence and my virginity arose and shouted that the thing was impossible, that no man could ever know all of me'), cloaking her distaste in a maidenly 'agony of shyness' but also, and significantly in view of what had already passed and was to pass between them, telling him that 'now thou wilt know that Christianity is not a religion of repression'. Constantine, for his part, was exuberant, covering his future wife with 'tenderness and caresses' and telling her that 'the chief end of his life' was to live in perfect harmony with her.[46]

Other matters too shouted of things than Chiara's reminder, spoken of an earlier fiancé, that 'one spends with one's husband not only days but nights'.[47] A premonition that although "the first beginning of love seemed private and unique – her sweetheart [had] said he loved as man never before", once she and Constantine decided to marry, poetry would "harden into prose". A feeling that

their nuptials would seem as "staged [as] … a dramatic performance" and that the "intense and persistent" sense of "Reality" which pervaded their courtship would be dissipated by the appearance on the marital scene of "necessary parts of the apparatus of [real] life"[48], such as furniture. A sense that like the heroine of Susan Ferrier's novel *Marriage* (a novel lent her by Susanna Venn but dismissed by adolescent Aelfrida as "very poor stuff")[49] she had made her marital choice (a choice forced on her because she had run out of excuses for not marrying) and, like 'Lady Juliana', would have to live with the consequences, among which was marriage to a young man so penniless that "friends and relations … took on the aspect of purveyors of cheques".[50] Knowledge that she was about to marry someone with whom she was not, in spite of protestations that 'my longing for Constantine is unbearable'[51] but as the palmist had warned her, passionately in love with and that she, as someone who 'couldn't bear to live away from Cambridge' because she could 'hardly breathe away from its hyper-refined atmosphere'[52], was about to depart Cambridge for somewhere far from 'Cambridgy' where, widened though her horizons might be by physical separation from the house and town of her birth, she might also find her freedom of thought and action curtailed by social constraints and by the dictates of the Foreign Office with regard to postings. (It was not until 1913 that Aelfrida, with two small children in tow and at a low point physically and emotionally, begged and received a posting for Constantine consonant with *her* life and wishes.) Not only this but there was also Constantine's personality to be taken into account: as bitter experience had shown, he was by no means the meek little boy of her own age who would not take up too much of her attention once envisaged as her future mate.

Constantine, son of a tall mother and a Mediterranean father, was himself rather short and consciousness of his lack of height may explain why he so often chose to be photographed sitting down or alone or standing on a step at the back of a group. (A picture taken at Fordfield shortly before his marriage shows Aelfrida towering over him as she stands beside him; he sits staring at the camera with the supercilious look he adopts on such occasions.) In fact it is rare to find Constantine and Aelfrida in the same picture and if they do appear together, either one or both are seated or Aelfrida bows her head to conceal the difference in height. (Their scenes in *Les Femmes Savantes* must have been all the more amusing for the sight of taller Bélise ardently pursuing shorter Vadius.) Together with lack of height, however, went the 'little man' syndrome, with all that that implies of enormous ego, boundless ambition, and a desire to dominate, a dangerous combination in a personality damaged by childhood insecurities which had left him as emotionally needy and as controlling as his future wife, and throughout their courtship Aelfrida had had ample proof of her fiancé's possession of such characteristics; indeed, she had positively encouraged the first two and, strong-willed herself, had only reluctantly submitted to the latter. But she had promised 'absolute surrender' and knowing what she did of Constantine's obduracy in matters of religion and sexuality, could only expect that he would hold her to her promises after marriage. On 18 January 1907, inspired perhaps by the lines of *Chanson de la Mariée* which warn a young bride about her husband, namely that for 'husband' (*époux*) she will have to substitute 'master' (*mâitre*) and that a man who promised to be easy-going (*doux*) will not live up to his promise[53], she noted grimly that 'everything is fairly begun now' and that a solo country walk from which she had just returned 'was [her] last bit of liberty'.[54]

Evidence of the apprehension lying below the surface of the forced tranquillity with which she approached her wedding ('I am perfectly happy and serene ... I have as far as possible been going on with my usual occupations, studying, writing, reading ... this seems to me the best preparation')[55] can be deduced from a sonnet and a diary entry of the time. The sonnet, *A Girl to her Lover Drowned at Sea*, was written on 12 January 1907 shortly after Constantine had been forced by Anatolia to spend his last bachelor Christmas with her in Paris and Aelfrida, knowing that he was prone to sea-sickness, had worried lest the Channel crossings be rough. Although ostensibly longing for Constantine's return, she herself, exhausted by a year's spiritual and physical malaise from which death had sometimes seemed her only release, desired death: but whose death – hers or Constantine's? Had Constantine drowned it would have been Anatolia's fault for forcing him to cross the Channel in midwinter but the wishful thinking would have been Aelfrida's: her fiancé's death at sea would have provided her with a "release from strife" comparable to that which her own death on land would have granted herself.[56] The date of the poem's composition is significant for other reasons too: 12 January was the day on which she bought herself a potentially lethal weapon, so death in some shape or form would have been in her mind; second, she was unhappy that Chiara's disclosure to Constantine of the rhythm method of contraception meant that her now having to give herself up to Constantine's embraces only during the 'safe period' of her monthly cycle would leave her as much 'without immediate hope' of the children she dearly wanted as would a sexless marriage; third, and most poignantly, 12 January was the day she referred in her diary to an accidental meeting of a fortnight earlier, asking herself 'why did I propose to John Forbes whom I did not in the least care for?'[57]

An incident involving John Forbes Cameron had caused her much distress during the preceding year. Not only was he now married, something Aelfrida always found unforgivable as far as former beaux were concerned, but a year following his marriage Chiara informed her that Elfrida Cameron had had a baby. Aelfrida's reaction to the news was angst-ridden ('I felt savage and miserable and jealous ... you know how I want a child') and in a distraught moment she informed Constantine. Later she felt ashamed: 'I suppose it was the cruellest thing I could say to a man in his position'[58] i.e. who had just committed himself to a long engagement and to a chaste marriage for the sake of his sisters' future and because his future wife had failed to disclose that she knew of the rhythm method of contraception.

When Aelfrida was unhappy, she was capable of acts of emotional cruelty towards another party, a means, it may be, of relieving her feelings by savaging someone else's. An accidental meeting with John Forbes Cameron on 29 December 1906 was not an occasion on which she was unkind – in fact she was more embarrassed than anything else by Cameron's radiant look when he met her – but it was the sequel to an event she had reason to remember with shame.

On Christmas Eve 1906 she and Julius (Constantine was in Paris) attended a lunch party at Castlebrae. Among those present were Mr and Mrs Cameron. In John Forbes' hearing, Aelfrida 'rose to the occasion and was malicious', taunting Elfrida Cameron with ignorance of her husband's earlier life and accomplishments:

> 'Mrs C: "I do not care for dancing".
> I: "*What* a pity! Mr Cameron dances so well".
> Mrs C (sharply): "Oh – does he?"
> I (a little dreamily): "Yes – he waltzes ..."
> I see John Forbes in the distance looking perfectly wretched, his eyes haggard.
> I: "Tell Mr Cameron not to listen, and then we can say more pretty things about him"'.

As the party broke up she engineered matters so as to cause John Forbes more anguish still, touching his hand as if accidentally. 'He said nothing but looked me full in the face with that melodramatic "Ah" look as though he were clutching at his heart after a bullet shot and crying "he has done for me!" Dudu and I went away laughing'. Only later did her conscience prick her: 'I am glad ... that John Forbes is ... happy – when I am out of the way. His wife is a nice little thing'.[59]

On 17 January Aelfrida wrote in her diary 'my thoughts are very simple – I am fulfilling the object of my creation and giving my whole life to love Constantine, calmly, deliberately and with perfect joy. He and I are doing *right'*.[60] (The object of her creation, she later informs us, was to be "hallowed as a temple of the Holy Spirit, made holy, ready for childbearing".)[61] It was fortunate, therefore, that regrets were so well concealed ('I see all that is in people's minds [but] … they see nothing in mine')[62] and that the serenity with which she went to the altar, even if assumed, was convincing: 'it is about an hour and a half before our wedding … Chiara and I have made up the bed Constantine and I are to sleep in and I have some time left to read my bible and have lunch. You see how quiet I am'[63], an artificial tranquillity imposed by reading a Goldsworthy Lowes Dickinson essay, *Shakespeare, Ibsen and Mr Bernard Shaw*, instead of thinking about what lay ahead. The day following the ceremony she wrote that she had been 'very happy all through our marriage … Constantine spoke up bravely and I too … We walked away to the vestry hand in hand – I *couldn't* have him offering his arm … as though he were a young man at a dinner party'.[64]

The ceremony, according to the *Cambridge Independent Press* was "witnessed by a crowded congregation, which included a number of friends from different parts of England".[65] (It also included a number of friends from a different social class, for Aelfrida had specifically invited 'a huge number of cherubs and poor people'[66] – Sunday School pupils and Cambridge Place mothers, for example, for whom a separate party was held at Fordfield Cottage – and in a ghostly echo of her long-dead brother, her godson, Conrad John, son of the Fordfield cook who alone of the family had had the courage and compassion to tell bewildered little Frida that Conrad Francis was dead, a boy who grew up to look uncannily like his namesake: 'a tall slender boy … pale and dreamy-looking … He looks as though he would either die young or live to be something unusual'.[67] He did neither.) Argyris and Helen Michaelides attended the wedding, the latter, for reasons ungiven, not as a bridesmaid; Anatolia and Irene did not. And to be able to punish Anatolia's rudeness and lack of consideration by excluding her from the wedding notice must have given Aelfrida immense satisfaction.

Lack of mention of a honeymoon is now revealed: there was none. Following the reception ('very beautiful … the only person who looked unhappy was Eric [Silvanus], and he – oh, very')[68] Constantine and Aelfrida 'drove away and pretending to go to the station, went to Mrs Verrall's' where they 'sat in the old schoolroom where I used to have lessons and eat (*sic*) a big tea and were very happy' before returning surreptitiously to Fordfield, though not before receiving a short homily from Dr Verrall on excavations on Vesuvius, the poor man being 'too much embarrassed to talk about anything else'.[69] The ostensible reason for this bizarre arrangement

**MARRIAGE OF MISS TILLYARD
AT ST. COLUMBA'S, CAMBRIDGE.**

There was celebrated at St. Columba's Presbyterian Church, Cambridge, on Saturday afternoon at two o'clock the wedding of Miss Aelfrida Catharine Wetenhall Tillyard, only daughter of Mr. and Mrs. A. I. Tillyard, of "Fordfield," Brooklands Avenue, Cambridge, and Mr. Constantine Graham, of King's College, Cambridge, only son of Mr. C. C. Michaelides, of Hessle, Yorkshire, formerly of Mytilene, known in Modern Greek literature as "Argyris Ephtaliotes." The bridegroom was placed first class in the first part of the Historical Tripos in 1903, and second class in the second part of the Moral Science Tripos in 1905.

The ceremony was witnessed by a crowded congregation, which included a number of friends from different parts of England. The bride, who was given away by her father, wore a dress of white crepe-de-chine over white silk, trimmed with old Limerick lace. She also wore a tulle veil and orange blossoms, and carried a long sheaf of white lilies and asparagus fern. Her bridesmaids were Miss Verrall, of Cambridge, and Miss Longstaffe, of Kensington, who wore dresses of white ninon over white silk, and white hats trimmed with Parma violets, and carried bouquets of violets—the colours of King's College. Mr. Eric Silvanus, of King's College, was the best man.

The service, which was fully choral, was conducted by the Rev. G. A. Johnston Ross, assisted by the Rev. R. Athol Cliff, of Hunstanton. Miss May Cliff, F.R.C.O., Mus. Bac. of Durham University, was at the organ. While the congregation were awaiting the arrival of the bride, the organist played the Occasional Overture of Handel, and Beethoven's Choral Symphony was performed while the register was being signed. The hymns used were " Come, Holy Ghost, our souls inspire," and " O, God of Bethel," and as the bridal party left the church Miss Cliff played Bach's Toccata and Fugue in D minor.

Following the ceremony a reception was held at "Fordfield." The newly-married pair will shortly leave England to take up their residence at Odessa, where Mr. Graham has been appointed British Vice-Consul.

was that between 26 January (the original date of the wedding) and their departure for Odessa, there was no time for Constantine and Aelfrida to have a honeymoon; in order, however, to bring the reception to a suitable conclusion and to persuade people that they had actually gone away, they arranged with Mrs Verrall 'to pretend we are having a proper honeymoon … [but] really return to Fordfield to make *our* room sacred'. The illusion was enhanced by the arrival of a carriage, by (empty) suitcases being placed in it, by Aelfrida entering it in a 'going-away' costume, and by enthusiastic farewells from the Learned Twins who were not privy to the deception.[70]

Another reason for the pretend honeymoon was that the wedding was originally intended to be held on one of Constantine's weekend visits, the groom finishing his studies at the Board of Trade on Wednesday 23 January and returning to his temporary lodgings in London on Monday 28 January two days after the ceremony. ('Better so!'[71] was Aelfrida's relieved comment.) The putting back of the wedding date to 19 January (the Foreign Office, it seems, was not so heartless as to force a new vice-consul to take less than a week's leave of absence for his nuptials) allowed for nearly two weeks' honeymoon but the opportunity was not taken and the farcical 'honeymoon' arrangement allowed to stand. Prior to their departure for Russia, Constantine and Aelfrida therefore spent a total of eight nights at Fordfield under the eyes of her parents and teenage brother (*and Julius*), three nights in London with Warren relatives, and two nights in Hessle with Constantine's father and sister, an arrangement notable for lack of privacy but for that reason possibly much to Aelfrida's taste. This may be deduced from her complete lack of reference to sexual behaviour from the day of her wedding until many months had elapsed (a description of 22 January of her and Constantine going to London on Foreign Office and Fisher Unwin business and being 'delightfully inexperienced and important'[72] relates to consular and literary, not sexual, matters), from the only entry for 20 January being a factual description of her wedding, and from there being no entry at all for 21 January. For a diarist whose entries for the preceding three years had been almost daily and often quite outspoken, Aelfrida's diary now appears like a brightly-lit stage in front of which a thick curtain suddenly descends.

There was, however, more to her reticence than maidenly modesty. (Or to Aelfrida, now twenty-three, feeling that although marriage as an institution was not all it was cracked up to be, the prospect of "being an old maid [was] so awful"[73] that she 'must' or 'ought' to go through with it.) For one thing she had persuaded herself (and a possibly reluctant Constantine) that she looked on Fordfield "as sacred and [wished] … all the most holy incidents of [her] life to take place under its roof"[74], a fact she may also have made known to her mother for Chiara entered the marital bedroom when Constantine and Aelfrida had retired to bed to pray at their bedside and to bless them before tucking them up as if they were children. For another – and possibly Chiara knew this too or else why enter the room of a newly-married couple who might have been in the throes of their first full sexual intercourse – Constantine and Aelfrida had arranged to pass a 'virgin bridal night'[75] and to leave their marriage unconsummated until the Sunday.

This, it seems, was something more than a wish on Aelfrida's part to lose her virginity on a 'holy' day or a literary conceit (Swinburne's poem *The Maiden Marriage*, known to Aelfrida from Constantine's readings-aloud, has Trystram of Lyonesse win his way to Iseult's "bride-bed" but nobly leave her "all night sleeping in her maidenhood")[76] and more to her belief that as a bride she was "something sacred", that the "lovely ceremonial" of her wedding was "not a kind of stage play with [herself] as the leading lady but a sacrament", and that because as bride and groom she and Constantine trod "holy ground" on their wedding night[77] both should remain celibate during

it. (Fordfield, of course, was already a 'sacred' spot because of its association with her parents' marriage; to hold her own there and yet to remain chaste on her wedding night would make 'our room sacred'[78] too; there was also, it seems, a rather confused association in her mind between earthly marriage and the church as composed of "the elect" and their relationship to Christ, as "the *Bride* of Christ"[79], she herself apparently having become a 'bride of Christ' also in going through the sacrament of marriage with Constantine, her marriage being so '*right*' in this respect too that she 'hardly need ask God's blessing on it'.)[80] But knowing how 'cruel' Constantine could be with regard to her particular brand of 'Christianity', she presented the matter to him as if she was suffering another maidenly 'agony', asking him to 'leave' her on their wedding night so that after consummation on their second night together she would not have to 'face' him again for several more. The Foreign Office's generosity in allowing Constantine a fortnight's honeymoon instead of only a weekend put paid to her plan and undermined her reasons (she never, in fact, tells us outright at what point her marriage *was* consummated) but it seems that Constantine was both 'resolute' that their marriage would be consummated on their second night together and yielded to her entreaty regarding the first night; indeed, he even affected not to 'despise' her for her 'shyness', covered her with 'tenderness and caresses' and told her that 'the chief end of his life was harmony with [herself]'.[81] And if Aelfrida, following a day which, if not the worst of her life, closely approached it (of her eleventh wedding anniversary, a day on which the existing cracks in her marriage were widening rapidly, she was to write that she was 'much happier now than … then'[82], 'then' being the day she had prophetically expected to 'loathe')[83] "ran upstairs to her room, flung herself on her bed and [wept bitterly]"[84], perhaps this too was attributed to bridal nerves and not to independence and virginity shouting that marriage was 'impossible'.

Her honeymoon over, Aelfrida said goodbye to what she knew and went away with her new husband to what she did not know.[85] Perhaps by now Constantine had showed her "how babies are made". Perhaps, stating that she was still "a little frightened", she had managed to postpone consummation. Perhaps she had even persuaded him that living in other people's houses as they currently were, it was preferable merely to "play … games"[86] and to postpone consummation until they were properly alone. But of one thing we may be sure and as the *CIP* account of the 'Marriage of Miss Tillyard' had it, the newly-married couple eventually left England "to take up their residence at Odessa where Mr Graham has been appointed Vice-Consul"[87], he to wear a uniform "calculated to uphold the dignity of the Empire", she, "patriotic to the hem of her … going away dress", but neither, one suspects, wearing the fanciful red, white, and blue costumes depicted on the *Fashions* page of the *Military and Civil Journal* for January 1907.

# Notes

1  *CIP* 25 January 1907. The cutting is pasted in the contemporary volume of Aelfrida's diary (GCPPT 1|1|14).
2  Tillyard, HCW. *The Letters of ACW Tillyard* (MTC) Letter from Aelfrida to Mina Kaufmann of 28 September 1907.
3  GCPPT 1|1|12  24 April 1904.
4  ibid. 28 January 1907.
5  ibid. 17 January 1907.
6  GCPPT 1|1|12  23 April 1905.
7  Tillyard, HJW. *The Letters of ACW Tillyard* (MTC). Letter from Aelfrida to Julius Tillyard of 5 February 1906.
8  GCPPT 2|2a September 1905 (*Lord Chesterfield's Advice to Young Men*) and January 1907 (*Applied Arts*).
9  Tillyard, HJW. *The Letters of ACW Tillyard* (MTC). Letter from Aelfrida to Julius Tillyard of 5 February of 5 February 1906.
10  GCPPT 1|1|14  23 November 1906.
11  ibid. 29 November 1906.
12  Tillyard, HJW. *The Letters of ACW Tillyard* (MTC). Letter from Aelfrida to Julius Tillyard of 10 February 1906.
13  GCPPT 1|1|14  7 December 1906.
14  Tillyard, Ae. *Marrying a Stranger* pp 22–23 (GCPPT 2|6).
15  GCPPT 1|1|13  12 July 1905.
16  GCPPT  2|2a. The *MCJ* of November 1906 contains "Major Michaelides" riposte (*The Archaeologist. A Satire*) to "Michael the Macharite's" *Legend*.
17  Tillyard, HJW. *The Letters of ACW Tillyard* (MTC). Letter from Aelfrida to Julius Tillyard of April 1905.
18  ibid. Letter from Constantine Graham to Julius Tillyard of 24 September 1907.
19  GCPPT 1|1|14  14 January 1907.
20  GCPPT 2|2a January 1907. *Carmen Sentimentale*.
21  GCPPT 1|1|14  14 January 1907.
22  GCPPT 1|1|13  5 May and 6 July 1906.
23  GCPPT 1|1|14  2 December 1906.
24  GCPPT 1|1|13  3 July ('June' in error) 1906.
25  Tillyard, HJW. *The Letters of ACW Tillyard*. (MTC) Letter from Aelfrida to Julius Tillyard of 5 February 1906.
26  GCPPT 1|1|14  29 October 1906.
27  GCPPT 1|1|13  6 July 1906.
    Tillyard, HJW. *The Letters of ACW Tillyard* (MTC). Letter from Aelfrida to Julius Tillyard of 20 February 1906.
28  GCPPT 1|1|14  20 December 1906.
29  ibid. 22 November 1906
30  ibid. 2 January 1907.
31  The sonnet, dated 23 December 1906, was later published in *To Malise* (p33).
32  ibid. 28 September, 4–8 October (single extended entry) and 31 October 1906.
33  ibid. 11 December 1906.
34  ibid. 19 November 1906.
35  ibid. 2 and 7 December 1906.
36  Tillyard, HJW. *The Letters of ACW Tillyard* (MTC). Letter from Aelfrida to Julius Tillyard of 13 April 1905. Aelfrida's ring was very up-to-date; diamonds had only just begun to replace pearls as the gem of choice for engagement rings.
37  GCPPT 1|1|14  11 December 1906.
38  ibid. 18 December 1906.
39  GCPPT 2|26|4(7).
40  KCA OB/i/1644 Tillyard. Letter from Aelfrida to Oscar Browning of 8 January 1907.
41  GCPPT 1|1|14  27 November and 27 December 1906.
42  ibid. 31 December 1906.
43  Tillyard, Ae. *The Glory of the West* p 252 (GCPPT 2|16|1Pt 2).
44  GCPPT 1|1|14  18 January 1906.
45  Molière. *Les Femmes Savantes* Act 5 sc iii.
46  GCPPT 1|1|14  31 December 1906.
47  GCPPT 1|1|8  16 September 1901.
48  Tillyard, Ae. *The Glory of the West* pp 8–10 (GCPPT 2 |16|3).
49  GCPPT 2|25|2(4). *Marriage,* first published in 1818 in two volumes, contains lengthy passages of almost incomprehensible 'Scotch' dialect; it is also heavily moralistic and dreadfully arch.
50  Tillyard, Ae. *The Glory of the West* p 8 (GCPPT 2|16|3).
51  GCPPT 1|1|14  24 December 1906.
52  GCPPT 1|1|10  13 September 1903.
53  Tillyard, Ae. *Le Livre des Jeux* p 58.
54  GCPPT 1|1|14 Entry undated but by context 18 January 1907.
55  ibid. 8 and 16 January 1907.
56  The sonnet was later published in *To Malise* (p 34).
57  GCPPT 1|1|14  12 January 1907.
58  GCPPT 1|1|13  5 June 1906.
59  GCPPT 1|1|14  24 December 1906. Aelfrida's comment on Cameron's prowess at waltzing was a reference to the ten dances she had with him at the Caius May Ball in 1902.
60  GCPPT 1|1|14 17 January 1907.
61  Tillyard, Ae. *The Glory of the West* p 10 (GCPPT 2|16|3).
62  GCPPT 1|1|14  17 January 1907.
63  ibid. 19 January 1907.
64  ibid. 20 January 1907.
65  *CIP* 25 January 1907.
66  GCPPT 1|1|14  7 December 1906.
67  GCPPT 1|1|17  5 February 1910.
68  GCPPT 1|1|14  20 January 1907.
69  ibid.
70  ibid. 14 December 1906.
    GCPPT 2|26|4 (2).
71  ibid. 14 and 31 December 1906.
72  ibid. 22 January 1907.
73  Tillyard, Ae. *Marrying a Stranger* p 162. (GCPPT 2|6).
74  ibid. p 146.
75  GCPPT 1|1|20  10 November 1914.
76  Swinburnian lines quoted by Aelfrida in *The Glory of the West* p 7 (GCPPT 2|16|3) are not from this poem but her association of it with a hero and heroine more usually known as Tristran and Isolde shows her familiarity with his poetry.
77  Tillyard, Ae. *The Glory of the West* p 7 (GCPPT 2|16|1). The passage is crossed out in manuscript so was presumably not intended for publication.
78  GCPPT 1|1|14  14 December 1906.
79  Tillyard, Ae. *The Glory of the West* p 7 (GCPPT 2|16|1).
80  GCPPT 1|1|14  17 January and 'Friday evening' (18 January) 1907.
81  ibid. 31 December 1906 and 8 January 1907.
82  GCPPT 1|1|22  18 January 1918.
83  GCPPT 1|1|9  11 September 1902.
84  Tillyard, Ae. *Just Alice* p 186. (GCPPT 2|19).
85  Tillyard, Ae. *The Approaching Storm* p280 (Author's paraphrase).
86  ibid. p 281.
87  *CIP* 25 January 1907.

# Absolute Surrender

*'At the house of the British … Consul, Odessa'*

The newly-married Grahams arrived in Odessa early in February 1907 following a journey through 'endless snow, plains and forests' to a town whose 'dim buildings, churches topped with cupolas shaped like blobs of cream, unlit streets bordered with hoar-frosted trees, hurrying men in sheepskins and fur caps, sleighs, and glass-sheeted pavements' fronted by a Black Sea so solidly frozen that they were able to walk out on the ice, seemed exotically different from anywhere either had ever been. A town, moreover, where, as they discovered shortly after their arrival, 'five policemen have been shot this week'.[1]

The Odessa in which Constantine received his baptism of fire as a very junior member of the Consular Service did not, during the greater part of the Grahams' ten-month posting, live up to its reputation as the Novorossian equivalent of a wealthy Western European city. Although New Russia's strategic and commercial capital and of sufficient importance to warrant a British Consulate, it had also been the scene of violent revolutionary disorders and a naval insurrection in 1905–6[2] and the 'disturbed state of the town'[3] continued into 1907 as a manifestation of the violent upheavals which had shaken Russia since 1901 and prefigured the Revolution of 1917.[4] It was therefore against this background of civil disturbance ('the town keeps up its reputation … five more bombs discovered … yesterday'; 'there was another bomb-throwing affair this morning and several people killed'; 'there has been a mutiny in the Black Sea fleet – if it is not suppressed Odessa will very likely be bombarded')[5] that Aelfrida recorded her earliest experiences of married life.

In spite of the presence of ultranationalist gangs ('Soyuzniks') roaming the streets offering violence to Odessa's large Jewish population, of gangs of boys armed with sticks demanding money from wealthy-looking citizens (Odessa swarmed with beggars who squatted in the caves and catacombs honeycombing the cliffs on which it stood), and of actual or attempted assassinations of government officials, the Grahams decided to adopt 'the English attitude [and] to ignore danger'[6] and to explore as much as possible. For all that, and although

**Charles Stewart Smith in Odessa**

it was only occasionally that they found themselves in potentially dangerous situations (visiting a polling station on the occasion of the convention of the second Duma on 10 February, they 'thought of bomb-throwing anarchists committing suicide on the street and so forth but … saw nothing'[7]; attending a service in the Cathedral to celebrate the Tsar's birthday, they 'drove away without a bomb having been thrown or Constantine having tripped over his sword'[8], he having worn dress uniform for the first time), worsening of the permanent state of tension brought an armed guard to their apartment, caused Constantine to load his government-issue revolver at night, Aelfrida to sleep with her dagger under her pillow, and the British Consul-General to describe Odessa as a 'bloody city'.[9]

The Consul-General was Charles Stewart Smith, described by Aelfrida as 'a naval officer of the best type' aged 'about sixty'. (Note added later: '*Wrong*, 48!')[10] The Grahams had been warned by the Foreign Office that Mr Smith was 'difficult to get on with' (they were also informed that he 'cared only for his children and his God')[11] but did not find him so, Aelfrida noting early in their stay that 'he likes Constantine [and] is getting very fond of me' (he called her, at her request, by her Christian name) and adding 'that as long as one is deferential … one can get as near as one likes'.[12]

As it transpired, Mr Smith was lonely, his wife and family being then in England. (His children were being educated there, their mother visiting them during the shorter holidays of the school year and they – or some of them – travelling to Odessa for the longer ones.) In spite, therefore, of Aelfrida playfully warning him that she and Constantine were 'extremely independent both in views and actions, and might offend him'[13], it was at his suggestion they shared the consular apartment to save expense and because of the difficulty of finding suitable accommodation elsewhere; given the disturbed state of the town it was safer as well, for in Otradnaya Street they benefited from Mr Smith's armed guard. The chamber allotted them was 'palatial, pillared and corniced [and] about three times as big as the King of Italy's sleeping apartment at the Pitti'[14]; to render it more homely, the Grahams bought a rocking chair and sofa and real and artificial plants and Aelfrida made a curtain ('*a hundred yards* of sewing')[15] to divide it into two more domestically-scaled rooms. A faded photograph pasted with her diary shows their living area exactly as described with the Grahams and Mr Smith seated between the plants in front of the curtain: his visiting their quarters was not surprising, given that he 'continues to father me and Constantine … [and] is being admitted to a good deal of our intimacy and we to his'. (The Consul-General's relationship with his vice-consul was more formal at the Consulate, Aelfrida finding their "Graham" and "Yes sir" exchanges rather amusing.)[16] In return, Aelfrida acted as hostess ("the consul-general's house is a large one and I have everything in my hands") but judging by her later description of herself as 'nothing but an unpaid housekeeper'[17], had no idea that in Mrs Smith's absence she was being trained by Mr Smith in the duties of a consular wife, that in marrying Constantine she had espoused his career as well, or that the married state, though it brought her status and rights, conferred responsibilities too, her lack of perception of her new role being implicit in her feeling 'a little unwanted having no official position'[18] at the dinner parties and soirées held at the Consulate for the intelligentsia, politicians, and merchants of a town which, though barely under the control of its Governor General, continued to function as a university, entrepôt, and seat of local government, and for the French, Italian, German and other diplomats *en poste* there. She also accompanied her husband and Mr Smith to receptions

and balls held by the Odessan élite in the winter and to the tennis parties which occupied the spring and summer months and, at Mr Smith's request, visited British nationals in the local hospitals, assisted in the repatriation of distressed British subjects, and entertained members of the Odessan sisterhood of English governesses. She also held her own At Homes on Mondays, visitors signing their names in her new Visitors Book.

The Odessan élite was not, however, the cultured company which Aelfrid expected. "The eternal rotter", she wrote, "is to be found in great quantities in Odessa"[19] and a letter from Constantine to Julius expands her statement: "I am dagoising in the midst of this most hybrid litter of unattached cosmopolitans that ever wagged their shiny, glittering, garish little selves in the midst of a shiny glittery pretence of culture and refinement. French is reduced to Esperanto …" In fact, amid "miserable coquetting and clucking females" and "clockworky little males", he was very happy ("the slanging is a way of showing it")[20], perhaps because Odessan society reminded him of the raffish circles in which he and his mother moved in Paris. Indeed, life in the Consular Service suited Constantine perfectly, steadying him and giving him a sense of purpose as his D'Annunzian view of life had not. Aelfrida was surprised at her new husband's "facile good manners and courtesy and the way in which he found just the right thing to say", noting that he was "at his best in … a crowd" and that, unlike herself whom crowds "cramped and restricted" (and possibly made to feel a little provincial, a quality hitherto attributed only to Constantine), a crowded social occasion bestowed unexpected "freedom of movement"[21] on him.

Aelfrida did not enjoy her new surroundings to the same extent. True, she did not go as far as Charles Stewart Smith who 'as so often with Englishmen abroad, [lived] entirely remote from the people here'[22] (his squiring of Constantine and Aelfrida to parties seems to have been unusual; Julius described him as despising Odessans and speaking very little Russian, and Constantine as "caring nothing for Russia" because he refused to look at it and consequently found it "dull and unsympathetic")[23] but she took little pleasure in socialising with people who, raffish though they were (she describes one as 'a fat fair lady hanging onto youth by two well-manicured hands' and another as 'a millionaire, a socialist, stingy, effusive and [with] "cad" written all over his face')[24], went out of their way to welcome the young bride in her pretty trousseau dresses. ('I suppose', she noted sourly, 'I cannot yet hope to be taken on my own merits!'[25], her linguistic fluency and skill at tennis not being insufficient to elevate one translated suddenly from social circles of which she was the centre to circles in which she was merely the wife of a junior vice-consul.) She preferred instead to hone her wit ("it's a duty one owes to one's mind to sharpen it on one's fellow creatures") at the expense of those to whom she learnt to speak platitudes and absorbed as 'copy': "I have … a lot of insight into character, coming from Cambridge".[26]

But in spite of visits to the Academy of Music ('I think Graham must have been locked up at the Consulate for Michaelides had a fine time at the concert')[27] and to her first operas ('*Eugene Onegin* shocked and hurt the puritan in [her]' because of the scene depicting 'a bedroom and a nightgowned lady', though *La Dame de Pique* afforded her 'only a few pangs of outraged sensibility' at the 'passionate love-making' therein[28]; she appears to have temporarily overcome her embargo on theatre-going) and of the excitement of working on her "Dago novel about Italy"[29] and of sending off the manuscript of *The Love of Money* to her publishers in England in March 1907, Aelfrida was not happy.

Some of her unhappiness stemmed from the darkness and cold of the prolonged winter of the Russian steppe ('like living in a dark room')[30] and the constant litany of Jew-baitings, knoutings, looting, soldiers marching with fixed bayonets, walls plastered with proclamations against rioting, and guarded churches depressed her spirits further: 'never, except in Russia, have I received such an impression of loneliness and desolation nor felt the possibility of believing in spirits of madness and of vacant horror borne on the wings of the wind'.[31] She was also desperately nostalgic for Cambridge, expressing her misery in a sonnet written on 10 May entitled *Homesickness* in which she describes the feeling of loss and longing which "… lengthens every weary street … / Drags out, like long-drawn sighs, the hours of day, / Cuts off the gleaming wings from fancy's feet"[32] and brooding longingly on the drawing-room at Fordfield with Chiara "pouring tea into the Crown Derby cups and [Julius] handing hot scones, and … his college friends laughing and talking", the vision being accompanied by "a pang … such as she had never known, a stabbing conviction that she had wantonly turned her back on all that was hers by right, on the place and country to which she belonged".[33] As *Homesickness* also makes clear ("I cannot raise my longing looks to God") unhappiness was of a religious nature too, for although the Grahams regularly attended a Protestant church – she found crowded Orthodox services frighteningly alien and feared that 'the barrier of ritual, pomp and circumstance' prevented her soul's 'free access … to God'[34] – discussions of religious matters were tabooed by her husband and she herself unable to confide to anyone else "the pain-swift thoughts that once quiescent lay" but now returned to haunt her. Worse still, it seemed as if "a

cloud, sucked up from the miasma of [her] earthly state" had interposed itself between herself and God, leaving only an occasional glimpse of Him.[35]

Such extreme unhappiness seems odd in a woman newly married to a man for whom she had expressed passionate feelings before her marriage and about whom she wrote of the months they had been married that they had afforded her 'a whole eternity of happiness'[36], but what is noticeable about the Odessan volumes of her diary is just how *few* references she makes to her feelings for her new husband and how brief and emotionally flat the references generally are, and letters home imply that Russian 'darkness' was metaphorical as well as climatic. Odd too is her sense of alienation from herself (a "queer feeling that she was … someone whom she had never met before. Cambridge, all her early life, seemed to have no connection with what was happening now")[37] and from her husband: "she did not feel a bit more intimate with him than she had done on the day when they became engaged". (Perhaps, she decided, "intimacy only came after months of marriage".)[38] It even seems that "a little devil said to her 'suppose you could leave your husband and go back to Cambridge, would you do it?'" and that her heart leapt in answer: "anything to get back". Her next feeling was one of self-disgust: how could she consider leaving her husband? Did she not love him? But the devil's second question: "do you love [him] so much that he can make up to you for the loss of everything that you care about – home, church, occupation, England? Do you *love* [him]?" (conspicuously absent is an unreserved 'yes') brought realisation that she had married Constantine for better, for worse, and that she "had better" love him because she had "got to".[39]

Were her feelings due solely to resentment that "she should have surrendered herself – which to a *woman* means surrendering everything"[40]? If so, what had Constantine done to hold her to her promise of 'absolute surrender'? And what had she surrendered that distressed her so much?

Her liberty of movement? Their stay in Odessa would not be prolonged, for junior members of the Consular Service changed posts frequently, and if unrest in the town prevented her from going out with or without a male escort, that irritating curb would be removed at subsequent postings where she could enjoy the greater freedom accorded to a married woman than to an unmarried girl. Her intellectual liberty? True, marriage to a vice-consul appeared to have condemned her to a relentless round of vapid socialising with people about whom she knew little and cared less. (Speaking very little Russian prevented her from making the acquaintance of 'the Russians we have been looking for, eager, tense, unconventional, occupation with the realities of life, instead of killing time with endless afternoon calls'[41] but her utter lack of interest in Russia's past and recent history – it included the Crimean War fought within her parents' lifetime east of Odessa and whose heroine, Florence Nightingale, was still alive – suggests deeper malaise than boredom.) But she had time to pursue intellectual pursuits of her own (of Charles Kingsley's *Yeast*, she noted that it 'had so stirred up' her mind that it had become 'a seething muddle … old problems, old interests set aside, new thoughts, science, I know not what' but said of a sonnet written on 9 June *On Reading "Yeast"* that the title was almost as stupid as the book – or her poem – or both)[42] and to continue with her 'Italian novel' though, as she told Constantine, writing of Italy reminded her of a country where 'my eyes were open, I *saw*', in contrast to the 'dark room' that was Russia[43] in which she neither 'saw' nor in many respects *wished* to see.

Loss of privacy, a loss that not even division of their room by a curtain could overcome? But was it only this which caused the metaphorical curtain which descended on her wedding day to be lifted just enough to provide tantalising glimpses of her thoughts and feelings? Or because Constantine had access to her diary – indeed, he even wrote in it – that her account becomes predominantly factual and unrevealing? But what is so striking about her account of her life in Odessa is not so much loss of interest in what she wears and how she looks (references to both are virtually absent, almost as if she no longer cared) or in people she meets except insofar as they provide her with opportunities for acerbic pen-portraits (of a Mrs Rinck-Wagner she wrote that she was "rather a Bluebeard in the matter of female friends and had a whole cupboard full of headless affinities")[44] which provided her with a means of simultaneously relieving her feelings and sharpening her wits, but sudden loss of *joie de vivre,* of which everything else is symptomatic. But not until twelve years later do we discover the reason.

In March 1919, shortly before Eustace's own marriage, Aelfrida decided that as his elder sister and a married women she ought to do what Chiara had done for herself and Constantine. She therefore asked Eustace 'if there was anything I could tell him that would be of use' but discovered to her surprise that 'he seemed to know a good deal more than [she] did'.[45] She also noted a book that Eustace was reading and decided to study it herself: Marie Stopes' recently-published *Married Love*, subtitled 'A New Contribution to the Solution of Sex Difficulties'.

Dr Stopes' 'wise and helpful book' opened Aelfrida's eyes:'much of the misunderstanding between Constantine and myself may have been due to no remoter cause than our lamentable ignorance in sexual matters. All my mother ever said to me was "never say you don't want to, or he will find another woman who does"'.[46] (Years later she wrote that apart from 'half-confidences' exchanged with Lucy Longstaffe, she was "almost unbearably ignorant of the physical side of love".)[47] The book also informed her that sexual intercourse might sometimes depend on the wife's desire for it, not solely the husband's, and that "each act of union must be tenderly wooed for and won, and that no union should ever take place unless the woman also desires it and is made physically ready for it".[48] That intercourse was intended to provide *mutual* pleasure had never occurred to her (of Constantine she noted that she 'just gave him what he wanted') while the idea that 'conjugal rites' (Stopes' preferred name for conjugal rights) should not be forced upon a woman undesiring of or unprepared for them was so novel as to be almost unthinkable. But she interpreted Stopes' views on the regulation of intercourse (three or four days' sexual activity followed by a few days intermission) so as to blame Constantine:'all unknowing, [he] over-indulged most terribly. At Odessa, for instance, every night for say three weeks on end and always twice, sometimes four or five times a night'. This, she decided, 'was to make [her] subconsciously start judging men to be "coarse brutes" and to give [her] a love of chastity such as a married woman is certainly happier without'. ("I felt", she wrote, many years later, "as if I had suddenly walked into an antechamber of Hell and found the devil there".)[49] Hence it was Aelfrida's equation of absolute surrender with Constantine's nightly violation of her body in acts tantamount to marital rape which caused her to shut down her emotions so drastically on what was effectively her honeymoon.

As usual, she turned to literature to express her feelings; not a hint of distress appears in her Odessan diaries. A passage in a later novel evokes her disillusionment ("Marriage seemed to promise not only personal happiness, but a wider horizon and an initiation into all sorts of glorious mysteries [but her husband] had taken her by the hand, and, bearing the lighted torch of Love, had led her – to [a] blind alley")[50] but it is perhaps in three poems written within a month of each other in Odessa that we should look for a reason for her predicament. The first poem, *My Puritanism* of 18 May, seems surprisingly gloomy given that the belated arrival of spring allowed the Grahams to 'peep into dacha gardens and steal … a sight of things growing'[51], but on reading it we discover that contrary to her later tendency to blame her husband's and her own 'lamentable ignorance' in sexual matters and Constantine's unbridled sexual appetite for later misunderstandings, from the earliest days of their marriage Aelfrida realised that more to blame than these was the 'puritanism' created by her peculiar brand of religiosity, this causing her to deny herself mirth, appreciation of "beauty on this earth", and sensual enjoyment by a young bride of her husband, in favour of a life bound by an "ugly law" which removed her heart from them (and them from her heart) and consigned them to the devil instead of dedicating them to God who bestowed them.[52] (As if in reparation she wrote – on the same day – a second poem entitled *Most obviously – à toi* [53] in which she tries "with speech and silence ... / To speak the love that lies within one woman's heart".) The third poem, entitled *The Empty Temple*, written on 16 June soon after a diary entry which states bluntly 'three years ago Constantine and I became engaged. *Voilà!* What else is there to say'[54], continues the theme but is written eerily but perceptively (and, as it happened, presciently) as if by Constantine:

"I made her heart a temple
And thought to dwell therein,
Bringing with me as offering
My laughter and my sin.
She said that in her temple
None e'er might dwell but God,
Its shrines stand still deserted,
Its pavements still untrod".[55]

It is hard to imagine Constantine's feelings on reading *The Empty Temple* only five months after his marriage to its author. That he might have done so can be deduced from a notebook in which poems and prose-poems by Constantine written between 1907 and 1909 appear at one end and poems by Aelfrida at the other with *noms de plume* used by both ('CC Michaelides', 'Aelfrida Tillyard', the latter adding 'Mrs Constantine Graham' in parentheses), privacy being assured only by the book being reversed as it passed between them. (The gap in the middle was used by Aelfrida for three later works.) It may be that Aelfrida's poems were transcribed into a notebook begun but abandoned by Constantine (in later years she used blank pages in his old college notebooks for some of her diaries) and that he was not privy to them at the time of composition but he may have had access to the poems as they were written and could compare their dated content with entries in his wife's diaries, a sobering thought given some of her revelations. (He certainly read them in *To Malise* three years later.) Possibly she *intended* him to make the connection, an even more sobering thought.

Apart from an adoring comment on the title page of the volume of her diary begun on 10 May 1907 (under his wife's signature 'Aelfrida CW Graham' Constantine wrote 'with a BIG LOVE. Oh *tant*'; the inscription above her name, '*d.d. HJWT Die Nativitatis 1906*', shows the volume to have been a birthday present from Julius, Constantine's rival in love), Constantine made two entries in Aelfrida's Odessan diaries, one a description of a spring fair attended by both in mid-May 1907[56], the other a strangely incoherent letter to his wife written after her entry of 19 July ('Constantine and I have been married three months – a whole eternity of happiness') implying that all was not well between them but that he continued to love her with 'BIG LOVE': "My own beloved one, What dost thou wish me to write here unless that I love thee which thou knowest ... I love thee most perfectly but sometimes the vision of the future baffles and the present is worn down till I see only the bare actual thee. And strange to say I love thee always more and more then. So I speak to thee the things in my mind not simply and without apology. But that comes with more perfect love. Then shall I love thee perfectly indeed. Constantine. Thy husband. God bless my treasure – now I see clearly what is – who is perfection. God bless my wife".[57]

We hear very little of Constantine's own voice in Aelfrida's life apart from these two entries, some poetry (as revealing in its way as his wife's) and a few letters. In Odessa, however, it becomes briefly clearer: his description of the fair, though rambling and muddled, is vivid and exciting; an undated poem, *Snow*, describing the steppes over which they journeyed to Odessa, complements Aelfrida's more factual description with its evocation of "long lithe waves of ... wind-curled drift" and "dark leaved hosts of silence-smitten trees, / The magic snow-wraith of the pine".[58] Other poems, in lighter vein, were written to cheer her up when she was ill.

In Odessa we first experience real sympathy for a young man whose D'Annunzian view of life has been as exasperating to read about as it must have been for others to experience. It cannot have been easy to begin a new career in a town where one might be robbed or assassinated on the way to work, in a country whose language was unfamiliar (French was the social and diplomatic lingua franca and Constantine's ability to speak Greek impressed local Greek-speakers but it was necessary to deal with monoglot Russians at the Consulate and elsewhere) when living in the same apartment as one's 'chief' (the Consulate was only open from 10am to 2 pm but Charles Smith rarely attended it, leaving the work to Constantine and a clerk), and married to a wife who, in spite of expressions of affection ('my *doux*') and of composition of a poem about his favourite composer (*To Beethoven*, of 29 May 1907), seemed so unhappy that it affected her health: by May 1907 she was recording 'bad neuralgic headaches' and by July that she was both 'unwell again' (this may be a euphemism for menstruation given that, to her distress, she had not yet conceived) and 'very thin'.[59]

The coming of spring, with its lengthening days and lightening of moods presaged another problem: Aelfrida's growing friendship with Charles Stewart Smith, whom she always very properly called 'Mr Smith'; indeed, the only really lyrical entries in her Odessa diary refer to a relationship which gave her "a feeling that life … might prove amusing after all".[60]

The friendship proper began early in May, Aelfrida noting that Mr Smith had been unwell and that she had perforce 'seen a great deal of him' while Constantine was at the Consulate. As the weather improved, Aelfrida and the convalescent Consul sat on the balcony; later they took walks by the sea and into the country. Constantine, possibly rather jealous, pointed out to his wife that she was behaving unconventionally by being seen alone with Mr Smith and that 'with [her] fatal wish to *make a difference* to people, [she] had been usurping the place that only Mrs Smith ought to occupy'. Aelfrida, who had only meant to be 'sweet and kind', was mortified by her breach of etiquette but secretly rather pleased at being told off: 'Constantine [was] very wonderful and luminous on the subject and such is my liking for psychological sensations … that I enjoyed his scolding, for all my contrition'. She decided, nevertheless, to 'draw back' from Constantine's superior though less for fear of upsetting her husband than because she had 'not yet solved the question of the friendship of the married'.[61]

Before the Grahams left England, an amusing fancy arose in Aelfrida's mind on the occasion of photographs being taken of Fordfield, a house 'most impressive in a picture', which, if shown to the right people, she half-jokingly hoped might further Constantine's career:

'Aelfrida: "Yes, that is a peep in the grounds".
Consul-General: "A very fine place, a very fine place, upon my word!"
Meanwhile Constantine charms the CG's wife – and promotion is the result!'[62]

But matters did not go quite as planned. There *was* no 'CG's wife' in Odessa for Constantine to 'charm' until shortly before the end of their stay and to such effect did Aelfrida 'charm' the Consul-General that he fell in love with her: 'I mean to ask no intimacy from Mr Smith. But he gives it, he gives it … he is getting intimate in a most determined way … You see, his body would never fall in love, but his mind might'.[63] A poem, *Love and Friendship*, composed on 14 May, expressed her dilemma: "Love

I know well enough, / Friendship I do not know …/ Love I see everywhere, / Friendship I cannot find…"[64]

In spite of Constantine's admonitions and her own uncertainties, Aelfrida and Mr Smith continued to spend time together, the latter, seven years into his consular service in Odessa and with (had he known it) six to endure, declaring that he wanted the Grahams to continue to share the apartment even after his wife's return. Initially, it seems, Aelfrida behaved to Mr Smith as she behaved towards her father ('I play chess with him, help him on with his coat and give him the quaint conversation he enjoys')[65] but the tenor of the relationship altered during the beautiful Odessan summer:

> 14 July: 'I had no idea he would allow me the privilege of so much friendship. He is *very* fond of me. The other day he took me to Arcadia for the evening …'[66]
> 1 August: (of a further visit to Arcadia) 'I received some confidences, babbled myself, and felt, as I generally do, that he ought not to be so fond of me. Still, the fondness is a beautiful one…'[67]

We do not know what confidences Mr Smith bestowed on Aelfrida and have only hints of those bestowed on him, but it is significant that it was in Odessa that she first turned to an older man with whom to maintain a loving but sexless relationship, a man, moreover, sufficiently mature not to overstep the bounds of propriety but willing and able to offer loving support to an unhappy woman younger than himself. Aelfrida's first experience of friendship with a man as chivalrous as Mr Smith, an ex-naval officer accustomed to responsibility, to taking command, and to remain professional in a crisis (he coped in a 'tender and so masterful a manner' when she was stricken with what she called 'heart pains' or a 'heart attack'[68]; the incident happened when Constantine was absent overnight on consular business but in spite of her love of 'scenes', she did not engineer it and was embarrassed during what was obviously a panic attack by Mr Smith having to assume her husband's role in ministering to her and by his presuming that she was pregnant) was to colour her future dealings with men (and a few women) to whom she turned for support when unable find it at home.

Masterful Mr Smith, however, also wished to help her with regard to her novels, in particular to Fisher Unwin's rejection of *The Love of Money* whose completion in February 1907 contributed to her depression: 'I feel as if the whole world has suddenly gone flat'.[69] Fisher Unwin 'declining absolutely' to publish a work into which she had put so much feeling ('it was a book dedicated to Chiara and to the glory of God. I wrote what I saw of this sad and wrong-acting world; of the love of money and of selfishness; with how they might be made better')[70] and for which Aelfrida had excitedly signed the contract shortly before departing for Russia, came as shock, particularly as the publisher vouchsafed no reason for rejection. Acrimonious letters then passed between London and Odessa, Aelfrida insisting that the contract be sent to *her* for annulment rather than that it be broken by Fisher Unwin; eventually Mr Smith took the matter 'into his own hands', settling it according to Aelfrida's wishes if not to her satisfaction.[71] His doing so created further friction between the Grahams, Aelfrida feeling that in taking over 'the Fisher Unwin correspondence', Mr Smith had 'usurped Constantine's place' and Constantine that Aelfrida's innocent intention of charming Mr Smith so that he would like both Grahams equally had resulted in her adversely affecting the relationship between 'chief' and subordinate and that he, as her husband, needed to reassert 'in a most restrained way' his rights over his wife. He therefore informed Mr Smith that Aelfrida's 'mission' of friendship was ended.[72]

A brief visit by Julius (he stayed in Odessa for sixteen days in July 1907 on his way back to England after a month on Mount Athos where he had been studying "Manuscripts of Byzantine Music")[73] could not have helped, his presence creating a *ménage à quatre* of three men and the woman with whom all three were in love. (Aelfrida putting everything else aside to devote herself to the brother who had written a plangent Latin lament on her departure from England and was shortly to compose a cheerful one in anticipation of her return cannot have endeared her to her other two swains – it was shortly after Julius' departure that Constantine wrote his loving but confused letter to his wife – though it may be said that Julius' inscription in the current volume of his sister's diary meant that a morsel of him was present throughout her stay in Odessa.) Fortunately for all concerned, Mr Smith departed for England a month later on leave and diplomatic business and was absent for nearly three. But instead of seizing the opportunity of a belated honeymoon (Mr Smith's brief absence on consular business in May had resulted only in 'some small difficulties … such as not kissing each other in the middle of dinner')[74], the Grahams squabbled: Aelfrida had unwisely informed Constantine of Mr Smith's adieus ("you have made all the difference to my life", said with a meaningful look which made her feel 'ill and a little tormented') and Constantine, 'not quite pleased with [her]'[75], 'play[ed] the Acting Consul-General … over his wife' as well as the Consulate.

His chief complaint was that Aelfrida had failed in her 'wifely duty' to himself because 'victim to a force stronger than [herself]' which made her 'establish some kind of "relations" between [herself] and men'.[76] (Constantine was not an entirely innocent party: he had embarked on another intense friendship with an older woman, Madame de Novikoff, 'a very grand Russian lady … who lives in a house all brown velvet and smoke' – Madame was a chain smoker – 'and who wears all her diamonds – I hope they *are* all – at 4 o'clock in the afternoon'; she was also 'ugly and almost middle aged' and she 'liked Constantine'[77] who visited her frequently.) Mortified by behaviour of which she was quite unconscious ('I cannot see what I do'), Aelfrida assured Constantine that she cared for no-one but him and 'his happiness, his approval' and agreed, albeit reluctantly, not to reply to affectionate letters sent her by absent Mr Smith.[78]

Freed from his superior's presence at home and at work, Constantine mellowed ('his charm and his brilliance are unrestrained … Mr Smith would not know him if he saw him now [for] being absolutely devoid of artistic perception [he] will never understand Constantine') and he turned to Aelfrida with love-making 'more tumultuous' than ever.[79] Having begun to find Mr Smith's attentions something of a strain, Aelfrida was 'so glad' of the respite that she responded more ardently than usual to the Acting Consul-General's love-making in the hope of achieving a 'perfectly serene honeymoon'[80] during the real Consul-General's absence. But serene it was not.

For one thing, the apartment was chaotic, Mr Smith having ordered its complete redecoration before he returned. For another, both Grahams were consecutively ill with chickenpox. ('Smallpox, I hold', noted Aelfrida who had recently visited a hospitalised British sailor who thereafter died of 'confluent smallpox'; she had been vaccinated but was nevertheless quite unwell and both Grahams were quarantined and the apartment fumigated.)[81] Then Odessa became 'rowdy [and] as wicked' again with bombings and killings, forcing Constantine keep his revolver at the ready 'with its magazine half in'.[82] He also received a letter from the Young Will, a pro-Jewish party, threatening to assassinate him if he did not call the diplomatic corps together to protest against anti-Jewish activities and informing that his movements were watched, Aelfrida noting 'every time I let him go to the Consulate … I wonder if he will come back' but consoling herself that 'consuls cannot be terrorised' and that Constantine was bound to survive 'to do his work and to give [her] children'. Constantine himself behaved with perfect sangfroid in public, handing over the threatening letter to the Odessan Governor-General and saying in disgust "To lose one's life for Russia!" but was privately troubled because 'it is not altogether pleasant for anyone as sensitive as Constantine to be told … that there are ten young men who have sworn … to kill him'.[83] (To be Acting Consul-General for three months after only six months in his first consular post must have boosted Constantine's not inconsiderable ego but as events proved, the position was no sinecure.) To crown it all, Acting Consul-General and Mrs Graham had to entertain the Bishop of Gibraltar as he passed through Odessa following a difficult and dangerous journey to Christian outposts in Turkey (to the bishop Constantine confided his doubts as to his fitness to take Holy Communion, given that his God was what his wife rudely called 'a smudge'; Aelfrida, though accorded an 'overwhelmingly special visit', preferred Mr Smith)[84] and General Sir John French and his aide-de-camp during the General's tour of inspection of the Black Sea area ('the occasion deserves at least a 10th class Victorian Order for Constantine!')[85], Mrs Graham encouraging Sir John to talk about South Africa and finding him 'simple-minded, blunt, uncultured, strong in character and very doggedly courageous …To me … paternal and very *galant*'. (Of the aide-de-camp she was dismissive: 'he is an aristocrat of the Lord Kitchener type, but coarse. Intelligent, yes, very adventurous, impudent, of, I should think, not very clean life … he only impressed me as a … less accentuated Ralph Paget. He has the camp virtues'.)[86] Luckily, and in spite of everything – and the list of what befell the Grahams between Mr Smith's departure early in August and his return late in October is not yet complete – time spent alone together permitted both privacy and fruitful discussions of their respective pasts and mutual future and was 'quite beautiful'.[87]

A further problem faced by Constantine at this time was his wife's worsening health. Earlier illnesses (bronchitis, a bout of malaria, 'neuralgic' headaches, 'heart pains', and 'chicken pox'), though unpleasant, were self-limiting. (In fact, she enjoyed being ill for Constantine particularly endearing at such times – 'quite perfect … suddenly revealing more love'[88] – and she obtained temporary respite from his overwhelming sexual demands.) In early October, however, she had to undergo surgery. Since her 'Florentine fever' in February 1904 Aelfrida had suffered, so she said, 'practically continuous' abdominal pain. (This is the first we hear of it.) An exacerbation in Odessa in September 1907 took her to Doctor Charles du Bouchet who diagnosed chronic inflammation of the appendix requiring immediate operation. The risks were high and Aelfrida, who considered her chances 'for life or death were even [and] perhaps expected death', wrote 'sweet letters [but] not goodbye ones', to her parents, her brothers, Lucy Longstaffe (recently married, now Mrs Henry Verey) and Constantine.[89] Thanks to the care of

Constantine Graham (left) as a vice-consul

Dr du Bouchet and her nurse Paulina Stanislovna, she survived, writing two weeks after her ordeal 'behold, I feel most fully and wonderfully alive. To the doctor it is usual, to me miraculous'.[90] Though much impressed by du Bouchet ('as a doctor he seems perfect with a rare combination of scientific coldness and real personal tenderness to his patients … [he] somehow makes us feel that he is there if we need him'[91]; coincidentally it would be to him, an American despite his name and a man whose good looks she appreciated almost as much as she admired his professionalism[92], to whom she turned for advice when she later encountered him in Paris), she also found him disconcerting: 'he *watched* us too much to be altogether charming. His looks were as bad as psychologising out loud'.[93] She later turned her experience into 'copy', reworking her diary record into two poems, a light-hearted one, '*Playing at Hospitals*', published in 1920 in *Verses for Alethea* and a more serious one, *Anaesthetic (Probably Ether)*, written on 1 December 1909 and dedicated to 'CW du B', in which she pertinently asked what, in the limbo of anaesthesia, constituted life and death.[94]

Charles Stewart and Anne Smith arrived in Odessa on 24 October 1907, the former with unwelcome news for Constantine – he was to be promoted, but only to Sebastopol – but with renewed affection for Aelfrida, telling her apropos the move "if I had my way I would keep you here always".[95] Aelfrida, though dreading 'another dreary Russian town'[96] and worried that Mr Smith cared for her 'too much' ('I have so jeered at Anatolia's "pure and beautiful friendships" and yet here I have one most truly pure and beautiful happen to me')[97], intuited that with his wife in Odessa, Stewart Smith 'wants me, does not need me, and has no time or place now for "all the difference" I made'. Noting his surprise at Constantine's request that the Grahams be allowed to leave as soon as possible, she confided: 'I prefer being alone with Constantine ... Let me go'.[98]

Severe illness thwarted her. On 27 October, she consulted Dr du Bouchet about 'catarrh of the bladder'.[99] Her next diary entry was made on 24 November: on 29 October cystitis had developed into 'inflammation of the kidneys', since when she had been 'very ill'. Anne Smith nursed her like a daughter in spite of her suspicions about the relationship between her patient and her husband. (During her absence, Mrs Smith may have received reports from her sister, Miss Macaulay, an 'extremely inquisitive [and] censorious' lady who visited Odessa soon after the Grahams' arrival, and it may have been so as not to offend his wife's sensibilities that Charles Stewart Smith forbore to visit Aelfrida's sickbed.)[100] Dr du Bouchet too was 'very attentive', Constantine 'by love and courage not only kept [her] alive but beautiful all [her] illness'[101], and she recovered, but it had been touch and go – as witness Constantine's heartfelt poem *To my Wife when she was ill,* with its intimations of mortality ("Thou hast been far /... And fast I strove .../ As who should strive with oar to stem a tide / Pathless that leads to an unknown sea ...") and its expressions of deeply felt emotion: "Thou art my wife whom words cannot express .../ My love whom I do love so tenderly'.[102] Aelfrida's own two poems *To Death* and *Death at Sea,* the first of which describes death as sweet (in that it promises rest) and bitter (in that it would part her from Constantine) and the second vividly evoking her bodily death at sea but her soul's returning "unto the God who made it", are indicative of how near death she believed herself to have been[103] or had been (or, given that in the first lines of *To Death* she describes Death's arms as strong and "very sweet" and notes that he "did'st insistently [his] call repeat", may have wished to be), for years

later she described a near-death experience in which her 'spiritual body' appeared hovering above her physical one but attached to it 'by a misty navel-cord' and noted that it was only because Constantine seized her wrists in Odessa and forbade her to die that she did not.[104]

By the beginning of December more than just Aelfrida's health began to improve: Boston USA replaced Sebastopol. Constantine 'accepted urgently' and began paying 'PPC' (*pour prendre congé*) calls. Aelfrida was assured by Dr du Bouchet that, provided she did not conceive before she was fully recovered, having a child would 'right [her] constitution' and that he was certain that she would conceive before long.[105] (Considering Constantine's frenetic love-making, it is strange she had not done so already but depression and ill-health may have prevented conception.) She was overjoyed: desperate for children even at the cost of surrendering to her husband's sexual demands, she had earlier had a vision of a 'ray of light'[106] penetrating her womb and had informed Constantine that she had conceived – but had not.

The Grahams left Odessa early in December, Aelfrida torn between wanting to go and finding it 'hard to go for I have taken root here more than I thought I had'.[107] (Her remark is surprising given that later accounts of her brief sojourn describe supra-normal horrors too: 'I knew that ... the air [was] full of devils waiting to possess human beings ... and to stir up horrors'[108], horrors and devils, it seems, other than those inhabiting the 'antechamber of Hell' which was sexual intercourse but which contributed to the development of such intense physical symptoms that she equated them with 'heart attacks'. It was in Odessa, however, that for almost the first time in her life since the Perse, she was 'obliged to' do things she did not want to do: domestic chores –'never more, *never,* NEVER, not so long as I live'– if the maid was absent, attend diplomatic functions and act as hostess at others, and so on, 'heart pains' occurring the day after such an episode[109] and again three days later.) She was consoled by 'goodbye talks' with 'the only people I care for here', a remark written on the same day as she noted that she and Constantine had been married for nine months, 'a very long time'[110]: Charles du Bouchet whose hand she kissed in gratitude, and Charles Stewart Smith, the latter leaving the room 'much *émotionné*' on being informed that she felt only 'disinterested affection' for him.[111] Both Grahams were relieved to see the last of 'the murders, strikes, outrages and distresses of this unhappy country'[112], Constantine in particular leaving 'all the effects of Odessa behind in Odessa' and reverting to 'his own sweet self, brilliant without solemnity, happy without having to count his mercies'.[113] Aelfrida's penultimate parting comment was succinctly ironic ('O Odessa, what a charming place you are')[114], her last, 'goodbye to Russia for ever'.[115] But it was neither 'goodbye' nor 'for ever', for Russian experiences haunted her for years to come.

The Grahams' leave in England lasted from mid-December 1907 until early February 1908 and was less peaceful than Aelfrida hoped. Several factors conspired to upset her. (Dick the dog was long dead; he had become crotchety and his death did not occasion much sorrow.) The first and worst was that both parents appeared to have rejected her. Chiara, the 'perfect mother', had sold Aelfrida's beloved four-poster bed, the bed which had been Henry Joseph Wetenhall's and Emma Barrett's bridal bed and death bed, the bed on which Chiara herself had been born and in which her daughter and Constantine had spent their wedding night[116], and had moved the Grahams to the East Room on the first floor. She had also crossed out pages and paragraphs in Aelfrida's 'Italian novel', completed and sent home in late September 1907. (She had refused to comment on the novel on first receiving it, her being 'so un-understanding' causing Aelfrida to feel that 'silence meant distance'.)[117] The Oracle had been censorious about *The Love of Money*, 'scorning it as impure' and, with Julius' agreement, suggesting 'drastic changes'.[118] Stormy scenes with both parents ensued.

It does not seem to have occurred to Aelfrida that her father's condemnation of *The Love of Money* and Fisher Unwin's volte face might have been connected and that it could have been at Alfred Tillyard's request – or even demand – that the firm 'declined absolutely' to publish it. (The fact that Fisher Unwin wished 'to be identified with the author's work in the future' may support this hypothesis.)[119] There may also have been collusion between Alfred Tillyard and Constantine, Aelfrida wanting the manuscript returned to her in order to '*see* what the Oracle so much objected to' but her husband advising against it; defiantly, she sent for it because 'it made [her] mad with misery not to have it'.[120] Reviewing it, she (reluctantly) admitted (to her diary) that 'I knew it was too outspoken … but I had no idea … I had succeeded in conveying an absolutely false impression' – she had made it appear as if her heroine, a 'selfish and immoral person', expressed the author's sentiments instead of her own – adding sadly 'I must be rather a fool for all my cleverness. I evidently had not got my theme in hand. They kindly attribute this to my state of health and I am inclined … to agree with them'.[121] Her real feelings were probably nearer those of a character in a later novel: "I always get treated like a naughty child and fed on bread and water to make me good".[122]

Chiara's comment to Constantine that Aelfrida's 'Italian' novel had made her wonder if her daughter

'were not a little, just a little, mad' ('do I strike you as mad?' Aelfrida asked her diary) provided an accurate summary of the latter's behaviour during the Grahams' sojourn in Cambridge. Aelfrida thought she was 'nothing worse than occasionally unreasonable'[123], in fact, her behaviour verged on the irrational: a 'fit of hysterics' on Christmas Day; 'a bad hysterical fit of crying' on 9 January 1908 followed by an hysterical fugue a few days later during which 'I feared I should go mad. My eyes saw blazing lights when I shut them and I had that impulse of taking the pots off my chimney piece and throwing them against the wall … or scream[ing] until my screams broke'.[124] No wonder her family described her as 'nervous'.[125]

What happened in England – apart from withdrawal of unconditional parental support, obviously equated by Aelfrida with loss of love – to affect her so terribly?

First came realisation of her emotional dependence on Constantine, for following her parents' defection and her own recent relinquishment of two mature supportive male friends whom she might never see again, Aelfrida believed that she had no-one to whom to turn and that to absolute surrender of her body to her husband, she had added absolute emotional reliance too. This was something other than the love a young wife might persuade herself she felt for her husband ('I wonder how I came to marry anyone so wonderful as Constantine … here in England he is not restrained … as he was in Odessa. He is high-spirited, impassioned, easy to put to a blaze') for it contains an hysterical note absent from earlier assertions that she could not be happy in Constantine's absence; apropos his temporarily abandoning her to visit Anatolia she wailed 'I do not know how I shall live without him', adding histrionically, 'why do I not go too? I was not asked – they do not want me. I am not strong enough to stand Paris'. She was also, it seems, 'afraid': eulogising her husband's physical beauty, character, broadmindedness, and understanding nature, she adds that he is uncompromising, has 'a naughty temper', and sometimes makes love to her so ardently that he becomes 'cruel'. ('I fear him then', she states.)[126] And as she was soon to discover, absolute surrender to a man who had already bruised her feelings by his 'cruelty' over her obsession with Roman Catholicism and who now displayed a 'naughty temper' with regard to male friendships and lovemaking did not augur well for married life.

Second, was that she had not yet conceived, the likelihood being lessened by Constantine's absence in Paris but improved by his impetuous decision to return after ten days because of concern for his wife's emotional health, itself worsened by a letter from Anatolia saying that she and Constantine spoke constantly of 'dear Frida' "with infinite tenderness" and by one from Constantine informing her that she was not mentioned at all.[127] A 'perfect orgy of looking over baby-clothes' early in the New Year did little to calm the nerves of one 'dreadfully set on having a child'[128]; at that point she could not have known that she had in fact become pregnant just before Christmas. Ten days later she knew: 'we have been married a year today … and today I have the crowning happiness of expecting a child … You know how perfectly and wonderfully happy we have both been (sic) … [this] was the one thing needed to make all the rest complete'.[129]

Her happiness at becoming pregnant at last – the delay, she felt, was inexplicable, especially in view of the vision she had had of 'the bright soul that I wanted for my child' which 'a few days later I felt at our union … came into my womb'[130] – was tempered by having to 'fight and fight against a longing for death'[131], a longing enhanced, it may be, by Constantine's wholly inappropriate Christmas present: Robert Burton's *Anatomy of Melancholy*.[132] Even the happiness of Christmas at home, with its presents ('a magnificent pair of fur gloves from Mr Smith')[133]; new clothes ('a voile dress, black, trimmed with Russian lace')[134]; churchgoing; visitors (Lucy Verey, 'inclined to be embarrassingly confidential about her conjugal relations'[135], Eric Silvanus, now teaching in Hampstead and 'very handsome, very sad and much less able to live in a dream world than before [and] rather more conventionally Bohemian as a result'[136], John Forbes Cameron, 'certainly not in love with me now and what a mistake to conjure up the spirits of the dead! It is so dull')[137]; a first meeting with 'Swab's friend Searle'[138]; the excitement of Julius winning a prize for his book *Agathocles* and her husband's twenty-fifth birthday ('he is now quite a respectable age to be married')[139], all failed to cheer her. 'In spite of everything … my better health, my happiness, Constantine, the hope of a child … the longing seizes me'.[140]

She had little time to brood. Constantine returned from Paris 'almost distraught with rows… dreadfully thin and nervous [and] said he felt as though he had been living through months of strain'[141] (which he had) and must have shared his pregnant wife's desire 'not to be intellectual nor problem-mongering [but] to live in a garden and see nothing but flowers and trees and sky'[142] but enjoyed only brief respite, if respite his leave could be said to be. In late January 1908 he was told to proceed to Boston 'at once', this precipitating 'a hurry of packing and good-byes'[143] prior to embarkation for the Atlantic crossing on 4 February. Given her relationship with Anatolia, Aelfrida's comment as she began her next round of pay, pack, and follow was predictable: 'I may like America, even Americans, but *not*, but *never*, Americanism!'[144]

An Atlantic crossing, she decided, was '*the most infernal waste of time*'. Though agreeing with American humourist Mark Tapley that '*any* land would do for [her]' after so much water', landing failed to compensate for unfortunate impressions of her new home: 'I dislike what I have seen of America … the America of vulgar display, of roses at two dollars apiece … of rush, of shallowness, of everything that is large and flashy and repulsive … [and] it is cheap and new [and] is undignified'; worse still, America seemed 'peopled with Anatolias and caricatures of her'. 'I shall not', Aelfrida vowed, remembering with nostalgia her 'big house' in Odessa, her servants 'to order about', and the feeling that in Russia she had after all been 'someone', 'get Americanised'.[145]

She later wrote of marriage that "one gives up all the things one's nature cares for, all the people and life and interests, and one gets just one man and nothing else in return. Sometimes one does not get the whole of him either. Just that – and exile. *Exile*".[146] Exile too, because in spite (or possibly because) of her familiarity with Americans in the shape of her mother-in-law and her Shipway relatives, she experienced a greater sense of alienation from an English-speaking culture derived from her own than she did in Odessa where everything was foreign to her. In Boston too, there was no Mr Smith to cheer her up by lending her naval log-books 'where the most blood-curdling adventures [were] told in the quietest manner possible' with 'admirably English'[147] sangfroid; in Boston there was only Constantine who immediately started work at the Consulate (the Consul, Captain Wyndham, was on leave), leaving her alone from 9.30 am to 7 pm in the apartment building she called 'that little Gehenna, The Coolidge'[148] (actually a modern building of restrained neoclassical design, standing in the Boston suburb of Brookline) which provided their first American home. 'Great fits of depression' ('I dread going out or getting to know people for fear that their Americanism should jar on me unbearably – and yet I feel it that I know no-one and count for nothing')[149] were worsened by having to wrestle with the American way of life ('a perfect nightmare of a "department store" [with] one of those beastly elevators')[150], by dismay at finding herself in a 'wicked and irreligious country' where business went on as usual on Good Friday[151], and by discovering that Constantine waxed 'enthusiastic over everything here'.[152]

He did; the vice-consul was enjoying himself. Son of an American whose Michigan family he had visited as a boy, Constantine had the best of old and new worlds, literally and metaphorically speaking the language of one while retaining the novelty and charm of his European upbringing and education. (Aelfrida, by contrast, refused to learn the language literally *or* metaphorically, mocking it in the *MCJ* and unfavourably contrasting the United States in general and Boston in particular to England and Cambridge in letters home.) The discovery that one of his ancestors had come over on the *Mayflower* opened doors that might otherwise have remained closed, as did his having graduated from the English university for which Harvard University in Cambridge, Massachusetts, expressed fraternal feelings, and he was soon 'taken up' by the best families of Boston such as Professors Lowell and Barrett Wendell of Harvard (the latter and his wife, said Aelfrida, received 'quietly interesting people … who do not sum you up at so much a yard as the Coolidge people do')[153] and even the Cabots. ('Cabots are awfully "it"'.)[154] He was subsequently interviewed and 'snapshotted' in his Russian fur coat and cap as a 'prominent individual', this causing his wife to comment sourly that she was 'always pleased when America lives up to its reputed absurdities'.[155] And in spite of Captain Wyndham's prolonged absence (he did not return to Boston until July 1908) and problems at the Consulate with which he felt ill-prepared to cope, Constantine was free from the ever-present threat of random or personal violence which blighted his stay in Odessa, enjoying instead the kind of introductions singularly lacking in provincial Russia: to George Santayana, for example ('the Spanish writer on aesthetics', according to Aelfrida's understated description, though when she herself met him she was more expansive: 'an intellectual aesthete …who shrugs his shoulders at the world's ugliness and expects very little understanding from his fellows')[156] and William James. Of the psychologist supporter of psychical research Constantine reported '[he] seems to be a nervous wreck'; Aelfrida herself described James as 'so much possessed by an *idée fixe,* either his own importance or the fear of going out of his mind' that he was extremely rude to one who completely failed to captivate him.[157]

As in Odessa, the coming of spring cheered Aelfrida enormously and gloomy questionings ("what was she going to do with herself all today – and tomorrow – and the day after and the day after that. There did not seem to be anything to do")[158] gave way to a return of optimism felt immediately prior to departure for America ('forward again to the fascination of a new uncertainty')[159] and to realisation that as a writer she 'ought … to be able to get *something* out of Boston'.[160] What she 'got' forms the subject of what follows.

Mrs Barrett Wendell's 'taking-up' of Constantine Graham opened doors for Aelfrida too: 'her unctuously-pronounced words "wife of the British Acting-Consul" seemed to impress … I have six weeks, I should

say, in which to become "it"'. ("Have we not sometimes … whispered in our souls I too … would throb, radiate, emanate, tangibelize (*sic*), BE success, … success is BEING IT".)[161] Her 'it-ness' engendered visits to The Coolidge by cultured Bostonian ladies whose intellectual company she enjoyed even if she derided their appearance ('I never saw so many ugly women so beautifully, really beautifully, dressed')[162] and to receive invitations to homes where she enjoyed the kind of conversation 'one might have heard at the real Cambridge'[163] even as she deplored the appearance of Harvard itself: '[it] looks like a collection of small lunatic asylums, cheap schools and provincial museums situated in a slum'.[164] (Returning hospitality, Aelfrida, used to academic dinner parties in 'real' Cambridge, found them 'not at all difficult to cope with'.)[165] She was no more polite about Bostonian socialites, describing one lady as 'so rich she seemed to have thrown her money on the floor and plastered it all over the walls' and her guests as bedecked in 'sheath costumes … and other eccentricities of the latest fashion'.[166]

Her snobbishness derived in part from feelings of inferiority rarely experienced in Cambridge, England, and her prickliness ('if the people here object to our being poor, *tant pis*'; 'I noticed Mrs Wendell taking stock of my … dress … before she acknowledged us'[167], and so on) blinded her to the fact that notoriously snobbish Boston ladies were doing her the honour of including her in their social occasions. She responded more graciously to cultural benefits brought to Boston by what she regarded as the vulgar wealth of its foremost families: a private view of French art of the 1830s at the Barrett Wendells; a performance of Beethoven's Choral Symphony ('sacred' because of its association with her wedding)[168] by one of Boston's famous orchestras; a visit to Mrs Jack Gardner's house, Fenway Court, to see her Raphael Room ('you step straight from Boston into Italy … all the lessons I had learnt in the galleries at Florence seemed suddenly to bear fruit and I awoke to a blaze of enthusiasm and insight')[169], and a visit to the theatre where she was overwhelmed by *Hedda Gabler*, writing that 'it was even more than I expected … I cried a little for the emotion of it'. (Pangs of Presbyterian conscience – 'I have kept away from the theatre for so long and with such motives that it gives me pain rather than pleasure to go'– were salved by the thought that acting of such calibre elevated the performance to the level of a sacred rite to which she felt it 'good and right to go, though never for mere amusement'.)[170] With all this and with 'spring making Brookline beautiful'[171] she was less able to complain of being 'hungry for beauty'.[172]

She was also cheered by confirmation of her pregnancy, feeling the child 'leap and flutter' so that she 'knew

**The Coolidge, Boston**

April shortly after she began letting out her dresses and bought 'a most embarrassing maternity corset'[180] and shortly before acquiring her first proper maternity dress of 'blue shimmery stuff … with a big wide collar of real lace', of which Constantine showed his admiration 'and love of me in it'[181] and the question posed by a lady visitor who enquired if the presence of a baby in her life would not be 'an interruption to [her] intellectual pursuits?' received the answer that no intellectual pursuits in the world were worth more than 'one baby of one's own!' though she had to admit that 'being with child certainly makes us women incapable for any intellectual effort'.[182]

But not for long. Besides helping Constantine with his Commercial Report, an official undertaking for which she did considerable research, Aelfrida also worked on projects of her own. A visit to the editor of the prestigious *Atlantic Monthly* looked promising as far as publication of essays on Italy (and one on Boston) was concerned, albeit he was 'humorously discouraging about [her] poetry' and later rejected her essays in a 'very buttery letter'.[183] Houghton Mifflin, the American publishers to whom she sent *Our Lady of the Grove* (presumably the version expurgated by Chiara) were complimentary but thought it better published in England [184], but neither Constable nor Grant Richards wanted it. (She had no better luck with her poetry, Grant Richards informing her, not altogether correctly, that poetry was *always* published at the author's expense[185]; in fact everything written by her and by Constantine at this time was rejected and it seemed they must start saving to pay for publication themselves.) She was equally unlucky with *The Love of Money,* for on beginning to revise it in the light of Julius' and the Oracle's comments, she found revision difficult: 'I thought it would be quite easy to make it pure merely by cutting out a few paragraphs … Then I came to a paragraph that was essential – and crude'. An appeal to Constantine for help merely provoked his anger; he settled the matter 'by taking the manuscript right out of my hands and telling me that I was wicked and selfish to work at my novel when my child required all my strength'. Weeping, she let him take it.[186]

She expressed unspoken thoughts in more than thirty poems (at least two were scissored out of the notebook used for fair copies) written between 27 February 1908 and 22 December 1909, thoughts which, she noted, 'I could write down … but, knowing my nature as I do, I have always forbidden myself that kind of thing'.[187] (A strange prohibition, indeed.) But write them down she did, albeit it is only by reference to events recorded in her diary that we can fully appreciate their significance; furthermore, she later published them in 'diary' form

with reverence and awe *that it was my child and that it was alive*'.[173] On arriving in Boston she consulted a doctor who informed her that it was too soon to be treated as a 'maternity case' and refused her even 'the certainty of having a child'[174], and this, and ignorance of how soon pregnancy should show ('I look at my little belly miserably and wonder if there is room for a child in there')[175] and absence of morning sickness made her fear that so much did she long 'to hear is that I am to have a child. Oh please, *please!*'[176], her pregnancy might be a false one. Constantine, she knew, 'could still be happy' were she not but she herself would deem herself unqualified for happiness until she was.[177] Feeling the child 'leap and flutter' was a positive sign even if a figment of her imagination so early in her pregnancy, as was the kindness of female acquaintances, discovery of a sympathetic doctor (Francis Denny, like du Bouchet, 'the kind of man whose presence gives you courage')[178], and Constantine being 'so sweet always', bringing her so many presents that she 'hardly dare cry for the moon for fear he should disarrange the whole universe in getting it for me!'[179] Her optimistic mood was reflected in a poem *A Woman's Thoughts Before the Birth of her Child,* composed on 21 i.e. in the same order in which they were composed. Changes of word or phrase between manuscript and printed versions are minor but significant – a few words added to a title to make it more impersonal (*A Woman's Prayer that She May Have a Child* instead of *Prayer that I May Have a Child*); a minor change in a dedication (*The Mother,* of 7 August 1908, is dedicated 'to Chiara' in manuscript but to 'C.S.T' in print); removal of a too-graphic verse in *A Shoe for a Child* of 1 August 1908, the colour of the shoe changing from "…laughing red / For the blood that must be shed / When each baby comes to birth" to a prettier though less dramatic "… radiant blue… the sign that love is true". There is also the splendidly ambiguous dedication of her poem of 10 March 1908, *The Blind Greek,* to 'C.C.M' which leaves us wondering if the 'Greek' is her husband or her father-in-law (Cleanthes Constantine Michaelides) until we discover that at a Spiritualist meeting attended by both Grahams on 5 March 1908, Aelfrida was greeted by a member of the group as a medium ('Usapia Paladino told me so', was her misspelt response)[188], that Constantine was writing a novel of Cambridge undergraduate life (*The Intellectuals*) concerning which his wife commented that 'as a mere maker of novels Constantine has everything to learn. But he can *see*'[189], and that the poem concerns a seeker after "a light more perfect or what men / Have called the Truth" who at the moment of vision ("I saw all Truth") is "stricken blind" by the brightness of the revelation, a revelation whose religious connotations are lost on a 'blind Greek' who can observe life but not see God[190] and whose eyes are so focused on the mundane that, unlike his wife, he is no 'seer' of a more perfect 'Light' or of any 'Truth' beyond what himself believes to be true or as illuminated by a wholly worldly light.

The theme of willed or involuntary loss of sight and the search for whatever for the blind or blinded seeker or seer constitutes ultimate Truth is developed in at least seven of Aelfrida's American poems. (*The Past and the Future, The Blind Greek, Fear of the Sea, The Way We See,* and *Perplexity,* all of 1908, and *Who Sings of Truth –?* of January 1909, with one poem, *À la Mort* of 4 April 1908, combining this theme with another of her favourites: death. Apart from *À la Mort,* three poems, all in their way significant, have death as their primary subject: *Old Age. A Mood Picture* of 3 May 1908, in which she still longs for death in spite of happiness at being pregnant, *The Ballad of Hailstone Hall* of 17 October 1908, with its references to the death of a child, and *The Sea Lady* of 22 December 1909 whose curious echoes of *To Her Lover Drowned at Sea* include a reference to the drowned man having been only "a thing of a day and a year" in the life of the female writer of the poem.)[191] The way she develops the theme

is also interesting: beginning with *The Blind Greek,* we discover that the blindness to which she refers is not only that induced by the burning-out of the seer's or seeker's vision by the brightness of his 'vision' but is also that which develops in the eyes of someone who does not wish to see or who has allowed his eyes to become clouded by focussing his sight on things which, though valuable in themselves, are only means to an end, not the end itself.

All this forms part of Aelfrida's growing realisation that she and her husband have different 'visions' and different ways of 'seeing'. Both are 'seers' in their own way, Constantine 'seeing' through music ("To some men Beauty comes arrayed in sound"), she through the eye of faith ("Sight is my soul's gift") but their ends are different.[192] Constantine seeks personal fame through his writing and his career; indeed, it is obvious that the efficiency with which he coped with problems inherent in the position of Acting Consul-General in Odessa after only a few months in the Consular Service and the competence with which he ran the Boston Consulate during Captain Wyndham's extended absence and, following the latter's retirement in October 1908 and the raising of the Consulate's status from Consulate to Consulate-General, as Acting Consul-General until the appointment of Captain Wyndham's successor in January 1909, had been noted by superiors who marked him down as a high flier. For Aelfrida, a career as novelist and poet is a means to an end, a way of clarifying her blurred thoughts on the nature of Truth and what constitutes Truth *for her*. (It took five more years and some harrowing personal experiences before she felt sufficiently confident to write that 'Truth is not an answer to a riddle, i.e. something one can *find out*, but The Path one walks from Man to God, and the Way is the Truth'.)[193] But she is still working through her ideas on the subject and not until 11 January 1909 and using the metaphor of song and imagery remembered from adolescent religious experiences is she able to conclude a sequence of sonnets on Truth with a poem entitled *Who Sings of Truth –?* whose last line reveals all: "*Truth is myself and God*".[194] And not until 1921 does she confirm that it was indeed *Constantine* who was the 'blind' Greek who 'for his blindness … cannot see'[195] and not until half a century has passed does she admit that 'it was at the time of … perfect *human* happiness that [she] was most conscious of agonised longing for … *personal* knowledge of God'[196] and that although in Boston she was full of '*good*' love for her husband, 'longing for … closer knowledge of God'[197] took precedence in her mind and heart. And it was also in Boston and within just over a year of marriage that it became clear to Aelfrida that Constantine would never share her vision or even admit that she had one, that he intended to ignore or disparage what he regarded as mere mental aberration, and that because he would not even *try* to see what she tried to reveal, namely the "moment's sight of God" which was for her the most important 'vision' of all, he would remain a 'blind' Greek, eternally unsatisfied and unfulfilled unless he allowed himself to come to God by another (and for Aelfrida, inferior) path.

Hence she also came to realise that in spite of ostensible happiness together, she and her husband had never shared an interest in spiritual matters in spite of Constantine's pretence of having one and her own delusion (because so blinded by the 'light' of his 'genius') that he had one. But whether it was concern for her husband's feelings or for revenge that she revealed her own in a volume of verse dedicated '*à toi*' i.e. to the 'blind Greek' himself, she does not say. (Perhaps his earlier comment that she was "a poetess but no novelist"[198] had some bearing on the matter – as witness the fact that Aelfrida enclosed a copy of *The Blind Greek* with a letter to Julius in which this comment appears.) Whether Constantine was so 'blind' that he was unable to deduce all this from the poems is something she also omits to tell us but if he *did*, as his later behaviour leads us to believe, he must have been deeply distressed by his wife's public proclamation of her disdain for his 'blindness'. Possibly he *could* not, for publication of the sonnets in order of composition interspersed with poems less germane to her theme may have concealed their significance even from one attuned to her way of thinking. If he *would* not, one wonders why she went to the trouble of publishing them at all.

Another manifestation of the dichotomies between Constantine's and Aelfrida's beliefs appears in a comparison of poetry written by each (in the same exercise book) during their stay in the United States. True, there are some correspondences which may or may not be intentional, that between Aelfrida's *Commonplace Thoughts on the Birth of a Child* of 4 October 1908 with its sombre vision of a young mother's realisation that "Who soweth life, the seeds of Death must sow. / And as with God's inexorable breath, / I gave thee life, and needs have given Death"[199] and Constantine's poem, *Death,* written sometime in early October and described by Aelfrida as 'like a flash of light, a foretaste of what his best work will be'[200], being a case in point. Other poems, however, point to discrepancies in their views at the time of composition, as witness Aelfrida's light-hearted poem of 4 January 1909 *Why One Would Rather Have a Boy* ("I said if the child is a boy / All his life shall be spent in joy") and Constantine's gloomy *Sonnet* of the same date ("Man is imprisoned in the toils of life / And from her bonds he struggles to be free ...")[201], though the latter could

be attributable to the recent arrival of the new Consul-General and to his informing the Foreign Office that under Acting Consul-General Graham, the Consulate had been both dirty and disorganised.[202] Other poems point to concordances of subject, if not of interpretation, as witness the Grahams' respective versions of a poem about the Massachusetts' woods, both written in June 1908, Constantine's *The Forest of Massachusetts before the Coming of the English* evoking prelapsarian beauty, Aelfrida's *The Forests of Massachusetts*, personification of a forest as a heavily-pregnant woman wilting in the heat of a New England summer and longing for delivery (storm-tossed though the birth may be) and for cool relief when the first snows of winter fall[203], a subject chosen shortly after Aelfrida noted 'we have found the country!'[204] and added an excited description of the Grahams' discovery of Boston's still-rural hinterland. The poems were also written shortly before their move from Boston to the township of Arlington Heights eight miles away, but it was less a desire to escape Boston as quickly as possible which inspired a poem written shortly after arriving there (*The City Speaks to the Country,* of 17 March 1908) than a desperate feeling that she herself had become a city in the midst of whose rush, heat, clamour, and mercantile activities there was no "silent aisle for prayer"[205] which inspired it.

In spite of her description of The Coolidge as a 'little Gehenna' because of its snobbish residents and communal dining arrangements, Aelfrida was perhaps not as miserable there as she pretended. This is shown by her diary entry of 20 February 1908 headed 'In our very own rooms' and by her noting that she was 'very happy in my first really own sitting room which grows prettier almost every hour' because of the 'beautiful green things' bought in the 'nightmare' department store (the Grahams carried small domestic items from posting to posting but bought or hired other items locally); indeed, she revelled in 'domesticated in almost every possible way'[206] in the first private place the Grahams had inhabited in a year of marriage and when the prospect of motherhood forced a move to spacious accommodation '*not* Coolidge'[207], wrote regretfully 'this is our last day in [our] little green home where I have been very happy in spite of my disapproval of apartment houses'.[208]

118 Hillside Avenue to which the Grahams moved on 2 July 1908 was 'a ten-roomed house [with] a sweet ragged garden' occupying an elevated position in an 'exquisite' neighbourhood encompassing 'hills, woods, lakes, and the people look real New England'.[209] Arlington Heights was then one of the pleasant small settlements ringing Boston – its population in 1906 was less than a thousand – served, conveniently for Constantine, by the Boston

and Maine Railroad. It contained a few factories but was chiefly known for its market gardens and, because of its salubrious situation, for its sanatoria, one of which, under the care of the Doctors Ring, a husband and wife team of 'mind-doctors', occupied the house next door to the Grahams'.[210] The house too was 'real New England', being of white-painted clapboard and with the benefit of a veranda, which, following local custom, Aelfrida called a 'porch'. On 5 July she wrote contentedly 'here I am sitting on our own porch as happy as I can be … the room that the child will have looks south and smiles … I love being here'.[211] A 'lady help', engaged by Chiara in England, soon joined the household ('I tell Constantine that his kingdom is increasing. This time last year he had only a wife to rule over but soon he will have a child and a maidservant as well!')[212], Aelfrida deciding that towards employees she would be 'both gentle and exacting and I *will* have my household arrangements perfect' and that 'fastidious Constantine' would soon agree with her. It appears he did but only after a show of 'naughty temper' over rental and other expenses: 'the household machinery is running smoothly and I have proved that I can manage with due economy. So let us say no more of the matter!'[213]

An interesting light is thrown on this episode of domestic friction by a letter from Aelfrida to Julius, the latter in Russia once more ("one may say what one likes … if one does not mention the Czar", his sister warned him) in pursuit of Byzantine manuscripts in general and those containing Byzantine music in particular. Describing the qualities required of a wife – patience, believing that one's husband's feelings are of "supreme importance" and that intimacy with him should be regarded as a kind of "Kingdom of Heaven", a wish to share all one's husband's interests (and he his wife's) – Aelfrida adds personal riders: that she herself ought to be treated as "reasonable" (i.e. of sound judgement) "even when I appear least so"; that she should not have to "beg and cajole"; that she is within her right to show feelings of disapproval because by doing so she will help Constantine get the better of his faults. And, she adds, were *she* a man whose character was occasionally "too feminine and unreasonable", she would expect to be thrashed even by a wife as "prepared to be as reasonable" as herself.[214] What this says of the woman who once professed herself willing to become a man's slave, of the mind of a woman whose own mother had recently described her as a little 'mad', of Constantine's true nature, and of the state of the Grahams' marriage hardly bears thinking about.

As her pregnancy wore on, Aelfrida was transformed into someone quite unlike her usual self:

14 June 1908 'I am getting lazy about diary writing' (there had been no entry for five days) 'which means that I am very lazy indeed'.
21 June 1908 'I am leading a very lazy life now, full of dreams and sunshine. The child in my womb never lets me forget it'.
19 July 1908 'I read … and let the world go on its own way'.[215]

And following Chiara's arrival on 4 August 1908 to superintend the birth of her first grandchild:

9 August 1908 'I do not suppose I ever had a such a happy time before, with a mother and husband to pet me … We have the most perfect days … Constantine [is] radiant as though her coming and our child and all our happiness were of his manufacture, as I verily believe they are'.[216]

The only problem was Anatolia who, on a brief visit, went 'chirruping about the house in a rather aggressive manner'.[217]

To add to her contentment, she and Constantine 'loved each other more than ever [and] have more than ever to say to each other … we have been married a year and a half – only that and all that'.[218] (A contributory factor may have been the sexual abstinence practised during Aelfrida's pregnancy, though it seems Constantine's sensuality had evoked some response in his wife for she noted following the birth of her child that she hoped loss of sexual desire would soon return 'since I adore and love him more than ever'.)[219] As she neared term, Aelfrida's lethargy gave way to a burst of activity. Spurred on by the local carpenter's comment that "these young things have never done a hand's turn of work before they came here, either of them"[220], she occupied herself with picking 'blackberries and peeling apples to make many pots of jam' while Constantine ('more *doux* than ever') was inspired to pick cherries and weed paths ('I … stand by and applaud')[221]; essentially, though, everything seemed to be waiting for one event: 'my time draws near and I begin to be impatient to hold my child in my arms'.[222]

Chiara and Constantine hoped for a boy; what Aelfrida wanted she does not say. Poems written before and after the child's arrival are male-orientated ("Word of God to baby boy"; "Lord, make my son to be the peer of kings"; "The child is here. His cry has answered mine")[223] but a significant conversation between a fictional couple in a later novel is not: the wife, pregnant with her first child, informs her husband that she wants a girl "of my very own, to play with and talk to, and educate all on my own theories", adding that "a girl would be more mine, I should talk to her about what I used to do when I was little, and about home and all the things I love, and she would understand … I used to think I liked boys best because girls sometimes giggle and are silly, but now I know I must have a girl". Her husband accuses her of loving him less than she did ("you are telling me in so many words that I am not enough for you, that you need a girl-child to fill the gap") and asserts that the coming child will be a boy: "the von Thieles always have a son first".[224] Constantine and Aelfrida's real-life son was to be called Constantine after his father and grandfather, Immanuel ('God with us')[225], and Wetenhall ('Chiara is very anxious that the name be perpetuated')[226] Graham.

"God sent a girl". Elizabeth Mary Alethea Graham was born on 22 August 1908 possessed of auburn hair, blue-grey eyes 'like a quiet sea on a cloudy day', a firm jaw, and an air of 'health and intelligence'.[227] Though Aelfrida later liked to think that her daughter's first two names had biblical connotations, Elizabeth being that of the mother of John the Baptist whose child leapt in her womb at the Visitation because he recognised Godhead Incarnate in Mary's and Mary that of the Mother of God with whom Aelfrida identified insofar as she believed that *her* child's spirit had entered *her* womb in Odessa in a kind of mystic Annunciation, they were also those of maternal and paternal relatives[228]; her third, deriving from the Greek word '*aletheia*', meaning Truth, was probably of deeper significance, 'Truth' being both God and Aelfrida's path to Him. And although Alethea's mother suffered labour pains 'such as I had not thought earth or hell could produce' (on 28 July she had recorded that Constantine did not want her to write him 'a love letter in case I died in childbirth', consoling herself that 'the child itself would be the only consolation' because emblematic of 'our love's eternal continuance' but sentimentally thought it 'unwise to omit anything that might … mitigate so great a sorrow; she wrote her spiky sonnet *The Way We See* instead)[229] and her grandmother spontaneously expressed her disappointment at the child's sex ('a *girl*!'), Aelfrida was delighted: '[Alethea] was *mine*'.[230]

September 1908 was one of the happiest months in Aelfrida's life to date. The new baby's Greek great-aunt and godmother Eurydice (Dr Denny's sister stood proxy at her baptism) sent thirty yards of white hand-made silk for tiny Alethea's future wedding dress. Chiara, concealing her chagrin, wrote immediately to Ancifera Gregory painting 'a lovely picture of our happiness' and behaved 'very grandmotherly' towards her first grandchild. Constantine was 'enthusiastically loving and a little stern'.[231] (A photograph taken at the time shows Alethea's father holding her and looking supercilious and detached; 'grandmotherly' Chiara bends over them looking like a woman who 'may sit on endless committees

and … believe in Higher Education for Women but she is an emotionalist when all is said and done'.)[232] Aelfrida 'felt watchful and tender and as though [she] had an infinite capacity for patience with the child', though when Alethea cried she cried too, thinking, in the manner so typical of her, 'of all the pains that she would have and that I could not make better'[233] and discovering to her surprise that 'my self-confident self is distrustful of my own powers of looking after Alethea adequately. And yet she is healthy and I am intelligent'.[234] To allay her fears, Dr Denny sent her Chavasse's *Advice to a Mother*, which she described in the foreword to a later work as a book to be "read and *used*, much like a cookery book"[235]; to Constantine he gave a talk on 'What a Young Husband Ought to Know' ('Constantine said "disgusting" to suggested expedients for defeating the ends of nature')[236] in order to prevent a second pregnancy too soon after his wife's first. Aelfrida was cheered and encouraged by being deluged with presents from Arlington Heights neighbours who had taken a friendly interest in her pregnancy and by visits from Boston acquaintances who 'all treat me protectingly and rejoice over my home'[237]; Constantine also showered her with gifts and began to 'court' her again after nine months abstinence: 'I am grown vain and wear my best clothes for fear that he should love me chiefly as the mother of Alethea … I wore my pink silk dress for dinner and was specially charming'.[238] Following Chiara's and the monthly nurse's departure in late September, she revelled in their regained intimacy, preferring after the excitements of pregnancy and delivery to be alone with her husband and baby.

Reality, in the shape of Anatolia Michaelides, interrupted the idyll. Apart from her flying visit in August, during which she 'talked a good deal of twaddle about her own nobility and her boundless love for Argyris' but had otherwise provoked '*no rows*'[239], Anatolia had not met Aelfrida since the latter's marriage to her son, a marriage Anatolia refused to attend. A longer visit in October 1908 did not pass off so smoothly. Anatolia did not try to conceal her aversion for her daughter-in-law (she also gave her son an 'insulting' message from 'Juanita', the content of which Aelfrida does not relate)[240] but appeared mellowed by the new baby: 'I love to see Anatolia with Alethea. My child brings out all that is good in her … Anatolia and I can love each other over Alethea'.[241] But with Anatolia, seeming truce was merely prelude to renewed warfare. Disregarding circumstances which might have suggested more pacific behaviour – if Constantine was absent, 'sometimes she almost forgets that I am the woman in possession'– when Constantine was at home, she became so 'miserably jealous'[242] that although Aelfrida hoped that the presence of Constantine's child and his mother's first grandchild might have 'reconciled' them, rows broke out, the latter informing her son that he had no love left in his heart for *her*.[243] Skirmishes continued after her departure, Anatolia combining in one and the same letter a panegyric account of how no one could 'get beyond the reach of her sublime love' and abuse for her son over some trivial incident. 'I had thought all that was over for ever', wrote Aelfrida resignedly.[244]

With Anatolia departed and Constantine away all day, Aelfrida revelled in solitude and her daughter, declaring her to be 'beautiful and loving' (prophetically, she also wondered 'whether I shall have so much joy from her when she is older')[245] and noting that 'if I do not write of her perfections … I have nothing to say'[246] and that 'in having her, in tending her, in seeing her perfectly well and happy, I have found peace'.[247] But if we do not hear much of Alethea in what follows, it is not because Aelfrida did not write about her; like her mother before her, she began a record of her daughter's 'being, doing and saying'. Details of Alethea's life went into the 'baby book', leaving the incorrect impression that she was peripheral to her mother's, an impression underlined by Aelfrida refusing to leave her with anyone else for the first nine months of her life and then only because unable to breast feed any longer and because Constantine demanded social life together. What little we have of baby and toddler Alethea in Aelfrida's diaries is limited to her daughter's sociability ('she is as friendly as she is fat')[248], to games played ('we have fine times together in the snow')[249], to vignettes of Alethea aged nineteen months 'helping' with domestic duties and, when able to enunciate, informing the world that her surname was "Graeme".[250] Her Greek Orthodox christening 'with all its gorgeous ritual most strangely evoked in this prosaic land'[251] went un-chronicled because Aelfrida was ill and because she did not feel moved to record it later; it may be, however, that preparing for 'the happiest Christmas Day that Constantine and I have ever spent'[252] and composition of two poems to celebrate Constantine's 26th birthday on 29 December (*To Malise* and *The Song of Big Love*)[253] took up all the time not dedicated to her daughter. But although the contrast with Aelfrida's hysterical behaviour on Christmas Day 1907 is remarkable, the Christmas dinner eaten in 'joy and peace' in 1908 was marred by a display of Constantine's 'naughty temper': he called his wife 'cravenly unselfish' in her attempts to do work more properly that of the 'lady-help' and followed his criticism by a 'tremendous scolding'. Luckily Aelfrida merely felt 'horribly inclined to laugh' and immediately after the diary entry recording the episode (it is odd to think of Constantine reading his wife's description of

the scene) Constantine wrote 'Mantalini or Micawber – which?' as a reference to and possibly an apology for his petty behaviour.

Although Aelfrida was prone to regard events which did not engage her emotions as unworthy of record (witness the comment 'oh diary, what a long record of unimportant events do I make in you!'[254] made soon after the Graham's arrival in Boston when social life revolved round entertainment of Constantine's new colleagues and their wives, a chore and a bore as far as she was concerned), it is obvious that the rural life she coveted proved too 'quiet and countrified' and that in spite of assuring Julius' 'Minnchen' that "babies do not make one stupid, they only make one apply one's intellectuality to practical life", the arrival of Alethea in the life of one who "wanted to be a mother ever since I was 13"[255] failed to engage her intellect as well as her emotions, that her visitor's question concerning her intellectual pursuits was more prescient that the questioner knew, and that it was not long before sewing Alethea's flannel petticoats provoked the feeling that she must 'throw them down and run away and write [a] novel'.[256] This she duly did, beginning *The Spanish Swindle* on 3 November 1908 and *The Mother* on 22 April 1909. (Her poetic output diminished but did not cease.) She sums up her feelings in one of the first entries in the volume of her diary begun in December 1908: 'here I am with a perfect husband, an adorable baby and a lovely home … and nothing happening'[257]; a poem written two years later puts it more bluntly: describing "a tiny baby-girl / Who taught my restless wings to furl", Aelfrida reflects bitterly that she has lost "the open road" and that "life's not life if it isn't free", a sentiment which was to materially affect the baby girl's life in the future. A subsequent novel contains an even more portentous comment: "When I have children … I shall love them a great deal but they won't be my intellectual equals … And of course one can't love people who aren't one's equals in mind as much people who are".[258]

News from home broke the monotony: Eustace's nineteenth birthday; Lucy Verey (née Longstaffe) whose first child was a boy; John Forbes and Elfrida with 'another little Cameron', recorded without bitterness as a future playmate for Alethea; Eric Silvanus' new teaching post in Ireland; Irene Michaelides engaged at eighteen to a Karl Hillerns described by his future sister-in-law as 'just the kind of German I dislike, soft outside and hard inside and … looks just like a grocer's assistant'.[259] Julius' appointment as Professor of Greek at Edinburgh University at a salary of £300 a year, though regarding Wilhelmina Kaufmann, three women had reservations: his mother, 'overjoyed'[260] that Julius had been unsalaried and could not entertain thoughts of marriage until he was, Mina herself undecided – she had not yet accepted his pro-posal – and Aelfrida, with whom Mina had stayed at the Coolidge, gently critical: "her faults are such as do not jar on one's nerves or shock one's refinement … [but] she would be not good in society".[261] (A further com-plication was Dudu's 'little Russian wild-cat'[262] still, after three years, on the geographical-emotional periphery of his life.) Domestic problems, however, tried Aelfrida's patience sorely: 'I rebel at having to spend so much time on the preparations for living … and minding one's own house and making little arrangements'[263]; worse still, one who had always declared she 'never *would* have a Servant Question'[264] (a gibe at Lady Frazer, who had perennial 'questions' with hers) found herself obliged to find another English 'lady-help', the first having proved unsatisfactory. (The new incumbent read Aelfrida's diary, leaving little notes in it saying that her mistress should not be so rude about people.[265] That household man-agement entailed a good deal of work behind the scenes had never been grasped by Chiara's coddled daughter, Aelfrida admitting that she gave little thought to maids 'except when they are tiresome'.)[266] 'New peace' even-tually descended on the Graham household and she was able to turn her 'much enduring mind' to the 'many other subjects' which also occupied it.[267]

Within six months of Alethea's birth, therefore, and eighteen of the move to Arlington Heights, Aelfrida was more than a little bored with bucolic existence in gen-eral and the minutiae of motherhood in particular (visi-tors' harping on the subject of babies drove Constantine 'frantic with boredom' and made herself 'fairly sick of the subject' too)[268] and the pattern of the Grahams' domes-tic life was set: he at the Consulate all day and at func-tions in the evening, she in voluntary exile in a personal space (involuntarily intermitted by domestic chores and concerns) where she could think and write but was also resentful at missing the cultural and social life so impor-tant to her in the 'real' Cambridge. ('I wonder if forced unselfishness is real', is a pertinent comment made about this time, though a later comment that Constantine was 'dining with the Wendells. Not me; as usual' shows resentment lingering long after the end of her self-im-posed postpartum exile.)[269] A letter from Constantine to former mentor Oscar Browning also speaks volumes: "British Consulate, Boston. Dear OB … We live really in the country which is wild and untamed.[270] We have our child who is now eight months old. Her name is Alathea (*sic*) and she is very beautiful and intelligent … We both of us write and read and see those friends whom we can lure to Arlington Heights … I have my fill of theatres and concerts …[271] Yours ever, Constantine Graham *né* Michaelides".[272]

Dr Denny having informed her in March 1909 that she had a duty to herself as well as to her child and Constantine's insistence that she play the part of consu-lar wife, caused Aelfrida 'break out of 'the magic circle around our hill' and re-emerge 'into ordinary life'.[273] First came calls on other 'Arlington Heighters', then trips to Boston, one a five day stay with Dr Denny's sister while Constantine visited the Shipways in New York ('actually off my hill … it was just what I wanted, only I do not find it any easier … to live without Constantine'[274]; she does not say why she did not accompany him), another a lecture by Goldsworthy Lowes Dickinson ('to hear [this] English voice and perfect language was like having a draught of water in the desert'), after which Dickinson clasped Constantine 'warmly by the hand and looked at him with that kind of noble love that men sometimes have for other men'.[275]

Once off her hill and increasingly sorry to return to household duties when longer or shorter absences were over, Aelfrida discovered that increased freedom came at a price. Constantine, who had once found her attraction for men amusing, saying that 'in a quarter of an hour's tête-à-tête' she could have a man at her feet[276] was more and more inclined to possessiveness, allowing her just one dance with a Harvard lecturer (a friend of Julius' whom Aelfrida had met in Cambridge) and that 'with an air of allowing [her] just so much rope' on the unlikely basis that young Kirkwood was in love with her. True, Kirkwood had 'looked things unutterable' but as he had earlier confused the Frida of Fordfield days with a sister she never had, the Aelfrida of the Harvard Class Day Ball shrugged him off, confronting her husband with his daughter as someone 'much less trouble to talk to' and not given to 'unutterable looks'.[277] She was, however, allowed to maintain her correspondence with gentle-men friends safely ensconced in Europe: Charles Stewart Smith wrote frequently, Charles du Bouchet occasionally, and Gian Falco meekly to tell her that he was both mar-ried and the father of a baby daughter ('he has not even the spirit left to be proud of his defeat'), she replying with single-word sympathy to imply that she too under-stood what absolute surrender entailed: "*Capisco*".[278]

Constantine, on the other hand, was beginning to show that, devoted to his wife though he appeared to be, he was not impervious to the attractions of younger members of the opposite sex. Although Aelfrida was no longer concerned about Vally Crocius who was 'fatter and gloomy …[and] had another Romance'[279], she began to worry that Constantine being now 'so strong, so radiant, so much more master of his life, his passion, his genius'[280] while retaining his youthfulness might make him even more attractive to women; indeed, she had two direct instances of this, the first, occurring when she herself was heavily pregnant, causing her to write of a female friend's interest in her husband that 'I only wonder that more women have not done it here. He is more beautiful and intelligent than ever'[281], the second, occurring at a time when she herself was unwell, causing her to describe the ex-Radcliffe girl who 'flirted rather crudely with Constantine' as 'a little chit with a wide mouth and a snub nose and eyes big enough to make the man she is being nice to call her pretty'.[282] Realising that neglecting Constantine in favour of her child (Alethea, she wrote 'has *never* been naughty – though *I* have been stupid')[283] was insufficient recompense for nearly a year's chastity on his part and that the charms of a wife who had 'silver candlesticks and other pretty things on the table'[284] might not outweigh those of flirtatious younger women, Aelfrida not only got off her hill but accompanied her husband to Grand Rapids, Michigan, to visit the Graham side of his family.

The journey there and back encompassed Detroit, Montreal, Niagara Falls, the St Lawrence River, the Great Lakes, and parts of New England, but was dismissed by Aelfrida in few words. (Of one of North America's natural wonders, she wrote 'saw Niagara'; eleven years earlier, rhapsodising over a Welsh waterfall, she had written 'I think I should *die* if I saw Niagara'.[285] Manifestly she did not.) Nor was she, initially at least, impressed with stolid Michigan Scots-Dutch farmers who had not seen Constantine since he was ten, who called him 'Cosie', and who so enjoyed having a British vice-consul to show off that he was written up in the local paper under the headline 'The Gift of Tongues' because of his command of foreign languages. (Aelfrida herself, though she spoke to or wrote of her husband in terms of endearment – '*my doux*' – never called him by an affectionate diminutive or nickname, an odd feature in one coming from a family so given to these.) She also felt intimidated by ranks of relations 'grim and censorious or jovial and ill-at-ease in their best clothes' summoned to meet the exotic English import whose appearance and character had doubtless preceded her to Grand Rapids in the shape of unfavourable reports from Anatolia, joking that 'little did I think when I first met him that he had such relations – I thought they would all be sky-rockets or balloons!'[286] The presence of Alethea and her mother's acceptance by Constantine's grandparents overcame the family's suspicions (perhaps the riding technique of the former Lausanne '*amazone*' counted in her favour) and by the end of the fortnight's visit she had won them over; indeed, she even admitted that 'I am getting to like being here … I have more respect for America since going to Grand Rapids'.[287] But although the feeling that

**Aelfrida and Constantine Graham with Alethea Graham 1908**

'I could not live here … I am too civilised' caused her to experience unexpected sympathy for her mother-in-law, revelations concerning 'our Parisian Anatolia' (she had run away from home and had treated her mother badly) caused Aelfrida to note that her original judgment of her mother-in-law had been so inaccurate that she would not attempt another.

Travel on a wider scale than Michigan and considerably further than visits to Sleepy Hollow Cemetery or to a small Massachusetts town was in the air in terms of Constantine's career. (It seems that Aelfrida's dislike of all things American did not extend to two American writers: Ralph Waldo Emerson, transcendentalist campaigner against contemporary culture as too materialistic and present religion as too intellectualised – he advocated intuitive religiosity instead – whose grave she visited, and Louisa May Alcott, author of *Little Women,* whose former home was already a place of literary pilgrimage and whose idealised view of family life lived in concord and Concord revealed undercurrents of discontent, frustrated desires, self-centredness, and sickly piety familiar to Aelfrida from her own home-life and whose depiction of these in four sisters' personalities may have inspired two of her own later novels.) In February 1909 the Grahams had decided to try for a new post later, calculating the pros and cons of Bergen, Brest, Livorno, Spezia, Bremerhaven, and Emden, 'the last two less desirable'.[288] An offer from the Foreign Office of a salary of £700 pa to set up a consulate 'at Kasai in the Congo, a place not even on the map!' was an honour but was rejected for Alethea's sake (she would have had to remain in England, 'probably to become an orphan in a few months', Constantine having been warned by a colleague that he would be a 'damned idiot' if he accepted because not for nothing was West Africa known as the White Man's Grave) but the thrill 'of having had the chance' remained.[289] Fortunately for mother and child, Aelfrida's concerns regarding separation from her daughter were pacified by a November offer of Emden. Constantine bore his disappointment well; Aelfrida was first grateful ('Emden … means not leaving Alethea behind') then pleased ('I like the idea of Emden more and more … I want a garden and to be near the sea'; in the event she lacked the one and only felt the effects of the other) then ecstatic: 'also – if you want more news – I *may* be making another child. Think how glorious!'[290]

During the Grahams' stay in America Aelfrida's health was generally good. Although she had written shortly after their arrival that she wondered if she would ever be really fit, problems had been mostly of a minor nature and apart from a single recurrence of malaria, the psychosomatic headaches and 'heart attacks' of Odessan days disappeared, and though she felt very tired at times, this was only to be expected of a young mother with a ten-roomed house to service assisted by a single and somewhat unwilling servant. Aware, however, that Constantine, loving and caring though he was when she was unwell, found physical illnesses rather repulsive, she tried to play down pains in her womb and pain on intercourse ('pain in tail', she coyly termed it) experienced after Alethea's birth.[291] The pain on intercourse, Dr Denny believed, could be cured by surgery or by her having another child to rupture what he diagnosed as vaginal adhesions, but he had no suggestions regarding treatment for her uterine discomfort; Aelfrida, for her part, declined surgery and was therefore delighted to find herself pregnant again for more reasons than merely wanting another child. For Constantine's sake, however, and because 'desire' caused her so much discomfort, she tried a more immediate but unconventional cure.

Hugo Münsterberg, Harvard professor of clinical and experimental psychology and champion of behaviourism (including the power of prayer and autosuggestion) was, metaphorically speaking, on her doorstep, and with her interest awakened by de Sarlo's lectures in Florence, Aelfrida wrote asking if 'pain in tail' was 'amenable to that kind of treatment' and noted that she was 'not … ill-displeased at the prospect of testing it'. With Constantine's consent (did he too suspect that there might be a psychological element in his wife's symptoms?) she visited Professor Münsterberg who after asking her 'intimate' questions and arriving at a 'right comprehension' of the cause of her problem, gave her 'a little sermon … for taking too gloomy a view of life and for letting my conscience tell me things that are not true' ('at least he *said* they weren't', she added, albeit without enlarging further on the professor's diagnosis and 'sermon'), thought it likely that 'pain in tail' might yield to psychotherapy. Hypnotising her there and then, he told her "Ze pain vill go, ve vill haf no more pain, all vill be djoy etc, etc". Stifling a desire to laugh at his accent, Aelfrida found, somewhat to her surprise, that 'the pain *is* better'.[292]

Only one more hypnotherapeutic session took place because the Professor, advising 'prolonged treatment' (the pain had recurred within a few days), felt that as an academic rather than a clinical psychologist he could hardly continue to treat her. Aelfrida was not too put out (perhaps Münsterberg had told her things about herself she preferred not to hear), noting that 'I have the experience and he has had an extra case to tabulate, so we ought both to be pleased'.[293] In the event, Constantine being 'so good [when] we make love'[294] succeeded in overcoming both her pain and her inhibitions and her 'glorious' second pregnancy was the 'djoyful' result.

More joy was occasioned by the Grahams' imminent departure for England, their passage being booked for 12 January 1910. Aelfrida was so impatient to leave that the upheavals of packing and boring rounds of farewell calls paled into insignificance: 'I think this had better be my last *American* entry in my diary. I feel like writing it in letters of gold! It is no good, I am really *very* glad to leave. I *hate* the American spirit and it intrudes almost everywhere and spoils almost everything … I don't *ever* want to come back'.[295] (Writing to Mina Kaufmann shortly after the latter's return to Germany from Boston, she put it more strongly: "when I leave America I shall never, *never,* NEVER set foot in it again".)[296] Her final 'American' poem was written on 21 December 1909; entitled simply *England,* it evokes the love she feels for her native land and in particular for the East Anglia of her birth and of happy childhood holidays spent in a "… dream of mist, soft-flung o'er dune and fen".[297] Constantine, on the other hand, looked forward to the challenge of a new post but departed America with regret, the superior pose adopted in his letter to OB ("I… watch the thick-skinned puritans scratch themselves against the fence of art … a pathetic and ludicrous sight, by the Gods")[298] belying his obvious enjoyment of everything America had to offer. *His* valedictory poem, written on 28 December 1909, was curiously prophetic ("Out of the eastern sea, out of the mist …/ The sun arises to a glorious tryst / with the new world …")[299] because it was to that same New World he would shortly return to spend first one year, then ten more. But for Aelfrida 'the tremendous joy of being a Yank no longer' was about to begin. 'To Yank', she wrote feelingly, 'is to have trouble with your servants, to be cheated by all your tradesmen and wash females' (thieving washerwomen were a perennial problem), 'to hear of endless "graft" and to see vulgar headlines in newspapers, to be deluged with false culture … to hear the Almighty slapped on the back in church …Oh no, never again. Goodbye America, and may we *never* see each other more'.[300] They never did.

Her diary entry for 23 January 1910 was joyous: 'Home! We did get here, we really did!'. But her joy at returning to the 'real Cambridge', at no longer feeling 'busy or harassed'[301], at seeing her husband enjoying freedom from responsibility (of a visit to Goldsworthy Lowes Dickinson, she noted that Dickinson 'does not treat *me* as though I had much separate individuality but he thinks I am quite an adequate wife for Constantine')[302], at being able to attend church with people who cared for religion, at Eustace reading Classics at Jesus College and 'doing the thing properly' by living in college and by being 'a kind of Ideal Undergraduate'[303], at social life with people she loved or respected, at meeting new young men ('Swab's friends' with, at a tea party on 11 February, another meeting with Willie Searle), and at Alethea being 'most amusing and conversational'[304], was tempered by unease with regard to other aspects of her life.

The first was Alethea herself who, at Constantine's insistence, had been provided with a nurse, Olive Turner (Ovvie), Aelfrida herself admitting to utter fatigue and to the fact that her second pregnancy had upset her more than the first, but regretful at relinquishing sole care: 'I shall do it gradually but it must be done'.[305] She worried, too, that she either would not or could not love the coming baby as much as she loved Alethea, the girl destined by God to "be a mother" herself[306], for she had not had the same visionary experience prior to its conception.

There was too her growing sensation of rootlessness, for although they regarded Fordfield as 'home', even there the Grahams continued their practice 'of living in other people's houses, or on their furniture, and often at their expense'.[307] Her sense of dislocation was heightened by discovering that 'one always finds that things [have] changed after one has been away and always minds in just the same way'.[308] (In a novel she put it more graphically, her heroine feeling "passionately eager to see

all the familiar streets and colleges and houses again and to assure herself that everything was exactly as she left it. A new house, a change of wares in a shop window, annoyed and offended her beyond words".)[309] She was also out of touch with friends who had developed interests of their own in her absence and who did not seem to care if she went abroad again. And Chiara seemed distant and pathetic, her children's independent lives leaving a gap in a life which good works failed to fill.

Alfred Tillyard too was not his usual imperturbable self because his 'CIP affairs were all wrong again'.[310] They had begun to go wrong in 1908, Chiara informing her heavily-pregnant daughter shortly before the birth of 'Constantine Immanuel' that 'the dear old CIP no longer yields profits and the Oracle has had to contemplate giving it up'. Because proprietorship of the *Cambridge Independent Press* constituted Alfred Tillyard's chief source of income, relinquishment might entail 'the unbearable calamity of leaving Fordfield'[311], a misfortune diverted by the expedient of the Oracle leasing the CIP to Captain AC Taylor, owner of the *Cambridge Daily News*, he himself continuing as editor on a seven-year contract. It now appeared that 'that cad Taylor' had asked her father to resign and that the Oracle was uncharacteristically undecided as to what to do.[312]

Fisher Unwin also proved a disappointment, for in spite of recommendations that Aelfrida's books be published in England, not America, Mr Unwin himself declined to do so, saying that although he personally liked her work, professional 'readers' who reported on submitted manuscripts did not. (He may also have recalled the furore over the original version of *The Love of Money*.) This left Aelfrida wishing she had disobeyed Constantine's instructions about holding the publisher to his contract but, as she ruefully concluded, 'one must obey one's husband'.[313]

The said husband left for 'less desirable' Emden on 1 February 1910, Aelfrida noting that 'before he went he said the kind of things that one would give a life-time of devotion to hear'.[314] Missing him already, she dared not wish time go faster before joining him in Emden later the same month because the prospect of leaving Alethea at Fordfield with Ovvie and her parents while she found suitable accommodation made her unhappy. (As it was, she could hardly bring herself to leave her daughter when the time came: 'I had one moment of horrible despair in which I felt I *could not* – but of course I did … such is life as a consul's wife!')[315] But in spite of wishing that the Grahams could have stayed in Cambridge for 'eight months at least' before beginning to 'wander again'[316], she departed for East Friesland as arranged having spent less than a month in England.

# Notes

1 GCPPT 1|1|14 5 February 1907.
2 *Encyc. Brit.* Vol. 20 pp 3–4. The 'insurrection' was in fact the mutiny by the crew of the Russian Navy's premier battleship *Potemkin*.
3 GCPPT 1|1|14 8 February 1907.
4 Wood, A. pp 30–35.
5 GCPPT 1|1|14 4 and 10 March 1907.
   GCPPT 1|1|15 20 May and 13 June 1907.
6 GCPPT 1|1|14 5 February 1907.
7 ibid. 10 February 1907.
8 GCPPT 1|1|15 19 May 1907.
9 GCPPT 1|1|14 19 and 21 February 1907.
10 ibid. 5 February 1907. Charles Stewart Smith (1859–1934) entered the Royal Navy in 1871, retiring as Lieutenant Commander in 1888. After vice-consular service in Mombasa, Zanzibar and Bilbao, he was appointed Consul-General in Odessa in 1900, remaining there until 1913. (*Who Was Who* Vol.3).
11 GCPPT 1|1|15 25 November 1907.
12 GCPPT 1|1|14 5, 6 and 11 February 1907.
13 ibid. 19 February 1907.
14 ibid. 5 February 1907.
15 ibid. 22 March and 19 April 1907.
16 ibid. 11 February, 29 March and 7 April 1907.
17 Tillyard, HJW. *The Letters of ACW Tillyard* (MTC). Letter from Aelfrida to Mina Kaufmann of 28 September 1907.
   GCPPT 1|1|15 25 October 1907.
18 GCPPT 1|1|14 8 February 1907.
19 Tillyard, HJW. *The Letters of ACW Tillyard* (MTC). Letter from Aelfrida to Julius Tillyard of 23 April 1907.
20 ibid. Letter from Constantine Graham to Julius Tillyard of 28 September 1907.
21 Tillyard, Ae. *Marrying a Stranger* p 125. (GCPPT 2|6).
22 GCPPT 1|1|14 6 February 1907.
23 Tillyard, HJW. *The Letters of ACW Tillyard* (MTC). Introduction, and letter from Constantine Graham to Julius Tillyard of 28 September 1907.
24 GCPPT 1|1|14 11 and 15 January 1907.
25 ibid. 8 February 1907.
26 Tillyard, Ae. *Marrying a Stranger* p 127.
   GCPPT 2|2a September 1907, very Russian in tone, includes *Extracts from the Diplomatic Reminiscences of Lord Augustus Fitzmuffin* edited by "Lieutenant Wetenhall" i.e. Aelfrida herself.
27 GCPPT 1|1|14 24 April 1907.
28 GCPPT 1|1|15 22 and 25 May 1907.
29 Tillyard, HJW. *The Letters of ACW Tillyard* (MTC). Letter from Aelfrida to Julius Tillyard of 23 April 1907.
30 GCPPT 1|1|14 11 April 1907.
31 GCPPT 1|1|22 19 June 1918.
32 The poem was later published in *To Malise* (p 5). It was dedicated to 'CSS' i.e. Charles Stewart Smith.
33 Tillyard, Ae. *Marrying a Stranger* p 45.
34 GCPPT 1|1|12 5 November 1904.
35 Tillyard, Ae. *The Fruits of Silence* pp 117 (GCPPT 2|18).
36 GCPPT 1|1|15 19 July 1907.
37 Tillyard, Ae. *Marrying a Stranger.* p 34.
38 ibid. p 33.
39 ibid. pp 63–64.
40 ibid. p 33.
41 GCPPT 1|1|14 24 April 1907. GCPPT 2|2a September 1907 includes an article by "Lieutenant Wetenhall" entitled *Russian by the Direct Method in one Lesson.*
42 GCPPT 1|1|15 19 July 1907. The poem was later published in *To Malise* (p 8). *Yeast: A Problem* by Charles Kingsley was published in 1881. In his preface to the novel Kingsley wrote that it was written "to call attention to the questions … now agitating the minds of the rising generation" and of the need to provide solutions before "the faith of our forefathers" crumbled before their onslaught. The more thoughtful young men and women of the day, he continued, are "wandering either towards Rome, towards sheer materialism, or towards an unChristian and unphilosophic spiritualism … [and] sinking out of real living belief into … dead self-deceiving belief-in-believing … parent of the most blind, dishonest and pitiless bigotry", sentiments with which Aelfrida probably concurred. The fact that the novel's plot hinged on choice and its consequences may also have been of relevance.
43 GCPPT 1|1|14 11 April 1907.
44 Tillyard, HJW. *The Letters of ACW Tillyard* (MTC). Letter from Aelfrida to Julius Tillyard of 23 April 1907.
45 GCPPT 1|1|23 7 March 1919.
46 ibid. 30 March 1919.
47 GCPPT 2|25|3 (8).
48 Stopes, M. *Married Love* p 60. The chapter in which these lines appear is headed 'Mutual Adjustment'.
   Marie Stopes (1880–1958) established Britain's first birth control clinic and was an early champion of women's rights.
49 GCPPT 1|1|23 30 March 1919.
   GCPPT 2|25|3 (8).
50 Tillyard, Ae. *Marrying a Stranger* pp162–163 (GCPPT 2|6).
51 GCPPT 1|1|14 1 May 1907.
52 The poem was later published in *To Malise* (p 6).
53 The poem, lacking its (or any) title, appears in *To Malise* (p 38).
54 GCPPT 1|1|15 31 May 1907.
55 The poem was later published in *To Malise* (p 39).
56 GCPPT 1|1|14 His description appears immediately after Aelfrida's entry for 10 May 1907 and continues to the end of the volume.
57 GPPT 1|1|15 Letter from Constantine to Aelfrida, written after her entry for 19 July 1907. A partly illegible line inserted after 'know-est' mentions "all the [?evil lessening] clouds that sometimes pass and strange melancholy has come over me". Constantine's writing, small and legible when he began to write to OB, soon became flamboyantly large (with a Greek ε) and very hard to decipher. This, his peculiar English and his tangled syntax often makes him difficult to interpret; Aelfrida herself blamed his incoherence on the fact that he not only used highly metaphorical language but also visualised each metaphor as he used it (GCPPT 1|1|14 19 November 1906). It may be for this reason that she helped him with his reports.
58 GCPPT 2|2 The manuscript is unpaginated.
59 GCPPT 1|1|15 13 June and 14 July 1907.
60 Tillyard, Ae. *Marrying a Stranger* p 125.
61 GCPPT 1|1|14 19 May 1907.
62 ibid. 26 September 1906.
63 ibid. 19 May 1907.
64 The manuscript version of *Love and Friendship* (GCPPT 2|1) is dated 14 May 1907, the published version (*To Malise* p 37) 28 May 1907. The discrepancy may be intentional and is certainly significant: on 25 May Mr Smith left for a week's visit to the Crimea, leaving Constantine and Aelfrida alone for the first extended period in their married life.
65 GCPPT 1|1|14 10 February 1907.
66 GCPPT 1|1|15 14 July 1907. Her reference to going to 'Arcadia' has no sexual connotations; Arcadia was a resort on the Black Sea Coast two miles from Odessa.
67 ibid. 1 August 1907.
68 ibid. 4 August 1907.
69 GCPPT 1|1|14 15 February 1907.
70 GCPPT 1|1|15 27 August 1907.
71 ibid. 21 July and 9 August 1907.
72 ibid. 4, 5 and 27 August 1907.
73 Tillyard, HJW. *The Letters of ACW Tillyard* (MTC). Letter from Aelfrida to Mina Kaufmann of 28 September 1907.

74  GCPPT 1|1|15 27 May 1907.

75  ibid. 5 and 6 August 1907.

76  ibid. 6 August 1907.

77  GCPPT 1|1|14 14 February 1907. Madame de Novikoff had a Cambridge connection; in 1884 she came to England where she met members of the Society for Psychical Research.

78  GCPPT 1|1|15 27 August 1907.

79  GCPPT 1|1|14 7 April 1907.
    GCPPT 1|1|15 6 August 1907.

80  GCPPT 1|1|15 27 August 1907.

81  GCPPT 1|1|75 31 January 1959.

82  GCPPT 1|1|15 27 August and 3 September 1907.

83  ibid. 5 and 6 September 1907.

84  ibid. 16 October 1907.

85  ibid. 18 October 1907. Sir John French (1852–1825) was appointed Inspector General of British forces in late November 1907; I have called his visit to Odessa a 'tour of inspection' in default of a more accurate term as Sir John was still Commanding Officer at Aldershot in October 1907. His earlier service in the Boer War must have endeared him to Aelfrida immediately.

86  ibid. 19 October 1907. The aide-de-camp ('Lord Brooke') was Maurice Brett (1882–1934), second son of the second Viscount Esher, who acted as aide-de-camp to Sir John, a friend and colleague of his father, from 1904 to 1912. Aelfrida's hints of a 'Ralph Paget' personality were perceptive: Maurice Brett had had a rather intense relationship with his bisexual father while a pupil at Eton.

87  ibid. 27 August 1907.

88  GCPPT 1|1|14 20 March 1907.

89  GCPPT 1|1|15 26 September and 16 October 1907.

90  ibid. 16 October 1907. It was only seventeen days into her convalescence that she and Constantine entertained Sir John French.

91  ibid. 16 October 1907.

92  In a letter to Julius written on 23 April 1907 Aelfrida describes 'Dr de Bushey' (*sic*) as "a most fascinating man … extremely handsome and most human in spite of spending most of his time removing appendices from all nationalities".(Tillyard, HJW. *The Letters of ACW Tillyard*. MTC).Du Bouchet, with his Russian wife and his daughter, was expelled from Russia in 1908, moving to Paris where he obtained a post at the American Hospital. (GCPPT 1|1|15 10 March 1908; GCPPT 1|1|16 24 May 1908). During the Great War he was on the hospital's Transport Committee, organising the provision of ambulance cars and trains for the front; he also drove an ambulance car himself. (Minutes of the American Hospital August 1914 – April 1915, American Hospital Archives, Paris, Samuel Watson Collection).

93  ibid. 15 September 1907.

94  The poem was later published in *To Malise* (p 73).

95  GCPPT 1|1|15 24 October 1907.

96  ibid. 19 October 1907.

97  ibid. 24 October 1907.

98  ibid. 25 October 1907.

99  ibid. 27 October 1907.

100 GCPPT 1|1|14 15 February 1907. The Macaulay sisters, daughters of the Rev SH Macaulay, were related to a well-known Cambridge academic family and it is possible that intimations of Charles Stewart Smith's *tendresse* for Aelfrida reached home before she did.

101 GCPPT 1|1|15 24 November 1907.

102 GCPPT 2|2. The poem is undated but its context can be inferred by reference to events. Constantine was a dreadful poet – derivative, mixing his metaphors, careless of scansion, plonkingly bathetic and sometimes so incomprehensible as to make it seem as if English was not his first language but his imagery is often very vivid and his sentiments always heartfelt, as here.

103 Both poems appeared in *To Malise*. *To Death* (p 9) was written on 24 November 1907 and *Death at Sea* (pp 40–44) on 25–26 November.

104 GCPPT 1|1|75 31 January 1959.

105 GCPPT 1|1|15 24 and 29 November 1907. Dr du Bouchet was obviously of the persuasion that pregnancy was a palliative for all female problems, a notion that persisted well into the twentieth century.

106 GCPPT 1|1|57 22 August 1939.

107 GCPPT 1|1|15 27 October 1907.

108 GCPPT 1|1|52 7 October 1936.
    GCPPT 1|1|61 3 July 1943.

109 GCPPT 1|1|15 1 August 1907.

110 ibid. 14 December 1907. It is impossible to judge whether she intended the remark humorously or sadly or if it was a disguised reference to her not yet being pregnant.

111 ibid. 19 October and 14 December 1907.

112 ibid. 27 October 1907.

113 ibid. 14 December 1907.

114 ibid. 29 November 1907.

115 ibid. 24 November 1907.

116 ibid. 5 December 1907.

117 ibid. 17 and 20 September 1907.

118 ibid. 27 August 1907. Neither novel was published and the manuscripts appear to have been destroyed.

119 ibid. 21 July 1907. That Aelfrida she bore Fisher Unwin no ill-will is shown by her sending subsequent novels to the company; all were rejected.

120 ibid. 1 September 1907.

121 ibid. 17 December 1907.

122 Tillyard, Ae. *Marrying a Stranger* p 260 (GCPPT 2|6).

123 GCPPT 1|1|15 14 December 1907.

124 ibid. 25 December 1907, 9 and 12 January 1908.

125 ibid. 14 December 1907.

126 ibid. 29 December 1907.

127 ibid. 6 January 1908.

128 ibid. 9 January 1908.

129 ibid. 19 January 1908.

130 GCPPT 1|1|18 4 March 1912.

131 GCPPT 1|1|15 29 January 1908.

132 Burton's book, first published in 1621, had been recently (1896) re-issued; its discussion of the definitions, causes and symptoms of melancholy (including 'religious' melancholy) as written by a man whose self-composed epitaph described him as a man who had dedicated his life (and death) to 'melancholia' can hardly have elevated Aelfrida's mood but nor, as we shall shortly see, did his recommendations of travel and the pleasures of country life as cures for melancholy help her either. Traces of Constantine's other present (St Augustine's *The City of God*) may be seen in Aelfrida's subsequent comparison of "wicked" Odessa with "perfect" Cambridge (Tillyard, HJW. *The Letters of ACW Tillyard* (MTC). Letter from Aelfrida to Julius Tillyard of 15 March 1908) and in her use of the Augustinian term 'devils' to retrospectively describe evil spirits she believed to be active in early 20th century Russia.

133 GCPPT 1|1|15 26 December 1907.

134 ibid. 17 December 1907.

135 ibid. 6 January 1908.

136 ibid. 23 January 1908.

137 ibid. 31 January 1908.

138 ibid. 14 January 1908.

139 ibid. 29 December 1907.

140 ibid. 29 January 1908.

141 ibid. 12 January 1908.

142 ibid. 31 January 1908.

143 ibid. 25 January 1908.

144 ibid. 1 December 1907.

145 GCPPT 1|1|13 20 February 1906.
    GCPPT 1|1|15 14 February 1908.

146 Tillyard, Ae. *Marrying a Stranger* p 193.

147 GCPPT 1|1|14 15 March 1907.

148 GCPPT 1|1|16 26 October 1908.

149 GCPPT 1|1|15 24 February 1908.

150 ibid. 17 February 1908.

151 ibid. 17 April 1908.

152 ibid. 14 February 1908.

King's College *Annual Report* of 17 November 1934 notes that in Boston Constantine was "particularly happy".

153 GCPPT 1|1|15 1 March 1908. Barrett Wendell (1855–1921), a Bostonian by birth, was a Harvard scholar and lecturer, his subject being American literature.

154 ibid. 5 March 1908. In June 1908 the Grahams were invited to a 'sacred Cabot enclosure' (it would now be called a compound) and were driven home afterwards in the Cabots' car, 'a most luxurious one … we felt opulent'. (GCPPT 1|1|16 2 June 1908).

155 GCPPT 1|1|16 22 March 1908.

156 GCPPT 1|1|16 18 March 1908. George Santayana (1863–1952) was a graduate of and professor of philosophy at Harvard. Also a critic and poet, in 1893 he underwent what he called '*metanoia*', literally speaking, a sudden alteration in the course of one's life for better or worse but either way with suggestions of rebellion against established order; in Santayana's case it involved a change of lifestyle from one actively engaged with the world to one of disengagement from it, this prompting Aelfrida to call him a 'recluse'. His withdrawal may have been influential on her own later one.

157 GCPPT 1|1|16 31 March 1908.
GCPPT 1|1|17 10 April 1909.

158 Tillyard, Ae. *Marrying a Stranger* p 77.

159 GCPPT 1|1|15 1 December 1907. A poem written on 27 February 1908, *The Past and the Future*, describes Aelfrida's meeting with both; from the former, who "never turned my waiting hands to fill", she herself turns with expectation to the latter, only to discover that "his wide-oped eyes were blind". The poem later appeared in *To Malise* (p 10).

160 ibid. 24 February 1908.

161 ibid. 5 March 1908.
GCPPT 2|2a June 1910 contains a spoof of an American self-help book entitled *The Path to Personality*.

162 GCPPT 1|1|15 11 March 1908.

163 GCPPT 1|1|17 31 May 1909.

164 GCPPT 1|1|16 17 March 1908.

165 ibid. 15 May 1908.

166 GCPPT 1|1|17 3 April 1909.

167 GCPPT 1|1|15 5 and 11 March 1908.

168 GCPPT 1|1|17 2 May 1909. Excerpts from the Choral Symphony had been played during the signing of the register by "Miss May Cliff FRCO, Mus Bac. Of Durham University", Aelfrida's cousin, and daughter of Athol Cliff who co-officiated at the ceremony. (*CIP* 25 January 1908).

169 The visit was paid sometime between 28 March and 2 April 1909 (GCPPT 1|1|17). Fenway Court's interior was designed to resemble a Venetian *palazzo*; it is now the Isabella Stewart Gardner Museum and contains, besides the Raphaels, pictures by Botticelli, Rembrandt and Titian.

170 GCPPT 1|1|16 7 May 1908.

171 ibid. 1 May 1908.

172 ibid. 18 March 1908.

173 ibid. 24 March 1908.

174 GCPPT 1|1|15 28 February 1908.

175 GCPPT 1|1|16 21 March 1908.

176 GCPPT 1|1|15 1 March 1908. A poem composed on 1–2 March 1908, *Prayer That I May Have a Child*, begs "Breathe on my earthly love, O Holy Ghost, / Till of its formless gold a child be made. / I only

ask a child…" The title of the poem was amended to *A Woman's Prayer that she may have a Child* prior to publication in *To Malise* (p 11).

177 GCPPT 1|1|16 22 March 1908.

178 ibid. 24 April 1908.

179 ibid. 7 April 1908.

180 ibid. 19 April 1908. The poem was later published in *To Malise* (p 13). The manuscript version (GCPPT 2|2) bears the more revealing title *Thoughts before the Birth of my Child*.

181 GCPPT 1|1|16 2 June 1908.

182 ibid. 21 April and 2 May 1916. In a poem written on 23 April 1908, *The Fear of the Sea* (*To Malise* p 14.) Aelfrida shows her fear of the sea as equivalent to the fear mankind in general has of death and notes that seeing the sea reminds her of everything she dreads. Although a possible 'dread' at this time was death in childbirth the poem seems anomalous in view of her happiness at having her pregnancy confirmed until one realises that the lady visitor was the same Mrs Cox who nursed her in Florence when, so she said, she nearly died of malaria.

183 ibid. 23 and 28 March 1908.

184 GCPPT 1|1|17 15 February 1909.

185 GCPPT 1|1|17 13 December 1908.

186 GCPPT 1|1|16 25 March 1908. In the course of her stay in America Aelfrida worked on at least two novels, a new novel 'about my lower middle classes in Cambridge' (GCPPT 1|1|16 8 November 1908), possibly *The Spanish Swindle*, a novel she describes as completed a year later (GCPPT 1|1|17 2 December 1909) and a novel entitled *The Mother* which she describes as a 'real one' (GCPPT 1|1|17 22 April 1909), stating that she will work on it and *The Spanish Swindle* alternately. (Neither was published and no manuscripts survive). This hardly squares with her declaration to her doctor that she had given up writing in order to concentrate on looking after herself and her baby (GCPPT 1|1|17 2 March 1909).

187 GCPPT 1|1|17 10 December 1908.

188 GCPPT 1|1|15 5 March 1908.

189 ibid. 7 March 1908. Aelfrida was more charitable as work progressed, noting on 23 March 1908 (GCPPT 1|1|16) that 'of course the whole book must be re-written but it is a great advance on Ralph' (i.e. *An Interlude*, the novel about Ralph Paget on which Constantine worked in Odessa) and on 19 September 1908 (GCPPT 1|1|16) that the revised novel was now 'a flawless work of art – excuse jargon!' Neither *The Intellectual* nor *An Interlude* was ever published.

190 *The Blind Greek,* with its dedication 'to CCM' was later published in *To Malise* (pp 45–47).

191 All poems listed were later published in *To Malise* in sections labelled 'sonnets' and 'other poems'. They are by-lined with the date and place of composition and are interspersed with poems written in England and Odessa.

192 In *The Way We See* of 30 July 1908 (*To Malise* p 167) Aelfrida puts this into telling verse: "As each man Beauty, so he Truth must see" but implies that her way is right, Constantine's wrong, and that though her way will bring her only "one moment's sight of God", his way will "torture" him. In the published version of the poem 'torture' is transmuted into 'beckon'.

193 GCPPT 1|1|19 27 September 1913.

194 *Who sings of Truth – ?* appears in *To Malise* (p 20).

195 GCPPT 1|1|26 18 August 1921.

196 GCPPT 1|1|73 1 May 1956.

197 GCPPT 1|1|74 15 July 1957.

198 Tillyard, HJW. *The Letters of ACW Tillyard* (MTC). Letter from Aelfrida to Julius Tillyard of 15 March 1908.

199 The poem was later published in *To Malise* (p 57).

200 GCPPT 1|1|16 5 October 1908. The poem describes Christ killing Death but becoming in His turn Death Incarnate because of His own incarnation as a man (GCPPT 2|2).

201 GCPPT 2|2 Aelfrida's poem was later published in *To Malise* (p 57).

202 GCPPT 1|1|17 4 January 1908. A photograph of the Consulate interior gives it the appearance of a wooden shed.

203 The poem, entitled '(my idea of)' *The Forests of Massachusetts* in the manuscript (GCPPT 2|2) later appeared in *To Malise* (pp 53–54). Constantine's poem appears in shortened form in Aelfrida's anthology *Cambridge Poets 1900–1913* and in full in GCPPT 2|2.

204 GCPPT 1|1|16 13 April 1908.

205 The poem, dedicated in *To Malise* (p 12) to 'FMT and ART', her Tillyard aunts Fanny and Mary who had direct experience of the hell of life in London's East End, contains an interesting reference to a poem written by Constantine in Odessa *To My Wife When She Was Ill* (GCPPT 2|2, undated) in which he writes of pain's "living light falling on naked eyes / That cannot close their lids"; this may be an instance of Aelfrida deriving her imagery from one of her husband's poems in the same notebook. The last line of her own poem substitutes 'shameful' for 'man-made' in the published version.

206 GCPPT 1|1|15 17, 20 and 21 February 1908.

207 GCPPT 1|1|16 19 May 1908.

208 ibid. 1 July 1908.

209 ibid. 28 May 1908.

210 Dr Barbara Ring once tried some 'experimental psychology' on Aelfrida who was rather dismissive, writing of Dr Ring that she 'pretends to sum up your character afterwards'; trying word-association on her own maid, however, Aelfrida achieved 'a splendid result!' (GCPPT 1|1|16 29 November 1908) in terms of her servant associating every word with a moral maxim.

211 GCPPT 1|1|16 5 July 1908.

212 ibid. 9 June 1908.

213 ibid. 5, 10 and 12 July 1908.

214 Tillyard, HJW. *The Letters of ACW Tillyard* (MTC). Letter from Aelfrida to Julius Tillyard of 17 June 1909.

215 GCPPT 1|1|16 14 and 21 June and 19 July 1908. Aelfrida nevertheless wrote seven poems in the period covered by the diary entries here, three, as one might expect, to do with her pregnancy (*The Forests of Massachusetts* on 30 June, *A Shoe for a Child* on 1 August and *The Mother* on 7 August) and three on religious themes: *The Ascete* of 23 June with its grim reference to there being "no greater prize than knotted scourge of cords", *After reading Adonis, Attis, Osiris* of 25 June, dedicated to 'JGF' (the book's author, James Fraser, husband of the Strawberry Eater) and *The Way We See* of 30 July. Only one poem, *A Very Feminine Argument* of 26 July, is lighter in tone. All were later published in *To Malise*.

216 GCPPT 1|1|16 5 and 9 August 1908.

217 ibid. 13 August 1908.

218 ibid. 31 May and 19 July 1908.

219 ibid. 1 November 1908.

220 ibid. 10 July 1908. Constantine's departing predecessor at the Consulate had informed the Grahams that they were 'two babes on the wood and far too young to be allowed to attempt life on [their] own' (GCPPT 1|1|15 20 February 1908).

221 GCPPT 1|1|16 19 and 25 July 1908.

222 ibid. 13 August 1908.

223 GCPPT 2|2. *A Shoe for a Child* (1 August 1908), *The Mother* (7 August 1908 dedicated to Catharine Tillyard 'CST'), and *Commonplace Thoughts on the Birth of a Child* (4 October 1908). All later appeared in *To Malise*. The 'mother' of Aelfrida's eponymous poem must surely be Mary Mother of Jesus (in Greek, *Theotokos*) for there are distinct echoes in the poem of *Isaiah* 9:6, a verse describing the attributes of the child 'born to us', and of the vision of the prophet Daniel of the 'dominion and glory' given to the 'Son of Man' (*Daniel* 7:13 and 14 KJV).

224 *Marrying a Stranger* p 144–145 (GCPPT 2|6).

225 "Behold a virgin shall conceive, and bear a son, and shall call his name Immanuel". (*Isaiah* 7:14 KJV). It is also possible that the child's

226 second name was derived from the surname of Constantine's aunt Eurydice Immanuel, a lady in whose charge he spent some of his childhood and who still 'stood for a great deal with him (GCPPT 1|1|17 24 May 1909). Aelfrida's first choice of name was Damien, possibly after the convent of San Damiano in Florence founded by St Clare, spiritual sister of St Francis, but her choice was vetoed by Catharine Tillyard.

226 GCPPT 1|1|16 10 July 1908.

227 GCPPT 2|2 *Why one would rather have a boy* written on 4 January 1902, published in *To Malise* (p 63). GCPPT 1|1|16 14 September 1908.

228 GCPPT 1|1|57 2 July 1939. Noting that the date was that of the Visitation, Aelfrida described it as 'a festival that should be especially Alethea's as she is named both Elizabeth and Mary' but it is only at this point that she openly notes the happy coincidence of names.

229 GCPPT 1|1|16 28 July and 14 September 1908. A poem written in Cambridge on 14 June 1911, dedicated to Alethea and later published in *The Garden and the Fire* (p 47) throws a more positive light on Aelfrida's first experience of childbirth: "They told me that I should forget / The pain I felt in bearing you. / Never! I love you all the more, / That pain alone makes dreams come true".

230 GCPPT 1|1|16 14 September 1908.

231 GCPPT 1|1|58 10 September 1940.

232 GCPPT 1|1|16 19 September 1908.

233 ibid. 15 September 1908. In *Commonplace Thoughts on the Birth of a Child,* written on 4 October 1908, Aelfrida puts her anxiety into verse, writing that "all these my pangs shall not spare thee one pain". (*To Malise* p 57).

234 ibid. 23 September 1908.

235 Tillyard, Ae. *Messages* (second foreword).

236 GCPPT 1|1|16 26 October 1908.

237 ibid. 21 October 1908.

238 ibid. 15 September and 5 October 1908. It was on 17 October 1908 shortly after these entries that Aelfrida wrote *The Ballad of Hailstone Hall* in which a child drowns while its mother dallies with her lover.

239 ibid. 13 August 1908.

240 ibid. 12 October 1908.

241 ibid. 12 and 21 October, 1908.

242 ibid. 15 and 17 October 1908.

243 ibid. 17, 21 and 25 October 1908.

244 GCPPT 1|1|17 15 July 1909.

245 ibid. 22 December 1908.

246 ibid. 16 January 1909.

247 ibid. 22 February 1909. Aelfrida's versified feelings concerning her "firstborn [and] holiest hush of love" for whom she (correctly) prophesied "the vision too / Of God the which for many years I strove", can be found in *What a mother feels about her first born* written on 18 June 1909 and dedicated 'to EMAG'. The poem was later published in *To Malise* (p 78) and placed as written in Cambridge, an impossibility as the Grahams were still in America in June 1909.

248 ibid. 2 April 1909.

249 ibid. 21 January 1909.

250 Tillyard, Ae. *Messages*. Foreword.
Tillyard, HJW. *The Letters of ACW Tillyard* (MTC). Letter from Aelfrida to Wilhelmina Kaufmann of 4 December 1909.

251 GCPPT 1|1|17 16 and 20 November 1908. Chiara had worried that a Greek Orthodox baptism might reflect badly on Constantine's career (GCPPT 1|1|16 5 August 1908) but the ceremony may have been at Argyris' instigation.

252 ibid. 27 December 1908.

253 *To Malise* appears as the dedicatory poem in the printed version of Aelfrida's current poetry but there is no manuscript version; *The Song of Big Love*, subtitled 'for the birthday of Malise' appears in both versions. The poems are dated 29 December 1908, the latter by-lined in

both versions as written for Constantine's birthday. The first poem, however, contains lines which accord rather oddly with a 'birthday' poem written by the ostensibly loving wife of the second: "I watch thy ways and know not where they go. / Nearest of all am I, yet not too near".

254  GCPPT 1 | 1 | 16 27 April 1908.

255  Tillyard, HJW. *The Letters of ACW Tillyard* (MTC). Letter from Aelfrida to Wilhelmina Kaufmann of 19 September 1908.

256  GCPPT 1 | 1 | 16 28 October 1908.

257  GCPPT 1 | 1 | 17 10 December 1908. It is as an addendum to this entry that Aelfrida tellingly 'of course I could write down thoughts but knowing my nature as I do, I have always forbidden myself that kind of thing'; she put them in a poem, however, expressing her discontent in *Variety in all* written on 1 January 1909. The poem is misdated '1906' in *To Malise* (p 62) but gives Arlington Heights as its place of composition.

258  GCPPT 2 | 5 *A Tramp*, written in Emden on 9 March 1911. The poem remained unpublished.
Tillyard, Ae. *Marrying a Stranger* p 92.

259  ibid. 20 May 1909.

260  GCPPT 1 | 1 | 16 14 March 1908.

261  Tillyard, HJW. *The Letters of ACW Tillyard* (MTC). Letter from Aelfrida to Julius Tillyard of 15 March 1908.

262  GCPPT 1 | 1 | 17 20 May 1909.

263  ibid. 25 October 1909.

264  ibid. 12 February 1909. Aelfrida's witty poem *From a Symposium on the Servant Question*, with its verses parodying Blake's *The Tiger* and others of his verses, appears in *To Malise* (pp 92 and 93) in the section entitled 'Poems not to be taken quite so seriously'. In later life Aelfrida recalled Lady Fraser writing a handbook entitled *First-Aid to the Servantless*, adding "now that the Servant Question has been answered by the disappearance of the servant, the handbook ought to be reprinted" (GCPPT 2 | 26 | 2 (1)). The *ODNB* (Vol. 20 pp 894–5) describes Lady Fraser's handbook, published in 1913, as "a witty and indeed prophetic description of middle-class life without servants".

265  GCPPT 1 | 1 | 17 26 July 1909.

266  ibid. 15 April 1909.

267  ibid. 20 February 1909.

268  ibid. 3 April 1909.

269  GCPPT 1 | 1 | 16 3 October 1908.
GCPPT 1 | 1 | 17 19 December 1908.

270  A poem written by Aelfrida on 23 February 1909, *A Warning to the Massachusetts Hills,* ostensibly suggests that the primordial purity of Constantine's *The Forests of Massachusetts* will soon disappear: ("Guard all your secrets ever safe untold, / Lest on your soil, men come to dig for gold. / Accurs'd are you if ever bought or sold …/ Men love the hills for what the hills can yield") but is also a metaphor reflecting her own sentiments about herself and her surrender to Constantine. (*To Malise* pp 70–71).

271  Among the 'theatres and concerts' attended by Constantine was the not-too-highbrow *Merry Widow* and Loie Fuller's danced version of Beethoven's Seventh Symphony. (On the latter occasion Aelfrida remained crossly at home, entertaining a dry Wesleyan Minister and his wife.) A year earlier Constantine met the famous actress/producer Olga Nethersole (1870–1951), the meeting earning the acid comment from his wife that Miss Nethersole 'was pleased to see the Acting Consul … as meaning social recognition by the solidly respectable' (GCPPT 1 | 1 | 16 21 March 1908).

272  KCA OBi/A: Graham CC.132. Letter from Constantine to Oscar Browning of 18 April 1909.

273  GCPPT 1 | 1 | 17 19 April and 2 May 1909.

274  ibid. 2 April 1909.

275  ibid. 10 April 1909. Fifty years later, having read a recent biography of Dickinson by an author met for the first and only time in 1912

Aelfrida noted that both 'author and subject [and] the OB … and I daresay others [were] homosexuals' and that Constantine must have been one of the men by whom Dickinson was 'moved intellectually and emotionally'. (GCPPT 1 | 1 | 73 3 November 1956).

276  GCPPT 1 | 1 | 13 27 July 1906.

277  ibid. 27 June 1909. Aelfrida had re-acquainted herself with the 'rather charming young Canadian' soon after arriving in Boston, noting that 'when he found out that my sister was I, he had no difficulty in transferring his tenderness'. (GCPPT 1 | 1 | 16 26 April 1908).

278  GCPPT 1 | 1 | 17 15 February 1909. Papini had in fact married his cook which is possibly why Aelfrida received no details of his wedding.

279  ibid. 26 September 1909.

280  ibid. 2 May 1909.

281  GCPPT 1 | 1 | 16 17 June 1908.

282  GCPPT 1 | 1 | 17 19 December 1909.

283  ibid. 16 January 1909.

284  ibid. 22 March 1909.

285  GCPPT 1 | 1 | 4 21 December 1898.
GCPPT 1 | 1 | 17 14 May 1909.

286  GCPPT 1 | 1 | 17 20 May 1909.

287  ibid. 20 and 31 May 1909.

288  ibid. 7 February 1909.

289  ibid. 6 March 1909.

290  ibid. 3 and 9 November 1909.

291  ibid. 3 August 1909.

292  ibid. 3 and 5 August 1909. By a curious coincidence Hugo Münsterberg also met Eusapia Palladino later the same year as he met the woman Eusapia had earlier hailed as a medium (Blum, D. pp 307–310). Eusapia he declared an impostor; Aelfrida, it seems, he diagnosed all too accurately.

293  ibid. 10 August 1909.

294  ibid. 14 October 1909.

295  ibid. 9 January 1910.

296  Tillyard, HJW. *The Letters of ACW Tillyard* (MTC). Letter from Aelfrida to Wilhelmina Kaufmann of 12 April 1908.

297  The poem was later published in *To Malise* (p 21).

298  KCA OBi/A Graham CC. Letter from Constantine to Oscar Browning of 18 April 1909.

299  GCPPT 2 | 2 *Sunrise*.

300  GCPPT 1 | 1 | 17 9 January 1910.

301  ibid. 1910.

302  ibid. 29 January 1910.

303  ibid. 23 January 1910.

304  ibid. 7 February 1910.

305  ibid. 19 January 1910.

306  GCPPT 2 | 2 *Why one would rather have a boy.*

307  ibid. 3 November 1909.

308  ibid. 25 January 1910.

309  Tillyard, Ae. *Marrying a Stranger* p 252.

310  ibid. 1 February 1910.

311  GCPPT 1 | 1 | 16 5 August 1908.

312  GCPPT 1 | 1 | 17 1 February 1910.

313  ibid. 15 February 1910. A black-edged card tucked into her current diary lists publishers to whom she has sent *The Love of Money*, *Our Lady of the Grove* and *The Spanish Swindle*. (There is no mention of *The Mother*). The (undated) list includes Fisher Unwin, Houghton Mifflin, Grant Richards, Methuen, John Lane and Heinemann. (Not all novels were sent to all publishers). As none of the above novels was, published a mourning card seems entirely appropriate.

314  ibid. 1 February 1910.

315  ibid. 3 and 19 February 1910.

316  ibid. 25 January 1910.

# Emden and Eric

Aelfrida's 'Emden novel' to which she gave the title *Marrying a Stranger* as it neared completion, was begun sometime in autumn 1911 and finished, so she said, on 27 November 1913. It is impossible to assign an exact starting date but an episode which took place in Emden on 6 October 1911 involving herself, Constantine, and a cripple at whom a crowd of jeering boys were throwing stones may have provided an inspirational moment: on 25 October she recorded that she was writing a novel about 'Friesland and Socialism' in which a 'creepy cripple' would appear.[1] The novel's ostensible date of completion is also problematic, given that its dramatic ending comes after, and is precipitated by, the onset of the Great War on 1 August 1914. Unusually, too, Aelfrida makes little or no reference in her diary to the novel's progress other than noting jubilantly on 16 February 1912, 'the gayest of all days', that 'my novel grows'.[2]

A possible explanation for the secrecy surrounding what is perhaps the most overtly autobiographical of Aelfrida's extant published or unpublished novels is that it is a *roman à clef* so intensely personal and so revealing of her own and other's motives and actions that secrecy was essential; indeed, it appears to have been written as an alternative version of her diary and of numerous poems composed between her arrival in Emden in mid-February 1910 and her final departure in May 1912. She had already tried to conceal how much of herself she put into her novels by telling Constantine that although her poems were 'self-expressions', novels were 'mere oratory'[3]; read without recourse to her diaries, that is what they are: 'oratory – to a blank wall', to complete her remark. Read with recourse to her diaries, however, they are her life. Hence plot and personae of *Marrying a Stranger* tally closely with what we already know of Aelfrida's past and will shortly discover of her immediate future: 'Elizabeth Lavington' and her brother 'Jerome' live with their widowed mother in Cambridge. 'Elizabeth' meets and impulsively marries a German engineer, 'Max von Thiele' and moves with him to Emden. 'Max' becomes an ardent Socialist and he and 'Elizabeth' become increasingly estranged as a result. Following a stillbirth during which she nearly dies, 'Elizabeth' returns to England but with her mother dead and 'Jerome' about

Eric Silvanus c1906

to enter the Catholic priesthood, is forced back to her husband. The marriage ends tragically: 'Max' is stoned to death by miners whose cause he has supported.

To seek the 'keys' to characters in *Marrying a Stranger* is both fascinating and dangerous; fascinating because of what one discovers of Aelfrida's life and dangerous because she left no written proof of her derivations. But judging by the clues she gives, what follows may not be too far from the truth. 'Elizabeth' is of course herself as Aelfrida Tillyard and as Mrs Constantine Graham. 'Jerome' is Julius. 'Mrs Lavington' is Chiara. So much is clear. Other characters represent more than one person. 'Max', for example, is both Hans Peter the young German engineer to whom Aelfrida became engaged on a whim, Constantine with regard to his relationship with Elizabeth/Aelfrida and Aelfrida herself in his almost religious adoption of good causes.[4] 'Max's' friend 'Victor' is Eric Silvanus insofar as he acts as mentor to Max/Constantine and extends his fondness to Max/Constantine's wife. The chaste relationship between 'Frauke', 'Max's' housekeeper following 'Elizabeth's return to England, echoes the brother/sister relationship

Aelfrida would have liked to lead with Constantine and that existing between Julius and Aelfrida herself. (Frauke, though this not revealed until the last pages of the novel, is Max's half-sister.) 'Cirksena', the miners' crippled leader, owes something to Goldsworthy Lowes Dickinson in the way in which both hail Max/Constantine as a 'coming Messiah'[5]; there is also an echo of Oscar Browning's fulsome praise of 'Micky' in the words 'Cirksena' uses to describe 'Max's' role in the new Socialist society 'Max' is to found and more than an echo of Anatolia's 'higher twaddle' in 'Cirksena's' political oratory. 'Cirksena' is Anatolia too in his rejection of Max/Constantine when the latter sides with his English wife rather than with the comrades into whom he has failed to infuse 'life and the desire to rise'.[6] (Significantly, Anatolia, OB, and Lowes Dickinson are as distorted in their relationships with Constantine as 'Cirksena' is in body.) 'Cirksena' is not, however, the only cripple in Aelfrida's 'Emden' novel: just as 'Elizabeth feels crippled emotionally and socially by her marriage to a man she now regards as a stranger, so Aelfrida begins to feel crippled insofar as creativity is stifled by the demands of her growing family and by having absolutely surrendered to Constantine's demands: 'I suppose one cannot help looking at the other side of things … sometimes I feel bitterly at not being able to throw [myself] recklessly into writing novels … Of course I do not mean that I am not really content that things should be as they are …' (A long dash signifies an unwritten *but*.) 'I could write now', the diary entry continues, '[but] I cannot put my life into [a] book'.[7] Yet between October 1911 and sometime in 1914 that is exactly what she did and *Marrying a Stranger* is the result.[8]

In spite of her dismay at leaving Fordfield so soon ('it is the dearest place on earth to me and I felt I could not, could not, could not come away', written of another departure)[9], Aelfrida enjoyed 'the sweet small sleepiness of Emden'[10], a town more Dutch than German with its irregular cobbled streets, canals, red brick or pastel-stuccoed houses with stepped gables, and mediaeval town hall. Then too, the 'long earthwork thing'[11] which encircled it (its former rampart, known as The Wall) was planted with trees and compensated for the garden lacked: the Grahams had rented two floors of the building in which the Consulate was situated, a convenient but somewhat confining arrangement. Nor was the sea as close as she hoped, being two miles away at the end of the Ems canal (a dramatic episode in *Marrying a Stranger* involves 'Max' and his workmen carrying out emergency repairs to a leaking caisson dam on a major canal in a storm) but the wide skies over the flat landscape, the protective dykes which lay between Emden and the sea, and the churches on hillocks in which people and cattle took refuge

during floods, reminded her of Cambridgeshire, particularly when East Friesland, like its East Anglian counterpart, was lashed by North Sea storms or shrouded in clammy mist: 'I love this place', she wrote apropos the 'golden light' of good days or the 'flaming sky … like some allegorical picture of terrible meaning' of imminent tempest.[12] She also took pleasure in becoming so fluent in German and so perfectly integrated into small-town life that she was invited to join the local *Frauenverein* whose object was the raising of money for charitable purposes and in discovering that the entertainment (and 'copy') provided by a ladies' afternoon *Kaffee Klatsch* or a fancy dress ball at the local barracks (Aelfrida went as the Duchess of Fordfield with Constantine in cricketing attire as her wayward son Lord Hessle) outweighed in importance issues with wider implications such as the women's suffrage movement.[13] No wonder she wrote of liking Emden 'more and more [because] the quaint prettiness of [the] place, and the simple kindliness of the people … soothes me and makes me happy'.[14]

The move to Emden created other happinesses. When Constantine was studying for the Consular Service he and Aelfrida met only at weekends and in Boston and Arlington Heights they were parted for the greater part of the day; in Odessa they met for lunch but lived in the company of omnipresent Charles Stewart Smith. In Emden, on the other hand, Aelfrida commented cheerfully that 'Constantine and I are … seeing a great deal of each other, more … than we have ever done before …'[15] The novelty of her husband's undiluted companionship was exciting: in America, he had been absent for so much of the day and evening that she often forgot to 'chronicle' his movements.[16]

There was, however, another side to a world which had "shrunk to you and me".[17] No hint of this appears in Aelfrida's diary and only in two poems written between her arrival in Emden in February 1910 and her departure for England in April 1910 for the birth of her second child can we see that even in a 'wonderfully picturesque' town where the 'very sunlight [was] so much more peaceful than in America'[18], there were darknesses in her mind. The first stems from the fact that she was once "young and free" and is now nearly thirty and confined by marriage and child-bearing to a world shrunk to "a time of weariness", or, in a nautical analogy appropriate to a town whose harbour was large enough to accommodate ocean-going ships, narrowed to a mast on which there hangs a single "brooding light".[19] The second arises from the decline of physical intimacy between herself and a husband whose 'charms' she continues to hymn but whose praise "upon [her] lips grows cold" because of his "chill command" that they limit their family for economic reasons.[20] In the diary to which Constantine had access she wrote something quite different, however: 'I have the pleasure of seeing what a beautiful thing is love between husband and wife when it is not lessened by desire being for a time impossible' because of her second pregnancy and because 'our desire … seemed an immense part of love but now our love is no less. It is very wonderful …'[21]

Even more wonderful was the proximity of Emden to England, for much as Aelfrida might rhapsodise about her 'little green home' in The Coolidge or the homely delights of a frame house in Arlington Heights, it was her childhood home, Fordfield, which was *home*. (The corollary, of course, was that the place where she lived with her husband and children was not and never would be 'home'.) The veneration with which she regarded Fordfield is put into the mouth of 'Max von Thiele': "I look on this … house as sacred, and I wish all the most holy incidents of our life, such as the birth of our children, to take place under its roof".[22]

Given an opportunity to 'drift back unconsciously to Fordfield'[23], Aelfrida seized it for a total of eight months during Constantine's 26-month posting. Her first stay in Emden lasted two months and was followed by a four month visit to Fordfield during which she gave birth to her second child. From this somewhat lengthy visit (she had, after all, a nurse to care for her children and a local girl to help in the house) she returned with both children and 'Ovvie' for a period of just over seven months before 'drifting back' to Fordfield with 'two babies and thirteen pieces of luggage'[24] towards the end of May 1911. Her second four-month stay in Cambridge was purely recreational (Constantine returned alone to Emden after a month's leave) albeit her return was unavoidably delayed by illness. Although it is possible that extended absences from Emden were substitutes for the shorter and more frequent holidays to which she was accustomed but were now made inconvenient by sea-crossings with babies and luggage, Aelfrida was never in a hurry to leave a home where she surrendered nothing but her burdens ('one is very grateful for such luxuries … and one longs, or I do, for a few more. I want a … big garden, and endless flowers and specially fine sheets and daintily served meals')[25] to return to a 'home' shared with husband and children and with a servant whose deficiencies were a constant irritation. (Her third and final stay in Emden lasted seven months, her premature return home being due to problems with her health.) Of her joy at returning to Fordfield in time for the birth of 'Two' she wrote: 'that first spring when [Constantine] and I were engaged and gathered flowers together in the garden here at Fordfield I said to myself "This is the best time of my life" … Now I can see

no greater happiness than is mine now, with a husband and child and another coming, and the summer before me in my own home with all my family around me!'[26]

Aelfrida's second child and second daughter, Aelfrida Catharine Agatha Graham — it seems Chiara did not mind if the Wetenhall name was not perpetuated by girls — was born on 12 July 1910 in the presence of her father, her maternal grandmother, and her great-aunt Fanny, the latter acting as midwife. Like her sister, Agatha was received into the Greek Orthodox Church, the name by which she was usually known being the feminine of '*agathos*' meaning goodness or good. Undeniably pretty, she owed her looks to her paternal grandfather, her mother writing in a brief note two weeks after her birth that 'I call her my little Dago baby because she is dark and Greek-looking'.[27] Perhaps it was because Agatha looked so unlike her Wetenhall forebears that Aelfrida found it harder to bond with her second daughter than with her first: 'there is not the same affinity between me and her as there is between me and [Alethea]' and noted that baby Agatha (concerning whom her mother took pains to emphasise that she loved her as much as Alethea in spite of the stronger intimacy she felt with her first-born) preferred her father — 'and he her'.[28]

Both parents had wanted a son, Aelfrida in particular because, having achieved the girl who was *'mine'*, she hoped for a boy to assuage the disappointment felt by Chiara and, it seems, by Argyris with his atavistic desire for 'male descendants'. Aelfrida herself believed that 'Two' would be a boy because the coming baby was so 'lively' when she was examined by her English doctor, now Dr Ingle of nearby Shaftesbury Avenue[29], but was studiedly neutral when describing a prenatal experience in which she felt her thoughts enter 'the soul of the unborn child [which] takes them and weaves them into itself'[30] and the poem inspired by the event whose last two lines ("Forge into words the drifting light of dreams / To make a crown unto thy poet head / And to thy mother rear a graven stone")[31] are significantly sexless; indeed, their emphasis lies more in Aelfrida's hope that 'Two' will grow up to be a wordsmith like herself, inherit everything she holds dear ("…the beauty of the world, / The peace of home, the radiancy of love, / The mystic joy of pain"), and live long enough to immortalize her.

As always when approaching childbirth, Aelfrida worried lest she not survive the event, writing on 19 June that she hoped she would not succumb because 'I don't think I *could* die while [Alethea] wants me … no-one can ever understand Alethea as I do, unless she finds a second Constantine for a husband'[32] but that in the event of her succumbing, Alethea and 'Two' should stay at Fordfield: 'the Oracle is so strong and so gentle and Chiara is unselfish – then there is the garden and everything that loves me and that I love'. ('Of course', she added, 'the children would be Constantine's first … but they do not belong to the other side of the family. They never wanted me, and my children are not theirs'.)[33] Her worries were groundless; she survived to write devotedly that 'my life is my two babies'[34] and to decide that she would care for them herself as much as possible once re-installed in Emden: 'I won't be cheated out of my babies by the mere fact of having a good nursemaid'.[35]

Aelfrida, only daughter of a comfortably-off family whose Presbyterian ethic precluded the taking of a cab unless one was in fragile health or evening dress but whose disposable income permitted prolonged summer holidays, found it hard to comprehend that a vice-consul's salary, already stretched by the expense of renting a duplex apartment, by paying the salaries of two employees, and by providing for a wife and two children, did not also stretch to the five children on which she set her heart. Although they were not forced to economise to the extent that Constantine's strictures on household management suggested – 'we always *do* have enough money', his wife noted[36] – it never occurred to her, besotted as she was with the idea (if not the practicalities) of having children, that income was a finite commodity. Nor did she stop to think that monies earned by her husband might be better saved or spent on family needs; in Emden, it seems, she regarded thrift as selfishness and wished to give away surplus. A scheme to build two rentable cottages on land owned by her mother but reverting to Aelfrida on Chiara's death, was discouraged by Constantine on the grounds that an investment of that kind was not 'perfectly safe' and his refusal to consider it provoked 'rather a scene', Aelfrida informing her husband that 'he prevented me too often from doing things that I believed to be right, such as … joining the Roman Catholic church and trying to do good … I am afraid I made him and myself rather sad'.[37]

Her belief that it was her right to have five children dated from Boston days. Constantine, on being informed, told her that she was not 'strong enough' to have five, though whether physically or mentally she does not say.[38] Given that her emotional health was excellent during her first pregnancy, the latter seems unlikely; her second pregnancy, however, was beset by minor illnesses so that when Constantine reiterated in Emden that she was 'not strong enough' to bear five children, Aelfrida took it to mean that he meant bodily, albeit she added 'I think I take things too much to heart'[39], Constantine having perhaps intimated that one who returned from Odessa 'a little mad' might be too mentally frail to cope with that number of children. (She expressed the thought

that Constantine's refusal to allow her five children also represented rejection of her love in a poem written on 31 December 1910 entitled *The Passing of Love* whose last two lines "So love had gone. But pain, like night's dark wall / Wears still the stars that love had scattered there"[40] are particularly evocative.) But although she also realised that five children (two girls and three boys) were incompatible with a literary career, a fact she had denied in Boston when pregnant with Alethea[52], she persisted so strongly in her belief that she would be 'right' to have that number, the last at thirty-six, that Constantine made her 'map out [her] baby-having programme' in detail in order to dissuade her on financial grounds if health grounds proved unconvincing and informed her that her plan was 'ill-considered'.[41] A 'rather sobering enquiry into our financial situation' brought realisation that more than two children on a vice-consul's salary 'might be a trifle rash', though Aelfrida did not exclude the possibility of a happy accident.[42] Thwarted in her desire for a large family and aware that 'Two' might be 'Last', she did the next best thing: in the third trimester of her second pregnancy she conceived a book. *To Malise,* an anthology containing virtually all her poems written between 1906 and the summer of 1910, appeared on 2 November 1910, Aelfrida noting of it that 'this ought to be a great day for me, for … I have held a copy in my hand and written therein a dedication to my husband. I felt quite shy before Constantine…'[43]

But why 'shy'? And why 'ought'? Shyness was not one of Aelfrida's notable traits; indeed, the diary entry quoted continues 'I think my poems are better than those of any English woman-writer … better than Christina Rossetti and "dearest Ba"'[44], and a request from the editor of *The Biographer* for a biography of the author of *To Malise* was described as 'a drop of fame towards the ocean yet to come!'[45] Shyness, it seems, stemmed from being 'ashamed that I should publish sooner than he'[46], not a difficult feat, one would think, for an author who, in default of a publisher, decided to publish her poems by subscription and to recoup her costs by limiting copies to friends and relatives who indicated their willingness to subscribe.

But what of 'ought'? From contemporary diary entries it is clear that Aelfrida's joy was diminished by the reactions of her subscribers. Although Argyris was complimentary, informing her that "you are a greater artist than I. I wish I had your emotions" ('I was *touched*', wrote Aelfrida, at praise from the author of *Tales from the Isles of Greece*)[47], other people were not. Her having created 'something of a stir!' should have warned her that her 'sacrifice of [her] deepest feelings to [art]' might be misconstrued because the personal nature of the poems, though she was more concerned that a vanity publication might be taken as merely gratifying her vanity; otherwise, she wrote, she would have refrained from 'hawking her soul around at half-a-crown'.[48] In fact, Lucy Verey and Aelfrida's immediate relatives thought the poems 'too personal for publication' and had no hesitation in saying so.[49] (Catharine Tillyard, receiving a copy inscribed 'to my mother with all the love in the world', did not even cut the pages but the alternation of uncut sections with pages visible when the book was opened cannot have pleased her: opposite *The Mother* with its dedication 'to CST' she would have found *Perplexity* with its leading question "shall my mind, a thing most strong and sane / Be worthy but of pitying disdain?"[50] and opposite D'Annunzio's *Il Piacere*, *A convert to the Catholic Church*.) Criticism from people she loved and respected did not, however, dissuade her from immediately beginning another batch of poems which would not only say 'exactly what I meant'[51] but would also relieve pent-up feelings arising from publication of her first.

*To Malise* was dedicated '*A toi*', the affectionate superscription in books given by Constantine to Aelfrida during his courtship, and Constantine's own copy 'to my perfectly beloved husband – this and everything else that I have to give'. His reaction to a dedication which is simultaneously fulsome, truthful, and duplicitous, to poems which treat in intimate detail of his courtship of, and early wedded life with, Aelfrida, and to a verse noting that as his wife, she not only "watch[es] his ways and know not where they go" but is also "nearest of all … yet not too near"[52], was not recorded in her diary. Was he more hurt or more angry at what are as much *poèmes à clef* as her novels are *romans à clef* in their delineation of his fiancée's and wife's feelings of recent years? One of the perils of being married to an author who has no inhibitions about putting her private thoughts and feelings into verse and prose which she then publishes is that one may find oneself represented therein in less than flattering or loving terms; for Constantine to find himself in an anthology which charts in desperate detail the beginning of the decline of his relationship with his wife – for this is what *To Malise* essentially does – must have been both horrifying and humiliating, for although he himself possessed a '*clef*' to the content of poems which might appear impersonal or baffling to an uninitiated reader, enough personal detail was provided to allow anyone with the smallest '*key*' to the poems' true meaning to interpret them, and the insights provided into his marital affairs must have occasioned enormous embarrassment to a man in a public position and as sensitive to slights as Constantine Graham.

Perhaps his most hurtful discovery lay in the section of the book entitled 'poems not be taken quite so seriously', the said poems being described by their author as 'reprinted from the *Military and Civil Journal*.' The *MCJ* of June 1910, devised about the time of Aelfrida's outburst regarding investment in property, was described by her as nobly maintaining the Tillyard 'tradition of cheap wit' (in parenthesis she added 'Constantine cannot altogether approve. He was never young in that particular way')[53] but her inclusion of certain other poems in this section of *To Malise* (with the implication that they were examples of 'cheap wit' unappreciated by her husband) was a particularly vicious action: as John Forbes and Elfrida Cameron had discovered, Aelfrida was liable to revenge herself on other parties when she herself was miserable and at this point in her marriage could no longer conceal her pent-up resentment with regard to Constantine denying her further children and foiling her benevolent or religious instincts. And in *To Malise* she took her revenge in more durable form than dinner party chat: she published it.

Her later assertion that her 'message' was 'best to be found in my poems and … therefore they must be published whatever else is not'[54] is seen at its cruellest here. Although the ostensible content is innocent enough, Aelfrida makes sure that Constantine knows at whom her barbs are pointed by writing the majority of them in French, the language the Grahams frequently used to each other (they *tutoyer*-ed each other even when speaking English) and by dedicating two poems specifically 'to GCC' (i.e. ostensibly to minor French poet Guy-Charles Croz but more likely a reversal of 'Constantine Cleanthes Graham'), a dedication which does little to disguise the dedicatee and much to demean him insofar as it reflects the reversal of his wife's feelings for him. Aelfrida's description of five of the poems as being from *Les Auteurs Français* and the other (written in Italian) as deriving "from the Opera of San Diavolone" also provides little comfort to one who has, in Rimbaudian terms, the 'key' to this poetic '*parade sauvage*': is not she herself an '*auteur français*' insofar as she wrote *Le Livre des Jeux* in that language and does not Italian have special connotations for the Grahams insofar as it is the language of her husband's one-time favourite author and one she herself speaks fluently?

None of the poems in this section of *To Malise* are dated (they may be dated approximately by the volume of the *MCJ* in which they appear; in any event, none can have been written later than mid-October 1910 as *To Malise* would have been in proof soon after that) but the relevance of the date or dates on which the relevant six were written is for once unimportant. What we have here is a poetic account of Aelfrida's belief that absolute surrendering herself to Constantine, though it resulted in the birth of the children she desired, also resulted in spiritual, emotional, and lifestyle imprisonment from which she now wished to be free. And if the price of freedom was money spent on publication of *To Malise* (she does not say if subscriptions covered expenditure), so be it; it would be money well spent.

The first poem, *Il mio Cuore*[55], begins the darkling theme which runs through the first four poems and which does not begin to lift until the end of the fourth and beginning of the fifth. The poem, ostensibly a lament for a lost lover ("*l'ora presente è priva di te*") reads like a metaphorical description of Aelfrida's relinquishment of God as result of Constantine's unremitting emotional pressure: "*Tutto finisce, / La gioia vanisce, / La mattina per altri è notte per me*". The poem's subtitle ('from the Opera of Santo Diavolone') may provide a clue. Although the phrase seems to refer to an operetta, *Fra Diavolone*, performed in Paris in the 19th century (the 'Brother Devil' of the title was an anti-Napoleonic French freedom fighter disguised in a monk's habit), Constantine is the 'diabolical' personage whose 'task' (*opera*) it has been to separate Aelfrida from God, the '*te*' (in this context, more properly 'Thou') of the poem. (The '*toi*', Italian '*te,*' to whom the poems are dedicated is, confusingly, also Constantine but the ambiguity may be deliberate.) If so, this throws new light on Aelfrida's assertion that in Florence she had allowed the devil to turn her aside from her former life of devotion to God, the devilish being who poured 'words of doubt into her ears' being her future husband.

The second poem, *Victor Hugo*, seems at first sight adaptation of one of Hugo's favourite themes, the misery of the human condition exiled from home and from liberty of thought. In fact, it describes Aelfrida's deep despair at the state of spiritual exile in which she finds herself, her personal "abyss" (*abîme*) being one of absolute surrender of thought and right action to one who has rendered her prisoner, body and soul, by the administration of repeated sexual, spiritual, and emotional blows (*coups*) and the imposition of an alien way of life upon her.

The third poem in the sequence, *La Nuit,* though it repeats the nocturnal theme of the preceding two, develops a regenerative, spiritually-lightening motif which will eventually lead to Aelfrida offering Constantine his physical freedom in return for her spiritual and emotional liberty. She begins by equating night with a rose ("*rose bleu de mon désire*"), then with a virgin ("*vièrge languissante*"), and finally with the soul ("*âme, d'un tendre souffle créée*"), the last attribution being one which she begs the moon to bestow on her: "*donne-moi ton âme*". But there is no such thing as a *blue* rose, so what does that

say of her desire? And why is she a languishing virgin? And why does she lack a soul?

The answer to our first question may be found in another poem, *A Fragment of Decadent Verse*, written in Arlington Heights on 9 November 1908 in which Aelfrida describes desire as a melancholy phenomenon (*le triste désir*), an appropriate reference given her current pain on intercourse[56] but whose deeper nuances may be reminders of an 'antechamber of Hell' entered in Odessa and to two references in the fourth poem *A la soeur que j'aurais dû avoir*. Here we discover that the 'sister' that Aelfrida *ought* to have had is an "*âme douce ... pure et chaste*" and that because she lacks a sweet, pure, and chaste sister-soul she also lacks chastity of heart: "*un plus chaste coeur*". She lacks spiritual chastity because she has surrendered her physical virginity to Constantine but her desire for bodily chastity (currently satisfied by Constantine's insistence on abstinence as a form of birth control) is at variance with the "*rouges désirs*" he has aroused in her and which are currently frustrated by his curt refusal to have more children. Her warring emotions are summed up in the poem's last two lines ("*Ô soeur, ô âme, ô tête, ô pureté, / Ô paroles sourdes, silences et chasteté*") with their contrasting of what she lacks (purity of soul, clarity of mind, and spiritual chastity) and what she has: hollow promises, brooding silences, and enforced physical chastity. No wonder, then, that she languishes.

The tone of the fifth poem, *Amour et Destinée*, subtitled '*poème moderne*', is gentler and sadder. In it Aelfrida bids farewell to a beloved friend (a female friend, given that it is an '*amie*' to whom she speaks, possibly the same '*petite soeur*' to whom the previous poem is dedicated), a friend to whom Aelfrida owes much because it is she who has directed her budding faith (*naissante foi*) to God in the form of the Holy Trinity (*le mystique nombre trois*), and is the loved and loving friend destined to taste (spiritual) pleasures denied to one whose own soul remains mired in self-love. Or so it seems; the poem is capable of more than one interpretation and it is only because of its being placed in its present context that the above interpretation is possible.

The last poem, *A qui la Gloire?*, climaxes Aelfrida's poetic tirade. Once, she says, she was ecstatic at the sound of Constantine's voice (*divin ramage*, as it were the warbling of a bird) and when contemplating his genius (*ésprit du sage*) but no longer; now, she realises, he is only an upstart eaglet (*fier aiglon*) whose song, an ugly croak (*difformé ramage*) bears imputations of moral as well as physical deformity. Constantine, she continues, the 'eaglet' whose writings are so minor in comparison with those of his 'eagle' father, should flee ('*fuir*', punning on the '*fier*' of the previous line) in search of a new and more effulgent song (*un radieux language*) even if this means leaving herself behind, a songbird caged by domesticity ("*je suis un oiseau dans une cage*") or a mouse gnawing a rind of cheese, rind being all that is left of their former life together. This is not the life she hoped for ("*la vie est loin*") but for the moment it is all she has. Yet she is not completely without hope. Though she will keep silent concerning the reasons for their separation ("*mon silence est la gage*") and though crouched submissively in absolute surrender and aware of the loss of security (gage) his absence will create in her life, she herself is also "*sans gage*" because once liberated from her '*aiglon*', she will revert from passive pawn to a woman with a voice and a language of her own. And, she threatens, she will look for a new master to adore: "*je cherche les ravissements du mage*".

With the poems in mind, Aelfrida's summary of the good things happening to and around her on her twenty-seventh birthday on 5 October 1910 immediately prior to publication of *To Malise* rings very hollow: 'My parents and brothers and husband and … two splendid intelligent children are all alive and well and happy, and so I am … I have plenty to do; and I love Emden; and I have a book coming out … and the world really does seem to be getting better … Just now I am very, very happy. I wonder if I shall ever be quite as happy again' and the contrast between buoyant diary entry and a poem written three weeks later is marked: "I loved and yet I cannot love again …/ I said goodbye, and weep to feel no pain. / Thy kisses turn my passive lips to stone. / Thy words fall lifeless as the autumn leaves. / Yea, time has garnered all the golden sheaves / Of bliss, and all the summer days are gone. / When love has perished, there is death indeed".[57]

Constantine's reaction to the revelation of his wife's true feelings for him explains a good deal about his otherwise inexplicable behaviour towards her between November 1910 and April 1912. His discovery of the hypocrisy of a wife who professed to love him and to welcome his sexual advances at the same time as she wrote and had the temerity to publish such terrible poems (and to send them to reviewers, as a diary entry of 24 November shows)[58] provides an excellent reason for the apparently heartless way in which he behaved towards a woman whose pretty children were an asset in *gemütlich* Emden and who behaved for once as a vice-consul's wife should by assiduously cultivating the wives of local officials in order to overcome anti-British sentiments expressed in contemporary Germany. His immediate revenge (he did not, it seems, take his wife's poems 'not quite so seriously') was swift and appropriate, involving as it did one of Aelfrida's own poems and another woman. The poem was *About an Italian Student of*

*Marine Biology* and the woman Igerna Brünnhild (Hilda) Sollas.[59]

Since arriving in Emden, both Grahams had 'been occupying [their] thoughts somewhat with "little friends"'.[60] Aelfrida had thought of starting a 'little friendship' with 'slain' Geoffrey Hatten who had written to her about *To Malise* but in practice continued epistolary friendships with established correspondents such as Gian Falco and Charles Stewart Smith. (A 'pure and beautiful friendship' with an Emden medical practitioner did not 'come off' because although the doctor concerned was 'tall and fair and imaginative and strong and quite disposed to admire [her]', his refusal to play by the rules of the game and the likelihood of this 'making everyone concerned very unhappy' – Dr Kessler was married – made her desist, though she was shortly to note apropos 'little friends' that she and Constantine were 'serenely sure of each other – and of ourselves'.)[61] Constantine 'occupied his thoughts' by corresponding with Madame Novikoff of Odessa days (her family later visited him in Hessle) and, rather unusually for someone who preferred older women, with 'young ladies, who are afraid of his charm and respond stiffly or queerly according to their nature'.[62] (How did Aelfrida know? Did she spy on him? Her earlier obliviousness seems to have given way to obsessive watchfulness: 'I can almost sift every one of his thoughts through my fingers. I often wonder whether he watches me as much as I watch him …')[63] Hilda Sollas, however, fell into the category of older women, being born in 1877.

Miss Sollas[64] first appeared in Aelfrida's diary in 1905 when she and Constantine visited her at Newnham where she was a don. Aelfrida's initial impression was favourable but gently critical: '[she is] small, pretty in a soft elusive way, a person of delicate perceptions and of a … harmonious pale grey, lilac and mauve character'. She also noted that beside Miss Sollas she felt 'rather large and poppy-like' and that there was 'not a shadow of doubt' that Miss Sollas was in love with Constantine.[65] A second visit in January 1908, at a time when 'poppy-like' Aelfrida was in a highly 'nervous' state following the Grahams' return from Russia, resulted in Constantine becoming even more attracted to someone 'sweet and wise and childlike' who was equally attracted to him.[66] A visit to Fordfield in June 1910 showed Miss Sollas to be deeply in love with Constantine. Aelfrida, heavily pregnant with Agatha, watched Hilda watching her husband: 'there was something in [her] hungry and passive attitude that gave her away as completely as if she had shouted her feelings out loud … if Constantine had got up and kissed her on the lips she *could not* have pushed him away'. (Of Constantine she wrote 'I am confident he will act wisely [and] be careful not to see her too

Cleanthes Michaelides (Argyris Ephtaliotes) with Michael Hillerns

much ... He is, of course, absolutely to be trusted'.) Her unnerving discovery ('I had never before seen a woman absolutely defenceless, and ... it was a rather terrible sight')[67] prompted her to poetry. On 3 August 1910 she wrote *About an Italian Student of Marine Biology* (the word 'Italian' in the title does not appear in the manuscript version and may have been inserted to disguise the poem's subject) in which Hilda Sollas' strange eyes (described as "grey–green ... and the light in them spun and twisted like a spark of sunlight on the sea")[68], though of "grey mist ... of subtle spell" and "full / Of love" for Aelfrida's husband when bent on him, became "silver swords" which "stab and ... kill"[69] when turned on Constantine's wife.

Following publication of *To Malise,* Hilda Sollas wrote to Constantine complaining that the poem was aimed at herself. (Aelfrida's comment was 'she would have richly deserved it, if it had'.) Constantine, ripe for revenge, made his wife write to Miss Sollas apologising for the supposed libel. This she did, commenting acidly that the letter 'pleased him, bored me, and goodness only knows what effect it will have on ... poor Miss Sollas'. (She also noted that 'I daresay it is rather good for Constantine to have ... females adoring him, but it is occasionally tiresome for his wife to have to be so careful of their feelings'.)[70] Miss Sollas, anxious to smooth things over, replied that it was all a mistake and that she had thought

another poem, *Minerva of the Grey Eyes,* referred to her instead.[71] This Aelfrida regarded as 'rather humorous' but at the same time recognised that Constantine's revenge had made her look 'a mild kind of fool'[72] for having published the poems in the first place. She had the last word, however. Knowing that Hilda Sollas was a Christian Scientist, a religion Aelfrida found rather repellent, she wrote another poem omitted from the manuscript version of *To Malise* but composed, from diary evidence, sometime in June 1910, entitled *The God of the Christian Scientists,* whose first line of only three reads "Within my mind there is no thought of sin". The poem is ostensibly dedicated 'to Mrs McKH'[73] but its real subject is surely the 'poor Miss Sollas' of whom Aelfrida subsequently commented that it was rather odd that one so chaste and seemingly so aloof should allow herself to become enamoured of a married man. The man in question, however, anxious that the Sollas affair be brought to a conclusion, intimated to Hilda that the friendship would be discontinued unless his wife was included in it[74] (this did not preclude his having tea alone with Miss Sollas in her room at Newnham to the disgust of students shocked 'in spite of their somewhat advanced views'[75] at their tutor's behaviour); the friendship, however, continued.

But why, in the last poem of the sequence of six poems discussed prior to revelation of Constantine's revenge and his means of retaliation, does Aelfrida describe her husband as "*un héros sans bagage*"?[76] Has he expressed a desire to be free? And if so, from what physical, marital, or emotional impediments does he wish to be freed? To discover the answer we must return to the beginning of the Grahams' stay in Emden.

On the night of the 10/11 April 1910 Constantine suffered an attack of retention of urine, an unusual event in a man not yet thirty. Aelfrida, about to leave for England to await the birth of 'Two', managed to relieve his discomfort by 'suggesting' him as Münsterburg had 'suggested' her but later sent him as a precaution to Dr Kessler who reassured him that there was nothing physically wrong. Aelfrida herself attributed the attack to Constantine's nerves being 'strained', saying that her husband had had 'no proper holiday for years' (one could say, not since his brief visit to Dorset in August 1906 when he and Aelfrida 'let the sleeping dogs of Realism and Idealism lie' and devoted themselves 'to love-making', brief interludes between postings having been fraught with problems of his wife's and mother's making) and had had 'endless responsibilities and anxiety'. Now in Emden, 'the house [and] getting his bearings in a fresh place, all have told on him'.[77]

It is hardly surprising that Constantine was bored and resentful at a move which removed him from the acting-consular status of previous posts and from the cultural delights of Boston and placed him in a vice-consular position in a 'petty and a stupid little town'[78] where there were few resident British subjects and an even smaller transient British population and in which the contrast between calls on the Customs Inspector and the editor of the local daily newspaper hardly compared with those paid on Lowells and Cabots in Boston or to Madame Novikoff in Odessa. A visit paid by Constantine to Berlin during which he conducted diplomacy of such secrecy that he could not describe it even to his wife[79] and a visit from a British naval attaché who enthused about the active diplomatic life of towns like Copenhagen or The Hague made him realise what a backwater Emden was and imbued him with a desire 'to get away and be out in the world and work to the utmost'; in Emden, he complained, his powers were 'dormant'. (Aelfrida, on the other hand, revelled in 'the calm waters and still joys of the little place', calling Emden a 'dear little backwater' where she enjoyed 'happy quiet times with [her] babies' and discovered that she preferred 'obscurity' to Constantine's desire to 'get on'.)[80] To family members, however, she justified the posting as important to a government cognisant of Constantine's special qualities because of Emden's strategic position in the fields of international politics and commerce[81]; even so, Constantine's consular activities took up so little of his time that he was able to spend hours on novels whose writing had been postponed *sine die* in busy Boston. If to this we add jealousy of his wife's social success and of her having now published *two* books and realisation from flying visits to Cambridge of what his life might have been had not academic success eluded him, his now taking a kind of perverse pleasure in denying his wife further children (as Aelfrida noted, without realising the full implications of what she wrote, namely that her husband might no longer find her attractive, 'Constantine has something of the ascete in him [and] takes some kind of pleasure in restrictions')[82] and the boredom he displayed after only a few minutes of his children's society[83], demonstrates that life in Emden was singularly unsatisfying in all respects. It also explains why Aelfrida thought apropos the 'brilliant boy' she had married and made to 'settle down' that 'next time Constantine gets a move he will go away by himself'[84]: to be "*un héros sans bagage*", in fact.

A reading of Aelfrida's diary pertaining to the first part of the Grahams' stay in Emden with its assertions of happiness and of her boundless love for her husband and his for her ('our love … is very wonderful – I suppose more wonderful in Constantine than in me')[85] glosses over tensions and it is only occasionally that acerbic comments show the real state of affairs. A particularly telling comment made apropos Constantine's optimistic remark that 'the first crucial time of marriage … is over for us and we have emerged triumphant' is truer of Aelfrida's actual feelings than his: 'I am glad he thinks so. Certainly we love each other more than ever – but he seems to have forgotten that he said we were to prove to the world *that two persons can be one*, and have not done it … But though he failed he does not seem to mind'. (The corollary, 'that *I* could never become anyone else'[86] – had she forgotten that she had once written 'we both feel we have but one soul, as one day we shall have but one body?[87] – she had already expressed in bitter terms in a sonnet written two months prior to the diary entry just quoted :"The years have judgement given. They have done / Slowly to death the hope that was in me / That I could fuse my life with life of thee …/… all myself was never mine to give".)[88] To one who felt this way, it was safer to express her feelings in verse, beginning on 23 October 1910 with a sonnet *Modern Poetry* ("unbidden comes to men the gift of song") and ending on 24 August 1913 with an *Unofficial Biography* of the 'magus' whose 'ravishments' she sought. The nearly forty poems produced during that time (one or two were suppressed by being cut out of the manuscript) represent her *real* state of mind so accurately that they provide a poetic account running parallel to prose versions in her diary.[89] But without reference to her diary they are incomprehensible.

Further intimations of the rift widening between the Grahams appear in a diary entry of May 1910. Aelfrida was in England awaiting Agatha's birth when she received a letter from Constantine stating that he was about to abandon the teetotalism accepted in deference to herself. Aelfrida was cross; this was a decision they should have made together: 'I had been very reasonable in promising not to mind if he offered wine to our visitors in Germany but I do not think I have deserved to be treated as though I were hopelessly unreasonable'.[90] Not wishing to upset his heavily pregnant wife, Constantine agreed to defer his decision until he was thirty[91] and his arrival in Cambridge on 27 May meant that 'all shadows of misunderstanding vanished', albeit Aelfrida noted that because of the 'wine question', she and Constantine had 'not borne the separation as well as [they] ought to have done'.[92] Aelfrida's unilateral decision that Constantine read the Church Service at the Consulate on the first Sunday of every month also provoked disagreement. In spite of tiny congregations, usually only Aelfrida herself and two or three others, the services continued until January 1912 at which point Constantine used his mother's arrival in Emden as an excuse to give them up and possibly to abandon family prayers also.[93] The decision prompted a short bitter poem from his wife ("I'm look-ing for the well of life / And joy's eternal springs …/ The springs [I] seek deep hidden lie / Beneath the pools of death")[94] but no further diary comment.

A third intimation arose as a result of Constantine's (and possibly Anatolia's) post-*Malise* decision to exclude Aelfrida from Michaelides family occasions as far as pos-sible. He attended Irene's Paris wedding to Karl Hillerns alone, the ostensible reason for Aelfrida's non-attendance being that had the wedding been held in the summer instead of the spring of 1911, Agatha would have been weaned (she was nine months old at this point) and she and Alethea could have been left at Fordfield, but from the self-pitying tone of her diary entry (she describes Irene as blindly selfish for not arranging her marriage to suit her sister-in-law's convenience), it seems that little effort was made on anyone's part to encourage her to attend.[95] She was therefore forced to content herself with sending an epistolary blessing to Irene and was only somewhat consoled by receiving 'a sweet childlike' reply from her 'loving sister, Irene' expressing her regrets at Aelfrida's absence and her joy that baby Agatha looked so much like her aunt Helen at the same age.[96]

A brief visit to Hessle early in June 1911 seemed to confirm Irene's new-found friendship for her sister-in-law in spite of 'nasty digs'[97] aimed at Aelfrida by Anatolia and only to be expected following the publication of *To Malise*. (Constantine's visit lasted longer than Aelfrida's, the latter noting on his return that he came back 'rather Anatolianized' and that their own relationship would 'jar a little' until the effect wore off; in fact, a lengthy row ensued on the subject of self-realisation versus self-sacrifice which left them both 'pretty well tired out'.)[98] Aelfrida's own visit almost did not take place for Constantine refused to allow her to accompany him, using as his excuse that he could not afford the double fare, a plan thwarted by Aelfrida selling one of her two copies of Dante's *Vita Nuova* to raise money. His real reason, one may guess, was 'the kind of constraint' the Grahams experienced when once more in their respec-tive family circles as a result of the pretence maintained by Aelfrida (and by Constantine when at Fordfield) that their marriage was 'perfect', a constraint stemming from Aelfrida feeling physically and emotionally rejected by her husband ('I am not allowed to love [Constantine] with all of me') and Constantine refusing to resume mar-ital relations for fear of another pregnancy[99]: 'I wanted him to take me back but he said he could not afford it.'[100] Having to share a room at Fordfield (the Tillyards pro-vided twin beds) and possibly a bed at Hessle may have compounded the problem, for a comment in Aelfrida's diary that in Hessle 'Constantine slept near me again

and it was very beautiful'[101] suggests separate sleeping arrangements in Emden. 'Constraint' is also supported by Aelfrida's comments concerning a second visit to Hessle by herself and the children, Constantine's work requiring his earlier return to Emden: Anatolia, 'gay and natural and loving' in the absence of a married son whose pres-ence induced angry and jealous feelings, took delighted charge of her granddaughters and Aelfrida herself, 'quite at [her] ease and happy' in Anatolia's company as a result (an unusual state of affairs), was able to spend time alone or quietly in the garden. Argyris, though complimentary about 'the babies … and [her] poetry', was 'with us but not of us – he cares [only] for his writing and his roses'.[102]

Although conversations with Anatolia had involved some 'feline amenities'[103], Aelfrida was so lulled into thinking that the two women could actually become friends that a letter from Irene to her brother written fol-lowing both Grahams' return to Emden took her by sur-prise: following her departure from Hessle both Anatolia and newly-married Irene ('a sledgehammer in Anatolia's hands', with Anatolia as 'motive-force') had written to Constantine 'pitying him for his miserable marriage and urging him to wrest his children from his wife's clutches'.[104] Aelfrida was understandably furious and in spite of Constantine urging silence, wrote a lengthy reply (quoted verbatim in her diary) in which she poured out bitterness pent-up since her first meeting with Anatolia and her daughters in June 1904.

Too long to quote in full, even a summary conveys the disgust its writer feels for the machinations of Anatolia and a daughter who so worships her mother that she calls her her 'goddess': '*ma déesse*'.[105] Ostensibly written in Constantine's defence but in fact as Aelfrida's own response to the 'cold hostility' towards herself expressed therein, the letter is intended for Irene but aimed at Anatolia and Aelfrida's ostensible reason for writing it, namely that she is trying to make peace (*sic*) between Irene and her brother, is actually revenge for the unkind letters sent to Constantine by Irene and her mother on the subject of his wife and children. Beginning with an attack on Irene's comment that in marrying Aelfrida, Constantine has "fallen so low" ('*tombé bien bas*', an expression accredited by Aelfrida to Anatolia), an accu-sation which Aelfrida refutes by describing herself as "his equal in birth and education" and as someone who brought him interests in politics, social reform, and edu-cation that he never had before, the letter continues with references to other benefits bestowed on Constantine by herself: "passionate adoration and two beautiful chil-dren". (Irene's attack on the way Aelfrida raised her chil-dren is responded to with tigress protection: "As for my babies, dear child, don't trouble! … Constantine says that

I give them *too much* tenderness and that a little wholesome discipline would be good for them! … Such happy, fearless children are not produced by gloomy restraint".) Irene, the letter concludes, has no right to treat a brother eight years older than herself and her superior in intelligence and experience in this manner and in its writer hoping that there will be no more scoldings "as though he had forged a cheque or run off with his neighbour's wife". It is signed: "Yours affectionately, Aelfrida".[106]

If Aelfrida's response to Irene's and Anatolia's persistence in treating married Constantine as Lucifer ("how hast thou fallen … son of the morning")[107] seems overwrought for one whose usual response to attacks of this nature was placatory or dismissive, it can be explained by the occurrence of three separate but interconnected events during the preceding four months.

The first took place in July 1911 between Aelfrida's first and second visits to Hessle and shortly after Constantine's return to Emden and involved the latter's best friend and best man, Eric Silvanus. On 6 July Aelfrida received 'a strange letter' from Eric whose tone and content suggested that it was more appropriately aimed at Constantine than herself, he having visited Eric when passing through London on his way to Emden.[108] But Eric, like 'Victor Stein' his similarly pipe-smoking alter ego[109] of *Marrying a Stranger,* had fallen in love with her. (This, said her father, had been obvious since Eric proposed accompanying the Grahams to whichever posting they were assigned.)[110] But unlike 'Victor', who believed that loyalty to 'Max' would prevent him "losing his head" over 'Elizabeth'[111], Eric had lost his head over Aelfrida and wished to declare it. His choosing this moment may have been suggested by his having read *To Malise* and, knowing what he knew of both Aelfrida and her husband ('Victor', unbeknown to 'Elizabeth', "watched both her and Max and how it was faring with their love")[112], realising from tensions expressed therein that all was not well between them. He therefore chose Constantine's absence to express emotions of his own, an event which Aelfrida herself had seemingly predicted six years earlier when she confided that Eric, though 'beautiful and loveable is, between ourselves, a bit of a rotter!'[113]

Mystified and embarrassed by Eric's declared passion – she had thought his 'caressing indulgence'[114] was directed more towards Constantine than herself but should have been warned by his letter of September 1906 declaring that he loved her very much – Aelfrida nevertheless found Eric's attentions and declarations during a weekend spent in Cambridge as 'passing sweet' as her feelings but decided that 'the sensible thing … is to do nothing, just manage not to see Eric very often'.[115] Eric's two-day visit to Cambridge was therefore spent with Eric behaving 'as though all barriers save one were down' and Aelfrida feeling ill at ease because under the same roof as her father and children (Chiara, Julius, and Eustace were absent), though she managed to clear up 'what had been the barest, barest suspicion, or shadow of suspicion' by asking Eric 'has Anatolia been your mistress?' and was delighted to hear him deny it.[116] A bicycle ride with Eric brought them to 'a little wood made out of sunlight and beech boughs somewhere up the Roman Road way'[117] where she accepted his praise for *To Malise* and allowed him to 'look long, long into [her] eyes as though a look were a touch' in a manner incapable of misinterpretation even while 'trying to persuade myself that Eric is *not* in love with me'.[118] A poem written later in the day suggests otherwise ("When gazing deep down in your eyes / I feel your look is like a touch / To wake the love that sleeping lies. / When gazing deep down in your eyes / I see the limbs of love arise / And shrink back lest I see too much")[119]; indeed, it rather suggests that Aelfrida too and in spite protestations that she loved 'no man but Constantine'[120], might herself have behaved 'as though all barriers but one were down'.

The weather at the time of this torrid episode was exceptionally hot. On 15 August and with return to Emden imminent, she wrote a second poem *Two Things.* In it she asks of an unnamed man that he do two things for her when she is dead: to forget her, or if he cannot do that because "From out my sombre life I flung …/ Such strains as woke your song to answer mine", to remember and praise her and render herself and her poetry immortal.[121] At this juncture, 13-month old Agatha became gravely ill with 'acute inflammation and catarrh of the bowels' and in spite of Dr Ingle's ministrations, became rapidly worse.[122] An inarticulate and much-altered poem written of 20 August shows why Aelfrida thought this had happened: "Let even my conscience sore accusing be / For all myself/my life I killed and marred and lost.'[123] Fortunately for her mother's conscience, the child recovered.

A sense of divine retribution, that listening to Eric's outpourings of love constituted a sin, and that the consequence of sinning was condemnation to even greater physical and emotional 'loneliness' than she now experienced, was expressed in two further poems, both written on 9 September. In the first she poeticised a vow made at Agatha's bedside 'to give up pure and beautiful friendships' ('as far as possible') if Agatha recovered and transmitted to Eric in a letter informing him that he was not to consider himself *her* special friend but a friend of herself *and her husband.*[124] In the second, *Goodbye,* she asks Eric to "go now," adding that her parting gift is solitude (described here as "… an interlude / Twixt strife and strife, and never-ending rude / Voices of passion and of will, a moan / Of strong men checked") and notes that even loneliness can be "power-imbued".[125] The joy of Agatha's recovery and Aelfrida's return later in September to 'the sweet small sleepiness of Emden' was enhanced by news received in October 1911 that Eric had found – as a result, Aelfrida hoped, of her advice about leading his own life, not clinging on to other people's – a 'cultivated female friend', Maude Taylor, to whom he soon became engaged.[126] Aelfrida's valediction took the form of a poem but whether she sent it to Eric, she does not say: "I have got my happiness. Now take yours. / Goodbye. I have a husband, children too. / I never even thought of love with you. / But there are days not anchored to the shores / Of one's reality, days when one soars / Like ship of cloud across a sea of blue, / And it was you that made me know it true … / Such was the hour which you had best forget'. Her next meeting with Eric would be on a day when the last line of the poem ("Timeless and bright as death's eternity") seemed about to come true.[127]

The second event occurred four days before Aelfrida's reference to Maude Taylor and the day after her own twenty-eighth birthday on 5 October.

Strolling through Emden on 6 October, the Grahams came across a crowd of boys taunting and throwing stones at a cripple. In spite of Constantine warning her to keep out of trouble, Aelfrida berated the boys roundly and succeeded in distracting them from their target long enough for him to escape. Returning to the spot where she had left her husband, she discovered that Constantine had walked away. She scolded him for abandoning her; he retorted that she had been mad to interfere, that she had no business to disobey him, and was 'altogether furious'.[128] Returning home, they began to discuss the matter calmly and rationally, 'trying to be very gentle, for we love each other with a big love', but that discussion escalated into major row can be surmised from a diary entry four days later: 'Constantine and I agreed that … we discussed things too much. Thoughts that are quite gentle often become sharp and sword-like in words. It is not that we have agreed to differ … but simply that we shall understand better if we don't discuss … Of course, all this is nothing new – but one does not say anything even to one's diary. I don't want, you see, our married life not to be perfect…'[129] But it was as a result of this episode that Aelfrida began her revealing 'Emden novel'.

Her feelings were so strong that she also spoke out to her diary. (She also described the gulf between the Grahams – it had existed for some time but she preferred not to reveal it – in a poem written on 8 October, *Malise Speaks. I Answer,* which metaphorically describes the difference in their present view of the world and

how far apart they have moved since 1905/6.)[130] In a bitter outpouring she listed everything that caused her unhappiness. Constantine, she wrote, 'wished to be a kind of Oriental despot and deny me even a soul. He *says* he wishes me to be free [but] he will not even give me as many children as I want and he always opposes every suggestion I make, even in the little things … the whole of our life is planned as [he] wishes it. I *hate* our spending even as much as we do on food or books – I think we ought to give the money away – but because *he* thinks it right I say nothing. Oh, and the little we go to church, and our giving wine at dinners are *all* in accordance with his wishes'. With particular reference to her rescue of the cripple she stated that Constantine wished her to surrender to him not only their common life but also her conscience: 'Constantine, whose head is filled with the idea that he must be master at all costs, says that I must obey him even when my conscience says he is asking something I believe to be wrong … The thing is impossible. I *cannot* do what I know to be wrong … When it is a question of my own personal conduct, I *must* follow my conscience. Otherwise I cannot live'. She valued her conscience (or, rather, 'the blood of Puritan ancestors in [her] veins [which had] made conscience a law of nature with [her]'; of course, she adds, 'I often *slip* but I *can't* deliberately go wrong', a nice equivocation) so highly that in support of it she could even give up writing novels. (Though not poetry, a psychological necessity quite unlike the '*voulu*' activity of prose.) But, she concluded, there were two things in her life that she would never surrender: 'my sense of right and my babies'.[131]

Though some of Aelfrida's grumbles verge on the ludicrous – how could she expect Constantine to accede to her request that the Grahams give away surplus income while demanding that he give her five children and why did she not go to church alone if Constantine declined to go with her? [132] – two points made in the course of her diatribe are of particular significance relative to her own and Constantine's post-*Malise* behaviour.

The first arises in connection with what Aelfrida regards as Constantine's despotic behaviour; to keep the peace, she says, she usually yields to him, adding smugly 'of course I generally get my own way – but never, alas, by asking for it openly'. The second and ultimately more important point was trying 'to influence him to what I believe to be right'[133], as witness her attempts to impose Teetotalism and insistence that Constantine attend public and private religious ceremonies to which he, nominally Greek Orthodox and certainly irreligious, felt no personal or doctrinal allegiance.

Teetotalism was, as we know, an integral aspect of Aelfrida's life. She refused alcohol if offered but unlike her father whose teetotal mayoral banquet (his 'Water Banquet') caused a councillor to call successively for champagne, sherry, claret, beer, and on finding there were none, for his hat [134], she rarely tried to impose her beliefs on others in her immediate social circle. (Outside it, she did.) To the young engineers in Finhaut her views were delivered in the course of general flirtation ('I told them just what I thought, coquettishly of course and as charmingly as I knew how') [135] and were accepted by one in the same manner: "Mademoiselle … to win your admiration I would renounce the spirits for all my life".[136] Towards Hans Peter, however, she was intransigent, first suggesting he become a total abstainer for her sake in spite of her mother pointing out that this was too much to ask of any man and that Aelfrida had no right 'to make him yield to [her] in this matter'[137], then insisting that she could not be happy with a man who was not a teetotaller.[138] Enrico, pleading that abstinence from alcohol would ruin his career, initially submitted to her wishes; so too, initially, did Constantine. Shortly after the Grahams' arrival in Emden, however, he explained that it was an embarrassment to a man in a public position not to be able to offer wine and beer to his guests and to join them in what Enrico termed 'the pleasures of conviviality', but it is not until many years later that Aelfrida reveals that dissention between the Grahams 'on the subject of wine'[139] had begun earlier – in Odessa, in fact. That Constantine chose to announce his abandonment of Teetotalism by letter during Aelfrida's absence in England spoke volumes about the moral blackmail he knew he would face: 'you care more about your success than you do about my happiness … What right have you to ask me to be unhappy?'[140] With neither man did it occur to her to ask if Enrico or Constantine might be made unhappy by *her* behaviour. And provided they conformed to *her* particular morality, would she have minded if they were?

The same question could be asked with reference to her second point. Not only did she try to *influence* Constantine's behaviour with regard to what she thought was right but she also tried *impose* her views: 'I tried to teach Constantine to be a man when he was only a boy *and might have been made to obey me*'.[141] But opening Constantine's eyes to matters never experienced before[142] (Mission Settlements, Sunday Schools, Cambridge's 'lower middle classes') on the grounds that he was a man "utterly unformed with all his questions unanswered, some even unasked [and] all his roads unchosen"[143] and that it was her duty to direct him, was one thing but to try to remake him in her own image with regard to his religious beliefs (or lack of them) while protesting that she was helping rather than directing, quite another.

With the exception of Silvia Myers whom she had bombarded with religious advice and marked-up texts from *The Imitation of Christ* during their girlhood friendship ('I will do anything to will her to God') before deciding that it was 'no use ramming the Gospel down her throat'[144], Aelfrida made no attempts to preach to or convert members of her own social class and discussed religious matters only with those she knew to be sympathetic. With Constantine, however, things were different (he had received a copy of Aelfrida's favourite religious treatise on 31 May 1905 but was then so besotted with her that he failed to regard the gift as a warning), for in his eagerness to win her he professed an interest in religion he did not feel: 'he wishes me to teach him to be a Christian [and] prays everyday as I wished him "Oh Lord, make me and Aelfrida good"'.[145] His interest waned rapidly during and possibly because of Aelfrida's obsessional interest in Roman Catholicism in 1905/6, so much so that the Bishop of Gibraltar's visit to Odessa prompted him to ask if it was proper to take Communion 'when his God was not personal nor his Christ divine'.[146] (The Bishop's reply was emollient; Aelfrida's comment was that she had not ceased to wonder at Constantine's request for an interview but whether it was because of his request or his question she does not say.) By the time of his January 1912 decision to abandon organised religion altogether, his religious beliefs had reverted, according to Aelfrida, to 'self-realisation instead of self-sacrifice, [to] a vague kind of smudge instead of God', and to 'a set of theories which he never applies to his life' imposed on him by Anatolia ('he thinks he works it all out for himself, but she put it there years ago')[147], to whose influence and with the passing of time and waning of physical desire for his wife, he had become susceptible once more. Unable to appreciate that attempts to convert him to her way of thinking were bound to fail because Constantine's mind-set was too different from her own, Aelfrida also failed to realise (it only became apparent some years later as a result of her readings on a subject other than religion) that in marrying someone who sought to make him obey her by imposing her ideology on him and who rewarded him for compliance by granting him sexualised favours, Constantine had in effect married his mother.

Considering this in the light of a behavioural theory much employed in later years by Aelfrida herself ('psycho-analysis', she wrote in 1924, 'is certainly … illuminating. It quite explains Constantine's conduct. There is no doubt that he had a very strong Edipus (*sic*) complex')[148], we discover that Constantine, Anatolia's 'more than son' towards whom she behaves in a sexualised manner, moves out of his mother's geographical and emotional orbit when he comes to Cambridge. In Cambridge he meets a young woman remarkably like his mother in height and bearing and pronouncements on matters of religion, the latter bearing considerable resemblance in tone and sometimes in content to Anatolia's 'higher twaddle'. He acts with her in a play in which sexualised behaviour is de rigueur ('kiss me like where Vadius kissed Bélise') and falls passionately in love with her. She meets his mother and a clash of wills ensues, after which Constantine sides with his 'new' mother (a woman who though chronologically younger than himself, looks older) and distances himself from his 'real' mother. Constantine and his 'new' mother marry; their wedding is boycotted by his 'real' mother who further distances herself from her son as a result of his desertion.

Constantine's attempts to restore the emotional bonds between himself and his 'real' mother, already loosened as a result of his growing up (going to university, falling in love, failing to obtain the first-class degree which might have allowed him to lead the life of a Cambridge don, a life Anatolia hoped to share) and by his marriage to Aelfrida are unsuccessful. Attempts to restore lost bonds by inducing a mother-substitute to bond with him give rise to childish exhibitions of jealousy and anger when they too are unsuccessful. But once, as he thinks, successfully bonded with Aelfrida by her act of absolute surrender, he decides that 'two persons can be one' and is happy. The unconditional mother-love he sought and thinks he has found in Aelfrida comes to an end, however, when he realises that Aelfrida's love is conditional on his behaving as *she* wishes and that what she wishes him to think and do is at variance with the moral code instilled in him by the mother for whom he has substituted a woman sufficiently like her to allow him to subconsciously believe that he has regained possession of her. Realising that in publicly rejecting his 'real' mother's unconditional love by marrying her substitute and that by not conforming to his mother-substitute's demands he has lost *her* unconditional love too, and unable to re-create the intense emotional bonds formerly established with his wife, he switches his emotional allegiance back to Anatolia ('he is as susceptible to her influence as ever'[149], notes his wife), a woman whose behaviour throughout his relationship with Aelfrida has been directed towards separating son from wife and winning him back to herself. Significantly, however, Aelfrida never, then or later, seeks – or perhaps prefers not to seek – an explanation for her own emotions and behaviour except to note that Constantine's falling in love with her seems inexplicable; indeed, and even after subjecting the Grahams' relationship to 'psycho-analysis', she prefers a physiological to a psychological explanation, stating that Constantine's 'irrational hostility' to his father was due to his having been 'turned

against' Argyris' masculine body odour when taken as a small boy into his parents' bed and that it was only because of this that he transferred his affections to his mother.[150]

The presence of two small girls in this sorry tangle of Oedipal emotions complicates a complex situation, soon to become more complicated still with the occurrence of a third significant event. In June 1911 Aelfrida, on leave in England, and about to receive the 'strange letter' from Eric Silvanus in which he declares his love for her, consults Dr Ingle, about recurrent backache and 'some displacement or weakness of the womb' which makes walking difficult, commenting ruefully that Constantine will inevitably use her new ailment 'as a reason for [her] not having another baby yet awhile'. But, she adds, ominously 'the sea of longing is beginning to rise'.[151] On 25 September, safely back in Emden after Eric's revelations and Agatha's life-threatening illness and reunited with a husband described on her return as 'sweet', Aelfrida records her happiness after 'some very loving converse' with him the previous night.[152] A month later she notes 'I *may* be making another child … there would be something in me that could not help being pleased but Constantine and I cannot help feeling somewhat dismayed. We did not intend it. Neither his income nor my health allows it'.[153] Significantly, however, she is keeping to the schedule of pregnancies unilaterally decided upon when pregnant with Agatha she intends to have babies at age 24, 26, 29, 34, and 36: 'five in all and very moderate'.[154] Alethea is born when she was twenty-four, Agatha when she is twenty-six. The new baby is slightly ahead of schedule but will be born when her mother is in her twenty-ninth year.

Poems record her mixed feelings. The first, *To a Baby That Might Like to be Born,* was written on 15 October 1911 and in manuscript bears an undated note written in red ink (a colour used by Aelfrida to denote great events in her life) 'I was with child then, though I did not know it'.[155] She was being disingenuous; a later diary entry which retrospectively describes her Odessan experience of Alethea's soul arriving in her womb and her lack of realisation of the moment of Agatha's actual or spiritual conception, notes that 'at a given moment of passion, something in me cried "a child, O God, a child!" and I felt a soul dart into my womb like a flame and said to myself "I have conceived", so now I fancy the child as a child of fire and want to call her Agneta'.[156] Other poems reflect less happy thoughts, prompted as much by the argument with Constantine on 6 October over the 'creepy cripple' about to appear in her novel 'about East Friesland and Socialism' and by the resentful thoughts arising from that event (*Malise speaks, I Answer* was written on 8 October) as by her feeling 'so ill': 'my heart is quite ready – but I do … find it so hard not to be gloomy and cross'.[157] Three poems, *One Winter's Night* of 3 November, in which she tosses her soul into the winter sky to shine as a star but sees only "a pack of storm-clouds", *Monotony* of 12 November, which compares her to "the average workman" waking to "heavy consciousness of dawn", and *Fragment, written when I was ill* (dated only 'November 1911') with its escapist hope that someone will "Take me away to a place of forgetting / Set me down on an ocean of dreams …"[158], represent a state of mind made more sombre still by the arrival of Irene's infamous letter of 11 November. (It also accused Constantine of 'baseness' with his new sister-in-law, Rose Hillerns.) Reading 'to try and quiet [her] brain' was unsuccessful; morning sickness and pervasive sadness gave way to a sensation of her brain being 'on fire', the fire fuelled by obsessive 'questioning'. Of what she does not say; she does, however, express concern that obtrusive thoughts could not be good for 'Baby-to-be'.[159] But it was to be more than fiery thoughts[160] which affected embryo Agneta.

Before her first pregnancy but following her serious kidney infection, Dr du Bouchet had warned Aelfrida that it would be unwise for her to become pregnant before she completely regained her health, adding that were she to do so the baby would be still-born and her health 'ruined for ever'.[161] Desperate for a child, Aelfrida ignored his advice; fortunately for herself and for Alethea all went well. Agatha was conceived at a time when Aelfrida's health was generally good but a 'sharp attack of malaria' following her birth impeded her mother's recovery.[162] Agatha was born healthy, the malaria having recurred after the critical first trimester of her mother's pregnancy; Agneta's conception, on the other hand, was followed by attacks of malaria every night or every other night for two weeks in November 1911, by sharp attack in December, and by attacks in January 1912 severe enough to curtail a social life less curtailed by pregnancy and breast feeding in domesticated Emden than in socialite Boston. It was not, however, recurrent malaria which worried Aelfrida but a prolonged bout of 'influenza' which occurred in late March 1912 and during which Dr Kessler informed her that there was 'some danger of Baby-to-be being born too soon' and that her illness had left the foetus 'very weak'. Complete rest was advised: 'I am not allowed to stir until it gets stronger … I love it all the time, believing that to be the best way of making it live'.[163]

Domestic chaos arising from enforced invalidism was unconducive to peaceful pregnancy. Nor was the behaviour of Constantine and his mother. The former complained bitterly that 'he would have given half a year's

Constantine, Agatha and Alethea Graham with Harry Shipway c1913

pay not to have the baby, [that] children are not worth the price you give for them'[164] (this is an expurgated version; what he actually demanded was what his wife meant by "spawning another brat")[165] and that he could hardly bear to think of a wife who did not make him happy ('oh, not *my* fault, he says') because he no longer enjoyed her uninterrupted attention and companionship. (A brief visit from Rose Hillerns had reminded him of 'how different things might have been'.)[166] Adding insult to injury, Anatolia arrived in Emden in January 1912 bent on revenge for the 'peacemaker' letter written by her daughter-in-law to Irene (inaptly, 'Peace') in November 1911.

She wielded an effective weapon over a sick and pregnant woman: another woman. What happened next was recorded by Aelfrida in her diary but Constantine, reading what she had written, made her cut out the relevant pages.[167] (She had earlier informed him that 'I would rather he did not read my diary. I hated to do it but what can one do? One must tell something or someone and a diary is better than a person'.)[168] A year later she replaced, in abbreviated form and with added comments, the destroyed entry: Anatolia, she said, had arrived in Emden with the intention of forcing her son to write to 'Juanita' (of whom Aelfrida had once written 'Constantine, it hurts me that you should have loved such a woman')[169] to tell her 'that he loved her as much as ever'. Aelfrida asked him to defer sending the letter, saying that he would be wiser when Anatolia had gone. He refused. She then 'made him a scene, got hysterical, begged him for the child's sake ... He was hard and quite unmoved ... Finally he altered the letter, but did not show it to me. It was a cruel unnecessary business'.[170] (It may be that the letter was in reply to one from 'Juanita' brought to Emden by Anatolia, a letter in which, so Aelfrida said after accidentally lighting on a cache of her husband's correspondence some years later, 'Juanita' 'poured out her whole soul to him'; she also discovered Juanita's reply to Constantine's 'memorable [letter] from Emden' in the same cache, but does not disclose its contents.)[171] Constantine's heartless behaviour (his exact words during the 'scene' may have been "oh dry up! ... I hate melodrama ... You'll be ill again if you work yourself up like that")[172] towards an ill and pregnant wife who lacked 'the weapon of desire' to assist in her fight against renewal of Anatolia's malignant influence over her husband, was underlined by the behaviour of that 'selfish and detestable' person herself[173], for Anatolia, not content with using another sexualised mother-figure ('Juanita', a woman of her own age) as a weapon, also informed her son that it was his duty to rescue his children from Aelfrida's 'blighting influence' and that she herself would do everything in her power to help him.[174] With what one hopes was unconscious irony she also proclaimed that she had reached such a pitch of goodness that she was unable to think an ignoble thought or do an unworthy action; Aelfrida, hearing this, wrote that Anatolia sang her own praises 'like a patent medicine' and retired to bed 'for sheer lack of ability to face her' any longer and even wondered if Anatolia possessed the gift of the evil eye.[175]

Anatolia's departure on 11 February heralded a change in Constantine's behaviour, Aelfrida noting that he was 'giving up his little-boy attitude and ... behaving like a man again'.[176] (That she rather regretted his 'grown-up' behaviour is evident from two comments made earlier, one in January 1911 that 'grown-up' Constantine had become 'a little hard', though not, she hastened to add – erroneously as it turned out – to *her*[177], the other in January 1903 when she wrote that she hoped to marry 'some meek little boy of my own age who won't take too much of my time'[178]; sadly, the 'meek little boy' she married had turned against her, one of his reasons being that she accorded him too little of her time.) Noting, too, that she and Constantine had found 'the most beautiful of harmony again', that her 'Emden novel' grew, that Agatha and Alethea were 'radiant', and that 'baby-to-be

leaps in my womb for joy'[179], two poems demonstrate her real feelings: *A Little Song,* written on 28 January 1912, whose joyful beginning belies its sombre ending ("the path to joy" leads to "the pools of death") and *Trying to be Brave* written on 4 February 1912[180] in which she notes that in spite of her belief that 'you may hide love and trample on it and curse it – but I have yet to discover a way to kill it'[181], Constantine's inconsiderate behaviour and contention that he had done nothing wrong had caused her to fall suddenly and completely out of love with him – or, more correctly, with Constantine Graham; Constantine Michaelides she loved still.

Medical advice notwithstanding Aelfrida decided her third child must be born in England, and with her children and Ovvie and escorted by Chiara, left Emden for Cambridge, arriving there on 4 May 1912. Constantine, nearing the end of his current posting, remained behind to close up the apartment and hand over the Consulate, arriving in England later the same month to find his wife lamenting not his arrival, but his imminent departure for his next posting: Panama.

To that posting, Constantine made it clear he intended to go unencumbered by wife and family. Aelfrida had often thought that 'next time Constantine gets a move, he will go away by himself' but had 'prayed frantically' (so she said) that 'it might not be so'; now she resigned herself to letting him go to 'be young and adventurous' on his own.[182] (Had she not written prophetically early in their courtship that she hoped she would be 'great enough to wish him, later on, to go away of his own accord without pain' and that Constantine, for his part, would realise 'when – or may I say if – he has failed and ... go?' Unfortunately, he did not go away 'proudly [and] sublimely'[183] but pettishly and selfishly, 'sick of Emden and bored with domestic life'[184], the 'practical things'[185] which seemed so charming during his courtship having lost whatever charms they had and domesticity having become confining to his spirit.) Realising too that after the domestic crises of the previous year, she herself needed the physical and spiritual rest afforded by a quiet year at home with her parents and children but racked nevertheless by thoughts of separation, Aelfrida resigned herself to parting: 'I am so unhappy because Constantine is going away. I think of it all the time ... as though it were some kind of black shadow that followed me'.[186] But the 'black shadow' which dogged her footsteps was the shadow of the Valley of Death and a month later she would be on the threshold of the most absolute surrender of all: that of life itself.

In the early days of her first pregnancy and on the eve of the Grahams' departure for Boston, Aelfrida wrote of not wanting to be 'intellectual or problem-mongering' but living instead in a garden with 'nothing but flowers and trees and sky'.[187] In May 1912 she had her wish, writing of Fordfield that 'here everything is very quiet … I lie in the garden on the sofa and think …' But whether it was because her head was 'overstretched with merchandise for which I am not allowed to find an outlet' or because she had 'nothing to do but sit in the garden and dream'[188], she began to see ghosts.

One, a haunting presence if not quite a ghost, was Hilda Sollas, who, hastening to greet Constantine on his arrival, appeared looking 'queer and shadowlike in black'.[189] Another, a true revenant, was Henry Joseph Wetenhall, Aelfrida noting on 12 May that on six occasions since returning 'home' she had caught sight of 'a tall stately old man with rather long silver hair and a brown suit of somewhat peculiar shade, walking about the garden'. Checking with Chiara if Henry Joseph such a suit, she elicited from her shaken mother that her description would 'quite apply to grandpapa – whom of course I have never seen'. Do the dead, she wondered, 'perhaps leave parts of themselves in places that they love?'[190]

She did not, however, regard the presence of her dead grandfather as ominous, concentrating instead on Rupert Brooke's poems, published the year before. Reading them prompted her to versify on 22 May, *Tout pour toi!* being full of elliptical references to an unnamed poet who twists a "wild sweet wonder into words" and to herself taking the magic of his song "to breathe it afire upon the lips I love". (Whether the lips are her husband's or Eric Silvanus', she does not say but there are references to "woods at midday quivering all alight / Alive with maddening mysteries…".)[191] She also enjoyed visits from 'all kinds of callers, mostly men'[192], one, 'a tall lanky young man, quite undistinguished-looking in an ill-fitting flannel suit and soft collar' with an 'irregular profile and a long nose … his mouth, half hidden by a weak moustache, is very sensitive as are his long rather ugly hands [but] he has a pair of expressive blue eyes, the blue eyes of a minor poet … he looks very delicate, as though observation has rather taken the place of life', being the 'celebrated novelist' EM Forster[193], another an Irish–Armenian student with 'a brilliant fervid mind' who was 'a good deal mad' and whom Aelfrida decided she would like much better 'were [he] not so swarthy and … washed more'[194], another still Eric Silvanus with his fiancée in tow, the latter informing Aelfrida 'almost in so many words, that she was jealous of Eric's intimacy with me, but I explained that it was only [an] extension of his intimacy with Constantine'.[195] Much cheered by the visits, she stated that as long as Agatha, Alethea, and Constantine remained 'well and happy' and 'Baby-to be

[was] a strong little boy', she would 'ask no more of fate – for the present!'[196]

There is a gap of a month in Aelfrida's diary account following Eric and Maude's visit. The next entry, written on 27 June, demonstrates what fate had had in store for her: 'the baby has been born dead and I have been very ill'.[197]

Experiencing what she was sure were labour pains on the day following Forster's visit, Aelfrida consulted Dr Ingle who assured her she was mistaken: the baby was not due for some weeks and her obstetric history ran to late deliveries. On 28 May, however, the day of Eric Silvanus' visit, she went into labour proper: 'I was taken ill at midnight and suffered for an hour all alone, feeling at first unwilling and then unable to call anyone. But at last I managed to rouse Constantine and he called Chiara. Of course he went at once for the doctor, leaving us to face things as best we might. I kept as quiet as I could, fearing to awaken the children, and that made it all the harder to bear. At one point I felt the baby's soul leave me and said to Chiara "It is all over – there is not going to be any baby" but of course she did not understand. Then the baby came, and I said "It is dead, isn't it?" Chiara answered "It does not cry and it is very tiny". I heard myself say – I still hear myself say – "Oh poor little dead baby". And then I lay still and did not say any more.

When Dr Ingle came there was plenty for him to do. Presently Dr Bowen appeared too.[198] The haemorrhage could not be stopped.[199] Chiara was in the room, Constantine [and] afterwards a great angel with grey wings, near the foot of the bed. I knew it for the angel of death and was neither sorry nor surprised, but only full of anguish because I wanted to say things to Chiara about Alethea and Agatha … and though I fought against my weakness, I was speechless and prayed for life then [so as] not to leave the children. Dr Ingle left me suddenly and drew Dr Bowen away with him out of the room. I heard him say in quick almost angry tones "Is there *nothing* we can do?" And Dr Bowen, quiet and grave, "No. We have done everything we can". After that, I am told, Dr Ingle said to Constantine that the end would probably be in a few minutes. He (Constantine) came and took hold of my hand – I thought he must have seen the angel, for he walked round it so carefully.[200] I remember telling the doctors to go and have some breakfast for they must be tired and hearing them say "presently". Perhaps I lost consciousness after that, for an hour or more must have passed when I looked up and saw that the angel was no longer there … Dr Bowen, with his hand on my pulse, shifted his position stiffly, as though he had been sitting there a long time. Then I heard the children's voices overhead and thanked God that my prayers had been answered.

It was the beginning of that long, that interminable day, when I was lying motionless and living through the dreadful hours of the night again, that I suddenly felt a touch of tiny finger on my cheek, and, looking up, saw my dead baby there. She was tiny and pale with soft straight golden hair and "new-born blue" eyes. She laughed at me with eyes and mouth and told me – not speaking, of course – that her name was Agneta and that she loved me ... Then I saw, above her, Dear and Aunt Gregory and Conrad, all looking so radiant and serene. They smiled at her and she went away to join them. So they vanished, leaving me happy too, in spite of the long weariness of that endless day'.[201]

# Notes

1 GCPPT 1|1|18 25 October 1911.

2 GCPPT 1|1|18 16 February 1912. In September 1914 Aelfrida began 'revising' *Marrying a Stranger* in the light of current events, completing it sometime in October. The novel was rejected by Grant Richards in November 1915 (GCPPT 1|1|21 20 November 1915). She continued to revise it during the Great War but it remained unpublished.

3 GCPPT 1|1|17 11 December 1910.

4 Aelfrida's initial inspiration for Max's Socialist proclivities came from the father of an Emden acquaintance, 'a Socialist idealist who dedicated himself to his party instead of earning money for his family' (GCPPT 1|1|18 25 October 1911) but her description of Max's first speech to the miners owes much to her own speech to the Swavesey Band of Hope (GCPPT 1|1|9 22 April 1902).

5 GCPPT 1|1|17 1 February 1910.

6 Tillyard, Ae. *Marrying a Stranger* p 281.

7 GCPPT 1|1|17 6 March 1910.

8 Aelfrida added no later interpolations to the volumes of the diary which cover the Grahams' Emden posting, possibly because she felt no need to do so, comment and amplification appearing instead in *Marrying a Stranger* and in the poetry she wrote during this time. There are no interpolations in the diaries covering Odessa, Boston, and Cambridge intermissions either, possibly for the same reason.

9 GCPPT 1|1|17 6 September 1910.

10 GCPPT 1|1|18 19 September 1911.

11 GCPPT 1|1|17 20 February 1910. Aelfrida's description of Emden predates but is very similar to that of the 1911 *Encyc. Brit.* Vol. 9 pp 331–332.

12 GCPPT 1|1|17 20 February and 16 October 1910 and 8 March 1911.

13 Cambridge and Catharine Tillyard were much exercised over women's suffrage though Aelfrida herself showed only a mocking interest in the subject. She exercised her right to the franchise in later years.

14 GCPPT 1|1|17 6 September 1910.
   GCPPT 1|1|18 23 September 1911.

15 GCPPT 1|1|17 24 March 1908.

16 GCPPT 1|1|15 1 March 1908.

17 The quotation comes from *An Evening Picture,* a poem published in *To Malise* (p 80) but of which no manuscript version exists. In the book it is dated only 'Emden 1910'; it was probably written sometime between 19 February and 22 April 1910.

18 GCPPT 1|1|17 15 April 1910.

19 *An Evening Picture* (*To Malise* p 80) dated only 'Emden 1910'.

20 The poem *As a fall'n Coal* (*To Malise* p 22) from which these lines are taken appears in the manuscript version of *To Malise* (GCPPT 2|2) as *Sonnet (Méthode Directe)* a title which reminds us of the means by which

Aelfrida taught French and the forceful manner in which Constantine made his point.

21 GCPPT 1|1|17 28 February 1910.

22 Tillyard, Ae. *Marrying a Stranger.* p 146.

23 GCPPT 1|1|18 20 May 1911.

24 ibid.

25 GCPPT 1|1|17 28 March 1910.

26 ibid. 27 May 1910.

27 ibid. 29 July 1910.

28 ibid. 12 November 1910. Aelfrida's 'affinity' with Alethea is described in the poem written on 18 June 1910 entitled *What a mother feels about her first-born though she could never tell him*; the manuscript version (GCPPT 2|2) is more explicit, containing as it does the dedication 'To Alethea. If she only knew (though I could not possibly tell her)'. The poem begins with a curious echo of Anatolia's letter to Oscar Browning in which she describes Constantine as 'more to me than son', namely "thou art not merely as a child to me" and continues with Aelfrida's description of her own feelings about and hopes for a child whom she, like Anatolia, believes to be her 'dearest friend and companion', a child whom she admits, she almost idolises (GCPPT 1|1|17 28 February 1910) and whom she later describes as 'more to me than the whole universe' (GCPPT 1|1|17 16 June 1910).

29 GCPPT 1|1|17 19 June 1910.

30 ibid. 3 June 1910.

31 In the manuscript of *To Malise* (GCPPT 2|2) the poem is entitled *Poem to "Two"*: in the printed version (*To Malise,* p 77) it appears as *Poem to an unborn Child,* dedicated 'to ACAG'. The poem was written on 12 June 1910, nine days after Aelfrida's prenatal experience. A Girton College copy of *To Malise* contains Aelfrida's hand-written dedication of the volume to Agatha 'who is the best poem I ever made'.

32 GCPPT 1|1| 17 19 June 1910.

33 ibid. 3 June 1910.

34 ibid. 19 August 1910.

35 ibid. 10 March 1910.

36 ibid. 1|1|17 25 February 1910.

37 ibid. 22 June 1910. An article in the woman's column of *The Baptist Times* of 8 July 1910 on the subject of "getting and keeping" refers to an article of 1 July by the same author on the subject of "a building scheme as a good investment for the money of Free Church people" and is, judging by tone and context by Aelfrida herself; indeed, she notes in her diary (GCPPT 1|1|17 7 June 1910) that she was currently writing for two temperance journals, the *CIP* and the *Baptist Times.* Catharine Tillyard ran the woman's column of the *Baptist Times and Freeman* (to give it its full title) under the by-line 'Eleuthera' ('freedom') and it seems that her daughter occasionally wrote the column under the same pseudonym. The scheme may have been inspired by the 'Learned Twins' who not only performed good works by stealth but also bought up properties which they let at low rents to people in need (Soskice, J. pp 274–275). The Twins, however, were wealthier than the Grahams were ever likely to be.

38 GCPPT 1|1|17 17 March 1909.

39 ibid. 8 January 1911.

40 GCPPT 2|5. The poem was never published.

41 GCPPT 1|1|17 18 March 1910.

42 ibid. 20 March 1910.

43 ibid. 2 November 1910.

44 ibid. 'Dearest Ba' refers to poet Elizabeth Barrett Browning, so addressed by her husband Robert.

45 ibid. 2 March 1911. An unpublished short poem, undated but by context written sometime between 13 February and 5 March, notes that "From thoughts unstirred comes sense of power to man. / There's much of greatness in an untried span" (*Feeling great!* GCPPT 2|5). A longer poem (*Surtout pas trop de zèle* of 6 March 1911) expresses less optimistic sentiments.

46 ibid. 2 November 1910.

47 GCPPT 1|1|18 13 June 1911.

48 GCPPT 1|1|17 19 August 1910.

49 ibid. 24 November 1910.

50 *Perplexity* was written in Arlington Heights on 5 November 1908. (*To Malise* p 19).

51 GCPPT 1|1|17 18 March 1911.
   GCPPT 2|25. The poem remained unpublished.

52 *To Malise*, the dedicatory poem of Aelfrida's anthology was written on 29 December 1908 in Arlington Heights, poem and anthology having as its author 'Aelfrida Tillyard (Mrs Constantine Graham)'. It seems that Aelfrida had abandoned her proposed nom-de-plume 'Aelfrida Michaelides' prior to her marriage for all her books are by-lined 'Aelfrida Tillyard' ('Mrs Constantine Graham' is optional); Constantine retains his former surname in a literary capacity, possibly because it was as Michaelides that he was known at Cambridge but as Constantine Graham in the Consular Service.

53 GCPPT 1|1|17 19 June 1910.

54 GCPPT 1|1|20 15 July 1915.

55 The poems quoted appear in sequence in *To Malise* pp 83–88 but were as far as is known (not all volumes of the *MCJ* still exist) not written in that order. Of those of which we can be sure, *Amour et destinée* appears in Vol 2 No 3 October 1903 (this, of course, was prior to Aelfrida's first meeting with Constantine Michaelides and so may have been written with John Forbes Cameron in mind; its subtitle, *poème moderne*, however, was added for publication as if its author wished it to apply to Constantine also), *Victor Hugo* in the *MCJ* of September 1905 and *La Nuit* and *A la Soeur* in that of June 1910, both as 'after' Guy-Charles Croz (GCPPT 2|2a).

56 The poem also appears in *To Malise* p 60.

57 GCPPT 1|1|17 6 October 1910. The poem, of 31 October 1910, was later published in *The Garden and the Fire* (p 23) under the title *In Autumn*.

58 GCPPT 1|1|17 24 November 1910. Unnamed reviewers apparently described them as "pleasant" or "choicely expressed"; they also (ironically) described them as containing "hardly a trace of personal feeling"; there were, Aelfrida hoped, 'more sensible reviews to come'.

59 The fashion for unusual female Christian names extended beyond bestowal of a feminised version of a father's name (Alfred/Aelfrida) to include names derived from Arthurian legend, Wagnerian opera, Norse myth, and so on.

60 GCPPT 1|1|17 1 December 1910.

61 ibid. 30 September and 2 and 21 October 1910. Dr Kessler was only the first of several medical practitioners with whom Aelfrida's relationship transcended the professional.

62 ibid. 11 March 1911. One of the 'young ladies' may have been Rose Hillerns, a sweet pretty girl shortly to become Constantine's sister-in-law. His sister Irene castigated him over this friendship but Aelfrida regarded it as 'a most harmless P. and B.F. of which I quite approve' (GCPPT 1|1|18 11 November 1911).

63 GCPPT 1|1|17 2 October 1910. An interesting comparison may be made here with lines (quoted earlier) from the dedicatory poem of *To Malise* of the same title: "I watch thy ways and know not where they go, / Nearest of all am I yet not too near". The poem is dated 29 December 1908 but the sentiments apply more closely to 1910; could it have been written nearer to the book's date of publication (2 November 1910) and backdated to make it appear as if written contemporaneously with *The Song of Big Love*? There is no reference to either poem in diary entries either date.

64 Hilda Sollas (1877–1965) graduated from Newnham in 1901; in 1910/11 she was lecturer in Zoology there. (*NCR* vol 1 1871–1923).

65 GCPPT 1|1|12 25 May 1905.

66 GCPPT 1|1|17 20 May 1910.

67 ibid. 20 May 1910.

68 Tillyard, Ae. *A Little Road-Book for Mystics* p 77.

69 GCPPT 2|1 and *To Malise* p 79.

70 GCPPT 1|1|17 1 December 1910.

71 The poem appears in *To Malise* (p 69) in a section entitled 'Some Gods'. It is only two lines long: "Pain I know not, nor hateful lust,/ Nor motherhood. I know the Truth".

72 GCPPT 1|1|17 10 December 1910.

73 GCPPT 1|1|17 6 June 1910. Mrs McKendrick Hughes was a neighbour of the Tillyards who had recently converted to Christian Science. Aelfrida, pumping her for information, decided that 'I was glad ... to find that in Christian Science there is a noble if untrue philosophical concept to counterbalance the absurd physical side'. The poem appears in *To Malise* (p 68) on the page preceding *Minerva of the Grey Eyes*.

74 GCPPT 1|1|17 26 May 1911.

75 ibid. 24 May 1911.

76 *A qui la Gloire?* (*To Malise* p 88).

77 GCPPT 1|1|17 11 April 1910.

78 GCPPT 1|1|18 11 November 1911.

79 ibid. 8 December 1911.

80 GCPPT 1|1|18 13 October 1911. An unpublished poem, *Malise and I*, of 14 December 1910 expresses her sentiments during the Emden years: "For thee – the windless nights of higher thought ... / For me – the labour over little things, / Wrought in the shadow of an angel's wings" (GCPPT 2/5).

81 Emden, according to the contemporary edition of the *Encyclopaedia Britannica* (Vol. 9 pp 331–332), was strategically important not only as the commercial capital and military centre of East Friesland but also as the North Sea outlet of an extensive canal system, as an *entrepôt*, as the home port of deep sea fishing fleets, as a manufacturing town, and most importantly in view of what was commonly regarded as a coming war between England and Germany, as the station for undersea cables connecting Germany with England, Spain, and North America. Aelfrida makes little mention in her diary of the difficult relationship then existing between England and Germany other than remarking on her relief that England was not (yet) at war with that country (GCPPT 1|1|17 6 October 1910), that international politics had replaced Balzac in her husband's conversation (GCPPT 1|1|17 24 March 1910), and that both she and Constantine were subjected to anti-British comments from the chief administrative officer (*Landrat*) of the Emden district (GCPPT 1|1|18 8 December 1911). She does, however, describe German imperialism and warmongering at some length in *Marrying a Stranger*.

82 GCPPT 1|1|17 29 October 1910.

83 ibid. 9 September 1910.

84 GCPPT 1|1|18 13 April 1912.

85 GCPPT 1|1|17 28 February 1910. The title of an unpublished poem of 18 January 1911 *Sonnet to the effect that when one has given all to Love it needs no further fuel, but will burn untended for ever* would seem to support her view until one reads just *how much* Aelfrida feels she has sacrificed for Love – and how little recompense she has received. (GCPPT 2/5).

86 GCPPT 1|1|18 15 December 1911.

87 GCPPT 1|1|13 18 November 1905.

88 *That two persons cannot be one* was written in Emden on 23 September 1911 and was marked 'A++' in manuscript to mark its importance to her; it was later published in *Cambridge Poets 1910–1913* (p192).

89 GCPPT 2/5 consists of fair copies of poems written between October 1910 and August 1913. Although the poems do not appear in the manuscript in strictly chronological order, the fact that each poem's date and place of composition is given makes it easy to relate it to contemporary diary entries. Several poems appear later in *Cambridge Poets* (1913) and *The Garden and the Fire* (1916).

90 GCPPT 1|1|17 12 May 1910.

91 ibid. 16 May 1910.

92 ibid. 26 and 27 May 1910.

93   GCPPT 1|1|18 28 January 1912.

94   GCPPT 2|5 *A Little Song* was written 28 January 1912 and remained unpublished.

95   GCPPT 1|1|17 7 April 1911.

96   GCPPT 1|1|17 16 April 1911.
      GCPPT 1|1|17A Irene's letter, dated 10 April 1911, was delivered to her sister-in-law by '*le petit Bonhomme*' (i.e. Constantine) and is one of the few letters Aelfrida preserved from later holocausts.

97   GCPPT 1|1|18 13 June 1911.

98   ibid. 21 and 24 June 1911.

99   ibid. 3 June 1911. A rough calculation shows that in their 4½ year marriage the Grahams had refrained from sexual intercourse (for various reasons) for almost half the time.

100  ibid.

101  ibid. 13 June 1911.

102  ibid. 26 July and 2 August 1911. Aelfrida's poem *The River of Life (after the Greek of Argyris Ephtalotis)* was written in Hessle on 4 August 1911; it was published five years later in *The Garden and the Fire* (p 23) in the section entitled 'songs about love'.

103  GCPPT 1|1|18 6 August 1911. Anatolia may have been annoyed by attentions paid by Aelfrida to another of her mother-in-law's house-guests, Michel de Calvocoressi (1877–1944), the Greek writer, critic, linguist and musicologist.

104  ibid. 11 November 1911.

105  GCPPT 1|1|18 11 November 1911.

106  ibid.

107  ibid. The quotation is taken from *Isaiah* 14: 12: "How art thou fallen from heaven, O Lucifer, son of the morning!" As usual, Aelfrida misquotes.

108  GCPPT 1|1|18 6 July 1911.

109  A pen and ink sketch of Eric Silvanus inserted into the back of the contemporary (GCPPT 1|1|18) volume of Aelfrida's diary depicts him pipe in mouth. The sketch is drawn on the back of a fragment of an undated love poem, written in French and initialled 'EMS'. Contrary to her usual custom, Aelfrida did not stick the sketch into her diary but inserted its corners into four slits cut into the page. The relevance of sketch and poem is enhanced by its appearing contiguous to photographs of Charles Stewart Smith and Constantine. Constantine's photograph, taken at an Emden wedding on 2 July 1911, is inscribed 'There is delight in remembrance' and signed with an illegible but probably female signature. It is significant in that it shows Constantine smiling; no photographs exist which show him smiling in the presence of Aelfrida or his children.

110  GCPPT 1|1|18 11 July 1911.

111  Tillyard, Ae. *Marrying a Stranger* p 171.

112  ibid. p 152.

113  GCPPT 1|1|13 22 August 1905.

114  Tillyard Ae. *Marrying a Stranger* p 116.

115  GCPPT 1|1|18 11 July 1911.

116  ibid. 10 July 1911.

117  GCPPT 1|1|13 14 June 1906. Aelfrida's previous visit to the small forest on the slope of the Gog Magog hills south of Cambridge had been with Constantine during their courting days.

118  GCPPT 1|1|18 12 July 1911.

119  The poem appears in GCPPT 2|5 with the title *Triolet* and the dedication (later crossed out) 'EMS'; its date and place of attribution are Cambridge 10 July 1911. In *Cambridge Poets (*p193) it appears under the title of *To a King's Man* without dedicatee. The last two lines of the poem are reversed from the manuscript version, probably to provide a stronger ending.

120  GCPPT 1|1|18 14 July 1911.

121  The poem appears in GCPPT 2|5 with the crossed out comment 'most pretentious!' It was subsequently published in *Cambridge Poets* p 197. Aelfrida's reference in the penultimate line to her hope that

Eric's "unforgetting praise" of her would constitute his "priest's attire", refers to his having told her that as a fair-haired Welshman he came of priestly caste and to her replying that in that case she envisaged him 'as a bard sitting all alone on the top of a Welsh mountain playing a golden harp!' (GCPPT 1|1|18 10 July 1911).

122  GCPPT 1|1|18 30 August 1911.

123  GCPPT 2|5 The poem was written on 20 August 1911 and remained unpublished.

124  GCPPT 1|1|18 8 September 1911. The poem appears in GCPPT 2/5 under the title *This is the vow I made –*, and is dedicated 'to Agatha'. In *The Garden and the Fire* (p 43) it has no dedicatee and appears under the title of *The Vow of Olga Stanislovna* in order to disguise it as the vow made by a Russian woman (whose name closely resembles that of Aelfrida's nurse in Odessa) to her lover: "This is the vow I made when you were ill – / That I would look no more into men's eyes, / And watching see them with desire grow dim. / It was a vow I made. Have I the will / To make it law, and not a worthless whim …" The answer to Olga/Aelfrida's question is 'no'.

125  GCPPT 2|5 9 September 1911. Perhaps worth noting in this context is that 'go now' is the formula for dismissing spirits one has conjured up but for whom one now has no further use; because they have been formally conjured up, so they must also be formally dismissed.

126  GCPPT 1|1|18 20 December 1911.

127  GCPPT 2|5 The poem, entitled *To – on his Betrothal* is dated and placed Emden 21 January 1912; there is no dedicatee but worth noting is that the Eric episode generated six poems (of which three were published in two separate anthologies) and characters in *Marrying a Stranger* and *Haste to the Wedding*.

128  GCPPT 1|1|18 6 October 1911

129  ibid. 6 and 19 October 1911.

130  GCPPT 2|5 *Malise Speaks. I Answer* was later published in *The Garden and the Fire* (p 53) in the section entitled 'Borderland Poems' to signify its creation on a significant cusp in the Grahams' relationship: the 'Malise' and 'I' of the title are "looking on sunset pageant of the west" together but 'seeing' different things (ships and eagles v. God's armies and angels); once, says Aelfrida, they looked on the 'selfsame sunset sky' and saw the same thing. That the Grahams could put up a united front in the face of the enemy however much they might differ in private is shown by Anatolia twice informing Aelfrida that 'Constantine agrees with you in everything' (GCPPT 1|1|18 20 November 1911).

131  GCPPT 1|1|18 6 October 1911.

132  The Emden custom of paying calls on Sunday mornings may have precluded Sabbath attendance at church particularly if Constantine wished Aelfrida to be 'at home' to callers at that time.

133  GCPPT 1|1|18 6 October 1911.

134  GCPPT 1|1|4 11 March 1900.

135  GCPPT 1|1|8 11 August 1901.

136  ibid. 22 August 1901.

137  ibid. 27 August 1901

138  ibid. 16 September 1901.

139  ibid. 17 August 1901.
      GCPPT 1|1|52 4 July 1937.

140  GCPPT 1|1|8 16 September 1901.

141  GCPPT 1|1|18 6 October 1911.

142  'Max', Constantine's fictional alter ego, hoped that 'Elizabeth' would not "try and explain British Municipal Politics" to him, noting ruefully that her intellect "was a thing to be admired … but kept at arm's length" (Tillyard, Ae. *Marrying a Stranger* p.14.)

143  Tillyard, Ae. *Marrying a Stranger* p.18.

144  GCPPT 1|1|5 4 and 14 June 1900.

145  GCPPT 1|1|11 12 June and 13 July 1904.

146  GCPPT 1|1|15 16 October 1907.

147  GCPPT 1|1|18 28 January 1912.

148  GCPPT 1|1|28 14 July 1928.

149 GCPPT 1|1|18 28 January 1912.

150 GCPPT 1|1|28 14 July 1924.

151 GCPPT 1|1|18 28 June 1911.

152 ibid. 25 September 1911.

153 ibid. 5 October 1911.

154 GCPPT 1|1|17 18 March 1910.

155 The poem as published differs from the manuscript version by one line; the line which runs "Yet guarding life as men their treasures keep" in the published version (*The Garden and the Fire* p 47) is given as "Giving your life into another's keep" in GCPPT 2|5.

156 GCPPT 1|1|18 4 March 1912. The name Agneta probably derives from Sanscrit works lent to Aelfrida by Mrs Venn (GCPPT 2|25|2(4)) in which Aelfrida would have discovered that Agni is a god particularly associated with the fire on the altar which, in consuming the sacrifice, acts as mediator between gods and men.

157 GCPPT 1|1|18 8 November 1911. The sentence continues '… and then I get homesick and want Fordfield teacakes and silly things like that', a sentiment expanded into exiled Elizabeth's thoughts in *Marrying a Stranger*.

158 GCPPT 2|5 The three poems quoted were never published.

159 GCPPT 1|1|18 5 December 1911.

160 Significantly, perhaps, Aelfrida's poem *Malise Speaks, I Answer* of 8 October 1911 is full of 'burning' imagery: "a golden ship with flame aboard"; "the flaming armies of the Lord"; an eagle leaving his "fiery nest".

161 GCPPT 1|1|15 29 November 1907 and 12 January 1908.

162 GCPPT 1|1|17 7 and 19 August 1910.

163 GCPPT 1|1|18 18 March and 8 April 1912.

164 ibid. 8 April 1912.

165 GCPPT 1|1|21 24 September 1916.

166 GCPPT 1|1|18 8 April 1912.

167 ibid. 12 February 1912. The entry continues without a break, so was obviously rewritten later. Other entries were cut out following diary entries for 25 February and 9 September 1910; Aelfrida makes no comment regarding these.

168 ibid. 1 February 1912.

169 GCPPT 1|1|11 9 August 1904.

170 GCPPT 1|1|18 21 March 1913.

171 GCPPT 1|1|22 10 May 1918.

172 Tillyard, Ae. *The Centaur* p190 (GCPPT 2|21|1).

173 GCPPT 1|1|18 28 January 1912.

174 ibid. 1 February 1912.

175 ibid.

176 ibid. 10 February 1912.

177 GCPPT 1|1|17 19 January 1911.

178 GCPPT 1|1|10 7 January 1903.

179 GCPPT 1|1|18 16 February 1912.

180 GCPPT 2|5. The poem remained unpublished. It is dedicated to Marjorie Lülser, an Englishwoman recently married to a German husband and already regretting her decision; it may be that Marjorie Lülser was another model for the character of 'Elizabeth' in *Marrying a Stranger* and, together with other Marjories known to its author, gave her name to 'Marjorie Lane' in the same book. A poem written on 8 April 1912, *Wind at Emden,* later published in *The Garden and the Fire* (p 48) continues the 'wind' theme of *Trying to be Brave* but with the wind now grown into a malevolent force (as it were, Anatolia) "straight from the troubled womb of sea... Seeking some pretty living thing to maim ... / Destruction is the only garb you wear".

181 GCPPT 1|1|9 22 December 1901.

182 ibid. 13 April 1912.

183 GCPPT 1|1|11 14 and 26 May 1904.

184 GCPPT 1|1|18 13 April 1912.

185 GCPPT 1|1|11 23 July 1904.

186 GCPPT 1|1|18 26 April 1912.

187 GCPPT 1|1|15 31 January 1908.

188 GCPPT 1|1|18 7 May 1912.

189 ibid. 7 and 12 May 1912.

190 ibid. 12 May 1912. This was not the first ghost in a brown suit seen by Aelfrida in recent times; in March 1911 she saw the ghost of a man in a brown suit in the drawing room of the Emden apartment. Not recognising him and 'not wanting to have anything to do with spooks', she shut the folding doors on him and 'sat down to write' (GCPPT 1|1|17 11 March 1911).

191 GCPPT 2|5 *Tout pour toi,* with its comment 'after reading Rupert Brooke's poems', remained unpublished.

192 GCPPT 1|1|18 29 May 1912.

193 ibid. E M Forster, like Constantine, was a protégé of Goldsworthy Lowes Dickinson; Constantine had met Forster at King's on 24 May 1912, inviting him to Fordfield the following day. Although Aelfrida's description of Forster is somewhat more flattering than that of Rose Macaulay, met in Cambridge the year before ('a young woman of thirty or so, plain, with ... a thin virginal figure and large flat feet' (GCPPT 1|1|18 30 May 1911), an earlier critique of *A Room with a View* shows lack of insight: "What is the matter with E M Forster is that he ought to get married. Then he would either write much better novels or none at all. Forster once made a great discovery which [has] faded into – bathing with nothing on is much more god-like than wearing a top hat … Let him get married … he can still bathe and be god-like if he wishes" (Tillyard, HJW. *Letters of Aelfrida C W Tillyard* (MTC)). Letter from Aelfrida to Julius Tillyard of 25 November 1908.

194 GCPPT 1|1|18 17 May 1912.

195 ibid. 28 May 1912.

196 ibid. A poem written on 22 May 1912 entitled *My Son* ("God sends to me a son, a child of song") had its title subsequently crossed out and a note added ' no, better call it *The Poet's Mother*' (GCPPT 2/5). It remained unpublished.

197 ibid. 27 June 1912.

198 William Bowen (1878–1963) qualified at Guy's Hospital, London in 1901. Appointed FRCS in 1903, he worked at The Royal Ear Hospital, London until 1910 when he was appointed to Addenbrooke's Hospital, Cambridge as Assistant Surgeon with a special interest in aural surgery. He lived at 24 Lensfield Road about a mile distant from Fordfield. Robert Ingle lived in Shaftesbury Road just across Brooklands Avenue.

199 It seems that Aelfrida suffered placental abruption ie rapid, premature detachment of the placenta from the uterine wall. Signs of placental abruption are the onset of sudden intense labour pains followed by haemorrhage and collapse. The baby is almost always stillborn.

200 One of only two extant poems written between 29 May and 27 June 1912 (there is a page cut out of the manuscript version between this poem and a sonnet written on 23 July 1912), it was written on 7 June 1912. Entitled *To Anyone,* it speaks in fact to Constantine: "Sometimes your eyes wore an expectant look, / As waiting for a step that never came. / Who then the laggard guest? Love, riches, fame, / Fair crowds of words to prison in a book?" and goes on to warn him that "one day at dawn" he too will look up to find "an angel by your side". The poem later appeared in the 'poems about death' section of *The Garden and the Fire* p 37.

201 GCPPT 1|1|18 27 June 1912.

# Bright Cup of Pain

'Recovery', wrote Aelfrida on 5 July, 'has been slow'. It was complicated by a 'severe return of haemorrhage'[1] five weeks after the traumatic events of 28/29 May and her 'struggle back to health' seemed to take a very long time. With Constantine's departure for Panama imminent, he and she 'had some very beautiful times together, and we are … managing to be very brave and not spoil what is by the thought of what is to be'.[2]

Touching as this picture is, Aelfrida's diary record for the period 26 May to 27 June 1912 (the account of Eric's visit on 28 May was written retrospectively) paints another picture and is remarkable for what it omits. Omissions cannot be attributed solely to her having nearly died on 29 May and by her having recovered sufficiently to write a detailed account on 27 June of events surrounding the stillbirth but subsequently suffering a 'severe' secondary haemorrhage sometime between that date and the entry of 5 July and being too weak to write; diary entries when eventually made are lengthy, coherent, and in a steady hand and two poems composed during this time (*To Anyone* of 7 June and *The Prayer* of 20 June)[3] are carefully constructed and, in the latter instance, several pages long. Perhaps the most glaring omission among other unrecorded events (why, for instance, was the Oracle absent from the anticipated deathbed of his only daughter?) is unrealised by a reader of her diary until one comes to Aelfrida's 5 July entry in which she notes almost in passing that Constantine went to Hessle 'ten days after [her] illness'[4] and stayed there a month. (He returned on 6 July and left for Panama less than three weeks later on 24 July 1912.) When we remember that during his wife's 'illness' Constantine had been informed that 'the end would probably be in a few minutes', departure for Hessle soon afterwards seems callous even by the standard set by his recent uncaring behaviour – a contemporary photograph shows him seated with Irene on the lawn at Ephtalon, both laughing as if her critical letter of November 1911 had never been written – and barely explicable by a desire to see his parents and Irene (Helen was in America) before departing for a part of the world known for the prevalence of serious and sometimes fatal diseases. The gap can be filled, however, with the help of a later diary entry and a non-diary literary source which provide as much information about what happened in

Constantine Graham (back row, third right) in Panama 1913

the immediate aftermath of the stillbirth as Aelfrida's near-contemporary diary entries and her poetic interpretation of the event tell us of the stillbirth itself.[5]

A fictionalised account of the stillbirth and its sequel appears in *Marrying a Stranger*:

Elizabeth is very ill after giving birth to a dead son. Recovery is impeded by auditory hallucinations and obsessive thoughts during which she relives the birth of her child again and again: pains so sudden and so much sharper than she expected, the silence when the child came, her own voice asking "It does not cry does it?", imperfectly-heard reassurance blotted out by her cry "Oh poor little dead baby!" Everything else seems very dim. She remembers that two doctors had come and that she felt sorry for them because they seemed so worried about her. She remembers, too, that Death was a sea, a grey, grey sea, towards which she floated quite passively[6]. Again and again she hears the sound of her own voice but as if coming from outside herself: "Oh, poor little dead baby", it says, "oh, poor little dead baby". Her nurse bends over her telling her "Your husband is here" and asking "Would you like to see him? Shall I ask him to come in for a minute?" But Elizabeth refuses to see Max because she feels only blind resentment: it was all his doing. He had killed the child.[7]

That this was Aelfrida's own reaction is shown by a diary entry of March 1913 in which she paraphrases pages cut from her diary on Constantine's instructions during Anatolia's Emden visit of January 1912: '[Anatolia] made him write a letter to Juanita in which he said that he loved her as much as ever. Of course this wasn't true [but] I made a scene … begged him for the child's sake – the unborn child – for my reason's sake [not to send it] … He was very hard and quite unmoved. It killed the child'.[8] If, therefore, Aelfrida actually accused Constantine of causing Agneta's death, it is no surprise to find him leaving Fordfield for Hessle soon after almost becoming a widower.

Before he went, however, he and his wife appear to have reached a degree of rapprochement. His first visit to her is described by Aelfrida in *Marrying a Stranger* in terms of 'Max's' first visit to 'Elizabeth':

> He had borne his banishment from her with resigned impatience but on … hearing that she was well enough to sit up in bed he declared that he absolutely must be admitted to her room. She was there, frail and white, supported by many pillows, looking somehow far-away and other-worldly, as though death had breathed on her and the white mist of his breath veiled her even now. Max flung himself on his knees by the bedside and covered her hands with kisses.
>
> "My wife", he cried, "my wife".
>
> Elizabeth looked at him languidly. "This is my husband", she thought …
>
> "Thank God thou art better!" Max murmured, "My darling! Oh my darling … How do you feel?"
>
> "I feel as though there were a great big empty world inside my head. Sometimes at night things with wings, black wings, fly about in it and make a kind of rushing noise".[9]

Having reassured himself that Elizabeth/Aelfrida is not going to die (everyone assures him that she is "going on as well as could be expected")[10], Max/Constantine has to decide what to do next – to stay with a wife who is his "personal responsibility" (but who, in Aelfrida's case, has people to look after her) or to follow his star: Socialism in 'Max's' case, the Consular Service in Constantine's. Both men opt for the star, 'Max' to live with the miners he hopes to lead, Constantine for a prestige posting in Panama.

Aelfrida herself was already resigned to Constantine going to Panama without her and makes no comment, bitter or otherwise, concerning his decision to do so within two months of her near-death experience. 'Elizabeth', on the other hand, is enraged by 'Max's' decision to place Socialism before herself and a scene ensues which may mirror the parting between Aelfrida and Constantine prior to his visit to Hessle, a scene in which the couple mutually accuse each other of unreasonable behaviour. It ends with Max/Constantine turning coldly away, leaving Elizabeth/Aelfrida, tears running unheeded down her cheeks, "alone with her own voice that hovered about in the misty light" ("Oh poor little dead baby, oh, poor little dead baby") and believing that there was little point in her confiding in anyone because no one could 'hear' her.[11]

Catharine Tillyard's worries concerning her sick daughter are expressed in a letter to Ancifera Gregory written sometime in June/July 1912. Frida, wrote Chiara, "is going on quite well but slowly … she still seems lifeless [and] does not wish to see anyone or to make any effort … It is very sad to see how invalidish she is and what a number of invalid ways she has acquired". (One of Aelfrida's 'invalid ways' was to complain about her ears; Chiara does not state if her complaint included auditory hallucinations. An appended note by Julius – "while staying in Cambridge, Aelfrida had a miscarriage and a severe illness from which she never fully recovered" – merely refers the reader to the 'mystical vision' associated with the event.) Yet although she also noted that her daughter's health had not been good prior to "the crisis" and that she realised the importance of restoring her daughter to "normal ways" before the latter embarked on "an independent life" again[12], Chiara, it seems, was ignorant of the emotional upheavals suffered by Aelfrida during her pregnancy. (Aelfrida's pretence that her marriage was 'perfect' had been too plausible; as she herself said apropos visits to Fordfield from Emden, 'we have talked chiefly about Things in General, Things that Matter being a little too vital'.)[13] She therefore failed to recognise that the deep depression into which Aelfrida had fallen had any cause other than physical frailty consequent upon a complicated still-birth.

From Aelfrida's own description of her feelings it is easy to deduce that during the latter half of 1912 she suffered from severe post-natal depression, a then unrecognised syndrome exacerbated in her case by the loss of a much-wanted baby. She describes her symptoms in another fictionalised account of the still-birth and its aftermath written six years later: "I was very ill. The baby, to whose coming I had looked forward with so much joy, was born dead. I myself was not expected to live".[14] Following a description of the still-birth itself, the speaker ('Catharine Sutherland') continues with a textbook account of the hopelessness, helplessness, lack of motivation, anxiety, and feelings of guilt and inadequacy experienced by a sufferer from the condition: "It seemed, however, that I was not to be given back completely to human existence. Months passed and I failed to get into touch … [People] did not seem real. Some deep instinct made me concern myself with the little details of my children's welfare but I felt no tenderness towards them and the sight of them evoked no pleasurable emotion. My own weariness, my own soul-sickness, obsessed me", this latter symptom in particular leading 'Catharine' to believe "I should never be well [but] make everyone who came near me full of sadness".[15] (Not being privy to the background to the conversations which took place at this time between the Grahams, Chiara still favoured her son-in-law, noting in her letter to Ancifera Gregory that "it is so sad for Constantine to be always considering how much she can stand".)[16] Auditory hallucinations also figure in 'Catharine Sutherland's' account, as does preoccupation with "strange phrases" ("the vasty halls of death", with accompanying visions of enormous, silent, gloomy, cold, vaulted chambers)[17] and a sensation of flying "through endless spaces, seeking I know not what".[18] Later the same year Aelfrida also wrote of how "… the vault of darkness mocks your noise, / And silent heaven broods o'er a silent deep"[19], of how she had "… followed my thoughts to the churchyard / And covered each wish in its grave" (a wish which cried "through the night and the morning" just as her own thoughts cried "oh poor little dead baby") and of how, driven by obsessive thoughts and echoing hallucinations, she, like 'Catharine', "tasted the music of madness".[20]

Her failure to "get in touch" with people who "came in and out of [her] room"[21] – she says they spoke to her "cheerily", but it seems that only one actually did – was not entirely her own fault, the said people's behaviour being repetition of the Tillyards' conduct in similarly stressful circumstances immediately after Agatha's near-fatal enteric illness of August 1911 when Aelfrida, shattered by this and by Eric's unexpected declaration of love, felt that she had no strength left to care about anything but her children. (Looking back on Eric's declaration and her daughter's illness, believed by Aelfrida to be divine retribution for dalliance with her husband's best friend, she wrote 'when Agatha was ill, I prayed that the next illness … in the family might come to me – and it most certainly did'.)[22] At that time too, the Oracle had shown more concern for his failing business than for his daughter and sick grand-daughter, Julius and Chiara, returning from a visit to Russia, had been respectively 'gloomy' and 'dazed with all she had seen and felt'[23], and Eustace, the recent recipient of a first-class degree and the Craven Scholarship and shortly bound for Greece[24],

was more interested in 'statues, … cameras, Greek grammars, trains and so forth'[25] than with the concerns of a sister to whom he was not particularly close. It is ironic, therefore, to look back on Aelfrida's comment of April 1905 concerning her 'own nearest ones' and 'how perfectly united we all are'[26] and at her diary account of the events of August 1911 to discover that the only factor which united the Tillyards in the terrible summer of 1912 was their seizing the opportunity of disburdening themselves of worries by offloading them onto a family member imprisoned at Fordfield by physical weakness and 'the music of madness' and of demonstrating by their actions a monumental indifference to her sufferings.

Chiara, always the 'perfect' mother, was, it seems, 'quite splendid', but a grandmother who had recently dealt single-handedly with the stillbirth of a third girl seems to have been so impatient to return to normality in the shape of 'her too numerous committees'[27] that she spent little time at the bedside of a daughter who apparently wished to be left alone but who might have confided her problems to a sympathetic listener had she been present. Aelfrida makes no further comment in her diary concerning Chiara's behaviour but we may infer that she required more support than her mother was willing or able to provide from Elizabeth/Aelfrida's despairing thought when Max/Constantine visits her after her stillbirth "I wish mother was here".[28] It may also be inferred from Aelfrida's description of 'Mrs Lavington', the Chiara figure in *Marrying a Stranger*, that she had become more critical of and clear-sighted about a mother whose ostensible aim in life was 'to devote herself and to be appreciated'[29], for although 'Mrs Lavington' believes herself able "to ignore her own feelings where the happiness of her children was concerned", she prefers to concentrate on unimportant matters over which she feels she has some control at the expense of more serious matters concerning which she might, at worst, protest "in a ladylike manner" before resigning herself to the will of God or, at best, pretend with an air of "gentle dignity and unobtrusive obstinacy" that they never existed.[30] Mrs Lavington/ Chiara's behaviour with regard to a marriage suddenly revealed as far from perfect between a son-in-law she regarded as a second Conrad and a daughter who, though "a little too definite in her tastes, with none of that beautiful smudginess of character that would have so won her mother's approval"[31], had nevertheless smudged sufficiently to cause the latter to believe the marriage to be as idyllic as she pretended, was therefore only to be expected: unable any longer to ignore the tension existing between her daughter and a son-in-law accused by his bereaved wife of de facto, if not *de jure,* infanticide, she took refuge in good works.

The Oracle, for his part, brought 'full accounts of [his] endless worries over the *CIP*' to his daughter's bedside, worries now four years old and no nearer solution than before. The problems were manifold: the 'low section of the Cambridge Liberals who wanted a flattering and servile paper' and whose damaging behaviour had caused the newspaper to run at a loss and forced its alliance 'with that scoundrel Taylor'[32] were still causing problems to its ex-proprietor and present editor ('they want a dirty vulgar rag – and he *won't* give it to them') and the resulting clash between the 'low section' and an editor who wished to run Cambridge's only Liberal newspaper with reference solely to respected Liberal doctrines and to university news of little interest to 'townees', caused all but the most senior local Liberals to turn against him. Squabbles with Captain Taylor over the newspaper's premises also broke out, Aelfrida concluding that her father had not been appreciated ('he is one of those for whom the Beatitudes were written') and that he felt his failure deeply[33]; indeed, severing of editorial connections with the *Cambridge Independent Press* took place at an unspecified date in 1912 and seems to have resulted in diminution of family income though not to the extent feared earlier in connection with loss of Fordfield.

Of all her visitors, Julius was the worst, his 'dreadful pessimism' driving Aelfrida 'perfectly frantic'.[34] To discover the reason for his gloom we must go back ten years to September 1902. While the Tillyards were in Worthing with convalescent Eustace, Aelfrida received letters from twenty-year-old undergraduate Julius, then spending a few weeks in Lahr to improve his German. In Lahr Julius made the acquaintance of Wilhelmina (Mina) Kaufmann, who, according to his sister, was 'neither beautiful nor accomplished' but to whom, as a 'protestant, sensible and lively' young lady, Julius found himself attracted. Contemporary letters to Aelfrida read oddly, for he wrote that he was 'afraid' he was falling in love with Mina, that he was much fonder of his sister than of 'Minnchen' and that Aelfrida was not to tell their parents. Aelfrida's replies read equally oddly. She was, she said, so 'alarmed' by Julius' confidences that she treated the matter 'seriously, [writing] him pages of sympathy and good advice' and telling him to wait a year before making any further moves. To herself, she commented that she thought it unlikely 'his little passion, if such it may be', would last, adding 'I did think he was above such little weaknesses'.[35] Be this as it may, Julius, returning to Cambridge for the next academic year, found his feelings for Mina unchanged, though, as Aelfrida put it, 'he quite expects they will!'[36]

Time passed. Julius' lukewarm affection for Mina continued, letters between them hinting at future marriage.

In December 1905 Julius, then in Athens, wrote to Aelfrida asking her to ask Chiara if Mina could stay at Fordfield to improve her English. Chiara initially considered the matter 'vaguely but favourably', then gave a decided no (Aelfrida says of her parents that 'they *froze*' when she told them of Julius' feelings for Mina)[37], and it was not until May 1906 that, Julius being still abroad, Mina was invited to Fordfield and, Chiara being really or diplomatically unwell, given the standard Tillyard tour of Cambridge by Aelfrida, Eustace, and the Oracle. Aelfrida's description of eighteen-year-old Mina as serene, dignified, and intelligent, 'ethical and romantic' rather than 'artistic or worldly', shy, 'very maternal [and] deeply religious'[38] makes her seem an ideal wife for a young man whose own personality traits were contemporaneously described by his sister as having been accentuated by postgraduate travels in Italy, Greece, and North Africa: 'he is more reserved, more fond of books and less of life, more gentle, more home-loving, even more modest'.[39] The following year, however, she noted that if Mina married someone else, Julius would not mind; she noted too that he still loved herself 'better than Minnchen'.[40]

Julius' parents' dismay at discovering their elder son's feelings for Mina *may* have stemmed from their earlier experience of Aelfrida's abortive engagement to Hans Peter (another foreigner) or from a desire that Julius not embark on marriage until he completed his studies abroad and gained a Cambridge fellowship and an income sufficient to support a wife and family, but it is also possible that both they and his sister recognised something in him that made marriage impossible. Aelfrida, for her part, wrote him a letter, poignant in what it expresses of her own relationship with Constantine, in April 1905: "Oh, Dudu, don't make love to Minnchen or to anyone else unless you really and firmly believe that you could not be two but one. It is not enough to be very fond of anyone and to be adored in return, or merely to understand them psychologically or to have 'tastes in common' … Of course all that is very desirable, but far more is both possible and right … And until thou seest the possibility of agreeing with me thou hadst best continue in thy present unlovelike state of mind or thou wilt make mess of it."[41] His parents' views are mediated through the medium of Aelfrida's diary but in view of her description of what happened next, we may guess that their 'freezing' at the news of Mina's presence in their son's life was based on something more than economics; indeed, Chiara's delight at Julius' being obliged to undertake a second *Wanderjahr* because neither his 'fellowship nor his life as a don in Cambridge'[42] had transpired, may indicate that intimate knowledge of her son led her to believe his nature to be unsuited to marriage with anyone. (Julius,

**Julius Tillyard and Wilhelmina (Mina) Kaufmann 1913**

for his part, though disappointed at not gaining a fellowship, seemed singularly unworried about the uncertainty this cast over his future life with Mina.) It may also have been for this reason too that Catharine Tillyard accompanied her son to Russia in June 1911 on the trip from which she returned 'dazed' and he 'gloomy'.

On his way to Sicily during his first *Wanderjahr* of 1905–6, Julius met and was 'flirted with' by the Russian girl, Nadja Laptchinski, later referred to by Aelfrida as 'Dudu's little Russian wild-cat'.[43] That he was conscience-stricken both for having looked at another woman besides Mina and for having flirted with *any* woman, is shown by a consoling letter written to him by Aelfrida in February 1906: 'it is absurd that thou should'st reproach thyself for having admired a lively Russian. Thou could'st *never* desire even superficially one who was not chaste and pure in mind'.[44] His relationship with Nadja Laptchinski continued in tandem with his tepid courtship of Wilhelmina Kaufmann: Nadja had more experience with men than Julius with women and it seems that her frankness and fearlessness about sexual matters attracted him and put him at ease in her

presence.[45] His trip to Russia with his mother was therefore to enable him to make a decision: should he marry Nadja or cleave to Mina?

Shortly before Aelfrida left for Hessle for the visit on which she and Anatolia exchanged 'feline amenities', she and the Oracle, recovering at Fordfield from Eric Silvanus' visit, received news from Russia that Julius and Nadja were engaged. Aelfrida had premonitions which turned out prophetic ('to make love to Nadja must be glorious – but marrying such a woman is a terrible risk')[46] for on 9 August she received a letter from her brother in which he spoke of such 'revulsion of feeling' for Nadja that he was unable to kiss or even touch her and of his consequent feelings of 'bitterest self-tormenting and anguish'. Aelfrida's reaction to the news ('he must not, cannot marry her – or anyone else')[47] shows that she too wondered if Julius lacked the capacity 'to really love anyone' because he suffered from 'some kind of self-distrust or want of primitive energy … that holds him back and spoils his happiness' and made him 'not altogether a man'[48] and explains why Aelfrida's tête-à-têtes with Julius over the cot of convalescent Agatha were 'somewhat gloomy' (he expressed 'the blankest pessimism about everything'), the only light relief being provided by Aelfrida's response to the doctor's diagnosis of Julius' symptoms as merely a response to 'intense sensations' and curable by marriage to a dull wife: "well … at least you will have plenty of choice!"[49]

It seems, however, that Julius did not lack the capacity to love but that, as Aelfrida perceptively wrote of his alter ego 'Jerome Lavington', "the person he loved most in all the world was his sister".[50]

Julius, as we know, was always very close to his sister but it was not until he and she ran into each other's arms on being reunited after the death of Conrad that he became exceedingly – indeed, excessively – fond of her. References to his 'very loving' behaviour towards her occur regularly throughout her diaries up to the time of her marriage and while these might be taken as part of normal affection between a brother and sister drawn together by a traumatic childhood event, there is something in their tone which gives pause for thought, a sense of Julius wooing and Aelfrida consciously or unconsciously responding.

Although we have very little of Julius' actual correspondence with his sister during his or her extended absences from Fordfield and can only guess the depth of his feeling for her from poems in the *MCJ*[51], letters quoted by Aelfrida in her diaries speak of his almost doting love for her while hers to him (or such as survive) include terms of endearment more appropriate to young lovers than to a brother/sister relationship:

28 March 1905. "Come home soon if thou canst. I miss thee more than I can say".

9 July 1905. "*Je t'aime et je t'embrasse*. Don't forget me."

5 February 1906. "…hear that I love thee and think about thee every day and pray for thy safety and admire thy enterprise and long to see thee …"[52]

Events recorded in her diaries provide even stronger evidence. In November 1901, for example, with Julius an undergraduate at Caius and Aelfrida recently returned from Lausanne a 'finished young lady' sexually awakened by Enrico's embraces, we find brother and sister scandalising a Newnham student by their 'quite indecent' behaviour towards each other (she took them for sweethearts)[53] while in December a walk home in the dark from an At Home to which Julius had squired his sister was accompanied not only by singing and conversation but also by their 'now and then stopping to "| • ___ ", Aelfrida commenting naïvely 'Dudu seems really to enjoy kissing me! Queer, isn't it?'[54] Or again, three years later in Soham, she endeavouring to revive the village's flagging interest in Temperance while studying the 'lower middle classes' and Julius reading Roman Law, after which 'we walked about hand in hand … and I would say "isn't this lovely" [and] he would gaze into my eyes and answer "Isn't *this* lovely?" or kiss me … it was like a honeymoon – Dudu's and mine!'[55] Significantly, perhaps, it was only three months after their Soham 'honeymoon' that Aelfrida had her vision of herself, Constantine, and their children, the boy characterised by his 'abnormal sensitiveness' smiling up at his sister with 'infinite tenderness'[56]; seven years after that, Aelfrida, describing Julius' 'revulsion of feeling' with regard to Nadja also refers, it seems, to her feelings for Constantine ('one needs desire to … give one the courage to come very near to another human being') and ends the sentence with a sigh: 'Oh, Dudu, Dudu …'[57]

There is, too, evidence that Julius' depression deepened after the appearance in Aelfrida's life of a more serious contender for her affections than Lord Kitchener (of whom Aelfrida wrote that, unbeknown to Julius, she 'loved someone a thousand times better than my own dearest brother')[58] or Enrico (with whom Aelfrida was not in love) or John Forbes Cameron with whom she only pretended to be in love: Constantine Michaelides. A letter written by Julius to Aelfrida during her stay in Lausanne and quoted by her in its entirety because it might be of use 'to the great Julius Tillyard's future biographer' (and, one might say, to her own) notes that "the time may be short in which I shall hold first place in your heart of all young men".[59] (He was obviously unaware of his sister's deep feelings for Archie Stent.) Constantine'

arrival on the scene during Julius' last year at Caius therefore posed such a serious threat that Aelfrida refrained from telling him about Constantine's 'lovemaking' until her brother completed his examinations lest the news upset him too much.[60]

Julius' 'coming back from Greece' a year later and his sister's assertion that she 'must be with him'[61] gave rise to a battle of wills between the brother who loved Aelfrida 'better than he does anyone else in the whole world' but who now looked at her 'a little wonderingly' because in his absence she had 'known and felt something he had not'[62] and the young man who had failed to obtain a First but gained (with some reluctance on her part) Julius' sister's hand, if not her heart. Battle was engaged by Julius being 'more than usually loving and good' to a sister currently recording in her diary that 'Constantine and I are more one than ever'[63] and by attempts to reinstate himself in his sister's affections whenever Constantine was absent: 'I had a long walk with Dudu and a talk like those we used to have at Soham. It was inexpressively sweet'.[64] Julius and Constantine were eventually 'able to be intimate' (the intimacy may have been more on Constantine's part than Julius', the former signing his letters to the latter 'ever most loving' and 'infinite love')[65], though references to Aelfrida's impending marriage hurt Julius deeply ('he said "Oh!" as though he were deeply shocked')[66] and he found it difficult to be near her when she was pregnant with 'Agatha unborn'[67], an unambiguous manifestation of Constantine's sexual activities with his sister.

Aelfrida's marriage, the Grahams' consular postings, and his own appointment as research fellow and lecturer in Greek at the University of Edinburgh in 1908 removed Julius from his sister's immediate orbit; his gaining a position also removed his excuse for remaining unmarried on the grounds that he could not support a wife and family. His rejection of Nadja and the tendency of Edinburgh mothers with eligible daughters to 'aunt' a thirty-year-old bachelor lecturer on their behalf turned his thoughts again to Mina, inaccurately described by Aelfrida as a 'very earnest young woman indeed … something like myself [but] without so much passion'.[68] It was therefore a sense of having been driven into a corner by circumstances (including, it may be, by the near-death of his adored sister) and by the continuing presence in his life of patient Mina with whom Aelfrida now urged marriage that brought Julius almost to breaking point in the summer of 1912 ('he thinks the world a wicked and miserable place, and everywhere he sees some kind of … horrible and depraved sex-instinct instead of love and need for human companionship')[69] and to the bedside of his sick sister. Convalescent Aelfrida, driven 'perfectly frantic' by his 'dreadful pessimism', escaped to The Avenue to walk Psalm 119, each tree and verse representing a stage in her affliction and, ultimately, in her recovery as she moved along the road from madness to sanity and from despair to acceptance:

"Daleth: My soul cleaveth unto the dust …
Nun: I am afflicted very much …
Resh: Consider mine affliction and deliver me …
Tau: Let my cry come near before thee, O Lord …
    Let my supplication come before thee;
    Deliver me according to thy word.
    Let thine hand help me …
    Let my soul live." [70]

Finding comfort and succour lacking in members of her own family – even Eustace, though he brought no problems to her, was more concerned with 'beautiful photographs and still better stories and enthusiasms' brought back from Greece and with wooing a 'little friend' [71] of his own, Phyllis Mudie-Cooke, a Girtonian now teaching in London, than with an ailing older sister whose recent 'crisis' he had missed – Aelfrida turned to those on whose quiet professionalism she had recently and rather less recently relied.

The first was the nurse whose 'brave and eager and tender' [72] care was instrumental to her recovery; ironically, only a paid outsider had Aelfrida's interests exclusively at heart during the terrible month following the stillbirth, but even she refused to be drawn into discussions of her patient's near-death experience (Aelfrida, having never previously imagined death "in proximity to [herself]" was keen to engage in discussions concerning "life after death – if there is any"; she also, it appears, "wanted to call [her] nurse's attention to [herself] and [her] own interesting speculations" on the subject) [73] and was noted by her patient to be regarding her quizzically as if she doubted her sanity. It is likely, however, that the "calm method" [74] of a trained nurse brought a measure of tranquillity to the shattered household and to Aelfrida herself.

The second was Charles Stewart Smith, 'very blue-eyed and naval, white hair … adding to the charm of his appearance'. He arrived alone and the two met for the first time in nearly five years: 'that his feeling for me is love admits no doubt; and I gathered that he felt sad that he had not the right to protect me – since that is the way I chiefly appeal to him … his sympathy for my troubles was so deep and true it nearly made me cry'. [75] Her tears, it seems, were more for Constantine than for Agneta to whom at this point she rarely refers though she certainly said 'something bitter' about the dead child, for Mr Smith cried "Don't, don't! I can't hear you speak like that". [76] (Constantine had departed for Panama on 29 July, leaving Aelfrida numb with grief and shattered with the effort of willing herself to be brave so that her husband would remember her 'not as an invalid but as someone quite gay and well in a white linen dress and a new big black hat most "scruciating becoming"' [77], but assumed cheerfulness occasionally broke down.) She refused, however, to accept Mr Smith's proffered kiss (her exasperated mother's comment was "why don't you let him? He's old enough to be your father!") lest she break down completely or reopen old emotional wounds when her present ones were so raw. But she agreed to call him 'Stewart' and allow herself to feel 'gravely glad that he had been'. [78]

The third person to whom Aelfrida turned was William Bowen, one of the doctors to whom she dedicated the poem provisionally entitled *The Two Doctors* and to whom, together with Nurse Mildred, she gave a copy. She describes him as a 'plain grave young man' (he was thirty-four) with a solemn professional manner 'and good in a crisis' [79], and confided to him verbally and by letter her admiration of his care for her and, it seems, something of her troubled marital relationship. But hopes that Dr Bowen might become a 'Little Friend' ('though I really prefer to know my doctors only professionally') because 'he seemed to take such an intellectual interest in me', were shattered by her discovery on 5 July during an ostensibly professional visit that Dr Bowen had fallen in love with her: 'his hand trembled so when he tried to feel my pulse that he had to give up the attempt and walk away to the window to compose himself'. [80] A brief absence on holiday only increased his ardour and in spite of his stating at a meeting early in August that "if a man wants to get on in his profession he must not have too much to do with women" and Aelfrida agreeing ('and especially a doctor, don't you think?'), this was not, as she thought, 'the last of Bowen'. [81]

Dr Bowen's subsequent behaviour towards a patient who had recently lost a baby, who had nearly died herself, who was extremely fragile both physically and emotionally, and whose husband was stationed across the Atlantic (a telegram saying "Arrived" reached Fordfield on 13 August, Aelfrida recording that Constantine's arrival in Panama was the first step towards his coming home) [82] was disgracefully unprofessional but emotionally understandable. Although decorum was maintained on both sides, albeit with some difficulty on Dr Bowen's, transcendence of the appropriate doctor/patient relationship ('he touched me as though I were the relic of a saint and evidently could not bring himself … to examine me thoroughly') [83] delayed diagnosis of uterine prolapse which, if treated earlier, might not have become a chronic problem, and it was not until some months later that Aelfrida was referred to a male London gynaecologist who diagnosed 'a severe displacement of the womb, probably needing an operation'.[84] Dr Bowen, a surgeon himself though not a specialist in women's complaints, preferred conservative treatment but eventually referred Aelfrida to a female Cambridge gynaecologist, Dorothy Hare. Dr Hare, described by Aelfrida as 'charming and very womanly' and '*good,* not caring about doing or being anything wonderful but just about helping people'[85], also opted for a conservative approach and became a supportive friend – though not a Little Friend, for Little Friends were invariably male. Pending referral to Dorothy Hare, however, Dr Bowen prescribed a long seaside holiday and suggested that Aelfrida 'neither write a book nor have a baby for several years', leaving her to ponder: 'when God called me back to life [I felt] it must be for something special, but [as] it isn't at present for a husband or a baby or a book – what then?'[86]

Dr Bowen's advice with regard to two months by the sea, together with Aelfrida's own wish ('I *must* go away')[87] to escape members of her family resulted in her taking not the "lovely and expensive holiday" envisaged by 'Max' for 'Elizabeth' under similar circumstances in the 'Emden Novel'[88] but in a series of short visits to friends and relations. Sadly, all but one of these increased her sense of failure and isolation and another (a visit to Hessle by Agatha and Alethea accompanied by Chiara and Ovvie, during which Anatolia tried without success to win her eldest granddaughter's affection away from her mother) contributed to her distress.[89]

The first took place early in August 1912 and was to her Aunts Fanny and Anna in Letchworth where, retired from nursing, they were now leading 'the simple life with great vigour', rising early, taking cold baths, and eating 'horrid, chilly vegetarian products' tasting 'not good at all'.[90] Great-aunt Rachel Tillyard now lived in Letchworth too, and it was during her stay that Aelfrida first heard Rachel's stories about her Tillyard ancestors ('*la parenté*'), composing the poem *Heredity* shortly after her return.[91] Aunt Rachel, Aelfrida later recalled, was 'so tender' to her that sad summer, eulogising her after her death in February 1913 as 'the last of that generation … of so many noble and gracious women … of such beautiful faith and character'[92], among whom she also listed two who appeared in her 'Agneta' vision of the previous year: Eliza Gregory and 'Dear'.

The second took place at the end of August and was not a success. During a week spent with Lucy Verey in London, the former Lucy Longstaffe displayed not the 'faintest interest in anything I said, [or] asked about my writing or … any of my concerns'[93], leaving Aelfrida

**Nadja Laptchinski**

feeling much as she had when confidences to her friend concerning Lord Kitchener met with little response and coming to the same conclusion as her sixteen-year-old self, namely that 'we all have to live our own lives, bear our own pain, [and] I am very lonely though it seems wickedly ungrateful to say so'.[94] That seven months pregnant Lucy might have other things on her mind did not enter Aelfrida's head; more poignant still, Lucy was later delivered of a boy of whom Aelfrida wrote 'I fought hard to look at him without envy, but something would tug at my heartstrings'.[95]

Visits to the Fordhams at Odsey in September 1912 and April 1913 were difficult for other reasons and contrasted with earlier and cheerier sojourns. George Fordham, still pompously obsessed with the minutiae of local government, was now a widower and insisted on confiding his troubles to Aelfrida, culminating one evening in 'the kind of sudden outburst reserved people treat one to at times'.[96] It also appears that George Fordham walked into her 'magic net' ('how useful is that phrase of Anatolia's')[97] but Aelfrida, frozen by grief and by Constantine's harsh behaviour towards her, found herself unable to respond. Molly and Marjorie Fordham, on the other hand, were being alternately courted and rejected by young Irish poet Billy Henn, described by Aelfrida as having 'wonderful deep-set blue eyes [and] a whole range of colour in them like the sea' and concerning whom she felt moved to write a poem[98] because he was such a 'very taking person'.[99] Both young women unburdened themselves to her, Aelfrida finding Molly's confidences particularly difficult her own present distaste for the subject: 'Molly's chief pre-occupation in life is sex. I know I used to think a certain amount about young men but I vow I never thought about sex until Constantine made me'.[100] *The Crypt of Idols*, written at Odsey on the same day as her poem about Billy Henn, includes "Lust, in flame and ragged robe arrayed" in a list of "gods to whom I never prayed".[101]

With unhappiness unalloyed by absence from Fordfield and only marginally by the presence of 'taking' Billy Henn, Aelfrida turned before and after her final holiday to means of communication towards which she formerly felt distaste or which she had sworn to abandon: the supranormal and the Roman Catholic Church, the first, it may be, an attempt to contact her dead baby, the second an attempt to find the consolation family and friends seemed unable to provide but which contact with God through well-loved rituals might invoke. Both failed. Crystal-gazing ('a form of auto-hypnosis, I suppose') provided only a glimpse of graves strewn with violets[102], 'automatic writing' some Anatolian 'higher twaddle' ('what we want is love etc., etc.') which *seemed* to arise from her subconscious self but more probably emanated from 'this world … not from the other'.[103] (Her heightened state of consciousness also allowed her to intuit the content of a 'momentous letter' from her husband before she opened it[104] but, like other practices, no real contact with the absent.) Two nights' spiritual conflict and a desire for the comforts of religion (there were, it seems, no others forthcoming) persuaded her 'to see whether the Church could take me and my doubts too'.[105] She therefore paid a visit to Father Kay, assistant priest at Our Lady and the English Martyrs, and admitted to feeling 'solemn and hopeful' as she came away.

Informing her father of her renewed attraction towards the only church in which she thought she might find peace of mind led to a storm of protest from Alfred Tillyard ("Is not Christ enough for you?") and of tears from Chiara and to Aelfrida herself finding herself prey to 'all the tumult [gathering] round me again, menacing if not active' and to dreaming that 'the devil came and made a prostitute of me'.[106] Parental opposition, possible

thoughts of her husband's wrath, and her being informed by Father Kay that the Catholic church demanded 'faith implicit and explicit in all her doctrines' (a fact of which Aelfrida was already aware)[107], led to her explaining to him that previous doctrinal difficulties had returned to haunt her ('the Church demanded beliefs that I had not got') and that she wished to proceed no further. (To her diary that she admitted that she was not strong enough to 'face the pain of having things put before me and wanting to believe and not being able to do so'.)[108] But she continued to feel that God, though doctrinally concealed in "shroud of Sacrament and Mass", would eventually triumph over ritual and that the Roman Catholic Church was inherently and personally the only true one.[109]

Perhaps the worst symptom of post-natal depression is the sufferer's belief that the only escape from a desperately negativistic state of being is death: "Last night I dreamed the magic face of death. / Her eyes were silver as the crescent moon / And all the scent of flowers was in her breath. / She beckoned me, she bent and whispered 'soon'".

*The Suicide,* from which these lines are taken, was written in Emden on 13 February 1911[110] at a time when its author, though plagued by minor ailments and worries about her parents and tenure of Fordfield relative to the fluctuating fortunes of the *Cambridge Independent Press*, did not seem to be unduly depressed. Yet if the poem reflects her true feelings in early 1911, how much worse were her feelings in late 1912 and how much more evocative of them is her invocation of the thoughts of a would-be self-destroyer.

Aelfrida's revelation of late October 1912 that she intended to kill herself comes as something of a surprise, her earlier reference to going on 'doing just usual things as one would wish to before one's death'[111] being apparently more of a desire that Constantine in Panama should remember her assumed air of composed cheerfulness than determination not to survive her dead daughter. Yet the 'terrible images of madness and suicide' to which she referred during a marital crisis a year later[112] seem to have haunted her to such an extent in autumn 1912 that in spite of an increasingly active social life ('as usual a little admiration of my cleverness went to my head … when I am quite well I find it easy to watch myself but in weakness I am too easily excited … Perhaps Constantine would prefer that to my thinking about problems all day')[113] and growing responsiveness to the kindness of perceptive acquaintances (a Mrs Fay, for example, allowed Aelfrida to nurse her own newborn for half an hour: 'did she guess that my arms ached to hold a baby, that she let me have hers so long?')[114], Aelfrida fixed her thoughts on death:

"*October Evening, Trumpington Road.*
The windswept sky, the windswept sky –
On such a night I mean to die.
With ne'er a winking star to peep,
Or wild-eyed moon to stir my sleep,
But only clouds of wind-swept grey
To snatch my restless soul away.
The storm shall lift me like a sea –
I shall be free, I shall be free!" [115]

She gives no indication of her chosen means of destruction. Opium is a possibility; it was cheap, easily available, and an item in the Fordfield medicine chest and she was aware of its soporific effects from her experience of 'accidental' overdose during her relationship with John Forbes Cameron. There is, too, literary evidence for her choice in a later book, *Vision Triumphant*, in which the stricken hero demands of 'Catharine Sutherland' who recalls with dismay that she once held forth to a group of Cambridge undergraduates – of whom he was one – on "the right to suicide" [116], that she provide him with poison ("opium, I think") and her response that she herself had made the same – fruitless – request of her doctor following her stillbirth. [117] Drowning is another possibility and a more likely one, given Aelfrida's long-standing preoccupation with and repeated literary references to death by drowning, usually at sea: "And thee, mysterious one, thou white-armed sea …/ Have lured me too, and promised deepest peace …" [118] In *Marrying a Stranger* too, 'Frauke', whose celibate relationship with 'Max von Thiele' abruptly ceases after 'Elizabeth' returns from England and is reconciled with her husband, drowns herself in a nearby canal wearing her oldest clothes and leaving a note explaining her actions [119], circumstantial details which may reflect Aelfrida's own plans for the stormy night on which she meant to die: "I fear the snake-like river 'neath the bridge. / 'Tis flowing, flowing, and it calls me 'Come!.. / Between my quiet banks there lies thy home'". [120]

The apparently happier frame of mind which allowed her to rejoin Cambridge social circles in the autumn of 1912 and the somewhat frenetic gaiety she exhibited there may have deceived her family but did not deceive her doctor: deeply depressed people sometimes display a lightening of mood immediately prior to attempting or committing suicide because they have fixed on a means of escape, and Aelfrida, it seems, had fixed on hers. Though reckless of her own life, she was, however, concerned for her daughters' well-being and involuntarily revealed her intentions to Dr Bowen by asking him if he would take charge of their health in the event of her death. But on her adding 'sometimes I feel angry

with you for … having saved my life' ('I was thinking aloud, foolish me!'), Dr Bowen realised the implication of her request. Exclaiming "Mrs Graham, I can't hear you say such things!" [121], he answered her unconscious cry for help by prescribing an urgent visit to the Isle of Wight (it seems she left in such a hurry that she forgot her diary), a visit from she which did not return until early December.

Ventnor, wrote Aelfrida, 'is pretty – and I loved my solitary roamings by sea – but depressing, for half the world seems sick and the other half in attendance on it'. [122] But because she gives no details of 'St David's', the house in which she stayed, we are left to ponder its function: private house taking paying guests or nursing home? In fact, the whole Ventnor episode is rather odd, given that sending an unaccompanied suicidal woman to the seaside where opportunities for death by drowning would be easy does not seem a sensible move on the part of Dr Bowen or her family. Given too that there are no references to 'St David's' in contemporary directories and that Aelfrida's name does not appear in lists of arrivals published in local newspapers, it is possible to ask: did she actually go to Ventnor? Diary evidence seems conclusive, but given the stigma attached to mental illness and that she omitted to take her diary with her, a short stay in a private asylum at Ventnor or elsewhere might explain discrepancies in her account. Her gloomy impression of the place chosen for emergency therapeutic intervention was, however, ameliorated both by her removal from Fordfield and its insufferable inhabitants and by a friendship she made in the place to which she went or was sent.

Before she left Cambridge for Ventnor, Aelfrida (her account was written retrospectively) 'had second sight about someone [she] was to see there, a tall striking-looking woman … who spoke Italian'; she also 'heard' a voice bidding her give a copy of her poems (possibly *To Malise* but the entry could equally refer to unpublished poetry) to the lady from whom she would receive something in return. 'And behold', she writes, 'the first person I saw at St David's was she!' [123] Mrs St George (of whom there is also no record in Ventnor) was the widow of an Anglo-Irish aristocrat and a cultured person with whom Aelfrida held long conversations about literature; more to the point, Mrs St George was familiar with conventual life, having attended retreats as an aspect of her vocation as a Franciscan tertiary. And, as predicted, Mrs St George later sent Aelfrida 'a quaint little book' which provided the latter with welcome 'spiritual insight'. [124] The two ladies also attended an Anglo-Catholic church together, Aelfrida later writing a poem dedicated to Mrs St George (FKStG) concerning an incident which occurred during a Mass in which Aelfrida saw her own 'torments' reflected.[125]

In a curious echo of the Fiesole convent, she also became embroiled in discussions with a High Church curate, Father Berry, their talks like 'being back in the Middle Ages' because of the topics discussed: church matters, religious orders, Satanists, and the devil. Inspired by Father Berry (he had, she wrote, 'a fine trained intellect' and a 'fine ascetic face' but was something of a 'fanatic') she studied the Thirty-Nine Articles, the defining statement of Anglican doctrine, and argued interminably with him on these, on other ecclesiastical matters, and on the subject of what she called 'religious truth'. (Discussions of this nature were dismissed by the Oracle as mere 'intellectual dissipation': 'is he right?' she asked herself.) Too much thinking, however, re-opened 'the R.C. question too' and, given her precarious mental state, caused Aelfrida to wonder if 'brain-fever' might not follow the 'constant wraith' of emotional and spiritual pain which haunted her and tempted her to suicide.[126] She therefore returned Father Berry's loaned books and decided not to begin a 'pure and beautiful friendship' with a man whom she could not consider as a 'Little Friend' because he was a priest and therefore something less than a man. (And married, with a wife and child under the same roof.) But before leaving Ventnor she knelt for his blessing and rose feeling 'as though something had happened'.[127]

Coincidentally or not, a definite lightening of postnatal depression occurred during Aelfrida's extended holiday (shortly after her return she wrote a poem *Each Man Must Meet God Alone* which begins in desolation but ends by describing the comfort she is once more able to derive from Deity)[128], though it was not until two years later that she suddenly realised that the 'solid black wall of misery that I couldn't get past or over' had finally disappeared, leaving only 'a black cloud destined to break or roll away'.[129] (It is notable, however, that several poems contain references which serve as reminders that the 'black wall' might be re-erected at any time – "I am too tired for faith or hope, / For love I am wearier far. / Faith is a wind o'er scorching sand / And love a cold blind star" – or infer that the "bright cup of pain" which might be seen as "the mystic chalice of the Grail" or as the "mad moonshine" which sometimes rendered her lunatic, had not wholly disappeared.)[130] Poems written between mid-November 1912 and late January 1913 chart the course of her recovery. In *Truce!*, written on 15 November 1912, she explicitly states her readiness (not without misgivings, for a truce is only an intermission in war, not an end of strife) to "make my peace with life again", while in *Treasure of Earth and Treasure of Heaven* the refrain ("And now I must die") of the first two verses

changes in the last two to affirmation that she 'must' and 'shall' *live*.[131] She also sought rapprochement with the estranged husband whom she 'honestly' (*sic*) though she loved 'more than ever'[132], writing poems which spoke of re-awakened affection: *Thanks to Malise* of 26 December 1912, *Roundel* of 27 January 1913 with its refrain "Love me again", and Constantine's imagined reply in *I, N. take thee M* of 25 January 1913: "Now for all eternity thou art my wife". The poems, if sent to Panama (her diary entry is ambiguous) must have given Constantine food for thought, especially *Triolet* of 25 January 1913 which states: "I'd like to have a baby every year".[133] She does not record his response, if any.

Returning home just before Christmas 1912, Aelfrida was further cheered by Dr Bowen's decision to adore her only 'from afar'[134] (a decision with which she concurred, he having written thrice during her stay in Ventnor, two formal letters and one telling her that what she needed was 'affection and respect'), by a visit from Anatolia ('quite civil and not at all absurd')[135], by Julius' news that he was 'content with his bargain with Mina' and looked forward to 'calm happiness' with her[136], and by the arrival of letters from gentlemen friends: Charles du Bouchet, now in Paris who thought 'often and affectionately'[137] of her, Charles Stewart Smith in Odessa and Gian Falco in Italy, and from married Eric Silvanus, a man of whom Aelfrida, noting the propensity of erstwhile admirers to go away and forget her (*sic*; the evidence of diary entries contradicts her), wrote 'look at Eric, who has quite dropped me now'.[138] Wishing that she had more time to cultivate friends from her past and possibly in hopes of a more enthusiastic response from her present husband (in *Marrying a Stranger*, 'Elizabeth', in England following her traumatic stillbirth, writes to 'Max' at weekly intervals "long affectionate letters such as one might write to a brother" to show that there was "no definite rupture between her and her husband". Max replies "with equal regularly, telling her about his work and the new life he was leading")[139], Aelfrida was as yet unaware that recent acquaintance with younger members of the opposite sex were soon to blossom into 'Little Friendships' of great significance for the future and that it was these friendships, together with a surrogate child, which were to form the next phase of her recovery.

## Notes

1 GCPPT 1|1|18 5 July 1912.

2 ibid. 18 July 1912.

3 The close thematic and temporal relationships of the poems are disguised both in their manuscript version (GCPPT 2/5) where they are separated by a seven page gap and by their subsequent publication in two separate books, *The Prayer* in 1913 in *Cambridge Poets* (pp

190–192) but without reference to its original dedication to 'the two doctors', and *To Anyone* in *The Garden and the Fire* (p 37) in the section entitled 'Poems about Death'.

4 GCPPT 1|1|18 5 July 1912.

5 *The Prayer*, written on 20 June 1912, is paralleled by Aelfrida's diary entry of 19 June, albeit the poem ends inconclusively and lacks the dialogue between the doctors (Aelfrida's original title for *The Prayer* was *The Two Doctors* but she depersonalised and disguised it for publication in *Cambridge Poets*) and the description of her dead great aunt, dead grandmother, dead brother and dead child. It may be that she was too overcome by physical or emotional frailty to complete the poem or that the vision seemed too personal for publication so soon after the event (the poem ends in mid-sentence with "the doctor / Sitting stiffly, his fingers on my pulse …") or it may have been the impossibility of putting into blank verse an ineffable experience of this nature which prevented her: many years later she noted the similarity between Isaiah's vision of God 'high and lifted up' and her own visionary experience 'at the moment of death'. (GCPPT 1|1|72 14 December 1954).

6 *The Prayer* is full of watery imagery: an 'ebbing tide', a 'remorseless sea', a 'drowsy stream', and so on.

7 Tillyard, Ae. *Marrying a Stranger* pp 222–225 (GCPPT 2|6).

8 GCPPT 1|1|18 21 March 1913.

9 Tillyard, Ae. *Marrying a Stranger* pp 231–232.

10 ibid. p 233.

11 ibid. pp 222–225.

12 Tillyard, HJW. *The Letters of ACW Tillyard*. (MTC) Undated letter of June/July 1912 from Catharine Tillyard to Ancifera (Annie) Gregory.

13 GCPPT 1|1|18 20 May 1911.

14 Tillyard, Ae. *Vision Triumphant* pp 109–115. Aelfrida's description is clearly based on those given in her diary and *The Prayer* but now places her vision of the dead Agneta at the point at which the doctors take Constantine aside to inform him that her death is imminent and immediately before she hears her children's footsteps overhead and prays to live. In the context of the book – Aelfrida's fictional alter ego 'Catharine Sutherland' is trying to persuade a young man maimed and blinded in the Great War that life is worth living using her own experience as an example – rearrangement of events makes better dramatic sense.

15 Tillyard, Ae. *Vision Triumphant* pp 109–115.

16 Tillyard, HJW. *Letters of ACW Tillyard*. (MTC) Undated letter of June/July 1912 from Catharine Tillyard to Ancifera (Annie) Gregory.

17 In a later novel *The Approaching Storm* (p 208) Aelfrida quotes the Matthew Arnold poem *Requiescat* in which the phrase occurs and intimates that she learnt it at school. She also misquotes: Arnold's 'hall' is singular.

18 Tillyard, Ae. *Vision Triumphant* pp109–115.

19 GCPPT 2|5 *The Unknowable*, written at Fordfield on 15 October 1912 The poem was never published.

20 GCPPT 2|5 *Treasure of Earth and Treasure of Heaven*, written at Ventnor on 1 December 1912. The poem remained unpublished.

21 Tillyard, Ae. *Vision Triumphant* pp 109–115.

22 GCPPT 1|1|20 8 May 1915.

23 GCPPT 1|1|18 30 August 1911.

24 ibid. 21 June 1911.

25 ibid. 30 August 1911.

26 GCPPT 1|1|12 24 April 1905.

27 GCPPT 1|1|18 5 July 1912.

28 Tillyard, Ae. *Marrying a Stranger* pp 231–232. 'Mrs Lavington' had in fact died during 'Elizabeth's' first pregnancy.

29 GCPPT 1|1|16 13 August 1908.

30 Tillyard, Ae. *Marrying a Stranger* pp 20 and 23 (GCPPT 2/6).

31 ibid. p24.

32 GCPPT 1|1|17 2 May 1909.

33 ibid. 1 February 1910.

34 GCPPT 1|1|18 5 July 1912.

35 GCPPT 1|1|9 24 September 1902.

36 ibid. 29 October 1902.

37 GCPPT 1|1|13 6 December 1905.

38 ibid. 5 May 1906.

39 ibid. 25 June 1906.

40 ibid. 6 July 1907.

41 Tillyard, HJW. *The Letters of ACW Tillyard* (MTC). Letter from Aelfrida to Julius Tillyard of 13 April 1905.

42 GCPPT 1|1|12 16 October 1904.

43 GCPPT 1|1|13 6 July 1906.

44 GCPPT 1|1|17 20 May 1909. Tillyard, HJW. *The Letters of ACW Tillyard* (MTC). Letter from Aelfrida to Julius Tillyard dated 2 February 1906.

45 GCPPT 1|1|18 26 July 1911.

46 ibid.

47 ibid. 9 August 1911.

48 GCPPT 1|1|18 6 and 30 August 1911. 'Jerome Lavington', Julius' fictional counterpart in *Marrying a Stranger,* has been in love with, but rejected, his cousin 'Marjorie Lane', telling her "I have not as much control over my feelings as I do over my actions … forget me as soon as possible" (p 263).

49 GCPPT 1|1|18 8 September 1911.

50 Tillyard, Ae. *Marrying a Stranger* pp 22–23.

51 The *MCJ* of June 1910 (GCPPT 2|2a) contains an untitled poem by Julius written while Aelfrida was in Emden whose first line runs "*Hic ego miser in Anglia langueo*".

52 Tillyard, HJW. *The Letters of ACW Tillyard* (MTC). Julius' notes to this volume rightly suggest that some of Aelfrida's high-flown terms of endearment derive from *An Englishwoman's Love Letters* by L. Housman, published in 1902 and described by her as 'a study in exaggerated sentimentality' (GCPPT 1|1|16 26 May 1902). While this is certainly true of some of the letters (on 8 July 1902, quoting from the book, she calls Julius "my share of the Universe"), other letters, even if stylistically derivative, express sentiments which Aelfrida sometimes hesitates to commit to paper: "I often think out letters to thee. I scarcely know why they never get written …"

53 GCPPT 1|1|9 7 November 1901.

54 ibid. 17 December 1901.

55 GCPPT 1|1|11 16 April 1904 Aelfrida's recollection of this idyllic time may be reflected in an unpublished poem written in Emden on 12 May 1911 entitled *Morning in Spring,* though the picture she paints is, she says, 'near Fulbourn' (GCPPT 2/5).

56 GCPPT 1|1|11 24 July 1904.

57 GCPPT 1|1|18 6 August 1911.

58 GCPPT 1|1|6 1 November 1900.

59 ibid. 1 November 1900.

60 GCPPT 1|1|11 1 June 1904.

61 GCPPT 1|1|13 20 June 1905.

62 ibid. 25 June 1905.

63 ibid. 21 July 1905.

64 ibid. 22 August 1905.

65 ibid. 12 July 1905.

66 GCPPT 1|1|14 7 December 1906.

67 GCPPT 1|1|18 21 June 1911.

68 GCPPT 1|1|17 16 January 1911.

69 GCPPT 1|1|18 5 July 1912.

70 Pages 25–28 of Aelfrida's *The Night Watches* of 1938 (subtitled Thoughts for Sick Folk) describe a time when her soul was like "a dark, empty hollow... void of everything" and when, as a consolatory spiritual exercise, she read Psalm 119, visualising it as a long tree-lined avenue of which individual trees represented a verse of the psalm and bore that verse's Hebrew letter of the alphabet.

71 GCPPT 1|1|18 21 June 1911.

72 ibid. 6 July 1912. The nurse probably came from the Cambridge Nursing Association operating out of premises at 13 Fitzwilliam Street. The C.N.A., founded in 1875, carried out the intentions of a Miss Hutton's Benefaction, these including provision of private nurses for Cambridge families.

73 Tillyard, Ae. *The Approaching Storm* pp 208–209. Aelfrida made much use of her near-death experience as 'copy', writing two poems on the subject and putting it into two novels and a homiletic work.

74 Tillyard, Ae. *Marrying a Stranger* pp 226 (GCPPT 2/6).

75 GCPPT 1|1|18 3 August 1912. In Emden on 18 December 1911 Aelfrida wrote a poem *The Son of a Great Woman*; beside it are written in pencil the initials 'C.S.S'. (GCPPT 2/5). Its tone and content evoke Charles Stewart Smith exactly. A photograph of him pasted in the back of the contemporary volume of her dairy (GCPPT 1|1|18) shows her description of him to be accurate.

76 GCPPT 1|1|18 15 December 1912.

77 ibid. 23 July 1912. A photograph taken prior to Constantine's departure is pasted in the back of this volume of her diary. Willie Searle had come to supper on 22 July and 'we all sat together ... and were merry' but if the photograph was taken on this occasion they look anything but merry. Seated close together on a bench in the garden are, from left to right: Constantine, with his usual glum and slightly superior expression; Aelfrida grim-faced in white, feet on a stool and arms laced over her abdomen; Chiara expressionless and elegant as ever; and Willie, serious – his brother Walter had drowned the previous year, Aelfrida commemorating his death with a poem *Love not the Dead O'ermuch* (GCPPT 2/5 with the pencil dedication 'to Willie'); the poem later appeared in *Cambridge Poets* (p 196).

78 GCPPT 1|1|18 3 August 1912. Chiara was privy to Mr Smith's feelings for her daughter, having met him in London during his lengthy leave in 1907. Aelfrida later commented on their meeting that 'he seemed not to dare to say how fond of me he was' (GCPPT 1|1|15 14 December 1907).

79 ibid. 6 July 1912.

80 ibid.

81 ibid. 3 August 1912.

82 ibid. 13 August 1912.

83 ibid. 13 October 1912.

84 ibid. 19 December 1912.

85 GCPPT 1|1|18 25 April 1913.
GCPPT 1|1|20 19 December 1914. Dorothy Hare (1876–1967) qualified as a doctor in 1905 at the London School of Medicine for Women (Royal Free Hospital). From 1910 to 1916 she practised privately in Cambridge. She was described by one of her clinical students as having a calm and impressively confident manner. For further details of her interesting career see the *ODNB* Vol. 25 pp 245–246.

86 GCPPT 1|1|18 13 October 1912.

87 ibid. 14 October 1912.

88 Tillyard, Ae. *Marrying a Stranger* p 333.

89 GCPPT 1|1|18 22 August 1912. Anatolia's behaviour was recorded by Aelfrida in her diary but not, for obvious reasons, in the separate records she kept of her two daughters.

90 ibid. 4 August 1912.

91 *Heredity* with its references to "sires and dames long dead" was dedicated in manuscript (GCPPT 2|5) to 'Aunt R'. Written in Cambridge on 12 August 1912, it was later published in *The Garden and the Fire* (p 54) in the 'borderland poems' section, dedicated 'to my father'.

92 GCPPT 1|1|18 1 February 1913.

93 ibid. 31 August 1912.

94 GCPPT 1|1|5 11 June 1900.

95 GCPPT 1|1|18 19 December 1912.

96 ibid. 16 April 1912. Aelfrida's poem *The Widower* of 14 April 1913 (GCPPT 2/5), written at Odsey in George Fordham's voice, reflects many of her own feelings for dead Agneta: "Men say that Time shall wear away my cares / And laughter leap upon me unawares / And hide the death, the bed, the flowers.../ Dead, dead ... I must believe that she is dead." The poem was never published.

97 GCPPT 1|1|19 18 May 1913.

98 GCPPT 1|1|18 4 February 1913. Aelfrida's poem *The Irish Poet*, dedicated in manuscript (GCPPT 2|5) to 'F W Baron Henn', was written at Odsey on 10 September 1912 and was later published in *Cambridge Poets* (pp 194–195). William Henn came from an aristocratic Anglo-Irish family and was at the time a Cambridge undergraduate. His younger brother later described him as a writer of "excellent light verse". (Henn, T. p 22).

99 GCPPT 11|18 4 February 1913.

100 ibid. 17 September 1912.

101 GCPPT 2/5 *The Crypt of Idols* was never published.

102 GCPPT 1|1|18 23 December 1912.

103 ibid. GCPPT 1|1|18 10 January 1913. A poem, *The Gods O'ertake Us* , written the same day, expresses Aelfrida's despair over the death of her baby and her loss of physical and emotional communication with Constantine ("blood lies / Our blood, our kisses maimed, our slaughtered words") and strangely presages a dream recorded the following day (11 January) in which Constantine arrived home early and was very loving, an event which did not take place. The poem later appeared in *The Garden and the Fire* (p 24) in the section entitled 'Poems about Love.'

104 Aelfrida does not disclose the letter's contents but a subsequent meeting with a beautiful young woman and her jealous older husband, a woman of whom she wrote that Dita Mallet-Pringle 'was so good to [Constantine] in Panama ... [that] if I had been a man I should have fallen madly in love with her, and how Constantine managed to remain unstirred is more than I can understand' (GCPPT 1|1|19 6 December 1918) makes one wonder if Dita was not its subject and that if so, if Aelfrida was being deliberately disingenuous.

105 GCPPT 1|1|18 15 December 1912.

106 ibid. 14 January 1913.

107 ibid.

108 ibid. 6 and 19 February 1913.

109 The poem later appeared in *The Garden and the Fire* (p 66) in the 'borderland poems' section, with a dedication 'For Valentine', the nickname given by Aelfrida to a pen friend, a pupil–teacher named Gladys Sanderson, later a Roman Catholic and later still a nun. Aelfrida's 1905 comment regarding Gladys: 'I liked to hear her talk about confession and retreats and Anglican sisterhoods' (GCPPT 1|1|13 15 August 1905) did not prevent her from mocking Gladys' pious behaviour: Gladys' idea of a 'perfect holiday' according to the *MCJ* Vol 2 August 1904 (GCPPT 2|2a), was of an opportunity to improve her mind and cultivate her talents. Although the manuscript version (GCPPT 2/5) notes that the poem was written 'after reading a dismal speech by the president of the Free Church Council', it is entirely appropriate that a poem about Aelfrida's beloved local Catholic church was dedicated to a convert to Catholicism.

110 GCPPT 2/5 The poem was dedicated to Gian Falco and remained unpublished.

111 GCPPT 1|1|18 23 July 1912.

112 GCPPT 1|1|19 23 November 1913.

113 GCPPT 1|1|18 18 October 1912.

114 ibid. 26 September 1912. An unpublished poem written on 15 October 1912, *The Unknowable,* combines references to a sleeping child with references to "stiffened features of the dead" and contrasts the joy inspired by the "sunlight" of God's grace with the overarching

"vault if darkness" which makes a mockery of "joy's most soaring wings" (GCPPT 2/5).

115 The poem was later published in *The Garden and the Fire* (p 37) in the section entitled 'poems about death'.

116 Tillyard, Ae. *Vision Triumphant*. p 107.

117 ibid. pp 106 and 109.

118 GCPPT 2|5 *The Suicide* .The poem was never published.

119 Tillyard, Ae. *Marrying a Stranger* p 288. The mill pool in Cambridge with its deep water and dangerous currents was a favourite suicide spot for desperate local women, the Cam itself being too shallow. Gwen Raverat (1885–1957), Aelfrida's near-contemporary, once witnessed a bunch of bedraggled undergraduates carrying an unconscious woman into a neighbouring public house: "Drowned in the river? That was my first thought" (*Period Piece* pp 170–172), and Aelfrida could have heard of the episode from Gwen herself or, more likely, from Silvia Myers who attended the same art class as Gwen; a passage in a much later novel, *Just Alice* (GCPPT 2|19 p 243), describes a very similar episode, the woman involved being a prostitute. Or she may have got the idea from stories of attempts presided over by her magistrate father, attempted suicide being then a crime.

120 GCPPT 2|5 *The Suicide*.

121 GCPPT 1|1|18 31 October and 15 December 1912. Aelfrida reported most of the episode retrospectively. The *Vision Triumphant* version (pp 109–115) has 'Catharine Sutherland' asking her doctor directly "what was the easiest way of taking my life", adding "his look of horror told me how my request struck him".

122 GCPPT 1|1|18 19 December 1912 (retrospective description). Ventnor, then a popular watering-place on the Isle of Wight was regarded "as one of the best resorts in England for … invalids". It contained a number of convalescent homes and some seaside homes attached to London city missions (*Encyc. Brit.* Vol. 27 p 1012).

123 GCPPT 1|1|18 19 December 1912 (retrospective account).

124 ibid. 28 December 1912. The book was *Especially,* EB Buckle's hagiographic account of the latter days and death at sea of WE Collins, the Bishop of Gibraltar met by Aelfrida in Odessa in 1907 whose last words were, reportedly 'the fellowship of loneliness'. The book went into several editions, the most recent being that of February 1912.

125 Dated 17 November 1912, *Mass – and a Kensit Row* (later published in *The Garden and the Fire* pp 56–57 in the 'borderland poems' section) describes the violent intervention in a Mass by followers of John Kensit (1853–1902), organiser of public protests against Catholic places of worship. The incident went unrecorded in Aelfrida's diary and was not noted in the local newspaper. According to the poem, the police were called to remove men Aelfrida describes as 'desecrators'.

126 GCPPT 1|1|18 19 December 1912 (retrospective account). GCPPT 2/5. *The Suicide.*

127 GCPPT 1|1|18 19 December 1912.

128 The poem, written on 11 December 1912, is dedicated 'to SCV' (Susanna Carnegie Venn), a strange dedicatee given Aelfrida's earlier derogatory remarks about Archie's mother. The reason for the dedication becomes clear when we discover that three years later and prior to the poem's publication in the 'Borderland' section of *The Garden and the Fire* (p 253), Aelfrida discovered that Mrs Venn's affection for her arose not only from her wish to have her as a daughter-in-law but also because Mrs Venn was a mystic 'who for some reason had never realised her full florescence' but who, recognising Aelfrida as someone who shared her spiritual proclivities, hoped that Aelfrida would achieve what she herself had failed to do (GCPPT 1|1|20 22 February 1915).

129 GCPPT 1|1|20 15 January 1915.

130 GCPPT 2/5. *The Quest,* written in Cambridge on 18 February 1913 remained unpublished; *The Bright Cup of Pain,* written in Cambridge on 29 December 1912 and dedicated to 'the memory of WE Gibraltar', was later published in *The Garden and the Fire* (p 45) in the section entitled 'poems about all sorts of things'. The phrase 'mad moonshine' is taken from *The Quest.*

131 GCPPT 2/5 *Truce!* is subtitled 'written after illness and sorrow by the sea'; *Treasure of Earth* was also written in Ventnor, on 1 December 1912. Neither poem was published.

132 GCPPT 1|1|18 1 February 1913.

133 GCPPT 2/5 The poems remained unpublished.

134 GCPPT 1|1|18 19 December 1912 and 18 February 1913. An unpublished poem, *Early days of Love* (GCPPT 2/5), written in Cambridge on 8 January 1913, suggests that Aelfrida was perhaps as attracted to William Bowen as he to her: "Somewhere within this self-same little town / The road rings merrily beneath your feet. / Perhaps this very day I'll walk the street / And see you – oh, my heaven comes singing down!" Or perhaps it was meant as *his* message to *her.*

135 ibid. 22 January 1913.

136 ibid, 3 January 1913.

137 ibid. 15 December 1912.

138 GCPPT 1|1|20 24 July 1914.

139 Tillyard, Ae. *Marrying a Stranger* p 252.

# Little Friends and Cambridge Poets

Although Aelfrida and her younger brother were generally on no more than the 'best of distant terms', it was from apparently uncaring Eustace that she received practical and appropriate help at this juncture.

Dr Bowen having read her 'a long sermon on [her] failings' during which he informed her that she 'played' with her emotions too much (she agreed, reluctantly)[1] and that she should stop ruminating about religion and the past, prescribed an active and amusing social life. Trying to be '"Bowenesque" and to *have* fun', she invited a group of Eustace's friends to dinner and read them a short play on which she had been working. Although she regarded the occasion as rather highbrow – among other subjects discussed was 'the problem of social intercourse with the lower classes' – she was rather put out when Eustace informed her that the young men were more interested in herself than her 'curtain raiser'.[2] His determination to treat her like a normal human being instead of a neurotic invalid and the rewards reaped by his helping her to 'have fun' (the dinner party, and university and collegiate events to which she was subsequently invited caused her to write that 'men's admiration is worth something even in these degenerate days')[3] made her appreciate a brother who, helped by Phyllis Mudie-Cooke (described by her future sister-in-law as 'gentle, reserved, intelligent and wealthy' and apt to look at Eustace 'as though she expected him to propose')[4] had finally 'struggled through to manhood'.[5] She and Eustace also became better friends because he lacked Julius' 'gloomy intensity of feeling' and morbid introspectiveness and possessed qualities which were right for her at that moment: exquisite taste, intellectual alertness, and a sunny smile[6]; he also, like her, valued friendships with people outside the family circle, a quality Julius lacked. It was, therefore, with assurance of Eustace's continuing presence and support (a first class degree and a year's research in Greece had earned him a Jesus College fellowship) and in spite of assertions of semi-invalidism and of her absent husband representing the only romantic element in her life, that Aelfrida discovered early in 1913 that she was enjoying an 'Indian Summer of youth – … and "little friends"'.[7]

As a woman who once recorded that 'men either fell in love with me or I do not affect them at all'[8], she

**Hubert Henderson with the Grahams 1914**

revelled in having a bevy of young male companions, diarising in June 1913 that 'boys, somehow, adore so frankly; and it does make one feel wonderful when they are so intensely interested in all the shades of one's feelings' and deciding that it was 'all so thrilling'[9] and that she was 'in a fair way of getting [her] head turned'.[10] Her *cavalieri serventi* were fascinated in turn by an older woman prepared to devote time and energy to their callow but to them important concerns.

Relationships with members of the opposite sex conducted by Aelfrida in the spring and summer of 1913 were quite unlike superficial flirtations carried on as a young single woman, being fewer in number and in several instances developing into classic *amitiés amoureuses*. There was, too, something of a mediaeval Court of Love about them, she sitting in judgement on questions of amatory matters brought to her by younger esquires in a feminine, cultured, chivalric and chastely amatory context in which a youth might swear devotion to his chosen lady in person or in letters or poems, though a lady who, while acknowledging his devotion, was not expected to reciprocate; indeed, in the realm of Courtly Love, as in that of Little Friendships, the woman controlled the relationship, encouraging the young man's enthusiasms or damping his ardour as occasion (*her* occasion) demanded. There were also no expectations of sexual congress on either side, a theme dear to Aelfrida's heart with respect to Constantine with whom she would have infinitely preferred a chaste and cerebral (and loving) marriage.

Her influence over her Little Friends was entirely beneficial. On the one hand she acted as mother-confessor to young men she accepted for what they were (not, as in the case of Constantine, for what they might become if persuaded to adopt her own notions) at a time when, constrained by doubt, distance, or convention, they were unable to confide in members of their own family or in friends of the same or opposite sex.[11] On the other hand, she taught them how to make love (in the socially acceptable sense of the expression) to a woman if that was where their inclination lay and allowed them to gain experience and confidence in doing so in safe and structured environments: at Fordfield, where she lived with her parents and children and at the University whose round of lectures, college societies, sporting fixtures and meals in hall was familiar to her from her brothers' recent experience of them. She was also happy to refute Julius' accusations of 'phallus worship' (*sic*) by informing him that her relationships with Little Friends were 'chiefly intellectual' (she did not dwell on the fact that several felt more than cerebral attraction for her, for this would have supported Julius' contention that she only had to say 'good morning' to a man for him to fall in love with her) and that she was prepared to bet him that no Little Friend would elope with her 'even if they got the chance'.[12] To herself, she admitted that 'the young men feel more free to be pleasant because they aren't afraid they might have to marry me'[13] championing 'the cause of comradeship between men and women' to the Oracle when he wrote critically of Little Friendships the following year.[14] To her father's dismay (it seems he not only 'watch[ed] disapprovingly[15] but vocalised his disapproval too), Constantine approved of her friendships: indeed, it seemed as if he actively *wished* her to have men friends and enjoyed her accounts of them. Given his propensity to control all aspects of Aelfrida's life, approval of her undergraduate friends (of whom she artlessly fed him information) seems odd but probably stemmed from a desire to use (if need be) her information as future

ammunition or find a means of diverting suspicion from his own friendships (little or otherwise) with women in England and abroad. Or perhaps it was from a desire to return to a more cheerful and less alienated wife that he encouraged what he might otherwise have condemned or forbidden.

Of the five Little Friendships which occupied the greater part of Aelfrida's time and emotional energy in 1913/14, one was to lead to a romance, one to a lifelong relationship; of the other three, though intense at the time, two dwindled into conventional but affectionate friendships, one fizzled out altogether.

Eustace's friend, William Searle, once a frequent visitor to Fordfield – he was on such familiar terms with the family that he dropped in whenever he felt inclined[16] – was now articled to a solicitor in London and more rarely seen. He was, however, a weekend guest on the occasion of Aelfrida's 'Bowenesque' dinner party, his visit causing her to record her interest in a young man whom she found rather puzzling: 'I can't make Willie out. He looks like some ardent fanatic or visionary [but] he talks like anyone else'; she must, she decided, 'get to the bottom of Willie'.[17] Eustace, however, counselled caution, informing his sister that if she 'noticed' Willie at all he would certainly fall in love with her because he was 'far too much interested' in her already.[18] Receiving an 'intimate' letter from Willie soon afterwards, Aelfrida therefore replied with a 'kind but choking-off-some reply'; she also noted that she did not want Willie 'in the magic net and he seems halfway in already'.[19] Willie responded with determination to continue the correspondence, describing Aelfrida as 'a siren' whom he intended to 'make sing a little more'. At this point and having difficulty in regarding Willie as anything other than a friend of her younger brother, Aelfrida closed (as she thought) both correspondence and episode by replying that the only 'siren' she meant to be was one on a departing steamer.[20]

That Aelfrida's Little Friends discussed her among themselves and were not above boasting to each other of the progress each made in his respective relationship with her, is evident from what happened next: 'now Altounyan writes', saying that he 'has "heard from Willie" that [she is] in "great form"'. Aelfrida answered the letter as 'cleverly' as she could, but warned Altounyan that a second letter risked being unanswered; his second letter, however, arrived on the day on which she tried to discourage renewed advances from Dr Bowen by informing him that having her for his 'ideal' might be good for him but was 'very bad' for *her*.[21]

Perhaps she was insufficiently 'clever', for Altounyan merely replied that her letter 'had "put a song in his head all the day"!'[22] and persisted with his protestations, turning up at regular intervals to discuss 'poetry and love in his usual wild way'.[23] Aelfrida was still in two minds about the Irish-Armenian she had earlier described 'as a man I should like … better if he were not so swarthy and if he washed more' but something in his being, with his 'brilliant, fervid mind, a little, no a good deal mad'[24] and his having undergone a mystical experience in 1911 so intense and life-altering that he could not resist sharing it with his tutor and his friends (whereupon he was treated by his doctor as one mentally ill and 'shipped … off to America' to recover; Aelfrida, so she said, wrote to him at the time reassuring him that he was not but there is no record of the incident in her diary)[25] drew her to one she realised was a kindred spirit mature beyond his years and possessed of a religious spirituality akin to her own.

Tommy Altounyan was friends with another member of Aelfrida's Court of Love, John Layard, reading Anthropology during a fourth year at Cambridge. Aelfrida did not take Layard's protestations of love as seriously as she did those of other Little Friends, recording that he was 'fond, but it won't last'.[26] She was therefore surprised when 'simple Layard, who has no moods, but who adores all the time quite openly', declared his love for her during a prolonged interview on a Cambridge common on 14 June. The interview, described by Aelfrida as 'very futile and very touching' (and so prolonged that she caught 'some sort of chill [from] lying on the grass' and was unwell the following day)[27], was followed by further protestations on 17 June, after which Aelfrida told him 'not to be an idiot, to stick to the Ten Commandments, and to try and grow up', 'whereat', she added, he became 'very glum'.[28]

Finding Layard's attentions somewhat overwhelming, she turned to the Little Friend who, with Layard, became the most famous of her 1913 coterie: Hubert Henderson[29], recent graduate of Emmanuel College and former pupil of Maynard Keynes, who had remained in Cambridge after graduation to teach Economics to members of the Workers' Education Association. Aelfrida's first contact with Hubert was in 1912 when as President of the Cambridge Union, he sent her tickets for a debate accompanied by 'a charming little note'[30], but sunk in post-natal depression and desperate to leave Cambridge, she made no further moves towards friendship at that point. It did not, however, escape her that 'boyish-looking intelligent' Hubert 'was obviously at the first well-known stage the other day'[31] i.e. had said good morning and fallen in love with her. Contact was resumed when Aelfrida needed 'backing' during the visit from Anatolia which took place shortly after her return from Ventnor, Henderson 'playing up' brilliantly by hanging

over Aelfrida 'with lover-like solicitude' and gazing at her with 'undisguised admiration'. (Anatolia was 'much impressed'.)[32] Spring and summer 1913 saw Henderson 'getting to like [her] exceedingly'[33] (Dr Bowen exhibited signs of jealousy) and becoming so 'tremendously stirred' during a discussion on the ultimate nature of the universe (exemplified for Aelfrida by Love) that she had to remind herself to be careful lest, presumably, the conventions of Courtly Love be forgotten.[34] This did not, however, prevent her from taking Hubert, 'very eager to talk and to admire',[35] for a tête-à-tête in the 'gardens-at-the-back' during a Fordfield tennis party and from describing her delight in his 'straight and noble nature' and 'clean, strong, simple, sweet' mind.[36]

The fifth of Aelfrida's Little Friends of 1913 had none of these attributes. He never tried to make her 'sing' and nor did his admiration bear the febrile tint of a *folie à deux*; nor was he a Hubertian character *sans peur et sans reproche*[37] or, like Tommy Altounyan, keen to marry and have children. Like Aelfrida herself, he was dismayed by the physical and spiritual constraints imposed by sharing one's life with another but unlike her, he professed no interest in religion, being too egocentric to consider adherence to a belief-system which did not have himself as its focal point. But because his mind, especially in its darker moments, was so like her own and because he relieved and relived his anguish in the literary medium (poetry) which Aelfrida believed best expressed her own inner griefs and yearnings, it was with Frank Woodyer Stokoe[38] that she conceived her most profound and enduring Friendship.

Unlike other Little Friends, Frank Stokoe was a man of her own age. Born on 21 October 1882, he was almost Julius' twin and filled the gap left in her life by Julius' physical and emotional defection. Now living away from Cambridge and about to separate himself still further from his sister by marrying Mina Kaufmann, Julius had provided little or no support in the aftermath of Agneta's death; indeed (and as Frank Stokoe himself was later wont to do), he assumed the role of emotional incubus, draining his sister of emotional energy at a time when her vital forces were dangerously depleted. Stokoe, on the other hand, had much to attract her: for many years he lived accessibly in or near Cambridge, he was never attracted to other women, he was an intellectual who shared her love of, and fluency in, modern languages, and he showed interest in Agatha and Alethea, saying of them "I had not expected anything as lovely"[39] and composing fairy stories for them.

In fact, it was as a fellow author that Aelfrida first became interested in 'Fidelio' as she later called him[40], writing on 20 February 1913 'last night Stokoe the poet came to dinner … his poetry at its best is fairylike and fantastic, at worst chilly and inarticulate'.[41] (Not everyone appreciated Stokoe's poetry, Aelfrida recording that 'Dr Bowen called … and had some of Fidelio's poetry read to him. He bore it heroically'.) She also noted that 'Fidelio knows far more about poetry than I do and is very keen', that on reading him some of hers, 'he passed a few very just criticisms and once exclaimed a bit was "magnificent! Simply magnificent"'[42], and that the unusual title of one of his poems (*Tollkopf on Dreams*) moved her as she 'sat and watched [Stokoe's] grave handsome profile' to think 'what queer things he must think about when he is alone since he writes such odd verse'.[43] A poem written on the same day as the diary entry expands insight gained by reading and listening to his poetry: that Stokoe was 'one of the people whom nature intended to be lonely'[44], that his poetic inspiration depended on his being able to keep aloof, and that it behoved her not to intrude into his solitude lest inspiration desert him.[45]

For this reason and although Stokoe was 'infinitely attracted' by and 'moderately in love' with her[46], she decided his feelings spoke more of spiritual affinity than of the 'glamour' of sensuality, a belief shared, it seemed, by Stokoe himself, for when Aelfrida suggested that one of his poems was written with her in mind, 'he did not seem to think I appreciated him in quite the right way'.[47] But with examinations looming, Altounyan and Layard begged Aelfrida to withdraw her company from Fidelio because she 'excited' him too much; indeed, she gathered from some of Layard's remarks that 'the affair is serious' and that Stokoe wanted to make her some kind of 'declaration'.[48] Perhaps he did, but a disclosure the previous day that he hated Cambridge and was going away for the summer because he could neither work nor write there did not, it seems, stem from a belief that Aelfrida herself was the cause of his discontent but from two (possibly) unrelated causes, one to be disclosed in due course, the other being his mother.

Alice Stokoe, a doctor's widow living in reduced circumstances, appears to have moved to Cambridge for the same reasons as Mary Tillyard, i.e. her son's admission to the university.[49] Regarding Frank as 'a mixture of a god and a baby', she was much alarmed by his friendship with Aelfrida, seeing her as a distracting influence with regard to academic work and in spite of Layard's and Altounyan's protestations to the contrary, as a 'designing female who would ruin her son's life'.[50] Luckily, Aelfrida met and disarmed Mrs Stokoe, reassuring Frank himself that his and her relationship was too important to be disrupted by other people; indeed, they went so far as to swear a 'compact of friendship'[51] to be broken only by death and sealed with ironic significance by Fidelio

borrowing Constantine's hood for his degree ceremony on 17 June 1913, the loan being to someone whose relationship to Constantine's wife would outlast her husband's.

When 'Elizabeth von Thiele' née Lavington returns to England following the rupture with her husband, a visit to Cambridge demonstrates just how little former friends care about her. She also finds them changed in unexpected ways: one, formerly an untidy and aggressive Girtonian, is now an internationally famous speaker on Feminism, another, a "nobody, a dunce at school", now organises "classes for cripples and Boys Clubs in a masterly manner"; a third, 'Editha St George', once despised as a flirt, is "surrounded by a circle of young men each with his verses in his pocket".[52] And it was with the help of 'Stokoe, the poet' that Editha/Aelfrida embarked on her next literary venture: of the day following her first meeting with Stokoe, she recorded excitedly 'I had an idea to publish an anthology of Cambridge verse 1911–13 with Stokoe as co-editor. I wrote to him at once … He is very enthusiastic'. Together they visited the Eagle Press in Cambridge's Market Square 'to ask about publishing'.[53]

Although Stokoe's appearance in her life acted as Aelfrida's immediate inspiration for her proposed anthology, three other factors are also relevant. The first may be deduced from comments that Little Friends' attentions were going to her head, that she ought to have '*heaps* of babies' to divert her energies into more proper channels[54], and that socialising was all very well 'but think how *much* better a baby would have been'[55], the anthology being in some measure a substitute for dead Agneta. The second may stem from Aelfrida's need to show her father that she was not to be regarded solely as Constantine's wife and her daughters' mother, for Alfred Tillyard's important *History of University Reform* was nearing completion with a view to publication in late 1913 and although his daughter fails to mention his *magnum opus* in her diary, it may be that his literary endeavours spurred her own. The third stimulus was less personal, namely the appointment of Arthur Quiller-Couch as King Edward VII Professor of English Literature in 1912 and his delivery of the first of a series of lectures on 29 January 1913.[56]

'Q's' lectures took Cambridge by storm, Eustace Tillyard describing him as 'public lecturer No 1 in attraction'.[57] Dressed unconventionally in a 'shepherd's plaid suit [and] ordinary waistcoat'[58], his craggy good looks, upright bearing, and *bonhomie* also contrasted markedly to the effete aestheticism of so many dons and to the physical appearance of a predecessor so crippled with arthritis that he had to be carried into the lecture theatre. Aelfrida herself (she makes no mention of having attended his lectures but could have read full and enthusiastic accounts of them in *The Cambridge Magazine* or received verbal reports from Little Friends) appreciated his 'exquisite use of the English language' and his familiarity with 'all the sequestered gardens of English literature'.[59]

'Q' also related easily to women and was eager to help undergraduates; more importantly, he had recently edited *The Oxford Book of Victorian Verse* and had stated in his second lecture that the prime duty of a Professor of English was to encourage appreciation of English Literature of the past and production of it in the present, with a special plea to his audience that "it is to the universities … that we must look to keep alight the flame of English poetry".[60] In his third lecture 'Q' went even further, urging his Cambridge listeners to rival Oxford "and take the lead in English poetry once more"[61]; to such good effect did he plead that a *Cambridge Magazine* article written shortly after his fourth lecture noted a "decided increase in the output of Cambridge verse" and asked "can it be that those who listened to Sir Arthur Quiller-Couch's lectures last term are already acting on his advice?"[62]

Fired by the general excitement – for was she not also a Cambridge poet – Aelfrida 'called, by appointment, on Sir Arthur Quiller-Couch in Jesus' (not having a Cambridge college of his own, 'Q' was appointed Professorial Fellow at Eustace's) to show him 'an account of [her] scheme of Cambridge Poets'. Her scheme 'found favour in his sight', 'Q' also stating that he would be 'delighted to write the introduction'. Having already made contact with a possible publisher, she 'raced to Heffer's and told [her] victory'[63] and she and 'Young Heffer' began to make plans.

Ernest Heffer[64], with his greater knowledge of the world of publishing, was undoubtedly aware that an anthology entitled *Oxford Poetry 1910–13* was due out later that year; he therefore suggested that Aelfrida widen the scope of her own to include poetry written by Cambridge poets between 1900 and 1913. The prospect excited her: 'it will be a much bigger thing than I thought'.[65] So too did Heffer's financial terms: he offered, 'if we get together a really good book', to bear all the expenses and to divide the profits with her; this, she wrote jubilantly, was 'quite handsome'.[66] He also required an 'independent opinion' on the book before drawing up a contract but on Maynard Keynes declining to provide one, settled for 'Q's blessing instead'.[67] With that, Aelfrida 'tactfully' asked Stokoe to resign from his position as co-editor, saying his mother feared anthologising would distract him from his studies but privately adding that this was only just as she had done all the work so far and Stokoe little or none.[68]

She gives no details of how she acquired poems for her anthology beyond taking malicious pleasure in criticising two poems submitted by Maynard Keynes on behalf of a friend[69] and noting that she was 'deluged with letters'[70] from poets keen to be obey Quiller-Couch's commands. It is probable she was helped by Ernest Heffer's familiarity with publishers of verse by more established authors, for the anthology was to include work already in print and a poet had only to have lived in Cambridge between 1900 and 1913 to qualify for inclusion. A university connection helped but was not obligatory; in practice, only two poets (Frances Cornford and Aelfrida herself) lacked academic credentials, the former being already a recognised poet and the latter doubtless hoping that anthological association with published poets or with poets whose alphabetically-listed names added that of their Cambridge college to their own would add lustre to what was *au fond* a vehicle for publishing more of her own verse at someone else's expense.

Quiller-Couch also advised her on which poets to include or exclude ('our tastes usually coincide though he is more severe on technical mistakes than I. We both dislike vague sentiment entirely!')[71] but although Aelfrida records no remarks concerning her own poetry, 'Q's' introduction suggests a wish to dissociate himself from the contents of the volume he himself had inspired. Critics, he writes, "– middle-aged ones especially – will find much amiss …; and the fault … will lie with … the critic's years [at least as much] as with the [poets'] lack of them". Pleading an age-related inability "to pick and choose for commendation" the poems "gathered together by Mrs Graham", he proceeded to attack the overly subjective nature of the anthology's constituent verses and damned with faint praise the "poetic *impulse*" of which the "small but sufficient volume" gave evidence.[72]

An advertisement in *The Cambridge Magazine* of 15 November 1913 announced the publication of a volume containing selections from the work of thirty-eight authors. Aelfrida herself was ecstatic: 'I have just received my copy of *Cambridge Poets 1900–1913* and it is so beautiful! … It makes me feel very happy to think what a good chance I am [giving] to all these young poets – and even the established ones will be pleased at seeing themselves in print!'[73]

Cambridge poets represented in Aelfrida's anthology are an interesting mélange. Some wrote their poems and moved on, becoming wives and mothers, stockbrokers, academics, missionaries, magistrates, journalists, civil servants in England and her colonies, school teachers, secretaries to men of letters, atomic scientists, and leading figures in international politics. Others followed literary careers or poetised in their leisure time. Two at least, Rupert Brooke and James Elroy Flecker (an Oxford graduate, Flecker qualified for inclusion because of post-graduate studies at Gonville and Caius for the Consular Service), were soon to die. Some graced Aelfrida's diaries: Harold Monro promised to publish two of her poems in his *Poetry and Drama* as a quid pro quo[74] but reneged on his offer; Ferenc (Francis) Békássy, 'a Hungarian, with a fine mass of yellow hair'[75]; Esmé Wingfield-Stratford, 'rather bear-cubby in a gentlemanly way and more intellectual than a poet'.[76] Frank Stokoe, whose proximity to Aelfrida was serendipitously alphabetical and emphasised in print that, her brothers excepted, he was the man with whom she sustained the longest relationship of her life, was accorded the honour of five poems and Aelfrida's appropriation of a stanza from *Ode to Earthly Joy* for use in two of her future books and, one could say, for her epitaph:

> "I followed ever, where by land and sea
> Vanishing lovely shapes have haunted me,
> Swift touches, sounds, and gleams –
> Hints of a perfect splendour…"[77],

for, as she presciently wrote apropos Marie Feyler's criticisms of *The Ending of the Way*, 'perhaps … my life will be a success but I shall never get what I care for above all'.[78]

The provenance of Aelfrida's own contributions to *Cambridge Poets* has been discussed with reference to all but four poems and has revealed some interesting facts about her life and feelings at the time of writing. The four poems not so far discussed – *A Mother on her Son's Twenty First Birthday, Architecture, The Difference,* and *For my Mother's Journey* – were written in 1911, the first two in Emden, the others in Cambridge[79], and they too demonstrate much of their author's frame of mind when she wrote them.

The first poem, composed on 5 March 1911, does not initially appear to refer to any particular mother or son celebrating (or in the mother's case, regretting) the latter's coming of age. Although the poem could well describe Chiara's emotions on the twenty-first birthdays of her sons (Julius in 1902, Eustace in 1910), an inspection of Aelfrida's diary entries for the weeks immediately preceding its date of composition provides several clues: on 8 January Constantine informed her that she was not strong enough to bear more children ("…but I – but I / I need a child"); on 1 February Constantine received an abusive letter in which his mother accused him of having 'no soul, no generosity'[80] as a result of his marriage to Aelfrida ("I made his soul and with it did entwine / My soul, my life, my very self – and yet / He is not I…"); on 27 February Aelfrida began weaning Agatha, a time regretted because it marked the end of dependent

*Cambridge Poets 1900–1913*

babyhood: "He loves me but he needs me not". What we have here, then, are two, or possibly three, mothers' laments for babies they have lost to Time, Aelfrida's own being for her 'little boy' Constantine ("He cannot see I made him as he is") and that she herself is no longer "the god on whom [his] eyes are set".

The second poem, *Architecture,* composed on 31 March 1911, was written when Aelfrida was tired and bored and resentful at being unable to accompany Constantine to Paris for Irene's wedding and because Chiara had postponed the date of the Grahams' summer holiday in Cambridge lest the presence of young children distract Eustace from his examinations.[81] Whether Aelfrida paid a specific visit to an Emden church is not known but because the poem was written around Easter it is likely; more pertinently, on 3 March she and Constantine went to Larrett, a small village in the fens beyond Emden in whose 'little church on the hill … people took refuge during floods'.[82] Hence to the idea of a real or metaphorical church whose "stall and arch and stone" provided real or metaphorical protection from "the world's deep anguish", she added stormy and watery imagery ("…a roar, / That beat in many a wave against the door, / As if some sea of torment sought reprieve. / I almost feared the flood of sound would cleave / My gates …"), imagery which might suggest to the poem's critical dedicatee ('AWG') that its writer has also been through a "sea of torment" since her marriage and that it was what Ancifera Warren Gregory had termed religiosity which enabled her "to face the world's deep anguish unafraid". But given Aelfrida's contemporary need to 'write a really sublime poem that said exactly what I meant'[83] and the appearance in *Cambridge Poets* of a poem whose title can be taken to mean *either* a real or a conceptual structure *or* man as the 'architect' of his own fate, together with a poem (*Myself*) written on Easter Day 1911 which describes her vision of her own psyche ("Something of joy I feel and something fear / When to my soul's own depths I gaze adown"), what we have here is a dramatic and revealing representation of an unhappy woman's mind.

*The Difference*, the first of the two poems written in Cambridge, was composed on 21 May 1911 shortly after the Grahams' arrival in England, Eustace's examinations notwithstanding. Constantine has been occupying himself 'writing letters to young ladies' and is about to resume his interrupted friendship with Hilda Sollas, a woman Aelfrida knows is in love with him. Aelfrida has been having a '*very* mild flirtation' (Constantine, she says, is 'amused' and refuses to take it seriously) with Dr Kessler who is in love with her and they have had a sentimental parting on a balcony, he 'quite thrilled' at being near her, she feeling 'high-spirited and naughty inside'.[84] The poem may therefore express Aelfrida's thoughts on how differently she and Constantine would behave were either physically unfaithful to the other, she tenderly and forgivingly, he justly but sternly, but may have deeper implications.

The last poem, *For my Mother's Journey*, written on 30 June 1911, seems the simplest to decipher. Chiara is about to leave for Russia; Aelfrida, worried at her travelling so far and to such a chaotic country, cannot sleep, so gets up, writes the poem, and feels better, even though she 'can't help wondering whether I shall ever see [Chiara] again'.[85] But Chiara is going to Russia with Julius to meet the girl to whom he hopes to become engaged but from whom he will recoil in physical and emotional disgust and Aelfrida, "born to see her loved ones go" (as Constantine is showing signs of wishing to do), is left in "sudden loneliness" hoping her love will be strong enough to ensure their return.

These four and her other seven poems in the anthology provide a vignette of Aelfrida's life between the publication of *To Malise* in 1910 and that of *Cambridge Poets* in late 1913. The two anthologies therefore provide a versified diary-equivalent of her life from just before her marriage to the summer following her near-fatal stillbirth; the publication of *The Garden and the Fire* in 1916 will complete the trilogy and close a decade during which Aelfrida chronicles events and her emotional reaction to them in parallel formats, one private, the other revealing only if one possesses the key. (A reader lacking the key can only confront the poems for what they are: the introspective and opaquely-subjective products of a very minor poet.) An anthology published by private subscription need not, however, be exposed to public view, though Aelfrida, it seems, ensured that it was; an anthology designed for public exhibition is open to review – and reviewed it was, in many cases so harshly that her baby-substitute was subjected to critical infanticide.

*The New Age* was the first to open fire, noting with justification – it is unusual for an anthologist to include his or her own poems in a collection of which they are the editor – that the anthology's compiler was "a lady … who might be accused with every reason of having rather too great personal interest in a book which contains no fewer that eleven of her hitherto unpublished poems" and that the book was no more than the expression of "Aelfrida Tillyard's likes".[86] *The Literary World*'s reviewer criticised Aelfrida's injudicious selection ("the inclusion of Mr Rupert Brooke sets a rather high standard to judge others by")[87]; the *Manchester Guardian,* though praising the note of "vigorous sincerity" demonstrated by the anthology, wrote damningly of the "sad, mad" poetic lapses it contained.[88] *The Morning Post* regarded too many of the poems as "poetical exercises" typifying Cambridge's obsession with poetry for poetry's sake and suggested that "poetical eugenics" should have been practised on the "gay to gaudy blossoms" culled by Mrs Graham.[89]

Edward Thomas' review in *Poetry and Drama* was kinder. Comparing Aelfrida's anthology with the contemporary *Oxford Poetry 1910–1913* introduced by Gilbert Murray, Thomas, quoting Murray, approved of the fact that the Cambridge poets were all "in touch with … the moving impulses of contemporary poets" – some, indeed, were among the formative forces behind the impulses – and that their poetry derived immediacy from personal experience, pleasant though tending to "mere clamouring for ecstasy" rather than ecstatic experience as such, and unpleasant: "scratchy [and] censorious-angry".[90] Both Thomas and Murray believed that *Cambridge Poets* had the edge over *Oxford Poetry* in its inclusion of women poets, Murray in particular noting that Aelfrida's compilation possessed "a normal human atmosphere in which women are treated as fellow-workers and not as freaks of nature [and] in which men and women met and talked and knew one another", and contained less of the "virginal atmosphere of … absolutely uncontaminated College", less "extreme religiosity", "less of the grotesque or fantastic [and ] less… pure pursuit of insipid beauty". He also praised *Cambridge Poets* for the "refreshingly firm and clear" metrical treatment of the poems it contained and for the said poems' "bony structure" of genuine and interesting thought.[91]

Although Aelfrida had noted that reviews of *To Malise* were favourable even if comments from family and friends were not, she makes no reference at all to reviews of her own verse as published in 1913 (*Cambridge Poets*) and 1916 (*The Garden and the Fire*) nor does she appear to have kept press cuttings. An indication of her dismay at the virulent or lukewarm reviews of *Cambridge Poets* may, however, be discerned from the appearance in *The Granta* of a review, *The Puff by Parody*, by-lined 'AT'. It is not often, 'AT' begins, "that an author or editor has the good fortune to review his own work but … it falls to me to give an appreciation of my own anthology", explaining the parodic element of her 'puff' by saying that although "a review of verse ought to consist almost entirely of quotations, [because] I have [given] away the twelve copies that the publishers sent me, [I] have to rely entirely on my memory for what I wish to quote…"[92]

Francis Békássy's "brave and supremely intelligent poem" *Fragmentary Views* is parodied in terms of his coiffure, already commented upon in her diary: "Thou living hair! Upstanding there / A-tiptoe with exuberance of Thought!" (Or, as Békássy himself put it: "Thou living water! Settled softly there, / Proud with the proud reality of Thought".) Dermot Freyer, described as 'aesthetic and amiable'[93] and liable to 'lionise' her, whose poem *Chrysanthemums at Night* is praised as a "quaint, frieze-like … impressionistic and picturesque … imitation of the French", she parodies as *Rugger Blues at Afternoon*, poetry far removed from Freyer's decorous *In Lavender Covers* of 1912.[94] She is kinder to Rupert Brooke's *When love has changed to kindliness*, stating that Brooke was "too well known from the slander suit that the united villages round Cambridge brought against him in consequence of his poem on Grantchester to need any advertising from [herself]" but notes that *When wit has changed to Donnishness* embodies "so exquisitely [his college's] attitude to existence".

Further revelations arose as a result of Aelfrida's parody of Frank Stokoe's *Three Songs to Fidelio*. The revelations were not made until the summer of 1915 but it is possible that it was as a result of her unwitting disclosure of Stokoe's predilections that they were made and that the 'declaration' Stokoe failed to make in midsummer 1913 concerned them.

Aelfrida, as we know, was capable of acts of emotional cruelty towards innocent parties when she herself was unhappy. At the time of publication of *Cambridge Poets* in November 1913 she was in a highly-elevated state of mind (the reason will be discussed shortly), soon to be followed by Constantine's refusal to allow her to continue a friendship with a man (*not* a Little Friend) discovered through the medium of her anthology, but it is possible that her 'puff by parody' *was* an act of revenge, a poem by Stokoe entitled *The Mad Magician* having been published in *The Cambridge Magazine* of 6 June 1913 at a time when he was trying to steer her away from involvement with the man in question. This being so, it is hard to see why Aelfrida includes *The Mad Magician* in *Cambridge Poets* (it cannot have been for its poetic qualities) unless as a manifestation of her delight in risky behaviour, but its inclusion goes some way to explaining her cruel parody of January 1914.

Aelfrida's parody of Stokoe's contribution to *Cambridge Poets,* a contribution she describes as having "brilliance, a kind of fairy-like elusiveness and iridescence [and] something gem-like, as of a diamond" (the Walter Pater phrase 'gem-like' is probably intentional) consists not, as one might expect, of *The Mad Magician* but of the trilogy *Three songs to Fidelio* and of the poem *Ode to Earthly Joy.* Her *Ode to an Earthly Boy* from *Three Songs for Giornalio* has Stokoe "madly pursuing the unattainable, in the shape of the boy with the evening paper" and concludes with the hope that Stokoe "never catch that which you are seeking, for if you did we should be many poems the poorer". Luckily, Aelfrida's innocent (or was it so innocent – had she not once written in a moment of exasperation at his amatory dilatoriness 'what's the matter with the man?')[95] revelation of his sexual orientation did not result in arrest for criminal behaviour.[96]

Exigencies of their respective lives separated Stokoe and Aelfrida until August 1914 and it was not until he and she were meeting regularly once more that Stokoe visited to announce that what he was about to tell her would 'shock and disgust' her. 'He told me', she recorded, 'that he was attracted by boys, not by women, that it was horrible, that he loathed himself [and] that he was in Hell very often'. Aelfrida, to her credit, did not recoil in horror or even judge him harshly. ('How could I, knowing nothing of the matter'.)[97] Realising this and aware of the benefits of cathartic disclosure to a discrete and supportive person, Stokoe then sent her a lengthy letter, explaining 'exactly what manner of Hell he inhabits' and on a subsequent visit, indulged in 'self-revelation on a large scale'.[98] Having formerly regarded him as 'pure as flame'[99], Aelfrida was moved by her friend's capacity 'for evil and for suffering' ('his words and his look scorch like corrosive fluid') and by the torment it engendered in a man 'so quiet and gentle'[100], but retained sufficient sense of proportion (and humour) to note apropos Stokoe's belief that 'his only chance lies in being with a boy, loving him purely and having his affection' that 'this does not seem to me to be a perfect solution of his problems'.[101] Of more practical value was her decision to act as confidante for as long as Stokoe required one (a decision, as it happened, which enabled Stokoe to follow an academic career and to abandon recurrent thoughts of suicide) and to trust him sufficiently to invite him to Fordfield where he could meet children (of both sexes) in a protected family setting.

A Cambridge poet with whom Aelfrida had sustained a more intimate relationship was her husband Constantine 'formerly Michaelides', under which name three of his poems were included in his wife's anthology[102]: *The Red Admiral Butterfly* of September 1907[103], *The Forest of Massachusetts* of June 1908, and *To My Father* of 9–11 October 1909. The latter two poems (and their named author) were awarded a rare favourable mention by the reviewer of *The New Age*, a possible source of chagrin for Aelfrida whose own poems had been savaged and who must have been hyper-sensitive to adverse comments from any source after *To Malise*. This may explain why an apparently gentle *Granta* parody of *To My Father* (*To My Tutor*) has such a sting in the tail, for not only does the parody hint at Constantine's relationship with OB but *To My Tutor* is said to be 'by another King's man', a particularly poignant gibe because one of Aelfrida's own poems in *Cambridge Poets* is entitled *To a King's Man* and because the 'King's man' in question is the 'other' King's man in her life, Eric Silvanus.[104]

How much Aelfrida discussed *Cambridge Poets* with her husband is not known (it is to be hoped that she consulted him with regard to alterations made to *The Forest of Massachusetts* and *To My Father*)[105] but his reaction to her own poem, *The Prayer*, in which she describes Constantine as "him whose love had made / My life an ecstasy of joy and pain" may be gauged by remarks made apropos the second tranche of verses and the novel (fortunately unpublished but probably read by him) in which his stormy relationship with his wife is revealed: it may be *Marrying a Stranger* to which Constantine referred when he upbraided Aelfrida for her 'fifth rate novels' and to the eleven poems of *Cambridge Poets* when he castigated her 'third rate verse'.[106]

Aelfrida, however, took her revenge (in spite of professions of love for her husband, she knew exactly how and where to hurt him) by publishing three years later a poem written on 29 April 1914, *Critic and Poet,* in which she represents herself (as 'Poet') as 'inspired' and

Constantine (the consular official once nicknamed by the Tillyards 'the Poet') as merely 'hired'.[107] Revenge being a dish best tasted cold, a study of her diary explains otherwise incomprehensible references to 'Critic's' behaviour and to why he should be asking prosaic questions about form, content, and metre of a 'Poet' whose inspiration comes from a source other than and superior to himself, he being only the conduit through which the "soul of the earth"[108] speaks: *The Quest* had recently published *The People of God,* a poem in which Aelfrida stated that man's nature is divine because it partakes of God's divinity[109] and it may be to this poem that 'Critic's' questions refer. But 'Critic's' apparently out-of-context admission ("Peccavi! I have sinned") may relate to Constantine's most recent 'little friend', Ethel Poncelle, described by Aelfrida as very beautiful and very much in love with him who, as was his wont, he invited home to meet his wife[110], or even to mutual accusations of extra-marital peccadilloes, wrangling over which might have ended, like the poem, with the weary statement "turn on the light. We'd better sup".

Although Aelfrida looked forward to Constantine's return from Panama with excitement ('I love him – oh so much') she admitted (to her diary) to feelings of trepidation too: 'I am afraid I may be unwise ... and have another try at making two people into one'.[111] Although this could be taken to refer to her desire to mould Constantine's moral character so that it conformed more closely to her own, it may also refer to the vexed question of conjugal relations practised with or without contraceptive measures (and if without, with the possible risk of another stillbirth and further physical and emotional damage to herself) or maintained as a chaste brother and sister relationship which went against all Constantine's 'Greek instincts' and regarding which cogitation had led to the only conclusion possible for her: 'But *no* ... I have had time to reconsider my whole view of life [and have decided that] love between man and woman is indeed glorious but at its best when not too closely related to sex'.[112] Still apprehensive in spite of her unilateral decision and of a further decision 'not to bother if we disagree – and [to] argue as little as possible'[113], she nevertheless sought reassurance (of a kind) from a source other than that of Little Friends who knew nothing of the problems of married life or of Dr Bowen to whom she felt she had confided too much of her relationship with her husband. Her choice was not the wisest but given that a visit to a man who had expressed his admiration for her in the strongest possible terms would reassure her that she was still attractive to men in general and in particular to a husband from whom she had been physically and emotionally estranged for over a year, possibly the most appropriate. On 11 May 1913, with Constantine due in Cambridge at any moment, Aelfrida visited archetypal 'little friend': John Forbes Cameron.

John Forbes, the first man to whom she awarded the then derogatory title and whose rejection sent her rebounding into the arms of 'Vadius', appeared 'contented [but] with all his dreams gone'. A brief conversation showed this not to be the case; indeed, so swiftly and effectively did Aelfrida prove that she still possessed the power to enchant that she decided not to prolong the interview lest words and even kisses be exchanged which both parties might regret. Then with disingenuousness one can only hope was real, she returned home to 'innocently' inform her family of her visit, to find her parents 'horribly shocked' at what she had done, and to have Eustace point out the adverse effect of her action on Cameron himself, something which had not crossed her mind.[114]

'Alas', she wrote three days later, 'for romance!', she and Constantine having met on the stairs at Fordfield when he 'strolled in' at 8.15pm on 14 May 1913 to find her gone to her room for a soda-mint because pent-up excitement had given her indigestion. In spite of Chiara urging that Constantine be allowed his conjugal rights, Aelfrida was determined that she and her husband would maintain nothing more than a loving but chaste relationship and was prepared to suffer 'any torments of desire than so debase the beauty of physical love' by douching after intercourse as a form of contraception. But having decided that 'a little asceticism' would 'add lustre to [Constantine's] intellect'[115], she proceeded to do 'a rash thing'. Taking Constantine out into the garden one evening 'where the air was all just scent of flowers and things were oh, as nearly as possible what they used to be' in their courting days (she even wore a significant cloak) she 'loved him quite wildly' until she stirred him ('just as I try *so* hard not to do with other men') into giving her 'a real, *real* kiss!'[116] The following day Constantine left for his next posting, having spent ten days in England, eight with his wife.

Aelfrida 'hardly minded at all'. For one thing '*this* parting was so much less terrible than the last'[117] because she and the children were shortly to re-join him; for another, she was too busy selecting type and paper and correcting proofs for *Cambridge Poets* to care very much about her husband's comings and goings. Lastly, chastely amatory attentions of Little Friends like John Layard (of whom she wrote in the same diary entry which described her husband's 'real, *real* kiss' that Layard had written 'four incoherent pages' begging her not to invite him to Fordfield until his examinations were over because she excited him 'too much [in] body and mind' but adding

that a postcard would 'bring him to [her] feet at once')[118] were preferable to her husband's sexual advances (such as they were, he seems to have been 'boyish and ... coaxing' rather than sexually demanding) and certainly to his indifference: 'he didn't seem to notice me much'.[119]

Constantine had not gone far. On 22 February 1913 Aelfrida had recorded in her diary 'Last night a sudden thunderclap of joy "*Accepted Paris. Graham*". I cabled back "Superb". I feel all in a whirl – to see him again, ye gods, how sweet!'[120]

On her way back to Cambridge from Ventnor/'Ventnor' Aelfrida paid a visit to Lord Dufferin in London ('I quite enjoyed getting into a taxi ... and saying "Foreign Office"')[121] to inform him that because her state of health did not permit her to join her husband in Panama, 'could Lord Dufferin perhaps bring him back a little nearer home?' Lord Dufferin, unmoved by Aelfrida's 'best brown things' and musquash coat, informed her that there were then no European posts vacant but unbent sufficiently to note her suggestion that when the next moves were made, Constantine be allocated a more suitable one.[122] Receipt of Constantine's telegram three months later therefore caused her to write 'Constantine has *me* to thank for his Paris appointment – and I, I, how I thank Lord Dufferin!' On 28 February she received 'a very friendly note from Lord Dufferin' confirming her impression that 'it *was* my doing. I am so proud of myself and happy!'[123] Whether Constantine knew or approved of his wife's pulling strings on his behalf is not recorded.

If 'Max's' fictional feelings on being deserted by 'Elizabeth' are anything to go by, Constantine's departure for Panama in July 1912 found him regarding himself as "a man set apart and consecrated by loneliness and by suffering"; Constantine being Constantine, "this aspect of the situation pleased him and his mind dwelt on it at some length"[124] and "he had found it a little difficult to come down from ... contemplation of himself as a martyr and a superior being".[125] (Photographs preserved in the current volume of his wife's diary show him looking dashing in tropical whites and surrounded by smiling women; his martyred pose and status as temporarily sole but safely married man must have added lustre to Panamanian friendships with members of the opposite sex.) A vice-consular position at Panama and the additional status accruing from early promotion to Secretary to the Legation soon cheered him up, Aelfrida enthusiastically informing future readers of her diary that 'you must read [his letters] and see'.[126] (She did not preserve them.) It seems, too, that in Panama Constantine found a position exactly suited to his talents (his cosmopolitan background and linguistic powers would have chimed perfectly with Panama's multicultural and polyglot population) and that it was for this reason that neither Lord Dufferin nor Aelfrida ('you must not let any wishes of mine ... stand in the way of my husband's best interests and advancement in the service') wished to recall him too soon.[127] It is possible, therefore, that Constantine did not view his return to Europe and domesticity with the same eager anticipation as his wife, for in spite of Aelfrida's hope that Paris would 'content' her husband and her determination that, once there, Constantine 'shall go where he likes and do what he likes'[128], it was less than a year since he had escaped from Emden's petit bourgeois society and his wife's surveillance to be *'un héros sans bagage'* across the Atlantic. In Paris, too, the ex-Secretary of Legation would be merely one of two vice-consuls, and this and unresolved problems inherent in the Grahams' sexual relationship and Anatolia's presence in Paris for eight months of the year, did not augur well for acceptance of Lord Dufferin's 'superb' posting. Aelfrida, on the other hand, was 'unspeakably happy' at the prospect of re-joining her husband and in spite of her belief that 'there will be much that I must condemn [there]', decided not to 'fuss about Paris and the future in the least', writing joyfully on 7 July 1913 'off to Paris tomorrow!'[129]

But why 'condemn'? Everyone, as Kathleen Adler notes, "had their own vision and fantasy of Paris: its beauty, its light, its myriad attractions, its vibrancy. The combination of old and new building, the splendours of the new boulevards and the Bois de Boulogne, the profusion of cafés, the theatres, the contrasting opulence and seediness of the city, its strange ways ... all these aspects of the city exerted a spell on visitors"[130]; what could Aelfrida possibly find to condemn in an exciting place loved since she first encountered it as an adolescent? It was not, however, Paris itself she 'must condemn' but people she would be obliged to meet there. Specifically, Americans. More specifically still, her American mother-in-law, Anatolia Michaelides, now calling herself 'Lila' and living (or believing she lived) *la vie de bohême* in a tiny apartment ('the Anatolian flat sounds as uncomfortable as the Anatolian atmosphere')[131] at 132 Rue d'Assas on the Left Bank to which a daily visitor was a man young enough to be her son (he was thirty-five to Constantine's thirty) of whom Aelfrida wrote in September 1913 'he dangles after [Anatolia] all the time and they flirt as though they were both eighteen'.[132] (It was not until later that, recalling Anatolia, 'painted and bedizened', kissing his lips again and again 'in a kind of sentimental rapture'[133] horribly reminiscent of the way in which she used to fondle her son, that Aelfrida realised that Guy-Charles Croz was her mother-in-law's gigolo.) Knowing she would be bound to see much of Anatolia and having

resolved that in Paris she would try to understand before she condemned because 'perhaps seemingly the worst of people are following the best they know'[134], Aelfrida decided on a final conquest of her mother-in-law 'by fair means or foul' in order that peace might reign during their sojourn in the same city. Believing – wrongly, as it turned out – that the conquest would be 'absurdly easy', she looked forward to being 'displayed to Paris as the latest acquisition in the "magic net"'.[135]

The "permanent colony of Americans in Paris", writes Erica Hirshler, "was described as 'a little city within a big one – having its own social cliques and customs, its charities, clubs, churches, shops and *pensions*".[136] (And its own hospital where Charles du Bouchet now worked.) As the colony grew, membership became more a matter of preference (many Americans "had no patience for it and kept it at arm's length")[137] than an aspirational attempt to absorb the culture of Europe's most glittering city in the company of sympathetic fellow-countrymen. There was also a language problem, for many members of the colony spoke little or no French (Aelfrida mocked Anatolia's pronunciation and vocabulary and rejoiced when Helen Michaelides ordered from artist Lucien Monod[138] not a sketch – *un ébauche* – of herself but *'un débauche'*) but poor command of French notwithstanding, Anatolia felt more at ease in Paris than in Hessle: "American women ... found unprecedented autonomy in Paris, for not only had they escaped the strictures of their own society, but, as foreigners, they were also free from the customs and rules of behaviour that applied to French women"[139], hence, perhaps, her uninhibited behaviour with Guy-Charles. It was to louche aspects of life in the American Colony that Aelfrida therefore took exception (she described an earlier visit paid by Constantine to his mother as consisting of meetings with 'crazy people, *exaltés* – mostly women – pseudogeniuses, cosmopolitans, mystics [and] poets')[140], noting that the freedom of action she was about to grant her husband would not apply to herself. She opted instead for 'a little house at St Cloud or Versailles, my children, and peace – not crowds of Anatolia's immoral friends'.[141]

The 'little house' into which the Grahams moved on 30 August 1913 was in Le Vésinet, a commune situated in a loop of the Seine seven miles west of Paris. The area had once been 'a great park with waterways and gardens and avenues' but was now a suburb whose tree-lined lanes divided bosky gardens in which 'quaint villas, each different, [hid] themselves modestly behind trees'[142]; the Grahams' own 'quaint villa', *La Cigogne* at 10 rue Villebois, was 'a tall, gentle, welcoming little house' standing in a 'quiet, intimate, enclosed garden'.[143] After the upheaval of settling two small girls, their nursemaid, and Ovvie's sister, Dorothy Turner, the cook-house-keeper, into an unfamiliar setting – it was two years since Aelfrida had had to undergo the process, and she noted ruefully that 'one feels each time like a soul going to another incarnation' – she 'shouldered the burden of life again'[144] and began to enjoy 'the housework, the marketing, having the children down to dinner and talking French to them'.[145]

With the wings of 'our little *Cigogne* ... beautifully smoothed'[146] in spite of the departure in early 1914 of both Ovvie and Dorothy necessitating the appointment of a French nursemaid-housekeeper, Octavie Berruè[147], Aelfrida made every effort to rebuild a relationship with daughters she had effectively rejected for a year following Agneta's death, insightful reflection shortly before Constantine's return from Panama having suggested to her that 'one realises oneself in self-sacrifice' and that an important aspect of self-sacrificial development of one's higher self at the expense of largely or wholly self-centred desires was putting one's children's spiritual and emotional welfare before one's own.[148] She therefore devoted herself to playing with and instructing six-year-old Alethea and four-year-old Agatha, inventing endless stories, taking them on nature walks in the vicinity or on the banks of the Seine a short tram ride away, teaching them housewifely duties, and providing 'play-lessons' in French, poetry, history, and geography. Nor was music neglected, she and the girls gathering round the piano to sing songs of the kind included in her own *Livre des Jeux* or she accompanied the girls' Dalcroze eurhythmics ('cosmic games', Aelfrida calls them) during which they pretended to be waves of the sea or stars going round the sun.[149] The children responded gratefully to a regime in which they were '*never* punished and hardly ever talked to gravely' by blossoming into 'brown and well and good and intelligent'[150] little girls whose mother almost regretted keeping separate record books for them because this meant that she did not record their 'sweet doings' in her diary as they grew 'more interesting, more enthralling, every day'.[151]

Staying at home with the children and being 'oh, so happy' as a result[152] did not entirely preclude a social life, for Aelfrida paid and received calls (local British residents were 'not thrilling')[153], founded the Vésinet Anglo-American Society in March 1914 in an unsuccessful effort to 'screw people up one peg higher'[154], and held dinner parties for consular officials and their wives. She also renewed acquaintance with Odessan friends: Dr du Bouchet, still 'the same fine handsome presence' fond of both Grahams and delighted to meet the children he had been sure they would have[155], and Charles Stewart Smith, 'still naval, still blue-eyed, still absurdly like himself' but to

Aelfrida's relief, 'less *emotionné*' about her than before[156], on his way from his Odessan 'captivity of Babylon' to his new post in Barcelona.[157] Some visitors were less congenial (Anatolia and Guy-Charles, for example), some were forbidden altogether: Giovanni Papini, passing through Paris early in 1914, was warned off by Constantine.[158] One in particular occasioned Aelfrida much disquiet: Déla Bernet, a friend of Anatolia's, introduced to Constantine with the intention, it seems, of fostering discord between her newly-reunited son and daughter-in-law. At Constantine's insistence Aelfrida invited Déla to tea, describing her as 'not pretty but with fine hair and eyes, powdered cheeks and lithe expressive body. I never saw a being so *physical*, she seems ... to have sensations where other people have thoughts'[159], but although she initially believed the relationship to be, if not wholly platonic, at least going no further than kisses on the lips, Constantine's habit of visiting Déla in the evenings, the classic *cinq-à-sept* of the married Parisian *flâneur*, and Madame Bernet being an older woman, later caused her to suspect that Déla had offered her person to her husband and that he had accepted it.[160] At the time, however, she did and said nothing ('I ... just let him hurt me') though she agreed with her parents that being forced by Constantine to meet a woman who was possibly more than merely one of her mother-in-law's 'queer friends' was both wrong and insulting. She continued to act the part of *femme complaisante*, however[161], with regard to the little friendships of one to whom she had accorded freedom to go where he wished and see whom he wanted, particularly if, as in the case of Ethel Poncelle, Constantine, though 'enormously attracted' lacked opportunity 'to pursue the acquaintance further' because Ethel was married to a watchful husband.[162]

Rather oddly for one who had a vested interest in keeping his wife in seclusion in the suburbs while he pursued life and women in Paris (and who would have preferred not to stir from her 'woods and streams and meditations' in any case)[163], Constantine, initially at least, insisted on Aelfrida's presence at his side on visits joining 'a sense of duty ... to a sense of the inevitable'[164] but to which she, a fluent Francophone, could contribute much. Visits to 'Anatolia's celebrated "little nest"'[165] and consular At Homes were categorised as duties, though a formal Christmas lunch with the Consul-General and his wife was appreciated as an opportunity for entering a world in which 'a decent veil of ladylikeness and gentlemanliness' was drawn around the 'naked realities of life'[166], and during a visit to Paris by George V and Queen Mary in April 1914 Aelfrida enjoyed being escorted by her husband, a 'distinguished-looking gentleman in uniform', to a gala performance at the Opéra in honour of the royal

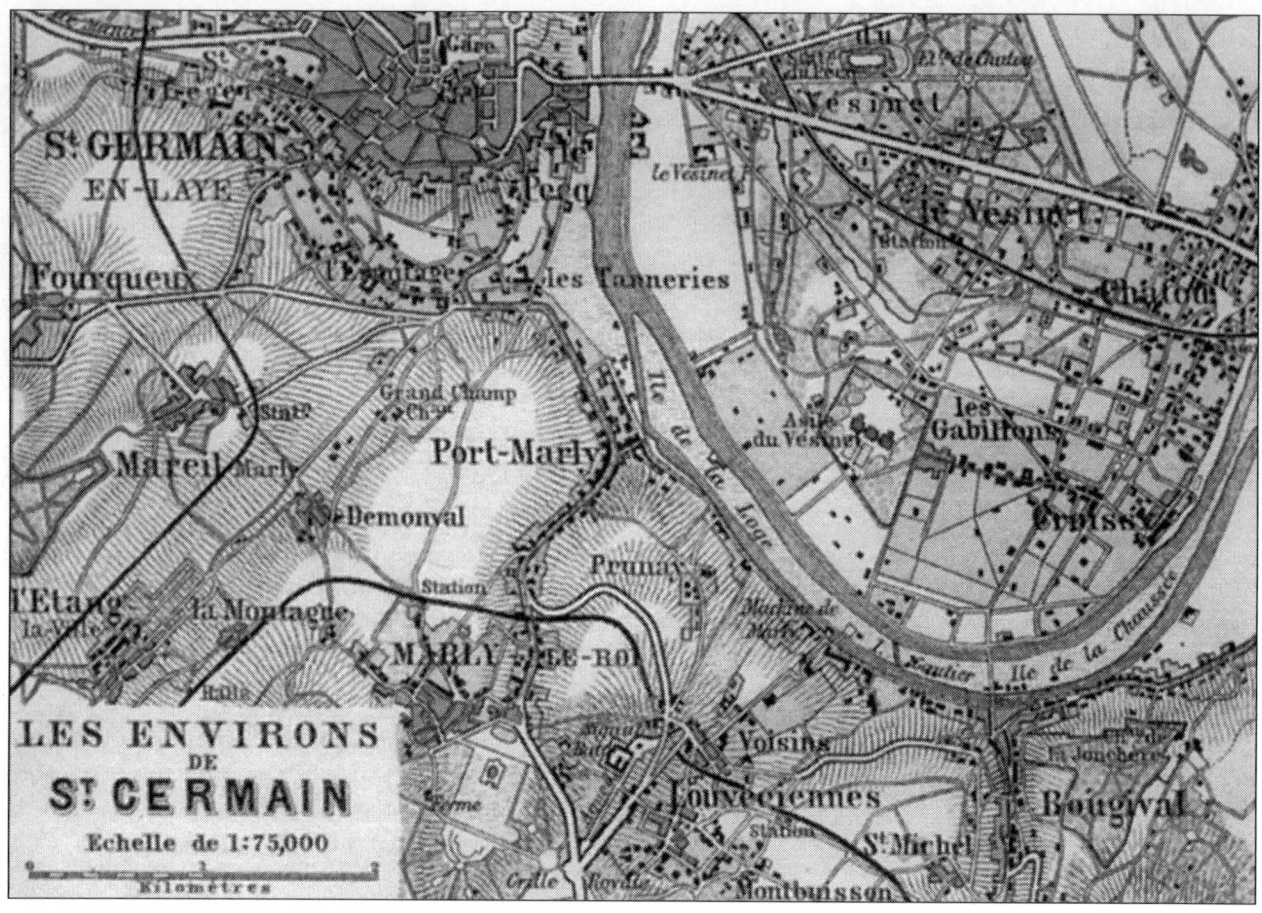

**Le Vésinet 1896**

couple. (Catching sight of herself *en grand tenue* reflected in a mirror, she decided that she looked 'absurdly like a celebrated authoress incognito!')[167] Modern art, however, was not her forte – visiting the *Salon des Indépendents,* she described Futurist, Cubist, and Post-Impressionist paintings as providing 'enough bad dreams to last us a twelvemonth'.[168]

Sufficient nightmares to last the Grahams' twelve-month stay in Paris arose from other sources too, it being during their post-Panama reunion that their married life began to demonstrate that dissensions which disturbed it in Emden and threatened to split it altogether in May 1912 remained unresolved in spite of Aelfrida's resolutions to the contrary. On 26 December 1913, after Christmas festivities described by her as 'mutually loving'[169], Constantine left for six weeks' leave in England. Before he left he kissed his wife passionately, telling her that he loved her more and more and that harmony between them was restored. (Or so his wife said.)[170] This, and Aelfrida's earlier description of the 'idyllic time' she and Constantine passed together during the early days

of their stay in Paris ('he has been – oh, everything that he always was, and more')[171] before the arrival of the children and the move to Le Vésinet caused 'intimacy [to be] perforce lost in domesticity'[172], might lead us to believe that reconciliation had been effected, but diary evidence provided by a thwarted nocturnal burglary on 17 September 1913 during which Aelfrida discloses that the Grahams have separate bedrooms, suggests otherwise.

A major cause of dissent (there were two; the other will be discussed in a subsequent chapter), was, of course, the continuing dichotomy between Aelfrida's unassuaged desire for more children ('I wonder – when *my* turn will come for another child', she wrote on 8 April 1914 on receiving the news of the birth of a son to her sister-in-law Irene)[173] and her belief, formulated the previous year and enforced in Paris, that love between a man and woman was indeed glorious but should not be too closely related to sex. She was not unaware of or unsympathetic to the strain which 'enforced chastity' occasioned her husband and the effect it had on their relationship ('his perpetual irritation with me [has] filled me with grave apprehension ... for our married happiness') but in spite of this found herself unable to face the notion of artificially preventing conception and 'degrading the sexual act ... into the satisfaction of an itch'.[174]

Matters came to a head in May 1914 when Aelfrida consulted Dr du Bouchet about a minor but persistent gynaecological problem. Following his examination and discovering that du Bouchet looked on her as 'a cool oasis in the desert of worldliness' of the American Colony and that this '[sent] his heart towards [her]', she stayed to chat about 'poetry and ideals and things'. The relief of finding a sympathetic listener after Constantine's continual carping caused her to confide in du Bouchet without meaning to: she and Constantine, she revealed, had had separate rooms for two years and a half. ('It's more, really', she noted in her diary; the term 'separate rooms' being a euphemism.) Du Bouchet's response that she was doing 'very wrong' and that 'not only Constantine's temper but also his health would suffer', depressed her on two counts: first, because, so she said, 'chastity has not been easy for me either', and second, because although she had prided herself 'on being a superior being and meekly putting up with [her] husband's tempers', she herself was chiefly at fault. Consoling herself with the thought that it was preferable for herself rather than her husband to be in the wrong ('I have ideals and "illusions" about him, and they *matter*'), she decided to grasp the nettle and 'talk to Constantine seriously'.[175]

This she did on 25 May with devastating results and what she learnt was to cause a diametric shift in her view of human relationships and to have repercussions for years to come. Informing Constantine of her conversation with du Bouchet, she received the bruising reply that chastity had not been difficult for him as he had long ceased to find her physically attractive. (A possible reason for this but one which did not occur to Aelfrida then, is that a man who hated even the thought of illness and disease but who had nursed his wife through surgery and numerous illnesses, who had witnessed two normal deliveries – an unusual occurrence for the time – and who had been present at his wife's gruesome near-death-bed might find physical attractiveness waning as medical interventions increased, du Bouchet's diagnosis of chronic inflammation of the womb being only the most recent but to an enforced and fastidious celibate like Constantine, a particularly repellent and ironic one.) Aelfrida was aghast: 'it was odd how it hurt – how primitive one is in matters like that. Of course I had guessed ... but to have it put coldly like that by the man one loves, the man who deliberately roused all one's passions with words and gestures of an eternity of love ...' Her then asking if Constantine did not still love her for her mind

brought the chilling response that her 'intellectual interests' made her even less attractive: "I never believed in women thinking ... it only unfits them for their proper function of being charming". Devastated but aware of the imminent arrival of visitors (Anatolia, the Lucien Monods, and Edith Poncelle), Aelfrida closed her heart to human affection and by an enormous effort of will decided 'to replace person-desiring by desires for God and humanity', appearing so 'serene if not joyful' that Edith, ignorant of what had just transpired, was moved to congratulate her hostess on her ability to rise above dependence on friends and to exist in a tranquil world of her own making. Aelfrida, intent on withdrawal into a private place where no-one, least of all Constantine, could hurt her so much again, manoeuvred her visitors in such a way as to allow Constantine a tête-à-tête with Edith and to later vote the evening a 'great success'.[176]

Manifestations of Constantine's worsening behaviour towards his wife, evident in Emden but now involving both verbal abuse ("bloody idiot") and, as we shall see, physical violence, were attributable, however, to something more than sexual frustration. As he grew older, Constantine dealt with problems by reverting to his most enduring role-model, namely his mother; indeed, it is easy to see that his manner of interspersing 'grumbling and lecturing and ... sermonising'[177] with sugary endearments (telling his wife that she grew more *doux* every day)[178] as a means of punishing or rewarding behaviour which pleased or displeased him was adopted directly from Anatolia. Aelfrida seems unaware of this; had she realised, she might have worked out a means of dealing with his behaviour instead of allowing it to erode her confidence and to shred her nerves with its unpredictability. But instead of standing up to her husband, she adopted the role of willing victim (one might almost say, accomplice), blaming herself ('it is all [my] fault from the beginning')[179], never defending herself or exhorting her husband to improve his behaviour ('my criticisms I keep for my diary')[180], and maintaining her belief that Constantine was a genius and that his good points outweighed his bad by admiring him 'all I can'.[181]

Complicity was essential because she was financially dependent on Constantine and depended on keeping him by her side if there were to be any more of the children she craved, but in seeking to preserve her sanity, her emotional integrity, and her spiritual purity by distancing herself as far as possible from her husband's consular and Parisian life, her behaviour ensured the exact opposite. Her habit of secluding herself at Le Vésinet and making it obvious that she preferred the company of Agatha and Alethea, her compulsive writing (*Marrying a Stranger* occupied much of her time), and her plans of founding an association of young men and women engaged in nourishing 'the "life of the spirit" within one'[182], led to a scene in which Constantine accused his wife of no longer caring for him or his work and described himself as 'only an episode' in her life. Although Aelfrida denied this ('he, the one love of my life, an episode …')[183], Constantine was absolutely correct and it is significant that one of two poems written immediately after the event (*Winter,* on 28 April and *Critic and Poet* on 29 April 1914) accurately states that "between my heart and yours there lies infinity".[184]

It was around this time too that Aelfrida became aware that grave problems existed in a marriage other than her own. At the end of May 1914 the Grahams and their daughters returned to Cambridge on leave. Constantine did not spend all his leave in Cambridge and returned to Paris ahead of his wife but was probably still at Fordfield when Chiara told Aelfrida a story which made her believe that not only was her brother's marriage as unhappy as her own but also that her husband had had a hand in making it so.

Julius and Wilhelmina Kaufmann having become engaged in August 1912, a visit by Mina to Cambridge in the October of that year showed her to be 'most tremendously in love'[185] with a man of whom his sister had commented earlier that 'it seems a little odd … that anyone should be so much in love with Dudu, but I suppose sisters often feel that way'.[186] Julius had seemed 'placidly content with his bargain, and looking forward to calm happiness' with Mina[187] but soon disclosed to his sister that placidity was because Mina had agreed to a 'brother and sister' life .[188] Julius and Mina were married in Lahr on 8 April 1913, his sister recording that 'the wedding was German and solid and gorgeous'.[189] (Aelfrida did not attend, perhaps because unable to stand the strain of travel and festivities while recovering from her stillbirth of the previous year but her absence seems odd nevertheless.) Mr and Mrs Julius Tillyard then returned to England to spend their honeymoon at Fordfield before Julius took up his Edinburgh post once more. Having vacated both her bedroom and her home in favour of the newly-married couple (hence her second visit to Sir George Fordham, the gloomy widower of Odsey), Aelfrida wrote sentimentally that 'it was in [my] room, in my bed, that the marriage was consummated … Let me … rejoice that Julius' pessimism is over'.[190]

She was wrong on both counts. On 1 August she discovered that Julius and Mina were 'not living as husband and wife at all' (nor, of course, were she and Constantine) and that so intolerable did Julius find married life that he almost ran away.[191] A visit to his sister in Paris the following month reassured Aelfrida on one score ('Dudu is

much better … For Mina he seems to have steady brotherly love. Perhaps that is enough for them both') but worried her on another, for Julius was brooding on the 'sex question' and regarded physical expressions of love with 'fear and distaste'.[192] No more was said, however, until June 1914 when Chiara confided to her daughter the terrible events of the previous February.

It appears that Mina, unhappy with her *mariage blanc,* confided in Constantine in January 1914 and asked his advice on how to remedy the situation. (It is unlikely that she knew that Constantine too was an unwilling participant in a similar marriage, for the Grahams had not disclosed the matter to anyone in England.) Constantine 'urged Mina to insist on her rights as a wife'.[193] This she did 'just for once', with the horrifying result that Julius tried 'to take his life by means of an overdose of sleeping draught'. He failed, but 'conjugal relations were not renewed'.[194]

Aelfrida does not (perhaps dared not) speculate on the underlying reasons for Julius' unwillingness (and if her diary is to be believed, inability) to consummate his marriage, possibly because to do so would raise questions with regard to his feelings for herself. She dwelt instead on the fact that 'Dudu has all the material for happiness and [yet] his life is a torment to him' and on the fact that her husband might have encompassed her brother's death. Unwilling to proffer advice lest it precipitate another tragedy, she resolved to write 'loving letters and pretend not to notice'[195] (a tactic adopted in relation to her husband too), though a comment written just before her own marriage to the effect that 'I pray every day for Dudu's happiness but God does not agree with me evidently'[196] had never seemed so true until now.

The Grahams' summer holiday was not without delights. Of a morris dancing display (English folk songs and dances were enjoying a revival), Aelfrida recorded that she had Constantine on her right, Hubert Henderson (more in love with her than ever) on her left, John Layard ('still [looking] like a sentimental parrot') at her feet, and a new admirer, Eardley Davidson ('simple and modest, with a tremendous capability for hero worship)[197] whispering in her ear, and asked herself 'I didn't do badly, did I?' Other Little Friends also appeared ('Constantine doesn't mind. [They] ask him to lunch …')[198] though their visits were hard work: Frank Stokoe, 'extraordinarily fond of me … there does seem a chance that Fidelio should care for the real me' (as opposed to Constantine who 'says he loves me as much as ever but … I know it was not I whom he loved, but his own glorified imaginings')[199], and Tommy Altounyan, regarded as 'having such great spirituality' as to be above temptation but anxious to confide that 'there were times when he had not wished to live ... and just clutched at pleasure to cheat his pain'. (But 'how terrible were the forces of evil if even he could not withstand them'.)[200] Little wonder that she noted 'quiet at Le Vésinet will be – adorable! I can't stand all this intimacy'. Only Willie Searle, 'smile, sweetness and all', was uncomplicatedly supportive.[201]

Toward the end of her stay in England Aelfrida, Agatha, and Alethea spent two weeks in Hessle with Anatolia. (The latter passed the summer months in Hessle to avoid Paris's sultry heat and to assure local Mrs Grundys that she had not wholly deserted her husband.) Thinking she had effected a rapprochement, Aelfrida was surprised to find Anatolia 'particularly nasty'[202]; the coincidence between Anatolia's attitude and Constantine's recent solo visit to Hessle (he had returned to Fordfield on 29 June and left for Paris the following day) must have struck her because information imparted by son to mother provided ammunition for Anatolia's wounding remarks. Discovery inspired a lengthy poem in which she describes in terms more flowery but no less expressive than those of *Winter* or *Critic and Poet* the divergence of interests between herself and her husband, one of whose bullying tactics was 'pulling me up by the roots to see how I am growing'.[203]

*Kingdoms*, subtitled 'A dialogue of no particular time or place', is written in the form of a blank verse playlet with two characters, a king and a poet. The poet is Aelfrida herself in the guise of a rosy-cheeked youth; the king is Constantine, whom the Oracle and Chiara had once called 'Constantine the Great', giving him a picture of the Emperor Constantine to underscore the joke. The poem begins with the king asserting his power over the poet: "Beggar, salute your king! ... I am the king / And here within my kingdom's ample bounds / All things are mine' but ends with the king's reluctant admission that powerful as he is, he is not free, and that the poet owns a boundless kingdom of the spirit and of the imagination in which he is both all-powerful ("where I live / I reign") and free, owing allegiance only to his creator and inspirer, the "God of all worlds".[204] As a refutation of Constantine's behaviour and a demonstration of her own spiritual (if not emotional or physical) freedom, the poem could hardly be more revealing.

*Kingdoms*' reference to the "mutterings of distant wars" which keep the king awake at night (the poet enters "the crowded halls of sleep" where he dreams vividly) intimated an end to the Grahams' Parisian sojourn and contributed to further deterioration of their relationship. On 1 August 1914 Aelfrida wrote 'it seems almost wicked to write about one's own little affairs with this cloud of impending war ... hanging over us', though she recorded that on her arrival at Le Vésinet the previous day (in view of the worsening political situation, she left her daughters in Cambridge) Constantine had received her 'rapturously' and had given her the impression that he needed her by his side.[205]

Arriving in Paris after a crossing illuminated by 'searchlights flashing across the water from battleships', she found chaos: 'soldiers guarding the stations and panic everywhere ... a partial famine of provisions ... everyone in a stew either about their men folk ordered to join the colours or their investments'. At 5.30pm an official paraded the streets of Le Vésinet proclaiming the mobilisation order due to come into force at midnight 'so things must be pretty bad'; at 6.30pm Constantine returned from the Consulate to tell her that the First Secretary had said "We have done our utmost. We are now in the hands of God". ('When First Secretaries begin to talk about God', Aelfrida noted, 'one knows that matters are serious'.) He also informed her that she and Octavie must leave for England immediately and that he himself would remain *en poste* for the time being. Aelfrida and Octavie therefore 'turned the key in the door of our little house and left everything as it stood, furniture, silver, clothes, everything'[206] and with what they could carry in two handgrips caught the last boat train to leave Paris.

Although a comment made on 4 August 1914 ('I was not a long time in France, was I?')[207] suggests that Aelfrida's Parisian episode was over, she remained spiritually in Paris for the rest of her life. Like Constantine, albeit for a wholly different reason, she 'accepted Paris' and although she disapproved of much of what she found (it was not only Anatolia who associated with 'crazy people, *exaltés* – mostly women – pseudogeniuses, cosmopolitans, mystics and poets' there), what she found was to remain with her and influence the tenor of her life forever. The Grahams' stay in Paris, though relevant to their complex marital situation, was more relevant still insofar as it formed the *mise-en scène* for one of the most significant events in Aelfrida's life to date, more significant in view of what was to transpire than discovery of her husband's flirtations or that he no longer found her physically or intellectually attractive: in Paris, Aelfrida was to find the 'magus' whose '*ravissements*' she sought in the last line of *A qui la gloire?*

*A qui la gloire?*, written sometime prior to 1910, was published in Aelfrida's anthology of that year, *To Malise*. The anthology was reviewed apparently sympathetically but actually (and especially if one knew the true identity of the reviewer) tongue in cheek by one 'AC Hobbs', his review appearing in Volume 1 No10 of a new magazine, *The Equinox*. Compared to other lukewarm reviews and in particular contrast to comments from family and friends (and possibly worse from

Constantine), 'AC Hobbs" review of Aelfrida's volume of "sonnets serious and not so serious", those "not so serious" to be enjoyed by readers "blessed, or cursed with a strain of gentle flippancy" and those serious "portraying spiritual yearning with impelling earnestness and artistic imagery" and manifesting a "palpitating thrill of womanhood in its highest sense"[208], must have cheered her immensely. (She makes no comment in her diary. Hobbs' review may or may not have been one of the 'more sensible reviews' she hoped would be written by reviewers to whom she or Ernest Heffer – given the provenance and content of *The Equinox*, of which 'young Heffer' as a bookseller and publisher would have been aware, more likely Aelfrida herself – had sent review copies, but the omission itself suggests duplicity or deliberate disingenuousness or both: curious references in *Tout pour toi!* to "maddening mysteries", to "magic" songs, and to visions of "forms" so "dazzling bright" that "every dullard man" who experiences them becomes a "seer" and her inclusion of no fewer than ten poems by 'AC Hobbs', himself a 'Cambridge poet', in her next anthology suggest inside knowledge and a quid pro quo.) Under his real name 'AC Hobbs' (the initials were his own) would also be the man about whom was written the last poem in Aelfrida's manuscript collection of poems composed between 1910 and 1913, a poem dated 24 August 1913, the day on which she, holidaying in Cambridge, noted with breaking heart that she felt obliged to conceal from her parents her suspicions concerning her husband's friendship with Déla Bernet[209], concealment perpetrated both to protect Constantine and to maintain the farce of the Grahams' 'perfect marriage', a marriage into which AC Hobbs' intrusion would cause their lives to diverge even further. Three years after publication of her threat to "*cherche les ravissements du mage*", Aelfrida would find her '*mage*' (or had she already found him but does not say?) and would celebrate her discovery in verse and prose, most of which would enter the public domain.

The last line of *A qui la gloire?* ("*je cherche les ravissements du mage*" is the penultimate) reads in part "*Qu'on tourne la page!*", the French equivalent of one of Aelfrida's favourite phrases ('ah well, turn over another page') used to denote the closure of one 'episode' in her life and the opening (or so she hoped, a life without 'episodes' being not worth living) of another. But the 'page' she was about to turn and the 'episode' she was about to describe were unusual even in a life crammed with incident and though brief (eight months of living-through, a mere paragraph in a life of seventy six years) were to prove life-altering: in finding her '*mage*' she would find God again and finding God would lose not only her husband, but her children too. The name of her '*mage*' was Aleister Crowley.

## Notes

1 GCPPT 1|1|18 4 February 1913.
2 ibid. 9 February 1913.
3 ibid. 14 October 1912 and 22 January 1913.
4 ibid. 20 May 1911.
5 ibid. 21 June 1911.
6 GCPPT 1|1|19 19 June 1913.
7 GCPPT 1|1|18 11 February 1913.
8 GCPPT 1|1|13 13 August 1906.
9 GCPPT 1|1|19 11 June 1913.
10 GCPPT 1|1|18 26 April 1913.
11 A letter from 'Silvia Barrington' to 'Catherine Sutherland' in *Vision Triumphant* describes the confessional role played by the latter relative to undergraduate 'Noel Ashton', 'Noel' having informed Silvia that "quite a lot of men he knows go to [Catharine] for advice about spiritual difficulties". (Tillyard, Ae. *Vision Triumphant* p11.)
12 GCPPT 1|1|19 18 September 1913.
13 GCPPT 1|1|18 26 April 1913.
14 GCPPT 1|1|19 28 January 1914.
15 ibid. 26 May 1914.
16 William Cavendish Searle, born in 1887, was the second son of a former Master of Pembroke College whose elder son, Charles, later a doctor, was Julius' contemporary at St Faith's. Aelfrida's *Sonnet written because Willie and "Bun" came to see us just as Constantine was leaving* describes an occasion when Willie's welcome was subdued; Constantine was about to leave for Panama, so impromptu visitors interrupted what Aelfrida had hoped would be an evening of 'tender farewells'. ("Bun" Worthington tactfully did not stay long but Willie lingered.) The unpublished sonnet, written on 23 July 1912, expresses Aelfrida's current difficulties with maintaining friendships when she is grief-stricken but determined, for Constantine's sake, to "strike up a brave full chord / On laughter's lute".
17 GCPPT 1|1|18 9 February 1913.
18 ibid. 11 February 1913.
19 ibid. 12 February 1913.
20 ibid. 15 February 1913.
21 ibid. 18 February 1913. Ernest Raik Riddell ('Tommy') Altounyan (1889–1962), surgeon and poet, was then an undergraduate at Emmanuel College. He later worked in the eponymous Altounyan Hospital in Aleppo, founded by his father. (Details of Tommy Altounyan's life are taken from the *ODNB* entry of his son, Roger Altounyan. Vol 1 p906).
22 GCPPT 1|1|18 20 February 1913.
23 ibid. 6 May 1913.
24 ibid. 17 May 1912. So swarthy was Tommy's skin that on being awarded his MD at Cambridge in 1916, he was congratulated by the Regius Professor of Surgery on his excellent command of English! (GCPPT 1|1|21 31 October 1916).
25 GCPPT 1|1|19 4 July 1913.
26 GCPPT 1|1|19 11 June 1913.
27 ibid. 1 and 16 June 1913.
28 ibid. 17 June 1913.
29 Hubert Douglas Henderson (1890–1952) was an economist whose lengthy and distinguished academic and political career is described in the *ONDB* vol 26 pp318–320. Reference will be made to episodes relevant to his relationship with Aelfrida as they occur.
30 GCPPT 1|1|18 22 October 1912.
31 ibid. 18 and 22 October 1912.
32 ibid. 22 January 1913.
33 GCPPT 1|1|19 31 May 1913.
34 ibid. 1 June 1913.
35 ibid. 4 July 1913.
36 ibid. 11 June 1913.
37 Père Hubert, the French army padre in Aelfrida's 1919 novel *Vision Triumphant*, owes more than his name to Hubert Henderson.

38 Frank Woodyer Stokoe (1882–1952) graduated from Caius College, Cambridge, with a degree in mediaeval and modern languages. His life as an academic was spent largely in Cambridge, where he acted as supervisor in modern languages to various colleges; he was appointed Lecturer in French in 1930. Before and after graduating he wrote and published poetry.

39 GCPPT 1|1|18 10 March 1913.

40 The name was probably derived from Stokoe's poem *Three Songs to Fidelio,* shown by him to Aelfrida in the spring of 1913. She must also have read his poetry in *The Cambridge Magazine.*

41 GCPPT 1|1|18 20 February 1913.
GCPPT 1|1|19 29 June 1913.

42 GCPPT 1|1|18 20 February 1913. Fidelio was less enthusiastic over poems included in Aelfrida's 1916 anthology *The Garden and the Fire,* informing her that some were "bad – bad – very bad" and saying of another that "if the object of poetry is to produce a slight feeling of vertigo, you had better put *this* in". On this occasion Aelfrida deemed him 'over severe', albeit with faultless taste (GCPPT 1|1|21 8 September 1916).

43 GCPPT 1|1|18 10 March 1913. *Tollkopf on Dream and other Poems* by F W Stokoe was published in 1922.

44 ibid.

45 Aelfrida's perspicacious poem *The Moral Tale of a Man of Gotham whom Nature intended to be lonely* (GCPPT 2/5), dedicated 'to Fidelio', was written on 10 March 1913. She does not say if she showed it to the man who inspired it; it remained unpublished.

46 GCPPT 1|1|19 4 June 1913.

47 GCPPT 1|1|18 25 April 1913.

48 GCPPT 1|1|18 6 May 1913.
GCPPT 1|1|19 14 June 1913.

49 Street directories have Mrs Stokoe domiciled at 157 Chesterton Road where her son was visited by Aelfrida in the early years of the Great War. In 1918 she was living in lodgings in Maids' Causeway in the house, according to Aelfrida, in which her own mother, Catharine Wetenhall, was born (GCPPT 1|1|22 8 July 1918).

50 GCPPT 1|1|19 14 June 1913.

51 ibid. 16 June 1913.

52 Tillyard, Ae. *Marrying a Stranger* p 253 (GCPPT 2|6).

53 GCPPT 1|1|18 22 February 1913. Two of Aelfrida's comments are significant in this context: 1911–13 was the period covered by poems written after the publication of *To Malise* in 1910 and to find a publisher to bear the cost of a subsequent anthology was important for she had insufficient money of her own to pay for another subscription edition; attempts to raise money 'to publish more poems' by writing 'vile pot-boilers' for popular magazines do not seem to have met with much success (GCPPT 1|1|18 13 January 1912). It is unlikely, however, that the popular magazine and the 'pot-boiler' to which she slightingly refers were respectively *The Cambridge Magazine* and the amusing article *A Guide to Modern Verse* (by-lined 'Elfred Kendal', as it were 'Elfrida Likened') which appeared in it early in 1913, but revealingly, of the five poems given as exemplars of how to write 'modern verse', the first is a pale imitation of almost any of her own, the second (*The Mystic*) a poem which like many of hers, "suggests ineffable things". The third, a "New Art" one "throw[ing] over all trammelling conventions of meter and rhyme", with its American–Indian theme may be a spoof of Constantine's Bostonian verse. The fourth describes "a little town in Hants" which is "awfully jolly" and may refer obliquely to her visit to 'Ventnor'; the fifth (*The Irish*) spoofs her own *The Irish Poet*. The article concludes with the sentiment that "to write poetry is easier than you thought" and encourages its reader to collect and publish his or her own poetic efforts, especially as "it is … most impressive to sign your name in its fullest form" (as Aelfrida herself did) "when your anthology is published" (*The Cambridge Magazine* vol II No 9 18 January 1913 pp 218–219). From the article's concluding lines it is possible to deduce

that Elfred/Aelfrida had a second anthology in mind prior to meeting Frank Stokoe for the first time on 21 January 1913 and that their meeting was the catalyst rather than the inspiration for her preparing to do so.

54 GCPPT 1|1|18 18 October 1912.

55 ibid. 6 March 1913.

56 The appointment of Sir Arthur Quiller-Couch (1863–1944) to a chair whose previous incumbent had been the respected scholar Arthur Verrall (obit 1912) caused some consternation in Cambridge University circles, for 'Q' was both an Oxonian and better known as a novelist and anthologist. Eustace Tillyard's *The Muse Unchained* (p 39) suggests that 'Q's' appointment was politically motivated, being a reward for services rendered to the Liberal Party.

57 Tillyard, EMW. ibid.

58 GCPPT 1|1|18 28 February 1913.

59 GCPPT 1|1|35 14 November 1928.

60 *The Cambridge Magazine* vol II No 13 15 February 1913 p 319, review of Quiller-Couch's second lecture by 'C.M.A.'

61 ibid. vol II No 15 1 March 1913 pp 395–396.

62 ibid. vol II No 19 26 April 1913 p 483, article entitled *Cambridge and the Poets.* 'Q's' lectures were later included in his book entitled *On the Art of Writing,* published in 1916.

63 GCPPT 1|1|18 28 February 1913.

64 Ernest Heffer was the son of William Heffer, founder of the eponymous Cambridge firm of publishers, printers, and booksellers.

65 GCPPT 1|1|18 23 February 1913.

66 ibid. 28 February 1913.

67 ibid. 6 May 1913.

68 ibid. 3 and 10 March 1913. Aelfrida did, however, thank Frank Stokoe in her preface for his "helpful criticism and advice".

69 KCA JMK|PP|45|123|1. Letter from Aelfrida to Maynard Keynes of 21 July 1913.

70 GCPPT 1|1|18 19 April 1913.

71 ibid. 25 May 1913.

72 *Cambridge Poets 1900–1913* Introduction pp xiii–xv. 'Q's' savaging of Aelfrida's anthology did not go unavenged, a reviewer writing on 1 January 1914 that "Sir Arthur Quiller-Couch seems to be entirely out of sympathy with the poets of his new university. Possibly he was only called in because he is such an experienced hand at writing introductions to popular anthologies" (KCA RCB|X|82 Cutting from *The Literary World*).

73 GCPPT 1|1|19 10 November 1913.

74 GCPPT 1|1|19 24 May 1913.

75 ibid. 18 May 1913.

76 GCPPT 1|1|18 2 June 1911.

77 Stokoe's *Ode to Earthly Joy* may have been the poem Aelfrida liked to think was written for her, in which case it would have special significance as an epigraph (she later quoted the four lines in *A Little Road-Book for Mystics* p 17 and in *Can I be a Mystic?* p 14, in each case without attribution), but another poem (*We two are on the self-same planet*) in *Cambridge Poets* (p178) seems more appropriate insofar as it refers to an "ineffectual song" sung by one of "we two" to another in "Cambridge town", and yet another (*Sonnet,* in *The Cambridge Magazine* vol II No 19 26 April 1913 p 490) more appropriate still given that in it 'FWS' informs his reader that his heart "were yours with little pains" but suggests that should 'reader' refuse, it will be *his* (or her) loss as well as his own. All five of Stokoe's poems from *Cambridge Poets* were reprinted in *Tollkopf on Dream*; of those, two (*Three songs to Fidelio* and *Ode to Earthly Joy*) first appeared in Aelfrida's anthology.

78 GCPPT 1|1|7 7 June 1901.

79 None of Aelfrida's poems in the printed version of *Cambridge Poets* (pp 189–197) are provenanced; all are dated and placed in manuscript (GCPPT 2/5). In all three anthologies thematic similarities are disguised by the relevant poems appearing on widely separated pages in different sections or even in different volumes published several years apart.

80 GCPPT 1|1|7 1 February 1911.

81 ibid. 25 March 1911.

82 ibid. 8 March 1911.

83 ibid. 18 March 1911

84 ibid. 18 March 1911.

85 GCPPT 1|1|18 30 June 1911.

86 KCA RCB|X|82 Cutting from *The New Age* of December 1913. The reviewer was also harsh about 'Q's' introduction and deplores the appearance in the anthology of poetesses from Newnham and Girton, Cambridge's "parasitical colleges".

87 ibid. Cutting from *The Literary World* of 1 January 1914.

88 ibid. Cutting from the *Manchester Guardian*, of 11 February 1914.

89 ibid. Cutting from *The Morning Post* of 4 December 1913.

90 *Poetry and Drama* Vol. I June/July 1913 pp 489–491.

91 *The Cambridge Magazine* vol 3 No. 9 6 December 1913 p 221.

92 *The Granta* vol XXVII No. 605 24 January 1914 pp 143–144. Of the article, Aelfrida's diary records 'there is a mock review of *Cambridge Poets* with parodies, all written by me, in this week's *Granta*. What price versatility!' (GCPPT 1|1|19 30 January 1914).

93 GCPPT 1|1|18 26 April 1913.

94 Freyer's chief claim to fame as a publisher's reader was his rejection of James Joyce's *Ulysses*, another work far removed in spirit from his own.

95 GCPPT 1|1|19 14 June 1913.

96 Fidelio's reaction to Aelfrida's *Puff by Parody* may be gauged by a poem published three months later, *An Unspoken Dialogue,* which describes the hurt inflicted on him by an unnamed person and the indifference shown by that person to his sufferings. Aelfrida was, of course, in Paris when the poem appeared but she appears to have had access to *The Cambridge Magazine* (and *The Granta*) and could hardly have remained unaware of the poem's significance. Her lack of comment is on a par with her omission from her diary of any mention of the stinging reviews of *Cambridge Poets* or of positive or negative reactions to her 'parodies'. *An Unspoken Dialogue* appears in *The Cambridge Magazine* vol III No. 19 25 April 1914 pp 514.

97 GCPPT 1|1|20 20 July 1915.

98 ibid. 22 July and 4 September 1915.

99 GCPPT 1|1|19 6 August 1913.

100 GCPPT 1|1|20 4 September 1915.

101 ibid. 22 July 1915.

102 Aelfrida avoids charges of nepotism by disguising the relationship (at least as far as reviewers were concerned) by using her and Constantine's former surnames as pen names and by calling herself Mrs Constantine Graham in her bibliography. Apart from two articles in the *Independent Review,* Constantine's contribution to Cambridge Poets constitutes his entire published *oeuvre* and this, one suspects, only because his wife was the anthology's compiler.

103 *The Red Admiral* by 'Major Michaelides' first appeared in the *MCJ* of September 1907 (GCPPT 2/2a); it also appears in GCPPT 2/2 in conjunction with poems written in Odessa. Aelfrida refers to Constantine reading this and another poem aloud in Arlington Heights on 29 July 1909 (GCPPT 1|1|17).

104 *To a King's Man* (originally *Triolet*) is the poem written on 10 July 1911 during Eric Silvanus' tempestuous visit to Cambridge in which he declared his love for Aelfrida. The manuscript version (GCPPT2/2) is marked with a cross to show that it must be published 'whatever else is not' and an 'alpha plus' to show its importance.

105 The published version *The Forest of Massachusetts* omits 26 lines of the manuscript version (GCPPT 2/2). The omissions provide the poem with a tautness and thematic flow lacking in the earlier version but Aelfrida does not state whether she or Constantine revised the poem to better effect. A comparison of the manuscript and published versions of *To My Father* shows that some alterations were made at the time of composition, others before its appearance in *Cambridge Poets.*

The earlier alterations are certainly by Constantine; the later ones may be his or his wife's.

106 GCPPT 1|1|21 9 March 1916. By context, Constantine's criticisms were earlier than Aelfrida's diary entry.

107 The poem appears in *The Garden and the Fire* (p 49) in the section entitled 'poems about all sorts of things'.

108 It is probably significant that the line of the poem in which this phrase occurs is so arranged that it begins with the capitalised word 'Soul'; an aspect of Christian doctrine as believed by Aelfrida was that God (for her, the 'Soul' of the earth) 'breathed' life into men's souls while they were still within the womb. Also of significance is that 'Poet's' reference to being the 'pipe' through which 'thought' is channelled may refer to the Hindu belief that sound (*shabda*) is a manifestation of the single impersonal Absolute (*brahman*) in words and that only in this way can Godhead be revealed and made comprehensible.

109 *The People of God*, written in Cambridge on 20 June 1913, was later published in the 'Mystical Poems' section of *The Garden and the Fire* (pp 70–71) under the title *Fundamental Differentiations of the Absolute.*

110 GCPPT 1|1|19 25 May 1914. The 'Peccavi' reference is to Sir Charles Napier's (possibly apocryphal) coded telegram concerning British annexation of a portion of Indian territory (Sind) early in the nineteenth century.

111 GCPPT 1|1|18 4 May 1913.

112 ibid. 19 April and 4 May 1913.

113 ibid. 19 April 1913.

114 ibid. 11 May 1913.

115 GCPPT 1|1|19 14 May 1913.

116 ibid. 24 May 1913.

117 ibid. 25 May 1913.

118 ibid. 24 May 1913.

119 ibid.

120 GCPPT 1|1|18 22 February 1913. Constantine's appointment dated from 1 February 1913.

121 ibid. 19 December 1912 (retrospective account). Lord Dufferin was diplomat Terence Hamilton-Temple-Blackwood (1886–1918), second Marquess of Dufferin and Ava.

122 GCPPT 1|1|18 19 December 1912 (retrospective account).

123 ibid. 22 and 28 February 1913.

124 Tillyard, Ae. *Marrying a Stranger* p 271.

125 Tillyard, Ae. *Marrying a Stranger* p 271.

126 GCPPT 1|1|18 3 September 1912. The letters were later destroyed.

127 ibid. 19 December 1912 (retrospective account). Aelfrida records that the Foreign Office later praised Constantine 'in the highest terms for [his] work in Panama' (GCPPT 1|1|19 24 May 1913).

128 GCPPT 1|1|18 22 February 1913.

129 ibid. 6, 7, and 10 July 1913. The entry for 6 July is mistakenly headed '6 June'.

130 Adler, K. et al. p12.

131 GCPPT 1|1|15 6 January 1908.

132 GCPPT 1|1|19 30 September 1913.

133 GCPPT 1|1|22 20 February 1918. Guy-Charles Croz' initials (GCC) are those placed by Aelfrida above two poems (*La Nuit* and *A la Soeur*) which appear in *To Malise* as coming 'From Les Auteurs Français'. Aelfrida had not then met M. Croz but may have heard of him from Anatolia during her recent visit to the Grahams in Emden. Guy-Charles may have been a poet; his Franco–Algerian father certainly was.

134 GCPPT 1|1|19 10 July 1913.

135 ibid. 17 August 1913.

136 Adler, K. et al. p71, quoting Ford, M. *American Society in Paris* in *Cosmopolitan* May 1893 vol 15 pp 72–79.

137 ibid. p 71.

138 Lucien Monod, described by Aelfrida as looking like 'an emancipated puritan' (he was of Huguenot descent), a man with whom she 'got

intimate in about ten minutes' (GCPPT 1|1|19 12 July 1913) had an American wife of Scottish descent.

139 Adler, K. et al. p 84.

140 GCPPT 1|1|15 6 January 1908.

141 GCPPT 1|1|18 22 February 1913.

142 GCPPT 1|1|19 3 September 1913. Le Vésinet, though 'practically country' (GCPPT 1|1|19 12 July 1913), stood in the same relationship to Paris as Arlington Heights to Boston and, like Arlington Heights, was conveniently accessible by train from the metropolis. The area had formerly encompassed a forest-park set out by Henri IV but derelict since the revolution of 1789. With the coming of the railway in 1837 Le Vésinet developed into a fashionable suburb of garden city appearance.

143 GCPPT 1|1|19 12 July and 3 September 1913.

144 ibid. 30 August 1913.

145 ibid. 8 September 1913.

146 ibid. 3 September 1913. A '*cigogne*' is a stork, hence the allusion to 'wings'.

147 Octavie was later the subject of a poem (*In France*) in Aelfrida's *Verses for Alethea* (p 5): "I had a nurse called Octavie / Who came from Couy, Cher". Octavie, an unmarried mother, was apparently 'very sweet with the children' (GCPPT 1|1|19 15 April 1915).

148 GCPPT 1|1|18 19 April 1913.

149 GCPPT 1|1|19 14 November 1913 and 21 January 1914. Emile Dalcroze (1865–1950) a Swiss composer and pianist, invented the practice of rhythmic gymnastics (eurhythmics) as an adjunct to the teaching of music but later developed it into an educational system in which harmonious body movements to a musical accompaniment were supposed to instil into the practitioner both bodily grace and a sense of rhythm sympathetic to, and deriving from, the rhythms of nature. Aelfrida had made much use of the Dalcroze method in her French classes at the County School for Girls, particularly with reference to songs (of which Dalcroze composed more than a thousand) and was now educating her young daughters along the same lines. Dalcroze eurhythmics, usually termed 'music and movement', remained popular in the education of girls well into the twentieth century.

150 GCPPT 1|1|19 29 April 1914.

151 ibid. 12 May 1914.

152 ibid. 11 January 1914.

153 ibid. May 1914.

154 ibid. 11 March 1914.

155 ibid. 26 September 1914.

156 ibid. 26 May 1914.

157 ibid. 4 November 1913.

158 ibid. 19 March 1914.

159 ibid. 18 July 1913. Déla Bernet had been for seventeen years the mistress of Franco-Algerian author Paul Margueritte (1860–1918) but had been deserted by him not long before her introduction to Constantine Graham.

160 GCPPT 1|1|22 18 February 1918.

161 GCPPT 1|1|19 24 August 1913.

162 GCPPT 1|1|22 18 February 1918.

163 GCPPT 1|1|19 24 April 1914.

164 ibid. 6 October 1913.

165 ibid.

166 ibid. 22 December 1913. The Consul-General of the time was Everard Huddlestone Gastrell. He was commissioned in 1916, joined the Indian Army and ended the war as a lieutenant-colonel. Although biographical details in *Who Was Who* describe his post-war career in the Consular Service, no mention is made of his pre-war Parisian post. Seemingly still *en poste* in March 1914, he appears to have left Paris soon after for both then and in 1913 Constantine describes himself as Acting Consul-General.

167 GCPPT 1|1|19 24 April 1914.

168 ibid. 8 March 1914.

169 ibid. 20 December 1913.

170 ibid. 26 December 1913.

171 ibid. 24 July 1913.

172 ibid. 30 August 1913.

173 ibid. 8 April 1914.

174 GCPPT 1|1|18 19 April 1913.

175 GCPPT 1|1|19 23 May 1914.

176 ibid. 25 May 1914.

177 ibid. 3 February 1914.

178 ibid. 6 March 1914.

179 ibid. 25 May 1914.

180 ibid. 12 February 1914.

181 ibid. 12 February 1914.

182 ibid. 11 March 1914.

183 ibid. 27 April 1914.

184 The poems were later published in *The Garden and the Fire*, (pp 27 and 49), *Winter* in the section entitled 'Songs about Love' (the poem, though complete as it stands, appears unfinished; Aelfrida recorded on 27 April that Constantine's 'episode' declaration had interrupted composition of a poem); *Critic and Poet* in 'Poems about all sorts of things'. No manuscript version exists of either poem.

185 GCPPT 1|1|18 10 October 1912.

186 ibid. 3 August 1912.

187 ibid. 3 January 1913.

188 GCPPT 1|1|18 8 January 1913.
GCPPT 1|1|72 9 June 1955.

189 GCPPT 1|1|18 16 April 1913.

190 ibid. 16 August 1913.

191 GCPPT 1|1|19 1 August 1913.

192 ibid. 18 September 1913.

193 In *Marrying a Stranger* (p267) 'Jerome' tells 'Elizabeth' apropos 'Max' that "St Augustine said that wives should insist on their rights in these matters" and that "there are ways that a wife has of enforcing her arguments".

194 GCPPT 1|1|19 1 June 1914.

195 ibid.

196 GCPPT 1|1|14 14 January 1907.

197 GCPPT 1|1|19 29 and 31 May 1914.

198 ibid. 24 June 1914.

199 ibid. 24 June 1914.

200 ibid. 27 July 1914.

201 ibid. 28 July 1914.

202 ibid. 5 July 1914.

203 GCPPT 1|1|19 27 April 1914.

204 *Kingdoms,* written at Hessle on 7 or 8 July 1914, was later published in *The Garden and the Fire* in a section of its own.

205 GCPPT 1|1|20 1 August 1914. The assassination of Franz Ferdinand in Sarajevo on 28 June 1914, the event which precipitated the onset of the Great War, passes unmentioned in Aelfrida's diary and is dismissed by Elizabeth (p297) in *Marrying a Stranger* in a few words "Who cares about a murdered Arch-Duke?". The Germans mobilised on 1–4 August 1914, an event vividly described in *Marrying a Stranger* pp 295–297.

206 GCPPT 1|1|20 1 and 4 August 1914.

207 ibid. 4 August 1914.

208 http:||www.|the-equinox.org/vol1/no10/eqi10091.html

209 GCPPT 1|1|19 24 August 1913.

# Aleister and Sarasvati

At 4.15am on Friday 9 January 1914 Aleister Crowley, student of the occult and practitioner of Ceremonial Magic, a procedure and belief system whose "rituals and processes" aimed at "stimulating and developing the will or latent spiritual powers of the Magician"[1], recorded "a wonderful and repeated dream". Two women figured in it: "Clairbelle (Lady Walkoski)"[2] and "Aelfrida Tillyard, the beloved disciple". In the course of it, Crowley, "much to the expressed wonder and alarm of Ae.T" (*sic*), kept "reducing symbols to the Lingam and Yoni, and thence destroying them. … I remember catching up an old felt hat and explaining to Ae.T, Sarasvati, the beloved disciple, that it was only to be destroyed by first perceiving it as a disguise for the Yoni".[3]

That Aelfrida was known personally to Aleister Crowley prior to January 1914 is obvious from her appearance in the passage quoted but where and how they became acquainted needs to be examined in detail; indeed, without access to Aelfrida's diaries it is difficult to trace the connection between Crowley and a 'disciple' so 'beloved' as to be called by a ritual cognomen and with whom he was on sufficiently familiar terms to be able to discuss sexual symbolism without the necessity for explanations of the Hindu terms for the male and female genitalia. It seems, however – Aelfrida's diary entries are ambiguous – that it was through one of Aleister Crowley's acolytes that she first made his acquaintance.

Among the 'Cambridge poets' who deluged her with letters early in 1913 was Victor Neuburg, late of Trinity College, concerning whom Aelfrida commented 'he has taken up shoe-blacking as an alternative to suicide' and that Neuburg had written her 'mad letters … about his life and the state of his soul'.[4] (Seven of Neuburg's poems were to appear in *Cambridge Poets*.) On 26 April, however, she recorded excitedly that 'I have discovered *one* genius for my book, Aleister Crowley, Victor Neuburg's master … his poetry is *marvellous*… mystic or sensual or singing or majestic – and once in a way downright beastly'. (She also recorded something of Crowley's past: 'there are odd legends about him; how he used to kneel for hours in his room at Trinity so thick with incense that you could not see across; how he eloped with a clergyman's daughter and was so persistently unfaithful to her that she took to drink and they had to separate – and

**Aleister Crowley 1911 by Augustus John**
© Bridgeman Art Library

I know not what besides'.)[5] In early May she noted that Crowley himself had seized the opportunity afforded by inclusion of nine of his poems in her anthology to discuss not only how he wished them to appear but his views on 'life and being' also.[6]

That Aelfrida fell rapidly under Aleister Crowley's spell is shown by inclusion in her anthology of only two fewer of his poems than of her own and in what was intended as an anthology of Cambridge poetry written between 1900 and 1913 of a man who was a Cambridge alumnus but had left Cambridge in 1898 and paid only brief and controversial visits since then and whose chosen poems were not all written after 1900. But although inclusion could be explained by Crowley's continuing influence on Cambridge poets and poetry (the quantity of poems included was nevertheless disproportionate)[7], what reviewers chiefly objected to was Aelfrida's inadequate exercise of editorial control in devoting twenty pages to his "overblown rhetoric" (*The Manchester Guardian*) or selection from "Aleister Crowley's … strange and mystical books" poems contemplated "with considerable astonishment but little admiration" (*The Birmingham Post*; *The New Age* referred to "Mr Crowley's dusty, musty – we would like to say razzly-dazzly – mystagogery")[8], this obliging her to spring to Crowley's defence and by extension to defend her choice of him as a 'Cambridge poet' worthy of inclusion in a volume of Cambridge poets better qualified than himself in terms of chronology or literary ability.

On 12 November 1913, therefore, and shortly after the anthology's publication, she wrote a brief *Note on Ceremonial Magic* for *The Cambridge Magazine*[9], the *Note*, though she fails to note it, being ostensibly an explanation of only one – but possibly the most contentious in the present context – of Crowley's poems: *The Palace of the World*.[10] Initially rejected, supposedly because it mentioned Crowley by name, the *Note* eventually appeared on 24 January 1914 albeit without identifying the author of the poem or a book, also by him (777, defined by Aelfrida as containing "the tabulation of the data of comparative religion, with the Quabbalistic Tree of Life as a basis"), to which she refers her reader for further information. Explanation is necessary, she writes, because "so many people" have asked the meaning of the author's or editor's reference to the "lesser ritual of the pentagram", here defined by her in a spirit quite contrary to Crowley's (he defined magic as the "science and art of causing change to occur in conformation to the Will")[11] as an act performed by a 'magus' who, "having banished intruding thoughts and understood them … now waits more or less passively for … grace from on high".

The *Note* also contains a defence of Ceremonial Magic, according to Aelfrida both the precursor of experimental psychology and a practice whose aim is *"union of the soul with God"*, an exposition of the relationship of Ceremonial Magic's rituals and devices to those of Roman Catholicism, and an explanation of the poem itself. The latter section is perhaps the least convincing, not least because Aelfrida expounds the poem's meaning and imagery in wholly Christian terms, a device which leaves her reader in some doubt (as Crowley himself possibly intended) as to which 'Trinity' he refers: the Holy Trinity or Hermes Trismegistus ('thrice-greatest'), the Hellenised version of Thoth, the Egyptian god believed to deify mankind by endowing it with knowledge. She also has difficulty in convincingly associating the 'magician' or 'magus' who officiates at a Ceremonial Magic ritual with a poem whose context she describes as Christian. Furthermore, her elucidation of the poem's imagery shows that she is somewhat disingenuous in her attempts to explain it in Christian rather than Ceremonial Magic terms and in her insistence that she herself is not a magician and so is "very little acquainted with the whole subject".

The consternation felt by Aelfrida's immediate family on reading Crowley's poems with their references to a "necromantic hymn" and to "fatuous phantoms of desire"[12], her own explanations of terms used and "secret symbols" described in *The Palace of the World* (the "mother-mediator", the "holy lotos flower", the pentagram as a "symbol of man considered as microcosm of the universe") and her use of terms which do not appear in the poem itself ("*Sahasrata Chakra*", "*Malkah*", "*Binah*" etc.) but serve to show how many of Crowley's works she must have read in order to be able to elucidate his '*marvellous*' poetry, and her anthology's final poem (*Epilogue*) with its reference to "we … poets" daring to believe in and even to see the God who gave "voice and vision to their need", a poem signed pseudonymously but stylistically and contextually by their sister, daughter, or wife, can only be imagined. (Inclusion in her anthology of nine poems by a man whose literary reputation alone had something of the decadent about it was also a risky undertaking for a married woman whose family and friends had been upset by *To Malise* and whose husband was slowly climbing the ladder of promotion in the Consular Service, a service which maintained records not only of its employees' conduct but also, though less formally, of their wives'.) Furthermore, her inability to keep silent on the subject of Crowley's 'genius' outside her family circle may have resulted in information from other sources filtering back to Fordfield to increase the circle's consternation.

Friends, Little and otherwise, with whom she 'discussed Crowleyism'[13] were worried by her enthusiasm for and increasing spiritual reliance on a man whose reputation they believed dubious at best and sinister at worst. John d'Aubray Bell of Caius, whose *Spring in Montparnasse* would shortly appear in *Cambridge Poets*, told her frankly "he's the most famous – or infamous – man in England … He has a temple in London where they worship him. That's what he's doing, taking advantage of people and leading them on … And I've heard tales about him – oh, unspeakable!" Pressed further, d'Aubray Bell described Crowley's magico-mystical practices as "nothing but intellectual curiosity" and his poems as "a macédoine of words", to which Aelfrida responded "yes, but they speak straight to one, like music, without … intermediary". D'Aubray Bell's perceptive response, that her soul must be 'attuned' to Crowley's if she had no need of words to communicate with him, brought her up short and she tried to laugh the matter off ('isn't that a little startling!'), at the same time realising that d'Aubray Bell was right. With Hubert Henderson too, she found it 'a little difficult to argue' because his request that she 'throw over Crowley and his ways' chimed with her own feelings that there were 'useless and useful' practitioners, that Crowley might be one of the former, and if so, she should have nothing more to do with him. Frank Stokoe, whose poem *The Mad Magician* (soon to appear in her anthology) with its description of a wizard who builds "a palace high up in the air" and sets out to find "a darling" to inhabit it, is probably a coded reference to Crowley's on-going enticement of his friend, was blunter. Informing Aelfrida that he was 'dead, *dead* against it', warning her 'of madness etc. etc.', he begged her to abandon her own 'experiments', something which would afford him 'absolutely perfect joy'.[14]

At this point Aelfrida should have remembered both her tendency to become obsessed with 'one man … and then another' and her Molière, for Act 2 scenes 3 and 4 of *Les Femmes Savantes* contains a significant exchange between Bélise and her brothers Chrysale and Ariste, the latter warning her that the fancies ('*chimères*') she entertains are dangerous, to which she replies that they are *not* '*chimères*' ("*chimères, moi?*") but even if they *were* (and she does not believe that they are: "*je ne savais pas que j'eusse des chimères*") she would still delight in them. Hearing this, Chrysale informs Ariste that their sister is mad (*folle*); Ariste agrees, adding that her madness is increasing every day. And increase each day Aelfrida's 'chimeras' duly did though oddly interspersed with domesticity: '8 June 1913 I alternately darned Constantine's socks and read Aleister Crowley's verse – which I now understand'.[15]

There was, however, as Fidelio's reference to Aelfrida's 'experiments' shows, more to her association with Aleister Crowley than literary affinity, for by her own admission 'profoundly dissatisfied' with her spiritual state at this time, she had begun 'a kind of "yoga"' under Crowley's written direction, 'yoga' she did not consider 'religious except insofar as the mantra is sacred but useful as teaching concentration'.[16] (Her mantra was 'And in Jesus Christ, his only Son our Lord'.) On 28 May she noted that work on her 'mantra' was proving 'intensely absorbing and giving wonderful results' in terms of 'queer sensations, mind-pictures, slight loss of consciousness etc. etc'. and that mantra-induced experiences culminated 'in

a great peace, in nearness and reality of the other world and in greatly increased health and vitality'. Perhaps, she added hopefully, 'I shall grow peaceful and good without being obliged to compel myself to Roman Catholic doctrine – perhaps [even] find the church not made with hands'.[17]

The 'kind of yoga' practised by Aelfrida under Crowley's direction and as expounded by him in 1911 in the book to which she refers in a diary entry of 13 July 1913 in which she notes that she has spent 'a quiet morning with the New Testament and *Book 4*'[18], was that on which he embarked during a visit to Ceylon (now Sri Lanka) in August 1901, a visit satirised by Aelfrida in a poem entitled *The Unofficial Biography (Aleister Crowley)*: "then we hear of him in Kandy where the Buddhists came in handy / Teaching him as much of yoga as would satisfy an ogre".[19] As practised by Aelfrida under Crowley's direction, yoga involved the holding of prescribed positions, the practice of breathing exercises, the repetition of a chosen phrase (Aelfrida's 'mantra', hers being usually but not exclusively Christian) and concentration of the mind, sometimes with the assistance of a material or imagined object, a candle, say, or a coloured shape, or a crucifix. On Crowley's instructions she also embarked on a course of meditations on a chosen object or subject, sending brief written descriptions of the results of 'mantra-yoga' and meditation to him for perusal and comment.

For a woman wracked with postnatal depression, an ability to "become more of a master inside [her] own head", to shut out the "unwanted thoughts … [and] the stream of pictures, sounds and words that whirled … and whirled … day and night"[20] there ('poor little dead baby', 'the vasty halls of death'), and to overcome the 'blackness' behind which hovered the 'terrible wings of madness and suicide'[21], must have proved invaluable therapy and by conscientiously practising exercises designed to aid mental concentration by means of mental, postural, respiratory, and relaxation techniques (she recorded how much time she devoted to each), Aelfrida became able to dismiss the compulsive thoughts which tortured her. (She also, it seems, regained the ability to visualise colours 'outside the prism', something she had been able to do as a child but for which she had lost the facility as she grew up.) She also found herself able to ask her mind to ask specific questions and to receive appropriate answers while ostensibly asleep, a faculty which gave rise to a curious and unnerving coincidence: a request for a somnial answer to the meaning of a particular magic symbol was followed by feeling impelled on waking to pick up the particular volume of *The Equinox* in which the explanation appeared.[22]

In all this, of course, she was not far removed from the contemporary conviction that the basis of human life was mysterious but could be configured if one found the correct key, be this Anglo-Catholicism, Kabbalah, Buddhism, Christian Science, Theosophy, astrology, the occult, or parlour games of serious intent such as the palmistry practised on or, on a notable occasion in the Fiesole convent when her perspicacity upset a visiting priest, by herself. (Palmists, wrote Crowley, believe that the palm of the hand mirrors the man and that "there is a correspondence or analogy between ... the seen and the hidden", a sometimes unnerving example of the doctrine of correspondences or "signatures".)[23] Hence it is unsurprising to find her agog for guidance in the hope that further "psychological discoveries"[24] would enable her to command her mind to an even greater extent. But what such control mechanisms also implied was that for the first and only time in her life she lost sight of what was for her the only legitimate key to self-discovery, namely the Christian faith, in favour of a means which, as she herself was shortly to admit, could be regarded as an end in itself with all that that implied of spiritual danger to the enquiring soul. She was nevertheless determined to pursue it, but whether her still solely epistolary relationship with Aleister Crowley would have developed further had Constantine not left for France on 24 May can only be guessed at. But it was in Constantine's absence and just over a month since her first recorded contact with Crowley that Aelfrida underwent a spiritual experience more intense than that of finding herself weeping beside the bedside of a dead or dying man, of 'seeing' and 'hearing' herself and Constantine with their future children, or of 'seeing' Christ while taking Communion. She called it 'the most *real* experience of [her] life' and so shattering was its effect that although she continued to flirt with Ceremonial Magic for some months thereafter, her own particular brand of Christianity ultimately won the day.

The 'most real' experience took place on the night of 28/29 May 1913 and was recorded in her diary in real time. She began her '"Mantra Yoga" or whatever you call it' by lying on her back, arms spread out in the form of a cross. Her account then continues:

'8.55–9.05. Sense of peace strong; meditation become infinitely precious.

9.45. Read Aleister Crowley's letter.

10.00. Try to sleep. Longing to meditate unbearably strong; resist.

11.20. Can resist no longer… *Something is going to happen*. Waiting … Mantra faster and faster; visualise a great wooden cross; stinging pain in palms very keen. And then, oh my God, the cross is under

me and I nailed to it, unable to move. Pain of the nails appalling. Then with a great blaze of light Christ's essence comes down to me and wells up within me, giving spiritual joy unspeakable …'

By midnight the vision was over. Bewildered, she asked 'What has happened? I feel blinded. How can one live with God so near?' The pain in her hands persisted till morning, at which time she noticed a small bluish bruise on the palm of her right hand.[25]

Early June brought humiliation: Aleister Crowley, in the shape of '"Frater Perdurabo", as he calls his "higher self"', responded harshly to her 'Vision', advising her to give up thinking about religion for three weeks and to practice 'a little severe mind-discipline'[26] to counterbalance the intensely transcendental nature of the experience. (He also prescribed mental exercises in which he selected a symbol and bade her visualise a door with the symbol painted on it, then to imagine herself passing through the door and 'seeing' on the other side what was supposed to bear relation to the symbol.) His chief criticism was that she had failed to distinguish between the 'inessential' (the crucifixional) and 'essential' (the union with Christ) aspects of her vision, though this, said Aelfrida, was a misjudgement because she *knew* how to distinguish one from other and that 'the "inessential" was necessary … as the chalice into which the sacred wine was poured'.[27] Subsequent communications resulted in Crowley's admission that she had achieved both the trance-like meditative state which both called '*dhyana*' and the ecstatic state of *Samadhi*, 'a state of consciousness in which the soul knows nothing but God'.[28]

The experience remained with her in spite of an active social life, greater involvement with her children, tête-à-têtes with Little Friends, and hard work on *Cambridge Poets*; indeed, not only had her meditations suddenly become so 'absolutely religious' that 'meditating on the personality of Jesus Christ' had completely replaced 'prayer that is mere begging' and left her wanting 'to empty myself that Christ may fill me', but the 'Vision' had also 'dwarfed' everything else.[29] She seemed, too, to have entered a state of "perpetual *Samadhi*" or "super-consciousness", later defined as one in which "God dwells in us and looks at the world through our eyes" or, in a more graspable analogy, in which "we are the flute and He the breath that puffs through us".[30] Resolving, however, to remain silent about her 'Vision' (she did not even discuss it with Tommy Altounyan who, it seems, had himself achieved *Samadhi* two years earlier, for fear that she too be thought 'mad' and sent away), she noted that, thanks to Aleister Crowley, she was now definitely committed to the 'Mystic Way'.[31]

The 'mystic way' to which Aelfrida believed herself committed will be described in detail in a later chapter but her reference to the idea that she might be someone to whom was vouchsafed unmediated communion and communication with God first appears in her diary in late 1902 at the point at which she borrowed William James' book *The Varieties of Religious Experience* whose lengthy chapter on Mysticism begins with the portentous words "personal religious experience has its root and centre in mystical states of consciousness".[32]

She seized upon James' statement (and chapter) with delight for in it she found confirmation of what her idiosyncratic and subjective religiosity included of the irruption of transient but ineffable and illuminative experiences into her daily life and mundane world; subsequent discussions with people she trusted would take her questions seriously demonstrate her conviction that she had found an explanation at last. (And this even though an attributed statement – "Mysticism? All bosh. Mystic's only another name for lunatic!"[33] – must have given her reason to pause and to decide not to publicise her experiences lest she too be thought 'lunatic'.) It was therefore 'full of [a] new thirst for *mysticism*'[34] that eighteen months later she entered the Florentine Duomo to pray. To find in Aleister Crowley (or think she found; his article entitled *The Dangers of Mysticism* with its references to mystics combining the "morphino-maniac's feeling of *bien-être*" with the delusions of a tertiary syphilitic or feeding themselves on their own imaginations and persuading themselves of their own "attainments" i.e. of having achieved knowledge of a realm so far beyond the boundaries of everyday thought that they eventually appear as "moral and spiritual narcissi [perishing] in waters of illusion"[35] cannot have made happy reading in 1913), a man who not only underwent extraordinary experiences himself but had also begun to instruct her in the complex rituals by means of which she could achieve even more numinous experiences *at will,* brought comfort and joy and convinced her that here indeed was the '*mage*' she sought.

Three letters and a present later, reciprocated by Aelfrida with the offering of a gold necklace and other gifts, her enthusiasm for Crowley increased: 'I have been reading the truly marvellous account of his Quest for Truth, his study of mysticism in many lands … The man is a great religious genius … [his] psychology is marvellous, he seems to have all the wisdom of East and West in one; he is certainly an adept at handling the human mind. And certainly he has devoted more energy and courage to the task of Union with God than the rest of us'. In spite of this, she expressed doubts concerning Crowley's association of Mysticism and Magic: 'why choose magic? … surely these complicated *means* … are very dangerous snares to the human soul?' Perhaps, she rationalised, 'magic is merely intended as a training and as a *test*', deciding, in spite of being 'infinitely prejudiced against magic', to reserve judgement until she delved deeper. It was only as she did so, using the contents of the 'present' (it included nine numbers of *The Equinox*, journal of the A∴A∴, the occult brotherhood founded by Crowley in 1907/8, and the copy of 777 referred to in her *Cambridge Magazine* article and described in her diary as 'the table of correspondences of religious symbols of all nations')[36] that she lost her scepticism. Loss was encouraged by another 'most wonderful mystic experience' nine days after her first, an experience 'more wonderful, though less dramatic, than the other'.[37] It was not, unfortunately, recorded in a diary whose reader was referred instead (as elsewhere during this period of Aelfrida's life) to 'records', later, alas, destroyed, or reproduced only in etiolated form.

At this point too, she gained a name for her own 'higher self'– Sarasvati – a name 'not chosen by Fra. P. nor by myself but miraculously "given"'. By whom she does not say, but anxious lest it 'turn out to be something laughably unsuitable', she turned to the *Encyclopaedia Britannica*. Sarasvati, she discovered, was in Hindu mythology 'a goddess of rivers and woods' (a sacred river also bore her name but in keeping with the life of the woman who bore its eponym, it is now classified as 'lost', its course invisible save to satellite imagery), wife of Brahma of the Hindu Trinity, and mother of the Vedas, books containing Hindu sacred lore.[38] Sarasvati is also the goddess of wisdom and learning and in one of the aspects (an older woman of spotless beauty) in which she appears at different times of day a symbol of the Light seen at the moment of ecstasy by one in an advanced stage of spiritual development i.e. 'the light of mystic illumination'[39], by extension the presence of God "apprehended as light", light subsequently worshipped as a divinity in its own right "by ignorant men".[40] Pursuing the subject in Edouard Schuré's *L'Évolution Divine*, Aelfrida discovered not only that 'the mystic way was not without lamps' but also that Schuré's description of Sarasvati's symbolisation of the divine Light exactly expressed that of which she herself believed her 'mystical communion with the divine' had always consisted, namely a supernatural light penetrating to the core of her being and giving rise to inexplicable felicity.[41] And it was as 'Sarasvati' that she composed her epilogist poem in *Cambridge Poets*.

By 1 July 1913 Aelfrida's longing to *meet* Crowley was intense: he 'has been the means of my learning so much … I *must* see Crowley for myself. *Can* his words be so good … and the man so contemptibly and yet so superbly bad?'[42] Dreaming about him on three successive nights, she decided 'to get to the bottom of this Crowley mystery' and to 'dream true' about him. ('Dreaming true' involved willing herself into a state of somnolence in which she dreamed about a chosen subject; though unable to control the course or imagery of the dream, both were invariably appropriate and sometimes even predictive.) In a 'true dream' carried out on the night of 22/23 July, she describes her 'astral body' or ethereal alter ego travelling to a small temple on whose walls there were 'curious signs … and a life-sized crucifix'. Crowley appears in 'rather impressive white robes' and offers her a crystal cup of unidentified liquid which she refuses to drink but inhales instead. At this she feels 'an ecstasy of fire and wonder run through [her] veins'. Clasping the crucifix she experiences Christ's soul passing into hers 'most divinely filling [her] with perfection'. Turning to Crowley, she flings away the goblet because it is 'tinged with the physical', telling him 'I know there is still sensuality in your soul. I am called Sarasvati, the light of the pure soul. Listen to me and renounce power over others!' The dream ends with Crowley's disappearance, the arrival of two angels, one white, representing Crowley's 'Holy Guardian Angel', the other black (in occult lore, 'the Guardian of the Threshold', an entity which deliberately conceals his goal from a seeker of a vision of the astral world), the shattering of the temple, and the re-entrance of Aelfrida's astral body into her physical one. Her flippant but rather frightened comment on waking 'isn't it just a little too odd' shows that this initial experiment of 'dreaming true' about Aleister Crowley worried her more than she liked to admit; she would, she added, give up yogic practices for the time being and be 'purely critical and rational'.[43]

Two further 'true dreams' involving Crowley occurred on the night of 11/12 September. In the first, Aelfrida finds herself in a time and place 'where everyone believed that he was a prophet'. She is struggling to understand one of his books when her maid (who, with the inconsequentiality of dreams, is doing the dusting) comments scornfully that they are no harder to understand than the Book of Revelations or Mary Baker Eddy's Christian Science magazine *Science and Health,* adding wisely that 'people won't grasp that they must offer *all* themselves to God, evil and all, not just pick out the little bits of themselves that they happen to think are good'. At this point Crowley appears, looking very ill. He lies on the floor and brings up black vomit and 'a thin roll of paper' containing a 'sublime poem'. The first dream ends here. The second dream begins with Crowley at Fordfield demonstrating 'magical instruments' to Aelfrida and her father. (The Oracle is sceptical of their genuineness.) Aelfrida

and Crowley walk out onto a bare hillside together; he asks her "Sarasvati, what do you think of me?" She replies "If you can teach men how to use their faculty of apprehending God, that is enough. If you can do that well, no more would be required of you". Crossing a bridge over a gulf, she gives him both her hands in farewell, but stumbles; he saves her from falling. She walks away from him. Turning to bid him farewell, she finds him aiming a pistol at her: "No answer but death", she decides, "so be it then". But Crowley merely waves and departs and she wakes for the second time. On the breakfast table next morning she found *The Collected Works of Aleister Crowley* and *The Book of Lies.* 'Presents, I suppose … what shall I say?!!!'[44] Of the latter she wrote that it was 'either mad or written in a language that I do not understand – possibly both!' but that it nevertheless 'contains some profound sayings!'[45]

Before leaving Cambridge for Paris, Aelfrida received a letter from Crowley which seemed to provide evidence (as opposed to inaccurate or highly coloured stories) that her current idol might have feet of clay, being both 'insane' and in marked contrast to letters received earlier which were 'sane and very spiritual. This is neither!' (Frank Stokoe, to whom she showed it, suggested that Crowley was drunk when he wrote it.) Disillusioned, she continued 'Crowley has been the means of my learning so much … And it is through the hands of this man that I have had some of the most wonderful revelations of my life! … But Crowley is lewd! … Of course Crowley has a "dual personality", the mystic and the sensualist. I did but see the mystic … It is bad enough to see a fool go wrong – but a master mind! Such genius, such power, and yet –!' On 17 August she returned Crowley's letter to him: 'I wonder whether he will answer'.[46]

On 8 September, now in Paris, she received her reply, Crowley assuring her that his letter was "a try-on, a joke" because as a "Guardian of the Sanctuary" it was his business "to keep out the unworthy at all costs". (Aelfrida's comment was 'this sounds rather feeble. I reserve my judgement, however, until we meet'.) She was also, she noted, 'addling [her] brains' by reading *The Equinox,* some of which she decided was mad, some unintelligible, some 'marvellous and tragic'. (It must have been around this time that a photograph was taken of her brooding sombrely over a copy of it.) She subsequently decided 'after thinking and thinking and *thinking'* that there was 'just one use for Crowley – to answer the question "Is there a special facility to apprehend God, and, if so, how is it to be developed?"'[47] On 13 September she received a second letter in which Crowley stated "I am really innocent of pulling your leg" and announced that he did not want to be thanked for the 'mountains' or blamed for the 'valleys' experienced as she lurched between highs and lows of spiritual experience or attained or failed to attain the next stage of her quest for enlightenment, that he only wanted her "to do what you said you had done and eliminate me altogether", and that far from trying to stop her penetrating further into Ceremonial Magic, he was trying to see whether "you will allow me to keep you out". To this perceptive interpretation of her wildly fluctuating feelings vis-à-vis himself and the experiences his teachings promoted, Aelfrida replied humbly that she was 'grateful for both mountains and valleys' and enclosed in her letter 'the poem I wrote about him *By Broken Wings*'. ('He can make what he likes of it!' she confided to her diary.)[48] What Crowley 'made of' it was a poem, *The Tyler* (possibly never read by Aelfrida, but how mortifying if she did) in which he warns "chaste women of the baser sort", otherwise called the "unworthy sows" who read his works with "frowning brows", that he deliberately interlards his pronouncements with "obscene allusion" in order to confound them with "complete confusion" but that, conversely, his "Priapic epigrams" are garnished with "Virgin garlands from an angel's brow" in order to make them intelligible.[49] His immediate response, however, was to send her 'an absurd poem', *The Disciples,* dedicated to (among others) 'A.C.W.G. and H.E.H.' ('Her Excellent Husband'), a joking reference to Constantine's vice-consular position. Perhaps he was too busy to do more: he had been in Russia from early July to early September 1913 as impresario to the troupe of Ragged Ragtime Girls headed by musician Leila Waddell, during which time he had had a passionate affair and had written compendiously, his writings including his famous *Hymn to Pan* [50], and on his return to England, had had to prepare the tenth and last and longest (223 pages) part of the first volume of *The Equinox* with its 244 page supplement containing his translation of Eliphas Lévi's *The Key of Mysteries*. Aelfrida's receipt of this three months later must have made bitter reading in the light of their recent correspondence, for it contained Crowley's appended warning that "the A∴A∴ and *The Equinox* and all the rest of it are a stupid joke of Aleister Crowley's. He merely wished to see if anyone were foolish enough to take him seriously. Several have done so …" As also must reading of the 'absurd poem' with its references to her easily-identifiable married initials and to the credulity, scepticism ("an ingenious blind!") or prudishness ("a filthy insult") of those who professed to be "disciples" of "an Adept of the Holy Order", for the poem itself appeared in the same tenth part as Crowley's warning.[51]

At the time of her arrival at the Villa *La Cigogne* on 30 August 1913, Aelfrida was therefore thoroughly confused in her efforts to reconcile what she regarded as the sacred and profane aspects of Aleister Crowley's personality as revealed in his books and letters. On the one hand, he appeared to agree with her that only complete surrender to God was capable of giving answers concerning the how, why, what, and wherefore of human life on earth which ratiocination alone was too poorly equipped to provide; on the other, and in spite of believing he had 'unalterable love in every fibre', Crowley was a hater of many things she respected or held dear. Furthermore, her earlier admission of being 'prejudiced against magic' still held true insofar as 'adeptship' tended to evoke prideful or posturing behaviour and 'magick' procedures illusions which not only took on the appearance of 'reality' but were also capable of creating the satisfying belief that they evoked a 'c.w.g.', Aelfrida's shorthand for 'a closer walk with God.'[52] Worse still, on 27 September she had another 'true dream' about Crowley which she refused either to record or to relate to him because to do so would force her to admit that she was 'too far in'. Her feeling obliged to compose a letter to Herbert Adams, a would-be disciple of Crowley's, in which she employed a 'mixture of commonsense and Christianity disguised as Karma-Yoga and Bhakti-Yoga … designed to choke him off', exacerbated her anxieties, for was not Adams' view of Crowley exactly the same as hers but without her insight into the latter's baser nature? 'People', she wrote acerbically, 'shouldn't be such earnest and admirable fools'[53]; scepticism did not, however, prevent her from becoming more of an 'admirable fool' herself. Influenced by Evelina Garnier, an American friend of Anatolia's domiciled in Paris and married to a Frenchman, whose enthusiasm for Theosophy had given rise to an interest in Aleister Crowley, Aelfrida adopted Garnier's name for him: 'the Guru'.

5 October 1913 was Aelfrida's thirtieth birthday. ('I don't mind a bit'.) The following day she received a telegram: 'a silly thing … with "I am Hermes" and a caduceus inside it. If it means that Crowley is coming to Paris why doesn't he say so?'[54] Two and a half weeks later she recorded excitedly: 'who do you think walked into the Consulate yesterday? Aleister Crowley!' Constantine met him and they briefly discussed mutual interests: 'the anthology and Cambridge'. Constantine's immediate impression of Crowley was of a rather pathetic person 'cut off … from ordinary human relationships'. (This, noted Aelfrida, 'does not sound at all like the Big Red Devil of the legends'.) On 24 October she received a telegram from Crowley inviting himself to dinner that evening ("*Viendrai ce soir*")[55] and dashed out to find ingredients. She gave him roast chicken.

The evening began conventionally with the Grahams and Crowley talking about Cambridge. (Did Aleister and Aelfrida discover that they had been very near each other between 1885 and 1888, he at the Rev D'Arcy Champney's Plymouth Brethren boarding school at 51 Bateman Street, she playing with Conrad and Julius, later Crowley's near-contemporary at Tonbridge School, in Fordfield's garden a third of a mile away? Or that both had met Eusapia Palladino, he in Naples in December 1911[56], she in Cambridge with Frederic Myers? Or that between 1895 and 1898, Margaret Verrall had been Aelfrida's teacher and her husband Crowley's tutor, and given that "during Dr Verrall's tutorship generations of undergraduates were welcomed at Sunday luncheon" or to the 'open house' held in Selwyn Road afterwards[57], adolescent Frida, staying there during Eustace's attack of chicken pox, might have met undergraduate Edward Alexander – self-styled Aleister – Crowley on one of these occasions[58] and may have read his earliest ventures into verse in undergraduate magazines?) Aelfrida's initial impressions of Crowley were of 'profound sadness' ('*Mon Dieu, qu'il a souffert*') and 'extraordinary humility', evidence, she thought, of Crowley identifying his will with God's. (He also seemed rather shy.) 'As for his Don Juan reputation – yes, there are marks on his face of early excesses', but Constantine's exclamation when Crowley had gone that 'I would trust thee alone on a desert island for twenty years with him' suggests that Crowley's behaviour was irreproachable on this occasion. Physically Crowley was described by Aelfrida as 'a little shorter than I am, ugly, ungainly, growing bald on his forehead and looks ten years older than he is'. (He was just thirty-eight.) She also noted his 'extraordinary' eyes, alternatively 'wistful' and 'very piercing'.[59] Furthermore, though familiar with Crowley's appearance from photographs sent on 9 October and from illustrations in the volume of his *Collected Works* filched (after devious manoeuvres) from Ernest Heffer, she found it astounding that his physical reality as he sat talking to her in the Villa *La Cigogne* accorded exactly with his appearance in her 'true dreams', even to the brown suit he wore.

Postprandial discussions, however, produced a dramatic change in Crowley's appearance from 'sadly humble' to magisterial, a change initiated by Aelfrida asking 'how am I getting on?' Beginning shyly but becoming more animated as he spoke with 'calm authority', Crowley answered "I don't know. You have all along been a great puzzle to me". He also admitted that he found it disconcerting to have a pupil "who knows so much more about the subject than her master does", that Aelfrida had had "more spiritual consolations in a fortnight than most mystics get all their lives … higher spiritual experiences than St Paul or anyone I have ever heard of", and that because of this he rejoiced for her "in quite a

wonderful way". He also decided that she must be "an elemental, an undine" because of the way in which her soul reflected impressions of supernatural reality, an accolade Aelfrida rejected because elementals were supposed to be purely mirrors, throwing back interpretations but having no experiences of their own, and undines spirit-women who gained a soul only by marrying a mortal man and bearing his child. Lastly and perhaps significantly in view of what he already knew or had deduced about her (visualisation exercises not only enable a '*chela*' to learn something about himself but also allow a master to learn something of his pupil's "subconscious mind")[60], Crowley informed her that he had nothing more of any importance to say to her but that he was happy to continue to meet her socially because he had taken a liking to her.

Crowley's mixture of appreciation and flattery was received by Aelfrida with delight. And with scepticism: 'of course I know this is absolutely preposterous'.[61] (Constantine's views went unrecorded but preposterous was a word much used by him.) He followed it with communications on 26, 29, and 31 October in which he apologised for underestimating his pupil at the expense of his opinion of himself ("I cannot think of myself as a champion Guru with a star Chela") and sent her a 'Secret Holy Book', probably *Liber Cordis Cincti Serpente*, "an account of the relationship of an Aspirant with his Holy Guardian Angel", dictated to Crowley by Aiwass (the Holy Guardian Angel of his description) in the winter of 1907.[62] (Aelfrida's gloating comment on receiving the book was 'so now we shall see what more there is in Initiation!' albeit with the rider 'not that I am joining the A∴A∴ – oh no!')[63] Crowley also declared her "seven times blessed" and predicted that people would come to her for teaching for "you are the Light and yourself the Begetter and Manifester of Light'.[64] At this point Constantine had second thoughts regarding his wife's relationship to her 'Guru' and banned her from seeing him again. He relented sufficiently to agree to her inviting Crowley to the Villa *La Cigogne* on one further occasion after Aelfrida (who suddenly remembered that as a girl she used to perform what Crowley called 'rising on the planes' nearly every night, adding that 'I was quite as much at home on the astral or spiritual planes as I am here')[65] took her husband 'on an astral' (i.e. on a controlled out-of-body voyage, not unlike that undergone in April 1906 when, 'in a mad freak', she half-hypnotised him) during which he saw, so she said, 'peacocks and stars'. (She was much amused next day to receive a letter from Crowley asking her to take the 'dullest fool' she knew on an astral trip 'to see if I can guide –'.)[66] Crowley's and Aelfrida's second and probably last meeting (her account contains ambiguities) took place in Constantine's presence on 9 November, Aelfrida being gratified to find Crowley gazing at her 'with the loving pride of an artist in his work' and Crowley seizing the opportunity to proselytise both Grahams, giving them 'an intensely interesting lesson on 777', not all of which Aelfrida understood ('I can follow him … when he is talking psychology. The Universe is beyond me!') though she appreciated the magnitude of the gigantic task he had set himself namely of discovering 'the … machinery of the Universe and the workings of the human mind'.[67]

The immediate results of Crowley's second visit were Constantine having 'serious thoughts' of breaking up the relationship between Crowley and his wife because he felt the latter's behaviour vis-à-vis the former was 'too discipular'[68] and Aelfrida herself 'doing an astral' on Crowley as a consequence, she intimates, of having received letters – from whom she does not say – 'warning [her] against him'. Although she failed to describe the 'astral', noting only that it was 'quite satisfactory, but might have been all out of [her] own mind – probably was'[69], she describes in vivid detail an astral experience pre-dating her second meeting with him by five days: '4 November 1913. I had been meditating on what Frater Perdurabo said about getting *Samadhi* on the astral plane, and so, without realising the full import of what I was doing, I tried. Acting on an idea I got from his last letter I made myself a "body of light" and willed to rise straight to the highest point of that same vision'. Feeling the plane 'too high' for her but holding herself together 'by will', she heard a voice cry "To await Thee is the end not the beginning". Words failed her in her effort to describe what happened next: 'And – what? God knows! The rushing together of all the hosts of Heaven – ecstasy – *Samadhi* … the fundamental and final something, Alpha and Omega, the darkness whence light sprang – I don't know –'.[70]

Ten days after Crowley's second visit the storm broke. On 22 November Constantine, on a visit to Anatolia, met Samuel and Mina Mathers, self-styled Count and Countess Macgregor. (It is possible that the meeting was deliberately engineered by Anatolia who, ever ready to make trouble between her son and Aelfrida, had had to be placated by her daughter-in-law after a disagreement over a trivial subject: the payment of taxi fares.) The Count had sued Aleister Crowley in 1909 for breach of supernatural copyright and for exposing the private rites of the esoteric Order of the Golden Dawn (of which Mathers was co-founder) to public view in *The Equinox*; Crowley won the case on a technicality and was awarded costs. As 'noted enemies' of Crowley, the Mathers were therefore only too happy to enlighten Constantine with

regard to his guest's reputation: 'from them', Aelfrida's diary notes, '[Constantine] learned tales of sadism and other horrors. I could not believe it'. (Her husband had to explain what 'sadism' meant.) Beside himself with rage, Constantine offered physical violence to his wife, flinging her to the ground so hard as to bruise her quite severely; he also threatened to kill her: "*je suis capable de te tuer*". ('He looked it too', she added.) A hideous row followed, during which Constantine banned her from seeing Crowley again or even corresponding with him, saying that because she could achieve *Samadhi* at will, she had no need of a teacher. He also stated that if she did not agree, he would turn her out, deprive of her daughters, and never see her again.[71] Further conditions followed: Aelfrida was not to send Crowley a copy of recently-published *Cambridge Poets* nor were she and Crowley to publish, as intended, their correspondence.

Next day, Constantine offered two concessions: one, Aelfrida might see Crowley again if the latter was able to clear his name or, failing that, to behave in such a way as to rebuild his shattered reputation; two, she could write to Crowley to explain the imminent rupture in their relationship. A draft of the letter in Aelfrida's lengthy diary entry for this momentous day runs as follows: "Dear Frater Perdurabo, my husband wishes me to write to you. He is not dictating this to me but it will reach you in a form approved … by him. He adds that I am probably writing to you for the last time … He considers that you have too much influence over me and that the influence is … of an undesirable kind … My husband will not … let me see you but he has no objection to my receiving a letter from you. Or, of course, you could call and see him at the Consulate. Always gratefully, Sarasvati". In spite of Aelfrida's pleading that the letter not be sent if only because it showed that she and Constantine were at odds (she also noted that both Grahams had known of Crowley's reputation before he ate their 'bread and salt' and that his behaviour towards them had been impeccable), the letter was posted on 25 November. But whether Crowley received the sketch, reproduced in her diary, of a cross surmounted by the word LVX and beside it the Biblical annotation '*lux lucent in tenebris*'[72], is not known: Constantine, asked to send it with a covering letter, refused, not perhaps believing as his wife did that Crowley had 'from the hell of his own nature … looked up and seen God' or that 'God [had] come to dwell in [Crowley]' either.[73]

Although Constantine stopped short of accusing his wife of physical infidelity, he regarded her dealings with Aleister Crowley quite differently from Little Friendships. And with good reason. Aelfrida's admiration for Crowley was based on a different kind of attraction and expressed in quite different terms to those used for Little Friends. Although admiration for certain Little Friends was expressed rather fulsomely (she described Frank Stokoe as 'tall, handsome, with the looks of an actor ... and a poet – with a good deal of "temperament"')[74], her feelings for a man (other than Constantine) had not been so torrid since Lord Kitchener days; hence when Crowley stated that he regarded her as almost as great an adept as himself and, in spiritual terms, as equivalent to First Wrangler, a person placed first in the Cambridge mathematical tripos[75], admiration went to her head. At the same time, however, she felt liberated from Constantine's desire to control her actions and even her mind for she had entered, without his permission or the necessity of swearing an oath to believe or not believe according to his wishes, into a compact with a man more powerful than her husband. Her subservience to Crowley therefore has something of liberation about it and it seems that it was loss of liberty rather than Constantine's physically and verbally aggressive attempts to regain control which distressed her most. Sadly, however, Crowley was not, whatever the tenor of his poem *The Challenge* might have suggested to the compiler of *Cambridge Poets* ("Back from my lips, back from my breast! / I hold you as I always will / ... unprofaned and uncaressed")[76], an advocate of Courtly Love or content to engage at a polite distance or to behave like Charles Stewart Smith and William Bowen, 'honourable Christian gentlemen' with whom she could trust herself alone on a desert island (ironically, the same phrase used by Constantine of Crowley) even when expressing their love for her, had an attractively evil reputation as far as women were concerned, a reputation underlined by Mathers' disclosure to Constantine of a newspaper article referring to Crowley as 'an unspeakably immoral being'.[77]

Aelfrida was undecided about what to do. Her immediate impulse was to placate Constantine because 'what good could come of disobliging [him]?', a move which met with such success that on 1 December the Grahams passed 'a lovely quiet Sunday together'. To this was added reluctant admiration for Constantine's protectively uxorious behaviour, recorded with unconscious irony in view of subsequent events as 'we do love each other!'[78], and realisation that she could not be angry with a husband trying to do the right thing for a wife he believed to be 'horribly deluded and perverse'. ('Who knows?' she asked, 'he is ... as likely to be right as I'.) She was however, convinced of two things: the validity of her 'mystical' experiences and that the experiences themselves were not 'dependent' on 'Crowley or Crowleyism', the latter comment being particularly significant given that it was now that Aelfrida, the dominant partner in

friendships with men, suddenly realised that she had allowed herself to adopt a subordinate and submissive role vis-à-vis her 'Guru'. Another thought was that there was 'no harm in my breaking with my Guru'[79] because although Crowley was 'absolutely sincere in his search for truth', 'a strange distortion might well occur in the brain of a Plymouth Brother' (as Crowley had once been), the strain of his investigations having brought him 'to the verge of lunacy'.[80]

So far so good, but it is obvious from Aelfrida's diary entries for November and December 1913 that she had no intention of giving up 'Crowley' or 'Crowleyism'. Her devious behaviour did not stem solely from her fascination with Ceremonial Magic but also from annoyance at Constantine's attempts to thwart her intellectual freedom: 'I am less depressed than I thought I should be at being deprived of my Guru ... Besides, I plan looking elsewhere for initiation'. She therefore played for time by seeming to acquiesce with Constantine's demand that she sever all connection with Crowley, giving as her excuse 'I rather want ... to read *The Equinox* ... and get a more thorough acquaintance with the whole business!'[81]

On 27 November, however, Mathers appeared at the Consulate with evidence of other lawsuits against Crowley. Aelfrida's comment 'it seems impossible to see where the truth lies (it almost looks as if truth did lie!)'[82] shows her still in two minds about Crowley as a person; next day, coincidentally or not, Crowley sent Constantine a pamphlet on the Order of the Golden Dawn and herself 'a gentle and quite sane note ... saying he can clear himself of scandal and will if I like'.[83] A further letter arrived on 4 December, written to Aelfrida but demanding from Constantine an apology for having slandered him. Constantine, not unnaturally, was furious. Aelfrida, unbeknown to her husband, replied to Crowley, telling him that he was mistaken – Constantine had no intention of slandering him – and warning him 'I told you months ago that my husband might at any time break off all relations between you and me ... please do not write to me again'. She also diarised that she feared further physical violence when Constantine discovered what she had done.[84]

Her fears were justified. The following day she showed Crowley's letter to her husband. Constantine erupted in fury, declaring Crowley to be 'the devil incarnate' and insisting on locking away Aelfrida's copy (her 'key to Initiation') of Crowley's *Liber Cordis Cincti Serpente*. (He had asked on 1 December that Crowley send no more books, a request precipitated by the arrival of the issue of *The Equinox* containing the poem dedicated to 'A.C.W.G. and H.E.H'.) Then in spite of Aelfrida's desire that he not do 'these violent things', Constantine struck her on the face, sending her into a mood of 'blackness and humiliation'. (He subsequently asked forgiveness.) Her new ability to induce intense spiritual experiences at will allowed her to re-establish a modicum of tranquillity by means of a vision of a peaceful 'sea of light' (she noted in passing that Constantine's accusations of delusion had no basis in fact, the vision being 'real, real, *real* … and if there was any illusion I would discover it') but the frightening-flattering realisation that husband and 'Guru' were 'fighting a duel for what can and never will belong to either of them', namely control of her soul[85], remained with her.

Victory appeared to be Constantine's. On 8 December he and Frater Perdurabo met at the Consulate where he 'stonewalled [Crowley] with perfect politeness' and they parted 'without hostility' but also without shaking hands.[86] (Is it too much to think that Aleister Crowley was relieved at ridding himself of an increasingly inaccessible acolyte whose Christian faith was unlikely ever to render her properly malleable and of her anything-but-complaisant husband?) Coincidentally or not, on the same day that Crowley and Constantine parted at the Consulate, Aelfrida received an unexpected visitor in Le Vésinet: 'Crowley's faithful prophet'[87] Victor Neuburg who, in the guise of Frater Lampada Tradam, had arrived in Paris to assist Crowley with "the series of sexual magical operations, later known as the *Paris Working*".[88] After discussing 'magick, adeptship, initiation, etc. etc. at some length', Neuburg's comment that Aelfrida was 'marked out for adeptship' brought the swift rejoinder that *her* will would remain in her own (and God's) keeping, 'not in Crowley's or anyone else's' and if that was what initiation entailed, she 'must do without'; she added, however, that she would always acknowledge Crowley as her 'Guru'. Then the curiosity which had led her one evening when Constantine was out to draw a 'Pantacle' with 'some very lovely symbolism'[89] (not, alas, reproduced in her diary) prompted her to ask Neuburg 'to see how much in earnest he was and how the thing struck [her]' to perform the Lesser Ritual of the Pentagram with her red ruler (a rectangular rod, it seems) as a wand. Her only comment at the completion of the Ritual was 'it did not create much impression on me, though I appreciate the symbolism of it'.[90]

The following day she owned up to Constantine, who calmly told her to write to Neuburg severing relations with him as well. Her letter, ostensibly to Neuburg but actually to Crowley, spoke 'magickally' to the latter, urging him 'to live in conformity with conventional standards of sexual morality', an ironic request given that the *Paris Working* on which he and Neuburg were about to embark would involve the ritual sodomisation

of Frater Perdurabo by Frater Lampada Tradam. She emphasised the importance of her request by swearing 'by my Holy Name (Sarasvati) and by all that it means to me, that this thing has got to be'. ('Of course', she confided to her diary, 'it is a bit of a "try-on" this speaking his own language to him'.) Then having wielded her 'magick will' over Crowley, she went on to spend a 'delightfully domesticated day' with Constantine[91] as if none of the earlier commotions had occurred. And from the tone of subsequent diary entries one can deduce that she was relieved to have been rescued from entanglement with Crowley regardless of the fact that entanglement and rescue had happened at great emotional cost to herself and her husband.

This was, however, far from the end of the matter. Between 9 and 20 December Aelfrida was to engage with Ceremonial Magic to a greater extent than before and to undergo one of her longest and most intense mystical experiences as a result.

Her first engagement took place on the evening of the 'delightfully domesticated day' when Constantine was out and everyone else busy or in bed. Getting out her red ruler and the issue of *The Equinox* in which the rite was described, she performed the Lesser Ritual of the Pentagram for herself 'both invoking and banishing'. (The Ritual's first aim was isolating the celebrant from ambient distractions, its second to protect him from invasion by other entities, its third, purgation of undesirable energies, its fourth, production by means of mental exercises of visions which were subsequently "examined, tested and recorded for agreement with known facts about the astral realm".)[92] Admitting that the Ritual was 'beautiful …when you understand it', she described the result as 'rather flat', adding that she hadn't *expected* it to produce a 'goblin'.[93] (Or, as she later put it, when using 'Crowley and Crowleyism' as 'copy', "ritual … isn't a kind of magic which would blow you up or turn you into a goat if you do it wrong" but existed for the psychological effect it had on its practitioner.)[94] On 20 December, Constantine being again absent, she declared 'I am going to do the Lesser Ritual of the Pentagram. My red ruler and *The Equinox* are beside me on the table. Why do I do it? Oh, just to affirm my resolution – to keep me "recollected," not for magic, at least not what most people mean by magic'.[95] She recorded neither ceremony nor results.

Between these two episodes was an even odder one. The day after the performance unproductive of 'goblins', Aelfrida went to bed feeling 'curiously elated' as if 'something joyous was going to happen on the morrow'. The feeling persisted when she woke up and she began the day 'with the keenest expectations' that something extraordinary was about to occur. (The fact of her, a strict teetotaller, going out to buy brandy for the Christmas pudding is only an amusing coincidence.) After sitting down to read Eliphas Lévi (probably Crowley's translation of *The Key of Mysteries* as it appeared in Vol. 1 No. 10 of *The Equinox*)[96] and pondering over a lecture she hoped to give in Cambridge on *Mysticism as the Basis of Religious Unity*, a flash of understanding allowed her to grasp 'what ... intuition and imagination had known – the truth behind all religions, philosophies, and sciences, the *Light* in which all things are harmonised'. With this, she stepped, as she put it, into the '*Arcanum Arcanorum*'[97], i.e. into an ecstatically visionary state of mind in which she was rewarded not only with "enormous lucidity, a supreme intuition in regard to the one thing on which the ... interest has been set"[98] but also, as a consequence of this, with revelation of the secret (the *Arcanum Arcanorum*) thought to be behind all revealed systems of belief, including astrology, alchemy, magic, and Christianity itself. Lucidity also featured in emotions associated with the vision, there being none of the 'blackness' behind which hovered 'the terrible wings of madness' which provided the basis of her warning to Evelina Garnier that 'studying "occultism" out of curiosity sends one to the madhouse'.[99]

Her immediate reaction to her vision (she describes others in her diary, abbreviated here for reasons of space, in which she found herself blazing 'into one light of unspeakable glory' with the Holy Spirit in the form of a silver dove as her guide or passing through a 'great fire'– a kind of 'magical oath' ceremony, she thought – or achieving a yogic trance 'of the nature of Shivadarshana' in which nothing was perceived 'as anything'; no wonder she felt impelled – 'I do want things to blaze up' – 'to take a staff and a mystic robe and go and tell ... people' what she had seen)[100] was that it was so indescribably joyful that she could not confide it even to a future reader of her diary because unless they too had followed 'step by step the way I have gone' they would be incapable of understanding it. Two days later, she relented: 'I have decided that I ought to record how the *Arcanum Arcanorum* appeared to me'.[101] In spite of this, her account stops abruptly after a few pages as if her customary fluency deserted her; she did, however, succeed in putting across to Constantine her theory that man possesses both a universal and an individual consciousness and have him tell her that (for once) she had been thinking 'sanely and clearly' and had reached a conclusion 'of real value' even though in coming to it she had by no means achieved knowledge of 'the ultimate nature of reality'.

The *Arcanum Arcanorum*, according to Aelfrida, essentially consisted of the notion that 'Godhead is universal

**Aelfrida Graham holding *The Equinox* 1913**

consciousness'. Man, she continues, possesses two kinds of consciousness: individual consciousness and universal consciousness. The average man's universal consciousness is vestigial and only a 'saint, adept, [or] mahatma' possess universal consciousness of higher degree; Christ, being simultaneously man and Godhead, has individual and universal consciousness in equal degree. This, she notes, is the thing to aim at: to become so at one with Christ as to be able to share not only His man-ness (with all that that implies of individual consciousness) but also His 'God-ness', i.e. His universal consciousness. The easiest, but not the only, way of achieving universal consciousness is through an 'ecstasy or mystical experience' during which one becomes spiritually one with Christ. And just as the Fall of Man led to man's acquiring individual consciousness because now no longer one with God's universal consciousness, so man's development of individual consciousness is the means by which he can regain the universal consciousness lost in falling. Seen in this light, heaven is nothing more or less than 'the final merging of all individuals ... in the universal consciousness'. Achievement of universal consciousness in the guise of Heaven (or vice versa) therefore provides a man with 'joy, peace, power (over people, since you touch them from above), and love'.[102]

Her *Arcanum Arcanorum* experience, though lucid at the time (to a reader of her diary it appears very confused; the above is interpretation and clarification) seemed less clear in retrospect; reading it over a year later she added a note: 'This does not seem so clear as it did then! To speak of God as "Father", the source of all souls, is simpler and nearer the truth'.[103] She also emphasised that '*a mystical state has no moral value in itself*' and that the nature of ecstatic vision is personally and culturally pre-ordained. This second insight led her to conclude not only that the 'light in which all things are harmonised' will incarnate itself in different forms (Vishnu, Buddha, Christ, even Satan) but also that because the ecstatic's *mind* is the medium through which the Light flows, the vision he sees will be coloured by his 'instincts and intentions': 'the pure in heart ... see God. The wicked see the devil'. Both, however, have in their own way 'touched universal consciousness'.[104] It was therefore because of the innate differences in their respective 'instincts and intentions' that Aelfrida felt herself out of sympathy with Aleister Crowley's view of universal consciousness though she respected his ability to achieve it; she also worried that he might not use his achievement for 'perfect good' because lacking the necessary purity of heart. She did, however, add that she herself deserved no praise 'for having got a taste of the Universal Consciousness' and that whether she made good or bad use of her 'taste' was entirely in her own hands.[105]

Aelfrida's later statement that 'my "message" is best to be found in my poems and therefore they must be published whatever else is not'[106] is particularly significant when experiences of 'Crowley and Crowleyism' recorded throughout 1913 and the early part of 1914 are studied in the context of poetry written during the same period. Fortunately for us and almost certainly with intent on Aelfrida's part, relevant poems (all of which appear in *The Garden and the Fire,* the anthology of her own poetry published in 1916) are dated and placed and it is easy to associate them with entries in her diary and to regard them as extensions of it. (We also know that she sent Crowley poems several over and above *The Unofficial Biography,* one at least being written after she had officially broken with him.) In the context of biography, a detailed analysis of each poem would remove us from life-story to literary criticism but a salient point or two from each will indicate how much matter lies concealed in Aelfrida's odd and, without reference to her diary, inexplicable poems on the subject of Aleister Crowley and Ceremonial Magic.

The earliest poem in the series, *Ecstasy,* was written on 27 July 1913 when the Grahams were living in a Parisian *pension* prior to moving into the Villa *La Cigogne.* Aelfrida was already deep in correspondence with Crowley whom she had twice tried to telephone while passing through London on 8 July, only to find he was in Russia; she had also recently received 777, *Book 4,* and nine issues of *The Equinox.* Other recent events included bestowal of her cognomen, Sarasvati; assiduous practice of yogic exercises; assurance by John d'Aubray Bell (who had met Crowley but refused to be drawn further on him) that her soul must be 'attuned' to Crowley's, an event followed closely by her sudden remembrance of the 'vision I had when I was 14 or 15' of an unknown man beside whose deathbed she wept, a man she now thought might have been Crowley[107]; and recurrent 'sensible' or 'true' dreams about him.

*Ecstasy,* one of Aelfrida's longest poems, follows the rite of the Lesser Ritual fairly closely. Beginning with the scene-setting so important to a practitioner of Ceremonial Magic and moving on through the stages of isolation and purgation, she becomes receptive to whatever experience will ensue. A pause follows, as it might also in a rite. Suddenly she is roused by a "silver ray / Stabbed through my heart" and senses the mysterious presence of One under whose influence she feels herself borne aloft towards an ecstatic vision of "God who Is and yet is Not". The vision does not, however, appear as brilliant as one might expect given the imagery surrounding it (the Moon's "maddening light", a "blazing spire of stars", a "white-flamed spirit", and so on) but as a silence and darkness within which only her own soul ("one fragile spark") provides illumination. Crowley, to whom she sent the poem with its curious mixture of pagan beginning ("Cynthia calls the spirits down") and Christian climax ("All living things must die, that God alone may live"), was puzzled by the second line quoted and asked what exactly did it mean? Aelfrida's reply was that it meant 'the in-drawing of the breath of God'[108] cannot have enlightened him; perhaps even she herself did not fully understand it.

Though Crowleyian references can be traced in almost every instance to Aelfrida's correspondence with him or to readings of his works, one reference in particular is worth considering at more length: the "fire-plumed swan" between whose wings she is borne higher and higher until a vision of the perfect splendour of "God Who is and yet Is Not" is manifest.

Given that Aelfrida has recently 'become' Sarasvati in terms of her 'higher self', the swan "with wings of fire" to which she refers as a manifestation of breath emitted by an unnamed spirit-being describable only in terms of its manifesting itself in "trees or hills or sea" or in the perfume of "dew-encrusted poppies" or as the force which "stirs the birds to wing" or rouses "the sleeping sea" to waves of ecstasy[109] may be the 'vehicle' of her 'consort' the god Brahma, the creative aspect of the Hindu trilogy who "sets the planets ordered way", who "first divided night from day", and called herself "from the clay".[110] Brahma, however, though capable of artistic representation[111], is a more abstract deity than Vishnu or Shiva and less commonly represented than they, but neither is he "the God Who Is and yet Is Not" to whom she gives her very "Self" at the poem's climax. While therefore, as 'Sarasvati' she is happy to make use of her Hindu spouse's 'vehicle' to enable her to come close to God, as Aelfrida Graham née Tillyard, direct communer with Deity, the Brahmanic 'vehicle' she uses as a means of achieving Him remains a vehicle only, to be discarded like her 'husband', cognomen, 'higher self', and Aleister Crowley once she has completed her apotheosis and achieved union with the god who is for her the only true god, the Christian one.

There is, however, even more to the poem than this. The poem's original title as given in another of Aelfrida's rare diary references to current versifying was *Atmadarshana*. (She also notes that it was written at white heat in only twenty minutes – and gave her prolonged indigestion – and describes 'an extraordinary occurrence, possibly *Samadhic* in a higher form or even *Atmadarshana*' which took place on 11 July 1913, some days prior to its composition. The 'occurrence' itself was written up in the separate record which she kept of her spiritual experiences but was transcribed into her diary the following day.)[112] On the morning of 11 July she and Constantine quarrelled over the seemingly trivial matter of the position of the day and night nurseries at the Villa *La Cigogne*, the event being described by Aelfrida as 'a great emotional crisis' which left her 'utterly exhausted and beaten'. (The quarrel may in fact have concerned the Grahams' sharing or not sharing a bedroom, Aelfrida pleading the need for two nurseries on the first floor in order to obtain a separate bedroom for herself elsewhere.) After lunch, she and Constantine retired to their room where, in an attempt to regain control of her feelings, she lay back in her chair with her arms above her head in the yogic position '*Aum tat sat Aum*' ('God which is God'), at the same time repeating to herself a sentence which had been 'speaking itself' in her mind for an hour: 'the essential is the elimination of the Ego'. (The sentence, she noted, bore some relationship to Constantine's accusations during their quarrel, humorously paraphrased by her as "thou hast got rather more than thy share of ego".) Using as her mantra 'the Name of God', she found that 'all material things fell away into the abyss', Time and Space

following, until she found herself 'alone with God, God as Fire, as Blackness, as the Nothing that is All – *and the Ego was annihilated*'. As the vision faded, she heard Constantine's voice as from an immense distance, 'very gentle and pitying'. Making a great effort she 'got back' and on opening her eyes found her cheeks wet with tears. Because the nature of the 'extraordinary occurrence' seemed to transcend even contemplation (*Samadhi*) she described it as '*Atmadarshana*' or ecstasy.[113] The poem's title is therefore only to translate (and disguise) her original title: A*tmadarshana*.

Aelfrida's second poem, *The Magician Poet*[114], was written on 26 August 1913 during a brief visit to Cambridge to collect her daughters and domestic staff prior to moving into the Villa *La Cigogne*. It is also the poem, then entitled *By Broken Wings*, which she sent Crowley on 13 September from Le Vésinet, that being the day she received a reply from him justifying his 'lewd' letter of the previous month. Knowing this, its content is easily decipherable: the guru whose "potent words" have so impressed her has, she now realises, aspects of his nature so "shamelessly a-wrong" that they negate the "starry things" he teaches and even deny him entry to the "starry throng" which he aspires to join "by broken wings" while flinging the resonant and potent phrase to heaven "*Aum tat sat Aum!*" It also warns her that, "wingless" though she too is, she must not 'buy' "broken wings" like his in order to emulate him.[115]

On 13 September she also wrote two other poems. The first, *The White Horse Inn,* was dedicated to 'FWS' (Frank Woodyer Stokoe) who had repeatedly warned her against Crowley. Its subject – the choice of a suitable mount from the inn's stables for the author's "ride into tomorrow", the seven horses' names (Love, Need, Laughter, Care, Hope, Power, and Sorrow) indicating both their characters and the manner in which they should be ridden – seems irrelevant to Aelfrida's current doings, until one comes to the name of the eighth horse (Death) and realises that the poem was written the day following her second 'true dream' about Aleister Crowley in which he turned a pistol on her and she thought 'no answer but Death'.[116]

The other poem, *Dieu Fait son Métier*, is in three parts: 'A misty morning', 'Midday in summer', and 'A starlit night with lightning'. Its ostensible subject is God, craftsman of the human soul, nature, and time but its tripartite scheme is also suggestive of the Hindu Trimurti: Brahma, creator of the universe as a manifestation of himself; Vishnu, the preserver or redeemer, a solar deity; Shiva, the Bright One, who destroys and re-creates and inspires; indeed, the verses themselves with their misty, generative, and fiery imagery suggest successively the worlds of emanation, creation, and re-creation from destruction. The third part is the most relevant, for although Aelfrida's ostensible reference is to the Christian Deity (God "working in the forge of time" and "beating out the circle of Infinity"), the 'god' to whom she actually refers who dances within a flaming aureole in whose endless circle all opposites are reconciled and who drums as he dances, is Shiva as reconciler of death and resurrection and as implacable Lord of all that pertains to new life, a deity personified in Aelfrida's eyes as Aleister Crowley, destroyer of everything that was negative in her religiosity and inspirer ("blown sparks rise / And shower new stars and suns about the skies") of the 'mystic' way she was shortly to follow.[117] *Dieu fait son Métier* can therefore be regarded as a vote of thanks to the *'mage'* who (as Brahma) has created her 'higher self' and (as Vishnu) preserved her from mental breakdown and even suicide and (as Shiva) has inspired her.

At first sight both poems appear to parody Crowley's high-flown style: "March through the dark-resounding halls of Magick… / With word and wand and smoking thurible"; "Behold I am the Pure Soul's flameless light, / The lamp within the great magician's hand". Given Aelfrida's quoted reactions, it might therefore seem that she was poking fun at Crowley (whom she had not yet met) in an attempt to play down his influence over her ('there's getting to be too much Crowley!' she had written on 22 July)[118] or that the poems were what she elsewhere described as 'a bit of a "try-on", speaking to him in his own language'. Imitating Crowley's style and imagery would not be difficult to one who (as the *MCJ* showed) was an excellent parodist and who was familiar with his prose and poetry and had his contribution to *Cambridge Poets* in front of her. (Crowley's bibliographical entry in the anthology has thirty-five entries, including one which must have horrified her parents: *Alice, an Adultery*, printed under Crowley's own auspices by the 'The Society for the Propagation of Religious Truth'.) Nor, according to the imagery of *The Magician's Birthday* with its evocation of Crowley's mountaineering exploits in the Himalayas ("Have I not climbed the icy peaks of pain / And stood alone amid unchallenged snows"), was she as ignorant as she sometimes professed about his past life; Crowley was adept at self-publicity and besides, if he and she planned to publish their correspondence, there must have been far more letters than those mentioned in her diary if the project was not to be derisorily short. But while *The Magician's Birthday* may be no more than parody (and if it was one of the seven poems sent by Aelfrida to Crowley on 29 October five days after their first meeting, one wonders what he made of it), the person whose 'birthday' the poem celebrates (if that is the right word,

given what follows) is Aelfrida herself and the agonised feelings attributed to the 'magician' her own: "have I not crossed the desert of despair", a line posed as a statement not a question; "from out the smoke / And ruins of my mind … I cry in vain / … unutterable darkness of the soul / Wave on wave, hath compassed me about". And for why? Because He for whom she crosses the desert of despair, He for whom she cries in vain ("yet hear me, Lord" ) is Deity – but Deity whom she cannot 'attain' (she is "Still seeking"), not because she does not know for Whom she seeks ("Thou, Thou hast been my quest") but because when she thinks she has found Him, what she sees is only "a vaster-imaged Self / With wide eyes open at [its] own dismay!" Hence her desolation ("perhaps for me, God keeps no promised land / Perhaps … no resurrection morn / Shall shaft her beams … / Upon my sealéd grave"); hence too her march "through the dark-resounding halls of Magick" where with the help of rituals akin to those of Roman Catholicism in their use of the "petal-plumed smoke / Of incense", she may attain at last to Him whose garment's hem she would stoop to kiss "so I did know it Thine".

In *Sarasvati* Aelfrida refers to her 'higher self' pseudonym, to her attributes as Sarasvati, to Aleister Crowley in his Shivan aspect and even to herself as Parvati, Shiva's consort, the eight lines of the poem conveying an esoteric message decipherable only by reference to her diary and to her readings of material provided by Crowley himself. (She refers to few books beyond this though this does not, of course, mean that she failed to read any; we know, for example, that she borrowed books on Theosophy from Evelina Garnier and lists of books preserved elsewhere suggest that she read widely.) Contemporary diary-recorded activities are the same as for *The Magician's Birthday*, the only difference being that on 6 October she visited Paris 'from a sense of duty joined to a sense of the inevitable'.[119] Perhaps her joy at returning from Anatolia's torrid 'little nest' to her own cool suburban one inspired her to write a poem in which she not only regards herself as "the Pure Soul's flameless light" and as "the Lamp within the Great Magician's hand" but also as one as indispensable to Crowley as Parvati to Shiva: "without my chrism is neither shrine nor rite / Nor any god at all", the presence of Parvati being essential to any Shivan rite and the rite in her absence invalid.[120] Conversely, in the poem's second verse Aelfrida, as herself, informs the 'great Magician' that *his* 'church' "must fall" and that God's, illuminated by herself as the light in an even greater 'Magician's' hand, will triumph.

A further poem, *Evening – Silence – a Shaded Lamp*, initially seems harder to place in context.[121] True, the days previous to its composition on 28 November 1913 have been dreadful: Constantine has received Mathers' account of Crowley's behaviour, Constantine and Aelfrida have had a terrible quarrel and the former has refused to send a message on her behalf to Crowley but has forced her to write in person to him stating that 'Sarasvati' and 'Frater Perdurabo' are not to meet again. But though seeming to acquiesce with Constantine's demands, Aelfrida is planning to look elsewhere for initiation. And how better to hone her skills than to perform a rite which may enable her to regain a measure of control over her unravelling life and at the same time to conjure up the simulacrum of a man whom she fears she may never meet again?

But the rite which Aelfrida describes here and which she initiates with raised arms and the stamp of a foot cannot relate to either of the occasions on which she performed a named ritual, for these (and Victor Neuburg's visit of 8 December during which he performed the Lesser Ritual of the Pentagram for her) took place on 9 and 20 December i.e. after the poem was written on 28 November. What we have here, then, could be a poetic evocation of a ritual derived from her reading of *The Equinox* (copies of which, we should remember, she received on 3 July, three weeks before writing a comparable poem *Ecstasy*) or part 2 of *Book 4* on Magic. Or it could be Aelfrida's description of a rite performed by her but unrecorded in her diary for fear of discovery, an unlikely event given that she now kept it under lock and key. (Or recorded in another notebook, later destroyed.) Or, the most likely explanation, it is Aelfrida's description of the event which took place in Constantine's absence on 14 November which she described rather flatly in her diary as 'quite satisfactory' and during which she drew a pantacle or magic-invoking disc containing 'some very lovely symbolism' before performing an 'astral' on absent Aleister Crowley.

The poem's imagery supports this view, including as it does Aelfrida's description of "the wonder I here inscribe" (i.e. the pantacle) with a pen which has "blossomed as Aaron's rod" and a book which becomes a "magic psalter" and lies on a table which has "grown an altar". Setting the scene is followed by a pause in which she describes the 'crumbling away' of the world outside and her focussing on the silent pool of light provided by her shaded lamp. Then she begins the 'astral', sending her "wandering wishes" to Crowley: "To find your house and to bid you come / Up the guarded path to the doorway dumb ..." (The "noisy chamber where others sate" might be the room where Constantine was at a formal dinner.) She then describes what must have been a shattering psychic event:

"Veil your eyes and avert your face,
For here the walls have a thousand eyes,
And blinding lights from the altar rise,
And all the air is a sea of motion
With incense waves from a spirit ocean.
The very ceiling becomes a star
White as the cup of a nenuphar..."

All in all, a 'quite satisfactory' experience indeed.

Tempting and fascinating though it is to essay a lengthy exegesis of the poem's dense and opaque symbolism, more profitable in the present context is to note that *Evening – Silence – a Shaded Lamp* constituted for Aelfrida both a research project for which she employed assistants (on his subsequent visit to Le Vésinet, Victor Neuburg not only explained – at her request – the astrological significance of certain zodiacal signs but also supplied her with information on symbols of whose meaning she had enquired[122]; it also seems she had supra-natural assistance in the form of an "airy tribe" of "angels, demons [and] elfin sprite[s]" conjured up in the course of the ritual) and a graduation ceremony (a "holy rite") carried out in the lamplit privacy of her own room in a Paris suburb on which a misty twilight has fallen. But whether Aleister Crowley, bidden come, came, she does not say (her bidding was metaphorical) nor does she note the similarities between her own poem and Crowley's *The House. A Nightmare*, written in Anuradhapura in Ceylon a few years earlier, whose ultimate words ("Beware! Beware!")[123] should have warned her of troubles to come.

Other 'Crowley' poems in *The Garden and the Fire* were written after Aelfrida's obsession with her 'Guru' had begun to wane but before it developed into repulsion for him and his works. The first was written on 15 February 1914, shortly after Crowley and Neuburg completed the *Paris Working* on the 12th. (It was on 9 January, eight days after beginning the *Working*, that Crowley dreamed his 'beloved disciple' dream about 'Ae.T'.) The poem, *Suleiman bin Daoud,* appears in the section labelled 'borderland poems', together with *The Magician Poet, Gems* (to be discussed shortly), *The Magician's Birthday, Dieu fait son Métier*, and *Evening – Silence– a Shaded Lamp*, in all of which Aelfrida appears as a liminal personality able to step at will over the threshold separating the physical and spirit worlds or as someone on the cusp of a period of their life where they are forced to look both forward and backward with a mixture of excitement and regret. (15 February was also the day on which Aelfrida noted in her diary that Crowley asked her to elucidate a line of *Ecstasy*.) Events immediately preceding the poem included Crowley having apparently administered drugs to Evelina Garnier with the object of producing a state of supranormal consciousness (he merely succeeded in making her very ill) and his carrying out a rite at which he had apparently sent three acolytes into cataleptic trances. There had also been discussions with Chiara (in person, in Paris) and the Oracle (by letter) concerning Crowley's influence over their daughter but at the point at which Aelfrida believed that she had reconciled her mother to Crowley by explaining to her 'how splendid and devoted my guru is' ('guru' with a small g, now) and that it was he who taught her to 'trust experience instead of authority', she received letters from her father censuring her 'feminine curiosity' about 'occultism' and attacking Crowley and her own 'writings' on the subject. (Alfred and Catharine's feelings on the subject of their daughter's recently published *Cambridge Poets* would have been interesting to know, given that her eleven poems refer in only slightly coded form to intimate details of Tillyard family life and that one of Crowley's provoked her *Mrs Graham Explains* article.) But in spite of pointing out to her father (he had discussed the matter with Constantine when the latter was on leave in England) that Crowley had 'only made a much more ardent Christian of me than ever, besides giving me a chance of mastering the storms of my own nature', Aelfrida was forced to admit that her 'troubles with Crowley' were not yet over.[124]

*Suleiman bin Daoud,* therefore has a valedictory tone for although it refers at the start to the wise king's enthronement in the course of a rite in which he "… grasps the rod / Of wisdom, and there lies o'er breast and knees / The robe of power, whereon are writ such keys / As make the man to know, and be as God", it ends with the king shorn of power, power which took the form of words which are "shed as leaves" until he is "stript and bare". To disguise the subject of her poem as 'Suleiman bin Daoud' is another of Aelfrida's tranformational tactics: Solomon, son of David, was no stranger to her in a Ceremonial Magic context, for *The Goetia of Solomon the King*, with its titular reference to wizardry and the working of miracles, was an esoteric tome translated by Samuel Mathers with notes, emendations, and an introduction by Crowley himself, published in 1904 and reproduced in issues of *The Equinox* thereafter.

*Gems* was written at Le Vésinet on 20 April 1914. Aelfrida had continued to meditate frequently with 'an "astral" once a week for a change'.[125] (*Sic.*) She was also studying Theosophy as part of a Crowley-inspired enquiry into Comparative Religion, aspects of which confirmed her belief in his powers[126] even as she turned from him with something of a feeling of gratitude towards Constantine for having rescued her from a situation in which she was rapidly becoming out of her depth.

The poem begins with a statement of Aelfrida's disdain for jewels: "I never cared for gems … / A jewel's vivid, soulless, proud". It then describes a vision she has had of a woman "clothed and girt about with gems" who showers her against her will with "glowing gauds" (as Constantine showered her with a diamond engagement and a gold wedding ring or metaphorically flung the 'jewel' of his genius into her lap) while informing her that "There's power within the gem … / A goal to set your hopes upon". Aelfrida rejects them, saying "their touch defileth me", but the woman continues to shower them on her, telling her: "I, Beauty, of my substance fashioned them …/ Bid them be lures and never satisfy / The pilgrim hearts of men".

Given Aelfrida's disenchantment with 'Crowley and Crowleyism' (but how amusing that it should be by means of *Hindu* gods and *Buddhist* spiritual exercises described or propagated by him that she found her Christian God again), what we have here may be allegory, the woman who personifies Beauty representing the glamour of 'Crowleyism' which Aelfrida now believes has lustre but no substance, the gems with their meretricious glitter Crowleyian doctrines to which she recently subscribed[127] but which are in truth only distractions from a Deity who is His own adornment (sapphires, diamonds, topazes and pearls may be specifically mentioned because of their magic connotations as explained by Crowley in the gemmological section of 777), and the woman's announcement that with her help Aelfrida has seen beauty not only in the "dull waste spaces of the earth" but also in "the ugliest soul that swells behind the eyes / Of man", a reminder that Aelfrida had (or thought she had) seen beauty Crowley's own soul.

Aelfrida used the months preceding her dramatic dash to England as France mobilised at the start of the Great War to discover more about the 'guru' whose power over her was waning and from whom she had physically separated herself for ever. (Crowley was to sail for America on 24 October 1914; before leaving he ritually cursed Victor Neuburg when the latter took his leave of a man he had come to regard as an impostor.)[128] Evelina Garnier and Tommy Altounyan provided her with information of a peripherally relevant nature, the former meeting Crowley on an Italian train, the latter playing chess with Crowley on three occasions (and possibly also visiting him in a medical capacity) after which he announced "there is too much difference between his theories and his practice".[129] Leila Waddell (referred to by Aelfrida as Leila Bathurst; her full name was Leila Ida Nerissa Bathurst Waddell; Crowley called her Laylah; by bizarre coincidence, her A∴A∴ name was 'Agatha')[130] proved more informative. On 2 January 1914, Aelfrida, whose curiosity concerning Crowley extended to his female acolytes, received a letter from Leila informing her that what the 'Master' needed was 'a band of devoted women who will stand by him'. She does not record her reply (if any) but in her diary she was scathing: 'that is all very admirable for her, I daresay, but … I for one do not admit his claim to be a "Master". A candidate for Buddhahood, if you like – no more'.[131]

A further letter followed on 19 February in which 'Laylah' defended Crowley's morals, saying "he has never to my knowledge, behaved badly to a woman and certainly never committed the varied abominations of which he has been accused". (Crowley's behaviour, Leila added, had been "absolutely beyond reproach" during the time she had known him.) She also informed Aelfrida that she (Leila) would be in Paris in April and would like to meet a disciple of whom Crowley had spoken "as one of amazing gifts spiritually and as the one person who naturally understands what he says". Aelfrida replied that Leila should not write to her again, that Leila and Crowley should go to the Consulate and arrange for Constantine to marry them (*sic*), that Victor Neuburg 'should not be worked too hard', and that the use of drugs and 'physical means' to attain spiritual ends should be avoided. (This begs the question: how much did Aelfrida know of the *Paris Working* and who told her?) As her diary entry for 19 February concludes 'I hope my guru will listen to me'[132], it is obvious that her letter to Leila was written for Crowley's eyes also. Constantine, whom Aelfrida later informed of the correspondence, commented that Crowley himself had persuaded Leila to write[133], a possibility in view of the coincident timing of Aelfrida's correspondence with Leila and Crowley's 'beloved disciple' dream of 9 January. But how interesting that Crowley's quasi-biblical (or consciously or unconsciously blasphemous – or perhaps merely truthful) description of his 'chela' occurs *after* he has been dismissed by her; perhaps he was in truth impressed by her as she by him.

Before and after leaving Paris Aelfrida continued to 'dream true' about Crowley. The first dream on whose content she expatiates was so vivid that she almost believed Crowley had visited her 'in the astral' to discuss Leila's second letter, Crowley saying he was unsure about marrying Leila before chiding Aelfrida for not working hard enough on psychic exercises and for thinking too much about perfecting herself; she was, he said, only the 'cruse' into which certain 'oils' have to be poured. (The oils, whose provenance Aelfrida checked later, probably in 777, were those of cinnamon, with its warm, positive, solar affinities; myrrh, negatively associated with sorrow, bitterness, darkness, and passivity, and galengal. Galengal is not named in 777 but may have been mistaken by

Aelfrida for galbanum, representing equilibrium.)[134] The second dream left her 'troubled' because it occurred shortly before Tommy Altounyan painted 'a quaint picture of Crowley ill … robed in purple with a cross on his breast … propped up by enormous cushions [and] round him disciples, foolish, adoring' at the point when Aelfrida herself had dreamed that he was unwell.[135] Her final dream took place on 4 November 1914. Once again she 'dreamed true about [her] guru'; once again she fails to describe the dream though after it, so she said, an intuition told her to 'sever the psychic connection' with Crowley because his influence over her was 'too hot'.[136]

The last lines of *Perdurabo*, Aleister Crowley's final poem in *Cambridge Poets*, hint that though an "exile from human kind" because his mind, "wrought / Into dark shapes of solitary thought" awakens "no answering love or pity" in his fellow men and that because of this he is mentally "crucified / … Tortured [and] cast out", he will also "abide".[137] And abide he did, the poem being symbolic of its author's enduring presence in Aelfrida's life, for although she had no intention of being his 'heir', she nevertheless perpetuated his memory (and so was in some sort his heir) by including references to his theories and practices in future works. In fact, references to Aleister Crowley, albeit without actually naming him, appear in books written years after she gave up writing (or at least publishing) verse and even more years after she recoiled in spiritual revulsion from 'Crowley and Crowleyism' and proclaimed the period of Crowley's influence over her as one akin to that undergone by the world during the Great War, episodes from which she hoped she and it would emerge 'purified'.[138]

Aelfrida's earliest and longest use of 'Crowley and Crowleyism' as 'copy' appears in *A Little Road-Book for Mystics*, a twentieth century *Pilgrim's Progress* first published in 1922 and re-issued, after revision by its author, in 1931. (It was also her only book to achieve a second edition.) The second stage of the pilgrim's journey describes his need for assistance at a point when he feels incapable of progressing further by his own exertions; chiefly, he requires the assistance of illuminative experiences: dreams, visions, intuitive insight, and so on. The pilgrim, described by Aelfrida as a 'mystic', will also require written help to elucidate his experiences; looking around, he will find along his way "some charming bookstalls" on which he will find 'road-books', among which she instances "volumes on mystical and ascetic theology or … the latest treatise on the Psychology of Religious Experience".

She continues with a parable which she calls *A Strange Experience*: the pilgrim, discovering "an old book, quaintly bound in red leather, marked with strange-looking signs", turns aside from the road, and sits down to read it. *A Hidden Way whereon Men may walk to God* speaks "of a primitive tradition of Holy Lore handed down in secret from adept to adept, preserved from the eyes of the profane in magic sign and symbol; of power to be conquered; … of ways of God more wonderful and more sure than that offered by the humble path of self-sacrifice and prayer" and "as he read he felt his heart grow hot within him and a mysterious surging of expectation made the blood sing in his temples. Surely this was the Road-Book for which he had been looking!" The pilgrim's reading is interrupted by the arrival of an old woman who invites him to her nearby garden "where she could speak better to him of the high secrets he sought to discover". Perhaps his eyes have been dazzled by the heavenly light that has shone on him during earlier stages of his journey or perhaps they have grown dim from studying the old treatise, but when the pilgrim follows his guide, he does not notice that he has left the high road.

The garden to which the old woman leads him is very beautiful. Lawns are cut in squares, circles, and triangles, yew trees are clipped into curious shapes, and narrow paved paths form a maze. Fountains gush out of the mouths of goblins and gnomes, flowers with heavy scents make drowsy the air, and great forest trees loom over all. Pilgrim and woman make their way to a quaint seven-sided summer-house, overgrown with briony[139] and other creepers. Before bidding him be seated, she traces a circle with her stick, whereat he wonders very much. He then sits down to listen to her story.

"Know then, fair traveller", says the old woman, "that there are two kinds of magic, the one black and the other white, and the secret of them both is Power. In black magic the evil man learns Power for evil, in white magic the righteous man acquires Power for good. This magic of which I speak is the basis of all religions, which are in themselves all equal when you have penetrated their depths. Shall I teach you Power?" "What must I do", the pilgrim asks, "if I become your pupil? I already have a teacher, who speaks to me of such things as simplicity, humility, love to one's fellow-men, courage, devotion to God, self-sacrifice, and the like". "That is all very well for beginners", the old woman replies, "but you must pass beyond that now. Promise me two things, Secrecy and Obedience, and I will show you the secrets of the gods".

The pilgrim hesitates, stating that he would like to hear more before he promises to obey her. The old woman lights a curiously-wrought lamp containing sweetly-perfumed incense whose trailing blue smoke ascends to the bower's roof. "Close your eyes", she commands, fixing her own glittering grey-green ones upon him, "breathe

long deep breaths and I will show you what you may become". The pilgrim obeys. Initially he sees nothing but a cloud of smoke. As he gazes, however, it rolls back and he sees a great hall, set for some magic rite. Figures of men and women in vivid clothes decorated with symbols move hither and thither in rhythmic patterns. In the centre of the hall is a man clothed in white and gold to whom they pay homage as chief, king, and dispenser of knowledge and power to them. The pilgrim looks at the man's face, noting its passionless self-control, its steely insight into other souls, its deep knowledge of the follies of men. It is a face without pity, without humility, without sorrow. With a cry of repulsion he springs to his feet for, as he looks, he sees the face become his own. The smoke-filled picture fades. Awakening from his dream, the pilgrim finds himself alone. Groping his way out of the garden back to the high road, he meets a friend who asks him where he has spent this last year; the pilgrim had thought himself to have been but an hour away.[140]

Why the story is inserted in a straightforward account of spiritual illumination and how to achieve it seems puzzling but to anyone familiar with Aelfrida's account of her involvement with Crowley, its meaning is clear. So too is its imagery, the lawns of squares, circles, and triangles suggesting the red triangles, white circles, and blue squares suggested by Crowley to Aelfrida as polarising devices on which to concentrate while exercising 'a little severe mind-discipline'[141] and the briony the magic described by the old woman: white briony with its remedial uses but with its suggestion of charlatanism (its roots were sold to the credulous as mandrake) and black with its purgative and wound-healing properties are both attractive plants whose medicinal use is therapeutic in moderation but toxic in excess.[142]

The presence of the parable also explains the appearance of a short section on the occult immediately after it.

Aelfrida begins by defining Occultism in almost exactly the same words as she used in *The Cambridge Magazine* to define Ceremonial Magic: "Occultism seems to me to bear the same relation to … religious psychology … that alchemy does to the chemistry of today". But instead of repeating her description of Occultism as one of several legitimate means by which the seeker after God can achieve spiritual union with Him, she now describes it as "a strange and bewildering mixture of sense and nonsense" in which the ability to keep a secret, to enjoy the vividness and immediacy of spiritual experiences, to make one's mind more receptive to impressions, and to gain better control of one's thought-processes (all legitimate mental practices) must be balanced against the risks of stimuli which produce only false impressions at best and result, at worst, in madness. Occultism's modus operandi, however, should not be ignored insofar as its psychological and psychotherapeutic elements can be utilised by the medical profession in general and by students of the workings of the human mind in particular (she makes special mention of the Society for Psychical Research in this connection); its teachings, on the other hand, should not be accepted for the following reasons: "the people who practise it … seem a weird, vain, windy-minded crew, a little crazed … and unfitted for ordinary life" ("of course", she adds, "there are honourable exceptions, some of whom I name now to myself in silence, with gratitude for what they have taught me"); although some "occult arcana" are "mystical treatises of great beauty and high spiritual value", some is neither; much of Occultism's attraction arises solely from its "picturesque paraphernalia … its wands and its cups and its pantacles, its signs, its perfumes, its vestments"; Occultism's object is Power, its result, Pride, an adept being more often than not "a tiresome being who considers himself more exalted than the rest of mankind" whose vanity is based on "secret pretensions" of unverifiable veracity rather than on the pureness of heart essential for true visions or visions of the truth. (For Aelfrida, Christian 'Truth'.) Occultists themselves believe that anyone having "control over the powers of his body or mind can raise himself up through the planes to commune with the Most High" and to this end "tamper with forces that they but imperfectly understand"; while it is therefore possible that they may be influenced for good "by the living or the dead", they are equally likely to dive "into great rivers of evil suggestions [where] they may be submerged or drowned". Lastly Occultism offers a short cut to a state of mind in which a weary seeker hopes his desire will be satisfied without too much effort and with the added lure of wonders in store. This is even more the case when the pilgrim on his progress towards God feels that God, so far supportive, is about to withdraw some of his consolations, for at this point he may feel "that he could more securely fasten God's presence to him by magic word and ritual than by … acts of everyday dull existence" ("it is so much more attractive to perform the Lesser Ritual of the Pentagram than to pay the bills and hash the cold mutton!") but the glamour associated with being one's own priest and performing one's own rites soon gives way to realisation that there is no romantic royal road to God and that "if Occultism proclaims that there is, Occultism lies".[143]

*Spiritual Exercises*, published in 1927 but written between 1923 and 1925, is Aelfrida's extensively researched essay on Comparative Religion, an interest awoken in Paris as a result her involvement in Ceremonial Magic. Here too one finds hidden references to Crowley

and to the 'year' during which she absented herself from her 'friends' because of him, for before moving on to discuss Hindu, Buddhist, Islamic, and Christian methods of training the soul for communion with the particular Absolute to which each belief-system aspires, she discusses the various means of establishing the conditions required before any form of spiritual exercise can be properly embarked upon. She also warns briefly against unsuitable practices, giving two examples. The first is that of "an American woman of my acquaintance" (obviously Evelina Garnier) who was "very anxious to experience super-consciousness and for many months used the meditations recommended in an American handbook; nothing happened, except that she felt a confused medley of exciting sensations. She determined to … use a drug which, she was assured, would produce the desired feelings. What the drug did produce was an illness which lasted several weeks and left her much disgusted with what she imagined to be mystical experience". The second refers to Aelfrida herself: "another woman I know, who spent long hours in Eastern Meditation, certainly succeeded in inducing unusual states of mind but she was neglecting her ordinary duties and becoming unfit for normal relations. In this case the motive which led her to take up meditation was intellectual curiosity". The passage concludes with a warning: "mere inquisitiveness, spiritual pride, the wish to raise oneself above the ordinary run of devout people or love of the strange and occult, lead the seeker to disaster".[144]

In spite of this and of her curious assertion in the second example that the woman 'had no teacher to guide her', Aelfrida had no compunction in quoting, without attribution, Aleister Crowley's poem *The Goad*, composed in Amsterdam on 23 December 1897. Lines from the poem, included in her own *Cambridge Poets* and attributable to him by anyone familiar with that book or with his *Collected Works*, are used as an illustration of the way in which meditation can merge, as a result of spiritual exercises undertaken by one attempting spiritual development, into a hypnotic state in which the participant, meditating on the Passion of Christ while contemplating a silver crucifix, joins with Him in convulsive collusion. Indeed, comparison of the passage quoted and the lines immediately preceding and following it demonstrate how much intense mystical experiences undergone under Crowley's guidance owe to him and his writings, particularly insofar as in her descriptions of vivid dreams and visions – as witness those of 28/29 May and 22/23 July 1913 in which she experiences crucifixion or finds herself clasping a crucifix while Christ's soul passes into her or achieves universal consciousness while concentrating on the Rosy Cross as type both of her quest and of the Crucifixion – Aelfrida uses imagery very similar indeed to that of *The Goad*.[145]

The third of her lengthy but unacknowledged references to Aleister Crowley appears in *Can I be a Mystic?* of 1930, a book describing in epistolary form the correspondence between a "middle-aged woman and a younger friend who asked for spiritual advice".[146] (The 'middle-aged woman', referred to as 'Author', is Aelfrida herself; the 'younger friend' with whom she corresponds is designated 'Stranger'.) Midway through their correspondence, 'Stranger', having been asked by 'Author' which books he has read in his quest for spiritual enlightenment, replies that he has been a voracious reader of "works on Occultism, Mysticism, Psychology and a dozen different 'religions'". (He has had a single brief personal encounter with true mystics, relying otherwise on "books without number … the tenets of so-called New Thought, Occultism, Theosophy … and the rest".)[147] But though the books provided "useful all-round knowledge", they did not produce the "inner peace" he sought. He therefore turned to 'Author' for help.

Aelfrida's, or rather, 'Author's', response is interesting. Although, she says, she initially visualised her correspondent as "one of that growing band who claim to be in touch" with "'a Master of Wisdom' – a relationship (or attachment, rather) I have never been able to understand or tolerate" (*sic*), she now realises that he is *not* one of those "who regard themselves as *chelas* to entities whom they … call their … masters"; indeed, she rather agrees with 'Stranger' in feeling impatience with people who arrogate to themselves the right to communicate with "a Master" and who "strut about wrapped in a ridiculous mantle of so-called occult knowledge" as a result.[148] The experience she wishes 'Stranger' to have, conversely, "is the reward not of magical ceremonies and mental gymnastics, but of dedicating one's life and thoughts to Christ".[149]

But why did Aelfrida allow herself to be beguiled by the attractions of Ceremonial Magic?

Her first (and unspoken and possibly even unconscious) reason is to be found in the old woman's teachings in *A Strange Experience*: the secret of all kinds of magic is Power and Magic is the basis of all religions. For someone who needs to be in control, this is heady doctrine: she will become power-imbued either by practising Ceremonial Magic ("the disciplined will of the Magician can achieve anything [and] is limitless")[150] *or* by committing herself to a 'mystic way'. Ceremonial Magic seeks to subordinate some higher power to the practitioner's will, a doctrine which must have appealed to Aelfrida at this particularly powerless period of her life, Christianity advocates becoming one with God's Will,

for Aelfrida, the most powerful will of all. Involvement with Ceremonial Magic, however, has brought her nothing but trouble; it may even send her or cause her to be sent 'to the madhouse'. She therefore opts for what she believes to be another kind of 'magic', namely Christian Mysticism, in the hope not only of 'acquiring power for good' but also of achieving power in a socially-acceptable way: no-one, surely, could accuse a wife and mother leading a piously prayerful domestic life with her husband and daughters (daughters on whose behalf she has abjured Ceremonial Magic) of *power-play*?

Her second reason is one of which she herself was aware, namely that the instinct which led her "to look down the bypaths of Occultism and see whether it be the straight road to Heaven" was not wholly wrong for one seeking "vividness and immediacy in religious experience". Her third lies in discovering that the "picturesque apparatus" of Ceremonial Magic helped her to deal with manifestations arising from beyond immediate consciousness which had been invading her mind for some time, culminating in the experiences which accompanied Agneta's birth and death and her own near-death; it also appeared to ratify the employment of "certain symbols" (in her case the Cross) as objects on which to concentrate her mental forces until the distracting (and in her case distracted) activity of her conscious mind died away, to be replaced by spontaneous or invoked images of enormous spiritual benefit, as for example, and, significantly in this context, her 'Vision' of herself "crucified before the Lord".[151]

Her fourth reason was her unresolved relationship with Roman Catholicism. (She was living during some of her relationship with Crowley, in a Catholic country whose religious services she attended surreptitiously.) Lacking the spiritual consolation the Roman Catholic Church had briefly afforded her, she turned instead to a creed which she believed could satisfy her emotional needs and took refuge in rituals enticingly similar to those of Roman Catholicism but promising greater spiritual rewards. (At the height of her infatuation with Crowley, she noted 'I don't think creeds will bother me any more now; and my intellect which smashed itself so despairingly against the walls of the RC church must learn to subdue itself to something higher'.)[152] The feeling that she had no one with whom she could discuss religious matters without acrimony also rendered her susceptible to someone to whom she felt she could open her mind on the subject, Aleister Crowley being a man who, far from seeking to curtail her religious freedom, taught her that with the help of physical and mental exercises derived from non-Christian religions she could achieve unmediated communion with God: he too had passed through a phase of seeking consolation in the rituals, if not the tenets, of the Catholic Church and he too had moved on to the study and practice of a belief-system independent of what he, like Aelfrida, now regarded as irrelevancies: formal prayer and "creed".[153]

Hence although disclaiming acquaintance with him in her books, in private she acknowledged how much she owed to Crowley, one of the three men with whom her life was intimately bound up in 1913–14, the other two being Constantine Graham and Frank Stokoe. All were flawed, Constantine because of his refusal to accept her personal mores as his own, Frank Stokoe because of his sexual proclivities, Crowley because Samuel Mathers' revelations left no doubt in her mind regarding the nature of some of his 'magic' practices. But it was Crowley, who should have been for her the most abhorrent of the three, who was responsible for bringing to an end the spiritual drought she had experienced since absolute surrender to Constantine had replaced prayerful submission to Deity. In fact, it was less than a month following the 'Vision' at the start of which re-reading a letter of Crowley's precipitated her from peaceful precious meditation into a state of ecstasy that she was able to see clearly what she had struggled to visualise for so long: 'the fundamentals of religion'.[154] And not just religion in general but the form of religion to which she now wholeheartedly subscribed and would continue to subscribe for the rest of her life: unmediated mystical communion with God.

But not God alone. God, for Aelfrida, was a triune Deity and the doctrine of the Trinity, the 'essential thing'. God ('of whom one can say very little but that He Is, [though] I do not suppose that God the Father is ever revealed to *us* here') is its head, Christ 'the point of contact [between] God and Man, God incarnated, God with all the sublimest of human attributes, Jesus whom we love', the Holy Ghost 'the gathered spirit of all life, who is we, whose temple our bodies are, God duly apprehended by philosophers who tell us that we are "fundamental differentiations of the Absolute"'. To better 'express her meaning', she 'wrote a poem about Christ … and one about the Holy Ghost', giving the titles in her diary. The poem 'about Christ', written on 4 June 1913, she called "*No Man Hath Seen God At Any Time*"; the poem 'about the Holy Ghost', written on 20 June 1913, she called (with a nod to John McTaggart's essay of 1893, *Further Determination of the Absolute,* in which the fundamental nature of spirit is defined as Love), *Fundamental Differentiations of the Absolute*. She dedicated the latter poem to 'EA', possibly Edward Alexander/Aleister [Crowley] but more likely Ernest (Tommy) Altounyan, whose *samadhic* experience had led him to try to live his 'vision' in everything he did as she too

hoped to do. Of God Himself she wrote no specific poem though His presence permeates both, saying only 'thank God for Mysticism'.[155]

It was Crowley, therefore, a man of whom she wrote that he, like her, had looked up from the hell of his own nature and seen God[156], who was the agent responsible for making her a more ardent Christian than ever before and who helped her to set foot on the arduous road which would lead her to a closer walk with God and to her stating proudly and publicly four years later "I myself, as I had better confess quite frankly, am a mystic".[157] In spite, however, of having informed Constantine that 'having seen, I know, and knowing must not keep silence', she felt unable to proclaim her belief publicly until 1917, partly, it seems, for fear of being thought 'lunatic', partly because she needed time to formulate her ideas. Instead, and though 'definitely committed to the Mystic Way', she decided to keep 'the visions and the discipline' private, revealing to Constantine and the world only 'a simple life of ordinary virtues'.[158] (A footnote added sometime in August 1921 reads emphatically '*Amen*' but much had happened in the intervening years to cause her 'simple life', her 'ordinary' virtues, and her 'so be it' to appear perversions of the truth.) To confirm her commitment she swore on New Year's Eve 1913 a solemn Oath of Obligation (i.e. a formal, binding acknowledgment that she was pledged to perform a particular action) to what she now saw as her '*Great Work*'[159] a work not to be confused with Aleister Crowley's ('the understanding of the whole machinery of the Universe and the workings of the human mind')[160] or Constantine's grandiose plan of writing novels 'made of the life of the whole world' (it was losing impetus because of the demands of his consular career), but one of her own devising which would allow her both to answer a question asked in September 1913 ('is there a special faculty for apprehending God and how is it to be developed?')[161] and help her to help others attain the faculty too.

With this in mind, she ceased work on *Marrying a Stranger* and began preliminary investigations into mystical states of being, but being enthusiastic concerning her discoveries, broke her self-imposed silence. Constantine's reaction was predictable, causing her to note sadly in her diary 'I have been a fool'. But after lamenting 'the loneliness consequent on there being no one in the wide world with whom I could discuss the Great Work', she decided to pursue her studies without support or encouragement from her husband or anyone else[162] and within a few days had so far recovered her equilibrium as to be able to write jubilantly 'Hurrah for the Great Work!'[163] and, encouraged by her Oath of Obligation, to record early in 1914 that 'the Great Work looks … at me from everything, the sky ... the faces of people I meet in the street, books and my own quiet house [and] from my children's eyes'.[164]

The outbreak of the Great War in August 1914 effectively terminated Aelfrida's personal involvement with Ceremonial Magic. Diary entries relating to Crowley virtually cease though it is obvious from six-year-old Alethea's revealing comment that Frank Stokoe was 'jealous of Mr Aleister Crowley'[165] that her mother continued to discuss him with one person at least. In 1918, however, with the end of the war in sight, Aelfrida's diary refers to him once again. On 29 July and after pondering for some months on her experiences of what she retrospectively described as 'that marvellous autumn at Le Vésinet' when the supernatural was 'so near'[166], she decided to relinquish her few remaining souvenirs of that time, giving Aleister Crowley's letters and 'secret book' to Frank Stokoe, he being, she said, a better judge of 'sensual evil' (*sic*) than herself.[167] (The book was probably Crowley's *Liber LXV. Liber cordis cincti serpente*, described by him as the "account of the relationship of the Aspirant with his Holy Guardian Angel" given to 'probationers'[168] and by Aelfrida as 'the "secret book" of the Probationers'[169], a book which, concealed from Constantine beneath hoarded wrapping paper in the bottom drawer of her bureau, she must have snatched up, together with Crowley's letters, prior to her precipitate flight from France.) Of other items, such as photographs of her 'Guru' and copies of *The Equinox* and of Crowley's other books, she says only that she was unable to recover certain 'papers' before she left or subsequently; perhaps Constantine destroyed them before he too fled France.

Although she later noted that she 'did not often think about' the man she still called her 'guru', Aelfrida certainly thought about him in 1918 and immediately after the Great War came to some interesting conclusions: that 'the episode of [her] guru' might have been more intelligible (whether to readers of her diary or to herself, she does not say) had she 'stuck to English words ... to describe [her] states of mind' instead of using 'queer foreign' ones, adding that she was afraid the 'pseudo-Eastern stuff' had made her experiences 'appear somewhat exotic' (*sic*)[170]; that while some of her dreams had been 'rubbish' and many of her waking experiences nonsensical ('why couldn't I enter the Mystic Way by a less fantastic gate')[171], both had contained a good deal of 'sense' and had provided a psychotherapeutic environment in which to work through recent traumas to an extent (a somewhat limited one, it is true) impossible before. Hence while anxious to assure herself and future students of her 'guru' episode that she had never let Aleister Crowley 'come right inside [her] soul'[172] (i.e. had never wholly

succumbed to '*les ravissements du mage*') and that she had been undecided whether he was 'bad or not' ('he was one of those', she concluded in a comment as true of herself as of him, 'who justify their passions because they cannot control them'), she remained 'eternally grateful to him' for having shown her the way to the 'Mystic Way'[173], a 'way' which, like the meditations which helped her onto and along it, consisted in climbing over a certain stile or opening a particular door or taking a specific turning and walking along a path of thoughts with here and there a pause to gather flowers ... until you get to God".[174]

## Notes

1 Crowley, A. *Diaries 1914–1920*. Introduction by K. Grant.
   Of the hundreds of books on Aleister Crowley I have chiefly relied on *Perdurabo* (Kaczynski, R. 2002 and 2010). Others are quoted as indicated.

2 'Lady Walkoski (or variants thereon) may be the 'Russian countess, voluble and *exaltée*' described by Aelfrida (GCPPT 1│1│19 2 November 1913) as visited by Crowley a few days prior to her diary entry.

3 Crowley, A. *The Equinox* Vol. V No 4 March 1981 pp 199–201 *The Paris Working* (The Seventh Working).

4 GCPPT 1│1│18 19 and 25 April 1913. For an amusing account of Neuburg's life at this time see Calder Marshall, A. *The Magic of my Youth* in which Neuburg, though unnamed, is referred to as the 'Vickybird'. Worth noting too is that two other 'Cambridge poets', Arthur Grimble and Gerald Pinsent, knew Aleister Crowley and it could have been from them that Aelfrida first heard of him.

5 GCPPT 1│1│18 26 April 1913. Rose and Aleister Crowley divorced on 24 November 1906.

6 GCPPT 1│1│18 2 May 1913.

7 Chainey, G. p 201 both refers to the anthology (wrongly given as *Cambridge Poetry 1900–1913*) and suggests a reason for Crowley's inclusion therein.

8 *KCA* RCB/X/82. Critics were not the only people displeased by Aelfrida's choice of poets: *A short dialogue between two Cambridge Poets (1900–1913)* which appeared in *The Cambridge Magazine* (vol III No 12 31 January 1914 p 302) shortly after the anthology's publication has one poet complain bitterly about his work being included in the same volume as the "dubious bard" Aleister Crowley and the other that his contribution has been downgraded by its appearing "next to that of Crowley". The poem's author is given as 'I. A. W' (Iolo Aneurin Williams) whose own rather strange *Love Demonic. A Grotesque* appears on p 211 of *Cambridge Poets* at the other end of the volume to Crowley's; the poet whose poetry is 'next to' Crowley's is either Frances Cornford or Norman Davey, the former a previously published poet, the latter (like Williams himself) not.

9 GCPPT 1│1│19 12 November 1913.
   *The Cambridge Magazine* Vol. III No 11 24 January 1914 p 284. The article, by-lined 'Aelfrida Tillyard', is entitled '*Mrs Graham Explains*'. Aelfrida does not explain why she chose her married name in this context; in view of disclosures made later in this chapter, it may have been revenge. She also added her current address.

10 The poem, originally entitled *The Soul of Osiris,* was written in 1901; it appears on p 204 of Crowley's *Collected Works* Vol. 1 of 1905 under the title *The Temple of the Holy Ghost*. The poem, under its most recent title, appeared in *Cambridge Poets* pp 62–65.

11 Kaczynski, R. p 477 (2010).
   Evelyn Underhill (*Mysticism* pp 152–153) defines it as "the extension

and practice of volition beyond the usual limits" or (pp 156–158, quoting AE Waite's *The Occult Sciences*) as the "synthesis of methods and processes" utilised by (and eventually developed into the "trained powers" of) a practitioner in terms of "a tremendous forcing-house of the latent faculties of man's spiritual nature" with a view to the achievement of power over oneself and over para-natural forces.

12 The phrases are taken from *Song* and *The Challenge* as reprinted in *Cambridge Poets 1900–1913* pp 55–57 and 58–59 respectively.

13 GCPPT 1|1|19 11 June 1913.

14 ibid. 2 May 1913. Frank Stokoe's *The Mad Magician* appeared not only in *Cambridge Poets* (pp 185–186) at a time when Aelfrida was safely out of England but also in *The Cambridge Magazine* (vol II No 25 6 June 1913 p 655), a magazine in which poems by him appear in virtually every issue, at a time when she was still resident at Fordfield. The poem must have been composed soon after her earliest intimations of her enthusiasm for Aleister Crowley and is written in the *faux naïf* style not infrequently employed by him, possibly as an attempt to dissuade Aelfrida from further dealings with her 'magician' by heaping ridicule on him.

15 GCPPT 1|1|19 8 June 1913.

16 ibid. 25 May 1913.

17 ibid. 28 May 1913.

18 ibid. 13 July 1913. The *Book 4* to which Aelfrida refers was only Part 1, published in 1911, its subject being Yoga. Part 2 on the implementation of magic, published in 1913, she describes as 'a marvellous work of symbolism and very inspiring but … quite impractical' (ibid. 10 July 1913).

19 GCPPT 2|5. The poem was written in Cambridge on 14 August 1913, Aelfrida's reference in the concluding lines to her heart 'aching' being because 24 August was also the day on which she informed her parents of Constantine's friendships with other women, notably Déla Bernet.

20 Tillyard, Ae. *The Centaur* p87 (GCPPT 2|21|1).

21 GCPPT 1|1|19 23 November 1913.

22 ibid. 3 and 21 October 1913.

23 Crowley, A. *The Magical Record of the Beast*. Introduction by K. Grant p ix.

24 Tillyard, Ae. *The Centaur* p 87.

25 GCPPT 1|1|19 29 May 1913. A sonnet written in Cambridge on 4 June 1913 entitled "*No man hath seen God at any time*" (the reference is to *John* 1:18 ) was almost certainly written in response to her Vision. In the ms version (GCPPT 2|5) it is dedicated 'to Fra P' but in the published version in the 'mystical poems' section of *The Garden and the Fire* (p 69) is without dedication.

26 ibid. 27 June 1913.

27 ibid. 1 June 1913.

28 ibid. 27 June 1913.

29 ibid. 31 May 1913.

30 Tillyard, Ae. *Spiritual Exercises* pp 56–58.

31 GCPPT 1|1|19 4 July 1913.

32 James, W. p 379.

33 GCPPT 1|1|10 4 February 1903.

34 GCPPT 1|1|12 17 October 1904. Author's emphasis.

35 Crowley, A. *The Equinox* Vol. 1 September 1911 pp 153–158.

36 GCPPT 1|1|19 3 July 1913.

37 ibid. 9 June 1913.

38 ibid. 3 and 14 July 1913.

39 GCPPT 1|1|52 13 March 1957.

40 Tillyard, Ae. *A Little Road-Book for Mystics* p 66.

41 GCPPT 1|1|19 14 July 1913. Edouard Schuré (1841–1929) was, *inter alia*, a well-known contemporary esotericist; his *Evolution Divine* of 1912 (subtitled '*du Sphinx au Christ*') in which he sought to study human evolution as influenced by esoteric cosmic forces ('*puissances*') of a Greco-Christian nature (p xiv) would have been a dangerously persuasive

book for Aelfrida to read at this point in her relationship with Aleister Crowley because of its association of Christianity and the occult.

42 GCPPT 1|1|19 22 July and 6 August 1913.

43 ibid. 22 and 23 July 1913. The phrase 'the Guardian of the Threshold' ('*le Gardien du Seuil*') appears in Schuré. E. p 379.

44 ibid. 12 September 1913.

45 ibid. 13 September 1913. *The Collected Works of Aleister Crowley* was published in three volumes in 1903, 1906, and 1907, *The Book of Lies* (subtitled *The Wanderings or Falsifications of the One Thought of Frater Perdurabo which Thought is in Itself Untrue*) in 1913.

46 GCPPT 1|1|19 6, 17 and 22 August 1913.

47 ibid. 8 September 1913.

48 ibid. 13 September 1913. The poem was written on 26 August 1913, three weeks after the arrival of Crowley's 'lewd' letter. It was later published in *The Garden and the Fire* (p 54) as *The Magician Poet*.

49 *The Tyler* was first published in *Olla* (p 46) in 1946, dedicated to 'Aelfrida Tillyard, Cambridge'. A 'tyler' in freemasonic terms is one who stands outside a Masonic lodge admitting to a meeting only those qualified to attend; as such, he remains outside but within earshot of the proceedings. The term therefore applies in this instance both to Aelfrida and to Aleister Crowley himself.

50 Booth, M. pp 308–310.

51 *The Equinox* Vol 1 No 10 October 1913 pp 91–92.

52 GCPPT 1|1|19 3 July and 22 August 1913. Aelfrida's idiosyncratic spelling of the word 'magick' suggests that she, like Crowley, employed the word to suggest specific acts or actions designed to bring about the result wished for by a practitioner of Ceremonial Magic; the word spelled thus appears in *The Equinox* Vol 1 No 1 in Crowley's lengthy supplement on 'magical retirement'.

53 GCPPT 1|1|19 26 September and 3 October 1913. Aelfrida's reference to different modes of philosophic meditation imply that she suggested to Herbert Adams that he practise first an act of piety (*kharma*, not in this sense the principle of causality), second, that he attempt visualisation of a particularly intense and blissful kind (*bhakti*) of the entity or deity on which his devotion was fixed.

54 ibid. 6 October 1913.

55 ibid. 24 October 1913.

56 Crowley A. *The Confessions of Aleister Crowley* pp 281–283. Crowley considered Palladino a fake but admitted that she was among the very few mediums to produce "evidential phenomena".

57 Harrison, J. *In Memoriam – Mrs AW Verrall*. Newnham College Letter 1916 reprinted in the *Proceedings* of the SPR LXXIV Vol XXIX December 1917 pp 376–385.

58 Aelfrida dedicated *Cambridge Poets 1900–1913* 'to the memory of Dr VERRALL; to Mrs VERRALL; and to all my Cambridge Friends', an interesting dedication in view of this possibility.

59 GCPPT 1|1|19 24 October 1913. In a poem written on 4 October 1913 at Le Vésinet entitled *The Magician's Birthday,* the subject of the poem states that he has lived "full forty years". Aleister Crowley was born on 12 October 1875.

60 Tillyard, Ae. *Spiritual Exercises* p 52.

61 GCPPT 1|1|19 24 October 1913.

62 Crowley, A. *The Equinox* Vol.1. No 10 October 1913 p 44.

63 GCPPT 1|1|19 29 October 1913. Aelfrida's *Unofficial Biography* of Aleister Crowley (GCPPT 2|5) runs in part "Now if you want to know the way to become / A Crowley in a day. You must join the A+ (–A)".

64 GCPPT 1|1|19 26 and 29 October 1913.

65 In his introduction to Crowley's *The Magical Record of the Beast 666*, K. Grant notes (p ix) "that there exists a timeless realm Called the Astral Plane … a plastic medium, more fluid that the real world,… [which] interpenetrates and supports the real or tangible world".

66 GCPPT 1|1|13 2 April 1906.
   GCPPT 1|1|19 31 October and 3 November 1913.

67 GCPPT 1|1|19 10 November 1913.

68  ibid. 12 November 1913.

69  ibid. 14 November 1913.

70  ibid. 10 November 1913.

71  ibid. 23 November 1913.

72  The transverse arm of the cross bears five V's; whether these were ornamentation or a secret reference to one of Crowley's magical titles (Frater V.V.V.V.V, from his Magister Templi motto Vi Veri Vniversum Vivus Vici) Aelfrida does not say. Also worth noting is that 'lux' as written by Aelfrida (LVX) has Ceremonial Magic connotations of which, having read *The Equinox,* she was almost certainly aware. For further details see Kaczynski, R. pp 168 and 511(2010).

73  GCPPT 1|1|19 23 and 25 November 1913. Constantine had exercised a veto over Aelfrida's correspondence once before in the case of Giunio Corsi, a more innocuous correspondent by far. The annual Christmas letters sent to each other by Corsi and Aelfrida were put a stop to by Constantine prior to his marriage, he himself writing to Corsi to inform him of this.

74  GCPPT 1|1|18 20 February 1913.

75  GCPPT 1|1|19 4 November 1913.

76  *The Challenge* appears in *Cambridge Poets* pp 58–59; it was not written to or for Aelfrida herself.

77  GCPPT 1|1|19 25 November 1913.

78  ibid. 2 and 25 November 1913 and 1 December 1913.

79  ibid. 23 and 25 November 1913.

80  ibid. 25 November 1913.

81  ibid. 25 and 27 November 1913.

82  ibid. 25 November 1913.

83  ibid. 26 November 1913.

84  ibid. 4 December 1913.

85  ibid. 5 December 1913.

86  ibid. 8 December 1913.

87  ibid.

88  Booth, M. p 313.

89  GCPPT 1|1|19 14 November 1913.

90  ibid. 8 December 1913.

91  ibid. 9 December 1913.

92  Kaczynski, R. p 45 (2002).

93  GCPPT 1|1|19 9 December 1913.

94  Tillyard, Ae. *Marrying a Stranger* p 256 (GCPPT 2|6).

95  GCPPT 1|1|19 20 December 1913.

96  Eliphas Lévi (Alphonse Louis Constant 1810–1875) of whom Crowley believed himself to be an incarnation, was a researcher into magic and the occult whose interest, as expressed in books published in 1860 and 1861, was fundamental to the later nineteenth century revival of interest in those subjects. For more on Lévi, see Underhill, E. *Mysticism,* chapter entitled 'Mysticism and Magic'.

97  GCPPT 1|1|19 10 December 1913.

98  Underhill, E. *Mysticism* p 363.

99  GCPPT 1|1|19 12 February 1925.

100  ibid. 21 October, 4 and 11 November 1913, and 11 January 1914.

101  ibid. 12 December 1913.

102  ibid. 10, 12 and 26 December 1913.

103  GCPPT 1|1|30 12 February 1925.

104  GCPPT 1|1|19 12 December 1913.

105  ibid. 24 October 1913.

106  GCPPT 1|1|20 15 July 1915.

107  GCPPT 1|1|19 22 July 1913.

108  ibid. 15 February 1914. The poem later appeared in the 'mystical poems' section of *The Garden and the Fire* (pp 72–75).

109  Tillyard, Ae. *Ecstasy,* lines 54–61.

110  ibid. lines 89–92. Aelfrida's imagery, though seemingly Old Testament Jewish and New Testament Christian, is almost certainly not; in this context it is more likely Brahma, Hindu creator of heaven and earth and everything therein, of whom she speaks.

111  *Encyc. Brit.* Vol IV pp 378–379.

112  GCPPT 1|1|19 12 and 28 July 1913. Worth noting in this context is that Diaghilev's ballet *The Rite of Spring,* with its Stravinsky score and Nijinsky choreography, took Paris by storm in 1913. Given Aelfrida's distaste for modern art in any form, it is unlikely that she saw it (of her only visit to the theatre she says nothing of the performance) but descriptions of the ballet's 'ecstatic' choreography would have been difficult to avoid and it is possible that her poem is in part a response to it.

113  GCPPT 1|1|19 12 July 1913. *Atma* means either the supreme spirit (for Aelfrida, the God whose Name she called) or the human self as it experiences itself as or at one with the single impersonal Absolute at the point at which temporospatiality and the material world fall away; *darshana,* the vision of deity seen by a worshipper on a ceremonial visit to the deity's enshrined image or (as for Aelfrida) the place where deity dwells.

114  *The Magician Poet* later appeared in the 'borderland poems' section of *The Garden and the Fire* (p 54). Its manuscript title (GCPPT 2|5) was *The Poet (Aleister Crowley).*

115  In a much later novel Aelfrida refers obliquely to Crowley as a small, feeble baby bat whose crippled wings cause an observer to wonder if it is harmful or merely pathetic or "quaint" (*Naomi da Costa* pp121–126. GCPPT 2|22).

116  *The White Horse Inn* later appeared in the 'borderland poems' section of *The Garden and the Fire* (p 63).

117  *Dieu fait son Métier* later appeared in the 'borderland poems' section of *The Garden and the Fire* (p 63).

118  ibid. 22 July 1913.

119  ibid. 6 October 1913.

120  Guy, J. et al. p 80.

121  *Evening – silence – a shaded lamp* later appeared in the 'borderland poems' section of *The Garden and the Fire* (pp 64–65).

122  GCPPT 1|1|19 8 and 9 December 1913.

123  Crowley, A. *Oracles* pp 112–115.

124  GCPPT 1|1|19 22 and 28 January 1914.

125  ibid. 13 March 1914.

126  ibid. 29 December 1913.

127  The poem's dedicatee (AWG) is Ancifera Warren Gregory, though why Aelfrida should dedicate this poem to that particular lady is not known; possibly Ancifera had chided her for failing to wear her engagement ring or items of jewellery given as wedding presents, adornments of this nature being now regarded by Aelfrida as contrary to ascetic practice.

128  GCPPT 1|1|20 9 September 1915.
     Kaczynski, R. p 221 (2002).

129  GCPPT 1|1|19 2 May 1914.
     GCPPT 1|1|20 15 June and 30 October 1914.
     Tommy Altounyan had been more sympathetic than Frank Stokoe to Crowley's theories but, like Aelfrida, expressed increasing disillusion with his practices (GCPPT 1|1|19 4 July 1913).

130  Kaczynski, R. pp 171–172 and 183 (2002).

131  GCPPT 1|1|19 2 January 1914. In her *Unofficial Biography* (GCPPT 2|5) Aelfrida noted jokingly that in Ceylon Crowley had "reached the grade of Babu" (i.e. 'Father', a title of respect) after which she gives him the punning name "Fra Perdu R'Abu", and that in this, as in other respects, the Buddhists of Kandy certainly "came in handy".

132  GCPPT 1|1|19 19 February 1914.

133  ibid. 1 May 1914.

134  ibid. 1 March 1914.
     Crowley, A. 777 pp 102–105.

135  GCPPT 1|1|20 30 September and 3 October 1914.

136  ibid. 4 November 1914.

137  *Cambridge Poets, 1900–1913* p 66.

138  GCPPT 1|1|20 3 August 1915.

139 In *O Passionate World* (GCPPT 2|11 p 328) Aelfrida describes briony as a wandering plant "not numbered among the ranks of the regular churchgoers but those who sought God in freer ways". It may therefore represent herself and/ or Aleister Crowley.

140 Tillyard, Ae. *A Little Road-Book for Mystics* pp 75–80.

141 GCPPT 1|1|19 27 June 1913.

142 Harris. E. and J. ed. pp 157 and 392. Crowley himself always denied involvement in 'black' magic (Kaczynski, R. p 377 2002).

143 Tillyard, Ae. *A Little Road-Book for Mystics* pp 80–84. To those familiar with Aelfrida's diary entries and associated poetry of 1913–14 this passage makes fascinating reading particularly because her 1922 exposition in *A Little Road-Book* is very different from Evelyn Underhill's thoroughly researched but impersonal account of magic, alchemy, and the occult in her compendious *Mysticism* of 1911. Aelfrida's version by contrast, is dramatically *personal* – she has been more deeply involved in *Materia Esoterica* than Mrs Underhill and has the emotional scars to prove it – but as a lengthy and approved quotation from Underhill's *The Spiral Way* (written as 'John Cordelier') shows, was not above extrapolating in her own words a short passage by Underhill herself on the subject of and dangers to an "insistent neophyte" of "wisdom [as] imparted [through] revelation". (Tillyard, Ae. *The Making of a Mystic* pp 17 and 25, quoting Underhill, an author described by 'Audrey Talbot' as "superior and sniffy" and liable to confuse psychology and religion but "frightfully interesting" nevertheless).

144 Tillyard, Ae. *Spiritual Exercises* pp 6–7.

145 GCPPT 1|1|21 5 December 1915. Aelfrida's choice of a Crowley poem in the context of a book on Mysticism (lines from *The Goad* appear on p 25 of *Spiritual Exercises*) can be explained by its being taken from a period in Crowley's life when much of his poetry was fervently – one might say perfervidly – mystico Christian in character. (*The Goad* appears in Vol. 1 of Crowley's *Collected Works* in a section entitled *Songs of the Spirit*). That Crowley was in Aelfrida's mind during the writing of the early pages of *Spiritual Exercises* is evident from two entries in her diary for June 1923, in the first of which she records Frank Stokoe telling her that Crowley had 'started some sort of community' in Sicily. Fidelio's information, though not exactly up to date (Crowley's 'Abbey of Thelema' near Cefalù was founded early in 1920) set off a train of memories which allowed her, so she said, to gather up 'threads that had come loose'; a week later it also caused her to identify 'waves' of 'world sorrow' coming, she thought, from the south, as it might be from Sicily (GCPPT 1|1|27 16 June 1923).

146 Tillyard, Ae. *Can I be a Mystic?* p 11.

147 Evelyn Underhill (*Mysticism* p153) defines the then fashionable tenet New Thought as "cheap American transcendentalism ... lightly called mystical by its teachers and converts". Aelfrida's own *Unofficial Biography (Aleister Crowley)* notes that anyone desirous of becoming "a Crowley in a day" must buy a "stupendous list" of books including Crowley's *Collected Works* ("mostly in rime and *very* holy") and an invented tome the "*Via Croliana Crucis*" (GCPPT 2|5).

148 Tillyard, Ae. *Can I be a Mystic?* pp 20–22.

149 ibid. pp 91–92.

150 Crowley, A. *The Magical Record of the Beast*. Introduction by K.Grant p ix.

151 Tillyard Ae. *A Little Road-Book for Mystics* pp 83–84.

152 GCPPT 1|1|19 27 September 1913. For an interesting exposition of the close relationship between Ceremonial Magic and Christianity, see Underhill, E. *Mysticism* pp 162–164. Influenced by AE Waite's interest in religion and the occult, Underhill was briefly a member of the Hermetic Order of the Golden Dawn, hence her interest in correspondences between the two.

153 Tillyard, Ae. *Sarasvati* (*The Garden and the Fire*, section entitled 'mystical poems' p 69).

154 GCPPT 1|1|19 22 June 1913.

155 ibid. Both poems later appeared in the 'mystical poems' section of *The Garden and the Fire*. (*Fundamental Differentiations* first appeared in *The Quest* Vol. 5 No. 3 pp 551–552 entitled *The People of God*, its publication being celebrated by a diary note of 1 April 1914). The manuscript version of *Fundamental Differentiations* (GCPPT 2|5) is entitled *To Everyone* with 'Mantra Yoga "Aum tat sat Aum"' added in brackets after it. This is interesting given that it was on 11 July 1913 while sitting in the 'God which is God' position that Aelfrida experienced the vision subsequently (2 July 1913) versified as *Ecstasy* and that on 26 August 1913, a month after composing *To Everyone* with its significant titular addendum, that she wrote *The Magician Poet* in which the mantra also appears. Her deliberate juxtaposition of poems in the 'mystical poems' section of *The Garden and the Fire* is also interesting: *Sarasvati* comes first, *"No man hath seen God"* second, a poem written in Emden on 2 March 1912 (*The Vanity of Life*, dedicated to 'FMT' i.e. Fanny Tillyard) third, *Fundamental Differentiations* fourth, *Ecstasy* fifth, and *Epilogue. The Curse of Duality* last; all, we can now see, are evocations of Aelfrida's 'new thirst' for unmediated communion with God, God the "Whole" of *Sarasvati* and the "Divine" of *Epilogue*.

156 GCPPT 1|1|19 23 November 1913.

157 Tillyard, Ae. Preface to *The Making of a Mystic*, a book dedicated (as if to underline the point) 'To my mother and my father'.

158 GCPPT 1|1|19 4 July and 23 November 1913.

159 ibid. 2 January 1914.

160 ibid. 10 November 1913.

161 ibid. 8 September 1913.

162 ibid. 16 December 1913.

163 ibid. 22 December 1913.

164 ibid. 11 January 1914.

165 GCPPT 1|1|20 20 August 1914.

166 GCPPT 1|1|23 29 December 1919.

167 ibid. 29 July 1918.

168 Crowley, A. *The Equinox* vol 1 No 10 October 1913 p 44.

169 GCPPT 1|1|23 29 July 1918.

170 GCPPT 1|1|22 3 March 1918.
GCPPT 1|1|24 17 July 1919.
Aelfrida is being disingenuous here: she was already familiar with words like *dhyana* and *Samadhi* from reading William James' *Varieties of Religious Experience* in 1902 but had not used the terms herself prior to 1913.

171 GCPPT 1|1|24 17 July 1919.

172 ibid. 13 June 1919.

173 GCPPT 1|1|23 29 July 1918.

174 Tillyard, Ae. *Messages*. Foreword.

# The Garden and the Fire

In August/September 1909 Constantine Graham composed a lengthy ballad, *The Crystal Gazer*, in which a beautiful woman stands amid gloomy "halls of wathlessness"[1] where there exists no living thing but herself. She carries a "crystal of glittering (*sic*) white" which emits a "mystic light". Gazing into it "as one might read a missal", she sees an "all-entrancing sight": a knight "full clad in silvery armour / As t'were the silver moon" and an "opened lattice" beyond which grows "a magic fruit-tree" from which the knight plucks a "dream-fruit" but holds it tantalisingly just beyond her reach. She tries to lure the knight into her arms but fails; maddened, she abjures him and he vanishes. In despair she strikes the 'dream-fruit' with a sword; it shrivels and dies. The next moment she finds herself "once more a bride" with a young man beside her to whom in happier times she had given her heart but whose face now reveals none of the glamour "that love's light gives love's noon". "Dark with sorrow", he kisses her then turns away to sink "dying as from a bitter wound". The lady asks the crystal what has happened to her "vain vision" but the crystal from whose "depths prophetic" a "dream-future" had lately appeared crumbles to dust in her hands, leaving her, "the sad death-weary ghost-form / Of her who loveless sinned", to contemplate "the bitter past" and a future which promises only "lightless ashes" and a life in which there will be no one to tend or adore her "and none her cries to hear".[2]

As a description *four years before they took place* of Aleister Crowley's *ravissements,* Aelfrida's response, and the consequences of this for the Grahams' marriage, Constantine's poem is uncannily prescient, the 'blind Greek' being perhaps more of a seer than his wife realised. Indeed, the poem even foresees Crowley's formal dismissal of her at the end of their first meeting, Aelfrida having informed him that she had achieved both ecstasy (*Atmadarshana*) and 'a taste of the Universal Consciousness' and Crowley responding that there remained 'nothing of any importance' for him to impart[3], a statement which goes some way to explaining the ease with which she abandoned him once Constantine exhorted her, with violence, to do so.

In fact, Constantine's desire to reassert dominion over his wife led him to relentless questioning about her involvement with Crowley and Ceremonial Magic: 'his

**Constantine Graham with the Sternebergs, Amsterdam c1916**

perpetual insistence on being admitted to all my inmost secret thoughts is sometimes terrible … I wish he would let me not answer at all but if I am silent he groans over want of confidence … It is not that I do not *wish* to tell Constantine everything. I do … but he simply does not understand my language'.[4] Her relief during brief intervals of escape was palpable (apropos a visit to a family unaware of recent events, she wrote 'it's lovely not to be "watched" and thought peculiar')[5], for Constantine now sided with Chiara in believing Aelfrida to be 'a little, just a little, mad'. (He preferred the sporting expression 'off the track'.)[6] But instead of offering sympathetic support to an emotionally and mentally afflicted wife, he behaved in another manner altogether.

Aelfrida's fictional version of her relationship with Crowley is even more interesting. Written while she was mentally working-through the momentous events of 1913 and the immensity of the spiritual awakening undergone as a result of association with him, the 'strange experience' she later turned into a parable in *A Little Road-Book for Mystics* appears in *Marrying a Stranger* as an allegory:

Elizabeth, having left Max following her stillbirth and near-death experience, is living in Weston St Stephen with Jerome, now a High Anglican priest. Suffering from "loneliness and self-pity", she is attracted one night by "a great stream of moonlight" which lures her out to discover "what the night felt like". In the garden "the lawn looked like a pool of black water with the paths for safer shore. All in and among the trees were twined and twisted long drifting strands of mist which the moonlight had silvered to look like angels' robes". "Beyond the garden, clear and firm and black, stood the church, seeming to defy the witchery of the moonlight and Elizabeth feels compelled to visit it. Passing through the gate separating garden from churchyard, she finds the latter transformed by the "moon's magic" into a bewitched place in which "marble crosses and broken pillars, stone slabs recumbent or erect" seem so pregnant with life that the dead reawaken to "some semblance of life". Entering the church she finds the building "not empty, but what filled it she could not say. The air was heavy with prayers made tangible, the … stalls full of … ghostly worshippers. And yet there was nothing one could touch, only … dim aisle and nave and … black carved wood [and] untrodden floor", a bronze cross on the altar, and some "star-like white flowers". In the hollow of a worn stone she catches sight of something "lying like wine in a cup – a tiny pool of blood … warm and a little sticky to the touch". Looking up in horror, she sees the face of St Stephen in the stained glass window over the altar transform itself into Max's[7]. She runs from the church; behind her, the windows suddenly blaze with light and the organ plays without help of human hands. Jerome, looking like a monk in his corded dressing gown, asks "Why these moonlight excursions?", answering her cry of "Why do you have such a dreadful church?" with rational explanations. Safely in the rectory, Elizabeth accepts Jerome's offer of a "sane … unemotional biscuit" and "somewhat ashamed … of the noise she made"[8], begins to plan her return to her husband.

Aelfrida's fictional description of her state of mind after Agneta's death and Constantine's departure for Panama, of her attraction by Aleister Crowley, of her exploration of Ceremonial Magic during which she studies books of occult lore and practices rites in which she sees her surroundings transmogrify themselves and in which strange sounds are heard and visions seen[9], of Constantine's intervention which opens her eyes to aspects of Crowley's nature she prefers to ignore, and of her abandonment of Ceremonial Magic and return to domesticity, is spine-chilling. It also suggests a happy ending, but, like Constantine's poem, does not have one. In *Marrying a Stranger*, 'Elizabeth' is reconciled with 'Max' and bears

him a son, but 'Max', like St Stephen, dies under a hail of stones.

As a small child, Frida was carried one night to a window to see the Aurora Borealis. The sky, "all afire with rose-gold light and … long quivering strands of pure gold" represented, she thought (or, rather, she thought as an old lady edifying the scene for publication; at the time she was merely 'quite sure it was something to do with God') the flaming sword of the angel which guarded Paradise after God expelled Adam and Eve for tasting the forbidden fruit of the tree of the Knowledge of Good and Evil. The Garden of Eden, she decided, "may have been east of Eden" but judging by the direction in which the Northern Lights appeared, "it was also north-north-west of Fordfield".[10]

Although adult Aelfrida does not say if she had this imagery in mind when she entitled her last published anthology *The Garden and the Fire,* her calling it by a title which incorporates connotations of celestial conflagration and earthly paradise is significant insofar as it reminds us of her awareness of what the words 'garden' and 'fire' signify in Abrahamic traditions underlying Judeo-Christian and Islamic lore.

Exoterically speaking, a garden of the kind envisaged as a terrestrial reflection of Paradise is beautiful because of its structured and disciplined nature. (The word 'paradise' derives from the Greek *paradeisos,* a term also used in *Genesis* to describe the Garden of Eden; to desert dwellers, it implies an enclosed, verdant, well-watered, formal garden surrounding a private house.) Esoterically it represents the state of a human soul as it contemplates the heaven it is entitled to enter because the life of the person it inhabits is characterised by the same qualities as the garden itself. Such right-living souls ("Companions of the Right") dwell after death in "repose and ease and a Garden of Delight"[11] because they are entities of whom God is mindful and to whom in remembrance of their fearing "the Station of God" before death He grants entry to paradisiacal "gardens / abounding in branches / therein two fountains of running water / of every fruit two kinds".[12] Fire, conversely, is envisaged exoterically as a terrestrial reflection of Hell ("Gehenna, that sinners cried lies to")[13], an unstructured, disordered, all-consuming state whose nature is echoed esoterically in the souls of "Companions of the Left" put out of mind by God or from whom God absents Himself because in acting unbecomingly or unworthily, they have taken "God's signs in mockery". In recognition of this, they are condemned to a Hell of "burning winds and boiling waters / and the shadow of a smoking blaze"[14] where they remain without hope of redemption, their only refuge being "the Fire"[15] itself.

Publication of *The Garden and the Fire* in 1916 is relevant insofar as the poems it contains cover a period during which Aelfrida felt herself alternately remembered or forgotten by God, evidence of His mindfulness being sweet even if thoughts of it were inspired by a man she now regarded as a tainted source and of His absenting Himself hurtful to one who had recently devoted herself at some personal cost to the 'Great Work' of attaining unmediated apprehension of Deity for her own and others' benefit. Writing on 18 November 1916, the day on which she fell with a cry of delight on 'my book! *The Garden and the Fire*'[16], she noted her happiness at seeing in print poems in which she had written 'of what I know, of love to all mankind, Beauty, the reality of the spiritual world' (and of much else besides, including revenge, which she omits to mention) and quoted the last two lines of the final poem: "Turn to God, O soul of mine. / Ye twain shall be the One, divine …"[17]

*Epilogue. The Curse of Duality*[18] by title and position summarised everything she hoped to express of themes regarded as 'the best justification of [her] existence'.[19] In it she also describes in imagery more fiery than paradisiacal ("sunset flame", "fiery petalled", "flaming sword") the anguish which overwhelms her when she considers the duality which exists on an earthly level between man and man (more specifically, between herself and Constantine) and, on a spiritual level, between man and God, expounding doctrines with which she was now familiar in verses redolent with personal relevance: those who, like Constantine, live wrongly (i.e. who reverence not God, but self) live under the curse of duality, the "two-edged … cleaving pain" which dooms them to existence on a multiplicity of earthly levels whereas a right-living person like herself escapes the curse by putting God before self and in so doing finds 'earthiness' depart and soul become one with the single, divine Reality which is God or God's. (Also important is that the duality which seemingly exists between God and man is illusory and may be overcome by spiritual exercises, chiefly meditation, as a result of which the meditator's mind becomes so permeated by Godhead that no sense of duality exists.) But it was with doubts as to whether a 'garden' or the 'fire' was to be her lot and her 'mystic way' a path of mastery over self or just another turning aside from the 'Thou' she sought that Aelfrida began the next stage of her life. And as events were to prove, there was to be more of 'fire' than of 'garden' in it for years to come.

Her initial reaction to the outbreak of hostilities in August 1914 was to deny their existence: 'I wish the babies and I could go to sleep and wake up when the war is over … cultivating "the higher indifference" seems to be the best one can do'; indeed, she cultivated it so successfully that her father commented that she was the only person he knew able to go about their 'ordinary business' unaffected by events.[20] But in spite of believing that 'this appalling war and one's anxieties for the whole civilised world' could be evaded by embedding herself at Fordfield in the 'quiet easy life of everyday' and by opening herself to 'the blaze of the glory of God and the stirrings of the spirit which must, surely, … show me how I can conform the outer life to the inner'[21], she found escape impossible. Transformation of Cambridge commons into army camp (three generations of Tillyards drove round the town to see the 'rows of tents, long lines of picketed horses, baggage wagons and guns, men drilling … all incredibly animated')[22] and the billeting of a Major Gregor[23] at Fordfield did not (except for what they portended) affect her very much. But the appearance of wounded soldiers in tented hospitals, together with news of death in action of erstwhile 'cherubs' and of former admirer Robin Smart, with the demeanour of men she had known as boys invalided home from the trenches (of one, a 'young Hercules' with whom Frida was paired off in cookery classes where she described him as 'horrid young Clay' because he was 'noisy and larked about', she wrote that in spite of his funny stories, 'his eyes looked as though he had seen things he could not forget')[24], with rumours of the imminent invasion of East Anglia, and the actuality of Zeppelin raids ('we heard the whirr of the machine, the crashing of the exploding bombs') left her uncomfortably aware of 'war at every turn'.[25] Worse still, war evoked a *Weltschmertz* so profound that she found herself 'unable to keep [her] mind from dwelling on the misery and sin of the world'.[26]

At home, there was a degree of happiness. Constantine ('my beloved, whom may God protect!')[27] from whom Aelfrida parted 'very quietly' on 1 August 1914 ('he had said "no goodbyes" and seeing him so brave I was very proud of him')[28], reached England without mishap in mid-September 1914 (Aelfrida had already 'renounced him' because of the likelihood of his being killed during a German bombing raid on Paris[29] but instead of resigning herself to war-widowhood, greeting his return with joy not unmixed with apprehension) and was allocated a Foreign Office position pending posting as Acting Consul to Amsterdam in neutral Holland. Agatha and Alethea were already ensconced at Fordfield where they were to live until young adulthood. Aged four and six, they found another parting from their father distressing[30], reacting to this, to their mother's preoccupation with matters other than themselves, and to tensions evident in their parents' relationship by becoming excessively good in the case of Agatha (she called herself 'Saint

Bam', 'Bam' being her nursery name) or turbulent and rude in the case of Alethea, a child 'not to be distracted from what she wants'.[31] Little Friends too were safe: Frank Stokoe because precarious mental health rendered him unfit for combat; Hubert Henderson, 'now "Mr Henderson of the Local Government Board"'[32], graded C3 (unfit for combat) when conscription was introduced because of stress-related problems induced by overwork; Tommy Altounyan training as a doctor. John Layard, inspired by social anthropologist WHR Rivers, left Cambridge for a year's solo anthropological field-work in the New Hebrides, returning early in 1916 'lonely and depressed' and suffering from malaria.[33] Willie Searle, formerly a pacifist, volunteered and fought through the war; Aelfrida's December 1914 description of him as 'very hale and fit and happy and quite absorbed in soldiering'[34] antedated his departure for the trenches but subsequent events left him so traumatised that when on leave he was unable to talk about or reflect on the terrible experiences he had undergone. Julius and Eustace survived, though not without occasioning their parents and sister much anxiety, the latter writing to Sir John French, now Commander of the British Expeditionary Force, on behalf of both. As it happened, intervention by the man charmed in Odessa seven years earlier proved useless in the case of the former and the latter took steps to help himself.

Julius, researching Byzantine Musicology with Mina 'somewhere in Serbia' in August 1914 ('a little danger', his sister commented acidly, 'may help him to value the life he sets so little store by')[35], managed to reach the comparative safety of his wife's home town but was interned, initially under the relaxed but tedious regime of house-arrest described by Aelfrida in her poem *A Letter from Lahr, South Germany*[36], then, after short spells in prison in Lahr and Berlin, in Ruhleben concentration camp near Kiel[37]; there he remained, not uncomfortably apart from shortages of food as the British blockade of German ports took effect, until May 1915 at which point he and Mina were allowed to return to England and both to Edinburgh where Julius gained his doctorate in 1918. Meeting Julius again, Aelfrida was happy to see that 'the mad horrible *something* that … once couched behind his eyes'[38] had gone, but a walk alone with her brother dashed her hopes, Julius, in 'a fit of depression on about his future' informing her that he would like to shoot himself. Persuading herself that 'the transition from the small sorrows of Ruhleben to the great sorrows of freedom' had temporarily overwhelmed him, Aelfrida was nevertheless so preoccupied with her own problems and so anxious that Julius not unburden himself again at her emotional expense that she was unwontedly brisk

and brusque: 'I … suggested that … if death were what he wanted, in war time no one need go the trouble of shooting himself'.[39] (To her diary she confided that Julius should be grateful that he was not 'lying in a trench with a bullet through his head or maimed for life'.)[40] A notable cooling in the siblings' relationship took place after this piece of sisterly advice and persisted for some years.

Asking her diary in May 1915 'are all the sacrifices one offers accepted, I wonder?', Aelfrida made two vows. The first, to barter 'any chance of fame' as a result of promulgation of her 'Great Work' if Julius was released, was answered ambiguously: Julius *was* released and she did not deliberately court fame (though was not displeased when a modicum came to her) but lasting renown escaped her. Concerning the second, she asked 'for Swab's safety, what could I offer?' Her answer – 'all my "spiritual consolations" perhaps' – is significant chiefly for its 'perhaps', for her next sentence recounts an uplifting vision experienced while supervising her daughters' bedtime prayers and it is obvious that when 'spiritual consolations' are weighed against Eustace's safety, the former will balance out the latter.[41] (Four months earlier she had written of Eustace that there had been 'every chance of his turning into a sleek and selfish don' but now, because he was so 'quietly splendid' as a soldier, his death in action would be worth the sacrifice.)[42] Fortunately for Eustace's career and Aelfrida's conscience, the brother who had been so supportive during the dark days of 1912/13 survived the war, was mentioned three times in dispatches, won the OBE and the Greek Military Cross, and came home to marry 'dainty and graceful … quiet and yet animated … simple and yet distinguished, warm-hearted, with plenty of commonsense *and* a temper, and very adventurous'[43] Phyllis Mudie-Cooke and to become one of the prime movers in "the revolution in English studies in Cambridge", an interest stimulated by discovering English poetry in the trenches and Shakespeare on sick leave.[44]

Eustace's war inspired his sister to prose and poetry. In epistolary novel *Vision Triumphant* she describes how 'Noel Ashton', awaiting his commission before he joins the British Expeditionary Force, gains experience by "putting in work" with the Cambridge University Officers' Training Corps ("good old OTC! We thought it was only a convenient form of [exercise] … and never thought what we learnt there would come in handy")[45], and in *The Garden and the Fire* we find *A Letter from Ealing Broadway Station* 'from EMWT'[46] describing a night-watch undertaken prior to embarkation for France. But though 'guarding Ealing Broadway station … made a man of [Eustace] and strengthened his character at the expense … of his boyish charm'[47], his (poetic) desire "to feel that [he] was helping / To send the German curs a'yelping" soon replaced 'Lieutenant Mandeville's' boyish talk of sticking Boers with bayonets with truly terrible reality.

Interspersed with excited descriptions of how her spiritual life is blossoming in spite of the enormities of war, Aelfrida's diary contains many references to her younger brother: his first letter from "Somewhere in France" (soldiers in the trenches could not disclose their whereabouts), comments about the camaraderie at the Front, and descriptions of trench life and of his first attack, the former amusingly macabre (a dead leg with a boot on sticking out of the side of the trench being used as a hat-rack)[48], the latter 'almost *too* vivid' for his sister to bear[49]; indeed, experiences undergone by 'Noel Ashton' before he is invalided home mirror those undergone by Captain Eustace Tillyard before his knowledge of Modern Greek and realisation that he had much to live for and that his chances of survival were "very small out here" persuaded him to apply for the post of intelligence liaison officer with the Greek Army.[50] His secondment in 1916 to Salonika whence he cheered his sister with descriptions of 'olive groves, dagoes and sunshine'[51] saved his life; his own modest comment concerning his life in the trenches as fictionalised in *Vision Triumphant* was that it took 'some living up to'.[52]

But what did Aelfrida, with her social conscience and her awareness of sacrifices made and dangers undergone by men near and dear to her, do to help the country of which she thought so fondly and patriotically when homesick in Odessa or exiled in the United States? With Constantine, Julius, and Eustace safe, her daughters attending a small local school and nurse-maided by Octavie, and her own needs supplied by domestic staff ably overseen by her mother, this was surely the moment to demonstrate the Christian principles which directed her life and to exert herself on behalf of her compatriots at home or at the front. But no, as she herself frequently said when confronted by issues or responsibilities she regarded as abhorrent. True, she continued with activities which she might (or usually did not) undertake in peacetime: playing Lady Bountiful by distributing produce from Fordfield garden to friends and relatives (man-power shortages – young men were in the trenches and school-leavers as young as eleven on the land – meant no garden boy to help Hubbard's successor)[53] or encouraging her daughters to make charitable gestures towards the orphan girls of the Cottage Home in nearby Shaftesbury Avenue or donating her profits from a small book of children's poetry (*Bammie's Book*) to Dr Barnardo's[54] or accompanying Chiara on an inspection of the 'dullard school'[55] to distribute cast-off clothing. (She described

her visit entirely without irony or intention of bestirring herself in terms of 'how I should *love* to go there often and do a lot ... I find [God] best when I am helping other people'.)[56] Other than this, she did nothing save suggest that hard-working people work even harder (e.g. that the teachers at the 'dotty school' keep the school open during the holidays to enable the dullards' mothers to contribute more to the war effort) and record wrote smugly that 'I often have the satisfaction of setting other people to work while I sit still and do nothing'.[57] Not even prickings of conscience moved her: of a harvest festival held at a school for 'the children of the poor' she wrote, knowing that her help would have been appreciated, 'I am not prepared to break my barrier and help in any way'.[58]

The 'barrier' was her conviction that war in general and the current war in particular were morally wrong, patriotic and jingoistic 'Lieutenant Wetenhall' of Boer War days having become an ardent pacifist who found it hard to come to terms with Eustace's and Willie's enlistment (and that of Eardley Davidson, her newer admirer) or her husband's consular contribution to desperate domestic conditions in blockaded Germany. (More courageously, she expressed unfashionable solidarity with ordinary Germans whose 'courage, devotion, bravery, intelligence, to say nothing of education and religion' she regarded as perverted to 'the service of the devil'[59]; she also took German lessons.) As the war wore on, however, and conditions in England became sufficiently uncomfortable to affect her personally (she was particularly exercised by the rigours of voluntary, then compulsory, rationing in 1917, noting 'we are beginning to learn what going short really means')[60], her sentiments became less charitable: 'our cause is the juster one and the world will be a better place if we win than if the Germans win ... better to be England now than Germany, a brutal, insolent, merciless country'[61] and her desire to retreat from 'the bewildering horror and vastness'[62] in which she was forced to live more pronounced.

Humanitarian principles notwithstanding, it was an early encounter with Belgian refugees[63], victims of Teutonic 'devils ten times over'[64], and with a group of orphaned Serbian boys[65] somewhat later which confirmed her determination to avoid any occupation which could be construed as 'war-work'; indeed, she mocked those who performed it[66] and was sharp with Constantine when he urged its suitability. Unable, however, to withdraw completely from a world she disliked, she decided 'to make [her] world tiny'[67] and to use as her excuse one which would attract sympathy for her plight, provide her with a perfect alibi, and conceal her closet pacifism and lukewarm patriotism ('war is wrong. Non-resistance is right [and] if non-resistance meant the annihilation of England, *tant pis*'![68], sentiments she shared with no-one in her immediate circle save Julius who also kept quiet)[69]: impaired health.

When Agatha suffered her near-fatal attack of gastro-enteritis in August 1911, Aelfrida vowed that if the child recovered, the next severe illness to attack the Grahams should be hers. *This* vow she kept.

Her diary for the years 1914 to 1918 is a litany of major and minor complaints. While these certainly impaired her health to greater or lesser extents and in the longer or shorter term (coughs and colds shared with Chiara and her daughters caused degrees of discomfort out of all proportion to their seriousness but were of little long-term consequence), other problems reinforce the impression that the good health enjoyed as child and adolescent deserted her following her 'Florentine fever' of 1903. Physical illnesses also mirrored fluctuations in her emotional health and although it would be inaccurate and unfair to attribute all ailments to psychological conflicts manifesting themselves as physical symptoms, it is true to say that an attack of illness was frequently precipitated by a specific worry or unpleasant occurrence, that bodily discomforts experienced even when not suffering from an identifiable illness were largely attributable to the state of tension and dismay in which she existed, and that although she agreed with Constantine when he scolded her for 'being ill and it being all [her] fault' ('perhaps it is', she added in parenthesis)[70]and with Anatolia that her ill-health was due to 'poverty of soul ('there is truth enough in what she says'[71], because she found it almost impossible to shake off the sensation of being physically and spiritually 'run down' as the current expression had it and desired nothing more than 'to go to bed and – metaphorically – turn [her] face to the wall')[72], neither the fault nor the poverty were *au fond* of her own making. In fact, they were largely attributable to the shock of Constantine's statement early in 1914 that her physical and intellectual charms no longer held any attraction for him, to the profound effect of his rejection on her emotional well-being, and to her repressing her anger at her husband's insensitive behaviour in favour of 'higher indifference'[73], a state of mind in which she allowed herself to feel 'innocent affection' towards people she believed deserved it but forbade herself to expect or accept any in return (her children always excepted), even from those who could have provided sympathy and solace.[74]

It was only by going to bed that she kept going at all. The 'two lovely quiet days'[75] a week spent there in addition to bed-rest enforced by intercurrent illnesses were pure escapism, and she was aggrieved if circumstances caused loss of one or both days. Self-confined to bed she was far from idle, however, using the time to meditate, to read, to maintain her voluminous correspondence, and to write, the woman too frail to contemplate 'war-work' working on no fewer than five books during this time: reshaping *Marrying a Stranger* between 1914 and 1918 to conform to her hopes that what began as a vengeful *roman à clef* would eventually be seen as a book 'promoting good feeling between England and Germany' in the post war period[76]; collating poems for and self-publishing *Bammie's Book* during 1915[77] and for *The Garden and the Fire* in 1916[78] and, in the same year, writing articles and poems for *The Cambridge Magazine*; conceiving, writing, and publishing her first book putting forward her 'Great Work', *The Making of a Mystic* in 1917, and conceiving and starting work on *Vision Triumphant* (originally entitled *A Soldier's Pilgrimage*) in 1918.

Nor was she wholly inactive during the five days spent downstairs. True, she did not go for long bicycle rides, a too visible sign, perhaps, of not being as ill as she wished to appear; instead, she walked at least two miles a day and was perforce active in the house, looking after the children during Octavie's time off ('two arduous days with the kiddies'[79] refers less to the physical work of caring for Agatha and Alethea than to annoyance at being prevented from doing what *she* wanted) and performing light housework as the exigencies of servant-life required. She also helped in the garden, 'picking and distributing fruit until quite exhausted'[80], mowing the tennis court area of the lawn ('I seem to have spent most of my time chained to the mowing machine', an activity which gave her backache, hay fever, and palpitations)[81], and watering vegetables with water from a bowser: 'twelve rows of potatoes and got a backache such as never'.[82] She also carried out informal classes for small children, tutored privately in Italian, and preached at Nonconformist services in Cambridge and surrounding villages, such activities not, apparently, coming under the heading of 'war-work'.

Recurrent references to backache remind us that, Constantine's and Anatolia's criticisms notwithstanding, Aelfrida suffered genuine ill-health during the war years. She was prevented from joining Constantine in Amsterdam in August 1915 not only by the presence of U-boats in the English Channel but also by a severe attack of cystitis[83], urinary tract infections having to be taken seriously since the acute nephritis to which a previous attack had led in Odessa; thereafter she suffered recurrently from bladder infections until Constantine's lengthening periods of absence abroad and a consequent diminution of sexual activities, renewed in 1914 after a three-year gap, alleviated the problem. She also developed a large boil on her buttock (boils were another ailment she shared with her mother and daughters) which required bathing and 'cupping', gave her 'swollen glands where I didn't know I had any (the groin, I think – anatomy shaky!)'[84], and forced her to stay in bed for a week. A 'horrid boil on [her] face' in April 1918[85] was even more worrying for septic foci in pre-antibiotic days could give rise to severe systemic infections with a high risk of mortality but was also symptomatic of an immune system affected by the reactive depression from which she seems to have suffered. Other 'horrid little ailments [to which] I ought to be used … now'[86] encompassed at least five bouts of malaria (in abeyance since 1912) and 'sick headaches' (migraines) more severe than those suffered in Odessa and Emden but like them, induced by tension and emotional fatigue. The pandemic 'influenza epidemic'[87] of 1918–20, on the other hand, receives only a brief mention in her diary (only one person she knew died of it and none of her immediate family); that it impressed itself on her mind, however, is evident from its reappearance as 'copy' in the form of a plague which devastates the world after a 'Great War' two hundred years in the future.

Conditions which affected Aelfrida's health in the longer term certainly began or worsened at this time. The first was rheumatoid arthritis, a disease which also affected her father and her paternal grand-mother. Although its gradual onset and diffuse symptoms, several of which were equally attributable to other ailments from which she continually or intermittently suffered, caused it not to be diagnosed until near the end of the war as 'rheumatism in my joints .. an active state of physical discomfort night and day'[88], the chronic systemic inflammatory disease with its tendency during exacerbations to make her feel as if she were burning up and the contemporary lack of effective medical treatment resulted in her suffering a remitting but relentless medical condition for the rest of her life.

Her reaction to the disease was multi-faceted. Inspired, no doubt, by her maternal grandmother's example, she used her illness as an excuse to distance herself from social occasions she did not wish to attend and from the strains and stresses of a marriage rendered unhappy by her husband's behaviour, but more significantly and unlike most sufferers from debilitating chronic pain, seems to have welcomed physical discomfort because its presence overrode emotional anguish. She also incorporated it into her esoteric personal religion, rheumatic pains being an intimate evocation of Christ's pain upon the Cross ("the mystic chalice of the Grail")[89] and an appropriate punishment for the pervasive but unaccountable sense of sin which beset her to such an extent that in the intervals of physical pain another kind of pain had to be invented for the purpose.

The second condition was gynaecological. Aelfrida's gynaecological problems began after Alethea's birth in 1908 and contained both psychological and physiological elements. The doctors' heroic efforts following Agneta's stillbirth in 1912 resulted in uterine prolapse exacerbated by the increased amount of physical work she was now forced to undertake but which eight weeks' enforced rest ('bed most of the day and no walks and no sitting up')[90] did nothing to alleviate. She also seems to have developed uterine fibroids or endometriosis or both but no firm diagnosis was ever made and some symptoms (pelvic cramps, severe period pains, backache, and heavy periods resulting in anaemia) are common to both; either way, what she coyly referred to as being 'indisposed' became a time of disabling abdominal pain and of such debilitatingly heavy menstrual flow that she sometimes had to take a taxi to her pupils' houses.[91]

Despairing of the persistence and multiplicity of her patient's symptoms, Dr Hare proposed a 'suggestion cure'.[92] But whether it was Dr Hare's lack of familiarity with the technique (she was, after all, a gynaecologist, not a Münsterberg) or lack of co-operation on Aelfrida's part – she used the sessions as a means of overcoming a period of spiritual aridity in which she felt herself alienated from, indeed, rather bored by, the thoughts of God which usually sustained her, using the second and third to re-open herself to the 'unseen world'[93] of the spirit, the fourth to will herself into a state 'where everything is perceived in spirit'[94], and subsequent sessions to meditate and even to receive visions: 'a great cross, as it were on fire [which] laid itself gently on me and I received it willingly'[95] – the 'cure' failed to cure her.

In diary entries describing 'suggestion séances', Aelfrida provides actual or hinted reasons for lack of co-operation: getting rid of her 'beastly afflictions'[96] would leave her unable to avoid war-work and prevent her from taking days in bed in which to practice and to expound in print spiritual exercises vital to her 'Great Work' of 'bringing man to the knowledge of the Divine within him'[97]; restoration of health would bind her again to the physical world of ambition and desire ('better sickness and pain than … rivalry and love')[98]; because she felt herself, as a member of the human race, to be responsible for the 'passionate and bitter suffering [of] people hurt by this war', she wished to suffer too. ('I want to serve, to atone'[99] – and how better to atone than by accepting physical discomfort as a substitute for asceticism difficult to practise under Chiara's watchful eye?) She therefore asked Dr Hare to discontinue the sessions, saying she was 'exactly where [she] used to be with regard to health' and if anything somewhat worse.[100] Dr Hare's perceptive response was that it was 'the will of God that people should be well' (Aelfrida begged to differ, saying that although she agreed it was God's will 'that people should be in health', she herself refused 'to dogmatise about particular cases')[101] and that Aelfrida was unconsciously clinging to illness 'through fear of the world', an observation the latter denied, saying that all her 'wishes and desires and instincts [tended] towards health' and that she hated 'the tepid gloom of invalidism'.[102] (This may have been true, but truer still is that from this point in her life and for the reasons stated, Aelfrida needed and enjoyed ill health.) There the matter rested, but Dr Hare's suggestion that her patient "have it as [her] ideal to be perfectly normal and commonplace"[103] perfectly expressed the exasperation of a busy doctor who had given up hours of her evenings to fruitless therapy.

A misery for which even Dr Hare's 'suggestion séances' would have failed to compensate was the Grahams' resumption of marital relations in 1914, Constantine informing his wife on his return from Paris that he was "tired of living a chaste life" and wanted ("Art thou not glad?") sexual intercourse. Noting resignedly that her body was 'his to do what he likes with' and that perhaps she 'was not meant to bear more children'[104], Aelfrida (reluctantly) agreed.

For Constantine too the years 1914–1918 had more of 'fire' about them than 'garden', in part because of his arrogance and intransigence, in part because his behaviour towards his wife resulted in alienation from wife and children alike. Returning to England in September 1914, he did not immediately obtain another posting. Though he affected to enjoy secondment to the Foreign Office ('the austerely aristocratic air of the FO suits him', Aelfrida wrote, 'and he revels in having no domestic responsibilities'; he stayed in town during the week and spent only weekends at Fordfield)[105], it was, in fact, an expression of his superiors' disapproval: not only had he, as Aelfrida suspected, been 'playing about' in Paris and 'doing things that would make the FO furious'[106] but he had also arrogated £540 of Consulate funds to his own account, possibly because he believed that acting as Consul during the Consul's absences in 1913 and 1914 and even, it appears, at the moment war was declared, he had been insufficiently remunerated. Whatever the reason, he was severely reprimanded by the British Ambassador, Sir Francis Bertie, and reverberations of '*l'affaire Bertie*' rumbled on for some months thereafter.[107]

Whether it was admiration for his wife's sangfroid on 1 August 1914 or a cynical appraisal of what might be revealed on the Grahams' return to the bosom of her family if he did not behave in a more uxorious fashion, Constantine's decision to resume marital relations led almost immediately to a very public revelation that all was not well between them. The prime cause was contraception.

The weekend before her thirty-first birthday was one which Aelfrida intended should pass off quietly ('I did not mean to tell Constantine what my conscience had decreed') because Anatolia was staying at Fordfield, but when the Grahams retired for the night was unable to stop herself blurting out her feelings. Constantine was understandably '*furious,* furious as only a man with his passions baulked can be', calling her a devil and a hypocrite, declaring that 'he would have his own way and on his own terms', and threatening her with a thrashing if she did not submit. Hearing Chiara outside escorting Anatolia to her room and terrified by Constantine's almost uncontrollable anger, Aelfrida pulled her mother into the room, crying "he has hit me before and if you go I am afraid he will hit me again".[108]

The scene degenerated rapidly from drama to melodrama ('I am not certain he would not have murdered me if we had been alone. He is not English') to (bedroom) farce: Constantine in pyjamas, 'handsome, bullying, absurd', wrapping himself in the Graham tartan rug and demanding his own way. The following day everyone 'pretended everything was all right', Aelfrida blaming Charles du Bouchet for encouraging her to submit to Constantine's embraces again but informing her husband that she would fall in with his wishes, Alfred Tillyard (forewarned by a note from his daughter placing the blame on herself) warning of the possible consequences of her behaviour ('an open scandal' and the risk that Constantine 'will probably go off with someone else'), and Constantine speaking gently of perhaps having another child when he achieved consular status and his wife recovered her health. That night, however, Constantine came into his wife's bed and 'instead of speaking words of love as is customary', verbally abused her and, having reduced her to a state of near-hysteria, raped her.[109]

Aelfrida's first thought on waking next morning (her mind was 'too full of wild thoughts' for sleep but having concluded that hell was to be 'powerlessly submerged in one's own emotions', she did) was "I hate him, I hate him", her second that she hated her husband because Constantine forced her to do wrong[110], her third (a lesson learnt from her father who also "like[d] to pose as a martyr")[111] that she must 'not hate but love'. So she parted 'affectionately' from her husband, he catching the 8.30 train[112], she to try to recover her equanimity.

We can only speculate whether Constantine acted as he did at Anatolia's instigation or whether, having earlier that year urged Mina to force Julius to consummate their marriage, he acted on his own advice, taking Julius' sister by force as an act of revenge for three years' celibacy and the prospect of more to come if Aelfrida proved adamant in her refusal to consider contraception. This time, however, no-one attempted suicide. Constantine returned to London whence he wrote abusive letters calling his wife a "tell-tale sneak"[113] and accused her of not loving him enough. ('Query, do I?' wrote Aelfrida, 'I think I do'.)[114] Aelfrida, in Cambridge, feeling 'too sore, too outraged, too humiliated for words to express', noted sadly that 'the "higher indifference" [was] having a very poor time'[115]and turned, as on those terrible evenings the previous year when Constantine inveighed against Aleister Crowley and offered physical violence of a less intimate kind (this time he inveighed, ironically under the circumstances, against Frank Stokoe, saying he 'is amorous and will have to go')[116], to spiritual consolation and to meditation: "'I" am not my poor body nor … these bitter emotions, but the eternal, the steadfast, the changeless … for if my Oath [of Obligation] holds good not even my own wrong actions, if forced upon me from without, can turn me from the path'.[117] Feeling "amazingly calmed and braced after resting in the presence of God" after what she described as a "very difficult and agitating"[118] weekend, only for a moment did she consider Constantine's position, noting 'what a nuisance' he must find her because having no room in his world for a wife with a mind and conscience of her own.[119]

Calm and braced she may have believed herself to be but judging by the immediate and later effects of Constantine's forceful overriding of her wishes, her loss of personal integrity and control as he raped her, and her conditioned response to traumatic events that 'everything was all right' when it manifestly was not, the onset of major ill health, withdrawal from the world, a tremendous increase in supernatural experiences (one might almost be tempted to say that the rape contributed to the 'making' of her as mystic), and the freezing of her emotions with regard to men and sex into a mould she was never able to break, it appears that Aelfrida was deeply traumatised by an event which echoed in intensity if not in detail one which had occurred in the same house and in the room above her own in 1888. But having heard a sermon on forgiveness and on rejoicing in affliction at age fifteen and remembered "how annoyed [she] had felt [at the time] because [she] had no enemies to forgive and no sorrows to rejoice in", she was gratified to discover fifteen years later that someone had done her "a most terrible injury" and certainly required forgiveness. And having opened the appropriate "memory drawer", she did.[120] Or persuaded herself that she had, difficult as this was: "with a start she remembered that she was a Christian and that

here was an opportunity for testing … her belief [but] sorrow had come [and] with it no power to rejoice … [and] as for loving her enemies, she felt in her … pain that she could not bear the sight of anyone…"[121]

To relieve her feelings she took refuge and revenge in poetry. *Dirge for Tatyana's Bridal Day* may seem a strange title for a poem which was soon to appear in the 'songs about love' section of *The Garden and the Fire* and 'dirge' an odd substitution for 'epithalamion', but Aelfrida had her reasons. *Dirge* was written on 6 November 1914, a month after her marital rape and at a time when diary entries demonstrate the perturbation whirling in her brain: her slipping 'quite inexplicably into *Samadhi*' while meditating after receiving a bitter letter from Constantine 'pointing out [her] likeness to the devil'[122]; the strain of Constantine's weekends at home during which hurtful comments alternating with amiability when he got his own way made her wish for life devoid of all company once the girls grew up; recognition that like a woman of her acquaintance, she was becoming "more enthusiastic than most people think decorous" about her particular form of religion, even to the extent of being "usually considered a little mad"[123] but also that she could achieve 'bright, rich and warm' spiritual experiences' within Fordfield's gloomy walls because of it; constant complaints of ill health echoing the horror of being taken by force: 'alas why have I a body!'[124] But it was with the most recent exhibition of Constantine's aggression in mind that she wrote the third of the poems in which she chiefly reveals her thoughts about her husband, the others being *The Blind Greek* and *The Prayer,* poems whose public manifestation she ensured by publishing them in three separate anthologies (*To Malise, Cambridge Poets,* and *The Garden and the Fire*) which appeared following behaviour on Constantine's part which she found intolerable; indeed, it is almost as if she hoped to drive him away but did not dare to say so openly: "Mothers are loving, but husbands are churlish; / Mothers will fondle, where husbands will beat …/ Better in arms of the earth to be sleeping / Than marry a husband and lie by his side".[125]

Having played cat and mouse with his wife's emotions during the winter and early spring of 1914/15, Constantine left for Amsterdam on 7 April 1915. 'The parting was … a wrench', wrote his wife, continuing without irony or a break 'only great love could achieve the miracle of harmony between two people so dissimilar'. (She was, in fact, more relieved than bereft: 'conjugal relations bring *him* nearer to me though I do not feel that they brought *me* nearer to him. Personally … I would rather refrain [because] such pleasure keeps me to the good things already known when I want to pass on to the unknown "senses of the soul"'.)[126] Left behind with her children, her elderly parents, her illnesses, her diary, and her philosophies, she took her revenge.

*The Cambridge Magazine*, it assured its readers, was happy to send copies to subscribers wherever they were posted abroad, an important factor in keeping up morale in wartime. Knowing this (for otherwise why publish retaliatory articles about one's absent husband in it?) Aelfrida wrote no fewer than seven articles for the magazine during 1916 alone. The first was composed following two letters from Constantine saying that if she did not keep within her £225 annual allowance he would "take measures to enforce [his] wishes". Already scrupulous as to expenditure ('I am going without things I need … I *know* I am not extravagant'), Aelfrida was deeply hurt ('I knew before I married him how he would hate this kind of thing … it is such a defilement to our love that he should behave so!'), asking her husband 'for a clear statement of our resources' and informing him that although *she* was prepared to scrimp and save, *he* was not to stint himself – to which he readily agreed.[127] She expressed her true feelings, however, in *Economy for Men*, a dialogue between 'Mrs Shelford', an older woman who wears "the anxious, purposeful expression of one whose life is passed at committee meetings", and 'Mrs Linton', a younger woman who "thinks herself clever":

Mrs Shelford:  "My husband is dreadfully depressed about Thrift. He says we cannot possibly win the war unless we take Economy more seriously".

Mrs Linton:  "Economy seems to have a kind of intrinsic absurdity, like mothers-in-law … I wonder why, though, it is the women who have to do the economising while men make cheap jokes at their expense …"

Mrs Shelford:  "… A man's only idea of Economy [is] cutting down the allowance of his wife and daughters".

Mrs Linton:  "Men [have] admirable reasons for doing what they want …" (the author then lists the reason given by men for not economising e.g. their official positions oblige them to entertain guests with wine and cigars in order to acquire information or clinch a deal)… "I'm wearing a coat and skirt that I got in a sale four years ago and [a] hat … I trimmed myself …"

Mrs Shelford:  "Yes, but so many men are patriotic in big things, you cannot expect them to deny themselves little things too".[128]

Possibly as a result of reading Aelfrida's satirical article (another reason will be divulged shortly), Constantine's letters from Holland during 1916 were 'dull and chilly', so chilly, in fact, that he appeared to be making very little effort to keep in touch with his wife and daughters. Stung by the thought that his love for her had 'burnt itself out as all the world said it would'[129], his wife took further revenge in six *Letters to Lucy*, the first of which appeared in *The Cambridge Magazine* the day after the diary entry just quoted. The letters contain references which immediately identify the author and the real subject of her satire: the names of her closest friend (Lucy) and one of her daughters, disguised as 'Althea'[130]; the subject of Constantine's Part 2 Tripos, Moral Sciences ('Moral Stinks', in undergraduate parlance); to Wagner (*Tannhäuser* was one of Constantine's favourite operas and he often played music from it on Fordfield piano) and to Goldsworthy Lowes Dickinson, his admirer. They also contain remarks which must emanate from Constantine himself ("if we must have melodrama … let's tone it down"[131]; "kill ten German babies for every English baby and you'll soon stop the Zepps")[132] and one attributable to Aelfrida, namely that people who figure in *romans à clef* (possibly *Marrying a Stranger,* which if Constantine read it prior to departure would not have endeared him to its author) are annoyed "not because their private lives are revealed to the world's curiosity but because they think their characters are badly described".[133]

1916, however, was also a year in which Aelfrida became less bitter and more insightful, albeit no less self-righteous. Between her ninth and tenth wedding anniversaries, she cogitated at length on her marriage and came to some interesting conclusions: 'I admit … that I love him now more as one loves a child than as one loves a husband – but my love is purer and more ardent so … I admit too … that I am happier at Fordfield than I ever was with him [because] … in all our married life I have never felt completely at ease with him, but always strained and watchful'.[134] Her unease, she believed, was due to Constantine greeting her every observation with 'chilling un-sympathy and criticism' and being 'completely indifferent to [her] interests and pursuits' ('it is difficult when one's husband says "I do not think thy opinion worth having" with an air of boredom and distaste')[135], to his discontent with married life in general and celibacy in particular, and to his failed hopes of a literary career. She nevertheless resolved 'to be a better wife to him than I have been' and that she would look forward, not back.[136]

Her resolutions were undermined by two events which also took place that year. During the first, Aelfrida's idealised view of her husband was tested to breaking point; during the second, her notion of herself as a perfect wife was considerably dented.

During a fit of introspection suffered in March 1916 Aelfrida confided to her parents that she believed Constantine as poet and writer to be a kind of 'priest or … prophet, born to reveal that aspect of God which is known to us as Beauty or Harmony' ('he thought so too', she added) and that she had 'spoiled a genius by marrying him'. To her surprise, the Oracle and Chiara rounded on her, telling her that she 'ought no more to have taken Constantine seriously when he said he wanted to be a genius' than she took little Alethea's intentions of being 'a farmer or a pastry cook'. The scales fell from her eyes: 'his claim, then, was the height of fatuity. As a genius he criticised my fifth rate novels and third rate verse and my religion and my ideals. As a genius he demanded concerts ad lib and kisses from Déla Bernet … perhaps it was my vanity that made me fancy I was to make a genius – but he was so sure of himself! … Well, thank God for a lost illusion. I shall not love Constantine less but God … the more'.[137]

The second event occurred in July. Aelfrida had taken Agatha and Alethea to visit their paternal grandparents in Hessle. Argyris was 'his usual sweet and loving attentive and thoughtful self'[138] but Anatolia, inspired perhaps by bombing raids across the Humber, was preparing bombshells of her own. Seizing every opportunity, she bombarded her daughter-in-law with home truths, telling her that she had 'no intelligence, no love, no passion, no tenderness, no devotion, no sense'; that she was 'a complete failure as a wife and mother' and 'the most absolutely selfish person' Anatolia had ever met; that Constantine had spent a great deal of money on her and received nothing in return; that houses run by her were 'always … nightmares'; that her ill-health was entirely her own fault; that Agatha and Alethea were badly brought up. Though she initially belittled Anatolia's accusations as 'grievances of ten and twelve years' standing, old grudges, old jealousies', Aelfrida later admitted 'of course there is truth enough in what she says. Selfish! Don't I know it? Yes, and of course I can't pretend to have been a perfect success as a wife'. Hoping to placate her mother-in-law, Aelfrida asked what could or should be done to remedy the situation. Anatolia opened fire with both barrels: boarding school for 'turbulent' Alethea and a mistress for Constantine.[139]

Aelfrida waited until 1922 before turning her diary account of Anatolia's tirade and her own response into homily, describing in *Can I be a Mystic?* an occasion on which an exasperated woman is saved from responding to another woman's criticisms ("M— started finding fault with me, saying I was censorious, self-righteous,

self-absorbed, no use to anybody etc., etc.") by a flash of insight in which she sees 'M—'s' soul "free from its poor, soiled, earthly wrapping, pure and flashing as it came from God" and by discovering as a result "that God loved [M—] as I might love a crippled child, more tenderly, it might be, because of her deformity… so I got up and kissed her and said … I hoped it would all be better in the future".[140] And in view of what transpired in Hessle in July 1916, it is probably as well that apart from a brief meeting at Eustace's wedding to Phyllis Mudie-Cooke in 1919, Aelfrida and Anatolia never encountered each other again.

On 26 May 1917 Aelfrida began a new volume of her diary. Informing her future readers 'you know where I stand – light within, darkness and war without, and in my immediate surroundings at Fordfield, peace and contentment'[141], she began (in spite of resolving not to do so) by looking back, writing on the thirteenth anniversary of her engagement 'the garden …looks much as it did then – all the lilac and laburnum and chestnuts full of blossom and the sun as golden as ever. I spent a while with ghosts … I think if Graham met Michaelides now he would not care for him'.[142] Looking forward as promised, albeit with apprehension, to Constantine's long leave later that year, she wrote 'suppose he should be in love with me again … Should I try to believe it all as I once did and speak the language of human passion, trying to believe *that* the gate of heaven, while only half beguiled? I tried to give myself wholly – to "see God in him" – tried and failed. I took the language from his lips, kindled something of a fire in me from his heart, but a part of me always remained apart, aloof, untouched … Have I anything to give him [now] that he will take and prize? He is all my romance, my earthly love …'[143]

The disparity between romance and religion continued to plague her but was resolved using arguments similar to those used during her engagement: 'there is, of course, no real opposition between one's love of God and of man. The antithesis is a false one and something is wrong with one's vision when it seems to exist. Synthesis, not choice, Aelfrida!'[144] Less easy to dismiss, however, was the thought that Constantine was 'unconsciously' (more likely consciously, for he was later to shout at her 'I come first') 'rather jealous of the children and very jealous of God [but] I can't help loving God best and the children second. And how can one of Constantine's temperament bear to be only third'.[145] But although she also noted that 'the divine in man may be loved with that complete ardour which marks one's love of God'[146], she did not then or later promote her husband to first place even if by doing so she might restore his love and preserve her marriage. Not even a 'short sharp lecture' from the

Oracle on the day of Constantine's return on the danger of trying to 'edify or uplift' her husband ('my reputation, evidently – a moral east wind')[147] caused her to falter: she would continue to love Constantine *third* and to blow easterly on him.

At first all went well. Constantine was 'very loving and in a mood to be pleased' and Aelfrida a 'very happy woman ... [for] he keeps, bless him, the most lovely ... freshness with regard to his intimate relations. Let it be accounted to him for righteousness that he has kept faithful to his wife *and* that he is not emotionally unmoved by coming back to her'.[148] Agatha and Alethea too were overjoyed at meeting their father again, recalling 'in the most charming way stories that he told and games that they had played together'.[149] The idyll did not last. Three things conspired against it.

The first was the change which had taken place in Constantine. To Aelfrida's amusement, her husband had become a dandy: 'when I first knew him he wore threadbare blue serge and looked like a young god. Now he wears the most elegant attire ... and looks like a man of the world'.[150] He was also 'a good bit stouter' and being 'a perfect fool over his health', sitting up to 'unheard of hours and [keeping] himself going with whisky when he is tired'[151], cardinal sins in a temperance household which believed in the moral benefits of early to bed, early to rise; he also showed 'all the symptoms of "brain fag" and will get really ill if he does not learn'.[152] More worrying still was the change in Constantine's character, he having become 'strong and masterful, a man among men, hard-worked, keen, intelligent, accustomed to command ... so absolutely bound up with the world and its ways [that] he has ... completely turned his back on all the things he used to care for [and] all his old idealism'.[153] He had also become intensely ambitious (his chief wish was to be appointed commercial attaché), expressing annoyance that his wife was not more use to him from the point of view of his career. ('And there ... I sympathise with him entirely', wrote Aelfrida, wholly unwilling to do anything to help.)[154] Nothing the Tillyards could do to demonstrate the charms of Cambridge life reconciled Constantine to the 'small beer' of existence in England beyond London. (He also showed little interest in Aelfrida's new book *The Making of a Mystic,* describing it as 'goupy'[155] i.e. as piously sentimental, and saying that he had neither time nor inclination to read it.) His world, concluded Aelfrida sadly, 'is not my world – it is the world of ambition and emulation, of power and rule and riches'.[156] Noting that although she did not want to criticise her husband but 'to love and admire him' ('may God deliver me from harshness and self-righteousness')[157], she added that his presence caused her 'more pain than pleasure' and that

even when 'Constantine Michaelides' was being 'quite human and companionable', perpetually superimposed on him was 'the Graham whom I so much dislike'.[158]

Early in November 1917 Constantine paid a solo visit to Hessle. Anatolia may have informed him of home-truths bestowed on Aelfrida the previous year (the latter had not imparted Anatolia's accusations to Constantine, describing her mother-in-law only as behaving towards her with her customary unfriendliness)[159]; Constantine certainly returned to Fordfield in a 'most unsympathetic and censorious mood'. He proceeded to attack his wife in very 'Anatolian' terms, accusing her of being a "luxurious ascetic" who took all she wanted and made a pose of denying herself things she did not care about ('his words had some truth in them', Aelfrida admitted, she having begun to eat detested foods 'for a little cheap asceticism' and, finding she now liked them, continuing to do so even as she jeered at herself for failing the test)[160] and of believing in a wholly subjective religion of mere "intellectual idiosyncrasy"; he also, she said, 'blamed' her for virtues (*sic*) she tried hard to attain, chiefly 'detachment' (her vaunted 'higher indifference'), detachment being in Constantine's eyes an excuse for utter disregard of himself.[161] He also attacked her attitude towards Agatha and Alethea, telling her that their lives were 'too quiet' and that she was imbuing them with unsuitable opinions, notably pacifism. Finally, he wished to know if she proposed to earn money from her books and on finding that she did not, suggested she was wasting her time by writing them.[162]

Had Constantine returned to Amsterdam at this point matters might have been settled sufficiently for the Grahams to maintain the pretence of a marriage. On 17 December, however, Constantine, preoccupied with Foreign Office matters since his return to England, delivered 'a bolt from the blue': not only was he not returning to Holland except briefly to settle his affairs but he had also been removed from yet another post.

Constantine's superior in Holland was Ernest Maxse, Consul-General to the Netherlands, with headquarters in Rotterdam.[163] Not having learnt his lesson from his earlier brush with Francis Bertie ('the cause of his having to leave Paris', according to Aelfrida), Constantine had quarrelled with Maxse over the 'far too independent and high-handed' manner in which he (CG) ran the Amsterdam Consulate, his inability to organise, his extravagance, and his quarrels with his staff having finally forced Maxse to request his subordinate's removal. Constantine, for his part, admitted to a 'divergence of policy' from his superior and agreed that he had blundered in complaining directly to the Foreign Minister that Maxse's conduct towards himself impeded the smooth running of the Amsterdam office; he also blamed 'his own impet-uous nature' and declared himself 'willing to eat a certain amount of humble pie' lest his next posting be Batavia: 'exile, not to say disgrace'.[164] The matter was settled by Constantine accepting a probationary posting to Lyons as acting vice-consul, 'a clear loss … of position, of pres-tige, of money', with promise of advancement to Consul or Consul-General when the present incumbent moved on, subject to satisfactory conduct in the interim. On 28 January 1918 Aelfrida received a 'short and charac-teristic' letter from Constantine, currently in Amsterdam winding up his affairs: "I have seen some old friends and found that all my arrangements have stood the test of absence and administration by others. I have no news … no knowledge of the future, a sense of the unspeakable bitterness of many things … a weariness of all but a very few things in life. I hope thou art well. Kiss the kiddies for me. With all love. Thy husband".[165]

Awaiting Constantine's earlier return from Amsterdam in October 1917, Aelfrida worried that instead of being 'in love with [her] again', he might have become 'cold, very consular and official' towards her. She also asked herself 'will that hurt me much?'; given his behaviour in Paris and her assumption of 'higher indifference', cool-ness towards her would be no more than normal behav-iour on his part and detachment an appropriate response on hers. Her next question, however, seems curiously disconnected from her first: 'is my place as secure as it now feels?'[166]

What did Aelfrida know or suspect that she did not impart to her diary? In fact, she did know, but preferred to laugh the matter off as an impossibility.

During her visit to Hessle in 1916, Anatolia took great delight in informing her that shortly after arriving in Amsterdam, Constantine had fallen in love with his landlady, Madame Sterneberg, later described by Aelfrida as 'a widow, cultured … and she keeps a boarding house for young ladies and has two children of her own, aged 14 and 16'.[167] (Photographic evidence shows Madame Sterneberg to be a handsome woman in early middle age; Aelfrida describes her as 'forty-two or three'.) Constantine, Anatolia continued, was extremely happy both with the relationship and with the fact that Fordfield and Tillyards notwithstanding, he had found 'a home … at last'.[168] (Contemporary photographs show him look-ing contented and at ease with his adopted family; in fact, Madame's 'handsome, sullen' children were sent to boarding school because they disapproved of their moth-er's liaison.)[169] Affecting to disbelieve the story, Aelfrida wrote to Constantine informing him of Anatolia's insist-ence that her son was in love with Madame Sterneberg; a subsequent letter sent while Constantine was winding

up his affairs in Amsterdam early in 1918 included 'an absurd picture' of his 'imaginary goings-on' with his (supposed) inamorata.[170]

A premonitory dream on 14 January 1918 should have warned her: walking through lovely countryside by the sea, the Grahams came upon a ruined church surrounded by fields full of graves, whereupon Constantine turned to her and told her he no longer loved her. Feeling 'cold all over', Aelfrida woke to a letter from her husband inform-ing her that he was 'more untameable than ever' and did not see how he could 'submit to the rules of a household again'. Worried by the dream but pleased because his 'young and untamed' attitude reminded her of happier times, Aelfrida replied with a 'spirited answer'; three days later she promised to 'look forward – not back'.[171]

This was as well on two counts. In January 1918 Aelfrida found herself unexpectedly pregnant for the fourth time at the age of thirty-four, right on sched-ule. (The Grahams, it seems, did not always take contra-ceptive precautions in spite of Constantine's decree that 'there must be no more children'.)[172] Her initial reaction was 'what unspeakable joy to have another little one to love!' but because the man who accused her of 'spawn-ing another brat' in 1911 was likely to be 'decidedly annoyed'[173] in 1918, and because thoughts of the conse-quences discouraged her (the discomforts of pregnancy and agony of childbirth, 'the care and weariness and anx-iety of a little one; money difficulties; the cold welcome accorded to the child' and, most important of all, having to abandon work on her 'Great Work' until it was old enough to be relatively independent, a stage reached by Alethea, now aged ten, and Agatha aged eight)[174], she left the matter in God's hands. God decreed miscarriage, Aelfrida noting 'alas, there is to be no baby!', but whether from natural or unnatural intervention, she does not say. (Nor does she say if she informed Constantine of her pregnancy and of its termination.) Adding that she did not know 'whether [she was] … disappointed or relieved', she decided that the creative energy which would have gone into making a child would be diverted into other channels: 'I am turning the baby into a book!'[175] (*Vision Triumphant* was published in 1919 when she was thir-ty-six, the age at which she had hoped to complete her 'five in all and very moderate' family.) Secondly, although Constantine's final departure from Holland and his arrival at Fordfield sent her into raptures ('I'm so happy … radiant with delight at having him safely back and full of love and eagerness'), the fact that her diary entry con-tinues without a break <u>Later. I feel dazed – stunned</u> sug-gests premature elation. A private conversation between husband and wife was to cause her life to unravel for the foreseeable future and cloud it forever:

Constantine: "I have something to tell thee".
Aelfrida:     "Very well. Tell me now".
Constantine: "I do not love thee any more".
Aelfrida:     "I suppose thou dost love Madame Sterneberg".
Constantine: "Yes …"
Aelfrida:     "Is she thy mistress?" [176]

She was.

Aelfrida's reaction ran a predictable course. She began moralistically ('thy action with regard to Mrs Sterneberg is wrong')[177], continued by blaming first herself ('I can't help thinking it must have been … my fault')[178] and by wondering at length what her fault could have been – her ill-health, her having encouraged Constantine's little friends? – without lighting on the obvious ones, then Anatolia ('she brought him up without principles and she has persistently worked against me')[179] and Argyris ('by inaction')[180], lastly Constantine himself: 'his conceptions of love were … un-English'.[181] Fury followed ('that he should have required my person of me and not … told me that his body had been given to the use of another woman')[182], then numbness ('such grief as I feel is *detached* … I wonder whether I shall grieve more later on')[183], then pain ('last night … I lay awake and *suffered* – oh, *suffered*'), pain more on Constantine's account than on her own because '[his] character had so deteriorated'[184], then Christian resignation ('God has been with me these days')[185], finally questioning acceptance ('I don't want him to be good in my way – do I?') and rationalisation: 'with my body I do not love him … how could I after the way he outraged it – but with my mind and my heart I love him more than ever'.[186] This last, at least, was true and it was to colour and ruin relationships with other men for the rest of her life.

Two wry thoughts persisted: that Constantine 'might have treated [her] better if [she] had borne him a son'[187], and that Crowley's prediction 'that sorrow would come to [her] through [her] affections' had come true, for on her informing him that she was ready to endure any sorrow provided it did not injure those she loved, he had repeated the phrase mockingly before announcing "how grimly smiles the universe at large! As for you, you can be hurt, and hurt you will be".[188]

Constantine travelled to Lyons in April 1918. For a man who had been Acting Consul-General for some months in Paris and Acting Consul in Amsterdam for two years, demotion to one of two vice-consuls was a severe blow (his present mood, he noted without irony, was 'one of considerable unbelief either in justice or fair play')[189] and he soon gained the reputation of being 'ambitious and touchy'.[190] To Aelfrida, he wrote of his revulsion from all 'inhuman things'[191] i.e. from any form of spiritual consolation for his present unhappiness; he also informed her that she herself was "bound in the cruel darkness of religious intolerance" and had "failed in thy duty as a wife for a very long time and wouldst without a word have allowed me to live in utter … desolation or even to die… except perhaps that thou wouldst have luxuriated in pious self-satisfaction".[192] Given that Aelfrida's diary entry for the same day (10 May) includes an account of her accidental discovery of 'hotly passionate' letters to Constantine from Hilda Sollas, 'Juanita', and others, her emotions must have defied description.

Rather than indulge in recriminations, Aelfrida preferred to 'turn aside from the clamour of the world-war' and from the antipathy between herself and her husband and to copy out for her biographer 'a letter written in more peaceful times by myself to myself' re-discovered that day in 'old papers':

12 October 1902
Fordfield, Cambridge.
"Dear Frida,
Are you still Frida Tillyard or are you someone quite different? I hope you don't mind me knowing your age, I who was nineteen just a week ago and who must seem to you a mere girl. If the years have been good, you should be proud of them. But I don't mean to preach, Frida dear, I wish to write you a word of cheer. Oh, if you are an old maid I am afraid your life is rather a cheerless one. Do you still spend your nights in hopeless longings for the man you used to love – so many, many years ago? Are your dear ones dead? Has your heart grown cold? Oh, I beg your pardon! You aren't so very old, after all …

If you are a happy wife and mother you will smile at the fears that I feel tonight. If you are a celebrated authoress, as I pray you are, perhaps you shake your head and say I have caught a glimpse of the future. Fame without love – is that your fate?

Or have you neither, Frida, neither? Now don't be angry with me. You see, I feel as though I knew you very well – once!

My love to your husband – if you have one – and to the chicks – if there are any.

Thine for auld lang syne,
Aelfrida CW Tillyard.

… PS. You needn't answer this letter. I am a ghost of your dead past". [193]

Premonitory or ironic though it was, Aelfrida read the letter in the spirit in which it was written: 'no, dear child, I have not forgotten you – even if I have forgotten Lord

Kitchener![194] I can look you in the face, clear-eyed, earnest young girl, and say that the years have been good [and] that I am not ashamed …'[195] Four days later she heard with 'sober thankfulness' that Germany had accepted the peace terms laid down by the President of the United States and was preparing to negotiate.[196] On 8 November she recorded that 'military representatives have arrived in France to arrange about the armistice'[197] and on 10 November that the Kaiser had abdicated. Writing her diary on 11 November 1918, she heard 'the sound of cheering and of bells … *the Armistice is signed!*'[198]

Not, however, for the Grahams. Hearing that Constantine was likely to remain in Lyons for some time, Aelfrida decided to join him at the earliest opportunity: not only did she profess to love him '*far* more than ever'[199] but she also needed to discuss their marriage in person instead of relying on the slow and unsatisfactory medium of letters. There was, however, unfinished business to complete in England first, for lying above and around the personal and universal disharmony which formed the 'fiery' antithesis to the serene and structured spiritual 'garden' in which she tried and wished to dwell, was knowledge that the years between 1914 and 1918 had created the perfect conditions for her to forge ahead with the 'Great Work' to which she solemnly swore her Oath of Obligation every New Year's Day and to place her feet firmly on the 'mystic way' she hoped to pursue. Scorched by the fires of marital warfare, ill-health, and heartbreak ("I was a warm well-tended cottage home – / A wreckage left when tides of war swept by")[200], she prepared to make her necessary journey through flames to a place where she could meet with other and perhaps more intimate 'mystical adventures'. But first, like the pilgrim in the 'Strange Adventure' recounted in *A Little Road Book for Mystics*, she must turn aside into territory almost as bizarre as the 'garden' described there.

## Notes

1 'Wathlessness' is a most evocative word in this context, a 'wath' being a ford or a dialect or obsolete version of 'wade'; the condition of 'wathlessness' therefore implies a state of mind or a place through which one passes only with great difficulty if, indeed, one is able to pass at all.

2 Aelfrida had not tried crystal gazing before October 1912 so could not have provided the inspiration for the poem; whether it inspired her scrying is not stated but the poem appears in the volume of manuscript poems shared by both Grahams (GCPPT 2/2). No events described in Aelfrida's contemporary diary records provide context for the poem's composition.

3 GCPPT 1|1|19 24 October 1913 with marginal emendations of December 1913.

4 ibid. 10, 12, and 16 February 1914.

5 ibid. 10 February 1914.

6 ibid. 18 February 1914.

7 Aelfrida's description of 'Weston St Stephen' church is an amalgamation of several churches near Linton, a village south of Cambridge in which she spent several holidays. Weston Colville seems to have provided her with details of 'Weston St Stephen's' situation and view of Ely Cathedral, its churchyard's pillared and tumbled tombstones acting as a model for those described in *Marrying a Stranger*. Holy Trinity church in Balsham more nearly answers her description of the church of 'Weston St Stephen'; the rectory too is close by, accessible by a small gate. Holy Trinity also contains windows in which are depicted large single figures of saints.

8 Tillyard, Ae. *Marrying a Stranger* pp 248–251 (GCPPT 2|6).

9 A full explanation of Aelfrida's imagery would be too lengthy but the 'tombstones' may represent books of occult lore, the pool of blood in its hollow stone an occult experience or a memory of postpartum haemorrhage; a childhood memory of milk for the cat being poured into a hollow brick outside the Fordfield gardener's cottage may be relevant too.

10 GCPPT 2|24|1. *Blessings.*
   GCPPT 1|1|45 12 June 1934.

11 *The Koran. The Terror* (56:8 and 45–50).

12 ibid. *The All-Merciful* (55:45–50).

13 ibid. *The All-Merciful* (55:44).

14 ibid. *The Terror* (56:40–43).

15 ibid. *Hobbling* (45: 32–33).

16 GCPPT 1|1|21 18 November 1916.

17 The printed version – there is no manuscript version – ends with the lines "Turn unto God, O soul of mine – / Ye twain shall be the one, Divine!' The change of emphasis in the last line (One/Divine) may be a result of Aelfrida having second thoughts (or a printer's error) but the diary version expresses her meaning better.

18 *The Curse of Duality* (*The Garden and the* Fire pp 75–76 section entitled 'mystical poems') was probably written in late August or early September 1916: in a diary entry of 8 September Aelfrida describes rescuing her manuscript from Heffer's printing works where it had gone to be typeset because she wanted to make a 'final revision' of the text, but as there is no reference in her diary to what is obviously a very significant poem, the exact date of composition remains open to conjecture.

19 GCPPT 1|1|21 8 September 1916.

20 GCPPT 1|1|20 11 and 13 August 1914.

21 ibid. 28 August 1914.

22 ibid. 19 August 1914. Visiting soldiers on the Cambridge commons was a spectator sport at that point in the war.

23 GCPPT 1|1|20 19 December 1914. Major Gregor died on active service.

24 GCPPT 1|1|20 6 July 1915. The 'young Hercules' episode appears in GCPPT 2|26|2(1). Jack Clay survived the war.

25 ibid. 21 January and 9 September 1915.

26 ibid. 9 September 1915.

27 ibid. 20 1 September 1914.

28 ibid. 4 August 1914.

29 ibid. 14 September 1914.

30 The only reference to Constantine ('Father', more usually 'Fuvver') in published poetry written during the war by Aelfrida for Agatha and Alethea comes in *Bammie's Book* of 1915 in which the last line of a poem entitled *Parents* declares that in spite of the noisy fun the girls have with 'Father' and the quiet times they have with 'Mother' (Aelfrida was invariably 'Mother') *two* parents – father *and* mother – are best.

31 GCPPT 1|1|20 7 August 1914.

32 ibid. 14 September 1914. The first poem in *The Garden and the Fire* (*In Time of War* pp 3–4, section entitled 'poems about the war') is dedicated 'to H D H'. Written on 13 November 1915 it describes Aelfrida's fears for England if the English win or lose the war (both, in her view,

harbingers of social upheaval) and her hope that, winner or loser, England turn to God when fighting ceases.

33 GCPPT 1|1|21 28 February 1916. Aelfrida's last meetings with this particular Little Friend persuaded her that 'New Hebridean manners and customs must be vastly superior to ours, for [Layard] is so much improved' (GCPPT 1|1|21 29 January 1916). They also provided inspiration for a poem *Her Lover, to Rosamund,* written on 4 March 1916, a day on which Layard had invited her to lunch and forgotten she was coming; Aelfrida ate whatever food she could find in his college rooms and departed, leaving him a 'mocking note' in the form of the poem whose refrain "I shall forget …" would remind him not only of a missed lunch but of other matters too: the moment, for example, when "your lips and mine were met". The poem, of which no manuscript version exists, was later published in *The Garden and the Fire* (p 27) in the section entitled 'songs about love'.

34 GCPPT 1|1|20 22 December 1914.

35 ibid. 4 August 1914.

36 *A Letter from Lahr* ('from HMWT') appears in the 'poems about the war' section of *The Garden and the Fire* (pp 10–11), Aelfrida recording in her diary entry for 21 October 1914 (GCPPT 1|1|20) that she had written an 'imaginary' letter from Julius which reduced both her and her mother to tears. Prior to its appearance in Aelfrida's anthology the poem was published in *The Cambridge Magazine* vol IV No 6 14 November 1914 p121 under the title *A Letter from a Young University Lecturer Detained in Germany.*

37 Ruhleben (usually referred to as a 'Concentration Camp' following the introduction of the term in a Commons debate of March 1901 to describe settlements instituted by Aelfrida's former idol Lord Kitchener during the Second Boer War of 1899–1902), was in fact an internment camp in which Englishmen over 17 and under 55 years of age caught in Germany at the outset of the Great War were housed in rows of brick or wooden barracks. Julius appears to have regarded his stay as a kind of monastic respite from the miseries of marriage during which he read books from the camp library, coached fellow internees for Cambridge entrance examinations, and wrote uncharacteristically light hearted poems for his nieces, three of which were published in *Bammie's Book* and a further possible two in *Verses for Alethea*. Further poems were read by Julius to the family on 11 May 1915 and described by Aelfrida as 'half-morbid, half-gay, bitter, humorous, sarcastic, ingenious – the strangest mixture' (GCPPT 1|1|20), Julius, like his sister, choosing to air his grievances in verse rather than let them fester inwardly or confront them openly.

38 GCPPT 1|1|20 11 May 1915.

39 ibid. 13 May 1915.

40 GCPPT 1|1|23 9 September 1918. Julius' former civil prisoner status later exempted him from conscription.

41 GCPPT 1|1|20 8 May 1915.

42 ibid. 15 January 1915.

43 ibid. 5 May 1915.

44 Tillyard, EMW. pp 11–18.

45 Tillyard, Ae. *Vision Triumphant* p14. The novel is dedicated 'to Eustace and Willie'.

46 The poem first appeared in *The Cambridge Magazine* vol IV No 2 p40 on 17 October 1914. To add verisimilitude it names two Little Friends ("The train to Bristol past me booms./ I wonder who has got my rooms! / I like to think that Frank is there/ and Willie in the basket chair…") and a distant cousin, "Ernest with his guileless looks" being Ernest Crundwell, descendant of Thomas Castle, Catharine Castle's brother. *A Letter from Ealing Broadway Station* appears in the 'poems about the war' section of *The Garden and the Fire* (pp 5–6).

47 GCPPT 1|1|20 7 November 1914.

48 The corpse built into the parapet was at Festubert of which Eustace wrote 'it was beastly, damp, and stinking there' (GCPPT 1|1|21 3 November 1915).

49 GCPPT 1|1|20 22 June 1915.

50 *NCO* Henderson Collection 20|7|6. Letter from Eustace Tillyard to Hubert Henderson of 3 August 1915.

51 GCPPT 1|1|21 23 March 1916.

52 GCPPT 1|1|23 13 February 1919.

53 In the first 46 years of its existence Fordfield had only two gardeners, Jervis and Hubbard. Hubbard retired when over 80 and was replaced by Parry who only stayed two years, leaving in disgust in October 1917 at the amount of work he was expected to carry out on his own. Parry was succeeded by Fordfield's fourth and final gardener, Church. For an account of Jervis, Hubbard, and Parry see GCPPT 2|27|2(3).

54 Thomas Barnardo (1845–1905), founder of the Barnardo homes for destitute children, relied entirely on charitable donations to fund his foundations. *Bammie's Book,* published in November 1915, whose profits Aelfrida informs her readers were to go to Barnardo's foundation, would have raised around £24 if all 500 copies had been sold; many were not.

55 GCPPT 1|1|20 9 July 1915.

56 ibid. 9 and 11 July 1915.

57 GCPPT 1|1|21 16 December 1915.

58 ibid. 16 September 1917.

59 GCCPT 1|1|20 3 November 1914.

60 GCPPT 1|1|22 19 December 1917. The Tillyards never, of course, experienced real deprivation; they merely disliked lowering the culinary standards to which they were accustomed (for descriptions of an ordinary and a festive tea see Tillyard, Ae. *Just Alice* pp 10–12) and the inclusion on their diet of surrogate foods. ("Sloe leaf tea", "margarine / That masquerades as butter", "tomato jam and lentil ham" are described by Aelfrida in *After the War*, a poem which appears in the manuscript version of *Verses for Alethea* (GCPPT2|8a) but not in the published version; it is unlikely that the Tillyards were reduced to substitutes such as these) or foodstuffs regarded as the province of the 'lower middle classes' e.g. black treacle and dripping instead of jam and butter or "a plate of cabbage soup … or half an inch of eel" (*Invitation au Festin* in *Verses for Alethea* pp14–15). Learning from Maynard Keynes, now a government economist, that there was a record rice harvest in 1916 Aelfrida had laid in supplies, only to worry later that the Tillyards might be accused of the criminal offence of hoarding food (GCPPT 1|1|22 9 and 10 Feb 1918). Chiara's American relatives also supplied them with staple and luxury foodstuffs ("barrels of white flour and of sugar, boxes of candy, boxes of stuffed dates, salted almonds and California plums". Tillyard, Ae. *The Approaching Storm* p87) until worries that they might be denounced as 'food hogs' caused the Tillyards to beg them to stop.

61 GCPPT 1|1|22 22 and 26 March 1918.

62 ibid. 16 March 1918.

63 Aelfrida describes the refugees as mostly the 'better classes from Antwerp' (GCPPT 1|1|20 18 October 1914) though in fact they came from every social class, the Belgian Refugee Committee in Cambridge making itself responsible for clothing and housing many of them. The University, moved by their plight, contributed funding and with the help of Margaret Verrall established a 'Belgian University in Cambridge' run by exiled lecturers from Louvain, Ghent, Liège, and Brussels. (For an interesting account of the Belgians in Cambridge, see Keynes, F. p 87 and Keynes, M. pp 183–187. Contemporary issues of *The Cambridge Magazine* also contain many references). Two of Aelfrida's own poems refer to German atrocities perpetrated during the invasion of Belgium: *Belgium. August–September 1914,* written on 27 September 1914 (the poem first appeared in *The Quest* Vol.VI No 2 of January 1915 with a footnote, omitted from the version published in 'the 'poems about the war' section of *The Garden and the Fire* of 1916 p 7, which enlarged on the poem's last line "Cry 'Thou art He!'":
" there is an Indian Mutiny tale which relates how a hermit, on being bayoneted by a British Soldier, broke the silence of fifteen years to

exclaim Thou too art He!") and *The Stones of Belgium* written on 13 March 1915 which first appeared in *The Cambridge Magazine* vol IV No 22, 22 May 1915 p427, then in Charles Forshaw's 1916 anthology *One Hundred of the Best Poems on the European War* (bylined ' by women poets of the Empire') and later that same year in *The Garden and the Fire* (pp 4–5), also in the 'poems about the war' section.

64 GCPPT 1|1|22 22 March 1918.

65 Aelfrida's reference to the 'little Serbians' temporarily housed at Cheshunt Theological College in nearby Bateman Street (GCPPT 1|1|21 23 April 1916) alludes to the group of 152 lads spirited out of Serbia in an attempt to save a few of the country's next generation of young men. (Serbia, at war for the third time in two years, was on the side of the Allies during the Great War). Aelfrida's efforts on behalf of the local Serbian Relief Fund were confined to supplying icons and to making the wholly inappropriate suggestion that Frank Stokoe be co-opted to teach the vulnerable youngsters. (Fortunately he refused, saying the post was 'just the wrong thing for him'. GCPPT 1|1|21 23 August 1916). A poem describing the desperate measures to which refugees were reduced, *An Incident of the Flight from Poland,* written on 2 August 1916, dedicated to 'CSS' (Charles Stewart Smith) and probably inspired by the fall of Warsaw (GCPPT 1|1|20 6 August 1915) appears in the 'poems about the war' section of *The Garden and the Fire* (pp 12–13).

66 In *Letters to Lucy,* a series of fictional letters which appeared in *The Cambridge Magazine* in the autumn of 1916, the anonymous author, by context and content Aelfrida herself, has the letter writer ('Althea') describe to her Newnham student friend 'Lucy' the 'war-work' the former undertakes (rolling bandages in Cavendish Square) at the behest of her 'Aunt Boadicea', work to and from which she is driven in a Rolls Royce (The tone of the *Letters* is heavily ironic). The letter quoted appears in *The Cambridge Magazine* vol 6 No 2 21 October 1916 p45.

67 ibid. 16 March 1918.

68 GCPPT 1|1|21 31 March 1916.

69 The only outsider with whom she shared them was Bertrand Russell, unseen (though not unheard of) for over ten years. Having written to him commenting on his newly published *Justice in Wartime* in which Russell criticised what he regarded as the barbarism of trench warfare and the misguided patriotism which condemned a generation of young men to premature death under savage conditions, Russell invited Aelfrida to his college rooms for a discussion. While there she asked his opinion of the merits or demerits of starting up a branch of the Women's International League for Peace and Freedom (founded in 1915) in Cambridge. (Russell advised against it on the grounds that it would only be hijacked by local Quakers!) On his enquiring about her own views on Pacifism she informed him 'cheerfully' that she was a 'religious fanatic and a non-resister' (GCPPT 1|1|21 4 May 1916) whereupon Russell brought the conversation to an early conclusion. As Russell was later deprived of his lecturer's post for advocating views set out in *Justice in Wartime,* Aelfrida's decision to remain silent was sensible even if not very brave.

70 GCPPT 1|1|20 6 March 1915.

71 GCPPT 1|1|21 27 and 28 July 1916.

72 GCPPT 1|1|20 1 March 1918.

73 ibid. 13 August 1914.

74 ibid. 5 December 1914.

75 GCPPT 1|1|21 30 March 1917.

76 GCPPT 1|1|20 15 October 1914. Aelfrida's hopes were singularly naive given that anti-English sentiments expressed by German military and civilian characters throughout the book are not exactly those the English wanted to hear before, during or after the war, England the "arch-enemy" and the "home of selfish grasping individualism" being contrasted with "the Fatherland, the country of devoted effort, of devotion of every man to the State" (*Marrying a Stranger* pp 119–121).

77 *Bammie's Book* is probably the only book of verse for children to receive the accolade of a review in *The Cambridge Magazine* (vol V No 8 4 December 1915 p159) and Alethea and Agatha the only little girls to be mentioned by name there: apropos the poem *Remember* ("Remember not to shout when talking / Or to point at men you meet") the reviewer comments "even the most weedy or exotic of undergraduates may surely pass them in safety". The poem begins with a strikingly unchildlike reminder ("Remember not to wake up crying") more applicable to Aelfrida at that time than to two young girls.

78 *The Garden and the Fire* appeared under the imprint of Cambridge booksellers/publishers W Heffer and Sons but is almost certainly a vanity publication. (The author's profits, Aelfrida reminds us, 'will be given to the Serbian Relief Fund'; judging by the number of copies remaindered the SRF did not receive much). The anthology was dedicated 'to Cambridge Poets. The Living and the Dead'.

79 GCPPT 1|1|21 18 September 1916.

80 GCPPT 1|1|22 10 September 1917.

81 GCPPT 1|1|21 6 May 1917. Much of the lawn was dug up for potatoes and the remainder left to revert to meadow.

82 GCPPT 1|1|22 23 June 1917.

83 GCPPT 1|1|20 19 August 1915. Worth noting here is the coincidence between Aelfrida's decision to join Constantine in Amsterdam in August 1915 and enactment of the National Registration Act on 15 July 1915. The Act enabled Local Government Boards to call on the services of compulsorily registered women aged 15 to 65 possessing relevant skills or eligible for work other than that on which they were currently employed. ('Home duties' was Aelfrida's description of hers). The Register was taken on 15 August 1915, three days prior to Aelfrida's proposed date of departure. Though 'convinced ... that I am doing the right thing [even though] I have never in my whole career as a mother ... put my wishes [and] interests before [the children's]' and though it was possibly only 'romance and adventure' she sought or 'God's Will [or] His plan' that she followed (GCPPT 1|1|20 12,16 and 19 August 1915), it is also possible that the prospect of further 'surrender' to Constantine outweighed the dubious charms of compulsory 'war work'. Ill-health intervened and with this as an excuse, she did not need to go.

84 GCPPT 1|1|20 26 August 1915. Cupping involved the application to the skin or to a septic focus of a small glass dome in which a partial vacuum had been obtained with the aim of drawing out 'impurities'.

85 GCPPT 1|1|22 13 April 1918.

86 GCPPT 1|1|21 14 December 1915.

87 GCPPT 1|1|22 10 July 1918.

88 GCPPT 1|1|23 30 January 1919.

89 The quotation is taken from *The Bright Cup of Pain* (*The Garden and the Fire* p 45, section entitled 'poems about all sorts of things').

90 GCPPT 1|1|20 28 December 1914.

91 Worth mentioning in passing (there is no concrete evidence to support the contention) is that some of Aelfrida's symptoms could be attributed to a sexually transmitted disease caught from Constantine who, as she was later to discover, had probably been unfaithful to her from the time of his sojourn in Panama. (Constantine's episode of urinary retention might also be attributable to this, as might Aelfrida's recurrent vaginal discharge, cystitis, and pelvic pain; even her rheumatoid arthritis could be similarly attributed). Furthermore, her later conviction that she had uterine cancer (for 'cancer' read 'chancre', a symptom of primary syphilis), obsession with moral and physical purity, abhorrence of diseases termed 'venereal', and fear of going or being thought 'mad' might stem from the same real or imagined cause.

92 GCPPT 1|1|21 1 October 1915.

93 ibid. 2 and 6 October 1915.

94 GCPPT 1|1|21 10 October 1915.

95 ibid. 6 December 1915.

96 ibid. 3 November 1915.

97 ibid. 2 January 1916.

98 ibid. 14 October 1915.

99 ibid. 6 December 1915.

100 ibid. 2 January 1916.

101 ibid. 23 December 1915.

102 ibid. 8 January 1916.

103 GCPPT 1|1|20 4 November 1914. Dr Hare's advice (and Aelfrida's apology for the manner in which her behaviour affected other people between 1913 and 1918) reappears in a speech attributed to a young woman in *A Little Road Book for Mystics* p96: "I know how I have gone wrong. I read all kinds of silly old books and did nothing but go to services, and neglected the most obvious duties. When I think of how I talked to every one about mysticism and was all the time as selfish as ever I could be at home, I feel sick. It is no good trying to be better than other people; you only turn out to be much worse. I am going home and going to be as commonplace as ever I can".

104 GCPPT 1|1|20 14 September 1914.

105 ibid. 10 December 1914.

106 GCPPT 1|1|25 1 November 1919.

107 GCPPT 1|1|20 1 and 22 September and 19 October 1914. Sir Francis Bertie (1814–1919) was British Ambassador to France from 1905 to 1917.

108 ibid. 5 October 1914 ('My birthday!').

109 ibid.

110 ibid.

111 GCPPT 2|2a Vol. 2 No 3 October 1903. *The Passive Resister.*

112 GCPPT 1|1|23 5 October 1918.

113 GCPPT 1|1|20 10 October 1914.

114 ibid. 15 January 1915.

115 ibid. 5 October 1914.

116 ibid. 10 October 1914

117 ibid. 5 October 1914.

118 In *Can I be a Mystic?* (pp 99 and 104–105) Aelfrida (as 'Author') provides "a specimen record of meditations from my ms collection" for 'Stranger' to compare with his own: "After a very difficult and agitating day I ... meditated as usual "O Infinite God, I adore Thee", and was at once lifted up in ecstasy". The lines closely parallel meditative experiences recorded after the events of 5 October 1914 but could equally apply to psychotherapeutic exercises undertaken by Aelfrida in November 1913 following rows with Constantine with regard to Aleister Crowley.

119 GCPPT 1|1|20 5 October 1914.

120 Tillyard, Ae. *Messages* pp 33–38.

121 Tillyard, Ae. *Marrying a Stranger* pp 150–151.

122 GCPPT 1|1|20 10 October 1914.

123 ibid. 25 October 1914

124 ibid. 8 October 1914.

125 *Dirge for Tatyana's Bridal Day,* subtitled 'Russian Folk-Song' (*The Garden and the* Fire pp 26–27, section entitled 'songs about love) first appeared in *The Cambridge Review* vol V No 4 27 January 1915 p159, prior to Constantine's departure for Amsterdam in April 1915 (No manuscript version exists). The poem's reference to "a-gathering mushrooms" in a forest by the light of "the magical moon" may relate to a dream Aelfrida had about Aleister Crowley on the night of 3/4 November 1914: Crowley used the hallucinogenic drug *Anhalonium Lewinii* (mescal, from the Mexican peyote cactus) to enhance his Ceremonial Magic practices, calling it "the elixir introduced by me to Europe" (Kaczynski, R. pp 176–177 2002). Though not exactly equivalent to 'magic mushrooms' (psitocybin), Aelfrida's reference is not too wide of the mark. There is no evidence she ever tried Crowley's 'elixir' herself.

126 GCPPT 1|1|20 7 April 1915.

127 ibid. 7 January and 25 April 1916.

128 *Economy for Men* appeared in *The Cambridge Magazine* vol V No 17 11 March 1916 p358. Its author's name is not given but internal evidence and reference to events described in Aelfrida's diary suggests that she wrote it.

129 GCPPT 1|1|21 1 and 20 October 1916.

130 A reading of Richard Lovelace's *To Althea from Prison* shows how apposite is this slight change of name.

131 *The Cambridge Magazine* vol VI No 7 25 November 1916 p175.

132 ibid. vol VI No 2. 1 October 1916 p45.

133 ibid. vol VI No 6 18 November 1916 p147.

134 GCPPT 1|1|21 30 December 1915 and 20 January 1916. A signed poem, *Parallel Lines,* published in *The Cambridge Magazine* (vol V No 14 19 February 1916 p313) exactly sums up Aelfrida's feelings: "Twin lines that bravely fare through chilly space / Are symbols of our human life to me; / Near, yet untouching; rigid; only free / To run a bare predestined race ..." While it is probable that the poem, dedicated 'to a mathematical friend' refers John Forbes Cameron whom Aelfrida occasionally met socially, a plethora of evidence pointing to Constantine (to "fugal airs"; to "problems solved," as they might be by one who studied commercial arithmetic for his consular career; to the "infinity" which his wife noted elsewhere now lay between their hearts) and to a recent reference by Alfred Tillyard to Euclid's proposition "that two straight lines cannot enclose a space" (*Stones of Stumbling* p 130, a book in process of composition), suggests that it was not only Cameron whom Aelfrida had in mind.

135 GCPPT 1|1|22 20 January and 20 November 1917.

136 GCPPT 1|1|21 17 January 1917.

137 ibid. 9 March 1916.

138 ibid. 31 July 1916

139 ibid. 28 January 1916.

140 Tillyard, Ae. *A Little Road – Book for Mystics* pp111–112.

141 GCPPT 1|1|22 26 May 1917.

142 ibid. 31 May 1917.

143 ibid. 11 September 1917. Neither here nor anywhere else does Aelfrida presume that Constantine was not a virgin when she married him. The evidence suggests otherwise; his sexualised pre-marital 'play' and aggressive sexual activity after marriage ('pushing passion to the verge of torture' GCPPT 1|1|22 22 February 1918) indicate a sexually experienced young man anxious not to shatter his fiancée's illusions with regard to his 'purity'. Possibly 'Juanita' did more than merely 'suggest' adultery to him.

144 GCPPT 1|1|22 15 September 1917.

145 ibid. 14 September 1917 and 19 February 1918.

146 ibid. 15 September 1917.

147 ibid. 22 October 1917.

148 ibid. 22 and 24 October 1917.

149 ibid.

150 ibid.

151 ibid.

152 ibid. 20 November 1917.

153 ibid. 22 and 29 October and 3 November 1917.

154 ibid. 29 October 1917.

155 ibid. 19 October, 7 and 20 November 1917.

156 ibid. 22 October 1917. Alethea, outspoken and observant, summed up her parents' relationship succinctly, stating on 10 November 1917 that "Fuvver is very ambitious ... he could never be satisfied" (GCPPG A1|1a *Alethea's Record Book*) and in December that "Fuvver and Mother ought never to have married – they have too different tastes" (GCPPT 1|1|22 19 December 1917).

157 GCPPT 1|1|22 22 November 1917.

158 ibid. 20 November 1917.

159 ibid. 28 July 1916.

160 GCPPT 1|1|21 6 December 1915.

161 In her contemporaneously written book *The Making of a Mystic* (pp. vi and 20–21) Aelfrida, in the guise of 'Catharine Sutherland', feels the need to defend 'detachment'. It is not, she writes, disillusionment with, and indifference to, the things of the world ("social position or wealth") but a positive quality resulting from renouncement of phenomena of the "transient shifting of the world" in favour of a clearer vision of the "spark of the divine life" incarnate in each and every aspect of it and especially in human beings. That she failed to make this clear to those she loved is shown by Frank Stokoe, a man more sensitively attuned to her way of thinking than Constantine, being unable to comprehend her 'higher indifference' and berating her for being cold and unloving as a result of practising it.

162 GCPPT 1|1|22 26 November 1917.

163 Ernest George Berkeley Maxse CMG was a soldier and diplomat of aristocratic descent. Appointed Consul-General to the Netherlands in 1913, he held the post until 1919. For details of his earlier and subsequent career see *Who Was Who* vol 4.

164 GCPPT 1|1|22 17, 22, 24 and 30 December 1917.

165 ibid. 28 January 1918.

166 ibid. 11 September 1917.

167 ibid. 17 February 1918.

168 ibid. 20 July 1916.

169 GCPPT 1|1|57 15 May 1940.

170 GCPPT 1|1|22 17 January 1918.

171 ibid.

172 GCPPT 1|1|20 14 September 1914.

173 GCPPT 1|1|22 24 January 1918.

174 ibid. 25 January 1918.

175 ibid. 28 January 1918.

176 ibid. 17 February 1918.

177 ibid.

178 ibid. 22 February 1918.

179 ibid. 17 February 1918.

180 ibid. 20 August 1918.

181 ibid. 22 February 1918.

182 ibid. 17 February 1918.

183 ibid. 18 February 1918.

184 ibid. 20 February 1918.

185 ibid. 22 February 1918.

186 ibid. 20 April 1918.

187 ibid. 18 February 1918. Constantine's married sister Irene Hillerns now had two sons, Graham, Constantine's godson, 'stolid and German-looking', and Michael, who looked 'absurdly like Constantine'. Aelfrida met the boys for the first and only time on her 1916 visit to Hessle.

188 GCPPT 1|1|22 3 March 1918. Crowley's prediction does not appear in the Parisian volume of Aelfrida's diary nor does she refer to it with regard to their correspondence. She does, however, refer obliquely to it in *The Closer Walk with God* (p125): "wizard's predictions are no more that clever guesses [but] suppose...one of these necromancers could actually foretell the future? ... If I ... had been told some years ago that I should be a target for so many arrows from the quiver of misfortune, I might ... have died from sheer apprehension".

189 ibid. 2 May 1918.

190 ibid. 31 July 1918.

191 ibid. 2 May 1918.

192 ibid. 10 May 1918.

193 GCPPT 1|1|7a. The letter was meant to be opened on Aelfrida's fortieth birthday in 1923 but she pre-empted the occasion by five years.

194 Lord Kitchener, whose portrait looked out from recruiting posters all over Britain during the Great War ('Your Country Needs You') and the man whose raising of three million volunteers for the 'Kitchener Armies' was a feat unparalleled in military history, drowned in June 1916 when the cruiser *Hampshire* on which he was sailing to Russia hit a mine and sank. Aelfrida dismissed his death in a few lines: 'I forgot ... to look on the matter as anything but a *national* disaster – forgot, I mean, that I had once loved him ... so completely do one's feelings change' (GCCPT 1|1|21 7 June 1916).

195 GCPPT 1|1|23 9 October 1918.

196 ibid. 13 October 1918.

197 ibid. 8 November 1918.

198 ibid. 11 November 1918. Aelfrida's unpublished poem *In Victory*, written in the back of this volume of her diary, is undated but must by context ("O England mine, be just today") have been written on or about 11 November 1918.

199 GCPPT 1|1|23 10 November 1918.

200 The quotation is from *The Stones of Belgium* (*The Garden and the Fire* pp 4–5), written in Cambridge on 13 March 1915 to appear later in the 'poems about the war' section of the anthology. The 'war' to which Aelfrida refers is not only, as the poem itself makes clear ("Her husband marched away and – God knows best"; "Peace is but a prim child-ridden spouse") the Great War but also the war waged between the Grahams.

# Mediumistic Cypher

One of several opprobrious epithets applied by Constantine to Aelfrida following their stormy passages at Fordfield early in October 1914 was that of 'mediumistic cypher'.[1] 'Cypher' was entirely appropriate: as a member of the Consular Service, Constantine would have been familiar with a word used to describe messages in code which only those who held the 'key' would be able to 'decipher' an encrypted message. Using the word as an absolutely correct term to apply to a wife he no longer understood but to whose writings he more than anyone held the key, a man whose curriculum for the Consular Service had included commercial arithmetic, would also have been aware that a 'cipher' is the symbol used to denote an amount of no value occupying a vacant space to add coherence to what

is expressed: 0.5 mgs, for example. To imply that his wife was a 'nought' or a 'cipher' as far as he and his life were concerned was therefore extremely hurtful even though (something Constantine may not have considered in his eagerness to hurt) that be she physically present or not, his life reverberated with her noughted or cryptic presence.

But why 'mediumistic'? True, Constantine was present when Aelfrida was asked if she was a medium at the Spiritualist Church in Boston and had heard her reply that Eusapia Palladino had recognised her mediumistic potential; he had also been present at her hallucinatory (or contrivedly hallucinatory) experience of 14 July 1904 during which she 'heard' and 'saw' herself with Constantine and their future children. But unless

The Old Rectory and church, Caldecote

she had told him something of her adolescent psychic experiences or informed him of more recent psychic events (a possibility, given her inability to keep silent), Constantine's propensity to belittle and criticise as abnormal behaviour by his wife which did not conform to his preferred norms might have given rise to an epithet which was no more than a veiled reference to 'Crowley and Crowleyism' or a gibe which happened to contain more truth than he knew.

On the other hand, enough evidence has been adduced to show that Aelfrida was, if not yet a medium, at least attuned to a world beyond the physical. Hypnopompic and hypnagogic experiences (of herself weeping beside the bedside of a dead man; her ability to 'dream true', to retain some control of the dream-events[2], and to be able to recall and record every detail on waking), visionary experiences of a religious nature, the ease with which she summoned up and dismissed spirits while practising Ceremonial Magic, all suggest an ability to step over the threshold between the real and the spirit world and to go about her business in the latter as easily as in the former.[3] Further examples of her ability are given throughout her earlier and wartime diaries: déjà vu experiences, during which she recalled previous existences as an adult in a chateau in France and as a child in classical Greece 'and the recollections are always the same'[4]; telepathic abilities, dating from before her marriage but particularly strong with regard to her daughters: 'with Alethea … I have always been able to *live inside* her mind. I can stroll across into her without feeling that here I end and she begins. This is generally true of me and Agatha [too] though at times she withdraws into some secret place…'; with Frank Stokoe she had 'no sense of *possession* [but] when he is here, and sometimes when he is not here, I enter into the strange world behind his eyes and there suffer or rejoice …with him')[5]; clairvoyance, as when she '*saw*' a young man and a 'dark pale intelligent-looking girl' talking together in a neglected garden and told the Oracle 'the next letter from Russia will announce Julius' engagement to Nadja'[6] (it did) or when, prior to leaving for Ventnor, she had 'second sight' about someone she was to see there: 'a tall striking-looking woman with grey eyes and black hair who spoke Italian … Mrs St George'[7]; premonitions concerning a particular person or that matters would turn out as she predicted (a 'feeling of impending calamity' in September 1915 that Eustace would be killed on 12 October was the only reported instance of her being mistaken)[8]; telekinesis, as when, mowing Fordfield lawn, she noticed the grass alongside the lawnmower being mown by an unseen agency, a phenomenon also witnessed by Agatha and Alethea (the former decided it was fairies, the latter 'an angel

sent by God') and checked for veracity by Frank Stokoe who, expecting 'an "attachment" to the mower which extended the width of its operation', tried and failed to reproduce the 'miracle', after which Aelfrida repeated her experience.[9]

More to the point in view of what follows is Aelfrida's ability to step over the threshold separating the living from the dead and to experience ghosts from the past. Apart from the brown-suited ghost of the Emden dining room and ghostly visitations from her grandfather in 1912, she also records the appearance of Henry Joseph Wetenhall's ghost in 1921 on the Fordfield veranda and in the corridor by the West Room and in 1922 'on the lawn …looking wistfully towards the house'.[10] There were also ghosts 'thick as smoke' during a children's party at Denny Abbey (a monastery, later a nunnery, but for centuries a private house) and particularly prevalent 'in the orchard by a shrine' which, had she been alone, she might have 'seen'.[11] Other ghosts 'crowded round to watch our progress or flitted quietly about their own business untouched by flesh and blood so near' at Catley Park Farm near Linton, a house visited by Aelfrida while holidaying with her daughters in the village[12] or, wearing fashions from an earlier age ('do other people see these things or only I?') worshipped alongside her in Clavering church in Essex.[13]

Relevant too, was Aelfrida's experience of automatic writing. Her first expressed interest in the subject was in 1902 when, inspired by a visit from Helen Verrall who discussed 'automatic writing and spirit rapping and wierd (*sic*) things', she tried it herself: 'my pen wrote "briny" and "briney" over and over again … I wonder what is the interpretation thereof!'[14] A visit from Helen in 1910 elicited the information that Helen's own experience of automatic writing had led her to believe that the messages she received came from her own mind or at most from another *living* person; Aelfrida too, said Helen, possessed remarkable psychic powers after her former schoolmate told her of her own clairvoyant experiences.[15] In January 1913 Mrs Verrall herself discussed psychic research with Aelfrida, mentioning messages received in dreams or trances or via automatic writing from 'a spirit world'. Relieved at being able to talk to someone who listened to her communications with sympathy and understanding (the meeting, significantly, took place within a month of her return from Ventnor), Aelfrida confided to her former tutor 'some of [her] real experiences about the spirit world' (she does not record which), described the process by which she 'dreamed true', and informed Mrs Verrall that she herself had received 'telepathic messages [albeit] from this world … not from the other'. On being told of Aelfrida's most recent experiment with automatic writing ('some "higher twaddle" about "what we want is love" etc. etc.', which seemed, she said, 'to come out of [her] own subconscious self'), Mrs Verrall described her as "very psychic".[16]

Although Aelfrida's later interest in automatic writing could have arisen as a result of reading the works of Madame Guyon (works dictated, so that lady said, by God to His amanuensis), she was in fact more interested in Guyon's relationship with Père LaCombe, seeing interesting parallels between it and her own relationship with Frank Stokoe.[17] A more significant influence might have been Susanna Venn who, coincidentally with her interest in psychical research, wrote novels dictated by a 'control', Susan Ferrier, daughter of a bailiff on the family estates, later an author and friend of Sir Walter Scott. Visiting her in 1898, Aelfrida had listened entranced to Mrs Venn's account of how she 'began to write not because she wanted to but because she felt as though someone spoke through her and she had to allow them utterance'[18] and her own subsequent belief that her poetry felt 'as though it were "impressed" from outside'[19] with herself as 'conduit' and that her novels seemed 'dictated' to her may have resulted from conversations with Archie's mother. But the possibility remains that they did not.

With this in mind and remembering that the majority of Aelfrida's psychic experiences occurred at times when she was in an elevated or depressed mood because of events in her quotidian life (and also that it was at such times that she wrote poetry and prose as if under some overwhelming compulsion to do so), it comes as no surprise to find her receiving and transmitting messages, all but two of which concerned people to whom something happened in the course of or as a direct result of the Great War.

Her first visitor was Frederic Myers, dead since 1901, the man who had offered to 'initiate' her into 'mediumism'[20]; her first proper communication from him took place on 8 October 1914 three days after the long diary entry detailing her marital rape and two months since the outbreak of war had sent her scurrying for Fordfield. (Myers, it now appears, had also visited her during Constantine's absence in July 1914, to ask her 'wise man! whether I knew Mrs Verrall'[21]; it may be that Constantine's gibe refers to this visit, a visit unrecorded in his wife's diary but concerning which she may have spoken to him, unlikely as this seems, given that she no longer told him anything which could be used as ammunition.) On 13 October she showed Mrs Verrall 'a document [she] was rather ashamed of – a page of automatic writing that the ghost of Myers had … bothered [her] into doing' five days earlier. But although she found both process and message interesting in the abstract, writing

of the former that 'one feels the writing-centre in one's brain [is] deliberately taken possession of by someone else' and of the latter that Myers now lived in a world where everything was ideas ("Plato, you know. It is not the highest, but it feels good"; Aelfrida's response was that no-one save Bertrand Russell could 'keep alive in a world of ideas!'), she hated the feeling of being taken over by forces outside her control ('I *loathe* being a medium')[22] and continued to profess distaste for Psychical Research.

In November 1914, with Julius incarcerated in Germany and Eustace about to leave for France, she received another 'fine automatic from "Myers"'.[23] She discussed it with Mrs Verrall a few days later, the latter being quite happy to talk about the world 'over there' now her former SPR colleague was working through her ex-pupil. (Aware how easy it is for a teacher to influence the mind of a pupil, Mrs Verrall, so Aelfrida said, had never 'talked psychism' before the latter confided in her in January 1913 but Aelfrida's own later admission that 'dreaming true' or a 'true dream' was a term used by Mrs Verrall to denote 'an authentic message, in symbolic form, from beyond' and her own use of the term prior to 1914 suggests that 'psychism' may have been a topic of conversation much earlier; Aelfrida herself later preferred to believe that Mrs Verrall, 'unknown to us both [may] have helped to turn me towards the little-known powers of mind that are now attracting me'.)[24] On this visit too Mrs Verrall also informed Aelfrida that yogic exercises recently resumed in an effort to calm her mind were 'first rate practice for that kind of introspection'.[25]

Aelfrida's next visitor was a young man, four of whose poems had appeared in *Cambridge Poets*; who had been parodied (very gently) in *The Puff by Parody*; whose poetry Aelfrida had been reading in the garden at Fordfield shortly before Agneta's birth and death and, inspired by it, had written her own poem *Tout pour toi!* on 22 May 1912; whose best-known poem about a place known to them both was written in the same month as *Tout pour toi!;* and of whose recent death in uniform if not in action on 23 April 1915 Aelfrida had written 'of all the wanton destruction wrought by the war none seems more wanton than the death of a poet'[26]: Rupert Brooke.

That a young soldier should be one of Aelfrida's earliest paranormal wartime correspondents seems entirely appropriate given that Rupert's first visit coincided with Eustace's preliminary communications from France, a pre-paid card on 6 May and a letter without identifying address other than "Somewhere in France" of 8 May 1915 bringing reassurance only of his being alive at the time of writing. On 9 May Aelfrida recorded her first meeting with the author of the sonnet beginning "If I should die, think only this of me"[27]: 'Rupert Brooke came to talk to me a few nights after his death'. Having initially thought – a typical Aelfrida touch – that Brooke had come to apologise for a missed luncheon engagement ('I never met him, you know') and annoyed at the arrival of 'more spooks, especially as there was nothing to be seen', she made the best of her ghostly visitor by asking him as an opening conversational gambit if he 'minded being dead'. Brooke said no, "it was glorious being free … and floating about looking at things"[28] and on Aelfrida asking him, a professed atheist, if there were 'any God "up there"', replied "no, not God exactly, but boundless light", a Buddhist notion with which Aelfrida was familiar but Brooke found puzzling. Quoting a line of poetry ('his own, I think, which I have forgotten') he departed.[29] A month later Aelfrida recorded that she had had 'quite a good "true dream" about Rupert Brooke who seems set on having a P. and B. F. now that he is dead' because "the others … are all so busy they won't listen to me".[30] Who 'the others' were, Rupert did not disclose but nor did his 'pure and beautiful friendship' with Aelfrida long endure.

On 19 June, two days after her 'true dream', Aelfrida had occasion to visit the Old Vicarage, Grantchester, where Rupert once lived. After describing the vicarage itself (she uses Brooke's own expression "the falling house that never falls") and the 'lovely green tangle' of garden leading down to the river[31] and being always sensitive to presences, she noted that 'Rupert must have loved the place for there seemed a lot of him about'.[32] On 22 June, the day on which she received an 'almost too vivid' letter from Eustace and with Rupert and Grantchester still on her mind, she received yet another visit (her fourth, she says; she does not record a third unless it was at the Old Vicarage itself) during which she collaborated with Rupert on a poem to be called *Settled Down*. Of this, she subsequently and annoyingly recalled nothing (of a poem dictated a week later she recalled only a fragment: "Light like the dreamy haze on distant hills / Of unimagined blue …")[33], though she remembered Brooke himself as 'too funny, so eager and so excited about the spirit world and so keen to get a listener'.[34] A week later she wrote of Rupert being in 'tremendous high spirits and … awfully amusing', enquiring of her diary 'did you ever meet a ghost with a sense of humour? Rupert is really witty'.[35]

A startling visitation took place on the night of 17/18 June: 'as I was going to bed Rupert made himself known and said Myers had just suggested automatic writing and would I please try'. She initially refused on the grounds that she had been re-reading Myers' *Human Personality* and that recent acquaintance with a posthumously-published book on the survival of personality after bodily death meant she was not in a 'properly detached frame

of mind'. (She did not appear to consider Rupert's visit to be an effect rather than a cause on this occasion any more than contemporary events in Eustace's life.) Her description continues 'Rupert seemed rather hurt but determined to get his way – so I went to sleep. Presently, as I thought, I awoke and heard Myers say "There! Now you've got it!" to Rupert while Gurney and Verrall looked on'.[36] Then, she writes, 'Rupert seemed to take possession of my brain and to make me dream and dream and dream about him and his new life. Again, as I thought, I awoke, took pencil and paper and obediently began the automatic writing'. At that point she really did wake up, recording what she could remember of Rupert's dictation: 'he plunged into the river of death and the drops sparkled on his golden hair. It is better thus than that he should have died in the noise of battle. He feels himself truly to be a victor'. Then, becoming aware of Rupert's presence in her room and 'of his glee at having got his way and of his great desire to continue', she took another sheet of paper and wrote at Rupert's direct dictation that he and she "are both seekers of living harmonies, though your rhythm is not so free and your cadence stiff. There is no doubt that you can listen, rather amusing I call it, in the case of one who talks as much, eh Sarasvati?", an accurate assessment of one who, by her own admission, lived 'with [her] thoughts on [her] lips' but disconcerting too insofar as Rupert knew the name of her 'higher self'.[37] Expressing a desire to wish her well in spite of her "incredible … stupidity", Rupert's message ended with a description of himself: "I don't feel like a discarnate spirit. I feel like me, Rupert, with wings to my soul instead of legs to my feet".[38]

Rupert paid his final visit on 30 June, asking Aelfrida to pass on a message to his mother: "Write to Mrs Brooke 24 Bilton Road, Rugby thus: I know, I love, I understand". (The message seems to have been a sequel to a longer one delivered by automatic writing the previous day.) Aelfrida, surprised at the message's lucidity, wondered if it had come 'from [her] subliminal self' but its precise content and what she described as 'practically an "auditory hallucination"' accompanying it (Rupert's voice saying: "not your desire but my imperious will, Rupert")[39] convinced her that it did not. Wondering if the address was correct and what Mrs Brooke's reaction would be to a message from her dead son, she nevertheless wrote as directed. Mrs Brooke's response was both encouraging and discouraging: 'the address was correct and [she] gave quite involuntary confirmation … of the genuineness of the communication' (it may have referred to the death in action in France of Rupert's brother William on 14 June) but not being a believer in Spiritualism, she intimated that it would 'give her great pain to have her son send her messages through a total stranger' and requested that no more be sent. (None were.) This 'closes the incident, I fancy', Aelfrida wrote.[40]

Feeling the need to confide her supra-natural experiences to someone who understood their significance, Aelfrida wrote twice to Mrs Verrall. Mrs Verrall's response was oddly muted given that (or perhaps because) her own dead husband appeared in one of them, for other than assuring Aelfrida that the messages were genuine and not a figment of her overwrought imagination, neither she nor Helen (who, if confided in by her mother, might have expressed a wish that Aelfrida publish her experiences in the Journal of the SPR) showed any interest in taking the matter further. Though their disinclination might be imputed to chagrin at the new medium's success or to a wish not to upset bereaved Mrs Brooke or because both women were so engrossed in cross-correspondences concerning communications between the protagonists of the Palm Sunday Case[41] that messages between two Cambridge poets seemed of minor importance, it may also say something of their long-standing knowledge of Aelfrida herself, a woman whose growing reputation for eccentricity might endanger investigations both Verralls took seriously and practised scientifically.

Aelfrida was deeply impressed by association with a man never encountered in life, a fellow poet of whom it was written that "nearly every one of his later poems … was inspired by his own experiences, though few of his friends knew of the heights and the depths of the emotional crises through which he passed"[42], a description as true of herself as of Brooke. Her interest is demonstrated by what followed during the late summer and early autumn of the year in which they 'met'.

On 11 July 1915 she noted that for the last few months (including, of course, the period of her association with Rupert Brooke) she had deliberately cut herself off from all but her immediate family with the aim of 'withdrawing into [herself and] going into the desert as far as might be to find God'. Yet on asking herself if she had found Him, she admitted 'sometimes, yes [but] sometimes I found nothing but my own loneliness'.[43] Whether it was loneliness that led her to Brooke (or him to her, as a 'detached other' in whom he could confide because she, unlike 'the others', was not too 'busy') or the absence of a 'guru' of Aleister Crowley's calibre ('I want to know whether I am getting on or not')[44] or her feelings regarding the current conflict ('a year of war – and no-one can … yet see the way out … time is long and people suffer so much')[45] or the sensation that things other than Rupert's visits were happening beyond her control ('sudden coldnesses and desolations; then equally sudden raptures when I seem taken out of

myself and plunged into the very heart of God')[46] or her first encounter with Freud's *Interpretation of Dreams* (an 'unpleasant book'[47] because she disagreed with Freud's emphasis on sexuality; possibly she also disliked the implication of this for her own supposedly 'pure and beautiful' friendships with Cambridge alumni younger than herself even than Brooke), by the middle of August she had reached 'a point beyond which one's will cannot spur one's body and that point I seem to have reached'.

To a modern Cambridge dweller, Caldecote[48], a village seven miles to the west, seems an odd holiday destination, but in 1915 as Edward Conybeare's description of its church suggests ("a retired little fane on the hillside …, a very oasis of devotional peace and quietude")[49], it was the perfect place for recuperation; accompanied by her daughters and Octavie, Aelfrida arrived there on 10 September. Feeling that it was becoming very hard 'to keep sane' in the days before her departure but relieved to know that by the time she returned 'this strange poignant summer will be over'[50], her first thought on arriving at the Old Rectory was 'well, here's a place – as good as your Old Vicarage, Rupert! – "to forget the lies and truth and pain"'.[51]

'You come', she wrote, 'to a cedar tree, a wide-open gate, a great chestnut behind which sleeps the grey tower of the little church; and then passing up the drive … you reach the house, a big rambling building tall at one end and low at the other, gabled and tiled and thatched, with creepers hanging over'. In the morning she sat 'by the south wall of the house facing the church and looked at whitewashed wall and rose-grown porch, a grey tower behind a privet hedge'; in the afternoon she moved to a little lawn overlooking 'trees and nettles and morning glory and struggling fruit and flowers'. The 'big bare room' where she slept faced west to a quiet glow of sunset over hills, meadows, and trees.[52] Wandering alone through nearby fields ('seas of green with buttercups as foam'), she had a strange experience, feeling her soul leave her body to mingle with the wind and go sweeping over the hills before returning to her purified and calmed[53], something she found enormously therapeutic: 'I let myself be overwhelmed by things … I won't brood and get morbid … I am here to rest and be still'.[54]

Good resolutions did not last long. On 18 September she recorded of the previous night 'I was excited and could not sleep … I was partly in pain, partly exalted [and] wrote three poems and heard all the world singing'.[55] Two poems, *A Load of Hay* (dedicated 'to O.P., hay woman', in fact Olga Pashler, owner of the Old Rectory)[56] and *Triolet*[57], are germane to Aelfrida's visit, the first being an evocation of a soldier in "far-off Alexandria / Or at some battle-ruined town in France" lifting down a "scented bale of hay" and being immediately transposed in thought to the gentle Cambridgeshire countryside with its "honeysuckle o'er the lattice trailed", "rose-crowned hedges / Sloping on upland hills", and grey-towered churches "asleep … / Above the grass and earth where lie the dead", the second, an evocation of her own lightening of spirit as she explores the local countryside: "The wind along a wider lea…/ Can set my stagnant spirit free …/ Can fill my heart with song".

The third poem, *The Old Rectory, Caldecote*, is relevant to Caldecote and to Aelfrida's recent relationship with the dead poet for whom it was a memorial and an elegy.[58] The poem, like Brooke's, begins with intimations of place: "a house with hanging eaves / A garden overgrown with leaves / Where roving morning glories climb" in her case, a Berlin café in his. Aelfrida's poem, however, soon loses its rapturous tone to become both a weary description of her present state of mind ("My eyes are blind, my lips are dumb / My heart is hot and dull with flame") and a valedictory enumeration of the natural wonders she wishes the 'you' who is 'gone' to enjoy: "lonely places", "spanless airs / Twixt height and height", and the "unimagined glory of the sky". Brooke's poem, on the other hand, after a brief digression into the present ("Here I am, sweating, sick, and hot"), moves on to rhapsodic descriptions of Cambridgeshire countryside not far from Aelfrida's Caldecote rectory ("And sunset still a golden sea / From Haslingfield to Madingley") and to tongue-in-cheek description of villages well-known to her from weekend rambles with Constantine ("Coton's full of nameless crimes"), from bicycle rides with Eustace and her parents ("Barton men make Cockney rhymes") and from the traumatic weeks which followed the death of Conrad: "there's none in Harston under thirty." Unlike Aelfrida, however, who writes "Far from my garden Beauty lies", Brooke hopes that in the deep meadows around Grantchester he will find Beauty ("And Certainty? And Quiet kind?") and "forget / The lies and truths and pain" so evident in Aelfrida's poem (and life) in spite of having retreated to a haven reminiscent of his own.

The elegiac mood of Aelfrida's poem does not, however, refer solely to Rupert Brooke, for there are curious resonances in it of other Cambridge poets gone from her life for other reasons. Of Constantine (physically absent for several reasons and equally absent on emotional and intellectual levels), lines from whose poem *The Forest of Massachusetts* echo in *The Old Rectory, Caldecote*; of Frank Stokoe, now ravaged by recurring mental breakdowns but not so self-consumed that he cannot, on a visit to Aelfrida at Caldecote, 'set the whole face of his character' against hers to denounce as a wholly wrong attitude

her goal of 'total annihilation of … individual personality' in favour of a 'higher indifference' to everything that makes life worth living: desires, ambitions, even possessions, an attitude so similar to Constantine's that Aelfrida complained 'it's enough to have one's husband try and destroy one's foundations'[59] much less one's best friend. Of Aleister Crowley, now living on his wits across the Atlantic, with regard to her having a "fairy name", Brooke's reference to 'Sarasvati' having recently reminded her of it.[60] Finally, of her own childhood, for lines in *The Old Rectory* describing the "lilied pool" which still exists in the rectory garden, may also refer to a cup-shaped pool in the New Forest discovered by Frida on a childhood visit to Lucy Longstaffe, a pool which provided her with a "sudden disclosure of Beauty … Beauty so exquisite as to seem divine" because of the lilies-of-the-valley which grew in profusion round it.[61] But the real and remembered pool also reminded her that youthful innocence, like Beauty, lay far from the "hot and airless" garden of her present mind and life and that vestiges of innocence (and certainty and quiet kind) were liable to be sucked up by the "burning ray" of fires of war and marital discord which had caused her heart to become "hot and dull with flame".

At The Old Rectory Aelfrida read Mrs Pashler and other paying guests one of her three 'Caldecote' poems, *A Load of Hay*; she did not read the other two, commenting 'no-one will care about the vision ones'.[62] Repeating the same sentiments in 1925 to Middleton Murry to whom she gave a copy of *The Garden and the Fire* after hearing him lecture in Cambridge, she noted apropos its 'mystical poems' (in which *Triolet* and possibly even *The Old Rectory* could be included) that it seemed she had succeeded in expounding her 'vision' 'but nobody heard!'[63] But by whom did Aelfrida mean 'nobody' and why did they not 'hear'? Aleister Crowley? Unlikely, given that she now disguised her connection with him during discussions with those to whom she thought revelation might damage her spiritual credentials. With fellow visionary Tommy Altounyan she appears not to have continued discussions on the subject after the beginning of the war. Frank Stokoe, in whom she felt able to confide, was not interested in the mystical aspects of her religiosity or poetry. Constantine refused to discuss the matter. But what, with regard to everyone else, did Aelfrida expect of a slim volume of poetry with a limited print run, published by a provincial publisher, containing verses by a poet whose first anthology was published by subscription and reviewed in *The Equinox* and whose second (with particular reference to her own poetry) was accorded scant critical acclaim and whose appearance in 1916 coincided with the slaughter on the Western Front, and even if due regard is given to its few 'patriotic' poems, of limited interest to a public unlikely to appreciate the esoteric nature of its contents? In any case, though 'patriotic' poems contain sentiments which would give them wider appeal, 'visionary' poems are so intensely personal that unless they are read in conjunction with diaries to which no-one but herself now had access, interpretation is difficult if not impossible. All in all, she should not have been surprised that nobody 'heard' the earliest published manifestations of her 'Great Work'.[64]

Rupert Brooke, however, was a fellow-poet with whom she had briefly shared life and experience and it is intriguing to speculate that had Brooke not died when he did and had Aelfrida been able to overcome her distaste for his 'Neo-paganism, she might have corresponded with him as someone who could sympathise with her on a more than poetic level because he and she were both, as Rupert himself said, 'seekers of living harmonies'.[65] References in *The Old Rectory* to the 'you' who has 'gone' and to Aelfrida's inability to accompany him ("I linger here and stay / Chained …") are therefore less likely to refer to living men from whom she was separated by circumstance and geography than to dead Rupert Brooke whom she cannot 'join' because she is still alive and whom she is unable to accompany on disembodied peregrinations because she is imprisoned in and by the physical world.

Her having been able to cross the threshold between life and death in her meetings with Brooke because of innate or acquired psychic abilities (her success in conjuration during the practice of rites pertaining to Ceremonial Magic is surely relevant here) is interesting insofar as it seems that in 1915 the Cambridge poet in question, though physically 'dead', was 'alive' insofar as he existed in the spirit world and, in his communications to and through her, in her own mind too. (Aelfrida herself was later to state categorically that "under certain circumstances communication between the living and the dead is quite possible and has taken place"[66] and in *Kingdoms* has the king taunt the poet "…Come, know'st thou aught of POWER? … Last night I killed a man … Could'st thou do that?" and the latter reply "Last night, O king of deeds most terrible, I called the dead to life … could'st thou do that?" "Dost thou recall the dead?" asks the astonished king, to which the poet confidently replies:"There are no dead".)[67] Then too, while it is possible Aelfrida was subconsciously prompted into dreaming about Brooke by news of his death and by reading Myers' book, corroboration of the contents of Rupert's message to his mother by *that very person* suggests that there was rather more to the episode than mere suggestion; indeed, evidence of the impression made by the

---

> THE OLD RECTORY, CALDECOTE.
>
> I've found a house with hanging eaves,
> A garden overgrown with leaves,
> Where roving morning-glories climb,
> And dandelions mark the time....

*The Old Rectory, Caldecote* (*The Garden and the Fire* 1916)

Brooke episode on Aelfrida's mind is to be found in her first book on Mysticism proper, *The Making of a Mystic* of 1917.

The book, a fictional correspondence between a would-be mystic and her spiritual director, contains a letter dated 1 October 1916 in which the latter expresses her grief that the husband of a friend of her protégée has been killed in the war and attempts to console her. Emphasising the need for human affection in a difficult world, the director warns her pupil that affection is not the same as slavish adoration or a self-seeking means of gaining approval from the loved one; it is love of the manifestation of the Divine in the loved one's personality. If, she says, we can serve those worthy of our affection or redeem those unworthy of it by loving them, our love partakes of the nature of divine love and we are able to experience something of the nature of the heaven where souls of the blest "Spend in pure converse our eternal day; / Think each in each, immediately wise; / Learn all we lacked before; hear, know and say / What this tumultuous body now denies; / And feel, who have laid our groping hands away; / And see, no longer blinded by our eyes".[68] The lines, although unattributed, are from Rupert Brooke's *Sonnet* (*Suggested by some of the Proceedings of the Society for Psychical Research*); by 1916, it seems, Aelfrida not only believed that new spiritual vistas were opening before her but also that she was more open to the spirit world because no longer 'blinded' by the physical one.

Rupert Brooke was her only revenant contact in 1915. But as if to underline her new openness to the paranormal she received four contacts in 1916; all were brief and related to current events. The first and last provided only fleeting contacts – a fragmentary message from a newly deceased neighbour concerning his widow and daughters ("I deeply regret their grief")[69] and an attempted materialisation by a young soldier recently killed in action who 'couldn't quite pull it off and swore in the most human manner possible!!'[70] – but are relevant because the soldier was Edward Spearing, known to Aelfrida as Eustace's friend and hero-worshipper, the news of his death arriving the day after she wrote in her diary that so many young men she knew had been killed that she no longer recorded all their names[71], and the older man, the Rev Owen Whitehouse DD, late principal of Cheshunt Theological College in nearby Bateman St, the father of a friend whom Aelfrida had attempted to comfort by describing her own near-death experience ('[I felt] my soul gradually withdraw itself from the body') in the hope that a description of a peaceful life-ending would help Lilian come to terms with Dr Whitehouse's sudden death.[72]

In August 1916, however, Aelfrida received a wholly unexpected visit from a complete stranger, a contact she found rather hateful though honesty compelled her to record it: two nights after his traitor's death by hanging in Pentonville Prison on 3 August 1916, she encountered Sir Roger Casement.[73] Although there was nothing in her immediate life to suggest why she should be visited by an Irish revolutionary nationalist, her only reference to contemporary Irish affairs having been made four months earlier apropos the Easter Rising of 2 April 1916 ('the news from Ireland makes the papers exciting reading')[74], her mind at the time of Casement's appearance was much exercised by another man with Consular Service connections, namely her husband. Casement made contact early a few days after Aelfrida's visit to Hessle during which she was informed by Anatolia of Constantine's was affair with Mme Sterneberg; August was also the month in which the Grahams, she in a state of denial, he desperate to conceal the truth, were simultaneously but independently attempting to hush matters up, he writing angry letters to his mother, she imploring Argyris to silence his wife lest her revelations damage Constantine's career.

Prompted, it may be, by news of Constantine's actual or supposed treachery, Aelfrida received 'a most vivid impression' of Roger Casement: 'I don't know whether he knew he was dead – anyhow he was not thinking of himself but of Ireland, Ireland'. Casement, 'a dreamer, a patriot if ever there was one', begged her 'to take and deliver a message about Ireland, [talking] (not out loud of course) for some time in an impassioned way, urging, insisting'. She refused, so he 'floated on, looking for a better and friendlier spirit' with whom to communicate. Aelfrida excused her refusal by asking if it was 'one's duty to be civil to ghosts one doesn't know' and by stating that she had 'a prejudice against ghosts'; she felt guilty nevertheless.[75]

Her astonishment at receiving Roger Casement was attributable less to lack of anticipation of a visitation from a man whose execution made headlines in the newspapers and more because she was 'half-expecting

a visit from Mrs Verrall'.[76] In early June 1916 Margaret Verrall, suffering from advanced cancer but philosophically regarding her imminent death 'as if it were a trip to America', made arrangements to visit Aelfrida from 'over there' once she had passed on.[77] (A more likely visitor might have been Lord Kitchener, whose recent death by drowning had been noted without emotion in Aelfrida's diary; a visit from the hero of her first novel and the object of her adoration for over seven years would have made fascinating reading.) On 4 July 1916 and now regarding herself as a fully-qualified medium, Aelfrida recorded that Mrs Verrall was 'dead, or so we say', adding half-ironically her supposition that Mrs Verrall was about to join 'the Myers-Hodgson-Gurney committee of the SPR[78] which holds its ghostly meetings "over there"' and sadly that because the Selwyn Gardens house was to be sold, she herself would never revisit the schoolroom where she and Constantine had held their 'honeymoon' tea.[79]

Unfortunately for psychical research, Aelfrida's post-mortem correspondence with Mrs Verrall never amounted to much. On 2 September 1916 the latter paid a brief visit to say she had indeed joined Frederic Myers, Edmund Gurney, and Richard Hodgson and her dead husband, "over there" and to ask Aelfrida to take down a message. Aelfrida pleaded a headache (she had just had a long session with Frank Stokoe during which he told her that his childhood fear of 'losing the thread of existence in sleep' had resulted in desperate efforts to keep awake lest he actually do so and that this had now transformed itself into abnormal expansions and contractions of consciousness during which he feared he was losing his mind) and asked Mrs Verrall to return at 9pm the following day.[80] (She did not.) Her final visit took place rather appropriately on All Soul's Eve[81], but although Aelfrida sensed her presence in the room and was able to talk to her, the lady herself remained invisible:

Mrs Verrall: "I have come, as I promised I would".
Aelfrida:  "You are dead, aren't you, and I alive? I want to make that quite clear".
Mrs Verrall: "Yes, I have been asleep and that is why I did not come before".

She then briefly described 'life' as lived after 'death' as 'uniting one's self with the Higher Self or purely spiritual part' before departing, never to return. The fact that Aelfrida's life in the autumn of 1916 was full of partings – Frank Stokoe to Oxford (before he left and hoping to make 'fewer mistakes in [her] dealings with him', Aelfrida asked for details of his past life; to her dismay he told her 'much more than [she] had ever wanted to know')[82], Tommy Altounyan to the RAMC, and Willie Searle, on sick leave from 'terrible experiences in France'[83], to the trenches after only a month in England – may be of relevance here insofar as all three men were, like Mrs Verrall, associated in some respect with disease and death and two were at risk of dying.

Aelfrida's 1917 visitation was from someone she had known and loved all her life, her aunt Fanny Tillyard, who had died under anaesthetic during an operation for appendicitis on 4 March. She had been unwell for only a few days but as a former nurse had realised the seriousness of her condition (it seems peritonitis had set in) and had a premonition that she would not survive. (According to Aunt Anna, Fanny found Aelfrida's poem *No Waiting* a great comfort: "So come thou, too, O Death, in thy good time…/ And kiss my lips – I will not say thee nay".)[84] Aelfrida was devastated (or so it seemed) at the news, describing Aunt Fanny as 'my ideal of goodness … I loved her humility [and] her wonderful power … of seeing good in the most depraved of human beings', adding that Fanny had had 'tremendous influence' over her. But the fact of her recording four days after Fanny's death that she had not dwelt on the sadness of the occasion (nor did she attend her aunt's funeral) because she had 'other things to think about'[85] (this was true but the 'things' described were not so important that they precluded attendance or mourning; they were, however, dramatized to make Aelfrida's presence appear indispensable) may have been the reason for her dead aunt visiting only twice, once in the summer of 1917 in the company of other (unnamed) 'blessed dead' and once to inform her in a 'true dream' that "The Path of the Righteous shineth more and more towards the Perfect Day"[86], a salutary reminder to Aelfrida who had written in the interim 'how little really *right* action comes from me! …The store of spiritual power is so soon exhausted…'[87]

It seems too that, following her psychic adventures of 1916–17, Aelfrida's mediumistic powers were temporarily exhausted, for she received no more messages until 1919. Inspired, however, by Aunt Fanny's communications she decided to inform a living proponent of psychical research of her experiences, namely Sir Oliver Lodge, President of the SPR following the death of its co-founder Henry Sidgwick and since 1900 Principal of the new University of Birmingham. Her reasons for doing so were two-fold. Inspired by her own paranormal communications, she had borrowed Sir Oliver's book *Raymond*, published in 1916, to see if what he described there of precognition of his son's death and of communication with Raymond after the latter's death in action in 1915 corresponded with her own observations. It did: she found the book 'entirely credible and none of it

preposterous'.[88] (It was also from *Raymond* that Aelfrida discovered Sir Oliver's belief that 'archetypes' of books existed, to be 'impressed' on the brains of authors when the time was right, relating her discovery to her own experience of writing poetry.)[89] On the other hand, and as a consequence of Sir Oliver having vetoed Julius' appointment as Professor of Latin at Birmingham University in 1918, she suggested to a mutual friend that he apprise Sir Oliver of her existence and inform him that she was in a position to show him 'messages [she] had had from the spirit-world'. (The conversation took place in front of her parents and caused them some surprise; she had hitherto divulged her experiences only to Mrs Verrall.) Her motive, however, was not disinterested: 'would Sir Oliver rise to it – quite a new medium! What an attraction! Would the desirable sister counterbalance the undesirable wife!!'[90] (Julius' German wife had been instrumental in Sir Oliver vetoing his appointment after it had been made, ostensibly on academic grounds but more likely because anti-German prejudice following Raymond's death affected his judgement; Aelfrida, hearing the news, had been furious: 'is *this* what men have been dying for – that small-minded prejudice should dominate?')[91] Mina's German origins continued to outweigh his sister's mediumistic attractions and Aelfrida's second effort – a personal letter to Sir Oliver in August 1918 – received acknowledgment of 'Myers communications'[92] but no more. Julius, however, after two years' exile as Professor of Latin at University College, Johannesburg, was elected Professor of Latin at Birmingham University in 1921, Sir Oliver having retired in 1919.

This was not, however, the last Sir Oliver heard of Aelfrida. In February 1919 the Spanish influenza pandemic carried off Lilly Grove, daughter of the Strawberry Eater. Poor Lilly had lived an unhappy life before breaking free from her domineering mother and going to live in Switzerland where she studied to be a teacher; Aelfrida, at James Frazer's request, had tried to befriend her in Cambridge days but had found Lilly's prickly personality too unsympathetic to persist. ('Few will regret her', she wrote on hearing of Lilly's death.)[93] Lilly came back into Aelfrida's life in February 1919, 'bothering [her] with a persistent presence'[94] even before the latter knew Lilly was dead. 'Desperately tired and depressed … because all one's friends seem either ill or dead'[95] but rejoicing that her usual Lenten fare of 'reading none but holy books and … thinking none but holy thoughts'[96] had so refined her sensibilities that she felt more able than usual to leave the 'world of sense'[97] behind, Aelfrida re-encountered Lilly as an interjecting presence in a dream in which Frederic Myers again attempted to communicate with her. Something of what he wished to say must have got through in spite of Lilly's inter-ruptions for Aelfrida passed on his message to Sir Oliver Lodge who passed it on to Helen Verrall, since 1915 Mrs WH Salter.[98] Comparing Myers' messages with her own records of spirit communication, Helen discovered that what he said corresponded with entries in her scripts, but apart from telling Aelfrida that this was so, does not seem to have taken the matter further. She did, how-ever, confide to the latter that other people's observations confirmed Aelfrida's own, in particular 'that there is a kind of little committee of the SPR sitting "beyond" to try and communicate with us and that all maintain the characteristics that they had on earth'.[99] Lilly herself did not appear again.

Aelfrida's penultimate message, again involving a dead son and a living mother, took place during family prayers on Armistice Day, 11 November 1920. In September 1920 the Tillyards, short of money because Constantine had temporarily defaulted on payment of Aelfrida's allowance, resorted to taking in a paying guest, Mabel Morris, a widow, one of whose sons (Jack) had been killed in the war. Aelfrida, vacating the East Room and its adjoining dressing room in Mrs Morris' favour, returned to her girlhood room on the second floor, the room in which she and Constantine eventu-ally (so she implies) consummated their marriage. This return to her old haunts brought back memories ('I can hardly see across the room for the ghosts of my dead thoughts and aspirations')[100] and it may have been prox-imity to ghosts of the past which made her aware of Mrs Morris' longing for her dead son during the Armistice Day prayers. She also became aware that Jack himself was present as 'a gay adventurer, rather immature but very keenly alive'. Jack, it seemed, wanted to tell his mother 'that she was not to consider him out of things' but in touch with family events such as his brother's recent engagement and impending marriage. Informing Jack that she 'hated being a medium' and asking him to leave her alone, Aelfrida was surprised to find herself 'swept' into Mrs Morris' room as she passed the door and unable to refrain (albeit with 'apologies and disclaimers') from delivering his message.[101]

Aelfrida's final ghostly visitant was, once again, Frederic Myers, and it was while staying in a house bor-rowed from Helen Salter in which Aelfrida saw ghosts whose clothing was of the period of the house's most famous reputed inhabitant, Nell Gwynne, that Myers' spirit pleaded with her "surely you will be willing to help us?" Aelfrida refused, though with something of a bad conscience ('is it very wrong of me *not* to be willing?') and citing her belief 'that I can do better work even than that'.[102] 'Better work' was, of course, prosecution of her 'Great Work' and it is to a consideration of the impor-tance of this to her life in the years 1914–1918 that we must now turn. Before doing so, however, it is important to note that refusal to consider Myers' plea arose not only from belief that she had 'better work' to do but also from conviction that exercise of miraculous (i.e. supernatural) powers such as "automatic writing and thought-transfer-ence, clairvoyance and communication with the spirits of the dead" might "prove a hindrance to the progress of the soul in true spirituality". Furthermore, she wrote, while certain men and women possess 'dormant' or 'latent' powers which may be evoked by deliberate train-ing of a non-religious nature or accidentally through the regular practice of spiritual exercises, for an aspiring mystic to use these powers in any way other than in the service of God reduces his or her spiritual status to that of 'magician', with all that that implies of deviance from "the main trend of the Mystic Way".[103]

There are, however, further aspects of Aelfrida's career as a medium which must be discussed before we move on to consider the 'better work' taken up by her in the course of the Great War, aspects un-discussed till now because she herself did not disclose them until some-time after her supposed relinquishment of 'communica-tion with the spirits of the dead' in 1921. (In fact, as we learn in due course, she never ceased communicating, albeit her capacity for doing so came and went; indeed, she was soon to discover that the 'spirit world' in the shape of Margaret Verrall was so reluctant to let her go that whenever she embarked on a course of meditation, repetition of her current mantra as she concentrated 'on the essence of the Deity' resulted in 'true dreams' about her dead teacher and even in reception of a 'message' in the same format as bulletins issued by the SPR (*sic*) on the subject of her living husband's 'state of mind and … how his actions appear[ed] to the spirits "up there"'.)[104] It is, of course, impossible to prove that Aelfrida actually underwent experiences she described (retention of Mrs Brooke's confirmatory letter would have provided objec-tive evidence) and no corroborative evidence appears to exist beyond the pages of her diary but one incident she describes is hard to dismiss.

Rupert Brooke was not the only 'Cambridge poet' to die in 1915: James Elroy Flecker, contributor of eight poems, died of disease early that year and Ferenc Békássy, contributor of three, was killed within weeks of Brooke himself and during the time when Brooke and Aelfrida were in spirit communication; it was not, however, until 1925 that Aelfrida described a post-mortem visit from the young Hungarian whose 'fine mass of yellow hair' she had parodied in her *Puff* and who by her own account had 'entangled himself in [her] "magic net"'[105]. An even later (1946/47) version describes how "a young poet … killed in the 1914–18 war asked a friend with psychic gifts to explain to his former tutor where a [manuscript] of poems had been put away and to arrange for their publication. The tutor, [however], believing that the poet was still alive, treated the communication as spurious".[106] The tutor to whom Aelfrida gave dead Békássy's message (she is irritatingly vague about dates, hence we have no means of relating her description to actual events or diary entries) was none other than Goldsworthy Lowes Dickinson (currently President of the SPR, though Aelfrida, so she says, did not know), the 'communication' he treated as 'spurious' was that in a bureau in a particular room in Békássy's family castle in Hungary there was a collection of poems which he wished to be published under the title of *Adriatica,* and his dismissal of Aelfrida's news was as an 'invention' of her own mind.[107] Some years later, however, the poems were "discovered in a secret drawer of an old desk at the poet's home, exactly where the spirit-message had located them"[108] and on 8 May 1925 Aelfrida found herself vindicated by the announcement in *The Times Literary Supplement* of the English publication of *Adriatica and other poems*. Naturally she sought corroboration; infuriatingly, she does not tell us if she found it.

But why, we may ask, did Aelfrida become a conduit for messages from the spirit world at this point in her life? Was it solely because 'deliberate training of a non-religious nature' by Aleister Crowley awoke 'dormant' or 'latent' powers which she proceeded somewhat unwillingly to exercise or because, traumatised by recent events, her subconscious mind did indeed 'invent' events as a means of releasing or diverting or disguising the mental and emotional anguish from which she currently suffered? Or was it because, always impressionable, she was influenced by the current *zeitgeist*, the fact that several of her contacts were victims in some way or another of the Great War being no more than a personal expression of England's incremental interest in Spiritualism as lists of those killed in action lengthened daily, proof of life after death providing solace for grieving families un-persuaded by pious propaganda that it was sweet and meet for their husbands, sons, and brothers to die for their country? Or were her mediumistic communications and revelation of them to Margaret Verrall and Sir Oliver Lodge (and to two bereaved mothers) attention-seeking behaviour indulged in with seeming reluctance in an attempt to divert attention from her Crowleyan escapade or to re-attract attention to herself as one recently returned from a seven year sojourn abroad who by her own admission had lost the important position in Cambridge society she once believed she had? And if

so, how better to accomplish her first aim than by establishing her mediumistic credentials among a group of people prominent in psychical research circles insofar as messages from those *known to be dead* (including members of the SPR) could hardly be dismissed as instances of telepathic communication between the living, messages which were in all cases and unlike those received by students of "cross-correspondences"[109] (i.e. fragmentary messages received via automatic writing by several practitioners, the sense of which was not immediately apparent and sometimes only became so when messages received at different times and places by different people were put together and their formerly enigmatic contents deciphered), cogent as and when received, and in some instances objectively verifiable? (Worth noting in this context that Aelfrida was friendly with Silvia Myers at the time of Frederic Myers' death in 1901 and privy to Silvia's hope that post-mortem messages might be received from him; that she was familiar with earlier and current SPR publications – the *MCJ* of June 1907 contains a brilliant parody, complete with spoof 'case history', of these[110]; that brief transcripts of SPR proceedings appeared in *The Cambridge Magazine* c.1913/14 and that it would not have been difficult for her to present her 'communications' in approved format or, conversely, for them to be influenced by what she read.) And how better to achieve her second aim (and to divert attention from recent eccentricities) by modelling herself on a local heroine known to her as a fellow actress in Lady Frazer's French plays and from her investigations of living conditions in Cambridgeshire villages: Eglantyne Jebb.

Similarities between Eglantyne's and Aelfrida's behaviour are notable: both were pacifists (Aelfrida's idea of a 'Peace Day' to be organised in England by British women in 1915 was discouraged by Eglantyne who informed her to her chagrin that steps had already been taken on an international scale to promote it)[111], both suffered the sudden onset of chronic ill health, both albeit for different reasons and Eglantyne with more justification (in 1913 she had been a relief worker in the Balkan War in often dangerous conditions) deliberately decided to live retired lives at home, and both received messages from the dead, in Eglantyne's case from a suddenly and recently deceased male friend whose messages she recorded and published as *Conversations with the Dead*.[112] But Eglantyne being regarded favourably in Cambridge circles from which Aelfrida felt more than ever excluded suggests that the latter's mediumistic activities might have been consciously modelled on Miss Jebb's and undertaken in in the hope of similar recognition.

But why did Aelfrida refuse to continue? Her ostensible reason – that she could 'do better work than that' – is true as far as it goes; her *real* reason, however, remained un-divulged for over ten years and was subsequently referred to only after another twenty years or in fictional form. In February 1932 at a time when someone close though not then particularly dear to her was so '*very ill*' that Aelfrida had begged the attending doctor not to fight to keep her alive[113], she noted in her diary that she could not remember (*sic*) if she had recorded her 'spiritualist' experiences in earlier volumes, giving as possible reasons for omitting them that she did not like her family knowing that she was 'psychic', that she disliked being 'thought psychic', and that her diaries '[would] perhaps be read after [her] death'. More importantly, however, she also noted that it had been 'an experience of a devil or devils trying to get possession of [her] emptied brain' which persuaded her to have no further 'communication with spirits'.[114] Fictional accounts enlarge on this, one describing a young man whose participation in séances finds him reporting accurately, rapidly, and "with perfect assurance" messages transmitted through him by a dead woman who acts as his 'control' but whose experiments with "automatic writing" are of more sinister import: "spirits collect in *crowds* and … think they've got a right over me and [that] I *must* take down their messages", after which, compelled by the spirits to continue, the devil appears and imprisons him in "a kind of well" from which he escapes only after sending up a cry for help to a "dim circle of light"[115] above his head, the other an older man, possessor of "mediumistic gifts", who breaks down under the strain of dealing with benign spirits who claim his services "as a right", then, offended at his dwindling enthusiasm, become "spirits of evil"[116] who drive him to his death. It is possible, therefore, that Aelfrida, afraid of "the mocking spirits of darkness" which tried to creep into her mind when she made it blank or who tapped at her "mind's windows" in an effort to "lure [her] soul out into the night" and thence into hands of "magicians and sorcerers, spiritualists and freak-religionists"[117], decided to desist. But was it only an instinct for self-preservation which prevented her from publicising the fact that the "solemn assembly of Myers and his Psychical Research Society friends" with whom she had been in communication had bidden her "inform scientists that all future discoveries would be *concerned with vibrations!*" or was she afraid of being thought an unreliable witness at best and at worst more than a little 'mad' or was it because, as Goldsworthy Lowes Dickinson surmised, her mind had indeed 'invented' them?

## Notes

1   GCPPT 1|1|20 10 October 1914. The preferred spelling is now 'cipher'.

2   GCPPT 1|1|18 10 January 1913.

3   Aelfrida's ability may have been inherited from both sides of her family. Mary Tillyard was psychic though she rarely displayed and never voluntarily used her gift (GCPPT 2|27|1(10)) and Louisa Warren, Catharine Tillyard's cousin, had 'psychic fits' during which spectral presences and poltergeist activities were manifest in the house in which she lived (GCPPT2|27|2(7)). A parodied version of 'Aunt Louie's' sayings and mannerisms (*Interview with Aunt L.*) appears in the *MCJ* of January 1907 with Aelfrida as author (GCPPT 2|2a).

4   GCPPT 1|1|18 4 March 1912.

5   GCPPT 1|1|22 9 July 1918.

6   GCPPT 1|1|18 26 July 1911.

7   ibid. 19 December 1912 (retrospective entry).

8   GCPPT 1|1|21 26 September 1915. Aelfrida makes no later comment regarding the inaccuracy of this particular prediction.

9   GCPPT 1|1|22 5 July 1917.
    GCPPT 1|1|65 26 February 1948.

10  GCPPT 1|1|25 19 February 1921.
    GCPPT 1|1|26 27 April 1922.

11  GCPPT 1|1|27 10 September 1923. Aelfrida may not have been as psychic here as she would have us believe: stories of Denny Abbey being haunted abounded, as did tales of secret passages.

12  GCPPT 1|1|22 18 June 1918. Catley Park began life as a Tudor manor house. It was enlarged and extensive gardens laid out around it in the seventeenth century but fell into desuetude in the eighteenth and was pulled down except for one wing which became Catley Park Farm. The house was gradually abandoned during the twentieth century and was demolished in 1978. Only fragmentary walls and dilapidated barns remain. For the full story of Catley Park see Stevens, RL et al *Linton, the Story of a Market Town* (1992).

13  GCPPT 1|1|26 28 August 1921.

14  GCPPT 1|1|9 22 April 1902.

15  GCPPT 1|1|17 7 February 1910. Helen Verrall, like Margaret Verrall, was the recipient of messages from discarnate entities by means of automatic writing. She began to receive messages in this manner in 1901, shortly before her first discussion with her former schoolmate.

16  GCPPT 1|1|18 10 January 1913. Margaret Verrall's own psychic powers post-dated her association with the SPR, members of the society later hailing her as a competent and trustworthy medium and a vigorous investigator of paranormal phenomena.

17  Jeanne Marie Bouvier de la Mothe Guyon (1648–1717) was a French mystic of Quietist persuasion with whom Aelfrida believed she had much in common : a preference for contemplative devotion and for passivity and of extinction of the will in one's relationship with God, for example, and a need to cultivate 'indifference' with regard to worldly things. Mme Guyon was rebuffed by her husband and family because of her beliefs and was later exiled from Paris where she had once wielded much influence at court and over the philosopher Fénelon. Her devoted disciple, Père LaCombe, a Barnabite monk, was subsequently imprisoned in the Bastille because of his association with a lady of supposedly heretical views. In *Can I be a Mystic?* (pp 166–167) Aelfrida describes Madame Guyon's life very much in terms of her own ("it was her marriage which turned her towards a life of piety. Desperately unhappy through her ill-treatment by her husband and mother-in-law … she suffered seven years of the most acute aridity"), going on to discern parallels between Mme Guyon's "soul struggle" and her own.

18  GCPPT 2|25|2(4).

19  GCPPT 1|1|22 29 July 1917.

20 Myers seems to have been particularly communicative after his death, often communicating through more than one medium (Katz, D. p130).

21 GCPPT 1|1|20 20 July 1914. It was after Myers' death in 1901 that Margaret Verrall first obtained significant results from her own experiments with automatic writing.

22 GCPPT 1|1|20 13 October 1914.

23 ibid. 28 November 1914.

24 ibid. 20 July 1914.
GCPPT 1|1|59 30 March 1942.

25 GCPPT 1|1|20 20 July 1914.

26 ibid. 1 May 1915.

27 Rupert Brooke's *The Soldier* was written in November–December 1914 when Eustace, a 'soldier boy in uniform', was guarding Ealing Broadway station and Aelfrida was writing of him and his friend Eardley Davidson that young men like them would not 're-emerge unchanged' from the coming conflict (GCPPT 1|1|20 7 November 1914).

28 Brooke's poem, *Clouds*, written in October 1913 just too late for inclusion in *Cambridge Poets,* ends with the lines "They say that the dead die not, but remain / Near to the rich heirs of their grief and mirth./ I think they ride the calm mid-heaven, as these, / In wise, majestic melancholy train, / And watch the moon and the still-raging seas, / And men, coming and going on the earth". Aelfrida does not say if she had read *Clouds* prior to Brooke's visit in May 1915 but she had certainly done so by 1919 for she refers to it in *Vision Triumphant* (p 81) in a passage in which two young soldiers under fire discuss "that poet-chap who bust up with sunstroke in Greece [who said] we were going to float about on clouds and watch our old friends down here walking out with their best girls".

29 GCPPT 1|1|20 9 May 1915.

30 ibid. 17 June ('July' in error) 1915.

31 The Old Vicarage and its river frontage were later to figure in the dramatic climax of Aelfrida's novel *The Young Milliner.*

32 GCPPT 1|1|20 19 June 1915.

33 ibid. 30 June 1915. The line as recalled by Aelfrida bears remarkable resemblance to AE Housman's "blue remembered hills" of *The Shropshire Lad,* sonnet 36.

34 GCPPT 1|1|20 22 June 1915.

35 ibid. 27 June 1915.

36 Edmund Gurney was one of the co-founders, together with Henry Sidgwick and Myers himself, of the SPR; Dr Verrall was associated with it only insofar as Margaret Verrall was his wife. All four men in Aelfrida's dream (Gurney, Myers, Verrall, and Brooke) were dead. For more on Gurney see Shultz, B. pp 288–291.

37 GCPPT 1|1|19 16 December 1913. How, we may ask, did Brooke know the name bestowed on Aelfrida by Aleister Crowley? Possible explanations are that he had, before his death, equated the 'Sarasvati' of *Cambridge Poets* with the anthology's compiler or that he knew of the passage in Crowley's *Paris Working* in which 'AeT … the beloved disciple' was identified as Sarasvati, but if Rupert, living, lacked information on either score (and we should remember that Aelfrida herself did not now publicise the Crowley connection and had never met Brooke himself), he called her by a name not generally known. We can only conclude that the 'Sarasvati' epithet came from Aelfrida's subconscious mind or that it was intuited by the spirit visitor then occupying it.

38 GCPPT 1|1|20 28 June 1915.

39 ibid. 30 June 1915. Aelfrida was familiar with contemporary writings on the 'subliminal self' in particular W. James' *Varieties of Religious Experience* in which is discussed the "discovery of a consciousness existing beyond the field or subliminally, as Mr Myers terms it". One of the effects of having a "strongly developed ultra-marginal life of this sort is that one's ordinary fields of consciousness are liable to incursions from it", "up rushes" into consciousness of energies originating in the subliminal parts of the mind, hallucinations of sight and hearing and the

direction of automatic writing being manifestations of them (op. cit. pp 233–234). James also refers his reader to Myers' essay on *Subliminal Consciousness* published in 1892 in the Proceedings for the Society for Psychical Research vol 7, an essay enlarged upon in *Human Personality* (James W. pp 511–512) which Aelfrida had recently studied.

40 GCPPT 1|1|20 2 July 1915.

41 For details of the Palm Sunday Case see http://www.prairieghosts.com/cross_corr.html

42 Keynes, G. Preface pp 8–9 to *The Poetical Works of Rupert Brooke.*

43 GCPPT 1|1|20 11 July 1915.

44 ibid. 14 July 1915.

45 ibid. 3 August 1915.

46 ibid. 14 July 1915. Aelfrida had a brief rapture ('a hesitation between word and word') while reading a Brooke poem aloud to her family but does not say which poem provoked it.

47 ibid. 19 August 1915.

48 ibid. 6 August 1915.

49 Conybeare, E. p271.

50 GCPPT 1|1|20 9 September 1915.

51 GCCPT 1|1|21 11 September 1915. The quotation (or, rather, misquotation, 'truth' for 'truths') comes from Rupert Brooke's *The Old Vicarage, Grantchester,* one of the four Brooke poems included in Aelfrida's *Cambridge Poets 1900–1913* (pp 25–30).

52 GCPPT 1|1|21 11 September 1915.

53 ibid. 21 September 1915.

54 ibid. 16 and 17 September 1915.

55 ibid. 18 September 1915. The three Caldecote poems later appeared in *The Garden and the Fire* with only one *(The Old Rectory)* bearing its ostensible date of composition, the other two (*A Load of Hay* and *Triolet*) being dated 21 September 1915. It may be that Aelfrida discarded two un-named poems written on 17 September though she contemporaneously records that she wrote *A Load of Hay* on 21/22 September.

56 Olga Pashler's husband had died, leaving her penniless, and she took in lodgers to make ends meet. During the war she was employed by the Government to requisition hay as fodder for horses serving in the British armies in countries where forage was in short supply. *A Load of Hay* appears in the section entitled 'poems about the war' in *The Garden and the Fire* (pp 8–9); it also appeared in *The Cambridge Magazine* vol V No19 15 January 1916 p207.

57 *Triolet* is dedicated 'to C.W.du B', Charles du Bouchet, whose warwork consisted of the organisation of ambulance and ambulance-trains to ferry the wounded back to Paris from the Front; the sound of these convoys was one of Eustace's first impressions on arriving in France. *Triolet* appears in the section entitled 'poems about all sorts of things' in *The Garden and the Fire* (p 44).

58 To demonstrate its importance in Aelfrida's life and 1916 anthology, *The Old Rectory, Caldecote* is accorded a section of its own in *The Garden and the Fire* (pp 31–33).

59 GCPPT 1|1|21 17 September 1915.

60 *Triolet* may also contain a reference to Crowley in its evocation of "the starry throng" to which Aelfrida felt herself lifted during the out-of-body experience of 16 September, a "starry throng of devas" (i.e. of divine or angelic persons) being one to which Crowley would find it hard to attain "by broken wings".

61 GCPPT 2|25|3(6a).

62 GCPPT 1|1|21 22 September 1915.

63 GCPPT 1|1|30 15 February 1925.

64 It is conceivable that Aelfrida self-published *The Garden and the Fire* in 1916 because she had been refused inclusion in *The Oxford Book of Mystical Verse* (also 1916), a refusal the more poignant because some of her own 'Cambridge poets' (including Aleister Crowley) appeared in it. Perhaps she hoped the avowedly 'mystical poems' her own anthology contained might be included in a later edition.

65  GCPPT 1|1|20 28 June 1915.

66  Tillyard, Ae. *Can I be a Mystic?* pp 94–95.

67  *Kingdoms* (*The Garden and the Fire* pp 17–20). The poem with its preliminary description of the garden and wider vista in which it is set, follows the format of short play-poems in *The Equinox* e.g. *The Ship*, "a mystery play by Saint Edward Aleister Crowley" in vol 1 No 10 October 1913 pp 59–79.

68  Tillyard, Ae. *The Making of a Mystic* p 77.

69  GCPPT 1|1|21 20 April 1916.

70  ibid. 17 December 1916.

71  ibid. 23 September 1916.

72  ibid. 20 April 1916.

73  Sir Roger Casement (1864–1916) was hanged in as a traitor, having been captured, tried, and stripped of his knighthood by the British following his negotiations with Germany on behalf of Irish Nationalists prior to the Easter Rising.

74  GCPPT 1|1|21 30 April 1916.

75  ibid. 8 August 1916. Aelfrida's 'prejudice' may have stemmed from the fact that excerpts from Casement's diaries detailing homoerotic dealings with Brazilian and Congolese natives were circulated prior to his execution to stiffen the resolve of those advocating commutation of the death sentence on the grounds that his consular career had been exemplary.

76  GCPPT 1|1|21 8 August 1916.

77  ibid. 7 June 1916. Margaret Verrall died on 2 July 1916.

78  Myers had announced in February 1901, a month after his death, that he had founded a branch of the SPR in the life beyond, with Henry Sidgwick (obit August 1900) as president. His communication was made through the American medium Leonora Piper (1859–1950) whose daughter Alta had been invited to tea at Arlington Heights (GCPPT 1|1|17 3 June 1909; her signature appears in Aelfrida's Visitors Book) albeit without a record being kept of their conversation. Richard Hodgson (1855–1905), the other member of Aelfrida's triumvirate, was an Australian lawyer with an interest in psychical research who was sent by the SPR to India to investigate the truth or otherwise (otherwise, as it turned out) of Mme Blavatsky's mediumistic claims. In 1895 while Professor of Legal Studies in Cambridge he met Eusepia Palladino but believed her fraudulent. He later moved to the United States where he co-founded the American SPR and became a full-time researcher into paranormal phenomena and a friend of William James. For further details see Schultz, B. pp314–315 & 701; Katz, D. pp128–130.

79  GCPPT 1|1|21 8 August 1916.

80  ibid. 31 August 1916.

81  ibid. 2 November 1916.

82  ibid. 30 September 1916.

83  ibid. 31 October 1916.

84  *No Waiting*, written in Emden on 8 March 1912 when Aelfrida was pregnant with Agneta, appears in the 'poems about death' section of *The Garden and the Fire* (p 40).

85  GCPPT 1|1|21 5 and 8 March 1917.

86  ibid. 30 March 1917.

87  ibid. 16 March 1917.

88  GCPPT 1|1|22 29 July 1917.

89  ibid.

90  GCPPT 1|1|23 30 August 1918.

91  ibid. 9 December 1918.

92  ibid. 9 September 1918.

93  ibid. 26 February 1919.

94  ibid. 26 February 1919.

95  ibid. 11 March 1919.

96  ibid. 4 March 1919.

97  ibid. 13 March 1919.

98  For a brief but informative biography of Helen Salter (née Verrall) see Bishop-Culpeper, N. *Mrs Salter: The Crown House Medium* (*Newport News* No 23 June 1985 pp 53–54). WH Salter, barrister and psychical researcher, was President of the SPR 1947–1948.

99  GCPPT 1|1|26 18 September 1921.

100  GCPPT 1|1|25 30 September 1920.

101  ibid. 12 November 1920.

102  GCPPT 1|1|26 4 September 1921.

103  Tillyard, Ae. *Spiritual Exercises* pp 195–196.

104  GCPPT 1|1|26 24 September 1922.

105  GCPPT 1|1|19 18 May 1913.

106  Tillyard, Ae. *Christian Old Age* p 103 (GCPPT 2|17).

107  GCPPT 1|1|30 9 May 1925.

108  Tillyard, Ae. *Christian Old Age* p 130. Békássy was killed on the Eastern Front on 25 June 1915. It is possible that Aelfrida heard of the manuscript's existence from Maynard Keynes who visited Békássy at Kis Sennye in 1911 (Skidelsky, R. pp 264–265) or that Békássy himself had told her, the latter being something which Békássy's inclusion in *Cambridge Poets 1900–1913* might seem to support, for a poem, *Fragmentary Views*, appears in both Aelfrida's anthology and in *Adriatica* and was also parodied by her in *The Puff by Parody*.

109  Schultz, B. p723.

110  GCPPT 2|2a June 1907 *Servant Personality* by 'FWH Myers', written by Aelfrida herself.

111  GCPPT 1|1|20 18 April 1915. It is possible that Aelfrida's 'Peace Day' was inspired by a contemporary movement, the National Mission of Repentance and Hope.

112  For details of the life of Eglantyne Jebb (1876–1928) between 1913 and 1916, see Mulley, C. pp 177–189 and 192–201. Details of her work during the Balkan War are given in chapter 8.

113  GCPPT 1|1|40 19 February 1932.

114  GCPPT 1|1|40 11 February 1932.
    GCPPT 1|1|72 2 August 1955.

115  Tillyard, Ae. *The Centaur* pp 142–151 (GCPPT 2|21|1).

116  Tillyard. Ae. *The Glory of the West* pp 300–304 (GCPPT 2|16|1 Pt 2).

117  ibid. p 300.

# Bloodhound on a trail

Aelfrida's comment of 15 August 1914 that everyone was doing something except herself was true insofar as it referred to 'war-work' carried out by other people but untrue with regard to herself. In fact, the years 1914–1918 saw her enthusiastically occupied with a project which, though it took place in the context of the Great War, was carried out on her own account and, in spite of disclaimers, chiefly for her own benefit. The project was, of course, the prosecution of the twin aims of her 'Great Work': her own spiritual development, phrased in terms of a journey along the Mystic Way, and the spiritual development of fellow-travellers on the Way and encouragement of those taking their first faltering footsteps on it, mystics being for her seekers after "some ultimate reality with which they can commune and in whose being they find satisfaction" (and as a result of this, those to whom "the spiritual world … is more real than the material world")[1] and the Mystic Way the "special road" taken by an individual in search for that which is sought.[2] How she began her 'Work' is the subject of this chapter.

A serendipitous coincidence of independent factors provided or promoted the conditions which enabled her to do so. On the one hand, Constantine's premarital promise to lead her 'through love to a new revelation' had 'finished in nothing at all', leaving her with an emotional void which she proposed to fill by 'passionately [returning] to the better way'[3] of focusing of emotional energy surplus to that lavished on her daughters and all her spiritual energy on her own spiritual development and that of sympathetic others. On the other hand, the Grahams being separated by inclination and events for the greater part of the war meant that Aelfrida, safely ensconced in a paradisiacal environment (for however much she complained, the fiery hell of war did not touch her greatly in a material sense) where time-consuming, distasteful, or physically-tiring domestic tasks were (mostly) consigned to other people, was able to indulge her bent for spiritual exploration to a greater extent than would have been possible in the presence of a husband, however supportive, and impossible in the presence of carping Constantine. When to this one adds her refusal to support aggression so widespread that it gave the 1914–18 war its epithet of 'great', it is easy to see how

Aelfrida Graham c1920

refusal, combined with unexpected freedom of action, allowed her to commit to a period of study in which vivid but hitherto inchoate intimations of transcendental Reality could be evaluated, then, with sense and teleology established, employed to furtherance of her 'Great Work'. Without the Great War, one could say, her 'Great Work' might never have been prosecuted.

The beginning of Aelfrida's compulsion to explore what it meant to be a mystic, a person that is to say, who, with or without the use of specific initiatory exercises is able to achieve unmediated spiritual union with God and who, as a possible precursor to and a hoped-for result of this, believes in and hopes to grasp a Truth which lies beyond mere sensory perception, dated from the year prior to her first meeting with Constantine. Discussing 'what he calls mysticism' with Julius in January 1903, she suddenly realised that she might be 'a bit of a mystic' herself, if only because of an emergent feeling that although she had not yet '*seen God*' (another possible definition of a mystic), she found herself more and more 'in tune' *with* God.[4] Involvement with John Forbes Cameron and Constantine Michaelides precluded further introspection and it was not until her arrival in Florence in October 1904 that, full of her 'new thirst for mysticism', she was able to devote time and energy to satisfying it. Illness, courtship, the necessity of earning money to support Constantine during his studies, marriage, foreign travel, motherhood, and a near-death experience intervened, and it was only after her crucial relationship with Aleister Crowley that she was able to surrender herself more fully to the embrace of omnipotent and omnipresent Deity. By 1914, however, separated by circumstances and by his own belief that he had nothing more to teach her from a 'guru' whose 'Great Work' diverged in aim and content from her own, Aelfrida realised first, that the (to her) 'strange and startling' results of mystical experiences undergone at Le Vésinet had awakened a desire and, indeed, a *need* to delve further into "the whole question of mysticism"[5] in order to find out whence, spiritually speaking, she had come, where she now stood, and whither she was going, and second, that, failing Crowley, she required the help of other agencies if she were to make progress with interiorised or exteriorised aspects of her own 'Work' and 'way'.

Once again the Great War came to her help. Wife, sister, and daughter of Cambridge graduates, sister of an unavoidably-absent fellow of a Cambridge college, and inhabitant of a university town in which so many undergraduates answered Lord Kitchener's call to arms that numbers of graduands plummeted to levels unheard for nearly five hundred years, Aelfrida was welcomed with open arms by underemployed academics eager to teach a woman known to be 'clever' and voraciously eager to learn. She therefore had the unhoped-for opportunity of fulfilling William James' dictum that the ideal qualification for a student of Mysticism was "to have first naively undergone spiritual experiences" and second, to be able to critically examine them "from a scientific point of view".[6]

Nor, from the academics' point of view, was she devoid of academic credentials. In Florence she had attended de Sarlo's lectures and visited his famous laboratory and in Boston she had been 'suggested' by Münsterberg himself; in addition, she had a quick mind and by adroit questions was able to acquire sufficient information to make her appear well-informed. (Talking to Granville Grove,

brother of Lilly, in July 1900, Aelfrida commented after a discussion which ranged from 'psycical (*sic*) research [to] Homeric controversy' that 'it sounds as though we had a very improving conversation, doesn't it? But I believe I could talk about bi-metallism and flirt at the same time'.)[7] Then too, she had been invited by the Heretics, a Cambridge society whose members regarded themselves as radical free-thinkers (a condition of membership was "the rejection of all appeal to authority in the discussion of religious questions")[8] to lecture on the subject *Can We See God?*, the invitation being a response to her *Cambridge Magazine* article of 24 January 1914 in which, as 'Mrs Graham', she explained Ceremonial Magic references in Crowley's *Palace of the World*. (She behaved 'as though [she] were publicly beginning a ministry' and was disappointed when Heretics present responded to her more in the spirit of intellectual enjoyment than in earnest pursuit of the truth.)[9] This fortunate concatenation of circumstances allowed her to prepare the ground for future exploration during her extended summer vacation of May – July 1914.

Within days of her arrival in England, she obtained a reader's ticket at the University Library ('I felt so *thrilled* walking through all those books')[10], an institution in which, 'though rather lost, both in the building and [her] subject'[11], she was to spend many happy hours ('the subject is opening out wonderfully')[12] and to realise what an opportunity she had lost in preferring motherhood (and its expected precondition, marriage) to the academic career to which she would have been ideally suited: 'had I eyesight and opportunity I believe I *could* be a scholar. There is a mingled repose and excitement in learning that fascinates me … And then the ardour of pursuing clues, the thrill of feeling one's mind grasp a subject – oh marvellous'.[13] But 'research and parties', she reluctantly decided on the day when, surrounded by admiring Little Friends, she watched the morris dancing, 'don't go together … something will have to be given up'[14]; the outbreak of war two months later made her decision easy. Prior to that, however, she had seized the opportunity afforded by Constantine's absence in Hessle for the greater part of June 1914 (he did not attend her lecture to the Heretics but as he disapproved of his wife speaking in public and because the occasion arose as a result of her association with a man on whose account he had physically assaulted her, this was probably just as well) and of her parents holidaying with Constantine in Le Vésinet for most of July, to visit Cambridge's newly established Psychological Laboratory.

Aelfrida's initial contact with the Laboratory was by letter, she having enquired of Charles Myers[15] if he knew of books on the psychology of 'mystics and the like'. Myers' response was to invite her to the Laboratory where he informed her that 'experimental mysticism' was an untapped subject and that 'a real mystic [had] never been brought under scientific observation' even though 'the psychology of the religious life [had] received a good deal of attention'.[16] On Aelfrida volunteering to have him observe her while she tried 'to get *Samadhi* in his presence'[17], Myers, so she said, 'simply jumped at it, [saying] that the most desirable thing would be for [her] to have a vision with him there'. She agreed to try, informing Myers of her Parisian experiences (she deliberately did not name Aleister Crowley or provide a full account) and that she was keen to try for a visionary experience under controlled conditions lest earlier ones arose solely 'from thoughts transferred from [her] teacher'.[18] Pending the experiment, she agreed to keep a record of visions (if any) experienced in the interim.[19]

The experiment took place on 19 June 1914 in Myers' office, Aelfrida being so 'supremely desirous' of demonstrating the credibility of the experience she was about to undergo that she felt 'neither awkward nor a fool'. Taking off her hat and gloves (a nice touch!) she lay down on the floor with Myers' coat and academic gown beneath her and a pillow under her head. Placing herself in the *Aum tat sat Aum* position, she closed her eyes, repeated a mantra, 'and passed into meditation'. From a meditative state she passed rapidly into *Samadhi*: 'my consciousness was first alone with God and afterwards merged in His … a sublime experience, an eternity of delight'. Her vision over, she sat up 'a little dazed' to hear Myers tell her that 'he did not know in the least what to make of it'. (Observing his subject closely, Myers saw that her expression hardly altered during the supposedly 'ecstatic' experience; Aelfrida herself remarked that she was aware of extraneous noises after entering *Samadhi*, something which suggests either that her experience was not as intense as she made it out to be or that the experience was both exclusive *and inclusive* insofar as percepts were embraced by it as enhancements of the whole.) Keen to repeat the experiment, Myers also asked her to dictate her experience to him while it was still fresh in her mind.[20] The events of August 1914, however, precluded further experimentation, Aelfrida recording on 22 October that Myers had 'gone to the war'[21] and she herself handed over to his demonstrator Bernard Muscio.[22]

Inspection of the Psychological Laboratory having reassured her that it was 'a nice friendly little room in which no one ought to be nervous'[23], she allowed Bernard Muscio to carry out experiments during which she had to comment on scenes 'witnessed on a cinematograph'. Muscio's conclusions, namely that her recall

of visual imagery was 'abnormally keen' and that she was able to reproduce vivid mental representations of sound, motion, and even smell, did not surprise her; she was aware of this from earlier visionary experiences and eventually came to the conclusion that experiments of this nature were rather 'silly'.[24] As a quid pro quo, however, she taught Muscio yogic exercises which enabled him to enter into the same frame of mind as herself when undergoing visionary experiences. But although she describes him as practising so enthusiastically that he not only had premonitory dreams but also developed the ability to view his experiences impersonally at the time of experiencing them[25], her attempts to persuade him to carry out the exercises in a 'religious' frame of mind foundered on Muscio's determination to remain dispassionate[26] (he was, after all, conducting scientific experiments) and possibly also on his belief that Aelfrida's introduction of Ceremonial Magic practices into the Laboratory (she writes of Muscio having achieved a glimpse of the diabolic 'guardian of the threshold' and comments that 'all this cabalistic stuff ought to suit him' because of his Jewish blood)[27] was a step too far to take even in the interests of research.

A later account of their experimentation appears in Aelfrida's *Spiritual Exercises* in terms of the difficulties encountered by psychologists "who "investigate the types of spiritual consciousness [or try to] identify types of mystical experience as found in different religions".[28] She also notes that "about a dozen persons here in Cambridge undertook, at my suggestion, an experiment in spiritual exercises. Half of them did so with devotional intention, the others merely as students interested in types of human consciousness. In no case did the seekers after religious experience fail to attain their object, and the results of their meditations were most varied and interesting. Altogether the experiments, though few in number, justify me, I think, in laying down as an axiom that *religious intention is essential to the successful performance of a spiritual exercise*".[29]

The student group included, besides an unnamed junior demonstrator and three students from the Laboratory itself, a theologian from Westminster College, a botanist from the Botanic Garden, and an Anglo-Swiss chemist[30], but only with the latter, George von Kaufmann[31], did she achieve her hoped-for results, the others rapidly losing interest or becoming too sceptical. Describing von Kaufmann as 'a fresh-faced boy [who] wants to devote his life to chemical research – and mystical adventures' and as her own first '*chela*', Aelfrida named him 'Siddhartha'[32] before guiding what she hoped were his initial steps on the Mystic Way.[33] After many 'fine, spirited arguments' on spiritual matters (her response to

'Siddhartha's' enquiry if 'complete chastity was necessary to the best kind of spiritual life' was that her preference was for 'normal behaviour combined with long periods of continence'[34], a state she herself had recently achieved because of Constantine's posting to Amsterdam and her inability to join him), Aelfrida felt sure enough of her '*chela*' to hail him as 'a child of [her] spirit' and as one who, younger by a decade and a man, would be able 'to do the works I cannot and go where I may not go'. She worried, however, that the potential 'saint and … prophet' lacked an essential something[35] but it was only following von Kaufmann's departure from Cambridge that she discovered her '*chela*' had not only kept several mistresses during his time at college ('I never suspected! I am … incurably simple-minded') but had even introduced one to her.[36] After that, there were no more '*chelas*'.

Even before the onset of the war which separated her from a husband who would have denigrated her efforts had he been present and of the appalling health which dogged her during the four years it lasted but which because of her insistence on spending so many days in bed, allowed her a vast amount of time for undisturbed reading and writing (behaviour in which her father colluded by taking out books for her from the University Library and even, to her surprise, encouraging studies concerning which he expressed only qualified enthusiasm), Aelfrida had begun research to enable her to ascertain the meaning of and role played by mystics and mystical experience in world religions other than Christianity. Although she was eventually to decide that such topics, though fascinating in themselves, did not provide the information she required and might result in dissipation of spiritual energy were she to engage with sectarian beliefs which did not fulfil her personal aim of achieving spiritual union with Deity or her wider aim of guiding others to deeper appreciation of the Divine, she nevertheless found the subject so absorbing that she expended an enormous amount of energy on it.

She began her research by visiting Stanley Cook, Reader in Comparative Studies of Religion, who informed her that her particular interest, namely how mystics of various nations and creeds were able to produce certain states of mind at will, was 'practically untouched by scholars' of the new discipline. Deciding that she would therefore be obliged to collate information from those who had made studies of specific religions, she wrote ecstatically 'I feel the lure of research – one is like a bloodhound on a trail!'[37] Further inspired by a visit to GRS Mead on 22 June 1914 from whom she obtained little information ('I think he has not recovered from having left the Theosophical Society')[38] but much encouragement ("Go on, go on. Read, think, study, write

… you *may* find something, who knows")[39] and though disappointed with recently-knighted Sir James Fraser because even he with his compendious (but exclusively theoretical) knowledge of Anthropology knew nothing about 'ecstasy in the higher religions'[40], she embarked on a course of study which would occupy her during the war years and for some time thereafter.

Among the mentors listed in the preface to *Spiritual Exercises* two names go unmentioned. The first is Aleister Crowley, whose innovative work on Comparative Religion (777, published in 1909) had been given her by its author. The second is Susanna Venn, now living the reclusive life of a tipsy widow but once the lady whose loan of 'sacred notebooks' to a teenage visitor thirsting for spiritual enlightenment had done much to stimulate her interest ("I longed … to know how much spiritual light God had vouchsafed to men … outside the Christian faith [and] I honoured the writers as genuine seekers after God") even while causing her to feel that in *their* pages she was unlikely to hear the voice of God speaking meaningfully to *her*.[41] Even more significant, however, was adult Aelfrida's wartime discovery that the Mrs Venn of whom she had once written "I used to stare at [her] and wonder whether Eastern literature had taught her to commune with God … I thought it probably had not",[42] was a mystic *manqué*.[43] Her belated tribute may have been inclusion among the "devout lay people" listed anonymously alongside "priests, monks [and] nuns" who preferred not to be mentioned by name or whom, as with Aleister Crowley, she preferred not to mention by name even when quoting his poetry in her book.[44]

Aelfrida's study of Comparative Religion encompassed a range of belief-systems. Each was seized upon with more or less enthusiasm according to her spiritual requirements of the moment or the rapport she felt with her current mentor but all, like her mentors, were subsequently discarded. With two she dabbled only briefly: Spiritual Healing, insofar as this was associated by GFC Searle[45] with the influence of mystical aspects of religious belief on mind and of mind on body ("'healing" is his line but he is just as keen on the spiritual uplifting of people')[46] though she baulked at Spiritual Healing's reputed ability to cure a prolapse as severe as hers and had a vested interest in not testing its efficacy on psychosomatic ailments; and Judaism towards which, for all her positive experiences with the Schechters, of being informed of 'passionately interesting things' about Jewish mystics[47] by a visiting rabbi, and of finding herself able to link her new knowledge with cabbalistic details imparted by Crowley, she felt little sympathy because of Jehovah's stern and unloving nature, a nature a little too like Constantine's in its impassivity and in its 'eternal obligation' that she submit with unquestioning obedience to its dictates.[48]

Her next interest (already awakened by Aleister Crowley), namely in the Hindu religion in general and the mystic aspects of Hinduism in particular, was further inspired by a mentor with whom she achieved early and immediate rapport because not only did he inform her that she had had a 'good guru' (Crowley, she noted excitedly, albeit without disclosing his name, 'certainly unlocked all manner of gates for me') and treat her – 'the foreigner, the woman!' – as one worthy to listen to sacred things, but also because he placed greater importance on *Samadhi* (and, of equal importance to Aelfrida, post-*samadhic 'return* full of blazing enthusiasm to the world') than on formalism and dogma.[49] Through him, therefore, she was able to achieve closer contact with the world of Hindu spirituality.

Aelfrida's initial meeting with Surendra Nath Maitra, an eminent Brahmin physicist from Calcutta working towards a Cambridge higher degree[50], took place on 4 June 1914 at a time when Constantine was still in England. Noting his wife's enthusiasm – Maitra had undertaken yogic studies in India and was deemed 'highly competent to give [her] information'[51] – and fearing a reprise of Crowleyan discipularity (Crowley was much on Aelfrida's mind during the early days of her relationship with Maitra because the latter's explanation of a 'symbol–astral' she had performed at Crowley's behest demonstrated, so Maitra said, 'a very complete account of [her] spiritual development')[52], Constantine allied himself with Alfred Tillyard to declare that there was '*no* common ground between us and the Indians'.[53] Their remarks failed to dampen her enthusiasm. Nor was it dampened by Maitra's information that the books she needed were in Sanskrit 'and that … nothing important was ever committed to writing'[54]; indeed, Aelfrida's joy at discovering a man between whose mind and hers 'there seemed no barrier … neither of race nor of creed'[55] not only moved her to record their conversations (the records no longer exist) but also to discuss with him visionary and ecstatic experiences undisclosed to anyone save Tommy Altounyan (and then only briefly and in rather general terms of the 'intolerable contrast' between her spiritual and her 'ordinary conventional life')[56] since Crowley himself. Because of their closeness she also felt able to read some unspecified poems to him (something she did only to trusted acquaintances like Frank Stokoe), paying homage to his interest and sympathy by including a version of the Brahmin Salutation to Light performed for her by Maitra on 19 June (the ceremony was 'only supposed to be done alone or with another Brahmin')[57] in the last eight lines of *Kingdoms* written

shortly afterwards. (She also dedicated the poem to him as 'SNM'.) As no further reference to Maitra appears after the outbreak of war in August 1914, it must be presumed that he returned to India at that point but that Aelfrida's interest in Hinduism persisted and that she read widely around the subject is demonstrated by her extensive use of references in the Hindu Meditations chapter of *Spiritual Exercises* and by the thanks she extends to scholars who provided her with information on 'ecstasy in Indian Literature'.[58] To one of them (Dr JD Anderson) she even dedicated a poem *To Amrita. Indian Love Song*, verses which refer not only to the "the great Lord Brahman" of whom both the "unsubstantial earth" and the lovers themselves are but "the pageant of his dream" and to "Lord Ishvara" (Shiva in his creative aspect but now also for Aelfrida the "personal" or, more correctly, personalised aspect of the divine spirit in man which enables him to contemplate and comprehend "Deity")[59] but also to Aleister Crowley in their evocation of "White Himalaya's crags and cloud-girt snows".[60]

Her next, or rather, concurrent enthusiasm was for Theosophy, an unsurprising interest given Mme Blavatsky's positing of the source of eternal wisdom as the Indian subcontinent.[61] On 24 August 1914, having had a 'true dream' connecting Letchworth and Theosophy (Ebenezer Howard's Garden City was well-known for the diversity of religious sects attracted to it) with Mme Blavatsky (dead since 1891) and her successor Annie Besant [62], she decided to join the Theosophical Society on the grounds that she too had achieved unmediated intimacy with God as a result of earlier ecstatic experiences. Unable, however, to afford the subscription, she contented herself with discussing Theosophical tenets with her father with predictable results: his stating that she was as bad as Mrs Besant and that, England being a free country, she could think what rubbish she liked but not to bother *him* with her thoughts, resulted in a moment of 'bitter [and] unrelieved loneliness'[63] on the part of the would-be Theosophist. A week's visit to Letchworth allowed her to contact local Theosophists, to borrow a biography of Swami Vivekananda whose books on yogic practices had been lent to her by Evelina Garnier in 1913, and to discover with delight that the Swami's *Samadhic* experiences bore strong resemblances to her own[64] but conflicting advice from people she respected that she would be a worthy successor to Mrs Besant, then firmly alive, not to 'be in a hurry' to become it[65] or Tommy Altounyan declaring, on Aelfrida telling him that she had dreamed that Mrs Besant wished her to be her successor in England, that Aelfrida was not 'strong enough to stand the racket' (sage advice from a doctor aware of her mental fragility)[66] did less to discourage her than a verbal attack from Constantine (then working at the Foreign Office pending posting to Amsterdam) whose antipathy to Theosophy had been revealed when, following a visit in December 1913 to Charles Blech, Parisian secretary of the Theosophical Society, Aelfrida had made no secret of her new interest. The Oracle too was anxious lest her latest enthusiasm lead his daughter into paths as strange as those of the Ceremonial Magic with which Theosophy, in his eyes, had much in common.

Aelfrida's interest in Buddhism lasted the better part of two years (October 1915–June 1917) with a further surge in 1923 when a chance meeting with Burmese student Ba-Han[67] provided her with material on Buddhist meditations at a time when *Spiritual Exercises* was nearing completion. The interest, already awakened by familiarity with Aleister Crowley's *Science and Buddhism* article in Vol. 2 of his *Collected Works* (a chapter whose sense and content she reproduced without acknowledgment in the Buddhist Meditations chapter of *Spiritual Exercises*), was based on sympathy for Buddhist tenets, in particular the Four Noble Truths (the world is filled with mental and physical suffering; suffering occurs because of too great attachment to objects of desire; by eliminating attachment one can eliminate suffering; attachment can be eliminated by following the Eightfold Path consisting of right understanding, resolution, speaking, action, living, effort, heeding and reflection, the key 'path' being the latter, otherwise known as meditation) because of their sympathetic resonance with her own beliefs. A coincidental meeting also provided assistance both literary and personal: on 14 October 1915, Aelfrida re-encountered Professor de la Vallée Poussin, a distinguished Orientalist previously met in Odessa but now a participant in the *Conferences Belges* set up under the auspices of Cambridge University so that lecturers and students among the Belgian refugees who flocked to England in 1914–15 could continue their teaching and studies. Professor Poussin, 'a fierce little man to whom learned controversy must be the breath of life'[68], was keen to help, arranging for Aelfrida to meet Japanese philosopher Hakuju Ui, 'a real, real Buddhist priest [who] belongs to a meditation sect … he was so interesting, so illuminating'.[69] EJ Thomas of the University Library, one of the most eminent Orientalists of the day[70] and whose *Life of Buddha as Legend and History* was among Aelfrida's core texts, was also enormously helpful in her explorations of Buddhist doctrines and their relationship to Christian meditation, so much so that in June 1916 she optimistically decided that on the basis of her own meditational and ecstatic experiences and studies of Buddhist tenets that she was qualified to give a series of public lectures on aspects of Buddhist belief.

She was dissuaded by being told by a professorial Orientalist whom she consulted on the subject that theology at Cambridge had nothing to do with religion but was 'merely a subject for academic learning'[71] and by discouraging remarks made by Caroline Ridding ('said to be a great scholar')[72] who opined that Aelfrida was unworthy of holding an opinion on Buddhism 'unless [she] knew Sanskrit, … Tibetan, Chinese, etc., etc.' and that she knew no more about Mysticism 'than [she] did about Pali'[73], the Indic language used in canonical Buddhist texts. (Aelfrida had not thought fit to inform Miss Ridding that she herself was 'something of a mystic'.) There was also a need to dissociate her former interest in Aleister Crowley (evidenced by material in the public domain) from her present interest in Comparative Religion in general and Buddhism in particular because of Crowley's current notoriety, he having been accused of producing anti-British propaganda while in America during the Great War. The need was underlined by a meeting with Kenneth Ward, one of Crowley's first probationers, recently returned from Rangoon, a place he was inspired to visit by his having taken up the study of Buddhism as a direct result, as his worried mother informed Chiara, 'of the bent given to his mind by Aleister Crowley'[74], who informed her that although Crowley had begun his 'Great Work' by 'earnestly imparting the science of meditation to his followers in an effort to regenerate mankind by revealing to it its true nature', once 'money failed and love of power grew' he had become more and more 'histrionic' and as far as Ward himself was concerned (though not in the eyes of 'silly women' whom Crowley 'duped'), less and less plausible.[75] Having been informed by her parents only two days earlier that she was an 'impractical visionary'[76], Ward's 'silly women' comment hit home.

There was, however, more to Aelfrida's abandonment of Buddhism than this. On the one hand, and rather surprisingly, given her current pessimism and views on sexuality, she regarded Buddhism as an inherently "gloomy system of philosophy which sees nothing but sorrow in the world and whose best hopes are for nothing more joyous than the cessation of desire".[77] On the other, and in spite of favourable comparisons of the Buddha to Jesus of Nazareth, she found Buddhism per se an unfocussed religion because of her innate need for an idealised male person on whom to worshipfully fix her thoughts, be this Lord Kitchener, Constantine, or Deity – and Buddhism lacked Deity.

Two Middle Eastern religious sects for which Aelfrida expressed particular sympathy were Sufism and the Baha'i faith. She approached the first during her momentous summer holiday of 1914 by acquiring information from eminent Orientalist RA Nicholson, 'an amicable but somewhat uncouth scholar',[78] and the other through interviews with Mirzà Issa Sadiq, Reader in Persian and 'a small copy of a king from an Assyrian bas-relief' who, though personally antagonistic to the Baha'i faith, was prepared to provide information on it, and on both with the help of EG Browne, Professor of Arabic[79], who expatiated on the influence of Neo-Platonism on Sufism and allowed her to attend lectures on Baha'ism illustrated by 'pictures cast on a screen by a wonderful lantern thing', an epidiascope.[80]

Sufism, to which Aelfrida felt particularly drawn [81] – the chapter ostensibly on Islam (Mohammedanism, as she terms it) in *Spiritual Exercises* actually panegyrises the Sufi faith – because as a mystical and tolerant form of Islam it placed particular emphasis on love of God and God's love for man and was a faith with which she could have remained were she not so adamantly Christian. Her sympathy for a belief-system whose evolution so closely mirrored her own spiritual development in its having arisen "in answer to a genuine need for spiritual experience which could not be satisfied by … theology, philosophy or ritual" and whose followers were "men and women willing to subject themselves to long and severe discipline both of body and mind in order to attain to conscious communion with the Divine" and who, during their quest, "made many mistakes …[because] led away by their love of the marvellous and the unusual" into "strange and forced" meditative exercises but who, as "genuine seekers after God [were] rewarded by feeling His Presence"[82], led her to delight in Sufism's ecstasy-inducing practices and in the poetic imagery employed by Omar Khayyám (a Sufi, she now realised, noting delightedly "Omar becomes comprehensible")[83] to introduce the seeking mystic to knowledge of God and to try to build its tenets into her own life. Indeed, her desire to follow the Sufic threefold path (abstinence, allied with material and spiritual generosity) and to live without being affected by other people's whims and desires, goes some way towards explaining behaviour during and after the war which seems at best ridiculous or impractical and at worst perverse: refusal to indulge in sexual activity; denying herself enjoyed foods but eating those she disliked even when not obliged to by rationing; lack of interest in her appearance; refusal to attend concerts where music she loved was to be played; refusal to take money matters seriously and giving to charity the proceeds of her books at a time when she was short of money herself; continual forgiveness of appalling behaviour on the part of her husband; seemingly harsh comments concerning her brothers' welfare and her insistence at whatever cost to others (except her daughters) on the practice of

'higher indifference' – all make sense in the light of Sufi doctrines imperfectly followed by one whose asceticism was, as Constantine rightly remarked, 'luxurious', whose philanthropic impulses were frequently over-ridden by self-interest, and whose 'higher indifference' proved fallible in the presence of men to whom she was attracted.

Something of this appears to have happened with regard to Mirzà Issa Sadiq, for Aelfrida's short-lived interest in the Baha'i faith – while meditating on the Baha'i Prayer for Unity (adherents believe that there is essentially only one God and one Truth and that different religions represent the different ways in which God reveals Himself and expresses His will)[84] she was 'caught up in a kind of ecstasy'[85] and in the course of 'two lovely quiet days in bed' wrote poetry ('perhaps some of my best work') based on the Baha'i saying "Ye are all drops of the same ocean", poetry (of which no trace remains) which seemed to stem from '*literal* inspiration … breathed into my ear' [86] – was further abbreviated by realisation that not only was her 'Assyrian bas-relief' falling in love with her but also that she herself enjoyed 'being made love to' through the medium of Persian love-songs and discussions of poeticised romances.[87] Her discovery during the summer vacation of 1917 that Mirzà Issa Sadiq was not travelling round England as the dervish as he professed to be but had come to Letchworth where she and the girls were on holiday expressly to see her and in hope of lunch[88], effectively ended their association, Aelfrida retaining profound respect for Baha'i tenets, if not for Sadiq.

An interest in Quakerism arose in part because of the respect in which she held Fanny Tillyard, that lady having joined the Society of Friends after retirement to Letchworth, in part because of the Society's readiness to find Mina paid positions in Quaker-run English orphanages during the war on the grounds that German origins were of minor importance when weighed against qualifications as a social worker. (Cambridge philanthropists had reacted in horror at the thought of the objects of their humanitarian gestures being forced to breathe air tainted by Teutonic exhalations.) Quaker pacifism also accorded with her own ('this appalling accumulation of slaughter makes one feel one should make what protest one can')[89], a position underlined by her first and only visit to the 'vast, decorous and horrible' First Great Eastern Hospital established in Cambridge for the treatment of wounded soldiers but where 'the unspeakable wickedness of these men having been stricken by their own brothers [seemed] to [her] a thing that shouted out its horror'[90], and because the Quaker doctrine of Inner Light (the notion that man is lit from within by the presence of God) accorded well with her new belief that she too was one of God's Illuminati.

CHRISTIAN MEDITATIONS 161

and, being all of one mind, wait upon the Lord and expect to receive His Holy Spirit.

Have you ever been to a Quaker meeting? The people assemble very softly, and take their places with no stir and bustle. At first there are a few sounds, a child fidgets, someone's boot creaks, you sit down and wonder when "it" is going to begin. If you are accustomed to meditation, you banish intruding thoughts and concentrate on some familiar words of Scripture, or try simply to fill your mind with God. In any case, don't listen for someone to speak, don't wonder when "it" is going to begin. "It" has already begun.

All around there is an atmosphere of waiting upon God. We take down the shutters of everyday preoccupations and open wide the windows of the soul to the sunlight of spiritual reality. The stillness deepens. You feel a subtle fellowship, a communion with these other quiet, expectant souls. Each seems to be helping the other in the search after God. Daily worries grow smaller, show how trivial they are in the light of eternity, vanish altogether. In the unseen and not in the seen, lies the centre of reality.

Now the little room is filled with light. What a hush, what a radiance, what an apprehension of peace and of joy! The sense of time is lost. Surely God is with us in our midst, and heaven is here and now! . . .

It is quite a shock when a man rises to pronounce the Benediction; an hour has passed and no word has been spoken. "A good meeting," you hear someone comment, as the little company disperses. At times, however, there is a good deal of talking; possibly garrulous brethren have to be asked in subsequent privacy whether they are quite sure they were moved by the Spirit and not by the love of hearing their own voices. Or it may be that the sense of communion between the worshippers shows itself by one after another "speaking to the condition" of troubled souls there present.

The persistent attempt to get in touch with the

11

*Spiritual Exercises*

Failing a Professor of Quakerism to whom to apply for information, Aelfrida visited the only local member of the Society of Friends she knew. To Aelfrida Graham's surprise, Elfrida Cameron received her coolly ('her talk about the "Inward Light" sounded a trifle remote'), pointing out that the Society of Friends had moved with the times and that 'modern 'Liberal' Quakerism might not fulfil Aelfrida's needs. Preoccupied with this thought and with the thought that she might have to fall back on 'the St Columba folk' with whom she felt Quakers had much in common or on Sufism whose state of being 'with God' bore resemblance to illumination with 'Inward Light', Aelfrida virtually ignored the appearance of '*Little* Friend' John Forbes Cameron himself: 'I was not, at the moment, interested in him and hardly spoke to him. I hope I was not rude. He seemed, I thought afterwards, rather puzzled and wistful'.[91]

Doubts assailed her after two more 'perfect days in bed' during which she read Caroline Stephen's *Quaker Strongholds* of 1871, one of several books lent by Elfrida Cameron[92] and 'wait[ed] in silence before the Lord', but eventually came to the conclusion that she was 'not at all bothered about the Quaker question' and that if she listened, God would tell her what to do.[93] Further study of *Quaker Strongholds,* however, 'uplifted me in a most wonderful ecstasy such as [has] not come upon me since the autumn at Le Vésinet' during which she felt 'as though the Light in which I dwelt must almost stream through my material self'[94], and this, together with exploration of Miss Stephen's *Light Arising* of 1908 and the Quakers' latest *Book of Discipline*[95], caused her to conclude that she might eventually join the Society of Friends. But not before attending a Quaker Meeting 'as a pupil ... to listen, not to speak'.[96]

Attendance at two Meetings caused a further change of mind. Although she regarded communal silence as 'quite wonderful ... I find it exalts one very much'[97], she was disappointed by the short spontaneous addresses given by members of the congregation moved by the Spirit to share their thoughts with others, calling them 'nice little pi "family talks" ... very sincere but very limited'. Having failed to find the spiritual home or uplift she sought and in spite of feeling 'much drawn' to Quakerism (she noted with unusual honesty that 'I always feel drawn towards whatever is good in whatever religion or sect I come across and none is *quite* perfect')[98], she decided that Quakerism's limitations (its lack of intellectual stimulus and challenge; the quiet certainty which did not meet the demands of a seeking spirit such as hers; silent meetings where brethren moved to speak but who spoke too often or too long were open to reproof, anathema to one whose 'Great Work' impelled her to speak out and at length) outweighed its spiritual benefits and never became one.[99] Her continuing sympathy for the Society of Friends is evident, however, in contemporary and near-contemporary writings, namely *The Making of a Mystic* of 1917 whose heroine is befriended by Quakeress 'Mercy Allen' who not only lends her the two books by Caroline Stephen named by Aelfrida in her diary but also acts as an edifying example in matters of Christian conduct, and *A Little Road–Book for Mystics* of 1922, in which Caroline Stephen herself is described as "a gentle priestess of the Inward Light".[100] In *Spiritual Exercises,* too, anyone reading her description of a Quaker Meeting ("a deliberate intention to reproduce as far as possible the conditions prevailing at Pentecost [so] that the faithful may be able to hear [God's] voice guiding them to a right life") and of "the striking humanitarian undertakings of the Society of Friends ... during and after the war"[101] will recognise the admiration she felt for the Society's actions and intentions.

Insight into the absurdity of feeling drawn to whatever she felt was good in whichever belief system seemed to satisfy her current spiritual, intellectual, or emotional needs nevertheless allowed her to poke fun at her penchant. In *Can I be a Mystic?* and following William Law's example[102], she invents 'portraits' of Christian 'types' whose personalities are based on characteristics of people known to her in real life. She herself is 'Adèle', a "delightful creature [who] changes her religion almost as often as a fashionable lady changes her clothes" and who, beginning as a "High Churchwoman [delighting] in elaborate ritual and … the finest ecclesiastical pageantry", tires of "ornate worship and [becomes] a Quakeress … very charming … in grey, very demure and pensive at "silent meeting"" until a need to commune more deeply with the unseen moves her to become an Occultist, a phase during which "ritual returned, this time performed by the lady herself, with cups and wands and symbols and other strange devices". Following a nervous breakdown, during which 'Adèle' is sent (*pace* Agnes Slack, a great frequenter of these) to a "New Thought Sanitarium", she becomes a Christian Scientist, but "an ankle sprained at tennis" and the attention lavished on it by her Scottish doctor[103] seems likely "to make a Presbyterian of her after all, unless she should chance to meet one of the Buddhist missionaries recently come to London".[104]

Although Aelfrida's enthusiasm for the study and possible practice of whichever religion currently attracted her had waned by late summer 1917, her freedom to explore the highways and byways of Comparative Religion would have been curtailed in any case by Constantine's return from Amsterdam in October and by her determination to be a better wife to him than hitherto. Disclosure in February 1918 of his affair with Mme Sterneberg diverted her mind from academic research to considerations of interpersonal relationships and it was not until seven years later that she 'FINISHED [her] book on Spiritual Exercises – and [felt] ten years younger!'[105], a book whose full title, *Spiritual Exercises and their Results,* and subtitle, 'an essay in psychology and comparative religion', demonstrated where her interests lay in the years 1914–1917.

Begun in spring 1917, *Spiritual Exercises* was intended as 'a work of scholarship'[106] on a par with those read during the formative war years and as a more rigorously-researched and formally-written volume than those in which the second aim of her 'Great Work' was to be promoted in the form of chatty discourses not at all dissimilar to the pious little 'family talks' criticised with reference to the Society of Friends. Yet although she

regarded *Spiritual Exercises* as an expression of her belief in the importance of Mysticism as a way of life and as the culmination of extensive research into the subject – and judging by the number of primary and secondary sources she quotes concerning the means by which followers of different religions practise or develop the faculty of immediate apprehension of whatever is meaningful for them in a world beyond matter, her reading round the subject was prodigious – it is, for several reasons, the least satisfactory of her books.

For one thing, it was so long in the making and so much happened to distract her in the meantime that the spirit which gave it life was killed by the letter of duration of composition. For another, dwindling enthusiasm for some of the spiritual exercises she had practised so assiduously occurred because of light thrown on them by "Freud and the New Psychologists" whose ideas on the significance of symbols and symbolism otherwise chimed with hers insofar as she and they appreciated "the place of symbols in the subconscious activity of the mind" and regarded them as "convenient form[s] of mental shorthand" and as entities whose evocative power was often greater than that of the spoken or written word (a cross, for example, giving rise to "more intense emotions than a word such as Sacrifice or Atonement" in the mind of a Christian)[107] but whose basic tenets she found distasteful because of their connection of baser with higher human instincts. Third, religious prejudices blinded her to the significance of certain non-Christian spiritual exercises for their practitioners: when discussing Buddhism, for example, she expresses puzzlement that a mind "however detached, however convinced of the non-existence of the ego, however well-trained in concentration, can be moved to rapture by considering … the loathsomeness of food"[108] but omits to note that a religion in which ecstasy may be achieved through contemplation of Deity in the form of a living man bleeding from wounds and nailed to a wooden cross or whose doctrines include the transsubstantiated consumption of the flesh and blood of a man-who-is-God (and vice versa) might appear both perverse and repugnant to one whose religion forbids violence towards living things and consumption of fleshly food in any form.

Other problems arose from the brief and interrupted time allotted by Aelfrida to basic research, a fact duly noted by Miss Ridding who suggested that 'a Pythagorean training in five years silence'[109] was required before she put pen to paper and that her inevitable reliance on translated sources might not capture the spirit of the original. Then too, and in part as a consequence of this, in part because of her tendency towards uncritical acceptance of evidence offered by a source on whom her enthusiasm was currently focussed, Aelfrida was liable to accept unquestioningly views held by academics whom she believed she met on equal terms, as witness her condemnation of James Haughton Woods' *The Yoga-System of Patanjali* ("terms used are in contradiction with those employed by other translators")[110] because it was disparaged by Edward Thomas. Or again, she introduced without preamble or discussion topics mentioned by her better-informed teachers e.g. that "Alexandrine Neo-Platonism was … influenced by Hinduism [and] Jewish mysticism" or that Neo-Platonic ideas influenced Christian Mysticism (a theory, so she said, "too well-known to need insisting on here")[111], less because she appreciated their significance or even, one suspects, fully understood them as concepts, than because they added (spurious) academic lustre to her book. (Borrowings are obviously copied verbatim from notes taken during discussions with the likes of Browne, Anderson, Nicholson, and Thomas; the − supposedly fictional − criticism of a doctoral dissertation which appears in one of her late novels, namely that it was a "paste-pot and scissors" job[112], may have been applied in real life and with justification to *Spiritual Exercises*.) Finally, she includes long lists of meditative practices without making any real attempt to discover what motivates the practice of these particular exercises in a particular religion and accords the same level of significance to St Ignatius' complex rigorous spiritual exercises (from whose own *Spiritual Exercises* her title obviously derives) and the effusions of Victorian mystic Frances Ridley Havergal[113] whom Aelfrida held in unwarranted respect because her hymns were said to be dictated by Deity and because some of Miss Havergal's mystical experiences accorded with her own.[114] All in all, *Spiritual Exercises* should be read less as an example of its author failing to become what she manifestly is *not* − an academic theologian − and more as the demonstration of a particular stage in the spiritual development of the mystico–religious enthusiast she manifestly *is*.

Diary and literary evidence for this stage of her life enhances the interest of a lack-lustre book based, as always, on Aelfrida's exterior and interior life to date. For one thing, it allows us to see how much of her interest in Comparative Religion arose from acts of homage and defiance. Homage to Aleister Crowley for unlocking gates and for setting her feet firmly on the Mystic Way, defiance towards Constantine in order to demonstrate that a despised and denigrated wife was capable of producing a book which was neither mystically 'goupy' (i.e. soppily religious) nor third or fifth rate poetry or prose with the help of personal tuition from respected academics from his own Alma Mater to whom she was careful to introduce him during his leave of 1917. Defiance, too, towards

a father who made it increasingly clear that he preferred sons becoming well-known in the fields of English Literature and Byzantine Musicology to a daughter who had not only made a mess of her marriage but as the only one of his three children to produce a family to date, had also failed to provide him with male descendants.

From the point of view of her interior life, however, it shows how far Aelfrida had absorbed the teachings of the Christian religion that "mystical states of mind" are not, as she had once held them to be, valuable for their own sake but because their end is to allow the mystic to "progress in humility and all the virtues" and to enable him to "come down from the heights of spiritual communion … to preach the good news that human and divine can meet".[115] It was with these important truths in mind that spiritual insights imparted during her foray into Comparative Religion inspired her to move on to the next stage of her 'Great Work': to preach the "good news" and, spurred into action by the precepts of "a God both Immanent and Transcendent … made in the Person of our Lord"[116], to try to illuminate and educate others by sharing her spiritual insights with them.

But prior to discussing Aelfrida's activities as educator and illuminator it is imperative to remember that *Spiritual Exercises* had a prequel in the shape of 'an investigation into certain mystical states' incorporating and illustrated by 'an attempt at classification of the experiences of some modern mystics'[117], and that it was in the inconspicuous notebook in which she recorded preliminary notes for her 'investigation' that she divulged the experience which was to transform her into one of the 'modern mystics' she proposed to describe.

Although her first diary entry regarding the 'scheme of [her] attempt at classification of mystic states'[118] does not appear until 27 November 1913 at the point at which she put aside her 'Emden' novel and 'began another book at once'[119], Aelfrida's first mention of her notion of 'classifying mystics' dates to the day following her second meeting with Aleister Crowley on 9 November 1913 during which he discussed the idea with her, designated it 'splendid' − and declined collaboration.[120] The idea must therefore have been maturing in her mind for some time before Crowley's encouragement inspired her to embody her thoughts on the subject.

Her 'scheme' as set out consists of a preface explaining the different ways by which the subject may be approached. An explanation of terms follows in order that 'mystic states' classified as *vedane* (i.e. as chiefly dependent on emotions and often with a strong sensory component), *dhyanic* ("the rushing together of subject and object", albeit with duality continuing to exist between them), *samadhic* ("universal consciousness", albeit still with a degree of separation of self and cosmos), *atmardashanic* ("the oneness of all") and *shivadarshanic*, described by Aelfrida here as a "very rare" vision of "the absolute zero"[121] or (in another notebook) "the Nothing that is All"[122], may be illustrated in terms of examples she will provide of each. Section three will include data concerning each mystic quoted (a short biography, predisposing factors including their current state of health, their use or not of artificial aids to meditation, and the consequences to them of a particular state or of such states in general, all to be supported by written evidence; in the event, only Anna Tillyard's character is delineated and little background evidence provided), section four, a case "for and against mysticism and teaching it in schools as a part of practical psychology and *savoir vivre*" (sic), section five, a description of "the development of mysticism in the ordinary person", and six, her conclusions. More interesting, however (and more relevant, given that her 'book' never progressed beyond its schematic outline), are the examples she provides, some by people she had met or knew well (on 9 January 1914 she noted that men and women had suddenly started confiding in her, something she attributed to her new-found 'vision'[123] but undeniably odd given that people who knew her well were aware and disapproved of her recent association with Aleister Crowley and were hardly likely to open their hearts to her as a result), some garnered from published sources, and one from Frédéric Amiel, first read at age fifteen and discovered then to have a 'type of mind' very similar to her own[124] but whose nomination as 'modern' was possible only insofar as her scheme allowed inclusion of mystics from '1800 on'.

Aelfrida's heterogeneous list of 'modern mystics' included her aunt Anna Tillyard (an odd inclusion given that it was *Fanny* Tillyard who was later described by her niece as entitled "to the high name of mystic")[125], Ancifera Gregory ('AWG', a down-to-earth teacher given to snubbing her younger relative's wilder flights of fancy), Catharine Tillyard (as 'Ch. dream'), Tommy Altounyan (as 'EA' whose 'vision' had brought him in touch with a "wonderful … Being … contemplation of whom [resulted in] a peaceful desire to walk quietly the rest of one's days", "*everything*" thereafter being "interesting and … loveable"[126], a great consolation, one would think, to a medical officer in the Great War), Gladys Sanderson ('Valentine') known since childhood, Caroline Dalmas ('CD') a Franco-American met in Paris and described by Aelfrida as a 'kindly, ponderous, intensely serious [and] typically Old–New–England' middle-aged 'dragon' who, though an unlikely mystic, could converse about 'mediums and cosmic consciousness' (Aelfrida she described as 'evolved', Constantine as

'less evolved')[127] and essay vivid histories of how she had gone out "into the unknown" there to "bathe and soar on the Infinite", to pass "beyond the stars", and to experience a "pure delight" ('*Extase*') describable only in terms of the nuptial flight of the bee in Maeterlinck's *La Vie des Abeilles*. (Aelfrida, listening enraptured to Caroline's plunge into the Infinite, classified the latter's '*extase*' as "*Samadhi*, rising to *Atmadarshana*".)[128] More prosaically, she also quotes "young American" Horace Holley[129] and an anonymous female contributor to the *Atlantic Monthly* of January 1919. A further female contributor ('Mlle J')[130], later described as a "French-speaking Sufi who is still living"[131], completes the list.

Aelfrida does not tell us why she discontinued her researches into 'modern mystics' at a preliminary stage (a 1921 letter from American psychologist James Leuba to whom she sent her examples which notes that, though interesting, none were "sufficiently carefully … observed and described"[132] to make a useful contribution, may have some bearing on the matter) but not wishing to waste collected evidence, she incorporated much of it into *A Little Road–Book for Mystics* and *Spiritual Exercises*, the former containing that of Horace Holley, of the anonymous contributor to the *Atlantic Monthly* (both in abbreviated form, one as deriving from 'the author's MS collection', the other from the magazine's 'contributor's column') and of Catharine Tillyard's 'dream'[133], the latter Frédéric Amiel's (quoted at length and in French in the section on 'Buddhist meditations' because his experiences seemed better classified with these), 'Mlle J's (classified as *samadhic*, headed "a Sufic ecstasy", and quoted at length, in French, and as from the author's MS collection), and Gladys Sanderson's, anonymously but as written by a woman of thirty who had recently converted to Roman Catholicism.[134]

More significant still is that Aelfrida's 'scheme' contains descriptions of two 'mystic states', one of which is almost certainly her own (it is headed "*an auditory phenomenon*", includes what may be the mantra – "*intra nobis regnum Dei*" – recited to inspire it, and is by-lined 'S', possibly 'Sarasvati'; its references to "penetrat[ing] all things even into the secret of men" and to the need for 'S' to destroy books "which stop the freedom of men" are pertinent to Aelfrida's life at this time)[135], the other identifiably so as 'ACWG'.

Riding home one day from Mrs Verrall's schoolroom at a time "when I was often troubled about religious matters and thought myself very unworthy, sometimes even to the point of wondering why God did not annihilate so useless a girl as myself", 'ACWG' suddenly saw a soft light in front of her "in shape tall and oval, about the height of a man". So astonished that she nearly fell off her bicycle, she looked more closely and "saw that within the light was the figure of Christ wearing ... a dress something like a Roman toga, anyhow white and with folds. It looked on me with divine love and I felt oh so happy. Then it was gone – but looking round me I saw that all the world was beautiful. I specially remember noticing how lovely blades of grass were – I don't think I had ever *seen* one before".[136] And suddenly adolescent Frida's religiosity, allusions, and seemingly inexplicable moods and actions become clear.

## Notes

1 Tillyard, Ae. *Spiritual Exercises* p 1.
2 Tillyard, Ae. *Can I be a Mystic?* p187.
3 GCPPT 1|1|22 26 November 1917.
4 GCPPT 1|1|10 11 January 1903.
5 Tillyard, Ae. *Spiritual Exercises* p 154.
6 ibid.
7 GCPPT 1|1|5 10 July 1900. Bimetallism, about which Aelfrida knew very little, was a concept derived from political economy and concerned the combined use of gold and silver coinage as standards of currency.
8 Tillyard, A.I. *Stones of Stumbling* p 38.
9 GCPPT 1|1|20 8 June 1914.
10 ibid. 28 May 1914. The University Library was then part of the Old Schools building next door to the Senate House.
11 ibid. 29 May 1914.
12 ibid. 4 June 1914.
13 ibid. 24 July 1914.
14 ibid. 29 May 1914.
15 For an excellent exposition of the life and work of Charles Myers FRS (1873–1946) and his connection with the Cambridge Psychological Laboratory, see Richards, P. pp 15–18.
16 GCPPT 1|1|20 5 June 1914.
17 ibid. 19 June 1914.
18 ibid. 5 June 1914.
19 GCPPT 1|1|20a contains a description of a vision experienced 'about June 1st' which Aelfrida wrote down at the time but omitted to date. If the date in question is 1 June 1914, the vision predated her visit to Myers but may have been recorded in anticipation of it. Four days prior to the visit, Aelfrida experienced a 'deep *Samadhi*' lasting two hours (GCPPT 1|1|20 15 June 1914) but does not relate if she included a description of it in her record for Myers.
20 GCPPT 1|1|20 19 June 1914.
21 ibid. 22 October 1914. Myers "spent the war in charge of shell-shock cases for the whole of France" (Richards, P. op. cit.) as Official Psychologist to the British Expeditionary Force. Shell-shock, a term coined by Myers himself, would today be classified as post-traumatic stress disorder.
22 Bernard Muscio, later Professor of Philosophy at the University of Sydney, Australia, took over Myers' work during the latter's absence 1914–18.
23 GCPPT 1|1|20 18 December 1914.
24 ibid. 3 June 1915.
25 ibid. 28 November 1914.
26 ibid. 3 November 1914.
27 ibid. 28 November 1914. In *Spiritual Exercises* pp 27–28 Aelfrida describes the results of experiments in which Muscio concentrated on Buddhist mandalas: "while concentrating his attention on these circles the student found passing in front of his eyes a series of symbolic

pictures, much like those in the Books of Daniel and Revelation. These images became so vivid that they amounted at times to visual hallucination. The experimenter professed to be much amused and not impressed by the result of his meditations. I could not, however, refrain from thinking that, since he was of Jewish origin, there remained in his subconscious mind that passionate interest in religion which persists even in the least orthodox or believing of Jews. The visual imagery, be it also noted, was Jewish rather than Buddhist, and was obviously determined by the student's mentality, and by his familiarity with Jewish symbols rather than by the associations connected with Buddhist circles".
28 Tillyard, Ae. *Spiritual Exercises* pp 26–27.
29 ibid. pp27–28.
30 GCPPT 1|1|20 10 December 1914.
31 ibid. 18 December 1914. George Adams von Kaufmann (1894–1963), an ardent pacifist during the Great War (he was briefly imprisoned for his convictions), later joined Rudolph Steiner's Anthroposophical Movement which sought to develop man's cognitive faculties by way of appreciation of transcendent or spiritual 'realities'. (Rudolph Steiner 1861–1925 was the founder of the German branch of the Theosophical Society but was expelled after expressing dislike of Indianising developments within the Society; he went on to found the Anthroposophical Society). Von Kaufmann's subsequent studies on projective geometry and path curves, though appropriate in terms of what we already know of the elliptical path of Aelfrida's life, is unlikely to have been inspired by his brief association with his 'guru'.
32 GCPPT 1|1|20 28 March 1915. Siddhartha (literally 'he who has attained the goal') was the given name of Gautama Buddha.
33 GCPPT 1|1|20 9 March 1915.
34 ibid. 3 June and 29 July 1915.
35 GCPPT 1|1|21 20 January 1916.
36 GCPPT 1|1|22 16 June 1917.
37 GCPPT 1|1|19 30 May 1914.
38 George Robert Stowe Mead (1863–1933) joined the Theosophical Society in 1884, acting as secretary to Helena Blavatsky (1831–1891) from 1889 until 1891, during which time he became an expert in gnostic and hermetic studies. He left the Society in 1909 after a disagreement with Mme Blavatsky's successor Annie Besant, founding his own quasi-theosophical movement, The Quest Society, dedicated to studies of the philosophy of religion and, later, psychical research, the same year. At least one of Aelfrida's poems appeared in the society's eponymous magazine prior to publication in her own anthologies.
39 GCPPT 1|1|20 26 June 1914.
40 ibid. 13 October 1914.
41 GCPPT 2|25|2 (4).
42 ibid.
43 GCPPT 1|1|20 22 January 1915.
44 Tillyard, Ae. *Spiritual Exercises* p 25.
45 George Frederick Charles Searle FRS (1864–1954) was a physicist working at the Cavendish Laboratory who became interested in Spiritual Healing after the illness and death of his wife. (See *ODNB* vol 49 pp 606–607 for details of his Cambridge career). In *Spiritual Exercises* (pp 187–188) Aelfrida quotes a book (Dorothy Kerin's *The Living Touch* of 1914) recommended by Dr Searle which describes the author's recovery from the last stages of tubercular meningitis as a result of a vision. Although she quotes Miss Kerin's account from the point of view of its visionary rather than its therapeutic content, it would appear from her doing so that Aelfrida was less dismissive of the idea of Spiritual Healing than her diary entries suggest.
46 GCPPT 1|1|20 17 June 1915.
47 ibid. 11 March 1915.
48 The references are to *The Difference*, one of Aelfrida's own poems in *Cambridge Poets* (pp 196–197) and *The God of the Jews*, her description of Jehovah in the section entitled 'some gods' in *To Malise* (p 64).

49  GCPPT 1|1|20 11 June 1914.

50  Surendra Nath Maitra was later appointed to a chair at Presidency College, Calcutta and was mentor to several well-known twentieth century Indian physicists.

51  GCPPT 1|1|20 4 June 1914.

52  ibid. 19 June 1914.

53  ibid. 11 June 1914.

54  ibid. 4 June 1914

55  ibid. 11 June 1914.

56  ibid. 15 June 1914.

57  ibid. 19 June 1914.

58  ibid. 19 September 1914.

59  Tillyard, Ae. *Spiritual Exercises* p 44.

60  *To Amrita* was written on 5 April 1916, its composition being recorded in Aelfrida's diary entry of the following day, an entry which also describes how a week-long attack of malaria had confined her to bed where she meditated 'and wrote a little poetry' once her symptoms abated (GCPPT 1|1|21 6 April 1916). The poem later appeared in the 'songs about love' section of *The Garden and the Fire* (p 28) so must have been written shortly before publication. 'Amrita', a name often bestowed on girls of Hindu origin, is literally, and importantly in the poem's context, a heavenly ambrosia which confers immortality on those who partake of it but given that *To Amrita* (possibly Aelfrida's most beautiful poem) is evocative of scents, an amusing coincidence is also worth noting: in 1916 Aleister Crowley apparently invented an aphrodisiac ointment while experimenting with "sex magick" during his wartime exile in America, the active ingredient of which was his own semen (Kaczynski, R. p238.2002). He called it 'Amrita'.

61  For an interesting discussion of Theosophy's connections with India and with the SPR, see Katz, D. pp 163–169.

62  GCPPT 1|1|20 24 August 1914.

63  ibid. 2 September 1914.

64  For details of Swami Vivekananda (1863–1902) see Katz, D. p 169. Vivekananda was one of the first to introduce yoga to the West, his books on the subject (*Karma-Yoga* and *Raja-Yoga)* appearing in 1896. (Aleister Crowley was, of course, responsible for Aelfrida's initial introduction to yogic practices). Aelfrida herself first heard of the Swami in 1903 when a friend had sent her a copy of *Anubis*, a journal of "occultism and advanced Buddhism" but her earlier reaction differed markedly from that of 1913/14: 'phew!! These people are more savage than a naked cannibal!!' She described the journal as 'written by lunatics for lunatics' (GCPPT 1|1|10 8 June 1903).

65  GCPPT 1|1|20 11 September 1914.

66  ibid. 18 October 1914.

67  GCPPT 1|1|27 21 March 1923.

68  GCPPT 1|1|21 14 October 1915.

69  ibid. 14 October 1915. Hakuju Ui is probably the 'Japanese priest' referred to on pp 78–79 of *Spiritual Exercises.*

70  For an interesting résumé of the long life of Edward Joseph Thomas see http:|| wwwquangduc.com/English/figure/18westerncontribution – 2.html

71  GCPPT 1|1|21 20 June 1916.

72  Caroline Mary Ridding (1862–1941) whose field of study was Pali and Sanskrit, was a former Girtonian working at the University Library, the first woman to be so employed.

73  GCPPT 1|1|20 29 September and 29 December 1914.

74  GCPPT 1|1|19 19 March 1914. For details of Kenneth Ward's association with Aleister Crowley see Kaczynski, R. pp 142,149,151,180 and 187(2002).

75  GCPPT 1|1|21 24 March 1916.

76  ibid. 22 March 1916.

77  Tillyard, Ae. *Spiritual Exercises* p65.

78  GCPPT 1|1|20 21 July 1914. Professor Reynold Alleyne Nicholson (1868–1926) devoted his life to the study of Islamic Mysticism.

79  GCPPT 1|1|21 1 January 1917. Edward Granville Browne (1862–1926), Orientalist and respected traveller in the Middle East, is best known for works on the Baha'i faith and its history.

80  ibid. 1 May 1917.

81  For an excellent exposition of Sufism see Chittick, W. *Sufism.*

82  Tillyard, Ae. *Spiritual Exercises* p152.

83  ibid.

84  For details of the Baha'i faith see Smith, P. especially ch2 pp16–41 (*Bahá'u'illá and the Emergence of the Baha'i Faith*). Aelfrida's sympathy for Bahá'u'illá (1817–1892), founder of the Faith, is obvious, he being not only a visionary (and for two years and even though married with a family, a hermit) but also a religious leader who claimed to have received divine revelations directly from God or via His intermediary, a luminous divine maiden. He was also a man who awarded himself titles ("He Whom God Shall Make Manifest"; "all-knowing Physician"), a writer of occasionally hermetic but generally accessible prose and poetry and a follower of a 'mystic way' with a strongly practical moral dimension. (And also a man who, though he demonised his enemies, accorded women equal status with men as exponents of the Faith.) Professor Browne had had an audience with Bahá'u'illá in 1890 and had been much struck by his noble appearance and his 'presence'; doubtless he conveyed this to Aelfrida together with other information on the Faith.

85  GCPPT 1|1|21 3 March 1917.

86  ibid. 30 March 1917.

87  ibid. 20 February 1917.

88  GCPPT 1|1|22 25 August 1917.

89  GCPPT 1|1|21 19 April 1917.

90  ibid. 23 April 1917. Aelfrida's visit probably inspired her description of mutilated soldiers in the nursing home to which blind and crippled 'Noel Ashton' is relegated in *Vision Triumphant.*

91  GCPPT 1|1|21 22 April 1917.

92  Caroline Amelia Stephen (1834–1909), youngest sister of Sir Leslie Stephen and aunt to Virginia Woolf, lived as a 'sisterhood of one', wearing plain grey 'Quaker' dress and writing extensively on spiritual topics. She and Aelfrida, though Cambridge contemporaries, never met.

93  GCPPT 1|1|21 27 April 1917.

94  ibid. 1 May 1917.

95  The *Book of Discipline* was a series of volumes of extracts from the Society of Friends' London Yearly Meeting which expounded or updated the Society's theological position.

96  GCPPT 1|1|21 9 May 1917.

97  GCPPT 1|1|21 15 May 1917.
    GCPPT 1|1|22 7 August 1917.

98  GCPPT 1|1|21 30 March 1917.

99  Albinski, N. p 87 describes Aelfrida as a Quaker, quoting in support Joan Slonczewski's *Still Forms on Foxfield* in which Aelfrida is described (p 90) as a "Quaker citizen" and as one of the "touchstones of Friend's tradition". Professor Slonczewski (personal communication 6 November 2004) cannot recall her source of information for this attribution.

100  Tillyard, Ae. *A Little Road-Book for Mystics* p 16

101  Tillyard, Ae. Spiritual *Exercises* pp 160–162.

102  William Law (1686–1761) was an English mystic (see King, U. pp 184–186 for a succinct account of his life and influence) whose book *A serious call to a devout and holy life* was first read by Aelfrida about this time.

103  While staying in Caldecote in 1915 Aelfrida met a Christian Scientist who 'in spite of everything being Mind, [had] gone ... to have a whitlow lanced [and] was decidedly cross at the failure of her ideals' (GCPPT 1|1|21 22 September 1915). Aelfrida's jibes at Christian Science are understandable coming from one who owed her life to medical intervention but are also reminders to Constantine (to whom she sent a copy of every book she published) of his involvement with

Christian Scientist Hilda Sollas. An even stronger jibe appears in *The Approaching Storm* (p 179) where a woman 'takes up' Christian Science until her son develops measles: "of course I agreed with my healer that there are no spots in the mind of God, but Peter was covered with them, and I just *had* to send for Dr Bryant!"

104  Tillyard, Ae. *Can I be a Mystic?* pp 161–162. Aelfrida's description of 'Adèle' may also owe something to RH Benson's *The Necromancers* of 1909 in which (p 24) a lady is described as "a New Thought kind of person ... a vegetarian last year [and] ... a sort of Buddhist five or six years ago. And then she nearly became a Christian Scientist".

105  GCPPT 1|1|30 26 February 1925.

106  GCPPT 1|1|21 26 May 1917.

107  Tillyard, Ae. *Spiritual Exercises* p 190.
     Tillyard, Ae. *A Little Road-Book for Mystics* p 74.

108  Tillyard, Ae. *Spiritual Exercises* pp 95–96.

109  GCPPT 1|1|20 29 December 1914.

110  Tillyard, Ae. *Spiritual Exercises* pp 59–60. Patanjali was the reputed 2nd century author of the Yoga Sutras, later introduced to the West by Vivekananda. JH Woods (1944–1935) was a Scottish-Australian historian, classical scholar, and Orientalist.

111  Tillyard, Ae. *Spiritual Exercises* pp 29–30.

112  Tillyard, Ae. *The Centaur* p251 (GCPPT 2|21|1). A review in *The Moslem World* (vol 19 January 1929 p93) is equally dismissive; concentrating on her chapter on Mohammedanism, it implies that Aelfrida is both derivative and inaccurate.

113  Frances Ridley Havergal (1836–1879) was a prolific writer of hymns and religious poems, some of which came to her through automatic writing. The youngest daughter of the then Rector of Astley in Worcestershire, her life, though shorter than Aelfrida's, bore certain similarities to it: continuing adult dependence on family, education and further travel in Switzerland, an interest in Temperance, extreme religiosity, life-threatening illness, etc; unlike Aelfrida, she never married.

114  Miss Havergal's 'musical vision' of September 1874 (quoted by her sister Maria Havergal in her hagiographic *Memorials of Frances Ridley Havergal* of 1882) is quoted by Aelfrida in *The Making of a Mystic* p 38 and in *Spiritual Exercises* pp 188–189. The 'vision' occurred on a Swiss train; one of the correspondents in *The Making of a Mystic* ('Catharine Sutherland', alias Aelfrida herself) informs us that she too "heard heavenly music, yes, and saw it too" during a rough channel crossing but although Aelfrida notes several such crossings in her diary, she nowhere describes such a vision.

115  Tillyard, Ae. *Spiritual Exercises* pp 154–155 and 211.

116  ibid. p 211.

117  GCPPT 1|1|19 27 November 1913.

118  GCPPT 1|3.

119  GCPPT 1|1|19 27 November 1913.

120  ibid. 10 November 1913.

121  GCPPT 1|3.

122  GCPPT 1|4. The notebook contains at one end a list of prayers for the week, some in English or French and one Jewish and at the other an extensive booklist. (Authors included are Swami Vivekananda, Annie Besant, Max Müller, Eduard Schuré, GRS Mead, Stanley Cook, Jane Harrison, and James Frazer, the latter represented by *Adonis, Attis, Osiris,* read by Aelfrida in Boston and celebrated by her with a sonnet, *After reading "Adonis, Attis, Osiris",* written on 25 June 1908 and dedicated 'to JGF' which later appeared in *To Malise* p 16. The sonnet, written during her first pregnancy, described as a harvest "sown in darkness to be reaped in pain", compares the joyfulness of primitive classical religion with the gloomier Christian belief in a god 'learnt' not from "need or fancy" but through bitter experience.) The list is accompanied by comments (of Richard Ingalese's *The History and Power of Mind* she notes 'I can't stand this Yankee stuff. He tells you to "meditate" on $100!!!'), by brief notes on her reading, by a list of 'visions' (astral, devotional etc), by brief notes classified in terms of the "wrappings of the soul, each to be got rid of in turn" before "pure consciousness" is achieved by the "manifestations of God (according to Annie Besant)" e.g. Brahma/Vishnu/Shiva or Father/Son/Holy Spirit and of 'yogas' (*raja, bhakta, mantra, kharma,* etc) representing, for Aelfrida, union with Godhead through will, love, speech, and work respectively.

123  GCPPT 1|1|19 9 January 1914.

124  ibid. 27 November 1913.

125  Tillyard, Ae. *A Little Road-Book for Mystics* pp 68 and 132–134 ('a portrait of a mystic').

126  GCPPT 1|3.

127  GCPPT 1|1|19 9 October 1923 and 20 April 1914.

128  GCPPT 1|3. Maeterlinck's description of '*le vol nuptial*' appears in Book 5 of *La Vie des Abeilles* (Book 6 describes '*le massacre des males*', something 'unevolved' Constantine Graham might have cared to note, given the current state of his marriage) and ends with a comparison between the experience of the sole male bee to win the queen and the ultimate truth (*la dernière vérité,* whatever that may be) for which men strive (p261) and the effect on each man's life and soul of the moment at which he finds it (p 322). Aelfrida does not say if she read this particular book of Maeterlinck's but her descriptions of her own later supranormal experiences may owe something to it.

129  GCPPT 1|3. Horace Holley (1887–1960) had been a follower of the Baha'i faith since 1909. A poem by him, *The Stricken King,* appeared in *The Oxford Book of Mystical Verse* (pp 626–627) of 1916 and his signature in Aelfrida's Visitors Book between that of Constantine Graham (*sic:* how odd for a husband to sign his wife's book but given that he now saw himself as an 'episode' in her life, perhaps not so odd after all) and Constantine's 'little friend' from Panama, Dita Mallet-Pringle.

130  From evidence provided elsewhere in her diary we may deduce that the first name of 'Mlle J' was Juliana (GCPPT 1|1|62 24 June 1944) and that she was a princess (GCPPT 1|12|73 21 January 1956). It is possible that she was a Russian émigré aristocrat encountered by Aelfrida in person or in print sometime in 1913/14, 'Juliana' being a popular name for girls in Russian society because of the earlier existence of an aristocratic Russian saint of that name. Irritatingly for a biographer, Aelfrida later pretends to 'forget' Juliana's surname but her inclusion of the lady in a sentence incorporating two other 'modern mystics' (Margaret Alacoque and Bernadette Soubirous) suggests that she was indeed alive in the early years of the twentieth century.

131  Tillyard, Ae. *Spiritual Exercises* p 149.

132  GCPPT 1|3 Letter from James Leuba to 'Miss Graham' of 18 November 1921.

133  Tillyard, Ae. *A Little Road-Book for Mystics* pp 58, 61 and 69–70.

134  Tillyard, Ae. *Spiritual Exercises* pp 106–108, 149–150 and 185–187.

135  GCPPT 1|3.

136  ibid. For a description of similar crystalline clarity of vision with regard to a commonplace and usually disregarded phenomenon, see *A Little Road-Book for Mystics* p 59: "every head [of grass] shone and glistened like pearls. I could hardly walk for the overwhelming sense of the Divine Presence ... I almost *saw* God".

# Knowing Him

Aelfrida's earliest recorded mystic experience took place in Fordfield garden when she was very young. (What she later liked to think of as her first ever 'mystical experience' was her toddler equation of the Aurora Borealis with 'something to do with God'.)[1] The garden, it seems, was regarded by her as something of a sacred space because of its association with 'angel child' Conrad and with Hubbard the gardener who not only 'walked with God' but was also the first person she met who wholly dedicated his life and thoughts to Christ[2], and it was in that same garden that she heard what she described as a "silent voice" calling her. Standing under a tree she gazed searchingly upwards but could see no-one. At the same moment she experienced a mysterious living current which flowed upwards through herself and the tree towards the entity which had spoken and whom she understood to be their mutual creator. Accompanying the disclosure was the sensation of a "warm glow of beneficence" streaming into her heart which seemed to emanate from the unseen entity whose voice she had heard. Running to her mother for an explanation, she received the reassuring reply that it was God Himself whom she had experienced and, young as she was, realised instinctively that Catharine Tillyard's words were true.[3] She subsequently made light of her childhood experience ("I was quite good and pi when I was *very* small and believed quite ardently in God and angels and all that")[4] and even admitted to forgetting all about it by the time she went to school (and discovered boys); indeed, a month before her fourteenth birthday in October 1897 while reading Canon Knox–Little's book *A Broken Vow* [5] in which mention is made of 'the nearness of the Spiritual World to this', she expressed regret that she, unlike the story's heroine, had never seen or experienced 'strange supernatural beings' such as angels or spirits of the departed and that much as she wished to, she felt the matter 'too great' for a girl of her age.[6]

Writing as an old lady, Aelfrida noted her lack of "genuine *personal* affection for Our Lord until [she] was twelve or thirteen", the point at which "consciousness of [her] own sinful nature was becoming agonisingly acute".[7] She fails to note the reason but given her inexplicable and global feeling of sinfulness and that, as she later noted, "the young are often deeply distressed by

THE MAKING

OF A

MYSTIC

AELFRIDA TILLYARD

CAMBRIDGE
W. HEFFER & SONS LTD.
1917

*The Making of a Mystic*

their varying religious moods"[8], it may be that lack of 'personal affection' compounded her guilt; the onset of puberty at thirteen may have also enhanced her negative feelings about herself. Prior to puberty, however, and again in retrospect, she noted of herself that she was "naturally religious" but also rather unquestioning concerning what she believed was "the rightness of all she had been taught" with regard to belief and morality and that she had been haunted by the notion that Sunday attendance at St Columba's, though "satisfying the need of worship" and engendering a frame of mind which was "wholly or even chiefly religious", smacked rather too much of social occasion and custom, a pleasing mood "of goodwill towards all mankind [as] one came home to Sunday lunch" [9] being her chief impression of the day. She felt too, and regardless of the 'magnificent sermons' preached by successive ministers, a sense that something was lacking, namely 'a sense of kinship with Christendom as a whole'[10] attributable, perhaps, to the sense of spiritual superiority engendered in and by a congregation which believed itself well rid in of Anglicanism and Roman Catholicism its preference for "simple Low Church Christianity".[11] And it was, of course, at the age of twelve or thirteen that Frida was moved by the all-pervading atmosphere of religion in an orthodox Jewish household and by the sense of kinship engendered in a family whose belief-system encompassed Jews collectively, irrespective of racial origin or tribe.

Then came her vision of Christ in a mandorla of light, later described as "the light of the Holy Spirit dawn[ing] on [her] soul".[12] (And more prosaically in 1913/14 as a vision ranked at the lowest *vedane* level because of its emotional and sensory components.)[13] Of this Damascene experience during which, as Renan's description of St Paul's on the road from Jerusalem to Damascus has it, "Jesus … had left his Father's right hand to come to convert and instruct him" and to provide by direct revelation of Himself the "basis of his faith … [as a] Christian untrammelled of all authority, believing only by personal conviction",[14] she provides no details beyond those which appear in a brief description fifteen years later and omits the date, the place, and her age when it occurred (from evidence provided elsewhere we can deduce that she was fifteen and that the experience therefore took place sometime between 5 October 1898 and her sixteenth birthday a year later), all three, one would think, of vital importance to an adolescent who had undergone a seminal experience. Why she omitted from her diary both the event and details which would promote its veracity, she does not say. Perhaps, as elsewhere, she believed it to be too prosaic a medium in which to record a spiritual experience of this magnitude; perhaps she was too overwhelmed by the magnitude of the experience to consign it to paper.

Or perhaps she did, but in fictional form. In August 1899 'when I was fifteen', Aelfrida spent the short holiday with aunts Anna and Fanny at Walberswick, chronicled in detail and including the group's resolution 'to "do" two churches each day'.[15] At this point Aelfrida's (much later) fictionalised account part company with her diary version. Out walking on her own one day, she writes, a thunderstorm obliges her to take shelter in an ancient church on a hill. Outside, "lightning flashed and thunder roared but [inside] the church remained quiet and very still … Each church has a special message for the listening soul. There was no mistaking the message of these voiceless stones, though I only understood it later – LORD, THOU HAST BEEN OUR REFUGE FROM ONE GENERATION TO ANOTHER". The storm over, she leaves the church, only to discover a large hole near the porch where lightning struck just as she reached shelter. (Another version of the story has a tree fall across the doorway.) As she departs, a man and a woman walking together ask her if she is all right: she reassures them and returns to where she and her aunts are staying. She says nothing to them of her adventure.[16]

As an allegorical description of a recent life-changing episode, Aelfrida's account speaks volumes because much her life before and after the event is depicted. She is alone, separated from her parents, here, literally, in real life emotionally. She has recently experienced several upsetting events including death and personal injury (chronicled in her diary) and has been emotionally vulnerable since Lord Kitchener's visit to Cambridge the previous year; now she receives a vision of and a 'voiceless' message from Christ and understands that in Him she will find refuge. It is as if a chasm has opened or an immoveable object fallen between her former and future lives. Her parents (the man and woman walking together) notice a change in her but other than assuring them that she is unharmed, she provides no explanation for it.

Or is she? She certainly found the experience exhilarating and began to feel that the "wonderful and dazzling" experience (it stemmed, she thought, from "quite outside [her] normal range of consciousness") had transported her "into a spiritual world more real than the material world to which [she] was accustomed" and resulted in her wishing to "make all [her] life [into] into offerings … and … [into] a ritual performed to the glory of God". But stumbling "almost by chance into religious experience" (the 'almost' is important; the experience, she later stated, "did not really occur suddenly, though it may have seemed to do so" but was "connected way back, with … childish intuitions and impressions" glossed here in religious terms) was not an undilutedly happy experience: "not knowing", she writes, "that my feelings were the most natural in the world and by no means unusual … I thought I was mad". (It may have been horror at the idea of being thought a "spiritual freak" which prevented her from confiding her experience to anyone.) It seems, too, that 'wonderful and dazzling' though her experience was (experiences, rather; she also seems to have seen "heavenly lights" and heard "divine words or music"), she tried to allay her frightened and frightening feeling of being so wholly "rapt" into a "new world" that her feet "ceased to touch earth" by touching the furniture in her room in order to "assure herself that she was still in the body".[17]

Eventually – and fortunately, given that it was not until two or three years later that she was able to broach the subject with anyone – the experiences diminished and disappeared but their effect on adolescent Frida's life was devastating. ("I somehow feel", she stated years later, "that I answered the spiritual call too readily, too completely".) From then on, she regarded "everything of the earth"[18] as a snare and banned meat from her diet (a slightly later *MCJ* refers to 'vege' food and to parental worries regarding lack of 'protene')[19] "and quite a lot of other harmless things"[20] from her life.

Vegetarianism and avoidance of theatrical performances were harmless manifestations of her response but others, described as occurring in the course of "a period of extreme exaltation", were not: "withdrawal from 'the world'" ("I preferred ... to be alone with my thoughts"), asceticism (chiefly diminution of food intake, and sleep deprivation), cravings for "intense feeling" ("a miser's store of rapture to be gloated over in secret"), and viewing religion "as an *escape*"[21], all point to an abnormal state of mind. She also indulged in "outwardly peculiar"[22] actions, so that when to all this was added a "taint of self-consciousness" and the mistaken belief "that when you *felt* good you *were* good"[23], no wonder her "pretensions" were laughed at, censured, and generally misunderstood.[24]

Worse was to come. Not only did teenage Frida now appear to possess "a vivid and personal appreciation" of Deity and an enlarged religious sensibility (neither a bad thing in itself but of more sinister import in view of her existing personality disorder), but she also developed an awakened conscience accompanied by "an excitable approach to sin and grace" and a conviction that she was almost irredeemably sinful. She also began to indulge in deliberately and self-consciously distinct "devotional forms" chosen to suit her "idiosyncratic devotional [palate]" and to create for herself an "ideological ghetto"[25] into which she withdrew less to be alone with her thoughts than to preserve herself from insidious and perfidious influences arising from the 'material' world which was no longer her 'real' world. Although she later liked to think she had eventually "come down from the hilltop" on which "the miracle happened" and was able to "walk once more in the ordinary ways of life"[26], she never, to her own and others' cost, was so able or did.

An important and probably the major reason for her inability was what she later (but too late) realised was a typical neophyte mystic's mistake: trying to conform "to an obsolete and unsuitable pattern of holiness"[27], for, not

daring to confide in anyone, she turned instead to what she described in an enigmatic and subsequently emphasised diary entry as 'books'.[28]

Aelfrida's choice of 'books' is interesting in what it tells us of her frame of mind at this point and exasperating because she does not explain why she turned to particular books i.e. whether her recent experience inspired her to do so or whether, reading them, she was inspired to behave as she did. Both are possible, even probable, but lack of diary reference and reference only by innuendo to spiritual matters makes it hard to be certain, especially as her obsession with Lord Kitchener, her meeting with and engagement to Enrico, her excitement at being 'a finished young lady', and activities deemed suitable for the 'finished' were soon to supervene; indeed, a superficial reading of diary entries between 1898 and 1901/2 might lead one to believe that her spiritual life consisted of little more than prescribed religious observance and degrees of religious fervour dependant on the charisma of St Columba's current incumbents. (Between 1893 and 1909 St Columba's appointed two particularly charismatic ministers, the Rev Halliday Douglas whose sermons "expounded Christianity as a reality, a history, a person, a belief, a theory of life, an ideal and a salvation" and provoked in his congregation a desire to wrestle with the profundities of their faith[29] – Aelfrida later wrote that it was he who first showed her the way to God[30] – and, from 1902 to 1909, the Rev Johnstone Ross, an inspirational preacher and instigator of a series of Bible lectures – 'the Founding of the Kingdom of God' and 'The Heart of St Paul' were among their titles – every word of which impressed itself on Aelfrida's mind.) The first book to which we know she turned (the event went unrecorded in her diary but was later disclosed with reference to her 1913 investigation 'into certain spiritual states') was Frédéric Amiel's *Journal Intime*, he being initially encountered as a diarist but later as a co-religionist whose opening diary entry ("There is but one thing needful – to possess God")[31] was all-embracing. Later entries describing the impossibility of being "outside God" (with its corollary that "the best is consciously to dwell in Him")[32] must also have appealed to the adolescent reader of a journal whose opening entry continues "religion is not a method; it is a life – a higher and supernatural life, mystical in its root and practical in its fruits; a communion with God" in respect of which "all our ... powers of mind and soul are ... so many modes of tasting and adoring the Divine".[33] Or, as Aelfrida's choice of mantra for a series of mediations begun in 1921 ran, 'Knowing Him, you know all'.[34]

Although Aelfrida's pre-1898 literary explorations of matters religious (Canon Knox Little's *Life of St Francis of Assisi* of 1877, for example, read when she was four-teen, Francis being probably the "sallow brown-frocked man"[35] whose ascetic vocation may have influenced her post-vision intentions and would have accorded with them) are probably relevant here, it was unfortunate that a young woman who now experienced "a terrible feeling of separateness"[36] from everyone and everything and who was looking for a guide or guide book who or which would reassure her that she was not going mad, chose the wrong man and the wrong book: Thomas à Kempis' *The Imitation of Christ*.[37] Realisation came later; at the time, she believed that this single volume had arrived at the right moment and had "added cubits to [her] soul's spiritual stature".[38]

Already conditioned by a surprising remark of her father's (surprising, because 'no man could be fonder of wife and family' than he) that *'compared with spiritual things, earthly things are nothing'*[39] (the remark was made in answer to a daughterly question as to why Christ rejected His mother and brethren in favour of closer kinship with His disciples), adolescent Frida seized on a doctrine which promised that to 'have God' meant He was *'all-sufficient'* and that she would henceforth require 'no human consolations'.[40] (It took her many years and several separations to discover that He was not and she did; perhaps that her multiple flirtations were a means of testing her resolve.) But whereas imitation of Christ's life on earth and emphasis on a personal relationship with and spiritual connection to Deity through imitation of His Son might have proved helpful to a girl as troubled as Aelfrida , adoption by such a troubled girl of concepts which included imagining herself in terms of an affec-tive piety as a spectator at the Crucifixion, despising this world at the same time as placing emphasis on the next, preferring silence and solitude to the company of fellow human beings, regarding revelations received in visions as more valuable than formal instruction, believing the Devil to be a real entity, meditating on death as leading to reunion with God, practising austerities and emphasis-ing the necessity for a joyless, comfortless, troubled, and painful existence on earth (pain encompassed both phys-ical pain and spiritual trials) in order to achieve Heaven after death was to prove disastrous to herself and to those on whom she tried to impose them. Knowing nothing of all this (Silvia Myers, having been force-fed Thomas à Kempis for several weeks, declared for atheism) or that her beliefs were based on mediaeval monasticism and the fourteenth century practice known as *devotio moderna* of which *The Imitation of Christ* is a notable example, others believed them to be her own invention or a manifesta-tion of what seemed increasingly akin to pathological religiosity – and reacted accordingly.

Imitation of the life of Christ as advocated by a fif-teenth century monk was one thing; living life in the real world of early twentieth century Cambridge quite another and by December 1902, Aelfrida, now nineteen, was 'torn by religious difficulties, both of belief and of practice'. 'How much folly may be excused if we plead our youth?' she asked one whom she felt had once stood where she stood now but how, she also wondered, could *she* achieve the 'peace of God which passeth all under-standing', the state enjoyed by 'dear old Thomas' when he wrote his *Imitation*? True, she achieved it sometimes ('God comes and then I can bow my head and say "Lord it is well"')[41] but 'sometimes', she told 'Thomas mio', was not enough.[42] Little of this appears in a diary whose unusually muted tone could be attributed to worries concerning her relationship with John Forbes Cameron were it not for this and a single other entry, though it seems that problems of belief were partially resolved by further recourse to 'dear old Thomas' ('I think I now fully *understood* that earthly happiness is an impossibility … we were never meant to seek it or even spend one moment in asking oneself if one possesses it. Surely we should bend our energies to glorifying God')[43], in par-ticular, if a common theme in her later spiritual life is indicative of the passage of the *Imitation* paraphrased in the diary entry just quoted, a chapter entitled 'On the Royal Road of the Holy Cross'.[44]

That the only road to oneness with God was that of following Christ's footsteps on the *Via Crucis* was difficult theology. Its emphasis on bodily, emotional, and spiritual suffering un-assuaged until God brings relief; in there being no road to God *other* than that of the Cross; on the fact that the further a man advances in the spiritual life the heavier and more numerous he finds his crosses "for his ever-deepening love of God makes more bitter the sorrows of his earthly exile", and on the fact that unless a man live a "dying life" (dying to self, that is) he will never begin to live to God, was wholly at variance with the life of a self-centred and pleasure-loving young woman and hard to grasp in its unrelenting severity, but grasp it (or, rather, grasp at it) Aelfrida did. Her doing so set the pattern for much of her life to come and explains features of it puzzling in their incongruity: her preoccu-pation with and longing for death even when happiest; her ready acceptance of ill-health and ill-treatment; the frequency and vividness of ecstatic visions in which the Cross itself appears; the undeviating manner in which she pursued her course and her 'Great Work' at whatever cost to herself and others – all are explicable in terms of that single chapter of Thomas à Kempis' *Imitation of Christ*. Furthermore (and under the circumstances, unfortu-nately), only a few days after deciding to deny herself earthly happiness, she was able to put à Kempis' precepts into practice: to her description of the occasion on which she spotted John Forbes Cameron on a visit to Elfrida Sturge, she added: 'I was able to triumph and to thank God from the depths of my heart for His teaching … He is showing me … how to withdraw my heart from all earthly things and to love Him alone. All the way home … I was full of gratitude and joy at the wondrous ways of God. To be near Him, that is all I want'.[45] Yet when Thomas à Kempis' austerities became too much to bear, she turned to the gentler consolations of the religion of Love to which she was later to feel drawn, discovering in Sufism's tenets of God-as-Love located not in some distant abstract 'heaven' but deep in every human heart and of God-and-Love as the mystic essence in which a seeker after union with God must immerse himself in order to achieve union *with* God, that Omar Khayyám ('certainly a mystic') 'understands one better than Thomas'.[46]

Difficulties of practice were less easily resolved. Although Aelfrida only hints at them – describing a younger friend's religious quandaries, she notes that Dorothy Smith (*not* 'Mr Smith's Dorothy') 'must beware of the Road to Rome' – she asks herself 'do all roads really lead there?'[47], a premonition, surely, of the longing to join the Roman Catholic church which was soon to beset her, to disrupt her relationship with Constantine, and to cause such anxiety to her parents, and which endured until dissipated by involvement with the man who appeared transiently but influentially in her life: Aleister Crowley.

Aelfrida's cryptic reference to 'books' may also include her own diary, the 'book' to which she 'confided … more indeed than to any human being', unmasking to it not only her follies and thoughts but also her 'very heart' and begging it that it 'keep [her] secret well'.[48] One such 'secret' may be deduced with reference to Lord Kitchener whose visit to Cambridge in July 1898 and the first intimations of her 'grand passion' for him in December 1898 neatly bracket her fifteenth birthday on 5 October and are immediately followed by enraptured descriptions which appear at first sight to refer to Welsh scenery visited in the course of a family Christmas spent in Barmouth, a visit followed in April 1899 by her baptism and first Communion. From then on, frequent and increasingly passionate references to Lord Kitchener appear in the diary, references which by early 1900 could apply equally or more aptly to God and His Son than to an earthly 'splendid commander'[49] of her heart and soul; indeed, from around the time of her hypnopompic experience and her starting on *The Ending of the Way* in June 1900 (a significant title given that thirteen years later Aelfrida admitted that subjects which preoccupied her mind since her early teens were, other than

'religious truth and forms of religion', 'God, [and] how I can bring myself near to Him', and 'death as the ultimate solution and triumph')[50] such entries may be regarded as referring in encrypted fashion ('I know the meaning though no-one else does')[51] to Deity. Read in this light, diary comments ostensibly referring to Lord Kitchener acquire greater poignancy: the 'Lord' to whom novelist Aelfrida refers is the Lord God and the 'Duke' to whom she refers in conversation with Percy Stanley and John Forbes Cameron (a man to whom she poured out what she wanted to say to 'Lord Kitchener' in the guise of saying it to him) is Christ, Christ to whom she awards a high hereditary title and concerning whom she informs Percy Stanley that her 'Duke' has a 'long pedigree', and to whom she is 'attached' because he is the sovereign prince on earth of the small state which is her soul. And whom having seen once on an 'unforgettable day', she now loves and always will.[52] In which case, is the 'Lord Kitchener' between whom and herself a 'black curtain' falls in Florence the Herbert Horatio whose death by drowning on 5 June 1916 touches her not at all because 'so completely do one's feelings pass'[53] or is it God and His Son between whom and herself Constantine Michaelides has interposed himself?

There were, however, and fortunately for a religious adolescent worried that although she 'held the Christian faith … blindly', she was in danger of going to her grave 'with all [her] questions unanswered'[54], people to whom she could turn for help, whom she could trust, who would take her religious difficulties seriously, and with whose help she might find an answer to a question posed, we now realise, as something more than the title of a later book: can I be a mystic?

Two men with whom Aelfrida felt able to discuss her problems were her distant cousin Robert Tillyard[55] and her brother Julius. Robert, a recent Cambridge graduate, was about to embark on a year of postgraduate studies in Theology and his being amenable to discussions of Aelfrida's religious doubts and certainties was a great help to one feeling her way in matters of belief. Julius, though himself beset (not for the first time) by 'fundamental difficulties of belief' and requiring help and comfort from his sister (Aelfrida advised him to resolve his problems by doing as she had done: 'rest in the perfect love of God'), was sufficiently aware of his sister's inkling that her religious bent might be mystical (something he himself, so he later said, would never be: 'my mind does not … work that way. *Mysticus nascitur non fit*') to encourage her 'pretensions', to support her belief that her newfound creed was neither a symptom of insanity nor the unthinking faith of a child but the 'reasoned conviction of a [rational] being'[56], and even to hail her as a mystic[57].

He also encouraged her initial reading of William James' views on Mysticism as expressed in the latter's *Varieties of Religious Experience* and bought her Khayyám in Edward Fitgerald's translation, reading which persuaded Aelfrida that, 'groping in the dark' like herself, Omar's hands too might have touched God's.[58] Julius (or more likely Robert) may also have been responsible for introducing her to 'one Barry, of Corpus' (otherwise known as 'The Corpus Protestant'), an Evangelical churchman ('one sees he lives with God') with whom Aelfrida felt able to discuss 'religious difficulties', they being now less difficulties of belief than 'wrong thoughts' with regard to men. Barry's advice, namely to take her difficulties to God and 'ask Him for a *reasonable* explanation'[59], may or may not have been followed but it is noticeable that her talk with him, together attendance at a sermon by Oswald Dykes, Principal of Westminster College, after which she understood that though her 'prayer life could be more real and more precious … than … work or family affections or anything else', it paradoxically added value to those 'other interests' (*sic*) by irradiating them with its light[60], served to lighten her mood. As also did a helpful experience, later classified as *samadhic*, undergone in 1901 or 1902 when, alone in the countryside, her soul "somehow got out of my head and floated away … until I lived in the air"; returning to her "quite suddenly", it brought with it "a wonderful feeling of *power*, almost as though I had felt what it was like to *be* God".[61]

Sitting by the fire soon after Christmas 1903 the mystic 'born not made' meditated on spiritual storms and stresses experienced earlier that year. (Her happier mood had not held, for the contrast between 'Flirting' and her attempts to 'force' the gates of Heaven by concentrating her spiritual energies on doing so, together with her parents' suggestion that 'being in love with God [was] irrational and morbid' and would, if not checked, result in her becoming 'a weird mediaeval thing', had rendered her both miserable and trapped in a 'ravaged zone' with God on one side and 'the world' on the other.)[62] Thanking God 'for increased knowledge of Him', she suddenly realised that if the passing of time brought such increase, growing older 'was no longer a thing to be looked on with fear and hate'[63], a revelation besides which her mother's worries that a woman of twenty not yet married or engaged was in danger of perpetual spinsterhood dwindled into insignificance. Then came *Les Femmes Savantes*. In mid-February 1904 Aelfrida went to a rehearsal 'with many good resolutions to behave'[64] but 'flirted gloriously with Mr Michaelides'[65] instead and all thoughts of religion were put aside until her 'thirst for mysticism' broke out afresh in Florence, a place where she may have undergone another but unrecorded

'experience'[66] as a letter to her father, ostensibly about Young Italy suggests: " I have seen a little, I may see more – indeed I have some faith in my own powers of … seeing".[67]

Ten years later and deprived of the presence of men with whom she could discuss the "immediate communion" now so precious to her (Little Friends had become absent friends, Constantine was mostly abroad and unsympathetic when at home, Robert Tillyard had emigrated, Julius was a prisoner of war, or, following rejection by Sir Oliver Lodge, teaching at Tonbridge until a university post became available elsewhere), to whom could she turn for help? (With the exception of Miss Ridding, Aelfrida never disclosed her mystic proclivities to Cambridge academics with whom she discussed Comparative Religion, and discussions with foreign fellow-travellers were intense but intermittent.) Having parted with 'guru' Aleister Crowley, the absence of a spiritual director began to distress her: 'no-one would *really* do except Jesus'[68] and He, it seemed, was unavailable. Help arrived, however, in the guise of a whole battalion of directors. In 1915 Aelfrida discovered she was not alone: from the anonymous 14th century author of *The Cloud of Unknowing* to well-known living practitioner Evelyn Underhill, there were other mystics out there, all of whom had trodden the same 'mystic way' and many of whom had recorded their experiences in vivid detail. She did not accept their evidence uncritically, rejecting 'signs and miracles'[69] and writers who lacked emotion and enthusiasm or who watered down difficult theologies for popular consumption, in favour of the teachings of St John of the Cross[70] ("there's a kind of sombre fire about him which makes me feel I'd do anything and dare anything to follow him")[71] or Stephen Grellet[72], and noting that it did her good to contrast her 'pharisaic "righteousness"' with their 'humility and ardour'.[73] Early in 1918 she also discovered that discussions of 'books and art, and criticism in the correctest style' were boring compared to *The Dark Night of the Soul* ('who cares what Quiller-Couch thinks about Thomas Hardy?')[74] or Henri Delacroix' psychological analysis in *Les Grands Mystiques Chrétiens*[75] of three 'great' mystics: St Teresa of Avila[76], Mme Guyon, and Henry Suso.[77]

The comforting realisation that she was just the most recent in a long line of mystics encouraged Aelfrida to acknowledge to herself that she was one of them and to publicly affirm she had joined their company. It also formed the basis of a lifelong study of the lives and thoughts of mystics of both sexes and all ages regarded by her as inspirational exemplars and as comrades to whom she could turn for solace in times of spiritual turmoil. She therefore seized the hour and in spite of demands on her time and energy which could not be denied, embarked on a course of action which allowed her to spend time with those spiritual exemplars towards whom she felt most sympathetically disposed. She also charted her spiritual progress, broadcast her discoveries verbally and in writing, and embarked on the second part of her 'Great Work'.

There was, however, another facet of Mysticism which attracted Aelfrida strongly, namely that Mysticism *per se* was, as Caroline Stephen put it, both "essentially individual" and "a personal peculiarity rather than a form of belief".[78] This being so, "what constitutes a mystic?" Mystics, according to Miss Stephen, "are those whose minds, to their own consciousness, are lighted from within" because they are in immediate inward communication with God. Consciousness of being lighted from within causes them to be "naturally independent"; indeed, so far are they "assured of the sufficiency … of possession of that inward guidance … felt by each one in his own heart" that they believe themselves intrinsically independent of external authority and even of each other.[79] This, of course, accorded so strongly with Aelfrida's own beliefs that she was persuaded to continue with patterns of mystico-religious behaviour of an individualistic nature and to believe that spiritual direction was superfluous for one naturally independent and encouraged by a fellow-mystic to be so. Only later did she realise that the spiritual pride which encouraged her to think in this way had given rise to serious errors of judgement with regard to her own spirituality and that of others.

Her own thoughts on what constitutes a mystic are expounded on the first page of the introduction to *Spiritual Exercises*. A mystic, she writes, is both a seeker "after some ultimate reality with which they can commune and in whose being they find satisfaction … [a] *man to whom the spiritual world* – that is, the world of religious experience – *is more real than the material world*" and someone who has cultivated a "set of faculties" differing in degree from those required for sensory perception in order to give concentrated attention to the spiritual world. Such "senses of the soul" (i.e. those "awake to receive messages or pictures believed to be divine") should, however, remain under volitional control, for only by an act of will can the mystic deliberately withdraw his attention from "the thoughts and scenes of everyday life" and concentrate it on "the subject of … meditation or on communications to be received from God". Hence the need for spiritual exercises, defined here as "practices designed to bring the aspirant into communion with ultimate reality".[80]

Aelfrida's description of spiritual exercises is interesting for what it tells us of her own. She begins by describing "systems of self-culture" used by mystics who, lacking a teacher or unaware of "the great mystical traditions", evolve for themselves (or are taught by God) methods ("prayer and meditation and a saintly life") which independently achieve the desired result.[81] It was, presumably, one such 'system' which saw her through the difficult period of her early spiritual struggles until Aleister Crowley's intervention allowed her to regularise her 'method' for she then discusses a mystic's need of a spiritual director to train his "religious consciousness", "regulate … ascetic practices, suggest suitable exercises … and restrain indiscreet ardour", albeit with the proviso that the director must himself be "versed in mysticism" in order not to do more harm than good to his pupil's spiritual development. An injudiciously chosen (or imposed) director "may paralyse the action of God on such chosen souls [keeping] them, contrary to their vocation, in an inferior state where they will mark time instead of making progress", a state in which "they will be fortunate indeed if this ignorant director does not welcome with a sceptical smile, perhaps with a jest and sarcasm … a veritable gift of God".[82] (Given that Constantine's scepticism had resulted in ten years' spiritual aridity – for who would not be discouraged by sarcastic remarks that only "autosuggestion" or outright "madness" would allow a woman to think that "God spoke to you specially and [that] you are above all others", to despise those "not led your way", to be credulous with regard to visions and divine "guidance"[83], and to neglect her domestic duties while she pursued chimeras – this may be yet another reason for Aelfrida's wartime decision not to practise what she preached by acquiring a spiritual director.) "Guru worship" by a disciple, on the other hand, can degenerate into superstitious awe which may actually prevent attainment of ecstatic union with God by the guru-worshipping *chela*.[84] Hence while close spiritual affinity between teacher and pupil is a precondition for achievement of *Samadhi* by the latter, "guru-worship" is not, and it may be that growing realisation that although it was with Aleister Crowley as her 'guru' that she first achieved *Samadhi*, over-reverencing him as a man verged on 'worship' and might preclude further spiritual development which allowed her to break away from him so effortlessly when Constantine's comment that she was too 'discipular' opened her eyes.

Interestingly in view of what transpired between herself and her husband in the years 1914–1918, Aelfrida includes a short passage on the ethical aspects of spiritual exercises in which she states that "it is expressly laid down in every religion that no man or woman in a state of sin" may undertake exercises relating to "the senses of the soul". In this respect, vows of poverty, chastity, and obedience are not merely "excellent in themselves" but also because they are conducive to the "serenity and detachment" required for proper implementation of spiritual exercises. Poverty and obedience she quickly dismisses – she was not then affected by one or subject to the other – but "the question of chastity is a more difficult one". Significantly in view of recent events, she answers it only by remarking that although "the absence of a wife and children keeps a man's mind free from anxiety", their absence also leaves him open to "the possibility of temptation" and by describing the benefits of chastity to the mystic only in terms of yogic practices or by stating that they did not come "within the scope of this book".[85] This being so, why raise the subject at all unless to remind Constantine yet again of the enormity of his behaviour relative to herself?

Asceticism as a form of spiritual discipline was regarded by Aelfrida with mixed feelings. On the one hand, ascetic practice as a preliminary to meditation "was formerly much honoured by mystics of all colours and creeds" because "indifference to bodily comfort … tends to detachment of mind" and because "extreme lucidity" resulting from certain ascetic practices, particularly fasting and sleep deprivation, is "peculiarly favourable to the development of mystical states of consciousness".[86] Her exemplar here, though she only hints that this is so ("to refrain from eating when one is hungry, to keep awake when one would like to sleep require more will-power than those who have not tried it can know") is her adolescent self as one who discovered the self-disciplinary strength induced by deliberate deprivation and her adult self who practised more subtle forms of discipline: "refraining from conversation about oneself" (always Aelfrida's favourite topic) and "not feeling self-righteous when one has succeeded".[87] She also distinguishes two types of asceticism. The first, she says, "proceeds from the conviction that the bearing of pain is in itself a meritorious act, either because it propitiates an angry Deity or because it is an act of warfare against that evil creature, matter"[88], but having suffered so much involuntary physical pain herself, she finds herself unable to agree with a tenet she describes as perverse and irrational even while agreeing that certain mystics found it a help.[89] (Henry Suso, for example, imposed appalling austerities on himself for fifteen years until ordered by God to desist.) The second proceeds from "the centring of love and of the powers of enjoyment on spiritual rather than on physical delights"[90]; with this tenet she agrees, regarding 'higher indifference' less as deliberate suppression of libido than an attempt to loosen every tie which binds her soul to earthly things, pursuing it even at the risk of possessing 'only … God' when she longs for 'fellowship' [91] and of

being rebuked by people whose opinions she respects: Frank Stokoe and Charles du Bouchet.

Meditation is a topic on which Aelfrida expatiates at some length in the introduction to *Spiritual Exercises* and again in the section on Christian meditations towards the end. Though she agrees that solitude, detachment, and the absence of worldly cares and preoccupations are vital for anyone "who would cultivate the mystic consciousness", she also emphasises that although "systematised spiritual exercises" are usually the preserve of those who have adopted the life of a religious, this should not discourage a keen layman from attempting them.[92] Detachment she was struggling to attain and absence of 'cares and preoccupations' was achievable by dint of rigorous exclusion of these from her life whenever opportunity arose and by whatever means, however unscrupulous, e.g. deliberate alienation of affection or stating that she was acting or refraining from acting at the bidding of a heavenly authority. Solitude was possible (though liable to interruption) by dint of days in bed in a "lonely room… empty save for the solitary contemplative … where the mystic, like a bride in the bride-chamber, may commune with God"[93] (while researching and writing *Spiritual Exercises* Aelfrida returned to her old room on the attic, ostensibly because this freed the East Room for paying guests but actually because it further removed her from the hurly-burly of life at Fordfield; she returned to the first floor only if she or her daughters were ill and then only for so long as it took for herself or them to recover) and by making the best use of times when she was unlikely to be interrupted (her favourite times for meditation were between six and seven a.m. and between nine and ten p.m.) and by ensuring that she and Constantine spent as much time apart as possible, in separate bedrooms, towns, or countries as occasion arose. This suggests that although there was, for Aelfrida, only one motivating factor which "justifies" meditation, namely "the desire to attune the mind for communion with spiritual reality, under whatever form spiritual reality may be conceived", "purity of intention", "the first essential for the man or woman who would be a mystic" (purity which should remain unsullied by "inquisitiveness, spiritual pride … or love of the strange and occult")[94], was sullied in her particular case by selfish needs (of compulsive intensity, admittedly) and achieved by manipulative means. When, therefore, she discusses Christian meditation in terms of its being carried out by one who must "love humanity" and the individuals of which it is composed, albeit "in such a way that he is not dependent on them for peace in his soul, their praise or censure [being] powerless to turn him from a course of action he believes to be right, his serenity untroubled by their love or aversion"[95], one should remember that it was not only at great cost to herself that she became 'detached'.

A "spiritual exercise", according to Aelfrida, consists of five interrelated components: adoption of a particular posture; quieting of the mind by means of deep regular respiration; banishment of intrusive thoughts; concentration; repetition of a "sacred sentence" or mantra.[96] Her subsequent discussion of each component is interesting for the light it throws on her own practice: with regard to posture, for example, she recommends an attitude "reserved for meditation and for meditation alone in order that an immediate mental connection should be established when the posture is taken up" and suggests that kneeling is particularly suitable.[97] (Diary accounts show that she herself usually meditated lying supine in bed – prone if she felt particular need for abasement in the sight of God – with her arms in the *Aum tat sat Aum* position[98] or crossed on her breast; more rarely she meditated reclining in a chair.) Breathing exercises she knew from her introduction to yoga by Aleister Crowley; she also employed them therapeutically. Banishment of intruding thoughts ("the power of concentrating the attention is indispensable to [one] who wishes to meditate")[99] was already a much-practised exercise, banishing itself being described here in terms of the withdrawal of attention from external objects, first by closing the eyes then by gradually withdrawing attention from other percepts (hearing being the most persistent) until one's mind is focussed on a chosen object, usually "a sacred object or symbol" of particular relevance to the meditator. (Aelfrida sometimes focussed on a cross or crucifix but more usually on a mental image of a cross within a circle variously representing "sacrifice, life and immortality, the Incarnation, the union of divine and human consciousness, the merging of the self in the Absolute, etc.")[100] "The mystic, closing the eyes and ears and putting worldly considerations from his mind", then allows his thoughts to dwell on "the attributes of God, on the work of divine grace in his soul, [on] Death and Judgement, [on] the Garden and the Fire".[101] (Aelfrida herself meditated on subjects as diverse as "God as Artist and we the medium" or as herself as a corpse in a coffin with two men chanting "death to desire, death to affection"[102] as they nailed down the lid; she also practised the formal Points of the Compass meditation[103] during which she meditated in turn on aspects of the world north, south, east, or west of her.) Repetition of a mantra (i.e. of a word or phrase endowed with sacramental energy) enhances concentration, its words being chosen because appropriate to the meditation or, more usually with Aelfrida, according to "the particular aspect of divine truth"[104] with which she currently felt particular spiritual affinity (e.g. the

omnipresence, power of bestowing inner light, or infinite nature of God)[105] or according to which of several sins predominated and required correction (most commonly, spiritual pride); the mantra even varied within a particular set of meditations, '*Om Mane Padme Hum*' reverting to 'knowing Him you know All' and back again.[106]

Only two overt examples exist of Aelfrida's own meditations[107] though she states that she kept extensive records of meditative experiences in order to note her spiritual progress or to refer to them in time of spiritual aridity when "written description of graces already enjoyed may be of incalculable benefit to [one] who has almost come to doubt that he has received any favours from God at all".[108] She did not, however, and in spite of her promise of October 1914 that 'I have been doing a little meditation every evening for some time past and mean to keep it up *always*'[109], always do so, for illness ('interruption, due to bad cold, etc.')[110], fatigue, and the intrusions of daily life frequently precluded anything but the most 'discursive' of meditations. (Discursive meditation differs "in no way from the ordinary manner of giving an interesting matter one's attention … except that the object of thought is a sacred one".)[111] It is evident, however, from her diary and from lengthy passages of meditations quoted in several of her books (in particular *The Making of a Mystic, A Little Road–Book for Mystics,* and *Can I be a Mystic?*) that she meditated frequently and that the examples she quotes are largely, though possibly not exclusively, of her own meditations. This may be deduced by comparing the content of diary entries with those of quoted meditations (direct correlation is difficult because she fails to include the year when dating and timing a particular meditation or notes only the day of the week and the time it occurred), a particularly vivid example being given in *Spiritual Exercises* where she quotes a "seer" (*sic*) accustomed "to meditate with great regularity and to keep a careful account of the results of meditation" whose meditation "was a consideration of the mystery of the Incarnation with the visualisation of a cross, accompanied by the words from the Apostles' Creed '*and in Jesus Christ His only Son, our Lord*'". 'Seer's' account of feeling compelled to meditate after reciting a mantra, assuming a supine position, discovering that concentration is 'almost perfect', and so on, is almost identical to her diary entry of 28/29 May 1913 describing 'the most real experience of [her] life'. Like it, too, 'seer's' account continues with a description of an 'infinitely precious' meditative experience during which and almost without realising it, 'seer' moves from meditation to participant experience and thence to 'blinded' return to self and to demanding to know 'how can one live with God so near'.[112] As 'seer', however, Aelfrida omits to say that she reread a letter from Aleister Crowley immediately before her 'visualisation'.

Not every meditative experience found Aelfrida slipping 'quite unexpectedly into *Samadhi*'[113] and although this was her unspoken ambition, it seems that most, though they provided her with 'the most vivid joy and peace'[114] or a 'wonderful feeling of mental exhilaration and physical lightness'[115], did not. Nor can one be sure that experiences described as *samadhic* were exactly what is meant in terms of the mystic's mind becoming "wholly assimilated into God in the beatific vision which it now enjoys"[116], for on several occasions she 'retained sufficient ego-consciousness to register the experience'[117] or, as in the case of her experiment with Charles Myers, remained aware of external stimuli, or had 'a *wonderful Samadhi* in my sleep'[118] which, given the circumstances of her life at the time, reads more like dream-fulfilment of physical desire for Constantine than 'mystical' experience. (She went so far as to attribute physical symptomatology and concurrent depression to 'the price one pays … for *Samadhi*'[119] even though reassured by Surendra Nath Maitra that there was nothing "*unnatural* or *supernatural*" about "this … most natural state … in [which] God dwells in us".)[120] She also tried to achieve *Samadhi* with 'eyes open' in the hope of studying it as she experienced it ('I want to see what one can do with supernormal consciousness') but found the experience too overwhelming: 'the wonder grows too great, one's soul melts in one, one is on the verge of ceasing to be' so was able to describe *samadhic* experiences only in terms of waves of '*light*' ('it looks like light … but it is understood as not being light or the imagination of light') filtering into her mind to 'reappear later as an indescribable apprehension of having been as one with the presence of God'.[121]

Another means by which she 'saw God' was that of spontaneous visionary experiences. Although she often describes 'visions' experienced while meditating or after entering a contemplative state, it is important to distinguish, as she does, visionary experiences arising as the result of spiritual exercises volitionally undertaken in private with the aim of detaching herself from the world in order to achieve direct communion with Deity from 'visions' which came to her unexpectedly and involuntarily, sometimes when she was alone in a public or private place, sometimes when in the company of family or strangers, and often when engaged in other activities.

The content of Aelfrida's involuntary visions (i.e. of those described in detail in her diary; not all visions were consigned to paper even if of 'overwhelming wonder and absolutely satisfying', because 'I simply haven't had time to write about [them]')[122] is interesting insofar as it appears to be derived from phenomena experienced in daily life (sitting in the firelight in the Fordfield drawing-room admiring the beauty of russet chrysanthemums set against a brown velvet curtain)[123] or from the subject matter of current research (a vision of herself begging God to 'let me be a Buddha [and] let me return again and again until the least of Thy creatures is saved')[124] or from the resurgence of childhood memories (pictures by early nineteenth century visionary artist John Martin) or from projections of mood-swings between paradisiacal and hellish emotions ('the earth, from being flames writhing in torment, turned to flowers')[125], or from objects handled or seen: the crucifix permanently hanging round her neck, or a beautiful meadow or sky. Indeed, for one engaged with a 'Great Work' of self- and other-enlightenment and whose diary, she hopes, will eventually be published to complement the homiletic works she intends to write, such seemingly involuntary visions are frequently so opportune and apposite with regard to content or timing or both that one wonders if she deliberately 'shaped' them to fit or that she employed them as literary devices to illustrate and support her current agenda, namely her 'making' as a 'mystic'. Either way, the visions are valuable for what they disclose of the way her mind was working at this point (and thereafter), though one should never lose sight of the fact that personality disorder drove much of her thought, for the way in which they allow us another pathway into that mind (a particularly valuable pathway if the visions were *truly* involuntary), for allowing us to gain glimpses of the other 'world' her mind inhabited, for providing us with a sense of 'place' in a mind whose placements are sometimes spectacularly awry, and because they may demonstrate instances of unconscious promptings from her surroundings, from past, present, or wished-for circumstances, or from the living or dead with whom she has dealings.

A study of the content of some of Aelfrida's visions is interesting when contextualised by reference to her diary. One occurring in conjunction with conversations with George von Kaufmann about the spiritual world involved her feeling 'all at once … the presence of God so intense, so vivid that [she] was filled with fear – but not fear terrible but joyful'.[126] Another happened shortly after a 'suggestion-séance' at the point at which she decided to ask Dr Hare to stop the sessions on the grounds that they were not improving her health and might even be hampering her spiritual development, this resulting in a vision of Christ's cross with huge heaps of skulls around its base symbolising 'dead hopes, dead desires, dead selves' which as she watched, 'changed, broke, blossomed into lilies of the purest white'.[127] A third occurred shortly after a series of visits from relatives drawn together by the awfulness of war. It began with 'a moment of "universal consciousness" when all the pain of the world seemed to be present in [her] mind at once' but as God's presence filled the shadowy room where she sat in firelight, the solid walls around her seemed to dissolve, releasing her spirit into the dark November night outside (a night made darker by the need to conceal lights for fear of Zeppelins) and into 'deep after deep of stars away to infinity, above, around, below'.[128] A fourth took place while she was speaking in public on religious topics: a Pentecostal vision of 'a shower of light around me and something above my head, whether flame or wings or light I do not know, but God was with me …'[129], a fifth while Constantine was in Holland in January 1918 ostensibly settling his affairs but actually saying farewell to Mme Sterneberg, and Aelfrida, pregnant but shortly to miscarry, was chatting to her parents: a vision of herself 'put to stillness by the glory and the presence of God', then branded by an angel on the forehead with 'a fiery cross', immediately after which she heard a voice saying "for every death a flower is given, for every wound a song" and found herself lifted up into a godly cloud of 'Light all around', there to hear His admonition "let your light so shine before men".[130] But whatever the content and regardless of whether the vision came to a natural conclusion 'just right for that particular time'[131] with Aelfrida herself 'coming back' joyfully in a state of praiseful exaltation or was abruptly ended by an irruption from the outside world ('twice or thrice God's Presence returned – and then someone came into the room')[132], she found such spontaneous and 'wonderful visions and experiences of God'[133] enormously satisfying, chiefly because after each 'a great peace possesse[d] me. I rested in God'.[134]

She voiced, however, three concerns with regard to her visions. The first involved the 'spiritual loneliness' which beset her because she had (by choice or circumstance) no-one to whom to confide them, a gap unfilled during the war because Frank Stokoe, her sole confidant, was largely absent from Cambridge and obsessed with recurrent mental miseries. Second, although she disguised her loneliness with the 'aptitude for talking clever nonsense'[135] cultivated as a 'finished young lady' and employed to devastating effect thereafter, she was concerned that there were 'other things one can't talk of' besides visions per se. 'I am used', she wrote ,'to the odd experience, generally momentary and generally accompanied … by some feeling of God [but] it is when all material things, walls and tables and chairs, become unsubstantial and exist only by reason of the spiritual reality behind them [that] one is left dazed and alone in a spaceless eternity'. Dematerialisation of *things*, though

worrying, could be coped with; more worrying was when people too became insubstantial: 'their individuality fades from me and they are seen only *as souls*, perfect but undifferentiated, glorious indeed but strange and unhomelike'. (In the course of a vision which occurred while she was talking to her parents, she had a sudden out-of-body experience during which she found herself looking down to 'see' the Oracle and Chiara as '*timeless, neither old nor young, as spirits do after death*' and as if their souls shone through 'the transparent substance of temporal matter'. (The vision lasted about two minutes, Aelfrida re-entering her body after a remark by Chiara broke the spell.)[136] More disconcerting still was the manner in which people outside her immediate family frequently ceased to be 'real' people, becoming not merely disembodied (a state with positive connotations because it implied a degree of *spiritual* perfection) but as if gone from her life, a negative condition which left her 'dazed and *lonely, lonely*'.[137]

Her third concern involved the closeness of her relationship with God as revealed through visions. In order to become as or at one with God, it was, she realised, necessary to perfect herself but, as she also realised with intense self-disgust, she fell far short 'of all I really admire': the ability to misprize 'the love which had its spring in the emotions' in favour of unemotional acceptance of 'people as they are and God as He is'[138] or to un-will herself in favour of filling herself with God's will, abilities which emotionally-needy and controlling Aelfrida knew would not be attained without a struggle and abdication of personal autonomy. Worse still was growing realisation that problems were rooted in '*sins*', particularly that of using God 'for [her] own spiritual advancement and for getting spiritual gifts from, instead of adoring Him for His own sake'. Sometimes, she wrote, 'I even feel that I am *good* to serve Him, instead of that *He* is infinitely gracious in deigning to use me. Sometimes I see my own meanness so vividly that I feel I should like to *kill* the self that could be so contemptible. Think … how I could be so full of complacency and self-satisfaction at my "mystical adventures"! Think of the way I have patted myself on the back. Oh, it is so *low*, so unlovely and puts God … so far away!'[139] Little wonder, then, that she begged God to 'destroy [her] will and substitute for it His own'[140] and to empty her 'of all but [Him]self'[141], but it was not until 1922 that she noted with regard to a vision which took place in church of 'a great cross, rising to Heaven with behind it a light and I in its shadow' and formed the climax of powerful persistent feelings of 'God-consciousness', that she comprehended that visions were 'of small *relative* importance [when] compared with the plain simple consciousness that *God is* and that I *am* in Him'.[142]

Lacking a spiritual director but increasingly aware of the difficulty of tracking her 'mystic way' without a guide, Aelfrida revived an earlier notion, that of possessing a 'guardian angel'. Her earliest reference to her 'Guardian Angel' is found in the same diary entry as that in which she records the burglary at Le Vésinet in September 1913 and inadvertently reveals that she and Constantine do not share a room: the 'angel', she wrote, came to her while she was meditating and helped her to rise through various planes of mental being until, attaining the plane of '*Binah*' (i.e. understanding), she grew frightened and refused to go any further.[143] A second reference occurs in November 1914: having 'dreamed true' about Aleister Crowley, she was informed by her 'holy guardian angel' that Crowley's 'mental temperature' was too hot for her, that he still exerted an influence over her, that one as 'non-attached' as she purported to be should not allow herself to be influenced, and that she should 'sever the psychic connection' immediately. (The angel also informed her that her 'wish to do good' by putting the second part of her 'Great Work' into operation was 'tainted by love of power over men's souls just as [Crowley's] is'; a perceptive angel indeed, and one whose advice was described by Aelfrida as 'perfectly just and reasonable … [even] if arrived at in a rather odd way'.)[144] Both visits are significant insofar as they occurred at times when Aelfrida was either in contact with Crowley and acting under his instructions or had broken with him but had him in mind because introducing Ceremonial Magic's methodology into studies undertaken with Bernard Muscio, for it was almost certainly from Crowley himself that she derived the notion.

As the latter noted in *The Tyler*, the poem dedicated 'to Aelfrida Tillyard, Cambridge', though she might 'read' him "in complete confusion" she would nevertheless "gain a fresh hold" of her "Guardian Angel" by doing so[145]; indeed, Crowley himself believed he possessed a Holy Guardian Angel named Aiwass. Aiwass, so Crowley said, dictated the Thelemic Holy Books to him, including, significantly, the *Liber Cordis Cincti Serpente* with its five chapters describing the relationship between an Adeptus Minor and his particular Guardian Angel.[146] Reflecting in 1945 on Aiwass' exact nature, Crowley wondered if he (He) was a "discarnate Being" or a real person able to exercise mental influence through time and space but concluded "I simply do not know and cannot reasonably surmise, because I do not know the limits of the powers of such a one".[147] Aelfrida herself described her guardian angel as a directorial "higher power (God) whose mode of working was obscure but very likely involved the use of discarnate spirits as intermediaries" and at some length in *Can I be a Mystic?*: "I like to imagine to myself that I have a friendly companion in the unseen world who is interested in my progress" who, when he gives an order, "always provides the means for carrying it out, [his] plans [being] invariably successful". (She does not at this point give her 'companion' a name.) Her guardian angel, she further posits, is "a force, a monitor, a power" guiding her life, whose directions, spoken in an "inward voice", are perfectly clear (though sometimes not what she wants to 'hear') and disobeyed at the cost of loss of peace of mind. Once accustomed to this constant but "unseen companion", she gained, so she says, "a wonderful sense of security and peace" and the satisfaction of knowing that "the sense of being directed by a higher power [was] the reward … of dedicating one's life and thought to Christ".[148] She also allotted him a day on which to specially remember and thank him, her choice of 2 October being neither random nor because that was the occasion on which her angel first manifested himself but because the Roman Catholic Feast of the Holy Angel-Guardians was celebrated on that date.[149]

Aelfrida's guardian angel played an important part in her life for the rest of her life, so much so that during one meditative exercise she felt him place his foot on her neck when she fell on her bed before him in token of submission.[150] Regarding him variously as "a conception of an Inward Light"[151], as an expression of the voice of conscience[152], or as an "inward monitor"[153], she (almost always) followed his instructions with regard to all aspects of her life, be these spiritual ("my guardian angel said I had better change the method of my meditation because the feeling of elation … which accompanies me all day is, to a certain extent, selfish … I obeyed")[154], literary (further revision of *Marrying a Stranger* instead of completing *Spiritual Exercises*)[155], or personal: 'my guardian angel has calmly suggested that I should go to Holland next week. I critically examined the proposal and there seemed nothing against it except that I don't want to leave the children, so I wrote to Constantine and applied to the Foreign Office for my passport' even though it was rumoured in August 1915 that a German invasion of East Anglia was imminent. Her intention of leaving the 'kiddies'[156] with a grandmother who threatened suicide should the Kaiser's soldiers enter Cambridge was, of course, thwarted by the serendipitous eruption of a septic spot on an intimate part of her anatomy.

Having been granted help by an agent who operated on both spiritual and mundane levels but of whom, lest she be derided as a 'spiritual freak', she preferred not to speak, Aelfrida now faced a problem which would become even more apparent in the post-war period, namely how to reconcile the difficulties inherent in living an intense inner/spiritual and a prosaic outer/earthly life simultaneously. Not (then) able to live retired from the world, she found it almost impossible to maintain continual awareness of 'the blaze of the glory of God and the stirrings of the spirit'[157] while coping with the care and education of her daughters, the fluctuating state of her health, and with problems posed by 'this appalling war' and her relationship with Constantine. Though endowing herself with opportunities for retreat into an inward life which provided "refuge from the ever-changing aspects of outward existence [and] from the multitude of cares and pleasures and agitations which belong to the life of the senses and the affections"[158], she led notwithstanding a 'queer double life' consisting of a state of "sensible devotion"[159] in which she experienced both her 'holy treasure of the Universal Consciousness' with all that that implied of a world-soul in which was reflected God's love for man and man's love for God (a soul or consciousness, moreover, to which in spite of Caroline Dalmas' warning that an individual "may no more claim … discovery of … universal consciousness than one may claim discovery of the sun when one first [sets] eyes on it" because "every soul at a certain point in its evolution experiences it"[160], Aelfrida continued to attach the personal pronoun 'my') and 'the going-out of personal desire'[161], and mundane existence in a world which was just itself and no more. Deciding in summer 1915 that 'a life of balanced meditation and activity is the best' (it might later be necessary 'to give oneself up entirely to one or the other' as circumstances demanded)[162], she nevertheless found it difficult to reconcile her 'inner' and 'outer' lives then and for many years to come.

Because so much of Aelfrida's 'outer' life between 1914 and 1918 was engaged with problems posed by major and minor illnesses, it is worth pausing here to consider the impact of these illnesses on her 'inner' life (with particular reference to her achievement of ecstatic and visionary states), for however much she declares herself to be *not* her 'poor body' but an eternal, steadfast and changeless 'I'[163], to that body her 'I' was irrevocably bound.

Evelyn Underhill believed the phenomenon she described as "mystic ill-health" to be "the natural result and not the pathological cause, of the characteristic activities of … mystics", "bodily rebellion against growing spiritual stress" being an essential aspect of the pattern of spiritual growth described by Aelfrida in terms of her personal 'mystic way'.[164] In the latter's case, association of 'mystic ill-health' and a 'thirst for mysticism' is possible, given that at least two intense spiritual experiences later realised to be 'mystic' in nature insofar as they evoked a private 'way' to God or which, as the etymology of the term 'mystic' or 'mystical' suggests (*muo,* in Greek, means to conceal) should be kept secret until she chose to reveal

them, antedated the onset of the chronic ill-health which plagued her thereafter. Given, however, that it was a severe attack of malaria early in 1905 which precipitated the decline in her health, that a comforting vision took place on the day she nearly died of postpartum haemorrhage, and that her subsequent postnatal depression is explicable in physiological and emotional terms rather than in terms of intense and overwhelming mystical experiences, it is more likely that the stress-related illnesses from which she subsequently suffered (migraine certainly, and possibly rheumatoid arthritis also) were manifestations of 'bodily rebellion' engendered by Constantine's attempts to damage her emotional and moral integrity than the result of 'spiritual stress' engendered by 'mystical adventures' which, though they might be fearful, brought happiness in their train because they created 'a well of light within me, bubbling up and overflowing no matter what the outward circumstances may be'. Indeed, the lifting in early 1915 of the 'solid blank wall of misery that [she] couldn't get past or see over'[165] which had formed the background to her life since 1912 (and, judging by her poetry and diary, since marriage in 1907) can itself be attributed to the happiness of knowing that God had revealed Himself to her and that the 'well of light' within her was a manifestation of His presence in her life.

Rather than describe Aelfrida as suffering 'mystic ill-health', we should perhaps regard 'characteristic activities of the mystics' as positively health-enhancing in her case, and in at least one instance, as curative. We can also see how cleverly she employed the excuse of physical ill-health to enable her to spend more time on spiritual exercises which enhanced both her spiritual and her emotional health and her physical health insofar as that was affected by circumstantial unhappiness; indeed, it is possible to argue that the effect of physical suffering on her emotional and spiritual health might have been greater had she not possessed and developed a consoling 'vein of mysticism' and to regard her deliberate use of yogic exercises as therapy as a precursor of techniques taught today to patients suffering from life-threatening or chronic illnesses as a means of alleviating emotional distress, controlling pain, and boosting immune systems damaged by disease, medication, or the stress of illness itself. It may be, too, that Aelfrida relied on yogic practices and the ecstatic release of tension afforded by the experiences in which they resulted to pull herself back from what she later described as 'the borderline between madness and sanity'[166], a liminal state or place first approached as an adolescent, re-encountered in the autumn of 1912 following Agneta's birth and death, and brought worryingly close again between 1914 and 1918 at times of mental invasion by discarnate spirits or marital discord.

A question which must also be asked in the context of Aelfrida's 'mystical adventures' is: did her numerous illnesses contribute to the occurrence, frequency, imagery, and content of her visionary experiences? From diary evidence there appears to be no connection: though she might have bad dreams when physically unwell, she did not have spontaneous visions and, knowing that illness impaired her ability to carry out the necessary preliminaries to willed events, she did not meditate or practise spiritual exercises at that time. While it is therefore tempting, given migraine's accompanying symptoms of abnormal sensitivity to light, sound, colour, and tactile stimuli and of hallucinations of vision and audition ('hearing' distorted speech or music, 'seeing' oscillating iridescent optic phenomena, experiencing ambient lighting as abnormally bright or colours as saturated with refulgence, etc.), to suggest that 'visionary' experiences were migraine-related, it is unlikely (though not impossible) that migraine was a predisposing factor or that her disabling migraines of the war years contributed to the content of visions occurring in close conjunction with attacks because migraines were rarer than visions were frequent and because (recorded) symptoms encompassed only severe headache and nausea.[167] Conversely, it could be argued that the 'fiery' imagery of contemporary visions derived from her being constantly beset by pyrexias accompanying recurrent infections or from the sensation of her body 'burning up' during exacerbations of rheumatoid arthritis.

There is also the question of how much opium Aelfrida consumed in order to abate the discomforts of earache, toothache, sore throats, migraine, cystitis, backache, gynaecological problems, and rheumatoid arthritis. Teetotalism precluded the use of alcohol (she does not say if she used alcohol-based tinctures of opium) but as one who carried opium tablets for pain relief when travelling and was familiar with opium's use as a home remedy (when Agatha, a toddler of fifteen months, had her 'bad attack of colitis' in August 1911, Aelfrida plied her with opium every three hours, noting to her own if not to our surprise that 'during her illness [Agatha] was asleep nearly all the time')[168], increased consumption of a cheap, effective, readily-available analgesic[169] by someone in constant pain of some sort is a definite possibility. Though vehemently opposed to deliberate use of drugs to enhance willed experiences of the supernatural, it is possible that, knowing of opium's hallucinogenic side-effects, she increased her usual consumption and that this provides another explanation for the increased frequency and extreme vividness of visions experienced during the war years.

Though not wishing to suggest that Aelfrida's accounts of visions experienced between 1914 and 1918 constitute the 'Confessions of an East Anglian Opium Eater' but mindful of her later admission that in times of trial she turned "to aspirin *or worse*"[170], it is interesting to discover similarities between recorded visions and those experienced by Thomas de Quincey when under the influence of a drug he described as producing "sympathy … between the waking and the dreaming states of the brain"[171]:

De Quincey: "space swelled and was amplified to an extent of unutterable infinity".[172]

Aelfrida: "the sensation … of being just a point with the infinite depths of star beyond star above, below and around me".[173]

De Quincey: "vast processions moved along … in mournful pomp".[174]

Aelfrida: "I became aware of people … driven by an unseen compulsion, seeking God, the whole creation travailing and seeking Him".[175]

De Quincey: "a theatre seemed suddenly opened and lighted up within my brain, which presented … spectacles of more than earthly splendour".[176]

Aelfrida: "I entered at once into the peace of God. His presence apprehended as *light*. I felt it not only around me, stretching out through wide luminous space into infinite distances, but penetrating the very depths of my being … The light was so great that I could not look (though of course my eyes were shut and it was dark in my room)".[177]

De Quincey: "Buildings, landscapes … were exhibited in proportions so vast as the bodily eye is not fitted to receive".[178]

Aelfrida: "Meadows of buttercups surrounded by trees laden with flowers … sea and white cliffs in dazzling sunshine; austere mountains, first grey, then snow-covered … the Divine Artificer was there attempting to build a magnificent cathedral".[179]

Or again, as an alternative explanation of Aelfrida's rapid changes of mood from 'serenity and exaltation' to 'passionate and bitter suffering'[180], one can cite parallels between de Quincey's elevated mood while experiencing tremendous opium-fuelled visions and the "deep seated anxiety" and "funereal melancholy" amounting to "suicidal despondency"[181] experienced as the effects of the drug wore off.

Notwithstanding the difficulties inherent in coming to terms with mood-swings as violent as hers or of discovering the implications of Aleister Crowley's pre-diction that the visions she experienced in Le Vésinet would be precursors of barriers 'much worse because infinitely stronger' between herself and God because the very act of experiencing them would tie her strongly to self ('I – I – I see, hear, adore, rejoice') and that her ability to *see* God would hinder rather than help her relationship *with* God unless she was willing and able to 'self-naught' completely (i.e. 'to empty oneself that one may be filled by God')[182], Aelfrida's mystical inner life brought her so much joy that in 1915 she confided to her diary 'I'm *happy*! It seems almost insane to be happy now but … I can't help it'.[183] Though the disappearance of her 'solid blank wall of misery' was not solely due to contemplation of the 'ineffable joy of God'[184] but owed much to earthly joys provided by Little Friends, her now waking so frequently in a 'golden haze' of happiness[185] was chiefly attributed to new-found abilities: to be able to turn to God whenever she wishes and to find in Him what she sought but lacked in real life ('light, space, perfection, freedom … passionate love and beauty, serenity and wisdom')[186]; to be able to feel God 'everywhere, *overwhelmingly*'; to be so 'unceasingly conscious of Him'[187] that she finds herself craving for sessions of meditation during which she achieves 'direct experience of God the Father in this life'[188]; to know for certain 'that *God was*'.[189]

Her letter of October 1902 to her future and older self contains a passage as yet unquoted:

> "One thing I must ask you", Frida writes, "are you 'walking worthy of your high calling'? Not your calling of authoress … or even of mother. I mean your calling of Christian, what is, and has been, and will be till death, the chief end of your life? I expect you are now well-versed in the wicked ways of the world – I don't mean that you are wicked but that you always *see* when other people are – … but if you don't know God … what's the use of all your knowledge. Shut up your books, leave off setting your neighbours to rights and down on your knees before your Maker!"

Opening the letter in October 1918, Aelfrida assured her younger self: 'I *do* know more of God'; in 1953, confirming her knowledge, she added a final note: '*Laus Deo*'.[190] But though happy to call herself a Christian and to believe she was following a 'Christian' calling and to spend much time on her knees before her Maker, she had no intention of shutting up her 'books' or of leaving off setting people to rights; indeed, she was to make the chief end of her life that of opening books and trying to do so.

## Notes

1   GCPPT 1|1|45 12 June 1934.
2   Tillyard, Ae. *Can I be a Mystic?* p 92.
3   Tillyard, Ae. *The Fruits of Silence* p15. Perhaps worth noting in this connection is the similarity between Aelfrida's childhood experience and that of the Buddha when he recalled sitting as a child under a tree in his father's palace garden and experiencing a moment of self-forgetfulness which prefigured his becoming the Awakened One at Bodh Gaya some years later. Aelfrida's study of Buddhism prior to writing *Spiritual Exercises* would have familiarised her with the story.
4   Tillyard, Ae. *The Making of a Mystic* p 18. Aelfrida speaks here in the voice of fictional alter ego 'Audrey Talbot'.
5   The third edition of the book, more properly *The Broken Vow, a Story of Here and Hereafter*, appeared in 1887. W J Knox-Little, then Vicar of Hoar Cross, Staffordshire, was contemporaneously described as a firm believer "in the Unseen World and in the possibility and likelihood of intercourse between the inhabitants of that world and us who are living here for a season" (Dix, M. p 82).
6   GCPPT 1|1|4 9 September 1897. Aelfrida later (date unknown) placed a √ beside the entry to denote its significance for her religious development.
7   GCPPT 2|26|4(9).
8   Tillyard. Ae. *Christian Old Age* p 50 (GCPPT 2|17).
9   Tillyard, Ae. *Marrying a Stranger* pp 61–62 (GCPPT 2|6). Aelfrida speaks here in the voice of fictional alter ego 'Elizabeth von Thiele'.
10  GCPPT 1|1|69 13 August 1951.
11  Tillyard, Ae. *Marrying a Stranger* pp 61–62.
12  GCPPT 2|26|4(9).
13  GCPPT 1|3.
14  Renan, E. p83.
15  GCPPT 1|1|4 22 August 1899.
    GCPPT 1|1|72 24 January 1955.
16  GCPPT 2|23 *The Watchword* September 1957.
    Tillyard, Ae. *Just Alice* p 156 (GCPPT 2|19).
17  Tillyard, Ae. *Can I be a Mystic?* pp 37–41 and 43.
18  ibid. pp 43–44.
19  GCPPT 2|2a *Vol 1 No 8* (undated but by context May 1900). *Without our protene we should die* by 'Capt. Tillyard'. Julius also became a vegetarian about this time.
20  Tillyard, Ae. *Can I be a Mystic?* pp 43–44.
21  ibid. p 48.
22  Tillyard, Ae. *A Little Road-Book for Mystics* p 25.
23  Tillyard, Ae. *Can I be a Mystic?* p 48.
24  Tillyard, Ae. *A Little Road-Book for Mystics* p 25.
25  Heimann, M. pp 139 and 142–146.
26  Tillyard, Ae. *Can I be a Mystic?* pp 39–41.
27  ibid. pp 55–56.
28  GCPPT 1|1|4 25 December 1899. The word 'books' is marked with a cross.
29  Knox, R.B. p24. The Rev Halliday Douglas was minister from 1893–1901.
30  GCPPT 1|1|9 15 June 1902.
31  Amiel, F. p 1. Entry dated 'Berlin. 16 July 1848'.
32  Pater, W. Review of Mary Ward's translation, quoted on htttp:||pater.the free library.com/The_Guardian/2_1
33  Amiel, F. Introduction p xli.
34  GCPPT 1|1|26 23 September 1921.
35  The quotation is taken from *The Blind Greek* (*To Malise* pp 45–47) written in Boston on 21 March 1908.
36  Tillyard, Ae. *Can I be a Mystic?* pp 43–44.
37  Thomas à Kempis (1380–1471) was an Augustinian canon in the monastery of Mount St Agnes of which his elder brother John was prior. His *Imitation of Christ* was probably written around the time of his

ordination in 1413. Worth noting in connection with what follows is that not only was Thomas à Kempis a monk from the age of about twenty and had therefore no adult experience of the joys of personal relationships but also that his childhood must have been darkened by the recollections of his slightly older and adult contemporaries of the death and destruction wrought by cyclical recurrences of the 'Black Death' which invaded Europe in 1348, 1361 and 1368.

38  Tillyard, Ae. *Christian Old Age* p 7.
39  GCPPT 1|1|73 10 June 1956.
40  GCPPT 1|1|48 19 July 1935.
41  GCPPT 1|1|9 11 November 1902.
42  ibid. 6 September 1902.
43  GCPPT 1|1|10 8 December 1902.
44  A Kempis, T. Book 2 (Counsels on the Inner Life) ch 12.
45  GCPPT 1|1|10 16 December 1902.
46  GCPPT 1|1|11 22 December 1903. An extended reference to Khayyám as a follower of a religion of Love, namely Sufism, appears in *Spiritual Exercises* pp 150–152.
47  GCPPT 1|1|19 28 August 1902.
48  GCPPT 1|1|4 23 May 1900.
49  ibid. 27 November 1898.
50  GCPPT 1|1|18 7 January 1913.
51  GCPPT 1|1|5 4 June 1900.
52  GCPPT 1|1|8 18 August 1901.
53  GCPPT 1|1|21 7 June 1916.
54  GCPPT 1|1|13 8 June 1906.
55  Robert Tillyard (1881–1937), son of Alfred Tillyard's cousin John Joseph Tillyard, matriculated at Queens' College Cambridge in October 1900 where he read mathematics, graduating senior optime in 1903. The early onset of rheumatoid arthritis proscribed the military career on which he had set his heart and in 1904 he began a fourth year of study reading Oriental Languages and Theology with a view to entering the church but worsening of his condition compelled emigration to a warmer climate. He later married Pattie Craske, Aelfrida's friend from Newnham College, she believing Robert and Pattie's marriage 'was of [her] making' (GCPPT 1|1|16 14 March 1908). Robert (as Robin) subsequently became a distinguished entomologist. For further details of his life see *Who Was Who* vol 13.
56  GCPPT 1|1|8 5 October 1901.
57  GCPPT 1|1|10 8 March 1903.
    GCPPT 3 Letter from Julius Tillyard to Aelfrida of 3 August 1947. In his introduction to *The Letters of ACW Tillyard* (MTC), Julius attributes inspiration for his sister's 'vein of mysticism' to teenage readings of W. James' *The Varieties of Mystical Experience*.
58  GCPPT 1|1|8 5 October 1901.
59  GCPPT 1|1|9 30 July and 4 August 1902.
60  Tillyard, Ae. *Christian Old Age* p 86.
61  GCPPT 1|3. A literary evocation of this experience may appear in a poem *Morning in Spring*, written in Emden in May 1911 but subtitled 'the picture is near Fulbourn', a small village to the southeast of Cambridge, two lines in particular ("Sorrow is strong but stronger still is joy / And I am rich in springtime strength today") evoke her empowerment (GCPPT 2|5). The poem remained unpublished.
62  GCPPT 1|2.
63  GCPPT 1|1|11 27 December 1903.
64  GCPPT 1|1|11 1 January 1904 'I make my good resolutions at the beginning of the *academic* year!'
65  ibid. 13 February 1904.
66  GCPPT 1|2.
67  GCPPT 1|1|72a Letter from Aelfrida to Alfred Tillyard of 21 December 1904.
68  GCPPT 1|1|21 6 December 1915.
69  ibid. 9 December 1915.

70  St John of the Cross (1542–1591), a Spanish Carmelite monk, was a follower and colleague of St Teresa of Avila. For a summary of his life and thought see King, U. pp 153–157.
71  Tillyard, Ae. *The Making of a Mystic* p25.
72  For a brief informative description of the life of Stephen Grellet (1773–1855) see http:|| www.famous americans.net/stephen grellet/
73  GCPPT 1|1|22 19 March 1918.
74  ibid. 20 March 1918.
75  *Les Grands Mystiques Chrétiens* was first published in 1908. An erudite and sympathetic analysis of the minds of those who "*doit appréhender immédiatement le divin, éprouver intérieurement la présence divine*" and who operate, as a result, in an exalted state "*où la personnalité ordinaire disparâit*" (op. cit. p vii), it is essential reading for anyone engaged in the study of mystics and Mysticism. Aelfrida speaks of it approvingly even when she disagrees with Delacroix' premise that mystics' mindsets are the product of their unconscious ('subliminal') minds rather than of omnipresent and omnipotent Deity; Evelyn Underhill, on the other hand, praises Delacroix because his conclusions were entirely free from theological bias (*The Mystic Way* p 7).
76  For details of the life of the Spanish Carmelite nun, Teresa of Avila (1515–1582), see King, U. pp 149–153.
77  Henry Suso (1295–1366) was a German Dominican monk whose asceticism is vividly described in his autobiography. See King, U. pp 110–114 for details of his life.
78  Stephen, C. *Quaker Strongholds* p 35.
79  ibid. pp 36–39.
80  Tillyard, Ae. *Spiritual Exercises* pp 1–2.
81  ibid. pp 2–3.
82  GCPPT 1|2.
83  Tillyard, Ae. *Spiritual Exercises* pp 3–5.
84  ibid.
85  ibid. pp 9–10.
86  ibid. p 11.
87  ibid. p 13.
88  ibid. p 12.
89  ibid. p 10.
90  ibid.
91  GCPPT 1|1|22 20 March 1918.
92  Tillyard, Ae. *Spiritual Exercises* p 5.
93  ibid. p 165.
94  ibid. p 7.
95  ibid. p 165.
96  ibid. p 15.
97  ibid. p 167.
98  GCPPT 1|1|26 Diary of Meditations. 22 September 1921 10pm.
99  Tillyard, Ae. *Spiritual Exercises* p 18.
100 GCPPT 1|1|26 Diary of Meditations. 22 September 1921 10pm. Tillyard, Ae. *Spiritual Exercises* p 20.
101 Tillyard, Ae. *Spiritual Exercises* p 19.
102 GCPPT 1|1|26 Diary of Meditations. 24 September (10pm) and 26 September (10 pm) 1921.
103 ibid. Diary of Meditations. 24 September 1921 10pm.
104 Tillyard, Ae. *Spiritual Exercises* p 22.
105 Tillyard, Ae. *Can I be a Mystic?* pp 103–104. The examples given ('Meditations from my MS collection') are largely Aelfrida's own. GCPPT 1|1|26 Diary of Meditations. 18 October 1921 (6.45am) and 22 October 1921 (10pm).
106 GCPPT 1|1|26 Diary of Meditations. 22 September 1921 (10pm) and 23 September 1921 (6.15am).
107 GCPPT 1|1|26 Diary of Meditations. 22 September 1921–29 September 1921. GCPPT 1|1|31 11 October 1925–5 November 1925.
108 Tillyard, Ae. *A Little Road-Book for Mystics* p 45.
109 GCPPT 1|1|20 10 October 1914.

110 GCPPT 1|1|26. Diary of Meditations. 6 October 1921. No time given.

111 Tillyard, Ae. *Spiritual Exercises* p 14.

112 ibid. pp 189–190.

113 GCPPT 1|1|20 10 October 1914.

114 GCPPT 1|1|26 Diary of Meditations. 30 September 1921 (10pm).

115 ibid. Diary of Meditations. 4 October 1921 (7.15am).

116 Tillyard, Ae. *Spiritual Exercises* p 197.

117 GCPPT 1|1|20 10 October 1914.

118 ibid. 10 December 1914.

119 ibid. 9 September 1915.

120 Tillyard, Ae. *Spiritual Exercises* pp 57–58.

121 GCPPT 1|1|20 31 August 1914.

122 GCPPT 1|1|21 30 June and 20 December 1916.

123 GCPPT 1|1|21 21 November 1916.

124 GCPPT 1|1|22 3 March 1918.

125 GCPPT 1|1|21 21 November 1916.

126 GCPPT 1|1|20 28 March 1915.

127 GCPPT 1|1|21 23 December 1915.

128 ibid. 21 November 1916.

129 GCPPT 1|1|22 7 July 1918.

130 ibid. 2 January 1918.

131 GCPPT 1|1|21 30 June 1916.

132 ibid. 21 November 1916.

133 ibid. 20 December 1916.

134 GCPPT 1|1|22 7 July 1918.

135 GCPPT 1|1|21 24 December 1916.

136 GCPPT 1|1|26 29 October 1921.

137 GCPPT 1|1|21 24 December 1916. Rather oddly, Aelfrida does not associate her experience of dematerialisation with concurrent experiences in the spirit world, Edward Spearing, for example, having been unable to 'materialise' properly a few days prior to this diary entry.

138 GCPPT 1|1|22 5 and 7 July 1918.

139 GCPPT 1|1|20 19 January 1915.
GCPPT 1|1|23 20 September 1918.

140 GCPPT 1|1|21 23 December 1915.

141 GCPPT 1|1|22 5 July 1918.

142 GCPPT 1|1|26 5 and 8 February 1922.

143 GCPPT 1|1|20 27 September 1913.

144 ibid. 4 November 1914.

145 Crowley, A. *Olla* p 19.

146 Kaczynski, R. p 138 (2002). Crowley's first experience of his Holy Guardian Angel was in March 1904 while in Cairo with his first wife, Rose Kelly, although it was not until some years later that he actually granted Aiwass a name as well as a title.

147 Letter from Aleister Crowley to Gerald Yorke of 9 March 1945 quoted by Kaczynski, R. pp 101 and 508 ref (2002).

148 Tillyard, Ae. *Can I be a Mystic?* pp 81–82 and 91–92.

149 The nature and role of 'holy angel–guardians' is described at some length in Alban Butler's *The Lives of the Fathers, Martyrs and Other Principle Saints*, first published between 1756 and 1759 and thereafter in many editions. Butler's description of 'angel–guardians' as spirits chosen by God "to be particular guardians to each of us", be we in a state of grace or among "sinners and infidels", and whose role encompasses both protective watchfulness and compassionate friendship (op. cit. vol. 3 pp 1183–1188) may have been read by Aelfrida while convalescent in the Fiesole convent ('too much Lives of the Saints made my head spin' GCPPT 1|1|12 27 February 1905) in which case she was already familiar with the concept of superior beings created by God acting "in various dispensations" towards beings inferior to themselves.

150 GCPPT 1|1|26 Diary of Meditations. 4 October 1921 (10pm).

151 Tillyard, Ae. *Can I be a Mystic?* p 91.

152 ibid. p 81.

153 Tillyard, Ae. *Marrying a Stranger* p 122.

154 Tillyard, Ae. *Can I be a Mystic?* p 108.

155 GCPPT 1|1|22 11 September 1917.

156 GCPPT 1|1|20 12 and 13 August 1915.

157 ibid. 28 August 1914.

158 Steven, C. *Quaker Strongholds* p 36.

159 Tillyard, Ae. *Can I be a Mystic?* p108.

160 GCPPT 1|3.

161 GCPPT 1|1|26 3 December 1921.

162 GCPPT 1|1|20 11 July 1915. Aelfrida may have derived this notion from Henri Delacroix' suggestion (quoted by Evelyn Underhill in *The Mystic Way* p 248) "that permanent consciousness of the Divine does not suspend practical activity". Although elsewhere Aelfrida dismisses Evelyn Underhill as " 'mixed pickles', religion and psychology mixed up" (*The Making of a Mystic* p 25), it is obvious that she was greatly influenced by Underhill's two recently published books, *The Mystic Way* of 1913 and *Practical Mysticism* of 1914.

163 GCPPT 1|1|20 5 October 1914.

164 Underhill, E. *The Mystic Way* p 149.

165 GCPPT 1|1|20 15 January 1915.

166 GCPPT 1|1|26 19 December 1921.

167 Given that it too can induce 'visionary' experiences, temporal lobe epilepsy could be postulated as another causative factor though one cannot, of course, prove that Aelfrida suffered from it. She herself was aware of the connection between physiological brain disorders and intense religious experience ("I once heard", she wrote, "a Swiss professor say visions were an early stage of epilepsy." *The Centaur* p 158 GCPPT 2|21|1) and that Paul's vision on the Damascus road was regarded by some as an epileptiform manifestation but never suggests it as a possible cause of her own; divinity not disease gave rise to hers.

168 GCPPT 1|1a *Agatha's Record Book* 6 September 1911.

169 Opium tablets usually contained 1, 2 or 3 grains of the drug, roughly equivalent to 6, 12, or 18 mg. (Children were given proportionately smaller doses, usually in liquid form.) 10 mg would be considered an average adult dose of modern opiates. Opium consumption was particularly high in fenland areas around Cambridge for the treatment of 'fen ague' (English malaria) prevalent until the early years of the twentieth century; its use as a sedative was also widespread. Opium in various forms was easy to obtain; indeed, it was often peddled door to door by local producers until successive Pharmacy Acts restricted its sale to registered chemists.

170 Tillyard, Ae. *Christian Old Age* p 114.

171 De Quincey, T. p 224. Thomas de Quincey (1785–1859) became addicted to opium as student after taking it to relieve toothache.

172 ibid p 224.

173 Tillyard, Ae. *Can I be a Mystic?* p101.

174 De Quincey, T. p 223.

175 Tillyard, Ae. op. cit. p 100. There is also a remarkable resemblance between Lovat Frazer's mournful illustration *Heaven's Full* in *The Cambridge Magazine* (vol 11 No12 8 February 1913 p 293) and some of Aelfrida's gloomier visions.

176 De Quincey, T. p 223.

177 Tillyard, Ae. op. cit. pp 100–101.

178 De Quincey, T. p 224.

179 Tillyard, Ae. op. cit. pp 100 and 106

180 GCPPT 1|1|21 6 December 1915.

181 De Quincey, T. p 224.

182 GCPPT 1|1|20 6 March 1915.

183 ibid. 15 January 1915.

184 ibid.

185 ibid. 6 March 1915.

186 GCPPT 1|1|21 6 January 1917.

187 GCPPT 1|1|20 7 June 1915.

188 GCPPT 1|1|21 14 September 1916.

189 ibid. 27 October 1915.

190 GCPPT 1|1|7a.

# Aelfrida Tillyard, Straightener

In answer to a "burning question" posed in 1902 "should women work?" Jane Harrison of Newnham, toiler in academic fields, answered "no, not as things are at present". Aelfrida, writing as 'Pertilote' in the *Cambridge Independent Press* of 22 August 1902, discussed the pros and cons ("a woman should not, because of some fanciful ideas about equality of the sexes, leave a home where she is really wanted and rush into employment for which she is physically unsuited. [But] nor should she … stay at home with her hands folded [as] a burden on her family") but concluded that a woman must decide "at the bar of her own conscience" whether or not to work outside the home. In March 1915 she joined the Cambridge branch of the National Union of Women Workers (its Cambridge branch was chaired by Florence Keynes; Catharine Tillyard joined in 1912, the same year as her friend) on the grounds that 'men have made such a mess of this world … 'tis time women taught them better'.[1] Ironic as this may seem with regard to one whose conscience forbade 'war-work' and who preferred to set other people to work while she sat still and did nothing (the irony, one hopes, was not lost on her mother to whom Aelfrida had recently suggested the benefits to education of even more meetings than Chiara already organised and attended), her justification for joining the NUWW seems to have been that she too was a worker, her 'work' being the 'Great Work' of bringing mankind 'to knowledge of the Divine in him'.

Two months after her *Arcanum Arcanorum* experience of 24 October 1913 Aelfrida described an urge 'to take a staff and a mystic robe and tell the people of [her] vision'[2] but knowing what Constantine's reaction would be if she did, she imposed silence on herself until his wartime absence abroad and her increasing sense of being 'thrillingly conscious of God' made her 'want to be *doing* for Him'.[3] Her 'want to be doing' was supported by dabblings in theologies which suggested that ordinary people like herself contained a representative spark of God's own nature, albeit muffled by the pressures of the physical world, and could achieve direct communion with God by blowing life into it. (And by removing the pressure.) Having achieved direct communion with God, they could then act – indeed, it was incumbent on them to act – as mediators between God and other people

### CAN I BE A MYSTIC ?

I. *From* the Author *to* the Stranger.

Cambridge.

YOU ask me, " Can I be a mystic?" I answer, " Yes, by the grace of God, you can."

Of course, I should like to know just what was in your mind when you put that question, but I think I can guess. You feel two things—a distaste, and a hope.

Let us consider the distaste. If I am wrong in my diagnosis, you must tell me so. Your letter, however, was so much like a picture of my own thoughts and aspirations some years back, that I cannot help thinking that we have heard the same call and responded in much the same way. This, I believe, is a very ordinary experience, and I am glad that it should be so. A mystic is not an odd, queer, out-of-the-way being, but a normal man who tries to commune with God.

Very well, then, Stranger. You are not satisfied with yourself. You are restless, you cast about this way and that for satisfaction, you are impatient, you long for peace in your soul. Yet the more you

13

*Can I be a Mystic?*

who wished achieve knowledge of the Divine in them. So she put her plan into action.

Believing with Evelyn Underhill that there was an "abundance of practical work" to do as "the direct outcome of [her] mystical experience"[4] and knowing herself to be a good teacher but disregarding both her father's criticism of her inveterate propensity for setting her neighbours to rights and St John of the Cross' strictures concerning beginners who "develop a desire somewhat vain … to speak of spiritual things in others' presence and sometimes even to instruct rather than be instructed"[5], Aelfrida launched her new career as mystico-theological lecturer, preacher, counsellor, and writer.

Writing in 1958 to Girton College librarian Helen McMorran, she explained why she began it by giving lectures: "I had no right to lecture on Mysticism at all but being parked [in Cambridge] during the 1914–18 war I wanted to attend lectures but there were none, so I gave them myself!"[6] In *Can I be a Mystic?*, however, she gives the real reason:"I had been studying Mysticism and the Psychology of Religion in a desultory (*sic*) sort of way for some time, when, in 1915, my guardian angel commanded me to give some lectures on Spiritual Exercises".[7]

Aware of the limitations of her knowledge of the theological background to what she was about to stand and deliver (something Miss Ridding pointed out in no uncertain terms) and suffering in consequence from unusual loss of confidence in speaking in public (something she had once loved to do because she believed it her moral duty), Aelfrida confronted her guardian angel, telling him "the thing was impossible". Excuses that "no-one would give me a lecture-room, no-one would come and listen to me, that I knew next to nothing of the subject, and so on" were discounted by the angel who told her "go and see Professor CS Myers". She did. "He received me as though his mind had been prepared beforehand to be specially courteous to me". Unable to disregard the angel's promptings any longer (he even, she said, rounded up her audience and instructed her to publish the lectures in book-form as *Spiritual Exercises*), she did her best: "the course was a complete success".[8] Whether her guardian angel also moved John McTaggart, the then University Recorder, to have her lectures placed on the official lecture list for December 1924 where her name joined those of eminent academics Arthur Pigou, Bertrand Russell, Arthur Quiller-Couch, and McTaggart himself or arranged for Frederick Bartlett of the Psychological Laboratory[9] to attend her lecture to the Heretics and to invite her to lecture on related topics in the Laboratory itself, she does not say.

Her guardian-angel-directed compulsion to lecture in the Psychological Lecture Room on Spiritual Exercises in the Higher Religions and their Psychological Results and concerning which she commented excitedly 'Cambridge University looks so impregnable from the outside [but] a few blasts of the trumpets, a little faith, and the walls of Jericho fall down!'[10], provided her with a further excuse for shutting out the horrors of war. Seeing her closeted in Fordfield study preparing for this and subsequent lecture-series 'as if the war did not exist', Willie Searle informed her that 'everybody ought to be interested in the war'[11] and Chiara wondered aloud if her daughter had 'not much heart'. Aelfrida herself affected boredom with the war and with discussions concerning

her 'qualities and defects', saying she would rather think about God[12], but from her keenness to proceed with a task which she found more intellectually and emotionally onerous than anticipated, one can deduce that escapism was as much a motivating factor as the behests of her guardian angel.

Her compulsion to tell people of her 'vision' was so strong that her first lecture series was held even before Constantine left for Amsterdam. (It was given on a weekday while he was in London so he was unable to attend. Aelfrida makes no comment with regard to her husband's reaction to her defiance of his earlier instructions not to speak in public or, indeed, with regard to her giving a course of lectures at all, but his chagrin at discovering that the wife whose intellect he despised was lecturing at his old university must have been acute. Worse still, she lectured as 'Mrs Constantine Graham'.) The title of her first lecture, given on 21 January 1915, cannot now be ascertained but seems from her comments ('it is too early to judge yet whether anyone really *understood*') to have been of an introductory and explanatory nature. Her guardian angel, she noted with relief, 'didn't play [her] false', for over fifty people including 'lots of undergraduates' attended and she herself 'was not all nervous [and] spoke well and clearly'.[13]

Her second lecture, on *Hinduism*, given on 28 January, was so well attended that she and her audience (it included Frank Stokoe, George von Kaufmann, Learned Twin Mrs Gibson, Frederick Bartlett, and don Jane Harrison) had to move to a larger room in the Physiological Laboratory which smelt disconcertingly 'of anaesthetics and dissected rats' and had a wonky blackboard. Undeterred by this and by the presence of an Indian undergraduate whose eyes gleamed with amusement at her mispronunciation of Pali, Aelfrida spoke glowingly 'of gurus with bands of devoted disciples in temple gardens' but failed to make her audience '*see*'; instead, 'they looked on and thought what queer horrid ways those funny Indian savages indulge in … I did want them to understand a little more'.[14] Her third lecture (4 February) on *Buddhism*, was more successful, her guardian angel having promised that 'as thy faith is so shall thy strength be' and Lilian Whitehouse to pick her up if she fainted.

Fidelio's enthusiasm, the fact that a combination of spiritual exercises and attendance at her first three lectures had transformed one of her student-experimenters (a theologian from Westminster College) from cocky undergraduate to someone forced to admit that 'he didn't quite know his way all round the mysteries of the universe' yet, and her guardian angel's admonition that she '*was*' to go on, persuaded the flagging lecturer to continue, her fourth lecture on *Mohammedan Meditation* on 12 February being 'quite a success'. It even began to seem, she and Dr Searle agreed, as if 'the world [was] on the brink of a great mystical revival'.[15]

Of her fifth lecture of 18 February on *Christian Meditations*, Aelfrida says nothing except that 'no-one but [God] will ever know what it cost me. May it be to His glory'[16], though it is obvious that lecturing to a largely academic audience on a subject close to her heart occasioned much emotional strain. Though she begged her guardian angel 'mayn't I have a holiday – oh *please*!'[17], it seems he refused, for her sixth and last lecture on *Modern Gnostic Cults* took place on 15 February. (Did she mention Ceremonial Magic, one wonders, or confine herself to Theosophy and the like? She does not say.) Unsure, in spite of a phenomenal amount of research in a very short time, as to 'whether the [lecture] was very brilliant', she was nevertheless gratified to discover people crowding round her afterwards 'wanting to ... talk it all over'. This led her to hope that ensuing discussions with interested parties would enable her to discover 'whether I have really been able to do as the Guardian Angel said'.[18] Bartlett being moderately enthusiastic and Aelfrida herself experiencing 'the same overwhelming sense of compulsion'[19] to lecture in spite of discovering that working so hard on her lectures meant that she had to give up meditating ('one can't work two sets of brain-centres ... at the same time, there isn't enough nervous energy to go round')[20], she arranged to deliver another series on associated topics early the following year.

Her second lecture series took place between 22 January and 27 February 1916. Due to the popularity of the first series, she and her band of devotees were promoted to the larger Physiology Lecture Room, a privilege accorded because she agreed to lecture on Saturday afternoons when the Department was otherwise unused. The *Cambridge Magazine*, "with a pleasure which will be shared by all who heard her course last year", publicised the new series of six lectures by "Mrs Constantine Graham (Aelfrida Tillyard)" under the title of *The Development of the Religious Consciousness in the East and West*[21], but were it not for the magazine also listing the contents of the lectures (*The Religion of Childhood; Conversion; Spiritual Exercises; Miraculous Powers attributed to Saints; The Devil; Two Modern Mystics,* and *Religious Development according to Eastern and Western Psychologists*), one would not discover from Aelfrida's diary on which topics she spoke and what she said.

She began the new lecture-series with trepidation. Having announced to Frederick Bartlett early in January that it was ready ('paper and sticks and coal ... waiting for the Divine Fire! ... one of my household similes so jeered at by Constantine')[22], she worried during her introductory lecture, given to nearly seventy people on 22 January, that she had 'laid [her] sacrifice on the altar but no fire from heaven came down to consume it'. (The absence of undergraduates, more of whom were in the trenches, deepened her despondency.) Lack of fire she attributed to her being currently 'far from God'[23] (migraines and rheumatoid arthritis had worsened, Dr Hare's suggestion therapy had failed, her sister-in-law Irene Hillerns had had a second son, Michael – he would later reappear in his aunt's life in unusual circumstances – and her ninth wedding anniversary had reminded her of Constantine's 'dissatisfactions', chiefly with herself)[24] but it may be that in pleading the necessity of applying a "scientific spirit" ("the humble and reverent desire to learn of facts")[25] to religious experience in order to discover of what the "development of religious consciousness" consisted, Aelfrida found the gulf between scientific rigour and mystic ecstasy too wide to bridge; indeed, a review by George von Kaufmann of her first lecture series concludes by making just this point.[26]

Of her second lecture *(The Religion of Childhood)* Aelfrida's diary fails to note if she included a topic of much interest to herself, namely American psychologist ED Starbuck's theory that the onset of puberty and the beginnings of a serious interest in religion, while not necessarily exactly coincident, tended to supplement and support each other, with girls who developed the interest ("converted") at thirteen or sixteen having their menarche at fourteen. (13.8 years to be exact; Aelfrida's 'conversion' at fifteen and onset of puberty at thirteen fitted Starbuck's theory exactly.)[27] Her *Cambridge Magazine* reviewer, however, emphasised her point that *all* children "have naturally a dim and obscure perception of a spiritual world" which fades as they grow up but reappears in adolescence as a "spontaneous awakening" and noted that "the most ordinary individuals see visions and hear voices at the time of religious awakening".[28] This suggests that Aelfrida used (without sourcing them) her own childhood and adolescent experiences as examples and possibly as psychologist-supported explanations for the more bizarre aspects of her behaviour at the time of her own 'conversion'.

Of the fourth lecture on 29 January she recorded that the 'sacrifice was accepted and my guardian angel spoke through me'. (She also noted that she had provided her audience with 'a decent amount of learning' so use of a university lecture room was not entirely farcical; Chiara, who attended all her lectures, suggested that she had been 'a little too sermony'.)[29] Her anonymous reviewer, expatiating on the content of this lecture, explained that spiritual exercises (especially those invoking the name of Deity) were devised "for the expansion of ... religious consciousness" and noted her recommendation of music as an aid to meditation[30], a point enlarged upon in *Spiritual Exercises* with reference to Sufism: "music is, of course, recognised in every religion as an aid to devotion. To the Sufi it is more than this; it is of the very atmosphere of the spiritual life itself".[31] Of her fifth lecture, *Supranormal Powers attributed to Saints*, she commented 'I thought it a little queer myself, and not particularly inspired'[32]; her reviewer, on the other hand, described it as an exposition of how holy men and women develop supernormal abilities, "some useful, some merely strange".[33] Following the lecture, Lilian Whitehouse was moved to describe Aelfrida as simultaneously "a kind of Buddha sitting on a high hill and giving an occasional dispassionate glance at the sorrows of the world" and "a thoroughgoing British matron", but although Lilian's description of the 'curse of duality' currently plaguing her was entirely accurate, Aelfrida regarded neither attribution as complimentary.[34]

Her sixth lecture on *The Devil*, held on 12 February, was somewhat sensational, for it included "some fine devil-stories"[35] given to an audience who 'wanted their ears tickled with private information about his Satanic Majesty'.[36] It was also the product of a good deal of research ('information on the devil in different religions and some half dozen fine theories of what experience of evil outside one's self might be')[37] and of (probably unacknowledged) personal experience. Eustace, who had recently experienced more than most people present of a phenomenon described by his sister's reviewer as "good men's experience of evil forces"[38] and who had become an agnostic as a result, attended the lecture in military uniform while home on leave, something which may have prompted her to write that "we have stood helpless watching men … perpetrate deeds which we recognised as diabolical. Had the devil been mere legend or symbolism such deeds would never have been done".[39] Her conviction that the Devil was a real entity was, however, derived from something more than fraternal descriptions of the horrors of trench warfare: Aelfrida had seen him, or, more accurately, experienced manifestations of the evil forces he controlled.

On the afternoon of 17 January 1902, the day after she attended a dance of which the now rather blasé debutante wrote dismissively 'all dances are very much alike. The … girls look nice in white and the … men look foolish … Chaperones all look bored and supper always *looks* nice and *is* nasty'[40], was resting on a bed in a darkened room. (The bed for some inexplicable reason was her father's, he being the man who had oracularly informed her in her early teens that 'devils' – and angels – 'really existed' and that he himself had once had direct experience of 'Satanic Majesty'.)[41] As she lay there thinking, so

she said, of the limitations of Christian knowledge, she experienced 'spirits – I cannot put it more plainly – … very close to me. I felt them all around … I called them to help me – to give me knowledge of things'. What happened next could barely be expressed: she seemed to be 'surrounded by fire. A spirit said "Look!" but I did not dare [because] I felt that the spirits were evil. For a second I believed I was lost. Then I breathed a prayer and the spirits vanished with a noise like crackling, while I lay back exhausted on the bed'.[42] If this teenage brush with forces of evil – she even made a Faustian pact to pay whatever price they exacted for providing her with 'knowledge of things' – was used without attribution as an example of that of which 'evil outside one's self' might consist, the immediacy of her description would have made her lecture even more absorbing to her listeners. (Unfortunately from the point of view of lecture material, her next recorded diabolic experience did not occur until January 1917 when, reflecting smugly on a good deed recently done, she suddenly 'hallucinated' – her word – a mirror in front of her 'in which my smiling, virtuous face was reflected – and then, ah! just behind me, a devil …'; convinced of the Devil's existence, she quickly assured God that she was 'more in love with [Him] than ever'.)[43] Her anonymous reviewer, however, was as unforthcoming as herself with regard to the content of what must have been a gripping lecture.

Neither does he refer to the content of her penultimate lecture, held on 19 February, nor name the 'two modern mystics' whose mystical experiences Aelfrida proposed to describe. One remains anonymous; the other was herself, her guardian angel having told her 'to speak of [her] own experiences'. Although originally intending to describe them as her own (whether of her own volition or at the bidding of her guardian angel, she does not say), her mother's suspicions were aroused when Aelfrida requested that she not attend this particular lecture so Chiara having begged her daughter to 'preserve a discreet anonymity', Aelfrida spoke of herself in the third person as 'Sarasvati'. No-one, she thought, guessed: 'perhaps [her] complete self-possession deceived them'. Fortunately, too, the audience, satiated with devil-stories, was 'rather small'. Complete self-possession notwithstanding, Aelfrida found the lecture 'a great ordeal', being unwell before and after it; lecturing in public on very personal matters was not, after all, something to which she was accustomed. In spite of this, of not yet having 'come out' as a mystic, and of never having experienced her 'queer division of personality' quite so acutely as when talking about herself in the abstract (part of her, she noted, coolly explained and discussed 'the material for an excellent psychological study' while another part

– a 'queer thing of fire'– stood beside her 'living all the explanations over again and burning with hope that they might be profitable' to her listeners), she found the experience worthwhile, first, because she felt herself more a 'part of humanity rather than an individual self' as a result of sharing pseudonymised experiences with other people, second, because her ordeal had been preceded by two overwhelming but reassuring 'experiences of the presence of God'.[44]

The 'experiences' (she fails to describe them) carried her through her last lecture on 26 February. (The Oracle was in the audience and 'intimidated [her] a little'.)[45] The lecture, billed as a description of 'Religious Development in East and West', was actually, as Aelfrida's reviewer pointed out, a description of the Mystic Way in general and of the Christian Mystic Way in particular. Aelfrida herself became so carried away with enthusiasm for her subject that she ended by prophesying that in course of time ordinary men and women would enjoy both 'that constant and intense sense of the presence of God … hitherto the privilege of saints' (or, as her reviewer put it more prosaically, "the normal religious person would develop the peculiar form of spiritual consciousness … hitherto the privilege of the few") and a sense of 'the unity of the human race as a *fact in consciousness*': "humanity is one".[46]

Her third lecture series took place in January/February 1917. Having been 'busy with Buddhism' for some time, she had already devised three lectures on *The Nature of Religious Experience in Buddhism* when her guardian angel 'stepped in' to suggest that lectures on *Practical Mysticism* might be more appropriate.[47] So 'practical mysticism' it was, supported by the presence at her lectures of Aelfrida's 'extraordinarily handsome' (and rich) young relative Ernie Crundwell[48] and by help and advice from Mirzà Issa Sadiq who overcame his dislike of the Baha'i faith sufficiently to chant a poem in praise of Behá'-u'-illá at a climactic point in the last lecture.

The series, actually entitled *The Practice of Mysticism,* began with its lecturer in the throes of depression: 'the war weighs heavily on everyone … there are moments when one realises how thin is the ice which separates one from calamity [and] there is nothing but to cast oneself on God, to go down into the dark if need be, trusting to find Him there [though] God, who ought to be one's life appears [only] as an escape'.[49] To begin a new series of lectures on the subject closest to her heart when she herself was oppressed by war-induced and personal woes (Constantine in Amsterdam 'posing as misunderstood'[50]; imposition of food-rationing reminding her of 'the pain of all mothers of starving children' and promoting 'universal consciousness' on their behalf

so agonisingly intense that the 'dreadful gripes in [her] inn'ards'[51] brought on by having to ingest porridge and potatoes instead of more delicate fare paled in comparison) did not augur well but her mood lightened almost as soon as she began and became positively jocular by the end.

The first lecture, held on 27 January 1917 with Dr Searle and Mr Strachan, the then minister of St Columba's, in the audience, was entitled *The Characteristics and Dangers of Mysticism*. Lacking George von Kaufmann's commentary (the conscientious objector had substituted Wandsworth Prison for Cambridge University), we are reliant on Aelfrida's diary for descriptions of the content of individual lectures but other than comments about her audience ('a queer odd and endy lot')[52], their reaction ('it went well')[53], her delivery ('I think I managed to be a little simpler')[54] and her subject ('I was touching on matters too high for me')[55], entries are so brief as to be uninformative. This is disappointing, given that the subject of her second lecture (3 February) was *The Relation of Mysticism to Ethics, Theology and Occultism* (a topic which may have formed the basis for *A Little Road-Book for Mystics*) and that the third, *The Psychology of the Beginner,* given on 10 February, included a discussion of different subjects for meditation (Universal Love, the Points of the Compass meditation, etc.) and what was entailed in the meditative Practice of the Presence of God.[56] Of the contents of the fourth lecture, *The Psychology of the "Proficient" and of the "Perfect",* of 19 February, she says nothing, a startling omission given that it must have comprised an exposition of St John of the Cross' three-staged Way of Perfection, a subject close to her heart because she felt that his description of beginners, proficients, and perfects in *The Dark Night of the Soul* mirrored her own spiritual struggle for complete communion with God.[57] Nor does she add anything to the title of the fifth lecture, *Christian and non-Christian Religious Experience,* given on 24 February, beyond the comment that 'Professor de la Vallée Poussin and Mr Thomas, two of the greatest living authorities on Buddhism were both there. How intimidating!'[58], leaving us to hope that much of what she said was reiterated in *Spiritual Exercises,* begun within a week of the lecture.

The sixth lecture, given on 3 March, is untitled in her diary but according to the calendar of events in *The Cambridge Magazine* was called *The Present Position of Mysticism*.[59] It included discussions of 'the essential one-ness of all spiritual religion' and 'the reality of the unity of man'[60] but beyond listing the points in her diary, Aelfrida does not enlarge on them. She tells us, however, that Mirzà Issa Sadiq's singing of it was intended to underline the importance for her and for her audience of the Baha'i Prayer for Unity which she read (in translation) as the climax of the lecture; earlier the same day while meditating on the Prayer she had become 'caught up in a kind of ecstasy'[61] whose essence remained with her while she spoke. Emotionally exhausted but happy to have expressed everything her guardian angel bade her and she herself felt compelled to say, she decided 'I don't want to lecture any more'.[62]

Her resolution was short-lived. In January 1918 she was invited to read a paper on *The Psychology of Meditation* at the 5th Conference of Modern Churchmen to be held at Girton College from 5 to 12 August 1918. She accepted immediately and on Chiara suggesting that her daughter stay at Girton for the duration of the conference to make a 'kind of retreat', wrote joyfully 'I should *love* it – beyond all words'.[63]

An invitation to participate in the Conference was an honour insofar as inclusion suggests qualification on the merits of a single book, *The Making of a Mystic*, published the previous year; she was also one of only three female participants, one of the few participants without formal academic qualifications, and a layman. Rather oddly, no mention is made in the Conference prospectus' biographies of each participant of Aelfrida's three lecture series on religious topics; not mentioned either is the fact that she was, in a sense, a 'Modern Churchman' herself: shortly after receiving her invitation to the Conference, she had felt moved to offer herself as part-time minister to the Free Church newly established in the Cambridge suburb of Cherry Hinton, noting 'I long to be accepted [but] if nothing comes of it I shall assume that I am not yet "advanced" enough to be able to preach … to others'.[64] The position, she was informed, was already filled but she hoped that 'an opening may be found for me somewhere. I have so much to say'.[65] Fortunately for the 'invalid' who was insufficiently ill to consider a part-time salaried position but whose alibi might have been discovered for what it was had she taken up regular paid employment, her guardian angel 'had the matter in hand'[66]: she was invited to preach and even to conduct services – fees went to charity – at several villages near Cambridge. She found the experience exhausting but exhilarating ('I love preaching much more than I do lecturing! Lecturing is so cold by comparison')[67] but declined an ancestrally-appropriate invitation from the Particular Baptists because exclusive sectarianism did not accord with her belief in religious unity.[68]

The joys and benefits of collegiate life soon became apparent to one who proudly headed her diary entry of 7 August 1918 '*Girton College, Cambridge*', adding 'I do *love* being here. It seems so wonderful to have a room all my own where I can read and write and do just what I like and to have my time all my own, and no-one to demand anything of me'.[69] She also revelled in informal discussions which took place over meals in hall or in the intervals between sessions ('people keep stopping me in the corridors to ask me things or make remarks')[70], in the formal discussions at the end of each group of lectures (some, discussions 'only by courtesy, being really a series of highly technical sermonettes')[71], in 'thrilling' lectures whose content complemented and expanded knowledge acquired during years of self-motivated research[72], in days which began with Holy Communion and ended with Evensong, in the joy of strolling alone in the college's beautiful grounds where 'the wind in the trees became the Spirit of God' and she herself rapt 'in an ecstasy'.[73] She was also able to explore topics of more personal interest: enquiring apropos Fidelio (she did not disclose his name) of GRS Mead, a member of the audience and 'an expert on the darker ways of psychology', about 'homosexuality', she noted that because Mead talked very seriously to her 'partly in theosophic language' and partly in very plain English, she 'learnt an enormous lot'.[74] There was also the pride of presenting a paper of her own researching and devising, though she had to omit 'great big bits of it because they were too long and too academic'.[75]

Although Aelfrida tells us little of the content of her paper on *The Practice of Devotion and its Psychological Value*, she informs us that in it she made two 'practical suggestions'. (Given that she found the majority of her fellow-participants 'well-meaning mediocrities … pathetically conscious of being out of touch or still more pathetically *unconscious* of being out of touch with ordinary humanity' who preferred talk of 'parishes and preferment' to 'Life … with a big L'[76], she may have included them at the last minute.) Her first suggestion – that 'meeting for silent prayer should be held among Christians of all denominations' – is obviously influenced by her attendance at Quaker meetings. Her second, that modern churchmen should organise 'panels' of qualified 'straighteners' ('I didn't use either of those words!' she confided) to whom people with religious quandaries 'might be referred', evoked a '*fine*' discussion but little actual support.[77] ("The Modern Churchmen", she tells us in 1930, "were not modern enough to agree with my scheme … that there ought to be a kind of Harley Street of religious practitioners to whom all people, sick or well, in need of advice could go. Some of these practitioners should be priests, others laymen and women of religious experience, all equipped with up-to-date psychological knowledge. They told me I was the *enfant terrible* of the Conference and proceeded to discuss other matters".)[78] The second suggestion is significant because her 'war-work' and 'Great Work' already included a form of religious counselling and her suggestion that "the experiment ought to be tried" [79] disingenuous because she had already set herself up as a 'panel' of one, was already calling herself a 'Straightener' (with a capital S), and had already given a lecture to the Heretics entitled *Soul-doctoring as a Profession for the Laity*.[80]

Having decided early in the Great War that she was not going to perform anything that could be construed as 'war-work' but conscious that she found God most easily when helping others (*sic*), Aelfrida devoted herself to other peoples' spiritual development in terms of spiritual 'straightening'. This, though not 'war-work' *as such* was certainly '*doing*' something[81]; indeed, she was extremely busy with a programme which would enable her to help and to inspire others to devise their own "right way of living".[82] This did not mean, so she said, that she intended to make someone 'good' on *her* terms but that the advice she gave them would encourage them to *become* good or, if departed from a 'right way', 'keep them up to the mark'[83] in terms of returning to it.

Keen to pursue the second aim of her 'Great Work', she saw no irony in describing herself as a 'professional' without having undergone a recognised form of training leading to formal recognised qualifications, the which might be inferred from her use of quasi-medical terminology, or in becoming a spiritual director at the same time as declaring herself independent of spiritual direction, or in pursuing a career which if not actually inspired by the onset of the Great War, certainly owed its earliest formal clients to it, or in promoting herself as an altruistic helper of humanity at a time when keener on *self*-development and *self*-preservation. Perhaps no irony was intended, her God-given 'vision' having laid open people's hearts to her and her achievement of 'Universal Consciousness' having enhanced a pre-existing telepathic faculty: 'people instinctively tell me what I know already'.[84] Perhaps closing her own heart to human affections as a result of Constantine's rejection underlined her desperate need to be needed, if not by her husband, then by people as needy as herself, 'higher detachment' deriving from the one combining with emotional neediness to so wholly replace 'person-desiring' with 'desires for God and humanity'[85] that she became altruistic by default at a time when people as needy as herself sought help from anyone who appeared qualified to provide it.

Lacking formal qualifications, what qualifications did Aelfrida possess? She was a mature woman whose demeanour made her look older and wiser than her years and as if she herself had suffered as much as her proposed clients, something which might suggest that having gone through 'fire' herself, she would be sympathetic to those in whose life there was currently little 'garden'. Abhorring 'priestcraft'[86], she seemed willing and able to help others explore the problems they brought to her in a religious context if that was what they wished. She was sufficiently dispassionate to remain objective but was able to give clients the sympathetic attention they needed. 'Straightening' sessions were private and confidential (carefully anonymised anecdotes concerning her clients' religious dilemmas were later used to illustrate a point in books written some time after the 'straightening' depicted) and took place at Fordfield, a detached house where clients' comings and goings could be disguised as social calls. She was known through her lectures as someone engaged in studies of spirituality and as a seeker after knowledge of a currently fashionable kind. Her connections with the Psychological Laboratory would have added to her credibility. Finally, her 1915 lecture series in particular provided exactly the information people sought in exactly the right language for them to understand and it was as a result of people crowding round at the end of a lecture to discuss points she had made, of earlier practice in counselling Little Friends, and of more recent experience of friends and family members suddenly confiding their 'inmost thoughts' (Eustace, though now an unbeliever, admitted to belief in an "Upward Tendency")[87], their spiritual problems (a Presbyterian minister's loss of faith), and private matters undisclosed even to a sister (Aunt Anna, by letter)[88], that she was inspired to adopt the title and profession of "Straightener or Soul-Doctor".[89]

Her reasons for using those particular terms may be deduced from what we know of her life to date. The term 'spiritual director' she uses only to disclaim it ("I am by way of being a spiritual director or, as I prefer to put it, a Straightener")[90], possibly on the grounds that the term was currently associated more with clergy than laity and with men than women, and because she had no wish to be compared with *grands mystiques* who became mystagogues. (It seems, however, that she chose to disregard St John of the Cross' warning of the "indiscreet zeal" and "very vain" desire to "speak of spiritual things in others' presence and sometimes even to instruct rather than be instructed" experienced by spiritual novices "so fervent and diligent in their … undertaking that a certain kind of secret pride is generated in them".)[91] The term 'guru' used in relation to George von Kaufmann (and, briefly, to Bernard Muscio) seems not to have been considered, possibly because too exotic even for broadminded Cambridge or because it had unfortunate personal connotations with regard to the 'Guru' who predicted in Paris that people would come to her for instruction because "you are the Light and the Begetter and Manifester of

Light".[92] Guru might also have equally unfortunate repercussions for one seeking to establish herself as a lay Christian adviser but who not long before had published an anthology containing poems by Aleister Crowley (a suspect mystagogue in some people's eyes) and, in a university magazine, an article defending Ceremonial Magic even though in it she had sought support from Evelyn Underhill's recently published assertion that Ceremonial Magic and psychotherapy were associated: "the ancient occultists owed much of their power … to the fact that they were psychologists before their time … Magic therapeutics, or as it is now called 'mental healing', is but the application of these principles upon another plane".[93] Hence although there was nothing inherent in the term 'guru' to prevent her using it (gender is irrelevant here; what is important is the guru's "reputation for spirituality")[94], she used the term only in the privacy of her diary.

Most commonly she refers to herself as a 'Straightener' ('Aelfrida Tillyard, Straightener, has been quite busy'; 'the Straightener had quite hard work yesterday')[95], having borrowed the term from Samuel Butler's novel *Erewhon* in which physical illness is described as a crime (and punished accordingly) and moral turpitude as the result of pre- or post-natal misfortune and treated (albeit with harsh remedies) by 'straighteners' who have themselves been obliged to practice each vice in turn until sufficiently confident of their ability to subdue it, at which point they are permitted to advise and treat 'patients'.[96] Then too, and although *Erewhon* was first published in 1872, a second edition, prefaced by Butler himself, had appeared as recently as 1901 and an even more recent association may have arisen because a lecture given to the Heretics on the subject of *Samuel Butler and Erewhon* on 12 April 1913 while Aelfrida, alone in England, (Constantine was in Panama) was heavily engaged with Little Friends, of whom Hubert Henderson, a Heretic himself, was one. It may also have been discussions of this event which inspired her to reply to Frank Stokoe's question of June 1914 as to what she proposed to do with her life that 'I would be a Straightener' and him to respond (he had come to see her 'declaring that he was in hell and that all his being was going into the melting-pot etc, etc.') "Aren't you something of that already?"[97]

Though anyone familiar with Butler's novel could relate to the term 'Straightener' or, if unfamiliar, could easily have it explained in relation to what Aelfrida hoped to achieve, her personal preference seems to have been for the term 'soul-doctor', a title lacking *Erewhon*'s association of 'straightening' with moral turpitude. This, though speculation, is supported by Aelfrida herself calling those who came to 'consult' her 'patients' (once 'cured' but still keen to continue discussions on spiritual matters, they became 'pupils'); by her proudly announcing to her diary in March 1915 that she had had her 'first experience as professional (*sic*) soul-doctor' the previous day[98]; by her declaration to Bertrand Russell who, during their 1916 interview asked her what she did "besides writing and all that", that not content with being a 'religious fanatic' (*sic*), she was also a 'Soul-Doctor'[99]; and by her stating in the first book in which she describes herself as 'Straightener or soul-doctor' that "many people are the better for a little soul-doctoring"[100], 'doctoring,' that is to say, rather than mere 'straightening'. The origin of the term 'soul-doctor' is also speculative but given that Aelfrida was impressed in spite of herself by Barbara Ring of the husband and wife team of psychotherapists who ran the sanatorium adjacent to the Grahams' house in Arlington Heights and that she described the Rings as 'mind-doctors' ('mind-doctor' is a reasonable translation of 'psychotherapist') it may be that she turned 'mind' into 'soul' and became a 'soul-doctor'.

Barbara Ring is important in another respect: she was a woman who treated male patients. Studies of Comparative Religion having taught Aelfrida that not only could a woman become a guru but also that women could "rise above the natural inferiority of [their] sex and … act as guru to a man"[101] and a woman act as guru to her son (the close relationship was regarded as particularly efficacious in terms of the latter's spiritual development)[102], it is unsurprising to find Aelfrida practising at the outset of her new career as 'Straightener' on younger men whom she already regarded as spiritual 'sons': Frank Stokoe, Tommy Altounyan, and Hubert Henderson. She behaved towards them, however, less as if pursuing a 'profession for the laity' (only with Fidelio did she act in this capacity and even then it was more in terms of listening patiently while he recounted his miseries than actively acting as therapist) and more as a 'wise woman' (*not* a mother-figure, having tried that approach with Frank Stokoe and succeeding only in alienating him) who treated them as the adult men they now were rather than as the callow undergraduates they had lately been. And, having learnt a salutary lesson from another 'son', namely Constantine, she did not try to mould their minds into conformity with her own but acted only as someone to whom they felt able to confide anything in perfect confidence (she confided what they told her only to her diary – and to her biographer) and from whom they received advice (if sought) and moral support.

In February 1915 Frank Stokoe suffered a mental breakdown, informing Aelfrida that he was "a little afraid of going mad".[103] Aware that Fidelio's 'peculiar states of consciousness' were pathological but lacking knowledge of their aetiology (judging by his symptoms, he suffered from bipolar disorder[104] which gave rise either to depression so severe that poetic inspiration and even the will to live deserted him[105] or to elevated moods in which he was able to write but was exuberantly careless of others' feelings and extravagantly spendthrift; his mother found her son's 'manic' episodes more upsetting than his 'depressive' ones because of the uncontrolled nature of his actions and reactions during that phase)[106], Aelfrida tried to reassure him but found him so tormented that her own 'little hells' seemed 'mild affairs with pink and lemon flames and operatic devils' in comparison with his.[107]

Disabling symptoms persisted for the greater part of the war, with Aelfrida rather than Mrs Stokoe (from whom Frank maintained an emotional and as far as possible a geographical distance) bearing the brunt of his problems for when absent from Cambridge Fidelio wrote frequently, his letters including lengthy descriptions of his tormented frame of mind: 'it is impossible to imagine a more tragic life than his'.[108] Attracted to Fidelio even during his darkest moods because she appreciated the friendship of a fellow writer whose ability to wring the utmost enjoyment from a situation when in an uplifted mood accurately mirrored her own and because even if depressed, he spontaneously understood thoughts she found it difficult to articulate, and though making light of her emotions ('I think I feel about poets – real ones! – as most young ladies do about curates') and wishing that she was in a position to ask Constantine 'oh *doux*, I'm not falling in love with Stokoe, am I?' and to receive his reassuringly grumpy reply ("*how* perfectly preposterous!")[109], Aelfrida realised how easy it would be to become emotionally involved with a man who by the summer of 1918 was sufficiently recovered to attempt poetry again (she sent him some verses of her own, *Words to a Lazy Poet,* to prod him into action)[110] and to tell her gratefully of how much 'peace and strength' he derived from their friendship.[111] It may be, however, that Stokoe did not always find Aelfrida's help as efficacious as she believed it to be; his poem, *Unspoken Dialogue,* quoted in a footnote with reference to Aelfrida's *Puff by Parody,* includes lines which could be taken to refer to a conversation between him and herself: although it begins with the other person's attempts to reassure him that he is not going mad ("I am in hell and you can set me free"/ "You are on earth and in the streets with me"), continues with them withdrawing from Stokoe's "place of doom" because they do not wish to join him there and ends in social niceties which reduce his distress to the level of a childish tantrum: "Here our ways part. When will you come and see me?"

Knowing that Frank Stokoe was 'extraordinarily fond' of her imparted 'unique charm' to a relationship which

because of his proclivities and her marriage seemed unlikely to develop beyond a loving friendship. But his caring for 'the real me' (unlike Constantine, who cared only for his 'glorified imaginings, for all that he said that he knew me')[112] added complications because although it was from the 'real' Aelfrida that Fidelio derived peace and strength, the 'real' Aelfrida of the Great War period was not the 'Aelfrida' with whom Little Friendships were initially forged; further complications arose as a result of their relationship having changed from one in which poet spoke to poet to one in which wounded mind cried for help to wounded soul. Realising the precariousness of Fidelio's mental state, Aelfrida (for once and with difficulty) put another's needs before her own in order to avert a tragic outcome. She also concealed the fact that she had transcended the boundaries of therapeutic intervention by falling in love with her 'patient' – and it is obvious that she *did* fall in love in spite of stating that she felt 'no trace of anything that could possibly be interpreted as love but only intense sympathy with his troubles'[113] – but in August 1918 recorded that 'the battle of "no human consolations"' had had to be fought again in relation to Fidelio and that 'it hurts *acutely*'.[114] The effort cost her dear ('I prayed that God would remove from me whatever kept me from being "non-attached" and I have not quite left off desiring that [Fidelio] should return my affection')[115] and it was not solely apropos an Italian academic towards whom she also felt herself attracted that she decided 'I must have no more friends … until I am indifferent whether or no they love me in return'.[116] Non-attachment won the day and she found herself able to offer Stokoe the supportive but impersonal therapy vital to the treatment of mental disorders.

Her decision was supported by a feeling which grew stronger the more she practised as Straightener, namely an innate dislike of exposing the inmost recesses of her mind and soul to those she regarded as 'patients' (something difficult to avoid when dispensing spiritual counsel based on her own experiences) because revelation resulted in emotional exhaustion, debilitating migraines, and recall of incidents she preferred to forget. Although self-centred Fidelio refrained from asking the probing personal questions posed by some 'patients', she persuaded herself that the 'affinity' (Fidelio's word) [117] which existed between them constituted a similar 'infringement' from which she should recoil. Hence though willing to discuss problems of a spiritual nature with him (e.g. what should she do when her guiding 'vision' seemed to fade – should she try to live by the memory of it? Fidelio sensibly suggested she find God 'in ordinary everyday things and people')[118] and to confide 'quite unreservedly' her hopes for her children or her 'little private dream of ending [her] days in a simple hermitage'[119], Aelfrida never spoke of matters too personal to be shared: her activities as a medium or her deteriorating relationship with a husband whose rejection of her had encouraged the 'detached' behaviour against which Stokoe railed without realising that it was precisely Aelfrida's ability to practise 'non-attachment'[120] which enabled her to help him through a terrible period in his life.

Fidelio's recovery from wartime attacks of bipolar disorder took place during the summer of 1918. Although both he and Aelfrida were aware that recovery was only remission and that sooner or later "everything [went] black and there [was] nothing – nothing" and that even during remission "the power of evil"[121] encompassed and tempted him (another factor, though she did not tell him, which persuaded her not to let herself come too close to him, for sexual proclivities once regarded as unfortunate character traits were now regarded with 'priggish [but] passionate' resentment as vices)[122], Aelfrida had already come to the conclusion that her ability to 'walk about' inside Stokoe's mind ('which he can't do, I am glad to say, in mine!')[123], though advantageous from her patient's point of view, was too emotionally draining from her own, that the 'complex feelings' existing between them were becoming a 'bore', and that it would be better for both if she took their friendship more 'simply'.[124]

A relationship in which 'there was never any physical attraction' and from which 'the emotional element' had been purged suited Aelfrida perfectly if only because there remained 'the … mutual wish to understand things together, to find out beauty together, to help'; indeed, her new relationship with Stokoe approached perfection because its 'detachment from earthly things' gave it a heavenly perfection of its own. Furthermore, the fact that it only *approached* perfection because 'only in God can my affections rest', allowed Aelfrida to cling to it 'because one would see if it cannot be more fairly wrought'.[125] ('I hope', she wrote, 'all this will be good practice for getting on with Constantine. But, after all, it is much easier to get on with a man on whom one has no claims and to whom one owes no obedience'.) Then too, a relationship so nearly heavenly in its perfection was both a precursor in the human 'here and now' of 'the intercourse which will be ours hereafter'[126] and a terrestrial reflection of a relationship with God 'capable of infinite development'. But 'would that I could say the same of my relationship to Constantine!' she added ruefully.[127]

With Tommy Altounyan, Aelfrida's relationship went beyond soul-doctoring for from it she derived almost as much benefit as he from her: "in your friendships", he told her, "you have such wonderful opportunities".[128] She was reminded of this on meeting John Forbes

Cameron early in the war, noting sadly that archetypal 'little friend' had 'settled down', that 'everyone settles down. Who says "everything burns"? … in most people nothing burns but their youth', that she herself prayed 'to be always on fire, even knowing as I do what it costs'[129] (after two years of war she still described herself as a 'thing of fire … burning with hope')[130], and that neither she nor Fidelio nor Tommy would ever 'settle down' because of their propensity for feeling 'alive to one's fingertips'.[131] Tommy's 'fire', however, was not of the same hellish calibre as Fidelio's, being a mixture of 'ardour and simplicity' leavened by a sense of humour and an ability to take an interest in 'the vibration of human beings other than himself'.[132]

In August 1915 Tommy became engaged. His future wife, Dora Collingwood, an artist from an artistic background (her father, WG Collingwood, was a painter friend of John Ruskin), was the sister of a woman whom Tommy might have married had Barbara not insisted on a chaste relationship devoid of the children he desired. At first 'bubbling over with happiness'[133] and so madly in love 'as Constantine used to be' that Aelfrida found herself 'living it all over again in him', she realised with clear-sighted dismay that for 'funny Tommy' his future wife was, like herself in relation to her own husband, 'just a peg to hang his fine feelings on and probably knows it as little as I did'.[134] Tommy married Dora in September 1915; Aelfrida neither attended the wedding nor commented in her diary, recording when they met the following year that Tommy appeared 'sad and changed and lustreless'.[135] He was, and his revelations of why (his wife had failed to recognise – 'how could she?'– that he had married her 'chiefly to have a baby', that he wanted her 'to develop her own personality' rather than try to merge her life with his, that he liked 'to be let alone') made Aelfrida thoughtful because the Altounyans' relationship closely reflected that between the Grahams and because it revealed to her where she had gone wrong: 'men say "give yourself all, all, every bit!" and you do. Then they are bored, complain that you have no "mystery" left and are a little shocked at your having given yourself … They want complete devotion on the woman's part and absolute liberty on their own'. Confident that none of the conversation would be transmitted to his wife, Tommy thanked Aelfrida for allowing him to unburden himself to her; Aelfrida, half in sympathy with Dora, hoped she herself might be a better wife to Constantine 'if I ever get another chance'.[136]

Her hope that there might be less unhappiness between the Altounyans (she described Dora as 'Victorian-looking [and] *narrow*' in contrast to her 'big tempestuous passionate' husband without realising that the description also applied to her own husband and herself)[137] was fulfilled when she heard in September 1916 that Dora was pregnant (a daughter was born in the early spring of 1917) and that Tommy was 'as ecstatic as Constantine was when I was first with child'.[138] (The following day she added the bitter memory of Constantine demanding what she meant by 'spawning another brat'.) Arriving in Cambridge in October 1916 to collect his MB prior to joining the Royal Army Medical Corps, Tommy confided that his marriage was on a happier footing, but her subsequently informing him that as a 'soul-doctor' she too knew 'the delights of having a "medical sense"' failed to cheer a 'Dr Tommy' emotionally burnt out after two years of front-line surgery during which he was awarded the Military Cross, a man who now stated that all he wanted to do was 'to write novels and live in a world of imagination'.[139]

For Hubert Henderson for whom Aelfrida remained 'the central reality of his life'[140] life as 'the kind of Briton who with a good-natured smile and an almost indolent manner manages to govern and build empires as though it were as natural as eating breakfast'[141] began to unravel coincidentally with his marriage to Faith Bagenall in October 1915.[142] Discontent derived primarily from the burdens imposed on him by the war (unable to work for peace, he was classified as too 'neurasthenic' and too physically unfit for active service) but it may be that his restless unhappiness owed something too to realisation that marriage to anyone but unavailable Aelfrida would be less fulfilling than their friendship. As with Tommy Altounyan, Aelfrida did not attend or mention Hubert's wedding, commenting on meeting his wife a year later that Faith made a rather 'smudgy' impression and that 'she would be pretty … except that instead of having a good chin she has two bad ones'.[143] (Aelfrida invariably criticised the women her gentleman friends married; her dislike was reciprocated by the women themselves, they doubtless hearing more than enough about her from their husbands.) Hubert's natural buoyancy returned with peacetime and he and Aelfrida resumed their friendship (though not, because of his wife, a Little Friendship) when he was appointed Lecturer in Economics (formerly a pupil of Maynard Keynes, he was now Keynes' colleague) and fellow of Clare College in 1918.

Hubert's earlier unhappiness may also have owed something to realisation that what Aelfrida now felt for him was 'a calm affection … which causes no excitement', 'higher detachment' and growing daughters having caused her to regard Little Friends less as soul-mates and more as potential sons-in-law.[144] Detachment and marriage caused something of a coolness between them, for after opening his heart to her in May 1915, Hubert,

while in Cambridge, met Aelfrida only in the company of his wife and she herself behaved circumspectly; the dreadful dinner party at which she taunted Elfrida Cameron in her husband's hearing was not repeated, for having been badly hurt by the presence of 'little friends' in Constantine's life, it seems she was now unwilling to hurt the wife of one of her own. But she parted from 'the lad' with 'a pang at losing a Little Friend, a very human pang'[145]; hearing of Gian Falco's wedding in 1909 she had 'rejoiced greatly', diarising jubilantly 'they all marry'[146] as if it was a tribute to herself that men did, but the marriages of two Little Friends within forty days of each other in autumn 1915 was no reason for rejoicing: 'freedom of detachment is very hard to get, O Aelfrida!'[147] With Hubert Henderson and Tommy Altounyan married and Frank Stokoe (when in Cambridge) liable to switch disconcertingly from talking morbidly but sanely to being 'away in the dark regions of the mind where no friendly interest can touch him'[148], 'Aelfrida Tillyard, Straightener' concentrated on soul-doctoring those who were not and never became Little Friends, even if, like Alfred Compton Rickett, they were intellectual and male or thought 'affinity' a good idea.[149]

Between 1914 and 1918 Aelfrida's real 'patients' i.e. those in relation to whom she acted as 'Straightener or soul-doctor' in terms of her description in *Can I be a Mystic?*, were women. There were, of course, few socially-acceptable young men to counsel in Cambridge during the Great War and if the mood prevailing there during the Second World War is representative, there was little inclination to introspection on the part of those able to continue their studies. It may be too, that the religious tone of her counselling sessions discouraged young men who, like the real Eustace or fictional 'Noel Ashton', saw their friends dying in the Flanders mud and temporarily or permanently lost their faith in a God who permitted such terrible slaughter. Women, on the other hand, came to Aelfrida precisely because the counsel she offered was couched in reassuringly religious terms. (In *Vision Triumphant* she describes a 'straightening' session with one 'Esther Cunningham', a young woman whose religious upbringing has left her ill-equipped to deal with problems stemming from the deteriorating relationship between herself and the unsympathetic father who inculcated her early beliefs. 'Esther' loses faith in God during the war and is sent to 'Catharine Sutherland' by a friend who has already availed herself of 'Catharine's' spiritual advice; though sceptical when 'Catharine' tells her to deliberately train her will and emotions towards restoration of her faith by means of daily meditations, part active – "thinking loving thoughts *of* God", part passive – "imaginatively receiving loving thoughts *from* God" – she agrees to try, succeeds, and is reconciled with her father on his death-bed.)[150] Such women ranged from students whose arrival at Cambridge taught them to think for themselves and hence to question beliefs held unquestioningly since childhood, a discomfiting state of mind at any time but especially so in wartime, through single women of Aelfrida's own age whose wartime lives were examined and found wanting, to older women whose prime need was reassurance that although the world as they knew it was coming to an end it was not the end of the world.[151] To the latter, Aelfrida's advice was brief and practical: to one whom 'the war had thoroughly upset … so she left off praying and got in a muddle', she suggested 'more prayer, not less'[152] and to a spinster in her fifties suffering a surfeit of prayer and religious exercises, a course of 'novel-reading and frivolity with prayers and churchgoing reduced to the barest minimum' ('my advice scandalised her a little … has the Straightener been wise?') until matters were restored to their proper perspective.[153] With students and with women of her own age she took more pains, though she was briskly dismissive of those she felt were wasting her time, writing of Elsie Rose, a woman of thirty-four whom she had known since adolescence, that 'being restless and unsatisfied, she tries first one thing and then another … some formula or set of doctrines which she calls "The Truth" … Dreaming over a bunch of white may is about her line'.[154] But no patient, however irritating or undeserving, was charged for consultations, the mystic born not made regarding as abhorrent receipt of money for spiritual services extended to others by virtue of God working through herself.

Four women – two Girton students, two teachers – comprised the central elements of Aelfrida's war-time 'soul doctoring'. With one she parted company before the end of the war; one maintained intermittent contact for the rest of 'Straightener's' life; one who already regarded herself as a friend became a much-mocked visitor to Fordfield, Agatha and Alethea guying her appalling taste in clothes and brash mannerisms. One, with whom Aelfrida felt a strong spiritual affinity, became a friend but was not admitted to her confidence.

Aelfrida's first 'patient', Lilian Whitehouse, aged thirty-four, daughter of the 'elderly and *very* learned' Dr Whitehouse whose fragmentary post-mortem message she had received as a medium, was not properly a patient at all. Describing Lilian as someone whose mind she 'saw' so easily that she worried that her ability to 'draw' Lilian's mind to herself might result in 'Straightener' imposing thoughts on Lilian 'from outside'[155] and she herself being engrossed in Psychological Laboratories investigations, she regarded Lilian more as an experimental subject than

a 'patient' and suggested Lilian do '"spiritual exercises," i.e. yoga, for [her] investigations and she agreed if Red Cross work does not interfere'.[156] Though tending to display an unseemly thirst for 'sensations', Lilian kept a record of the results of her meditations (e.g. 'a slight identification of self with figure of Christ on cross')[157], the results of which, wrote her mentor in November 1914, showed Lilian to be a serious student. The student herself felt somewhat out of her depth and was only encouraged to continue by attendance at Aelfrida's first series of lectures early in 1915: '[she] is longing to embark on the Mystic Way but doubts her courage'.[158] By June 1915, however, Lilian had decided that the Mystic Way was not a road she wished to follow ('her mind is all dark and wriggley (*sic*) in consequence', wrote her mind-reading mentor)[159] and being of a practical rather than a mystical bent, joined the Voluntary Aid Detachment. Her father's death in 1916 meant Lilian having to 'turn out and earn her living'[160] as Aelfrida smugly but ungraciously put it, little dreaming that she too might have to do the same four years later. But a relationship of sorts was forged on the basis of Aelfrida's supportive sympathy at the time of Dr Whitehouse's death, Lilian returning frequently to Fordfield to discuss her friendships with men (she settled for 'pure and beautiful' versions rather than marriage but tended to Bélisian delusions as to her charms) and her problems with a crotchety widowed mother and censorious older sister. (Lilian received a confidences regarding Aelfrida's troubled marriage in return; as one of the latter's few 'female admirers', perhaps Aelfrida felt that Lilian might take her part.) But although she also liked to think that she had 'straightened' Lilian, she had tried to set Lilian on a wholly unsuitable path and was surprised and disappointed when the latter failed to follow it.

She had only limited success with her next two 'patients', 'intelligent, a little perky and *very* young' Dorothy Wrinch and 'shy' Marjory Harrison[161], Girtonians who asked to see her after attending her 1915 lecture series and Anglo-Catholics who had discovered that their studies for the Mathematics and Moral Sciences tripos respectively had raised doubts in their minds (this 'saved them from smugness')[162] about which they came separately 'to consult the Straightener'.[163]

Of the two, Aelfrida found Dorothy the more interesting. Their relationship, however, never really recovered from a unfortunate session during which Dorothy declared "it would be so awfully lovely to have visions and that sort of thing" (Aelfrida acerbically suggested the meditation known as the Practice of the Presence of God in order to concentrate her mind)[164] and demonstrated an obsession with inessentials: could she as an Anglo-Catholic accept spiritual advice from a Presbyterian?

Although Aelfrida tried hard to make Dorothy 'see, not argue'[165] (an inappropriate tactic to adopt with regard to a Girtonian encouraged to question everything), her hope that Dorothy (pupil-name 'Roswitha')[166] would succeed in her quest for God was dashed in November 1915 when 'Roswitha' suffered total loss of faith following the stress of examinations and neither advice to 'go away for a holiday ... and let her soul take care of itself'[167] nor messages from Aelfrida's guardian angel that Dorothy was 'not [solely] herself but a part of the World-Soul given into her charge'[168], could persuade Miss Wrinch otherwise. Worse still, Dorothy fell under the influence of Bertrand Russell with whom she studied Symbolic Logic during a fourth year course in Moral Sciences and became *his* disciple instead of Aelfrida's (Aelfrida's statement to Russell in May 1916 that as a 'soul-doctor' she had to fight the influence of his 'sterile intellectualism' on the 'intelligent young' obviously refers to Dorothy)[169] with precisely the result anticipated by her 'guru': '[Russell] kills something in them, makes them ... dry and hopeless and academic'.[170]

With Marjory Harrison (pupil-name 'Amrita') Aelfrida had a longer relationship but limited success. Finding Marjory the embarrassingly adoring possessor of an equally embarrassing tendency to probe (Aelfrida refused to disclose details of her spiritual experiences lest Marjory think her 'very holy' to have been 'favoured with visions' and she herself use disclosure as 'an occasion for vanity')[171] and discouragingly unable to abandon spiritual 'curves and distortions' with regard to Dissenters[172], Aelfrida acceded to Marjorie's post-graduation request to discontinue consultations in favour of war-work on the land. (She described Marjory in January 1917 as 'milking cows' and 'more inarticulate than ever'.)[173] Marjory, however, persisted in regarding Aelfrida as 'invested with authority over her soul' (an authority Aelfrida vehemently disclaimed, though she was happy to continue as a 'guide'), informing the latter shortly before the end of the war that she wished to become a nun.[174] Aelfrida sent details of the Retreat House attached to the Convent of the Holy Cross at Limpsfield in Surrey because being a retreatant might help 'Amrita' decide if she had a vocation, but in the course of flying visits during 1918 and 1919 Marjory informed her that she had abandoned the idea after seeing the Limpsfield Sisters sitting indoors on a hot day crocheting and that she had decided to become a teacher instead. Finding 'Amrita' as 'vague, vacillating and self-centred as ever'[175], Aelfrida decided to remove herself from her admirer's orbit at the point at which Marjory asked her 'right out for a full account of all [her] spiritual experiences!!' Replying that if Marjory felt in need of special help and that if a description of any

particular experience of her own would be of use, she would be happy to oblige, she declined to satisfy mere curiosity because that it was not part of a Straightener's remit 'to be made a spiritual peep-show [or] a religious cinema'.[176] (She had no such compunction about illustrating her books with examples taken from her own 'spiritual experiences', however, and by no means all were anonymised.) Almost the last we hear of Marjory is that she is teaching at a 'crank school in Weybridge' and that Aelfrida is 'faintly bored' by their relationship.[177]

Aelfrida's most successful 'patient' was science teacher Evelyn Bales who 'would fain be mystical' and who asked the Straightener 'to shew her God' and 'to let [her] see Him as a living reality'. 'Straightener' 'gave her a few ideas, a warning or two, a great deal of sympathy and promised ... a meditation' and suggested the Practice of the Presence of God as suitable for a beginner[178], whereupon Miss Bales began to have 'subtle spiritual experiences', so subtle as to be 'almost unnoticed except in the effect they leave', but which left her serenely confident that she had 'found her soul'.[179] Pleased that one 'patient' at least had responded appropriately, Aelfrida encouraged Evelyn to continue, only to have to reassure her when spiritual exercises raised 'obscure forces of evil ... within the self or without' identified by Aelfrida as equivalent to Aleister Crowley's 'Guardians of the Threshold'.[180] (It seems that it was not only Lilian Whitehouse's mind that was 'all dark and wriggley' in June 1915.) By December 1915, however, Miss Bales, no longer a 'patient' but a 'pupil', required no further help because she was 'on the right road and doesn't need "straightening"'.[181] In spite of this, Evelyn maintained contact, informing her in 1919 that 'Straightener' had been correct in promising that in time of trouble Evelyn would derive comfort from her 'firm hold of God'.[182] In 1921, following a breakdown brought on by overwork, spiritual worries, and an unspecified personal tragedy, she again took Aelfrida's advice, namely that rest and travel would allow her 'to get a firm grasp on essentials' again[183], Aelfrida knowing that Evelyn was always, and in spite of everything, sustained by 'the splendour of her faith'.[184]

In November 1916 Aelfrida suffered an unusual 'fit of humility': 'I a Straightener – my God!'[185] (Would she, one wonders, have become one had Aleister Crowley not hailed her as a teacher? She certainly followed his methods of instruction.) Humility was called for, for her wartime career (or rather, 'vocation'[186], because she had been called by God to undertake it) was unsuccessful with regard to all but one of her few female 'patients' and she had made very little progress (and that of the wrong kind) with her sole male one. The reasons for this were curiously un-evident to 'Straightener' herself but may be summarised as follows: first, she had little patience with women (or with old-maidish men such as Compton Rickett) and was unlikely to feel sympathy for females who did not immediately and enthusiastically embrace the Mystic Way. Second, she was somewhat doctrinaire in the way in which she forced her beliefs on others as if there was no other path to take ("the Mystic Way – *tout ou rien*", as she wrote in *The Making of a Mystic*)[187], presuming that anyone who approached her for spiritual advice *must* have decided to pursue the same path as herself. Third, she was unprepared to adapt her 'doctoring' technique to particular 'patients', assuming, for example, that a meditational technique such as the Practice of the Presence of God would suit women as disparate as older and spiritually-mature Evelyn Bales and a younger student with a sharply analytical mind like Dorothy Wrinch. Nor would she brook discussion; indeed, as she wrote a few years later apropos the contrast between the results of her own spiritual exercises and the unseeing behaviour towards God she thought she discerned in others, 'sometimes I want to shake people and say "look, you fool, look *look*! *There* lies your true happiness. Can't you *see*, you double-dyed idiot!" (This was not, 'soul-doctor' later admitted, 'the way Jesus addressed the simple crowd'.)[188] Fourth, she was so sure of her 'vocation' that she set herself up as a 'soul-doctor' without taking counsel from anyone as to her suitability and her success with Evelyn Bales (chronologically, her first proper 'patient') blinded her to the fact that she herself lacked spiritual 'direction'; given, therefore, that she acted as she did, she was fortunate to do no spiritual harm to her patients, though one wonders just how efficaciously she 'straightened' ordinary women who came to her in spiritual distress. Lastly, her 'war-work', altruistic though it might appear, was essentially devoted to her own spiritual development, time, place, and circumstances affording her a perfect opportunity for self-centred and self-centring behaviour in which insights gained from her work as a 'soul-doctor' were used therapeutically for her own spiritual ends.

Was Aelfrida, then, a failure as a 'soul-doctor'? Insofar as she provided friendly advice to confused young men like Hubert and Tommy, she was not, for she handled them so deftly that she was able to ease them into marriage and, while keeping their friendship, gently disengage their love from herself in order to bestow it on another; she did this, moreover, without any mention of religion. She was of great help to Frank Stokoe in terms of a supportive dialogue which enabled him to pursue an academic career and prevented him from committing suicide (no mean feat in the context of bipolar disorder), albeit at some emotional cost to herself. (She also never alluded to her own grave personal problems of the war years,

problems which, had Little Friends but known, coloured so much of her relationships with them.) As a 'soul-doctor', however, she was less successful because as a 'modern mystic' and a decade-long pietist (someone, that is to say, who sought, like seventeenth century followers of the Lutheran doctrine of *Pietismus*, to practice an intensely personal piety superior in every way, to their way of thinking, to compliance with outward forms of religion), her inability to 'soul-doctor' in any other manner than that of earnestly-religious dispenser of mystico-Christian doctrines doomed her efforts from the start, and it may be that, realising this (and for the further propagation of her 'Great Work') she embarked on three books which show 'Aelfrida Tillyard, Straightener' (as herself or as her fictional alter ego 'Catharine Sutherland') in a more favourable light and as precisely how a textbook 'soul-doctor' should conduct herself in providing her 'patients' with sufficient spiritual comfort, information, and advice to enable them to work through their problems in a manner which makes the result right *for them*.

To herself, Aelfrida listed the three books as *The Straightener at Work* Vols I, II, and III; in practice they were entitled *The Making of a Mystic, Vision Triumphant,* and *Can I be a Mystic?* The first two, of 1917 and 1919 respectively, were conceived and wholly or partly written during the period 1914–1918 and have the Great War as an integral aspect of their plot; the third, published in 1930, was begun in June 1925 and has as its background the unsettled years to which the events of 1914–1918 gave rise. In *The Making of a Mystic* and *Vision Triumphant* the protagonists undergo spiritual trials as a result of living in time of war and come to 'Catharine Sutherland' for 'straightening'; in the third volume the 'Stranger' of the subtitle (Letters to a Stranger in Answer to his Question) is a journalist who fought through the war, has been troubled by spiritual doubts ever since, and comes to the 'Author' to whom he appeals for help by way of a book she has written in which he discerns the beginning of answers to his questions and a sympathetic person to provide them.

The format of all three books is similar: the protagonists write to 'Catharine Sutherland' or to 'Author' about their problems and she replies in epistolary form.[189] In the two earlier books, however, letters are interspersed with excerpts from 'Catharine's' diaries which both move the story on and echo the way in which Aelfrida herself dealt with Fidelio, conducted consultations, and described both in her diary. *Can I be a Mystic?*, on the other hand, is conducted solely by letter, echoing the fact that Aelfrida's post-war 'straightening' was carried out solely on 'patients' who had read volumes I and II of *The Straightener at Work* and whom she 'straightened' at a distance through the medium of 'many, many letters'.[190] But while this allowed her to embark on a "lifetime crusade to save the souls of strangers by post"[191] and afforded a greater degree of privacy (and a great deal of 'copy'), it also had the disadvantage of her remaining unaware of the subtle nuances of tone and gesture which provide a 'soul' (or any) doctor with vital information about a 'patient'.

The *Straightener at Work* series is interesting for another reason: it is intensely and intentionally autobiographical. For one thing, Aelfrida wrote little poetry after *The Garden and the Fire* so that apart from her diary we would have no other insight into her life and thought had she not put so much of both into books written after 1916. For another, her books, with very few exceptions, represent her progress as a mystic from enthusiastic young student to world- but not God-weary older woman. Third, Aelfrida, like so many mystics, believed that an important aspect of her role as recipient of unmediated experience of God was to share the content and richness of her experiences with those unable to achieve them for themselves because too inexperienced or too ill-equipped, spiritually speaking, to do so. And given that her 'message' was best expressed in her poetry which was why that must be published whatever else was not and that, for reasons unexpressed, her poetic output declined dramatically after 1916, it may have been essential for her to continue to broadcast her 'message' in prose.

Mystics' propensity to declare their experiences inexpressible only to describe them in detail and at length is one shared by Aelfrida. But a Julian of Norwich or Teresa of Avila she was not, for her writings lack the homely religious sensibility of the former and the dramatic religious sensitivity of the latter, characteristics which make them so consoling or so uplifting to read; they also lack Julian's quiet insight into and Teresa's dynamic depictions of visionary experiences, being more often than not reportage which so seldom transcends the personal that it is unlikely to achieve the universal. Worse still, her language shares characteristics which make contemporary mystics like Evelyn Underhill and Frances Ridley Havergal hard to read and easy to ridicule: archly cosy phraseology, tear-jerking sentimentality, and what Constantine called 'goupy' notions whose preciousness conceals their profound theological pedigrees, "alone with the Alone" being a case in point.[192]

It is nevertheless important to note that Aelfrida's 'Straightener' books in general and *The Making of a Mystic* in particular struck a chord with many people (mostly women) who found formal theology incomprehensible or too unrepresentatively masculine to answer their questions, their immediate response being to take

up meditation 'just as the Straightener in my books tells people to'.[193] Then too, her 'Straightener' books should be read not only as an important change of direction in her career as a writer or as prose representations of her 'vision' and 'Great Work' but also as manifestations of a new confidence in her own literary and spiritual abilities. And for all their apparent spontaneity, it is important to remember that all three were written at times of trial ('when I have helped someone I see so clearly [that] … *personal happiness does not matter*') and only after unremitting hard work ('nothing matters but that the purpose of God should be fulfilled in me')[194] by an unwell woman unused to writing books of this nature who diarised exhaustedly towards the end of the Great War that 'as for the words I hope to say and write as Straightener … it would be a relief if an angel came and told me that they were not required of me and that I might muse instead'.[195]

Short synopses of Aelfrida's first two 'Straightener' books show just how closely her life and those of her characters are intertwined. *The Making of a Mystic,* conceived in only three months, was her final baby-equivalent (she was thirty-four, right on her child-bearing schedule when it was published; conception of her last real but miscarried child must have taken place coincidentally with the book's publication) and was therefore more a 'child of her spirit' than erstwhile *chela* George von Kaufmann. She describes it as 'a kind of road-book for the Mystic Way in the form of letters'[196], an accurate description insofar it depicts in abbreviated and over-simplified form a young girl's progress along the road Aelfrida herself had tried to follow since adolescence:

February 1916. Audrey Talbot[197] is in her second year at Newton College, Camford. Audrey has two brothers: Sebastian, a prosperous businessman who has no use for religion, and Augustus, currently fighting in France, who at least believes in an "Upward Tendency".[198] Audrey attends lectures[199] given by Catharine Sutherland [200], a self-declared and 'detached' mystic, who offers to act as her Straightener. With Catharine's help, Audrey embarks on a voyage of spiritual discovery during which she reads recommended, meditates[201], worries about distractions ("why do mystics have exams?"), and has an ecstatic experience of God while visiting a local wood with a college friend, Quakeress Mercy Allen[202], an exemplar of how a Christian life should be lived. Early in 1917 things begin to go wrong. Augustus is killed in France. Audrey's parents die, leaving her with little money but unwilling to rely on Sebastian to whom she has never been close. She also suffers from spiritual 'aridity', a period during which Catharine feels she has failed her but decides that "it is better that God should be near her and help her than that I should". She entertains thoughts of becoming a nun "but I shouldn't like vows I couldn't keep and I always have a kind of feeling that Anglican Sisterhoods aren't *quite* the real thing". At this low point in her life, Mercy's father, a philanthropic businessman, offers her the position of Welfare Supervisor in a jam-making factory for which he has great schemes for improvement.[203] (Mercy is overjoyed, telling Audrey that her father practises "a kind of knight-errantry of commerce".)[204] After unexpectedly experiencing "Universal Consciousness", Audrey decides to work for her fellow men instead of following the Mystic Way for her sole spiritual benefit. She accepts Mr Allen's offer and, leaving behind the Celestial City of which meditation has allowed her a glimpse, returns to the "crowded haunts of men" with God as her friend and guide.

On 5 March 1918, following a 'dream or vision' in which she saw herself begging God to be allowed to reincarnate as a Buddha in order to help Him save 'the least of Thy creatures' (God agreed) and passionately 'eager to do His will'[205], Aelfrida began her second 'Straightener' book. As with her first, she felt an overweening compulsion to do so, a compulsion given added force by the receipt of a 'mere scrap of a letter from Constantine' (now in Lyons) and realisation that 'scraps' were all she was likely to receive in the future.[206]

*Vision Triumphant,* one of whose provisional titles, *By Different Ways*[207], echoes her earlier comment that Constantine's 'way' is no longer hers, is simultaneously the most and the least personal of her three 'Straightener' books. It is the most overtly personal because, begun shortly after her miscarriage of January 1918, it contains the lengthy description of Agneta's birth and death quoted earlier, a story confided to very few people (other than her readers and biographer), one of whom was Lilian Whitehouse. It is ostensibly the least personal because although it contains some of Aelfrida's pet theories such as the need to revivify England's 'decaying countryside' after the war[208], it is essentially a series of dialogues between 'Catharine Sutherland' and two young people whose lives are drastically rerouted as a result of the Great War and is illustrated by events which happened not to Aelfrida herself (with the important exception noted above and possibly one other) but to other people. Remembering, however, that the key to Aelfrida's writings lies in her diary, it is unsurprising to discover that one of the two young people represents Constantine as he is in 1918 and as Aelfrida would have

liked him to be in 1919 and the other in some respects herself as she was before Constantine rejected her and herself as she hopes to be after a reconciliation effected by greater insight into man/woman relationships:

> When the Great War begins, Noel Ashton[209] is studying theology at Cambridge prior to taking Holy Orders. He is engaged to Silvia Barrington[210], daughter of a local vicar with whom he reads theology during vacations. In October 1914 Noel enlists, telling Catharine Sutherland who has already acted as his 'Straightener' (Silvia knows this as "quite a lot of men … go to [Catharine] about spiritual difficulties") that he would feel a cad expending his energy "over Hebrew roots and Greek verbs while the Germans are murdering Belgians". Because of the terrible experiences he undergoes in the trenches and describes in letters to Catharine[211], Noel loses his faith. Feeling that Silvia would neither approve nor understand, he breaks off their engagement.[212]Silvia, heartbroken, turns to Catharine for advice, begging "find me something to think on − 'meditate on' as you say, a special big thought to hold on to, *tight*"; Catharine tells her to "hold fast to God" in a changing world. Silvia undertakes war-work where her attempts to practice "the Presence of God all the time" so impress her colleagues that they decide "to try some meditations [purely] as a scientific experiment". They are so affected by the results that one comes to Catharine for 'straightening'. Noel is wounded and, blind and missing a hand and a foot, is repatriated. Catharine visits him at his parents' request in the nursing home in Hampshire in which he is temporarily incarcerated: he is so depressed that he has become reclusive and suicidal. She tells him the story of her own near-death experience in childbirth and redemptive vision (she also gives him much practical advice as to how to manage his future) and he eventually decides to stop running away from God who, he now realises, has been with him even "in those desolate spaces of the mind" where he, like Catharine before him, has been wandering. He returns to Cambridge and with his parents' help resumes work on his degree. He is reunited with Silvia who, apprehensive of the burden she will bear as the wife of a blind cripple, turns again to Catharine for advice. Catharine reassures her[213], saying that Noel now *feels* things he only 'saw' before and will be a better priest as a result of his tribulations.

'Noel' and 'Silvia' are reunited; Constantine and Aelfrida were not. Aelfrida's final attempt at reconciliation took place in May 1919 prior to the publication of *Vision*

*Triumphant.* It failed, but she let stand the happy ending of *The Straightener at Work* Vol 2 to show what might have been achieved had Constantine not remained obdurately blind to her persuasions and spiritually crippled by his love of money and position.

The third book in which Aelfrida speaks directly as a 'Straightener' (all her homiletic books and most of her novels have 'straightening' as their theme, though not always by name) was published in 1930. It was begun towards the end of a period during which her life, apparently serene on the surface, was so fraught with difficulties that it was only by a great effort of will that she was able to make spiritual progress; indeed, lack of progress along her 'mystic way' contributed, she believed, to her now having very few 'patients' to 'straighten'[214], people being unlikely to consult a 'Straightener' as devoid of spirituality as herself. In fact, she had not ceased to provide spiritual advice to young men and mature women (an undergraduate with examinations looming who 'got the wrong end of the Theosophical stick' and was, as a result, on the verge of a nervous breakdown but who was able, as because of Aelfrida's sensible advice, to 'fix his eyes on God'[215], forget dogma, regain his peace of mind, pass his exams, and become a teacher; the matron of the Eton Union Workhouse who thanks to Aelfrida's written responses to her 'long outpouring of spiritual difficulties'[216], was able to compose herself and even to extend help in return) but a feeling that her 'vocation' had deserted her seems to have moved Aelfrida to write a book reassuring herself that this was not so.

*"Can I be a Mystic?"* writes Aelfrida in her preface, "is in reality what a former work of mine ... merely pretended to be ... a correspondence between a middle-aged woman and a younger friend who asked for spiritual advice".[217] This may be so – indeed, the publisher's blurb on the book's cover assures us that it contains "the actual correspondence which has passed between an earnest seeker and his spiritual mentor" and Aelfrida describes it as a 'collaboration book' written by herself and one Erle Lunn[218] – but the book was actually begun in June 1925[219] three years before she first mentions her 'new "goup"'[220] in her diary. There are, too, textual oddities which make one wonder how much 'collaboration' took place: 'Stranger' and 'Author' both speak (write, rather) in Aelfrida's voice and a letter from 'Author' to 'Stranger' written "in a field somewhere between Horningsea and Clayhithe"[221] is redolent of Evelyn Underhill's habit of writing letters "even in a pause on a country walk"[222]: Aelfrida invariably wrote at home, using trips to the country as opportunities to bond with her daughters or, if alone, to cogitate, or to commune with nature. (The 'field' between two Cambridgeshire villages was actually the scene of an idyll shared with Constantine Michaelides.) Other evidence, too, notably a diary entry describing how she has 'just finished writing another "Letter to a Stranger" for Erle Lunn' ('for', not 'to')[223] suggests that the book was less a collaborative effort than Aelfrida composing letters to a 'Stranger' whose conveniently-timed request for spiritual advice added verisimilitude to work-in-progress and adapting and incorporating his replies to suit her text. Then too, Aelfrida was anxious to maintain literary, actual, and metaphorical distance from a 'goup' so keen to have her as his 'pontifical and authoritative' advisor in spiritual matters that after making contact with her in January 1928 he began to shower her with presents (she asked him to desist because 'spiritual benefits must be bestowed without any return'), only to find her 'reticent and a little frightening' when he eventually met her because of her reluctance to acquire 'another intimate friend', especially one as 'half-educated'[224] as Lunn; indeed, it was not until after *Can I be a Mystic?* was published in spring 1930 that Aelfrida relaxed her guard somewhat and noted her happiness at being Lunn's 'spiritual director'.[225] It may also be that 'Stranger's' discomfort with what he describes as "low-brow literary work"[226] owes more to Hubert Henderson's dissatisfaction with editorship of *The Nation* in 1923 (he told Aelfrida he was 'not in the least suited to journalism and ought to have remained in Cambridge')[227] than it does to a man with spiritual pretensions whom Aelfrida did not meet until *Can I be a Mystic?* was well advanced.

Aelfrida's third 'Straightener' book follows the same literary and thematic format as her earlier two. 'Stranger' (demobilised in 1919, he has been married for five years and is thirty-three years old) approaches her because he has read *The Making of a Mystic, A Little Road-Book for Mystics*[228], and *Spiritual Exercises* and thinks she might be able to 'straighten' him. Aelfrida, no longer 'Catharine Sutherland' but impersonal 'Author', tells him what books to read[229], which philosophies to avoid, notably Occultism[230], and guides him through the difficulties he encounters as he struggles to find meaning in life. As 'Author', however, she is humbler than her earlier fictional counterpart, being "puzzled or clumsy or inadequate" rather than "always wise" and less a "Lady Almoner" than a "fellow pilgrim". The 'Stranger' whose spiritual journey she joins rather than directs, does not make 'Audrey Talbot's' "amazing progress" but is often discouraged[231]; indeed, he parts company with 'Author' for a year during which a friend, "a man of much spirituality", tells him that all he really needs to do is love God.[232] This, 'Stranger' does – but like 'Audrey Talbot' and 'Noel Ashton', he does not become a mystic. *His* love of God, like theirs, will be manifest in service to his fellow-men in 'exercises' of a less spiritual kind.

Before considering Aelfrida's life in the decade following the Great War – and if it seems that a disproportionate amount of time has been spent on her life during the years 1914–1918, this is not because those years were uneventful (the post-war years will be no less so) but because her patterns of thought and behaviour were so deeply affected by events which transpired during that time that in no aspect of her life, be this spiritual, intellectual, emotional, or sexual, was she able to move on; indeed, she became, as her perceptive elder daughter later noted, "in thought more stationary"[233] than anyone else Alethea knew – it is worth pausing to consider a poem written by her in the back of the current volume of her diary. (The volume had belonged to undergraduate Constantine Michaelides – Aelfrida used pages left blank – and still contains between its leaves a piece of blotting paper used by himself earlier and herself later, she preserving the side used by him by confining her blottings to the other; stuck in the back are contemporary photographs of stouter and nattily-dressed Constantine Graham on a charabanc trip to Chamonix.) The poem, inspired by 'the sound of cheering and of bells'[234] proclaiming the Armistice ending the war to end all wars, was entitled *In Victory*: "Thou, who through harsh unbroken days / Of dark defeat, dost go about thy ways / Serene of aim and with unbending brow …/ To greet a distant song thy eyes upraise. / Glory is thine whom no defeat could bow! / As thou hast steadfast been, now gentle be, / Take with a lowly heart thy victory"…

Apparently addressed to "England mine", the country its author loves and which she bids "be just today" and "be noble now" as other nations gather in retributive anger around Germany, it was never published. It is easy to see why: *To Victory* is Aelfrida's admonition to herself.

In everything she wrote for publication Aelfrida had an agenda, be this revenge or revelation or promulgation of her 'Great Work'. If *To Victory* is anything to go by, revenge and revelation were uppermost in her mind in November 1918 but as one dedicated to bringing man to knowledge of the Divine in him, she could hardly wreak one overtly or reveal too much of herself. The poem therefore remained concealed in a volume of her diary but its theme – magnanimity in victory – could be revealed immediately with regard to a husband who through the "harsh unending" (an alternative reading) days lived in England by his "prim child-ridden spouse"[235] had serenely gone about his ways in Amsterdam with Madame Sterneberg. On the other hand, revenge for Constantine's recent "intolerant and intolerable"[236] behaviour towards herself was too sweet

to pass over – and how better to revenge herself than in a poem to be read and, with luck, published by a future biographer?

Aelfrida's 'war-work', though hardly comparable in kind or benefits to that undertaken by her own mother and by virtually every other woman she knew, had been work nevertheless. It had been manifest in public lectures, in a conference paper, in research undertaken with the support of eminent Cambridge academics, and in the publication of two books, one (by subscription) by a local publisher regarding which Mr Heffer informed her that he had advance orders for 130 copies[237] and which resulted in its author receiving 'many appreciative letters'[238] (how gratifying that this should coincide with Constantine being on leave in England!) and in a group of Newnham students asking to be allowed to dramatize it[239], and concerning which Father Martindale SJ sent a commendatory note[240], the other by a London publisher and resulting in payment of royalties. On the other hand, insights into man/woman relationships derived from information confided by Tommy Altounyan and Hubert Henderson which 'Aelfrida Tillyard, Straightener' hoped to apply to her relationship with Constantine were never put into practice because disclosure of wartime (and, as we are about to discover, subsequent) infidelity prevented it. There was also the matter of revengeful articles in *The Cambridge Magazine* and of poetry disclosing marital disharmony in *The Garden and the Fire* written by one who had recently bidden herself 'be noble now', and as 'Mrs Constantine Graham' Aelfrida must have wondered if her libelled husband could or would overlook these and be 'just' in return.

There was too her coming out as a mystic ("I myself, as I had better confess quite frankly, am a mystic")[241] in a book later pronounced by Constantine (to Aelfrida's surprise: he initially dismissed it as soppy but given that in it 'Audrey Talbot' describes in girlishly rapturous terms a vision of "One, even Jesus … robed and girt in light" received as she kneels at midnight in the cathedral of which her father has recently become dean, One who descends from His cross to stand so close to her that she sees the prints of the nails in His hands as He bends towards her to touch her forehead[242], this is hardly surprising) to be 'rather good'.[243] (*The Making of a Mystic* was not, however, dedicated to Constantine but – revengefully – to Alfred and Catharine Tillyard, described in it fictionally but recognisably and respectively as "suave and severe and … tolerant in a way – and yet so narrow" and as a "perfect darling to live with" but unable to accept "any criticism … in religion"[244]; their comments on the book went unrecorded.) And how to come to terms with a wife who was practising as a 'soul-doctor' when in her husband's (and parents') eyes she was in need of 'straightening' herself?

Although Aelfrida may have hoped that 'in victory', life would be different – that she need no longer take thought for the morrow but could 'cultivate a spirit of adventure' instead, could be 'idealistic', 'grow', 'have zeal for souls', and joyfully accept 'change, sickness, bereavement' (but never 'sin')[245] – she was wrong, for in terms of interpersonal relationships at least matters would turn out otherwise. Hence although it was true that after travelling "for seven years round 'the circumference of the mystery of things'", she had "on 'just a bit of roadway'" found herself "caught suddenly into the luminous centre of the secret"[246] and realised that, as a mystic, she had won through, against that she had to weigh the decline of her marriage from a relationship filled with "joy as ne'er had been / On mortal earth" to one of "kisses maimed" and "slaughtered words" and to learn as she trod "down into despair"[247] that magnanimity was not enough and that her victory was hollow.

## Notes

1 GCPPT 1|1|20 9 March 1915.
2 GCPPT 1|1|19 20 December 1913.
3 GCPPT 1|1|20 4 April 1915.
4 Underhill, E. *Practical Mysticism* p184.
5 St John of the Cross. *The Dark Night of the Soul* Book 1 ch 2. Aelfrida, reading *The Dark Night*, was moved by St John's remarks on "some of the imperfections … possessed by beginners" to comment that they made her 'blush to [her] very soul', because she too had 'gone on just like that!' (GCPPT 1|1|21 8 January 1916).
6 GCAC 4|6|3|3 Letter from Aelfrida to Helen McMorran of 5 November 1958.
7 Tillyard, Ae. *Can I be a Mystic?* pp 82–83.
8 ibid.
9 Frederick Charles Bartlett (1886–1969), Charles Myers' successor as head of the Psychology Laboratory and Cambridge's first professor of Experimental Psychology, was then a relatively junior member of the department; having graduated in 1911 he was currently engaged in post-graduate research with Myers as his supervisor.
10 GCPPT 1|1|20 3 December 1914.
11 ibid. 22 December 1914.
12 ibid. 15 December 1914.
13 ibid. 22 January 1915.
14 ibid. 29 January 1915.
15 ibid. 5 February 1915. *The Cambridge Magazine* of 13 February 1915 (vol IV No 13 p 252) has Dr Searle quote a recent University Sermon in which it was stated that "in the religious trend of the hour the loud cry for mystical experience strikes one's ears"; he also invites his readers to attend Mrs Graham's next lecture, on Christian 'Mysticism', in fact 'Meditations'.
16 GCPPT 1|1|20 18 February 1915.
17 ibid. 5 February 1915.
18 ibid. 26 February 1915.
19 ibid. 24 July 1915.
20 ibid. 20 July 1915.
21 *The Cambridge Magazine* vol V No 19 15 January 1916 p186.
22 GCPPT 1|1|21 17 January 1916.

23 ibid. 24 January 1916.
24 ibid. 20 January 1916.
25 Aelfrida's own words are paraphrased in a brief anonymous review in *The Cambridge Magazine* vol V No 17 11 March 1916 p 382.
26 The review appears in anonymised form in *The Cambridge Magazine* vol IV No 15 27 February 1915 p 291 but according to Aelfrida's diary (GCPPT 1|1|20 2 March 1915) George von Kaufmann was the author. It may be that he also wrote the 1916 review in the same magazine.
27 Erwin Diller Starbuck was then Assistant Professor of Education at Leland Stamford University. His *Psychology of Religion* was published in England in 1899 with a preface by William James. James refers frequently to his fellow American in *The Varieties of Religious Experience.*
28 *The Cambridge Magazine* vol V No 17 11 March 1916 p 382.
29 GCPPT 1|1|21 29 January 1916.
30 *The Cambridge Magazine* vol V No 17 11 March 1916 p 382.
31 Tillyard, Ae. *Spiritual Exercises.* p 140.
32 GCPPT 1|1|21 2 February 1916.
33 *The Cambridge Magazine* vol V No 17 11 March 1916 p 382.
34 GCPPT 1|1|21 10 February 1916.
35 *The Cambridge Magazine* vol V No 17 11 March 1916 p 382.
36 GCPPT 1|1|21 12 February 1916.
37 ibid.
38 *The Cambridge Magazine* vol V No 17 11 March 1916 p 382.
39 Tillyard, Ae. *The Way of Praise* p 128.
40 GCPPT 1|1|9 17 January 1902.
41 GCPPT 1|1|73 1 May 1956.
42 GCPPT 1|1|9 17 January 1902.
43 GCPPT 1|1|21 1 January 1917.
44 ibid. 20 February 1916.
45 ibid. 27 February 1916.
46 GCPPT 1|1|21 27 February 1916.
   *The Cambridge Magazine* vol V No 17 11 March 1916 p 382.
47 GCPPT 1|1|21 19 August 1916.
48 ibid. 28 January 1917. Ernie Crundwell is the "Ernest with his guileless looks" of *A Letter from Ealing Broadway Station.* Aelfrida nicknamed him 'Bayard' after the '*Chevalier sans peur et sans reproche*' of French romances but subsequently (i.e. after his marriage) found him rather dull.
49 GCPPT 1|1|21 2 February 1917.
50 ibid. 4 February 1917.
51 ibid. 7 February 1917.
52 ibid. 10 February 1917.
53 ibid. 4 February 1917.
54 ibid. 19 February 1917.
55 ibid. 4 March 1917.
56 ibid. 10 February 1917.
57 According to St John, beginners seriously seeking God are still too attached to the things of this world and too afflicted with a desire for sensory gratification. Although the initial effect of their attempts to escape may result only in aridity (a sense of being alienated from God and unable to re-establish a relationship with Him), intense spiritual struggle will result in subjugation of the sensory by the spiritual life and a rediscovered ability to love God before self. Proficients are those who, by dint of actively purging themselves of psychophysical dross which remains even after the struggles of beginnerhood are over, find their mind centred on God. They therefore possess a sense of inner harmony not granted to beginners but because they continue to be afflicted by imperfections such as excessive attachment to their superior state of spiritual development, they too are unable to progress further. The perfect are those who in passively allowing themselves to become completely united with God (God being the active agent here, not the seeker after God) are 'perfected' or 'made perfect' insofar as being at one with God removes all trace of selfish and sense-orientated imperfection because the presence of God in them makes it impossible for imperfections whose origins are ultimately in the seeker's spirit to

exist there any longer. A perfect, therefore, is a seeker whose whole personality has been so transformed by the power of God's Love that he or she now exists with and in Him. For further exposition, see: http:||carmelitesofeldridge.org|juan29.html

58  GCPPT 1|1|21 25 February 1917.
59  *The Practice of Mysticism* by 'Mrs Constantine Graham' was announced in *The Cambridge Magazine* vol VI Nos. 10–15 Jan/March 1917 but no details were given other than the title of the series and of individual lectures.
60  GCPPT 1|1|21 4 March 1917.
61  ibid. 3 March 1917.
62  ibid. 4 March 1917.
63  ibid. 13 January 1918.
64  GCPPT 1|1|22 3 April 1918.
65  ibid. 10 April 1918.
66  ibid. 13 April 1918.
67  ibid. 5 May 1918.
68  ibid. 2 June 1918.
69  GCPPT 1|1|23 7 August 1918.
70  ibid. 9 August 1918.
71  ibid. 8 August 1918.
72  ibid. 9 August 1918.
73  ibid.
74  ibid. 11 August 1918.
75  ibid. 10 August 1918.
76  ibid. 9 August 1918.
77  ibid. 10 August 1918.
78  Tillyard, Ae. *Can I be a Mystic?* p 170.
79  ibid p 171.
80  GCPPT 1|1|21 6 November 1916. The Heretics advertised the lecture ('5 November at 8.30pm Mrs Constantine Graham on "soul-doctoring"') in *The Cambridge Magazine* vol VI No4 4 November 1916 p92; sadly no further account of it was provided. The title of the lecture, however, is the only real proof we have (other than Aelfrida's diary) that in describing 'soul-doctoring' as a profession which could be undertaken by someone who was neither a trained psychologist nor a priest, Aelfrida had pre-empted Sigmund Freud who in his *The Question of Lay Analysis* of 1926 put forward a remarkably similar view. Conversely one should also note that Aelfrida's view was neither published nor widely publicised until 1930 in *Can I be a Mystic?*, four years after Freud's theory first appeared in print.
81  GCPPT 1|1|20 4 April 1915.
82  Tillyard, Ae. *Can I be a Mystic?* p171.
83  GCPPT 1|1|19 2 May 1914.
84  ibid. 18 February 1914.
85  ibid. 25 May 1914.
86  ibid. 2 May 1914.
87  Tillyard, Ae. *The Making of a Mystic* p 13.
88  GCPPT 1|1|19 16 February 1914. It should perhaps be noted here that in spite of the inspiration provided by these personal approaches, Aelfrida rarely counselled family members. Though sorely tempted to counsel Julius and Mina ('if only she had a child and he a religion') she refrained from doing so lest 'havoc' ensue (GCPPT 1|1|21 27 April 1917) and other than suggesting that Julius too 'set out on the Mystic Way' (GCPPT 1|1|20 8 June 1915) or 'give up brainwork … and take a light job as a gardener' (GCPPT 1|1|22 26/27 June 1918), she held her peace. In the post-war years, however, her 'straightening' skills were made use of by the unhappy couple at Julius' request.
89  Tillyard, Ae. *The Making of a Mystic* p 6.
90  ibid.
91  St John of the Cross *The Dark Night* Book 1 ch 2 and ch 5.
92  GCPPT 1|1|19 26 October 1913.
93  Underhill, E. *Mysticism* p161. Aelfrida herself touches on this theme in *Spiritual Exercises* pp 62–63 in a section entitled 'Magical Powers'.

94  Tillyard, Ae. *Spiritual Exercises* p 37.
95  GCPPT 1|1|20 5 March and 5 June 1915.
96  Aelfrida's description of *Erewhon*, a land in which "illness was punished by imprisonment and Straighteners called in to treat sinners", appears in *The Making of a Mystic* p 6.
97  GCPPT 1|1|20 19 June 1914.
98  ibid. 2 March 1915.
99  GCPPT 1|1|21 4 May 1916.
100  Tillyard, Ae. *The Making of a Mystic* p 6.
101  Tillyard, Ae. *Spiritual Exercises* p 60.
102  ibid. p 38.
103  GCPPT 1|1|20 8 February 1915. It may be significant that this intimation of Stokoe's precarious mental state coincided with his being awarded the Tiarks Scholarship in 1914 and with a period of intensive research into the influence of German Romanticism on contemporary English writers.
104  The symptoms of bipolar disorder are graphically described in Aelfrida's diary record of the course of her friend's illness. The cause of the condition is uncertain but it is known to be strongly familial and stress-inducing events may trigger or worsen attacks. A supportive therapeutic environment, especially for those contemplating suicide because of the severity of their symptoms, can be of enormous benefit to a sufferer. (Geddes, J. *Bipolar Disorder BMJ* vol 332 7 January 2006 pp 32–33).
105  An introspective poem entitled *Epitaphic* written by Stokoe sometime before 1920 has the poet "pondering how I may say farewell to life". The poem, one of three, appears in *Cambridge Poets 1914–1920*, published in Cambridge in 1920 and dedicated, like Aelfrida's *Cambridge Poets 1900–1913,* to Quiller Couch. The anthology's co-editors consulted Aelfrida as to which poets their anthology should contain; she 'strongly advised [them] to limit themselves to *young* authors, though I excluded myself (*sic*) and I think my advice will be taken' (GCPPT 1|1|22 6 March 1918). Her poems were excluded.
106  Alice Stokoe poured out her concerns about him to someone she now described gratefully as "Frank's friend" (GCPPT 1|1|34 11 June 1927). She also confided to Aelfrida that of her three children, two suffered from mental illness, her daughter Ruth having been confined to a 'private madhouse' for some years (GCPPT 1|1|23 15 August 1918). Coincidentally or not, the onset of Frank Stokoe's symptoms occurred at the same time as the onset of his sister's.
107  GCPPT 1|1|20 9 September 1915.
108  GCPPT 1|1|21 4 March 1916.
109  ibid. 7 July 1916.
110  GCPPT 1|1|23 26 July 1918 The verses ('which you will find among my poems') no longer exist.
111  ibid. 29 July 1918.
112  GCPPT 1|1|20 24 July 1914.
113  GCPPT 1|1|21 7 July 1916.
114  GCPPT 1|1|23 19 July 1918.
115  GCPPT 1|1|20 21 February 1915.
116  ibid. 21 February and 3 June 1915.
117  GCPPT 1|1|23 12 September 1918.
118  GCPPT 1|1|21 9 July 1916.
119  GCPPT 1|1|23 31 July 1918.
120  GCPPT 1|1|21 10 July 1916.
121  GCPPT 1|1|22 22 July 1918.
122  GCPPT 1|1|23 12 September 1918.
123  GCPPT 1|1|22 22 July 1918.
124  GCPPT 1|1|23 12 September 1918.
125  GCPPT 1|1|22 16 July 1918.
      GCPPT 1|1|23 31 July 1918.
126  GCPPT 1|1|22 22 July 1918.
127  ibid. 16 July 1918.
128  GCPPT 1|1|20 2 October 1914.
129  ibid.

130  GCPPT 1 | 1 | 21 19 February 1916.

131  GCPPT 1 | 1 | 20 2 October 1914.

132  ibid. 3 October 1914. As Cambridge contemporaries, Altounyan compared himself to 'fire', Stokoe to 'air and water' and a third, more 'grounded', friend to 'earth' (Altounyan, T. p 14).

133  GCPPT 1 | 1 | 20 2 August 1915.

134  ibid. 4 September 1915.

135  GCPPT 1 | 1 | 21 20 June 1916.

136  ibid. 21 June 1916.

137  ibid. 22 June 1916.

138  ibid. 23 September 1916. Of Tommy's four children, Harriet (Taqui) became an author and Roger (1922–1987) a Cambridge asthma specialist.

139  GCPPT 1 | 1 | 22 20 May 1918. He partly achieved his wish, combining creative writing with surgery during a post-war career at the Altounyan Hospital in Aleppo.

140  GCPPT 1 | 1 | 20 9 March 1915. A letter of 8 March 1915 from Catharine Tillyard to Hubert Henderson includes the significant line "I meant to have seen you before you left but ... I saw you and Frida talking very earnestly over the fire so I stole away not wishing to interrupt". (NCO 20/7/9 Henderson Collection).

141  GCPPT 1 | 1 | 20 7 December 1915.

142  Faith Bagenall graduated from Newnham College, Cambridge. Also an economist, she married Hubert Henderson on 15 October 1915; they had three children.

143  GCPPT 1 | 1 | 21 17 October 1916.

144  GCPPT 1 | 1 | 20 7 December 1914.

145  ibid. 27 June 1915.

146  GCPPT 1 | 1 | 17 15 February 1909.

147  GCPPT 1 | 1 | 20 27 June 1915.

148  GCPPT 1 | 1 | 21 18 September 1916.

149  Alfred Compton Rickett (1869–1937), 'a weird elf-like being', was a Cambridge alumnus currently employed as an extension lecturer in English Literature and History in Oxford. (He may have been referred to Aelfrida by Frank Stokoe). Aelfrida 'sent him away comforted' but after receiving 'an affinity letter' discouraged further contact. (GCPPT 1 | 1 | 22 12 and 15 July 1918).

150  Tillyard, Ae. *Vision Triumphant* pp 98–101.

151  GCPPT 1 | 1 | 21 6 April 1916.

152  ibid. 7 February 1917.

153  GCPPT 1 | 1 | 23 6 April 1919. This particular piece of 'straightening' also appears in *A Little Road–Book for Mystics* (p 99): "a woman ... complained to me that she ... felt such repugnance against services, prayer and meditation that she was in despair about herself. I lent her a couple of novels and suggested that she should forget all about God for a week or two – knowing ... that she loved Him too faithfully to swerve in her allegiance ... To my amusement and relief the cure was instantaneous! The mere thought ... of putting God out of her mind ... had so horrified her that it had opened her eyes to the reality of her love for Him and had brought back to her the delight in Him which she had lost". What Aelfrida omits to mention is that her patient's repugnance was accompanied by 'a recrudescence of carnal desires' and that in her diary she mocks her as a 'mortified ... saint of fifty-two' (GCPPT 1 | 1 | 23 ibid) nor does she tell us for twenty-five years the same 'shy little saint' also sought advice from better known 'straightener' Evelyn Underhill (GCPPT 1 | 1 | 62 1 September 1944).

154  GCPPT 1 | 1 | 20 5 March and 8 June 1915. There is something of Elsie Rose in 'Adele' of *Can I be Mystic?* and 'Hermione' of *The Approaching Storm* (both quoted earlier with reference to Aelfrida herself) especially with regard to Elsie's trials of 'New Theology, Theosophy [and] Christian Science' (GCPPT 1 | 1 | 20 5 March 1920). It that seems Aelfrida was not alone in seeking 'The Truth' in troubled times and time of trouble by paths which later appeared divergent or dead ends.

155  GCPPT 1 | 1 | 20 8 August and 29 September 1914.

156  ibid. 8 August 1914.

157  ibid. 26 September 1914.

158  ibid. 26 February 1915.

159  ibid. 27 June 1915.

160  GCPPT 1 | 1 | 21 20 April 1916.

161  GCPPT 1 | 1 | 20 5 February and 5 March 1915. Dorothy Maud Wrinch (1894–1976) matriculated at Girton in 1913. After graduating in 1918 and following further studies at Cambridge between 1920 and 1923, she lectured in Pure Mathematics in Oxford and London. She subsequently became a respected theoretical biologist, researching the borderland between physics, chemistry and biology in England and America. Aelfrida, meeting Dorothy, 'now a very great person at Girton', early in 1921, thought her 'developed intellectually' (*sic*) (GCPPT 1 | 1 | 25 7 February 1921) but did not fully appreciate her former 'patient's' fame until she read the notice of her engagement to her first husband, Professor John Nicholson: 'she *must* be a celebrity – her picture was in *The Times*' (GCPPT 1 | 1 | 26 14 July 1922). Marjory Midsummer Harrison (b. 24 June 1894, which explains her unusual middle name) was at Girton between 1913 and 1916. She later married and became a teacher of music.

162  GCPPT 1 | 1 | 20 5 March 1915.

163  ibid. 23 April 1915.

164  ibid. 5 March 1915. The Practice was a spiritual exercise advocated by cleric Jeremy Taylor (1613–1667) noted for the excellence of his sermons and devotional writings.

165  ibid. 5 June 1915.

166  Roswitha (more properly Hrotsvith) was a learned 10th century Benedictine nun at Gandersheim. She wrote a series of plays in Latin on "pious and instructive themes" with particular reference to holy virgins, steadfastness under temptation, and constancy of religion when faced with martyrdom, and promulgated the virgin state as the ideal both for unwedded women and for wives who on conversion should eschew "the claims of natural affection" (A man should prefer "an unwedded life"). The quotations are taken from the introduction to Julius Tillyard's translation of *The Plays of Roswitha,* for whose sister's life Roswitha's precepts will be seen to have particular relevance.

167  GCPPT 1 | 1 | 21 10 June 1916.

168  ibid. 11 November 1915.

169  ibid. 5 May 1916.

170  GCPPT 1 | 1 | 22 16 June 1917. Aelfrida had her revenge: Dorothy Wrinch later appears in *Vision Triumphant* (pp 35–9) as 'Vera', an ex-pupil of Russell's who has suffered a nervous breakdown as a result of worrying over "philosophy and things".

171  GCPPT 1 | 1 | 20 5 June 1915.

172  GCPPT 1 | 1 | 21 22 October 1915.

173  ibid. 31 January 1917.

174  GCPPT 1 | 1 | 23 25 September 1918.

175  GCPPT 1 | 1 | 26 30 July 1921.

176  ibid. 5 February 1923.

177  ibid. 30 July 1921.

178  GCPPT 1 | 1 | 20 2 March 1915.

179  ibid. 1 April 1915

180  ibid. 30 June 1915.

181  GCPPT 1 | 1 | 21 4 December 1915.

182  GCPPT 1 | 1 | 23 28 February 1919.

183  GCPPT 1 | 1 | 26 12 November 1921.

184  GCPPT 1 | 1 | 23 28 February 1919.

185  GCPPT 1 | 1 | 21 9 November 1916.

186  GCPPT 1 | 1 | 30 16 February 1925.

187  Tillyard, Ae. *The Making of a Mystic* p11.

188  GCPPT 1 | 1 | 30 5 March 1925.

189  Books in epistolary form have a sound English pedigree but one foreign and one émigré example may be more relevant here: in 1906 Julius sent Aelfrida a copy of one of Verga's works, a supposed

collection of letters written by a girl destined for convent life to her best friend, and Mary Annette Russell's 1907 novel *Fräulein Schmidt and Mr Anstruther* with which Aelfrida was familiar was also written in the form of letters.

190  GCPPT 1|1|26 18 February 1922.

191  Chitty, S. p 115.

192  The phrase appears in Tillyard, Ae. *The Way of Praise* p 151 and in Underhill, E. *Practical Mysticism* p169. It is important to remember, however, that phrases which appear somewhat ridiculous to modern readers were pregnant with theological significance to contemporary writers and that 'to be alone with the Alone' actually describes a concept with awesome implications for someone who had involuntarily become 'alone' following her vision of Christ in a mandorla of light and who had deliberately made herself 'alone' by renouncing human consolations in order to adore God in isolation and to conduct a one-to-One relationship with Him. God, on the other hand, is 'the Alone', because, being uniquely and peerlessly Existent, He can be nothing else. As an 'alone' i.e. one who *is* alone but who also needs to *be* alone, Aelfrida would have considered herself not only a manifestation of God as archetypical Alone but also that her 'aloneness' was a manifestation of the Alone in herself. For a detailed discussion of the phrase, see Corbin, H. pp 121–125, 213, and 307 and for a devastating critique of the phrase, see Poem VIII of W H Auden's *Poems 1931–1936* in *The English Auden 1927–1939* (part IV pp 122–123) in the three verses beginning "Dare-devil mystics …" and ending "While the world flounders". See also Part III (*The Orators* Book III *Six Odes* Ode IV p105) in which Auden derisively describes the "poofy redeemer" who peddles such rubbish.

193  GCPPT 1|1|25 26 June 1920.

194  GCPPT 1|1|26 12 November 1921.

195  GCPPT 1|1|23 5 October 1918.

196  GCPPT 1|1|22 26 May 1917. *The Making of a Mystic* was begun at the same time as *Spiritual Exercises,* hence it might be said that Aelfrida's last (literary) conception was twins.

197  Impossible as it is to be sure about the derivation of names of characters in Aelfrida's books, 'Audrey' may be Aethelrida of Ely (locally called St Audrey) depicted in stained glass in the church of Our Lady and the English Martyrs, the Catholic church much frequented by Aelfrida in 1905/6. (The possible origins of 'Talbot' are too numerous to discuss here). 'Audrey Talbot' also has the same initials as Aelfrida Tillyard.

198  'Sebastian' owes something to Eustace who had "never quite forgiven father for giving him such an awful name" but more to Constantine Graham: he looks "plump and sleek … and superior and asks why do I bother my head about God?" (*The Making of a Mystic* p 13).

199  The lectures are those given by Aelfrida in 1915 as part of her first lecture series, lectures which, as she notes in her preface to *The Making of a Mystic*, resulted in her being "constantly asked for advice by men and women who wished to become pilgrims on the Mystic Way and felt the need for intense religious experience". 'Audrey', incidentally, attends what was Aelfrida's third lecture (on Buddhist Meditation) *before* she attends the second.

200  'Catharine Sutherland' probably represents Catherine of Siena (1347–1380), ascetic, councillor, and native of the 'southern land' of Italy where Aelfrida first declared her 'new thirst for mysticism'. 'Catharine' also has the same initials as Caroline Stephen, the Quaker mystic mentioned in this book.

201  Records kept by 'Audrey' of her meditations may be those kept by Aelfrida herself at a similar age, being much less mature in tone than meditations recorded in the 1920s.

202  The wood is probably Hardwick Wood, situated within easy walking distance of the Old Rectory, Caldecote. It may have been in or near there that Aelfrida underwent the visionary experience described in her diary record of her stay in Caldecote in September 1915, versified as *Triolet*. Mercy, a quality often twinned with Goodness, was a popular Quaker name for girls; it is an important Sufi tenet. Aelfrida's inspiration for 'Mercy Allen' may have been 'Miss Clark, the sweetest little Quakeress' observed during a Newnham debate on The Spirit of Quakerism in 1899 (GCPPT 1|1|4 3 June 1899, an entry later emphasised with a cross).

203  The Tillyards were friends of the Chivers who owned a jam factory in Impington just north of Cambridge. Although it was the Chivers, together with George Cadbury and his model factory/town of Bournville, that Aelfrida cited earlier as examples of good business practice (GCPPT 1|1|9 9 May 1902), her description of 'Mr Allen's' philanthropic venture probably owes more to AC Wilkin's Tiptree Village Estate founded on philanthropic principles in 1885. Incidental details also suggest a Tiptree connection.

204  In July 1917 Aelfrida had conceived what she called one of her idealistic 'Big Schemes' (Constantine preferred the adjective 'crackbrained') for 'a college to teach a kind of knight-errantry of commerce' whose aims were 'to rescue commerce from worldliness and selfishness', 'to reconcile capital and labour', and to make 'protectionism and trade war impossible' (GCPPT 1|1|22 24 July and 16 August 1917). As with all such schemes, she failed to raise any enthusiasm in people in a position to implement them so wrote it instead into *The Making of a Mystic* in the book's climactic pages. Her phraseology owes something to Charles Kingsley's 1848 poem *Elegy* in which the words the "joyous knight errant of God" appears (Chitty, S. p 129) and to economist Alfred Marshall's somewhat later exposition of "Economic Chivalry" with regard to commerce (Skidelsky, R. p 49).

205  GCPPT 1|1|22 3 March 1918.

206  ibid. 5 March 1918.

207  GCPPT 1|1|23 8 November 1918.

208  Tillyard, Ae. *Vision Triumphant* p 68. Although Aelfrida rhapsodised over the English countryside, she was a town-dweller at heart who feelingly described 'the boredom … and the stupidity of true country life!' (GCPPT 1|1|21 23 April 1917). Her ideas may have been inspired by Eglantyne Jebb's championship of "a new moral code and economic order", based on reformed land usage and farming practices, while she (EJ) was associated with the National Agricultural Organisation Society in 1914 (Mulley, C. p176).

209  'Noel' is so called because as 'Père Hubert', a French padre, reminds him "You have the name of the sacred birthday of Our Saviour" (*Vision Triumphant* p 83) because he was born on Christmas Day. Constantine's birthday was 29 December.

210  'Silvia' is probably Silvia Myers (Aelfrida knew no-one else of that name) and 'Barrington' because of the village's association with Dorothea Conybeare's father, its former rector.

211  Not all 'Noel's' descriptions are derived from Eustace Tillyard's letters. The longest and most dramatic event in which a group of soldiers pinned down by German fire while succouring an enemy soldier eventually make it back to their own lines at the cost of 'Père Hubert's' life (he is killed by friendly fire) is taken from an incident related by a George Anderson, recorded in Aelfrida's diary on 26 August 1916 (GCPPT 1|1|21). The content and epistolary format of *Vision Triumphant* also owes much to the wartime phenomenon of French 'war godmothers' (*marraines de guerre*) who took it upon themselves as a patriotic duty to correspond with 'soldier-godsons' (*filleuls*) who had no families of their own or who, isolated in the trenches, felt in need of womanly guidance and comfort. A book on the subject, *L'École des Marraines* by French author Jeanne Landre, was published in 1917; its depiction of an epistolary relationship between a 'godmother' and a 'godson' which is as significant for her as it is for him can easily be seen as foreshadowing that of 'Catharine Sutherland' and 'Noel Ashton'. Numerous books were later published about *marraine/filleul* relationships, some containing real letters, others fictional. Evidence to be discussed in a later chapter suggests that Aelfrida was familiar with Jeanne Landre's work; she could also have

heard about the *marraines* from Octavie whose fiancé was a *poilu*. For further details, see http:||www.worldwar1.com.franc/marr.htm

212 Aelfrida had recently communicated with Rendel Harris about her 'knight-errantry of commerce' scheme and had taken the opportunity of asking why he suddenly and inexplicably broke with Chiara, his almost-fiancée. Rendel Harris refused an explanation to Chiara's daughter.

213 Aelfrida herself offered supportive advice in 1918 to a Frenchwoman about to leave Cambridge 'to marry a lame and blinded soldier', speaking particularly of 'the extraordinary interest of "seeing" life through a blind man's eyes' (GCPPT 1|1|22 11 March 1918). Her sentiments and doubtless also *Vision Triumphant* owe much to a 1915 book by Abbé Felix Klein, *The Diary of a French Army Chaplain*, an account of his war service; among the patients he describes (p227) is "a blind man … by degrees resigning himself to [his fate and] helped to submit by an ingeniously sublime consort". The diary, written between 14 August and 31 December 1914, was translated and appeared in two English editions in 1915.

214 GCPPT 1|1|32 24 January 1926.

215 GCPPT 1|1|27 30 April and 7 May 1923.

216 GCPPT 1|1|32 3 February 1926.

217 Tillyard, Ae. *Can I be a Mystic?* p11.

218 GCPPT 1|1|35 17 April 1928. Erle Lunn, described by Aelfrida as 'a very sensitive aspiring soul … who writes to me for spiritual advice' (GCPPT 1|1|35 25 February 1928) but by Alethea as a man who 'writes "puffs" for novels he hasn't read to earn his living', who 'just missed being a gentleman', and who talked about himself 'pathetically and melodramatically' and 'almost exclusively in clichés' but was 'not without charm' (GCPPG A1.1 2 January 1930), was a reader for Hutchinson Ltd to whose attention he brought Aelfrida's 1928 novel *The Young Milliner* after she lent him the manuscript 'just to amuse him' (GCPPT 1|1|35 19 September 1928). Other than his association with Aelfrida, Lunn's sole claim to fame seems to have been the translation from the Danish (his wife was a Dane) of Kai Thorenfeldt's 1928 book *Round the World on a Bicycle*.

219 GCPPT 1|1|30 14 June 1925.

220 GCPPT 1|1|35 11 February 1928.

221 Tillyard, Ae. *Can I be a Mystic?* p 115.

222 Symonds, R. p 146.

223 GCPPT 1|1|35 14 April 1928.

224 ibid. 25 February and 29 September. 1928.

225 GCPPT 1|1|37 17 April 1930. In June 1928 Aelfrida's guardian angel had informed her that he had led her into corresponding with Erle Lunn because Lunn was 'capable of experiencing Universal Consciousness' (GCPPT 1|1|35 23 June 1928). This information doubtless encouraged her to continue a correspondence with a man who, though 'exactly what I want to help on the Great Work of the universal consciousness', was nevertheless 'a trifle commercialised [and] a common type' (GCPPT 1|1|35 19 September 1928).

226 Tillyard, Ae. *Can I be a Mystic ?* p 115.

227 Hubert Henderson was appointed editor of *The Nation* in 1923 at Maynard Keynes' behest. He left the post in 1929 to join Keynes as an economic adviser to the Government. His appointment and his sadness at leaving Cambridge academic life is recorded by Aelfrida (GCPPT 1|1|27 23 March 1923 and GCPPT 1|1|30 11 July 1925).

228 On p113 of *Can I be a Mystic?* 'Author' actually quotes a passage from *A Little Road–Book* as if 'Aelfrida Tillyard' were not also the author of the book in which letters to 'Author' appear. In *The Making of a Mystic* (p 84) Aelfrida quotes, without attribution, her own poem *Architecture* from *Cambridge Poets 1900–1913*.

229 It is amusing to discover how many of the books recommended by 'Author' to 'Stranger' (and by 'Catharine Sutherland' to 'Audrey Talbot') appear in a booklist published in *The Equinox* vol 1 No 10 pp iii–iv, the list being probably that guyed by Aelfrida in her 'unofficial biography' of Aleister Crowley himself.

230 Aelfrida was later distressed to find that *Can I be Mystic?* was reviewed 'almost exclusively by *dreadful* occult or semi-occult publications' (GCPPT 1|1|37 9 July 1930); in fact, the editorial review which appeared in *The Occult Review* of May 1980 (vol 51 No 5 pp 289–299) is deeply respectful, describing the book as one in which "the intimate recesses of the soul … are laid bare for the benefit of others" and as an "intensely interesting autobiographical record" of its author's spiritual exercises and her lectures thereon and of the existence of her 'guardian angel'. The publisher's blurbs which appears on the front and back flaps of the cover of *Can I be a Mystic?* are similarly commendatory (the book is described as an "intimate story of a questing heart") and might even from its tone and content have been written by 'Author' herself.

231 Tillyard, Ae. *Can I be a Mystic?* pp 11 and 91.
GCPPT 1|1|35 25 February 1928.

232 Tillyard, Ae. *Can I be a Mystic?* pp 175–176. 'Stranger's' defection (and something of his earlier life) owes much to John Middleton Murry's 1929 *God. The Science of Meta-Biology*, even down to both men's retirement at a particular point in their life to a Sussex cottage; it was not, however, Lunn's defection which upset Aelfrida so much as the man to whom he defected 'when he thought [she] was not helping him enough': Meredith Starr, 'a sort of minor Aleister Crowley', regarded by Aelfrida as 'a false prophet' preaching universal love who used 'specious language' and who accepted payment for his ministrations but who nevertheless achieved results because he was able to intuit the '*experience*' (generally 'some form of spiritual aggrandisement') his followers sought and to flatter them into believing that they had found it (GCPPT 1|1|54 18 and 26 November, 1937). For an amusing account of the brief association of Meredith Starr (Herbert Close) with Aleister Crowley, see Kaczynski, R. p 171(2002).

233 GCPPG A1.1 20 February 1930.

234 GCPPT 1|1|23 11 November 1918.

235 The phrase is taken from *The Stones of Belgium* (*The Garden and the Fire* pp 4–5) written by Aelfrida in Cambridge on 13 March 1915 three weeks prior to Constantine's departure for Amsterdam.

236 Tillyard, Ae. *A Little Road–Book for Mystics* p 25.

237 GCPPT 1|1|22 11 November 1917.

238 ibid. 1 January 1918.

239 ibid. 10 December 1917.

240 ibid. 19 December 1917. Father Martindale was an early biographer of RH Benson, a man whose literary and presence was recurrent in Aelfrida's life.

241 Tillyard, Ae. *The Making of a Mystic* p v.

242 ibid. p 90.

243 GCPPT 1|1|22 26 November 1917.

244 Tillyard, Ae. *The Making of a Mystic* p 4.

245 GCPPT 1|2.

246 *The Occult Review* vol 52 No 6 June 1930 p 412 quoting *The Sufi Quarterly*, a newly founded and self-entitled 'Journal of Mysticism'.

247 The quotations are taken from *The Gods O'ertake Us* (*The Garden and the Fire*, p 24, section entitled 'songs about love') written in Cambridge on 10 January 1913.

# Graham v. Graham

While it is true to say that Aelfrida did not have – indeed, did not want – a spiritual director during the Great War, she acquired one by default in April 1918 when she received 'a short ecclesiastical letter (with a little cross, and PAX on)'[1] from Dom Savinien Louismet of Buckfast Abbey. Her 'Benedictine Monk'[2] had read and appreciated *The Making of a Mystic* and sent her in return one of his books, *The Mystical Knowledge of God*, published in 1917. His action initiated a correspondence in the course of which he recommended further readings on Mysticism and, it appears, tried without success to convert her to Catholicism.[3]

It seems, too, that Aelfrida had been reflecting on the reasons for her estrangement from Constantine. She therefore confided to Dom Savinien that her own 'religious attitude' had been a contributing factor and asked his advice because being a monk 'nearer to God' than other men, qualified him to judge her case.[4] His reply was not what she expected: "If you were a Catholic coming to me for spiritual direction, the very first thing I would expect from you would be the laying-aside of all pretensions to higher knowledge and other-worldliness which have so incensed your husband … I would insist that your first duty of life, after that of loving God and obeying His commandments, is to make of yourself a good wife and a good mother, a loving, dutiful helpmate of him to whom you have pledged yourself before God; and if this entailed the giving up of some of your most cherished pursuits and personal preferences, I should say you ought not to hesitate to sacrifice them".

Aelfrida had been expecting sympathy instead of a lecture as full of home truths as any delivered by Anatolia but agreed (reluctantly) with everything Dom Savinien said: 'that is very sound and excellent advice. I hope I follow it to the best of my ability … lectures, preaching, all should be given up'. Then she began to argue the truth of it: '"pretensions" – have I pretensions? I have some expert knowledge of religions such as anyone can acquire … I have experience of God, first hand, [which] seemed "special" to me at the time [though] I soon discovered that my path was a familiar one, and [that] I had … many thousands of comrades where I had thought that I must walk alone'. As for other-worldliness, 'can I deny that I value spiritual things more than temporal

Aelfrida, Agatha, Catharine & Alfred Tillyard, Beatrice Zender Brown, & Alethea 1921

… could I renounce that? It would be to deny God! … and if *that* angers Constantine so much, can I do more than be silent over my joys and *never* contrast them with his?'[5] 'I *wish*', she wrote the following day, 'I could see my faults more clearly'.[6]

She nevertheless tried to follow Dom Savinien's advice, resolving on her thirty-fifth birthday in October 1918 'to be the right kind of wife to [Constantine] in the future, if future is given to me'.[7] Aelfrida being Aelfrida, however, she could not resist adding 'a few reflections' to her next letter to her husband, reflections described as "piffle" by their recipient and their sender as "no use to anyone". 'Is the misunderstanding between us hopeless?' she asked miserably.[8]

It was, for both parties to it were intransigent. Constantine, still savagely disappointed with relegation to vice-consul and consequent drop in salary and seriously considering leaving a Service which afforded 'no money, no opportunity, no nothing', was alternately 'begging pity of everyone'[9] and quarrelling with his superior as one hatching 'a plot against himself'.[10] (According to Chiara, questions had been asked in Parliament as to 'why so unsatisfactory a man was retained' in the Foreign Office's employment after the Amsterdam debacle.)[11] In a sentence remarkable for its emphasis on the personal pronoun, Aelfrida refused to entertain the notion of her husband entering the business world to make money ('I *very strongly* oppose this – I don't want us to be rich; I detest the commercial spirit, I love to think of him serving his country, I like life abroad … I wish he would stick to his work')[12] and had no hesitation in telling him so, describing earthly riches as 'very vulgar' and 'the riches to which we look forward [in] our heavenly home'[13] as infinitely preferable. (Events were soon to modify her views.) 'Quite bewildered' at Constantine contemporaneously blaming her 'for having failed him where he most needed comfort and for never having given him the kind of love he needed'[14] – for was not Constantine the guilty party here? – Aelfrida was even more hurt to find her husband writing to her parents (the letter arrived on 29 December 1918, his own thirty-sixth birthday and two weeks before her twelfth wedding anniversary) demanding that their daughter put himself before her 'mystical … and literary ambitions' and give him 'affection instead of principles'.[15] That settled it. Declaring defensively that she had *always* done her writing in odd moments and had '*never* put it before anything' (she intended, however, 'to put it aside *entirely* for a time and give Constantine *all* [her] strength'), Aelfrida went on the offensive: though prepared to abandon outward forms of worship 'if need be', nothing would induce her to 'give up God' no matter how jealous her husband.[16] She even went so far as to add to her annual oath of allegiance to her 'Great Work' a vow to 'seek *first* the Kingdom of Heaven within and without'.[17]

Mindful, however, of Dom Savinien's advice and encouraged by having taken Eustace into her confidence when he lent her Marie Stopes' *Married Love*[18], Aelfrida decided, not without misgivings ('the effect of his infidelity is to make me feel that I *never* could be his wife again') to inform Constantine that she wished 'to ignore the past … and begin again anew'. (To her diary she confided 'the hope, never quite stilled of another child' and that if any woman was Constantine's rightful mate it was herself.)[19] Catharine Tillyard, misled by and surprised at the apparent strength of her daughter's love for a husband whose absence she did not seem to regret but with reasons of her own for reanimating the Grahams' marriage (Aelfrida had not told Chiara of Constantine's liaison with Madame Sterneberg but to write that it was fortunate she had never given Chiara 'the slightest hint' that there was 'anything amiss' between Constantine and herself[20] was to underestimate her mother's powers of observation; however much Chiara behaved like 'Mrs Lavington', she could hardly have forgotten the dreadful weekend of 5 October 1914), urged that it was Aelfrida's wifely duty to leave her daughters and cleave to Constantine wherever he might be posted, 'to be the best possible wife to him, … keep house with him again, and live where and how he likes'.[21] Even Constantine who had been 'looking forward hopefully to the family ceasing to be the social unit'[22] in post-war society and to his wife and children remaining in England during his postings because 'it is cheaper to live at Fordfield'[23], seemed to be 'beginning dimly to want his wife and family and possibly even to wish that the past had been otherwise'.[24] The Oracle, too, so far forgot himself as to abandon *The Times* and 'interest himself in [his daughter's] affairs'.[25] Only Agatha and Alethea, anxious at losing the only parent who provided a constant presence in their lives, were reproachful at her impending departure: 'I feel I *cannot* leave the children to go to Constantine. They love and need me so …'[26] Aelfrida herself was in two minds about reconciliation ('I must go back to [Constantine] as soon as possible, though God alone knows how I dread it')[27] and because of other significant instances in her life.

The first involved rereading diary entries for the years 1904–1906 (and the addition of the passionately sad and resentful entries noted earlier, these including 'I have given him all, all my devotion and it has been lost like a drop in the ocean')[28], this occasioning expenditure of much anguish ('has it been *my* fault that he has changed? … O God, show me my faults and punish *me* for them') over a man who had been so sweet 'and so ardent and unworldly'.[29] But Constantine's insightful comments regarding himself ('I do not know if I am capable of always loving one woman')[30] should have warned her – indeed, judging by her own comments about Constantine throwing off his love as a woman throws off her cloak or, with regard to her fiancé's wish to give her perfect happiness, 'I do not know that he will'[31], *had* warned her – that suffering would certainly follow those glorious days when she was 'happy, happy, happy!' because she was young and beautiful and Constantine loved her.[32]

The second concerned visions experienced during the time of indecision whose content included imagery of an appropriately cardiac nature. Her heart, a much-exercised organ in Aelfrida's emotion-wracked life, was more frangible than usual because of the 'almost insoluble nature' of the problems that would confront her when she met Constantine again: 'I must neither condone nor condemn … doesn't God give tact and insight as well as virtue? Oh pray Aelfrida, pray!'[33] Her first vision was of the Sacred Heart, accompanied by an audition whose content she does not record.[34] The second, recorded on the day on which Constantine demanded priority over Mysticism and Literature, occurred at a time when Aelfrida felt the supernatural so near that she had difficulty in maintaining contact with ordinary life:

while in church (possibly, it being Sunday, St Columba's) she found herself ushered in a vision by her guardian angel to the foot of an enormous crucifix and, on raising her head to see Christ's face, saw a splash of blood from the wound in His side fall into her heart, a token whose significance was puzzling but whose presence ('it lies there still') was comforting.[35] On a Good Friday service the vision recurred, this time accompanied by 'heavenly music and … what some people call angels and which seem to me spiritual presences'.[36]

Having decided that she must join Constantine in Lyons and post-war conditions being now sufficiently stable to allow her to do so, Aelfrida pondered on the best means of effecting reconciliation. Constantine, she wrote, 'does not want to see the same wife whom he had wronged … but he may want to see someone new and interesting, with fresh ideas and varied experiences, a healthier body, new clothes, *quoi*?' Deciding that 'for his sake, perhaps, [she] ought to stoop to conquer'[37], she planned her strategy: 'I'm going to have some fun … pose as worldly, perhaps. Puzzle Constantine, if I can [but] not condemn him or anything he does'.[38] Therein lay a problem: suppose Constantine was so attracted by his 'new and interesting' wife that he wished to resume marital relations? Should she, if this happened, be 'gay and tender' towards him or should she, to prevent it happening, stand 'a little aloof'?[39] If she succumbed to Constantine's charms during her 'adventure to Lyons', a prospect already reawakening 'old desires and ambitions and lures'[40], would that lay her open to his being once more able to 'stroll about in [her] soul's garden in his contemptuous way and say what a poor sort of place it is'?[41] Deciding that on this occasion she required 'special help' and that even Straighteners sometimes needed to unburden themselves, she risked 'spiritual dissipation' (*sic*) and made 'a short and simple confession' ('short and simple' because she had no intention of having her confessor – a village vicar, singled out for his 'intense and burning spirituality'- probe 'in the recesses of [her] heart')[42], after which she received absolution for what, she feared, constituted a major impediment to reconciliation, namely the 'spiritual pride' which might prevent her from remaining 'humble to [her]self' while posing as enigmatic and worldly to her husband.[43]

A 'very persistent' vision on 1 May 'of [her] guardian angel offering [her] the choice between a chalice and a sword' which Aelfrida, disregarding its Freudian symbolism, took to mean that she was to perform God's will perfectly in Lyons or be punished[44], preceded her departure on 5 May: 'Goodbye Fordfield, good-bye dear ones … I only go because it is *right* – nothing else could take me from you'.[45] Carrying a virgin volume of her diary

(there was too much of her 'soul's garden' recorded in the previous volume and it was wiser to waste precious pages than run the risk of Constantine reading them) and somewhat depressed by an 'undefinable feeling of … the very soil itself having bled' as her train crossed the mutilated fields of northern France[46] (a short stopover with Zelle, her former nursery governess, restored her equilibrium)[47], Aelfrida arrived in Lyons on 7 May 1919.

At first all went well. Constantine met her at the station and escorted her to his apartment overlooking the Rhône. As wife of the popular English Consul-General – Constantine's paranoid fears of persecution by jealous rivals had been allayed by his having achieved his promised promotion late in 1918; mellowed by this, he was now enjoying life in a cosmopolitan city untouched by war[48] – Aelfrida was made much of by Lyonnais and expatriate society alike. She responded in kind ('I wore my pretty blue linen embroidered frock and chattered nonsense in French and Italian and felt very different from my home self … I made everyone laugh very much [and] had *a succès fou*. Constantine was pleased')[49]; she even danced. While Constantine worked she explored Lyons, lighting a candle for Dom Savinien at the shrine of the Virgin of Fourvière before descending the *colline sacrée* with its 'holy garden full of shrines commemorating the joyful and sorrowful mysteries'[50], this and a subsequent visit inspiring an Ascension Day repetition of her vision of the crucified Christ's blood falling on her heart.[51] On Sundays the Grahams attended the English church, though Constantine's tendency to discuss venereal disease in the American Army of Occupation instead of the sermon on the way home was indicative that church attendance was more keeping-up appearances on the part of the Consul-General than renewed interest in religious matters: 'his deadness on the divine side causes me unutterable pain'.[52] (It did more: at a Sunday luncheon held by the Grahams at a Lyons hotel with 'smart things to eat and plenty of wine flowing', the menfolk began to tell what Aelfrida primly called 'gentlemen's stories'. On her announcing that "considering it is Sunday, suppose we talk about something else", Constantine retorted "damn Sunday" and told another. Feeling 'insidiously invaded' by the general merriment, Aelfrida debated whether to walk out or to stay; she stayed but Constantine's put-down hurt her in a more than personal way: 'it was as if I had seen my Lord bound and blindfolded … and someone had struck him'.)[53] But this was of little significance beside the fact that Constantine 'eagerly took [her] as wife again' and successfully recalled to life 'that part of me which I have for the past year and a half been trying to kill'.[54]

The idyll – if idyll it was – did not last. Having reawakened his wife's repressed sexuality, Constantine then 'refused further union' because of the risk of pregnancy. (It is obvious from Aelfrida's diary account that sexual congress took place at the most fertile point in her menstrual cycle; possibly she was trying for another child and Constantine realised this.) 'Moved by much desire', Aelfrida agreed to contraception but was repulsed ('he really enjoyed the sight of my distress … he enjoys having people in his power')[55] and in a long diary entry written on the fifteenth anniversary of their engagement – a day made particularly poignant by Constantine's gift of a bunch of flowers – laid bare a relationship which even she realised was beyond redemption. The faults, of course, were Constantine's: his meanness with money (after showing signs of wanting to shower her with 'new hats and furbelows', he provided only centimes for spending money while lavishing expensive meals on people he wished to impress)[56]; his physical decline, over-indulgence at table having caused him to become 'stout about the stomach'; his conversational topics being limited to 'his ambitions for more money and more power and his endless grievances, sex, and gossip'[57]; his lack of interest in daughters whose weekly letters he no longer bothered to answer 'because they are girls'[58]; his despotic behaviour towards herself ('as long as I wear my best dresses, listen to all he has to say, go where I am told, ask no inconvenient questions and do not interfere with his life, he is very kind to me')[59]; his assumption of the moral high ground (a spot reserved for herself) whence he accused the Oracle and Chiara of adopting "a tone of moral superiority" towards himself and his family and of "bringing up and allowing to impose on others a woman whose parallel in wickedness and egoism [he had] never met", this monster of depravity being, of course, the wife whose behaviour during the Great War he described as "tantamount to desertion".[60] Finally, the sometimes bizarre behaviour of a man she had once described as 'splendidly sane'[61] during which Constantine accused her of urging him to take two wives or of having a 'secret compact' with Willie Searle to marry him after his (CG's) death or who, though never violent or brutal, acted in such a way as to seem barely responsible for what he did: at a meal during which he had (for once) drunk only water, he sang snatches of songs in different languages, raved about "alabaster palaces" and "ever-virgin houris", and finally sank down 'in a kind of coma' from which he awoke with no memory of the event.[62]

There was, too, the question of Constantine's relationship with his landlady, Madame Cochaud, a widow slightly older than himself, 'small and dark and slight, gentle yet lively in manner, [and] intelligent without being at all cultured'[63], and mother of four sons. At first well-disposed towards Madame Cochaud, it was not long before Aelfrida realised that her husband's landlady would be 'exceedingly glad to get rid of Constantine's wife'.[64] Though bent on magnanimity, 'suspicions … crossed [her] mind' that Constantine and Madame Cochaud were having an affair: they were 'very free of … each other's bedrooms' (Constantine and Aelfrida slept apart) and, his wife's presence notwithstanding, Constantine frequently kissed Mme Cochaud, addressed her as '*tu*', and talked 'endearing baby talk' to her while describing himself in the third person as '*petit Costi*'.[65] Madame Cochaud was even invited to accompany Constantine and Aelfrida and Constantine's vice-consul on an expedition to look at a house for the latter, an occasion on which Madame and Constantine became so engrossed with each other that Aelfrida wandered off alone to admire the villa's striking view over the Saône valley.[66]

In spite of everything – the *ménage-à-trois* at No 4 Place St Clair and Aelfrida's constraining presence (she generally kept her religious ideas and opinions to herself but made her husband subtly aware that they had had not changed; discussing Constantine's general conduct with her mother and father in November 1917, Chiara took Constantine's part, telling her daughter that she was 'too prone to make trivial things a matter of principle', a sentiment to which Aelfrida added 'true', while the Oracle suggested, correctly, that the fundamental and irreconcilable difference between the Grahams was that Constantine cared predominantly for this world and Aelfrida for the next)[67] – the Grahams parted amicably: 'he evidently wants me to take pleasant memories with me'.[68] In her heart of hearts, however, Aelfrida knew her marriage was finished, telling herself as her train pulled out of Lyons station 'your youth is over'[69] and describing as 'tragedy, tragedy!'[70] the fifteen-year relationship she was leaving behind.

Of Dom Savinien we hear little more beyond a couple of brief references in *Spiritual Exercises*.[71] An undated letter from him to Aelfrida (the otherwise illegible postmark bears the year 1919) appears to coincide with the period following her return from Lyons insofar as it refers to the possibility of maintaining some kind of relationship with her husband through the medium of their respective guardian angels and to Aelfrida's need to keep herself spiritually and emotionally "fit and healthy for the sake of your dear children".[72] But because no 'dust-cloud of metaphysical subtleties'[73] could console Aelfrida at this point and because the Benedictine who had 'assumed the office of spiritual director' had proffered only bad advice and because she had no intention of letting Dom Savinien or any other spiritual director 'come *right* into [her] soul', a place reserved for 'God alone'[74], she embarked without direction on life without the husband she was never to see again.

Given Constantine's past behaviour – and this, Aelfrida now informs us, included 'things which I was too loyal … even to put down in my diary'[75] – and his recent blatant proof of continuing infidelity, it is strange that Aelfrida allowed her marriage to continue as long as it did. As early as November 1917 Alfred Tillyard suggested legal separation but she had refused to consider it[76]; in July 1918, however, she all but confessed to Frank Stokoe that the Devil had suggested divorce, telling her "of course you don't want to do it yet but you had better get used to the idea".[77] Furthermore, in a diary entry recorded without emphasis but italicised here to denote its significance, she noted that when she refused to disobey Constantine by continuing her 'Great Work' under Crowley's guidance, Crowley had stated that it made no difference, '*that one could not escape one's Karma, and that I should only lose my husband some other way*'. (A 'chance hit', she asks, 'or did *his* subconscious know?')[78] But was it only because she had not yet got used to the idea that Aelfrida behaved so humbly towards her bullying husband but at the same time threatened to 'separate from him at once'[79] if he returned to Holland to bid farewell to Madame Sterneberg, only to fail to carry out her threat and even to make herself his accomplice by blaming herself for his wrong actions? Or was it because of what she would relinquish by moving from the position of married woman to that of 'someone "mixed up" in a divorce'[80] and from Consul-General's wife to a woman with 'no position and no status'[81]? Or because of the ignominy 'an open scandal'[82] would bring to her family or to herself as a 'soul-doctor' unable to 'straighten' herself sufficiently to keep her husband? Or that divorce would expose her 'perfect' marriage for the sham it was? Or because she did not want to deprive her daughters of their father? Or because in spite of everything, Constantine remained 'my beloved husband dear to me, my charge, my love, my only beloved'?[83] Or was it yet another manifestation of co-dependency, namely toleration of inappropriate behaviour in an effort to compensate for self-esteem lowered by a husband who, denigrating everything she held dear and criticising everything she did, caused her to love him '*as a slave should love*' and instead of defending herself to write him 'rather pathetic' letters 'putting [herself] in the wrong'[84], letters whose content could not have been better designed to alienate Constantine's remaining affections (such as they were) than if they had been written with the express purpose of doing so?

Constantine, however, smarting from realisation that Aelfrida had employed him as a stud to 'provide … babies' and that having borne two living children, she regarded him as a necessary but unfortunate episode in her life (an episode, moreover, whose perceived failings she had publicly reviled) and their marriage as a means of 'providing all other necessities of life'[85] (especially status: she continued to style herself 'Mrs Constantine Graham' long after she was legally entitled to do so), that she had and would always put God and her daughters before himself and his career, and that she continued (covertly now, rather than openly) to vaunt her moral superiority, behaved like Argyris, once described by Aelfrida as 'a real Greek who knows how to hate'.[86] Egged on by Anatolia who informed her son that his former inamorata Ethel Poncelle had recently divorced and suggested that it would be 'noble and free and wonderful' if he followed Ethel's example[87], Constantine set in motion proceedings which Aelfrida herself might have done no more contemplate.

The treaty which formally ended the Great War was signed on 28 June 1919; on 6 July Constantine opened fire by closing the Grahams' joint bank account, by refusing to pay his wife's quarterly allowance, by accusing her of extravagance because following Octavie's departure in October 1918, Agatha and Alethea, now seven and nine, had been cared for by what he termed 'useless and unnecessary' nursery governesses[88] (the second was dismissed on 30 July, Aelfrida having discovered her head to be '*alive* with beasties' and noting ruefully 'dear me! no time for the higher feelings in the midst of lice and tears!')[89] and by reminding his wife of her 'place and relative importance' in his life and that she would shortly find herself unable any longer to lead the life of a '*grande dame … in idleness*'.[90] His withdrawing financial support from his wife and daughters left them to subsist with the rest of the Fordfield household on income from Chiara's rental properties (the Oracle's income of some £580 a year from directorships and property was reserved for his personal expenses and to pay the minuscule wages of the boy who cleaned the knives and boots; Chiara's income was around £250 a year) and forced Aelfrida to sell some wedding present silver to pay outstanding medical and other bills. On 9 July he delivered his second broadside, writing to the Oracle to inform his father-in-law that matters were in the hands of his solicitors, that all communications were to pass through them, and that he hoped Aelfrida would divorce him. He also demanded custody of his daughters.[91]

Aelfrida was devastated, wailing in the privacy of her diary that 'all my personal joy in life is over for ever. I may have – have now – happiness in the children and my dear ones, in honest work well done, in religion, but no personal delight for myself … I feel as though I had concussion of the brain in my soul'[92]; she also declared that because Anatolia had 'polluted' Constantine, she herself would 'fight to the death' to prevent her innocent daughters from ever coming in contact with the 'moral contamination' exuded by their father and paternal grandmother.[93] She then demanded of God that He 'save Constantine' from becoming 'wicked' ('He *must*, He MUST') before resigning herself 'in darkness and blindness' to His will.[94]

Her mind 'grinding out the wheat of sorrow' and herself 'restless and miserable beyond words' and 'too unhappy even to cry'[95] (a tearstain blots Anatolia's name in her diary entry for 9 July), Aelfrida considered only briefly that the breakdown of her marriage owed much to her own faults as a wife (her single 'bad mistake' was 'to try and make a teetotaller of him')[96] before deciding to write to Constantine's vice-consul informing him that his superior was suffering from 'war neurasthenia' (unlikely in a non-combatant) and begging him to persuade Constantine to take home leave or to see a doctor [97] and to inform her father of Constantine's infidelity and ask him to act for her in all dealings with solicitors as if by doing so she could distance herself from the consequences of her own actions.

Alfred Tillyard stated that Constantine's infidelity put him "beyond the pale of forgiveness"[98] and he should be treated with the 'sternest justice'.[99] (Having 'the strongest objection to any legal proceedings except such as would give [her] the guardianship of the kiddies'[100], Aelfrida agreed – reluctantly.) Eustace was quietly supportive and provided practical comfort in allowing his sister and nieces the surrogate happiness of visiting his and Phyllis' first married home and of hearing the joyful news of Phyllis' first pregnancy. Julius, about to leave for South Africa, was not told because 'his nerves are not strong'[101] and appears to have been so pre-occupied with his own affairs that he failed to notice his sister's distress, a distress she concealed effectively in public ('my troubles – and this kind of edict of separation *is* a trouble – shall make no-one suffer but myself')[102] but expatiated on at length in her diary. Argyris, appealed to, replied that Constantine had not confided in him and that as the matter was in the hands of solicitors he did not propose to become involved.[103] Anatolia, having achieved a longstanding ambition, remained publicly silent but continued to plot and plan during Constantine's visits to her in Paris and Hessle. Chiara informed her daughter that she considered it 'disgusting' that Aelfrida had maintained a sexual relationship with Constantine after discovering his infidelity[104] and stated that the Tillyards were unlikely to hear anything more from Constantine unless it concerned financial arrangements; she also proffered sensible advice: the welfare of 'the kiddies' should be everyone's 'unique preoccupation'.[105] The little girls, it seems, were told nothing nor were they encouraged to ask questions and both became 'very naughty and wild'

as a consequence of their mother being 'troubled and anxious and perhaps a little inattentive'.[106]

Apart from Aelfrida – and it has to be said that the tone of current diary entries is so consciously 'tragic' that it verges on melodrama – the person most upset by Constantine's behaviour was her mother. Chiara had received 'such a loving letter' from Constantine while Aelfrida was in Lyons so was 'very much upset' on being informed of the breach between her daughter and son-in-law, more upset than Aelfrida expected of one who declared that the Tillyards should have 'no thought for Constantine or what is to become of him'.[107] True, she had written to Ancifera complaining how bitter and baffling it was to have Constantine behave as he now did and that this was the family's reward for lavishing "kindness, love and confidence" on a man whose earlier behaviour seemed to indicate how much he loved "Fordfield, our family life, our home, each one of us", and saying how hurt she was by her son-in-law's ingratitude to herself as the person whose influence had secured his career.[108] But it was not until later that she confided to Aelfrida the chief cause of her unhappiness: other than Rendel Harris, Constantine was the only person towards whom she had 'allowed her affections to flow unchecked' and Constantine having 'scorned and flouted and trampled on all she cares for and believed in', she was heartbroken.[109]

Besides her immediate family, Aelfrida also confided in Frank Stokoe. But Fidelio, then in a state of 'spiritual excitation' and having been told 'all that it was necessary for him to know', resented her having 'absorbing troubles' to the detriment of interest in his own; indeed, he suggested "detachment" ('very good advice', wrote Aelfrida tartly, 'but God has done all the "detachment" for me and I need not strive after it myself')[110] before absenting himself from her company (and, in August 1919, from Cambridge) though he wrote to say he would return 'if needed'.[111] Embittered and angry ('he is my very dear friend but he is not relevant to the present situation ... I do not need him; I will need, I am resolved to need, no-one but God')[112], Aelfrida turned to Willie Searle, on leave from the British Army of Occupation in Germany, and found him 'extraordinarily sympathetic': 'he understood more than Fidelio did ... it helped me very much to talk to him'.[113] She did not, however, tell Willie the whole truth about her marriage; that disclosure came later and not from her. After that there was nothing to do but end 'the most tragic volume of [her] diary' (to date; there will be more tragic ones) with the un-consoling thought that, though trying desperately not to hate Constantine, 'when I think of [his] ingratitude towards my people and the base injury he has inflicted on his loving trustful children, I get all hot with anger and have to pray *hard*, very hard, before I can forgive him'.[114]

Anxious to avoid the 'open scandal'[115] he predicted in October 1914 if Aelfrida's denial of sexual relations to her husband entered the public domain but keen not to prejudice the career of a son-in-law on whose continuing financial support his daughter relied, Alfred Tillyard drafted a private deed of settlement[116] but was overridden by a solicitor keener on divorce. 'Bitterly sad at bringing grief to [her] *dear*, dear family'[117] and with her health (as usual in a crisis) collapsing, Aelfrida reflected ruefully on 'the bitterness and difficulty' of her present and, it seemed, her future, existence as a dependent: 'since I am now admittedly incompetent to manage my own life [the Oracle and Chiara] treat me … as a child … but if Chiara pays the piper she will naturally call the tune'.[118] To her further dismay, the Oracle and Chiara (and possibly also Aelfrida herself who, on receiving the news that Constantine had been seen in Cambridge, asked herself 'what did he want? To kidnap the children? – shoot me?')[119] decided that the Tillyards should absented themselves from Cambridge for the duration of the divorce proceedings and to that end rented the seaside house of a family friend. Having recently felt that God had deserted her at a point when her life was already 'harder than I have ever known', Aelfrida was sustained shortly before departure by a 'triumphant vision of God' as she walked the long, dull length of nearby Bateman Street in pouring rain ('I don't think I have ever felt happier … than I did then. Oh, the reality of it!')[120], only to decide that it was 'a good thing that God's grace is inexhaustible' for she would need 'a perfect fortune of it' to sustain her in a North Norfolk seaside resort in winter.[121] Having rented out Fordfield complete with staff, the Tillyards decamped to 'Hunstanton Above All. Sea-air, Salubrious and Sanitary' (as advertisements had it) on 8 October 1919, their journey being made more distressing by their having to travel by lorry because strikers had brought the Great Eastern Railway to a standstill.[122]

'Small but habitable'[123] Burlington Cottage was a modern semi-detached villa on Austin Street. Though designed by architect Bertie Ibberson of the famous Holkham picnic as one of his 'New Art' houses (the sundial's motto on his own house a short distance away – "it is better to travel hopefully than to arrive" – must have made ironic reading to one who had just endured an eighty mile journey during which Alethea was repeatedly travel sick), by Tillyard standards the cottage was 'lower middle class' and apart from a charlady whose periodic absences resulted in strenuous working days for Aelfrida and her mother, was servantless: 'it is hardly life here, physically … after what one has been used to

at Fordfield'.[124] Chiara and Aelfrida divided the chores between them though ill-health made housework almost unendurable. Chiara hated life in Hunstanton even more than her daughter, was plagued by chronic indigestion, but generally managed to struggle on; Aelfrida, plagued by rheumatism, severe period pains, headaches, sore throats, backache, and 'neuralgia on [her] breasts'[125], regularly collapsed into bed 'to claim a couple of days' solitude with a clear conscience'[126] and deeply resented having to carry out her mother's tasks when Chiara herself was unwell. Having once declared that she would 'never, *never*, NEVER' carry out housemaid's work 'unless I am obliged to'[127], she frequently found herself obliged to, writing bitterly on the day Constantine sailed for his next posting as chargé d'affaires at Colon in Panama 'I wonder what [he] would think if he had watched me with my poor hands covered with broken chilblains trying to light a fire with damp [wood] or turning out the living room and sending clouds of dust into a poor eye half-closed with a big stye, or going out … all shabbily dressed to glean a few sticks!'[128]

The Tillyards' Hunstanton exile being a self-imposed penance made matters worse but in the midst of everything Aelfrida found consolations: realisation that her present 'hard life' was illuminated by the 'intimate joy' that she had risen to the occasion and could cope with physical and emotional adversity[129]; that, though distressed by 'dark groping longing' for Constantine and by dreams about a husband who either returned ready to resume married life or was 'mad and tried to murder [her] and the children'[130], she had set in train procedures which would free her from the presence which had overshadowed her life for nearly twenty years. Third, but possibly first in importance, that she was experiencing 'triumphant joy' arising from a renewed 'sense of God's presence' in her life[131] all the sweeter for having absented itself when she needed it most, and although descriptions of spiritual experiences are few and far between during her 'exile' (she was, she hinted, too busy to record them but it may be that sheer physical fatigue denied her what more leisured life permitted), she derived comfort from those she had: a 'marvellous dream of ecstasy' during which her soul 'soared up like an eagle and met with God'[132], or 'sudden escapes into Universal Consciousness [without which] life would be intolerable here'[133], which, though not entirely pleasant because of what they contained of the pain of the world, nevertheless allowed her to experience 'Immanent God' welling up within her.[134] She was also cheered by conversations with a local Baptist minister who had made a particular study of English mystics (his introducing her to Thomas Traherne resulted in an Easter vision of Traherne's

**Ibberson houses in Austin Street, Hunstanton**

"orient and immortal" cornfields 'breaking into songs of praise')[135] and who provided a sympathetic ear into which she could pour woes pent up in her parents' presence and unrevealed (she hoped) to her children.

Lastly, literary inspiration had not left her. While in Hunstanton she completed *A Little Road-Book for Mystics* (put aside in the summer of 1919 because the consolations of religion described therein had lost their savour), began and abandoned a book of short stories, and in May 1920 embarked with her guardian angel's permission on another novel, *All the Blessings of this Life,* whose self-willed hero was modelled on Alethea.[136] She also wrote some revealing poems: *Autumn by the Sea,* inspired by a perfect autumn day on Hunstanton beach which 'so put me in touch with poetry again [that] I had the great joy of being able to write ... after long months of being parched and dried up'[137]; *Go if thou wilt,* of 13 January 1920, addressed to Constantine ("Go if thou wilt. Thou canst not free thy heart / Nor rid thy sense of love that once had been / Twixt man and wife ...") and commented on wryly (and, as it transpired, inaccurately) five days later 'that poem might make you think that I want him physically. This is not so'[138]; *On the Road to Old Hunstanton,* of 20 March 1920, with its theme of spiritual renewal after a soul-winter when "the fields of life [lay] dead"[139]; and an untitled, undated poem beginning "I kneel unto a rose. Laugh on, O fool .../ You never saw God pass o'er hill and lea ..."[140] probably addressed to the 'blind Greek' from whom the law was shortly to separate her.

As news spread of the Grahams' impending divorce, Aelfrida received letters of condolence comforting during an exile 'among people who haven't heard of my books nor my lectures nor any of my talents and who are not interested in me in the least'.[141] Some correspondents – Phyllis' father Henry Mudie-Cooke, for example, and Dorothy Smith (not 'Mr Smith's', now a successful London dentist) offered financial support for herself and

her daughters.[142] Some, like Florence Keynes, were 'sympathetic but business-like'[143], Aelfrida's refusal to perform 'war-work' having been noted by that hard-working lady. Some came from 'unexpected quarters'[144] – Silvia Blennerhasset née Myers with whom, since Silvia had married and become a society lady, Aelfrida had had little contact, and James Stark, Julius' former school friend, who not only ordered a copy of *Vision Triumphant* but also told its author that she was not to consider herself as "having brought disgrace on your family", that he refused to believe she was disgraced ("someone else may be disgraced. Your greatest happiness is that *you aren't*"), that as a man "with a bad mother", Constantine could hardly be expected to respect women, and that instead of it being "vulgar and degrading" to have to worry about money, money worries were a blessing in disguise because being "compelled to be practical" helped keep one sane.[145] Others, particularly Lucy Verey, were '*most* loving and dear'.[146] (Hal Verey, Lucy's husband, was soon to represent Aelfrida in court.) Some, like Aunt Anna who had always regarded her niece as selfish and spoilt, were 'sympathetic and pious' but tended to lay the blame for her broken marriage at Aelfrida's door [147], a truth that caused the latter to note crossly how sad it was that 'people who have no pretensions to piety are not censorious and are much more spontaneous in their sympathy than those of conspicuous goodliness'[148], ironically that 'people tell me I ought to forget Constantine ... it seems to me that one may question whether I ought ever to have loved him!'[149], and sadly that letters of sympathy were a waste of time given that all 'love-happiness' was over.[150]

Early in November 1919 and exiled in the 'haven of refuge' which Hunstanton (and even Burlington Cottage) had become, Aelfrida wrote a letter to Constantine. It was so important that she transcribed it into her diary: "My beloved husband, I most earnestly entreat you to agree to a reconciliation ... My love for you is unalterable and I am sure that with good will on your side we could be very happy together. The children ask for their father. Can we not make a home for them? ... Oh my love, my love, come back to me! Aelfrida".[151] On 22 November she recorded Constantine's reply, written on 17 November 'c/o Mrs Michaelides. 147 Boulevard St Michel, Paris', his home pending his departure for Colon. It was not addressed to her but to his solicitor: "Dear Dr Jackson ... I do not intend to resume conjugal relations with my wife and nothing will induce me to do so". Shrinking from the letter's 'coarseness and brutality', Aelfrida blamed Constantine's behaviour on Anatolia: 'his mother has carried him off, body and soul, and she is now devouring him at her leisure'.[152] This, if nothing else, stiffened her resolve: divorce rather than legal separation.

There were, however, legal formalities to be gone through before that. On 19 December she took 'a petition for restitution and an affidavit' to be sworn in the presence of the local Commissioner of Oaths: 'I felt so bad at invoking the help of the law against my dear, dear Constantine [but] to see his cruel words there on the document so neatly engrossed – and my own cry to him to come back – and his curt brutal answer – O my God! My God!'[153] Her 'cry to him to come back' of 7 November was, of course, part of the legal process; she does not say how much was a cry from the heart.

Constantine sailed for Colon in January 1920 (having been advised by his solicitors that maintenance payments for his wife and children were legally enforceable[154], Aelfrida received £100 on 23 January, ten days after writing *Go if thou Wilt*), leaving his wife reflecting, like Job in the Old Testament, on the spiritual benefits of submission to God's will and of the exercise of patience and forbearance in adversity and that she should accept her husband's sins as her own 'to *bear* and try and *atone* for them'.[155] Her reflection was timely: on 15 February she received a letter from her solicitor asking for confirmation of Constantine's appearance ("the maid at the hotel describes him as …"), this causing her to ask 'oh what *has* he been doing to get free?'[156] What Constantine had done, of course, was to provide recent incontrovertible evidence of adultery as the law demanded. No wonder, then, that his wife's next vision was of 'impish spirits' taking her captive, dragging her away from the Mystic Way, and nailing her to a cross.[157]

On 2 April 1920 Aelfrida, represented by Hal Verey, appeared before Mr Justice Horridge in London to pray for restitution of conjugal rights, a legal move which would either compel her husband to return to her or, should he fail to do so, allow her to divorce him for desertion without further ado.[158] Describing herself as 'absolutely heartbroken at having turned the law against Constantine and put this further barrier between us'[159], she was further dismayed to find the case reported in the papers on 28 April as "A Respondent in the Consular Service. Graham v. Graham" and quoting in detail not only her letter of 7 November 1919 and Constantine's reply but also a formal letter received by her two months after her return from Lyons:

"British Consulate-General, Lyons, 7 July 1919.
Dear Aelfrida,
I have after many years determined to close once for all my relations with you [and] I propose to give you the opportunity of seeking divorce … I shall ask for the children, having concluded that you are criminally incompetent both as a wife and as a mother".[160]

Her dismay was only slightly relieved by the newspapers' omission of 'the worst part of Constantine's letters'[161] (the letter quoted must have arrived at Fordfield at the same time or shortly after the letter received by Alfred Tillyard on 9 July but Aelfrida makes no reference to its derogatory contents in her diary) but the shame and strain attendant on the episode turned her air 'quite white' (so she said; it later reverted to brown) and made her 'want to go away all by myself and cry where no-one will see me … but of course one can't'.[162]

Decree of restitution (costs to be paid by the defendant) was granted and Constantine judicially advised to return to his wife within three months, i.e. by the end of July 1920. But now safely *en poste* across the Atlantic (Aelfrida does not comment on the curious coincidence of her husband's *second* departure for Panama having followed *another* major breach in their relationship) and knowing that nothing Aelfrida might do would induce him to return, Constantine did not return. (Robert/Robin Tillyard, visiting from Australia shortly after the injunction expired, informed Aelfrida that Constantine was 'a dago who could never stick to one woman' and who would never want to see or hear of her again.)[163] The Tillyards, meanwhile, moved back to Cambridge in June 1920, a month before the injunction expired.

Although she rejoiced at returning to Fordfield and derived much peace from the cool green garden, Aelfrida felt the need to spring-clean her heart as well as the house. She therefore sold a large number of Constantine's books[164], sent four boxes of his belongings to his solicitors, cleared out the small room used by Constantine as a 'den', and burned the 'Michaelides Letters' sent by him to her during their courtship ('to think that of all his love there is nothing left but a little pile of ashes!'[165]; three years later she came upon the sole letter to escape 'destruction that I have so much regretted', describing it as 'a great treasure' she would one day steel herself to re-read)[166] and such of hers to him as were there. But though her motive for burning the letters may have been to 'get some of the dust out of [her] heart'[167] in order to be able to "look bravely forward"[168] instead of regretfully backward, it is also possible that she did so in order to destroy evidence which might be embarrassing to her if subpoena resulted in them being read out in court. (She may have disposed of Aleister Crowley's letters to herself by giving them to Fidelio in July 1918 because they might provide incriminating evidence of an infatuation she did not wish to become public property should legal separation from Constantine, the possibility of which had already entered her mind, come to pass. A fourth reason, given much later, was lest "a callous future biographer … nose out and publish them'.)[169] Having completed her holocaust, however, Aelfrida discovered to her dismay that she had destroyed evidence which might have brought her divorce to a speedier conclusion: the kind of 'hotel evidence' provided by Constantine before he left England was 'looked on suspiciously by judges' because it provided insufficient proof of longstanding infidelity.[170]

In spite of recurring dreams that Constantine, repentant, returned and was reconciled (a constant theme in Aelfrida's waking and sleeping thoughts for years to come, though pragmatically she knew that she would never allow him near his daughters again for fear of moral contamination), Constantine himself furnished sufficient 'evidence of misconduct'[171] early in 1921 to allow the case to proceed. On 21 February 1921 Aelfrida signed her divorce petition, learning, as she did so, the story behind the 'chambermaid' episode: 'one day in December 1919 Constantine committed adultery at the Midland Hotel, St Pancras with one Elizabeth Bartlett'[172], a woman picked up in a cinema and induced to spend a night with him 'in order to make evidence for the divorce' and also, 'for a consideration', to appear in court as a witness.[173] Small wonder, then, that she found herself 'passing through a time of great depression and discouragement'[174] during which she had a vision of her guardian angel slashing a cross on her heart before lifting it out of her body for her to see.[175]

On 27 July 1921 the divorce summons and extrovert Tom and Beatrice Zender Brown, distant American cousins of Catharine Tillyard, arrived simultaneously at Fordfield. (The Zender Browns left tactfully early on 1 August but not before taking a revealing photograph which demonstrates the toll on the family of the strain of the preceding two years: Aelfrida grim faced, the Oracle, tall, thin, and frail, supported by his small unsmiling wife, Agatha subdued, Alethea grown enormously fat.) On 28 July 1921 Aelfrida accompanied Hal Verey to the Law Courts in London to receive her divorce.

She dressed, as she had done in Lyons, for effect, in a 'Quaker dove-coloured costume and white blouse'[176] remarkably reminiscent of an outfit she had worn on a stage of a rather different kind two decades earlier one wet afternoon when she, Lucy Longstaffe, Lucy's reprobate brother Jack, Robin Smart, and Mr Dumville Smythe who knew 'the rules of flirtation', 'got up a play' in which Aelfrida, 'eyes downcast and [her] whole conversation eminently proper', wore a similarly sober dress.[177] The 'Quaker' costume donned in 1921, however, did not represent 'Mrs Debenham', matronly mother of an eligible daughter, but a wronged wife entering the witness box knowing that Elizabeth Bartlett was also in court. (She was described by Aelfrida as a lady of forty-five — Aelfrida was thirty-seven — gaudily dressed in the latest fashion and with a heavily powdered face, 'the hardest I have ever seen, harder even than Anatolia's'.)[178] Mrs Graham was treated with courtesy and sympathy by the lawyers present and after identifying Constantine's "fine bold handwriting"[179] in the hotel register (he had signed in Elizabeth Bartlett as his wife), was allowed to leave the court before Mrs Bartlett gave her evidence. Her decree nisi was granted and the 'horrible endless day' ended, the day, perhaps, which finally brought home to her that Constantine, "fastidious to a degree", now "hated her so much that he would do anything, however horrible, to be rid of her" and, "desperate indeed", had not shrunk from doing so.[180]

But what of Agatha and Alethea, then aged just eleven and almost thirteen? Having initially asked for custody (to which he was legally entitled) on the grounds of his wife's 'criminal incompetence' as a mother, Constantine, it seems, had second thoughts in view of his posting to Panama. The court therefore granted custody to Aelfrida, stating that "she has devoted herself to them entirely and taken greatest trouble with regard to their education". It further noted that "Mrs Graham [would] be prepared to give the fullest consideration to any suggestion which Mr Graham may make with regard to their education or bringing-up"[181], Constantine having stipulated that his daughters be reared commensurately with his status and position. (Constantine's standing with the Foreign Office, already lowered by unprofessional behaviour in Paris, Amsterdam, and Lyon, was not as high as he believed; following his divorce he did not receive another European posting until 1930.) He also agreed to pay Aelfrida an annual allowance of £240 to which was to be added an annual increment for his daughters' upkeep. This was not formal alimony, for which Aelfrida would have had to petition, but an ex gratia payment subject to Constantine's whim and her reliance on Constantine's generosity (never his strongest point) was to cause financial discomfiture in years to come, discomfiture made bitterer by the knowledge that had she not refused Chiara's advice to let the solicitors 'fight out the question of alimony' but had relied instead on Constantine's promises to increase the allowance as he saw fit (which he never did)[182], she would have received £1000 a year instead of £300. None of this was disclosed to Agatha and Alethea; indeed, Aelfrida's silence on the matter in both her diary and the girls' record books suggests that very little explanation was given — and that biased in their mother's favour — to account for the radical change in their circumstances. In fact, Constantine was so completely erased from their lives as to cause Alethea to write in 1922 apropos a visitor's innocent comment 'she seemed to think Fuvver was dead; I wonder whether Mother has never told us' and to decide not to ask because 'he was too nasty to her for me to care to know' and because 'if he is, perhaps he will be punished for his wickedness; if he isn't he may live to repent … therefore I hope, though rather coldly, that he is alive'[183], a bitter comment indeed for a girl of fourteen who, though privy to details of Phyllis Tillyard's mother's addiction to paraldehyde, did not know if her own father was alive or dead.

The court case over, Aelfrida was mortified to find herself congratulated by family and friends on her 'freedom' ("some people thought you had a good deal to put up with"[184], may have been one comment), noting bitterly 'how odd it is that everyone expects me to be so happy to get rid of Constantine'. But though critically clear-sighted about her ex-husband ('he was always an egoist. He liked to set the stage and see himself as the centre of it. He admired himself as *le grand poète, le grand auteur, le grand amoureux, le grand homme du monde,* each in turn [and] … he staged an unreal existence, generated a hot close air where I could hardly breathe') and willing to admit what hell her life with him had been ('I was always afraid of him in spite of the magic he could set going, … afraid of his passion, his exacting moods, his dark and fiery furies, his sarcasm … his contempt, his complaints, his unappeasable cravings … He was jealous if I had any life apart from him, bored if I tried to live to him alone [and] my motherhood, after just the first, disgusted him')[185], Aelfrida allowed no one but herself (and then only in the privacy of her diary) to say a word against him. Was this because she loved him in spite of everything ('with all [your] faults, how sweet [you] could be … I do not love your faults … but *you*')[186] and hated to hear her love decried or because "when the crash came and I lost Constantine in a sadder way than by death", it was she alone who truly understood "the blindness that was not his fault" and who alone was qualified to pardon? [187] Or was it because she now knew how to apportion blame – in which respect it is worth quoting again the postscript dated 21 January 1919 written at the end of the volume of her diary in which she noted in July 1904 of the day on which her still-unofficial fiancé left Cambridge at the end of the Long Vacation term 'I ought to be with Constantine … whom God has joined together let not man put asunder'[188], a postscript pregnant with significance in 1921: 'as I read this over, I am filled with an immense pity. Constantine and Aelfrida move blindly like figures in a Greek tragedy, impelled by some overmastering fate … on the whole, I prefer Constantine to Aelfrida – he is wonderful, beautiful, radiant – but he has lived too much in the atmosphere of French novels… As for Aelfrida, I admire her high spirits and her enthusiasms and the religion which … guides her through the

labyrinth [but] her blindness to her own faults … revolts me. She is always watching herself act and yet never sees what she is like'. A postscript whose penultimate line is bitterer and more introspective still: 'as for Constantine, is it my fault that he had so little of what he wanted of life?'

The Grahams' decree nisi became absolute on 6 February 1922. Aelfrida, still sad and still reluctant to believe that she had lost Constantine for ever but beginning to create a new life for herself and her daughters, described it as just 'one pang more'.[189]

How big a pang is open to question. Although Aelfrida, like her father when confronted with the Education Act, *liked* to "pose as a martyr"[190], she was, as evidence arising from her restitution and divorce actions shows, less a passive resister to the notion of separation than a passive–aggressive instigator of it in terms of behaviour designed to drive Constantine away and of deliberately-engineered moves to make herself, as plaintiff, appear as a wholly injured and innocent party.

The document issued on 6 February 1922 which absolutely dissolved the Grahams' tempestuous and disastrous marriage stated that the respondent "had been guilty of Adultery coupled with desertion of the petitioner he having failed to comply with a Decree of Restitution of Conjugal Rights dated 22 April 1920".[191] But accusations made by aunt Florence Boyle that Aelfrida had rejected her husband by not joining him in Amsterdam in 1915 and that she had provided only a "flimsy excuse"[192] (probably her daughters' health, for both fell ill after her departure, Aelfrida reacting with morbid alarm to what were evidently minor illnesses: 'my children, my children, how I long to be home … I'll never leave the children again')[193] for returning home after a single month's visit to Lyons in 1919, begs the question: who deserted whom?

Realising early on the terrible mistake she had made in marrying Constantine, Aelfrida effectively deserted her husband by refusing to share either a bedroom or his life. True, she invariably provided herself with excellent reasons for behaving as she did but these were both 'tantamount to desertion' and excuses rather than reasons, and in truth she was much happier living apart from her husband. As for Constantine's supposed desertion: Aelfrida, being a woman, required another reason besides adultery in order to gain her divorce; why therefore did she not use cruelty? Evidence of physical cruelty could have been provided by her diary and by servants who must have noticed bruising on their mistress's face and arms in Paris, and of mental cruelty by diary records of conversations and by letters (now inconveniently destroyed) from Constantine to his wife – but was not. With no other evidence forthcoming, Aelfrida was left with desertion – and how convenient that Constantine did not comply with the Decree of Restitution, for if he had, Aelfrida would have had to accept him back. In which respect, was Aelfrida's visit to Lyons – for a visit it was, as her diary makes clear – a pretext? As the newspaper report of restitution proceedings makes clear, Aelfrida was supposed to be *living* with her husband in Lyons, a supposition she herself later supported with "impassioned self-gratification" by stating that the house inspected by Constantine's vice consul for his own use was actually one inspected by her husband and herself to which they proposed to bring Agatha and Alethea[194], a version proved untrue by the evidence of her own diary. It seems, therefore, that the visit may have been made solely to establish Aelfrida's wifely credentials (hence her joy at the resumption of marital relations which would add verisimilitude to her claim; pregnancy would have added even more) and that it was with gratitude disguised as shock and dismay that she, having already decided on separation with or without divorce, received Constantine's letter stating his determination to close once for all his relations with her and that he proposed to give her the opportunity of seeking divorce.

Furthermore, though Constantine's departure for "Colon, Panama"[195] was serendipitously coincidental, it hardly *in itself* constituted evidence of desertion, but his recent promotion to chargé d'affaires and his slightly earlier promotion to Consul-General had resulted in increases in salary (the latter increase was noted bitterly by Aelfrida to be insufficient to allow her husband 'to have [her] at Lyons' but perfectly adequate for theatres and dinners and 'to take him to Chamonix')[196] and it may be that for the first time in his life Constantine found himself possessor of a salary[197] large enough to cover the expense of a divorce and to support separate households, regardless of whether or not Aelfrida and his daughters continued to live at Fordfield or chose to live separately. And, knowing his wife's inability to separate herself from Fordfield for long, Constantine also ensured the likelihood of her remaining there by providing her with a settlement so small that financial constraints ensured that she did.

All in all, the conventional legal description of Constantine's and Aelfrida's divorce as 'Graham versus Graham' seems eminently apt.

## Notes

1   GCPPT 1|1|22 10 April 1918.
2   GCPPT 1|1|24 10 June 1919.
3   GCPPT 1|1|22 26 April 1918.
4   ibid. 3 June 1918.
5   ibid.
6   ibid. 4 June 1918.
7   GCPPT 1|1|23 5 October 1918.
8   ibid. 20 October 1918.
9   ibid. 26 February 1919.
10  ibid. 7 March 1919.
11  GCPPT 1|1|25 12 May 1920.
12  GCPPT 1|1|23 30 November 1918.
13  ibid. 10 December 1918.
14  ibid. 7 November 1918.
15  ibid. 29 December 1918.
16  ibid.
17  ibid. 1 January 1919.
18  ibid. 7 March 1919.
19  ibid. 29 March 1919.
20  ibid. 8 April 1919.
21  ibid. 10 June 1918.
22  ibid. 21 August 1918.
23  ibid. 3 January 1917.
24  ibid. 19 November 1918.
25  ibid. 9 January 1919.
26  ibid. 13 April 1919.
27  ibid. 19 November 1918.
28  GCPPT 1|1|11 Entry at end dated 21 January 1919, Aelfrida's 12th wedding anniversary, a day on which Constantine had sent a telegram of congratulations which provided more pain than pleasure.
29  GCPPT 1|1|23 21 March 1919.
30  GCPPT 1|1|11 11 June 1904.
31  GCPPT 1|1|12 28 November 1904.
32  GCPPT 1|1|11 12 June 1904.
33  GCPPT 1|1|23 21 April 1919.
34  ibid. 4 December 1918. The vision occurred in St Botolph's Church. In *A Little Road-Book for Mystics* (p71) Aelfrida describes the service in some detail: "we had met together that winter afternoon for silent prayer. There were only half a dozen of us … and I was sitting so far forward … that I was not conscious of anyone else being present in the church … With eyes open, I had watched ghostly figures say Mass – for long ago the church had been Catholic … The grey-garbed monks moved and bowed and spoke, Christ moved in the powerful hands of the priest … At the end a voice cried *In hoc signo vincis* and I saw the crucifix above the rood screen flame into life …" The vision took place, she says, in "March 1919".
35  ibid. 29 December 1918. The vision, described at length in Aelfrida's diary, is quoted virtually verbatim in *A Little Road-Book for Mystics* (p 72) but omitting the presence of the guardian angel. The last lines of the published version expand on the puzzling episode of the splash of blood: "my heart opened to receive it, and, when the instant stinging pain was passed, closed as a casket closes over a jewel. So the vision faded, but there remained with me that drop of blood, His, my Lord's". In the published version, too, this vision is elided with the vision of 4 December 1918 to create a single visionary experience whose symbolism Aelfrida subsequently (pp 72–74) expounds, describing the Cross as a symbol of sacrifice and the splash of blood as indicating that "something of Christ's life" had passed into her, this enabling her to share in "the age-long sacrifice that God makes for His children", an interesting, though *ex post facto* interpretation of what was shortly to occur.
36  ibid. 19 April 1919.
37  ibid. 29 March 1919.
38  ibid. 13 April 1919.
39  ibid. 24 April 1919.
40  ibid. 26 April 1919.
41  ibid. 13 April 1919.
42  ibid. 26 April 1919.
43  ibid. 24 April 1919.
44  ibid. 1 May 1919.
45  ibid. 5 May 1919.

46 GCPPT 1|1|24 9 May 1919.

47 Zelle was now proprietress of a Vincennes *boutique* where she sold *tisanes* of 'mint-leaves and lime-flowers' and herbal remedies, 'sweet-smelling old-wives things' like the 'French herb pre-period medicine' she prescribed for Aelfrida (GCPPT 1|1|24 9 May 1919; GCPPT 1|1|25 30 June 1921). Zelle and Aelfrida had renewed acquaintance when the Grahams were living at Le Vésinet and kept in touch thereafter.

48 In *Who Was Who*, Constantine is listed as "acting vice-consul ... with local rank of consul" during his stay in Lyons 1918-1919.

49 GCPPT 1|1|24 9 and 23 May 1919.

50 ibid. 11 May 1919.

51 ibid. 29 May 1919.

52 ibid. 31 May 1919.

53 GCPPT 1|1|50 6 November 1935.

54 GCPPT 1|1|24 31 May 1919.

55 ibid. 31 May 1919.

56 ibid. 13 and 31 May 1919.

57 ibid. 31 May 1919.

58 ibid. 24 1 June 1919.

59 ibid. 31 May 1919.

60 ibid.

61 GCPPT 1|1|15 2 March 1908.

62 GCPPT 1|1|24 10 July 1919.

63 ibid. 9 May 1919. 'Note, too', wrote Aelfrida five years later, 'how older women attract him', citing Mme Cochaud as one (GCPPT 1|1|28 14 July 1924).

64 ibid. 1 June 1919.

65 ibid. 1 June and 10 July 1919.

66 ibid. 24 May 1919. Thirty years later Aelfrida gives a rather different version of the visit (GCPPT 2|27|2(4)). Describing the villa as a house to which she was shortly to move with her daughters, she continues "Constantine and I stood with our arms around each other as if we were lovers again, gazing out at that incomparable scene ... I was happy beyond words".

67 GCPPT 1|1|22 27 November 1917.

68 GCPPT 1|1|24 1 and 2 June 1919.

69 GCPPT 1|1|25 13 October 1920.

70 GCPPT 1|1|24 31 May 1919.

71 Tillyard, Ae. *Spiritual Exercises* pp 157 and 211.

72 GCPPT 1|1|25a. Undated letter from Dom Savinien Louismet to Aelfrida.

73 GCPPT 1|1|23 26 January 1919.

74 GCPPT 1|1|24 13 June 1919.

75 GCPPT 1|1|23 8 January 1919.

76 GCPPT 1|1|22 27 November 1917.

77 ibid. 22 July 1918.

78 GCPPT 1|1|25 1 September 1919.

79 GCPPT 1|1|24 6 July 1918.

80 GCPPT 1|1|30 25 May 1925.

81 ibid. 3 July 1925.

82 GCPPT 1|1|20 5 October 1914.

83 GCPPT 1|1|24 9 July 1919.

84 GCPPT 1|1|22 30 November 1917. GCPPT 1|1|25 25 June 1920.

85 GCPPT 1|1|36 29 September 1929.

86 GCPPT 1|1|21 1 October 1915.

87 GCPPT 1|1|24 31 May 1919.

88 ibid. 6 July 1919.

89 ibid. 28 July 1919.

90 ibid. 6 July 1919.

91 ibid. 9 July 1919.

92 ibid. 11 July 1919.

93 ibid. 9 July 1919.

94 ibid. 10 and 11 July 1919.

95 ibid. 12 July 1919.

96 ibid. 11 July 1919.

97 ibid. 11 and 12 July 1919.

98 ibid. 6 August 1919.

99 ibid. 23 July 1919.

100 ibid. 16 July 1919.

101 GCPPT 1|1|24 9 July 1919 and GCPPT 1|1|25 16 September 1919. Julius later described the eventful summer of 1919 as an impending crisis in the Graham's marriage which developed inexorably into "an open breach" after which "divorce followed" (Tillyard, HJW. Introduction to *The Letters of ACW Tillyard* (MTC).

102 GCPPT 1|1|24 19 June 1919.

103 ibid. 6 August 1919.

104 ibid. 6 August 1919.

105 ibid. 16 July 1919.

106 GCPPT 1|1|25 12 November 1919.

107 GCPPT 1|1|24 15 and 16 July 1919.

108 Tillyard, HJW. *The Letters of ACW Tillyard* (MTC). Letter from Catharine Tillyard to Ancifera (Annie) Gregory, written at Hunstanton in the autumn of 1919 but otherwise undated.

109 GCPPT 1|1|25 29 January 1920.

110 GCPPT 1|1|24 13 July 1919.

111 ibid. 5 August 1919.

112 ibid. 10 July and 5 August 1919.

113 ibid. 14 July 1919.

114 ibid. 8 August 1919.

115 GCPPT 1|1|20 5 October 1914.

116 GCPPT 1|1|24 8 August 1919.

117 ibid. 10 July 1919.

118 GCPPT 1|1|25 26 September 1919.

119 ibid. 28 July 1920.

120 ibid. 1 October 1919.

121 ibid. 26 September 1919.

122 GCPPT 1|1|25 28 September 1919. Aelfrida's comment that although she hated 'class and industrial war' as much as she did 'race war', her sympathy with the working classes was eroded by the lorry journey, is echoed in an ironic poem *Invitation à la Liberté* published in 1920 whose last verse is "Oh come my love and vote with me/ And share in Reconstruction./We're going to make Old England *Free*/ Without the least obstruction" (*Verses for Alethea* p16).

123 GCPPT 1|1|25 11 October 1919.

124 GCPPT 1|1|25 15 November 1919. One of the few advantages 'of living in a lower middle class way' was that 'the lower classes are so much more friendly'; the charlady, discovering Aelfrida's domestic ineptitude, gave her friendly advice: 'I learn a lot!' (GCPPT 1|1|25 14 June 1920).

125 GCPPT 1|1|25 15 November 1919, 20 February and 21 June 1920. Aelfrida's 'neuralgia' was probably mastodynia, i.e. breast pain attributable to pelvic pathology.

126 GCPPT 1|1|25 18 November 1919.

127 GCPPT 1|1|15 1 August 1907. The quotation on Ibberson's house (it comes from R.L. Stevenson's *El Dorado*) would have made even more ironic reading had Ibberson completed it: "and the true success is to labour".

128 GCPPT 1|1|25 10 January 1920.

129 ibid. 10 January 1920.

130 ibid. 6 December 1919.

131 ibid. 29 November 1919.

132 ibid. 20 October 1919.

133 ibid. 20 June 1920.

134 ibid. 6 March 1920.

135 ibid. 6 April 1920. The mystical works of Thomas Traherne (1637-1674) had been rediscovered as recently as 1896.

136 ibid. 12 May 1920.

137 ibid. 20 October 1919. The poem, according to Aelfrida, was written for Agatha as a summary of 'her impressions and mine'. An undated and unascribed poem, *Impressions*, obviously written by a child, (GCPPT 1|1a *Agatha's Record* Book 22 October 1919) is probably Agatha's version.

138 ibid. 13 and 18 January 1920.

139 ibid. 20 March 1920.

140 ibid. 20 October 1919. By context the poem appears to have been written after *Autumn by the Sea,* Aelfrida noting on 6 October that poetry was 'all there, on the bubble!' but that she had no leisure to write it down. None of the 'Hunstanton' poems were published.

141 ibid. 20 October 1919.

142 ibid. 21 December 1919. Henry Mudie-Cooke was particularly generous, even offering to pay for Agatha's and Alethea's education. (GCPPT 1|1|25 3 March 1920, and letter dated 29 February 1920 from him to Aelfrida in GCPPT 1|1|25a).

143 ibid. 29 November 1919.

144 ibid. 28 April 1920.

145 Tillyard, HJW. *The Letters of ACW Tillyard* (MTC). Undated incomplete letter from James Stark to Aelfrida. The letter, written by context in November 1919, was forwarded by Aelfrida to Julius so he must have been aware of his sister's impending divorce at this point.

146 GCPPT 1|1|25 4 November 1919.

147 ibid. 4 November 1919.

148 ibid. 28 April 1920.

149 ibid. 25 June 1920.

150 ibid. 23 July 1920.

151 ibid. 7 November 1919.

152 ibid. 22 November 1919.

153 ibid. 19 December 1919.

154 The Matrimonial Causes Act of 1857 had made it possible to order a man to make financial provision for an estranged or divorced wife.

155 GCPPT 1|1|25 22 January 1920.

156 ibid. 15 February 1920.

157 ibid. 19 March 1920.

158 Under the terms of the Matrimonial Causes Act, a husband had only to prove his wife's adultery but a wife had to prove that her husband had committed adultery and one of the following: incest, bigamy, cruelty, or desertion. The serendipitous assonance of Mr Justice Horridge's surname with 'porridge' was to inspire Aelfrida to comic verse: "The plaintiff recalled the first morning when the porridge was burnt / The morning when he had learnt / That he didn't *really* love his wife. / Thereafter there was war to the knife" (GCPPT 2|13).

159 GCPPT 1|1|25 23 April 1920 (dated by context as undated in diary).

160 Newspaper cutting from an unidentified newspaper dated in ink 28 April 1920 inserted in *The Letters of ACW Tillyard* (MTC). No such report appeared in contemporary Cambridge newspapers; probably Alfred Tillyard's influence kept it out.

161 GCPPT 1|1|25 23 April 1920.

162 ibid. 28 April 1920.

163 ibid. 12 August 1920.

164 In January 1926 while rummaging through a box of second-hand books outside Heffer's bookshop, Alethea turned up Paul Bourget's *Un Crime d'Amour* of 1886 and discovered her father's name inside. She bought the book and took it home but did not tell her mother. In her diary she wrote 'the situation strikes me as rather like Father's own in a way. I suppose it's merely coincidence and that I'm rather silly to care … I never realised I cared anything for the memory of a man who made my family miserable' (GCPPT A1.1 12 January 1926) The first volume of Agatha's diary (GCPPG A2/1, begun 1 April 1923) contains a family tree which lists 'Mother' as her sole progenitor.

165 GCPPT 1|1|25 3 July 1920.

166 GCPPT 1|1|27 2 May 1923.

167 GCPPT 1|1|25 10 July 1920.

168 Tillyard, Ae. *O Passionate World* p 410 (GCPPT 2|11).

169 ibid.

170 GCPPT 1|1|25 20 November 1920.

171 ibid. 13 February 1921.

172 ibid. 21 February 1921.

173 ibid. 28 July 1921.

174 ibid. 7 March 1921.

175 ibid. 19 February 1921.

176 ibid. 28 July 1921.

177 GCPPT 1|1|5 8 August 1900.

178 GCPPT 1|1|25 28 July 1921.

179 Tillyard, Ae. *O Passionate World* pp 216–217.

180 ibid. p 73.

181 GCPPT 1|1|26 Undated fragment of an official letter to Aelfrida's solicitors tucked into this volume.

182 GCPPT 1|1|26 15 October 1921.

183 GCPPG A1.1 2 September 1922.

184 Tillyard, Ae. *O Passionate World* p 41.

185 GCPPT 1|1|25 25 June 1920.

186 ibid. 25 June 1920 and undated note added in 1922 to GCPPT 1|1|13 10 October 1905.

187 GCPPT 2|27|2(4).

188 GCPPT 1|1|11 31 July 1904.

189 GCPPT 1|1|26 8 February 1922.

190 GCPPT 2|2a Vol. 2 No 3 October 1903 *The Passive Resister.*

191 Principal Registry of the Family Division of the High Court of Justice, Document no 128, 1922.

192 GCPPT 2|27|2(4).

193 GCPPT 1|1|24 19 May 1919.

194 ibid.

195 Tillyard, HJW. *The Letters of ACW Tillyard* (MTC). Cutting from an unidentified newspaper dated in ink 28 April 1920.

196 GCPPT 1|1|23 21 March 1919.

197 Members of the Consular Service had been salaried since 1825, payment being on a scale determined by position and seniority. In 1911 Consuls received between £600 and £800 a year and Consul-Generals between £800 and £1000, both with local allowances in addition; vice-consuls received between £350 and £450 a year without allowances. (*Encyc. Brit.* vol 7 pp 20–22). A decade later, salaries would have risen commensurately.

# The Perfect Peace of Fordfield

In September 1903 Aelfrida stated that there was 'no place like Cambridge' and that she could not conceive of wanting to live anywhere else.[1] In 1916, trapped in Cambridge by ill-health, domesticity, and the Great War, she longed to be 'up and away' and was so 'mad for another land, strange people, stronger voices' that she would willingly endure homesickness and exile.[2] By 1922 she was desperate to escape: 'if I consulted no-one but myself ... I would take my children right away to a new country and leave this house, this country, this Europe, so full of ghosts'.[3] Four years later she wrote despairingly that 'I feel ... so sick of ... the town that I sometimes I feel as though I should scream if I had to walk ... there again'.[4] What, we may ask, had happened to turn Cambridge in general and Fordfield in particular, once the 'dearest place on earth ... [from which] I felt I *could* not, *could* not, *could* not come away'[5] and

which even now she admitted to loving so much that she tried to compensate for her devotion by choosing 'detachment' as her ideal, into a prison in which she felt 'hopelessly enslaved'?[6] Was it *only* divorce from the man to whom she had promised 'absolute surrender' which had delivered her into a state of servitude so seemingly absolute that all she wanted to do was 'go away ... and be very quiet and build up [her] life again with solitude and prayer'[7] – but could not?

In part, yes, for whereas the wife who informed Miss Ridding 'my husband has deserted me' (Miss Ridding suggested 'a mystic's discipline and detachment' as a means of consolation[8]; they were no consolation at all) was treated with sympathy, a woman 'mixed up in divorce' was not.[9] Innocent party though she might be (on paper, at least, and in her own eyes), Aelfrida found it degrading to be treated by people 'who ought to know

Fordfield, with Aelfrida Graham, Catharine Tillyard, and Ancifera Gregory

better'[10] as if it was she rather than her husband who had 'disgraced the family', to discover that Italian lessons for children had to be given up once parents knew she was divorced[11] (one girl, Joan Thomson, was the daughter of Nobel prize-winner JJ Thomson of the Cavendish Laboratory and Master of Trinity College, a very important man indeed in contemporary Cambridge life, and Joan's removal from Aelfrida's class was a real blow), to experience an 'over and aboveness'[12] when people were nice to her as well as to her mother at parties she forced herself to attend in spite of finding them 'painful' and, worst of all, to realise that as a newly-single woman living at home, she had 'no position and no status'.[13] Even the consoling thought that she had clever daughters was marred when she was snubbed by the mothers of their school friends, when Agatha and Alethea were excluded from children's parties because of the scandal attached to their mother's name, and when parents of pupils at the school currently attended by the girls requested that they be expelled because of their father's reputation.[14] (They were not, though Agatha, being younger and more vulnerable, was victimised by a teacher.) But there was more to Aelfrida's sense of entrapment than the opprobrium attached to a divorced woman and other factors too prevented her from taking advantage of the freedom offered by the ending of the Great War and of her marriage.

The first was her health which, though it improved following Constantine's departure, continued to be indifferent. A visit to a woman friend during which the subject of Christian Science was raised reminded her of numerous ailments: 'backache with the usual discharge from the womb'; 'headache and eye-ache for some part of every day' (they were due to the tension of writing for hours at a time rather than the migraines which plagued her during her marriage); 'sore throat most of the winter'; 'swollen glands'; 'palpitations of the heart', probably due to anaemia exacerbated by vegetarianism and an ascetic desire to mortify her flesh by existing as far as possible on carbohydrate material spurned by the rest of the family as stale; 'indigestion'; 'varicose veins which swell and ache', these, like her backache, forcing her to spend much time in the semi-recumbent position recalled by one of her nieces as habitual; 'catarrh of the bladder'; 'constant rheumatism'; debilitating fatigue.[15] (Malaria, following a short, sharp attack in 1923, seems to have burnt itself out.) Hence tempting though it is to regard Aelfrida's frequent retreats to bed as escapism (as she wrote in Emden, 'I am grateful for not always being strong because it gives me quiet time when otherwise I should have to be rushing around doing things I don't want')[16] and her admission that 'I keep going splendidly and get a lot done!'[17] when too happily engaged in

activities to feel the need to escape as evidence that ill-health was exaggerated for effect, most of her complaints were genuine and she was rarely free from one ailment or another.

Feeling 'quite young again'[18]as a result of her divorce allowed her to ignore symptoms of her various diseases. She took renewed pleasure in physical activity, bathing in the Cam in summer and going on cycle rides at all times of year during which she rode short distances to the beechwood where she revelled in country quiet and her daughters' company instead of Eric Silvanus' hectic attentions[19] or marathons of thirty-two miles interspersed with picnics and visits[20], all accompanied by moments of ecstasy during which she became conscious 'the life hidden in the earth [and] of union with the essence and fulness of nature'.[21] Her improved mood was also due to the arrival in Cambridge in 1922 of 'new lady doctor' Joan Cooper who specialised in the diseases of women and children[22]: "A gentle-eyed doctor called Joan / Will listen to all that you moan. / But you have to obey / Her 'mayn't' and 'may' / She's got such a will of her own".[23]

Another problem was posed by Aelfrida's refusal of formal alimony. Her annual allowance remained the same as that paid by Constantine during the Great War and deemed by him sufficient for a wife living with two small children under her parental roof. (Given the fluctuations in his salary as he was alternately promoted and demoted, this was probably all he could afford.) Her post-divorce settlement and the girls' annual increments were barely adequate by 1921 and by 1925 Aelfrida was having difficulty in making ends meet and had it not been for financial help from her mother and for her own small earnings from language coaching and writing (she charged 6 guineas an hour for the former and only hints at income from the latter), she would have been hard pressed to support herself and her daughters in the style to which they were accustomed. True, she could have found a full-time job but her 'Great Work' took precedence even though, as she noted ruefully, 'my books don't pay'[24] and she was reluctant to leave the comforts of Fordfield for the cheaper discomforts of single motherhood in a small house in which the impracticalities of combining motherhood and Mysticism would be even more apparent.[25]

The comforts of Fordfield, however, came at a price and as early as September 1919 she complained of 'the bitterness and difficulty of living as a dependent'.[26] Enforced acceptance of 'a daughter's place' as a permanent feature of post-Constantine existence meant acceptance of parentally-imposed conditions: having to ask permission to have a friend to tea; having her correspondence 'enquired about and commented on [and] …

treated as more or less public property'; having to give a full account of all activities outside the house, however trivial[27]; being always at her mother's beck and call ('there is no romance in being the good daughter at home but it has the austere beauty of … inevitable duty')[28]; having to take her share of domestic chores ('I shall certainly … put "home duties" on the census paper!')[29]; receiving constant criticism with regard to the way she brought up her daughters; male friends being subjected to scrutiny and their visits curtailed or encouraged as her parents decreed; worst of all, it being taken for granted 'that [she] should be always serene and content'.[30] To all this, however, Aelfrida might have acceded willingly had it not been that the Oracle and Chiara were inclined to treat her 'as a dear little child … since I am now admittedly incompetent to manage my own life'.[31] Was there, she asked herself, nothing more to aspire to than 'being mildly useful in unimportant ways [and] putting on the Oracle's boots?'[32]

'Putting on the Oracle's boots' was not, however, a degrading activity devised by a sadistic father as punishment for 'incompetence'; it was a necessity. The Tillyards' return from Hunstanton in June 1920 coincided with a sudden deterioration in Alfred Tillyard's health, a decline so marked that on the occasion of his seventieth birthday two years later Aelfrida could only describe his existence as 'a triumph of the spirit over the body'.[33] Beset by digestive problems, by rheumatoid arthritis so severe as to render his hands almost useless and the rest of his body so feeble that on the daily walk on which he insisted he leant so heavily on Aelfrida's arm that her prolapse 'came all dragging down'[34], and by 'arterial sclerosis' which rendered him 'unutterably pathetic'[35] and would eventually kill him, he also went blind.

The first intimation of worsening sight occurs on 9 July 1919, the day on which Constantine informed him of his intention of divorcing his daughter; unable to read the letter himself, the Oracle handed it to Aelfrida who consequently received its contents in the form of an un-softened blow: 'life goes on its even way – we do our little daily tasks, say our prayers, hope for the future – and then …'[36] In fact, and although she does not say so at the time, the Oracle's sight had begun to deteriorate two years earlier: in July 1917 he was capable of independent existence but by December Aelfrida had to accompany him to directors' meetings of the *Cambridge Independent Press* and by May 1918 act as his proxy. By June 1918 she regularly read aloud to him although it was not until November that he consulted an oculist who told him he would 'gradually go quite blind'.[37]

The irony of the title of his third and last book being *Stones of Stumbling* cannot have been lost on a blind man

whose livelihood and leisure had revolved round production of the printed word, Aelfrida noting that it was 'infinitely sad to see a man lay aside the tools of life'.[38] There was too the inconvenience and indignity of having to rely on someone else's sight in order to hear words he could no longer read for himself; for some years he availed himself of the services of a paid reader but he otherwise depended on the goodwill and availability of members of his family. Sadder still was his being unable to see his first grandson, Eustace's son Stephen, born in July 1920. (He would be remembered by Stephen and his younger sisters as an unseeing old man who identified them by the feel of their hair.) Although Aelfrida frequently found her blind father irritating ('whatever muddle the house is in, *he* mustn't be neglected')[39], she found him curiously touching too: 'as he loosens his grasp on this life, he seems to get a firmer hold on life eternal … I can feel him moving among the real and everlasting things while his body grows weaker and his response to ordinary surroundings more imperfect. His little faults of character fall from him like leaves in autumn while his knowledge and understanding of God burn with a clear flame'.[40]

That was written in 1920. Six years later, having had an excruciatingly painful left eye enucleated at the Evelyn Nursing Home (the best in Cambridge')[41] in October 1926 and having become a bad-tempered recluse who preferred his study to the family drawing room, who took his meals alone, and who had to have a member of the family present in the house because he refused help from anyone who was not, the Oracle's 'little faults of character' had evolved into unpleasant character traits and he into someone described by Aelfrida as 'gloom personified'[42] and by Alethea as 'too grumpy for words'.[43]

His behaviour, in particular his lack of consideration for others ('he always has the best of everything … and is always considered first … [but he] doesn't *care*)[44], drove Aelfrida to diary entries whose irritability was as indicative of despair at her own as of her father's plight: 'I *don't* like waiting on Oracle! … I should not mind if [he] were satisfied but my ministrations scarcely ever please him … I do things for him … as well as they can be done and I take all the trouble I can and do them gladly [and] offer them as done to the Lord [but] I am frightfully bored with the minutiae [of his life], and the way he eats, clacking his false teeth and letting bits drop out of his mouth, makes me feel sick'. Should I mind, she then asks, 'if I loved him more?'[45], a question which demonstrates all too clearly the depths of her dislike for a man once fastidious in his habits and nicknamed 'Sweeter' because of his equanimity.

Indications that Alfred Tillyard was not the paragon Aelfrida once believed him to be had been in evidence for some time. As head of the household he had always put his own interests first and during the war had behaved selfishly, taking more than his fair share of such luxuries as graced the Fordfield table. Always a man of few friends, intransigent behaviour prior to retirement seems to have alienated those he had so that in later years he had few visitors on his own account; as a result, and though frequently introduced to family visitors (a description of someone 'being taken in to talk to Oracle' is a recurrent phrase in Aelfrida's diary), he had to contend with loneliness and lack of outside interests as well as ill-health, blindness, and depression.

In spite of Aelfrida's voluble complaints concerning the amount of time she had to devote to her father's needs when she was ill herself or busy with her writing, it is obvious – as she herself admits – that the burden of care fell largely on his wife. Obvious, too, is that Chiara's self-effacing attitude towards her husband ('Chiara … always assumes that her place is in the dust')[46] was a repetition of behaviour towards her sick and aged parents and that it reinforced her husband's worst personality traits to the detriment of her own health and temper: 'Chiara is looking very tired and the Oracle has a slave-driving fit on … I wish he would die suddenly because he is wearing [her] out'.[47] But if Aelfrida intervened in an attempt to spare her mother, Chiara turned on her, accusing her of 'wanting to boss the household'.[48] Hysterical crying or stony silences followed, these causing Aelfrida to record ruefully that 'life is very dreary when one's mother is cross!'[49]

Anything, in fact, which appeared to encroach on Chiara's position 'as mistress of [the] house'[50] infuriated her. 'Delicate adjustments'[51] were therefore required to keep the peace between Aelfrida and a mother who had not only endured Constantine's betrayal of her love and, shortly after the Tillyards' return from Hunstanton, the death of beloved friend and servant Ellen Ison, but who had also relinquished all outside interests (with the exception of the governing body of the Perse School for Girls to which she intended her grand-daughters to go) in order to be at her husband's beck and call. This resulted in Chiara becoming 'dreadfully depressed', 'nervy and worried about nothing in particular' (a notable character trait at the best of times), obsessional over matters of little import, tetchy if offered advice, and inclined to harp on 'one theme with endless variations', namely that nothing – England, servants, modern children – 'was as good as it used to be' and to ruminate sadly on memories of 'Dear and Dear Grandpapa' and of her 'false lover' Rendel Harris.[52] Little wonder, then, that Aelfrida, regarding her mother with newly perceptive eyes, noted that 'much inner turmoil went into the making of [Chiara's] life of devotion'.[53]

Deciding that Chiara needed a life 'with much more colour and movement in'[54] and that further problems might arise as a result of her being apparently 'bent on self-immolation'[55], Aelfrida, Eustace, and Julius held a meeting in April 1923 'on how to lighten [her] burden'.[56] Though neither parent was initially willing to change their morbidly co-dependent patterns of behaviour, the Oracle's intransigence was eventually overcome by the united efforts of his two sons and Chiara's by dint of Dr Cooper declaring that she '*must not* do so much'[57] and *must* take regular holidays. The elder Tillyards therefore settled down to a new routine. Chiara holidayed with friends and relations for longer or shorter periods (she once ventured as far as Cannes with Phyllis' parents) or enjoyed the company of her elderly but sprightly widower cousin George Warren. Julius willingly, and Eustace, less willingly and 'looking rather gloomy' when he arrived 'to take up his duties'[58], took turns to move into Fordfield to look after their father in Chiara's absence. Aelfrida lived out her invidious role of dependent daughter unable to vent the vexation of her 'irksome, exhausting and depressing' existence on anyone but her 'dear diary and safety valve'.[59] And the Oracle continued – in his sons' absence – on his selfish path (Eustace's gift of a wireless set transformed his days but did little to improve his behaviour) and extended his 'tyrannical exacting ways'[60] over Agatha and Alethea as well.

Earliest intimations of his change in attitude occurred during the family's sojourn in Hunstanton at a time when, cooped up in a small house, it might be expected that the chatter and bounce of children of seven and nine would irritate a man who was losing his sight and who had been forced by his daughter's unwise choice of husband to leave comfortable familiar surroundings. Hypercritical behaviour continued, however, after the Tillyards' return home, the Oracle complaining to Aelfrida that Agatha and Aelfrida were noisy, rude, and inconsiderate, and reminding her that Fordfield was his, not hers; he also informed her that 'everyone' wondered how he could put up with having her and her daughters in his house. Aelfrida tried to make light of his criticisms by reminding herself that problems were inevitable in a three-generation household, but she also warned Agatha and Alethea to be on their best behaviour in their grandfather's presence.[61] By 1923, however, the Oracle's attitude had become thoroughly unpleasant: 'he never speaks *to* [Agatha and Alethea] except to snub or find fault and rarely *of* them except to criticise. Yet he expects that they should always be ready to wait on him and give him the best of everything without thanks'.[62] Although such behaviour on Alfred Tillyard's part *could* be explained as a manifestation of a mild to moderate cerebro-vascular dementia caused by 'arterial sclerosis', the fact that his behaviour with Julius was perfectly acceptable, with Eustace, with whom he animatedly talked 'university shop'[63], a model 'of all that is amicable, reasonable and contented'[64], with visiting children tolerantly grandfatherly, and with adult visitors polite and interested, shows that there was no physiological cause for his unpleasantness towards Agatha and Alethea. Indeed, Aelfrida was moved to write '*why* Oracle, who is so patient about his blindness, is always so disagreeable to my girls I cannot understand'.[65]

The Oracle's chief criticisms were reserved for outspoken, impatient Alethea who, though Wetenhall/Barrett in appearance, had inherited her father's manner; quiet, compliant, pious (and very Greek-looking) Agatha did not escape censure but was not picked upon to the same extent. References in Aelfrida's, Alethea's, and Agatha's diaries (the latter begun in 1922 and 1923 respectively) to the Oracle's behaviour show how persistently and pervasively unpleasant it was; they also show that Chiara sided with her husband, their mutual intolerance of Alethea in particular increasing from mild grumbles about her upbringing to venomous and unjustified attacks on her morals: they called her (not to her face but to Aelfrida who then informed her daughter) 'disgusting, depraved, [and] loose' because she wanted to see a play of which they disapproved[66] and announced that her behaviour (aged seventeen) was completely 'out of hand'[67] when, caught up in the University Rag and late for an appointment, she accepted a lift from a man she knew only slightly. (Agatha, even when not a target, defended her sister hotly and was told off by her 'intolerable' grandmother for doing so.)[68] A family row which took place just before Christmas 1926 and arose as a result of the Oracle making life so unpleasant in the drawing room that Aelfrida and her daughters left the room to sit elsewhere, reveals that there was more to Agatha's and Alethea's unhappiness than vicious verbal attacks from a grandfather they were expected to revere and respect. Once alone with their mother, 'the girls vented their feelings, and from having a grievance about Oracle passed on to objecting to [her] as not wholly on their side', an absolutely just criticism given that Aelfrida was too scared of being asked to leave 'the dearest place on earth' to do more than protest feebly at the worst aspects of the Oracle's behaviour. 'Conscious of the hopelessness of [her] task in trying to make everything harmonious and lovely', she wept helplessly, wailing that 'if it were only a question of getting on with Chiara we should manage beautifully but the Oracle is hopeless'.[69]

**Agatha and Alethea Graham c1924**

According to Agatha, her mother wept 'because we didn't get on too well with Cara and Oracle just then' (the girls, both fluent Italian speakers, called their grandmother 'Cara', i.e. 'Dear') 'and *she* has to keep the peace'; she also summed up the stormy family relationship most perceptively for one so young: 'we love them and they love us but the difference in generations does make a huge difference … the Oracle won't realise that we've got any feelings because we are young and belong to the despised sex … he does despise all women except Cara'.[70]

Matters continued thus for a decade from October 1919 until the Oracle's death in October 1929, something to be borne in mind during descriptions of joyful events which happened during that time but beneath which surged undercurrents of unresolved anger and frustrated desires. His death was commemorated by Alethea with understated thankfulness ('we are in a way relieved')[71]; by Aelfrida coolly ('so that is the end … now one has a sense of rather desolate leisure')[72] and by advising her daughters 'not to plunge themselves into artificial gloom'[73]; by Chiara bewailing her late husband's "wonderful dignity and self-control" and his "long service of love and … precious companionship" being over[74], after which, her "allotted task" completed, she delegated financial and domestic responsibilities to Aelfrida, bought herself new clothes, and prepared to enjoy the rest of her life; and by Julius with reference to Fordfield and in Latin: *vacua et vidua domus*'.[75]

Empty though the house was of one of its longstanding inhabitants, the void left by the Oracle's death was soon filled with family squabbles and it was with Eustace, usually the peace-maker, that most friction occurred. In default of a husband, it was natural for Aelfrida to turn for help to a nearby brother when she required advice but to her dismay, the younger brother she had once treated like a servant was unwilling to be made use of except in emergencies. He also made it clear that his priorities were primarily his wife and family, his academic career, and his wife's parents (Phyllis' father, Henry, was hale but her mother' moods were affected by addictions to drugs and alcohol and she was estranged from Phyllis' sister Olive, a mentally and emotionally unstable artist) and only secondarily with a sister living on an allowance in the comfort of Fordfield who could have earned a living from teaching and writing had she been prepared to go about either in a systematic and professional manner, who was unwilling to sell her mystic birthright for a mess of literary pottage in order to create books that would sell, and who generally acted on a whim or at the bidding of her guardian angel. Furthermore, he declined to act as chauffeur ('they never take us out in their car')[76], provider of entertainment ('[they] don't ask us out as often as some relatives do')[77], chaperon (he refused to take his nieces to the theatre just because Aelfrida liked to go to bed early or expressed moral scruples with regard to theatrical performances or denied herself the pleasure of attending on ascetic grounds and if, as a favour, he did, expected his sister to pay), and even banker.

Although Aelfrida undoubtedly went without luxuries (and sometimes even necessities) in order that Agatha and Alethea lacked nothing (in September 1920 she wrote of 'trying to *squeeze* out enough money to buy Alethea a bicycle which means going-without for me')[78] and although she envied every penny earned by her salaried brothers and by the family of the present Fordfield gardener, Mr Church, whose grown sons earned good wages (their total annual income, she calculated, was nearly £800, adding sourly 'one doesn't grudge it … of course, if they *work* for it')[79], she is coy to the point of silence as to exactly how much she earned from language tuition and from her writings and from the fact that Agatha was able to write in July 1925 that 'we seem much richer than we used to be and we all three have nice clothes and can go for nice summer hols.'[80], it is obvious that Aelfrida was not as financially strapped

as she liked to appear and that repeated hints that she needed money did not go down well with a young academic with a wife and family to support. Nor did they go down well with his wife, Phyllis believing (possibly with some justification) that Aelfrida was hankering after a share of the money expended by wealthy Henry Mudie-Cooke on his daughter's behalf. Matters came to a head in September 1926 when Aelfrida approached Eustace and Phyllis for a contribution towards Alethea's initial requirements at university. Her request was badly timed for Henry Mudie-Cooke had already offered to pay half the cost of Alethea's books provided Julius or Eustace paid the other half and Aelfrida herself had recently returned from a five week holiday in France with her daughters during which she had spent money which Phyllis felt should have gone towards essentials. Furthermore, Phyllis and Eustace denied that they had ever offered financial help with what they termed 'whims and fancies' but Aelfrida deemed essentials, namely clothes, and noted that proffered help had been conditional on Alethea *not* obtaining a scholarship – which she had. Aelfrida, who had refused to allow Hal Verey to 'bother' Constantine for more money '[hers] by right' or to increase her language coaching fees because already paid 'all [she was] worth', had banked on family contributions to send Alethea to university in style and was surprised and hurt to receive a letter from Phyllis accusing her sister-in-law of being 'mercenary' and stating that she herself was fed up with Aelfrida's persistent wheedling after money. Telling herself that she had just received 'a superb picture of yourself as others see you'[81], Aelfrida replied in conciliatory fashion and, following a visit from Eustace, considered the matter closed. Eustace, however, also discussed the matter with his parents and Aelfrida received a severe scolding from Chiara: 'being in disgrace makes me feel just as I used to when I had bad reports from Mrs Verrall. Such a familiar discomfort!'[82] A frosty relationship ensued, made chillier still by Phyllis' scorn for someone who had 'neither to earn nor cook nor so much as order [her] own dinner' but lived instead in a world 'peopled with emotions and dreams and burning pains and joys' from which she looked down disdainfully on women burdened with 'horrid material things'[83] and by Aelfrida's jealousy of a married woman, mother of a son preferred by Chiara to Aelfrida's own daughters, wife of a rising star in the English Literature firmament, chatelaine of her own establishment, beloved daughter of a generous father, and possessor of a First Class classics degree from Girton which had not only allowed her to embark on a formal teaching career (interrupted by war and motherhood) but which might also open doors for her in the future, the latter a particularly bitter sentiment for one who had discovered in 1920 that the 'ancient and venerable University' which welcomed her with open arms in 1914 was too busy with the post-war influx of undergraduates to pay attention to an unaffiliated medium and mystic 'longing to do some more research'.[84]

As Constantine discovered to his cost, it was not a good idea to cross a woman prone to revenge herself for real or imagined slights in her next volume of poetry or prose. Possibly Phyllis had not read or grasped the import of Aelfrida's vengeful poetry or perhaps the fact that her sister-in-law now wrote only books of a religious nature or commissioned biographies of Temperance crusaders (*Agnes E Slack*) or Austenesque novels of nineteenth century Cambridge life provided a false sense of security. Either way, she must have been dismayed to find her child-rearing methods pilloried in Aelfrida's first novel *The Way We Grow Up*.

Before Stephen Tillyard's birth on 28 July 1920 Aelfrida was upset by his 'very modern' parents' insistence that the baby (if a boy) would be called plain 'Stephen' without reference to ancestral names on either side of his family and that he was to be devoid of baptism or religious upbringing.[85] She was even more upset to discover the following year that Stephen was being enthusiastically 'hardened' by being made to eat raw food, to sleep with his bedroom door and window open even in cold weather, to take tepid baths, and to wear what his aunt considered inadequate clothing. Believing such 'senseless hardening' made the child 'listless and ill', Aelfrida first 'sermonised' his nursemaid then wrote 'a pleading note' to Phyllis begging her to abate the rigours of her regime on the grounds that she was raising Stephen 'with more theories than sense'.[86] (She subtly undermined Phyllis' regime by coddling Stephen at every possible opportunity.) Though Eustace, ever the peacemaker, confessed that he and Phyllis 'had overdone the hardening'[87], the damage was done: Phyllis bore a grudge which undoubtedly contributed to the unpleasant tone of her letter of September 1926 (for a woman to criticise the way in which another woman brings up her children is a very personal form of attack and evokes primitive responses) and Aelfrida revenged herself by caricaturing theories which stated that it was good for a baby to 'be left alone to howl half-naked in a draught'[88] when commonsense suggested that such treatment might be detrimental to its physical and emotional welfare.

In October 1926, a month after Phyllis accused her of being 'mercenary', Aelfrida confessed that 'another book … is kicking about inside my head'; the book, written during 1927 and 1928, was published in early October 1929 with the comment that parts of it were 'intimately true'.[89] With regard to the theories which Aelfrida

considered had 'embittered Stephen's babyhood'[90], they certainly were and Phyllis cannot have been pleased to find herself depicted as 'Blanche Hildersham', a mother prepared to put principles so far beyond what Aelfrida regarded as proper maternal feeling (while noting her 'regretted tendency to criticise Phyllis'[91], she made no secret of the fact that she believed her sister-in-law to be 'entirely without maternal instinct' and liable to do 'the most unwise things' as a result)[92] that "her theories of discipline and hardening" cause her baby's death, and Aelfrida (as 'Daisy', the 'nurse-girl') as provider of "the extra vest, the warmer bath-water, the closed door of the night-nursery, the hot-water bottle in the perambulator on cold days, [and of] furtive hugs and kisses".[93]

Julius too created difficulties. Having returned from South Africa 'well and brown' in December 1921 (and with a tendency to address the Fordfield cat 'in Zulu and Afrikaans')[94] to take up his post as Professor of Russian at Birmingham University, he rapidly reverted to type, Aelfrida writing exasperatedly that 'if Julius were not my brother, what a cranky old bachelor I should think him'. His being willing 'to do any mortal thing Chiara wants'[95] and his willingness to take responsibility for his father for the better part of every university vacation somewhat redeemed him in his sister's eyes but his tendency to arrive, tired and pessimistic, to shed gloom over an already gloomy household and to continue in this vein until 'the magic of Fordfield' worked upon its 'devotee'[96], and his never contributing to household expenses during his lengthy visits drove her to record uncharitable thoughts in her diary.

His grumblings notwithstanding, Julius' presence at Fordfield might have lightened Aelfrida's load considerably had it not been for the antagonism he demonstrated toward Alethea, already the butt of her grandparents' displeasure. Whether he adopted this approach in emulation of his parents or whether it was the spontaneous reaction of a man dislodged from his sister's affections by the arrival of her first child, a reaction kept in check during Alethea's childhood but now revealed because of her resemblance to that of the man who had taken Julius' place in his sister's heart, it is impossible to say. Jealousy seems the most likely reason, for Julius manifested symptoms of displeasure relative to *both* girls (he was usually perfectly pleasant to Agatha) on the rare occasions when the Oracle and Chiara were away from home together, Aelfrida noting 'it is not always easy to keep the peace between Dudu and my daughters. They all want me [but] Dudu wishes my girls to get out of his way'.[97]

That Agatha (to some extent) and Alethea (invariably) rejoiced when Julius left is obvious from Aelfrida's description of Julius' verbally unpleasant behaviour towards her elder daughter ("hold your tongue", "don't be a fool", and "we don't want to hear *your* opinion" are some of the remarks she quotes), behaviour which engendered such strong dislike on Alethea's part that it was sometimes hard for Aelfrida to keep the peace. Dependent on her brother for help with the Oracle and unwilling to complain to a mother whose admonitions might have made him desist but who might equally have sided with Julius and asked Aelfrida to remove her daughters and herself from Fordfield, Aelfrida not only failed to rebuke her brother but also glossed over snubs by changing the subject as if by so doing she could persuade Alethea that unpleasantnesses had not happened and that Julius' niece would come to love the 'Dudu' Aelfrida remembered from childhood instead of resenting the grumpy uncle he had become. (Eustace was either unaware of tensions between his parents, brother, and niece or chose not to intervene.) Alethea, politely restrained in public, informed her mother only that "I don't like Dudu"[98] but was less polite in her diary: 'I don't think he's quite sane'.[99]

The 'Fordfield magic' which cheered Julius arose less from 'magic' emanating from the house or its inhabitants and more from the fact that in relieving Chiara he provided himself with an excuse for absenting himself from Mina. Mina, unhappy in her marriage and over the effect of the war on her homeland, had eventually persuaded Julius to allow her to adopt two children, a boy in 1922 named Conrad Walter after his adoptive parents' dead brothers (Conrad, died 1888, and Mina's brother Walter, killed in action in 1918) and a girl (Constance Emma) in 1924. This led to Aelfrida commenting bitterly about 'seeing my own daughters set aside' in terms of 'expectations of inheritance'[100], to visiting Aunt Luna[101] (who also catechised Aelfrida as to how much money the latter made from her books and on the size of her allowance from Constantine) noting sarcastically that if Julius and Mina *liked* "to spend their money on two little brats instead of on themselves that was *their* affair!"[102], and to the 'brats' adoptive father absenting himself as much as possible from their infancy and childhood.

The first pretence maintained by the Tillyards – so stoutly maintained that it deceived everyone who did not know them well – was that they were a happy, united, and Christian family. The second, that there reigned at Fordfield 'perfect peace' of a tranquillising and salubrious nature – the phrase was coined by a visitor, not an inmate – was maintained most stoutly by the person whose existence was possibly the least peaceful, who not infrequently found herself at the centre of the storm, who had the strongest interest in keeping up the illusion, and who invariably employed the phrase with

reference to the difficulty of keeping the peace unbroken or, when fractured by internecine warfare, of encouraging it to resume its sway, was not, as one might expect, Chiara, but Aelfrida.

Her thirty-seventh birthday on 5 October 1920 found her sunk in gloom, though following a litany of complaints – a streaming cold, another rejection of her 'Emden Novel', constant interruptions – she felt able to admonish herself with the words 'courage Aelfrida! Don't be trivial'[103] and to look on the brighter side of life, a side more often recorded in 'the kiddies' record-book'[104] to which Agatha and Alethea had access than in her own diary. By the following year, however, periods of feeling that 'sometimes one *must* be gloomy inside' but also that she did not want the unthinking sympathy offered by 'kind, stupid people'[105] had begun to be replaced by the ability to step back from the negative side of her existence (primarily the Oracle but also her inability to bestow money on others because she had barely sufficient for her own needs, because she wanted 'to teach the world to be wise' but it would not listen, and because her own behaviour fell short of her sainted mother's) and to count her blessings. Foremost among these was 'knowledge of God and constant communion with Him'. Second was her delight in watching her children grow up 'well and happy, intelligent, affectionate, competent'. Third, the 'serene and beautiful' (*sic*) life she led at Fordfield: 'the companionship of those I love, enough solitude, leisure to write (if not always strength), books, friends, letters, a garden, small but beloved duties of housework and sewing and reading aloud', 'memories of past raptures, sunsets, music sometimes …'[106], a life which led her to reflect 'what a happy woman I am. So blessed in my religion and my children and my other dear ones and my pleasant life'.[107] (The tone of such diary entries was not intended to be ironic though she frequently complained of wanting 'to write a good long grumble to relieve [her] feelings' but being 'too utterly weary and dispirited' to put pen to paper.)[108] Her fortieth birthday in October 1923 found her happier still. Reiterating earlier blessings, she enumerated more: 'the same sense of wonder, of power, of boundless possibility that I had when I was twenty … almost sufficient health [and] I look younger than I did four years ago'.[109] (Contemporary photographs show the truth of this last assertion; one, the first ever, even shows her laughing.) In February 1926 she went so far as to write that 'when the sun shines and I have Fordfield and all my dear ones … I want nothing'.[110] But she did. She wanted (in both senses of the word) Constantine.

The early 1920s saw Aelfrida commit to paper lengthy ruminations on and laments over the wreck of her marriage, laments so prolonged as to verge on the pathological. Not content with having rendered Constantine blind even to her good qualities or with having freed herself from his domination by driving him away, she now wanted him (or, rather, her idealised version of him) back but, unable to accept that he would never come back, preferred to believe that circumstances or a belated appreciation of her value to him or his own inability to live without her would bring him sooner or later to her side. Some laments (the minority) referred to her own part in the disaster and were chiefly concerned with the fact that her own behaviour had been morally inadequate: 'I ought to be such a person ... near whom goodness [was] so attractive that wickedness was unthinkable [and] wrong impossible'[111]; she even mentally composed a book 'which will probably never be written and certainly *never* published' entitled *Letters to my Former Husband* in which she expressed her continuing love and attempted to explain the 'attitude to life' which had alienated him from her.[112] Others – a recurring theme – referred vivid dreams in which Constantine repented and returned, 'radiant and unashamed', to a forgiving wife who 'of course ... opened [her] arms'.[113] (The Oracle and Chiara, though now less bitter about their son-in-law's defection for they too had had time to contemplate the fact that their daughter's behaviour had been largely responsible for the breakdown of the Grahams' marriage, had stated that should Constantine return, he would be refused entry to Fordfield. Aelfrida therefore decided that although she could not 'wish him back' at present, she could hope for reconciliation in the future 'if he were old or ill or lonely'.)[114] The majority, however, referred to physical and emotional longing for the man she continued to call 'my love, my love'.[115]

From 1919 to 1923 and beyond, Constantine was 'always there, either in the background or the foreground of [her] mind'[116] and she felt 'widowed' without him.[117] Did Constantine, she wondered, ever guess or even care how much she still loved him? (Re-reading a diary entry of October 1905 in which she noted how, ill at Fordfield with 'Florentine fever,' she was comforted by an adoring Constantine and recorded that 'we love wonderfully', she added a sad reflection: 'my love has lasted, Constantine. I do not love your faults nor your love of me, but *you*'.)[118] Or that she loved him in spite of his 'blindness' and wished that he could 'have those things which for his blindness he cannot see'?[119] Or that the mere mention of his name, though it hurt terribly, fanned into flame 'the longing for him that is always smouldering'[120] so that 'in the night ... passion catches me'[121], passion so strong that 'if Constantine ever beckons I must rise instantly and go to him?'[122] Or that not even the passing of time allowed her to forget him, either 'with my body [or] with my heart'[123] because she lived now as she did in the days when Constantine courted her ardently in a house and garden where 'the poignant vividness, the mingled sweetness and bitterness of the memories of twenty years ago ... seems as though it were the other day'?[124] Or that his daughters, 'sweet Agatha' and 'resolute, keen intelligent' Alethea[125] were growing up fatherless?

The 'perfect peace of Fordfield' was, it seems, a perfect sham.

## Notes

1  GCPPT 1|1|10 13 September 1903.
2  GCPPT 1|1|21 2 November 1916.
3  GCPPT 1|1|26 28 July 1922.
4  GCPPT 1|1|32 13 March 1926.
5  GCPPT 1|1|17 6 September 1910.
6  GCPPT 1|1|32 10 April 1926.
7  GCPPT 1|1|25 27 April 1920.
8  ibid. 4 December 1920.
9  GCPPT 1|1|30 25 May 1925.
10  GCPPT 1|1|27 8 July 1923.
11  GCPPT 1|1|26 14 December 1921.
12  GCPPT 1|1|30 3 July 1925.
13  ibid. 3 July 1925.
14  GCPPT 1|1|25 8 November 1920.
15  GCPPT 1|1|28 20 February 1924.
16  GCPPT 1|1|18 13 October 1911.
17  GCPPT 1|1|28 20 February 1924.
18  GCPPT 1|1|25 18 November 1920.
19  ibid. 3 July 1921.
20  GCPPT 1|1|27 5 August 1923.
21  GCPPT 1|1|28 2 June 1924.
22  GCPPT 1|1|26 10 November 1922.
23  GCPPT 2/2a *MCJ* February 1932 *Medical Number*.
24  GCPPT 1|1|25 26 September 1919.
25  Contemporary mystics quoted by Aelfrida had no such problems. Caroline Stephen was financially independent and had no dependents. Evelyn Underhill was married to a supportive husband who allowed her to lead an active spiritual life in conjunction with a public one; she was also well-to-do and childless.
26  GCPPT 1|1|25 26 September 1919. Mary Coleridge and Frances Ridley Havergal enjoyed childlike dependence on parents and siblings which allowed for, and even encouraged, mystical activity. Neither married, neither suffered financial hardship.
27  GCPPT 1|1|25 29 September 1919.
    GCPPT 1|1|26 10 September 1921.
28  GCPPT 1|1|32 30 October 1926.
29  GCPPT 1|1|25 18 June 1921.
30  GCPPT 1|1|32 21 August 1926.
31  GCPPT 1|1|25 26 September 1919.
32  GCPPT 1|1|32 15 May 1926.
33  GCPPT 1|1|26 5 April 1922.
34  GCPPT 1|1|28 5 December 1924.
35  ibid. 8 November 1920.
36  GCPPT 1|1|24 9 July 1919.
37  GCPPT 1|1|25 15 November 1919.
38  ibid. 27 November 1920.
39  ibid. 3 July 1920.
40  ibid. 27 November 1920. The theme of loss of vision leading to clearer 'vision' of God is, of course, expressed in Aelfrida's *Vision Triumphant*, a

novel which probably owes as much to Alfred Tillyard's real loss of sight as it did to Constantine's wilful 'blindness'.

41 GCPPG.A2.1 20 November 1926. The Evelyn Nursing Home was founded in 1921 by Charles Morland Agnew, a London art dealer, and named after his wife. It was situated in Trumpington Road a short distance from Fordfield and was much patronised by the Tillyard and Graham families. Alfred Tillyard probably suffered from arteriosclerotic retinopathy resulting in glaucoma.

42 GCPPT 1|1|27 16 March 1922.

43 GCPPG A1.1 13 March 1926.

44 GCPPT 1|1|26 14 and 19 October 1922.

45 GCPPT 1|1|32 22 November 1926.

46 GCPPT 1|1|30 3 October 1925.

47 GCPPT 1|1|26 26 November 1922.
 GCPPT 1|1|34 12 May 1927.

48 ibid. 12 May 1927.

49 GCPPT 1|1|32 22 January 1926.

50 GCPPT 1|1|27 28 March 1923.

51 GCPPT 1|1|30 8 November 1925.

52 GCPPT 1|1|28 1 March 1924.
 GCPPT 1|1|32 11 January 1926.

53 GCPPT 1|1|32 21 August 1926.

54 GCPPT 1|1|28 1 March 1924.

55 GCPPT 1|1|27 12 June 1923.

56 ibid. 21 April 1923.

57 ibid. 9 May 1923.

58 ibid. 6 July 1923.

59 ibid. 21 June 1923.

60 ibid. 22 July 1923.

61 GCPPT 1|1|26 14 October 1922.

62 GCPPT 1|1|27 21 June 1923.

63 GCPPT 1|1|32 22 November 1926.

64 GCPPT 1|1|27 22 July 1923.

65 GCPPT 1|1|32 21 February 1926.

66 GCPPG A1.1 13 February 1926.

67 GCPPT 1|1|34 27 February 1927.

68 GCPPG A2.1 9 December 1926.

69 GCPPT 1|1|34 12 December 1926.

70 GCPPG A1.2 18 December 1926.

71 GCPPG A1.1 11 October 1929.

72 GCPPT 1|1|36 9 and 12 October 1929.

73 ibid. 9 October 1929.

74 Letter from Catharine Tillyard to Julius Tillyard dated 8 October [1929] included in Alfred Tillyard's obituaries in Tillyard, HJW. *Synopsis of Diaries* (MTC).

75 Undated addendum to letter of 8 October [1929] quoted above.

76 GCPPG A2.1 12 July 1925.

77 ibid.

78 GCPPT 1|1|25 11 September 1920.

79 ibid. 11 September 1920.

80 GCPPG A2.1 12 July 1925.

81 GCPPT 1|1|32 10 September 1926.

82 ibid. 11 and 12 September 1926.

83 GCPPT 1|1|30 9 April 1925.

84 GCPPT 1|1|25 12 January 1920.

85 ibid. 14 July 1920.

86 GCPPT 1|1|26 1 October 1921. Phyllis may have been influenced by the child-rearing theories of Sir Frederick Truby King (1858–1938), the New Zealand Director of Child Welfare, who in 1907 instigated a mothercraft and child care movement dedicated to the bringing up of babies on scientific principles. Following his attendance in 1913 at the Child Welfare Conference in England, his doctrines were adopted, and sometimes over-zealously applied, by English women's organisations of which Phyllis was a member.

87 GCPPT 1|1|26 4 and 6 October 1921.

88 ibid. 31 December 1922.

89 GCPPT 1|1|36 8 October 1929.

90 GCPPT 1|1|26 31 December 1922.

91 ibid. 24 April 1922.

92 ibid. 24 August 1922.

93 Tillyard, Ae. *The Way We Grow Up* p 179. Aelfrida's denigration of modern methods of childrearing and eulogy of her own occupies two chapters (XVII and XVIII) of the book.

94 GCPPT 1|1|26 13 December 1921.

95 ibid. 23 December 1921.

96 GCPPT 1|1|32 4 March 1926.

97 ibid. 27 August 1926.

98 GCPPT 1|1|30 13 January 1924.

99 GCPPG A1.1 6 March 1926.

100 GCPPT 1|1|26 4 January 1923.

101 Luna Eady née Boyle was the daughter of Emma Barrett's sister Susanna, wife of Joseph Boyle, and the younger sister of formidable Florence Boyle. Known in her younger days (she was born in 1853) as "unashamedly and joyfully worldly", as "a lover of jewels, furs, lace, elegant food, dances, admiration [and] the limelight", and as "if not fast, at least somewhat *rapid*" (GCPPT 2|27|2(5)), by 1931 she was 'as pathetic a sight as you could wish to see [with] curled and dyed hair … and [a] skinny body exhaling a mixed smell of scent and spirits' (GCPPT 1|1|28 3 November 1924).

102 GCPPT 1|1|28 3 November 1924.

103 GCPPT 1|1|25 5 October 1920.

104 ibid. 23 October 1920.

105 ibid. 6 June 1921.

106 ibid. 20 May 1921.

107 GCPPT 1|1|26 30 August 1921.

108 GCPPT 1|1|25 6 June 1921.

109 GCPPT 1|1|27 5 October 1923.

110 GCPPT 1|1|32 26 February 1926.

111 GCPPT 1|1|26 24 January 1922.

112 ibid. 10 July 1922.

113 ibid. 6 August 1922.

114 GCPPT 1|1|25 12 December 1920.

115 ibid. 18 December 1920.

116 ibid. 4 December 1920.

117 ibid. 11 July 1921.

118 GCPPT 1|1|13 10 October 1905 with added note dated only '1922'.

119 GCPPT 1|1|26 18 August 1921.

120 ibid. 25 January 1923.

121 ibid. 30 August 1921.

122 ibid. 22 September 1921.

123 GCPPT 1|1|27 5 October 1924.

124 GCPPT 1|1|28 1 June 1924.

125 GCPPT 1|1|26 21 August 1921.

# Fidelio and Cousin Willie

Fidelio's return to Cambridge in 1921 was regarded with indifference by Agatha ('Mr Frank Stokoe, poet friend of Mother's', is almost the only reference to him in her diary)[1], without a trace of her former jealousy by Alethea who in August 1914 had asked Fidelio to go away because she wanted her mother to herself[2], and by Aelfrida with misgivings. Having decided in 1918 that she was 'as "detached" as ever [she] could wish', that 'if there was ever any glamour over him, it has all gone now', and that she could regard him as just another 'sinning suffering man down, down in the mire like the rest of us' (remembering an earlier diary entry in which she compared her feelings for Fidelio to those of young ladies for curates, she added 'even his being a poet makes no difference'), she turned with a 'passion of joy' to contemplate a being of 'seamless perfection' to whom it was perfectly permissible to attach herself, namely God: '*there* I may adore, *there* I may fearlessly devote myself'[3]. But for how long?

Her resolve ('I think I could trust myself however much I saw of [Fidelio] but I am told that the human heart is not to be trusted')[4] was strengthened by an Oracular decree that Stokoe was not to visit Fordfield until Aelfrida's divorce was over, Constantine's wife, like Caesar's, having to be above suspicion until due legal process was complete, a condition to which Aelfrida, a woman of thirty-five, agreed reluctantly: 'this is not my home, and … I must do, as far as I can, what my people like'.[5] Although she and Stokoe continued to meet surreptitiously (the latter was currently in a manic phase during which he wrote poetry consigned for safekeeping and comment to Aelfrida but was soon to revert to 'nervous misery')[6], his lack of interest in her current world of 'lawyers and divorces and settlements'[7] and his annoyance when her time was taken up by these and by domestic concerns made her hope that Fidelio would 'settle down to work, find plenty of friends and not need [her] so much'.[8] Then too, far from making her want to turn to anyone else, disillusionment with marriage and because she could only think of Constantine with 'grief and indignation' made her feel 'less drawn to be intimate with anyone whatsoever'.[9]

This being so, Aelfrida's misgivings following the 'pleasant intimate talk' which took place between her

**Willie Searle with Aelfrida and Alethea Graham 1924**

and Stokoe following his return to Cambridge in July 1921[10] seem unfounded, particularly as Fidelio was not attracted to women and, other than initially and probably inspired by John Layard's overwrought devotion, had never made a play for her. The problem rather lay with discovering that Fidelio's 'glamour' continued to attract her to such an extent that her guardian angel was obliged to warn her to get rid of 'glamour as well as resentment and desire'.[11] Stokoe's notion of settling in Cambridge to be near her – he was looking at rooms in Panton Street, 'much *too* near' Fordfield[12] – added to her dismay: 'I wish to be "detached" [because ] I have the utmost horror of depending on any individual for my happiness … I do not want to see him often'.[13] She was, however, happy to meet Fidelio provided this involved nothing more than responding to recurrent appeals to 'save him from restlessness and the cold of loneliness'[14] because that was consistent with 'detachment' and because 'the opportunity of devoting myself is the limit of what I ask'.[15] But the sight and sound of him reading his poetry to her (one poem in particular, *The Secluded Dwelling,* was, she thought, a veiled cry for help) awakened an all-too-familiar tendency to hero-worship which alarmed her so in spite of cautioning her diary and a future biographer 'don't be imagining "falling in love" … every capacity for *that* went [with] Constantine', that she was forced to remind herself that should Constantine ever beckon, she must 'rise instantly and go to him', that she must 'view things and people as they are in themselves and not as they are in relation to [herself]', and that devotion must be aimed at 'God, not man'. Supported in her resolve by her guardian angel warning her to keep herself free "for the work that God wishes you to do"[16] and that she must stop building castles in the air with regard to 'an old age with Constantine' or, failing that, adoption of an orphan 'with Fidelio to father it' (*sic*), and by the wonderfully bracing effect of a course of yoga and 'a little mild asceticism' which allowed her to overcome her 'deplorable outburst of emotionalism'[17], Aelfrida found herself slipping into the more comfortable role of literary adviser.

Although the start of Fidelio's academic career in Cambridge was blighted by a recurrence of 'melancholy' severe enough to make teaching difficult and research impossible[18], it was not sufficiently severe to prevent him from writing poetry or from publishing his anthology *Tollkopf on Dreams*. Describing the title as 'stupid' but conceding 'there's wonderful stuff in the book' and that Fidelio's poetry was much better than hers ('I have no personal vanity or feeling of any kind about my poems *as mine*'[19], wrote the diarist who once described her poetry as better than Christina Rossetti's or Elizabeth Barrett Browning's), Aelfrida wondered, 'as Fidelio is a genius', whether she ought to 'Boswellise'[20] him but decided that she lacked the energy to produce a life as compendious as James Boswell's of Samuel Johnson. (In fact she did, her diary from 1913 to 1952 being almost as much the story of his life as of hers.) She was honoured, nevertheless, by being allowed to read Fidelio's *journal intime* in which he recorded 'thoughts not of external events or even of other people [but] … a strange tragic mixture of sunshine and night, fall and rebirth, encounters with God and the Devil' and introspections into his own 'multiple states' written in a style 'curiously monotonous yet ever fresh'.[21] (A diary, it seems, remarkably like Aelfrida's own.) It was also to Aelfrida that Stokoe felt able to confide his continuing spiritual quest 'for something of which he gets strange alluring glimpses and which he must follow though he knows not what it is', a quest so remarkably like her own with regard to Deity that she was able both to sympathise and to enter with Fidelio into 'the Cloud of Unknowing where [I] usually [go] alone'. She did, however, inform him that *she* had already found what *he* sought: 'I told him right out that what he was looking for was God'.[22]

More worrying than fear of falling in love with a man for whom she felt such spiritual affinity was Fidelio's change of attitude towards herself following the granting of her decree absolute on February 1922, an event greeted by Aelfrida as 'one pang more' and by her legal representative as a subject for congratulation, Hal Verey informing her '"now you are free" as though he expected [her] to marry again forthwith'.[23] Fidelio's 'airs of proprietorship and ordering me about quite as if I were his wife!'[24] and tendency to behave like 'a man to whom much intimacy has been granted' (he called her 'Frida' and monopolised her in company) not only persuaded her parents (the Oracle and Chiara were unaware of his proclivities) that he wished to marry their daughter but also upset Aelfrida in case the unlikely event were true: 'I could not tolerate anyone near me who wanted to marry me'.[25]

Fortunately for both, Stokoe's proprietorial behaviour disappeared almost as suddenly as it arrived. Aelfrida gives no reason for this but there are at least two possible explanations. First, Stokoe underwent formal therapy sometime in the early 1920s (Aelfrida writes of his being 'cured of being a poet and turned into a pedant')[26] and his mental condition seems to have stabilised to such an extent that although he continued to suffer mood swings during which he greeted Aelfrida with 'the blue flame in his eyes that I hadn't seen for years', devised grandiose impractical schemes for his future which never came to fruition[27] or 'an entire new system of philosophy'[28], or declared, following an incident in which, 'looking for a change of mood', he almost drove his car off an escarpment while announcing that 'at last he found the journey's end he had been looking for'[29] (what that 'end' was, Aelfrida does not say), or informed her that he was 'nearer despair' than ever before because he realised that far from becoming a great poet, he was dwindling into a middle-aged don whose poetic abilities had deserted him, he was better able to cope with life without continual support from herself. (Aelfrida dealt with his highs and lows much as she had always done, rejoicing at any return of his old fire while discouraging his madder schemes and making 'stimulating remarks' when he was 'inclined to be tragic'; she also noted that 'poets ought to die young, like Rupert Brooke and Békássy'[30] and that 'Fidelio as a genius, has never fully flowered perhaps because he shrank from life … instead of opening his heart to it'.)[31] Second, a busy academic career, publication of his first and only academic treatise, *German Influence in the English Romantic Period 1788–1818* in 1926, and appointment as Lecturer in French in 1930 seem to have been therapeutic in their own way. (Neither the treatise nor *Tolkopf on Dreams* were dedicated to the woman to whom he owed so much in terms of literary and emotional support, possibly because, as Aelfrida suspected, he did not now value their friendship as highly as she did; he did, however, send her a copy of the treatise accompanied by a 'loving letter'[32] whose content she does not divulge but given the date of the diary entry in which she records its receipt, it may have incorporated birthday wishes as well as gratitude for support which enabled him to publish, albeit belatedly, an erudite if not absolutely original thesis.)Visiting Fidelio at his lodgings in the Cambridgeshire village of Comberton in June 1924, Aelfrida found him 'sane [and] happy' and noted that 'prosperity suits him'[33]; three months later, however, she noted that prosperity had added 'a coat of flesh to his mind'[34] too, a disappointment to one who believed Stokoe to be a genius. (There were also uncomfortable parallels between the new Fidelio and her former husband.) Visiting him the following year she found him so busy with examination papers that he had little time for her even while presupposing 'the same sympathetic interest in himself' on her part.[35] The discovery left her rather bereft though she rejoiced at his being 'so much more at peace with the world' and that his continuing sensitivity 'to all beauty, spiritual, intellectual, [and] natural' meant their friendship could continue albeit on a less intense level.[36]

There was, too, the fact that 'emotional friendship' of the kind she maintained with Fidelio was 'more to [her] taste than marriage' (though 'if you want babies you have to go a … *big* step … further!')[37] and that a 'kind of love without sex'[38] more closely approximated the sexless relationship she had envisaged between herself and Constantine. In fact, a relationship begun in the same 'unreal world, goblin- and fairy-peopled'[39] as that in which she first encountered Constantine had transformed itself into one which enabled both Stokoe and Aelfrida to maintain their freedom of thought and action[40] ('when Fidelio is not here I hardly ever think of him, or if I do, do not miss him in the least!') while remaining so much of one mind ('he understands me better than any of my other Little Friends have in spite of his being more interested in himself than in me')[41] that when they met they were 'just as affectionate and intimate … as if we had been seeing each other often'[42] instead of once or twice a year.

A friendship begun on the basis of a mutual interest in poetry also had interesting repercussions insofar as both participants moved on to novel writing, Fidelio producing one (and that unpublished), and Aelfrida several, some published.Whether or not Fidelio's was a *roman à clef,* Aelfrida does not relate; hers, however, were – and in them Frank Stokoe and his mother played a part. Alice Woodyer Stokoe's contribution (above and beyond the fact that keeping in touch with his mother allowed

Aelfrida to learn more about him than he himself was willing to divulge and to know when to make herself available should a psychotic episode require intervention) was of an indirect but important kind insofar as it provided Aelfrida with possible background information for two novels (*The Young Milliner* and *Haste to the Wedding*) written during the 1920s but set in the nineteenth century. Mrs Stokoe was, with good reason, rather depressing company but this did not prevent Aelfrida from adding her to a lengthy list of elderly ladies (blood relatives, relatives by adoption like 'Aunt Laura'[43], widows of academics and of St Columba worthies, and friends of Chiara's whose sons had once been beaux of her own) whom she visited assiduously, ostensibly as acts of Christian charity but more, one suspects, because she "turned to old ladies, as [she] turned to novels, in order to find out what life was like and what kind of spiritual and emotional adventures [she] might expect" for herself.[44] Some visits were paid expressly 'to look for "copy"'[45] but Aelfrida also used chance and regular acquaintances in this manner (an elderly Linton lady and her dog appear recognisably in *The Way We Grow Up*) and it seems that calls on Mrs Stokoe were not intended solely for the purpose of cheering her up.

Fidelio himself appears in an unpublished novel, *O Passionate World,* begun in 1930. In the guise of 'Alan George', a friend of the heroine's, Fidelio is depicted as a university contemporary of her estranged husband who tells her that for her children's sake she must divorce him ("the only pity is that he did not go sooner")[46], as a hard-hitting critic of her novels ("your books are not up to date")[47], and as a man "ugly to look at, delicate in health, a bachelor"[48] with "very little use for women"[49] whose innate pessimism leads him to declare that he "would end the whole silly show this very moment if [he] could".[50] And in an uncanny presaging of Stokoe's own death, 'Alan' dies of a heart attack, leaving the heroine to mourn the loss of "another human consolation"[51] but her daughter to declare that 'Alan' was better dead because "he was a sort of … parasite, hanging on to you like mistletoe on an oak tree … [he] had a cold and clammy soul and … was always trying to get near you and steal your warm soul".[52] Given that the remark was made by a character modelled on Alethea and the name given to that character – Vera – also means 'truth', an interesting sidelight is thrown on Aelfrida's relationship with Fidelio which may explain some of her relief when Stokoe began to distance himself in 1924. The remark may also, of course, form the revengeful coda of an otherwise sympathetic depiction which reveals Aelfrida's sadness that Fidelio did not now rate their friendship as highly as he did.

In keeping with Aelfrida's propensity for becoming 'preoccupied' with one man after another, there was present in her life at the same time as Frank Stokoe a man whom Alethea called first 'uncle' then 'cousin' Willie, namely Willie Searle. The young man Aelfrida had been advised by Eustace in February 1913 not to 'notice' because he was 'far too much interested' in her already but to whom she later confided some of her marital problems, had returned to England in 1920 to resume his interrupted career as a London solicitor. He had, however, several reasons for paying visits to Cambridge: surviving members of his family and his childhood friend Eustace Tillyard. Both his parents being now dead (his father had been over sixty and his mother over forty when he was born) Willie was 'adopted' by Chiara and often spent weekends at Fordfield as a 'son of the house'.

On 15 August 1920 Willie, accompanied (and, it may be, chaperoned) by his spinster sisters Nellie and Dorothy, came to tea, a visit described by Aelfrida as 'not at all a success' because the Misses Searle made no secret of their dislike of and their brother no secret of his liking for her, he sitting so close that 'the fear which has long existed vaguely became definite, namely that … he is beginning to want to marry me' and she panicked 'lest he should gradually be establishing himself here and it would be impossible to turn him out'. She therefore decided that making himself 'so much at home … must be stopped', first, because she herself was nearly forty with 'two big daughters'[53] (Alethea was twelve, Agatha ten) and Willie a contemporary of her younger brother, second, because in spite of Chiara urging her to marry again, the idea aroused 'the most passionate disgust'[54] because of her being unable to tolerate anyone near her who wanted to marry her and because she regarded marriage after divorce as 'legitimised adultery'.[55] Thirdly, *any* invitation by any man whatsoever to enter into 'a further spiritual intimacy' (even if this manifested itself as no more than a 'fatherly' interest in her essentially fatherless daughters) was to be treated with 'reticences and reserves' because she was unsure that her vaunted power of 'detachment' would prove sufficiently strong against the delights of even a spiritual friendship (Fidelio described her attitude here as 'morbid and over-scrupulous') and because renewed adherence to doctrines of 'no human affections' meant she was permitted to love other people for *their* sake only, not for any pleasure *she* might derive from their society.[56]

Few references to Willie appear in Aelfrida's diary between September 1920 and May 1922 apart from a cryptic comment made in November 1921 midway between her decrees nisi and absolute that 'much could be said about Willie!'[57] It seems, however, that reticence concerning a man whose continuing admiration made her more determined to treat him like a younger brother concealed Willie's determination to become her second husband, though it was not until a three-day visit made by her hopeful suitor to the Tillyards during the latters' lengthy stay in the Suffolk village of Clare in summer 1922[58] that he finally declared his love for her.

Having persuaded her mother that it would be unseemly for Willie to think of courtship so soon after divorce, Aelfrida had also warned Willie that she would behave towards him solely as aunt to favourite nephew, to which end she and Chiara stage-managed the visit so that Aelfrida and Willie were never alone together. On a short un-chaperoned walk, however, the 'little devil' which prompted Aelfrida to ride horses she could barely control, to flirt with married men, and to publish provocative poetry, prompted her to force Willie into making exactly the kind of declaration she did not (so she said) want to hear. She began by suggesting that he transfer his affections to Alethea on the (unspoken) grounds that Willie and Alethea much alike in being superficially gay and adventurous and fond of the good things in life but *au fond* serious and chivalrous and that fatherless Alethea would do well 'in the hands of a man [old] enough to be husband and father in one', she herself becoming Willie's mother-in-law. (That a London solicitor of thirty-four would be unlikely to be attracted by an overweight, hoydenish, and sulky adolescent twenty years his junior never entered the head of one keen to promote the cause of a daughter she proudly called 'handsome and brilliant' and to divert Willie's attention from herself.) To her – pretended – surprise, Willie reacted angrily (in an – again pretended – failure of her usual facility for total recall of significant conversations, Aelfrida wrote 'I can't report, even if I remembered [because] words … never look right') and stormed off, leaving Aelfrida to feel that she had been 'unspeakably tactless and brutal, imagining (*sic*) that Willie didn't care a bit because I want him not to'.[59]

After a wakeful night during which she was aware of Willie moving restlessly in the next room next and of the same 'little devil' asking her "why don't you get up and go to him?" (a thought she thrust from her with horror 'but it seemed to leer at me as it ran'), Aelfrida renewed her 'bitter contest between the desire for personal happiness and what I know to be right – detachment'. She also asked herself some hard questions ('why am I not honest? Why do I not admit my weakness?'), confessing at last what she might have suspected all along 'though I have only recently discovered it', namely that she was a highly-sexed woman who, though she 'rarely' (so she said) responded physically, became 'most quickly emotional' in the presence of particular men.[60] Shocked by her discovery, she felt obliged to take a day in bed following Willie's departure: 'I want, like one of Miss Austen's heroines, to become "tolerably composed"'.[61]

Apart from indulging in further discussion with the 'little devil' who reminded her when she declared 'I am not free [and] besides I love Constantine' that even though emotionally bound by love for a man who existed in only her imagination ("why spoil your life for a dream?"), legally she was now free to marry when and whomsoever she wished, Aelfrida also tabulated the pros and cons of marriage to Willie. Willie, she wrote, was 'the finest type of English gentleman', a man with a 'broad outlook on life' who had 'seen much of men and women', who had freed himself from 'academic scepticism' and from the narrowness of Nonconformist sectarianism, and whose character had been tempered in the fires of war. Furthermore, 'the children and my people like him immensely', 'he is well off and could give the children advantages', and he had been her faithful admirer for ten years; she also found him physically attractive, a definite advantage given that her very first point was 'I want another baby'. On the other hand, 'the more I like him, the less I ought to burden him with a wife four years his senior, delicate, opinionated, and with two big girls' who might 'detest him as a stepfather' as much as they liked him as an adopted uncle or cousin. Then too, she could never leave Chiara and the Oracle. But the first on her list of reasons for not marrying Willie and the escape-clause required in any relationship, was 'I have devoted my chastity to God's service'.[62]

This being so, one would think there was no point in continuing the relationship. Aelfrida and Willie would part, she to devote herself to her parents, her daughters, and Deity in ascending order of importance, Willie to marry a woman as like Aelfrida as possible (or as unlike, in order to forget her), to start a family, and to pursue a successful career. Aelfrida, however, had other ideas: she would ensure that her life pursued the course she planned while keeping Willie dangling in case a change of plan was needed.

She began by writing to him to explain her 'theories of "detachment"' and to ask him not to make things hard for her. Willie's reply that her '"weakness" did but make her more dear', that her "philosophy of life" was probably due to her sad experience of a man like Constantine and might mellow in the warmth of his love, and that, not wishing to order her life for her, he was prepared to wait for her to change her mind, was not what Aelfrida wanted to hear. She wrote back immediately, explaining her theory of 'detachment' at more length and, encouraged by a 'telepathic dream' during which she and Willie

discoursed on this in detail, also informed him that 'ever since she could remember she had felt like a stranger on this earth' and that it was only when she yielded to the 'exactions' of this strange sensation by detaching herself from people and things and attaching herself spiritually to God that she felt truly happy and at peace. Having done what she believed to be right by telling him what she had never told anyone else, she hoped that Willie would 'begin to think seriously of Alethea' and that even allowing for the fact that he was 'one of those men whom you instinctively obey' and that there was an enormous attraction in lowering her moral standards sufficiently to allow her to lay herself and her troubles in Willie's arms, she would 'never again be tempted as I have been by [him]'.[63] She also decided to throw herself 'passionately into prayer and meditation'[64] as the most efficacious antidote to Willie's charms and was happy to discover her guardian angel (curiously absent during the period of the 'little devil') taking so serious a view of an interlude of which she herself felt desperately ashamed, that he ordered her to undertake 'a course of meditation on Death' ('the one right subject just now') while 'lying in the attitude of a corpse', a course not to be abandoned until 'my guardian angel tells me I may leave off'[65] and chiefly memorable for its production of 'true dreams' about deceased Margaret Verrall and vivid dreams about living Constantine with whom, she reflected, she had had a 'romantic love match' in spite of the pain he caused her.[66]

Boxing Day 1922 saw Willie invited to Fordfield for supper. Although 'his eyes lighted on me – a simile is necessary! – like a bird alighting after a long flight'[67], Aelfrida avoided her would-be suitor as much as possible but unbent so far as to give him a copy of recently-published *A Little Road–Book for Mystics*. (She also sent a copy to Constantine, hoping that even if he did not read the messages to him concealed therein, sight of the cover might tell him she still loved him.)[68] She then compared Willie unfavourably to her former husband as he sat in the family circle 'resolute and masterful, where Constantine ought to be', feeling that much as she *liked* Willie she did not *want* him and wondering sadly why anyone 'should … want me – now?'[69], a woman of nearly forty, tainted by the opprobrium attached to divorcees, obliged to be 'so prudent for the children's sake'[70] lest they be tainted both by her disgrace and by her behaviour vis-à-vis men in general and Willie in particular, and curiously unprotected from predatory males because of her newly-single state.

In the middle of a wholly unrelated conversation with her mother which took place shortly before the Tillyards' flight to Hunstanton in October 1919, Alethea

*Constantine Michaelides.*

\*TO MY FATHER.

('Αργύρης 'Εφταλιώτης author of Νησιώτικες 'Ιστορίες

[*Tales from the Isles of Greece*], etc., etc.)

THE haunted image-bearing minds of men
  Born in these northern spheres,
Are blinded by the crowding of things dreamed
  Upon things seen. To us
Thought sinks not mistless on the shapes of things,
  Clear as the day; but harsh
And driven to boldness in the city-night,
  Straining beyond herself
She makes strange dreams of her bewilderment.
  Of such race are you not;
For you, untripped by unseen snares, in light
  Can see the simple truth
As it has been through centuries in those isles
  Which neither live nor die
But are immortal. The refrains of love
  And death and tragedy
Seem sad by very changelessness. The world
  In the forthflow of time
So new, is yet so hopeless and so old,
  That every tear we shed
Is but a repetition of those tears
  Which perhaps Sappho shed.
The same chant murmurs in the ageless sea
  As Homer turned to words,

128

**To my Father** by Constantine Michaelides (*Cambridge Poets 1900–1913*)

suddenly asked "how would you like Fuvver to have two wives?" before continuing to discuss a book on botany as if her 'queer subconscious mind' had never prompted the question[71]; it was not, however, until January 1923 that Constantine took a second wife.

Aelfrida began a new volume of her diary in February 1923 with the comment that although she had had the book several days, she had not begun writing in it 'from a feeling that something was going to happen. And [she] wanted to know what it was'. (She had also wanted to declare that only two things kept her from being perfectly happy: 'the sorrows of the world' which continued to afflict her during moments of 'universal consciousness', and 'ignorance of Constantine's life', a lack which troubled her even as she realised that although she had declared 'at the time I lost my beloved Constantine … that my personal happiness was at an end', the sense of release from tension she now experienced was enormous.) On 8 February she discovered something which allowed her to begin her diary and to fill a gap in her knowledge: 'this, then', 'this' being an announcement in *The Times*: "On the 8th January at the Union Church, Balboa, Panama.

Constantine Graham, His Britannic Majesty's Consul at Colon, to Mildred Seymour Swarz, only daughter of Henry Seymour … of Washington and Panama".[72]

Asking herself 'what do I feel?', Aelfrida surmised that she felt glad for Constantine and silently sent him a 'whole world full of love and blessings … with no bitterness, no wish to interfere' and hopes that he be happy in his new relationship.[73] (Agatha and Alethea 'received the news with complete indifference [because] their father means nothing to them. They never miss him now nor I believe think of him'[74]; neither mentioned his remarriage in their diaries.) She could not, however, prevent herself from pondering about her successor, hoping she was 'a good woman', deciding that she was 'probably a divorcée, as the announcement says nothing of a former husband', certainly an American, possibly rich, and 'I should think handsome'.[75] Hearing from Hal Verey that Constantine was in England in late February 1923 (perhaps he brought his new wife to meet his father; six months later 'dear, dear Argyris, who was always so good to me'[76] was dead), Aelfrida hoped for a message but resigned herself to silence, Constantine being 'no nearer to me than he was before, since his remoteness … cannot be expressed in geographical terms'.[77] She consoled herself with the thought that although she loved Constantine less 'now that he definitely belongs to another woman', should he ever need her, her love, 'more in abeyance than extinct', could 'flame into life again'.[78]

Words of sympathy (why sympathy?) came from Lucy, Charles Stewart Smith, and Fidelio and, more worryingly, from Willie: 'Willie wants to "console" me and … that is impossible [because although] he always touches and stirs me and I am very fond of him … I honestly wish he would forget me'. Replying to a 'most splendid letter', she therefore informed him that 'anything more than friendship' was 'out of the question'[79], only to receive a further letter 'surrounding [her] with consideration and affection' and offers of consolation should anything more occur to 'hurt' her.[80] So feeling exceedingly vulnerable because Constantine's marriage to Mildred had abruptly and publicly removed another reason for remaining single (Constantine might repent and return and she must be free to receive him), she temporised. Following a visit of 'three mortal hours' in March 1923 during which she felt extremely stirred by Willie's physical presence but was for practical reasons unable to practise the traditional remedies for temptation of fasting and mortification thereafter, Aelfrida decided the best thing to do was to acknowledge her physical and emotional weakness with regard to him and to ignore it because it did not affect her general conduct. Hence she need 'neither avoid Willie nor seek him out' nor discourage nor fight emotions repressed for so long and the spiritual struggle which would ensue would be valuable because 'this sort of thing keeps one humble'.[81]

Her belief that having looked 'the Willie-temptation in the face'[82], it would cease troubling her and that not even the possibility of having a son could induce her to marry him, Aelfrida was mortified to discover that not only was she still tempted 'just to stretch out [her] hand and take what he offers' (a move 'so easy and yet, to [her] mind, so utterly forbidden') but also that she was still prey to 'feelings to which my will in no way consents but [is] powerless to prevent'.[83] (Willie it seems, felt the same, for on Christmas Eve 1923 he informed her that he had given up worrying about his personal life and would immerse himself in work, politics, and Spiritualism instead, remedies often employed by those who had survived the Flanders killing fields; on Boxing Day, however, he added a "Barkis is willing" postscript to a letter.)[84] The 'war of the flesh with the spirit' raging in Aelfrida's heart continued unabated into 1924 and was evident even in sleep ('when I dream that Willie makes love to me, I also dream that I tell him I have put all thoughts of earthly love from me')[85] until it seemed that although her subconscious mind did not give consent, her body had developed a will of its own; describing a dream in which she and Willie kissed and from which she awoke 'in a glow of delight', Aelfrida wrote bitterly 'I do resent the effect that Willie has on me … why should my body be so intractable?' (She had, she added, 'no objection to dreaming about Constantine … nor to longing for him … for I do not see why a wife should not desire her own lawful husband'.)[86] Harder to fight than physical attraction, however, was the 'perfect chivalry' which prevented Willie from harassing her into marriage (harassment would be easier to rebuff) and the notion that 'faithful waiting' might easily slip into loneliness and loneliness into turning to someone else for consolation. Was her vow of chastity, she asked herself, 'merely a pious affectation' to which she had no right to sacrifice another's happiness ('if you *are* commonplace and sensual, Aelfrida, why try to be anything different') or was her desire for Willie as evidenced in a 'true dream' in which she and Willie figured (despairing of disentangling her thoughts without help, she had 'asked God for illumination in sleep') contrary to God's plan for her and, as her guardian angel told her, a manifestation of the hell-fire to which she would be consigned if she broke her vow?[87] But still she kept him dangling, for the presence in her life of a man who declared himself 'ready to offer … anything and everything [she] would accept' and was always "at your feet Frida"[88], made the woman of forty with a treacherous body 'thrill and glow' ('at my

age, to be so unmortified!') in spite of repeated assertions that she was 'deeply ashamed' of herself, that she wanted Willie 'to forget [her] and care for someone else'[89], and that she was 'waiting for a summons from God' either to perform some special work for Him or to die.[90]

The glow of Aelfrida's '"Indian Summer" wonder of being loved'[91] continued unabated (attempts to quench it were 'like trying to put out a fire with a spoonful of water')[92] in spite of intimations from Willie that he was not prepared to continue their relationship in its present unsatisfactory form. Resolving therefore that 'all this nonsense about Willie had got to be stopped'[93], she devised reasons why the 'nonsense' should cease.

The first and most pressing was that infatuation with Willie was a manifestation of 'getting slack in [her] spiritual life' as a result of relief and happiness at freeing herself from Constantine. Deciding that she must 'turn again to fasting and meditation' and hoping that with God's help her desire would incline once again to 'Him alone'[94], she was dismayed to discover that fasting was a 'perfect farce'[95] because meals were taken under her mother's watchful eye and because she continually sought 'earthly consolations' ('what I like to call "the devil" – as though it relieves me of … responsibility for my own weakness – remarks "why struggle? it is so *silly*!"') in spite of determination 'to *conquer* the temptation not just outgrow it'.[96] Meditation was more effective. With its help and by dint of days in bed to enable her to become 'recollected' and a mantra suggested by her guardian angel ("look up and adore, for God is everywhere!"), Aelfrida lay with her hands crossed on her breast as if in a coffin persuading herself that she was dead to all desire for personal happiness and that from now on her thoughts would fly 'instinctively to God'.[97]

They did not, of course, or at least not immediately. Sitting alone in springtime Cambridgeshire countryside 'dreaming of Willie and thinking of my vows', she asked herself how, 'being … very much in love', she could judge dispassionately of the right course of action? Was she, she wondered, preserving her chastity because of a preference for solitude and detachment which was in truth 'morbid and futile … medieval and perverse'? Was she trying for 'a higher kind of virtue than I am fit for … a false kind that is unnatural and displeasing to God?' Was mere bodily chastity worth anything when she dreamed of Willie 'all day long' and frequently at night? God, she decided, must tell her what to do even though His manifestation as Inward Light seemed to 'burn so dim' just now as to be no help at all. (Lucy Verey, in whom she had confided, told her briskly "vows and chastity, my dear [are] stuff and nonsense" and that she was behaving selfishly.) By the autumn of 1925, however, it being '*extraordinary* how a little meditation helps' especially when 'coupled with the trivial "mortification" of always eating what I like least at table'[98], Aelfrida had become 'absolutely at peace' with herself and the world. For the time being.

Another reason for her newly-regained serenity and for discontinuing her relationship with Willie was her growing belief that her attraction to him was no more than an expected but temporary aberration. Basing her premise on discoveries made during explorations in 'New Psychology'[99], Aelfrida began by attempting an explanation of Constantine's relationship with his mother ('psychoanalysis is certainly very illuminating … if he had gone to a psychoanalyst instead of to the divorce court, all might have been well')[100] before moving on to apply her findings to herself and to explain her attraction for Willie as 'volcanic eruptions of passion … natural at my age' because 'what I am after is a baby'.[101] (She had become aware of the ticking of her biological clock soon after her fortieth birthday, noting that 'my hands hold themselves out for another child'[102]; a year later, deciding that biological impulses must not be allowed to divert her from her spiritual pilgrimage, she decided to lay the blame for the 'Willie episode' on Nature rather than on herself or the devil, it being Nature who was 'ensnaring [her] to bear another child and bidding youth linger as long as might be'.)[103] In this respect, as she frankly admitted, Willie was only 'more or less of an occasion'[104] (i.e. a stud like his predecessor) to be disposed of as and when biology or God decreed.

They did not so decree immediately. For one thing, she liked Willie 'for himself' as well as for his reproductive potential[105]; indeed, and 'alas! Aelfrida, alas!'[106], hopes of disentangling her feelings from a man with whom she was 'in love' even if the love she had for him (she likened it to an exile's love for 'the fire on the hearth of his old home') paled in comparison beside the love she felt for Constantine (a love 'strange and exotic … that calls to the home-keeping heart to wander in the enchanted distances of the world')[107] was ultimately doomed. For another, 'silly' as it was, 'there always seems to be one man … and then another in whom I am interested [and] who somehow preoccupies me'[108] and, failing Constantine and Fidelio, it might as well be Willie Searle. Lastly, to forbid herself to think about Willie (her current preoccupation was that Willie had 'won something' from her in forcing her admission of why she could not marry him and that this was making him 'enormously proud' of himself)[109] might give her 'a "Willie complex" in the unconscious' (*sic*), a risk which could perhaps be averted by taking up 'some practical religious or philanthropic work … outside the family', continuing lecture series

notwithstanding. (Luckily, she lacked the strength to attempt it.)[110] Alethea's wise comment that her mother was 'emotionally very susceptible' to men and that she loved 'Cousin Willie in mind and body – and the two loves cannot agree', sums up Aelfrida's conflict accurately as far as it goes but it may be that the truth lies in her next sentence: 'And she loves God – more than either?'[111] The ambiguous question mark is a killer: if Aelfrida did *not* love God more than either, whom did she love? Was Alethea suggesting that the only 'god' her mother loved was Aelfrida herself?

Having explained her behaviour in psychological terms to her own satisfaction, Aelfrida proceeded to analyse Willie's in relation to herself in the hope that she might 'get to the bottom of Willie' more profoundly than in 1913. In view of what she discovered, her third reason for bringing 'all this nonsense about Willie' to a conclusion is possibly the most valid.

To enable her to delve more accurately into Willie's psychology, she asked advice of two other men: Eustace, who knew Willie well, and a Frenchman who had never met him but who, as an author and former soldier (he had fought and been seriously wounded in the Great War), might be expected to have considerable insight into the male psyche. The Frenchman, hearing Aelfrida's story ('I thought as I told the tale – well really … Willie and I are a couple of idiots. Such a waste of time and emotion!') declared the case to be a simple one: either Willie had a mistress he was unable to get rid of or he was 'sexually timid', most probably the latter in view of the fact that 'Willie has plenty of sentiment to give and even feels desire' (in which respect it is interesting to note that nowhere does Aelfrida say that she and Willie had physical contact of any kind) 'but when it comes to the point – he is too shy'. The Frenchman's sweeping statement provided food for thought for it seemed to explain Willie's 'almost exaggerated chivalry to women' and his timidity when obliged to confront them (he had boasted to Aelfrida that five or six women had been in love with him and that he had rejected them), characteristics evidenced by a remark made earlier in their relationship to the effect that he did not wish to be more to Aelfrida than a caring and consoling friend. Believing that Willie only needed 'the tiniest shove' to be 'put right', the woman whose activities as Straightener now extended to reassuring spinsters of a certain age that 'New Psychology's' belief in the primordiality of the sexual impulse was not necessarily the correct explanation of their particular hang-ups (or, though less dogmatically, of her own) and male undergraduates that their sexual impulses vis-à-vis women were healthy, not perverse, decided that in Willie's case she could (and, her escape clause, would) do nothing.[112] The following year, however, having updated her French confidant on the 'Willie business', he informed her that she had been having an affair with '*un perverte*' and that the only man she really loved was her husband.[113] In the meantime, however, Aelfrida had informed Willie that they should not marry (he, for reasons undisclosed, had agreed) because her mind was 'made up, irrevocably, on religious grounds'[114] (while meditating she had been 'suddenly overwhelmed by a sense of God's presence so intense as to be almost terrifying')[115] and because (though she did not say so) she believed the Frenchman's explanation to be correct.[116] Further meetings, however, caused 'much internal desolation, as though [she] were wandering among the charred ruins of a palace'.[117]

Charred ruins notwithstanding, there may have been another, unspoken reason for Aelfrida's readiness to agree with her French adviser over her *'affaire à perverte'*. Having discovered (to her manifest surprise) that she possessed (and exuded, a fact which also seems to have escaped her) sexual allure, it may be that Willie's physical reticence compared unfavourably with Constantine's sexually-charged 'lovemaking' during their engagement and hyperactive sexual behaviour in Odessa. True, Aelfrida had had scruples about the former and had not enjoyed the latter, regarding Constantine as a 'coarse brute' who 'over-indulged' and sexual surfeit the real reason for his subsequent 'distaste' for her[118], but he had undeniably awakened something in her which Willie's 'chivalry' failed to satisfy and which was unconsciously demonstrated in comparisons made between the man whose preferred position was at her feet and the man who had recently married someone else. Disillusionment with *both* men is, however, manifest in a bitter diary entry of June 1925: 'the Constantine I loved never existed … and Willie, whom I thought the perfection of chivalry, does not exist either. I see it only too clearly now … they are all tainted, these men, one way or another'.[119]

Early in 1926 Aelfrida turned to Eustace for advice as the result of a crisis precipitated by her having asked Willie if, given her refusal to marry him, he wished to remain friends. Willie turned on her, denying vehemently that he had ever said he loved her or wanted to marry her and, on being confronted with 'ardent remarks' written in love letters, became first disbelieving, then very angry; minutes later, he appeared to have forgotten the conversation and was puzzled by references to it. Discussing the event with Eustace and her parents, Eustace informed her that Willie was 'more ill than any of us know' because suffering 'shell-shock' as a result of wartime experiences, this being manifest *inter alia* in amnesia and in the 'flash-backs' common to this condition. Chiara agreed: Willie's

love for Aelfrida was unmistakeable but he often 'looked *tragic*' and his sisters had said that his behaviour since the war was sometimes out of character, his having prowled the house one day, gun in hand, being a case in point.

Reflecting on this the following day, Aelfrida agreed with Eustace's diagnosis: Willie's letters were sometimes so 'curiously agitated' as to be virtually incomprehensible[120] , his conduct was occasionally unaccountable, and the look which sometimes appeared in his eyes 'as of a soul dazed and baffled, shut in behind doors of anguish' reminded her of Fidelio 'when not quite sane' and of Julius 'when he came back from Russia' after breaking off his engagement to Nadja, they, like Willie but for different reasons, being 'mad in patches and quite sane everywhere else'.[121] In fact, had Aelfrida not been so blinded by her 'Willie-complex', she might have realised this earlier: in 1914 she had predicted that Willie would not 're-emerge unchanged after the war'[122], Willie had confided his anguish to her when home on leave, and she was familiar with Siegfried Sassoon's poignant poems (of which there was an example in nearly every issue of the anti-war *Cambridge Magazine* in 1916)[123] describing the effect of trench warfare on soldiers' minds and souls. But what should she do? She decided to do nothing, the 'soul-doctor' thinking it best (for her own sake though ostensibly for Willie's) to 'not write to him, nor help or console in any way'.[124]

Confiding her belief that Willie might recover if left alone, she was dismayed to hear her father proclaim grimly "you can't leave a man alone. You play with him as a cat plays with a mouse".[125] Alethea, who as a sixteen-year-old had been as puzzled as everyone else by her mother's ambivalent attitude to men in general and Cousin Willie in particular ('I wish I understood exactly what is the matter between him and mother … I'm sure he wants to marry her, … but she seems to *want not* to – or thinks she *ought* not to – marry again, though I'm equally sure that she loves him')[126] but was now a vastly more mature seventeen-year-old, took her mother aside to inform her that "you want some good advice and I am going to give it to you … You aren't going to marry Cousin Willie [because although] he is quite sane as long as he keeps to ordinary things, when he gets to *feelings* he is a little mad. You have a very bad effect on him … if you don't leave him alone, he will go mad".[127] Discovering a few days later that she also had her guardian angel's support in the matter (he 'always said "NO"' to her marrying Willie)[128], Aelfrida decided to end the relationship, be Willie 'shell-shocked or not'.[129]

She had, in fact, begun to do so during the previous year and in her customary manner: letters blowing alternately hot and cold ('I had let him see that he was a temptation to me and said I had better not write to him any more')[130]; ambiguous messages (she sent Willie flowers and her card with the comment "because there really is something of the woman about you and you rather enjoy your conquests"[131], regarding this as gentle chaff until a stony silence alerted her to hurt feelings); replying to an appeasing letter asking her to live with him in London "and [to] play at being sensible"[132] with the composition of 'an extremely witty and rather improper society farce' with Willie as the hero bombarded by love-messages from women whom he repulses gently but firmly[133], on receipt of which Willie sent 'a brief but furious letter' saying she had 'practically destroyed' his love for her.[134] (In the light of her Frenchman's disclosures, she later decided that to have sent a man like Willie a 'jeering play' and flowers were 'very brutal' moves on her part.)[135] Discovering too (or thinking she had discovered) that Willie had not lived 'a pure life' (with the implication that she had safeguarded her chastity while he had not), she informed him that they could not be friends because he had not 'lived as he should'.[136] (The fault, said Chiara tartly, was Aelfrida's for sexually frustrating him, not Willie's for being unchaste.) Her trump card, however, was to inform Willie that because a recent conference at Lambeth Palace had decided that re-marriage in church of divorced persons could not be sanctioned (a fact confirmed by a letter to her from the then Bishop of Ely to whom she had applied for advice), she 'would *prefer* not to do anything that *anyone* thinks is wrong'.[137] Concluding (to herself, not to Willie) early in 1927 that 'ecclesiastic considerations apart' there was 'a certain indelicacy' in marrying again which revolted her[138], that although her vow of chastity would mean 'never knowing a man's touch again or conceiving another child'[139], she was right to have made it, and that Willie, relative to Constantine, would have been 'a substitute, a very dear and adorable substitute ... but not quite the real thing'[140], Aelfrida decided that she had now mastered her feelings and would 'not even write about Willie' in her diary.[141]

She did, of course, and for four reasons. First, was her inability to keep her thoughts under control; trying to meditate, she drove them 'like an unwilling herd of swine up the steep heights of prayer and away they scatter and run screaming whither I would not ... into imagined conversations with Willie'.[142] Second, was Willie's persistence in maintaining a relationship of sorts long after Aelfrida made it clear that she had no intention whatsoever of marrying him, be this because of bishops, daughters (Agatha and Alethea were now antagonistic to the thought of Willie as a stepfather because of the deleterious effect of his presence on their mother's emotional life and hence on theirs), vows of chastity, a decision never to have her personal space invaded again by a man who might impinge on her 'peace of solitude and meditation'[143], worries that he might treat witnessed or reported visions as evidence of abnormality rather than manifestations of attainment of *Atmadarshana,* or insistence on domestic and social activities at the expense of writing and lecturing. There was, too, Willie's worrying inability (for whatever reason) to commit himself ('he would have said all manner of rash things – only ... to retract them in that incomprehensible way ...should I have tried to hold him to them')[144] while at the same time indulging in the 'sterile tormenting' of the woman he professed to love because he appeared to enjoy sending up Aelfrida's 'emotional temperature'[145] at the same time as he inhibited his own; in fact, by late 1929 mutual antagonism had resulted in a relationship heading for breakdown because chiefly based on a capacity for 'wounding and misunderstanding each other'.[146]

Third, was the unfortunate fact that the further Aelfrida and Willie drew apart, the more her brother and mother pressed her to marry him, Eustace stating mildly that "I should *like* Willie as a brother-in-law"[147] and Chiara urging the union on the grounds that Aelfrida might bear a son, that Willie's devotion ought to be rewarded, that she personally would like Willie as a member of the family[148], and that even if marriage meant Aelfrida's departure from Fordfield, it would be good for Agatha and Alethea to have a father, to which end she forbade her daughter to break with Willie even as she noticed the deleterious effect of the relationship on Aelfrida's physical health and emotional well-being.[149] (Chiara's attitude was ambiguous; she seemed keen to see Aelfrida married to a man of whom she approved but ensured that the couple were rarely left alone to develop their relationship – Aelfrida and Willie had to snatch precious moments together in the Fordfield garden or in the garden-behind-the-house and conducted much of their relationship by letter – possibly because with the Oracle declining rapidly in health, she was reluctant to let Aelfrida go.) The Oracle, though keen at first, became notably less so after the revelations of March 1926, the blind seer growling from his chair by the fire that if Aelfrida "had nothing to do with men, these troubles would not arise".[150] Julius' opinion, if any, is not recorded.

The fourth reason and the one which put an end to the affair ('Willie has had more "last appearances" than Nicholas Nickleby but this really *was* the last')[151] was news early in 1930 of Willie's engagement to a divorcee described by him as 'good and sweet' but not young, rich, beautiful, well-connected, or charming[152], the marriage to take place in a London register office on 1 May 1930. (Aelfrida was not invited and makes no mention of the occasion in her diary; Agatha's comment was "that is what I call coming to a bad end", Alethea's "just the sort of silly thing I should expect him to do!")[153] Aelfrida professed herself unconcerned by the news ('I had always imagined that when it happened it would be rather a blow and was quite astonished to find out that all I felt was a little mild surprise coupled with mild regret'), expressing instead a gloating *schadenfreude*[154] at her discovery that Willie had been persuaded to give up his liberty because he was tired of being pursued by women for themselves or by mothers for their daughters.

But in spite of stating that Willie's 'jealous and possessive nature' was masked by 'enough charm to enslave his wife and drag her unresisting through a maze of perpetual misunderstandings'[155], she was more upset than she cared to admit. (Perspicacious Alethea noted 'I'm not sure that Mother is pleased even though she didn't want to marry him herself. It is rather pleasant to feel that someone isn't getting married at all for love of you. But you can always pretend … that love is one thing and marriage another'.)[156] To disguise her feelings Aelfrida treated her married suitor and his new wife with sisterly friendliness to their faces and disdainfully in her diary, writing on the occasion of Mr and Mrs Searle's first visit to Fordfield that the couple looked 'as placidly devoted to each other as if they had been married thirty years' and that she found Tess dull and with 'no vitality, no glow of body or intellect' about her.[157] (Alethea described her as a 'big, beautiful-eyed, cow-like woman with ugly teeth, said to be dreadfully possessive'; Aelfrida called her 'his limpet of a wife – but feminine in the extreme' and noted that Willie looked 'small and crushed' beside his expansive and possibly rather plump – the word used by tall, slim, catty Aelfrida to describe Tess's most salient quality is '*épanouissement*' – wife[158]; she was, however, delighted to discover on a later visit that Willie, initially 'dull and heavy' and full of 'the latent antagonism that had always been there', displayed 'animation and eagerness' when she exerted her charm.)[159] Essentially, however, and in spite of her 'Willie-complex' having been 'so interesting and varied and thrilling', it had also (like her relationship with Aleister Crowley) been 'a wrong turning in life's maze'[160], valuable because it taught her humility[161] but disastrous because it caused her to waste time she could have devoted to God's service. So it was 'good-bye to all that … without regrets, goodbye'.[162]

But not quite yet nor quite 'goodbye'. Puzzled and hurt by Willie's behaviour which insofar as his marriage followed and emphasised his defection was not dissimilar to Constantine's (or to that of several men of her acquaintance), Aelfrida rationalised his behaviour and exacted revenge by depicting him as a character in *O Passionate*

**Constantine Graham c1920**

*World,* a novel begun around the time of his marriage. Unlike Fidelio, whose ungrateful desertion of one who had been "the beacon flashing out messages of courage, virtue and optimism across the dark sea"[163] of bipolar disorder may have caused her to kill off his fictional alter ego 'Alan George', Aelfrida does not arrange a premature demise for Willie's alter ego 'Richard Temple'; she mercilessly exposes his weaknesses instead. She does this by quoting almost verbatim the conversation of March 1926 during which Willie denied that he had ever loved her or proposed to her and asked her to leave him alone (says 'Richard Temple' "Have I ever asked you to marry me? … I have had all I can bear")[164] and by having her alter ego 'Carola' ask herself forlornly "why had Richard behaved so unaccountably … she *knew* he cared – too many men loved her for her ever to be mistaken".[165] She also makes 'Richard Temple' an indecisive, petulant, and rather weak character whose excuse for the sudden change in his behaviour from "delicate adoration" to brutal rejection is that he is a priest and priests do not marry[166] (he is a Church of England clergyman perfectly at liberty to marry), behaviour which graphically illustrates Aelfrida's belief that Willie Searle suffered from 'fear of life' and drew back in panic from moves made by women responding to speeches or actions on his part.[167]

Interestingly, however, it is not only on Fidelio and Willie that Aelfrida wreaks revenge in *O Passionate World*: it is also on herself. In the guise of 'Carola' she castigates herself for the "self-interested, self-absorbed" behaviour which has alienated men like her husband ('Adrian' has not only left her, he has re-married) and 'Richard Temple'. She realises too that she is both manipulative where men are concerned ("her own playwright") and her own "admiring beholder"[168], and that this, together with her tendency to stage-manage relationships, may be factors in their departure. 'Carola's' forgiveness of men-friends' wrong behaviour may also be regarded less as a magnanimous desire to maintain a friendship "too fundamental [and] too precious" to be damaged by "superficial humiliation"[169] and more as a selfish desire on her part to have a man (any man) in her life to provide her with the excitement she as "the all-conquering, the indispensable, the admired"[170] Aelfrida Graham craves and enjoys.

In real life, however, Aelfrida tried to rationalise her behaviour vis-à-vis Willie Searle in a manner more in tune with her religious beliefs. Writing in her diary in March 1932 during a three-week period in which she had had unusual leisure in which to indulge in 'long spells of consecutive thinking' (Chiara had been very ill and during her convalescence Aelfrida spent the day at her mother's bedside in 'almost continuous silence'[171] for Chiara was mostly asleep and, when awake, too frail to say more than a few words), she came to the conclusion that her belief that she had been in love with a man whom she had several times recorded that she loved and once that she loved him 'bitterly'[172], was a delusion. (With Fidelio, she added, forgetting earlier diary entries, 'I never made the mistake'.)[173] It was, rather, an aspect of her 'enhanced view of the beauty and value of individuals in the sight of God', a view which 'tormented' her into attributing quasi-religious significance to men like Willie and Constantine (or as she more accurately put it, to 'their portraits in the mirror of my perceptions'), something which caused men to respond at best with incredulity and at worst by denouncing her way of thinking as wrong. It was this view too which led her to believe herself profanely in love with a man when her love was more properly spiritual appreciation of the man's value in God's eyes.[174] Either way, the relationship ended in estrangement, men feeling they could not live up to her idealised view of them, she, crying 'no human affections', retreating into 'detachment' when they spurned her.

Be that as it may, and though it is possible that there was "an indefinable barrier which [he] himself was powerless to remove"[175] in Willie's character which made him unable to commit himself to a relationship with a woman in the immediate post-war period, there may have been other more prosaic reasons for his reluctance to marry Aelfrida and which would also explain the antagonism he frequently felt towards her. Her jeering at him in her 'witty and rather improper society farce' of March 1925 may have reminded him of her tendency to reveal marital discord in poetry and prose, a fate to which he had no wish to be subjected. His sisters, whose knowledge of Cambridge gossip would have been more profound than his (their dislike of Aelfrida seems to have pre-dated their brother's friendship with her) would have been delighted to warn Willie of what Aelfrida herself admitted was her 'queer reputation'[176] in Cambridge social and academic circles, her lectures on Mysticism and Comparative Religion having given rise to the belief that she was either a Theosophist or some kind of lay-nun, the latter impression supported by her sober dress, demure hair-style (she now wore her hair parted in the middle and pulled back into a pleat at the nape of her neck as she had formerly worn it only in the evening), and pectoral cross. Or perhaps Willie received a letter from Constantine accusing him of having a 'secret compact' with Aelfrida to marry in the event of his own death, a letter which might have put thoughts into Willie's head and would explain both 'Richard Temple's' cry of "have I ever made love to another man's wife?"[177] and his startled reaction to other disclosures, these leaving him "so amazed that he was not … capable of further astonishment".[178] ('Adrian' also tells 'Carola' that "when the decree nisi has been made absolute and Christian resignation is beginning to get a little stale you can marry Richard"[179]; Aelfrida does not transcribe into her diary the letter written by Constantine to her on the same day, 9 July 1919, that he wrote to the Oracle informing him that he wished to divorce his daughter but the sneering tone and content of 'Adrian's' letter may reproduce Constantine's actual words on this or another occasion.) Perhaps Constantine informed Willie of Aelfrida's involvement with Aleister Crowley (as unsuitable an involvement for the wife of a London solicitor as it had been for that of a vice-consul), this being a matter of which Willie, not being one of the Little Friends with whom Aelfrida discussed Crowley, was previously unaware. Or did he warn Willie that marriage to Aelfrida was likely to be sexless, a fact which could have been corroborated by Chiara or Eustace, with both of whom Willie was intimate and to both of whom Aelfrida had confided news of (if not the reason for) her *mariage blanc*?[180] Or was it because of the reason provided by Willie himself (a reason suggested by Alethea as early as 1925, namely that Willie's reluctance was attributable to fear)[181] when trying to explain 'the queer alternations of wanting and not wanting to marry' a woman who admitted that at age forty-five she could not spend half an hour in his company without it going to her head, namely that he loved 'dominating people' and was concerned that the 'power' Aelfrida already exerted over him become a desire to dominate, something to which he would never submit because he could not contemplate marriage to a woman whose personality was as strong as, or stronger than, his own?[182] Whatever the reason, Aelfrida eventually decided 'if I had married him, we should have been miserable' and wished him (in her diary) 'goodbye, and God grant you peace'.[183]

While in Lausanne and briefly attracted to Charles Cornay, Frida confided to her diary that 'as an authoress and a pietist' she should be above 'the usual weakness of [her] sex'[184] with regard to men. Recording her 'feelings on entering upon the twentieth [century]', a century she had begun 'on [her] knees ... asking for help to spend all of it ... as I ought to do', only to find herself 'being silly' with Cornay during New Year celebrations, she felt 'rather ashamed and vowed to do better'.[185] In 1904, reading over in Cambridge what she had written in Switzerland, the 'finished young lady' who had unofficially engaged herself to 'Mr Michaelides', added 'Oh you little humbug! What a pose!'[186] In 1924, apropos her infatuation with Willie Searle, she added a further note: 'your same old pendulum, Aelfrida. Men one side – God the other! tic-toc!'[187] So even before abandoning thoughts of marrying Willie, she swung the pendulum back to God.

## Notes

1 Agatha's diary (GCPPG A2.1) for the period 1 November 1923 to 11 April 1924 ends with a list of people mentioned in that volume, among them 'Mr Frank Stokoe'.
2 GCPPT 1|1|20 20 August 1914.
3 ibid. 21 June 1918.
4 GCPPT 1|1|24 14 June 1919.
5 ibid. 23 June 1919.
6 GCPPT 1|1|25 30 August 1919.
7 ibid. 11 August 1919.
8 GCPPT 1|1|24 18 June 1919.
9 GCPPT 1|1|22 21 June 1918.
10 GCPPT 1|1|26 12 July 1921.
11 ibid. 29 October 1921.
12 ibid. 10 August 1921. Stokoe's period of residence in Cambridge itself was brief. Apart from a few months in a cottage on Coe Fen Lane (now Fen Causeway) within easy walking distance of Fordfield, he lived in rented accommodation in nearby villages.
13 GCPPT 1|1|26 10 August 1921.
14 ibid. 21 September 1921.
15 ibid. 10 August 1921.
16 ibid. 22 September and 20 October 1921. For a short period in 1921/22 Stokoe had an eleven-year-old orphaned protégé regarding whom he appeared 'ever so proud and paternal' (GCPPT 1|1|26 23 December 1921). Although Aelfrida worried about 'the intense struggle between good and evil' that such an interest meant for Fidelio (GCPPT 1|1|26 7 March 1922), the relationship appears to have been loving but innocuous.
17 GCPPT 1|1|26 23 and 27 September 1921.
18 ibid. 5 November 1921.
19 ibid. 10 December 1921.
20 ibid. 12 April 1922.
21 ibid. 27 April 1922.
   GCPPT 1|1|40 1 July 1931.
22 GCPPT 1|1|26 5 November 1922.
23 ibid. 8 February 1922.
24 ibid. 17 September 1922.
25 ibid. 5 November 1922.
26 GCPPT 1|1|33 10 August 1926.
27 GCPPT 1|1|32 14 February 1926.
28 GCPPT 1|1|37 17 December 1929.
29 GCPPT 1|1|40 18 July 1931.
30 GCPPT 1|1|32 29 April 1926.
31 GCPPT 1|1|40 18 July 1931.
32 GCPPT 1|1|33 5 October 1926.
33 GCPPT 1|1|28 17 June 1924.
34 ibid. 29 September 1924.
35 GCPPT 1|1|32 24 December 1925.
36 GCPPT 1|1|30 29 May 1925.
37 ibid. 19 July 1925.
38 GCPPT 1|1|37 17 December 1929.
39 GCPPT 1|1|38 27 July 1930.
40 GCPPT 1|1|37 17 December 1929.
41 GCPPT 1|1|38 30 August 1930.
42 GCPPT 1|1|35 14 April 1928.
43 Laura Smith, Henry Julius Wetenhall's ward, led a peripatetic life as a governess before returning to Cambridge at the start of the Great War. The saga of her frequent changes of lodging and declining health occupied much of Aelfrida's time and diary between 1914 and Aunt Laura's death in 1930, at which point Aelfrida describes her as 'the only person who ever loved me with an absolutely uncritical affection' (GCPPT 1|1|37 18 January 1930).
44 GCPPT 2|25(4).
45 GCPPT 1|1|13 6 and 11 January 1906.
46 Tillyard, Ae, O Passionate World p 79. (GCPPT 2|11). There is no evidence in Aelfrida's diaries that Frank Stokoe ever made such a definite statement (he seems, rather, to have distanced himself from the whole business of her divorce) but the comment put into his mouth probably reflects those made by her family and friends.
47 ibid. pp 81–82.
48 ibid. p 76.
49 ibid. p 80.
50 ibid. p 83.
51 ibid. p 191.
52 ibid. pp 193–4.
53 GCPPT 1|1|25 15 August 1920.
54 ibid. 15 September. 1920.
55 GCPPT 1|1|17 31 January 1909. Aelfrida's belief is probably based on St Paul's dictum (Epistle to the Romans 7: 2 and 3) that if a woman "while her husband liveth ... be married to another man, she shall be called an adulterer".
56 GCPPT 1|1|25 23 March 1920.
57 GCPPT 1|1|26 15 November 1921.
58 The Tillyards rented Clare Hall from the beginning of May to mid-July

1922, Fordfield being taken over by officials from the Cambridgeshire County Agricultural Show. Although the visit occurred shortly after Aelfrida's decree absolute, it appears to have been more in the nature of a prolonged and overdue holiday for the whole family (or a source of income disguised as a holiday) than the flight to Hunstanton three years earlier. Aelfrida revelled in the beauty of the Suffolk countryside, an experience reproduced in her later novel *Concrete*.

59  GCPPT 1|1|26 6 June 1922.

60  ibid. 7 June 1922.

61  ibid. 10 June 1922. It may be significant that during this time Aelfrida was writing *The Young Milliner*, an Austenesque pastiche.

62  GCPPT 1|1|26 10 June 1922.

63  ibid.

64  ibid. 7 June 1922.

65  ibid. 13 June 1922.

66  ibid. 16 September 1922.

67  ibid. 26 December 1922.

68  ibid. 21 December 1922.

69  ibid. 26 December 1922.

70  ibid.

71  GCPPT 1|1|25 1 and 4 September 1919.

72  GCPPT 1|1|27 8 February 1923.

73  ibid. 8 and 10 February 1923.

74  ibid. 8 February 1923.

75  ibid. 8 February 1923. Mildred Seymour Swarz was indeed a divorcee and an American with two sons by her first husband aged 8 and 6 at the time of their mother's remarriage. She and Constantine were introduced by a mutual friend who, thinking that 'Constantine looked lonely without a wife and Mildred, having divorced her husband, needed another', deliberately 'brought them together' (GCPPT 1|1|38 11 December 1930). Constantine's entry in *Who Was Who* describes his second wife as 'Mildred Seymour daughter of etc.' but omits to mention her previous marriage. Rumour had it that Mildred was 'flighty' (GCPPT 1|1|27 9 February 1924) but she seems to have been a much better wife to Constantine than Aelfrida. She was also, as Aelfrida herself pointed out, another of the 'older women' to whom he was attracted (GCPPT 1|1|28 14 July 1924).

76  GCPPT 1|1|27 9 February 1924. Aelfrida learnt the news of Argyris' death from an unexpected source, namely the Strawberry Eater, Lady Frazer having, it seems, kept in touch with Anatolia Michaelides since meeting her in Cambridge in 1905. Cleanthes Michaelides died suddenly in Antibes on 25 July 1923 at the age of 84.

77  GCPPT 1|1|27 17 February 1923.

78  ibid. 21 February 1923.

79  ibid. 17 February 1923. An interesting parallel exists between Aelfrida's behaviour towards Willie Searle and that of 'Marian Tenterden', heroine of RH Benson's 1915 novel *Loneliness,* towards its hero 'Max'; 'Marian', a singer, parts company with religion at the start of her career but returns to Christ ("my knight!") after losing her voice at the climactic moment of *Tristan and Isolde*, the *Liebestod*. Thereafter she renounces 'Max', telling him that they must no longer be lovers but only friends. Aelfrida, already aware of salient details of RH Benson's religious career, was contemporaneously studying his life and works with a view to lecturing on him.

80  GCPPT 1|1|27 16 March 1923.

81  ibid. 18 and 21 March 1923.

82  ibid. 28 March 1923.

83  ibid. 4 September 1923.

84  ibid. 24 and 26 December 1923.

85  GCPPT 1|1|28 30 March 1924.

86  ibid. 21 May 1924.

87  ibid. 3 November 1924. In a postscript added to this entry Aelfrida wrote 'if this comes into the hands of anyone after my death, I beseech them not to let Willie know'.

88  ibid. 13 July 1924.

89  ibid. 19 July 1924.

90  ibid. 23 October 1924.

91  ibid. 13 July 1924.

92  ibid. 3 November 1924.

93  GCPPT 1|1|30 24 January 1925.

94  ibid.

95  ibid. 30 January 1925.

96  ibid. 23 January 1925.

97  ibid. 7 February 1925.

98  ibid. 11 April and 22 October 1925.

99  Adolescent Alethea's insightful comment regarding her mother's new interest was that 'I don't think it improves either her work … or her temper' but that it was not her place to say so (GCPPG A1.1 28 July 1924).

100  GCPPT 1|1|28 14 July 1924. Her interest was stimulated by attendance at lectures given in Cambridge on 25 and 26 October 1921 by American psychologist James Leuba (1867–1946). Attending what she thought would be lectures on the psychology of Mysticism and Religion, Aelfrida was shocked to discover that not only did Leuba tend to reduce mystic experiences to psychophysiological phenomena akin to epilepsy, 'neurasthenia', and drug-induced states of being but that he also seemed to 'connect mystical experiences with sex impulses'. This caused her not only to 'think and think' (GCPPT 1|1|26 26 and 27 October 1921) but also to become so preoccupied with Leuba's notions of the primordiality of the sexual impulse that she wasted valuable meditation time 'trying to think out' the implications for herself of what he had said (GCPPT 1|1|26 *Diary of Meditations* 27 10.21 9.45pm – 11.30pm). Unable to attend Leuba's final lecture, she asked him to lend her his lecture notes, which he did. (GCPPT 1|1|26 26 November 1921). This, and her description of Leuba as 'a nice, shy, gentle little man' (GCPPT 1|1|26 26 October 1921) makes amusing reading when one discovers in two letters from 'Author' to 'Stranger' in *Can I be a Mystic?* that 'Author' professes herself unaware of Professor Leuba's existence, let alone his theories.

101  GCPPT 1|1|32 14 January 1926.

102  GCPPT 1|1|28 21 May 1924.

103  GCPPT 1|1|31 9 August 1925. Although Aelfrida was not yet overtly menopausal, gradual diminution of her gynaecological problems suggests that her fertility too was waning.

104  GCPPT 1|1|32 14 January 1926.

105  ibid. 14 January 1926.

106  GCPPT 1|1|30 8 November 1925.

107  ibid. 7 November 1925.

108  ibid. 15 February 1925.

109  ibid. 6 April 1925.

110  ibid. 9 April 1925.

111  GCPPG A1.1 24 March 1928.

112  GCPPT 1|1|31 21 August 1925.

113  GCPPT 1|1|33 17 July 1926.

114  GCPPT 1|1|32 27 February 1926.

115  ibid. 26 February 1926.

116  ibid. 27 February 1926.

117  ibid. 12 November 1926.

118  GCPPT 1|1|23 7 March 1919.

119  GCPPT 1|1|30 22 June 1925.

120  GCPPT 1|1|26 17 September 1922.

121  GCPPT 1|1|32 4 March 1926..

122  GCPPT 1|1|20 7 November 1914. A curious coincidence exists between Willie Searle's symptoms of 1926 and Constantine's of 1919, the latter's irrational behaviour, restlessness, irritability, obsession with self and sexuality, 'depression and morbid thoughts', suspicion, withdrawal, impatience with positive suggestions (but not insomnia, memory loss, and 'flashbacks') being uncannily similar to the former's

(GCPPT 1|1|24 11 July 1919). With hindsight Aelfrida might have realised that *both* men, for different reasons, were suffering from 'neurasthenia', one war- the other wife-induced.

123 In December 1919 Aelfrida and Eustace had a 'grand argument' about Sassoon's poetry (GCPPT 1|1|25 22 December 1919); she does not tell us if she or Eustace sided with Sassoon. A particularly relevant poem, *Survivors,* was later included in Sassoon's *Selected Poems* of 1915: "No doubt they'll soon get well. The shock and strain /Have caused that stammering disconnected talk" in " Men who went out to battle grim and glad" but who have become "Children with eyes that hate you, broken and mad" as a result of their terrible experiences, could almost have been written with Willie Searle in mind, so exactly does it describe his symptoms.

124 GCPPT 1|1|32 2 March 1926.

125 ibid. 4 March 1926.

126 GCPPG A1.1 5 April 1925.

127 GCPPT 1|1|32 3 March 1926.

128 ibid. 7 March 1926.

129 ibid. 10 April 1926.

130 GCPPT 1|1|30 13 March 1925.

131 ibid. 18 March 1925.

132 ibid. 4 May 1925.

133 ibid. 5 May 1925. A slightly later diary entry (GCPPT 1|1|31 21 August 1925) describes the Willie of her farce promising himself to three women but as then deserting all three by fleeing to Timbuktu.

134 GCPPT 1|1|30 7 May 1925.

135 ibid. 17 July 1925.

136 ibid. 21 June 1925.

137 ibid. 13 July 1925.

138 GCPPT 1|1|34 19 January 1927.

139 ibid. 1 January 1927.

140 ibid. 19 January 1927.

141 ibid. 26 June 1927.

142 GCPPT 1|1|30 30 April 1925.

143 ibid. 13 July 1925.

144 GCPPT 1|1|34 20 September 1927.

145 GCPPT 1|1|35 21 May 1928.

146 GCPPT 1|1|36 22 October 1929.

147 GCPPT 1|1|30 1 July 1925.

148 ibid. 14 March 1925.

149 ibid. 20 April 1925.

150 GCPPT 1|1|32 2 March 1926.

151 ibid. 1 March 1926.

152 GCPPT 1|1|37 30 May 1930

153 ibid. 14 February 1930.

154 ibid. 10 February 1930.

155 ibid. 30 May 1930.

156 GCPPG A1.1 16 February 1930.

157 GCPPT 1|1|38 27 July 1930.

158 GCPPG A1.1 23 November 1931.
    GCPPT 1|1|40 25 December 1931.

159 GCPPT 1|1|40 22 November 1931.

160 GCPPT 1|1|32 27 February 1926.

161 GCPPT 1|1|32 19 November 1925.

162 GCPPT 1|1|37 10 February 1930.

163 Tillyard, Ae. *O Passionate World* pp 406–407.

164 ibid. pp 395 and 400.

165 ibid. p 403. These lines are crossed out in the only surviving copy of the novel. Did Aelfrida suffer pangs of conscience?

166 ibid. pp 397–398 and 403. These lines on pp 397–398 are also crossed out.

167 GCPPT 1|1|34 24 April 1927.

168 Tillyard, Ae, *O Passionate World* pp 406–407.

169 ibid. pp 403–404.

170 ibid. pp 391.

171 GCPPT 1|1|41 6 March 1932.

172 GCPPT 1|1|34 20 September 1927.

173 GCPPT 1|1|41 6 March 1932.

174 ibid.

175 Tillyard, Ae. *O Passionate World* p 29.

176 GCPPT 1|1|26 2 August 1922.

177 Tillyard, Ae. *O Passionate World* p 395.

178 ibid. p.31.

179 ibid. p 14.

180 Discussing Marie Stopes' *Married Love* with Eustace in March 1919, Aelfrida let slip more than she intended but admitted that 'the relief was … enormous'. She also considered asking Constantine's permission to confide further in her younger brother but later decided that Constantine's mind was so set against her that Eustace's intervention would be useless (GCPPT 1|1|23 7 March 1919).

181 GCPPT 1|1|31 21 August 1925.

182 GCPPT 1|1|35 30 October 1928.

183 GCPPT 1|1|37 30 May 1930.

184 GCPPT 1|1|6 12 December 1900.

185 GCPPT 1|1|6 2 January 1901.

186 ibid. The addendum is initialled 'ACWT'.

187 ibid.

# Spiritual Espousal

Though diary evidence might lead us to believe that Aelfrida's thoughts during the early 1920s were focussed on Constantine and her divorce, on Willie Searle (described by Alethea as 'mother's flirt'[1], thereby reducing a twenty-year relationship to the level of a passing fling – which, in a sense, it was, for Aelfrida if not for Willie), on the problems of single parenthood, and on keeping a three-generation household 'on good terms'[2] (on paper, if not in fact), she never lost sight of the blessing which took precedence over all others, namely 'knowledge of God and constant communion with Him'. Also evident, in spite of repeated grumbles about wanting 'to teach the world to be wise and it won't listen'[3] and about having 'no time for any affairs or interests of [her] own'[4], is that she certainly had sufficient solitude in which to turn her thoughts to God during 'long meditations'[5] and to promote her spiritual life and sufficient leisure to enable her to try to impart to others what she believed to be the 'important things in life'.[6] More evident still is that it was during this time that she took an important step towards independence from her parents' doctrinal domination of her life and towards the notion of 'vocation', a step so faltering at first as to seem a false start but later to constitute a pursuit marvellous in its intensity and hideous in its disregard for others.

Visions, rare around the time of her decree nisi (in June 1921 in the same entry as she noted apropos divorce proceedings that she felt 'widowed', she also noted a single episode of 'sensible devotion' during which she felt 'no longer myself but part of an innumerable host of departed saints and angels'[7], a comforting sensation to one soon to be subjected to social ostracism), became more frequent as 'God–consciousness'[8] returned around the time of her decree absolute, so much so that a month before that date she recorded such 'extraordinary feelings of rapture' at seeing herself in a vision 'holding a torch before the altar of the Lord' that she could 'hardly keep from dancing and shouting with joy from the sheer ecstasy of God's presence'.[9] (Her next sentence, 'Eustace and Phyllis to tea,' is strikingly bathetic in the context of visionary rapture.) As before, visions were frequently appropriate to time: an Easter Sunday twilight during which an angel with a golden trumpet (possibly a close relation of those on the chancel screen in King's

*Visions*

To many wayfarers, too, come those waking dreams which we call visions. The seer himself is apt to take these more or less as a matter of course. He has entered into a glorious world of wonders and would rather have been surprised if nothing unusual occurred. The bystander or hearer of the tale, however, is much puzzled and startled. That a man or woman should see saints and angels, even our Lord Himself, hear voices, and perhaps have his nostrils filled with the strange sweet odours of the Heavenly Garden—here, indeed, is cause for amazement.

The ignorant multitude are always prone to admire a saint for the number of his visions as for the celebrity of his " miracles." The psychologist, too, loves to study such holy men as have shown the most remarkable picturesqueness in their spiritual life.

The mystics themselves look on these visions as the commonplace of the inner life, however much they may have been elated the first time such an experience came their way. Vivid and revealing as the visions are, they are not fit to stand beside those secret and more loving touches of the hand of God, which the seer

*A Little Road-Book for Mystics* p 70

College chapel) 'suddenly … shot across the sky'[10] or an Ascension Day evening on which she became 'aware of the Presence of Our Lord' ('I could almost see him but not quite'), He telling her that He was going to His Father and bidding her, plunged into ecstasy, to follow.[11] And to place and circumstance: while on holiday in Suffolk among hedges 'white with thorn, larks singing, wind-blown skies and great distances flooded with sunlight'[12], a 'complex and vivid vision of God [as] … a fashioner of innumerable worlds, as near familiar presence, as force, as many things … mingling in one great blaze of light in which I was annihilated'[13] or in the midst of appalling winter weather during which she listed eleven concurrent physical ailments but concluded 'and yet I keep going quite splendidly' , a nocturnal vision of the solid walls of Fordfield melting away to disclose the garden white with snow and a woman walking there singing in 'a voice of more than human sweetness "Glory to the Lord! Glory! Glory"'[14] or, her offer of help having been rejected by the matron of the Ely Diocesan Maternity Home for unmarried mothers in nearby Bateman Street because she was a divorcee, of an angel thrusting a jagged sword into her heart, every tooth of which embodied 'the gathered sorrow of a whole nation'.[15]

'Sensible' devotion i.e. 'consciousness of God's presence amounting almost to ecstasy'[16] and the familiar sense of 'losing [her] identity in the perfect beauty of God'[17] were delights which also returned abundantly once the shadow of divorce proceedings was removed. Counting her blessings on her fortieth birthday on 5 October 1923 ('I have so much – my children, my dear ones, leisure, books, sufficient money, almost sufficient health'), Aelfrida decided that 'the best thing life has brought is the knowledge of God'.[18] Concluding the next volume of her diary in December 1924, however, she bemoaned the fact that 'the world and its cares and pleasures' (Willie Searle included) continued to throng so closely that she had made little if any 'sensible progress' in working actively for God or in her apprehension of Him.[19] March 1925 found her worrying that her love of and dependence on God were symptomatic of having set herself 'too difficult a task in wishing to communicate direct with [Him]' and that perhaps she should have 'let [her] religion centre more round the human Jesus', something she had previously avoided lest 'some admixture of human love [tincture] an admiration that should be purely spiritual'.[20] Recalling that this passage had been written in the same month as she recorded that 'the battle between the flesh and the spirit' with regard to Willie Searle had left her 'absolutely exhausted', that it was the 'consciousness … of being loved' – whether by God or Willie she does not say, but by context the latter – which made her look so young that even Ancifera commented on it, and that having 'burnt my boats when I told Willie of my vow of chastity, … if he had me now he would surely despise me'[21], caused her to decide during two bedfast days of 'solitude and meditation' occasioned by recurrence of 'constant rheumatic pains' that 'a long process of purification and preparation' would be needed before further spiritual progress could be made. Deciding too that the process ought to be 'proceeded with'[22] immediately in spite of feeling 'weary and tragicall' (*sic*)[23] because a publisher had rejected *Spiritual Exercises* (he recommended 'one or two little corrections and a study of a further authority on the most recent ideas about Nirvana')[24], she focused on her 'strong – if vague – sense of *vocation*' that God was calling her ('though I know not

to what', she added)[25] and made preparations to 'do some work'[26] for the His glory in lieu of trying to restore his youth to Willie and have hers restored by him.

Keeping to her on-going desire 'to bring light, as far as I can, to the world' by following the Eastern tradition which held that the best spiritual teachers were those whose authority derived less from caste or religious status than from their being endowed by Deity with a personal enlightenment which entitled them to preach and teach, but humbled by her coincident discovery that, though awake at midnight on New Year's Eve 1921, she had forgotten to renew her vow of allegiance to her 'Great Work'[27] of transmitting God to mankind, she decided that forgetfulness was symbolic of a new desire, namely to demonstrate less absorption in her own 'spiritual experiences and progress' and in what she termed 'the Higher Selfishness' (the reason, she thought, why God had not made more use of her in the post-war period) and more interest in educating people 'very young in their spiritual experience'.[28] The desire, and a feeling that a mystic whose every fibre of her being cried out in adoration of God should be doing more 'to set Him forth' ('oh, that my light would so shine before men that they would glorify *Him*')[29] and fortified by promptings from her guardian angel (more usually employed at this time in warning her against secular involvement with Willie Searle) that she should "desire not happiness, neither earthly nor spiritual, for thyself but for All"[30], eventually gave rise to two lecture series (1922 and 1924) and to two books designed for the spiritually immature in the case of the general public and the chronologically as well as spiritually immature in the case of her daughters, then just entering their teens.

University lecture rooms being now fully occupied by the post-war influx of undergraduates, Aelfrida's lectures were given at Cheshunt Theological College in Bateman Street. She prepared for the first series by 'doing a little mantra-yoga' (her mantra was "Oh God"), rejoicing to find that this provided her with an audition of 'the symphony made by different souls' realisation of God'.[31] (It was these preparatory sessions of 'mantra-yoga' which caused her to note exasperatedly 'why my repeating "O God, O God" and concentrating on the essence of the Deity should cause me to have true dreams about Mrs Verrall I have not the slightest idea'.)[32] September 1922 saw her researching in the University Library and distributing prospectuses announcing the first series (she was no longer accorded mention in *The Cambridge Magazine*), though the Oracle's selfish behaviour when she '*needed* to work at [her] lectures' led to teeth-gritting references to having to 'cultivate the higher stoicism'[33] with regard to him.

Aelfrida's first post-war lecture series consisted of six lectures carried out between 27 October and 29 November 1922. Lacking *Cambridge Magazine* reviews and a coherent account in her diaries, we can only guess their content, though brief references apropos the second (a young man asking for information on 'comparative mysticism')[34], the fourth ('chaotic notes on Mohammedan meditations')[35], and the fifth ('I felt *burdened* … with the weight of the message my guardian angel bade me deliver')[36], suggest they were essentially a rearrangement of those given during the war in the light of research undertaken for *Spiritual Exercises,* then in process of composition. The lectures were poorly attended save by her 'faithful few'[37], she herself blaming 'people not [being] interested in meditations' or being too busy or unable to find Cheshunt College or just 'bored with me'[38]; she even blamed the guardian angel who had earlier bade her 'speak as [she] was told'[39], noting after a particularly poorly attended session that 'perhaps [he] didn't want me to lecture' at all.[40] By the series' end she was so dispirited that she felt moved to record that 'God does not seem to call me to anything very definite yet'[41] and to refrain from talking on religious topics to any audience larger or more intellectually demanding than a Mothers' Union branch meeting for nearly two years.

Her second lecture series was more successful. Entitled *Christian Types*[42], the six lectures covered aspects of modern Christianity typified by a named practitioner. The first was Sundar Singh ('a Christian of no denomination') about whom she 'got quite eloquent' because 'a Christian of no denomination' was what Aelfrida (invariably, and in spite of her supposed Presbyterianism and successive attractions to other denominations) aspired to be[43] and because Singh was someone who spent long periods in prayer and meditation, who modelled his life on that of Francis of Assisi and on that advocated by Thomas à Kempis, and who underwent visionary experiences and received divine revelations[44]; the second, Robert Hugh Benson, author and priest, as an example of 'the acceptance of Authority as … the crucial decision for a convert to Catholicism'[45], something she herself had failed to do. Third was William Booth, Evangelical founder of the Salvation Army, for whose promotion of Teetotalism and support of the work of his 'soldiers' in slums of the kind familiar from her visit to her aunts' Mission Hospital, Aelfrida much sympathy if little desire for emulation. Stephen Grellet, Quaker reformer and missionary, came next: Aelfrida was contemporaneously studying his life with the help of Agatha and Alethea who were also allowed to attend the lecture ('they were *quite* thrilled! I would rather do them good than anybody else')[46]; fifth was Mary Baker Eddy, founder of

Christian Science, an odd subject given Aelfrida's dislike of both Mrs Eddy and her doctrine of healing the body by the power of mind, a dislike intensified by a visit from a 'patient' ten days before the lecture who informed 'Straightener' that she (Miss Tipping) had contracted a disease in India of which she had nearly died because her Christian Scientist practitioner told her it had been caused by 'the malicious Animal Magnetism of Roman Catholics'[47]. Last came George Tyrell, the Catholic Modernist whose desire to abolish unquestioning 'acceptance of Authority' (a point also stressed by Aelfrida in her lecture on Benson and Catholicism)[48] and of an abstract and impersonal theology in favour of a religion which recognised the importance of personal devotion and the reproduction in every individual life of the life of Christ led to his being both excommunicated and denied Christian burial.[49]

Although Aelfrida's audience demanded further lectures the following year and she even began to plan two series, one on female 'Christian Types' to include Quaker mystic Caroline Stephen and missionary Mary Slessor whose death in Nigeria in 1915 was widely reported, the other on *Religion and the New Psychology*, no further lectures took place, probably because Aelfrida realised that voluntarily or involuntarily restricting her teachings to a small band of female devotees was not the most effective way of reaching out to those 'very young' in terms of spiritual experience or development. She therefore resumed the didactic literary career interrupted by divorce, domesticity, and the joys of research into Comparative Religion, in the course of which (if we exclude *Spiritual Exercises*, an essentially academic treatise, *Can I be a Mystic?*, the third in her 'Straightener series, and the commissioned biography of Agnes Slack from which Miss Slack deliberately had her date of birth omitted)[50], she wrote two targeted volumes: *A Little Road-Book for Mystics*, published in 1922, aimed at adult readership, and *Messages,* published in 1924, aimed at "boys and girls in their teens".

*A Little Road-Book for Mystics* owes its concept and title to George Fordham of Odsey. Sir George, besides being a gloomy widower, was also a notable cartographer[51] who possessed a large collection of "Road-Books, relics of the old coaching days when each driver was provided with a road-book of the way"[52], the road itself running up the centre of the page with landmarks to either side: "here a farm; there a well; hard by, a manor house; yonder, a grove of trees".[53] From adolescence, therefore, 'road-books' had entered into Aelfrida's "imagination of spiritual things"[54]; they now inspired her to write her own. Modestly claiming that the book 'only [repeated] what all the mystics know'[55], she listed among her precursors "wise men and women [who] have written for our guidance Road-Books of the Mystic Way".[56] (Among others she lists St John of the Cross, Evelyn Underhill, and the Persian Sufi poet Farídu'ddín Attár[57] but amusingly in view of her distaste for psychoanalytic interpretations of the mystic's relationship with God, also acknowledges as mentor "a man who is no mystic but a scientist and dispassionate observer of the minds of men"[58], namely Henri Delacroix.) The greatest of all guides, however, was John Bunyan, who "knew every inch of the path and all the dangers that beset it".[59]

She began work in February 1919 immediately after despatching *Vision Triumphant* to the publishers. Writing a book 'which deserves all one's thoughts'[60] was a struggle maintained through a difficult period of her life (the break with Constantine, exile in Hunstanton, the onset of her father's blindness) but she managed to complete it just over a year later with the help of advice from her family to whom she read excerpts and constructive criticism from the Baptist minister in Hunstanton and to summon up 'acute delight and thankfulness' when she held the published volume in her hands in December 1922.[61] Delight and thankfulness, however, were due less to completion and publication than to having written a further book 'to the Glory of God' (in which respect it was her 'best-beloved book-child' to date)[62] and to her believing it (with hindsight) to be 'the wisest and truest of all [her] books' which she hoped might be 'reprinted again and again and remembered while the name of the author is forgotten'[63] if only because 'the best part of it was written by [her] guardian angel'[64] with herself as amanuensis.

*A Little Road-Book for Mystics* is interesting for two reasons. First, because it shows Aelfrida as she moves on from her original definitions of a mystic as "a man to whom the spiritual world is more real than the material world" or as "a seer who has fallen in love with God" or as "one to whom Union with God is the chief end of life" or as "a mortal with a capacity for living not only in Time but [also] in Eternity"[65] to the notion of a mystic as one engaged in a *quest for* God and for "the reality which will give meaning [to] the world where he has been born" because he has "fallen in love with God Unseen" and wishes to "see" Him[66]. Her 'modern' mystic henceforth becomes "a Knight-errant of the high adventure of the soul" and someone who tries to follow "the Living Way" (i.e. Christ) in daily life "as a pilgrim who has found the Kingdom of Heaven within" and now seeks its King.[67] Second, because of what it demonstrates of the effect of Aelfrida's personal life on her own pilgrimage at a point where she has freed herself from a stultifying marriage but during which she entertains other relationships which themselves threaten to divert her from her particular 'mystic way'[68]; indeed, and although her homiletic works use real people (including herself) as exemplars, it is perhaps in *A Little Road-Book for Mystics* that she reveals most clearly some of the spiritual problems which have recently and will continue to beset, her. As she told someone soon to prove more of a temptation than Willie Searle (of her relationship with Willie was now 'a wrong turning in life's most puzzling maze'[69] and it would be a long time before she forgave herself 'for having turned aside from the Mystic Way'[70]), production of a book based firmly on her own experiences meant she could '*never* plead an excuse' that she was ignorant of what she was doing, where she was going, or at which goal she aimed[71] or be unaware of how far she deviated from the path she had set herself to follow.

Another interest of *A Little Road-Book* lies in its emphasising to those who wish to use it as a guide that the Mystic Way is not to be traversed without difficulties and that these derive in large measure from the personality of the pilgrim who travels it: he may want "to be naughty … out of sheer perversity"[72]; believing himself "no longer accessible to the charm of the world", he may find that "ambition, love of ease and of power, even sensuality", attract him as never before; earlier temptations ("the society of worldly people", for example) may return to torment him "like a swarm of devils"[73]; as a result of prolonged and over-intense concentration on his subject he risks becoming "thoroughly bored with God".[74] The way in which these intrinsically personal traits develop is illustrated by Aelfrida in terms of vivid imagery with more than passing reference to her ex-husband: "when a man first becomes enamoured of a woman, he cries out that his love for her will never change. With the passing of time, however, mere familiarity lessens the charm of the beloved and if the man's love is only passion it is bound to become weaker. Very often he blames her for what has happened in himself and declares that she has changed when it is only his fancy that has played him false … The mystic, too, in the first ardour of his devotion to God is convinced he will never alter … He is quite sure that he is different from other people, more secure in his faith, nearer to God". Or, with reference to herself, "clouds gather" and the pilgrim, beginning with "passionate self-accusation", goes on to bewail sins "real and imaginary" and perhaps even to confess them to a priest before "upbraiding God [and] reproaching Him with not keeping His promises" and falling into a "deep dejection" in which he feels that God has forsaken him.[75] At the same time, however, as he discovers that naughtiness and old temptations fail to console his desolation, the pilgrim also discovers that his feet are still upon the Mystic Way in a stage "dark indeed ... but so well-known that it is clearly marked on every Road-Book"; even more consolingly, he discovers that he has "companions all along the road, even if he cannot see them" and that "as they persevered and finally triumphed ... he may do so too".[76] Further consolation derives from the pilgrim's discovery that although he himself is "in deep despondency and much perplexed about his inner life", other people, sensing that he too is or has been "struggling with difficulties ... and doubts", come to him for spiritual advice whereupon, speaking to them "out of the riches of his own experience", he surprises himself by the "calm confident ... tone of authority" with which he addresses his listeners, tone and authority persuading him that he has not only "externalised and objectivised" his own experiences in such a way as to be able to reassure himself that "God cannot have led him this far in safety [only] to delude and fail His servant at the end" but also that the help he has afforded others is proof that his troubles are transitory and his 'soul-doctoring' divinely inspired.[77]

As a summary of the way in which 'Aelfrida Tillyard, Straightener' discovered that the best way to help herself was to help others, this could hardly be bettered, but in the years immediately following the publication of *A Little Road-Book* the former Mrs Constantine Graham found herself struggling in the emotional Slough of Despond that was Fordfield and so benighted in the "gloomy valley" of spiritual disability that she became "terribly unfit to teach even ... the mere beginner [or] the humblest child the way to God".[78] Hence although she rejoiced when she had new 'patients' (though if she had had more, 'how much ... the Straightener ... would learn!')[79] and even, prompted by her guardian angel, wondered if she 'might set up as a Straightener in good earnest', she abandoned the notion, giving her parents' reaction as her excuse: 'the mere idea that I should ... have anything to do with psychoanalysis, which they know nothing about but seem to think a mixture of sex-perversion and occultism filled them with ... horror'.[80] Another problem was that 'patients' self-selected from spinsters of a certain age and social class praised her so effusively for 'straightening' them that she was liable to be turned aside from her 'vocation'[81] because swayed by 'human affections' which a properly 'detached' mystic should have ceased to feel towards anyone, "passionately loved" as a fellow-man though they might be.[82] Finally, she herself was a 'poor crooked Straightener'[83] because unable to put an end to the 'nonsense about Willie'.

Of interest relative to the spiritually immature to whom Aelfrida hoped to impart her message is her warning to readers of *A Little Road-Book* of "external trials" to be met along their various 'mystic ways' because such 'trials' closely resemble those encountered along her own. Among these she lists refusal of other people to fall in with the pilgrim's plans ("everything went wrong with the little drama that [I] had set out to stage ... the chief actor failed, the whole play was shattered, my choice nullified")[84], "loss of [one's] fair name", and "loss of friends" who reproach the pilgrim "with being [one of those] callous and inhuman beings who ...selfishly devoted themselves to the saving of their own souls" because his "having set his affections supremely on God makes men imagine that he has no love left for them".[85] The worst trial of all is that of the "fire of criticism, kind, sensible, intolerant and intolerable" aimed at him during which "the more [the pilgrim] is in earnest and the more his earnestness leads him to outwardly peculiar acts, the more will his dear ones quiz, laugh, advise, protest, censure, exclaim and fail to understand", telling him that he is "morbid and unnatural", that he is "giving way to an absurd medieval pose", that he is "suffering from vanity of a pietistic kind", that he is "wasting his time and spoiling his health by wanting to pry into the secrets of the Almighty", that he is "a loafer at the gates of Heaven instead of a useful and busy citizen on earth", and that "if he *must* be religious he ought to be content with the 'just trust' attitude and with ... services at dear St Tabitha's".[86]

Not content with this searing indictment of Constantine and her 'dear ones', Aelfrida proceeds to self-criticism in the guise of one of the "pilgrims" returning "travel stained and worn ... from where [the pilgrims themselves] believe the Heavenly City to be". Such pilgrims realise they have done wrong "in trying to rise above priest and sacrament and choose a more direct way to God" (to do so implies "a certain contempt for ... the Church and the wisdom of better men than [they]"), in "neglecting ... the most obvious duties ... while looking for more noble services to render to God", and in failing to recognise that their "most valued religious experiences" are "mere delusions, the cloudy forms of rising mania [and] sure signs of neurasthenia"; indeed, one returning pilgrim (a young woman) is so sickened by her behaviour ("I know how I have gone wrong ... I talked to everyone about mysticism and was ... as selfish as ever I could be at home ... I read all kinds of silly old books and did nothing but go to services") that she has decided to "go home and be as commonplace as ever I can".[87]

A possible inspiration for Aelfrida's second roadbook for the spiritually immature was a comment of Alethea's. Having asked her mother in November 1917 for a copy of *The Making of a Mystic* ('a kind of roadbook for the Mystic Way in the form of letters')[88] and saying how proud she would be to receive it, Aelfrida overheard her then nine-year-old daughter add wryly to her nursery governess "what a shame mother writes such boring books" (being a bright little girl, she said it in fluent French)[89], a particularly galling remark because of Alethea's concurrent behaviour with regard to her father ('she sits on his knee and makes baby-love to him'[90], telling him "you are much nicer, Fuvver, than everyone here")[91], a man whose intermittent presence in wartime Cambridge caused her mother 'more pain than pleasure' because of his worldly ambitions and his 'complete indifference to [her] interests and pursuits'.[92]

*Messages* was not, however, written solely as Aelfrida's delayed reaction to this episode or as a response to Alethea's earlier comment "why do you read so much about meditation? You ought to study something more useful"[93], a question referred to in the foreword to *Messages* addressed to "my own children": "you have sometimes been rather puzzled ... that your mother should do a queer thing called meditate".[94] On the other hand, it is possible she wished to compete with the Oracle, he being a 'dear one' unsympathetic to his daughter's religious stance and sufficiently audacious to produce two homiletic volumes of his own, *The Manuscripts of God* of 1919 being aimed at Cambridge undergraduates keen to examine the significance of religious issues "from the standpoint of evolution"[95], and *Stones of Stumbling,* published the year before *A Little Road-Book* (it was dedicated to "young persons who are beginning to think for themselves")[96], defending, explaining, and amplifying *Manuscripts.* On the other hand, she had been planning a book on *Adolescence* (subtitled 'a study of a girl's mind')[97] in Emden and had since given talks to children at the New Cherry Hinton Church in 1918 on *The Religion of Adolescence* and *The Right Side of the Bed*[98] and may have been inspired by a conversation which took place shortly before publication of *A Little Road-Book for Mystics* in which a Quakeress declared modern young people to be 'profoundly uninterested ... in their relationship to God'[99], this inspiring her to 'write a book to be called (provisionally) *Meditations for the Modern Child* ... it sounds preposterous but the idea is to show children how things that they are supremely interested in lead up to the most interesting thing in the universe – God'. (Her guardian angel, as excited as herself at the prospect of a 'hopelessly unconventional' tome, promptly 'dictated the foreword and outlined the scheme of the book'.[100] It remained unwritten.) Then too, Agatha and Alethea, now thirteen and fifteen, were entering puberty and might soon, if they had not already begun and James Starbuck was correct, experience adolescent religiosity akin to or even stronger than their mother's; it would therefore be appropriate to dedicate to and present them

with[101] a book to guide their footsteps along the proper path, the path, that is to say, their mother wished them to follow. (Aelfrida might have been disappointed had she read their diaries; her daughters' adolescent interests revolved round sports and school-friends and made no mention of religion at all.) Finally, it is probably significant that not only did Aelfrida record contemporaneously with the publication of *Messages* that she was 'always thinking of Constantine and sending him messages'[102] but also that she sent a copy of *Messages* to him in Panama[103], her chief message being, of course, that 'if I have done nothing else for the glory of God, I have at least seen that [Agatha and Alethea] have been well and Christianly brought up'.[104]

Trying, as she said, to put her daughters 'in such sort where they could grow in grace'[105], Aelfrida constructed the book 'in a language that children can understand'.[106] To illustrate her points as vividly and relevantly as possible, she included episodes from Chiara's youth and her daughters' childhoods (the building of Fordfield; Agatha and Alethea's beloved marmalade cat, Leo) and from her own life: the pain of childbirth being forgotten in the joy of having a baby; games played with Julius in Fordfield garden. She also divided it into four 'weeks', each containing seven 'days'. The first 'week' is devoted to school lessons (maths, history, science, etc.), the second to domestic life (houses, gardens, and families), the third to public life (streets, shops, museums, etc.), the fourth to "a few odd messages" (birthdays, keeping a diary, "a day in bed ...alone with God" and so on.)[107] Saturdays are devoted to recreation, socialising, and hobbies, Sundays to religion: "suppose St Paul came to stay ... and I took him for a walk ... right down into the town".[108] Each 'day' is illustrated by statements appropriate to day and subject, largely, but not invariably, with a religious slant: everyone has a guardian angel; a new house should be dedicated to God during a special service; a reminder that "where you cannot take Him, you should not go"[109], and the like. The book begins and ends with suggestions that the child study and ponder on a section each evening (they might even keep a diary in which to record their ponderings but not in term time when they are busy with homework; *Messages* was essentially a 'meditation-book for children')[110], only to discover that every aspect of their life brings a message from God to which they should learn to listen because of the importance of what it has to say.

Only rarely after publication of *To Malise* does Aelfrida give us the opinions of members of her extended family about her books; *Messages* is the exception. Ancifera, a High Church schoolteacher, thought it 'flippant'[111]; Phyllis' father, asked if he would like a copy for his birthday, replied that he could not fairly encourage occupation of time and waste of money incurred in writing books of this nature and that he was not alone in feeling that Aelfrida might profitably put time and money to better use.[112] (Aelfrida herself, though nursing hurt feelings on both counts, for Ancifera and Henry Mudie-Cooke were people whose opinions she respected, was not altogether pleased with her production, noting that *Messages* was 'rather a dull little book and I didn't feel the usual thrill in holding a new-born book-child [but] I daresay its soul is all right'.)[113] Agatha and Alethea, enthusiastic when read excerpts prior to publication ('I expected Agatha to be responsive but it was a real triumph to have interested Alethea')[114], were less so when *Messages* appeared in print. (Perhaps they were embarrassed at having their childhood and childish sayings exposed to their schoolfellows' scrutiny in terms of the sentimental evocations of affective piety beloved by their mother and proudly recorded in their Record Books.)[115] Agatha diarised 'I read a good deal of it yesterday'[116] but made no other comment. Alethea wrote critically '*Messages* is not altogether what I like – it doesn't seem to help nearly as much as the prayer book by itself or the old Catholic hymns', adding that she preferred not to talk to her mother about religion because if she did, Aelfrida 'would wish to put before [her] a whole lot of theological facts'[117] which would confuse her so much that further discussion was pointless.

Faced with *Message*'s barrage of advice as to her moral and spiritual conduct but surprisingly in view of her unenthusiastic comments about the book, Alethea (and Agatha who as usual followed her older sister's lead) took Aelfrida's advice literally; indeed, it seems that she took her mother's precepts concerning the central role of religion in a young person's life so thoroughly to heart that she came to a conclusion logical on her terms but dumbfounding on Aelfrida's, namely that she no longer wished to be associated with the same church as grandparents who may have "lived up to a high ideal of Christian duty and love … in their public lives"[118] but certainly did not do so at home. On the day prior to the diary entry in which she noted that *Messages* was not wholly to her liking, Alethea, accompanied by Agatha, 'cut church and went for a ripping bike ride'; their doing so, she added, went 'rather against the wishes of the family'.[119] That was an understatement. Alethea's action provoked fury in grandparents who informed Aelfrida that she should have 'forced' her daughters to accompany them to St Columba's and anguish in her mother: 'I must do some hard thinking about the whole question'.[120] She did, and the upshot was that mother and daughters abandoned Presbyterianism for Anglicanism.

Some of Aelfrida's reasons for doing so are explicit, some not. Those not may have included a desire to rebel against the 'Puritan' upbringing which contributed to the breakdown of her marriage and inhibited development of relationships with other men (at this point, Willie Searle, regarding whom she promised Alethea that she 'needn't expect anything romantic')[121], something which manifested itself at best as tendencies to euphemism and prudery ('naughty girls' for unmarried mothers; refusal to display photographs of her daughters in the modest bathing suits of the day because she believed that to be photographed thus was improper) and at worst as a propensity to '[build] a little wall round her mind and [refuse] to consider things except over the wall'.[122] Perhaps she wished to free herself from the perpetual 'daughter's place' assigned by her parents by demonstrating spiritual if not material or emotional independence or to distance herself from the prevalent association of Nonconformism with 'trade', membership of the Church of England being more acceptable to the class of men she hoped her daughters would marry. Perhaps she wanted to share religious as well as other experiences with her daughters as a means of controlling their lives, here as elsewhere. Explicit reasons, on the other hand, ranged from something as trivial as irritation with the 'booming emptiness' of the preaching of the current minister of St Columba's[123] to an increasing desire for 'harmonious surroundings in worship', a desire stimulated by a visit to an Anglican Sunday Service of which her 'Puritan ancestry and instincts' made her almost ashamed but which allowed her to achieve greater spiritual satisfaction through the more 'aesthetic' and more 'feminine' medium of a 'lovely service'[124] held in a Suffolk church than through the masculine austerity of Presbyterian St Columba's, 'a man-made thing … of the people and for the people … completing the series which includes school, law courts and town hall'.[125] She had, however, no desire to cut herself wholly adrift from 'organised Christianity' or from the 'priest and sacrament' she, a mystic in direct communion with Deity, sometimes seemed to regard as superfluities; indeed, she now suggested that 'one's beliefs are more likely to come to maturity in a religious atmosphere'.[126] Promoting Quakerism to anxious young men was one thing; she herself plumped for the Church of England as practised at St Botolph's church in Cambridge's Trumpington Street.

The atmosphere at St Botolph's had long appealed to Aelfrida and she and her daughters had been fairly regular attenders at services there for some years before Agatha and Alethea decided to become communicants. She had also visited the church by herself for private prayer or to attend morning service (several visionary experiences of the war years took place there), disguising her visits as shopping for her mother and almost certainly without informing either parent. (She also continued to pay numerous visits to Anglo-Catholic Little St Mary's just across the road, finding the retired little building with its bosky garden more conducive to meditation.) Services at St Botolph's, however, seemed 'to answer to something deep deep down in me which is satisfied and filled to the brim with peace'; they also gave rise to the feeling that she was a more active participant in the service than at St Columba's where congregations were passive spectators.[127] The building too provided her with a sense of history and permanence lacking in an edifice erected in her own lifetime: describing St Botolph's as 'almost like a bit of eternity'[128], she revelled in the knowledge that it had stood for hundreds of years and would likely stand for hundreds more 'dwarfing the puny mortal' who might sometimes 'creep in and worship there and creep out again'.[129]

Not content with attending services at St Botolph's, Aelfrida decided to join Agatha and Alethea in becoming communicating members of the Church of England there. (Changing one's denominational affiliation was a family trait, it seems.) But whereas for the girls, baptised into the Greek Orthodox Church, joining and being confirmed into the Church of England stemmed, their mother believed, from a religious sense which came 'as naturally as breathing' to Agatha or from Alethea's 'wish to live rightly'[130], for their mother it was at once less and more of an affair, less insofar 'as I have never felt Presbyterian (*sic*) [so] I don't propose to feel Anglican … [the dear Presbyterians] think I have "left the fold" [but] I merely feel that I have wandered off to another part of the fold and that it is a matter of no importance'[131], more insofar as 'the ceremony will be an occasion for a more complete self-dedication – my spiritual espousal at last perhaps! I pray so. PS Tea with Mrs Carless'.[132]

Compared to the mystic marriage on which her thoughts were fixed (or, rather, from which they continually 'flying off to Willie')[133], a temporal marriage to the said Willie who had recently intimated to her by letter that 'if he didn't get what he wanted, he didn't want anything else'[134] did not stand an earthly chance, an impression confirmed by her daughters' 'half-laughing, half in earnest' questions as to why she was so reluctant to commit.[135] Her resolve stiffened by a day in bed during which she meditated 'on "my spiritual espousals"' and on her determination that 'the barrier between Willie and me may be impenetrable' and by a vision of Christ showing her the wounds in His hands[136], Aelfrida joined Agatha, Alethea, and the Church of England in Fordfield drawing room on 1 April 1925: 'the walls … and all the

grave memories of the place certainly approved [but] I thought of Constantine and wondered what he would have said'.[137] The ceremony took place in the presence of the Oracle and Chiara whose comments went unquoted. (On an anniversary of her induction, Aelfrida described them as being 'generous and … understanding' and as never stating that their daughter 'ought not to have joined the C of E'[138], but because at this point in her life she also liked to recall them as 'perfect', it is hard to know what to believe.) After the singing of 'O God of Bethel', a hymn significant for having been sung at the wedding of Miss Tillyard and the girls' father, Alfred and Catharine Tillyard condescended to make friends with the vicar of St Botolph's who conducted the ceremony. Accompanied only by Chiara ('hardly any of our friends knew about it'; Eustace and Phyllis 'took no notice nor displayed any interest'), Aelfrida and 'the fruits of [her] earthly marriage' were confirmed the same day by the Bishop of Ely. Feeling 'a little Anglican thrill' at the Bishop's laying-on of hands because it betokened 'benediction in [an] unbroken chain from the apostles' and that she could go 'as a child and not as a stranger into all the parish churches and cathedrals of the land', Aelfrida nevertheless found the ceremony something of an ordeal ('I felt so keenly what I was renouncing and what my life must henceforth be'), abjuring herself 'now, little spouse of Christ, try and behave yourself. And if you can't be good, at least don't imagine yourself better than you are'.[139] (Salutary advice and, as usual, ignored: she also thought how much better it would be if she and her daughters were killed on the way home from the ceremony because they would go 'consecrated and free from future sin, straight to God'.)[140] Less than a week later she decided not to banish Willie lest she develop a 'Willie-complex', with all that that entailed of five more years' misery for both.

In spite of becoming 'a renegade or pervert or something to Anglicanism'[141], Aelfrida did not wholly turn her back on the church whose 'good wholesome Scottish flavour'[142] she tasted on rare occasions or when in need of consolation from a congregation who continued to make her (though not her daughters, one of whom was publicly snubbed as a 'heretic') feel like 'a daughter or sister of their loving family'.[143] She also discovered that Presbyterian services appealed more than before because of their 'vigorous and masculine tenor' (the fact that more than half the congregation of St Columba's were men probably added to the 'virility' of the atmosphere) and because the "intellectual level of preaching is probably higher than in any other denomination"[144]; an Anglican service's tendency was to be 'weakly devotional' and tolerable only 'by females over forty'.[145] (Of whom, of course, she was one.) On the whole, however, and in spite of Presbyterianism being 'fine for building up character', she stuck with Anglicanism because 'I ... like a liturgy best'.[146] And it was her preference for liturgy which was to contribute to the next stage of her pursuit of mystical or spiritual matrimony.

Throughout her life Aelfrida conceived many 'theories about setting the world to rights, schemes and plans and methods for every creature from the cradle to the grave'[147], theories usually termed 'Big Schemes' or 'Brilliant Ideas'. Those to date included not only the 'knight-errants of commerce' notion discouraged by Rendel Harris and the 'cottage scheme' dismissed by Constantine as impractical but also the 'Peace Day' to be held in 1915 during which women all over England would compose messages of sympathy to women in all countries currently at war with England, together with promises to unite with them to ensure that the current war would be the last', the scheme, or, rather, Aelfrida's 'most recent command from the Guardian Angel'[148], being abandoned at Eglantyne Jebb's urging, and a 'Pilgrimage of Prayer' during which pilgrims would parade through towns and villages 'asking people to pray and seek God'[149], an idea relinquished when Aelfrida realised she would have to organise the pilgrimage herself. She also schemed the division of Cintra House, a large building in central Cambridge, into 'apartments', a plan abandoned because it did not meet with support from local hotelier, Maurice Bradford[150], and, following the Tillyards' lengthy stay in rural Suffolk in 1922, two 'cracked-brained schemes' (as Constantine called them), the first 'an intensive study of the conditions of farm labourers, with the causes and possible cures of their discontent'[151] (a book never written because Aelfrida's co-author, a busy farmer, pleaded pressure of work) the second, a plan 'for helping agriculture and diminishing unemployment' by putting men on the dole to work on the land, being dismissed by the parliamentary candidate to whom she suggested it in a 'civil letter' promising only 'careful consideration' of her idea.[152]

But whereas Constantine tried to discourage his wife's wilder ideas by telling her not to 'talk such piffle'[153] and Ancifera carried 'a snub in her bag for Frida' with regard to schemes and plans lacking 'the epic importance' Frida was inclined to attribute to them[154], the Oracle and Chiara tended to '[listen] too indulgently and [applaud] my "brilliant ideas" too easily'.[155] Although their behaviour seems odd, given that it continued until Aelfrida was in her thirties, it may have been a way of coping with their daughter's sometimes bizarre behaviour (if the evidence of *A Little Road-Book* is to be believed, more bizarre than she acknowledges in her diary) by

humouring her in the knowledge that her butterfly mind would soon abandon the 'Brilliant Idea' of the moment only to light on another and to abandon that in turn or an attempt to patronise their matrimonially-incompetent daughter for purely selfish reasons: both were aging and infirm and might require the presence of a 'good daughter at home' to care for them. But their failure to discourage a 'Brilliant Idea' developed by Aelfrida contemporaneously with her obsession with Willie Searle and given impetus by the emotional charge attached to her 'spiritual espousal' was to have far-reaching consequences, for though the 'Idea' in question was of comparatively short duration, it inspired a sequence of events which had dire repercussions for Aelfrida and her daughters at a time when her parents were no longer present to contain her behaviour.

November 1923 found Aelfrida asking her diary why the accounts of 'external events' with which she chiefly filled it ('reading up ... for my lectures', teaching commercial English to foreigners, socialising at home and away, 'minor ailments' and, unusually in a diary where events of international importance were usually relegated to 'noises off', the Tokyo earthquake)[156] were so unimportant when compared to 'what is, to me, *personally*, the most real and important, namely the inner life and the constant reaching-out to God', and confiding that although she tried to use the 'trivial round' which she recorded so often (and so vividly) as 'a ritual in praise of God', her thoughts turned more and more to 'a conventual life'. She was unsure, however, whether this stemmed 'merely from love of the picturesque' or from 'a desire to be solely preoccupied with the service of God'[157] or was only (as she noted a few years later apropos her 'leaning towards the conventual life and all that it implied of asceticism and renunciation of earthly joys') reaction to Constantine's desertion[158], the latter a possibility given that in December 1923 she wrote of refusing to allow her thoughts to focus on Jesus lest 'something ... of unsatisfied human love might enter in'. (A statement emphasised by her next sentence: 'last night I dreamed most vividly again of Constantine'.)[159] It was not, however, until after her 'spiritual espousal' of 1 April 1925 that she first expounded an idea over which she had been mulling in relation to Willie Searle, namely that vows of chastity could be put to better use than that of torturing the man with whom she professed to be much in love.

During the conversation with Chiara in which the latter urged marriage to Willie for Agatha's and Alethea's sake and forbade breaking with him, Aelfrida tried to explain (without using the terms 'vows' and 'chastity') why she could not or would not obey her mother, informing Chiara that she should not be surprised at her daughter's preference for 'putting spiritual things first' because this was how she had been brought up. Chiara, taken aback, replied "if you were a man and had a vocation, it would be different" and was inclined to be dismissive until Aelfrida, perhaps remembering Constantine's 'luxurious ascetic' gibe, countered light-heartedly with "they wouldn't have me in a cloister … because my husband is still living and I wouldn't go because I couldn't give up my hot water bottle" but added "leaving aside the husband and the hot water bottle, I *do* feel I have a vocation".[160] What her 'vocation' was, she shortly began 'very dimly to see'.[161]

It was, she decided in May 1925, to be 'the founding of a very simple kind of religious house' called "The Servants of the Lord's Household"[162], its maxim ('I am uncertain of the spelling') being "*Nella sua voluntate è la nostra pace*".[163] Chiara, she hoped, would agree to be 'the first head of the convent'[164], though the Oracle being still alive might mean 'I … have to wait *years* yet'.[165] The Servants, for whom she also devised a mission statement and a habit, were to renew their vows annually and subscribe to a routine in which plain living was encouraged but (remembering the hot water bottle) 'asceticism … discouraged'. Half the year was to be spent 'in community' preparing 'by prayer and practical work' (e.g. organisation of retreats for girls about to marry) for the following six months during which the Servants would replace 'some tired mother … or teacher or social worker or someone who needed rest for soul or body', the latter entering the 'Community House' in order to recuperate and because, while there, they could be instructed in how to 'glorify God in the simple life' and could then indoctrinate 'people, especially the young' on their emergence.[166] (The following day Aelfrida attended a 'wild and charming' party at the Haddons and completely forgot that as 'someone who has been "mixed up" in a divorce'[167], she might not be regarded as the best person to preach 'vows and chastity' or that as someone who complained bitterly over the unavailability of servants, she was not the best qualified person to preach the virtues of the 'simple life' either.) On 17 June she recorded excitedly 'all my will and energy is set towards my vocation'[168]; at the same time, however, she noted Willie's refusal to be friends because, having informed him of it, he said he would rather not see her for a while, and with chagrin that 'I suppose one can't hope to keep one's rejected lovers as friends' and that she half wished she 'didn't have a vocation and might chase after happiness like other people'.[169] Which, as we shall see, she proceeded to do though not with regard to Willie.

Willie was not the only person she told. She also told Chiara ('she quite approves')[170], the Oracle

('unexpectedly sympathetic')[171], Dorothea Conybeare, who announced in her 'chill and virginal' manner that she was glad Aelfrida did not intend to remarry[172], and Fidelio, who hearing her state that she would be 'a poor sort of thing to undertake such a work', gave the bracing response that 'if the work needed doing and I believed God wanted *me* to do it, what business had I to think about myself at all'.[173] Father Tompkinson of Little St Mary's told her dauntingly that "the way most religious orders were founded was this – that people prayed for ten years and then it just happened". (Aelfrida flashed back "that is how I have begun".)[174] Julius admitted her 'convent scheme' was good but was 'grudging and unsympathetic' about her involvement, possibly because he seemed to 'distrust all enthusiasms'[175] but more likely at the prospect of losing his sister to 'the Lord's Household'. Eustace made no response – or was not consulted.

Having settled on her 'vocation', Aelfrida was assailed by doubts. (Or, given her wistful desire to 'chase after happiness', excuses for non-compliance.) Would poor health bar her from a life which would be as active as it was contemplative? ('I pray not'.) What of Agatha and Alethea to whom she must devote her time for years to come? ('I have no patience with saints who neglect their families!')[176] And 'suppose I *do* found a religious order and suppose after my death the dear sisters wish to write an edifying life of me and suppose they come across my diary – oh dear! What a shock awaits the dear sisters!!!'[177] Of more serious import was discovering that not only would no-one *join* a religious house founded by 'a woman in [Aelfrida's] position'[178] and that the 'ecclesiastical attitude to people in [her] position'[179] was harsh. Having written for advice to the Mother Superior of the Limpsfield Convent to which she had referred Marjory Harrison (a convent at which she herself had hoped to make a retreat but was prevented by circumstances from doing so), Aelfrida received the shattering reply that as a divorcee whose former husband was still alive, she was ineligible for life as a religious unless (in a strange echo of her premarital hopes) Constantine became a monk, a 'ludicrous idea' indeed, given his proclivities and remarriage. The 'great blow' upset Aelfrida considerably: 'I must have been … more attached to the idea of ultimately becoming a nun than I thought I was … It is curious what a sense of loss I have'.[180]

The Mother Superior's rejection also placed her in a difficult position – and not only because she had publicly announced her 'vocation'. Did such rejection also represent God's non-acceptance of her vow of chastity? If so, was the vow cancelled? If so, there remained Willie. Her escape-clause with regard to Willie vanishing before her eyes ('I know, of course, that religion and ordinary married life are not incompatible'), Aelfrida decided that though prepared to relinquish future thoughts of life as a religious if relinquishment would benefit Agatha and Alethea, she would not do so at any time to benefit Willie and, this being so, she 'had better leave Willie out of [her] calculations'.[181]

To anyone else, abandonment of yet another 'Brilliant Idea' was par for the course. For Aelfrida, however, it brought 'dread the loneliness of the Mystic Way … without the help of community life'[182] and realisation of how much a sense of vocation had steadied her and given her something to which to aspire.[183] Wishing on a day in October 1925 when the Oracle was particularly 'difficult and exacting' that she 'had [her] vocation back again'[184] and troubled because a visit from Willie demonstrated that in spite of their recent disagreement he continued to adore her 'in just his old way'[185], she 'turned passionately to meditation again', using as her mantra the phrase which would have formed the Servants' maxim had events not conspired against her: "in His Will is our peace". Calmed and braced ('it is *miraculous* what meditation does for me')[186] but wondering during a Sunday Communion at which she performed an 'act of resignation' (whether of Willie or her vocation, she does not say) 'what God *will* require of me?'[187], she felt relieved at ceasing to dwell on 'personal ambitions and desires'[188] insofar as these concerned her 'convent scheme'. But a question regarding life as a religious posed shortly after the rebuffing message from Limpsfield shows that her seemingly-abandoned 'Idea' was, far from being abandoned, her most 'brilliant' yet: 'I still wonder whether that may not, after all, be reserved for me'.[189]

There is, however, much more to Aelfrida's 'vocation' and 'spiritual espousal' than this, for the 'vocation' to which she feels called is one she had been considering for many years. The sight of a nun adoring the Blessed Sacrament in the Fiesole convent seems to have awakened 'the longing to be as close to God as she was', a longing which persisted 'all through the time of [her] greatest worldly happiness'[190], the phrase chosen to describe her far from 'perfect' marriage. And how better to become close to God than to become a Bride of Christ, spiritually espoused to Him in a white wedding dress and veil in a union symbolised thereafter by the wedding ring worn on one's finger? Hence the 'vocation' to which she now turns or, rather, returns, is not so much the next stage of her personal 'mystic way' but the re-treading of a path trodden prior to her marriage and never really lost sight of thereafter in spite of the "cloud, sucked up from the miasma of [her] earthly state" which interposed itself (i.e. which she allowed to interpose itself because "many sights and sounds allured [her]") between God and

herself and because of which she "paused among human joys and let [her] heavenward journey wait". Removal-by-divorce of her "earthly happiness"[191], though socially and emotionally a disaster, was not therefore a wholly miserable event because in liberating her from the bonds of earthly marriage, it qualified her (or so she thought until disillusioned by the Mother Superior of Limpsfield) for entry into the 'contemplative vocation' for which she felt an ever-increasing '*pull*' but from which she had 'by [her] own action shut [herself]' out.[192] (Was her conversion from Presbyterianism to Anglicanism preparation for this, Nonconformism not being a system in which convents existed?) But Constantine being unfortunately still alive and she a divorcee, all she could do at this point was invent a 'convent scheme' whereby she could live in community in company with other lay-women, a community from which she could (and would? A questionable point) sally forth at intervals to allow someone requiring 'rest for body and soul' to take her place.

Thwarted, however, of her 'convent scheme' but adamant that she *had* received a call 'to some form of the religious life', a call later described as heard only 'spiritually' but so clearly 'that it seemed to have objective sound' (she even remembered the exact spot where she heard it: 'I was walking along the high path past the Botanic Gardens gate (Cambridge, of course)'[193], she perforce answered it in the only way open to her by removing herself to a "lonely room … empty save for the solitary contemplative" where literally and metaphorically "like a bride in the bride-chamber"[194], she could commune with God. Or did she not answer the call in 1924 or 1925 (in 1939 she describes her 'call' as having been 'heard clearly' some fifteen years earlier[195] but not answered till now) for another, more compelling reason: the voice, she reported, not only called her 'to some form of the Religious Life' but also warned her "you will have to give up your *self*". Somewhat taken aback, Aelfrida answered ('in thought') "but I *can't* – it is the only self I have", only to be told "you will have to!" And thirty years later she was still asking 'have I?' and concluding not only 'not fully' but also that she 'might have tried harder'.[196]

But though unable to become a professed religious or a lay contemplative, as a mystic and a professed celibate she could follow the precepts of those who suggested that aspects of it were achievable in a secular environment: the Practice of the Presence of God could be carried out as a spiritual exercise even while ensnared in the toils of 'the perfect peace of Fordfield', and 'yearning for God'[197] was not incompatible with childcare, earning one's living, or even with the presence of one man after another in one's life. Then too, though her prayers might remain at a level described by Père Poulain as 'ordinary' insofar as they verbalised a devotee's simple intuitions, affections, and resolutions, there was a chance that by a "special action of divine grace" she might achieve a degree of prayerful "mystic union" culminating in the "spiritual marriage of the soul with God … a mystical state [of] … union that is almost permanent persisting even amidst exterior preoccupations and … in such a manner that the two different occupations do not interfere with one another".[198]

Celibacy it now appears, was not so much a post-divorce pursuit as a previous 'vocation' from which Aelfrida had been lured by her emotional neediness (and, it may be, by the thought that the prospect of being an old maid "*even with a vocation*"[199] was too awful to contemplate), a vocation decided upon at age fifteen at the time of the 'vision' of Christ seen while cycling home from school and confirmed on reading the lives of the saints in the Fiesole convent, the point at which she would have discovered that almost every female saint devoted herself to Holy Virginity as her personal and particular "portion of Christianity".[200]

Consecrated or Holy Virginity also had a lengthy and respectable pedigree, having been from early Christian times a profession adopted by educated young women as a means of leading a life free from the obligations of arranged marriage (or in Frida's case a means of escape from the male sex of whom she was scared and whom she did not trust) or because they felt truly called to a vocation of this nature. It was also led in a sheltered environment: unless the woman chose to join a community of like-minded women, she remained at home in simple but not impoverished surroundings (a degree of asceticism was expected but more in terms of disdaining jewellery, fine clothes, rich foods, and frivolous company than of material deprivation), there to maintain a private, secluded, and because of its religious connotations, a respected existence whose 'estate' exemplified a superior form of 'holy living'. Furthermore, though not a religious in the formal sense, a consecrated virgin was a nun in all but name and it was incumbent on her family not to force her into marriage. (Marriage, though also a suitable 'estate' for a woman, was a lower form of 'holy living' altogether.) Having once consecrated herself to Holy Virginity, however, the young woman was expected to remain in that state perpetually, a later change of heart or circumstances being insufficient excuse to permit return to unconsecrate existence.

At this point Aelfrida's maxim for her Servants of the Lord's Household ("in His Will is our peace") suddenly acquires significance – and even greater significance because quoted *in Italian*: what she omits to tell us but something easily ascertainable knowing both her fluency in that language and that she was emotionally overwhelmed by Dante's *Divine Comedy* on reading it as an adolescent, is that in the third part of the poem that very line appears.[201] The verses in which the line is embedded are of greater significance still for they tell the story of Piccarda Donati, first "a virgin sister in the world", then a professed nun "closed … in … habit's rule" "forced back into the world" by her family to make a political marriage.[202] Can it therefore be that following her vision of Christ in a halo of light, adolescent Frida made a vow of Holy Virginity but, pressured by her parents to marry and blinded by Constantine Michaelides' glamour, she broke it, only to announce that God was 'angry' with her because she had committed an 'unpardonable' sin and that because she herself had consented to the marriage, she had 'lost the light'[203] through her own fault and had been drawn away from God?

What then does this imply of her agreeing to absolutely surrender herself to Constantine, knowing that as a woman with a "virgin-nature" she will likely be very unhappy because unable to cultivate the "secret garden" of Holy Virginity "within the married state"[204]; of her swearing on the Bible not to become a Catholic with the aside that only she was aware of the implications of her oath[205]; of her statement that "a girl's dreams die" when she receives a kiss of love[206]; of her description of an occasion in the garden-behind-the-house during which she and Constantine watched the last flickerings of a bonfire: 'when the flames at last died down and the smoke had all gone up to heaven, I stretched out my arms and said quietly "*que … Dieu … accepte le sacrifice*" … oh, but it was pagan to the last degree and yet I felt that God … heard and understood'[207]; of the 'sister-soul' "*pure et chaste*" she should have had but had lost[208]; of the 'Marriage of Miss Tillyard' being the worst day of her life because on it she performed an act of treachery towards the Deity to whom she had once consecrated herself "in love, through all eternity"[209]? (Little wonder that in Odessa she '*knew*' that there were 'devils waiting to possess the wicked' and that she herself was no longer 'spiritually valiant enough' to fight them[210], for in breaking her vow of Holy Virginity she had laid herself open to their machinations.) And was her 1925 declaration of celibacy an attempt to re-establish herself as a 'holy virgin' by pretending that the 'Marriage of Miss Tillyard' had never taken place or, given the unfortunate presence in her life of two daughters by an earthly spouse, that as a divorcee she was free to declare for an 'estate' ranking above matrimony but below Holy Virginity and *spiritual* espousal because divorce had restored her 'virgin-nature' to her?

If so, she was following an accepted, albeit medieval, path. In early Christian times, a widow (which Aelfrida was not, though she felt – indeed, *had* to feel – 'widowed') who promised God to remain celibate following the death of her first (and therefore only) husband became both a "virgin mother"[211] (if she had children) and "a holy widow" symbolically dead to the world. She also became a woman whose virginity had been 'recuperated' by her promise and by her husband's death.[212] Furthermore, whereas as wife and mother she had surrendered her 'estate' of Holy Virginity in favour of an "honorary" virginity (a prestigious condition made more prestigious still if its possessor was able to insist on a regime of virginal "household" conduct too but contaminated nevertheless by "the moral contamination of the [Fall]"), as a 'widowed' divorcee following the 'death' of her marriage (if not of her former husband), Aelfrida could believe herself eligible once more for a 'holy' virginity and for its concomitant benefit of becoming an "active selector" of a "top-ranking" bridegroom, namely Christ.[213]

With Christ as bridegroom, no mere mortal man could compete, but Aelfrida's need to have a mortal man constantly in her life contemporaneously with her 'top-ranking' bridegroom, together with her recent discovery that she was highly-sexed, were bound to create conflicts in her mind and emotions. Fortunately, therefore, for one whose "technical" or "spiritual" virginity (with all that that implied of willed and technical bodily intactness) was constantly negated by amorous thought and come-hither actions, the "virgin estate" could be restored by constant "conceptual modification" during which continual repentance ensured continued restoration[214], a realisation and a process which underscored her relationships with men thereafter. And knowing this, how much more of her apparently irrational behaviour becomes clear.

# Notes

1  GCPPT A1.1 List of dramatis personae at end of volume covering 3 August–16 December 1926.
2  GCPPT 1|1|30 8 November 1925.
3  ibid.
4  GCPPT 1|1|30 8 November 1925.
5  GCPPT 1|1|25 27 June 1921. The extended sessions of meditation recorded in contemporary volumes of her diaries are evidence of her determination to persist in exercises designed as much as anything to calm a mind which became 'restless and worldly' if deprived of them.
6  GCPPT 1|1|25 2 June 1921.
7  ibid. 11 July 1921.
8  GCPPT 1|1|26 5 February 1922.
9  ibid. 8 January 1922. Aelfrida's sensations here strikingly resemble those of Teresa of Avila in whose *The Interior Castle* (the Sixth Dwelling pp

209–210) we find her noting that in the midst of "divine experience", God ("the Beloved") sometimes fills the mystic's soul "with feelings of exultation" akin to (Sufic) "inebriation" and so strong that in that state of "blessed madness" it experiences joy so great that its impulse is to indulge in "festivals and exhibitions" and to shout its joy "from the rooftops".
10  GCPPT 1|1|26 16 April 1922.
11  GCPPT 1|1|27 11 May 1923.
12  GCPPT 1|1|26 4 May 1922.
13  ibid. 7 May 1922.
14  GCPPT 1|1|28 20 and 21 February 1924.
15  GCPPT 1|1|27 21 August 1923. The Ely Diocesan Maternity Home was founded in a former seminary for young ladies in Cavendish House, Bateman Street, in response to the increase in number of unmarried mothers because of the presence of so many soldiers in Cambridge during the Great War. It closed in 1971.
16  GCPPT 1|1|30 25 February 1925.
17  GCPPT 1|1|27 21 August 1923.
18  ibid. 5 October 1923.
19  GCPPT 1|1|28 13 December 1924.
20  GCPPT 1|1|30 14 March 1925.
21  ibid. 13, 14 and 16 March 1925.
22  ibid. 5 March 1925.
23  ibid. 7 March 1925.
24  ibid. 17 March 1925.
25  ibid. 19 March 1925.
26  GCPPT 1|1|28 23 October 1924.
27  GCPPT 1|1|26 1 January 1922.
28  ibid. 26 December 1921.
29  GCPPT 1|1|28 20 June 1924.
30  ibid. 7 October 1924.
31  GCPPT 1|1|26 2 September 1922.
32  ibid. 24 September 1922.
33  ibid. 19 October 1922.
34  ibid. 1|1|26 2 November 1922.
35  ibid. 10 November 1922.
36  ibid 22 November 1922.
37  ibid. 15 November 1922.
38  ibid. 27 October 1922.
39  ibid. 29 November 1922.
40  ibid. 8 November 1922.
41  ibid. 3 January 1923.
42  GCPPT 1|1|28a Contains one of Aelfrida's 'notices' announcing dates and subjects of the six lectures constituting the series. Now divorced for two years, she continued to advertise herself as 'Mrs Constantine Graham' adding 'Aelfrida Tillyard' afterwards in parentheses; she sent one of her 'notices' to Constantine. The lectures were again held at Cheshunt College and again to a wholly or predominantly female audience.
43  GCPPT 1|1|27 31 January 1924.
    GCPPT 1|1|28a. It is possible that Aelfrida's view was influenced by that of Evelyn Underhill whose contemporary books on Mysticism make no mention of corporate worship and who herself, following a period of intense attraction to Roman Catholicism, did not become a formal member of the Church of England until 1921.
44  Sadhu Sundar Singh (1889–1929) was a Hindu mystic who converted to Christianity following a vision of Christ whom he had formerly despised. He then travelled throughout India preaching Christianity and combining "the ideals of the Hindu and of the Christian mystic" (Tillyard, Ae. *Can I be Mystic?* p140). Singh was, however, a rather more interesting person than Aelfrida's bald account suggests. Born into a Sikh family he had early contacts with Christian missionaries. Following his conversion on 18 December 1904 he was baptised on his sixteenth birthday 3 September 1905 and on 6 October the same year

adopted the saffron robe and mendicant ascetic life of an Indian holy man or *sadhu*. Between that date and his death in 1929 (walking in the Himalayas, he disappeared) and with the exception of a short stay at St John's Divinity College, Lahore, in 1909–1910, Singh travelled widely in the Indian subcontinent and in Tibet, Afghanistan, Malaysia, China and Japan in the evangelistic but ultimately forlorn hope that his undenominational mystic Christocentric Christianity would convert others. In 1919 he learnt English prior to visiting England, Europe, Australia and the United States of America in 1920 and 1922, countries in which he was made widely welcome and even, to his dismay, lionised. For more on Sundar Singh see Parker, A. (Mrs) *Sadhu Sundar Singh* (1918), Streeter, B. and Appasamy A. *The Life of Sadhu Sundar Singh* (1921), and Underhill, E. *The Mystics of the Church* (1915) pp 253–256.

45 GCPPT 1|1|27 6 February 1924. For details of the life of R H Benson (1871–1914) see *ODNB* vol 5 pp 200–201. Benson's own *Confessions of a Convert* was published in 1913.

46 GCPPT 1|1|27 19 February 1924. Agatha's comment was that the lecture was 'really very interesting' especially about 'Quaker Saints'. (Stephen Grellett, though certainly a Christian 'type', was hardly a 'modern' Christian, being born in 1773; perhaps his death in 1865 qualified him for inclusion). She also throws an interesting sidelight on Aelfrida's inability to stand for very long because of her gynaecological problems: 'Mother sits on the table to lecture' (GCPPG A2.1 23 February 1924).

47 GCPPT 1|1|27 18 February 1924.

48 ibid. 6 February 1924.

49 For details of George Tyrell's life, see *ODNB* vol 55 pp 802–804.

50 *Agnes E. Slack*, subtitled 'Two Hundred Thousand Miles Travel for Temperance in Four Continents', was researched and written in 1925–26. Though flattered and excited at being asked ('would I like to write her life … indeed I would!' GCPPT 1|1|30 8 May 1925) Aelfrida was dismayed by Agnes' refusal to allow her to include personal details, her insistence on omitting anything 'vivid and striking' in favour of 'chunky reports' of temperance conferences (GCPPT 1|1|32 8 December 1925), and her capacity for reducing 'thrilling stories about her travels' to a 'series of awful platitudes and dull events' (GCPPG A2.1 2 December 1925). The book was published in 1926 after many differences of opinion between Agnes and Aelfrida and Agnes and her publishers, Aelfrida noting vindictively that 'the book deserves to be a dead failure and I hope none of my friends will read it' (GCPPT 1|1|32 17 January 1926). Her wish was granted; many copies remained unsold.

51 George Fordham died on 20 February 1929, having first summoned Aelfrida to write for him what she disingenuously called a 'French letter' to thank the French Geographical Society for awarding him a gold medal for his cartographical expertise. Aelfrida considered it most unseemly that a man 'on the very brink of death' was more concerned with a medal than with 'considerations of eternity' but wrote the letter nevertheless (GCPPT 1|1|36 19 and 21 February 1929).

52 GCPPT 2|25|3 (10).

53 Tillyard, Ae. *A Little Road-Book for Mystics* p 7. The frontispiece of the second edition depicts "The Road Map of The Way" (i.e. the Mystic Way) "adapted from an English road book of 1675, kindly lent by Sir George Fordham" (The garden to which the pilgrim is led by the old woman in "A Strange Experience", quoted with reference to Aleister Crowley, is shown as a cul-de-sac opening off the main road). Road-books first appeared in England in the seventeenth century, the *Itinerarium* of William Stukeley (1687–1765) being perhaps the best known example.

54 GCPPT 2|25|3 (10).

55 GCPPT 1|1|38 15 November 1930.

56 Tillyard, Ae. *A Little Road-Book for Mystics* p 7.

57 Attár (died 1221) was, like Omar Kháyyám, a poet of the 'intoxicated' school of Sufi mystic poetry, 'intoxication' being the state of spiritual

inebriation entered by a seeker after God who is so overcome by the joy of finding Him that he loses the ability to discriminate between God and His creation, his own self included. Intoxication in this sense is not only "associated with expansion, hope, and intimacy with God" but also with "the human response to … God's compassion, love, kindness, beauty, gentleness and concern" (Chittick, W. p 26), characteristics for which Aelfrida felt enormous gratitude and through the agency of which she found no difficulty in abandoning herself to an identical inebriation. Attár's own 'mystic way' is described in a long poem, *The Language of the Birds*, of which a verse (quoted by Chittick p 93) gives a glimpse of the spiritual intoxication experienced by those who drink the "heart-opening wine" of God.

58 Tillyard, Ae. *A Little Road-Book for Mystics* p 9.

59 ibid. p 7. Aelfrida had been familiar with Bunyan's *Pilgrim's Progress* since childhood as "a kind of addition to the bible" (GCPPT 2|26|4(9)) and was mortified to find the editor of the Faith Press intent on describing her *Road-Book* as bearing the same relationship to the literature of the present day as *Pilgrim's Progress* to the literature of its time. Aware of how far behind John Bunyan's book her own lagged, she described Father Douglas' panegyric as 'fulsome drivel' and told him to omit it from his prospectus (GCPPT 1|1|26 2 May 1922).

60 GCPPT 1|1|24 8 June 1919.

61 GCPPT 1|1|26 16 December 1922.

62 ibid. 2 May 1922.

63 GCPPT 1|1|39 2 January 1931. *A Little Road-Book for Mystics* was, in fact, the only one of Aelfrida's many books to reach a second edition, being reissued to 'overwhelmingly good reviews' by a different publisher in 1931. Re-reading it in 1937, however, Aelfrida disliked it intensely, declaring that the book was so 'full of my worst qualities, shallowness, self-importance, [lack] of discernment and spiritual judgement' (there was also far too much 'I' in it) that she could only agree with her guardian angel's warning that 'bits … are not so bad but some of it is entirely wrong' and warn those to whom she lent copies that this was so (GCPPT 1|1|37 3 February 1937). She does not, unfortunately, tell us which 'bits' she and her guardian angel disliked.

64 GCPPT 1|1|40 16 July 1931.

65 Tillyard, Ae. *A Little Road-Book for Mystics* pp 9–10.

66 ibid. pp 1–12.

67 ibid. pp 9–10.

68 In her preface to *A Little Road-Book for Mystics* (p 7) Aelfrida lists three Roman roads ("Watling Street, or Icknield Way or the Dover Road") as roads particularly well marked in road-books. She was, of course, familiar with Roman roads near or bisecting Cambridge (Via Devana, Akeman Street, Ermine Street and the Icknield Way itself) and was doubtless aware of the contrast between their undeviating trajectory and her own wavering course. There is also a significant passage in one of Quiller-Couch's 1918 lectures which Aelfrida herself may have heard or read and taken note of, namely *The Commerce of Thought* pp117–118, in which 'Q' expatiates on certain named "old Roman roads" and equates the importance of a road's upkeep with "pious and meritorious works before God".

69 GCPPT 1|1|32 1 March 1926.

70 ibid. 7 March 1926.

71 GCPPT 1|1|39 17 February 1931.

72 Tillyard, Ae. *A Little Road-Book* for Mystics p 91.

73 ibid. p 102.

74 ibid. p 91

75 ibid. pp 90–92.

76 ibid. p 103.

77 ibid. p 100.

78 ibid. pp 100–101.

79 GCPPT 1|1|26 23 January 1923.

80 GCPPT 1|1|28 14 July 1924.

81 GCPPT 1|1|30 16 February 1925.

82  Tillyard, Ae. *A Little Road-Book* for Mystics p 117.

83  GCPPT 1|1|30 24 January 1925.

84  Tillyard, Ae. *A Little Road-Book* for Mystics p 127.

85  ibid. pp 116–117.

86  ibid. pp 25–27.

87  ibid. p 96–98.

88  GCPPT 1|1|22 26 May 1917.

89  GCPPT 1|1a *Alethea's Record Book* 10 November 1917.

90  ibid. 28 November 1917.

91  GCPPT 1|1|22 26 November 1917.

92  ibid. 20 November 1917.

93  GCPPT 1|1a *Alethea's Record Book* 7 February 1916.

94  Tillyard, Ae. *Messages* Foreword.

95  Tillyard, A.I. Preface to *The Manuscripts of God*.

96  Tillyard, A I. Preface to *Stones of Stumbling*.

97  GCPPT 1|1|17 11 December 1910. An unpublished poem originally entitled *A Little More Cheap Philosophy of Life* but later retitled *Alastair's Song* (incidental poem from *Adolescence*) (GCPPT 2|5) is Aelfrida's only other reference to a book which, had it been written, might have provided interesting insights into its author's adolescent religiosity. The poem, dated 15 August 1910, was written at Fordfield a month after Agatha's birth and four days before Aelfrida noted 'my life is my two babies' (GCPPT 1|1|17 19 August 1910). Its disillusioned tone ("was life worthwhile to give?") accords oddly with Aelfrida's joy in her children and excited expectation of the publication of *To Malise* but is all too prophetic of what was soon to ensue. *Adolescence* may have been influenced by G. Stanley Hall's 1904 book of the same name, Stanley Hall (1844–1924) being an American professor of paedagogy with a special interest in adolescent behaviour and the way in which secondary education could be carried out more sympathetically vis-à-vis the storms and stresses of that period of a young person's life.

98  GCPPT 1|1|23 25 November 1918. Notes for her talks (GCPPT 1|2) include several comments relating – without ascription – to her own adolescence, e.g. that adolescents are liable to develop 'morbid tendencies'. A poem entitled *The Wrong Side of the Bed* later appeared in *Verses for Alethea* (p11) along with others similar in tone to Aelfrida's later 'messages'.

99  GCPPT 1|1|20 14 December 1922.

100  GCPPT 1|1|27 4 March 1923.

101  *Messages* is dedicated 'to some children whom I love', the list of names which follows being headed by those of Agatha and Alethea.

102  GCPPT 1|1|28 29 May 1924.

103  GCPPT 1|1|28 2 April 1924

104  GCPPT 1|1|43 16 March 1933.

105  ibid..

106  GCPPT 1|1|27 9 June 1923. Her language and tone is, in fact, rather young for adolescents like Agatha and Alethea but judging by the inclusion in the book's dedication of the names of some of her nephews and nieces, it was intended to appeal to younger children too. A second foreword, addressed to "dear other peoples' children", recommended that *Messages* was a book to be read by them with the same excitement as *Treasure Island* or *The Jungle Book* and to be used by their mothers as they might use a cookery book or a guide to child rearing.

107  Tillyard, Ae. *Messages* pp 110–114.

108  ibid. pp 101–105.

109  ibid. pp 27–33.

110  GCPPT 1|1|27 26 May 1923.

111  GCPPT 1|1|28 20 May 1924.

112  ibid. 22 May 1924. On hearing that Aelfrida's book sold (albeit in small numbers) Mr Mudie-Cooke repented of his criticisms and promised to read *Messages* 'with an open mind' (ibid. 26 May 1924).

113  GCPPT 1|1|28 2 April 1924.

114  GCPPT 1|1|27 23 March 1923.

115  GCPPT 1|1a *Agatha's Record Book* 16 May 1913 has Agatha inform her mother that "I was one of Jesus' disciples and went about telling people to be good … it was *another* Bammie, very old." Family evidence, however suggests that pious statements attributed by Aelfrida to child members of her family may have been put into their mouths by Aelfrida herself (Angela Yaffey personal communication 23 April 2007).

116  GCPPG A2.1 21 April 1924.

117  GCPPG A1.1 28 July 1924.

118  The quotation is taken from Catharine Tillyard's obituary in the *Cambridge Weekly News* of 21 December 1932 (GCPPT 1|1|43a). A further irony is that the obituary was probably composed by Aelfrida herself, by a daughter, that is to say, who castigated her parents in her diary for professing but not practising Christian principles with reference to her grand-daughters and herself.

119  GCPPG A1.1 27 July 1924.

120  GCPPT 1|1|28 28 July 1924.

121  GCPPG A1.1 5 April 1925.

122  ibid. 7 August 1928.

123  GCPPT 1|1|32 5 September 1926.

124  GCPPT 1|1|27 21 April 1923.

125  GCPPT 1|1|35 14 October 1928.

126  GCPPT 1|1|27 27 May 1923. Following her 1921 decision to join the Church of England, Evelyn Underhill too became a staunch supporter of the Anglican Church; she also regarded her earlier dismissal of church membership as something not to be encouraged in other followers of the Mystic Way.

127  GCPPT 1|1|40 21 June 1931.

128  GCPPT 1|1|35 14 October 1928.

129  ibid.

130  GCPPT 1|1a *Alethea's Record Book* 7 January 1925.
     GCPPT 1|1|58 1 April 1941.

131  GCPPT 1|1|30 11 March 1925.
     GCPPT 1|1|37 22 May 1930.

132  GCPPT 1|1|30 11 March 1925. The expression 'spiritual espousal' may have been adopted by Aelfrida from *The Spiritual Espousals* by Jan van Ruysbroek (1293–1381) an Augustinian with whose writings on mystical theology she was already familiar. Also of relevance may be the chapters in Teresa of Avila's *The Interior Castle (The Sixth Dwelling)* on spiritual betrothal.

133  GCPPT 1|1|30 27 March 1925.

134  ibid. 11 March 1925.

135  ibid. 24 March 1925.

136  ibid. 1 April 1925.

137  ibid. 2 April 1925. Agatha had been received into the Greek Orthodox Church in that very room; her grandparents' comments on that occasion are not recorded and we do not know if they attended. Chiara had returned to England prior to Alethea's Greek Orthodox christening in Arlington Heights.

138  GCPPT 1|1|58 1 April 1941.

139  GCPPT 1|1|30 3 April 1925.

140  ibid. 4 April 1925.

141  GCPPT 1|1|42 3 October 1932.

142  GCPPT 1|1|35 23 October 1927.

143  GCPPT 1|1|42 3 October 1932.

144  GCPPT 1|1|37 25 May 1930.
     Tillyard, Ae. Preface to *Spiritual Exercises* p vii.

145  GCPPT 1|1|37 25 May 1930.

146  GCPPT 1|1|35 23 October 1927.

147  GCPPT 1|1|28 22 June 1924.

148  GCPPT 1|1|20 4 and 27 April 1915.

149  GCPPT 1|1|21 30 June 1916.

150  GCPPT 1|1|23 30 January 1919. This particular 'Brilliant Idea' may owe something to HC Lander's 1911 Letchworth Garden City

scheme for a block of service flats for professional people (with additional communal facilities) on the corner of Sollershot East and Spring Road. The flats were intended for "those numerous folk of the middle-class ... on a meagre income ... who require domestic help but can very ill afford it" (Miller, M. p65, quoting Lander). Did Aelfrida herself hope to live in adapted Cintra House in just such a flat?

151 GCPPT 1|1|26 21 July 1922.
152 GCPPT 1|1|26 3 November 1922.
   GCPPT 1|1|26a Letter from Edward Montague to 'Mrs Graham, Fordfield, Cambridge' of 1 November 1922.
153 GCPPT 1|1|22 20 October 1918.
154 GCPPT 1|1|42 24 October 1932.
155 GCPPT 1|1|22 20 November 1917.
156 GCPPT 1|1|27 5 November 1923.
157 ibid. 17 November 1923. Aelfrida's interest in the conventual life may have been stimulated by the arrival in Cambridge of an order of Carmelite nuns of whom she wrote 'I love to feel them accomplishing what I only attempt … I wake in the night and feel their prayer lifting mine' (ibid.) but was more probably revival of an interest dating from her stay at Fiesole.
158 GCPPT 1|1|36 7 May 1929.
159 GCPPT 1|1|27 2 December 1923.
160 GCPPT 1|1|30 19 April 1925.
161 ibid. 18 May 1925.
162 ibid. 24 May 1925. Aelfrida's notion may owe something to the Brothers of Common Life, medieval religious communities composed chiefly of laymen who worked among the poor as an aspect of their calling. (Thomas à Kempis lived in one such community between 1392 and 1399.) The communities re-entered contemporary consciousness in the early 20th century.
163 ibid. 28 June 1925.
164 ibid. 8 June 1925.
165 ibid. 24 May 1925.
166 ibid.
167 ibid. 25 May 1925.
168 ibid. 17 June 1925.
169 ibid. 11 and 15 June 1925.
170 ibid. 8 June 1925.
171 ibid. 23 June 1925.
172 ibid. 24 June 1925.
173 ibid. 30 May 1925.
174 ibid. 23 June 1925.
175 ibid. 1 June 1925.
176 ibid. 7 June 1925.
177 ibid. 14 June 1925.
178 ibid. 15 July 1925.
179 ibid. 18 July 1925.
180 ibid. 18 July 1925.
181 ibid. 18 and 21 July 1925.
182 ibid. 1 July 1925.
183 ibid. 19 September 1925.
184 ibid. 3 October 1925.
185 ibid. 11 October 1925.
186 ibid. 13 October 1925.
187 ibid. 15 November 1925.
188 ibid. 18 November 1925.
189 ibid. 11 September 1925.
190 GCPPT 1|1|73 1 November 1955.
191 Tillyard, Ae. *The Fruits of Silence* pp 14–17 (GCPPT 2|18).
192 GCPPT 1|1|46 2 February 1935.
193 GCPPT 1|1|72 'The Transfiguration' (6 August) 1955.
194 Tillyard Ae. *Spiritual Exercises* p 165.
195 GCPPT 1|1|57 5 October 1939.
196 ibid. 'The Transfiguration' (6 August) 1955.
197 Chapter 2 of van Ruysbroek's *The Spiritual Espousal* describes the living of one's life in terms of this 'yearning'.
198 Tillyard, Ae. *Spiritual Exercises* pp 198–200, quoting Augustin Poulain SJ, contemporary writer on mystical theologies. It is also possible, given hints in adolescent and later diaries, that Aelfrida was familiar with Richard Challoner's *The Garden of the Soul*, compiled round 1740 and with later editions in 1896, 1899, 1900 and 1902; originally sub-titled *Instructions for Christians who (living in the world) aspire to Devotion,*, it also described itself as *A Manual for Spiritual Exercises* aimed at placing quotidian life in a sanctified and sanctifying setting. For more on this, see Heimann, M. pp 68–79 and 83–86.
199 Tillyard, Ae. *Marrying a Stranger* p 162 (GCPPT 2|6). Author's emphasis.
200 Barrow, J. et al. Vol. 1 pp 447–448, Vol. 4 pp 61–62.
201 Dante. *The Divine Comedy: Paradise* canto III: l. 84 or, as Dante's thirteenth century Italian has it, "e'en la sua voluntade è nostra pace".
202 ibid. lines 46–123. Worth noting in this context is that it was from a Florentine convent of the order of St Clare that Piccarda was taken.
203 GCPPT 1|2.
204 Tillyard, Ae. *The Glory of the West* p 252 (GCPPT 2|16|1 Pt 2). Also of relevance in this context is Dante's inclusion of those who are not maritally chaste in the Circle of the Lustful (*The Divine Comedy: Purgatory* Canto XXV).
205 GCPPT 1|1|13 22 January 1906.
206 Tillyard. Ae. *The Florentine Movement* p 77.
207 GCPPT 1|1|11 18 July 1904.
208 Tillyard, Ae. *A la soeur que j'aurais du avoir.* (*To Malise* p 86).
209 ibid. *A very feminine argument.* (*To Malise* p 52). The poem was written in Boston on 26 June 1908.
210 GCPPT 1|1|52 7 October 1936.
211 Lane Fox, R. p367.
212 Wogan-Browne, J. pp 27 and 42.
213 ibid. pp 5,19,and 48.
214 ibid. pp 19,41 and 42.

# Seething Cauldron of Memories

With the ending of the Great War in November 1918 social life in Cambridge flourished once again, Aelfrida commenting delightedly that it was 'quite like old times'[1] to see teachers returning to Homerton, soldiers to their families, and the wives of masters of colleges to their social duties. Better still was to see 'real *whole* undergraduates in the streets'[2] instead of the physically maimed and the safe return of be-med-alled Captain Eustace Tillyard[3] who, donning tutorial responsibility for the new English Tripos, brought 'various young men to the house [who] make us feel the war is really over!' But if only, she sighed, 'the world would settle down and people all love each other, how happy and literary … we might all be!!'[4]

Entomological too, for one of Fordfield's first post-war visitors was Robert Tillyard (now definitively 'Robin' to the world) of whom Aelfrida wrote approvingly 'he used to be a very worthy but somewhat boring young man, too fond of talking about his temptations and chiefly admirable for his devotion to work and to Pattie Craske (now Mrs Robert)'.[5] (Robert's four beautiful little girls – Faith, Hope, Charity, and Prudence – appealed to her too.) On the occasion of a later visit in 1926 during which Robert, now 'the most brilliant living Entomologist', was 'lionised' during a series of lectures given in Cambridge (Aelfrida appears not have recalled – or chose not to recall – earlier derogatory remarks concerning her cousin's intellectual capabilities), she was more critical, writing that the atmosphere engendered by Robert and Pattie was 'a trifle strained and boisterous', something attributable to Robert's ill health ('he is only just alive – so bent and old and racked with pain') and to Pattie being 'high-spirited, energetic and a trifle self-satisfied'.[6] (Agatha found her 'loveable and great fun'.)[7] A visit in 1928 during which Robert received an honorary fellowship from Queens' College, passed without much remark for life in the Tillyard household was not easy during the last years of the Oracle's life, but elicited from eighteen-year-old Alethea the comment that her distant cousin was 'unbearably conceited', that she did not care for him in the least 'in spite of all the letters after his name and all the distinction he has brought on the family', and that she would 'change Robin for someone else any day'.[8]

**Constantine Graham (second left) 1927**

Comments concerning her mother's old flames were no more complimentary. Cousin Percy, last seen sitting lachrymosely at the piano contemplating the engagement of his beloved Frida to Constantine Michaelides, was now the Reverend Percy Stanley, headmaster and proprietor of 'a flourishing school of sixty little boys'.[9] Aged fifty-one to Aelfrida's forty-one when he visited Cambridge in November 1924, bachelor Cousin Percy decided to try his chances with divorced Mrs Graham but intimacies were rebuffed, albeit more gently than his earlier efforts: 'either I have grown more tolerant or he has improved but I like him much better than I did …

he is sensible and understanding, a little conventional … but full of the tolerance which comes from the sense of the pathos in human life'.

Having worried that Percy might be censorious about 'the mess I have made of my own life', Aelfrida was gratified to discover that she no longer cared what Percy thought because 'I have so little sense of continuity with the Frida he knew'[10] and that Percy's attempts at consolation were easily pushed aside because Percy's pity would be intolerable and because she had already received more pity than she deserved. She was, however, moved when Percy sang a song about loving an unattainable 'her' for ever 'with his eyes on me in just the old style [and] trembled so he could hardly get through it', asking herself afterwards 'how should a middle-aged woman fail to be touched by so much constancy!' (She also noted that 'Alethea and Agatha caught my eye and I was afraid they would laugh [but] they restrained themselves'[11]; Alethea said 'Percy sang excellently' but noted the extreme 'dullness of … mother's old admirer'.)[12] On another occasion 'poor Percy' was more cheerful ('one doesn't expect a voice from the dead, so to speak, to sing comic songs') but although Aelfrida laughed 'for the sake of old times and for Frida Tillyard whom I knew so long ago', she also, with a possible nod to Freud's definition of the Id, wrote bitterly that Percy had made her feel 'like an old witch bending over a seething cauldron of memories' and while admonishing herself 'silly old thing, Aelfrida, silly old thing … it none of it matters in the least'[13] was glad to receive 'a good scolding' from her guardian angel 'for being so vain and self-absorbed'; thereafter she was 'desperately penitent and promised to try and devote myself to … my higher calling'.[14] Percy, however, proved fickle, arriving unexpectedly at Fordfield in June 1933 with a bride in tow, 'a widow of fifty-five-ish … ridiculously overdressed in sky-blue', though he had the grace to admit to Aelfrida 'with some emotion' and in front of his wife that he had been "very much in love" with her. Not wishing to upset 'Mrs Percy' and hoping to persuade her that Percy's affection for herself was 'a mere boy and girl affair', Aelfrida made light of the half-dozen times she had refused Percy's offers of marriage by remarking blithely "I know you were; you used to come to tea in the nursery and argue with me about church heresies".[15]

Other encounters, too, restored the *amour propre* of a woman who had recently and publicly mislaid it, and though these brought back memories not all of which were happy, they helped Aelfrida to gather up threads 'that had come loose'.[16]

One such encounter took place in June 1923. During a chance meeting with John Forbes Cameron, Aelfrida discussed 'the Modern Parent' and received on parting 'a long look from his cool fathomless blue eyes, a look with no love in it but with much sweet remembrance and faithful friendship'. (That night she dreamed a poignantly vivid dream that Constantine came to renew friendship and to introduce his new wife.) She also elicited the fact that John Forbes himself was 'getting on' only 'fairly well', said in such a dejected tone that Aelfrida challenged him to 'say "wonderfully well", "extraordinarily well", "radiantly well" – anything but "fairly well!"' and was gratified when her former admirer 'woke up a little' and pursued a lively conversation.[17] Perhaps it was his dejection (or her wearing a 'modest but very becoming biscuit-coloured dress' and matching hat) which prompted her to tell him at a subsequent meeting that she had asked herself apropos the Downing College garden party at which their encounter took place "what person in Cambridge would I most like to meet and thought of *you*" (a 'spontaneous' remark prepared as soon as she saw him across the lawn), a compliment which evoked a talk about 'old times' and a comment that he was glad she was 'renewing her youth'. 'I couldn't help the illusion', Aelfrida wrote afterwards, 'that the years had not been', before concluding that perhaps she and Cameron had had rather too much 'fun' before their ways parted.[18]

Another old flame whose lambency had dwindled to a flicker was Geoffrey Hatten, a 'slain' whose admiration had conveniently bridged the gap between John Forbes Cameron's rejection and Constantine Michaelides' adoration. Geoffrey, alas, had grown 'painfully thin and absurdly legal-looking and all the fire and romance of youth [had] been knocked out of him'. (She does not record if the Southend solicitor fought through the war but appears surprised that almost all her former men friends seemed 'to have lost their sense of adventure and to have given up expecting the unexpected', a loss to which wartime experiences of any kind might have contributed; by contrast, she herself whose war had largely consisted of vibrant spiritual adventures, still lived 'with a vivid sense that something thrilling [was] waiting for [her] round the corner'.) She was happy to note, however, that Geoffrey looked at her 'with the same dog-like devotion' but the premature death in 1930 of a man described by Alethea merely as 'friend of Mother's'[19] passed without more comment than that he left four young children.

'A lovely cosy tea with Mrs Bowen and her new baby' in February 1919 brought Dr Bowen back into Aelfrida's orbit. On parting, the now-married surgeon gave her 'a long searching friendly look – to see if I am happy', a perceptive action on the part of a doctor to whom Aelfrida had confided her marital miseries in 1912 and to whose ears her later marital problems might have penetrated. She, for her part, hoped she concealed present unhappiness sufficiently to fool him[20] but the fact that when asked for favours during the 1920s (chiefly free medical examinations for Tillyard dependents) his tone said "anything for you, to the half of my kingdom"[21] and that at their rare meetings he appeared self-conscious 'as though he remembered old times'[22], encouraged her to keep their friendship on a purely professional level.

A reminder of another intense friendship arrived in September 1924 in the form of 'Mr (formerly Consul-General) Smith', as 'hale and naval' as ever in spite of his hair being a little whiter 'and his figure a little more portly'. Aelfrida found the visit reassuring ('he is one of the people whom one may reasonably expect to be just the same'), remembering gratefully how 'in a quicksand of ""East of Suez"-like society' Stewart Smith 'was a fine foothold' and how she had 'put up with his prejudices for the sake of his principles'. But whereas a visit in October 1914 had seen her refuse to see him alone less because he might have declared his continuing love for her and more because 'I might have confided in him about Constantine', in 1924 she felt able to talk freely about old times with a man of whom she remained 'very fond', and though mention of an ex-husband last seen by Stewart Smith as a honeymooning vice-consul revived her pain ('I long for Constantine as if I had just lost him')[23], it also reminded her that, having lost him, she was 'serener and happier than I should have thought possible'[24] and that although her family thought her visitor dull, she owed 'Mr Consul-General Smith' a debt of gratitude she could never repay. Aelfrida and Charles Stewart Smith never met again; his death on 23 February 1934 went unnoticed by one preoccupied with another's mortality.

In June 1927, overwhelmed by visitors ('some people I love and most people I like but I should both love and like not seeing anyone for a fortnight')[25] and desperate to finish revising *Spiritual Exercises* ('I am getting the scholar's passion for accuracy … but have only got to page 62!!')[26] in the light of Edward Thomas' helpful criticisms, Aelfrida discovered she possessed the power of melting the heart of an eminent scholar whom she had hitherto regarded not 'as a *man*, only as a sort of dictionary'. Not only did Mr Thomas 'haunt' her in the library (once or twice, she wrote, 'I looked him full in the face – and he was not a dictionary but only a small vocabulary of a particular kind!') but she had also seen him 'mooning about gazing at Fordfield in a lost sort of way'. Feeling 'grieved and penitent' at having unwittingly led him on but 'gratified and touched' by his admiration (it seems it was not only for his academic qualifications that she acknowledges in the book's preface her debt "to Mr Thomas of

the University library [of] more gratitude than I can well express")[27], she added to the entry in which she recorded his admiration a comment regarding her attractiveness to men made by her perceptive Frenchman: '*pour une femme comme vous il n'y a qu'une chose: vieiller*'.[28] But growing old – or at any rate, older – did not seem to deter men of any age, Aelfrida recording of post-war friendships that they were 'too interesting, too delightful … isn't it all thrilling and aren't I a fortunate woman!'[29] But a subsequent statement apropos a Little Friend's wife having evinced jealousy that 'if only she knew how little she need be! I am thoroughly middle-aged now where men are concerned, and glad to be so'[30] was to prove untrue: Aelfrida never became 'middle-aged' with regard to men. Nor they with regard to her, for once she ceased to be 'the central reality'[31] of their lives, adoration was transformed into affectionate regard.

In July 1927 Aelfrida made three diarised confessions, all to do with men. (Four if one counts her revelations about Edward Thomas.) Attending a Liberal Garden Party, she discovered first, that a public figure (Lloyd George, no less) could be 'self-conscious and bored and pettish', second, that arrogant Maynard Keynes could be 'very affable' if he chose, and third, that Hubert Henderson's greeting "How is life treating you now, Frida dear?" ('did he say "dear" or did I imagine it from his tone?') thrilled her greatly because in spite of 'vocation', vows of chastity, and protestations of 'detachment', she could not help 'being touched by men's homage': 'I try – I say it is all done – all over – but it happens again and I feel the same delight'.[32] Two years later, however, 'dear Hubert!', newly appointed secretary to the government's Economic Advisory Council, visited Fordfield where he talked Liberal politics 'at great length' to the Oracle's but possibly not to Aelfrida's delight; furthermore, the contrast between the charmingly boyish Hubert who graced a 1914 photograph of herself, Constantine, Agatha, and Alethea on Fordfield terrace and the present world-weary economist was too marked: Hubert, she wrote (and contemporary photographs bear her out) now looked like a 'broken-down Nonconformist minister'.[33] But a prediction made a few months after the Fordfield photograph was taken came true: 'there is a quiet force about Hubert – he ought to do great things if he isn't lazy'.[34]

August 1919 saw 'Dr Tommy MC' leaving England to join his father at the Altounyan Hospital in Aleppo. Finding him now 'quite Armenianised', Aelfrida worried lest Tommy's anti-British views indicated an unhealthy interest in 'Armenian intrigues' engendered by a manipulative father and by Tommy's impressionable nature.[35] She was even more disillusioned when she heard from Willie Searle in 1923 that Tommy, in England for a half-year course in surgery, was 'the two things I thought he never would be – rich and contented'; worse still, 'he dresses at the height of fashion and flings his money about lavishly'. Were it not for his 'four unattractive and unhealthy children', Tommy, no longer a eager young idealist with a 'vision', seemed so disconcertingly like Constantine that Aelfrida decided that she did not want to see him: 'Tommy with his wallet full of dreams was one matter, Tommy with his wallet full of banknotes quite another'.[36] A visit from 'dear Tommy' in September 1923 made her sadder still but for a different reason – the Little Friend who now professed himself happily married, worked at 'doctoring' twelve hours a day and spoke 'in a weary middle-aged voice' from which all 'dash and fire' had gone.[37]

Eardley Davidson, the 'simple and modest' and 'clever alert boy'[38] who whispered in her ear in May 1914, returned to England after the war as Major Davidson of the Royal Flying Corps to qualify as a doctor. Living in Cambridge while working on the theoretical part of his training, Eustace's friend (and best man) made it clear that he wished to resume his friendship with Eustace's sister too, so clear that he cycled a twenty-mile round-trip to the village where Aelfrida and her daughters were holidaying in April 1919 to assure her of the fact.[39]

'Wonderfully pure' and hero-worshipping Eardley had no intention, however, of transgressing the bounds of friendship because recently married to a woman who had her husband 'where she wants him'. ('Ought I to have brought up Constantine like that?'[40] Aelfrida pondered before deciding that instead of reproaching her husband when she met him in Lyons she would 'feel no resentment, only love and pity'.)[41] She therefore provided both Davidsons with practical and spiritual assistance, the former to a couple in the throes of moving house, the latter to Catherine Davidson who, following her first pregnancy, suffered badly from 'depression and morbid thoughts'.[42]

Disappointed that her post-war practice as a 'soul-doctor' had so few patients, Aelfrida was delighted to have Catherine Davidson come 'to consult the Straightener'. (The irony of 'an adored and cherished wife … turning for calm strength to me, the poor spurned one'[43] was not lost on someone whose husband had just announced his intention of divorcing her.) Her own experience of post-natal depression enabled her to provide the 'calm strength' Catherine needed; indeed, so effectively was she 'straightened' that recovery was relatively rapid. Further pregnancies, including one of twins, saw no recurrence of 'morbid thoughts' though Aelfrida later observed that a 'faint air of pathos and helplessness'[44] continued to cling around her former patient.

Once qualified, Eardley became a general practitioner in Watford. Frequent social visits to Eustace and Phyllis restored him to Aelfrida's orbit, albeit less as an acolyte and more as a 'medical man' with whom she could discuss 'Old Age … a subject which seems not to have received the attention it deserves'[45] and a particularly burning issue given that the Oracle was then 'so cut off from everything alive that being with him is like being half buried' and Chiara 'bent on self-immolation' until her old beau Rendel Harris visited, at which point she 'woke up and was quite young again'.[46] She was also glad to obtain free consultations with 'the kind of man who glows with delight when you ask a favour of him' though Eardley's chief success as unofficial medical adviser lay in his 'air of concern, of extreme interest in the patient's complaint, of being master of all the resources of science and full of enthusiasm to put them all at the patient's disposal'. His 'bedside manner', she continued, 'is worth £2000 pounds a year to him'[47]; to her, it was priceless because of its reminder of boyish devotion.

In 1931, however, Aelfrida was dismayed to discover that Eardley had acquired 'a slightly pompous … manner'. (His redeeming features were that he retained 'the same good doggy eyes' and was 'a real true *permanent* friend'.)[48] He was also as impervious to the blandishments of religion ('I have long wanted to make a Christian of him')[49] as Constantine ('if only [Eardley] could see God … his is a *very* precious soul')[50] and possibly for the same reasons: he seems to have regarded Aelfrida's prescription of Deity as a remedy for post-natal depression as inappropriate and was himself unwilling to be 'straightened' by a self-professed mystic who persisted in trying to (as the Quaker expression went) 'speak to his condition'.[51]

As if to console her for the gradual withdrawal of gentleman friends (Little and otherwise) from her life, men known for ten years and more to whom she clung as if by doing so she could recapture the joys of 'pure and beautiful' friendships without breaking recent vows of 'recuperated' virginity, there arrived on the scene a certain Thomas Henn, one of Eustace's 'young men' and a pointer to future relationships with men who had never known her as Constantine's wife.

Tom Henn[52] attracted Aelfrida's attention on his first visit to Fordfield in 1922, being the son of a former pupil of 'Aunt Laura's', a pupil and later a colleague of her younger brother[53], and the younger brother of Billy Henn, the 'Irish poet' about whom she had once written a poem[54] and the 'very taking man' met while staying with 'lonely widower' Sir George Fordham at Odsey in 1913 and to whom (in spite of his caddish attitude towards Molly and Marjory Fordham) she found herself unwillingly attracted while seething with anger and resentment towards her husband. Whether it was because Tom Henn's blue eyes reminded her of Billy's 'wonderful deepest blue eyes' or because she was delighted to discover someone other than herself and Fidelio who believed in fairies[55] or discovering that Tom (like Fidelio, Billy, and herself) was a 'Cambridge poet'[56], Aelfrida felt an immediate attraction to him. They had little time, however, to cultivate a Little Friendship, for soon after graduating in 1923 Tom joined the Shell Oil Company in Calcutta in an effort to restore family fortunes lost during the Irish Troubles ('he is going to work hard and try to buy back [the family home] for his elder brother')[57], and it was not until May 1925 that she and Tom ('Brandon')[58] met again.

Revival of interest in a man much younger than herself (Aelfrida was now forty-one, Tom twenty-three) was almost inevitable for a woman recently divorced from a husband to whom she was attracted when he was Tom's age but who, unlike Tom, did not then or later combine 'manliness with delicate feelings'.[59] But a stop appeared in the form of Tom's fiancée, Enid, who, being of an 'exclusive' rather than an inclusive nature, forbade her future husband to associate with 'old friends'.[60] Enid's desire for 'exclusivity' arose, it may be, for two reasons: first, Aelfrida was exhibiting overmuch affection for a man she pretended was a mere acquaintance, second, as a result of Tom's anxiety and doubt concerning his approaching nuptials; indeed, August 1926 found him confiding that 'marriage as a state did not attract him' – he even asked 'ought [I] to go on with it?' – and demanding to know how he could make a success of it. Pointing out that she herself 'could hardly be the authority'[61] on such matters, Aelfrida allayed his fears as best as she could because she 'intensely want[ed] him to be happy' but at the same time informed him (her guardian angel had bidden her go to early Communion and 'make once and for all an act of renunciation of such human affections as hold me back in spiritual progress') that his impending wedding 'must and ought to' make a difference to their relationship.[62]

Although Alethea later noted light-heartedly that 'Tom Henn's wild Irishness' had been tempered by matrimony[63] (Girton dons pronounced him "Henn-pecked")[64], it seems Tom found the early years of his marriage very hard work ('marriage has certainly taken all the sparkle out of *him*')[65] and though 'too chivalrous' to put his misery into words, he relied heavily on Aelfrida's support to see him through a period when Eustace too was concerned for his welfare. As with Frank Stokoe, Aelfrida put another's needs before her own (summer 1929 saw the 'perfect peace of Fordfield' more than usually liable to fracture and she herself wondering if 'the mystical position is tenable under modern conditions'; 'it is', she decided)[66], persuading 'Brandon' that life was worth living after all.

The adoration of a new male friend and the continuing camaraderie of older ones was not the only homage paid to divorced Mrs Graham. In March 1924 and much absorbed in 'psychoanalytical literature', she made three interesting discoveries: that 'it was sex that made me find men more stimulating than women'; that Anatolia's excessive love for Constantine and her desire to dominate him was both wrong and dangerous; that Julius' 'inability to be a husband' stemmed from 'excessive dependence' on Chiara.[67] (She excused Julius' and Constantine's inability to free themselves from their mothers by persuading herself that modern psychoanalysts' belief that the 'mutual love of mother and son is the most fundamental and everything else is a substitute for it'[68] was certainly true of them.) Her first two suppositions were probably correct, her third was not, for Julius' 'excessive dependence'[69] on his mother's approval stemmed less from 'mutual love' and more from survivor's guilt and fear of further rejection. But none of her readings of 'psychoanalytical literature' prepared her for the startling disclosure made by Julius to his sister in December 1924. Discussing Nadja ('the Russian girl who proved so attractive to Dudu')[70], Aelfrida asked Julius why she herself felt 'such affinity' for 'a remote Russian', only to have him reply "I fell in love with her because she [was] so much like you and it was because she was so like you that we could never marry".[71]

Aelfrida accepted Julius' revelation without shock or surprise as a manifestation of something she had known all along but had never before heard put into words. (She also chose not to question Julius further, hence remained puzzled as to why his suggestion to Nadja that their marriage entail a brother and sister relationship and Nadja's refusal to countenance it should have rendered him 'so utterly wretched and indignant'.)[72] From now on, however, the coolness which existed between Julius and Aelfrida since his return from Ruhleben disappears and she basks once again in the closeness of her relationship with 'my Dudu'.

Julius' disclosure of his love for his sister at this point was, it seems, less because Constantine's disappearance from it and the intrusion into it of another potential husband in the shape of Willie Searle made it imperative to assert his prior claim and more because of the reappearance in his life of the woman whose name precipitated disclosure.

Little had been heard of Nadja Laptchinski since Julius' return to England from Russia in the summer of 1912, following which his 'dreadful pessimism' as he sat by Aelfrida's bedside drove his depressed sister 'perfectly frantic'. His appointment as Professor of Russian at Birmingham in 1921 following his two-year sojourn in South Africa and his frequent trips to Russia between that date and his appointment as Professor of Greek at Cardiff in 1926 had worried Aelfrida because she believed his cultivation of 'all things Russian' demonstrated recrudescent love for Nadja. (She also believed that the influence on a man as 'gloomy' and impressionable as Julius of 'Russia as she was, with her cruelties, her madness, her charm [and] as she is now, dominated by idealism turned putrid and fine things distorted to hideous lunacy'[73] could be malign.) Nadja's arrival in England in November 1924 (now a teacher, she had been given leave by the Russian government to stay for a year to improve her English but was to remain for a decade) and lengthy visits to Fordfield (Chiara had met Nadja in Russia in 1912 and often invited her to Cambridge) provoked something of a crisis. Julius refused to meet her (his escapes were sometimes hairsbreadth: 'he was only just out of the house … when in she walked')[74], but Nadja and Mina met once, the former 'radiating charm and vitality, pathos and seduction … in her simple black dress [with] her magnificent hair crowning her proud head', the latter 'clumsy, badly dressed, complexion all spots, hair anyhow, no grace, no charm'. Asking herself (naively, in view of Julius' declaration) why Julius 'let Nadja go', Aelfrida wondered what Nadja and Mina thought of each other[75] (neither said) but was glad that Julius and Nadja never married: 'she is several sizes too big for him in every way'.[76]

Nadja's 'size' posed other problems, for although initially she seemed far from '*die wilde Russin*' of doubtful principles who had bewitched Julius[77], she soon proved to be "a tragedy queen, [a] femme fatale who never left you as she found you – if indeed a woman who *could* leave you … once she had determined to alter and subjugate you", a woman in whose presence "the demands of melodrama never relaxed", a woman with whom to live "would have been agony … you would have been forced to be heroic in your bath, exalted at breakfast, adventurous all the morning, passionate before you had had your dinner, noble and full of sublime thoughts on a chilly evening [with] every incident … a crisis, every dawn a red-letter day, every tune … a complete orchestra", a woman for whom "boredom was out of the question" so that "wherever she went, things began to happen [and] the world, instead of going on its usual way … began to revolve round her [and] nothing but the unexpected happened". A woman, in short, whom "men worshipped".[78] A woman, too, described by Alethea as 'a Romantic Russian Friend, with a past and a temperament'[79] whose promotion of 'a melodramatic Russian

atmosphere … was rather oppressive'[80] and departure ('whisper it') 'rather a relief'[81], comments which, were it not for their 'Russian' overtones (and Aelfrida's description of Russia 'as she was … and is' is also relevant here) could equally apply to her mother; a woman so like Nadja that it is no wonder Julius had been so violently attracted to her, that he dared not meet her again, and that Nadja herself said of Julius' sister "we are very much alike. There is an affinity between our souls".[82]

Nadja, however, had her uses. For one thing, she provided good 'copy'. Although Aelfrida never wrote the "Odessa novel with Nadja as heroine" that everyone suggested she write, she felt for Nadja "the interest of a novelist and an amateur psychologist"[83] and avidly absorbed her 'heartrending tales'[84] of a Russia about which Englishmen knew little or nothing: of the 'hunger years' during which people subsisted (if they were lucky) on coffee-substitute, black bread, gruel and wild berries[85] and slept on straw paillasses on plank beds with only a single blanket in the depths of winter[86], of 'shootings and prisons', of licentious behaviour, of 'the fornications of children in their teens'. Watching Nadja's eyes as she spoke, Aelfrida saw the 'pictures she sees' and lay awake at night thinking about them[87]. (Eight years later Nadja's tales of Russia's desolation under Bolshevism were to reappear in *The Approaching Storm*.) For another, she introduced Aelfrida to two of the 'real Russians' she and Constantine had longed to meet in Odessa but from whom circumstances effectively separated them: research fellow Peter Kapitza ('he looks like a jolly English stable boy')[88] and 'the famous Lydia Lopokova … the great *danseuse*', fiancée of Maynard Keynes, whose mother called her 'dear little Lydia' because of her 'simple and childish' manner.[89]

Exasperating though Nadja could be with her continual demands for attention and assistance, her knack of making others work on her behalf while she sat still and did nothing, and her penchant for outstaying her welcome and for criticising other people's behaviour while lacking insight into her own, she provided the Tillyards in general and Aelfrida in particular with a good deal of amusement at a time when the 'perfect peace of Fordfield' provided no amusement at all. But what neither they nor she seem to have appreciated was that in meekly submitting to behaviour so similar to Aelfrida's own (were it not for details specific to Nadja, Aelfrida's account of Nadja's life in England could be taken for autobiography) they were guilty of perpetuating it and in danger of becoming helpless victims of it. Then, too, Aelfrida's descriptions of Nadja's aptitude for being 'ever unsatisfied'[90] and of her idiosyncratic and self-dramatizing behaviour (and the recurrently unsatisfactory nature of her relationships with men) should have warned her of how exasperating she herself might be to live with and how bizarre her behaviour might appear to outsiders who knew less of her personal and family circumstances than she of Nadja's. Unfortunately, however, and in spite of Julius drawing her attention to similarities between sister and ex-fiancée, it did not, Aelfrida's 'affinity' for her 'affinity' preventing her from being sufficiently objective to see in Nadja reflections of her own dysfunction.

The Tillyards' priority was to find Nadja a job. Ever-resourceful Florence Keynes organised one at the Papworth Village Settlement ('the Papworth place for consumptive people')[91] in the establishment of which she herself had been instrumental. Nadja's teaching and nursing skills were made use of in the sanatorium and the sheltered workshops (she taught leather working), the Settlement being a place whose Medical Director (Pendrill Varrier-Jones)[92] and Matron (Miss Borne) had conceived "the bold idea of rivalling Davos ... with an English TB camp ... in the fens" where "the patients were ... inoculated with hope and enthusiasm as well as with drugs".[93] At first all went well, then, according to Nadja, Varrier-Jones fell in love with her and Matron, seemingly in love with Varrier-Jones herself, jealously accused Nadja of being his mistress, whereupon Nadja consulted a doctor (or three, accounts varied) who certified her virgo intacta and left Papworth in a huff. (Doubting 'the calumny as much as the fact', Aelfrida felt 'a sudden gasp of pity ... that Nadja, so highly sexed, should live and die a virgin'[94]; Florence Keynes, less sympathetic, informed Chiara that 'the jealously part is all moonshine ... the Matron likes Nadja exceedingly'.)[95] In truth, the 'Papworth Melodrama'[96] seems to have arisen as a result of Nadja's desire to marry an Englishman so as not to have to return to Russia; having been rebuffed (sic) by Varrier-Jones but before she departed Papworth 'in a tense and dramatic atmosphere'[97], she declared she had fallen in love with Willie Searle ('a look was enough!')[98] and he with her. Though this could have proved convenient to one whose guardian angel 'always said "NO"'[99] to Aelfrida marrying Willie herself, Willie's complete indifference to Nadja resulted in the latter wailing that 'all who loved her or whom she has loved have been bewitched [with] death, suicide, insanity [and] impotence'[100] and in the failure of Aelfrida's efforts to arrange a marriage of convenience with an elderly Fenlander canny enough to refuse her offer of £5.

Nadja's next post was found as a result of Aelfrida's activities as Straightener. One of her 'patients' was a Mrs Ablett, Matron-Supervisor of the Eton Union Workhouse, concerning whom Aelfrida wrote with Willie Searle in mind 'I take it that God wants me to be a Straightener rather than a wife'.[101] Mrs Ablett (her 'straightening' was carried out entirely by letter) had written to 'Aelfrida Tillyard, Straightener' in some perplexity after reading one of Aelfrida's books to ask why she, "a good Christian all her life, had been denied direct perception of God"[102]; a lengthy correspondence ensued. In November 1927, however, Mrs Ablett was able to provide practical help in return for spiritual advice. Nadja was staying at Fordfield pending the appearance of another job and Aelfrida was writing increasingly frantic letters to all and sundry when one evening 'at my meditation time, my guardian angel said "why do you fuss like this. Lie still and get into touch with someone"'.[103] (In Can I be a Mystic? in which the episode is used to illustrate the fact that Aelfrida's guardian angel never gave an order without also providing the means of carrying it out, the angel chides her more strongly: "really, Aelfrida, I am ashamed of you! All this fuss and worry ... instead of writing all these unnecessary letters and bothering your acquaintances to no purpose, why don't you listen?")[104] Flinging her thoughts far and wide, she "became aware that a Stranger-friend ... had a job to offer of just the kind needed" and on the basis of telepathic communication wrote to her the following day. Mrs Ablett's response was that Aelfrida's offer of Nadja's services "came as an answer to a prayer" and Nadja was duly dispatched to the Eton Union ("my guardian angel managed it all so neatly that I was charmed") and was soon "happily at work and the two women ... of the very greatest help and comfort to each other".[105] In reality, Nadja objected strongly to the menial tasks she was told to do and departed two years later following a real or imaginary assault by a fellow nurse.[106] She returned at Fordfield in June 1930 looking 'so wild and haggard [that] she seems to bring with her all the sorrows of the world' and refusing ('so Russian'[107], and so like Aelfrida at that time) to face the question of her future. The remainder of Nadja's life in England fluctuated between short-lived nursing posts, visits to Fordfield ('as always, interested in nothing but her own troubles'[108], wrote Aelfrida in exasperation, being currently beset with plenty of her own), and prolonged sojourns with compassionate Russian émigrés elsewhere. To Aelfrida's joy, Nadja became extremely religious ("her love of God and her desire for Him burned with a pure flame") but her concurrent "calm and steadfast desire for martyrdom" eventually effected a return to Russia whence a last letter arrived saying that she was in despair and begging Aelfrida not to reply because "one little letter from England might send her to Siberia or a torture-chamber".[109]

Memories seething in Aelfrida's emotional cauldron had not so far included people intimately involved with her wedding but were now to do so. In no instance did she meet – or meet again in life – the subjects of the memories (two men who had loved her, one woman who cordially disliked her) but their re-appearance in her life provoked emotions which ranged from indifference to anguish.

Her hope of 20 February 1919 that the world would settle down and people love each other included in its description of 'how happy and literary … we might be' the phrase 'and agricultural'[110], the only man of her acquaintance connected with farming being Eric Silvanus who, following his discharge from the army, hoped to take up an 'agricultural career'. Rather curiously for a man who had snubbed her before and both Grahams after his marriage, Eric (he had 'been through all [the] fighting and come out unhurt')[111], had written to Aelfrida in 1917 enclosing a studio photograph of himself in Royal Fusiliers uniform and a number of poems. Whether this was a genuine attempt to resume contact or a bid for immortality in the event of his death – were Aelfrida to edit another volume of *Cambridge Poets*, he would qualify as a 'King's Man' and his poems included – Aelfrida does not say, but mindful of the brusque way in which he discarded her she seems to have ignored his hints. Post-war references to him are rather derogatory: that he had twin daughters, lived in Bolton (of all places), and far from becoming a farmer, had taken up school-mastering again and could talk boringly of nothing else. She had not, however, heard the last of Constantine's best man and her own admirer, discourage him as she might.

Her unexpected meeting with Anatolia Michaelides at Eustace's wedding in March 1919 (Anatolia had refused to attend her son's wedding to Aelfrida, so why was she invited to that of Aelfrida's brother?) should have warned her that amicable though Anatolia appeared on that occasion, trouble tended to dog the rebarbative lady's footsteps. Hence although Aelfrida prided herself on bearing Anatolia 'no ill-will for having carried out her design of wrecking my married happiness'[112] and Anatolia disappeared from her life following the Grahams' divorce, she and her son were to re-appear a few years later with consequences which became as malevolently 'bewitched' as Nadja's as time passed.

In July 1924 Aelfrida received a letter from Anatolia, now shuttling between Paris and a villa at Cap d'Antibes adjacent to that of her daughter and son-in-law Irene and Karl Hillerns. The letter was addressed to 'Mrs Frida Tillyard': "Dear Frida, my thoughts are often occupied lovingly with thoughts of you and Constantine's children. I would like greatly to have news of them … nothing that has happened in life can prevent me from loving the two little girls so closely related to me. I have never

understood what Constantine would like me to do in the matter of his children – beyond the fact that he supports you and them, I have no information whatsoever – but I take it upon myself to put myself in relation with you and them". Asking that Aelfrida enclose a photograph of Agatha and Alethea in her reply and adding a brief passage of what Aelfrida, had she commented on it, would have termed 'higher twaddle', Anatolia concluded "tell the little girls my love … and let me have news of them".[113]

Aelfrida's first impulse was to take Anatolia's letter 'as an answer to all [her] prayers about Constantine and to read into it some evidence of his repentance', her second, 'to write at once and ask for news of him', her third, 'to consult the girls' even though 'the danger to them of any intercourse with Anatolia would be too appalling'.[114] (Since Anatolia's verbal attack during her visit to Hessle in July 1916, Aelfrida had consistently refused to allow Agatha and Alethea to meet their paternal grandmother because further contact with Anatolia would tend to moral corruption: 'I dare not expose the children to her influence … I *must* protect [them] whatever it costs me'.)[115] Her fourth was to ignore the letter, a move suggested by Chiara quitting the breakfast table in a storm of hysterical tears because Aelfrida refused to tear up the letter immediately, her fifth, to reply but to decline to enter into further correspondence.

To placate her mother, Aelfrida announced that rather than reply herself she would forward the letter to Hal Verey for him to deal with; to her daughters she proclaimed dramatically that she 'would rather see them dead than accepting Anatolia's ideas about life and conduct'.[116] In fact, she followed her final impulse and replied directly to Anatolia: "Dear Mrs Michaelides, Alethea and Agatha are well and happy. If I had no-one but myself to consider, I should welcome the opportunity you gave me of getting in touch with Constantine, whom I have never ceased to love. For the sake of my girls, however, it is clear that there should be no communication whatsoever with your side of the family".[117]

To underline her message, she signed herself 'Aelfrida Graham'. Neither correspondent mentioned Anatolia's recently-deceased husband.

Anatolia's letter had repercussions unanticipated by Aelfrida. In August 1924 during their first holiday abroad with their mother, Agatha and Alethea, no longer the 'little girls' of six and eight remembered by their grandmother but adolescents 'grown up physically and intellectually, and nearly grown up morally and emotionally'[118], pestered Aelfrida with questions about their father: 'what fault had he committed, with whom, [and] why?' Aelfrida, so she said, answered them 'frankly' but as the explanation she gave was that which she now gave to everyone and had even persuaded herself was true, namely that '[she had] had perfect happiness with him' and that Constantine's 'education' by Anatolia, not he himself, was to blame for his infidelity[119] (she did not explain why a man with a 'perfect' marriage should indulge in infidelities), the girls must have been more puzzled by the explanation than by events: 'the whole subject was … acutely painful to Agatha … Alethea thought that I was to blame for being so devoid of suspicion'[120], a double entendre recorded by her mother without further comment.

The following month Aelfrida received a greater shock: 'suddenly, at breakfast, a letter from Constantine'[121]; to her chagrin, the letter was addressed to Alethea, embraced both daughters, and did not mention herself at all. All three Grahams recorded the event in their diaries, Alethea immediately and with excitement ('a letter from Father – seven or eight pages written on both sides … it seemed affectionate and was rather more full of interest for us than I should have imagined probable … think of Father being Consul-General of Valparaiso!')[122], Agatha after reflection ('a letter from Fuvver! Full of Anatolia's spirit and it said, among loving things, that it didn't matter what sort of [life] you led as long as you lived it in the right spirit. So like Anatolia!'[123]; of the three, only Agatha suggests a possible connection between Anatolia's and Constantine's letters), and Aelfrida bitterly, noting that her ex-husband's 'very callous and jaunty letter'[124] was 'just like the old Constantine – confident, grandiloquent, poetical' with its hints that Cambridge was a backwater and that he himself inhabited 'a richer freer world' in which what was important was "not outward things" ('such as adultery and deserting your wife and children', she interpolated) "but the spirit in which any life is lived no matter what or where it is". Worse still, he also – and this was what caused the Oracle and Chiara to urge that the letter be instantly destroyed because 'prompted by the devil himself' – suggested that his daughters join him in Valparaiso.[125]

At this point Agatha indulged in indoctrinated and pious panic: 'Fuvver … wants to get us away from Mother and go and behave like he does with his side of the family, but of course we'd never, never go [because] Fuvver isn't a bit sorry and we … hope he won't write again until he writes to make it all up'.[126] Aelfrida, 'tortured [with] longing' by the fact of Constantine's 'dear handwriting lying close to [her]', decided, after trying to shuffle off responsibility on to the daughter to whom the letter was addressed (Alethea declined to accept it on the grounds that any decision she made would be overridden), that it would be unfair to 'the other Mrs Graham' for Constantine to have the children of his first marriage 'trailing around'.[127] (Alethea, noting that Mildred

Graham 'has some rights now … but it is bad luck on her to wish things were otherwise'[128], failed, like her mother, to note that it might have been 'the other Mrs Graham' who prompted Constantine's and Anatolia's letters in the first place.) She also stated that because Constantine's letter showed 'no contrition … for past sins' (her *sotto voce* comment 'perhaps one day he will repent' refers only to herself and does not consider that Constantine's letter to his daughter was his attempt at reparation with regard to them), neither she nor the girls would reply. She justified her decision by declaring that Agatha and Alethea 'must be kept as far as possible from [the] power and glamour [of] worldly contamination', to which end she would 'pray for them, oh pray, *pray*'.[129]

In May 1926 Constantine tried again. Reading in *The Times* that Alethea had been awarded a scholarship to Girton, he wrote to congratulate her and to send love to Agatha. Alethea being absent, Aelfrida opened the letter ('not a word to me', she noted sadly), ostensibly before passing it on to her elder daughter. But though deciding that 'relations of formal civility' between father and daughter 'could be no danger' to Alethea, pique at Constantine having ignored herself twice (though 'if Constantine wants to make amends I should welcome him with open arms … the past is dead enough for there to be no bitterness, no regret') overcame her better feelings and 'very sadly and with many prayers to God in case my action should be wicked in his sight', she burnt the letter without communicating its contents, an action justified as being a mother's duty to protect a 'clever daughter' from a father interested only in the 'new sensation' of possessing one.[130]

Believing, however, that Anatolia had forwarded to Constantine the letter in which she expressed her continuing love for him and feeling about him (so she said) 'only a calm and dispassionate and benevolent curiosity'[131] negated by a slightly later statement to the effect that 'how I still love the Constantine that used to be!', Aelfrida wrote direct to Constantine himself. 'I did it', she noted, 'from duty, not inclination [and] quite without emotion … beginning "dear Constantine" and ending "Aelfrida" … the contents were nothing but a little family news'.[132] To her chagrin, Constantine did not reply. In July 1927 she tried once more. Having dreamed about Constantine 'almost every night for a fortnight' and wondering if this presaged his presence in England, she wrote without much hope of a reply to the man 'I should love to see again'[133] but of whom she noted that by corresponding with them and even more by meeting them he was liable to 'corrupt Agatha and Alethea'.[134] (Her desire to resume contact with Constantine seems to have coincided with her decision that although she loved Willie Searle 'bitterly', there could be no marriage.) Constantine, inevitably, did not answer but by a strange coincidence she gained news of him by another route: via Jessie Stent, sister of long-dead Archie.

According to Jessie, who had travelled in Central and South America as a governess, 'much good and much bad' was spoken of Constantine in his various postings there; she also informed Aelfrida that 'the new Mrs Graham' was 'a great social success', a description taken by the first Mrs Graham to mean that her successor must be as 'hard and glittering' as Anatolia for Constantine with his Freudian 'mother-fixation' to be happy with her.[135] The information, and a Wagner concert on the radio, set her mind 'running on Constantine' again with particular regard to 'the tumultuous … melodies [he] played me before the birth of Alethea' and a motif from *Siegfried* ('so haunting, so full of poignant emotion') used as a whistled call-sign in the days of their engagement.[136] The memories combined with recent musings about her own body ('more youthful and supple than it was … and … has more acute desires and is capable of more exquisite gratifications')[137] to make her wonder if Constantine and Mildred had children of their own and to wish for more herself; at the same time, however, she realised that 'the Constantine I love is so dead that even God could not recall him … and if I saw Constantine as he is now and if some of the involuntary dreams that torment my sleep came true, that would only make the contrast between the present and the past more bitter'.[138] Little did she know when she wrote these words that within two months she would be receiving an account of him 'as he is now' and that had she not retired to bed when he was within half a mile of her, might even have caught a glimpse of him.

Following a minor road accident, the 'shock' of which gave her a temperature ('but I knew that Willie and Constantine had something to do with it'), Aelfrida took three days in bed to recover. (The shocked and febrile patient occupied herself with writing a foreword to a projected book about Stephen Grellet.) She also hoped to enjoy some much-needed '*quiet*'[139], but quiet, she noted ruefully, was 'not easy to get'[140]: a letter from Constantine's lawyers stating that their client, then on leave in England, wanted to meet his daughters, Alethea, now nineteen and about to start her second year at Girton and Agatha, aged seventeen, in her last year at the Perse School for Girls.

To say that Constantine's demand upset the 'perfect peace of Fordfield' is an understatement. Chiara and the Oracle became 'dreadfully agitated'.[141] Agatha wept, saying that she did not want to meet her father but that if he was remorseful it would be unchristian to refuse to see him. Alethea said she thought Constantine 'had

a right to see his own children and confessed to curiosity with regard to him'.[142] Aelfrida, convinced that Constantine would try to detach her daughters from her by means of emotional appeals made in the privacy of his hotel room, wailed tragically 'melodrama, champagne perhaps, … even Anatolia … I can't allow that!'[143] (The interview was eventually fixed for 15 October 1927 in the prosaic surroundings of Brookfield, Aelfrida's solicitor's house on the corner of Trumpington Road and what was now Brooklands Avenue; champagne was not served.) Privately, however, she expressed gratitude that she had *not* married Willie Searle for then Agatha and Alethea could have reproached her "you loved Willie and your own happiness more than you loved us, so why should we not turn to Fuvver?"[144]

Aware that Constantine steadfastly refused to meet her ('I wish I were seeing him too, not … because I should like show him how a Christian can forgive but [so that I could] talk to him in the most simple manner possible')[145], Aelfrida consoled herself with Beethoven's *Choral Symphony* whose 'supremest melody' had been their wedding march and with another Wagner concert, 'just the things that Constantine loved best'[146]; she also went to St Botolph's to pray '*extra* most suppliant prayers for [the girls] and me and him'[147] before retiring to bed again on 15 October: 'mercifully I have a real bad cold and can … be alone without anyone asking why'.[148] In bed she cogitated on the coming day ('it gives me a strange feeling of sweetness and tenderness that he should be here in Cambridge, seeing it a little sad and misty and autumnal … it must soften his hard heart a little'), on what might have been ('why was he in such a hurry to marry again? We might perhaps have knit up the ravelled sleeve of the past … But for his own action, he might have been here at Fordfield with us all')[149], and on Constantine as she intuited he now was: 'grown middle-aged and hard … so different from the young Greek god whom I loved'.[150]

Shortly before three o'clock on 15 October 1927 Agatha, 'much moved and agitated' and full of 'tempestuous loyalty' to her mother, and Alethea, 'cool and distant' and dressed 'with grave elegance'[151] (sent to Paris to perfect her French before reading Modern Languages at Girton, she seized the opportunity of transforming herself from gauche overweight teenager to *soignée* young woman; she also 'acquired the gentle art of small-talking'[152] and conducted it fluently in English, French, and Italian) set off for their short walk between the house where their mother waited anxiously ('what an ordeal awaits my daughters!')[153] and the parlour where 'the young Greek god' (no doubt equally anxiously) awaited them.

'Today', Agatha diarised, 'we have seen Fuvver ... I should hardly have recognised him. He is fat and placid and plain and wears horn-rimmed spectacles ... Before, he was beautiful – a genius – and ... he was Mother's and ours ... We had the real him – him in his beauty – and it is better so than if Mother had seen him get less beautiful'.[154] (She did; she pasted newspaper cuttings in her diary which show him exactly as described.) That was the first shock. The second was to find her father's 'other wife' there too and to discover her to be not the 'beautiful or wicked or dramatic'[155] creature of Aelfrida's hectic imaginings but 'sensible, intelligent, kind, capable [and] tactful'.[156]

'At first', wrote Agatha, apropos the encounter, 'I thought "what a dusty answer gets the soul / When hot for certainties in this our life"'[157] but then I thought it was better like that. He is a different man ... staid and plain, and he is [Mildred's] and they are happy. Since he is a different man it is natural he should have another wife [and] now perhaps mother won't mind someone else having him. She has got the man she married as much as ever and for always'. She was, however, deeply disappointed at the shattering of her illusions ('I had thought about him so much and he had seemed so magnificent [like] some glorious but inaccessible god ... Hundreds of times I've thought of seeing him – when there was music and beautiful things ... lovely and shadowy ... I had looked for him to come back so much that I felt he couldn't come back') but consoled herself that 'the coming back was in me' and that she still had her father 'as much as ever and for always'.[158]

There was, of course, a debriefing at Fordfield after 'the dreaded interview'.[159] Alethea had 'expected to feel some strange emotion'[160] on meeting her father again after nearly a decade but appears to have adopted her 'most suave society manner, without defiance or confusion [to show] how admirably she got on without him'; she also informed her mother that Constantine was 'without charm and rather a bore' and that she was 'well rid of him'. (By contrast, she extolled the second Mrs Graham's charms so hard that, hearing about her 'pleasant-looking [and] quietly dressed and exceedingly friendly' successor, Aelfrida was moved to the kind of snide remark more usually aimed at the wives of Little Friends: 'I suppose in America, where one marriage in seven is dissolved, one expects to be constantly meeting one's husband's children by former wives').)[161] But though Alethea suppressed her emotions in her diary and in public, Agatha expressed hers in dramatically evocative poetry.

Two traumatic events had already taken place in Agatha's short life at the corner where she and Alethea parted from a father they might never see again. Aged five, she had fallen six feet from a bridge spanning Hobson's Brook, to be rescued, tearful, wet, and muddy by Octavie[162]; aged sixteen, she was knocked down by a car within a few feet of and almost on the same date as her earlier mishap, emerging faint but otherwise unhurt from beneath the wheels[163]; on 15 October 1927 she watched her father disappear once more from her life:

*Mist on an Autumn Evening*
... "You were real when I saw you lately under the
    lamp-post,
Where round the circle of light the mist lay curled:
But now you have stepped into the mist and are
    transfigured,
And now you have vanished over the edge of the
    world ...
Whether you are of the dead or of the living,
When you shook off the light and stepped out over
    the fen,
My thoughts will always see you far and cloud-wrapped,
My vision never bring you back again".[164]

Aelfrida too committed her thoughts to paper but in melodramatic prose. Though prepared to believe that neither daughter found Constantine or his life-style beguiling (she had been concerned lest they feel a 'rush of affection towards the man who is after all, their father' and that 'vistas of [the] wonderful amusing worlds' he inhabited might lure them away from her)[165], she was nevertheless devastated by their account of lost glamour, stating sadly 'my Constantine is more dead than if he had been killed in the war'[166] and 'how much better if he had gone to the war and died a splendid pagan death!'[167] (And, one might say, have made a 'proper' widow of her.) And in view of what was to transpire as a result of Constantine's reappearance in his daughters lives, it might have been better for everyone had her wish been granted.

Before leaving England, Constantine made further overtures to both girls, asking them to meet him in London singly or together. Alethea refused point blank, saying she had no wish to see her father again and asked the Mistress of Girton to provide an alibi by refusing her an exeat, a request to which that lady, much amused, acceded. Agatha also refused but refusal rendered her 'sad and thoughtful'[168] because 'I don't want him to be sent away and think we didn't love him because then he would never come back to us at all'.[169] It was, significantly, to Agatha, his 'Greek' daughter, that Constantine addressed subsequent letters, congratulating her on winning a scholarship to Girton in 1928 ('his hand-writing', wrote Aelfrida, 'lacks the firm bold originality it used to have'; she was right and it was more legible and his thoughts more intelligible as a result)[170], and in 1929 sending 'a rather middle-aged letter' concerning which Agatha made no comment but which caused a tug at Aelfrida's heartstrings, for her Greek god, once 'the incarnation of youth, radiant and unconquerable', was now a spatted and spectacled mortal of forty-six who 'had left youth so far behind [that] he could not even remember what it felt like'.[171]

## Notes

1  GCPPT 1|1|23 25 November 1918.
2  ibid. 24 January 1919.
3  ibid. 6 February 1919.
4  ibid. 20 February 1919.
5  GCPPT 1|1|25 12 August 1920.
6  GCPPT 1|1|32 17 May 1926.
7  GCPPG A2.1 19 May 1926.
8  GCPPG A1.1 17 June 1928.
9  GCPPT 1|1|27 27 September 1923. A prescient joke in the *MCJ* (GCPPT 2|2a vol 2 no 2) of September 1903 details an advertisement for "Dr Emptyhead's Educational Establishment", the said doctor's qualifications being "6 years' residence at St Caths' and a 4th class degree".
10 GCPPT 1|1|28 8 November 1924.
11 ibid. 9 November 1924.
12 GCPPG A1.1 8 November 1924.
13 GCPPT 1|1|28 10 November 1924.
14 ibid.11 November 1924.
15 GCPPT 1|1|44 9 June 1933. An even more prescient joke appears in the October 1903 edition of the *MCJ* (GCPPT 2|2a vol 2 No 3). "Anubis Ltd" casts the horoscope of one "Sir Percival", describing men like him as "much inclined to bachelorhood, though they often end in marriage".
16 GCPPT 1|1|27 16 June 1923.
17 ibid.
18 GCPPT 1|1|30 4 June 1925.
19 GCPPG A1.1 7 December 1924.
20 GCPPT 1|1|23 28 February 1919.
21 GCPPT 1|1|27 23 January 1924.
22 GCPPT 1|1|30 16 November 1925.
23 GCPPT 1|1|23 14 October 1918.
   GCPPT 1|1|28 30 September 1924.
24 GCPPT 1|1|28 5 October 1924.
25 GCPPT 1|1|34 29 June 1927.
26 ibid. 13 and 19 July 1927.
27 Tillyard, Ae. *Spiritual Exercises* p vii. Edward Thomas is sympathetically depicted in one of Aelfrida's *romans-à-clef (Haste to the Wedding)* as 'Dr Ezra Gotobed', a middle-aged Cambridge geologist who woos the young heroine with presents of minerals and precious stones and is thoroughly dejected when she plights her troth to another man.
28 GCPPT 1|1|34 31 July 1927.
29 GCPPT 1|1|23 3 February 1919.
30 GCPPT 1|1|26 9 April 1922.
31 GCPPT 1|1|25 7 December 1920.
32 GCPPT 1|1|34 31 July 1927.
33 GCPPT 1|1|36 24 February 1929.
34 GCPPT 1|1|20 9 March 1915.
35 GCPPT 1|1|25 24 August 1919.
36 GCPPT 1|1|27 2 September 1923.
37 ibid. 7 October 1923.
38 GCPPT 1|1|19 31 May 1914.

39 GCPPT 1|1|23 21 April 1919.
40 ibid. 1 January 1919.
41 ibid. 4 January 1919.
42 GCPPT 1|1|24 25 August 1919.
43 ibid. 11 July 1919.
44 GCPPT 1|1|32 4 April 1926.
45 GCPPT 1|1|27 16 June 1923.
46 ibid. 12 June 1923.
47 GCPPT 1|1|32 4 April 1926. Alethea described Eardley Davidson as 'sympathetic, charming and amusing [and] a little whimsical', Catherine as fat, sweet and 'rather pathetic' (GCPPG A1.1 5 April 1926).
48 GCPPT 1|1|40 18 October 1931.
49 GCPPT 1|1|44 7 May 1933.
50 GCPPT 1|1|42 9 October 1932.
51 ibid. 20 September 1932.
52 Thomas Rice Henn (1901–1974) was the son of Francis Henn, barrister-at-law, of Paradise, Ennis, County Clare. After gaining a first in the Cambridge English Tripos in 1922, he became successively Fellow, Senior Tutor and President of his old college, St Catharine's. A specialist in Anglo-Irish literature, Henn later became the Cambridge Professor of English. His autobiography *Five Arches* (1980) provides an interesting account of life in Ireland and Cambridge but does not mention Aelfrida.
53 Tom Henn's description of Eustace Tillyard (*Five Arches* p 95) praises him as "a brilliant teacher, co-operating with his pupils rather than attempting to impose his personality upon them; infinitely wise and mature, with a love of all great literature which he invariably managed to communicate".
54 William Henn CBE MVO graduated in 1914 (he was an exhibitioner at Magdalene College, Cambridge when Aelfrida encountered him in 1913) and immediately joined the army. Wounded at Gallipoli, he later joined the Egyptian Civil Service and was promoted to Chief of Police at Alexandria. Tom Henn, from whose *Five Arches* (p 22) these details are taken, describes him as "good in a boat [and] he also wrote excellent light verse". A sample of Billy Henn's verse, *The Reefs of Aran,* which describes how "the long white reefs of Aran" swamp "the reeling curragh" can be found in *The Cambridge Magazine* vol III no 23 23 May 1914 p 633.
55 GCPPT 1|1|27 18 June 1923.
56 Tom Henn's *Selected Poems* were published in 1958.
57 GCPPT 1|1|27 5 December 1923.
58 GCPPT 1|1|30 17 May 1925. 'Brandon' is an earlier spelling of 'Brendan', the sixth century Irish saint and patron of sailors.
59 GCPPT 1|1|32 30 April 1926.
60 GCPPG A2.1 18 December 1926.
61 GCPPT 1|1|32 29 August 1926.
62 GCPPT 1|1|32 19 September 1926. According to Agatha, Tom asked Aelfrida if he could continue being friends with her as much as before 'because he is very fond of Mother and used to confide in her'; she also notes that of the four Tillyard women invited to Tom's wedding only Chiara went, Aelfrida and her daughters being actually or ostensibly unable to afford to do so (GCPPG A2.1 23 September 1926). Aelfrida herself makes no comment regarding the only recorded wedding invitation ever received from an actual or aspirant Little Friend.
63 GCPPG A1.1 17 June 1928.
64 GCPPG A2.1 18 December 1926.
65 GCPPT 1|1|36 7 July 1929. Poem V111 (*Grand Testament*) in Tom Henn's *Selected Poems 1958* in which the poet writes that his "life's plan [was] broken at twenty" because Ireland was then "a land of civil war", also describes how "only Tillyard's wisdom" helped him, a young man "Ignorant, fearful of women, and driven to hide [his] fear / In a dim worship of their power and strength and comfort", through the torments of his early Cambridge years. Notes at the back of the (unpaginated) volume state Henn's intention to "set ... out more fully and less equivocally than is usual" otherwise unexplained references in

the poems but leave his 'Tillyard' reference equivocal: Eustace Tillyard's 'wisdom' was certainly helpful in terms of tutoring and mentoring but it was to Aelfrida, a fellow poet writing under the name 'Tillyard', that Henn turned for help with regard to relationships with women.

66 GCPPT 1|1|36 8 July 1929.
67 GCPPT 1|1|28 3 March 1924.
68 ibid. 7 September 1924.
69 A poem written by 21-year-old Julius to and about his mother for her birthday ("to CST age 39, Sept 19th 1905"; she was actually 51) suggests that both are possible, *Katesbloom* being both a love poem ("Blossom nor fade! 'neath moonlight's pride / When golden sun to rest is laid / Katesbloom, with hues from both supplied / Blossom nor fade") and a reminder of the death of Conrad: "blooms that died … sleep soft beneath thy shade" (GCPPT 2|2a vol 2 No 2 September 1903). Like all 'Katie Wetenhall's' young men, though for different reasons, Julius' preferred postal address was 'Kateside' (GCPPT 2|27|2(2)).
70 GCPPG A1.1 20 November 1904.
71 GCPPT 1|1|30 27 December 1924.
72 ibid. 15 December 1924.
73 GCPPT 1|1|26 18 December 1921.
74 GCPPT 1|1|30 26 October 1925.
75 ibid. 17 November 1925. Nadja was aware of Mina's existence, having received from and sent to Julius "one or two letters" after their final parting; her last letter, ironically, was to wish Julius "joy of [his] betrothal" (GCPPT 2|26|3 *Nadja Laptchinski*).
76 GCPPT 1|1|28 23 November 1924.
77 ibid. 21 November 1924.
78 GCPPT 2|26|3 *Nadja Laptchinski*.
79 GCPPG A1.1 3 August–16 December 1926 in the list of dramatis personae which ends the volume. Nadja's life had always been difficult and often tragic. Born to wealthy and cultured parents, her father had died comparatively young and her mother reduced to penury by the Russian Revolution One of five siblings, Nadja became a nurse during the Russo-Japanese war of 1902/5, meeting Julius for the first time in November 1905 when in Naples recovering from her wartime experiences. (Prior to meeting Julius, she had been, so she said, engaged to four men, including a father and son, one of whom died of tuberculosis, the others by murder or suicide.) Following the breakdown of her engagement to Julius, the Great War, and the Russian Revolution, Nadja became a teacher in a Spartan co-educational boarding school in Petrograd. Escaping to England on the pretext of improving her English, she arrived wearing a superb fur coat over patched clothes and carrying the family jewels (entrusted to friends in Finland at the start of the war) from which she selected a gold and diamond crucifix and gave it to Aelfrida, who, in spite of her poetic assertion that she "never cared for gems", wore it conspicuously for years.
80 ibid. 21 November 1927.
81 ibid. 21 October 1925.
82 GCPPT 1|1|46 26 August 1934.
83 GCPPT 2|26|3 *Nadja Laptchinski*.
84 GCPPT 1|1|28 1 December 1924.
85 ibid. 21 November 1924.
86 ibid. 3 December 1924.
87 ibid. 25 November 1924.
88 GCPPT 1|1|30 18 October 1925. At the time of his meeting with Aelfrida, Peter Kapitza (1894–1984), described by her as a Russian aristocrat who had lost his fortune in the Revolution and his wife and children to typhoid before coming to England, was working at Cambridge's Cavendish Laboratory. In fact, he came from a professional family of Polish land owning descent and his wife (and her newborn baby) and young son had died of Spanish influenza and scarlet fever respectively.
89 GCPPT 1|1|35 8 November 1927. Lydia, an actress as well as a dancer, appears in Aelfrida's 1930 novel *O Passionate World* (p 90) as

'Lydia Andraeona', the leading lady in a play entitled *Silver Shoes* in which she is described as "more subtle than Sarah Bernhardt, more appealing than Duse, more starry and remote than Sybil Thorndike", none of whom Aelfrida had ever seen. For details of Lydia Lopokova and her relationship with Maynard and Florence Keynes, see Skidelsky, R. *John Maynard Keynes*.
90 GCPPT 1|1|30 13 October 1925.
91 GCPPG A2.1 17 September 1925.
92 Doctor (later Sir) Pendrill Varrier-Jones (1883–1941) was a Cambridge pathologist appointed County Tuberculosis Officer whose vision for the Papworth Village Settlement saw it become a thriving treatment and rehabilitation centre by the time of his early and sudden death. (For further details see Birks, E. *Papworth Hospital … Pendrill Varrier-Jones' dream realised*. 1999). Varrier-Jones was forty-three when he encountered Nadja, then in her late forties.
93 CPPT 2|26|3 *Nadja Laptchinski*. Aelfrida wrongly gives Matron's name as 'Bourn'.
94 GCPPT 1|1|39 24 April 1931.
95 GCPPT 1|1|32 11 February 1926.
96 ibid. 11 May 1926.
97 GCPPT 1|1|34 22 April 1927.
98 GCPPT 1|1|32 12 March 1926.
99 ibid. 7 March 1926.
100 ibid. 13 March 1926.
101 ibid. 3 February 1926.
102 GCPPT 2|26|3 *Nadja Laptchinski*.
103 GCPPT 1|1|35 25 November 1927.
104 Tillyard, Ae *Can I be a Mystic?* pp 83–84.
105 ibid.
106 GCPPT 1|1|37 29 January 1930.
107 GCPPT 1|1|37 7 and 10 June 1930.
108 GCPPT 1|1|44 7 May 1933.
109 GCPPT 2|26|3 *Nadja Laptchinski*. The version given here of Nadja's return to Russia differs in important details from that given in Aelfrida's contemporary diary entries. On 10 August 1934 Nadja arrived in Cambridge out of work and so deep in persecution mania as to be unemployable. Aelfrida, determined to rid herself of all encumbrances at this point in her life (Julius absented himself literally and metaphorically from his sister's dilemma), persuaded Nadja that it was her duty to return to Russia to attend her sick mother. (She also noted cruelly that because everyone in Stalinist Russia suffered from persecution mania, Nadja's would pass unnoticed). She was aided and abetted in this by Peter Kapitza who persuaded Nadja that conditions in Russia were not as black as painted (GCPPT 1|1|46 10 and 28 August 1934). (Ironically, Kapitza himself was recalled to Russia in 1934 on the same pretext and detained there for two years, much to the dismay of fellow Cambridge scientists, before being allowed to return to England). In December 1934, however, Aelfrida heard that a 'new Red Terror' had begun in the country to which she had just persuaded poor mad Nadja to return (GCPPT 1|1|46 6 December 1934); she therefore concealed her (and Julius') heartless behaviour by having Nadja recalled by the Russian authorities in her fictionalised version of Nadja's life, a life to which Julius contributed a short and expurgated version of his relationship with her.
110 GCPPT 1|1|23 20 February 1919.
111 GCPPT 1|1|22 6 April 1918.
112 ibid. 2 July 1918.
113 GCPPT 1|1|28 4 July 1924 Alethea describes the letter as 'gushing [and] very characteristic' (GCPPG A1.1 6 July 1924 ). Her account differs in tone and detail from Aelfrida's.
114 GCPPT 1|1|28 5 July 1924.
115 GCPPT 1|1|22 2 and 10 July 1918.
116 GCPPT 1|1|28 5 July 1924.
117 ibid. 16 July 1924.

118 GCPPT 1|1|29 23 August 1924.

119 GCPPT 1|1|34 19 June 1927.

120 GCPPT 1|1|29 9 August 1924.

121 GCPPT 1|1|28 24 September 1924.

122 GCPPG A1.1 24 September 1924. According to *Who Was Who* Constantine, had been successively chargé d'affaires at Panama and "with the legation at Santiago" for a year; he was now (1923–1930) HM Consul-General for the Republic of Chile at Valparaiso.

123 GCPPG A2.1 9 October 1924.

124 GCPPT 1|1|30 14 March 1925.

125 GCPPT 1|1|28 24 September 1924.

126 GCPPG A2.1 19 October 1924.

127 GCPPT 1|1|28 24 September 1924

128 GCPPG A1.1 24 September 1924.

129 GCPPT 1|1|28 24 September 1924.

130 GCPPT 1|1|32 25, 26 and 27 May 1926.

131 ibid. 25 May 1926.

132 ibid. 30 October 1926.

133 GCPPT 1|1|34 7 and 8 July 1927.

134 ibid. 24 June 1927.

135 ibid. 14 August 1927.

136 ibid. 22 August 1927. The notion, albeit with a different motif, was used as 'copy' in Aelfrida's 1931 novel *Haste to the Wedding*.

137 ibid. 20 August 1927.

138 ibid. 22 August 1927.

139 ibid. 20 and 24 September 1927.

140 ibid. 26 September 1927.

141 ibid.

142 ibid. 20 September 1927.

143 ibid. 26 September 1927.

144 ibid. 20 September 1927.

145 GCPPT 1|1|34 26 September 1927
GCPPT 1|1|35 14 October 1927.

146 GCPPT 1|1|34 7 October 1927
GCPPT 1|1|35 15 October 1927.

147 GCPPT 1|1|35 14 October 1927.

148 GCPPT 1|1|25 15 October 1927.

149 GCPPT 1|1|34 24 September 1927
GCPPT 1|1|35 15 October 1927.

150 GCPPT 1|1|34 24 September 1927.

151 GCPPT 1|1|35 15 October 1927.

152 GCPPG A2.1 9 December 1926.

153 GCPPT 1|1|35 15 October 1927.

154 *Agatha's Diary* [15] October [1927] (MTC).

155 GCPPT 1|1|35 15 October 1927.

156 *Agatha's Diary* [15] October [1927] (MTC). Agatha's handwriting is now very like her father's in his undergraduate days.

157 The entirely appropriate lines are taken from *Modern Love*, a poem by George Meredith (1828–1909), which runs in part: "Thus piteously Love closed what he begat: / The union of this ever diverse pair! / These two were rapid falcons in a snare,/ Condemned to do the flitting of a bat! / Lovers beneath the surging sky of May / They wandered once; clear as the dew on flowers: / But they fed not on the advancing hours: / Their hearts held cravings for the buried day. / Then each applied to each that fatal knife, / Deep, questioning, which probes to endless dole. / Ah, what a dusty answer gets the soul / When hot for certainties in this our life! / In tragic hints here see what evermore / Moves dark, as yonder midnight ocean's force". Rosamund Lehmann (1901–1990), at Girton shortly before Alethea, published her first and, for its time, sensational, novel *Dusty Answer* in 1927, and it is possible that Agatha's attention was drawn to Meredith's poem as a result of reading it.

158 *Agatha's Diary* [15] October [1927] (MTC).

159 GCPPT 1|1|35 16 October 1927.

160 GCPPG A1.1 14 January 1928.

161 GCPPT 1|1|35 16 October 1927.

162 GCPPT 1|1a *Agatha's Record Book* 21 August 1915.

163 GCPPT 1|1|32 29 August 1926.

164 *Mist on an Autumn Evening* appears in a group of poems entitled *Poems 1927* 'in order of writing' included at the end of the volume of Agatha's diary which covers 15 October 1927. Another poem appears in the same volume and by context was written shortly after 25 December 1927, the day on which Constantine sailed for South America. Although it does not appear at first sight to refer to Constantine, this and other resonances suggest that it does:
To an Island.
"We will always remember./ Your rocks of crimson stone / Shall stand out clear in the night of our forgetting / Once we have known./ We will never forget red. / Your cliffs will stand out red, / And your sad birds cry to us across the silence / When we are dead".
In 1926 Agatha, with Aelfrida and Alethea, paid a visit to Perros Guirec in Brittany, a place whose 'reckless masses of granite' of a vivid coral colour were remarked on by both Aelfrida and her younger daughter (GCPPT 1|1|33 20 July 1926). Agatha also remarked upon the fact that Constantine visited Perros Guirec as a young boy (GCPPG A2.1 'The Abroad Supplement' 15 July–13 August 1926). The Russian word for 'red' (*krasny*) is also used to describe something beautiful, a fact Agatha could have learnt from either Julius or Nadja. Is it therefore too fanciful to see in Agatha's poem Constantine as the once-beautiful 'island' his daughters "…will never forget …/ Though the torn waves roll between, / They shall not carry your darkened memory seaward once we have seen".

165 GCPPT 1|1|35 15 and 16 October 1927.

166 ibid. 16 October 1927.

167 GCPPT 1|1|34 24 September 1927.

168 GCPPT 1|1|35 23 October 1927.

169 *Agatha's Diary* [15] October [1927] (MCT).

170 GCPPT 1|1|35 5 July 1928.

171 GCPPT 1|1|36 22 January 1929.

# Universal Aunt

At some point during the volume of her diary covering the years 1925–26 Aelfrida wrote a reminder to herself inside the back cover: 'Discipline. Humility. Secrecy'.[1] Discipline seemed easy: 'I will … make a Rule for myself and live by it', the necessary escape clause being 'as far as I can'. Secrecy was difficult to one whose chief interest and topic of conversation was herself and because she felt impelled 'to help people if I can', something not easily done by stealth. Humility was more difficult: 'I have been subtly flattered at being thought an expert on Mysticism … that must stop'. (It did not, and humble or humbling tasks carried out for other people were recorded in her diary for a future biographer's benefit.) She did, however, 'try and be thought quite commonplace and ordinary … and live … without being noticed'[2], though had she not been 'noticed' she might have been annoyed. She was also bound to fail; indeed, one might go so far as to say that so comprehensively did she fail with regard to all three reminders that the years 1926 to 1930 were some of the happiest of her life for during that time she so far freed herself from 'personal preoccupations' as to be able 'to get on with the work of the world'[3] without too much repining. 'Go to it, Aelfrida, Universal Aunt'[4], she admonished herself – and 'to it' she went.

The change in Aelfrida's outlook on life was noted by outsiders as early as March 1925 and liberation was expressed in different ways. As late as the time of her decree nisi in August 1921, she dressed in the long skirts, demure blouses, and waist-cinching belts fashionable at the time of her abortive courtship of John Forbes Cameron and marriage to Constantine Graham; she also wore her hair in the now very old-fashioned 'aureole' arrangement adopted when she first 'put her hair up' in 1900. Inspired, it may be, by Constantine's attempts in Lyons to buy her more fashionable clothes, by public appearances in lecture room and divorce court, and by pressure from daughters clothes-conscious from childhood, Aelfrida raised her hems and updated her wardrobe by buying a new coat and skirt (the first since 1912) of putty-coloured gabardine with a cream crêpe-de-chine blouse to match.[5] Three years later she adopted the smock-dresses favoured by Phyllis, albeit Aelfrida's, as befitted one who wore a large cross on her bosom,

**Eustace and Phyllis Tillyard with Stephen Tillyard**

were more subdued in pattern and colour, and for everyday use the hairstyle 'parted in the middle and braided behind', previously worn only in the evenings. In May 1926, however, she had her hair bobbed ('shingled') in the then fashionable style adopted by her daughters, stating that short hair was more comfortable and convenient and that because of her current desire 'to pass as unobserved as possible' in the interests of discipline, humility, and secrecy and because a centre parting and braided hair, together with her ostentatious pectoral cross, made her look 'rather saintly' (a fact on which people had commented to Agatha), she felt she ought 'to have no pretensions, not even this unintentional hypocrisy'. And so, 'as "everybody" is shingled', she was shingled herself. Finding the hairstyle '*most* becoming'[6] (an inadvertent result at variance with her wish to be as little noticed as possible), she then adopted the style of dress worn by Agatha and Alethea which, with its cloche hats and columnar coats and dresses, showed her tall trim figure to great advantage and made her appear not so much 'saintly' as indistinguishable from her equally tall and modishly-dressed daughters.

A new look was accompanied by a new outlook on life. New Year's Day 1927 saw Aelfrida in a reflective mood quite different from that formerly lavished on rededications of her Oath of Obligation to her Great Work.[7] In some respects, she wrote, 'I have advanced, as perhaps one does automatically as one grows older. I have learned more of the art of communion with God'. (True.) 'I judge my neighbour less harshly'. (Untrue; of a recently-widowed lady, she wrote that the latter was 'much improved by … loss of her professor's-wife-status'.)[8] 'I am more careful not to give pain and readier to … plan small satisfactions for people'. (Willie Searle might have disagreed.) She was grateful, she added, for 'Fordfield and my dear ones' (i.e. the parents whose attitude towards another blessing, her 'splendid daughters', endangered the 'perfect peace' of the house they shared), for 'the blessings one took for granted when one was young' (a roof over her head, food for which she did not have to forage, and Chiara's money to pay for it all) and 'for the inner life which flows its deep quiet (*sic*) course'. On the other hand, 'I shall never know a man's touch again' (soon to be proved untrue), 'never conceive another child' (true, but there would be a quiverful of literary 'babies'), her books were a 'failure' (partly true, and soon to be partly remedied) and her message unappreciated: 'I suffer, but I submit'.[9] Then again, and in spite of substantial improvement in her health, having 'always … a pain somewhere' suggested abandonment of other physical penances[10]; indeed, she went so far as to decide that her former pride in disdaining comfort and convenience had resulted only in her 'getting ill and being a nuisance to everyone' and that it was better to do as she did now: restraining her taste for 'devoting' herself in favour of looking after herself 'as carefully as if I were my own child' and keeping 'out of the doctor's hands' as a result. Even the thought that self-protective behaviour might damage her character failed to dent her resolve: 'it is better to be saintly than to be sensible' and 'the fact is, I doubt my capacity for saintliness and I think I may as well be sensible'.[11]

Her twentieth wedding anniversary on 19 January 1927 gave rise to reflections on what she might have done, given her time over again, to have 'held' Constantine: 'if I had been a worse woman … capricious, exacting and tyrannical, less devoted to religion and babies, more given to spending money on myself and my personal adornment [and had] always put myself first and expected him to do the same … I might have pulled it off'. (Some people, she added with reference to flirtations with Little Friends, 'might have thought I gave him grounds for jealousy … but no! he knew me too well'.)[12] It was, she decided after 'serious' and revealing thinking, her devotion to religion in general and to 'detachment' in particular which even more than physical separation resulting from the Great War, was the basis of the rupture between her former husband and herself.

'Detachment' – or lack of it – was, and continued to be, 'the central problem of [her] life' and the basis of nearly 'all the mistakes [she had] made'. The problem, of course, was how to love her neighbour (or a husband or a would-be husband) 'ardently and sensitively' and yet preserve her relationship with God as an inviolate thing apart ('a flame in a windless place')[13]; worse still, it had been at times when she was 'striving most to be "detached"' that she fell in love with men she was to marry or not marry, with the result that not even an ability to rise above mere sentimentality could salvage relationships in which one party's 'detachment' appeared as indifference to the other. It was, however, a mistake 'to consider "detachment" as an *alternative* to human affections [and] as though the two great commandments ["thou shalt love the Lord thy God with all thy heart and with all thy soul and with all thy might" and "thou shalt love thy neighbour as thyself"][14] were 'an "either-or" proposition [for] if the heart tries to love God *instead* of human beings or to the exclusion of human beings, it either fails miserably or becomes inhuman or merely deceives itself'. It was equally wrong 'to flee the world, to try to keep oneself apart'; far better was to 'accept it … to know you are part of a humanity, to love all men [and] never feel … aloof or superior'. (And if 'the pain of loving them became too much', she added, pain must be accepted as a going-through of the fiery furnace 'with the Son of God at your side'.) Realising that she herself was 'utterly and completely incapable' of doing without 'human consolations', that she needed 'people to love as much as I need God to love', that she could never be 'altogether unhappy' as long as there remained one person in the world on whom she could lavish affection, and that having Agatha and Alethea to love made her 'utterly content', Aelfrida turned not so much away from God (because 'loving Him is the highest joy and good of which we are capable')[15] as towards the world she longed to embrace, noting in her diary how silly it was of fellow Cambridge poet Frances Cornford to talk of the "long littleness of life" when she herself believed life was 'amazing and awe-inspiring beyond words'.[16] And to be experienced with 'a wonderful zest and exhilaration in living'.[17]

*Joie de vivre* extended even to her visions which throughout this time were almost uniformly joyous; indeed, she records only two which recall earlier experiences of 'universal consciousness' of the misery of the human condition, one being 'crowds of black figures ... clinging to each other because of terror of death' (a vision which may have been inspired by the sight of 'vast wracks of jagged clouds scudding across the sky' as she walked on Coe Fen)[18], the other 'hours of almost agonised pain in which all the sorrows of the world seemed to pierce [her] like ten thousand swords' and which caused her to fret that she could do nothing 'to enlarge the bounds of compassion' except 'speak – write – urge people to be kinder, the one to the other'. But recognising her impotence in the face of such 'overwhelming sorrow', what could she do but turn to 'any foolish relief – fall in love, God knows what!'[19] to lift her mood. Happiness, on the other hand, expressed itself in luminously colourful visions and in a sense of bodily and spiritual elevation. She also experienced sensations of God conceived as pure invisible light and Jesus as a prism breaking up the light 'into glorious colours of attributes and virtues' (though having read 'too much psychoanalysis' she could never, she confessed, become 'a "Christo-centric mystic"' on the strength of visions like this because of a fear that her 'devotion was tainted with sensuality'); of God in His 'dazzling infinity and perfection' or as Light 'radiating out through an infinite concourse of spirits'[20]; in Little St Mary's, of 'all sentient beings in dazzling myriads upon myriads [bowing] down before God's holiness' ('it was quite difficult to make contact with the earth again and to get on my bicycle and ride home')[21]; in Brooklands Avenue, of God 'so intense, so burning, that I almost knelt there in the path'.[22]

Two experiences, described at length, were particularly impressive. The first took place after she had been 'lunching Miss Major'[23], 'a dear, in spite of wearing a very short skirt and very tight grey alpaca dress and being [Mistress] of Girton', and had later gone to church 'very contrite' to consider that her thoughts and attention were running more on Alethea's academic career than on God. She then found St Botolph's beginning 'to fade and blur and I knew I was going to have an ecstasy. I as it were said "oh *please* don't let anything happen that anyone could notice" [just] as everything ceased to be except God. He was felt chiefly as *light*, light wholly spiritual but shafting out to find me and surrounding me with a cone of light and saying "you are mine"'.[24] The second occurred while returning in sombre mood from sick-visiting in Romsey Town, 'one of the ugliest parts of Cambridge'. Crossing Mill Road bridge, she suddenly 'passed into another mode of existence [in which] matter

became insubstantial, unreal, spirit visible and coherent [and] spiritual light flooded the world and maintained it in being. As for myself, I was lifted ... with joy so that I could hardly press my feet to the ground. "Good heavens!" I said, "this is what levitation feels like. If I don't take care I shall be floating away over the railway lines and what a fool I shall look then". For a moment I was quite seriously alarmed'. The glory of the experience remained with her until she turned in at Fordfield gate.[25]

Visions like these, though isolated experiences, were representative of an elevated and energised mood which persisted for weeks at a time, weeks in which Aelfrida experienced both a 'continuous [and] wholly spiritual exaltation' interspersed with flashes of 'a flame of ecstasy and universal consciousness' during which she soared free of the world 'singing the praises of God' and from which she returned to find people around her 'attractive and loveable'.[26] There were also moments in which 'the usual quiet radiance ... of God's presence' burgeoned into an 'almost too dazzling glow ... as though I were touching the Source of Thought and Beauty [and had] a direct and immediate apprehension of God [and] of the very essence of life and creative being itself'.[27] But even more significant than a new relationship to God 'more vivid and real than love, more even than motherhood', was realisation that earlier leanings 'toward the conventual life and all that it implies of asceticism and renunciation of earthly joys' was reaction to Constantine's desertion, now placed in proper perspective: 'I am a mystic ... but I am not a nun. I love to watch life and the older I get the more I love to watch it. I find people ... simply too enthralling. Life is too fascinating, too vivid, too bewildering, too swift, too wonderful. Nuns oughtn't to feel like that!'[28] So she plunged back into the earthly joys and human affections she once sought to renounce but had never truly abandoned.

Joys began with nephews and nieces. On 29 July 1920 she had recorded 'great news – Stephen is born!'[29] Meeting her nephew for the first time she recorded that Stephen was '*most* intelligent-looking' and 'absurdly' like Eustace[30] of whom she noted that although 'a splendid father', he was 'a little solemnised by paternity'. (Of Stephen's mother she noted tartly that 'motherhood has aged Phyllis very much' but decided that her sister-in-law's preference for husbands over babies was something she herself should have emulated in her own marriage.)[31] Thereafter little Stephen and his secular and 'hardening' babyhood occupied much of her time, energy, and diary. Stephen 'has *blonde cendré* curls'[32], she recorded after one visit, and his short stays at Fordfield during his parents' absence on holiday made her positively rhapsodic: 'it is lovely having Stephen here ... it feels quite like having a son of my own. The world narrows when a baby comes into the house … *These* are the important things – one little human being and all the arrangements for his welfare'[33], arrangements, it has to be said, left almost entirely to Chiara and his nursemaid. (The entry is doubly ironic given that granting of her decree absolute two days later meant that the 'son of her own' who might have saved her marriage was unlikely to be engendered by Constantine.) Eustace and Phyllis' move to a larger house in Sawston in 1921 resulted in many bicycle rides back and forth, and the birth of Stephen's sister in February 1922 ('Chiara, of course, is disappointed that the baby is a girl; I feel nothing but delight … she is to bear the delightful name of Veronica') brought further happiness, particularly because Veronica was not 'brought up on such "modern lines" as her brother'.[34]

Having two babies to cherish made Aelfrida broody ('I have so much special baby-love to give')[35], the more so when she took charge for nearly three weeks in the summer of 1923 while Eustace and Phyllis holidayed in France: 'Phyllis' babies', she wrote, 'are so particularly charming'.[36] She was also delighted to discover that a third baby was due in July 1924 and even more delighted when the child was another girl (Chiara expressed her usual 'deep disgust' at the child's sex)[37], even though Angela was 'a very plain baby [with] a pug nose and a bucolic expression'.[38]

As 'Aunt Aelfrida' to three 'handsome, lively and sweet'[39] little Tillyards, Aelfrida 'could not help' making frequent visits, visits made easier by their parents' move to Merton House in Cambridge's Queens Road in late 1924. Presents, sometimes sweets, more often educational, made the children 'most pleased to see [her]'[40], unlike their mother, of whom she noted sourly 'I wish Phyllis would look a *little* more pleased ... when … I call'[41], 'Aunt Aelfrida's' barbed hints about the untidy state of their nursery doing little to endear her to a sister-in-law with three children under five.

Aelfrida seems to have visited Merton House less frequently following her epistolary disagreement with Phyllis of September 1926 on matters of expenditure; indeed, there seems to have been something of a conscious effort on Eustace's and Phyllis' part to distance 'Aunt Aelfrida' from her Cambridge nephews and nieces, chiefly because they disapproved of her religiosity but possibly for other reasons too. But diminution of contact as they developed into 'a very solemn little boy with a great sense of the importance of material possessions' who would perhaps be 'a great economist – though I destine him for the Church'[42] (Stephen became a teacher, then a librarian, and a Quaker) or 'quite the little schoolgirl'[43] (Veronica) or became merely 'less stolid than usual'[44]

(Angela), made Aelfrida sad: 'I see so little of them and they are so sweet'.[45]

'Adorable' Veronica was her favourite. In March 1931, Veronica being now nine and Aelfrida and Chiara having invited her to lunch (minus siblings) at Fordfield, her aunt recorded of Veronica and herself 'Oh! we understand each other and we love each other so much we just look at each other and *dream*!'[46]; eighteen months later, again over lunch, Aelfrida and the 'dignified, serene and charming' Veronica 'enjoyed our secret understanding to the full'.[47] It was, however, this 'secret understanding' which provoked further trouble with Veronica's parents.

In August 1933 Aelfrida paid a short visit to Merton House to look after Angela and Veronica in their parents' and brother's absence. Seizing an opportunity to 'teach the little girls … about religion'[48], she spent time praying with and over them, instructing them in religious matters, and giving them religious pamphlets ('little "Pax" books') to read in bed. 'Graceless Angela' was not much impressed but Veronica was, responding piously to Aelfrida's homilies and placing her pamphlet with other treasured items in a special chest.[49] Inevitably, Phyllis found out. Soon after her departure, Aelfrida received a not unexpected but nevertheless 'gentle and temperate letter' from Eustace asking her 'not to … influence the children in the matter of religion'.[50] She had, of course, acted wrongly and provocatively (she knew of Eustace's and Phyllis' views on religion and was aware that not only did she risk setting her brother and sister-in-law against herself but also that her behaviour put Eustace as brother and husband in a difficult position) but placed the blame squarely on the shoulders of her guardian angel, it being he who suggested that she ought to teach the girls 'about religion' and who informed her that the 'secret' shared by Veronica and herself was 'apprehension of God' and that whatever difficulties were to be overcome, Aelfrida was to have no fear: '[Veronica] will understand, *will* know'.[51]

Aelfrida does not say openly that she discerned (or thought she discerned) the makings of a mystic in Veronica or that she hoped to attract her niece's attention at an impressionable age in order to guide her first footsteps on the Mystic Way but in spite of protestations that the way the children were brought up was Christian in all but name, she was forced to submit; at a subsequent meeting with Phyllis at which aunt and mother discussed the 'Religious Education of the Young' ('I tried', wrote Aelfrida, 'to be much less opinionated than I usually am') it was decided that 'Aunt Aelfrida' should not air her religious opinions at Merton House and that it was for Eustace and Phyllis to bring up their children in the way they thought best. Aelfrida, however, won one point: Phyllis agreed to read *Messages* (a book whose dedication to "some children whom I love" included the names of Phyllis' brood) 'and there see what I had actually taught my own children'.[52] Her response was not the hoped-for one: Phyllis strongly objected to Aelfrida "dragging religion into everyday life" and to her "making it an obsession". Agreeing that their divergence of opinion was fundamental, Aelfrida informed Phyllis that she herself 'adopted the out-and-out mystical position'[53] and that she was amazed that Eustace and Phyllis did not want their children to follow the 'Christian' example set by their Tillyard grandparents, the reason for which was so startlingly obvious that only wilful blindness on Aelfrida's part could have persuaded her to overlook it.

A reference made in April 1922 to the fact that Mina would soon be blessed with 'a satisfactory orphan'[54] is Aelfrida's first intimation that she was to acquire another nephew and niece, Conrad Walter, 'chosen' in 1922, and Constance Emma in 1924. Aelfrida was delighted by the appearance and behaviour of both children, describing baby Walter as 'my new nephew ... grey eyed [and] fair haired with a good straight nose and firm chin'[55], little Constance as '*ravishing*' with 'masses of fair curls and the most enormous blue eyes'[56], and the conduct of both as vastly superior to that of Stephen, Veronica, and Angela because of Mina's 'wonderful *hausfrau* capacity'[57] for imposing discipline on her children.

Julius' professorships in Birmingham and Cardiff meant 'Aunt Aelfrida' saw less of his children than she did of Eustace's and in spite of her amazement that efficient former social worker Mina should be 'so baffled' by her first adopted baby that she had to be instructed by Phyllis how to 'manage' him[58], she restrained herself from the kind of derogatory comments made in 1920 with reference to Phyllis' childrearing techniques. She was, however, horrified ('I feel as though it were almost blasphemy')[59] at the refusal of *both* sisters-in-law to be overwhelmed by the experience of real or surrogate motherhood, Mina stating that she was not a 'baby-lover' and never would be, Phyllis making it clear that she regarded babies less as embodied spirits 'trailing clouds of glory' and more as 'little animals having to be fed', and neither believing themselves to be as 'glorified by motherhood' as Aelfrida herself.[60]

Though Aelfrida hoped that Mina would find greater contentment in her marriage once she had children to cherish, the presence of children seems to have driven Julius and Mina further apart; indeed, as early as 1923 she noted that 'Julius' relationship to Mina seems to present an insoluble problem'. Her suggestion that Mina find happiness in current and future babies and leave Julius 'to his own devices' especially when overcome by one of his 'fits of black melancholy' met only with rebuff from a wife who continued to behave towards her unloving husband in an over-solicitous manner which irritated him beyond belief.[61] It was, however, Mina's own 'depression bordering on melancholia'[62] which drove her to seek her sister-in-law's help in January 1930 – or which, it is truer to say, drove Julius to send Mina to Fordfield as a 'patient' for the 'soul-doctor' with regard to whom he made no secret of the fact that he preferred her company to that of his wife.

Aelfrida was not pleased at Julius' tactless action, lamenting 'alas! shall I ever have the "room of one's own" which Virginia Woolf says is indispensable to writing. I have a writing fit on [but] they have sent me Mina ... well, God give the Straightener strength and the author self-denial!'[63] A week of Mina's 'melancholia'[64] sufficed; pleading ill-health and the pressure of preparing a new lecture series, the Straightener continued her ministrations but had Mina removed to Merton House. Insightful enough to appreciate that Mina's trouble stemmed chiefly from her unsatisfactory marriage and from resentment at being tied by children to a husband who 'doesn't care a bit for her', Aelfrida did not blame her sister-in-law for behaviour which 'worried the family half out of their lives' (she noted caustically, however, that Mina seemed determined 'to get notice at any price', even to the extent of threatening suicide; possibly someone had once said the same of herself) and zealously administered 'moral support' until Mina's departure.[65] She did not, it seems, offer religious or other advice on this occasion but confined herself to allowing Mina to ruminate repetitively on her woes; unsurprisingly, therefore, March 1930 found Mina 'no better'[66] and April the likelihood of her drifting into 'hopeless melancholia', a state which so exasperated Julius that in spite of stating 'nothing *we* could do would be any good', he agreed to Mina becoming his sister's 'patient' once more in the hope that the 'perfect peace of Fordfield' and her 'loving ministrations' would effect a cure.[67]

Although Mina soon seemed 'marvellously better for Fordfield'[68] and 'quite herself again ... to all outward appearance'[69], she became 'as ill as ever' soon after returning home. Unable to face a third soul-doctoring session, Aelfrida resorted to straightening-by-letter, expatiating on the possible causes of Mina's problems (chiefly "marriage" – note the quotation marks – but also the scars left by her being a German in England during the war) and trying 'to put some heart in her' by making positive suggestions.[70] To Julius, however, whose next move was to pack Mina off to her parents in Lahr until able to do more than 'mope and lament' in Cardiff, Aelfrida suggested formal therapy: 'psychoanalysis' by 'a good nerve-specialist'.[71] Her advice was rejected; to subject

Mina to psychoanalysis would have risked exposure of painful family secrets.

An altogether happier family business was the Cambridge Steam Laundry with which Aelfrida was actively involved from 1929 to 1931.[72] The Laundry, founded by Alfred Tillyard in 1881, never played as important a role in his life as the *Cambridge Independent Press;* in fact, it seems to have been used by him more as a means of augmenting his income through a paid directorship than as a business over which he retained active oversight. In July 1929, however, and 'very grave over forthcoming loss of income'[73] in the event of worsening disability or death, he arranged for Aelfrida to take over his two remaining directorships, that of the Cambridge Steam Laundry being one and of the Barnwell Coffee Palace Company[74] the other.

Apart from attendance at Annual General Meetings at which she made suggestions for the comfort and safety of the commercial travellers who were the Coffee Company's chief clients and from accepting a 'very modest' salary[75] for doing so, Aelfrida showed little interest in the Coffee Palace; for the Laundry, however, she demonstrated both interest and enthusiasm. Her reasons for doing so were pragmatic (a director's salary would be useful in providing treats and possibly even an inheritance for her daughters and involvement in business would prevent her 'living too much in the clouds and finding this world too unreal compared with the spiritual') and philanthropic: she hoped to be 'of real use' to the 'girls' (mostly middle-aged and elderly women)[76] who ran and staffed the business with the help of a resident caretaker/engineer.

Aelfrida's joy – she found the Steam Laundry 'quite thrilling' and as early as January 1930 took an active interest in what went on ('I folded sheets and minded an ironing machine and talked to lots of the girls')[77] – was due not only to her being able to prove that membership of the NUWW was not a sham or to discovering that she had an eye for business (in March 1930 she visited a Laundry Exhibition in London and 'came away with [her] … head full of plans') but also because 'my Laundry'[78], as she now called it, provided her with a means of actualising one of her otherwise abortive 'Brilliant Ideas'.

Among several such 'Ideas' floated by her in January 1919 was that of a 'co-operative laundry'.[79] The idea of 'co-operative' businesses had been mooted in the early years of the twentieth century (schemes of this nature were also supported by the NUWW) in terms of mutual assistance rather than competition (Aelfrida's 'knight-errantry of commerce' idea owes much to this way of thinking) and in terms of the individual employed by such organisations striving for the good of his employer's business and being cared for in sickness and health by that person and body in return. The Cambridge Steam Laundry was run along 'co-operative' lines from its inception and was a business for which its employees felt much affection because of the paternal manner in which it housed them before and after retirement; management practices, however, had stagnated and facilities become less than satisfactory.

The Laundry therefore provided a brilliant opportunity to put at least one 'Brilliant Idea' into practice and, unusually for her, with Aelfrida herself as an active participant. In April 1930, having completed a review of existing practices and facilities and fizzing with further 'ideas [for] my laundry'[80], she enthused 'her' fellow directors into improving efficiency with the establishment of receiving offices in outlying towns and villages, into bettering working and recreational conditions, and into updating machinery and laundering techniques to increase throughput and improve quality. Imagining 'what it is like in big business [and] how easy [it is] to get absorbed in [work]'[81], she attended the Laundry almost daily, sometimes up to three times a day if she felt matters needed to be chivvied along. She also regarded involvement as wholly beneficial to a mystic such as herself: 'the *most* important thing for mystics is to be *conscious of God*. Nothing else really matters. On the whole it is best to be normal and practical because then the machinery of life runs smoothly and other people *leave you alone*. A laundry is an admirable disguise. Being a laundry-director … I can be a mystic [too] and no-one notices'.[82] (Visiting Fordfield one day, Lilian Whitehouse enquired of Agatha what it was like "having a mystic for a mother", to which Agatha replied "Mother leads a double life … we get endless amusement out of her Laundry, and her mysticism doesn't inconvenience us at all!")[83] Whatever her motives, by June 1930 matters had so far improved under Aelfrida's tutelage that the forewoman declared she didn't know of a 'better, airier laundry' and Aelfrida that she herself had not lived in vain.[84]

The idyll did not last. Manageresses appointed to promote efficiency were inclined to think (probably with justification) that Aelfrida interfered too much in the day-to-day running of the 'dear Laundry' (as she herself noted, 'I *want* my own way') though she justified intervention by stating that an impersonal director would not have the welfare of the 'dear laundry girls' at heart.[85] Then too, though far from antagonistic to reform, she adopted a somewhat Luddite attitude towards dismissal of ineffective personnel and abandonment of outmoded practices which such personnel persisted in pursuing even in the face of increasing competition[86]. She also tended to regard the Laundry more as a form of social service run for the benefit of its employees than as a business, a stance which became less and less rational when her vision of what the Laundry ought to be clashed with economic realities endangering its continuation as a provider of work, income, and housing. Fortunately for the Laundry, personal problems in 1931–32 and lengthy absences from Cambridge in 1933–34 reduced Aelfrida's involvement and by the time of her resignation from the Laundry's Board of Management in 1936, participation had dwindled from attendance at monthly meetings to attendance at Annual General Meetings only.

The Laundry episode, though brief, nevertheless demonstrates what Aelfrida might have achieved given another life and another *métier* and how successful and inspirational she might have been had her path not led her so unswervingly along her particular 'mystic way'. It is also interesting to note that it was at the same time as her involvement in the Steam Laundry that she once again manifested her ability to engage with and instruct the young.

Although Frank Stokoe had distanced himself both physically and emotionally from Aelfrida following his return to Cambridge in 1921, he showed his gratitude for her earlier support and complimented her linguistic prowess in Italian, French, and German by sending her students reading or about to read Modern Languages whom he considered 'in need of special stimulus'[87] designed to bring them up to the required standard. Aelfrida, a soon-to-be divorced lady whose quixotic refusal of alimony had left her at the mercy of Constantine's financial whims and dependent on her mother's financial generosity, was both grateful and regretful: hour-long tutorials on several weekdays during term resulted in 'loss of leisure for writing'[88] and led to complaints of having 'no time for any affairs or interests of [her] own'.[89]

A small but steady source of income and a degree of intellectual stimulation brought another delight in its train; the renewed presence in her life of young men to fuel her '*prehensile* love of admiration'.[90] And fuel it they did. One or two fell in love with her and had to be gently discouraged with the sad (but inaccurate) reflection that they were 'the last of my flock of admirers'[91]; some ('three such *unusually* handsome undergraduates')[92] were fêted like former admirers; some reminded her of happier days when visits to college rooms figured in her social calendar: tea (chaperoned by Agatha and Alethea) at Trinity College ('aren't we gay!')[93] or, with lots of 'hot stuff' and 'sticky cakes', a discussion of '"rags" and so forth' in the presence of another 'nice boy' and his equally 'nice' friend. [94] (Their mother's language coaching also

provided Agatha and Alethea with male admirers though whether their charms or Aelfrida's inspired their invitations, she does not say.) Undergraduate friendships of this time, however, were largely of a superficial and social nature and were deliberately kept so by a woman preoccupied with Willie Searle and 'spiritual espousal'; indeed, to one undergraduate who might have profited from greater moral support (a young man recently diagnosed with tuberculosis and in revolt against a possibly fatal disease because of the sacrifices his divorced and impecunious mother had made to send him to university), she gave only a copy of her poems (she does not say which; all were inappropriate in the circumstances), leaving compassionate understanding to Agatha ('no wonder he didn't think things were worthwhile ... they can't seem real at all ... when they are shadowed by death – or, rather, lit up brilliantly so that the unreality of things that seemed real is revealed. But they are real [and] I hope he'll see it')[95] and practical advice (to invoke Crane's Charity to pay his medical bills)[96] to the Oracle.

With only one young man (he was twenty-seven to her forty-two) did Aelfrida approach anything like Little Friendships of former days. He first entered Aelfrida's life in November 1925 but it was not until the following year that he and she became close friends. Initially described by Alethea as 'Mother's new Spanish "goup"'[97] and (more correctly) as 'a certain over-polite and informative and mystical young man from the Balearic Isles'[98], Aelfrida's elder daughter remained unimpressed by the man even Aelfrida felt impelled to describe as a 'goup', noting drily that Juan Mascaró 'gave up business to study mysticism, Sanskrit, Greek and old religious writings'.[99] Agatha, having a clearer perception of Mascaró's spirituality, described him as 'a wonderful person ... who ... felt that the only way to find out the meaning of life and a backstairs to Heaven is to read the Hindu scriptures in the original ... he looks like a shy wild thing of the woods ... and knows an amazing number of languages [already]'.[100] Aelfrida, alarmed to discover that as an adolescent, Mascaró had been briefly interested in Occultism, made it her mission to steer him away from 'the attraction of the psychic'[101] and to point him in the right direction 'to find out the Mystic Way' but was dismayed to discover that he was already engaged in spiritual exercises of a yogic nature and regarded herself as an 'adept'.[102] Worse still, Mascaró began to call her his '*amie espiritual*' and to press her to impart not only her 'ideas on mysticism' but her own mystic experiences also.[103] (It was with Mascaró in mind that she inscribed in her diary the key words 'discipline, humility, secrecy' and vowed that love of the subtle flattery of being thought 'an expert on mysticism' must be banished from her life.) Then again, as long as the conversation remained impersonal, she enjoyed 'talking about mysticism to Mr Mascarò' (she had no-one else with whom to discuss it at that point) though it was almost impossible to keep the personal out of a conversation in which one participant insisted (like Mirzà Issa Sadiq a decade earlier) in 'quoting ardent love-poetry to [her]' while there emanated from him the 'electric thrill [of] men who are feeling passion'.[104] (Six years later Mascarò, now in India, sent her 'an extraordinarily loving and admiring letter' which, had it been written by an Englishman, 'would have been a love letter'.)[105] She therefore tried to be neither feminine nor charming, only to find that Mascarò persisted in regarding her as Beatrice to his Dante, a compliment to one who declared (erroneously) that she was 'done with gratified vanity'.[106]

She nevertheless took pity on her Dante (had she not resolved 'to help people if I can'?) to the extent of 'talking goupism' when Mascarò suffered spiritual crises over his 'vocation' remarkably similar to those suffered in a different context by Frank Stokoe: 'temptations and trouble … so bitter that sometimes he feels he is being persecuted by evil spirits'.[107] She also listed points for him to ponder, using as illustration four anonymised spiritual experiences of her own whose significance she had come to appreciate: that a mystic should perceive the spark of 'the divine' in all things; that perception results in such an intense sense of communion between 'the divine' within all things and the Divine from which such 'divinity' derives that all sense of separateness is lost; that men who experience this expansion of consciousness become as and at one with all sentient beings in which 'divinity' is manifest; that the development of such 'universal' consciousness enhances men's sense of communion with God. (Realising how little her views had altered over the years, she added 'when I was fifteen I was carrying on exactly this kind of correspondence with Silvia Myers'.)[108] In order to provide him with 'spiritual insight' and to 'hold him before God' during his absences from Cambridge (Mascarò had embarked on simultaneous degrees in Cambridge and Madrid), Aelfrida also arranged to perform 'parallel meditations' with him once or twice a day at set times on mutually-agreed subjects (the Lord's Prayer, the Star of Bethlehem, 'Spirit is God', and so on), meditations which, though not as fruitful as those carried on with Erle Lunn (another 'goup') in October 1929[109], resulted in Mascarò 'beginning to feel his consciousness stretching out and touching God's'[110] and Aelfrida herself as even more mind-expanded than usual. To her relief, Mascarò's departure for India in December 1930 closed the episode ('he thinks his "Spiritual Friend" does not see enough of him [and]

Mina and Julius Tillyard with Walter and Constance Tillyard and Mr and Mrs Kaufmann

wanted much counsel and alas! self-revelation … to take with him … well, I just *can't*)[111] but did not wholly sever their Spiritual Friendship, for Juan's 'lonely, proud and sensitive [but] too introspective' soul[112] continued to reach out to hers across the miles and years.

A 'Spiritual Friendship' with Mascarò and a desire to live 'without being noticed' was one thing but with Alethea and Agatha entering or about to enter tertiary education, Aelfrida needed 'to earn more money'[113] to support herself and her daughters. 'Content to be passive in the hands of God' but with her 'eager brain always devising plans' and aware that naïve hopes that, failing Constantine, God would provide financial as well as spiritual assistance, seemed unlikely to be fulfilled, she decided that too much humility and secrecy were not conducive to earning a living. Aware too that Fate had a habit of 'kicking over'[114] some of her more 'brilliant' ideas, she nevertheless embarked on a series of didactic activities of a sacred and, more significantly in view of assertions that she did 'try!'[115] to earn money, of a secular nature.

Fate certainly kicked over her first scheme. Six short lectures "for Overseas Students on Present-Day England" by "Mrs Graham (Aelfrida Tillyard)" inspired by lectures attended by Alethea at the Sorbonne, promised to be interesting (topics ranged from English society, through local and national politics, government, and education to the "position of women" and "the Press and its influence")[116] but attracted only three students. A second 'Brilliant Idea', to start a School of English for Foreigners, met with even less success, for lecturers approached by Aelfrida were more interested in furthering their own careers than hers and the Local Examination Syndicate only if Aelfrida was prepared to 'hitch' her scheme onto its own, and because Aelfrida herself, while protesting 'I wish I could earn more'[117], was reluctant to give herself up wholly to a money-making concern because 'I *must* keep time for thinking and lecturing and writing books'.[118]

The appearance in Aelfrida's papers of a prospectus for Cambridge University's Board of Extra-Mural Studies vacation course for foreign students of 1927[119] signifies a more successful venture. Feeling 'vivid and unorthodox' among the 'pedants' who taught it[120] (no 'commonplace and ordinary' pedant, she!) Aelfrida took part in three such 'Summer Schools' in July 1927, 1928, and 1929 and was, by her account, a great success. She taught using the Direct Method, instructing the dozen men and women in her class in colloquial English through the medium of games, debates, poetry readings (chiefly about Cambridge, though her own poetry featured too), novels, plays, and *The Times,* advertisements and all; no wonder her classes '[throve] amazingly' and that her pupils were 'most responsive': 'they love the lessons and so do I!'[121] At the end of each School she invited her pupils to a garden party at Fordfield at which she presented them with copies of *Verses for Alethea* (of which she still possessed a large number) and received the gift of a book or a bouquet in return.

Although the diary volumes covering the years of her role as 'Universal Aunt' contain fewer references to her spiritual life than those which immediately precede or follow them, Aelfrida's preoccupation with things of the spirit had not disappeared. Thinking, usually in the form of meditation on topics such as 'saintliness' ('utterly beyond me')[122], was carried out whenever she had time: early mornings, late evenings, when keeping company with her father, and during days in bed 'earned after a most strenuous weekend'[123] meeting new pupils or entertaining family callers. 'Writing books', a 'money-making concern' with a moral as well as a pecuniary purpose, took up much of her time but will be considered as a topic in its own right in a separate chapter. Lecturing took place throughout.

Some – a few – lectures were entirely secular: *The Poetry of Rose Macaulay* and (with reference to Middleton Murry) *Shall we abolish the literary critic?* in March 1929 and February 1930 respectively at the Letchworth Settlement, an adult education centre opened in 1923[124]; others, such as a lecture at the Letchworth Quaker Meeting House on *The Buddhist Contribution To Spiritual Religion* to 'a most receptive and responsive audience'[125] were on subjects closer to her heart, as also was a lecture series carried out in Cambridge between 4 February and 9 March 1928 entitled (with a nod to William James) *The Psychology of Religious Experience*. This latter

series encompassed, along with some unnamed topics (unnamed, it seems, because Aelfrida was suffering from 'acute eczema' of the perineum which she decided was her guardian angel's way of punishing her for 'getting too much absorbed in the … pleasures of this world' as exemplified by 'lustful feelings' for Willie Searle)[126], some of her favourite subjects: the religion of childhood, conversion, human affections, and death, the latter 'rather solemnising'.[127] A feeling, however, that she was ignoring the second part of her Oath of Obligation in being so 'universal' an aunt caused her to decide to verb the noun and to 'aunt' specifically for the most important entity in her life, namely God. She did this in a series of enthusiastically delivered (and better attended) lectures given between 27 January and 4 March 1930 in St Botolph's vestry, the vestries of Cambridge city centre churches being often used for religious educational purposes because more private – and warmer – than the nave.

Aelfrida regarded the lectures as a burden put on her by God ('another effort in a world of effort')[128] and as a further opportunity, as the titles of the lectures showed, to demonstrate that she was indeed 'an expert on Mysticism': *Mysticism and Action,* an appropriate title given that she was currently administering moral support to Mina; *Mysticism and the Intellect*, a useful antidote to a strenuous morning in the Laundry but also one described rather flatly by Alethea as an exposition of 'the spirit of the universe in everything'.[129] (Aelfrida herself saw it as provoking an 'enormously valuable' discussion which showed 'where my conception of divine things [has] been crude and inadequate'.)[130] Then followed *Mysticism and Art,* after which a university professor delivered a commentary completely misunderstood by Aelfrida who described it as 'dull, technical and vague … in spite of his obvious sensitivities to Beauty'[131] and by Alethea as revealing how fossilised her mother's thought-patterns had become since the Great War and that they ran on narrowly theological lines 'with mysticism as a kind of holiday'[132]; *Mysticism and Comparative Religion,* after which there was an 'amazingly broad-minded' discussion[133], and *Mysticism and Psychology* whose content might have been fascinating had Alethea seen fit to enlarge upon it and Aelfrida not become so concerned lest she had been 'gadding about too much' that she confined subsequent diary entries to Lenten meditations on 'the soul as a bit of God given us to tend'.[134]

A secular lecture given on 2 December 1929 evoked her youth. In the shape of 'over half an hour's Italian without notes!'[135], it was delivered to the Cambridge University Italian Society, of which Alethea was then secretary, on the subject of Gian Falco. Gian Falco ('my old friend Papini'), though judging by his letters, 'something ponderous, middle aged and successful' (he was forty-six and a well-known author)[136], had continued to correspond faithfully though intermittently with Aelfrida, the latter being amused to discover that the godless socialist reformer of the *Circolo Filosofico* had embarked on a 'Romeward journey'[137] and by 1923 had become a 'successful Catholic writer who boasts that over eight hundred articles have appeared in Italy alone on his *Vita di Cristo*'. ('I suppose', she noted on hearing this, 'we all tend to grow old along the same route and to pass from knight-errantry to orthodoxy!')[138] Thanks to Constantine's prohibition, Aelfrida and Gian Falco never met again but Alethea had seen him while in Florence in April 1929 on a visit during which attendance at meetings of Young Fascists amusingly but less consequentially mirrored that of her mother at Young Italy's, and in an account written shortly after returning home had noted how pleased she and Gian Falco had met because of 'Mother and him having been friends for so long'. She also noted that in marrying his cook 'Papini chose well', that he was as ugly, if not uglier, than photographs suggested, and that his writings were 'now [as] religious with passion as [they were] once atheist with passion'[139], and, reading over Aelfrida's diary of her own Florentine adventures, that naïve Signorina Tillyard obviously had no idea 'how to behave' vis-à-vis Italian men.[140] Aelfrida agreed, and during the lecture inspired by Alethea's visit (Aelfrida makes no mention in her diary of her daughter's meeting with Papini) read aloud 'some carefully-selected extracts of my diary of long ago which amused people enormously', commenting afterwards 'dear me, what an innocent little blue-stocking of a minx I was!' and, on hearing from an Italian present at the lecture that another admirer, '*piccolo* Assagioli', was now 'a celebrated psychoanalyst with a large clientele among ladies!!', that 'I haven't changed so much ... as I ought to have done ... either'.[141]

Aelfrida's final (and last ever) lecture series took place early in 1932 at a time when the 'happy days' of which she had once written regretfully 'why do you go so fast!'[142] had almost gone, never to return. Unusually for her, the lectures were a co-operative effort, she giving a brief introductory exhortation on Mysticism and invited speakers following her with dissertations: on 'Human Affection' by 'a Westcott House man' (Westcott House being a theological college, what he said was described by Aelfrida as 'rather too much like a sermon')[143], on 'Science' by Alethea's fellow Girtonian Helen Megaw[144] ('I felt rather lost having to be chairman to a discussion on a subject of which I knew nothing')[145], and on 'Spiritualism' by a local Spiritualist of whom Aelfrida noted dismissively that 'the experiences which led her to Spiritualism might just as well have led her to the Salvation Army' and after which some 'rampant Spiritualists' in the audience were quashed by Aelfrida arguing (rather unusually given her earlier animadversions against the SPR) for psychical research conducted scientifically 'rather than by a spiritualist church' and (she knew whereof she spoke) 'against amateur dabbling in the occult'. (Even more unusually, for she never spoke publicly about her abilities as a 'psychic', she supported her argument with descriptions of her own mediumistic experiences, dismissing them as 'merely a by-product of "spiritual exercises"'.) The last three lectures were less controversial (Aelfrida had been relieved that 'the bitterest wind I ever remember outside Russia [had] kept some *fierce* Spiritualists away' from the third)[146], being on *Mysticism and Education* ('I was a little too vehement ... but I felt so intensely that the chief end of man was to know God and ... education had ... largely made it impossible')[147], on *Mysticism and Health* (an appropriate title given that Cambridge was in the grip of an influenza epidemic; Dorothea Conybeare conducted the 'health' part on the strength of being a masseuse), and on *Mysticism and the Church*, her own 'small contribution towards a mystic revival'.[148] The approach of Lent, however, reminded the lecturer who six years earlier had promised to 'live without being noticed' (difficult in front of an audience of sixty, all 'agog to discuss')[149] and to discipline herself for being 'subtly flattered at being thought an expert' on Mysticism that, apropos the lecture series, she needed to repent '*very specially* ... of ... spiritual pride' and of her continuing belief that 'possession of a developed mystical sense implies moral excellence in the possessor'.[150] Ironically, however, the repentant 'alas and alas!' which ended the sentence was soon to be applied to graver events than merely breaking her vow of 'Discipline. Humility. Secrecy' in order to propagate her Great Work.

In the meantime, and beginning with Alethea's matriculation in October 1926 and continuing after Agatha's in October 1929, there was more university life to be enjoyed vicariously. The fact that both Agatha and Alethea attended a Cambridge college made this easier, as also did their insistence that Aelfrida join their social and, as far as possible, their collegiate life: 'they were so perfect to me, always wanting me to be there'.[151]

'There' was not only the college to which Aelfrida frequently repaired ('Oh, it *is* lovely up at Girton ... happy girls to be there')[152] to gossip with young women and pretend she herself was 'about twenty' ('though at night when I have ... pain which keeps me awake ... I feel ninety')[153], to attend garden parties ('sunlight! And flowers! And music! So festive')[154], and to be lunched at high table where, flanked by Miss Major and Mary Lloyd Thomas, lecturer in English, she was disconcerted by the latter's opening gambit "Are you interested in the higher regions of physics?" ('I wasn't going to say no', wrote the mystic, 'so I made play with Haldane … and Einstein and red-herringed as soon as I could') but was gratified to be congratulated by Miss Major on her 'two outstanding daughters' and especially on Agatha with her 'magnificent brain'.[155] 'There' also encompassed pride in Alethea opening the debate in French at the French Society, the first woman ever to do so[156]; enjoyment of balls and boat races in May Week during which 'the whole world seemed festive and Cambridgy and exhilarating'[157]; meeting the girls and their friends for 'elevenses' at Cambridge's new and fashionable tea shop, The Whim in Trinity Street, and, on 'one of those lovely days which make me wonder if I am not *too* happy'[158] (Aelfrida's 'puritanical conscience' invariably smote her when leading 'too happy a life'[159] at the expense of spiritual development but she assuaged it with penances e.g. staying at home with her father instead of going on a river picnic); a tea-party à *deux* with one of the undergraduates who confided in her and consulted her on their choice of career but concerning whom Agatha chided her ('[she] doesn't approve of young men paying me attention!!')[160] because she considered it improper for her mother to visit young mens' rooms unchaperoned, particularly as she and Alethea were forbidden to do so. No wonder Aelfrida wrote exhaustedly 'once term begins, life is too full and too interesting'.[161]

Protesting 'if only I weren't so tired, how I should enjoy life!'[162] – fatigue did not prevent her from doing what she enjoyed but provided a reason for excusing herself from unwanted invitations – Aelfrida's reflections on her forty-fifth birthday were entirely positive: 'you know the proverb "*si la jeunesse savait, si la veillesse pouvait*"? [Well], as far as my brain goes – not my body which is an inefficient machine – I *sais* as if I were old and I *peux* as if I were young!'[163] (Credit for this, she noted, should go to God whose presence she still felt so strongly that returning from a visit to Girton she found it 'a tremendous effort to withdraw my mind from heavenly things and bicycle all down Bridge Street and Sidney Street where one *must* pay attention to the traffic'.)[164] Her elder daughter, however, was less sure, writing of her mother at this time that 'her life has been one struggle between mysticism … and the desire to be admired and loved'. But even Alethea admitted that it was the struggle between Mysticism and desire which, together with 'a goodly mixture of sensuality and conceit' and 'infinite charm', made Aelfrida so unlike other women of her age, they having 'settled down to a pure maternal ordinariness'[165] which excluded dressing in modish clothes (of Lucy Verey, Aelfrida asked 'why does she dress so old … in a black "matron's" hat [and] a plum … crêpe de Chine dress?')[166] or partying enthusiastically with young people half their age and included more conventional 'good works' than directing a laundry, lecturing on Mysticism, and writing spiritual 'road-books' and *romans-à-clef*.

Notwithstanding efforts made during snatches of 'precious, precious solitude'[167] to be 'more "recollected" in the sight of God'[168], Aelfrida was too busy with 'pleasant external activities' do more than cherish her inner life in 'the secret chamber of my heart where I shut the door and am alone with God' whenever she could; indeed, she was busier at home than away because surrounded by 'dear and charming' young people[169] brought to Fordfield by her daughters. But to a woman who felt able to understand the young and to keep up with them as if she were one of them (at a tea-party held in January 1927 she sat gossiping on the hearthrug 'as if I were another schoolgirl'[170] and had to apologise for monopolising the conversation) this was very heaven: a house filled with female language students on exchanges or as paying guests, with daughters teaching themselves (and her) those daring new dances the foxtrot and the quickstep (the Charleston, they decided, was indecent) to records played on their new gramophone (it is not recorded what the Oracle and Chiara thought of this but their reaction may be gauged by the venom with which they continued to attack Alethea), with sons of old friends (Oswald Barkway, eldest son of the Anteater; Lucy's son, Philip Verey, 'a lout … and Eton too!')[171] and with fascinating male undergraduates (females were tolerated, in a ratio of 1:2 or 3) was more than adequate recompense for the dreariness preceding (and surrounding) the present time. But, wrote Alethea sadly, 'at Fordfield it's always hectic and Mother is almost too solicitous and arranges things more than I'd like [and] jars on one with her purposefulness'.[172]

Sundays were especially joyful because Agatha and Alethea invited particular friends home for tea: Helen Megaw, the girls' second cousin Ruth Warren (a Girton contemporary of Alethea's), Olga Liebowitz ('a clever Jewess'[173], Alethea's particular friend) and Prudence Wilkinson, Agatha's Girton contemporary, chiefly represented the women. Among soon-to-be-famous young men were Michael Redgrave, later a well-known actor but then 'one of the Magdalene aesthetes'[174] who Aelfrida mistakenly believed had fallen in love at first sight with Alethea and lionised at a Fordfield tea (she scared him silly) because as an influential figure in the world of Cambridge undergraduate poetry, Michael had bestowed favourable reviews on poetry written by Alethea prior to graduation or arranged for it to be published in magazines including *Granta* and *The Cambridge Review*, and 'Alethea's latest young man', artist Julian Trevelyan[175], who seemed 'amazingly fond' of a daughter 'pleased to be admired'.[176] (And admire: Alethea bought one of his pictures and kept it all her life.) And Douglas Davidson, one of Maynard Keynes' circle of bright young economists, addressed by Aelfrida as 'dear Douglas' (he had, she wrote, 'no word or look for anyone but Alethea' but scandalised Agatha by his 'worldliness')[177] and coached by her in Economics from a textbook written by Hubert Henderson which she studied assiduously so as to keep just ahead of her student. (She was amused to discover that Davidson's father referred to her as his 'professor'.) And 'a charming fresher from Trinity ... with beautiful manners [but] cynical and *very* argumentative' by the name of Donald Maclean who expatiated between sets of tennis with Agatha on how he wanted to 'reconstruct society on a new basis'.[178] (He later tried to do so by passing British intelligence secrets to Russia.)[179] No wonder that with visitors like these, Aelfrida described Sunday teas as consisting of 'gay conversation and strolling and lounging in the grass'[180] and, thinking of Fordfield in later years, chiefly remembered 'parties like these – the garden all sunshine and vivid green; people playing tennis; friends from overseas'.[181]

Aelfrida was not, of course, the only attraction: there were also her 'sweet daughters [with] their vitality, their good looks, their wit, their charm'[182] (a remark prompted by a visit from Helen Megaw when much water had passed under many bridges since those happy days), Alethea being 'amazingly animated' and Agatha 'beautiful and gay'.[183]

To believe that God wished her 'to share innocent pleasures with [her] girls [and] to rejoice with them in all the happiness of their youth'[184] was in keeping with Aelfrida's notion of herself as 'Universal Aunt'; the other side of the coin, however, and almost certainly the reason why her 'purposefulness' jarred on Alethea, was that the 'Universal Aunt' who exhorted herself to 'go to it', abandoned humility and secrecy to impose on herself the discipline of 'aunting' for husbands for her daughters as assiduously as her own and Elfrida Sturge's mother had 'aunted' John Forbes Cameron. Sunday teas provided the perfect opportunity but Aelfrida was so keen to see Agatha and Alethea married that she had had 'aunted' possible candidates for several years before the girls' matriculations at Girton provided her with further opportunities.

Both girls had been attractive to men from their midteens. Alethea, in spite of being 'pretty big and pretty fat'[185] at that point, had had three serious admirers by the age of sixteen, Agatha a serious suitor at fifteen, rejected by Aelfrida only because her daughter was still at school but kept in reserve because hoping Agatha 'could get engaged young to some good man'.[186] Both girls were at ease in masculine company, Agatha subsequently acquiring so many followers that 'quite frankly, she does not know [her] own mind [and] is afraid of making a clean sweep ... and having none left'[187], and Alethea, 'though she had nothing of the flirt about her'[188], attracting so many young men with her Parisian poise, 'quiet, self-reliant manner and ... knack of dressing with simple effective elegance'[189] that Aelfrida had 'very gently to suggest moderation in all things – though I *love* her to be admired'.[190]

While at Girton both girls received offers of marriage, one a definite proposal, the other an unofficial engagement. Alethea's proposal came from a man described as 'the product of a wealthy ... intelligent and well-educated family'[191], John Hamilton Wedgwood, son of Sir Ralph Wedgwood and his authoress wife[192] and descendent of the Josiah Wedgwood whose foreman Samuel Barrett was Alethea's own ancestor. Aelfrida described him as 'dark and clever and political'[193] and wished Alethea liked him more (she herself preferred 'dear Douglas'), which she shortly appeared to do for within six months of their first meeting John was paying 'what used to be called "marked attention"' to her[194] and Alethea, 'usually quiet with young men'[195], glowed and looked so happy in his presence that all at Fordfield remarked on it. Four months later, however, John's parents 'interfered to put a stop to his friendship with Alethea'[196] and although he told Aelfrida that he meant to marry Alethea once he was sure she would not refuse him (and actually proposed two years later), Alethea decided she found him 'a little monotonous'[197] and broke off the friendship. Agatha's somewhat longer relationship was with Ruth Warren's younger brother, Humphrey, who embarked on a chaste courtship during his time at Cambridge (he did not kiss her for two and a half years) but behaved as if engaged by putting a ring on the third finger of her left hand and dallying with her unchaperoned in Fordfield 'snug'.[198] Agatha was in two minds about him, replying either 'no, no! I can't!'[199] to her 'aunting' mother's questions or proposing that she and Humphrey wait a while after his graduation to give him a chance to find his feet in the world; they later parted by mutual consent.

So busy was Aelfrida sharing 'innocent pastimes' with her girls that it seems she did not enquire too deeply into the failure of her 'aunting'; indeed, she appears to have no inkling that failure was attributable to her own actions until it was thrust upon her a few years later in a manner she could not ignore. In the meantime she placed the blame squarely on her daughters' shoulders. (The one exception was her own inverted snobbery: because 'I don't like knowing people grander than myself'[200], she begrudged Alethea the attentions of young men with titled parents.) Agatha, she decided, was too immature for sustained relationships. Alethea, though 'quite fit to stand alone'[201], was inclined to snub 'forward young men' ('but why snub them? Why not enjoy their attentions!!')[202] because she did not want to marry too soon 'in order to see what she could accomplish as an independent woman first'; she would also, she informed her mother, have to be 'immensely fond of a man'[203] to relinquish her independence early or at all, warning the latter that she was "not to blight our young lives by wanting us to marry".[204]

There was, however, more to the matter than this. For one thing Aelfrida's keenness to see her daughters 'settled', together with her own sexual reawakening as she neared middle age, caused her to 'aunt' so assiduously that she lost all sense of proportion (her guardian angel, she said, rebuked her 'for making too many plans and clinging too much to schemes of my own')[205] and to pretend that her daughters, like herself in younger days, 'made a conquest of every man they [met]'[206], a view Alethea found odd considering her mother's own 'tragic mistake in the way of falling in love'[207] and embarrassing insofar as in relationships with men, she herself preferred lasting friendship to passing passion. For another, but something which Aelfrida chose not to remember or to regard as important, there was her own dubious reputation, for the Wedgwoods' response to news of their son's association with Alethea probably stemmed less from their discovery that she was not moneyed than from information imparted by their Cambridge relatives the Darwins (who not only knew the Tillyards but everyone else who mattered too) that Alethea's mother was a self-confessed 'religious fanatic' who wrote and lectured on topics not far removed (in their eyes) from Spiritualism and Theosophy, who published *romans-à-clef* detailing her relationship with a husband whose Consular Service reputation was tainted and whom she had divorced in scandalous circumstances[208], and who as a 'Cambridge poet' had been associated with Aleister Crowley, dubbed by periodical *John Bull* a "seducer, devil doctor and debauched dope fiend".[209]

Aelfrida's 'aunting' for Agatha and Alethea was not, we also learn, carried out solely with the altruistic aim of seeing them established in stable relationships with good men, able to enjoy 'their fair share of normal human happiness'[210] at last. (Her description of the perfect husband was that he should be "eugenically perfect, morally blameless, cultured, charming, a gentleman", a lover of home life, children, and simple things, and not a grumbler i.e. as unlike Constantine as possible. He must also

be motherless, because, thanks to Anatolia, she regarded mothers-in-law as mischief makers and gadflies.)[211] It was also carried out for purely selfish reasons: she wanted grandchildren ('a promise of the future, of hope that I might … see *their* children')[212]; she wanted freedom to do what *she* wanted ('perhaps when the girls are "settled" I may venture to be spendthrift of my poor store of energy')[213] i.e. to enjoy lengthy periods of 'almost complete solitude' in which to work ('and rest a bit', of course)[214] and to experience 'that freedom of spirit which seems to accompany chastity and loneliness' (a freedom she now valued 'more than children')[215]; and she wanted to be free from distraction in order to indulge religious practices and experiences which 'like a scarlet thread'[216] guided her along the sometimes labyrinthine path of her personal 'mystic way' and which, in truth, provided the only clue to which she could cling when lost in labyrinths of spiritual or emotional turmoil. Her daughters, however, seemed determined to thwart her wishes.

Although, as she admitted, 'if they marry and go, it will need much grace to enable me to rejoice whole-heartedly'[217], Aelfrida's desire to be free of encumbrances manifested itself as soon as Agatha and Alethea were old enough to travel without her; indeed, as she noted in April 1927, though 'never quite happy when my girls are out of my sight, … I am continually making plans … to send them away'.[218] And send them she did every Easter and summer vacation on holidays or language exchanges in France, Italy, Switzerland, Holland, and Germany, leaving immediately school or university term was over and returning immediately before the next started. Absence from home was ostensibly for the girls' benefit, being 'good for their health, good for their intelligence, good for their character'[219] but it was more in hopes of solitude for herself (or as much solitude as Fordfield afforded out of term; Chiara tended to fill the house with visiting friends and relations) that Aelfrida dispatched her daughters so briskly and consistently and even when unhappy or unwell. (Her strange reference to absence from Cambridge being good for their 'health' may be taken as an echo of Henry Joseph Wetenhall's belief that Cambridge's climate was enervating but may also be interpreted as representing a desire to separate the warring generations at Fordfield in order to provide 'perfect peace' for both sides; it may also have arisen from awareness that the predatory nature of her affection for them or the over-dependent nature of theirs for her was potentially harmful and ought to be mitigated by frequent physical separation.) Hence it was with growing dismay that the 'Universal Aunt' regarded daughters who seemed determined to put career prospects before marriage ('*I think a right marriage is a woman's best career*')[220], who shortly after graduating from Girton 'had disposed of all [their] admirers'[221], and who declared that the 'unity of the three of us was so close' that they would not be the first to break it and that if Aelfrida did not remarry they themselves would never marry. ('What a terrible responsibility for me!')[222] It is therefore against this background of Aelfrida's realisation that 'Universal Aunting' had its disadvantages – 'if in ten years' time they were still here – unmarried – it would be much less good'[223] – that her description of a promenade taken with her daughters along the Backs one autumn day should be read: 'Cambridge these days of mist and sunshine is so lovely … the crimson of the creepers, the nearby trees all gold and green but far away vaporous like puffs of smoke, the bridges in the distance seeming insubstantial like skiey architecture come to earth, the lizard-green river, the grave grey buildings … we walked in enchantment, Alethea and Agatha and I'.[224]

## Notes

1 GCPPT 1|1|32 undated note at end.
2 ibid. 5 May 1926.
3 ibid. 24 January 1926.
4 ibid. 9 December 1925.
5 GCPPT 1|1|25 6 July 1921.
6 GCPPT 1|1|32 28 May 1926.
7 GCPPT 1|1|34 1 January 1927.
8 ibid. 16 February 1927.
9 ibid. 1 January 1927.
10 ibid. 4 March 1927.
11 ibid. 1 January 1927.
12 ibid. 19 January 1927.
13 ibid. 21 June 1927.
14 *Matthew 22: 37–39.* (KJV).
15 GCPPT 1|1|35 29 August 1928.
16 GCPPT 1|1|34 20 August 1927. The quotation is taken from Cornford's poem *Youth*, quoted in *Cambridge Poets 1900–1913* (p 42): "A young Apollo, golden haired, / Stands dreaming on the edge of strife, / Magnificently unprepared / For the long littleness of life".
17 GCPPT 1|1|32 3 October 1926.
18 ibid. 12 November 1926.
19 GCPPT 1|1|36 6 May 1929.
20 GCPPT 1|1|32 1 and 6 June 1926.
21 ibid. 17 June 1926.
22 GCPPT 1|1|34 3 December 1926.
23 Edith Helen Major read History at Girton 1885–1888 and after a teaching career elsewhere, was Mistress 1925–1931.
24 GCPPT 1|1|34 26 May 1927.
25 GCPPT 1|1|35 18 September 1928
26 GCPPT 1|1|36 6 August 1929.
27 ibid. 20 March 1929.
28 ibid. 7 May 1929.
29 GCPPT 1|1|25 29 July 1920.
30 ibid. 18 September 1920.
31 ibid. 4 August and 27 November 1920.
32 GCPPT 1|1|26 12 September 1921.
33 ibid. 5 February 1922.
34 ibid. 10 and 19 February 1922.
35 ibid. 22 February 1922.
36 GCPPT 1|1|27 20 November 1923.
37 GCPPT 1|1|28 10 July 1924.
38 ibid. 8 September 1924.
39 GCPPT 1|1|34 8 December 1926.
40 GCPPT 1|1|32 3 September 1926.
41 GCPPT 1|1|30 5 November 1925.
42 GCPPT 1|1|41 1 July 1932.
43 GCPPT 1|1|36 29 September 1929.
44 GCPPT 1|1|34 26 December 1926.
45 GCPPT 1|1|38 25 November 1930.
46 GCPPT 1|1|39 30 March 1931.
47 GCPPT 1|1|41 7 August 1932.
48 ibid. 30 August 1933.
49 GCPPT 1|1|44 1 August 1933.
50 ibid. 28 August 1933.
51 ibid. 30 August 1933.
52 ibid. 17 September 1933.
53 ibid. 7 October 1933.
54 GCPPT 1|1|26 24 April 1922.
55 ibid. 6 January 1923.
56 GCPPT 1|1|34 23 March 1927.
   GCPPT 1|1|39 27 January 1931.
57 GCPPT 1|1|35 10 January 1928.
58 GCPPT 1|1|26 24 November 1922 and 3 January 1923.
59 ibid. 24 November 1922.
60 ibid. 24 April and 21 November 1922.
61 ibid. 9 January 1923.
62 GCPPT 1|1|37 15 January 1930.
63 ibid.
64 ibid. 21 January 1930.
65 ibid. 28 and 29 January 1930.
66 ibid. 14 March 1930.
67 ibid. 9 April 1930.
68 ibid. 24 May 1930.
69 ibid. 6 June 1930.
70 ibid. 18 June 1930.
71 ibid. 6 July 1930.
72 The Cambridge Steam Laundry occupied a plot on Cherry Hinton Meadows, south-east of Cambridge; next door was The Grange, a similar-sized plot also owned by Alfred Tillyard and consisting of a small house and an orchard. Behind the Laundry lay open fields; more orchards and the spacious grounds of Cherry Hinton Hall lay to the east. The laundry buildings were situated to the rear of the site; drying grounds, a well, and employees' cottages lay between them and what then was a semi-rural road leading to Cherry Hinton village. Urban development in the 1950s and 1960s left only a vestige of what was once a well-known business: a cul-de-sac (Laundry Lane) providing access to garages belonging to the houses which now cover the site.
73 GCPPT 1|1|36 4 July 1929.
74 The Barnwell Coffee Palace Company ran an establishment in Cambridge's East Road known as the White Ribbon Coffee House and Temperance Hotel. The day-to-day-running of the establishment was taken over by the Salvation Army in 1932.
75 GCPPT 1|1|46 23 November 1934.
76 GCPPT 1|1|37 12 December 1929.
77 ibid. 8 and 31 January 1930.
78 ibid. 28 March 1930.
79 GCPPT 1|1|23 30 January 1919.
80 GCPPT 1|1|37 7 April 1930.
81 ibid. 9 April 1930.
82 ibid. 13 April 1930.

83  ibid. 2 May 1930.

84  ibid. 27 June 1930.

85  GCPPT 1|1|41 23 April 1932.

86  ibid. 21 June 1932. Several other laundries opened in Cambridge about this time, some offering facilities, such as dry-cleaning, not offered by the Cambridge Steam Laundry.

87  GCPPT 1|1|30 16 October 1925.

88  ibid. 9 November 1925.

89  ibid. 8 November 1925.

90  GCPPT 1|1|32 29 November 1925.

91  ibid. 6 March 1926.

92  ibid. 7 November 1926.

93  GCPPT 1|1|28 4 December 1924.

94  ibid. 25 November 1924.

95  GCPPG A2.1 9 May 1927.

96  Crane's Charity was a fund from which grants-in-aid could be made to undergraduates whose parents earned less than £500 a year. Founded in 1612 by John Crane, a Cambridge apothecary whose estate was bequeathed to the relief of sick and poor scholars, it was administered in the 1920s by respected Cambridge surgeon Arthur Cooke, together with the University's current Vice Chancellor and the Regius Professors of Divinity, Law, and Physic.

97  The term 'goup' seems to have developed as a result of Constantine's using it adjectivally to describe *The Making of a Mystic* but by the early 1920s had become an active or passive verb – to goup or to be gouped – and a noun – goup, goupism – used somewhat pejoratively by Agatha and Alethea to indicate their mother's more spiritually-inclined visitors, how she behaved towards them, and the topics they discussed: Alethea's diary entry for 25 November 1929 (GCPPG A1.1) describes a Fordfield tea party at which a visitor was 'gouped by Mother, quietly', Agatha describes a student arriving to 'talk goupism with Mother' (GCPPG A2.1 14 November 1926).

98  GCPPT A1.1 1 March 1926.

99  ibid. 9 March 1926. Juan Mascaró (1897–1987), linguist, translator, and philosopher, came of Majorcan farming stock. He arrived in Cambridge in 1925 to read Modern and Oriental Languages, including Sanskrit and Pali, in order to further an interest in Mysticism inspired by earlier reading of the *Bhagavad Gita*. While in Cambridge he lectured on the Spanish mystics, a subject close to Aelfrida's heart and one which he was to discuss with her in later years. Following his departure from Cambridge, Mascaró became successively Vice-Principal of a college in Jaffna in what was then Ceylon and Professor of English in Barcelona. Moving to England as a result of the Spanish Civil War, he became Supervisor of English at Cambridge while working on magisterial translations of the *Bhagavad Gita* and the *Upanishads*. For further details see Mir, G. pp 9–37.

100  GCPPG A2.1 28 June 1926.

101  GCPPT 1|1|32 28 February 1926.

102  ibid. 5 March 1926.

103  ibid. 22 May 1926.

104  ibid. 20 June 1926.

105  GCPPT 1|1|41 28 May 1932.

106  GCPPT 1|1|31 15 October 1926.

107  GCPPT 1|1|35 25 January 1928.

108  GCPPT 1|1|32 21 June 1926.

109  GCPPT1|1|35 11 February 1928.
GCPPT 1|1|36 28 October 1929. A 'parallel meditation' carried out with 'my Stranger' (i.e. Erle Lunn) in November 1928 on the difficulties of 'out-of-work miners, tramps, etc.' (*sic*) resulted in Aelfrida receiving 'universal consciousness … of such terrible intensity' that she nearly screamed aloud and had to wrench herself free because 'I felt the anguish would have killed me' (GCPPT 1|1|35 29 November 1928).

110  GCPPT 1|1|37 27 December 1929 and 17 January 1930.

111  GCPPT 1|1|37 29 June 1930.
GCPPT 1|1|39 16 December 1930.

112  GCPPT 1|1|37 29 June 1930.

113  GCPPT 1|1|32 18 November 1926.

114  ibid. 26 January 1926.

115  ibid. 18 November 1926.

116  GCPPT 1|1|32a. The object of the lectures, Aelfrida's prospectus noted, was not "to glorify England at the expense of other countries" but "to explain to overseas students the mentality, standards and habits of ordinary English men and women". The fee for the course was 15/-, single lectures 3/-.

117  ibid. 18 November 1926.

118  GCPPT 1|1|35 7 December 1927.

119  GCPPT 1|1|34a. International Summer Schools for Foreigners were organised by Cambridge University's Board of Extra-Mural Studies. First held in 1923, the courses were primarily intended for European teachers of English or English-related subjects and included sessions on English Language and Literature and British history and institutions.

120  GCPPT 1|1|34 29 July 1927.

121  GCPPT 1|1|34 29 July 1927
GCPPT 1|1|35 11 August 1928.
GCPPT 1|1|36 27 July 1929.

122  GCPPT 1|1|37 15 February 1930.

123  GCPPT 1|1|36 28 January 1929.

124  For a history of the Letchworth Settlement see Miller, M. p 80.

125  GCPPT 1|1|36 28 January 1929. For a history of the Quaker presence in Letchworth see Miller, M. p 83.

126  ibid. 22, 24 and 26 February 1928.

127  ibid. 9 March 1928.

128  GCPPT 1|1|37 28 January 1930.

129  GCPPG A1.1 18 February 1930.

130  GCPPT 1|1|37 11 February 1930.

131  ibid. 18 February 1930.

132  GCPPG A1.1 20 February 1930.

133  GCPPT 1|1|37 25 February 1930.

134  ibid. 8 March 1930.

135  GCPPT 1|1|37 5 December 1929.

136  GCPPT 1|1|34 3 January 1927.

137  GCPPT 1|1|26 27 June 1922.

138  GCPPT 1|1|27 26 March 1923. Papini's book, more properly *La Storia di Cristo*, was published in 1921 and was widely read in Italy and (in translation) abroad.

139  GCPPG A1.1 28 April 1929.

140  GCPPT 1|1|36 28 April 1929.

141  GCPPT 1|1|37 3 December 1929.

142  GCPPT 1|1|32 30 September 1926.

143  GCPPT 1|1|40 27 January 1932.

144  Helen Dick Megaw was then in the final year of her Natural Science Tripos. After gaining a PhD in 1934 she pursued a distinguished career in London, Oxford, and Vienna as a crystallographer. In 1946 she was appointed Director of Studies in the Natural Sciences and lecturer in Physics at Girton.

145  GCPPT 1|1|40 4 February 1932.

146  ibid. 11 February 1932.

147  ibid. 17 February 1932.

148  GCPPT 1|1|41 1 March 1932.

149  GCPPT 1|1|40 4 February 1932.

150  ibid. 9 February 1932.

151  GCPPT 1|1|47 19 May 1935.

152  GCPPT 1|1|37 21 May 1930.

153  GCPPT 1|1|32 16 and 19 October 1926.

154  GCPPT 1|1|37 12 June 1930.

155  GCPPT 1|1|35 25 April 1928.

156  GCPPT 1|1|34 21 November 1927.
157  GCCPT 1|1|36 4 June 1929.
158  GCPPT 1|1|35 28 April 1928.
159  GCPPT 1|1|34 1 June 1927.
160  GCPPT 1|1|35 24 November 1927.
161  ibid. 23 April 1928.
162  GCPPT 1|1|34 28 April 1927.
163  GCPPT 1|1|35 5 October 1928.
164  GCPPT 1|1|32 12 November 1926.
165  GCPPG A1.1 31 July 1929.
166  GCPPT 1|1|35 22 June 1928.
167  GCPPT 1|1|34 4 May 1927.
168  GCPPT 1|1|32 10 November 1926.
169  ibid. 21 February 1927.
170  ibid. 30 January 1927.
171  GCPPT 1|1|35 11 November 1928.
172  GCPPG A1.1 10 June and 9 July 1929.
173  GCPPT 1|1|32 20 October 1926.
174  GCPPG A1.1 18 June 1929.
175  GCPPT 1|1|37 15 May 1930. Trevelyan's autobiography *Indigo Days* (pp 14–20) provides an interesting account of Alethea's Cambridge contemporaries, including those mentioned in her mother's diaries, but does not mention the three Graham women.
176  GCPPT 1|1|37 9 May 1930.
177  GCPPT 1|1|35 3 and 20 May 1928.
178  GCPPT 1|1|41 8 May 1932.
     GCPPT 1|1|43 13 February and 15 March 1933.
179  Amusing as it would be to discover Aelfrida hosting, all unwittingly, *two* of the 'Cambridge spies', it seems that the 'A. Blunt' of Alethea's visitors' book, diary, and photograph album was 'a clever boisterous Rugbeian' by the name of Arthur Blunt not Marlburian art historian Anthony Blunt. Alethea did, however, know Anthony Blunt who edited *The Venture*, a Cambridge literary magazine in which one of her poems appeared, but there is no record of him appearing at one of her mother's Sunday teas.
180  GCPPT 1|1|37 8 June 1930.
181  GCPPT 1|1|36 8 May 1929.
182  GCPPT 1|1|47 19 May 1935.
183  GCPPT 1|1|36 12 May 1929.
184  GCPPT 1|1|35 19 January 1928.
185  GCPPG A1.1 summary written after 13 September 1922 addressed to 'Ye / Who find my diary after I am dead'.
186  GCPPT 1|1|34 7 April 1927.
187  GCPPT 1|1|38 24 November 1930.
188  GCPPT 1|1a *Alethea and Agatha Joint Record Book* 2 May 1927.
189  ibid. 15 October 1927.
190  GCPPT 1|1|35 27 January 1928.
191  GCPPG A1.1 21 November 1927.
192  Sir Ralph was the President of the Iron and Steel Institute and a director of the LNER; his wife wrote novels about industrial life. John (1907–1989) was educated at Winchester prior to matriculating at Trinity College, Cambridge. He succeeded to his father's baronetcy of Etruria in 1956.
193  GCPPT 1|1|35 21 November 1927.
194  ibid. 4 February 1928 (written in error as 1927).
195  GCPPT 1|1|30 26 April 1925.
196  GCPPT 1|1|35 4 June 1928.
197  ibid. 26 November and 7 December 1928. John Wedgwood married in 1933 and had five children.
198  Humphrey Warren (1910–1978) was more forthcoming than Aelfrida's lukewarm description implies. A keen rower when at Cambridge, he later rowed for Britain in the 1936 Berlin Olympics. He was also awarded the Air Force Cross as a fighter pilot during World War Two.
199  GCPPT 1|1|41 28 July 1932.
200  GCPPT 1|1|37 7 February 1930.
201  GCPPT 1|1|32 30 April 1926.
202  GCPPT 1|1|34 28 January 1927.
203  GCPPT 1|1|38 8 December 1930.
204  GCPPT 1|1a *Alethea and Agatha Joint Record Book* 8 November 1929.
205  GCPPT 1|1|36 30 May 1929.
206  GCPPT 1|1|32 30 April 1926.
207  GCPPG A1.1 1 July 1924.
208  The Wedgwoods' reluctance may also have stemmed from an unpleasant divorce which took place in 1918/19 involving John Wedgwood's uncle Joseph Clement Wedgwood and his wife Ethel Bowen. Joseph Wedgwood, though the innocent party (his wife had left him) chivalrously provided evidence enabling her to divorce him and was publicly reviled. Only after granting of his decree absolute was he able to defend and rehabilitate himself. (For further details see Wedgwood, C. pp 126–136.) It may also have stemmed from the association of one of John's more distant male relations James Ingall Wedgwood (1883–1951) with Aleister Crowley.
209  *John Bull* 27 April 1929, quoted in Kaczynski, R, p 349 (2002). Considerable public revulsion was expressed against Aleister Crowley in the late 1920s and early 1930s; it therefore behoved Aelfrida to keep very quiet about her connection with him lest she (and her daughters) be tainted by association.
210  GCPPT 1|1|41 29 July 1932.
211  Tillyard, Ae. O *Passionate World* p 263 (GCPPT 2|11).
212  GCPPT 1|1|47 19 May 1935.
213  GCPPT 1|1|30 9 April 1925.
214  GCPPT 1|1|35 5 July 1928.
215  GCPPT 1|1|34 20 August 1927.
216  GCPPT 1|1|11 Postscript to volume added 21 January 1919.
217  GCPPT 1|1|35 23 December 1927.
218  GCPPT 1|1|34 3 April 1927.
219  ibid. 30 June 1927.
220  GCPPT 1|1|41 22 June 1932.
221  GCPPT 1|1|40 22 August 1931.
222  GCPPT 1|1|39 29 May 1931.
223  GCPPT 1|1|35 23 December 1927.
224  GCPPT 1|1|36 1 November 1929.

# Rubbish that will sell

*Spiritual Exercises* was published in 1927. To all intents and purposes – and with the exception of *Can I be a Mystic?*, third and last of the 'Straightener' series begun in 1917, Aelfrida published nothing but novels from 1927 to 1935. But why novels? Her reasons for such a dramatic about-turn – she had not seriously attempted a novel since *Marrying a Stranger* in 1913/14 and had destroyed all manuscripts save that – are four-fold and throw interesting sidelights on her life in the interwar years.

The first was economic necessity: 'books on mysticism', she noted bluntly in May 1920, 'won't help me bring up the family'.[1] Necessity included a desire to provide Agatha and Alethea with good things in life to compensate for the lack of a father ('everything … from Parisian clothes to affection has been amply provided')[2] and with an allowance until they married or were earning their own living.

When Constantine asked Aelfrida in 1917 how much money her books brought in (a question prompted, it may be, by early considerations of how to free himself from an impossible marriage), she replied blithely 'not a penny'.[3] Two years later in answer to a question posed by a hypothetical reader of her diary as to how she proposed to support herself and her children without a husband, she replied bluntly: 'my books don't pay'.[4] The

**Aelfrida Graham (with book) with Summer School pupils 1929**

contrast between her two statements was occasioned by Constantine's withdrawal of her allowance following her return from Lyons as a way of forcing her to file for divorce (Mrs Graham, he informed his solicitor, was not 'entirely dependent on her husband'; Aelfrida's replied 'Mrs Graham certainly has no money of her own and finds the present state of affairs highly inconvenient'[5], so inconvenient, in fact, that she had to sell wedding presents in order to have 'a little cash in hand'[6] because cheques were dishonoured; her laudable but improvident habit of giving money to good causes when least able to afford it did not help) and by her discovery that until Constantine obeyed a court order ensuring regular financial support for his wife and children *pendente lite* (i.e. until the divorce was absolute), she must rely on remittances of varying amounts arriving at irregular intervals. There was, too, the problem of supporting her daughters in the middle-class manner to which they must remain accustomed when she herself by virtue of diminished income had descended almost to the level of the 'lower middle classes' so useful as 'copy' but patronised because of their defining habits of being 'in trade' and living in suburban villas, a decline underlined by the humbling thought that a woman who had entertained Sir John French and the Bishop of Gibraltar, who had been briefly 'It' to the Boston Cabots, who had attended the Paris opera in the presence of royalty, and who affected to despise those motivated by the love of money (the root of all evil, so the Bible informed her)[7] was reduced to living on her mother's charity.

Charity had its drawbacks. Not only was it humiliating to receive (Aelfrida, it must be said, always overcame her moral scruples when Chiara offered to underwrite all or part of a particular expense) but reliance on Chiara was subject to conditions. Furthermore, although Catharine Tillyard's rental and invested income was sufficient for the upkeep of Fordfield and to support Aelfrida in times of need, she found herself financially embarrassed as the 1920s and 1930s wore on because her investment portfolio was mismanaged by an adviser retained less for his financial acumen than for sentimental reasons and because her philanthropic refusal to raise the rents on Staffordshire Street properties inherited from Emma Wetenhall did not provide her with enough money to maintain the houses properly; indeed, the former mayoress suffered the indignity of being forced by the city council to have houses stoutly built by Samuel Barrett a hundred years earlier but now declared unfit for human habitation, 'put into perfect order'[8] at her own considerable expense.

There was too the matter of Aelfrida's own expenditure. Her income, apart from her allowance from Constantine (once fixed, and with a new wife and two stepsons to support, Constantine never thereafter raised it) came from language coaching (an occupation taken up only because her parents suggested it as a means of earning money) and from fees earned by teaching at Summer Schools, from her directorships of the Coffee Palace and the Steam Laundry (although she jeered at the 'sleek cupidity' of their shareholders[9], she took over the directorships from her father specifically for financial reasons), from book reviewing for *Theology* (house journal of the SPCK), and from royalties. Books of a religious nature sold at 3/6d, the cheapest category (only pamphlets and children's books cost less) and, like her books of poetry, did not sell well. Novels, however, sold at around 7/6d so that in spite of her fictional alter ego 'Carola' complaining that novel-writing was not "as profitable as is commonly supposed"[10], when royalty cheques for sums ranging from £50 to £150 began to arrive following the appearance of her first published novel, Aelfrida was happy to receive them.

Expenditure, apart from payment to Chiara for her own and her daughters' board and lodging, chiefly concerned Agatha and Alethea. They lacked nothing: long summer holidays abroad with their mother; trips abroad singly or together as exchange students (or occasionally as 'holiday governesses', in which case they earned a pocket money salary); pretty clothes made initially by Aelfrida (matching dresses in Graham tartan, for example), later by Fordfield's 'home dressmaker'. As they grew up they received generous dress allowances which they spent in Cambridge department stores, in Harrods, and even at minor Parisian couturiers, and with private education culminating in a joint total of seven academic years at a Cambridge college. There were also unexpected but unbudgeted-for expenses such as medical bills, a major item in the early 1930s with regard to both girls but an on-going expense because of Aelfrida's chronic ill-health. No wonder then, that shortly before his death in the autumn of 1929, the Oracle accused Aelfrida of being 'very extravagant' and insisted that she gave him a full account of recent income and expenditure.

His accusation arose as a result of his refusal or inability to hold to an earlier promise that he would help with Agatha's college fees if required: unlike her sister, Agatha was not granted a state as well as a college scholarship. Aelfrida was furious, contrasting her father's meanness ('it is bad enough to feel that Constantine grudges every penny without feeling that the Oracle does too') and his 'horrible inheritance of killjoy Puritanism' with her own (rather recent) view that 'when money can purchase knowledge and health and freedom from worry, it *ought* to', but some of his criticisms hit home: she *had* spent money without thought for the morrow ('though what extravagance is possible when one keeps within an income which ... has never exceeded £300 for three people I cannot understand'), she *could* have made greater efforts to earn money (though 'with all the burdens laid on me in this house I am taxed beyond my strength to do what I do'), and because of the Oracle's accusation would now feel like a criminal over every penny she spent. But being 'humiliated and unhappy beyond words'[11] was one thing; discovering the following day that the unpaid balance of Agatha's fees had been paid (by which parent she 'did not dare ask')[12] quite another, for Aelfrida had known the expense was imminent, had made no attempt to budget for it, and preferred to remain in childish ignorance as to who paid the outstanding amount so long as she herself was not expected to recompense them.

Quite why Aelfrida's insouciant attitude to money took the form it did is hard to ascertain: possibly her disdain for domesticity meant she had no idea how to budget; possibly life in a well-to-do middle-class family suggested that money was always forthcoming; possibly she had been taught (*pace* James Stark) that to show an interest in financial matters was vulgar and degrading; possibly having been forced into a state of childlike dependence on her parents she decided to think and act like a child and spent money like pocket money; possibly she believed that she herself need take no thought for the morrow because God really would provide; possibly she followed Sufi precepts to an absurd extent. She hints at all, and it was for one or several of the above reasons that growing realisation that she must not only preach but also practise economies took so long to materialise. It came as a shock when it did: the unwelcome discovery in 1929 that she was expected to pay income tax on her allowance was followed by realisation that she was expected to pay 'every year again' after paying off arrears of £35.[13]

A second reason appears in *O Passionate World*. According to 'Alan George', 'Carola' writes fiction as a drug to numb the pain of 'Adrian's' desertion: as 'Carola' admits, "I can't just sit and think about Adrian all the time and turn the screw to see how much I can stand".[14] Then again, "sorrow was said to be an arouser of ... talent" and it seems that Carola/ Aelfrida felt an "unusually urgent need for expression"[15] as a result of grief occasioned by the breakdown of her marriage (pages and pages of diary and novel devoted to this traumatic event bear witness to a need to express emotions repressed in public) and discovered (or, rather, rediscovered) the novel to be an appropriate medium. Novels were also escapism[16], for Aelfrida often 'told [her]self stories' on days when she went to bed with 'nerves all frayed'[17] by the strain of papering over the cracks in the 'perfect peace of Fordfield'. She also wrote novels as a form of mental discipline amounting to spiritual punishment: noting in late May 1930 after a series of particularly enjoyable social occasions and further emotional entanglements with men, that her 'soul was getting slack'[18], she gave herself 'a real good scolding' next time she went to church and was rewarded by a 'peace-after-absolution feeling' and by the discovery that 'hard work at several more novels'[19] provided as excellent a cure for 'slackness', however induced, as it did for emotional unhappiness.

Like an addict when a drug is withdrawn, escaper when escape is thwarted, ascetic unable to practice his favourite mortification, or nympholept unable to achieve ecstatic release, Aelfrida exhibited considerable irritation when unable to give free rein to her talent: 'how *can* one "produce great works of Art" when all one's energy *must* be diverted into other channels'[20], being one complaint (the 'channels' were chiefly childcare, running errands for her mother, and reading aloud to her father), another that with 'a writing fit on', all she wanted to do was to 'sit down to a fresh sheet of lined paper' but was prevented from doing so ('poor me') by visitors and business until evening at which time, though physically fatigued, she felt better because she was able to get 'some of [her] ideas on paper!'[21] at last. A third complaint was no 'room of one's own'[22]; it seems she was not allowed to shut herself away in case she was needed, 'a good hour and a half's work with only four interruptions' being accounted 'quite unusual luck'[23] and to be able to write three novels in eighteen months a praiseworthy effort given that constant intrusions prevented her from counting on an unbroken hour's work 'at a stretch'.[24]

There was too, the fact that Carola/ Aelfrida felt compulsively driven to create at a time when everything in life reeked of loves lost and bridges burnt: "write she must. The need for expression was there, unusually urgent".[25] The need was more than that of having an occupation beyond the drudgery of 'kiddie-minding' or playing the part of the 'good daughter at home'; it was an urgency to commit to paper the "plenty of books queuing up in her mind"[26] because more than one novel at a time was '[hanging] ripe on the tree of [her] imagination'.[27] As evidence of her 'need', she worked on ten novels in a dozen years (during that time she also wrote *Messages*, *Can I be a Mystic?*, and Agnes Slack's biography, and revised *Spiritual Exercises*), five being published, three completed but rejected by publishers, and two begun but abandoned. To fulfil her need she was more unscrupulous than usual about taking days in bed: 'I always get more work done in bed than anywhere else [and] I have made up lost time[28] ... if I wrote all the books I think of, what a library there would be! I always think of a new one when I have a day in bed'.[29] This applied even when genuinely unwell: 'feeling my bones ache and my temperature go up, I retired to bed [where] I have written many pages of [my] novel', ill-health being such a conveniently coincidental event that she wondered 'whether when I have a writing fit on, my … *very* … unconscious self kindly provides me with an ailment so that I can take a day in bed and really get something done'.[30]

Perhaps it was also her 'very unconscious self' which provided her with the 'night stories' and 'fantasies' from which she wove the plots of her novels, stories which so occupied her waking mind too that she 'sometimes failed in [her] … resolution to give [all her] thoughts as far as possible to God'.[31] Worse still, her compulsion to write diverted mental energies from 'thinking about God as much as [she] did'[32], this making her so 'dissatisfied' with herself ('I cannot meditate … [and] my soul goes all untended')[33] that she asked her guardian angel 'whether I ought to be writing [a] novel or meditating'[34] and even tore up (after a night's delay in case he changed his mind) a 'new novel' begun at the angel's behest.[35] But novel-writing took precedence if only because the necessity of taking up her writing 'at odd moments' and constant interruptions to her train of thought when she sat down to do so meant the parallel necessities of living '*in* my novel so as to be always ready to write should I get any spare time' and of being 'so far advanced with the book that one practically has it by heart'[36] before committing it to paper.

Aelfrida's third reason for writing novels is not explicitly stated but may have been to prove that she *could* write books which would sell. As early as 1905 she had proclaimed her intention of making her fortune by her pen, albeit with the disclaimer that 'authorship in my family should [properly] belong to Constantine' and that she herself 'would make any sacrifice' rather than become 'that curious anomaly, "the lady novelist"', but after 1920/21, needs must; she even had hopes of becoming 'a Woman with a Public'.[37] Then too, freed from Constantine's censorship of what she wrote (and even of what she said – it seems she was not allowed to exchange ideas with Fidelio unless she first checked with Constantine to see if they were acceptable and was banned from doing so if he 'definitely rejected them')[38] and disdain for what she published ("Adrian called [her books] 'circulating library stuff' [and] did not bother to do more than riffle the pages") she, like 'Carola', would be able to write "novels, serious and yet high-spirited … full of belief in life and human nature, books about brave and splendid people … honest pictures of life" and which she would love as "if they had been her children".[39] There would also find delight in writing novels

accepted for publication as Constantine's sole completed novel was not, the 'Messiah of Literature's' literary career having foundered after two articles in the *Independent Review*.

Aelfrida's fourth and last reason was didactic, a point underlined by her excuse for forgetting, though awake, to renew her Oath of Obligation to her 'Great Work' at midnight on 31 December 1921; seeming absent-mindedness, she stated, was actually symbolic 'of my wish to forget myself, even my own spiritual progress, in my desire to bring light, as far as I can, to the world'.[40] (It was for this reason too she was 'far more hurt than [she] ought to have been' by Henry Mudie-Cooke's description of *Messages* in particular and her religious writing in general as a waste of time and money and why she informed him that she did not write 'for Art's sake or Self-Expression but to *preach*'.)[41] But bringing light to the world in the shape of books was not enough. Because 'I know so much … of what is good and beautiful and true … I must write, tell people … plainly so that they cannot mistake'[42], she was prepared to imperil her immortal soul ('novel-writing might be a snare')[43] to get her message across. Her switch from 'road-books' and epistolary 'straightening' to works of fiction therefore stemmed from a conscious decision to entice her 'wayward public' into listening to 'some of what I want to tell it about God' by concealing 'the pill of [her] truths' in 'the jam of the story'.[44] (Her not doing so in verse in spite of finding herself 'in touch with poetry again'[45] during the Tillyards' exile in Hunstanton may be attributed to her previous lack of success in getting her 'vision' across in this medium or because, as she cryptically noted but did not enlarge upon, there were other reasons why she wrote 'poetry when … young, prose when … older'.)[46] There is, too, a hint that she turned to novels because after so many homiletic volumes she felt spiritually written out: 'I would rather be writing books on mysticism than novels [because] in novels all I can give is a flash of the truth here and there … but I could not [now] write … mystical books and not *one* that was adequate'.[47] Deciding that a 'flash of the truth' was better than no truth at all, she turned to novels instead and the palmist's prophecy of 1903 came true at last.

Her first thought, given her domestic circumstances and that constant interruptions would make "the sustained effort of a novel" hard to maintain, was that short stories might be easier ("no weight of heavy story-fabric, no long-drawn-out strain of nourishing her characters … on her thoughts and emotions")[48], but having decided that short stories were not her forte (the fact that her 'night stories' and 'fantasies' were in serial form probably influenced her decision), began a novel instead.

Because she (like 'Carola') was "not interested in murder and adultery and [hated] psychoanalysis and worries about money and lunacy and [didn't] want to write about passionate peasants or sheiks or the corrupt aristocracy" (Aelfrida was not, it seems, an admirer of DH Lawrence, EM Delderfield, or Elinor Glynn) and was beginning a new phase of her Great Work, Aelfrida decided to write books which would make the "average person" say "life is like that. I have always thought so but I haven't had the opportunity of putting it into words".[49] Her first post-Constantine novel was therefore entitled *All the Blessings of this Life* (no irony was intended), its hero 'Daniel Archer' achieved 'universal consciousness'[50] – and it bombed.

Aelfrida herself found it absorbing ('I am living in the novel … all the people are alive') and was grateful to her guardian angel for putting her on the right track.[51] The story, begun on 12 May 1920 and written at white heat in Hunstanton, was completed on 25 October 1920 with the promise that, if published, it would be dedicated to Constantine. It was submitted for a £500 prize but to her chagrin (she needed the money for her family and the winning as an 'excuse' for writing more novels, though with Constantine decamped to Panama, 'what could [fame] mean to me, now that I cannot lay it at [his] feet?'), it failed to win.[52] Subsequently rejected by two publishers, one being Fisher Unwin of unhappy memory, Aelfrida re-submitted the 'poor little book … in which I put so much of my best'[53], only to find it fail again. A firm of literary agents having informed her that the novel was 'powerful but amateurish' ('which I knew already')[54] and publisher John Long (visited while in London for her decree nisi) that "there is Literature in your book … but we don't want Literature. We want rubbish that will sell … Go home and write …what you think the public will like" (and, more encouragingly, "you *can* write – it's in you")[55], she went home and did some hard thinking.

She began by reading 'modern novels … to compare with mine'[56] (she had, she said, read very few because 'I hardly ever have time to open one')[57], finding hers 'superior in drama, in meaning, [and] in a certain intensity of feeling, but very inferior in technique', particularly when compared to those of Rose Macaulay (met for the first and last time in 1911 but lectured on since) because of the contrast between her own rather dated technique and Macaulay's 'perfectly deft, absolutely up-to-date, humorous, human … clever [and] indecent in a clear bright shameless utterly modern way' manner of writing. (Macaulay, she added, made her feel 'about fifty-two' – Aelfrida was then thirty-seven – 'a hopeless age for a would-be successful novelist!')[58] Discouraged by her brief foray into the modern novel, she decided not to write 'rubbish that will sell' but to stick to her own long-running saga – 'the diary of a nobody!'[59] It seems, however, that following her discovery of a kindred spirit in the shape of 'May Sinclair', she decided to persevere.[60]

The 'diary of a nobody', however, appears as the basis of all Aelfrida's subsequent novels (possibly even *Aaron Lord, Communist,* begun 'without enthusiasm' in March 1920 because 'one must work on something' and as a result of reading Maynard Keynes' essay *A Short View of Russia* but abandoned because although she 'knew' her hero 'from the inside by direct perception', he was also 'a prophet who worshipped at the wrong shrine' and she 'did not feel at home' with him)[61] and as the source of much of her inspiration and most of her characters. Her novels therefore portray her 'vision' through the medium of people and places not wholly imaginary in themselves but 'imagined' by her into situations and relationships which illustrate the Truth (as she saw it) as comprehensively as examples taken from 'a manuscript in the author's collection' or as exemplary stories about herself and people she knew in overtly homiletic works. They also act as duplicate diary and gain immediacy and relevance thereby.

Aelfrida's next novel was begun in May 1921 and completed, after many interruptions, in June 1924. (It was not published, however, until 1927 because having been sent to a publisher in 1926 and returned with the comment that it was not 'bad enough … to be popular nor good enough to charm the jaded elite', a criticism she agreed was 'very just', it was subjected to further revision.)[62] *The Young Milliner* was described by its author as 'a placid romance of Cambridge a hundred years ago'[63] and as 'charming, though of course not powerful [but] it isn't intended to be'.[64]

Placid is an unusual adjective to apply to a novel whose plot involves much emotional heart-searching, whose climax occurs during a storm of unusual intensity, which was written by an author whose life in the years of its writing and revision was anything but tranquil, and whose theme of women's abandonment by men and their need to achieve financial independence in order to rise above a life of genteel poverty was one close to Aelfrida's heart in the early 1920s. Yet placid and escapist it is insofar as by removing her story from the angry present to a time recounted in 'stories of old Cambridge'[65] by elderly relations and ladies visited for 'copy', a novel about the 'romance of Cambridge a hundred years ago' must have seemed as soothing to Aelfrida's mind as opium to her nerves.

Remembering that Constantine had once stated that her best work 'should be as good as Jane Austen's'[66], it was to Jane Austen she turned in her first attempt to be 'popular', specifically to Austen's first novel *Pride and Prejudice*, written between 1796 and 1797 but, rejected by publishers, unpublished until 1813. (The setting of Aelfrida's own novel can be dated to around 1819, a character visiting London seeing "the infant princess [Victoria] who might one day be called to occupy the throne".)[67] Adopting Austen's style and language so exactly that she could be accused of plagiarism were not her homage so clearly expressed ("You consider, then, that a woman has more to gain than a man by matrimony?" "Indeed, is that not universally admitted?")[68], Aelfrida also adapts Austen's plot, albeit with embellishments and settings with which she herself is familiar:

Mrs Foxton of Newlands Manor in Cambridgeshire is left a widow with four unmarried daughters: Euphemia, Sophia, Clarissa, and Letitia. The estate is entailed to an unmarried male relative[69] on whom she feels it would be unseemly to impose. But what should she do and where should she go? Retire to a small cottage and live in "pinchbeck gentility"[70] in the hope that some decent men will meet and marry her dowerless daughters? No, declares Clarissa, the family will move to Cambridge and in "that part of Trumpington Street some now call Trinity Street"[71] they will set up a Millinery and Fancy Goods Emporium ("*Trade!*" cried Mrs Foxton. "My poor Clarissa, do my ears deceive me? Are you suggesting that we should engage in trade?" "Yes, ma'am, indeed I do".)[72] The shop is a success and after many adventures, the girls marry: Euphemia ('of good report'), the Reverend Timothy Orwell whose prophecies concerning the imminent end of the world result in himself, Euphemia, and his disciples proceeding in haste "even unto the hill that is called Gog-Magog, there to enter into Paradise"[73]; Sophia ('the wise'), a London publisher encountered while arranging for the publication of her book for children *The Green Reticule or Virtue Rewarded* (she later becomes a successful author); Clarissa ('the one who clarifies') and after many misunderstandings ("the moment when she should hear a declaration of affection on the lips of a man whom she could respect as well as love had come and gone, but after its brief budding and flowering had left no fruit, nothing but the withered petals of sterile regret")[74], a Hertfordshire gentleman, Francis Ashwell, whose brother Ralph, a rackety undergraduate[75], elopes with Letitia during the thunderstorm which forms the story's climax but is drowned when his carriage overturns into the mill pond at Grantchester; and Letitia (after this sobering incident, no longer 'the light-hearted one'),

the Reverend James Alfriston, vicar of Grantchester, whose vicarage lies close to the river. All save coldly pious Euphemia have children. Mrs Foxton marries the inheritor of Newlands Manor and moves back to her old home.

A summary, however, provides only the bare bones of a witty, pacey, and dramatic novel whose set-pieces make gripping reading. It is also impeccably researched (that every detail is accurate can be proved by recourse to documentation) and several incidents are based on historical events (e.g. the Cambridge ascent of an "air balloon", the great storm which battered Britain on 24 January 1809, the keeping of a tame bear by an aristocratic undergraduate)[76] though liberties are taken with time and place to suit the story. Topical references (to Cowper's poems, for example) add verisimilitude, as do polite nineteenth century language ('tay' for 'tea', 'courtesy' for 'curtsey') and local dialect. To amuse her Cambridge readers without spoiling the fun for those who did not know them, Aelfrida also inserts a delightful portrait of the 'Learned Twins'[77] in the guise of the "Misses Abigail and Amelia Twistle".

The book is accurate in another respect also: the 'Foxton' girls are allegorical representations of aspects of Aelfrida herself. 'Euphemia', whose religiosity blinds her to the truth, pursues false prophets; 'Sophia' writes religious tracts designed as entertainment (the first part of the title of her book for children will arouse their interest, the second assure their parents of its moral suitability), bears daughters, and boasts that she will be a "happy wife"[78] but her husband plays a smaller part in *The Young Milliner* than any other character; 'Clarissa' sees clearly what everyone else ought to do but lacks insight into her own motives and is apt to ride roughshod over other people's feelings in pursuit of her own ends, yet her loving care for a crippled neighbour enables the lad to pursue a successful university career; 'Letitia's' headstrong nature leads her to choose the wrong man and the brief relationship ends in tragedy.

"The first experiment in fiction of a writer who has hitherto sought expression through other literary forms"[79] was a success, *The Times* hailing it as "an admirable change for readers suffering from a surfeit of unnatural thrills or depressing problems", the *Daily Telegraph* as "an enchanting work of art … rich in irony and wit", and *Queen* as a book "worth more than all the hectic modern-girl type novels put together"[80]; author and critic Gilbert Frankau called it "epoch-making". ('How nice and idiotic of Gilbert Frankau' was its author's response.)[81] Though she made light of it, Aelfrida was pleased by the novel's reception and enjoyed activities associated with publication ('proofs! proofs! coming by every post')[82] and being 'lionised' (it made her 'want to giggle')[83] by Mrs Stokoe and others. To her diary, however, she confided hopes that her guardian angel was 'not displeased that I have strayed down a flowery path of literature instead of keeping to the main road' and assured him that her pen was still 'vowed and dedicated'[84] to the service of God. Beset by further qualms ('can I write according to my conscience [books] that would bring me in money?'), she nevertheless decided to 'concentrate on novels'[85] because she needed the money for Agatha and Alethea; indeed, as early as August 1923 she began another, based once again on 'one of my old night-stories' with characters 'familiar to me for many years'. Initially entitled *The Square* or *The Selfish Woman* [86], it was published in late 1927 as *The Way We Grow Up*.[87]

*The Times'* critic who reviewed *The Young Milliner* and looked forward to 'Miss Tillyard's' next volume being in the same vein as her first, may have been disappointed to discover that it was not. True, it begins and ends in Cambridge, but this is twentieth century Cambridge (Aelfrida shows the same accurate ear for modern speech as she showed for nineteenth century diction) and as Hutchinson's synopsis (possibly by Erle Lunn) notes, her plot has a modern note too:

> "Roy Hadstock, the founder of an undergraduate society called the Square ... is convinced that the vital struggle of the future is not of Capital against Labour or of one nation against another but of Youth against Age. He is determined that he and his ... friends shall always be on the side of Youth. This is the story of how life takes hold of these men and, using women as its instruments, forces them to face its realities".

Aelfrida was absolutely correct in stating that the characters in *The Way We Grow Up* had been familiar to her for many years for among the most important ones are, more or less disguised, herself, Phyllis, Julius, Mina, and Constantine. Phyllis' role as the mother whose Spartan methods of child-rearing result in the death of a child has been noted earlier. Julius and Mina appear in the guise of 'Andrew Keith', a cynical, disillusioned Trinity don and author of a *History of Pessimism,* and of 'Lois Pennefather', a Quakeress whom 'Andrew' hopes will be "a safe companion in the perilous ways of life"[88], but they are Julius and Mina leading the kind of 'ideal' life they might have led had circumstances and personalities been different. (Of the pages in which 'Andrew Keith' figures, pages which appear to have had particular significance for Aelfrida and which unlike much of the rest of the book are written without malice, their author stated that 'here and there ... real beauty is

achieved'.)[89] Constantine is 'Roy Hadstock' (the undergraduate discussion group 'Roy' founds is known as 'The Square' because it has four members but "it is really the Hadstock Admiration Society")[90], a charming and irresponsible young man who has just scraped a third-class degree, who intends to write but never completes his Balzacian novel about "the struggle of men against circumstances"[91], and whose high spirits perceptive 'Andrew Keith' fears "[will] soon tarnish and he would grow peevish and middle-aged".[92] Seeking 'copy' for his novel by staying as the paying guest of the Free Church minister of a Suffolk village, 'Roy' meets and impetuously marries an older woman, 'Blanche Hildersham', "beautiful, ... but self-righteous in the extreme, ... cold-blooded ..., and as proud as Lucifer"[93], and changes his name to hers. 'Blanche's' thwarting of her new husband's concerns for impoverished local families and mutual recriminations following the death from pneumonia of their first child result in 'Roy' informing her that she is the most selfish person he has ever met. He leaves her and impetuously signs up as photographer on an expedition to Nigeria during which, separated from his companions and delirious with fever, he is rescued by English missionary 'Honoria Clinton-Stapylton' who tells him that his "Peter Pan pose is simply silly"[94] and persuades him to return to England. ('Honoria' has given up the man she loves because Christ commanded her to "come out into the waste places of the world with me"[95]; she is also 'Blanche's' cousin.) 'Blanche' realises how much she was to blame for the breakdown of her marriage: "Roy's gay youth had been given into her keeping and by her censoriousness, her pride, her chill complacency she ... had driven him away ... not Roy's doing but hers had been the wrecking of their married happiness".[96] In the novel, as never in real life, Aelfrida/Blanche and Constantine/Roy are reconciled, 'Blanche' begging for forgiveness and 'Roy' declaring that "youth is a childish ailment, like measles, and best got over as soon as possible".[97] The reviewer who found *The Way We Grow Up* to have "an interest beyond that of mere plot and circumstance"[98] was closer to the mark than he knew.

Further interest is provided when we discover that in her 'modern' novels too Aelfrida is an unashamed plagiarist. Her admission prior to writing *The Young Milliner* that it was necessary to read some modern novels in order to model herself on them and statement that she regularly resolved 'to fast from novels in Lent' but hardly found it a privation because 'I hardly ever have time to open one'[99], might lead us to believe that she read few novels anyway; in fact, she seems to have been an avid reader of novels published before and just after 1900. Their style and content being deeply out of fashion in the 1920s and 30s (they would have been popular with the parents of the readers to whom she hoped to appeal), it must have seemed safe to mine them for plot and character, a practice made less liable to detection by her habit of not maintaining (or of destroying) notes of work in progress, of never noting her sources in her diary, and of rarely if ever noting the titles of novels read (there are comparatively few references to books on religious topics either, though from book lists and notes of books reviewed we can deduce she read many) once Constantine ceased force-feeding her his favourites. It is therefore only through intuitive guesswork, serendipitous discovery, or by conscientiously following up the slightest hints that one is able to discover her sources at all.

Three novels were mined for *The Way We Grow Up*: *Yeast* (1849) by Charles Kingsley, read in Odessa and the subject of a sonnet written there; *The Babe BA* (1897) by EF Benson; and *The Helpmate* (1907), an early work by May Sinclair – and they were mined assiduously.

*Yeast* provides ideas for plot, name, and character and unwittingly hints at interests in Aelfrida's later life: 'Lancelot Smith', when at Cambridge, founds a club called the 'The Navvies'; he subsequently breaks a leg and is cared for by 'Honoria Lavington'[100], the gentle and pious half of a pair of sisters, the elder of whom, 'Argemone'[101], he later marries. 'Argemone' has "four new manias every year" (Greek drama, German philosophy, High Church ceremonial, etc.) and is fond of visiting a little chapel for "an hour's mystic devotion, set off by a little graceful asceticism".[102] 'Lancelot', finding his idealistic urge to engage with people morally and materially poorer than himself thwarted by his snobbish wife, leaves to become an impoverished but spiritually-fulfilled artist. He later receives news from 'Honoria' that 'Argemone' is dying and returns in time for a deathbed reunion. 'Honoria' too dies in edifying circumstances.

*The Babe BA* is interesting on several levels, not least because in referring to it as a "back number"[103], Aelfrida provides a rare hint of where to look. It is a *roman à clef* ('Mr Stewart' is Oscar Browning; a minor character, 'Leamington', may be Aleister Crowley, born in Leamington Spa); it includes a dog which plays a significant role in disclosing character and moving on the plot (the dog in *The Way We Grow Up* bears the name of one known to Aelfrida; its owner was also known to her) and a 'Lord Grantchester' whose 'local' name may have inspired Aelfrida to do the same, and it centres on a group of Cambridge undergraduate friends whose focus "an imperishable child"[104] round whose charming but futile flippancy the story revolves. It is also, judging by a comprehensive list published in a 1929 *Cambridge Independent Press* article entitled *The Universities in fiction. Do modern heroes come to Cambridge?*[105], one of many 'Cambridge' novels written in the late nineteenth and early twentieth centuries which describe the development of a young man's character as he progresses through university and after[106] – in which connection it is interesting to note that Aelfrida herself is named as one of "several women writers [who] have turned their attention to Cambridge in recent years" and to discover that not only was she writing about a subject on which she was well informed but also that she was following a well-trodden path.

The similarities between Aelfrida's life to date and May Sinclair's novel are so startling that it seems likely Aelfrida based her first 'modern' novel on *The Helpmeet* for this reason:

> Annie Majendie so strongly associates profane with sacred love that she demands that the man she marries must be as Christ-like as possible. She is therefore devastated to discover that her husband's behaviour falls short of the standard she has set and "consciously withdraws into … communion with God as her spiritual husband" as a result, to the extent of becoming a "saint in love with her own sanctity". Endowed at the same time with "healthy animalism", she represses this knowledge as an unwanted truth but her desire for motherhood is so strong that she eventually bears a daughter to the husband she treats disdainfully. The child, used by Annie as a device to keep her husband at arms' length, dies young; Walter Majendie leaves his wife and declines into alcoholism but, broken in health, returns home to find Annie, "still a religious devotee but … shocked… from being a proud and cruel wife into becoming a kind and forgiving wife".[107]

Aelfrida's third novel widens the circle of associations further. She began work on 19 September 1928 and at intervals thereafter 'fell on [her] "religious" novel and worked at it frantically'.[108] She completed the first draft by 2 November (a day on which she recorded in her diary how much she wished she could 'write the day-by-day of the inner life as I do the outer' because, though 'too elusive for trite daily description', her inner life was 'so much more thrilling')[109] and its revision by 30 December. The novel, originally entitled *Alaric*, had by February 1929 acquired the 'not … very happy title' of *Concrete. A Story of Two Hundred Years Hence*.[110] Published in April 1930 on the same day as *Can I be a Mystic?* (the *Daily Telegraph* noted that "Miss Tillyard may be said to have executed a very difficult task with complete success" and that one who had been poet, biographer, children's author, and lecturer on Comparative Religion, displayed "astonishing versatility" in writing science fiction)[111], *Concrete* nevertheless fell 'very flat'. Aelfrida blamed this on her publisher, Hutchinson's books not being taken seriously because 'known to be circulating library trash'[112] but the truth lay elsewhere: though written to earn money 'to launch Alethea in a career'[113], *Concrete* was primarily 'part of [her] contribution to the Great Work'[114] ('my guardian angel wrote some of it', Aelfrida noted)[115] and in her anxiety to entice the wayward public to listen to what she had to say (the *Telegraph*'s review also noted that 'Miss Tillyard' was *inter alia* a 'mystic'), she employed insufficient 'jam' to conceal the 'pill' of the truths she wished to express. This, together with inconsistencies of plot and unconvincing characterisation, ensured that this particular attempt to bring light to the world ended in darkness.[116]

Following the World Revolution of the Proletariat in 1950-51, England has been reconstituted along Utopian lines: "mankind built, and built nobly. War was outlawed … science, tamed and repentant, sought to teach men the Art of Living … the Eugenist Party came rapidly to the fore and dominated all the new legislation … the unfit were eliminated and a strong healthy stock evolved. Men were taught to live by Reason and to guide their private and public life according to what was best for the race".[117] Christianity, associated with the previous Age of Unreason, has been abolished and avowed belief or speculation in matters of religion made punishable by death.[118] In 2126, however, apathy prevails and spiritual lassitude infects all areas of life in England's materially-advanced but over-regimented society. Utopia has become dystopia and in an attempt to escape the pervading anomie men turn to recreational drugs[119] or even to voluntary euthanasia[120] by means of a death-dealing agent (thanatine), specially tailored to be fatal only to the would-be suicide. It is against this background that two young people, Alaric and Eleuthera, meet and mate.[121]

Alaric edits the *Aesthetic Review* for the Ministry of Aesthetics ("man cannot live by Reason alone")[122]; Eleuthera is a teacher. They mate (i.e. marry) at a mass-ceremony presided over by President Childeric, Alaric's father, and live in a mating-bungalow in Suffolk[123] whence Alaric commutes by private plane to London. Eleuthera bears the regulation number of children[124] and sinks happily into motherhood but Alaric feels trapped by domesticity. Eleuthera's grandfather gives her an illicit copy of *The Book of Common Prayer* and she finds herself irresistibly drawn to Christian doctrine. Alaric is warned by his mentor Manlius, Chief Secretary of State for Reason, a man

he calls "Big Brother"[125], that Eleuthera is "under observation" because she possesses a book in which God's name is reverenced and because she foolishly proclaims her interest but she persists in practising rituals which bring her closer to God. She is overheard by sinister Miguel, Registrar of Euthanasias, who informs her that she is subject to the death penalty. Eleuthera persuades Alaric to flee with her and their children in his plane.

Landing on a distant island they discover and are welcomed by a Christian community, descendants of refugees who fled Cambridge during the World Revolution.[126] Eleuthera enters into the religious life of the community but Alaric, discontented son of the Age of Reason, is unwilling to do so. Torn between loyalty to his wife and revulsion from what he regards as the magical nonsense believed by all save him, he breaks down. A soul-doctor recommends a period of isolated introspection as the only means of resolving the conflict in his mind. Alaric's vigil ends with acceptance of God and baptism into the Christian faith.

As synopsis shows, *Concrete* contains many elements derived from Aelfrida's personal history, many more, indeed, than those noted here; it is also a disguised attempt to disseminate her moral message of the redemptive power of religion. Diary references to the novel forming an important part of her 'Great Work', to her guardian angel having written some of it, and to her disappointment at its lack of success, acquire greater significance in view of an entry made in October 1930 in which she notes that a friend who read *Concrete* in manuscript asked her if 'Alaric's' religious experiences were based on her own. Aelfrida replied evasively that no-one would dare write about such things 'unless one knew something about them from the inside' but added that experiences of the kind described were 'more usual than was commonly supposed'.[127] Further investigation suggests that she *did* indeed know something about 'Alaric's' experiences 'from the inside': they were her own, they occurred at a pivotal point in her life, and they influenced the course of her life thereafter.

Aelfrida, so she says, underwent a religious conversion-experience at the age of fifteen but did not describe it in her diary because her inner life was 'thrilling but too elusive for trite daily description'. Clues provided by the relevant chapter (*The Vigil*) in *Concrete* and an examination of concurrent events suggests that this was the first but not an isolated experience and reveals a possible time and place for another 'thrilling' experience of an equally visionary nature. In December 1898 the Tillyards holidayed in Barmouth on the Welsh coast; their lodg-ings overlooked splendid vistas in all directions and a short uphill walk provided extensive views of the town below with its sandy beach glittering 'like silver and gold' and of ranges of mountains culminating in Cader Idris.[128] On 21 December the family set off to explore the locality, discovering first 'a tiny little waterfall … with a pretty little cupful of water that did its best to make spray and splashing' which 'filled us with rapture', then, while walking along 'all raptures', another stream over everyone exclaimed ('we may have been silly to be so rapturous but it was so lovely'), finally 'the most heav-enly view', at which point Frida 'sat down … overcome by the beauty of it all'. Only after resting was she able to go on 'but I felt as if I had been allowed a peep into paradise'.[129]

This could be no more than an impressionable ado-lescent's enthusiasm at her first sight of mountain scen-ery (she had not then been to Switzerland) were it not for four things. First, reiterated emphasis on the 'raptur-ous' nature of her experience; second, belief that she had been granted a glimpse of heaven; third, her noting after a gap of nearly two weeks (a period covering Christmas, a day usually described in detail and unusual that year insofar as the Tillyards were away from home) that she had been neglecting her diary because 'the scenes I would write about are far, far too lovely for … a person of my limited vocabulary'[130]; fourth, concrete evidence which also went unrecorded in her diary because she did not then regard spiritual experiences as 'proper material' for inclusion. One Sunday during the Tillyards' stay, the family attended a Presbyterian chapel where services were held alternately in English and Welsh. Discovering too late that the service was in Welsh but thinking it improper to walk out, the family remained – without, of course, understanding a word of what was said. The sermon, nevertheless, 'was extraordinarily dramatic and look and gesture told that the tale of Our Lord restoring sight to the blind man by putting clay on his eyes was the subject. The preacher said that when *we* prayed for light, God often replied by an intensification of darkness *then* gave an opportunity for obedience, and through obe-dience light came. I remember following intently and only at the end realising that the sermon had been in *Welsh*', the preacher's thought having gone 'straight from his mind to [hers]'[131] without impediment.

It seems Aelfrida was so overwhelmed by her expe-riences and by the rapturous feelings they engendered that she needed spiritual and emotional space to think them through; from 14 January to 3 April 1899 her diary is blank because 'such a lot of things have happened [and] I only wish I could give you an account of them'.

She does, however, record that some time during those months (she did not record the dates) she has been bap-tised and has taken Holy Communion twice and that this makes her feel 'happy … and yet how solemn!'[132]

This is significant insofar as the months prior to Frida's 'peep into Paradise' had evoked conflicting emotions, some (as the Tillyard expression had it) 'happifying', some not. A bicycle accident resulted in nasty facial injuries but 'won her the hearts of the Cambridge public'[133] for her courage in acting the same day in one of the Strawberry Eater's French plays; she had measles but gained a 'new accomplishment! I have learned to use a typewriter'[134]; she paid her first visit abroad, staying with Ancifera at the Hotel de France in Dieppe (the 'delightful cup of *café au lait*' partaken then was Frida's first taste of a beverage thereafter regarded as rather risqué and later as almost sinful)[135]; and having been entered by Mrs Verrall for the Junior Local Examination, she had to do holiday lessons in preparation for the '*beastly*'[136] event instead of spend-ing time with beloved Dudu. These, of course, were no more than the normal ups and downs of adolescent life – save for two things: in November 1898 she fell in love with Lord Kitchener, with all that that entailed of unre-quited affection and hopeless longing for an unattain-able being and nascent religious impulses were so sti-fled by 'stuffy and rather uninteresting' addresses from ecclesiastical dignitaries expounding theology 'without even mentioning the Church of Christ'[137] that she found herself in the state of spiritual dissatisfaction emphasised in an appended note of November 1904 'I was *miserable* when I wrote this … and yet they talk of the happy days of childhood!'[138] It is at this point that Aelfrida's and 'Alaric's' lives coincide and that the former in the guise of the latter describes and conflates some of her earlier religious experience and places them in a 'Barmouth' setting:

> Alaric, warned by the soul-doctor that he needs to "resolve the conflict in your soul" and to "unify" his divided self, goes alone to a peak on the north shore of the island[139] where he finds a spring of water "rising out of the ground … pure and cold, [running] away in half a dozen tiny rivulets". Suddenly, the spring becomes a beautiful fountain at which Alaric gazes rapt in adoration; in the spray he descries the figure of a man "with face infinitely tender and strong, stern and yet full of love" who holds out "scarred hands" towards him. Alaric, kneeling and bowing his head, hears "with the ears of his soul" the man's voice relat-ing the parable of the Prodigal Son and realises that "here beside him stood Jesus, He who carried the eternal into the temporal and brought the mysteries

of infinity into the grasp of all who wanted to know God". Kneeling by the spring, Alaric decides "here he … would be baptised and the priest should be none other than the Son of God". He bends his head and the cool drops touch his brow. In his heart he hears soundless words: "In the name of the Father and of the Son and of the Holy Ghost" and prays "stay with me, O Son of God, even unto the end". Knowing that there exists a God whom he can adore, a God inescapable, universal, and infinitely majestic, Alaric descends the mountain to re-join his family.[140]

Aelfrida's and 'Alaric's' shared experience (and they share more than just the former's 'Barmouth' experience for 'Alaric's' vision of Jesus is very similar indeed to Aelfrida's vision of Christ seen when cycling home from school) has two life-changing effects. The first arises because the "urgency" of what they 'saw' and 'heard' liberates their "creative energy" and impels them to describe their "vision" in poetry and prose.[141] The second is a desire to proselytise and to open "men's hearts to God"[142]; both accept the challenge regardless of possible consequences: family opprobrium in Aelfrida's case, danger of enforced euthanasia in 'Alaric's' if he returns to Cambridge. Both decide to act alone, Aelfrida because she has spurned 'human consolations', 'Alaric' because he fears a companion may divulge the island's location and it will be invaded by "all … the blessings of modern civilisation".[143] Both decide to begin their mission in Cambridge, through force of circumstance in Aelfrida's case, in 'Alaric's' because "in Cambridge, if anywhere, there was youth and an open mind to be found".[144] Aelfrida spreads her message by means of books and lectures, 'Alaric' by preaching to male and female undergraduates. Then their lives diverge. Aelfrida remains safely in twentieth century Cambridge; 'Alaric' is escorted to twenty-first century London by 'Manlius' to confront the President. 'Childeric' threatens to consign his son to immediate euthanasia if he continues to propagandise but relents on one condition: 'Alaric' will state his case for God and 'Childeric' his case against, with 'Manlius', Minister for Reason, as adjudicator. The loser will be handed a thanatine-soaked kerchief lethal to father or son because they are of the same blood. Both speak persuasively. As midnight strikes, silence falls and 'Manlius' hands the poisoned kerchief "to the man on his left".[145]

A dramatic ending (does the man for Christ or the man against Christ prevail?) but not, alas, an original one. Aelfrida had been familiar with the mystical fiction of RH Benson[146] for some years before she wrote *Concrete* – her lecture series of February/March 1924 on *Christian Types* had Benson as its 'type' for 'the acceptance of *Authority*'

as a crucial decision for a convert to Catholicism[147] and as 'Catharine Sutherland' she quoted one of his books in *The Making of a Mystic*, prefacing her quotation with an adulatory description of "Father Hugh's manner of devotion"[148] – so it is unsurprising to find her turning for inspiration for much of her plot, a good deal of her imagery, and for her ambiguous ending to Benson's 1907 novel *Lord of The World*.[149] Parallels between Benson's novel and *Concrete* are too numerous to list here; more pertinent are Benson's final pages in which he depicts the forces of Antichrist in the shape of 'Julius Felsenburgh' ("la Prezidante" in Esperanto, the common language of a world in which "dogmatic secularism" was established in 1959)[150] ranged against a small group of men headed by Englishman 'Percy Franklin', Pope Silvester III, a man who walks "no more by faith but by sight" for he has received a "Vision of God"[151], he and the group being all that remains of Christ's church on earth. In an apocalyptic climax, the man for Christ and the "Prince of rebels, the creature against God" confront each other on the plain of Armageddon while the earth, "rent in its allegiance", shrinks and reels "in the agony of divided homage". The novel ends with the line "Then this world passed and the glory of it" but whether "this world"[152] is the world of Christ or of Antichrist is left unclear: the "Lord of the World" who prevails may not be the man we think and hope he is.

The title of Aelfrida's next novel is taken from a poem by Frances Cornford, reprinted in *Cambridge Poets 1900–1913*, of which the second verse begins "O passionate world; O faces of my friends! / O half-grasped meanings, intricate and deep!" The quotation is appropriate, passions of varying sorts and degrees being interwoven in a plot which is both intricate and deep in being a *roman à clef* on a par with *Marrying a Stranger* and in containing *petit-romans*, the meanings of which are so privily symbolic that they can be deciphered only with reference to her diary. Even the poem's title (unquoted by Aelfrida) is significant insofar as her novel is an attempt to tie "*A Certain Knot of Peace*" between herself and an ex-husband who made it clear in October 1927 that although delighted to see his daughters again, he had no desire whatsoever to meet his ex-wife.

Aelfrida's comments on *O Passionate World* are telling. Shortly after beginning it in June 1930, she described it as 'a very personal and intimate novel'[153]; six weeks later, with fifty pages written, she noted how much she enjoyed 'plunging into a new story' and that she had lived 'a lot of lives … in another (not necessarily a better) world' since doing so.[154] Living other lives reminded her so vividly of Constantine that she had a '"coming-back" dream' about him, 'so simple and vivid it seemed it *must* be true'[155] (it was not) and, working on her novel in Fordfield garden where he had once courted her, was moved to send him (he was now Consul-General in Hamburg, a brief posting omitted from *Who's Who*) 'snapshots of us all together with a brief note suggesting that we might as well be friends'. ('I hardly think he will answer', she added sadly.[156] He did not.) Nor was recollection of past lives as consoling as she hoped: the novel was 'about myself and Constantine [and even] though I am not *quite* Carola nor he Adrian', the act of writing it 'opened old wounds' and restored to consciousness hurtful memories long consigned to her subconscious.[157] Then, too, because the novel was '"a psychological" one dependent for its effect on emotional tension'[158], writing it was more difficult than that of any previous book and the 'effort of carrying such a depressing child'[159] induced 'black fits of depression' unusual at this otherwise cheerful period of her life. She was therefore very glad when the strain of working on such a draining book ended early in 1931.

Aelfrida was keen to see the book in print for several reasons: it was (supposedly) an act of reparation for her behaviour towards her former husband; because (a debatable point) she portrayed him in a better light than she portrayed herself[160]; because, reading it, Constantine would be able to see 'how I loved him and him alone', again a debatable point, given that much of the emotional stimulus for writing it was provided by a younger and more ardent suitor than Willie Searle.[161] Given the picture she paints of the Grahams' relationship (the novel is deeply vengeful though Constantine is not its only victim), it is fortunate that Constantine was spared the embarrassment of reading it. In September 1931 Alethea asked Aelfrida not to send *O Passionate World* to her agent on the plausible grounds that publication might damage Constantine's career. Aelfrida agreed, reluctantly ('I [do not] think that people should ask authors to publish or to refrain from publishing [but] I love Alethea infinitely more than my books, so I consented')[162], but as with *Marrying a Stranger,* preserved the manuscript because of its significance and because of what it might (with luck) reveal to a future biographer of the Grahams' life together and of her (idealised) love for the 'stranger' she married.

Because *O Passionate World* was essentially written 'for an audience of one'[163] (the 'audience' being Constantine), Aelfrida included in it incidents personal to the Grahams themselves: the clandestine sale of unwanted wedding presents to provide themselves with funds[164]; Constantine stripping off on a secluded Dorset beach to run naked into the sea[165], an incident which suggests that she was more familiar with the naked male

form than most unmarried girls of her age and class; a letter written in the "Arabian Nights" style favoured by wooing Constantine and adopted by Aelfrida for her replies ("so the Princess wrote to the Prince as follows …") whose "fancy-dress and curiously-wrought"[166] style was accurately and uncannily representative of the play-acting relationship maintained with her fiancé until 'the Marriage of Miss Tillyard' opened her eyes to reality.

She also reproduces private conversations between herself and Constantine which in the context of his career and their divorce were better left unpublished. The conversations, some a quarter of a century old, appear to be reproduced verbatim. This begs several questions: were they reproduced so accurately because she recorded them soon after they occurred? If so, where? Or did she have such complete recall that, as she noted apropos a lady who remarked on Aelfrida's 'wonderful memory', that it was 'only too good, I fear, for my own affairs'?[167] Or can it be that what we have here are not the 'Michaelides Letters' i.e. love letters written by Constantine to Aelfrida during their courtship, but 'Graham Letters' written in the course of their marriage in which Constantine tells Aelfrida the truth as he sees it, letters she subsequently destroys but not before making copies of relevant passages with an eye to 'copy-as-revenge'? In all events, the conversations have a ring of truth about them. Some of Constantine's remarks have been quoted already in relation to Willie Searle, others (e.g. "your first business in life is to be charming")[168] can be related to specific times and places (Paris 1914, in this instance), others still can be seen as representative of complaints that Aelfrida's religiosity made life with her seem "like a wet Sunday … in the countryside" and was, in any case "pose, mere pose"[169] because she mistakes the "sensuous enjoyment" she derives from church services for "saintliness" ("you like caresses on your soul") and in persistently clinging to what she knows in her heart of hearts is a mistaken view of religion, she makes "a matter of principle out of [her] obstinacy".[170] The most poignant quotation occurs towards the end of the novel:

Carola is alone. Following the Le Maitres' divorce whose proceedings are described in detail and through Carola's eyes, Adrian has remarried and lives abroad. Gentlemen friends are dead or refuse to have anything more to do with her. Her daughter Vera has married an older man who wishes her to sever all connection with her mother. Her son Robin[171] has gone away and Carola does not know if he will ever return. She decides to leave her country house and to move to Adrian's old flat in London while she comes to terms with her "passional vicissitudes" in relation to men.[172] On the night of her arrival she dreams that Adrian returns and holds out her arms to him. She is woken by the real Adrian's arrival: a playwright, he has returned only to look for a missing manuscript. Carola is anxious to talk to him but Adrian dismisses her brusquely – "save your sermons for a more appreciative congregation"[173] – and departs, leaving his ex-wife to muse that the event was "tragically different from the scene that she dreamed and longed for".[174]

In spite of 'Carola' being an authoress who includes details of her life in her books (even the titles of her novels echo Aelfrida's, *The Lady of the Manor, Evan Jones, Miner, Speculation,* and *Dark Waters* being respectively *The Way We Grow up, Aaron Lord, Communist, The Love of Money,* and *Marrying a Stranger*), it is also in the context of two plays by Constantine's alter ego 'Adrian Lemaitre' that his and Aelfrida's lives are written. *Ten Million Dollars* concerns "men who sold their souls and women who sold their bodies for money [and] small bourgeois who lived for what money could buy and bought it and spent the rest of their lives paying for it"[175] and may be a synopsis of Aelfrida's novel on the same subject, *The Love of Money,* the novel 'which thanks, I believe, to my guardian angel, never got published', as she noted shortly before beginning *O Passionate World*.[176] 'Adrian's' other play, *Silver Shoes,* is even more relevant, given that it is an allegorical representation of Aelfrida's married life:

> Princess Morning-Glory is to marry Prince Dear-Delight. On her wedding day a pedlar sells her a pair of magic silver shoes which she puts on and, forgetting the Prince and accompanied only by her faithful dog Ma-Chiao[177], goes to seek the Jewelled Islands beyond the Western Sea. After many adventures, in all of which she is a hapless victim[178] and during which she loses one of her silver shoes (it is rescued, ragged and tarnished, by Ma-Chiao), the Princess returns to her father's court. The King, incensed by her disobedience, orders her death. Ma-Chiao carries the tarnished shoe to the Princess's grave and dies there too.[179]

What seems at first sight a farrago of such imbecility that in real life it would have been booed off the stage, is easily decipherable in terms of what we know of Aelfrida's life ('Princess Morning-Glory' is herself, born at 8.20am, 'Prince Dear-Delight' is Christ, the 'pedlar' is Constantine and so on; even the 'silver shoes' can be provenanced)[180] and when it does not depict what has already happened, is often remarkably prophetic concerning what will shortly occur. (This is not necessarily due to Aelfrida's prophetic abilities, though some of her guesses are uncannily accurate, but because although she completed *O Passionate World* within a few months of beginning it, she continued to revise it in the light of subsequent events so that, as with *Marrying a Stranger,* sections were added or re-written almost in real time.) It is also noteworthy that neither Aelfrida nor 'Carola', distraught as they are, actually die as a consequence of the misadventures they have undergone; though both entertain thoughts of suicide, they turn instead to the consolations of religion, Aelfrida in the manner described in earlier chapters, 'Carola', in need of "the healing touch of Christ"[181], looking for illumination in the works of Thomas à Kempis, St John of the Cross, and Julian of Norwich, and being vouchsafed a vision in which "a soft luminous haze" glows round her and she hears a voice telling her "Fear not, for behold I am with you always". (She also feels "a nail from the True Cross" pierce her palm.) No longer a "stricken thing" but "the beloved child of the Great Spirit", she decides that quasi-conventual life is what she needs and takes the first steps to enable this to happen.[182]

The decision is made as a *result* of 'Carola's' divorce; although Aelfrida mentions in passing that her alter ego was already accustomed to regular communion with God, religion is not as fundamental to the breakdown of 'Carola's' marriage as it was to Aelfrida's. For Aelfrida, to whom a 'relationship to the Divine [was] more fundamental than the greatest of human love'[183], her vision of Christ in a mandorla of light (she may even have heard His voice telling her to "Fear not, for behold I am with you always") was *causal,* but did one not know this already one might be led to think that in her case, as in 'Carola's', mystico-religious experience was a sequel, not a prequel, to divorce. Yet in a sense it was, for although she had already embarked on anamnesic transformations of the truth to suit present circumstances, in this instance she was speaking the truth: it was not until her divorce had taken place that she, like 'Carola', was able to move steadily forward along her 'mystic way' and to take steps towards membership of a religious community.

Aelfrida began her next novel in March 1929 between assuming her father's directorship at the Laundry and giving a talk to a local Mothers' Union during which she felt her guardian angel 'push' her aside and, the subject of the talk being 'Presents', speak with amazing eloquence through her on 'the greatest Gift of All'.[184] The title, taken from that of an old tune, was *Haste to the Wedding* and its heroine was called by the '*lovely* name [of] Cassandra Fazakerley'. Cassandra being also the name of Jane Austen's sister, it comes as no surprise to discover that *Haste to the Wedding* was another 'period' novel[185], a form of escapism popular during the bleak years of the Depression. As usual, she wrote swiftly, and after a panic when Hutchinson seemed reluctant to publish (a worrying possibility because *The Young Milliner* had sold well but attributed by Aelfrida to her guardian angel not wanting her to write novels, 'even religious ones'), found herself completing one novel while correcting proofs of *The Way We Grow Up*; this, she noted, was 'like starting a new baby before you've weaned the other!'[186] The 'new baby' was published in 1931.

Aelfrida, it seems, enjoyed writing *Haste to the Wedding* – it has fewer of the dark over- and under-tones of previous novels – and its essentially joyous quality represents the golden years when Agatha and Alethea were at Girton and she herself acting as 'Universal Aunt' to a succession of handsome or interesting young men. Set in early nineteenth century Cambridge once again and, as before, correct in every historical detail, the novel begins enticingly:

> "A wayfarer, approaching the town of Cambridge from Trompington (*sic*), may see, not far beyond the modern building of Addenbrooke's Hospital, a handsome redbrick house … This edifice faces the garden and grove of St Peter's College and may be considered a most suitable abode for any gentleman of easy, but not ample, circumstances. It had, nevertheless, stood empty above a year when it was purchased by Dr Thomas Fazakerley, an opulent widower recently returned from the Indies … Concerning the gentleman and his daughter Cassandra, a sweet and blooming girl just turned twenty, the tongues of the gossips were busy …"[187],

and continues with the amatory adventures of its heroine and a young man met under unusual circumstances: 'Douglas Arlesey' has ridden his horse up the stairs to his college room and it has panicked and refuses to descend until 'Cassandra' blindfolds it with her kerchief and tempts it down with a piece of sugarloaf. The course of true love does not run smooth because 'Dr Fazakerley' objects to 'Douglas's' refusal to obey his mother's wishes and become a clergyman (Douglas himself hopes to be a doctor); all ends well, however, after a series of ingenious turns and twists which demonstrate that Aelfrida was a deft novelist when covering her 'message' with sufficient 'jam'.

Describing *Haste to the Wedding* as it neared completion, Aelfrida wrote 'I have lived with my characters until I know them better than I know most living people because I know them from the *inside*'.[188] She did indeed; 'Cassandra Fazakerley' is herself in several important respects.

Julius' introduction to his compendium of some of his sister's letters makes explicit something which Aelfrida (in her diary, at least) does not: her refusal to enter higher education because her sole aim in life is 'marriage and motherhood'. (She also, of course, wanted to write novels.) But having persuaded herself that childbirth, "the common lot of women, was the supremely great experience"[189] because it encompassed the incarnation of an immortal heaven-born soul (the idea certainly adds a new dimension to Constantine's role as stud), Aelfrida did not, unfortunately – though she refers to it in *Haste to the Wedding*[190] – heed God's warning to Eve that, following eviction from the Garden of Eden, He would "greatly multiply thy sorrows and thy conception" and that she would be forced to submit to a husband who "shall rule over thee".[191] Alfred Tillyard, however, had other ideas, sending her to Lausanne to study European literature and to Italy to perfect her Italian and encouraging her to teach at the County Schools with a view, it may be, to persuading her that there her vocation lay. It may be, too, that he regarded Constantine as an unsuitable husband (and Anatolia as an unsuitable mother-in-law, for the lady had unquestionably led a 'very odd' life[192], and this and her treatment of Aelfrida may have prompted repeated but fruitless attempts to ban her from Fordfield) and hoped to divert his daughter's attention from marriage to teaching. Either way, he failed, opposition serving only to increase Aelfrida's determination to organise her life along lines ordained by herself and God. It is, therefore, not entirely coincidental that in *Haste to the Wedding* she adopts a theme from May Sinclair's novella *The Cosmopolitan* of 1910, in which appropriately-named 'Frida Tancred'[193], a young woman who acts as secretary to her father and leads a rather isolated life as a result, is encouraged to act independently by an ardent young artist:

> Sir Thomas Fazakerley is engaged in "the compilation of an *Encyclopaedia of Human Knowledge* designed to enlighten the curious reader [about] the achievements of the human race in all branches of learning, sacred and profane". Cassandra, who rarely leaves his side and who feels towards her father "a dove-like meekness mingled with a most tender regard", is initiated by Sir Thomas "into the secrets of Natural Philosophy"[194] and copies out pages of his magnum opus under his direction. It is, therefore, as much to Douglas Arlesey's intention of separating him from his daughter as to the young man's supposed 'wildness' that Sir Thomas objects. He separates the lovers; Douglas leaves Cambridge to train as a doctor and eventually goes abroad; Cassandra's repinings affect her health and Sir Thomas is obliged to track him down and allow the pair to marry.

Little Frida believed her father "knew all there was to know" and it was only as she grew older that Aelfrida realised "being informed is not the same as being wise".[195] The comment applies as much to the Oracle as it does to his alter ego 'Thomas Fazakerley' with reference to both fathers' opposition to the man on whom their daughter has set her heart, for the man on whom Aelfrida set her heart was not Constantine Michaelides but Christ Incarnate. It may be, therefore, that 'Sir Thomas" overcoming of scruples regarding 'Cassandra's' marriage to 'Douglas Arlesey' and of his selfish desire to keep his daughter at home as reader and amanuensis represents Alfred Tillyard's acknowledgment that he could no longer prevent his daughter from living her chosen life of self-confessed mystic. Or it may not, for 'Thomas Fazakerley' may also represent Aleister Crowley (both have a 'great work' in progress, both pursue knowledge by means of experiments which sometimes end in disaster, both keep a woman in thrall in the hope that she, with him as her guide, will "traverse … the greatest highways of philosophy")[196], in which case 'Douglas Arlesey' may represent Constantine Graham (or 'Maurice Durant' in *The Cosmopolitan*), a man who liberates a woman from the clutches of a magus–figure by forcefully exerting his own will. Or he may represent God the Father, for everything Aelfrida writes has multiple layers of meaning, is capable of multiple interpretations, and should never be taken at face value (the palmist's prophecy that she would be a writer of fiction came particularly true with respect to versions of her own life), and one of many ironies was that once her feet were planted firmly on the Mystic Way by Aleister Crowley, she found herself able to fulfil her father's wishes (albeit belatedly and not in the way he envisaged) by pursuing a career in education not far removed in aims (though certainly in practice) from that he once encouraged her to bestow on Sunday School 'cherubs' and 'Hooligans'. Furthermore, 'Thomas Fazakerly's' diktat that 'Cassandra' keep herself "untrammelled for [her] noble task" by becoming a kind of "vestal virgin" dedicated to the acquisition and guardianship of knowledge, is mirrored in Aelfrida's decision that she remain chaste within and after marriage in pursuit of a "high destiny"[197] of an equally epistemological kind.

May Sinclair also included supernatural elements in some of her short stories; *Haste to the Wedding* is Aelfrida's only novel of this period to do so but inclusion in it of two supernatural characters materially affects the plot. The first is a 'fairy fiddler' who appears from nowhere to act as bearer of letters between 'Cassandra' and banished 'Douglas Arlesey' (he announces his arrival by playing the old country tune which gives the novel its title)

but who disappears mysteriously into a mill pool at the moment of Douglas' restoration. The second is the 'gambalony man':

> Cassandra Fazakerley meets the "gambalony man" moments after she has been informed by a fortune-telling gypsy that something significant is about to happen to her. Attracted by his colourful costume and by the number of musical instruments he plays simultaneously, Cassandra follows him across Cambridge market place to "where the old houses cling to the flank of Great St Mary's church".[198] At this point she loses him but discovers at her feet a letter which will shortly result in her first meeting with Douglas Arlesey. Hearing Douglas declare his love for her, Cassandra fears the gambalony man may be an "emissary of the Evil One sent to tempt me from the duty I owe to dear Papa"[199] but later forgets about him as he seems to have gone from her life. He reappears, however, on her wedding day, dressed as before and with pipe and cymbals, bells and drum, makes merry music for the wedding party before disappearing for ever.

Given Aelfrida's inclusion of accurate source material in her historical novels (there was, for instance, a local Grantchester legend concerning a 'fairy fiddler'), it is odd that the only detail which cannot be verified in this particular novel is the 'gambalony man' himself. True, itinerant musicians of the kind she describes are not unusual – one was seen regularly in the streets of late twentieth century Cambridge close to where 'Cassandra' first meets hers – and it may be that a member of her family told her stories of such a man in early nineteenth century Cambridge or Norwich. But there is more to the 'gambalony man' than this:

> "His costume displayed a pleasing variety of gaudy colours, while from his wrists, knees and ankles hung tiny bells which chimed when he moved. Upon his head was a high, pointed rose-coloured cap, likewise garnished with bells. In his left hand he held a pipe of graded elder stick which he moved hither and thither along his lips, while with his right hand he vigorously belaboured a small drum … From his cap dangled two triangles of metal which danced and rang and danced again as he agitated his head.'[200]

By his accoutrements and his colourful dress and unusual ornaments, it is easy to guess that the 'gambalony man' represents Shiva Nataraja, Lord of Dance, who dances while he beats his drum to call the world into creation, Shiva Alamkara adorned before the act of '*darshan*', the sacred viewing of the deity by his worshippers as they prepare to receive the transfer of grace, and Shiva 'the restless one', an appropriate epithet for a deity who deals with transition, transmutation, and transitoriness – and it was, of course, as an avatar of Shiva that Aelfrida sometimes envisaged Aleister Crowley. By 1930, however, Crowley himself was *persona non grata* (hence, possibly 'gambalony', 'balony' implying foolish talk or nonsense and 'gam' being a polite version of a Constantinian description of Ceremonial Magic as 'damn balony'), but she has the grace to remind us here that it was with Aleister Crowley's help that she first set her feet properly on her particular 'mystic way' and that it was under the influence of a letter from him that she had a 'Vision' so powerful that she received the stigmata. She further underlines her point by having the 'gambalony man' appear later in the story to 'Thomas Fazakerley' himself, albeit divested of his outlandish clothes and holding a pistol in his hand, just as she herself once beheld Crowley in a dream.

The 'gambalony man' and the slave trade, Ceremonial Magic and Quakerism, seem odd bedfellows but were all subjects Aelfrida researched during her travels along the Mystic Way; all, therefore, were equally worthy of inclusion in *Haste to the Wedding* and it is through the person of 'Douglas Arlesey' that one leads to the other:

> Separated from Cassandra by parental decree, Douglas leaves Cambridge for London to become an apprentice doctor with William Allen and to attend the latter's lectures at Guy's Hospital.[201] Attending a Quaker Meeting with Allen, Douglas meets "one Stephen Grellet from America, a French Quaker of remarkably elegant address and person".[202] So moved are both men by Grellet's account of his proselytizing travels "the entire length and breadth of the American Continent … and Eastward to Muscovy and the countries beyond"[203] that they accompany Grellet on his next preaching venture to the "Low Countries, Russia and Turkey, returning by way of Italy and Switzerland"[204], and, in the novel, Spain and France. It is in the liminal zone between Spain and France that Douglas is met by Thomas Fazakerley shortly after the latter is menaced by the gambalony man and is escorted to England to marry lovesick Cassandra.

Stephen Grellet had long been one of Aelfrida's heroes and the years 1927 to 1930 saw her involved with projects concerning him: planning 'a new book *The Mystic's Quest* contrasting the lives of Stephen Grellet and Marie Lataste'[205] (aristocratic Frenchman turned proselytising peripatetic Quaker, French peasant girl turned ecstatic mystic) for which she wrote only the foreword before interrupted by Constantine's first post-divorce visit to his

daughters and by attempts to find a suitable British husband for Nadja. Lectures, inspired by her guardian angel, entitled the *Psychology of Religious Experience* and given in February/March 1928, were 'based on the lives of Stephen Grellet and of William Allen'[206]; she also began a biography of Grellet himself for which she researched enthusiastically on 'lovely portfolios' of unpublished letters held at Friends' House in London[207] before realising that she would have to visit America to inspect Grellet material there (something she could not afford to do and a country to which she had sworn never to return), that life in Cambridge was 'too full and too interesting' (and too tiring) to allow embarkation on a long-term research project, and that her need for present money was more pressing than hope of future fame. She therefore consoled herself by putting collated material into a novel, a novel, moreover, which began and ended in Cambridge, a town connected with early Abolitionists and with rejected suitor Archie Venn, descendant of the Rev John Venn, "the catalyst of the Clapham Sect"[208] of abolitionist Evangelicals.

Aelfrida's last novel of the 1920s and 30s is a prequel to *Concrete* and underwent several changes of title before she announced in October 1932 that '*The Approaching Storm* is out!'[209]:

> London lies in ruins.[210] Following the long war which brought about the World Revolution of the Proletariat of 1950/51 and the Great Death which followed it[211], world population numbers have dropped 75%. Ten years of Dancing Sickness are about to begin: "by day, by night, in hunger and in rags, amid ruin and desolation unspeakable, men and women, old and young, had danced … in mad measure until they dropped".[212] Orphan children Leopold and Jacinth scramble from the underground shelter which has been their home and leave London to avoid contagion. Travelling westwards they discover an isolated manor house inhabited by elderly widower Frederic Ellicott and his staff of three. They are taken in and kindly treated and eventually Sir Frederic tells them the story of his life, a life led in an England which could not be more different from the one they know. Once old enough to do so, Leopold and Jacinth go through a ceremony of marriage and produce a son, Walter, emblem of hope for the future.

Conceived contemporaneously with *Concrete* and described in her publisher's synopsis as another "vivid glimpse into a frightening future"[213], its initial title was *Out of the Ruins*.[214] Subsequently altered to *The Phoenix*, an even more positive title given the novel's upbeat ending but one heavily ironic too, given that the intimate isolated utopia it depicts will soon be subsumed in totali-tarian dystopia, both titles were later abandoned, possibly because of similarity to those of other contemporary or near-contemporary publications. The title was altered yet again in June 1932 to *The Man Who Ran Over a Child* (the story of 'Frederic Ellicott's' life which occupies the greater part of the novel hinges on a transformational moment: as an undergraduate showing off to an older woman to whom he is in thrall, he knocks down and kills a child while driving too fast through a Cambridgeshire village)[215] before its final transformation in September 1932 prior to publication.

As usual with Aelfrida's novels, *The Approaching Storm* is full of personal allusions (to Fordfield and Catley Park Farm as models for 'Frederic Ellicott's' house[216], to sheltering from a downpour in a haystack on the way back from visiting Nadja at Papworth[217], to visiting a Cambridge police court with students from a Summer School[218], to 'motoring' at speed as 'reckless [and] selfish – and deeply enjoyable'[219], and so on) and as usual it is a parable, a fact Aelfrida (unusually for her) admits in her introduction: "Dear Public, I do not write to please you and yet I want to please you when I write … you read my serious books and you read my light novels [but] you do not altogether appreciate my serious novels. So here is a book which may be read for the story or for the meaning or both".[220] She enlarges on this in two almost identi-cal diary entries, the first made on the day she sent the typescript of '*The Phoenix* alias *The Man Who Ran Over a Child*' to Hutchinson, the second apropos a speech by Stanley Baldwin in November 1932 to the effect that of all the countries in the world, only England and Japan were not immeasurably worse off than in 1931. Both express her feelings forcibly: 'if anyone thinks from read-ing this diary (which I dare say no-one ever will read) that I am interested in nothing but myself, let them study *Concrete* and let them see how deeply I care about the state of England and of the world' [221] and 'what a world! … and all because individuals and nations would not *first* seek the Kingdom of Heaven (as known to them.) I may seem careless of these things, writing in my diary of noth-ing but my own affairs, but if you read *The Approaching Storm* you will see that they are deeply felt'.[222] But even with an explanatory preface in which she notes that 'Frederic Ellicott' as the man (or, rather, 'The Man') who ran over the child "symbolises … modern civilisation" (towards the end of the novel she enlarges on her state-ment by noting that modern civilisation in the person of 'Frederic Ellicott' is guilty of murder because "impelled by fate [it takes] human life") and that the women in his life are, respectively, an "unattainable ideal of Beauty", the "incarnation of his baser nature", and the "*femina*

*medicatrix,* the woman who heals" (or in 'Sir Frederic's' case, fails to heal because his spiritual unease is a symp-tom of the Zeitgeist), one would be hard put to it to discover the point she is trying to make; indeed, she even trivialises it by appearing to suggest that the windmill against which she tilts is contemporary England's 'vul-garity'[223], not its immorality.

More to the point, Aelfrida's *femina medicatrix* was a living person aware that she was included in the novel and who agreed to her inclusion but who 'disagreed with [her] portrayal' in it[224] (and who vetted chapters from 'the medical point of view'), namely Dr Joan Cooper. This interesting fact went undisclosed by Aelfrida until the novel had been in process of composition for two years and her decision to base the character of *femina medicatrix* on a woman known to her since 1923 and now an inti-mate friend was not taken until April 1932 and resulted in a good deal of last minute revision: 'the woman the hero marries may as well be Doctor Joan … out and out'. (Her next sentence 'I hardly ever draw direct from life but let the characters rise from my unconscious like Aphrodite from the waves!!' may be what she believed but is manifestly untrue.)[225] The following month she stated explicitly: 'I put Doctor Joan as … Nurse Sarah Rose, afterwards Lady Ellicott'[226], and, following pub-lication, more explicitly still: 'she is Sarah the Femina Medicatrix'.[227] The book went to press 'with the name *Sarah* unaltered'[228], a fact whose significance was known only to herself and 'Doctor Joan', 'Joan' being a pseu-donym adopted as the result of a traumatic childhood incident involving 'a thieving servant', also called Sarah, and it was only with reluctance and because of their close friendship that Dr Cooper divulged it.[229] Aelfrida was much relieved ('I had always resented her having a common cacophonous name'; 'Sarah' was 'good and dignified and beautiful')[230] and such was her devotion to 'Sarah-Joan' (at Dr Cooper's request, Aelfrida did not call her 'Sarah') that she proceeded to indulge in her first and only love-affair with the woman of whom she was later to note that it was not only *men* who had taught her "the beauty of romantic love".[231]

By 1930 Joan Cooper was a well-known and well-re-spected Cambridge general practitioner/anaesthetist holding consultations at Wytherton, a house built to her own design in Newnham Road. Aelfrida does not record if anyone suspected that the 'Nurse Sarah Rose' whom she describes so recognisably and whose family history she records with only a few details altered was Dr Cooper (family members were aware but kept silent) but it seems no Cambridge people penetrated her secret. 'Nurse Sarah Rose' becomes 'Sir Frederic's' nurse after he sustains a head injury severe enough to require surgical intervention, marrying him on his recovery and becoming the mother of two children, 'Leopold' and 'Daisy', who may or may not be the father and mother of 'Leopold' and 'Jacinth' respectively. Introspective reclusive 'Sir Frederic' prefers spiritual engagement to engagement with the world and philanthropic 'Lady Ellicott' immerses herself in service to society; they are Aelfrida and Joan Cooper to the life and the 'Ellicott's' marriage bears marked similarities to Aelfrida's relationship with 'Sarah'. Her description of Joan Cooper as "a dear little squirrel of a thing, shy and auburn-haired and bright-eyed, and yet firm and *quick* and with plenty of character" also tallies so closely with that of 'Sarah Rose'/'Dr Joan' herself as "a personality … rather below middle height, neat and compact in figure" whose "hair … was auburn-brown [and] her eyes … very direct in their gaze"[232] that it is strange no one guessed.

In April 1931 Aelfrida recorded that not only was Dr Cooper fully 'established as a beloved friend of the family'[233] as a result of numerous supportive visits to herself and her daughters (Dr Cooper, she wrote, 'envelops us all three in a maternal tenderness')[234], but also that it was unusual for her to feel 'so ardent a drawing of sympathy towards a woman'.[235] By August 1931, however, she had drawn Dr Cooper into her 'magic net' by dint of asking personal questions and inviting confidences and Dr Cooper had begun to reciprocate, making 'shy advances towards friendship'[236] on her own account. Although she continued to act towards Aelfrida as doctor to patient, advising her that many of her physical problems were menopausal in origin and refusing to mince her words when she thought her patient was behaving wrongly (she informed Aelfrida that she was 'spoilt by [her] family [and] … too fond of disposing of [her] own time'[237] and that 'the amount of repression' she exercised on herself was damaging her health)[238], progress was made in mutual intimacy: 'she got the Dr Cooper part [of her visit] over very quickly and lingered to be Sarah'. Aelfrida was chiefly the wooer ('I amused myself by laying siege to her affections … I want to make her like me more, and it is a new experience to make a woman like me') and Dr Cooper the wooed, being 'quite coquettish [and] playing up most responsively'.[239] (Joan exhibited her newly-fashionable camiknickers; Aelfrida sent Valentines to 'Sarah-Joan' and her dog[240], invited her to intimate suppers, cultivated her elderly father in order to gain entrée to Wytherton without seeming to intrude, and was even willing to '[set her] cap at' at Joseph Cooper in order become stepmother to the woman she called '*my* Sarah'.)[241] She did not, however, attempt to proselytise because unable to decide if Deity or romantic interest was more lacking in her friend's life.

Aelfrida's description of Joan Cooper as '*my* Sarah' is interesting insofar as it demonstrates an important difference between Joan Cooper and 'Nurse Sarah' who is openly religious and because of what it demonstrates of Aclfrida's desire to make a conquest of her. Although at pains to emphasise that her affection for Joan Cooper was 'as little possessive as any affection can be', what she actually felt for 'Sarah-Joan' were 'fresh schoolgirl raptures'[242] amounting almost to the 'grand passion' of a schoolgirl crush – though there was, she hastened to reassure a future biographer, nothing of the physical in this; indeed, it was positively refreshing to maintain a relationship in which not even 'the most careful scrutiny'[243] could detect a hint of sexuality and in which only the rare chaste kiss was exchanged because 'I don't suppose Dr Joan is any more lavish of her kisses than I am'.[244] What she felt for Joan Cooper, she insisted, was 'a mixture of gratitude and moral admiration', a feeling seldom experienced because of her 'profound distrust and distaste' for emotional friendships between women.[245] But mention of 'raptures' and knowing Aelfrida's propensity to possessiveness and need to be in control, it comes as no surprise to discover that the 'emotional temperature' between the two women rose so high that she began to wonder if she could 'bear the weight of so much affection' (affection bestowed by Joan Cooper because of the 'big gap of loneliness at the very heart of her'[246], a gap into which Aelfrida had wormed her way) and to worry that she had 'somehow … overdone it with Dr Joan [and] made her love me too much'.[247] Too much love, of course, might result in her being as 'possessed and dominated' by Joan Cooper as Joan Cooper by her: "I couldn't stand Jane Coldham", says a female character in a novel written many years later when Joan Cooper and Aelfrida met after a decade's separation, "talk about being possessive! … What *she* wanted was to have Roma all to herself [to] devour at leisure". "That isn't fair", replies the novel's hero, "Dr Jane supplied the steadying that Roma needed". "No", retorts his interlocutor, "she was a dragon".[248] And when we realise that 'Roma', the hero, his female friend, and 'Dr Coldham' are aspects of Aelfrida herself, how much more significance do we find in her description of Jane/Joan Coldham/Cooper.

Unwilling to be as 'possessed and dominated' as she had been by Constantine, Aelfrida concluded that Joan Cooper must be 'no friend of [hers]'[249] or she of Joan Cooper and proceeded to do a most unkind but absolutely typical thing. Pleading to her diary that friendship with 'Sarah-Joan' was making her own mother and daughters jealous (Agatha tried so hard to break up the relationship by informing her mother that the latter was becoming addicted to Joan Cooper's 'sympathy and …

charm as one might … to a drug' and that Dr Cooper was 'an ordinary little thing and the more I know her the more I shall be struck by her ordinariness' that Aelfrida began to believe her, recording that 'allowing for Agatha's tendency to be picturesque', the suggestion of addiction was true and that the 'real' Sarah did not live up to 'the "Sarah" in my book') and that her guardian angel had pointed out to how much possessiveness remained in one who had foresworn 'human consolations', Aelfrida wrote to Dr Cooper informing her that she had no wish to become a 'Dr Joan addict' and that she intended to reduce the temperature of their friendship forthwith. (She also stated that her rejection was not to be considered 'a tiresome caprice' but as part of a 'serious philosophy of life'.)[250] Visiting Wytherton the following day to confirm the news, she blew 'dear Sarah' a farewell kiss and 'went away quickly, feeling already a weight off [her] mind'.[251]

What 'dear Sarah' herself felt is not recorded but from her immediate reaction ('she looked so blank as she said "Oh, I see!"')[252] and subsequent insistence that it was solely as *'femina medicatrix'*[253] that she wished to stand in relation to a woman in need of her friendship as much as of her professional services, we may deduce she was deeply hurt. (Her hurt was unappreciated by Aelfrida until the day when, 'exhausted in body and soul' by nursing her sick mother, she requested an urgent visit, only to be informed by Dr Cooper's secretary that Dr Cooper would call 'later in the week'.)[254] Dr Cooper also came to regard her former confidante with the 'tinge of contempt' that Aelfrida feared she might[255], the incident having alerted her to the problems inherent in a doctor becoming emotionally involved with a patient and to the very real danger of becoming involved as a private person with a woman who possessed the dangerous traits of emotional neediness, a desire to dominate, and utter carelessness of other people's feelings. And who enjoyed new experiences because of the excitement and entertainment they provided, not for their intrinsic merit or importance to others than herself.

There may, however, be more to Aelfrida's breach with Joan Cooper than this. Aelfrida, as we know, was always on the look-out for 'copy' and although she began *The Approaching Storm* before making what can only be described as a pass at Dr Cooper, it is significant that 'Sarah Rose' did not assume 'Sarah Cooper's' mantle until the novel was well advanced, until, that is to say Aelfrida realised what good 'copy' her friend provided. Her abrupt dismissal of 'Sarah-Joan' following publication of *The Approaching Storm* may therefore be regarded as typical of her loss of interest in a completed work: 'to finish a novel always makes me feel dreadfully flat … the characters are

dead, so to speak. Or at least lost to me'.[256] The end of Dr Cooper's period of use as 'copy' also coincided with 'a mother to tend and daughters to adore'[257] and a guardian angel's advice to heed with regard to spiritual matters more intently than of late and it may be significant that 'Sarah Rose' (as 'Lady Ellicott') is killed towards the end of *The Approaching Storm* and that 'Sir Frederic', though regretful, is not grief-stricken because he and his wife lead such different lives that little common ground exists between them. Can it be that Aelfrida ended her friendship with Joan Cooper not only because she had served her literary purpose but also because realisation dawned how little she and Joan Cooper had in common beyond Dr Cooper's intrinsic loneliness and her own emotional neediness and desire to dominate, and used as her excuse reasons more compatible with religiosity than the truth?

Though unhappy to find herself using Dr Cooper as a 'drug', Aelfrida also used her as an antidote. Stating that she could never 'so far lose [her] self-respect as to adore anyone unhesitatingly'[258], she had recently done precisely that with a young man ('my mind', she wrote, 'dwells insistently on our last caresses'), something which horrified her so much that she could only 'offer the turmoil to God' and decide, while 'psychoanalytically analysing [her] feelings', that she had been 'trying to ease the strain of over-affection for Anthony by affection for Sarah' ('an indefensible proceeding', she had the grace to add), a deduction which both begged the question: 'how much real affection [do] I feel for Sarah?' and provided the answer: 'I do not know'.[259]

## Notes

1  GCPPT 1|1|25 7 and 8 May 1920.
2  GCPPT 1|1|35 21 October 1927
3  GCPPT 1|1|22 26 November 1917.
4  GCPPT 1|1|25 26 September 1919.
5  ibid. 5 September 1919.
6  ibid. 23 September 1919.
7  *Timothy* 6:10 (KJV).
8  GCPPT 1|1|30 10 March 1935.
9  GCPPT 1|1|40 11 November 1931.
10  Tillyard, Ae. *O Passionate World* pp 81–82 (GCPPT 2/11).
11  GCPPT 1|1|36 1 October 1929.
12  ibid. 3 October 1929.
13  ibid. 25 April and 12 July ('June' in diary) 1929.
14  Tillyard, Ae. *O Passionate World* p 157.
15  ibid. *O Passionate World* p 148.
16  ibid. p 154.
17  GCPPT 1|1|35 26 August 1928.
18  GCPPT 1|1|37 31 May 1930.
19  ibid. 1 June 1930.
20  GCPPT 1|1|26 16 September 1921.
21  GCPPT 1|1|37 22 April 1930.
22  ibid. 15 January 1930.
23  ibid. 13 May 1930.

24 GCPPT 1|1|36 1 October 1929.
25 Tillyard, Ae. *O Passionate World* p 148.
26 ibid. p 160.
27 GCPPT 1|1|37 1 June 1930.
28 GCPPT 1|1|36 18 March 1929.
   GCPPT 1|1|37 19 April 1930
29 GCPPT 1|1|28 10 October 1924.
30 GCPPT 1|1|41 22 and 23 July 1932.
31 GCPPT 1|1|28 21 April 1924.
32 GCPPT 1|1|27 10 September 1923.
33 ibid. 23 September 1923.
34 GCPPT 1|1|26 19 September 1921.
35 ibid. 10 October 1921.
36 GCPPT 1|1|27 10 and 23 September 1923.
37 GCPPT 1|1|12 23 October 1904.
38 GCPPT 1|1|26 10 August 1921.
39 Tillyard, Ae. *O Passionate World* pp 75–76.
40 GCPPT 1|1|20 1 January 1922.
41 GCPPT 1|1|28 22 May 1924.
42 GCPPT 1|1|41 26 April 1932.
43 GCPPT 1|1|21 20 November 1915.
44 GCPPT 1|1|35 12 January 1929. It may be significant in this context that 'Lancelot Smith', hero of Charles Kingsley's *Yeast*, a book much in Aelfrida's mind at this time, felt impelled to speak out in order to engage people's hearts and minds on religious and moral subjects but was unsure how to go about it.
45 GCPPT 1|1|25 20 October 1919.
46 GCPPT 1|1|43 11 February 1933.
47 GCPPT 1|1|41 17 July 1932.
48 Tillyard, Ae. *O Passionate World* p 148.
49 ibid. pp 377–378.
50 GCPPT 1|1|25 4 December 1920. 'Daniel Archer', she tells us elsewhere, was based on 'self-willed' Alethea, the 'chief preoccupation of my subconscious mind' (ibid 26 May 1920); possibly also of significance is that 'Daniel Archer's' initials, like those of 'Douglas Arlesey', are the same as Dante Alighieri's. The book's title is taken from the General Thanksgiving recited in the Anglican Church.
51 GCPPT 1|1|25 12 May and 5 June 1920.
52 ibid. 23 April 1921.
53 GCPPT 1|1|26 10 September 1921.
54 GCPPT 1|1|27 29 June 1923.
55 GCPPT 1|1|26 28 July 1921.
56 ibid. 30 August 1921.
57 ibid. 2 March 1921.
58 ibid. 30 August 1921. Rose Macaulay (1881–1958), Aelfrida's almost exact contemporary, had just published her first novel *Dangerous Ages*.
59 GCPPT 1|1|26 30 August 1921. Aelfrida's reference to G and W Grossmith's *Diary of a Nobody* is ironic given that its hero, Mr Pooter, leads the lower middle class life she derides but to which, financially-speaking, she has herself almost descended.
60 'May Sinclair' was the pen name of Mary Amelia StClair (1862–1946). Sinclair, like Aelfrida, took up her pen to support her family, writing poetry, non-fiction and novels, the latter often *romans-à-clef*. She also introduced 'psychological' and 'supernatural' themes into her work as a result of an interest in Freudian analysis and the SPR, was responsive to Eastern religions, and wrote perceptively about women's emotional lives within and outside marriage (her fictional autobiography *Mary Olivier* in which such themes are developed was published in 1919) and she too suffered protracted ill-health. (For a fuller exposition of her life see Boll, T. *Miss May Sinclair: Novelist*). Also worth noting in the present context is that Sinclair's *A Defense of Idealism* of 1917 included a chapter on 'The New Mysticism' in which she noted that although 'detachment' was an "indispensable condition of mystical experience", it was also a "very dangerous state" because by its very nature separated from reality. Hence it was liable to lead to what French psychologist Pierre Janet (1859–1947) called 'dissociation' and to neurotic and even psychotic states of mind. She also noted that there exists in all mystical practices a "dubious borderland" between desire and expectation, on the cusp of which a mystic may experience seemingly supernatural powers (clairvoyance, clairaudience, therapeutic intervention, even control of matter) and perhaps "miracles": the 'borderland', it seems, encompasses psychic powers common to Magic and Mysticism. Once here, however, the mystic may also find him or herself in "a region of the utmost uncertainty and danger" (op. cit. pp 282, 290–291, and 293), particularly with reference to his or her ability to return to reality and to function adequately there. The analogies between Sinclair's 'borderland' and Aelfrida's 'borderland poems' in *The Garden and the Fire*, also of 1917 (and, one might say, between Sinclair's 'borderland' and what we know and will discover of Aelfrida's life as a mystic) may be no more than coincidental but are striking nevertheless.
61 GCPPT 1|1|32 11 March 1926.
   GCPPT 1|1|40 30 September 1931.
   GCPPT 1|1|61 7 February 1943.
   Keynes' essay, it seems, inspired a 'night story' and the novel developed from that (GCPPT 1|1|45 11 November 1933).
62 GCPPT 1|1|32 26 February 1926. The same criticism was applied to *Marrying a Stranger*.
63 GCPPT 1|1|25 11 May 1921. A Mothers' Union session taken by Aelfrida four years later was treated to a discourse on the same topic (GCPPT 1|1|30 3 June 1925).
64 GCPPT 1|1|28 21 June 1924.
65 GCPPT 1|1|41 26 June 1932.
66 GCPPT 1|1|13 10 August 1905.
67 Tillyard, Ae. *The Young Milliner* p188.
68 ibid. p134. *Pride and Prejudice's* famous first line is, of course, "it is a truth universally acknowledged that a single man in possession of a good fortune must be in want of a wife". Also worth noting here are thematic and nomenclative parallels between *The Young Milliner* and Austen's earliest novel *Frederic and Elfrida*. Austen's juvenilia remained unpublished until 1955 but Aelfrida could have heard of *Frederic and Elfrida* (written c. 1786/7) from Eustace's colleague IA Richards, introducer of new critical techniques to English literature, who was himself influenced by RW Chapman's contemporary (1922–1933) collation of Austen's works. Aelfrida herself did not rate Richards highly, including him, together with TS Eliot and Rose Macaulay, in her list of "people considered by Cambridge to be important" (*The Way We Grow Up* p45) but may not have been above making use of information imparted by him.
69 The inheritance laws of the time did not allow a man's widow or daughters to inherit his estate: in the event of his death and in the absence of sons it might pass to a distant male relative with no interest in relicts or female dependents.
70 Tillyard, Ae. *The Young Milliner* p 39. Pinchbeck, an alloy of copper and zinc resembling gold, was invented in 1732. It was used to make cheap jewellery.
71 Custance's map of Cambridge of 1798 shows it as Trumpington Street; by 1830, however, *Pigot's Directory* calls it Trinity Street. It was a popular street for milliners' and dressmakers' establishments in the early nineteenth century.
72 Tillyard, Ae. *The Young Milliner* p 36. Catharine Castle must have passed on to her daughter Emma the extensive knowledge of fabrics, colours, and haberdashery terms exhibited by Emma's grand-daughter in *The Young Milliner*.
73 Tillyard, Ae. *The Young Milliner* p 243.
74 ibid. p 100.
75 The incidents in which 'Ralph Ashwell' is involved provide an accurate picture of town /gown battles of the time and of low-life pursuits (cockfighting, for example) indulged in by contemporary undergraduates.

76 A tethered hot air balloon ascended from Parker's piece in 1834 to celebrate the accession of Queen Victoria; Aelfrida has it ascend from Midsummer Common in the presence of the Mayor and provoke a town/gown riot. The bear was Lord Byron's; having discovered in 1805 that Trinity College statutes forbade the keeping of dogs in college he procured a bear instead. Aelfrida has 'Ralph Ashwell' ride a bear for a wager and fall injured in the 'Foxton's' doorway, whence he is rescued by 'Letitia'.

77 Vera Brittain, reviewing *The Young Milliner* in *Time and Tide* (Vol. 10 No5, 1 February 1929 p116) notes that "if this tale, as the publishers announcement states" , is actually based on "true incidents" from the author's family, "Miss Tillyard is fortunate in commanding so gracefully rounded a set of facts upon which to base her agreeable reconstruction of the past", but is not, of course, privy to the fact that the book's characters derive less from Aelfrida's ancestors than from her own life. Though the 'Learned Twins' would doubtless have enjoyed Aelfrida's portrayal of themselves, her depiction was posthumous: Margaret Gibson died in January 1921, Agnes Lewis, in March 1926. For an account of the Twins' last days see Soskice, J. pp 291–292.

78 Tillyard, Ae. *The Young Milliner* p 238.

79 *Time and Tide* Vol. 10 No 51 February 1929 p 116.

80 Publisher's blurbs on end page of Aelfrida's second novel *The Way We Grow Up*.

81 GCPPT 1|1|35 12 January 1929.

82 ibid. 9 November 1928.

83 GCPPT 1|1|38 24 November 1930.

84 GCPPT 1|1|35 8 January 1929 ('1928' in diary).

85 GCPPT 1|1|27 27 August 1923.

86 ibid. 30 August 1923. The novel seems to have changed its title several times in course of composition, being at one time *The Art of Living* and at another *The Way We Grow Old* 'and I forget what else besides'. (GCPPT 1|1|36 23 January 1929).

87 *The Way We Grow Up* was published on the day of Alfred Tillyard's death (8 October 1929) which may explain Aelfrida's lack of enthusiasm for the finished work.

88 Tillyard, Ae. *The Way We Grow Up* p 166. The two chapters and twenty-one pages devoted exclusively to 'Andrew Keith's' meeting and relationship with 'Lois' end ambiguously – he kisses her but does not actually propose marriage.

89 GCPPT 1|1|36 19 October 1929.

90 Tillyard, Ae. *The Way We Grow Up* p 10. Constantine, when at King's, founded a society for reading Balzac's novels aloud in French.

91 ibid p16. 'Roy's' literary pretensions are also mocked in a conversation which suggests that poems published since he went down are only "T S Eliot and water. The usual thing" (ibid p 251); they appear in periodicals "kind enough to print verse without paying for it" (ibid. p104).

92 ibid. p 168.

93 Tillyard, Ae. *The Way We Grow Up* p 126. Aelfrida's earlier statement that characters in her books are 'seldom charming' (GCPPT 1|1|17 23 November 1909) is particularly apt here.

94 Tillyard, Ae. ibid p 273. J M Barrie's play *Peter Pan* opened in London in 1904 and was followed by a novel, *Peter and Wendy*, in 1911.

95 ibid. p 272.

96 ibid. p 236.

97 ibid. p 282.

98 Review of *The Way We Grow Up* quoted in the publisher's blurb to *Haste to the Wedding*. While it is possible to discover the provenance of almost every reference or incident (even down to minor details such as the name of 'Blanche Hildersham's' mother's dog), wholly invented characters ('Sir James Ashwin' for example, an Etonian Tory landowner) are unconvincing.

99 GCPPT 1|1|26 2 March 1922.

100 Aelfrida also uses the name 'Honoria' in *The Young Milliner* and 'Lavington' in *Marrying a Stranger*. It is possible, however, that the use of the surname in *The Way We Grow Up* is homage to her friend the economist Frederick Lavington (1881–1927) who died prematurely of bowel disease while the novel was being written.

101 'Argemone' is the name of an American poppy with showy white petals; 'Blanche' Hildersham is an 'Argemone' in name and nature and dresses in showy white clothes.

102 Kingsley, C. *Yeast* pp 24–25. Worth noting in the context of Kingsley's novels is that his *Alton Locke* (also of 1849 and a twin to *Yeast* in its sympathy for the rural or urban poor and its preaching of the folly of going to extremes) has as its hero a tailor who becomes a sizar (an undergraduate who supports himself financially by waiting on his richer fellows) at Cambridge – as does the crippled boy 'Phil' (son of a tailor) befriended by 'Clarissa' in *The Young Milliner*.

103 Tillyard, Ae. *The Way We Grow Up* p 15.

104 Benson, E F. *The Babe BA* p 169. The 'real' Babe was Herbert Pollitt, close friend of Aleister Crowley; there is no evidence the Aelfrida knew this but equally she may have done and omitted to say so.

105 *CIP* 4 November 1929. It is eminently possible that Aelfrida was the article's author: the style of writing is very like hers, the article mentions her at some length, and she was currently researching and writing *The Way We Grow up*. The article is initialled 'MS' – can it be that Aelfrida disguised authorship under May Sinclair's initials?

106 Constantine's novel *The Intellectuals* was a 'novel on Cambridge' disparaged by Aelfrida as 'chaotic scenes from university life … too life-like to be interesting [and] about too peculiar a kind of man to be real' written 'in journalese of which the *Daily Mail* would be proud'. (GCPPT 1|1|15 7 March 1908.)

107 Boll, E. pp 190–192.

108 GCPPT 1|1|35 29 October 1928.

109 ibid. 2 November 1928.

110 GCPPT 1|1|36 26 February 1929. The title derives from H G Wells' 1898 novel *When the Sleeper Wakes* in which a man who falls into a trance in 1894 wakens to be told that he has been asleep for two hundred years and reflects in surprise that though he been "prepared to hear of a vast repose … these concrete centuries defeated him" (op. cit. p26). The man's name is Graham; Aelfrida neither notes the coincidence nor reveals the source of her title, but nor does she note the coincidence of salient points in her own novel (e.g. British towns retain recognisable features even though drastically altered in other ways) with those of her inspiration. She even goes so far as to describe *Concrete* as "a novel about the future, written long before the fashion started" (GCAC 4|6|3|3 Letter of 11 October 1958 to M L Cartwright, Mistress of Girton) and to omit to mention that she was familiar with the works of one of the founding-fathers of the genre. She did, however, have the grace to note later that it gave her an 'odd feeling' to see *Concrete* advertised in *The Times* 'just as if I were … Wells' (GCPPT 1|1|37 7 April 1930), which in a sense, she was.

111 The review appears in Hutchinson's publicity material added to Aelfrida's next novel *Haste to the Wedding*.

112 GCPPT 1|1|37 9 July 1930.

113 ibid. 7 April 1930.

114 GCPPT 1|1|36 3 September 1929.

115 GCPPT 1|1|37 27 February 1930.

116 *Concrete* was originally submitted for a religious novel competition organised by publishers Hodder and Stoughton, the company subsequently making an offer for it (GCPPT 1|1|36 26 February and 3 September 1929). Although Hodder and Stoughton's readership might have been more appreciative than Hutchinson's of a 'religious novel', Aelfrida (possibly from gratitude) offered first refusal to Hutchinson who, probably influenced by Erle Lunn, agreed to publish it. A review in *The Occult Review* (vol 50 No 5 May 1930 pp 289–299), though admiring (*Concrete* is described as "a story of deep insight"), inadvertently explains the book's unpopularity: contemporary readers of

futuristic novels were unlikely to appreciate its also being "a vehicle for the presentation of deeply spiritual truths". An inappropriate Cubist dust jacket cannot have helped either.

117  Tillyard, Ae. *Concrete* p111.

118  Aelfrida wrote *Concrete* when 'oppressed with the secularisation of "the World"' (GCPPT 1|1|40 22 September 1931). In *The Way of Praise* (p161), published in 1937, she addresses her audience along much the same lines: "imagine a secularised England. Twenty-five years ago such a contingency would have been unthinkable. Who dares say that it is unthinkable now? You and I may live to see religion outlawed and martyrdom the price of faith".

119  The drug of choice is 'heroline'. (Aleister Crowley had been addicted to heroin since it was prescribed for his severe asthma in 1920; his novel *The Diary of a Drug Fiend* appeared in 1922). So worried were the authorities about the increased use of heroin and other recreational drugs that the Dangerous Drugs Act was passed in 1922 in an attempt to outlaw their illicit use. Given that Aelfrida herself may have taken opium experimentally earlier in her life, it is interesting to find that a character in *Concrete* with whom she identifies admits to taking 'heroline' out of "curiosity [and] the desire for a new sensation" (pp 253–254).

120  Aelfrida herself was pro-euthanasia especially for those who, without hope of recovery from illness, ardently wished for death. (GCPPT 1|1|41 23 June 1932.)

121  Alaric was King of the Goths until his death in 410 AD. Like Constantine, he was a Christian but of Arian (cf Greek Orthodox) persuasion; like Aelfrida on occasion, he was said to have heard an insistent 'voice' urging immediate action of a specific nature. 'Eleuthera' was, of course, Chiara's *nom-de-plume* when writing for *The Baptist Times*.

122  Tillyard, Ae. *Concrete* p 51.

123  The 'mating-bungalow' is situated between Clare and Cavendish in unspoilt countryside familiar to Aelfrida from family holidays. A pivotal scene is set in nearby Ovington churchyard, a place identical even today to her diary description.

124  Albinski, N. (pp 78–80) posits women's utopias of the twentieth centuries as centring on "women's right to be something other than breeding machines" but notes that this right sometimes conflicts with the male domination of societies "which dictate woman's reproductive behaviour, whether ... to restrict or to enforce pregnancy". Aelfrida, as we know, was opposed to any form of birth control on religious grounds (to prevent conception was to prevent the birth of a child made in God's image) and it was Constantine who imposed its use on her.

125  George Orwell's 1949 novel *Nineteen Eighty Four* also refers to a 'Big Brother'. Both his and Aelfrida's earlier novel describe a subversive nonconformist reacting against the confines of a totalitarian state, a fact which makes the coincidence of nomenclature even more curious.

126  Island utopias have a lengthy pedigree but Rose Macaulay's *Orphan Island* of 1924 in which the descendants of an earlier shipwreck perpetuate the mores of the society their ancestors left behind is probably the most relevant here insofar as Aelfrida's island society is both Christian and governed "as a University is governed" (*Concrete* p 226), the 'University' in question being Cambridge itself.

127  GCPPT 1|1|38 12 October 1930.

128  GCPPT 1|1|4 23 December 1898.

129  ibid. 21 December 1898.

130  ibid. 5 January 1899.

131  GCPPT 1|1|52 7 June 1937.

132  GCPPT 1|1|4 4 April 1899. The diary entry is marked with a cross to remind her of its significance.

133  ibid. 10 May 1898. Julius' account in his introduction to *The Letters of ACW Tillyard* (MTC) notes that the accident was the beginning of

'a long train of discomfort and suffering' because his sister's broken teeth were splinted by 'a pioneer in dentistry but a ruthless manipulator', the metal plates remaining in place for 'many months'. Aelfrida stoically does not mention the 'plates' at all.

134  ibid. 31 March 1898.

135  ibid. 3 September 1898.

136  ibid. 11 August 1898.

137  ibid. 4 April 1898.

138  ibid. 22 January 1898.

139  Tillyard, Ae. *Concrete* pp 249–250.

140  ibid pp 256–257. Aelfrida is paraphrasing *Matthew* 28:20 (KJV) here: "Lo I am with you always, even unto the end of the world".

141  ibid pp 261–262. A significant but undated poem appears in the next volume (1|1|5) of Aelfrida's diary. It describes how she and her "Sorrow" sit alone "far above the world" dejected because God "will not draw nigh" and prayers do not reach Him. Suddenly Hope flies down from Heaven, crying "Look up". They do, and "God's Son from out the sky" descends to dwell with her. Some years later, in the context of visions seen by her as an adolescent but not described in her diary, Aelfrida noted of the poem (which she now called the *Vision of Sorrow*) that it was a 'form of *Samadhi*' (GCPPT 1|3).

142  On 9 January 1900 (GCPPT 1|1|4) Aelfrida noted her 'wild wish' not only to be a 'celebrated authoress' but also 'to do good' by her stories.

143  Tillyard, Ae. *Concrete* p 270. Aldous Huxley's last novel, *Island*, published in 1962, describes how a religious island community is destabilised by such an intrusion. This, and other parallels between Aelfrida's *Concrete* of 1930 and Huxley's *Brave New World* of 1932 would repay further study. Huxley is known to have read Aelfrida's *Spiritual Exercises* (GCPPT 1|1|54 14 August 1937) and it is possible that he read her novels too.

144  Tillyard, Ae. *Concrete* p274. 'Alaric's' Cambridge is recognisably Aelfrida's but with significant differences: King's and Trinity are now 'President's' and 'Lenin' college respectively, "fine houses in Grange Road" have been blown up "as being the homes of capitalists", and meadows have replaced "the dreary streets ... beyond Mill Road bridge" (ibid. p 273).

145  Tillyard, Ae. ibid. p 288.

146  Robert Hugh Benson (1871–1914) was a brother of EF Benson, author of *The Babe BA*. A Cambridge graduate, Benson was initially ordained as an Anglican priest, his 1903 conversion to Roman Catholicism being a high-profile affair which stimulated much contemporary interest at a time when Aelfrida's own inclinations were towards that faith. Even more influential in terms of her 'Great Work' was his self-imposed mission "to try to interpret the old religion of the centuries to the English people of today ... to guide men, if he could, to appreciate the beauties of a faith which completely satisfied the yearnings of his own soul" (*In Memoriam Robert Hugh Benson* in *The Cambridge Review* vol XXXVI No 889 28 October 1914 p 40).

147  GCPPT 1|1|27 6 February 1924. Aelfrida was approached after this lecture by Dom Bede Camm OSB (1864–1942), then Master of Benet House in Cambridge and earlier an important figure in the Anglo-Catholic revival movement, who informed her that he not only knew RH Benson but had also collaborated with him on some of his books.

148  Tillyard, Ae. *The Making of a Mystic* pp 85–86.

149  *Lord of the World* was written during Benson's later period of residence in Cambridge (1904–1908) at a time and in a place where Aelfrida was herself undergoing spiritual trials akin to those Benson graphically describes.

150  Benson, RH. *Lord of the World* p xvii. Esperanto, an artificial international language invented by L. Zamenhof in 1887, was much in

vogue at this time; an International Esperanto Congress, attended by Zamenhof himself, was held in Cambridge in 1907.

151  ibid. p 341.

152  ibid. pp 351–352.

153  GCPPT 1|1|37 1 June 1930.

154  GCPPT 1|1|38 18 July 1930.

155  ibid. 19 August 1930.

156  ibid. 20 August 1930.

157  ibid. 27 July 1930.

158  ibid. 25 July 1930.

159  GCPPT 1|1|39 16 January 1931.

160  GCPPT 1|1|40 12 June 1931.

161  GCPPT 1|1|39 16 January 1931.

162  GCPPT 1|1|40 28 September 1931.

163  GCPPT 1|1|39 16 January 1931.

164  Tillyard, Ae. *O Passionate World* p 51. Aelfrida's placement of the episode shortly after 'Carola's' marriage suggests that disposal of wedding presents dubbed by her new husband an "aesthetic crime" was based on a real incident. The Grahams probably used monies raised in this way to equip themselves for Odessa.

165  The incident probably took place on 4 August 1906, the day on which Aelfrida and Constantine explored an isolated chine 'where the land breaks suddenly and the crumbling cliffs are cut by a tiny stream'. (GCPPT 1|1|13 25 August 1906). The scene as described in *O Passionate World* (pp 286–287) is very similar but Aelfrida gives no hint in her diary of the incident as described in the novel.

166  ibid pp 411–413. The letter may be the one described in *A Little Road-Book for Mystics* p 11: "I have heard how, long ago, the Prince Diadem … heard of the fair renown of Donia, Princess of the Isles of Camphor and of Crystal …" It may also reproduce the sole 'Michaelides letter' saved from Aelfrida's post-Hunstanton holocaust.

167  GCPPT 1|1|46 11 February 1935.

168  Tillyard, Ae. *O Passionate World* p 8.

169  ibid. pp 2 and 8.

170  ibid. pp 2–4 and 8.

171  'Robin', though a boy, is essentially Agatha. He is given a bird's name because at the time of writing (1930/31) Aelfrida usually referred to Agatha as 'Temu'. 'Temu' was a name adopted by Agatha when a little girl engrossed in the 'Birdie Book', an ornithology inherited from her mother. It seems she adopted the seamew as her totem and that 'Temu' (pronounced 'Teemew') was her childish attempt at correct pronunciation.

172  Tillyard, Ae. *O Passionate World* pp 406–407. Of note in this context is the plot of May Sinclair's 1904 novel *The Divine Fire* in which a young man becomes involved in relationships with women of very different kinds while seeking to discover who he really is. Boll (pp 177–178) describes it as a "psychological romance", an apt term, too, for *O Passionate World*.

173  ibid. p 419.

174  ibid. pp 422–425.

175  ibid. pp 345–346.

176  GCPPT 1|1|35 1 September 1928. May Sinclair's *The Divine Fire* also included three poems and a verse-drama ostensibly written by its hero (a poet, later a novelist) as representative of different stages of his emotional development. Aelfrida takes the process a step further by having 'Adrian' write one play based on an unpublished novel of her own (*The Love of Money*) and another which is an allegorical depiction of 'Adrian's' real-life counterpart's wife's life.

177  Ma-Chiao may represent Aelfrida's guardian angel, his name deriving from 'chi', the Greek letter X, first letter of 'Christ' with the addition of 'alpha' and 'omega' as representing Christ as "Alpha and Omega, the first and the last" (*Revelation* 1:11) but there other possible etymologies.

178  The adventures undergone by the hapless princess are allegorical descriptions of episodes in Aelfrida's married life, a bandit camp

179  Tillyard, Ae. *O Passionate World* pp 87–89.

180  The play's title derives from a pair of silver brocade shoes worn by Alethea with her Parisian couture dress (GCPPG A2.1 1 January 1927) but their mystical significance for 'Princess Morning-Glory' transcends the prosaic nature of the objects which inspired their inclusion. Also worth noting is the coincidence between Aelfrida's 'silver shoes' and the silver slippers worn by 'Dorothy' in Frank Baum's widely reviewed story and musical of 1900 and 1902 respectively and between the plot and characterisation of 'Adrian LeMaitre's' play and Baum's. And of course Aelfrida may have been having a quiet laugh at her readers' expense: a poem by Ethel Archer entitled *The Fairy Fiddler* which appears in *The Equinox* of March 1913 (vol 1 No 9 p 115) describes its subject as "bound by the far faint rune / Of the Fairy Fiddler's silver shoon".

181  Tillyard, Ae. *O Passionate World* p 91.

182  ibid. pp 121–123.

183  GCPPT 1|1|39 9 January 1931.

184  ibid. 27 March 1929.

185  ibid. 25 March 1929. The name 'Cassandra' has other allusions of interest in this context, *Cassandra* being also the title of a novel by Florence Nightingale. Written 1850-53 but only recently (1928) available to the general public, it immediately became a focal feminist text for women writers such as Vera Brittain and Virginia Woolf (both read by Aelfrida) with whom Nightingale's tale of the stirring of creativity in one expected to be a "daughter at home" resounded strongly. (For more on this, see Bostridge, M. pp 177–180, 374 and 533–535). Also in this connection one might note that Homer's Trojan prophetess Cassandra was doomed by the gods who cursed her with the gift of prophecy but of never being believed. More prosaically, 'Fazakerley' may derive from the surname of one of Alethea's contemporaries at Girton, a source used elsewhere by her mother.

186  GCPPT 1|1|36 3 September 1929.

187  Tillyard, Ae. *Haste to the Wedding* p 1. The 'Fazakerley's' house is now the Master's Lodge of Peterhouse. The 'grove' to which Aelfrida refers was then a deer-park belonging to the college.

188  GCPPT 1|1|36 3 September 1929.

189  Tillyard, Ae. *O Passionate World* pp 298–299.

190  Tillyard, Ae. *Haste to the Wedding* p 61.

191  *Genesis* 3:6 (KJV).

192  GCPPT 1|1|16 16 September 1908.

193  Boll, T. p 175.

194  Tillyard, Ae. *Haste to the Wedding* pp 10–11.

195  GCPPT 2|23 *The Watchword* June 1957.

196  Tillyard, Ae. *Haste to the Wedding* p 61.

197  ibid.

198  Tillyard, Ae. p 18–20.

199  ibid. p 157.

200  ibid. pp 18–20.

201  For details of William Allen (1770–1843) and the background to much of what follows see Hochschild, A. *Bury the Chains. The British Struggle to Abolish Slavery.*

202  Tillyard, Ae. *Haste to the Wedding* pp 185–187. Here, as elsewhere in this section of *Haste to the Wedding*, Aelfrida is (as she admits in a postscript to the novel) quoting virtually verbatim from William Allen's journal, read in November 1927 (GCPPT 1|1|35 2 November 1927).

203  Tillyard, Ae. *Haste to the Wedding* p194.

204  ibid. p 256.

205  GCPPT 1|1|34 21 July 1927. Aelfrida describes the life of Marie Lataste in emotive detail in *Spiritual Exercises* pp 202–208.

206  GCPPT 1|1|35 4 February 1928 ('1927' in diary).

207  ibid. 20 April 1928.

208 Annan, N. pp 334–337.

209 GCPPT 1|1|42 28 October 1932.

210 In a talk given to a Mothers' Union meeting on Armistice Day 1925 concerning the devastating effects of what she called the 'next' war, Aelfrida graphically discussed 'Zeppelins hovering over Cambridge and flinging down poison gas' and colleges, churches, schools and homes reduced to 'monuments in one vast graveyard, where there were no living to bury the dead' (GCPPT 1|1|30 11 November 1925). Although it may be with this in mind that she embarked on her description of London, her material is chiefly derived from Nadja Laptchinski's descriptions of revolutionary Russia and the dreadful years which followed ('la bête humaine is revealed so disgustingly in free Russia' GCPPT 1|1|22 3 February 1918), from stories retailed by Russian friends of Chiara's reduced to 'sweeping Moscow streets when not imprisoned' (GCPPT 1|1|25 22 February 1921) and from Julius' visits as Professor of Russian to 'the land of the Bolshies' (GCPPT 1|1|32 12 June 1926).

211 'Now comes God's punishment', wrote Aelfrida of the Spanish Influenza epidemic which followed the Great War (GCPPT 1|1|23 26 October 1918).

212 Tillyard, Ae. Concrete p111. Although Aelfrida disapproved of several of the popular dances of the 1920s, her notion may also derive from a curious epidemic prevalent in Germany, Austria, Hungary, Russia, and the Netherlands in the aftermath of the Great War. Popularly known as the "sobbing sickness", it seems to have been a neurological or hysterical condition affecting all ages and both sexes whose symptoms were uncontrollable attacks of sobbing leading in some cases to choking attacks, to epileptiform fits, and even to loss of consciousness. (The Cambridge Magazine vol 8 No 40 12 July 1919 pp 841–842 quoting the New York Literary Digest of 8 May 1919). Unlike Aelfrida's 'Dancing Sickness', the 'sobbing sickness' was not fatal.

213 HG Wells' novel The War of the Worlds (1898) included the phrase "the gathering storm" but Aelfrida, as usual, makes no reference to her sources. Wells himself led a campaign for world peace in the 1920s based on his belief that if everyone were alerted to the nature of social problems and to the dangers inherent in using war as a means of solving them, the world would be a better place, and it may be that Aelfrida's two novels on these subjects were inspired by his ideas. A comparison of The Approaching Storm and Aldous Huxley's Ape and Essence of 1948, with its vivid depiction of Los Angeles after World War Three, would also repay study.

214 GCPPT 1|1|37 1 June 1930. Out of the Ruins is also the title of the first story in a collection of stories of the same name published in 1927 by Aelfrida's own publisher, Hutchinson. Of Philip Gibbs' story, details from the first two may have been adapted by Aelfrida for use in her own current novel, e.g. Gibbs' description of "the dancing disease, a kind of madness" (The Wandering Birds p 54).

215 Aelfrida's story-within-a-story may derive from Hugh Walpole's 1912 novel The Prelude to Adventure which depicts the life of a Cambridge undergraduate "darkened by the memory of a crime" and his decision that only by doing something for society can he "win his way back to citizenship". (The Universities in Fiction. CIP 4 November 1929). Also noteworthy in this context is that a character in RH Benson's 1914 novel Initiation (pp 245–250) runs over a child while driving with his fiancée.

216 Tillyard, Ae. The Approaching Storm pp 43–46.
GCPPT 1|1|22 19 and 26 June 1918.

217 GCPPG A2.1 26 August 1926.

218 GCPPT 1|1|35 11 October 1927.

219 GCPPT 1|1|14 2 November 1906.

220 Tillyard, Ae. The Approaching Storm p 9.

221 GCPPT 1|1|41 1 June 1932.

222 GCPPT 1|1|42 5 November 1932.

223 Tillyard, Ae. The Approaching Storm pp 9–10 and 284.

224 GCPPT 1|1|41 30 May and 2 June 1932.

225 ibid. 20 April 1932.

226 ibid. 30 May 1932.

227 GCPPT 1|1|42 31 October 1932.

228 GCPPT 1|1|41 30 May 1932.

229 ibid. 28 April 1932. Dr Cooper's birth certificate shows that 'Sarah Annie Cooper' was born in Ayr in Scotland on 31 October 1892, the daughter of Joseph Cooper, Wesleyan Minister, and Annie Elizabeth née Beattie. Her later adoption of the name 'Joan' was apt in that it paid tribute to both parents: Jo-an. Dr Cooper's original name was, of course, known to the father who shared his daughter's house at the time of the latter's friendship with Aelfrida but was never disclosed by him. Nor did Dr Cooper herself disclose it to anyone other than Aelfrida, friends and colleagues being amazed and incredulous when informed of the fact.

230 GCPPT 1|1|40 6 February 1932.

231 Tillyard, Ae. The Fruits of Silence pp 27–31.

232 GCPPT 1|1|39 29 March 1931.
Tillyard, Ae. The Approaching Storm p70.

233 GCPPT 1|1|39 9 April 1931.

234 GCPPT 1|1|40 5 July 1931.

235 GCPPT 1|1|39 25 April 1931.

236 GCPPT 1|1|40 1 August 1931.

237 ibid. 7 August 1931.

238 ibid. 20 January 1932.

239 GCPPT 1|1|41 28 February 1932.

240 GCPPT 1|1|40 14 and 19 February 1932. Superior Valentine for Dr Joan appears in the undated MCJ Medical Number (GCPPT 2|2a) composed shortly after Valentine's Day 1932; it was written expressly for and contributed to by Joan Cooper herself.

241 GCPPT 1|1|41 8 June 1932.
GCPPT 1|1|62 10 August 1944.

242 GCPPT 1|1|41 27 June 1932.

243 ibid. 30 June 1932.

244 ibid. 15 July 1932.

245 ibid. 30 June 1932.

246 GCPPT 1|1|42 3 November 1932.

247 ibid. 28 October 1932.

248 Tillyard, Ae. The Centaur p 91 (GCPPT 2|21|1).

249 GCPPT 1|1|43 9 March 1933.

250 ibid. 43 11 and 20 November 1932.

251 ibid. 21 November 1932.

252 ibid.

253 ibid. 13 November 1932.

254 ibid. 15 December 1932.

255 ibid. 22 November 1932.

256 GCPPT 1|1|17 23 November 1909.

257 GCPPT 1|1|43 23 November 1932.

258 ibid. 22 November 1932.

259 ibid. 23 November 1932.

# O Passionate World

The Frenchman with whom Aelfrida discussed her '*affaire à perverte*' with Willie Searle was prolific poet, dramatist, novelist, biographer, and autobiographer Albert Erlande[1], encountered for the first time in August 1925 when she and her daughters stayed for a month as guests of the Erlande family, Alethea's hosts during her pre-Girton visit to Paris, at the family's rented summer villa at Grandcamp in the Calvados area of Normandy and at the point in her relationship with Willie Searle when she decided for the first (but not the last) time that 'the Willie episode' was finished and that she should press on with her 'spiritual pilgrimage'.[2] The pleasant surroundings of a fishing village cum resort would, it seemed, provide the perfect place to forget him.

Arriving on the 1st, by 3 August she had been 'led into literary tête-à-têtes with M. Erlande', albeit with the warning 'Aelfrida, be good!' because Erlande, a 'quaint, ugly little man, brilliantly clever [and] full of sympathy and humour', nine years older than herself and 'cynical, of course', was 'not good' for her to know because of his 'love of power [and] knowledge of women'. Hence, too, her initial reluctance to confide in a man who 'would like to hear all about my experiences of life and I do not wish to tell him'.[3] Three other factors also made her hesitate: Erlande's books were 'not quite sane'; wartime experiences had affected him mentally and there were times when 'all sense of his own personality left him'[4]; because Erlande had a reputation for behaving like 'a perfect savage'[5] in pursuit of every woman he met.

'Vocation', vow of celibacy, and 'spiritual espousal' notwithstanding (remember in what follows that the latter event took place only three months earlier), Aelfrida found herself succumbing to her half-wish to 'chase after happiness like other people' and enormously attracted to a man more hot-blooded than 'sexually timid' Willie Searle. ('I am incorrigible in wanting instinctively to interest the nearest male!') What happened next was inevitable: literary tête-à-têtes (he admiring her poetry, she reading and commenting on his novels) became exchanges of confidences (the 'Willie problem', 'universal consciousness', 'human love', and so on)[6], then sexually-charged behaviour (Erlande said mutual attraction between a man and a woman was a force not to be resisted[7]; Aelfrida pleaded religion as a force stronger

**Alethea and Agatha Graham with Albert Erlande 1926**

still; he said or hinted "come, you are a woman, I am a man – you stir me – you know it") climaxing in one author pursuing the other on walks, around the villa, and even into her bedroom to inform her that nothing mattered except Sex and that by the feel of her cheeks, lips, and thighs ('I forget the descriptive adjectives') she too was 'made for love'. Aelfrida concurred: 'there was just enough truth in what he said [for] part of me thoroughly enjoyed his caress [and] part of me is not at all insensible to his fiery southern charm'.[8] Deciding therefore, that she must be 'jolly careful' because she had no wish to upset Madame Erlande and because Erlande's embraces made her belief that 'religion matters more than anything' hard to maintain but also that she did not object to 'providing him with a few stray thrills to help him with the book he is writing'[9], her next move was to write an essay in immaculate French on the subject of her favourite author.

The essay, given in full in her diary, expatiates on Erlande's literary style ("*il doit se donner beaucoup de peine pour trouver le mot juste*"), characterisation ("*dans ses pages, il n'y a pas un personnage qui ne soit vivant, pas une situation qui ne répond à la vie même*"), unique ability to study a fellow human being like an anatomical specimen laid out for dissection, voice ("*tantôt épée, tantôt caresse*"), and effect on women: "*Erlande est acier et feu – de l' acier quand il vous regarde, de feu quand il vous touche*".[10] She then gave a copy to the essay's subject who, skilled *littérateur*, steely of glance, and fiery of touch though he might be, was known to be disinhibited (adultery, he said, should be enacted as a sort of sacrament) and of whose wife she was currently the guest.

The holiday ended a few days later, both parties conducting themselves (with difficulty) with sufficient restraint not to upset Madame Erlande. (The latter confided to Aelfrida that her husband always behaved in this extravagant manner towards women, that she believed him to be completely faithful to her, and that she found his behaviour distressing nevertheless.) Erlande also asked Aelfrida to write to him as woman to man, not author to author, and on her departure kissed her hand and then her arm 'long and ardently' ('I ought to have been shocked and displeased. I was not', for, as she noted, had she been asked if she would like Albert Erlande to fall in love with her, she would have 'said *no* … but since he did, the woman in me is bound to be gratified')[11]; Aelfrida promised to make Erlande 'known in Cambridge'.[12]

This she did. Believing herself to be 'quite an authority' on Erlande's 'style, ideas and personality'[13] on the basis of superficial acquaintance with his works and some illicit and much-enjoyed embraces, she prepared a lecture on 'my "discovery" of a great French novelist'[14] (Erlande sent five books to assist her research dedicated "*à Madame Graham … charmante femme*" which led her to believe that she might have with him the same kind of 'thoroughly satisfactory literary friendship' she enjoyed with Gian Falco)[15], delivering it on 27 May 1926 to the Sophists, an undergraduate society whose members 'tried to be as clever as they could [and] being young and eager and bright … succeeded in being very clever indeed'.[16] (What she did *not* tell them was that the 'lady' she quoted who said of Erlande that he was '*acier et feu*' was herself and that her essay formed the basis of the lecture she had just delivered.) And as if to underline her latest 'tic-toc' from saintly to secular behaviour, the day following her lecture was the one on which she had her hair 'shingled' for the first time.

There remained Willie, the man who commented caustically shortly before her departure for Grandcamp and Erlande's 'fiery southern charm' that the charms of Cambridge soon wore off and that it was a relief to be able to criticise it 'without emotional bias' ('I am not a fool', wrote his hearer, 'for "Cambridge", read "Aelfrida"')[17]; whose psyche had been dissected by Erlande to Aelfrida's satisfaction; who had been maliciously apprised by Alethea of 'M. Erlande's attempted love-making'[18]; and concerning whom Aelfrida was to confide that 'the mere presence of a middle-aged London solicitor' still caused her 'intense feeling'.[19] Is it surprising therefore, to find Willie's ardour cooling to such an extent that he ceased writing to her, or to think that among the several reasons for his breaking with her the arrival of a rival might be one?

A year later Aelfrida decided to play with fire again ('why *is* mother so attracted to M. Erlande?' wrote Alethea despairingly)[20], she and her daughters joining the Erlandes in Brittany in newly-fashionable resort Perros Guirec. There she rediscovered that M. Erlande was more interested in amatory than literary friendships (walking back from a swim *à deux,* she asked herself 'was he making love to me all the while? It was so subtly done that I hardly knew')[21]; he also tried to lure her into his room or to assail her in hers, provided graphic descriptions of what he would do if he and she were alone on a desert island, suggested that she ought to take him as a lover ('he has no reticences') and that he and she "go off together [for] five years of happiness" ('why five, I ask myself?')[22], and generally made such vehement approaches that she did not know whether to impute his behaviour to the wound in his head or to 'the incurable wound of genius'.[23]

But still she encouraged the man whose attentions she described as 'tiresome' and of whom she was 'rather afraid'[24], and increasingly dramatic scenes took place over spirit lamp and teacups in the Erlandes' beach hut. The sessions inspired two poems ('*vers très libre!*') unlike any written by Aelfrida before – or thereafter:

A Bathe at Perros Guirec
"… a bathe? Why not?
Alone? Yes.
A swinging gesture. Flinging the peignoir down.
Fling off convention, rule, restraint, the clinging garments of a dusty age.
Call of the sea, call of the pure translucent blue …
Like the first touch of love, silent, alluring …
Waist deep, breast-high, deeper deeper –
Plunge, as I plunged into life"[25],

and, following a further scene 'too intricate (alas!) to be described':

"Pick up the peignoir. Shiver across the beach …
'So cold?' A hand upon my waist.
A touch.
What wide-flung magic born of wind and wave
Narrows sudden to a single stab,
Sharp, acrid, tipped with flame? …
I am shut out for ever from the touch of man.
Sterile, sterile.
'So cold?' Yes".[26]

After which, the woman who later described holiday diaries as 'dull'[27], placed both poems in Erlande's room. (Fortunately neither his wife nor his teenage children found them.) During a third 'somewhat dramatic' beach-hut session, Aelfrida 'listened to a good deal that I ought not to have listened to'[28] and found herself responding physically to Erlande's advances. At this point she realised the danger inherent in provoking a brain-damaged man disinhibitedly addicted to 'dangerous behaviour' with regard to women[29] and drew back, noting that 'the worst of keeping a diary is that one is … on one's honour to speak the truth, however humiliating'[30] (*sic*) and that along with that to which she ought not to have listened, she had heard some home truths: she was 'too much interested in men' for a woman of her age ('oh dash! why am I so incorrigible? Forty-three next birthday – it is really getting beyond a joke')[31] and that like a spoilt nun (*une nonne ratée*) she had God in her head and the devil in her body.[32]

So what did she do? She began a novel, written in French but entitled in English *Clash!,* in which she has the 'heroine' tell the 'villain' that he has 'aroused her feelings but by grace etc. etc.'[33] she will elude him. She then gave it to Erlande to read, with predictable results: he made a serious pass at her ('a vulgar trick … too much in the yokel and milkmaid style')[34] and when she repulsed him ('dear guardian angel, keep close to me'), addressed her as '*chérie*' even while making bitter remarks about her chastity.[35] In a belated attempt to excuse herself, she addresses a future biographer as follows: 'I hope you don't think from anything I have written that M. Erlande has any kind of affection for me … partly for love of danger, partly for the sake of his books, he deliberately submits himself to the charm of every attractive woman he meets [and] if there is anything doing I daresay he – does it. With me there is nothing doing'. 'I wonder', she added, 'if I am the first woman who has ever said no to him'.[36]

Furious rows then broke out between the Erlandes. Aelfrida (to exculpate herself) took Madame's side, only to find the Erlandes playing one another off against herself. Monsieur Erlande became 'very grumpy'[37] and Aelfrida suffered an attack of morality ('sin is performing an action, deliberately and with intention, which you believe to be wrong')[38] which lasted (with reservations, because the episode had 'heartened and refreshed' her) long enough to see her home. At Fordfield she bade goodbye to 'holiday Aelfrida' and returned 'to [her] quiet normal life'.[39]

At first regretful ('I miss M. Erlande [and] the tone of his voice when he said "*chérie*"'), then wistful ('I would not, of my free choice, hear [his voice] again … but if I did I should enjoy it'), then self-deluding ('I am glad that God knows all my weakness [and] that people round me do not'[40]; judging by excoriating comments in Agatha's diary about 'people who call themselves Christians'[41] and in Alethea's concerning the way in which Erlande had seemed 'to worm his way into mother's mind'[42], her daughters, at least, were aware of their mother's recent behaviour), then philosophic ('what I value most is not a pleasant sensation but a consciousness of life being very vivid [as a result of] the clash of personalities'), then smug ('I feel now that I can turn happily from my own enjoyment and help other people to bear the burden of life')[43], Aelfrida finally realised the enormity of her behaviour. Dismay, however, was not because of damage inflicted on a marriage already under strain because of M. Erlande's behaviour (he admitted that he was mentally ill but refused medical intervention because literary inspiration might disappear at the same time as the source of his overpowering sexual urges)[44] or because she had encouraged behaviour whose basis was pathological but because she had been guilty of moral weakness: 'I have turned with horror from the very thought of M. Erlande … [with] horror, *horror* because he aroused physical sensations to which my will did not (*sic*) consent. How far I was … to blame I have not the faintest idea (*sic*) [but] feeling as I do the intense and overwhelming beauty of holiness and saintliness, why am I so bad? Alethea to the dentist this morning'.[45]

'Horror' was heightened by an incident which took place within a short time of her return. The day following Agatha's motor accident and Tom Henn's disclosure that marriage did not attract him, an admirer whom Aelfrida had barely noticed when he was in Cambridge – there are two brief diary references to him in October 1906, both derogatory – gave it to her 'hot and strong', informing her that 'friendship without passion' was impossible between a man and a woman like herself and that it was conceited of her to believe her charm intellectual 'when the physical is so overwhelming'; chastened, Aelfrida decided it was 'detestable to be an elderly *ingénue*' and that she must be 'amazingly ignorant of men and their passions'.[46] A letter from M. Erlande received in February 1927 elicited further shudders at having been 'in the least degree sensitive to his odious charm' and the statement 'I have sometimes wished to burn that volume of my diary but it is better there to keep me humble'.[47]

Given her remorse, why did Aelfrida behave as she did? Perhaps because having 'rather overdone … humility' in response to disgust at having contemplated 'the possibility of marrying Willie'[48], (*perverte* or not), her response to Erlande's 'particular temptation of the moment'[49] was nothing more than attraction to a rampantly heterosexual male. Perhaps, as she herself recognised, the similarity between Erlande and her former husband (a man divorced only four years earlier and with whom, as Erlande trenchantly observed, she was *au fond* still in love)[50] caused her to feel 'so much at home with him' that she felt impelled to refashion Erlande's 'wrong' behaviour until it accorded with her own moral code (and to persevere in this in spite of manifest lack of success), in which respect her comment that 'modern society makes no allowance for men naturally polygamous (*sic*) like Constantine and Erlande and judges them just as severely when they go wrong as if they were Eustace or Julius'[51] makes curious reading, given that it was written wholly without irony and that she had been (and still was) very ready to castigate promiscuous behaviour in Constantine and others. Then too, it seems that a woman in her early forties who had recently admitted to possession of a physically passionate nature and who liked to live dangerously (and if this meant provoking a 'scene', so be it) but whose life now revolved round domesticity and the care of elderly parents, was 'bound to be gratified'[52] by the ardent attentions of the first man since Constantine to arouse her sexually. Gratification was also to be gained from the discovery that she was not the physically and intellectually unattractive person rejected by him, a discovery made with regard to a man similar to himself. (And, as with Constantine, initial physical and emotional attraction transmogrified itself into physical and emotional repulsion when the man who proposed that she be his 'Complete Confidante'[53] was discovered to require more from her than friendship.) Lastly, 'holiday Aelfrida's' activities took place away from Cambridge, a town where she had to be 'discreet' for her daughters' sake and from Fordfield where she lived under her parents' watchful and disapproving eyes. But they also took place when she herself, though vulnerably spouseless, was protected by the presence of Madame Erlande from Monsieur's more outrageous advances, Erlande's wife being her escape-clause.

But 'horror, *horror*' notwithstanding, fifteen months later she was once more willing (and more than willing) to abandon thoughts of spiritual espousal and to relegate God to second place in favour of a man who represented everything that Constantine had been when she first met him – young, ardent, and idealistic – and to try to recreate with him the relationship she had had with Constantine Michaelides before censorious disillusioned Constantine Graham replaced him. The man she chose, however, possessed two qualities lacked by her former husband: a sense of honour and a future in which financial integrity was of paramount importance and practised with absolute probity. He was also so tall that instead of towering over him, she could rest her head on his chest; he was motherless, so she would not be hag-ridden by another Anatolia; and he was chaste. So, much as she disliked people who fell in love more than once and 'would much rather have gone on loving Constantine'[54], she fell heavily in love with yet another Cambridge undergraduate and was only prevented from abandoning ideals of Courtly Love and Little Friendship by a twist of fate unforeseen at the start of their relationship.

Anthony Wrightson, 'pleasant, tall, leggy, bespectacled … very serious-minded, good, quite pleasant to talk to' but 'very staid … you would think he was forty'[55] (his brothers called him 'grandfather'), was a friend of John Wedgwood's brought by the latter to tea at Fordfield on 1 March 1928. The young man with 'no charm, just great honesty and a good intelligence' attracted Aelfrida so much that she sat herself next to him and 'approved of him visibly'.[56]

Anthony's maturity and restfulness was just what she needed in a world which included Willie Searle 'send[ing] up the emotional temperature' when weekending in Cambridge from which Aelfrida fled to that 'blessed haven of refuge', meditation, to seek not ecstasy but '*steadying*'.[57] It also included the Wedgwoods' intervention in John's friendship with Alethea, teaching at Summer Schools, a book to write (*The Young Milliner*, of which she noted that "even if I do not produce great works of art I know what it feels like to produce them!" … After all, the greatest geniuses are only the best shorthand typists of the Almighty')[58], a forty-fifth birthday spent in bed with a feverish cold ('the best place' because 'why I should I not be happy?')[59], and busy days filled with trivia: housekeeping, paying calls, cycling to Merton House with Agatha, shopping, the flower rota at St Columba's, and coping with Nadja, 'Aunt Laura', and Agnes Slack. October 1928, however, saw Anthony visiting Fordfield for solo French lessons, and November, 'lively' parties at Trinity, ostensibly for Agatha's benefit (Aelfrida had already earmarked 'dear, slow, good, thoughtful, dependable Anthony'[60] as a suitable husband for her younger daughter) but actually because Aelfrida felt drawn to a man so different to Constantine, to Willie Searle, and to Albert Erlande.

Motherless Anthony himself felt drawn to an older woman in whom he could confide and by May of the following year (the month in which Aelfrida confided to her diary that she felt inclined to turn to 'any relief – fall in love, God knows what!')[61] and 'in a very bad state of health' because of impending Finals, had become a regular visitor to Fordfield; to calm his 'oh! so delicate' nerves, Aelfrida took him into the garden where they chatted and she read him two chapters of the novel (*Haste to the Wedding*) on which she was currently working. Anthony, however, became 'so confidential and so affectionate that I really… thought he was making love to me'[62], an impression enhanced by the 'rather wistful'[63] young man continuing to haunt Fordfield until term and his time at Cambridge ended and he departed for a position in the family insurance company in London. (Aelfrida herself was 'happy to meet someone quite new' who with his 'aesthetic without being effeminate, courtly [and] charming' air reminded her of 'a more English Constantine': Michael Redgrave, Alethea's new 'admirer'.)[64] There then followed a summer retrospectively described by Aelfrida as 'happy' because of her having experienced 'consciousness of the Presence of God which gives deep deep peace *glowing* all the time' but marked in her diary by complaints about everyone and everything, a summer during which Anthony wrote increasingly ardent letters ('for a long time he [has] been "yours affectionately"')[65], culminating in a suggestion that they meet at his flat next time she was in London. So they did.

In London on 3 September 1929 to greet her daughters on their return from their respective vacation occupations, Aelfrida met Anthony as suggested and 'the emotional temperature began to go up'. He began by discussing his feelings for her ('half of me wanted to stop him and half of me wanted him to go on') but progressed to protestations of adoration and even to hints of marriage. She, though tempted to make him commit himself, was so aware of the quarter-century discrepancy in their ages and her own chequered past that she asked him to keep his distance: "if you try to come too near and know too much I shall drop you altogether". As she prepared to leave, however, Anthony drew her into his bedroom. Confronted by 'pink pyjamas set out and a copy of *Verses for Alethea* on the chest of drawers', Aelfrida did not know whether to be 'puzzled [or] downright shocked' at his presumption. With a reproachful conscience, she took her leave.[66] (A year later another young man, also given to signing off letters with protestations of affection, invited Aelfrida to stay at his flat while his wife was away; to Erle Lunn, she answered 'as distantly as [she] could', it being 'so *vulgar* to write like that to your spiritual director'.)[67] Some 'rather tender letters from Anthony'[68] followed her home.

'Grave, mature [and] sweet' Anthony spent a day at Fordfield in December. Chaperoned by her daughters and Chiara, he and Aelfrida lacked opportunity for exchanging sentimental passages but Agatha and Alethea later teased her about his obvious devotion. Remembering her 'age and dignity', Aelfrida had said nothing to her daughters of the London episode[69] but Chiara was both aware of it and beginning to urge marriage as 'a relief … to her mind' and 'an advantage to

the girls'[70] because marriage, even to a man close in age to her elder *grand*-daughter, would regularise Aelfrida's position in society and improve Agatha's and Alethea's marriage prospects. A further meeting with Anthony early the following year ('delight such as I have no right to expect at my time of life and which I vow I took no advantage of')[71] left Aelfrida in a quandary: 'it would be so lovely to marry Anthony … his youth gives him enormous charm … he values all that I have to give [and] I could make him very happy', but the thought that she would look extremely silly if she married a man young enough to be her son made matrimony 'a temptation to be fought tooth and nail'. Could she, she wondered, persuade Anthony to marry Agatha, closer to him in age?

Crying "no girl would want to marry Anthony unless she liked being an old man's darling"[72], Agatha urged that Aelfrida '*must* marry Anthony', the latter's 'preoccupation'[73] with Anthony and his fondness for her having been drawn to her own and Alethea's attention by former Cambridge contemporaries, one of whom, Douglas Davidson, shared Anthony's 'apolaustic' bachelor flat in Pembridge Crescent. (Disapproving of his friend's penchant for Alethea's mother and hers for him, Douglas played 'Spinster Aunt' rudely and pointedly during one of Aelfrida's visits.)[74] Being unwilling or unable to decide whether to marry Anthony in spite of her doubts and his friends' disapproval or to give him up, Aelfrida declared herself 'passive in the hands of God', perfectly detached from 'little affairs'[75], happy to be advised by her guardian angel, and determined not to marry ('I shall not go there again in a hurry')[76], and set out on her usual course of playing cat and mouse with a man's affections.

During the ensuing year Aelfrida chided herself for becoming increasingly 'tender' over Anthony. (Her feelings included 'gratitude and astonishment that he should care' and, unconscionably, 'physical passion too, which a middle-aged woman apparently is prone to feel for a … man'[77] young enough to be her son; she and Anthony had done no more at that point than exchange handshakes.) Descriptions of her feelings for Anthony read oddly when interspersed with practical plans for the Steam Laundry but indicate her capacity for compartmentalisation; it seems, however, that she had almost come to the conclusion that 'human love' *could* make 'this world a paradise' and was preparing to act accordingly.[78] Then doubts set in: practical, sexual, and religious.

Practical doubts chiefly concerned chronology and finance. Anthony, though 'a City Magnate already!' and desperate to marry 'someone who would look after him … and to whom he could "pour his heart out"' (he also wanted someone with whom he could be 'restful', an unlikely state of affairs if married to Aelfrida) was not yet in a position to support a wife and would not be, he thought, for six or seven years. Aelfrida, crying "ah, Anthony, if I had been twenty years younger", decided that she would then be 'quite definitely too old': 'a woman of fifty is impossible'. (She also informed her diary 'I have no intention of marrying him'.)[79] Sexual doubts were more pertinent, for Anthony had begun to question her on the subject of marital relations and to complain she was too reticent on the subject: a woman who replied '"very true" in as non-committal a tone as possible'[80] to questions about spending nights as well as days together from a young man who had made his feelings for her 'obvious to everyone' was hardly encouraging, though Anthony was now so besotted that even this failed to discourage him, Aelfrida noting of daily love-letters that 'I am afraid this kind of thing can't go on ... I suggested being his favourite Aunt!'[81]

Anthony, it seems, did not want another aunt, favourite or otherwise: he wanted a wife. Meeting Aelfrida as she passed through London on her way to a holiday in France with Alethea, he kissed her cheek on parting, an experience which provided her with 'one of the most exquisite experiences of my life', which 'enhanced my feelings of individuality', which 'made me feel more alive', which 'sharpened my taste of life', which 'made all the colours of existence brighter', and which was only outshone by 'one of the most superb, purest experiences of God-consciousness that had ever come to me', experienced in Braquemont church soon after arrival, an experience which not only freed her from individuality, limitation, blindness, disharmonies, and strivings (for the time being) but was also 'as much more *real* than a man's kiss as eternity is more *real* than time'. No mere man and his mere mortal kiss could compete with being steeped 'in the being of God'[82], and this and concurrent work on her latest novel, *O Passionate World,* made Aelfrida extremely thoughtful. Comparing the three men whom she had recently loved, Fidelio (met in an 'unreal' world inhabited by elfish or fairy elements), Willie (for whom she felt a 'sisterly affection which he fanned momentarily into passion'), and Anthony, she came to three conclusions: that her feelings for Anthony were 'mostly maternal'[83]; that Anthony was just a charming symbol, valued 'for what he brings and what he stands for'; that whatever feelings she had for Anthony paled in comparison to those experienced in relation to the man of whom Anthony (and Fidelio and Albert and Willie) was but a poor imitation: 'mine, my share of the universe, my man, the only one I have ever loved'[84]. (Constantine Michaelides, not Julius.) But she refused to let him go, for asking herself what really made her happy, she listed

three things: 'the presence of God, chiefly'; 'the love of my dear ones', next; lastly, 'a kiss from Anthony'.[85]

In January 1931 Anthony spent the weekend at Fordfield. After everyone but themselves had gone to bed, he took Aelfrida in his arms and embraced her until 'the flame caught me too and I put up my mouth to be kissed and he kissed me on the lips, twice', after which he 'walked away to the other end of the room saying "that is enough"'. Torn between relief and dismay, Aelfrida 'lay awake till dawn wondering whether it had been wrong' to allow Anthony to kiss her where he kissed her (twice) and if it were not 'pure sensuality, especially ... disgusting in a woman who pretends to be pious' to allow him to do so and to enjoy it when he did. (She had recently begun to allow him to kiss and even fondle her but had not returned his caresses; this was the period at which, Alethea noted, her mother talked compulsively about 'what she called sex ... with a rather disgusted air'.)[86] She then consoled herself with three such outrageously hypocritical consolations that had she not recorded them in her diary, it would be hard to credit them: first, 'now I *know* and am in touch with God, many things and much liberty are permitted which were not permitted before'; second, Anthony's love was only a foolish indulgence ('*une gâterie*') on a par with the many little treats she allowed herself in order to survive life at Fordfield; third, she hadn't liked to spoil his fun. Before he left for London she therefore informed him that 'what you did last night is the traditional way of leading up to – something else', that she had no intention of performing 'something else' with him, and that there must be '*no more*' intimate kisses.[87] To her diary, she added that she felt 'extraordinarily happy' nevertheless[88]; Anthony's feelings as he entrained back to a bachelor flat 'devoted to enjoyment' can only be imagined.

Religious doubts were few and easily assuaged. Having decided in May 1930 that she did not 'really want to form any more earthly ties' (*sic*) but desperately wanted 'to be lonely and to test [her] capacity for being all alone with God'[89], Aelfrida was delighted to discover the escape-clause she needed: at the Lambeth Conference held in August 1930, three hundred bishops, conveniently 'believing themselves to be guided by the Holy Spirit', decided that not even the innocent party in a divorce had a right to re-marry in church – and Aelfrida would never contemplate a Register Office. 'Well', she wrote with relief, 'that settles it finally about marriage as far as I am concerned ... happiness is nothing compared with doing what is right'. (In parenthesis, she added 'you may say I would not have married Anthony anyway ... but the temptation was very much there'.)[90] Four days later she noted 'how much easier decisions are when they present themselves in the form of a choice between *right* and *wrong* rather than between inclination and disinclination … as soon as it became a question of right and wrong, the decision made itself'. 'Light-hearted'[91] at her escape, she informed Anthony that marriage between them was impossible and that she would brook no argument on the subject. (She did not, however, tell him that her decision to hide behind the bishops was because she was liable 'to be ruled by passion and expediency' or that knowing she could easily '*make* [Anthony] want with all his being', she had even considered 'companionable marriage' – cohabitation '*à l'americaine*', as she put it, adding 'my … opinions are scandalous'[92] – so that he and she could enjoy a few years' happiness together before she became too old or convention or God intervened.) They therefore decided to meet '*only seldom*'[93], though Anthony, subjugated but not convinced (on a recent visit to Fordfield and in spite of her refusal to reciprocate, he had kissed her soundly in a 'gust of passion')[94] by Aelfrida's pleas and by her also resurrecting her 'idea of "detachment"' ('considerably modified since the old days': *sic*) as a deterrent, found his inamorata's decree inscrutable and suspected that unresponsiveness stemmed from something more than matronly reserve.[95] He would have been even more upset had he heard her declaration that she thought of him only as a 'charming symbol' and regarded his love for her as 'a mere shadow' compared with God's.[96]

January 1931 saw Aelfrida suffering from the 'black fits of depression' which parallel meditations with Juan Mascaró, en route to India, did little to assuage and which she attributed to the strain of finishing her 'difficult novel' (*O Passionate World*), to appalling weather, to the economic depression 'through which the whole world was passing'[97] whose ramifications affected Chiara's investment income, to the 'deplorable state of trade'[98] responsible (so her agent said) for non-publication of a compendium of essays on Mysticism and Modern Life, to Alethea's absence in Paris (she had obtained the position of sub-editor of the English edition of *La Semaine à Paris*, a position taken up as soon as university examinations were over and of which her mother noted sourly 'I would much rather she got a husband')[99], and to a 'humiliating and recurring … fight against physical desire'[100] with regard to the young man whom she had sworn never to kiss again and certainly not to marry. By Ash Wednesday, however, her mood had improved and she felt able to list the ways in which she intended to keep Lent: to give up eating sweets and reading novels ('I hardly touch sweets anyway and don't read half a dozen novels in the year'); to deny herself alimentary luxuries ('my fare is already the extreme of simplicity'); to try not

to talk about myself' ('but [I] don't succeed'); to refrain from neglecting 'some other duty' in favour of attending services at St Botolph's (the current cold and sleety weather may have influenced this resolve); to practice more intense self-examination ('I am too much given to that already'), and to continue with her current meditation '*Spirit is God*'.[101] She did not include Anthony.

That none of the above involved much in the way of self-denial was brought home to her on 3 March when fate, God, or her guardian angel having taken a hand in the direction her life was to take, she remembered a dream sent by the latter on Shrove Tuesday but unrecorded at the time. Unable to think of an address for a women's meeting at Cherry Hinton Free Church, Aelfrida had asked her guardian angel to help her; this he did, bidding her tell the assembled women that "we do not know until we are in trouble how good people are", that "we cannot truly feel for others until we have felt for ourselves", that "we do not notice the beauty of everyday mercies until for a time they have been withheld", and that having to cast ourselves "*utterly* on God" is one of life's most valuable experiences. Aelfrida had dismissed his suggestions with a flip comment ('the platitudinous is often the appropriate!')[102] and it was not until the dreadful events of Lent 1931 began to unfold that she realised the angel's dictated 'sermon' had contained both advice and a warning.

On 21 February 1931 Agatha, then in the second term of her second year at Girton, came home to be nursed through tonsillitis. In pre-antibiotic days spread of infection was a risk and on 22 February she developed 'cruel earache' (we are not told which ear) which hot fomentations prescribed by Dr Cooper failed to cure. Incision of her eardrum by 'Dr Walford, the ear specialist'[103] released pressurised pus but afforded only temporary relief to a patient 'wailing and sobbing with … pain'. By the evening of 28 February she was so ill that she was taken by ambulance to the Evelyn Nursing Home where Mr Walford, with Dr Cooper as anaesthetist, performed a mastoidectomy. On 5 March Aelfrida noted that 'Precious Temu'[104] was improving but five days later that she was 'not fully satisfied with [Agatha's] progress towards health'. Nor was Alfred Walford, who feared 'another abscess in the bone and [that] he must operate again'. That night Agatha returned to the operating theatre where Mr Walford removed infected material from a large vein adjacent to the site of his earlier surgery.

By this time, Aelfrida was so beside herself with worry that she did or omitted to do three things. She did not pray and her remarkably few references to Deity included two ejaculations, one – "God give me strength!" – being very strong language indeed for one who never took God's name in vain, though she did have a vision of 'being united to God and through Him to all that ever had been and was and ever would be … lovely and good in the world', including her younger daughter.[105] She retired to bed '*indisposée*', weepy, headachy, and suffering from a severe sore throat, and was relieved when Dr Cooper diagnosed tonsillitis and provided her with a valid excuse for staying there, whereupon she enjoyed 'peace and solitude', read *The Times*, reviewed the second volume of a history of Spanish Mysticism for *Theology,* and wrote 'quite a lot of letters'.[106] She also made a vow remarkably similar to that made with regard to Eric Silvanus[107] on the occasion of a potentially fatal illness suffered by the same daughter twenty years earlier, namely 'that if Agatha came through … I would never kiss Anthony again or let him caress me', his kisses and caresses being 'the sweetest *personal* thing that I am free to give up'.[108] But like 'Olga Stanislovna's' vow of 1911, Aelfrida's vow of 1931 'to give up Anthony's caresses' was conditional and contained an escape clause: 'you may say that the … instinct to offer a precious possession … was purely pagan [and] of course one does not bargain with the Almighty but … have I offered something which is not mine to give – Anthony's pleasure in me?' So because his feelings for her remained so strong that since their last meeting they had decided to avoid tête-à-têtes 'yet awhile' (*sic*) 'for fear of sin' and because her vow of chastity would be 'good discipline for both of us', it was only as an afterthought that she hoped Agatha's recovery would enforce both vow and discipline.[109]

Though it would be interesting to speculate how Aelfrida might have behaved towards Anthony (or Eric) had her daughter *died*, Agatha did not – though she came close to doing so on 10 March and on 13 March closer still. At the time of Alfred Walford's third surgical intervention, Aelfrida had gone so far as to resign herself to Agatha's death: 'people say that in this world nothing is perfect, but my relationship with Agatha has been … If she lived longer, would her character grow more lovely? It would be enriched by more experience but it could hardly be more beautiful … For her sake, which is better, to die or to live? This is a hard and cruel world and yet … she has taken everything that is beautiful and good and left the ugliness, not unknown, but untouched … I do not pray either way [but] surely God alone knows how I love her and want her!'[110] On 13 March, death seemed close as Agatha underwent 'another operation, the fourth, the worst of all': ligation of a major blood vessel to prevent dissemination of infected thrombus into her cardiovascular circulation. (Anguish notwithstanding – 'again, the same torment again'[111] – Aelfrida's obvious enjoyment of the 'Agatha drama'; her account is melodramatic, not

distraught – and her casting of Alfred Walford and Joan Cooper in the roles of intrepid surgeon and supportive handmaiden, of Agatha as saintly sufferer, and of herself as distraught, devoted, devoutly-trusting mother, suggests that she viewed the episode as potential 'copy' and wrote her diary rendition accordingly.) Agatha's fourth operation entailed heroic pioneering surgery ('[it] *was* something remarkable … Dr Walford was marvellous beyond words … and … not another doctor in England could have saved Agatha then', was Aelfrida's rendition of Joan Cooper's account)[112] and a description of Agatha's post-operative appearance as 'lifeless and remote … her neck swathed in blood-stained bandages'[113] did not augur well for recovery. But she did, and was soon able to make jokes 'which didn't somehow seem like "last words"'[114] and to return 'in triumph' to Fordfield a month after she left it.[115] Whereupon, after the 'somewhat agitating ups and downs of convalescence'[116], she made a full recovery. On Good Friday 1931 Aelfrida went to church for the first time since Lent and her ordeal began, feeling that in spite of 'preoccupations with Agatha's illness', she had been living 'among things of the spirit'. With one important exception: 'desire for Anthony, more insistent and more poignant than I could have imagined', so forgetting that 'physical preoccupation' might lead to breaking her recent vow, Aelfrida decided not to fight it (desire was 'not *wrong* – only distracting') and to let her relationship with Anthony 'flower into images and so fade and go'.[117]

Though Anthony's image and Aelfrida's desire *were* destined to 'fade and go', both underwent interesting developments before dissolution and departure. The process began before Agatha left the Evelyn ('I am glad I did not pray for her recovery but resigned her fully into the hands of God … that way alone lies inward peace')[118] on a day when Aelfrida, confined to bed with a 'bad headache' (migraines had returned with the stress of Agatha's illness), read and reflected on a poem of John Donne's, which, she decided, 'explains some of me to myself'. Quoting the opening lines of *Air and Angels* ("Twice or thrice had I loved thee / Before I knew thy face or name / So in a voice, so in a shapeless flame / *Angels* affect us oft, and worshipped be"), she commented 'that is just it. Sometimes I wonder if I have loved any man at all and not just that *shapeless flame* which stands round now this, now that, human being. It is certainly not mere physical desire, for it touched Fidelio who is physically slightly repulsive, and once a woman, my nurse when the dead baby was born. And so many men: Lord Kitchener, Archie Stent (not Enrico, Cameron, Mr Consul-General Smith) – I can't even remember them all [though] Constantine *was* [once] the elusive thing I had always loved and would always love [but] when the glow [had] left [he was] like a rocky landscape when the sun has gone, bleak and stark and lifeless. The "shapeless flame" is round Anthony now … I wish I understood … *what* it is that makes one man luminous and vivid beyond all others'.[119] And with Anthony as the latest embodiment of Donne's "lovely glorious nothing", she resumed her pursuit of her most recent 'flame'; indeed, she did not so much pursue him as to prepare to throw caution (almost) to the winds.

She was therefore somewhat annoyed to discover that Anthony's initial reaction to the vow of which she informed him during a stroll in the nearby but public surroundings of Cambridge's Botanic Garden, was tender and respectful acceptance. ('Part of me would rather he had protested … I am amazed that I mind so much, but I do'.)[120] She was even more annoyed when, following an earthquake that night (a real, not an emotional, 'rocking and heaving')[121], the justifiably bitter parting words of a man once described as a '*gâterie*' were "you get a lot of amusement out of a lot of people, don't you?"[122] and that although absence of physical expression would make no difference to his love for her, they 'had better not meet till the autumn'.[123]

Anthony's rebuttal sent Aelfrida 'tic-toc' back to the arms of God. Deciding not to waste spiritual energies by 'allowing [her] life-force to flow towards Anthony' (or more generically, towards the 'chaos of worldly passions')[124] but to sublimate her passion by re-consecrating herself to Him, she practised 'detachment' so assiduously that she believed she had 'no business of [her] own, only God's'.[125] She also undertook displacement activity in the shape of 'an orgy of [her] beloved Laundry'[126] and embarked on her 'drawing of sympathy' towards Dr Cooper whose 'almost divine compassion for the sorrows of others'[127] had been so important in recent weeks but towards whom she might not have felt so attracted had Anthony not been brusque.

'Very turbulent thoughts'[128] concerning the relative merits of Deity and Anthony persisted during the intervening months: if she married Anthony she would be forbidden Holy Communion ('little as I agree with the bishops … I should lose more than I should gain')[129]; she had 'not thought enough about God' and her meditations had been 'brief and perfunctory'[130]; it was 'strange that the effort to conquer my … desire for Anthony and substitute thoughts of God should [keep] me awake half the night'[131], and so on and on, and it was with relief that the problem of where to take Agatha to complete her recovery was solved by her guardian angel telling her to stop 'fussing' and to wait for the right place to present itself.[132] Which it obligingly did, through the agency of Anthony himself.

Ellen Wrightson, one of Anthony's many aunts, owned and ran a religious retreat house at St Mary's Abbey at Leiston in Suffolk[133]; hearing from him of Agatha's illness, she offered a furnished cottage 'right *in* the precincts'[134] for her and her mother's use. Aelfrida had 'longed for … many years'[135] to go to a retreat house to 'think things out'[136] but for financial and domestic reasons had been unable to do so and on receiving Miss Wrightson's offer experienced 'powerful drawings … to a retreat at St Mary's Abbey'. (And 'the hope that I may ultimately go and live there'.)[137] Delighted at the prospect of a peaceful cottage in sanctified surroundings where she could 'think things out' with regard to God and to Miss Wrightson's nephew, she arranged for herself and her daughter to stay at Leiston for a month from 30 August 1931. Alethea joined them shortly afterwards; having been dismissed from *La Semaine à Paris* in February 1931 because of a breakdown brought on (supposedly) by pressure of work, she had arrived at Fordfield depressed and dismayed to find herself ignored by a mother whose energies were concentrated on her desperately ill sibling. It was at Leiston, however, and with Miss Wrightson's help that Alethea was able to decide the direction *her* future was to take – and that it did not include her mother. Or her sister.

While Alethea went for therapeutic walks and rides and convalescent Agatha revelled in the presence of her older sister and her impending return to Girton, Aelfrida entered fully into the life of the Abbey, attending sessions of the retreat currently in progress and twenty-eight services. She also enquired closely into details of the habit worn by Miss Wrightson and Miss Madden, her sister-in-religion and sole helper, and into the 'Rule' to which the ladies adhered (its rules of conduct including regular attendance at Divine Office and lengthy periods of silence but involved 'no definite doctrinal obligations' and only 'limited enclosure'), a 'Rule' Aelfrida described as 'not too exacting' and under whose jurisdiction she could envisage herself living[138] once free from daughters who stubbornly refused to leave her or returned broken in spirit when they did.

In her anxiety to live at Leiston ('the decision is made … my vocation lies here')[139], she overlooked two things: Leiston closed in winter so she would be homeless for part of the year and Miss Wrightson (she called herself Leiston's 'lady abbess' though St Mary's was not a religious house nor she herself a professed religious) seemed curiously unwilling to have her there again and this even though a third person would enable St Mary's to become a regular 'Community'. Without stopping to ask herself why – it transpired that Miss Wrightson had several concerns, namely that Aelfrida's presence 'spoilt the harmony of the place'[140] (Aelfrida agreed); that she distrusted women who presumed to set themselves up as spiritual directors; that she suspected Aelfrida of Theosophist or Spiritualist 'leanings', Aelfrida having informed her that she espied the 'shapeless flame' which surrounded Anthony around his aunt also (and around Joan Cooper and Veronica Tillyard though she did not inform *them* of this), this being in Miss Wrightson's eyes too reminiscent of 'demonic experiences' from which she herself had recoiled in horror during earlier dabblings in Spiritualism[141]; that although not quite a 'fallen sinner' there was something suspect about Aelfrida's profession of chastity ('I am not complete ... without a man', the latter protested indignantly); that in pursuing Miss Wrightson's favourite nephew Aelfrida was by no means the 'virtuous matron' she ought to be; and (one of the greatest snubs Aelfrida ever received) no one of the latter's temperament 'should presume to aspire after the religious life'[142] because *'wanting'* it was not the same as being *called to* it [143] – Aelfrida saw her way clear. She would dispossess herself of her daughters as soon as possible, would leave Fordfield ('one needs to be a bit of a *grande dame* there and I would rather not'), and would never marry Anthony ('it would be treason of the worst kind') because in order to fulfil God's purpose for her she must begin by living alone in the 'outer courts of the heavenly city'[144] (i.e. Leiston) in a cottage as embedded in the abbey's fabric as her life would be in the Body of Christ. With eyes 'still a little dazzled by the wonder of the threshold of Heaven' but 'steadfast' in her resolve[145], she returned to a world plagued by her daughters' 'uncertain future'[146] and by Anthony professing himself 'busy with family affairs' and unable to visit 'for some time'[147], to begin the long and onerous process of disentangling herself from the 'human affections' to whose acquisition she devoted so much time and emotional energy. She also embarked on a 'night-story', significantly entitled *Peace Within Thy Walls*.[148]

Doubts immediately assailed her. Having made up her mind 'to go ultimately to Leiston – *Deo volente*', could she 'renounce' Cambridge or would she, in leaving it, merely 'go somewhere where I should hope to be better employed'? What was it about her that caused 'unusual' men like Anthony Wrightson and Albert Erlande to fall in love with her and could a woman with God in her head and the devil in her body consider 'leaving one's passions on Leiston doorstep'?[149] Why should a visit to a retreat house result in a revelatory 'sight of myself as I really am'? ('It isn't so much the blackness of my sins as the dirty-grey state of my virtues!')[150] Should she 'repent' of her 'attachment to Anthony' (Alethea had said she was "spoiling his life") and the bitterness and 'repression' this caused him?[151] Could she divert his attention to Agatha, thereby killing three birds with one stone: Agatha's

'uncertain future' would be settled, Anthony relieved of 'repression', and she herself free to return to Leiston?

Anthony dashed her hopes. Her suggestion that he marry someone else was 'choked off' (unusually, Aelfrida was 'instantly silenced')[152] and she was heaped with reproaches: he was 'hurt and angry' at her attraction to St Mary's[153], 'apprehensive that I might sacrifice him to get what I wanted', finding the 'strain of repression ... very great', and convinced that Aelfrida was 'trying to take the best of both worlds in an unjustifiable manner'. ('Am I? I may be', was her disingenuous comment.) She therefore decided that rather than suffer the indignity of a letter from Anthony 'saying *stop*'[154], she would 'stop' him first.

Though feeling 'rather selfish to be taking a day in bed' on the day of Alethea's discharge from the Evelyn Nursing Home (she had had her appendix and an ovarian cyst removed), Aelfrida took the opportunity to send Anthony his *congé* in a letter reproduced verbatim in her diary and posted (with a few minor amendments) in time for him to receive it as a Christmas present. The letter is unusual in its conventionality: having listed Anthony's good qualities (especially his height: 'I have to look up and up at you'), Aelfrida noted how much he meant to her and her gratitude that he alone among men 'who might have cared more but with such a mixture of illusion and desire' that their affection was 'comparatively worthless', had really tried to get to know her, asked that they remain good friends, and pledged continuing affection. Unconventionally but predictably, it also contained two particularly cruel comments: her feelings for him had always been fundamentally 'maternal' ('if you were an altogether-wise Anthony you would call me "Mother Aelfrida"'), and, well as he thought he knew her, there were 'plenty of unexplored places ... whole tracts of territory where you have never been'.[155] (And would never, she hinted, be allowed to go.) It is to Anthony's credit (Aelfrida was his first love) that his reply was 'very tender', so tender, in fact, that her relieved sigh 'that is over' (Alethea describes her as 'very tired and nervous and dreadfully "on edge"' at this juncture)[156] was instantly transmuted into feeling unable 'to write *Finis*' just yet.[157]

At this point Aelfrida's life, rarely a pattern of tranquillity, took an even more complicated turn: a year to the day after Agatha's near-fatal mastoiditis, Chiara developed pneumonia (it was largely due to Dr Cooper's skilled medical attention and Aelfrida's devoted nursing that she recovered) and Anthony, in a 'very understanding' letter, begged Aelfrida to spend a night at his flat in Elgin Avenue ('could I? Would it be wise? My vows!') as she passed through London on the way back from a holiday in Dorset with her daughters. (It was on this holiday that Aelfrida paid her second and last visit to the grave of another young man round whom the 'shapeless flame' had flickered, namely Archie Stent, noting that 'the place was too full of ghosts – I almost wished that I had not gone' but also that she was 'very happy now and ghosts cannot hurt me'.)[158] Vows or no vows, she agreed, though she insisted on booking a room at her usual hotel in case of emergency.

After dinner (described in *O Passionate World* in terms of lunch with 'Richard Temple') during which Anthony imbibed Dutch courage in the shape of half a bottle of Sauterne, he and Aelfrida discussed 'indifferent things, more or less successfully, till nine o'clock'. (They may have been indifferent to her but they were important to Anthony: his intense and, to Aelfrida, unreasonable jealousy of her other 'friendships', notably with 'Dr Joan', and his intention 'in a few years' to marry a 'housemate' but to continue to give Aelfrida 'all that is really valuable in his love'; he also spoke some loving words 'perhaps not here to be written' but including 'the prettiest compliment I have ever had in my life'.) At nine o'clock, however, 'things became impossible'. Anthony sat on the floor by her chair in the firelight while Aelfrida stroked his hair ('the caress that his mother used to give him and that he missed so much … the only caress I allowed myself') but it rapidly became borne on her 'that if I had said "take me" he would have done so then and there, without thinking twice, not wantonly but gravely and confidently', and in spite of Anthony's cry "come and see my bedroom", she fled. ('Our parting was rather confused', she added.) Lying awake at the Pembridge Gardens Hotel, she thrilled at what had taken place ('whatever it costs, love is very wonderful. To be loved at my age, doubly so!') but realised with horror that to have given herself to Anthony would have made it 'impossible for [her] to go to St Mary's Abbey'.[159] (Broken vows and Miss Wrightson's scorn were not to be lightly disregarded: '*suppose* he and I had both taken wine and our self-restraint had been loosened … should I not have sinned – we were appallingly near – only the grace of God saved us'.)[160] There was also the thought that Anthony was already 'proud beyond words of the power he has over me'[161] (he had pursued her to Leiston on the pretext of visiting his aunt) and that agreeing to sexual intercourse would only increase his dominion. It would also endanger the emotional carapace erected around herself after Constantine's rejection of her physical and intellectual charms, a carapace rationalised in religious terms as 'detachment' or as having risen above mere 'human' affections.

Deciding, therefore, that 'if ever I am to fit myself to cross the threshold of St Mary's Abbey' she must take immediate steps to break with Anthony ('I dare not go on as I am going on now … I am very tired and preposterously thin [but] if body fails under the struggle between spirit and flesh I cannot help it'; her next sentiment, that 'it would be funny if it did not happen to be so serious'[162], was not shared by poor Alethea on whom the brunt of her mother's 'confidences and worryings' fell)[163], Aelfrida took two sensible steps. First, she immersed herself in work (her current novel, her Laundry, and strenuous domesticity), then in spite of protestations that she must overcome desire for Anthony with no help but God's, sought professional advice from 'Dr Joan'.

Aelfrida had already consulted 'Dr Joan' (shortly to be discovered to be 'Sarah') on 'the Anthony problem' and much of the consultation consisted of Aelfrida's side of the conversation with Anthony which took place on the momentous evening described above. Dr Cooper, it seems, had earlier informed Aelfrida that she must explain to Anthony at the earliest opportunity that his feelings for her were not love but 'maladjustment' arising from 'a sensitive child's longing for his dead mother' manifesting itself in 'a grown man's love for his [first] woman' and that, understanding this, he would be able to be 'merely friendly' or would cease to love Aelfrida altogether. This was not what Aelfrida wanted to hear because 'being loved means so *terribly* much to me', but intending 'to do what was right at whatever cost to [her] self'[164], she had set off for Anthony's flat in April 1932, Chiara's illness and her own holiday having occasioned the delay. Trying to break the subject as gently as possible by informing Anthony that their present relationship was detrimental to their health, that they should cease to emphasise 'the aspect of [the] relationship which cannot be permanent'[165] (i.e. sexual attraction), and that a mother/son relationship would be best for both, she aroused Anthony's ardour by stroking his hair – and their 'rather confused' parting was the result. Rather confused herself, for on another occasion 'Dr Joan' had said that she should marry Anthony at once because his 'mother fixation' would make him an ideal husband for an older woman, because middle age was no bar to satisfactory 'physical intercourse', because Aelfrida's 'repression' of her natural instincts was unnatural, and because no-one, least of all her medical adviser, expected her to be "100% virtuous"[166], Aelfrida's post-Elgin Avenue consultation found her being told briskly that she was too 'severe' with herself, that she was in real danger of physical and mental breakdown, and that 'much of the difficulty [was] owing to [her] "time of life" and to family anxieties'.[167]

To have the love of her middle years reduced to a combination of 'mother fixation' and menopause ('the Straightener straightened', as Aelfrida put it wryly)[168] did nothing for her morale. (Alethea noted that she did not believe such 'confessions' were good for her mother because they neither relieved her feelings nor produced 'clarity and … action' and resulted in 'one introspection [leading on] to another and [to] a jumble of worries'.)[169] At this point too Aelfrida's health began to crack under the strain. Joan Cooper's diagnosis that some of her problems were 'largely time of life' was correct as far as it went, for palpitations and depression could be attributed to hormonal fluctuations (Aelfrida was nearly fifty) or to concern for her daughters (Agatha had developed asthma and Alethea, still moping at home, 'was not as well as she ought to be')[170] or for an elderly mother whose health and spirits were failing, but exacerbations of rheumatoid arthritis and migraine suggested she was "burning [herself] up" emotionally and that in spite of protestations of being 'able to cope with things'[171] and that Anthony did not disturb 'anything essential'[172], she was close to breakdown. To make matters worse she began to suffer 'womb problems'[173] which by mid-September 1932 resolved themselves into pains of agonising severity, 'a feeling of congestion'[174], and continuous blood-stained vaginal discharge, and Dr Cooper's initial diagnosis of benign uterine polyps which might require diagnostic and probably curative minor surgery hardened into one of probable cancer requiring urgent major surgical intervention.

Aelfrida was delighted. Here was the solution to all her problems, and death, should it occur, would be 'a nearer way – if you see what I mean'[175] to God. Delight manifested itself in a 'strange ecstasy' during a church service in which she saw 'the way clear from me to Him' ('perhaps soon there will be my funeral at St Botolph's', a homecoming after a life full of 'sin and folly in plenty')[176], in a sense of being so 'surrounded by God like a bird surrounded by air' that her soul 'sang and sang'[177], and such intense happiness that 'St Andrew's Street in the rain seemed like the streets of the New Jerusalem'.[178]

A joint consultation with Dr Cooper and gynaecologist James ('Robin') Canney[179] took place on 12 October 1932. (Aelfrida's account, longer even than her account of Constantine's physical violence in Paris or of her marital rape in October 1914, is unconsciously very funny for, practised at consorting with medical men at moments of crisis, she casts Mr Canney as the 'terribly formal' doctor won over by the charm and pathos of a woman brave and insightful enough to say forthrightly 'the trouble, of course, *is* cancer of the womb'[180] and herself as a character out of *The Model Patient's Handbook* who so far retains a sense of humour that she is able to amuse her doctor with an account of '*illnesses I have had*'. Joan Cooper, 'shivering with apprehension and sympathy'[181], is relegated to the role of handmaiden.) Aelfrida's

self-diagnosis and Dr Cooper's urgings notwithstanding, Mr Canney decided to perform diagnostic surgery first and to proceed to hysterectomy only after histological confirmation of malignancy.

Having a week to kill prior to admission to a 'quiet room with a serene [view] of poplar trees' at the 'haven of peace and rest'[182] otherwise known as the Evelyn Nursing Home, Aelfrida prepared herself for an edifying death-bed. ('Willie once told me that my greatest fault was always wanting to improve an occasion. I certainly want to now! If *only* my light can so shine before men that I glorify my Father'.) Pausing just long enough to note that it was 'best not to be presumptuous' because even *she* could hardly say '*look* what a good advertisement I am for Christianity'[183], she proceeded to say so. Efforts to publicise her 'golden serenity of the spirit'[184] in the face of death paid off handsomely. Eustace reacted with practical sympathy, Julius ('who always finds life difficult') with gloom, Alethea with sensitivity, Agatha cheerfully (she was not informed of the probable severity of her mother's condition), Chiara with 'pathetic resignation', Fidelio with diversions ('his idea of comforting me is … to talk about himself' and to read some 'not notable' poetry), Lucy Verey with a loving visit[185], and Anthony (to whom she had written in early August that 'the struggle was now over and that my will does at last dominate my emotions and so on and so on')[186], with an urgent request to see her.

Aelfrida was happy to accede but not before comparing herself to the Bishop of Gibraltar ('Collins', in case we had forgotten) whose last words as reproduced in a hagiographic biography were '*the fellowship of suffering*'. (Her pain having increased in severity, she pondered on 'how by pain one might enter somewhat into the fellowship of the Cross'[187], an extension of the idea deriving from her post-miscarriage poem dedicated to the said Bishop in which she stated that "pain is the mystic chalice of the Grail".) She also visited Merton House where, for Phyllis' special benefit, she tried 'to be [her] most charming, animated, intelligent and affectionate self' ('and it is not for me, ahem! to say whether I succeeded or not')[188], enjoyed what she believed would be her last birthday on 5 October, and said a fond farewell to Cambridge, with particular emphasis on the particular spot on the Backs from which she could gaze across the Cam at Constantine's former rooms in King's. And with memories of Constantine Michaelides' youth 'and eagerness and aspiration'[189] in mind, she turned to his successor.

Anthony arrived at Fordfield on 15 October 1932, to encounter Dr Joan ('so my two dear friends *have* met'; fortunately 'they liked each other') and to demonstrate both 'retrospective jealousy of Constantine' ('I could not say anything against the Constantine of those days or the beauty of our love', Aelfrida noted)[190] and that he had forgotten an earlier promise that his love for Aelfrida transcended 'physical passion'.[191]

That evening, the family being in bed, Aelfrida informed Anthony that 'he might caress me again, if he wished to, for the last time', giving as her excuse that 'there was an evening *owing* to him, for at the time of my vow I had never intended to deprive him of *that* and now the time had come to enjoy it'. (*Sic.*) Concern that a young man might not *want* 'to caress a woman of forty-nine ... suffering from some disease of the womb' was unfounded – Anthony very much wanted to caress her and caress her he did 'in every way – one only excepted – that passion could suggest'. Aelfrida professed herself sufficiently aroused to give Anthony 'whatever he wanted'; indeed, she 'let him have his way, only now and then begging for release when ... too exhausted', but it seems from her description that in spite of protestations that 'I could not have given more, even if we had been married and I could legitimately do so', she pleaded ill-health as a reason for prohibiting full sexual intercourse. When it was all over, she said "it has been very good"; Anthony said nothing beyond protesting vehemently when told that 'this must be the last time'.[192] Knowing that she would never do so again, Aelfrida allowed herself to rest her head on Anthony's chest as they said goodnight.

Easy as it is to poke fun at Aelfrida and her pretensions – indeed, it is sometimes the only way to vent one's exasperation at her stupidity, her insensitivity, and her monstrous egocentricity – it would be possible to guy this scene as the grotesque gambolling of a menopausal woman with a lonely and naïve young man whose lack of experience with women prevented him from grasping the fact that she was playing with him for her own emotional ends. But there is more to the scene than that.

For one thing, Anthony was twenty-five when Aelfrida's second and almost-absolute surrender took place and Constantine had been in his twenty-fifth year when 'the Marriage of Miss Tillyard' took place. For another, the scene took place in the same setting (Lucy Verey had commented on her recent visit that 'Fordfield was so unchanged')[193] as Aelfrida's staged scene of 'absolute surrender' a quarter of a century earlier. Third, the scene seems almost a replay of one which took place before Anthony was born: on 16 July 1904, a day described by Aelfrida as 'the most beautiful that ever the sun beat out of his rays to be a golden setting for the ... god of youth', she and Constantine lay down together on a pile of mown hay in a remote corner of Fordfield garden to eat cherries and read Swinburne's *Tristan and*

*Iseult*. Suddenly, she writes, 'Constantine flung away the book and lay down by my side ... I could feel all his body quivering against mine while he kissed my lips again and again. His kisses scorched me like live coals and the blood in my veins was like fire. It seemed like a merging of life and death. I do not know how long we lay like that but presently he rose and, understanding, said "You would like me to go?" I have written to him telling him that we must not again'.[194] Is what we have here, then, a conscious or unconscious attempt on Aelfrida's part to re-enact the passionate embrace of the man of whom she had written 'my youth is over' when she said goodbye at Lyons in 1919, the man to whose ghost she had recently said final farewells as she gazed across the Cam? If so we should perhaps regard her behaviour not as just another example of her wish to make life 'very vivid' or of her propensity to behave dangerously (suppose her mother, her daughters, or the maids had entered at the moment of climax, for Anthony, if not herself, became orgasmic; suppose Anthony had become so carried away that he took her by force?) for she herself seems to have regarded and described the event in terms of it being a profoundly spiritual occasion (almost a 'spiritual espousal') and as if it were the fulfilment of the vow taken on her fortieth birthday: 'I do not want to forget [Constantine] neither with my body nor in my heart'.[195]

The following morning Aelfrida attended Holy Communion: 'you may have thought what I chronicled overleaf was a very bad preparation ... but it was not so [because] not done in wantonness or for the mere pleasure of physical sensation ... but to express love not otherwise expressible ... so I went forward eagerly to [a] Communion ... more preoccupying than anything that was behind'. She then held 'a real proper Sunday tea party', after which she and Anthony parted quietly 'with nothing but a handshake'. On Monday morning she 'wrote to Anthony to explain lest he should be misled' that 'physical love was now definitely over and might be relegated to the place of memories'.[196]

In this respect she was correct; in others, not. For one thing, the biopsy showed 'it *isn't* cancer'. ('I owe an apology to the Consolations of Religion for having invoked them when they were not needed'.)[197] Feeling rather foolish ('perhaps I ought not to have told anyone that it was even early-stage cancer until there had been more confirmation')[198], Aelfrida resigned herself to life: 'I feel unequal to decisions [and] responsibilities. God give me strength'.[199] For another, she did not end her days at Leiston; her question 'will the dear Lady Abbess ever have me!'[200] being answered with a decided no. And as for Anthony and dramatic though it would be to say that he and Aelfrida never met again, they did; in fact, the affair rumbled on in a desultory fashion for another year before reaching a conclusion.

Her appetite for 'sensations' dulled by the events of the past eighteen months, Aelfrida decided that she would rather not see Anthony again if a meeting would force her 'to endure [once more] the blaze of emotion that marked our last contact'.[201] But meet they did, once under dramatic circumstances, once 'accidentally'. In the first instance, she and Anthony met in March 1933 in a nursing home where, too ill to talk because of complications following an appendicectomy, he lay with 'light and joy [welling] up from within' as she held his hand and talked gently to him, albeit without revealing that 'I love him as much as ever'.[202] In the second, passing through London in 1934, Aelfrida asked herself 'am I enough "detached" to go and see Anthony?' and on discovering that she was but that he was not in his office, strolled along Leadenhall Street in the hope of bumping into him. She did, and Anthony, 'so eager and so moved', stood her tea and they talked, chiefly about himself, for Aelfrida, aware that 'physically, the old fires are not dead', had 'no desire to stir them or ... provoke any response in him'.[203] (There was, too, the matter of Anthony being now a married man, Aelfrida having promised earlier not to 'poach on anyone's preserves'[204] should Anthony find another woman; he did, informing Aelfrida in October 1933 that he had become engaged to and was shortly to marry 'a girl from Exeter, a friend of the family', Elizabeth Bernays. More upset than she liked to admit, Aelfrida waxed philosophical, telling him that in finding Elizabeth, he had given her 'someone else to love' and consoling herself with the thought that Anthony had learnt from her 'some of the fine shades of the Art of Loving'.)[205] 'Dear Anthony', she reflected as they parted, 'we can leave it at that. I might have done him so much harm. No credit to me that I did not'.[206]

Anthony and Aelfrida never met again but Aelfrida never wrote FINIS to her love for him; indeed, she always described their relationship in very much the same terms as she wrote of hers and Constantine's: 'what I have had, no-one can take away while I have life and memory – and that has been more than my share'.[207] To underline what Anthony had meant – and continued to mean – to her, she inserted a chapter about him in her on-going novel O Passionate World:

Carola, deserted by Adrian, has decided never to "set sail again on the vast sea where the winds of desire and repulsion blew so strangely and so strong".[208] On holiday in Brittany, however, she meets twenty-five-year-old doctor Hector Branthwaite [209] whom she initially regards as a possible husband for her daughter

but, realising that he has fallen in love with herself, tries to discourage by telling him she is too old ("you are about 11am and I am about four o'clock in the afternoon – teatime I suppose")[210], by mentioning her continuing love for her former husband, and by informing him of her belief that "a woman whose husband is alive must not ... consider remarriage".[211] Undeterred, Hector declares that Carola is "the most enchanting woman on earth", that his sole aim in life is to make her happy, and that "it's only a convention that a woman mustn't be older than her husband".[212] Carola is tempted ("why don't I take the plunge and start a new life with him? I might even have a baby")[213] but eventually decides she cannot marry a man whose first kiss she treasures "as one of the loveliest moments of her life ...complete in itself, needing no future to make it perfect"[214] and whose love for her has been "the last and sweetest triumph of her womanhood".[215] They part, Hector to further his medical career in Labrador, Carola to realise "how powerfully the whole current of her life had set towards the cloister".[216]

O Passionate World was not the only novel generated by Aelfrida's relationships with men during the 1920s and 30s. A fragment of a projected novel and some novellas exist, none written but all inspired by her; one portrays her in a minor but pivotal role, the others as one or more character. Though not invariably unkind about her personality and appearance, they depict her behaviour as it might appear to an objective and not altogether sympathetic observer. The authors are her younger daughter and Albert Erlande.

Agatha, as we know, did not approve of young men who paid her mother what she regarded as unseemly attentions or of her mother in responding to them. But it was not until the appearance in Aelfrida's life of serious admirers like Juan Mascarò and Anthony Wrightson that she began to demonstrate jealousy over the amount of emotional energy her mother expended on them and dislike of being 'aunted for' so that her mother could keep Anthony near her without having to marry him herself. Like her mother, she expressed her feelings in prose.

In April 1928, a month after Anthony's arrival in Aelfrida's life and two years after that of her 'little ... goup from Majorca', Agatha diarised 'I have begun writing a book'.[217] (Aelfrida, lighting on it by accident or design, noted that her daughter was writing a novel in secret – 'en cachette' – but did not comment on its content.)[218] The novel's hero is 'John Habbington', a young, bored, languid, cultured, tall, delicate, and wealthy orphan engaged to a woman older than himself. His fiancée's overween-ing behaviour towards him enervates him so much that he first consults a 'mind-doctor', then decides to try the therapeutic effect of a long voyage. Before leaving, he visits his fiancée who, jewelled turban, and dangling ear-rings apart, is Aelfrida to the life: "a romantic woman between thirty and forty but with enough – or nearly enough – of her glamorous youth left for her to … lie among many-coloured cushions gazing at men mysteri-ously from under her white eyelids while forgetting she was not as slim or as fascinating as she used to be". As if this description were not cruel enough, Agatha continues "yet in her strangely charming way she made men feel she was a priestess of some mysterious goddess of love [who] talked about purity and real love and … said she was leading [her] worshippers up to some higher better thing. And all this when she was flirting with her wor-shippers and was really selfish, self-worshipping, impossi-ble".[219] For this accurate but unflattering description to have survived is amazing, given that Aelfrida later burnt many of Agatha's literary effects. Perhaps she retained it as an example of Agatha's talent as a writer or as a salu-tary reminder to herself of how she appeared in other's eyes; either way, it is one of very few extant examples of third party opinions of a woman who considered herself so interesting that she consigned her own diaries and surviving literary productions to a place of safety where they would run no risk of destruction after her death.

Agatha's fragmentary novel remained unpublished; Albert Erlande's novellas first appeared in 1927, the year in which Aelfrida shuddered with 'horror, *horror*' at having fallen victim to his 'odious charm'. The earli-est, *Le Trajet de la Foudre*[220], may have been begun soon after Aelfrida and Albert's first meeting in August 1925 (her comment that she did not mind providing him with 'a few cheap thrills [for] the book he is writing' was made on 23 August, with the proviso that she hoped not to see herself portrayed in it as '*la grande Anglaise*')[221] and completed or revised during their reunion of 1926. (Aelfrida describes Erlande as 'writing notes'[222] for an unnamed novel.) It is also possible that, being only a hundred pages long, it was written rapidly immedi-ately after her second visit (*Clash!* may have inspired Erlande to record his own version of their relationship) for inclusion in an anthology of short stories by himself and others published early in 1927.

We do not know if Aelfrida read *Le Trajet* but for two reasons we may conjecture that she did. First, she responded in the same medium and in a form recog-nisable by Erlande if circumstances allowed him to read what she wrote. The novella preceding Erlande's in the anthology is by Jeanne Landre; entitled *Les Idylles de*

*Pont-aux-Muses*, it describes the lives of retired actors and actresses living in Pont-aux-Muses, a residential home where well-known actors with whom they have appeared form the chief topic of conversation, 'Frédéric LeMâitre' being one of these. Is it purely coincidental that both parts of the name appear in novels written by Aelfrida shortly afterwards, 'Frédéric' in *The Approaching Storm* (without the accents and lacking the final 'k' of common English usage) and 'Lemaitre' (without the cir-cumflex) in *O Passionate World*? Second, cries of 'horror, *horror*' recorded in her diary in the same year (1927) in which *Le Trajet* appeared may have arisen less from disgust at finding herself sexually aroused by Erlande's caresses than from discovering that he *had* used her as 'copy', this placing her in the invidious position of biter bit and forc-ing her to see that what had begun as a flirtatious 'literary friendship' had transformed itself into public betrayal of secrets hitherto confided to no one but her diary:

*Le Trajet de la Foudre* describes the final stages of a loving friendship between an older writer, Dominique Dancrès, and a younger married woman, Denise Grampe, whom we first encounter at the Parisian salon of an émigré Russian, Princess Nadia Nachkine. Nadia is a striking figure dressed dramatically in green and silver robes which serve to disguise her extreme emaciation and to enhance the aura of magic and mystery which surrounds her, her personality being so captivating that all who know her fall immediately under her spell. Her story is a sad one: having cached her family valuables abroad in the early stages of the Russian Revolution, Nadia returned to Russia to be with her husband; she later escaped and now lives in widowed penury on the proceeds of the sale of her jewels. To amuse her visitors she reads aloud excerpts from memoirs written to enliven her otherwise futile existence, memoirs she hopes to publish one day in order to earn money to support herself and to expose the horrors of life in contemporary Russia.

Dancrès escorts Denise home; the night is dark and foggy and she turns up the collar of her coat less because she feels cold than to disguise her identity from acquaintances who might see her in intimate conversation with a man not her husband. Once home, she wraps herself in a black and gold kimono and, reclining on a chaise longue in her boudoir, gives herself up to reverie. In a strange mood half-dream-ing, half awake, she summons phantoms in whose presence she feels as if she has entered a mysterious country where anything might happen. It does: the spirit of Nadia appears. Denise hails her as a magi-cian and describes her life to her: she is married to a businessman who, disillusioned by the Great War, now glories in nothing but making money; the war, however, did not disillusion Denise herself but opened up to her a realm of spirituality and the supra-normal. Though keen to pursue her studies, she is forbidden by her husband to involve herself further with matters and instructors he finds abhorrent. When he discovers that she is not only pursuing her interests in secret but is also devoting the greater part of her time to them, M. Grampe is furious – he threatens to throw her out and forbids her on pain of separation from her child to continue her studies; he also forces her to help him entertain business colleagues with whom she has nothing in common.

Denise's reverie is rudely interrupted by her husband bursting into her boudoir whence, after a hectoring speech in which he further asserts his authority over her, he carries her protesting to her bedroom and takes her by force.

We know, of course, that Aelfrida confided in Albert Erlande with regard to Willie Searle and it is unsurprising to find him well-informed about Nadja Laptchinski, given that Nadja arrived in England in November 1924, was domiciled more or less continuously at Fordfield until moving to Papworth in the summer of 1925, and would have provided Aelfrida with a dramatic topic of conversation. (In fact, Erlande's description of 'Nadia's' appearance, particularly her emaciation, fits Aelfrida perfectly, for in the years following her divorce she was very thin indeed and both Erlandes commented on this and on how little she ate.) More surprising, given her usual reticence on the subject, is how much of her own recent history Aelfrida confided to Erlande, including her involvement in Ceremonial Magic ('Denise's' outcast and opium-addicted but supportive uncle is an obvious portrait of Aleister Crowley) and her troubled relationship with Constantine, the latter in such detail that Erlande's account of 'Denise's' marital rape is virtually déjà vu.

Aelfrida never discloses *why* she felt so compelled to confide in Albert Erlande about her relationship with Constantine, though a woman who had spent her married life and the years since her divorce concealing her emotions must have found it cathartic to disclose secrets hitherto confided only to paper: that she did so and in considerable detail is evidenced by Erlande's novella. (Aelfrida and Gina Erlande exchanged confidences concerning their respective husbands though more on Madame's part than Aelfrida's; short of reading her diaries, there was nowhere else Erlande could have acquired his information. During her first encounter, Aelfrida was guarded, telling him only 'some of the things in my life that were *not* love – lectures, preaching etc'[223], but during her second seems to have confided more.) From diary evidence we may deduce how it happened.

First, there was much in Erlande's personality which reminded her of Constantine, a man in whom she had confided until reduced to silence by jeering criticisms, and of Aleister Crowley's, a man to whom she confided secrets un-divulged to anyone else. Second, Erlande was a fellow-writer who informed her that "only authors can understand other authors"[224]; indeed, it seems he understood her so well that he informed her that all her feelings went into her books and that, though superficially a passionate woman, she was *au fond* frigid.[225] Fourth, Erlande was one of those people 'who "take" you at once' and who by intuitively grasping 'fine shades of meaning'[226], quickly realised the import of what she was trying to tell him; indeed, apropos another woman visitor to Perros Guirec who by name ('Madame Longue'), demeanour (tall, thin, handsome, and with unquiet eyes), and by the fact that she was the mother of two well brought up daughters (*"femme que j'avais déjà remarqué à cause de son élégance et de la gentillesse de ses fillettes"*, says a male character in *Le Trajet* of 'Delphine Avart' whose '*fillettes*' though French, bear the English names 'Martha' and 'Jane')[227] we may infer is actually herself, Aelfrida confided 'one felt he had gone straight to the unguarded secret of [her] nature … and that she was [unwittingly] revealing to him all her inmost feelings [and] the secrets of her married life'.[228] Fourth, Erlande was 'more like a doctor listening to a patient … than anything else'[229] when confided in and, in contrast to his usual behaviour, gentle to a woman who found herself pouring out confessions interpreted by Erlande so as to make out 'that one has said – or thought – more than one has'.[230] Lastly, of someone whose passion was '*the vivisection of character*'[231], Aelfrida could only say 'what a psychoanalyst the man would have made!'[232] Hence she felt compelled to return to Albert Erlande for further 'therapy' and why, having done so, experienced such ambiguous feelings towards a man she regarded as both father-confessor ('when I confide in Erlande he is … paternal – no, sacerdotal [and] he calls me "*mon enfant*" or "*mon petit enfant*"')[233] and a would-be seducer who boasted 'that no woman has ever denied him'.[234] Perhaps it was not only chastity which made 'some things … unthinkable' with regard to Erlande's suggestion that they become lovers.[235]

Erlande's motives for putting Aelfrida into subsequent novellas are unknown. Was it for love or for revenge? At first reading, revenge seems likely: he had been spurned by a woman who had led him on by actively participating in what she admitted were 'dangerous games'[236] and who, in spite of protestations to the contrary, had come very close to succumbing: 'fire, that man with whom it is dangerous to play'.[237] He was also a man whose powers of self-control had been rendered precarious by wartime injuries and who was unlikely to be inhibited by the risk of hurting his wife's feelings, of embarrassing Aelfrida by exposing in print matters told to him in, as it were, the confessional, or of revealing to Aelfrida's daughters facts about her marriage that their mother might prefer them not to know. The same man and for the same reasons and knowing that his intimate knowledge of Aelfrida's character (her being a '*nonne ratée*' and still in love with her husband and, an even more perceptive and prophetic comment, 'one of those people … who would enjoy being crucified')[238] had placed her in his power ('M. Erlande is not good for me')[239], might lack compunction in exercising that power by featuring her in future works, rendering of aspects of her personality, appearance, and circumstances sympathetically in the persons of 'Nadia', 'Denise', and 'Delphine' but caricaturing her as a dried-up old Englishwoman ('*vieille Anglaise sèche*') wearing a calico smock and spectacles, '*la nurse*'[240] to 'Denise's' small daughter, a caricature both cruel and accurate because Aelfrida wore such smock-dresses at this time and, something much disliked by Constantine because it made a wife who looked older than himself look even older (there is only a single mention of her wearing glasses in her diaries), reading glasses.

Or is *Le Trajet* a letter to a woman with whom Erlande has genuinely fallen in love by a man who suspects he will never see her again? His portrait of 'Denise Grampe' is very tender and uses the same tone and language reportedly used to 'Madame Longue'. He includes objects (e.g. kimonos, presents from the Shipways to Aelfrida), occasions (the scene in 'Denise's' boudoir resembles an occasion when Erlande erupted into Aelfrida's bedroom while she was reading in a reclining chair), phrases ('so cold', said twice, in her second Perros Guirec poem of 27 July 1926 becomes "*avez-vous froid?*" and "*j'ai froid*"[241] at a poignant moment in the novella), and endearments unrecorded in Aelfrida's diary ('Delphine', for example, calls 'Dancrès' her "*grand ami*"[242], as it might be that a man several years older than Aelfrida would be a 'big' rather than a 'little' friend) but piquant because known only to herself and him. Or is this to see treason where none exists? Is it rather, that Erlande discovered in Aelfrida some excellent 'copy' and made the most of it by putting it into not one but several books?

Judging by her revulsion, Aelfrida regarded *Le Trajet* as an act of revenge and betrayal, revenge because of her having made clear to Erlande as early as August 1925 that she would always cleave to the spiritual rather than the material world and to the soul rather than to the body however much he tempted her to act otherwise (his reply was "what a pity"), betrayal because the novella dealt with her private property; worse still, he portrayed both in the same medium as her own revenges. (In parenthesis it is important to remember that Aelfrida knew that Erlande was writing a novel in which she might appear and that, seen in this light, her 'horror, *horror*' reaction is disingenuous; she may, however, have hoped that Erlande would portray her as she preferred to appear, i.e. as the morally superior heroine of *Clash!* rather than as a woman who wilfully misinterpreted his intentions towards her – as he told her, "*vous méprisez beaucoup trop la matière*"[243] – in the interest of maintaining the proprieties and her 'recuperated' virginity.) If, therefore, Aelfrida truly believed *Le Trajet* to be a revengeful rather than a romantic gesture (given that she said of Erlande's literary technique that "every word is considered, every phrase weighed and measured"[244], it may have been both), one can understand why she was so upset by it. Her rejection of Erlande nevertheless acquires a certain poignancy when we discover towards the end of *Le Trajet* in the chapter in which 'Denise Grampe' and 'Dominique Dancrès' part for ever, that 'Denise' tells her lover wistfully that she will always be grateful to him because he has given her back her soul: "*vous m'avez donné mon âme!*" 'Dancrès', however, replies bitterly that all he has done is to make ready her soul so that she can bestow it on someone else: "*j'ai préparé votre âme pour un autre*".[245] As Dancrès/Erlande had indeed done – with Anthony Wrightson its first recipient, Deity its second.

There are, however, other twists to the relationship between Albert and Aelfrida. In 1927 Erlande published another novella: *La Vipère Dorée*. As with *Le Trajet*, *La Vipère* tells the story of a woman's disruptive effect on other people's lives. This might be coincidental were it not that characters in *Le Trajet* appear in, or are referred to, in *La Vipère*: 'Nadia Nachkine' (in a lesser role), a 'Doctor Gorcier' (in a more important role), and a 'Madame de Targes' more prominently. In *Le Trajet* 'Madame de Targes' introduces 'Denise Grampe' to the beliefs which alienate her from her husband; in *La Vipère*, however, she is portrayed as a woman who counsels young men in an attempt to assuage her grief at the premature death of her husband. (The novella's hero, 'Élie de Versangues', is even described as her 'son of the house': *fils adoptif de la maison*')[246] Madame has much of Aelfrida about her in other ways too: not only is she "*une conseillère … attachée à ceux qu'elle nominait ses clients*" to whom young male 'clients' owe their happiness and sense of direction, but she also, like Aelfrida herself at the least hint of "*indélicatesse*" or even "*par caprice*" because they have ceased to entertain her, abruptly drops 'clients' she has previously 'counselled'.[247] Other echoes of Aelfrida's life also appear: an eighteen-year-old girl is begged by her mother to be 'normal' (as Aelfrida may have been begged by Chiara and certainly was by Dr Hare) and even becomes engaged in an effort to be so, but after her marriage finds herself in a kind of spiritual limbo until her faculties are re-awakened (in Paris) as a result of books she has read, whereupon she finds herself surrounded by the phenomena (spectres, gesturing hands, deafening cries etc.)[248] described by Aelfrida in *Evening. Silence. A Shaded Lamp.* 'Élie' too, describing his infatuation for the 'viper' of the title, uses phrases which Erlande himself may have used to Aelfrida during their passionate sessions at the beach hut and elsewhere[249] or might have used after reading Aelfrida's poetry: "*au diable ce journal de déséquilibrée; les poèmes russes, anglais, italiens et allemands; les songes prophétiques*".[250]

All this might be conjecture, particularly when we discover that *La Vipère Dorée* was begun in July 1914 and completed in August 1921 before Aelfrida and Erlande met, but it seems that as an aspect of his relationship with her, Erlande transformed an earlier unpublished work into a prequel to *Le Trajet* (*La Vipère* makes no reference to the Great War and by context occurs before it) albeit with the alteration or addition of certain names and characters ('Nadia Nachkine' being a case in point, but there are others) which would render it immediately recognisable by Aelfrida for what it was. Not only this, but Erlande's placement of an unbalanced, psychic, multilingual poet and diarist among the 'hysterics and madmen' noted by her as typical of his characters[251] demonstrates the clarity with which he perceived her. Furthermore, Erlande's third novella of 1927, *Ils Jouaient de la Vie*, appeared in a series of '*cahiers illustrés*' published in Paris on the first and fifteenth of each month; it is possible, therefore, that it also formed the subject of his letter to Aelfrida of February 1927, a letter which elicited both a shudder and regret that she had been 'in the least bit sensitive to his odious charm'. The story begins with a small girl waking in a strange bed to be told that her mother has been taken ill, that she has been carried to a neighbour's house fast asleep, and that the son of the house with whom she is good friends will come to comfort her. He does – and the girl, whose mother dies the following day, becomes so emotionally close to him that she calls him 'brother'. The boy's name, Jean, begins with the same letter as Julius'; the girl's, like Aelfrida's, is a feminised masculine: Gilberte.

How ironic, therefore, that as the first and only person with whom Aelfrida felt able to discuss the craft of novel writing, who agreed that 'people in one's books were more real than people in real life', and who was seemingly the first person to 'notice' (and praise) her poetry, Erlande was also the first to betray her confidences in print.[252]

Ironic too, is that Erlande may have continued to send literary messages to Aelfrida until shortly before his death on 16 May 1934. (His death passed unrecorded in her diary, but as she remained in contact with Madame Erlande after that date, she can hardly have been unaware of it. As with Charles Stewart-Smith who died 23 February 1934, lack of comment may have been due to preoccupation with the death of a man closer to her than they.) The messages refer to events in their relationship or to what Aelfrida had told him of her past to date. *Dongiovanninesca,* a surrealist novella of 1929, begins with a row of beach huts, once crisply white but now faded and rust-spotted, contains a character who knows someone living in Panama, describes Satan smoking opium in a green kimono embroidered with 'silvery storks' (*cigognes argentées*), and refers bitterly to damnable women who delight in poisoning the lives of deserving men through sheer devilry.[253] The plot of *Si belle en ce miroir,* also of 1929, revolves round the revelatory reading by a masculine third party of an account of entangled relationships written by one of those involved, a woman who purposely leaves it where he will alight on it.

Also ironic in this context is Aelfrida's comment in the foreword to her 1924 book *Messages*: writing of meditation, she describes it metaphorically as running along a path made of thoughts "with here and there a pause to gather flowers".[254] Are Albert Erlande and Anthony Wrightson therefore no more than 'flowers' paused over, gathered, and discarded before she continues on her way? Or are they men about whom, in her damaged and imperfect way, Aelfrida was briefly but truly passionate?

## Notes

1 'Albert Erlande' (1874–1934) was the nom de plume of Albert-Jacques Brandenburg. Born in Marseilles, Brandenburg was the son of a Frenchwoman and an engineer, Maltese by birth but a British subject by right (his grandfather was an Englishman) who, failing to interest their son in a suitable profession, allowed him to go to Paris where he lived *la vie de bohème* with financial support from his doting mother. Aged 28 and beginning to establish a reputation as a writer, Brandenburg married a childhood friend, Gina Baudoin, and, moving back to the South of France, lived an idyllic bucolic existence with her and their three children until the outbreak of the Great War. In 1914 he enlisted in the French Foreign Legion under his pen-name (adopted c. 1900) of 'Albert Erlande' but was invalided out in 1915 with shell shock and a head injury so severe as to incapacitate him for some time and to bring on pathological character changes, evidenced by erotomania, unfounded jealousy of his wife, and heavy drinking, traits which contributed to the break-up of his marriage in 1930. His injuries, however, liberated something in him which allowed him to

become a successful writer and he and his family moved to Paris where a regular stipend from his publishers removed the necessity of earning his living other than by his pen. (Biographical details from GCPPT 1|1|31a and from brief entries in Aelfrida's later diaries. Further biographical details may be gleaned from F. de Paemelaere's Introduction to Erlande's 1928 'novel for children' *Coup de Pif*. The *Dictionnaire de Biographie Française* p1381 contains few biographical details but provides a useful bibliography).

2 GCPPT 1|1|31 9 August 1925.

3 ibid. 13 and 23 August 1925.

4 ibid. 10 August 1925.

5 ibid. 21 August 1925.

6 ibid. 13 August 1925.

7 ibid. 7 August 1925.

8 ibid. 23 August 1925.

9 ibid.

10 ibid. 25 August 1925.

11 ibid. 4 September 1925.

12 ibid. 30 August 1925.

13 ibid. 10 August 1925.

14 GCPPT 1|1|30 6 September 1925.

15 ibid 9 October 1925.

16 16 1|1|32 27 May 1926.

17 GCPPT 1|1|30 25 July 1925.

18 GCPPG A1.1 30 August 1925.

19 GCPPT 1|1|32 21 December 1925.

20 GCPPG A1.1 7 August 1926.

21 GCPPT 1|1|33 21 July 1926.

22 ibid. 24 July 1926.

23 ibid. 22 July 1926.

24 ibid. 16 July 1926.

25 ibid. 26 July 1926

26 ibid. 27 July 1926. The second poem is entitled *Swing to the soundless rhythm of all created things.*

27 GCPPT 1|1|39 28 May 1931.

28 GCPPT 1|1|33 1 August 1926.

29 ibid. 2 August 1926.

30 ibid. 6 August 1926.

31 ibid. 1 August 1926.

32 ibid. 4 August 1926.

33 ibid. 6 August 1926. Aelfrida records that she continued to work on her 'Perros novel' after her return (GCPPT 1|1|32 15 September 1926) but soon seems to have abandoned it. In January 1930 she resumed work, but not, it seems, for long (GCPPT 1|1|37 15 January 1930). Completed or not, we hear no more of *Clash!* and the manuscript appears to have been destroyed in one of her periodic holocausts.

34 GCPPT 1|1|33 7 August 1926.

35 ibid. 8 August 1926.

36 ibid. 2 and 10 August 1926.

37 ibid. 10 August 1926.

38 ibid. 7 August 1926.

39 ibid. 14 August 1926

40 ibid. 21 August 1926.

41 GCPPG A2.1 31 July 1926.

42 GCPPG A1.1 7 August 1926.

43 GCPPT 1|1|33 14 August 1926.

44 ibid. 10 August 1926.

45 ibid. 29 September 1926.

46 GCPPT 1|1|32 30 August 1926.

47 GCPPT 1|1|34 24 February 1927.

48 GCPPT 1|1|33 29 July 1926

49 ibid. 28 July 1926.

50 ibid. 17 July 1926.

51 ibid. 10 August 1926.

52 GCPPT 1|1|31 4 September 1925.

53 GCPPT 1|1|33 27 July 1926.

54 GCPPT 1|1|30 30 October 1925.

55 GCPPG A1.1 18 January, 8 February and 10 June 1928.

56 GCPPG A1.1 12 May 1928.
GCPPT 1|1|35 12 March 1928.

57 GCPPT 1|1|35 21 May 1928.

58 ibid. 23 September 1928.

59 ibid. 5 October 1928.

60 ibid. 5 December 1928.

61 GCPPT 1|1|36 6 May 1929.

62 ibid. 23 May 1929.

63 ibid. 9 June 1929.

64 ibid.

65 ibid. 3 September 1929.

66 ibid.

67 GCPPT 1|1|38 21 October 1930.

68 GCPPT 1|1|37 8 November 1929.

69 ibid. 2 December 1929.

70 ibid. 13 April 1929.

71 ibid. 7 February 1930.

72 ibid. 13 April 1930.

73 GCPPT 1|1|37 25 April 1930.
GCPPG A.1.1 19 February 1930.

74 GCPPT 1|1|37 15 June 1930.

75 ibid.

76 ibid.

77 GCPPT 1|1|38 27 July 1930.

78 ibid.

79 GCPPT 1|1|37 26 April 1930.
GCPPT 1|1|38 6 August 1930.

80 GCPPT 1|1|37 9 May 1930.

81 ibid. 4 May 1930.

82 GCPPT 1|1|38 16 September 1930.

83 ibid. 27 July 1930.

84 ibid. 29 November 1930.

85 GCPPT 1|1|39 3 January 1931.

86 GCPPG A1.1 Undated entry written between 17 and 24 September 1930.

87 GCPPT 1|1|39 25 January 1931.

88 ibid. 26 January 1931.

89 GCPPT 1|1|37 9 May 1930.

90 GCPPT 1|1|38 15 August 1930.

91 ibid. 19 August 1930.

92 ibid. 15 August 1930.

93 ibid. 24 November 1930.

94 ibid.

95 ibid. 10 August 1930.

96 ibid. 29 November 1930.

97 GCPPT 1|1|39 9 January 1931.

98 GCPPT 1|1|40 20 August 1931.

99 GCPPT 1|1|37 10 May 1930.

100 GCPPT 1|1|39 9 January 1931.

101 ibid. 18 February 1931.

102 ibid. 3 March 1931.

103 ibid. 23 February 1931. Alfred Walford (1899–1979) was appointed Clinical Assistant to Addenbrooke's Hospital Ear, Nose and Throat department in 1927 and promoted to Honorary Assistant Surgeon the same year following William Bowen's resignation.

104 GCPPT 1|1|39 5 March 1931.

105 GCPPT 1|1|39 11 March 1931.

106 ibid.

107 Eric Silvanus appears in *Haste to the Wedding* (pp 221–222) as 'Leverington', a dissolute friend of 'Douglas Arlesey', who, pretending

to be the fairy fiddler with a letter from her lover, entices 'Cassandra' into the garden where he kisses her before she has time to recoil from "the ill-favoured lineaments and leering eyes of her lover's quondam boon-companion". The novel was, of course, written prior to Agatha's illness.

108 GCPPT 1|1|39 23 February 1931. In May 1932 Aelfrida completed *The Approaching Storm* and began another novel, *Victoria's Vow*, later rejected by Hutchinson and of which no manuscript survives. Although ostensibly to do with 'women and their ideals for higher education' (GCPPT 1|1|41 1 May 1932), her own vow of 23 February 1931 might have featured in it.

109 GCPPT 1|1|39 12 March 1931.

110 ibid. 10 March 1931.

111 ibid. 13 March 1931.

112 ibid. 29 March 1931. A letter, amusing under the circumstances, appeared in *The Cambridge Review* of 10 February 1933 (vol LIV no.1326 p232). Referring to the Evelyn Nursing Home, it notes how "the most admired surgeon in Cambridge [performed] a series of wonderful operations on one of my children [there] and [came] at half past eleven one snowy night to tell me how the patient had stood [the most recent one]". The letter is signed 'Gratias Ago' (i.e. 'I give thanks') by a writer whose initials –A(CW)G– are oddly similar to 'Gratias Ago's' but whose diary version (GCPPT 1|1|39 14 March 1931) is both more and less dramatic: the night, though frosty, was not 'snowy'.

113 ibid. 14 March 1931.

114 ibid. 15 March 1931.

115 ibid. 31 March 1931.

116 ibid. 4 April 1931.

117 ibid. 3 April 1931.

118 ibid. 23 March 1931.

119 ibid. 27 March 1931.

120 ibid. 7 June 1931.

121 ibid. The tremor, a manifestation of Britain's largest (magnitude 6.1) twentieth century earthquake, was epicentred under the North Sea off the Humber estuary and was, according the *CIP* of 12 June 1931("Earthquake shocks Cambridge. Giant Hand in Silken Glove") "a veritable zephyr among earth tremors. The 'zephyr' was nevertheless strong enough to ring a bell on Queens' College and cause wheeled beds in Addenbrooke's Hospital to roll across the ward.

122 GCPPT 1|1|39 7 June 1931.

123 GCPPT 1|1|40 8 June 1931.

124 ibid. 6 August 1931.

125 ibid. 9 August 1931.

126 ibid. 11 August 1931.

127 GCPPT 1|1|39 25 April 1931.

128 GCPPT 1|1|40 26 June 1931.

129 ibid. 21 June 1931.

130 ibid. 23 June 1931.

131 ibid. 24 June 1931.

132 ibid. 14 July 1931.

133 St Mary's Abbey was founded at Minsmere (also in Suffolk) in 1182 by an order of Augustinian Canons and transferred to Leiston in 1363. After the Dissolution of the Monasteries in 1536, St Mary's became a farm, the farmhouse being constructed within the ruins themselves. House and ruins were bought by Miss Wrightson in 1928. At her death in 1946 the estate passed to the diocese of Bury St Edmunds.

134 GCPPT 1|1|40 14 July 1931.

135 GCPPT 1|1|32 27 February 1926.

136 ibid. 11 February 1926.

137 ibid. 4 January 1931.

138 GCPPT 1|1|40 18 September 1931.

139 ibid. 3 and 4 September 1931.

140 ibid. 25 October 1931.

141 GCPPT 1|1|40 27 October 1931.
    GCPPT 1|1|41 16 March 1932.

142 GCPPT 1|1|40 16 October 1931.

143 GCPPT 1|1|44 18 March 1933. "A vocation is not a *wanting*, it is being called", a lady abbess tells 'Carola', the latter having decided to embrace conventual life because divorce, desertion, death and the marriage of her daughter have conspired to make her feel unwanted. Snubbed by the abbess, 'Carola' decides to marry 'Richard Temple', only to find that he has no desire to marry her (*O Passionate World* pp 384–388).

144 GCPPT 1|1|40 2, 4, and 18 September 1931.

145 ibid. 21 September 1931.

146 ibid. 27 September 1931.

147 ibid. 3 October 1931.

148 ibid. 27 September 1931. The title is taken from Psalm 122: 7; it begins with the significant lines "I was glad when they said until me: we will go into the house of the Lord" (KJV).

149 ibid. 16 October 1931.

150 ibid. 18 October 1931.

151 ibid. 25 October 1931.

152 ibid. 7 November 1931.

153 In *O Passionate World* (p 258) Aelfrida has 'Carola' inform 'Richard Temple' that she wants to become a nun because "they live in *eternity*. We only live in *time*", only to have 'Richard' tell her that it is futile to model herself on them because "you are so ... human. It is a mere affectation to try and be anything else".

154 GCPPT 1|1|40 25 November 1931.

155 ibid. 16 December 1931.

156 GCPPG A1.1 26 December 1931.

157 GCPPT 1|1|40 30 December 1931.

158 GCPPT 1|1|41 undated entry written between 17 March and 2 April 1932.

159 ibid. 2 and 3 April 1932.

160 GCPPT 1|1|50 15 March 1936.

161 GCPPT 1|1|41 2 April 1932.

162 ibid. 5 April 1932.

163 GCPPG A1.1 4 April 1932. 'I wish the girls still kept diaries. I am sure their diaries would be just as interesting as mine', Aelfrida wrote (GCPPT 1|1|40 20 September 1931), not knowing that Alethea still kept hers (Agatha had stopped in July 1928 shortly after leaving school) and would continue to do so until February 1934; how much she would have enjoyed Alethea's insightful depiction of her mother's personality is open to conjecture.

164 GCPPT 1|1|40 2 February 1932.

165 GCPPT 1|1|41 2 April 1932.

166 GCPPT 1|1|40 20 January 1932.

167 GCPPT 1|1|41 7 April 1932.

168 ibid.

169 GCPPG A1.1 4 April 1932

170 GCPPT 1|1|41 20 April 1932.

171 ibid. 16 April 1932.

172 ibid. 20 April 1932.

173 ibid. 16 April 1932.

174 GCPPT 1|1|42 13 September 1932.

175 ibid. 1 October 1932.

176 ibid. 2 October 1932.

177 ibid. 6 October 1932.

178 ibid. 19 September 1932.

179 James Robertson Campbell Canney (1883–1967) was a Cambridge general practitioner/anaesthetist who, following service with the RAMC in Cambridge's 1st Eastern General Hospital during the Great War, was appointed Honorary Assistant Surgeon in Addenbrooke's Hospital Department of Gynaecology from 1920 until his retirement in 1948. Aelfrida's description of him accords well with that of his

erstwhile partner in general practice, the latter writing of him that Canney was a "tall spare Scot … a deft and gentle operator whose cases did well [but who] did not suffer fools gladly and [who] could be disconcertingly forthright". (Salisbury Woods, R. p65.)

180 GCPPT 1|1|42 7 October 1932.

181 ibid. 12 October 1932.

182 ibid. 17 October 1932.

183 ibid. 17 and 22 September 1932.

184 ibid. 13 September 1932.

185 ibid. 20, 22, and 29 September and 11 October 1932.

186 GCPPT 1|1|41 9 August 1932.

187 GCPPT 1|1|42 19 September 1932.

188 ibid. 23 September 1932.

189 ibid. 11 October 1932.

190 ibid. 16 October 1932.

191 GCPPTT 1|1|41 9 August 1932.

192 GCPPT 1|1|42 16 October 1932.

193 ibid. 29 September 1932.

194 GCPPT 1|1|11 16 July 1904.

195 GCPPT 1|1|27 5 October 1923.

196 GCPPT 1|1|42 17 October 1932.

197 ibid. 28 October 1932.

198 ibid. 22 September 1932.

199 ibid. 27 October 1932.

200 GCPPT 1|1|40 16 October 1931.

201 GCPPT 1|1|42 6 November 1932.

202 GCPPT 1|1|43 15 March 1933.

203 GCPPT 1|1|45 10 July 1934.

204 GCPPT 1|1|40 16 December 1931.

205 GCPPT 1|1|44 3 and 31 October 1933.

206 GCPPT 1|1|45 10 July 1934.

207 GCPPT 1|1|39 8 June 1931.

208 Tillyard, Ae. O Passionate World p232.

209 The Iliad, Book 6, describes Hector as an altogether admirable son, husband, and friend whose farewell to his wife Andromache before he goes out to fight Achilles and to die is most movingly expressed; 'Branthwaite' is a surname inscribed in the Odessan pages of Aelfrida's Visitors Book.

210 Tillyard, Ae. O Passionate World p271.

211 ibid. p 324.

212 ibid. pp 322–324.

213 ibid. p 378. This paragraph is crossed out in the manuscript.

214 ibid. pp 323–4.

215 ibid. p 329.

216 ibid. p 390.

217 GCPPG A2.1 8 April 1928.

218 GCPPG 1|1a Alethea and Agatha Joint Record Book 1 June 1928. The 'novel' to which Aelfrida refers may have been begun in late 1927 for fragments appear in Agatha's diary of that date but other and equally undated versions, provisionally entitled O Rest and The Son of Consolation, exist among her papers (GCPPG A2. 3 and 4).

219 GCPPG A2.1 1927. Undated fragment of novel included in this volume.

220 Trajet implies a passing, crossing or course, foudre a manifestation of an electrical storm or, figuratively speaking, a sudden calamity; the significance of Erlande's title is explained in his text but can be noted briefly here as describing a short sharp shock whose effects, though actually instantaneous, may not become manifest until the initial cause is forgotten. A coup de foudre is, of course, a description of the effect of love at first sight.

221 GCPPT 1|1|31 3 August 1925.

222 GCPPT 1|1|33 30 July 1926.

223 GCPPT 1|1|31 26 August 1926.

224 ibid. 21 August 1925.

225 GCPPT 1|1|33 6 August 1926.

226 GCPPT 1|1|31 13 August 1925.

227 Erlande, A. Le Trajet de la Foudre p 201.

228 GCPPT 1|1|33 3 August 1926.

229 ibid.

230 ibid 1 and 17 August 1926.

231 GCPPT 1|1|31a. Notes made by Aelfrida for her lecture to the Sophists.

232 GCPPT 1|1|33 3 August 1926.

233 ibid. 17 July 1926.

234 ibid. 6 August 1926.

235 ibid. 29 July 1926.

236 ibid. 2 August 1926.

237 ibid. 28 July 1926.

238 GCPPT 1|1|31 29 August 1931.

239 ibid. 23 August 1925.

240 Erlande, A. Le Trajet de la Foudre p 217.

241 ibid. pp 213 and 306.

242 ibid. pp 217 and 293.

243 GCPPT 1|1|31 28 August 1925.

244 GCPPT 1|1|31a.

245 Erlande, A. Le Trajet de la Foudre p 297.

246 Erlande, A. La Vipère Dorée p103.

247 ibid. pp 15–16.

248 ibid. pp 90–92.

249 ibid. pp 44–45.

250 ibid. p 99.

251 GCPPT 1|1|31 25 August 1925.

252 ibid. 4 and 26 August 1925.

253 Erlande, A. Dongiovanninesca . Mercure de France vol CCIX No 735 1 February 1929 pp 549–576.

254 Tillyard, Ae. Messages Foreword.

# Approaching Storm

Aelfrida's last published novel, prophetically entitled *The Approaching Storm,* seems to have been conceived (she is, for once, vague about dates) shortly after she began *Concrete* in September 1928, so probably existed in some shape or form early in 1929. Appearing in print in October 1932, the novel therefore coincides almost exactly with the sequence of events to be described in this chapter and although this is also the period during which she experienced 'Indian Summer' happiness with Anthony Wrightson, its title strangely and accurately heralds the tempest which broke over her head in 1933, which was to alter the tenor and course of her life, and from which it took her years to recover. The story, even more coincidentally, begins and ends with a cat, a death, and a dose of morphine.

February 1929 was bitterly cold. Alfred Tillyard, victim of advanced arteriosclerosis, his wife's insistence on unheated bedrooms, and of his own predilection for daily walks whatever the weather, suffered a severe epistaxis on the night of 3/4 March ('bleeding most violently from the nose' for an hour)[1] and another at 5.30am on 10 March ('more alarming than ever … the blood poured out'), the latter requiring medical intervention to stem the haemorrhage[2]. Thereafter, though frailer than before (it was at this juncture he asked Aelfrida to become a director of the Steam Laundry) and even more demanding of his wife, Alfred Tillyard insisted on maintaining his usual routine. Alarmed by the episodes and exhausted by her husband's increasing nocturnal restlessness but fixated on martyrdom, Catharine Tillyard became 'violent and abusive' when Aelfrida suggested extra help, declaring that if her daughter introduced a 'strange woman' into Fordfield, she would be 'turned out of the house' forthwith.[3] Exasperated beyond measure by her parents' intransigence, Aelfrida retired to bed to revise the novel then rather appropriately entitled *The Way We Grow Old* and to congratulate herself on missing Fordfield's annual 'Spring Cleaning Festival'.[4]

Matters continued thus until 1 October, the day on which Aelfrida and her father argued over her extravagance and payment of the balance of Agatha's college fees. (Aelfrida's forty-sixth birthday four days later was a rather muted occasion.) On 6 October the Oracle took his usual evening walk in the 'gardens-at-the-back'; at

**Aelfrida, Agatha and Alethea Graham with Anthony Wrightson 1929**

9.30pm on 7 October, however, he groaned and collapsed after 'terrific vomiting' and the doctor was called. A diagnosis of indigestion was made (given Alfred Tillyard's medical history, a heart attack seems more likely) and two injections of morphine administered in an attempt to alleviate his pain.[5] At 8am the following day, Chiara asked Aelfrida to administer a third dose, left by the doctor for the purpose; this she did, noting that her father looked 'ill but not desperately so'.[6] A newspaper proprietor to the last, Alfred Tillyard had extracts from *The Times* read to him before falling into an uneasy sleep with his wife and daughter at his bedside. At 5pm Aelfrida noticed a change in his breathing, at 5.30pm his condition deteriorated and at 5.45 he died in his seventy-eighth year 'with that wonderful dignity and self-control he always had'.[7] (This may have been so, but Aelfrida's comments with regard to 'the tragic indignity of death' and to the 'physical humiliation'[8] suffered by her father suggests otherwise.) As Alfred Tillyard expired, Bushie, Chiara's grey Persian cat, successor to Leo who died young, ran 'distractedly over the house mewing incessantly'.[9] At 2.30am on the day following his funeral Aelfrida heard her dead father's characteristic footsteps mounting the stairs to his bedroom door; half an hour later they descended and 'all over the house there was complete silence'.[10]

Reverberations of his death continued nevertheless. Julius, summoned in haste from a visit to Patmos, was sad but not overwhelmingly so, for although his *vacua et vidua domus* comment accurately reflects the funereal Fordfield atmosphere ('the house is sad without its master, even though its master was old and ill and blind')[11], his allegiance was to his mother. Eustace, a reluctant participant in caring for his father, seemed more upset by his death than anyone else. Agatha and Alethea, having been told not to plunge themselves into gloom, sorrowed more for their mother and grandmother 'than for any great personal loss'[12] though Alethea noted perceptively that in spite of her grandfather's propensity to ride 'rough-shod over our feelings and [to leave] us in tears', he had been 'fond of me and Agatha' in his own way; she also noted how rootless the all-female household felt without him: 'we miss … his physical presence, his moral hold over us'.[13] Chiara, engrossed in funeral arrangements and in bewailing the loss of 'precious companionship', was already 'looking forward', talking excitedly of what she going to do now she was free.[14]

Aelfrida, for her part, wished that the Fordfield women-folk had been left in peace to grieve (the death of a once well-known Cambridge figure with an extended family made that impossible) because she would have been able to shut herself away to 'mope' and to try to penetrate the 'mysterious stillness that covers Oracle'[15] and because she needed to do some serious thinking. Had her pecuniary irresponsibility precipitated (or even caused) her father's death ('I *am* glad I never said to him any of the things about money that I wrote in my diary')[16] and why, and 'in spite of all his exactions and his little ways' (a tremendously muted description of the Oracle's tyrannical behaviour, much of which has been omitted for the sake of brevity), did she find it so hard to mourn sincerely one who left her with a sense of 'rather desolate leisure' rather than any real sense of loss? Why, too, did she only now realise how much she was her father's daughter? 'Some of the things I don't like in myself', she wrote, 'came straight from him', adding that although the Oracle 'was fonder of Julius and Eustace

than he was of me', she herself was closer to his essential nature even when they disagreed ('perhaps even closer then') and that this explained why he behaved as he did towards one whose personality was so similar to his own and for the same reasons: by "childhood's troubled maze", by a "godward vision", and by a "dread of sin" manifestating itself in 'kill-joy Puritanism'.[17]

As soon as it was decently possible – even, one might think, before – Aelfrida and her daughters resumed an active life of 'interesting and varied things'.[18] Alethea dallied with her circle of admirers, joined in the 'funny, clever, endless Fordfield talk' which she found 'tiring but loveable',[19] and attended a Social Studies course at Bishop Creighton House in London.[20] (She also received a 'strange hard letter' from Constantine in which he wrote of his deceased father-in-law that he had 'kindly memories of the old man but his austerity was perhaps of another age', and recommended, in a possible reference to their mother, that his daughters depend only on themselves and look to no-one else for help.)[21] Agatha, 'very white and tired'[22] (it seems her grandfather's death, the first in her lifetime to disrupt the close family circle, hit her harder than her mother realised), embarked on her first term at Girton, reading Geography. Aelfrida exchanged 'some rather melodramatic letters' with Willie Searle[23] and received tender letters and a comforting visit from Anthony Wrightson (then in the early stages of his infatuation), wrote her father's obituary for *The Times* (the last line describes herself as "Mrs Constantine Graham who is carrying on the literary tradition of the family")[24], and planned a series of lectures refuting Middleton Murry's concepts of mystical experience 'at its bleakest and barest'[25], an interesting occupation in view of recent criticisms of her dead father and her own preoccupation since age fifteen with 'bleakest and barest' Mysticism and with the same kill-joy sense of sin and 'puritanism'. Chiara, now suffering from reaction and 'frail in black, clinging, aimless, infinitely pitiful', suddenly became 'terribly reliant'[26] with regard to even the most trivial matters; she also drove her daughter demented with her pessimism ('it does not matter what happens to her now')[27] and petty (to Aelfrida) worries over burglars (what Aelfrida describes jokingly as The Great Fordfield Burglary – it was a minor break-in and only the Oracle's peppermints were stolen – had taken place two years earlier)[28], and (with more justification) matters of finance. Luckily, however, a short visit to Ancifera Gregory saw her become 'much more herself'.[29] But which self?

'The other day', wrote Aelfrida in March 1930, 'Chiara remarked "we are quite different people … since Oracle died"'. Aelfrida agreed, particularly as far as her mother was concerned: 'now she does not need to be a ministering angel she has gone back to her natural self, moody, wayward, impulsive, given to saying sharp and clever things … restless in everything … [given] to sudden outbursts of doing unpleasant duties [but] spirited and adventurous [and with] none of the serenity and detachment of old age'. She also, and this upset Aelfrida who was currently rather sensitive on both topics, made 'nasty remarks about men, and sex'.[30] Alethea, even more perceptively, noted that not only was her grandmother 'rather sprightly (in a disparaging sense) and unkind in the things she says about people' but also that 'men, for her, have been no source of joy – an amusement when she was young and had … friendly flirtations with them; then, let down by Rendel Harris, she married Oracle whom I don't believe she loved. But duty and religion … made her devoted. Now that he is dead she has relaxed the tension'.[31] As a portrait of the Tillyards' relationship this is undoubtedly accurate (it is supported by a short passage in *The Approaching Storm* in which 'Sir Frederic Ellicott' notes of his American mother, "a woman of strong passions, stern principles and powerful intellect" obviously modelled on Chiara, that he never saw her "offering [his] father a kiss or receive any sign of affection from him")[32], but even more significant in the context of Aelfrida's life is that both Alethea's and her own description of widowed Chiara apply with uncanny accuracy to Aelfrida herself, the only difference being that Constantine was still alive. (Divorce, we must remember, made Aelfrida *feel* widowed.) They also go some way to explain the hollowness at the centre of the Tillyard and Graham marriages and how Chiara particularly and the Oracle to some extent sought to disguise this by compulsive preoccupation with good works which went far beyond the call of duty which a middle-class sense of service might provoke and Aelfrida and Constantine by equally compulsive preoccupations with things of the spirit and other men or women. (Aelfrida herself acknowledged this hollowness with regard to her own marriage, writing as 'Carola' that the initial harmony between herself and 'Adrian' was "a mere glamour-casting trick of Nature" in order to perpetuate the human race and that once children appeared, the "something solider" which ought to form the basis of a true marriage was revealed as lacking; her insistence on the 'perfect' nature of her marriage was, of course, another manifestation of her desire to conceal this from the world and from herself.)[33] Even more uncannily accurate is Aelfrida's slightly later description of Chiara's 'reticences' ('certain delicacies and fine shades that I think I sometimes missed') and 'hidden life in Jesus', and that sentimentalising over her devotion to duty blinded people to 'how *spirited* she was[34], for it is only by reading Aelfrida's diary, poetry, novels, and letters

with an intuitive eye that one comes to realise how much she omitted or only hinted at and how necessary (and how difficult) it is to track her own 'fine shades' of meaning to their lairs in order to discover what she *really* thought and the true motives for her actions. In March 1930, however, it was 'spirited' Chiara who packed her trunks and sailed for America, leaving Aelfrida alone at home (alone, that is apart from the gardener, two maids, and the charwoman) to cogitate on how different the house was without her mother: 'she and the house seem part of the same personality, she the active busy part, Fordfield the part that steadies'.[35]

The Oracle's death, Chiara's extended holiday in America (there are no references to her in Aelfrida's diary for the entire period of her visit), Alethea's absence in France at *La Semaine à Paris,* and the fact that Agatha's life now revolved chiefly round Girton, allowed Aelfrida a measure of leisure and solitude never experienced before: 'being here alone at Fordfield, I … commune with the place and … feel the intimate connection between a human being and the place where he was born … I have had long peaceful hours in the garden … letting the Divine within commune with the Divine without. I feel as if nothing could ever disturb the serenity of that inner sanctuary … I think I should be quite happy to live here alone always …'[36]

The world impinged in the shape of paying guests, Anthony Wrightson, Sunday teas, visits from family and friends, and attendance at church and at the Laundry, but for almost the first time in her life Aelfrida was able to indulge in long periods of uninterrupted reflection – and learnt a good deal about herself as a result. She was helped in this by Miss Wrightson's recent snub and by a 'joyous day in bed' during which she wrote '*pages*' of *The Approaching Storm* and received 'flashes of devastating insight into [her] own nature' occasioned by her guardian angel being 'perfectly frank' about what she must relinquish to achieve spiritual perfection.[37] But although the angel was rather vague with regard to exactly *what* Aelfrida must give up before she embarked on the next stage of her quest, be this retreat-life at Leiston or something else, she herself was well aware: her besetting sins of neediness for love, of egoism, and of pride.

Throughout her life, she noted, she had been 'too greedy of affection'.[38] Lacking the insight necessary to realise that this greed stemmed from what had seemed like sudden, and to a small child, inexplicable rejection by her parents in 1888, she formulated the first of her besetting sins as stemming (as in a sense it did, but not for the reason she gave) from the 'chaos that passion had made in [my] heart'. It was this 'inward tempest'[39] she thought (again correctly, but not for the reason she gave), which not only made '"detachment" a hopeless ideal' for [her][40] but also caused her to choose 'objects of devotion' for their actual or apparent ability to slake her 'greed for affection' rather than for their own sake[41] or for the sake of qualities specific to themselves. It was also for this reason that bouts of 'detachment' were so transient and so unreal (of one, experienced in August 1931 while heavily involved with both Anthony Wrightson and 'Dr Joan', she wrote that she 'watched it as though it belonged to someone else')[42] and why her frequent resolutions 'to be free from all human desires and conscious only to be used for the purposes of God'[43] were equally frequently broken within days of being made. So rather than hold to a 'hopeless ideal', she decided to be '*disinterested*' instead.[44] Sad to relate, this watered-down version of the Four Noble Truths assimilated (and to some extend practised) in the 'Buddhist' phase of her life with regard to the pain of the human condition and probable causes of that pain (in her case, a craving for affection) did not bring about cessation of pain, for 'disinterest' was an equally unattainable ideal because renunciation and disengagement were impossible for one so resolutely engaged with herself and the world.

Aelfrida had, in fact, realised this even before her short sabbatical from family cares allowed her a deeper period of introspection than had been possible for many years. In *Can I be a Mystic?* begun in 1925 and published six months after her father's death, she notes that "very few people, in the spiritual life, dare to be themselves" but embark instead "on a long and tedious process of crushing the round peg of [their] individuality into the square hole of ... medieval types of goodness" with the result that they become both exceedingly unhappy and unable to provide other people with an example of the "particular kind of goodness" required by the modern world. "I made this mistake myself", she admits, in trying to assimilate Thomas à Kempis' *Imitation of Christ* as "my chief spiritual food" and in trying "to model myself on the monastic ideal ... based on ... detachment, denial, austerity" but as she now realises, she needs engagement with the world in all its "richness and enthralling interest" in order to articulate "a sense of *vocation*" and to discover "what new place God is expecting [her] to step into".[45] In *A Little Road-Book for Mystics*, re-issued in 1931 with a revised last chapter, she goes even further, noting that "some mystics walk on the sunny side of the road, ... some on the shady side ... some go by the *voie de lumières* or way of delights ... and some by the *voie de foi pure* or way of faith alone ... The sunny side is full of visions ... of ecstasies, raptures, flights of the spirit [but] the man who walks on the shady side ... is ... one who enjoys no supernatural states of mind and who is capable

of no overwhelming feelings of fervour ... For my own part I prefer the way of wonder in spite of all the dangers that it brings of vanity and over-exaltation".[46]

Realisation that in forcing herself to take the 'shady side' (the *via negativa)* of the Mystic Way rather than the 'sunny side' (the *via positiva*) which accorded with her own nature and inclinations, she had taken, in effect, the *wrong* side, made Aelfrida even more thoughtful. She even went so far as to wish she had never modelled herself on Thomas à Kempis 'and the monastic virtues of austerity and detachment' because in fancying herself able to do so, she had succeeded only in deceiving herself and in 'preparing pride before a fall' because 'in exercising one's affections on human beings, one learns to love God' ('one *cannot* love people too much if one loves them disinterestedly', the latter something she entirely failed to do), and because disinterested love of people did not preclude 'the solitary meeting of the soul with God – the flight of the alone to the Alone' but enhanced the experience insofar as in both cases one loves one's neighbour as oneself and as a manifestation of the God in oneself whom one loves with one's whole heart.[47] She consoled herself, however, with the thought that she had 'travelled [far] from the Thomas à Kempis view of life' and that 'the satisfaction which I find in loving individuals ... is much less in degree but similar in quality to the satisfaction which I find in loving God' but was sufficiently insightful to ask if her 'loving' was really a giving and not a demanding of love.[48] As events were to prove, her doubts were justified.

Egoism had its good and bad points. On the positive side, egoism '*does* keep one amused. I don't feel as though I should ever be bored as long as I had myself to live with ... you see, I *do* find myself so interesting – I never have a dull moment!'[49] On the negative side, egoism made her 'rather callous' and it was only 'the multifarious experience of [her] own life' that allowed her to transcend the bounds of self and 'enter into other people's sorrow and happiness'.[50] (Her callousness, she added, was underlined by its contrast with Joan Cooper's compassion and altruism.) It also allowed her to indulge in two particular pleasures (she called them 'faults'), 'love of authority and love of being the centre of attention'[51], neither of which, dismayingly, could be indulged in were she to subject herself to Miss Wrightson's authority in the increasingly unlikely event that the 'lady abbess' allowed her to live at Leiston.

Aelfrida had, of course, sought to control her life since experiencing a frightening sense of powerlessness when sent away from home suddenly and without explanation in 1888, and it was this loss of autonomy which formed the basis of her dislike of ever finding herself, in fact or imagination, in anyone's 'power', however benevolent that person's feelings towards her might be. (This may also go some way to explaining Aleister Crowley's attraction for her, for although he briefly exercised considerable power over her, it was from him that she heard his Law of Thelema: "do what thou wilt … thou hast no right but to do thy will. Do that and no other shall say nay", one's will being that to which a person must devote himself to the exclusion of all else, barring activities such as sleep, food, and work which made such devotion possible.)[52] Her enjoyment of being the centre of attention (especially gentlemen's) predated the diphtheria episode, of course, but became an uncontrollable character trait as a result of it in order to ensure that she was never again marginalized and that she was always in a powerful position within the Tillyard family dynamic. It also goes some way to explaining why it took her over forty years 'to come to the conclusion … that I am [an] egoist' and to formulate her belief that 'good egoist or … bad egoist', she would never be able to transcend egocentricity even though this might deter her from achieving her current aim (Miss Wrightson, she noted, 'distrusts people who are interested in themselves [because] they might spoil the theocentric spirit of St Mary's')[53] or spoil the perfection of other plans God might have for her. Hence try as she might 'not to be an egoist'[54] and to '*forget* myself a little more'[55] ('what I want most of all … is *self-forgetfulness*'), for one who admitted that, although consciousness of God was the greatest blessing she had, 'solitude when I am conscious of no-one but myself' was 'well worth having', was never going to be someone who even if 'very gravely dissatisfied' with herself[56], was going to be able to relinquish her most engrossing topic of thought and conversation (God *not* excluded): '*Myself*'.[57]

Not content with two 'besetting sins', she contemplated her third: '*Pride,* Aelfrida, *Pride*'. But for one for whom self-abnegation was never going to be her forte, attempts to 'track the horrid thing to its lair' were bound to fail. For one thing, she became distracted ('on the way I see God and forget everything in adoration of Him')[58], if not by God, by Anthony Wrightson: 'I have so much to repent of … chiefly the Anthony episode … did I not think myself above some ordinary human weakness and fall lower in consequence?'[59] For another, and in spite of her tendency to believe that 'possession of a developed mystical sense implies moral excellence in the possessor' and to want '*very specially*' to repent of spiritual pride in consequence[60], she persuaded herself that it was 'much more important that God should be adored than that [her] character should be tinkered at'[61] like a faulty piece of machinery. Then again, she was not as proud as she had been: 'when I think of how I indulged in spiritual pride at

the time I was being taught by Aleister Crowley and, later on, when I was making wonderful discoveries for myself, I am overwhelmed with confusion' ('I *have* seen [and] I *do* know the Presence of God', she added pridefully)[62], so that although 'always having to begin *de novo* ('alas! Aelfrida, how you try the patience of your guardian angel!')'[63] in her efforts to track pride to its lair and to '*remember* that … I am nothing'[64], there was *some* improvement in *one* 'besetting sin' at least. But perhaps not as much as she hoped. Rereading *Vision Triumphant* in August 1931, she congratulated herself on being 'as wise and as experienced' as alter ego 'Catharine Sutherland'[65] before realising with horror that her liking 'to lead and teach and "straighten" and be prominent and wise in the sight if others' was hardly representative of spiritual humility; 'failing in humility one fails in all', she concluded sadly, adding that perhaps her greatest fault in this respect was 'spiritual presumption'.[66] So as an aspect of her new insights into earlier behaviour, insights which were salutary but not so salutary as to make her change her ways or even to accept that she was wholly unable to do so with or without supernatural assistance, she now focused her mind on her earlier role as self-proclaimed 'Straightener'.

The contrast between Aelfrida's current comments on her role as Straightener and the blithe manner in which she first donned the mantle of 'soul-doctor' is marked. She herself found it humbling and frightening: 'why … ever did I set up as a Straightener? To think I was competent to instruct other people because I had had a few mystical experiences was like pretending to be a music teacher because I had been to some concerts'[67]. (A Straightener, she now wrote, 'should *never*, NEVER pretend to be wiser or more competent than one is'.)[68] She also believed she had been 'too officious'[69] in trying to force 'patients' to take the spiritual path *she* dictated rather than guide them gently along the path that was right for them ('all I try to do now is to clear away a little rubbish', she wrote, though she always aimed 'to put a soul in touch with God')[70], in presuming to seek out 'patients' to 'soul-doctor' rather than letting them come to her (if, indeed, they came at all) and, insight occasioned by meetings with a trained psychologist, too 'tainted with self-love'[71] to operate effectively. In the context of present attempts at self-humiliation that was perhaps the most salutary revelation: 'the Straightener who considered herself so competent … years ago … [now sees] herself so small [but] I *like* it for the less there is of *me*, the more there will be of God in me'.[72] In all respects, she concluded, it was a good thing that as a Straightener, she had had a 'somewhat feeble career'.[73]

She remained, however, reluctant to accept all blame for it and in the course of attempts to justify it, criticised 'goups' who '*will* assume that a Straightener knows the backstairs to heaven' ('true', she added, 'I knew the way to God [and] that is [still] the case now [but then] I had vision but not holiness')[74] and who, in encouraging their Straightener's 'vanity, presumption and weakness'[75], persuade them to continue in a profession for which they had no training and for which their qualifications were inadequate. Mrs Ablett, Aelfrida's 'spiritual child' from the Eton Workhouse, was a case in point, but when she wrote to her 'spiritual mother' for advice after several years' silence, she found that 'mother' as keen 'to "speak to her condition"' as before (Aelfrida had obviously kept to her recent resolve 'to be a Straightener when people want me to be'[76], vanity, presumption, and feebleness notwithstanding) and to believe herself better qualified than before because 'so rich in the experience of [her] humbling'.[77]

Consulting 'Dr Joan', the 'perfect Straightener', about 'one of the rheumatic attacks I thought I was not going to have any more'[78] and about 'the kind of cramp' occasionally experienced in her chest[79] (the first was dismissed as a menopausal symptom, the second as evidence that Aelfrida's chronic uterine inflammation had affected her heart), she confided that she had tried to be a Straightener herself.[80] (She had recently turned for 'soul-doctoring' to a local cleric but found him more lenient to her faults than she was herself; 'that was not why I chose him!', she added hastily.)[81] She made it clear, however, that in spite of her pressing need for 'straightening', she had no intention of relinquishing her self-imposed career ('if anyone, man or woman, asks me for help, I am bound to give it')[82] in spite of family and amatory problems having rendered her 'temporarily useless'.[83] She even complimented herself on her fitness to practise 'by what I know' in spite of being disquieted 'by what I am' ('a Straightener should [be] one who has not only his actions but also his emotions under control … he should *transcend* rather than *repress*')[84], a rare moment of insight in one whose whole adult life had consisted of attempts to transcend or repress spontaneous emotion and natural instincts, and congratulated herself on the fact that she, unlike Mrs Besant, had never thought of leading 'religious sects' (true, though The Servants of the Lord's Household might have become a sect of sorts) or undertaken 'public ministry' (untrue) where her advice might have done as much harm as good.[85] Joan Cooper's side of the conversation is not recorded; her thoughts on the subject would have made interesting reading.

Aelfrida's intention of continuing her 'straightening' career was influenced by more than a sense of obligation to those who asked for help; it was also to be continued on the strength of her own 'holiness' and 'enlightenment'.

Holiness was a recently-acquired virtue of which she became aware in 1930 after borrowing a book on Zen Buddhism from 'Mr Thomas of the University Library'. Having delved into it with the same enthusiasm as that currently expended on 'besetting sins', she suddenly realised 'that [she] was one of the Enlightened' who had 'no need to go East or West, enter this church or that, study under any great teacher, for whatever any religion has to teach, I *know* [and] by thinking, by feeling, by working [and by] constant mystical communing with God … I can always touch ultimate reality', ultimate reality in this instance being Deity as 'light irradiating the universe from *within* and a timeless delight that brings eternity into now'. So because she 'could no longer charm any man at will' (untrue, as we shall see), she would detach herself from 'transitory, mortal … superficial [and] inessential self' and remain rapt in this new and 'wonderful' state of being[86] for ever. She did her best, writing a fortnight later that achievement of 'Enlightenment' provided her with 'warm-embracing peace in [her] soul' and with 'a strange, airy detachment … from outward observances (though I love going to church), … intellectual beliefs' (she continued to enjoy 'intellectual arguments'), … human affection (though I adore my daughters), … even the desire for personal immortality', the latter with the escape-clause 'I am a firm believer in survival of bodily death'. Best of all, in achieving 'Enlightenment' she had accomplished the first part of her 'Great Work': 'I know, I see … Many roads lead to God but Jesus is mine'. But as the enlightened one hastily reminded herself, 'it is so easy to forget. I will try and be very simple [and] very Christian'.[87]

She forgot. So keen to impart news of her discovery that she forgot that in describing herself as 'one of the Enlightened', she was providing an extreme example of 'pride, Aelfrida, pride', she informed Julius ('the Perfect Listener – it is amazing that a brother should find his sister so interesting')[88], then 'in the course of an extremely pleasant call', Frank Stokoe. Fidelio, however, a man who 'really understands me better than any of my other Little Friends', administered a douche of intellectual cold water to one who now knew how to go 'straight to the essential meaning of *any* mystical teaching, whether Christian or Buddhist or what not': "I am glad you *know* [provided] you treat knowledge as a starting-point".[89]

Enlightenment did not, however, make her a better Straightener with regard to Erle Lunn of whom she had the grace to ask two years later if she 'really helped people like [him] very much?'[90] By 1932 Erle Lunn, formerly a 'very sensitive aspiring soul'[91] believed by Aelfrida (and her guardian angel) to be 'capable of experiencing universal consciousness' and so 'desperately in earnest about finding God' (a 'common type, I dare say')[92] that he was the perfect person to help forward part two of her Great Work in the shape of *Can I be a Mystic?*, had reverted to what he had always been: 'one of the half-educated'[93], lacking ambition (at one point he was reduced to the role of "Aunt Wendy" in the children's supplement to *The Queen* magazine), and hopeless with money: 'I am glad I am his spiritual director and not the keeper of his privy purse'.[94] He was also prone to disobey her with regard to books read[95], to dabblings in Evangelical Christianity in the shape of Frank Buchman's Oxford Group[96], and to the Occult in the shape of Roland Meredith Starr.[97] July 1932 therefore saw Aelfrida demonstrating lack of sympathy for a 'goup' who had recently informed his spiritual director that he was "dying spiritually", it being 'only his vanity and his love of marvels and the unhealthy parts of his soul' that were dying[98] (as, she hoped, were her own) and distaste for a man who had insisted on accompanying her to Anthony's flat, only to be seen by him walking hand in hand with her. The problem was, of course, that she had encouraged in Erle Lunn precisely the pretensions which accorded most closely with her own (his writing 'very bad verse'[99] for the *Occult Review* which failed to publish it and his notion of going into the church, to which Aelfrida replied enthusiastically '*yes*'[100] because a close family member had just announced her intention of becoming a nun), pretensions which, in Lunn's case at least, should never have been encouraged because of his manifest unfitness for the roles he hoped to play. Realising this in later years, Aelfrida wrote ruefully 'Straighteners aren't as much use as they think they are', particularly when immature in spiritual terms but 'very much in earnest'.[101]

As with Erle Lunn, so too with those (and too late to repair damage done) with whom she had entered into intimate emotional relationships, but it was, oddly enough, her (unsuccessful) 'straightening' activities of 1930 with regard to Mina whose outbursts of utter misery were described unfeelingly by Aelfrida as 'sulkiness and ill-temper'[102] vented on herself and on Chiara (possibly they contained unpalatable home-truths), which helped her to understand something of what lay behind Constantine's defection.

Her cogitations were stimulated by the sight of Mina's mental malaise ('it's *terrible* for a man to have a wife who is ill or sickly. At first he can be gentle and pitiful but … unless he is a saint, he grows weary') and by extrapolation of this onto her own (physical) ailments: 'I [too] was often ill'. Then came realisation that 'since I had not found the way to God I was not as light-hearted as I am now …

I used to try and keep up with Constantine's desire for gaiety and brightness but it was no good'[103] (an astounding rationalisation given that it was *marriage* which temporarily quenched her own 'gaiety and brightness') and recognition that she had been 'too crude with too many principles too hastily applied, too much of the "Law" and not enough of the Holy Spirit' for Constantine's love to survive the onslaught. (These and other insights also appear in *O Passionate World*, written during this period of her life.) There were, however, other matters concerning Constantine which caused her to extend her cogitations to include the happy/unhappy subject of a man who, though he had put 'all his beauty' into loving her, had been unable to withstand the pressure of his wife's as yet unperfected character[104], matters happening in the present but imbued with the past.

In August 1930 Constantine exchanged South America and the 'showy social life … which … he enjoys' for a short-term consulship in Hamburg ('the Nordic spirit does not appeal to him')[105] whither Aelfrida sent photographs of herself and the girls, together with a suggestion that she and Constantine 'be friends'.[106] (Her wish to 'be friends' may not have been entirely spontaneous: Eustace had recently informed her that if she met Constantine now he would find her 'more charming and congenial and be sorry he left her'.)[107] Evincing no desire whatsoever to 'be friends' (a suggestion that they meet in London was rebuffed by a telegram stating bluntly "meeting quite impossible")[108], Constantine again showed a lively interest in his daughters and insisted on meeting both, Agatha in England, Alethea in Paris.

Reunions with Agatha in London and at Girton – she gave her father an 'apolaustic tea' of caviar sandwiches[109] – passed off smoothly in spite of Constantine's refusal to meet his daughters unless accompanied by Mildred, for Agatha expressed more sympathy than Alethea with her father's disillusioned feeling that he had spent his adult life 'pulling down the dreams of his youth'.[110] (She informed her mother, however, that Constantine was a bore and 'a spoilt baby' who should not be taken too seriously[111] and Mildred 'mildly vulgar'[112], though whether this was her own opinion or what she thought her mother ought to hear is open to question, given that she herself no longer kept a diary.) Meetings with Alethea however, were more problematical, for Alethea, it seems was reluctant to meet her father again.

Aelfrida's account of their meeting is rather flat ('her father came to Paris with Mildred and saw a good deal of her. At first Alethea was much agitated … but afterwards they got on well')[113] but reveals a fraction of the story, and it is only after a comparison of Aelfrida's and Alethea's diaries and Alethea's letters home (proudly written on *La Semaine à Paris* notepaper and largely paraphrased in Aelfrida's own account) that the difficulties of the situation become clear.

The first hint of trouble arose when Constantine intimated that because Alethea was now earning her own living, he proposed to dock Aelfrida's allowance of the portion allotted to his elder daughter's upkeep. (It is unclear if he fulfilled his threat but Alethea blamed herself for not being 'sharper than [she] was' with regard to Constantine's probing questions about her – very small – salary.)[114] The second hint was rather more than a hint: 'Anatolia invaded the office and gushed over Alethea'.[115]

Now domiciled entirely in Antibes, Anatolia had been visited at Villa *La Farandole* by Constantine from whom she discovered that a granddaughter unseen since 1916 was not only in Paris but also employed by a magazine with offices in the same Rue d'Assas as her former 'Anatolian flat'. She therefore came to Paris and, entering the offices of *La Semaine à Paris*, 'embraced Alethea and declared that this was the moment she had been waiting for all these years'.[116] Worse still, she arranged a lunch date.

All might have passed off smoothly – Alethea knew nothing of her grandmother's eccentric past and only an expurgated version of her stormy relationship with Aelfrida and had been prepared to treat with disinterested kindness 'a rather boring old woman whom she does not, for politeness sake, wish to offend' (Anatolia was admitted even by her family to be 'a bit cracked')[117] – had Aelfrida not reacted as she did, shrieking hysterically (to her diary) that the presence in Paris of one so 'morally corrupt' constituted an 'evil coming near my beloved Alethea' and (to her daughter) that 'as I hope for mercy at the last'[118], Alethea must cancel further meetings with her grandmother because she could not bear to think of them together. (A contemporaneous and 'most vivid "intellectual vision" of the *reality* and *power* of evil' was attributed neither to Anatolia's nor to Constantine's moral corruption but to 'the power of evil'[119] at large in the Soviet Russia to which she was soon to condemn poor Nadja.) Trapped through no fault of her own in the web of conflict between her mother and grandmother, Alethea cancelled the lunch at the risk of offending a father with whom she was reluctantly endeavouring to re-establish a filial relationship but recorded unhappily in her diary that although she personally felt no antagonism towards Anatolia, she also felt obliged to dismiss her grandmother quite brusquely because of the misery she herself had unwittingly caused her mother in agreeing to meet Anatolia again.

The third hint constituted a real problem with far-reaching repercussions. When Alethea suffered the breakdown which resulted in her dismissal from *La Semaine à Paris* (a breakdown to which the events described above contributed), she became so 'nervously ill' (moments of 'exaltation' led to 'helpless tears and then [to] complete exhaustion')[120] that her employers contacted a doctor at the British Consulate to advise on medical care and urgent repatriation. Alethea, it seems, confided in the doctor who then asked a vice-consul to inform Phyllis (the latter, knowing that Aelfrida was preoccupied with Agatha's mastoid surgery, had volunteered to escort Alethea home) that Alethea should sever all connection 'utterly and completely' with her father.[121] This surprising statement had nothing to do with Alethea's health; it seems that Constantine's character had 'gone so utterly to pieces', that he had become 'corrupt through and through' (the vice-consul's next sentence was that 'a man like that' needed 'a smart woman to keep him in order')[122], and that as a punishment he was being sent, not to Batavia as threatened for earlier misdemeanours, but to Liberia, 'a horrible place full of foul slave-driving Negroes with an appalling climate'.[123] He was to remain there for nearly two years during which time, it is to be hoped, he purged his guilt for whatever misdemeanour he had lately committed.

Aelfrida was devastated for 'poor, poor, Constantine's sake'[124] and for her own: 'I cannot tell you how sad it makes me to think that Constantine is bad through and through. I did *want* to think the best of him!'[125] Encouraged by Chiara who had long wanted to cut Constantine 'out of our life'[126], she took a unilateral decision: Constantine's daughters 'should cast him off' because he had 'failed to make them love him' and because they were clear-sighted enough to discern in him the 'shallowness and worldliness and self-indulgence'[127] which resulted in exile in Liberia. (With an irony that would seem improbable even in a novel, Goldsworthy Lowes Dickinson, at Constantine's request, had invited Agatha to tea shortly before she became ill, only to say sympathetically "how sad for you that your mother and father are going to Liberia". Aelfrida was glad 'that Constantine keeps up with his old friend' but the comment made her 'very confused'[128]; her confusion was nothing compared to Agatha's.) Her next move was to ask Hal Verey to write to Constantine 'as gently as possible', ostensibly for the sake of Alethea's emotional health though possibly in retaliation for having had her own offer of friendship rebuffed or because she did not want Constantine's interest in his daughters to divert theirs from herself, to sever 'all connections' between Constantine, herself, and their daughters.[129] In doing so she took a calculated risk, for Constantine might have stopped her allowance forthwith; fortunately he did not, though he wrote protesting

**Catharine Tillyard 1931**

(with some justification) that Aelfrida had poisoned the girls' minds against him, and that it was 'owing to [her] undue influence that they had agreed (*sic*) not to see him any more'. And there the matter ended – or appeared to end. Aelfrida said nothing of the matter to anyone, not even to Anthony Wrightson ('loyalty to the past and my love for Constantine as he was, forbids')[130]; Constantine was never to know how much she minded 'cutting the last thread that bound us'[131]; life, after all the upsets of the recent months became '*almost* normal' insofar as Agatha's health and Alethea's happiness were about to be restored[132] and insofar as it seemed remarkable how little their father's dismissal mattered 'in the minds of these daughters of ours'.[133] But life did not return to normal, Agatha's health and Alethea's happiness were not restored, the thread that bound the girls and their mother to Constantine remained unbroken, and all four were to meet again in tragic circumstances with tragic consequences.

Aelfrida's next sequence of cogitations on and comparison of her past and present spiritual states naturally turned to the importance of God in her life and to fluctuations in her relationship to Him. She had been cogitating on this fascinating subject prior to the Oracle's death but it was following his demise that she tried to clarify her often chaotic ideas.

Three months after 'holiday Aelfrida' returned to England following the second session of a relationship necessary to prove to a divorced wife that she is not the worthless creature her ex-husband believes her to be (and has persuaded her she is) and that she still has the power to attract men, she tic-tocked back to Deity. (Interestingly, she behaved in the same way two months after her first session by embarking on the intensive course of meditations noted earlier and lasting from 11 October to 5 November 1925; she recorded them in the back of the same volume of her diary as the Grandcamp holiday.) Writing in November 1926 and possibly inspired by revision of *Spiritual Exercises* prior to publication, she cogitated on the 'motives which send men to God' and on her own in particular.

Her list is lengthy ('I am driven to God by every motive which it is possible for a human being to feel in seeking the Divine')[134] and interesting for what it includes and omits and for the order in which it is written. Her first reason is the unexpected one of obtaining 'intellectual satisfaction', a revealing notion given the satisfaction she derived from researching *Spiritual Exercises* and from discussions which followed her lectures on Mysticism, and one which points to a fulfilling academic career had she not set her face resolutely against it. Her second, that of obtaining 'spiritual peace', is a given, given her 'restless mind' and 'unquiet body'.[135] 'Spiritual peace' increases in 1930 when she hears of Willie Searle's engagement to 'one of the eight women who proposed to him'[136] and begins to feel 'blessed with a particularly radiant sense of the Presence of God' ('otherwise, nothing special to relate', she adds rather oddly)[137], 'peace' becoming successively a marvellous awareness that 'the Presence of God round one [is] like immense peace still and deep and yet vibrating with power and love'[138]; a 'contentment too perfect for expression, a peace ... utterly beyond words'[139] at the point at which she receives 'Enlightenment'; a sense that living in God 'as the birds live in the air' or as in 'the air one breathes' provides 'the light that makes life visible', spiritual happiness and freedom never experienced before ('religion is not something you can put into a compartment')[140]; and a sensation of the peace in her soul reaching out to touch the Infinite Peace of 'the *eternal stillness* of God'[141] of which it is a dim reflection.

Given such 'peace', it is odd to find Aelfrida's next motive to be 'fear of God's judgement'. (She is also, she states, motivated 'by fear of my own passions', a likely motive given her continual battle between 'Puritanism' and sensuality and the fact that the early 1930s was the period of her infatuation with Anthony Wrightson.) Her 'fear' has three equally significant components. The first is 'fear of [God's] majesty [and] fear of His omnipotence'; the second, 'fear of ... wholehearted surrender' to God's will[142], the third, fear that '*Time is Short*' and that she will die before she has fulfilled God's Will for her.[143]

Her fears are very real. Of the first she writes that 'some mighty *force,* wholly good, is trying to express itself through me' and that far from being a '*comforting*' sensation, her chief feeling is of being 'quite overwhelmed [with] *awe*'[144]; she even has visions 'of the *overwhelmingness* of God' which lead to her feeling completely 'passive in [His] hand'[145], an uncomfortable and even panic-inducing sensation in one who preferred to lead from a position of power. Hence her fear of 'whole-hearted surrender' to God's Will with all that that implies of relinquishment of 'the last atom of freedom', for Aelfrida an absolute and ultimate surrender.[146] (At the same time, however, she lists as another motive, her need for 'the bracing and disciplining of God's sternness, God's dazzling righteousness'[147], qualities lacking in her life as the

Oracle's moral force declined into petty tyranny.) Fear that time is short haunts her even more. Her forty-eighth birthday finds her worrying that 'so little time remains' for her 'to grow in holiness', to 'write all the books I want to write' (i.e. to proselytise) and 'to learn'.[148] (1931 is, of course, the year in which Agatha faced death and she herself believed she did: 'I hear God calling so clearly ... all I can do now ... is to prepare myself'.)[149] Her conviction that she has only a short time to live ('the few years that remain to me of life'; would it have pleased or distressed her to know she had twenty-eight more?) in which 'to meditate more, to progress more in the intimacy of God and to help make a place where other people can do these things' leaves her wanting to 'begin *soon*'[150] in case she dies 'before [her] vocation is accomplished'[151] and with a growing conviction that she 'ought not to spend so many hours in merely doing what is pleasant'.[152] (Or as Anthony Wrightson has recently put it, in 'trying to get the best of both worlds', the sacred and the secular, 'in quite an unjustifiable manner', a sentiment with which she half-heartedly concurs.)[153] This goes some way to explaining a curious statement made early in 1932 to the effect that St Botolph's Church 'is the only place where I feel quite safe at the moment'[154]; perhaps, being psychic, she has premonitions that time is indeed short, not in terms of her own lifespan but in terms of impending calamities.

A longing 'for the beauty of holiness' and, 'having tasted earthly joys up to a certain point' (*sic*), for 'that which is more subtle, more spiritual, more complete'[155] than they, forms another motive. This is difficult for one who has failed so piteously in 'detachment' and in 'no human consolations' (she had just bought a copy of à Kempis' *Imitation of Christ* for Anthony's birthday when she wrote this)[156] for she has discovered that the practice of spiritual exercises 'leave[s] one's lower nature more free to assert itself when one's attention is elsewhere and that one's very aspiration makes one all the more exposed to temptation'. However, 'one *must* persevere even if one dies for it'[157], 'it' being a desire to lose herself in 'God Unmanifest'[158] or even, her ultimate longing, to be granted the 'Beatific Vision[159] usually enjoyed only by those at the point of death: an unmediated sight of God in the glory of Heaven.

All motives, however, are encompassed and explained by one hard to put into words; 'I turn to Him by a kind of inner compulsion', she writes and 'when all is said and done I cannot explain the instinct which forces me to seek God [but] I am miserable when I resist it, happy when I yield to it'. This 'instinct' she is powerless to disobey, both because she is 'confused [and] bewildered, uncertain of myself and everything' if she does not and because in submitting to it she becomes so conscious of God that she 'melt[s] like wax in a strong fire and everything ceases to be save God above'.[160]

Mystics, as Constantine found to his cost, make bad bedfellows; they also, as he knew too well, find themselves hard to live with. Easter Day 1920 had found Aelfrida, exiled in Hunstanton pending formalisation of the Grahams' de facto and soon to be *de jure* separation, informing herself that in spite of tribulations amounting to martyrdom she was 'far from being a saint'.[161] Ten years later she was still asking herself 'why am I not a better woman?' ('this is not the usual problem', she added, i.e. 'why are we all sinners?' but her 'special problem'), a worthwhile enquiry given that she had now 'received enlightenment [and] realised oneness' and could therefore approach God either through 'Jesus Christ and in Nature [or] more dimly, in art, people, thought, action' or 'directly lose [her]self in Him', a fact which 'gives reality to all the rest'. She continued to find herself very far from '*very* good', however, chiefly because her interests remained focussed on herself and her earthly wants ('another kiss from Anthony') and pleasures (compliments on her business acumen with regard to the Laundry) instead of on 'graver preoccupations'[162], particularly the state of her soul. Her silver wedding day ('I wonder if Constantine remembers …') in January 1932 found her disconsolate at lack of spiritual progress ('I seem to have all the faults I had twenty-five years ago') and at being 'possibly a bit more spoilt' than before because 'so more-than-contented' with her life, having, as Alethea put it, "your books and your daughters and your Laundry and your Anthony".[163] 'O Aelfrida', she chid herself, 'how very human do you still remain!'[164]

She decided early in 1930 that 'Saintliness' was 'utterly beyond [her]' and that, given her all-too-human failings, it was to her credit she had kept out of the pub (not difficult, given her rabid teetotalism) and had not been confined 'to prison, the workhouse … the hospital [or] the madhouse'.[165] With prison unlikely, the workhouse likely only through her own negligence, and the madhouse an unknown quantity, Aelfrida remembered something she had been told as a child: 'all Christians without exception are called to be saints'. She therefore decided that as a Christian and a mystic it doubly behoved her to become one and that in 'holding this clearly before [her] eyes', there could be no spiritual presumption in believing it possible. She therefore prayed a prayer so fervent in its demand that it equalled and even surpassed any prayed earlier: 'Lord, make me a saint, even me, and do not spare me in the making'.[166] And in case God did not hear her the first time, she repeated her request with increasing vehemence: 'Lord, make me a saint and do not

spare me in the making' (prayed after a vision in which 'some light formed itself into a cross and came down and laid itself on me … and there was no obstacle between myself and *God*')[167]; 'Lord make me a saint and do not spare me in the making' ('my *best* prayer', prayed with unconscious irony immediately after noting her present preference for Thomas Traherne's doctrine of God's love over the austerities of Thomas à Kempis)[168]; and, while reading proofs of *The Approaching Storm*, 'God! I hunger and thirst after righteousness. Make me a saint and do not spare me in the making'.[169] Hearing such heartfelt importuning, could God refuse her request? He did not. The question as to whether or not He made her a saint is for a better qualified person than a biographer to answer but as to whether or not He acceded to her request not to spare her in the making, one can only reply: He did. And did not.

At first, however, and rather surprisingly given that she was in direct communication with Him, Aelfrida wilfully or involuntarily misunderstood His response; indeed, she seems to have regarded God's plan for her solely in terms of current events rather than one which might – and would – reshape her future. This is understandable if rather short-sighted, given that she had received a warning from her guardian angel on All Souls Eve 1930 that she should '*Prepare for Suffering*' ('I wondered for *what* … I hope nothing to do with the girls'), rather confusingly amended on All Souls Day to 'prepare "for *sacrifice*" – not "suffering". ('I don't know what the sacrifice *is*', she added, 'but I do my best'.)[170] The warning was followed so immediately by the arrival of Anatolia in the offices of *La Semaine à Paris* that Aelfrida decided that it referred only to the '*coming trial*' of Anatolia's lunch date with Alethea, 'a very sore trial indeed'[171], and in spite of having recently published a book in which she informed 'Stranger' that a guardian angel's directions are always perfectly clear[172] (but also in another contemporary work and her role as 'Carola' theorised that not only did one's guardian angel hold out "the right thing to you at the right time" but that he was also always ready "with exactly the kind of humiliation of which you were most in need" when "specially tempted, over-elated, or riding the high horse of spiritual pride")[173], took the shorter rather than the longer view and forget the warning once the immediate danger was past. (Her capacity for precognition seems to have been in temporary abeyance.) It is also understandable, given her continuing preoccupation with her health ('I [always] have something to put up with … a good deal of physical fatigue and lassitude, pain sometimes and so on')[174] and subsequently with her daughters' physical or emotional collapse and her own supposed 'cancer of the womb'[175], that in this instance – and with good reason – she was more alert to earthly than to spiritual suffering. It is even more understandable given that she had always dismissed as 'morbid' the 'attraction of suffering for Christ's sake'[176] and now believed it neither 'right nor wise' to '*ask* to be led by the way of Suffering even if it were the way to great moral heights'. (In the light of what was to transpire she would abandon one tenet and cleave to the other.) Luckily, she thought it best 'to accept whatever God sends'[177]; God, His warnings apparently unheeded, decided to reveal Himself more clearly and to begin with someone more closely related to Aelfrida than her daughters: her mother.

Chiara's return 'much more herself' from her brief visit to Ancifera Gregory in November 1929 made Aelfrida vow to put her mother 'first in everything' for the rest of that lady's life and her own love of 'solitude and dreaming'[178] aside for as long as that life lasted. Chiara's return in September 1930 from her visit to America, however, found her looking so '*ghastly*'[179] in the aftermath of suspected typhoid that Aelfrida booked a nurse to care for her and in spite of her vow, left Julius and Ancifera in charge of weary and feverish Chiara while she herself departed next day for six days solitude in France prior to meeting Alethea in Dieppe for a further six-day vacation *à deux*. Returning on 16 September 'home to this', 'this' being the maids on leave, the house to run, Julius to be entertained, 'my bed not aired [and] my mattress given to Ancifera', Ancifera and Dr Cooper to be discouraged from respectively inducing 'a sickroom feeling' in Chiara and terrifying her with 'professionalism', Aelfrida decided that vow or no vow, she would not '*let* [Chiara] have the invalid mentality! She *shall* be her own brave spirited … self!'[180] and dismissed son, friend, and nurse forthwith. Whereupon (or coincidentally) Chiara 'suddenly got tired of being an invalid'.[181]

1931 was, of course, Aelfrida's *annus horribilis,* at the end of which she wrote (or thought she wrote) Anthony his '*Finis*' letter and made 'no special good resolutions' because 'tired of my silly old sins and feeling they were best forgotten' but, apropos a fire at the Laundry's local receiving office, wondered if the family's run of bad luck was or was not over; she also hoped in spite of everything that 'ship 1932' would 'set sail bravely over the uncharted sea'.[182] It did, but shipwreck was near. In February 1932 Chiara usually 'so brave, so vivacious' when compared to her daughters-in-law Phyllis and Mina, one of whom was unwell, the other melancholic, developed the prevailing 'influenza, I suppose'[183], as Aelfrida recorded laconically. By 21 February, however, and within a year almost to the day of Agatha's mastoiditis, Chiara had become '*very* ill' with pneumonia[184] and was raving with fever, though how much of her confusion was due to

infection and how much to the first alcohol to pass her lips for forty years – Joan Cooper had prescribed brandy as a cardiac stimulant – is open to question. (To further complicate Aelfrida's life, this was the point at which Anthony asked her to spend the night at his flat; Fidelio, though 'too stout now' to be an 'aetherial poet', provided more seemly comfort: 'poetry and his affection'.)[185] Chiara eventually made a very slow recovery[186] (Aelfrida, anxious to be free but inhibited by propriety from saying so, had hoped that Chiara would not survive her doctor's 'wise obstinacy'[187] in forcing brandy and other treatments on her patient and privately considered that Dr Cooper had been wrong to do so), so slow that as late as 29 May and with her mother even 'more of an *invalid* and less of a *convalescent*', she reluctantly decided to 'put aside all dreams and plans and devote my self to [Chiara] as she devoted herself to Oracle'.[188] Devotion to her mother, however, was not tested for as long as her mother's to her father.

Chiara's illness brought 'ship 1932' close to foundering for other reasons too. Expenses occasioned by Aelfrida's, Alethea's, and Agatha's hospital bills of 1931 had been high relative to family income and although Joan Cooper and Alfred Walford (certainly) and Mr Canney (possibly) remitted some of their fees and were happy for Aelfrida to pay outstanding bills by instalments, Chiara's sense of honour and hatred of indebtedness resulted in her paying the balance from dwindling income. She also took measures to reduce expenditure, suggesting that Agatha become an out-student during her third and last year at Girton, a suggestion acceded to by the college on health grounds, by Aelfrida as a face-saving gesture, and by Agatha with relief: she had been subjected to a lesbian assault by a close friend immediately prior to the onset of her illness and had no wish to live in college again. ('I never thought of [Girton] as a place where one picked up a nasty Freudian complex'[189], wrote a mother whose naiveté with regard to female homoeroticism was pronounced.) Chiara's pneumonia of February 1932 put further strain on the family's precarious finances and even prompted spendthrift Aelfrida to con her mother's accounts 'to find out what life here really costs her [and] … how poor we really are'.[190]

Faced for the first time in forty-eight years with knowledge of how much it cost to maintain a comfortable standard of living in a large house with extensive grounds and to pay the wages of staff essential to maintenance of standards, house, and garden alike, and with the horrid truth that Chiara was no longer a cash-cow to be milked as occasion demanded, Aelfrida was horror-stricken: '*IF*' ('the "IF" is a big one') no repairs were needed to Fordfield's fabric, no more investments failed, none of Chiara's properties required expensive upkeep, and no-one fell ill, 'she will *just* be able to make ends meet'.[191]

Shocked to the core, she cast around for what to do at least inconvenience to herself. (She and the girls continued to take regular holidays during this time, though with a nod to economy they did not go abroad.) Her suggestion that she and Chiara move to a smaller modern house nearby and donate Fordfield to the Perse School 'in memory of Oracle'[192] was shot down by Chiara and her sons. The possibility of selling up was never considered, though Aelfrida went so far as to suggest letting out 'poor Fordfield'[193] and Chiara to propose that Agnes Slack be invited to over-winter as a paying guest[194], but neither lady made moves in the direction of serious economies until one of them was forced to confront reality; the other, by this time, was past caring.

Though Aelfrida herself had no intention of making a greater financial contribution than she did ('I think I already do all I can'[195]), her energies being diverted to more important matters, namely the 'mystical approach to God … both in myself and to help other people'[196], world events had already reduced her own income and were soon to do so further. Publishers of past and proposed religious books were so alarmed by a general falling-off in sales that they declined further offerings until trade improved and even Hutchinson, a successful publisher of popular novels, expressed concern (with particular reference to recently-completed *Victoria's Vow*) that Aelfrida's novels were never going to be commercial propositions. (They 'sell books as a butcher sells *meat*', wrote their author indignantly, adding 'I suppose [they] simply *cannot* understand that I don't want to write a "best seller"!')[197] Puzzled by 'the bad luck I have had with my books'[198] but buttressed to some extent by Chiara's money, she came to the conclusion that she preferred possible penury to the actual ignominy of supporting herself and her dependent daughters and of contributing more to the upkeep of her family home by forcing herself to write more 'rubbish that will sell'. She therefore agreed with Hutchinson – the firm had options over 'several future novels'[199] – to terminate her contract by mutual consent in August 1933.

She rationalised the blow to her self-esteem ("the author sees his writings as they glowed in the fire of his thought [but his readers] see broken ash and burnt out coal")[200] and to her desire to enlighten others by stating, first, that she was now too busy 'to "save innumerable mankind"' by producing "great works of art" ('if I wrote about it all I shouldn't have time to do it!')[201]; second, that because she herself had achieved enlightenment, the first part of her 'Great Work' was accomplished[202]; third,

that 'once one has "realised Unity" … one feels a certain serene indifference as to the way God chooses to make use of one. Activity or passivity, fame or obscurity … makes no difference'[203]; fourth that she was happy to step aside for a short time because she had had 'all the light that I can as yet bear' for the present, it being better for her to remain quietly in God than to proselytise actively on His behalf.[204] (Or, indeed, do anything to remedy the family's dire financial situation by undertaking formal paid employment.) To this startling but typical example of the spiritual pride she was trying to avoid and of the indifference for her own and others' welfare which characterised her dealings with the world, she added that in future she would 'try and be very simple' and a better Christian and to remember that 'many roads lead to God'.[205]

Simplicity and appreciation of others' viewpoints not being two of Aelfrida's salient features, she soon forgot her resolve, deciding with reference to simplicity that although 'living in the world' made devotion to 'Perpetual Adoration' difficult, she would complicate her already complicated life by trying to achieve it[206] and to being a better Christian that she was reluctant to relinquish the 'little pleasures and satisfactions' with which she humoured herself 'as if I were one of my own daughters'[207] even if this meant conducting herself in an unchristian manner towards her 'dear ones'. (With regard to 'innumerable mankind', however, she remembered that although she now preferred to travel her 'mystic way' silently and secretly rather than vocally and publicly[208], she was still bound by the second part of her Oath of Obligation and, that being so, and although force of circumstances had caused activity in this area to be put aside temporarily, it was not wholly abandoned.) With her 'wonderful' or 'too good' (depending on how one looked at it) memory she should also have recalled her reiterated (and continuing) pleas to be made a saint and not spared in the making, though a train of events which began in May 1932 was soon to remind her. It was also to test to destruction the 'serene indifference' professed with regard to God's purpose and will, the 'peace in my soul and … life that suits me exactly'[209] being both about to disappear, one for a long time, one for ever.

On 19 May 1932 Chiara announced that she had had a 'heart attack' during the night, a diagnosis pronounced by Dr Cooper to be 'serious as a warning though not serious in itself'. (She later sent Aelfrida 'by way of delicate attention' a bottle of bromide mixture, though whether the sedative was intended for herself or her mother the former does not say.)[210] The 'heart attack' (it was in fact the onset of atrial fibrillation, an arrhythmia which affects the pumping action of the heart and ability to work as effectively as it should; digitalis was the drug of choice and what Dr Cooper prescribed) rendered Chiara 'limp and depressed' and her daughter '*desperately* depressed', in the latter's case because she suddenly saw her future as consisting of 'endless supporting of Chiara's failing health and spirits' and herself as 'inadequate to the task' and with her habit of preparing 'little satisfactions' for herself severely curtailed.[211] Worse still from everyone's point of view was that enforced rest and delegation of the running of Fordfield to her daughter not only worsened the agitated depression which had afflicted Chiara since the onset of her husband's blindness but also allowed her unwelcome leisure to give full rein to ritualised behaviour regarding to the safety of her home. Both rendered Fordfield hard to live in for those who (like Aelfrida) felt the cold or who (like her granddaughters) were trying to lead independent lives, Agatha as a student and Alethea, emerging from her post-Parisian depression, to plan a 'career of Social Service'[212] with the aid of a bursary from the Katherine Low Settlement in London but bitterly criticised by her grandmother because it would bring her into contact with undesirables. Harassed Aelfrida's one consolation in the midst of '*fuss*' and unwanted and unwonted domesticity ('I am … desperately tired … there seem endless little things to be done')[213] which left her with little time to write and reduced her to venting her frustration on long cycle rides, was Fidelio, the only person in her current life with similar problems and anxieties because his own mother was ill with suspected gastric cancer, in fact, 'nervous indigestion' of which Aelfrida asked without realising the relevance of her question to her own about-to-be-misdiagnosed 'cancer', 'will Mrs Stokoe rejoice or merely be cross!!' when she was informed of the diagnosis.[214]

Aelfrida's admission to The Evelyn Nursing Home in October 1932 provided her with a 'constant succession of devoted nurses to douche me, swab me, feed me and do everything imaginable to make me happy and comfortable'[215] and Chiara with an opportunity to re-establish control of household management. It was unfortunate, therefore, that an argument with Agatha one day and over-exertion on others resulted in 'heart attacks' severe enough to occasion transient loss of consciousness (both granddaughters acted in a 'serenely competent'[216] manner during these crises, probably because they thought their grandmother foolish to disobey her doctor's orders and possibly because they thought she was shamming) and in Chiara's refusal to accept further treatment from Dr Cooper, a woman of whom she was jealous and a doctor she disliked because she insisted that her instructions be carried out. Aelfrida's return home, though marred by regret that had she not with Joan Cooper's connivance

extended her stay in the nursing home, she might have been able to 'save [Chiara] from herself', nevertheless found her mother 'astonishingly rallied' under the care of the Oracle's erstwhile general practitioner, though Dr Parsons, like Dr Cooper, regarded his frail and now gently confused patient as having a very poor prognosis indeed. 'And *The Approaching Storm* is out!' wrote Aelfrida on the day she received this news[217]; a month later, and with impeccably awful timing given what was about to happen, she repudiated Joan Cooper (as a friend, not as a doctor) on the grounds that she was becoming 'addicted' to one whose supportive sympathy had seen her through many vicissitudes.

Chiara continued to be physically and mentally 'exacting'[218] until a slight stroke on 28 November announced the beginning of the end; a more severe one on 10 December caused her to deteriorate rapidly. (A stroke is a possible complication of uncontrolled atrial fibrillation; Aelfrida hints that Chiara had failed to take digitalis in defiance of prescribed treatment.) Lucid intervals during which she signed over power of attorney to Aelfrida, said goodbye to her Cambridge grandchildren, and wrote her *Confessio*[219], were succeeded by lengthening periods of alternating stupor and confusion which necessitated the appointment of a night nurse, Aelfrida, with Phyllis and Agatha providing occasional and reluctant relief, looking after her mother during the day. This was not easy, for Chiara, though not expected to rally, was tenacious of life, even to crying out at one point "I don't want to die!"[220], and Aelfrida, who had enjoyed long periods of sunlit or sunset meditation at her sleepily convalescent mother's bedside in the spring ('[I] look up and adore God [then] sink into the depths of my being, below the volcanic surface-personality into the region of calm [in which] there is deep contentment')[221], now found herself crouched in winter gloom over a barely-lit gas fire (illumination disturbed Chiara and the fire-glow ignited morbid fears of Fordfield being burnt to the ground but Aelfrida insisted on a modicum of warmth and light), bereft through her own heartlessness of Joan Cooper's friendship (her cry for help in 'dire need' elicited the cool reply from Dr Cooper's secretary quoted earlier; 'I recognised the hand of my guardian angel', wrote Aelfrida miserably)[222], and enduring 'a period of spiritual aridity, blank and complete'[223] ('if I prayed that God would make me a saint and not spare me in the making, certainly He is not sparing me')[224] with only Bushie the cat for solace and company.

The days dragged on. Desperate to 'lay down the burden of care' and with her thoughts turning longingly 'to quiet places where one could meditate and study'[225] free from financial, personal, and domestic worries,

Aelfrida prayed that when Chiara died it might be with 'merciful suddenness'.[226] But she did not. Periods of semi-consciousness during which she seemed to understand Aelfrida's comforting assurances that 'Dear, Conrad and Oracle [were] waiting for her' and that once dead she would be able 'to worship God without distraction' (strange comfort for one who cried out for 'more life [and] more enjoyment')[227] were succeeded by intervals during which Chiara lay immobile or exhibited emotional distress so severe ("Frida is dead" was one of her cries) that Dr Parsons prescribed morphine elixir. Mid-December found Aelfrida almost at the end of her endurance: 'I have sat here until the last drop of anguished sympathy has been wrung out of me … how heartrending it all is … if only the agony could be over'.[228] A plea that Dr Parsons increase the dose of morphine was refused on the grounds that he had already prescribed all he legally could. (It seems too that Chiara was 'abnormally resistant to drugs'[229]; had she, like her daughter, sought oblivion in opium during prolonged years of bondage and misery and was some of her agitation and depression attributable to it being obtainable only on prescription after Acts of Parliament in the 1920s prevented easy access to such solace?) So Aelfrida, having already disobeyed Dr Parsons' orders by withdrawing nourishment from her dying mother, took the law further into her own hands and moved by who knows what motives – fear that family finances would not stretch to long-term care, that untold years of devotion to a confused paraplegic would interfere with her spiritual life, a desire to sever the knot of co-dependency which bound her to a mother who had lately engendered more exasperation than love, compassion for one whose 'poor body lay there like some inexorably wound up mechanism' in a room 'already filled … with the odour of corruption'[230] – herself administered the *coup de grâce.*

Aelfrida had been a believer that an individual should have '*the right to die*'[231] at a time and by the means of their own choosing since witnessing the extended cancer-induced death of a woman acquaintance in 1914 (and even, one might say, since contemplating suicide herself in 1912), but it was not until she became the unwilling witness of her father's long decline that she became a proponent of assisted suicide in the form of the 'good death' offered by euthanasia. In *Concrete*, written during the period when Alfred Tillyard's arteriosclerosis entered its final stages, she describes how 'Eleuthera' lovingly and at her own request administers a tailored dose of 'thanatine' to one of her pupils, a small boy deemed by the 'Registrar of Euthanasias' to be so eugenically imperfect that death is the only solution[232], and of a visit to Aunts Alice and Anna midway between Chiara's pneumonia

of February 1932 and her strokes of November and December the same year, she wrote of frail blind Alice and bedridden Anna that she could not help thinking 'how merciful euthanasia would be for those who, with full understanding and belief that it was the will of God, desired it'.[233] On 16 December, therefore, having sat 'keeping [her] vigil' at the bedside of the 'dear patient' whom it seemed would never die ('twelve hours or more in the sickroom is something of a strain'; an unnecessary martyrdom too, given that Chiara now had night and day nurses but perhaps an act of expiation for selfish behaviour during the Oracle's later years), Aelfrida made life imitate art ("I shall do everything that is necessary", says 'Carola' to the nurse in the final pages of *O Passionate World* when she sits at a deathbed closely modelled on Chiara's)[234] and administered to her mother a lethal mixture of morphine and bromide elixirs. Chiara accepted it gratefully, her last words being 'my name, twice repeated and, when I gave her the draught, "thank you"'. (Let us hope for Aelfrida's sake that this was true, for in almost the same breath she describes her mother's soul as having 'already returned to its maker' though her body laboured on: a woman whose torturous breathing was ebbing rather than flowing might have been beyond speech and certainly not of 'full understanding' in the matter of consent.) Then she sat down in the dark with Bushie on her knee to recite 'prayers for the dying and for the dead … there [being] nothing else to do'.[235]

And still Chiara did not die, her wiry constitution and resistance to drugs keeping her alive well into the night. In the small hours of 17 December the night nurse roused Aelfrida with the news that her mother was dead at last. 'I feel a kind of triumph', she wrote, 'that I have done all that Chiara could have expected of me and if clumsily … seen that she had a quiet passing'.[236]

Obsequies and epitaphs followed, the latter composed by Aelfrida and, as usual, seized as opportunities to praise her own literary talents. Longing for '*quiet and solitude*' to enjoy 'sacred and solemn … memories' of her mother, her wish was granted on Christmas Day when, at her request, she spent the day absolutely alone[237] *sans* daughters or domestic staff. Attending St Botolph's on Boxing Day, she 'dedicated whatever remains of my life to God'.[238] On 26 January 1933 she had a vivid, almost a 'true' dream about her dead mother in which she envisaged Chiara as 'strangely aetherial' and with her face showing 'neither age nor youth but the beauty of both youthfulness and maturity'. The dream continued with Chiara informing her that although she herself now lived in a place 'where all discords were resolved and whence this world looked comprehensible and full of beauty', she was allowed to return 'to comfort dear ones' when they had need of her.[239] Cheered by this vision of Chiara as '*strong*' and peaceful, Aelfrida confided it to Agatha a month later – only to have her daughter turn on her for needing 'a dream as a prop to lean on': "*Do* you need such things? Aren't the living enough for you? *Do* you miss Cara so much?"[240]

She did indeed. If the Oracle's influence on Chiara had been 'wholly steadying'[241], how much more had Chiara's been over Aelfrida, and if Agatha and Alethea missed their grandfather's 'moral hold' over them, how much more would Aelfrida miss her mother's over herself. And if Chiara, no longer required to be a 'ministering angel', reverted to her 'moody, wayward, impulsive [and] restless' natural self, how much more would Aelfrida, freed by her own hand from ministering angelhood, revert to hers. But now, sheet anchor gone and, as she had once written prophetically and appositely with reference to 'Elizabeth's' feelings on hearing of the death of 'Mrs Lavington', with "everything she had most clung to crumbled away" and before her only "desolation beyond everything she had ever imagined"[242], Aelfrida found herself early in 1933 rudderless on the sea of life, a sea in which she had often floundered before escaping shipwreck in the haven of Fordfield with Chiara as harbourmaster and, at nearly fifty, forced to confront the world she had created for herself without Chiara to pay her debts, to accept blame for her actions, and to allow her to withdraw from it by taking days in bed. She did not like what she saw.

Nor did Bushie. The cat which ran 'distractedly' round Fordfield as the Oracle died seems to have accepted Chiara's death tranquilly, but he too received a *coup de grâce* at Aelfrida's instigation. On 15 June 1933 'poor loving little Bushie' submitted to 'gentlest kindest death'[243] by chloroform in the room in which Chiara had died six months earlier and Aelfrida began a descent into madness ('everyone is so concerned about my health', she noted [244], not realising that it was her mental health that was in question) almost as distressing to read about as it must have been to endure. Or, as she would have preferred to put it, set out on the next stage of her idiosyncratic 'mystic way', asking only one thing of the future: that she be allowed 'renew [her] "*closer walk with God*"'.[245]

## Notes

1 GCPPT 1|1|36 4 March 1929.
2 ibid. 10 March 1929.
3 ibid. 10 March 1929.
4 ibid. 18 March 1929
5 ibid. 8 October 1929
6 ibid. 9 October 1929.
7 Letter from Catharine Tillyard to Julius Tillyard dated 8 October [1929] (MTC).
8 GCPPT 1|1|36 19 October 1929.
9 ibid. 9 October 1929.
10 ibid. 12 October 1929.
11 GCPPG A1.1 9 December 1929.
12 GCPPT 1|1|36 9 October 1929.
13 GCPPG A1.1 3 December 1929.
14 GCPPT 1|1|36 10 October 1929.
15 GCPPT 1|1|37 2 December 1929.
16 GCPPT 1|1|36 9 October 1929.
17 GCPPT 1|1|36 1 and 12 October 1929. The quotations are from Aelfrida's poem *Heredity* dedicated (most perceptively, given that it was written in 1912) "*to my father*".
18 GCPPT 1|1|37 2 December 1929.
19 GCPPG A1.1 30 December 1929.
20 As the Reverend Professor Mandell Creighton, Cambridge Professor of Ecclesiastical History, he and his family had lived at Langdale Lodge next door to Fordfield. Professor Creighton was later appointed Bishop of London, dying in 1901.
21 GCPPT 1|1|37 10 December 1929.
22 ibid. 7 December 1929.
23 ibid. 22 December 1929.
24 *The Times* 10 October 1929.
25 GCPPT 1|1|37 4 November 1929.
26 GCPPG A1.1 9 December 1929.
27 GCPPT 1|1|37 9 November 1929.
28 GCPPT 1|1|35 30 November 1927.
29 GCPPT 1|1|37 14 November 1929.
30 ibid. 11 March 1930.
31 GCPPG A1.1 16 March 1930.
32 Tillyard, Ae. *The Approaching Storm* pp 68–69.
33 Tillyard, Ae. *O Passionate World* p 201 (GCPPT 2|11).
34 GCPPT 1|1|5 2 December 1936.
35 GCPPT 1|1|37 13 June 1930.
36 ibid. 25 and 27 June 1930.
37 GCPPT 1|1|40 30 October 1931.
38 GCPPT 1|1|47 3 March 1935.
39 GCPPT 1|1|40 5 August 1931.
40 ibid. 1 December 1931.
41 GCPPT 1|1|47 2 and 3 March 1935.
42 GCPPT 1|1|40 6 August 1931.
43 ibid. 8 August 1931.
44 ibid. 20 December 1931.
45 Tillyard, Ae. *Can I be a Mystic?* pp 55–57.
46 Tillyard, Ae. *A Little Road-Book for Mystics* p121.
47 GCPPT 1|1|40 27 September 1931.
48 GCPPT 1|1|43 20 February 1933.
49 GCPPT 1|1|37 24 May 1930. GCPPT 1|1|40 23 June 1931.
50 GCPPT 1|1|43 24 April 1933.
51 GCPPT 1|1|41 7 August 1932.
52 Kaczynski, R. p 102 (2002). The quotation "Do what thou wilt ..." is taken from Crowley's *Book of the Law* (*Liber Al vel Legis*).
53 GCPPT 1|1|40 10 October 1931.
54 GCPPT 1|1|37 24 May 1930.
55 GCPPT 1|1|40 23 June 1931.
56 ibid. 23 July 1931.
57 ibid. 19 January 1932.
58 ibid. 21 November 1931.
59 GCPPT 1|1|41 5 May and 22 July 1932.
60 GCPPT 1|1|40 9 February 1932.
61 GCPPT 1|1|41 24 July 1932.
62 ibid. 28 June 1932.

63  ibid. 21 July 1932.
64  ibid. 28 June 1932.
65  GCPPT 1|1|40 5 August 1931.
66  GCPPT 1|1|41 5 and 22 May 1932.
67  GCPPT 1|1|47 6 October 1936.
68  GCPPT 1|1|41 22 May 1932.
69  GCPPT 1|1|39 27 December 1930.
70  GCPPT 1|1|52 7 May 1937.
71  GCPPT 1|1|44 16 August 1933.
72  GCPPT 1|1|45 15 March 1934.
73  GCPPT 1|1|44 16 August 1933.
74  GCPPT 1|1|41 22 May 1932.
75  ibid. 14 June 1932
76  GCPPT 1|1|38 4 November 1930.
77  GCPPT 1|1|41 28 June 1932.
78  GCPPT 1|1|45 17 March 1934.
79  GCPPT 1|1|41 7 April 1932.
80  ibid. 9 April 1932.
81  GCPPT 1|1|37 6 June 1930.
82  GCPPT 1|1|41 14 June 1932.
83  ibid.
84  GCPPT 1|1|41 22 May 1932.
85  ibid. 14 June 1932.
86  GCPPT 1|1|38 8 August 1930.
87  ibid. 24 August 1930.
88  ibid. 10 August 1930.
89  ibid. 30 August 1930.
90  GCPPT 1|1|41 14 June 1932.
91  GCPPT 1|1|35 25 February 1928.
92  ibid. 19 September 1928.
93  ibid. 29 September 1928.
94  GCPPT 1|1|37 17 April 1930.
95  As 'Stranger', Erle Lunn expressed a liking for the novels of Algernon Blackwood (1869–1951) whose often fantastic themes hinted goth-ically at the supernatural and occult, and for 'Fiction' (*sic*) such as *In Tune with the* Infinite, the seminal work by Ralph Waldo Trine (1866–1958), founder of the American New Thought movement, writing to 'Author' that they had helped him "more than I can say" (Tillyard, Ae *Can I be a Mystic?* p90).
96  GCPPT 1|1|44 30 September 1933. Frank Buchman (1878–1961) was an American Lutheran priest who moved to England to prose-lytise in 1921. His Oxford Group movement, so-called because its activities achieved particular popularity there, preached zealous devo-tion to Christianity, repentance of and restitution for harm done to others, the importance of a daily period of reflection during which one could receive divine guidance, all tenets towards which Aelfrida could – and did – feel sympathetic, and the importance of public and private confession of sin for which she felt no sympathy at all. She nevertheless attended and even addressed meetings of the St Ives group in 1932/33 but disengaged herself thereafter (Buchman's pro-Fascist stance may also have discouraged her). The movement was renamed Moral Re-Armament in 1938.
97  GCPPT 1|1|54 14 August 1937. Roland Meredith Starr (1890–1971) was the pseudonym of Herbert Close, psychologist, home-opath, student of the occult, and reviewer for and contributor to the *Occult Review*, probably the magazine disdainfully referred to by Aelfrida with reference to the publication of *Can I be a Mystic?* For information regarding Starr's relationship with Aleister Crowley see Kaczynski, R. p171 (2002).
98  GCPPT 1|1|41 5 July 1932.
99  GCPPT 1|1|54 14 August 1928.
100  GCPPT 1|1|43 12 April 1933.
101  GCPPT 1|1|52 1 February 1937.
102  GCPPT 1|1|37 17 January 1930.
103  GCPPT 1|1|40 14 February 1932.
104  GCPPT 1|1|43 14 November 1932.
105  GCPPT 1|1|38 2 August 1930.
106  ibid. 20 August 1930.
107  ibid. 20 October 1930.
108  ibid. 2 and 4 December 1930.
109  GCPPT 1|1|39 30 January 1931.
110  GCPPT 1|1|38 9 October 1930.
111  ibid. 4 December 1930.
112  GCPPT 1|1|39 31 January 1931.
113  GCPPT 1|1a *Alethea and Agatha Joint Record Book* 11 November 1930.
114  GCPPG A1.1 4 November 1930.
115  GCPPT 1|1|38 11 November 1930.
116  ibid. 8 November 1930.
117  ibid. 13 October and 10 November 1930.
118  ibid. 6 and 7 November 1930.
119  ibid. 13 October 1930.
120  ibid. 23 February 1931.
121  GCPPT 1|1|39 2 March 1931.
122  ibid. 26 February and 9 March 1931. *Surtout pas trop de zèle* (the phrase is adapted from one attributed to Talleyrand), written, accord-ing to its subtitle, "in Frau Olga Leinberger's copy of *Malise*" and dated "Emden 6 March 1917" (GCPPT 2|5) suggests that in her role as 'devoted wife' Aelfrida was warning off one of Constantine's con-quests or prospective conquests; it also suggests that his womanising predated Panama and Paris.
123  GCPPT 1|1|39 25 January 1931. Constantine may have been sent to Liberia in disgrace but he was not demoted; as his entry in *Who Was Who* shows, he was Consul-General and chargé d'affaires there.
124  ibid.
125  ibid. 2 March 1931.
126  GCPPT 1|1|38 6 November 1930.
127  GCPPT 1|1|39 9 March 1931.
128  ibid. 9 February 1931.
129  ibid. 12 April 1931.
130  GCPPT 1|1|40 12 June 1931.
131  GCPPT 1|1|39 14 April 1931.
132  ibid. 10 April 1931.
133  GCPPT 1|1|41 20 April 1932.
134  GCPPT 1|1|32 27 November 1926.
135  GCPPT 1|1|38 21 November 1930.
136  GCPPT 1|1|37 10 February 1930. This is not as odd as it sounds; there was a shortage of eligible men after the Great War because so many had been killed.
137  GCPPT 1|1|37 9 February 1930
138  GCPPT 1|1|37 9 July 1930.
139  GCPPT 1|1|38 8 August 1930.
140  ibid.13 and 21 November 1930.
141  ibid. 27 November 1930.
142  GCPPT 1|1|42 4 September 1932.
143  GCPPT 1|1|40 5 October 1931.
144  GCPPT 1|1|39 20 January 1931.
145  GCPPT 1|1|37 26 April 1930.
146  GCPPT 1|1|42 4 September 1932.
147  GCPPT 1|1|32 27 November 1926.
148  GCPPT 1|1|40 5 October 1931.
149  ibid. 8 November 1931.
150  ibid. 6 November 1931.
151  ibid. 15 November 1931.
152  ibid. 27 November 1931.
153  ibid. 25 November 1931.
154  ibid. 31 January 1932.
155  GCPPT 1|1|32 27 November 1926.

156 GCPPT 1|1|38 27 September 1930.
157 GCPPT 1|1|41 7 April 1932.
158 GCPPT 1|1|40 14 August 1931.
159 GCPPT 1|1|38 27 September 1930.
160 GCPPT 1|1|32 27 November 1926.
161 GCPPT 1|1|25 6 April 1920.
162 GCPPT 1|1|38 4 and 6 November 1930.
163 GCPPT 1|1|40 19 January 1932.
164 GCPPT 1|1|25 6 April 1920.
165 GCPPT 1|1|37 14 February 1930.
166 GCPPT 1|1|49 14 October 1935.
167 GCPPT 1|1|41 7 August 1932.
168 GCPPT 1|1|42 23 and 26 September 1932.
169 GCPPT 1|1|42 7 October 1932.
170 GCPPT 1|1|38 1 and 2 November 1930.
171 ibid. 8 November 1930.
172 Tillyard, Ae. *Can I be a Mystic?* p82.
173 Tillyard, Ae. *O Passionate World* p137.
174 GCPPT 1|1|38 10 December 1930.
175 GCPPT 1|1|42 7 October 1932.
176 GCPPT 1|1|41 7 August 1932.
177 GCPPT 1|1|38 10 December 1930.
178 GCPPT 1|1|37 18 November 1929.
179 GCPPT 1|1|38 3 September 1930.
180 ibid. 16, 18, and 23 September 1930.
181 ibid. 28 September 1930.
182 GCPPT 1|1|40 1 January 1932.
183 ibid. 15 February 1932.
184 ibid. 21 February 1932.
185 GCPPT 1|1|41 26 and 28 February 1932.
186 ibid. 25 February 1932.
187 GCPPT 1|1|25 29 February 1932. The 'Medical Number' of the *MCJ*, created in February 1932, seems to have been composed in collaborative gratitude for 'Dr Joan's' medical assistance to the whole family.
188 GCPPT 1|1|41 29 May 1932.
189 GPPT 1|1|42 6 September 1932.
190 GCPPT 1|1|41 20 July 1932. Less than a year later, Aelfrida (as 'Gratias Ago') wrote feelingly of how "people budget for rent, food, clothes, holidays, amusements and, we assume, charity [but] ... look on medical charges as extortion". (*The Cambridge Review* vol LIV No 1326 10 February 1933 p232).
191 ibid. 20 July 1932.
192 ibid. 1 August 1932.
193 ibid. 29 June 1932.
194 ibid. 24 June 1932.
195 GCPPT 1|1|40 11 September 1931.
196 GCPPT 1|1|41 17 July 1932.
197 GCPPT 1|1|44 3 August 1933.
198 GCPPT 1|1|41 29 May 1932.
199 GCPPT 1|1|42 28 August 1932.
200 Tillyard, Ae. *The Approaching Storm* p 65. Aelfrida's tendency to blame her readers and not herself for her failure to enlighten 'innumerable mankind' shows just how unenlightened she was as to the real reason for her being absolutely forgotten as an author: she did not identify, or identify with, her audience. Men of any class would have been unlikely to read the kind of novels she wrote; educated middle class women like herself would be unlikely to read novels whose homiletic content would have rendered them (in their eyes) suitable only for their servants, or which were so far removed from their own experience as to be almost incomprehensible. (Aelfrida's two 'historical'

novels sold well because they were escapist; rigorously edited prior to publication, *Marrying a Stranger* and *O Passionate World* might have succeeded because they speak more to twentieth century woman's condition). For an interesting discussion of the social background to Aelfrida's failure as a novelist see Beauman, N. p3.
201 GCPPT 1|1|38 30 September 1930.
202 GCPPT 1|1|38 24 August 1930.
203 GCPPT 1|1|38 30 September 1930.
204 GCPPT 1|1|41 27 July 1932.
205 GCPPT 1|1|38 24 August 1930.
206 GCPPT 1|1|41 24 July 1932.
207 ibid. 1 May 1932.
208 GCPPT 1|1|44 21 July 1933.
209 GCPPT 1|1|41 1 May 1932.
210 ibid. 20 May 1932.
211 ibid. 30 and 31 May and 1 June 1932.
212 ibid. 11 June 1932.
213 ibid. 4 and 8 June 1932.
214 GCPPT 1|1|42 21 September 1932.
215 ibid. 21 October 1932.
216 ibid. 22 October 1932.
217 ibid. 26, 27and 28 October 1932.
218 GCPPT 1|1|43 26 November 1932.
219 The *Confessio*, written on 26 November 1932 in a shaky hand quite unlike Chiara's usual firm script, begins with the opening lines of Psalm 23 and the phrase 'God bless my darling children' and ends with a profession of faith. It was sealed in a small envelope (GCPPG A1.3/3) marked with a cross and the name 'Alethea', but when or by whom is not known.
220 GCPPT 1|1|46 4 September 1936.
221 GCPPT 1|1|41 16 March 1932.
222 GCPPT 1|1|43 15 December 1932.
223 ibid.14 December 1932.
224 ibid. 5 December 1932.
225 ibid. 27 November 1932.
226 ibid. 9 November 1932.
227 ibid. 10 and 13 December 1932.
228 ibid. 10 December 1932.
229 ibid. 11 December 1932.
    GCPPT 1|1|46 4 September 1936.
230 GCPPT 1|1|43 17 December 1932.
231 GCPPT 1|1|20 22 July 1914.
232 Tillyard, Ae. *Concrete* pp 95–97.
233 GCPPT 1|1|41 23 June 1932.
234 Tillyard, Ae. *O Passionate World* pp 422–423.
235 GCPPT 1|1|43 16 and 17 December 1932.
236 ibid.17 December 1932.
237 ibid. 19 and 25 December 1932.
238 ibid. 26 December 1932.
239 ibid. 26 January 1933. An interesting coincidence exists between Chiara's post-mortem appearance and RH Benson's description of a priest rapt in prayer: his face, says an observer, possessed "neither youth nor age [but] was ageless as are all those who look upon Him who inhabit eternity". (*Over the Gateway* in *The Light Invisible* p62).
240 GCPPT 1|1|43 17 February 1933.
241 GCPPT 1|1|37 11 March 1930.
242 Tillyard, Ae. *Marrying a Stranger* p150 (GCPPT 2|6).
243 GCPPT 1|1|44 15 June 1933.
244 GCPPT 1|1|42 17 December 1932.
245 GCPPT 1|1|43 28 and 31 December 1932. The quotation is from a hymn by William Cowper (1731–1800).

# Weary and Tragical

Early in January 1932, soon after the day on which she urged 'ship 1932' to 'set sail bravely over the enchanted sea', Aelfrida sat down to reflect on the 'fabric of [her] life' and to ask herself if she could discern 'the pattern God means to be there'. Some 'threads' she named: Constantine, Anthony, Agatha, Alethea; others, unnamed, concerned 'people half forgotten, incidents woven in', but overall 'the colours [grew] brighter' as she became more intensely aware of God and the way in which His Light shone 'more and more towards the perfect day'.[1] Temporally speaking, and by contrast, she was 'a dull harmless unobtrusive citizen' (*sic*) who lived simply, paid her debts, gave away what she could afford, 'didn't hate anyone', held pacifist principles, and who formed the "backbone of England".[2] (She was also decidedly annoyed to find herself unable to have 'breakfast in bed every day for a fortnight'[3] as prescribed by Dr Cooper for fatigue because other members of the household were unwell.) Less than a year later, Chiara's funeral found such certainties fled: 'the future – what? One begins, even now, to ask'.[4] Ten days later she rallied: 'the future does not worry me in the least though the New Year dawns so uncertainly!'[5]

Though such positive thinking was in keeping with earlier philosophies concerning the need for 'joyous acceptance of change, sickness, even bereavement' as part of God's plan for one's spiritual growth and for cultivating a spirit of adventure ('the "take no thought for tomorrow" spirit') in the face of adversity[6], an itemised list compiled as an aide memoire for the Oracle's obituary should have reminded her that the path which led to 'The Future' often began with 'money'.[7]

Engrossed in replying to letters of condolence ('I try in each case to make Chiara stand out as more beautiful than even the writer of … the letter had felt')[8], Aelfrida's *belle indifférence* towards 'The Future' did not apply to where she was to live. Shortly before Chiara departed for America in June 1930, she informed Aelfrida that she had made testamentary provision for her by leaving Fordfield to her in the event of her own death. Aelfrida, though 'most solemnised' by the bequest (the house itself 'took on a grave new beauty') and less inclined than ever to marry Anthony because she was now (or, rather, potentially) a woman of property, was also rather

**Agatha and Alethea Graham 1930**

horrified as one 'who [has] done my best to divest myself of all earthly possessions, who [has] no jewels, no valuables' (they were deposited in the vaults of Barclay's Bank), 'hardly any books, a stick or two of furniture [and] who never expected to possess the smallest cottage of my own'.[9] So although happy to continue living at Fordfield 'the [house] that steadies', the house where she was born, the house 'all dim with ghosts' whose familiar spirits of place 'are very peaceful and have healing in their hands'[10], the house in whose gardens she had strolled on 'green-walled paths' with men 'whose names I can now hardly recall'[11], she decided to consider herself its future guardian, not its owner, and as an indication of her preference for spiritual over real estate, to dispossess herself of it as soon as possible, even, it seems, prior to Chiara's death.

Whether her decision was motivated by her stated notion of adhering 'to the ascetic ideal of having as few possessions as possible'[12] or by an unspoken desire to rid herself of an expensive mausoleum crammed with

Victorian bric-a-brac preserved by Chiara as a shrine to her dead parents, she formulated her decision as renunciation of 'something that I love so much' that to retain it would be selfish. On Chiara's return, therefore, and as soon as she was fit to hear the news, Aelfrida announced that not only did she not want 'so precious a place' to be exclusively *hers* but also that (another 'Brilliant Idea') it should become 'a home for many people, a place where learning and piety might combine and the tradition of the place could be carried on' and that to this end Chiara ought to will it to the university as a hostel for male and female students 'with some special arrangement for Julius and Eustace and Alethea and Agatha having priority if they want to stay' and with Aelfrida herself appointed as (unpaid) principal of 'Wetenhall House'.[13] Chiara greeted this manifestation of idealistic brilliance by agreeing that though Fordfield *was* 'too precious for private possession', she would leave it to Aelfrida as planned for her to dispose of as she wished. (Chiara and the Oracle had earlier suggested that Fordfield be sold after their deaths and the proceeds divided between their three children and neither Aelfrida's horrified reaction – 'Fordfield sold … just to anyone as though it were just any house that might be treated as one liked!' – nor her suggestion that it was their children's 'duty' to ensure that the house was used for educational purposes in memory of their parents' interest moved them to regard her as anything but an 'impractical visionary' who would be glad of the money for herself and her daughters when the time came.)[14] A Leiston-inspired suggestion that Fordfield become a 'retreat-house' was also dismissed ('I could see that [Chiara] would *much* rather I married Anthony')[15], as was the notion that it be donated to an existing educational establishment in Chiara's lifetime. The future of Fordfield, still pervaded by dead Chiara's presence but in Aelfrida's eyes "as bare, as dull, as unresponsive as a house in which no-one had ever been"[16], therefore remained unsettled at the time of the former's death.

Although Aelfrida pretended ignorance ('Fordfield … and garden are, it seems, to be mine')[17] because Julius and Eustace were not privy to Chiara's disposal of it, her shock on formally receiving the property was all too real: Chiara had promised both Fordfield and 'all the money she legally could to keep it up' but had left her daughter only a life interest and insufficient funds to maintain it and the remainder of her estate was to be sold and the proceeds divided equally among her children. Furthermore, although Aelfrida might let the house if she wished, if she sold it the proceeds were to be divided equally between herself and her brothers. Pretending to be 'glad, really' (note the placing of the comma), Aelfrida stated that she 'hated the idea of having so much more than the

others' but was privately exasperated at Chiara's lack of forethought. ('Wills are tricky things aren't they?')[18] She was also dismayed, for she 'who never wanted material possessions or cared about them'[19] was faced with the prospect of Fordfield hanging like an expensive albatross around her neck or, if let, giving rise to complicated business dealings and leaving her homeless to boot, or, if sold, homeless with only a third of the proceeds to put towards a new home. The only thing in her favour was Eustace's and Julius' generous suggestion that she 'remain at Fordfield' while she made up her mind what to do, an invitation more ultimatum than request for although they had no legal right to remove her, they also knew she could not afford to live there. Hence their further insistence that she remain only for as long as it took (six months, they estimated) to wind up Chiara's affairs.[20]

'Business conversations' ensued, each family member offering conflicting advice. Julius, happy to substitute a sister who loved him for a mother whom he had spent his life since age six trying to placate for being the son who did not die, was keen that Aelfrida '*should* stay [at Fordfield] and make a vacation home for him', so keen, in fact, 'that he would contribute financially'[21], something he had never done. Alethea, too, valued Fordfield as a place for holidays and weekends, but now, it seems, thought more 'of serving her generation than leading a pleasant life'[22] and less of a house in which little of her life would be spent; indeed, she seemed so wrapped up in social work in Battersea (Aelfrida described her as having 'a kind of "St Francis" joy'[23] about her which made her so 'gay and unselfconscious' that it seemed Aelfrida might become 'the mother of a saint'[24] before achieving sanctification herself) and in her concurrent studies at Bedford College for a Social Science Diploma (Aelfrida informed her daughter that 'a right marriage [was] a woman's best career'[25]; Alethea ignored her) as to have virtually removed herself from the family circle. Eustace was against his sister remaining at Fordfield, advising her 'to launch out in some other way', not least because for her to do so would put a stop to Julius' tendency to link himself 'with death rather than life for he is psychologically substituting Fordfield for Chiara'.[26] (Julius was not alone in this: Ancifera Gregory, Anna Tillyard, and Agnes Slack were also showing signs of doing so and this, more than anything else – for she had no intention of nursing any more elderly ladies through their dying days – provided Aelfrida with a powerful reason for 'going away'.)[27] Agatha said she thought her mother needed a husband.[28]

Aelfrida herself was brimming with 'Brilliant Ideas': 'I have thought of five lives I could live perfectly happily', the only problem being that she could see 'an insuperable obstacle to each'.[29] 'Marry Anthony?' (A 'brief but troubling' letter from the man soon to announce his engagement to someone else reminded her that *she* had renounced *him* and that he was not sure he ever wanted to see her again.)[30] Retreat to Leiston? ('Miss Wrightson would not have me' and was unlikely to change her mind no matter how many retreats Aelfrida attended.) 'Live with Dr Joan?' ('Our friendship is too emotional', wrote Aelfrida, oblivious to the fact that Joan Cooper no longer considered herself Aelfrida's friend and was unlikely to share her house with someone who had ended their friendship so brusquely.) 'Build myself a tiny house' on a pightle of land overlooking Wytherton to share with Mary Allen, the soon-to-retire Principal of Homerton and long-standing friend of her parents? (Miss Allen pleaded family commitments elsewhere.)[31] Unable to find a husband to support her or to persuade possible Chiara-substitutes to share a home with her, she considered a fifth life: 'live with the daughters'.[32] This she rejected because 'at their age they should stand alone' and because 'I should burden them with the weight of my affection and accept from them too much … devotion'.[33]

With five possible lives impossible, Aelfrida settled for 'the alternative which attracts me less and may not be feasible either'[34]: to let Fordfield and live elsewhere on her own. She nevertheless continued to cast about for ways and means of keeping Fordfield in the family but was unsuccessful. Julius wanted a bolt hole, not a permanent residence; Eustace, offered the property rent free, declined point blank on architectural and associational grounds ('how strange to dislike one's ancestral home so much'[35], wrote Aelfrida who could hardly have been unaware that Eustace did not share her sentimental view of Fordfield as a Christian house inhabited in perfect peace by a united family but saw it for what it was: a gloomy and outmoded pile in which unhappy people preyed on each other's miseries), a refusal behind which Aelfrida saw the hand of Phyllis who cared nothing 'for the Tillyard Lares et Penates'.[36]

Inspired, perhaps, by pigeons preparing to nest in Fordfield garden, Aelfrida's guardian angel interested himself in rehoming the family gods and herself, suggesting that she too 'build [her] nest high up' in a place where she was already 'near the stars' with nothing but space and sunsets, trees and solitude, to keep her company: her attic bedroom. Aelfrida thought this a brilliant idea – 'with a little pulling about and building on [Fordfield] could be turned into two separate dwellings, a small top flat for me, and an ample two-storey house below'[37], her flat to be called 'Fordfield Heights' or 'Fordfield Above'. Presented with her 'alterations scheme', Eustace was at first agreeable, then disagreeable, informing his sister during one of their many 'business conversations' that

her 'lofty-home plan'[38] could not be carried out without his and Julius' consent and that of her trustees (Chiara had not considered Aelfrida sufficiently responsible to act alone), that a divided house with its owner living in the attics would be difficult to let, that Fordfield, a big house with a large garden in a now unfashionable street and lacking that sine qua non of middle-class living, electricity, was already proving hard to dispose of[39], and that because she herself was to pay the £500 cost of the alterations, she would 'be "temporarily short of cash" for many years to come'.[40]

Bereft of 'Fordfield Above' Aelfrida decided to quit Fordfield altogether: 'I will go and live at The Grange (with a few conveniences put in)', a plan 'much better than doing the conventional thing and living in a poky characterless modern house' in one of the new middle-class areas of Cambridge. The prospect of his sister living in an even older house without any modern conveniences whatsoever (Aelfrida describes it as 'uncomfortable but … intimate and charming')[41] in the middle of five acres of semi-derelict orchard in Cherry Hinton did not appeal to Eustace at all, primarily because the property had been willed by Alfred Tillyard to Chiara in life-interest only and by her to their three children jointly but also because he was keen to raise capital at the same time as ridding the family of another encumbrance by selling the land to a town council looking for sites to develop for working-class housing. With this Aelfrida was forced to concur, for though she disdained money, she had just received 'rather inopportune news': Constantine, newly returned to Europe as Consul-General in Berlin and for reasons undisclosed even to his solicitor, was about to reduce her allowance. This, she wrote, would leave her with only 'a small but sufficient'[42] annual income of around £340 derived from her (reduced) allowance, royalties, directors' fees, investments, and from the tiny rents provided by properties inherited from her parents.

Though this might prove sufficient to live on, the question of where to live remained unsolved. A visit to architect HC Hughes 'at his quaint little office in Tunwell's Court'[43] produced two eminently practical ideas. The first, that the gardener's cottage be converted for her use, was rejected on the grounds that it was too small and that she did not want to dispossess the Churches, a family whose longstanding loyalty to Fordfield should not be rewarded by loss of their tied cottage. The second, that she build her own cottage 'at the west end of the garden'[44], was deemed by Eustace the perfect, and by Aelfrida, a stop-gap solution 'that would suit me well enough – it would anyway be a place easy to leave if I got "guidance" to go elsewhere – in this world or the next'.[45]

'Wetenhall Cottage' provoked much enthusiasm in Eustace and Mr Hughes but very little in herself: 'they were full of zest and enthusiasm [and] wanted to settle all my little house for me ... I tried to be too ... but I felt little except sadness. Wetenhall Cottage ... means nothing but NO Fordfield'.[46] A week later she was both miserable and cross: 'if it wasn't for the daughters ... needing a home to come to, how much simpler and more seemly if I just slipped off ... somewhere without any fuss. Who am I that trustees, brothers, lawyers, architects and so forth should be busying themselves over my welfare. However, *some* of them get paid for it!'[47] The sight and sound of the western end of the garden being staked out and building materials delivered reduced her to migraine and despair and were it not for promising that the 'dear Fordfield Lares and Penates *shall* be well housed'[48], she would have opted out altogether and left the matter in Eustace's and Phyllis' hands because 'they are so much more interested in my arrangements than I am myself'.[49] There was, too, a moral aspect to having a house built specially for her and the incompatibility of this with her desire for a 'closer walk with God': 'everyone assumes that what one wants is to be as comfortable as possible – and I say to myself, is everyone not justified in their assumption? How genuine *are* my aspirations towards some kind of "heroic virtue" when I say to myself "I *must* have a home the daughters can come to" or "I *must* take care of my health ..." Are these genuine and valid reasons or mere excuses?' One thing, however, was absolutely clear: 'my conscience would not allow me to live at Fordfield even if I could afford it'[50] because she was 'so ashamed that I have so much while others have so little'.[51]

The future of Fordfield was still unsettled but there too a solution presented itself. Aelfrida's efforts to dispose of it philanthropically to the Association for Promoting Retreats (founded by Anthony Wrightson's mother) as a retreat house 'together with rates, repairs, upkeep of garden ... and my services as housekeeper'[52] or, at Miss Wrightson's suggestion, to the Bishopric of Ely as a diocesan retreat house[53] met with no success. She was therefore relieved when a married couple, he an architect, she an 'enthusiastic nurse', arrived 'to see it if would do for a nursing home'.[54] Encouraged by Joan Cooper and by Veronica's comment that 'Fordfield is a lovely place to be ill and to get better in', Aelfrida decided that transformation into a 'haven of rest for old people, chronic invalids and the like'[55] would be entirely suitable, that 'the dear home' would enjoy 'watching over sick people', and that she herself would 'look at it encouragingly' over the low fence dividing it from Wetenhall Cottage.[56] In keeping with her strictures on the vulgarity of money and her

optimistic belief that God would provide, Fordfield was leased to the Fordhams for £4 a year ground rent and Aelfrida prepared to depart.

A 'nightmare of activity' ensued, the brunt of it falling on herself. 'I have to make ... the arrangements about Fordfield etc., etc., by myself'[57], she wrote crossly, having discovered to her chagrin that home ownership involved responsibilities. (Arlington Heights excepted, she had removed herself from the hassle of setting up or dismantling a rented home by taking herself to another country, leaving Constantine to find and rent accommodation and buy, rent, or dispose of furniture.) Sorting china, taking the family silver and some 'Not-very-Valuables'[58] to the bank for safe-keeping, sending off surplus bedding for use by the unemployed, organising the removal and storage of furniture required for Wetenhall Cottage, turning out cupboards and sorting books, scattering so many hoarded lives ('a whole morning ... bringing [down] an astonishing number of assorted objects ... family daguerreotypes, dolls' furniture, ornaments and bric-a-brac of various kinds'[59] was reproduced in *O Passionate World* as a description of a Victorian house in "which no monument of bad taste was wanting: wool mats and wax flowers under glass shades ... horsehair chairs [and] whatnots ... belongings old and new, useful and useless, curious and comic ... vast quantities of miscellaneous possessions"),[60] arranging for furniture requested by Eustace and Phyllis to be taken to Merton House and by Julius to be packed and sent to Cardiff, left Aelfrida dirty and exhausted. And emotionally exhilarated, for the 'nightmare' was cathartic and it was not only Fordfield whose soul was cleansed after seventy years pell-mell muddle was cleared away.

Although Aelfrida waxed surprisingly unsentimental with regard to dismantling Fordfield ('I thought I should wake ... to heaviness and oppression. But no! I woke to thoughts of God, to a strange exaltation, to the wide freedom of the spiritual world'), 'stabs of sadness'[61] assailed her when it came to distributing Chiara's effects as dictated by her late mother. Giving her 'good clothes' to 'Bosey', the family nurse now living in the Royal Albert Almshouses next door, brought on 'attacks of cramps in [her] heart'[62] and discovering of a cache of letters from Constantine to Chiara, secreted in a box marked 'Receipts', made her wince and tear them up without looking at them.[63] Presentation of the portrait of their common ancestor Thomas Castle to Ernest Crundwell ('Bayard') made her happier ('I like to ... distribute gifts in [Chiara's] memory – I love giving and that sort of giving specially')[64] but occasioned uncomfortable reflections: doing 'kind things' cost her nothing and left her tainted with the spiritual kudos she now professed to detest; in building Wetenhall Cottage, she was leading a 'self-indulgent life'; in looking forward to the 'wide freedom of the spiritual world', she was 'letting good thoughts take the place of good deeds'[65], and so on. And excuses of needing to 'gather strength' for the next stage of a journey whose initials so closely reflected her own (TCWWG/ACWG) and of having to be 'self-indulgent' because of her health[66] looked feeble when compared with demands to be made a saint and not spared in the making.

Concern for her health was not confined to herself. Although Aelfrida expressed puzzlement as to the unusual amount of 'women's devotion' extended to her by people like Lilian Whitehouse, Dorothea Conybeare, 'sweet and understanding' Florence Keynes[67] whose presence as an old friend and as Cambridge's first lady Mayor at the funeral of a former mayoress had been much appreciated, Miss Allen (her sympathy 'remained unspoken but not unshown')[68], and by the wives of 'dear Presbyterians' from St Columba's who had known Aelfrida since girlhood and now 'overwhelmed [her] with sweet words and tender feelings'[69], it is obvious that in spite of Agatha's attempts to make light of the matter (the ladies hovered round, she said, only because Aelfrida represented '"life" and romance and all that sort of thing' to them)[70], all feared complete mental breakdown following the death of a mother on whom she had depended. (They were right, as it happened, but the breakdown did not happen immediately and was not solely due to Chiara's death.) Joan Cooper, 'solicitous and worried'[71], visited often (in a medical capacity, not as a friend, for as she bitterly informed a patient showing signs of emotional neediness, she now placed "no reliance" on Aelfrida's protestations of affection)[72] because 'troubled and [made] apprehensive'[73] by the latter's behaviour.

'Doctor Joan' was right to be worried, for Aelfrida's behaviour was at the extremity of normal grief-reaction. On the one hand, she veered wildly from manic physical activity to utter physical prostration compounded by episodes of illness ("psychologists tell us that the state of our body is merely the reflection of our state of mind", wrote 'Stranger' to 'Author')[74] from which she, a lifelong teetotaller willing to risk her marriage for the cause, dragged herself up with the help of nips of brandy. On the other, her moods ran the gamut of emotion from juvenile hilarity manifest by a Valentine to Joan Cooper entitled *The Ballad of Wytherton Way*[75] which could be taken merely as a tension-relieving device were it not that earlier and later evidence reveals it as an attempt to divert attention from deeper issues, through sudden 'wonderful and unexpected' sensations of God 'flooding full-tide' over her soul or of 'God's peace' pervading her

**Alethea Graham c1930**

being[76], to a morbid desire to divest herself of everyone, even – one might say, especially – of the 'sweet daughters' who could have comforted her most, in a desperate search for solitude.

Aelfrida's latest longing for solitude may be seen as a natural reaction to Chiara's death and to the terrible events which preceded and precipitated it. It began with her sending Agatha and Alethea to Merton House so that she could keep Christmas 1932 alone as a 'solemn and sacred' occasion on which to remember her mother, and in an attempt to regain her spiritual and emotional equilibrium ('solitude has a wonderful healing power')[77], to Bournemouth for two weeks after that. Their absence in January 1933, however, saw her not only 'alone all day and [loving] it' (alone, that is, apart from her domestic staff) but also *for the very first time in her life* 'all alone in a locked house' during an entire night.[78] After that, however, 'the taste for Solitude [grew]'. Solitude, she decided (Solitude with a capital S, not mere absence of people) was the path she was to follow in the future, for only in Solitude could she spend her time in uninterrupted communion with God. This new sensation of having 'no need at all for any kind of human society'[79] was stronger than any attempt to live in 'Fordfield Above' 'to enjoy [her] solitude'[80] or at The Grange to 'devote [her]self to Solitude', for the call to that state was now 'stronger than anything I have heard for many a long day'.[81] It was to endure for the rest of her life and to have important repercussions.

As usual with any decision made, Aelfrida was immediately assailed with doubts, the most important being 'if I lived alone could I be continuously conscious of God?' ('One can but try!' she added, the escape clause being 'if circumstances allow'.)[82] There was, too, the problem that solitude was, as early Christian hermits found to their cost, 'a great arouser of physical desire', a subject she probably did not raise when writing lyrical letters to unresponsive Anthony 'in praise of Solitude'[83] or fourteen 'edifying' pages on Solitude at the request of Richmond Theological College.[84] Then again, and much as she looked forward to having time to 'think and dream [and] worship' quite alone, to 'trace the guiding hand of God' in her life, and to enjoy a 'still, brooding existence' cut off from the world, was she being selfish to want to move on that stage of her life[85] regardless of her daughters' possible need of her? This last doubt almost (but not quite) swayed her into to putting aside thoughts of Solitude as a 'vocation' she could shuffle off her responsibilities and claim her right to choose it, for it was at this time of seeming spiritual indecision that Aelfrida was actually engaged in making important decisions with regard to herself and her future, a future in which obligations to others played a small and unimportant part. Her period of solitary reflection over, she prepared to abandon Solitude for as long as it took to make the necessary arrangements to achieve it and moved on to what she regarded as completion of the next stage of her plan: to rid herself of the last vestiges of the encumbrance that was Fordfield.

On 24 May she found herself 'trailing round after the men who catalogued furniture'[86] for the sale of items unwanted by the family. On 6 June a notice affixed to the gate announcing the date of the sale (20 June) 'made [Eustace] feel quite wretched'[87] but moved Aelfrida not at all because she herself was 'bruised with too much emotion'[88] for a wholly unexpected reason: the unconsidered effect on the emotions of those more affected than herself by breakup of the family home. Ancifera, 'very sad' at losing her childhood link with 'Little Katie'.[89] Julius, distraught at 'saying goodbye to Fordfield for ever'.[90] The 'Merton House children' whose only memories of Fordfield were happy ones. Lilian Whitehouse, 'a restless creature' since her own mother's death two years earlier, who looked on Fordfield and Aelfrida 'with a very strong and reverent affection'.[91] Frank Stokoe, who had once revelled in 'the bright, rich and warm experience outside

the world of books'[92] experienced there and who lived up to his nickname of Fidelio by coming to bid adieu to his former refuge. Church, the gardener, 'a bit grumpy'[93] (an understatement) at being evicted from a cottage and a job Aelfrida had rashly promised would always be his because Mrs Fordham did not wish to retain his services and because Mr Fordham had earmarked Fordfield Cottage for his architectural practice. 'Warm-hearted but tactless' American cousins Tom and Beatrice Zender Brown who visited often and 'rubbed [her] up the wrong way each time' but were 'hushed into being tactful'[94] by the awfulness of death and dissolution. Bushie, put down at this juncture with the epitaph 'better so'.[95] 'Poor little Temu … sad at leaving Fordfield … and full of a deep and sensitive awareness of the inherent tragedy … of human affairs'.[96]

Although Agatha had appeared least affected of all by the 'emotional … muddle and anxiety' surrounding Chiara's death, she was in truth leading a life of quiet desperation. Her last year at Girton had just begun. She had switched from Geography to a more congenial subject, namely English Literature, but although she produced essays 'up to a First Class tripos standard'[97], she had had a possible thesis rejected by Eustace and by 'old English don'[98] Hilda Murray because her scheme was 'too vague and philosophical'.[99] She was revising for Finals in a house made chaotic by her mother's frenetic clearances and alternately elevated and despairing moods (she achieved an upper second, correctly described by Aelfrida as 'very creditable … considering all the circumstances')[100] and had no idea what to do after that. Rejecting Eustace's suggestion that she lecture for the Workers' Educational Association[101] but making very little sustained effort to find an occupation, she wept to Aelfrida that she 'felt quite futile', that 'the best she could do when term was over was just to get out of the way' ('I knew just how she felt and honoured her for it'[102], wrote a mother who also noted that she had no idea what Agatha really felt because 'the habit of solitary brooding'[103] was growing on her daughter to such an extent that she had become virtually silent) because she was neither 'very well nor very useful'[104] as and where she was.

Useful she was forced to be, for Aelfrida, feeling 'far too sensitive' to confront Eustace and Mr Hughes as they planned 'the new demure … Wetenhall Cottage'[105], employed Agatha as protectress, a role formerly taken by Alethea. Unwell, she was; for the stress of losing Alethea to a career which would inevitably separate the sisters more and more, of being separated after brief reunion from a father whose special daughter ("Fuvver's Agata") she had always felt herself to be[106], of her own near-fatal illness ("my ear the ivory door / lets in the noise of floods and I am drowned")[107], of her mother's much-trumpeted and sister's mysterious illnesses and the dramatic deaths of her unloved grandparents, of losing the only home she could remember and in which she had lived for twenty-one years, and of finding herself deposed within a short space of time from 'precious, precious Temu' to a 'good daughter at home' infinitely less precious than Solitude, caused recurrent attacks of asthma of such severity that medicines prescribed by Joan Cooper 'at her grimmest and most professional'[108] were of limited efficacy. Hearing Agatha 'tugging for breath'[109] made Aelfrida thankful that she herself seemed to have avoided the 'breakdown' feared by Dr Cooper but also led her to declare (to her diary, not to her daughter) that she did not 'want *Agatha* to be ill'[110], good though suffering would be for the latter's character, lest it upset her own plans.

All too soon, however, it was 'the *last* this, the *last* that'[111]. The last Sunday tea party. The last May Ball. (Aelfrida refused to celebrate May Week: 'my memories … were too poignant'.)[112] The 'last weekend of "togetherness" at Fordfield' before mother and daughters went their separate ways and 'here am I not able to see this page for tears', wrote Aelfrida as she recorded Alethea's parting words.[113] The last pang of regret: 'last night the house spoke as old houses will and would not let me go to sleep. My room began "see, Aelfrida, this is the room where you were born … and this was your room when you were a girl … here you spent your wedding night and your mother came and knelt by your bed, the big four poster bed with the red damask curtains. And this was your children's nursery – you can see them running about in their scarlet dressing gowns – and so on and so on through every room in the house until I could neither sleep nor pray'.[114]

Aelfrida's account of the last five days of Fordfield's life as a family home has her by her own wish 'alone [there]' (that she had breakfast in bed on at least one of those days suggests otherwise), having packed Agatha off to Merton House and resisted everyone else's offers of company. Late one warm June evening she explored her 'domain' ('dear garden, dear house!') for the last time[115] before going upstairs to sleep in her 'bare dismantled room'.[116] Her very last evening and night were spent genuinely alone with only coffee and biscuits for supper: the parlour maid had been dismissed with a bequest from Chiara, 'faithful charwoman' Mrs Thompson and Georgina the cook whose services were retained for Wetenhall Cottage, had been found temporary positions[117], and Church, shortly to be re-employed as jobbing gardener to Wetenhall Cottage's smaller garden and to maintain a reduced 'garden-at-the-back', had removed

himself to a small house in Romsey Town. She penned a farewell letter to Julius in an attempt to convince him and herself that she had done the right thing, telling him that 'the joy was greater than the sorrow, that all we had of Fordfield in the past still lived on somewhere as treasure in heaven and so forth and so forth' until her eyes were so full of tears that she finished hastily because 'in danger of dropping them all over the paper'. Then she took a final walk round the garden looking up at the house's 'poor shuttered windows' before mounting the carpetless stairs to dream of what might have been ('I had hoped to see Alethea married from Fordfield and I know Anthony hoped to sleep in this room with me'), to listen to the silence ('the house is very quiet now – the voices are still – the ghosts are laid'), to anticipate the future ('the dear place seems to be ready for a new life and to be hopeful rather than sad'), and to leave blessings 'for the sick folk, the nurses, the doctors'[118] who were to move in.

On 20 June 1933, 'glad enough to go' but requiring the admonishment 'now, then, Aelfrida! Courage!'[119], she left the house of her birth to begin an odyssey during which she slept under thirteen different roofs, sometimes by herself, sometimes accompanied by one or both daughters (Alethea lived largely in London, Agatha was farmed out to family and friends and even, at her own request and in an attempt to assert her independence, to 'a … very sedate and rather charming … students' hostel place'[120] in London), before returning to Cambridge in late October 1933 to find Fordfield, 'all clean and fresh and white and blue'[121], reincarnated as The Brooklands Avenue Nursing Home[122] and Wetenhall Cottage waiting for herself.

But an event took place between the day of Chiara's death and Aelfrida's arrival eleven months later at the 'dear little house' that her 'third daughter' Veronica Tillyard hoped in childish innocence would be 'lucky' and that her aunt would 'enjoy [herself] very much' in[123], an event which reduced her courage to nothing, rendered her too 'weary and tragical' to supervise the move into Wetenhall Cottage (that was left to 'too sweet for words' Agatha with the comment 'suppose I had *two* daughters who were saints …')[124], and sent her spinning into an hysterical fugue during which she retired to bed, refused food, and addressed impassioned and incoherent supplications to the Deity of whom, though 'even to pray to be *made* a saint savours of extreme presumption', she had so often begged 'take me at my word … and beat me into shape'[125] and not to spare her in the making. The event, however, was only the sequel to one which had taken place earlier the same year.

On 27 March 1933, Aelfrida paid a short visit to London during which she met Alethea for dinner.

Alethea, her mother wrote, 'seemed somehow out of touch with everything' but so radiant that it seemed as if her serenity outstripped Aelfrida's 'with an ease and sureness which left me praising God that I was the mother of a potential saint'.[126] On 29 March Aelfrida and Agatha set off to Cornwall for a spring holiday. Lodging two miles inland they explored 'such dunes, such cliffs, such sands!' by train and on foot, having 'lovely times and talks together' in spite of Agatha's asthmatic cough. On 4 April, while returning from from St Ives, Aelfrida suddenly felt 'sorrowful unto death' and as if 'something was going to be asked of me which I did not know whether I should be able to give'. Was it, she wondered, news of Anthony (her visit to London had been to see him in the nursing home where he had been so ill) but Anthony was now so well recovered as to make this unlikely. On 5 April, however, she received a letter which, though 'most beautiful', sent Agatha weeping to bed for three days with asthma and anguish and Aelfrida herself to pace the shore in 'deep deep thought'[127]: Alethea had met someone with whom she hoped to spend the rest of her life pursuing her mother's ideal of a 'best career' for a woman, namely marriage. But although her future husband was exactly "the sort of man [Aelfrida] should want [her] daughter to marry"[128] ("eugenically perfect, morally blameless", fond of children and simple things[129], a clean-living and a tender lover, and 'a man who would be husband and father in one')[130], Alethea, though 'bred up to be the mother of children'[131], would leave her mother without hope of becoming a grandmother. She had decided to enter a contemplative order of Benedictine nuns, there to become a Bride of Christ.

## Notes

1  GCPPT 1|1|40 9 January 1932.
2  ibid. 2 January 1932.
3  ibid. 4 January 1932.
4  GCPPT 1|1|43 20 December 1932.
5  ibid. 31 December 1932.
6  GCPPT 1|2 Notes for services taken by Aelfrida at the New Cherry Hinton Free Church in 1918.
7  GCPPT 1|1|37a.
8  GCPPT 1|1|43 21 December 1932.
9  GCPPT 1|1|37 12 June 1930.
10  ibid. 25 June 1930.
11  GCPPT 1|1|22 22 July 1918.
12  GCPPT 1|1|38 18 August 1930.
13  ibid. 21 September 1930.
14  GCPPT 1|1|21 16 March 1916.
15  GCPPT 1|1|40 7 November 1931.
16  Tillyard, Ae. *O Passionate World* p 381(GCPPT 2|11).
17  GCPPT 1|1|43 19 December 1932.
18  ibid. 22 December 1932.
19  ibid. 19 December 1932.
20  ibid. 20 December 1932.

21  ibid. 22 December 1932.
22  GCPPT 1|1|41 28 February 1932.
23  GCPPT 1|1|42 24 September 1932.
24  GCPPT 1|1|41 4 May 1932.
25  ibid. 22 June 1932.
26  GCPPT 1|1|43 22 and 23 December 1932.
27  ibid. 28 December 1932.
28  ibid. 22 December 1932.
29  ibid. 20 December 1932.
30  ibid. 24 May 1933.
31  ibid. 20 December 1932.
32  ibid. 2 January 1933.
33  ibid. 15 November and 8 December 1932.
34  ibid. 20 December 1932.
35  ibid. 8 December 1932.
36  ibid. 30 August 1933.
37  ibid. 2 January 1933.
38  ibid. 4 January 1933.
39  ibid. 12 January 1933.
40  ibid. 28 January 1933.
41  ibid. 10 January 1933.
42  ibid. 20 January 1933.
43  Henry Castree Hughes (1893–1976) was a well-known Cambridge architect specialising in domestic architecture at that stage of his career but soon to embark on buildings for Cambridge town and university. He had been a friend of Eustace and Julius since youth and was described by Aelfrida as 'fat and amiable' when she made his acquaintance in Tunwell's Court. (GCPPT 1|1|43 7 January 1933). For details of Hughes' career prior to and after his work for Aelfrida see Calladine, C. *Fen Court* in *Peterhouse Annual Record* 2002/3 pp77–94. For an (incomplete) list of houses designed by Hughes in Cambridge in the 1920s and 30s, see http:||www.cambridge2000.com/cambridge2000/html/architect_builder/HC_Hughes.
44  GCPPT 1|1|43 9 February 1933.
45  ibid. 13 February 1933.
46  ibid. 10 March 1933.
47  ibid. 19 March 1933.
48  GCPPT 1|1|44 3 September 1933.
49  GCPPT 1|1|43 14 April 1932.
50  ibid. 13 February 1933.
51  GCPPT 1|1|28 14 May 1924.
52  GCPPT 1|1|43 5 March 1933.
53  ibid. 7 March 1933.
54  ibid. 11 March 1933.
55  ibid. 21 March 1933.
56  ibid. 21 and 25 March 1933.
57  GCPPT 1|1|44 9 June 1933.
58  ibid. 2 June 1933.
59  ibid. 22 May 1933.
60  Tillyard, Ae. *O Passionate World* pp 363–364 and 401.
61  GCPPT 1|1|44 16 June 1933.
62  GCPPT 1|1|43 12 January 1933. Rose Prior was not a Cambridge resident; her admission to the almshouses was probably due to her association with the Wetenhall/Tillyard family, itself associated with the RAH since its foundation in 1860/1. For further details, see Atkins, K. p19.
63  ibid. 16 January 1933.
64  ibid. 4 January 1933.
65  ibid. 1 February 1933.
66  ibid. 1 and 2 February 1933.
67  ibid. 11 February 1933.
68  GCPPT 1|1|44 25 December 1932 and 12 June 1933.
69  ibid. 15 June 1933.
70  GCPPT 1|1|43 4 February 1933.
71  ibid. 5 January 1933.

72  ibid. 20 February 1933.
73  GCPPT 1|1|44 17 June 1933.
74  Tillyard, Ae. *Can I be a Mystic?* p7.
75  GCPPT 1|1|43 22 February 1933.
76  GCPPT 1|1|43 20 December 1932.
     GCPPT 1|1|44 15 and 16 June 1933.
77  GCPPT 1|1|43 28 December 1932.
78  ibid. 8 January 1933.
79  ibid. 10 January 1933.
80  ibid. 2 January 1933.
81  ibid. 3 and 10 January 1933.
82  ibid.
83  ibid. 15 January 1933.
84  ibid. 26 February 1933.
85  ibid. 27 January 1933.
86  GCPPT 1|1|44 24 May 1933. The sale of "Furniture and Effects" was advertised in the *CDN* of 13 June 1933. It included Alfred Tillyard's roll top desk, the grand piano on which Constantine played Beethoven, and dining room furniture which must have proved hard to sell: a "massive" carved oak buffet, two sideboards, 12 chairs, and several side tables. An elaborate chair came to rest in Cambridge's Folk Museum.
87  ibid. 6 June 1933.
88  ibid. 12 June 1933.
89  ibid. 2 June 1933.
90  GCPPT 1|1|43 21 April 1933.
91  GCPPT 1|1|44 9 and 12 June 1933.
92  GCPPT 1|1|20 8 August 1914.
93  GCPPT 1|1|43 12 April 1933.
94  GCPPT 1|1|43 18 December 1932
     GCPPT 1|1|44 15 June 1933.
95  GCPPT 1|1|44 15 June 1933.
96  ibid.
97  GCPPT 1|1|42 3 November 1932.
98  GCPPG A2.1 4 May 1927. Hilda Murray, described more flatteringly by Aelfrida as a white-haired lady 'prim … but gracious' existing 'in a kind of cultural heaven of unemotional learning' (GCPPT 1|1|30 21 October 1925) was then vice-mistress of Girton and Examiner for the English tripos.
99  GCPPT 1|1a *Alethea and Agatha Joint Record Book* 17 July 1933.
100  GCPPT 1|1|44 15 June 1933.
101  GCPPT 1|1|43 1 January 1933.
102  ibid. 11 March 1933.
103  ibid. 16 March 1933.
104  ibid. 3 March 1933.
105  ibid. 5, 10 and 11 March 1933.
106  GCPPG 1.1a *Agatha's Record* Book 16 November 1911.
107  GCPPG A2.5 Undated *Poem for Music.*
108  GCPPT 1|1|43 24 January 1933.
109  GCPPT 1|1|44 6 September 1933.
110  GCPPT 1|1|43 24 January 1933.
111  GCPPT 1|1|44 4 June 1933.
112  ibid. 7 June 1933.
113  ibid. 18 and 19 May 1933.
114  ibid. 12 June 1933.
115  ibid. 15 June 1933.
116  ibid. 16 June 1933.
117  ibid. 18 May 1933.
118  ibid. 19 June 1933.
119  ibid. 19 and 21 June 1933.
120  ibid. 25 and 30 September 1933.
121  ibid. 17 September 1933.
122  A contemporary entry in the local *Register of Cambridge Nursing Homes 1928–1947* describes the Brooklands Avenue Nursing Home as having three rooms on the ground floor, six ("including operating theatre") on the first floor, and three on the second floor, and deems it suitable for "General, Medical and Surgical cases including occasional Maternity cases attended by a doctor". Fordfield itself is described as "brick built and slated" which hardly does justice to its polychromatic splendour and decorative features and larger rooms must have been subdivided to achieve six rooms on the first floor.
123  GCPPT 1|1|43 21 March 1933.
124  GCPPT 1|1|44 30 April 1933.
125  GCPPT 1|1|43 19 March 1933.
126  ibid. 11 April 1933. Aelfrida's account was written retrospectively.
127  ibid.
128  Tillyard, Ae. *O Passionate World* p312.
129  ibid. p 263.
130  GCPPT 1|1|26 6 June 1922.
131  GCPPT 1|1|43 11 April 1933.

# Unfortunate Victims

Elizabeth Mary Alethea (Truth) born in Arlington Heights on 20 August 1908 and Aelfrida Catharine Agatha (Goodness) born 12 July 1910 in Cambridge, led peripatetic lives before the onset of the Great War in August 1914 brought them back to Fordfield for twenty years. Details of their doings recorded in 'their respective chronicles'[1] on a regular but not a daily basis, together with numerous photographs of one or both (usually both) children, provide a comprehensive record of their development from babies to toddlers to schoolgirls and beyond, and their own and their mother's diaries and other writings flesh out the picture.

The 'chronicles', however, were not the private documents that Aelfrida's diaries became after 1912 and what is written there must be read with reference to other documents if the truth is to be ascertained. Statements concerning the children's appearance and behaviour (aged three and one, they were 'handsome, intelligent, big and not the least bit shy', Alethea being the general favourite because 'her charms are more obvious')[2] and the pretty things Agatha said are probably accurate ("when I am an angel I shall have a halo made of fire – *just like a Christmas pudding*"[3] seems a rather precocious remark for a toddler and one made at five made her mother uneasy: "I don't ever wish to be big. I would rather be an angel before I am big")[4]; others are contradicted by Aelfrida's diary. Constantine, she writes in Emden, 'cares surprisingly little for the society of his children. I think he likes having them – it gives him a certain weight – [but] he is in the Consulate flat all day except for lunch … [so] he barely sees them … and can [only] enjoy about five minutes of their company [before] he gets bored'[5] yet their *Record Books* show that Constantine spent time with his children in the evening and at weekends, amusing them with poems and songs dedicated to each girl individually and taking an interest in their moral and physical welfare. Then, too, Aelfrida's cry 'one never gets a moment to one's self!'[6] suggests that 'the babies' occupied her from morning till night; in fact, she left them largely in Ovvie's care so as to have time for as little household management as she could get away with and for as much of her own reading and writing as possible, 'baby-minding' occupying only an hour and a half in the afternoon and an hour at bed time.

**Alethea and Agatha Graham 1932**

Pregnant for the third time, Aelfrida worried about Agatha, feeling that her younger daughter, though seemingly 'strong and well', might sooner or later slip away like the baby whose survival to term seemed precarious: 'I sometimes wonder whether I shall keep her'.[7] Alethea's sturdy presence was comforting when Aelfrida found herself confined to a sofa with disquieting symptoms shortly after Anatolia's departure and the terrible 'Juanita' row of mid-February 1912, Alethea having recently stated that she would never marry because she wanted to 'live near Mother *all* the time'.[8] She also played quietly or lay beside her mother talking so perceptively that Aelfrida noted 'a strange, almost uncanny, sympathy'[9] between herself and her elder daughter.

We do not know what the two little girls were told about Agneta's birth and death in May 1912. Agatha was probably too young understand but Alethea's 'very touching' sweetness to her desperately ill mother [10] and her later comment regarding her surviving sister ("Bammie is *sure* to go to Heaven − she is *ever* so good")[11] suggests comprehension of the sad event. The children were not, of course, sent away from Fordfield without explanation and were surrounded by familiar figures (Ovvie, their grandparents, and their Uncle Eustace) but their father's departure for Panama (and a year is a long time in the life of little girls of four and two) and their mother's temporary absence in Ventnor and prolonged emotional absence with severe post-natal depression, scarred both for life. Although Aelfrida later wrote a short parable to explain her 'distant' demeanour to daughters unable to comprehend the change in her behaviour[12], the damage was already done. Agatha became almost parasitically dependent on Alethea; Alethea, later to become rude and boisterous in an attempt to evoke a response in a mother preoccupied by her husband's wartime malpractices and request for divorce, became withdrawn and watchful, subduing her own anxieties in an effort to take care of her mother "while Fuvver is away".[13]

A mother who wrote dully two weeks before her request to Dr Bowen that he look after her daughters' health in the event of her death and who was shortly to be packed off to Ventnor (or 'Ventnor', but either way, a further deprivation for her daughters) that her feelings for her living children amounted only to 'serving' them[14] was not, however, wholly neglectful of them. Agatha was old enough to invite Dr Bowen and her mother to a nursery tea party (somewhat to Aelfrida's embarrassment, both little girls regarded him as a father-figure, their insistence that he visit being at odds with her own desire to discourage his attentions) and Alethea to walk with Aelfrida along the Backs to hear how her great-great-grandmother, great-grandmother, and grandmother 'each in their turn used to walk [there] with their little girls and tell them how they, when they were grown up should do so too' and that she too would one day take *her* little girl to walk there[15], but it was not until after her return to Cambridge that Aelfrida demonstrated overt enthusiasm for her 'splendid' children.[16]

Though lifting depression allowed her 'to have … the children with [her] more' (her prediction 'I wonder whether they will always give me the supreme joy that they do now or will it, in the end, be "no human consolations"?' would come true twenty years later)[17] and, prior to Constantine's return from Panama in spring 1913, to note that 'parents must put their children first'[18], her happiness was due less to her children than to the 'Indian Summer of youth' afforded by Little Friends ('it is when Constantine is harsh to me that the temptation to friendship with other men is so strong'[19] was her

excuse for associating with them) and to her championship of Cambridge Poets in general and Frank Stokoe and Aleister Crowley in particular.

Preoccupation with persons not her daughters when emotionally distanced from them for nearly a year did not augur well for Paris. Nor did a comparison between her (ostensible) preference for 'self-sacrifice' and Constantine's desire for 'self-realisation'[20] cause her to wonder if pursuing an unmediated relationship with God might result in Agatha, Alethea, and Constantine being sacrificed, not herself. Hence although Aelfrida spent more time with her daughters in Le Vésinet and recorded the 'sweet doings' of the 'enthralling' little girls in their respective *Record Books*[21], the *concentrated* nature of time spent in their company suggests she compressed it as much as possible in order to leave more for her own pursuits. True, this might have been so of any middle-class mother of that era, but Aelfrida's pursuits were not those of an ordinary middle-class mother: writing her 'Emden novel' as an impassioned exposé of her married life to date; practising 'mantra yoga' and the Lesser Ritual of the Pentagram; reading 'Crowleyana'; undergoing overwhelming spiritual experiences ('*Atmadarshana*' on 11 July 1913; the '*Arcanum Arcanorum*' epiphany of 10 December 1913); corresponding with Little Friends whose letters suggested she was "not as far away from [their] thoughts as [she] ought to have been".[22] While, therefore, she was physically present in her daughters' lives, it seems she remained as preoccupied and as emotionally disengaged as before.

How much the children knew of her 'Guru's' influence over their mother is open to conjecture (there are no photographs of him in her diaries and albums though she tells us he sent her at least one) but that Alethea at least knew of him is demonstrated by her curiously mature remark of August 1914 that Frank Stokoe was 'jealous' of 'Mr Aleister Crowley'. Evidence is also provided by the 'Lily-Billy book', begun in Paris in November 1913[23] shortly after Constantine forced his wife to break off her 'discipular' relationship, in which Aelfrida recounts and illustrates a parable explaining her recent behaviour: 'Billy' is caught by a 'string-tree' in a magician's garden. 'Lily' asks the magician to free him. The magician, whose robes bear symbols associated with Ceremonial Magic (zodiacal signs and those for male and female, pentagrams, snakes, the sun and moon, geometrical figures, even the *lingam* and *yoni*), calls on the star, wind, fire, and water fairies in turn but none is able to do so and it is left to 'scissor-fairies' to cut him loose.[24]

There is, too, a curious lack of comment in Aelfrida's diary concerning Constantine's reaction to the publication (also in November 1913) of *Cambridge Poets*

*1900–1913* in which Crowley's poems figure so prominently. Although she notes her delight in showing a copy to daughters who 'seemed to appreciate what it was all about'[25], omission of comments by her husband suggests his reaction was less appreciative than theirs. With what embarrassment must Constantine have read Crowley's poem *The Challenge* ("Your lips are gathered up to mine / Your bosom heaves with fearful breath") even if assured by his wife that the lady in question was not herself and that the poem was written long before she met Frater Perdurabo, or Frank Stokoe's *The Mad Magician* ("Now you have seen me – now the surprise / Dawns in the dark of your dreaming eyes"), knowing that his wife and Crowley had met? (There were, too, Aelfrida's own poems hinting at real or possible infidelities with another 'King's Man' and that the man "whose love had made / My life an ecstasy of joy and pain" was her husband.) It must have taken a determined effort on the Grahams' part if their daughters enjoyed the Christmas (almost their last together as a family) described by their mother as 'all of us … being mutually loving and keeping each other's hearts warm in the way one must in winter'[26]; indeed, one wonders if it were not more of a winter of discontent than a season of goodwill and if girls of five and three were not more aware of discord between their parents than their mother would have us think.

The discord may have been apparent to Ovvie too (she had, after all been in the Grahams' employment during the 'Juanita' row in Emden, Aelfrida's accusations of infanticide levelled at Constantine following Agneta's death, and arguments ending in physical violence triggered by Aleister Crowley's presence in her mistress's life, and may have guessed at or seen something of the latter's yogic and 'magick' practices), for she left at very short notice in January 1914 shortly after Constantine departed for England on Boxing Day 1913; her sister Dorothy left in April 1914 during the period of wrangling which followed Constantine's return, saying she was 'wanted at home'.[27] Octavie alone replaced them.

Constantine's departure so soon after Christmas on 'leave' (he was absent for over five weeks) may have been genuine but circumstantial evidence reads oddly when reviewed in the light of Alethea's and Agatha's childhood. Aelfrida and the girls did not accompany him. He did not visit Hessle but stayed at Fordfield conferring, it seems, with the Oracle and Chiara about their daughter's recent behaviour in relation to Aleister Crowley and his disclosures resulted in the Oracle writing a critical letter to Aelfrida concerning her conduct and Chiara coming to Paris to observe it for herself. In his absence Eustace arrived at Le Vésinet, having been sent to stay with his sister while Constantine conferred with her parents and,

pending Octavie's and Chiara's arrival, to ensure that she took proper care of Agatha and Alethea and did not re-align herself with Aleister Crowley or take up with another unsuitable 'guru'. And for the next twenty years Aelfrida was never left alone for more than a few hours, a conspiracy, it may be, on the part of parents anxious to ensure that she could never again lapse into behaviour as deviant (in their eyes) as that she exhibited in Paris for fear of the harm it might cause to her young daughters.

It may be, too, that her behaviour in Paris was so manifestly strange that, far from abandoning her in Le Vésinet, Constantine was forced to forbid her to leave unless under his supervision (it also seems that he intercepted her mail, returning correspondence of which he disapproved to its sender) but that even then she behaved inappropriately: having informed her husband that during visionary experiences she had received wisdom concerning which she '*could* not rightly remain silent', she then admitted that in not keeping silent, she had 'been a fool'.[28] Perhaps she expatiated on her 'Great Work' or "preach[ed] to people" connected with the Consulate or "hand[ed] tracts about at the Ambassador's dinners"[29], actions which would make matters worse between herself and her husband and lay him open to official rebuke. It may be too, that preliminary explorations of her 'mystic way' *had* unfitted her 'for looking after [her] girls'[30], possibly to the extent of her becoming as negligent in supervising their care as she was over seeing that her husband's boots were mended 'and all that sort of thing', and that it was not until Constantine forcibly pointed out deficits in her wifely and motherly duties (from hinted evidence in a later poem of his wife's we may deduce that he filed an affidavit during divorce proceedings in which such deficits were listed) that she became aware of how negligent she had been (a point underlined in 1916 by Anatolia, a frequent visitor to Le Vésinet, in her comment regarding the disorganised state of the house) and tried to make amends by becoming 'dreadfully particular'[31] in one respect and by writing the 'Lily-Billy' story in another. If this is so (and though conjectural, it is supported by evidence provided by Aelfrida herself), the outbreak of the Great War in August 1914 was fortunate in one respect: it removed Aelfrida and her children to Fordfield, a house in which the girls' welfare could be supervised by their maternal grandparents.

Even so, two bright girls were unlikely to be oblivious of increasing tension between their parents, for the emotional magnitude of the row and rape of October 1914 and Constantine's admission of adultery in February 1918 must have sent shocks through their mother's sensibilities sufficient to make them aware that she was both unhappy and concealing something from them ('we all pretended everything was all right') and that 'this cloud of impending war hanging over us'[32] referred as much to internecine as to international battles. There was, too, the unsettling effect of more 'goodbysomeness': in January 1915 the girls' Uncle Eustace departed for the trenches ('"Dadi" in uniform delighted [Alethea and Agatha] beyond measure')[33] and in April 1915 their father ('Father, never Daddy')[34] to Amsterdam, not to return for over a year. ('Uncle Dudu' returned from civilian imprisonment in May 1915 but did not then play as important a role in the girls' lives as their bachelor uncle and would-be bachelor father.) Aelfrida too was frequently absent in mind or in body, for 1915-1918 were years of gripping 'mystical adventures', of the start of her lecturing, 'straightening', and writing careers, of her unwilled experiences as a medium, and of the onset of severe ill-health, and 'kiddie-minding' in Octavie's absence was an unwelcome chore. Perhaps it seemed to Agatha and Alethea that their mother had more time for other people (chiefly 'Dr Tommy', 'dear Hubert', and Fidelio) than themselves, a reason calling her 'horrid mother', 'seldom [caring] for petting', and showing a preference for 'being noticed' to 'being loved'.[35]

Materially, the girls lacked nothing; indeed, their childhood seems as rich as that enjoyed by their mother and uncles. Pets (guinea pigs, tortoises, goats, and Leo, the 'marmalade soodler ... nicer than any other cat in the world and more beautiful and cleverer'[36], whose early death upset them far more than Olive Mudie-Cook's very recent suicide)[37], lavish presents, bicycles, and private tuition in music, dancing, and Swedish drill (gymnastics) were provided. The large Fordfield garden was their playground. Stories were read aloud to them (*The Would-be-goods* rather than *The Water Babies)* by a mother sitting in the same chair as the one in which Chiara sat with Conrad on her lap to read to his older brother and sister. Poetry books were written for and about them[38] and they were introduced to eminent visitors, Sir James Frazer taking 'benevolent notice'[39] of them long after the girls' unprompted rendition of the entire list of illustrations in their 'Birdie Book' ('they know all the bird's names by heart and can chant them like a psalm') caused the bemused anthropologist to exclaim that the performance (it lasted ten minutes) was "exactly like a primitive incantation".[40]

Aelfrida was (almost) correct in telling Fidelio that her 'ruling passion' was love of her children[41] – they came second to God, of course, with Constantine third – but it was now that her passion to rule every aspect of their lives first made itself manifest. (Alethea, 'loving [but] a child who has to fight her battles alone'[42], was harder to rule than 'little Bam' who, self-styled 'Saint Bam', was 'too good ... her actions are all sweetness'[43] and unlikely to give her mother the same cause for 'bitter reflection' as her elder sister.)[44] Her child-rearing methods, modelled on Chiara's, relied chiefly on moral pressure, a satisfactory measure so long as Agatha and Alethea were brought up in a manner in which 'good things'[45] were expected of rather than imposed on them but easily transformable into moral brain-washing by someone of Aelfrida's temperament. Hence although the girls were '*never* punished and hardly ever talked to gravely'[46] by their mother and only Constantine and Chiara administered timely smacks, it may be that short sharp shocks were preferred by two small girls insufficiently mature to cope with indoctrination: in Aelfrida's world (as 'Vera' tells 'Carola') "everything [was] labelled either "Right or Wrong" instead of, as "in most people's world ... Nice or Horrid "[47] and 'Carola' being so "morally exacting" meant that she expected her daughters "to rise to great moral heights" unattainable by children of four and six. ('Carola's' response was to state firmly that she was "not a bit exacting"[48] and that 'exaction' applied only to money or material goods, a wilful misunderstanding of 'Vera's' statement.) But Aelfrida's "strongest instinct [being] to alter people I love and try and pull them into the shape I fancy"[49] was one thing and her statement that her children were not corrected because correction afforded an opportunity for "the exercise of power" quite another, and although believed she corrected them "wisely and with tender restraint"[50], in practice she enacted one and exercised the other by the same peculiarly unpleasant means employed by Henry Joseph Wetenhall with regard to 'Little Katie' and by Catharine Tillyard to herself i.e. by withdrawing into brooding silences easily misinterpreted by little girls as a withdrawal of love which might never return. Though her silences were later dismissed by Aelfrida (as 'Carola') as mere "mistakes of tactics"[51] (Constantine, she wrote, was 'antagonised' by silences imposed by his 'cock-sure and opinionated' wife when he failed to meet her morally exacting standards)[52] which no sensible person could possibly take for "mistakes of love"[53], it is obvious that insidious and invidious moral pressures interspersed with disapproving silences and overladen with an all-pervading religiosity caused Agatha to become piously 'good' in the hope of retaining her mother's affection and Alethea to begin her retreat into a protective shell where neither withdrawal nor restoration of affection could disturb her, a shell given physical expression by the layer of fat which now began to surround her.

The girls' paternal grandmother may have noticed what was happening and tried to prevent it. During her tirade of July 1916, Anatolia accused Aelfrida of being a 'complete failure as [a] mother', of bringing up her daughters badly, and of being devoid of common sense, accusations to which Aelfrida (reluctantly) assented because Anatolia, though prone to eccentric pronouncements ("there is no Gawd but the Gawd within us [and] *I am* my own Gawd"[54] being one and not the oddest), was perspicacious about and 'loving and natural'[55] with her granddaughters and her recommendation that Alethea go to boarding school may have an attempt to separate mother and daughter to the latter's benefit. Realising the truth of this and of Anatolia's other accusations, Aelfrida's refusal to take Agatha and Alethea to Hessle two years later can be seen less as a desire to punish her unfaithful husband by thwarting his wishes ("I do not write orders for fun or to be passed over in silence [regarding] our children's visit to my people", he wrote furiously)[56] and more as an intention never to allow Anatolia (always 'Anatolia', never 'grandmother'; Argyris was 'grandfather', never 'Argyris') the opportunity to 'embitter' (*sic*) Agatha and Alethea by exposing the myth of their parents' 'perfect' marriage and the role their mother played in its failure. It may be, too, that it was less because the girls might be exposed to Anatolia's peculiar brand of religion (proclamations about 'Gawd' could be easily refuted) that Aelfrida 'dare not expose [them] to her influence'[57], pleading 'the patriotic duty of not travelling', 'the danger from the flu epidemic', and 'expense' and more because she felt she '*must*'[58] protect her children from learning the truth about herself. She succeeded; Agatha never met Anatolia again and Alethea only briefly before Aelfrida prevented further contact by a timely fit of interventional hysterics.

Anatolia's admonitions could be dismissed as no more than further manifestations of her desire to disengage her son from his 'miserable marriage' to a woman of whom she had never approved (we are never told the reasons for her disapproval; it arose soon after prospective mother-in-law first met prospective daughter-in-law) and to remove her grandchildren from their mother's 'clutches' and 'blighting influence'[59] (we are never given details of the 'blight'), were it not that the girls' maternal grandparents too began to urge a degree of separation. They began by insisting that the girls enter formal education at Cambridge schools.

By September 1914, Alethea, aged six and already 'mature and dignified' ('and big'), was beginning to resent being a girl-child expected to be one of the "dear little things"[60] among whom her 'dainty looking'[61] younger sister with her ability to make herself 'adorably pretty'[62] was already numbered. The Oracle's suggestion that Alethea attend the kindergarten class at the Perse School for Girls was dismissed by Aelfrida because she did not

want her 'mature' daughter 'to dawdle over baby-lessons and think it work'[63] but her own plan of sending Alethea early in 1916 to small morning classes run by an ex-Newnhamite who had 'thoroughly sensible ideas about teaching' ('I rather mind letting Alethea's education out of my hands but … must be the virtuous and self-effacing parent')[64] did not gain Alethea's approval. She reacted by becoming 'turbulent and rude' at Mrs Chapple's and more and more withdrawn at home.

To Mrs Chapple, Aelfrida pretended that Alethea's turbulence was due to boredom and asked that her daughter be 'worked a little harder'[65] but to herself acknowledged that her own distant and distancing behaviour was a contributing factor. She therefore decided to spend more time with her elder daughter (Chiara spent more time with both girls than their mother) but other than noting that 'children need their mother's constant love as plants need sunshine', took few practical measures to remedy the situation.[66] She then discovered that the child described as 'a lovely radiant girl'[67] weighed twenty-one pounds more than was normal for her age, seemed to hate 'to feel or show any emotion'[68], and would only let her mother close when she had 'little' (*sic*) sorrows. (Aelfrida and Agatha, on the other hand, shared '*special intimacies*'.)[69] A move in January 1917 to a larger school 'patronised by the elite of Cambridge'[70] proved more successful, Alethea becoming less 'turbulent' in a more structured environment. Agatha, beginning formal education at the same school at the same time, revelled in escaping 'play-lessons' at home and in being placed in a class of girls up to three years older than herself. Both overrode Aelfrida's insistence that they not do homework (lest, presumably, they react as paranoidally to it as she had at their age) by begging to be allowed to do it because they enjoyed independent study so much.

The improvement in Alethea's behaviour was dramatic. Although Mrs Berry's school was (according to Aelfrida) a 'go-as-you-please' institution and Alethea (like Agatha) attended for only two hours a day (Aelfrida does not say whether this was for health or financial reasons), she was suddenly transformed into a 'wonderfully handsome and intelligent' girl demonstrating a tomboyish love of sport and considerable creativity, including poetic composition. Her tenth birthday on 22 August 1918 found her temper 'much improved', her personality more expansive (she had been 'too solemn and too wise' two years earlier), and in excellent health. (Her faults, Aelfrida noted, without realising how similar they were to her own, were selfishness, a tendency to exaggerate, 'want of consideration in little things', censoriousness, and a noted '*esprit de contradiction*'.)[71] But Alethea's statement that "when I am grown up … I mean to be independent – more independent than you think possible"[72] predicted storms to come and reads ironically when juxtaposed to an almost contemporary statement by Aelfrida that both children were 'nearly always good and reasonable now' because they had regained 'complete confidence' in her and that as a result she herself was 'a *very* happy mother'.[73]

Constantine's 'edict of separation' was heralded by not wanting to see much of his daughters when on leave in spite of their being 'sweet and loving and prettily behaved' (he was also afraid of his elder daughter's 'outspokenness' with regard to his relationship with her mother)[74] and by looking forward 'to the family ceasing to be the social unit'[75], but as early as October 1918 his intention of separating himself from his own 'family unit' was manifest by his omitting to reply to Agatha's weekly letters. (Aelfrida received a 'torrent of abuse' regarding his daughter's 'lack of respect' when Agatha refused to write to him if he did not write to her.)[76] Within a few months both girls' 'Sunday letters' were returned unopened if Aelfrida addressed the envelopes. Alethea's eleventh birthday on 23 August 1919 was ignored completely and shortly thereafter communication ceased.

Aelfrida does not say how (or indeed if) she explained to her daughters the need for 'exile' in Hunstanton from October 1919 to June 1920. It is possible she provided no explanation at all, explaining their 'naughty and wild' behaviour in terms of her own mental unrest ('I don't think I've been *outwardly* cross or snappy but … I have been troubled and anxious and perhaps a little inattentive')[77] instead of the uncertainty felt by two young girls suddenly removed from familiar and spacious surroundings and the company of doting grandparents to a cramped and unfamiliar house in which formerly strong and gentle Oracle became frail, blind, and crotchety and serene and competent Chiara sickly and shrewish at the point when their grand-daughters needed extra stability and support. School helped, for although Aelfrida was derogatory about their 'simple school' with 'absurdly old fashioned' teaching methods[78], it seems they enjoyed the change from Mrs Berry's educational hothouse to one where they mixed with ordinary Norfolk girls.

Even in Hunstanton – or perhaps, given closer proximity to their mother, *particularly* in Hunstanton – Agatha and Alethea realised something was amiss. In spite of Chiara's insistence that the girls should be everyone's 'unique preoccupation'[79], the shoal of letters which arrived following newspaper reports of Aelfrida's application for restitution of conjugal rights and her own 'profoundly distressed thinking' about her daughters ('what sorrow awaits them!') penetrated Alethea's consciousness at least. Her mother's frantic question 'how shall I ever

tell them!'[80] being answered by the decision to tell them nothing, Alethea, "apparently … absorbed in her school and her friendships and her games, was terribly well-informed concerning the relationship of her parents".[81]

Although Alethea later complained that Aelfrida had 'kept [her] pretty much in the dark as regards your affairs and Fuvver's' [82], the fact that her elder daughter had been 'so particularly loving and sympathetic' in her 'recent troubles' demonstrates that Alethea had 'guessed' (possibly even discovered) a 'great deal'[83] of what had transpired, something which would not have been difficult for an intelligent girl and because the family's return to Cambridge preceded the Grahams' divorce. Their return also resulted in attendance at Miss Borrer's school in Trumpington Street whose 'short hours, small classes and "intensive" teaching' may have 'suited them exactly'[84] but where the presence of a divorcee's children created something of a furore. From servants' gossip, school friends' tittle-tattle, or overheard conversations between adult members of the family from which details (omitted from her diary) of Aelfrida's appearance in the divorce court could be garnered in seedy detail, much could be learnt: Constantine (as 'Adrian') consorting in the Midland Hotel at St Pancras Station with a complaisant "cashier from a restaurant", Aelfrida (as 'Carola') having to identify her husband's "fine bold handwriting" in the hotel register ("Mr and Mrs Adrian Le Maitre")[85] or listen to her own begging letter read out in court, a letter which Hal Verey (as 'Mr Greene', 'Carola's' lawyer) wished had been "a trifle more – conventional".[86] And which appeared in the press.

Feeling 'widowed' as a result of her divorce, Aelfrida did what many widows do: she began "to burden her older child … with confidences and responsibilities … not easy for [her] to bear"[87] and to cast a daughter whose personality and mannerisms were like Constantine's in the role of surrogate 'husband'. (In *O Passionate World,* it is 'Carola's' boy-child 'Robin' who is expected to adopt 'Adrian's' role as paterfamilias but who feels inferior because unable to do so to 'Carola's' satisfaction; his role is subsequently taken over by older and more dominant 'Vera'.) Not only this, but as a result of being treated as incompetent by her own parents, Carola/Aelfrida lost all belief "in her own competence [and] in her power to deal high-handedly with life"[88] and turned to 'sturdy Alethea' to be "steadied and braced"[89], Alethea responding by surrounding her mother with "protective solicitude, as though she had been the mother and [Aelfrida] the vulnerable child".[90] It seems, too, that seeing her sister cast in the role of protector, it was to Alethea rather than to Aelfrida that Agatha turned for support when 'precious Temu' became aware that "home was not as it used to be [and] mother was under a cloud"[91] and Alethea who informed her sister of their father's departure from their lives and organised diversions to prevent her from moping.

The effect of enforced role reversal on Alethea was dramatic. Subduing her own emotional needs in favour of expending emotional energy on her mother's behalf forced her to make the kind of decisions that adult Aelfrida should have made for herself. She also bore the brunt of Aelfrida's thwarted desires and consequent mood-swings, not all of which were confided (as they ought to have been) solely to her diary or to another adult, and provided insightful dissection of her behaviour: "you aren't meant to be a widow or a spinster, or whatever it is you are going to turn into. Any man who happens to be near sees that [and] if there's a gap he wants to fill it ... It isn't their fault or yours, it is just the way you are made".[92] At the same time she was left to fight the battles of adolescence alone, Aelfrida behaving towards her surrogate 'husband' exactly as she had behaved towards her real one, making herself unavailable when support was needed and showing irritation when Alethea played 'at being a little girl again' and shadowed her exasperated mother round Fordfield like a pet dog[93] to attract attention. She also, having discovered that 'rude and boisterous' behaviour failed to engage her mother positively, tried to behave more like her 'saintly' younger sister, but failing to maintain so foreign an attitude, reverted to behaviour verging on the hoydenish.

When Constantine threatened to exert his legal right to custody of his children, Aelfrida began to evince extreme anxiety at the prospect of separation from them even if for only a short time and if aware that either or both were in a place of safety, according them less independence than she herself had enjoyed at their age. (Once persuaded by her guardian angel that her children would be all right without her, Carola/Aelfrida "would have unhesitatingly taken her own life" in the dark days following her divorce.)[94] The threat of Constantine removing her daughters from her care having receded following his departure for South America, Aelfrida's fears abated though she remained 'never *quite* happy'[95] when Agatha and Alethea were out of her sight or felt 'happy *all through*'[96] until they were restored to it. Uneasiness manifested itself in dreams in which Constantine tried to abduct his daughters and to shoot her when she resisted[97] ('I hope', she added, 'this does not mean that he thinks hate-thoughts of me. Why should he?') but did not prevent her from sending them abroad as they grew older and she wanted time to herself. (And the likelihood of abduction receded. She continued to act over-protectively by letter, however.) The years following her decree absolute also saw her become more and more emotionally enmeshed with her daughters as she disengaged her emotions from her ex-husband ('I feel absolutely lost when my girls are away [even] for a day')[98] with predictable results: she herself began once again 'to live [only] through them'[99] and Agatha and Alethea became so ensnared by their mother's emotional neediness that they exhibited anxiety symptoms whenever she threatened, openly or by implication, to break the chains of co-dependency which bound them to her.

None of this was apparent to people who congratulated Aelfrida on the 'intelligent and industrious' daughters[100] in whose company she was conspicuously seen in the hope that their presence would ease her back into Cambridge society. Alethea's thirteenth birthday on 23 August 1921 found her mother describing her as 'strong and handsome, resolute, keen, intelligent, quick of perception, warm-hearted, always vivid and interesting'[101] but as having 'many a hard lesson to learn for she is self-centred for all her generosity and her intellectual interests and her powers of affection' and that 'life will have to teach [Alethea] what I can't'.[102] (It did, and Aelfrida was not to approve of what it taught.) When Alethea reached puberty, Aelfrida also noted the development of 'shy depths of nature'[103], of which depths, however, she was largely ignorant because Alethea took care to conceal them from her. Of 'sweet Agatha'[104] we hear less, chiefly because a child of eleven who seemed 'to have been born in sympathy with God and with everyone she meets'[105] did not pose the same problems as a pubertal daughter concerning whom her mother emphasised that she was in spite of everything and a qualifying 'quite', a 'normal child'.[106]

Seizing the occasion of her first lengthy separation from Agatha and Alethea since her visit to Lyons in 1919 (the girls had been allowed a short holiday in Farnham with great-aunt Norah Crundwell during which Agatha wept copiously, Alethea behaved stoically, and their mother would have pined more had she not been about to embark on a lecture series), Aelfrida thought long and hard about how best to bring up her 'sweet kiddies'[107] in the absence of a father. Having 'got new light on the way to be the wisest possible mother to them'[108] as a 'Single Parent', she listed the means by which she intended to achieve this. Some were wise ('to foster their interest in everything that is lovely'; to encourage them to do 'what is comely' by putting 'the right paths before their eager feet', and to provide 'the right books' to enable them to follow those paths) but some seem sinister: to decide their 'amusements [and] occupations' and even their 'conversations' for them and 'to perfect their relationship' to herself, relationships with family, friends, strangers, the world, and even Deity taking second place.[109]

Alfred and Catharine Tillyard's 'constant criticism' of Aelfrida's arrangements for her daughters' education intensified as Alethea neared thirteen and the question of secondary education arose. Aelfrida herself was violently opposed to 'the noise and promiscuity and "bounce" of the modern High School'[110], chiefly because it had not suited herself and because she believed that secondary education concerned itself too much with social values (e.g. the importance of team-work and of service to others) at the expense of spiritual values and encouraged the training of mental faculties (the ability to organise, concrete thinking, and so on) at the expense of those which dealt with 'spiritual exercises' and with the growth of the spirit. Chiara's determination that both granddaughters attend the Perse School for Girls won the day: Aelfrida 'succumbed to the commonplace'[111] (reluctantly), sending first Alethea, then Agatha, to what she called 'a poor place but the best that Cambridge can provide'.[112]

Alethea, entering the Perse in September 1922, took to its noise and promiscuity and bounce like a duck to water, her mother noting with puzzlement two months later that her elder daughter was 'a good deal younger than she was a year ago' and wondering why.[113] A peep at Alethea's diary would have told her; volumes supposedly filled with religious cogitations occasioned by the spiritual awakening which complemented even if it did not exactly coincide with the onset of puberty, were crammed with girlish interests: team games, body awareness ('yes I am pretty big and pretty fat')[114], intense friendships (significantly, Alethea was attracted to 'gentle, womanly … maternal'[115] girls rather than to the popular or flamboyant objects of the usual schoolgirl 'crush'), teachers' foibles, lessons, holidays, animals, clothes, and, eventually, boys. In fact, she blossomed as never before, for the Perse provided welcome respite from her overpowering but dependent mother, clinging sister (there is little about either in contemporary volumes of her diary and nothing about her absent father save the wonder if 'Fuvver was dead' and a description of her feelings – 'they tell me I'm like him in character'[116] – on discovering one of his books on a Cambridge bookstall), hypercritical grandparents, and disagreeable Uncle Julius. Agatha's comment of September 1925 says it all: 'from being a rather plain and quite clever little girl [Alethea] has come to be handsome and [brilliant]'.[117]

A mother who regarded her elder daughter more as 'the Venus de Milo than a fashion plate'[118] and who believed Alethea when she said she was 'not in the least intellectual'[119], was surprised when a neighbour described her daughter's hair, skin, and hands as "wonderfully beautiful"[120] and when one of Alethea's thoughtful imagistic poems (*The Wanderer*) was chosen for *The New Cambridge*,

an anthology published in May 1925.[121] She was relieved however, that fifteen-year-old Alethea's 'passion [for] Literature'[122] was 'so much … saner and healthier'[123] than her own obsessions at that age and that 'Alethea's adolescence [was] so little like adolescence in books – or like mine was' (Alethea, unlike adolescent Frida, seemed to have 'no morbid feelings, no tendencies to gloom and queer phantasy')[124], though a woman who once believed she possessed the faculty of walking around inside her daughters' minds had to admit that mothers of adolescents 'don't see everything'.[125]

What Alethea's mother did not (or chose not) to see (or was prevented from seeing by Alethea herself) was the way in which her attitudes to men and to religion affected her daughter's. A comparison of their respective diary entries concerning an undergraduate (a recent 'patient' of the 'Straightener') attracted to Alethea shortly before her sixteenth birthday demonstrates the first only too well, Aelfrida warning her daughter 'about young men and friendship and love' and being particularly anxious (with her Greek blood, there was a danger of Alethea being highly sexed) lest Alethea mistake 'receiving attention' for 'serious affection'[126] (her next entry noted with horror the presence of a 'man' in Cambridge who advised young men on sexual matters and advocated 'complete unrestraint with the use of contraception to prevent consequences' and the danger of such unbridled conduct to 'my girls')[127], and Alethea noting coolly that considering her mother's 'own tragic mistake in the way of falling in love'[128] and her odd behaviour with regard to Willie Searle, her own dispassionate view of interpersonal relationships was infinitely preferable. (As she informed her mother, "I do not understand women who want to make a conquest of every man they meet. Most men's admiration is not worth having".)[129] So effective was Alethea's pose (and that it *was* a pose was recognised even by her mother: 'some people think Alethea *hard* … but her affections go down to the roots of her being')[130] that Aelfrida was (almost) persuaded to treat her elder daughter 'as a woman', to avoid further 'moral counsels'[131], and to stop ordering her about. It is therefore ironic that Aelfrida (as 'Carola') then decided that the only way for Alethea (as 'Vera') to "avoid her mother's mistakes" with regard to men would be for her to seize control of her daughter's life and to "earnestly and enthusiastically … set about building her future" (with a "perfect husband", of course)[132] and that Alethea avoided her mother's mistakes by excluding men from her life altogether, bitter experience being about to teach her that "love is tricky".[133]

Alethea's apparent indifference to religion – and particularly to her mother's brand of mystical religiosity – was a source of distress to the latter. Noting the day following Alethea's seventeenth birthday in 1925 that although her elder daughter was 'grown up physically and intellectually and nearly grown up morally and emotionally', in terms of spiritual development Alethea had not even 'been born' because her 'spiritual awakening' seemed further off than ever and 'the idea of dedicating herself and her life to God' un-thought, and her own feeling that she would feel 'much *safer*'[134] (*sic*) if she was sure Alethea was a committed Christian, Aelfrida was overjoyed to discover four months later that *both* daughters intended to join the Church of England: 'if they are *really* Christian I could die happy'.[135] Although her contemporaneous 'spiritual espousal' took precedence in her mind, life, and diary, she noted apropos Alethea that while the girl had a 'wish to live rightly' she had (as yet) 'no capacity for mystical experience'.[136] (On Alethea's eighteenth birthday Aelfrida noted that although her elder daughter had 'what the Americans call "poise"', she lacked 'mysticism'[137], but not having read entries in Alethea's diary emphasising that the latter had no intention of following her mother along the latter's 'mystic way' and that she concealed her religious beliefs from someone who muddied their clear waters by expounding idiosyncratic theosophies, she continued puzzled.) Apropos Agatha, whose bed was strewn with 'holy books' and whose piety was encouraged by her mother's gift of a 'holy medal' (Alethea received a book on tennis)[138], Aelfrida noted that to an 'introvert' like her younger daughter, mystic communion with God happened 'as naturally as breathing'; it did not, however, occur to her then and only dimly later that supposedly 'extrovert' Alethea, with her 'strong and noble' (but private) moral principles was genuinely and deeply religious, and that pious, compliant, and 'wonderfully spiritually minded'[139] Agatha manifested only a paler version of her mother's religiosity. Lacking the insight which would have enabled her to discriminate between Alethea's sterling religious qualities and Agatha's meretricious ones, Aelfrida was to be devastated by her discovery that a belief system so strong that it sustained her elder daughter through heavy trials was in her younger daughter's case so lacking in substance that Agatha would sink beneath the weight of lesser ones.

A major, and for all parties concerned, a significant switch in Aelfrida's affections took place soon after Alethea joined the Perse School in September 1922. Resentful, it may be, that the confines of Alethea's world had expanded to embrace an ambience different in almost every respect from that which she herself endeavoured to create and to maintain at Fordfield and of the diversion of Alethea's attention from herself to members of an institution she despised, and worried lest Alethea's 'hoydenish' behaviour result in the Grahams being asked to remove themselves from a house in which they lived on sufferance (the volume of the Oracle's complaints increased noticeably at this time and a five-hour tennis tournament for twelve Perseans held at Fordfield in May 1923 cannot have appealed to him), Aelfrida withdrew her affection from Alethea and bestowed it on Agatha instead. Agatha, she now believed, had 'the sweeter nature' of the two sisters[140], was 'strong in body and mind, high-spirited, intensely loving [and] intelligent' and 'spiritually minded'[141] and, unlike Alethea who was sometimes 'wilful' and exhibited 'carping and critical' moods unpleasantly reminiscent of her father's[142], was always co-operatively 'animated and talkative'.[143] She also began to evince towards 'infinitely precious Agatha' a love 'so intense that it hurts'[144] and to ensnare her younger daughter in the 'magic net' of her controlling affection to a suffocating extent.

Agatha began her diary (a gift from her mother) shortly before attending the Perse in September 1923. Much of it was devoted to school life ('topping', 'jolly', and 'swish' are favourite adjectives) but unlike Alethea, Agatha felt unable to 'put all [her] feelings and inmost thoughts into … diaries'.[145] (Some she did, admitting in September 1926 that she did not want to be either 'commonplace' or formidably 'highbrow' like her male Tillyard relatives.)[146] It was for this reason but using as an excuse that her life was transcribed in letters to absent members of the family, that she abandoned it shortly after leaving school on 30 July 1928. This is a pity insofar as we lose her voice at a significant period in her life (we find it again in her poetry but without the dimensionality and ease of dating afforded by diary entries) and because we lose everything but the earliest manifestations of what might have been a fruitful career as a writer, for Agatha, as her vivid and amusing letters demonstrate, was a wordsmith and was beginning to be aware of her capabilities as a poet – as witness her comment apropos travel by Underground that 'there is no fun going up an escalator' but that "*facilis descensus Averno*" ('the descent is rapid and agreeable') and her informing her mother (the recipient of the letter in which the phrase occurs) that 'you might well think that sentence is for future use'.[147]

Agatha's menarche in March 1926 was manifest by the onset of 'more excitable [and] less *balanced*' behaviour[148] worrying enough in itself but exacerbated by Alethea's departure in April to pursue pre-Girton studies at the Sorbonne. (Agatha, Aelfrida noted, looked 'pathetic' during her older sister's absence[149], as well she might, deprived of moral support and consigned to the exclusive and claustrophobic devotion of a mother in her early forties and to elderly grandparents who resented her presence.) The dramatic transformation in Alethea's appearance as a result of her Paris sojourn (it also manifested transformations rather more than skin deep) and her subsequent departure for a more independent life at Girton, caused Agatha and Aelfrida to feel 'desolate'[150] and the latter to suffer a psychosomatic recrudescence of rheumatoid arthritis. At this point Aelfrida decided her younger daughter needed 'more watching'[151] and set herself to do so. And to endeavour to become 'more intimate' still with the 'single daughter'[152] left at home.

An interesting portrait of the Graham girls at this juncture in their lives drawn by an acute and independent observer is found in Albert Erlande's novel *Edmée Combres,* conceived between January and April 1926 and published in 1927. Aelfrida and her daughters had spent several weeks with the Erlandes in 1925 and, following Agatha's and Aelfrida's arrival in Paris early in July 1926, they and transformed Alethea ('elegant without becoming vain or silly' and described by elderly Zelle to a woman she still called 'petite Frida' as a 'pearl of a daughter')[153] travelled to Perros Guirec for the holiday during which 'Madame Graham' had her second momentous encounter with M. Erlande. Alethea having stayed with the Erlandes during her sojourn in Paris, Albert Erlande must have noted her transformation with a connoisseur's eye but one of Aelfrida's excuses for flirting with Erlande, namely that it would prevent him making a pass at her slimmed-down, shingled, and sexy elder daughter, was either effective or unnecessary, for Erlande made no amatory move in Alethea's direction. He put her (and her sister) in a novel instead.

*Edmée Combres* describes the devastating effect on a Parisian family of a female visitor whose domineering influence blights the lives of its members and how the mother realises too late that her complaisance has contributed to the tragedy. Erlande's depiction of the family's two sons is fascinating insofar as it appears to depict the Graham girls as Agatha and Alethea were at that time. Alethea/Oliver is described as rather heavily built (*un peu lourd*, which 'Venus de Milo' Alethea was still), rosy cheeked, curly haired, dimpled (her *fossettes* were one of Alethea's most charming features), and with a candid gaze, Agatha/Lucien as thinner, more highly strung (*plus nerveux*), dark-eyed like her/his father, and given to regarding the world in a speculative manner.[154] Not content, however, with depicting her daughters, Erlande also depicts their mother as 'Denise', a woman takes pride in proclaiming her partiality (*faiblesse*) for her children, declares that she always takes their part, never punishes them or allows them to be punished, rarely requires them to take responsibility for their actions, and never reproaches them for misdemeanours.[155] At the same

time, however, her allowing 'Edmée', her elder sister, to wrest control of her children's lives from her demonstrates how cleverly, here as elsewhere, Erlande depicts different aspects of Aelfrida's character – in this instance the greedy, the sentimental, and the controlling – in different characters in the same story[156]; he also bases his physical description of 'Edmée' on Aelfrida as a woman in her forties, grey-haired, and wearing reading glasses. Even more significant is that 'Lucien's' suicide note begs his now-widowed mother *not* to behave towards 'Olivier' as his "pal" (*camarade*) but as his "mother and friend" (*sa mère et son ami*) because it is axiomatic that a 'pal' lacks the maturity of judgement with which a friend or mother should guide a child's behaviour.[157] Possibly in the hope that Aelfrida would read and heed his advice, Erlande wrote in a disclaimer placed prominently on the first page of the novel that although *Edmée Combres* could be read for pleasure as one might read a newspaper article (*un simple faits-divers*) or a character-study, those inclined to look on the dark side of life (*les esprits plus chagrins*) should take it as an object-lesson (*un enseignement*) in how not to behave.[158] Aelfrida may have read the book; she certainly failed to follow Erlande's advice.

Her initial attempts to control Agatha's excitable and unbalanced behaviour took the form of continually advising her daughter to rest, advice which exasperated the sporty adolescent ('I am always treated as if I were delicate [and] expected to be exhausted')[159] and produced no perceptible results. Agatha herself attributed her changed behaviour to the onset of severe pain in her grandfather's eyes early in October 1926 (probably glaucoma induced by atherosclerotic hypertension), this making the Oracle 'snap'[160] at her more viciously than usual and resulting in the enucleation of his worst affected eye, and causing her to state that she 'depended just then on school for my amusement and was noisy [there] because I couldn't be at home'. But, she added, 'Alethea's going to Girton made a difference [too]'.[161]

In fact, Alethea's departure for Girton (three miles distant but a world away as far as her younger sister was concerned) induced separation anxiety in a sister with whom she had had an almost parasitically close relationship (a relationship which Agatha now felt obliged to defend on weekend visits whose amusing and gossipy 'Sunday teas' were spoiled by 'horrid and uncomfortable' feelings induced by Chiara's and the Oracle's intolerant behaviour towards Alethea)[162] and who was now suffocating under the weight of undiluted affection from a mother who had previously preferred her older sister. There was also Agatha's recent rediscovery of the father whose favourite 'Agata' she had been but whose first epistolary contact was with her sister, an event bound to increase the emotional ambivalences by which she was surrounded.

Unwilling or unable to express herself to people, Agatha tried to relieve her feelings in her diary ('I wish I were healthier – and the wishing [itself] is unhealthy. I don't mean I am morbid …')[163] but could barely be bothered to do so. (She attributed this to feeling 'horribly lazy' as a consequence of influenza early in January 1927 but her tendency to be 'languid and disinclined to do what I was told' antedates this.) In the same entry she describes her behaviour between October and December 1926 as 'moody [and] rather rebellious' and notes that she 'got into a good many rows [at school] and was altogether made to feel rather a rebel' as a result. (Erlande's perceptive eyes discerned the change in Agatha's behaviour as early as August 1926 and, much to her surprise, for she regarded herself as a conformist, nicknamed her "Agatha *la revoltée*".)[164] Aelfrida, preoccupied with the deleterious effect on her own health of her fragmenting relationship with Willie Searle, noted only that Agatha had become 'grave beyond her years'[165] but awoke early in 1927 to the fact that the real reason for the change in her younger daughter's behaviour stemmed less from being "sensitive and not gifted with over much self-control"[166] and more from missing Alethea 'so much'.[167]

Believing that the best means of curing the 'grave' mood which had overtaken her younger daughter and worried, it may be, that Agatha's symptoms indicated an inclination towards the 'morbid' frame of mind which had attacked herself at the same age, Aelfrida settled on a cure: 'to see that [Agatha and Alethea] see lots of each other' during the long university summer vacation.[168] To achieve this, however, it was necessary for Agatha 'to get out of school'[169] early in order that both girls might be together for two weeks in Switzerland (Aelfrida's admission that she sent the girls abroad for their 'health' gains yet another dimension here) but this required a doctor's certificate. Joan Cooper was therefore asked to provide Agatha with both a certificate and an alibi. (Aelfrida does not say if she confided her worries concerning her younger daughter to Dr Cooper but curious gaps in her narrative suggest she did.) Somewhat to Agatha's puzzlement, for she was of upright carriage and completely asymptomatic, Dr Cooper found her spine 'wasn't straight', diagnosed latent scoliosis as the cause of her being 'languid and lazy', and predicted that with the help of remedial 'gym and massage' by a local 'medical gymnast', she would return from Switzerland 'very energetic and all'.[170]

Miss Lavén's treatment[171] was successful almost immediately ('I am much better and I'm feeling very cheerful')[172], as well it might be on someone whose postviral lethargy had lifted and whose spine was essentially normal, but Aelfrida remained worried because of the financial implications of a lengthy course of treatment (Agatha was to continue 'remedial exercises' for five years, albeit more and more resentfully) and because of the implications of Agatha's 'curvature of the spine'.[173] (The euphemism employed by Aelfrida with regard to her younger daughter's emotional problems has interesting connotations: her concern regarding the condition of 'Agatha's back' seems to be a projection of her fear that Agatha was growing up psychologically 'crooked', would never be 'perfectly well' and, failing marriage to some 'good young man'[174], would lack sufficient 'backbone', as the expression went, to make her own way in the world.) Not daring to subject Agatha to psychotherapy for fear of what this might reveal of her own and Constantine's role in their daughter's emotional 'curvature', Aelfrida decided to protect her as much as possible for as long as possible by ensuring that Agatha be 'not allowed to *stand*'[175] alone, literally for a short time and metaphorically for years, regardless of the emotional cost ('every atom and particle of one's love … vibrates in anguish')[176] to herself. And to Agatha.

For Aelfrida to make sacrifices on Agatha's behalf was one thing; for her to sacrifice Alethea's happiness on Agatha's behalf quite another, but this she now proceeded to do. June 1927 began with everyone 'gay and in high spirits'.[177] Agatha seemed happier and a play written, produced, and acted by herself and her best friend Helen Tansley was voted by the Perse 'a *grand* success'. Alethea was predicted (and achieved: 'Great rejoicing!')[178] a first class pass in the first part of her tripos. Fidelio, absent from Fordfield for many months, returned 'as intimate as if he had been here every day for a year'.[179] Aelfrida herself was 'contented and passionately grateful'[180] that things were going well. Then the blow fell. On 11 June, Alethea's 'most intimate friend Olga Liebowitz was killed in a motor accident'.[181]

Olga Liebowitz was the 'pleasant, intellectual, quiet little Jewess'[182] who graced Fordfield Sunday tea-parties and Alethea's 'tender, fantastic, wholly delightful' friend and confidante with whom she had recently spent a happy holiday in France and to whom she was so devoted she was 'afraid of loving [Olga] too much'.[183] Olga's 'sudden and cruel'[184] death devasted Alethea not only because of its unexpectedness but also because 'all sorts of things combined to make the day specially pathetic': 11 June was Olga's birthday and Alethea had sent presents which Olga did not live to receive; Saturday being the Jewish Sabbath, Olga should have attended synagogue, but being 'too *complaisante*', was 'talked into' a trip to London with two male undergraduates and another 'Girton girl and having been refused an exeat by Miss Major, should not have been in the car at all; Alethea had begged her not to go and blamed herself for not insisting that Olga stay behind.[185] Worse still, the accident need never have happened: "an unconfirmed report says that one of the girls was offering the driver some chocolates and he let go of the steering wheel for a moment", the car skidded, mounted the kerb, overturned, and Olga and one of the undergraduates was killed.[186] Worst of all, the girl who distracted the driver was Olga herself.

Alethea, wrote her mother, 'feels Olga's death very deeply … she says very little but … goes away quietly and cries'.[187] So what did she do? Finding the girl in tears, she pretended to think her sorrowing daughter was suffering from a cold and rather than offer her quiet time at home to grieve, sent Alethea and Agatha as previously planned to Switzerland two weeks after Olga's death on a trip on which it had been intended that Olga go too, salving her conscience with the thought that it was '*right* that the girls should go' because it would be 'good for their health [and] for their character'.[188] There was, it seems, no question of the trip being cancelled – it was more important that Agatha and Alethea 'should spend some time together' – and besides, Aelfrida herself wanted time and space to revise *Spiritual Exercises* and to prepare for her first Summer School.

Though pleased that Olga's death or the Swiss holiday or both brought Agatha and Alethea 'closer to each other' again, Aelfrida was soon aware that a new barrier had been erected between herself and nineteen-year-old and seemingly 'self-reliant' Alethea: there were now even fewer exchanges of intimacies between them and the girls being 'closer to each other' did not mean that one of them was closer to her mother.[189] In spite of this she blithely began a new volume of her diary by informing her future biographer that although it was difficult to predict 'what is "special" and what isn't', at the time of writing she had 'nothing special to say'.[190]

She soon had. On 15 October 1927 and within a few days of Alethea's return from a visit of condolence to Olga's mother, the first 'interview' for nine years between Constantine and his daughters took place, after which Agatha watched her father shake off the light, not knowing in the misty twilight if he was of the dead or of the living but fearing he had vanished over the edge of the world never to be seen again. (Constantine, of course, had no idea of Alethea's misery or Agatha's disturbed mood and would probably have acted as he did in any case.) Agatha reacted to the episode by composing poems describing her emotions on meeting and parting from her father and other poetry so dark that its tone surpasses that of ordinary adolescent angst: in *Prayer* she wanders "lost" in "dark wildernesses alone"[191] (an expression also

employed by Aelfrida when suffering postnatal depression); elsewhere she is compelled by a curse (the phrase 'the curse of Graeme which I made' appears in this volume of her diary) to walk the path of life[192] on which dreams which might be her "saving grace" desert her and she can find "no revelation, no awakening / No passing gleam".[193] And if a curious entry in her diary written late the same year ('I must start again. I have not been brave. I have deceived myself and tried to cheat fate. I have not gone in for amulets and charms but spiritual ones in a way and it seems to be that by illegal ways I have tried to make sure for me the good things of heaven and earth')[194] is read in conjunction with a startling degree of knowledge of the rituals and character of Ceremonial Magic demonstrated in her later *Chanson Macabre for Medicophils*[195] ("At Hermes Trismegistus' shrine … / A blue flame burns, the light is dim / A mandrake root shall chant the hymn / And in the censor night and day / A sulphur candle burns away"), it may be that Agatha tried to open a channel of communication with her absent father by 'magick' means, a sobering thought in relation to an adolescent girl showing signs of mental instability.

How much of this Aelfrida knew is open to conjecture (she certainly read the *Chanson Macabre*) but the decision she made a few days after Agatha's encounter with Constantine suggests that worries concerning her younger daughter's emotional state had re-asserted themselves: Agatha, she decided, was not 'nearly mature enough in mind or body'[196] to enter Girton in October 1928 and must postpone matriculation until October 1929. Agatha herself was not consulted because 'such a babe!',[197] Aelfrida announcing her decision when Agatha was naked and defenceless in the bath: "I have been deciding your future. Would you like to hear about it?"[198]

Agatha acquiesced (having been presented with a fait accompli, she had little choice), noting that she was to take a year off between leaving school and matriculating at Girton in order to 'do all sorts of nice things before applying [her] nose to the grindstone'.[199] During the year she developed a 'thirst for culture' evidenced by attending public lectures (almost always accompanied by her mother), travelled abroad (alone) on language exchanges, became a 'child of wonderful spiritual perceptions' as a result of studying Spanish mystics[200], and began the covert novel featuring her mother and the latter's new beau, Anthony Wrightson. Unfortunately she also settled into a life of learned dependency (Agatha, her mother wrote, is 'as satisfied with my company as I … with hers')[201] which would endure until the point at which Aelfrida, desperate to free herself from a co-dependency she herself had engendered, decided that the daughter she described in 1928 as 'the sweetest … most brilliant, most loveable child on earth'[202] now constituted such a drag on her progress along her 'mystic way' that her company must be actively discouraged.

Contrasting views of the relationship now existing between the Graham women are expressed in their respective diaries by two participants in the drama: Aelfrida and Alethea. Aelfrida finds Alethea 'challenging'[203] and in spite of her elder daughter being 'wonderfully good' by including her in Girton life, feels that being in Alethea's company imposes 'a certain strain' because Alethea 'expects more vitality of me than I possess' resents Aelfrida's withdrawals into 'dim recesses of [her] nature to brood'; indeed, she believes that her mother uses them as a means of eluding her. Assuring her diary that '*of course* I love [Alethea] as much as I do Agatha', Aelfrida immediately dispels the illusion by stating that her relationship with Alethea had been 'perfect' until the onset of Agatha's gap year[204] (a fallacy refuted by evidence provided by herself in earlier volumes) and by her effusions over the 'perfect' relationship she now has with her younger daughter: 'I am', she writes, 'more completely at my ease with Agatha than I have been with any other human being'.[205] Human beings including members of her family, Julius because of his pessimism and his being 'intellectually very arrogant' (a savage criticism indeed from his doting sister), Eustace because 'his lack of interest in religion [is] a real barrier to intimacy', and her parents because she can only engage with them on 'certain grounds' and towards whom the only sentiment she feels is pity. To Agatha, however, she feels '*very* close', closer even than to Constantine 'when we loved each other most', sharing private jokes with her and loving 'God and people' in the same way, and although they rarely exchange confidences, Agatha, unlike Alethea, knows when Aelfrida wants to be 'quiet' and respects her privacy at such times.[206] In fact, Aelfrida's only worry, other than the question of Agatha's future, is that perhaps it is not 'wholly good' for an adolescent 'to live so close to a middle aged woman' of whom even Aelfrida realises Agatha will never be emotionally quit however wide the physical distance between them.[207]

Alethea's view of the relationship between mother and sister demonstrates how similar they are and how closely Agatha's behaviour mirrors Aelfrida's. It is written during a holiday spent together in March/April 1928 when Agatha is in the middle of her gap year. Aelfrida has heard from Phyllis' parents how they inadvertently travelled to South America on the same ship as Constantine and Mildred (Henry Mudie-Cooke found Constantine 'coarse'), and this has rendered her 'very highly strung', particularly as she received the news in Willie Searle's presence.[208] Alethea is recovering from an episode of stress-induced aphonia, her complete loss of voice having been treated by Dr Cooper with 'cocaine and strychnine and other evil drugs' (as her sister gleefully reports) to such good effect that she is now 'vociferous and cheerful'.[209]

Cheerful and vociferous perhaps, but judgemental too: her mother and sister, she writes, have become 'almost disquietingly' similar. They share likes and dislikes; in spite of their 'critical spirit', they suffer 'uncritical passions'; they demonstrate innocence amounting to naiveté with regard to other people; they esteem themselves and each other as 'almost a genius' but lack (without realising it) the qualities required to be one; they possess a capacity for metaphysical experiences which pragmatic Alethea believes is hysterical in origin; they enjoy ill-health insofar as 'minor ailments' make them 'interesting'; they adopt an 'interesting' look in company and must be the focus of attention, 'especially with men'. 'Mother and Agatha', she concludes, have to be 'the centre of the world they live in'.[210]

Although Aelfrida liked to believe that Girton's green and flowery loveliness was symbolic of her daughters' happiness there, both girls' sojourn was blighted by unhappiness, of some of which she herself was the cause and the depths of which she deliberately chose not to plumb lest it disturb the tenor of her spiritual friendship with Juan Mascaró or her more earthly one with Anthony Wrightson or prevent her successful 'aunting' of potential husbands for the girls themselves.

Agatha's Girton 'future' as decided by her mother was initially scientific. It may be that Aelfrida was inspired by former 'patient' Dorothy Wrinch or by Alethea's friend Helen Megaw, but Agatha's Carlisle Scholarship having been granted for her 'rare brilliance and originality' rather than her 'accuracy'[211] and Agatha herself having decreed the thought of science 'intolerable'[212], Aelfrida and Miss Major settled on Geography with Anthropology instead. For Aelfrida, Anthropology had particular charms because of its sentimental associations (Dr Haddon teasing her about her romantic conquests, the earliest of which was his own son; John Layard inviting her to lunch but forgetting the invitation, leaving her to forage for food and to write *Her Lover, to Rosamund*, with its refrain "I shall forget"[213]) but being a subject chosen preponderantly by men, it would also ensure Agatha's placement in good 'mating' territory. But although Agatha's supervisor in Geography described her pupil as 'brilliant and competent'[214], it seems (Aelfrida herself is curiously silent at this point and we have lost Agatha's diary voice) that after a year's work, she was allowed to follow her aptitude and inclination in the more congenial field of English Literature.

Aelfrida herself blamed Agatha's lack of success in the subject chosen for her (her statement that Agatha 'will read' Geography says it all)[215] on the physical ill health which afflicted her daughter as soon as she left home. During her first year at Girton, Agatha suffered numerous 'freshers' colds and, more seriously, from dental abscesses which lost her weeks of work. (Her severe mastoid infection occurred in her second year.) Any illness, however mild, caused her mother to react with exaggerated concern (it is at this point in her diary that Agatha reverts to being 'Temu' or, when unwell, to 'precious Temu'), to attribute the normal fatigue of starting university to something sinister, and to insist that Agatha required 'careful supervision'[216] in *all* aspects of her life, not just the academic.

She was right to worry. During her time at Girton, Agatha, though 'so witty, so girlish and so womanly and so elusive and so utterly and completely bewitching [and] whimsical'[217], manifested a hectic and brittle gaiety beneath which lay dark moods bordering on the pathological and attributed by her mother to Agatha being troubled by the wickedness of the world and by a faltering in her relationship with God ("Him whom I knew / I now shall never know / Since I am Judas / Though I never knew")[218] and because 'that brilliant little brain of hers'[219] was inclined to think along worryingly 'unorthodox lines'.[220] (She fails to note that Agatha's Girton years were bracketed by mortalities, her grandfather's within days of her matriculation, her grandmother's within months of her graduation.) Poems written between 1928 and mid-1932 only one of which is known to have been read by Aelfrida unless she took the opportunity of her daughter becoming an out-student to pry into her papers, demonstrate the darkness within Agatha's soul, some being melancholic ("but here / silence and dark. / We are shut in, we drown. Oh who will hear / And light our flickering spark?"), some hag-ridden ("myself … poor and haunted / By unreality, by gnomes, by shadows / By the appalling fear of my half-waking"), and many dense with images of death.[221]

There was too, the question of Agatha's sexuality, a question which seems to have convinced Aelfrida that Agatha was unlikely to marry. Although Agatha never regarded Humphrey Warren (or anyone else) as a *parti sérieux*, his declaration of August 1932 that physical desire was a 'sin' from which he must 'flee' and that because he could never allow himself to 'want' Agatha in that way, he could never marry her either[222] came as shock but also as something of a relief for, as Aelfrida had suspected but now realised, Agatha was sexually timid to the point of inhibition. (Hence her cry apropos Humphrey "I can't marry him. I can't. I can't! It wouldn't be fair to him"

and her fears that 'circumstances' i.e. her mother, were 'pushing her towards marriage'.)[223] A belief that she was somehow sexually abnormal in her negative response to the opposite sex combined with disgust at a close friend's lesbian advances ('I always wondered on which rock that friendship split', wrote Aelfrida on receiving the news at the same time as she and Agatha discussed Humphrey's declaration) seems to have increased Agatha's emotional burden: she had disappointed her 'aunting' mother and sexual frigidity with regard to men (but not women; there are hints that a girl referred to in *Finis Terrae* as 'perversely loved' may be Helen Tansley) would ensure the blighting of heterosexual relationships in the future. Her revelations had one salutary effect however; they made Aelfrida question her competence as a parent for the first time: 'I have not been able to keep either [Agatha] or Alethea in perfect bodily or mental health … why did things go wrong?'[224]

Aelfrida asks herself this question in August 1932. She, Agatha, and Alethea are holidaying together for the first time since recuperative visits to Leiston and elsewhere of the previous year. Alethea's bodily health is imperfect and will be so for some time (she suffers from pelvic pain, eventually diagnosed as psychosomatic) but she is emotionally buoyant at the prospect of a life of social service. She is also buoyed up by 'High Church enthusiasm', a post-Leiston interest her mother describes disparagingly as 'not altogether wholesome'.[225] She is, however, 'far more light-hearted'[226] than Agatha, whose bodily health is perfect but who is brooding over her unsatisfactory relationship with Humphrey Warren and bored by Alethea's new interest (Alethea seems able to talk about nothing else), and who dislikes having her elder sister's attention diverted once again from herself. Aelfrida worries that the Graham tri-unity assiduously cultivated since Constantine's departure is fragmenting ('we do not form the unit we once did') but rather than seek the truth, ascribes this to divergence of interests. She also feels that openly religious though Alethea now is, she herself cannot follow her daughter 'all the way'; indeed, though she admires the way in which religion has 'beautified' Alethea's character, she also pities her because a twenty-four-year old woman who has been 'much admired and sought after'[227] ought to be more interested in finding a consort than consorting with priests.

To discover the reasons for Alethea's 'High Church enthusiasm' we must return to a time when she found life 'more delightful and congenial than anything she has experienced before': 'life at Girton'.[228] That life, however, remained 'delightful and congenial' only up to the moment of Olga Liebowitz's death, then it became burdensome. The blame for this cannot be wholly attributed to Aelfrida but much can, first, because of her embarrassingly obtrusive 'aunting' of potential husbands, second, because her insistence that Alethea read Economics as a second subject (a subject for which Alethea herself had no aptitude) resulted in the girl achieving not the expected First but 'only a 2:1' in her Finals, a degree which 'disappointed the family and college immensely'[229] and reduced Alethea herself to bouts of inconsolable weeping. (Her 21st birthday on 22 August 1929 was virtually ignored and one cannot help feeling that this was Aelfrida's way of punishing her.) Third, because Alethea's happiness was deliberately sacrificed for the sake of Agatha's mental health.

Agatha matriculated in October 1929. As part of her campaign to protect her 'babe' at whatever cost to herself and others, Aelfrida decreed that Alethea undertake a fourth year of study in order that the elder sister's fourth year overlap the younger sister's first. (Aelfrida does not admit this directly but her anguished squeals lest Alethea not achieve an extension of her Carlisle Scholarship make it obvious that this was what she had in mind.) She also decreed, over her elder daughter's protestations that she loathed 'the idea of doing Economics'[230], that Alethea read Economics with Italian as a second subject. Alethea, 'wistful and pathetic'[231] after the fiasco of Finals, was reduced to such a state of emotional prostration ('unkindness withers her at once and could … in a short time make her quite ill', wrote her mother, adding that she herself was 'almost sorry' that Alethea – sic – 'had decided to stay up another year')[232] that she was exempted by Joan Cooper's decree from the Economics Qualifying Exam. It was in this sad frame of mind that she began her fourth year by calling it 'an unpleasant necessity'.[233]

But why did Aelfrida insist on her 'doing Economics'?[234] True, Economics was as fashionable a subject at Cambridge in the 1930s as Sociology at the new universities of the 1960s; especially true was that Alethea's penetration into the charmed circle of economists surrounding Maynard Keynes (several of whom, like CR Fay and 'dear Hubert' Henderson, were known to her mother) might ensure a share of their academic kudos. But Alethea informing her mother that Aelfrida was not to blight her 'young life' by wanting her to marry 'yet'[235] demonstrates the truth of the matter: Aelfrida pushed Alethea into reading Economics because she hoped her daughter would attract a husband whose academic interests she could share – and where better than Economics, a field of study in which the majority of Alethea's admirers had been engaged? Alethea therefore endured a year of Economics whose gloom was lightened only by her Italian studies, fainted from anxiety during one of her examinations, achieved a creditable

Lower Second in spite of this, and in June 1930 departed for *La Semaine à Paris* with what Aelfrida regarded as unseemly haste as soon as term and its inevitable social commitments were over. She also believed her daughter to be singularly ill-equipped 'to go out and launch her boat on the big oceans of modern life'.[236]

Alethea's 'boat' began to founder within a short time of her arrival in Paris. She began work immediately, discovering that the job which had seemed so 'interesting and promising'[237] (the salary was small but she was engaged for only two days a week) entailed concentrated hard work, often till 2am, on the English edition of *La Semaine* of which she was sole reporter and editor, and much research (visiting restaurants, attending plays and exhibitions, etc.) in her free time. (Alethea, wrote Aelfrida, had 'really mastered the Art of Living'[238] but was blinded by the glory of her daughter's position to the deadening effect of dining alone night after night in search of 'copy'.) Then too, having moved out of Madame Erlande's apartment (the Erlandes were now living apart) in search of independence in a small flat on the Left Bank, Alethea found herself too tired and too shy to make new friends and although she pretended to her mother by letter and in person on brief visits home that all was well ('[Alethea] has work that she loves, which she found for herself [and] she enjoys her independence immensely') and only hinted that she was 'sometimes lonely and [had] little "society"'[239], her description of 'wild loneliness' and of feeling oddly detached from the world 'as if there was no future and the past was escaping [her]'[240] speaks of greater malaise than nostalgia for family and friends in Cambridge. Nor were loneliness and isolation assuaged by such 'society' as she had: John Wedgwood, defying his parents, travelling to Paris to propose marriage and being rejected; Anatolia forcing her way into the offices of *La Semaine*, an incident which so agitated Aelfrida that it moved her to declare that in spite of the years which had passed since Constantine had threatened to take his daughters away, her instinct was 'to keep the daughters near me always, to arrange every moment of the day, all that they do [and] to choose their friends, pursuits and beliefs for them' and that the hardest thing for her to do was to 'let them go away into danger, whether physical or moral'[241] and to worry that Constantine and Mildred might lure Alethea away when her mother was unavailable to 'shape' her conduct[242]; M. de St Cyr, director of *La Semaine*, making a determined pass at her, kissing her 'so sensually'[243]; a female friend unexpectedly declaring 'a perverse passion'[244] for her, a declaration which Alethea handled coolly and sensibly but about which she felt 'rather wild and angry and incoherent'[245] nevertheless. Yet although these unfortunate occurrences exacerbated her unhappiness, the real reason for it and for her precipitate departure from Cambridge lay elsewhere. It arose as a consequence of Aelfrida's decision to sacrifice her elder for her younger daughter's welfare and involved some curious twists of plot and circumstance.

On 24 June 1930, shortly after her arrival in Paris, twenty-two-year old Alethea met a man of forty-three with whom she had been, and continued to be, desperately in love – and he with her. They spent a gently romantic day together during which they danced cheek to cheek to a café orchestra and had long intimate conversations; then they parted, she to work, he to his family in Italy. Had circumstances been different, he might have been the man she married but he was already married and too honourable to behave dishonourably towards Alethea or towards his wife and this, together with Alethea's own moral principles, meant all that ever passed between them were tender passages exchanged in snatched moments of intimacy in Cambridge gardens or his college rooms. But Alethea's poetry and diary show the depths of her emotion, their plangency made all the more poignant by the sense of hopelessness pervading them. He was not, however, the man who awakened Alethea's sexuality (that honour went to an Italian neurologist who took advantage of the presence of a holiday governess to kiss and embrace her so ardently that had it not been for Alethea's common sense in a 'difficult situation' and because the doctor's interception of a letter from Aelfrida to his wife revealing her husband's 'unwelcome lovemaking' brought him opportunely to his senses, the situation might have become 'difficult and delicate indeed')[246], nor was he the first man towards whom she was attracted (that was Tom Henn, but Tom, the only man to take a serious and kindly interest in her at that stage of her life, was emotionally engaged with her mother and officially to someone else and Alethea was sad but relieved when marriage and Mrs Henn removed Tom from her orbit), but he was the first and last man with whom she could be herself 'emotion to emotion, no veiling artifices ... not shy or ridiculous' and in whose presence she felt 'sincere, charming, lively, truthful, young and loveable'.[247]

Raffaello Piccoli, appointed Serena Professor of Italian in 1929[248], first met Alethea in 1914 when she was six. As a Cambridge lecturer in Italian with an interest in spiritual matters, he had attended Aelfrida's lecture *Can We See God?* given to the Heretics on 7 June 1914 and, keen to continue the discussion, was invited to Fordfield on several occasions thereafter. At Fordfield he discussed Mysticism with Aelfrida, played card games with Agatha and Alethea, and went for walks with Constantine. In 1915 he attended Aelfrida's lecture series on *Spiritual*

*Exercises in the Higher Religions* and updated her on Aleister Crowley, 'not altogether pleasant hearing'.[249] Although Aelfrida later described Piccoli to Alethea as no more than a 'semi-goup' who wanted 'a Pure and Beautiful Friendship' 'for discussing philosophical problems etc.'[250], she had found his 'mixture of ardour and scepticism' (not to mention his 'wonderful black eyes')[251] '*molto simpatico*' and had experienced her usual desire 'to arouse his interest [even] more'.[252] Constantine's presence in England prior to his posting to Amsterdam counselled prudence, and on Piccoli arriving to 'seal a compact of friendship', Aelfrida felt obliged to dismiss him (with regret, for 'I felt that in his case ... I was giving up a great deal'), informing him 'quite frankly that my guardian angel has bidden me ... do without human sympathy ... because I am too dependent on it and I must have no more friends'.[253] Piccoli acquiesced (reluctantly), a 'coolness' ensued, and following his departure from Cambridge later that year, did not meet Aelfrida again until 23 April 1929 when she ran unexpectedly 'into my old friend Raffaello Piccoli' newly returned to Cambridge to take up his professorial chair[254], and, moments later, into Alethea and John Wedgwood.

To Alethea's joy, 'Piccoli remembered me when I was tiny ... and I was flattered ... and I liked [him]'.[255] A week later Piccoli visited Fordfield and Alethea fell suddenly and deeply in love (in a statement curiously like her mother's, she noted that 'being very feminine, there must always be for me a man "in the ascendant"') and he with her. She also noted that 'it's rather dangerous ... and I shall be unhappy'[256] and that 'it seems funny ... the same man being very attractive ... to [Mother] and then to me'.[257]

A superficial reading of Aelfrida's diary suggests she knew nothing of the relationship between daughter and Piccoli but although Alethea herself did not confide details of it to her mother, it is obvious from Alethea's own account and from cryptic allusions in Aelfrida's (e.g. to Piccoli asking her if he had 'annoyed' her or, apropos Alethea having 'disposed' of admirers of whom Aelfrida approved, that 'the others were all impossible – married or dago or something')[258] that Aelfrida was fully aware of what was going on but preferred to model herself on 'Mrs Lavington'. Her motives for doing so are interesting. First, she herself was enjoying her 'autumn love affair' with 'a man who never has been young'[259] but whose age relative to her own was almost exactly that of Alethea's to Piccoli and, preoccupied with Anthony Wrightson, preferred to attribute Alethea's moodiness to examination fatigue and to too much partying. Second, and more significantly, her allowing Alethea to read Italian as her second subject with Piccoli as her supervisor would console her for (and might even ensure her acquiescence in) having to endure a fourth year at Girton reading Economics. Hence instead of trying to 'shape' Alethea's 'conduct' with regard to a relationship of which she disapproved (at one point she accused Alethea of 'vamping' Piccoli)[260], Aelfrida acted as procuress, inviting Piccoli to 'Sunday teas' at Fordfield and including him in social occasions elsewhere.

Although Alethea's goodbye to Piccoli in Paris was known by both to be au revoir rather than adieu, so much was it the occurrence by which subsequent events were coloured that even had they not happened, her breakdown would only have occurred later rather than sooner. In fact, as early as mid-September 1930 she frequently found herself in tears or sleepless (several diary entries are written in the middle of the night); by late October her 'mind and emotions' were 'tired' and she desperately needed someone in whom to confide.[261] Hermine de Marclay, her immediate superior at *La Semaine*, knew something of her misery and suggested that Alethea take a short holiday, but arriving in Cambridge on 24 December she discovered that 'the unfortunate Professor Piccoli'[262] had been admitted to the Evelyn Nursing Home two weeks earlier with pneumonia. Alethea returned to France shortly after Christmas; Piccoli remained in the Evelyn and by 7 January 1931 was so ill that his wife was sent for from Italy. Alethea's earlier comment that Piccoli had 'something in him so alive and burning'[263] proved prophetic: pneumonia was a symptom of tuberculosis. Although he recovered sufficiently to meet Aelfrida and Alethea when the latter ('a little depressed, not quite her usual sunny self'[264], wrote her mother with masterly understatement) was allowed another short visit home early in February, he did not leave the Evelyn until a few days prior to Agatha's emergency admission later the same month. Returning to Paris while Piccoli was still in hospital, Alethea broke down completely, diagnosing herself as 'nervously ill' but soldiering on at *La Semaine* until 'moments of exaltation leading to helpless tears'[265] rendered her incapable of functioning. The doctor from the English Consulate declared her 'thoroughly strained and overwrought' and liable 'to break down completely' so Mlle de Marclay asked that she be escorted home to England.[266] Arriving at Fordfield 'looking amused and confident' to find Agatha in bed with incipient mastoiditis and her mother wilfully believing that Alethea '*isn't* as ill as all that … there is no sign of loss of balance or self-control', Alethea proved Aelfrida wrong by bursting into 'a bad fit of hysterical crying'[267] before being consigned to her bedroom (and in Aelfrida's contemporary diary entries to virtual oblivion) while her mother concentrated her energies on 'precious Temu's' illness and recovery.

In later years Aelfrida played down Alethea's emotional collapse ('rest and a little bromide soon put her right')[268] but it is obvious that, having sacrificed Alethea's welfare to Agatha's once again, she was horrified by what she discovered when able to divert her attention from her younger to her elder daughter: 'the normal Alethea is a tower of strength – that is why her condition when she returned from Paris was so peculiarly distressing'.[269] But having realised that for all her physical 'sturdiness', Alethea was 'rather breakable and strainable'[270] and that she was suffering from a 'mysterious [sickness which] must have been hatching for years in her subconscious [and which] may wreck her whole life if not wisely dealt with'[271], Aelfrida did nothing. Rather than delve into the truth or pay a doctor to do so (Alethea, she wrote, was 'a little bored and depressed but what can one do?')[272], she blamed the latter's breakdown on a 'serious Freudian complex' induced by Constantine's behaviour towards herself and used this as her excuse to sever all connection with him, something Alethea let her do on the grounds that this explanation was as good as any and would obviate the need for further explanations.[273] Alethea was therefore left to cure herself as best she might without help (she was, wrote Aelfrida, 'pathetically anxious to be "good" and give as little trouble as possible'[274]; convalescing at the Crundwells, Alethea told her mother she was 'being VERY CAREFUL … and not getting too tired and being a good, good girl, so good so good')[275] and became in due course, so her mother persuaded herself, 'more reasonable [and] more pleased with life'.[276]

A possible reason for the encouraging change in Alethea's demeanour made itself manifest in April 1931. Entering Alethea's room one day to discover Pascal's *Pensées*, St Augustine's *Confessions*, and other books of a religious nature by her bed, Aelfrida advised her "if you don't do it already … put yourself and all your worries into God's hands". Alethea looked her mother straight in the eye: "How do you know I don't?" Nonplussed for once, Aelfrida kissed her daughter and held her peace.[277] Alethea, in fact and as her diary shows, had begun to turn to God even before leaving Paris and by the time of Aelfrida's discovery was leading a quietly religious life of her own choosing, a life so consoling ('for God hath not given us the spirit of fear but of faith and of power and of a sound mind')[278] that she found herself able to engage with the world again to the extent of undertaking language coaching and translating and contemplating journalism in order to further her wish to become a writer. Then she and her mother and sister went to Leiston and her life changed direction for ever. For once, Aelfrida's intuition was correct: 'I always used to feel that the whole world of mystical religion was unknown to

Alethea … but now, though she has not said anything, I am conscious that she is beginning to explore [and] she is happier in her soul'.[279]

'For an account of Agatha's grave illness and four operations, also of Alethea's illness and loss of job; and for the account of the happy issue out of all our troubles, see my diary'[280], wrote Aelfrida in June 1931 in one of the rare entries now made in her daughters' *Joint Record Book*. A 'happy ending' seemed assured. Agatha, 'as intelligent and as sweet as she is well'[281], celebrated her twenty-first birthday on 12 July 1931 with a family party and returned to Girton 'almost mobbed by adoring friends'.[282] Alethea, now twenty-three but seeming 'so *young*' and more like a child than a woman-of-the-world who had earned her own living in Paris, a change correctly attributed by her mother to 'beloved Leiston'[283], lived at home pending the start of her social work career and filled her time by teaching disadvantaged girls. Aelfrida, burnt out emotionally by the traumas of the past year, was pleased that she and her daughters were reunited under the same roof in a 'unity which is more than the sum of three parts separately'.[284] She also hoped for time to herself to explore 'divine things'[285] and to indulge in some spiritual heart-searching but which judging by the paucity of diary entries referring to her daughters, did not include them. Then everything began to go wrong.

On 1 September 1932 Alethea, still absorbed in religion, embarked on her career of social service. Both factors occasioned her mother's dismay ('this change in her … I feel is somehow my fault')[286] for Aelfrida had recently discovered that Alethea was now 'by way of being an Anglo-Catholic'[287] and had begun to attend confession at Leiston on retreats organised independently of her mother and with a spiritual director in Cambridge, Dr Weekes of Sidney Sussex College. On 16 October 1932 Aelfrida and Anthony Wrightson held their firelight tryst and parted. On 16 December 1932 Aelfrida administered the *coup de grace* to Chiara, her death setting in train the disposal of Fordfield and its contents and rendering Agatha and Aelfrida temporarily homeless. On 4 April 1933 Alethea announced her intention of becoming a nun.

A reason for the timing of her announcement is not hard to find. In 1931 Alethea's emotional and Raffaello Piccoli's physical health had collapsed simultaneously but whereas she, with the resilience of youth and with her newfound faith to sustain her, eventually made (or appeared to make) a complete recovery with 'vitality and zest for life unimpaired'[288], Piccoli's tuberculosis rendered him 'a very sick man' and in November 1931 he was granted two terms' leave to travel to Switzerland in hopes of a cure.[289] In May 1932 he returned to Cambridge,

squiring Agatha and Alethea to May Week festivities, visiting Fordfield for tea and supper parties, and treating the three Graham women 'as if we were one friend who was very dear to him'. He was also so lacking in vitality as to be unable 'to be in love with Alethea'[290] any more, a revealing comment given Aelfrida's supposed ignorance of Piccoli's relationship with her daughter. Although *The Cambridge Review* announced that Professor Piccoli would recommence his lectures on 19 October 1932, it seems that shortly thereafter his health declined rapidly and he was obliged to return to Switzerland. He died in Davos on 21 January 1933; on 23 January 1933 Aelfrida read his obituary in *The Times*. (Alethea's brief and impersonal account notes that she was 'grieved' to hear of 'Dear Piccoli's' death, would never forget their friendship, and that 'one is really sad to let him go'.)[291] Three months later and having completely deceived her mother as to her true feelings (her 'vitality and zest', it seems, was actually 'the pathetic brightness of one who conceals a secret sorrow')[292] and her intentions, for Truth was as adept at concealing the truth as she was at revealing it as 'Vera', Alethea announced that Christ was now the 'man in the ascendant' in her life, and, adopting the Benedictine emblem of a Calvary cross surmounted by the word PAX, chose from "the many roads of the Spirit", the "quiet road Peace".[293] To the cloister.

## Notes

1 GCPPT 1|1|18 20 May 1911.
2 ibid. 26 July 1911.
3 GCPPT 1|1a *Agatha's Record Book* 5 January 1911.
4 ibid. 30 September 1915.
5 GCPPT 1|1|17 9 September 1910.
6 ibid. 19 September 1910. A page has been cut out of Aelfrida's diary in the middle of this entry which suggests a comment she did not wish Constantine to see or that he made her destroy one of which he did not approve.
7 GCPPT 1|1|18 7 March 1912.
8 ibid. 7 January 1912.
9 ibid. 8 April 1912.
10 ibid. 5 July 1912.
11 GCPPT 1|1a *Alethea's Record Book* 3 September 1912.
12 In the parable 'Lily' and 'Billy' are rebuked by their father for making a noise outside the closed door of their mother's room. A 'horrid mother' then comes in place of their own mother and mistreats them and they run away. Enquiring of a wise owl where their real mother is to be found, they follow a trail of flowers to a cave where she is lying asleep, surrounded by 'naughty thoughts' (Hieronymous Bosch-like figures) and with a fire burning at her feet. 'Lily' and 'Billy' make 'good thoughts' (haloed female figures with stars on their heads) which drive the 'naughty thoughts' away. They then wake their mother who returns with them and 'drives the horrid mother away' (GCPPT 2|3a pp 20–27). *The Lily-Billy Book* was a book in which Aelfrida recorded the stories and poems she recited to her children. It also contained illustrations and short pictorial stories drawn by Aelfrida and coloured in by Agatha and Alethea and seems, from a surviving copy, to have

been a less sophisticated version of the *MCJ* and of magazines produced by Julius and Aelfrida during their own childhood. Poems from *The Lily-Billy Book* appear in *Bammies Book* (*The Hut* pp 12–13) and *Verses for Alethea* (*Burglars* pp 13–14).

13    GCPPT 1|1|18 29 July 1912.

14    ibid. 13 October 1912.

15    GCPPT 1|1a *Alethea's Record Book* 16 September 1912.

16    GCPPT 1|1|18 23 December 1912.

17    GCPPT 1|1|19 31 May 1913.

18    GCPPT 1|1|18 19 April 1913.

19    ibid. 7 January 1913.

20    ibid. 19 April 1913.

21    ibid. 12 May 1914.

22    ibid. Letter to Aelfrida from Hubert Henderson paraphrased on 17 October 1913.

23    GCPPT 1|1|19 14 November 1913.

24    GCPPT 2|3a.

25    GCPPT 1|1|19 10 November 1913.

26    ibid. 20 December 1913.

27    ibid. 15 April 1914.

28    ibid. 16 December 1913.

29    Tillyard, Ae. *The Way We Grow Up* p 271.

30    GCPPT 1|1|30 15 February 1925.

31    GCPPT 1|1|19 5 March 1914.

32    GCPPT 1|1|20 1 August 1914.

33    ibid. 22 January 1915.

34    GCPPG A1.3.

35    GCPPT 1|1|21 6 October 1915.

36    GCPPG A2.1 22 September 1925.

37    Artist Olive Mudie-Cooke (1890–1925) drove an ambulance during the Great War and between 1916 and 1918 drew striking sketches of her experiences in chalk, charcoal, and watercolour. (The pictures were later displayed at Merton House, Aelfrida taking exception to the starkness of Olive's style and grimness of her subject matter.) It was, however, post-war relationship problems which caused her to shoot herself.

38    *Bammie's Book* (1915) and *Verses for Alethea* (1920) provide interesting supplements to the girls' *Record Books*.

39    GCPPT 1|1|27 11 February 1924 ('1923' in error).

40    GCPPT 2|52|2 *Dr Frazer and the "Birdie Book"*. Sir James' visit may be that described by Aelfrida as having taken place on 13 October 1914 (GCPPT 1|1|20).

41    GCPPT 1|1|23 31 July 1918.

42    GCPPT 1|1|20 20 July and 7 August 1914.

43    ibid. 20 July and 26 August 1914.

44    ibid. 7 August 1914.

45    GCPPT 1|1|23 7 November 1918.

46    GCPPT 1|1|19 29 April 1914.

47    Tillyard, Ae. *O Passionate World* p 240 (GCPPT 2|11).

48    ibid. p 198.

49    ibid. p 257.

50    ibid. p 407.

51    ibid.

52    GCPPT 1|1|52 31 October 1936.

53    Tillyard, Ae. *O Passionate World* p 407.

54    GCPPT 1|1|18 1 February 1912.

55    ibid. 2 August 1911.

56    GCPPT 1|1|22 10 and 23 July 1918.

57    ibid. 2 July 1918.

58    ibid. 10 July 1923.

59    GCPPT 1|1|18 11 November 1911 and 1 February 1912.

60    GCPPT 1|1|45 4 May 1934.

61    GCPPT 1|1a *Agatha's Record Book* 12 April 1911.

62    ibid. 16 April 1916.

63    GCPPT 1|1|20 24 September 1914.

64    ibid. 9 September 1914.

65    GCPPT 1|1|21 16 and 18 February 1916.

66    ibid. 20 October 1916.

67    ibid. 23 August 1916

68    GCPPT 1|1a *Alethea's Record Book* 13 March 1917.

69    GCPPT 1|1|21 30 June 1916.

70    ibid. 17 December 1916. The school was owned and run by Edith Berry, a clergyman's daughter married to university mathematician Arthur Berry.

71    GCPPT 1|1a *Alethea's Record Book* 22 August 1918.

72    ibid 6 October 1918.

73    GCPPT 1|1|22 15 May 1918.

74    ibid. 22 October 1917.

75    GCPPT 1|1|23 21 August 1918.

76    ibid. 20 October 1918.

77    ibid. 12 November 1919.

78    ibid. 11 and 15 October 1919.

79    GCPPT 1|1|24 16 July 1919.

80    ibid. 8 August 1919.

81    Tillyard, Ae. *O Passionate World* p 24.

82    GCPPG A1.4 9 November 1930.

83    GCPPT 1|1a *Alethea's Record Book* 30 July 1921.

84    GCPPT 1|1|25 6 July 1921.

85    Tillyard, Ae. *O Passionate World* pp 213–217. 'Adrian's' name has interesting resonances: Roman emperor Hadrian (Adrianos) was known as 'the Greekling' for his love of all things Hellenic and 'LeMaitre' suggests half-Greek Constantine's determination to 'master' Aelfrida.

86    ibid p 73.

87    Bowlby, J. *Loss* p 293.

88    Tillyard, Ae. *O Passionate World* p 209.

89    ibid. p 168.

90    ibid. p 299.

91    ibid. p 163.

92    ibid. p 177.

93    GCPPT 1|1|34 16 December 1926.

94    Tillyard, Ae. *O Passionate World* p222.

95    GCPPT 1|1|30 8 July 1925.

96    GCPPT 1|1|26 28 July 1922.

97    ibid. 21 May 1922.

98    GCPPT 1|1|27 5 November 1923.

99    GCPPT 1|1|18 30 August 1911.

100    GCPPT 1|1|25 6 July 1921.

101    GCPPT 1|1|26 21 August 1921.

102    ibid. 24 January 1922.

103    ibid. 21 August 1921.

104    ibid. 31 July 1922.

105    ibid. 24 January 1922.

106    ibid. 30 January 1922.

107    ibid. 28 July 1922.

108    ibid. 8 August 1922

109    ibid.

110    GCPPT 1|1|25 14 March 1920.

111    GCPPT 1|126 7 October 1921.

112    ibid. 30 January 1922. There was no question of the girls attending the County High School for Girls where Aelfrida herself had briefly taught; that was for hoi polloi.

113    GCPPT 1|1a 7 November 1922. Rather confusingly, comments concerning one daughter appear in the other's *Record Book* at this stage in their lives.

114    GCPPG A1.1 2 September 1922.

115    GCPPT 1|1a *Agatha's Record Book* 8 October 1924.

116    GCPPG A1.1 12 January 1926.

117    GCPPG 2.1 11 September 1925.

118  GCPPT 1 | 1a *Agatha's Record Book* 29 September 1924.
119  ibid. 7 September 1925
120  ibid. 22 September 1925.
121  ibid. 21 May 1925.
122  ibid. 1 January 1925.
123  GCPPT 1 | 1 | 27 22 August 1923.
124  GCPPT 1 | 1a *Agatha's Record Book* 27 February 1924.
125  ibid. 8 October 1924.
126  GCPPT 1 | 1 | 28 16 June 1924.
127  ibid. 17 June 1924. The man to whom Aelfrida refers was probably Noel Teulon Porter, resident at 5 Little St Mary's Lane between 1917 and 1934, a man known to hold "advanced" views on "the importance of sexual psychology and the need for more widespread knowledge of contraception" and whose "willingness to promote these views in the student population" led to Newnham and Girton Colleges banning their female students from attending the 'open house' he kept there. For further details see *On the Game* by Philip Pattenden in the *Peterhouse Annual Record* 2005/6 pp 103–122, quoting Harry Godwin.
128  GCPPG A1.1 July 1924.
129  GCPPT 1 | 1 | 32 30 April 1926.
130  ibid. 13 March 1926.
131  ibid. 9 July and 9 October 1926.
132  Tillyard, Ae. *O Passionate World* pp 262–263.
133  ibid p 325.
134  GCPPT 1 | 1 | 28 23 August 1924.
135  GCPPT 1 | 1 | 30 25 December 1924.
136  GCPPT 1 | 1a *Agatha's Record Book* 7 January 1925.
137  GCPPT 1 | 1 | 32 22 August 1926.
138  GCPPT 1 | 1 | 27 29 June 1923.
139  GCPPT 1 | 1 | 30 30 March 1925.
140  GCPPT 1 | 1 | 28 3 June 1924.
141  GCPPT 1 | 1a *Agatha's Record Book* 14 July 1924.
142  GCPPT 1 | 1 | 31 23 August 1925.
       GCPPT 1 | 1 | 32 12 April 1926.
143  GCPPT 1 | 1 | 28 13 September 1924.
144  GCPPT 1 | 1 | 32 30 August 1926.
145  GCPPG A2.1 28 March 1925. The line preceding this entry is occluded but whether by Agatha's or another's hand is uncertain.
146  ibid. 23 September 1926.
147  GCPPT 3 | 2 Undated letter from Agatha Graham to Aelfrida in which she quotes Virgil's *Aeneid*.
148  GCPPT 1 | 1 | 32 30 August 1926
149  ibid. 25 April 1926.
150  ibid. 9 October 1926.
151  ibid. 30 April 1926.
152  ibid. 25 April 1926
153  GCPPT 1 | 1 | 33 16 July 1926.
154  Erlande, A. *Edmée Combes* p 29.
155  ibid. The fact that Erlande calls the 'Aelfrida' figure in both *Edmée Combes* and *Le Trajet de la Foudre* by the name of 'Denise' is surely intentional.
156  Bowlby, J. *Loss* p294 notes that a widow's modes of discipline "are likely to be over-strict or over-lax" as a result of widowhood making her "anxious and emotionally labile" and that the modes swing frequently "from one extreme to the other". (Aelfrida was, of course, a self-styled 'widow'.) He also notes that many of the particular difficulties experienced by children after the loss of a parent are attributed to the effect of that loss "on the surviving parent's behaviour towards them".
157  Erlande, A. *Edmée Combres.* p126.
158  ibid. p1. In the preface to *Coup de Pif* (1928), a novel written for and about his own children, Erlande describes *Edmée Combres* as satirical i.e. as an attempt to expose the follies of its characters. He also lists it among several *romans à péripéties* (novels describing sudden reverses of

fortune or the vicissitudes which through their own fault or no fault at all beset men's lives) written by him around this time.
159  GCPPG A2.1 15 July 1926.
160  GCPPT 1 | 1 | 32 16 October 1926. The pain was probably glaucoma induced by atherosclerotic hypertension.
161  GCPPG A2.1 3 December 1926.
162  ibid. 9 and 18 December 1926.
163  ibid. 5 February 1927. The entry is incomplete; there are several pages torn from this volume.
164  ibid 18 April 1927.
165  GCPPT 1 | 1 | 34 24 December 1926.
166  Tillyard, Ae. *O Passionate World* p 98.
167  GCPPT 1 | 1 | 34 26 February 1927.
168  ibid. 28 April 1927.
169  GCPPG A2.1 18 April 1927.
170  ibid.
171  Miss Lavén hailed from Stockholm and ran a 'Swedish Gymnasium' in Union Lane in a house adjacent to the Conybeares'. Dorothea Conybeare was a masseuse herself and may have recommended Miss Lavén to Aelfrida.
172  GCPPT A2.1 9 May 1927.
173  GCPPT 1 | 1a *Alethea and Agatha Joint Record Book* 6 April 1927.
174  GCPPT 1 | 1 | 34 7 April and 22 May 1927.
175  ibid. 10 April 1927.
176  ibid 22 May 1927.
177  ibid. 12 June 1927
178  GCPPT 1 | 1 | 34 18 June 1927.
179  ibid. 23 May 1927.
180  ibid. 34 1 June 1927.
181  GCPPT 1 | 1a *Alethea and Agatha Joint Record Book* 11 June 1927.
182  GCPPG A1.1 20 October 1926.
183  ibid 24 April 1930.
184  ibid. 8 April 1928.
185  GCPPT 1 | 1 | 34 12 June 1927.
186  *CDN* 11 June 1927 headlined "Undergraduate and Girton girl killed. Car overturned".
187  GCPPT 1 | 1 | 34 17 June 1927.
188  ibid. 30 June 1927.
189  ibid. 7 and 8 September 1927.
190  GCPPT 1 | 1 | 35 9 October 1927.
191  *Agatha's Diary 1927* (MTC) section entitled *Poems 1927* 'in order of writing'.
192  ibid. *The Yoke.* Agatha may have borrowed the 'Graeme' cognomen from Alethea who as a small child called herself 'Aweta Graeme'; the 'curse' must have been written sometime between 22 May 1927 and 22 March 1928, the period covered by that volume of her diary.
193  Ibid. *The Yoke* and *Fen Evenings.*
194  *Agatha's Diary* 16 December 1927 (MTC).
195  GCPPT 2 | 2a Undated *MCJ (Medical Number)* almost certainly compiled in February 1932. The poem, like several in the booklet, is in Agatha's handwriting and is composed in characteristic language and style.
196  GCPPT 1 | 1 | 35 21 October 1927.
197  ibid. 22 March 1927
198  ibid. 21 October 1927.
199  GCPPG A2.1 1 May 1928.
200  GCPPT 1 | 1 | 35 6 August 1928.
201  ibid. 12 April 1928.
202  ibid. 28 August 1928.
203  ibid. 30 August 1928.
204  GCPPT 1 | 1 | 36 14 April 1929.
205  GCPPT 1 | 1 | 35 30 August 1928.
       GCPPT 1 | 1 | 36 30 June 1929.
206  GCPPT 1 | 1 | 36 14 April 1929.

207 GCPPT 1│1│35 30 August 1928.

208 GCPPG A1.1 24 March 1928.
GCPPT 1│1│35 24 March 1928.

209 GCPPG A2.1 27 March 1928.

210 GCPPG A1.1 31 March 1928.

211 GCPPT 1│1a *Alethea and Agatha Joint Record Book* 7 April 1928.

212 GCPPG A2.1 3 May 1928.

213 The poem, composed on 4 March 1916, later appeared in *The Garden and the Fire* (p27) in the section entitled 'songs about love'.

214 GCPPT 1│1│37 25 April 1930.

215 GCPPT 1│1a *Alethea and Agatha Joint Record Book* 18 May 1929.

216 GCPPT 1│1│37 25 April 1930.

217 GCPPT 1│1│38 9 October and 28 November 1930.

218 GCPPT 1│1a *Alethea and Agatha Joint Record Book* 12 January 1931.
GCPPG A2.5 *Finis Terrae*.

219 GCPPT 1│1│41 21 July 1932.

220 GCPPT 1│1│39 21 December 1931.

221 GCPPG A2.5 The poems (all but one undated and many fragmentary and untitled) are written in the same volume as notes on English Literature; Agatha also seems to have used some pages as a commonplace book. Poems written shortly before she left school which exhibit the same tendencies appear in the back of the volume of her diary ending 30 July 1928.

222 GCPPT 1│1│42 31 August 1932.

223 GCPPT 1│1│41 28 July and 16 August 1932.

224 GCPPT 1│1│42 27 August 1932.

225 ibid.

226 GCPPT 1│1│41 1 July 1932.

227 GCPPT 1│1│41 1 July 1932
GCPPT 1│1│42 27 August 1932.

228 GCPPT 1│a *Alethea and Agatha Joint Record Book* 5 November 1926.

229 GCPPT 1│1│36 15 June 1929.
GCPPG A1.1 16 June 1929.

230 GCPPG A1.1 4 July 1929.

231 ibid. 17 September 1929.

232 GCPPT 1│1a *Alethea and Agatha Joint Record Book* 13 August and 17 September 1929.

233 GCPPG A1.1 30 December 1929.

234 GCPPT 1│1│38 18 June 1926. Aelfrida's fictional version of her activities with regard to Alethea make interesting reading. Deciding post-divorce that "the essential drama of her own life had already rung down the curtain" but that there was still "Vera's very important play to be acted", 'Carola', hoping that "Vera will avoid her mother's mistakes", earnestly and enthusiastically sets about "building Vera's future" (*O Passionate World* p261).

235 GCPPT 1│1a *Alethea and Agatha Joint Record Book* 8 November 1929.

236 GCPPT 1│1│36 10 July 1929.

237 GCPPG A1.1 9 May 1930.

238 GCPPT 1│1│38 16 September 1930.

239 ibid. 7 December 1930.

240 GCPPG A1.1 4 and 12 July 1930.

241 GCPPT 1│1│38 9 November 1931.

242 ibid. 24 October 1930.

243 GCPPG A1.1 24 December 1930.

244 GCPPT 1│1│38 26 November 1930.

245 GCPPG A1.1 4 October 1930.

246 GCPPT 1│1a *Alethea and Agatha Joint Record Book* 14 July 1928.
GCPPT 1│1│35 4 July 1928.

247 GCPPG A1.1 24 June 1930.

248 Raffaello Piccoli (1886–1933) was of Venetian/Neapolitan extraction. Academic studies in Padua, Florence, and Bologna led to his appointment as Lecturer in Italian in Cambridge in 1914. During the Great War he fought in the Italian army and was wounded and captured at Caporetto. He was later appointed to the School of English

Literature at the University of Naples. Chiefly remembered in Italy as a poet (only his *Sonnetti ad Ariel* were published) and for his magisterial work on Benedetto Croce, he was admired in England for his translations into Italian of TS Eliot's *Ash Wednesday,* James Joyce's *Anna Livia Plurabelle*, Thomas Browne's *Urne Buriall* and two Shakespeare plays, *Hamlet* and *Othello*. He was married with two sons.

249 GCPPT 1│1│20 16 March 1915.

250 GCPPG A1.1 13 May 1929.

251 GCPPT 1│1│20 24 November 1914. According to his obituary in *The Cambridge Review* (vol LIV No 1325 3 February 1933 p 209), Piccoli had "large, conspicuous and mobile eyes set forward in wide … temples". He also seems to have been devastatingly good-looking ("tall, slim, graceful and distinguished in bearing … with a countenance like a statue's in strength of line"), "incomparably alive", "penetrating, unillusioned and tireless [in] spirit" and intellect, and speaker of exotically accented and phrased English. No wonder Aelfrida found him '*simpatico*'.

252 ibid. 21 February 1915.

253 ibid. 3 June 1915.

254 GCPPT 1│1│36 24 April 1929.

255 GCPPG A1.1 28 April 1929.

256 ibid. 30 April and 4 May 1929.

257 ibid. 13 May 1929.

258 GCPPT 1│1│39 19 February 1931.

259 GCPPT 1│1│40 22 August 1931.

260 GCPPG A1.1 4 July 1930.

261 ibid. 17 and 22 October 1930.
ibid. 22 October 1930.

262 GCPPT 1│1│39 12 December 1930.

263 GCPPG A1.1 24 December 1930.

264 GCPPT 1│1│39 11 February 1931.

265 GCPPG A1.1 23 February 1931.

266 ibid. 6 March 1931.

267 GCPPT 1│1│39 24 and 26 February 1931.

268 GCPPT 1│1│50 3 May 1936.

269 GCPPT 1│1│42 22 October 1932.

270 GCPPG A2.1 7 March 1924.

271 GCPPT 1│1│39 2 March 1931.

272 ibid. February 1931.

273 ibid. 2 and 9 March 1931.

274 ibid. 5 April 1931.

275 GCPPT 3│1 Letter from Alethea Graham to Aelfrida of 8 June 1931.

276 GCPPT 1│1│39 20 March 1931.

277 ibid. 18 April 1931.

278 GCPPG A1.1 18 May 1931.

279 GCPPT 1│1│40 15 September and 8 October 1931.

280 GCPPT 1│1a *Alethea and Agatha Joint Record Book* 5 June 1931.

281 GCPPT 1│1│40 17 August 1931.

282 ibid. 10 June 1931.

283 ibid. 8 October 1931.

284 GCPPT 1│1│43 4 February 1933.

285 GCPPT 1│1│41 24 July 1932.

286 ibid. 29 July 1932.

287 ibid. 24 May 1932.

288 GCPPT 1│1│43 4 February 1933.

289 GCPPT 1│1│40 3 November 1931.

290 GCPPT 1│1│41 10 July 1932.

291 GCPPG A1.1 1 February 1933.

292 GCPPT 1│1│26 30 November 1922. The phrase was employed by Aelfrida to describe Olive Mudie-Cooke prior to the latter's suicide.

293 The quotation is taken from *Primavera*, written by Alethea on 11 January 1930 (GCPPG A1.5). The poem, with minor alterations (as quoted here) appeared in *An Anthology of Cambridge Women's Verse* (*Hogarth Living Poets No 20* 1931).

# Malling

Aelfrida was furious, writing snidely in the final entry in her daughters' *Joint Record Book* of 'Alethea's religious vocation and determination to become a nun at the Anglican Benedictine convent of St Mary's Abbey, Malling, Kent'[1] that 'the secret of her vocation is known only to herself and God – but that it is a genuine call I think no reasonable (*sic*) Christian can doubt'.[2]

There were several reasons for her fury: Alethea had neither informed her of her decision nor asked her advice; by entering a convent Alethea had freed herself from her mother's clutches and could no longer be manipulated for her mother's (and sister's) ends; there was now no prospect of Alethea producing little pieces of God Incarnate for Aelfrida to mould into mystics as she had tried and failed to do with Veronica. Worst of all, in the eyes of one whose own inclinations (like 'Carola's') had long "turned towards the conventual life" but who had concealed from her daughter "that her mother was preparing herself, however remotely, for the cloister"[3], Alethea had both pre-empted and surpassed her mother in announcing in the most public and irrevocable way that her devotion to God was so strong that she intended to abandon home and family to follow Him and that she intended to enter an enclosed order where she could devote herself exclusively to His service.

As a self-proclaimed Christian and mystic, Aelfrida could hardly express her anger in public or even to Alethea, so after the initial shock caused by her elder daughter's 'most beautiful letter' of 5 April 1933, she 'wrote Alethea the most loving letter [she] could' and made the best of it. There was, after all, a certain amount of kudos accruing to 'the mother of a potential saint'[4], especially as the potential saint had outstripped her mother with unforeseen 'ease and sureness', and defending Alethea's decision to leave the world would provide her with an opportunity to rehearse arguments she herself would employ when it came to announcing her own. Furthermore, Alethea's unexpected defection so soon after Chiara's death and during the dismantling of Fordfield, would make Aelfrida 'interesting' again to family and friends who might have fallen away once house and chatelaine had gone. No wonder, then, that Aelfrida spent 5 April sunk in 'deep deep thought' (she also finished *Victoria's Vow*, a surprising accomplishment

**Mother Magdalen Mary, Malling**

for one who 'if it hadn't been for Agatha' would have asked God 'to take me to a better world for I could bear this one no longer' but less surprising in one about to be freed from the coils of one dependent daughter and hence a step nearer 'conventual' life of her own) before stating on her return to Cambridge that the event was 'the Will of God', that Alethea had 'rightly discerned' His Will, that she herself had received God's permission 'to *say* … that my precious daughter … will be more to me … in the cloister than under [one] roof', and that her feeling this way made Alethea 'very happy. A laundry meeting this afternoon'.[5]

Alethea, meanwhile – we lack a full account of what passed between her and her mother when they met in Cambridge on 10 April though Aelfrida promises a future biographer that 'someday, perhaps' she will 'tell you what we said' (unable to keep such important revelations to herself, she soon informs us of the reasons given by Alethea for her decision: 'the death of Olga, whom she loved far more than I [knew]', Constantine 'and all that that implies' of Alethea offering herself as a scapegoat for her father's supposed sins, the 'cooling of her feelings for John Wedgwood' and, not uncoincidentally, the arrival of Raffaello Piccoli, 'married already and on the brink of death', a very strong motive but one 'which I do not want to stress unduly')[6] – continued her studies at Bedford College and her practical work at the Katherine Low Settlement 'just as if she were not thinking of becoming a nun'. But even while looking 'radiant [and] extremely pretty'[7] in 'a very French-looking hat' and a pink silk dress, she assured her mother she was so sure of her vocation that she would pursue it even if Aelfrida 'opposed it vehemently'.[8] She also received an encouraging note from Abbess Magdalen Mary with an enclosure containing words of encouragement for Aelfrida: "it is not often that one has the joy of meeting so courageous, unselfish and understanding a mother".[9] Buoyed up by this and basking in Alethea's refulgence, Aelfrida celebrated Easter: 'living by Alethea, seeing her effortless gaiety and joy I cannot but be happy … [at] her high calling, … that she had been preferred before me (for my "vocation" was not accepted), … that my prayer Lord – do not spare me in the making has to this extent, been heard … I have never felt happier or more serene – with a joy wholly supernatural. How marvellous is the Grace of God!'[10]

Happiness and serenity, however, hid sadness and anxiety more accurately indicative of Aelfrida's mood: 'what is asked of me is harder than anything that has ever been asked before … harder than to be deserted by Constantine, harder than to lose Oracle and Chiara, and immeasurably harder than to face death (as I imagined) last October'.[11] She also had 'dark forebodings' about the 'physical austerities' Alethea would face ('I can't believe God exacts perpetual asceticism – no! Simplicity, yes – but not self-torture … my nonconformist blood revolts against these senseless and cruel anachronisms … so contrary to the spirit of Jesus')[12] but worse than foreboding was knowing that in spite of protestations to the contrary, she had indeed put pressure on and exacted from Alethea and 'told her that this or that was expected of her'[13] and that it was her own distorted view of human love and sexuality which made her 'a complete failure as a mother' because she had 'brought up [Alethea] with an inhibition which prevents her from complete development'.[14] ("Alethea ought to see a psychologist!" was Joan Cooper's blunt response to news of the girl's vocation.)[15]

There was also realisation that because she herself had 'staked all [her] existence on "the world" being in the wrong and on the spiritual being more real than the material', Alethea's action was 'entirely justified' insofar as it fulfilled her mother's message. 'Nothing remains for me', wrote Aelfrida, 'but to be heroic'.[16]

Heroism, however, could wait a little longer. Having compared herself to her daughter 'in the light of Alethea's vocation to the religious life' and found herself severely wanting ('I have mistaken a capacity for religious emotion for definite spiritual progress … my mental prayer has been of very poor quality because my heart and my life have been full of distractions')[17], Aelfrida tried to redeem herself (and to outstrip Alethea) by suggesting 'once by word of mouth and twice in writing' that she enter Malling instead of her daughter, not, Constantine being inconveniently still alive, as a 'fully-fledged nun' but as a lay-sister. She also tried one more exaction, informing Alethea that, this way, Alethea 'could look after Agatha when [she herself] was dead', but adamant Alethea refused in words 'not to be transcribed here'. Aelfrida's final suggestion, that Alethea 'was in a way going into the cloister' instead of her mother because the latter's vocation 'had been so slow in maturing' and that if Alethea was prepared to delay her vocation it would give her mother a chance to fulfil hers[18], also failed to move her.

There remained the problem of what to do with Agatha, 'so sad, so sad' because of the dismembering of her home and because Alethea had once more deserted her for someone else, namely Deity: "So from my side you crept / And died to me / Though you had died before / And shown me only shadow and my passion wasted … / In your inevitable sad departing. / Should I forget you left me?"[19] Possibly Aelfrida was too busy negotiating with or gloating over Alethea or playing the part of 'courageous, unselfish and understanding mother' to comprehend the depths of Agatha's sorrow or she was, as she herself admitted at this point, 'born rather callous' and that callousness prevented her from entering fully into 'other people's sorrow'[20]; either way, and for whatever reason – and another important reason will emerge shortly – even before Alethea announced her defection, Aelfrida had begun to reject her younger daughter too.

The process began in February 1933 on the evening when Agatha accused her mother of using dreams of dead Chiara as a 'prop to lean on' because she and her sister provided inadequate support. On Aelfrida replying that she *had* needed dreams as a prop but now regarded them as a completed aspect of her mourning for her mother, Agatha, it seems, tried to atone for her verbal attack by reading one of her poems aloud. For her to do so was both unusual ('Agatha does not show her poems') and an honour, the poem being 'the best she had – a long poem which had taken … three years to write'. Agatha read her poem sitting on the hearthrug in the firelight in the Fordfield drawing room, its gloomy spaces still reverberating from Beethoven's Violin Sonata played on the gramophone. Aelfrida found the reading 'a strange experience': here was 'Constantine's genius living again' in the shape of his 'Greek' daughter in the very room in which he had wooed her mother with Beethoven's music and his own literary creations. But instead of praising Agatha for 'the passion of tenderness and sympathy that made her bring me her secret poetry to fill the gap that death had made', Aelfrida launched into a critique using, one hopes, kinder words that those employed in her diary: that the poem contained 'flawless passages' and genuine emotion but was also 'in parts obscure, in parts redundant' and elsewhere 'preposterously Wordsworthian'.[21] And if the poem was, as manuscript evidence suggests, *Finis Terrae*, a poem expressive of profound unhappiness, its 'callous' critic also chose to ignore the fact that Agatha's expression of pent-up emotion was as much a cry for help as an attempt at consolation. (The very next entry in her diary describes an emotional session with 'Dr Joan' in which Aelfrida, sensing her friend's 'essential loneliness', tried to 'make her hard little self melt' but refrained when Joan Cooper went 'dead white' on hearing of Aelfrida's intention of mothering her.)[22] It may be too that Aelfrida, burnt out emotionally by the events of the preceding three months, was unable to respond appropriately or unable to bear another's emotional baggage as well as her own or that on being reminded that her younger daughter too suffered from 'an inhibition' which would prevent her from marrying and from producing little pieces of Incarnate Deity ("Alas my love was without sister, without child / And as she was without child, I also am childless")[23], suddenly came to regard Agatha as a useless and expensive burden. Whatever the reason, her chilly response was deadening and it is at this point that Agatha began her descent from despondent co-dependency to darkest and deserted despair.

Aelfrida, by contrast, embarked on an emotional high for the Lady Abbess had both invited her to Malling and written gushingly that she had "always been interested in Aelfrida Tillyard [as a writer] and little dreamt that God would give her to me as a friend".[24] But although Aelfrida found it 'quite *abashing*' that a 'saintly Lady Abbess' called her by her Christian name, she was also concerned that the same Lady Abbess wanted to make an Anglo-Catholic of her, something which Aelfrida did not then feel called to be ('the Lady Abbess, I fear, judges me from my books and not from my life … and

I had to pull her up pretty sharply … that sort of misconception makes one feel a fool and rather shook my faith in the dear lady's insight into character'), chiefly because of what it implied of having to make confession.[25] Confession, of course, was something on which Aelfrida rarely ventured in a religious context, particularly since epistolary confessions to Father Savinien had resulted in his unfortunate prescription of reconciliation and relinquishment of her religious and literary ambitions, and never in a secular one since disclosures to Albert Erlande occasioned different but equally unfortunate results. Her reluctance to make personal disclosures did not, however, prevent her from staying overnight at Malling Abbey guest-house early in May 1933, from taking Communion in the visitors' chapel attached to the convent church, and from having two lengthy interviews with the Lady Abbess ('she looks very stern but is a dear, not at all alarming') in the course of which the ladies discussed Alethea's health, 'character, talents, tastes and hopes' and conventual routine, and Aelfrida's belief that the Lady Abbess would be the 'mother to [Alethea] that I have always tried to be and have not succeeded in being … a true Mother in God'. With the Lady Abbess' commendation ringing in her ears ("I have never met so brave a mother") and herself feeling not merely 'heroic' but that 'it *was* so'[26], she returned to Cambridge to continue the dismemberment of Fordfield.

She left Fordfield on 29 June 1933, departing from Cambridge the same day in order to escape the dreadful finality of the sale of its remaining furniture and to 'enjoy a respite from intense emotion' ('let nothing thrilling happen all summer!' she pleaded)[27]; indeed, so strong was her determination to distance herself from the house and town to which she constantly 'drifted back', that she preferred the awkwardness of 'not having a home as a basis of operations'[28] to the anguish of remaining within sight and sound of Fordfield's transformation into a nursing home and Wetenhall Cottage's into her own home. In the interim she lived free or as a paying guest in thirteen different places, each described in more or less detail as circumstances dictated. (Of the whereabouts of 'poor little Temu', sad at leaving Fordfield and even sadder 'about Alethea'[29], we hear very little.) She also, something which made 'respite' difficult, had to endure the comments of family and friends on Alethea's decision: Lucy Verey's utter incomprehension; Ernest Crundwell's grim disapproval ('Bayard' was now forty-five and the pompous father of three small children); aged aunts pointedly ignoring the topic but making it clear that they regarded their great-niece's vocation as 'a personal loss too bitter to talk about'.[30] Of all the family, Eustace alone supported Alethea's decision; what Julius thought we do not know, but the fact that he and his niece effected a degree of rapprochement at this time suggests that he was not displeased at the removal of an obstacle between his sister's affections and himself.

From 17 to 31 July, however, Aelfrida again had the consolation of being received as a welcome guest at Malling ('it makes me feel quite queer to be called "darling" by a Lady Abbess'), a place which seemed in spiritual terms like 'the antechamber to Urbs Zion Aurea' and in physical terms 'like the battlements and walls of Heaven'.[31] She chose not to say why she chose this particular time to make an extended visit to Malling but several motives may be imputed to her. She was temporarily homeless and two weeks living cheaply in a convent guesthouse would both help her straitened resources and provide an opportunity of impressing her religious credentials on a Lady Abbess already predisposed to like her, something which might ease her path to eventual lay sisterhood. Or was it an attempt to force God's hand ('I *wanted* the religious life and [He] passed me over') or to so ingratiate herself with the Abbess that though 'passed ... over in favour of Alethea'[32], she would appear a more suitable candidate for admission (albeit only as a lay-sister) than her daughter, who, supplanted, would be forced to take up an alternative career and support Agatha? Or a possessive mother's attempt to pursue an escaping daughter to the very grille that would finally separate them? Or a fore-taste of the joys she herself might enjoy once Constantine was dead and her daughters safely disposed of even though her life at Malling was a 'farce' compared to that of a professed contemplative: '"a mortification" for me is going to two services and waiting half an hour before getting any breakfast [and] as for silence, that is no mortification at all'.[33]

She did, however, derive three benefits from her stay: for the first time in her life she found herself in an environment where mystical experiences (she had several voluntarily or involuntarily while there) which 'would be counted "queer" outside in "the world" are just the normal and natural thing' and during which she felt sufficiently secure 'to "let go" and fall into ecstasy' rather than beg God that He prevent it; she discovered the joys of the 'intimacy of common experience'[34]; and she was able to unburden herself of an accumulation of emotional and spiritual debris.

The cathartic effect of doing so was achieved only with difficulty. In the course of several meetings with Abbess Magdalen Mary, the latter proceeded to question her, to admonish her, and 'to lay her finger on just the correct places' ('she has no illusions about me now', noted Aelfrida ruefully)[35], to humble her by informing

her after Aelfrida had described her visionary and ecstatic experiences at considerable length and asked "why me?", that she was "not the only pebble on that shore", then to advise her concerning a vision Aelfrida had had of her guardian angel pressing a cross over her heart, that acceptance of the religious life 'means suffering', 'suffering from what [you] give up' *and* because she would have to experience something of Christ's sufferings. ('I looked at the suffering', wrote Aelfrida, 'and loved it and wanted it', so this at least was no hardship.)[36] Finally, and reluctantly, Aelfrida described details of a 'wonderful grace given me some nineteen or twenty years ago and refused in panic because of what it implied'[37]: her 'Vision' of 28/29 May 1913.

Kneeling in front of the Abbess, 'bathed in perspiration from head to foot' and with her face hidden in the Abbess' lap, Aelfrida tells her story: 'I had been doing various Indian meditations and I wanted to get to the heart of Christianity. I had had a little religious experience [and] I decided to meditate on the death of Christ. I did not meditate as peacefully as I do now [but] violently, in extreme tension of mind and body, beating with cries upon the gate of heaven'. Lying in the form of a cross and repeating 'the most tragic thing in history', Christ's cry of "*Eloi Eloi*", she feels a stab of pain in her side 'as if something sharp had been thrust in'; looking at her hands she sees the marks of the stigmata. Deciding afterwards that what she has experienced 'is either hysteria or a clear call from God to a closer relationship with Him than I am capable of', she 'dare not go on'. So she '[leaves] off that meditation, pushes all thoughts of the vivid marks on [her] hands' vehemently away and turns away from 'the great grace' with a feeling that in doing so she has committed her 'worst sin'. 'Suppose', she adds, ' I had not been a coward and suppose I had accepted the grace of the stigmata (its physical manifestations being of no importance but its spiritual significance profound) and suppose I had [had] the courage to persevere in the way I was called to walk, what should I have been by now[?] A saint probably. And I must be content to go a very long way round before I reach the Celestial City'.[38]

A comparison of Aelfrida's 1933 account of her 'Vision' with that of 1913 is interesting on several levels, first, because of what she omits ('I did not explain mantra-yoga' or the breadth and depth of earlier spiritual explorations or, we may be sure, the fact that she received the stigmata immediately after reading a letter from Aleister Crowley), second, because of what she now includes (the words of her mantra, the stabbing pain in her side, the fact that the marks on her hands remained vivid for three days and took three weeks to fade), third, because of her ingenuous disclaimers: 'I may not have written it in my diary … which omission, I see, … somewhat discredits the diary as a whole or the story itself', and fourth, that being 'so anxious' to forget what had happened she 'put it persistently out of [her] mind'[39], so 'persistently', in fact, that she not only discussed it with Fidelio in person and Aleister Crowley by letter and hinted at it in *O Passionate World* but reproduced it virtually verbatim in *Spiritual Exercises* as well.

The Lady Abbess, it seems, took these startling revelations in her stride, going along with Aelfrida's explanations and interpretations without disputing the truth of them. But having listened to her informal confession, she informed Aelfrida that formal confession was the next step. Aelfrida agreed but so reluctantly that her guardian angel had to speak to her severely: "really, Aelfrida, I have taken a great deal of trouble to get you the one man in England that you thought you would like as a confessor [so] you might at least let *him* direct you for six months before you see whether you can do better yourself".[40] So on 26 July Aelfrida made her confession to the 'one man in England', Dom Bede Frost of Nashdom Abbey, a noted Benedictine author and spiritual director.

Having already described her 'Vision' to the Lady Abbess, she felt too physically and emotionally exhausted (she was on several occasions quite unwell during her stay at Malling with fatigue so extreme that she had to miss services, with nocturnal 'cramp in [her] heart', and with 'a violent upset in [her] inside' during which she 'fortified [herself] by brandy')[41] to repeat it in detail to Dom Bede – it was, after all, unusual though not unknown for a modern middle-class woman to undergo St Francis' experience of being supernaturally branded with the marks left on Christ's body by crucifixion. She was even more exhausted by having to produce 'the story of [her] life' and a list of her sins for his prior perusal, for this, said Dom Bede, was an essential preliminary to a general confession: unless a "full and frank account of one's life, circumstances, difficulties, graces received, etc." was provided to a confessor beforehand, the soul seeking to "advance in the way of perfection" would be "an unknown region in which, consciously or unconsciously, lie the roots of sins confessed", this of itself preventing development of the "true peace … without which no progress can be made".[42]

We have no record of the version of 'the story of [her] life' given by Aelfrida to Dom Bede so cannot tell how far it differed from the version given in her diary but the list of her sins is extensive; it is also fascinating for what it reveals of past and more recent behaviour. Beginning with the sin of 'not responding to the grace of the stigmata'[43] and ending with two sins 'that I am most ashamed of!' ('flashes of jealousy when other

> The Religious seems to come straight from the Presence of God, bringing a knowledge of His closer dealings with the soul—a knowledge in which I may share.  In this Presence all that is bad in me, and petty and selfish, seems to shrink back ashamed and to grow less powerful, while all my aspirations towards goodness seem to lift their heads like flowers towards the sun. The Religious helps me, not by scolding me or lecturing me or arguing with me, but by loving me in God and for God, and, above all, by showing me how our fallen humanity may be redeemed and transfigured in Him.

*The Closer Walk with God* p 101

people possess virtues I long for or when they are praised for virtues I think I have' and 'wishing my good deeds might somehow come to the eyes of those whose opinion I value'), the list contains no fewer than *fourteen* other 'faults', of most of which we are already aware, intuitively or because Aelfrida has informed us of them: vanity; 'liking to order people about [and] to be the centre of attention'; spiritual presumption ('thinking I am more advanced than I am'); impatience; 'self-righteousness [and] having my own standards rather than God's'; 'intellectual snobbery'; 'occasional pride of class or race'; 'possessive affection towards two (*sic*) people … Anthony and Sarah-Joan' ('going to see Anthony that evening when there was nothing but the grace of God between me and mortal sin', was a sin emphasised during her confession); 'love of comfort'; 'fastidiousness'; 'indiscipline and liking to go my own way'; 'blindness with regard to my own faults and great ingenuity in finding excuses for them'; 'knowing that I … care for God supremely … and allowing my thoughts and affections to be wasted on lesser things' ('lesser things', she admitted two days later, included her children); 'too great a love of religious consolations'.[44]

As befitted one with this enormous list of sins, Aelfrida was prepared for (and, it may be as one who according to Albert Erlande, needed to be crucified, hoped for) 'a very heavy penance' and much 'severity'. She was therefore surprised, if not delighted, to be told to 'go away and *rejoice!*' by repeating the *Te Deum* and Psalm 103 which describes "the Lord … who forgiveth all thine iniquities".[45] In fact, and at all times, Dom Bede, increasingly aware as he must have been the more he interviewed Aelfrida that he had before him a woman on the brink of breakdown, handled her gently but firmly, suggesting that someone as spiritually advanced (and as well-read) as herself did not require "much direction" but also that her meditations should be on more abstract subjects (e.g. the Trinity) than heretofore, that she should not meditate (as she intended) on Christ's Passion 'as a penance for graces refused' but as symbol of His Humanity, and that in all her devotions she should remember the watchwords '*Simplicity* and *Patience*'. By six o'clock the following morning, however, she had disobeyed him by dwelling impatiently on the fact that although her sins were ('of course') forgiven, Christ Himself might still be grieved with her, and by meditating so intensely on the Passion that she had to stop after ten minutes because 'I had identified myself too closely with Our Lord – the anguish of mind … was simply more than I could bear', though not soon enough, for her hands became stigmatised once more.[46] And as we shall see, her behaviour vis-à-vis Dom Bede typified her relationships with all future spiritual directors and fathers confessor save one.

To Aelfrida's (diarised) dismay, Alethea and Agatha arrived for a short visit on their own account three days prior to her departure; she nevertheless disguised her chagrin so effectively that the Lady Abbess, disarmed by Alethea looking '*radiant*' and Agatha 'shy and sweet and receptive', declared mother and daughters to be a 'wonderful trio'. Comforted by the Abbess' concern for her younger daughter ('she will help Agatha as no-one else can … if it were the will of God I could send [her] here with my blessing'; she was not, however, to dispose of her younger daughter so easily) and by the 'beauty of holiness'[47] with which she herself had been surrounded, Aelfrida returned briefly to Cambridge where she was congratulated by Mr Hughes on her ideas for Wetenhall Cottage (he 'has never *had* such a client', she reported, innocent of double entendre), and provoked her famous row with Eustace and Phyllis by trying to influence Veronica and Angela in matters of religion.

She also took further steps to liberate herself from what seemed to be lingering emotional bondage to 'Sarah-Joan', ostensibly because she now had her love 'better in hand'[48] but actually because she now no longer required 'Dr Joan' as or to 'mother'; in fact, Aelfrida's desire to 'mother' Joan Cooper had lasted less time than her need for 'copy' and by the time of Chiara's death had transformed itself into a need to be mothered. But not having foreseen the possible consequences of her dismissal of Dr Cooper's friendship, January 1933 found Aelfrida literally and metaphorically motherless, Chiara being dead and Dr Cooper's affections alienated. She was therefore delighted to find a new mother in Mother Magdalen Mary, a Mother by title and position and motherly by nature ('a Mother in God', in fact, to

be addressed by Aelfrida as 'Lady Mother') who treated her with a loving but impersonal '*caritas*'[49] quite unlike Chiara's conditional affection or 'Dr Joan's' emotion. Realising too the deleterious effects on her conduct and personality of Chiara's absence – and also, it may be, that she was once more in danger of stepping over the 'borderline between madness and sanity'[50] – Aelfrida turned to the Lady Abbess as someone in whose presence she could pass in safety over the 'borderline between religion and the world'[51] (religion now representing sanity and the 'world', insanity) and, having done so, could then pass with complete assurance from the safety and sanctity of Malling to the dangerously uncertain secular world, all the time knowing that at Malling, as formerly at Fordfield, there was a mother-figure to whom she could turn for advice and shelter.

Aelfrida spent the two months between her second visit to Malling and her arrival for Alethea's clothing as a postulant in hoping against hope that Alethea would have second thoughts (sadly, her vocation showed 'no signs of wavering')[52], in discussing the cloistered life with her daughter ('the hardest thing', declared Alethea, 'would be the impossibility of doing little things on impulse')[53], and in making further disquieting discoveries concerning her daughter's motives for entering the religious life, Alethea having stated that a major reason for her doing so was that she was '*afraid of the power of evil*' and of the way in which that power had 'disintegrated'[54] her father's character. (This did not prevent her from writing to Constantine around the time of her twenty-fifth birthday to inform him of her plans or from concealing the fact of her having done so from her mother.) Hearing her daughter's confession, Aelfrida was 'a good deal … troubled' because of doubts it instilled regarding the nature of Alethea's 'vocation', because she believed Alethea's fear might lead to 'religious melancholy'[55], and because although a visit to Alethea's spiritual director in Cambridge suggested that Alethea had 'certainly not been influenced by any one person in making her decision'[56], of the three people from whom Alethea might have gained her impression that Constantine was 'evil', the Oracle and Chiara were dead and only Aelfrida herself with her hints of her husband's 'depravity' remained. (It is interesting in the context of Alethea's 'vocation' that Aelfrida was unusually reticent about 'setting forth' in her diary matters discussed by herself and her elder daughter but her comment that Alethea's fear of the 'power of evil' made her doubt 'whether she is acting wisely' in entering a contemplative Order but that, entry being inevitable because 'opposition would only strengthen her resolve', Alethea may have chosen the cloister because only there might she feel 'safe', speaks volumes.)[57] She also worried, though differently, about Agatha, hoping that if her younger daughter read her mother's diary after her death she would 'not think that [she] loved her or her sweet society less' because she longed 'with almost unbearable intensity' for Malling'[58], and listened, though without linking her daughter's symptoms to her own behaviour, to Agatha enduring severe attacks of nocturnal asthma, attacks which Aelfrida treated by dosing her with an unnamed medication which sent the girl into a profound sleep. But a sleep from which she, unlike her grandmother, awoke.

As her diary demonstrates, Aelfrida's state of mind as 25 September drew near was increasingly clouded; she misdated entries (always a sign of stress in one to whom the exact day, date, and even time of religious and other experiences was of paramount importance); she frequently retired to bed with minor illnesses (Dr Cooper suggested she enter the Evelyn Nursing Home to rest but Aelfrida refused, saying she could not afford to), and she pretended that she (and Agatha and Alethea when they were with her) was 'very happy' while worrying lest she (and they) concealed 'sad thoughts' from each other.[59] (She was right to be concerned: the 'desolation of spirit'[60] which she feared might attend Alethea's entry into the convent was suffered not by Alethea but by Agatha, the latter's poem *Apostasy*, crammed with conventual imagery, being, though she speaks in Alethea's voice, her own 'postulant lament' for a lost sister.)[61] She also, in an effort to prevent her thoughts lapsing too far over the edge of 'borderland', embarked on a series of meditations based on St Ignatius' scheme of spiritual exercises (expounded at some length in *Spiritual Exercises*) devised when he himself was in a state of spiritual perturbation, structured in such a way that the meditator acts as his own spiritual director, and resulting, if carried out correctly, in spiritual resolution and discovery and in deeper commitment to Deity.

Aelfrida's account of her own thirty day exercise follows her literary description fairly closely but a month of structured cogitations on topics such as 'have my actions been such as conduce to right prayer?' resulted in her becoming so enmeshed in Hegelian abstractions (the necessity of 'making [a] spiritual and moral synthesis', for example) at a time when she was incapable of thinking clearly, that she was forced to revert to her more usual form of meditation on a chosen mantra (in this instance 'O God – Thy Infinity!') which might or might not progress to contemplative experiences of an ecstatic and revelatory nature. She also, and significantly in view of the approaching 'sacrifice' of her elder daughter, underwent spontaneous and rather distressing visions of 'Christ being nailed to the Cross'[62] (these may have

been influenced as much by her regular meditations on the Passion as by memories of 'Ignatian' meditations on cathartic but distressing subjects: "the height, the breadth, and the depth of hell"; "the groans of ... millions of the damned"; "the *torment of eternity*")[63] which led her to believe that the 'vicarious suffering' of the stigmata such as she experienced on almost every occasion were manifestations of an absolute experience of the 'essence of the Cross'.[64]

Three days before Agatha and Aelfrida accompanied Alethea to Malling for her clothing, Aelfrida returned briefly to Cambridge where she re-read *Messages* in order to provide herself with ammunition in her current fight with Phyllis and to reassure herself that it was as a result of Alethea reading her mother's 'messages' as an adolescent that she was now following her 'vocation'[65], a fine but unappreciated ambiguity. She then joined Agatha and Alethea in Canterbury where she composed a surprisingly cheerful 'Negro spiritual' ("Oh how I love the Crucified! / We'll gather by His piercèd side")[66] and attended early service in the cathedral with her daughters after a night of 'pain of body and anguish of mind', the latter proving evidence, or so she hoped, that 'my prayer to suffer vicariously for Alethea [is] being answered already'.[67]

From 21 to 24 September 1933 she also reflected on the prospect of life without Alethea. Embroidering 'red As' on Alethea's 'trousseau', she noted that 'if one may speak for three [we are] as happy as if we were marking a trousseau for an earthly wedding ... There seems no sad feeling that these are "last days"'.[68] Then, reflecting on how few regrets Alethea had at leaving the world and that nothing, 'no person, no ambition, no pursuit seemed to draw or hold her back'[69], she indulged in a burst of introspection: 'how, *how* Alethea's vocation has put me to shame ... If I were to read over my diary ... I think I should die of shame, my vanity, my presumption! ... I feel I have not a shred of self-respect left ... I, *I*, the mother of a nun!' Yet just as Alethea was putting her to shame by choosing 'the hidden life' of an enclosed religious, so too would she choose but in choosing go one step further: 'I have always sought out the external manifestations of religion and talked, written and so on, in the public eye [but now] I am going to have a new "devotion" – the hidden life of Christ'.[70]

Reality hit hard on 24 September: 'this is Alethea's last day "in the world" ... I feel all numb'.[71] On 25 September she accompanied Alethea to Malling, making sure that she and not Alethea greeted Mother Magdalen Mary first by running on ahead to embrace her. Then she walked Alethea to the threshold of the guest parlour where 'we just smiled at each other and said goodbye'.

**Ancifera Gregory**

At 5.30pm she wrote 'at this moment the new postulant is being received – may the blessing of God be upon her'. Then she had supper alone (Agatha left before the ceremony to return to London, saying 'it was what she wanted')[72] before suffering a night of insomnia unalleviated by spiritual consolations of any kind. On 26 September she sat at her 'Lady Mother's' feet to hear her describe 'the ceremony of the new postulant being received and … about the younger nuns who will be Alethea's companions' and to receive reassurance that 'Alethea has a vocation and will stay'. She then attended Compline in the visitors' chapel with Alethea nearby but invisible in the adjacent nuns' chapel: 'I thought of [her] there and felt peace but no joy'. Then she made her confession, not to Dom Bede but to a 'wonderfully gentle and fatherly' priest, accusing herself chiefly of 'pride. Pride of opinion. Pride because of God's graces. Presumption. Egoism' and, rather surprisingly but not without justification, 'lack of faith in God's power to cure

[her] faults'.[73] On 27 September she left Malling and Alethea and travelled to Ancifera's house in Sunnyside Road, Ealing, where her reiterated prayer (last uttered on 21 September) 'God, make me a saint and do not spare me in the making'[74] received two earthly answers: on 3 October she was informed by Anthony Wrightson that 'a marriage had been arranged' between himself and 'a girl from Exeter' and by Mildred (via Agatha) that Aelfrida's 'beloved husband, the best of whom seems by the magic of love still to remain in my keeping', was seriously ill in Berlin and not expected to recover.[75] On 5 October, her fiftieth birthday, she began to break down and by 8 October, to Ancifera's alarm, was raving.

The doctor, summoned urgently to a patient who acted as if she was and felt herself to be 'thousands of miles away', diagnosed influenza; Aelfrida herself, delighted that she now had 'an excellent excuse for feeling rotten', decided that her problem was 'more mystic ill-health than flu' and that if she ate less (in fact, 'the Sacrament and nothing else') and prayed more she would quickly recover.[76] Ancifera's vicar, summoned to give Holy Communion to a woman he had been told was 'very ill', found the supposed moribund sitting up in bed so 'deeply absorbed' as to be conscious only that she was taking the Sacrament *as if* I were Constantine' atoning 'for all his sins' ('not recognised as such – my dear love! He did not know') with respect to Elizabeth Barrett ('the co-respondent in the divorce', she breaks off to remind us) 'and other women whom I do not know'.[77] Then she began to rave in earnest: about Constantine as Michaelides ('he was so wonderful and strong and full of vitality and … he hated illness … and I have always loved him, yes, and love Anthony too, who had he known, would have waited')[78]; about Wetenhall Cottage ('suppose [Constantine] dies and I can't afford to keep [it] up … [it] must be given up and the Fordfield Lares and Penates can have none but a spiritual home … all the time that Wetenhall Cottage has been building I have said to myself "£1,200 spent on me – and the Son of Man had not where to lay his head"')[79]; about the 'Lady Mother' who immediately refused Aelfrida's request that she be allowed to live at Malling 'for a few months' to recover from her shock at hearing of Constantine's illness ('she would rather see me in the last extremity of need, sorrow, sickness and every other diversity if she could thereby make a saint of me') because her presence in the precincts 'might [unsettle] Alethea'.[80]

The Abbess' refusal and Communion undertaken '*as if*' she were Constantine were responsible for Aelfrida's gradual return to normality and she began to think of others: of Alethea, 'who ought to have had calm for the beginning of her vocation'[81]; of Mildred, 'who thinks it is her duty to *pretend* to [Constantine] that he is getting better [even though] he is *dying*': Constantine had been ill with kidney stones since his arrival in Berlin in January 1933 and surgery had proved unsuccessful; of 'poor Agatha', who 'does so hate having no home of her own', she having declared that although wherever her mother was, was '*home'*, she always felt herself to be a visitor 'here', wherever 'here' was[82]; of 'poor Julius' who 'wanted Wetenhall Cottage as a Little Fordfield'; of 'poor Church' and 'all the people I was going to make welcome'. The only person about whom she did not worry was herself: 'not poor me, not if my guardian angel brings me to my desired haven', the 'desired haven' at this point in her life being death, or failing death, Malling.[83]

Closing her diary on pages and pages of more or less coherent cogitations on spiritual subjects ('that is what Hell is like … a place *where prayer is no longer any use* … hell is an actuality that can be *felt* in consciousness'), on religious schemes abandoned as soon as thought of ('what can I offer for Constantine? … can I bear to be put away entirely from [God] for a while, for Constantine's sake?')[84], on having 'pastured' both mind and body on 'heavenly things' instead of food because 'when I don't eat I feel all warm and nourished and when I eat I feel faint'[85], and with an increasing 'horror of the unusual and the abnormal'[86] manifesting itself in her mind (the doctor's incredulous response to her explanation for fasting – 'he looked at me as if I were a lunatic!'[87] – may have had a salutary effect), Aelfrida stepped back over the borderline between madness and what at this time passed for sanity and began to listen to sensible advice offered by members of her family regarding her immediate future. The most persuasive, because the most perspicacious, was Alethea's: "I know … your longing for leaving 'the world' but the 'Fordfield tradition' – which you mean to keep at Wetenhall Cottage – means more than almost anything … to Dudu, Stephen, Veronica [and] Angela [and] you ought to try and stay [there]".[88]

Aelfrida was consoled in her decision to do as Alethea suggested by something already agreed between her 'Lady Mother' and herself, namely that at some point in the future when Agatha needed her less or 'when life has disciplined [her] a little more!', she would become a Malling 'oblate-living-in-the-world', practising 'outside the cloister as far as possible the life of contemplation that Alethea will live in the cloister'[89], to which end she was already studying 'the rules for an oblate of St Benedict'[90] with a view to establishing 'a very simple rule of life[91] to be begun on her fiftieth birthday on 5 October and practised until such time as she was fully admitted. Events intervened. But that she was 'of the Benedictine family' and 'anchored at last'[92] provided enormous consolation

at the time of her breakdown and within a few days of her recovery she sat down ('and a London suburb seems an odd place in which to pursue the study') to '*understand* as well as to *feel*' the different aspects of her 'simple rule': to 'grasp with my intellect … how … God as King of Kings and Lord of Lords, High, Almighty, Wonderful, Omnipotent …can be so and in what way … true' and how Christ's love for sinners 'was in its essence and manifestation divine' ('the *"amor intellectualis Dei"* attracts me most powerfully', she added); to sustain 'the full blaze of the Presence of God' while willing herself, in the interests of intellectual rigour, 'to remain conscious and observant'; to become like God in her heart in order to draw nearer to Him; to discipline herself by 'simplicity of life [and] by clinging to the normal and usual'.

All this, she felt, her 'rule' could easily encompass, with one exception: however intellectual, godly, simple, conscious, observant, and normal she might will herself to be, she would be unable to prevent 'the *intensity* of the given grace' sweeping her 'altogether off [her] feet' to experience 'the highest and intensest form of joy known to human experience' or stop herself experiencing the 'intense rapture in "letting go"' as she relinquished consciousness of self for consciousness of God.[93] To prove her point, she attended an Anglo-Catholic service the following day and 'in a red brick church in Ealing' was 'with angels and archangels chanting before the Throne of God … dazzled and transported in an ecstasy of adoration and worship – and happy! So happy!'[94], after which and having decided that '"mystic ill-health" was a silly business'[95] and that she had better pull herself together before Ancifera broadcast her 'queer' behaviour round the family, she partook of a somewhat bathetic Sunday lunch. The following day, her guardian angel 'having quietly closed all other avenues'[96] and she herself having decided that her duty was 'to go and live at Wetenhall Cottage and to enjoy it', she left Sunnyside Road 'to take up the burdens of ordinary life again'.[97]

## Notes

1   St Mary's Abbey was founded c.1092 as one of the new wave of English Benedictine nunneries built following the Norman Conquest. The convent was dissolved by Henry VIII in 1538. What is now the Malling Abbey Community of Anglican Benedictine Nuns was founded on 22 July 1891 as an active sisterhood in North London. In 1906 the Community moved to a remote village in Somerset in order to follow an enclosed Benedictine contemplative life. In December 1916 the Community moved to Malling Abbey. For further details see *Living Stones. The Story of Malling Abbey* ed. Sister Mary David OSB.

2   GCPPT 1|1a *Alethea and Agatha Joint Record Book* 28 May 1933.

3   Tillyard, Ae. *O Passionate World* pp 232–233 (GCPPT 2|1).

4   GCPPT 1|1|43 11 April 1933. (retrospective account)

5   ibid.

6   GCPPT 1 | 1 | 43 11 and 17 April, and 27 May 1933.

7   ibid. 'Good Friday' (14 April) 1933.

8   ibid. 12 April 1933.

9   ibid. 14 April 1933.

10  ibid. 14, 15, and 16 April 1933.

11  ibid. 14 April 1933.

12  ibid. 13 and 21 April 1933.

13  GCPPT 1 | 1 | 39 2 March 1931.

14  GCPPT 1 | 1 | 43 26 April 1933.

15  ibid. 22 April 1933.

16  ibid. 26 April 1933.

17  GCPPT 1 | 1 | 44 30 April 1933.

18  ibid. 1 May 1933.

19  GCPPG A2.5 The lines are taken from one of several verses of an undated poem *Finis Terrae*. This and other versions include further veiled references to Alethea, "delighting in her garment of pale pink silk" being one.

20  GCPPT 1 | 1 | 43 24 August 1933.

21  ibid. 17 February 1933.

22  ibid. 18 February 1932.

23  GCPPG A2.5 *Finis Terrae*.

24  GCPPT 1 | 1 | 44 12 May 1933.

25  ibid. 18 May 1933.

26  GCPPT 1 | 1 | 44 7 May 1933. Aelfrida's description of the Lady Abbess appears in a list of 'nuns at St Mary's Abbey' at the back of this volume of her diary.

27  ibid. 6 July 1933.

28  ibid. 17 August 1933.

29  ibid. 15 June 1933.

30  ibid. 21 June and 10 and 18 July 1933.

31  ibid. 18, 19, and 23 July 1933.

32  ibid. 18 July 1933.

33  ibid. 21 July 1933.

34  ibid. 22 and 24 July 1933.

35  ibid. 24 July 1933.

36  ibid. 3 September 1933.

37  ibid. 25 July 1933.

38  ibid. 26 July and 3 September 1933.

39  ibid. 25 July 1933.

40  ibid. 26 July 1933.

41  ibid. 26 and 30 July 1933.

42  Frost, B. *The Art of Mental Prayer* p222. We know from her diary that Aelfrida was reading this book in June 1933 (GCPPT 1 | 1 | 44 6 June 1933) and it may be that her visit to Malling was made expressly to meet its author. Aelfrida's own copy, inscribed "For Aelfrida Graham with my blessing. Bede Frost", can be found in the library of the Convent of the Holy Cross, Tymawr, Gwent; it contains underlinings and marginal notes most likely made by Aelfrida herself, the passage quoted being one of these.

43  GCPPT 1 | 1 | 44 26 July 1933.

44  ibid. 26, 27, and 28 July 1933.

45  ibid. 26 July 1933. A full reading of the psalm demonstrates the appropriateness of Dom Bede's choice.

46  ibid. 27 July 1933.

47  ibid. 29, 30 and 31 July 1933.

48  ibid. 1 August 1933.

49  ibid. 24 July 1933.

50  GCPPT 1 | 1 | 26 19 December 1921.

51  GCPPT 1 | 1 | 21 11 August 1916. The phrase is taken from Aelfrida's description of the parlour of the Mother Superior of St Mary's Convent in Bateman Street in Cambridge, the first place in which she experienced sensations of this nature.

52  GCPPT 1 | 1 | 44 21 June 1933.

53  ibid. 21 August 1933 (by context, 22 August).

54  GCPPT 1 | 1 | 43 17 April 1933.
    GCPPT 1 | 1 | 44 6 July 1933.

55  GCPPT 1 | 1 | 44 6 July 1933.

56  GCPPT 1 | 1 | 43 17 April 1933.

57  GCPPT 1 | 1 | 44 6 July 1933.

58  ibid. 7 and 26 August 1933.

59  ibid. 11 September 1933.

60  ibid. 10 September 1933.

61  GCPPG A2.5 *Apostasy* is a long undated poem which begins coherently enough but soon fragments into incoherencies and eventually transmutes into another poem altogether, *The Camera Obscura of the Mind Looking Backward*.

62  GCPPT 1 | 1 | 44 8, 12, 13, August and 4 and 5 September 1933.

63  Tillyard, Ae. *Spiritual Exercises* pp175–179, quoting St Ignatius' own words.

64  ibid. 18 September 1933.

65  ibid. 14 and 17 September 1933.

66  GCPPT 1 | 1 | 44a. The poem is undated but may have been composed on 21 September 1933, a day on which Agatha played records of Negro spirituals on the gramophone, or on 22 September, a day on which Aelfrida described Canterbury as 'full of ghosts … of pilgrims'.

67  GCPPT 1 | 1 | 44 23 September 1933. Aelfrida describes the Grahams' attendance at Communion in *The Closer Walk with God* pp 37–38 at the start of a chapter called, rather appropriately, "Character-building", but disguises her daughters as "two friends" of hers, one of whom "was just about to enter a religious order". Her literary description follows her diary account closely.

68  GCPPT 1 | 1 | 44 21 and 22 September 1933.

69  ibid. 24 September 1933.

70  ibid. 21 and 22 September 1933.

71  ibid. 24 September 1933.

72  ibid. 25 September 1933.

73  ibid. 26 September 1933. Aelfrida's confession is preserved in 1 | 1 | 44a.

74  ibid. 21 September 1933.

75  ibid. 3 October 1933. A newspaper cutting announcing Anthony's engagement is preserved in 1 | 1 | 44a.

76  ibid. 3 and 8 October 1933.

77  ibid. 11 October 1933.

78  ibid. 10 October 1933.

79  ibid. 3, 10 and 12 October 1933.

80  ibid. 7, 13 and 14 October 1933.

81  ibid. 10 October 1933.

82  ibid 7 and 10 October 1933.

83  ibid. 10 October 1933.

84  ibid 5 October 1933.

85  ibid. 9 and 11 October 1933.

86  ibid. 8 October 1933.

87  ibid. 11 October 1933.

88  GCPPT 3 | 6 Letter from Alethea Graham to Aelfrida of 15 October 1933.

89  GCPPT 1 | 1 | 44 14 and 27 September 1933.

90  ibid. 29 September 1933.

91  ibid. 3 October 1933.

92  ibid. 19 October 1933.

93  ibid. 20 and 21 October 1933.

94  ibid. 22 October 1933.

95  ibid. 8 October 1933.

96  ibid. 12 October 1933.

97  ibid. 8 October 1933.

# Wetenhall Cottage

Aelfrida's well-honed knack of absenting herself from the felicities of moving house stood her in good stead in relation to Wetenhall Cottage. Though living in Cambridge for five days prior to 30 October 1933, the day on which she took possession of her new home, she avoided 'the burdens of everyday life' and it was Agatha, assisted by staff inherited from the 'First House' (as Fordfield was now affectionately called) who bore the brunt of the upheaval. Hence although she wrote rapturously of 'the fascinating muddle out of which order and charm will emerge'[1], it was not due to her efforts but to those of her daughter, Georgina, Mrs Thompson, and Mr Church that 'order and charm' emerged at 'Little Fordfield'.

As always, she found excuses for non-participation, chiefly 'weariness at all the problems of the future'.[2] The major problem was her indifferent health but there were also her 'vocation' and the role to be played by Malling in furthering this, of Agatha's unhappiness and as yet undecided career (Aelfrida had devised a plan of training her up 'to be a Laundry Director'[3] with a view to running the Steam Laundry but after a few sessions the Girton alumna decided that other people's dirty linen was not her forte), and, most pressingly, given she was now a homeowner, of finance. Finance, of course, was largely depended on Constantine's health, now entering a desperate phase (he was now 'semiconscious and screaming and moaning with pain, under opiates all the time')[4], for

**Wetenhall Cottage**

Constantine, according to his solicitors, was financially embarrassed as a result of his long illness ('he ought not to be, he ought to have saved'[5], wrote his ex-wife, forgetting that she herself had squandered money allocated to doctors' fees on daughters who resolutely refused to repay her by marrying wealthy men or by embarking on well-paid careers) and it seemed likely that her allowance would soon be cut more drastically still. Confident that God, as always, would provide, Aelfrida wrote several times to Constantine's solicitors asking that they convey her sympathy to 'Mrs Mildred Graham' and assurances of her 'unaltered affection' to Constantine himself (this latter message was not passed on, Mildred deeming it too upsetting for Constantine to hear); she also enclosed a cheque for £25 made out to Constantine himself (what she called 'my last love letter' was returned un-cashed and she received a scolding from Hal Verey for sending it) and begged to be told 'at once' in the event of his death.[6] In the meantime and having nowhere else to go, she moved into Wetenhall Cottage.

Two letters from Alethea greeted her, the first wishing Wetenhall Cottage "a happy life" and her mother "a happy life in it" ("and think how much less housework to do")[7], the second sending "a big love to begin with in Wetenhall Cottage" and saying how glad Alethea was that the new house "welcomes you so warmly in all ways".[8] It did, Aelfrida describing it as 'a sweet gentle welcoming [and] a modest friendly helpful'[9] little house which she couldn't help loving because it was designed by herself and 'even more beautiful than [she] had expected'.[10]

To one who 'never expected to possess [even] the smallest cottage of [her] own'[11] but now found herself in possession of one, Wetenhall Cottage grew 'sweeter and prettier every day'; it was also 'as comfortable ... as can be'[12] because everything Fordfield was not: compact, airy, uncluttered, convenient, warm and, best of all, electrified. It was also quiet, standing well back from the street and having the 'garden-behind-the-house' at the back. The cottage itself was L-shaped with interconnecting dining and drawing rooms to the front and kitchen quarters to the rear on the ground floor and four bedrooms on the first.[13] All rooms except the north-facing kitchen received sun for all or part of the day and enjoyed views over a lawn, over trees planted by Henry Joseph Wetenhall, and over new flower beds stocked with Aelfrida's choice of seasonal blooms. (She loved the Fordfield garden so much that she took a good third of it for herself. Because only a low fence separated 'Little Fordfield' from the 'First House', the occupants of the former could almost persuade themselves that they occupied the whole of the grounds while remaining so embowered that privacy was maintained.) And there was

colour too, not just in the garden where lilies and sweet peas replaced laurels, yews, and ivies and where the sun glowed on little copper roofs over the French windows, but inside too, where white walls acted as a foil for tiles, upholstery, and curtains of powder blue, rose pink, and leaf colours of russet and green.

The Fordfield Lares and Penates, whether 'visible and tangible entities' (a portrait of 'Little Katie' over the drawing room mantelpiece, Catharine Wetenhall's writing desk, the copy of Andrea del Sarto's *Madonna del Arpi* bought by Aelfrida in Florence in 1904) or as 'invisible spirits', seemed happy too, welcoming Agatha and Aelfrida 'quietly and serenely' to their new abode. The former rejoiced in being once more "in our own house instead of other people's"[14] and the latter noted with amusement that under the influence of so much concentrated beauty and tranquillity (the cottage, she wrote, 'seems already to have learnt the Fordfield peace')[15], she would soon 'be behaving and living exactly as "the world" thinks an elderly (*sic*) lady of slender means *ought* to behave'.[16]

But even though (or because) Wetenhall Cottage grew 'sweeter and prettier' and more 'comfortable' every day and its owner found her heart singing over her blessings (a 'short period of adoration' in Little St Mary's; 'having Alethea at Malling'; 'Agatha and everyone being so sweet')[17], Aelfrida was disposed to grumble: life was 'all too *comfortable*' ('I don't approve of asceticism for its own sake – but ... richness of inner life seems to demand *poverty* of outer life')[18] and it was becoming 'a hard fight to keep [her] desire steadfast'[19] and to practise her not very strict 'rule' in the hope of becoming an acknowledged oblate of Malling. Second, although her present life was interesting and enjoyable ('I don't mean Constantine being ill, I mean all my pursuits', she added hastily), she really wanted 'to be at Malling ... alone with God'[20], 'stripped of everything in life that I care for [so that] I could enter [fully] into the meaning of the Passion'.[21] Deciding therefore that Wetenhall Cottage was 'too lovely' and that she enjoyed it 'too much'[22], she planned to leave as soon as she could a house which already seemed so much a part of herself ('I, through Mr Hughes, have produced a real Work of Art ... to conceive in one's own brain and then to make visible and tangible ... is a great joy')[23] that it possessed a 'tradition'[24] as deep and rich as Fordfield's.

Aelfrida had once written of life at Fordfield that, beset by personal problems though she was, she had 'the companionship of those I love, enough solitude and leisure to work ... books, friends, letters, a garden, small but beloved duties of housework ... music sometimes'[25], a passage, judging by her lyrical descriptions of life at

Wetenhall Cottage, truer of 'Little Fordfield' than its predecessor. Why then, religious preoccupations apart, did she leave? The truth is, she never intended to stay, for having panicked on hearing of Constantine's illness that she would be unable to afford to live there in the event of his death (and Phyllis pointing out '*how* economical one could be if one tried'[26] was little use to a woman who could not conceive of life without servants), she used this excuse to publically justify her decision to 'let the house furnished' as soon as she could, she and Agatha then to follow their 'separate stars'.[27]

How far Agatha agreed to this arrangement – it seems the duo's stay at Wetenhall Cottage was originally intended to be only a matter of weeks – Aelfrida does not say. What she does tell us, however, are her real reasons for leaving: she wanted so desperately to partake in the fellowship of Christ's suffering that she needed to live as ascetically as was compatible with survival and 'to bear the discomforts as best I could'[28]; she felt guilty because 'the Son of Man had not where to lay His head' and she had a custom-built (and expensive) roof over hers; family, friends, and Agatha notwithstanding (while still at Ealing Aelfrida had decided that her remaining daughter was 'best flung out into the great world, to sink or swim'), she herself had now 'no call or duties anywhere'[29] and could live as selfishly as she pleased in pursuit of spiritual oneness with Deity; 'whether [she] ever … became a hermit or not, God [had] made [her] a *solitary* in soul' to whom people, however loved, were a distraction.[30] Finally she wanted to return to Malling to 'adore God there without interruption all day long'.[31]

But if Wetenhall Cottage was no more than a costly material impediment placed by fate and her brothers to block her path along her 'mystic way' or a luxurious present created with the help of Mr Hughes and inherited money as repayment for years of austerities voluntarily and involuntary practised at Fordfield or a means of persuading herself that austerities incumbent on an oblate-elect could be undertaken in congenial surroundings, why did Aelfrida go to the trouble of dedicating the rooms to positive virtues and emotions, of placing a religious motto above the front door, and of having the house ceremonially consecrated to God?

The answer is found in her first homiletic book for several years on whose subject and title (*The Closer Walk with God*) she had been pondering since Chiara's death in December 1932, the moment that is to say, at which she found herself able to 'renew [her] "closer walk with God"'[32] because free at last to tread single-mindedly ('for myself, nothing else')[33] the path she yearned to follow. It was not, however, until July 1933 that she had time and leisure to write a short foreword 'really to Anthony

because as *I* can't give him earthly joys I would like to give him heavenly ones' ('at least', she added honestly, 'I should probably like to give him both but very likely the former would preclude the latter')[34] and thereafter to continue (with interruptions occasioned by changes of abode and her breakdown at Ealing) until she settled at Wetenhall Cottage in October, after which ideas flowed more freely. By early December 1933 she had reached Chapter 3 (The Need for Saintliness), at which point she 'had [her] mind illuminated from within [and] dominated and possessed by certain ideas'[35], chiefly that Wetenhall Cottage was less a stone of stumbling than a springboard from which to launch herself into "a new beginning".[36]

"Downstairs, over the main entrance", she begins without preamble in chapter 1 of *The Closer Walk with God*, "are the words THE LORD BE WITH YOU"[37] ("I bloody well hope he is", said the postman on reading this)[38] "and the room where I now write is called SERENITY (PRAISE, JOY, and FIDELITY are in sequence along the corridor)".[39] (The rooms' names derive in part from Aelfrida having called her 'upper chamber' at Fordfield 'PEACE' and in part from her having discovered that rooms at Leiston were named in this fashion.)[40] SERENITY was Aelfrida's bedroom, serenity being less a present attribute than a quality she hoped to achieve as a result of her 'closer walk'.[41] The largest in the house, it faced south and west and contained, besides several pictures of a religious nature, the canopied bed from Fordfield's East Room used by the Grahams when in England between their return from Odessa in late 1907 and Constantine's departure from Fordfield in 1918. (Had Aelfrida hoped when she designed Wetenhall Cottage that Constantine would one day return to her and was another reason for her imminent departure the result of knowing that he never would?) PRAISE was the spare room, though Aelfrida worried lest occupants such as Julius, who had little to praise at this point in his life, might find the attribution tactless. An even more tactless attribution was that of JOY, given to Agatha's room. 'I *knew* she would mind – I know she finds Joy as hard to achieve as I find Serenity and I knew that the name would hurt her', wrote Aelfrida watching her younger daughter weep bitterly (Agatha's sad little comment " I know that there *is* joy, joy so great that one hardly dares think of it", may have inspired her mother, ever keen to point a moral, to name chapters 9 and 10 of *The Closer Walk with God* 'Joy' and 'Spiritual Joy' respectively), though she consoled herself that she had named it 'for the sake of courage and for the joy that [Agatha] *will* have'.[42] (But having discovered the name of her room, is it any wonder that Agatha, like her mother, longed 'to renounce … to give up everything, to go away')?[43] FIDELITY was Georgina's room, aptly named for a faithful servant.

In *Messages*, written long before Wetenhall Cottage was conceived, Aelfrida describes the building of a family home and the excitement engendered in those who are to occupy it. (Her description probably owes much to her mother's account of the building of Fordfield in 1868/69.) A month after completion, "when everything was in order", the family hold a "Dedication Service" of which Aelfrida gives imaginary details; she also notes how she herself "would love my [own] house to be blessed" and how "if I were cross or sad or lonely or ill", she would remember the words of the service "and they would comfort me".[44] (Years later she was 'still haunted' by the fact that 'there was sadness too, as well as love' at Wetenhall Cottage.)[45] On 18 November 1933 she wrote proudly 'the Blessing of Wetenhall Cottage is accomplished and the Lares and Penates are satisfied', as were, she added, 'the dear spirits of the dead'.[46]

The form of service she devised mentions neither 'the author and mistress [of] the exquisite little house'[47] nor its architect, also present at the ceremony, but includes Henry Joseph Wetenhall 'and Emma his wife', Alfred Isaac Tillyard 'and Catharine Sarah his wife', the children to whom *Messages* was dedicated (Alethea, Agatha, Stephen, and Veronica) and two others, Angela and Constance, unborn when the book was conceived.[48] To honour the occasion, Aelfrida wore 'an old Parisian dress of Alethea's' ('I was never so well dressed in my life before!'); she also 'loved the whole thing, the dear people present, [and] the ceremony'. And yet, she added, 'I would gladly take off my Paris dress and say goodbye to everyone and everything to go away and be a hermit'.[49]

How many of the 'dear people' present at the ceremony guessed her intention is open to conjecture; probably very few. (Eustace, Phyllis and their three children attended; Julius, on whose birthday the house was consecrated, did not, though he and Walter visited later.) And if Aelfrida hoped shortly to 'go away to be a hermit', she had first to endure shoals of visitors happy to see her settled in her own home at last but: childhood friend Dorothea Conybeare (but not, it seems, Lucy Verey), former admirers (Eardley Davidson, Ernest Haddon, Juan Mascaró), wives and mothers of admirers (Kathleen Bowen, Alice Stokoe), rejected admirers (Joan Cooper), relations (Frank Tillyard, Ancifera Gregory, Ruth Warren), and voices from the past: Agnes Slack, Florence Keynes, and Conrad John, Aelfrida's godson, now a married man with a son of his own. 'The Visitors Book prospers!' she wrote in January 1934.[50] There was also 'a letter from Papini'[51], of whom Aelfrida noted gratefully 'to think we

only had *one* (sic) conversation 29 Years ago and he still writes to me and sends me books … my friends are very faithful'.[52] Former Little Friends (Hubert Henderson and 'of course, Fidelio')[53] also made contact in person or by letter and it is indirectly to a Little Friend that we owe a contemporary description of Frank Stokoe.

The 'T. Altounyan' who signs Aelfrida's Visitors' Book is not, however, Tommy but Tommy's daughter Harriet (Taqui), now aged sixteen and completing her education in England. Aelfrida is not particularly interested in (or complimentary about) Taqui Altounyan except insofar as she is 'Tommy's eldest daughter'[54] and Taqui's interest for us lies chiefly in her description of Fidelio – but what a vivid description it is! "A bachelor", she writes, "[with] thick grey hair in a quiff at the front and a tuft at the back of his head which made him look like an elderly boy … Sometimes he had what we called 'hermit moods' which used to come on very suddenly and inconveniently like an attack of migraine. When this happened we knew … to leave him quite alone until the clouds passed". A man so shy that he travels first class on trains to avoid people but who engages in "cushion fights" with the Altounyan children, his "adopted family". A man whose study is a welter of letters, papers, gramophone records, and tobacco and who lays down "hermit rules" so as not to be disturbed when composing lectures. A lecturer who "hated lecturing and made no attempt to communicate with his students, [saying] 'I just go in, look down at my paper, read the lecture and … come home'".[55] And the only man among Aelfrida's visitors who asks her 'about Constantine and my feelings towards him'[56] because only Fidelio knows that Constantine is dying.

Aelfrida ate Christmas dinner 'all alone in [her] kitchen' at Wetenhall Cottage (the menu was simple and vegetarian as befitted an aspiring oblate), joining Agatha and Eustace's family at Merton House afterwards. She was 'not moping or sulking', it was just that after everything that had happened recently (the first anniversary of Chiara's death, for example), she 'couldn't quite face'[57] too much festivity. This was true, for much *had* happened even since her move into 'the new little house'[58] towards which everyone who crossed the threshold felt 'a real movement of affection' because the cottage seemed to 'take [them] into its heart'.[59] Some was good: Julius' first visit ('he loves the little house already')[60]; news of Anthony, very happy with 'his Elizabeth'[61]; the first of many appearances of a kingfisher dubbed 'my blue flame, my Assurance of Beauty' and symbolic, she thought, of how she and Agatha and Alethea 'co-existed … independent of time and space in the Kingdom of Heaven'.[62] Some was bad: a 'septic mouth'[63] which sent her to the Evelyn Nursing Home for an 'orgy of tooth extraction' and where, to the accompaniment of appropriate prayers ("*aperi, Domine, os meum*"), a dental surgeon did indeed open her mouth but only to have his patient, far from showing forth praise, complain that he had left her a 'toothless hag' with a 'splintered' jaw in his efforts to extract upper incisors heroically repaired following her teenage bicycle accident. ('Fiendish pain' did not, however, prevent her from writing an article for the Faith Press or from nicknaming her replacement and 'quite presentable' denture "Beau Gnash".)[64] Bad too was Agatha, with 'more shadows on her life' because lacking 'a worthy object of devotion' (a man, presumably, not God) 'and a channel into which she can turn the energy of that dark-bright nature of hers'[65], because she disapproved of her mother being 'under discipline' as an oblate, and because she was the recipient of 'sad sad letters' from her stepmother complaining that Constantine had "lost his splendid confidence"[66]; 'poor, *poor* Constantine, ill and unhappy' and beset by financial problems which Anatolia refused to alleviate[67]; Alethea, supposedly 'very ill' with abdominal adhesions but diagnosed by a London gynaecologist as having nothing organically wrong and moved temporarily to the Abbey guest house where her mother was not allowed to see her because Alethea must 'keep her enclosure'.[68] 'What can one do when these heavy blows fall?' wrote Aelfrida, 'nothing but accept them with humility, believing in the infinite love of God Who deals them'.[69]

Some were mixed blessings, some concerned with Malling, some not. Those not were letters from Constantine to his daughters, they having re-established contact following Alethea's letter informing him of her impending postulancy. At first Constantine was too ill to write himself but passed messages via Mildred to Agatha or to Alethea (he was, he said, sorry to hear of Chiara's death as he had been 'so fond of her')[70], a fait accompli at which Aelfrida connived because it was the only way, other than through solicitors, that she herself could gain news of him. (Though feeling 'very helpless and cut off', she refrained from writing because warned by Alethea that 'Mildred censors everything'[71]; Alethea, however, reassured her mother that 'Fuvver does … know we're praying for him … caring and not forgetting'.)[72] A few days before his fifty-first birthday on 29 December 1933, Constantine rallied sufficiently to write 'in his own dear handwriting'[73] to both daughters. Agatha's letter was not preserved but Alethea's, full of insight and expressing profound affection, was forwarded by Alethea to her mother, preserved by Aelfrida because 'such a precious letter'[74], and eventually reclaimed by its recipient. It begins with Constantine comparing the Benedictine PAX to the SPQR borne on the standards of Roman armies and continues with assurances that he fully supports Alethea's decision to take up a "monastic career", that he loves her, and that he himself is "thank God, better and gradually taking my place among the living". It ends "God bless you, dear … Your loving Father".[75]

Constantine's transmitted reassurance of impending recovery (there was even talk of going to Spain to convalesce) allowed Aelfrida to revisit Malling with a lighter heart as soon as she received permission to do so. (Mildred, she decided, had 'pretended that Constantine was much more ill than he was' as a ploy to have Aelfrida's allowance cut and, in January 1934, stopped altogether, in order to spend the money on frivolities for herself.)[76] What she found there did not altogether please her. Alethea, she discovered from short interviews with the girl herself and (through the grille) with the Mistress of Novices, though manifesting 'a real Benedictine vocation'[77] and 'spiritually impatient'[78] to progress from postulancy to novitiate, was 'tired through her nerves … not hysterical or strained … but a little oversensitive and … a little muddled intellectually'[79], the latter in particular leading the Lady Abbess to talk guardedly of the onset of 'religious melancholy' and to hint that unless Alethea made a full and rapid recovery, it 'would not be wise' to commit herself to the life of an enclosed religious.[80] Then too, although Alethea's health problems had briefly given rise to the hope that Aelfrida herself might replace her daughter at Malling for six months or so (or even permanently, she secretly surmised), in part to give Alethea a chance to recover and to see if God could be persuaded to call her 'back into the world' to 'prove right and *happy*' there with a husband and children (though 'of course if she *has* a vocation, God forbid that I should interfere'), in part to allow Aelfrida an earlier escape from Wetenhall Cottage (already in the hands of a letting agent) on the grounds that 'someone is needed to pray for Constantine' (*sic*) but actually because she wished vehemently 'to be alone with God … to ease my heart of its burden of adoration'.[81] But realisation on meeting Alethea at Malling that the girl was so set on her new life that it would be '*brutal*' to suggest substitution[82], caused Aelfrida to reflect sadly that 'Alethea and I have both got to have no plans, no hopes, no desires of our own, nothing, nothing but the Will of God'.[83]

There was also the matter of exactly what was entailed in becoming an oblate, for in spite of 'golden words' from the Lady Abbess that an oblate-elect must 'hide [herself] in Christ' and practice humility and 'detachment from *self*'[84] (always Aelfrida's intention but usually forgotten in her desire to exact from Christ His agreement that she be made a saint and not spared in the making or to compel God to do *her* will), Aelfrida discovered to her horror that there was more to oblation than the 'not too exacting' Rule practised at Leiston or the undemanding vegetarianism and leisurely readings of Compline and Terce carried out by herself in Cambridge. There was, for example, the possibility that (as the Lady Abbess warned her) God might take all 'consolation' from her as part of her spiritual education and 'for Constantine's sake and for the perfecting of [her] soul'[85] and that bodily as well as spiritual mortification might be expected for the same reason.[86] Then too, Dom Bede reminded her, Malling oblates were expected to attend early Communion fasting, Aelfrida's usual attendance unfasting at noon being highly unsatisfactory because it negated the idea of redemption 'body and soul'. ('An interesting idea on which I meditated', she wrote, before privily deciding that such rigorous devotions were not for her 'except now and again'.)[87] There was also the problem of attending regular Confession ('always an ordeal') and the worry that a confessor (in this instance, Dom Bede, though Aelfrida's worry was generic not specific) might 'interfere with [her] personality' or deal with her as priest to penitent rather than as spiritual equals. An 'hour after hour' nocturnal experience during which God 'took [her] away into an inner chamber and shut the door on everything but himself' having consoled her only in part, Aelfrida, unwell and sick at heart, left Malling a day early to return to the 'dear blessed Wetenhall Cottage' she said she could no longer afford and to the news that Constantine had suffered a serious relapse.[88] Six days later the blow fell: 'Constantine is dead'.[89]

'I grieve, I cannot tell you how I grieve. I mourn over everything', wrote Aelfrida on the day she heard the news. Though 'everything' included 'the promise of our happiness unfulfilled … the possibility of reconciliation gone for ever … his great gift misapplied … the books he should have written' ('to think that I said "Homer – Dante – Shakespeare – Michaelides!" and believed it too')[90] and 'the sons he ought to have had', most of all she grieved over Constantine's soul: 'he knew the higher and chose the lower' ('he got drunk to annoy me', was one of her complaints, undisclosed to her diary at the time because 'I wanted *not* to see')[91], 'he believed in self-gratification, arrogance and self-assertion' (he was not alone in this but Aelfrida was temporarily blind to her own faults) and 'though not without affection', was careless of the effect of desertion of his wife on Chiara and the daughters over whom he later 'sentimentalised'.[92] Worse still was that in dying, as she suspected, without having received the Sacrament, 'symbol of the pardoning love of God', Constantine had 'shut himself out from God forever' and it was only through her own prayers that the good in him could be 'garnered and treasured' and channelled

into grace.[93] Worst of all, because Constantine's real or imagined sins were many and heavy ('oh that I could believe him to have been good') and because her 'Greek' had been 'blind' to so much that she asked herself frantically how could Constantine 'see God' given that he was unlikely to have repented before his death ('*one* act of contrition would start him on the right road but has he made it?') and, that being so ('O Constantine, Constantine is it too late?'), he might be already 'beyond the reach of [her] prayers'.[94] So, with the memory of a recent visionary meditation on the Passion still vivid in her mind ('I watched the descent from the Cross, followed Christ to the tomb and knelt before His body in the dark … while His Spirit sought the souls of the dead in Sheol')[95], Aelfrida decided that 'vocation' must now include atonement for Constantine's sins by means of reparative practices carried out 'either in the world or in the cloister'[96] for as long as she or God deemed necessary.

She may have watched Christ's descent from the Cross two days before Constantine's death (her meditation took place on 26 January 1934, Constantine's death on 28 January), but Aelfrida had certainly described Constantine's (literary) death-bed, expanding the ending of *O Passionate World* in which 'Carola' and 'Adrian' meet accidentally in the London flat and 'Adrian' rejects her and departs, to encompass 'Adrian's' death:

> Adrian is knocked down by a car following his precipitate parting from his ex-wife. Mortally injured, he is taken to a nearby nursing home whose matron, checking his belongings, finds the telephone number of the flat and informs Carola. Reflecting how tragically different her last meeting with Adrian would be ("she was now going to see him die") from "that she had dreamed and longed for", Carola comes to sit dying Adrian's bedside as the light fades and rain beats down outside. Reflecting on Adrian's affinity with water and air and how she "saw him once poised on the edge of the sea with the wind blowing in his hair", she hears a child crying "softly and submissively" –

and the novel segues into *An Evening Picture,* written in Emden in 1910 and published in *To Malise,* a poem in which evening is both "time of weariness" and "time to seek redress" and where "the crying of the tired child on my knee" blends with "the murmur of the tired sea".

> Adrian's condition worsens and Carola realises that although "she had guarded the harbour light, believing that one day he would return to haven", he is now "launching out on an unknown sea, setting his ship towards an unseen port, far … beyond her reach". Dismissing the hovering nurse –

"For now the world has shrunk to you and me",

Carola resigns herself to loss –

"Give me the narrowing weariness of night / That merges into hush and sleep at last".

> Adrian rouses briefly, recognises her – and dies. Carola accepts that "Adrian must go … beyond the reach of her forgiveness, beyond the reach of her love, beyond all possibility of reconciliation" and that she must leave him to God "who would receive him more wisely than she could do". The scene ends with Carola's realisation that she must now "accept and bear not only her own sorrow but the sorrow of the whole world" and with an epigraph: "O passionate world! O faces of my friends! / O half grasped meaning, intricate and deep. / Sudden, as with a child, the tumult ends, / Silenced by sleep".[97]

Revising *O Passionate World* in the dark days immediately following Constantine's death and contemplating the strange coincidence between the story's ending and current events, Aelfrida declared herself mystified as to how she could have written the death-bed scene of a man she always assumed would outlive her (she attributed it to her 'subconscious self' having known all these years 'how it would be'[98] but the coincidence of events leaves us unsure whether she rewrote the ending to conform – 'Adrian', like Constantine, dies in January and 'Carola's' decision to bear the sorrows of the world curiously echoes one Aelfrida has just made in relation to Constantine – or whether it was inspired by earlier events, Chiara's death occurring shortly before Georgina was involved in a road accident. Possibly both – but what she really wrote was Constantine's epitaph.

Aelfrida, as we know, regretted that Alethea had dissuaded her from publishing *O Passionate World*, chiefly because Constantine, seeing her printed apology for sins committed against his person, would realise that she had moved on from the vengeful poems of *To Malise* (and from not scrupling to report his cry "at the full tide of his passion … 'I am thou!'")[99] to 'seek redress': 'it would show him how much I loved him and how I could understand his point of view without in the least agreeing with him … [and] it shows my faults and could make people allocate blame more justly, giving me my share'. ('Not', she reminds us hastily, 'that Adrian is exactly Constantine or Carola myself [but] there are parallels'.)[100] Now seeking post-mortem redress, Aelfrida also includes Constantine in her current book, describing in *The Closer Walk with God* how "a man chooses a career, studies, trains, begins his work", how "success comes and is maintained for a few years", how his power fails and "swiftly or slowly, but

nonetheless inevitably, the end approaches", and how at last the "man who was so full of vitality lies there on his death-bed. The doctors and nurses have done all they can but the angel of death will not be gainsaid. Now only the lifeless body lies there under the sheet". And remembering, it may be, Constantine's last letter to Alethea, she adds that there are "few symbols more lovely and more significant than the Benedictine PAX … peace in the very centre of sorrow".[101] But whereas restless, dissatisfied, suffering Constantine was now at peace, Aelfrida herself was not, for having centred herself in reparative sorrow on Constantine's behalf, she was soon to find herself more sorrowful still on her own and another's behalf and very far indeed from 'lovely and significant' PEACE.

There were, of course, other formal and informal obituaries.

'From the *Telegraph* (put in by Mildred) "on January 28th, in Berlin, after a long illness, CONSTANTINE GRAHAM, His Majesty's Consul-General, beloved husband of Mildred Seymour"'.

'From the *Cambridge Independent Press* (put in by me) "Graham – in Berlin, Constantine Graham (Michaelides) sometime scholar of King's College, Cambridge, aged 51 years"'.[102]

From the King's College *Annual Report* of 17 November 1934: "CONSTANTINE CLEANTHES MICHAELIDES (later Graham) [remembered] with affection as a charming ebullient rather enigmatic figure … [who] loved the College and revisited it in recent years".

From Alethea: "now Fuvver isn't afraid any more, not of death or pain or anything".[103]

Agatha said nothing but 'wept bitterly that her father died' (Aelfrida herself did not – 'I wish I could' – though at night she lay awake grieving)[104], and, rather more worryingly and like her Greek grandfather, accepted tragedy 'almost as if it [was] beautiful'.[105]

But although Alethea wrote sweet and peaceful letters, she herself was heading for breakdown as further information from her gynaecologist and Dr Cooper revealed. Alethea, they said, would never be mentally whole unless she agreed to see Cambridge psychiatrist Dr Bannister, problems stemming from her parents' divorce and her fearful attitude towards her supposed vocation being bad signs as far as diagnosis and prognosis were concerned. Aelfrida did not know whether to be alarmed in case Alethea would be unable to continue conventual life or optimistic insofar as God might take this as a sign that she herself was to replace her daughter at Malling, but consoled herself that because Constantine's death had absolved his elder daughter of having to make further sacrifices for a father Alethea believed had been granted space for amendment because of them, Constantine's former wife was now free to make spiritual 'sacrifices' for him at Malling or elsewhere. She therefore assented with good grace and just a hint of impatience to being burdened by her elder daughter again at the moment she seemed to be about to achieve liberation from her younger: Agatha had accepted a residential teaching post near Arundel. So Alethea returned to Wetenhall Cottage in mid-February 1934.

Though Alethea, as her mother noted, 'felt it a great relief when Constantine died'[106], she arrived home too soon to escape his obsequies. On 1 February Mildred had written to Agatha asking that Constantine's ashes be buried at Malling or at King's but Aelfrida decided for reasons unstated (hatred of Mildred as usurper of her place and of Constantine's affections, or a final act of revenge towards Constantine himself?) that 'of course, both were out of the question' and 'instructed Agatha to write and say that the Tillyard vault was at Mildred's disposal … or [that] there was the town burial ground on the Girton road'.[107] Mildred having opted for the vault, Aelfrida proceeded with the 'sad, sad task' of making arrangements for Constantine's 'little dust in an urn' to return to the town where he and she had met, wooed, and all too briefly loved.[108] She also – for Mildred's letters showed the second Mrs Graham to be in 'a very hysterical state of mind but one cannot wonder after all she has been through' – added a note to one of Agatha's thanking Constantine's widow 'for her devotion to [him]'.[109]

Constantine's 'dear ashes – yes, I think, *dear*' – came to Cambridge on 14 February (Ash Wednesday, as it happened), the day on which Aelfrida decided that her 'vocation' was to reparation. (It was also the day on which, bizarrely, she sent a Valentine to Joan Cooper.) On 27 February 1934, Aelfrida, accompanied by Agatha and Alethea and with Alethea's former spiritual director Dr Weekes to conduct the service, was driven to Histon Road cemetery. There she held the urn containing Constantine's ashes 'until the actual words of committal', remembering as she did 'how often I have dreamed that Constantine came back … but always before I could clasp him or even tell him that I loved him, I would awake'. 'And oh', her diary entry continues, 'how merciful that all these years the future was hidden and that no premonition told me that I should indeed clasp him in my arms as I did this morning by Chiara's and the Oracle's open grave'. The ceremony over, she walked home alone, knowing that even if Anthony were still free and still wanted to marry her, she could not bring herself to accept him: 'I have now held Constantine in my arms, closed the circle of his love and mine and made it impossible that anyone else should enter'.[110]

When Agatha and Alethea were thirteen and fifteen respectively, Aelfrida asked herself sadly if she would always be present in their lives 'to kiss away [their] tears' and what would happen if they had tears 'I cannot kiss away'.[111] Both girls now wept such tears but Aelfrida, though not bodily absent from their lives, was so spiritually distanced from them as to be effectively absent. But in a strange reversal of events, it was towards Alethea that Aelfrida, when not wrapped up in her own concerns, felt closest and Agatha whom she put aside. And both daughters in different ways rejected her.

Although Aelfrida hoped that Alethea would be put 'under obedience' by the Lady Abbess to co-operate with her psychotherapist[112], it seems that the girl, skilfully handled by Drs Bannister and Cooper, was only too happy to co-operate once assured that Dr Bannister was not a 'Freudian' analyst of the kind quoted by her mother, that neither doctor wished to 'try and detach her from her vocation', and that both wished 'to make her capable of carrying out what she believed to be right [for her]'.[113] Somewhat to Aelfrida's surprise, however, she found herself (and to a lesser extent, Agatha) included in an early example of family therapy ('we shall all have to co-operate to give the right atmosphere'), Dr Cooper informing her that although Alethea appeared to drop back unhesitatingly into her place in what even Aelfrida admitted was an 'odd family', the Graham women's 'unity' was not 'precious'[114] but pathological and must be broken. (If this were really so, wrote Aelfrida pathetically, Dr Bannister 'must do his best to break it' regardless of the fact that his doing so would involve 'great *great* sacrifice' on her own part.)[115] She also stated that Aelfrida was not to influence Alethea's choice in any way (Aelfrida had already purchased pretty new dresses in an attempt 'to prejudge Alethea's future [and] to interfere with her vocation') and that Alethea was to be allowed to do exactly as *she* liked 'in all her weekday and Sunday occupations'.[116]

Alethea herself, though happy 'about coming home to get well'[117], was 'tense and defiant'[118] towards her mother because, as she rightly suspected, Aelfrida was so keen to replace her at Malling that she was doing her utmost to act as 'a fetter and snare' to separate postulant from cloister. ('She is so like Constantine sometimes', noted Alethea's mother on being accused of this, 'entirely oblivious to the pain she is causing'.) Although Aelfrida temporised, pleading that Alethea not make 'premature choices' with regard to her future (though Alethea did not know it, Aelfrida had her elder daughter's future planned: Alethea would either live at Wetenhall Cottage 'looking after me [and] earning money so that I could afford to keep it on' or she would 'work for God *away* from me' as a teacher or missionary in South Africa), Alethea was adamant: 'the choice is already made, … God wants her at Malling'.[119] She also attacked Aelfrida on a more personal level, being '*very* exacting'[120] with regard to what she considered the 'unorthodox' and 'self-indulgent' nature of her mother's efforts to live as an oblate-elect: attendance at St Botolph's whose doctrines were 'much too broad' (she urged a 'real' Anglo-Catholic Mass)[121], Communion not being taken fasting (Aelfrida pleaded recurrent 'cramp in the heart' as a reason for having a cup of tea prior to attendance – if it suited her – at early service and that 'communion of God in [her] soul' and His 'imparting of Himself to [her]' was much more important than 'fasting Communion' and adherence to the letter of the law)[122], and a tendency to abandon other religious observances (reading Compline and 'all the Day Hours')[123] when Agatha was at home or if interrupted by callers. (Fidelio, for example, briefly 'sympathetic and understanding' but soon back 'in his own world … and making hardly any contact with mine'.)[124] Devoid of further excuses, Aelfrida could only reply that she had altruistically decided on 'no external "keeping"'[125] of oblate practices until Alethea recovered.

Her decision that for Alethea's sake her 'mortifications' must be 'inward'[126] had one unfortunate corollary: embarkation on a course of spiritual and physical mortification which was to preoccupy her to a more or less morbid extent for the next decade, which would result in spiritual or bodily suffering or both, and which was really only the latest manifestation of her propensity for ascetic practices which might help her atone for her own sinful nature. Her new 'vocation' to reparation, however, manifests the beginning of a less egocentric (but no less controlling) view of how she ought to behave insofar as by atoning for others' sins, she could smooth their spiritual path to God regardless of their personal circumstances, their belief or disbelief in Deity, and their not knowing or caring that they were the object of her activity. Prior to Constantine's death, however, Aelfrida, so she said, had always regarded reparative practices as 'rather morbid'[127] but his death or, it may be, a certain spirit of competition (in a perspicacious speech to Aelfrida which emphasises just how many character traits – a tendency to shirk responsibility and to repress anger, for instance – she and her elder daughter shared, Dr Bannister divulged that Alethea had consciously embarked on practices of this nature for her father's soul while unconsciously rejecting both him and them), persuaded her that she herself must bear the burden of practices too heavy for Alethea. (And for which there was now no need on Alethea's part: 'her task is *done* – it finished with Constantine's death'.)[128] Informed, however, by her guardian angel (he stopped her 'in the street … on [her] way down town') that even oblates-elect were expected to pray 'in faith [without]

sign or assurance' not only for those they loved (as she did Constantine) but also for those they did not know or 'do *not* love'[129], Aelfrida embarked on reparations pertinent to two specific women also: Mildred Graham and Anatolia Michaelides.

Meditating on reparation in general and on her own 'vocation' in particular, Aelfrida decided that she had '*got* to offer' herself for Constantine's wife and mother as much as for Constantine himself and this 'with real compassion and affection, *caring* and appreciating the beauty of their souls which no superficial ugliness can spoil'. ('As I see it', she added, 'it is a stern business being an oblate. And when I offer something I expect God to take it'[130]; one hopes He did.) Quite what Mildred had done to require Aelfrida's prayerful intervention other than marrying her ex-husband is puzzling, but a reading of the New Testament (Aelfrida's personal 'road-book') makes all clear: St Matthew states firmly that "Whosoever shall put away his wife except it be for fornication and marry another, committeth adultery; and whoso marrieth her which is put away doth commit adultery"[131] (Constantine had 'put away' Aelfrida and Mildred her former husband so both were sinners in this respect) and St Paul's fulminations about fornicators and adulterers and his strictures regarding marriage[132] were taken very seriously by Aelfrida with regard to her own and Constantine's peri- and post-marital behaviour and to Mildred's with or without marriage to Aelfrida's former husband. Anatolia, however, had 'sinned' in 'corrupting' Constantine and in behaving to Aelfrida as she did, and because she had never evinced the slightest desire to atone for this, it was up to her former daughter-in-law to make reparation to God (not 'Gawd') for her former mother-in-law's iniquities.

Yet although Aelfrida's guardian angel informed her that God had accepted her reparative prayers on Mildred's behalf and Aelfrida herself felt 'something happening [because] there is good stuff in her somewhere' and continued to 'feel for' and to pray for Mildred for several years on the grounds that reparative activity would help Constantine's widow as much as it helped him, we hear nothing of Mildred hereafter; indeed, as Aelfrida herself noted, 'the only "gesture" of mine that she will ever be aware of … was my paying for Constantine's funeral'.[133] With regard to Anatolia, on the other hand, she felt 'nothing. A blank', imputing this less to Anatolia than to herself ('perhaps in my unconscious there is resentment?')[134], but a chance encounter between Alethea and an Englishman who knew 'dashing old' Mrs Michaelides in Antibes set Aelfrida pondering ('will my prayers and offerings touch her? Would she jeer if she knew?') and to feel such unexpectedly 'wistful tenderness'[135] for

Constantine's mother that she decided to keep Anatolia in her prayers and herself informed as to the latter's whereabouts and well-being.

Spiritual trials, however, consisted of more than lack of response from Anatolia Michaelides and, as Aelfrida was about to discover, becoming an oblate was a sterner 'business' than she had anticipated. Noting on Good Friday 1934 that there were 'rocks ahead that may wreck me before I am even a secular oblate', the rocks being, *inter alia,* the unorthodox nature of some of her religious practices, Aelfrida was dismayed to receive a message from the Lady Abbess that she must undergo 'a "rather searching examination"' before being admitted. Her response was threefold: to deny that her beliefs were 'unorthodox' while privately admitting that they were ('I do not and cannot believe in Salvation by Correct Belief [because] it is not on my orthodoxy that I base my hopes of heaven', Alethea's and the Lady Abbess' strictures recalling all too clearly 'the bad old days when I was considering the claims of Rome' whose final stone of stumbling was submission to 'Authority'); to hope that Alethea's mind would be 'broadened' by Dr Bannister and that in her own particular case the Lady Abbess would be 'merciful' (i.e. broadminded) also[136]; to write to the Lady Abbess exculpating herself from blame for 'the events round Chiara's death' by telling her that she had acted in good faith but had experienced such 'horror and revulsion' afterwards that she would never act in the same way again. The Lady Abbess' response was not what Aelfrida wanted to hear: in practising euthanasia she had behaved in a wholly un-Catholic fashion and could not become an oblate unless repudiating the thought of it, that her not confessing her action to Dom Bede was 'very wicked'[137], that she believed Aelfrida did not "really want to be a Catholic" because of her dislike of anything 'partisan or sectarian', and that her 'clothing' as an oblate would not be a 'reward of merit' or a sign that she had reached 'a certain standard of virtue' but recognition that she came to Malling as a 'penitent, … God's mercy [being] greater than His judgement'.[138] No wonder, then, that even at this early stage in her preparations Aelfrida decided that she had already undergone what Stephen Grellet described as 'deep baptisms' and that she was 'very much exhausted' as a result.[139]

Deeper baptisms were to follow, for she was only now beginning to realise that 'the Way of the Cross' implied much more than 'just talk or feeling'[140], that her visionary experience of Christ's temptation in the desert in which she saw Him struggle 'to bring His human will into perfect conformity with the Divine Will' was indicative of the struggles she too would undergo, and that although God already seemed 'to act more than I do'[141]

in her prayers and meditations, such 'commerce of God in [her] soul', though accompanied by raptures in which she heard His voice 'calling [her], saying "*Come*"'[142], was not an invitation to relax into knowledge that, Anthony and Constantine having fallen by the wayside, there was now a more important male figure in her life than they. It was, rather, rendering herself vulnerable to God, laying-open her soul to a higher authority than her own desires, acceptance of responsibility for her own actions such as she had never faced before, and loss of every hiding-place she had ever invented. She accepted the challenge, however – and within two years it nearly killed her.

Battle commenced. But 'six solid hours' meditation and a four-page fugue on 'Authority or Orthodoxy' after which she found nothing 'unchallenged or final' when compared to 'holiness … and the spirit of God'[143] were nothing compared to hours of the night, 'night after night', during which 'God takes me and deals with me in *sterner* fashion' than ever before, showing her 'the essential triviality and cheapness' of her nature and how '*this* is not fully yielded, nor *this* nor *this*', '*this*' being pride, complacency, and self-satisfaction respectively, until she turned in desperation 'to the Cross to forget [her]self in union with the Crucified'.[144] And is it purely coincidental that Aelfrida's extreme and bitter self-analysis was carried on at night under the same roof as that under which Dr Bannister analysed Alethea during the day?

Even here she found little consolation, discovering to her dismay that, following 'an evening of God's "shewings" ('Himself, His very Self, in majesty so great that I seemed to melt like wax') from which she '*ought to* emerge wholly sanctified' but did not, that the tenacity of her sins would make her unable to sustain the intensity of the experiences which God now bestowed on her[145], experiences she could not ignore ('I *have* to listen … it is not a *passive* experience') because 'when He imparts Himself to me … my mind and spirit are *intensely* active [with] an activity in God not in itself'.[146] Nor could she obtain respite in gentle meditations on God's love for her, for the extreme intensity of the 'shewings' suggested that 'nothing else [would] do' at this point but reinstatement of exhausting meditations on the Passion and that if God chose to set His seal on her by endowing her with stigmata[147], exhausted and stigmatic she would be.

She recommended meditations on the Passion with trepidation because these were contrary to the Lady Abbess' recent instructions and because she wondered if stigmata which appeared on the palms and backs of both hands immediately she began (she describes them as barely visible, purplish, circular, and slightly indented 'scars' which made her palms 'tingle and burn' and sometimes gave rise to 'stabbing pains') were manifestations of 'pure hysteria' attributable to her distressed state of mind. Deciding that they were *not* 'the result of hysteria' ('I hope') but signs of God's 'overwhelming … honour'[148] and that she should not ask Him to spare her while making her a saint, she continued her meditations, only to discover that greater mortification awaited her: her guardian angel's insistence that she was to *sleep* in the same position as that in which she meditated on the Passion and in which she had first received the stigmata in 1913, lying flat on her back with arms outstretched in physical imitation of the Crucified.

To her credit, she tried, though not before protesting that she 'thought it would be impossible and anyway what was the point' and that she did not want to do anything 'silly' that would damage her health. But on her guardian angel telling her that the unnatural posture was to remind her that she took too much 'natural' pleasure in her association with Malling and that her 'love of being noticed … *must* be eradicated', she acquiesced, noting that the cruciform position altered the quality of such sleep as she had, making it as 'light and sensitive as though one's soul were surely with God while one's consciousness of it slept'. Gratifying though this was to one striving for continual 'union with the Crucified', she soon decided that to meditate on the Passion 'to the utmost limit of [her] endurance' (i.e. for around two hours) and then to sleep in the same position was 'unwise' because conducive less to 'deep, deep peace in the utmost recesses of [her] soul' than to insomnia and exhaustion which 'left none of [her] for ordinary life'.[149] (She also worried lest people notice stigmatic marks on her hands; it seems that no one did, not even observant Dr Cooper.)[150] One consolation, however, she received: attending noon Communion unfasting at St Botolph's and feeling '*outcast*' because unable to communicate as a result, she underwent the amazing experience of Christ giving her 'the Elements Himself, His spiritualised Body and Blood … a real and lovely grace to me unworthy' and of beholding Him 'like the picture on the Turin Shroud but with His face glorified not "marred"', an image which would remain in her mind's eye for ever and render her impervious to reproof from her guardian angel that she took overmuch delight 'in supernatural things'.[151]

'Supernatural things' became a greater joy and preoccupation at Whitsuntide 1934 as a gap in her diary from 10–19 May demonstrates: on 11 May she was allowed (after some hesitation on the part of the Lady Abbess and only for a week) to return to Malling.

The week was remarkable for three things. The first was confession to Dom Bede Frost during which Aelfrida failed to mention her mercy-killing of Chiara

but informed him in circumlocutionary fashion ('the result you expect') that she had received the stigmata on several occasions. (She did not, it seems, mention Aleister Crowley's letter.) Father Bede's response to this startling news was that she must ensure that 'shewings' of this nature increased humility, not spiritual pride; he also informed her that reparative practices must be carried out in 'soberness and moderation', advice Aelfrida chose to ignore almost as soon as tendered. The second involved lengthy discussions with 'my Lady Mother whom I love more than anyone else in the world' during which Aelfrida soberly confessed or the Lady Abbess pointed out sins as yet unresolved: '[her] love of admiration and of being the centre of attention'; that her love of Solitude had less to do with being alone with God and more to do with finding herself 'the best company in the world'; that a supposedly 'detached' affection for other people was largely love of seeing herself mirrored in their admiration for her, 'and so on'. (After one conversation Aelfrida's guardian angel appeared holding a mirror in which he made her 'look at myself as I really was … all night'; she did not like what she saw.) The Lady Abbess also informed her that because she was 'so spoilt' she would have to be 'sent away somewhere' to be 'disciplined' by someone 'used to the contemplative vocation', a proposition to which Aelfrida agreed provided Alethea no longer needed her and that she went at a time of her own choosing because 'I must be with Agatha'. She also stipulated that if sent to a convent it was to be 'as an unknown penitent, not as the widow (*sic*) of a consul–general or as Aelfrida Tillyard who writes books' because she was 'in *desperate* earnest' and like 'Tom' in *The Water Babies,* '*must* be clean'.

The third event was perhaps the most unexpected, the Lady Abbess accusing her of not keeping her rule, now spelled with a capital R. (Aelfrida protested that she had done so 'with the greatest exactions'; the evidence of her own diary refutes her statement.) After Compline on 17 May 1934 she was clothed as an oblate.

The service, throughout which she was obliged to kneel, was fortunately short. In the course of it she received a scapular 'drenched in Holy Water' which she wore by day and placed under her pillow at night, the name of 'Placida' (5 October, her birthday, was St Placid's Day, he being an early Christian martyr), a patron saint (St Thomas Aquinas) in whose writings she was to find 'an excellent definition of my chief sin *presumption*' (or as he put it, "*expecting to have the vision of God without taking the trouble to lead a saintly life*"; 'you have it exactly', Aelfrida noted), and a motto 'chosen for me by my guardian angel so that I *know* that it is right': "*Glorificate et portate Deum in corpore vestro*".

There was yet another privilege to be accorded the oblate so happy at bearing and glorifying God in her own person 'that I can hardly bear myself': that of being allowed to pray alone with the Lady Abbess ('a great favour'), Aelfrida in the visitors' chapel, the Lady Abbess behind the grille. But what began as privilege ended as revelation. As she knelt, very conscious at first of 'the discomfort of [her] position, [of] cold and fatigue' and of extraneous noises (the rustle of the Abbess' habit, a bird singing loudly outside) but determined to 'push away all thoughts of [her]self and [to begin] to adore God', a wonderful thing happened: 'my soul', she writes, 'began to mount and mount. I was for a moment aware of the tabernacle, blazing like a sheaf of light … but all that faded and all consciousness of self except what was needed to know that I met with God'. Meditating on her experience three days later, she assured herself that 'there could be no question of delusion': she had, for a moment, received a hint of perfect splendour in a beatific vision of Godhead. No-one 'but God Himself', she added, 'could have brought about an experience' – 'a trance', she called it – in which 'every particle of my being was claimed and taken' and during which she loved without emotion, apprehended without thought, and experienced the 'bare knowing that I was touching God'. 'Coming back' was agony: 'to judge from the difficulty I had in moving and breathing, I must have been motionless without breath'. (For twenty or thirty minutes, she later calculated.) She 'even had a moment of panic too lest [she] should never be able to make contact with the world again'. Stumbling out into the open air she was greeted by 'novice-oblate' Sister Bathida ("Sister Placida, is it not?") and comforted with restorative hot milk in the guest-house by Sister Ethelburga, both ladies recognising that Placida had undergone a major mystical experience in the darkling chapel. The following day she returned to Cambridge 'absorbed in the wonder of it all, God in me and I in Him … to Him be praise!'[152]

At Wetenhall Cottage, Sister Placida was deluged with disapproval. Eustace, having made practical enquiries as to the 'time of probation before one was an oblate' and receiving the reply that Aelfrida had been a 'postulant' for six months and would now be a 'novice' for a year, told her firmly to 'draw back before it was too late as I should … never tolerate the implied infringement of my personal liberty'. (Placida replied placidly that she was perfectly willing to give up certain things such as writing novels – the Lady Abbess was shortly to forbid publication of O Passionate World, giving no reason for her diktat – because being an oblate was 'something quite serious'; as she had already disengaged herself from Hutchinson and Co, this was

hardly a hardship.) Julius said he thought becoming an oblate was an 'archaism' but wrote "God bless thee in all the windings of thy earthly pilgrimage". Mina pronounced her sister-in-law's new life "rather strange and meaningless". Lucy Verey seems to have been non-committal. Joan Cooper implored her not to give way to "anti-social instincts" ('what does she mean?' Aelfrida asked, 'anti-social instincts suggests bootlegging and speakeasies or worse!')[153] Alethea and Agatha remained silent – or their comments went unrecorded.

Family disapproval was not, alas, the only disciplining the new oblate was obliged to undergo, for within days of returning from Malling, Placida found herself subjected to rather more than 'implied' infringements of her personal liberty. The first was a strong hint from the Lady Abbess that she use a rosary, a hint which set Aelfrida's Nonconformist teeth on edge ('I have not so far been able to bring myself to [do so]')[154]; the second posed even more of a problem. While Aelfrida was at Malling, the Lady Abbess informed her that 'nuns took the discipline "as a matter of course"' but did not suggest that Aelfrida follow suit; indeed, she was horrified when she later discovered that Aelfrida had 'taken' it too. Following her return home, however, Aelfrida took it upon herself 'as an oblate' to attempt self-chastisement as a form of mortification through physical punishment. Lacking a proper scourge, she used a narrow leather strap to give herself '25 good cuts just above [her] left knee (an easily accessible place)' and, two hours later, '50 more, so that the skin was all raised in weals'. The discomfort, she decided, was negligible compared to that of the stigmata or her omnipresent backache or to the physical and mental pain of a two-hour meditation 'in the attitude of the Crucified … trying to see the world from the point of view of the Cross' which separated one bout of 'discipline' from the other, but the spectacular bruising which discoloured her thigh the following day was alarming. She was also revolted by the very notion of a scourge because 'slapping myself with a strap makes me … feel an archaistic fool' (the scourging took place shortly after Julius' talk of 'archaism') and because she wondered if regular scourgings ('a kind of spite') might cause her to hate her own body, an entity which should be prized because it provided the medium for 'eyes to see Beauty and ears to hear Truth'. Furthermore, she was already subjecting herself to pain by meditating on the Passion for as long as and in the position she did ('the pain felt in meditation … may be merely imaginative sympathy but is extraordinarily real') and although infliction of pain in this way might seem 'far more morbid than the use of the discipline', it was this and not a leather strap which disciplined her will, enlightened her intellect, kindled her affections, and prepared her 'for the Beatific Vision'.[155] So she desisted – for the time being.

The third 'infringement' was the severest of all. The Lady Abbess's statement that because Aelfrida was so 'spoilt' that she would have to be sent away 'to be disciplined' was not an idle threat; she had a 'disciplinarian' in mind. (She herself was forbidden on health grounds to act as spiritual adviser to extern oblates and Father Bede was not, rather curiously, 'considered adequate'.)[156] Aelfrida, she now wrote, was to be handed over to Father Lucius Cary SSJE, 'one of the Cowley Fathers at Oxford'[157], Father Carey writing shortly afterwards to put himself at Aelfrida's (as she put it) 'disposal'. Telling herself that she had just received "one of the most important letters you have ever had in your life" (and also a favourable impression of Father Cary's 'cultivated language [and] his simplicity'), Aelfrida decided (though 'it will be *very* hard') that she would 'not mind as desperately as [she] thought … having to talk to him about [her] spiritual experiences'[158], an impression confirmed on meeting Father Cary while on retreat at St Ursula's Convent in Chiswick.

Father Cary, she wrote, was 'very, very wise', adding 'I am sure he is a saint for he makes no display of his fine intellect and his great oratorical gifts, [his] appeal is solely to the *spirit* and for God's sake alone'. In the course of two private sessions, she made her confession (she does not tell us what she said but from a message from the Lady Abbess passed on via Alethea reprimanding her for her 'constant craving for attention', her obsessive interest in her 'own states of mind and spiritual experiences', and for false humility – Aelfrida, she said, was more interested 'in the experience of humility' than being humble[159] – we may guess what passed), informed Father Cary that she had been sent to him to be disciplined and told him 'something of [her] circumstances and dispositions' and of her 'religious experiences', the latter with the greatest possible reluctance and only because she was 'under obedience' to do so. (Father Cary's advice was to practise '*Simplicity*' and to eschew 'meditation that might lead to physical results'.) Discovering that her first meeting with her new spiritual director had lifted her 'above the mists and miasmas of personal preoccupations into the clear air of the Spirit' but also that she had time to kill in London before the departure of her Cambridge train, Aelfrida returned to 'mists and miasmas' by asking herself if she was 'enough "detached" to go and see Anthony?'[160] Discovering that she was, she engineered the meeting with him described in an earlier chapter.

The fact that her spiritual director was based in Oxford was precisely what Aelfrida wanted because not entirely irrelevant to her present life. For one thing, she had already decided to spend the winter of 1934–35 there, possibly as a guest of Dorothy Smith, the latter having moved her dental practice from London to Oxford. For another, the visit to Oxford with Agatha and Alethea in August 1932 on which she realised her incompetence as a parent following Agatha's disclosures concerning her sexuality had predisposed Aelfrida to life in a 'sister university … so much like Cambridge … in beauty, in peace, in spirit', the presence of Somerville and St Hilda's notwithstanding. (Oxford's women's colleges were 'very inferior' to Girton and Newnham.)[161] Even more relevantly, Alethea's spiritual director at Malling was Father O'Brien, the then Superior of the SSJE, and perhaps a spirit of competition spurred her mother on in this respect. Most importantly, Father Cary's presence in Oxford and herself 'under obedience' to place herself in his hands, provided her with the perfect excuse to leave Wetenhall Cottage, a step not so much retrograde (as in the case of Father Savinien who had urged her to return to a husband from whom she was doing her unacknowledged utmost to detach herself) as a stride forward on her 'closer walk with God'. Nor could anyone complain that she had allied herself with another unsuitable 'guru': the Cowley Fathers were a respected Community of which Father Cary was a senior member. But if Aelfrida thought life as his pupil was to be one in which a compatible intellectual equal placed himself at her 'disposal', she could not have been more mistaken: Father Cary was to prove rigorous and uncompromising and an intellectual and spiritual *force majeure* such as she had encountered only once before.

Aelfrida returned to Cambridge from Chiswick more determined than ever to consider her new mode of life less in terms of the suffering it might bring (whether to herself or to other people is not stated but given that she had earlier complained of Alethea's 'holy selfishness'[162] in putting herself and her vocation before her mother's interests and welfare, we must assume to herself) or the joy it might bring to herself and more as '*the Will of God for me*'.[163] She was, however, dismayed to find common sense in the shape of the devil (rarely, unlike Deity, granted a capital letter) warning her that she had accomplished nothing so far by her efforts to transform her soul from '[her] own private house' to a chapel for God to dwell in' in which 'many things that would have done … as furniture for [her] own private house are entirely out of place'[164] and asking her "why make yourself miserable by trying? You only deprive yourself of natural joys and get nothing in return". She agreed ('so it seems sometimes')[165] but pressed on regardless: 'if only I had known years ago, that [God] would impart Himself to me … I would have tried much harder to be good … I would have trained myself more strictly and paid less attention to … worldly preoccupations'.[166]

Trying to silence her 'craving to *feel myself good*' ('a dreadful taint') or to 'find out how good I am or whether I am even good at all'[167], she realised the magnitude of her task and abandoned it until under Father Cary's direct supervision. Humility did not come easily either though she attempted it by 'never talking about myself and saying as little as possible about myself in my letters'. She would even, she decided, 'try and not write about myself here'[168] (i.e. in her diary) but as her next entry shows (it is five paragraphs long; three begin and are littered with the personal pronoun and the fifth is introspective), 'not to talk about oneself' required such exhausting and constant 'vigilance'[169] that she abandoned it as a 'silly business'[170] which might alienate her from a biographer and from herself. How fortunate that she failed, for otherwise biography might have ended here.

Not having sufficient 'deep baptisms' to endure, her physical health, precarious before and since Chiara's death, broke down further. An attack of cystitis, attributed by Dr Cooper to attendance at early service in cold weather and by Aelfrida to Alethea's insistence that even a draught of water constituted breaking her fast, was taken as another mortification, her only consolation being (for with Chiara dead and her daughters preoccupied, there was no-one to 'pet her up') that Alethea had given up *her* 'invalid ways'[171] as a result of Dr Bannister's treatment. In bed with one of her 'rheumatic attacks' and having closeted herself in SERENITY to keep a retreat and commune with God, an episode of 'cramp in [her] heart … and in [her] throat' so severe that she expected to die there and then of 'suffocation'[172] (a worrying symptom if attributable to angina) caused her to wonder how she could offer herself as an extern oblate while 'such a poor thing'.[173]

As Dr Bannister and Aelfrida herself recognised ("you *have* been buffeted about haven't you?" he asked sympathetically on hearing her version of recent events), she was once again close to breakdown and this, and realisation that she was living, emotionally speaking, on borrowed time, enhanced her desire to escape to healing silence and solitude in Oxford. What might have happened had she been unable to leave Wetenhall Cottage is hard to tell but increasing panic that Agatha and Alethea would never leave her was certainly counterbalanced by the hope that one of them (preferably Alethea) would realise her 'need of a daughter'[174] to look after her when she was 'at [her] familiar occupation of a day in bed'[175] or in the event of her suffering another mental breakdown. But because not even 'Cambridge [and] this perfect house and garden'[176] tempted either daughter to stay, she

had to rely on physical illness for temporary respite from intolerable spiritual and emotional pressures pending her departure for Oxford, though this was only to remit the inevitable intellectual, spiritual, emotional, and bodily breakdown predicted by Dr Cooper after Chiara's death of which Aelfrida's brief but total collapse in Ealing was a precursor.

Life at Wetenhall Cottage during the late spring and early summer of 1934 was unconducive to recuperation, for the house was not the happy place Aelfrida pretended it was. Though visitors (particularly if male) were met with smiling faces by the three Graham women, their vaunted unity was destroying itself from within. Never can the names of their respective rooms have seemed so ironic to Aelfrida suffering spiritual torments in SERENITY, to Agatha weeping in JOY, and to Alethea, her girlhood gone and her religion 'so joyless, so austere' in comparison to Aelfrida's 'all shining with God's presence felt'[177], grimly keeping her vocation in PRAISE. Of Georgina in FIDELITY we hear little, though her comments on the 'odd family' for whom she worked would have made interesting reading, and it may be that Aelfrida's suspicion that Georgina (like Church and Mrs Thompson, for all that the latter was Conrad John's aunt) was inspired less by devotion to her employer than by respect for Chiara's daughter was correct. But if, as Aelfrida hoped, un-praising Alethea or joyless Agatha would elect to remain with her, she was wrong.

Alethea's final session with Dr Bannister took place on 4 May 1934, whereupon he declared her (so she told her mother) "fit to go anywhere and do anything"[178] but suggested that she take a holiday or take up a "holiday post"[179] before returning to Malling. (She did both.) Aelfrida, 'sad, sad, sad that Alethea goes'[180], expressed grave concerns for her daughter's future, for not only had the Lady Abbess already hinted that although Alethea undoubtedly had a vocation, she would 'very likely never be able to fulfil it'[181], but Dr Bannister too was reluctant to pronounce her cured ("that is for the patient's subsequent history to declare") and it seems to have been contrary to his instructions (he prescribed a year's 'activity of body and mind … in "the world"' and preferably away from home before she returned to conventual life)[182] that Alethea, still harbouring suspicions concerning her mother's intention of supplanting her at Malling or of inveigling the Lady Abbess into placing her 'under obedience' to remain 'in the world and earn money for [her mother]')[183] or perhaps just desperate to escape from the smothering atmosphere of Wetenhall Cottage and the brooding 'First House' next door, acted as she did, returning to Malling in September 1934 after four months' absence.

Agatha, too, departed, only to return and depart again. On 16 February 1934, 'looking rather mournful' (she had no wish to enter the teaching profession) but furnished with glowing references from Eustace, she had attended Tortington Park School in Sussex for an interview. Her mother, seeing her off, noted that although Agatha had plenty of courage, she lacked 'physical (*sic*) strength' and prayed to God 'to give her as much of both as she needs'.[184] She also prayed that Agatha might 'marry here in Cambridge' and take over Wetenhall Cottage in order that she herself could 'dispose of it without wronging the Lares and Penates' but added that not even the return to Cambridge of one of Agatha's admirers was likely to overcome her younger daughter's 'inhibition' with regard to men[185], 'aunt' for Hugh Janisch though she might.

Agatha left for Tortington on 16 April, keen 'to show what she can do in the world'.[186] (An earlier comment that her 'favourite kind of embroidery [was] not *petit point* [but] *point du tout*'[187] should have warned her mother that 'Temu's' negativistic view of life extended to more than stitchery but Aelfrida chose to attribute the remark to wit.) Tortington Park was not, however, the best school for an unwilling and inexperienced teacher – its policy was laissez faire, no punishments were imposed, staff turnover was high, and the girls were not encouraged to be academic – and within a month 'precious little Temu', though 'managing beautifully in lessons which interested her', was being 'ragged' in others (she was unable, she said, to 'impose Authority for Authority's sake' on spoilt rich children termed by her mother 'plutobrats') and had been warned by the headmistress that early dismissal was likely.[188] It was. Agatha returned to Wetenhall Cottage on 9 June to acid comments from her elder sister that this would teach her humility (humility, said Aelfrida severely, was not to be confused with discouragement) and to rueful regret ('I *did* want a little peace and quiet … [and] I hate to see life disciplining my Temu') and a certain chagrin ('it was hard to tell [Eustace] of Agatha's debacle … one does like one's children to do well')[189] from her mother.

But although Agatha seemed cheerful on her return, dismissing dismissal as a matter of 'minor importance', it is obvious from the inertia which regained its hold over her and from her comparison of her life to a walk in a wood "heavy and oppressive with evening and apprehensive as if every opening in the trees and every dark vault and shadow [housed] spirits … and shadows", that a young woman soon to celebrate her twenty-fourth birthday was both depressed and distressed. (Aelfrida, wilfully blind to a daughter inside whose mind she still professed to be able to walk about, merely noted that Agatha was better fitted 'to write Poetry [than to] teach little Plutobrats'.)[190] She was also as keen as her mother

to leave a house which even now the latter persisted in believing to be 'a haven of peace' in which 'the three of us' could be '[so] happy, just quietly here'.[191]

Going was difficult, for Wetenhall Cottage, so cosy and comfortable in winter when compared to the real or enforced rigours of Fordfield, was exquisite in summer. Embowered among 'trees and flowers and birds' in a way that Fordfield 'lofty and aloof on a terrace'[192] had never been, the Cottage was agreed by Agatha and Aelfrida (though not by Alethea who seems to have regarded it as a prison or as a snare set by her mother) to be 'all that a house should be, a bit of perfection in an imperfect world'.[193] It was the 'prettiness of the garden'[194], however, which particularly called upon them to stay, the garden on which Church expended as much devotion as he had on that of the 'First House', where Aelfrida reclined 'basking in the heat' while she read and wrote and recited 'all the Day Hours'[195] and watched swallows feeding their young in nests under the eaves, and where Agatha slept outside at night beneath the white chestnut planted by her great-grandfather, so that when possible tenants came to view and Alethea 'urged *yes*', Agatha and Aelfrida, cried '*no, no*'.[196]

There was also Julius to consider, for the man who had regularly returned to Fordfield 'tired and discouraged'[197], now retreated to Wetenhall Cottage where, 'settled and happy', he found 'some of the "perfect peace of Fordfield" [which] caresses and soothes him as nothing else can'. (Alethea observed tartly that he would be 'better without it'.) But whereas in May Aelfrida had believed that 'if anything could make me … feel that I ought to try and go on living here' it would be 'my Dudu'[198], by mid-July she was so keen to place herself under Father Cary's direction that her attitude hardened and Julius became 'tired and discouraged' for another reason: his sister had found tenants for Wetenhall Cottage and Dudu's happiness was to be sacrificed to hers.

Having decided that 'the one place I want to go to is a convent'[199] and that, failing Malling, Oxford would have to do, Aelfrida wrote to the Mother Superior of 'a small, poor and simple' convent there asking if she, 'a widow (*sic*) aged fifty, with simple tastes' could overwinter there in order to 'keep a simple rule'.[200] The convent, unfortunately, 'had no room for [her]'[201] (it seems, too, that Dorothy Smith evinced no great eagerness to have her stay) so she was forced to make other arrangements. But it was not only the Convent of the Holy Childhood which snubbed her; it appeared that Father Cary was about to do so too.

'My guardian angel', wrote Aelfrida indignantly on 18 July 1934, 'is pleased that I should be humiliated'. (He must have heard her plea of two days earlier that she be made 'more disciplined [and] more submissive'.)[202] The angel's pleasure was manifested by two letters, one, 'very courtly', from Father Cary informing Aelfrida that she would not be 'comfortable' in a small convent and that it was not worth her while coming to Oxford to submit herself to him, the other, from the Lady Abbess of Malling, informing her that Father Cary had told her that Mrs Graham did not know how to use a spiritual director and that she was very disappointed at her new oblate's lack of humility.[203]

Aelfrida was furious. She had let Wetenhall Cottage in obedience to the Abbess's commands so was imminently homeless and the Lady Abbess had been 'high-handed' in sending her to Father Cary when she did not want to go: 'I dislike and do not believe in all this turning one's soul inside out [and] to go and prate to any man, priest or monk though he may be, of God's dealings with [my] soul seems to be sacrilege. I can't see that it is either right or seemly to go and tell anybody what should be a secret between me and God … If I had known [she] would make me tell other people, I would certainly have kept silence'.[204] Then realising that her rant was hardly submissive or indicative of a wish to associate herself with a Community where she would be not so much 'understood' as '*disciplined*'[205], she recanted – a little: 'the one kind of discipline I should feel would be to find myself in a situation where … nobody special wanted to be bothered about me … no, *no*, I am not complaining, I am merely rejoicing that my guardian angel is so delicately adjusting the punishment to fit the crime'.[206]

Father Cary, being a man, got off lightly. First, he was correct: 'I *don't* know how to use a director'.[207] (Had nobody instructed her or was she too arrogant to learn?) Second, looking at Father Cary's refusal dispassionately, she was 'immensely relieved that I should not have my soul *messed about* by anyone' – though 'of course', she admitted, 'left to myself, I make mistakes'. ('But that is how one learns', she added.) Regarding his refusal from the point of view of an 'indocile'[208] oblate was a different matter: to put herself in Christ's hands to be '*broken* as well as blessed by Him' was the only thing that might give her value in God's (and Cary's) eyes. Her resolve was strengthened by a vision of a crown of thorns placed on her head by invisible hands and by sudden consequent realisation that 'He *will* break me. I know He will … Now I must help Agatha wash up'.[209] He did.

None of this augured well for relationships to be sustained with Abbess or Father. Comparing herself to Alethea (her daughter, she wrote, had once and would again 'quietly hand over her will and her conscience to the Community and … just obey'), Aelfrida noted that she gave 'conformity' rather than 'obedience' and that

whereas 'I may in each separate occasion obey promptly and willingly … I always retain my critical intelligence [and] therefore I am always … a potential rebel'.[210] And with that the 'potential' rebel arranged to submit herself to Father Cary and to live at another 'small, poor and simple' convent in Oxford, initially in its guesthouse but as soon as a rented house in the precincts became available, to move into the 'poor little place' which was 'just as [she] meant it to be'.[211]

There was, however, her immediate future to be provided for: Wetenhall Cottage was let from 1 August and it was now mid-July. At that point Aelfrida remembered that a small Cambridge convent to which a student hostel was attached also took paying guests and decided that she and Agatha would move there pending her own departure from Cambridge (Alethea was to leave for Elfinsward, a Malling retreat house, on 23 July prior to returning to Malling itself in September) and until Agatha found a more permanent lodging in which to pursue (with Eustace's help) her interest in English literature. But when Agatha discovered her mother's plan she wept bitterly, for she had already approached the convent with a view to living in their hostel as a means of breaking with her. Informing Aelfrida that she loved her 'much too much', that while she and her mother lived under the same roof she 'would never do anything but run to [her]', and that 'she *must* try and live on her own', Agatha stormed against the Lady Abbess, the priesthood, and the mother who now seemed to be thinking of reasons why she should delay 'going'.[212]

Agatha was right; with departure imminent, Aelfrida panicked: 'I am *afraid* [but] I cannot now go back'. Not going back was less for practical reasons (though in disposing of her house, one can detect a whiff of burning boats) than for spiritual ones: 'in this strange work that God seems to be doing in me … He calls me to go on'. Going on, however, involved stripping herself of 'all pleasures in which there was an admixture of *self*'[213]: masculine company (of a 'sudden inspiration' on Fidelio's part to visit Wetenhall Cottage, she wrote 'seeing him made it harder to go')[214]; her house ('I felt that really it *was* rather splendid of me to be willing to give up anything so charming')[215]; her ability to enmesh strangers in her 'magic net' by laying herself out to attract them[216]; her love of attracting attention (attempts to divest herself of this particular sin are described as a kind of 'virtuous hide and seek')[217]; her 'naughty ways' of opting out of unpleasant tasks and of providing herself with little 'treats' (of which she noted that Alethea would probably say of attempts at penitence that her 'ashes were not thick enough and [her] sackcloth mere fancy dress'[218] – and at this point in the career of the extern oblate, Alethea was quite right); even her last hope of matrimony to, of all people, 'Dr Joan's' elderly father, Joseph Cooper having recently hinted that he and Aelfrida might enter a 'marriage of companionship'. (This last temptation, she decided, was really no temptation, merely 'an added reason for feeling that I do well to go to a convent'.)[219] Nevertheless she summoned sufficient strength to dismiss Georgina and Mrs Thompson (she retained the services of Church as jobbing gardener to her Wetenhall Cottage tenants) and prepared to leave the house of which she pretended that 'Fidelity, Joy, Praise and Serenity have been ours'.[220]

Her mind made up, her mood lightened. Eustace attributed this to excitement 'at the prospect of fresh adventures', Julius to his sister's natural desire to 'take Oxford by storm' *à la* Zuleika Dobson.[221] (A lady, we should remember, who left a train of suicides in her wake.) Aelfrida herself, noting that 'it might dawn on Julius and Eustace by degrees that I mean … to lead the life of a nun'[222], wrote that though hard 'to face separation and departure'[223], she had made the right decision. Significantly, perhaps, her farewells were said less to people than to places: the 'Cambridge blue sky' shining over 'green water "green as a dream"' (she did not complete the line from Rupert Brooke's *The Old Vicarage, Grantchester* "and deep as death"), the 'grey-green willows, flame-green grass'[224] of the meadows beside the river which had so many associations for her, the cottage commemorating her Wetenhall name and ancestry. The last night of her Cambridge life was spent there alone, walking through 'the beloved little house' to say goodbye to each and every room as she had done only a year before at Fordfield. For an hour or two she lay awake 'to look through some of my treasure-house of thoughts – ghosts (not sad ghosts) of children in the garden, [of] Little Katie, and Constantine, and so many others'[225], before deciding 'we must go out into wilderness'. But God, she added firmly, 'goes with us [and] all three of us, the sweet daughters and I, have given ourselves completely into His hands'. And, a final consolation, 'I am sure my guardian angel is arranging everything beautifully.[226]

## Notes

1 GCPPT 1|1|44 24 October 1933 ('29 October' in error).

2 ibid. 15 October 1933.

3 ibid. 27 October 1933.

4 ibid. 24 October 1933.

5 ibid. 25 October 1933.

6 ibid. 14 and 16 October 1933.

7 GCPPT 3|1 Letter from Alethea Graham to Aelfrida of 30 October 1933.

8 ibid. Undated letter written after 30 October and before 12 November 1933.

9 GCPPT 1|1|44 23 October 1933.

10 ibid. 27 October 1933.

11 GCPPT 1|1|37 12 June 1930.

12 GCPPT 1|1|44 2 November 1933.

13 H C Hughes' original plans for Wetenhall Cottage differ somewhat from the house as built.

14 GCPPT 1|1|44 31 October 1933.

15 ibid. 1 November 1933.

16 ibid. 29 October 1933.

17 ibid. 6 November 1933.

18 ibid. 31 October 1933.

19 ibid. 2 November 1933.

20 ibid. 27 October 1933.

21 ibid. 29 October 1933.

22 ibid. 31 October 1933.

23 ibid. 3 November 1933.

24 ibid. 1 November 1933.

25 GCPPT 1|1|25 20 May 1920.

26 GCPPT 1|1|44 12 October 1933.

27 ibid. 14 October 1933.

28 GCPPT 1|1|28 14 May 1924.

29 GCPPT 1|1|44 12 October 1933.

30 GCPPT 1|1|49 15 August 1935.

31 GCPPT 1|1|44 11 October 1933.

32 GCPPT 1|1|43 28 December 1932.

33 ibid. 31 December 1932.

34 GCPPT 1|1|44 3 July 1933.

35 GCPPT 1|1|45 8 December 1933.

36 Tillyard, Ae. *The Closer Walk with God*. p 2.

37 ibid. p 1.

38 Angela Yaffey, personal communication 23 April 2007.

39 Tillyard, Ae. *The Closer Walk with God* p 1.

40 GCPPT 1|1|41 7 August 1931. Aelfrida may have derived the name of her Fordfield attic room from John Bunyan who in *Pilgrim's Progress* has Pilgrim spend the night in an upper room in House Beautiful following his ascent of Hill Difficulty; waking at dawn, he calls the room 'Peace'.

41 GCPPT 1|1|40 26 June 1931 records that Aelfrida won a prize in a "Modern Collect" competition held by the *Church News*. Her collect ran in part "For serenity. Grant, O Lord … a serene and quiet spirit [that we] may possess a joy … no calamity can take from us" (GCPPT 1|1|40a. Undated cutting from *Church News*).

42 GCPPT 1|1|44 3 and 4 November 1933. Tillyard, Ae. *Messages* pp 27–33.

43 GCPPT 1|1|44 5 November 1933.

44 Tillyard, Ae. *Messages* pp 39–40.

45 GCPPT 1|1|58 28 August 1940.

46 GCPPT 1|1|45 18 November 1933.

47 ibid.

48 GCPPT 1|6 Wetenhall Cottage Consecration November 18 1933.

49 GCPPT 1|1|45 18 November 1933

50 ibid. 3 January 1934. The book, with its cracked wooden cover, still exists (GCPPT 1|1b).

51 ibid. 20 December 1933.

52 ibid. 1 January 1934.

53 ibid.

54 ibid. 20 November 1934.

55 Altounyan T. pp171–182. Frank Stokoe, together with John Rickman (1880–1951), psychiatrist, Freudian psychoanalyst, and friend of Tommy Altounyan since medical student days (he was the 'earth' element of Altounyan's comparison, Stokoe being 'air and water' and he himself 'fire'), acted *in loco parentis* to the Altounyan children when they were at school in England. Stokoe and Rickman separately accompanied the children to the Lake District during school holidays where they and the children appeared in fictionalised form in Arthur Ransome's *Swallows and Amazons* books, the latter as themselves, the two men as different aspects of the children's friend 'Captain Flint'.

56 GCPPT 1|1|45 19 December 1933.
57 ibid. 25 December 1933.
58 ibid. 6 November 1933.
59 ibid. 28 December 1933.
60 ibid.
61 ibid 5 December 1933.
62 ibid. 15 November 1933.
63 ibid. 22 December 1933.
64 ibid. 21, 26 and 29 November and 5 December 1933.
65 ibid. 15 and 25 November 1933.
66 ibid. 5 December 1933.
67 ibid. 20 November 1933.
68 ibid. 15 and 17 November and 2 December 1933.
69 ibid. 15 November 1933.
70 GCPPT 3|1 Letter from Alethea Graham to Aelfrida of 10 October 1933.
71 GCPPT 1|1|45 5 December 1933.
72 GCPPT 3|1 Letter from Alethea Graham to Aelfrida of 11 November 1933.
73 GCPPT 1|1|45 1 January 1934.
74 ibid. 4 January 1934.
75 GCPPG A1.4 Letter from Constantine Graham to Alethea Graham of 29 December 1933.
76 GCPPT 1|1|45 9 November 1933 and 5 January 1934.
77 ibid. 23 January 1934. Aelfrida was at Malling from 19–22 January 1934; her account is written retrospectively.
78 ibid. 17 November 1933.
79 ibid. 23 January 1934.
80 ibid. 11 January 1934.
81 ibid. 12, 13, and 14 January 1934.
82 ibid. 23 January 1934.
83 ibid. 11 January 1934.
84 ibid. 6 November 1933.
85 ibid. 23 January 1934.
86 ibid. 24 January 1934.
87 ibid. 28 January 1934.
88 ibid. 23 January 1934.
89 ibid. 29 January 1934.
90 GCPPT 1|1|38 9 October 1930.
91 ibid. 7 November 1930.
92 GCPPT 1|1|45 29 January 1934.
93 GCPPT 1|1|44 29 October 1933.
94 GCPPT 1|1|45 29 and 30 January 1934.
95 ibid. 30 January 1934. 'Sheol' was the Hebrew abode of the dead from which return was impossible, a fate Aelfrida feared for Constantine unless he repented his sins and turned to Christ, the (apocryphal) 'harrower' or spoiler of Hell following His crucifixion.
96 GCPPT 1|1|45 14 February 1934.
97 Tillyard, Ae. *O Passionate World* pp420–426 (GCPPT 2|11).
98 GCPPT 1|1|45 10 February 1934. Aelfrida quotes the concluding lines of *O Passionate World* (pp 425–426) in this diary entry, agreeing with 'Carola' that nothing was now possible but "to accept the Will of God".
99 Tillyard, Ae. *A Little Road-book for Mystics* p 138.
100 GCPPT 1|1|45 3 February 1934.
101 Tillyard, Ae. *The Closer Walk with God* pp 171 and 173.
102 GCPPT 1|1|45 Newspaper cuttings inserted in back of volume with additional comments by Aelfrida.
103 GCPPT 3|1 Letter from Alethea Graham to Aelfrida of 30 January 1934.
104 GCPPT 1|1|45 30 January 1934.
105 ibid. 1 February 1934.
106 ibid. 22 February 1934
107 ibid. 1 February 1934.
108 ibid. 9 and 10 February 1934.
109 ibid. 1 February 1934. Aelfrida's own distraught frame of mind is evidenced by the disorderly state of contemporary diary entries.
110 ibid. 27 February 1934.
111 GCPPT 1|1|32 18 April 1926.
112 GCPPT 1|1|45 7 February 1934.
113 ibid. 20 and 24 February 1934.
114 ibid. 19 February 1934.
115 ibid. 12 March 1934.
116 ibid. 20 February 1934.
117 ibid. 15 February 1934.
118 ibid. 20 February 1934.
119 ibid. 15 and 17 April 1934.
120 ibid. 9 March 1934.
121 ibid. 6 March 1934.
122 ibid. 25 February 1934.
123 ibid. 19 March 1934.
124 ibid. 8 February 1934.
125 ibid. 13 February 1934.
126 ibid.
127 ibid. 14 February 1934.
128 ibid. 9 March 1934.
129 ibid. 5 February 1934.
130 ibid. 2 March 1934.
131 *Matthew* 19:9 (KJV).
132 *Corinthians* 1:6 and 7 (KJV).
133 GCPPT 1|1|45 1 and 11 April 1934.
134 ibid. 11 April 1934.
135 ibid. 20 May 1934.
136 ibid. 30 March 1934.
137 ibid. 20 April 1934.
138 ibid. 21 April 1934.
139 ibid. 1 April 1934.
140 ibid. 5 February 1934.
141 ibid. 15 February 1934.
142 ibid. 25 February 1934.
143 ibid. 2 April 1934.
144 ibid. 6 March 1934.
145 ibid. 12 March 1934.
146 ibid. 21 March 1934. Aelfrida's use of the archaic word 'shewing' to denote visions of a particularly intimate and revelatory nature is interesting insofar as it reflects an early Christian belief concerning visions of this nature (the contemporary term was 'ostensio', Latin 'ostentatio') but is probably derived from Julian of Norwich who used the term to describe individual spiritual experiences incorporating both sensory and supra-sensory images.
147 ibid. 17 April 1934.
148 ibid. 20 and 24 April 1934.
149 ibid. 22, 25 and 25 May 1934.
150 ibid. 30 April 1934.
151 ibid. 6 and 7 May 1934.
152 ibid. 19 May 1934. Retrospective account.
153 ibid. 29 May and 1 and 10 June 1934.
154 ibid. 26 June 1934.
155 ibid. 5 June 1934.
156 ibid. 11 June 1934.
157 The Cowley Fathers, more properly the Society of Mission Priests of St John the Evangelist (usually abbreviated to SSJE), was founded by Father Richard Meux Benson in 1866 at 16 Marston Street in a suburb of Oxford named after the village and common engulfed by the south-west spread of the town in the second half of the nineteenth century. An Anglo-Catholic Benedictine foundation, its aims were two-fold: for the Fathers, an ordered communal life of liturgical prayer with added emphasis on solitary prayer and a degree

of asceticism as enhancing a life dedicated to God and, towards the world, educational and missionary endeavours involving the setting up of parochial missions in England, India (1874) and South Africa (1883). For further details and details of the life and charismatic persona of Richard Benson (1824–1915) see *ODNB* vol 5 pp 196–197 and *Benson of Cowley* ed. Martin Smith SSJE (OUP 1980).

158 GCPPT 1|1|45 11 June 1934.
159 ibid. 14 June 1934.
160 ibid. 10 July 1934.
161 GCPPT 1|1|42 27 and 29 August 1932.
162 GCPPT 1|1|45 27 April 1934.
163 ibid. 1 July 1934.
164 ibid. 10 April 1934.
165 ibid. 22 June 1934. It seems that in this context Aelfrida's 'devil' was not an evil spirit in the Augustinian sense but a classical '*daimon*' i.e. an inward mentor warning against unwise courses of action.
166 ibid. 19 March 1934.
167 ibid. 16 and 26 June 1934.
168 ibid. 11 June 1934.
169 ibid. 16 June 1934.
170 ibid. 22 June 1934.
171 ibid. 27 March 1934.
172 ibid. 12 April 1934.
173 ibid. 30 March 1934.
174 ibid. 26 May 1934.
175 ibid. 20 May 1934.
176 ibid. 26 May 1934.
177 ibid. 4 May 1934.
178 ibid.
179 ibid. 29 May 1934.
180 ibid. 23 July 1934.
181 ibid. 20 April 1934.
182 ibid. 27 April 1932.
183 ibid. 24 April 1934.
184 ibid. 16 February 1934.
185 ibid. 4 and 10 March 1934.
186 ibid. 26 April 1934.
187 ibid. 13 March 1934.
188 ibid. 24 May and 9 June 1934.
189 ibid. 3 May and 3 and 9 June 1934.
190 ibid. 5 June 1934.
191 ibid. 20 July 1934.
192 ibid. 17 April 1934.
193 ibid. 29 July 1934.
194 ibid. 10 May 1934.
195 ibid. 16 June 1934.
196 ibid. 10 May 1934.
197 ibid. 10 July 1934.
198 ibid. 5 May 1934.
199 ibid. 18 July 1934.
200 ibid. 13 July 1934.
201 ibid. 19 July 1934.
202 ibid. 16 and 18 July 1934.
203 ibid. 16 July 1934.
204 ibid. 19 July 1934.
205 ibid. 7 June 1934.
206 ibid. 18 July 1934.
207 ibid. 19 July 1934.
208 ibid. 19 and 22 July 1934.
209 ibid. 22 July 1934.
210 ibid. 8 June 1934.
211 GCPPT 1|1|46 7 August 1934.
212 GCPPT 1|1|45 19 July 1934.
213 ibid. 24 June 1934.
214 ibid. 26 July 1934.
215 ibid. 22 June 1934.
216 ibid. 3 June 1934.
217 ibid. 11 July 1934.
218 ibid. 3 June 1934.
219 ibid. 15 July 1934.
220 ibid. 25 July 1934.
221 ibid. 30 July 1934. Zuleika Dobson, heroine of Max Beerbohm's eponymous novel of 1911, is "a woman of really passionate fibre" who has never given her heart to anyone even though "strong in her were the desire and the need that it should be given". ("To be able to love once – would that not be better than all the homage in the world?"). But as a conjurer with men's affections and an "omnisubjugant" woman before whom men fall "fatuously prostrate" (op. cit. p 19), Zuleika is unlikely to encounter a man who meets her exacting standards. Having broken the hearts of all the undergraduates in Oxford, she prepares to move to Cambridge in pursuit of further victims and her *beau idéal*. The bereft Oxford undergraduates commit mass suicide by throwing themselves into the river.
222 GCPPT 1|1|45 30 July 1934.
223 ibid. 20 July 1934.
224 GCPPT 1|1|46 28 August 1934.
225 GCPPT 1|1|45 1 August 1934
    GCPPT 1|1|46 2 August 1934.
226 GCPPT 1|1|45 25 July 1934.
    GCPPT 1|1|46 2 August 1934.

# Being Nobody

Before she left Cambridge for Oxford in August 1934, Aelfrida's guardian angel 'promised to find me a place. I said all right, only it must not be too noisy'. The angel waxed 'quite indignant' at this criticism of his capabilities as an estate agent so she gave him carte blanche: 'he … found me *6 Osney Lane*'.[1]

6 Osney Lane was not, however, quite the 'poor little place' her description implied. Contemporary photographs show it as a substantial two-storeyed brick dwelling with a small walled garden to the side. The terrace of which it was one formed the southern boundary of the grounds of St Thomas' Convent, so when Aelfrida informed Ancifera that she was now living in 'convent precincts'[2], she was correct: the convent owned the row, renting it out to people like herself who wanted to live a conventual life without conventual restrictions or the enforced communality of the convent guesthouse.

The terrace of which the cottage formed the eastern end was inhabited by the convent's chaplain, guest mistress, and a floating population of 'pious ladies': elderly widows with husbands long dead or women who, widowed in the Great War, found themselves eking out small pensions in what the Victorians called 'shabby gentility', or spinsters of a certain age deprived by the same war of hopes of marriage and forced to support themselves by becoming teachers, missionaries, or nurses but who, once retired, were pensionless or existed on the tiny savings their poorly paid careers had permitted. There were, too, a number of single women whose fiancés, closet homosexuals anxious to escape 'aunting' or to disguise what were then criminal inclinations, declared for celibacy at the point when marriage could no longer be postponed on the pretext that the man was making his way in the world, leaving the girl, now in her late twenties, bereft of the hope of a husband because there were currently so few eligible men.[3] Constantine's premature death was therefore only one agency which caused his divorced wife to join the company in early middle age as a single woman neither widow nor spinster (for Aelfrida to term herself a 'widow' was as much to do with expedient respectability as it was with her belief that she was his true wife) whose penury was relative in comparison to theirs[4]; she also stood something apart from the company in having both a vocation and an occupation. The 'pious

**St Benedict's, Oxford**

ladies' nevertheless regarded her as one of themselves, a band of women silted up in the precincts of various convents, living vaguely discontented lives in sheltered and sometimes subsidised accommodation (Malling supported 'holy widows' to the tune of £400 a year), their lives given up to gossip, interpersonal rivalry, and increasing eccentricity. Though determined *not* to join a group she described as floating 'like amiable shellfish … around the shores of the religious life' because God required 'something *sterner*' of herself, and though sure they were 'good women … and there may be saints among them', Aelfrida proceeded to do just that, comparing the 'flavours' of the different convents with which she was associated exactly as the 'pious ladies' did and assuring herself that she was as 'well employed and happy'[5] as they believed themselves to be.

It seems, too, that her desire to achieve a 'closer walk with God' by moving to 'quiet places where one could meditate and study'[6] and to a conventual 'quiet place' as the only tolerable sort of refuge[7] for someone who 'needed rest for soul or body', was less a rationalisation of circumstances forced on her by Constantine's death or an ascetic desire to remove herself from comfortable middle-class life in Cambridge than a need to escape the draining effects of her daughters' emotional demands on her fracturing self: given her current mental disequilibrium, it was also a terrible mistake. First, she had no intention of settling in Oxford ('Oxford first, *quite* temporarily', she noted, 'but solitude after that'[8], Oxford being just another staging post for a "pilgrim for ever on some road divine")[9] at a point in her life when she needed nothing so much as stability. Second, by escaping to Oxford instead of remaining in Cambridge among people alert to oddities in her behaviour who could intervene if required, she was able to condemn herself to a life so Spartan that it broke her health and – almost – her spirit before she was rescued.

The convent she or her guardian angel chose was not entirely congenial. St Thomas' was 'in a poor quarter quite close to the station [with] no dignity or space' and lacked the 'overwhelming spirituality [of] Malling'. It housed twelve nuns 'with no charm' but plenty of 'goodness' because they belonged to an active order and worked hard in and for the poor parish in which they lived. (Aelfrida later described herself as living "in the slums of Oxford".)[10] The chapel, erected in 1889, was 'too Victorian to be beautiful' and the chaplain an old man whose down to earth joviality was not what she expected of a man in his position, though he was, she conceded, 'more educated than the nuns' and, having worked in South Africa, more interesting to talk to. The convent, however, had benefits apart from provision of cheap accommodation (her rent was twelve shillings a week; her Wetenhall Cottage tenants paid one guinea), for she was permitted to use its garden, library, and chapel, and a midday meal was available even to those with kitchens of their own: 'everything necessary for body and soul', as she put it.[11]

The house came with 'a bare minimum of very plain and rather ugly furniture' augmented by cutlery and linen bought cheaply from pawnshops and sales by a tenant who doubted 'whether bride sewing her trousseau put more love and happiness into it' than she into her 'convent cottage'[12], but it boasted electric fires and an 'electric bath' (i.e. an immersion heater: 'the one luxury') and the possibility of adaptation to suit her lifestyle without the need to consider other people's because larger than implied; Aelfrida describes it as having only 'four small rooms'[13] but from diary entries one can discern that it had three ground floor rooms and a scullery and

three bedrooms and a bathroom upstairs. Leaving the ground floor unaltered, she adapted the first floor as her living quarters, using the front south-facing bedroom as a study-sitting room, the north-facing bedroom overlooking the convent garden as her bedroom, and the third bedroom, little more than a box-room, for visitors. (She did not, as at Wetenhall Cottage, name individual rooms.) By living upstairs, however, she condemned herself to the variable warmth of coal fires (electric fires were installed only on the ground floor) to heat a north-facing room and a room which, though it faced south, was overshadowed by taller buildings in winter, compounding her discomfort by importing her deckchair with a rug thrown over it on which to sit. (A Windsor chair was lugged upstairs for visitors.) On the walls, apart from a silvery star (a present from Walter), were a crucifix and a religious picture, the overall impression being, as visiting Ancifera put it, "so beautiful, ... but so bare, so conventual". (Her further comment that "there are no *things* about" was gently mocked: 'Ancifera's room is all objects *pas d' art*!')[14] But bareness was what Aelfrida wanted: 'my bare room, my crucifix ... and peace in my soul'.[15] The first two she achieved; the third eluded her, for though enlightenment achieved in Oxford contributed to the 'Knowledge' of which she had boasted to Fidelio, it was neither negation of desire nor a 'going-out' from the self which tormented her.

Living 'in a tiny cottage' was one thing, bearing the discomforts 'as best [she] could'[16] quite another, for the cottage had many: mice, black beetles, a scullery which flooded inches deep in heavy rain, 'brown dust that blows in from the cattle market and oily black dust from the coal yards'[17], and, worst of all, noise. All her life Aelfrida had been acutely sensitive to noise and though Fordfield's proximity to Cambridge's railway station, cattle market, market depots, and a major thoroughfare must have meant a far from soundless existence, the opening of Brooklands Avenue to motor traffic in the 1920s transformed it from a gated path used only by walkers and cyclists into a public road and gave rise to complaints that PEACE was not as peaceful as hitherto. But Osney Lane noise was of a different dimension: 'jangles of wireless and gramophone' which continued late into the night, cars hooting, engines puffing, children's voices as they played in the street or attended the nearby school, clatter (and smell) from a visiting fish and chip van, and 'the poor in the street never seem to *talk*, they shout, they 'oller, they storm, they halloo ... and they whistle, they cry and [they] scream'. So although Aelfrida jokingly described her new home as an 'almshouse', she also found her first extended experience of life in a working-class area something of a shock ('the noise distresses me acutely ... [it is] such torture that every few minutes I break out into profuse perspiration') and added the torments of insomnia to those of jangling nerves. Only Saturday nights and Bank Holidays were quiet, the culprits (they chiefly inhabited the tenement block called New Christchurch Buildings in nearby Hollybush Row) departing for the cinema or seaside, leaving Aelfrida to hope that she would soon become 'too much "recollected"'[18] to notice the racket. Frank Tillyard's summary of her surroundings is as revealing as hers: "she built herself a very nice house", Aelfrida overheard him say to a family member, "but she wouldn't live in it, she preferred to go to the slums of Oxford and inhabit a horrid ... dark cottage with no damp course ... in fact, with not much of anything".[19] It was, however, in this 'horrid ... dark cottage' that she proposed to live according to her 'Rule' as 'Sister Placida, a Benedictine oblate'. She called it 'St Benedict's'.[20]

The word 'oblate' derives from the Latin *oblatus*, past participle of the verb *offerre*, to offer. In religious terms an 'oblation' implies something offered to a divine being (bread and wine in the context of the Christian Eucharist), an 'oblate' someone who offers themselves to the religious life, possibly but not invariably, in a monastic setting. Aelfrida, of course, had no intention of becoming a nun (the possibility of her having to relinquish her 'hope of the contemplative life' in order to bring her 'blind Greek' to 'knowledge of his vocation whatever that may be', his vocation being that 'in which he can most perfectly fulfil God's intentions on his behalf'[21], did not, *O Passionate World* notwithstanding, imply profession as a religious but, rather, a hope that at some point in her life she might achieve 'all the leisure she [could] sustain for contemplation' of God)[22] though she had for many years entertained the idea of becoming an informal 'lay sister' of the kind met at Whitchurch in 1906[23] or, more formally, a tertiary in the Third Order of St Francis, a confraternity of lay persons who lived the fundamental principles of Franciscan life without withdrawal from the world. Becoming an oblate at Malling can therefore be seen less as a spur of the moment decision and more as the achievement of a long-standing ambition.

Something of Aelfrida's state of mind on being accepted as an oblate is expressed by Marion Fry in *Reflections on being an Oblate, Tertiary, Companion or Associate*. An oblate, says Fry, is a person who lives "an ordinary secular [life] of Christian faith and service" in terms of a formalised link with a religious community. They have arrived at this point in their lives as the result of a visit or visits to a religious community offering retreats or informal attendances during which the visitor is able to join the community at worship, to talk

with a member of the community and (a particularly important aspect for someone like Aelfrida) to "let go of tensions" in an atmosphere where a desire for silence and solitude are regarded as the norm rather than idiosyncrasies; such visits also provide the visitor with a means of focussing their hitherto rather unfocussed longings for greater spiritual satisfaction than that obtained from private devotions and regular attendance at a parish church. Formal commitment to the community should not, however, be undertaken without "a persistent sense of vocation [and] of being called by name to undertake such a commitment"; it must also be accompanied by a belief on the part of the community that the would-be oblate's commitment is right for that community. The process which results in formal oblature should not, therefore, be hurried (as Aelfrida's seems to have been) but should proceed along the same lines as that of becoming a monk or nun with an initial period of probation ('discernment') during which either or both parties may decide not to proceed, followed by a novitiate of about a year's duration after which the oblate-elect is formally clothed. Formal admission means that "both parties are committed to supporting one another through prayer whilst sharing the same governing intention", shared intention being the *raison d être* of the community and its extended family (of which the new oblate is now part) and "mutual prayer" its bonding cement.[24]

The remarkably short interval between Aelfrida's first visit to Malling and her being clothed as an oblate (she seems to have been under the impression that her probationary period followed rather than preceded the ceremony but it may be that she mistook the ceremony during which she received her scapular and the name 'Placida' for the ceremony of acceptance, a definite possibility given that she was not in touch with reality at the time) left her joyful and thankful but lacking humility, so much so that after privately informing members of her family of her new status, she could not help publicising the fact that her move to Oxford was to a new life in the religious as well as in the literal sense. Try as she might (and mood and decision meant she did not have to try very hard), she nevertheless found herself a centre of attention before leaving Cambridge with particular regard to the 'dear faithful Scotties'[25] of St Columba's and to Florence Keynes, the latter using her position as family friend to oversee a woman whose actions, though logical in her own eyes, seemed increasingly incongruous and inexplicable in other people's. In fact, so much attention did Aelfrida's decision command – she implies that she was reluctant to discuss it but the fact that she also appears to have convinced people 'of her value and her charm' as a member of Cambridge society and of the loss to society her departure for Oxford would occasion – that she resorted to whipping herself as a reminder that 'oblates simply *must not* commend themselves even silently to other people'. (Twelve lashes 'if [she] noticed what [she] was doing and didn't stop *at once*', six 'if [she] didn't notice', and if in doubt, 'chastisement to be administered … jolly hard'.)[26] On informing the Lady Abbess of this and of her new home and Rule, she received both a rebuke (the Abbess 'strongly disapproved' of her 'taking the discipline') and a commendation – 'dear, dear blessings on [her] Oxford life'[27] – but a life with which the Lady Abbess refused to engage in any practical way because the responsibility was Aelfrida's alone and should she try it and fail, it would teach her humility[28] before she returned from the 'anteroom' that was St Benedict's to 'the dear, dear Abbey'.[29]

Shared intention, Dr Fry reminds us, "is lived according to a Rule"[30], a Rule which, far from assuming sacrifice of freedom and flexibility, implies both freedom from spiritual restlessness because of the rhythm and regularity imparted to a restless and rootless life by its becoming more and more focussed on God's love and grace through the structuring of its yearly, daily, and even hourly regimes by means of religious practices carried out in seclusion or in common, and flexibility because each individual's Rule is created (usually in consultation with the religious community concerned) so that it not only conforms to the individual's circumstances at the time of creation but also expands to accommodate spiritual growth developing as a result of adherence to it. From this it can be seen that a Rule does not prescribe "uniform practice … for all regardless of personal circumstances" or "a seeming 'invariable'… such as weekly or more frequent attendance at the Eucharist" or "prescriptions" for spiritual reading, prayer and service, but is intended to include "variables" and should be regarded as an elastic structure within which an individual lives and worships rather than a rigid construction in which he or she is confined.

Aelfrida, of course, had begun to think of making a 'Rule for myself' and of 'living by it as far as I can' as early as May 1926[31], the year in which she inscribed 'Discipline. Humility. Secrecy' in the back of her current diary, but was hindered from doing so because distracted by being a 'Universal Aunt'. Visits to Malling, however, refocused her thoughts on the value of a Rule to a mind as disordered as her own and she devised 'a very simple rule of life' for herself before submitting a copy to Dom Bede Frost for comment and approval. (She also informed him that in drawing up the 'rule' she had no intention of becoming 'one of those dull and pious females of whom there are too many already'[32];

fortunately for a future biographer there was no danger of that.) From this and from later comments, we know the 'very simple rule' was committed to paper, but rather oddly with regard to so important a document, no copy was retained to add lustre to the version of her life which Aelfrida wished to present to the world. Whether this is more to do with humility or with secrecy is open to conjecture but given her radical departures from the 'simple rule' originally devised, her need to cover her tracks insofar as those departures nearly killed her and insofar as they went against spiritual advice proffered by religious advisers of on several occasions, secrecy seems more likely; there is also the possibility that her eventual 'Rule' departed so far from the precepts laid down by the saint, Benedict of Nursia, on whose paradigmatic Rule it was supposedly based, that she preferred secrecy to revelation of the extreme disciplines to which she submitted herself and which she only disclosed to or hinted at in her diary. She does, however, note the importance of a 'Rule' as an important 'road-book' for the Mystic Way because it "gives one's day a rhythm and harmony which, even if a trifle artificial, has beauty and significance"[33] and puts the mystic traveller in tune with the daily and calendrical rhythm and ceremonies of the Christian Year; indeed, the book on which she was contemporaneously working devotes a chapter (the second, that on God's Presence being the first) to a description of "a simple but quite definite Rule of Life", one of whose objects was "the performance each day of so many acts pointing to God that your consciousness of him is unbroken".[34]

Of what, then, did Aelfrida's 'Rule' consist? With diary help, we may conjecture the following. Woken at 6am by the convent's Angelus bell reminding its hearers of Christ's incarnation (it also rang at noon and sunset, the sound of the bell punctuating her day), she got up at 6.45am to wash and dress, to drink some water (a preventative recommended by Dr Cooper following another attack of cystitis), and to recite the *De profundis* as her initial act of reparation of the day[35]; she then attended Mass at 7.10am, daily if well enough and if the nuns were not in retreat. (She was begged by the convent's Mother Superior *not* to attend Mass daily because this implied excessive devotion and dependence but asking herself 'what have I come here for if I don't?'[36], she did.) At Mass she took Communion 'as radiant as if it were [her] first and as solemn as if it were [her] last'[37] and as quietly as she could as Father Cary had bidden her, all the time 'looking up at God and ignoring myself'. (She did not always succeed; sometimes 'the *Splendor Domini Dei*' shone round her 'so poignantly … that it seemed [her] soul must melt in the fire of it'.)[38] Then came a light breakfast ("simple meals, with a grace before them to turn your thoughts to the giver")[39], after which she revelled (so she said, and it is probably true of early days at St Benedict's) in 'hours spent on housework and carrying home a heavy shopping basket'.[40] ('Can one shop at Woolworth's for the glory of God?' she asked herself, deciding that one *could* though 'chiefly in one's subconscious mind!')[41] The morning was occupied with writing 'undeterred by the gramophone across the road'[42], with research in the Bodleian Library, and with re-reading "the writings of holy men and women": Thomas à Kempis' *Imitation of Christ*, William Law's *Serious Call to a Devout and Holy Life*, Julian of Norwich's *Revelations of Divine Love*, François de Sales' *Introduction à la Vie Dévote* ("so much to be preferred in French"), Thomas Traherne's *Centuries of Meditation,* and the Bible. ("Naturally".)[43] She also meditated, feeling as she did so 'an awareness of God clearer and purer than I should have once have dreamed possible' when engaged with 'the world' and hoping by such means 'to "die daily" … to be nothing … to give up my old ways of spiritual aggrandisement [and] by the *common* ways, the *ordinary* means of grace [and] by the Rule' to feel God working in her. Spiritual exercises of all kinds were 'done and offered *first* for His glory and in … second place only for [her own] sanctification'.[44]

All this took so much time and energy that her intention of attending 'most of the Hours in chapel' was modified for 'spiritual and physical' reasons to exclude those which involved getting up too early (Prime at 7am), staying up too late (Compline at 8.30pm) or took up too much of a morning dedicated to her Rule (Terce at 10am); she did, however, attend Sext and None 'most days' at 12.40 and Vespers at 5.30pm 'sometimes', Hours not attended being read instead of, as originally intended, reading *one* and attending the rest. Midday dinner was taken at the guest-house except on Saturdays, a day on which she remained '*alone* with God'[45] because "the Jewish custom of 'preparation for the Sabbath' is psychologically a sound one"[46], or on days when the convent closed its doors to outsiders. Immediately after the meal (and sometimes later in the day also), knowing that at that time there was no fear of interruption, she spent thirty minutes in the conventual chapel dedicated to the Blessed Sacrament venerating the consecrated Host, a procedure which often inspired 'a light trance' whose onset she need not resist because she was alone and during which she experienced God's Presence as a 'strange and awe-inspiring *intensification* of that which is everywhere' brought to her in 'the pure stillness of spiritual intercourse'. (Her father, she noted in passing, would have derided this portion of her Rule as misdirected reverence.)[47] Afternoons were devoted to her garden (its gate opened onto the convent's larger one in a

manner whose symbolism did not escape her), to writing (even before finishing *The Closer Walk with God* she had made notes on what was to be her next book, *The Way of Praise*, its title suggested by her guardian angel's comment that she use '*Laudate!*' as her first St Benedict's mantra)[48], and to walks during which she explored Oxford and the surrounding countryside. The desire to write her diary seemed 'almost entirely to have gone'; fortunately for a future biographer, she kept it up 'from habit and a sense of duty'.[49]

Her keenness to explore begs the question: why Oxford? Negatively speaking, because almost anywhere would have done provided it was not Cambridge with its memories of mothers, homes, and lovers lost; because Cambridge, though 'close to my heart, never relinquished, unforgettable, a part of me' (but not that 'close' a 'part'; swathes of the town remained resolutely unvisited)[50] was where she had lived 'the long years of my presumption when I was taking part (never all, no I was not as wicked as that) of the credit of my religious experiences to myself … and indulging my love of admiration' and working out how to 'get the best out of both worlds'[51], sacred and the secular, and because Cambridge meant dependence on Joan Cooper and an 'idiotic habit of running to [her] whenever I am in a difficulty'.[52] Positively speaking, for several reasons, none revealed to her diary but capable of interpretation in view of her moving there: Oxford, cradle of the nineteenth century Movement to which it gave its name, would be a sympathetic milieu ('Oxford seems full of convents')[53] to one turning towards Anglo-Catholicism and a semi-conventual life. It was also home to the Cowley Fathers to whom she would be physically closer than Alethea, immured at Malling, a fact underlined by attendance at sung Mass at Cowley on Sundays and at Confession on Saturdays. (Sung Mass was held late on Sunday morning so allowed her one morning a week of self-indulgent rest in bed; she rarely attended the parish church adjoining the convent as neither the preacher, the architecture, nor the congregation were to her taste.) Then, too, Oxford was "more of Cambridge in another place"[54], a university town full of 'men looking so typically undergraduate one feels one has met them all before'[55] and of excellent libraries, beautiful colleges, and open spaces (Christ Church Meadows was a particular favourite), the towpath along the Oxford canal being frequently visited because it provided glimpses of kingfishers ('my Assurance of Beauty here too!')[56] and an excuse to abandon 'Bodleian and shopping' and thank God for sending 'sunshine to [her] soul'.[57]

After Vespers, Aelfrida had a frugal supper and sat down to self-examination. Had she performed her duty towards herself, her neighbour, God? Had she remembered not to grieve God by wrong actions? Had she shrunk from "the high seriousness of [her] Christian calling?" Had she performed certain obligations "even if not as eagerly as they should have been?" What had been her "besetting sin" that day?[58] (Hers was self-love, "*myself* ... my *good* self, my high-minded intelligent, cultured, sensitive, exceptional and immensely interesting self, with all its aspirations, ambitions, qualities and noble desires" being "the dearest idol I have known"; she did *not* worship, she hastened to add, her "*bad* self", a self left coyly undefined.)[59] Compline was read in bed, an item of furniture whose hardness constituted a penance of its own, beseeching God to lighten her darkness and of his great mercy to defend her from the perils of the night. Then she settled to sleep 'within twenty-five yards of the Blessed Sacrament' and the holy ground where her soul loved 'to take off its shoes and walk barefoot'.[60] She also read the Night Hours of Lauds and Mattins but not in the middle of the night 'though [she] was tempted to try'.[61]

Aelfrida's Rule, insofar as it was based on anything other than her self-seeking (but in view of recent events understandable) desire to shrug off responsibility in silence, solitude, and congenial surroundings (and if this sounds cynical, an alternative view of Aelfrida's Oxford life shows it to have been the pre-determined intention of a wholly selfish woman determined to lead the life she wished regardless of the hurt, bewilderment, and worry she knew it would cause others), was derived, so she said, from that of St Benedict as mediated through the medium of a 'precious little book' sent from Malling.[62] (She was interested in the founder of Western monasticism[63] only as author of the 'Rule' she followed – or pretended to follow – though she usually remembered to celebrate 21 November as the day on which Benedictine oblates privately renew their vows.) Oblates, *The Oblates of St Benedict* would have informed her, though living in 'the world', are subject to and are to be guided by their founder's Rule as much as if they lived claustrated, and are to adopt it as their way of life within the life 'the world' obliges them to live. Like a monk or nun, however, they too are expected to seek God daily by living the doctrine of Benedictine spirituality: the *opus Dei* (the work of God expressed through spoken or silent prayer solitarily or in community), *lectio divina* (the mind applied to study and, particularly important for oblates, the prayerful reading of Scripture), and manual labour, an inclusive category encompassing ploughing and housework, the three together providing the day with the unity and balance of the *via media* for which St Benedict's Rule is renowned.[64] Most importantly from the point of view of Aelfrida's currently disordered mind was that life under

Benedictine Rule "separates us from the variable action of our own wills in dealing with the world".[65] But her wilful departures from it were to take precedence over its precepts to a horrifying and deleterious extent.

Therapeutic silence and solitude were, of course, what Aelfrida thought she needed at this time and if to acquire them meant exile from Cambridge and subjecting herself to a Rule, so be it; if they also led to uninterrupted communion with God, so much the better. And if to raptures, better still: on 30 October she records that at 7.45pm the previous evening while obeying the precept laid down in the book on which her Rule was based to "quiet your mind ... before you compose yourself to sleep and listen, if you can, to God speaking"[66], the 'whole splendour of Heaven seemed to descend upon me ... all of a sudden [and] God seemed to flow over me and *into* me like a river of spiritual life penetrating every corner ... of my soul [and] especially taking possession of my will'.[67] In fact, she records surprisingly few mystico-spiritual experiences during the early months of her stay in Oxford; perhaps she was too overwhelmed by the newness of her new life to have them.

Her craving for a way of life where she could be solitary and silent was not, however, a new one, and her desire 'to go to Oxford and settle down and keep my Rule and be quiet ... and spend my time in prayer [and] a life of contemplation'[68] was only the most recent expression of a long-expressed wish; indeed, and although one of her earliest diary references to this ('the modern world has no use for me. I'm too serious. I ought to be a hermit', confided to John Layard with the private addendum 'so I ought')[69] dates from mid-1913, it is probable that it was first formulated in her teens or early twenties. Marriage intervened. While still married and bound to ask 'what would become of Constantine' if she proceeded with her intention of leading a reclusive contemplative life, she decided on 18 October 1914 (the date is probably significant given that the episode of marital rape took place two weeks earlier) that she 'would like, if the children grew up and no-one wanted me, to be a hermit up on the Gogs', sallying thence in the brown 'frock' denoting eremitical status to 'teach people'.[70] In August 1915 after a year of war and the period of alternating desolation and rapture that was shortly to drive her to Caldecote to rest, she broached the subject to Fidelio, a fellow-solitary, informing him that problems in making her 'outer' and 'inner' lives conform were causing her to dream of doing something desperate; on seeing Fidelio's alarm (he thought she was suggesting that they elope), she hastily informed him that what she meant was to live 'as the poor do' or to retire 'at the age of fifty to a hermitage on the Gogs'.[71] (Is it purely coincidental that her fiftieth birthday fell only a few months after her decision to move to Oxford?) In July 1918 while she and Stokoe walked together in the garden-at-the-back and he begged her to tell him of 'an easy path' out of his 'strange tormented life', she confessed herself unable to suggest anything but faith and prayer[72] (activities pertinent to her own situation with regard to Constantine) and reiterated her 'little private dream of ending [her] days in a sort of simple hermitage … all alone'.[73] The Girton Conference reinforced the 'dream' in a material way: 'it seems so wonderful to have a room all my own where I can read and write and do just what I like and … have my time all my own [and] rejoice in my solitude'.[74] Then Constantine came home from Amsterdam and the 'dream' was placed in abeyance for over a decade, though her wry comment apropos her appearance in court to demand restitution of conjugal rights that she wanted to 'go away all by myself and … be very quiet and build up my life again with solitude and prayer'[75] was no less apposite then than it was fourteen years later when, sitting by sick Chiara's bedside, her thoughts turned longingly 'to quiet places where one could meditate and study'[76] and to realisation that after her mother's death she could begin to live her life the way she wished: alone, in silence, and in prayerful activity. In the meantime she expressed her 'dream' in fiction, having 'Audrey Talbot' inform 'Catharine Sutherland' shortly after the deaths of her parents and favourite brother that "the one thing that seemed to me desirable was to go and be a hermit or something and meditate until the spiritual air was all clear round me". (She even, 'Audrey' added, "[had] serious thoughts of the Contemplative Life".)[77] 'Père Hubert', too, informs 'Noel Ashton' that his ideal life would be that of a Carthusian monk: "the solitary cells and tiny walled-in garden; the silence; … the walk once a week which is the only glimpse they get of the outside world … the procession by the light of their lanterns to the chapel for the midnight Mass … *dans le Paradis, moi, je serais Chartreux*".[78]

'Carthusian' though she tried to be in her solitary cell and walled garden and much as she enjoyed attendance at chapel, closer association with conventual life did not inspire Aelfrida to become a religious. Unprepared to offer obedience ("I shouldn't like vows I couldn't keep"), she retained 'Audrey's' belief "that Anglican Sisterhoods aren't *quite* the real thing"[79] and adhered to 'Author's' admission to 'Stranger' that while she did not disapprove of "convents and monasteries" as such because "for a certain type of character they offer exactly the right life and they help the world enormously by presenting the sight of companies of devout people who care for nothing but God", she regarded claustral life per

se as anti-Christian because based on "fear of the world, detachment, denial, austerity" instead of love of mankind. Possibly as a 'modern' mystic, she preferred to *dare to be herself* in her spiritual life, a "pioneer, exploring the possibilities of communion with God … *now*, in the present day, under modern conditions" instead of crushing "the round peg of [her] own individuality into the square hole of … medieval types of goodness" (as she feared Alethea was doing) because she would be unhappy and would deprive 'the world' of an exemplar "of the particular kind of goodness which it now needs".[80] Possibly she believed it wrong to "flee the world"[81] as completely as Alethea had done, oblation and St Benedict's providing a liminal stage between 'detachment' and severance: "I can see much beauty and rightness …in the life of the cloister [but] there are many ways to God".[82] Possibly she felt unable "to mount the stairs of renunciation"[83] because too physically and emotionally frail (or too 'luxurious') to do so or because Agatha might have need of her. Possibly comments from friends and family had hit home: that if God was, as she believed, omnipresent, she had no need to attach herself to a religious community or even to leave Cambridge to find Him; that given her domestic problems, she was an escapist coward who wanted 'to go into a convent and forget everything and everybody'[84]; that life at St Benedict's was less a 'new life' than a Never-Never Land in which she could toy with "romantic notions and dramatic ideas and dream [her] life away" among "mawkish women" practising "sham holiness".[85] Possibly because she regarded St Benedict's as a place where she could carry out an extended retreat of the kind described and directed by Evelyn Underhill[86] and briefly experienced herself at Leiston and St Ursula's, a retreat longer than those an oblate attended annually (one or two weeks was the norm) during which she like 'Audrey Talbot', could clear her 'spiritual air' and, as she informed Joan Cooper who had warned her that uninterrupted communion with God would make her 'queer' (she was right), acquire 'balance' again.[87]

For Aelfrida to believe herself unbalanced at this point demonstrates unusual perspicuity, for although she often felt out of step with the rest of the world and sometimes had difficulty adjusting her 'outer' to her 'inner' life, only rarely (and with good reason) did she describe herself as lacking 'balance'. Believing, however, that she herself was the best person to re-balance herself, she turned her back on the 'piercing charm' of the Benedictine *via media* as lived in convents, rationalising her decision by telling herself she 'would rather have a little house as a hermitage' than have her life 'balanced' by other agents. Lastly, and notwithstanding her 'House of the Servants of God' scheme or Constantinian criticisms that in going to "mumble litanies in a hermitage" instead of acting as Christ did ("he upset the Stock Exchange … and ran a highly successful open-air clinic")[88], she was not following her ostensible role model, she had no intention of rebalancing her life by working for others as the Mission Sister at St Thomas' did because working for others had been one of the causes of her loss of balance and because in a house associated with a convent but not subject to its edicts she could combine 'freedom [of action] with contemplation'[89] and neither with social service.

Aelfrida's decision to lead the life of an anchoress at St Benedict's was in keeping with the life of St Benedict himself, he having followed the Pachomian tradition of eremitic life[90] at Subiaco for several years before becoming a leading figure in cenobitic life there and at Monte Cassino. She was, however, more in sympathy with Mother Julian who lived from age thirty as an anchoress in a cell attached to St Julian's church in Norwich[91], and it may be that it was with unspoken reference to Julian as much as to the sight of swallows nesting under the eaves of Wetenhall Cottage that she decided that, following her extended retreat at St Benedict's, she would return (God willing) to Malling to live as a 'hermit' in a cell with a window opening onto the chapel, so that 'by day sitting in my chair and by night from my bed I could see the altar and the sanctuary lamp' and even if ill 'should still be *there*, still hear daily Mass, still not miss one of the Hours'.[92]

The hermit with whom Aelfrida identified most closely was not, however, Julian of Norwich but Charles de Foucault.[93] De Foucault, born in 1858, became first a soldier then a missionary in Algeria in the early years of the twentieth century, dying there for his faith on 1 December 1916. His life (he was the subject of numerous biographies, one of which, René Bazin's *Charles de Foucault, Hermit and Explorer,* she read while researching *Spiritual Exercises*)[94] bore resemblances to her own (aged seventeen, he was "all egotism, vanity and impiety [and] as it were mad"[95]; he had a "guru" (*sic*)[96], concerning whom he remained silent even when helped to change his life from licentiousness to piety; he made several retreats, one at least in a Benedictine monastery, before becoming a Trappist monk[97], a life he left in 1897 to follow a religious calling of his own, and so on) and it may have been re-reading Bazin's biography in the terrible year of 1931 which stimulated her decision to go out into the English equivalent of the Sahara desert (hardly a flattering description of Oxford but she was shortly to make a 'desert' of St Benedict's) to lead 'a strange life' in close and private pursuit of the Deity 'always … in the tabernacle of [her] heart'.[98]

Hermits and anchoresses, however, need a life support system if they are to devote themselves to a life of prayer. Julian of Norwich had a maid, de Foucault a convert-servant, Pachomius and Benedict fellow monks who provided food, and although St Benedict's Rule directed its followers to '*laborare*' as well as '*orare*', Aelfrida clove to the eremitic assumption that some human or supernatural agency would relieve her of necessary aspects of human existence. And as one accustomed to servants from childhood, could not envisage life without one ('I should like to be a hermit [but] I should want a maid')[99] and had no intention of carrying out the harder or dirtier work of running her hermitage herself. (She could never decide whether to be disgusted or amazed at the Zender Browns' willingness to run their large house in Cambridge without help.) To ensure the cleanliness of her Franciscan 'bower of Lady Poverty' (the holy nuptials of the '*poverello*' and 'Lady Poverty' are depicted by Giotto) and that she herself had ample time for a prayerful life, she employed a charlady at eight pence an hour. Daisy Allen, a young woman from the noisy tenement nearby was trained up to her own exacting standards (by November 1934, Daisy had the house in 'exquisite order')[100] and her absences found extremely provoking.

Then too, she had always been, as Constantine pointed out (possibly in response to her confiding to him her wish to exchange the marital bed for the solitary's) a 'luxurious ascetic' and at St Benedict's saw no need to deny herself luxuries ('a deck chair and a hot water bottle'[101] were two of these, though she did give up coffee) or to make her 'simple hermitage … too uncomfortable'[102] (it was high summer when she moved in) or to do more than wonder in false humility (for if she really felt that way, she should have rented a room) if 'four rooms and a kitchen' constituted 'giving up enough for God'.[103] She even planned her future 'cell' at Malling so as not to have to live 'exactly like anchoresses in the Middle Ages' who were probably cold and certainly dirty: 'I should need a stove and a bath'. The cell would also have 'a door opening onto the garden so I could have walks' and a window onto the chapel 'so when well enough I could take [my] place at Divine Office', the fact that Malling was a closed community being of little account because by then she would be wearing ('of course') a habit of some kind herself.[104]

Domestic chores, however, were as nothing compared to the problems posed by people, for to the natural curiosity of fellow 'pious ladies' regarding the lifestyle of one who was and yet was not one of them, was added the solicitude of the convent's Mother Superior for her newest tenant, a tenant who, though she had earlier stated her inability to achieve 'perpetual silence', now needed to 'bathe in it to keep [her] soul clean'[105] and who was adamant that she intended to add more silence still to a

Rule under which she socialised only one day a week and spoke as little as possible at any time in order to break her craving for interaction with other people and to devote herself solely to God. (She did not, however, stop writing letters because she must in keep touch with 'spiritual children' or 'anyone [else] … who wants my letters'[106], concerning whom she was not always polite: Elsie Rose's letter contained 'some of the worst drivel I ever read'.)[107] Local visitors such as Father Barrett the convent chaplain (he came by invitation, an occasion she intended to be 'serious, almost … religious' but which turned out 'entirely social' and secular)[108], the curate of St Thomas' church (acceptable because he was an 'extremely intelligent and friendly young man' and because she was able to offer her services as Straightener to one living 'at too great tension' because desperate to conceal his homosexuality)[109], or Dorothy Smith (soon to become her dentist and her only friend in Oxford), could be confined with more or less success to Sundays. (Her question 'why must I have people to tea' was answered honestly 'I enjoy it', and although she complained of lack of 'holy solitude', 'secular activities', she admitted, 'were good'.)[110] Family, however, could not: a visit from Jessie Stent 'was fun in a way and warming – but all the time I was longing to be alone with God'[111]; Julius, already showing a tendency to visit his sister during vacations and mournful that in moving to Oxford she had 'snapped the last link' binding him to Cambridge (so much for Eustace!), made her hope he might retire to Wetenhall Cottage, God reserving 'a habit or a cell' for herself there[112]; Mina, seeking friendship, not 'soul-doctoring'. 'Oh dear, oh dear', she wrote resentfully, 'now I understand why hermits … [push] further out into the desert, [retire] deeper into forest and fen!'[113]

Though revelling in 'being Nobody'[114] (it felt odd 'to have no Tillyard tradition behind [her], no position as consul's wife, no status as author or lecturer'[115] though she was not *too* reluctant to let people worm information out of her) in the 'deep peace [and] golden calm in the soul, intenser and quieter than anything I have ever known'[116], and in being by herself even on her birthday, 'the first … ever spent alone', in order to 'plunge [her] mind into God'[117] in solitude and silence, Aelfrida was not averse to abandoning 'desert' for 'fen' as directorships or Wetenhall Cottage business demanded, these being among the sources of income supporting her sojourn in 'Lady Poverty's' bower. Two visits of several days' duration were paid to Cambridge between her arrival in Oxford and Christmas 1934 and were much enjoyed in spite of Joan Cooper's refusal to believe that Aelfrida could prefer Oxford and solitude to Cambridge and company, and Phyllis' to allow her stay at Merton House in spite

of Aelfrida's protestations that years spent being 'more charming than Phyllis (and she knows it)'[118] should not be held against one who hoped to take advantage of her sister-in-law's hospitality to save the expense of an hotel.

Cambridge visits also provided an opportunity to check on 'precious Temu' (Aelfrida's November visit was spent under the same roof as her daughter), for although Agatha paid short visits to Oxford, she was 'eager to stand on her own feet as even Temus should'[119] and to prove that she too could make a life for herself away from her mother. Aelfrida was therefore delighted to hear that just as Alethea was 'blooming' at Malling, so her younger sister was brimming with 'Cambridge delights'[120] such as riding with Hugh Sykes Davies (a fact noted happily by her mother, for Hugh was a scholar, a writer, newly divorced from poet Kathleen Raine, and a man known to the Graham sisters from undergraduate days) until she remembered: prospective husbands were now 'quite impossible'[121] as topics of conversation and 'aunting' absolutely forbidden.

Father Cary, however, was always a welcome visitor. Over seventy when Aelfrida first met him, Lucius (or Lucien: his given names were Henry Lucien but he used Lucius and Lucien interchangeably) Cary, 'large and bulky with the three-fold cord of poverty, chastity and obedience round his waist' and wearing the black habit and 'monkish cloak' of the Cowley Fathers[122], was a commanding figure to whom Aelfrida was much attracted. (Father Cary, for his part, made no secret of the fact that he felt at ease in the company of women.) The Malling nuns regarded him as 'a saint in the making'[123]; on an earthly level, he was the scion of a well-known West Country family and a clergyman's son whose health broke down under the strain of study at Oxford. He was awarded only a pass degree and was forced to support himself by private tutoring in England and abroad; he subsequently joined the SSJE, working in two slum parishes in London before moving to Cowley.[124] What Cary did *not* tell her but Aelfrida discovered from other sources was that while holding a senior position at Cowley, he suffered a severe breakdown from overwork, was hospitalised for over a year, and spent two further years recovering.[125] All in all, he seemed an ideal person to guide her at this point in her life, not only because his mind and his spirituality were in tune with hers but also because as someone who had broken down under the strain of the life he led, he was well placed to minister to someone in a similar situation. He was also, by virtue of having been in a position of authority (he had been second in command at Cowley at the time of his breakdown), an ideal person to guide a strong-willed woman and by virtue of his personality, a man not easily intimidated. The Lady

Abbess of Malling and Dom Bede Frost had, it seemed, made a wise decision in sending Aelfrida to him.

But was he in fact Aelfrida's spiritual director? Given that he had already declined to act in this capacity, it is odd to find her noting in October 1934 that it was a 'wonderful privilege' to have Cary as her spiritual 'director' because he was 'almost exclusively' a *conventual* director and devoted only an hour a week to his 'penitents'[126] (i.e. to women who came to him as their father confessor) and in February 1935 that she hoped Father Cary would be her spiritual director 'for ever and ever'. It may be, however, that a relationship described by her as one of spiritual 'direction' was more likely one of spiritual guidance or 'discernment' (a word Aelfrida herself uses in this context), Cary proffering spiritual advice as she responded physically, emotionally, and intellectually to life-events, and Aelfrida responding to his concern and to firm but sympathetic suggestions as to how to behave but in spite of his outlining 'what the perfect relationship between director and penitent is' and her agreeing wholeheartedly though in rather general terms ("yes, just that … in every way, what you said")[127], going her own way as usual. It may be too that Aelfrida promoted Father Cary to spiritual director in an act of self-aggrandisement, for to have him appear as her director rather than her confessor (the two are not necessarily synonymous) would add lustre to her oblature and single her out from the large number of 'pious lady' 'penitents' who attended his confessional: having waited thirty minutes in a queue of such ladies before making her own confession, she noted wrathfully 'if I had known he was so much sought-after I should have protested even more vehemently than I did when the Lady Abbess first suggested that I should be directed by him'.[128] It would seem, therefore, that while Aelfrida presented herself (even to herself) as one 'directed' by Father Cary, she was in truth one of a number of 'penitents' who came to him for confession and advice, an altogether different matter given that a confessor hears sins committed, assigns penance, and gives absolution but a director enters into a spiritual and moral compact with the directed to supervise and direct their reaction to the workings of the Holy Spirit within them in order that they may reach their chosen spiritual destination in the best possible (or least deleterious) manner.

That Cary saw himself as Aelfrida's adviser and father confessor rather than her spiritual director (he may even have gone along with her belief that he *was* her director in order to be allowed near enough to contain her perturbed spirit to the best of his ability) is shown by evidence provided by her diary and other writings. Alethea's comment that if Father Cary was truly her mother's

spiritual director, she should ask his advice as to what she should read, evoked surprise from Aelfrida because this was 'a thing which would never have occurred to [her]'[129], and, during a chat with the chaplain of a retreat-house attached to a Torquay convent who evinced surprise that Aelfrida's spiritual director did not plan her time, tell her what to read, and advise her on how much time to spend in prayerful activity and what methods to use, she 'reluctantly' revealed that 'Father Cary left [her] free to do as [she] liked',[130] something no true director would have done.

Fictionalised accounts of visits paid by Father Cary to Aelfrida at St Benedict's support this contention. (Cary visited Aelfrida at home on several occasions following her move to Oxford, particularly if she was too ill to attend confession, this perhaps persuading her that this was how spiritual directors behaved; what Cary was really doing, of course, was conducting domiciliary visits to check on her physical and mental welfare, a duty more usually carried out by a doctor or a parish priest than a spiritual director.) As an old lady looking back over her past, Aelfrida published a number of articles describing in appropriately pious tones (the articles appeared in a journal published by a society one of whose precepts was 'bodily infirmity as a power of witness for Christ')[131] incidents and people of significance to her life and spiritual progress, three of which are particularly relevant in the context of Father Cary and St Benedict's. In each brief dialogue 'Amanda'[132], a grumpy elderly lady in indifferent health, is visited by 'Theodore' (literally, 'God-loving'), a seventy-two-year-old priest. ('Theodore' was a pupil in 'Amanda's' Sunday School class when he was six, she twelve, his the first name in the 'intercession book' given her at her confirmation, and 'Amanda' has remembered him in her prayers since the day he signed it.) 'Theodore's' present role in 'Amanda's' life is that of counsellor; he gently but firmly points out her faults (spiritual pride, self-righteousness, and a tendency to pessimism), reminds her of God's blessings, reassures her that she *is* making spiritual progress even when she seems not to be, and informs her of what she is doing wrong: living her spiritual life in too great isolation and brooding over herself too much. He also, and this is particularly significant in view of the confused state of Aelfrida's mind at the time ("it's all a muddle to me", 'Amanda' complains), suggests that he and she "go back to the beginning and see whether you have made any mistakes which can, even at this late hour, be remedied".[133]

Conversations between 'Theodore' and 'Amanda' mirror closely in tone and content conversations between Cary and Aelfrida soon after her arrival in Oxford. In one of the earliest (it took place after the 'great ordeal' she made of confession, writing that 'I doubt whether I shall ever get used to it'), Cary told her that she '*must* learn to be less sensitive' and must discipline herself mind, body, and soul 'to listen to God more quietly and simply' or she would fail to make spiritual progress.[134] Given, however, that many of Aelfrida's supernatural experiences were unwilled, not induced, and that it was at this point that they became vivid and frequent once more, Cary's advice was at best impractical and at worst disingenuous. (Two months later he went so far as to forbid 'additional solitude or silence'; 'so that's that!' commented Aelfrida who was busy planning how to include more of both in her already quite stringent regime.)[135] Not only was it impossible for her to listen to God 'quietly and simply' but a vision the following day during which the glory of God descended on her with such overwhelming majesty that she believed herself on the brink of physical death – "I hope Agatha won't mind very much", was the thought that flashed across her mind as she gave herself up 'to the intense joy of apprehending God while waiting for cessation of consciousness' – convinced herself that she had undergone a form of 'mystic marriage'. (Ten minutes later she was sufficiently 'back in the world' to hear the Compline bell, wash up her supper dishes[136], and confide the vision to her diary – though not to the 'spiritual director' who, gratifyingly, did not 'interfere with' her soul.)[137] Given too her propensity for deriving visionary content from current events, it is amusing to discover that a royal wedding took place that same month and that she had been recalling her own, All Souls' Day on 2 November having reminded her that she 'ought to have prayed … much more when he was alive' for her ex-husband's soul and that 'husband (*sic*) and wife [being] *one*', she could continue to make her communion '*as* Constantine'.[138] Her not informing Cary of this particularly significant vision was to have serious consequences, for Aelfrida's conclusion that God had so penetrated her being as to cause her to feel 'changed, marked, possessed' and belief that the painful intensity of the experience had given her 'a kind of divine knowledge of intimacy' with God's Son also, an intimacy 'which only comes to those who share His suffering' (suffering to be shared through devotion to the Cross and Passion), led her to decide to follow Christ by leading 'as hard a life as I am conveniently (*sic*) able to bear without being ill or gloomy'.[139]

It seems, however, that Father Cary guessed her intension of leading an even more ascetically anchoritic existence. She therefore received further instruction (couched in rather more dictatorial tones than usual though promulgated on a home visit during which she and Cary shared 'tea and elegant conversation') as to the proper nature of the 'Christian character'[140] and, after confession at Cowley,

an exordium on what was required of those living 'the contemplative life … in the world', chiefly 'forgetfulness of self', 'complete abandonment to the Will of God so that one makes no plans and has … no *choice*' (not, perhaps the wisest advice to one in Aelfrida's circumstances), and only such meditations as would not 'upset the balance' of her spiritual life.[141] All of which she chose to ignore, regarding Father Cary's instructions as impersonal recommendations which, though they 'set the seal on [her] vocation'[142], were not to be taken personally. She also made it clear (to her diary, not to Cary) that God was the only spiritual director she intended to obey.

A particularly striking example of disobedience relates to reparation. Aelfrida had, of course, practised a version of this since Constantine's edict of separation, writing in 1920 that she must try to bear and to atone for his sins ('*Christ* them, if that does not sound too presumptuous')[143], but having intensified her efforts after her 'husband's' death, sought Father Cary's views on the matter. Somewhat surprisingly given Cary's positive feelings toward the practice but unsurprisingly in view of what she may have told him (that she loved Anatolia and Mildred 'as myself', that she proposed to transform their 'foolish and wrongheaded and lost' souls by extending the 'shining beauty' of hers upon them[144], and that recent readings on the subject had persuaded her that offering oneself 'to be immolated with Christ upon the Cross' in 'the fellowship of His suffering' was a practice 'most suitable for an oblate')[145], his advice was sensible and succinct: "let there be no exaggeration in this. Offer your coming trials for these two souls but let that be enough". Aelfrida was disgusted ('I do not conceive of *limits* or bounds to "*caritas*"'), her next statement exemplifying both Cary's earlier remarks that she did not know how to use a spiritual director and her own spiritual arrogance: she would offer '*whatever*' pain of body or mind was required for Constantine's and Anatolia's salvation in whatever manner she thought best and if she lacked Cary's support for the venture, well, she had 'the prayers of nuns' to assist her.[146] So with her mother's example before her, for Chiara had sacrificed herself for a living husband as Aelfrida proposed to do for a dead one, she then became as 'ill and gloomy' as Chiara did and she feared she might and was powerless to prevent 'coming trials' from driving her deeper into madness.

The first and least soon manifested itself: November weather and her bedroom being 'only 40°[F] … this morning'.[147] Though her spirits had risen during her first Oxford summer, the onset of autumn made getting up for early Mass and Communion (something unavoidable in Oxford given her insistence that she had moved into convent precincts for this purpose) 'a real test of one's vocation'.[148] Worse still, 'little St Benedict's', though not 'too uncomfortable' in summer, became dark, damp, and cold as days shortened, temperatures dropped, and moisture rose up the walls, and this, and the onset of Aelfrida's usual winter gloom (itself exacerbated by walks curtailed because of bad weather), coincided with worsening of the minor but irritating illnesses which had plagued her since arriving in Oxford and with a recrudescence of rheumatoid arthritis. Her first 'rheumatic attack' occurred shortly after All Souls' Day, was severe, and was accompanied by delirium (her room, she wrote, was 'full of shapes of people … who were dead and I … too feverish to distinguish dream from reality') so she stayed in bed, attended by 'shock-headed' Daisy Allen twice a day and with only 'picnic food' to eat (bread, and grapes brought by the Mother Superior), 'aching all over and alone and no good to anybody' but surprisingly full 'of an immense contentment': 'God sent for me to come here. I came … now surely I am serving Him *hidden* as he wanted [and] what happens to me is for Him to say'.[149] Five days later she was 'up and about [and] pleased at getting Communion again' (she had been too ill to attend and the convent had been closed for a retreat) and even more strongly resolved never to return to 'ordinary life' because her enforced rest had been 'so calm, so *holy*'.[150] A second attack on 11 December, however, made her realise that 'ordinary life' had much to recommend it: daughters to pet her up (Daisy, she wrote, waited on her 'faithfully if not always intelligently'), a mother in attendance (the Mother Superior visited rarely), a doctor who knew her ailments intimately (her Oxford general practitioner, 'intelligent young Scotchwoman' Mary Frazer, showed no desire to become her friend), and peace and quiet ('traffic noise is fiendish here when one is ill'), and appreciate that 'assorted pains in [her] inside', 'rheumatic chills', and feverish confusion ('I thought the angelic hosts appeared round my bed')[151] were better experienced at Fordfield or Wetenhall Cottage than St Benedict's. Her guardian angel thought so too, providing her with a new mantra: '*self-sacrifice is true praise*'.[152]

Then, too, she was lonely, for in spite of unwanted visitors, one who had lived her life surrounded by people (so surrounded that she prayed for solitude) found being '*alone with God*'[153] brought human loneliness in its train (loneliness made more poignant by visits to Cambridge) and that being silent for the greater part of the day and week caused one who hitherto had lived with her heart on her lips to develop 'an odd longing for conversation'.[154] Hence, and in spite of protestations that solitude and silence allowed her 'to *feel*, to know, to understand that [she] must turn to God only'[155], that she had no desire to return permanently to Cambridge, and that

she was almost '*too* happy' at the prospect of being 'all alone'[156] (a statement made while Agatha was staying with her), her need to persuade herself (and her biographer) that she *was* happy suggests that 'being Nobody' in silence and solitude was hard to endure. She also began to feel increasingly divorced from reality and as if living in a dream-world from which she would suddenly awaken to find herself at Fordfield again 'with Chiara and Oracle still alive and Alethea and Agatha … little girls'.[157]

A further factor exacerbated the instability of a mind worsened by eremitic isolation and perturbed the emotions of a woman whose life had hitherto relied on the emotional impact she made on other people (and they on her) to provide it with 'reality'. Having noted in *Can I be a Mystic?* that she *needed* engagement with the world in order to cultivate her vocation and to discover "what new place" God expected her to step into, she had deliberately stepped out of 'reality' into the 'new place' she believed God had found for her and re-embarked on the "long and tedious process of crushing the round peg of [her] individuality" into the square hole of monastic ideals based on "denial [and] austerity".[158] The knowledge that she had already made this mistake in trying to assimilate Thomas à Kempis' model into her life thirty years earlier did not prevent her from making it again; indeed, it was to be as the closest possible imitator of Christ's physical suffering that she continued on her 'closer walk with God'. At St Benedict's she therefore left the "sunny" side of the Mystic Way but, unable to dare to be herself because of what recent events had revealed of capabilities when *being* herself (matricide, infliction of emotional damage on innocent parties), moved to the "shady" side, the "*voie de foi pure* or way of faith alone". Or so she said, for even here she discovered a source of tension which further perturbed her disordered mind: her involuntary inability to deny herself the "visions … ecstasies, raptures, flights of the spirit … supernatural states of mind [and] overwhelming feelings of fervour" which should never be enjoyed by one "who walks on the shady side"[159] but which had hitherto played and were to continue to play an important role in her relationship with God.

Assorted pains in her inside, however, were less a manifestation of ecstasies and raptures than of another 'trial': recurrence of postmenopausal bleeding. During a visit to Cambridge, Aelfrida included in 'odds and ends of business' a consultation with Joan Cooper to discuss her 'pains' and the unexpected resumption of her periods[160] but further bleeding in early December and a feeling that there was 'mischief brewing in [her] womb again'[161] drove her to consult Dr Frazer too and that lady to prescribe 'rest and douches' in an Oxford nursing home pending referral to a London gynaecologist. (Aelfrida would have preferred 'the cool austerity of the Evelyn'[162] but believed return to Cambridge would tempt her to renew her friendship with Joan Cooper and that God having invited her to closer intimacy with Him, the invitation was 'to Aelfrida Placida *alone* ... not to *Aelfrida Placida and Friend*'.)[163] Admission to a Woodstock Road nursing home provided respite from the winter austerities of St Benedict's and 'the "spiritual opportunity" of making a "Retreat" on which one can – indeed, must and should – carry out an important "Spiritual Exercise"[164] and of meditating in comfort on how the 'spread' of 'cancer' would allow her 'to share and understand Our Lord's sufferings' and to demonstrate holiness by bearing her burden joyously and 'glorifying God thereby'.[165]

Returning to St Benedict's on 29 December 1934 feeling less '*ephemeral*' but as if she lacked courage to bear the next burden about to be laid on her 'physical body'[166] (her conviction that she had not long to live was underlined by a new mantra from her guardian angel: '*non loquendo sed moriendo*')[167], Aelfrida was cared for by Agatha. Agatha, she decided, as her daughter cooked, shopped, made brilliant and witty remarks, read 'solid books', and wrote notes for what Aelfrida called her 'thesis' but was actually an entry for a literary prize, was a 'very remarkable person [with] her power of patient and sustained thought', the 'illuminating quality of her perceptions', and her ability to penetrate deeply 'into the heart of things'.[168] She was also 'a real tower of strength, so capable, so strong, not *Poor Little Temu* at all ... for she can arrange her own doings beautifully'.[169] In spite of this, Agatha seemed uncertain as to future plans, informing her mother that she was looking for a job but '*just a job* ... not a vocation or even a career'[170], a statement which made Aelfrida wish that her tendency to 'prevent' Agatha in all her doings (prevent 'in the old-fashioned sense of the word!' i.e. to anticipate) was not such a bad thing after all[171], to beg Agatha's guardian angel to 'keep very close to her for there is so little I can do'[172], and to notice with apprehension that 'wonderful' as her daughter was, she was rapidly growing away from her mother and 'hardly *mine* at all'.[173]

In the meantime her pain intensified (it was so bad on one occasion that she 'fainted right away', returning to consciousness feeling 'rather like a quantum theory atom must feel turning up again without having existed at all in the meantime') and sleep became full of experiences pursued 'in rather a tormented way'.[174] She also worried about the cost of 'the big operation'[175] predicted by Dr Frazer (the thought that 'operations and all that' had already played an important part in her 'sanctification'[176] was no consolation under the circumstances) and the effect on her daughters (particularly Agatha, but

Alethea too, who, so the Lady Abbess reported, had been weepy of late) of her diagnosis, prognosis, and probably imminent demise. One thing she did *not* do, however, was publicise her illness. Hence, although she told Lucy Verey who came 'to enquire tenderly ... after the details of [her] indisposition'[177] and the Lady Abbess of Malling who informed her that no, she could *not* visit Malling until she was better (a message which caused Aelfrida to wail 'the dear Abbey ... must I perhaps die without seeing it again?')[178], and hinted at 'coming trials' to Father Cary, she lacked the emotional outlet provided by earlier histrionics. This led to further gloomy introspection ('I expect I am ... to know the extremest weariness of flesh and spirit and to hold to God with the blind clinging of the will. So be it')[179] and to lying awake till 3am wrapped in her 'wedding garment'[180] scapular communing with the God she expected to meet very soon in the spirit as well as in the flesh.

Aelfrida's appointment with eminent London gynaecologist William Gilliatt[181] took place on 17 January 1935 and was thoroughly anticlimactic. Having poured out '[her] whole soul in adoration of God' on the train journey to London, she was brusquely dismissed by Gilliatt who told her that although she *might* have had 'symptoms of cancer', she had not got cancer ("there is nothing there", were his exact words) and that even if she had, he would not operate until the 'septic condition' of her mouth and teeth was dealt with.[182] He was also dismissive of the pain she was supposed to have suffered ("did you have any pain? I never heard about it")[183], something which supports Dr Frazer's diagnosis of 'hyperaesthesia'[184] and suggests that the pain, though perfectly real to Aelfrida, was psychogenic rather than physiological and may have been exacerbated by the presence of an observer, namely Agatha. (Agatha, in fact, returned to Cambridge within a few days of her mother's visit to Mr Gilliatt in spite of Aelfrida's protests that she was 'not really well enough to be left alone'[185]; she also seems to have treated her mother with unusually restrained affection while in Oxford.) Returning disappointed to St Benedict's, Aelfrida discovered to her surprise and joy that her pain had disappeared.

Was this, she asked herself, a miracle brought about as result of intense 'adoration of God' on the train or God's acceptance of reparative adoration for Constantine and his mother and (real) widow? Then common sense and because news of the 'miracle' was received very coolly by Father Cary and Mother Superior prevailed: 'as to my health, there has been no miracle ... I suppose my feeling so much better [is] due to a kind of spiritual exaltation which [makes] me ignore the claims of the body'.[186] And after all, 'a miracle of healing' was hardly an appropriate answer to the prayers of one who continued to demand to be made a saint and not spared in the making, for 'to have been thus spared would have spoilt both me and the making'.[187] She was nevertheless cheered by her guardian angel adding a fourth mantra to the 'wonderful sequence' already provided, the phrase "I am the Resurrection and the Life" taken from the Order of the Burial of the Dead in the Book of Common Prayer promising new hope for 1935 and neatly heralding the likely prolongation of her existence as the threat of premature death receded.[188] But what neither her guardian angel nor the 'wonderful sequence' revealed was that she would soon be bereft of anything to praise, that sacrifice would be involuntary, that the person not speaking but dying was not herself, and that the words of the burial service would be recited over another's coffin.

A further opportunity of acquiring 'the knowledge that I hope suffering will bring me' presented itself in the shape of the recurrent oral sepsis referred to by William Gilliatt and although 'dentistry [didn't] seem a very promising "school for saints"'[189], who knew what might not transpire?

What transpired was dentures. Aelfrida had undergone regular dental extractions for many years and by 1934/35 can have had few intact teeth left. Remembering the extreme discomfort she suffered after her previous extraction, she convinced herself that she would have 'a bad time with pains in my jaw and … all my bones' again and that 'such unpleasant physical things … if gladly accepted' could only increase her 'spiritual knowledge'.[190] Entering Oxford's Acland Nursing Home on 26 January 1935, she prepared for the worst, only to discover that pain was minimal, that she was prevented from increasing her spiritual knowledge by Dorothy Smith's prescription of an analgesic ("I'm not going to have you in pain for the good of a soul that is hypothetical"), and that even her guardian angel had lost patience with her, informing her perspicaciously and 'considerably to [her] astonishment' that she had 'for years been proud of having "hyperaesthesia" of body and soul' and that she 'ought to consider that it makes me a nuisance and attracts attention to me' and that should she ever achieve her 'swallow's nest' at Malling, even there she would 'sometimes manage to be a bother to somebody by attracting attention'. He also told her to meditate on the idea that Christ passed beyond His disciples' human sight in order that the Holy Spirit might open their spiritual eyes at Pentecost, a thought recently developed by Aelfrida with, it seems, dental clearance in mind: 'I see God wishes to prepare me for the complete process of "stripping" [and] will make *no* concession to my human weakness but will take everything from me'.

Then recalling that this was precisely what she besought Him to do, she asked anxiously of her guardian angel 'if human nature can bear this?' His answer made her shudder: "it is not meant to".[191]

Aelfrida left the Acland on 29 January to return, not to St Benedict's, but to the Woodstock Road Nursing Home to convalesce; 28 January having been the first anniversary of Constantine's death, she was gratified to learn that Alethea and the Lady Abbess had remembered him in their prayers. (The anniversary passed unrecorded in her diary though she had thought about him on his birthday, 29 December, in terms of how much spiritual benefit might accrue to her if she managed to identify so closely with the souls of sinners alienated from God but entrusted to her 'special care' that she too would share something of Christ's agony on the Cross[192] – and after all, did not this 'special care' derive from having been a sinner herself, alienated from God during the years of 'absolute surrender' to a *human* husband?) Neither novice or abbess, however, were privy to her next comment ('of course that kind of remembrance never comes amiss but I am somehow against anniversaries of deaths, especially sad ones like his', a strange comment by someone who said the '*De Profundis*' for Constantine daily), though she admitted to pondering on Constantine's 'unfulfilled promise' and to asking herself 'who can say that any of us have flowered as we should have done?'[193]

While still at Woodstock Road and interrupted only by nurses bearing mouthwashes and by Dorothy Smith taking impressions for new dentures ('"Mr and Mrs Nash", wonderfully becoming' but begging the question '*can* new teeth be worn patiently for the glory of God? … It is asking rather a lot!!')[194], Aelfrida undertook a major meditation on the Passion. The meditation is interesting for three reasons: because it was 'quiet' (she did not place herself in a cruciform position); because of what she experienced during it; and because of the detached way in which she described what was happening to her.

She begins her meditation by focussing on Christ sinking under the weight of the Cross as an aid to banishing thoughts of self. Then, she writes, 'there comes a point where I do not know whether I behold or experience [because] I cannot say how much is visual, auditory [or] tactile imagery, how much direct spiritual apprehension'. She then summons a feeling of the Cross beneath her and is 'conscious of men … holding hammer and nails and can hear the blows and feel the pain in my hands which increases as the meditation goes on'. Darkness surrounds her so that what she experiences is 'more felt than seen' and she senses the presence of 'the holy women [and] the crowd' more in terms of 'the clash and tension of their varied participations' than of their physical being. Presently, she continues, 'nothing seems to remain but Our Lord and again I do not know whether I behold or experience for I am not conscious of myself and yet consciousness is somewhere'. A pause follows during which she considers 'if I have … strength to bear the *drag* of flesh down by nails and all the bitterness of abandonment' before an even greater darkness representing 'the darkness and horror of [the] sin and rebellion … of mankind against God' descends. In the midst of this darkness there suddenly 'brims up … a fountain of perfect love, [of] adoration and communion, a commingling of essence with God the Father', a fontal *Atmadarshana* which turns on itself and flows downward as '*caritas*, compassion, pure love'. At the fountain's heart she discerns '*peace* [and] perfect equilibrium' and realises 'this is what I am seeking … it is *there* … that I wish to be and to abide'. Then she returns (or is allowed to return) to 'the world', knowing that after such a consummation 'nothing further can be accomplished'.[195]

The experience left her an exhausted but 'very happy Aelfrida Placida'.[196] Feeling that 'life ought to be plain sailing'[197] from now on, she returned to St Benedict's on 19 February. Then Daisy Allen caught mumps and changed the course of two lives.

The woman who had assured the Lady Abbess of Malling that she was willing to undertake tasks no-one else wanted, even cleaning lavatories, decided that there was nothing she wanted to do less than clean her own lavatory and, Phyllis having made it clear she was not wanted at Merton House and the nuns at St Thomas' Convent that she was not welcome either (the Community was decimated by illness), wrote to the Community of the Holy Family to see if she could be accommodated in their hostel pending Daisy's recovery. She could, and Aelfrida joined Agatha in Cambridge on 20 February 1935.

September 1934 had seen Aelfrida writing joyfully that she loved to think 'that we are all three going to convent precincts', Alethea to Malling, herself to St Benedict's, and Agatha to the 'House of Study' attached to the convent of the Holy Family in the Chesterton area of Cambridge.[198] Having decided that Agatha should be flung out into the world 'to sink or swim'[199], she was delighted to discover in February 1935 that Agatha, 'all by her precious little self', had not only 'found her way back into the stream of idealism and reverence for education [on] which both Chiara and I have in our generation floated'[200] (Agatha's so-called thesis was entitled *The Idea of Freedom in English Literature* and she professed herself happy at being able to 'study and to think without lectures or exams to break in on her private cogitations')[201] but was preparing to launch herself from a hostel on a hillside above the Cam founded by a friend of her grandmother's: in 'the old days of Higher Education for women', Agnes Mason had been a pupil of Henry Sidgwick, moral philosopher and champion of women's education. Sitting 'at the feet of Professor Sidgwick', Agnes met 'the Verralls and the Myers'[202], it being in Professor Sidgwick's house, Hillside, that some of the earliest experiments of the Society for Psychical Research took place following the Professor's marriage to Eleanor Balfour in April 1876.[203] Some years later, following Agnes Mason's profession as a nun and the Sidgwicks' move to Newnham, Hillside became the Anglican convent of the Sisters of the Community of the Holy Family with 'Mother Agnes' as its Superior[204], its 'Hostel for Students' providing sheltered accommodation for female scholars and a source of income for the convent. At the time of Agatha's stay, the convent's Superior was Newnham graduate Lilian Slater, since 1899, Sister Lilian of the Community of the Holy Family, and it was to her and to two of her nuns, Sisters Rose and Florence, that the former Girton scholar felt particularly drawn, they in turn admiring 'her brilliance and her wit'. She was also 'petted up' by the convent housekeeper, Hetty Bullimore.

Hillside as Agatha and Aelfrida knew it (it was, coincidentally, a near neighbour of 'Castlebrae' of 'Learned Twins' fame) was a tall yellow-grey house towering above the junction of Chesterton Lane and Chesterton Road, overlooking the river. On earlier visits, Aelfrida felt as if she had 'stepped back sixty years, the atmosphere was so thick with Victorian culture' and she was surprised that Agatha was content to live there because she found it creepy and claustrophobic with 'ghosts crowding in a little too close'.[205] (She promised her mother that if the atmosphere invaded her room too much she would 'seek quarters elsewhere'.) It seems too that Hillside, built in 1875, reminded Agatha of Fordfield, its near contemporary and the house of her birth left so sadly two years before, and her daughter's return 'to so familiar a place' made Aelfrida feel that Agatha's 'independent little path' had led her 'almost too forcibly' back to her beginnings.[206] It was, therefore, into this old-fashioned, quiet, intellectual, haunted, and pious place so like and so unlike Fordfield that Aelfrida erupted on 20 February, pleased to be reunited with her daughter, nostalgic for 'days that are no more' of which she was reminded by a glimpse of Fordfield as her train pulled into Cambridge station[207], already planning to spend the following winter at Hillside away from the rigours of St Benedict's, and sporting, rather self-consciously and not very comfortably (her gums were sore), her new dentures.

She found Agatha 'rather preoccupied' but no more than one would expect of a student busy with a 'thesis' and keen to assure her mother that she was eating and sleeping well, was 'very happy' at Hillside, and did not regret leaving Wetenhall Cottage. She also informed Aelfrida that she had an introduction to Eric Gill 'sculptor, printer of fine books, publisher, [and] disciple of Maritain'[208] and had arranged to visit his Guild of St Joseph and St Dominic on 23 February to arrange an apprenticeship in fine printing. Aelfrida gave her blessing to her daughter's new venture (the guild members were tertiaries of the Third Order of St Dominic) but worried that it might interrupt work on her 'thesis'. Apart from this and from one significant conversation, she does not record what further discussions, if any, took place between her daughter and herself (did they, for example, note that 27 February 1935 would be the first anniversary of the burial of their former husband's and late father's ashes?) but given that Agatha maintained 'long frequent silences' in between 'leaping, flaming outbursts of thought'[209] and that Aelfrida was trying to keep 'as much of my Rule as I can'[210], only small talk too trivial to record may have passed between them.

On 22 February Aelfrida, who had been 'looking forward to lovely times at Merton House' with her nieces, was informed by Eustace that all was 'infection and gloom' there (members of the family were ill and there was what the Strawberry Eater called a 'Servant Problem') and that there was nothing she could do to help; she therefore remained disappointedly at Hillside. That evening Agatha came to her room to discuss St John of the Cross whose works she had been reading. Aelfrida had only said a few words regarding St John's 'strength and greatness' when Agatha 'emphatically cried out' that it was 'our weakness and not our strength that God wanted and used'[211], that 'the greatest of the saints were nothing without Him', and, quoting St Teresa's maxim that "without God there is nothing in Teresa that anyone can depend on", ran out of the room in tears. Aelfrida did not follow her but cogitated happily on what she believed was Agatha's 'new and lovely humility' ('her one fault', she added, 'had always been a touch of conscious spirituality', inherited, one presumes, from her mother) and on how 'immeasurably' 'precious, precious Temu' had progressed in spiritual development since leaving Wetenhall Cottage. Then a thought struck her: had something *hurt* Agatha and had it 'hurt much' if it gave her such 'admirable knowledge'? She did not enquire further, being content to deem her daughter 'ready for God'.[212]

On Saturday 23 February 1935, Agatha left Hillside just before 9am. Aelfrida spent 'a very dreary day' in 'unaccountably low spirits' until a telegram arrived at 5.45pm: "Not back till after supper. Pleasant but undecisive day. Agatha".[213] During the next twenty-four hours she was to undergo an experience as intense and shattering as that undergone during her meditation on the Passion and as harrowing throughout as the passional one had been at the start. But it did not end in peace and equilibrium discerned at the heart of a fountain of perfect love nor by a lizard-green river on whose banks she and her daughters had once walked in enchantment but by waters deep as death beside which she would find herself living out her 'favourite nightmare': 'wildly hunting for a lost child'.[214]

At 8pm, the time Agatha could be expected to appear, Aelfrida '*felt* her near and grew terribly restless, watching, watching [but] she never came' (*Aelfrida frustra expectans diu vigilante expectans diu vigilare*[215]), the world seeming to narrow "to one preoccupation – when would [Agatha] come home? … The concentration of all her attention, all her desire, on one point was bitterly painful [and] ugly possibilities … tormented her until she felt frantic with impotence and longing".[216] Sometime later she undressed and went to bed to rest, not to sleep, two of the nuns keeping vigil beside her. The three women waited until 1.45am on Sunday morning, the time of arrival of the last train from London, then Aelfrida said "someone must go and telephone the police". One of the nuns volunteered to do so. (*Tandem tertia hora a.m descendit.*) 'I heard her open the front door', wrote Aelfrida, 'but she was back in my room in a minute with a folded paper in her hand'[217], retrieved from the threshold where someone had flung it. (*Litteras in limine invenit.*) "Dearest, dearest Mother. I love you more than words can say. Goodbye. By the time you get this, I hope I shall be dead".[218]

Aelfrida's first thought was for herself: 'I thought I had been as unhappy as it is possible to be. But no. This is far and away the worst. Oh! If these torments are necessary for my sanctification … purely as suffering I accept them with all my heart'. Then she remembered her daughter: 'Agatha has *disappeared* … she thought she was out of her mind and … was going to drown herself in the river'.[219] (*Nunc in flumine mortem oppetani.*)

"Dearest, dearest Mother … I have been gradually going out of my mind and apparently have no strength to prevent it … This is why I left you last autumn to try and get cured of [it but] my actions today have shown me still more clearly that I am not rational … I am wandering and hardly know what I do or say … Misery creeps on me like a kind of shadow and even when I walk the earth I am a ghost … If I had any hope of getting better I should try to be patient. But I am like someone who struggles in a marsh. I see nothing but horror to myself and no good coming to you. But death may *possibly* be a path to good, a desperate one, but the only one I can see".[220]

Everything, down to Agatha signing off with a quotation (or, rather, misquotation) from Milton's *Lycidas*[221], spoke of death by water so Aelfrida 'got up, dressed and went out along the river calling her name, very loud, all the way'. Having gone downstream as far as the nearby lock and found nothing, a journey during which she had the presence of mind to alert river workers and a night-watchman, she returned to nearby Hillside 'to see if there were tidings', only to find 'two assize men with lights', alerted by the nuns, 'all ready to go out and drag the river'.

Out she went again through the cold February night to nearby Merton House where Eustace came down at once in answer to her frantic ringing. (*Soror fratrum vocat*.) 'I thought he would have fainted when I told him', wrote Aelfrida, 'but he dressed with incredible speed and came out with me along the Backs ... then on to Newnham Mill and back again over Silver Street bridge ... There was a moon shining out between the black clouds and the trees were so still and dignified. But ... the water was gleaming and repulsive – oh! if she has drowned herself, she must be mad indeed'. (*Ambo vigiles. Frustra in ripis eam errantes petunt*.) Hoarse from calling and not knowing what else to do, Aelfrida returned to Hillside where she lay down in her clothes to think that on such a night she too had meant to die and to wish a quicker and an accidental end for her daughter ('oh! if [God] would have flung her under the wheel of a car rather than let her be guilty of her own death')[222] than prolonged self-slaughter by the very means she herself might have chosen. By 9.15am, however, she was up again, had eaten some breakfast 'for I may need my strength', had said Prime (did Constantine receive his *De profundis* or did her mind run too much on 'Fuvver's Agata'?) and was waiting for Eustace: 'God grant that this suspense be broken soon'.[223] It was. Five minutes later Eustace entered with the words "bad news"[224] on his lips: unlike her mother who was then only playing at 'being Nobody', Agatha had become 'nobody'.

Twenty years later, Aelfrida was sorting through family papers when she came upon a small notebook. Opening it at random she discovered a fragment of 'Agatha's rough copy of part of her last message ... the message flung down on the doorstep at Hillside before she went away to die'. Horrified at the thought that Agatha might have 'kept those words in her heart, God knows how long, before they were committed to writing', Aelfrida resolved to destroy the notebook. (In the event, she added an incomplete postscript to her diary entry 'I *couldn't* let the precious...'[225] and kept the page on which the message was written.) Agatha had indeed gone away to die. But she had not drowned.

'You know', wrote Aelfrida towards the end of that terrible February day, 'I always used to like the noise that ... *friendly* ... trains made. But when I was [in Oxford] ... I *hated* it. It said death – death – death [and] I used to wonder why ... But now I know'. She did indeed. The 'bad news' brought by Eustace was that Agatha's body had been found on the railway track just south of Cambridge. (*Mane nuntiant vigiles corpus in via ferrata ... esse.*) 'They told him ... death must have been instantaneous'.[226]

## Notes

1  GCPPT 1|1|46 7 August 1934.
2  GCPPT 1|1|48 30 May 1935. For a brief history of the Community St Thomas the Martyr, see Whitehead, J, pp 50–53, 58, 84–88 and 102, and Anson, P. (pp 285–288), the latter describing its conventual buildings of "mellowed red brick ... crowded together alongside the cemetery at the mediaeval church of St Thomas" (It was also in close proximity to the Great Western Railway and Oxford Station). The Community was founded in 1851 and had occupied the site since 1861.
3  For a lengthier discussion of the wider implications of this social phenomenon see Nicholson, V. *Singled Out*. Nicholson, however, makes only one reference (pp 247–248) to twentieth century conventual life in this context and may not have been aware of how many women whose lives were impoverished by loss or lack of husbands as a result of the Great War, lived in convent precincts.
4  Aelfrida's income at this time derived from directorships (soon to be relinquished), from investments, from rental income (Fordfield, Wetenhall Cottage, and properties inherited from her parents), from royalties (a small and dwindling amount) , and from articles and reviews written for the Faith Press and the SPCK.
5  GCPPT 1|1|51 28 June 1936.
6  GCPPT 1|1|43 26 November 1932.
7  GCPPT 1|1|30 24 May and 22 June 1925.
8  GCPPT 1|1|43 2 January 1933.
9  GCPPT 1|1|33 25 July 1926 includes a third 'Perros Guirec' poem (*A "Pardon"*) in which this line occurs. The poem was inspired by a religious procession witnessed by Aelfrida on one of the rare occasions when she was not accompanied by Albert Erlande.
10  GCPPT 1|1|46 7 August 1934 and undated cutting from the *Oxford Times* pasted into the back of GCPPT 1|1|48, by context written sometime between 30 May and 11 August 1935. Although signed only 'NEMO', this and the letter's content reveal Aelfrida's authorship.
11  GCPPT 1|1|46 7 August 1934.
12  ibid. 8 August 1934.
13  ibid. 7 August 1934.
14  GCPPT 1|1|48 30 May 1935.
15  GCPPT 1|1|46 7 August 1934.
16  GCPPT 1|1|28 14 May 1928.
17  GCPPT 1|1|46 16 and 20 September 1934.
18  ibid. 13 and 15 September 1934.
19  GCPPT 1|1|51 26 August 1936.
20  GCPPT 1|1|46 5 October 1934.
21  GCPPT 1|1|22 20 April 1918.
22  GCPPT 1|1|46 5 October 1934.
23  GCPPT 1|1|13 27 August 1906.
24  The full text of Dr Fry's article can be read on http://www.orders.anglican.org/arcyb/2000–MarionFry.html
25  GCPPT 1|1|46 13 August 1934.
26  ibid. 12 August 1934.
27  ibid.1 September 1934.

28  ibid. 5 September 1934.

29  ibid. 2 September 1934.

30  Fry, M. op. cit.

31  GCPPT 1|1|32 5 May 1926.

32  GCPPT 1|1|44 3 October 1933.

33  Tillyard, Ae. *A Little Road-Book for Mystics.* p39.

34  Tillyard, Ae, *The Closer Walk with God* p 11. There is no direct evidence in any of Aelfrida's writings that she knew of Richard Challoner's *The Garden of the Soul* (c1740, with many later editions) but, given that its subtitle was *A Manual of ... Instructions for Christians who (living in the world) aspire to Devotion*, that it was both a treatise on the spiritual life and a collection of spiritual exercises by means of which daily life may be sanctified, that it refers frequently to St Francis de Sales, that one of Aelfrida's later pronouncements appears to be lifted from it and that, referring to Garden Blaikie, she hints that her 'garden' is not him, it is possible to assume that she did.

35  GCPPT 1|1|46 5 September 1934. The first words of Psalm 180 are also the title of a Mass for the dead.

36  ibid. 13 September 1934.

37  ibid. 15 November 1934.

38  ibid. 28 September 1934.

39  Tillyard, Ae. *The Closer Walk with God* p13.

40  GCPPT 1|1|46 30 September 1934.

41  ibid. 17 September 1934.

42  ibid. 21 October 1934. The foursquare tenement block of Christchurch Buildings stood over a hundred yards distant and only just visible over the rows of terraced houses between it and the convent so one can only assume that others besides its inmates were noisy, that Aelfrida would not have objected to the 'jangles' had they been Beethoven, that she was exaggerating for effect, or that her nerves were so taut that the slightest noise upset her.

43  Tillyard, Ae. *The Closer Walk with God* p 18.

44  GCPPT 1|1|46 9 August 1934.

45  ibid. 27 October 1934.

46  Tillyard, Ae. *A Little Road-Book for Mystics* p40.

47  GCPPT 1|1|46 30 May 1935.

48  ibid. 23 November 1934.

49  ibid. 5 December 1934.

50  GCPPT 1|1|45 28 August 1934.

51  GCPPT 1|1|46 5 October 1934.

52  ibid. 26 August 1934.

53  ibid. 7 August 1934.

54  Undated cutting from the *Oxford Times* pasted into the back of GCPPT 1|1|48.

55  GCPPT 1|1|46 16 October 1934.

56  ibid. 28 September 1934.

57  ibid. 23 October 1934.

58  Tillyard, Ae. *The Closer Walk with God* pp 20–21.

59  ibid. pp vi and 58. Chapter 6 is entitled "The dearest idol I have known" after a line of the William Cowper hymn from which the title of the book is derived.

60  GCPPT 1|1|46 6 October 1934.

61  ibid. 5 December 1934.

62  ibid. 15 November 1934.

63  Benedict of Nursia (480–547AD) gave his name to a Rule devised in 527AD for his monks at Monte Cassino in southern Italy. The monastery later became the headquarters of the Benedictine Order and Benedict's Rule the pattern for monastic rules generally. A strict but not an unnecessarily severe Rule, it was devised so that an earnest-minded person could keep it without undue physical, mental or spiritual strain, its key precept being moderation in all things.

64  For further discussion of the Rule of St Benedict, see Parry and de Waal's preface and introduction to *The Rule of Saint Benedict* and http:||www.douaiabbey.org|office.htm

65  Benson, RM. *Instructions on the Religious Life* p10.

66  Tillyard, Ae. *The Closer Walk with God* p 21.

67  GCPPT 1|1|46 30 October 1934.

68  GCPPT 1|1|45 17 and 22 August 1934.

69  GCPPT 1|1|19 11 June 1913.

70  GCPPT 1|1|20 18 October 1914.

71  ibid. 5 August 1915.

72  GCPPT 1|1|22 22 July 1918.
    GCPPT 1|1|23 29 July 1928.

73  GCPPT 1|1|23 31 July 1918.

74  ibid. 7 August 1918.

75  GCPPT 1|1|25 28 April 1920.

76  GCPPT 1|1|43 26 November 1932.

77  Tillyard, Ae. *The Making of a Mystic* p 105.

78  Tillyard, Ae. *Vision Triumphant* pp 50 and 83.

79  Tillyard, Ae. *The Making of a Mystic* pp 105–106.

80  Tillyard, Ae. *Can I be a Mystic?* pp 55–56.

81  GCPPT 1|1|35 29 August 1928.

82  Tillyard, Ae. *The Making of a Mystic* p 76.

83  Tillyard, Ae. *O Passionate World* p 144.

84  GCPPT 1|1|38 8 November 1930.

85  Tillyard, Ae. *O Passionate World* pp 146 and 156–157.

86  In her *Light of Christ* (pp 102–107) Evelyn Underhill expatiates at some length on a person's "need of retreat" in an atmosphere where he or she can "dwell quietly ... in the atmosphere of God", clinically, to requicken "the spark of the soul ... which has grown dull and dead" and practically in terms of "spiritual welfare work" to relieve "the pressure and demands of the social ... machine". Underhill's book was not, of course, published until 1945, but she had led retreats for some years prior to that, chiefly at Pleshey, at which the addresses which form the basis of the book were given (Pleshey was a pre-Reformation religious foundation revived as a convent in 1902 by the Community of the Servants of Christ but subsequently a Retreat House when the community outgrew it), but also at places like Leiston. Aelfrida does not refer directly to Evelyn Underhill with regard to her 'hermitage' but she knew the latter's work and books and reports of Underhill's addresses were circulated in journals with which Aelfrida was familiar.

87  GCPPT 1|1|43 12 January 1933.

88  Tillyard, Ae. *O Passionate World* p 156.

89  GCPPT 1|1|22 20 April 1918.

90  Pachomius (329–346 AD) was converted to Christianity in 314 AD and subsequently lived an eremitical life at Tabennisi near Dendera in Egypt. He is generally credited with being the founder of Christian eremitic existence as a means of intensifying communion with God in silence, solitude and a degree of material privation. Aelfrida may also have heard of eremitical existence from the 'Learned Twins', Mesdames Lewis and Gibson having visited several hermits on their 1901 visit to Egypt (Soskice, J. pp 272–273) and from her later readings of the lives of saints; of particular relevance here is Etheldritha who became a hermit at Croyland in Lincolnshire c. 793 AD (an abbey with a strong eremetic connection) following her husband's death. Although she must also have read Aleister Crowley's rude (and in her case, prophetic) poem *The Hermit* in *The Equinox* (vol 1 No 1 pp 137–138 1909) with its description of a hermit as one who "laughed and heeded not" when God sent tribulations but continued to build his "Donkeydom" until "people certified him insane", given her present state of mind she was unlikely to have been deterred by it.

91  For details of Julian's life (c.1342–c.1423), see King, U. pp 133–132. Worth noting in this context is that when an anchoress entered her cell a requiem was sung as an indication of her now being 'dead' to the world.

92  GCPPT 1|1|45 9 January 1934.
    GCPPT 1|1|46 13 December 1934.

93  For a recent exposition of de Foucault's life see Fleming, F. *The Sword and the Cross.*

94  GCPPT 1|3. The notebook in which Aelfrida copied out relevant passages from Bazin's work of 1923 is also that in which she made notes on 'the experiences of some modern mystics' in 1913.

95  Bazin, R. p 6.

96  ibid. p 66.

97  ibid. pp 74–79

98  GCPPT 1|1|40 17 August 1931.

99  GCPPT 1|1|20 18 October 1914.

100  GCPPT 1|1|46 23 November 1934.

101  GCPPT 1|1|20 18 October 1914.

102  GCPPT 1|1|23 31 July 1918.

103  GCPPT 1|1|46 16 October 1934.

104  ibid. 13 December1934.

105  GCPPT 1|1|35 17 June 1928.
     GCPPT 1|1|46 23 October 1934.

106  GCPPT 1|1|46 23 October 1934.

107  ibid. 26 December 1934.

108  ibid. 25 September 1934.

109  ibid. 12 November 1934.

110  ibid. 18 September and 18 November 1934.

111  ibid. 23 September 1934.

112  ibid. 5 October 1934.

113  ibid. 25 September 1934.

114  ibid. 31 August 1934.

115  ibid. 30 September 1934.

116  ibid. 14 November 1934.

117  ibid. 5 October 1934.

118  ibid. 31 August 1934.

119  GCPPT 1|1|45 16 August 1934.

120  GCPPT 1|1|46 23 October 1934.

121  GCPPT 1|1|44 5 November 1933.

122  GCPPT 1|1|46 20 December 1934.

123  GCPPT 1|1|47 5 March 1935.

124  GCPPT 1|1|47 5 March 1935.
     GCPPT 1|1|49 28 August 1935. Biographical details are garnered from Aelfrida's diaries and must be presumed accurate; the SSJE is reluctant to divulge information.

125  GCPPT 1|1|50 16 May 1936.

126  GCPPT 1|1|46 7 October 1934.

127  ibid. 17 February 1935.

128  ibid. 22 September 1934.

129  GCPPT 1|1|48 24 July 1935.

130  GCPPT 1|1|50 11 January 1936.

131  The Society of Watchers and Workers, originally called the Guild of Invalids, was established in 1879 with the object of recognising sickness "as a bond of Christian fellowship" and "bodily infirmity as a power of witness for Christ".

132  The original of 'Amanda' was an ugly child, Amy Sale, teased by Aelfrida and Lucy at Littlehampton in 1892. They nicknamed her 'Amanda Carter' and because "'Amanda' means 'meet or fit to be loved', so we detested her". (GCPPT 2|25|2 *Littlehampton and Lucy*).

133  The three articles from which this paragraph is derived are entitled *Theodore and Amanda meet again* (GCPPT 2|23|1 *The Watchword* September 1909). *Theodore visits Amanda again* (GCPPT 2|24|2) and *Theodore gives advice to Amanda* (ibid). The first named article was published anonymously but is signed by Aelfrida in her copy 'Aelfrida Tillyard'; the second and third exist as proof copies only. *Theodore visits Amanda again* is also interesting insofar as in it 'Amanda' gives 'Theodore' news of two other pupils of hers, twin brothers 'Charles and Cosmo MacLeod', one of whom ('Cosmo', known as 'Cozzie') has been killed in the Great War; the other ('Charlie') was ordained and became in turn a slum curate, a missionary in Central Africa and,

following a breakdown in his health, a chaplain in France, Switzerland, and Madagascar. 'Charlie' has now retired to England where he pays a surprise visit to 'Amanda', informing her that he intends to live nearby in 'Theodore's' parish. 'Cosmo' is, of course, Constantine Michaelides, known to his American relatives as 'Cozzie', his death in the war being that wished on him by Aelfrida; 'Charlie' is Constantine Graham, whose life has been largely spent abroad and whose ashes have recently returned to England.

134  GCPPT 1|1|46 22 September 1934.

135  ibid. 24 November 1934.

136  ibid. 25 November 1934.

137  ibid. 24 November 1934.

138  ibid. 31 October and 2 November 1934.

139  ibid. 29 November 1934.

140  ibid. 20 December 1934.

141  ibid. 18 February 1935.

142  ibid. 20 December 1934.

143  GCPPT 1|1|25 22 January 1920. Of possible relevance in this context is the publication in 1914 of Stewart McDowall's *Evolution and the Need of Atonement*. McDowall was a Cambridge graduate whose ordination in 1909 resulted in his writing several books in which parallels are drawn between the development of Christian belief and Darwinian evolution. (He had read Natural Sciences before working in the Cambridge Zoological Laboratory in 1904). More significant from Aelfrida's point of view is publication of McDowall's work at a time when she was pursuing research on her own account (and privy to her father's; *Manuscripts of God* and *Stones of Stumbling* have an 'evolutionary' theme very similar to McDowall's), McDowall's belief (p132) that sin is "voluntary antagonism to the will of God" and that the only way for a man to free himself or one of his fellow-men from sin is by means of such close identification with "the Incarnate God" (p 171) that he achieves atonement through "the Atoning Death of Christ" (p 153) being remarkably similar to Aelfrida's statement with regard to her 'Christing' of Constantine's sins.

144  GCPPT 1|1|46 10 January 1935.

145  ibid. 5 February 1935. Aelfrida was particularly impressed by *Les Ames Hosties, Les Ames Victimes* by Abbé Paulin Giloteaux, published in 1927. The book will be discussed in more detail in a later chapter.

146  ibid. 18 January 1935.

147  ibid. 1 November 1934.

148  ibid. 30 October 1934.

149  ibid. 4 November 1934. Aelfrida may have had in mind here St Paul's message to the Colossians "for you are dead and your life is hid with Christ in God" (*Colossians* 3:3 KJV).

150  ibid. 9 November 1934.

151  ibid. 11 December 1934.

152  ibid. 23 November 1934.

153  ibid. 13 October 1934.

154  ibid. 15 January 1935.

155  ibid. 6 October 1935.

156  ibid. 28 September and 1 October 1934.

157  ibid. 2 November 1934.

158  Tillyard, Ae. *Can I be a Mystic?* pp 55–57.

159  Tillyard, Ae. *A Little Road-Book for Mystics* p 121. In this at least Aelfrida had much in common with the Illuminati, men and women (particularly women, including Teresa of Avila) for whom only ecstasies and visions provide experience of Deity. Anti-formalist adventures of this nature laid their practitioners open to charges of heresy.

160  GCPPT 1|1|46 13 October 1934.

161  ibid. 11 December 1934.

162  ibid. 16 December 1934.

163  ibid. 20 December 1934.

164  Tillyard, Ae. *The Closer Walk with God* pp 32–36. The nursing home described here is the Evelyn.

165  GCPPT 1|1|46 16 and 18 December 1934.
166  ibid. 18 December 1934.
167  ibid. 10 January. 1935
168  ibid. 31 December 1934.
169  ibid. 12 January 1935.
170  ibid. 5 January 1934.
171  ibid. 12 January 1935.
172  ibid. 5 January 1935.
173  ibid. 31 December 1934.
174  ibid. 10 January 1934.
175  ibid. 20 December 1934.
176  ibid. 11 December 1934.
177  ibid. 3 January 1935.
178  ibid. 12 January 1935.
179  ibid. 4 January 1935.
180  ibid.15 January 1935.
181  William Gilliatt (1884–1956), later Sir William Gilliatt KCVO FRCP FRS FRCOG, President of the Royal Society of Medicine and surgeon-gynaecologist to Queen Elizabeth, wife of George VI, was then a consultant surgeon at King's College Hospital. Aelfrida saw him at his consulting rooms in Harley Street.
182  ibid. 17 January 1935.
183  ibid. 20 January 1934.
184  ibid. 28 December 1934. 'Hyperaesthesia' implies hypersensitivity of nerve endings but the term is sometimes used by doctors to denote the pain of patients whose described discomfort does not tally with their doctor's clinical findings, something which may suggest an element of exaggeration of their symptoms in order to attract sympathy. (Their reasons for behaving in this way may not be obvious even to themselves). Hyperaesthesia in Aelfrida's case may therefore be seen as her response to overwhelming psychological (social, emotional, and spiritual) stress expressed as very real (to her) physical pain and her seeking medical advice as a cry for help, a cry so well disguised that it went unanswered.
185  ibid. 22 January 1935.
186  ibid. 19 January 1935.
187  ibid. 20 January 1935.
188  ibid. 1 and 12 January 1935.
189  ibid. 20 January 1935.
190  ibid. 25 January 1935.
191  ibid. 31 January 1935. Aelfrida's enthusiastic adoption of the term 'hyperaesthesia' to describe psychophysical states of being was shortlived; perhaps an Acland nurse enlightened her as to its possible connotations.
192  ibid. 29 December 1934.
193  ibid. 2 February 1935.
194  ibid. 13 and 15 February 1935.
195  ibid. 10 February 1935.
196  ibid. 18 February 1935.
197  ibid. 13 February 1935.
198  ibid. 7 September 1934.
199  GCPPT 1|1|44 12 October 1933.
200  GCPPT 1|1|46 11 September 1934.
201  ibid. 23 November 1934.
202  GCPPT 1|1|46 11 September 1934.
203  Schultz, B. pp 299 and 302.
204  GCPPT 1|1|46 11 September 1934.
205  The ghosts ('imaginary guests, please!') to which Aelfrida refers were presumably those raised by the activities of the SPR. Schultz, B. (p766) records that some of Hillside's older neighbours recalled that the house was said to be "haunted".
206  GCPPT 1|1|46 11 September 1934.
207  ibid. 21 February 1935.
208  ibid. 23 February 1935. The views of French Catholic philosopher/theologian Jacques Maritain (1882–1973) on the necessity for a revival of the spirituality inherent in the material world and its subsequent expression in works of art were enthusiastically adopted by Eric Gill and his Guild. They would also have evoked sympathetic resonances in Aelfrida's mind.
209  GCPPT 1|1|49 8 October 1935.
210  GCPPT 1|1|46 22 February 1935.
211  GCPPT 1|1|49 16 August 1935.
212  GCPPT 1|1|47 15 March 1935.
213  GCPPT 1|1|46 23 February 1935.
     GCPPT 1|1|69a contains Agatha's telegram dispatched from King's Cross Station, London at 5.23pm, received in Cambridge 5.33pm, and annotated by Aelfrida 'her last wire'.
214  GCPPT 1|1|21 17 January 1917.
215  This and other Latin interpolations are taken from Julius Tillyard's account of the circumstances surrounding his niece's death, written on 25 February 1935 (*Synopsis of Diary.* MTC).
216  Tillyard, Ae. *O Passionate World* pp 297–298, These apposite sentences were probably written to commemorate an earlier episode during which Aelfrida feared that Alethea might have been kidnapped by her father (in fact she was helping Lilian Whitehouse search for a lost dog) but it is also possible they were added later.
217  GCPPT 1|1|46 23 February 1935. The latter part of this entry was, of course, written on 24 February, a day for which there is no separate entry in Aelfrida's diary, a day coincidentally described by her in relation to Agatha's illness of three years earlier as 'strange, unnatural [and] horrible' (GCPPT 1|1|39 24 February 1931).
218  GCPPT 1|1|46 1 March 1935. Agatha's letter was undated; 1 March is the date on which Aelfrida copied the letter into her diary before she destroyed the original.
219  ibid. 23 February 1935.
220  ibid. 1 March 1935.
221  ibid. 1 March 1935. The last and commonly misquoted line of Milton's poem has "fresh woods", not "fresh fields".
222  Agatha had written in her suicide note of having tried earlier that day "to throw myself under a bus … but it stopt (*sic*) too soon" (GCPPT 1|1|46 1 March 1935), a form of death which could have been made to appear accidental.
223  GCPPT 1|1|46 23 [24] February 1935.
224  GCPPT 1|1|48 8 July 1935.
225  GCPPT 1|1|69 13 May 1952.
     GCPPT 1|1|69a.
226  GCPPT 1|1|46 23 [24] February 1934.

# Finis Terrae

Inquest on the body of Alfreda Catherine Agatha Graham aged 24 years (a student) of "Hillside", Chesterton Lane Cambridge (home address – Whitenhall Cottage, Brookland's Avenue, Cambridge) daughter of the late Constantine Graham, British Consul, who was found dead on the L.N.E.R. railway line in the parish of Great Shelford at about 7.15 am on Sunday 24 February 1935.[1]

*What is my pain, that I should recognise*
*Only when I must kill this ardent life?*[2]

Information of Witnesses severally taken and acknowledged ... touching the death of Alfreda Catherine Agatha Graham ... before Jasper Lyon, Esquire, His Majesty's Coroner ... on view of the Body of the said Person lying dead ...

*What is my pain, that I should recognise*
*Only when I must kill this ardent life?*
*What is my pain, that I might kill unknowing?*

Hetty Bullimore ... states "about 8.50 am on Saturday 23 February I was in the main hall at 'Hillside' ... when I saw Miss Graham leave ... That was the last I saw of her".

*And when I hoped, despair*
*Forbade*
*And made me walk in life ...*
*"I go because I must": this who can say*
*Has no remorse.*

Sidney Hinkins ... states "I was working the 7.10 am train from Cambridge ... on Sunday 24 February when I noticed something on the down road between Shepreth Junction and Trumpington and when passing saw that it was a woman's body. I stopped at Shepreth Junction signal box and informed the signalman".

*I go because I must: this who can say*
*Has no remorse.*
*But hopes to ride so to his deathly ending.*

Charles Henry Chalkley ... states "I am a signalman employed by the L.N.E.R. At about 7.16 am on Sunday 24 February ... the driver of the 7.10 am ex Cambridge stopped and told me there was a man lying dead in the four foot on the down line ... I informed the Cambridge Platform Inspector. When I went off duty at 7.35 am I went to where the body was lying and ... saw that it was the body of a female. I ... waited there until [the police] arrived".

*Thus far have I come*
*Here and no further.*

Edward Sussum, police sergeant, [states] "Sir, I beg to report that at 7.40 am on Sunday 24 February 1935 I was informed that the body of a woman was lying on the line about ¾ of a mile Cambridge side of Shelford Station ... I went at once to where the body was lying ... in the four foot way of the main down line. There were blood marks and bruising on the face and legs and the body was quite cold".

*Thus far have I come*
*Here and no further.*
*My solitary footsteps strayed*
*And had not strayed so far*
*Except necessity with an iron rod*
*Drove me beyond my utmost longing*
*Beyond my life ...*

Eustace Mandeville Wetenhall Tillyard on his oath saith "I identify my niece Alfreda Catherine Agatha Graham age 24 ... spinster and ex-university student".

*Here the aimless but driven wandering has end ...*
*And everlasting darkness shall consume my wasted hours.*

I, Jasper Lyon, one of the Coroners of our Lord the King do say "that the said Alfreda Catherine Agatha Graham on the 24 February 1935 ... whilst of unsound mind placed herself on the L.N.E.R line and was run over by a train travelling thereon ... The cause of her death was fracture of the base of the skull".

*Now there is nothing more to say.*
*Bright clouds that cast their shadows like a net ...*
*Are gathered now together and tiredly fall*
*In swollen piles, sagging and overladen,*
*Dragging dead children in their wombs to graves of silence.*

## Notes

1  Quotations in Roman type are taken from the Coroner's notes and associated material pertaining to the inquest held on 25 February 1935 at the Railway Inn, Great Shelford, Cambs. Errors of spelling and syntax are the clerk's. (GCPPT 1|7. Original documentation held at the Coroner's Office, Cambridge.)

2  Quotations in italics are taken from *Finis Terrae* (GCPPG A2.5).

# Reality of Death

Confronted in May 1927 by 'Timothy' White, the undergraduate newly diagnosed with tuberculosis and convinced that his illness was mortal, Agatha was simultaneously sympathetic ('no wonder he didn't think things were worthwhile. I should think they can't seem real at all … when they are shadowed by death … But they are real [and] I hope he'll see it though when brought near to the reality of death … it is hard to see it') and concerned at her ignorance: 'what do I know about it'.[1] Now, she knew.

Aelfrida knew too, or thought she did: 'I am sure that those who loved God (and Agatha did with all her soul) have a vision of God at the moment of death and that is why they are calm and radiant'.[2] But as her diary shows all too clearly, her sympathy and concern were for herself: 'they tell me I am too brave … but what can I do? If I feel calm in the strength of God … how else can I behave? Each wound that He makes in my heart is a channel through which He imparts Himself [and] with great joy I [receive] Him'.[3] And, as ever, she enjoyed the attention: nuns weeping over her (not *with* her, she remained dry eyed); Joan Cooper 'sad and … full of compassion'[4]; Phyllis, with memories of her own sister's suicide melting her usual stern attitude, 'endlessly kind'. (Of Eustace, who had had to identify the bodies of niece and sister-in-law and who knew or suspected that both young women had been hag-ridden to death by their mothers[5], we hear little; of Fidelio, to whom Aelfrida had been so supportive in times of trouble, nothing, though he wrote later – on a wholly unrelated topic.)[6] Julius, himself a suicide *manqué,* on a flying visit (he did not stay for his niece's funeral), 'so sad that [she] could hardly bear it … other people's grief is intolerable'.[7] The Lady Abbess of Malling and Father Cary praising her conduct 'as if [she] were a saint already'.[8] 'A man from the coroner'[9] to interview. Her nieces to impress as they gazed thoughtfully at her ('I want them to see the reflection of God in me as one might see the reflection of the sunset in a puddle that in itself is nothing but a little muddy water'), then, anguished thought, that they were not thinking 'lovely thoughts' about their aunt but remarking her ill-fitting false teeth instead.[10] Sedatives administered. Holy Communion brought to her room. 'A constant stream of letters'.[11] ('Those that said "what a wasted life"'

✠

**AGATHA**

IN HORA MORTIS MEÆ
VOCA ME

*The Closer Walk with God* (dedication)

and 'those that suggest[ed] Spiritualism as a consolation' were the ones that hurt.)[12] The Steam Laundry's Annual General Meeting to attend two days after Agatha's death, there to receive 'magnificently chivalrous' condolences from the directors and 'vulgar shareholders' which made the meeting 'the pleasantest ever'[13] (*sic*). 'I want to be like the "Melancolia"', she had written in a fit of adolescent angst in 1900 in Lausanne; her older self wrote 'why? ACWT 1904'.[14] In 1935 she knew why and was wringing every drop of pathos from the part.

Of course, and once the initial shock and sedative-induced numbness wore off, she suffered 'oh incredible grief for Agatha'[15], noting that she lived 'in a fire and torment of loneliness and longing … the pain of it – God! the pain of it'. Nor, she added, did she think 'that such a wound can ever heal [because] it is not *natural* for children to die before their parents'. All this, no doubt, and in spite of highly-wrought and melodramatic phraseology reminiscent of descriptions of Agatha's near-death experience four years earlier, was genuine grief ('how is one to spend one's days when one is so sad one is quite dazed with the pain … it hurts and hurts')[16] but Aelfrida's foremost feeling was a 'conviction that [Agatha's] death is a liberation for her *and for me in accordance with laws of the contemplative life'*.[17] Naturally, this rather extreme example of wish-fulfilment needed reinforcement – and who better to reinforce it than the dead girl herself: 'I seem to feel Agatha's spirit near me … , caressing me like soft air and saying "it is better so, isn't it?" and I say, yes, yes, better so'.[18] This, most of all, reinforces the impression that Aelfrida's chief emotion on learning of Agatha's death was one of relief that the burden of "the dear dignity of parenthood"[19] and of a dependent and depressive daughter had been lifted and that she was free to continue her 'closer walk untrammelled: 'every morning when I wake, I remember my guardian angel's command "*Laudate*" [and that] however sad I feel … God *must* be praised'.[20]

Relief, it may be, also explains Aelfrida's curious lack of curiosity concerning the circumstances surrounding Agatha's death, for as her diary and information provided at the inquest show, there are many unexplained or inexplicable features surrounding that event. Possibly she is so numb with shock that she never thinks to ask; possibly, given the relief of knowing that Agatha is dead, she does not want to know accepts without question the discrepancy between Agatha's intended and actual manner of death. Nor does she express the anger which often follows initial denial when a beloved person dies suddenly and hideously; instead, she accepts without question – almost, one might say, without surprise – that Agatha is dead and died in the manner in which she did. She is also more concerned that Agatha's suicide renders her ineligible for a Church of England burial service ("the office … is not to be used for any that … have laid violent hands upon themselves")[21] than that the daughter to whom she felt closest, whose personality was most like her own, and whom she loved "with the brooding inward-turning love that one gave to oneself"[22] is dead. Odd, too, is the fact that so much of her diary imagery is predicated on Milton's *Lycidas*, a poem brimming with *watery* imagery (waves, rills, fountains, streams, and tears), that it seems as if she is trying to persuade herself (and us) that Agatha *did* drown because, prolonged and painful though such a death might be, drowning could be passed off as accidental (like that of Lycidas) whereas death on a railway line could not. Not only this, but Agatha's coffin, adorned with 'a huge spray of yew … and daffodils'[23], is white like those used for children, possibly because Aelfrida regards her dead daughter as a child in the eyes of God because she did not live long enough to develop her full spiritual potential but possibly also to disguise the enormity of the adult action of one whom Aelfrida described and treated as a 'babe', a 'babe' not being responsible for its actions.

Agatha was buried in the family vault on 28 February 1935, a year and a day after she and Alethea watched their mother place their father's ashes in the selfsame tomb. (Before the burial and after Vespers for the Dead, a Requiem Mass, and a funeral service of some kind were conducted by a local priest in the Hillside chapel in the presence of the nuns, Aelfrida, Eustace, Phyllis, Hetty Bullimore, and Mr Church amid 'banks of flowers' sent in spite of Aelfrida's plea that there be none save hers,

Aelfrida had 'prayed and prayed' privately beside Agatha's bier.) At the cemetery she found 'the moment when the priest flings the handful of earth on the coffin … almost unbearable' but it was not grief which struck her to her knees as when she held the urn containing Constantine's ashes in her arms; it was 'God's presence [felt] so blindingly that [she] had to kneel'. She attributes her reaction to the service not being 'Agatha-some' insofar as her vivacious daughter was not accurately represented by a ceremony for the dead and had already 'turned away Godward' to be held eternally by her mother 'in some place deeper than memory'[24], but seen in the context of her statement that Agatha's death was in accordance with her own unspoken wishes, it is possible to regard her action as gratitude that the daughter whose life had been the single factor which stood between her mother and her goal was gone and that she herself was free to resume her 'closer walk' with an more important person than Agatha, namely Deity.

On 8 March Aelfrida ordered an oak cross (stone was too 'cold and formal') to be placed above the vault. It bore a bronze inscription:

"Aelfrida Catharine Agatha Graham
Born July 12 1910
Died February 23 1935
*In hora mortis meae voca me*".

At the base of the cross, also in letters of bronze, was a further inscription: "The ashes of her father Constantine Graham (Michaelides) who died in Berlin January 1934 aged 51 rest here". 'It seemed right', she wrote in her diary on the day she ordered the cross, 'to connect Agatha and Constantine [because] I have had so much of her and he so little'.[25]

Aelfrida, of course, had long wished to restore communications between herself and Constantine, if only because what she intended to be her edifying deathbed would 'help' his spiritual development, but his refusal to communicate with her and his pre-deceasing her (and how ironic and how prescient that 'Max', his fictional alter ego in *Marrying a Stranger,* is stoned to death and that Constantine himself died of kidney stones) forced her to resign herself to do so only through the medium of daughters in whom the best of her 'mixed with the best of him' would allow her to 'help' Constantine by proxy.[26] Having therefore decided to 'reach [Constantine] only through [her] daughters' ('and through my prayers', she added)[27], she was overjoyed that the daughter so conveniently dead and who in her own poetry had promised never to forget him "when we are dead"[28] was now available to act as intermediary: 'I have [had a] thought – that Constantine is needing her and she was called to go to *his* help and to teach him things that he could only learn through his little Bam'. Perhaps too, she thought, she herself had 'done wrong in rejoicing in a unity with sweet daughters in which he had no part', her 'mistake' being now remedied by Agatha's post-mortem reunion with her dead father.[29]

Perhaps so, and perhaps she found the thought comforting as she bargained with God and her conscience over her daughter's death. But other, contemporary, discoveries were less agreeable, and although Aelfrida had dwelt lovingly just prior to Agatha's death on 'the knowledge that I hope suffering will bring me'[30], the knowledge she was about to acquire brought suffering in its train.

One of the witnesses 'touching the death of Agatha Graham' was Joan Cooper, called in her capacity as Agatha's general practitioner. From her, the inquest learnt the following: "I have known Miss Graham for … ten years … In November 1934 a psychologist reported to me that Miss Graham had sought advice on account of depression. From that date psychological treatment was carried out and reports sent to me at intervals. The last report received on January 21st gave evidence of definite progress".[31] Furthermore, something unstated in the report of the inquest but emerging from newspaper reports of the event, was that the coroner delivered his verdict ("suicide while of unsound mind") only *after* "he had a private conversation with Dr Cooper".[32]

The (unnamed) psychologist was known to Aelfrida, being the same Dr Bannister who had interviewed herself and Agatha at the time of Alethea's breakdown, though neither he nor Dr Cooper, bound as they were by medical confidentiality, had been in a position to divulge information to Agatha's mother. How, therefore, can Aelfrida's diary contain the information that Dr Bannister's most recent session with Agatha took place on the day of her mother's arrival in Cambridge and that, far from expressing optimism concerning his patient's progress, he was dissatisfied with her overall condition because 'the trouble was much deeper in the unconscious than it was with Alethea'? The answer is that she learnt this during an interview with Dr Cooper on 24 February during which the latter, no longer bound to secrecy because her patient was dead, informed her that Agatha had begun to experience 'inclinations towards suicide' following Constantine's death. Not being privy to Agatha's poetry in general and to *Finis Terrae* in particular, Dr Cooper could not have known that Agatha's death-wish was worsened, not precipitated, by that event but Aelfrida did ('I knew her feeling for I had it for a week or two (*sic*) after the birth of my still-born baby. It is not a dreadful feeling [but] a still sombre attraction towards the unknown [and] I see now how much

of Agatha's thinking was steeped in it') for she herself had heard Agatha recite *Finis Terrae* two years earlier. Her subsequent statement that she was 'astonished … beyond measure'[33] at hearing of Agatha's depressive illness is therefore hard to credit, for although Agatha went to Dr Bannister without telling her mother, Aelfrida's worries concerning Agatha's mental health long antedated the latter's suicide. Dr Cooper knew this too, and it was this that moved her to point out, 'quite calmly in cold blood' within days of Agatha's burial, that Aelfrida was 'the most egotistical and self-centred person she [had] ever met'[34] and incapable of 'seeing things and people as they are in themselves but only in relation to [herself]'.[35]

Although Aelfrida shrugged off Dr Cooper's criticisms, remarking insouciantly that she loved to think that lady had 'no illusions about me'[36], 'Dr Joan's' criticisms cut deep, so deep that they provoked in their recipient an unusual, if not entirely accurate, degree of insight and a remarkably (for her) guilty conscience. Agatha's suicide, she decided, was provoked by 'a sudden gust blowing her towards her fate and it swept her along', the 'gust' being, of course, 'the fear of my death [which] stirred up dark mists which since the time of Constantine's defection have lain at the bottom of her unconscious mind'. But while it is true that Agatha 'centred too much of her devotion'[37] on her mother (a contention supported by Aelfrida's discovery when sorting through Agatha's effects that her daughter had kept 'all my letters, all my presents, however trivial, all the little poems I used to write to her')[38], it is more likely that Agatha's feeling of being pursued wherever she went by the incubus-mother she was trying to escape and particularly by the precipitate and unexpected arrival of that mother at Hillside, not the fear of that mother's death (Aelfrida's supposedly 'mortal' illness had been recently disproved by Mr Gilliatt), which formed the real 'gust' which 'blew' her towards the 'LNER railway line'.

We do not know what Aelfrida 'prayed and prayed' for or about beside Agatha's white coffin but from contemporary entries in her diary we may guess: forgiveness. On the one hand, she writes (briefly, 'for it is very bitter'), 'I have done harm to Agatha … yes, and Alethea too … not by what I *did* but by what I *was*', explaining and excusing her behaviour by adding that while her conduct towards both girls 'has been, as far as I can see, perfect', she did wrong by 'unconsciously' (*sic*) exacting 'far too much of their affection' and by diverting what could and should have been expended on 'sweethearts and husbands' onto one who only now realised that wisdom had been folly.[39] But though this might be taken as insightful appreciation of former foolishness, we have the evidence of her diaries and other writings to refute it: she was always aware of what she was doing (though not always conscious of the reasons which impelled her to act as she did) and as early as 1911 when Agatha and Alethea were very young and she herself not yet thirty had noted in an anguished poem that all her life she had "killed and marred and lost" everyone and eveything she loved (including some of the better aspects of herself), a terrible and perceptive admission for which her conscience was "sore accusing"[40] – but not so sorely accusing that she was prepared to alter (even if she could) her modus operandi. Hence although she took care to pretend that it was 'God's Wisdom' which had called 'one [daughter] to the cloister and another to death'[41] because to pretend otherwise would demonstrate that it was not His call or His wisdom which impelled them to act as they did, she herself knew very well why both young women felt driven to escape lives their mother had 'marred'.

In her defence, one can say that Aelfrida was perhaps not as oblivious to Agatha's plight as Dr Cooper thought, for in a later diary entry she noted apropos her unhappy daughter that 'I used to beg her to tell me what there was she was holding back' (there is no contemporary record in her diary of her having done so) but that Agatha with 'shining eyes' would insist 'that there was nothing wrong'. Hence even though she 'guessed at obscure travails of the soul', she did nothing, giving as her excuse that she did not dare 'intrude'[42] into the mind of one in which she had once claimed to walk freely. This may be so, but as (potentially) one of the saints with whom she professed to have no patience because they neglected their families[43], she proceeded to do just that, dallying like the lady of Hailstone Hall of her 1908 ballad with a 'cavalier' (Deity, in 1934/35) while her child 'drowned'.[44]

Dalliance with Deity may have been one reason why Aelfrida absented herself when Agatha or Alethea required comfort and support, but there is another, and it is in her comment that she wished her daughters had been 'more normal' that it is to be found. Aelfrida, as we know from *O Passionate World*, believed she had come into the world in order that an immortal heaven-born soul might be incarnated through her; on her terms and in terms of her daughters it was. (A later description of the putative moment of Alethea's conception in which 'a ray of light … brought her into my womb [and] she was born nine months after on the exact day that I expected her'[45] makes obvious reference to the Incarnation. It is also factually inaccurate.) Unfortunately for them and for her, Agatha's and Alethea's failure to marry and produce further incarnations resulted in their mother casting them off as unfit for purpose – and, it may be, because their continuing presence in her life reminded her of years wasted in 'absolute surrender' to their father's sexual demands (a surrender undertaken only insofar as it was the socially-approved way of incarnating souls) when, had she known that incarnation would stop with herself, she could have devoted her life to Holy Virginity and Deity instead of to unchaste behaviour and Constantine.

There may be another reason too for her rejection: if, as Albert Erlande's disclosures in *Edmée Combres* suggest, Chiara had begged her religion-obsessed daughter to 'normalise' herself by marrying, we are provided with a valid reason for Aelfrida's (reluctant) submission to her mother's wishes, her dramatic cry of 'absolute surrender' being a demonstration of how far she was prepared to go to achieve 'normality'. Marriage, unfortunately, failed to 'normalise' her – emphasising her 'perfect' marriage when evidence showed otherwise may have been a desperate attempt to prove to Chiara how 'normal' she had become, and her parents' unpleasant behaviour following Constantine's 'edict of separation' evidence of their fury that not only had she failed to 'normalise' but also that their efforts to 'normalise' her by marrying her off had failed too – and it may be that her subsequent behaviour towards Agatha and Alethea was an attempt to demonstrate how she, 'abnormal' though she was, could produce 'normal' children whose very 'normality' would suggest that she herself was not as 'abnormal' as people seemed to think. Unfortunately, and largely because of the manner in which she tried to achieve this, Aelfrida damaged her daughters irreparably and instead of making them 'normal', rendered them almost as 'abnormal' as herself. Rejecting them one after the other at times when their 'abnormality' was most manifest because their manifest 'abnormality' reflected badly on herself, but wishing to disguise her daughters' (and by extension, her own) 'abnormality', she blamed physiology (Agatha's scoliosis, Alethea's gynaecological problems), continuing to do so even up to the point of Agatha's suicide, the latter, in spite of legal and literary evidence to the contrary, not henceforth to be imputed to Agatha being of 'unsound mind' but to the physiological consequences of physical illness.

One of the most distressing tasks undertaken by Aelfrida in the days following Agatha's death was that of sorting out Agatha's effects. Deciding that it was best to give away nearly everything, she retained only objects of sentimental value and Agatha's literary productions. What she discovered among the latter would have provided ample evidence, if more were needed, of Agatha's abnormal state of mind (many years later she sorted through the material again, discarding 'some of the more illegible poems' but keeping many 'I cannot bring myself to read')[46] but one statement might have supported a 'physiological' basis for Agatha's suicide as interpreted in the light of Aelfrida's preferred hypothesis: "in the body the first trace of unhealthiness is apt to be more destructive (though more slowly) than an accident in a car".[47]

Although Agatha had seemed to take her near-fatal mastoid infection calmly, evidence available to her mother shortly afterwards but wilfully unrecognised by her then shows Agatha to have been deeply affected by this premature intimation of mortality, so much so that in the 'medical' *MCJ* dedicated to 'Dr Joan' she not only included references to her own (possible) death at the hands of a doctor who snatched her from her "pleasant fields" only to strap her "in a wooden box / And [send her] soul to wander among shades" but macabre jokes too: "doctors will tell you that corpses will float". Aelfrida, it seems, seized on this as evidence that Agatha's suicide was physiological rather than psychologically induced, proclaiming that Agatha had suffered 'anaemia of the brain' since undergoing ligation of her jugular vein at the time of her fourth operation.[48] (That this physiological impossibility did not constitute a valid reason was not, it appears, something Dr Cooper thought it appropriate to tell her at this time.) Having therefore 'proved' that she herself could not be held responsible for Agatha's suicide, Aelfrida proceeded to add to her re-invention of her life to date (her 'perfect' marriage, Constantine's unfortunate 'heredity', her being a 'widow') the cause of her younger daughter's death: 'cerebral anaemia'.

Though comforted by hearing a sermon on 'Beauty' at Mass a week after Agatha's death, Aelfrida was reminded by the hymn (appropriately and ironically "Love Divine, all loves excelling") of 'another crisis in [her] life'.[49] Though this particular crisis remained unidentified – the hymn was neither of the two sung at 'The Marriage of Miss Tillyard' – the 'crisis' of Agatha's suicide was shortly followed by two more, one arising from Agatha's own life, one, rooted in the past, now manifest in the present.

Going through Agatha's papers Aelfrida alighted upon a letter, written while Agatha was at Tortington Park, the 'strange school' at which her 'cerebral anaemia' (supposedly) first manifested itself[50], to a young man, Robert Fitzgerald, of whom we hear nothing in Aelfrida's diary but to whom Agatha had been sufficiently close to inform him that "I suppose my family to be under a curse like the House of Atreus. And in this generation misfortune is brought to a head".[51] What the 'curse' entailed, Agatha did not divulge (or Aelfrida suppressed) but given that Agatha had conceived her 'curse of Graeme' in 1927 and had confided to Robert that she must consult a doctor because the 'melancholy madness' ('*insania melancholia*', as Julius, himself given to 'fits of black melancholy', described it)[52] to which she was 'wedded' was growing rapidly worse, it seems that the 'curse' may have been

that to which the Tillyard side of her family were prone, namely endogenous depression. Alternatively it may have been an expression of her terrible Wetenhall legacy in which family members alternately battened emotionally on or rejected each other in relationships simultaneously and confusingly loving and unloving. Or it may have been a dreadful admixture of the two, from which the spiritually stronger of Aelfrida's daughters was in process of breaking free but to which the weaker succumbed, only to break free by the most drastic means of all.

Aelfrida does not say if Agatha's letter to Robert Fitzgerald was an unsent original or a draft or copy but either way it must have rung alarm bells in her mind for in it Agatha also wrote frankly of how she had tried to live apart from her mother but found herself unable to do so and of how she was reluctant to return home to "one of the most charming and welcoming houses in the world"[53] without her elder sister being there to share the burden of their mother's smothering devotion. But if Agatha was so frank to Robert, how much more frank might she have been to Helen Tansley (devastated by her death), to Humphrey Warren ('bitterly remorseful'[54] when he heard of Agatha's suicide; had she frightened him off with talk of a family curse, he concocting a story in order to escape the relationship and chivalrously placing the blame on his own shoulders?), to friends from university days any one of whom might have read newspaper reports of her suicide and recalled snippets of information concerning her mother's eccentricities[55], or to more recent admirers, one of whom, described by Aelfrida as 'rich, well-connected and intelligent [and] a *parti sérieux*'[56], might have 'normalised' her had she felt able to respond to his wooing.

If this seems improbable, we have the evidence of Aelfrida's diary to support it. Less than three weeks after Agatha's death, Aelfrida recorded (with maddening lack of detail) that a Father de Jonge of St Alban's House, Holborn, had 'suppressed' a newspaper item containing 'things about me which would be painful to me and to Alethea and to the Lady Abbess if they were allowed to appear'.[57] She was so horrified by the news that she could not (so she says) bring herself to enquire as to (or divulge) its content, but given that it might have affected her reinvention of herself as a pious 'widow', her recent oblation, or her attempts to ingratiate herself with the Lady Abbess of Malling on her own and precariously-postulant Alethea's behalf, we may conjecture something of its content and even of its provenance.

Published details of Agatha's suicide made no reference to her mother (or sister) but information may have been provided a quick-witted journalist who made the connection between the Eustace Tillyard who identified the body and Aelfrida Tillyard, author of tracts and novels in which religiosity was a prominent feature and compiler of an anthology in which her association with Aleister Crowley and his 'razzly-dazzly' beliefs was made clear. Or the perpetrator may have been someone who knew the Grahams and disliked Aelfrida (or loved Agatha) enough to supply material exposing Agatha's mother, not as the respectable 'widow' she pretended to be but for what she was: the divorced wife of an adulterous embezzler. Either way, material merely embarrassing to Alethea could have proved fatal to her mother's religious ambitions, this alone causing her to regard these particular sequelae of Agatha's death as a 'crisis' in her own life.

There was, however, another crisis looming, this one affecting Aelfrida's relationship with her elder daughter, a crisis which could only have confirmed her contention, written at the time of the Oracle's death and supported by Agatha's, that 'death precipitated you into a whirl of harrowing duties'.[58]

Alethea's voice was unheard in the clamour surrounding Agatha's death. She did not attend her sister's funeral but whether this was because she was a member of an enclosed Order or because Aelfrida pleaded that 'enclosure must not be broken for *my* private reasons' is unstated. (She also noted that she did not *need* Alethea at this juncture; she *needed* 'no-one but God'.)[59] The question of how Alethea was to be told and where ('oh pray, *pray* that she may have enough strength to bear it', wrote her mother dramatically, adding 'how I fear for her!')[60] was settled by the Lady Abbess assuming the task and Alethea being 'heroic in her acceptance and her calm'.[61] On 4 March, however, Aelfrida herself went to Malling ('*home*, my spiritual home, the dearest spot on earth')[62], only to be confronted with the reason for Alethea's unemotional reaction to her sister's suicide: Alethea was the only person – with the possible exception of the Lady Abbess who supervised all correspondence between the nuns and 'the world' – who was not deluded by Agatha's 'pathetic brightness'[63] (so similar to Olive Mudie-Cooke's prior to the latter's suicide a decade earlier, an event described by Aelfrida as 'long premeditated and planned')[64] into believing that her sister was recovering and who knew or suspected what Agatha with her penchant for dramatic gestures was about to do.[65]

Aelfrida's feelings on discovering that Truth had once again concealed the truth from her and that her 'Lady Mother' may have been complicit in concealing the fact that 'so happy' Agatha was 'happy' only insofar as she had determined to die, can only be imagined. But had she not been focussing so intently on her own future, she might have acted on hints from Malling that all was not

well with Alethea who had, as the Lady Abbess put it, "a look [of fear] in her eyes" and a tendency to weep quietly when she believed herself unobserved. On learning this, Aelfrida jokingly ascribed Alethea's unhappiness to having to work in the convent laundry ('that should be sobering!') but privily admitted that she was 'deeply uneasy'[66] on Alethea's account. She also – and the timing of this may be significant given that it was in November 1934 that Agatha first consulted Dr Bannister – noted in December 1934 that the only cloud in the blue sky of her halcyon early days at St Benedict's (other than those of noise, winter weather, and rising damp) was dreaming of Alethea in tears, something she attributed to Alethea's problematic menstrual cycle and to the Lady Abbess' fear that Alethea would not be strong enough to sustain the rigours of the contemplative life than to causes of which she herself preferred to remain ignorant. Had she probed more deeply she might have discovered the probable cause of Alethea's fear but to do this might also have deflected her from her course – and besides (the inevitable escape clause) Alethea was now the Lady Abbess' responsibility.

But not for much longer. Aelfrida's letter to the Lady Abbess asking her to tell Alethea that her sister was dead crossed with one from the Lady Abbess to Aelfrida informing her that Alethea was 'too energetic for the contemplative life' and 'could not be kept at Malling'.[67] Aelfrida was horrified, exclaiming to her diary that she 'hardly [knew] what to think or hope'[68] at the prospect of being burdened once more with an unmarriageable daughter. (A sleeping draught administered by 'Dr Joan' proved ineffective against a 'crisis' of this proportion.) She went, however, to Malling as planned where she was informed by Acting Superior Dame Frideswythe (the Lady Abbess had suffered a heart attack shortly after informing Alethea of Agatha's death) that Alethea would '*never* be really strong as to nerves' and could never endure the contemplative life because she found silence 'trying' and there was not enough outlet for her energy.[69] The news panicked Aelfrida so much that she persuaded Dame Frideswythe to postpone decisions about Alethea's future until the Lady Abbess was sufficiently recovered to join them and to keep Alethea at Malling in the meantime on the grounds that, Agatha being dead, the girl now had no distractions from 'outside' to prevent her from concentrating her energies on life in the cloister.[70] But having talked to Alethea thrice through the grille, she began to worry that not even an active order would suit her too-energetic daughter and to make contingency plans: should Alethea join her at St Benedict's as a secular oblate, there to 'pick up some coaching' to earn money or 'perhaps, ultimately', to marry 'in the hope of having little priests and nuns' (*sic*), or should she and Alethea 'take the gatehouse' at Malling as 'extern oblates, devoting ourselves to the Community but free to a certain extent to come and go'?[71] (To her diary she admitted that '*personally* I would rather build my swallow's nest … and have "no human consolations" but Alethea must come first – I helping or standing by according to her need … and yet I can say *truly* that I *need* no-one but God'.)[72] On three points, however, Aelfrida and her surviving daughter apparently agreed: 'Agatha never *belonged* to this world, … and … what has happened is *right*'; that in spiritual terms Agatha had not '*gone*'; that the 'unity of the three of us is unbroken'.[73] What Alethea *really* thought, Alethea kept to herself.

Forced to leave her 'spiritual home' by the imminent closure of the Malling guest house for refurbishment, Aelfrida returned to Cambridge to find herself unwanted there too. The Hillside Community had found recent events and Aelfrida's continuing presence too stressful for her to return ('it is the weaklings who are sent there', she wrote scornfully)[74] but though Phyllis and Eustace agreed to accommodate until Daisy's period of quarantine was over and she could return to St Benedict's (a letter from Daisy provided the one spark of humour in all this, that 'dear, devoted child' seeking to console her mistress with the immortal phrase "I must say your luck is out … but still, look on the bright side, it will turn one day")[75], attempts to provide a shining example of 'the reflection of God in me' at Merton House were doomed to failure at the point at which she retired to bed for three days to nurse the family cold which she, 'being feeble [got] … much worse' than anyone else. (Feebleness may have been enhanced by the concurrent arrival of Father de Jonge's letter.) Confronted by a sister–in–law who refused to be at the beck and call of a *malade imaginaire* ensconced at the top of a large house run solely (so his sister said)[76] for benefit of the silent hero of the whole sad affair, Eustace Tillyard, not all God's reflection in herself could prevent Aelfrida from penning some exceedingly acid comments concerning Phyllis' mode of life, personality, and unwillingness to 'pet up' a mother recently bereaved of a daughter whose life she had always felt would not be long.

Before leaving Cambridge, Aelfrida performed two further actions. First, she made a new will leaving £50 each to Malling, Julius, Eustace, and Girton College (Girton was also to receive her diaries) and her personal effects to Veronica if Alethea were 'a Religious or dead'[77] at the time of Aelfrida's own death, then she walked once more along the Backs, now in the full glory of springtime flowers ('wood anemones, … crocuses as if Flora herself had passed … primroses and scillas and daffodils

and almond trees and blackthorn in blossom' reminiscent of lovely descriptions of "flowerets of a thousand hues" of Milton's *Lycidas* written, as it happened, within a short distance of where she stood) as if to console herself that Agatha did *not* drown in the river of which her mother had so many happier memories and to remind herself that Agatha, like Lycidas, now inhabited God's "blest Kingdoms meek of joy and love": 'Agatha there, I here, God joining and not sundering us'.[78] Then, Daisy's quarantine period being completed, she returned to Oxford.

## Notes

1 GCPPG A2.1 9 May 1927.

2 GCPPT 1|1|46 23 February 1935.

3 ibid. 25 and 26 February 1935.

4 ibid. 23 February 1935.

5 Lest this judgement seem harsh, it is worth noting the following passage from *The Times* of 19 April 1914 (quoted by Beauman, N. pp 53–54), a passage which must have been read by Aelfrida, an avid reader of that newspaper: "every day a host of human vampires drain the life blood of those who are their nearest and … dearest … the most usual species is the widowed mother with a daughter of any age between twenty and fifty. The longer she stays on with her mother the more impossible it is for her to break away … The vampire ('such a devoted mother, my dear!') has them by the throat and slowly but surely squeezes them of youth and joy and hope".

6 GCPPT 1|1|47 8 March 1935.

7 GCPPT 1|1|46 26 February 1935.

8 GCPPT 1|1|47 3 March 1935.

9 GCPPT 1|1|46 25 February 1935.

10 GCPPT 1|1|47 10 March 1935.

11 GCPPT 1|1|46 26 February 1935.

12 GCPPT 1|1|47 17 March 1935.

13 GCPPT 1|1|46 26 February 1935.

14 GCPPG 1|1|6 14 November 1900. Melancholics were traditionally blessed with intellectual ability and artistic creativity, positive attributes which outweighed the darker aspects of their personality, and were generally depicted in pensive pose and as condemned to menial occupations. (Durer's 1514 *Melancholia* graphically depicts this.) Burton's *Anatomy of Melancholy*, however, read by Aelfrida in 1907, associates 'melancholia' with other mental phenomena which may be pathological (delusions, hallucinations, generalised fearfulness, supposed Satanic possession, and so on) as well as with visions, auditions, and parasomnial experiences, all of which, if known to third parties, might expose the melancholic to accusations of 'melancholy–madness'. Strong religious belief was supposed to be efficacious in the treatment of 'melancholia', as also was scourging if the melancholic was particularly oppressed by a sense of sinfulness. The pertinence of all this to what we already know and will eventually discover about Aelfrida is interesting, particularly insofar as she was prone to model herself on books read at impressionable points in her life.

15 GCPPT 1|1|46 26 February 1935.

16 GCPPT 1|1|47 10 March 1935.

17 ibid. 3 March 1935. (Author's italics.) Aelfrida may be referring obliquely here to mystic Angela of Foligno (1248–1309) who felt so constrained by family life that she prayed for her mother's, husband's, and children's deaths in order to be free to devote herself to God and to lead an impoverished and penitential life. Their subsequent deaths were therefore experienced by her as consoling rather than tragic events.

18 GCPPT 1|1|46 23 February 1935.

19 Tillyard, Ae. *The Fruits of Silence* pp 27–31 (GCPPT 2|18).

20 GCPPT 1|1|47 12 March 1935.

21 The quotation is taken from *The Order of the Burial of the Dead* from *The Book of Common Prayer*.

22 Tillyard, Ae. *O Passionate World* p 298 (GCPPT 2|11).

23 GCPPT 1|1|46 1 March 1935.

24 ibid.

25 GCPPT 1|1|47 8 March 1935.

26 GCPPT 1|1|38 24 October 1930.

27 ibid. 20 October 1930.

28 *To an Island* in the 1927 volume of Agatha's diary (MTC) in which she describes her and Alethea's meeting with Constantine entitled *After a long time.*

29 GCPPT 1|1|46 1 March 1935.

30 ibid. 19 January 1935.

31 GCPPT 1|7 Coroner's notes and associated material pertaining to the inquest held on 25 February 1935.

32 Undated (by context 26 February 1935) and unprovenanced newspaper cutting headed *Girton Student's Rail Death After Treatment by Psychologist* (MTC). The *Cambridge Daily News* report of 25 February 1935 makes the same point.

33 GCPPT 1|1|46 account dated 23 February 1935 though completed on 24 February.

34 GCPPT 1|1|47 3 March 1935.

35 ibid. 15 March 1935.

36 ibid.

37 GCPPT 1|1|46 23 February 1935.

38 GCPPT 1|1|47 10 March 1935.

39 ibid. 2 March 1935.

40 GCPPT 2|5 The quotation is taken from the poem *To Agatha, when she was ill* written on 20 August 1911.

41 GCPPT 1|1|47 2 March 1935.

42 GCPPT 1|1|50 14 December 1935.

43 GCPPT 1|1|30 7 June 1925.

44 *The Ballad of Hailstone Hall* was written in Arlington Heights on 17 October 1908 and later published in *To Malise* (pp 58–59) but only in February 1935 does its premonitory relevance become clear.

45 GCPPT 1|1|57 22 August 1939.

46 GCPPT 1|1|47 13 May 1952.

47 GCPPG A2.1 includes notes made from other literary sources, usually unattributed, but extremely relevant in the present context e.g. "the classical honour of suicide".

48 GCPPT 1|1|47 8 March 1935.

49 ibid. 3 March 1935.

50 GCPPT 1|1|52 4 July 1937.

51 GCPPT 1|1|46 25 February 1935. The 'curse of Atreus' of Greek legend was that imposed by avenging gods as a result of the eponymous perpetrator having committed murder, his action initiating a series of terrible family events culminating in his own death.

52 GCPPT 1|1|26 9 January 1923. The Latin description appears in Julius Tillyard's diary account of Agatha's suicide 18 March 1935 (*Synopsis of Diaries* MTC).

53 GCPPT 1|1|46 25 February 1935.

54 GCPPT 1|1|52 11 July 1937.

55 A case in point is that of Rosamund Lehmann's 1944 novel *The Ballad and the Source* with its theme of "love corrupted with viperous hatred; of friendship betrayed; of treachery begetting treachery; of incestuous concupiscence … of vital energies crushed into monstrous courses; of strength and beauty deformed to become violence, madness, malignity, despair" (West, J. Introduction pp vii–viii), all this personified in its heroine 'Sybil Jardine' and in her treatment of her Greek-named daughter 'Ianthe'. 'Sybil Jardine' is Aelfrida to the life, a woman who "cannot be defeated or cow[ed] or crushed", who has "instincts of survival, conquests and revenge", whose gift and burden it is "to see others but … never to see herself" and to be beyond anyone's help (ibid. p xiii), and unfortunate 'Ianthe', a would-be suicide by drowning who has earlier sought refuge in a nunnery and has also suffered severe post-natal depression, an amalgam of Agatha, Alethea, and Aelfrida. Lehmann herself was a Girtonian (1919–1922) of the student generation preceding Alethea's and Agatha's, but her younger brother John (1907–1997) was a Cambridge contemporary of both girls (he is mentioned in Alethea's diaries) and it may be that it was his stories of the Graham women's relationships which inspired his sister's novel, a novel she herself described as "half fiction, half recollection" (ibid. p ix). What is also interesting is that West describes the plot in terms of it being "an ancient myth … the force of [whose] passions had lost nothing in the passage of time" (ibid. p x), a myth, (as it might be) that of the Atreids or the 'Graemes'. A reader of the novel will discover other interesting resonances to support my contention.

56 GCPPT 1|1|44 5 November 1933. The admirer referred to by Aelfrida – he was later to describe his recreations (*Who Was Who* vol 8) as "hunting and horse trials, both at ground level" – was John (later Sir John) Ainsworth (1912–1982), Irish baronet and historian.

57 GCPPT 1|1|47 13 March 1935. St Albans's House was the residence attached to the church of St Alban the Martyr in London's impoverished Holborn area. The Anglo-Catholic church, founded in 1863, was also served by nuns from the nunnery of St John the Baptist at Clewer, and it may be that they or the St Alban's fathers were familiar with Aelfrida's religious writings and anxious to repress statements damaging to her reputation in this sphere of her life.

58 GCPPT 1|1|36 9 October 1929.

59 GCPPT 1|1|46 26 February 1935.

60 ibid. 23 February 1935.

61 ibid. 27 February 1935.

62 GCPPT 1|1|47 4 March 1935.

63 GCPPT 1|1|26 30 November 1922.

64 GCPPT 1|1|30 12 September 1925.

65 Julius' diary account of 18 March 1935 (*Synopsis of Diaries* MTC) has it that Agatha confided in no-one but Alethea; in his haste or distress he also describes Alethea as Agatha's 'wife' (*uxor*) and places her 'in Africam', a country she had not yet visited.

66 GCPPT 1|1|46 5 November 1934.

67 ibid. 26 February 1935.

68 GCPPT 1|1|47 2 March 1935.

69 ibid. 4 March 1935.

70 ibid. 8 March 1935.

71 ibid. 'Ash Wednesday' (6 March) 1935.

72 ibid. 4 and 6 March 1935.

73 ibid. 4 March 1935.

74 ibid. 2 March 1935.

75 ibid. 16 March 1935.

76 ibid. 13 and 16 March 1935.

77 ibid. 12 March 1935.

78 ibid. 18 March 1935.

# St Benedict's

'19 March 1935 *St Benedict's Oxford*. It is such a relief and joy to be back to my bare rooms and my crucifix; my solitude, my silence and the sound of the convent bells … I went across to the chapel and kneeling before the Blessed Sacrament offered myself once more to God', wrote Aelfrida finding herself once again in a cottage filled with spring sunshine. Heartened by flowers and letters from sympathetic guesthouse ladies and by a 'lovely welcome'[1] from Daisy Allen, she made plans for new carpets and crockery and to have the windows cleaned and garden tidied. (The 'hermit' did not deny herself the services of a jobbing gardener.) In fact, 'if it wasn't for the noise of the traffic and … the wireless going full blast in the tenement opposite' (and even that might be regarded 'as a salute' to her return), life would be perfect: 'I am so glad to be here, so glad, so glad'. Then she entered the small bedroom she had decorated and furnished for Agatha. What it evoked was so 'unbearably sad'[2] that it awakened associations she had successfully suppressed till now.

Given her ability to compartmentalise her life, her tendency to treat people as 'episodes', her pronouncement that Agatha's death was beneficial both to her tormented daughter and to herself insofar as Agatha's anguish 'interrupted' (*sic*) her mother's devotions by creating a reminder of worldly problems from which she thought she had escaped[3], and her comment on returning to Oxford that 'life which might be unbearably sad for me as a private individual is full of joys for the oblate'[4], one might be tempted to think that Aelfrida's sorrow, though certainly real, was not as 'unbearable' as she wishes us to believe. In fact, return to St Benedict's found her consumed with a guilty grief which was to colour everything she thought and did for the next two years and to make the remainder of her stay in Oxford as 'dark and sinister'[5] as Agatha had found St Benedict's itself.

Within a few days she was beset by oppressive thoughts concerning her blameworthy behaviour towards her daughter, thoughts which disprove earlier assertions that she knew nothing of Agatha's distress and underline the culpable manner in which she behaved towards her: 'I think and think about Agatha … I knew she was facing difficulties … *why did I not do something*

**Aelfrida Graham at St Benedict's 1955**

*to help?*' But what, she asked herself, could she have done, given that she also knew that Agatha wished to face her difficulties alone and '*wished* to be away from me … otherwise [so] she said … she would be a baby all her life'[6] and that she had persuaded herself Agatha was 'well situated in Cambridge' with 'Dr Joan in the background' and 'Merton House' (primarily Uncle Eustace, whom Agatha specifically thanked in her suicide note) to welcome her?[7] Then, finding herself unable to answer her own first question, Aelfrida was forced to ask herself three more: 'where would [Agatha] have gone? To whom would she have turned? … *How much did she suffer*?' and to provide her own reply: 'better that I should grieve all the days of my life' than continue to dwell on such morbid things. Better too, to console herself with 'this little house of refuge, my Rule, the hope of being less and less Aelfrida and more and more Sister Placida'[8] and with the thought that instead of her mother's fruitless efforts (such as they were: 'I tried to share my courage with her'), it was now God who 'comforts [Agatha] and who wipes all tears from [her] sweet eyes'.[9]

She then tried to rationalise her daughter's suicide by blaming other people: Constantine ('the core of [her] weakness came from mixed blood')[10] and Constantine's desertion of his children; Prudence Wilkinson and Humphrey Warren who prevented her from making 'normal adjustments'; Alethea, 'breaking our unity' by entering a convent; Deity, even ('perhaps it is wisest to say that God cast a darkness over her and out of the darkness, called'), but when rationalisation became too difficult to sustain, herself. But only to show herself in the best light. Agatha's death, she decided, must have been caused by fear that her mother would disappear from her life 'by death' (unlikely, given that Aelfrida's cancer scare was unfounded though 'of course I was prepared to die and was doing my best with every possible kind of foresight to provide for [Agatha] financially, physically, emotionally and spiritually [but] I think it was my death she dreaded and wanted to be there first to greet me' – (*sic*) or 'by vocation', a more likely event given Aelfrida's move to St Benedict's, though even then Agatha 'must have known' her mother would never have felt it right 'to go beyond the sound of her voice, so to speak'.[11]

As it happened, she did not. On 25 March, walking near the Botanic Garden and 'interspersing thoughts of Agatha with thoughts of kingfishers'[12], Aelfrida glimpsed an 'assurance of Beauty'. Although many places in Oxford reminded her uncomfortably of the holiday spent there with both daughters in 1932 and of having explored them in Agatha's company, she regarded the kingfisher as an omen that her younger daughter was not far off. So it proved. Of the night of 29/30 March 1935 she recorded 'I was in bed – the mode of my consciousness altered [becoming] more a trance than sleep, that is [I was] more alive to the other world and dead to this, except insofar as this world might relate to that [but] I did not expect that Agatha should be sent to talk to me but … it happened'.[13]

Aelfrida had, of course, received earlier visitations from 'beloved dead', most memorably when 'at the point of death at that stillbirth and saw Aunt Gregory and Dear and Conrad'[14], but also following the deaths of Chiara and the Oracle. (The latter instance had included a wish that instead of returning, her father 'stay dead' to spare himself and his family the pain of reliving a life which was a burden to him and them, and a reminder to herself, now truly prophetic, that she herself had once written a poem stating that one should not love the dead 'o'er much' but spare one's tears for the living who really needed

them.)[15] There was also the matter of mediumistic experiences during and after the Great War, these including people known to her but not 'beloved' and those unmet in life though certainly known of, all of which caused her to state firmly that she was a 'believer in survival of bodily death'[16] and that 'if we happen to hear messages from our blessed dead, we should listen'. (Apropos appearances from outside her immediate family, however, she noted that 'the whole business of mediumship' filled her with 'fear and misgiving'.)[17] She also saw ghosts at times of trial, and at St Benedict's and 'so often [she] hardly paid attention to it', saw a ghostly figure in the convent garden (a monk of former Osney Abbey, she thought), in this as in all cases noting that such apparitions 'never give [her] the creeps' because ghosts per se were harmless and because those she saw 'seem as ordinary as ordinary people until I come to reflect on it'.[18] It seems, however, that in spite of her belief that Agatha would 'never go very far' from her in spiritual or emotional terms (she had once declined to take a photograph of her mother on a trip abroad, saying she would rather take Aelfrida's 'soul')[19], Aelfrida was unprepared for the first of several post-mortem visits from a presence manifesting itself less as 'Little Bam' or 'my mature Agatha' than a 'timeless radiance'.[20]

In March 1932 in the course of a conversation with Frank Stokoe on the subject of Spiritualism, Agatha stated that she would "rather have interesting conversations with the living than dull conversations with the dead".[21] We have no way of knowing if she found post-mortem conversations with her living mother interesting or not but Aelfrida herself was agog, asking first "can you tell me what it is like where you are?" and on Agatha informing her that "there is more of every kind of light [and] we can see what goes on in the world if we want to but it doesn't bother us", venturing a second question "what do you *do* all day?" Agatha, she wrote, looked at her with that 'tender roguish look' that was 'so specially hers', only to exclaim mysteriously "'I *wonder!*" … one of her pet phrases when she doesn't mean to tell'. Then, casting a beauteous look around her, she departed, leaving her mother so joyous that her heart 'sang and sang'.[22]

How much of Aelfrida's experience was derived from SPR doctrines concerning survival of human personality after bodily death or because Spiritualism, for all she condemned it, had percolated her mind to such an extent that she regarded Agatha's death less as an ending and more as a transitional state from which 'Temu' would emerge transformed into the kind of person her mother had vainly hoped she would be (i.e. mentally healthy, energised, and capable), is open to conjecture, but it is obvious that she believed after-death contact with her dead daughter to be perfectly possible. Though it would be unfair to number Aelfrida at this time among the 'hysterical widows' and 'weak-headed women' whom she said made Spiritualism ridiculous and brought scientific investigation into disrepute (she also noted her belief that "communication between the living and the dead" was perfectly possible "under certain circumstances" but had no intention of making a "religion"[23] out of it), certain coincidences are worth noting in connection with Agatha's visit. First, Aelfrida's mediumistic powers returned (but only with regard to 'precious Temu') at a point in her life when she, like Leonora Piper the American medium, had recently suffered severe physical discomfort (in both cases abdominal in origin, though Aelfrida had other symptoms too) and had, though for reasons other than Mrs Piper, recently sustained a severe shock, both facts noted by Amy Tanner of the American SPR to be conducive to the encouragement (and possibly also to the initiation) of "mediumistic power" in a suitable subject.[24] For another, Agatha's first post-mortem appearance bears remarkable similarities to Rupert Brooke's twenty years earlier in terms of luminosity and insofar as she and Brooke were 'Cambridge poets' subjected to 'wanton destruction'. Third, and even more interesting, is the remarkable similarity between Agatha's first and later visits to her mother and the visit made a decade earlier by Katherine Mansfield to John Middleton Murry two months following Katherine's death in January 1923 at a time when her grieving widower was living alone in a remote cottage in a Sussex forest, an experience described by him in the same book (*God. The Science of Metabiology*) as that from which Aelfrida adopted elements of 'Stranger's' history in *Can I be a Mystic?* This, of course, may be no more than coincidence, for spectral consolation probably takes much the same form in many cases, particularly when a visitor from 'over there' convinces the bereaved that all is well with them in the hereafter (there is no doubt that Aelfrida found Agatha's visit an emotionally healing experience), but it is nevertheless interesting how much Agatha's first and subsequent visits owe to books read or to experiences undergone earlier by a 'mediumistic' mother who, like Margaret Verrall, regarded death as a 'so we say' situation, not finality.

Consoling as Agatha's spectral visit was, it also caused further anguish, for when asleep Aelfrida dreamed 'about Agatha [seeing her] in various fantastic settings [or] that she is still alive and … has told me of her impulses to suicide and asked me to help her', a request which brought bitter thoughts 'that Agatha … never allowed me the privilege – surely a mother's prerogative – of suffering with [her] … surely such intense love as mine

*must* have been useful' (the same, of course, had applied to, and been evaded by, 'Alethea [when] in Paris')[25] and an awareness that Agatha's new 'closeness' to her mother ('this isn't Spiritualism, *no*') stemmed from shared experience of another kind: how on a night 'years and years ago' the latter too had meant to die – and very likely by drowning.[26] And in the depths of renewed despair, not even a belief that Agatha's depression (unlike a recent exacerbation of Mina's, attributed by Aelfrida to the menopause) was 'madness out and out'[27], could make her mother anything other than 'sad, *sad* [with] longing for her – Temu! Temu!'[28]

However much she ruminated about her dead daughter, Aelfrida admitted to not always recording 'the result of [her] thinkings out'.[29] She does not disclose her reasons for the omission but we may essay a guess: perhaps it did not do to admit to herself or to a future reader of her diary that much as her eyes, ears, and arms ached for the sight, sound, and touch of Agatha's 'sweet self', her mother 'never, never wanted her back'[30] and though reluctant to bestow the epithet of 'episode' upon her, that she was undismayed at how quickly Agatha became one. (Worth noting in this respect that although Aelfrida performed a three hour Watch for the Dead on the night of 22/23 February 1936 but was surprised to feel '*no* sense of [Agatha] coming here and being near me', it was not until she checked her engagement diary (*sic*) that she realised she had mistaken the night and celebrated the first anniversary of Agatha's death twenty-four hours too soon.)[31] What she *did* achieve, however, as a result of Agatha's visit, was a kind of closure.

In August 1936 Aelfrida returned briefly to Cambridge to pack away 'diaries and papers' in the attic of Wetenhall Cottage, to collate and distribute small silver items and linens surplus to the requirements of one vowed to 'Lady Poverty' (an action as cathartic in its way as the dismantling of Fordfield, for once rid of 'that weight of stuff' – 'stuff' both material and emotional – she felt 'more light hearted' than she had done for some time) and to present to the baby daughter of her Wetenhall Cottage tenants, now her own god-daughter, 'the Panama gold necklace and a string of corals [and] Agatha's silver mug when the name has been changed'[32]: dead Agatha Graham living on in Annette Barron.

The laying to rest of guilty grief for Agatha did not, however, assuage that for another of Aelfrida's 'beloved dead', nor could moments of 'almost anguished but deep, *deep* penitence' for the 'sin-burdened human race' in general and herself in particular[33] erase 'thoughts to think and prayers to pray'[34] concerning the death of one of those (the Oracle, Constantine, Agatha, and, a month later, Aunt Alice) 'gone within so short a time'[35]: Chiara.

Placed in the balance, negative actions with regard to the death of her younger daughter were outweighed in terms of guilty associations by actual matricide, euthanasia not being counterbalanced by the consoling thought that Chiara was near death anyway. Hence though happy to give thanks to God within three months of Agatha's death for 'this wonderful year [and] for His forgiveness'[36] (*sic*), it was in respect of Agatha's and not her grandmother's death that God was forgiving; indeed, several years were to pass before Aelfrida achieved closure with respect to Chiara and it was more as a 'sinner and a penitent … sick at heart with remorse and sorrow'[37] with regard to a dead mother whose end was 'better not dwelt on'[38] than with thoughts of repentance for three lives (Agatha's, Alethea's, and Constantine's) marred by her insatiable search for a personal 'mystic way' that Aelfrida was soon to decide to depart Oxford in the hope of taking up an even more rigorous life elsewhere.

Seen in this light, her 'special vocation' for the practice of which (her guardian angel, so she said, was very clear on this point) she had been 'led' to Oxford[39] may have been inspired less by a need to atone for the sins of the human race in general (a privilege granted to her by God in the shape of 'universal consciousness' or arrogated to herself as a result of certain supernatural experiences having persuaded her that she possessed a kind of super-consciousness) or, more specifically, for the real or imagined sins of her former husband and his mother, and more by a need to atone for her own all-too-real ones in relation to those who had been blameless victims of her overwhelming desire to liberate herself from them in order to devote herself to Deity. Seen in this light too, Aelfrida's surprise at discovering that Agatha believed her family to be under a curse ('I had no idea')[40] should have come as no surprise, given that she herself had once described the dominant theme of Albert Erlande's novels as one of "sin bearing within itself the seeds of its inexorable punishment".[41]

To live in a house belonging to a convent dedicated to St Thomas the Martyr must have seemed entirely appropriate to one whose life there was to be devoted to 'the most austere, the most sacrificial'[42] vocation of reparative adoration and much of what Aelfrida performed there but which otherwise seems an unnecessarily severe 'martyrdom' self-imposed on one already bowed with grief and in poor health is explicable in this light. Hence when we find her standing braced against a wall, arms outstretched in the shape of a cross, for as long as she can bear to do so[43] we should remember that not only does she already possess an inclination (*un attrait*) towards reparation but also that in posing like this she is putting herself affectively and effectively in the position of the crucified Christ towards whom she now develops an *attrait* not seen before in one who deliberately set herself against Christocentric forms of worship because these smacked too much of the physical. Added to this, her preference for the phrase '*adoration réparatrice*' (reparative adoration) over the single word 'reparation' implies both her new veneration of Christ crucified *and* a feeling that 'what is [only] reparation *here* is adoration *sub specie aeternatatis*'[44] i.e. is also adoration seen in a more universal perspective with the crucified Christ as its object and exemplar.

Aelfrida's adoption of the notion of 'victim souls' (*âmes victimes*) as expressed by Abbé Paulin Giloteaux in 1927[45] seems at first sight wholly alien to one of Presbyterian lineage but is wholly explicable in terms of Albert Erlande's perspicacious comment that she was "one of those people … who would enjoy being crucified". (The remark was made on the occasion of her giving him the cheap crucifix she wore when travelling and his affixing it to his watch-chain.)[46] Although Aelfrida omits to tell us if Erlande enlarged on this rather startling statement (he may, after all have meant by it only that she enjoyed the emotional frisson provided by spiritual, emotional, or mental pain because it added interest to her life and provided good 'copy'), it may be that the truth lies in her need to 'atone' for those she had 'killed and marred and lost' and that by adopting a practice in keeping with earlier attempts at self-punishment (deprivation of food and sleep, to which she had recently added flagellation), 'enjoyment' of the penitential device of spiritual crucifixion as a 'victim soul' was so enhanced that she did indeed 'enjoy' it.

"Victim souls", according to Abbé Giloteaux, can be defined as "volunteers of suffering" who, following Christ's footsteps, ascend a Calvary of their own making in order to deliver those they define specifically or generically as "sinners".[47] (Or, in Aelfrida's own words, "go up to Calvary right willingly" provided they may attain "union with God" in the end.)[48] "Victim" or "reparative" souls therefore act in such a way as to "interpose themselves between Heaven and earth" as *âmes hosties* who, shouldering crimes committed by sinners whom they have made their particular "object of intention", endeavour to expiate them by metaphorically "[nailing] themselves to the Cross, filling that side unoccupied by Jesus".[49] In doing so they not only shoulder an immense load of responsibility but also offer themselves for chastisement, so much so that they actually enter a "victim state", the *summum bonum* of their life of reparation, a state which begins with adoration of the crucified Christ they seek to emulate ("Jesus-Victim" as archetypal "victim soul" suffering for the sins of the whole world) and ends, after numberless formal and informal rituals (in particular those pertaining to the Passion, to the Blessed Sacrament, and to the Sacred Heart of Jesus but also including those specifically designed by a victim for him or herself, all enhanced by supplicatory prayers and bitter sufferings) in expiation of the sins and regeneration of the souls of those for whom propitiatory rites have been enacted and they themselves suffered.[50] Vocation to the "victim state", Giloteaux also emphasises, comes as a "*secret individual invitation from the Holy Spirit*" to a particular, pre-ordained (because already self-surrendered) soul invited to "*total immolation*" in expiation of sins committed by others. For this reason alone, the "victim state" is not one to be entered "from mere caprice or out of love of suffering" and, prior to becoming a "volunteer of suffering", a potential "victim soul" must present an act of oblation in which he or she (chiefly, it seems from Giloteaux's lists of "victim souls", she) offers both to bear chosen sinners' penalties "as merited" in order that such sinners may "find salvation"[51] and to adore Christ while doing so.

Although Giloteaux emphasises that reparative adoration is carried out by "victim souls" for sins "which they themselves have *not* committed"[52], it is interesting that the prime object of Aelfrida's admitted reparations, namely Constantine, though acted-for primarily for the sake of his own sins, is also acted-for by his ex-wife in a manner which suggests that entering a "victim state" was as much for absolution of her sins relative to him as his relative to her. Admitting on her twenty-ninth wedding anniversary that she had been 'so unfitted for the task of being [Constantine's] wife' that she ought never to have married him (she pleaded lack of insight at the time and, remembering that 19 January was also Willie Searle's birthday, that what she felt for the man she now describes as 'yet another philanderer' (*sic*) was 'sheer passion … and a weak longing for the haven of some man's love')[53], she began to castigate herself "for having failed to be a better wife" and to punish herself as if by doing so, mourning for a lost love, recently renewed in strength by Constantine's death, would become a "sacred duty … by means of which [she] could make retribution".[54] Her admission also explains an un-expounded statement made a year later, namely that it was 'much sadder that Constantine should be dead than that Agatha should'[55], primarily because his being dead meant she had no means of knowing if reparative exercises were efficacious and so would have to continue her "victim state" indefinitely. Agatha's first (and subsequent) visitations, on the other hand, persuaded her mother that a "victim state" relative to Agatha could be abandoned because she had successfully atoned for sins committed towards her dead daughter.

Giloteaux's insistence that "victim souls" choose *specific* "objects of intention" for whom to immolate themselves is reflected in a lengthening list added to by Aelfrida as occasion demanded – and a curious and interesting list it is. Some of those included (Constantine, Anatolia, and, rather unjustly, Mildred Graham) were chosen chiefly with regard to sins committed in relation to herself, others because they revealed unpalatable truths, because they lived 'immorally', or because they spurned her religious blandishments.

As examples of these others we may quote Phyllis Tillyard, a prime candidate because she, like Anatolia Michaelides, Ancifera Gregory, Florence Keynes, and other clear-sighted women, saw through Aelfrida's religious pretensions to the unregenerately selfish and self-centred woman beneath. (Aelfrida was, of course, unregenerate because essentially and irreparably damaged but they, unaware of the motives for her behaviour, saw only its manifestations.) The reason for Phyllis joining Aelfrida's list of 'objects' was a series of letters exchanged between the sisters-in-law in October 1935 in which Phyllis accused Aelfrida of being a *malade imaginaire,* of liking to live 'in idleness and luxury at other people's expense', of being nothing but a 'spoilt little chit' incapable of appreciating others' concerns, of being a person with 'pretensions to spirituality' who claimed to be a 'devotee of higher things' but was actually more concerned with earthly matters such as trying to control her remaining daughter's life by continually 'fussing' over her presence at Malling in order to keep Alethea in 'complete dependence' on herself, and of indulging in escapist 'flights from occasion' as occasion demanded.[56] Aelfrida could not but agree ('Phyllis is unknowingly God's instrument to humble me as I deserve')[57], but her sister-in-law's 'scathing criticisms' with regard to her spiritual pretensions hurt so much (even these, she admitted, had 'some truth' in them)[58] that she felt obliged to add Phyllis and her 'fault-finding'[59] to her list forthwith.

A rather more unusual 'object' was Agatha's friend Helen Tansley. Helen's and Agatha's ways had parted during Agatha's gap year when Helen matriculated at Somerville College. Her return to Cambridge four years later coincided with deepening of Agatha's depression but, as Aelfrida noted bitterly, Helen was then involved in an affair with a married man and 'not interested' in supporting her unhappy friend.[60] Although she was later to console herself that Helen turned to religion following Agatha's gift of St Augustine's *Confessions*, Helen's spiritual and emotional struggles since Agatha's death, coupled with loss of direction in life so severe that she moved restlessly and hopelessly from one dead-end job to another, suggest otherwise. Unable too, to forgive

Helen's 'immoral' behaviour, Aelfrida condemned her for behaving badly without asking why, and when Helen turned to her for help (Aelfrida, she said, was the only person she *could* turn to), gave her platitudinous advice ('try and calm down … do nothing in a hurry') of a religious nature ('listen to the Holy Spirit') while pretending that in helping Agatha's friend she was helping 'a little bit of Precious Temu' too.[61] This may have been consoling – to Aelfrida, if not to Helen – but it seems Helen was added to Aelfrida's list less for sins of omission or commission than because she now, like Agatha earlier, had enormous spiritual and emotional problems.[62] While these, however, hardly constituted a reason for Aelfrida becoming a "victim soul" on Helen's behalf, it may be that seeing Agatha in Helen, Aelfrida extended expiatory practices for sins she herself had committed in relation to Agatha to include the young woman in whom she saw her dead daughter reflected.

Aelfrida's final 'object' of reparative adoration at St Benedict's was Dorothy Smith, her former pupil and present dentist. Given that Dorothy's continuing efforts to make Aelfrida's dentures fit properly and to cure the sore mouth which was the cause rather than the result of this ('my mouth has been behaving worse than ever … there is no end to dentistry!')[63] met with little success (the reason will be disclosed in due course but is relevant to her "victim state"), one can imagine Aelfrida regarding Dorothy's endeavours as machinations and adding her to her list accordingly. This, however, would be to impute to Aelfrida a tendency to act on 'mere caprice' (as Erlande correctly noted) or because she enjoyed being crucified, something irrelevant to her actions here. The reason she decided to offer *adoration réparatrice* for Dorothy Smith's 'soul'[64] was because 'in the intervals of dentistry' she was trying to save it – and because Dorothy was being indecisive (could she contemplate God and remain a dentist, was one of her questions)[65], then 'half-hearted', and finally, her partner having decreed '*no religion*', intransigent.[66]

Much had happened since adolescent Dorothy and early-twenties Aelfrida had strolled along semi-rural Hills Road in Cambridge, ostensibly to learn or teach conversational French, actually, we discover thirty years later, to argue about religion: "dear Theodora" (as Aelfrida now addresses her) "do you remember the walks we used to take together? … I have forgotten why we went … was I supposed to be teaching you French? … Be that as it may, you tried to make a Churchwoman of me for your father was a clergyman and mine a Presbyterian elder … But I was a couple of years older than you (*sic*) and entirely satisfied with my own judgements [and] a Presbyterian I remained".[67]

It seems from contemporary diary entries that Aelfrida and 'Theodora' did indeed discuss 'Church and Dissent'[68] but given that Dorothy's French lessons were conducted between 1902 and 1905 when Aelfrida was in thrall to Roman Catholicism, it may be that the 'dissent' preached by the latter was not Presbyterianism but 'non-conformism' of a kind strongly disapproved of by Alfred Tillyard and that Dorothy's subsequent parroting of Aelfrida's words[69] showed that she too was some way along the road to Rome herself. Dorothy's life, however, took a very different course to her teacher's. During the Great War she qualified as a dentist and by the mid-twenties ran a successful practice in London's West End. Alethea describes her as 'a fashionable … dentist [and] a most charming woman, quiet and mellow', altogether different from her own 'tired and nervous and dreadfully "on edge"'[70] mother, but Dorothy's manner belied her circumstances: her mother was often ill and died comparatively young (as did her sister), she was alienated from her brother, and her father was a womanising drunkard. In 1932 she quarrelled with her London partner and moved to Oxford where Aelfrida, wishing to socialise with no-one there but urgently in need of dentistry, availed herself of Dorothy's services.

Why she felt it necessary to proselytise a woman who admitted she was "spiritually blind [and] lacking any capacity for God"[71] because put off religion by her drunken promiscuous clergyman father's 'crimes'[72], Aelfrida does not say. Possibly she regarded Dorothy as a challenge; possibly, given that she began to do so within three months of Agatha's death, she needed to prove that, though a failure as a mother, she was still a skilful 'soul-doctor'. (Even here she hesitated, believing Dorothy's soul to be 'too delicate for [her] clumsy ministrations'.)[73] Possibly her enthusiasm as an oblate blinded her to Dorothy's reluctance[74]; possibly she wished to discharge a debt of gratitude for Dorothy's "concern for my soul when we were girls"[75]; possibly – and this seems likely, given that on completing the revised version of *The Closer Walk with God* she began its companion volume on 23 February 1935, the day of Agatha's suicide, but found herself unable to continue until 'this weight … of grief to bear alone' provided 'the necessary tension'[76] (*sic*) for her to continue with a volume to be called *The Way of Praise* – she required the presence of another Joan Cooper to provide 'copy', to add a personal dimension to her work (anyone knowing Aelfrida Tillyard would easily penetrate 'Theodora's' disguise), and to support her at a time when physical discomfort compounded emotional distress.

But although Dorothy Smith provided a peg on which Aelfrida hung the notion of a means of turning away from self towards God in order to adore Him[77] – 'the way of praise – *Laudate*'[78], Dorothy herself returned the manuscript of the book in which she figured without reading to the end, saying she 'had no capacity for God'.[79] (Or as her disappointed mentor put it, was 'so determined to avert her eyes from God, so fixed in her decision that she cannot even see'.)[80] Whereupon Aelfrida, already praying 'exceedingly tiring intercessory prayers'[81] for Dorothy's enlightenment, decided to pray harder and to add a reparative element in order to land Dorothy's soul 'safe in heaven'.[82] *The Way of Praise* is therefore an act of reparative adoration in literary form ('a very great work to accomplish in one small book')[83] made on behalf of one who, like Constantine (and for similar reasons) refused to succumb to its author's efforts to 'put her in touch with God'[84] – or because she preferred not to engage with a person who notably failed to practice what she preached and who behaved insensitively in pressing religion upon her. (Unlike Constantine, Dorothy was spared public revelation of her failure to conform to Aelfrida's ideals.) Dorothy was, however, sufficiently professional not to abandon a patient in the middle of a course of treatment, though Aelfrida's belief that Dorothy's actions (Dorothy also suggested that she not charge for her services) were evidence that the latter did not resent her prayers more likely stemmed from memories of former friendship and from pity for Aelfrida's recent tragedy and declining health than from gratitude for any 'interest' her patient took in her soul.[85]

To one called to (or who had arrogated herself to) the "victim state", two events which happened shortly after Aelfrida's return to Oxford following Agatha's funeral must have confirmed her view that she was both a "victim soul" and a victim of circumstance.

Easter 1935 passed beautifully and happily at Malling according to letters written by Alethea to her mother and ecstatically in Oxford according to Aelfrida's diary, its writer undergoing 'spiritual experiences' during which 'God seemed almost to overwhelm' her with assurances that He *was* the Resurrection and the Life as she 'walked dry-shod' towards Him through 'hours of adoration' and 'times … of almost anguished … penitence' like the Israelites through the parted waters of the Red Sea.[86] A month later Aelfrida celebrated the first anniversary of her clothing as an oblate by renewing her promise ('which you will find on page 33 of the Oblate's book') in the presence of the convent chaplain ('I prayed very very earnestly that my oblation might be solely and entirely to the glory of God'), an action for which she did not ask prior permission 'at the dear Abbey'. Noting truthfully that she was 'much more fit to act on my own than as a member of a community'[87]

and that because of this she might have done something wrong, she was unsurprised to find herself in disgrace for failing to renew her oblature at Malling itself and for having 'advertised the oblature' without permission. With 'Dr Joan' having recently condemned her 'for not leading a life of active service' and the Malling community now appearing less welcoming than before, Aelfrida felt herself doubly unwanted. She also began to worry about Alethea who not only wrote 'such *childish* letters as though she never used her brain at all' (this was true, for Alethea's letters then and later are very flat, a fact which, together with her new, characterless 'convent' handwriting, makes them appear as if written by a dull but dutiful child) but also seemed prone to asking any available priest to say Masses for Agatha's soul. ('Sheer superstition', according to Aelfrida, because 'strangers' would 'misunderstand' Agatha's chosen mode of death.) Was Alethea, her mother asked herself, 'troubled in her mind' again ('the consequences of such anxiety might be appalling'), before praying that 'nothing hurt [her] beloved Alethea' and that 'if there were any blows to fall, *all* fall on me'.[88] They did. The 'Aelfrida Placida who loves being an oblate'[89] was to cease being one and the daughter she thought safely stowed at Malling was to be sent away, to become her unwilling mother's responsibility once more.

What is surprising at this juncture is Aelfrida's real or assumed surprise, for Alethea's stay at Malling had been prolonged only at her mother's request pending the Lady Abbess' return from sick leave, and confirmation of her own oblation (already postponed) seemed increasingly unlikely given her recent behaviour. What transpired following the latter's return to Malling ('*home* … dear dear place, antechamber to Heaven, sweetest and most beloved spot on earth, precious to me above all the rest of the world') on 13 July 1935 nevertheless came as a shock to one who believed that "after all the years of wandering she had found the right altar on which to lay her gifts of devotion".[90]

Although the Lady Abbess, in frail health but good spirits, had seemed inclined to allow her troubled postulant to try her vocation a little longer provided Alethea did not 'get discouraged'[91], the strain of saying goodbye to her friend and cousin Ruth Warren on 15 July prior to the latter's departure for Madagascar to become a missionary (Ruth had been supervisor of Spanish studies as Girton from 1930 to 1934 but had tired of being 'the good daughter at home' since then) was the last straw as far as 'beloved Weta'[92] was concerned. On 17 July and forewarned by God's answer of '*not yet, not yet*' to her prayer the previous day that she be given the 'solitary life', Aelfrida was informed by the Lady Abbess that she must remove Alethea from Malling 'at once' and, rather oddly, must 'see that she doesn't get too much religion'.[93]

Passing within twenty-four hours from believing, after a talk with the Lady Abbess and a shorter one with Alethea, that as a 'heroic' mother she herself had again undergone 'the greatest renunciation that God has called me to make – that [Alethea] should go her spiritual way and I mine and meet only in God'[94] – to discovering that she 'must lay aside all other considerations and put [her] self entirely at Alethea's disposal', Aelfrida found herself 'dazed from the shock … and so weary, so spiritless'. Unlike Alethea, however, she was far from mute: Alethea, she wrote, in the melodramatic terms employed at times of crisis, was 'holding on to two things in the darkness – the Will of God and her mother's hand'. She was unsure, however, of her own abilities in this respect or of God's intentions for herself: 'and I? and I? God help us both'.[95]

He had need to. On 17 July Aelfrida found herself subjected to 'another blow': following a further talk about Alethea with the Lady Abbess, the Abbess, probing Aelfrida's feelings with regard to her 'intense longing to be "out of the world" [leading] a life of solitude', announced that God did indeed 'intend [her] for a solitary' and that it would be best 'if [her] connection with the Abbey were severed'. 'My face', wrote Aelfrida, 'must have shown what a sword thrust that was'.

Though seeming to concur with the Abbess' decision – life as a solitary at St Benedict's would, she said, be better for her in every way and in particular insofar as it would teach proper abandonment to the Will of God – Aelfrida was in truth bitterly hurt. ('One's spiritual affections long to fold their wings and rest – but it must not be'.) She was also bitterly resentful: 'ever since [the Abbess] asked me to be an oblate, I have ceased to look on myself as a private individual and have ordered my days, spent my money, and chosen my grave as befits a Benedictine oblate … how can I "sever my connection"? I took *irrevocable* vows in my own heart [and] can no more cease to be an oblate than I can become a maiden again having been married'.[96] The wound still festered three years later, Aelfrida noting that 'the person who hurt me most in my life was the Lady Mother when she made me give up being an oblate. Nothing else, not Constantine's infidelity, not Agatha's death, hurt as much as that'[97], an interesting sidelight on priorities but explicable insofar as the Abbess' action related to her life in religion, not to her role as wife or mother.

But although this was the end of Aelfrida's oblation, it is not quite the end of the story. In the course of her dismissal the Lady Abbess also stated that Aelfrida was not confirmed in her oblation 'for one reason alone – that she wanted it too much'[98], a curious comment which

neither lady enlarged upon at the time but whose significance is revealed in a statement made shortly afterwards by Aelfrida herself who, agreeing that she had been 'too eager', noted that her 'fatal love of admiration' had been responsible: 'I … wanted for God's sake to be the best possible oblate but I did want to be noticed being a good oblate'.[99] Also significant is a comment made by the Lady Abbess to Father Cary: Aelfrida, she wrote, though 'too far advanced [spiritually] to need props', was using Malling as an emotional 'prop' and was in danger of becoming 'too much attached to Benedictinism as such' and of losing sight of the end in the means; it was therefore in the interest of Aelfrida's spiritual 'growth and expansion that … uprooting was decreed'. There were, however, two consolations: it was love rather than condemnation which prompted the Lady Abbess' decision, and God was in the process of calling Aelfrida on, not turning her back.[100]

All this, as Aelfrida acknowledged, was true but there were other reasons too for her dismissal. A letter received eight years later in answer to a belated query as to why the Lady Abbess had behaved towards her in such a hurtful manner states that the impression received at Malling during Aelfrida's "noviceship as an oblate" was that she was "too new a Catholic to take on the obligations of an oblate".[101] This, it may be, was a tactful way of stating that Aelfrida's life was then too lacking in balance or that Alethea or another member of Aelfrida's immediate family had intervened on her behalf without informing her because they were so worried about her mental state, but it also suggests that there was something lacking in her understanding of and submission to the discipline and obedience expected of an oblate beyond her failure to ask permission to celebrate the anniversary of her clothing; as Aelfrida herself admits, she was prone to disobey the Lady Abbess's pronouncements as to how she ought or ought not to regulate her life. (She even went so far as to defy her openly: on the Lady Abbess informing her that because Aelfrida already endured so much physical pain, she would almost certainly prohibit the use of a discipline, Aelfrida laughed in her face saying "we shall see!")[102] On the other hand, as is obvious from her first visit to Malling, Aelfrida was, as the lady Abbess informed Father Cary, too much attached to her personally.[103] This, it seems, was not entirely Aelfrida's fault, for although the Lady Abbess was by all accounts a loving person who evinced spontaneous sympathy for the former's past and present spiritual and emotional travails, she should perhaps have structured their meetings more formally (e.g. by not entering Aelfrida's bedroom for evening chats and by always maintaining a physical distance between them) if she wished to prevent a woman who had recently lost a mother on whom she greatly depended from casting another 'Mother' in the same role. And it was chiefly because of the Lady Abbess' rejection of her as a 'daughter' that Aelfrida spent the night of 17/18 July sunk in 'indescribable darkness'[104], only to have her own doubly-rejected daughter handed back to her the following day and to find herself and Alethea 'adrift again'.[105]

'To have tried, to have spent all but two years trying to [be an oblate] and to have failed – that is how it looks to me'[106], wrote Aelfrida despondently on returning to St Benedict's on 18 July 1935. To her credit, however, for diary entries show how much she resented Alethea's reappearance in a life concerning which she was already on the defensive (and with good reason) 'lest anyone should pry'[107], Aelfrida for once put her daughter's interests before her own. 'Someone', she had written eighteen months earlier on the first occasion of Alethea being sent away from Malling (and her statement was no less applicable now), 'someone must give Alethea her release because there are two things she must not feel, namely that God has failed her and that she has failed Him'. 'The way Alethea was ejected from Malling was *brutal*'[108], she had added indignantly (she did not then know that she herself would be similarly 'ejected') though it is possible she realised that her daughter – as later herself – had been involved in a process of discovery in which strength of vocation or suitability as a member of a Community is tested and if found lacking, terminated in a manner in which common sense rather than a sense of failure should prevail. But though she herself was ultimately philosophical about her dismissal (she could read her Office and practice her Rule anywhere and if unable to receive Holy Communion, why, 'God … would impart Himself to [her] specially, directly, inwardly'), Alethea, 'stripped of her old interests' and utterly unable to face a world whose joys now meant nothing to her[109], would be utterly unable to share her mother's consolations.

Finding Alethea 'tired and sad but not hysterical in any way'[110], watching her 'placidly knitting' in the convent garden, and, 'encouraged by pretty frocks', already regaining some of her former 'bloom and … vigour'[111], Aelfrida began to plan her daughter's future: Alethea should over-winter with her mother at St Benedict's with some paid coaching to provide pocket money then 'take a real proper job somewhere'.[112] But Alethea was not 'placid', she was numb with shock. Then she became 'thoroughly unreasonable and argumentative'[113], then so lacking in resilience and so uninterested in life that Aelfrida began to worry that the precarious nature of her daughter's 'mental balance' (*not*, she reassured herself, 'mental *illness* as with Precious Temu')[114] might leave her prematurely deprived of *both* daughters. Then too,

Alethea, placed by God and the Lady Abbess back in her mother's hands, had no intention of remaining there a moment longer than she had to; indeed, she found and made life at St Benedict's so unpleasant that she and Aelfrida were glad to part for longer or shorter periods as circumstances dictated.

Matters continued thus for fifteen months. Alethea moved restlessly from shared accommodation (she and her Girton friend Helen Megaw, then at Somerville, were lent a flat belonging to Dorothy Wrinch, alias 'Roswitha', one of the 'Straightener's' former female 'patients'), to holidays alone or with Lilian Whitehouse (no longer the freakish figure who hung around smoking and drinking with undergraduates half her age, but sympathetic and supportive), to convent guest houses, and to country rectories which accommodated people whose emotional equilibrium was frail. She remained, however, within easy reach of her spiritual director at the SSJE and equally inevitably within her mother's orbit, for at the age of nearly thirty she was once again financially dependent on Aelfrida and obliged to not alienate her too absolutely by her behaviour. In spite or because of this, Alethea's brief forays back to St Benedict's were unhappy occasions. As at Wetenhall Cottage, she was contemptuous of Aelfrida's 'piety' (particularly with regard to 'the way [she] behaved with Anthony')[115] and critical of her 'Rule', and mutual recriminations took place with regard to spiritual exercises performed and mortifications practised by both women to a greater or lesser, temporary or permanent, extent, each accusing the other of laxness (Alethea wanted 'rules and regulations to make the present moment as acceptable as possible' whereas Aelfrida felt that if she said her Office 'in the spirit of devotion and "recollection"', minor mistakes did not matter very much)[116] or over-severity ('too great a tendency to excessive penances'[117], for example, though there was an unspoken element of competition here) according to what each discovered or admitted concerning their respective practices at particular times of the church year.

Aelfrida found Alethea's antagonism upsetting and bewildering and wondered if it might not have been better to have kept *both* 'sweet daughters' near her in order to provide the affection in which they basked and flourished[118] (or, as Phyllis put it, in order to keep them 'in complete dependence on [her]self' as Aelfrida now seemed to be doing to Alethea, a criticism underlined by Alethea herself describing Phyllis as an 'understanding' person – to which her mother would have *liked* to retort "well, she doesn't understand *me*")[119] instead of thrusting them away husbandless, childless, and loveless into the world in order to pursue her own interests and save her own soul. She was also peeved that when both women inhabited St Benedict's, Alethea made it clear that she was counting the days till she could leave (Aelfrida, of course, was equally desperate for 'all the solitude that circumstance and Father Cary will allow')[120] and that, physically unwell herself, Alethea was not prepared to 'pet up' a mother of whose own declining health she could hardly claim ignorance even as she denied it (to her mother's annoyance) to Father Cary.

The unsatisfactory state of affairs eventually came to an end. In spite of Father Cary having written to Aelfrida suggesting that it would be a good idea to "disentangle [herself] from making plans for other people" and from her "general preoccupation with ways and means" if she wanted to develop her "own form of contemplation" and noting that the more she scrabbled after a future "which is not ours to play with", the less energy she expended on the Kingdom of Heaven (the letter was described by its recipient as 'extremely plain spoken')[121], Aelfrida herself had already devised a plan for Alethea's future which would remove her daughter from her immediate orbit for some months.

Inspiration, it seems, came from Julius who had spent the academic year 1935/36 in Johannesburg and it may have been enthusiastic letters received from him (letters forwarded to Alethea by her mother) which suggested to Aelfrida that it might do her dejected and desperate daughter good to over-winter in the hot sunshine and under the wide skies of South Africa in order to put 'more events between her and Agatha's death'.[122] Bearing in mind, too, Ruth Warren's recent departure for Madagascar to take up a teaching post at a mission school, Joan Cooper's earlier suggestion that Alethea's 'vocation' was 'far more suited to the mission field'[123] than to enclosure in a contemplative order, that Aelfrida had recently visited a missionary exhibition in Oxford which described the 'wonderful ... work' done on South Africa missions (the African landscape, however, she described as 'nature at its *least* desirable', though this did not deter one who had been planning to persuade Alethea to go to South Africa as a missionary since Wetenhall Cottage days), and that the SSJE and St Mary's Convent at Wantage jointly ran a mission there (St Cuthbert's, near Tsolo[124] in Transkei Province), it seemed positively providential that 'God's own plans for Alethea'[125] coincided with her mother's and that Alethea herself became 'dead set on' visiting a place 'where there are *Cowley* Fathers'. ('It seems too silly to travel to the ends of the earth to find *them*', wrote her mother acerbically.)[126] 'Full of energy'[127], Alethea made plans for departure and after three failed bids for freedom (one in Paris, two at Malling) broke away from her living mother's and

dead sister's clutches on 16 October 1936. Travelling by sea and land, she eventually found herself on the same continent as that to which her father had been sent in disgrace and to which he had once refused a prestigious posting for his baby daughter's sake.

Alone at St Benedict's, Aelfrida noted that it was 'all over' and that Alethea had 'gone' – meaning, it seems, much more than her words implied; she also noted that although she had never felt so close 'in spirit' to Alethea as in the days before she sailed because 'we [both] wish to give our best to God', she was 'glad to be alone' at last because she preferred solitude and because she was sure solitude was 'God's will for [her]'.[128]

Elected Solitude was one thing, unintended loneliness another. As Aelfrida discovered even before Alethea left for South Africa, although "the elect" (among whom she numbered herself) enjoyed "the everlasting 'Flight of the alone to the Alone', that secret intercourse of the creature with the Creator"[129], loneliness "shuts up a man in a prison house and leaves him peering restlessly from behind the bars". Solitude, therefore, was "as much to be desired as loneliness [was] to be feared" because only in solitude could she break down "the cruel walls of selfhood" and in "ceasing to be aware of [her]self [know] only Him". Loneliness, on the other hand, was a "loneliness of the heart" which could find "no human affection in which to rest", its effect made worse in her case by its stemming as much from voluntary incarceration in the 'prison house' of St Benedict's as from the fact that having rejected 'the world' in order to pursue her 'mystic way', so 'the world' rejected her in return: "round every man there grows a desert of his own making", he and he alone creating "the great gulf across which even those who love him cannot pass". Even worse was realisation that loneliness was her lot in life for as long as her personality traits (pride, lust for power, envy, cruelty, meanness, possessiveness, slyness, coldness, censoriousness, and self-seeking; the list is unsparing) repelled those whom she thought of as 'dear ones' ("either people will remove their physical presences from [me] or while giving [me] their company ... will shut [me] out of ... their real interests and preoccupations"), that though people were nice to her, they would not "feel the esteem they show", and realisation that what she minded most about being lonely was *"not being wanted"*.[130] But sadly and in spite of insights gained during her time at St Benedict's, it was not until ten years later (the passage quoted was written in 1945) that Aelfrida realised with extreme clarity the implications and consequences of anchoritic rejection of 'the world' and of those who composed it in favour of 'secret intercourse' with Deity; in 1935, however, it is possible that she did not even realise that she was lonely

– or if she did, pride prevented her from committing it to her diary – and it is only by piecing together hints and allusions that one realises how much loneliness accompanied elected solitude.

Loneliness manifested itself in many ways. In exploration of Oxford colleges, ostensibly to escape 'that perpetual loudspeaker opposite jazzing away'[131] but actually to remind herself of happy days in Cambridge when she was feted and admired 'Miss Tillyard' or a 'Universal Aunt'. In friendships she would never have countenanced before: with common Daisy Allen (during an involuntary incarceration when Dorothy Smith 'carried off [her] teeth' in order to adjust Aelfrida's painfully un-wearable dentures, the latter doubted if she could bear to be 'without even Daisy to exchange a word with'[132] for the two days they would be gone), with Georgina her cook-housekeeper from Wetenhall Cottage with whom she stayed when in Cambridge, with the custodian of the ladies' conveniences in Oxford city centre, and with the 'coaxiest and most insinuating of all cats', a stray she called 'Randolph' after the hotel outside which she found him but relinquished because cats were forbidden in convent precincts.[133] And in the need to remind herself not to dwell on 'the old days and people I loved – still love' because although such 'episodes' (her word) were not wrong in themselves ('mostly', she added)[134], they distracted her from her closer walk with God.

It was, however, interruption to her compulsive need to *communicate* that Aelfrida found intolerable, a compulsion so strong that she was prepared to break her Rule to fulfil it. (Unnecessary infractions of silence were explained as 'it seemed the right thing to do' or in terms of there being no available conversationalists on the one day a week when she allowed herself to talk[135]; she also used her diary as a "recipient for superfluous feelings"[136], filling four volumes between March and December 1935.) In fact, she was so desperate 'to hear the sound of the human voice'[137] that she took to reading the Office aloud, the sound of her voice breaking the silence making her feel less lonely. Worse still, conversation, when permitted, increased her loneliness because it was reduced to the petty concerns of 'pious ladies' and to 'conventual small talk' which faintly bored her.[138]

Because of this and because even as a 'hermit (or whatever the feminine is)'[139] and as one who wished so fervently for the merest hint of the Beatific Vision that she spent days 'turning from one aspect of religion to another' while never seeming 'to get to the end of spiritual consolations' (all she had at this point in her life), Aelfrida decided not to relinquish 'the power of being interested in the daily paper … or in news of [her] friends'.[140] The hermit vowed to silence was therefore

dejected beyond measure on cold dark days when, hastening back to St Benedict's to be alone with God, she received a double blow: 'the fires were out and there were *no letters*'.[141]

Letters from 'goups' like Mrs Ablett were valued both because they demonstrated that 'the more solitude I have, the more God makes use of me'[142] and because they reminded her of being in demand as a Straightener; others, such as the eleven received in one day in April 1936, though they brought news of family illnesses, were evidence of people including her in family doings rather than (as they more likely were) duty letters written in response to one of hers asking for information. Frank Stokoe, emerging from a bout of depression occasioned by his mother's fatal illness was, however, gently discouraged, ostensibly because Aelfrida felt that having been 'so strangely … relieved of all family responsibilities' (*sic*) she wished to dedicate herself '*entirely* to God' (a 'joy beyond words', which nevertheless and significantly lay 'heavy on [her]')[143] but actually because Fidelio was currently 'much taken up with the Altounyan children'[144] and she, it seems, was jealous. This, and the reluctance of other friends to do more than reply briefly to letters of seasonal or birthday greetings (and some to ignore her altogether, as witness 'dear Hubert' Henderson, a research fellow at All Souls in Oxford since 1934, something Aelfrida discovered from a third party) meant she was often reduced to writing letters 'so they know where I am should they want to turn to me' or so as not to 'cut myself off from my friends altogether'.[145]

Even irregular correspondents became enormously important because they broke into the 'hermit's' lonely solitude to remind her that though she was (by choice) 'alone with the Alone', there were human beings from Arlington Heights to the Antipodes keeping open "a channel of affection" between themselves and herself, something important for a 'hermit' (who professed to be more 'detached' than ever before) because "the sheer delight of telling news and of sharing … the dramatic incident, the absurd situation, the family event, the journey to unfamiliar places" kept her grounded in 'the world' from which escape was increasingly accompanied by realisation that eccentricity (at best) and madness (at worst) accompanied her flight. For this reason if no other it seemed legitimate for the 'hermit' "to stretch out … and clasp the hand of a friend".[146]

The importance of continuing to stretch out her hands by letter in the hope that people would not slip through her fingers as a result of cutting herself off from them in person is also shown by the way in which she actively sought them out even while proclaiming her happiness at the 'hiddenness'[147] of St Benedict's and in wondering if she ought to don a 'habit' to underline the importance of being left alone to be 'Sister Placida'. (Of Christmas 1935 she wrote that she was '*so sure that God want[ed] her to be alone with Him on that day*' that she refused to 'turn to human consolations', only to attend a festive meal at the convent guest house, giving as her excuse that 'human consolations' were '*given*, not sought' in this instance.)[148] But it was, it seems, the company of young people she missed most, for Sundays, her only (official) 'talking-day', reminded her poignantly of Sunday teas at Fordfield and of the fact that with Agatha dead and Alethea unlikely to marry she herself had no 'promise for the future [or] of hope that I might live to see *their* children'.[149]

Loneliness may have been responsible for visits made to Cambridge between October 1934 and July 1935; nostalgia for her old life may have been another. ('I am glad to be here [in] … Cambridge – dear Cambridge'.)[150] And realisation that anchoritic existence in the slums of Oxford was both Spartan beyond the call of duty and unsuitable for one whose health was worsening day by day: of the reasons given for her visits (chiefly 'odds and ends of business')[151], only attendance at the Steam Laundry necessitated her actual presence (and even that was given up in December 1935, largely because she felt too ill to make the journey but also because Eustace assured her she had sufficient income from other sources) and it may have been the charms of houses so 'wonderfully spacious and quiet and elegant after Osney Lane'[152] as much as her need for company and stimulating conversation that lured her back.

It was, in fact, on an extended visit in July/August 1935 that the 'hermit' nearly succumbed to temptation. For all her protestations that God had made her 'a *solitary* in soul', that the more she loved people the more she lived only for God, and that 'the fellowship of [Christ's] suffering'[153] at St Benedict's was preferable to the delights of 'dear Cambridge', a few days respite in temporarily untenanted Wetenhall Cottage (a 'sweet house, so lovely and peaceful and welcoming, beautiful, serene [and] harmonious'[154] as unlike her primitive, noisy, dark, empty, even tomblike, house in Oxford as it could possibly be) gave common sense in the guise of the devil another opportunity to attack: 'what a fool I was to leave Wetenhall Cottage and give up my director's salary and a place where I was loved and admired … to go and ruin my health with a life too hard for me among people who did not care if I stayed or went'.[155] (The devil may have been prompted by overhearing Frank Tillyard's comment two days earlier concerning his niece's stupidity in leaving Wetenhall Cottage for St Benedict's.) But she resisted, noting that every time she went away – and apart from one momentous occasion,

her visits to Cambridge were soon to cease for many years – and no matter how much she had enjoyed herself, she was 'more and more glad to come back [to the] dear convent, dear little St Benedict's where I am alone with God and would like to be more alone … Not all at once, of course, but as I am able to bear it'.[156]

Alone with God, she discovered further loneliness in the shape of further deprivation. Suffering 'agonised contrition' over her failure to be 'the right kind of oblate' because submission to '*the spirit of Benedictine obedience*' required 'an attitude and a disposition entirely at variance from [hers]', Aelfrida put herself 'unreservedly in God's hands' and sought advice from Father Cary.[157] Sending an account of her interview with him 'happily and confidingly' to Malling, she was horrified to receive a reply addressed not "dearest child", but "my dear Aelfrida", informing her that playing off Mother against Father (as she had sought to do) was the action of a 'naughty child', that she wholly lacked the 'Benedictine spirit', that the nuns did not want her at Malling ever again, and that she must return her scapular, medal, and oblate's book forthwith.[158]

Her initial reaction was to blame Mother Magdalen Mary ('if I had offered *myself* it would have been different but she *asked* me and knowing my faults she clothed me'), her second, to blame herself ('I *know* I should be impossible as a member of the community … I am far too independent and self-willed'), her third, to justify herself ('in enclosure, one *must* be of the pattern of the community … but outside, do these fine shades matter?'), her fourth, to submit: 'if it be Thy will, take my connection with the beloved Abbey from me … But Eustace is coming to stay and I must make preparations. I've bought a ptarmigan'. Then she wept 'some of the bitterest tears I have ever shed'[159] and 'in spite of the extreme spiritual anguish' from which she suffered, 'managed to dish up … some very good meals, sharp to time'.[160] Eustace gone, she parcelled up 'the *symbols* of the Benedictine spirit *willingly*', even eagerly ('the "inward spiritual grace"', she added, 'remains with me'), for walking back from Holy Communion across the convent garden, 'God spoke to [her]'. Although what He said was not to be disclosed to anyone but the Lady Abbess and Father Cary, she nevertheless confided it to a diary written for publication: she was to be 'completely indifferent' as to whether or not she was granted permission to offer her oblation again, she was to keep her Rule, and she was to regard the Lady Abbess' rejection as 'a *perfect* instrument for the mortification of self-will' and as a means of leaving herself '*entirely* at God's disposal'.[161]

Leaving herself entirely at God's disposal, however, left Aelfrida lonelier still, for not only did 'all the joy of life' depart with the parcel for Malling (she sealed the parcel using the plain cross she wore in preference to her former flamboyant one; the cross was now replaced with a small crucifix) but a spiritual darkness fell over Oxford as if 'God was bidding [her] leave it'.[162] Having nowhere else to go, she stayed, though years later she recalled the 'exact spot … where, pausing for a moment in the teeth of an east wind as night fell, exhausted with sorrow over the past and fears for the future', she had sent up 'a wordless prayer to God'[163] asking for further directions. What He replied – or even *if* He replied – she does not say, but it seems that in order to punish herself for being not only the wrong kind of oblate but not now an oblate at all, she decided to widen the scope of her Rule to an extent unapproved by St Benedict by including in it spiritual and bodily mortifications severer than those practised before. That this might cause her to become dangerously unwell or 'nothing but an odd elderly widow – quite mad'[164] she was, if not unaware, uncaring.

Aelfrida, as we know, required the presence of 'one man and then another' in her life and no more so than when the road on which she walked with God "took on a new aspect". But because she had now left "the easy and devious path" of 'friends, lectures, coaching, influence, all the pleasant life into which I seemed to fit so well' in favour of "stony ways" ("the well-worn highway of the saints", not an "untrodden desert", she added hastily), a road which, though 'stony', represented "Christ Himself"[165] and so would bring her with the help of reparative adoration more quickly to her goal of union with Deity, the man on whom she settled had to be appropriately qualified. And who better qualified in both respects than masculine monkish Lucius Cary.

It was, as Aelfrida herself noted in her current book, *The Way of Praise,* necessary for her to have a spiritual guide to help her achieve a perfect balance between preoccupation with Christ's Humility or Divinity and experiencing His twofold nature, to educate her in the art of self-examination, to discourage "orgies of repentance" based on "remorse which is half pride" (a revealing comment) at the expense of spiritual development by quieter, humbler means, who would not (a vital quality in a spiritual guide for one as spiritually advanced as she believed herself to be) "stand between" herself and God or insist on helping her when she did not need help or telling her things she already knew.[166] It was unfortunate, therefore, that this radical change in outlook with regard to spiritual direction involved an attraction to Lucius Cary the man rather than an '*attrait*' to Father Cary SSJE and that subsequent disillusion with Cary the man would lead to deterioration in her relationship with Cary the monk at a time when she most needed his supportive presence.

Although Aelfrida noted on first meeting Lucius Cary that his appeal was 'solely to the spirit'[167], it was by no means solely to her spirit that he appealed, and although Alethea had noted of her mother apropos the supposed ending of her relationship with Anthony Wrightson early in 1932 that she would actually be 'happier without a man, being by nature solitary' (Aelfrida noted 'so be it' without actually agreeing)[168], Aelfrida (as 'Carola') was still "*chiefly* occupied with her own passional vicissitudes and [in] pursuing relationships with various men"[169] three years later at a time when recent 'passional vicissitudes' might have dampened her ardour for *any* man. It was not long, therefore, before the 'shapeless flame' which once flickered round Archie Stent, Constantine Michaelides, and Anthony Wrightson (two of whom were now dead and one absent) began to flicker round tall, dark, handsome, living, and physically-present Lucius Cary.

Although there were practical reasons for Aelfrida's attendance at Sunday Mass at Cowley St John above and beyond those of convenient timing, it is obvious from her diary that Cowley St John had attractions above and beyond the quality of its services: 'I … did not mean to do anything except worship God but there was Father Cary's profile on the direct line of vision between me and the high altar …'[170] Attendance at Mass or Evensong in the visitor's chapel at the enclosed Anglican Carmelite Convent of the Incarnation at Iffley (known as 'Fairacres' after the Victorian house in which it was situated)[171] of which Father Cary was spiritual director, found her manoeuvring to sit as close to him as possible because Cary was 'the most remarkable human being' she had ever come across, because his look was 'celestial', and because a 'radiance [emanated] from him [like] a clear soft glow of tenuous flame'[172], and it was not long before *any* contact with Cary, be this at Cowley St John, at Fairacres, or on retreats conducted by him at St Thomas' Convent, promoted lengthy diary eulogies extolling 'Saint Lucius'' virtues, sanctity, and miracle-performing potential. She even went so far as to proffer gifts and to believe, Bélise-like, that Lucius Cary the man was as much attracted to her as she to him – as witness his lengthy visits to St Benedict's when she first went to Oxford and his now signing letters to her "Yours affectionately" ('a slip but … a revealing slip … it seems so odd to get love from a monk')[173] as Anthony Wrightson once did.

But something happened which made her draw back. Attending Mass at Fairacres, she caught a glimpse of the nuns' faces as they gazed on Father Cary as he pronounced Benediction and realised that their attitude, expressive of 'intense, almost abandoned devotion'[174], might also represent an 'absolutely uncritical "doormat" adoration' and an 'uncritical cult of [his] divinity'[175] on a par with 'Dr Joan's' lady admirers for Joan Cooper. Her horror was compounded by a conversation the following day with the 'pious lady' residing in another convent cottage who informed her that Father Cary's 'penitents' went "quite silly over him" and that their deity was Father Cary, not God the Father.[176] Being already ill-disposed towards silly women who hung on the words of their "pet priests"[177], Aelfrida decided not to become a lay *'extension'* of Father Cary's personality, reminding herself that she was 'a *solitary*' at heart and that the closer she approached people the more she felt that 'the only open road … is towards God'.[178]

At Fairacres, too, Aelfrida had been struck by Father Cary's *'authority'* and by the way his personality *'dominates* these holy women'[179] and though she hastened to assure herself that Cary had no wish to 'authorise' or dominate *her* (and that she would not allow him to do so were he to try), the fact that she sometimes found him 'overwhelming'[180] may have reminded her of an earlier relationship with a similarly charismatic figure entered into following the death of another daughter (the parallels between Lucius Cary's and Aleister Crowley's personalities and Aelfrida's feelings for both men are obvious to a reader of her diary) and of her difficulty in extricating herself from it. Being now a more 'dispassionate' witness, she also noted that Father Cary's personality was so powerful that even when apparently self-effacing, he was able not only to make his penitents to, spiritually speaking, 'see', but also to make them see 'the vision that *he* beholds'.[181] She therefore decided 'to go [her] own way' and to accept Father Cary's help only insofar as it accorded with what *she* believed *God* demanded of her.[182]

There were, too, uncanny resemblances between Lucius Cary with his beautiful voice, expressive hands, wit, sophisticated manners, and 'exquisite appreciation of feminine nature and of feminine lacunae waiting to be filled' and another man by whom Aelfrida had been 'seduced' (in a small wooden beach hut not unlike a confessional) into confessing intimate details of her life, namely Albert Erlande; indeed, so marked was the resemblance that she herself commented on it. Noting that both men were 'endowed with a special knowledge of and affinity with women' and that if Father Cary had been 'turned towards wickedness' he could have been as much of a *grand séducteur* as Erlande, she decided to resist the blandishments of a man who even at seventy was 'irresistible to all but the most virtuous'.[183] (Among whom she numbered herself.) To this she made Father Cary privy in a letter informing her possibly rather surprised mentor that what she felt for him was 'a wholly spiritual affection, independent of his presence or absence', that she had no wish to seem possessive of him, and that she

preferred to meet him only in the confessional.[184] (To herself she added that her discoveries meant that she was now free of any desire wish to root herself 'in the Cary garden' or to join the 'harem' maintained at Fairacres by a man whom nasty-minded psychologist James Leuba would doubtless describe as a 'spiritual polygamist'.) She noted too (again to herself) that however much it dismayed Father Cary that she still considered confession to be an ordeal and shrank from telling him about her religious experiences or about the 'hard life' she now led[185], there were good reasons for her reluctance. What she failed to state was what they were.

Having to confront demons in the shape of a man whom, she assured herself, she loved 'incomparably more than I have ever loved anyone' ('spiritually', she hastened to add)[186] did nothing for Aelfrida's already tortured mind; indeed, she admitted, Cary's presence in her life wound her up to such an extent that 'things [went] better' and the tenor of her life was 'quieter' when he was absent.[187] It was therefore doubly unfortunate that the man to whom she turned in Oxford for support and advice was unwittingly responsible for increasing rather than decreasing tensions experienced there, a fact of which her noting in November 1935 that 'things are much harder since I am no longer an oblate' and that she now needed 'more steadying'[188] provides further evidence: the safe, enclosed, feminine atmosphere of Malling and the maternal 'steadying' offered by her 'Lady Mother' had provided the support which no man ever could because of Aelfrida's uncontrollable tendency to become 'excited'[189] in the presence of the opposite sex. Deprived, therefore, of the influence of a steadying Chiara-substitute and refusing to be 'seduced' by an Erlande-substitute into being 'steadied' by him, Aelfrida embarked on the only course (as she saw it) open to one who had hitherto busied herself (to her spiritual detriment) with 'nourishing [her] personality [and] enriching [her]self in all manner of ways' (e.g. by striking up intense friendships with men) and by acting 'as though [she] did everything for [her] own satisfaction and [her] own glory: *abandon complet à Dieu*'.[190]

But in order to achieve such absolute 'self-naughting' (i.e. 'being nothing that God may be All')[191], it was necessary to transform her life into a cross between a prison and an anchoress's cell ('I have forged my own fetters, built my own … walls, darkened my own windows')[192] and to live incarcerate until God Himself completed the 'steadying' process and set her free. What she did not unfortunately ask herself in her rush to imitate Christ (God incarnated in a *man*) was how much the excitement of allowing herself to be 'seduced' by Him (the archetypal *grand séducteur*) might exacerbate the emotional imbalance from which she suffered or if a different mode of life (one more inclusive of the feminine, for example) might prove more steadying. But rather than cast about for alternatives, she decided her only way to achieve 'absolute surrender' to God was to crucify herself on a cross of her own making.

## Notes

1   GCPPT 1|1|47 19 March 1935.
2   ibid. 19 and 21 March 1935.
3   ibid. 26 April 1935.
4   ibid. 21 March 1935.
5   ibid. 19 March 1935.
6   ibid. 22 March 1935.
7   ibid. 27 March 1935.
8   ibid. 22 and 27 March 1935.
9   ibid. 22 March 1935.
10  ibid. 22 March 1935.
11  ibid. 25 March 1935.
12  ibid.
13  ibid. 30 March 1935.
14  ibid.
15  GCPPT 1|1|36 26 October 1929. The poem quoted, *Love not the dead o'ermuch,* appears in *Cambridge Poets 1900–1913* (p196).
16  GCPPT 1|1|38 24 August 1930.
17  GCPPT 1|1|40 27 October 1931.
18  GCPPT 1|1|52 26 December 1936.
19  GCPPT 1|1|35 30 August 1928.
20  GCPPT 1|1|47 30 March 1935.
21  GCPPT 1|1|41 3 March 1932.
22  GCPPT 1|1|47 30 March 1935.
23  Tillyard, Ae. *Can I be a Mystic?* pp 94–95.
24  Blum, D. p 307.
25  GCPPT 1|1|47 5 April 1935.
26  GCPPT 1|1|50 28 November 1935.
27  GCPPT 1|1| 48 19 June 1935.
28  ibid. 30 May 1935.
29  ibid. 22 June 1935.
30  GCPPT 1|1|50 1 November 1935.
31  ibid. 23 February 1935.
32  GCPPT 1|1|51 21 August 1935.
33  GCPPT 1|1|47 24 April 1935.
34  ibid. 1 May 1935.
35  GCPPT 1|1|49 1 November 1935.
36  GCPPT 1|1|47 18 May 1935.
37  GCPPT 1|1|52 4 and 6 November 1936.
38  ibid. 17 December 1936.
39  GCPPT 1|1|51 15 August 1936.
40  GCPPT 1|1|47 22 March 1935.
41  GCPPT 1|131a. Biographical and literary details appended to Aelfrida's lecture to the Sophists on Albert Erlande.
42  GCPPT 1|1|51 24 July 1936.
43  ibid. 28 July 1936. This particular mortification was not devised by Aelfrida herself but adapted from a list given in vol 2 (pp 302–306) of *The Degrees of the Spiritual Life* by Abbé A. Saudreau, a book with which she had been familiar for twenty years. Among the mortifications practised by her since first reading it we find: keeping silence, never complaining (especially about aches and pains), always appearing cheerful, choosing food least liked (accompanied by dry bread if this could be done unobtrusively), accepting food disliked, and opting for minimal luxuries and uncomfortable seating. (Was her deck chair a mortification?) At St Benedict's she adds "keeping guard of the eyes when out walking", a custom begun 'in the middle of the summer sales' (*sic*) but abandoned 'when I cross the road' (GCPPT 1|1|48 26 July 1935) and striking or hurting herself "when guilty of a fault" . Gazing at the beauties of nature was allowed because they were aspects of God's creation.
44  GCPPT 1|1|51 3 August 1936.
45  Giloteaux's work, *Les Ames Hosties, Les Ames Victimes,* was translated on publication by L. Bond whose translation is used here.
46  GCPPT 1|1|31 28 and 29 August 1925.
47  Giloteaux, P. p 40.
48  Tillyard, Ae. *A Little Road-Book for Mystics.* p 9.
49  Giloteaux, P. pp 42 and 152.
50  ibid. pp 49–51.
51  ibid. pp 142,146 and 150.
52  ibid. p 42.
53  GCPPT 1|1|50 19 January 1936.
54  Bowlby, J. *The Making and Breaking of Affectional Bonds* pp 118–119. Interestingly in this context Bowlby suggests that this manifestation of guilty mourning is most likely to be seen as a result of an ambivalent marriage relationship (possibly because the husband resented his wife's "possessiveness") or as a result of an intense emotional relationship (amounting to co-dependency) entertained by the sorrowing spouse relative to the deceased.
55  GCPPT 1|1|47 6 May 1935.
56  GCPPT 1|1|49 2 and 27 October 1935.
57  ibid. 2 October 1935.
58  ibid. 5 October 1935.
59  ibid. 24 October 1935.
60  GCPPT 1|1|47 27 March 1935.
61  ibid. 26 May 1935.
62  GCPPT 1|1|49 19 September 1935.
63  GCPPT 1|1|47 11 and 20 May 1935.
64  GCPPT 1|1|49 8 September 1935.
65  GCPPT 1|1|47 11 May 1935.
66  ibid. 18 May 1935.
67  Tillyard, Ae. *The Way of Praise* "Epistolary Introduction". Dorothy Smith's real and fictional names both mean 'gift of God'.
68  GCPPT 1|1|11 9 September 1904.
69  GCPPT 1|1|9 28 August 1902;
    GCPPT 1|1|13 18 September 1905.
70  GCPPG A1.1 26 December 1931.
71  Tillyard, Ae. *The Way of Praise* "Epistolary Introduction".
72  GCPPT 1|1|18 5 July 1911.
73  GCPPT 1|1|47 11 May 1935.
74  ibid. 20 May 1935.
75  Tillyard, Ae. *The Way of Praise* "Epistolary Introduction".
76  GCPPT 1|1|47 9 May 1935.
77  Tillyard, Ae. *The Way of Praise* p 3.
78  GCPPT 1|1|46 11 December 1934.
79  GCPPT 1|1|51 18 July 1936.
80  GCPPT 1|1|48 6 July 1935.
81  GCPPT 1|1|47 11 May 1935.
82  GCPPT 1|1|50 14 March 1936.
    GCPPT 1|1|51 18 July 1936.
83  GCPPT 1|1|50 14 March 1936.
84  ibid. 25 May 1936.
85  GCPPT 1|1|46 23 January 1935.
86  GCPPT 1|1|47 24 April 1935.
87  ibid. 17 May 1935.
88  GCPPT 1|1|48 5 June 1935.
89  ibid. 20 June 1935.
90  Tillyard, Ae. *O Passionate World* p 358 (GCPPT 2|11).
91  GCPPT 1|1|48 13 July 1935.

92  ibid. 16 July 1935.

93  ibid. 17 July 1935.

94  ibid. 16 July 1935.

95  ibid. 17 July 1935.

96  ibid.

97  GCPPT 1|1|55 30 June 1938.

98  GCPPT 1|1|48 17 July 1935.

99  ibid. 26 July 1935.

100  GCPPT 1|1|49 7 September 1935.

101  GCPPT 1|1|61a. Letter from Dame Osyth OSB to Aelfrida of 21 August 1948. Dame Osyth, who succeeded Mother Magdalen Mary as Abbess in 1951, wrote on the latter's behalf, the Mother being unwell as she so often was at this time.

102  GCPPT 1|1|48 17 July 1955.

103  GCPPT 1|1|49 7 September 1935.

104  GCPPT 1|1|48 18 July 1935.

105  ibid. 17 July 1935.

106  GCPPT 1|1|49 7 September 1935.

107  GCPPT 1|1|48 16 July 1935.

108  GCPPT 1|1|45 7 February 1934.

109  GCPPT 1|1|48 17 July 1935

110  ibid. 18 July 1935.

111  ibid. 19, 20, and 21 July 1935.

112  ibid. 21 July 1935.

113  GCPPT 1|1|50 5 April 1936.

114  ibid. 2 May 1936.

115  GCPPT 1|1|51 3 July 1936.

116  GCPPT 1|1|49 21 September 1935.

117  GCPPT 1|1|46 21 September 1934.

118  GCPPT 1|1|48 2 August 1935.

119  GCPPT 1|1|49 2 October 1935.

120  ibid. 21 September 1935.

121  GCPPT 1|1|50a. Letter from Father Cary to Aelfrida of 'St Augustine's Day' (27 May) 1936.

122  GCPPT 1|1|50 31 May 1936.

123  GCPPT 1|1|45 25 April 1934.

124  GCPPT 1|1|50 25 November 1935.

125  GCPPT 1|1|51 10 June 1936.

126  ibid. 25 and 26 June 1936.

127  GCPPT 1|1|52 7 October 1936.

128  ibid. 16 and 17 October 1936.

129  Tillyard, Ae. *The Glory of the West* p 179 (GCPPT 2|16|3).

130  ibid. pp 287–293 (GCPPT 2|16|1 pt 1).

131  GCPPT 1|1|47 21 June 1935.

132  ibid. 26 March 1936.

133  GCPPT 1|1|51 9 July 1936.

134  GCPPT 1|1|48 4 June 1935.

135  ibid. 27 June 1935.

136  Tillyard, Ae. *The Glory of the West* p 174 (GCPPT 2|16|3).

137  GCPPT 1|1|49 21 August 1935.

138  ibid. 8 October 1935.

139  ibid. 25 August 1935.

140  GCPPT 1|1|48 24 June 1935.

141  GCPPT 1|1|50 6 February 1936.

142  ibid. 22 February 1936.

143  GCPPT 1|1|52 19 October 1936.

144  ibid. 21 October 1936.

145  ibid.

146  Tillyard, Ae. *The Glory of the West* pp172–175 (GCPPT 2|16|3).

147  GCPPT 1|1|46 30 September 1934.

148  GCPPT 11|50 25 December 1935.

149  GCPPT 1|1|47 19 May 1935.

150  GCPPT 1|1|48 8 July 1935.

151  GCPPT 1|1|46 13 October 1934.

152  GCPPT 1|1|51 18 August 1936.

153  GCPPT 1|1|49 15 August 1935.

154  ibid. 13 August 1935.

155  GCPPT 1|1|51 28 August 1936.

156  GCPPT 1|1|48 14 June 1935.
      GCPPT 1|1|49 21 August 1935.

157  GCPPT 1|1|48 29 July 1935.

158  GCPPT 1|1|49 4 September 1935.

159  ibid. 4 and 5 September 1935. The diary entry for 5 September is misdated 4 September.

160  ibid. 6 September 1935.

161  ibid.

162  GCPPT 1|1|61 29 April 1943.

163  Tillyard, Ae. *The Fruits of Silence* p17.

164  GCPPT 1|1|50 5 November 1935.

165  Tillyard, Ae. *The Way of Praise* Foreword pp 1–3.
      GCPPT 1|1|50 5 November 1935.

166  Tillyard, Ae. *The Way of Praise* pp 133–143.

167  GCPPT 1|1|45 10 July 1934.

168  GCPPT 1|1|40 14 January 1932.

169  Tillyard, Ae. *O Passionate World* pp 406–407 (GCPPT 2|11).

170  GCPPT 1|1|47 6 May 1935.

171  The convent was founded in Oxford in 1906 by Father George Hollings SSJE, moving to Fairacres in 1911. The original house was enlarged and a chapel added in 1922.

172  GCPPT 1|1|47 6 May and 7 June 1935.

173  GCPPT 1|1|48 7 June 1935.
      GCPPT 1|1|50 24 December 1935.

174  GCPPT 1|1|48 7 June 1935.

175  GCPPT 1|1|43 9 March 1933.

176  GCPPT 1|1|48 8 June 1935.

177  Tillyard, Ae. *Marrying a Stranger* p 261 (GCPPT 2|6).

178  GCPPT 1|1|48 7 June 1935.

179  ibid. 12 May and 7 June 1935.

180  GCPPT 1|1|51 9 June 1936.

181  GCPPT 1|1|48 7 June 1935.

182  GCPPT 1|1|47 12 May 1935.

183  GCPPT 1|1|48 7 June 1935.

184  ibid.

185  ibid. 7 and 8 June 1935.

186  GCPPT 1|1|50 22 February 1936.

187  GCPPT 1|1|51 21 June 1936.

188  GCPPT 1|1|50 12 November 1935.

189  GCPPT 1|1|49 23 September 1933.

190  GCPPT 1|1|50 31 December 1935. '*Abandon complet*' was a tenet propounded by St Francis de Sales with whose writings Aelfrida was familiar; it was also upheld by French 17th and 18th century mystics.

191  GCPPT 1|1|60 9 November 1942. It seems Aelfrida had forgotten Crowley's mischievous reminder (*The Dangers of Mysticism. The Equinox* vol 1 No 6 September 1911 pp 153–158) that the 'formula' of a mystic is zero (1–1=0) because assiduous self-naughting results in *reductio ad absurdum* (i.e. subtraction of self from person leaves only a hole where the person has been), and that the Fool of the Tarot (a blind-folded figure with an elevated expression about to step over a precipice) is portrayed with a nought above his head. Aelfrida herself had quizzed his article ("to make the sum work out at [nought], these books (see infra) must be bought") in her 'unofficial biography' of him (GCPPT 2|5).

192  GCPPT 1|1|50 12 November 1935. Aelfrida's reference is to the *Ancrene Rewle*, the thirteenth century guide for anchoresses.

# To Live as Living Crucified

Going "forth from the house of [her] selfhood … to worship [Christ] upon the Cross"[1], Aelfrida marked the beginning of her new life by designing her 'habit': a plain navy blue dress, linen in summer, wool in winter, a navy coat, augmented in cold weather by a short cape, and a black hat. ('Lady Poverty's bower' included a seamstress; dresses were bought but coat and cape tailored for her.) A crucifix and, when attending Mass, a white veil, completed the outfit. (The 'finished young lady' who had admitted to never enjoying herself unless she was '*suitably*' clothed, was now a middle-aged lady with 'an exceeding great longing' for a mode of dress suggested by her guardian angel as a means of keeping herself 'recollected' and as a 'kind of "enclosure"' in which she 'could be apart without offending anyone or hurting their feelings'; there was, however, no question of her adopting clothes whose 'inconvenience and discomfort' approached that of the Malling nuns or of leading a life in which the wearing of a 'habit' would not be 'seemly'.)[2] Once suitably clothed, she proceeded on her closer walk with God from the point at which Agatha's death had distracted her, doing so in such a way as to recapitulate the synopsis written in 1919 (another 'crisis' in her life) for *A Little Road-Book for Mystics*: seek God regardless of the pain; realise that in doing so "you have not so much withdrawn from earthly things, they have withdrawn from you"; "seek God in loneliness"; "consecrate your whole being to God" with the help of spiritual exercises, chiefly meditation; open yourself to visionary and ecstatic experiences ("suddenly … the light breaks"); walk now "by will where before you walked by sight" until you reach the glorious point at which "you *conquer* [and] begin here on earth your everlasting life".[3]

Her spiritual progress is described contemporaneously in *The Way of Praise*, the Oxford sequel to *The Closer Walk with God* (the latter book, begun in Cambridge and completed at St Benedict's in 1934, is dedicated to Agatha and bears the same inscription as the cross on her grave), both books forming 'little road-book' versions of her recent and present life; like her diary at this time, they omit or conceal as much as they reveal. They also, unlike her diary, paint a rosier and more tranquil version of the events which inspired their writing, for it was while composing them that Aelfrida decided to live her

**Convent of St Thomas the Martyr, Oxford**

life entirely on her own terms and to work out her own salvation in her own way.

In order to enhance reparative adoration, to return to a Thomas à Kempis' 'imitation' of Christ, and "to live as living crucified" with all that that implied of living "all through Jesus-Victim, all with Jesus-Victim, all in Jesus-Victim"[4], she resumed practices forbidden by a Mother and Father who had once had her spiritual welfare at heart but who had now, it seemed, rejected her: flagellation, briefly but as a foretaste of things to come, and stigmatic meditation on the Passion regularly and intensely.

Following the painful episode with the leather strap, Aelfrida had attempted flagellation with a tasselled cord but soon abandoned the practice as ridiculous, difficult, and dangerous. The cord, however, reappeared at St Benedict's tying up her Odessan fur coat, forwarded from Cambridge early in 1936 to help her cope with some exceedingly cold weather, but horrified at this reminder of 'luxurious asceticism' ("carry neither gold nor silver nor money ... nor bag nor two coats nor sandals"[5]; unlike St Francis, whose call this was, she did not go barefoot) and of how she had shirked the infliction of pain, she threw away the cord and gave the coat to a parish worker. Six months later, however, asked by Alethea prior to the latter's departure for South Africa to look in her suitcase for items of clothing required in the meantime, Aelfrida discovered (the items were concealed but she burrowed deeper than necessary) 'a small scourge of knotted cord' and 'a knitted girdle of horsehair about six inches wide'. She tried both, twenty strokes of the discipline (much less painful than the strap, she decided) and an hour's wearing of the girdle while meditating on the Passion: 'horrid, of course', but nowhere near as painful as the stigmata.

Recalling Phyllis' recent gibe that her sister-in-law's life was self-indulgent, Aelfrida decided that providing she could use the 'instruments' without exhausting herself too much and without taking pride in doing so, she would.[6] Delving deeper still in the suitcase, she discovered 'a great heavy scapular of horsehair' (a sleeveless hair shirt) which she tried out during another meditation on the Passion. Not, it seems, as appreciative of this form of mortification as of the girdle and discipline, she returned it to Malling with a covering note saying that it might have been wiser 'for God to choose His own "austerities" in His own way' than for them to be permitted to Alethea by the Lady Abbess[7]; she also wrote to Father O'Brien, accusing both him and the Lady Abbess of '*trop de zèle*' with regard to a young woman whose life was now and as a result of their excess of 'zeal', a 'delicate adjustment of last straws'.[8] Her actions, not unnaturally, brought down the wrath of both Alethea and Alethea's spiritual director on her head, the more so in the case of the former when she discovered that Aelfrida had appropriated girdle and discipline for her own use. Father Cary, consulted by letter, sanctioned certain mortifications but not, it seems, these, and the matter closed with Alethea, disregarding her mother's pleas, removing the 'instruments of discipline'[9] from St Benedict's forthwith.

Once re-established in Oxford after the turmoil surrounding Agatha's death but before Alethea's expulsion from Malling, Aelfrida had recommenced meditations on the Passion. Her first meditation, on the night of

21/22 March 1935, was so gripping ('I had difficulty leaving off [and] participation was too intense'), so overwhelming ('God taking me and infusing Himself into me ... a little more and the blaze of glory would have melted me like wax'), and so psychosomatically impressive (it rendered her hands stigmatic for twenty-four hours) that she resolved not to meditate on the Passion every night.[10] On the Feast of Corpus Christi, however, she allowed herself the 'beloved meditation', using as mantra 'He was wounded for our transgressions'. Feeling 'rivers of spiritual light' surge into the depths of her being[11], she held her pose supine on her bed with arms outstretched (an earlier experiment of lying supine on the floor proved more supportive of her arms but too 'draughty to the back of [her] neck')[12] from midnight to 1.30am at which point she began to experience cramps in her arms. At 1.50am she began to shiver convulsively 'which means I am really doing myself harm' and at 2am, unable to continue until the 6am Angelus as she hoped, she stopped, noting that 'the first minutes when one stops are terribly painful'. Following a feat remarkable in a sufferer from rheumatoid arthritis, she then slept till 5.30am before attending Mass in the convent chapel at 7.10am and High Mass at Cowley St John at 11.00. (Stigmatic pains in her palms persisted until after early Mass but she did not experience – as she had done the day before while meditating in bed though not passionally – 'that stab, just once in my side' first experienced, so she said, during her stigmatic 'Vision' of 1913 but of which there is no contemporaneous record.) That same day she also recited her Office (it was otherwise spent in 'almost complete silence'), passed two hours 'communing with God', adored the Blessed Sacrament for thirty minutes, and retired to bed at 6.30pm 'quite worn out'.[13]

A third, and perhaps the most intense, experience after which she abandoned meditations on the Passion for some months on the grounds that they were 'not good' for her, that there was 'no *magic* in the posture' (an interesting comment, given her earlier practising of incantatory postures), and that adoption of the 'position of the Crucified' was no more than 'a way of signifying that I long to have Christ formed in me'[14], took place on the night of 25/26 June 1935 when, having felt 'called' to perform it because 'a great longing took hold of me to come closer to Our Lord on the Cross', she employed the same mantra at 11pm and by 11.30pm (she was not clock-watching; she timed herself by bells chiming hours and quarters) was 'in bondage to the will of God'. This time, however, an element of competition or of the Psychological Laboratory entered her devotions, for noting that she had been unable hitherto to sustain passional meditations for the three hours of

Christ's Passion, she now determined to do so if she could. Within half an hour, however, 'intense physical weariness and … the tension at one's hands as though one's arms were actually holding up the body's weight' proved almost too much for her and she 'cried to God to give [her] strength'. Immediately, she writes, 'two angels in gleaming white raiment came, each bearing an arrow with which he pierced one of my hands. After that no movement except a very slight turn of the head was possible … so I lay motionless but wonderfully peaceful'. Angelic transfixion, however, was inefficacious in preventing the onset of painful cramps in her arms and shoulders or in alleviating the 'sheer pain of body and soul' accompanying the meditation but because the arrows represented her 'love to God', she 'gladly endured' until the sound of bells striking 2.30am told her she had won through. Afterwards, though there were only slight marks on her hands, she was unable to quieten the throbbing and burning of her palms except by pressing them together (her feet, she noted, hurt during the meditation but not thereafter); she also felt 'the ridge of the Cross' persisting along her back. (Neither phenomenon, however, prevented her from choosing new linoleum for the kitchen floor.) More impressive even than physical symptoms was the effect on her mind: 'peace and a calm tireless joy' in the deepest depths of her spirit, thoughts 'rising up from me Godwards or imparted … from Him', moments 'when thought seemed to go out like a blown candle and nothing but an awareness of God remained' (an interesting elision of Buddhist and Sufic interpretations of her condition) and, the following day, a feeling of 'great serenity … as if the arrows had indeed fastened [her] where [she] desired to be'.[15]

On 29 July she informed Father Cary of her recent experiences after, not during, a 'very brief confession'. (He seemed, she said, rather surprised at the angels.) Carefully reporting 'the three hours meditation' as matter-of-factly as possibly, she asked permission to meditate on the Passion daily. (Her asking permission is interesting, for since her 1913 'Vision' – and possibly since her vision of Christ at age fifteen – Aelfrida appears to have consciously or unconsciously shaped her life by excluding distractions, enacting rituals, undergoing physical practices known to induce higher states of consciousness and emulating men and women who had undergone similar experiences, and all this in such a way as to virtually ensure repeat performances; why she now asked permission to do so may have been a means of demonstrating her mystico-spiritual credentials to Father Cary rather than a belated decision to obey the instructions of her spiritual advisor.) Cary agreed, but on condition she not do so for more than ten or fifteen minutes; he also

gave her an 'instruction' on the importance of '*Serenity* in all things', particularly "in your life of adoration and reparation".[16] Aelfrida, for once, did not wholly disobey his advice but noting that if, nun-like, she had a 'title' it would be *Aelfrida Placida of the Holy Passion*[17], decided to sleep in the 'crucified' position though probably unable to endure it every night. (Henry Suso, the fourteenth century mystic whose penitential life-style was known to Aelfrida, endured twenty years' extreme asceticism as part of his *abandon absolu à Dieu*; during this time he penetrated his flesh with nails, flagellated himself, and slept supine on a large wooden cross.)[18] This proved true, and although she tried and, indeed, found the few minutes' sleep she obtained were such that she woke 'feeling I had been among the angels', the effort of remaining motionless in the appropriate posture without mantra or meditation was too 'stern' for her to maintain for more than a few minutes.[19] Lack of proper sleep also led to such utter fatigue that, regardless of the spiritual benefits of 'a very light sleep in which some sort of touch with God is maintained', she abandoned the effort in favour of maintaining the mental attitude of *abandon complet* awake or asleep[20] and of standing in a 'crucified' posture against the wall for as long as she was able during the day.

The 'bad, *bad*' pain she endured as a result of meditating or trying to sleep in the Passion-position, though sent, she believed, by her guardian angel to enhance the efficacy of reparative adoration, was so frightening that Aelfrida asked him if she ought to stop, but on the angel replying that reparative adoration was a privilege, not a duty, and that she could stop if she wished, she decided to continue – whereupon he increased the pain. Reluctant to 'shirk' pain (she refused analgesia stronger than aspirin) and to discuss physical problems with Father Cary, Aelfrida decided that the pain was God 'scourging' her and that it was her joyful duty to continue to bear it; not only was it God's Will but a manifestation of 'His hardest Will' also.[21] For an *âme victime* what could be better? So although she preferred a state of 'adoration [and] awe … before the overwhelming majesty and beauty of God', as a '*penitent*' she turned 'more easily to the Crucifixion'[22], forcing herself to remain in the shadow of the Cross in spite of the joy experienced at being wholly abandoned to God's Will in its more delightful aspects.

One of these aspects was His allowing continuation of the ecstatic visionary experiences she was too weak to resist or to exclude from her increasingly ascetic Rule. Two at least were directly associated with meditations on the Passion, one which occurred the afternoon following the meditation during which God 'infused' Himself into her being a sensation of the Holy Spirit coming upon her 'in light and peace' and in the reading room of the Free Library 'of all places'[23], the other occurring during Compline (overheard, not attended) three hours prior to the meditation of 25/26 June: 'the Holy Trinity as a mountain [with] God the Father as the summit … inferred … rather than seen and yet *known* with absolute certainty [and] God the Son showing himself in clear form and outline to be paths and ways for us … upwards'. (In a continuing metaphor which she finds 'startling', she describes the Holy Spirit less as spirit than as 'the ground beneath our feet, the ground of our ascent'.)[24] Other experiences arose independently of passional meditation or of adoration of a sternly reparative nature and it is obvious from Aelfrida recording them at length that they were one of (possibly the only) means by which she encouraged herself along the 'shady' side of the Mystic Way walked at St Benedict's.

In the main, however, visions and ecstatic experiences occurred as alternatives to passional meditation and as augmentations of the adoring aspects of life as a 'victim-soul'. As usual, experiences of this nature were 'given', not willed or requested[25]; they also, a new phenomenon, became part of a 'mystic way' manifesting itself more as a 'continuous calm indwelling' of the Holy Spirit and less as a series of 'sudden raptures' or 'periods of being "with God"' erupting into everyday life.[26] This did not, of course, make them any less rapturous, particularly when circumstances were propitious – at Holy Communion for example, or when '*coram sanctissimo*'[27] adoring the Blessed Sacrament – at which times 'a little gasp in [her] soul' preceded 'sudden blazes of illumination' during which normal consciousness changed, spiritual knowledge was 'infused' or 'revealed'[28], and 'the Presence' (that 'strange and awe-inspiring *intensification of That* which is everywhere') called her to 'the pure stillness of spiritual intercourse'. (Her father, she noted in passing, would have called such devotions 'superstitions'; she herself called them 'religion' because with their help she was able to apprehend Deity 'through His own supremest manifestations'.)[29] Some occurred on particularly relevant days (on All Souls Day, an 'intellectual vision' without sensory or emotional elements of 'the redeemed' as an abstract 'outflowering' of Christ's Humanity[30]; on the Festival of the Transfiguration, a 'Julian' vision of the world 'shrunk to the size of a little ball' … [and how] God by one touch of His hand … could annihilate it all')[31]; some as a result of an auditory stimulus (the Angelus bell giving rise to a sensation of her guardian angel ringing her round with the 'spiritual fire' emanating from his wings as he enfolded her in them)[32]; some when reading an Office (at Lauds, 'Jesus Himself was there, not visible but just by me, a spiritual presence, taking my adoration and lifting it up to the Father')[33]; some in response to weather phenomena: a vision of Christ 'all ablaze' on a huge cross following a storm preceded by flashes of 'silent lightning'.[34]

Somewhat surprisingly in view of her dedication to "Jesus-Victim", Christ did not figure largely in the visions, but a significant appearance occurred in September 1935 while Aelfrida was reading rather than attending Communion. (Her excuse for non-attendance was devotion to Alethea, who, having been sent away from Malling weeks earlier, was in bed with a cold.) Suddenly, she writes, 'I saw our Lord standing in front of me … He came near and, leaning over me, gave me Communion in both kinds Himself. It was so extraordinarily *real* that I opened my lips and swallowed what I seemed to have received'.[35] (The arrival of Phyllis' accusing letter three days later must have seemed incomparably unimportant by comparison.) The Holy Spirit, however, was manifest while Aelfrida was attending Communion in the convent chapel: 'I felt the Holy Spirit descend into me *in all His plenitude* [as] the perfection of spiritual life, something which I did not think could exist in this world at all … nothing but perfect tranquillity at the indwelling of the Spirit [with] none of the movement and emotion and ferment that I am accustomed to see [when] looking into myself'.[36] ('Who could have dreamed', she wrote of this and similar episodes, 'that in a world where my senses are continuously bringing me news of motors hooting and jazzing gramophones … and aches and stabs of rheumatism and rain lashing against the windowpane … that pure intercommunication of spirit should be possible? *And real.* And oh! joyful and lovely beyond hinting at!') The third member of the Trinity also put in an appearance: at Communion, '*suddenly* Heaven seemed to sweep down on me like a mighty wind of sweetness and love … I felt I was in the centre of the eternal with God' (she did not mention this experience when confessing to Father Cary next day, he having kept her on her knees for twenty minutes already)[37] and, when adoring the Blessed Sacrament on Trinity Sunday, 'the veil that separates us habitually from God parted and He lifted me up … *there*, in *Sinu Patris* where Pure Being and Pure Love are one'.[38] And having recorded that, she ended the current volume of her diary two pages early as if, finding herself in the inmost heart of God the Father, she could write no more.

To one as blessed as this it did not seem strange when miracles began to happen. The first occurred in December 1935 when Aelfrida was standing to recite the 6am Angelus in front of a representation of the angelic host praising God, a picture affixed to the wall above the fireplace in her sitting room. Lifting up her heart 'with a wonderful feeling of exhilaration', she suddenly felt herself raised some six inches from the floor and kept there 'till the Angelus was done' at which point she was 'gently set down again'. Feeling rather foolish, she 'peeped down at [her] feet to see whether they *were* solidly planted on the carpet' (they were) and though professing not to 'see the point of that sort of thing', was convinced she *had* levitated because she had found herself level with a picture to which she normally looked *up*. There was no witness to her experience and it seems she told no-one of it but a possible inspiration had taken place very recently: Alethea, then living at St Benedict's, owned a likeness of St Teresa of Avila taken from her death-mask. Aelfrida was much impressed by the expression on the dead saint's face ('she has neither age nor youth and the eyes which are closed to earthly things are open to behold the light of eternity'; it also recalled Agatha's 'eager and yet satisfied' expression when alive)[39] and this may have reminded her that St Teresa, when enraptured, sometimes found not only her soul "carried away" but also her "whole body … lifted from the ground … without [her] being able to prevent it", a manifestation, the saint believed, of God's favour expressed in "outward and visible signs".[40] As Aelfrida herself made no further comment regarding her own lifting from the ground, we do not know if she regarded her experience in the same light but knowing that she dreaded falling into a trance when rapt in worship in public lest anyone notice, she, like Teresa (some of whose enraptured experiences happened in public and were observed by others), may have begged God to send her no more such favours and kept quiet about this one too. She may also have kept silent knowing that at Malling her guardian angel had reinforced Dom Bede's message that she be as 'Simple and Patient' as possible, warning her that in 'the world' she should keep to 'ordinary duties and … elementary virtues' instead of allowing herself the indulgence of *spiritual* levitation or she would come 'crashing down'.[41] Having disobeyed both priest and angel at St Benedict's, perhaps she hoped to avert a further 'crash' by neither disclosing nor dwelling on *bodily* levitation.

A second supernatural occurrence took place in early March 1936 when Aelfrida, recently '*in Sinu Patris*', suffered a severe sinus infection and was referred by Dr Frazer to 'pleasant young Scotch surgeon, Dr Macbeth'. (He did *not*, she noted, appreciate references to Shakespeare's play.)[42] Macbeth proceeded to perform minor surgery using cocaine as a local anaesthetic. Unfortunately for his patient, Aelfrida reacted badly to it (she returned to St Benedict's feeling 'remarkably queer' and spent a wretched night thereafter)[43] and on 'Doctor Macbeth' decreeing more extensive surgery, opted for admission to the Acland Nursing Home and rectally-administered

sedation instead. Operation and sedation passed off uneventfully but two days later Dr Frazer took the opportunity of Aelfrida being hospitalised to treat her patient's recurrent uterine bleeding with what the latter described as 'vaginal injections' but were probably pessaries, given that they were to remain in situ overnight. In response to the first of these, however, Aelfrida suffered anaphylactic shock, a severe allergic reaction of which she gives an accurate description of the symptoms from a patient's point of view (difficulty in breathing, fluttering heartbeat, and dwindling level of consciousness), during which she hoped she was dying but from which she recovered after a 'scalding hot douche' removed the offending material.

Given her overwrought state of mind, she found no difficulty in transforming a medical emergency into a metaphysical miracle, describing it as 'one of those "mystic deaths" … from which one rises up in clear spiritual light more *alive* in God'.[44] (During the crisis she had been aware of 'a great blaze of light' which, given the circumstances and time of night, was probably electrical; she, however, convinced herself that it was divine '*bestowal* of strength' of overwhelming '*bareness* and *intensity*' and so powerful that for several days she remained 'in a kind of dream, looking down at life from … the immeasurable heights of God's love'.)[45] Lengthy reflections followed, leading her to conclude that 'mystic death' had not only led her into 'a new way of appreciating God' ('Our Lord seems to be using me as a place *in which to think His thoughts*')[46] but had also resulted in God '*indwelling*' in her '*on his own plane*' so completely ('By Him, with Him, in Him – I in Him, He in me', a gift 'utterly beyond [her] powers or dreams') that she had become a true contemplative '*infused* [with] *certainty*'.[47]

On this occasion, however, Aelfrida *did* discuss her 'mystical' experience with Father Cary, having bombarded him with letters beforehand because explanations proffered by her guardian angel were inadequate. On 8 April, following confession, she therefore demanded of her spiritual mentor if experiences such as hers were '*familiar* to him?' and on Cary answering no, asked "usual, then?" Cornered, Cary replied "no, … but given certain circumstances, perfectly *en règle*". He then informed her 'not sternly but gravely' that she *must* discipline her 'imagination and intellect' and be 'less interested in [her] emotions and [her] thoughts' because this was *not* how proper contemplatives behaved.[48] (He may also have been aware, as she herself certainly was, that her 'mystic death' took place on the eve of Passion Sunday and that her cogitations thereon climaxed on – though they continued after – Easter Sunday. Also worth noting is that before and during her convalescence at – appropriately – the Holy Trinity Convent in Woodstock Road, Aelfrida had been reading *The Oxford Book of Mystical Verse* with particular reference to John Donne's 'divine' poems, one of which, *The Cross*, exactly expresses her desire to extend her arms and be her own "Cross" and even her own "Crucifix". She omits to mention that the volume also contained RH Benson's *The Teresian Contemplative* and several poems by Aleister Crowley.) She promised to try, deciding to 'lay aside preoccupation with [her] feelings and reactions' even if this meant providing herself with distractions (chiefly household matters and gardening, Alethea's 'thoroughly unreasonable and argumentative' presence more marginally) but also that something so utterly against the grain of her nature would prove impossible to achieve.[49]

As indeed it did – and for good reason. Daisy Allen suffered from valvular disease of the heart and was often too unwell to perform her daily chores. Aelfrida responded unsympathetically to Daisy's absences (cleaning grates and carrying coals were not proper occupations for an anchoress) and enlisted the help of Daisy's sister Rhoda when they were prolonged beyond a couple of days. On 4 April 1936, two days after Aelfrida's Easter Sunday cogitations on how Christ now seemed to be using her as the mind in which to think His thoughts, Daisy, currently off sick, suffered a severe syncopal attack (possibly a cardiac arrest) from which she was revived by her doctor (fortunately present at the time), he injecting her with coramine, a new cardiac stimulant drug. Though his presence and presence of mind might be deemed miraculous, Aelfrida, full of newfound spiritual 'strength' as a result of her 'mystic death', arrogated to herself the privilege of Daisy's recovery on the grounds that had she not laid hands on and prayed over the unconscious girl pending the latter's removal to the Radcliffe Infirmary (clad in Sister Placida's nightdress and rosary for good measure), Daisy's recovery would have owed less to Dr Bailey's skill at intracardiac injection and 'artificial respiration' and more to intervention by a handy 'soul-doctor'.[50] She did not inform Father Cary of her intervention, however; possibly she feared a further reprimand, possibly, as Teresa of Avila said of *her* spiritual directors, she felt he did not understand her.

Although, like St Teresa with her raptures, Aelfrida regarded her stigmata as 'outward and visible signs' of God's favour, she never described them as miraculous per se even though they, like levitation or 'mystical death', were extraordinary events attributable to a supernatural agency. Possibly she regarded them as such overwhelming (and private and personal) signs of God's favour that they transcended the merely wondrous but her obsessive need to meditate on the Passion so intently as to be rendered (or render herself) stigmatic suggests that

there were other reasons why she ensured that no-one saw the marks and why she was so reluctant to discuss them with men and women in a position to proffer advice as to their aetiology and on how best to subsume them into her spiritual life. For one thing, and far from being solely 'outward and visible signs' of God's favour, it may be that stigmata were 'outward and visible signs' of release of enormous emotional and spiritual tensions occurring as isolated or repeated incidents according to degrees of tension currently experienced. It is also possible – for Aelfrida does not always reveal in her diary what she does not wish a reader to discover – that they were manifestations of self-harm, an action resorted to by those who feel unable to relieve negative emotions in any other way and who, moreover, make every attempt to conceal the wounds they inflict. (Self-inflected 'stigmata' could, of course, be regarded as an aspect of reparative adoration but this explanation does not hold good for pre-1935 manifestations.) It is also curious that stigmatic Aelfrida makes so *few* references to other stigmatics, for self-harmers not infrequently model themselves on other practitioners. True, she had special feelings for Francis of Assisi and was aware of Catherine of Siena (like herself, a lay member of a religious order, an ascetic, and a visionary)[51] but she either ignored or made little effort to relate to twentieth century stigmatics; indeed, it is not until 1946, when she herself had almost ceased experiencing (or self-inflicting) stigmatisation, that she noted the existence of two well-known modern stigmatics, Padre Pio and Thérèse Neumann, and then as if she had only just discovered the existence of the former and preferred not to dwell the latter, lest, it may be, that she be regarded as 'strange' as Neumann.[52] Padre Pio, of course, was a a monk whose stigmata bled profusely[53] so may have been someone with whom Aelfrida chose not to identify too closely, and Thérèse Neumann, though a Franciscan tertiary, was widely claimed to be a fake[54], but Aelfrida's relief at discovering the existence of other mystics besides herself is not paralleled by delight in discovering contemporary stigmatics. Perhaps she had thought herself or had hopes of being thought unique; perhaps, given that the stigmatics she mentioned were extraordinary public figures and that it was important to her to be thought 'ordinary', she did not wish to invite comparisons at the time, leaving disclosure to a future biographer. Perhaps she did not wish to be considered 'quite mad'.

Not all Aelfrida's 'supernatural' experiences were celestial; some were diabolic. Common sense questionings and natural doubts regarding the suitability of her life in Oxford continued to plague her in the guise of the devil: "why bother with Malling and the impossible exactions of the oblature"? (Her response was to become 'more exact over [her] Office … and work and speech, the guard of [her] eyes and thoughts'; had she been lax?)[55] Why had she made so little spiritual progress? (God Himself had recently said "I Myself will teach you" and she knew she needed to press on with her 'hard life and arduous prayers'.) Why did she persist "in being an idealist instead of looking facts in the face"? ('I will praise God where He set me and as He taught me even if I never [have] a spark of joy [again]'.)[56] If she had known what was in store for her when she came to Oxford, would she have gone on? ('Probably not, I should not have had the courage'.) "*Sensible* people do not mind admitting they have made a mistake – don't *you* think you have made one?" (No reply.) Worst of all, perhaps, was his suggestion that "God only respects those who stand up and face Him. Once you *humble* yourself, He puts His foot on your neck and … *squeezes*. Just look how he has treated you. He has killed your husband and one of your daughters. He nearly killed the other and now He has taken her away [and] He has deprived you of health, home, status, and half your fortune", but as Aelfrida herself had been His agent in all this she could vouchsafe no reply except to stammer that 'there *is* no help except in God'.[57] After this last and particularly pertinent gibe, she sought Father Cary's advice; she does not record his response but hints that she informed him not only of the devil's initial challenge ("so you want to fight me, do you?") and threat ("of course, I can come between you and God if I wish to") but also of the actual "ghostly" words spoken by her adversary, translated into human speech for Father Cary's benefit.[58] She also swore to tell no-one *but* Father Cary but nevertheless took particular care to preserve the volumes of her diary in which demonic interviews were recorded.

Rather more serious, however, were occasions on which the devil made 'physical attacks' on her, in two instances tipping her bed so violently that she nearly fell out, in one 'rushing' at her in an atmosphere of 'horror and malignancy'. On each occasion Aelfrida made the sign of the Cross and the manifestation stopped, but the presence in her room of a malign influence made her ask herself if the visitation was of the devil 'who is supposed to dislike hermits' or stemmed from the fact that she herself was 'alas! psychic' and that psychism might cause some 'mysterious vitality' in herself to 'take queer outlets' when not 'worked off on other people'. (She does not, interestingly, apply this explanation to her experience of levitation but confined it to 'levitations and prancings of the furniture'.)[59] Cary, consulted about all three episodes, reassured her that such visitations were "all in the course of things"[60], a curious statement given

that he seems not to have specified whether they were '*en règle*' in the general sense of being experiences any hermit might undergo or whether they were specific to Aelfrida's distorted sensibilities of the moment; either way, his attempts to defuse the situation failed to explain 'diabolic' experiences destined to disturb a disturbed mind in the future.

There was, however, more to Aelfrida's 'diabolic' episodes than this. During the tirade in which he spoke slightingly of God, the devil also accused Father Cary of being "a *fanatic,* a member of a group of fanatics" (an unflattering and inaccurate description of the Cowley Fathers) and informed Aelfrida that her confidence in Cary was so misplaced that she ought to "quietly drop him [and] find someone less exacting". Discussing the episode with Cary himself, Aelfrida 'couldn't help adding' ('for one must have a gleam of amusement if one can') the devil's gibe at 'the group of fanatics' to which he belonged (the gibe, she said, was prompted by 'the memory of ancient defeats')[61] but did not, it seems, tell him of the devil's advice with respect to Cary himself. Unfortunately for her peace of mind, Cary spoke at some length on "our ghostly foe" and his "tremendous reality" during a Retreat attended by her contemporaneously with her diabolic and sacerdotal conversations. In the course of his lecture Cary sought to disabuse his listeners of taking comfort from rising above situations in which the devil was likely to attack: the devil, he said, merely changed the *mode* and *strength* of his attacks and it was the "aweful (*sic*) intensity" of this transmogrified combat that "the [Christian] warrior [was] expected to sustain". Noting the 'dark dark abysses of agony' in Cary's eyes as he spoke, Aelfrida swore '*never*' forget his words.[62] Nor did she; obsessional brooding concerning her own and others' vulnerability to diabolic attack be-devilled her for years.

Following her return from Cambridge to St Benedict's in March 1935, Cary confronted Aelfrida with the need for the 'material, purpose, effect etc. etc' of regular confession.[63] She attended Cary's confessional every Saturday thereafter unless prevented by illness or absence from Oxford, timing her arrival so as to be last in the line of his 'chickens'[64] in order to have the opportunity of a chat with him following absolution. For the first year all went well, Cary proffering sensible advice and attempting to calm and control Aelfrida's seething mind, Aelfrida consulting him on everything from her sins to her social life, though not always obeying his instructions. His religious directives were succinct: her future was to be complete abandonment to the will of God and she was to take care lest '*any element of choice* … or taste creep in to mar it' ('italics *mine*!')[65]; she was to 'press on to purer spiritual life'[66]; 'the royal road to pure contemplation' was by way of 'keeping your eyes … steadfastly on [God and] to be eager to respond to the slightest intimation of what He would have you do'[67]; 'partial and immediate loyalties' should be avoided; '*God only*' was required of her.[68] In practical matters his role was advisory and admonitory: to give up 'prolongation of meditation'; to sleep 'in as restful and natural a manner as possible'[69]; to continue a life of solitude and silence but not to call herself a 'solitary' and not to withdraw her interest wholly from the world because "we live in the world for which Christ died"[70]; to carry out her Rule 'with simplicity [and with] the *sancta hilaritas* that would become a good nun' (working in her 'wee walled garden … feeling like a mixture of a Trappist [monk] and a nice little girl' was, Aelfrida joked, holy hilarity in action)[71]; to refrain from 'anything more in the way of physical self-discipline' because her life was already 'on the hard side'[72]; to regard her Malling oblation less as a failure and more as a stage in her spiritual progress and to reflect on how much she had learnt from it that she could not have learnt elsewhere[73]; to be grateful that the Holy Spirit was teaching her '*true* humility' – 'and painful the process is', noted Aelfrida, perhaps remembering Erlande's definition of the *Esprit Saint* as a fierce falcon (*un vif émouchet*) not a gentle dove (*une douce colombe*)[74]; to refrain from acting '*unreflectingly*'[75]; to remember that confession should not be regarded as 'an ordeal' but as 'the everlasting mercy'[76], and, very importantly, given her propensity to brood, 'to leave the past with God'.[77]

Eventually, however, and in spite of his expressing satisfaction with her Rule, her serenity (*sic*), and her 'love of *la vie dévote*'[78], a note of exasperation enters Father Cary's responses to Aelfrida's obsession with real or imaginary sins (he did not know of the sin which weighed most heavily at present: Chiara's *Nunc Dimittis* by bromide and opiate), with 'serious … sins, much worse than usual' listed for his delectation at confession, and with what he regarded as matters of 'secondary importance': membership of religious orders, devotional practices, 'and the rest'.[79] There was also her practice of bombarding him with letters (probably daily, possibly several times a day) witnessed by his to her apologising for not having replied and pleading pressure of work, for it never seems to have occurred to Aelfrida to spare the spiritual energy of an elderly man whose physical and possibly mental health was at risk of breakdown because he was unsparing in the service of others; indeed, by 1936 her need for continual spiritual reassurance reached such a pitch that she even pursued Cary when he was on leave, demanding – by postcard! – that she be allowed to use Alethea's hair girdle each time she meditated on the Passion and whip herself fifty strokes a week with Alethea's 'discipline'.[80] Perhaps the last straw was her decision to conduct a short retreat at St Thomas's Convent for six Church Missionary Society students without consulting him. Although Aelfrida herself enjoyed it ('I believe I *have* conveyed to those dear girls something of the True Light [and] it has meant so much to me to have them here')[81] in spite of feeling 'trepidation'[82] at emulating that well-known conductor of retreats Evelyn Underhill, the fact that Father Cary was 'delicately sarcastic' on the subject of her retreat in particular and on women conducting retreats in general and his declining to discuss the matter further because unable to spare the time[83], provide ample demonstration of disapproval of her conduct. (He had also worried lest her lectures be theologically aberrant or overly personal.) His disapproval did not, of course, result in her cancelling the Retreat, something she could easily have done given that she had a valid excuse: rapidly worsening health.

Cary's own health gave way in June 1936 and he was absent from Oxford until early August. (His absence was the occasion of Aelfrida noting that she sometimes found him 'overwhelming' because 'he [was] so close to God [and] so intent on one's sanctification' and that she was rather glad to be without him for a while.)[84] A gentle note sent in late July hoping "that all is going … reasonably well"[85] quite different in tone from 'extremely plain-spoken' letters received earlier[86] augured well for their reunion, as also did Cary's comment at confession on his return on the strength of Aelfrida's vocation 'to a life of silence, solitude and adoration' ('God's choice', she wrote; her own would have tended towards 'preaching or teaching or writing')[87], but two weeks later the storm broke. Detaining Father Cary after confession on 15 August, Aelfrida demanded answers to recent letters on the subject of reparative adoration, only to discover he had not yet read them; Cary, losing patience, snapped at her, called her 'ungenerous' when she suggested he had plenty of time before his mid-day meal to hear her recount their content, and stormed off. Aelfrida fled to the Lady Chapel to regain her composure and after reflecting that 'pious elderly females and their peccadilloes are rather a bore to priests', sent Cary a grovelling letter of the kind she sent to Constantine after provoked a 'scene', assuring him that she was 'deeply ashamed' of her behaviour ('much to blame', she crossed out), that she hoped to be 'less exacting' in future, and that she realised even the 'greatest of saints' could be 'testy'. Fortunately for both parties, Cary and Aelfrida spent the next month apart, he in Oxford, she in Cambridge and South Wales. (In a written apology for his rude behaviour to a penitent Cary offered 'anxieties and demands … behind the scenes'[88] as his excuse; the devil's comment that 'even Father Cary couldn't … hear [her] out in patience'[89] is probably nearer the mark.) But it is obvious that from this point Cary sought to disengage himself from his importunate 'chicken' and that a degree of frostiness entered his relationship with Aelfrida which time and separation never thawed.

Disengagement took the form of Cary enquiring if Aelfrida had thought of returning 'with further light and new strength' to her previous life now she had had practice 'in the *technique* of the good life' (she was not, he added, 'proficient' but the '*intention*' was there)[90], frostiness in a rebuke: her besetting sin, he told her, was "*playing up to people as soon as you feel that they have begun to notice you*", a criticism so apt ('*le mot juste*', she agreed, underlining Cary's words in her diary) in its application to her relationships with men and women in general and himself in particular ('I have a bad record'[91], she admitted) that rupture was inevitable. Though Aelfrida denied 'playing up' and assured Cary that, having ensured she had nothing to which to return, she only awaited God's revelation of His future plans for her[92] (she herself had already put out feelers of which Cary did not approve), it is obvious that she too sought disengagement: Cary, it seems, had nearly served his purpose.

Too clear-sighted to be subjected to manipulative behaviour and too monastic to allow himself to be caught in Aelfrida's 'magic net', Cary did not, to his credit, abandon her when it became clear he was in danger of becoming the focal point of aspects of his 'penitent's' disordered personality. To enable him to keep a watching brief while disengaging himself from her spiritual and emotional clutches, he arranged for another of his 'chickens' to befriend her, to monitor her behaviour more closely than he as a man and a monk could do, and to report back on her health and behaviour.

Eileen Kermack, wife of an Indian Army colonel, had returned to England to supervise the education of their daughter Pamela, 'a sweet only child' aged ten.[93] Mrs Kermack and Aelfrida had met at St Ursula's Convent in 1934 and Aelfrida had since noticed her worshipping at St Thomas's Convent 'so radiant in her prayer [that] her devotions have often helped mine'.[94] Bestowing the name of 'Philothea ('God-loving')[95] on her befriender, she was fascinated by the 'unusual person' Eileen turned out to be: though an associate of Fairacres who attended Mass and Vespers there daily and who spent much of her day in spiritual exercises, in doing church embroidery, and in offering practical help to the nuns, she could transform herself in an instant from a 'penitent' with 'a long black veil on her head and … her [mind] running on such subjects as … the unique excellence of the contemplative life'[96] to a colonel's lady clad in 'faultless tweeds', owning a flat, and running a car. Aelfrida envied her, for Eileen led the life she herself would have loved to lead: moneyed, independent, respected, and with an absent but adoring spouse who appreciated his wife's religious vocation and did not object to her friendship with a male director. Eileen in return envied Aelfrida's life in convent precincts where she could be as solitary or as silent as she wished but, as Aelfrida rightly noted, loved 'the life I lead, not the person I am'. Acting only 'under obedience' to Father Cary, she made no effort to maintain the friendship after Aelfrida left Oxford[97] but was enormously supportive during the months which elapsed between the latter's return to Oxford in March 1935 and her departure in November 1936, chauffeuring her to Mass, visiting St Benedict's when she was unwell, comforting her after Alethea's departure for South Africa, and, as we shall see, introducing her to the next staging-point on her closer walk with God.

It was, it seems, chiefly with reference to Aelfrida's health that Lucius Cary asked 'Philothea' to watch over her, for within months of her arrival in Oxford in late summer 1934, her health began to decline, a decline attributable less to a depressive reaction to Constantine's death, Alethea's desertion, and Agatha's suicide (though these certainly contributed) or to the cold and damp of St Benedict's and more to the reparative practices of a "victim soul" whose need for reparation for her *own* 'sins' formed the unspoken focus of her "victim-state".

Mindful that one of the four mantras recently suggested by her guardian angel was 'self-sacrifice is true praise', Aelfrida decided that though it was 'rash and presumptuous' to pray further prayers to be made a saint and not spared in the making (God, of course, had not yet wholly responded to that particular plea, Agatha's death being then three months away), it would be in order for her 'to lead as hard a life as I am conveniently able to bear without being ill or gloomy'.[98] It was therefore unfortunate that when she added the stringencies of reparative adoration to the hard life she believed God ordained for her without 'concession to … human weakness'[99], her already precarious physical health became very precarious indeed and she rapidly became both ill *and* gloomy.

Dental sepsis had beset her since August 1933 but she declined further surgery because reluctant to appear at Malling looking 'an Object and a Fright'[100] and it was not until William Gilliatt refused to entertain the thought of even exploratory gynaecological surgery until the 'septic condition'[101] of her mouth was dealt with (a sensible precaution in pre-antibiotic days) that Aelfrida and Dorothy Smith mutually decided that dental clearance should be undertaken as soon as possible. The arrival of dentures 'Mr and Mrs Nash' in February 1935 resulted in their becoming less and less comfortable as time went on because 'the bone and gums of my lower jaw seem to be … a kind of pulp and get ulcers and sore places all the time in the most painful and revolting way'[102]; indeed, so uncomfortable did her 'poor squashy gums'[103] become in spite of Dorothy's repeated ministrations that Aelfrida was forced to remove her teeth when she ate 'which seems … vaguely improper like sitting about without any knickers on!'[104] She was no better a year later, reporting 'perpetual neuralgia, "toothaches", sore places on [her] gums, swollen tongue and so forth' on every visit to Dorothy but noting too that continual oral pain was appropriate for one seeking to imitate "Jesus-Victim" and that further pain could be 'sought or inflicted on one's self with profit'.[105]

Recurrence of rheumatism was naturally attributed by Aelfrida to her cold damp house and to God using her *petites misères* as penitential aspects of reparative adoration.[106] Harder to attribute to Deity or to problems with her 'bower of Lady Poverty' were persistent bruising to and delayed healing of an elbow wound sustained in October 1935 after being knocked down by a cyclist[107], an inflamed Achilles' tendon which, though strapped up by Dr Frazer, caused her to hobble to church 'like a pilgrim going to Canterbury with peas in [her] shoes'[108], periods of indigestion or diarrhoea attributed to being 'too tired to digest [her] food'[109], 'eczema' as one of an 'absurd collection of minor ailments' which plagued her in June 1936[110] (the time at which she began to use Alethea's 'knitted girdle of horsehair' so unlikely to be 'eczema' as generally understood), and recurrent 'cramp in[her] heart' ranging from 'bad' to 'severe' ('I don't mind, of course, but it is a trifle inconvenient')[111], a litany of complaints individually debilitating but when taken together symptomatic of something more sinister.

So too with other new or recurrent complaints. Lower abdominal pain associated with blood-stained vaginal discharge and even with haemorrhage ranging from 'slight' to 'quite alarming' to 'excessive' which rendered her 'so dizzy [she] hardly dared to have a bath' and faint 'as if some invisible hand turned off the current of [her] being' and convincing her, in spite of Mr Gilliatt's reassurances, that 'something *has* gone wrong'.[112] Lassitude, beyond that attributable to leading a 'hard life' while struggling with the effects of chronic blood loss, ranging from complaints of being merely 'tired, so tired' to being so 'dazed with fatigue' (too dazed even to write her diary, she wrote) that she hardly felt she could continue because 'Brother Ass gets very weary'.[113] Weight loss so dramatic in one whose weight hovered on the lowest percentile suitable for a woman of her height that, seeing herself in a dress shop mirror, she was moved to note that though she did not look '*ill* exactly', she certainly looked '*insubstantial*' and 'as though [her] body were being purged of grossness'. (She also looked 'so much older'[114], a statement substantiated by a contemporary photograph in which she appears white haired, thin cheeked, and as if she had somehow shrunk into herself.) Acute on chronic infections of the throat and nasal passages giving rise to debilitating symptoms ('being on the verge of the Shivers all the time', worsening headaches unattributable to migraine, earache, 'my face as if … all run through with burning wires', coughing up 'a huge lump of blood') and to a diagnosis by Ronald Macbeth of her sinuses having been 'thoroughly infected for years and years' and of continuing to be so in spite of surgery.[115] And so on and on through several volumes of her diary.

That her health was indeed bad is also evidenced by the fact that, admissions for surgery excepted, Aelfrida spent some four weeks in total in nursing homes or convent guest houses in Oxford and elsewhere between early October 1935 and mid–April 1936 on Dr Frazer's orders and three days on her own account at a private house where two 'pious ladies' had 'tired people to stay and make them happy'.[116] This astonishing amount of absence from the 'cell' in which she professed to be so happy was, however, rather more than a medically-sanctioned extension of her habit of taking days in bed to escape from the rigours of life (of which there were many at St Benedict's) which reduced her to moans of self-pity when particularly unwell; it was an absolute necessity for one who was 'so desperately tired' that all she wanted to do was to 'lie still and be waited on', so 'limp from sheer starvation'[117] that nurses administered 'velvety French soups' to feed her up, so anaemic that she was prescribed douches in order to stem her vaginal bleeding[118], and who was eventually sent to convalesce with other 'elderly and invalidish' ladies on the English Riviera. ('If you like resorts, I suppose Torquay is very beautiful. I don't'.)[119] In fact, and as Aelfrida herself realised, something had indeed 'gone wrong'; what she refused to admit was that every aspect of her appalling health was attributable, directly or indirectly, to a single cause: she had rendered herself scorbutic.

Scurvy is a disease more commonly associated with conditions conducive to severe dietary deprivation than with the lifestyle of middle-aged middle-class ladies living in an English university town, but knowing that a lady answering this description was currently recording in her diary that whenever she trusted herself to do the right thing 'in [her] own best efforts', the outcome was invariably 'disastrous'[120] and that she had reached a point in her life at which she felt justified in being 'reckless' of her health[121], comparison of the signs and symptoms of severe vitamin C deficiency with Aelfrida's demonstrates that scurvy was indeed the condition she had induced. Not that, most unusually for one who liked to flaunt (often inaccurately) her medical knowledge, she ever openly admitted to being scorbutic for this would expose the enormity and stupidity of her actions; indeed, it was not until the onset of nyctalopia (damage to the eye resulting in poor vision at night or in dim light but permitting adequate vision during the day or in bright light; she herself merely described her eyes as 'weak')[122] which so badly affected her ability to read and write (activities vital to her spiritual and psychological welfare) that she had recourse to a reader and acted on the instructions of nutritional expert Vernon Mottram whom she approached with regard to 'diet in relation to eyesight as that is his special "shop"' and made sensible adjustments to her own as a result of his declaring himself 'shocked' by her revelations.[123] Only much later did she admit (to her diary) that 'in Oxford, I gave up, as a mortification, all fresh fruit'.[124]

Inadequate nutrition involving very low levels or absence of vitamin C has markedly detrimental effects on the human body's immune system and connective tissues and on the ability of the blood to clot.[125] Its chief symptoms, extreme fatigue and bodily weakness, ulcerated gums and oral sepsis, delayed healing of even minor wounds, loss of weight, intermittent fevers, swollen and painful joints and the structures associated with them, a tendency to spontaneous bruising and to delayed resolution of traumatic bruising and to the likelihood of spontaneous bleeding from any mucosal surface (including that of the lining of the uterus and gut) exacerbating the anaemia, faintness, and pallor caused by the deleterious effects of the disease on the sufferer's blood (haemorrhage exacerbated in Aelfrida's case by excessive consumption of anticoagulant aspirin as an analgesic and to counteract feverish 'Shivers') were all suffered by Aelfrida to a greater or lesser extent during her stay at St Benedict's. But given that she was neither a slum dweller, an ancient mariner, an alcoholic, a sufferer from malabsorption syndrome, nor institutionalised (all predisposing factors), how, other than by omitting fresh fruit from her diet, had she managed to induce the disease?

True, she did not like the food served at the convent guest house ('all slabs and chunks with cabbage like damp seaweed')[126] and avoided it when possible, but in spite of having earlier declared that she 'never could or would cook'[127], she could and did provide nourishing meals for visitors and must have partaken of them too in order to avoid arousing suspicion. True, too, and in spite of complaints of penury, she had sufficient funds

Alethea (far left, back row) as a postulant

to buy nutritious food and was rarely ill enough to be unable to shop; visitors, too, frequently brought food, saying she needed 'feeding up' after recent tribulations. But while avoidance of luxury foods could be explained as an aspect of her and St Benedict's Rule (she lived, she told one donor, 'on calories and vitamins under Father Cary's direction')[128], her giving away donated food to Daisy Allen or to the guesthouse was symptomatic of something other than generosity of spirit or a desire for alimentary "frugality".[129] In fact, her diet was extremely restricted ('what I set before myself is … monotonous and … unappetising')[130]: eggs (her only form of protein other than a little milk, but only at midday), bread and butter, cake (often stale), a bowl of rice (regarded as a meal), a penny-worth of potatoes, a halfpennyworth of carrots, and a two-penny packet of stock as '[her] dinner for three days!'[131] Meat she continued to avoid altogether, less from moral principles than because she found consumption unconducive to meditation and because the Benedictine Rule, following St Paul's admonition that "meat commendeth us not to God"[132], advised its followers to "refrain entirely from eating the flesh of quadrupeds.[133] But as she herself recognised, 'not eating enough' as an aspect of 'rather overdoing the hard life' on the grounds that it was 'very difficult to know where to draw the line when one is trying to give *everything* to God', particularly when it resulted in her feeling 'trembly

[and] *pas très solide'* and liable to faint even when lying down, was one thing, and 'sanctified common sense' quite another when it came to being 'called to [the] *unusual* vocation [of being] *nothing*'[134], and although her symptoms waxed and waned according to whether she was at St Benedict's or being looked after elsewhere, the overall trend was an inexorable decline in her health.

What, therefore, were Aelfrida's reasons for behaving as she did? In order to understand her rationale we must return to an important section of *A Little Road-Book for Mystics*, revised in February 1931 less than four years before her move to Oxford to a house where for the first time in her life she could wholeheartedly practice what she had hitherto only preached, earlier attempts at semi-starvation having been thwarted by her mother. "As the mystic hurries on his way", she writes, he or she may meet "a number … of men and women engaged in incomprehensible practices … At first sight they seem all to be activated by the same motive, namely by some kind of spite against the body". Later, however, the mystic realises that the men and women with whom he has joined company are not all activated by the same motive, some believing "that the bearing of pain is [both] meritorious for its own sake and automatically brings sanctity with it", others that pain or deprivation are to be used "as a means to an end". She herself is an ascetic of the latter kind, one of those who believe that "even when pushed to unwise extremes", asceticism is "right and reasonable" (it does not, for example, stem from a belief that "matter is inherently evil" and that God is a Being "capable of vindictive anger … who needs to be propitiated") and that its practice "satisfies a real need of the religious life". The "need", she continues, is to be able to concentrate all one's attention on the loving and benevolent Deity in whom this kind of ascetic believes in order to be better able to devote all one's desires to Him, the "end" being "full union with God".

This is not to suggest, however, that such asceticism, however right and reasonable its nature and however carefully graded the means by which the mystic exercises it, cannot become as pathological as the first because there may be "crises" in the mystic's life when "the body's wishes must be disregarded" in favour of harnessing and training the mind to cease gambolling over "the fields of frivolity" or relaxing in "admiring contemplation of the Ego". But when asceticism which began as a positive reminder (e.g. of "what Friday symbolises to the Christian's heart") or as "an intrinsic part of consecration" (i.e. of oblation or Holy Virginity) comes to regard everything irrelevant to the "one-pointedness" of the mystic's quest for God as "*ipso facto* bad", practices regarded by the mystic as "the most natural in the world"

are transformed into the "weird artificiality" of "self-inflicted mortification" akin to that practised by those who believe the infliction and bearing of pain and deprivation for their own sake is automatically pleasing to God.[135] And so it happened to Aelfrida herself four years after she revisited these words.

One-pointedness apart, there were other reasons for her exaggerated asceticism with regard to food, all of which are referred to in or deducible from her diary. First and foremost was the important role played by asceticism in reparative adoration, "victim souls" of necessity being expected to offer "substantial proof of genuine immolation".[136] To Aelfrida as a "victim-soul" desperate to expiate her own as well as others' sins, immolation by food deprivation came naturally – she had, after all, practised it intermittently, secretly, and to varying extents since adolescence and had been encouraged to do so by it being a mortification increasingly easy to incorporate into daily life – but particularly interesting in 1934/35 is her connection of a desire to purge herself of the grossness of her sins with a desire to purge herself of physical 'grossness' by reducing the quantity and quality of what she ate. Then, too, reduction in quality and quantity of food could be regarded as a necessity for one seeking to disentangle herself from an appetite for power, praise, sanctity, and 'the world' in general which had been the cause of so much 'sin', a point brought forcibly home in August 1935 by the devil asking why she had 'let Anthony go', a question which provoked so many reminders of her continuing dependence on spiritual mentors, on 'dear human companionship', and on 'visions or "shewings"' as manifestations of God's encouragement of her 'closer walk', that she decided to be both 'more exact over my Office … and work and speech' and 'more strict over food'.[137]

She also evinced a desire to emulate and possibly surpass other "prayerful souls" for whom mortification of the flesh was an "absolute necessity" if they were to "pray well", austerities primarily inflicted "out of a spirit of penance" providing support for the mind of one whose "faculties of the soul" (understanding, memory, will, etc) were to be bent as assiduously as positive "motions of the human heart" such as joy and hope (and even negative ones such as fear and grief, the latter a particularly prevalent emotion in Aelfrida's life at this time) to patient advancement of the soul in relation to God.[138] Hence although she wrote apropos her brief abstention from food while staying with Ancifera in October 1933 (an abstention which can now be seen as the beginning of her attempt to save Constantine's immortal soul, a soul which she, as the 'Undine' descried by Aleister Crowley, could be said to have fatally cursed as a punishment for his infidelities) that tales of fasting saints exasperated her[139], because she was already aware that the saints of whom she wrote found fasting 'a help'[140] in achievement of sanctity, she too decided to walk her 'closer walk' with the same assistance.

Aelfrida had, of course, many exemplars in her desire to "[force] the gates of Heaven" using semi-starvation as a battering ram with which to concentrate the "whole energy of [her] organism on one point[141]: St Paul ("I keep under my body and bring it into subjection lest … I find myself a castaway")[142]; Egyptian hermits who existed on minimal rations of bread, water, salt, and occasional dates taken once or twice a day when not altogether abstinent; St Benedict, among whose "Tools of Good Works" were "to punish one's body" and "to love fasting" (though not, of course to take it to extreme lengths, "a diminution in [the usual quantities] of food and drink" being all that was required)[143] and who, as a hermit, had sought refuge fasting 'among nettles, thorns and briars'[144] but who later recognised that "the just claims of the body must be considered and its demands for a sufficiency of food satisfied"[145], a point conveniently forgotten by one seeking refuge among metaphorical nettles, thorns, and briars at St Benedict's; St Francis, who, with his 'Brothers and Sisters of Penitence', deprived 'Brother Ass' of fodder; St Catherine of Siena whose self-starvation effectively shortened her life. Thérèse Neumann claimed to eat and drink nothing but the Holy Sacrament (Albert Erlande, worried that Aelfrida did not eat enough, joked that she did not need food because she ate only "*le pigeon du Saint-Ésprit*"[146], a bon mot even more apt a decade later), something which may have inspired Aelfrida to attempt the same: 'many of the Saints existed on the Blessed Sacraments and nothing else [and I too] feel an *attrait* towards a saintly fast … so strong that it cannot be resisted'.[147]

Fasts, saintly or not, give rise to hunger pains. Pain, even if (or, one might say, especially if) self-inflicted stimulates the body to produce endorphins, a natural form of analgesia chemically related to opiates. Can it be that Aelfrida, already accustomed to the effect of ascetically-induced endorphin production by means of minor degrees of food deprivation and, more recently, by means of whippings with belts and cords, found herself so euphoric as a result of being 'strict over food' that she became stricter still in order to quell distracting hunger pains and symptoms of scurvy and because endorphin-induced euphoria enhanced both content and awareness of visions, 'shewings', and 'spiritual emotions' (enhancement further enhanced by the metabolic disturbances of malnutrition) and this at a time when she was by her own admission and through every fault of her own suffering 'so much in [her] soul'?[148] (She was not, of course, aware of euphoria-producing *mechanisms,* only of *results,* but must have realised that the euphoria she experienced as a result of semi-starvation was remarkably similar to that induced by consumption of opium; she may also have realised that stigmatic pain, however induced, also gave rise to euphoria, something which would have encouraged her to continue meditations on the Passion so obsessively and for so long.) Reiterated protestations that she is 'so happy' when she should have been deeply unhappy can therefore be seen not only as ecstatic responses to spiritual events (which *au fond* they probably are) or attempts to convince herself that she has not made (as the devil suggested) a terrible mistake in living where and as she does, but as also indicative of chemical 'happiness' mistaken for true happiness but no less 'happifying' (as Aelfrida herself would say) for all that.

If, as it seems and as she had every reason to be, Aelfrida was also a victim of severe reactive depression while at St Benedict's, the presence of natural 'opiates' would have helped to lift her mood. Indeed, for someone who had already passed through the earlier stages of grief (denial, anger, and bargaining as to cause, effect, and blameworthiness) with regard to recent deaths and desertions and who now entered the next stage, namely depression, exacerbated in her case by "morbid and pernicious" asceticism (the latter derided by Aelfrida as akin to "religious melancholy and other … sad types of insanity")[149], recourse to means by which gloomy thoughts which seemed 'to push [her] down into that darkness [which] if it should become *worse,* something might snap'[150] (as it had done for Agatha, had almost done for Alethea following dismissal from Malling, and almost did for herself at this time) could be transformed quickly and easily into more positive ones seems entirely appropriate.

Depression may have inspired her to self-starvation for another reason. Having settled on 'being nobody' and having discovered that not only did nobody care about her 'being nobody' but also that they expressed relief at her being 'alone with the Alone' in Oxford instead of plaguing their lives in Cambridge, and always anxious to attract attention to herself, Aelfrida embarked on a course of action which would ensure attention because of its dramatic effects on her health and appearance. (Worth noting here is that it is characteristic of depressives "frequently to engage in behaviour that has the effect of arousing the anxious concern of those around them yet doing so in ways so indirect and unacknowledged that their purpose remains concealed".)[151] Although she later attributed the decline in her health at St Benedict's to having to 'get up from a sickbed … into a damp, cold and lonely house and set about getting one's own frugal tea'[152] (she vacated the house, she later wrote, because 'I was never well there')[153], it is obvious that, thwarted of her second attempt to be crucified on the cross of cancer, Aelfrida made just sufficient 'fusses' over the effects of her inadequate diet to ensure that people noticed: 'I don't wonder … that everyone is so sweet to me. I should be if saw anyone so changed'.[154] Did she perhaps hope that someone with sufficient authority would realise from 'fusses' whither her guilt had led her and, like Dr Bowen a quarter of a century earlier, step in and save her, and this in spite of promising to 'do something drastic and try and get better' because it upset people to see her so ill, a promise she had no intention of keeping if only (and as if the two were incompatible) because from the spiritual point of view 'it is better to be saintly than to be sensible'?[155]

The presence of Aelfrida's 'fusses' begs the question: why was she not diagnosed sooner? In the course of her two-year stay at St Benedict's, she was seen by two general practitioners (Joan Cooper, briefly, and Mary Frazer, frequently) a dentist (Dorothy Smith), and two surgical specialists, William Gilliatt and Ronald Macbeth. Of these only Dr Frazer was sufficiently perceptive to discern a single aetiology as the basis of her patient's polysymptomatic complaints, to decide that Aelfrida's problem was essentially nutritional, and to recommend a balanced diet as its cure; indeed, as early as April 1935 Aelfrida noted in her diary that Dr Frazer had expressed concern for her 'general health'[156] and in October that Dr Frazer was about to order her 'a few days *complete rest* in a nursing home' (and 'feeding up' while sufficiently immobilised not to be able to burn off calories by taking long walks) on the grounds that she did not take sufficient care of herself. ('I resist', wrote her gratified patient, 'the temptation to impress this on Phyllis'[157], Phyllis, of course, having recently accused her sister-in-law of being a *malade imaginaire*.) Visited by Dr Frazer and 'Philothea' soon after her discharge from the nursing home, the former to inspect her mouth and nose for residual or recurrent signs of mucosal haemorrhage and ulceration, the latter to enquire anxiously if she were feeling better, Aelfrida found it difficult to convince either lady that she looked after herself 'properly'.[158] A month later Alethea, not then resident at St Benedict's but visiting regularly with gifts of food, was 'so troubled'[159] about her mother's general condition that she contacted Dr Frazer herself. Dr Frazer promptly prescribed the addition of meat and beer to Aelfrida's diet but she, having teetotally refused beer and heroically tried bacon (it gave her 'unromantic biliousness [and] a *vile* headache')[160], refused meat altogether on the grounds that it 'clogged' her 'soul'[161]

– at which point her exasperated general practitioner packed her off to Torquay to see if two weeks in a convent guest-house could make her patient see sense and eat properly.

It did not, but nor did Aelfrida's attention-seeking behaviour have the desired effect as far as family and friends were concerned. Eustace, though 'affectionate and brotherly'[162] on flying visits, had disengaged himself. Father Cary, with whom she discussed 'the food I eat' as part of her 'somewhat hard life'[163], was solicitous of her health in general terms but did not enquire in detail. Lucy Verey, 'all excitement and busy-ness, and so happy and maternal'[164], was more concerned with her children's marriages and with the arrival of grandchildren to do more than bring eggs to one who sourly noted that 'some people would say that all has gone well for [Lucy] and wrong with me [and that Lucy's] life seems to widen and mine to grow narrower and darker'.[165] (And whose fault was that?) Alethea, aware that her mother was self-harming through semi-starvation, ignored her 'fusses' as the latter had done to herself and her sister in *their* hours of need and departed to a new life on another continent. (To compound her revenge Alethea 'rashly'[166] – Aelfrida's word – informed Father O'Brien that yes, her mother *did* look after herself – and told her mother what she had said.) Julius was too wrapped up in his own concerns (Mina's inexplicable '*tristitia*'; his impending year in South Africa) to offer advice even though informed by Daisy as early as December 1934 of the decline in her mistress's health[167] and was, in any case, too easily fooled by his sister putting on 'a good show of excellent health'[168] to disguise the cause and effect of her present illness.

For Dr Frazer to have ascertained as much as she did of the cause of her patient's protean illness is remarkable, given Aelfrida's guarded response to questioning for, attention-seeking 'fusses' excepted, the latter strove to conceal the nature and severity of her symptoms by affecting indifference to the pain of joints distended by bloody effusions and of anaemia-induced angina by dismissing new symptoms as if they were merely recurrences of pre-existing diseases, by dramatizing symptoms of lesser importance (hobbling heroically into church with an inflamed heel when she had been expressly ordered to rest; ostentatiously sniffing smelling salts during one of Father Cary's lectures) while failing to disclose others of greater significance ('a huge lump of blood' coughed up without warning) on the grounds that she 'did not need to tell anyone'.[169] She also, as with Dr Cooper, tried to divert Dr Frazer's attention from her symptoms by composing and passing round a sequence of light-hearted '*Eatmore*' poems inspired by her doctor's admonition that Aelfrida 'eat more' nutritious food, each poem being dedicated to a different foodstuff: fruit, meat, fish, eggs, porridge, and bread and butter.[170]

Aelfrida's reasons for behaving thus are implicit in her diary account of her illness and best summed up by an overheard conversation between Daisy and Rhoda Allen when both sisters were caring for Aelfrida while she was bed-bound with 'sharp rheumatic pains and severe cramp in the heart': "poor dear", she records one as saying, "*she's* not long for this world, I'll be bound".[171] That, of course, was the point – depressed and burdened by guilt, she had deliberately embarked on suicide-by-starvation.

Even when 'very happy and full of plans' Aelfrida had always longed to die. Noting that she frequently experienced 'a curious sense of *waiting*', she noted too that what she supposed she was waiting for was 'death'[172], for only by dying could she 'come nearer to the Beatific Vision'[173], rarely if ever revealed prior to death because "God's glory [veils] Him from our view".[174] (As 'Audrey Talbot' reminds 'Catharine Sutherland', "you would tell me that if we knew the glories of the other side, we should all commit suicide to reach them".)[175] Seeing herself so 'insubstantial' in the dress-shop mirror reminded her of this: 'I don't look unhappy … but wistful … and anxiously *expectant* as though I were listening for a soft call that I should be glad to hear'[176], a call whose imminence might be announced by her guardian angel's production of a mantra suggesting that death was to be regarded as a positive rather than a negative event: *Mors tua sit mihi vita indeficiens.*[177]

St Benedict's Rule, of course, advised her "to keep death daily before one's eyes"[178] as one of the 'tools of good works' of her personal Rule and she herself, in attempting to live by it, tried 'to "die daily"' in the sense of giving up her 'old ways of spiritual aggrandisement' in order to become a 'nothing' by whom good 'works' (prayer, meditation, the *opus Dei,* even housework and shopping) were performed and offered primarily for God's glory and only secondarily for her own 'sanctification'[179], but what Aelfrida was now attempting was physical, not spiritual: 'I will own up to something … I was trying to … find out how much food and of what kind was really necessary to sustain life [but] I [didn't] eat enough to keep body and soul together'. She did not do this, she added, for self-improvement or as a discipline or in imitation or because she believed in a God 'who hates human enjoyment', but as a kind of experiment which left her alive but 'rather badly undernourished'. Though aware that 'what [she] was suffering from … was as much starvation as anything else', she did not desist. Rationally, she could not condone her conduct; she was, rather, 'quite prepared to be even more strict if [she] should

find it possible' and that to continue 'to go that way if [she] could'.[180] Finding she could, she did, to the extent of almost becoming her "own executioner".[181]

What motivated her to attempt slow suicide at this particular juncture Aelfrida does not admit, though she notes some years later with probable reference to her life in Oxford that "much remains of necessity unuttered, audible to the ears of God only"[182] and that her mood was so dark that not even feelings of "deepest peace" which followed "dazzling flashes of ecstasy" during which she achieved "profound appreciation of the Triune God" were sufficient to overcome her "longing to be gone"[183], but by reference to her own and others' actions and to oblique references given when writing ostensibly of other things we may guess.

In spite of denying that she starved herself for self-improvement, discipline, imitation, or fear, it seems she was motivated by all of these: self-improvement by purging herself of 'grossness'; discipline by subjecting her unwilling body to a specific drastic mortification in order to bring it into subjection so that it would be forced to abandon the 'sunny' side of the Mystic Way altogether and take its closer walk with God on the 'shady' side; mortification, by its Latin roots (mors, *death; mortificare,* to kill) suggesting the means to take, namely fasting unto death; imitation of ascetic saints and of Jesus of Nazareth fasting in the wilderness; fear of a God who had 'killed' her 'husband' and one of her children and who if not properly propitiated, might take the other because He hated 'enjoyment' of one human being by another. Perhaps, too, she wanted to re-join her 'beloved dead', particularly Agatha ('I feel so sure that if Agatha had known that Alethea would come back from Malling and that I should be here too, she would not have left us')[184] and Constantine as "free[d] from the almost inevitable faults of the earth"[185], towards both of whom she still felt love so possessive that she was prepared to kill herself in order to repossess them. Perhaps, knowing her propensity for revenge, she regarded suicide as a means of wreaking it on living people who had in different ways rejected her: Phyllis Tillyard, Joan Cooper, Frank Stokoe, Alethea Graham, Lucius Cary, and the Lady Abbess of Malling. Perhaps, realising that with Alethea's departure to South Africa she was free of her last encumbrance, she knew she could die if she wished and chose a slow but certain means.

There was also her unfortunate tendency to accept uncritically doctrines propounded in the homiletic books she read, be these Charles Kingsley ("I must be clean. I must be clean", cries little Tom before he "drowns" into "the quietest, sunniest, cosiest sleep he ever had in his life")[186], Thomas à Kempis ("Christ speaks: naked I hung on the Cross ... offering myself freely to God the Father for your sins, My whole Person a sacrifice of divine propitiation ... I offered Myself wholly to the Father for you: I have given My very Body and Blood ... I require nothing less of you")[187], Paulin Giloteaux whose pernicious doctrine of reparative adoration suggested that "victim souls" could achieve as their supreme oblation "sacrifice fully perfected ... sacrifice of life itself"[188], an enormous temptation to one who though ostensibly acting in expiation of others' sins, was submerged in guilt with regard to her own, or virtually everyone quoted in James' chapter on 'Saintliness' in *The Varieties of Religious Experience*. Whatever the reason, it is important to remember that Aelfrida embarked on self-starvation as soon as she went to Oxford, *prior,* that is to say, to Agatha's death but following Constantine's and Chiara's but *after* Alethea had reneged on her obligations as one third of the unholy Graham 'trinity', only to increase her 'sacrifice' after the death of her favourite daughter brought home to her the enormity of her actions relative to all four.

What she did *not* do, perhaps because by now too mentally disequilibriated to be able to think straight or because she could not bear to see herself reflected in the mirror held up to her by a man she admired, was to compare her condition with that of Ignatius Loyola in his eremetical retreat at Manresa, a man who, like herself, had entered retreat in the throes of a breakdown as deep as and of markedly similar aetiology to her own; Loyola, about whom she had written at length in her own *Spiritual Exercises* and then, like herself now, "a textbook case of religiously induced psychic crisis, with classic symptoms of deep melancholia, unbearable anxiety over damnation and suicidal temptations [experiencing] acute scruples over meeting the exacting demands of full contrition that were made of [a] penitent so as to render the Sacrament of Penance effective". A man who, "abstemious, vegetarian, and moderate" when he began his retreat, "attempted to solve his problems by means of a hunger-strike against the Almighty, exacerbating his problems rather than solving them" and suffering delirium, hateful visitations, and near-death experiences as a result. A man who disregarded his confessor's practical and spiritual advice in favour of "reliance on visions for ... instruction". A man whom "devout ladies" watched over and looked after.[189] (As a 'luxurious' hermit Aelfrida did not, however, take self-neglect to an an Ignatian extent; indeed, she later wrote of St Margaret of Hungary that the dirty and verminous saint had 'neglected her person' in a most '*revolting*' manner.)[190] It even seems she was tacitly trying to out-Loyola Loyola by subjecting herself to the same "complicated disciplines", though less in the hope of "rising to the heights of contemplation or of experiencing ecstasies" than in order that she "*might have her sense of sin increased*"[191] (and even her death encompassed) and it was only by a twist of fate that 'devout woman' Eileen Kermack unwittingly saved her life.

## Notes

1  Tillyard, Ae. *The Fruits of Silence* p23 (GCPPT 2|18).
2  GCPPT 1|1|5 28 May 1900.
   GCPPT 1|1|46 16 February 1935.
3  GCPPT 1|2.
4  Giloteaux, P. p 275.
5  *Matthew* 10: 7–10 (KJV).
6  GCPPT 1|1|51 20 June 1936.
7  ibid. 22 June 1936.
8  ibid. 2 July 1936.
9  ibid. 24 July 1936.
10  GCPPT 1|1|48 22 March 1935.
11  ibid. 20 June 1935.
12  GCPPT 1|1|47 29 March 1935.
13  GCPPT 1|1|48 19 and 20 June 1935.
14  GCPPT 1|1|50 5 June 1936.
    GCPPT 1|1|51 17 June 1936.
15  GCPPT 1|1|48 26 and 27 June 1935. Aelfrida's stigmatic symptoms are explicable in terms of the symptomatology of rheumatoid arthritis and/or in terms of artefactual impressions made during attempts to alleviate the worst of her pain by massage, but so potent were her spiritual experiences that supernatural or psychosomatic causes cannot be easily dismissed.
16  GCPPT 1|1|48 29 July 1935.
17  ibid. 6 July ('June' in error) 1935.
18  Delacroix, H. pp 313–314.
19  GCPPT 1|1|48 25 July 1935.
20  ibid 11 July 1935.
21  ibid. 14 June 1935.
22  ibid. 12 May 1935.
23  GCPPT 1|1|47 22 March 1935.
24  GCPPT 1|1|48 25 June 1935.
25  GCPPT 1|1|50 20 November 1935.
26  ibid. 21 February 1936.
27  GCPPT 1|1|51 16 June 1936.
28  GCPPT 1|1|52 28 October 1936.
29  GCPPT 1|1|48 30 and 31 May 1935.
30  GCPPT 1|1|52 1 November 1936.
31  ibid. 'The Transfiguration' (6 August) 1936. From this point on, Aelfrida frequently heads diary entries with the name of the festival celebrated on that day, leaving her reader to guess the date from preceding or subsequent (dated) entries. Unlike her vision of the frailty of the world relative to God's might (a vision entirely appropriate to her circumstances at this time), Julian of Norwich's vision of "all that is made" as "a little thing, the size of a hazel nut" leads her to ponder on the world's endurance "because God loves it" (*Revelations of Divine Love* p 47).
32  GCPPT 1|1|50 8 May 1936.
33  GCPPT 1|1|49 28 September 1935.
34  ibid. 23 and 28 September 1935.
35  ibid. 30 September 1935.
36  GCPPT 1|1|48 19 July 1935.
37  GCPPT 1|1|47 5 May 1935.
38  GCPPT 1|1|50 8 June 1936.
39  ibid. 15 December 1935.
40  Teresa of Avila *Life* p137. It should, perhaps, also be noted that Eusapia Palladino too was said to have levitated (Lind, F. p78), a fact mentioned

in Spiritualist literature and possibly discussed within young Frida's hearing on one of her visits to Silvia Myers.

41  GCPPT 1|1|44 30 July 1933.

42  GCPPT 1|1|50 2 March and 9 April 1936.

43  ibid. 11 March 1936.

44  ibid. 30 and 31 March 1936. Aelfrida's account of the event was written two days after it occurred.

45  ibid. 3 and 6 April 1936. The latter date is erroneously written as '5 June' in her diary.

46  ibid. 11 and 12 April 1936.

47  ibid. 24 April 1936.

48  ibid. 8 April 1936.

49  ibid. 5 and 8 April 1936.

50  ibid. 14 and 17 April 1936. An article from the *Daily Sketch* of 17 April 1936 giving an account of Daisy's 'miraculous' recovery is preserved in GCPPT 1|1|50a. Aelfrida's diary account is reminiscent of the Biblical account of Christ's reanimation of Jairus' dead daughter but its rather peevish tone suggests disappointment that her presence at Daisy's bedside was not picked up by the press.

51  For details of the life of St Catherine of Siena (1347–1380) see King, U. pp 83–86.

52  GCPPT 1|1|63 5 March 1946.

53  For details of Padro Pio (Francesco Forgione (1887–1968), see www.padrepio.net and numerous other sites.

54  For details of Thérèse Neumann (1898–1962) see http:||members.chello.nl/~l.de.bondt.ThérèseNeumann.htm and numerous other sites.

55  GCPPT 1|1|48 11 August 1935.

56  GCPPT 1|1|51 28 August 1936.

57  GCPPT 1|1|52 17 November 1936.

58  ibid.

59  GCPPT 1|1|50 23 December 1935.

60  GCPPT 1|1|52 13 November 1939.

61  ibid. 17 November 1936.

62  ibid. 13 November 1936.

63  GCPPT 1|1|47 7 April 1935.

64  'Father Cary's chickens' was the name given by Aelfrida to his 'penitents' in a punning reference to 'Mother Carey's chickens', the name given by sailors to the stormy petrel; under their maritime nickname stormy petrels figure in *The Water Babies* and it is probably from this source that Aelfrida derived hers.

65  GCPPT 1|1|47 23 March 1935.

66  ibid. 5 May 1935.

67  GCPPT 1|1|48 5 August 1935.

68  GCPPT 1|1|49 19 October 1935.

69  GCPPT 1|1|48 5 August 1935.

70  GCPPT 1|1|49 29 August 1935.

71  GCPPT 1|1|47 11 and 24 May 1935.

72  ibid. 25 May 1935.

73  GCPPT 1|1|49 19 October 1935.

74  GCPPT 1|1|50 26 November 1935. The quotation is taken from Erlande's short story of 1929 *Dongiovanninesca* p564.

75  GCPPT 1|1|50 10 February 1936.

76  GCPPT 1|1|47 25 May 1935.

77  GCPPT 1|1|50 16 March 1936.

78  GCPPT 1|1|47 25 May 1935. Aelfrida's reference is to François de Sales' *Introduction à la Vie Dévote*.

79  GCPPT 1|1|48 5 August 1935.

80  GCPPT 1|1|51 22 June 1936.

81  ibid. 12 July 1936.

82  ibid. 13 June 1936.

83  ibid. 16 June 1936 and letter from Father Cary to Aelfrida of the same date (GCPPT 1|1|51a).

84  GCPPT 1|1|51 19 June 1936.

85  ibid. 28 July 1936.

86  GCPPT 1|1|50 27 May 1936.

87  CPPT 1|1|51 6 and 8 August 1936.

88  ibid. 15 and 16 August 1936.

89  ibid. 28 August 1936.

90  GCPPT 1|1|52 10 November 1936.

91  GCPPT 1|1|46 8 February 1935.

92  GCPPT 1|1|52 10 November 1936.

93  GCPPT 1|1|49 23 September 1935. Aelfrida was very fond of Pamela Kermack, giving her bound copies of *Bammie's Book* and *Verses for Alethea* (ibid. 2 September 1935) and dedicating a delightful poem to her entitled *Perplexities about Pamela* (GCPPT 2|13).

94  GCPPT 1|1|47 20 April 1935.

95  Philothea (in French, Philothée) meaning 'she who loves or is loved by God', was ostensibly Louise de Charmoisy, the lady to whom François de Sales addressed his *Introduction à la Vie Dévote,* but actually represents the soul as it aspires to devotion.

96  GCPPT 1|1|47 28 April 1935.
     GCPPT 1|1|52 22 October 1936.

97  GCPPT 1|1|47 28 April 1935.
     GCPPT 1|1|48 24 June 1935.

98  GCPPT 1|1|46 29 November 1934.

99  ibid. 31 January 1935.

100  GCPPT 1|1|44 17 August 1933.

101  GCPPT 1|1|46 17 January 1935.

102  GCPPT 1|1|47 5 April 1935.

103  GCPPT 1|1|48 6 July 1935 ('June' in diary).

104  GCPPT 1|1|47 5 April 1935.

105  GCPPT 1|1|50 3 January 1936.

106  GCPPT 1|1|47 29 May 1935.
      GCPPT 1|1|51 1 August 1936.

107  GCPPT 1|1|49 17 October 1935.
      GCPPT 1|1|50 3 November 1935.

108  ibid. 28 and 29 December 1935.

109  GCPPT 1|1|51 13 July 1936.

110  ibid. 25 June 1936.

111  GCPPT 1|1|49 22 October 1935.

112  GCPPT 1|1|48 16 June 1935.
      GCPPT 1|1|50 7 November and 17 and 19 December 1935.

113  GCPPT 1|1|49 12 September 1935.
      GCPPT 1|1|50 3, 10 and 11 November 1935. 'Brother Ass' was St Francis' name for his body of which, when dying, he begged pardon for having mistreated it because of the hardships he had imposed on it.

114  GCPPT 1|1|47 7 May 1935.

115  GCPPT 1|1|50 24 February, 12 April and 22 May 1936. 'The shivers' was a colloquial terms for a shivering fit; Aelfrida's capitalisation may have been inspired by the Grimm fairy tale *The Boy Who Left Home to Find Out About the Shivers.*
      GCPPT 1|1|51 6 July and 26 September 1936.
      GCPPT 1|1|52 22 October 1936.

116  GCPPT 1|1|51 20 June 1936.

117  GCPPT 1|1|46 25 January and 8 February 1935.

118  GCPPT 1|1|49 12 October 1935.

119  GCPPT 1|1|50 9 and 24 January 1936.

120  GCPPT 1|1|49 14 October 1935.

121  ibid. 25 September 1935.

122  GCPPT 1|1|54 18 January 1938.

123  ibid. 13 February 1938. Vernon Mottram (1882–1976) physiologist and nutritionist, was first known to Aelfrida as the husband of one of her 'goups'. After graduating in Natural Science at Cambridge in 1901, Mottram researched and wrote extensively on food and nutrition. When Aelfrida asked his advice he was Professor of Physiology at King's College for Women in London (See *Who Was Who* Vol. 7 for further details of his life).

124 GCPPT 1|1|59 29 July 1941.

125 For an excellent description of the signs, symptoms and causes of scurvy see http:||www.medscape.com/viewarticle/405856_3

126 GCPPT 1|1|46 16–29 December 1935 (exact date of entry unascertainable as account written retrospectively).

127 GCPPT 1|1|47 17 April 1935.

128 GCPPT 1|1|48 2 June 1935.

129 *The Rule of St Benedict* p 67 (ch xxxix *The Measure of Food*).

130 GCPPT 1|1|46 18 December 1934.

131 GCPPT 1|1|49 11 September 1935.

132 *Corinthians I* 8:8 (KJV).

133 *The Rule of St Benedict* p 67.

134 GCPPT 1|1|49 30 August and 3 September 1935.

135 Tillyard, Ae. *A Little Road-Book for Mystics* pp 29–33. There are interesting parallels here between Aelfrida's ideas on asceticism (especially in relation to food) and Edward Goulburn's *Thoughts on Personal Religion* (1862), a treatise on the Christian life 'in its two chief elements', devotion and practice, in particular his chapters on 'the High Prerogative of Suffering' (pt 3 ch 9 pp 280–293) and 'on Fasting' (pt 2 ch 7, pp 121–123). Edward Goulburn (1818–1897) was an influential English churchman whose sermons as dean of Norwich were read in published form and her pious old age by Aelfrida's maternal grandmother Emma Wetenhall; that they were also read by Aelfrida herself at an impressionable age is evident both from her habit of quoting them and from her tendency to take Goulburn's precepts literally.

136 Giloteaux, P. pp 155–156.

137 GCPPT 1|1|48 11 August 1935.

138 Saudreau, A. pp 183–184, 272–273 and 316–317.

139 GCPPT 1|1|44 8 October 1933.

140 GCPPT 1|1|20 6 March 1915.

141 GCPPT 1|2.

142 *Corinthians I* 9:27 (KJV), quoted by Goulburn, E. p xviii.

143 *The Rule of St Benedict* pp 17 and 79.

144 GCPPT 1|1|58 21 March 1941.

145 *The Rule of St Benedict* p59.

146 GCPPT 1|1|31 27 August 1925.

147 GCPPT 1|1|44 8 October 1933.

148 GCPPT 1|1|48 11 August 1935.

149 Tillyard, Ae. *A Little Road-Book for Mystics* p30.

150 GCPPT 1|1|50 23 February 1936.

151 Bowlby, J. *Loss, Sadness and Depression* p237.

152 GCPPT 1|1|50 14 November 1935.

153 GCPPT 2|62|3 *Nadja Laptchinski*.

154 GCPPT 1|1|47 7 May 1935.

155 GCPPT 1|1|50 13 November 1935.

156 GCPPT 1|1|47 26 April 1935.

157 GCPPT 1|1|49 5 October 1935.

158 ibid. 24 October 1935.

159 GCPPT 1|1|50 16 November 1935.

160 ibid. 30 November 1935.

161 ibid. 6 January 1936.

162 GCPPT 1|1|49 6 September 1935.

163 GCPPT 1|1|47 11 May 1935.

164 GCPPT 1|1|52 7 January 1937.

165 ibid. 12 December 1936.

166 GCPPT 1|1|49 11 September 1935.

167 Tillyard, HJW. *Synopsis of Diaries* (MTC) Entries for 15 and 17 December 1934.

168 GCPPT 1|1|48 1 July 1935.

169 GCPPT 1|1|52 22 October 1936.

170 GCPPT 2|13. *The Eatmore Series*. Apart from their immediate significance one poem is interesting for other reasons also: *Eat More Porridge* refers to evidence given during Aelfrida's divorce (e.g. that she had "just not bothered" with regard to domestic matters) but omitted by her from her diary account because of the unfavourable light in which it shows her.

171 GCPPT 1|1|49 22 and 23 October 1935.

172 GCPPT 1|1|27 3 March 1923 ('1928' in error).

173 GCPPT 1|1|35 11 February 1928.

174 Tillyard, Ae. *"No man hath seen God at any time"*. Sonnet written 4 June 1913 in Cambridge and published in 1916 in *The Garden and the Fire* p 69.

175 Tillyard, Ae. *The Making of a Mystic* p100.

176 GCPPT 1|1|47 7 May 1935.

177 GCPPT 1|1|48 11 July 1935.

178 *The Rule of St Benedict* p18.

179 GCPPT 1|1|46 August 1934.

180 ibid. 18 December 1934.

181 Saudreau, A. p 186.

182 Tillyard, Ae. *Christian Old Age* p 82 (GCPPT 2|17, manuscript version).

183 ibid. p111.

184 GCPPT 1|1|49 2 September 1935.

185 Tillyard, Ae. *Christian Old Age* (GCPPT 2|7, manuscript version).

186 Kingsley, C. *The Water Babies* p51. Kingsley's book was much in Aelfrida's mind at this time as references to Mrs 'Bedonebyasyoudid' and Mrs 'Doasyouwouldbedoneby' show; she even describes Father Cary in terms of the 'Good Fairy' who in various guises guides Tom on his journey to 'cleanliness'.

187 À Kempis, T. p 196.

188 Giloteaux, P. pp 154–155.

189 Mullett, M. pp 80–81.

190 GCPPT 1|1|63 28 July 1945.

191 Tillyard, Ae. *Spiritual Exercises* p 155. Author's emphasis.

# Incipit Vita Nova

When in former and happier days Aelfrida pointed out to Agatha and Alethea 'picturesque little ruins as a good spot to retire to', her daughters responded with teasing, telling her she had no work to retire *from*, so could hardly expect to retire *to* anywhere. Both, however (so she said), 'felt the seriousness of hope that was in [her] unconscious mind' and her surviving daughter was therefore unsurprised when her mother, now in Oxford, announced that she hoped 'gradually to withdraw [further] from the world'[1]: 'the hermit', as she put it, 'to her hermitage'.[2]

The date of Aelfrida's pronouncement is significant: September 1935 found her newly burdened with a daughter and deprived of the possibility of establishing a 'swallow's nest' at Malling. (Deprivation also brought a 'wonderful sense of ... liberation and expectancy' as if turning the page on Malling allowed her to pursue her vocation in 'solitude ... communing with God'[3] or in a community even more 'contemplative'[4], if that were possible, than Malling.) A conversation with one of her Osney Lane neighbours during which Mrs Illingworth commented tartly that 'considering how devout' Aelfrida was, she was 'astonishingly little interested in other people', put the 'hermit' on the defensive – she was, she said, too *much* interested in other people and that was why she needed to be alone – but caused her to reflect that this interest had been 'the chief hindrance to ... complete union with God'.[5] God, she therefore decided, was asking her to found an 'Order of Solitaries' (The Order of the Transfiguration, 'if the name is not already taken')

Tymawr

of which she would be if not its prime mover (ostensibly because she would 'spoil *everything* if I mixed anything of *myself* in my new hopes' but actually because she had no intention of doing anything save join the order once the work of setting it up had been done by someone else, preferably the SSJE), at least its first member.

Inspired by Psalm 84 ("the sparrow hath found an house, and the swallow a nest for herself … even thine altars, O Lord of Hosts")[6] and by recent visions of 'adoring angels' and a huge Cross ('intimations of what the "Solitaries" are to concern themselves with chiefly')[7], Aelfrida sent Father Cary 'a very bare and simple outline'[8] of her (or, rather, the Cowley Fathers') project, only to be told that 'Cowley as Cowley' would not involve itself in the matter. Disappointed but not discouraged, she decided to wait a year before trying again (this would give the SSJE time to look out for other potential 'Solitaries') and to 'tighten up [her] Rule a bit' in the meantime.

Father Cary, however, had not quite finished with her. As part of a move within the Anglo-Catholic hierarchy to regularise existing Communities and advise on new ones, it had been decided that 'hermits are not to be allowed'. (Ladies seeking to emulate Julian of Norwich had created problems of archiepiscopal dimensions, it seems.) In Aelfrida's case, therefore, 'no sort of [official] encouragement could or would be forthcoming' but provided she behaved discreetly 'without labels or outward signs', Cary had no objection to her leading the life to which she felt called.[9] (The Lady Abbess of Malling, to whom she also confided her scheme, was less accommodating; she had *never*, she wrote, wanted Aelfrida to be solitary, a reprimand which left her former oblate speechless: had not the Lady Abbess agreed only three months earlier that 'God intended [her] for a solitary' on hearing of Aelfrida's longing to be 'out of the world'?)[10] Deciding that she did not mind 'if I am not an oblate or a solitary or … any of the things I want to be', she settled for contemplation: 'contemplation suffices me'.[11]

But not for long. Early the following year she decided that although her favourite occupation was 'just being still and communing with God', God Himself required something more of her. What this was she could not discern but thought it might be something to do with her 'hermit-plan'[12] or with a newer 'Brilliant Idea': 'Houses of Prayer' in which men and women who would like to become monks or nuns but were unable to do so could live together, 'serene and silent', without vows or habit but keeping a Rule and offering assistance to the 'sick spiritually' or to the 'indifferent', in places already endowed with '*a living heart* of devotion'.[13]

Discussing her new scheme with Father Cary, Aelfrida was told firmly to stop 'making plans' of this nature.[14] He was equally dismissive of suggestions made by the newly-appointed Superior of St Thomas' that Aelfrida take the three-fold vows of poverty, chastity, and obedience (Mother Cecilia was obviously unaware that Aelfrida's Rule encompassed them already and Aelfrida's response is interesting: though she needed someone 'to order [her] about' and 'there would be no difficulty about Poverty and Chastity', 'what about Obedience?')[15] and that with her 'unusual vocation' to be a 'solitary', ought she not 'to be in a religious Community'.[16] Aelfrida, said Cary firmly, should not be 'mixed up' with *any* Community and having someone ordering her about would interfere with the 'very delicate operations of the Holy Spirit'[17] within her.

Undiscouraged by Cary's advice – she had already decided that what she needed was 'to love humiliations and being ordered about and made to do what I don't like'[18] and was beseeching God to send her someone (preferably a woman) 'to order me about, that I may learn obedience'; Father Cary, she thought, 'can give one's life *direction* but … not insist on details'[19] – Aelfrida decided not to appear 'too eager'[20] and to wait for a 'sign'.[21]

She received three. The first took the form of a personal message from Deity that she was 'to seek more solitude and [her] "swallow's nest"'. (He did not make clear whether the 'nest' was to be 'a here and now reality' or 'one of those eternal habitations', though He advised her that if she saw 'an opportunity to be a solitary and live always near the Blessed Sacrament', to take it.) The second involved a meeting in Cambridge with the priest who had conducted Agatha's Requiem Mass, during which Father Vidler, noting her vocation to silence and that God was obviously calling her to the religious life ('he can't *know* how I long for it') also stated that although she should not seek out 'social occasion[s]'[22], neither should she shun them. The third, however, was the most significant: Eileen Kermack had recently stayed at Tymawr, a 'wee Community somewhere near Monmouth', 'a mixture of St Benedict's and St Jeanne Chantal's [communities, both] … models of their Rule', whose aim 'if they were more numerous' (there were only five professed nuns) was perpetual adoration of the Blessed Sacrament. Hearing this, Aelfrida's heart 'leapt up': 'might there be a place for me there? [In] this remote spot … I might perhaps be a hermit at last!'[23]

Then she began to worry: would her 'pillar of fire and cloud lead [her] thither and then stand still'? Would eagerness to follow it disqualify her because to go there would be an expression of *her* will, not God's? ('For myself, it is the one earthly desire I have … but oh! dear Lord … if it *is* Thy Will that at long last I should be Sister Placida of the Holy Passion… even to be a humble oblate would be a joy unspeakable … I hardly dare pray'.)[24] A request to the Mother Superior of the 'wee Community' asking 'if there *should* be a place for [her] there' evoked the cool response that she was welcome to stay for a few days in September.[25] So to Monmouthshire she went.

'11 September 1936. *Convent of the Holy Cross, Lydart, Mon*. The land is green and wooded and gracious – green hills, valleys with streams and rivers running along them, lovely distances with soft … mists resting on them. The convent stands on a banked up terrace, a large solid grey stone house with a rather austere chapel … built at right angles'. The chapel, she continued, 'is very bare, with a large wooden crucifix just above the high altar on which the Blessed Sacrament is reserved. The floor is bare stone – there are a few chairs – [a] vase of Michaelmas daisies … gave the only touch of colour'. Both chapel and convent, however, gave the impression that Tymawr was 'a dear place, a *house of repose* for Our Lord, a place where He is truly loved'. Overwhelmed with fatigue and emotion, she retired to bed, only to find that the novelty of the experience kept her awake 'practically all night'.[26]

The next day, a day of 'streaming rain' characteristic of Wales, she spent in retreat, keeping silence at meals 'among guests who talk'. (There were four other guests besides herself and a Miss Hilda Harrison, a lady in her late fifties, who presided at meals and 'seems more or less to live here'.)[27] The following day she attended services, explored the surrounding countryside, and met the Mother Superior, 'a most unconventional and fresh and forthcoming woman' of about her own age who had read *The Closer Walk with God*. She also told Aelfrida something of the Community's history[28], informed her that she looked 'very ill' (Aelfrida, in the grip of scurvy and coughing up 'hard blackish stuff', was surprised and dismayed to find that ill-health might prevent her from living at Tymawr '[but] perhaps I shall come here sometimes for my health'), and introduced her to the Convent's Warden, Father Hubert Northcott of the Community of the Resurrection at Mirfield, who was '*very* contemplative' but lacked Father Cary's charismatic manner and appearance.[29] It was on the latter rather than on the Mother Superior (whose answer to Aelfrida's request that she become a tertiary at Tymawr had been firmly 'no') that Aelfrida decided to focus her attention in the hope that a man her guardian angel had obviously arranged for her to meet might be more sympathetic to her coming to live where 'there is perfect peace without the blaze of spiritual light that radiates from a large and fervent Community', where the sisters were 'very earnest and "recollected"', and where she found the 'atmosphere' so congenial[30] that the angel had already advised her to over-winter there to be '*tempered*' into a more perfect instrument of God.[31]

At this point Aelfrida's hopes seemed about to founder in a morass of alasses. Not only did the angel rebuke her by reminding her that at Tymawr she was 'thinking about [herself] and her "reactions" instead of worshipping God' ('ought I to be an oblate of even the humblest community … alas! It is too good for me', was one 'reaction'), a criticism with which she concurred ('I was, alas!')[32], but Father Cary's reaction to her proposal provoked another. Aelfrida had not bothered to consult him prior to departure, partly because she thought he might forbid her to go (his advice would have been to devote herself 'to adoration and prayer' but at the same time to remain 'accessible to people who want you for legitimate reasons')[33] but chiefly because she had not thought to ask him. In fact, the first intimation Father Cary received of her intentions was a letter posted the day of her arrival at Tymawr asking if she '*might*' aspire to become a member of the Community, on which receipt of which he was rightly furious, telling her that if she wished "to hitch your wagon to a nightlight, by all means do so" ('which is not encouragement … is it?' wrote his penitent perceptively) and suggesting that she was free to place herself under someone else's direction because it was clear she had lost her 'illusions' about him and had decided that he was not, spiritually speaking, good enough for her.[34]

Knowing that she would have to face him in person, Aelfrida returned to Oxford in chastened mood: would Cary dismiss her altogether and if he did, would another Father take her on? After confession on 19 September she therefore hastened to abase herself, informing Cary that he alone was her 'spiritual father' and that if he cast her off she would 'never have another one'. Somewhat mollified, Cary replied that what had chiefly angered him was the 'hasty' way she was 'trying to become a tertiary of the SSC' and that he was unhappy at her associating herself with 'a Community of which he knew nothing, with which he was not in touch', and which was 'only just emerging from the experimental stage' and had been 'rather odd and queer until Father Northcott … had taken it in hand'.[35] He did not, however, knowing that whatever he said was likely to be disobeyed, forbid her to make a further visit but told her that during her stay she must follow Father Northcott's advice to the letter, must regard her visit 'as an interlude for discipline' rather than as an opportunity to join the Community, and must act as a 'solitary' and not 'get mixed up with the Convent Life [or] convent affairs'. Lastly, he informed her that he had taught her all he could and that now she need not refer to him so much.[36]

Disregarding Cary's obvious but tactfully phrased dismissal (she had been concerned lest he dismiss her *before* she had a chance to tell him of her plans) because a further sojourn at Tymawr was a fait accompli – she had already consulted Dr Frazer about the desirability of wintering there away from the 'lake-dwelling' that was St Benedict's (Dr Frazer's advice was that she 'might get quite well … if [she] led a healthy life there')[37] and had arranged with the Mother Superior to do so ("I should like", wrote that lady, "to be certain that your Director as well as your doctor approves")[38] – Aelfrida was delighted to see her pillar of fire and cloud moving of its own volition but with a nudge from herself towards Monmouthshire: 'it does look as if [God] wanted me at Tymawr'.[39]

He may have wanted her there – and it can be inferred from Aelfrida's diary that once there, she had no intention of disobeying His orders by leaving – but there were practical matters to deal with first: Alethea to dispatch to South Africa; Anthony Wrightson to be told in "the kind of letter a favourite aunt might have written"[40], together with Julius ("*soror adhuc in monasterio loco Tymawr commoratur*")[41], Eustace (who probably regarded his sister's announcement as no more than another 'Brilliant Idea', abandoned almost as soon as thought of), Mother Cecilia of St Thomas' who 'received the news in the cool sweet equable way in which she receives all news'[42], and her wide circle of correspondents. There was also St Benedict's to sublet, not dispose of, for imminent departure from Oxford was not without anxieties. Would her precarious health stand up to the rigours of convent 'bareness'? (But how infinitely worse if her pillar of fire and cloud had led her 'to a husband' or 'to a school or an office' as 'an opportunity for good works'[43], for one of which she felt no inclination and for the other, even as a means of augmenting her meagre income, no enthusiasm, though this begs two questions: would she have followed it if it *had* led to husband and was her '*attrait*' to the *opus Dei* nothing more than a means of avoiding 'good works' of another kind?) Would she be spiritually able to bear 'the constant presence of God on [her] soul … out among the hills, in the convent, with no relief of lesser interests?'[44] Unless she knew with absolute certainty that 'it was the Will of God' that she go to Tymawr, could she bring herself to leave Oxford where she felt so '*safe*'? ('O fool, Aelfrida, fool, fool, fool!', sentiments occasioned by the devil's visit during which he stated bluntly that "*sensible* people do not mind admitting they have made a mistake".)[45] Worst of all, 'if my Lady Mother sent me away from Malling and if Father Cary has found me a burden, what security have I that God will not shut me out of His Presence?'[46]

This last thought led to questioning '*why* it could be that the most saintly people I know find me

unacceptable'.[47] Was it because she fell so short of 'the ideals to which I would aspire [and the] standards of spirituality whose existence I am just beginning to recognise' (reading Richard Meux Benson's *Instructions on the Religious Life,* 'a stern and terrible book, but … I too would walk that way' inspired the query)[48] that she affected Father Cary 'like a musical instrument that is out of tune?'[49] Or because, as Alethea perspicaciously suggested, that she thought too much and did not pray enough[50], making so many demands on Cary's time and patience by overwhelming him with reiteration of 'peccadilloes' over which she tended 'to hark back and to go over things in my mind' but which would have been better consigned to her diary ('if I write them down I get my release [and] I can go on … towards God unentangled') than paraded relentlessly in front of a priest bored to distraction by them?[51] Was it because she consistently disobeyed instructions (Father Cary's most recent advice had been to raise herself above the temporal, to quiet her emotions, and 'certainly not' to use a discipline)[52] and if so, was it too late to still the 'clamour of selfhood' by removing herself from 'the charms and distractions of Oxford' to a place where she could be subjected to '*proper* obedience' instead of indulging in 'isolated acts of acquiescence and submission'?[53]

Deciding that 'after a time it [was] *weakening* to be constantly applying to one's director for advice' and that it was not too late to be 'called to a vocation of pure praise'[54] in a contemplative Community, Aelfrida prepared to follow the devil's advice with regard to Cary ("you are going away – why not quietly drop him? … you can easily find someone less exacting")[55] by disengaging herself from him as far as possible. She also, in an act of public revenge for Cary's refusal to continue as her spiritual mentor (an act un-perpetrated until she was safely clear of Oxford but planned within days of her departure)[56], published an anonymous article in the SPCK journal *Theology*. She called it *The Spiritual Director.*[57]

It begins by emphasising the importance of distinguishing "between the priest in the capacity of *confessarius* and the priest as spiritual director" and by hoping that its readers do not think "these lines are written [to suggest] that nice kind clergymen … encourage pious elderly ladies to … talk endlessly about themselves" and continues with an exposition of how "the difficult and delicate task of spiritual direction" should be carried out "in the sphere of the supernatural", by whom (a prayerful man with the capacity to stand "in the centre of a penitent's soul"), and to what end: conduction of that soul "along the road which leads to union with God". It then castigates Father Cary's dealings with herself. (He is unnamed but from what we know and by her reference to Eileen Kermack's comment that as a spiritual director Father Cary had no *method* as such but taught by the example of his "life of prayer", he was obviously the object of condemnation.) A spiritual director, she writes, should not act as a psychoanalyst or psychotherapist[58] (i.e. should not "apply the New Psychology"), for psychotherapy is only "a fairly efficient technique of catharsis" ("the Cambridge psychologist", she quotes here is, of course, Dr Bannister), not a way of teaching the "penitent" that "the *real* is the spiritual". Nor should he seek to apply his own "theories or ideas" to his "penitent" (penitents, she adds, are not to be equated with "mystics and contemplatives") but should try instead to discern the movement of the Holy Spirit in the penitent's heart and, once discerning it, stand aside so that the Spirit alone may act therein. Lastly – and here she addresses her anonymous director directly – "you, Father, must recognise that however experienced, however wise, however holy you may be, you cannot know the exact pattern to which God wishes each of your penitents to conform" and if "the aspect of the Christ-life" to which that penitent conforms is different to "your idea of what the Christ-life is", then *tant pis,* Father, here our paths part.

As always with Aelfrida's literary productions it is important to explore the burden of her text in order to ascertain why she expressed the views she did. This is particularly important in the context of the *Theology* article because some of what she wrote with particular reference to a mystic's need for a guiding teacher who, if not a mystic himself, at least possesses in-depth appreciation of mystic practices and experiences (if he does not, he may "paralyse the action of God on such chosen souls") was a tenet she had held for over twenty years; because views expressed here regarding "the New Psychology" are diametrically opposed to those expressed a decade earlier in *Spiritual Exercises*; and because this change of heart tells us something of Aelfrida's real but unexpressed needs in Oxford.

"The up-to-date priest", she writes in *Spiritual Exercises*, "is not too proud to study modern psychology and will supplement his knowledge of ascetic and mystical theology by reading Freud [and] Jung"[59]; why, then, does she criticise Lucius Cary for trying to be her 'soul-doctor' as well as her spiritual mentor? Is this because Cary (who had been under the care of psychotherapists and knew something of their methods) had acted less as spiritual mentor and more as mental therapist? Realising this, does she criticise him for trying to be what he is unqualified to be (something recognisable from her own career as self-styled 'soul-doctor'), imputing the fact that after two years in Oxford she is no better psychologically

(and possibly much worse) to his lack of psychotherapeutic expertise? (A spiritual mentor who told her to walk away from unresolved conflicts and to "leave the past with God"[60] but did nothing to help her resolve problems amenable to psychotherapeutic intervention, was possibly the worst person to guide her at this point in her life.) In all respects, it is interesting to discover that although Aelfrida was then studying the life of Margery Kempe and writing of her that she wished that 'a good doctor … could have helped control [Margery's] excessive susceptibility'[61], she herself made no attempt to find a 'good doctor' of her own, possibly because she did not realise that she *had* a problem but more likely because, recognising that she had, she was afraid of what therapy might reveal of a psyche she preferred to conceal even from herself though happy to analyse those of others: 'the clearest possible case of an Oedipus-complex with jealousy neuroses', written of a seven-year-old boy she barely knew.[62] Or was it because, with Erlande's betrayal in mind, she was reluctant to reveal her deepest secrets to anyone? Or because she thought she knew what was best for her and preferred to work out her own salvation in her own way at her own pace? Whatever the reason, it says much for Lucius Cary's stature as a priest and a gentleman that there was no 'open breach' between himself and her (something, said the devil, best avoided for the sake of both parties but for hers in particular; he also stated that she was 'too sensitive' to be subjected to more of Cary's heavy handling)[63] even after publication of her article in April 1937.

Other than pillars of fire and cloud, a desire to end her relationship with Father Cary, and a pressing need to work out her own salvation, there were several reasons for Aelfrida's precipitate departure from Oxford in November 1936. Some were real, some rationalisations, some explicit, some hinted at, some practical, some spiritual, but all are interesting because of what they reveal of her current state of mind and past and present preoccupations.

Foremost was realisation that having rendered herself very ill in pursuit of reparative adoration, she needed to be with people who would 'pet [her] up a little' on a daily basis. Daisy Allen having proved unreliable, Alethea (while in Oxford) unwilling, and Aelfrida herself reluctant to employ a full-time housekeeper in 'Lady Poverty's bower', it was nevertheless with 'considerable surprise' that she heard her guardian angel ask "Why complain? This is what you asked for … the Fellowship of His Suffering", a remark which left her both 'marvellously serene'[64] at the thought of sharing Christ's dolours and weeping with exhaustion because too fatigued even to eat or drink. Then too, cooking, shopping, and housework had lost their novelty and such chores as she performed ('dinner to get', 'Vimming the bath', 'Ronukking the floors', and so on)[65] took longer time and greater effort to carry out. Osney Lane noise too, took increasing toll on one rendered insomniac by bodily pain ('I never get more than six hours [sleep] and always with interruptions') and who hoped to 'sleep more at Tymawr'.[66]

There was also the future of St Thomas' Convent to consider, for the premature death of Mother Cecilia's predecessor in October 1935 had left the 'poor little Community' of middle-aged or elderly nuns without a Superior.[67] Closure was averted when the convent was adopted by St Mary's Wantage, with a Wantage nun, Sister Cecilia, installed as Mother Superior, but Aelfrida suspected Wantage might disperse the inhabitants of the convent's cottages and guest house and that, this being the case, 'I, too, may be swept away'.[68] Having therefore decided that if forced to leave St Benedict's, she 'would … build [herself] a swallow's nest and try and discipline [herself] to perpetual adoration'[69], she must have been delighted to discover a quiet convent where she could both build and adore and, she believed, be cared and catered for in sickness and in health.

It was not, however, the threat of ejection or the rigours of St Benedict's which suggested that she leave it: she had come to love her little house 'too much' (i.e. as much as she had loved Wetenhall Cottage) and although it would be 'bitterly hard' to go, if God called her, go she would. She had also become as fond of Oxford as she was of Cambridge and of 'things at Oxford … which are not God'[70], a curious remark given her isolated existence until we discover that she was beginning to feel herself 'esteemed', Eileen Kermack having described her to a mutual friend as 'a genuine "holy widow" of unapproachable sanctity'.[71] She must therefore 'leave off noticing' (an impossibility) 'or go where I shall be less considered'[72] (her excuse for leaving Cambridge two years earlier), to live as God wanted her to be: 'isolated', plunged into the 'completest possible … solitude and silence'.[73]

Detachment from "the clash of suffering and pleasure one has in one's relationships to people"[74] was, of course, one of Aelfrida's (ostensible) aims in life. Having decided that Oxford's 'admiration' had 'no place in the devout life', that detachment per se was farcical if one did not (would not or could not?) 'leave off noticing', and that 'war to the death' against 'human consolations' would be 'a dreary business' (her guardian angel, unprompted, said it wasn't dreary, he enjoyed it!)[75] if conducted in a town where people were sweet and kind to her in spite of everything she did to discourage them, she believed that a move to isolated, austere Tymawr would allow her to win it. Her decisions are also interesting in the context

of contemporary diary entries on seemingly other but actually related topics (money and men) in which aspects of 'the world' she was anxious to escape seemed destined to delay her departure.

Financial concerns were chiefly to do with her own income and with Alethea's upkeep in South Africa. The moral difficulty of being simultaneously a landlord and a proponent of Franciscan poverty "carry[ing] neither gold nor silver nor money"[76] could be overcome by considering payment for board and lodging as providing financial support for the Community (Aelfrida is once again coy about costs but from diary hints we can deduce that she paid between £1 and £2 a week at the beginning of her stay and between £2 and £3 later) but plans to make over monies accruing from the rent of Wetenhall Cottage (or even the property itself) to Alethea provoked an outcry from her trustees on the grounds that it would leave her with a very small income indeed and would discourage Alethea from earning her own living. Common sense and a feeling that the latter point constituted a powerful argument persuaded her to make Alethea an allowance of £100 a year and hope 'the requirements of Holy Poverty' would be satisfied thereby[77], an equivocation indeed, given that at the time of her departure for Tymawr, Aelfrida was receiving rents from several tenanted properties in Cambridge and one in Oxford.

Men posed another problem. Two seemed intent on renewing acquaintance, the first reminding her of a sexually-charged escapade, the second of a spiritual friendship which had made too many demands on her to be sustained.

Interesting though it might have been to renew acquaintance with Eric Silvanus when he wrote in March 1936 offering 'sympathy for many sorrows' and asking for details of Constantine's later life, Aelfrida cut him short. Telling him in another re-working of the past to regard Constantine as 'a brilliant but bewildered child' for whom 'the world was too cunning and too strong', she remained 'perfectly reticent' about herself and broke off the correspondence when Eric showed signs of wanting to see her.[78] Juan Mascaró, on the other hand, who wrote to her from Algiers in October 1936 informing her that he had fled the Spanish Civil War and would like to come to England, she helped by proxy by asking Eustace and Frank Stokoe to help him but evinced no desire to meet her amie espirituel again in person.[79] (On an earlier visit to England Juan had arranged to meet Aelfrida in Cambridge but she pleaded ill-health, sending him instead to Dom Savinien Louismet at Buckfast Abbey in the hope that Juan would find 'the peace that he has been seeking all these years'.)[80] Her reluctance to meet Mascaró also suggests that one of her reasons for moving to an all-female environment was that she would be able to exclude the male sex, other than priests and incarnate Christ, from her life and thoughts.

Spiritual detachment from 'human consolations' was one thing; physical detachment from a world she found increasingly unsympathetic quite another. Aelfrida's views on the Jazz Age are already known; she also disliked the way suburbia was spoiling unspoiled English countryside with "£500 specimens of 20th-century architecture"[81] and in which moral values inculcated in her Victorian childhood and Edwardian young womanhood were abandoned in favour of those of the 'lower middle classes' – or lower. There was, too, the deteriorating political situation at home ('wicked, wicked Jew-baiting in the East End')[82] and in Europe ("the next war is likely to come without warning")[83], the rise to power of Hitler and 'Mussolini! (alas!)'[84], and the prospect that 'wars of the future will be between Fascism and Communism'[85], with Russian totalitarianism a particular bugbear. ('Is humanity *utterly incorrigible?*'[86] she asked, an accumulation of bad news having given rise to her question; in 1936 she offered Lenten prayers for countries in which she had once lived though she excluded the United States as, presumably, irredeemably incorrigible.)[87] So where better to escape to than an isolated Welsh convent where 'war news' (in contrast to the Great War of whose impending arrival she had seemed uncaring, Aelfrida now read *The Times* avidly) and even war itself was unlikely to disturb her 'life of prayer', her need to satisfy 'her soul's thirst for God', and her desire to help keep 'certain traditions of saintliness' alive.[88]

'Traditions of saintliness' manifest themselves in different ways and several such ways formed the remaining motives behind her decision to leave Oxford. The hope that acceptance at Tymawr would purge away 'the last drops of bitterness … from [her] thoughts of Malling'[89] – and serve, of course, as a massive snub to the Lady Abbess – and that Tymawr itself might serve as an earthly substitute for 'the fires of purgatory', a place or condition where 'a sinner and a penitent' like herself could be spiritually cleansed ('one *must* be good to stand before God')[90] after purging her own and others' guilt by atoning reparatively and adoringly. (She looked forward to Tymawr 'bravely' as well as 'gently' for she was afraid that without divine assistance she would find the task 'unendurable'.)[91] She also wondered 'if it would take a great deal of courage' to betake herself to prayer in the hope 'that by the intensity of one's worship and consecration something may be accomplished', though if the alternative was 'rushing around trying to set people to rights' as she had formerly done, the opportunity to lead 'an apparently selfish life' at Tymawr was infinitely preferable.[92] (And if Ancifera

Gregory made awkward enquiries as to what her distant relative 'meant to *do* all day' in a remote convent, so be it: 'I couldn't say *pray*, could I?'[93] To which one can only reply: why not?) There was also her growing realisation that God had answered her plea 'that He take away what He will' (albeit with the proviso 'so long as He gives me Himself')[94], for Alethea's departure for South Africa marked the end of an era: everyone Aelfrida loved was now dead, married, or lost to her and she had no hope of descendants (would they have kept her from Tymawr if she had?), the tradition begun by Catherine Castle and passed on to Emma Barrett, to 'Little Katie', and to 'Little Frida' of mothers and daughters strolling along the Cambridge Backs while remembering those who had walked there and dreaming of those to come having been passed on to Alethea but was 'there to end'.[95] And appropriately given that St Benedict's had been 'The Shelf' before Aelfrida renamed it, her having noted years ago with reference to Christ becoming more and more 'the centre of [her] thoughts' that she was reluctant to centre Him there because 'something … of unsatisfied human love' might enter into what should be a purely spiritual relationship and that consecration of oneself to 'God made known by Jesus'[96] implied at worst "an old maid becoming the Bride of Christ because no one else wants to marry her"[97], suggests that she, like elderly babushkas seen crossing and prostrating themselves during Russian Orthodox ceremonies in Odessa[98], was now so bereft of suitable human masculine company that she was forced to kiss the holy icons because she had nothing left to kiss and that 'the thought of a life where one does nothing but worship God'[99] beat on her mind less as vocation than last resort. (It may or not be relevant that three former admirers – Constantine Graham né Michaelides, Charles Stewart Smith, and Albert Erlande – died in 1934 shortly before Aelfrida embarked on eremitic existence.) Lastly, publication of Helen Waddell's *The Desert Fathers* seems to have encouraged her to further acts of dietary asceticism (her habit of giving away bunches of grapes presented by worried friends may have been inspired by what she read there) and to think that life in a 'swallow's nest' created by and for herself (as the desert fathers did their cells) in remote Monmouthshire would enable her to become "perfect in holiness" by sharing their "holy living"[100] in "an atmosphere and conditions in which, with the minimum of distraction [she could] attend to and realise God".[101] So like Charles Foucault, a modern 'desert father', she prepared to move to a "*forsaken*" place "deep in the mountains"[102] and to make Tymawr her Tamanrasset.

A month after having been 'so strangely … relieved of all family responsibilities' by the departure of her last family responsibility to South Africa ('*incipit Vita Nuova*', her guardian angel reminded her at Mass)[103], Aelfrida departed for Tymawr in Eileen Kermack's car. But though joyful 'beyond words', she experienced a sense of foreboding because about to "dedicate [herself] *entirely* to God', a feeling emphasised, it may be, in a character sketch written ostensibly of an Osney Lane neighbour but, as was to happen so often in the future as to suggest that this was Aelfrida's way of describing herself without seeming to for the benefit of future readers of her diary, applying closely to herself as well. Florence Fisher, she wrote, was 'born to rule without having any empire provided for her' and as 'a born mystic' could not understand 'why everyone has not the freedom of the spiritual world in the same way she has': she also had 'dark times of remorse though normally ... feels she did right'. And having been briefly an Anglo–Catholic religious, Florence expressed 'good natured contempt for pious ladies who play at being nuns'. Aelfrida, conversely, deemed Florence 'too delicate, too moody ... [and too] critical' to 'fit in a convent'.[104]

19 November 1936. *Convent of the Sacred Cross*: 'we turned down the lane and through the white gate, up to the convent – and here I am – in haven at last, I wonder? ... if I have *courage*, how joyful I shall be here ... God give me strength'[105]; two days later, in spite of weather so cold that she wore both coat and cape or fog so thick as to confine her indoors, she wrote 'this place has affinities with the Garden of Eden'.[106] She was right, it had, but like Eden, the Convent of the Sacred Cross contained not only the voice of the Lord God but also subtle serpents, temptations, knowledge of good and evil, and a gatekeeping angel by the name of Winifred Donkin.

As Mother Guenvrede, Winifred Donkin had been Mother Superior of the Convent of the Sacred Cross since its establishment at Tymawr. Of Yorkshire extraction, she was born in 1886 in Nova Scotia, the Canadian province to which her father had removed his wife and family a few years earlier. As a farmer's daughter, she was ideally qualified to oversee and partake in the running of the Tymawr demesne: she is described as studying "diet and cows and hens and pigs, estate management, car maintenance, batteries to supply electric light, pumps to fetch water up from the valley and, it seemed, a hundred other things", as well as actively practising "the life of prayer".[107] As head girl of St Katherine's School, Wantage, following the Donkins' return to England in 1898 (her nickname was 'Kruger' because she was 'so managing!!')[108] and following further studies and teacher training at Leeds, private tutoring in England and Argentina, and the founding of a school for evacuee children in 1914, she was admirably qualified to guide members of the Community's 'third order' as well as her own aspiring and professed nuns. As a person she was "a woman of remarkable character, clear vision and strong determination"[109], impatient of contradiction and who did not suffer fools gladly, and though three years younger and an inch or two shorter than Aelfrida, was sufficiently strong-willed not to be intimidated by her and sufficiently careless of her feelings to be absolutely indifferent as to whether Aelfrida liked her or not; that Aelfrida submitted to her authority was enough. As a religious, she won Aelfrida's respect and admiration; as for the rest, a fight was about to begin from which one lady emerged victor of the battles, the other of the war.

As for the nuns, Aelfrida found them 'very ordinary ... people'. Sister Monica, second in seniority, she had already met; now she encountered young Sister Jeanne, elderly and infirm Sister Katherine (one of two founder-sisters of the Society of the Sacred Cross in Cirencester), Sister Hilda with whom she had few dealings then or later, Novice Sheila (a former missionary whose brother was Bishop of Madagascar and knew Ruth Warren) and the convent's two postulants. But 'ordinary' as its members were, Aelfrida was impressed by the intensity of the Community's spiritual life ('its *for-God-ness* is ... unmistakeable') and by the way it offered 'without ostentation in the simplest and humblest way ... *a living sacrifice to the Cross*' infinitely preferable to Malling's 'stately magnificence' or to Fairacres as 'an extension of Father Cary's personality': 'where the human element is ... less, the divine is more *éclatant*', she declared.[110]

Meeting Father Amos, the resident chaplain noted for his spirituality and sense of fun, Aelfrida was critical in private and patronising to his face, describing him as 'rather porcine' in appearance, making sure 'he quite understood ... he was wanted to be a confessor and not a director' (Father Cary, she told him, had 'only taken [her] on as a favour'), and refusing to give him 'unnecessary information'[111] about her Rule or herself. She also found him forgetful, and inaudible in chapel. His only redeeming feature was knowing Cambridge.

Father Amos, it seems, was no fonder of her than she of him. The following month, with Father Cary ordered 'absolute rest and no correspondence till further notice' and she herself worried about getting into 'spiritual muddles'[112] for want of advice, Aelfrida was forced to ask for 'counsel', begging him "please don't spare me". Amos took his revenge, giving her 'what I should vulgarly call a "dressing down"' ending "now go away and don't think so much about yourself". Aelfrida, to put it mildly, was livid – though she also admitted that it would be good to have a confessor 'who will not spare me'[113] – and matters were not improved by Father Amos' subsequent instructions to reduce her time 'alone with God' to not more than two or three minutes a day ('I try and spend the *whole* of my waking hours … in God's Presence, alone with Him', wrote his flabbergasted penitent)[114] and to "polish [her] prayers" instead of starving her body.[115] (Mother Guenvrede knew of Aelfrida's ascetic eating habits from the latter's pleadings for less to eat; it seems her confessor did too.) Following these exchanges and though privately noting how much she missed Father Cary's advice, Aelfrida decided to mend matters with Father Amos by being 'less distant' (*sic*) at confession (less *de haut en bas* is implied but it seems she was also keen that he not think her 'a notable contemplative'[116] of such perfect humility that she no longer required the services of an advisor), a decision made easier by her discovery that Amos had 'a prodigious belief in intercessory prayer'.[117] Hence although she sometimes felt 'as though he were talking to someone else' ('but it doesn't matter, I overhear!'), his 'general advice' was 'excellent' and she noticed 'gradual increase of intimacy with our Lord' ('one … actually comes to live in Him and He to live in [me]') and a 'gradual liberation of the spirit' from 'preoccupation with [her] own states of mind and experience'.[118]

Aware before she left Oxford that life at Tymawr would expose her to greater contact with people, Aelfrida was dismayed to discover how much contact she had – and why. For one thing she was inevitably thrown into the company of Hilda Harrison by reason of their both being resident, Hilda being an unhappy and unsettled person without a home of her own (an adored brother had died and she was not on good terms with her sister) and one of the 'pious ladies' who floated around the shores of the religious life. (Aelfrida had first encountered her at St Raphael's in Torquay.) Hilda also aspired to be a tertiary but was unable to accept the rules of conduct; she also – an eventual cause of her relegation from guest-mistress to paying guest – insisted on leaving the convent every three months because "we get very *narrow* here … we don't see people [so] we need to go away a lot"[119], a belief which Aelfrida found incredible but which she would have done well to regard as relevant to herself as well.

For another, and particularly galling to one who sought solitude and silence and was already aware that she and Hilda would rarely be alone in the convent guest wing, a longer stay demonstrated with just how *many* people (private retreatants, SSC Associates and Tertiaries, maiden or widowed ladies in search of inexpensive holidays in congenial surroundings, clergy and religious on retreat, and group gatherings, the latter, with some of the others, being housed in Woodbine Cottage across the lane from the convent gate) with whom she would

have to consort at mealtimes in the library (the residents' and guests' sitting and dining room) or in chapel. A male visitor was greeted with delight ('of course I cheerfully began to talk to him')[120] or with subtle teasing ('all great fun')[121] in her best Cambridge manner. Female visitors, on the other hand, if not Eileen Kermack ('*enthusiastically* … of the opinion' that Aelfrida had been 'brought to the right place', Father Cary now apparently concurring)[122] or 'animated and delightful' (i.e. cultivated or with Oxford or Cambridge connections) ladies like herself, were treated coolly (she preferred them 'in retreat' so she was not obliged to talk to them)[123] and subjected to savage diary criticism which demonstrated that beneath the 'holy widow' image she cultivated so assiduously, Aelfrida remained as bitchy as ever. (Of a visiting nurse, also a 'psychic' and a 'solitary' with whom she might have had much in common, she wrote – perhaps with reference to herself, for in the same entry she comments on her own 'little pious arrangements and devotional practices' – that although 'a very good and devoted woman', she was 'far too much interested in herself and her own affairs', 'viewy' in the sense of having peculiar ideas, and full of 'pious "little ways"'[124]; another she described as 'convent-struck', and a third as having 'too many views and notions … and she talks a lot and very assertively'.) It is noticeable, however, that the tone of her diary quickly becomes less gloomy as she renews contact with 'the world' as met at Tymawr and much space is devoted to detailed descriptions of people she meets – and, too, to thoughts that perhaps she *had* 'indulged in arrogant spiritual isolation'[125] at St Benedict's and was having to atone for it by leading a less secluded life at Tymawr.

Atonement rapidly assumed practical and physical form. In December 1936 Hilda Harrison was diagnosed with breast cancer and left for Bristol to submit to mastectomy. (Aelfrida, it seems, was less concerned with Hilda's diagnosis than that she herself would be 'entirely and completely alone with silence all day long' during Hilda's absence, convent-imposed silences being 'definitely a strain' already.)[126] Hilda returned on 31 December looking 'as though she had been through a great deal' and was 'installed in elegant invalidism'[127] with a personal nurse and meals in bed, whereupon Aelfrida found herself expected to take Hilda's place as guest-mistress and to undertake domestic duties relevant to the comings and goings of visitors. She had bargained for neither but undertook both as 'a kind of test' set by Mother Guenvrede. In spite of complaints (to her diary) that her hands were 'all over broken chilblains which does not make housework easy'[128] and mild protests (to Mother Guenvrede) that 'something very hard is being asked of me … I went to St Benedict's for solitude and silence because God called me but there was not enough of either so I came here'[129], she carried out assigned tasks enthusiastically, sweeping and polishing like any house-maid, presiding at meals in her best Fordfield manner ('tea is very lively when I talk [but] very little is said … when I don't – or was it, she wondered, that people did not appreciate 'flippant remarks in the Cambridge style'?)[130], and greeting and bidding farewell to 'our' visitors at the top of the steps leading from the drive. But though she performed her duties with good grace ('blessed be holy Obedience … I *am* so glad I obeyed') and was pleased when Mother Guenvrede praised her ("you *are* getting on!") and when she discovered ('Oh wonder! Oh joy!') that such activities aided rather than distracted from rec-ollection, she only passed the test by making a 'game' of it, by enacting the part of an 'I-under-obedience', and by promising herself that as soon as God called her to return to 'my silence'[131], she would obey *Him* even if it meant disobeying the Mother Superior.

At this point Mother Guenvrede made two discover-ies: that Aelfrida was more spiritually advanced than she thought (she knew 'how to pray' and her prayers were 'in tune with the prayers of the Community')[132] and less tractable than she had been led to believe: 'too much of an individualist and too egocentric'.[133] Aelfrida agreed.

The first bone of contention was the degree of silence and solitude to which Aelfrida subjected herself accord-ing to her Rule, she, it seems, seeing no reason to change her mode of life to comply with the convent's. Following Mass at 7.30am at which she spoke to no one because the convent's twelve-hour Greater Silence pertained, she remained silent through breakfast and lunch even when engaged in domestic duties (she communicated by writ-ing or gesture) until four o'clock tea: 'my only talking during the day except on Sundays when I can talk as much as I like'. Nor did she speak to anyone before or after the three Offices for which she attended the chapel (Terce, Vespers, and Compline, the latter only 'if I feel energetic enough'), and her day otherwise consisting of a solitary morning walk, privately reading Lauds, Prime, Sext, None, and *The Times*, writing her diary or letters or the current work in progress (if any), studying 'good books', and prayer. Kneeling on a prie-dieu, she also took one or two half-hour watches alone in chapel ('a great privilege') as her share of the Community's perpetual adoration of the Blessed Sacrament.[134]

Even to one invited to 'long stretches of silence' this regime seemed oppressive, and in order that 'silence may not be heavy and dead', she divided her day into three parts: from Terce to None, *'the silence of penitence and rep-aration'*, 'till after Vespers … *the silence of adoration'*, and for 'the rest of the clock … *the silence of communion'*.[135]

Persuading herself that she loved it, she was gratified to discover that a two-day convent-decreed silence (broken by confession) had not seemed 'trying'. (She broke a second such silence twice, giving as her excuse that she had to treat a visitor's poisoned finger but had already discerned her inability to maintain complete silence without 'distractions'.)[136] But so much self- or con-vent-imposed silence also made her painfully aware of 'the almost crushing sense of God's presence out among the hills and in the chapel' and of 'strange vast spaces' in her soul from which neither silence nor solitude pro-tected her, and even when safely ensconced in room or chapel, experienced 'the loneliness and darkness and still-ness of God taking possession of His own'. [137]

As usual with Aelfrida, any activity undertaken was taken to extremes and solitary silence was no exception. Asking herself if she could keep silent all week (including teatimes) or even all the time except for 'great festivals' in order to quieten her 'still noisy clamour of selfhood'[138], she rejoiced when officially allowed to maintain silence during Holy Week 1937 and on conventual 'No Talking' days. (She also prescribed herself a 'Lenten Rule' which proscribed certain food and drink, flowers in her room, and the reading of letters immediately on delivery, and included the keeping of a 'holy hour' of meditation late at night two days a week and five minutes cruciform posture against the wall daily.)[139] She was nevertheless aware that not talking even when her own or the con-vent's Rule permitted it appeared 'selfish', replying rather defensively when Hilda Harrison (to whom the silent solitary had been reading aloud during the latter's con-valescence!) asked her why she was 'in silence' so much, if being so was an act of penance, and if her 'obvious enjoyment of conversation' was play-acting. Silence, Aelfrida replied, far from being a penance, was both an *'attrait'* and something God required of her[140], an expla-nation repeated to Mother Guenvrede ('it is not that I dislike talking or am in *any* way less interested in people than I used to be; it is just that God *calls* me to silence') when the latter said she thought her 'individualist and … egocentric' guest 'had better behave like everybody else and give up [her] silence Rule' and inquired if Aelfrida wanted to be a 'hermit'. Aware that her actual behaviour hardly tallied with her expressed desire to be closely asso-ciated with the Community, Aelfrida temporised, saying she had never made 'and never intended to make' a vow of absolute Silence but that perhaps when her health improved and if God required it of her, she would 'spend most of [her] time, not *all*, alone with Him'. Privately, however, she was 'appalled' that a Mother Superior might be able to order someone called to Silence to talk to particular people or on 'holidays of obligation' knowing that silence would be the hardest thing for Aelfrida to give up.[141] 'O passio Christi conforta me!' she prayed, feeling in this if no other respect that her 'portion' at Tymawr would be 'nothing but the shadow of the Cross'.[142]

As usual when spiritually elevated or emotionally fraught, she experienced ghostly visitants: the Angel Gabriel, 'with great wings that almost stretched across the chapel' *making ready* for Christmas' in December 1936 ('in a place like this … we should see angels all the time')[143], and a spectral nun (probably Sister Mary, Sister Katherine's co-founder) who walked through the fence surrounding the convent cemetery (the Campo Santo, named by Mother Guenvrede after that at Pisa) rather than through the gate inscribed *Mors Janua Vitae* before vanishing on top of her grave and appearing later in chapel in a place where no-one customarily sat but vanishing when Aelfrida looked more closely. ('I don't quite like being psychic but I can't help it'.)[144] And a young woman also believed by Aelfrida to have passed through the gate of death to eternal life: Agatha. Agatha visited twice, once on Christmas Day 1936, Aelfrida receiving the impression that her dead daughter was 'robuster [and] all glowing with joy [and] much stronger in spirit and personality'[145] (Agatha, she hoped, knew and approved of her mother being at Tymawr for, following a teenage visit with Alethea to Charles Stewart Smith, retired and living in Herefordshire, the girl expressed a wish to live 'on the hills above the Wye Valley')[146], once on Easter Monday 1937 when 'Precious Temu' was begged to 'look after Alethea'.[147]

Alethea arrived at St Cuthbert's in January 1937 after a circuitous journey during which she wrote weekly letters to Aelfrida describing sights seen and things done. (What she did *not* tell her mother was that the South African religious community considered her unsuitable for conventual life because 'too introspective and scrupulous' and because lacking sufficient 'sense of proportion and humour' to be able to withstand the rigours of life dedicated to 'the Three Vows'.)[148] Hearing from Alethea of her warm welcome at St Cuthbert's and of how happy and useful she was there (the information arrived on a postcard of St Francis receiving the stigmata: 'it comes appropriately', noted its recipient), Aelfrida suggested that her daughter stay 'another year'.[149] Her reasons were not entirely altruistic – she was deep in negotiations regarding her own future and would have been inconvenienced had Alethea's natural homesickness persuaded her to return sooner – but when Alethea, with her spiritual director's agreement, cancelled her return passage, was most upset: 'I *know* it is the right thing for both her and me … but I could not help feeling dreadfully desolate … I could only offer the pain to God and tell Him I have no will but His'.[150]

Alethea's decision forced Aelfrida to realise that loneliness experienced when living alone at St Benedict's was nothing compared to the loneliness of life in community at Tymawr. In Oxford, aloneness with the Alone, though interrupted by intrusive human contacts, was essentially controlled by Aelfrida herself but now, deep in the Monmouthshire hills and in spite of pleas to the Mother Superior that she be treated as 'that important Biblical character, the Stranger within the gates' (i.e. as an included and beneficent person able to invoke blessings on the Community)[151], Aelfrida found herself living alongside women whose life in religion took place behind a grille in a parallel universe from which she was excluded: 'they … *live* the religious life – I wander round the edges'. Leaving Mother Guenvrede to wonder whether lack of physical or moral fibre caused her would-be tertiary to announce that she was not 'strong enough' for a 'vocation'[152], Aelfrida found herself lonely in the midst of people.

As at St Benedict's she derived a modicum of companionship from animals (the convent cats, even sheep and cows encountered as she traversed lanes and footpaths) and from chance meetings with local people, to all of whom, forgetting her *attrait* to silence, she talked. She derived still more from her guardian angel and from her copious correspondence even if the news it contained was upsetting. 'Goup' Mrs Ablett, dying of stomach cancer. Anthony Wrightson unwell but recovering after a blood transfusion 'from a Bristol policeman'.[153] Her childhood friend Ruth Schechter now practising 'legitimised adultery' through having left her husband to marry her 'paramour', a term of opprobrium recently added to Aelfrida's repertoire. (She also added Ruth to her list of those for whom she made reparative adoration[154] but does not state if she added the Duke of Windsor whose abdication for the sake of a twice-divorced American she deplored.) The death of Robin Tillyard in a motor accident, Robin who (as Robert) had provided sympathetic support during earlier religious crises and her divorce, whose interest in the supra-natural mirrored her own, who also suffered chronic ill-health, and whose early retirement from active life in 'the world' was precipitated by 'deep depression' brought on by 'overstrain' and resulted in a 'breakdown [from] which he never fully recovered'.[155] But it is obvious from diary entries that it was lonesomeness rather than bad news which weighed more heavily on the 'solitary'.

Loneliness was assuaged by brief visits from Julius, since 1926 Professor of Greek at Cardiff University, whose Welsh home provided welcome proximity to an adored sister and to whom, called to Silence or not, she talked animatedly, but was emphasised by a reminder of her gregarious life as a Universal Aunt. Juan Mascaró, now domiciled in England and currently living at Tintern two miles away, aged thirty-eight and no longer slim but as before 'too sensitive, too responsive, too imaginative, too restless intellectually and spiritually' (a true '*ami espirituel*' still, in this), paid a five-hour visit early in February 1937 to tell her of everything he had felt, thought, done, and experienced since they last met ('I feel as if I had been sitting under a millwheel!') and by his 'warlike' views (he had had friends killed on both sides of the Civil War) to remind her how much spiritual space now lay between herself and him. So Juan was added to the list of those for whom she performed reparative adoration with the wry thought that as a result of his visit she was *obliged* to stay at Tymawr 'even if [she] *hated* being here and longed to go back to the world' in order to make reparation to God Himself for 'insults done to His honour'[156] in the name of nationalism.

Aelfrida's determination to become an SSC tertiary was also less a means of tempering herself or of clarifying and calming her muddled mind than a way of reinstating a family and social network dispersed by death or desertion in order to assuage the 'darkness of loneliness' in which she found herself: 'I hate the feeling of an empty house round me', she noted and though it was of an actual house she wrote, it was metaphorical mansions she had in mind.[157] Reluctant to let 'Alethea or Julius or people' know how utterly 'alone'[158] she felt even when conversing with members of the Community on 'talking days' (she had little contact with postulants and novices), she was delighted when Father Cary, aware that consent to or rejection of her request was immaterial to one who usually disregarded his advice and from whom he had withdrawn his spiritual jurisdiction, informed her in January 1937 that she had his permission to 'offer [herself] as a tertiary'. Without more ado, Aelfrida put her request in writing to Mother Guenvrede.[159]

An interview with the Mother forced Aelfrida to provide a brief – and expurgated – history of spiritual endeavours to date: how she had felt called 'to some form of the religious life'; that she been an oblate at Malling but had not proved 'humble enough' to continue; that she had been a 'hermit' 'under Cowley' in a 'house of prayer' 'under Wantage' (she made no mention of Leiston or of Miss Wrightson's poor opinion of her); that God had finally 'brought [her] to Tymawr'.[160] (She declined, however, to provide more than minimal information about herself and her personal circumstances beyond those already confabulated about her immediate family and omitted all mention of emotionally-charged relationships with men and women and of being 'magickally' directed by Aleister Crowley.) Mother Guenvrede having

provided her with a copy of the SSC Rule 'on which tertiaries base their individual Rule', she experienced joy 'not of the emotions but of the heart and will' ('*incipit vita nuova, alleluia*')[161] and was '*awestruck*' at the way in which everything seemed to be happening according to God's (and her own) plan: 'I feel sufficiently overwhelmed that Father Cary should deign to occupy himself with me but when God, *God* does it – oh I cannot tell you …!'[162] Too happy to sleep and with the marks of the stigmata burning and aching '*there* underneath the skin'[163], she was even more delighted to discover that her 'new life' would be the 'same life [as before] … lifted up to God'[164] and to hear from Passion Sunday until Holy Saturday 1937 Christ call her by name several times ('*Placida of the Holy Passion*', perhaps in answer to her 'want' that 'Our Lord Himself … add "of the Holy Passion" to [her] name'), this seeming to imply 'He *wants* me here'.[165]

Warning herself 'I must be very *watchful*' (whether this was lest she reveal details better left unrevealed or because she feared that promotion to tertiary would create a resurgence of earlier 'faults', namely 'pride, presumption and … stupidity', she does not say), she was brought down to earth by a further interview with Mother Guenvrede to whom she gave a copy of her Rule 'in its present form'[166], for that lady still showed an inordinate propensity to 'poke about in the rubbish heap' of Mrs Graham's past. ("Who are you? How have you lived?" as a fictional Superior asks a fictionalised version of herself[167]: had Mother Guenvrede been enlightened by Father Cary or others concerning Aelfrida's recent "outburst of insanity", the "instability" of her present "mental threshold", and her tendency to become "excited emotionally" in the presence of other people or by ideas she alone regarded as "brilliant"?) She also, aware of Aelfrida's fragile physical health, enquired as to her being able to lead a harder life than she already did, implying distaste for applicants whose illnesses prevented them from living a life of semi-enclosure ("would any sane Superior look at you?") and refused to countenance instruments of discipline other than the instrument of doing what she was told. She may also have warned Aelfrida not to dispose of her "possessions" prematurely lest her stay be "temporary".[168]

Confession to Father Northcott was less of an ordeal (he 'got in touch with me at once … and I with him') but at the interview which followed (an obligation, Mother Guenvrede informed her, prior to acceptance as a tertiary) Aelfrida was subjected to searching questions concerning her 'life, past history and circumstances, disposition and methods of prayer' and informed that preparation for becoming a tertiary would involve being 'treated like a child', that tertiaries were accepted as residents (as Aelfrida hoped and intended to be) only if they were 'the right sort', that her having found Tymawr a happy experience so far 'was no guarantee that [she] should always enjoy it', and that sanctification was carried out by the action of the Holy Spirit 'deep down in our souls and often unknown to ourselves', not by the tertiary herself.[169] Recording Father Northcott's homily without comment, Aelfrida found herself subject to further instruction from Mother Guenvrede 'in the spirit of the Community' (from the peevish tone of her diary entry, it seems Aelfrida felt further instruction unnecessary for one as spiritually advanced as herself) with regard to 'reparation' and the need to give a life (i.e. her own) to save a life. ('So *this* is where I have been brought', she wrote in horror, uncomforted by reassurances that adoration took priority at Tymawr.) She was also to remember that 'visions and consolations' were 'conditioned and made possible by *other people's* prayers'. ('So there! Aelfrida'[170], wrote the snubbed diarist who correctly described her next vision – of her soul as a piece of iron in the forge of the Holy Spirit lifted up and plunged into the furnace of Christ's heart before being taken 'all glowing' to an anvil to be beaten into shape – as a 'gift' from God clarifying the Mother's message.)[171] Mother Guenvrede's final message – that one did not just 'become' a tertiary but must have a 'tertiary vocation' and that the 'vocation of a tertiary' was a much '*humbler*' vocation than it seemed (it did not, for instance, involve becoming 'an inferior kind of choir nun' but electing to become *abjecta* i.e. obscure, humble, demeaned, and powerless) because only in that way '*and no other*' would God be satisfied – was the point with which Aelfrida felt most sympathy, deciding that the tertiary's '*humblest* vocation' was to be hers even if it involved 'rougher and harder work' ('the *opus Dei* of the tertiary') than she had strength to bear.[172]

That she took 'rougher and harder work' to mean merely or chiefly housework or chapel 'work' was her undoing, for having suggested abjection, Mother Guenvrede, on whose 'lovely nature' Aelfrida had commented while begging that lady to call her 'Aelfrida' rather than 'Mrs Graham'[173], 'requested' that Aelfrida give up saying her Office in Latin because the SSC used the English Diurnal. 'Very much taken aback and considerably distressed' but recognising the Mother's 'request' for what it was ('sacrifice as such and obedience as such'), Aelfrida argued (Latin was 'so much more natural to [her]'; she preferred the 'more beautiful originals' to translations etc.)[174] but acquiesced; in private and in defiance, she used Latin. So much, one might say, for the 'promise of obedience' she assured Mother Guenvrede she 'hoped' to make 'as a tertiary'.[175]

Mother Guenvrede, believing that particular battle won, informed Aelfrida that she loved her '*very much*'[176] and allowed her to participate in the ceremonies of Holy Week. The tertiary-elect did so enthusiastically, contributing a crown of thorns plaited from bramble and wild rose to the veiled 'altar of repose' to which the Sacrament was temporarily removed[177] and noting that she wanted 'Our Lord *Himself* to add "of the Holy Passion"' to the 'Placida' still concealed from Mother Guenvrede in spite of that lady's probing. She also experienced two, as she thought, deeply symbolic visions, the first of her soul 'all on fire [rushing] heavenwards where it touched – I hardly dare say God', the second of Christ putting out 'arms of love …to draw me to Him', another sign, she thought, that 'He *wants* me here'.[178]

Christ may have wanted her at Tymawr, others were less enthusiastic. Julius, though 'filled with awe' at his sister's 'new vocation', was dismayed for selfish reasons.[179] Eustace acknowledged 'without a comment' ('that hurt') the news that Aelfrida was to be a tertiary then said he thought her 'genius' was 'evangelical … not contemplative'[180]; that, and because neither he nor Phyllis blessed her new endeavour, hurt too. Alethea, unaware that her mother had 'offered God, if he let me be a tertiary here, to give up all that I care for most', including her daughter and (a lesser consideration) 'being able to write books for Him', was 'doubtful', saying that, tertiary or not, she hoped Christ would take Aelfrida into the wilderness and 'teach' her. (This 'sounded a little *bleak*'; Aelfrida preferred her own version: 'I will go with Thee into the wilderness'.)[181] The devil, who invariably visited 'just [as] I am attempting a step forward', visited twice, once 'ghostly' to say that rather than let her 'build [herself] into a Religious Community', he would carry her off and devour her, once 'pretending to be [her] guardian angel', to say she would 'always be able to sneak a little self-satisfaction for herself' and that he would 'to point out the opportunity'.[182] He was right on both counts; so, on hers, was Alethea. So, on his, was Eustace.

In April 1937 Aelfrida paid a brief visit to St Benedict's during which she renewed acquaintance with 'innumerable dear, dear friends and relations' and revelled in the 'gay and animated' Oxford scene.[183] She also read the chapter on 'Life in Community' in Father RM Benson's *Instructions on the Religious Life* (she described what she found there as 'pretty drastic' and noted that she had 'a *vast* amount … to learn … as a member of the SSC')[184] and had God respond to her request 'with regard to silence': 'Our Lord made it plain to me that my special "portion of labour" within the Community to which He calls me is adoration of Him in *His Silences* and particularly in His Silence on the Cross'.[185] (This did not accord well with a 'sweet letter' from Mother Guenvrede bidding her 'tread the *common* way' as if she were an '*ordinary* postulant'[186], Aelfrida having already expressed surprise that she was expected to undergo a probationary period. It had also never occurred to her that she might be sent away to undergo it elsewhere, the Mother having once said that she expected Aelfrida would stay at Tymawr 'always'.)[187] She was, however, disappointed when, wishing to make 'an *extra thorough*' (*sic*) confession to Father Cary, she discovered he was 'unavailable' (her anonymous but easily attributable article *The Spiritual Director* had appeared in that month's *Theology*)[188], a subsequent and 'rather distressing' letter from him making it clear that she was Father Northcott's responsibility and that Cary had no desire to meet her again. Next day he relented but quoting virtually verbatim from her article, emphasised that he had relinquished his position of spiritual mentor, reminded her that as a tertiary she must obey Mother Guenvrede's orders to the letter and must employ 'the Community instead of self as the unit of reference' ('of course, I agreed'), and warned her that she had 'a long and grim fight' before her. ('I know'.)[189] Nor was Mother Cecilia of St Thomas' more consoling; though 'rejoicing greatly' in Aelfrida's 'hopes of being a tertiary', the Mother warned her that 'Authority' would 'swoop down suddenly with its demands', that its demands might seem irrational but were 'a test', and that of the Triple Vows, '*obedience* is the hardest'.[190]

'To my amusement', wrote Aelfrida on returning to Tymawr in late April 1937, 'I notice that I am expected to conform in various ways now'[191], she having recently agreed with Father Northcott and Mother Guenvrede that '*obedience*' (not silence) was 'the only course at the moment'.[192] (It seems the SSC expected a quid pro quo for altering its Constitution to accommodate her.) She was less amused to discover that Mother Guenvrede had arranged her formal admission as a tertiary for the Feast of Corpus Christi (27 May) as her own special 'offering' on the festival commemorating the institution of the Eucharist, a privilege Aelfrida, seemingly so keen to join the Community, could hardly ask to be deferred for her convenience. (She had intended to await Alethea's return from South Africa before 'fixing myself definitely here' and felt spiritually and physically unready to do so.)[193] It was therefore ironic that both ladies' intentions were thwarted, Aelfrida's by Alethea making it clear in her few letters dealing with 'Things that Matter' as opposed to 'Things in General' (visits undertaken on horseback 'to strange but remarkably polite and hospitable heathen in various places'[194], for example) that she intended to remain in South Africa for as long as it took to work out her salvation, Mother Guenvrede's by a bacterium.

Two ways in which Aelfrida was expected to 'conform' at Tymawr concerned what she ate (or did not eat) and her physical well-being. Scorbutic on arrival, her general health improved with sensible food and regular meals (examining her in Oxford, Dr Frazer found her 'better than ever she expected [her] to be')[195] in spite of taking every opportunity to eat less by pleading a small appetite or that fatigue necessitated retirement supperless to bed or by denying herself nourishing as well as luxury items during Lent. (Butter and Oxo, for example, beef extract being not apparently unconducive to meditation; forgetting that these had constituted her daily diet at St Benedict's, she grumbled that dry bread for breakfast and a hard-boiled egg and cold rice pudding for lunch on Good Friday were 'sufficiently penitential' without having to do her own washing up as well.)[196] She also fasted whenever official or unofficial opportunity arose and was peeved that conformity required of a prospective tertiary included obedience to the monastic Rule 'of eating what is set before [one]' (she was allowed to omit meat) 'and not the simpler food I prefer'. 'The tertiary', she noted sadly, 'has a pain in her inside [from eating] what the others eat' and it would 'save a lot of trouble' if she could undertake extended fasts[197]; unfortunately, 'one's own little pious arrangements and devotional practices' must be subordinated to 'a conventual Rule … kept in the right spirit'.[198]

'Eating what was set before [her]' resulted in violent, painful, bloody diarrhoea and in protracted vomiting (in fact, she had been unwell since returning from St Benedict's) so she was allowed not to have to eat 'something of everything … set before [her]' and to return to her bland restricted diet.[199] 'Careful dieting – fasting mostly' did not, unfortunately, put matters right and she remained in bed with 'horrid pains in [her] innards' and Sister Monica to look after her.[200]

Earlier and minor bouts of ill-health had been treated by Mother Guenvrede and Sister Monica (a former nurse) less than sympathetically ('one isn't spoilt here … when one isn't well')[201], the former scorning 'soft or self-indulgent' people prone to fussing over 'ailments' ('say I to myself, Aelfrida, … as long as you have a hot water bottle you will be thought nothing of *here*')[202], the latter taking her multifarious complaints 'remarkably calmly'.[203] (Tymawr, it seemed, was not to be like the Evelyn Nursing Home, with nuns replacing nurses.) Even her sick-bed conspired against her, being 'a real *plank* bed' with a very hard mattress; requesting firm support for her perennially aching back, Aelfrida had received 'St Laurence's gridiron … a real mortification [and] if it hadn't been for the crucifix on the wall over [it] I must have asked for some alleviation'.[204] Eventually, however, even hard-hearted Mother Guenvrede realised that her would-be resident tertiary was seriously ill (she also complained of fever and a productive cough) and called the doctor. Aelfrida herself diagnosed 'gastric ulcer or catarrh of the stomach' due to 'being hostess here and talking at table when I am used to silent meals … with unsuitable food as a contributory cause'. (She also worried – needlessly for once – that Mother Guenvrede might think 'I am just trying to get my own way'.)[205] The doctor diagnosed 'acute colitis'. Mother Guenvrede stated – much to Aelfrida's relief – that the latter would not be clothed as a tertiary until she recovered. Eileen Kermack being conveniently to hand, Aelfrida had herself driven to Oxford, then by chauffeured car to Cambridge where, the Evelyn being fully booked, she was nursed at the Brunswick Nursing Home under the care of 'Dr Joan'.[206] And there, had it not been for Joan Cooper 'marshalling her forces to do battle against disease'[207], her 'Vita Nuova' and even her life might have ended, for Dr Cooper's 'grimness' concerning her patient's condition and 'uncompromising condemnation' of the lifestyle which caused it was justified: Aelfrida, it seems, 'was all full of streptococci, very unusual and rather serious' and, in pre-antibiotic days, unlikely to recover.[208]

She survived. Exhibiting *belle indifférence* to the severity of her symptoms ('suffering has been added to prayer and *adoration réparatrice* … I am very happy') and even to the possibility of dying ('the streptococci might suddenly turn virulent [but] I will … rejoice in whatever [God] sends me, death or life')[209], she refused Father Vidler's offer of Extreme Unction: she had set her mind on becoming a resident tertiary at Tymawr and had already received confirmation from God Himself that He wanted her there, so had no intention of celebrating her 'heavenly birthday' just yet. (She also, while at the Brunswick, received a message, from Christ: '"*tabitha cumi*", arise, be well'.)[210] Even so, given her as yet imperfectly-cured scurvy, she was fortunate to survive streptococcal septicaemia at this point in her life.

Recovery, as from post-partum haemorrhage, was slow. Discharged from the Brunswick early in June 1937, Aelfrida went first to Foxton Hall, a convalescent home near Cambridge where she declined spiritual healing from the proprietress on the grounds that although Mary Guillemard probably had 'the gift', she herself 'preferred to leave the matter to God'[211], then, her tenants being abroad, to Wetenhall Cottage under Georgina's care, then to – of all unsuitable places – St Benedict's. Her two month stay in and around Cambridge, however, besides providing her with the idyllic experience of being 'lazy and comfortable' in attractive surroundings with a soft bed and 'eatable' food (and of not having to attend Holy Communion early in the morning, 'tired and cold', and fasting)[212], also gave her time to reflect on her future at Tymawr and to consider what to do if prevented by ill-health or other circumstances from returning.

Although, medically speaking, she was soon 'astonishingly better' (she had been virtually force-fed at the Brunswick on the grounds that 'your stomach has got to get *used* … to food again after all those months of starvation')[213], Mother Guenvrede addressing her in letters as "my dear little tertiary-to-be"[214] was indicative of problems to come. Barely convalescent, Aelfrida discovered that she was already expected to 'conform' again and that pressure was being brought to bear to ensure that she did: she must be '*eager* to be well' because ill-health would constitute a barrier between herself and the SSC [215]; plain fare and avoidance of meat would be honoured but food fads would not; she was to 'renounce any say in Alethea's affairs'[216]; she was to realise that even a *resident* tertiary could not rely on her stay at Tymawr being permanent; she was *not* to take reparative adoration to extreme lengths; and 'self-inflicted … pain', being so 'dangerous and unusual', was 'negatived entirely'.[217] And she was not, absolutely not, to try to put 'Brilliant Ideas' into practice: finding Foxton rather unspiritual ('*stolid,* you know – not wicked')[218], she had decided to found a 'House of Prayer' there under SSC auspices in order to have somewhere to live in the event of being unable to return to Tymawr itself, had already involved the local vicar in her scheme, and had begun to sell possessions to raise money for it.

Mother Guenvrede's anger on this last score was devastating. Aelfrida, she wrote, was wholly deficient in 'interior silence', presumptuous in thinking she could found a '"daughter-house" of the SSC', idiotic in believing she was qualified to undertake 'the spiritual care of as many fools as [she could] collect to listen [her]', and in danger of being 'sent away altogether' if she persisted in her attempt. Aelfrida grovelled by post but privately decided not to think 'critical thoughts [of] the dear Mother' because, essentially, it was not Mother Guenvrede's decision that mattered, but God's.[219]

A further missive in which the Mother accused her dear little tertiary-to-be of instability, capriciousness, and of using illness as an excuse to escape the rigours of convent life and asked her where she would like her 'belongings and "comforts"' sent, brought Aelfrida to her senses. ('Comforts' included her hot water bottle and deckchair and a prayer mat fashioned from a small Turkish carpet, the resulting strip being used, tripled, as a kneeler or, extended, as a runner on which to prostrate herself.) Privately noting that Mother Guenvrede's view of her character and motivation was 'not altogether wrong', she hastened to make amends, assuring the Mother that '[she] had never for a moment wavered in [her] determination to live at Tymawr'.[220] Encouraged by a 'spirit talk' with Agatha who told her that, delighted though she was to find her mother at Wetenhall Cottage, 'the hills above the Wye' were where she ought to be[221], and in earnest of good intentions, she then made 'a clean sweep of things' by confessing her sins to priests in Cambridge and Foxton and by destroying 'possessions': 'all my manuscripts [of] novels. Plays, precious books, the whole lot', 'quantities of letters and documents' except for 'two perfectly sane letters of precious Temu's' and a 'mad' one from Constantine on the subject of alcohol, on reading which she thanked God that her former husband's love had 'failed' because had it not, Constantine might have 'infected' her with more 'queerness' than he did, and 'all the daughters' childish drawings and stories that [she] had treasured'[222], anything, in fact, which might contaminate her new life or tempt return to her old one. 'My memories', she wrote, 'are [now] in order, as far as I can make them, … assimilated and built in [and] repented of … and so … the way is *quite* clear'.[223]

Returning to St Benedict's by hired car on 22 July 1937 (she was tired of waiting for connections at intermediate stations and with her Wetenhall Cottage tenants paying a substantial rent, did not feel obliged to practice Holy Poverty to an absurd extent), Aelfrida made several important resolutions. To do only what *God* wanted of her. To practise reparative adoration. To contemplate 'our Lord in His *Silence* upon the Cross'. To 'seek solitude … and love suffering and to rejoice only in what Christ would have rejoiced in and not in anything else'.[224] To 'learn, with the Holy Spirit's help, what "internal silence" meant'. (That it entailed more than merely the 'sinking down of … the "clamour of selfhood"' in favour of having 'all one's being *hushed* while God imparts Himself without images, words or feelings being aroused in the soul'[225], she knew already.) To humble herself 'again and again until I *stay* humble otherwise the dear Community will not be able to assimilate me' and, for the dear Community's sake, to learn 'what "spiritual poverty" means'. ('Utter dependence on God', she later decided.)[226] To root out her '*secret desire to think well of myself*'.[227] To free herself from 'futile activity' by recording only 'spiritual' matters ('not … house cleaning … and so on and so forth!') in what was to be known henceforth as her '*Spiritual Journal*'.[228] She broke them all.

Goodbyes remained to be said, most already spoken in Cambridge, one important one to be said in Oxford, some to be said for the last time. To Wetenhall Cottage, 'mine and not mine', 'now commended to its guardian angel' but with the pleasure of discovering that 'dear godchild' Annette Barron had JOY as her playroom and that SERENITY glowed with her parents' 'human affection'.[229] To Mr Church, 'the "old family retainer" type'.[230] To Eustace, '*much* distressed' to see his sister return to Cambridge so ill. To Phyllis, 'handsome in a garden party frock', and to Veronica, now fifteen, with whom 'the mysterious link' still held.[231] To Julius, who would prefer her to settle at Wetenhall Cottage with 'all [her] pretty things around [her]' so that he could spend his holidays there.[232] To Ancifera Gregory, aghast at the thought of 'the model of all mollycoddlers' practising austerities in a convent.[233] To uncle Frank Tillyard. To the Zender Browns who as usual at any serious juncture unwittingly provided the comic element. To 'Dr Joan' with whom Aelfrida believed she enjoyed a purely 'spiritualised' friendship.[234] To childhood friends Lilian Whitehouse, Dorothea Conybeare, and Lucy Verey, towards whom 'consciousness of losing touch' hurt even though parting from them already constituted 'a kind of "enclosure"'.[235] Even Constantine paid a final farewell: 'shortly before midnight, I woke to the sound of Beethoven's piano sonata Opus 90 most *celestially* played … when I was quite awake the music still continued and lest I should not quite understand, [his] hands, his beautiful hands were visible, playing … I understood that he was close to me and wondered whether I might speak to him or he to me. But it was forbidden … Only I was made aware that *prayers* – Chiara's and Oracle's, Alethea's … Agatha's … [and] my offering of *adoration réparatrice* – were all strands in a cable of love which had [dragged] his soul out of the mire. So now … I have the assurance that all is well with him'.[236]

Aelfrida's (as she thought) last but actually penultimate meeting with Father Cary took place in Oxford on 27 August 1937. It was very brief – 'one little "no"' and his blessing 'and that is Goodbye'[237] – and occurred at the end of a Retreat conducted by him. (At this point Aelfrida recalled something she already knew but had conveniently forgotten: that spiritual mentors, like medical practitioners, corresponded with regard to their penitents/patients and that abnormal or unsuitable behaviour was circumspectly noted and passed on.)[238] Having already informed Aelfrida that if she wished to correspond with him, she could (she did '*indeed*')[239] and that although he did not regard her letters as a burden, he would not necessarily reply to any or all of them[240], Father Cary kept his promise: though he wrote infrequently, guardedly, often belatedly, and never spontaneously, he kept in touch until his death.

Aelfrida's brief stay in Oxford – Mother Guenvrede had issued an ultimatum: she expected Aelfrida 'home' on 9 September or failing that, not at all[241] – was marred by bickering with her tenant at St Benedict's (recorded at length in her supposedly 'spiritual' diary) but blessed by spiritual experiences (recorded more briefly) which enhanced the feeling that her pillar of fire and cloud was truly tending westwards: on 30 July, 'a vision of Our Lord on the Cross' as a reminder to 'seek solitude' but never to '*isolate*' herself [242]; on the Feast of the Transfiguration, a vision at Communion of Christ 'in His shining white garments and [of] a misty gold light [which] enfolded [her] … like spiritual arms', after which she begged God to hide her virtues from her ('because everyone has *some* virtues, of course') and reveal 'only [her] faults'[243]; a 'shewing' during which her guardian angel stated 'in spirit-talk very difficult to transcribe' that she must '*use* each tiny incident of each day and hour and moment … to perfect [her] adjustment to the Spiritual'[244]; while meditating on the Holy Passion, an invitation from the Holy Spirit which 'scorched'[245] her soul to '*enter into* … our Lord's pain as He experienced the sin and suffering of the world'; while adoring the Blessed Sacrament, a vision of 'the Holy Trinity … all three Persons, in Holiness, Life and Serenity'.[246]

'One problem', however, remained: the 'hard life'[247] God and Mother Guenvrede expected her to lead once re-absorbed into the Community. But longing for 'loneliness and …dark and … spiritual pain'[248], for silence, for the opportunity to fulfil God's purpose and, most of all, for 'a quiet place for prayer' where she could be '*at home and safe*'[249], Aelfrida decided no such negative thoughts should 'act as obstacles on [her] Jerusalem way'[250] and made ready to return. A letter from Mother Guenvrede encouraged her: "you will slide into your niche once more but far more easily … because of [enlightenment] given and lessons learnt. How wonderful are His ways". Aelfrida's response was wry: '*so far, so good!*'[251]

# Notes

1  GCPPT 1|1|49 16 September 1935.
2  GCPPT 1|1|50 11 April 1936.
3  GCPPT 1|1|49 11 September 1935.
4  ibid. 7 September 1935.
5  ibid. 25 September 1935. Agnes Illingworth knew whereof she spoke, being the widow and friend of clerics and an active lay missioner. (Whitehead, J. pp 85–86).
6  *Psalm* 84 v3 (KJV).
7  GCPPT 1|1|49 28 September 1935.
8  ibid. 3 October 1935.
9  ibid. 19 October 1935.
10  GCPPT 1|1|48 17 July 1935.
    GCPPT 1|1|49 25 October 1935.
11  GCPPT 1|1|49 1 November 1935.
12  GCPPT 1|1|50 22 March 1936.
13  ibid. 7 February 1936. Aelfrida's idea was not without precedent. Living in Oxford she would have known of John Henry Newman's

Littlemore, a 'house of prayer' founded in an Oxford suburb ninety years earlier. Other possible sources of inspiration are St Etheldreda ('Audrey') who having vowed herself to a life of Holy Virginity, was married against her will but, escaping, founded a 'house of prayer' in AD 673 in the Isle of Ely, and Selina, Countess of Huntingdon (1710–1791) whose South Wales seminary/'house of prayer' was moved in 1792 to Cheshunt, then in 1905 (as Cheshunt College) to Cambridge's Bateman Street to a building in which Aelfrida conducted some of her lectures. More recently (1908) author Florence Converse, of whom Aelfrida knew through one of her 'goups', had published a children's book, *The House of Prayer*, in which she describes how a small chapel deep in woods becomes a little boy's 'house of prayer' with an 'angel-verger' as his guardian.
14  GCPPT 1|1|50 16 May 1936.
    GCPPT 1|1|150a Letter from Father Cary to Aelfrida of 'St Augustine's Day' (27 May) 1936.
15  GCPPT 1|1|50 8 May 1936.
16  ibid. 19 April 1936.
17  ibid. 16 May 1936.
18  ibid. 18 April 1936.
19  ibid. 7 May 1936.
20  ibid. 8 May 1936.
21  ibid. 17 May 1936.
22  GCPPT 1|1|51 30 August 1936. Alec Vidler (1899–1991) was then an Anglo-Catholic Ritualist. He later became a controversial Cambridge theologian.
23  ibid. 19 July and 27 August 1936. St Jeanne de Chantal (1572–1641) founded the Order of the Visitation based on the precepts of her spiritual director St Francis de Sales. For interesting parallels between the lives of Aelfrida Tillyard and St Jeanne de Chantal, see King, U. pp 163–166 and Giloteaux, P. p 237.
24  GCPPT 1|1|51 27 August and 3 September 1936.
25  ibid. 22 July and 24 August 1936.
26  ibid. 11 and 12 September 1936.
27  ibid.
28  The Society of the Sacred Cross was founded in Chichester on 8 December 1914 by the Anglo-Catholic rector of a local church, Ernest Augustus Glover, as a means of encouraging "a disciplined life of prayer and study among [his] parishioners". Over the next four years the Society developed into "a confraternity of the 'hidden life'" with Father Glover as Warden and Chaplain. In 1918 the SSC rented a house in which a small group of women lived in community as "a Body with a definite Rule" but in 1922 "signs of the Contemplative Life" appeared and the SSC divided into three groups, one composed of those who wished to follow that life, the other two of future tertiaries and associates. On 9 February 1923 a House of Prayer, soon to become the Convent of the Sacred Cross, was founded at Tymawr, a large house situated on a south-facing hillside a few miles from Monmouth. The four members then left "home and employment" to establish the new Community in rather primitive conditions in a house which, though it already possessed a small chapel, was surrounded by an extensive curtilage encompassing gardens, meadows, and plantations which the nuns proposed to work themselves with minimal outside assistance. A larger chapel, together with a priest's room and vestry, was added in 1928–29. The new Community's Rule and Constitution were formulated in 1932 at which point it became a fully-fledged contemplative community with Father Glover as its first Warden. The Bishop of Monmouth was appointed as Visitor, the Community thereafter receiving "constant and caring support" from the diocese. (GCPPT 1|1|57a. SSC Summer Newssheet 1959 and *The Tymawr Community*, a pamphlet issued by the present-day Community).
29  GCPPT 1|1|51 13 September 1936. Father Northcott succeeded Father Glover in 1934, it being he who consolidated the Community's Rule and Constitution.

30  ibid. 12 September 1936.

31  GCPPT 1|1|52 13 November 1936.

32  GCPPT 1|1|51 11 September 1936.

33  ibid. 12 September 1936.

34  ibid. 11, 12 and 19 September 1936.

35  ibid. 19 September 1936. Father Cary was a member of an Advisory Council on the relationships between bishops and religious Communities, so knew whereof he spoke. His *Called of God*, published the following year, speaks (pp83–88) of how the Council wished to discourage "the multiplication of small Communities and Societies" chiefly because their "comparative isolation" and the absence of a larger Community from which to draw "strength and vision" often resulted in their placing overmuch emphasis "on matters … of comparatively superficial importance" at the expense of essentials and on the temporal and conditional at the expense of the sacred and eternal. For further details of his dealings with anchoresses and ecstatic stigmatics, see Yelton, M. *Anglican Papalism* pp 98–99 and 113–116.

36  GCPPT 1|1|51 19 September 1936.
    GCPPT 1|1|52 13 November 1936.

37  GCPPT 1|1|51 16 and 26 September 1936.

38  ibid. 18 September 1936.

39  ibid. 16 September 1936.

40  ibid. 3 October 1936.

41  Tillyard, HJW. *Synopsis of Diary* (MTC). Undated entry for period covering October – December 1937.

42  GCPPT 1|1|51 23 September 1936.

43  ibid. 17 September 1936.
    GCPPT 1|1|52 14 November 1936.

44  GCPPT 1|1|51 14 and 21 September 1936.

45  GCPPT 1|1|52 17 November 1936.

46  GCPPT 1|1|51 8 September 1936.

47  ibid.

48  GCPPT 1|1|50 25 March 1936.

49  GCPPT 1|1|66 20 June 1948.

50  GCPPT 1|1|51 3 September 1936.

51  ibid. 15 September and 4 October 1936.

52  ibid. 3 October 1936.

53  ibid. 21 September 1936.

54  ibid. 3 October 1936.

55  GCPPT 1|1|52 17 November 1936.

56  ibid. 25 November 1936.

57  The article appears in *Theology* (vol XXXIV No 202 April 1937 p228–233) by-lined "A Penitent". It owes much to Paulin Giloteaux's exposition of the role and qualifications of spiritual directors as expressed in Part II ch 4 pp 132–137 of *Victim Souls* and Bede Frosts *The Art of Mental Prayer* Pt3 ch4 on the direction of souls, especially pp 212–213.

58  Aelfrida's account differs from Giloteaux's here insofar as the latter regards it as very important that a spiritual director be "first and foremost a psychologist" who will conduct a "spiritual diagnosis" of "the person who desires his counsel and instruction" (Giloteaux, P. pp 132–134) before entering into a spiritually directive relationship with them.

59  Tillyard, Ae. *Spiritual Exercises* pp 4 and 157–158.

60  GCPPT 1|1|50 16 March 1936.

61  GCPPT 1|1|52 6 November 1936. For details of the life of itinerant mystic Margery Kempe and her relationship with Julian of Norwich see King, U. p137. Worth noting in this context is that although Kempe's book is ostensibly the autobiography of a devout peregrinating laywoman, her illiteracy meant that it was dictated to several scribes, some of whom may have had their own agenda for setting it down as they did. Also worth noting are the parallels between Kempe's life and Aelfrida's, especially with regard to both women's numerous supporters ('goups', to Aelfrida), exhibitionist behaviour, emotional need for frequent Holy Communion, spiritual restlessness, and tendency to behave like widowed vowesses even when married.

62  GCPPT 1|1|66 17 May 1948.

63  GCPPT 1|1|52 17 November 1936.

64  GCPPT 1|1|49 18 September 1935.

65  GCPPT 1|1|47 21 May 1935.
    GCPPT 1|1|52 17 October 1936.

66  GCPPT 1|1|52 31 October 1936.

67  GCPPT 1|1|48 7 August 1935.
    GCPPT 1|1|49 10 October 1935.

68  GCPPT 1|1|50 7 February and 21 March 1936.

69  ibid. 8 February 1936.

70  GCPPT 1|1|51 14 September 1936.

71  ibid. 22 July and 2 August 1936.

72  GCPPT 1|1|45 5 February 1934.
    GCPPT 1|1|52 2 August 1936.

73  GCPPT 1|1|51 14 September 1936.

74  Tillyard, Ae. *O Passionate World* p 384 (GCPPT 2|11).

75  GCPPT 1|1|52 25 October 1936.

76  St Francis' call to poverty is taken from *Matthew* 10: 7–10 (KJV).

77  GCPPT 1|1|52 21 July 1936.

78  GCPPT 1|1|50 2, 8 and 15 March 1936.

79  GCPPT 1|1|52 27 October 1936.

80  GCPPT 1|1|44 23 August 1933.

81  GCPPT 1|1|48 Newspaper cutting of Aelfrida's 'NEMO' 1935 letter to the *Oxford Times* stuck in the back of this volume. 'NEMO' suggests that an Osney field be preserved for those who live "in the slums of Oxford" as a beautiful natural area for them to enjoy instead of being used for housing. The letter was written at a time when three million houses were built in Britain during the 1930s, construction peaking the year after Aelfrida's departure from Oxford.

82  GCPPT 1|1|52 19 October 1936

83  *CN* 16 November 1934 quoting Wickham Steed, former editor of *The Times*.

84  GCPPT 1|1|49 19 August 1935.

85  GCPPT 1|1|52 27 October 1936.

86  GCPPT 1|1|49 3 October 1935.

87  GCPPT 1|1|50 26 February 1936.

88  GCPPT 1|1|51 17 September 1936.

89  GCPPT 1|1|52 20 October 1936.

90  ibid. 31 October and 4 November 1936.

91  ibid. 17 October 1936.

92  GCPPT 1|1|48 24 June 1935.

93  GCPPT 1|1|52 4 November 1936. Aelfrida's response is notable insofar as a pamphlet entitled *The Religious Life: Contemplative and Enclosed* written by the Lady Abbess of Malling suggests (pp 9–11) that the response to the question "what do you do all day?" should be "all the day is for a kind of prayer for recollection in the presence of God". Aelfrida's own copy of the pamphlet, annotated "Aelfrida Placida. St Benedict's Oxford" is preserved in Tymawr Convent library (PAM box 443–464. Pamphlet 444).

94  GCPPT 1|1|44 15 October 1933.

95  GCPPT 1|1|65 17 January 1948.

96  GCPPT 1|1|27 2 December 1923.

97  Tillyard, Ae. *A Little Road-Book for Mystics* p59.

98  GCPPT 1|1|14 17 February 1907.

99  GCPPT 1|1|27 10 September 1923.

100  Waddell, H. pp 14 and 80.

101  Underhill, E. *Light of Christ* pp 102–107.

102  Fleming F. p 199.

103  GCPPT 1|1|52 19 October 1936. Aelfrida's guardian angel knew his Dante, 'incipit vita nuova' being a phrase lifted by him from the first paragraph of Dante Aligheri's *La Vita Nuova* of c1292–94. The phrase with the addition of 'hodie' (today) also appears on p 72 of Aelfrida's *Haste to the Wedding* in the form of an encouraging note from 'D.A.' ('Douglas Arlesey'/Dante Aligheri) to 'Cassandra' delivered by the

'fairy fiddler' at a time when the girl, sunk in gloom and deeply in love with her banished suitor, is bemoaning her lot as a "vestal of learning", a career to which she has been dedicated by her father without her consent.

104  ibid. 29 October 1936.

105  ibid. 19 November 1936.

106  ibid. 21 November 1936.

107  For further details of Mother Guenvrede's life see *Gleanings: Extracts from Mother Guenvrede's Writings* (foreword pp vii–viii) in PAM Box 225–272. Pamphlet 230 Tymawr Convent library.

108  GCPPT 1|1|55 6 May 1938. Septimus Kruger (1825-1904), autocratic President of the Transvaal, notoriously pronounced apropos his opponents "this is my country, these are my laws. Those who do not obey my laws can leave my country". *Encyc. Brit.* vol 15 pp 931–932.

109  O'Ferrall, R. *Early Memories of Tymawr* in box file headed *Religious Communities*. Tymawr Convent library. In an unpublished novel *Just Alice* (GCPPT 2|19 pp 260 and 266), Aelfrida's description of 'Miranda Honeyburn' in later life is a thinly veiled portrait of Mother Guenvrede: as 'Lady Heacham', 'Miranda' dresses in black, moves "with dignity and grace", and holds herself "like a lady … accustomed to exercise authority".

110  GCPPT 1|1|52 24 November 1936.

111  ibid. 22 and 27 November 1936. The Rev John Amos joined the community on its move to Tymawr. From 1926 he lived at Michaelgarth, a house built expressly for his use a short distance from the convent. For a more positive appraisal of his character than Aelfrida's, see O'Ferrall, R. *Early Memories of Tymawr.*

112  GCPPT 1|1|52 19 December 1936.

113  ibid. 24 December 1936.

114  ibid. 8 January 1937.

115  ibid. 22 January 1937.

116  ibid. 22 November 1936 and 8 January 1937.

117  ibid. 26 January 1937.

118  ibid. 20 and 21 February 1937.

119  ibid. 8 February 1937.

120  ibid. 13 December 1936.

121  ibid. 11 January 1937.

122  GCPPT 1|1|53 8 March 1937.

123  ibid. 4 April 1937.

124  GCPPT 1|1|52 24 and 25 November and 31 December 1936.

125  ibid. 2 January 1937.

126  ibid. 6 December 1936.

127  ibid. 31 December 1936.

128  ibid. 27 November and 7 December 1936.

129  GCPPT 1|1|53 31 March 1937.

130  GCPPT 1|1|52 31 December 1937.

131  GCPPT 1|1|53 31 March and 2 April 1937.

132  GCPPT 1|1|52 5 January 1937.

133  GCPPT 1|1|53 31 March 1937.

134  GCPPT 1|1|52 19 and 25 November 1936.

135  ibid. 20 November 1936.

136  ibid. 27 November and 3 and 6 December 1936.

137  ibid. 3 December 1936.

138  ibid. 15 December 1936.

139  ibid. 12 February 1937.

140  GCPPT 1|1|53 3 and 28 March 1937.

141  ibid. 2 January and 31 March 1937.

142  GCPPT 1|1|52 31 December 1936.

143  ibid. 9 December 1936.

144  ibid. 26 December 1936 and 17 February 1937.

145  GCPPT 1|1|52 25 December 1936.

146  ibid. 7 January 1937.

147  GCPPT 1|1|53 29 March 1937.

148  ibid. 20 March 1937.

149  ibid. 1 and 2 February 1937.

150  ibid. 2 and 17 March 1937.

151  GCPPT 1|1|52 7 December 1937.

152  GCPPT 1|1|53 25 and 31 March 1937.

153  ibid. 3 and 4 March 1937.

154  ibid. 7 February and 17 March 1937.

155  ibid. 15 January 1937. The announcement in *The Times* of Robin Tillyard's death on 13 January 1937 was preserved by Aelfrida in the current volume of her diary; a faded patch on the entry quoted marks the place. Robin Tillyard's breakdown occurred very publicly at an international conference in 1933, forcing his retirement in February 1934. Aelfrida later hints that Robin's interest in Spiritualism may have contributed to his breakdown. (*The Glory of the West* pp 300–304 GCPPT 2|16|1). His death, however, was not (as she also hints) suicide, but attributable to the driver of the car in which he was a passenger losing control in bad weather.

156  GCPPT 1|1|52 8 and 9 February 1937.
    GCPPT 1|1|53 24 February and 17 March 1937.

157  GCPPT 1|1|67 19 April 1950.

158  GCPPT 6 December 1936.

159  ibid. 20 January 1937.

160  ibid. 21 January 1937.

161  GCPPT 1|1|52 27 January 1937.

162  ibid. 21 January 1937.

163  ibid. 22 January 1937.

164  ibid. 27 January 1937.

165  GCPPT 1|1|53 14, 23, 24 and 27 March 1937.

166  GCPPT 1|1|52 24 November 1936 and 21 and 27 January 1937.

167  Tillyard, Ae. *The Centaur* pp 302–304 (GCPPT 2|2|1).

168  ibid. pp 302–307.

169  GCPPT 1|1|52 2 February 1937.

170  ibid. 1, 3 and 6 February 1937. Author's emphasis.

171  GCPPT 1|1|53 8 March 1937.

172  ibid. 13 and 14 March 1937.

173  GCPPT 1|1|52 15 February 1937.

174  GCCPT 1|1|53 14 March 1937.

175  ibid. 31 March 1937.

176  ibid. 22 March 1937.

177  The 'altar of repose', erected when the main altar was stripped in preparation for Good Friday, customarily stood against the north wall of the chapel. A previously consecrated Host (there was no Mass on Good Friday itself) was placed in a pyx and in or on the 'altar', itself covered with a linen pall and with candles burning in front of it. The Host was removed early on Easter Sunday and the main altar restored; the 'altar of repose' might remain longer. Aelfrida's wreath was appropriate for an 'altar' alternatively known as a 'sepulchre' or 'altar hearse'.

178  ibid. 24, 25, and 27 March 1937.

179  GCPPT 1|1|52 6 February 1931.

180  GCPPT 1|1|53 23 February and 4 March 1937.

181  ibid. 2 and 12 March 1937.

182  GCPPT 1|1|52 31 January 1937.
    GCPPT 1|1|53 3 April 1937.

183  ibid. 7 and 18 April 1937.

184  ibid. 17 April 1937. Some of RM Benson's comments on the Religious Life must have seemed 'drastic' indeed to one as centred on selfhood as Aelfrida: that obedience is a "living power" not just avoidance of disobedience; that "head knowledge" of that life is in no way equivalent to "inspired knowledge" deriving from obedience to the "infused gift" of an "exercised vocation" (*Instructions on the Religious Life* p 9); that a religious "must not merely have the uniform of poverty but the heart of poverty" (ibid. p 24); that setting aside the world or being set aside by it does not necessarily mean that "God … takes us up" (ibid. p 25).

185  GCPPT 1 | 1 | 53 19 April 1937. The paragraph quoted is emphasised in Aelfrida's diary by a double vertical hatchment.

186  ibid.

187  ibid. 29 March and 6 April 1937.

188  ibid. 9 and 10 April 1937.

189  ibid. 23 and 24 April 1937.

190  ibid. 7 and 27 April 1937.

191  ibid. 29 April 1937.

192  ibid. 1 May 1937.

193  ibid. 9 and 18 May 1937.

194  ibid. 21 April 1937.

195  ibid. 12 April 1937.

196  ibid. 27 March 1937.

197  ibid. 27 and 29 April 1937.

198  GCPPT 1 | 1 | 52 24 November 1936.

199  GCPPT 1 | 1 | 53 6 and 9 May 1937.

200  GCPPT 1 | 1 | 52 18 January 1937.
    GCPPT 1 | 1 | 53 10 and 12 May 937.

201  GCPPT 1 | 1 | 53 13 March 1937.

202  ibid. 1 March 1937.

203  ibid. 19 March 1937.

204  GCPPT 1 | 1 | 52 19 November 1936.
    GCPPT 1 | 1 | 53 13 March 1937.

205  GCPPT 1 | 1 | 53 13 and 16 May 1937.

206  ibid. 22 May 1937. The Brunswick Nursing Home overlooked Midsummer Common, a view familiar to 'Little Katie' Wetenhall from her childhood in Maid's Causeway. Its matron and proprietress, Jane Emerson Jones, was a friend of Joan Cooper's and it was Nurse Emerson Jones' 'absolutely uncritical "doormat" devotion' to her friend which provided a reason for Aelfrida breaking off her own intense friendship with 'Dr Joan' lest she too join the 'cult of her divinity' (GCPPT 1 | 1 | 43 9 March 1933).

207  GCPPT 1 | 1 | 53 23 and 28 May 1937.

208  ibid. 22, 29 and 30 May 1937. An undated poem entitled *A Stir at the Evelyn* probably refers in its punning last lines to Aelfrida's illness: "Take heart. Not lost are those/ Kept by a valiant Cooper from the bier!" (GCPPT 2 | 19). It is possible that Aelfrida was treated with sulphonamides, newly developed in 1935, and used specifically for the treatment of infections by the coccal group of bacteria, and that with their help Dr Cooper and Deity effected a rapid and seemingly miraculous cure.

209  GCPPT 1 | 1 | 53 30 May 1937.

210  ibid. 8 June 1937.

211  ibid. 18 June 1937.

212  ibid. 16 June 1937.

213  ibid. 23 May 1937.

214  ibid. 25 May 1937.

215  ibid. 18 June 1937.

216  ibid. 16 June 1937.

217  ibid. 18 June 1937.

218  ibid. 19 June 1937.

219  ibid. 6 July 1937.

220  ibid. 9 July 1937. The description of Aelfrida's prayer mat is taken from *Just Alice* p326 (GCPPT 2 | 19).

221  ibid. 12 July 1937. 12 July was Agatha's birthday: her revenant appearance occurred the previous evening.

222  ibid. 4 July 1937. 'All' did not, of course, mean *all,* as material preserved in Girton College archive and elsewhere demonstrates. Agatha's and Constantine's letters appear to have been destroyed later.

223  ibid. 8 June 1937. It was in the mystic tradition to destroy by burning an account of one's life to date written (usually) at one's spiritual director's request, as earnest that one had put one's past life behind one.

224  GCPPT 1 | 1 | 54 27 July 1937.

225  ibid. 27 and 28 July 1937.

226  ibid. 1, 2 and 26 August 1937.

227  ibid. 6 August 1937.

228  GCPPT 1 | 1 | 53 27 July 1931.
    GCPPT 1 | 1 | 54 16 August 1937. Following abolition of auricular confession at the Reformation, many Puritans kept 'spiritual diaries' as a substitute. Aelfrida, of course, attended confession *and* kept a diary but seems to have confessed more to her diary and in alternative, fictionalised accounts than to any human confessor save unpriested Albert Erlande. And, possibly, Aleister Crowley.

229  GCPPT 1 | 1 | 53 29 June and 22 July 1937.

230  ibid. 22 May 1937.

231  ibid. 22 and 28 May 1937.

232  ibid. 14 July 1937.

233  ibid. 6 July 1937.

234  ibid. 3 July 1937.

235  GCPPT 1 | 1 | 54 5 August 1937.

236  ibid. 23 August 1937.

237  ibid. 27 August 1937.

238  ibid. 8 August 1937.

239  ibid. 31 July 1937.

240  GCPPT 1 | 1 | 53 24 April 1937.

241  GCPPT 1 | 1 | 54 17 August 1937.

242  ibid. 31 July 1937.

243  ibid. 6 August 1937.

244  ibid. 17 August 1937.

245  ibid. 19 August 1937.

246  ibid. 30 August 1937.

247  GCPPT 1 | 1 | 53 8 June 1937.

248  ibid. 10 June 1937.

249  GCPPT 1 | 1 | 53 9 July 1937.

250  GCPPT 1 | 1 | 54 17 August 1937.

251  ibid. 3 September 1937.

# Sister Placida

'9 September 1937 *Convent of the Sacred Cross*. God has brought me back here as He promised He would. It is almost exactly a year since I was first led hither … I remember how strange I felt and yet how God made His Will plain to me and saw that this was my spiritual home … And now there is a place for me – *what* place I do not yet know .

The Mother says "great changes are pending in the Community"'.[1] The Mother was right.

*Book of Acts* 1937 "On Sunday October 31 at Vespers of the Eve of All Saints Aelfrida Graham was admitted as Tertiary Sister Placida".[2]

'Ten years ago today', wrote Aelfrida in October 1947, 'I was admitted a tertiary … I suppose that on that memorable evening I hoped to be raised to great heights of sanctity'.[3]

Great heights or not – and in view of what was to follow, probably not – she underwent the ceremony in a soberer frame of mind than that of 'the "flight of the soul" along a pathway of light … experienced when … made an oblate'. Feeling instead 'the burning up of the natural in the sublime fire of the spiritual [and] the slow infiltration of the Holy Spirit into [her] spirit'[4] (in chapel the previous day she received a premonitory vision of 'God, Father, Son and Holy Spirit' during which she 'chose and entered into that which is spirit'[5] but from whose dazzling glory she had to avert her eyes), she seems to have gone through it "with the rather sad dignity that came to [her] help on formal occasions"[6], Mother Guenvrede on her right and her guardian angel on her left. ('*Almost* visible, I could feel him clearly'.) She emerged from the chapel wearing a veil 'of a blue like the sky at night with [a] white [Jerusalem] cross to come on one's forehead'[7] and resolved to 'give up any status that Mrs Graham had and [to] become something much humbler. *Elegi abjecta esse*'.[8] Celebrations followed: a 'festive jelly' made by Sister Sheila, verbal encouragement of her 'very clear vocation' from Sister Monica, notes and flowers from all making her room a 'kind of *Benedicite*' – and a reprimand from the Mother who, noted by Aelfrida to be looking 'anxious' before the ceremony, quashed her new tertiary's first bid for independence (during the ceremony Sister Placida had also received a 'command … to

**Mina and Constance Tillyard with Sister Placida, Tymawr c1940**

seek more solitude and silence') by insisting she take tea with Father and Mrs Amos at Michaelgarth because 'it is part of our cross … to put aside, at times, our extreme wish to be alone with God'. Recognising that she had lost the battle between her own 'call to solitude' and the Mother's prerequisite of 'holy obedience', Aelfrida noted 'well, well. If I go on quietly I daresay opposites will be synthesised after the manner of the Hegelian dialectic'.[9] Synthesis, however, was not to be achieved without a struggle, for Mother Guenvrede's thesis on how a resident tertiary should comport herself was the antithesis of Placida's.

Within days of the latter's return to Tymawr, Mother Guenvrede and Sister Placida met to discuss what was expected of her: she could keep her 'silence rule' provided it was maintained unobtrusively, not as an ostentatious 'pious practice'. She could have supper in her room to enable her to enjoy 'perfect quiet and solitude' from 4.30 pm one day until 8.30 am the next but other meals were to be taken in company and she was to talk on Sundays.

She was to remember that the duty of a contemplative was to keep open channels of communication between God and humanity even if 'ignored and un-thanked' and she was to behave in a 'recollected' manner '*all the time*'.[10] She was also to remember that she was 'a *beginner* in spiritual things', to 'think and pray before I speak or write' (a point also emphasised by her guardian angel)[11], to avoid 'drastic remedies' in favour of 'quiet yielding of myself to the action of the Holy Spirit and the keeping of my Rule'[12], that the elevated mood experienced early in tertiary life would fade leaving her 'to go on and on by endurance', and that 'people who … have an intense *desire* for the religious life usually have no vocation'.[13] There were also the matters of obedience ("[tertiaries] don't do as they like, they do as they are told"), of "penances" for misdemeanours, and of making herself "useful about the place" ("visitors are apt to imagine that … angels do all the work and [we] spend [our] time going into raptures. I assure you this is not … the case")[14] in order to support the Community and because "full occupation of time" gave "as little opportunity … as possible … for the devil".[15] Her '*duties*' were to consist of gardening, "ordinary office work"[16], plain sewing, translation from the Latin of texts such as "the Benedictine or Monastic Night Office"[17] for use in the convent chapel (a long term project of Mother Guenvrede's) and, as befitted the author of books on religious themes, writing, 'an intrinsic part of the Community's vocation' but 'perforce neglected' to date.[18] Finally, following interviews with Fathers Northcott and Amos who assured her that the SSC was happy to accept her as a tertiary *provided* her health held up and that she did not deliberately draw attention to herself in any way or allow 'misunderstandings' to occur[19], she was informed that she was to be known 'as Sister Placida *here* but still Mrs Graham to the world' and was to be treated as a probationer-tertiary (her veil was that of a novice) 'for the regulation period of three years', the minimum time required for 'letting the "clamour of selfhood" die down'. Of which clamour, said Mother Guenvrede, Sister Placida had 'alas, more than [her] share'.[20]

Aelfrida's initial response was as anticipated: humbled 'and yet … joyful' at the prospect of diminished selfhood[21]; anxious not to be 'amusing and entertaining'[22] for the sake of (or at the expense of) other people but keen to be 'obedient and entirely reasonable'[23] in her dealings with them; resolved to be watchful of her health in order not to be a burden, with the escape clause 'even if [God] does not give me the health to live the life here'[24], following which, and immediately after the interview with Father Northcott at which her health was discussed, she retired to bed with a cold; keen to 'write as I *ought* to' so that she might contribute something

worthy of the Community's acceptance of her[25] – she would have preferred the position of librarian as her 'Community job' but settled for scribe; agreeable that *complete* silence was 'not sensible at all' because she might 'mope'[26]; philosophical ('well, I must take what God sends and be thankful') on receiving the Mother's warning that 'spiritual life becomes arid after the early days'; impatient ('yes, of course, I know that') on hearing the Mother's views on religious vocations; determined to 'go on and on by endurance'.[27] Inwardly, however, she was horrified: 'I am only just beginning very dimly to realise the implications [and] it is more solemnising than words can tell. Unless I were absolutely convinced that I am called of God and that I *dare* not draw back I could not presume to go on'.[28]

She should have known, for she did not lack prior information. Had not 'dear old Thomas' à Kempis warned her that "it is not easy to live in a Religious Community and remain without fault … The habit … [by itself is] of small significance: it is the transformation of one's way of life and the complete mortification of one's passions that make a true Religious … nor can any remain long at peace who does not strive to be at least a servant of all. You have come to serve here, not to rule [and] no one can remain here unless he is ready to humble himself with all his heart"[29], and another, more recent, Thomas (Thomas Thellusson Carter) that as a novice-tertiary she was entering her new life with all the faults "to which she has become liable" and that though there had been a "momentous change in her circumstances", her "tendencies and dispositions" were unchanged except insofar as they now assumed "a religious aspect".[30] ("Living in Community", said a later Mother Superior of the SSC on reading an earlier draft of this chapter, "it is *impossible* to conceal one's defects of character".) But – and her wistfulness at being greeted calmly and quietly on her recent return to Tymawr instead of with the acclaim due to 'people in [her] position'[31] (a convalescent prodigal, a 'clever [lady] who [writes books]'[32], an erstwhile oblate of a larger and better known Community) should have warned her – it seems she had not properly considered that in subjecting herself (at her own request) to conventual 'tempering', she would be "under … immediate control, subject to a constant minute discipline [and] liable to be called to account at any moment for the slightest breach of rule or lack of observance" ("the very purpose and condition of a novitiate") and expected to play an active role in "the exercise of self-denial".[33]

There was also some doubt concerning her role in the Community. Though now accorded the privilege of being seated next to the novices in chapel, a position Placida regarded as insufficiently abject[34], she was not, veil notwithstanding, to be regarded as a nun at any stage of a nun's life as a religious. Then again, and apart from initial instruction, she seems to have been left to find her own way (Mother Guenvrede seems not to have fully formulated the role of *resident* tertiary and was feeling her way as much as Aelfrida was hers) as a member of but not *of* the Community (she was never invited beyond the grille, for example, as foundation tertiaries were) in a parallel universe she did not fully understand until transgression brought reprimand in its train and made it seem as if Mother Guenvrede exercised 'arbitrary authority for the sake of power'[35] instead of sustaining her tertiary's faltering footsteps by positive reinforcement and instruction. (Sometimes, it appears, the Mother did exceed her brief as, for example, when she forbade Tertiary Placida to eat between meals; Aelfrida, desperate to restore her health – and particularly her eyesight – by following Professor Mottram's dietary advice, responded by secreting food in her room and brewing extra drinks on a paraffin stove.) Matters were further complicated by Mother Guenvrede putting Placida '*under obedience* not to speak to [her] without asking permission first' (and by imposing the public penance of begging her pardon if she forgot)[36], a practice which led to the exchange of numerous letters, copies or the originals of some being preserved by Aelfrida in her diaries, and to misunderstandings which might have been readily solved had the Mother been more forthcoming and more approachable. Only to Sister Jeanne did Aelfrida feel she could turn 'when much was cold and strange'[37], but Jeanne, twenty-five years her junior, was regarded more as a daughter than a confidante and advisor. With Sisters closer to her own age she felt little rapport and, too proud to ask for help, made her way alone.

Placida, on the other hand, had not allied herself with the SSC solely to embrace the Threefold Vows or because she wanted 'to love humiliations and being … made to do what I don't like'[38] or because she needed 'someone to order me about'.[39] She had allied herself because she realised that her disordered personality and inability to look after herself properly required that she live in a structured, peaceful environment within which she could commune with God at a time and in a place of her own choosing (liberty to absent herself physically or spiritually was an essential aspect of her life as a mystic) while enjoying the material benefits of life in a 'family' setting offering both emotional and intellectual support and the removal of physical burdens of existence: Fordfield, as it might be, recreated at Tymawr.

The most problematic aspect of her 'new life' lay in its innate selfishness, and just as Aelfrida had actively or passively manipulated the routines and inhabitants of

Fordfield until she achieved (as far as possible) the life *she* wished to lead, so Placida sought to establish the life she wished to lead in a Community headed by another 'mother', Mother Guenvrede. In doing so, as in other respects, she paid only lip-service to St Benedict, likening herself to a cenobite living in community with all that that implies of input into the Community as well as support from it, while more and more removing herself from the Community in spirit and in fact in order to live as the 'hermit' or 'anchoress' she had tried (and failed) to be in Oxford. She even, as further readings of St Benedict's Rule should have reminded her (she was so familiar with it as to be able to use it as ammunition against Mother Guenvrede), acted more and more like men and women particularly abhorred by Benedict himself: "Sarabaites" who "shut themselves up in their own sheepfold … and whose law consists in yielding to their desires: what they like or choose they call holy and they reckon illicit whatever displeases them" or Wanderers, "never stable throughout their whole lives but … always roving and never settling … receiving hospitality in the monastic cells of others [and] following their own wills"[40], or, as she herself put it, 'I *know* I should be impossible as a member of a Community … I am far too independent and self-willed and undisciplined … I am much more fit to act on my own'.[41] And so she was, and if her 'dear Sisters in Christ' initially found her 'quiet in house and in chapel'[42], it shows just how devious and how good an actress Aelfrida was and how easily her 'dear Sisters' (Mother Guenvrede usually excepted) were hoodwinked: as soon as she was admitted as a tertiary and as unobtrusively but as firmly as possible (her course, she wrote was 'quite clear and plain and simple')[43], Placida devised ways and means of satisfying her personal requirements.

The most vital thing was to win over Mother Guenvrede, for at this stage in their relationship Aelfrida was unsure if lack of synthesis between herself and the Mother was due to the clash of two strong personalities or to the latter's efforts to perfect and discipline an errant 'child of God'. As self-styled 'child of God', Aelfrida like to think of herself as humbly walking with Him as a small child walks holding his father's hand[44] but her motives here, as elsewhere, were mixed: children, whether 'of God' or not, have much to learn, and when young and ignorant ('*beginners*') are not held responsible for their actions and the consequences thereof but when older must expect to be disciplined for deliberate infractions and praised and rewarded when they behave well. So Aelfrida was careful to behave well ('I grubbed up ground elder … instead of enjoying my usual walk')[45] and to be seen to behave well by working on the kitchen garden overlooked by the nuns' quarters (she preferred Woodbine Cottage in whose more isolated garden one whose childhood ambition was to be a 'lady gardener' weeded, pruned, and planted in perfect solitude and silence) and by assiduous attendance at Holy Communion (she recorded in her diary and recounted to Mother Guenvrede the number of weeks uninterruptedly attended) and 'the rest of the *opus Dei*'.[46] Hence although she noted as early as 1938 that 'love of the "pat on the back" is ... far weaker than it used to be'[47], it is obvious from the manner in which she behaved like a small child trying to attract its mother's attention, that frequent pats on the back were what she required and that if she failed to attract Mother Guenvrede's attention by behaving well, she drew it by behaving badly, reprimand being better than being ignored because it provided reassurance that the Mother continued to 'notice' her. She even went so far as to consciously elide Mother Guenvrede with her own dead mother, writing on Mothering Sunday 1938 that not only had she received a posy ('I also being a mother!') from Mother Guenvrede in return for a posy and a copy of *Concrete,* but also that she had done well 'in the matter of parents' by having had *three* mothers: 'Chiara, the Lady Abbess, and my Mother here'.[48]

Reprimands, however, were not always as unjustified as perhaps Placida believed. Although Aelfrida tried hard to be 'recollected' ('sleepless' hours[49] on her planked bed were supposed to help but manifestly did not), outbursts of enthusiasm (for a prolific crop of mushrooms, for example, during which 'fungi ceased to be mere food supply [and] became an object of scientific investigation'[50]) or 'Brilliant Ideas' (to turn a derelict mill fed by the same stream that watered Tymawr into a wayside shrine) or even 'an instant of absolute panic'[51] on smelling smoke in the middle of the night after which she broke the Greater Silence by raising the alarm (the sisters were fumigating the death-chamber of recently-deceased Sister Katherine but had not thought to warn residents that smell and smoke might percolate into the guest-house), were met with severity on the Mother's part (tempered with a spice of humour, though that was soon to change) and by grovelling apologies on Aelfrida's. Hence statements such as '*renunciation* has got to be more complete than I had understood'[52] (apropos mushrooms); 'God ... help me never to look at *anything* that lies outside my vocation'[53] (apropos the mill); 'there must be a specially irritating kind of *pride* in me that makes the Mother angry' – anger, she thought, was a greater flaw in the latter's character than pride in her own – but 'this is how tertiaries learn ... that they are Nobody and Nothing', apropos 'furious women who burn sulphur at midnight'.[54] Incidents like these, though

minor in themselves, were indicative of behaviour in which Aelfrida would act less spontaneously and more calculatingly (she does not disclose her reasons for this until much later) and the Mother responded by informing her tertiary of how 'out of tune'[55] Sister Placida was with 'the Spirit of the Community', a statement so similar to that made by Miss Wrightson apropos 'spoilt ... harmony' that Placida should have noted it. It appears, however, that Aelfrida was 'out of tune' in more ways than this, for having been warned by Father Amos that she was not to deliberately draw attention to herself, she proceeded to do just that by behaving eccentrically in chapel.

Mother Guenvrede's and Father Northcott's insistence that she be '*ordinary*' on returning to Tymawr in September 1937 puzzled Aelfrida so much ('how [could] they have got it into their heads that I *wasn't*?') that she mentioned the matter to Father Cary at Confession shortly before rejoining the Community. She also informed him that she had told Mother Guenvrede about her guardian angel and, 'thinking ... guardian angels came and went familiarly in convents', that he often spoke to her. Mother Guenvrede, it seems, was 'astonished'; Father Cary, knowing his penitent's foibles better, was admonitory: "you mustn't go round talking like that ... or you will be thought very odd". (Aelfrida's response was 'isn't it *odd* that one *should* be?')[56] But neither the Mother's nor the Father's reaction prevented what happened next: having once noted with distaste that a 'holy widow' living in the Malling guest-house had distractingly singular 'habits of devotion in chapel'[57], Aelfrida, ostensibly 'a 'holy widow' herself, proceeded to display some of her own.

Using a Turkey carpet 'prayer mat' and praying with hands folded on her left knee was one thing; falling into what she called 'trances' quite another. Her 'trances', according to Aelfrida, were 'an intense form of consciousness above thought [in which] the mind is perfectly steady, fixed unwaveringly upon the ... object of contemplation', the object being 'the supreme object ... God'. Trances were therefore to be regarded as gifts from the Deity who created in her 'a state of profound attention to the spiritual order' and who 'immobilised' her mind and body 'in order to detach [her] attention from everything that is not Himself'. (They were *not,* she emphasised, manifestations of 'bodily weakness under great spiritual stress'.)[58] Trances early in her stay during which she felt herself to be 'the object of God's purposive action'[59] seem to have gone unobserved (on 2 October, adoring the Blessed Sacrament, she became caught up 'into some great stream of power and might and ... *used* for some purpose of which [she] had no cognisance') but later ones were not: given that during trances her body became 'stiff and cold' and she herself apparently 'out' of it until 'gently replaced' at the conclusion of the experience, it would have been difficult for anyone present not to have noticed. But although trances experienced in company or alone worried Aelfrida considerably (on 18 November, for example, she had one 'bright, so bright' during Adoration, one 'dark' to which she was 'invited' after Vespers), on no occasion did she seek spiritual guidance for fear of being thought 'odd and queer', a sad comment given that she wondered if all 'aspirants' had 'such happiness' but explicable insofar as she worried about Mother Guenvrede's reaction if approached for advice on this particular score.[60]

Having had the Sisters' attention drawn to her odd and apparently involuntary behaviour, Aelfrida was annoyed to find the matter handled by Mother Guenvrede in the manner most calculated to upset her. Instead of enquiring privately if Aelfrida was suffering from 'strain'[61] (she later did so, receiving the reply that, far from being 'overdone', Aelfrida had found her soul 'infinitely refreshed' by her 'shewings'), she commented – and, as Aelfrida realised, the conversation had really nothing to do with a pregnant cow whom Aelfrida admitted she had hugged – "if anyone saw you … they would think you absolutely dotty".[62] She then set members of the Community to spy on Placida as she went into trances 'immobilised in [her] usual attitude … quite motionless' and 'came back' twenty or thirty minutes later. ('*Tant pis* [to the] Sisters noticing me'[63], was Placida's response, she having decided at Malling that experiences such as these were the 'normal and natural thing' in convent precincts.)[64] On hearing their reports (she had also sent Aelfrida on walks with Sister Monica on 'festival' days when Sister Monica was at liberty to talk and leave the convent and asked Hilda Harrison to ask probing personal questions, fruitless tasks since Aelfrida was adept at fending off unwelcome enquiries or insisted on walking in silence), Mother Guenvrede herself checked on her by 'happening' to be in chapel adjusting the sanctuary lamp at a time when she knew Aelfrida would be there for 'adoration *coram sanctissimo*'.[65] Placida duly went into a trance during which, so she said, she remained aware of what went on around her, and though nothing more was said, Mother Guenvrede ensured that, unless it was unavoidable, Placida never prayed 'wholly in isolation' but was unobtrusively supervised by a professed nun, a novice, or a postulant.[66] By early 1939, however, she seems to have been left uninvigilated, though she does not say if this was because there were now too few sisters to supervise her or because, having demonstrated that the Community now included a veritable (and verifiable) mystic, 'trances' no longer required public presentation,

or because she was deemed safe to be left alone. (Aelfrida herself had thought her 'trances would be over' when she became a tertiary and was somewhat surprised when practices associated at St Benedict's with 'shewings' continued unabated at Tymawr.)[67] But was it that she was in such a state of heightened sensibility in the early months of her *vita nuova* – something which premonitions some weeks before the event concerning the circumstances and even the date of Sister Katherine's death would seem to support[68] – that 'trances' continued involuntarily? Or did she no longer try to control them by a conscious effort if people were present? (She had always been able to control 'entranced' behaviour when worshipping at St Botolph's for fear of drawing attention to herself and may have done so at Tymawr once she realised the danger of it causing her to become even more 'out of tune' with the Community's spirit when and where being 'in tune' really mattered.) Or was 'entranced' behaviour eventually deemed harmless? (Mother Guenvrede told her not to 'desire' trances[69] but did not forbid her to undergo them.) Or were trances figments of a disturbed imagination 'tangling itself up with *God's* demonstration of holy mysteries'[70] and a manifestation that as a result of life-events brooded upon during two years of semi-isolation at St Benedict's, she had indeed become 'quite mad?'

In one respect, however, Aelfrida and Mother Guenvrede were united: that in order to sustain the rigours of her new life, the former should 'take reasonable care of her health'.[71] Placida was keen to do so for several reasons, primarily because poor or declining health might force departure but also because, even though deemed well enough to remain, she would be unable to endure increased silence and solitude without the consolation of being able to read and write. She was therefore concerned to find that scorbutic problems continued to affect her eyes well into 1938 ('eyesight not good enough to read'[72]; 'eyes too tired' or 'hurt'[73]; 'eyes bad again'[74], and so on) and although she consoled herself that an inability to read (and, so she said, write; lengthy diary entries continued but she professed herself unable to write books because unable to research) '*does* make for a hush in one's soul so that one can "think God" instead of thinking *about* Him'[75] and revelled in such silence (if not always solitude) as she was able to command on a daily basis ('Hilda and I have silent breakfast and lunch, talking tea and separate supper')[76] and during Holy Week ('I haven't spoken a word to anyone except when I forgot myself and mewed to one of the cats!')[77], it is obvious that diminution of scorbutic symptoms as her diet improved cheered her immensely.

Issues with food, however, continued to plague her. Her eventual desire to take all meals in her room can be

The library, Tymawr

attributed to something other than a desire for solitude for she had always hated eating in public and avoided it whenever possible, presumably because portion size and inclusion or exclusion of ingredients were difficult to control; sensitivity about her false teeth later added to her dislike. In spite of augmenting her still very restricted diet ('dinner' at midday was always a baked egg, vegetables, and stewed fruit, 'supper', bread and biscuits; her guardian angel, she said, 'preferred' her to eat thus even on festival days as a 'little mortification')[78] by nutritious ingredients recommended by Professor Mottram, she remained somewhat underweight (a contemporary photograph shows her as round faced and big breasted) and Mother Guenvrede banned 'serious fasting' in Lent because Sister Placida kept Lent 'all the year round' and probably did not 'get enough nourishing food' in any case.[79]

From the point of view of her general health, however, some of Aelfrida's symptoms ('always a headache' and 'two or three kind of aches at a time')[80] can be attributed to the stress of her new life (Mother Guenvrede said they were God-given signs 'of a contemplative vocation' or a penance)[81] but it seems that rheumatoid arthritis was exacerbated by the wild weather which even in summer and particularly in winter might rage round a convent exposed at a height of eight hundred feet on a Welsh hillside. Contrasting her 'insufficiently heated' room and the 'notable gale' raging wetly outside with Alethea's descriptions of walks along sunny South African beaches strewn with beautiful shells and bordered by exotic flowers, Aelfrida gritted her teeth ('God called me here')[82] even while complaining that she had to tend her room and paraffin stove herself (and if she did not, her bed remained unmade, her slops unemptied, and her room chilly) and that 'in contrast to the high noonday of inward light', Tymawr was frequently 'dreary'[83] with a cold which penetrated to her very bones: 'I shiver in chapel, I shiver in my room … I shiver out of doors'.

Then she pulled herself up: 'child of God is very much ashamed … that she grumbled in her diary about the cold … after all, when one espouses a Community … for better or worse … it is pure selfishness and folly to expect all "better" and no "worse"!'[84]

Other puzzling symptoms asserted themselves too, not always when Aelfrida felt unhappy. One of these, paraesthesia (pain *and* numbness) along her left arm, together with a feeling that any additional 'shocks' would result in a stroke, was attributed by her doctor to neuritis due to 'deficient diet' but should have raised suspicions of cardiac disease in a middle-aged woman with 'slightly above average blood pressure', intermittent 'cramps in the heart'[85], and a family history of arteriosclerosis. But 'fainting' while lying flat in bed seems improbable until one reads concurrent descriptions of nights of 'darkness and confusion' of a wholly unspiritual nature and of feeling 'very odd' when she 'came round'[86] and can deduce the probable cause.

Although she hated the cold, Aelfrida had an aversion to central heating and soon after her initial arrival at Tymawr asked to change rooms because the room allotted her was 'stuffy'. (She also, whatever the weather, slept with her window open, and her tendency to open the library window to "let out the smell of soup and toast" and let in some "chill fresh air" drove Hilda Harrison and Mother Guenvrede to distraction.)[87] That the temperature of her room was to her taste was important to one who spent much time there but although delighted to move to a room which answered her requirements better, its being both south-facing and adjacent to the kitchen chimney resulted in it being 'baking' in summer and this, together with 'the long-sleeved substantial blue dress [she] chose as suitable to a tertiary'[88], meant that a third room change (engineered by Mother Guenvrede for her own ends) brought a degree of relief. The West Room, however, also gave rise to complaints, for it too had central heating in the form of a hot pipe running below the window seat ('I detest it … it does not seem like holy poverty or good hygiene'; it also confused her 'moral sense' to be comfortably warm)[89] and, facing west, required a blind at the window in order to cut out heat and glare. (Aelfrida, so she said, 'forgot' to ask permission before installing one and Mother Guenvrede was 'very severe' as a result.)[90] More to the point, the '*very* uncomfortable and inconvenient' West Room had a fireplace whose chimney inadvertently interconnected with that of a boiler in the basement two storeys below and 'fumes from central heating' sometimes percolated in.[91]

Proximity to an antiquated flue whose erratic performance must have been exacerbated by the swirling downdraughts of a windy Welsh hillside gave rise to symptoms which the local doctor attributed to 'vernal catarrh'[92] (in spring) or to an allergy to pollen emitted by the chapel flowers (in mid-winter when there none; perhaps he meant incense) but which by their nature (recurrent headaches quite unlike her rarer migraines, nocturnal 'fainting', nights so 'dreadful with asthma I thought I should suffocate'[93], disturbed sleep from which she woke 'very tired and muddled in the head')[94] can be attributed to the presence of toxic products of incomplete combustion to which Aelfrida did not entirely succumb because of her insistence on open windows even when the convent was surrounded by snowdrifts. Eventually, but only after suffering upper respiratory tract problems ('rhenitis'[95], more properly, 'rhinitis') which gave rise to such severe inflammation that she complained bitterly of 'the Vesuvius inside [her] face' and that she felt 'really ill'[96] and the topical application of 'weird looking' cultures of 'all the nasty germs that inhabit noses'[97] which made her so unwell that she was packed off to bed, did she make the connection between symptoms and environment, reacting with less panic to the former and making sensible adjustments to the latter. In spite of this, she then and later underwent physical and spiritual experiences attributed, with comic or serious consequences, to causes other than the obvious one of carbon monoxide toxicity, some of which had serious implications for her life in the Community.

Just how much of Aelfrida's ill health during her early years at Tymawr was real, how much psychosomatic, and how much exaggerated for effect is hard to ascertain. (She was obviously jealous of the 'petting up' accorded Hilda Harrison when the latter's mastectomy was followed by radiotherapy and cross that Mother Guenvrede, who never gave in to physical weakness herself, did not visit 'with arms outstretched' whenever Sister Placida was unwell.)[98] Mother Guenvrede certainly accused her of 'misrepresenting' the doctor's diagnoses 'in order to get her [own] way'[99], and occasional comments which intersperse graphic descriptions of her symptoms that her health was better at Tymawr than 'all [her] life before'[100] do not suggest that, once fully recovered from scurvy, Aelfrida was as ill as she liked to think; indeed, after nearly two years at Tymawr she reported happily that her general health was 'definitely better'[101] and began to pride herself on how rarely she saw the doctor. Then, too, matters other than improving health conspired to make her 'better': she had fallen in love with the West Room and wrung a major concession from Mother Guenvrede.

The West Room, though 'a mixture of a poor student's college room and a hermit's cell', had notable assets: it was near the chapel; it had a marvellous view 'of an expanse of gardens … [and] one of the most magnificent beeches'; it overlooked the convent burial ground shaded by a sycamore tree to whose trunk was affixed a figure of the crucified Christ, a tree which filled her field of vision as she lay in bed and a piece of ground conducive to reparative adoration and its wider outlook, 'most harmonious and peaceful', was of hills beyond which the sun 'set in a blaze of glory'.[102] It had, of course, its inconveniences: by reason of the bed standing against the wall (there was no other place for it) it was impossible to spread her arms when meditating on the Holy Passion, any noise she made was clearly audible by Hilda Harrison next door, and there was so little storage that she was forced to live out of suitcases and boxes, but having reduced herself to the single room of her own to which she aspired, Placida was prepared to submit to the inconveniences of a 'cell' containing a bed and bedside table, a washstand, a table by the window at which she sat to eat or write on 'Father Cary's' Windsor chair imported from St Benedict's, and the ubiquitous deck chair in which she reclined to rest, read, meditate, or say her rosary.

Although Aelfrida's attitude towards mortification of the flesh as a 'soul discipline'[103] had been 'lukewarm'[104], in part because 'it would … be noticed', in part for fear 'it would make me ill'[105], in part because she regarded mortifying devices as 'senseless and cruel anachronisms', and in part she could not believe that God 'exacts … self torture'[106], her need to augment reparative adoration with the help of traditional mortifiers (and to score off Father Cary and the Lady Abbess of Malling, both of whom had forbidden her to use them, and possibly even Alethea who had used them herself) drove her to begin again at Tymawr. The 'traditional remedy of fasting'[107] having been vetoed by Mother Guenvrede, Placida settled for scourging instead.

She began surreptitiously, using a small strap as punishment for misdeeds ranging from rudeness to or about her tenant at St Benedict's (it frequently 'warranted a real good whipping')[108], through those committed unwittingly as a 'child of Christ' ('talking down' to visitors who resented her '*perfectly* unconscious assumption of superiority'[109] or, when in silence, reaching across the table for commodities she should have waited to be offered), to more major transgressions ('thinking of Chiara … and of how I must always be a penitent')[110], but on Mother Guenvrede learning of and apparently approving the practice, began to use it officially on a daily basis. She did not, however, obey the Mother's command that it be used 'moderately' – seven strokes a day were the limit – but immediately doubled the number.[111]

Mother Guenvrede not only acquiesced in her errant 'child's' use of a discipline but, on learning that Aelfrida used a strap, gave her an approved model (i.e. a scourge) as a damage-limitation exercise; this Placida kissed on receipt and before each use, dubbing the 'knotted cord' 'Saint Guenvrede' and noting that *'great* joy … a real *vita nuova'*[112] accompanied its use. Not having been taught the correct use of a discipline, she took it as usual on her back. Reluctant to relinquish 'so *great* a privilege' but worried about the resulting 'nerve pain in [her] spine', she sought Mother Guenvrede's advice, only to discover that 'Saint Guenvrede' was supposed to be used 'just above the knee' and *'certainly not'* every day or 'too hard' or in double figures unless Sister Placida felt 'a special call to reparation'[113], which, of course, Sister Placida frequently did. (She noted too that '14 good strokes of the discipline' fortified her – 'it *is* odd, it does!' – when she was so tired and dispirited she felt she could not go on.) She also and, it seems, quite easily, won other concessions (e.g. using 'the discipline, every Friday, properly, on my back')[114] and in spite of occasional disagreements (Placida pressing for longer sessions because during them she found it easier to unite herself with Christ at His scourging – 'my sacrifice for His'[115] – and Mother Guenvrede attempting to curb excesses), continued to take the discipline daily for years to come.

A short visit to Oxford followed this early manifestation of concessions granted, for Aelfrida had made appointments with her oculist (he misdiagnosed nyctalopia as 'conjunctivitis' and warned of its persistence), her dentist (Dorothy Smith did not mention the book in which she featured, now in print), and with Dr Frazer whom she consulted for a second opinion saying 'we had all been rather mystified about my health' but who, mystifying symptomatology notwithstanding, declared her former patient 'twenty years younger', something Aelfrida attributed to 'daily Communion, the regular life and perfect contentment'.[116] She had also to dispose of St Benedict's, Mother Guenvrede having proclaimed it God's Will that the house be relinquished and Mother Cecilia that relinquishment was in accordance with Holy Poverty. Two Mothers Superiors acting in unison constituted *force majeure,* and Mrs Graham was 'ejected unceremoniously from St Benedict's without even a month's legal notice'. (Sister Placida 'saw things quite differently' for, the house given up and its contents stored or disposed of, she could experience *'singleness of desire'* without distraction[117]; she also retired 'into the cell of [her] heart to pray' and longed for her pillar of fire and cloud 'to move back to Tymawr' for yet another 'fresh start'.) Ejection notwithstanding, Mrs Graham enjoyed 'the charm of Oxford' immensely, conducted business and socialised enthusiastically, and even paid a flying visit to Cambridge where she revelled in 'Cambridge conversation' and the

'company of children'. (Angela and Veronica were then fourteen and sixteen.)[118] More pertinently (one might almost say impertinently in view of earlier conversations), she once more played off Father against Mother, informing Father Cary that Mother Guenvrede allowed her the use of the discipline. His response was measured: her desire for it was merely a stage in her spiritual development and the instrument itself one of several 'recognised helps in the spiritual life'. He also recommended 'tact and humour' and 'the exercise of patience and humility' at Tymawr and that Aelfrida *not* justify her actions to the Mother unless the latter wanted to dismiss her[119], advice immediately forgotten when Placida proceeded to lose herself *'once and for all'* (and once again) 'in adoration … of God's Beauty and Holiness'.[120]

Encouraged, however, by Father Cary's comment regarding 'recognised helps' and by what she considered an easy victory over Mother Guenvrede with regard to one 'saint', Aelfrida set out to acquire two more.

Acting on her guardian angel's suggestion that she adopt the practice of wearing a hair girdle but 'much dismayed' at the thought of having to do so[121], she approached Mother Guenvrede, not for permission, for guardian angels took precedence, but for advice. (She also begged that she be allowed to attend Mattins – 'they spell it with one "t" here', though she herself continued to spell it with two as more 'canonical' – at 8.45pm as a 'spiritual' mortification but discovering that an hour standing or kneeling at the foot of the Cross gave her backache, desisted even though her guardian angel, currently very vocal, proclaimed that she allowed herself 'more sleep than is necessary' and that too much sleep was 'gross', to which end she mortified herself more comfortably by lying awake beyond midnight.)[122] Mother Guenvrede's advice was succinct: there were no hair girdles at Tymawr and 'hard work [was] better than hair shirts'[123], but Aelfrida might ask Malling for advice as to how to obtain one. Warning her that Mother Magdalen Mary was "very Benedictine in the manner of corporal austerities"[124] and implying that Placida should not demonstrate *trop de zèle* with regard to 'recognised helps', Malling referred her to the weavers of Eric Gill's Ditchling community. (She does not comment on the coincidence of Eric Gill and what would have been Agatha's twenty-eighth birthday but judging by a concurrent increase in diary references to her dead daughter, it seems not to have passed her by.) On discovering the cost (16/6d, 'a "luxury" penance'), she sent for some 'hair yarn' in order to knit her own, adding that 'when it is made we shall see whether [the Mother] feels moved to let me wear it'.[125] Being first presented with the yarn as 'an act of humility' and subsequently with the finished product ('the plastron goes in front and the girdle wraps round', the plastron being a small apron–like panel attached to the end of the girdle)[126], Mother Guenvrede asked for divine guidance before informing Placida that the girdle could be worn immediately and without restriction. This was as well, for Aelfrida's guardian angel had already issued instructions: she was to wear it at tea-time (and only at teatime) to teach her to keep interior silence 'however much I talk'; she was to wear it 'humbly and *gratefully*' ('he insisted on that', Mother Guenvrede having already accused her of 'self-will' in the matter); and she was not to think about it when not wearing it for fear of 'spiritual pride and physical apprehension'.[127]

Spiritual pride is understandable in one whose self-admonishment 'pride, Aelfrida, pride' had been so regularly (and unavailingly) repeated in former days but physical apprehension requires explanation. Since childhood Aelfrida had, so she said, experienced 'repulsion from hairy things' (one of Constantine's attractions was his smooth skin, one of Erlande's detractions, his hairiness), so that when it came to wearing the 'horrible object', she began to 'shiver with repulsion'[128] and it was only by an enormous effort of will that she overcame 'leniency' towards her 'temperament' and the 'sick and shivery' feelings which beset her as soon as she donned it.[129]

Why, therefore, did she wear it, given that given her discipline and her restricted diet, she wondered if it was wise to afflict her body further? Her answer is interesting – and unexpected. Although she wore it as an aspect of reparative adoration in order to be 'bruised', like Christ, for 'our iniquities'[130] (her own and other people's) and as a means of reminding herself that unless she first rid herself of 'a vast quantity of useless lumber in the way of prejudices, views, tastes, preferences, etc., etc.' she would never develop a 'pure capacity' for Him[131], she chiefly wore it because her body, now in 'quite good health', was becoming more and more 'rebellious', objecting strenuously to 'food, bed and time table' and to her Triple Vows (even 'to *Chastity* – !! At *my* age – but it *does*') because it did not like 'the road [her] soul ha[d] taken'.[132] Use of a hair girdle was therefore an attempt on Placida's part to overcome Mrs Graham's sexuality by '*spiritualising [her] body*' into becoming 'a fitter instrument of [her] soul' by donning a garment that would remind her ('I need a goad') and '*toughen*' her.[133] To reinforce the girdle's message Aelfrida promoted it to 'cincture' and gave it a name: 'Saint Rose of Lima'.[134]

Not content with two 'helpful instruments', Placida tried for a third: could she, she begged Mother Guenvrede, wear a 'hair shirt' too? Mother Guenvrede had already reacted with distaste to 'Saint Rose' ("you don't mean to tell me you want to wear *that* every day?")[135] and refused,

telling Aelfrida not to be impatient and to let the matter rest until Lent 1939. The latter, however, having tried on Alethea's scapular ('rather like a bit of stair carpet')[136] at St Benedict's three years earlier, disregarded both the Mother's and the Holy Spirit's advice ("ask for no more privileges either in the way of penance or anything else but … set yourself to live the life as quietly as possible [and] put [your] trust in God [and] let Him act") and even that of her guardian angel (the scapular, he said, was something to be 'longed for' and she had sufficient supplementary penances at present), and by September 1938 had received permission to wear 'Saint Rose' at Mass (a practice forbidden by her guardian angel) and to knit a 'Carthusian' 'hair scapular … to be called Saint Bruno'.[137]

Knitting 'Saint Bruno' with needles called 'Penitence' and 'Praise' was a more arduous task than knitting 'Saint Rose'. Begun on 6 October 1938, the "wondrous object" (Mother Guenvrede's description)[138] was not completed until late January 1939. Donning it for the first time on 7 February, Placida felt 'no repulsion on putting it on and the first half hour called for very little endurance' but after forty-five minutes 'every hair seemed made of fire' and she was 'much exhausted afterwards'.[139]

Though still intent on 'beating [her] rebellious body into submission', Aelfrida seems to have regarded 'Saint Bruno' less as an instrument of subjection (a scapular is a symbolic yoke) than of reparation. Noting on the day she first wore it that not only was she much calmer since rooting herself 'in this beloved Community' but also that the Holy Spirit, in 'assuming control of [her] prayer life and through it of all [her] thoughts and words and deeds', was more efficacious in every respect than any material 'instrument' (the process, she also noted, 'is not … of course … complete – never can be' ; there was plenty of the old Adam in Mrs Graham yet), it is obvious from comments made while knitting it that wrongs committed by herself in relation to other people weighed on her mind: towards her daughters ('I … wonder God has spared Alethea to me so long for when He took Agatha I wondered whether it would not be better for the sisters to be together') and, on what would have been their thirty-second wedding anniversary, to Constantine, 'always beloved, more beloved the more I pray'.[140] But though she had now come to terms with the deaths and departures of these 'beloved dead', one death still required expiation.

References to 'always' having to be a 'penitent' with regard to Chiara are reminders of how much euthanasic matricide preyed on her mind in spite of admission five years earlier to the Lady Abbess of Malling while attempting to justify 'the events round Chiara's death' that '[she had] acted in good faith but ... felt horror and revulsion ... [and] would not do it again'. (But, she added, 'how far I could bear to see my dear ones suffer I do not know').[141] Hence while it is possible to regard 'Saint Bruno' as another 'recognized help' employed by Aelfrida as a means of keeping herself 'recollected' (or, more cynically, of proving to Mother Guenvrede the devoutness of the tertiary now 'rooted' in her Community, in which respect it is interesting to speculate what other 'helps' Placida might have employed had events not precluded usage: the chains recommended by Abbé Giloteaux, perhaps, 'he going even further' than she would in favour of mortifications such as these)[142], it is surely significant that within a year of beginning to wear it, she felt able to enter the last stage of grieving – acceptance – and, on the seventh anniversary of Chiara's death, to take 'what [she] did amiss ... to the foot of the Cross and [leave] it there' with the words 'it cannot be undone but it is forgiven'.[143]

Placida's employment of 'useful saints' as symbols 'of my Lord as He perpetually offers His sufferings for the sins of the world' and of 'self-naughting'[144] ("mortification allows one to travel light")[145] were the subject of negotiations with Mother Guenvrede for some years. ('Saint Cadoch', the prayer mat now named after a Welsh saint, and 'Saint Thomas Aquinas', her chapel reading-desk[146], though equally 'useful', were purely utilitarian objects.) Aelfrida, as expected, pressed for more and more privileges because they provided so much progress 'into the Light'[147] and the Mother, as usual, advocated discretion and moderation on the grounds that 'grace of office' enabled her to know what her 'child of God' could bear.[148] Aelfrida countered that she was 'invited' to wear the 'helps' by the 'Saints' themselves and that she experienced 'a *genuine* attraction' to their use even though usage was accompanied by 'an intense shrinking of the flesh', and by increasing or decreasing usage according to her own feelings of what was currently appropriate. (At this point Mother Guenvrede resorted to prayer.) Placida did, however, follow Mother Guenvrede's instructions occasionally ('a quarter of an hour of Saint Bruno' on Fridays and 'Saint Guenvrede as usual')[149], if only to pacify her or when it seemed that the privilege might be withdrawn altogether if she transgressed too blatantly ('an hour of Saint Rose is better than nothing'), giving as her reason that although she found the devices 'curiously exasperating to the nerves', compared to physical pains experienced in the past, their discomfort was '*nothing*'.[150] Furthermore, such 'penances' were 'part of [her] vocation' and 'demands made on her by God'[151] to which adequate response must be made.

Self-naughting was one thing, physical burdens added to those already voluntarily undergone for the sake of

reparative adoration quite another, and within three years of beginning to wear 'Rose' and 'Bruno' Aelfrida was forced to relinquish them, 'Rose' because although she had hoped to wear it daily (if not all day) 'until the day of [her] death', the cincture gave rise to 'violent nerve pain' and to 'an open wound ... swollen and raw and running' in the area of her navel[152], and 'Bruno' because intermittant wear gave rise to an eczematous rash on her back[153], the conditions recurring even if the two 'Saints' were given a 'holiday'[154] until the problems resolved. Complaints of 'eczema' on her scalp, however, makes one wonder if she had not been experimenting with a crown of thorns also; she was certainly capable of plaiting one, having done so in Holy Week 1937.

There were other reasons too for Placida's abandonment of 'Bruno' and 'Rose', some explicit, some implicit. For one thing, because Aelfrida remained a 'luxurious' ascetic, Placida found it more and more difficult to resume her 'Saints' after a break, particularly 'Saint Rose' for which she felt 'sheer physical loathing'[155] but 'Saint Bruno' too because of the skin condition to which it gave rise, a particularly distressing condition because her stained underwear was laundered by the nuns themselves. (Walter Tillyard, aged seventeen and camping in the area in May 1939, enquired if there was 'self-torture' in religious communities but was given no hint 'that hair shirts and disciplines exist at Tymawr'.)[156] For another, and having had to contend with her spirit being willing but her flesh a 'poor coward thing'[157], Erlande's "*nonne ratée*" with God in her head and the devil in her body, found herself assailed by a 'malignant presence'. The devil's attempts to '*press out* all apprehension of God' or to frighten her by 'belching black horror' over her (a description one hopes is metaphorical, given Aelfrida's problems with flues) or by rocking her bed as part of 'a definite personal attack ... to prevent [her] taking a step forward'[158], were dealt with by sprinkling holy water or making the sign of the Cross (Father Northcott's advice to resist 'any wish to add to your Rule or to take any further step' as being temptations of the devil had naturally been disregarded – with predictable results)[159], but the devil in her body seems to have frightened Aelfrida so much that it was easy to relinquish 'Rose' and 'Bruno' when physical symptoms provided an excuse.

It seems she experienced revulsion less because 'Rose' and 'Bruno' gave rise to unpleasant skin conditions but because their use resulted in sexual arousal. ('Saint Guenvrede', applied 'just above the knee', does not seem to have done so – or was not recorded as having done so.) Arousal manifested itself initially as feelings of 'frivolity' during which Placida became so talkative and witty at teatime that 'the Library' (as she collectively called

Hilda Harrison, residents, and visitors) became 'helpless with laughter' and she herself prone to enquire 'ought I to afflict my body further [because] my life is not at all in tune with the Holy Spirit'[160], but subsequent use of expressions with sexual as well as religious connotations ('get my release'[161], with regard to 'Saint Bruno') and comments that 'psychologists would have been absolutely certain' that 'somewhat oversexed' Mrs Graham was 'sublimating the sex instinct' by turning 'naturally' to language and emotions in which she expressed how her ' whole ... life [was] lifted to a higher ... spiritual ... level' and experiencing physical gratification from instruments whose ostensible use was to *subdue* carnality, suggest something more. The difficulty she experienced in 'calming [herself] down' after one such 'fiasco'[162] ('Saint Rose' seems to been the chief offender), coupled with references to her battles with '*Chastity*!!' and with memories of certain psychologists' comments on the connection between Mysticism and sexuality probably provided her with another motive for discontinuing the use of 'Saints' which, though 'helpful' in one respect, had unwonted or wanted effects in another.

Other – unspoken – reasons must be considered too. Possibly, as Father Cary predicted, Placida passed through the stage of spiritual development requiring recourse to 'helps' and to what were essentially trappings; possibly common sense prevailed, 'it [being] best ... that my "vocation of praise" should be the first charge on what strength I have'[163]; possibly it was her keen sense of the ridiculous, for descriptions of Cambridge attempts to procure a suitable 'discipline' ('a ... bit of rope ... the kind of thing that the horrid sea–captain beats the apprentice with' but, finding 'nothing thicker than sash cord', having recourse to the 'substantial silk cord dressing gown girdle with heavily weighted tassel' which was to make an unwanted and unwonted appearance at St Benedict's)[164] would have made amusing retrospective reading; possibly with 'Catharine Sutherland' in mind, she remembered that "the idea that one can acquire merit by bearing self-inflicted pain is a mistaken and barbaric one"[165] and decided that she couldn't 'see anything religious in it at all, even when it is done with religious intention'.[166] Possibly, while understanding and sharing 'the spirit that makes one wish to identify oneself with the sufferings of Christ', use of 'Bruno' and 'Rose' became 'mere misapplication' of energies better reserved for adoration than reparation; possibly physical side effects made them less 'picturesque or interesting'[167]; possibly – and in spite of having written a poem thirty years earlier whose opening lines describe Christ as Him who "to my vain renouncements dost award / No greater prize than knotted scourge of cord – / That

lashèd doubts may seem a faith's increase"[168], she came to regard her 'Saints' as diversions from the true path of her 'closer walk with God'. Possibly too, the onset in September 1939 of strife which made 'fusses' concerning the use of cincture and scapular appear paltry made her stop, for their use declined as war with Germany began to seem inevitable in spite of her misplaced confidence in Neville Chamberlain, a man whose 'guardian angel had sent him on wings of peace ... to persuade Hitler to desist from his mad and warlike schemes'[169] and diminished further in 1940 when her confidence in the persuasively pacific powers of guardian angels was severely shaken.

Although Placida seems to have relinquished 'Rose' and 'Bruno' of her own volition (Mother Guenvrede appears to have left her to come to the decision in her own time or, tiring of her resident tertiary's religious foibles, concluded that there were more pressing matters to attend to with regard to the Community as a whole), keenness 'to write as I ought' on the Community's behalf died even earlier and though supposed to be an intrinsic aspect of her own and the Community's 'vocation', was never resurrected on their behalf.

The only book published by Aelfrida when at Tymawr, *The Night Watches*[170], must have been conceived soon after her return in September 1937 and was certainly in print by mid–1938. (In contrast to progress reports on earlier works, there are only two brief diary references to it, one quoting reviews, the other noting donation of a signed copy to a visitor[171]; Julius, as an inscribed copy in Girton College shows, received it on 18 December 1938.) In contrast to the extant volumes of her 'closer walk' trilogy, Aelfrida makes two significant points. First, "in the following pages 'I' is to be thought of as referring to the reader, not to the writer, of [these] meditations".[172] Second, she no longer pictures her spiritual life as a "pilgrimage"[173] because peregrination is no longer necessary: her spiritual life is now "*my life in God*", God in whom she lives and moves and has her being[174], and because she has arrived at the point at which she wants to be: "here-and-now communion with Thee" in which her spiritual life "*is* my life in Thee" and "*Thy life in me*".[175]

It seems, however, that some or all of Placida's 'meditations' for *The Watchword* crept into *The Night Watches,* for in spite of the book's serenely philosophical tone, it is subtitled *Thoughts for Sick Folk* and contains numerous references to its author "being ill" or "an invalid" and, worse still, an encumbrance. On the other hand, the writer is at last in the right place for her (Tymawr; implied, not named), a place which is God's choice of setting for her, somewhere she can obtain "visions of towers and pinnacles of the City of God"[176], and somewhere she can use "pains of body and ... heaviness of soul" as reminders of His loving kindness in finding the right place for her in her hour of need.[177] In spite, therefore, of physical and spiritual discomforts, she will put pain-engendered insomnia to good use, long "night watches" reminding her of Christ's Holy Passion and teaching her to be more aware of Him during the day as well.[178]

Aelfrida was already a chronic insomniac, an incapacity dating back to days of deliberate sleep deprivation in adolescence (a practice resumed at Tymawr in July 1938) and possibly to the 'night terrors' which beset her childhood. Voluntary or involuntary sleeplessness was exacerbated by telling herself rousing 'night stories', by retiring very early because physically but not mentally exhausted, by deliberately choosing uncomfortable beds as mortifications (though the presence of planks beneath a thin mattress aided 'recollection' by irresistibly calling her attention to the Cross and reminding her she was a 'penitent', her Tymawr bed also induced 'many sleepless hours' because she too was 'thin')[179], and of meditating (a mentally energising though physically calming activity) in bed on subjects which gave rise to out-of-body experiences and sometimes to physical manifestations. Lying in bed was also associated with unpleasant experiences: the burning pains of rheumatoid arthritis, visits from the devil, Constantine's sexual demands or erotic tortures occasioned by their cessation, and with obsessive rumination over sins or wrongs, none of them activities associated with restful sleep. At Tymawr, however, insomnia assumed a more positive aspect because it extended waking hours of adoration: "I have remembered thy name, O Lord, in the night ... / "At midnight will I rise to give thanks unto thee ..."[180]

Psalm 119 from which these lines are taken is that from whose verses Aelfrida derived comfort as she drifted deep in post-natal depression from tree to tree (*aleph, beth, gimel* ...) along Brooklands Avenue in 1912. Now mourning the death of another child in whose death both she and Constantine had played a part ("Life – a thing ... that man can so easily destroy and ... so often wantonly does destroy")[181], she derives comfort from the psalm once more – but this time she is able to move beyond the point (verse *Caph*) where the psalmist turns from pessimism to optimism and from feelings of affliction to hopes of succour until, paraphrasing as she goes, she reaches the last triumphant verse: "let my soul live".[182] Furthermore, however reminiscent one daughter's death is of another's, she now has no need of recourse to an earthly 'Guru' (she ignored her guardian angel's contemporary suggestion that 'at some convenient opportunity' she inform Mother Guenvrede

'about [her] meditations with Aleister Crowley'[183] and only later recalled how Crowley, 'a man who did not know the difference between right and wrong ... out of his ignorance ... did help me' and decided he 'must be prayed for')[184] because she has God Himself to guide her.

Following *The Night Watches* Aelfrida wrote nothing save letters and her diary for six years; she also gave away her stock of manuscript paper lest she be tempted to do so. Her reasons were largely unspoken but may be surmised. Perhaps after so many years' intensive authorship she felt written out; perhaps she preferred a hush in her soul to acclaim as a 'clever lady who wrote books'[185]; perhaps writing books as a means of easing her mind had been important but having come to terms with events which inspired them, writing could be confined to her diary. Perhaps, with one daughter dead and the other living cheaply in Africa and with rents from Wetenhall Cottage and elsewhere providing an adequate income and her own expenditure (apart from postage) negligible, she was less driven by a need for money. Perhaps with Hilda Harrison's strictures on *The Way of Praise* underlining her own re-readings of *A Little Road-Book for Mystics* (crammed with 'shallowness ... lack of discernment and spiritual judgement ... and far too much "I"')[186] and *Can I be a Mystic?* ('hopelessly on the wrong track ... all directed towards ... spiritual self-aggrandisement')[187], she now believed that 'most of [her] edifying remarks were nothing but pious chatter'.[188] Perhaps spiritual life took precedence over being 'too set on making everything perfectly clear to [her] intellect and on putting everything into words'.[189] Perhaps, as once in Lausanne, she was so busy absorbing impressions that she found it impossible to 'put out' at the same time ('my own books ... can go. And they probably will!'), saving her energies for performing 'the *opus Dei* with my sisters-in-the-Lord'.[190] Perhaps, as official writer-in-residence, she found herself unable to write to order, memories of a commissioned literary effort, *Two Hundred Thousand Miles Travel for Temperance,* being revived by a visit from Agnes Slack herself, 'old and tired, the former fierce Agnes quite gone'.[191]

Perhaps all of these but chiefly because acting on a command from Lucius Cary, 'Saint Lucius' having seen fit to take very human revenge for *The Spiritual Director* during Aelfrida's recent visit to Oxford. "Do you", he asked her, with reference to book reviews written for the same journal (*Theology*) in which her article had appeared a year earlier, "find that exercising your cleverness on other peoples' books helps you in your spiritual life?"[192] (She had recently reviewed 'three large intellectual books, one in French' for the journal.)[193] Furthermore, "writing ... numerous letters or reviews or books constituted a leakage [of spiritual energy]" and "a breach of spiritual silence". Aelfrida, dismayed, cried out "but what outlet should I have?" "PRAYER", Father Cary replied sonorously, 'as if to say "there is your path. Take it"'.[194] So she followed both path and advice. But only up to a point.

Though forbidden to 'seek an audience by publication', Aelfrida was allowed to write 'to clarify [her] mind'[195], a concession she interpreted liberally. True, she gave up reviewing books altogether and did not begin another book of her own until 1944, but the flow of 'numerous letters' never ceased: letters to Father Cary, to 'goups' old and new, male and female, in England and abroad, and to family and friends across the world. In one thing, however she followed Cary's advice implicitly. Cary, she informed Mother Guenvrede, had told her to ask herself 'does this help me spiritually?' before performing or not performing an action, a question she now used as an excuse to do or not do (ringing the bell for chapel, she said, put a 'stop in [her] mind' and prevented full participation in the service which followed) just what she did or did not want. "I suppose", was Mother Guenvrede's acid rejoinder, "you don't want to do anything useful. You are the one person who … is no good to the Community at all".[196] And already one senses it was not only about bells that she spoke.

Aelfrida's brief but delightful visit to Cambridge in May 1938 found her 'more susceptible to the *tug* of the old life' than she realised: an 'elegant and comfortable environment' (Phyllis had relented: she stayed at Merton House), 'together with … intellectual pleasure [and] human interests and emotions, make a great contrast to the bareness of the life [here]'. Finding itself confronted at Tymawr with a midday meal 'to be eaten … out of a chipped brown dish such as one would give to a dog and [off] a plate … of the kind one keeps bits on in the pantry', her 'natural self' decided to contest 'every inch of the ground' of the life her spiritual self was creating for itself. Realising, however, that life at Tymawr would be 'intolerable' if Mrs Graham tried to live it 'for myself and in my own strength', Placida decided to live it for God in *His* strength ('God help me'), to see in it 'perfect beauty and rightness', and 'to try not to be so silly in future'. (In an undated note Aelfrida added 'it was *very* naughty of me to write all that'.)[197] Then she looked for compensations.

Compensations were required for other reasons too. Mother Guenvrede submitting to Sister Placida's wish for increased silence and solitude (or perhaps testing her tertiary's resolve) by vigorous enforcement of privileges already accorded and by the addition of some of her own choosing if she thought Mrs Graham's tendency to sociability required curbing. (Fear of being 'contemptuously

**View from the West Room, Tymawr**

dismissed' if she rebelled kept Aelfrida compliant.)[198] The unexpected onset of *tedium claustrae* as Placida began to experience 'boredom' in 1938 ('the sheer monotony, day after day the same, [is] very trying'[199]; she rationalised it as 'the old restlessness'[200] which overtook her in early spring as she emerged from winter-induced gloom) or her soul wanting 'to slip its leash'[201] of unremitting existence in the world of the spirit in order to revisit the 'real' world. So notwithstanding reassurance by Mother Guenvrede that these feelings attacked 'most Religious' at some point and were to be regarded as 'a *temptation*, not a sin'[202], Aelfrida succumbed to temptation, first, by keeping open channels of communication between herself and her former 'world', second, by intensive exploration and enjoyment of the 'world' in the vicinity of Tymawr.

The Sister Placida who, even before Cary's latest admonition, had decided that writing novels, travel, and interest in 'any news over and above what is needed for prayers' (a let-out clause to enable her to read *The Times*; she assuaged her conscience by reading the convent copy a day late, at which point she could also read it at leisure and cut out articles she wished to keep) was 'wrong' because it represented 'a "tug" away from things spiritual to things material' and who continually reminded herself to 'HUSH'[203] and that she '*must not* … write … pages and pages [of her diary] about *people*', continued desperately lonely in the midst of spiritual consolations. Feeling the lack of the human consolations she was supposed to have given up, Aelfrida made sure she experienced them by proxy. Having decided not to write about 'people here' (lengthy descriptions of Sister Katherine's death, requiem Mass, and burial follow this entry), she consoled herself with the thought that 'people who write and ask for spiritual advice' could not be ignored; nor, of course, could 'all [her] friends and things that happen to them'. With regard to the latter she decided that keeping in touch would show them that 'their relationship to God' and her wanting them to be 'where His holy Will places them' was desperately important to her, though there was to be, she reminded herself, none of her former attitude of corresponding with people solely 'as a field of potential conquest' or in order 'to be thought well of … for my charm' or because letters provided an opportunity to criticize and gibe or a means of keeping people 'near me if I liked them and a long way off if I didn't'.[204] Not content, however, with having received letters every day since her return to Tymawr in September 1937, she ordered or sent off *two hundred* presents, letters, or cards ('to the glory of God', of course)[205] in the weeks before Christmas 1937 and judging by 'the vast quantities of letters and cards'[206] received in return, not many fewer in 1938. As a sop to conscience, however, and as a way of keeping Christmas Day inviolate, she opened them as they arrived, not on the festival itself.

Such derogation of silence (inner *or* outer) and of solitude (actual *or* postal), though much enjoyed at any time of year, made Placida feel so guilty ('this flood of news – all these dear people claiming my attention to their affairs and wanting news of me … oh! how it hurt!')[207] that she decided to try much harder at 'living out of the world'. To some extent she succeeded, requesting that only immediate family send presents, by limiting travel to places within walking distance, and by refusing to enter any building save Penalt post office and Trellech village shop[208], but assertions that she '*dare* not, no *dare* not shut the door of my cell, *myself*' to correspondents show how little in earnest she was. ('But oh! if God would do it *for* me', was her escape clause.) In spite, therefore, of agreeing with Mother Guenvrede to write fewer and shorter letters with 'none … to be used … as an opportunity for being expansive'[209], continuing guilt concerning the receipt of letters demonstrated that she continued to write and to reply to far too many and her need to alleviate claustral tedium and to redress loneliness was pressing.

And, of course, she continued to write 'pages and pages about people' in her diary, people about whom she could only have heard by letter: former suitors of Agatha's (including Humphrey Warren) married or engaged; Uncle Frank and Aunt Anna, both disapproving of her new life; Ruth Connolly (née Warren) embarking on marriage and motherhood in Madagascar; 'Philothea' Kermack now deeply involved in 'national activities'[210]; Lucy Verey and her extended family; George Warren, with whom the Grahams had spent part of their strange honeymoon, dying at ninety-five, Daisy Allen

prematurely of heart disease; Eardley Davidson divorcing the wife whose post-natal depression Aelfrida had unsuccessfully 'straightened', an event which Aelfrida, herself a divorcée, treated censoriously and by adding Eardley (together with Aleister Crowley) to her list of those for whom she made reparative adoration.

Assisted by Tymawr's proximity to Cardiff, she also entered a new and very loving phase of her relationship with Julius, for dispossessed of daughters whose affections were reduced to a 'stretching-out … from another region', Aelfrida turned more and more to the man who had always provided comfort and who, even when absent, remained a 'presence' in her life. Julius reciprocated, visiting Tymawr at regular intervals to spend the day with a sister whose joyful welcome and undivided attention brightened a life embittered by lack of academic recognition, by Mina's 'black gloom'[211], and by dread of another global war. (Mina, accompanied by Constance, visited once during Aelfrida's early days at Tymawr and at intervals thereafter; of the 'Merton House folk', Eustace visited twice and Phyllis and Veronica once apiece; Angela and Stephen not at all.) Julius' visits were greeted by his sister with wild excitement ('a glorious day together … we talked and talked and talked')[212]; indeed, she sometimes became so wildly excited that she suffered a physical reaction 'post hoc' and had to retire bed. Wishing because of this and for more spiritual reasons (she had had to miss Communion and abandon a short 'retreat' on which she had unilaterally embarked) that she 'did not get excited when he comes'[213], she worried on another score also: 'do I love … his own most beloved self … only "in God"? I don't know'[214], a question she did well to ask given that descriptions of walking and talking with him read uncannily like those of the brother/sister 'honeymoon' spent in Soham. Hence although she prided herself on having 'no "particular affections"' for anyone and there being 'no-one' who made her 'pulses beat faster'[215], there was one man for whom she had and they did: her elder brother. Another thing, too, pleased her enormously: the change in Julius' personality since Chiara's death and the dismantling of the mausoleum that was Fordfield: 'dear, dear Dudu grows stronger in character … better in every way now than he was then, stronger in health [and] *goodness*, depending more closely on God [and] continually planning for other people's happiness'[216], chiefly, it seemed, her own.

Although Mother Guenvrede did not actually *forbid* Placida to receive letters and visitors (possibly she realised that, deprived of such outlets, Aelfrida's precarious mental health might degenerate), she seems to have discouraged visits from anyone not immediate family, saying that as Mother Superior she did not like '"just people" about the place'. Aelfrida was forbidden to invite Juan Mascaró again in order to 'help him spiritually', on the grounds that "he was only trying to get you to marry him and other things were a pretext", something which had not occurred to her before[217] but was also forbidden to visit ninety-year-old Ancifera Gregory when that lady suffered a stroke (God did not want Aelfrida to go, she informed her; Placida described the Mother's action as a 'test case')[218], a deprivation understandable in terms of Mrs Graham's current need for a stable environment and as few reminders of the past as possible, but curious too in its seeming heartlessness.

The 'piercing charm of the contemplative life' longed for by Mrs Constantine Graham in 1918 but thirty years later found to contain measures of claustral tedium unanticipated by Sister Placida could also, as the latter realised with regard to 'boredom', be enhanced by means other than writing and receiving letters or receiving visitors in a manner which exactly accorded with her 'Rule', namely by undertaking a daily walk combined 'contemplation with 'freedom'.[219]

While still at St Benedict's, Aelfrida realised that if she ever led a more 'enclosed' life than there, it would be impossible to rid herself of 'that adventurous restlessness which can never see a hill without wanting to peep over [it] or a horizon without longing to reach it'.[220] With other outlets for 'restlessness' curtailed (or maintained in secret in the case of her diary, for at Tymawr one accustomed to living with her heart on her lips perforce confined it mainly to her pen), Placida turned to physical means of ridding herself of surplus mental energy: 'I have … a mind that … runs off after … things that I don't *really* care about but which give it something to chew'.[221] Gardening, however assiduously carried out, did not provide the degree of 'freedom' required (though 'profitable spiritually', it was 'merely …an outlet for ill-regulated natural energy')[222], so in the course of her regulation daily walk, she turned to exploration.

Monmouthshire in general and the environs of Tymawr in particular form an area of historical and archaeological interest whose monuments date from the Neolithic to the modern era.[223] Aelfrida began her explorations by seizing on what seemed most relevant to her new life, namely evidence of the sixth century Cadoch after whom she named her prayer mat, his local life and ministry being evidenced by the presence of several churches named after him.[224] She then convinced herself on the basis of a modicum of physical evidence, local legends, and her own 'psychic intuitions' that Cadoch had constructed a 'cell', if not on the site of Tymawr itself (a '*colline sacrée*', she thought, on whose slopes a druidical sacred grove had been supplanted by

a Christian foundation)[225], at least in the vicinity, and though informed by Mother Guenvrede that the 'ruin' she fixed on as Saint Cadoch's 'monastery' was a ruinous fortified manor house of which there were numerous local examples[226], dubbed it her 'House of Defense' and repaired there at regular intervals to commune with God in 'sacred enclosure'.[227]

Having subsequently sanctified every stone wall, sheepfold, and spring in the vicinity as further evidence (chapels, cells, holy wells) of Cadoch's activities in the area, Aelfrida suddenly found herself meeting an even more distant past: 'Prehistory'. Exploring round the 'House of Defense' one day, she laid her hand on a 'huge flat round stone' and was 'suddenly in touch with *ghosts* … of strange fierce men of very *very* long ago'.[228] 'Monmouth stones' thereafter 'thrilled'[229] her and 'Prehistory' became an enthralling interest verging on obsession. Some of her discoveries (Neolithic implements, a Roman sarcophagus used as a watering trough) were verified by Julius or Eustace but when the 'big stones' called her and she set off like a bloodhound on the trail of 'psychic scents'[230], common sense deserted her and her mythologised version of local history began to rival that of an earlier 'pre-historian', twelfth century Geoffrey of Monmouth.

For someone who now lived physically on the borderland between England and Wales and had always lived spiritually and emotionally on metaphysical 'borderlands' (sacred/secular, sanity/madness, carnal/mystical), transitional places such as Aelfrida discovered – or imagined she discovered – were imbued with terror ('savage presences' who made 'human sacrifices')[231], with mystery ('strange men doing acts that I could not see')[232], and with human interest: 'what *happened* to the civilisation on these hills? Did God sweep the whole race away? Or are the people … whom I see every day their descendants?'[233] Finding 'the whole place dotted with remains'[234], she also found herself peering into the past: into 'hewn chambers and pits'[235] ('pit-fortresses', some of them); at circular sacrificial 'altars' with V-grooves and central holes to let the blood run off, some accompanied by 'caches' of conical 'weapon stones'[236]; at 'sacred' oak groves where 'some priest-chieftain' officiated at shamanistic rites (snake-worship, she thought); at 'aligned upright stones' pointing to forgotten places and events.[237] Hilda Harrison, informed at 'talking tea' of her discoveries, was sceptical, accusing Aelfrida of reconstructing civilisations on the basis of 'stones' and the adders with which the area abounded. (And, one may add, on the basis of natural caves or of chambered wells – of which the 'Virtuous Well' at Trellech was a notable example – or of quarries for building stone or ironstone, or of millstones whose upper surfaces are incised with dovetailed runnels through which flour emerges and which are centrally pierced to accommodate the mill-shaft, together with the conical stone wedges used to lever or incise them[238], or of abundant trees planted as fuel for furnaces for the mediaeval iron industry and then and later for the production of charcoal, or of 'packing stones' on which itinerant salesmen rested their packs, or of socket stones for wooden crosses destroyed at the Reformation: 'every archaeologist', Aelfrida admitted, 'should have a sceptic on his … expeditions').[239] But at this liminal period of her life when she was Mrs Graham to the world and Placida of the Holy Passion at Tymawr, Aelfrida, it seems, was crossing other thresholds too. What they were she does or dare not reveal yet (she even went so far as to attribute a bout of ill health to God's punishment 'for having talked about prehistoric secrets')[240] and over a decade was to pass before she did.

Mindful, however, that poking about in 'Prehistory' constituted another leakage of spiritual energy and breach of spiritual silence ('I must be *very* careful not to turn into an archaeologist instead of a tertiary'), she laid aside her researches during Advent ('no archaeology until after Christmas')[241] and Lent. At other times she regarded 'Prehistory' as a glamorous snare to which a 'Cambridge upbringing' and 'intellectual curiosity' attracted her but which was designed to lure her away from her path of 'Penance and Praise'[242], and tried to restrain her enthusiasm. (Significantly, perhaps, Mother Guenvrede did not; she even encouraged her tertiary's activities on the grounds, it may be, that surplus energy was better expended on 'Monmouth stones' than on the Community.) On the other hand, 'Prehistory' *might* be a 'spiritually profitable' pursuit because it brought Placida face to face with '*one* aspect of God: incomprehensibility'.[243]

God comprehensible, however, was grasped in a manner equated by Placida not with breaches or leakages but with manifestations of 'the Light of His Presence'[244] in the world: Deity incarnate in Monmouthshire countryside. Aelfrida, of course, had been familiar with rural England from childhood but never before arriving at Tymawr had she lived in continuous proximity to deep countryside like that which now surrounded her. Venturing beyond the convent curtilage, she found her surroundings 'beautiful beyond words'[245] (even the snowfall which accompanied 'Siberian winds' created 'a world of white and gleaming beauty')[246], less because of its intrinsic loveliness than because it was "charged with the grandeur of God".[247]

Pursuing 'Prehistory' along lanes bordered by hedges of honeysuckle and wild rose, through forests of beech and oak, through bluebells and bracken, up hills, down dales, and across streams, Placida discovered that 'God was with [her]'[248] on each and every walk and in Trahernian tones proclaimed that 'the world showed itself [to me] like the Garden of Eden, a paradise of sunlight and fresh springing green and of gentle kine'.[249] She also enjoyed 'Garden of Eden encouragement'[250] from wild and domesticated animals and even seems to have acquired strange authority over them, for they allowed her to draw near and did not move away until she withdrew her attention from them: adders charmed by whistling the hymn *Jerusalem, my happy home*; foxes with their 'glorious red-gold coat shining in the sun'; 'a *very* baby white lamb' which came to her to be '*cuddled*'[251]; a pair of owlets perched on a gate, 'solemn and hardly afraid'.[252] She valued them not only not merely because they provided comfort and companionship but also because with clearer and clearing eyes she could see "all creatures full of deities" and the piece of earth they inhabited as undertaking the "office of a priest".[253] Modelling herself on Saint Francis who loved Nature for the same reason and who called on his 'brothers' and 'sisters' in God's creation to praise their mutual Father, she addressed trees as family, calling the white chestnut which sheltered the summer house 'Sister Castanea' and the 'magnificent beech' seen from the West Room window 'Brother Fagus'. And under the spell of countryside "Peace and Beauty" ('the valleys seemed like deep pools of His stillness'), she became aware of its calming effect on her "inner turbulence"[254] and believed that God too was bestowing 'interior' silence on herself. But it was, alas, '*Tymawr* quietness, *not* Aelfrida quietness'[255] He bestowed.

## Notes

1  GCPPT 1|1|54 9 September 1937.
2  *Book of Acts* (Record of happenings in the Society of the Sacred Cross) 31 October 1937.
3  GCPPT 1|1|65 'Eve of All Saints' (31 October) 1947.
4  GCPPT 1|1|56 23 March 1939.
5  GCPPT 1|1|54 31 October 1937.
6  Tillyard, Ae. *The Centaur* p317. (GCPPT 2|21|1).
7  GCPPT 1|1|54 1 November 1937.
8  ibid. 31 October 1937.
9  ibid. 31 October and 1 November 1937. Aelfrida's readings in McTaggart's *Studies in Hegelian Philosophy* while on 'honeymoon' with Julius in Soham in April 1904 might have been the reason for her wry comment four years later that "even Soham might be dull after one had been there a month". (Tillyard, HJW. *The Letters of ACW Tillyard* (MTC); letter from Aelfrida to Julius Tillyard of 15 March 1908.
10  GCPPT 1|1|54 12 September 1937.
11  ibid. 20 September 1937.
12  ibid. 30 September 1937.
13  ibid. 24 and 25 October 1937.
14  Tillyard, Ae. *The Centaur* pp302, 304 and 306.
15  O'Ferrall, R. *Early Memories.*

16 Tillyard, Ae. *The Centaur* p 305.
17 GCPPT 1|1|67a SSC Newsletter 'Christmas 1949'.
18 GCPPT 1|1|54 30 September 1937.
19 ibid. 14 and 27 September 1937.
20 ibid. 20 and 30 September 1937.
21 ibid.
22 ibid. 22 October 1937.
23 ibid. 14 September 1937.
24 ibid.
25 ibid. 30 September 1937.
26 ibid. 14 September 1937.
27 ibid. 24 October 1937.
28 ibid. 21 September and 22 October 1937.
29 À Kempis, T. pp 45–46. Chapter entitled 'On the Monastic Life'.
30 Carter, TT. *Spiritual Instructions: The Religious Life* pp117–118.
31 GCPPT 1|1|30 18 May 1925.
32 GCPPT 1|1|54 30 October 1937.
33 Carter, TT. op cit pp 66 and 120.
34 GCPPT 1|1|54 1 November 1937.
35 GCPPT 1|1|45 8 June 1934.
36 GCPPT 1|1|57 'The Transfiguration' (6 August ) 1939.
37 GCPPT 1|1|55 'St John the Baptist' (24 June) 1937. Sister Jeanne, then aged 32, was English by birth but French by extraction. A former masseuse, she was described by Aelfrida as 'a born contemplative' and praised for her lovely voice; she was then the Community's cantress.
38 ibid. 18 April 1936.
39 ibid. 7 May 1936.
40 *The Rule of St Benedict* p 7 ch 1 'The Kinds of Monk'.
41 GCPPT 1|1|47 17 May 1935.
   GCPPT 1|1|49 7 September 1935.
42 GCPPT 1|1|54 14 September 1937.
43 ibid.
44 GCPPT 1|1|44 27 September 1933.
   GCPPT 1|1|54 3 March 1938.
45 GCPPT 1|1|54 29 April 1938.
46 ibid. 13 February 1938.
47 ibid. 21 April 1938.
48 ibid. 27 March 1938.
49 ibid.12 September 1937.
50 ibid. 14 October 1937.
51 GCPPT 1|1|54 21 December 1937.
52 ibid. 14 October 1937.
53 ibid. 28 April 1938.
54 ibid. 21 and 23 December 1937.
55 GCPPT 1|1|54 28 February 1938.
56 GCPPT 1|1|54 8 August 1937.
57 GCPPT 1|1|44 23 July 1933.
58 GCPPT 1|1|54 29 March 1938.
   GCPPT 1|1|55 28 May 1938.
59 GCPPT 1|1|54 20 September 1937.
60 ibid. 2 October and 19 November 1937.
61 ibid. 19 November 1937.
62 ibid. 21 and 22 November 1937.
63 ibid. 19 and 21 November 1937.
64 GCPPT 1|1|44 22 July 1933.
65 GCPPT 1|1|54 13 December 1937.
66 GCPPT 1|1|56 20 November 1938.
67 GCPPT 1|1|54 8 November 1937.
68 ibid. 7 December 1937. There is no contemporaneous mention in Aelfrida's diary of these '*given*' intuitions and she informed Mother Guenvrede of them only after the event (ibid. 11 December 1937).
69 GCPPT 1|1|55 17 June 1938.
70 GCPPT 1|1|56 11 December 1938.
71 GCPPT 1|1|54 12 September 1937.
72 ibid. 1 January 1938.
73 ibid. 8 November 1937 and 15 January 1938.
74 GCPPT 1|1|55 25 August 1938.
75 GCPPT 1|1|54 18 January 1938.
76 ibid. 4 February 1938.
77 ibid. 'Maundy Thursday' (14 April) 1938.
78 ibid. 26 November and 26 December 1937.
79 ibid. 28 February 1938.
80 ibid. 12 November 1937.
81 GCPPT 1|1|56 25 May 1939.
82 GCPPT 1|1|54 1 and 15 January 1938.
83 GCPPT 1|1|56 16 May 1939.
84 GCPPT 1|1|54 3 and 5 January 1938.
85 GCPPT 1|1|5 4 2 April 1938. There is also a known correlation between rheumatoid arthritis and cardio-vascular disease.
86 GCPPT 1|1|54 13 November and 20 December 1937.
87 The quotations are taken from *Lay of the Valetudinarian* (GCPPT 2|13), composed at Tymawr on 18 February 1938 (GCPPT 1|1|54) or 27 January 1939 (GCPPT 1|1|56) after arguments with those ladies.
88 GCPPT 1|1|55 14 June 1938.
89 GCPPT 1|1|56 21 and 24 October 1938.
90 ibid. 15 January 1939.
91 Ibid. 4 December 1938.
92 GCPPT 1|1|54 4 April 1938.
93 ibid. 18 March 1938.
94 GCPPT 1|1|56 23 December 1938.
95 ibid. 9 April 1939. Worth noting here is that aspirin, taken to excess, can also cause rhinitis and bronchospasm ('asthma').
96 GCPPT 1|1|55 1, 3 and 4 September 1938.
97 GCPPT 1|1|56 23 December 1938.
98 GCPPT 1|1|54 21 March and 4 April 1938.
99 GCPPT 1|1|55 6 May 1938.
100 GCPPT 1|1|54 4 April 1938.
101 GCPPT 1|1|57 22 July 1939.
102 GCPPT 1|1|56 15 October 1938.
103 GCPPT 1|1|26 23 September 1921.
104 GCPPT 1|1|21 29 January 1916.
105 GCPPT 1|1|26 27 September 1921.
106 GCPPT 1|1|43 13 and 21 April 1933.
107 GCPPT 1|1|27 21 March 1923.
108 GCPPT 1|1|54 23 January 1938.
109 ibid. 28 February 1938.
110 GCPPT 1|1|56 17 December 1938.
111 ibid. 28 February and 5 March 1938.
112 ibid. 5 and 10 March 1938.
113 ibid. 5, 6, 7 and 23 March 1938.
114 ibid. 16 and 28 April 1938.
115 GCPPT 1|1|55 8 June 1938.
116 ibid. 11 May 1938.
117 ibid. 29 January 1938.
118 ibid. 14 and 21 May 1938.
119 ibid. 9 and 14 May 1938.
120 ibid. 14 May 1938.
121 ibid. 4 July 1938.
122 ibid. 5, 6, and 9 July 1938.
123 ibid. 10 July 1938.
124 ibid. 9 July 1938.
125 ibid. 'Trinity V' (16 or 17 July) and 21 July 1938.
126 ibid. 31 July 1938. A sketch of girdle and plastron is appended to this entry.
127 ibid. 26 and 31 July 1938.
128 ibid. 31 July and 1 August 1938.
129 ibid. 1 and 2 August 1938.
130 ibid. 31 July 1938.

131 ibid. 21 July 1938.

132 ibid. 'Trinity V' (16 or 17 July) 1938.

133 ibid. 6 and 9 July 1938.

134 St Rose of Lima (1586–1617) was a mystic and ecstatic Dominican nun who practised extreme physical mortification from an early age: sleeping on a bed of stones, thorns, and potsherds, wearing a spiked metal crown (disguised as a rose garland) and a chain cincture; she also endured lengthy fasts and died young.

135 ibid. 1 August 1938.

136 ibid. 'Trinity V' (16 or 17 July) 1938.

137 ibid. 3 and 31 August 1938. St Bruno (c1031–1101) founded the austere Carthusian order near Grenoble in 1084 in what was then a very remote area as a result of a vision of a secluded hermitage in which communion with God could be experienced without interruption; he later withdrew to an even more remote area in Calabria where he founded further religious houses. Carthusians, Aelfrida was delighted to discover, wore hair scapulars as 'of obligation' as part of their habit (GCPPT 1|1|56 26 October 1938). She was further delighted to discover that Saints Bruno and Placid shared a day 'since every day in convents begins the day before' at Mattins/Matins (ibid. 6 October 1938), St Bruno's Day being 6 October. St Bruno as the patron saint of those whose minds are supposed to be possessed by demonic forces may also have had some significance for her, given her own diabolic visitations.

138 GCPPT 1|1|56 24 November 1938.

139 ibid. 7 February 1939.

140 ibid. 17 and 19 January 1939.

141 GCPPT 1|1|45 21 April 1934.

142 GCPPT 1|1|46 8 February 1935.

143 GCPPT 1|1|57 17 December 1939.

144 GCPPT 1|1|57 12 May 1940.

145 Mother Magdalen Mary. *The Religious Life: Contemplative and Enclosed* pp 3–5.

146 GCPPT 1|1|54 25 January 1938.
GCPPT 1|1|55 2 August 1938. 24 January was St Cadoch's Day and Thomas Aquinas her patron saint.

147 GCPPT 1|1|54 6 March [1937].

148 GCPPT 1|1|56 21 October 1938. Of interest in this connection is Aelfrida's contemporary discovery of Edith Peacey's *Saint Birgitta of Sweden* (GCPPT 1|1|56 17 and 21 October 1938). Birgitta (1302/3–1347), a widowed noblewoman, became a Franciscan tertiary following her husband's early death. A visionary ecstatic prone since childhood to exaggerated acts of penitence, Birgitta's first attempts at monastic standards as a tertiary made her so ill that her spiritual director put her under obedience to live less rigorously. Peacey's definition of a Christian mystic as one who sees God "through a temperament" (op. cit. p95) fits Aelfrida exactly.

149 GCPPT 1|1|57 16 July 1939.

150 GCPPT 1|1|56 2, 6 and 27 October, 'All Saints' (1 November) and 4 November 1938.

151 ibid. 6 March 1939.

152 GCPPT 1|1|56 3 November 1938.
GCPPT 1|1|57 11 August 1939.

153 GCPPT 1|1|56 'Shrove Tuesday' (21 February) 1939. Aspirin in very large doses can also give rise to urticaria but the localised nature of Aelfrida's 'eczema' militates against this.

154 GCPPT 1|1|57 24 December 1939.

155 GCPPT 1|1|56 4 March 1939.

156 ibid. 30 May 1939.

157 ibid. 2 June 1939.

158 GCPPT 1|1|54 3 November 1937.
GCPPT 1|1|59 4 March 1939.

159 GCPPT 1|1|54 3 February 1938.

160 GCPPT 1|1|55 2 August 1938.

161 GCPPT 1|1|57 16 July 1939.

162 ibid. 26 and 27 October and 8 November 1938.

163 ibid. 30 March 1940.

164 GCPPT 1|1|45 24 January 1934.

165 Tillyard, Ae. *The Making of a Mystic* p21.

166 GCPPT 1|1|45 24 January 1934.

167 ibid.

168 The lines are taken from *The Ascete,* written in Brookline, Mass. on 23 June 1908 as one of the series of searingly introspective sonnets composed during Aelfrida's first pregnancy (GCPPT 2|2). It was later published in *To Malise* (p15).

169 GCPPT 1|1|55 16 September 1939.

170 Aelfrida's title may derive from any one of several psalms in which the phrase appears (e.g. 63:6) but in the context of the book most likely derives from 119.

171 GCPPT 1|1|61 29 July 1943. Published reviews were, so Aelfrida said, favourable, *The Guardian*'s noting that "in the writings of A-T-" (sic) the "fine flower of Anglican mystical devotion" bloomed again. (GCPPT 1|1|55 17 June 1938).

172 Tillyard, Ae, *The Night Watches* (Title page). The author's name is given as 'Aelfrida Tillyard'.

173 As epigraph to *The Way of Praise* Aelfrida chose a phrase from Psalm 119 (*Zain* 54) "Thy statutes have been my songs in the house of my pilgrimage", a mantra suggested to her by her guardian angel (he Latinised it) on 6 June 1935 (GCPPT 1|1|48) while she was composing the book. A favourite mantra during the writing of this and preceding volume of her 'closer walk with God' trilogy, Aelfrida does not use it again now she has, as it were, reached her goal.

174 Tillyard, Ae. *The Night Watches* pp 1–4.

175 ibid. pp37–40 and 45–49.

176 ibid. pp 5–8. Worth noting in this context is the similarity of Aelfrida's description to two pictures by visionary painter John Martin, *The Plains of Heaven* (c1845–1853) and *The Celestial City and Rivers of Bliss* (1841), in which the City of God appears glowing in the sky above a beautiful landscape. Aelfrida had been familiar with Martin's doomy pictures since childhood but may have seen reproductions of his 'celestial city' ones too.

177 ibid. pp 9–12.

178 ibid. pp13–16.

179 GCPPT 1|1|54 12 September 1937.
GCPPT 1|1|55 6 June 1938.

180 Psalm 119 *Zain*:55, *Cheth*: 62(KJV).

181 Tillyard, Ae. *The Night Watches* pp 45–49. Pages 25–28 of this book are those in which Aelfrida describes her Brooklands Avenue walks of 1912.

182 Psalm 119 *Tau*: 175(KJV).

183 GCPPT 1|1|55 10 July 1938. Aelfrida's *Eat More Mushrooms* poem, written only months before her prevarications concerning Aleister Crowley, also refers to a 'wizard' who picks them at cock-crow.

184 GCPPT 1|1|56 14 January 1939.

185 GCPPT 1|1|54 31 October 1937.

186 GCPPT 1|1|52 3 February 1937.

187 GCPPT 1|1|54 18 November 1937.

188 GCPPT 1|1|47 22 April 1935.

189 GCPPT 1|1|54 16 March 1938.

190 ibid. 18 March 1938.

191 GCPPT 1|1|56 7 May 1939.

192 GCPPT 1|1|55 6 May 1938.

193 ibid. 19 April 1938.

194 ibid. 6 May 1938.

195 ibid.

196 ibid. 'Pentecost' (5 June) 1938.

197 ibid. 1 June 1938. The entry is paraphrased closely in a novel (*The Centaur* p325 GCPPT 2|21|1) written in 1951 whose hero, revisiting Cambridge before entering a monastery, realises that though

life in Cambridge "was sweeter than anywhere else", he himself has chosen "something sterner, colder [and] harder … where there was darkness and silence and pain and the fight against … evil powers in the world and in himself".

198  GCPPT 1|1|55 29 May 1938.
199  ibid. 2 January 1938.
200  ibid. 4 March 1938.
201  ibid. 2 January 1938.
202  ibid. 4 March 1938.
203  GCPPT 1|1|54 14 October 1937.
204  ibid. 28 November 1937.
205  ibid. 17 December 1937.
206  GCPPT 1|1|56 23 December 1938.
207  GCPPT 1|1|54 26 December 1938.
208  ibid. 5 March 1938.
209  GCPPT 1|1|56 24 November 1938.
210  ibid. 8 August 1939.
211  GCPPT 1|1|54 25 December 1937 and 1 January 1938.
212  ibid. 'Lady Day' (25 March) 1938. Julius' reaction was more prosaic: *"sororem visi in coenobia"* (*Synopsis of Diary* 24 March 1938 MTC).
213  GCPPT 1|1|56 14 and 26 February 1939.
214  ibid. 2 and 22 October 1938.
215  GCPPT 1|1|54 5 March 1938.
216  ibid. 1 January, 25 March and 8 April 1938.
217  GCPPT 1|1|57 19 August 1939.
218  ibid. 30 June 1939.
219  GCPPT 1|1|22 20 April 1918.
220  GCPPT 1|1|48 24 June 1935.
221  GCPPT 1|1|56 7 November 1938.
222  ibid. 20 April 1939
223  I am particularly indebted in what follows to Stuart Piggott's *Ancient Europe* (1973) and to Cyril Fox's *South Wales and Monmouthshire* (1955), but have also made use of privately printed and often anonymous booklets and monographs on subjects of local historical interest held in the SSC library at Tymawr.
224  St Cadoch (c500–580 AD) was born and raised in Monmouthshire, though his major shrine, a hermitage later expanded into a monastery with Cadoch as Abbot, was at Llancarfan in Glamorgan. A Norman church dedicated to him was founded on the ruins of the Roman legionary headquarters at Caerleon near Newport and a chapel bearing his name survived the dissolution of Monmouth priory until the later seventeenth century.
225  GCPPT 1|1|52 23 January and 26 October 1937.
226  Fortified manor houses were common in the turbulent Welsh Marches in early mediaeval times though many later fell into disrepair; traditional fortifications were imitated in rudimentary form in Tymawr's battlemented parapet.

227  GCPPT 1|1|54 22 March and 23 April 1938. The name is derived from a phrase in the *Book of Common Prayer*: "Thou O Lord … hast set thine house of defense very high".
228  ibid. 23 April 1938.
229  GCPPT 1|1|67 3 January 1950.
230  GCPPT 1|1|55 10 September 1938.
      GCPPT 1|1|56 20 April 1939.
231  GCPPT 1|1|56 12 February 1939.
232  GCPPT 1|1|61 28 March 1943.
233  GCPPT 1|1|56 13 February 1939.
234  ibid. 15 November 1938.
235  ibid. 4 November 1938
236  ibid. 12 and 14 February 1939.
237  GCPPT 1|1|61 28 March and 4 April 1943.
238  The area round Tymawr was famous for the manufacture of millstones used locally in flour and other mills and across the Wye in cider presses.
239  GCPPT 1|1|56 'St Mark's Day' (25 April) 1939. For more on the archaeology of the Trellech area see
      www.lostcityoftrellech.co.uk
      http:||www.celiahaddon.co.uk/standing%20stones/wales.htm
      http:||www.data–wales.co.uk/trellech.html
240  GCPPT 1|1|56 12 February 1939.
241  ibid. 4 and 24 November 1938.
242  ibid. 12 and 20 April and 15 November 1938.
243  ibid. 14 February 1939.
244  GCPPT 1|1|57 9 August 1939.
245  GCPPT 1|1|54 'St Francis' Day' (4 October) 1937. Because the conventual 'day' began before midnight, St Francis' day would blend into St Placid's on 5 October.
246  GCPPT 1|1|56 20 December 1938.
247  The quotation is taken from Gerald Manley Hopkins' *God's Grandeur*. A comparison of the worldly and spiritual lives of the two mystics (Hopkins, born in 1844 and dying in 1889, was of the generation preceding Aelfrida's) gives rise to interesting parallels. Aelfrida, though aware of Hopkins' verse, mentions him only rarely.
248  GCPPT 1|1|54 7 April 1938.
249  GCPPT 1|1|61 28 March 1943.
250  GCPPT 1|1|54 26 October 1937.
251  GCPPT 1|1|56 14 March 1939.
      GCPPT 1|1|61 28 March 1913.
252  GCPPT 1|1|57 7 July 1940.
253  Traherne, T. *Dumbness* (*The Oxford Book of Mystical Verse* pp 68–71).
254  GCPPT 1|1|54 13 March 1938.
      Tillyard, Ae *The Centaur* p 8.
255  GCPPT 1|1|54 3 October 1937.

# This Child of God

On 5 March 1927 while fretting over 'weary and heavy-eyed' Tom Henn (he was overworked and his wife was pregnant)[1], talking Temperance to mothers at Cambridge's Parkside Baby Clinic ('I was so eloquent that [they all] wanted to sign something')[2], waiting up 'to turn out in the rain' to fetch her daughters home from a dance[3] (an unnecessary martyrdom; Alethea was nearly twenty and at Girton, Agatha nearly nineteen), suffering always 'a pain somewhere [so] I don't think I need undertake any physical penances'[4], and dreaming wistfully that she and Constantine were reconciled ('the dream stopped short – they always do – of physical union but such as it was, was very sweet'), Aelfrida dreamed of joining an Order where she enjoyed 'wonderful and exalted religious experiences'.[5] Ten years later Sister Placida had and did, experiences described at length in her diary (some entries consist only of these) but frequently so wonderful, so exalted – and so numerous – that she found herself unable to describe them in detail ('I had a "shewing" yesterday [but] I just can't write it all down')[6], an inability unusual in one adept with her pen but a manifestation, if one were needed, of their spiritual immensity. Feeling less empowered than usual to describe 'things that happen', 'trances', 'shewings', 'an intense spiritual activity and *awareness*', God 'near, *near,* pressing on [her] soul'[7] and less and less able to tell what she saw, but experiencing, as always, a compulsion to unburden herself, 'this tertiary, this Child of God, this Placida of the Holy Passion' was forced notwithstanding to her diary. A Mother Superior who considered her 'odd', a confessor 'not in touch with [her] soul'[8] because unsympathetic to her reparative need to dwell repetitively on the burden of sin she carried (her own sins in this instance, 'which with weary boredom reappear')[9], or a Visitor who, though he gave good advice ('go on quietly and accept everything that God sends … with gratitude and humility', do not 'analyse' or wonder 'why to *me?*'), also warned her that in her relationship to God she, unlike the shepherds of the Nativity, should not need 'the whole orchestra of Heaven' to rouse her[10], were all three impossible confidants.

She took some heed, it is true, of her guardian angel (once wont to stand beside her while she prayed, now enveloping her 'so that I kneel in his immaterial form

**Father Amos**

as one might stand in light')[11] when he too counselled humble acceptance of experiences given rather than casting about for an adequate response[12] and of Father Cary when he told her bluntly to refrain from fruitless attempts to 'understand' and from 'making *grande chose*' of visions and 'shewings'.[13] Then too, Father Northcott's practical advice made her aware that 'dazzling spiritual experiences' were only incidental to '*the life itself*' (a life to which she was 'called by God Himself' as a channel of mankind's 'Godward longing' but in which 'God and what is due to Him, stands first')[14] but when he also warned her that elevated feelings 'more and more full of wonder, more *absorbed*, more *drawn into God*'[15] constituted the '*fervor novitiorum* which God sends to mark the spot where He wishes you to be' but would not endure and that, the fervour of the novitiate having dissipated, "all sorts of things happen", Placida was dismissive: 'Of course. I shall see in time'.[16] (She did.) She even turned perforce to Mother Guenvrede and although she increasingly disliked and distrusted her as a person chiefly because passages of arms between them persuaded her that the Mother's judgemental response to her tertiary-mystic's inadvertent or supposedly minor misdemeanours was wilfully unpleasant or wholly unjustified, found her spiritual advice helpful. Her first major request for assistance happened after receiving a vision, rapturous beyond description, of 'God Himself' seen 'imageless [as] light … by pure spiritual perception' (her guardian angel had suggested that she pray to be taken 'into the heart of divine love') but which nevertheless troubled her so much (was she, she asked herself, 'deluded'?) that she invoked higher authority. Mother Guenvrede's comments – Aelfrida actually went so far as to show her the diary entry describing the experience, an unrepeated action for much of her diary before and after the event was extremely critical of Mother Guenvrede and other members of the Community and a wholly 'spiritual' diary it was not – was sensible and (up to a point) reassuring: Sister Placida *had* seen "as much as we can see of God in this life", such visions were given to *all* God's children even to those 'who are not even "good" people', and recurrent experiences of this nature were inherent in the contemplative life and privileges which could be withdrawn.[17]

Authors too were valued, chiefly for their support of views already held: Richard Meux Benson, for example, on the meaning of the religious vocation[18] (Placida should have heard his warning that "any peculiarity of religious devotion" was liable to develop the individual at the expense of the oneness of the Community to which he or she belonged[19] but did not, though she noted that his text as a whole opened 'the vast prospect of what vocation means' and made her 'surer than ever' of her own[20]), or Thomas Thellusson Carter on the difference between spiritual and sacramental communion[21], a reading of which underlined for her the importance of the latter in and to her present exalted experiences. In fact Thellusson Carter's exposition of "spiritual communion" as involving the communicant attracting Christ to himself with all the "drawings" of which he is capable and opening channels of communication of his own designing (something of which Aelfrida was aware of having done prior to entering Tymawr), and of "sacramental communion" as being that in which Christ "gives forth

Himself according to His own full and absolute purpose … after His own way … [possessing] us and making us his own" during donation of the Bread of Life which "needs to be received day by day" (not once a week or only on festivals) in order to underline its significance as a symbol or "antepast" of "the Eternal Communion" to be enjoyed after death[22], both explains and supports Placida's enthusiasm for daily Communion[23], her utter misery ('a black cloud … covered my spirit')[24] if there was 'no daily bread for the child of God' (consolation could be achieved nevertheless through 'spiritual communion' only: 'Christ feeding me with His own Body and Blood')[25], her conviction that 'she had to fight … against an odd kind of restlessness such as [she] used to have in the world'[26] if unable to take Communion in either form, and her insistence to Mother Guenvrede that she be allowed to pray 'never to miss Holy Communion or the Hours until the day of [her] death'.[27] Yet even now and despite advice it seems she continued to believe that by demonstrated devotion and faithful exercise of chapel duty she could achieve the sanctification signally un-granted by earlier demands that God make her a saint and not spare her in the making.

As before, 'wonderful and exalted' experiences occurred as a response to events. A visit to the chapel (as advised by Saint Benedict after travel) on returning from Oxford and Cambridge in spring 1938 inspired a vision of 'spiritual fire' descending from heaven to consume her 'spiritual sacrifice'[28], and at Christmas services 'the veil that separated us from the unseen' parted to disclose the heavenly host manifest as 'strange colours such as no earthly rainbow holds which I have seen from childhood' and 'sounds that usually lie just beyond our mortal ears'.[29] (The 'strange colours' suggest Aelfrida may have been an unrecognised migraine sufferer since age eight or nine; at Tymawr, migrainous headaches became rare, attacks diminishing to 'dazzles' whose oscillating iridescence seems remarkably similar to optical effects seen as a child.) Some, however, occurred spontaneously as she went about her daily routines in house and garden ('God touched me and poured His Grace upon me'[30]; 'God comes leaping down … snatching my soul away into regions beyond the reach of the mind')[31] spite of efforts to be as 'centred down' (a Quaker expression) as her spiritual advisers wished. The majority, however, occurred when, alone in chapel after Vespers '*coram sanctissimo*', she adored the Blessed Sacrament for the thirty minutes of her allotted watch.

'When I pray [in front of the Blessed Sacrament]', wrote Aelfrida at St Benedict's, 'I feel as if I am doing what I am most *meant* to do. I go in, I kneel down, I … push away everything that is not God' (this action is not, she emphasises, 'a mere bit of technique' akin to that undertaken prior to a Ceremonial Magic ritual) 'then I gather myself together and with all the fervour at my command, pour out myself in worship … make quietness, calm all the waves of emotion and thought, give up hopes of sweetness, try and pray. If all goes well the Holy Spirit stays with me … in a perfect stillness of mind, body and soul' (this is 'not a trance', she reminds us) '[and] in that stillness there begins a kind of subtle movement, an outpouring from above, a welling-up from within … an overwhelming intensification of the Presence [of] God … a kind of spiritual instinct which says "Rest here, this is *ultimate*".[32] Stillness, however, was harder to achieve at Tymawr even with the help of 'useful saints'; indeed, it seems that during Aelfrida's first year as Sister Placida and well into her second, some of her perpetual tiredness can be attributed to the frequency and intensity of spiritual phenomena experienced shortly before going to bed and wakefully meditated upon thereafter: suddenly (in a 'shewing' of twenty-five minutes duration) 'the power of God came upon me with great weight and vehemence … as if he would *eject me from myself* … to make room for His Spirit'[33], or when during a 'shewing' twenty-minutes long (it was preceded by a talk to the Mother about handkerchiefs 'because last week poor nose required fifteen!'), God 'swooped down on me … as an eagle might swoop down on its prey … I felt almost annihilated'.[34] A vision of a seraph 'made of golden light' shooting an arrow through her heart to pin her to her place, symbolic, she thought, 'that I am *attached* here' in a 'spiritual "vow of stability"'. ('Written down like that the incident looks quite incredible'; perhaps it was.)[35] A 'shewing' prior to which 'Placida of the Holy Passion' had begged Christ 'to burn up everything in me that is not Christ-like (a big blaze, I fear!)' and was rewarded by finding herself consigned to a *fornax ardens caritas* to whose flames she gave herself eagerly, only to find herself reduced by the refining fire to 'a tiny bit of gold' representing 'what had been in me of disinterested love, *caritas*' and whose microscopic nature shamed her into making 'a mental note to see, later on, what further good actions [she] could do'.[36] (None were recorded till *much* later.) A vision of the Christ Child during which she lost all sense of time and even, she thought, consciousness, only to find herself 'gazing on him as angels and archangels gazed'. (Subsequently, however, she wondered if what she had thought '*was so*' was merely '[her] own imagination … tangling itself up with *God's* demonstration of holy mysteries'.[37] Or, she asked herself, was she creating mental images from material "provided by [her] study of … the Golden Age of Monasticism" or even "picking up a dream" as it passed through someone else's mind?)[38] A

vision of 'our Lord, speaking in "spirit speech" … asking me if I desired that He should plant His prayer in my heart' to enable her to 'lay self aside entirely to live solely for … God' (she qualified her reply 'yea Lord' by warning Him that 'I *know* I shall go away and forget and be vain and wilful and opinionated and self-centred' and 'un-Christ-like'; she also admits that the conversation was not reported verbatim but as 'from memory') and, the prayer being implanted, rejoiced that 'yet another Vita Nuova' seemed to open before her: 'Oh! the wonder and the joy!'[39] And many, many more.

Rejoicing too that she had every intention of embarking on each new life as God presented it to her (or on each new aspect of that life as she discovered it and rejected the old) and that she was dominated by a sense of having been singled out, for Mother Guenvrede's response to Aelfrida's question 'why to *me*?' that all God's children saw God in different ways did not convince one who believed herself singularly favoured – as witness her reception of so many and such intense manifestations of His favour – Placida also rejoiced that she continued to be called 'to the beloved meditation' whose eponym she bore.[40] Invitations to meditate on the Holy Passion resumed soon after clothing as a tertiary in September 1937 but no mention of receiving the stigmata appeared for nearly a year. In late May 1938, however (significantly, perhaps, during her visit to Oxford and just after having noted how she longed to return to Tymawr for yet another 'fresh start'), she once again recorded the sensation of 'sharp pains of Our Lord's wounds' and recurrence of highly-visible palmar stigmata. Believing these to be reminders from the Holy Spirit of the 'quietness and detachment' He had endeavoured to create in her over the preceding months (with some success, she reckoned, her ability to be 'recollected' not being at variance with exalted spiritual experiences and the *fervor novitiorum*) and realising now that such signs were as '*nothing*' compared to exceptional manifestations of God's favour (e.g. His indwelling in her, as demonstrated by her 'shewings'), Aelfrida asked Lucius Cary if she 'need' (her word) inform Mother Guenvrede and Father Northcott. (She was, it seems, concerned that the marks on her hands might be noticed by the Community; the 'very clear marks' which also appeared on both feet remained concealed and pain, 'sometimes dull aching, sometimes stabs, in hands and feet and side'[41], could be attributed, if she was seen wincing, to arthritis.) Father Cary's response (if one was forthcoming) is not recorded but three months later Aelfrida's guardian angel suggested she confide in Mother Guenvrede.

On 10 July 1938 she did so, informing her that stigmata (she 'did not use that word, it sounds presumptuous', calling them the 'marks of the holy passion' instead) to be either a gift from God ('an *invitation*, not a reward') or, interestingly, 'some effect of [her] own sensitiveness' and emphasising that 'no marks of His Passion, however precious', could approximate in joy to daily sacramental Communion. She further stated that stigmatisation provided her with 'deep and solemn joy' *only* if no-one – Lady Abbesses, Mothers Superior, and spiritual Fathers excepted – knew she had them and that it was important for her to receive them because they reminded her that she had already refused the Cross twice, once following her initial stigmatisation in May 1913 when, as she told the Lady Abbess of Malling, she had committed her 'worst sin' by not responding to the 'great grace' bestowed on her, once on an unspecified occasion but most likely on or around 19 January 1907 at the point at which she broke her vow of Holy Virginity by consummating her marriage, and did not wish to do so thrice.[42] Mother Guenvrede's response was not recorded (nor, it appears, did Placida of the Holy Passion inform Father Northcott of her 'marks') but it seems that within a twelvemonth of her confession, increasing tranquillity of mind or, it may be, adoption of external pain-inducing devices which rendered actual or artefactual stigmatisation unimportant, or diminution of guilt when viewing her unmarked palms because guilt-inducing events no longer requiring that she see Christ gazing in "gentlest reproof" at palms that "bore no mark of pain"[43], occasioned diminution in the severity and frequency – though not the complete disappearance – of such physical manifestations. Or perhaps she simply refused further 'gifts'.

Refusal is supported by decisions made as a result of an extremely disconcerting event. At some point during chapel services held at Easter 1939, Sister Placida found herself praying involuntarily with hands uplifted as the nuns did, instead of folded on her knee. She continued the practice voluntarily but whether this was because it made her feel more at one with her 'Sisters-in-Christ' or because she found the posture more reverential or because the pose proclaimed her piety, she does not say. What she does say, however, is that her palms were painful and 'burning'[44], a manifestation, she thought, of Christ's passional presence within her. (Elevation of the hands is also a recognised way of easing the pain of arthritic symptoms or of localized contusions.) Two months later, however, and following the appearance of unusual manifestations on her left hand (two concentric circles, the inner much darker than the outer) which Aelfrida was convinced anyone with 'normal' eyesight would notice (is there a hint of disappointment that they did not; surely not all the inhabitants of Tymawr were myopic?), Placida was horrified to perceive during Mass on, significantly, the Festival

of the Precious Blood, that her left hand was 'pierced right through' and that blood dripped from it onto her missal. So vivid was the impression ('the sight stabbed me') that she actually tried to staunch the bleeding. Then realisation dawned: 'the wound was not "really there" in the sense that the wounds are sometimes' but a hallucination – or, as she preferred to put it, '*my translation* of something that my crucified Lord wished me to perceive [as] a *part* of His indwelling'.[45] Either way the experience rattled her – did she fear the onset of overt haemorrhages *à la* Padre Pio? – and she decided to 'refuse' invitations to meditate on the Passion in an effort to prevent or minimise further real or supernatural manifestations. (It may or may not be significant that she suffered a brief recrudescence of vaginal bleeding around this time.) Further distress occurred when she discovered that pleas of fatigue (a more acceptable excuse than fear) resulted in reprisals: a scolding from her guardian angel for refusing such 'a gift for the Community', horrible dreams 'like *Concrete*, only worse', and a terrifying 'shewing' at Mass during which 'everything … became insubstantial': people, 'familiar material objects', even 'status and achievement', leaving Placida 'a naked soul in the Presence of the Judge'.[46] Whatever the reason – and if refusal, this would have meant a mighty act of will in Aelfrida's part – stigmatisation declined in frequency and severity.

That Aelfrida was able to bear experiences of this nature without breaking down is evidence not only of her noted ability to compartmentalise her life (the entry quoted above ends with the anguished cry 'oh, for the sake of the glory of God I *must* be better, I must try, try, and try', the next begins 'there is a by-election at Monmouth and all the household, Sisters included, went by car and voted … I thought our business was to pray not to vote'; she herself stayed behind)[47] and to consider a matter closed once she had unburdened herself of it, but also of the therapeutic effect of living in a Community whose spiritual aims were the same as hers though individual personalities might jar and Community practices differ. Never before had Aelfrida found herself a member of a supportive Community like the SSC. At the Perse School and in every Consular Service posting save Emden she been an outsider, a feeling enhanced by her own excluding behaviour. At Malling, though made lovingly welcome, she remained on the periphery of an enclosed order. But as resident tertiary at Tymawr she felt 'the spirit of the Community' (and the spirit of community) enfold her to such an extent that she found indescribable happiness 'in this most beloved place'[48] and noted the beginnings of 'a hush and serenity in my soul … such as I never thought would be possible to me'.[49] This was not to say, of course, that she declined further 'emotional fervour', for life, however joyous, luminously still, and lacking 'spiritual self-consciousness', would be a trifle dull without '*any* glimpse of the Most High' through visions, auditions and 'shewings'[50], but with her physical health improving in tandem with increasing emotional and spiritual tranquillity Placida found herself seeing more clearly 'the relative importance of things in [her] spiritual life' and able to reflect on how her spiritual priorities had altered 'since [she] came here': 'God and what is due to Him stands first'[51], reparation and intercession second, and herself ('*ancilla Domini,* the *bondswoman* of the Lord') last.[52]

So strong was her desire to feel as and at one with the Tymawr Community that she forgot – or disregarded – Father Cary's advice not to become overly enmeshed with it. Her desire, heightened by loneliness ('you live in a Community, you share the spiritual life of the Community but your neighbour in the next cell is a sealed book to you')[53], by the interest she always took in 'people' and, it has to be said, by her love of meddling, impelled her to concern herself more with the Community than perhaps an electively-abject resident tertiary should. Much of her involvement was benign, even if at times misguided or reminiscent of Mrs Graham at her most managing, and to this Community and visitors responded warmly. Her obvious joy at being allowed to participate in the *opus Dei* ('as ritual becomes more familiar, its beauty throws an ever brighter light on the spiritual significance of its meaning') and in liturgical festivals (the Rogationtide procession around the convent grounds was a particular favourite for its associations with springtime and nature though, appropriately for a member of a Community dedicated to the Sacred Cross, she felt 'most at home on Good Friday')[54], and her appreciation of being permitted to share the Community's sorrows (the death of Sister Katherine, the departure of one who had 'no vocation for the enclosed life')[55] as well as its joys (the admission of postulants and their subsequent clothing as novices, novices' professions as nuns, the taking of life vows by professed nuns) was rewarded by the Community including her in celebrations punctuating the conventual year. Admission to the occasion on which Sister Jeanne presented her with a white rose from the 'bridal wreath' the latter wore when taking life vows in September 1939, a ceremony watched with much emotion by Mrs Graham (it reminded her of her own wedding day, or, rather, of the sentimentalised version she preferred) and described with spiritual insight by Sister Placida as 'an eternal relationship actualised in time'[56], was particularly appreciated.

The Community's positive feelings for Placida were reciprocated by the latter's 'unspeakable' thankfulness that her newfound ability to yield herself completely to God was due to her new life as a member of the particular Community to which God had called her.[57] An equally newfound desire for inclusivity in one who, even when actively promulgating the social aspect of her Great Work, trod a private pathway to God, does not seem to have been singled out by Aelfrida as odd or unexpected; instead, as Placida, she embraced (or believed she embraced) inclusivity wholeheartedly and enthusiastically, noting that she must align herself rigorously with the Community's '*purpose*'[58] and that for the first time in her life she felt 'rooted'.[59] She also – and this was very important to her as a 'member' (a reiterated word) of the SSC – liked to feel that she 'represented' it whether in chapel as a tertiary 'called of God' supporting her 'Sisters-in-Christ' on a day of continuous prayer[60] or as 'a part of the Community's welcome'[61] when groups of miners' wives from Tredegar colliery visited for a few days' rest and recuperation, or as a visionary 'fulfilled with grace for the benefit of the Community' receiving 'the power of the Lord' during a fifteen minute 'shewing' *coram sanctissimo*.[62]

There was, however, another side to this which was soon to have darker resonances: as Placida herself noted within months of her clothing, she lacked 'certain elements … as a member of the Community'[63] and possessed a marked tendency to deviate 'from the Community spirit'.[64] Although she did not make '*grande chose*' of this ('my guardian angel … has told me already … well, I must just persevere!')[65] and on occasion even joked wryly about it ('I confess … that when one holy maiden … reads aloud to a concourse of other holy maidens St Ambrose on *Virginity* I ask myself what possible right have I to be there')[66], it is obvious from her private and public behaviour (her continuing use of the Latin breviary, for example, or her interruption of the Sisters' annual Retreat in November 1938 by sending a note into enclosure demanding that someone – Sister Monica as it happened and in silence – pay attention to an ankle sprain so trivial that, though it occasioned the acid remark that the nuns obviously cared more for *their* souls than *her* body, did not prevent attendance at chapel)[67] that she remained as self-centred and as 'individualist' as her guardian angel said.[68] She also reacted antagonistically to instructions issued at Lent or Advent which did not coincide with her particular 'intentions' and huffily to occasions (the Bishop of Monmouth's quinquennial Visitation; a meeting between the Sisters and a group of Chichester retreatants) which as a tertiary she felt she had every right to attend but to which she was not invited by reason of her being neither a religious nor a member of the Chichester confraternity.

Notable, too, though less overtly expressed, were feelings of superiority towards members of the Community insufficiently privileged to receive 'sudden inrushes of the Holy Spirit' or 'tidings of another world, messages in another language' because their souls, unlike hers, were insufficiently 'attuned', for in spite of protestations that she was increasingly 'Nobody and Nothing'[69] relative to the Community, Aelfrida remained convinced that she, once called by God to preach and teach but now invited to greater intimacy with Him in solitude and silence (an invitation Mother Guenvrede seemed determined to thwart with her insistence that Placida act as guest mistress during Hilda Harrison's absences and entertain visitors at other times) was, spiritually speaking, a cut above the 'very ordinary people' comprising it, Mother Guenvrede possibly excepted. Was she not, she hints, a trained observer of supernatural phenomena, a yogi experienced in spiritual exercises and particularly so in achieving what she formerly called 'Samadhi', an adept of the spiritual life with highly-developed powers of penetration and absorption, an ecstatic who could see God more clearly than people bound by the confines of a physical body because of His having personally endowed her with the ability to do so, a mystic with whom the Holy Trinity was on intimate terms?

Though such elevated views of herself could be explained by saying ruefully 'I simply do not see myself as I am'[70], insight acquired into her motivations as a result of recent events makes it hard to believe that deviant behaviour was entirely unintentional. A possible reason is provided by Aelfrida herself: she had begun to suffer 'temptations to want a holiday from being good'[71] and, as in nursery days, to be naughty out of sheer perversity.

'Holidays' took the form of trying to control or to stir up trouble between people and hence to create a 'scene' within the Community or in a wider context than life in Monmouthshire and began with Alethea. Having earlier agreed with Mother Guenvrede and Father Northcott that she not interfere with Alethea's life in any way and more recently with Mother Guenvrede that Alethea could be prayed for and advised on religious matters by Sister Placida but was under no circumstances to be forced to take Mrs Graham's wishes into account[72], Aelfrida began once again to plan her daughter's future. Should Alethea, she wondered, become the SSC's 'missionary tertiary' ('she seems to have a missionary vocation')[73] with a view perhaps to her being 'ultimately … led hither' (i.e. to Tymawr) as a nun[74], a notion encouraged by Placida 'living through' the ceremony of a postulant being clothed as a novice and hoping that one day she might witness Alethea undergoing the same ritual in the same chapel (and what a snub for Malling that

**Hilda Harrison**

would be) or arising from a suggestion by her guardian angel that she invite Alethea to Tymawr ('I keeping my Rule the whole time') in order that her daughter could have 'quiet to know what her vocation is to be'.[75] But interesting though developments might have been had Alethea adopted her mother's suggestions, she did not, nor did Mrs Graham's approaches to Alethea's spiritual director prove any more fruitful: Alethea, said Father O'Brien firmly, was 'to settle down at St Cuthbert's' and put all thoughts of conventual life out of her mind 'for the present'.[76] A year later – and from Father O'Brien's statement one can deduce that Mrs Graham continued to plot and plan – the scope of the cordon sanitaire flung round Alethea by the Cowley Fathers to protect her from her mother had widened: furlough (if any) was to be taken on a return ticket; the missionary life suited both her emotional health and her natural aptitudes; she was forbidden to 'test her vocation'; 'married life would not appeal to her'.[77]

Thwarted of her daughter, Aelfrida turned her attentions to a woman close enough in age to be her sister and to the woman she regarded as her third mother.

Hilda Harrison was a former social worker with whom in later years Aelfrida became fast friends, but during her earlier years at Tymawr she kept Hilda at arm's length, in part because she regarded the latter's probing into 'past sorrows'[78] as intrusive (but how did Hilda know about them if Aelfrida did not hint at them? she eventually vouchsafed her version of Constantine's behaviour and Agatha's death but only after Hilda herself confided that she believed breast cancer to be a form of reparation for her brother's misbehaviour), in part because she was wary of forging another fervid female friendship[79], and in part because she did not want Hilda to discover her instruments of mortification ('anyone would hate having that known')[80], these now including the planked bed which had transformed itself from a means of alleviating backache into a Benedictine device to aid recollection. She need not have worried, for friendship between Hilda and herself was strictly regulated by Mother Guenvrede (the two women had to ask permission to visit each other's rooms and were told when they were permitted to take walks together) and Hilda herself appeared to have little wish for intimacy with a person she regarded as 'mysterious and inscrutable'[81], of whose 'prehistorical' discoveries she was deeply sceptical, and with whom she squabbled childishly over her tendency to regard Woodbine Cottage garden as her 'private and particular hobby' instead of an impersonal 'portion of labour'.[82] (It must have been difficult to start and maintain tiffs when one party to the quarrel was 'in silence' but the ladies managed; possibly it was this 'clash of temperaments' with the only person at Tymawr with whom Aelfrida felt inclined to pursue friendship as much as 'stories of need and hardship at Tredegar' related by the miners' wives which prompted Placida to entertain 'vague questionings as to whether [she] ought not to be doing something different somewhere else', a rhetorical question, surely, since she had no intention of leaving.) It is also obvious from Aelfrida's comments regarding the relationship between Hilda Harrison and Mother Guenvrede (they 'do not fully understand or trust each other')[83] that she took delight in sowing discord between them, inveigling the doctor into declaring that Hilda's health was now sturdier than her own prior to reporting the conversation to one who still tended to treat Hilda as 'delicate' and Aelfrida as a weakling clinging to 'deckchair, cushion, hot water bottle and so on'[84], or when she sided with each lady in turn when one sought her support and advice relative to the other.

Aelfrida played a subtler game with regard to Mother Guenvrede, alternating grovelling apologies (e.g. that she had 'forgotten' her 'recent determination … *never* to try and create a personal impression' when the Mother accused her of putting on 'a "come and see me being

nice to these people" air' with the Tredegar wives, an air which Aelfrida freely admitted she had formerly adopted expressly to annoy Phyllis Tillyard[85] with obviously false assurances that she valued the Mother's reprimands highly or by 'lying low' in the hope that the Mother not discover what she had done (she '*may* be furious!!')[86] when perpetrating a deed of which she knew Mother Guenvrede would disapprove. Then too, in spite of pious reminders to herself that Mother Guenvrede was right or in the right ('*Placida*. Don't forget!')[87], Mrs Graham deeply resented being made to apologise and submit: 'I was *very* much taken aback [and] it felt very odd to be "under obedience" entirely at variance with my own opinion [but I said] "you shall be obeyed" [and bowed and withdrew]'. (As an afterthought and because she felt obliged to, she added 'I am *glad* to obey'.)[88] It is also clear that she indulged in and took pleasure in indulging in a campaign of civil disobedience amounting almost to vendetta against the Mother (seeking outsiders' advice, inferring and accusing, withholding information, etc.), a campaign to which she then drew its victim's attention in the guise of asking Mother Guenvrede's advice or by expressing exaggerated concern for her welfare. ('Could I have done more – ought I even to have done so much – to try and prevent her having a breakdown?' when Mother Guenvrede was suffering from smoke inhalation following a brush fire on the convent plantation; Placida, not to be outdone, was inspired to receive a vision *coram sanctissimo* of the Tabernacle slowly opening – 'my eyes, of course, were shut' – to reveal 'a fire all glowing … [a] "spiritual fire" of love' reaching out 'a long strand of flame' to kindle 'a tiny heart … beginning to be on fire'[89] in her own breast.) The result of what seems to have been a deliberate attempt to undermine the Mother's (and the Community's) confidence in her physical and mental capacity as Mother Superior of a young, isolated, and impoverished Community had the desired effect and Mother Guenvrede did indeed suffer some kind of breakdown. It also had an undesired and unforeseen one: it demonstrated how easily Placida of the Holy Passion, Christian mystic, *ancilla domini,* and child of God, could become a bully.

Talking with Hilda Harrison in November 1938 Aelfrida was surprised and dismayed when Hilda accused her of being 'very selfish': she had arrived, said Hilda, out of the blue from goodness knows where and she had made 'a nice little niche' for herself in which she 'lived [her] own life'.[90]

Hilda was correct in all respects; by the end of her first probationary year ('the tertiary is a year old today … far and away the most blessed year of [her] life')[91] Placida had indeed created a niche for herself in which she lived, if not entirely the life she would like to lead, as close an approximation as circumstances allowed. (The comment made, so Aelfrida says, by Father Amos to Mother Guenvrede and passed on by her to Aelfrida and by Aelfrida to Father Cary that Sister Placida was not taking life at Tymawr 'seriously'[92] is revealing in this context.) True, she had had to surrender some liberty of choice and action and her demonstrated lack of 'the spirit of Benedictine obedience' (acquisition of which would mean 'a battle that [would] last the remainder of [her] life'[93] and a change of attitude at variance with a disposition such as hers) frequently led to trouble. True too, her desire for increased silence and solitude (Father Cary called it "intensified claustration")[94] was often thwarted by the exigencies of life in community because 'too much happens – there are too many distractions, even here'.[95] But when one considers how much she *had* achieved, the truth of Hilda's statement becomes clear.

For one thing, she now enjoyed a level of solitude and silence only slightly below that enjoyed at St Benedict's and, when in retreat, above, because no longer interrupted by visitors or domestic chores; she was, moreover, supported in this by Mother Guenvrede herself ("we are responsible for you and we have to see you through as best we can") who not only scolded Hilda when she explained Placida's taciturnity by saying derisively "Sister Placida only talks at tea" instead of noting gently that "Sister Placida is in silence till Sunday" and potential candidates for postulancy (who should have known better) when they tried to make her break silence during communal meals[96], but also arranged for her to lead a life of seclusion unless needed on Community service. For another, she was allowed to maintain her outside interests through correspondence and study (to be reduced to what Mother Guenvrede described as "a real tertiary's job" of putting 'little pads on the end of the chapel chairs' legs'[97] to stop them grating on the stone floor must have seemed menial and tedious to one as widely travelled and as used to 'Cambridgy' conversations as Mrs Graham), to take a daily walk, to receive visitors, to practise (within prescribed but not always adhered-to limits) what Lucius Cary termed "the self-immolation and austerity" which represented for him and for Aelfrida a "peculiar devotion to the Sacred Passion in its sacrificial appeal"[98], to make Woodbine Cottage garden her own provided she helped elsewhere if required, and to pay visits locally as health or shopping demanded. Lastly, she had been allowed to create (or had so insidiously created that no–one realised) the conditions which suited her best: a roof over her head of which she was not the householder; board and lodging provided cheaply with some small financial input from herself as a sop to conscience; freedom from the demands of dependents ('arduous days with the

kiddies', a pernickety husband, sickly parents)[99]; a room of her own to which she could withdraw uninterruptedly for hours at a time; and care if she was ill.

Throughout her early married life Aelfrida longed for Fordfield, the home to which she invariably 'drifted back' and from which she tore herself with difficulty. Looking back from the nearest place she ever found to her 'dearest place on earth', she transformed (as she transformed so much else) childhood traumas and their aftermath and the grim decades from 1914 to 1934 into a golden age, a lost paradise always sought but never found (not even 'in [her] own little homes with Constantine') until Tymawr: 'all our love for each other at Fordfield where natural and spiritual affection was closely interwoven was preparing me … for the spiritual love in this beloved place'.[100] (A question and answer session with Walter Tillyard during his visit throws interesting light on the subject, Walter asking "how does one find one's way to a place like this?" and "how do you know when you have got … to the right one?" and his aunt replying "you pray" and that you followed a pillar of fire and cloud and "where it rested, [you] stayed".)[101] It may be too, that Fordfield's successor as 'beloved place' reminded Aelfrida of a convent which lovingly received her at a time when marriage to Constantine and departure from Fordfield seemed dismal duties, not the beginning of a new life, and, when, broken in health and confused in mind, she perforce sought refuge: the convent of the Little Sisters of Mercy in its hillside garden at Fiesole where the nuns were 'peaceful and cheery and … very kind' and where the atmosphere was 'so restful' that she felt 'quieter and stronger already' and as if 'the beauty of it must make [her] well'.[102]

At Tymawr, doubly beloved because of its associations with Fordfield and Fiesole, the 'child of God' also discovered a family: the sisters she longed for but never had but for whom she was not responsible because they were only sisters 'in the Lord'; a Eustace to deride (Father Amos); a stern father to respect and against whom to rebel (Hubert Northcott); the real Julius, closer now than for thirty years; a mother-substitute in Mother Guenvrede with whom she now conducted the same loving/hating passive/aggressive relationship as that conducted with her mother.

That Aelfrida, even when bullying her, relied enormously on Mother Guenvrede, is evident from panic experienced if the latter was away or temporarily absent from the *opus Dei*, reliance expressed in letters to Father Cary and evidenced by the tenor of his replies: "fortunately either your angel or the kind Mother seemed to have intervened quite satisfactorily"[103] (on Sister Placida having detailed recent 'shewings' and instructions concerning interior silence issued by her now hyperactive and hyper-vigilant guardian angel) and gladness that Mother Guenvrede was keeping a "watchful eye [on] the measures of seclusion that she approves" because Sister Placida had no *advocatus diaboli* "to criticise or censor her requests".[104] (She did not need a devil's advocate; she had the devil himself as an immanent, unmediated, and sometimes physically manifest agent in her life.) It is evident too that she relied on Mother Guenvrede for the tough love which Chiara had meted out to little Frida and to adolescent Tit and in this respect at least did not overly resent the Mother's assurance that although she respected Placida's religious attitude and aptitude, she did *not* love 'child of God's' 'natural self [which was] useless and a nuisance' and reminder that it would be much simpler if Mrs Graham remembered to live, socially speaking, 'unplaced' at Tymawr instead of reverting in company to being 'an authoress or a consul's wife'.[105]

All might have continued in this Hegelian vein with Mrs Graham/Aelfrida/Placida achieving a modus vivendi if not an absolute synthesis with Mother Guenvrede, had not events occurred which provided the former with opportunities to enlarge her niche and to live the life she wished to lead to an even greater extent, a life which combined that of 'a hermit and [an] "extern oblate" allowed to go for walks [and] to join the Community at recreation sometimes if [she] could not bear complete solitude'.[106] The events themselves put such severe strain on Mother Guenvrede that that redoubtable lady often became overwrought; indeed, had they not happened, it is possible that Mother Guenvrede (who seems to have taken a slightly malicious pleasure and very human delight in disciplining – at the latter's request, of course – 'the lady of 54, the authoress of pious books, Father Cary's penitent etc., etc.')[107] might have succeeded in bringing her recalcitrant, egoistic, indiscreet, manipulative, and frequently hypochondriacal 'child of God' to heel, but happen they did – and Aelfrida seized the moment.

The first event seemed minor but was to have major repercussions: in October 1938 Mr Donkin died and Mrs Donkin (an SSC Associate) came to live at the convent for longer or shorter periods, moving in on a permanent basis a few years later. Describing her as someone who possessed 'every virtue except repose'[108], Placida noted with admiration how much effort had gone into the creation of Mother Guenvrede's calm demeanour given that she and 'the Reverend Mother's-Own-Mama'[109] were so similar in other respects. The second event was economic: the SSC was, as Aelfrida knew, desperately poor, so poor, in fact, that in December 1938 Mother Guenvrede had to turn away three prospective postulants because they

brought no dowry. Such small-scale income-generating schemes as the convent undertook were barely sufficient to increase income generated by residents, visitors, and retreatants to economic levels or to offset the rising costs (a notable feature of the later 1930s) of 'overhead expenses'[110], of hired labour (the gardener-handyman whose wife helped in the laundry), or of commodities the Community did not produce itself. The third event was the worst of all and had the most profound consequences: the outbreak of the Second World War in September 1939.

Although Mrs Graham was more concerned with personal problems (censoring of visits and visitors, disposal of St Benedict's) and Aelfrida with enjoyments ('prehistory', her 'niche', Julius' visits), 1938 saw Placida facing the fact that in spite of Mr Chamberlain's assurances and of her own hope that 'war will be averted' ('but so I thought in 1914'), war was 'inevitable'.[111] Asking herself 'can one poor tertiary do anything?', the writer of homiletic novels mourned that books written specifically 'to warn [her] country'[112] (i.e. *Concrete* and *The Approaching Storm*) had proved ineffectual. (They were to prove prophetic of much to come.) Placida set herself to '*pray* [and] *pray*' over 'the state of Europe – the plight of the Jews and … Hitler trying to gobble up Austria'[113] and 'wicked Japanese bombing Chinese towns' and to see a vision on Michaelmas Day of Tymawr chapel filled with warrior-angels flowing outwards on oceans of light to conquer the powers of darkness.[114]

Contrasting the convent in general and the chapel in particular as a 'Place of Light' set against the wicked world outside and the peaceful spirit of Tymawr[115] with that of an England about to spend £350 million pounds on armaments, prayerful Placida came to an expected and an unexpected conclusion: 'there is only *one* solution to international differences – seek ye *first* the Kingdom of God' and, a remarkable volte-face in one whose divinely-inspired pacifist beliefs had – so she said – prevented participation in any form of war-work in 1914, that 'pacifism as a purely "this world" expediency is useless'.[116] She also, and as if she realised prayer would prove as ineffective as her books, began to undergo 'dark' ecstasies *coram sanctissimo* of Christ's sufferings on the Cross, but 'shilly-shallied and hung back'[117] when invited to meditate on the Passion as if she could not bear to identify too closely with His (and through His, the world's) sufferings. She also experienced 'universal consciousness' whose negative aspects (there was much in it of persecution, of sin, of '*suffering* love')[118] were more reminiscent of visions experienced during the Great War than representative of the fewer but positive and '*wonderful*' visions 'shewn' since[119], and filled pages of her diary with gloomy and somewhat confused cogitations and doom-filled prognostications concerning the fate about to overtake a godless world.

Early in 1939 Sister Placida, whose 'poor self [was] mortgaged already over again' (what, we might ask, had happened to the 'plenty of *space* for intercessory prayer' she believed she possessed now she no longer pleaded 'for emotional satisfaction in prayer'?)[120], added another name to her heterogeneous list of those for whom she offered reparative adoration: Adolf Hitler, the first and only member of the list whom she did not know personally and envisaged with a devil on his back 'inciting him to evil', who had just violated the Munich Agreement by invading Czechoslovakia. (She did not offer herself as 'victim-soul' for Mussolini because she regarded him as misguided rather than evil, and so great was her hatred of Communism that she never considered offering it for Stalin.) Inspired by '*waves* of terror and dismay coming from the newly-annexed territories' and by a vision of a bier between her and the altar and of grey angels of death surrounding her while she prayed alone after Vespers[121], she persuaded the Community to undertake a nine-day devotion of penitential prayers for peace (Placida herself usually held novenas for particular people), at the end of which she realised with horror that her assumption that she had plenty of time to 'play about and indulge [herself]' (*sic*) at Tymawr while sanctification happened automatically (an interesting statement, given Father Amos' earlier comment that she was not taking life at Tymawr seriously) was mistaken and that nothing but *abandon complet* would suffice to save her soul[122], much less avert a war.

A second concern was the safety of her immediate family. Julius, after an anxious moment in 1938 when it seemed that 1914 might be about to repeat itself and he be interned as an enemy alien (as before, he had been researching Byzantine music in the Balkans) was home again in Cardiff with Mina, herself recently returned from travels in Germany. Eustace and Phyllis, both of whom had first-hand experience of wartime battlefields, were about to vacate Merton House for a cottage in Hadstock, a small village south of Cambridge. Of the younger generation, Stephen and Walter were of an age to render them eligible for compulsory military service (a Bill to this effect – 'oh sorrow, sorrow and shame' – was going through Parliament as Aelfrida wrote)[123]; Stephen, in fact, and much to his *ci-devant* pacifist aunt's disgust ('if he does not think it right to bear arms … he ought to stay and testify to his belief and then do Red Cross or land work', a rich comment from one whose Great War membership of the NUWW had been purely nominal)[124], was about to return to the United States where he had already embarked on academic life, but Walter, hoping to go to Cambridge, remained in England. (Constance, Angela, and Veronica, still in secondary education, became in the course of the war a nurse, an evacuee to Canada and, on returning, a land worker, and a Girton student respectively.) Alethea, who had booked furlough for April 1940, was forced to cancel, much to her mother's delight: 'if a war should come upon us … I don't want her back. I want her as far away as possible … in South Africa [and] I am glad Agatha is in heaven', heaven being a place of safety to which her mother in another transformation of the past had 'given' Agatha to God rather than God having 'taken' her.[125]

Although Aelfrida was able to note on a 'serene and glowing evening' in July 1939 on which Tymawr appeared at its most celestial 'how far off do war and preparations for war appear!', neither were far off, a prospect underlined by the imminent arrival of evacuees at Woodbine Cottage and by rumours that 'Saint Cadoch's Grove' might be felled for an aerodrome. The latter possibility provoked protests from Placida that there would be aircraft overhead day and night and lanes infested with lorries and motorcycles to disturb her silence and solitude. (Mrs Graham's offer to Mother Guenvrede to 'use [her] influence to block the scheme – the aerodrome not the war!' by 'writing various letters and stirring up the influential' was sharply and publicly rejected as evidence of Placida's selfish desire to defend her 'niche'.) She also worried that in the event of an 'almost inevitable' German victory, religious orders would be dispersed or secularised and that even if England were not invaded, the Community would be unable to maintain 'this great house and estate' and would render her homeless.[126] Worse still, Aelfrida was aware that at Tymawr she had neither 'ring-fence' to protect her because in denuding herself of family responsibilities in favour of '*abandon complet à Dieu*' she had unwittingly laid herself open to secular civic duties in the form of the wartime support services expected of non-combatants, nor enough 'personal preoccupations' to furnish a 'hedge' against terrible thoughts of what might happen 'if war comes to Europe'.[127]

Other 'preparations' upset her too: 'up there among the stars … the long fingers of searchlights feeling the sky', a sight which provoked both her vision of her Malling oblature as 'the "flight of the soul" along a pathway of light' and 'a sudden sense of something *evil*' and that even at Tymawr there was a 'tense and horrible psychic hush before an Approaching Storm'[128], the weather, prophetically appropriate, being wild and stormy with gales blowing, thunder booming, lightning flashing, and 'torrential showers'; Hilda's return from an Air Raid

Precautions lecture on 'poison gas bombs' followed by the 'incongruous [and] revolting' arrival of two young men to measure members of the Community for gas masks: 'may the Prince of Peace keep us from ever needing them!'[129] prayed Placida who was first to try one on. (Because she was keeping her 'silence-rule', she remained silent until commanded by Mother Guenvrede to "say something" in order to check if one '*could* say the Office while wearing one'. One could.) 'Virgilio' the gas mask thereafter proved his worth but not with respect to 'poison gas bombs'.[130]

On the night of 24/25 August 1939, *The Times* having declared that "war is imminent", Aelfrida lay sleepless: having over- and mis-heard Sister Jeanne talking on the Tymawr telephone, she had convinced herself that 'German aeroplanes' would appear overhead within the hour. (She had also refused to join Father and Mrs Amos and 'the Library' – of whom, besides herself, there were then only two members, Hilda Harrison and a new resident tertiary, formerly a nun, 'both very quiet and good [with] no sign of fuss but ... very anxious' – round the Michaelgarth radio and was about to spend a day in retreat so could not ask what was happening; anticlimactically, the only invaders encountered were mice 'trying to carry off [her] sponge'.) The following day dawned in 'tranquil autumn sunshine, beautiful beyond words' but even this failed to calm her: Brother Ass, she feared, was 'a coward and a sybarite and very likely had "nerves" too'; would she, she wondered, 'be able to control him in actual danger?' (Sister Monica, 'naturally timid', looked 'abjectly mis[erable]'; Mother Guenvrede, 'born to be a "warrior saint"', looked both grave and exhilarated.) Spiritually, of course, she would behave as she had done at the start of the Great War: 'to think as little as possible of the actual details of events [and] in quietness to draw waters of peace from ... everlasting wells'.[131]

On 1 September 1939, 'just after Sext, Hilda came up to me and said "I suppose you have heard that war has begun" ... I said nothing – there was nothing to say [but] I felt a strange sense of *awe* – God has spoken'.[132] What He said His 'child' does not relate but judging by her own thoughts and by a quoted remark from Mother Guenvrede, He decreed that it would be best for the future of mankind if 'the forces of destruction should destroy each other without delay' and that "purification may be necessary – there may be no other way".[133]

## Notes

1   GCPPT 1|1|34 16 February 1927.
2   ibid. 21 February 1927.
3   ibid. 1 March 1927.
4   ibid. 4 March 1927.
5   ibid. 5 March 1927.
6   GCPPT 1|1|55 17 September 1938.
7   GCPPT 1|1|54 27 and 28 March 1938.
8   ibid. 18 February 1938.
9   ibid. 13 November 1937.
10  GCPPT 1|1|56 21 January 1939.
11  GCPPT 1|1|54 3 March 1938.
12  GCPPT 1|1|56 3 October 1938.
13  GCPPT 1|1|55 16 and 17 September 1938.
14  ibid. 23 September 1938.
15  GCPPT 1|1|54 25 December 1937.
16  ibid. 3 February 1938.
17  GCPPT 1|1|55 27 and 30 June 1938.
18  RM Benson's instructions as given to the fledgling SSJE in 1874–1875 in the form of an exposition of the principles of the Religious Life, were published in 1939 under the title *The Religious Vocation* with an introduction by Lucius Cary.
19  Benson, R.M. op. cit. p251.
20  GCPPT 1|1|56 23 March 1939.
21  TT. Carter's *Spiritual Instructions* on various topics were originally given as discourses to the nuns at Clewer. His discourse on Spiritual and Sacramental Communion appears in Chapter 7 of *Spiritual Instructions: The Holy Eucharist*.
22  Carter, TT. op. cit. pp 65–68.
23  A more prosaic reason for her enthusiasm may stem from Aelfrida's Nonconformist upbringing. As she herself later noted (*Christian Old Age* p 99 GCPPT 2|17) "the nonconformist who is content with ... a simple memorial service once a ... month has no idea of the ardour which brings many ... to the Lord's Table every morning spiritually to receive our Lord Himself". No cubes of bread and tots of grape juice handed round by an elder at St Columba's could compete with this.
24  GCPPT 1|1|54 16 October 1937.
25  ibid. 8 February 1938.
26  GCPPT 1|1|56 20 March 1939.
27  GCPPT 1|1|55 'Eve of Corpus Christi' (15 June) 1938.
28  ibid. 25 May 1938.
29  GCPPT 1|1|56 'Christmas Day 9.30pm' (25 December) 1938.
30  GCPPT 1|1|55 21 July 1938.
31  ibid. 29 August 1938.
32  GCPPT 1|1|51 13 June 1936.
33  GCPPT 1|1|56 17 October 1938.
34  GCPPT 1|1|57 9 August 1939.
35  GCPPT 1|1|54 5 March 1938.
36  GCPPT 1|1|56 26, 27 and 28 March 1939.
37  ibid. 20 December 1938.
38  Tillyard, Ae. *The Centaur* p279 (GCPPT 2|21|1).
39  GCPPT 1|1|54 12 March 1938.
    GCPPT 1|1|56 4 April 1939.
40  GCPPT 1|1|54 21 October 1937.
41  GCPPT 1|1|55 28 May 1938.
42  GCPPT 1|1|44 26 July 1933.
    GCPPT 1|1|55 10 July 1938.
43  Tillyard, Ae. *The Making of a Mystic* p 90.
44  GCPPT 1|1|56 'Ascension Day' (18 May) 1939.
45  GCPPT 1|1|57 'The Precious Blood' (1 July) 1939.
46  ibid. 22 July 1939.
47  ibid. 22 and 25 July 1939.
48  GCPPT 1|1|55 23 September 1938.
49  GCPPT 1|1|56 27 October 1938.
50  GCPPT 1|1|55 23 September 1938.
    GCPPT 1|1|56 27 October 1938 and 26 March 1939.
51  GCPPT 1|1|55 23 September 1938.
52  GCPPT 1|1|56 27 October 1938.
53  GCPPT 1|1|54 21 March 1938.

54  ibid. 'Easter Day' (17 April) 1938.

55  GCPPT 1|1|56 24 January 1939.

56  GCPPT 1|1|57 17 September 1939. Petals from Sister Jeanne's rose were preserved by Aelfrida in an envelope tucked into the current volume of her diary.

57  GCPPT 1|1|56 8 December 1938.

58  GCPPT 1|1|54 18 February 1938.

59  GCPPT 1|1|56 7 February 1939.

60  GCPPT 1|1|54 'Fiery Cross Day' (23 November) 1937.

61  GCPPT 1|1|57 30 June 1939.

62  GCPPT 1|1|54 3 November 1937.

63  GCPPT 1|1|55 15 September 1938.

64  GCPPT 1|1|54 21 March 1938.

65  GCPPT 1|1|55 15 September 1938.

66  ibid. 24 July 1938. She did well to ask, Thomas Thellusson Carter (*Spiritual Instructions: The Religious Life* p5) having expressly noted that the Religious Life implied "a virgin, or, as included in the same idea, a widowed chastity" with "our Lord, Himself a Virgin, of a Virgin born" as paradigm. St Ambrose himself placed great emphasis in his teachings on the Perpetual Virginity of Mary as *Mater Dei*.

67  GCPPT 1|1|56 19 November 1938.

68  ibid. 25 May 1939.

69  GCPPT 1|1|54 23 December 1937.

70  GCPPT 1|1|56 21 February 1939.

71  GCPPT 1|1|57 'The transfiguration' (6 August) 1939.

72  GCPPT 1|1|54 11 October 1937.

73  ibid. 1 March 1938.

74  GCPPT 1|1|55 22 May 1938.

75  ibid. 18 August 1938.

76  ibid. 22 May 1938.

77  GCPPT 1|1|57 8 August 1939.

78  GCPPT 1|1|54 7 November 1937.

79  GCPPT 1|1|54 16 March 1938.

80  GCPPT 1|1|55 'Whit Monday' (6 June) 1938.

81  GCPPT 1|1|54 7 November 1937.

82  GCPPT 1|1|57 16 July 1939.

83  ibid. 24 June 1939.

84  GCPPT 1|1|54 4 April 1938.

85  GCPPT 1|1|57 30 June 1939.

86  GCPPT 1|1|55 12 July 1938.

87  GCPPT 1|1|56 24 October 1938.

88  GCPPT 1|1|57 28 July 1939.

89  GCPPT 1|1|56 'Corpus Christi' (31 May) 1939.

90  ibid. 15 November 1938.

91  ibid. 'Eve of All Saints' (31 October) 1938.

92  GCPPT 1|1|55 6 May 1938.

93  GCPPT 1|1|48 29 July 1935.

94  GCPPT 1|1|55a Letter from Father Cary to Aelfrida of 16 September 1938. Father Cary's extant letters to Aelfrida at Tymawr are addressed to 'Mrs Graham' and begin 'my dear Aelfrida'; he never styles her 'Sister Placida'.

95  GCPPT 1|1|57 26 June 1939.

96  GCPPT 1|1|55 16 and 27 May 1938.

97  ibid. 6 August 1938.

98  Cary, L. *Called of God* p20.

99  GCPPT 1|1|21 3 September 1916.

100  GCPPT 1|1|57 'The Visitation' (2 July) 1939.

101  GCPPT 1|1|56 30 May 1939.

102  GCPPT 1|1|12 18 February 1905.

103  GCPPT 1|1|55a Letter from Father Cary to Aelfrida of 16 September 1938.

104  GCPPT 1|1|56 9 March 1939.

105  GCPPT 1|1|57 18 and 21 June 1939.

106  GCPPT 1|1|56 30 September 1938.

107  ibid. 13 November 1938.

108  GCPPT 1|1|55 1 September 1938.

109  GCPPT 1|1|57 1 December 1939.

110  GCPPT 1|1|56 16 May 1939.

111  GCPPT 1|1|55 25 September 1938.
     GCPPT 1|1|56 28 September 1938.

112  GCPPT 1|1|54 26 March 1938.

113  GCPPT 1|1|54 13 March 1938.
     GCPPT 1|1|56 3 November 1938.

114  GCPPT 1|1|54 30 September 1937.

115  GCPPT 1|1|56 11 November and 17 December 1938.

116  GCPPT 1|1|54 3 March 1938.

117  ibid. 13 and 14 March 1938.

118  GCPPT 1|1|56 4 April 1939.

119  GCPPT 1|1|55 18 July 1938.

120  GCPPT 1|1|54 9 October 1937.

121  GCPPT 1|1|56 16 and 17 March 1939.

122  GCPPT 1|1|57 16 July 1939.

123  GCPPT 1|1|56 27 April 1939. Conscription for those aged between 18 and 40 was introduced in May 1939. I am indebted for this and other details of World War II as references to that event appear in Aelfrida's diaries to Calder, A. *The People's War, Britain 1939–45*.

124  GCPPT 1|1|57 29 August 1939. In an undated and unsent letter to a Tymawr Associate, Aelfrida later noted that she did not deserve the title "pacifist" because although she believed that "*war in itself* is always an evil", she now also believed that "it may be the *lesser* of two evils" and that with regard to the coming war "we are bound to *try* and chastise the Germans for *their* good as well as our own", "our good" implying that it was preferable ("right") for England to be at war than to be accused of "indifference or cowardice" (GCPPT 1|1|58a. Letter from Aelfrida to a Mrs Scrace).

125  GCPPT 1|1|54 13 March 1938.
     GCPPT 1|1|55 25 September 1938.
     GCPPT 1|1|57 11 July 1939.

126  GCPPT 1|1|57 26 and 28 July 1939.

127  ibid. 8 July 1939.

128  GCPPT 1|1|56 20 and 23 March and 12 April 1939.

129  ibid. 6 October and 26 November 1938. In 1939 ARP wardens were warned of the possible use of poison gas by the Germans and decontamination centres were set up and mass graves dug, the latter to be used for air raid shelters or for trench warfare if poison gas bombs did not materialise. In July 1939 Aelfrida sold inherited shares in Imperial Chemicals because the company was involved in armament production 'including poison gas' (GCPPT 1|1|57 8 July 1939), but whether she did so wholly on moral grounds (she probably saw gassed soldiers during her only hospital visit during the Great War and was much distressed by reports of the use of 'poison gas' by the Italians in Abyssinia in 1936) or merely wanted to make sure of her money (£267) in case the stock market crashed, she does not say.

130  GCPPT 1|1|57 31 August 1939. 'Virgilio' is Roman poet Virgil (70–19 BC) whose 4th *Eclogue* was supposed to foretell the coming of Christ. More relevantly in the present context, Virgil was Dante's guide through Hell and Purgatory in the first two books of the *Divine Comedy*, advising the latter to "take me for thy guide and pass with me through an eternal place and terrible" (*Hell* Canto 1: 113–114).

131  ibid. 25 August 1939.

132  ibid. 1 September 1939.

133  ibid. 25 August 1939.

# Peace Within Thy Walls

'1 September 1939. Everything is very quiet, our visitors have gone … there is a solemn hush over the convent, one feels the intensification of prayer, the more earnest self-consecration. God help and keep us all'.

'2 September 1939. I do not know, after all, whether England *is* at war or not. War conditions, however, have begun'.

'4 September 1939. England is now definitely at war – and we shall not be exempt from suffering'.[1]

And having come to that unhappy conclusion, Placida prepared to make her 'niche' as snug and secure as possible.

Life was not going to be easy: house and chapel darkened at dusk by blackout curtains; warning sirens disturbing the peace of the countryside; the air 'humming with planes', probably 'enemy'; 'spy signalling' from the hills[2] ('fifth columnists', she thought, a term adopted from the Spanish Civil War); six schoolgirl 'refugees' moving into Woodbine Cottage (Mrs Graham, 'the only mother on the premises', was forbidden to comfort sad little girls: two were so homesick that they returned forthwith to Birmingham, the remainder being removed to somewhere less isolated and primitive to be 'dealt with' by someone more maternal than Mother Guenvrede)[3]; 'very rigid censorship of news'[4] and 'of letters going abroad'.[5] Confession to Father Northcott ('he treats me as if I were about three') concentrated Placida's mind on essentials: 'not to *fuss* over this little sin and that but to repent *all the time* over my bias to self-love', to 'maintain quietness', and to decide 'what God requires of me now, in wartime'.[6]

What God required of Placida, namely to ensure that 'the work of the Community … should continue … as pure, as ardent, as untroubled as possible'[7] and 'to strive to be *nothing* but a capacity for adoration and a channel of God's love'[8] and what Aelfrida herself required were related but different things. Primarily, she must make herself indispensable and ensure she was not sent away – and if in achieving her aims she made mountains out of molehills, failed to maintain interior or exterior quietness to such an extent that, as she noted of histories of Religious Orders, a visitor to Tymawr would see

**Mother Guenvrede**

'how rare and fugitive' was peace of any sort, particularly '*external*'[9], and exasperated Mother Guenvrede by prioritising what Placida believed to be God's requirements for herself at the expense of the wartime Community's, so much the worse for the Mother and that Community, the fault, if fault there was, lying not in Aelfrida, Placida, or Mrs Graham but in her 'Sisters-in-Christ'.

To make herself indispensable, Placida became more Benedictine than the Benedictines: 'my duty is … plain – manual labour and prayer, as tradition decreed'.[10] Prayer was easy: not only had her guardian angel spread his wings over her and promised to guide her 'wonderfully' lest she be led by self-love 'to where the rebel angels are'[11] but Christ Himself had also called her again by name three times and she, making 'wordless response of love and readiness', felt '*straightened*' by this further manifestation of God's Love.[12] Manual labour, though less welcome, was entered upon assiduously, 'kitchen garden weeds' being particularly gratifying to uproot because their proximity to the chapel made them more 'numinous' than those at Woodbine Cottage[13]; 'Miss Harrison's azalea bed which I am deep digging for her while she is away'[14], a shining example of 'doing an "our" job instead of a "my" job' ('though I don't really look on the cottage garden with any sense of proprietorship!')[15]; 'gathering sticks for the Mother's pile of kindling', a task 'very tepidly performed heretofore'[16] because reminiscent of one to which she had been reduced at Hunstanton in 1919 and beneath the dignity of a consul's 'widow' twenty years later. But '*laborare*' she must as well as '*orare*' for if she did not, compulsory war-work awaited an 'elderly' woman of fifty-five as men volunteered for or were conscripted into the Forces. Luckily, it was easy to make spectacular gestures while not really doing very much at all.

Ensuring she was not sent away was harder. A marginal note to her diary entry of 24 September explaining that 'of course, the Community *cannot*, in the nature of the case, be wholly responsible for tertiaries as it is for Sisters' and that if she became destitute or chronically unwell, she would have to leave, demonstrates two of her anxieties at this time.[17] Meanwhile she enjoyed 'the disposal of [her] own money'[18] and a home of her own at vacant Wetenhall Cottage – the Barrons, as American citizens, had removed her small god-daughter from a potential war zone, but Aelfrida was 'fortunate indeed'[19] to find new tenants quickly and for a higher rental. The departure of a novice 'to do war work' in late September 1939 and the promptings of her guardian angel as soon as war broke out regarding the desirability of making a public "*promise of stability*", sent Placida to Mother in haste. Phrasing her request in conventually acceptable terms ('you see, I think there will be difficulties and darkness, exterior and interior, for me here and a promise to remain might the best provision against them')[20], she received an ambiguous answer: a promise of stability was to a Community, not to any 'special place' and the Community agreed 'not to send [her] away except for reasons for which the Sisters would be sent'. Comforted by the Holy Spirit's Vesperal promise later the same day that the Lord promised His blessing and '"life for evermore" … *here*'[21], Placida failed to take three things into account: that if she behaved very badly she *would* be sent away; that in making promises of *any* kind she was expected to abide by them; that Mother Guenvrede meant what she said.

There was something else to consider too – during an extended 'shewing' lasting from 7pm on 28 September until 3am on 29 September, Placida received another message: "He hath made fast the bars of thy gates"[22], the gates being, she thought, those of her soul and the bars those locking her (with God) into Tymawr. Only later did she realise that she, God, the war, and a fourth factor to be discussed in due course, had also made a prison for her, a prison to whose gates Mother Guenvrede held the keys, locking her in *or out* as Placida's behaviour determined. She had also forgotten that the devil had some say 'in the matter of any promise to be here always'. Arriving on 29 September, the 'rebel angel' reminded her 'in the most reasonable manner possible of the folly of giving up most of the things that have hitherto made life attractive in favour of an existence that is both dull and uncomfortable'. Pleading that *God* had called her to an existence lacking in comfort, interest, and 'accreditation' (or did she mean credibility? Neither a compliment to Deity, one would think) and that He had inspired in Mother Guenvrede a wish to keep her at Tymawr, Aelfrida encountered utter fury: he could and would, the devil informed her, make darkness around her, beginning on her fifty-sixth birthday, St Placid's Day, 5 October 1939.

Day and date were significant for another reason too: three days prior to Aelfrida's latest conversation with the devil, Mother Guenvrede informed Placida that her final promises would be made then. We do not know why the Mother decided to allow her to make them after two years' probation, not three (and, as Aelfrida put it, at 'the fag end of a more or less selfish life')[23] but may guess that, spiritually speaking, Sister Placida had made such progress in muffling (if not absolutely silencing) her 'clamour of self-hood' that Mother Guenvrede believed her to have reached the point at which "our work … will begin"[24], and, more pragmatically, the Mother needed Aelfrida's presence as peacekeeper between warring factions in the 'Library' (her 'Own Mama' now being one) and Mrs Graham's money.

Imminent vows and a three-day retreat beforehand made Placida thoughtful ('the more I read, the more I see how I fall short of the minimum requirements of the novice' e.g. 'self-regarding impulses' from which she turned 'with *loathing*'[25] but continued to cultivate as assiduously as cottage or kitchen garden) and the prospect of making a general confession to Father Amos on 4 October even more so. Her confession (it encompassed only the years since her first contact with the SSC so did not present as great a problem as that made to Dom Bede at Malling) is a revealing document. Because 'details [would] have taken too long … [she] grouped sins under headings' as summaries of the poor picture 'this child of God' presented to her Heavenly Father. Sins 'Towards God' included 'taking credit for His gifts', 'trying to serve Him in my own way', and being sometimes 'perfunctory, slipshod and grudging in His service'; sins 'Towards the Community', 'thinking too much of myself and my own needs, comfort and tastes [and] liking my own way', 'being inconsiderate towards the Reverend Mother' and 'slow to understand the nature of Holy Obedience'. Sins 'Towards Mankind in General' included 'thinking myself superior … because of advantages of birth, education and opportunity'; sins 'Towards Individuals' a 'critical spirit' which blinded her to 'the image of God in them', 'lack of tact and understanding', and 'reluctance to put [herself] out'. Sins 'Towards Myself' (only one is listed) was that of 'being too easily satisfied [and] content with too low a standard of goodness'.[26] Adoring the Blessed Sacrament after confessing the lengthy list (abbreviated here but perusable in full in Girton College archive), Placida experienced 'a strange [and] cleansing sprinkling of [her] soul with the Precious Blood', a sprinkling repeated at intervals during the almost sleepless night which followed. (She does not say what penances Father Amos imposed before pronouncing absolution.) On the morning of 5 October she was '*ready* – the Holy Spirit had prepared me'.[27]

Standing in front of the altar facing Father Amos 'in cope and biretta' with Mother Guenvrede on her right ('the Mother said I shouldn't have a martyrdom like Saint Placid's' – Placid was killed outright by barbarians in Sicily in 541 AD – 'mine would be bit by bit'), her guardian angel (who 'had *said* that if I was to be a tertiary, it must be *here*') grouped with the Sisters' guardian angels (her 'bridesmaids'), and with 'the Holy Presence round us', Placida received scapular and crucifix (the latter 'like the Sisters' only smaller') from the Chaplain and from the Mother a choir veil with a blue cross (embroidered by Hilda Harrison) instead of her former white one. Thus accoutred, she was 'held and accepted – the call clearly heard more than fifteen years ago … answered at last'.[28] (The SSC Book of Acts provides a more pragmatic account: "1939 October 5 … Sister Placida was admitted a life Tertiary".) Mass, Holy Communion, cards, flowers, kisses, and breakfast completed the occasion. But if we look back to the momentous but unrecorded occasion in the early 1920s when Aelfrida received the call, we realise how little her life has changed as a result ('what troubles me most', she wrote then, is that, feeling as conscious of [God] as I do, with every fibre of my being crying out in adoration of Him, I cannot by my life set Him forth more clearly [because] I [so] often find myself guilty of petty meanness in thought and action, of little wrigglings out of plain duty')[29] and note with apprehension the implications of this for her life as a resident tertiary.

On the evening of 5 October Placida reviewed her day: 'I have just done *usual* things … collected apples and worked in the kitchen garden … but always with the Presence surrounding me. It is so wonderful that God Himself prepared a place for me here'.[30] A week later – she had been 'too happy, as well as too busy, to write in [her] diary' – she recorded that though expecting to feel a 'deeper sense of peace' and 'more complete resting in God' (and, significantly, an 'eager desire to go … whither He calls me'), she was surprised to experience '*a sudden liberation of the spirit*' and a sense of 'great spaces' opening above her into which her soul 'took wings and soared and soared'[31], spaces interpreted correctly as promoting spiritual enlargement and incorrectly as portending increased freedom of action on earth.

On 15 October Mrs Graham received a trunk and suitcase forwarded from St Thomas' Convent and held another holocaust of 'manuscripts of my books [and] sheets of my writings'[32] – and if among these was the uncompleted manuscript of a Leiston novel *Peace Within Thy Walls,* how symbolic, for, disregarding the rest of the quotation ("for my brethren and companions' sakes I will now say, Peace be within thee")[33], Aelfrida set out to make life as dark for herself and as un-peaceful or others as the devil prophesied, and in the mistaken belief that being a life tertiary meant she was safely stowed at Tymawr for life, proceeded to behave as if there were no danger of ever being removed.

Fortunately for Placida but unfortunately for the SSC, the opening stages of her campaign against the Community in general and Mother Guenvrede in particular took place during the period of the 'phoney war' during which, though civil liberties were eroded to an extent envisaged in *Concrete* ('England has been made a "totalitarian state"')[34], identity cards issued (Aelfrida makes no mention of receiving one though she must have done, and a ration book as well), and petrol rationing imposed (something regarded by Placida as a bonus because less traffic meant increased silence), there were so few indications of extramural conflict at Tymawr that Mrs Graham was able to consign thoughts of world war to the far corners of her mind and to concentrate on planning a personal war of alternating aggression and attrition.

Minor skirmishes marked its onset, Placida receiving a 'sharp reproof' for addressing a Sister before midday because general silence was maintained till then (she forgot that she herself was supposed to be 'in silence' till tea-time), Mrs Graham for bothering Mother Guenvrede with gifts of books and garments from her St Thomas' hoard when the Mother was busy, and Aelfrida for two unspecified matters[35], but these were par for the course for one who professed herself dissatisfied with herself in spite of 'great and glorious certainty of progress' made as she approached her 'second birthday' as a tertiary.[36] Nor did they disqualify her from inclusion – a great privilege; Placida was one of only two non-nuns to attend, the other being also a life tertiary – in the conventual Retreat conducted by Father Northcott in early December 1939.

Placida's report of the Retreat (she found 'the privilege of being in chapel with the Sisters ... a little overwhelming')[37] is fascinating for what it reveals of lack of insight, of arrogance, and of dissatisfaction. Taking as his theme *Romans* 8:19-21[38] (a theme of enormous relevance to Aelfrida had she appreciated it), Father Northcott delivered two addresses a day: on God ('*very* beautiful'); on Death (he demonstrated 'an unfamiliarity with Heaven' which took Placida 'aback somewhat')[39]; on Ananias and Sapphira as examples of the danger of keeping anything back 'of a gift that one need not ... have made' (an interesting point, given the devil's recent remarks to herself), and of the wickedness of 'any sort of hypocrisy, pose or ... wilful unreality ... in the spiritual life' (ditto: the practical outcome of this particular discourse was Aelfrida's energetic gathering of kindling and her comment about sneaking a little back afterwards)[40]; on the Fellowship of the Mystical Body of Christ; and on the Community as a living organism, during which Northcott spoke 'gravely and sternly' as if 'there had been dissensions here'(hearing this, Aelfrida felt 'sad and ashamed and [as if] I ought not to be present', not because she felt Father Northcott's criticisms were aimed at *her* – how could they be? – but on the Community's behalf: 'perhaps it is that they are all very tired')[41]; on suffering as a *privilege*, a topic related to his preceding discourse; on acceptance of the Holy Spirit's guidance and rejection of 'false "guidance"' and on how God's hierarchy 'from the highest angels to ourselves ... as contemplatives' must engage in spiritual warfare between the hosts of light and of darkness[42], an Manichean doctrine which Aelfrida was to embrace wholeheartedly with reference to Mother Guenvrede.

Confession to Father Northcott during the Retreat was more of an ordeal than confession to Father Amos. Placida, it seems, did not tell him that she was 'intellectually disappointed' with addresses whose lack of coherence contrasted with Father Cary's and emotionally disappointed when comparing the Warden's 'clinging to earth' personality with Lucius Cary's 'unearthly radiance and fragrance'[43] or (something confessed only to her diary) that she was 'chilled' by Northcott preaching to her of '"ordinariness"' and on taking care of [her] health'. Although she 'prayed and prayed ... that [she] might receive his admonitions with deep humility' and agreed (up to a point) with those concerning her health (her restricted diet included daily vitamin C and 'Saints Rose and Bruno' were used only rarely), Aelfrida waxed indignant with regard to his insistence on '"ordinariness" *for*

*me*' (biographer's italics): 'if he means *hiddenness,* simplicity, absence of pretensions on parade, I agree entirely ... but it isn't *honest* to pretend that I am leading or want to lead (*sic*) an ordinary life'.[44] (How could she, given that she conversed with angels and the devil, saw 'heavenly light' shining everywhere while out walking on a dark and dreary day[45], experienced in a trance *coram sanctissimo* 'the burning pain of His dear wounds in my hands'[46], and on receiving a vision of Christ planting His prayer in her heart, experienced it as 'life reaching out to Life' and as 'yet another *Vita Nuova*'[47] opening before her?) 'I *do* behave like an ordinary person at tea-time', she wrote (i.e. for thirty minutes a day) 'but the end of my cogitations [is] that God [has] given to Father Northcott not a great intellect nor the gift of understanding middle-aged ladies'.[48]

Worried that by 'ordinary' Father Northcott was hinting that she ought to return to 'life in the world', Placida tackled him again. To her relief, '*ordinariness*' meant 'Community ordinariness, not worldly ordinariness, taking [her] share in manual labour and so on' ('of course, I agree') and that she should 'persevere in silence'[49], an effective means, he may have thought, of keeping her quietly 'ordinary' while letting her think she was doing God's Will. But a 'silent' (i.e. unspeaking) Placida was not 'silent' at all and resorted to parlaying loudly and frequently on paper instead. And with results remarkably similar to those noted earlier with regard to Lucius Cary.

Mother Guenvrede's comment regarding the Retreat that retreats constituted 'something of a *disturbance*' to a contemplative but 'a necessary disturbance as, without it, one's prayer would grow thin' did not have its intended effect on Aelfrida but was seized upon enthusiastically by Placida ('a ray of divine light had been pressed on my soul rousing in me an almost *agonising* desire to ... to do nothing but pray ... and to sweep out of the way all occupations that usurp the place of prayer') as an excuse to continue creating the 'niche' she wished to occupy 'as far as humanly possible'. Her guardian angel, however, 'was very cool about it', telling her 'to go on as usual, only making better use of [her] privileges and God in His own time would give [her] more silence and so on'.[50] His advice failed to suit the life tertiary engaged in enhancing her own life regardless of others', so she disregarded it, taking matters into her own hands in the hope of chivvying Deity along.

Attendance at Retreat and admission as life tertiary having boosted confidence in her infallibility in spite of Mother Guenvrede having accused her of 'deliberately twisting what she said about my always being here so that it fitted my own ideas' (an episode described as one of the 'strange misunderstandings' inevitable in a convent and to which the Mother was particularly prone)[51], Placida proceeded – but only after actively concerning herself with 'other people's plans' for their lives inside or outside the Community without consulting Mother Guenvrede, this earning her both a stern rebuke ('this is *her* convent and we ought to be humbly thankful that we are allowed to be here') and accusations of disloyalty and untrust-worthiness met with real or assumed incomprehension by Aelfrida whose conscience, she wrote, was clear[52] – to ensure the minimisation of occupations which usurped the place of prayer, of silence, and of solitude.

The winter of 1939/1940 was the coldest for a century. Aelfrida's descriptions of the ice-storm which hit southern Britain on 27 January 1940 (a manifestation, surely, of God's displeasure with England) are so dramatic that they might be taken for exaggeration were they not corroborated by meteorological evidence. The conditions worsened a cough (probably tubercular, was her diagnosis) which had beset her since the autumn (her cough, like her unusually rosy face, a classic symptom of carbon monoxide poisoning, was attributable to fumes from the boiler flues whose inefficiency was compounded by overzealous stoking with unseasoned wood and by blocking of the chimneys by snow being piled so high on the convent roof that the Mother and one of the novices had to climb up to dislodge it)[53] and certainly contributed to Placida's reluctance to run errands through snowdrifts eight to ten feet deep and involving journeys which in normally took an hour's quick walking to accomplish. The intense cold also gave her 'sharp attacks of cramp in the heart' when working outside, attacks of which Mother Guenvrede was aware though so far had relations between them deteriorated that she regarded Aelfrida as 'idle and disobliging [and] shamming'[54] and refused to send for a doctor until the Placida staged a dramatic collapse at Vespers, a 'heart attack', she says, but her ability to repeat even when lying 'semiconscious' on the library settee "*Christ for all our sakes became obedient unto death, even the death on the Cross*"[55] and to record the phrase in her diary for her biographer's edification lest she succumbed, should arouse our suspicions, given the circumstances precipitating the 'collapse' itself.

Early in March 1940 Mother Guenvrede asked Aelfrida to clear debris from the long herbaceous border stretching from the library to the Campo Santo. Placida undertook the task grudgingly because she was already responsible for the care of the cottage garden (the border was Hilda's responsibility but Hilda had pleaded ill-health; she had also been absent so frequently and for so long that she provoked jealousy in Aelfrida's breast – Aelfrida had not been enjoying the fleshpots of Cheltenham as

Hilda had – and was demoted from guest-mistress forever) but Mother Guenvrede was adamant: she need do no more than ten minutes a day; was to regard those ten minutes as an 'obedience'; 'the task of the long border … must be *done*'. This to Aelfrida smacked less of 'obedience' than coercion, and to coercion she reacted as formerly to compulsory schooling with headaches, nightmares, and panic attacks, of which her 'collapse' in chapel may have been one for her description of 'the knock-knock-knock of [her] heart'[56] and notable lack of pain during the episode is reminiscent of attacks suffered when coerced or about to be coerced into doing something she did not wish to do. (Her earliest description of psychosomatic symptoms brought on by being sent to the Perse School appears here.) Realising, perhaps, that her 'holding back from the task' was due to 'temperamental disability' rather than 'physical weakness' (sufferers from rheumatoid arthritis experience genuine lack of stamina regardless of their willingness to undertake or complete a task; this may have been a contributing factor in Aelfrida's case but was not the predominant one), she nevertheless professed 'physical weakness' in preference to admitting to a 'temperamental' weakness which might result in being sent away. In view of what transpired, however, she might have done better to plead 'temperament' and 'a pathetic attempt to escape from the need of facing up to life'[57], for her attempt to 'sneak a little back' by pleading ill health cut no ice with Mother Guenvrede.

Informing the Mother (by letter) that Father Northcott had warned her during confession that she was to be 'very careful of [her] health and to consider it a sin against the Community to do anything which [she] knew to be unwise', Placida received the reply that she could behave exactly as she wished "or you will develop some new disease". (It does not seem to have occurred to her that Mother Guenvrede might report to Warden Northcott on the health and character of those under her authority and receive advice from him as to her dealings with them, but Aelfrida's guardian angel's whispered warning that some of her 'privileges' might be withdrawn if she did not obey opened her eyes to the dangers of playing off Father against Mother under the circumstances.) Having written her usual grovelling note of apology, a note so phrased that it could only irritate Mother Guenvrede further ("I would rather be ill than disobey"), Placida then cornered the Mother in the library in order to explain further. The rebuke she received was delivered 'lovingly and sweetly' (and, one suspects, through gritted teeth, for Mrs Graham was a paying guest and the Community's financial state, as Mrs Graham knew, parlous)[58] but rebuke it was:

- "You plan things and when any interruption occurs you are [put] out [because] there is a streak of self-will in you [which has] never [been] corrected".
- "You become tired whenever … put to work [you] don't like".
- "You never learnt to dominate your body by your mind [and although] you aren't a bit strong", there is difficulty in discerning how much ill health is real and how much assumed for effect.
- "You have been overdoing *silence*" (Father Northcott had permitted Placida to keep total silence on weekdays during Lent, something which, as Mother Guenvrede correctly surmised, provided too much time to brood over real or imaginary wrongs) "or you wouldn't have made so much fuss about all this".
- If she were a novice and did not try to "overcome" her faults (as Placida manifestly did not) she would be "sent away".
- "Alethea has the same traits" (Aelfrida submitted Alethea's letters to Mother Guenvrede for perusal in the hope of demonstrating to her what a 'saint' her daughter had become under her mother's tuition but did not otherwise submit letters unless she chose) and that is why she "could not stand the grind of the Religious Life".

Receiving this last comment, Aelfrida 'flared up maternally and denied it'; afterwards she wondered (as much, perhaps, of herself as of her daughter) if what Mother Guenvrede said were not 'true'.[59]

Confessing to Father Amos later that day, Placida received cold comfort from him too. (We all find work we dislike more tiring than work we enjoy, he told her, adding that it was sensible to balance the Sacraments and the *opus Dei* "by the other sort of work".) She therefore decided to tackle the 'long weary flowerbed' by mentally dividing it into the Stations of the Cross and by meditating on each as she worked along it, 'ministered to' by her guardian angel when symptoms of panic threatened to overwhelm her. On 13 March she staged her 'collapse' in chapel.[60]

The necessity of describing this particular episode at length (there are many to follow but these can be described more briefly as a result) becomes apparent when we consider what it reveals of Aelfrida's damaged personality, of her continuing mental and emotional instability, and of the power games she continued to play even when ostensibly under no necessity to do so. It shows too how soon clear-sighted Mother Guenvrede took her measure and decided that if she wished to be 'disciplined', disciplined she would be. It was therefore in this particular, and as we shall see, in every other power-broking or insubordinate instance, not (much as it

pleased Aelfrida to think so) and never would be Mother Guenvrede who was defeated, something Placida should have reflected on as Lent 1940 came to an end 'calm and full of "wisdom" all through … in spite of outward events and spiritual ups and downs'.[61]

Or perhaps she *did* reflect, as witness her noting on seeing the Mother completing Placida's allotted task that her 'chiefest sin' of the moment was 'strong instinctive self-will brought out by an unexpected demand or check', that she *could* have 'learned to dominate [her] body in the interests of [her] soul' if she had 'taken it in hand' sooner' (the perfect escape clause), and that there was always 'an element of truth' in the Mother's judgements.[62] Then shutting her reflections in a compartment of her mind, she proceeded to behave as if the Mother's reproof had never occurred: by requesting a weeks' leave of absence from the *opus Dei* (not, *nota bene*, from Communion lest she break her unbroken record of attendance, currently standing at forty weeks) to prove that her collapse was physical, not temperamental (in her diary, however, she attributed her 'collapse' to a 'breakdown' rather than to physical illness)[63]; by holding conversations with the Mother during which she tried to put the latter (torn between 'compassion and anger', Aelfrida was pleased to note) in the wrong and herself in the position of martyr[64], and by insisting that Sister Monica chaperone her when she was examined by the doctor so that a nurse could report back to Mother Guenvrede 'on his diagnosis'.[65] It seems, however, that neither Sister Monica nor the doctor took her seriously, the former having sent 'collapsed' Placida briskly off to bed with the advice that a drink of water would cure her symptoms and the latter, noting Mrs Graham's unconcern about her 'heart attack' and inappropriate gaiety had it really been one, replying to her question "does imagination enter into the case … were pains and tiredness *real* pains – *real* tiredness?" by answering "oh no" without intimating to which part of the question his answer applied.[66]

Having tried and failed to fool or manipulate her second Mother/mother and Father/father as well as a nurse and a doctor, Placida turned to Father Northcott, not because she wished to confess to him (far from it; she asked the Mother to dispense her from confession on the grounds that 'it is best not to see Father Northcott *at all* … because he asks very searching questions' and because although this might lead to her implicating Mother Guenvrede in 'the events that led to[her] having a heart attack', it might equally lead to trouble for herself because, as Northcott might point out, she had been disobedient in gardening for *more* than her allotted ten minutes and she had *not* reported her 'cramp in the heart' to the Mother which, as in matters of health, she was 'under obedience' to do) but because she wished to discuss with him (by letter) Mother Guenvrede's latest ruse: that Placida 'ought to have a change as I am ... so unwell'. Declaring that the only 'change' she could countenance was removal after death to the Campo Santo and that going away 'just because I am run down etc.' might unsettle the Sisters 'for whom "stability" is hard' so that 'for their sakes ... I would stay', Aelfrida found herself checkmated by Father and Mother acting in unison, the former declaring that convalescence away from Tymawr did not constitute 'instability' and the latter reminding her that 'tertiaries were not allowed to bind themselves', a statement hastily twisted by Placida into avowal that she herself could never *promise* never to leave.[67]

Privately, however, she raged, and in a four page denigration of Mother Guenvrede exposed what she described as the 'flaws' in that lady's character without admitting that they also existed in her own :

– 'She was born with an intense longing for personal affection and personal domination – the need to possess the inmost citadel of other people's character ... up to a point she is conscious of this but it is mostly in her unconscious mind, so much so that any victory was delicious to her ... [as] the essence of pure human triumph'.[68]

(It was the Mother's need to possess Aelfrida's 'inner citadel' that particularly frightened her for it reminded her not only of Father Cary's wish to dominate as well as direct, a possible reason for deciding to break with him, but also of Constantine who 'always wanted to possess the inmost core of my personality', his failure to do so being 'the ultimate cause of his deserting me', another rationalisation but entirely appropriate in one who had refused to yield up her inmost 'shrine where I worshipped God'[69] and informed her husband of this in a published poem.)

– 'She seems, in dealing with people, to mark them down, to watch them, to see when they are vulnerable, to strike; if she fails, to withdraw and look the other way, to watch again, to close in more carefully, to strike a blow that disintegrates the inmost citadel, to establish herself there ... to rule with the utmost generosity'.

(At one point during their library session of 8 March Aelfrida felt that the Mother had 'tricked' her into admitting 'something [she] did not really believe'; wisely, perhaps, she does not say what it was but asked herself instead if she was *really* guiltless 'of a wish to put her in the wrong and be right myself?' She also admitted that at the end of the session Mother Guenvrede had consoled her with the words "don't think of this as your will against mine".)

– She did not encourage people to adore her but tried to make them 'see the world through her eyes'.

(The session over, Placida had professed herself 'touched and so eager to obey ... my very dear Mother-in-God' but later wondered what her obedience was really worth – 'does not my unconscious self murmur "as long as it does not interfere too much with my comfort or convenience"' – and if she, unlike Sister Jeanne, would ever be able to 'obey perfectly, love her Mother-in-God – and [remain] perfectly detached'. She also asked herself if her only reason for remaining at Tymawr was admiration for the way in which the Mother was 'perfectly yielded to the Will of God and His chosen instrument for His work here'.)

– 'She is the most inscrutable person I have ever met and the more one knows her the more does one have to adjust one's impressions', a statement with which Aelfrida's biographer must concur.

Deciding at this point that the devil would press her very hard if she persisted in character assassination and risky behaviour, Placida decided to 'put the whole thing out of [her] mind'.

The episode, however, provided further ammunition. Mother Guenvrede, she noted, though callous towards 'sick people', was herself vulnerable to mental collapse if pushed too far ('and collapse she does, for all her fortitude')[70] and though she no longer seemed as 'much in evidence as Superior [with] a certain consciousness of position and ... a way ... of being pleased with her own personality [and] her whimsical ways and words'[71] (an apt description of Placida too) but more aloof and more apt to delegate, underneath her stalwart exterior lay insecurities to be played upon by someone whose love of power was similar to her own. The Mother, she also noted, was vulnerable to 'outbursts of what she calls "vehemence" and what Hilda refers to ... as '"temper"'[72] during which her behaviour verged on the abnormal (was it, she wondered, the Mother's 'Kruger' personality which was the reason for the Community being still so small twenty years after its foundation?)[73], something which could be reported to higher authority disguised as 'outward loyalty' to one she ostensibly defended 'with earnestness and sincerity'.[74]

'Happified' by the outcome of her first serious engagement with Mother Guenvrede and springtime allowing 'a little gardening' on a voluntary rather than a coerced basis, Placida proclaimed 'vocation of praise' more important than internecine warfare. She therefore used a 'talking day' to thank the Mother 'for a happy Lent'[75] and to beg her to report the 'collapse' to Father Northcott 'if it is her duty to make a fair report, even of humble tertiaries'. The Mother's reply was brusque: her time, she said, "was fully occupied in discussing more important matters".[76] It was indeed. Scenting an *odour of wickedness* spread abroad', Sister Placida discovered a day later than everyone else (the penalty of fully silent days; she also refused to listen to the wireless and continued to read *The Times* when 'everyone else [has] read it first')[77] that the 'phoney war' was about to end: Germany had annexed Denmark and invaded Norway.

A vision *coram sanctissimo* ('an "imaginary" one, picture clear') of a dark cloud over the altar blotting out the crucifix from whose 'purple depths emerged a great arm dark too but very distinct … '*God in His Aspect of Power*' alarmed her but the silver chalice it held 'tipped so that one could see the precious Blood of Our Lord [and] the blood of those who have suffered in union with His Passion' reassured her, for in that 'red wine … full mixed' she perceived Tymawr as 'a tiny drop, held safely in the hand of Almighty God – *safe in suffering*'.[78] But Tymawr, 'peaceful beyond words', was peaceful only in comparison to Holland (invaded soon after 'poor Norway'), to Brussels ('bombed'), to northern France ('overrun'), and to the 'invasion of England'. ('Expected'.) 'Vibrations of horrible events, the devil defying God Almighty', came closer still: 'Churchill, the boaster, the Godless militarist is Prime Minister'[79]; football pools and greyhound racing allowed to continue and the black-out used as cover for crime ('and I myself? Could I read through my diaries without the deepest shame? … Thank God … I *have* repented')[80]; a National Day of Prayer, inefficacious 'if England merely calls on [God] to get her out of the tight corner into which her own stupidity has landed her' ('stupidity' manifested by 'betting', 'road-hogging', 'childless marriages', and 'neglect of God'), but as she feared, the King's speech gave 'no hint of the need for repentance'. (Placida kept the day in retreat 'except for tea' with 'a little fasting' and Saint Guenvrede twice to keep her recollected; 'Saint Bruno was forbidden'.)[81] France, in decline because 'the 1914 war damaged her terribly' and because 'birth control, VD, alcoholism and so on have sapped her vitality'[82], setting up a collaborationist government in Vichy.

And closer: the 'reverse' of Dunkirk ('it is impossible to read without emotion … how 350,000 British troops were saved and embarked for England … the coolness, the courage, the heroism of all')[83]; Malling evacuated to Fownhope, 'a house lent them at Hereford' whence mutual visits between the two Communities occurred.

('*Delighted* to hear how dear Alethea is still to them', Aelfrida contributed £1 to removal expenses because 'in the midst of a mass-evacuation of civilians, cashing cheques might be impossible' – but only £1 because 'my little fortune may prove to have wings … and I may come to know Holy Poverty of an almost Franciscan bareness'.)[84] A letter from the Orphans' Home near Fordfield telling of barbed wire entanglements in Brooklands Avenue, pictures in *The Times* of 'a wrecked row of houses [in] *Cambridge itself*'.[85] Monmouth, a quiet little market town, enlarged by 'barracks'[86] for nine thousand soldiers and erection of an ordnance factory and depot nearby. Placida asked not to leave the convent grounds 'for fear of raids' but wangling the concession of two or three walks a week 'because I am so busy – for me! – in the garden'.[87] The chapel bell silenced 'by military orders, to be used only to give warning of invaders, not for holy use'.[88] 'Aerial combat' over the convent announced by '"take cover" warnings' from sirens and accompanied by 'searchlights, planes and the guns firing'. ('I am *glad* we have our share of the common danger, I would be ashamed to be in a perfectly safe place' but 'how tiresome if a bomb fell on the kettle … when we are waiting for tea'.) Mother Guenvrede saying philosophically "bombs will not fall on us unless they are intended to"; Placida praying that 'if a bomb is destined for Tymawr, it may fall on my corner of the guest house [not on] the dear Sisters … *Mors Janua Vitae*'.[89]

Death may be the gate of life but neither Aelfrida nor Placida (nor Mrs Graham, somewhat in abeyance at the moment given Mother Guenvrede's recent rebukes) were ready to close the gate behind them yet. They were too busy with letters to write and receive, people to see, prayers to pray, a 'night story' to compose, and revenge to plot.

Letters from Father Cary, balm to the soul of one who felt 'uninspired' without him, glad to know "that all goes well with you in the best kind of way … in the matter of conditions and environment"[90], an unintended irony, surely, given that Placida appears to have concealed disagreements with the Mother from him. Letters to and from Alethea, Aelfrida informing her daughter that although nationalist feeling in South Africa was being stirred by Nazi propaganda, her mother's wishes were 'God's Will first … not "safety first"' (a gibe at Eustace for sending two of his three children away and for asking his sister, through Julius, to use her 'influence' – her wide circle of correspondents – to enable him to send Veronica too)[91] and Alethea, in answer to a 'maternal letter about "her future"' written during the 'long border' incident (Placida, in grave danger of cardiac 'collapse' and being sent away from Tymawr, was doubtless hoping for a daughter to care for her in either event), stating firmly that it was God's Will she remain at St Cuthbert's. Letters to and from Fidelio who, holidaying nearby, requested a meeting: showing his letter to Mother Guenvrede whom she was currently keen to placate, Aelfrida described Fidelio as 'a French lecturer, a poet and a solitary' with whom she had been friendly since 1914 and as a man who had never been in love with her; she also intimated that, though reluctant to 'shirk the obligations of friend-ship', she preferred 'to be alone with God', a point acted upon by the Mother when she cannily suggested that in view of Sister Placida's recent ill health it would be wiser if Mr Stokoe did not visit. (The suggestion provided Aelfrida with an escape-clause at the same time as it infuriated Placida: 'I did think I ought perhaps to see him because I might help him spiritually'.) In the event she replied in a letter (submitted to Mother Guenvrede who read it before forwarding it without comment – or with-out recorded comment) combining 'a lot of irrelevant friendly talk from the Aelfrida he knows', saying noth-ing about Fidelio visiting the convent ('all I said was … "greet Juan for me; he can enlighten you about visits to Tymawr"') and signing herself ('of course') 'Placida. Ter. SSC'.[92] (No wonder, added Mrs Graham in diary pri-vacy, that 'the atmosphere I bring [to Tymawr] seems … more redolent of Cambridge than of heaven!')[93] Letters to and from 'goups', correspondence which did not, it seems, 'breach' 'silence' or create an outlet for pent-up emotions during which one could give 'free rein' to 'nat-ural expansiveness' (the latter an aspect of her 'clamour of selfhood', so Mother Guenvrede and her guardian angel informed her) but part of a 'prayer pattern' woven by the Holy Spirit from 'spiritual connections' transcending distance and nationality.[94]

Visits 'redolent of Cambridge' occurred too. In the early stages of the war Julius visited thrice, the first time on 22 September 1939, a meeting described by Aelfrida as 'the happiest of all … because our relationship *is* becoming spiritualised'. (She now, so she said, experi-enced 'no *doux épanchement*, no desire to receive sym-pathy or comfort' from him but only the sweet increase in 'spiritual poverty' with regard to affections recom-mended by her guardian angel while reciting Prime – in Latin – in her room.)[95] On his second visit on 29 April 1940, Julius, like her contemporary medical visitor, noted his sister's abnormal gaiety ('*sororem viso, quam satis hilarem sed parum validam inveni*')[96] and agreed, to her joy ('Julius is supremely faithful to the Fordfield tradition and to all that was good in the old ways and days. *He* should go there – not I, not Eustace')[97] to move with Mina to Wetenhall Cottage on his retirement. His third visit on 16 July 1940 constituted 'a perfect brother-and-sister

day' during which 'dear *dear* Dudu' bemoaned 'the sin and folly and suffering of mankind' (his sister thought him 'brave and unselfish [and] doing his duty': he was now an ARP warden) and Aelfrida (described by Julius as 'robust and serene') refrained from embarking on a description of her latest disagreement with the Mother.[98] Eustace, miserable and angry because war was upsetting his 'happy disposition and fortunate circumstances' (his sister could never resist a dig at her younger brother, even in wartime), visited on 11 December 1939 (a visit pre-pared for by Aelfrida with prayer; diary entries antici-pated antagonism but found '*natural* affection intensified' instead)[99] on his way to arrange for storage of goods in Cardiff 'in case the eastern counties are evacuated and he and his household have to flee (Fordfield and Wetenhall Cottage are immovable!)'.[100]

Prayers to pray included Anthony Wrightson, prayed for but not written to, and people and entities not prayed for hitherto: France (reparative adoration, it seems, as Placida's prayers involved 'penance')[101] and 'Mevrow Sterneberg of Amsterdam [and] Madame Cochard of Lyons' ('I think they were both Constantine's mistresses'), ladies of her own age living in occupied countries who provoked the comment 'is that twenty years ago? It is very vivid still but it stirs [only] a yearning pity'.[102] Even prayers for Conrad 'my baby brother … ripe for heaven so young'[103], though why Aelfrida prayed for a baby brother dead for fifty years at this point in her life, she does not say.

Ripeness for heaven at the 'fag-end' of her 'more or less selfish life' appealed to Placida too, her hopes being formulated in the form of a 'night story'. Although most of Aelfrida's published and unpublished novels were ini-tially conceived as or in the course of 'night stories' and took the form of re-interpreted events from her own past or extrapolated hopes or fears for the future, this particular 'story' is firmly rooted in the present:

> It is a beautiful summer morning in June 1940. Placida is working in the garden of Woodbine Cottage. She has just finished nailing up a section of trellis which has come loose under its weight of roses when she hears voices in the lane. *German* voices. Screened by the hedge, she listens intently. What she overhears horrifies her. The Germans are parachutists, dropped during the night on the plateau above the convent. They plan to take over the convent as a base for spying and for raiding parties, activities to be conducted dis-guised in the habits of the nuns they will first have to kill. Conferring amongst themselves, they move off down the lane towards the convent gate. Trug in hand, Placida slips silently into the convent grounds by a

field gate, hurrying past the Campo Santo and along the length of the herbaceous border. About to enter the convent by the French windows of the library, she stops aghast. She has arrived too late. The Germans, pistols drawn, are running up the drive. Standing at the top of the steps where she has greeted visitors in happier times, Placida confronts them. Addressing them in halting but grammatically-correct German, she asks them to kill her if kill they must but to spare her sisters-in-Christ. Disconcerted by the apparition of a frail elderly woman in the habit (as they think) of a religious (alerted by her guardian angel, Placida had the foresight to don her tertiary's veil before setting out), the soldiers look to their captain. "Kill her!" he commands. Falling to her knees, Placida offers them hammer and nails from her trug. "Crucify me!" she cries. They drag her to one of the oak trees gracing the convent garden and nail her to it through the stigmatic marks glowing on her hands and feet. Fixing her eyes on the Figure affixed to the living tree[104] overhanging the Campo Santo, Placida prays before she dies "Father, forgive them, for they know not what they do". Overcome with remorse, the soldiers take down her lifeless body and surrender it and themselves to Mother Guenvrede. After a beautiful Requiem Mass in which nuns and soldiers join, the corpse is borne through the gate inscribed *Mors Janua Vitae* to a hastily but reverently dug grave.

This poignant example of a Christian martyr attaining the premature but longed-for achievement of her heavenly birthday does not appear anywhere in Aelfrida's extant personal papers and it is perhaps presumptuous of a biographer to present it as if written *by her,* but that the story *was* conceived may be deduced from material she chose to preserve. Conception probably took place at the time of her comment concerning 'vibrations of horrible events' of 12 May 1940, a comment inspired by news of the imminent invasion of Belgium whose sufferings in 1914 (they included rumours of the pillaging of convents and raping of nuns) had been graphically depicted by Mrs Graham in two Great War poems, *The Stones of Belgium* and *Belgium. August–September 1914.* Would Tymawr, Placida wondered, suffer a similar fate? Could she, to avert this and as a supreme example of reparative adoration, offer herself as an examplar of 'my Lord as He perpetually offers His sufferings for the sins of the world'?[105] Hence though 'mortally afraid' of the prospect of invasion ('I used to be physically brave – I doubt if I am now')[106] but believing every rumour of Fifth Columnists disguised as nuns and the impossibility of defending the locality "if enemy parachutists descended

on the plateau"[107], Placida decided that if it was God's Will that nuns were to be 'crucified in Thee'[108], she and her 'sisters-in-Christ' should meet the German soldiery 'with hammers and strong nails so that they might crucify us on the oaks'.[109] What she did *not* tell the bishop to whom she later disclosed this startling piece of information was her intention that only she herself should meet them (nor did she disclose the fact that Mother Guenvrede, on being informed of her tertiary's sacrificial intentions, received her suggestions with scorn) though a subsequent diary entry modifies her account to suggest Community rather than individual heroism: 'the Mother … would have stood firm and I hope none of us would have failed her'.[110]

Hinting to Alethea in her weekly letters that martyrdom was a distinct possibility but that 'this last week has been the most serene and happy *sub specie aeternitatis* that I ever remember'[111] (Alethea's response went unrecorded) and encouraged in her project by discovering a 'German spy' snooping around Woodbine Cottage ('there must be hundreds scouring the countryside for quiet and defenceless spots where parachutists can lie in ambush') but undeterred by discovering that the 'spy' to be 'Mr Duveen the former Bond Street art dealer' who had rented the cottage for his stepdaughter's use, Placida decided to brush up her German in case she should be required to act as intermediary ('porteress') in the event of 'invaders' arriving at Tymawr. Snubbed by Mother Guenvrede who, far from praising her tertiary's 'obscure but very strong instincts' to protect the Community, told her to put her silly notions aside and to 'live more completely in the supernatural'[112], Placida found herself torn between 'an intense attraction towards martyrdom' (she did not 'dare pray for it … for fear of presumption' but felt that, failing martyrdom, her allowance of an hour a week of 'Saint Rose' – 'hair cincture', in case we had forgotten – was a poor substitute)[113] and diminishing eagerness 'to attain the "holy death"' she longed for because 'for the sake of the Community … I want to see them through the rough waters and out into the calm again'.[114] Fortunately, she never had to choose.

Revenge – or as far as she dared to go in the matter – took literary form: *Note on the Tertiary's Vocation,* composed on 24 July 1940 as a sequel to yet another skirmish with the Mother.

On 16 July, the day of 'dear, *dear* Dudu's' latest visit, Mother Guenvrede accused Aelfrida of going for a walk without permission and withdrew permission for all walks whether inside or outside the convent curtilage. The likelihood of invasion had already limited Placida's walks to 'the damp and dreary meadows'[115] of the Tymawr estate but she had invented an 'errand' and slipped out, excusing herself when found out that 'having [her] liberty restricted weighed on [her] very much'. (The 'errand' was to inform the Local Defence Volunteer of 'something suspicious' discovered on an earlier walk: a pool of 'mustard-gas', later discovered to be petrol leaking from an LDV motorcycle.) Attempts to justify her action (she had disobeyed the Mother in breaking bounds, and in passing on "wrong and distorted" information had talked both "unwisely" and in defiance of her own self-imposed 'Rule of Silence')[116] resulted in closer confinement ("tertiaries are *entirely* under my jurisdiction … [and] as head of household … I have expressed my wishes")[117] and in further deterioration of the relationship between Mother and 'child of God'. They also resulted in a revealing letter on the part of the imprisoned tertiary: "Dear Mother … I … beg that you will allow me my walks again. I use [them] partly for getting rid of natural restlessness, partly for thinking out various questions and problems but mostly for a kind of communing with God that I get no other way … You see, one needs an *outlet*. I have given up writing books; teatime chatter affords very little outlet, walks give me exactly what I need … Please … undo what you have done and allow me my liberty again". Then, realising that expressing anguish might occasion further accusations of 'temperament', Placida played her trump card: "You are laying upon me a burden which I have not the strength to bear [and which] constitutes a real spiritual obstacle … These last two or three days … I have been beset by horrible temptations [as] when I was overdoing penances [and] you said it was dangerous and I must stop … at once [and] this morning … for the first time, I loathed my prayers. I can walk the whole trouble off in an hour. *Mayn't* I? … I am trying to keep the spirit as well as the letter of obedience [but] don't you think the glory of God would best be served by our letting the whole matter drop … In all humility, your loving child in Christ". ('Oh dear', she confided to her diary, 'how I LOATHE the fusses that women-alone get themselves into'.)[118] So the matter was dropped and Placida resumed her walks.

The Mother, however, unwittingly provided further ammunition. First, she seems to have discussed the matter with Sister Jeanne and Father Amos, both of whom concluded that she had been overly harsh. Unable to express their feelings directly, the former intimated to Aelfrida that Mother Guenvrede was so angry that a 'furious letter turning her out of the house'[119] might be expected unless she quickly confessed her error (this gave Placida time to think out her strategy) and the latter provided a 'fatherly and comic bit of advice' after a confession during which, 'in great distress … and labouring under a strong sense of injustice', she informed him that she

was 'threatened with expulsion': "you won't be a doormat, will you?"[120] (A statement of fact or an instruction?) Second, she demanded of Placida a copy of her Rule.

Placida, it appears, had not kept (or said she did not keep) a copy of her original (Malling) 'Rule'. Informing Mother Guenvrede of this, she handed in a copy of 'the Rule I had kept at Oxford', this being the same as the one kept 'only slightly modified' at Tymawr (she does not list the 'modifications' but some were probably dietary) and in which, she emphasised, '*walks* are specified under the heading "occupations"'.[121] In view of the Mother's recent 'contemptuous' conduct, she also reminded the Mother that 'the nature of [a] tertiary's obedience' did not include giving up 'their property or their liberty of movement'; that in 'restricting [her] movement' Mother Guenvrede was doing something 'unconstitutional'; that she herself was 'not a Sister but only a tertiary' and could not attain the standards of a choir nun 'because she had no such exalted vocation'. (To her diary she confessed 'I *know* I could never bear enclosure nor having my whole time arranged by Authority. God has not called me to this'.)[122] Then, thinking that perhaps she had humbled herself too much, given that it was Mother Guenvrede, not she herself, who was in the wrong, Mrs Graham reminded the Mother that qua tertiary she was superior to the usual run of pious women: 'I was a consul-general's widow [and] had been in Class I in the Foreign Office "Book of Wives" (as Lord Dufferin himself showed me) and so on and so forth'.[123] Lastly, she threatened ('wondered whether she ought') to appeal to Father Northcott[124], whereupon Mother Guenvrede, addressing her as '*Sister* (very correct)' instead of as usual '*Sister Placida, dear*', accused her of being in a "goaty mood"[125] and demanded an account of conduct Placida believed proper for a tertiary.

Having ascertained that goatiness did not imply a tendency 'to *butt* people' but was characteristic of an animal which 'put in the middle of good grass … breaks its tether and wanders off … to nourish [itself] on brambles'[126] (Aelfrida denied the former definition but accepted the latter), Placida sat down to '[think] out the implications of a tertiary's vocation'. As by no means all the 'implications' appear in her final draft, it is worth noting those omitted before we read it: she could never conform to the ideals of life in enclosure and to 'hourly obedience' because she was constitutionally opposed to imposed Authority and because she preferred to 'plan [her] days … within the framework of [her] individual Rule' rather than being 'tied by Community Rule and Mother's orders'; having bound herself to the Community by vows taken in 1937 and confirmed in 1939, she had discovered too late that 'the Common Life … makes small acts of private self-indulgence almost impossible'; she found the 'sense … of being [continually] under observation … oppressive'.[127] There was, too, 'a *call* to being misunderstood' inherent in her vocation so it was 'probably *best* that people should assume one's Rule is *choice* rather than *vocation*'[128], a cryptic remark whose import will not become clear for some time.

With this and the preceding pages in mind, let us now enjoy Sister Placida's *Note on the Tertiary's Vocation*[129]:

"The vocation of a tertiary in its broad outlines will be the same as the Community to which she is attached. If the Community is called to adoration and reparation and to a desire for the fellowship of Our Lord's sufferings, so too is she.

She must always bear in mind, however, that the vocation of a tertiary is a much humbler one than that of the choir nun, and that she is specially called to *humility*. The tertiary is not asked to give up her property or her personal liberty – her status, therefore, is not as honourable as that of nuns, who have nothing that they can call their own, and who live in enclosure. She knows that this degree of sanctity is not for her, and she must therefore always remain very lowly in her own eyes.

The tertiary may nevertheless, without presumption, believe that she is specially called to live in direct dependence upon the Holy Spirit. The nuns' life is more rigid, there is little element of choice for the individual – the Community's Rule and the daily orders of the Superior cover almost all their ground. But the tertiary, who has more freedom, needs to be extremely sensitive to the monitions of the Holy Spirit if she is not to live a life of pious self-pleasing. Her comparative freedom from interruptions and the stretches of time that she can call her own should be used for a continuous awareness of God's Holy Presence, and for sustained thought on divine things.

The tertiary is called to spiritual solitude. She should detach her attention and her affections (except in so far as she needs knowledge for her prayer and for seeing everything and everyone in God) from the world outside. Nor should she desire too close a contact with her Sisters in Christ. "Commune in your heart and in your chamber and be still", are words that apply with special force to her.

The chief danger to the tertiary (possibly a danger shared by the nuns) is that of *not pressing forward*. Silence, abstinence, manual labour, and a position of inferiority, all bitter at first, become sweet through use, and beloved for the graces that they have brought. The tertiary is tempted to be satisfied with territory conquered especially if she should lack a stimulating director.[130] The same is true of spiritual matters. Her wonder and joy at God's gifts must

not prevent her seeing that He has ever fresh bounties to bestow.

Communities have been likened to gardens, in which some are called to be trees, some flowers, some grass, and so on. If such a comparison were being considered, the tertiaries would be the grass – good to be trodden under foot, but good also to give a sense of rest and spaciousness to the eye.[131]

A Community, though, is something more than a harmony of beautiful objects, it is a living organism, and its life flows from one member to another. Communities are valuable, not because of their numbers, not because of their active work, they are valuable because of the quality of their prayer. Has the Community offered acceptable praise to God? Has it duly lifted up before Him the sin and the anguish of the world: Is it an unobstructed channel for his grace?

There should be two elements in good prayer – intensity and spaciousness. The nuns would chiefly contribute the former, the tertiaries, the latter. Nuns and tertiaries are mutually dependent. If the nuns' prayer is growing narrow perhaps the tertiaries are partly to blame. If the tertiaries are lukewarm, the nuns may be in a measure responsible. Or mutual love may be deficient. The more the nuns and the tertiaries love each other in God, the more bright will the fire of the Holy Spirit blaze up in the Community".[132]

If Placida was disappointed at the Community's reaction to her *Note* with its implied rebukes and barely concealed warnings, she does not show it. Mother Guenvrede merely remarked that its tone was 'too self-conscious', a comment with which Aelfrida agreed: 'one day I shall cease being interested in myself and be wholly absorbed in God. But not yet awhile, I fear!'[133], and Father Northcott that it was better to be simple and patient than try to conform to a mental image of 'the ideal tertiary'.[134] The latter comment made her thoughtful: 'it is *selfish* of me to … live in an atmosphere of romantic mediaeval conventualism if what the Mother wants is a little twentieth century common sense'.[135] So she set out to provide it.

The twentieth century, however, had other ideas. While Placida was doing her best to disturb the peace within Tymawr's walls, Adolf Hitler was busy shattering whatever vestiges of romantic mediaevalism remained without.

The months immediately preceding Sister Placida's latest skirmish with Mother Guenvrede found her reading and much impressed by Edward Leen's book *The Holy Ghost*, especially, she informs us, page 134. Page 134, on which Placida ruminated over the course of several days (e.g. 'how far can a man become "giveable" to another human being when he is "owned" by God?', with the corollary that she herself had not been 'give-able' to Constantine, but only partially 'gifted', a flash of illumination into 'a mental fog that has lasted for 30 years')[136] suggests that not only does God have a "benev-olent purpose ... in bringing intellectual and reasonable creatures into existence" i.e. that of giving them *Himself* "to the full measure in which they can participate in Him", but also that in order for God to be able to give Himself to man, man must use his will (and is created by God expressly for that purpose) to unite himself to God "by bringing [his will] into conformity with His".[137]

This, of course, was fine as far as it went but 'present history'[138] intruded. Ruminating on God's relationship to England and England's to God in time of war, Placida declared she 'must not allow the war to dominate [her] mind' because a tertiary's business was 'to praise God and to become more and more united to Him in will and love'. She also found herself forced in spite of herself 'to think out the whole question of divine intervention in wars and so on'[139] – and for a moment her faith wavered: if, as she believed, 'the whole of a nation's civilisation should be based on its relationship to God'[140], how 'give-able' was Germany, or for that matter, England? And if, as Edward Leen stated, the Holy Ghost had a mission "to take up His abode ... in the souls of the just [in] an inchoate form of the perfect possession of God that is enjoyed by the blessed in Heaven"[141], who, in the present context, constituted "the just"? To this question Placida had no answer, except to note that after 'nearly two thou-sand years of Christianity ... civilized men [should] have moved to a higher plane' and that she herself felt nothing but gratitude 'to army, navy and air force, bulwarks that I may write here in peace under the spreading branches of a huge white chestnut'.[142]

Write in peace though she might, diary entries were anything but peaceful:

– 20 June 1940. 'I felt no fear only a detached inter-est' as a 'raiding plane' circling overhead set local dogs barking.[143]

– 26 June. Standing on 'Prehistory' surveying 'the far-flung view', she received a message '"there shall no evil happen unto thee, neither shall any plague come nigh thy dwelling" – but whether the promise is spiritual or material ... I have no idea!'[144]

– 29 June.'One takes it all as a matter of course already'[145], written of warning sirens and distant gunfire.

– 1 July. 'I had not meant to write ... about raids but unless I put down last night's terrors, I shall keep reverting to it in my mind ... The enemy ... wish gradually to poison all our air ... the horror of dark-ness was very close ... it must be poison gas ... I

thought I would see if gas mask gave relief, got it (in the dark) and tried – it was like walking out of a smoke-filled room into outer air ... "Father, forgive them for they etc."' (at this point, seeking martyrdom, she removed 'Virgilio') 'and then the all clear sounded and I went to sleep'.[146]

– 2 July. 'After I had written all that stuff in my diary I came to the conclusion that I am a bit of a coward ... I must pray for *fortitude*'.[147]

– 12 July. 'Life flows on serenely – in spite of the enemy [but last night] a whole big show – raiders, search-lights, guns, bells ... bombs and what I took to be machine gun fire'.[148]

– 13 July. 'War is *here* ... not as something remote and unthinkable but ... as part of the normal experience of our earthly pilgrimage ... I hate war, conflict, dis-harmony – but I cannot stand apart from it'.[149]

– 14 July. 'Of all the people here the Mother is the one with whom I feel at home spiritually ... yet superfi-cially she does things I cannot understand and which grieve me', notably a demand that Aelfrida store Vichy water drunk 'to keep inside clean' in a disused shed at Woodbine Cottage because water imported from col-laborationist France must not pollute the convent.[150]

– 23 July. '1am. Four bombs explode very close making the convent *shudder*. I said "this is the end", folded my hands over my little silver cross, commended my soul to God ... 1.20am [Two more bombs fall] 'I drew down the blind, lit a discreet night light, partly dressed, got into bed and said Compline ... a smell of gunpowder (reminding me of cap pistols!) drifted into the room ... Outside our cows were bellowing frantically [but] everything was quiet throughout the house'.[151]

– 29/30 July. 'How close danger is. And how calm it leaves one's heart when one's mind is stayed on God ... I found myself writing to Alethea "everything has been very peaceful here since I last wrote"!! ... I sup-pose I was thinking of convent quietness and of peace in my heart'.[152]

– 31 July. 'Last night I thought that the devil had a spe-cial grudge against the Mother and sent one of his emissaries to bomb the convent ... it was very bad indeed [the bombs] sounded like the devil striking his heel on the ground ... the enemy roamed at will'.[153]

If one of Aelfrida's reasons for choosing Tymawr was that of being as far as possible from the coming war without actually leaving her natal land, she had not chosen well. The convent, though isolated, lay beneath the path of German aircraft flying from northern France to bomb the entrepots and great industrial centres and rail net-works serving them situated, because of their proximity to the South Wales coalfields, along the Glamorganshire coast to the west; Bristol docks lay across the Severn estuary to the east and the Wye and Severn rivers provided excellent landmarks even at night. To the north, Liverpool docks and the urban conglomerations of the Midlands also lay within reach of invaders whose planes, encountering their first real resistance from English fighter aircraft (the convent pigs were named 'Spitfire' and 'Hurricane' in their honour) and from barrages of anti-aircraft fire from guns situated on the hills above the Severn, Wye and Usk valleys, were forced to retaliate on inward and outward journeys, sometimes to the point of releasing their bomb-load in order to effect their escape. Hence even when not actually aimed at structures in the vicinity of Monmouth (known locally as 'Little Woolwich')[154], bombs fell and gunfire was experienced very close to Tymawr, so close, indeed, that Placida's West Room 'hummed and vibrated like a sounding box'[155], incendiary and high explosive bombs were 'nightly sprinkled around'[156], 'a huge hail of shrapnel' regularly rattled on the roof [157], and Mother Guenvrede, feeding the chickens, became the target of 'machine-gunning from aloft' and had to dash to safety in the turkey shed.[158]

The onset of the Battle of Britain and the Blitz in August/September 1940 widened the scope of Aelfrida's worries. Raids on London ('*sic transit gloria mundi* the bombs seem to say as they fall')[159] reminded her of family there; Ancifera, now ninety-one, alone in Ealing save for an elderly servant, the Stanleys, such as still lived in Nightingale Lane, all older than Aelfrida by some years; and of friends, particularly Anthony Wrightson: 'I fear he is in great danger … I pray for him.[160] Julius, in Cardiff, dealing with the aftermath of 'big scale bombing' ('*multas bombas*') but 'facing all his manifold duties with fortitude, even with zest', wartime action being an excellent antidote to depressive introspection. (On a brief visit to Tymawr, Julius recorded that his sister was well in spite of '*periculi*' from '*multi aeroplani*'; Aelfrida did not tell him of the machine-gunning episode.)[161] Mina, a blood donor: 'love-in-action of a *very* noble kind'.[162] Eustace, sleeping in college despite 'bad air-raids on Cambridge' and 'bombs dropped all round Wetenhall Cottage'. Phyllis, in Hadstock, having a 'miraculous' escape (a 'spiritual message', Aelfrida hoped) when two time-bombs fell in the back garden, or running the gauntlet of metropolitan 'ruins and raids' to visit her dying mother in London.[163] Churchill prophesying at least two more years of war: 'always "the frantic boast and foolish word" of pride and vainglory – it makes me shudder'.[164] Father Amos praying '*unhesitatingly* for victory [but] I *can't* … I can only pray "Thy will be done" [but] of course my human self longs for dear England to win'.[165]

There were, of course, consolations. A visit from Agatha on her mother's fifty-seventh birthday to wish her happy returns in the ironic tone she always used because she disliked that particular '*formule de politesse*'.[166] The beauties of Nature: 'a glimpse of wild duck on the wing … spindlewood and wild guelder rose berries in the hedges – the shaded colouring of bracken … mist and shadows, sombre sunsets with cloud monsters black against pale-apricot sky … autumn flowers, purple, crimson, gold – everything inexpressively lovely, all touched with supernatural light'.[167] The supernatural, manifest in 'shewings' and visions and auditions, fewer now but still vivid and precious when they came: a vision at Vespers of standing on the world ('a little globe all dark and black') with her guardian angel formed of 'pure spirit' protecting her and finding 'my feet on earth, my spirit in heaven [amid] God's Triune Love flowing and flowing … *life* … far beyond human comprehension'[168] or, just before Compline, God calling her 'deep deep into His Infinity [there] to feed [her] spirit on His Omnipotence and His Love'.[169] 'In the midst of night's turmoil' of bombs and machine-gun fire, God gives her 'a hush in my soul and makes Himself known to me … I have been *in Him* and He *in me* more fully these … nights than ever, I think, before'.[170] At Communion, 'my Lord [placing] His pierced hands on my head in blessing, keeping them there until the chalice had been given me'.[171]

But nights were now so terrible that ghostly comfort notwithstanding, Placida changed her prayer routine. Instead of donning her small silver cross and saying Compline until the 'all clear' sounded (Compline, even in Latin, did not seem 'quite adequate' now), she donned her larger 'tertiary's cross' when 'night raiders' came over and repeated 'a few *triumphant* hymns'. The ritual, and prayers that she and the Community were using 'as weapons against the devil and his angels', gave her such a 'perfect hush in [her] soul – bombs or no bombs' that she was able to '*rest in the Lord*' if not in her West Room.[172] She even endeavoured to say Compline 'for Jerry'[173] i.e. for the souls of young German airmen 'on their way to bomb Liverpool' but intercepted and possibly killed on the way.

Some nights were so terrifying that Aelfrida was 'left to [her] own weakness' and in spite of 'many prayers … had no consciousness of God and was very desolate'. (Only now did she fully appreciate Agatha's almost-last words "it is our weakness, not our strength, that God wants".)[174] Placida, however, behaved both calmly and bravely because '*parata sum et non sum turbata*'[175] and buoyed up and prepared for death in the face of real and present danger by her faith in God, reported only one real moment of panic: 'I was reading yesterday's *Times* and sucking a peppermint when a raider came trundling by quite close … A terrific noise rocked the house and nearly tipped me out of my chair … A second explosion brought me to my feet … "I ought to be in chapel" so I put my unfinished pep (*sic*) on a plate … and went downstairs as fast as I could … [where] safe and happy on prayer mat, I opened my Prayer Book'[176] – only to be 'sharply' reproved by Mother Guenvrede for entering chapel at a time when she was not permitted to be there, inconsistent behaviour on the Mother's part because she had already given permission for Placida to do as she thought best 'in case of an air raid': pray in chapel, remain in her room, or seek shelter outside.[177] She also made use of 'battle nights' as a kind of '*Purgatory to me*' of temporary suffering during which she could expiate venial sins too trivial for reparative adoration and vent herself of 'everything I don't like [such as] feeling helpless in the face of the world's pain – and bombs – and minor ailments and inconveniences – and my own tiresomeness and stupidity' in order to 'hurry things up a little on the other side and once across the waters of death, make no slow tarrying'.[178] An ability to dissociate herself from material terrors with the help of spiritual exercises in order to enter into the intense spirituality of the supernatural world helped too: 'the centre of Reality shifted [and] the veil that hides Heaven … parted'.[179] She was also buoyed up by hopes of being 'called home' to the perfect union with God for which she had 'longed with anguished longing' for so long.[180] ("Don't make any mistake", said Mother Guenvrede when informed after Hours for the Dead recited on All Souls 1940 that Placida hoped her turn would come soon, "you have a long way to go yet".[181] She was right.) And by assiduously willing herself to quietness, she *became* recollected to an extent unimaginable in peacetime when people and events conspired – or in her anguished mind, seemed to conspire – to thwart her 'closer walk with God'.

But not yet as recollected as she wished. The Community's Retreat of November 1940 was conducted by 'refreshingly familiar' Oxford priest, Father Pridham of the SSJE. Father Pridham (he had the inestimable merit of having been instructed by Father Cary) conducted the Retreat entirely to Placida's satisfaction by exemplifying in his discourses 'all Our Lord's words and deeds as *portals* through which our soul may pass'. This, his suggestion at 'a *good* confession' ('true contrition on [her] side and wise counsel … on the confessor's') that Placida replace self-centredness with "God-consciousness"[182], and maintenance of complete silence during the Retreat (when it ended, 'there were six copies of *The Times* waiting to be read')[183], reminded Aelfrida that she had not yet passed through two 'portals' (Silence and Solitude) as far as she would like. But having decided

during a three-day retreat of her own devising that the 'shining path' leading to these particular 'portals' had become 'much clearer' (but also 'alas and alas!' that it was 'so sweet to be *good in one's own way*')[184], Placida found her path booby-trapped at Christmas 1940 by the discovery that even at Tymawr there was 'too much of the secular' mixed up with what should be an entirely sacred festival. Persuading herself that 'the Library's' traditional Christmas dinner was too redolent of secularity she had sought to avoid since 'Christmas Days at Fordfield' (it must have been borne on Agatha and Alethea at an early age that a mother who counted every card and present she received and was aggrieved if anyone forgot her but who eschewed Christmas fare in favour of bread and butter and avoided festivities by withdrawing to her room to 'meditate', was not as other mothers), Placida 'feasted in her heart' as she ate her frugal meal alone in her room and retired early, giving as her excuse (for excuse it was, as her diary makes clear: Christmas Day being a festival, she could and should 'under obedience' have socialised) that she had a '*very* bad headache'. She then decided that God's continuing call to Silence (and to its necessary adjunct for a compulsive communicator, namely Solitude) could no longer be ignored and because Silence was 'His choice for me, not mine for myself', she dare no longer delay the next stage of her 'earthly pilgrimage'.[185]

## Notes

1  GCPPT 1|1|57 1, 2 and 4 September 1939.
2  ibid. 4 September 1939.
3  ibid. 2 September 1939.
4  ibid. 9 September 1939.
5  ibid. 2 September 1939.
6  ibid. 9 and 17 September and 2 October 1939.
7  ibid. 2 September 1939.
8  ibid. 2 October 1939.
9  ibid. 4 September 1939.
10  ibid.
11  ibid. 2 October 1939.
12  ibid. 23 September 1939.
13  ibid. 4 September 1939.
14  ibid. 11 October 1939.
15  ibid. 1 June 1940.
16  ibid. 5 December 1939.
17  ibid. Marginal note 'NB Dec 13' added to entry for 24 September 1939.
18  ibid. 10 September 1939.
19  ibid. 14 November 1939.
20  ibid. 24 September 1939.
21  ibid. 26 September 1939.
22  ibid. 'Michaelmas Day' (29 September) 1939.
23  GCPPT 1|1|54 24 September 1937.
24  ibid. 30 September 1937.
25  GCPPT 1|1|57 10 September and 2 October 1939.
26  ibid. 4 October 1939 and 1|1|57a 'I will keep the paper – here it is'.

27  ibid. 5 October 1939.

28  ibid. 24 September and 4 and 5 October 1939.

29  GCPPT 1|1|28 20 June 1924.

30  GCPPT 1|1|57 5 October 1939.

31  ibid. 11 October 1939.

32  ibid. 15 October 1939.

33  *Psalm* 122:7 and 8 (KJV).

34  GCPPT 1|1|57 24 May 1940. Aelfrida's reference is to Defense Regulation 18B of the Emergency Powers Act which temporarily removed the right of habeas corpus.

35  ibid. 15 and 19 October 1939.

36  ibid. 31 October 1939.

37  ibid. 3 December 1939.

38  Verses 19–21 of St Paul's *Epistle to the Romans* run as follows: "For the earnest expectation of the creature waiteth for the manifestation of the sons of God. For the creature was made subject to vanity, not willingly, but by reason of him who hath subjected the same in hope, Because the creature itself also shall be delivered from the bondage of corruption into the glorious liberty of the children of God". (KJV).

39  GCPPT 1|1|57 4 December 1939.

40  ibid. The story of Ananias and Sapphira is recounted in *Acts* 5: 1–11.

41  ibid. 5 December 1939.

42  ibid. 7 December 1939.

43  ibid. 3, 4 and 5 December 1939.

44  ibid. 4 and 5 December 1939.

45  ibid. 1 November 1939.

46  ibid. 29 October 1939.

47  47 GCPPT 1|1|56 3 and 4 April 1939.

48  GCPPT 1|1|57 5 December 1939.

49  ibid. 5 and 7 December 1939.

50  ibid. 9 December 1939.

51  ibid. 22 December 1939. This was the '"incident" not worth recording' noted by Aelfrida in the 13 December marginal note added to her diary entry of 24 September 1939.

52  ibid. 22 and 23 December 1939.

53  ibid. 27 January and 16 and 17 February 1940.

54  ibid. 5 March 1940.

55  ibid. 14 March 1940.

56  ibid.

57  ibid. 6 March 1940.

58  GCPPT 1|1|59 23 January 1942. Commenting that the Community was 'in *very* low water' in 1940 ('prayer turned the tide', she added happily) Aelfrida fails to make clear if the 'low water' was financial, spiritual, numerical, or all three. By context, she means financial but numerical also applies; spiritually she elsewhere implies.

59  GCPPT 1|1|57 8 March 1940.

60  ibid. 9 and 14 March 1940.

61  ibid. 22 March 1940.

62  ibid. 19 and 26 March 1940.

63  ibid. 8 April 1940.

64  ibid. 14 March 1940.

65  ibid. 15 March 1940.

66  ibid. 'Palm Sunday' (17 March) 1940.

67  ibid. 2 and 4 May 1940.

68  ibid. 'Passion Sunday' (10 March) 1940.

69  ibid. 4 June 1940.

70  ibid. 10 March 1940.

71  ibid. 4 November 1939.

72  ibid. 10 March 1940.

73  ibid. 9 November 1939.

74  ibid. 10 March 1940.

75  ibid. 'Easter Day' (24 March), 30 March and 6 April 1940.

76  ibid. 1 May 1940.

77  ibid. 12 April 1940.

78  ibid.

79  ibid. 12 May 1940.

80  ibid. 17 May 1940.

81  ibid. 19 and 26 May 1940.

82  ibid. 19 June 1940. VD was a euphemism for 'venereal disease'. Aelfrida's censorious views owe much to Alec Vidler's polemical *God's Judgement on Europe* of 1940 in which (p 98) the war is described as a consequence of "Europe's detachment from its [Christian] foundations". The book does not, however, include specific examples of Europe's moral disintegration, Aelfrida's parade of pet hates (betting, contraception, promiscuity, alcohol, and motoring malpractice) being her own view of what constituted 'disintegration'.

83  ibid. 21 May and 6 July 1940.

84  ibid. 19 May 'Corpus Christi' (22 or 23 May), 28 May and 3 August 1940.

85  ibid. 9 (*sic*) and 22 June 1940. So overcome was Aelfrida at this news that she misdated entries, one illegibly and two as '9 June'. 118 high explosive bombs and 1000 incendiary bombs were dropped on Cambridge during the war; 29 people were killed. Brooklands Avenue's proximity to the goods yards near Cambridge station and to an important bridge made it particularly vulnerable though houses there sustained little or no damage; the church of Our Lady and the English Martyrs sustained some damage in 1941.

86  ibid. 20 May 1940.

87  ibid. 20 and 21 May 1940.

88  ibid. 15 June 1940.

89  ibid. 22 and 23 June 1940.

90  ibid. 26 December 1939. Father Cary's letter dated 'St Thomas 1939' is preserved in 1|1|57a.

91  ibid. 17 December 1939 and 7 July 1940.

92  ibid. 4 June and 8 July 1940.

93  ibid. 15 June 1940.

94  ibid. 23 December 1939, 9 May and 4 July 1940.

95  ibid. 22 September 1939 and 9 February 1940. The italicised 'is' is the author's; Aelfrida, surprisingly for such an important statement, leaves it unemphasised.

96  Tillyard, HJW. *Synopsis of Diary* 30 April 1940 (MTC).

97  GCPPT 1|1|57 30 April 1940.

98  GCPPT 1|1|58 16 July 1940.
    Tillyard, HJW. *Synopsis of Diary* 16 July 1940 (MTC).

99  GCPPT 1|1|57 12 December 1939.

100  ibid. 19 May 1940.

101  ibid. 15 June 1940.

102  ibid. 15 May 1940.

103  ibid. 2 October 1940.

104  GCPPT 1|1|56 1 April 1939.

105  GCPPT 1|1|57 10 and 12 May 1940.

106  ibid. 17 May 1940.

107  Tillyard, Ae. *The Centaur* p8 (GCPPT 2|12|1).

108  GCPPT 1|1|56 12 April 1939.

109  GCPPT 1|1|68 12 August 1950.

110  GCPPT 1|1|73 16 May 1956.

111  GCPPT 1|1|57 17 May 1940.

112  ibid. 25 May 1940.

113  ibid. 19 June 1940.

114  ibid. 17 June 1940.

115  GCPPT 1|1|58 20 July 1940.

116  GCPPT 1|1|58a. Undated note from Mother Guenvrede to 'Mrs Graham', by context written 16 July 1940. Aelfrida refused to read it because not addressed to 'Sister Placida', returning it marked 'returned unread'. Mother Guenvrede sent it back 'with "*Important*" on it' whereupon Aelfrida returned it (still unread) with the further inscription 'Sister Placida asks your love and charity as you are answerable to God', noting in her diary 'to think that all this fuss is

for *no cause*'. Mother Guenvrede then placed the note in an envelope addressed to 'Tertiary Sister Placida' whereupon Placida decided that 'if the Mother put "Tertiary Sister P." on the envelope I ought to read the contents'. To her diary she confided 'I am afraid [the Mother] is losing her sense of humour and sense of proportion … [but she] isn't herself – the anxieties of the war must have got on her nerves' (GCPPT 1|1|58 16 and 21 July 1940). Aelfrida unwittingly condemns herself by preserving the Mother's letters and copies of her own side of the correspondence.

117 GCPPT 1|1|58a ibid. The LDV force, started on 14 May 1940, was renamed the Home Guard on 22 July.
GCPPT 1|1|58 21 July 1940.

118 GCPPT 1|1|58 20 and 21 July 1940.

119 ibid. 21 July ('June' in error) 1940.

120 ibid. 20 July 1940.

121 ibid. 21 July and 4 August 1940.

122 ibid. 21 and 22 July 1940.

123 ibid. 29 July 1940. Aelfrida's statement contains three untruths: she was *not* a Consul-General's (or anyone else's) 'widow' and Lord Dufferin could not have shown her, spontaneously or at her request, a non-existent "Book of Wives".

124 ibid. 21 July 1940.

125 ibid. 25 July 1940.

126 ibid. 18 September 1940.

127 ibid. 24 July 1940 and GCPPT 1|1|58a.

128 ibid. 26 July 1940.

129 The *Note*, dated 24 July 1940, is preserved in GCPPT 1|1|58a.

130 This piece of gratuitous nastiness concerning Father Northcott is made more poignant by his making it obvious to her during a session of 'counsell (*sic*) and confession' on 9 October 1940 at which she expressed distress that the Mother was 'disappointed' in her (a comment later relayed by Placida to Mother Guenvrede) that he knew Mother Guenvrede could be difficult (GCPPT 1|1|58 9 October 1940).

131 The simile is taken from a discourse given by Father Northcott during the 1939 Retreat – "what would a garden look like if all the flowers were roses and lilies? Suppose we are meant to be blades of grass?" (GCPPT 1|1|57 7 December 1939) – developed here by Aelfrida in terms of tertiaries being a 'lawn'.

132 GCPPT 1|1|58a The dig at Mother Guenvrede in her final paragraph probably stems from the fact that two novices had recently left, one to do 'war work', the other to follow a former fiancé, now in the RAF. It was also Placida's way of hinting publicly why 'postulants and even novices don't stay' (GCPPT 1|1|58 14 September 1940).

133 GCPPT 1|1|58 6 August 1940.

134 ibid. 9 October 1940.

135 ibid. 29 July 1940.

136 GCPPT 1|1|57 4 June 1940.

137 Leen, E. *The Holy Ghost and His Work in Souls* p 134.

138 GCPPT 1|1|57 6 June 1940.

139 ibid. 9 and 10 June 1940.

140 ibid. 1 June 1940.

141 Leen, E. Foreword pp v-vii.

142 GCPPT 1|1|57 4 June 1940

143 ibid. 20 June 1940.

144 ibid. 26 June (misdated entry, by context 27 or 28 June) 1949. The source of Placida's 'message' is *Exodus* 12:13 (KJV).

145 ibid. 29 June 1940.

146 ibid. 1 July 1940. For a graphic description of exposure to 'poison gas' see Wilfred Owen's poem *Dulce et Decorum Est*. HG Wells, with whose works Aelfrida was familiar, had envisaged the overhead release of 'poison gas' on defenceless civilians from enemy aircraft in the course of future wars.

147 ibid. 'The Visitation' (2 July) 1940.

148 ibid. 12 July 1940.

149 ibid. 13 July 1940.

150 ibid. 14 July 1940. Vichy water was an effervescent alkaline mineral water popular with dyspeptics.

151 GCPPT 1|1|58 23 July 1940. In 1940 the convent owned 2 cows, 2 'heifer calves' 12 hens, 36 pullets, 7 turkeys, 5 cats and 2 pigs. (Donkin, W. p 36. PAM box 225–279 Pamphlet 230).

152 GCPPT 1|1|58 29 and 30 July 1940.

153 ibid. 31 July 1940. This entry was written on Mother Guenvrede's birthday, Placida seeing no contradiction in praying 'very loving prayers for my Mother-in-Christ' and assuming that the devil had a 'special grudge' against her as a person.

154 ibid. 17 August 1940.

155 ibid. 26 August 1940.

156 ibid. 1 September 1940. Bomb craters remain visible in fields near the convent.

157 ibid. 29 November 1940.

158 ibid. 8 and 10 November 1940.

159 ibid. 8 September 1940. For details of the London Blitz see Calder, A. ch 4 pp163–227. The Tymawr Community later received first-hand information concerning the devastation of London's East End by incendiaries and high explosive from a Sister working in Poplar at the time. Hearing her account Aelfrida wrote poignantly of 'fire and ruins' and of how 'still the raiders come [and] the bombs fall [on] ruined churches and houses [and] poor homeless people' (ibid. 14 September 1940).

160 ibid. 3 October 1940 'Anthony's birthday'.

161 162 GCPPT 1|1|58 4 August and 12 November 1940. Tillyard, HJW. *Synopsis of Diary* (MTC) entry written between 16 August and 3 September 1940 and dated entries of 12 November 1940 and 2 January 1941.

162 GCPPT 1|1|58 27 November 1940.

163 ibid. 3 September and 15 and 17 October 1940.

164 ibid. 22 August 1940. Aelfrida's low opinion of Churchill's rallying speeches in Parliament was not shared by others.

165 ibid. 9 September 1940.

166 ibid. 6 October 1940.

167 ibid. 25 September 1940.

168 GCPPT 1|1|57 8 July 1940.

169 GCPPT 1|1|58 26 July 1940.

170 ibid. 26 August 1940.

171 ibid. 6 October 1940.

172 ibid. 17 and 19 August 1940. Lest Placida's statement seem to demonstrate the 'frantic boast' she disliked in Churchill, a poem by Sister Jeanne (*October Thanksgiving*) written on St Placid's Day, 5 October 1940 puts her statement in conventual perspective: "For membership of Placid's team of *peaceful fighters* … Benedicamus Domino" (GCPPT 1|1|58a, author's emphasis).

173 ibid. 22 December 1940.

174 ibid. 30 August 1940.

175 ibid. 7 December 1940.

176 ibid. 31 October 1940.

177 GCPPT 1|1|57 22 June 1940.
GCPPT 1|1|58 1 December 1940.

178 GCPPT 1|1|58 2 September and 'All Souls' (2 November) 1940.

179 ibid. 1 September 1940.

180 GCPPT 1|1|57 22 June 1940.

181 GCPPT 1|1|58 'All Souls' (2 November) 1940.

182 ibid. 17 and 20 November 1940.

183 ibid. 27 November 1940.

184 ibid. 24 October 1940.

185 ibid. 25 and 26 December 1940.

# Intensified Claustration

Not content with plagiarising R H Benson's "terribly sensational" novel *Lord of the World*[1] as Aelfrida Tillyard, Placida, it seems, set out to model her life on the hero of another Benson novel, *Richard Raynal: Solitary.*

Although Thomas à Kempis' precepts on Solitude and Silence must have been recalled by one who practised other of his precepts so assiduously (e.g. "control the appetite and you will … control all bodily desires … undertake manual employment with discretion"), a statement enjoining avoidance of "unnecessary talk" and prescribing "withdraw[al] from the crowd [to] live an inward and spiritual life with Jesus" ("choose rather to serve God in solitude … [for] God with his holy angels will draw near to him who withdraws himself")[2] provided splendid justification for one who had already warned Mother Guenvrede that she intended to spend most of her time alone with Him and had proclaimed in her *Note* that she was not only "called to spiritual solitude" but desired not too "close a contact" with her Sisters-in-Christ either. (And had not Father Cary advised her not to get 'mixed up' with convent life, advice conveniently forgotten when it suited her but equally conveniently remembered now?) It was, however on Benson's 1906 novel that Placida now seems to have modelled her life – even, one might say, her entire post-divorce life, for ruminations regarding life as an eremitic contemplative recorded in the 1920s proclaim adoption of a solitary's mode of life long before events of 1932–35 precipitated the emotional crisis which brought her to St Benedict's.

Benson's fictional life of 'Richard Raynal' was itself inspired by that of 14th century mystic Richard Rolle ("Hermit Richard"), regarded by Aelfrida as "a type of all the mystics who at the outset of their career have to contend with the shocked surprise of those who had hitherto approved and loved them".[3] 'Hermit Richard's' career took him from Oxford via Paris to a decision that academic life was not for him, to a sojourn in a cottage built for him on a friend's estate, to life as a contemplative and writer in increasingly remote 'cells', and finally to association with a Cistercian monastery and is so similar to Aelfrida's (Tymawr, for example, declared itself to be Benedictine in form and "Cistercian in spirit")[4] that it is possible she modelled her eremitic career upon it, adopting themes from Benson's account of "Master

**Father Hubert Northcott CR**

Richard's"[5] self-devised hermit's dress, and his woodland 'cell' with its little garden and friendly wild life as she followed her pillar of fire and cloud from Cambridge to cottage to 'cell' to convent. (Note also with regard to recent and future events in Aelfrida's life, Benson's description of 'Richard Raynal' taking shelter in a monastery while on a journey, only to find himself "hardly treated and flouted, for professed monks like not solitaries [calling] them self-willed and lawless and pretending to a sanctity that is none of theirs".)[6] But what prompted Placida sometime in late 1940 and early 1941 to emulate 'Hermit Richard'/Richard Rolle more closely than before?

Possibly the spectacular disagreements which took place between Mother Guenvrede and herself during the year reminded her that although she had longed for a woman 'to order [her] about'[7], the Mother's conduct (like that of the anonymous spiritual director in her essay for *Theology*) was disturbing the very delicate operations of the Holy Spirit within her, disturbances more easily avoided in a state of "intensified claustration".[8] Possibly Placida believed that isolation in spiritual Reality would prevent her being 'more conscious of physical discomfort and of the tangles and discords of the world than ... of anything celestial', for to the 'thought of going on day after day, year in and year out, whipping up Brother Ass [and] enduring ... the monotony of existence' in the real world of Tymawr ('here', her guardian angel reminded her tartly on her complaining of this, 'one lives by divine grace and the more clearly one sees the impossibility of finding purely natural satisfaction in a convent the better')[9] was now added the all-too-real discomforts of life in wartime: food rationing (Aelfrida, so she said, suffered 'pangs of hunger', an unusual complaint for one whose ostensible diet was ascetic but it was the lessened availability of biscuits, jam, sugar, and cheese, and her being supplied 'with more or potatoes or something plain' to compensate[10] that formed the real burden of her complaint) and, a particular bugbear to Mrs Graham, introduction of 'daylight saving' with clocks kept one hour ahead of Greenwich Mean Time in winter and two in summer: 'we shall be getting up at nominal 7, real 5 am'.[11]

Possibly she secluded herself so as not to be infected by others' fear, for air raids continued unabated ('the house shook, my room was lit with ... the flashes of bursting shells ... I cried "*in hora mortis meae voca me*" and rededicated myself to God')[12] and, said Mother Guenvrede and Father Northcott, German invasion was imminent. On hearing that in the event of invasion, 'guest house ladies' were to take shelter in the basement furnace room, Placida refused to join them unless allowed to lie on a mattress at the top of the stair leading to it. ("There's nowhere to run to but I am healthy-minded and [will] save our lives if [I] can", was Mother Guenvrede's reply.) She then asked permission to remain above ground to be 'martyred', stating that confinement in a subterranean space with 'scarcely standing room ... and nowhere to sit except on dirty steps' would be bound to bring on a 'heart attack'[13] (i.e. a panic attack); she failed to state, however, that it was only by practising private propitiatory rituals (Compline in Latin, prayers for 'Jerry', and repetition of 'all the hymns about heaven that [she] could remember')[14] that she remained 'recollected' in public. Both suggestions provoked Mother Guenvrede's wrath: "we have all thought for some time that you were the one person in the house likely to give trouble in a crisis and have been waiting to get rid of you and now I shall take the first opportunity *of writing to your brother and telling him to ... take you away*".[15]

Mother Guenvrede's statement begs an interesting question: Aelfrida would be neither homeless nor penniless (something her trustees had already ensured) if sent or taken away; she was also free to leave whenever she wished, for the 'resident' aspect of her tertiary life in no way bound her to live there always. Why, therefore, did Julius (if it was he, not Eustace) need to be informed of the Mother's decision and 'told' to 'take' his sister away? Can it be that, unrecorded by one known not to record everything in her diaries, Aelfrida had been *consigned* to conventual surroundings for however long it took to restore her physical and mental health?

But consigned by whom and with whose collusion? Consider the facts: Aelfrida's return to Cambridge in the summer of 1937 scorbutic and septicaemic must have alerted Eustace and Julius (as visits to St Benedict's had not) to their sister's parlous physical and mental state, a state to which information provided by Ancifera Gregory regarding Aelfrida's mental breakdown at Ealing three years earlier would have opened their eyes further, particularly in view of family events which occurred in the years immediately preceding and following her stay in Sunnyside Road. A frantic family conference may have ensued with probable medical input from Drs Cooper and Fraser and spiritual input from Fathers Cary and Frost and Mothers Magdalen Mary and Cecilia (it is obvious from Aelfrida's diary that the latter handled her in a manner more appropriate to a mentally disturbed than to a sane person, humouring her and calming her by turns), as a result of which and with the agreement of Father Northcott and Mother Guenvrede, Aelfrida was presented with an ultimatum: voluntary or involuntary admission to a mental hospital or incarceration at Tymawr until well enough to resume independent existence.

With memories of Ruth Stokoe's lengthy incarceration in an asylum from which she wrote 'Frank's friend' perfectly sane letters ('frantic' letters to Frank and his mother, on the other hand, may have aroused Aelfrida's 'intense sympathy [for] the mentally ill', given that in them Ruth begged to be restored to liberty)[16] and certainly knowing of Mina's refusal to accept anything other than spa treatment for 'melancholia' lest she too be incarcerated, Aelfrida, it seems, opted for confinement in the Community with which she had already established spiritual ties. She therefore entered Tymawr for reasons of therapeutic containment presented to those unaware of the truth as 'vocation'.

If this seems improbable, consider further. Father Cary's sudden and inexplicable agreement to association with the SSC and his later noting his happiness that all went well with her "in the best kind of way" because Tymawr provided "what [she] might not elsewhere have found in the matter of conditions and environment".[17] Mother Guenvrede allowing 'Placida' concession after concession (but forbidding her to use that name outside the convent) as, it may be, a means of keeping her paying 'patient' where the latter's brothers wished her to be (possibly Eustace and Julius contributed something over and above Aelfrida's modest amount for the privilege of having their sister cared for in a tranquil isolated environment under the care of good women who could, as Quakers put it, 'speak to her condition'), and this to the extent of making her a life tertiary after a truncated period of probation and in spite of Aelfrida's manifest unsuitability for conventual life or oblation. (In May 1940 after an episode of disobedience and threats of dismissal, Aelfrida asked Mother Guenvrede 'if she really *wanted* me to go', the Mother replying that she would '*much* rather' Aelfrida stayed because, as noted earlier, "we are responsible for you and we have to see you through as best we can"[18] – though she also, because of pressure placed on her by her 'patient's' bizarre behaviour, took irrepressible, if reprehensible, delight in threatening to send away someone not at liberty to leave because of what would happen to her if she did, something which would explain Aelfrida's insistence on geographical 'stability', a mental hospital being the alternative.) St Benedict's being taken back by Mother Cecilia before the end of Aelfrida's tenancy to prevent her return. Conditions laid down by Father Northcott with regard to not meddling with Alethea's life (surely none of his business except insofar as the Cowley Fathers were trying to protect Alethea from a mother whose mental health was problematic) and by Mother Guenvrede as to Aelfrida's return to Tymawr by a specific date regardless of the latter's state of health, a stumbling block to returning until then. Julius' (and, later, Mina's) frequent visits and less frequent (and unusual given the geographical and emotional distance between older sister and younger brother but not so unusual if the above is true) visits from Eustace, visits which often coincided with manifestations of disobedient or bizarre behaviour. The Sisters keeping Aelfrida's 'trances' under observation until satisfied that forbidding them would cause more harm than allowing them to continue. Mother Guenvrede allowing her to roam unattended away from convent precincts once satisfied she was unlikely to abscond and revoking her ban on 'walks' for fear Aelfrida might abscond if thwarted.

It is easy, of course, to see conspiracy where none existed but Aelfrida's 'meek little' notes of apology and attempts to divert the Mother's anger from herself by attributing it to 'the strain of responsibility in wartime' suggest otherwise. (Privately, she accused the Mother of demonstrating the 'true Dictator mentality' because 'she suspects me of independence'; conversely, she also expressed concern because 'she *does* turn people out'.) She also came to two important conclusions: 'never again' to exchange 'agitated letters' with Mother Guenvrede 'as I did when she deprived *me* of my walks' (Hilda Harrison had not been deprived of hers) because to do so could be taken as signs of mental instability, and 'to keep away from her as much as possible lest I provoke her'.[19] In both respects, intensified claustration would serve an important purpose.

An unstated but often hinted-at reason for withdrawing further from communal life at Tymawr was pressure of people. Visiting Associates who 'brought nothing of that kind of curiosity which, however sympathetic, jars so much when outsiders come for the first time even though one *wants* them to come … and to understand'[20] were one thing, though their 'coming and going' at major festivals disturbed one 'alas, so easily disturbed'[21], but the influx of "elderly gentlewomen of slender means … who enjoyed indifferent health" and whose conversation was chiefly composed of "laments for present ills coupled with forebodings of worse to come"[22] who arrived at Tymawr accompanied by quirks and foibles and mountains of luggage because deprived of their homes by wartime conditions and with every intention of staying 'for the duration' (as the saying went), quite another. Although Aelfrida found them individually delightful ('I am *glad* Miss Lowe is here … she is very devout'; Miss Lowe was also 'much travelled, an excellent linguist, a shrewd observer of human nature, and not without a spice of malice' so she and Aelfrida got on excellently)[23], collectively they tried her patience. 'Feminine cross currents' which did not seem to emanate from anyone in particular but which made everyone 'so miserable' made Aelfrida decide 'to get right up *above* them'[24] by removing herself spiritually from their 'worldly conversation'[25] and literally to the West Room. To provide herself with an excuse for absenting herself from a library reminiscent of 'the waiting room at King's Cross'[26], Placida pleaded that 'chatter – delightful as it is – [seemed] like sacrilege', that much as she enjoyed it, it 'broke up' interior silence, that she *needed* silence to help her sustain the power and 'spiritual pain' of her 'shewings', and that, the ultimate excuse, 'silence seems to be God's Will for *me*'.[27]

Her reasons notwithstanding, Aelfrida continued to talk to local people towards whom she felt sympathetic and it was the *quality* not the *quantity* of library 'chatter' to which she chiefly objected: 'of course I say nothing against *talking* ... people *should talk* – with intelligence, with brilliance, with tenderness and so on ... What good and lively talks we used to have at Fordfield!'[28] Another reason was importation by 'the Reverend Mother's Own Mama' of ('horrors!') a 'radiogram' and 'we had it on *loud, at tea*'. (Its arrival coincided with Father Northcott's Retreat of December 1939, an event employed by Placida as ammunition in her battle to have it removed: 'it seemed like the voice of "the world" ... invading our holy precincts'[29]; 'the *wireless* brings *worldliness* to the library' and should be banished 'from this dear house of prayer'; it disturbed the Greater Silence[30], and so on.) But though she herself refused to listen to it and was mightily annoyed when 'listening-in' made Mother Guenvrede late for None and Vespers or if the broadcaster's 'self-satisfied blatant male voice ... giving out such *specious* war news, not false exactly but selected' (and worse still, announcing 'sensuous dance music' and 'tidings of ... football matches') percolated into the West Room, her efforts to have 'the instrument' banished met with failure *and* with removal of *The Times* for a month until Placida ceased lamenting and criticising 'Authority'.[31] Removal of *The Times,* coinciding as it did with Aelfrida's battle with Mother Guenvrede over the 'long border' and with the Mother's insistence that 'heart attacks' in chapel and dead faints in deck chairs 'for exactly the duration of Terce'[32] notwithstanding, Placida complete her allotted ask, was the last straw: 'I can make no further protests [but] oh! how precious are ... Fridays!'[33], the day Placida was allowed to remain in silent seclusion all day.

Having failed to silence the 'radiogram' ('I wish that silence extended all over the guesthouse ... for my sake, that is – I don't mean that I would try and enforce it')[34], Aelfrida was faced with another manifestation of 'Authority' in the shape of her fellow resident tertiary, now appointed guest mistress. Sister Monica's earlier insistence that Placida run 'some innocent errand or other' when she would rather have been resting, reading, or meditating had driven her to recite 'Penitential Psalms'[35] in chapel to atone for naughty thoughts concerning that particular Sister-in-Christ but to be obliged to undertake domestic duties at the behest of Sister Christine (former nun though she was) was too much.

This particular reason for Placida's intensification of silence and solitude stemmed from the departure of two novices early in the war, one of whom, a former Girtonian, undertook domestic chores only under obedience, the other, a non-academic, more willingly. The subsequent departure in November 1940 of the 'temple child', an unpaid helper brought in to remedy the deficit

in the convent workforce, resulted in Placida being asked to take over the 'washing up of the tea things'. This for several reasons she would not do: first, it looked like being less of a temporary task than 'a burden as long as I am here'; second, the task 'occupied time ordinarily given to meditation and thought ... though I try to meditate as I do it'; third, when there were visitors (there were eight at Epiphany 1941) 'the task was harder'; fourth, she had no intention of following Sister Christine's 'real Domestic Science Demonstration of how to do it'; fifth, Mrs Graham would not undertake a chore which involved kneeling with bowls of water *on the bathroom floor*. Aelfrida therefore pleaded a 'pathetic' (Mother Guenvrede's description) inability akin to that suffered with respect to flower borders, Mrs Graham (who had had to endure Sister Christine's lessons on conventual etiquette, e.g. 'on the proper way to talk to people') ensured continuation of her stay at Tymawr by informing Mother Guenvrede that though she did what she could ('*so little*') for the Community, she was not strong enough to wash cups and saucers, Placida underlining her point by 'collapsing' again after Mass (to her chagrin, 'only Hilda noticed' but the Mother was notified and proved surprisingly solicitous) and by lying 'like a log all day' in bed thereafter and by confessing to Father Northcott that she was a 'poor drone who couldn't even wash up the tea things!'[36]

Having blatantly disregarded Richard Meux Benson's admonition that participants in the Religious Life "have to work with persons whom [they] do not find congenial" and must carry out work to which they were not "naturally suited" ("let there be no self-will as to forms of usefulness")[37], Placida continued to plan for intensified claustration with care and cunning. She began by asking Father Northcott (to whom she praised the Mother's generosity to 'the poor drone') if she could '*attempt*' a silent Lent (it was, she said, God's Will for her but she would relinquish the attempt 'if circumstances should make Silence impossible or if it were too great a strain')[38] and having gained his consent, tackled Mother Guenvrede. On that lady agreeing to what was essentially a fait accompli, albeit with the warning that a forty day silence would be 'very very difficult' and that Placida must rely '*entirely* on God' to see her through[39], the latter embarked on it, albeit not without misgivings: she would, she realised, be more exposed than usual to 'those piercing rays of divine justice which – especially when one is in retreat – flash into the depths of one's soul there to burn up pretensions and complacency and subterfuge'.[40] Encouraged, however, by her guardian angel and by a vision *coram sanctissimo* of herself standing alone in the cloud (the weather was currently foggy) that rested on the Mount of the Transfiguration 'with Jesus only … after Moses and Elias had gone' listening to 'the Words of God'[41], she began her attempt: 'and now Silence'.[42]

Silence – outer silence, at least – lasted five days. Although she informed no one but Mother Guenvrede that she proposed to pass 'a whole Lent in silence', hints to 'the Library' that she intended 'to be alone with God' so as to be able to draw the world into her heart and present it to the Holy Spirit as an oblation at the same time as she '*shut out*' aspects of it (chiefly the war, though 'a *huge* explosion [which] made the house *rock*' and nearly threw her down made this so difficult that she forgot 'to pray for Jerry' until later) and hence would feel much more *one* with 'all the dear people here' than if she joined them for tea, seem to have been effective insofar as its members did not appear to find her silence 'unfriendly'. (Silence was supported by silent good deeds: taking Hilda Harrison 'butter and lozenges and a book' when Hilda was in bed with a cold, and Miss Lowe extra wood for her bedroom fire 'from the cottage pile'; perhaps Placida recalled Aleister Crowley's criticism of mystics who "shut themselves up completely" for lengthy periods of time, namely that their selfish removal of their good example from society demonstrated only absence of all human virtue.)[43] Mother Guenvrede was more of a problem, for on attempting to discuss provision of eggs for Julius and Mina and finding Placida, 'mindful of Lenten silence', unwilling to reply, she upbraided her for 'doing other than the Community does'. Breaking silence, Placida reminded the Mother of her concession and Father Northcott's permission. Mother Guenvrede stated that she had only conceded *weekdays* in silence, that she was 'very unlikely' to concede more, and that that day being St David's Day and therefore a festival, Placida was under obedience to talk.[44] Another unseemly wrangle took place (by letter) but Placida won her point, Mother Guenvrede first allowing her to remain 'in retreat' until 24 March, then on that date permitting her 'to continue [her] God-given silence until the end of Lent'[45], at which point Placida broke her silence, enjoyed 'a lively tea with everyone … and lots of *petit mots*', and was dispensed from everything except Mass 'on health grounds' for a 'rest-week' with 'talking allowed all the day long'. But although she enjoyed the 'friendly chatting', God, she said, was 'calling [her] towards more silence' and it was only necessary to await 'the Mother's permission' before she obeyed. Her joy at having triumphed over Mother Guenvrede, over the 'dear good ladies of "the Library"' (they were not, she noted, 'penitents on behalf of a sinful world' as she was; a stricken marginal note reminds her 'I ought not to have said that – how do I know?'), and over her 'poor thing' natural self, was further enhanced

by a visit from 'dearest and best "Brother Julius"' during which brother and sister spent 'the happiest time'[46] together.

Interior silence was harder to achieve and less profound than it ought to have been. For one thing, a tertiary ostensibly in retreat seems to have been remarkably well informed about the war (the British Army winning 'victory after victory' in North Africa; 'German U-boats playing havoc with our shipping'; 'the swastika flying over Athens'[47], and so on) which suggests *The Times* was not laid aside. For another, she was fully conversant with conventual comings and goings: the arrivals of a new 'tertiary-sister', of two new 'permanent guests', and of Myfanwy, a land-girl; a visit paid by Sister Christine to Edinburgh, behaviour 'not a bit like a tertiary keeping Lent'; the departure of Mr Duveen's step-daughter, 'a poor thing completely dominated by the kind people who arranged her life'[48] – or, as it might be, Aelfrida's own, for Miss Lowengaard too was temporarily incarcerated in an isolated spot under the watchful eye of a 'companion' because of a mental incapacity not at all apparent to Placida when the two chatted in Woodbine Cottage garden.

Lastly, correspondence continued unabated, this including letters between herself and Julius which could have waited until after Lent but were answered because they referred to publication of 'his new book on Byz. Music', *The Hymns of the Octoechus*. Publication occasioned a heart-felt comment from Aelfrida as to 'how long and valiantly he has pursued his research and how little recognition he has had' and that Julius had learnt '*humility*, *reverence* and *charity*' from 'ancient saints and hymnographers'. This latter news alone was worth breaking inner silence: 'Brother Julius', formerly somewhat disengaged with regard to religion, was now a fellow-traveller "in the service of the Prince of Peace and His holy Church" ('a *Nunc Dimittis* is it not?' wrote Placida of this quotation from his book)[49] on a journey which, though it led by more intellectual paths and through 'fires of affliction' different to her own, was bringing him to a place where he and she could achieve a spiritual relationship akin to that of Saints Francis and Clare or François de Sales and Jeanne de Chantal.

But although Placida revelled in her lengthy retreat and in its ever-deepening 'Lenten silence' ('the joy of opening one's lips … only to praise God is beyond all description') and in the opportunity it afforded for long quiet periods of thought, she did not find it the engrossing spiritual experience she expected or derive from it the spiritual benefits she hoped for: God, she wrote, had not lifted her 'up to heaven'. True, she had been 'extraordinarily happy' in discovering God '[stooping] *down*' to show her 'Truth in flashes'.[50] (Insight that she was 'important' to God insofar as she possessed an 'immortal soul', not because she 'gave lectures, wrote books, and was admired and sought after' and was connected 'as daughter, sister, wife and mother with other more admirable and more important persons than [her]self'[51] presumably came as a result of one such 'flash' and realisation that spiritual progress required obstacles in its path in order that God's 'spiritual tide flowing over ... selfhood' could eddy and cascade into still waters[52], another.) True too, she was granted visions, perhaps not as many as she hoped but valuable nevertheless because they helped her to pour out before her Lord the 'reservoir of praise' with which 'the silence and quietness of Lent' in retreat and the '*wonderful*' experience of Christ calling her by name and demonstrating to her 'the infinite Vitality of '[God's] Perfect Love'[53] had filled her soul to overflowing with joy. She had, too, had opportunities for walks along nearby Whitebrook with its weirs and fish hatcheries (hence her watery metaphors) and through spring countryside 'all sacred, all God's'[54] and of working in the convent garden 'in [the] spirit [of] blessed Father Benedict' and as a '*sacramental*' expression of God as the 'Giver of Life'.[55] But as a way of life alien to the gregarious and loquacious existence preferred by her 'natural self', this brief but representative example of the continuous silent communing she intended to pursue filled Placida with foreboding and it was with difficulty that she persuaded herself that extreme fatigue experienced following her forty-day 'retreat' was due to transformation of a former rubbish heap ('Perseverance Hill') to tilth ('*sacramental*' expression had encompassed hard digging in the kitchen garden as well as gentle pottering in Woodbine Cottage's) rather than spiritual exhaustion. Would intensified claustration actually be '*bad*' for her, she wondered, insofar as it might 'dry up [her] soul' instead of refreshing it?[56] But a physical 'pointer' in the direction 'of further silence and solitude' (an attack of stomatitis which left her mouth so sore that she was unable to talk or eat and had to live on 'Horlicks and rusks') and a letter from Father Cary hoping that spiritual experiments in solitude and silence went well in the 'quiet laboratory' that was Tymawr, encouraged her to seek an interview with Mother Guenvrede in the seclusion of the summer house to plead for 'retreat all day always'.[57]

To this Mother Guenvrede might have consented if only to remove her turbulent tertiary from the daily life of the Community (she wished, she said, that the convent was so arranged that 'the oblates never see the Sisters') but angered by discovering on a visit to the evacuated Malling sisters that Aelfrida had in 'breach of confidence and lack of reverence for the spirit of the Community' informed them of a Tymawr novice's defection, not all Placida's grovelling (on her knees, on bare earth, and 'very silly I looked I daresay') could persuade the Mother to grant more than absence from library tea except on festivals and Sundays and the passing of all 'ordinary days' in retreat. 'God leads me a step at a time', noted Placida, 'unhappified' by another person taking responsibility for the decision as to how 'God's will can ... be obeyed by me'.[58]

Following confession to Father Northcott early in May 1941 during which Placida raised 'the question of Silence' and Father Northcott urged '*adoration* and thanksgiving' rather than something his penitent felt 'exactly ... called to do', namely penance, Aelfrida was gratified to discover (what follows must be paraphrase) that her desire 'to be in retreat every day except Sundays and festivals' was *not* 'some silly notion' of her own ('I wanted to be *quite* sure – one must be *specially* careful when one feels drawn to do something a little unusual') but response to God's call.[59] Mother Guenvrede's advice, tendered when Aelfrida asked her 'informally' on a day which was neither a Sunday nor a festival if it was the will of God that she now 'add ... extra silence to [her] Rule', was to go on as before till Holy Cross Day before enquiring further as to 'God's Will'. That Placida had had to break silence ('alas!') for such 'necessary business' when a note would have sufficed was presumably a cross to be borne, as also were 'business letters' (ordinary letters, though 'a great tax physically and spiritually', were regarded as gifts 'given for the glory of God' and never, even now, curtailed)[60], the tendency of visitors to chat away to her 'silent self', and the necessity of acting under obedience ('in spite of being in retreat ... I *do* seem to get a lot of talking') by speaking to people outside the Community, notably Mrs Amos and a local farmer's wife from whom Placida bought extra bread to augment a diet deprived of luxuries. Even so, she wrote happily, 'I *do* get long periods of solitude and silence'.[61]

Nor, of course, were family visits curtailed; indeed, Eustace's visit of July 1941 included a walk and a chat (but *no* chapel visits or religious talk) with a 'dear, dear [brother] who so bravely keeps the flag of learning aloft' and a 'very gay ... "library lunch"'[62], as also did later ones from 'dear, dear Brother Julius' whose new beard made him 'look like a mixture of George V and the Oracle'[63] (and even more 'oracular' as he grew older and the beard longer and whiter) or Mina and Constance. Little wonder, then, that Mother Guenvrede was dubious about the legitimacy of Placida's "Rule of Silence" or that she reacted to protestations that intensified claustration was God's Will for Placida with "amusement more than any other feeling". She also described Placida's 'vocation' as a "*farce!*"[64]

Placida, of course, did not regard her behaviour as a 'farce' but as a heaven-sent opportunity for getting her own way: 'I *am* a hermit'.[65] Within a year she had managed to exempt herself from talking on Sundays too ('the *quietness* [is] glorious') ostensibly in order to 'mortify [her] love of knowing what goes on here' ('my mind', she wrote, 'is like a fair or a market place') 'and [her] natural expansiveness'[66] (i.e. behaving 'like a gracious and experienced hostess' in the library) but actually for reasons which will become apparent shortly. Mother Guenvrede, speaking, it may be, with forked tongue, agreed that 'extra silence' added to Placida's Rule 'helps the Community'.[67]

Reparative adoration at this point in the war was to be offered less for specific persons (with one important exception) than generically on behalf of a sinful world with England ('*not* repenting', in spite of Placida's prayers) and Germany as its particular (and 'callous and … blind') representatives. A 'shewing' on 15 April 1941 inspired by the bombing of Belfast by 'aerial messengers of wrath' during which God reminded her of Christ 'taking the unfelt remorse of the sinful unto his own sinless self' in order to grieve over 'the shame that the shameless ignore', persuaded her of the necessity of employing reparative vocation on a wider scale than that of moral misdeeds perpetrated by herself and those who offended her. It also removed her spiritually as well as physically 'from the pleasant gentle atmosphere of "the Library"' (currently fraught with dissention as its inhabitants squabbled among themselves) 'to [her] own cell and the chapel'[68] – and, she hoped, closer to Sisters of a Community whose Cistercian isolation, Benedictine practise of the *opus Dei*, Carthusian preference for silence and contemplative prayer, and Carmelite association of penance with adoration closely reflected her own Rule.[69]

The exception to Placida's generic reparation and adoration was Mother Guenvrede for she took very seriously the Mother's threat to tell one or other of her brothers to 'take [her] away'. (Apart from a minor tiff during which a letter from Tertiary Placida to Tertiary Christine complaining that the latter's unpunctuality in chapel disturbed the former's devotions was intercepted by the Mother and returned with the superscription "mind your own business"[70], Aelfrida did not provoke another major row until March 1942.) Not only did she try to analyse the reasons for the Mother's bad temper (heredity, loss of a 'sweetheart' during the Great War, 'enclosure' preying on the mind of one whose disposition was 'adventurous', and 'comparative inactivity' – *sic*, Mother Guenvrede had recently added bottle-rearing a calf to her already immense burden) but she also decided that reparation made kneeling accompanied by the use

of 'Saint Guenvrede' 'as hard as [she] could' might gradually 'enlighten and sanctify' a woman who was 'with the exception of Anatolia, the most unkind and unjust woman I have ever met'.[71] Then, worried that God might not forgive this harsh judgement of her 'Mother-in-Christ' and that she herself might 'unconsciously' (*sic*) 'drift into blaming and judging … the Superior of a Contemplative Order', Placida vowed (but only after her guardian angel stated 'that if [she] cultivated more reverence for the Mother as [her] Superior and thought less about her faults as a person, it would be much better') to offer Mother Guenvrede (though not Winifred Donkin) 'all the love and loyalty … that I can give'.[72] She broke the vow before a year was out.

Having abandoned two of her 'useful saints', Placida returned to alimentary asceticism as a means of mortification. She had begun to practise this earlier in the war when a dearth of imported fruit meant that the 'one orange a day' ordered by Professor Mottram became unavailable, limiting herself to stewed fruit and 'a little fruit juice'[73] but never touching on principle any of the abundant fresh fruit provided by the Tymawr estate. By 1941, however, she again began to show symptoms of vitamin C deficiency (ulcerated mouth, 'the Shivers', enlarged 'armpit glands', a heart not 'working properly', neuritis, 'eyes bad'[74], and so on) which might lead to premature ejection from 'the sacred precincts'. Visits to Monmouth to dentist and optician ('I can't afford an oculist', a pitiful remark did we not know that Aelfrida sent numerous books, items of clothing, insecticide, and £50 worth of Defence Bonds to Alethea during the war *and* bought the gelding the latter rode on visits to outstations, misplaced generosity if Placida was really as poor as she likes us to think) and discovery there that her *clothed* weight (in August, admittedly a cold wet month, she was wearing, besides her substantial tertiary's dress, a thick winter coat and wool-lined boots) was well below eight stone ('I can see that I am pretty much of a skeleton but the actual figures came as rather a surprise')[75], brought her to her senses: out walking one '*enchanted*' day, she allowed her guardian angel to feed her 'manna … in the shape of wild raspberries'. Thereafter she subsisted on 'wild fruit, taken in solitary places' because her need for fruit was 'so great'[76], a ruse which also ensured that her official ascetic diet could continue without interruption or addition.

Depriving herself of the – as she herself admits – abundant convent produce 'so as not to deprive other people' not only included depriving herself of (rationed) butter which she took – in what she tried to pass off to Mother Guenvrede as an act of piety when the latter discovered what she was doing – to an elderly couple living nearby with whom the 'silent' tertiary enjoyed frequent chats[77] but also complaints of undernourishment to Alethea. From food parcels subsequently delivered from South Africa she extracted things she craved (sweets, marmalade, and tinned cheese) before donating sugar 'for "unrationed jam"' and a portion of other items such as tea (she kept a good deal for herself), noting in her diary both her 'great delight' in gifting the Community and her chagrin at not being thanked for pious donations which were (as her diary makes clear) bribes to keep Mother Guenvrede sweet ('obviously I am not being ejected yet awhile!') or a means of making that lady feel guilty at not behaving better to a tertiary trying to prove worthy of the Community by stating 'I generally prefer not to be thanked for anything that I do because thanks make me feel [as if I were only] a visitor'.[78]

There was, however, more to Placida's disordered behaviour with regard to food than this. Mortification apart, one might almost believe she was merely following Father Meux Benson's instructions to willingly forego superfluities, to disregard inconveniences caused by absence or diminution of "necessities" like food and drink, to "accept … times of privation with thanksgiving" and to endure them for Christ's sake[79] were it not for inconsistencies in her complaints: that her thoughts did not 'run to food' at a time when she was suffering 'pangs of hunger' and begging Mother Guenvrede for more to eat (and complaining to her diary that 'no more food had, to date, been provided')[80]; that meals already 'as plain and as ascetic as [she] was able to endure' but which she now enjoyed because she was so hungry were too luxurious for wartime and that in eating them her greed and self-indulgence meant others went without, a plaint so manifestly ridiculous in one living in the midst of 'good wholesome food' provided by a well-stocked smallholding that Mother Guenvrede's assurance that Placida had 'no more than what is necessary for health' was superfluous[81]; that the 'pangs' of hunger which promoted fatigue and undernourishment also promoted emotional euphoria ('my heart sings and sings')[82], a welcome discovery for one for whom intensified claustration was not proving to be the grand spiritual experience she had anticipated; that consumption of food, especially in wartime when 'one's thoughts wander too easily' to it, could acquire religious connotations (the association of bread with the 'Blessed Sacrament', for example)[83] and be employed as a kind of spiritual exercise undertaken in private because other people merely regarded food as food; that a 'sudden vision of a bier being carried out of the vestry door … to the Campo Santo' was less the culmination of a 'night story' than the expression – as indeed was the 'night story' – of a death wish: 'dear Lord, if thou wilt gather one soul this year – take me'.[84] And of

something else too, barely manifest yet but later to manifest itself to an alarming extent as intensively claustrated Placida paid less and less attention to the real world and more and more to the 'reality' inside her head: paranoid thoughts focused on Mother Guenvrede.

Although Aelfrida tried to persuade herself that being 'undernourished' was a 'nonsense – just a wile of the devil to make one greedy and demand more to eat'[85], complaints of diminution in amounts of food allocated to her manifested a deeper worry: was Mother Guenvrede trying to starve her out – or into submission? Seen in this light, the Vichy water episode and the Mother's earlier attempts to dictate what Aelfrida ate gained sinister connotations in the mind of one known for her ability to transform dietary (and other) stupidities into religious practices, so much so that Alethea's food parcels came to be regarded less as a means of restoring luxury items essential, given Aelfrida's extant dietary restrictions, for maintenance of weight and nutrition, and more as a means of thwarting Mother Guenvrede's supposedly sinister designs; indeed, it is noticeable with what gratitude they were received, Aelfrida evincing none of the scruples exhibited during the Great War with regard to Harry Shipway's donations. Then too, comments that she could trust the Mother not to 'spoil' (an ambiguous word in this context) her or 'allow' her to become 'under-nourished' can be read as attempts to reassure herself that the Mother dare not provide her with less food 'than what is necessary for health' and to persuade herself that it was unnecessary 'to be deluded'[86] with regard to the Mother's behaviour and to become 'quieter in [her] thoughts'[87] as a result. But other signs too begin to point to lessening 'quietness': lengthening gaps between diary entries imply that obtrusive thoughts are not being consigned to paper and confusion concerning day and date worsens to such an extent that the sixth anniversary of 'sweet, sweet Temu's death' reverts unnoticed to 22 February.[88]

Hilda Harrison's warning that unbroken residence at Tymawr made minds 'narrow' should have been borne in mind by one intent on removing herself from Tymawr's 'world' for spiritual reasons, but Aelfrida's refusal to do more than visit dentist and optician ('neither shopping nor sightseeing tempted me') and to rush into chapel 'like an exile coming home' immediately on return because shocked 'seeing the world again through the eyes of the ordinary person'[89], suggests that those of her correspondents who informed her that she was fortunate 'to be placed so that [she] could shut out the world and its sorrows and enjoy [her] own peace'[90] were more perceptive than she cared to think and less perceptive than they ought to have been with regard to her mental welfare. Then too, as aerial warfare moved away from

Monmouthshire (it was to return briefly later in the war) and peaceful nights succeeded peaceful days, Placida became more and more intent on removing herself further and further from the real world in order to enter 'the fellowship of the Mystery'.

Fellowship of the Mystery, for all its Crowleyan connotations, had nothing to do with Ceremonial Magic and everything to do with Placida maintaining herself in 'a *state* of prayer' in which to concentrate her mind on '*the pulsation of the Eternal*, the movement of Love within the Godhead, [and] the interchange of communion between the Persons of the Most Holy Trinity'. In this prayerful state, the 'Mystery' (a religious truth, that is to say, not something merely puzzling) would be revealed, so Placida hoped, by Christ opening 'His Sacred Heart wherein the Mystery lies' to a mystic so completely surrendered to Him as to be able to comprehend immensities beyond mere human understanding.[91] Quite what she meant by these esoteric and idiosyncratic reflections is unclear (was she implying, for instance, that, as a mystic, she was able to eavesdrop on Trinitarian communications?) but what she makes clear is that the experience and the spiritual exercises which led up to and maintained it were preceded and accompanied by recurrence of 'the pains of His dear wounds' and of stigmatic manifestations 'clear, so clear and coming up as it were from a deep wound'. Other comments made in this connection have worrying connotations: one, that the '*pain*' was 'supernatural' because 'the physical stabs [had] a spiritual quality [though] the visible marks *may have a natural cause*'; two, that she was 'called to solitude' in case 'someone *saw*' the marks, marks which she couldn't '*bear*' people to see[92] because, it may be, they might suspect artefactual enhancement or, what was worse, realise that she found intensified claustration such a strain that only by injuring herself could she release the emotional tension it generated.

Another possible reason for Placida to augment stigmatisation by artifice (this is the only occasion on which she comes close to admitting it) was disappointment with the intensity and duration of the spiritual exhilaration which should have arisen as a result of 'fellowship' with Christ's 'Mystery', rather than, as formerly, with the 'Suffering' to which there are notably fewer references in her diary now than heretofore. Hence what should have constituted the next (illuminative, ecstatic) stage of her spiritual pilgrimage was experienced as a state of spiritual stasis which, though illuminative in its own way, evoked dissatisfaction rather than delight.

Placida had, of course, been warned by Father Northcott and Mother Guenvrede that the sensation of God gradually withdrawing 'the blaze of light' which shone over her life might follow *fervor novitiorum* but had been convinced that God would not allow it to happen to herself. She was therefore surprised and dismayed to discover that withdrawal into solitude and silence gave rise to the precise sensation about which she had been warned and though she professed herself understanding of *why* the 'blazes of light' diminished in intensity (the blaze, God told her, was an aspect of '"the clamour of selfhood" [and] it was *best* it should go') and happy (or rather, 'I don't mean … I am not happy') that the key motif of her spiritual life henceforth would no longer be 'how happy I am here!' but 'how great is the Glory of the Lord!'[93], the fact that efforts made to enhance 'personal holiness'[94] had resulted only in *God's* glorification came as something of a blow to a supreme egoist.

The revelation, supported as it was by marked diminution in the number and intensity of visions and 'shewings' which, though it might imply that she no longer needed them as illuminative means of conveying impressions of God and that Christ's 'peace and silence' had indeed descended on her soul, might also mean withdrawal of spiritual favours from one still 'tainted with selfhood', was salutary: 'I want … no spiritual pretensions – no spiritual claims[95]… all my life has been *tainted* [with] spiritual and moral blindness [and] weakness'.[96] Insight thus provided – and enhanced, it may be, by her not being invited to join the Community's 1941 Retreat (the Father conducting it did not want outsiders; Placida preferred to think exclusion was 'God's Will')[97] and by the devil renewing his threat to darken her existence at every opportunity by creating a 'strange day of temptations' during which he caused her to become 'a prey to violent physical desire' and to dwell on 'past scenes … with pictures vivid to hallucination' and emphasised 'how *bare* the life is here' ('people who come here see … lovely ceremonies and catch glimpses of our joy in offering them to God but the dark hours are hidden')[98] reminded her that she, like Mina, needed 'a new orientation of her whole character' and that instead of 'brooding secretly over her troubles'[99], she must provide it without intervention by priest or 'soul-doctor'.

Orientation or, in Aelfrida's case, re-orientation of character, though ultimately 'to be made plain to [her] in prayers', seemed to involve 'greater fervour of adoration'[100] and concomitant diminution of reparation, so much so that in one of her now-rare 'shewings', Placida, awaiting the call to Midnight Mass on Christmas Eve 1941, was granted a vision of a 'brilliant blue-gold light' emanating from a Roman lamp 'rather like a squashed teapot' ('the flame comes out of the spout!') whose symbolism was clear: 'my sanctuary lamp, my steadfast prayer of adoration lighted by the … prayer of the Incarnate

Son before His Father's throne'[101] illuminating the path she was to take. 'One used', she wrote, 'to approach religion with the attitude "I must pray in order to live a better life". Now I [say] "I must live so as to be able to say better prayers"', to which end she must extirpate everything that that did not 'remotely or proximately' contribute to it. ('Can I live up to this?' provided the necessary escape clause.)[102] Better still, illumination provided by her fifty-eighth birthday (her 'happiest birthday' because in spite of not being fond of herself any more, she had disembarrassed herself of aspects of her past life for which it was necessary to offer reparation)[103] and the fourth anniversary of her becoming a tertiary imbued with God's Life ('oh, the WONDER of it!') meant that what had seemed like spiritual stasis was rationalised as the beginning of another *vita nuova* in which 'the wonder of my Lord living in me [and] giving me … His Silence' took priority over personal glorification[104] and in which appreciation that she, a 'bride of Christ' insofar as she had now 'died to the world', had to be of '*marred countenance* like [her] Lord' (i.e. as He was depicted on the Turin Shroud) before she became acceptable to God.[105] Two things, however, marred her enjoyment: first, apprehension on Father Cary's part 'lest [her] "way of silence" should be beset with dangers and [she] not notice' (significantly, perhaps, Placida did not keep the letter in which these 'dangers' were listed), together with the hope that Placida's 'wise Superior' was doing everything necessary 'in the way of protection and corrective vigilance' (*sic*), and second, that her Superior's behaviour towards her, protective and corrective though it might be, now took the form of public and private humiliation 'as if Sister Placida's "pious platitudes", bright ideas, little ways and general oddness were the greatest joke in the world'.[106]

What was it about Placida's current behaviour which made Father Cary apprehensive of the intensified claustration of which he had formerly approved and laid her open to ridicule from Mother Guenvrede and from 'the Library' who, following the Mother's lead, now teased Placida 'mercilessly' for her 'spiritual pretensions' to such an extent that she wondered if she could 'stand fast in time of persecution'?[107] True, there was the obvious dichotomy between avowed withdrawal from 'the world' and all-too-obvious engagement with it when it suited her; true, too, her faddiness over food, obsession with 'Prehistory', disdain for ordinary leisure pursuits, habit of taking long walks only to plead fatigue when faced with chores, posturing in chapel, tendency to talk when she should not and refusal to talk when she could, constituted 'little ways' of striking 'oddness', but what constituted 'pious platitudes' and 'bright ideas' and how were these manifest?

Of 'bright ideas' we have few examples other than those already discouraged by Mother Guenvrede but pious platitudes are plentiful in her diary (e.g. 'memory of my old sins came to me *most* poignantly … how one wishes one could *disown* one's evil deeds')[108] and might have been vocalised. Platitudes, however, were nothing new; what *is* new is the appearance of extended passages of homily of the kind formerly expressed in books but now, because of relinquishment of writing for publication, confined to it. But *were* they so confined? Did Placida, if not 'preach to' or 'write books for' the ladies of 'the Library', at least try 'to *convey* to them … all I know', and did they, ordinary women trying to lead lives as normal as possible under wartime conditions, resent assumption of superiority in matters spiritual in one manifestly flawed or, if already 'persons trained in spiritual consciousness'[109], find Placida's idiosyncratic interpretations of good and evil unoriginal ("the present evils in the world are due to the failure of nations and peoples to carry out the will of God")[110], ridiculously idealistic ("put a Christian at the head of the Reich instead of Hitler and all might turn to the glory of God")[111], hopelessly Utopian ("Christian parents [should] breed Christian children immune from the virus of worldliness"), or so far removed from reality (Monmouth, she wrote, on the basis of a few abbreviated visits, must be a grossly unspiritual place because it had many pubs and few churches and those few were labelled "Public Air Raid Shelter")[112] as to provide evidence only of "exaggerated awe … solemnity of diction … vanity of archaic phrases, a false veil of holiness upon the unclean shrine, [of] phylacteries increas[ing] about the hem of the perfect prig, prude and Pharisee"[113] – and a notable failure of common sense?

Or did Placida, realising her present impotence, decide to preserve themes inspired by spiritual experiences and pondered on at length in silence and solitude in order that what were (supposedly) 'spiritual diaries' charting her spiritual progress might be studied by a biographer more sympathetic than Mother Guenvrede or 'the Library'? (Her papers were, after all, intended for *eventual* publication.) Or did she decide to make her mockers feel guilty by behaving towards them as the Bible said, by turning the other cheek to their verbal blows, each manifestation of saintly or martyred behaviour ('I … give them presents … I offer remedies, send flowers [and] delicacies to anyone who happens to be unwell … I *love* petting people up, [and try] to be "Little Providence" to them', practices, she noted, contrary 'to the spirit of [her] vocation' because they drew attention to herself and were performed less in the spirit of charity than as means of capturing people's affection; no wonder she later confessed to Father Northcott her 'intense contrition' at performing 'Good Works … to [her] own credit, in [her] own way, to [her] own liking') being accompanied by 'pious platitudes' in the form of 'nice … little letters'?[114] Or was her behaviour merely revengeful (being nice to her detractors would make them feel guilty) or another example of her 'need' to be 'crucified'?

But if Placida behaved like this because keen to prove that wanting to be a "new creature" through and through … [and] good with [her] Lord's goodness'[115] was a genuine desire and Mrs Graham because she was terrified of being sent away (to which end she worked '*very* hard in vegetable and cottage garden', as references to 'sowing carrots' and 'lifting the beet crop' show)[116], Aelfrida herself evinced no improvement at all. Indeed, one might conclude that as outward silence ("valued and practised") and inner Silence ("the soul's waiting upon God") deepened, "moral Silence" (the wish not to censure, disparage, or even comment on Community matters)[117] dwindled to such an extent that dangers associated by Father Cary with her 'way of silence' must have included crabbiness, censoriousness, and hostility.

Crabbiness was chiefly directed toward members of 'the Library': Miss Lowe, now deemed 'fussy and tiresome' and prone to writing 'little notes and getting into little huffs if she couldn't arrange other people's ways to suit her convenience'[118] (a comment realised by Aelfrida to apply to herself too) and to 'trailing [an] atmosphere … of fashionable piety … *Christianity without the Cross*, the devil's most subtle and most potent temptation' (Aelfrida's 'piety' was 'disguised [and] sugar-coated with intellectualism'[119], the Cross, one might say, without Christianity), and Mrs Donkin 'not really … *persona grata* anywhere … so discontented and restless that everyone – the Mother most of all – finds her a great trial'.[120] (Like Aelfrida herself.) Censoriousness is best represented – though there are many instances, notably that vented on a potential postulant whose 'whims, moods, nerves, restlessness and egotism' were as nothing compared to her 'gift for perverse and often scandalous argument' i.e. she was a proponent of abortion[121] – when Placida stumbled 'unawares into a corner of the Black Market' (Trellech village shop) where she spotted Father Amos, aging and unwell and nursing a sickly wife, 'acquiring' an extra pot of jam. Her behaviour on this occasion did not do her credit: she denounced the shop (anonymously) to the local branch of the Food Office but said nothing to Amos himself, not even to warn him that he might find himself 'in the dock for Black Market purchases', and not all her begging Mother Guenvrede for the privilege of wearing 'St Bruno' for thirty minutes 'for some sinner's special need' or castigating herself for being as tainted with the world's 'guilt and greed' as Father Amos or transforming

The chapel, Tymawr (exterior)

his misdeed into a message that she too ought to 'look to [her] own and work out [her] own salvation in fear and trembling'[122] absolves her from of having behaved in an unpleasantly underhand and unChristian manner.

Hostility seems to have been aimed – in the privacy of her diary but who knows how much of this (and of crabbiness and censoriousness) showed in her demeanour – at Sisters disliked as people but tolerated as Sisters-in-Christ ('what is the use of women being nuns when … they fail to rise to the ordinary level of courtesy', on Sister Monica having chided her 'as no *lady* would speak even to a black servant')[123] or those who, as actual or potential postulants, were more intimately connected with the Community than herself, remarks whose lack of charity ('she had no vocation, she wouldn't be a help here'; 'did she come here out of some freakish love of experiment?')[124] is underlined by being made on a 'festival' day celebrating a novice's profession or during a Retreat from which Placida was excluded. As for Tertiary Christine, her departure in April 1942 to marry an old friend occasioned diary entries written with such a poisonous pen that not even Mrs Graham sending the 'ex-Sister' a 'lovely' wedding present[125] can excuse them. Even Sister Jeanne, 'a true Religious [who] always brings the Presence of God with her' (she had been promoted to 'novice mistress and also a saint') whose advice she often sought in preference to Mother Guenvrede's (could one who 'normally … only read religious books – and *The Times*, briefly' read secular books as well?), was sneered at for '*second rateness*'[126] when she composed a poem for Placida's birthday.

Although prone to joke that even as a tertiary, 'great stretches of *heathendom*' existed in her unconscious mind[127], comments seething with anger, resentment, and jealousy, are not those of a soul brimming with interior silence or a woman at peace with herself and God. They are, rather, reminiscent of diary entries written during the dreadful decades when Aelfrida felt herself ill-used, over-burdened, and under-appreciated by those for whom she toiled begrudgingly and thanklessly at Fordfield, and though there was much in her life in the grim years 1939–1942 to cause her to write bitterly (Walter, aged twenty, 'called to the colours suddenly' and who 'because of this accursed war … may have fewer years to live than I'[128]; walks less beautiful because 'enchanted woods' were being felled for timber; the onset of severe and 'incurable' tinnitus which filled her head with the noise of 'sirens [and] telephone bells'[129], a probable symptom of excessive use of aspirin, with hypertension and carbon monoxide toxicity as contributing factors; 'weariness and weakness' of body worsened by 'privation' as food rationing was extended and fuel rationing introduced. But diary entries displaying a 'critical and carping spirit' show that 'heathendom' was due less to the disordered state of the world or 'bitter and barren' weather[130] than to a metaphorical winter of spiritual discontent regarded by Aelfrida as encompassing both 'privilege and privation'[131]: privilege because on good days she felt herself safely cradled at Tymawr as a member of a Community whose life, like hers, was structured and buttressed by 'the Benedictine framework of the *opus Dei*' and as an individual, drawn more and more to 'Our Lord's hidden life [of] silence and … prayer'[132], privation because on bad days she felt insecure and unwanted.

Although the war years caused generalised diminution of interest in organised religion, they also occasioned a strengthening of faith in those inclined to belief (particularly women) apparent even at remote Tymawr where a 'rising tide of postulants' threatened to float the guest house ladies 'right out of the convent'.[133] The presence of nine aspirants hoping to become postulants sent a shiver down Placida's spine: was she in danger of being ejected to make room for them and if so, would God make plain to Mother Guenvrede that He 'desired [Placida's] presence here'?[134] That 'floating out' was no idle threat can be ascertained both from Aelfrida's frequent descriptions of the clothing of postulants of all ages and social classes (and of widows, eligible because relicts) and from the upheavals which took place as the conventual area of the house was expanded to accommodate them. Convinced she would be '*miserable* if the Mother even suggested … [she] should go away'[135], Placida became distraught (confused religious musings support her contention

that she was not thinking clearly), less at the thought of leaving Tymawr ('if the pillar of fire and cloud moves, I follow')[136] but lest she be relegated, together with Hilda Harrison and Miss Lowe, to Woodbine Cottage, 'always on the Spartan side' because of its cold taps and outside privy.[137] It being preferable to stay on in the convent with its indoor sanitation and hot water (the bathroom, alas, had disappeared behind the grille, but warm water was available) even if this meant relegation to a 'most inconvenient' L-shaped north-facing 'cell' where life might be 'more bare and hard' ('I *want* things to be hard sometimes', she reminded herself, 'it is my vocation')[138] and 'condemned to silence always' because there would be no 'Library' left to talk to[139], but so desperate not to be exiled to Woodbine Cottage that she was prepared to offer herself as a postulant, ineligible though she was because a divorcee and certainly not a relict and because 'I could not live the life … I [see] *no* way of being able to offer obedience'[140], Aelfrida was relieved when Mother Guenvrede decreed that Placida, Hilda, Mrs Donkin and the land girl (other residents decamped rapidly when Mother Guenvrede's scheme was made public, the land girl shortly afterwards) might remain in the reduced guest-house area of the convent, with visitors relegated to the Cottage. But the 'wave of unrest'[141] engendered by the upheaval took a long time to settle and nowhere more slowly than in Aelfrida's mind, for though she comforted herself that the new arrangement, 'inconvenient as it is for us in what remains of the guest-house', was conducive to 'holy calm' because there was more convent and less guest-house[142], she waxed indignant at the thoughtless manner in which Mother Guenvrede carried out her plans 'with no thought of the damage [she] does as she pursues them'.[143]

Not liking being done by as she had done to others, Placida returned to her 'lonely breakfast' of 'Virol on … bread to eke out the jam ration'[144] to brood on real or imagined wrongs: 'lack of "Community sense"' and of the '*atmosphere of love*' noticeable at Cowley and Malling[145] as this affected herself as a 'humble tertiary' whose affinities lay with the Community rather than the 'dear *dear* people … of the Library"' and, what was worse, on the 'subtle process of separation'[146] initiated by Mother Guenvrede between her 'humble tertiary' and herself.

The 'subtle process' manifested itself by the feeling that Placida now lived at Tymawr on sufferance ('I am, so to speak, allowed to occur') and that 'often and often' the Mother was 'pushing [her] away'.[147] Was this due, she wondered, to increased separation of convent and guest-house as former grew and latter dwindled (a good thing in one way, because separation might help Mother Guenvrede 'overcome her temper')[148] or to the 'inescapable clash of temperament'[149] which made the Mother find fault with Placida and accuse her unjustly? In the course of meetings with Mother Guenvrede she tried to explain her feelings: although Mother Guenvrede's 'spiritual understanding' was almost on a par with Father Cary's (a compliment indeed) and her 'humble tertiary' both respected and trusted her and turned to her 'again and again ... even when [she] hurt [her]', she dreaded the Mother's anger, crumpled 'at the merest hunt of displeasure', and while 'in disgrace' suffered 'partial excommunication', and she could love and respect her more if the Mother apologised for unjust dealings or acted towards her as if she were truly 'a member of this dear *dear* Community' instead of an irritant sooner or later to be ejected.

Mother Guenvrede's response is interesting and revealing, the more especially when Aelfrida reacted to 'annoyance – atmosphere' with panic attacks (*not* 'nerves', she hastily assures us)[150] and noisy demonstrations of emotion such as sobbing loudly through None, choir practice, and post-practice prayers until she attracted the Mother's attention because frustrated at being unable to arrange her life as she wanted[151], an inappropriate response for a woman in her late fifties. "I know I hurt you", Guenvrede says, " I think I *have* to". Aelfrida's reply is equally interesting and revealing: "Yes ... I think so too. It doesn't matter. I am *glad* you should". But being hurt by someone of such 'spiritual understanding' – and standing – for her own spiritual good (in terms, for example, of the achievement 'of an even more complete surrender of self' in one currently experiencing a '*very intense*' but not a joyful 'action of God on [her] soul')[152] was one thing; reception of confusing messages by a damaged personality increasingly uncertain of status and stability with regard to the SSC quite another. ('Evidently', she writes of being excluded from late evening parts of the *opus Dei*, 'it is not for me [because] it does not belong to a tertiary's vocation'.) But on informing Mother Guenvrede that she 'dreaded' her anger, she was told "you *must not* be so upset by what you call my anger. It is only *stage* anger and I find it very useful at times ... When I am really *angry* ... I go all hard and cold and depart ... into my room. I have *never* been really angry with you and ... never could be".[153]

Aelfrida knew better, for Mother Guenvrede had often been 'really *angry*' with her and had departed abruptly behind the grille to prove it, but either by way of testing the Mother's protestations or in an act of incredible stupidity at this juncture (she had already admitted to herself that Sister Christine's departure might make 'the position of the remaining resident tertiary very difficult'), she wrote to Mother Guenvrede ostensibly asking

if she might put some 'further questions about tertiaries' ('one is so betwixt and between') but actually ('incidentally') to let her see a recent letter from Father Cary 'as I vaguely (*sic*) felt she ought to see what he had written'.[154] What broke over her head as a result was not '*stage* anger'; it was real and justified fury.

Aelfrida had tried to maintain as low a profile as possible since May 1941 and apart from the minor occasion concerning Sister Christine's lateness for chapel, appears to have succeeded in doing so. In September 1941, however, Mother Guenvrede's acceptance of a postulant lacking the 'dowry' desperately needed by an impoverished convent prompted Placida to write a letter (as from Wetenhall Cottage and probably as 'Mrs Graham') to the editor of the *Church Times* on the subject of 'financial difficulties' faced by Religious Communities, together with a suggestion as to how these might be alleviated. The editor, begged by its writer not to publish the letter as it stood, 'made a nice little paragraph out of it' which, when read by Mother Guenvrede – the letter's style and references it contained made it unmistakably Aelfrida's – was described as an evasion and a 'breach of silence' because it revealed the Community's plight. There was, however, more to letter (and 'paragraph') than this: it also contained barely-concealed criticism of the Mother's generosity (or lack of common sense and financial acumen) in admitting a postulant 'unprovided with means of support' when the Community was hard-pressed to provide existing members 'with adequate food and fuel'. To compound her felony, Aelfrida herself endowed the postulant (her gift was supposed to be anonymous but the postulant's silent gratitude showed someone revealed its source) with sufficient funds (£5) to cover her first year, noting for a future biographer's edification that it was a '*privilege*' to provide a little money for [the] saint-in-embryo'.[155]

This first instance of Aelfrida criticising not the Mother's actions with regard to herself but with regard to management of the convent, was followed in March 1942 by an even more serious instance: an attack on a very personal, hurtful, and deceitful level on the validity of the Mother's authority as Superior of the Community to which 'humble tertiary' Placida was attached. It was this second attack – again involving letters and reference to outside agencies – which brought down the full weight of Mother Guenvrede's wrath on her head.

On 21 March 1942 Aelfrida recorded in her diary that the SSC had been granted the honour (unique in the Anglo–Welsh church) of possessing licence and faculty for Exposition of the Blessed Sacrament at Benediction on Sundays and festivals. At this point, Placida's innate 'puritanism' rebelled at what it regarded as the flummery (seven-branched candlestick, Sanctus bell, white brocade draped over the monstrance, elaborate vestments, prostrations, and so on) which on certain days interrupted the convent's quiet 'Devotions': the 'Sacramental Presence', she wrote sourly, 'is more clearly seen in the eye of the soul and better apprehended by the spirit when the tabernacle is closed and the Host hidden'. ('PS', she added, 'fuel has apparently given out ... *very* penitential' and though she tried to regard 'the cold of our unheated convent' as further evidence that God would give her 'of His strength' to bear the cold and the 'severer pains' induced by Exposition, the icy chapel and unseasonably wintry weather did nothing to improve the luxurious ascetic's temper and may even have made it more 'critical and carping' than usual.)[156] Concomitant blessings of a nocturnal visit from Agatha who read a poem in which an imaginary child limps into Heaven "with a gash in her soul", is tended by angels, and declares herself both "glad to be dead" and "*utterly* content at last ... with full radiance of joy"[157], and of two visions vouchsafed while kneeling with eyes shut (so as not to see the flummery) before the Exposed Sacrament, the first of 'the very Throne of the Holy Trinity round the monstrance as it stood above the tabernacle'[158], the second of Christ lifting her 'in the strong arms of His prayer' to present her to God 'not all foul and world-stained as I am now but purified and *acceptable*'[159], failed to mollify her and it was in a spirit of rebellion that she wrote (twice) to Father Cary.

Cary's replies, though phrased so as not to "betray bias", made it clear that he too disliked the "increasingly common ... practice".[160] Aelfrida does not say which reply she 'incidentally' forwarded to Mother Guenvrede; though either would have aroused her anger, the tenor of her response suggests that it was more likely the first with its implied criticism of local ecclesiastical authority for granting the privilege. The resulting row ran its predictable course. Mother Guenvrede opened the attack with canonical and spiritual justification for Exposition, continuing with a fusillade of complaints about tertiaries in general (they did not 'justify their existence') and Placida in particular: she was a 'gatecrasher', a 'pressman keeping the outside world continuously informed of convent happenings', a physical and inspirational drag 'on the spiritual family [God had] given [her] for [her] own', someone who should 'pray more before acting' and so careless of what she did and thought when alone that the privilege of intensified claustration might be withdrawn. Aelfrida regarded the Mother's criticisms as an irrelevance but the threat caused Placida a night of suffering akin to those known to the 'writers of

the Penitential Psalms' ('waves of terror met over my head ... I don't think I have ever suffered so much'; 'here', added as an afterthought) after which and four pages of anguished self-justification later, she decided 'to serve the Community in its way, not in mine [and] not to be afraid to suffer for it'; to be more deferential to Mother Guenvrede as her Mother-in-Christ ('if she requires deference, deference I must for the love of Holy Obedience, give') but to treat Winifred Donkin 'as an ordinary human being, not as a Potentate'; to 'avoid the *cause* of trouble with the Mother' (her own 'unsatisfactoriness' ranged against the unscrupulous behaviour of a 'typical tyrant') by withdrawing her attention from her. (The feeling that Placida's eyes were always on her made Mother Guenvrede feel 'challenged, brought to book, spied on [and] noted down'.)[161] By avoiding 'the Library' except when under obedience to talk (times and days enthusiastically enjoyed because of their contrast with silence and seclusion) because even limited contact with co-residents and visitors (Placida continued to act as spiritual adviser to at least one regular visitor) was criticised by Mother Guenvrede as an attempt to usurp the Superior's place ('that *is* a tendency of mine', Aelfrida admitted, adding 'I have no *conscious* wish to run the Community')[162] and to win peoples' sympathies away from her by sheer force of personality, something particularly noticeable in the case of Hilda Harrison. To meet the Community '*only* in God' and if it pleased God to send her back into 'the world' for the Community's sake, to be 'ready at any moment to go'.[163]

There was, however, more to Placida's desire to keep out of the Mother's way than this: her presence, she noted, drove Mother Guenvrede 'almost frantic sometimes' and although the latter's violent reactions ('her rages terrify me, I feel ... like David Copperfield before Mr Murdstone') could be explained as exaggerated responses to 'many preoccupations' and to the 'never-slackening stress of [wartime] circumstances', they might also be evidence that the Mother was going 'out of her mind'.[164]

Having failed to appease Mother Guenvrede ('I love her spiritually [but] personally I don't care for her a bit!')[165], Aelfrida was consoled by a visit from '*very* dear Dudu' (unlike Mother Guenvrede, he was growing 'gentler, more patient, more tolerant [and] wiser' as he grew older)[166] to whom his sister had dropped hints regarding the Mother's harsh and sometimes threatening behaviour towards herself.[167] On the basis, it seems, of the contrast between brother and Mother she then decided that the 'silliness [and] conscious malice and perversity'[168] prevalent in her relationship with the latter must stem from defects in the Mother's mental health and that the 'sense of *rightness*' she experienced during the Mother's absences was attributable to this instead of to 'anguish and turmoil'[169] generated in the Community by her own passive–aggressive behaviour towards its Superior. Supported in her belief by the Mother's reaction to a spell of 'invalidism' self-diagnosed by Aelfrida as 'slight heart strain, mild gastroenteritis and nephritis … and some uraemic poisoning' but more likely a nervous reaction to the Exposition episode accompanied by an upset stomach and a urinary infection (Mother Guenvrede accused her of bringing trouble on herself by unspecified 'disobedience')[170], she sought the opinion of others. (She also hinted obliquely to Father Northcott that 'problems' had arisen between Mother Superior and tertiaries.) Though finding a degree of justification in their response (but only a degree, but also an excuse for the Mother's rages: '*cruel* treatment as a child')[171], Aelfrida failed to realise what a dangerous game she was playing with her insinuations of madness. Possibly she believed herself immune from reprisals because deemed by her family so mentally incompetent that she required incarceration in an environment from which, for Christian and therapeutic reasons, she was unlikely to be ejected. Possibly, status being 'part of the game' when she was a consul's wife[172], such behaviour as a consul's 'widow' was assertion of 'status' versus 'tyranny'. Possibly – and though this seems an unlikely conjecture, future events will demonstrate some truth in it – she was revenging herself on someone who belittled (as she thought) her attempts at spiritual advancement by behaving towards her in a manner which would ensure a breakdown.

As she entered the sixth year of her stay at Tymawr, mitigating circumstances for Aelfrida's otherwise inexcusable behaviour arose, two events occurring in the troubled year 1941/42 providing proof that all actions have consequences and that even when intensively claustrated in a convent, she could not escape her past. The first concerned a person she thought (indeed, secretly hoped) never to see again, the second a life she believed she had left behind.

In August 1941, the month in which Aelfrida noted the ravages of her 'starvation' diet, Alethea announced she 'was trying for a postulancy' at the Convent of St John the Divine at Maritzburg, Natal Province, a teaching order formed in 1887. (Father Northcott said "*not* SSJD Maritzburg, I hope"[173] when informed of this.) Aelfrida expressed only moderate delight at her daughter entering a convent 'very Cowley in spirit' and with a better balance of the active and contemplative than Malling[174] but was 'happified' by letters from Maritzburg showing 'none of the *strain* about her life' evinced (for reasons known to her mother but unmentioned here)

during Alethea's earlier postulancy.[175] The departure of Sister Christine in spring 1942 and of novices whose acceptances and clothings had delighted her prompted her to hope that Alethea (at least, and this time) would '*stay* where she is [and] *persevere*'[176] but the philosophical tone with which she greeted a brief resurgence of local air-raids and the elevated sentiments ('what a high calling for me – to be the mother of a saint')[177] expressed on hearing of 'Novice Alethea's' clothing at Whitsun 1942 ('it is very solemnising to me that my very own Weta should wear the religious habit')[178] gave way to anxiety at the point at which Mother Constance SSJD wrote hinting that although Alethea was "perfectly strong [and] had no doubt at all about her vocation", she was suffering from "nerves" which needed "stabilising".[179] This, together with a warning from Aelfrida's guardian angel that Alethea would not remain at Maritzburg and a long gap in Novice Alethea's letters, augured poorly for perseverance: in December 1942 Alethea and the SSJD parted company.

Although Aelfrida wrote consolingly to ex-novice Alethea that she should regard her stay at Maritzburg as a 'course in spirituality' rather than another failure, that God must want Alethea to '*offer* the life [of a nun] but not to live it', that Alethea must be 'supple in His hands, to follow this way and that as He calls' and should now set herself 'to get thoroughly strong so as to be able to do the next work that seems to be God's Will for her'[180], diary entries demonstrate barely-concealed fury: 'alas! I fear I have a restless daughter who is unable to stick at anything' (a trait inherited, she thought, from Constantine, though she herself admitted to being as 'emotionally' restless as Constantine was socially)[181] and who, at thirty-four, needed to learn to 'manage herself a little better [because] people who rush from one work to another are … a nuisance'.[182] She then wrote to Alethea to suggest 'very gently' (*sic*) that 'she would be better and happier earning her own living and not in any way dependent on me for money' but confided to her diary that if Alethea did not respond to this 'gentle hint', she would harden her heart and stop her daughter's allowance: 'now she is free to earn, she *should*'.[183] She was too late; Alethea had already returned to St Cuthbert's where 'she won't be self-supporting … but … God has spoken and I concur … if He needs her there it is my privilege to help. So that is that'.[184]

God may have spoken; Alethea certainly did. In one of the few letters to her mother which spoke of personal matters (a deliberate policy on Alethea's part), Alethea begged her mother "please do not try to give me spiritual direction. I know you mean to help me … [but] it is almost impossible for you who have not seen me … for nearly seven years and at such a distance to … advise me".[185]

Aelfrida's comments regarding the failure of Alethea's conventual life also hint at the diminishing success of her own. Remarks already quoted show this clearly even as they demonstrate the positive aspects of life at Tymawr (that life in a convent in which physical work and prayer-work were balanced was healthier than a purely contemplative one; that good mental and physical health was a sine qua non for one who wished to follow a spiritual life; that if God called one to perform a 'next work' one should be prepared to follow) but Aelfrida's emphasis on the need to '*persevere*' in spite of 'emotional restlessness', 'weakness from strain', the tendency of one's spiritual director to impose a 'particular way-of-approach to God' on his penitent without considering if it was the right one, and meanness, discomfort, and inflexibility with regard to 'food, clothes and routine'[186], suggests that she now regarded her *vita nuova* at Tymawr as a 'course in spirituality' of finite rather than infinite duration. Not only this, but remarks attributed by Aelfrida to Alethea (the latter, it seems, had admitted to 'hesitations and disillusions' even before being clothed as a novice and had felt 'unhappy … unwell, unsatisfied [and of] little use' since) and descriptions of how conventual life was '*very* bad for Alethea' because its rules, though 'necessary, of course', made her so full of 'fears and scruples' that 'she *wilts*', suggest that it was as much of herself as of her daughter that she wrote, a suggestion underlined when we find her adding that 'there was a good deal of "escapism"' in Alethea's need for claustration: 'she shrank from the world and shirked its difficulties'.[187] On the other hand, it might not be wholly Alethea's (or her own) 'psycho-physical make-up'[188] which rendered (or might render) both women unsuitable for life in complete or partial enclosure; it might also be the fault of the Community to which they committed themselves, 'narrow-minded tiresome … women pleasing to God because they love Him and serve Him to the best of their ability' but who created 'a mental atmosphere in which free spirits like Alethea' (and herself) could not 'breathe' because it lacked 'mental stimulus [and] opportunity for initiative' and was therefore 'bad for health and brain'.[189]

Other comments reveal further similarities between mother and daughter: that Alethea's nature was subconsciously 'clamouring' for a sexual relationship ('marriage', as Aelfrida euphemistically put it)[190]; that 'difficulties and dangers' did Alethea no harm but that 'it is monotony she can't stand'; that Alethea was 'by temperament unfitted for … the Religious Life'; that Alethea needed 'more *freedom* in order to develop her life of service to God'; that although appropriate for Alethea

to try her vocation again (if she had one: her mother now expressed doubt and even a little smug satisfaction because 'God [has] given to *me* – worldly little *me*! – the grace of vocation … and withheld it from Alethea who is so much better and purer than I'), it was now 'entirely right for her to go'. (And if going meant eventual return to England[191], so be it.) There was also Fordfield, dear to Aelfrida because so 'many precious people' connected with it (chiefly her grandparents, 'Dear', and Ellen Ison) 'lived the good life in the world almost to perfection' in a 'beloved home' filled with '*God's* Peace', a life and peace and building linking past with present: 'Alethea, I fear', she wrote entirely without irony, 'is homesick for what she can never never have … [her] ordered and sheltered childhood [and] the peace and security of Fordfield'. (And, of course, the presence of her mother, though as Aelfrida admitted, 'as Alethea's mother I am best away from her'.) There remained one question, a question she found herself unable to answer with respect either to her daughter or herself: 'is it *my* fault that these things are so?'[192]

A life left behind caught up with Aelfrida about the same time as she recorded joyously of Alethea and Maritzburg that her daughter was '*Really There*', teaching 'senior orphans' and walking 'small orphans' in the children's home attached to the convent.[193] Constance Fordham, matron and proprietress of the Brooklands Avenue Nursing Home, died suddenly early in 1940. Mr Fordham kept the Home open but in July 1940 'gave it up as a bad job', sold off the equipment, and, renting out the flat created for him and his late wife in what would have been 'Fordfield Above', moved into the former gardener's cottage whence he ran his architectural practice. The first Aelfrida heard of this was letters from Mr Fordham written over a year later asking her permission to dispose of the remainder of the lease 'to an RC Nursing Community' and from a 'psychologist at Addenbrooke's', Dr Noble, asking if he could buy '"the former nursing home at Fordfield" as a medico-psycho nursing home'.[194]

Lengthy and increasingly acrimonious correspondence ensued. Mr Fordham was reluctant to relinquish Fordfield Cottage. Dr Noble wished to buy Fordfield for £2,500 and to lease Wetenhall Cottage as a nurses' home. Julius vacillated before washing his hands of the matter and Eustace and Aelfrida were left battling it out, she keen to sell and lease, he (or, 'truthfully … Phyllis') 'angry and bitter' at his sister thinking only of herself but forced to concede that her life interest in Fordfield allowed her to sell the house provided she shared the proceeds equally with Julius and himself and that she could do as she wished with Wetenhall Cottage, her own property. Mother Guenvrede suggested that Placida practice Holy Poverty by selling *all* her 'real estate' but not if it would cause 'family … coolness'. Aelfrida herself decided that if 'family coolness' was what she deserved as a result of unspecified 'Bad Old Days', she would receive it 'with all meekness' ('my godly ancestors would *curse* me if I allowed property-ownership to make trouble in the family') but also to turn the affair to spiritual profit by showing Eustace how 'Christians and tertiaries' behaved under trying circumstances and by demonstrating 'the overwhelming importance of the *opus Dei*' relative to 'worldly affairs'. Unfortunately for herself and for Mr Fordham whom Dr Noble had already 'bustled' out of the gardener's cottage but fortunately in terms of potential family 'coolness', Dr Noble broke off negotiations (the valuation price of Fordfield was more than his offer), leaving Aelfrida to wonder if 'an imperceptive secular psychologist' who had caused 'much inconvenience and some expense to a lot of people' was fit to 'mess sick souls about'.[195]

There was, however, more to Aelfrida's renewed interest in '*property ownership*' than a desire to rid herself of Fordfield or to 'persuade … to go' the architect by whom she believed she had been treated very high-handedly and with whom she had had many battles over Fordfield's antiquated heating system in the early days of the Brooklands Avenue Nursing Home: she had plans of her own. Instead of 'waiting to be turned out of [Tymawr] by the Mother', she decided to adopt an 'inviting suggestion' made by the devil (masquerading, she later realised, as an 'angel of light') that she 'gently persuade' her Wetenhall Cottage tenants to move out in order to install herself there 'as "Straightener" to the new nursing home'. Elaborating on this 'most alluring' idea, she also decided to co-opt Hilda Harrison and a Tymawr Associate as joint 'reception-clerks' at 'the new nursing home' (Dr Noble's opinion was not sought, but as he was known to be irascible that was probably as well) and, in an echo of her Foxton scheme, to found in Wetenhall Cottage a '*House of Prayer* as daughter house to Tymawr', the Cottage's drawing room becoming its chapel with Mass conducted daily by an 'aged priest' imported for the purpose. (His room was to be SERENITY.) But having 'thought the thing out in [her] mind', she was beset by doubts: 'all the old love of Cambridge and Fordfield surged up in me'; 'I prefer making my own arrangements to falling in with other people's'; 'I noticed how the idea of *being in authority* attracted me', and so on, and with her soul blushing for shame at this demonstration of her 'deepest and most fundamental weakness' (i.e. a desire to impose her '*moral standards*' on others)[196], she both abandoned the idea and admitted to Mother Guenvrede

(without, however, admitting as to what prompted the admission) that she had succumbed to 'the lure of my old fondness of … having my own way [and] of "meddling with souls" and the unconscious but powerful *pull* of old associations and of places deeply loved'.[197] In this last respect, at least she was prophetic.

Dr Noble having 'bustled' Mr Fordham out of Fordfield and reneged on his offer to buy it, the house stood empty, 'a great risk in wartime'[198] because rendering it liable to compulsory purchase by the government for public use; luckily and in spite of this, it remained vacant. Sometime in 1942, however, Aelfrida received intimations from 'the Cambridge "Public Assistance" department' that if she did not use the house herself, it would be compulsorily purchased for housing 'God's poor'.[199] She immediately took steps to have it occupied by people of more suitable social status, offering it to the Evelyn Nursing Home for the use of "sub-acute and chronic cases" not requiring intensive nursing. The Evelyn, though currently so full that it had a waiting list for admission (conscription meant that many of those who either did not wish or were unable to look after themselves moved into nursing homes for the duration – not then predictable – of the war because lacking the domestic staff to enable them to remain at home), declined Mrs Graham's offer because it was short-staffed – many nurses were in hospitals or the Forces – and could not run "a satellite establishment" in addition to its own. More helpfully, it referred her to a "Nursing Sisterhood in Bateman Street" (possibly the same 'RC Nursing Community' referred to by Mr Fordham) who might be keen to avail itself of her offer.[200] Currently feeling 'thoroughly ill' (she had just received news of Alethea's departure from Maritzburg), Aelfrida was delighted to discover ('*that* is what I have been praying for') that the Bateman Street 'Sisterhood' wished to 'take on or buy Fordfield' as an annexe to or a replacement for its present premises in order to 'make special provision for the needs of the aged'. She was even more delighted when the 'Sisterhood' (more properly, the Sisters of Hope) took Fordfield on a five-year lease early in 1943[201] and after carrying out some very necessary alterations and renovations, moved in on 24 June 1943, Fordfield becoming the Hope Nursing Home at 'Hope House'.[202]

One February day in Lent 1942 Placida sat down to record the tribulations which made Lent particularly penitential: 'the weather, arctic, black frost and east winds day after day'; war news more and more chastening; the Community not now fasting on Fridays but performing the penitential psalms kneeling instead, an action deemed 'very tiring, all that time on one's knees … but the best possible expression of what is in one's heart this year'; Mother Guenvrede and three Sisters off sick; her own 'minor ailments': 'head noises [and] broken chilblains on all [her] fingers', sciatica from heavy digging; the world 'bewildering' because there were 'too many events in [her] own life'. ('Can I have lived only 58 years?' she asked herself.) She was also, in spite of claustration as intensified as she could tolerate and Mother Guenvrede permit, 'overwhelmed as I have never been overwhelmed before by the *multiplicity of things*'[203], so overwhelmed, indeed, that she suffered 'distractions in chapel about it'.[204] And how ironic it must have seemed to one re-reading Father Cary's description of Tymawr as a 'quiet laboratory' in which 'the furnaces and crucibles of God'[205] were extracting from the drossy core of Aelfrida's soul the purer metal which would, with His help, enable her to live a saner and holier life[206], when as Placida had recently discovered to her cost, laboratories are also places where explosions occur if equipment and materials are handled improperly.

## Notes

1   The description is Benson's own (*Lord of the World* preface).
2   À Kempis pp 48-51.
3   Tillyard, Ae. *A Little Road-Book for Mystics* pp 25–26.
4   SSC pamphlet *The Tymawr Community. Our Life Together.*
5   Benson, RH. *Richard Raynal: Solitary* p 31. For details of the life of Richard Rolle (c1290–1349) see www.ccel.org/ccl/rolle
6   Benson, RH. op. cit. p77.
7   GCPPT 1│1│50 8 May 1936.
8   GCPPT 1│1│55a The phrase appears in a letter from Father Cary to Aelfrida of 16 September 1938.
9   GCPPT 1│1│57 26 December 1939.
10  GCPPT 1│1│59 20 April 1941.
11  ibid. 4 May 1941. Aelfrida's views on early rising are expressed in *Christian Old Age* p50 (GCPPT 2/17): "convents look very romantic places and visitors who wander round [their] precincts on a summer's day ... think how easy goodness must be in such numinous surroundings. But the ... nuns who rise ... to say Mattins and Lauds in an unheated chapel with Prime and Mass to follow at dawn ... are not I imagine ... conscious of much glamour or romance ..."
12  GCPPT 1│1│59 31 May and 1 July 1941.
13  ibid. 31 May and 'Whitsunday' (1 June) 1941.
14  ibid. 1 July 1941.
15  ibid. 1 June 1941. (Author's emphasis).
16  GCPPT 1│1│58 22 July 1940.
17  GCPPT 1│1│57 26 December 1939.
    GCPPT 1│1│57a Letter from Father Cary to Aelfrida of 'St Thomas' Day' (21 December) 1939.
    References in *The Night Watches* to "being ill" or "an invalid" suffering not only physical pains but "heaviness of soul" (pp 9–12) suggest that Aelfrida herself was one of the "sick folk" included in its secondary title *Thoughts for Sick Folk.* Her further comment that as a sick person she has tried to get well and failed but is still hopeful of recovery and is now where she ought to be to ensure recovery (and that this is God's choice of setting for her) also speaks volumes, as does her statement (ostensibly with reference to Deity) that she "no more [sets] out into far countries of [her] *own choice*" (ibid. pp5–8; author's emphasis).
18  GCPPT 1│1│57 12 May 1940.

GCPPT 1│1│55 27 May 1938.
19  GCPPT 1│1│59 'Whitsunday' (1 June) and 2 June 1941.
20  GCPPT 1│1│58 'Christmas' (25 December) 1940.
21  GCPPT 1│1│66 2 April 1949.
22  Tillyard, Ae. *Haste to the Wedding* p263.
23  GCPPT 1│1│58 11 January 1941.
24  GCPPT 1│1│59 14 June 1941.
25  GCPPT 1│1│58 11 January 1941.
26  GCPPT 1│1│57 6 April 1940.
27  GCPPT 1│1│57 'St Matthias' (24 February) 1940.
    GCPPT 1│1│58 23 August 1940.
28  GCPPT 1│1│57 'St Matthias' (24 February) 1940.
29  ibid. 1 December 1939.
30  ibid. 16 April 1946.
31  ibid. 1 December 1939 and 16 April 1940.
32  ibid. 8 April 1940.
33  ibid. 16 April 1940.
34  ibid. 1 December 1939.
35  ibid. 29 October 1939.
36  GCPPT 1│1│58 2, 4, 5 and 22 January 1941. Apropos washing up, Aelfrida seems to have forgotten Crowley's description (*The Dangers of Mysticism. The Equinox* vol 1 No 6 September 1911 pp 153–158) of how "the nun Gertrude when it came to her turn to wash up ... used to explain that she was very sorry but at that particular moment she was being married with full choral service, to the Saviour". For the reason for Crowley's distaste for Gertrude (1263–1303), see the anonymous hagiographic *Life and Revelations of St Gertrude* published in 1879.
37  Benson, R M. *Instructions on the Religious Life* p 65.
38  GCPPT 1│1│58 22 January 1941
39  ibid. 18 February 1941.
40  ibid. 22 February 1941.
41  ibid. 29 January 1941.
42  ibid. 'Ash Wednesday' (26 February) and 27 February 1941.
43  ibid. 'Ash Wednesday' (26 February) and 21 March 1941.
44  ibid. 2 March 1941.
45  ibid. 9 and 3 March 1941.
46  ibid. 'Easter Monday' (14 April) and 16 and 18 April 1941.
47  GCPPT 1│1│58 5 April 1941.
    GCPPT 1│1│59 29 April 1941.
48  GCPPT 1│1│58 6 and 23 March and 'Palm Sunday' (6 April) 1941. The Women's Land Army to which 'land girls' were drafted worked on farms during the war in place of men away on war duty. Like the 'temple-child', the 'land girl' was probably recruited by the SSC to fill the gap left by Novices Philippa and Helena.
49  GCPPT 1│1│58 6 March and 'Maundy Thursday' (10 April) 1941. The book of Julius's referred to by Aelfrida here was the most recent of several written by him on the subject of Byzantine music; it refers to the *Octoechus* of St John of Damascus, a liturgical schema based on the eight modes of medieval Greek music (Tillyard, HJW. *Byzantine Music and Hymnography* p20). Julius's 'fires of affliction' were also literal: in March 1941 Aelfrida described him as being 'in the thick of the Cardiff raids [helping to] put out incendiary bombs while high explosive bombs burst all round him'. (ibid. 10 March 1941.)
50  GCPPT 1│1│58 13 and 29 March 1941.
51  ibid. 3 April 1941
52  ibid. 2 March 1941
53  ibid. 3, 10 and 29 April 1941.
54  ibid. 2 March 1941.
55  ibid. 21 March 1941.
56  ibid. 2 and 21 March and 8 April 1941.
57  ibid. 'Easter Monday' (14 April) and 18 April 1941.
58  GCPPT 1│1│58 18 April 1941.
    GCPPT 1│1│59 20 April 1941.

59  GCPPT 1|1|59 5 May 1941.
60  ibid. 20 May and 24 June 1941.
61  ibid.19 and 20 May 1941.
62  ibid. 11 July. 1941.
63  ibid. 3 September 1941.
64  GCPPT 1|1|58a July 1940. Notes from Mother Guenvrede to "Mrs Graham".
65  GCPPT 1|1|59 14 June 1941.
66  ibid. 21September 1941 and 22 February 1942.
67  ibid. 22 September 1941.
68  ibid. 18 April 1941.
69  ibid. 15 July 1941.
70  ibid. 30 August 1941
71  ibid. 2 and 27 June 1941.
72  ibid. 2, 5 and 24 June and 15 August 1941.
73  ibid. 29 July 1941.
74  ibid. 6 April, 10 May and 27 July 1941.
75  ibid. 22 April and 13 August 1941.
76  ibid. 29 July and 30 August 1941.
77  ibid. 11 and 20 May and 29 July 1941.
78  ibid. 31 May and 2 and 3 June 1941.
79  Benson, R M. *Instructions on the Religious Life* pp 19–22.
80  GCPPT 1|1|59 20 April 1941.
81  GCPPT 1|1|58 18 February and 2 April 1941.
82  ibid. 29 March 1941.
83  ibid. 'Palm Sunday' (6 April) 1941.
84  ibid. 29 March 1941.
85  ibid. 2 April 1941.
86  ibid. 18 February and 2 April 1941.
87  GCPPT 1|1|59 8 June 1941.
88  GCPPT 1|1|58 22 February 1941.
89  GCPPT 1|1|59 22 April, 10 May and 13 August 1941.
90  GCPPT 1|1|58 17 January 1941.
91  ibid. 18 March 1941.
92  GCPPT 1|1|59 29 June and 15 July 1941. (Author's emphasis).
93  ibid. 20 December 1941.
94  GCPPT 1|1|40 10 October 1931.
95  GCPPT 1|1|59 7 November and 23 December 1941.
96  GCPPT 1|1|58 18 March 1941.
97  GCPPT 1|1|59 10 November 1941.
98  ibid. 14 September 1941.
99  GCPPT 1|1|57 28 February 1940.
100  GCPPT 1|1|59 15 July 1941.
101  ibid. 'Christmas Eve' (24 December) 1941.
102  ibid. 4 October 1941.
103  ibid. 'St Placid's Day' (5 October) 1941.
104  ibid. 29 November 1941.
105  ibid. 11 September 1941.
106  ibid. 23 December 1941.
107  ibid. 29 November and 23 December 1941.
108  ibid. 18 November 1941.
109  ibid. 10 May 1941.
110  GCPPT 1|1|58 22 December 1940 in which Aelfrida quotes a letter to *The Times* from the Archbishops of Canterbury, Westminster and York.
111  ibid. 13 March 1941.
112  GCPPT 1|1|59 29 April and 10 May 1941.
113  Crowley, A. *The Dangers of Mysticism* (*The Equinox* vol 1 No 6 September 1911 p 156).
114  ibid. 30 August and 'St Luke's Day' (18 October) 1941.
115  ibid. 'St Luke's Day' (18 October) 1941.
116  GCPPT 1|1|59 21 October 1941.
      GCPPT 1|1|60 16 and 21 April 1942 ('1941' in error).
117  Benson, R M. *Instructions on the Religious Life* p59.
118  GCPPT 1|1|59 'All Saints' (1 November) 1941.
119  GCPPT 1|1|60 31 May 1942.
120  ibid. 10 June 1942.
121  GCPPT 1|1|59 31 August 1941.
122  GCPPT 1|1|60 23, 24 and 27 July 1942.
123  ibid. 16 April 1942.
124  GCPPT 1|1|59 18 September and 18 November 1941.
125  GCPPT 1|1|60 1 May and 14 June 1942.
126  GCPPT 1|1|59 21 October 1941.
      GCPPT 1|1|60 21 August and 18 October 1942.
      Aelfrida's own rare poetic effusions of the Tymawr years are themselves derivative, hymns composed by Frances Ridley Havergal being their obvious model. Father Cary politely refers to one written for Good Friday 1942 ("In anguish I renounce the sins / That sent Thee to the Tree") as "a little hymn of devotion … rather reminiscent". (GCPPT 1|1|60 27 February 1942 and letter from Father Cary to Aelfrida dated 'Thursday in Passion Week' 1942 GCPPT 1|1|60a).
127  GCPPT 1|1|54 31 January 1938.
128  GCPPT 1|1|59 26 April 1941.
      GCPPT 1|1|60 25 April 1942.
      Walter Tillyard joined the Signal Corps and in spite of his aunt's gloomy prediction survived the war.
129  GCPPT 1|1|59 14 October 1941.
130  GCPPT 1|1|60 28 March 1942.
131  GCPPT 1|1|59 29 September 1941.
132  ibid. 6 August 1941.
133  ibid. 20 September 1941.
134  ibid. 22 September 1941.
135  ibid. 30 January 1942.
136  ibid. 22 September 1941.
137  ibid. 22 August 1941.
138  ibid. 29 September 1941 and 30 January 1942.
139  ibid. 14 January 1941.
140  ibid. 29 September 1941.
141  GCPPT 1|1|60 26 April 1942.
142  GCPPT 1|1|59 22 September 1941.
143  ibid. 22 August 1941.
144  ibid. 30 January 1942.
145  GCPPT 1|1|60 13 May 1942.
146  GCPPT 1|1|59 14 June 1941.
147  GCPPT 1|1|60 13 May 1942.
148  GCPPT 1|1|59 14 June 1941.
149  GCPPT 1|1|60 13 May 1942.
150  ibid. 27 May and 17 July 1942.
151  ibid. 26 May 1942.
152  GCPPT 1|1|59 29 September 1941.
153  GCPPT 1|1|60 18 July 1942.
154  ibid. 7 June 1940.
155  GCPPT 1|159 10 September and 2 December 1941. The *Church Times* paragraph, dated 29 November 1941, is preserved in GCPPT 1|1|59a.
156  GCPPT 1|1|59 18 and 21 March and 'Passion Sunday' (22 March) 1942.
      GCPPT 1|1|60 28 and 30 March 1942.
157  GCPPT 1|1|60 30 March 1942.
158  ibid.
159  ibid. 28 June 1942.
160  GCPPT 1|1|60a Letters from Father Cary to Aelfrida dated 'Tuesday in Holy Week' (31 March) 1942 and 30 May 1942.
161  GCPPT 1|1|60 7 and 8 June 1942.
162  ibid. 'Epiphany' (6 January) 1943.
163  ibid. 7 and 8 June 1942
164  ibid. 8 and 23 June 1942.
165  ibid. 22 September 1942.
166  ibid. 16 September 1942.

167 Aelfrida's complaint appears in the entry for 3 September 1941 in Julius Tillyard's *Synopsis of Diary* (MTC). Although Mother Guenvrede ('*abbatissa*') is described there as an '*acerba*' and '*minata*' head of household ('*domina*'), Aelfrida's own diary makes no mention of her having complained to Julius then or earlier of the Mother's harsh or threatening attitude towards her.

168 ibid. 28 March 1942.

169 ibid. 19 June 1942.

170 ibid. 18 and 29 August 1942.

171 ibid. 20 August 1942.

172 ibid. 8 June 1942.

173 ibid. 14 December 1942.

174 GCPPT 1|1|59 13 August 1941.

175 ibid. 22 February 1942.

176 GCPPT 1|1|60 21 April 1942 ('1941' in error).

177 ibid. 3 June 1942.

178 ibid. 7 August 1942.

179 ibid. 22 July 1942.

180 ibid. 16 and 21 December 1942.

181 ibid. 14 December 1942.

182 ibid. 21 December 1942.

183 ibid. 18 January 1943. Alethea, as witness the entry in Aelfrida's diary in which Alethea's outlay on 'charities', 'presents', and 'clothes' (photographs show her as always very smartly dressed even when living on a remote mission) is listed to the nearest shilling, had to account for every penny spent from her allowance of £100 a year (GCPPT 1|1|58 19 October 1940). It should be noted' however, that her allowance *doubled* her annual income: she also received £100 a year stipend from St Cuthbert's, £50 of which was deducted at source for board and lodging leaving her £50 for necessities. This £50 being insufficient to cover holidays, subscriptions, and presents, Alethea gladly accepted a further £100 a year from her mother. At Maritzburg she was expected to pay ('i.e.', wrote Aelfrida, 'I shall pay') £4 a month for her keep (GCPPT 1|1|59 12 December 1941).

184 ibid. 27 January 1943.

185 GCPPG A1.4 Letter from Alethea Graham to Aelfrida of 20 March 1943.

186 GCPPT 1|1|60 14 and 21 December 1942.

187 ibid.

188 ibid. 10 January 1943.

189 ibid. 14 and 21 December 1942.

190 ibid. 14 December 1942.

191 ibid. 14 and 17 December 1942 and 28 January 1943.

192 ibid. 11 September and 14 and 17 December 1942.

193 GCPPT 1|1|59 12 December 1941.

194 ibid. 27 September 1941. Dr Noble had been appointed head of the Cambridge Psychological Department and Child Guidance Clinic in 1934. In early November 1934 he inspected Brookfield (former home of Aelfrida's solicitor Mr Ginn, with a view to running it as a private 'nerve clinic' when widowed Mrs Ginn moved to the Brooklands Avenue Nursing Home the following year. Local general practitioners already admitted 'nerve cases' to the Evelyn and baulked at this; Brookfield was subsequently leased to an Addenbrooke's physician as his private house (Mann, S. *A Wonderful Thing for Cambridge* p38). Dr Noble lived and consulted at Langdale next door to Fordfield, the latter being even more suitable than Brookfield for his 'clinic'.

195 GCPPT 1|1|59 27 September, 14 and 24 October and 'Eve of All Saints' (31 October) 1941.

196 ibid. 27 September 1941. Aelfrida's reference to the devil disguised as 'an angel of light' refers to St Paul's warning (*Corinthians* 2.11:14) that this was how Satan might 'form' himself to delude Christian believers. She might also, in the present context, have read the preceding verse with regard to "deceitful workers".

197 ibid. 29 September 1941.

198 ibid. 14 October 1941.

199 Tillyard, Ae. *The Centaur* p318 (GCPPT 2|21|1).

200 My account of correspondence between Aelfrida and the ENH is based on the minutes of the Home's House Committee for 20 November 1942; nothing of this appears in Aelfrida's diary.

201 GCPPT 1|1|60 16 and 17 December 1942 and 1 January 1943.

202 The Roman Catholic Sisters of Hope were a branch of the Association of the Holy Family founded in Bordeaux in 1821. The designated apostolic activity of the Sisters of Hope was nursing the wealthy sick in their own homes, monies raised being donated to branches caring for those less financially favoured. The Holy Family of Bordeaux expanded into England in 1868, the Sisters of Hope establishing a nursing home (Hope House) in North London in 1876 where they cared for the sick and looked after a small group of elderly ladies. Fifteen Sisters and a number of elderly 'Lady Boarders' were evacuated to Cambridge on 17 October 1940, living in two rented houses on opposite sides of Bateman Street. The practical and financial problems posed by existence in two houses separated by a busy street lasted three years; Aelfrida's offer of Fordfield must have seemed serendipitous. For further details see Flanagan M-B. *A Good Man Has Passed this Way* and Mann, S. *The Hope Nursing Home*.

203 GCPPT 1|1|59 20 February 1942.

204 ibid. 24 October 1941.

205 GCPPT 1|1|58 'Easter Monday' (14 April) 1941.

206 GCPPT 1|1|60 4 and 22 May 1942.

# Furnaces and Crucibles of God

Pressing forward on her 'pilgrimage' in the spring and summer of 1942 (her journey towards God had not yet, it seems, reached its destination), Placida heard 'our Lord calling [her] away from ordinary meetings-with-people more deeply into his silence and prayer', a further step, she thought, 'along the mysterious road of His choice'.

His choice it may have been but a 'warily' phrased request to the Mother that Placida be allowed to withdraw from communal life altogether because at '*solitary meals*' God granted her the privilege of 'never eating bread without it reminding [her] of the Blessed Sacrament' – a 'sign' not granted at 'library tea' – was made chiefly because dissention in 'the Library' had reached such a pitch that it was unpleasant to be there. Her ruse was noted by Mother Guenvrede whose immediate response was a written request to pick redcurrants ('a task I don't like as it tires me very much') though she later relented, saying that it was "a good idea to avoid the crowd".[1] A decision, prompted by her guardian angel, not to press the Mother on this (or any other) point at present seemed sensible lest her request be refused: 'I must show her that I *can* go on quietly not asking for any change yet'. It also provided an opportunity to 'nourish *interior* silence more carefully [and] look out for more opportunities of little mortifications' e.g. 'being content with a mere glance at *The Times*'. There remained, however, the comforting thought that 'when I am *ready*, Our Lord will date His invitation – it is *undated* now'[2] and a comforting experience *coram sanctissimo* of 'universal consciousness' ('*not* sympathy or imagination [but] … multiple consciousness … with infinite boundaries') of herself as 'all human beings … who had ever worshipped God the *fons et origo* – I AM'.[3] Father Northcott too advised a woman as cardiologically and renally compromised as Aelfrida had recently declared herself to be 'to *wait* for some definite sign of God's will'[4] (the 'most benevolent smile'[5] smiled by Mother Guenvrede a few days beforehand suggests collusion between Mother and Father with regard to 'child of God'), so following 'a call to the nation to *humble itself*' during the 11am Service broadcast on 3 September (Placida had steeled herself to listen to the wireless) after which, duly humbled and declaring total submission to God, she received (at equally reviled

**The chapel, Tymawr (interior)**

Exposition) a vision of 'the Throne of Glory' from which flowed 'a deep gold river of liquid light' filling the chapel before streaming out over the world 'to slake parched souls and fructify barren hearts'[6], she bided her time. But barely a month later she received a call 'so clear, so urgent, to leave the *city of myself* … and go out into the unknown, deeper into the heart of God [to] lose *myself* in Him, commune with Him with fewer breaks [and] pray and pray and *pray*'[7], a call accompanied by a strong sense of having so successfully sloughed off pretensions that peace lay 'broad and deep in [her] soul', that Placida prepared for departure. The only thing to blight her joy was 'being not a bit *well*' with 'sciatica, and bronchial cough, poor circulation and so on and so forth'.[8]

A reason was not hard to find: the absence of fulminated-against central heating. Firing the furnaces of God did not now include firing the guest house boiler, her unheated room making Aelfrida wonder if Mother Guenvrede, having unsuccessfully tried to starve her out, was now trying to freeze her out.

Common sense informed her that it was fuel shortages ('*deficente ligno et carbone*', as Julius noted when Aelfrida wrote to him complaining she was frozen)[9], fuel rationing, and a series of government decrees that central heating be used as little as possible or not at all, not frigidity of personality which caused Mother Guenvrede to reduce the inmates of the guest house to portable heaters only, but to a sufferer from rheumatoid arthritis, lack of background warmth proved troublesome because paraffin stoves did little to alleviate the damp chill which pervaded Tymawr even in summer: 'if only [my] more *docile* body [didn't] object so violently when its feet are cold'. (And with cold feet 'all sorts of ailments begin to occur'.)[10] But even with 'kidney stones' added to her cough (her cough, said Mother Guenvrede, was due to Placida not wearing enough clothes) and with her room not much above freezing and its soft furnishings 'clammy to the touch'[11], Aelfrida proved stubborn: she would *not* demean herself by laying, lighting and cleaning the grate of a fire in her room nor would she join 'the Library' for tea, preferring to remain in her 'remarkably chilly and damp bedroom' than return there after having become thoroughly warm elsewhere.[12] Mother Guenvrede's brusque response to a request for a second stove ("you had better go to a nursing home or your relations") prompted a propitiatory note, two diarized queries ('is she quite sane? … can one propitiate the unbalanced?') and a prayer ('Lord, plead *Thou* my cause') but a Mother Superior callous 'to everyone who is not Community' (the latter an interesting comment insofar as Placida had hitherto represented herself as 'Community') proved equally callous with regard to resident tertiaries. The convent's central heating, however, was *not* turned off ('of course, I *am* glad they are warm')[13] and that of the guest house, in which the visiting priest's room was situated, turned on only when there was a priest in residence, the latter eliciting a wry comment from Mrs Graham: 'I can't help being amused that delicate elderly ladies' (she was fifty nine) 'are supposed to … bear frost and snow but a monk should be kept warm'.[14] Only the thought that she lived in 'a Paradise regained in perfect "creature-liness" [with] God [her] Saviour'[15] kept Placida warm and refusing 'to be unhappified' in spirit if not in body, and prevented Aelfrida from complaining more bitterly than she did about the absence of 'Brother Fornax' or, on a rare warm day, about heating which made the chapel 'like an American hotel'.[16] But, and an important but for one who hitherto had desperately tried to achieve that "humble obedience" which would enable her to live "in unity of purpose" with her Superior, Placida now found herself unable to enter "the sepulchre of obedience"[17] and to give Mother Guenvrede 'full obedience in [her] heart'[18] because, it seems, that lady had interfered with a luxurious ascetic's creature comforts once too often and to too great an extent.

As usual in matters pertaining to 'Authority' in general and room temperature in particular, Aelfrida's quarrel was as much with her own dead mother as with living Mother Guenvrede. But although the barely-heated West Room may have reminded her of Fordfield winters in which Chiara's decree that bedroom gas fires were never

to be lit meant her daughter being forced to freeze in glacial PEACE if unwilling to join her parents and daughters by the drawing room fire, it was to Anatolia (a not dissimilar personality) and Nadja (her alter ego) and not to Chiara herself that she consciously compared Mother Guenvrede, noting how their 'noise and swashbuckling' had made her feel 'wedged into a small corner of the universe' while they occupied all the rest of the room.[19] Yet if those ladies had such an effect on herself, how much more did Aelfrida have on Mother Guenvrede in terms of noisy refusals to understand the reasons for the latter's actions or see that they were the result of wartime shortages and government policy, not a desire to dominate? In fact it was left to Alethea to hint to her mother that her behaviour exceeded the norm; having learnt of a comment made by the then Bishop of Capetown, she quoted it in a letter home: "Tillyards terrify me. There is one, Aelfrida [who] ought to be '*Dictatrix Mundi*'".[20]

Alethea's reference to her mother's global desire to dominate (the latter regarded the Bishop's remarks as a compliment) is significant, for a serious row was about to take place between Aelfrida and the daughter whose life she tried to dictate. Though 'much more buoyant'[21] since returning to St Cuthbert's (she had been greatly missed and received a warm welcome), Alethea was understandably sensitive concerning her release from Maritzburg because having now been sent away from conventual precincts twice, no Mother Superior would accept her in the future. Aelfrida's 'gentle hint' that Alethea was now thirty-four and would be better and happier earning her own living cannot have been well received by someone whose brief secular (and salaried) career had ended in breakdown. It is also possible that Aelfrida compared Alethea detrimentally to her younger cousins: Walter in the Forces; Constance, a nurse, and as attractive to men as her aunt at her age; Stephen, with a Master's degree from Columbia, returning to England to declare himself a conscientious objector and to work with the Society of Friends; Veronica with a 2:1 from Girton, about to become a teacher but unlike her aunt at her age, was not preoccupied with 'religion and young men'[22]; Angela, back from Canada, now a land-girl but intending to matriculate at the same college. Nor can Aelfrida's subsequent letter bidding Alethea 'be simple' (a rich comment from one who consistently ignored her spiritual adviser's advice to be likewise) and lay aside any self-imposed Rule (she herself, she wrote, would be 'answerable at the Day of Judgement' for her daughter's spiritual default)[23] have appealed to one who regarded her mother as a piously parasitic dweller in convent guest houses. Aelfrida therefore received a sharp reply, in which, though revealing that she believed herself badly treated at Maritzburg because unable to sustain the 'rush and scramble [and] *heavy* physical work'[24] there, Alethea forbade '*Dictatrix Mundi*' to interfere: Aelfrida, it seems, had not only discussed 'Novice Alethea' with her conventual Superior but had written to Alethea's spiritual director in South Africa as well.

Worried lest her 'eagerness to help' alienate Alethea completely ('how far should a daughter be allowed to make mistakes that a mother's experience, foresight or intuition could have prevented?'; she conveniently forgot that she herself had encouraged Alethea to enter Maritzburg), already planning for an old age which increasingly looked as though it would not be spent at Tymawr and which for that reason if no other could re-encompass the presence of a living daughter recently envisioned 'all warm and glowing with life' in a dress of dark power-blue[25], Aelfrida hastened to make amends by air-gram and letter. To her diary, however, she put the question '*would* it have been better to [give] Alethea no advice?' before deciding that if Alethea could not take advice 'on a religious matter' from her tertiary mother, the fault must lie with – rather surprisingly – herself: Alethea, she wrote, had watched her mother practise 'Christianity without the Cross' and what reason had she to think her behaviour different now? And if as Alethea's mother she had been so blind to her own sins, was she (as Placida) less 'obtuse' about them now? If not, perhaps 'silence of the pen' was called for. (Placida had, of course, no intention of desisting from letters written for the benefit of *other* recipients: 'tranquil letters – *silent* letters – letters that convey His peace – loving letters – beautiful letters'[26], letters, in fact, quite unlike the grovelling, threatening, self-justifying, and childishly petty ones with which she bombarded Mother Guenvrede.) It was not needed. Alethea accepted her apology, replacing bitter reproaches with lyrical descriptions of South African scenery.

A problem nearer home and one irresistibly reminiscent of Chiara's later years, was Mrs Donkin, 'of all the hard, self-righteous, self-centred, censorious and cantankerous old ladies ... the worst', herself her only topic of conversation and the standard by which she judged others, a lady of eighty-two whose 'delusions about herself are farcical' and (the only characteristic in which she differed from her critic) going senile to boot.[27]

The departure of residents when the convent area was expanded to house the influx of postulants which coincided with the onset of the 'real' as opposed to the 'phoney' war' had left only three permanent members of 'the Library'; the grille, however, was moved back to its original position in November 1942 when the Community's numbers dwindled following the departure

of disenchanted novices and postulants earlier that year.[28] Two factors, however, combined to persuade Hilda Harrison and other residents to leave: the continuing absence of central heating and the permanent presence of the Mother's 'Own Mama'. They left, Hilda to return for festivals and holidays, Miss Lowe for ever, accompanied by scathing remarks from Mother Guenvrede about 'people who come to Tymawr or ... stay on at Tymawr largely for their own convenience' (Placida, oblivious to the gibe, noted that *she* was there because 'God chose the place')[29] but not before dissention rocked the convent. ('I *know* when [the Community] is disturbed – and God keep me from disturbing it myself', wrote Placida; Aelfrida, hearing recriminations ricochet round the bathroom following its re-appearance from behind the grille, said nothing: 'peace is more precious than hot water'.)[30] They also drove the Mother 'almost distraught with all the demands' they made on her.[31]

Placida tried to 'fast from sociable walks and talks ... and betake [herself] to prayer and penance alone' but was inevitably drawn into quarrels 'too silly and odiously feminine for words'.[32] (She noted gleefully, however, 'who says life is dull here!'[33] and even seems to have enjoyed her 'efforts at peace making'[34] because of the exciting 'scenes' which arose as a result.) In her diary, however, and in letters to Mother Guenvrede who had asked Aelfrida's advice as to how to deal with the quarrelsome ladies, she wrote revealingly of herself in the guise of describing 'pious old maids ... full of suppressed complexes and vain regrets over the past' ('married women', she added without irony, 'are less taken up with themselves')[35], pre-occupied with building bulwarks against the world behind which they brooded on 'loneliness, minor ailments, past failures, slights and misunderstandings', taking 'perverse pleasure in being catty'[36] and, though 'deeply religious' (and 'cultured and charming'), believing 'that one can have Christianity without the Cross', a belief of which 'it takes a long time to get the poison out of one's views'. ("*Thank you. Exactly*", was Mother Guenvrede's reply to Aelfrida's last comment, her tertiary having played right into her hands.)[37] She also, and even more revealingly, described Hilda Harrison as someone who missed the masculine element at Tymawr (she had a 'crush' on Father Amos but he did not otherwise count) and who was happiest when accompanying 'a man or men on an adventure' as 'a "good companion" type of woman' (i.e. in a platonic relationship) and another 'pious old maid' as a 'harem-type' who would love a man 'to visit her by night but [wants] him out of the way in the daytime'[38], the latter an interesting comment from one who had recently written of God in terms which Professor Leuba would have regarded as supporting his views on the connection between sexuality and religion: 'how I *long* to let Him have his way with me, in me, through me'.[39]

Hilda's departure left tantrum-prone Mrs Donkin to her own devices. Mother Guenvrede, already ruffled by 'the Library's' disgraceful behaviour (at one point she had accused Hilda and Aelfrida of "behaving as if the place belongs to you" and had announced that, post-war, she would "have no more 'permanent people' here at all")[40], was forced to ask for help to keep her mother amused. Placida seized her opportunity. Having rashly offered to keep Mrs Donkin company for tea and found her offer accepted with alacrity, she negotiated hard: *if* she agreed to 'take duty' with Mrs Donkin 'for a bit on Fridays' and *if* her guardian angel did not consider 'taking duty' to be a breach of silence (he did not), would Mother Guenvrede allow her extra penance as a quid pro quo?[41] Mother Guenvrede agreed. The extra penances (very occasional use of 'St Bruno' and further concessions on silence) were duly practised by a tertiary who so much enjoyed 'the privilege of inhabiting holy precincts … the glory of the Sacramental Presence … the unity with a Community of dedicated – even if perhaps uncongenial – persons' and of living a life 'physically … *liveable*'[42] (but only just) that she disregarded the Mother's threat regarding the probable impermanence of 'permanent people'; indeed, she was so pleased at hearing the Mother invite Father Amos into the (as she thought) empty library with the words "there is nobody here" that she felt sufficiently confident to note '*good*! If I am nobody the Mother won't … send me away, *ever*!!'[43]

But matters other than Mrs Donkin conspired to make Aelfrida thoughtful. Two were prompted by visits from Julius, one by reading a twentieth-century author.

In May 1942 Julius and Aelfrida discussed diaries. Noting how difficult it was to record 'memories of Greece' in a manner vivid enough to make them worth reading by anyone but himself, Julius confided that he was 'no good as a diarist' because unable to "*pose before myself* in the interesting way that true diarists do". Aelfrida 'blushed inwardly': it had never occurred to her that qua diarist she 'posed' before herself but now, she realised, she did.[44] Believing hitherto that her diary was merely a 'rubbish-heap'[45] on which she dumped the detritus of the day and forgot about it (a statement less true now than in earlier days when compartmentalisation had been easier because it had not yet been borne upon her that actions have consequences) or that 'putting things on paper *steadies* me' (true, because once consigned to her diary they did not '[turn] sour or get the moth inside [her] head!'[46] though by 1943 'putting things on paper' in her diary was beginning to prove insufficient outlet for sourness or 'moth'), Aelfrida

looked at herself posing – and looked away. The thought, however, remained, a thought less concerned with being a *poseur* even to herself (something of which she was already aware but preferred to ignore) or, a *poseur's* other self, 'something of a fantasist' (by March 1943 and contrary to Sister Jeanne's advice, Placida was reading secular as well as religious books, significantly in this context Opal Whiteley)[47] and more with finding other outlets for her souring mind. Was silence, she therefore asked herself, the most appropriate estate for her, even though in a seminal talk unmediated by guardian angels God had asked Placida if she had *heard* His call to silence and on her answering "yea Lord", asked her why she had not obeyed?[48] (Aelfrida made no direct response to God's second question but given that she now felt she was living her spiritual life 'too much in isolation' and had begun to believe 'self-naughting' to be 'contrary to nature'[49], perhaps she was beginning to regret her 'vocation' and to realise that although abstention from speech and avoidance of company might promote a "hush of the soul" and the "stilling of individual claims and desires"[50], they had not prevented one prone to give way to temptation from falling or beginning to fall 'into the old pits that … the Evil One … had digged for the vain and the self-willed'[51] or from needing other and perhaps more therapeutic outlets as well.) Or was it because she had 'a mind more apt at distorting … truth than most people's do' (*sic*) that God 'called' her to silence as a 'drastic purgation and recreation'[52] of mental processes so disordered that it was only through His imposed Silence and not her own feeble attempts at taciturnity that damage-limitation could be exercised? In which case, was Mother Guenvrede inspired by God to give her 'permission to retire into silence' because neither Aelfrida nor Placida were 'fit' to talk?[53]

Doubts as to the rightness of her chosen path were underlined by reading CS Lewis's newly-published book *The Screwtape Letters*; she found it 'fascinating' but 'did not enjoy it … and it gave [her] bad dreams'.[54] Given that in it a senior devil ('Screwtape') alternately encourages and admonishes a junior devil ('Wormwood') regarding a 'patient' of the latter's who has recently become a Christian, advising 'Wormwood' to bring his 'patient' to "a condition in which he can practice self-examination … without discovering any of those facts about himself which are perfectly clear to anyone [else]"[55], the book cannot have made comfortable reading for one who posed to herself as a Christian, a mystic, a contemplative, and a hermit, whose "fasts and vigils and … crosses" might well be "only a façade"[56], whose Puritanical contempt for the physical might be "mistaken for purity"[57], and whose beliefs concerning "irresistible and all-excusing

'Love'" might easily induce her to marry – with disastrous results, as "overweening asceticism" strove with "sexuality".[58]

Furthermore, 'Screwtape's' description of 'Wormwood's' patient's mother as a woman who suffers from "the gluttony of Delicacy" and whose life is "enslaved to this kind of sensuality" ("formerly she had other pleasures to distract her") fits Aelfrida perfectly. The woman's 'gluttony of Delicacy', says 'Screwtape' consists in wanting "what … is smaller and less costly" than food set before her[59] ('tepid remains', noted Sister Placida, 'are a good mortification'[60], the phrase applying as much to life as to potatoes) even while not recognising *as* gluttony "her determination to get what she wants however troublesome it may be to others".[61] (In October 1942 the Community began to take their main meal in the evening, reciting None immediately after a snack at 12.30; Placida, however, insisted on having *her* main meal at 12.30 as usual, stating that it was 'not *much* [trouble] to the cook' and that *her* evening meal consisted only of 'Horlicks, etc.' in bed[62]; she also, of course, insisted on her usual 'Lenten fare' regardless of the Community's meal choice of the day and recoiled in horror when obliged to confront a full Christmas dinner, her revulsion aptly illustrating 'Screwtape's' comment that "the particular state of delicacy to which [she is] enslaved is offended by the sight of more food than she happens to want".) Lastly, the delicate glutton believes she is practising "temperance"[63] ('baked egg or soup, warmed up vegetables, a little stewed fruit')[64] when what she is really doing is indulging her appetite for *power*. (This, of course, throws new light on Aelfrida's attitude to food at Tymawr: she is behaving towards Mother Guenvrede exactly as she did to Chiara when, fifty years earlier, her mother forced her to go to school.) But having read the book, Aelfrida dismissed it; considering the books by which she *was* influenced, it is a shame she did, for there was more in it she could have taken profitably to heart.

The second of Julius's visits to render his sister thoughtful took place a year after the first. The occasion was not as cheerful as usual for Julius was 'tired and sad and war-weary' (a recent air raid on Cardiff had shaken him, and Walter, it seemed, might be sent on active service over his adoptive mother's native country as bomber air crew) and expressed a hope that euthanasia might soon be legalised and that if it was, he would seriously consider it as a means of escaping old age, sickness, or long-drawn-out dying. To her diary (and possibly to '*very* dear Dudu' too) Aelfrida expressed horror and disbelief, noting vehemently that it was wrong for a Christian 'whose life and death are in God's hand' to pre-empt Deity's designs. ('For "humanists", perhaps, a lower code of ethics is permissible'.)[65] This diametrically opposed view and lack of reference to her earlier belief in the benefits of euthanasia is significant insofar as it demonstrates a change of heart occasioned by the remembered horror of an episode during which she had overridden her guardian angel's objections in order to be free (a never-admitted reason; it was preferable to think she had liberated her mother) but whether she told Julius then or ever of the reasons for her horror, she does not say.

For someone who now (so she said) read *The Times* only cursorily and was supposed to be cultivating inner silence, Placida continued remarkably well-informed about the progress of the war. Her comments, as one might expect, are mostly moralistic: 'Sunday fighting is sacrilege'[66]; 'is it really necessary to drop two ton bombs at the rate of one a minute on Turin?'[67]; 'I know we *must* beat the Germans but is their death agony to be an entertainment for our tea table?'[68], written of 'heart-rending' broadcasts which drove her from 'library tea' even on Sundays. ('God forbid', she added later, 'that I should be obscurantist and conservative'; even she appreciated that post-war reconstruction might involve more than obedience to Old and New Testament precepts.)[69] Some comments are factual (in 1942, shipping losses to German submarines, the fall of Singapore, Japanese ill-treatment of British prisoners, and the Jews' 'ghastly sufferings'[70]; in 1943, 'starvation etc. etc. in Europe'[71], the defeat of Hitler's 6th Army at Stalingrad, the St Nazaire raids and 'Berlin in flames!'[72]), others are inaccurate or wishful thinking or veiled complaints: fewer clothing coupons 'because garments we might have had are on their way to Russia' and less chocolate because supplies were 'being "vitaminised" for Europe's starving children for when peace comes'.[73] Some, for a professed Christian, are positively vindictive: 'Mussolini has "resigned owing to ill-health". *Sic transit gloria mundi*'[74]; 'the Germans have had their "Dunkirk" … God's Justice has been done'.[75] Others still are summed up by Placida's arrogant reaction to Father Northcott quoting lines from Frederic Myers' 'grand second rate' poem *St Paul* ("desperate tides of the whole great world's anguish / Forced through the channels of a single heart"), namely that 'the anguished desire of the whole world for God seems to force itself through me'.[76] (Her Lenten 'special intention' of 1943 was 'to pray for those who are God's enemies' – not the whole world, it seemed, desired God – those, that is to say, who 'from conviction or ignorance or wickedness or lunacy declare themselves "anti-God"', among whom we find Constantine while married to Aelfrida, it being Mr Graham who provided the model for 'Aaron Lord, Communist' in his wife's unfinished novel.)[77] But perhaps her most significant comment concerns the British victory at El Alamein in November 1942. By government order, church bells (and the Tymawr chapel bell) were pealed and on Mother Guenvrede's instructions the Community sang the 150th psalm after Mass ("Praise ye the Lord, praise God in His sanctuary ... Praise all His mighty acts"); later, they gathered 'much excited' round the wireless to hear the news in full. Only Aelfrida was gloomy, noting lugubriously that 'our chastisement is not over yet' and that 'repentance and trembling hope' were more suitable emotions than exaltation.[78] And perhaps Churchill's warning that the victory was not the end or the beginning of the end but only the end of the beginning provided a timely warning (or a source of inspiration?) for Placida too.

Gloom might, of course, be taken as no more than Aelfrida's disenchanted response to what she described as the all-pervading 'war-tension'[79] which waxed and waned as Britain experienced victory or defeat but it also seems that increasing disillusion with her '*vita nuova*' influenced her description of Britain as 'waiting for the "*Go*"'.[80] Apparently unrelated activities bear witness to this: thoughts of Fordfield's suitability as a 'house for aged gentlewomen' (she was nearing sixty and had considered herself elderly since fifty), sorting out stored books to send to Alethea, and comments that 'the British public' (of which she was willy-nilly one) were 'becoming impatient'[81] with the hard life they were forced by circumstances and authority to lead. Then again, personal 'war-tensions' were due to a local, not a world, war, and in 1943 she too would discover 'chastisement' prevailing over 'trembling hope', suffer defeat at a Stalingrad of her own making, and find herself waiting for the '*Go*'.

Since her last major engagement with Mother Guenvrede, Placida's life had not, in spite of complaints, consisted solely or even largely of 'furnaces and crucibles'; indeed, it seems that the 'holy calm'[82] which descended on Tymawr in May 1942 following Tertiary Christine's departure and, somewhat later, that of warring factions from 'the Library', she actually enjoyed such company as she permitted herself: a Sunday walk with one of the rare visitors, a week of 'talking days' at Christmas and a brief 'tea-time talk' at Epiphany which 'might have been at Cambridge' with a teacher from Cheltenham Ladies' College.[83] News too, was good: of the Connollys in Madagascar (the war in the form of the island's recapture from the Vichy French had penetrated even there)[84]; of Anthony Wrightson, reported in *The Times* to have a daughter now as well as a son[85]; of Fordfield, concerning which the Sisters of Hope kept her informed 'with the greatest dignity and sweetness'[86] of their confidence that they and their patients would be happy as her tenants

and of how they would "keep and care for the place as though it were their own".[87]

Interior and exterior life had pleasant aspects too: visits from Mina 'singularly serene' between bouts of 'melancholia' because her wartime 'life of duty' eased, as her sister-in-law noted perspicaciously, 'the ache of love within'[88]; gardening, termed by Julius her '*labor rusticus*'[89] and approved of by Father Northcott because rustic labour 'balances well with silence'[90] and by Placida because 'hard work down at the [cottage] garden' counterbalanced rarefied existence as a mystic.[91] Visions too though described briefly and in unemotionally ('my Lord stood by me ... and for a minute placed His hands on my head')[92] were occasionally 'perfect, awe-inspiring, beyond speech'[93] and only sparingly 'intellectual' because including both visual impressions ('tiers of adoring angels') and auditions: 'thousands of voices out in the garden and all round me, in choirs, ... softly murmuring [the] Communion Service'.[94] There was even a flash of humour rarely associated with spiritual experiences: 'a *good* week' spent in February 1943 because between prayer and gardening she had 'spent most of my time on my knees (that sounds like Anatolia!)'[95]

If this sounds too good to be true, it was. Trouble began again late in 1942 when Mother Guenvrede informed Aelfrida (and Hilda Harrison, returned for a brief visit) that because the Community was 'tired', outsiders would be excluded from its November Retreat. Worse still, she intended to close the guesthouse during the Retreat, Hilda to keep away and Placida to stay with Julius in Cardiff. ('Everything', wrote Aelfrida on receiving the news, 'went dark and confused but I cling to the certainty that God wants me *here*'.) Pleas failing to move the Mother, she tried moral pressure ('stability, continuity, an unbroken Rule are of the essence of the contemplative life'; the Mother could not point 'to a single voluntary absence from Office') and bribery: 'a *huge* box of nuts ... gathered and cleaned and ripened for the Community'[96], '2 wheelbarrows full of my best books ... from Cambridge – and £10 for fuel'[97], and, on St Guenvrede's Day, 'a pot of my best geraniums' and a note informing the Mother that her tertiary was keeping a novena for her.[98] Having prayed for advice, Mother Guenvrede relented ('surely *propter hoc!*' wrote Aelfrida, feeling that the novena had swayed the balance)[99] and Placida enjoyed a pleasant private Retreat during which, as if to show whose side He was on, she heard a voice saying "come thou bride of Christ, receive the crown which the Lord hath prepared for thee" and again experienced Christ Himself lifting the crown of thorns from His head to 'let it rest ... for a moment'[100] on hers.

Whether it was the Mother's inconsistent behaviour in trying to send away (albeit only for a month) a tertiary once refused leave of absence to visit a sick relative, or the stark contrast between Hilda's stay in a cosy comfortable house and her own Retreat in a single room whose windows were so iced up that she could not open them till midday, or aggrieved feelings at not being 'the first tertiary to be called home' ('I thought *I* should have been', though the fact that even a foundation-tertiary received a 'Low Mass' instead of a 'beautiful Requiem' consoled her)[101], it was, it seems, at this juncture that the iron entered Mrs Graham's soul. (Or, as she preferred to put it, 'the same darkness over [Tymawr] as there had been over Oxford when God was bidding me leave it'.)[102] She therefore began to contemplate a strategic retreat.

She did not make concrete plans at this stage; indeed and instead, she fought to remain – the war was not yet over and she herself liable for war-work if she left – but from the general tenor of her diary we sense growing disillusionment with conventual life and a growing need to move beyond its confines. Then too, and although Mother Guenvrede congratulated her on her quietness during the Retreat (Placida attended the *opus Dei* but spoke to no-one), the focus of her injured feelings increasingly rested on that lady. Hence although Placida continued to respect her, Aelfrida did her best to exasperate her and to undermine her authority because 'God must discipline' Mother Guenvrede for injustices inflicted on her innocent tertiary.[103] Deeming insinuation less likely to see her sent away than accusation, when Father Northcott enquired at post-Christmas confession about Placida's relationship with the Mother, he received the ambiguous response that although Mother Guenvrede was helpful when approached directly, indirectly she acted so as to inhibit her tertiary's 'luxuriant spiritual growth'.[104] But on Northcott wilfully or unwittingly ignoring her hint that all was not well between tertiary and Superior, Aelfrida stepped up her attack.

She began by humbling herself before the other members of the Community as a hint to that though they, as spiritually superior beings, were able to bear Mother Guenvrede's oppressive regime, 'I am not'[105] and, following a spat with the Mother (Placida had obliterated tractor access to a neighbouring field with a new flower border) by informing Hilda Harrison (now, since Aelfrida saw her only intermittently, 'the most congenial of all the women who have been here' and much missed as a result) that though 'mad or sane' Mother Guenvrede had yielded her will to God, she was now showing symptoms of 'persecution mania' and was liable to go 'quite mad'.[106] What Aelfrida did not appreciate, however, was that the Mother's supposed 'mania' was fuelled

by Placida's incremental mental unease (an unease exacerbated by Hilda Harrison's lengthy absences and by her own solitude and silence, isolation and incarceration being liable to lead to emotional hypersensitivity and even to frank psychosis in predisposed subjects) and that when Placida withdrew into herself ostensibly to answer a 'further demand for Silence [and] intimate self-sacrifice' because 'right at the core of [her] being there was still noise … displeasing to God'[107], it was actually to brood on the increasing 'madness' of a woman very like herself and to forget how Mrs Graham had been taken in desolate and scorbutic by the very Community she now set out to harm in the person of its Superior. Given that it was hard to find concrete evidence of the Mother's supposed insanity – she was, Aelfrida admitted, as 'masterly over business as she is with the hay cutter'[108] (a machine ridden in full habit) and exhibited a sense of humour even when exasperated by Placida's behaviour, "No. Boo! Go away! You are in Silence!" being her retort to the latter's offer to help cock the hay[109] – all might have gone well because it was God's Will that Placida 'try and order [herself] lowly and reverently to … [her] betters'[110], had not an incident, trivial in itself but symptomatic of Aelfrida's increasing distaste for conventual life, caused a blitzkrieg all its own.

In August 1943 Aelfrida's sleep and Mrs Graham's moral sense were disturbed by the night games and scrumping of convent fruit by a troupe of Boy Scouts from the Cardiff slums camped in a nearby field. Instead of informing Mother Guenvrede, Placida complained directly to the scoutmaster who himself complained to Mother Guenvrede. Aelfrida pleaded innocence ('I was completely at sea … I couldn't see what all the fuss was about … my conscience is perfectly clear') then, as usual and after accusations from the Mother of presuming to act without her permission, contrition ('dear Lord … make me teachable, submissive, wise') but was inwardly furious. Fury at the Mother's seeming injustice ('she is always telling me not to bother her') was, however, tempered with fear ('my natural self is afraid … I have started to slip down into the old pits') for as part of her 'scolding' Mother Guenvrede had informed Aelfrida that she had told 'someone' (probably the scoutmaster) that Placida was "not quite responsible" (touching her forehead as she spoke) and although Aelfrida professed to take this lightly ('she and I are agreed on the matter of my sanity') it seems that this and earlier statements that Placida was 'odd' because thoughts tended to turn 'sour' inside her head[111] in the absence of adequate outlet, gave rise to greater resentment: who was Mother Guenvrede to deem her tertiary mad when she was 'not quite responsible' herself? An alternative feeling that perhaps her own 'tiresomeness' and the Mother's rages (the Boy Scouts incident was only the most recent 'tiresomeness') had paradoxically brought them closer through mutual forgiveness[112] and that the peaceful period which preceded the incident was indicative that both ladies had unhooked their malevolent 'attention' from each other[113], lured Placida into a state of false security. In late August 1943 she received a severe shock: Mother Guenvrede intended to close the guesthouse 'for all October' and to send away her resident tertiary and 'own Mama'. Enquiring why, Placida received the chilling response "the Community wants the place to itself" and, on enquiring if she herself was not 'Community', the chilling rebuff "No. Not in that respect".[114]

Having lain awake till 4am 'just *suffering*', Aelfrida marshalled her forces. First she objected on principle 'to taking a completely unnecessary journey in wartime'. Then she asked 'what would become of the Cottage garden if no-one touched it for a whole month'. Then she tried bribery: £5 as a thank offering for not having missed Mass for a year. Then she pleaded physical frailty: she was 'not strong enough to … travel'.[115] Then, having had a 'shewing' at Mass of 'the Mother's spirit in glory' and heard a voice telling her to love Mother Guenvrede 'as the embodiment of the Community with the very love wherewith the Persons of the Holy Trinity love each other', she regaled her with the news at a subsequent 'audience' (not, be it noted, 'a nice motherly chat') as a reminder that it was not a mere tertiary but a visionary mystic who was being rejected 'just as in marriage … a man can put away his wife when he is cross and call it incompatibility'.[116] Ruses having failed, she decided to act on her guardian angel's advice to 'just disappear' into a 'quiet room at Trellech' near the church (preferably in the rectory itself) where she could behave outwardly 'just as Mrs Graham (sister of Professor Tillyard of Cardiff)'[117] while inwardly keeping her Rule, but her plan was inadvertently revealed to Mother Guenvrede by the rector himself. (The Mother was insistent that Aelfrida 'say nothing' to anyone 'of what goes on here'[118] because only *she* had the authority to do so; she was also afraid that Placida would prattle and had begun to censor her outgoing letters, a move circumvented by Mrs Graham posting them in a distant mailbox instead of the convent's.) She then resorted to manipulation in the course of which she successively involved Chaplain, Warden and Visitor. Then, having achieved nothing but a dressing-down from 'testy, censorious and impatient'[119] Father Northcott and a series of increasingly 'adamant' letters from Mother Guenvrede ("from 30 September to 30 October day to day exact we want the place to ourselves … I do *not* give my permission for you to go

to any place or home except a convent guesthouse or your brother's. You need not visit your relatives if you don't want but book quickly [elsewhere] *or* you will find yourself roofless … if you stay anywhere in the neighbourhood I shall take you off the list of tertiaries and not have you inside Tymawr again … and if you don't arrange for a convent … I shall ask Brother Julius to come and fetch you on the appointed day")[120], she capitulated – but not before pointing out that 'Julius's house, though a sweet spot' (a lie; she regarded it as Teutonically gloomy and crammed with kitsch German artefacts) 'is still "the world"'[121] and that going there would compromise interior silence, tertiary stability, and spiritual poverty. On 10 September 1943 she wrote to Julius asking him to 'let me occupy his big attic and keep my Rule as best I can under his roof [as] October is the Community's rest month'. (She appears to have given him no hint of the battle raging between herself and Mother Guenvrede when he visited on 8 September.)[122] On 30 September she departed for Cardiff, leaving Woodbine Cottage weeds 'abashed'.[123] Before leaving, however, she came to two conclusions, one with regard to Mother Guenvrede, the other to herself.

During a retreat conducted by Father Cary in Oxford in 1936, Aelfrida heard him discourse with 'tremendous reality' on the devil. Calling the devil mankind's 'ghostly foe', Cary stated that no-one, however spiritually 'seasoned', could escape him, for the devil, encountering such a person, '*intensified*' his attack or changed his mode of attack, 'the seasoned spiritual warrior' with whom he strove finding him or herself engaged in combat of truly 'aweful (*sic*) intensity'. So impressed by the fervour of Father Cary's discourse that she vowed '*never*' to forget it[124], August 1943 (coincidentally or not on the very day that Mother Guenvrede announced temporary closure of the guest-house) found Aelfrida recalling Cary's message with reference to Mother Guenvrede who, judging by her 'shattered' demeanour must be, if not actually diabolically possessed, pressed closely upon by her 'familiar devil'.[125] Remembering too that during Cary's discourse she had been struck by the 'dark dark abysses of agony' behind his eyes[126], Aelfrida drew parallels between Cary's earlier mental breakdown and Mother Guenvrede's impending one and recalled a warning received from God earlier that year that she herself might be '*used* against the powers of darkness'. Deciding, however, that the Community would be terrified if the news became common knowledge, Placida appointed herself 'my beloved Mother-in-Christ's *bodyguard*' (she had, she wrote, been trained by Lucius Cary for this 'special work') and prepared to open battle 'against the power of evil that beset her'.[127]

This, of course, says more about Aelfrida's state of mind than Mother Guenvrede's but is unsurprising given a belief in the existence of the devil and diabolic forces which long antedated Lucius Cary's sermon, its content in this respect being supportive rather than inspirational. Her views derived from adolescent readings of Thomas à Kempis whose *Imitation of Christ* stated that "the Devil never sleeps … but prowls around seeking whom he may devour", that (something particularly relevant to her present life) there was "no Order so holy nor place so secluded" that Satan could not penetrate, and that one of the practices of a "Good Religious" was to arm himself "manfully" against the foe.[128] It says something too about Placida's current thoughts concerning herself and her surroundings, namely that there was 'ugly' and 'wicked' noise, displeasing to God, 'at the very core of [her] being'[129] ('ugly' and 'wicked' were very strong words in her vocabulary and by 'noise' she does not mean lack of silence) and that the devil was abroad in the world, the latter sentiment underlined by a vision during which Christ forced her to look upwards directly at God (an action she 'could not sustain') then backwards 'at the Evil One and his legions', at 'Satanists', and at books which made 'evil seem more real and the powers of darkness more active'. And is it purely coincidental that the man to whose books, life and legions Aelfrida could conceivably be referring was staying less than twenty miles from Tymawr, he having sought temporary respite from London bombing raids on 17 June 1943 at Tredegar Park near Newport with fellow practitioner of Ceremonial Magic, Evan Morgan, 2nd Viscount Tredegar? The man was Aleister Crowley.[130]

Being sent to Cardiff at this juncture naturally horrified Mother Guenvrede's 'bodyguard', particularly as the latter's 'familiar devil' had recently won a 'great victory' over one whose supposed mental instability seemed to support Richard Meux Benson's contention that there was "no place Satan will attack so much as a religious House" and that this being the case, there would be "a gathering of the powers of darkness [over it] such as nowhere else".[131] Espying from a worsening of the Mother's symptoms (stubbornness, love of power, cruelty, 'she *enjoyed* making *me* suffer', etc.) that 'the welfare of an immortal soul [was] at stake' and that the Mother's 'precious, precious soul' was in grave danger ('ah! not to outer darkness, dear Lord, let it not be, my pen shudders, my eyes are full of tears'), Placida pleaded that God arm her to fight as she had never fought 'for anything or anyone' before. Her weapons, primarily '*prayer*', were also to include penance (though the Mother 'would be suspicious if [she] asked for Saint Bruno'), '*humour*' ('the light barbed arrow can pierce'), and 'willingness to suffer' in such a good cause.[132]

Her conviction deepened on receipt of Mother Guenvrede's notes, notes which must have been 'dictated by the devil who holds the outskirts of her personality'. In need of earthly help against the '*frantic*' powers of evil gathering over Tymawr, 'bodyguard' turned to Father Northcott. Composing letters in which she confined herself to 'facts [not] feelings' (*sic*) and approaching the matter 'from the viewpoint of one who has seen the Mother's soul as it will be in glory' but aware that she had taken an 'extremely serious step' in complaining of Superior to Warden, she also declaimed (in her diary) that she had '*defied the powers of evil*' for the sake of Mother Guenvrede's soul and for the glory of God 'must not ask for any profit for [herself] and no wages except pain'.[133] And pain was what she received in the form of Father Northcott's 'testy, censorious and impatient' reply and body-guarding profited her nothing, for 'without protest, heartbroken but grateful for privileges [received]', she left for Cardiff as planned. And it cannot have sweetened her departure to see Mother Guenvrede looking relieved and '*radiant*' at Placida's surrender to someone whose position gave her every right to enforce it.[134]

That, of course, was the crux of the problem but as Aelfrida's comments show, there was more to the matter than this. Her panicky reaction to threats of being sent away in 1942 and to being actually sent away (albeit temporarily) in 1943 was, as she herself dimly realised, a reaction to being forced into doing what she did not want to do but was powerless to prevent: surrendering to a man's sexual demands, weeding a flower bed, ringing a chapel bell, attending school, or being sent by a 'cruel' mother and a 'testy impatient' father to Other Dear's house in Harston, a place which, though 'sweet' and inhabited by beloved and familiar people, was not home. It was not, therefore, solely Mother Guenvrede having informed the Trellech rector that Mrs Graham was 'mad' or Placida that she 'trusted' Julius[135] (to look after his mentally-compromised sister?) though both comments were undoubtedly relevant, which made Aelfrida suddenly snap out of her delusion on 11 September: 'of course [all] this may be just my imagination'. It was also realisation 'that there is something wrong with *me* [because] all these cross-currents rouse too many echoes in my brain'.[136] Realising too that in reliving a 'tragic tale'[137] suggestive of earlier tragedies, she had been in a very dark place, Aelfrida came to her second conclusion: to restore her sanity she needed therapy. So, defying Father Cary but with Mother Guenvrede's instant approval of 'authorship for me', she began a book. 'The relief was instantaneous!'[138]

Her decision to do so shortly before leaving for Cardiff is all the more significant given that only a month earlier she had informed the former curate of St

Thomas' Church, Oxford (now 'Father Lucas of Swanley, Kent', on retreat at Tymawr for a week; at his request Placida was allowed a talk with him) that "No, no, *no!*" she had no intention of writing any more books and her diary that 'I don't think I shall ever write again'.[139] But her request two weeks later that the rector of Trellech find her a room 'near the church and quiet, where [she] could write a book'[140] suggests a sudden change of mind. For the rest of her life she wrote compendiously and almost uninterruptedly, updating her spiritual autobiography tome by tome and providing her biographer with material hitherto omitted from or only hinted at in her sixty-one volumes of diary to date.

In forcing her to write only letters and her diary, Cary had exacted more perfect revenge on his disobedient penitent than he knew. (Or had he, as Aelfrida suggested in *The Spiritual Director*, been ignorant of what really motivated her, his ignorance arising more from lack of knowledge of or misinformation about her earlier life than from spiritual arrogance causing him to think that he knew what was best for her?) In forbidding her to write the *romans à clef* or homiletic books in which so much of her life was expressed, Cary effectively condemned her to further madness for letters were henceforth confined to pious platitudes and her diary, even when written at tedious length, could provide only limited release for one who needed to put her thoughts into fictional or literary form before properly confronting them. What he had not foreseen, however, was the dreadful effect his ban would have on others besides Aelfrida, in particular the SSC and Mother Guenvrede, though worth noting in Cary's defence is that even after turning again to 'authorship', Aelfrida's behaviour did not improve to the expected extent and that it was this as much as her behaviour towards Mother and Warden in September 1943 which determined the subsequent course of her life in Monmouthshire. Aelfrida herself, with good reason, was now keen to absolve Father Cary from blame, noting that she had 'forgotten' his advice that she '*should* put things on paper' (a fact omitted from her contemporary account of their interview) and that because she had 'stupidly … connected … ideas of writing and [of] publication', had stopped writing altogether. Be this as it may, she retrieved her 'most enchanting pile of manuscript paper' from Hilda Harrison and began work: 'I have got a lumber jam of half a dozen books inside my head [but] I needn't write six, one will let the current flow steadily again'.[141]

Noting how 'very improvident and extravagant' it was to start a new book on new paper in wartime when every scrap of paper was precious – her subject, appropriately under the circumstances, was *Hell and the Powers of Darkness* and her theme that 'exclusion from the Divine Presence is sole and sufficient punishment' for transgression and guilt nothing but choosing 'darkness' – Aelfrida also noted two important points. The first was that the process of putting her thoughts on paper – and even the thoughts themselves – was still 'too much charged with emotion to be worth much yet' and that both process and thoughts would have to have their 'temperature' reduced before they were worth developing, the second, and more important, being that the moment she put pen to paper and thoughts began to flow, her 'mental temperature' went down to normal (a debatable point) and she experienced enormous '*catharsis*'. (The cathartic effect of relieving tensions pent up for five years was enhanced by not writing on 'odd scraps' of paper, a clean sheet and a new leaf indeed.)[142] Catharsis was coincidentally enhanced by the breaking-up in huge thunderstorms of the sultry weather which had accompanied her delusions and by the opportunity of confession to the current Visitor (now Bishop O'Ferrall, Sister Sheila's brother) during which she gave no inkling of what recently transpired between herself and Mother Guenvrede beyond noting that the difficulty she had in 'getting in touch' with the Mother was not a spiritual one but because the latter was 'in the last stage of physical and mental exhaustion'.

Having made it clear to Chaplain, Warden and Visitor that, catharsis or no catharsis, she considered the Mother mentally unhinged and believing that '[even] if I never know what lies behind all this … I *have* done my Master's beloved will'[143], Aelfrida looked forward to her sojourn in Cardiff. ('The thought of helping Mina with the washing up is very attractive'[144]; can it be that it was as much from a desire to remove Aelfrida from the rarefied world in which she lived and to remind her of the real world of wartime England as from a desire to relieve the Community of an irritant, that Mother Guenvrede sent her to Cardiff and that Aelfrida herself realised the wisdom of this?) She took missal, diurnal and 'Saint Guenvrede' with her but left her guardian angel behind as proxy 'bodyguard'.[145] *Hell and the Powers of Darkness* remained unfinished (traces appear in later works) but the act of authorship alone had begun to free her from her demons: 'there is so much that I cannot see but I feel that the powers of darkness have had a defeat. (Perhaps they were threatening *me* and I never saw them.)'[146] Her parenthetical remark forms the most notable part of her statement.

Leaving Tymawr, however, she took with her not only books of devotion, discipline and Rule, but 'furnaces and crucibles' too, discovering in Cardiff that escape from God's 'quiet laboratory' was impossible. She also experienced 'the tug of the world'[147] more strongly than ever and Julius fell in love with her all over again.

# Notes

1  GCPPT 1|1|60 30 July 1942.
2  ibid. 2 July 1942.
3  ibid. 7 July 1942.
4  ibid. 1 September 1942.
5  ibid. 5 July 1942.
6  ibid. 4 September 1942.
7  ibid. 2 October 1942.
8  ibid. 14 October 1942.
9  Tillyard, HJW. *Synopsis of Diary* 30 March 1942 (MTC).
10  GCPPT 1|1|60 24 July 1942.
11  ibid. 30 October and 'All Souls' (2 November) 1942.
12  ibid. 25 October and 7 November 1942.
13  ibid. 'All Souls' (2 November) 1942.
14  ibid. 18 January 1943.
15  ibid. 25 October 1942.
16  GCPPT 1|1|60 18 January 1943.
   GCPPT 1|1|61 'Holy Cross Day' (3 May) and 10 May 1943.
17  Benson, RM. *Instructions on the Religious Life* pp 115–116.
18  GCPPT 1|1|61 28 April 1942.
19  GCPPT 1|1|60 26 December 1942.
20  GCPPT 1|1|61 26 March 1943.
21  GCPPT 1|1|60 27 December 1942.
22  GCPPT 1|1|61 7 February 1943.
23  GCPPT 1|1|60 31 January 1942.
24  GCPPT 1|1|61 4 March and 5 May 1943.
25  GCPPT 11|57 28 November 1939.
26  GCPPT 1|1|61 8, 13 and 14 May 1943.
27  GCPPT 1|1|60 12 January 1943.
28  Writing to Aelfrida in December 1942, Cary attributed their dissatis-faction to there being "too many Superiors liking to exercise author-ity who would be better as simple Sisters" in larger Communities, too "numerous small convents each with its chaplain and apparatus of worship" and "too many Superiors of small Orders fishing in the small available pond for postulants" (GCPPT 1|1|60 23 December 1942). Aelfrida's only comment was 'I wonder'; she does not appear to have shown this letter to Mother Guenvrede.
29  ibid. 12 January 1943.
30  ibid. 8 December 1942 and 2 February 1943.
31  GCPPT 1|1|61a Draft of a letter from Aelfrida to Hilda Harrison of 23 January 1944.
32  GCPPT 1|1|61 2 January and 14 February 1943.
33  ibid. 12 May 1943.
34  GCPPT 1|1|60 25 January 1943.
35  ibid. 12 January 1943.
36  ibid. 18 January 1943.
37  ibid. 28 January 1943.
38  GCPPT 1|1|61 24 February 1943.
39  GCPPT 1|1|60 2 October 1942.
40  GCPPT 1|1|61 27 April 1943.
41  ibid. 25 May 1943.
42  ibid. 9 May 1943.
43  ibid. 21 May 1943.
44  GCPPT 1|1|60 9 May 1942.
45  ibid. 23 July 1942.
46  GCPPT 1|1|61 30 July 1943.
47  Opal Whiteley (1897–1991), American nature writer and diarist, pub-lished her childhood journal as *The Story of Opal* in 1921. Whiteley was convinced that her parents were adoptive and that she was actually the daughter of Henri d'Orléans (obit 1901). Marie Bashkirtsev's pub-lished diaries, read by Aelfrida as an adolescent, are also prime examples of someone posing to herself.
48  GCPPT 1|1|61 29 April 1943.
49  GCPPT 1|1|60 7 and 9 November 1942.
50  Tillyard, Ae. *Christian Old Age* p 86 (GCPPT 2/17).
51  GCPPT 1|1|61 3 August 1943.
52  ibid. 18 May 1943.
53  ibid. 30 April 1943.
54  ibid. 3 August 1943.
55  Lewis, CS. p 21.
56  ibid. p 112.
57  ibid. p 99.
58  ibid. pp 99 and 105.
59  ibid. pp 86–88.
60  GCPPT 1|1|60 4 November 1942.
61  Lewis, CS. pp 86–88.
62  GCPPT 1|1|60 31 October 1942.
63  Lewis CS. pp 86–88.
64  GCPPT 1|1|60 31 October 1942.
65  GCPPT 1|1|61 19 and 21 May 1943.
66  GCPPT 1|1|60 2 August 1942.
67  ibid. 25 November 1942.
68  ibid. 1 February 1943.
69  GCPPT 1|1|61 4 March 1943.
70  GCPPT 1|1|60 23 December 1942.
71  ibid. 24 January 1943.
72  GCPPT 1|1|61 4 March 1943.
73  ibid. 16 July 1943.
74  ibid. 26 July 1943.
75  ibid. 15 August 1943.
76  GCPPT 1|1| 60 18 January 1943. Myers' *St Paul* poem of 1867 was written after his 1865 'conversion' from Hellenism to Christianity; his life at the time of composition sounds remarkably like Aelfrida's later one, involving as it did "prayer, self-discipline and inner rap-ture" (*ODNB* vol 40 pp 59–62) In 1869 Myers, influenced by Henry Sidgwick, abandoned Christianity for Spiritualism.
77  GCPPT 1|1|61 7 March and 'Ash Wednesday' (10 March) 1943.
78  GCPPT 1|1|60 15 November 1942.
79  ibid. 9 August 1942.
80  GCPPT 1|1|61 30 May 1943.
81  GCPPT 1|1|60 4 and 12 August 1942.
82  ibid. 22 May 1942.
83  ibid. 1 January and 'Epiphany' (6 January) 1943.
84  ibid. 9 May 1942.
85  ibid. 18 October 1942.
86  GCPPT 1|1|61 28 February 1943.
87  ibid. 19 June 1943.
88  ibid. 24 February 1943.
89  Tillyard, HJW. *Synopsis of Diary* 8 May 1942 (MTC).
90  GCPPT 1|1|61 18 May 1943.
91  ibid. 9 June 1943.
92  ibid. 10 May 1943.
93  GCPPT 1|1|60 11 November 1942.
94  GCPPT 1|1|61 15 August 1943.
95  ibid. 20 February 1943.
96  GCPPT 1|1|60 30 October 1942.
97  ibid. 31 October 1942.
98  ibid. 'St Guenvrede's Day' (3 November) 1942.
99  ibid. 9 November 1942.
100  ibid. 22 November 1942.
101  ibid. 18, 22 and 25 November 1942.
102  GCPPT 1|1|61 29 April 1943.
103  GCPPT 1|1|60 24 November 1942.
104  ibid. 18 January 1943.
105  ibid. 5 February 1943.
106  GCPPT 1|1|61 27 and 28 April 1943.
107  ibid. 15 June 1943.

108  ibid. 8 July 1943.

109  ibid. 29 June 1943.

110  ibid. 29 July 1943.

111  ibid. 29 July, 1 and 3 August 1943.

112  ibid. 10 July 1943.

113  ibid. 20 April 1943.

114  ibid. 23 August 1943.

115  ibid. 23 and 26 August and 8 September 1943.

116  ibid. 10, 17 and 19 September 1943.

117  ibid. 6 and 7 September 1943.

118  ibid. 14 May 1943.

119  ibid. 18 November 1943.

120  1|1|61a. Undated notes from Mother Guenvrede to Aelfrida labelled by the latter 'notes from the Rev. Mother SSC'.

121  GCPPT 1|1|61 8 September 1943.

122  GCPPT 1|1|60 10 September 1943.

123  ibid. 'Michaelmas' (29 September) 1943.

124  GCPPT 1|1|52 13 November 1936.

125  GCPPT 1|1|61 23 August 1943.

126  GCPPT 1|1|52 13 November 1936.

127  GCPPT 1|1|61 28 June and 23 August 1943.

128  À Kempis, T. pp 39–41, 48 and 80.

129  GCPPT 1|1|61 15 June 1943.

130  ibid. 15 and 28 June and 3 July 1943. This was not the only coincidence occurring in summer 1943. On 31 May a '*grande dame* … old frail and wistful' but looking 'as if she might be Somebody' (GCPPT 1|1|61 31 May 1943) arrived at Tymawr. Maud Graham was the widow of Douglas Graham JP of Wonastow Court near Monmouth and she was 'wistful' because she had been obliged to evacuate her house on it being requisitioned for army use. Distressed by her loss, Mrs Maud Graham poured her 'pathos and problems' over Mrs Constantine Graham 'like a flood' and although the latter complained to her diary about the 'fresh burdens she had to bear on [her] heart', that conversation with her namesake unfitted her for 'listening to the voice of God', and that if God spoke she might miss 'some of what He asked of [her]' (ibid. 10 July 1943), it is obvious that she enjoyed Maud Graham's 'genuine "county" conversation' (a fact noted by Mother Guenvrede and subsequently held against a tertiary who pleaded for more '*Silence*') for though Aelfrida felt happier when relieved, as now, of Hilda Harrison's 'moods and difficulties', Hilda had been 'something of a "woman consolation"' (ibid. 31 May 1943) of the kind once derided but clung to now. Maud Graham, however, did not stay long, leaving on 28 July to return home and accompanied by a signed copy of Aelfrida's *Night Watches* inscribed to "to dear Mrs Graham". Her departure after only two months seems strange, given that once the army requisitioned a house it usually remained requisitioned until the end of the war, but its release may have come about because of action taken by Maud's near neighbour, also a JP, Viscount Tredegar. Can it be that, hearing from him of Mrs (Maud) Graham's recent vicissitudes and discovering that a Mrs Graham lived at Tymawr (a fact that the Viscount, who took his public duties very seriously, could have derived from other sources) and eliding or confusing the two ladies, Crowley wrote to 'Mrs Graham' commiserating with her problems and expounding a few of his own and that Mrs Maud Graham received the latter and passed it on to Mrs Constantine Graham, she promptly complaining of the weight of 'other folks' (in the plural) troubles bearing on her heart? (It was not only Maud Graham's troubles of which Aelfrida wrote though that lady is the only 'folk' specifically named). Can it also be that Aelfrida replied to Crowley's letter but instead of offering him the same spiritual and material assistance that he had generously and willingly offered to her in 1913, spurned him rudely, accompanying her rejection with edifying remarks and pious platitudes employed in letters to those she believed might be impressed by them and with descriptions of her life as a tertiary and of how she now practised reparative adoration in silence and solitude for her own and others' (including his) sins instead of the Lesser Ritual of the Pentagram with the aid of a red ruler?

131  Benson, R.M. *The Religious Vocation* p 219.

132  GCPPT 1|1|61 7 September 1943.

133  ibid. 9 September 1943.

134  ibid. 10 September 1943.

135  ibid.

136  ibid. 11 and 12 September 1943.

137  ibid. 9 September 1943.

138  ibid. 12 September 1943.

139  ibid. 16, 21 and 25 July 1943.

140  ibid. 6 September 1943.

141  ibid. 12 September 1943.

142  ibid. 12 and 13 September 1943.

143  ibid. 13 September 1943.

144  ibid. 28 September 1943.

145  ibid. 7 and 28 September 1943.

146  ibid. 16 September 1943.

147  GCPPT 1|1|62 9 August 1944.

# Tug of the World

Churchill's description of November 1942 British victories in North Africa as "not the end … not even the beginning of the end [but] perhaps the end of the beginning"[1] applies to Aelfrida's state of mind in late 1943. *Her* Alamein, however, was a battle lost, for Mother Guenvrede's insistence that Mrs Graham visit Cardiff was both a victory over her tertiary-adversary and an event with repercussions for Placida's future as a member of the Community.

Placida's view differed, she writing even before departure that she had come to Tymawr 'seeking the quenching of [her] spiritual thirst' and 'oh! how abundantly that has been satisfied' but that it now seemed 'time to go' and '*is* the pillar of fire and cloud moving on?'[2] That the pillar *was* 'moving on', albeit slowly, for she had no intention of leaving Tymawr permanently until the end of the war, she deduced from 'the return of the impulse to write' and from 'a strange "*nunc dimittis*" feeling' that God was bidding His servant depart (in peace, if possible) according to His word. It also seemed that 'a … "*consummatum est*"' not of her seeking or doing had been achieved and 'as if some chapter in the Community's history were over'.[3]

A feeling that she and Tymawr were nearly 'over' each other is clear from her exposition of what seven years' residence had 'made plain' of tertiary life. That it had taken all that time 'for the forging of a tertiary and for making her an instrument of God's Will'. That she now possessed 'the 'definite tertiary's vocation in all its suppleness and mobility', interesting adjectives given her former inflexibility and determination not to be removed and that insofar as tertiary 'presence' was spiritual not geographical, there was no further need to 'stand firm *here*'.[4] Three further entries support her contention, one noting that Hilda Harrison (or as it might be, herself) had evinced both gladness at the prospect of leaving Tymawr and eagerness to be gone[5], the second a serendipitous coincidence of events (or possibly a parable) during which out on 'a "Te Deum" walk' during which she thanked God that she and Mother Guenvrede were now in accord, she liberated a rabbit from a snare with the words "you are now free and well. You may go" before pushing the snare deep into the ground lest it inflict pain on another creature.[6] The third and most significant was that it behoved

The Figure on the Tree, Campo Santo, Tymawr

her to behave as Mother Guenvrede's 'thorn in the flesh' because, 'from the heavenly point of view', it was as a 'thorn' that she kept the Mother humble. Qua 'thorn', she also provided a nail to fasten the Sisters 'to the True Cross' insofar as 'thorny' behaviour upset the Mother so much that her anger affected the whole Community, and because in personal terms behaving as a thorn '*intensified*' her own love through the infliction of pain: '*the more I was hurt, the more I could love*'.[7]

This truly terrible explanation of her conduct explains much about Aelfrida's relationships with other people:

because she could only love when hurt, she had to behave hurtfully in order to be able to love people who, loving her, were hurt by her behaviour towards them and hurt her in return. (Had Constantine suspected this – and what new light this throws on Aelfrida's sentimental feelings towards him after the breakdown of her marriage – and not married her, how much unhappiness might he and his children have been spared. Willie Searle and Anthony Wrightson did not hurt her – though her 'cat and mouse' behaviour towards both men gave them plenty of opportunity, they did not take it – so she could never have truly loved them. Albert Erlande certainly hurt her; did she therefore love him?) But if Aelfrida felt compelled to exist in a perpetual state of enmeshed hate and love, what does that say of her relationship with God? Did He too have to hurt her before she loved Him? And if He had not hurt her (as she believed He had), would she have been able to sustain her belief in Him and love Him as she did?

It was necessary, of course, for Aelfrida to rationalise thoughts of departure so as to present them in a good light to herself and others. She therefore phrased them as altruistically in terms of the *Community*'s future with only a hint at her own: because there was to be 'no *private* building till long after the war' (Mother Guenvrede was already planning for post-war expansion) and because there were once again aspirants queuing for admission, Placida would be blocking a room if she stayed and be unmissed if she went; if she stayed and if the guest-house was empty of visitors or used as an overflow 'convent', 'it would mean complete silence' for which she was not yet spiritually ready, and so on. Then having decided that 'where the pillar of fire and cloud goes, there I will follow'[8], she followed it (in the first instance) to Cardiff.

'It *was* sunshine at [Cardiff] – sunshine of "human consolations" but my guardian angel … *allowed* them so I had no hesitations', wrote Placida of 'sunshine' rationalised as '*a test of detachment*' from which she would emerge able 'to *use* "human consolations" without being bound by them'. Reading between the lines of her retrospective account, however, we realise that Aelfrida enjoyed every moment of her stay: hot baths every night, congenial company ('dear Julius [and] dear Mina … full of graciousness and *caritas*', their intellectual friends, and their lodgers, one a retired French-speaking consul with whom Mrs Graham achieved instant rapport, the other a student suffering a nervous breakdown from 'loneliness and overwork' to whose condition the former Straightener believed herself sent by God to speak – and speak she did), walks during which she 'chattered away' to 'dear Dudu', keeping her Rule but not so Silence and Solitude obtruded overmuch.[9] On one matter she says nothing: her sixtieth birthday on 5 October 1943, the

day on which she became eligible for the old age pension and ineligible for 'war service.'

Returning to Tymawr on 30 October to 'a "Benedictine" welcome as if [she] had not been away' ('a few kisses and a few words of welcome, that is all'; did she expect more?) Placida expressed delight that 'the spirit of discord and suspicion' prevalent prior to her departure had been ejected by '*prayers*' and an intention of being 'so quiet, so quiet that … the Mother won't send me away again'. But 'dear me!' she added, 'I have had to mortify my curiosity': Sister Monica had been absent ('!???!!') and Novice Isabel's query "I suppose you have heard about our goings-on while you were away?" sent her into paroxysms of frustration: '"goings-on" ??!!! – I didn't ask, tried not to want to know!'[10] But the 'tug of the world', that 'unconscious but powerful pull of old associations and of places deeply loved' was renewed just as she thought it vanquished[11] and was accompanied by reflections that Placida, like the Community, had passed through her 'first wonderful period of enthusiasm' and through a 'period of organisation [and] consolidation' and had now entered a 'period of waiting' in which the fire of initial enthusiasm burned so low that only 'spiritual quickening' from elsewhere could re-ignite it.[12]

Tugs took several forms but all involved the quickening effect of 'human consolations' Placida believed she had put behind her for ever. They began with the most unlikely person: during her absence in Cardiff, 'the Reverend Percy Stanley called'. Though touched that her suitor-cousin should want to see her again, Aelfrida professed herself glad to have missed 'another old "*prétendant*"'.[13]

Men, whether suitors for her hand or claimants for her attention were a commodity in short supply at Tymawr (a convent, she noted apropos a visitor who developed a 'g.p.' on Placida herself, was 'not exactly the place!!' for a woman whose lifelong tendency was to surround 'one man after another … with a haze of illusion'[14] nor for a woman whose male contacts were limited to her brothers or to celibate monks or priested married men whose opinion of her was low) but having missed a '*prétendant*', being barred by Mother Guenvrede from further meetings with Juan Mascarò and having to dissuade Frank Stokoe from visiting fretted one whose self-esteem rose and fell in conjunction with the degree of masculine admiration she was accorded and whose silent and solitudinous dialogue with Deity had not yielded the anticipated spiritual rewards. She was therefore not altogether displeased to receive a Christmas letter from Fidelio begging her to resume their lapsed correspondence.

Affecting dismay that time spent away from Tymawr had 'in some way involved [her] in *that* again', Aelfrida wrote a 'friendly but impersonal' reply saying that 'if he felt in the mood and wrote [her] a midsummer and a midwinter letter, [she] would answer'; secretly she was flattered – Fidelio, she noted, was saddened by the death of his (still incarcerated) sister Ruth, and had written to his old friend and confidante 'as one longing after the spiritual truth that I know'. She nevertheless disguised her longings for masculine company by stating that as Fidelio's former 'soul-doctor' she could not ignore his cry for help[15], by presenting his request and justifying her response as arising from telepathic interaction of their respective guardian angels, and by noting that although she felt duty bound not to "fuss or fret over him" ("his troubles… it may be … are the very discipline he needs"), she must "mark where the stresses of life irk him" and offer him "crystal clear … disinterested affection". Maybe so, and maybe Placida truly believed that disinterested affection focussed on Fidelio (an unbeliever) "the rays of Our Lord's love"[16], but a ration of two letters a year provided small comfort to one in such anguish of mind as he. Furthermore, her comment that she was prepared to "go with" and "feel with" her bereaved friend[17] disguised the fact that she had no intention of meeting Fidelio again to extend the personal comfort which meetings can and letters do not always provide. A 'very wistful letter' from Fidelio received in December 1945 reminding her that he – and surely she too – felt sure that "God blesses the communion of friends" and asking to meet her should he revisit the Wye Valley (he had just resigned his Cambridge lectureship in order to spend his retirement 'in the search after truth') softened her heart: 'I have answered that if he *does* come … I will ask the Reverend Mother for permission'.[18] He did not come (perhaps her tepid response discouraged him) but in the masculine wasteland of Monmouthshire, Frank Stokoe's attentions were welcome.

Julius, however, was both a suitor for her heart and a claimant for her attention and, God excepted, had then no real rival, and it is obvious that *malgré* Aelfrida's protestations that her 1943 visit to Cardiff was both '*a test of detachment*' and a pointer as to how 'to use "human consolations" without being bound by them', the fact that Julius had tears in his eyes when saying goodbye and had taken her 'closer into [his] heart than ever before'[19] was proof that he was her real '*prétendant*'. Hence in spite of assuring Father Northcott that being at Tymawr was '*life* in a way that existence elsewhere was not' and that she never wanted to leave or be sent away (assurances put forward in a letter written at her guardian angel's prompting in which she tried to exculpate herself from blame for the fact that she had 'unwittingly' – *sic* – given the impression that she wished to get Mother Guenvrede

into trouble), Aelfrida felt obliged to confess that although she was a member of the 'dear dear Community', lack of 'human consolations' was increasingly a burden and that she had enjoyed spending time with her brother. (Enjoyment, she added, had not distracted her from 'life here' but the fact that Julius had actually *thanked* Mother Guenvrede for sending his sister to him suggests how much enjoyment Aelfrida derived from being with 'dear Dudu' and he with her.)[20] Closer acquaintance, however, reminded her of Julius' faults ('despondency', and a tendency to 'extreme individualism'[21], the latter a trait shared with his sister) and his suggestion that he stay at Monmouth occasionally in order to walk with her more often[22] was vetoed as incompatible with her desire for silence and solitude in general and during Lent and Advent in particular. But as Placida hastened to point out to Mother Guenvrede, should she continue to interrupt silence and solitude 'to pour out tea for "Mrs D"', she would expect a further quid pro quo: 'if Brother Julius … wants to come he should do so, as usual'[23], he being the sole 'human consolation' she refused to forego.

October 1944 saw Aelfrida sent to Cardiff again, a bigger bribe (£25), an exaggerated minor illness, and protestations that Mother Guenvrede had not consulted her notwithstanding. ("I have already arranged with Brother Julius that you are to spend October with him", she replied, the matter having been decided between them on one of his visits.)[24] This time the 'tug of the world' was stronger, for in spite of *ex post facto* assurances that she had kept guard of her heart so well 'that human affection was no temptation even when I had been sorely wounded by my Sisters-in-Christ here' (the set-to which accompanied Placida's protestations had involved other members of the Community too), Aelfrida enjoyed her '*wonderful* stay'[25] even more than the first. She met friends old and new, 'revel[led] in Beethoven!', enjoyed 'sweetness and kindness beyond description' from Mina and Constance, and spent much time with Julius, he reading aloud a 'lively Greek novel' in process of composition, she vocalising an impromptu sequel, and both composing a 'whimsical adventure story'[26] reminiscent of those on which Dudu and Tit collaborated in childhood days. Julius' subsequent letter complaining that "everything [had] been flat as a pancake" since she returned to Tymawr ('evidently', wrote his sister, 'I did just what Father Benson says the Religious *shouldn't* do [namely] "add to the natural brilliance of society"!!')[27] reminded her of Julius' need to have her near to illuminate a life 'shadowed' (his word) by 'sorrows and trials' ('but *has* he had more … than I?' his sister wondered) and to cheer with her accepting philosophy a man of sixty-two 'dreading old age intensely'.[28]

A third visit to Cardiff in October 1945 proved 'the most precious, the most interesting and profitable' of all because 'most of [her] walks and talks' were with Julius. (Mina was 'brooding over the woes of her country', Constance in a 'confused emotional state' with regard to certain young men, and Walter, home on leave, 'prepared to be extremely nice to Aunt Aelfrida as long as she kept off religion'.)[29] It was also precious because Mother Guenvrede allowed Placida to 'take "St Guenvrede" on a holiday' too, though as before her diary was left behind because it was growing 'too worldly' and required the company of saints 'Rose' and 'Bruno' 'to teach it better!!'[30], an interesting comment seeing that Placida ventured only muted protest at the prospect of departure, retired to bed for three days prior to departure only because she caught 'the Prevailing Cold [which] has been attacking us all'[31], and put sentiments into visiting Hilda Harrison's mouth (she was 'so to speak on tiptoe with wings outspread for flight ever since she last came back, so that only her bodily presence [was] here' and was 'hoping to go away and never to live here anymore')[32] which exactly reflected her own.

Revealing comments in diaries covering 1944–1945 also demonstrate Aelfrida's growing need for greater intellectual stimulation than that provided by Silence, Solitude, and the contemplative life in an isolated convent. Spiritual stimulation she had in plenty but though she still felt 'Sunday-fied every day of the week which is what you have to do in a convent'[33], 'thrills [came] from outside'[34] in the shape of academic honours heaped on her brothers and enjoyed by their sister by proxy but yearningly as if she would not be altogether sorry to abandon rural meditations on the Kingdom of Heaven for academic life in an urban "Kingdom of Thought"[35], namely Cambridge.

Julius, whose 'congenital pessimism' led him to regard professorships in Edinburgh, Birmingham and Cardiff as exiles to be endured until he could return to Cambridge, was delighted to discover in 1945 that he was 'at long last reaping the reward of all his labours for Byz. Music' in terms of 'unlimited funds', publication by the prestigious Clarendon Press, and conferences in Oxford.[36] Eustace too had books appearing, his *Shakespeare's History Plays* of 1944 being 'greeted with acclaim' and his revised *Poetry Direct and Oblique* reissued to glowing reviews. (His sister's belief that he had 'seriously turned to the study of Christianity' was wishful thinking; since age three Eustace had maintained a healthy scepticism with regard to Bible truths and did not seem "to have any use for religion". What baffled Aelfrida was not Eustace's lack of need for religion but that he got on "so happily without it".)[37] He had also been appointed Master of

Jesus College: 'I am so very *very* glad', wrote Aelfrida, 'he will fit the post as the key fits its lock'.[38] (The oddness of learning the news from *The Times* does not seem to have struck the future Master's sister.) The new Master's description of ceremonies accompanying his installation in October 1945 ("something of a great day" and "quite exciting" even to one rather overwhelmed by "antique behaviour" expected of him at the time) was forwarded by Aelfrida to Alethea with the comment that Master of Jesus though Eustace might be, the 'Master Eustace' he would always remain to his sister had chosen 'such brittle paper' that she feared it would 'hardly survive the journey to St Cuthbert's'.[39] But then and later Aelfrida was happy to bask in reflected glory as the sister of a Master of a Cambridge college.

'Thrills from outside' of such a thrilling kind stimulated worldly tugs from other members of the extended Tillyard family; having dissociated herself from them when she left Cambridge for Oxford in 1934, Aelfrida, it seems, now wished to reunite herself with them. A brief visit from Phyllis in August 1944, however, filled her with trepidation beforehand and exhausted her afterwards because 'all the imperfectly-sublimated Cambridge-complexes suddenly became alive and made [her] mind seethe', and though interaction with "our kin generally"[40] were, as she reminded Mother Guenvrede, important for their spiritual welfare and her own, the prospect of more permanent reunion with 'kin' was both desirable and daunting.

The tug asserted itself as much because of deaths as because of 'thrills' generated by the living, mortality reminding Aelfrida of the passing of time and the impossibility of deathbed reconciliations if she continued her present mode of life: Aunt Anna, dying in December 1944, whose work as a nurse in the 'indescribable slums' of London's East End was 'all done to the glory of God'[41], something noted with perhaps not wholly unconscious irony given that Anna Tillyard lost her faith at the end; 'Aunt Agnes' Slack in January 1946, still, in her ninetieth year, associated with if no longer active for the Women's Temperance Union[42]; and, perhaps the greatest break with the past, 'Auntie Ancie', Aelfrida's distant relative Ancifera Gregory, in February 1946. Noting that it was 'very solemnising when dear ones die', Aelfrida was even more solemnised to discover that Ancifera had bequeathed her only an ebony and silver crucifix and £200, a sum much smaller than her £1000 bequest to her servant Leah. (Placida added the crucifix to her growing collection, the £200 she renounced in favour of Alethea in order to double the latter's own legacy.) The death of one her 'childhood playmates', Maynard Keynes, in April 1946 made her wonder 'why *I* am still alive'[43] and fret that much dearer people might die before she tugged herself free from claustration: Alethea, reported well and happy but a long way from England, or 'Uncle Frank' Tillyard, 'in fine form'[44] according to Eustace but elderly nevertheless.

It was, in fact, Frank Tillyard who unwittingly underlined the importance of allowing herself to respond to 'the tug of the world' and a dilemma she would face if she did: glancing down the list of Birthday Honours in *The Times* on 15 June 1945 Aelfrida saw 'Uncle Frank's name among the knights'. Her initial feeling being one of 'dismay' because receipt of honours was '*not at all* in the Tillyard tradition', she directed congratulations to his wife ('a dutiful wife must be delighted when her husband receives *condign* honours'), not the culprit himself. But addressing her letter to 'Lady Tillyard' pulled her up short: 'honours in the family give me a horrid feeling that the world would like to lure me back', a feeling enhanced by letters recently received which asked '"won't you want to stay at … [Jesus] Lodge?" and so on'. 'Lord *hold me fast*'[45], she prayed, but, as we shall see, was not unduly disappointed when He did not.

That He did not is also evidenced by 'tugs' from the world being replicated by 'pushes' from within. 'Pushes' fell into three categories: clashes of personality, physical and mental health or ill health, and the position of tertiaries, resident or not, within the SSC.

Aelfrida's return from Cardiff in November 1943 saw relations between herself and Mrs Donkin established on a more equable footing for the 'tantrums'[46] of the previous winter seem to have arisen as a result of personality clashes with Hilda Harrison, now only intermittently resident; indeed, Placida began to hope that God's renewed promise of '*interior silence*' could be maintained even during tea with 'the Reverend Mother's Own Mama' because all Theodora Donkin required was the presence of some 'kind lady' to listen to her reminiscences, the said 'kind lady' being able to carry on 'familiar colloquies with Himself'[47] while lending an ear to her companion's earthly chunterings. The happy footing diminished as Mrs Donkin more and more reminded Aelfrida of the 'mama' whose earthly existence she had helped to terminate. Not only did 'Own Mama' now rest 'the whole weight of her personality' on Aelfrida as they sat or took short walks together ('maybe', wrote the latter apprehensively, 'I shall need that kind of psychological support … when I am [old]', not realising that she herself had behaved that way most of her life) but her formerly interesting conversation (never as intellectual as Chiara's at the best of times but colourful nevertheless) deteriorated into 'perpetual grievances'[48] concerning her daughter's unfriendly behaviour towards her and

the dreadful state of the world. By January 1944, with Mrs Donkin's behaviour 'worse, memory worse, temper worse, grumbles worse'[49], Aelfrida was driven to exasperation and to fill pages of her supposedly 'spiritual' diary with abusive descriptions of 'Mrs D's' personality; she also realised with horror that she was trapped at Fordfield-Tymawr with another Chiara. (She did not actually contemplate euthanasia but noted that keeping Mrs Donkin in bed for one day a fortnight 'under sedation' would be an excellent idea.)[50] Even more reminiscent of Fordfield days when friends and relations, deluded by her assumed devotion, congratulated her on how perfectly she 'managed' her 'own dear ones when they were old' ('dear ones' now loved sentimentally because they had hurt her), Mother Guenvrede praised her for keeping Mrs Donkin 'happy' and hinted that Placida might 'be drawn back into "the library"' as guest mistress. But no, 'I *couldn't*', declared Placida, giving as her excuse that if God called her away from people, how could she seek their company[51]; in truth and with Mrs Donkin becoming increasingly 'cantankerous'[52], Aelfrida had no intention of spending more time with her than was necessary not to be sent away before she completed preparations for departure.

Worse even than this – and here Aelfrida might have made more allowance for Mother Guenvrede than she did, given that she herself had experienced the foibles and phobias of an elderly mother – was that the Mother was showing signs of becoming a mixture of her 'Own Mama' and Aelfrida's: making 'all sorts of little rules and regulations designed to prevent anyone ever feeling at home'[53]; forbidding Placida's enjoyment of little treats ('sweet Saint Guenvrede, extra')[54]; becoming 'very very forgetful' of Aelfrida's 'good deeds' and because of her 'strange and warped' nature[55], harping on the bad ones; demonstrating inconsistency, ungratefulness, and an 'inability to receive suggestions'; being charming to visitors who, when they commented to Mrs Graham 'how "sweet"' Mother Guenvrede was, made Mrs Graham feel 'quite cynical'[56] and to note apropos a visitor but more properly of herself that it was not lack of physical comfort but lack of 'psychological support' which was pushing her away from Tymawr[57] and that it was not only Winifred and Theodora Donkin who acted like 'caged lionesses.[58] But though Placida consoled herself that if Mother Guenvrede '*must* have her knife into someone', it was better for the Community if that 'someone' was herself, and with a vision of Christ telling her in 'spirit language' to welcome feelings of despondency engendered by the Mother's unfriendly behaviour towards one who no longer felt like a 'child of the house' because such feelings constituted her '*bridal* wreath, thorns of

His crown'[59], Aelfrida (though she tried to deny it) felt both bitter and resentful, a state of mind which led to revengeful outbursts on paper or in word or deed and to doomed attempts 'to be as unobtrusive, respectful, *complaisante* and inwardly (*sic*) obedient as I can' and to make as few demands as possible on a woman whose chief request was that Mrs Graham 'let [her] alone'.[60] But unable to let anyone alone in spite of reminders to herself not to meddle and of awful examples of what happened when she meddled vivid in her mind (Agatha's and Alethea's responses to her meddling must have constituted an 'imperfectly-sublimated Cambridge complex' of a particularly unhappy kind), Aelfrida continued to harass Mother Guenvrede verbally and by letter.

Intimations of trouble began in March 1944 with regard to Aelfrida's continuing tendency to demonstrate what she described as her 'unusual gift for getting in touch with people, in a friendly way and spiritually' and Mother Guenvrede as socialising with visitors 'here for spiritual reasons alone' and as usurping her own position by proffering 'spiritual counsel'. Driven to tackle Placida directly about these unfortunate traits – she found it difficult, she said, to 'get in touch' with her resident tertiary so was forced to speak plainly – Mother Guenvrede found Placida 'only too happy' to desist (she was interested in people, she explained, 'from a novelist's point of view' but her deepest desire was silence, not friendship) but unable to comply because of the 'very strong flavour' of her personality. Of this 'very strong flavour', continued Mother Guenvrede, 'we get too much … at times'. (As they must have, given that by Aelfrida's own account she had not spoken a word to 'anyone … for ten days and didn't *feel* that [her] silence was being noisy'.) Noting that the Mother's scolding was both 'perfectly right and eagerly accepted' (and that in the matter of disruptive behaviour there was little to choose between Nadja's at Fordfield and her own at Tymawr), Placida embarked on a 'calm and wonderful ecstasy' but an ecstasy which 'cannot, I think, last'.[61]

It did not; Aelfrida made sure of that. Instead of embarking at God's request on 'a process of *spiritual purgation*' during which 'a lot of me will have to be thrown overboard' if she was to become ('as far as possible') '*nothing but a soul at prayer*' conveying to the Community 'a sense of His Presence' and nothing of her own[62], Placida wrote a deliberately provocative letter to Mother Guenvrede incorporating needling comments ('I understand that on Mothering Sunday it is the correct thing to send good wishes *only* to *you*'), reminders of old injustices ('last September … when I was nearer to complete discouragement than … ever … before'), hints that she herself was spiritually superior to her Superior ('Our

Lord came … with the Father and the Holy Spirit and *took up His abode in me*. Since then He has been, so to speak, able to direct me without raising His voice'), and niggles ('I must give up inviting people for walks – but are walks to be given up altogether or would you send us or should people be allowed to invite?')[63] guaranteed to exasperate a woman trying to run a convent in which "during these five years of war it has … taken every scrap of strength and time to keep up the regular round of worship and prayer [and] to live and to look after the spiritual and material needs of numerous guests"[64], one of whom was Mrs Graham, the other the Mother's cantankerous mother. Only the onset of Lenten silence prevented further verbal or epistolary skirmishes.

Later the same year Aelfrida took advantage of Mother Guenvrede being distracted (Sister Jeanne was suffering from exacerbation of a chronic painful neurological condition affecting her left leg and side, Sister Monica was now 'permanently off duty' with hypertension[65], and the convent was in such dire financial straits that cows and outside help were temporarily relinquished) to ask remission from the few 'Library' duties she performed. This time Mother Guenvrede made no attempt to conceal her feelings: "Oh, do as you like! … I should like to shake you for *never* giving a thought to anyone but yourself" and, on Placida replying self-righteously that she was 'always in touch with other people' (that, of course, was the problem) and reminding the Mother that a few weeks earlier the latter had advised her to 'live in the convent as if [she was] the only person there' (an unnecessary admonishment, one would think), actually shook her before exiting.[66] The sirens and gunfire forming the background to this episode (the 'Little Blitz' hit South Wales and other areas of Britain in 1944) underlined the fact that Placida's belief that 'peace and love reign here, war or no war'[67] was as deluded as that concerning the 'perfection' of her marriage as her relationship with Constantine fell apart.

A brief lull in the strife between two ladies never apparently destined to achieve an Hegelian synthesis (Placida's prayerful comment on the twenty-first anniversary of the convent's dedication 'Peace be within thy walls' ends in an exclamation mark)[68] was attributed by Aelfrida to Mother Guenvrede noticing her tertiary's assiduous work on the 'vast weeds' afflicting the cinder path by the vestry door, to prayer, and to helpful attempts at '*quietness*'[69], but aerial combat currently making 'a good deal of noise' by night and day[70] (another reason for Mother Guenvrede's distracted behaviour, had Aelfrida cared to notice) symbolised warfare to come.

Finding that tactics employed in 1943 were no more efficacious in 1944, Placida's behaviour took a more sinister turn. She began by writing a letter to Mother Guenvrede guaranteed to wind up the latter's strained nerves to breaking point:

"Dear Mother, you once told me that you had a 'Lewis Carroll streak' so here is a suggestion for a holiday joke … instead of sending me to Cardiff this year will you please send me to Coventry? … since P[lacida] would be in Coventry there would be no need to cook anything for her but the Ancient Monastic Custom of setting out a *Beggar's Portion* … in the hall … might be revived. (*Pittance* or *Caritas*.) Beggar would return crockery washed up … Prayer-Mat would be vacant and for a whole month P's voice would not be heard in chapel. (Wouldn't that be nice?) But if someone crept in at the back … that would be the grateful Beggar … At your feet in tears of longing or laughter, Placida *Tertiary SSC*".[71]

Then, hearing Father Amos pray at Mass that Mother Guenvrede be strengthened 'in body and mind'[72], she informed him that she had noticed 'some … disturbance' in the Mother's mind (in her diary, she recorded that Mother Guenvrede was 'delusional' insofar as she suspected Placida of trying to 'usurp her place' and 'of writing to all and sundry saying she is mad') and asked his advice. On Father Amos letting slip that 'there *had* been "trouble like that"'[73] in the past, she tackled Father Northcott. Having decided following 1943's 'lamentable fuss' that she had a low opinion of Northcott's 'human wisdom and insight'[74], she should not have been surprised when, on repeating to him what she had recently told Father Amos, 'the storm', as she put it, 'came'. Demanded why she interfered with Mother Guenvrede's management and why she stayed if she wasn't happy and hearing her self-justifying replies, Northcott 'went off the deep end' ('I think [that] is the right phrase') with regard to what he termed accusations and insinuations concerning the Mother's 'mental illness' (Placida's description, not Northcott's) and after putting 'the worst possible construction on [her] words', declared her to be 'a liar and a lunatic (not in quite such plain English)', sneered at her 'as I have never seen anyone sneer', and told her it would be better if she left Tymawr forthwith. ('Is it my duty to remove myself permanently … if my presence is what gives rise to the delusions?' Aelfrida asked herself, perhaps seeking an excuse for doing so[75], then, remembering 'when he was in a rage with me an alien personality seemed to look out of his eyes', wondered if Northcott too was not suffering from 'nervous breakdown'[76] at 'the mere idea of a tertiary seeing anything wrong with her Superior's mind and saying so'.)[77] 'What a coil', she wrote at the conclusion of this lamentable scene, 'a gentleman, a

priest and a religious to behave so to his penitent'. Then, tension relieved after a more massive 'scene' than any previously staged at Tymawr (and pages and pages of contemporary diary entries show that Mother Guenvrede's reported statement to Father Northcott that Aelfrida's mind was '"far too active" i.e. that [she] was mad' was not far from the truth at this point), Aelfrida saw at last that she had 'brought it on [herself]' and that 'it would have been better to have prayed and said nothing' and hoped that God would now fill the 'dear dear' convent with His peace'.[78]

He did not, alas, Placida made sure of that. Even while assuring Mother Guenvrede that she was 'never going to make fusses about anything anymore', Aelfrida continued to pester her about visits to Cardiff, only to be told that the Sisters were exhausted and needed a break and that they would 'get on better without [her]'. She also, in spite of determination on '*quietness*', plagued Mother Guenvrede with her concerns that Mother and tertiary might be 'out of touch', only to be put off with the reply "I am rather busy … if you want to find me … you must look for me in God".[79] (The Mother 'is pushing me away whereas before she had drawn me in', Aelfrida deduced correctly, adding that if she had to go, go she must 'without a murmur'.[80] And from her tone one realises that it is not only Cardiff to which she refers.) Then under the impression that 'bloodshed' erupting between herself, her Superior, and the Visitor was over, she assured Father Amos that all was well between them; in private, however, she added the sly, vindictive, ironically humorous and extremely revealing comment that she 'was not nearly as sorry as [she] ought to be'[81] for the trouble she had caused.

At this point she retired to bed with 'flu', presented to the doctor as 'a little heart trouble'.[82] Sister Monica being now released from "the activities of the daily round"[83], Sister Jeanne was detailed to 'wait on' (Aelfrida's phrase) the invalid. Only 'the minimum of waiting on' was provided (or required) and on Aelfrida remarking on this ('I am so used to love and devotion from whoever had looked after me [even] from coolly competent professional nurses'), Sister Jeanne, more ill than Aelfrida, proved unsympathetic, saying 'she had been ordered to [Placida's] bedside against her will'. ('Has the Mother told her I was shamming?' asked Aelfrida of herself.) She also lost her temper: neither she nor anyone else, she cried, would do anything 'for *you*'.[84]

Sister Jeanne's attitude shook Placida 'more, almost, than any experience I had ever had … where was my little saint who these eight years has been my friend?' Rationalise it how she would (was Sister Jeanne 'mentally afflicted' or merely a 'Spoilt Beauty'?)[85], realisation that her behaviour had resulted not only in personal animus on the part of Mother Guenvrede but also in alienation from her favourite 'Sister-in-Christ' constituted another and a very strong 'push' and upset her deeply. (Thirteen diary pages describe the episode.) Worse still was realisation that the Community as a whole (now described as 'a very haphazard set of women' whose 'spiritual unity' was vaunted rather than apparent and whose value as an 'anchorage' had lost its 'attractive power')[86] was itself pushing her away by withdrawing its support from one who herself valued membership of it less and less.

Accosting Mother Guenvrede yet again on the subject of Cardiff holidays, Aelfrida received both cold comfort (the 'anguish of longing' for Tymawr was something to offer God; family duties were owed whether to Mrs Donkin – a 'martyrdom', her daughter admitted – or to Julius and Mina; it was not beyond Placida's capabilities to close the sluice-gates of 'natural affection' in order to direct the full flow of her spiritual energy into 'a Godward channel', and so on) and another reason why the Community wanted to be rid of her: she was a 'solitary' and although the Sisters understood and respected her desire to be one, they found it difficult to cope with someone who simultaneously depended on and acted independently of them. Aelfrida, conveniently forgetting the rest of the conversation, added 'go I must, I fear' to her diary entry.[87]

Colder comfort and plainer speaking occurred during a visit paid by Mother Guenvrede to the West Room which, because it took place shortly after Sister Jeanne's 'outburst', would have made a less self-centred person than Aelfrida realise the damage she had done to the therapeutic community which had sheltered her for nearly a decade and seriously consider rather than merely 'wonder' if there was 'something amiss with *me* that the Mother should *want* to send me away?'[88] The visit included 'one of the most unusual conversations' Aelfrida ever had, Mother Guenvrede giving her the full benefit of her 'tyrant-self which hates and fears me' and expressing her own views in the guise of the Sisters':

– "they think you are *queer* and they don't like to have queer people about".
– "they think you are queer because you like to have your own way".
– "they think you are queer because you ask for things and want things different".
– "[they] think the *life* you lead is queer".
– "they think you talk when you like".
– "[they] may not want you to *return*".

Then as an afterthought ('see omission added overleaf') another 'queerness': "keeping quiet for a long time and then suddenly … doing something", which, though

she disputed the accuracy of other accusations, Aelfrida admitted was 'true, but the suddenness is only apparent, it is … the climax of a long process of maturing'.[89] And had Mother Guenvrede read Placida's diary on a regular basis, the truth of Aelfrida's assertion would have been immediately apparent.

Although she tried to brush off the episode with 'well, now did you ever!!', Aelfrida was more shaken by the Mother's measured words than by Sister Jeanne's spontaneous outburst. Had Mother Guenvrede, she wondered, told the Sisters as well as Father Northcott that Placida was 'mad'? The thought worried her so much that she consulted her doctor when he confirmed that 'hardening of the arteries' notwithstanding, she was (alas) fit to travel, informing him that she sometimes showed 'signs of excitement' (*sic*) which she could not control and 'which made people think [her] queer'. Dr Hunt's reply, though reassuring on the one hand ("you can't control them … because they are not in your control … tell people to let you *be* – you'll be all right then"), was worrying on the other: might her 'longing to be alone' be 'not as spiritual as [she] thought' but a symptom of mental pathology exacerbated by being 'watched and whispered about and suspected' when she tried to achieve peace of mind by 'stand[ing] alone in God's Presence?' But if she *were* 'mad', how could 'holy people' like Mother Guenvrede and Father Northcott treat a 'lunatic' so cruelly? ('I hope the ungodly are more merciful to … patients in mental hospitals than the godly are outside'.) Or was it only 'the devil who wants me out of Tymawr' speaking through the 'godly's' lips?[90]

Admission that she was, if not frankly 'lunatic', at least mentally abnormal, begs several questions: was Aelfrida in truth 'mad' at this time? And if she *was* 'mad', was Mother Guenvrede's 'mental illness' real or merely a reflection and figment of her own?

Mother Guenvrede was certainly so distracted by Aelfrida's presence as to act quite irrationally – at one point she accused her of felling a bay tree, a cupressus, and a syringa in the garden of Woodbine Cottage, 'a notable trio for Freud to interpret', wrote the irrepressible 'under-gardener' some years later though she found the episode less amusing when she showed Mother Guenvrede the trees still flourishing and the latter remained unconvinced[91] – but her tendency to accuse people of being 'not quite normal'[92] is hardly indicative of abnormality in herself. Then, too, her habit of blanking Placida 'as if [she] were an inanimate object'[93] was more likely indicative of preoccupation or a wish not to be pestered by an importunate 'child' than of mental illness and her removal from the library of 'half a dozen of Aelfrida Tillyard's books'[94], together with Aelfrida's copy of Father Cary's recent pamphlet *Hortus Inclusus* describing the contemplative life as lived by the Sisters of the Love of God at Fairacres ('my [own] soul's [garden] is more *incultus* than *inclusus* I fear!' noted its recipient correctly)[95] more likely attributable to the unsuitability of their contents for her novices and antipathy to a man whose spiritual advice Placida sought in preference to her own, than to 'delusions'. And, as Aelfrida's diary demonstrates, Mother Guenvrede's 'suspicion' that her 'child of God' was 'writing to all and sundry saying she was mad' was correct: in spite of Placida's protestations that she '[hadn't]said a word to anyone'[96], she had written to Hilda Harrison and Miss Lowe warning them of new restrictions imposed by Mother Guenvrede's 'tyrant-self' on 'the Library' and touching on the 'queerness' of the Mother's present behaviour[97] and to Sister Frances, a Tredegar tertiary, 'disseminating' (as irate Mother Guenvrede put it) 'convent news again to all and sundry' when expressly forbidden to do so.[98] She also drafted and kept for her biographer's benefit (it showed 'another milestone [she had] reached') a revealing letter to Hilda Harrison in which she stated that had the convent guest house been as it now was at the time of her first visit, she would have 'gone, never to return'; that Mother Guenvrede was deliberately courting mental illness ("one has to offer everything to God, even one's reason"); and that the Mother's 'queerness' was premature senility.[99]

Though Mother Guenvrede must have been comforted by meeting Sister Cecilia, Superior of St Thomas' Convent during the greater part of Aelfrida's tenure of St Benedict's, and by having "some good laughs over you and your ways" (judging by Aelfrida's hurt comment that the two Superiors 'made merry at [her] expense'[100], 'laughs' may have included a description of how, suffering the side-effects of cocaine administered by 'Dr Macbeth', she returned to the convent acting as if she had imbibed 'an overdose of alcohol')[101] and by discovering that Placida's eccentric behaviour antedated her arrival at Tymawr, it seems she was now so worried by the latter's 'religious fervour' (fervour unmoderated by advice from herself, Fathers Northcott, Amos, and Cary, visiting priests, and the convent doctor)[102] that she decided to send her away permanently because 'fervour' was further disrupting Placida's fragile mental equilibrium. Her decision may have been strengthened by another comment from Sister Cecilia, namely that Placida invariably 'crashed' (Aelfrida's word) when she 'tried to be *active* for God' instead of peacefully contemplating His attributes ("the alabaster box", Sister Cecilia had told her comfortingly, "*must* be broken [before] the fragrance fills the whole house")[103], Mother Guenvrede at last realising

**Julius Tillyard c1942**

that regular 'crashing' was inherent in Aelfrida's personality, that others might suffer collateral damage from the 'crash's' fallout, and that she herself with her Community's help had done as much as they could to release Aelfrida's imprisoned 'fragrance' from its spiritual and emotional 'box'. Or possibly she decided that Aelfrida's personality was so irretrievably shattered that no further action on her part or the SSC could repair it.

To be rejected by one real and two surrogate mothers, especially as rejection by the surrogates was caused by her behaviour relative to them, must have been devastating for one reliving her childish terror at being sent away from home instead of being '*at home* [and] safe'[104] as she had believed herself to be as a small child at Fordfield or an adult 'child of God' at Tymawr (Aelfrida's newest recurrent nightmare was of being confronted by Mother Guenvrede in secular dress and of not being able to find her way back to, or around the interior of, the convent) and noteworthy of the 'Cardiff' episodes of 1943 and 1944 is that her overwrought response was mediated by an event which took place nearly sixty years earlier. But her behaviour overall manifested eccentricities not all of which could be attributed to this or to 'religious fervour': the replacement of books' dust jackets with pieces of wallpaper might be dismissed as mild eccentricity and refusal to accept more than 'two silver leaves and a fragment of icing' from a nun's 'bridal' cake because she herself was 'a married woman who [had] had both a cake and a husband' as rather silly[105], but who could have regarded her as anything other than the 'odd elderly widow, quite mad' she feared to become when behaviour conspicuous in a quiet rural area (scrambling maniacally across the landscape in pursuit of 'Prehistory', embracing livestock, or as she strode the lanes, declaiming or muttering as she mentally composed letters to Mother Guenvrede or 'thought things out' or prayed aloud) was noticed and commented on by those who met her outside the convent, including her doctor?

Being thought 'mad' by Mother Guenvrede worried Aelfrida intensely, for she had already known occasions when 'the terrible wings of madness'[106] hovered over her mind. But whereas in September 1943 she decided that 'if staying on here meant that the Mother would accuse me of lunacy and send me to a madhouse', she would accept the risk because a 'madhouse' might be part of God's plan for her[107], by April 1944 her attitude had changed: 'far better to lead a perfectly ordinary life in the world than indulge in queer practices on one's own account and out of presumption and delusion', practices which went beyond anything attributable to mere 'pious eccentricity'.[108] Hence, for example, increasing reticence 'about [her] being *used* to fight against the forces of darkness' currently assailing Mother Guenvrede (she must 'keep things in proportion', she reminded herself when deciding not to address her concerns to the obvious person, Hubert Northcott)[109] and her decision to 'exercise [herself] in silence' when seeking to thwart the devil's 'designs' on the Community. What these statements say of her current state of mind is worrying in itself, given that she had begun to regard Father Northcott's scoldings as yet another aspect of the devil's machinations[110], but fear of being thought 'mad' by people in authority over her (particularly if she had been placed in Tymawr in lieu of a 'lunatic asylum', of which there was a notable example near Cambridge) and of actions they might take as a result, must have inspired a desire to leave before 'pushed' somewhere she had no desire to be.

Two further factors may have influenced her decision to separate herself from the Community. The first was a message from one Muriel Pont, formerly Tertiary Teresa of the SSC but now alienated by Mother Guenvrede's behaviour from further association with it. (Muriel too was happy to practice 'Poverty [and] Chastity' with 'any amount of enthusiasm' but had 'no capacity for obedience' whatsoever.)[111] Muriel had recently informed

Aelfrida of a pair of elderly anchoresses from the Isle of Wight who had 'gone quite mad', so mad that they had to be taken in by a local convent; the information made Aelfrida 'think *hard*': 'so much mental trouble among those who … give themselves to contemplation. What *is* wrong?'[112] She may also have wondered if she herself, though cured by 'Tymawr peace' of the 'madness' which beset her after Chiara's, Constantine's and Agatha's deaths, was now beset by 'madness' occasioned by overindulgence in Silence and Solitude, one of whose manifestations was belief in the diabolic possession of her current spiritual directors.

The second factor is conjectural but plausible. Two of RH Benson's books (*Lord of the World* and *The Necromancers*) describe battles between the forces of good and evil. *Lord of the World* portrays the battle as taking place between two men, one personifying good, the other evil; *The Necromancers*, on the other hand, portrays them as taking place *in the mind* of the female protagonist personifying goodness. Evil, "an enormous Power external to herself yet approached in an interior way", is eventually overcome by force of mental prayer but not before the heroine's mind becomes so "saturated" with it that she almost succumbs to its "malignity", entering a state "in which two personalities [face] one another, welded together in a grip that lay on the very brink of fusion" before she begins "internally to pray" and wins through.[113] Can it be that Aelfrida saw herself as 'Maggie' and Mother Guenvrede as 'Laurie', the demonically-possessed hero for whose soul 'Maggie' battles (a likely contention, given that her descriptions of 'possessed' Mother Guenvrede agree closely with Benson's of possessed 'Laurie') and believed that she too was falling (or had already fallen) captive to the devil and that it was this captivity which made her behave 'madly' and suffer sensations of powerlessness and terror so strong that prayer seemed inefficacious? (A further indication, if one were needed, of an evil presence within her.) If so, 'tugs' from 'the world' might deliver her from the convent to a place of safety, a place to which, ironically, the devil's presence at Tymawr was already pushing her.

How much of this is delusion, how much the escape-clause negotiated by Aelfrida whenever subject to temporal or spiritual authority, how much self-fulfilling prophecy, is impossible to say. Worth noting, however, is that there may be a physical explanation for some of her mental oddities.

Carbon monoxide toxicity had certainly contributed to ill-health suffered at Tymawr but the onset of the 'Little Blitz' of 1943–44 and news reaching England that 'poison gas' had been used in German concentration camps for the 'disposing of prisoners'[114] and of the

German boast of 'secret weapon[s] *now* being used and … more extensively in the future'[115], convinced her that the further appearance in her room of 'evil-smelling smoke' indicated the presence of arsenic-based 'poison gas' disseminated 'on quiet nights' by fiendish German devices, the gas giving rise to 'widespread lassitude and discouragement' experienced in daylight. Fear of further accusations of 'madness' prevented her from asking anyone's advice and her wish to keep 'Brother Ass' from panicking from enquiring after 'war-news' (lack of information in *The Times* merely meant 'people [preferring] to keep it quiet if it *could* be hushed up') but eventually common sense prevailed: the impracticality of using 'poison gas' where there was 'too much air' and awareness of the quirks of Tymawr flues put paid to this particular delusion. (And she 'felt rather a fool' for framing it.) But medication taken to alleviate one of the symptoms ('rhenitis') caused by fumes from 'anthracite and green wood'[116] may have given rise to others.

In 1943 (probably) and 1944 (certainly) Aelfrida suffered nocturnal hallucinations. Quasi-ecstatic experiences she subsequently (and correctly) attributed to bursting star-shells and to searchlights illuminating the night sky but others involving 'the feeling that the air was … murmuring "tremble, tremble, tremble! Hitler, Hitler, Hitler" like a plane-borne ventriloquist' and the impression of 'weird swastikas dancing on [the] walls' (projected, she thought, by 'a kind of magic lantern' from a German plane)[117] could not be attributed to sudden changes in air pressure, to the 'results of too energetic gardening', or to the effects of 'war tension'. On Sister Jeanne stating that she too experienced '"*something* very queer" in the atmosphere surrounding the Convent'[118], Aelfrida attributed her own visions and auditions to manifestations of the "crafts and assaults" of the devil as described in the Litany and decided to summon up prayerful power against him and them on Mother Guenvrede's and the Community's behalf. Recording the incident twenty years later she remained convinced that 'the devil [had] called up his legions' and that the air had become so full of 'tension' that other Sisters noticed it too, asking Placida if she, like themselves, felt the presence of 'evil influences'.[119] In Aelfrida's case, however (there is no evidence of the truth of her statements concerning the Sisters) 'tensions' may have stemmed less from 'influences' than from overuse of a sympathomimetic drug prescribed for 'rhenitis'.

Ephedrine, prescribed for Aelfrida under various proprietary names, is a nasal decongestant whose action mimics that of 'fight or flight' hormone adrenaline.[120] Used to excess because perennial rhinitis made her 'heavy in mind and body'[121], it caused the very symptoms

suffered by her at this time: headache, tachycardia ('heart knocking all night, pulse 126 this morning')[122], anxiety ('tremble, tremble, tremble'), restlessness (described in spiritual terms as her soul soaring on 'wings')[123], insomnia, and tremor ('war-tension'); it must also be used with caution in patients suffering from known hypertension and possible cardiac disease ('cramps in the heart'; 'heart not working very well' and 'choking waking-up heart-beats')[124] as Aelfrida did. Definitively, however, it causes an abuser's hands and feet to feel extremely cold, something she noted on several occasions as impossible to alleviate even with a hot water bottle. It may also have exacerbated the tinnitus which gave rise to 'weird sounds' afflicting her 'without intermission'[125] and of which 'plane-borne ventriloquists' may have been a manifestation, and caused paranoid thoughts about Mother Guenvrede.

If this seems improbable, consider two things. First, Aelfrida's 'most unusual conversation' with Mother Guenvrede's 'tyrant-self' only a month after the former's hallucinatory dreams of July 1944, in the course of which the Mother repetitively accused her of abnormal behaviour and Aelfrida tried (unsuccessfully) to justify it; second, the strange fugal state entered by Aelfrida just prior to those dreams shortly Mother Guenvrede insisted on her Cardiff visit of 1944, a state during which Placida appealed to St Bruno (her 'invisible director') for support and received admonitory advice from him concerning misbehaviour of which she was well aware. (She even lists it, adding '*mea culpa, mea maxima culpa*', and intimates that Mother Guenvrede was fully justified in wanting to eject her from the Community.)[126] Whether it was 'St Bruno or conscience'[127] that restored her to her senses or 'a real good thrashing with Saint Guenvrede' (scapular 'Saint Bruno' was aired on a hot water bottle pending permission to wear it, but not, it seems, worn)[128] but the coincidence of 'silly [kinds] of dream', of the appearance of St Bruno (not a 'hallucination', but a 'perfectly clear experience … of … that great saint'), of an exacerbation of 'rhenitis', and of Mother Guenvrede's warning made Aelfrida ask herself '*exactly how much* objective truth' pertained to her statements 'about Jerry … and about St Bruno' (and, we may ask, about Mother Guenvrede), to note that 'truth is a very elusive thing', and (the necessary escape clause) blame her 'delusions' on the war.[129]

Admitting to 'delusions', war-induced or not, suggests that Aelfrida had begun to realize that other people were not invariably wrong or in the wrong or she herself invariably right or in the right, that she saw the world reflected in the distorting mirror of personality disorder, that her view was sometimes so distorted as to qualify her as 'mad' in other people's eyes (people whose view of her *might not be wrong*), and that distortions might be attributable to her particular brand of religiosity and to over-enthusiastic self-medication. Realisation is interesting on four counts. First, that if she is really as 'mad' as respected insightful people imply, she risks formal diagnosis and formal psychiatric intervention. Second, that because she is unable as yet to face the full truth about herself, she blames aberrant behaviour on an event over which she has no control, namely the war, or on maltreatment by other people. Third, that because she has learnt (or begun to learn) an important lesson about herself, she is free to leave a 'school' which has no more to teach her. Fourth, that pending departure, she must embark on some kind of interim therapy.

Having decided to 'take up [her] writing' (as she put it after a later 'crash' rendered her temporarily incapable of rational thought)[130], Aelfrida's decision to write herself sane was adopted enthusiastically. Frenetic literary activity started early in 1944 ('I began, some weeks ago, a wee book … I think it out mostly on walks but sometimes lie awake at night deliberately and let it well up in my mind')[131] and continued until completion of two books by July 1945 'refreshed [her] in body and mind'[132] more than 'jotting down … thoughts' in her diary, the latter constituting mere 'intellectual and moral *pottering*' ('ugh!') and not a very 'sensible'[133] occupation for one as prone to delusions as herself. Then, too, setting herself to 'write a definite book' ('the question of publication could be settled later') justified 'tugs' from without: 'I had given up "the world" and writing, of course, but having been sent back, partly, to "the world", authorship may have been included in new duties to it', a marvellous justification for both 'tugs' and her need to write. (The 'noise of the world' is 'very loud, down here'[134], she wrote, after one visit to Cardiff; it would become even louder after more.) And as usual with Aelfrida, an element of revenge may have played a part: one of the 'pushes' from within was Mother Guenvrede banning all her books *except* her 'silly novels'[135] from the library, it being her writings on Mysticism which Placida valued most.

Whatever her reasons for beginning another round of intensive literary activity, rounds invariably followed or accompanied periods of emotional stress. (Poetry as a young woman dedicated to Holy Virginity but overwhelmed by broken vows and a husband's sexual demands; homiletic books when other men, aging parents, and troubled children put pressure on her soul; novels when financially pressured and her 'Great Work' ignored.) Furthermore, whenever Aelfrida led a profoundly contemplative life, so active did her mind remain (in part spontaneously, in part because inspired by reading writers seized upon as inspirational and confirmational) that, like Augustine Baker[136], she became compelled to abridge her prayer life in order to unburden her teeming thoughts on paper.

Literary activity at a particular stage of her spiritual life was not, of course, peculiar to herself, for in behaving as she did she followed the same path as countless other author-mystics, but Augustine Baker's personality and experiences are particularly relevant here[137]: his being "of a contemplative temperament, inclined to solitude and quietness"; his use of contemplative prayer as an important spiritual tool[138]; his insistence that the ability to enter a "life of introversion" was the aim of all spiritual exercises and that to achieve this the would-be contemplative must lead an "ascetical life … hidden with Christ with God" (a Pauline reference much favoured by Aelfrida)[139]; his noting that bodily, spiritual, and emotional mortifications were essential adjuncts to prayer in the achievement of such a life; his belief that vocalisation and "corporal motions" were demonstrations of the Holy Spirit working through corporeality and of "the state of the spirit" as a mystic's body "accommodated" it.[140] Of particular significance is that after several years' contemplative life during which Baker expressed abhorrence at the "notion of writing any long discourse", spiritual activities which accompanied his prayer life went, as he put it, "into his head", there to cause an "alteration" from preponderantly spiritual existence to an active existence involving the "penning of books", "abridgement" of contemplation being unimportant in comparison to the "exercise of writing".[141]

Aelfrida's 'exercise of writing' expressed itself in two volumes written consecutively on seemingly different but actually interrelated topics.

The first, entitled *The Fruits of Silence*, was begun early in 1944 (she does not provide the exact date but notes early in March that she had begun 'a wee book … some weeks ago') at a time when 'many other books' were 'asking' to be written; *The Fruits of Silence*, being 'very short', was given priority. It was given priority for other – unspoken – reasons too: it was to be an inward-looking (introverted, almost), retrospective, and personalised account of her life as a silent solitary, to which end she included (sometimes almost verbatim) diarised instances of spiritual experiences and insights (her diary from 1941 to 1945 reads like a work in progress, in this instance 'explorations into the positive aspects of Silence')[142], and if, as reviews of *The Way of Praise* had hinted, her pre-war homiletic books represented the "fine flower of Anglican mystical devotion", did she not have a duty to God to write further books for Him to 'use' as He wished?[143] If so, she was right to ignore Father Cary's 1938 injunctions regarding breaches of spiritual silence and leakages of spiritual energy and begin.

Injunctions notwithstanding, inspiration for her title came from an article published in the November 1939 edition of the Cowley *Evangelist* in which Cary wrote of Silence predisposing the soul to receive the gifts of the Holy Spirit, of one of its 'fruits' as the ability "to perceive with a spiritual perception that which lies beyond the scope of … natural intelligence at its best", and of "the spiritual energy … stored in silence" which enables the silently contemplative soul to "absorb into its depths the grace of the Sacraments by which its supernatural life is evermore renewed". Placida, recently promoted to life tertiary, was moved by Cary's words, noting that, blinkered though she was by consciousness of self' and 'in spite of many lapses', silence of the quality he described did indeed lead her 'right *into* [God's] Being … more and more'.[144] By June 1941, and in spite of further lapses, she had made some progress, believing that one of Silence's most important fruits *for her* was the novel ability of abandoning her 'tendency to … look at myself and enquire how I am getting on' in favour of looking to God and asking if she were doing both '*His Will*' and His Will to the best of her ability.[145] Failure to do so other than imperfectly was later to cause her to nickname her new book 'the *Scum* of Silence' because 'it is what I skim off in order to leave clear depths below'.[146]

Did one know nothing of what brought Aelfrida to Silence and Solitude at Tymawr or of events taking place there during the spring, summer, and early autumn of 1944 which culminated in Placida's second and most severe reprimand from Father Northcott and her decision to stop behaving 'like a naughty child' in accusing Mother Guenvrede of injustice and in insinuating that the latter suffered from diabolically-induced mental instability and to 'exercise [herself] in silence' instead of turning 'this way and that for this reason or other'[147], one might think from reading *The Fruits of Silence* that she was indeed the holy person she pretended to be. Foreknowledge, however, illuminates the state of her soul as she writes her book and because of what she reveals therein of past and present 'lapses' ('*Scum*'), redeems her in part even if it does not wholly reveal or persuade us of 'clear depths below'.

Silence, she notes, has many manifestations. There is, for instance, the Silence of Longing (God being "the thing I long for")[148]; of Reverence for God as "*fons et origo … semper agens, semper quietus*", phrases used by Placida when describing Deity as "Fount and Origin" and as the "infinite activity and infinite rest" of the "balance and unity" she struggled to achieve[149]; of Penitence, so needful for a sinner like herself; of Sympathy for the sufferings of Christ and mankind; of Pondering in one's heart like the Virgin of the Annunciation what God's words might

mean. The Silence, too, of Bewilderment when one cannot clearly discern one's spiritual path; of Acceptance of God's Will; Self-Forgetfulness (departing "the house of … selfhood")[150]; of Enlightenment ("in Thy Light I see Right")[151]; of Gratitude "for the gift of Thyself"[152]; of Detachment, so hard to attain. Paradigmatic of human silences is "Our Lord's own Silence", the "silence of eternity interpreted by love"[153] of John Greenleaf Whittier's hymn.

Each short section on a different manifestation of Silence is illustrated in terms of her own experience. (Had Hilda Harrison read the manuscript, she might justifiably accuse its author of inserting too much of herself.) In Pondering, for example, we find the story of Little Frida in the Fordfield garden looking for the "Unseen One"[154] whose silent voice calls her when playing with her brothers – and realise that if she was, as Aelfrida would have us believe, five years old, the event must have taken place between 5 October 1888 and 5 October 1889, soon after Conrad's death and sometime before or shortly after Eustace's birth. It is, of course, difficult to be absolutely accurate about the exact timing of childhood happenings, even significant ones, particularly when one's mother is no longer alive to corroborate timing or event (a mother whose record of her children might have referred to it had it happened in Frida's fifth year but before Conrad's death) but Aelfrida's keenness to illustrate her latest book with a telling example of childhood piety begs two questions. Did the event actually happen? Or has she transformed a commonplace childhood experience into one of religious significance? Ten years later she will see (if she did) Christ appearing in a mandorla of light and, fifty years later still, will publish her book anonymously as an 'Anglican Tertiary' but ensure that the sole copy she preserves is inscribed 'Sister Placida Tertiary SSC' in order that there is no mistaking the identity of the child or 'child' to whom the experience (is said to have) happened.

Self-Forgetfulness also contains revelations, for it is while still embroiled in self-hood that Little Frida and adult Aelfrida sin. Frida sins the kind of childhood sins described in *Little Frida is Tempted*: picking and eating two "most seductive … most luscious" strawberries from the kitchen garden, only to be found out and banished for two weeks from the "garden of Eden" and from "Olympus, the serene home of the Gods".[155] Is this episode, representative, as Aelfrida would have us believe, of how a sin might appear to a little girl as "natural, excusable, caused by circumstances" and to an adult who trusted herself "not to bite deeply into the fruit" as something which "could not really do much harm … just to taste and see what a very little experience of one attractive and often-committed sin was like", or does it represent, as *The Fruits of Silence* suggests, an argument on the part of an adult woman that "the desire for experience was legitimate" and that, being the highly moral person she is, she "could not be attracted by anything really foul"?[156] Yet it seems she was, for though she never actively *desired* "the strange and the unusual ... in human ... experience" (or in "spiritual experience"), God, she says, "bestowed" them on her and, judging by her next line ("I recall now, in silence, before Thee, things of which I cannot write", 'things' which, if spiritual, were understandably unrevealed but if not, best left undescribed), she succumbed.[157] No wonder, then, she notes the "devious course" of her life's path (at the time of writing she was grubbing up 'vast weeds' from the cinder path in the hope that Mother Guenvrede might be 'more inclined to think her tertiary *has* some sort of vocation' than if merely 'informed' of 'God's gifts' to Placida) and prays for all who try to direct men's souls. (Directors include 'false prophets of whatever persuasion'.) Her escape-clause, however, is to say that it was *God* who, seeming to set her down in a maze, was, in fact, setting her feet on "a quiet and unerring ... way" to Him.[158]

Other pertinent statements refer to events in Aelfrida's immediate or distant past. In the Silence of Detachment she prays "disentangle me, Good Shepherd, from the wish to influence my fellow men or from the wish to make myself a leader on the pilgrim-road to Heaven. Let me be content that other men should write books" (*sic*: six books and numerous articles follow *The Fruits of Silence*), "preach the sermons, direct the penitents and organise the good works". ("These are hard lessons. I have not learnt them yet", she has the grace to add.)[159] She also refers obliquely to herself as "a human soul ... perchance ... through no fault of its own ... damaged by circumstances, bitter, vindictive".[160] In the Silence of Penitence she disingenuously states "I have no desire for power"[161], though she also notes "I abhor ... my assertiveness, my pride, my belief in myself and in my own judgement, my delusions as to the purity of my motives and my desire to set the world to rights", negative qualities due, she realises, to "the turmoil at the core of [her] being".[162] In the Silence of Bewilderment she describes how she 'trusted in men and they ... failed me' and how 'the passage of time has not blurred the impression nor dulled the pain'"[163], and in the Silence of Sympathy notes that "there was a time ... when I ... used to turn away my eyes (whether of the body or the mind) from the sight of pain ... not of set purpose or wilfully but unconsciously to barricade myself against the invasion of the world's anguish [because] if I had no opportunity of bringing help why should I concern myself with what

other persons endured?"[164] Some references predict or promise (in the Silence of Longing, "it is for the young to seek adventure and romance"[165]; in the Silence of Enlightenment, "all my tawdry pretensions shall go [and] my complacency, my self-regarding")[166], promises and predictions destined to be broken or manifestly untrue. Some are requests (e.g. "space for amendment"), some recognition that she needs more time.[167] References to current events show how her current book reflects her life: to Lent and Holy Week 1944 and to having read St John of the Cross during 'Silences' of Self-Forgetfulness and Pondering because "it delights me to study ... Theologians and Divines and then ... to go away among hill and forest where solitude and nature stimulate my mind to make its own decisions"[168] (and, one might say, led her to strange conclusions); in the Silence of Gratitude to her being a 'half-blind and illiterate Beggar'[169] and to her letter of 24 July 1944 begging Mother Guenvrede to send her to Coventry; to a vision experienced on 24 June 1944 while praying *coram sanctissimo* ('the mystical experience par excellence') at which there occurred 'an as-it-were "blood transfusion" of Spirit into spirit ... an experience of the undifferentiated Godhead ... common to mystics of all religions' ('though of course only the Christian can fully interpret the vision')[170], transcribed virtually verbatim as "some mysterious blood-transfusion of the Spirit"[171] in the section on Our Lord's own Silence. References to Silence as an important spiritual quality in a book devoted to its 'fruits' are also of an immensely personal nature: "my child, I have called thee to Silence", says God in the Silence of Reverence[172], and His "I bade thee offer me Silence and the fruits thereof"[173] in the Silence of Bewilderment echoes Placida's initial feeling that "Silence was but [her] own personal abstention from speech" in order to create "a hush in her soul", that personal silence later "merged into Community Silence, [her] portion of labour in our Contemplative prayer", and that only now does she realise "it [is] Thy Silence, O Crucified, that I must keep"[174] in a Silence of Gratitude.

Writing her first book for some years can also be seen as an attempt to move on to the next stage of her spiritual progress, as an indication of the 'fruits' she hoped to enjoy there, as a Newmanian 'apologia' for inconsistencies apparent in her behaviour as she edged her 'mystic' way along a 'way' whose course was as indistinct as her own was uncertain, as an attempt to find space for amendment, as a means of silencing the noise of 'the world' which rang in her ears 'very loud' as 1943 merged into 1944 (louder even than 'bangs' from 'Jerry' or the 'weird noises' in her ears)[175] or of proving that Mother Guenvrede's 'Anglican Tertiary' had achieved interior silence. She may also have regarded it as liberation from what she increasingly regarded as spiritual captivity i.e. less an escape *to* God than escape *from* the demands of senile Mrs Donkin, emotional Hilda Harrison, and claustration.

Fortunately for Aelfrida's mental and the Community's spiritual equilibrium (though the positive effect of intensified claustration was to imbue spiritual experiences with supernatural significance, the negative effect was that of turning emotional susceptibilities into intellectual certainties and these to delusions), Placida's next intention, namely to withdraw into total silence, was thwarted by the very people she hoped would support it.

Although she had recently expressed fear of living a life of complete silence even if this was God's Will for her[176] and was even prepared to amuse Mrs Donkin if totality could be avoided in this way, the coincidence of Agatha's 'heavenly birthday' with Ash Wednesday (a Community 'silent day') in February 1944 persuaded her that she, like Agatha, ought to be (but while still alive) nothing but the 'soul at prayer'[177] recommended by Augustine Baker to the nuns at Cambrai. Being now well into writing *The Fruits of Silence*, she decided that God Himself also desired her to be '*nothing except a soul at prayer*' (with the human escape clause 'as far as is possible'), He having announced this Himself by sending her a vision at 10.50am on Sunday 9 July 1944, a day on which He called her into chapel (the weather was too wet for a walk) to manifest Himself 'in His modes of Power, Love and Silence', to allow her to experience 'His Will for [her]' by causing her to become a purely prayerful soul, and to inform her that she was to convey to the Community 'a sense of His Presence' rather than her own.[178] (It may or may not be relevant that it was in January 1944 Aelfrida decided to keep a low profile and make no demands on Mother Guenvrede lest she be asked to leave permanently and that it was in February 1944 that the Mother began hinting about Placida being 'drawn back into "the Library"'.) Conscious, however, that she was about to demand something of Mother Guenvrede, she began her campaign by making no demands on her at all while seemingly obeying her instructions: Silence, she explained (in writing) to a visitor, 'could be broken at any time at the call of charity' but Placida must have the Mother's dispensation to break it.[179]

Mothering Sunday 1944, however, saw 'Placida Ter. SSC' writing her deliberately provocative letter to Mother Guenvrede. It also challenged her authority: "We agree that *Religious Silence* [constitutes] silence of the lips and of the soul in [God's] Holy Presence … an intense awareness [and] a gift from Him … Last September … Our Lord came … with the Father and the Holy Spirit and *took up [His] abode in me* … [He] further explained

to me that He wishes me to be *nothing but a soul at prayer* [but] what I want to know is, how is this to be worked out in practice? … [but] if it is God's Will, I MUST do it … I hope all this is quite clear".[180]

Mother Guenvrede's (verbal) response was that she was 'inclined' to 'agree with' Placida's request (Aelfrida crossed out 'to grant my request' as too definite a version of what the Mother did or did not say) that she be allowed to maintain total silence till Easter or even until Whit Sunday six weeks later (Placida privately determined to hold out till Holy Cross Day in mid-September then, 'if allowed', to make a promise of a year's silence with the exception of Christmas, Easter, one other major festival, and 'the inevitable breaches' created by visits from Julius and 'other kin') but was worried that silence made Placida's mind 'act queerly'. Aelfrida hastened to reassure her: silence 'was the only thing that seemed to give [her] mind all the room it needed' and it was 'the pressure of other people's personalities' on her own which caused her to act 'queerly'.[181]

Her request was not solely spiritual: Hilda Harrison was due for an extended Easter visit and although Aelfrida now expressed 'solid woman friendship'[182] with her, she had no intention of listening to Hilda's woes again. An opportune sore throat and 'Authority' ordering her to bed till Palm Sunday provided an excuse for Placida's 'act of moral cowardice'[183] but, as she also recognized, a forty-day Lenten silence was already creating a mental vacuum into which surged disturbing thoughts concerning 'bombs and bombs and *bombs*' raining down again over Cardiff, 'non-military casualties' described unemotionally by *The Times* to the horror of someone so wrapped in her quest for personal salvation that she had failed to give thought to them, and the contrast between the 'friendly and unsuspicious' natures of animals (and people) met away from but not now inside the convent. 'I must not get frantic', she wrote, 'my business is prayer and silence'; even God, giving into her keeping 'some of His own Silence', warned her not to attract attention to herself by behaving 'queerly' again.[184] And Placida's quietest ever Holy Week ensued.

Having discovered that continuous silence was not only an 'intensely luminous' and a 'not unnatural' state of being but also 'something my spirit has always longed for without knowing it'[185], Placida appealed to Father Northcott, currently at Tymawr for the triennial election of a new Mother Superior. (Aelfrida dreaded the 'utter impossibility' of opening her soul 'to a *new* Mother'[186] and was relieved when Mother Guenvrede was re-elected.) Their interview took place on 30 April 1944, when, having explained 'the whole question of [her] silence' to him (reported statements mostly begin

One of Sister Placida's letters to Mother Guenvrede

with the first person egotistical: '*I* suggested / put it to him / proceeded to tell him', and so on), Placida was gratified to hear the Warden agree that she was certainly moving 'in the direction of perpetual silence' but less pleased concerning his comments on her intention: she was not promoting *interior* silence properly ('you [have] a large correspondence …cut that down''; she did not) and though it might be possible to 'offer a year's silence' ('of course it isn't, cannot be *complete*', noted Placida, joyfully listing the reasons why it couldn't be), he would have to discuss the matter with Mother Guenvrede first, a lady who, so Aelfrida said, 'thinks I am just a freak and that it is less trouble to let me do as I like than it [is] to check me'. PS, she added, 'of course I said nothing to Father Northcott about my being *used* to fight against the powers of darkness …'[187], a wise decision given that silence undoubtedly made her mind 'act queerly' and that Father Northcott almost certainly knew it.

Armed with further ammunition Placida tackled Northcott again (her guardian angel had warned her 'very insistently *not* to run to the Mother [with] enquiries as to [her] fate'), informing him that the chapter on Solitaries in the newly published *Directory of the Religious Life* 'confirmed' that the unusual vocation existed and recommended that 'the Solitary should be attached to a Community'.[188] She therefore begged him 'to authorise the Mother' to admit her as a Solitary ('class V', according to the *Directory*) with a Rule of perpetual silence except on 'necessary occasions as should be agreed between [herself] and the Mother'. She did not, she added confusingly, wish to live in *absolute* silence, Carthusian and Trappist 'keeping apartness' (*spatiamentum*) being something she dreaded more than the kind of 'perpetual' silence she envisaged for herself. In any case, even 'anchoresses are allowed conversation'.[189]

An informal chat with 'most friendly-disposed' Mother Guenvrede in mid-May failed to raise Placida's hopes, the former declaring herself 'as … prejudiced against Silence as Father Northcott [was] prejudiced in its favour' (*sic*) and that Placida was 'slower than most people in learning to talk while maintaining interior silence'.[190] Pending Father Northcott's still unspoken approval of the scheme ('I am afraid I puzzle him. And I don't wonder!')[191], Placida decided to let the Mother settle the matter 'then she can't say I am obstinate'. She added, however, that the Mother had obviously forgotten that Silence was Placida's 'portion of labour' for the Community (Placida's idea, not Mother Guenvrede's) and that what she and the Mother meant by 'interior silence' were thesis and antithesis, one believing it to be personalised recollective Practice of the Presence of God as advocated by Brother Lawrence and carried out 'even when consorting with one's fellow men', the other something originating with God and God-bestowed as a 'hush in the soul' in a soul which '*must* be alone' to receive and respond to it.[192] On 17 May (and probably after consultation with Mother Guenvrede) Father Northcott gave his decision: he did not 'altogether approve of Solitaries' and was not, *pace* the *Directory,* convinced of their 'expediency', so as Placida already enjoyed a 'degree of silence and retirement such as few others can enjoy … [she] had better be satisfied with that'.[193]

Aelfrida expressed herself 'well content' to return to 'Sundays-and-Festivals-talking' and to making better use of the silence intervening; privately she responded by withdrawing her current 'portion of labour' (planting potatoes), by pleading fatigue (she was not too tired to enjoy 'the best of all the Deardududays' exploring 'Prehistory' some distance from the convent), and by beginning a letter in which she implored Mother Guenvrede to 'let [her] be in Silence for a year'.[194] The letter was never sent. While composing it under the shade of 'Saint Castanea', she was accosted by Hilda Harrison who lectured her 'directly and earnestly' on the 'Undesirability of Silence' from 'the Library's' point of view: 'the Library', she said, did not like Aelfrida's 'goings-on', thought she was 'putting too much strain' on herself, and regarded her desire for silence as 'merely Pride ... coupled with a love of being conspicuous'. (Her further comments that Aelfrida's company was 'wanted' and that no-one *really* believed that Trappists and Carthusians were more pleasing to God than anyone else, suggests a degree of collusion between Hilda, Mother, and Warden.) The onset of a thunderstorm prevented Aelfrida from replying but Hilda's words brought her up short: 'doubtless there *is* a huge store of pride hidden in my unconscious'. She therefore decided to 'happify the Library and maintain interior silence [even] when exterior silence must be broken'.[195]

Then a thought struck her: was Silence *really* God's Will for her or was it, as Hilda said, a manifestation of egocentricity and eccentricity? Two days later she received a reply, though not quite the one she expected. Praying after Vespers *coram sanctissimo*, she felt the Holy Spirit take her '*into* my Lord's Silence as He hung upon the Cross', there to perceive 'that in the *centre* of [His] Silence was infinite peace and contentment' and 'into *that I entered*'. This sudden realisation that hopes of achieving the perfect splendour of the Beatific Vision (a vision which, like Silence and Solitude, was only a pointer or a means to an end to what she sought) were nothing compared to what she had never been – *at peace with and at peace within herself* – was one of the most important moments of her life: 'O loving Spirit', she prayed, 'transform me into that which I behold'.[196] And suddenly we realise that the Beatific Vision for which she hopes is that of the perfect splendour of mental peace and equilibrium and that although her hope is couched (as for Aelfrida it must be) in religious terms, it does not depend on Deity for fulfilment.

But peace within Aelfrida's heart and mind in summer 1944 was less likely than world peace for, thwarted of 'perpetual' silence, Placida tried a different stratagem. Hoping, as she put it, that replies to letters written might be used as '*sparks* to kindle a fire'[197], she began by trying to set Mothers against Mother. A letter to the Reverend Mother 'of the Fordfield Community' received no or an unsatisfactory (and therefore unrecorded) response; a letter to Mother Magdalen Mary of Malling received a reply from Sister Osyth, a redoubtable religious writing on her behalf. From her reply, we can deduce questions put: what was the difference between 'recollection' and 'interior silence' and what were the Lady Abbess' views on 'the question of Silence'?[198] But if she hoped for ammunition – her inclusion of a bribe in the shape of making over royalties from *The Closer Walk with God* to Malling suggests she hoped for largesse in return – Aelfrida was to be disappointed. The Lady Abbess, said Sister Osyth, did not believe that "interior silence" was

a "technical" subject on which people should introspect at length, prayer and "the *doing* it", not "the science of prayer", being what mattered. As to Aelfrida being a "solitary", the life she was currently leading "attached to a Community but not actually living in it" was sufficient – and in any case being a "solitary" as described in the *Directory* was "perhaps rather too fashionable these days!" Furthermore, in currently bearing "a large portion-of-labour of the Community's silence", Aelfrida was doing "quite enough in this way." Finally, an appeal: "she says '*couldn't* you go down ... oftener to the poor guests?' With my love in Christo. Dame Osyth OSB".[199]

Phyllis' visit to Tymawr prevented her sister-in-law from taking the matter further. (The irony of her comment that Aelfrida "so obviously belong[ed]" at Tymawr seems to have been lost on its recipient.)[200] But having pondered Sister Osyth's proxy remarks, Placida wondered if obsession with 'the science of prayer' could not be subsumed into 'the Silence that my Lord enjoins' and decided that *pace* Malling, unofficial claustration 'alone with the Alone' might be in order.[201] She therefore tried another tactic: while ostensibly agreeing that Mother Guenvrede really *did* need to take her down 'several pegs' (a work in progress, surely?) and that as 'Aelfrida – Placida – whatever you call yourself', she was 'second rate, third rate possibly, and boring to the Saints in heaven'[202], she wrote to a saint on earth: 'Saint Lucius' Cary.

But if she hoped to set Saint and Father against Mother and Father she failed, for far from supporting her with heavy artillery, Lucius Cary peppered her with admonitory shot: "terminology" ('recollection', 'interior silence', and so on) was "full of traps"; devotion had both uses *and dangers* insofar as an individual such as herself might misinterpret or fail to properly assimilate the "spiritual sentiment" of the Community to which they were attached; silence per se was no antithesis to "lightmindedness" nor did it "act as an antidote to evil", evil which could be ("is it not?") "hatched out" as much in silence as without it; silence as self-discipline (*ascesis*) might serve a purpose but was essentially a "contributory condition to other spiritual values that are in themselves [more] positive", loving one's neighbour as oneself being a case in point. Finally, whether or not a year's silence "would ... promote Sister Placida's sanctification" was an irrelevance in terms of her spiritual development and, this being so, he would *not* encourage her "intention". And, his parting shot, rather than refer to him, "Sister Placida *must* refer to those who have immediate oversight of [her] life and insight into its arcana".[203] Shot down in flames rather than sparking a fire, Aelfrida conceded defeat.

This 'push' from Father Cary may, however, have added fuel to the fire which was soon to rage between Mother

Guenvrede, Father Northcott, and herself with regard to her latest visit to Cardiff; it may also have prompted two remarks made in the period which followed his letter and preceded her departure. The first, made within days of the former while pondering on a notion conceived during her 1943 visit that if Mother Guenvrede had told her that she could return to Tymawr if she walked barefoot, she would have set out immediately, caused her to ask in 1944: "should I? I wonder!!"[204] The second, made while wondering where to go if, following her 1944 visit, she was not allowed to return (Leiston, possibly, recently reopened as a retreat house after closing earlier in the war) was that the thought of life away from Tymawr might be less a 'temptation' than a 'signpost'.[205]

Aelfrida began her second book, *The Glory of the West*, on 9 December 1944, a month after returning from her second visit to Cardiff. Although its immediate inspiration may have been Anna Tillyard's death, the idea for and title of the work had been present in her mind since June 1930 as a contemporary diary entry shows: 'the discipline I want and need is hard work … at least three [books] hang ripe on the tree of my imagination and will only deteriorate if not plucked'. The first of these (*O Passionate World*) was about to be written, and the third (*Out of the Ruins*, 'a grim and fantastic story of England after the *next* great war') would be *The Approaching Storm*. The second, already entitled *The Glory of the West* and described after the manner of Vera Brittain's '*Testaments*' of *Youth* and *Friendship* of 1933 and 1940 as her 'testament of Beauty'[206] (Brittain's and Aelfrida's testaments of '*Experience*' were written in the following decade), was delayed for fifteen years until the moment she decided to write 'a definite book on something sensible'[207] in order to write herself saner even than with *The Fruits of Silence,* none of whose fruits, so she then thought, were pathological.

Aelfrida's reasons for writing this second and quite different book, outward and forward-looking and though still referring back to a golden age, keen to press on to an even more golden future – even the style is liberated from archaically 'pious' language inherited from literary models regarded by herself (and others) as suitable for intercourse with and interpretation of Deity – can be deduced from the book itself and from an earlier occasion in her life at Tymawr. The occasion occurred on Ash Wednesday 1941, the point at which Aelfrida bestowed her manuscript paper on Hilda Harrison 'and with it all my unwritten books, my unborn children' so that she herself would not be tempted to write – and, notably, so that Hilda too with Aelfrida's admonition in her ears ("write down absolutely everything … don't leave out a single point – externalize the lot") could

'unfuss' herself from the 'dark clouds' of her past by committing to paper a 'truthful history' of her life. (That by Hilda she also meant herself is evident from two further comments: Hilda, she wrote, 'ought to have married a Christian gentleman and brought up a large family of splendid children', and someone who has made "a big book" of their past in this way should give it to a person whose judgement they respect to read "and then burn it").[208] In 1945, however, and having reclaimed her precious paper (Hilda's life remained un-externalised and fussed), Aelfrida developed the idea of 'unfussing' oneself by writing diaries ("useful recipients for superfluous feelings") or letters ("a channel of affection" constituting a legitimate means of "stretch[ing] out [to] clasp the hand of a friend … [or] regular correspondents")[209], or a book in which one can release one's pent-up emotions and ideas and enable others to do the same by travelling through "the wide and fertile fields" of the writer's knowledge, the latter a particularly important activity for a reader whose mind is "morbid, discontented, queer" because confined by "stale imaginations" and "fed on propaganda"[210] (*sic*) disseminated by those whose concepts of man's relationship with God are based on an outmoded emphasis on monastic life.

Even more significant, perhaps, is Aelfrida's emphasis on "mental health". If, she writes, "you have been spending a life that lacks balance … you cannot expect … to enjoy perfect … mental health when you are sixty". Lack of 'balance' may manifest itself as the mild "eccentricity" people are prepared to tolerate in themselves because it distinguishes them from the "flatly commonplace", but if not checked may become a symptom of serious mental trouble. This is particularly likely in someone shut up in an "unwholesome" atmosphere of introspection in which "the distorting medium of his … personality" creates a "morass of grievances and miseries" or in someone suffering "thwarted desire" because "squeezed into shape … by circumstances" and unable to expand to "the full size of his personality". Writing as one who has "not even had what is euphemistically called a 'nervous breakdown'" (*sic*), she warns her readers not to "delight in toying with the fantastic lures of madness" as such people tend to do but to distract themselves by performing "ordinary everyday" tasks (including, inevitably, "regularity in … religious practices"), by reminding themselves that belief in God "keeps us sane" (*sic*), and by asking themselves "what figures do [we] cut in the light of heaven's sanity?" Lastly, she assures her readers that "it is not such a disaster [if] … you should … become a little unwell mentally" because "fear of insanity" is often worse than insanity itself (dwelling on one's fear, she adds, tends to "actualise" it) and modern treatments for those who are "unwell mentally" are "rational and kind".[211] And what better plea for reassurance of her own sanity under adverse circumstances and for support of her intention to respond to 'the tug of the world' to complete the process could she have written?

The tone and content of Aelfrida's diary changes as she composes her latest volume of 'spiritual autobiography'.[212] Quietly optimistic in spite of the volume of war news recorded, it contains few records of internecine warfare, of recording-breaking attendances at the *opus Dei*, of visions, of Christmas 1944 or even of Lent 1945 ('the *silentest* of all Lents I have ever had', something for which Mother Guenvrede was to express thanks for having been able to '*forget all about*' her resident tertiary for once; Placida, she noted, had had a '*quieter* silence' instead of her usual 'noisy' one)[213] because Aelfrida was both enjoying a 'good spell'[214] of work on *The Glory of the West* and rediscovering the extent to which the physical act of writing and literary composition constituted '*catharsis*'.[215] Writing 'THE END on p343' on 22 July 1945, she noted that instead of being exhausted and voided as she was wont to be on completion of a book, she felt 'refreshed … in body and mind'.[216]

Subtitling it "A book on Old Age", Aelfrida described *The Glory of the West* as a 'mixture of [the] commonplace, irony, humour, good advice, and mysticism!'[217]; it is also the sanest and most practical of all her books to date. Having travelled with her through near-death experiences, thoughts of suicide, self-harm, 'madness', and despair, it is wonderful to find her winning through to a place where she 'can see far and wide in all directions'.[218] Though ostensibly describing the vistas opened around the convent after wartime felling of surrounding woodland, metaphorically speaking she has rid herself of so much mental and emotional 'dead wood' that she can see remaining 'trees' outlined in 'bronze–gold radiance'[219] and at their feet 'bright flowers' springing up which never grew before because smothered by 'undergrowth' and deprived of 'light'. And so it is with Aelfrida's life as she traverses the pages of a book which, unsurprisingly under the circumstances, '*has been writing itself*.'[220]

She begins by addressing her audience ("dear and gentle reader, on December 28 1944 I began to think seriously about old age … being old is very interesting [and] … I am sure that my ideas on old age will be more lucid and more correct on the other side of the grave [but] I cannot … afford to wait so long") and a future biographer ("if a thread seems to have slipped out of my fingers, I shall know that is safe in yours and that it will be woven in again bye and bye … the finished product shall serve either as fireside rug or a magic carpet or as a prayer mat … have it as [you] will')[221], then she

plunges into her theme: "old age as an antechamber to heaven".[222]

As with *The Fruits of Silence,* she illustrates her text with examples taken from her own life. Her need for solitude (as opposed to loneliness) as a quality which "breaks down the cruel walls of a man's selfhood and gives him back the boundless country from whence he came".[223] Her need to remind and reassure herself (as during childhood worship in a side aisle of St Columba's she could not) that she is now one of "the elect [who] enjoy the everlasting 'Flight of the Alone to the Alone', that secret intercourse of … creature … and creator".[224] Her spiritual experiences: "the sycamore stretches its branches over holy soil and there is the bronze figure of the Crucified, nailed to the living tree. And have I not in thought seen our Lord Himself lying stretched under the oaks as once in Gethsemane, bowed beneath the demands of His Father?"[225] Her thoughts on channels of communication opening between herself and God: channels of repentance, trust, pain, beauty, thought, daily tasks (hers – attendance at Holy Communion – is over before breakfast, a new and excellent excuse for opting out of 'portions of labour' allotted by Mother Guenvrede), human affections (a new and significant addition), and the most vital: prayer.[226] Her thoughts on the devil, of whom she asks "is [he] *real*?" before answering that he *is* in the sense of being "of the same fabric" as her guardian angel ("always near", but of whom she prefers to "say nothing") and that in the form of "mocking spirits of darkness", he can "tap at the mind's windows and lure the soul out into the night", an interesting admission, given that there is a correlation between the devil's visits and her bouts of mental imbalance and that what she describes as physical manifestations of his presence (choking darkness, her bed being shaken violently) may be metaphorical descriptions of her mind becoming temporarily unhinged to such an extent that when she looks at her reflection in a mirror (or at herself reflected in Frank Stokoe or Nadja Laptchinski), she sees, not a "friend", but "an alien and malignant personality". But "look steadily and pray", she adds, "and you will see behind the alien personality the beloved soul" of the person you know, albeit a soul temporarily "chained and bound".[227] A poignant plea, indeed, given what we know of her life to date.

The greater part of *The Glory of the West*, however, is a road-book for the over-sixties. (Aelfrida turned sixty-one while writing it.) Practical hints flow from her pen: "open the doors of your mind" to the world; if you cannot sleep on "a hard mattress laid over boards", do not brood on infirmities or injustices but enjoy "moments transparent of eternity" by turning your thoughts to happy memories, distant friends, and God; "say as little as possible about [your] ailments, even to [your] most sympathetic friends"; keep good books to hand (Thomas à Kempis, Julian of Norwich, and Francis de Sales are among those listed); keep active ("what admirable outlets ... do housework and gardening provide!") ; regularly undertake "a grand stocktaking and [spring] cleaning of ... your thoughts and ways" in order to clear your mind of "supposed complexes ... neuroses and phobias"[228]; make your will under legal supervision, make it accessible to your executors, and "think of the effects that your bequests are likely to have".[229] Presciently she also foresees the deleterious effects on society of populations containing "more citizens over sixty than under"[230] and of welfare state payments creating a "lack of incentive to do anything". (A rich comment from one who now received the "old-age-allowance" and had received a "maintenance-allowance" for fifteen years.) She also asks if "Feminist movements" "pay any attention to the masculine point of view or [are] ... only occupied with women and *their* rights and claims?"[231] and even invents the University of the Third Age in the form of 'summer schools' for the old "whose courses are "Spiritual, Intellectual, Occupational [or] Recreational" but "you can have a sort of mixed grill"[232] if you prefer.

Her favourite chapter was entitled 'From Dawn till Dusk'. Beginning at dawn when "Sister Castanea, the chestnut, [Brother] Fagus, the huge beech, wake up and glow in the light", it continues with a lyrical description of a Tymawr day and ends at dusk when "one solitary gleam of crimson lingers still beyond where an oak tree makes a rough cross with trunk and extended boughs, ... the meaning of the day distilled into a single thought: the mystery, the glory of the west".[233] The day described is also her own life from childhood to the moment at which she sits in the West Room on 'Father Cary's chair' alternately expressing "in rhythmic words"[234] what she feels about 'Things that Matter' and gazing from her window at the 'heavenly-lovely sunset' which has coincided with the anniversary of Agatha's 'Heavenly Birthday'.[235] Sunset is her own thoughts as she prepares to go west (as the contemporary expression had it) towards death, the "last obstacle to be overleapt before we emerge into life that is life indeed" – though not, in 1944/45, as proximate an obstacle as she hoped.

The changing appearance of the sky as the sun sinks behind the Welsh hills symbolises aspects of her personality: "steadfast fire from the heart of a lonely prophet who spoke truth when no-one listened" (Mrs Constantine Graham, authoress and lecturer); "rays of light from a crown of thorns" (Sister Placida of the Holy Passion); "blood-red streams from a tall black cross" (Aelfrida

Tillyard, mystic and visionary); "some gleam from the eyes of a *mater dolorosa* who has turned her grief into love towards all the world" and for whom it takes "pain as well as joy to make the glory of the west"[236]: Agatha's 'Mother'. As the sun sinks below the horizon, Aelfrida also compares herself to a ship, battered but still afloat after a thousand voyages, sailing along the path of the "Light Perpetual" which creates the true 'glory' of the west and will lead her to harbour with God in "Ageless Eternity", a ship whose crew has "thrown overboard the rubbish and kept the treasure; got rid of the vanities and the petty exultations and kept the warmth of love and the wish to be good; flung out the possessiveness and preserved the generosity; cast away the self-seeking and retained the longing after God".[237]

But if, dear and gentle Reader, you believe that the author of *The Glory of the West* has followed her own advice and become a nicer person, dear and gentle Reader, you are wrong. There are eleven volumes of diary to come and not until the penultimate does the fight go out of Aelfrida – and even then she is not quite as transformed as she would like to have us think into the person she describes above. But how dull the remainder of her biography would be if she had behaved henceforth as *The Glory of the West* suggests.

## Notes

1 Excerpt from a speech made by Prime Minister Winston Churchill on 10 November 1942, reported bathetically by Aelfrida as 'the war seems to be going better' (GCPPT 1|1|60 11 November 1942).
2 GCPPT 1|1|61 'Holy Cross Day' (14 September ) 1943.
3 ibid. 'Holy Cross Day' (14 September) 1943 and 17 September 1943.
4 ibid. 16 September 1943.
5 ibid. 28 September 1943.
6 ibid. 24 September 1943.
7 ibid. 16 September 1943. Author's emphasis.
8 ibid. 'Holy Cross Day (14 September) 1943.
9 ibid. 'Vigil of All Saints' (31 October) and 'All Saints' (1 November) 1943.
10 ibid. 'All Saints' (1 November) 1943.
11 GCPPT 1|1|59 29 September 1941.
12 GCPPT 1|1|61 9 March 1944.
13 ibid. 6 November 1943.
14 ibid. 20 February 1944.
15 GCPPT 1|1|62 27 December 1944.
16 Tillyard, Ae. *The Glory of the West*. pp 44–45 (GCPPT 2|16|3).
17 ibid.
18 GCPPT 1|1|63 21 December 1945.
19 GCPPT 1|1|61 6 November 1943.
20 GCPPT 1|1|61 23 November 1943.
GCPPT 1|1|62 'Christmas Day' (25 December) 1944.
21 GCPPT 1|1|61 18 November 1943.
22 ibid. 16 February 1944.
23 GCPPT 1|1|61a Draft of letter from 'Placida Ter. SSC' to Mother Guenvrede of 19 March 1944.
24 GCPPT 1|1|62 31 July and 2 August 1944.

25 ibid. 2 November 1944.

26 ibid.

27 GCPPT 1|1|62 22 November 1944.

28 ibid. 18 November 1944.

29 GCPPT 1|1|63 31 October and 1 November 1945.

30 ibid. 30 September 1945.

31 ibid. 22 and 28 September 1945

32 ibid. 22 and 28 September 1945.

33 Tillyard, Ae. *Naomi da Costa* p 48 (GCPPT 2|22).

34 GCPPT 1|1|62 21 February 1945.

35 Tillyard, Ae. *Naomi da Costa* p 198.

36 GCPPT 1|1|63 25 February and 1 November 1945. For interesting discussions of Julius Tillyard's past, current, and future 'labours for Byz. Music', see Tillyard, HJW. *Byzantine Music and Hymnography*, Wellesz, E. *A History of Byzantine Music and Hymnography*, and Benson, C. *Egon Wellesz (1885–1974) Chronicle of a Twentieth Century Musician*. Aelfrida's first mention of one of Julius' two chief collaborators in the study of Byzantine musicology appears on 25 November 1941 (GCPPT 1|1|59). Describing Wellesz as an 'Austrian Jew' and typically misspelling his name as 'Wellerz', she mentions him occasionally thereafter; Carsten Høeg of Copenhagen, Julius' other collaborator, she mentions more rarely. The 'unlimited funds' to which she refers came from 'inspired millionaire', 'Dr Whittemore', described by her as 'the Illustrissimus Donor' (GCPPT 1|1|59 25 November 1941 and GCPPT 1|1|62 21 February 1945) but more properly Thomas Whittemore (1871–1950), archaeologist-founder of the Byzantine Institute of America in 1930.

37 GCPPT 1|1|62 21 February 1945. In *The Making of a Mystic* (p13) Aelfrida describes Eustace (as 'Sebastian') as disbelieving the story of Noah because sure "all those animals could not have got into the ark".

38 GCPPT 1|1|63 6 June 1945.

39 GCPPT 3|4 Letter from Eustace Tillyard to Aelfrida of 7 October 1945. The letter, sent from Merton House, begins "Dearest Frida" and is signed "Swab" and appears to have been written on pages from an exercise book. Aelfrida forwarded it to Alethea on 12 October 1945 and it survived its journey, reappearing much later 'in the Family Archive'.

40 GCPPT 1|1|61a Draft of a letter from 'Placida Ter. SSC' to Mother Guenvrede of 19 March 1944.
GCPPT 1|1|62 2 August 1944.

41 GCPPT 1|1|62 15 December 1944.

42 GCPPT 1|1|63 21 December 1945. Agnes Slack's obituary notice (GCPPT 1|1|63a) describes her as a widow, she having married late in life. 'She did not live long to enjoy married life – or … was it the death of her?' was the acid comment of a biographer whose inability to discover her subject's age until the subject died rankled still.

43 GCPPT 1|1|63 15 and 26 February and 29 April 1946.

44 GCPPT 3|4 Letter from Eustace Tillyard to Aelfrida of 7 October 1945.

45 GCPPT 1|1|63 15 June 1945.

46 GCPPT 1|1|61 14 November 1943.

47 ibid. 'All Saints' (1 November) and 6 November 1943.

48 ibid. 14 and 18 November 1943.

49 ibid. 15 January 1944.

50 ibid. 16 January 1944.

51 ibid. 18 November 1943 and 22 February 1944.

52 ibid. 1 January 1944.

53 ibid. 14 November 1943.

54 ibid. 25 November 1943.

55 ibid. 15 January 1944.

56 ibid. 23 January 1944.

57 ibid. 17 November 1944.

58 ibid. 8 December 1943

59 ibid. 18 November 13 and 16 January 1944.

60 ibid. 16 and 23 January 1944. Draft letter from Aelfrida to Hilda Harrison.

61 ibid. 1 and 3 March 1944.

62 ibid. 6 March 1944.

63 1|1|61a 19 March 1944 contains the first draft of a letter from 'Placida Ter. SSC' to Mother Guenvrede. The draft was apparently 'abbreviated' before the letter was sent.

64 GCPPT 1|1|62a *SSC Newsletter* 8 December 1944.

65 GCPPT 1|1|62 4 May and 23 September 1944. Aelfrida describes Sister Jeanne's condition as 'a kind of elephantiasis of the left leg and side' but it was more probably reflex sympathetic dystrophy, a debilitating neurophysiological syndrome with pain and swelling as its chief features.

66 ibid. 18 June 1944.

67 GCPPT 1|1|59 3 May 1941.

68 GCPPT 1|1|62 15 August 1944.

69 ibid. 10 July and 17 August 1944.

70 ibid. 11 and 17 August 1944.

71 GCPPT 1|1|62a Letter from 'Placida. Tertiary SSC' to Mother Guenvrede of 29 July 1944.

72 GCPPT 1|1|62 31 July 1944.

73 ibid. 6 and 7 August 1944.

74 GCPPT 1|1|61 23 November 1943
GCPPT 1|1|62 2 August 1944.

75 GCPPT 1|1|62 9 August 1944.

76 ibid. 15 August 1944.

77 ibid. 9 August 1944.

78 ibid. 9 and 10 August 1944.

79 ibid. 4 September 1944.

80 ibid. 2 August 1944.

81 ibid. 9 and 14 September 1944.

82 ibid. 25 September 1944.

83 GCPPT 1|1|63a *SSC Newsletter* of April 1945.

84 ibid. 24 September 1944.

85 ibid. 24 and 27 September 1944.

86 ibid. 13 July and 8 November 1944.

87 ibid. 2 August 1944.

88 ibid. 13 July 1944.

89 ibid. 25 September 1944.

90 ibid. 25 and 27 September 1944.

91 GCPPT 1|1|73 22 January 1956.

92 GCPPT 1|1|61 12 February 1944.

93 ibid. 16 January 1944.

94 GCPPT 1|1|62 13 July 1944.

95 GCPPT 1|1|61 9 February 1944. Father Cary's pamphlet is undated but a letter from him to Aelfrida thanking her for her letter of appreciation dated 14 February 1944 (GCPPT1|1|61a) provides context. Though Father Cary's 'brochure' (as he termed it) was removed from the library by Mother Guenvrede in July 1944 (coincidentally or not about the time of arrival of another letter from Cary to Aelfrida), it was later reinstated as a catalogued item.

96 GCPPT 1|1|62 7 August 1944.

97 GCPPT 1|1|61 13 March 1944.

98 GCPPT 1|1|62 19 December 1944.

99 GCPPT 1|1|61a Draft letter from 'Placida Tertiary SSC' to 'dearest Hilda' Harrison of 23 January 1944.

100 GCPPT 1|1|63 8 November 1945.

101 GCPPT 1|1|50 11 March 1936.

102 GCPPT 1|1|63 15 November 1945.

103 GCPPT 1|1|53 22 July 1937.

104 ibid. 10 June 1937.

105 GCPPT 1|1|62 12 January 1945.

106 GCPPT 1|1|19 23 November 1913.

107 GCPPT 1|1|61 16 September 1943.

108  GCPPT 1|1|62 29 April 1944.

109  ibid. 2 May 1944.

110  ibid. 21 and 23 August 1944.

111  GCPPT 1|1|72 30 August 1955.

112  GCPPT 1|1|62 2 November 1944.

113  Benson, R.H. *The Necromancers* pp 299–306. There are early editions of several of RH Benson's books at Tymawr, including *The Necromancers* and *Richard Raynal* but excluding *Lord of the World*. There are also copies of AC Benson's books but not *The Babe BA,* a work plagiarised by Aelfrida somewhat earlier.

114  GCPPT 1|1|61 27 December 1943.

115  GCPPT 1|1|62 5 July 1944. The 'secret weapons' were V1 flying bombs and the V2 rockets now falling (or soon to fall) on London and south east England.

116  GCPPT 1|1|61 27 December 1943.
     GCPPT 1|1|62 8 July 1944.

117  GCPPT 1|1|62 6 June, 14 and 30 July 1944.

118  ibid. 6 June 1944.

119  GCPPT 1|1|73 22 January 1956.

120  *BNF* No.50 p551.

121  GCPPT 1|1|62 21 May 1944.

122  ibid. 'Monday' (25 September) 1944.

123  ibid. 30 July 1944.

124  ibid. 14 and 22 July 1944.

125  GCPPT 1|1|61 27 December 1943.

126  GCPPT 1|1|62 12 and 13 July 1944.

127  ibid. 18 July 1944.

128  ibid. 13 July 1944.

129  ibid. 14 July 1944.

130  GCPPT 1|1|73 8 April 1955.

131  GCPPT 1|1|61 3 March 1944.

132  GCPPT 1|1|62 22 July 1945.

133  ibid. 9 December 1944.

134  GCPPT 1|1|61 23 February 1944.
     GCPPT 1|1|62 9 December 1944.

135  GCPPT 1|1|61 3 March 1944.

136  For details of the life and thought of Father Augustine Baker (1575–1641) see the *Confessions of Venerable Augustine Baker* ed. J McCann, *The Life of Father Augustine* Baker (Salvin, P. and Cressy, S.) and Baker's own *Holy Wisdom or directions for the Prayer of Contemplation,* edited and reissued in 1911 by Abbot Sweeney OSB. Baker, as pp 39–40 of *The Making of a Mystic* show, was known to Aelfrida when writing her first homiletic book.

137  Augustine Baker was born David Baker at Abergavenny less than 15 miles from Tymawr, underwent the life-changing experience of near-drowning in a river near Monmouth, became a Benedictine monk, suffered much ill-health, was widely travelled, and by reason of his powerful personality caused dissention in a religious community for nearly ten years.

138  Salvin, P. and Cressy, S. p xxiii.

139  ibid. p xi. *Colossians* 3:3 (KJV).

140  Baker, A. *Confessions* p105.

141  ibid. pp 114–126.

142  GCPPT 1|1|61 3 March 1944.

143  GCPPT 1|1|55 17 June 1938.

144  GCPPT 1|1|57 8 November 1939. Quotations from Father Cary's article are taken from this diary entry.

145  GCPPT 1|1|59 24 June 1941.

146  GCPPT 1|1|62 1 September 1944.

147  ibid. 23 August 1944.

148  Tillyard, Ae. *The Fruits of Silence* pp 3–5 (GCPPT 2|18).

149  ibid. pp 5–8.

150  ibid. pp 20–24.

151  ibid. pp 24–27.

152  ibid. pp 27–31.

153  ibid. pp 36–39.

154  ibid. p 15.

155  GCPPT 2|23 *The Watchword* March 1957.

156  Tillyard, Ae. *The Fruits of Silence* pp 22–23.

157  ibid. p 30.

158  Tillyard, Ae *The Fruits of Silence* p 25.
     GCPPT 1|1|61 25 February 1944.
     GCPPT 1|1|62 10 July 1944.

159  Tillyard, Ae. *The Fruits of Silence* pp 32–35.

160  ibid. pp 31–36.

161  ibid. pp 8–9.

162  ibid. pp 8–9.

163  ibid. p 17.

164  ibid. pp 10–12.

165  ibid. pp 3–5.

166  ibid. pp 24–27.

167  ibid.

168  ibid. pp 12–14 and 20–24.

169  ibid. pp 27–31. The 'Beggar' allusion was not a new one; Aelfrida describes herself in much the same terms in the last line of *Can I be a Mystic?*

170  GCPPT 1|1|62 24 June 1944.

171  Tillyard, Ae. *The Fruits of Silence* pp 36–37.

172  ibid. pp 5–8.

173  ibid. p 17.

174  ibid. pp 27–31.

175  GCPPT 1|1|61 23 February and 4 April 1944.

176  ibid. 19 September 1943.

177  ibid. 23 February 1944.

178  GCPPT1|1|61 6 March 1944.
     GCPPT 1|1|62 10 July1944.

179  GCPPT 1|1|61 22 February 1944.

180  ibid. 19 March 1944

181  ibid.

182  ibid. 28 March 1944.

183  ibid. 27 and 29 March 1944.

184  ibid. 28 March and 4 April 1944.

185  GCPPT 1|1|62 23 April 1944.

186  ibid. 29 and 30 April 1944.

187  ibid. 30 April and 2 May 1944.

188  ibid. 2 May 1944.

189  ibid. 5 May 1944. RH Benson's *Life of Richard Rolfe* in his *Book of the Love of Jesus* (pp 217–227) may have influenced Aelfrida's views here and with regard to her 'swallow's nest' at Malling. Anchorites or anchoresses, Benson states, invariably live enclosed in a cell which they never leave but are "far from being without human society". They sing instead "as a caged bird might, confined within bars through which men … look" because an important aspect of their role is to advise those who come seeking spiritual help. (Nor, doubtless to Aelfrida's relief, are they under obedience.) A hermit, on the other hand, such as Aelfrida pretended to be at St Benedict's (though with much confusion over the respective roles of hermits and anchoresses), sets him or herself apart by habit and habitation and generally but not always exclusively keeps silent in solitude; he or she is therefore "more of a solitary [but] less of a prisoner." (Nor is he or she under obedience.) Both anchorites/anchoresses and hermits, however, devote their lives "wholly to the direct praise and glory of God"; both generate an enormous "spiritual power" whose "moral effect" on others is marked; both may appear "idle and grotesque or at the best mistaken".

190  GCPPT 1|1|62 14 May 1944.

191  ibid. 10 May 1944.

192  ibid. 15 May 1944. Brother Lawrence of the Resurrection (1611–1691) preached "an entirely practical spirituality, [the] practice of the

presence of God" in marked contrast to that of an "intellectual who has to work out reasons and methods" (King, U. p 171). Aelfrida, as is evident from her advice to 'patients' in her days as a Straightener, preached Father Lawrence's doctrine to others (his advice, promulgated in letters addressed entirely to women, was published posthumously as *The Practice of the Presence of God*) but did not always follow it herself, in part because she absented herself as much as possible from the domestic tasks which occupied the Carmelite lay brother's working hours and whose execution he employed as a means of simply and directly approaching God, in part because her personality was such that she felt compelled (as he did not) to work out reasons and methods in order to achieve certainty of authority over relationships, be they with God or man.

193 ibid. 17 May 1944.

194 ibid. 17, 22 and 31 May 1944.

195 ibid. 31 May 1944.

196 ibid. 2 June 1944.

197 ibid. 28 June 1944.

198 ibid. 26 May and 28 June 1944.

199 GCPPT 1|1|62a. Letter from Dame Osyth OSB (at Fownhope Court, Hereford) to Aelfrida of 24 June 1944.

200 GCPPT 1|1|62 2 August 1944.

201 ibid. 21 July 1944.

202 ibid. 27 July 1944.

203 GCPPT 1|1|62a. Letter from Father Cary to Aelfrida of 29 July 1944.

204 GCPPT 1|1|62 2 August 1944.

205 ibid. 1 September 1944.

206 GCPPT 1|1|37 1 June 1930. Vera Brittain (1893–1970) was a writer whose relationship with her brother Edward (killed in the Great War) was as deep as Aelfrida's with Julius.

207 GCPPT 1|1|62 9 November 1944.

208 GCPPT 1|1|58 'Ash Wednesday' (26 February) 1941. In a later novel (*Rich Man's Choice* p 250. GCPPT 2|21|2 Pt1) the hero advises a mentally disturbed colleague (as Julius once advised adolescent Aelfrida) to "write down absolutely everything [about himself] … don't leave out a single point – externalise the lot. Make a big book of it, give it to me to read and then *burn* it". Bearing in mind Aelfrida's own holocausts, one wonders what revelations, valuable to a biographer, were similarly burnt.

209 Tillyard, Ae. *The Glory of the West* p 172–5 (GCPPT 2|16|3) The book is contained in three folders in the Girton College archive (GCPPT 2|16|1 Parts 1 and 2 and 2|16|3). I have indicated against each reference the folder in which it appears.

210 ibid. p 56. It is perhaps also significant that during the period of her writing *The Glory of the West* the scope of Aelfrida's reading widened to include books by contemporary writers on religious topics.

211 ibid. pp 65–93.

212 GCPPT 1|1|58 'Ash Wednesday' (26 February) 1941.

213 GCPPT 1|1|62 6 March 1945.
GCPPT 1|1|63 15 April 1945.

214 GCPPT 1|1|62 9 March 1945.

215 GCPPT 1|1|63 5 June 1945.

216 ibid. 22 July 1945. The typed version of *The Glory of the West* ends with a colophon

★

FINIS

and is signed 'Sister Placida of the Holy Passion'. The dashes presumably represent the five wounds of Christ; the star over the central cross is typed in red to emphasise that this is Christ's on Calvary. The book was never published but was retained by Aelfrida among her personal papers; it seems that it was the writing of it rather than its appearance in the public sphere which was important. The book's anonymous author (should it be published) was originally given as 'one poor widow'; the 'widow' subsequently changed her mind and called herself 'Aelfrida Tillyard', her usual pen name.

217 GCPPT 1|1|62 27 February 1945.

218 GCPPT 1|1|63 11 April 1945.

219 ibid. 25 November 1945.

220 GCPPT 1|1|62 9 December 1944.

221 Tillyard, Ae. *The Glory of the West* pp 1–6 (GCPPT 2|16|1 Pt1). Correcting her typescript, Aelfrida crossed out whole pages and chapters, marking them 'omit'. As these sections contain much interesting and revealing information, I have obeyed instructions issued elsewhere and woven them into my account. She also intended that Julius should be her collaborator in order to provide the "masculine point of view" (ibid) but the bitter and pessimistic tone of his contribution repelled her and she wrote alone 'to the glory of God and [for] the comfort, the *strengthening* [and] the enlightenment' of her readers (GCPPT 1|1|62 9 December 1944 and 20 March 1945).

222 ibid. 1|1|62 9 December 1944.

223 Tillyard, Ae. *The Glory of the West* pp 291–292 (GCPPT 2|16|1 Pt1).

224 ibid. p 179 (GCPPT 2|16|3).

225 ibid. p 387 (GCPPT 2|16|1 pt 2). Aelfrida's description derives from a diary entry of 2 January 1945 (GCPPT 1|1|62) in which she describes a recurrent vision of it being dusk and she, looking out of the West Room window down the garden towards the oak trees near the Campo Santo, sees 'prone among the brown leaves, Our Lord … lying [with] His head … pillowed in his left arm [and] His right arm … stretched out upon the ground … tense with pain, … agonising under the weight of our sins'. So vivid is her impression that she even sees 'a drop or two of blood' on the leaves.

226 ibid. pp 1–6 (GCPPT 1|16|1 pt 1) and p 388 (GCPPT 2|16|1 pt2).

227 ibid. pp 297–318 (GCPPT 1|16|1 pt 2.) It is surely significant that two of the longest chapters in *The Glory of the West* deal with mental illness and that some of what she writes reads remarkably like RH Benson's *The Necromancers* e.g. that the person possessed by "spirits of darkness" may be lured by them into hands of "magicians and sorcerers, spiritualists and freak-religionists" (ibid. GCPPT 1|16|1 pt2) as she herself now believed she had been by Aleister Crowley.

228 ibid. p 37 (GCPPT 1|16|3).

229 ibid. pp 331–333 (GCPPT 1|16|1 pt2).

230 ibid. pp 1–6 (GCPPT 2|16|3).

231 ibid. pp 277 (GCPPT 2|16|1 pt2).

232 ibid. pp 214 and 253 (GCPPT 2|16|1 pt 2).

233 ibid. pp 385–401 (GCPPT 1|16|1 pt2).

234 ibid. p 146 GCPPT 1|16|3).

235 GCPPT 1|1|63 23 February 1946.

236 Tillyard, Ae. *The Glory of the West* p120 (GCPPT 2|16|3) and pp 402–414 (GCPPT 2|16|1 pt 1).

237 ibid. p 402–414 (GCPPT 2|16|1 pt 1).
ibid. p 117 (GCPPT 2|16|3).

# *Itinerarium*

To preach philosophical acceptance of trials and tribulations inherent in growing old was one thing but to suffer them gladly herself quite another when irritations and deprivations which, though looming large at times, could be dismissed as unimportant in the wider spiritual scheme of things, assumed the aspect of unbearable burdens when illuminated by the afterglow of faded *fervor novitiorum*. Then too, Aelfrida had failed to heed warnings by earthly and heavenly advisors regarding the unsuitability of a silent, isolated, monotonous, and spiritually-pressurised environment for one whose mind craved variety, human interest, and intellectual stimulation, and whose *joie de vivre* for the real world was irrepressible even in the presence of the Real. In all respects, Pierre Charles' *La Prière de Toutes les Heures* must have made poignant reading. Why, the writer implores God, do You ask such sacrifices of me? Why do You drive me to utter abnegation of self, imprison me in a vocation for which I am not suited, and ruin my health as a result? Why do You put me to the test while at same time delaying my just reward? Protect me from myself, I beseech You. Set me free to continue my pilgrimage.[1]

Aelfrida's 'abnegation' may have been in part a learned trait inherited from two generations of unhappy women. Emma Wetenhall, widowed at sixty-two, had already abandoned an active social life for a valetudinarianism in which she displayed her piety to her immediate family and her social inferiors (but how odd to conceal her Bible and prayer book from visitors as if religion was something shameful) and ensured the unChristian captivity of her only child. Catharine Tillyard, 'widowed' de facto if not *de jure* by her blind husband's reclusiveness, withdrew at sixty-seven into penitential seclusion broken only by enforced holidays and by Sabbath displays of piety at St Columba's while treating her own captive daughter abominably. Aelfrida, 'widowed' by divorce before she was forty but tied to 'the world' until her daughters dispossessed themselves of her, retired ostentatiously into religious enclosure (intermitted by voluntary or inflicted holidays) at fifty and treated an adopted 'mother' appallingly. Can it be that Emma Wetenhall's over fifteen-year retirement from which she was freed by death, Catharine Tillyard's ten-year withdrawal from which she was freed by her husband's death, and Aelfrida's (as is soon to

**Mors Janua Vitae**

transpire) twelve-year retreat from which after 1943 she did her utmost to ensure her 'sending ... away'[2] were different manifestations of seemingly self-sacrificial behaviour in which the outward trappings of religion were used to conceal – with varying degrees of success – the revengeful power-broking which is so often the chief pursuit of women 'unhappified' by the men with whom they agree to spend their lives? And if we include Aelfrida's masculine Deity in this category, what does this imply of earlier abnegation and an increasing wish to escape?

Aelfrida's enforced visit to Cardiff in October 1945 passed off without 'bloodshed', her only protests being one to Mother Guenvrede that she wished she need never go beyond the range of the chapel bell and one to her diary that it 'puzzled' her that she had to go at all[3], but it is obvious from her enjoyment of a visit described as the 'most precious ... most interesting and [most] profitable of all'[4] that she could never now be at peace at Tymawr because in such a 'divided state', hankering after 'the world' when in the convent and after the convent when elsewhere.[5] So, like Hilda Harrison, she proceeded in her work of sending herself away.

The majority of Aelfrida's complaints as 1944 became 1945 and 1945, 1946 were so petty that her recording them at length indicates a carping state of mind determined to find fault with everything to do with conventual life. A postulant singing plain chant in a 'tara-ra-boom-de-ay voice … as if it was a comic opera, with a tremolo and flat on the top notes'[6] to whom Placida later sent 'biscuits and a pious [birthday] card', the faintest sneer accompanying her description as if 'pious' was now a pejorative term.[7] The food, about whose quality and quantity she complained bitterly (she justified her voluntarily-restricted fare as not 'depriving Europe' of food, as if her 'boiled egg … and half an orange' dispossessed starving millions of their only meal but enjoyed the contrast between her abstemiousness and the fat goose 'and a lot of sausages' enjoyed by the convent at Christmas 1945)[8]: no fresh eggs when the convent hens stopped laying in winter and the 'monotony of badly cooked and tepid food' featuring the 'greyish yellow … slime (which looks like dog's vomit) of "reconstituted dried egg"'[9] which replaced them. Hunger when her trayed meals were briefly delayed by the Sisters' busyness elsewhere or when she believed that conventual fare was reduced below 'the recognised minimum standard' for financial reasons, something she herself might have helped to alleviate by giving the £200 left her by Ancifera Gregory to the SSC (who needed it) rather than to Alethea (who did not) instead of grumbling about having her charges raised and 'almsgiving' the convent less than usual on Shrove Tuesday[10] in revenge. The weather, no worse than that endured earlier but worsened in her mind as 'a Siberian east wind' percolated into her (west-facing) room in spite of restored central heating and as rain poured through the convent's war-damaged roof on to the landing outside a 'cell'[11] whose own ceiling bore ominous cracks. Mother Guenvrede insisting on bright lighting in chapel on a day when Placida suffered a rare recurrence of 'blue lightenings' accompanying a migraine.[12] A young couple about to occupy Woodbine Cottage, he to act as convent handyman, she with her new baby 'to enjoy the use of the garden' to the exclusion of the 'Undergardener' (Christ, of course, being the Gardener) who had expended 'so much labour'[13] and her own money on it. Only one complaint was justified because it impinged on her Rule: Mrs Donkin, now a 'crazy old woman' who wandered about the convent muttering to herself 'like an old witch' or pestered Aelfrida with questions whose gesticulated or written replies were incomprehensible to her (Placida remained ruthlessly silent), who became physically or verbally aggressive when thwarted, and who was now left largely to Mrs Graham to watch over, the latter feeling ground between 'the upper and nether millstones' of the reciprocal dislike of a 'senile … domineering old woman' and a 'rebellious daughter' in whose 'Institution' she herself was imprisoned in a manner uncomfortably reminiscent of Fordfield. (It was not only Winifred and Theodora Donkin who 'longed

for a separation'.)[14] And not all Father Northcott's gentle homilies 'on being thankful for small inconveniences' or an invitation to attend his appropriately-timed and 'very beautiful instruction on Mortification'[15] could persuade Aelfrida in 1945 that life at Tymawr was worth living.

Father Northcott, in fact, constituted another reason for 'separation'. Mid-1945 saw him severing relations with the SCC when he left England to establish a new Community of the Resurrection priory on a 'Native Reserve' in South Africa and his replacement as Warden by another Mirfield Father.[16] Though grateful for 'all he had done for [her]' and for the fact that '[their] stormy interviews of last September [had] dropped entirely out of sight'[17], Aelfrida was not entirely sorry to see him go because of what had passed between them with regard to Mother Guenvrede and because Father Northcott had recently prohibited 'perpetual' Silence. But if Placida hoped that a new and younger spiritual director would be easier to manipulate by someone tutored by Lucius Cary (a recent letter from him reminded Placida to avail herself of 'useful scrutiny and criticism' from the convent's Warden in order to augment the 'oversight' exercised by Mother Guenvrede of which, he supposed, she had a 'certain amount'; 'oh yes! certainly!' was Aelfrida's ironic response)[18] and as spiritually experienced and mystically attuned to Deity as herself, she was wrong. Not only did Father Barker preach against 'the kind of *religious exclusiveness* into which a Contemplative … might so easily lapse' and note that 'earth-contacts were essential to heavenly vision' and that 'personal satisfaction' was a 'by-product' not the end or object of religion (to serve the purposes of God was that)[19], he was also dismissive of her pretensions. On Placida informing him that her '*one* spiritual difficulty' (*sic*) was herself and that she was constantly nourishing her selfhood 'even in spiritual matters', he told her brusquely to desist from enquiring as to her spiritual progress (Christ, he said, would see to that) and to stop trying to rush the process of sanctification.[20]

It was, however, another Mirfield Father who brought home to her the likelihood of being unable to continue at Tymawr for physical reasons. Joining the Community's Retreat in November 1945, Placida received an unexpected response to her query at confession as to why she found herself increasingly 'unable to respond when God intensifies His Presence upon me'. This, said Father Curtis who, recently recovered from a severe head injury, knew whereof he spoke, was because she was "simply too tired" to respond and was consequently "caught between the millstone of Austerity and the millstone of physical weakness". Had not her doctor and her spiritual directors, he then asked, advised her to "moderate [her] religious fervour?" ('I *did* think that an odd question!' commented

Aelfrida without thinking that Father Curtis might have been primed by Mother Guenvrede to ask it, a distinct possibility given that only a few months earlier the Mother had said of aging Hilda Harrison, always 'poised for flight if she could find somewhere she liked better', that she wished Hilda "would find a permanent place" other than Tymawr "to flop into")[21], before advising her, as his own Community had advised himself, "to give up all austerity and accept the humiliation of helplessness instead". 'So that', wrote Aelfrida flatly, 'was that'.[22]

As might be expected, she disobeyed Father Curtis' instructions ('dear Saint Guenvrede, dear boards under my thin mattress … I need not give them up yet')[23] and even spurned an eiderdown lent by Mother Guenvrede during a spell of bitterly cold weather because 'a bed with a thin mattress placed over boards so that the … edges can be felt through and a luxurious eiderdown on one's shoulders' were mutually incompatible, that acceptance of added warmth was out of harmony with her need to offer 'hardness and physical austerity … in the spirit of [the] convent', and that what she ejected from her room after one night was less a quilt than a temptation 'to give up … the business of warring against the flesh … on the excuse that I am old and weak'. Weeping, she got out her discipline 'and with love to my Master nerving my arm, took the usual 14 strokes' – and twenty-eight more, fourteen for each of two days missed when unwell (the reason for her request for warmer bedding beyond her usual two blankets) and to assuage her guilt at having enjoyed the quilt even for one night. Only then did she feel thoroughly 'straightened' out'.[24]

In practice, however, it was not so much Placida warring against her flesh as her flesh warring against Placida – and with more vehemence than usual – which provided another 'push'. November 1944 found Aelfrida suffering from 'acute rheumatism or something' in her right knee[25], the pain puzzling both herself and Sister Monica because it differed in type and severity from the generalised aches and pains of rheumatoid arthritis and in duration from the strains and sprains of overenthusiastic gardening. By summer 1945 the joint was so painful that walks were severely curtailed and gardening activities restricted. (She was not too disappointed, regarding release from her horticultural 'burden of labour' as a heaven-sent opportunity to impose 'very drastic revision' on *The Glory of the West* because it contained too much 'self-importance'[26]; on her guardian angel's advice she also restricted her walks to the vicinity of the convent and to monthly trips to Trellech or Penalt.) Visiting Cardiff in October 1945, she consulted Julius' doctor who deemed her 'unfit for gardening or housework' because of her still-undiagnosed but probably 'incurable' ailment whose

pain was one of her 'penances'; by Christmas 1945, however, her knee had become permanently swollen and her pain fluctuating in severity but continuous.[27] Who then can blame Mother Guenvrede for wanting to rid her Community of one who, though less combative than formerly (Aelfrida's diary records only a single minor 'contest of wills between me and Authority'[28] since starting *The Fruits of Silence*) had transformed herself from foot-soldier to non-combatant or Aelfrida from deciding that she had become 'too old and too weak' to lead a 'physically … hard' life any longer or 'drive Brother Ass' any further and would be a 'burden and an anxiety to … the beloved Community … if [she] stayed'. (Her chief complaint was having 'to get up at 5.45am GMT every day and descend to a chapel 'that may be icy cold'; she did not now complain of spiritual anguish if infirmity or Mother Guenvrede forbade attendance at early Mass.)[29] So, imitating Hilda Harrison's propensity for 'sending herself away', she began to 'make excuses to herself' (e.g. Tymawr was bad for her health)[30] and prepared to do likewise.

But should she have to 'go away and never … live here anymore'[31], she, unlike Hilda, had a home to go to, as comments in February 1946 that 'family affairs' needed 'much thought and prayer' and that she had 'rather too much outside business to attend to' demonstrate.[32] Although she had 'let Fordfield go without a pang' to the Sisters of Hope because Christ had claimed it as His own once He in the guise of the Blessed Sacrament 'took up his abode in the chief room of the house' (her parents' bedroom, not the drawing room)[33], Aelfrida still owned Wetenhall Cottage from which her present tenants were willing to depart as and when occasion demanded. Having recently persuaded Julius to move to Cambridge for a year after his retirement, the latter's tendering of his resignation to Cardiff University early in 1946 and decision to let his Cardiff house and move into Wetenhall Cottage later that year provided his sister with a Cambridge pied-à-terre and with assurance of further income, it being her intention that Julius' and Mina's use of the Cottage be as rent-paying tenants, not as grace and favour lodgers. She therefore gave notice to her current tenants and began to sort out her effects.

'Cambridge books' were to be donated to the SSC to edify future users of 'the Library' and Father Cary's Windsor chair could grace another room: Mrs Graham would take only clothes and personal items including her tertiary's veil, scapular, and crucifix and would leave everything else for Community use.[34] 'Saint Cadoch' too would remain because no longer needed as a buffer between the chapel's stone floor and Placida's knees, and of her three 'useful saints', only 'Saint Guenvrede' would accompany her. With regard to 'spiritual' diaries covering "two years at Oxford and nearly ten here", Aelfrida wrote on 6 March 1945 to the current Mistress of Girton College, Kathleen Butler, reminding her of the promise made in 1935 by her predecessor, Helen Wodehouse, that the college would accept the gift of "£50 and [her] diaries".[35]

The decade intervening between earlier and present correspondence had altered Aelfrida's perception of her bequest to posterity. She now intended to place 'spiritual' diaries in Girton's safekeeping should she leave Tymawr, unspiritual volumes, currently stored in the attic of Wetenhall Cottage, joining them after her death as originally planned. Miss Butler, recalling "some very delightful tea parties" at Fordfield shortly before Alethea matriculated, was delighted to accept, her only regret being that the twenty-five-year embargo stipulated by Aelfrida in letters to herself and to her predecessor would prevent her from reading them.[36] The thought of *anyone,* much less the Mistress of Girton, reading her 'spiritual' diaries made Aelfrida pause: 'those diaries! I suppose if I were to reread them – *what* a penance! – I should now be most ashamed of just the things of which I was most proud'[37]; writing to Miss Butler the following year, she therefore requested that *all* donated volumes, regardless of the significance of their "psychological, historical, religious [and] possibly literary" content, remain "*unread* until all *personal* interest in them is entirely passed away".[38] ("Some parts", she noted, "are very lively reading indeed"[39], a point with which readers thereof wholeheartedly agree.) Miss Butler acquiesced, and when four registered parcels containing the "ms diary of Mrs Aelfrida Graham née Tillyard (sister of the Master of Jesus, mother of two Girtonians, one of which is dead)" arrived at Girton in June 1946 they were stored with a note added by Helen McMorran, the then librarian, emphasising that they were "to be kept unopened for an indefinite period".[40]

But if Aelfrida was making arrangements to detach herself from Tymawr, so too was the SSC making moves to detach itself from her, for even as it allowed her to remain a life tertiary, it moved to rid itself of tertiaries (and particularly resident tertiaries) altogether. In July 1943 Mother Guenvrede had chilled Placida's blood with her 'ultimate' threat: 'to abolish tertiaries'. The terror this threat provoked saw Placida extend grovelling apologies for her latest misdemeanour (complaining of the antics of the Boy Scouts camped nearby) and try to sweeten the Mother's temper with a gift of brown sugar from one of Alethea's food parcels[41], but it was not until 1944 and from another source that her fears were confirmed. In the course of letters exchanged between herself and

Muriel Pont (Tertiary Teresa) that year, Aelfrida discovered that tertiaries *were* to be abolished 'for good and all', to be replaced by oblates 'with a somewhat different part to play in the Society'.[42] Because this information coincided with Placida's decision to quote chapter and verse of the *Directory of the Religious Life* in order to become a 'Solitary' embedded in the Community like 'a jam-pot in an aquarium!!', her guardian angel's insistence that she not 'run to the Mother and ask for explanations and enquiries as to [her] fate and future' assumed greater significance, and although she tried to persuade herself that she was prepared for anything and worried by nothing ('*parata sum*', implying readiness for something, even, in this instance, departure), Aelfrida panicked: 'and I? Suppose I was asked either to be an oblate or go?' Her panic was worsened by the inaccurate belief – later rectified, though rectification brought its own dismays – that as an oblate she would be obliged to wear 'a hateful stuffy habit' and live in enclosure, neither of which she would be able to bear.[43]

Muriel Pont, as Placida discovered, had several axes to grind with regard to Mother Guenvrede (she had not been elected a life tertiary even after three years' probation and complained of lack of spiritual guidance and that the Mother was practising a 'policy of elimination' with regard to someone like herself who had a life and career outside the Community) and was not averse to playing off Placida against Superior. (Having read *Concrete* and *Can I be a Mystic?*, lent by their author, Muriel compared Aelfrida's teachings and vocation to Evelyn Underhill's and expressed regret that Mother Guenvrede prevented visitors to Tymawr from contacting 'the only Tertiary … we could meet' able to translate her vision into 'practical teaching'.)[44] Her comments, however, worried Aelfrida considerably. If, she asked herself, the SSC found it difficult to 'assimilate' tertiaries living in 'the world', what did this suggest of her continuing relationship with it should she choose to leave? Was Mother Guenvrede pursuing a 'policy of elimination' with regard to her resident tertiary too? Why was Muriel allowed to publicise her connection with Tymawr when Placida was not, even to clergymen?[45] A permitted talk with Muriel in July 1944 during one of that lady's visits provided more and even less 'happifying' information. The Mother, said Muriel, had issued a six-point *Oblates' Rule* which stated that not only must oblates be Anglo-Catholics, keep all religious obligations pertaining to Anglo-Catholicism including confession and receiving advice from a spiritual director with whom they were to agree a personal Rule, and be free to withdraw at any time or to suffer dismissal by the Mother Superior (with none of which points Aelfrida had much or any quarrel), but also that they must devote all their time, work, and money to the SSC.[46] With this last point Aelfrida, hearing from Hilda Harrison that oblates had to donate £20 or £30 a year, strongly disagreed ('I had no idea ... that there was to be a "property qualification"')[47] and it may be that the question of involuntary as opposed to voluntary contributions that made her look for '"pointers" to know God's Will for His tertiary', pointers ostensibly to do with 'more or fewer human' contacts[48] but actually to do with money and property, and to wonder if, like Muriel's, her pillar of fire and cloud was not moving away from Tymawr, 'bereft' though the Community would be of her spiritual and pecuniary 'gifts' if she departed.[49]

But even while reflecting that if, like Muriel, she withdrew from the Community because no longer able to regard it as her 'spiritual home' and hence to '*devote*' herself to it as she ought[50] and, that that being so, transformation from a source of strength into one of weakness constituted another reason for 'sending herself away', especially since she had already failed to become the kind of tertiary required by Mother Guenvrede (one, that is to say, who would 'mediate the spirit of the Community in due proportion to guests') but had always – and given her propensities and personality, could hardly have done otherwise – made herself 'personally acceptable' instead[51], Aelfrida began to pester Mother Guenvrede with questions about her future. The Mother's replies were non-committal to the point of saying she did not know what 'God's desire' for Placida 'in two years' time'[52] would be, a statement which suggests that compulsory visits to Cardiff may have been informal releases from the convent-asylum in which a sick spirit had been confined to a halfway house from which Julius (his sister's temporary guardian) reported back to Mother Guenvrede on her patient's progress and fitness (or otherwise) for discharge.

The SSC Newsletter of December 1944 provided even less comfort, for in answer to "questions asked from time to time" regarding "Tertiaries, Associates and Oblates", it defined Associates as "friends and relations ... associated with the Community's life and work [who] help in any way they can" (this category included demented Mrs Donkin) and Oblates as those who "work for or support the House in material things and in return are ... partakers in the spiritual works and oblations of the religious"; it also noted that although the SSC "grew out of the tertiary band, it looks as if in time they will die out".[53] 1945 Newsletters enlarged on this theme; indeed, it seemed that as Placida removed herself from the Community spiritually and emotionally, so it moved itself literally and metaphorically from her. The April Newsletter, for example, noting the imminence of Sister Sheila's final vows and announcing a May novena "for the Increase and Development of the Religious Life", also announced that the "special intention" for the year was for "the Blessing of God on ... the growth of the Community ... and of [its] Oblates and Associates"[54] – and not only was there no mention of tertiaries, but Placida's copy of the Newsletter was 'forgotten'. ('I like to be forgotten', she noted ruefully, '[and] mustn't complain that [I am]'.)[55] But if, as she believed, separatist behaviour now and in the past did not constitute 'a kind of invisible ... barrier' between herself and 'the rest of "us"' and that the Religious Life as lived at Tymawr would be 'weakened' if she, though a 'mere tertiary', broke a single strand of the spiritual cable binding them[56] by 'sending herself away', she was wrong. As the April arrival of 'new black habits of fine broadcloth'[57] and the positive tone of the Autumn 1945 Newsletter showed (its tidings included two new oblates admitted "after due probation" in September, the purchase of two in-calf heifers, the arrival of the Woodbine Cottage tenants, and the need to reduce guest rooms to three in order to make room for an influx of postulants[58], the latter news provoking a further nightmare during which the Mother in secular dress stated firmly "we have all got to pack up and go and you will have to go as well")[59], the Community was looking forward to whatever demands might be made on it in the future, demands which seemingly excluded those made on it by its resident tertiary. That Aelfrida 'trembled at the hint' but was preparing for separation is clear both from words she puts into Hilda Harrison's mouth ('she loves the chapel life here but [is] otherwise far happier away [and] is more at ease among her own folk than at Tymawr' and that 'the Library [was] no place for *residents* now'[60], Mother Guenvrede having noted the benefits of the Carthusian custom of curtailing a guest's stay after ten days on the grounds that longer stays "do not work")[61] and from her placing less emphasis on her need for geographical stability, the range of the chapel bell being now metaphorical.

Whether Aelfrida was at heart one of the wanderers whose peripatetic lifestyle horrified St Benedict because it destabilised settled communities and undermined the idea of commitment to a particular Community or was more Franciscan than Benedictine in her desire to preach and teach wherever the Spirit moved her (as Eustace perceptively remarked) is hard to discern, but given her unstable temperament and her continued but unspoken desire to fulfil the second part of her Great Work, probably both. But whereas in 1937 and devoid of emotional, spiritual, and intellectual balance, she regarded geographical instability with disquiet because it paralleled her mental instability and was resigned to never seeing Alethea again or being unable 'to write books for Him'[62] so long as she could rebalance herself by becoming a resident tertiary at Tymawr for the rest of her life, by 1943 (possibly) and by 1945/46 (certainly) she, with the SSC's support (and with the help of an outsider, though we do not learn this for some years), had recognised both the truth of Thomas à Kempis' warning that even a "devout hermit" could not promise him or herself security "in this life"[63] and that, mentally and emotionally stabilised and secured, she herself no longer required physical anchorage in a single spot. Tertiaries not being 'allowed to bind themselves'[64] was therefore irrelevant, geographically speaking, because, internally stabilised (in her own eyes, even if not in those of an impartial observer) she felt sufficiently secure to move independently along her spiritual 'way', leaving behind the institution to which she had bodily and spiritually consigned herself (and, if our surmise is correct, had been consigned) because liberated (as she thought) from 'madness' by the Community's love and care.[65]

A further reason for feeling able to move on was coming to the end of the period in her life in which reparative adoration played a dominant part. (An indication of this is the diminution of ghostly visits from Agatha after October 1940 – there was to be only one more – it being, perhaps, that her mother now regarded sins relating to her younger daughter as purged and did not require further spiritual assurance of Agatha's love and present happiness.) By 1946 the need to purge her guilt relative to others, aided, no doubt, by the passing of time and interposition of actual and metaphorical distance between herself and those for whom she acted proxy victim, seems to have diminished, and though she continued with 'intercessory prayer'[66] (as she now preferred to call it) for those she considered in need or worthy of it, she now confined it to Friday mornings.

Of those named to date, some no longer required active intervention: Constantine, who though he offered nothing of 'repentance and sacrifice' when alive (and, more specifically, while living with Aelfrida) had achieved purgation because of the 'mysterious "space for amendment"' hinted-at by and shared only with Alethea (to his 'widow's' chagrin, for she could not and must never ask)[67]; Phyllis, now deemed 'full of a "natural" goodness' and 'what a Christian she would make!')[68]; Agatha's friend Helen Tansley, now baptised, confirmed, and married to 'a good young man'.[69] Some were irretrievable: Hitler; Ruth Schechter, 'atheist and Communist', living in legitimised adultery[70]; Mrs Donkin, 'not persona grata anywhere'[71]; Eardley Davidson, cast off following his divorce and second marriage; Juan Mascaró, who would not follow what Aelfrida decided was God's call and

become a monk, for a call ("Juan, Juan") heard *coram sanctissimo* described as 'tender, peremptory, searching, quickening' and as couched in 'both human and divine terms'[72], reached her ears only. Some were unfinished business: Aleister Crowley; Albert Erlande; Dorothy Smith ('"Theodora", for whom I [still] offer *adoration réparative*')[73]; Mother Guenvrede; and, most tantalisingly unfinished of all, Anatolia Michaelides.

Although she was later to write that 'Constantine's relations and their acts and standards' now seemed to her as remote as 'people in a book'[74], July 1940 had found Aelfrida so concerned for her former mother-in-law's welfare that she even thought of lending her Wetenhall Cottage.[75] Whether this was prompted by genuine concern for Anatolia's welfare or by Aelfrida's propensity to revenge herself on those who behaved towards her in a 'very odd' manner (she had recently noted that Anatolia's, Phyllis', and Mother Guenvrede's 'somewhat contemptuous estimate' of herself as a 'vain, shallow, self-centred woman' was 'entirely accurate'[76]; what she fails to note is that 'odd' behaviour by other women towards herself almost certainly stemmed from their intuitively feeling what an 'unhomely' – Aelfrida's translation of *unheimlich*, more usually translated as 'uncanny' – person she was) by being '*extra* nice to them' as 'a sort of last-nail-in-the-coffin'[77] blow, is unclear. (Her statement that she would help Anatolia 'with great *great* joy'[78] could be interpreted either way.) A letter to her former father-in-law's solicitors stated that no news regarding 'Lila, widow of Cleanthes Michaelides' had been received since 1939[79], so other tactics were called for.

Early in 1941 Aelfrida wrote to Lady Frazer, the 'Strawberry Eater' of childhood days and of a world 'crumbling with astonishing speed'[80], who, it transpired, had received no news of Anatolia since 1938 when the latter visited her undergraduate grandson Michael Hillerns (matriculated 1936) in Cambridge. ('And I never knew'[81], wrote an aunt whose chagrin may have stemmed less from missing a nephew by marriage met only once than from realisation of how much information Anatolia might have garnered from Lady Frazer regarding the contemporary exploits of her former daughter-in-law.) A report in *The Times* in June 1942 of Michael Hillerns' marriage allowed her to ask his bride's mother for information concerning a 'very dear friend' (*sic*) of whom she had lost sight 'since the Germans invaded France' of whom Michael 'must be' the grandson.[82] A single letter from Lieutenant Hillerns of GHQ Liaison Regiment ('there may be many, many reasons why he should never write again'[83], Aelfrida reported without irony, his being killed in action on 19 August 1942 being perhaps the least ironic and the most tragic) stated that he couldn't 'place' her (under what name, one wonders, had she written?) and provided news of Anatolia – she still lived near his parents at Cap d'Antibes and had recently suffered a nervous breakdown[84] – and Aelfrida with the ammunition she currently required.

She fired her first fusillade to demonstrate the excellent light in which the news placed a forgiving daughter-in-law relative to a tyrant mother-in-law, a parable which Mrs Graham could retail to Mother Guenvrede in 'perfect confidence' that the latter would draw parallels between Anatolia and herself. (Placida and Mother Guenvrede had recently clashed over the former's correspondence with Father Cary regarding Reservation and Exposition of the Blessed Sacrament, the latter accusing Aelfrida of being a 'newspaper-reporter' and reminding her that tertiaries did not justify their existence, were still on trial, and that prior even to Mrs Graham's arrival, the decision had been taken to abolish them.)[85] Her second, though it pertained chiefly to the positive effects of reparative adoration, could also be fired in relation to Mother Guenvrede insofar as the former in the course of an amazing instance of rationalisation (mediated, so she said, by her guardian angel) noted that Anatolia's breakdown was due to '*remorse*' at 'spoiling' Aelfrida's life and that she had cried out in anguish "if only I could know that Aelfrida has forgiven [me]", a cry overheard by Placida in the course of 'My Lord's *own* Silence' but misinterpreted as pertaining to Mother Guenvrede. (Further prayers on Aelfrida's part apparently reached their target, Anatolia regaining 'an inner calm and certainty' from them though she remained in need of further prayerful activity lest, presumably, she backslide.) Furthermore, Anatolia's 'cruelty' could be said to have been 'turned by God into an instrument of [Placida's] highest good' insofar as it helped the latter to detach herself from 'the world' and led her to Tymawr.[86] Receiving a letter from Aelfrida enclosing the note from Michael Hillerns on the basis of which this phantasmagorical edifice was constructed (it also detailed her thoughts on the subject of cruel mothers-in-law – or 'in Christ'), Mother Guenvrede thanked her – and never referred to the matter again. Aelfrida, however, convinced of the correctness of her deductions, continued to be plagued by lack of information about 'poor Anatolia'[87] because unless able to contact Anatolia in person, Anatolia (like Mother Guenvrede) would never know how much Aelfrida wanted to teach her 'what *caritas* is'.[88]

God, on the other hand, had arranged that Mother Guenvrede (like Anatolia) should hurt Aelfrida as she did for '[her] soul's good', the Mother '*not being*' as 'blameworthy' in this respect[89] as Anatolia. (The Mother's soul', Aelfrida noted, '[was] all right' even if her temper and personality were not.)[90] Possibly as a result of Aelfrida's

cogitations concerning Anatolia, a degree of mutual respect now developed between thesis and antithesis. Although Mother Guenvrede continued to remind Placida that not every 'spiritual bright idea' that came into her head was put there by her guardian angel[91] and to remark that it was useless giving her advice on spiritual matters because unless she came to the same conclusion herself, she ignored it[92], and Aelfrida to refuse to creep to Mother Guenvrede as Miss Lowe with her 'let-me-imbibe-this-draught-of wisdom' air had irritatingly done (she would defer, she wrote, but only with regard to spiritual matters)[93], it seemed that in spite of one lady's 'tiresomeness' and the other's 'rages', synthesis in the form of 'mutual understanding' had been achieved and mutual *caritas* developed from mutual forgiveness.[94]

But what Aelfrida had forgiven with regard to Mother Guenvrede's treatment ('I am so *content* now to be under the Mother', she wrote in May 1945) was nothing compared to the "purposeful endurance" ("control of anger, resentment, censoriousness [and] anxiety")[95] Mother Guenvrede had practised with regard to Aelfrida. Hence although Aelfrida now believed (and continued to believe) that she *had* 'helped and steadied' Mother Guenvrede by her prayers[96], a diary entry made eleven years later demonstrates the extent to which her behaviour contributed to the Mother's negative qualities during the war years.

Writing at a time when she was driving yet another Superior distracted by recalcitrant behaviour and the spoken and written word (and for much the same reasons), Aelfrida noted how similar that Superior's behaviour was to Mother Guenvrede's under similar circumstances. (She blamed it on 'the devil … getting partial possession' of both ladies' minds.) She also discloses that at some point during Placida's stay at Tymawr (1943, diary evidence suggests), Mother Guenvrede was briefly hospitalised with 'persecution mania'[97], more likely the cumulative strain of running a small wartime Community containing a 'mad' tertiary. Seen in this light, Placida's belief that she herself 'of all people' was 'fitly chosen to help … to keep devils away from the Mother'[98] can be seen for the fallacy it was, it being largely her own behaviour vis-à-vis Mother Guenvrede which precipitated the latter's breakdown.

By early 1946, however, having received intimations that the Community intended to move on without its resident tertiary and that Mother Guenvrede had every intention of 'cutting [Placida] off from people'[99] instead of, as earlier, hoping for her participation in their stay, Aelfrida seems to have decided that if she wished to remain (or, she tried to convince herself, if 'God bids me stay') on 'holy ground [and] … built as a living stone into the Community'[100], she would do well to paper over some of the cracks appearing between that edifice and herself. She may also, though given her persisting conviction that she was in the right and the Mother, devil or no devil, in the wrong, this seems less likely, have suffered pangs of conscience and wished to atone for previous bad behaviour for, as she realised, Mother Guenvrede had been a mother superior to any real or surrogate 'mother' met before and it was largely due to her superior maternal efforts that Aelfrida herself had been granted nearly ten years of increasing serenity.[101] She therefore began to seek rapprochement by behaving (as she thought) immaculately in relation to her so as to reassure her that suspicions regarding her tertiary's motives were unfounded.

She was successful on the first count (the Mother, she wrote of one meeting with her, was 'in great form, … talking to me in the most lively and affectionate way … when I think of all that has happened during these nearly-nine years that I have been here … she … on the borderline of collapse and I on the brink of being sent away – well! [But] now … at long last there is … true spiritual affection and understanding between us')[102] but unsuccessful on the second. Following a trivial incident (an Easter card expressing 'collective good will' sent to 'rebel and deserter' Hilda Harrison, signed by everyone except the Sisters and Mother Guenvrede, was organised by Placida without the Mother's permission and Hilda's reply 'innocently' forwarded to her)[103], Placida received both a reproof and a '*shock*', Mother Guenvrede's response ("you will have to go") making it clear that 'spiritual affection and understanding' notwithstanding, she did not trust Aelfrida any more than formerly and that she fully intended Mrs Graham to leave. (Aelfrida's interpretation was that something was '*pushing* [her] away from the convent', that it was '*hostile*', and that it would be '*dangerous*' if she stayed.) But not all Placida's reassurances that the Mother's lack of trust was due to a 'a bogy invented by the devil'[104] and the Mother's laughing response could override the latter's determination to remove Mrs Graham at all costs: "this is my country, these are my laws", said President Kruger, "those who do not obey my laws can leave my country" – and Mrs Graham, knowing of both President and nickname, should have taken heed.

The something dangerous and hostile pushing her away from Tymawr was not, of course, Mother Guenvrede but that which Mother Guenvrede embodied: Authority. And though Aelfrida invariably used the word metonymically ('I could not bear … having my life arranged by Authority, God has not called me to this'[105]; 'Authority has just ordered me to bed'[106]; 'I hope I was

not wanting my own way but, rather, Authority's mandate to follow Our Lord's way'[107], and so on), it is to Mother Guenvrede she refers.

Though Catharine Tillyard's description of toddler Frida as 'the embodiment of contrariness'[108] may have described a character trait, adult Aelfrida's antiauthoritarianism chiefly transpired from a traumatic childhood incident. Later in life she remained ignorant of *why* she frequently found '*no* way of being able to offer obedience'[109] and suffered the consequences of failure to do so (her 'failure to be the right kind of oblate', for example)[110] and although she commented censoriously on Stephen Tillyard's wartime creed of 'philosophical anarchism' with regard to the 'organised compulsion' of the call-up ('would he allow tax-paying to be voluntary – and education?')[111] and Hilda Harrison's technique of 'subtly opposing Mother all the time'[112], she attributed contests of will between herself and 'Authority' ('*l'affaire* Pixie', for example, a contest of wills regarding treatment of the convent cat)[113] to the machinations of the devil or to her own 'Nonconformist upbringing with its bias towards independence'[114] or to her "sturdy practical independent nature" which grew best "in Free Church soil".[115] To anything, in fact, than to her emotional need of '*being in authority*' lest she be forced to fall in with 'other people's arrangements' once again.[116] Significantly, however, and apropos Mother Guenvrede's supposed 'denigration' of tertiaries in the SSC Newsletter of December 1944, Aelfrida comes close to admitting her absolute inability to place herself 'docilely and unreservedly' under authority, though not the reason or, rather, not the real reason: God's authority, she writes, is the only authority to which she will submit, not the Mother's, not a husband's, not a spiritual director's. One thing, however, she notably does not ask: why was she prepared to submit to *God's*? Mothers Superior, spiritual directors, and even husbands were, in her eyes, God's representatives in varying ways on earth; why then submit to His authority if she could not submit even in part to theirs? Because He represented the ultimate, perfect Authority behind whom she could hide when forced by human authority to leave home, to go to school, to abandon creeds she wished and others did not wish her to follow, into marriage to make her 'normal', to entertain people she did not wish to meet, to assume responsibilities she wished to avoid: God as the ultimate escape clause? Or was her inability to submit any part of herself to anyone 'however great or wise'[117] a manifestation of her inability to submit wholly even to *God's* Authority and her life a battle between her craving for the wise calm authority of a superior force to order her disordered personality and her adamant refusal to submit to *anyone* after the events of that dreadful summer night in 1888? Though had she never encountered Christ in a mandorla of light, what would have become of her? Remove Deity from her life, where and what would she have been? But because, as she told a later confessor, her 'whole life [had been] built on … belief'[118] in God (and by extension in His Authority) it was in theistic contexts (in the widest sense) that she chiefly rebelled and though it was her expressed *need* for "rigid discipline for intellect and action"[119] which brought her to Tymawr, it would be her inability to submit to 'Authority' there that would send her away.

Aelfrida, of course, was unable to recognise her oscillating flight from one 'authority', be this spiritual, emotional, marital, doctrinal, or conventual, to another for what it was. (She herself described it as tic-tocking between God and man, which in a manner of speaking it was.) Having settled on or in the orbit of one 'authority', she immediately began to fight it, then fled it for another in the guise of following a pillar of fire and cloud. In religious terms – for Aelfrida there was no other way to put it – "the most terrible of all problems" was the problem of "*Authority*" with its diktats "Submit" and "Obey" and although she did in great measure achieve at Tymawr "the vision of the serenity which would be [hers] … in all its surpassing beauty" (in part because in the shelter of an Anglo-Catholic Community she was able to "pour out all [her] energies in one undeviating stream of adoration to God", to go some way to achieve her "desire for absolute certainty", and to assuage "the thirst for perfection" which never left her), her inability to submit to *any* authority gave rise to the (as she put it) "and yet and yet …" pertinent to whichever 'Authority' to which she was prepared to submit for as long as she could bear it but whose authority she continually questioned even as she submitted to it: "[had] it never failed?" "[Had] it never been mistaken? [Were] all its judgements righteous?"[120]

Applying this to Mother Guenvrede, we find a revealing diary entry made in 1956 when time and distance allowed Aelfrida to formulate a possible reason for cleaving to and separating herself from the Mother: 'at Tymawr', she writes, 'I made the mistake of thinking that Rev. Mother must be a second St Teresa in experience and wisdom [and] expected impossibilities of her'.[121] But having fought the Mother's 'Authority' every inch of the way and having discovered her 'second St Teresa' to be as fallible as herself, she bade Mother Guenvrede farewell and went out "once again into the sunny road", there and from "the airy substance of [her] visions, [to] fashion some [new] palace of … belief".[122]

She did not, of course, see it quite like this. 'I was not', she wrote in an attempt to justify her actions, 'a nun … and I [had] kinsfolk and friends and the work had to go on in "the world"'. But neither justification nor the Mother's failure to live up to her expectations prevented her from admitting 'what I needed most was *discipline* and she gave me that in full measure'.[123]

That, of course, was what she *thought* she needed and what she certainly and up to a point received. The word discipline, however, has more than one meaning and the '*discipline*' she received or hoped to receive from Mother Guenvrede was of more than one kind. The least important, perhaps, was that of spiritual training: Placida was already advanced in this and needed only advice, advice which in any case she rarely followed. To have her disordered mind brought under control was more important and though it need not have occurred in a conventual context, that context was best guaranteed to succeed given Aelfrida's religious proclivities and distaste for psychoanalysis: at Tymawr she found an environment so structured by daily performance of the Office, by Holy Communion each morning, by time alone *coram sanctissimo* every evening, by regular confession, and by allotted 'portions of labour' that a degree of psychological stabilization was bound to happen. (And if over-indulgence in Silence and Solitude and pre-existing psychopathology prevented her from achieving it completely, let us be thankful she achieved a modicum.) Furthermore, her real or imagined burden of guilt and her intense need to be relieved of it by spiritual and physical self-punishment or, if unable to sustain it, by means of some another punitive agent, required enforced submission to the very 'Authority' she detested. She even attached herself to surrogate 'mothers' and 'fathers' in order to achieve it.

The most important mortification for someone as spiritually proud and personally egoistic as Aelfrida was humiliation and it may be to humility to which she refers in her enigmatic statement of May 1938: 'I am so very, *very* happy – God had procured something … that I wanted and *needed*'.[124] In order to be humiliated, however, there has to be a humiliating agent, provided in this instance by (or set up by Aelfrida to provide, for she behaved in exactly the same way to other people) Mother Guenvrede. It is, however, difficult to humiliate a person whose behaviour relative to 'authority' does not warrant it so she ensured humiliation by behaving in such a way as to ensure it i.e. by courting it. This, of course, explains her 'rejoicing in humiliations'[125] and in having 'a most *lovely* humiliation'[126] prepared for her and in behaving in such a way (or as she preferred to put it, having a constant *call* to being 'misunderstood')[127] that she was forced, in Richard Meux Benson's words, "to … think badly of [herself]".[128] (There is, however, something equally authoritarian in Aelfrida's perverse delight in being humiliated, for in continually setting herself up as an apparently powerless 'victim' of the Mother's rages, she controlled Mother Guenvrede, the *real* victim here, by forcing her to behave in the disciplinarian manner her 'victim' required.) The desire to be a 'victim-soul' relative to 'Authority' can therefore be seen less as intimation of a desire to imitate "Christ's Way of the Cross"[129] and more as the manifestation of a 'need' to be crucified (by 'Authority', in this instance, and by being humiliated) and of finding (or making) her own 'Cross' and bearing it abjectly.

In 1945, however, Aelfrida was far removed from the woman who paced the woodland walks of Girton College with feet whispering "hu-mil-it-y", "hu-mil-it-y" as they brushed the grass to remind her of the virtue she lacked most. (A woman, too, whose desire to keep herself 'low' was countermanded by pride in being a speaker at a theological conference and in being 'caught out of [her-self] in an ecstasy and plunged into the Infinite' as she walked.)[130] What she now required was to be, like Christ Himself, judged, mocked, scourged (tongue-lashed, that is to say, not physically beaten unless by her own hand, for she had no intention of imitating Giloteaux's "Jesus-Victim" *too* closely), despised, and rejected by Mother Guenvrede, and to this end Placida of the Holy Passion set herself up. And was she also trying to imitate Christ in the sense of living (as she had always lived, to achieve her aim) the Beatitudes[131], particularly those expounding humility and humiliation, mourning, spiritual poverty ('I am such a *poor thing*,'[132] she constantly reminds us), meekness (in the sense of suffering injury submissively), and being reviled and persecuted. (Hungering and thirst-ing after righteousness and being pure in heart were easy; being merciful and a peacemaker were not.) And all this in the hope that God would make her 'a saint' and men perceive her as a light shining before them as an exemplar. Or, as she preferred to put it, a medium through which the Holy Spirit could flow over the 'loathsome' state of mankind in order to purify it as she herself, infused with God Transcendent, was '*purified*'.[133]

And was – as we may hope and she believed – her sojourn in her Monmouthshire Montserrat a catalytic Ignatian experience extended over years rather than weeks, in the course of which God – as Alethea had hoped He would – took Aelfrida into the wilderness and taught her? As to what He taught, perhaps it *was* a kind of humility of which the earliest intimations were seen at Leiston where Aelfrida mistakenly 'thought [she] had a vocation [and] … was doing the choosing'[134], further intimations at Malling when Mrs Graham first became conscious of her 'presumption', and later intimations early in her stay at Tymawr when, writing of the coming war and presciently of herself, Placida noted that it was

necessary for 'forces of destruction' to mutually destroy themselves if 'mankind' was to enjoy a happier future and in Mother Guenvrede's words, discover that "purifica-tion may be necessary – there may be no other way".[135] If so, perhaps Father Cary was correct when, writing his Christmas letter to Aelfrida in December 1943 at a time when realisation was growing that what she *really* wanted and needed was 'peace at the heart of things'[136] (and if this meant war with Mother Guenvrede because a woman who could only find love through hate, could only find peace through warfare, so be it), his message including the comforting words "you seem to find at Tymawr what you had so long been seeking … that [in itself] is something to make substance of your Bethlehem this year".[137]

Although visionary activity diminished overall during Aelfrida's stay at Tymawr as her mental imbalance rec-tified itself, 1943 saw it increase around the time of the first of her two enforced visits to Cardiff, only to taper off (but not cease) after her third. Four of these later visions are worth describing briefly, three, because they demonstrate how much she owed to RH Benson, one, for what it says of her wish to be free.

The first three, though differing in context, occurred when Placida was praying in the convent chapel: after None on 23 November 1943, a vision of Christ calling her into the 'dark brightness' described by St John of the Cross, where, silently and 'in his own way, [He] con-summates the mysterious espousals of His own making', an experience which consisted in Benson's words of a spiritual fact presented "clearly and vividly to the intel-lect" *only*[138] and which, given the vision's coitional asso-ciations, Aelfrida is at pains to emphasise that it contained 'no imagery … nothing but the complete surrender of Spirit to Spirit'[139]; awaiting Holy Communion at Epiphany 1944, she looked up at the crucifix above the altar 'and saw the Figure not, as it is, carved of wood but of living flesh and blood … lighted up from within'[140], and on Easter Saturday 1946 while watching before the altar of repose, her 'heart opened and Our Lord invis-ibly came forth from it as from a tabernacle and there began a mysterious *pulsation of life* between Him and His sacramental Presence on the altar'[141], both notably Bensonian images. The fourth occurred on the night of 24/25 August 1944. Mother Guenvrede had recently informed Aelfrida of arrangements made for her to go to Cardiff that year. Aelfrida was convinced that the devil wanted her out of the way in order to strengthen the 'foothold' gained at Tymawr since her acceptance as a tertiary; she was also worried that at Cardiff she might set herself afloat on the tide of 'human sweetness' again. An opportune 'shewing' of a road broken by 'a lovely dewy ravine' over which God Himself was building a 'spiritual bridge', convinced her that it was possible to visit ravine and bridge simultaneously, i.e. to leave Tymawr for 'the world' without having to relinquish the 'joy above rapture' of life with and within God. And it may not be solely of the impending visit to Cardiff that she wrote, her vision having been presaged by a prescient dream of which she noted 'I was a lay-sister in some religious community where we all enjoyed in an extraordinary manner the sense of the presence of God. One day one of the nuns said to me "dear Sister, when you are within our enclosure with us, I feel very happy ... but I tremble for you when you go out into the world". I showed her a cross such as is borne in processions and announced "you need have no fear, Sister, for I take this with me. No-one sees it but myself. And the consciousness of God's Presence never leaves me".[142]

Two 'Bethlehems' unforeseen by Father Cary graced Aelfrida's final years at Tymawr. The first occurred late in Advent 1945 and concerned a woman whose presence in Bethlehem was to change religious history. The second, on 7 May 1946, though no less miraculous, was significant insofar as 'Bethlehem' translates as 'house of bread'.

The spiritual experience which assailed Aelfrida on 21 December 1945 (it went undescribed in her diary until 24 December because it was 'queer' and because she hesitated to commit it to paper) saw her become aware of 'a most beautiful fragrance' in the West Room just after she finished saying her rosary, a fragrance like a mixture of roses and violets but 'fresher and purer' and more '*alive* and *spiritual*' than either and which had '*attached*' to it associations with the Virgin Mary as a fragrant presence which 'seemed to invite response'. Trying to explain what she called a 'Strange Experience', she noted that, being Advent, there were no flowers in the convent to which she could attribute the fragrance, that no one in the convent was wearing scent, that the 'great gale of rain and wind and sleet' blowing outside was unlikely to waft perfumes with it, and that 'vague Protestant inhibitions where the BVM [was] concerned' had prevented her from feeling sympathy for the Virgin's 'distinctive spirituality'.[143]

21 December 1945 was not, however, the first time Aelfrida overcame 'Protestant inhibitions' with regard to the Mother of Christ. For one thing, she had received spiritual comfort from praying in front of a statue of the Virgin and Child in the Lady Chapel of Our Lady and the English Martyrs in Cambridge during the period of her intense attraction to Roman Catholicism and had even persuaded herself that she had seen tears of sympathy in the Virgin's eyes. For another, something (the statue of the Virgin in Tymawr's Lady Garden, perhaps)

moved her to read Bede Frost's book *The Mystery of Mary* early in her stay, to meditate Mary's special significance at Christmastide[144] (a ritual repeated several Christmases thereafter), and to incorporate some of Frost's themes into her own diary and patterns of thought e.g. that she was a handmaid of the Lord (she preferred it in Latin: '*ancilla Domini*') as well as a ('recuperated') virgin and a mother and, like the Virgin, a channel transmitting God's grace to mankind. Lastly, she had already met the Virgin in person (in a vision) at a time when she was in danger of losing a 'mother' to whom she was emotionally attached at another of these borderland periods in her life at which earlier actions on her part forced her life into new paths, paths not necessarily wished-for but invariably accompanied by intense mediumistic or spiritual experiences.

July 1935 had seen Aelfrida returning '*home*' to the 'antechamber of heaven' otherwise known as St Mary's Abbey, Malling. Arriving on 13 July as an oblate, she departed on the 18th shorn of oblation and accompanied, to her horror and dismay, by 'beloved Weta', until 17 July, postulant Alethea.[145] '*Home*', however, had changed in material ways since Aelfrida's previous visit, the convent having embarked on a building programme which did *not* meet with the approval of an anchoress sworn to Holy Poverty: the new accommodation, she wrote, with its parquet floors and its 'labour-saving electrical gadgets', suggested not so much 'Religion' as 'an extremely well-equipped modern nursing home' and she considered it positively unChristlike to live 'in the midst of [such] ... expensive surroundings'. ('God keep me from being censorious', she had the grace to add, though she considered it divine punishment when extensive underpinning of the convent's older buildings was required almost as soon as the new ones were completed.)[146] Deciding but unable to put the new buildings out if her head, she retired to her 'Benedictine bed' with its straw mattress in an uncharitable but also 'vaguely expectant and restless' mood, feeling as if 'someone was coming to see [her]'. Someone was, but not perhaps the person she was expecting. After an hour's unusually peaceful meditation on the Passion she sensed 'without opening [her] eyes' the presence of someone standing by her bed: to her 'intense surprise' and, she owned, 'considerably to [her] embarrassment', it was the Virgin Mary.

The Virgin, she wrote, 'stood in the midst of roses, not roses such as you might pick in this garden' ('oh! roses, *roses!*' she had written of the convent grounds on arrival) 'but roses of her children's love. She ... [had] a very s*trong* face and *still*, ... secret and beautiful ... She stood considering me ... as if she enquired what I was meaning. Then she commented "you do *well*" and after that, very clearly, "*this place shall be much blessed*"". Musing on the vision, Aelfrida decided that because Malling was dedicated to the Virgin, it was 'probably accustomed to her familiar presence' and that compared to what she had just 'seen', parquets and gadgets paled into insignificance. On the other hand, '*something* had [died] in [her] love for the Abbey' which had little to do with either and everything to do with the severing of her own and Alethea's physical 'connection' with it: 'the soul that seeks Perfection cannot rest *here* … I would have had *this* flawless but it cannot be'.[147] Then after a night of intense spiritual darkness unmitigated save for five aspirins, she returned to 'little St Benedict's', a house on which she now resolved to spend as little money as possible.

In March 1943 Aelfrida enjoyed three visions on the same day on the same theme. At the first Vespers of the Annunciation, at Mass, and just before Terce she '*perceived*' the Angel Gabriel before her in the form of a 'filmy fire' and realised she herself '*was*' the Virgin Mary to whom Gabriel 'gave his message … in the spirit language'. Pondering 'what does it all *mean*?', Placida came to no (or does not relate that she came to a) conclusion but her noting a few days beforehand that what unhappy Miss Lowe needed was 'a home and children and normal joys'[148] may indicate retrospective regret for what Mrs Graham had lost. Seen in this light, her 'strange experience' of 21 December 1945, though certainly odd, does not constitute quite the 'strange' (i.e. unusual) experience she would have us believe.

It was, in fact, the first of many new ones, these beginning three days later. On Christmas Eve 1945 'a great "*bouffée*" of the same celestial storm' gusted into the West Room as Placida prepared to attend Sext, localising itself in a column a little taller than herself. Worries lest this second manifestation be 'a wile of the devil … to make me think myself a saint', she made the sign of the cross and asperged the room with holy water, only to experience a 'gentle reproachful feeling … as if Our Lady … said "Placida, don't you *know* me?"' Deciding that the Virgin had come to spend Christmas with her 'for love's sake … not for any merit of [her] own,' Placida descended to the chapel, the perfume transforming itself into 'a sweet reverent hush in [her] soul' as Sext proceeded. The contrast between the gently supernatural nature of the episode and the scene which confronted her when she was called to the library later that day to receive a present, a scene which turned her 'sick and faint' though whether it was the 'carnal and worldly' (*sic*) nature of the occasion, the contrast between the Community's festive meal and her own 'solitary tea', or the affront to her vegetarian sensibilities of a fat goose 'and a lot of sausages'[149] which occasioned the megrim, we are left to imagine.

Further episodes followed, some relevant to task (writing her first letter of 1946) or place (in chapel for Vespers, intensifying during the Benediction), or calendar (on the day celebrating the Seven Sorrows of the Blessed Virgin, the 'mysterious perfume appeared in three places')[150], others (the presence of 'a mingling of many unknown flowers, a melody, a song in scent', quite distinct from the lilac blooming outside her room) perhaps related to current preoccupations: a message, for example, from her guardian angel, exasperated by pleas for 'more silence', telling her sternly to stop 'wanting to know every minute what [she was] being used for' and to stop pleading for "sensible sweetness".[151] To all of which – and there were to be more episodes to come – Aelfrida could only respond that the whole experience was '*odd*'.[152] But given that in 1915 Bernard Muscio of Cambridge's Psychological Laboratory noted her ability to reproduce 'abnormally keen'[153] sensory impressions, it would be interesting to know what other 'scented' associations filled her mind at this and other relevant times.

Aelfrida's second and even stranger experience – she headed her description '*A miracle!*' and drew double marginal lines beside the diary entry for emphasis – occurred as a single event on 1 February 1946 on a day when 'mysterious perfumes' floated faintly around her as she worked, 'wonderfully serene and happy', on *The Glory of the West*. As befitted one who took her meals alone and lived in silence, communications with nun-caterer Sister Sheila took place by means of notes left on the tray when Aelfrida returned it to the table in the hall whence she collected it. A note requesting more bread (she was perpetually hungry these days because the sweet foods she craved were in shorter supply than before) was removed by wandering Mrs Donkin, so she was forced to ring at the grille and ask for some. As she carried the very small piece of 'box-shaped loaf' upstairs she suddenly saw the substance of the bread 'moving and working' like milk coming to the boil. Placing the bread on her table by the window she saw its crusty top rising too until it gained an inch in height. On picking it up she found the loaf 'quite definitely *heavier*' and so much larger that it sufficed for seven and a half meals instead of four. Initially stupefied by what she had witnessed (more stupefied, in fact, than by her earlier experience of levitation) and as unable to explain the event as when 'fairies' helped her to mow the lawn at Fordfield during the Great War (an event witnessed by both daughters and Fidelio but never described as miraculous), Aelfrida moved from amazement ('the bread rose so naturally!') through puzzlement ('why for *me*?') to modestly disclaiming 'any merit or share in the happening'. Tasting what she called the 'over-and-above' bread and finding it real, she decided the miracle must be evidence of God's 'tenderness' towards her and that she must rededicate herself to Him at the Eucharist next day.[154]

Three months later and on her guardian angel's instructions, Aelfrida informed Mother Guenvrede. (She never, it seems, told anyone about her episode of levitation and it was not until later that she revealed her 'miraculous perfumes'.) Receiving her note, Mother Guenvrede visited Aelfrida in the West Room. The latter recounted the 'bread-miracle story … almost word for word the same' as she had recounted it in her diary but added that she had felt '*fear*'.[155] (She *had* exclaimed "depart from me Lord for I am a sinful man"[156] but had not recorded feeling afraid.) The following conversation ensued:

Mother Guenvrede: "It was a miracle. But what you felt was not fear".

Aelfrida: "No, not fear in the ordinary sense [but] what the soul experiences in the presence of omnipotence".

Mother Guenvrede: "Exactly".

Aelfrida: "What puzzles me … is that the occasion did not seem to warrant a miracle".

Mother Guenvrede: "God does these things for His glory and our encouragement".

Comforted by the Mother's sensitive response, Aelfrida handed over the miracle 'for which [her] need for bread [had] provided the occasion' to the Mother as her own and the Community's.[157]

A touching story – but is it true? Certainly it reads true at first telling and Aelfrida's comment that perhaps miracles like hers were 'not so unusual in convents'[158] parallels her earlier belief that it was perfectly all right to discuss guardian angels in conventual settings because convents were their normal environment, but doubts arise when one considers it more closely. Why, for example, did she call no-one as witness and destroy the evidence by eating it? (Material evidence of speaking the truth would have gone far in rehabilitating her in the Community's eyes.) Did she worry that people would think her 'odd' if she recounted the event? Why did the occasion not 'warrant' a miracle? Was it too commonplace? But surely the commonplace events which initiated it i.e. her martyred reaction to receiving insufficient (unrationed) bread to last her a day, were the criteria required for material proof of God's 'tenderness' towards her – and if not, what criteria *would* need to be fulfilled before a miracle of this extremely symbolic nature occurred? Why disclaim all 'share in the happening' if it were true? Why call it a 'story' when the word suggests something invented? And why wait three months before handing the 'miracle' to Mother Guenvrede?

Possibly it was too much 'a tenderness of God towards *me*'[159] for immediate sharing. Possibly she now believed that although 'the slightest manifestation of God's presence used to throw [her] into disturbing raptures and emotions', after nine years in a therapeutic Community she could cope calmly and alone with an extraordinary manifestation of God's 'everyday presence' in her life.[160] But when we consider what happened during the six months preceding the February 'miracle' and in the three months intervening between it and Aelfrida recounting it to Mother Guenvrede, we may uncover her true motives for delaying communication of an episode reminiscent of Christ's parable of the Kingdom of Heaven working like leaven in the measured 'meal' of men's souls.

Descriptions of conventual life and the springtime countryside around Tymawr acquire a particular poignancy early in 1946 as Aelfrida's sojourn in Monmouthshire neared its end. In the light of recent visionary and miraculous events this news seems not to have distressed her unduly, for miracles and other manifestations antedated her arrival and there was no reason to expect their cessation on her departure. She had also achieved an armistice with Mother Guenvrede and was looking forward to her own future 'flowering' as, when and where God should bid her blossom[161] for there were now so many aspirants 'clamouring' (as Mother Guenvrede put it) to join the Community that Aelfrida would be failing in her duty (as Placida put it) as resident tertiary if she 'put any obstacles in the way of its increase'[162] by continuing to occupy the West Room. The reason for this sudden 'clamour' was, of course, the ending of the war whose approaching storms had formed one of Mrs Graham's reasons for fleeing to Monmouthshire in 1936/37 and whose cessation and concomitant indications of increasing prosperity at Tymawr (a convent, Aelfrida would have us believe, maintained throughout the war almost entirely by her own financial contributions) also provided her with valid excuses for leaving.

Her diary provides a dramatic account of the final months of hostilities, albeit one biased in terms of her own preoccupations:

February 1944: of Monte Cassino 'now a heap of ruins', 'I wonder [if] St Benedict …will be consoled if we start a monastery at Michaelgarth'.[163]

12 April 1944: the Russians 'are back in Odessa – or in the ruin that was once Odessa'.[164]

10 May 1944: waking at 3am to 'great rivers of sound [pouring] in wave after wave over our roof … aircraft, flying in formation with lights on … an awe-inspiring portent … that some great events were pending'[165], the 'great rivers' portending

'the "Big Push"' of D-Day, 6 June 1944, bathetically described by Hilda Harrison as 'a landing in Normandy'; Aelfrida, dreaming in French, remembers holidays there with her daughters – she does not mention Albert Erlande – and is grateful that the future was hidden from them then.[166]

4 June 1944: the Allies enter Rome on Trinity Sunday, 'God … sweeping aside the forces of evil on this festival', a festival greeted by Aelfrida six hours prior to their arrival with such a vivid vision of the Holy Trinity filling the whole universe that even on a 'talking day' she keeps her room 'alone with God … in the darkness of His Majesty and Mystery'.[167] (On 8 June she woke in the night feeling 'the intense pain of [Christ's] wounds, particularly in the hands' and suffered her hallucinatory impression of plane-borne ventriloquists.)[168]

14 August 1944: 'Walter is in France …'[169]

21 August 1944: an Allied landing at Cap d'Antibes; Constantine, Aelfrida believes, 'is helping me pray for his mother [and] … we are united in loving her and wishing her well'.[170]

25 August 1944: 'a *levée en masse* of the inhabitants … freed [Paris]'[171] – and Zelle, as Aelfrida later discovers to her joy, is still alive though her son has been murdered by the Germans.

8 November 1944: 'surveying the World Prospect … the future of religion is bleak'.[172]

17 November 1944: Churchill displays 'wisdom and generosity'[173]; indeed, so far has Aelfrida's opinion of him improved that by July 1945 he is 'the man who saved England'[174] and by 1955 is endowed with 'stalwart English virtues'. And 'some outstanding English faults'.[175]

21 April 1945: 'Heartrending pictures' of Belsen suggest a reparative fast day (dry bread only) and extra 'Saint Guenvrede' but Mother Guenvrede refuses, telling Aelfrida she is 'past that now [and] too old and infirm for penances'. Aelfrida agrees.[176]

1 and 2 May 1945: Mussolini shot by partisans ('I will … pray for his soul') and Hitler commits suicide. Should she pray for *his* soul? 'No'.[177]

8 May 1945: on 'Victory Day' she feels 'no movement of patriotic triumph only a deep, deep sense of thanksgiving that England has survived'.[178]

10 May 1945: 'if a visitor from abroad … dropped down on our plateau … I do not think he would have guessed that there had been either war or peace'.[179] (An earlier confession to Father Amos during which Aelfrida said she could discover no 'anti-Authority motives' in herself[180] does not ring true in this – or any other – context.)

8 July 1945: Alethea says there is 'no chance' of her being able to book a passage home for at least two years; 'I had not realised how many plans I had made', notes *Dictatrix Mundi*.[181]

9 August 1945: Hiroshima brings memories of the 'stir … in Cambridge when Rutherford split the atom … and now … an *atomic* bomb has … been dropped on a Japanese [town] causing devastation of a scale hitherto unknown … Alas! Mankind [seems] on the road to destruction. Can *prayer* bring it back?'[182]

15 August 1945: at midnight, the sound of bells 'in a dancing measure … over and over again … there could be no doubt. *Peace had come.*'[183]

Aelfrida, Placida, and Mrs Graham greeted the news with trepidation. Life at Tymawr was sometimes hard but if she left would she be subjected (like England after cessation of American Lease-Lend) to 'severe privations?' (But if 'poverty it *must* be, it shall be Holy Poverty'.)[184] If so, would she, like everyone else, clamour for more food and tire of being 'heroic?'[185] Would election of Labour candidate Clement Attlee as Prime Minister result in the 'secular Utopia' whose sinister aspects she pilloried in *Concrete* and whose stupefying tendencies she ridiculed in *Invitation à la Liberté*[186], a poem of 1920 which, though referring to conditions in England under a Liberal government after the Great War, accurately foretells the deadening effect on initiative and aspiration of governmental micromanagement? Would she have to suffer the sight of 'wicked Soviet Russia' imposing 'Russian Communism'[187] on other countries? Would she be forced to grieve 'every day, many times a day, over the dark cloud of brutishness and ungodliness' which now hung so heavily over the human race? (Particularly over those 'who go to dog races'.)[188] She would.

By May 1946, therefore, and within a month of the last diary entry quoted above, Aelfrida had at least two motives for informing Mother Guenvrede of her 'bread miracle'. (To prevent being sent away can be excluded; in spite of everything, she was raring to go.) The first was that of persuading Mother Guenvrede that her tertiary's sometimes bizarre behaviour in relation to herself had been essentially protective insofar as it was she alone who recognised the devil's intrusions into the Mother's mind and sought to combat them – in which respect it was fortunate that on entering the West Room to discuss the 'miracle', Mother Guenvrede unwittingly played into Aelfrida's hands by complaining of oppression 'by a sense of the *power of evil* in the world'. Seizing her opportunity, Aelfrida reassured the Mother that aspects of her tertiary's behaviour about which the latter had complained most bitterly were the same 'bogies' as those 'invented by the devil' for the Mother's torment and for her tertiary's unhappiness as a result of the Mother 'flying into a temper'; privately, however, she noted that a supposedly private 'miracle' had in fact been sent by God to the Mother as a 'manifestation of [His] omnipotence in a little thing' in order to support her through the devilish 'onslaughts' which oppressed her in terms of the 'power of evil' at large in the world and even affected her belief in 'God as Almighty'[189], and, by extension, her belief in the spiritual worth of a tertiary to whom His Son spoke 'from the Crucifix and from the Tabernacle' to 'shew' her 'the brightness of His Divinity [and] His Divine Nature …*infinite and eternal*'.[190]

Her second motive was to remind Mother Guenvrede of the spiritual value to her 'heterogeneous and undistinguished' Community of the presence of a mystic through whom was demonstrated 'our Lord's power upon [it]'[191] – and if earlier 'trances' had failed to convince the Mother of this, perhaps a 'miracle' would. And what sweet revenge to vouchsafe this on the point of being sent away.

On 16 May 1946 Aelfrida received two invitations concerning departure, the first potential, the second imminent. Both involved Donkins. On 15 May she became 'agitated' when Mrs Donkin was overtaken by violent vomiting and the following day, herself suffered a heavy nosebleed, both events predictive to the Oracle's daughter of the 'longed-for invitation to [her] heavenly birthday'. As she correctly surmised, the actual date was 'a good way off yet' but expectoration of two 'enormous' clots of blood ('instant death if they had gone to heart or brain') led her to warn Mother Guenvrede (already alerted to impending catastrophe because Aelfrida had used the convent's entire supply of hot water to wash her blood-soaked handkerchiefs) that should she suffer a stroke, Mrs Graham (should she survive) was to be consigned forthwith 'to the nuns at Fordfield' and Sister Placida (should she succumb) to the Campo Santo after a beautiful Requiem culminating in the Community giving each other 'a kiss of peace all round'. But Aelfrida's reflections on her readiness for 'the summons' (if summons it was) and on how Alethea would rejoice 'in having a mother in heaven or on the way there!' were rudely interrupted by a message from Mother Guenvrede: she was to vacate her room by the end of July and plead though Placida might, her decision was irrevocable.[192]

Though she described the news as 'expected', Aelfrida was so taken aback by the 'unexpected' brevity of her remaining sojourn at Tymawr – two and a half months – that she maintained diary silence (at her guardian angel's bidding) for a fortnight, recording on 30 May that she had been 'suffering such anguish at the thought of uprooting that [she] was altogether like a wound that cannot bear to be touched'. The wound, however, seems to have been to her pride, not her soul, for on hearing Mother Guenvrede's diktat she had protested only a little (to her diary she confided that she knew her time at Tymawr was 'nearly over' so was perhaps not as surprised as she made out) and anguish notwithstanding, was already making plans for life after Tymawr. Such detailed plans, in fact, that when God eventually led her 'to a place that He is preparing' the ground work would have been done and her future, 'at first completely bare', clarified in general terms if not in particulars. Forward planning also ensured that Mother Guenvrede's attempts to mitigate the severity of her pronouncement by informing Placida that the latter could return if the expected influx of aspirants failed to materialise were countered by Mrs Graham stating that if she went 'it would be for good', disguised though her sentiment might be (Mother Guenvrede's diktat provided a perfect escape-clause but it was also necessary to make the decision appear her own) in terms of failing health ('the life here is now too hard physically'; she did not intend to lead an easier life in the future but chose not to make that known) or a pious wish to promote the welfare of the Community at the expense of her own 'even if it meant me turning out'.[193]

With regard to the Community, however, Aelfrida's most poignant thoughts concerned her relationship with it. How, she asked herself, had she '*failed*' with respect to it? Had she failed in being too '*personal*' (a curious statement not enlarged upon but meaning, perhaps, that she had indulged in too much 'clamour of selfhood'[194] or had made herself too prominent as a person or as the personality complained of by Mother Guenvrede) and by not giving 'perfect love' to God, to the Community, to the Mother, or to life as a resident tertiary? (She had, she said, given love 'to the limits of [her] capability' and 'as spiritual as [she] knew how to give'.)[195] She had also tested God's and Mother Guenvrede's patience to the limit with her 'sins, negligences, and ignorance' (His and the Mother's patience in bearing with them moved her profoundly)[196], had not achieved '*perfect* contrition' or 'unfeigned love of the Cross' ( an ambiguous remark: did she *dislike* being a 'victim-soul' or was she, as in Florence, only 'playing' at religion?), and she remained 'unmortified in self-regard'.[197]

More positively, and in spite of worrying that in the Community's eyes she was 'just … a "goup"'[198], she had learnt much. The Community, she noted, had 'drawn away all the *emotionalism*' from her prayer-life and provided purer and simpler apprehension of the religious truths she sought, and by allowing her to share its spiritual life, had bestowed so much '*caritas*' upon her that 'frailties … either my own or other people's … [were] no longer stumbling blocks'. (If by '*caritas*' Aelfrida meant the theological virtue sometimes rendered as the 'love' or 'charity' bestowed by God on mankind as a gift to those who share His life to the best of their ability, her intention to practise it with regard to other people's frailties did not long survive her resolution.) And when she asked herself if the religious life had suffocated or liberated her and if in trying to live it she had felt '*closed in and weighed down* or set free', she replied that she had never had enough spiritual 'room' until she came to Tymawr.[199] So 'most *intensely* grateful for the blessed years here'[200], she would leave quietly with love in her heart to lead a life of 'Continuity and Silence' (and *caritas*) elsewhere.[201] But – and with Aelfrida there is always a but – however much it pleased God to send her back into the world for the Community's sake and however ready she was 'at any moment to go'[202], her presence had imposed a spiritual (and physical and emotional) burden on the Community so great that, as she had once written of another convent entered at another crisis point in her life (and from which she also returned to Cambridge), when she asked herself if she was 'more capable, more interesting, more lovable, better for all [her] experiences' there, she could only answer 'perhaps'. And this being the case and though it had been a 'wonderful [and] glorious' experience, she could not stay because she had suffered 'and others too'. And for that reason, if no other, she was 'glad to go'.[203]

Departure, of course, meant another series of letters explaining why she was about to leave the place to which her pillar of fire and cloud had led her and in which she had intended to remain for rest of her life. Aelfrida does not tell us what she said but we may gauge people's reactions by what she reports of their response. 'Bayard' Crundwell may have been surprised to have her hint obliquely that Cambridge 'drew her children back' even as Aelfrida assured him that she herself was not one of them.[204] Alethea expressed regret and asked if anything had gone wrong, but as Aelfrida (so she said) had never even '*hinted*' at problems, she was able to reassure her daughter with a clear conscience.[205] (Elsewhere, however, she makes the telling comment that it was 'with intense relief' that she went because she disliked the prospect of being snubbed for her pretensions when, as seemed increasingly likely, she and Alethea met again: 'it will be infinitely best that she should never meet Sister Placida'.)[206] Julius visited on hearing the news, '*jubilant*, though he was very discreet! at my exodus from what he evidently considers some kind of bondage', to offer

a 'welcome … at Wetenhall Cottage' until arrangements already in train were completed. Eustace invited her to Jesus Lodge though she declined his offer because 'not well enough'. (To her diary she described the Lodge as 'a most unsuitable place for a tertiary!')[207] Father Northcott, now in South Africa, wrote tactfully of his regret at Sister Placida being "uprooted" from Tymawr but assured her that parting was "inevitable once the Society began to expand"; he also noted that she seemed to be taking the parting in the right spirit "as an indication of God's Will for [her]".[208] But Aelfrida's comment on her erstwhile director lacked *caritas*: he had been, she growled, 'too timid' to object when Mother Guenvrede sent her thrice to Cardiff.[209]

Goodbyes had to be said to inanimate objects and to people. To 'beloved places' and her West Room, 'all full of the Presence of God and of prayers and thoughts of Him'.[210] To 'useful saints' 'Rose' and 'Bruno' ('Saint Guenvrede' was to accompany her), buried piecemeal ('I couldn't bury a *whole* hair shirt or … girdle so I cut them up') under gorse and dead bracken at the 'House of Defence', there to be guarded by 'Prehistoric Stones', by 'a most exquisite snake … the *Genius Loci,*' and by the sign of the cross made over them.[211] To Father Amos, 'old and apathetic' with a sick wife and coping at Michaelgarth with the assistance of a devoted housekeeper, but said only 'for courtesy's sake'[212] after her final confession to him. To Sister Jeanne in a talk of a 'mostly spiritual' nature and nearly an hour[213], Aelfrida being now reconciled with the 'little saint who [had] been [her] friend'[214] for the greater part of her stay and who was now 'quite her dear self again'[215] after their spat of 1944 when Aelfrida feigned illness and Sister Jeanne, 'on the verge of a nervous collapse'[216], was sent to 'wait' on her. To Associates and other members of the Community and to Bishop and Mrs O'Ferrall. And to Mother Guenvrede.

During the fifty-five days which elapsed between Aelfrida receiving the 'expected-unexpected' news and her departure, Placida reprised her behaviour during the preceding nine years towards her Superior. Prompted, it may be, by loss of face – she would have liked to pre-empt Mother Guenvrede by saying she '*ought*' to go because her 'pillar of fire and cloud [seemed] ready to move' – she decided that the reason why Mother Guenvrede now avoided her 'pointedly' was because the latter's conscience pricked her at sending away an aged invalid in a 'too precipitate a manner'[217] and 'prematurely a 'child of God' whom she had promised to 'see through' spiritual difficulties but had 'forgotten' to do so ('her mind has *gaps*')[218] because of pressure of work, 'some physical deterioration in [her] brain', or the promptings of the devil. Hence it was not because Aelfrida sought 'relief' from

God's intensification of His Presence upon her ('His Holiness *burns*')[219] by deliberately picking a final quarrel with the Mother; it was because she was burning for revenge.

Knowing that Mother Guenvrede's withdrawal of attention and her suffering one of her 'most strained and restless moods'[220] was because the Community had been struck with "a run of ills"[221] requiring extensive and expensive treatments which withdrawal of Mrs Graham's financial contribution of over £100 a year would adversely affect 'even if I give them presents as I hope to do' (failure to gauge the Mother's desperation to rid herself of a thorn even though it deprived the Community of income indicated Mrs Graham's egocentricity)[222], Aelfrida fired her parting shot. Deliberately choosing 'a very inopportune moment', she wrote Mother Guenvrede a letter concerning a novice's 'lateral curvature of the spine' unnoticed by the novice or anyone else. Timing the letter so that Mother Guenvrede would have the Greater Silence 'in which to recover from … annoyance' at her interference, Aelfrida prepared to grovel but found herself, to her chagrin, confronted by Sister Sheila, bearer of an insulting message: "Mother wishes me to tell you to mind your own business and to leave the convent to manage its own affairs".[223] So she did, but not before hinting (by letter) to Bishop O'Ferrall that she was 'anxious about the Mother' and that his sister as second in command needed his 'help and counsel'[224] and (verbally) to members of the Community that Mother Guenvrede being 'exhausted and nervous' was symptomatic less of exhaustion than of a recurrence of 'mental trouble'.[225] In her diary, however, she noted what she believed to be the true cause of the Mother's distress: the Mother having recently commented to her that everything seemed '*evil* just now' and that she had had to choose 'the lesser of evils [and] walk by faith' and that Aelfrida must do the same[226] (a hint not taken) provided ample proof that not only had the devil got his foot firmly 'in the Community door'[227] (something which distressed her more than the thought of leaving, for she would no longer be there to 'protect' the Mother) but also that it was he who, having threatened to 'dislodge' Placida when she stood between him and Mother Guenvrede, had planted 'delusions and suspicions and forgetfulness in the Mother's mind' and thereby caused her to 'fail' Aelfrida by sending her away.[228]

To all this Mother Guenvrede, 'exhausted and nervous' though she was, responded with a degree of *caritas* Aelfrida would have done well to emulate, with charity and love, that is to say, indicative of great spiritual strength in the face of physical and emotional adversity. (Her response – though Aelfrida was too firmly fixed in her obsession with diabolical interference to see this – also refuted the possibility of the devil's presence within the Community.) As her 'gentler self', Mother Guenvrede made encouraging remarks: Aelfrida, she said, had "grown out of all recognition spiritually" during her years at Tymawr and in acknowledgement of this would be the object of a Benedictine farewell on the Sunday preceding her departure, a ceremony which would enable her to (as Aelfrida put it) leave 'not under suspicion for imaginary (*sic*) misdeeds but as a beloved member of the Community'.[229] As Winifred Donkin, however, the Mother could not resist a final dig: Mrs Graham, she said, would '*love* being once more admired and petted and able to have [her] own way' (Mrs Graham agreed, noting privately that although she had valued the Mother's *fortiter in re*, 'a little more *suaviter in modo* would have been a good thing but … I know she can't *help* the harshness') and must therefore ensure that she was subjected to discipline and severity wherever she settled. To which Mrs Graham responded that she 'dreaded' returning to the 'charm of Cambridge and the warmth of … human affections' and that in her heart she had already 'renounced houses and lands and kinsfolk'.[230] And if she really thought so at this point in her life, who could gainsay her?

> 7 July 1946. 'I could never believe that my last Sunday here could be anything but anguish [but] today has been radiant in the Holy Presence'. After None, Mother Guenvrede, dismissing the novices and junior Sisters, knelt with Sisters Sheila, Hilda, Monica, and Jeanne behind Aelfrida at the back of the chapel to recite the *Itinerarium,* the Benedictine prayers for a religious who is being sent on a journey and for Aelfrida an honour and a ceremony which 'bound [her] in closest spiritual fellowship with the beloved Community'.[231]
>
> 9 July 1946. 'At Mass, God drew me into His Infinity, His Omnipotence, His Peace. The Little Hours are over – now there will be only Vespers which I hope will not be put off, as it was last night, till 9.15pm because of cutting the hay'. After Vespers, 'each one of the Community bade me a separate goodbye … one or two were in tears … The Mother's goodbye was the best [for] when the Community had filed out past me … [she] stopped, put her hands on my shoulders [and] … laid her cheek against mine whispering goodbye'.

On 10 July, up at 5.45 to be ready to leave by 6.15am, Aelfrida 'went off alone'.[232] Her departure went unrecorded in the convent's *Book of Acts.*

'I was happiest', she wrote, consciously or unconsciously paraphrasing John Henry Newman's letter to

Henry Wilberforce of a century earlier as she looked back on her years at Tymawr a decade later, 'surrounded by those who tried to live for God alone – happiest with my "useful saints" … happiest in the ordered life … happiest with the hard bed and the scanty meals and the long hours of silence, happy at the consciousness of God's presence', happiest, perhaps, as 'Sister Placida [whom] the tether to the beloved Community still holds'.[233]

"I have tried", wrote Sister Jeanne in 2003, "to put together what I [remember] about Aelfrida Tillyard – Sr Placida … I understood that she wished to live here as a praying presence in a contemplative environment … earning from the writing and sale of her books … She came to every Office and Eucharist and spent much time in Chapel … As far as I know, the difference of opinion between M. Guenvrede and Placida came over the shutting and opening of windows [and] Placida's passion for *personal total silence* on big Feast-days, Professions, etc., *and breaking it on a Community silent day.* [Also] giving unsuitable gifts (books) to Novices and … sudden determination that her room must be changed … There was a grille which in a sense protected [her] from us and us from [her] and both sides willingly accepted the ways of life protecting silence. Yet she was *not* dotty … And a great deal of affection, generosity, patience and kindness was … evident on both sides. She left after the war and I'm afraid I have *no* idea where she went".[234]

## Notes

1 Charles, P. Vol. II pp 114–115 (Author's translation.) Of the three volumes of Charles' work in the Tymawr library, volumes I and III have most pages cut; Volume II has fewer cut but those cut include the significant passage quoted.
2 GCPPT 1|1|57 30 December 1939.
3 GCPPT 1|1|63 22 and 25 September 1945.
4 ibid. 31 October 1945.
5 ibid. 25 November 1945.
6 ibid. 27 January 1946.
7 ibid. 18 February 1946.
8 ibid. 'Christmas Eve' (24 December) and 'Christmas Day' (25 December) 1945.
9 ibid. 15 November 1945. Anyone forced to eat reconstituted powdered egg will sympathise with Aelfrida's complaint.
10 ibid. 'Shrove Tuesday' (5 March) 1946.
11 ibid. 10 January and 'Ash Wednesday' (14 March) 1946.
12 ibid. 13 January 1946.
13 ibid. 8 August and 22 September 1945. *John* 20:15 tells the story of Mary Magdalene mistaking the risen Christ for the gardener of the garden in which His sepulchre was situated.
14 ibid. 22 December and 'Christmas Eve' (24 December) 1945 and 14 March 1946.
15 GCPPT 1|1|62 14 and 17 March 1945.
16 Details of Father Northcott's departure and of his successor are taken from the SSC's Autumn 1945 Newsletter (GCPPT 1|1|63a) and from Aelfrida's diary (GCPPT 1|1|63 15 August 1945).
17 GCPPT 1|1|63 14 March and 15 August 1945.
18 ibid. 2 April 1946.
19 ibid. 15 August 1945.
20 ibid. 2 April 1946.
21 ibid. 'St Benedict' (11 July) 1945.
22 ibid. 15 November 1945.
23 ibid.
24 ibid 22 January 1946.
25 GCPPT 1|1|62 26 November 1944.
26 ibid. 22 July and 1 August 1945 and 14 February 1946.
27 ibid. 1 November and 15 December 1945.
28 GCPPT 1|1|62 28 January 1945.
29 GCPPT 1|1|63 16 May 1946.
30 GCPPT 1|1|57 30 December 1939.
31 GCPPT 1|1|63 22 September 1946.
32 ibid. 14 February 1946.
33 ibid. 2 and 12 November 1945.
34 GCPPT 1|1|64 28 June 1946.
35 GCAC 4|6|3|3 Letter from Aelfrida CW Graham to Kathleen Butler of 6 March 1945. Kathleen Butler was Mistress of Girton 1943–1949.
36 ibid. Letter from Kathleen Butler to Aelfrida Graham of 10 March 1945.
37 GCPPT 1|1|62 14 March 1945.
38 GCAC 4|6|3|3 Letter from Aelfrida CW Graham to Kathleen Butler of 13 June 1946.
39 ibid. Letter from Aelfrida CW Graham to Kathleen Butler of 6 March 1945.
40 ibid. Envelope labelled "correspondence relating to 4 registered parcels etc" by-lined "Miss McMorran June 1946".
41 GCPPT 1|1|61 29 and 30 July 1943.
42 GCPPT 1|1|62 2 May 1944.
43 ibid. 3 May and 18 June 1944.
44 GCPPT 1|1|62a Undated letter from Muriel Pont (Tertiary Teresa) to 'Sister Placida'.
45 GCPPT 1|1|62 13 June 1944.
46 ibid. 5 July 1944.
47 ibid. 18 June 1944.
48 ibid. 14 August 1944.
49 ibid. 13 June 1944.
50 GCPPT 1|1|61 9 March 1944.
51 ibid. 29 June 1943.
52 GCPPT 1|1|62 2 November 1944.
53 GCPPT 1|1|62a SSC Newsletter of 8 December 1944.
54 GCPPT 1|1|63a SSC Newsletter of April 1945.
55 GCPPT 1|1|63 3 May 1945.
56 ibid. 22 January 1946.
57 ibid. 2 April 1945.
58 GCPPT 1|1|63a SSC Newsletter of Autumn 1945.
59 GCPPT 1|1|63 17 May 1945.
60 ibid. 10 and 15 June 1945.
61 GCPPT 1|1|61a Undated letter from Mother Guenvrede to Aelfrida on the subject of Hilda Harrison.
62 GCPPT 1|1|61 14 May 1943.
   GCPPT 1|1|53 2 March 1937.
63 À Kempis, T. p 50.
64 GCPPT 1|1|57 4 May 1940.
65 I am indebted for my ideas on monastic stability as it relates to Aelfrida's years at Tymawr to ch 6 (*Stability and Change* by Mother Abbess Mary John OSB) of *Living Stones.*

66 GCPPT 1|1|54 9 October 1937.

67 GCPPT 1|1|59 'All Souls' (3 November) 1941. A "story" narrated by Aelfrida in *The Closer Walk with God* regarding two (male) friends, the "wrong" done one to the other, and the way in which the wronged man assures himself that the "vocation of sorrow" to which he cleaves on his wronger's behalf will ensure that the latter makes his peace with God during his last illness, can now be read for what it is: a parable.

68 GCPPT 1|1|57 14 November 1939.

69 ibid. 27 January 1940.

70 ibid.

71 GCPPT 1|1|60 10 June 1942.

72 GCPPT 1|1|59 25 November 1941.

73 GCPPT 1|1|57 20 February 1940.

74 GCPPT 1|1|72 19 January 1955.

75 GCPPT 1|1|57 15 July 1940.

76 GCPPT 1|1|59 27 July and 21 October 1944.

77 ibid. 28 June 1941.

78 GCPPT 1|1|58 19 October 1940.

79 ibid. 31 October 1940.

80 GCPPT 1|1|59 10 May 1941. The words were written three months after Aelfrida's last contact with Lady Frazer on the day the former learnt that elderly ailing Sir James Frazer had died and that Lady Frazer, throwing herself on her husband's corpse, died 'a few hours after [him]'.

81 GCPPT 1|1|58 31 October 1940 and 18 February 1941.

82 GCPPT 1|1|60 10 June 1942.

83 ibid. 4 August 1942.

84 ibid. 10 June 1942.

85 ibid. 8 June 1942.

86 ibid. 10 June 1942.

87 GCPPT 1|1|61 23 December 1943.

88 GCPPT 1|1|62 17 August 1944.

89 ibid. 18 July 1944.

90 GCPPT 1|1|61 23 January 1944.

91 ibid. 10 July 1943.

92 GCPPT 1|1|63 18 November 1945.

93 GCPPT 1|1|60 16 June 1942.

94 GCPPT 1|1|61 10 July 1943.

95 Donkin, W. *Gleanings*: note written during Lent 1946.

96 GCPPT 1|1|63 3 May 1945.

97 GCPPT 1|1|73 22 January 1956.

98 GCPPT 1|1|63 25 November 1945.

99 ibid. 25 April 1946.

100 ibid. 12 September 1945. Aelfrida's 'living stone' reference derives from the *First Epistle of Peter* 2:5 (KJV). Had she read verse 8 she might have noticed the analogy between her position at Tymawr as a "disobedient … stumbling block and a rock of offence".

101 Tillyard, Ae. *The Glory of the West* pp 1–3 (GCPPT 2|16|3).

102 GCPPT 1|1|63 29 and 31 July 1945.

103 ibid. 26 and 27 April 1946.

104 ibid. 27 April 1946.

105 GCPPT 1|1|58 20 July 1940.

106 GCPPT 1|1|61 28 March 1944.

107 GCPPT 1|1|62 18 June 1944.

108 Tillyard, CS. *Record of my Children* 24 July 1887 (MTC).

109 GCPPT 1|1|59 29 September 1941.

110 GCPPT 1|1|48 29 July 1935.

111 GCPPT 1|1|61 28 September 1943.

112 GCPPT 1|1|62 2 July 1944.

113 ibid. 28 January 1945.

114 ibid. 9 August 1944.

115 Tillyard, Ae. *Vision Triumphant* pp 73–74 (GCPPT 2|7).

116 GCPPT 1|1|59 29 September 1941.

117 GCPPT 1|1|62 7 December 1944.

118 GCPPT 1|1|73 23 September 1956.

119 Tillyard, Ae. *Vision Triumphant* pp 73–74.

120 Tillyard, Ae. *A Little Road-Book for Mystics* p 23.

121 GCPPT 1|1|73 14 August 1956.

122 Tillyard, Ae. *A Little Road-Book for Mystics* p 24.

123 GCPPT 1|1|73 14 August 1956.

124 GCPPT 1|1|55 27 May 1938.

125 GCPPT 1|1|59 29 May 1941.

126 GCPPT 1|1|58 21 July 1940.

127 ibid. 26 July 1940. As an example of her hearing the '*call* to being misunderstood', note her behaviour of 15 August 1940. On the day that the South Wales airfields first experienced the full might of the Luftwaffe (London had begun to experience it a few days earlier, so the avid reader of *The Times* could not plead ignorance), Aelfrida's concern was that she was forbidden to leave convent precincts (she had already broken bounds by doing so against the Mother's express instructions) is also, we can now see, an invitation to censure and humiliation, not merely a need for freedom.

128 Benson, RM. *Instructions on the Religious Life* pp 54–55.

129 À Kempis T. pp 172–173.

130 GCPPT 1|1|23 9 August 1918.

131 For Christ's Sermon on the Mount in which these are enumerated see *Matthew* ch. 5–8.

132 GCPPT 1|1|57 4 July 1939.

133 GCPPT 1|1|61 17 December 1943.

134 GCPPT 1|1|44 12 October 1933.

135 GCPPT 1|1|57 25 August 1939.

136 GCPPT 1|1|60 19 June 1942.

137 GCPPT 1|1|61 20 December 1943. Aelfrida did not keep the letter from which she quotes.

138 Benson RH. *The Light Invisible*, story entitled *In the Convent Chapel* pp 110–111.

139 GCPPT 1|1|61 23 November 1943.

140 ibid. 'Epiphany' (6 January) 1944. Aelfrida's use of the capitalised word 'Figure' (e.g. 'the Figure nailed to the living tree' of GCPPT 1|1|56 1 April 1939) probably derives from RH Benson's short story *The Watcher* in which a small penthouse sheltering a crucifix ("the Figure on the Cross") plays an important part. (*The Light Invisible* p 27). The chapel crucifix at Tymawr had formerly hung on the 'living tree' in the Campo Santo but being wooden had begun to deteriorate so was moved to the chapel and replaced by a metal one.

141 GCPPT 1|1|63 'Easter Eve' (20 April) 1946. This vision appears to be a greatly compressed version of that described in Benson's *The Convent Chapel* in which an observing priest becomes aware of intense spiritual reverberations passing between the Tabernacle and the heart of a nun taking the watch in front of it but cannot tell from which source the "power" emanates. (*In the Convent Chapel* pp 110–126; the convent concerned, though Benson does not say but Aelfrida knew, was Malling). Aelfrida herself quotes Benson's story in *Spiritual Exercises* p 166.

142 GCPPT 1|1|35 9 March 1928.
   GCPPT 1|1|62 23 and 25 August 1944.

143 GCPPT 1|1|63 'Christmas Eve' (24 December) 1945.

144 GCPPT 1|1|56 7 December 1938. *The Mystery of Mary* was published in 1938.

145 GCPPT 1|1|48 13 and 16 July 1935.

146 GCPPT 1|1|48 15 July 1935.
   GCPPT 1|1|54 10 February 1938.

147 GCPPT 1|1|48 14 and 17 July 1935.

148 GCPPT 1|1|61 21 and 26 March 1943.

149 GCPPT 1|1|63 'Christmas Eve' (24 December) 1945.

150 ibid. 13 April 1946.

151 ibid. 14 May 1946.

152 ibid. 1 January 1946.

153 GCPPT 1|1|20 3 June 1915.

154 GCPPT 1|1|63 1 February 1946. There is a possible though unmiraculous explanation for Aelfrida's 'bread miracle': insufficiently baked bread contains still-live yeast which continues to work after the bread is removed from the oven. The bread will therefore continue to rise but will rapidly denature and become inedible. Beyond informing us of the 'miracle', however, Aelfrida makes no comment as to the keeping qualities of her piece of loaf except to note that it lasted her several meals.

155 ibid. 5 May 1946.

156 ibid. 1 February 1946.

157 ibid. 5 May 1946.

158 ibid. 1 February 1946.

159 ibid. Author's emphasis.

160 ibid. 15 December 1945.

161 GCPPT 1|1|62 10 May 1944.

162 GCPPT 1|1|63 16 May 1946.

163 GCPPT 1|1|61 18 February 1944. The idea of Michaelgarth housing a monastery was an SSC scheme which never reached fruition.

164 ibid. 12 April 1944.

165 GCPPT 1|1|62 10 May 1944.

166 ibid. 6 and 11 June 1944.

167 ibid. 4 June 1944.

168 ibid. 8 June 1944.

169 ibid. 14 August 1944.

170 ibid. 21 August 1944.

171 ibid. 25 August 1944.

172 GCPPT 1|1|62 8 November 1944.

173 ibid. 17 November 1944.

174 GCPPT 1|1|63 28 July 1945.

175 GCPPT 1|1|73 21 February 1955.

176 GCPPT 1|1|63 21 April 1945.

177 ibid. 1 and 2 May 1945.

178 ibid. 'Victory Day' (8 May) 1945.

179 ibid. 'Ascension Day' (10 May) 1945.

180 GCPPT 1|1|62 18 August 1944.

181 GCPPT 1|1|63 8 July 1945.

182 ibid. 9 August 1945.

183 ibid. 15 August 1945.

184 ibid. 28 and 29 August 1945.

185 ibid. 5 September 1945.

186 ibid. 28 August 1945. *Invitation à la Liberté* appears in *Verses for Alethea* (pp 16–17).

187 ibid. 2 April 1946.

188 ibid. 13 April 1946.

189 ibid. 5 May 1946.

190 ibid. 13 April 1946.

191 ibid. 16 April 1946.

192 ibid. 16 May 1946.

193 GCPPT 1|1|63 16 May 1946.
GCPPT 1|1|64 30 May 1946.

194 GCPPT 1|1|64 17 June 1946 ('July' in diary).

195 ibid. 30 May 1946.

196 ibid. 17 June 1946.

197 ibid. 9 July 1946.

198 ibid. 17 June 1946.

199 GCPPT 1|1|63 12 May 1946.

200 GCPPT 1|1|64 30 May 1946.

201 ibid. 17 June 1946. ('July' in diary).

202 GCPPT 1|1|60 8 June 1942.

203 GCPPT 1|1|12 11 March 1905.

204 GCPPT 1|1|64 4 June 1946.

205 ibid. 11 June 1946.

206 ibid. 16 May 1946.

207 ibid. 30 May and 4 June 1946.

208 GCPPT 1|1|64a Letter from Hubert Northcott CR to Sister Placida of 22 July 1946.

209 GCPPT 1|1|64 17 June 1946.

210 GCPPT 1|1|63 14 May and 22 June 1946.

211 GCPPT 1|1|64 7 June 1946.

212 ibid. 2 July 1946.

213 ibid. 7 July 1946.

214 GCPPT 1|1|62 24 September 1944.

215 ibid. 10 January 1945.

216 ibid. 28 September 1944.

217 GCPPT 1|1|64 16 June 1946.

218 ibid. 17 June 1946.

219 GCPPT 1|1|63 14 May 1946.
GCPPT 1|1|64 26 June 1946.

220 GCPPT 1|1|64 16 June 1946.

221 GCPPT 1|1|64a. The SSC *Newsletter* for September 1946 describes "a run of ills through the convent" beginning at the time of Aelfrida's 'expected-unexpected' news and continuing throughout the year and beyond.

222 GCPPT 1|1|64 22 June 1946.

223 ibid. 21 and 22 June 1946.

224 ibid. 23 June 1946.

225 ibid. 22 and 26 June 1946.

226 ibid. 4 June 1946.

227 ibid. 22 June 1946.

228 ibid. 17 June 1946.

229 ibid. 3 June and 6 July 1946.

230 ibid. 4 and 7 June 1946.

231 ibid. 7 July 1946. Chapter LXVII of the Rule of St Benedict recommends that "Brethren who are being sent on a journey" commend themselves to the prayers of the Community and that "in the final prayer of the Work of God" those who are absent should be commemorated. The *Itinerarium* itself usually consisted of a canticle, versicles and collects, and the Benedictus.

232 ibid. 10 July 1946. Aelfrida's description of her last Tymawr Vespers was written on 10 July but is given here as 9 July for the sake of clarity.

233 GCPPT 1|1|74 29 August 1957. Newman's letter of 15 December 1846 describes himself as "happy at Oriel, happier at Littlemore, as happy or happier at Maryvale – and happiest here" i.e. at Birmingham Oratory (Turner, F. p 637).

234 Undated letter (by context written August 2003) from Sister Jeanne SSC, then aged 98, in answer to the author's request for information about Aelfrida. Sister Jeanne's memory was at fault with regard to her not knowing where Aelfrida went; she and Aelfrida corresponded regularly until the latter's death.

# Holy Poverty at Lolworth

'Always having to begin *de novo*'[1] was one of Aelfrida's regular complaints though more usually couched in terms of having to start anew on her spiritual pilgrimage than in terms of physical departure and arrival. Departure from Tymawr and arrival in Cambridge, however, had different emotional and domiciliary connotations because she had been asked to leave a beloved place in which she had lived uninterruptedly, brief exiles in Cardiff notwithstanding for during them she remained at Tymawr in spirit, to return to a place from which she had deliberately distanced herself. Her 1946 '*de novo*' was therefore less a joyful '*vita nuova*' than – as she had once written of enforced moves as a consular wife – a going forward to a new uncertainty.

An uncertainty perhaps but not an uncertain future, for less than three weeks after receiving Mother Guenvrede's 'expected-unexpected' dismissal, Aelfrida had found herself a new home and a new occupation. Following what she believed was God's Will, she wrote to the then Bishop of Ely enquiring 'whether any priest in the diocese, say in some remote country village in the fens, who was feeling discouraged by lack of response among his flock … would like a tertiary to … live in or near the vicarage and pray for his work'.[2] The Bishop replied cordially, promptly, and positively but it was her guardian angel in the shape of Dorothea Conybeare who directed her to a 'suitable incumbent … [at] Lolworth Rectory'.[3] Aelfrida was delighted: Father Lovell celebrated Mass daily in the village church and the Little Hours (Prime, Terce, Sext, and None) privately 'in an oratory at home'; better still, he and Mrs Lovell were Franciscan tertiaries. Informed of this, the Bishop wrote again, noting his gladness that someone would 'give the Lovells the help and encouragement they need'.[4]

Neither the Bishop's veiled warning nor information provided by Mrs Lovell (one bath a week, no electricity, board and lodging at £2-2-6d a week slightly cheaper than Tymawr because of that) deterred one convinced she was doing God's Will and that Lolworth rectory would be 'a lovely place for Alethea to come to' when able to obtain a passage because it was only six miles from Cambridge and 'much homelier than a convent'.[5] (And *not* a convent, a happier situation for both women.) A letter from Father Lovell saying sadly that he was "up

**Aelfrida Graham at Lolworth Rectory c1948**

against a blank wall of materialism and indifference" decided her: 'Yes, that is the *kind* of parish to which I felt God was calling me'.[6]

Aelfrida's choice of parish and of parochial service was deliberate. She had long harboured a 'vague notion' of becoming some kind of 'deaconess', originally because she might gain entrée to Leiston that way, subsequently because the lay diaconate might quality her 'for work in some country parish'.[7] (She had, of course, no real intention of putting herself forward and subsequent events deflected her from this particular path.) In 1936, however, she was stimulated by an article in *Theology* in which the editor wrote of a "moving comment" sent in response to an earlier editorial by a rural parish priest who, calling himself one of the "poor relations of the Church", wrote despondently of dwindling congregations, of "country people" not now wanting "the things of God", and of his attempts to inspire his congregation falling "quite flat"[8], to write six stories for the SPCK entitled *Parish Tales (The Vicar's Household*.) Beginning in April 1936 within days of the 'mystic death' occasioned by anaphylactic shock and completed three months later at the moment when 'Philothea's' visit to Tymawr inspired her to go there herself, *Parish Tales* netted Aelfrida £50 but like the villages where "nobody cares", seem not to have been cared for sufficiently by their author to warrant keeping copies.[9] Having subsequently entered Tymawr, a place whence she intended never to depart, Aelfrida put notions of parish work aside, though a reference in Alec Vidler's *God's Judgement on Europe* to England being in danger of drifting into a state of "post Christian secularisation" akin to wartime Germany's[10] may have kept the dormant notion alive until such time as the necessity of finding a new home (Wetenhall Cottage was now occupied by Julius and Mina and their children, 'all rejoicing to be there')[11] prompted her to revive her earlier idea of becoming an incumbent's assistant if not an actual deaconess.

Aelfrida's initial feeling on returning to Cambridge was 'joy indeed' ('the first signpost saying *Cambridge* was a great thrill … Cambridge, still there, alive with its old life, after all the dangers that have beset it') and as her hired car neared "the outskirts of the town [her] heart warmed towards the dear place [and] it was pleasant … to reach [her] old home".[12] Her 'old home' twice over, for following lunch and tea at Wetenhall Cottage 'whose rose pink and powder blue curtains waved a welcome in the breeze' and 'whispered "the Lord be with you"' to an owner who never thought to visit her 'beloved little house again'[13], Aelfrida was welcomed '*home* to "Fordfield"' (now Hope House or the Hope Nursing Home) where she went as planned 'as a patient to be under observation for a few days'[14]; it was not only Julius, it seems, whose ambition in life was to be 'at his best loved Cambridge and come home to Fordfield'.[15] (Admission was probably an arrangement made by herself in order that proper assessment might be made of her physical condition; she had little faith in Monmouthshire doctors.) Entering the Home, she was interviewed by the Reverend Mother in what had been part of the drawing room but was now the Mother's 'parlour' and shortly thereafter ensconced in the former night nursery on whose floor she had once crouched weeping over her sins.

Joy indeed was short. The following day she retired early and in tears from 'sheer exhaustion, plus bitter longing for Silence and Solitude and … a sense of utter inability … to meet all righteous demands made on [her] … by God and man'.[16] Not only this, but changes at 'Fordfield' (the West Room, 'always [reserved] for the Master of the house' and now the chapel, had its altar on the exact spot where she had eased the Oracle and Chiara into death; its vestry, appropriately, had been the Oracle's dressing room)[17] were accompanied by changes elsewhere. 'Dr Joan's' locum, 'a very jaunty Modern Girl kind of doctor … with rouge on her lips and a wedding ring on her finger' (Dr Cooper herself was off sick with 'a bad breakdown') 'blew in to see me, agreed with my diagnosis, ordered me the 4 days rest I had planned to take and blew out' – and was unsympathetic to one whom, were it not that admission to the Hope required medical sanction, her patient would have dismissed outright because she also 'suggested' that Aelfrida *not* take to her bed.[18] Hope House's second sister expressing hopes that Mrs Graham 'convert' to Roman Catholicism, an odd thing to do given that the Sisters of Hope ('*perfect ladies* as well as good Religious and excellent nurses') made a point of not obtruding their views on 'patients' own preoccupations', be these physical or spiritual[19], but understandable given that Aelfrida attended Mass with the 'unselfconscious, informal, intelligent, dignified gracious and harmonious sisters' who 'waited on' her and with whom, though they made her feel a '*spiritual vulgarian*'[20], she felt an affinity.

Returning to Wetenhall Cottage on 15 July, Aelfrida enjoyed a 'delightful … family union', finding Julius 'master of the house here' as never in Cardiff, Mina 'happy and hospitable', Constance 'all prettiness and charm' and studying music, 'plain but friendly' Angela at Girton, Stephen 'elegant in looks … but altogether inscrutable', Phyllis 'chatty', Eustace 'mellow and dignified' as Master of Jesus, Walter still in the army but soon to matriculate at Emmanuel, and Veronica a 'handsome and dignified' teacher.[21] She also met or made a point of meeting outsiders: Mr Church, now 'a wee little old man of 81', with whom she walked round the 'garden-at-the-back'[22]; 'Timothy' White, once the tuberculous undergraduate for whose fear of death Agatha felt so much sympathy (Agatha, it seems, was not referred to at 'family unions' though she must have loomed large in everyone's minds as well as her mother's, the latter referring to her twice in her diary in as many days; Alethea was scarcely mentioned), now 'a stoutish, handsome man bearded and sunburnt'[23]; Alfred Walford (also careful not to mention Agatha) prescribing penicillin for an attack of sinusitis, an experience Aelfrida found 'quite thrilling' as the 'stuff' conquered her 'germs', though she expressed concern lest the exciting new drug postpone her 'Heavenly Birthday'[24]; Florence Keynes, physically frail at eighty-eight but her mind 'strong and astonishingly accurate', showing her visitor photographs of recently-dead Maynard ('[he] was hideous!') and proofs of a book on 'old Cambridge'[25] to be called *Gathering up the Threads*, 'threads' which unaccountably failed to include

Fordfield or the Tillyards; Lilian Whitehouse, 'much mellowed'[26]; Louisa, Eustace's former nurse, still living in the Albert Homes next door; Dorothea Conybeare, as spinsterly in fact and outlook as always. And the Matron of the Orphans' Home in Shaftesbury Avenue (where Aelfrida, though we do not discover this until much later, had sponsored a girl since 1942) who declared that Mrs Graham 'hadn't changed a bit!'[27] She was right. Aelfrida had hardly changed at all.

Yet in spite of Julius' obvious delight in his sister's company (talking with her in the Wetenhall Cottage garden with 'quietness and beauty all around', he sighed "the perfect peace of Fordfield" and Aelfrida 'knew that he was happy')[28] and of her own pleasure in revisiting old haunts (King's, with 'everything as it was when Constantine was [there]', though 'in the chapel, the blackout spoke of war years')[29], in 'natural' things (an elegant lunch at the Cottage 'with a white damask tablecloth', Jesus Lodge 'a delight to behold' and 'the garden has the unique charm of college gardens')[30], and in being 'petted up' when 'poor knee [was] bad again'[31], Aelfrida found being in '"the world" even where it is *good*'[32] very trying. For one thing, it seemed extremely noisy to one whose life had been lived in more or less silent solitude for nearly a decade and though some of the noise was pleasant (Walter, Constance, and Mina playing Handel trios), sounds made by people moving around the house late at night and early in the morning irked her immensely (she tried not to grumble 'even to [her] diary')[33] because it disturbed one who liked to meditate and pray without interruption and because it reminded her of the 'pressure' family members exerted on her soul. For another, there was 'so much talking' to do that she complained of 'great weariness' and of an 'almost unbearable' longing for imposed or voluntary silences at Tymawr.[34] ('Isn't it strange', she noted, 'no one asks me any questions about the convent'![35], a lack of curiosity due, it may be, to all members of her immediate family except Stephen and Angela having visited her there or, perhaps, to embarrassment at meeting again a mentally-unstable relative consigned there – as they hoped – for ever or, in outsiders, to a resigned response to one known to be religiously eccentric and given to wild enthusiasms of which, it seemed, conventual life had provided yet another example.) How could she, she asked herself, maintain awareness of God and of herself 'as a chosen instrument for work of which I know nothing except that it is God's' in the midst of so many unpleasant (and pleasant, of course; she loved being a 'favoured guest') distractions?[36] The only thing to do was to offer 'no rebellion' and her pains to God – at which point, and probably significantly, she reverted to 'my old meditation on the Holy Passion,

lying on my back with arms outstretched', a meditation and position largely unsought at Tymawr but now turned to 'with vehement longing', with relief of tension, and with intense gratitude because 'the pain in my hands begins a few minutes after I unite myself in spirit with my crucified Saviour'.[37]

She also paid a flying visit to Lolworth, the 'tiny village' (it had only a hundred inhabitants and twenty-four houses) over which her pillar of fire and cloud now hovered some six miles beyond Girton and a short distance off the road to Huntingdon. 'I shall love being at Lolworth', she wrote enthusiastically, '... as [I] drove along I caught sight of a fine church tower against a background of huge trees ... The rectory is so deeply embedded in trees that we drove past it without noticing!' It should, she added, 'be really quiet here for ... Lolworth [is] a cul-de-sac [without] through traffic [and] no aerodrome near'.[38] But was she being disingenuous or had she forgotten? This was not her first visit. In May 1928 she and Agatha cycled to Lolworth during the latter's gap year. 'You seem', Aelfrida wrote then, 'to go back fifty years ... [to] a couple of prosperous-looking farms and its own little schoolhouse and such a beautiful old church'. Meeting the rector, she found him a 'wild-eyed' practitioner in cassock and biretta of an 'earnest popery' which 'thoroughly bewildered' the 'indifferent' villagers, though when shown by him round the rectory garden, she enjoyed a redeeming view of 'exquisite green distances'.[39] Returning after nearly twenty years she found little had changed save the rector – and even he resembled his predecessor in several ways.

Father Lovell, she wrote, is 'about 45' ('no, he is 52' is added later in the purple ink favoured by the rectory) 'with ... thin cheeks and dark "visionary" eyes'; Mrs Lovell she described as 'plain, gentle [and] welcoming and a good deal younger than her husband'. ('She is 42', in the same purple ink.) The household also included Mrs Lovell's sister, Ivy Baker, known to all as 'Auntie Ivy', who 'helps in the house' and who acted as housekeeper and hostess during the Lovells' frequent absences on holiday, on retreat, or at conferences, and the Lovells' daughters, Mary, aged twelve and at boarding school, and Clare aged seven, one of the ten pupils in the 'little schoolhouse'. But although 'everything was quickly arranged' and her new room discovered to be 'about twice the size of [hers] at Tymawr' and enjoying 'a green and restful view over the garden', the rectory itself was 'large and inconvenient' (the rooms, too, though 'spacious ... well-furnished [and] beautifully clean, [were] rather shabby') and she was 'a little dismayed to hear of Mass at 6.30am and the church unheated ... except on Sundays' (Father Lovell promised a later start and 'to use his oratory for Mass in winter') and that Oakington 'aerodrome' was only two-and-a-half miles away (another purple ink addition), a blow to one who 'longed' for quiet.[40] Still, she could hardly renege on an arrangement deemed God's Will for her or refuse to go to a place to which she had been directed by guardian angel and fiery/cloudy pillars in a move sanctioned by the Bishop of Ely, albeit with a warning regarding "the deadness of Lolworth", a subject on which he would be interested to hear her views "when you have been there some time".[41] So on 15 August 1946 she went to Lolworth.

When meeting new people, especially men, Aelfrida was disposed to think well of them. Father Lovell, she decided, would make an excellent spiritual director had not problems encountered at Tymawr dissuaded her. She was happy, however, to confess to him, enjoyed the way he conducted services 'very slowly and reverently', and regarded his sermons as 'lofty and spacious, clearly expressed … and delivered with great sweetness of manner'.[42] His being a tertiary also helped, as did his having been a missionary in Borneo, and she soon dubbed him 'Brother Henry'. (His 'dear little wife' became 'Sister Lilian'[43]; although a hint of prurience entered Aelfrida's diary with regard to a pair of tertiaries, supposedly sworn to chastity, begetting two children, she had too much respect for a marital relationship conducted as she would have liked to conduct her own to speculate further.) This, and closer acquaintance with 'very saintly …and so humble' Father Lovell made her feel he ought 'to have been a monk or a celibate priest' instead of a husband and father; she also wondered if 'Manual Labour in a monastery' would be better for him than closeting himself in his study all day at Lolworth[44], emerging only for meals and services. Then too, though she respected his 'special devotion to Our Lord's Second Coming', she found his '*very* definite ideas' regarding the imminence of 'a reign of righteousness on earth' both tedious and impractical, noting 'I wish he would brood less over the Second Advent … and take more trouble over his garden'[45] (the rectory garden was a wilderness) but what else could one expect of a mystic (as she, being one herself, instantly divined he was), 'conversant with the highest reaches of prayer' and able to preach 'memorably' on St John of the Cross[46] but oblivious to the practicalities of life on earth?

Although Aelfrida thought highly of Father Lovell as 'a priest and a mystic', as a person she regarded him as 'strangely muddle-headed'. For one thing, he was an 'astonishingly indifferent father' to Mary and Clare, taking little notice of his daughters other than to insist that both attend church on Sunday morning and the latter Sunday School in the afternoon but also given to encouraging

horse-mad Mary's attendance at Newmarket races. (To Aelfrida, such sporting activities were anathema and she had no hesitation in saying so: 'if he thinks me a grumpy old Puritan, I can't help it'.)[47] For another, he and his family were ineluctably lower middle class with an ineluctably 'bad accent'. ('I must not be put off by a little thing like that', wrote Aelfrida who replied to Father Lovell's query at her first confession if she had 'any difficulties to submit?' by saying no, she was just putting herself in God's hands.)[48] There was also the matter of sharing a house with a man for the first time (apart from brief visits to relations) since the Oracle's death in 1929 and although she generally referred to the 'rectory folk' as 'dear people'[49] and expressed no distaste with regard to co-habitation with 'Sister Lilian' and Auntie Ivy, Father Lovell's resemblance to the Oracle was irksome: he was intensely but joylessly religious, censorious, selfish, demanding, sickly, reclusive, and had unpleasant personal habits, and it was this as much as anything which caused her to complain to his wife on numerous occasions, to take all meals other than Sunday tea in her room, and to avoid him unless worship or confession threw them together.

What she – naturally – failed to take into account (in spite of 'privations' and the dangers inherent in living under the flight paths of enemy bombers, Aelfrida, leisured, solvent, free from family responsibilities, living in a Community of like-minded women, with nourishing food available if she chose to eat it and central heating generally available if she chose to use it, had had a much easier war than most Englishwomen) was that Father Lovell was a tired and under-nourished middle-aged man whose war had been one of little privilege, some danger, and much privation. He was also rector of an isolated rural parish, paid a small stipend, living in a 'poor old house … falling to bits and damp and draughty as an abandoned barn'[50] lit by candles and oil lamps and heated by ranges and stoves burning rationed fuel and whose kitchen with its temperamental equipment was the domain of a harried wife and sister-in-law who had had to care for two small girls and for evacuee children lodged in the drawing room. A man, too, burdened with a mentally 'afflicted' sister domiciled at Fulbourn Asylum as a voluntary patient but occasionally released 'on parole' (as Aelfrida put it) to stay with her brother, and by the periodic appearance of his wife's extensive family in search of cheap holidays in the country. No wonder then, as the Bishop of Ely warned her, Father Lovell required Aelfrida's 'help and encouragement' and that she came to regard him as a man whose mind was 'very delicately poised and might all-too-easily have its balance upset'.[51]

There was also, as Lovell himself 'ranted' to her, the 'indifference of his own parish'.[52] Forewarned by Mr

**Lolworth Church**

Church that Lovell's predecessor had been 'wonderful High Church and people didn't care for it', Aelfrida initially attributed the villagers 'unresponsiveness' to Anglo-Catholicism[53] to its having been imposed by Robert Stapylton, rector from 1895 to 1909, when he purchased the advowson of the living and influenced its religious tenor by presenting it to what she (inaccurately) described as the 'Society for the Defense of the Faith'; she therefore offered what she regarded as helpful advice, saying 'at the convent we just prayed and prayed without looking for results'.[54] The villagers' 'indifference', however, was attributable less to Anglo-Catholicism and more to the prickly nature of the present incumbent. Furthermore, as an article on *Country Parishes* in the June 1936 volume of *Theology* pointed out (together with possible reasons for the decline in churchgoing in England since the Great War: "country people have *never* wanted 'the things of God'", attendance at church was no longer regarded as "the solid basis of any respectable life", and people could listen to services on the wireless in comfort at home), he was also "too centred on [him*self*] in [his] attempts to 'get hold of ... people'", too prone to employ "bullying" tactics as the man "running the show", so "obsessed by 'results'" that he forgot to "walk by faith and not by sight" and to remember that "pastoral activities must be founded on a view of our fellow men not as possible converts and communicants but as ... a human soul created by God". Therein it seemed, lay Father Lovell's problem, but what he failed to do, as the article recommended he should, was not demand something *of* his parishioners but want something *for* them, namely that they find God "for themselves" under his guidance – in which respect, it was also his "business" that in "the pilgrimage of the soul to God", his own journey should be the exemplar.[55] But with these problems Aelfrida's pious platitudes and

determination to live a life as identical as possible to that at Tymawr were no help at all; indeed, receiving soon after her arrival and after confession with a visiting priest (the Lovells were on holiday) a 'vague and rather disturbing warning' about the dangers besetting an 'unattached Sister' living in a parish (a warning, he said, not to be taken personally but when he read in the *Church Times* of such a one wanting "parish work", he said to himself "poor Sister – and perhaps poor parish!", a comment noted in Aelfrida's diary with '!?!!' after it), she noted huffily 'I am *not* a Sister *or* unattached *or* here to do parish work'.[56] Wrong on the first count – Sister Placida of the Holy Passion made no secret of the fact that she was an SSC tertiary and always wore her tertiary's veil to church services – Aelfrida was confounded by the second and correct on the third.

Shortly after arriving in Lolworth, Aelfrida offered to talk to the local branch of the Mothers' Union on 'Alethea's missionary work'. Knowing Mrs Graham to be a mother herself and therefore eligible for entry to the Union, 'Sister Lilian' provided her with an entry form and a copy of MU rules and regulations. 'To my horror', wrote Aelfrida on reading them, 'I saw that no one who had been through the divorce court is eligible'. Her own divorce, she continued as if in mitigation, was so 'deep buried in [her] mind' that she had somehow (*sic*) 'forgotten' it and the time which had elapsed since then ('27 years ago, is it?'; actually, twenty-five) was hazy – and in any case 'the ten years at the convent were so *vivid*, so much more real than all other life, that I tried to think of myself just as Ter[tiary] Sister Placida SSC [and only] after that as a widow (*sic*), as the mother of a missionary, and so on'. Nor, she admitted, had she told anyone the truth there, 'not the Mother, not Miss Harrison, no one', giving as her reason 'loyalty to Constantine' and (the real reason) 'a feeling that [she] dare not'. But having lived a lie for so long, what should she do? Conceal her past or own up 'to the dear people here?' She had no choice and for a reason that had not occurred before: her past was known to certain Lolworth villagers, Mr Church having family connections with the village and the postmistress being a relative of a former Fordfield cook. Knowing that Cambridge servants gossiped as assiduously on their carefully-synchronised days off as their mistresses did at their weekly At Homes, Aelfrida found herself living in proximity to people familiar with her previous existence and dared not conceal a divorce which might be intentionally or inadvertently revealed by someone aware of her scandalous past.[57] Unable, however, to bring herself to actually speak to Mrs Lovell of the matter ('it *hurts* very much to be classed with the "bad goats"'), she communicated by letter – and was much relieved to receive instead of the expected 'shut door [and] exclusion from the company of the virtuous' (a possible but hitherto unrevealed reason for leaving St Columba's?), 'sympathetic acceptance' by someone who noted that it was 'a joy to have you with us … bringing extra Blessing and Peace to this place' – and an invitation to speak to the Mothers' Union, 'bad goat' or not.[58]

Discovery, however, provided both an escape clause and a revelation. Was the episode 'an indication that God did not want [her] to do any *active* work at Lolworth because the "spiritual water" offered to Mothers' Union members "should be of unquestioned purity"'? (She had obviously forgotten that she had talked happily as a known and recent divorcee to the York Street Mothers' Union in Cambridge; her Lolworth talk went ahead on 7 November regardless.) As for revelations, the 'flood of thoughts about Constantine' promoted by the episode ('on these rare occasions when I think of him outside prayer-time it is with love and gratitude towards one who taught me Love and Beauty and Romance, who gave me children and the perfection of purely-human happiness'; had she forgotten the physical violence, the marital rape, the jeering, the betrayals?) reminded her that in the 'sad days' surrounding her divorce she found solace in believing 'the sin more heinous but the sinner less culpable'. So she 'shut the door on the past' ('better so') and prepared herself for Harvest Festival.

The divorce itself was not so easily forgotten: 'if [only] I *could* be just a soul at prayer and not a human being with all the chains of past actions … to bind me!'[59] It was not until some months later, therefore, and only after one of several vivid visions heralding a new stage in her life and the emotional upheaval that accompanied it of being lifted by God 'into His Infinity' to be shown 'a golden light growing and burning which [revealed] itself as His Son' and a 'company of celestial beings' who asked her 'in spirit language' if she had heard 'of the joy that there is over one sinner that repents?' that 'the chains of sin' fell from her leaving 'a lightness and a freedom behind', that Aelfrida achieved release from the secret burden she had borne so long. Realisation too that '*repentance* [and] *perfect contrition*' (the intensity of her feelings can be gauged by the number of underlinings here and in what follows) were more pleasing to God than the '*emotions*' inherent in the practices of a 'victim–soul' intent on reparative adoration for the 'sin' of divorce also lightened her heart, so much so that during the General Confession in church five days later she realised that 'perhaps' she '*was* sorrier for [her] sins', albeit not '*wholly* sorry' because such a state of 'perfection … could not be retained' and anyway there was 'a big parcel from Alethea' to open.[60] But she continued to style herself 'widow'.

Nor did she intend to actually involve herself in 'parish work'. This was in part a desire not to encroach on Father Lovell's parochial preserves, overtures of friendship made by village women soon after her arrival prompting her to ask herself if she was meant 'to know each and all of them or just to pray for the parish as a whole and keep aloof?'[61] She therefore informed him that a courteous greeting would suffice and, if pressed, a brief visit ('no *hospitality*, of course' to be accepted) on Sundays or festivals[62] and that while 'prayers for individual parishioners'[63] were acceptable, prayers for the parish were for Father Lovell to perform. But being no longer in the position of having to undertake physical labour she disliked (prayer and only prayer was *her* 'portion of labour'), avoidance of 'parish work' assumed another aspect and when Father Lovell asked her to act as sacristan, problems were bound to arise.

Assuring him that she would 'love to if [she] had the strength' ('the elderly tertiary does not at all resent being ordered about but she is doubtful of her ability')[64], Aelfrida set about her duties with enthusiasm. The church, she wrote, is 'dedicated to All Saints, for which I greatly rejoice [and] … it is most dignified and impressive with that air of timeless patience and wisdom which only *very* old churches possess'.[65] (Its venerable beauty was later to give rise to an ecstasy during which she perceived 'half-seen forms of worshippers' in all modes of dress from mediaeval to modern extrude themselves from the ancient walls and pass through the altar 'out and up into ever brighter and brighter light, light so dazzling I could not look and opened my eyes'.)[66] The Blessed Sacrament was reserved on the 'High Altar' and a 'lovely little lane' lined with venerable elms with vistas of 'dewy meadows' to the right 'and low hills afar off and sunlight everywhere' to the left[67] lay at the bottom of the rectory garden to conduct her to it.

The church, however, had four defects: it was cold (the reason for Aelfrida choosing to sit in the second row from the front on the left instead of centre front row as usual becomes apparent when one visits: she positioned herself directly behind the only radiator); a 'noisy American organ'[68] played inexpertly by dead Father Stapylton's spinster daughter accompanied the hymns; 'Catholic' importations ('statuettes and whatnot') and glazed polychromatic plaques depicting the Stations of the Cross adorned it, the latter provoking the comment that such aids to religion were 'more suited to village worshippers' than to a *habitué* of 'our convent' (Mother Guenvrede deliberately kept the chapel clear from what she regarded as distractions) and that services including them were 'curiously savage [and] suited only to peasants'[69]; and it was both untidy and '*filthy*'.[70] So the 'elderly' tertiary rolled up her sleeves and cleaned it, an event celebrated spiritually by a vision at Evensong of a stream of living water flowing from the Tabernacle to join a second stream inflowing through a permanently-closed door, along whose banks the white-robed and golden-haloed saints of the church's dedication processed with dancing gait.[71]

By 'Michaelmastide' the church was pristine[72] and Aelfrida had relinquished most of her duties and was about to divest herself of the rest. The reason, of course, was not lack of 'strength' or 'ability' but resentment at being 'ordered about', she having discovered that priests, incumbent or visiting, were 'far too fond of exercising Authority'[73] with regard to setting out vestments or ringing the Angelus bell and that being 'a Doorkeeper in the House of the Lord' involved far too many responsibilities. So she pleaded physical frailty and resigned the position, but given how much time and energy she had expended on the interior fabric of the church and how on fine days she strode out (more slowly and for shorter distances, it is true) along local driftways to watch 'great cloud galleons … chasing each other across the sky'[74], Father Lovell, like Mother Guenvrede ignorant of the real reason for his sacristan's inability and not yet attuned to Aelfrida's vagaries, seems to have regarded her as both lazy and disobliging. She continued to haunt the church, however, attending Mass and Holy Communion at 7.30am ("the Nonconformist who is content with … a simple memorial service … once a month has no idea of the ardour which brings a woman …to the Lord's Table every morning spiritually to receive Our Lord Himself")[75] and Evensong at 5pm. She also paid a daily visit to worship the Blessed Sacrament *coram sanctissimo* ('solitary worship' in a preReformation church 'has so much to say to the soul … the sense of the Holy Presence is almost overwhelming')[76], this and the two services being, she assured Father Lovell, 'about all I can manage'.[77]

The rectory to which 'lovely little' Church Lane led was of Georgian construction with Victorian additions. Drawing and dining rooms, Father Lovell's study, a small subsidiary sitting room, and kitchen quarters occupied the ground floor and a number of bedrooms the first, the Lovells' with its attached oratory being the largest. The south-facing garden was mainly laid to lawn with shrubs and flower beds but also contained a 'loathsome evil-smelling pond'[78], a vegetable garden, an orchard, and a tin hut housing the Parish Room. Aelfrida's room was on the rectory's northern side but had an east-facing window whose view encompassed a group of ancient houses (Clare Cottages) and the Cambridge to Huntingdon road running parallel to the foot of the gentle escarpment on which Lolworth

stood. Beyond the road, flat fenland fields stretched to the horizon.

Her room, though shabbily furnished and not receiving much sun in winter, had sufficient space for her few possessions: clothes (still chiefly her navy tertiary's dress), a rug-draped deck chair, a paraffin stove, books, and an attaché case containing writing materials for her voluminous correspondence (the Post Office was only a few yards away), manuscript paper, and the current volumes of her diary. ('Spiritual' diaries were now at Girton.) It was therefore to see his sister in her new quarters that Julius paid his first visit to Lolworth in September 1946, accompanied (unusually) by Mina. After lunch and tea with the Lovells, meals at which 'much animated conversation on wholly suitable topics' took place (e.g. Professor Tillyard's visits to monasteries in search of 'Byz.Mus.'), Julius and Aelfrida had 'a good talk in [her] room' while Mrs Lovell took Mina blackberrying.[79] Ten days later, Eustace and Phyllis lunched, behaving 'perfectly' ('the Master's Lodge was never mentioned – you would have thought they came straight from Hadstock!') and 'quite [appreciating] the charm of Lolworth'.[80] But what Aelfrida with her snobbish disdain for the lower middle class Lovells does not relate was poor Mrs Lovell's attitude to her paying guest's self-invited visitors'[81] (and there were to be many more, all expecting refreshment when rationing of foodstuffs was still in force) or Father Lovell's to a tertiary who pretended to regulate her life so as to spend it in the Silence and Solitude imposed by a Rule (now slightly modified but still encompassing solitary meals on a tray, Bible study of a chapter a day, 'Office, said in my room', 'time for brief adoration', a walk, meditation and private prayer, reading books and *The Times*, and writing)[82] to which she proposed to adhere at the same time as she entertained numerous visitors.

The onset of autumn, however, reminded Aelfrida what a 'poor old house' she had chosen to live in, a house as 'damp and draughty' and 'ghostly' as abandoned Catley Park. (Lolworth ghosts, however, were 'good and holy presences' like 'the faithful departed … crowding rooms holding dusky candles' on All Saints Eve; she was unsure how much 'objective reality' the presences possessed.)[83] Rain 'dripping through [her] ceiling down on [her] floor'[84] in September 1946 heralded increased suffering from '*cold* … in [her] damp and semi-heated room': 'I am unheroic and do not rejoice in my pains even if I offer and accept them'. (There was no question of a fire but whether this was due to asceticism or fuel rationing or her refusal to perform housemaids' work, she does not say.) 'Aches and pains and shivers' ('may all the saints who have shivered for the love of God, help me!')[85] arrived with November and December and, following a day's visit to cosy, elegant Wetenhall Cottage, the grim discovery that 'leather objects' grew green mould and that 'even with the oilstove at its warmest' she could not 'coax' her room up to a liveable temperature. At this point 'endurance' gave out, she pleaded for warmer quarters, and was moved to a 'smaller [and] shabbier' (it was identical in size to the one vacated) east- and south-facing room next door, 'cosier' because sun shone in nearly all day and because it received some heat from the fire burning in Father Lovell's study directly below.[86] But a letter received from Father Cary in answer to a request "for a word of benediction on [her] new venture" (he aspired, he wrote, to be her "honorary as well as [her] honorific Father") noted that although her description of Lolworth made it sound "very attractive in itself and suitable for that purpose and manner of life to which you have been led", he hoped she would not find "the winter months too trying [because] the English countryside makes its demands on endurance in the cold wet days and months". (Strength would doubtless be given her to endure it, added "yours affectionately in Christ, Lucius Cary".)[87] A horrified comment made by a former St Cuthbert's missionary ("are you *really* going to spend the winter here?" in a rectory so 'dark and dank and dilapidated' that if Miss Laura Tillard herself was forced to stay there, 'she would drown herself in the pond')[88] should have persuaded Aelfrida to change not just her room but her habitation too before winter set in in earnest. She did not. Instead, she compromised: Christmas at Lolworth followed by two nights (30 December–1 January 1947) at Wetenhall Cottage would see her through.

'I shall always remember Epiphany at Lolworth … the bitter cold … and [the] icy wind from Russia [and] snow falling, the flakes tossed and swirled by the wind', wrote Aelfrida early in January 1947[89]; from 'Nature Notes' recorded on the last pages of her current diary we can deduce that post-Christmas weather was nothing compared to the horrors which followed:

7–8 January 1947: 'Lolworth under … heavy snow'.

20 January: 'v. cold, hoar frost etc.'

29 January: 'mercury disappears into bulb of thermometer!!! More snow too!'

31 January: 'the Cam is frozen over, there have been zero temperatures over England so … I may be excused for shivering'.

19 February: 'this ghastly weather … when snow and ice and frost last for weeks and weeks and there is such shortage of coal that … domestic heating is curtailed … Well! it *is* pretty miserable [and] my "natural feelings" [do not] like getting up every morning in a [freezing] room. And oh! the church! How one shivers!'; indeed, so cold was All Saints that she had to give up Evensong in spite of Father Lovell 'bothering' her to attend – she was his only congregation – because the icy building induced severe 'cramp in [her] heart' and because her sleep was so disturbed by chill-induced numbness that she felt too tired and ill to attend. (Spiritually, of course, 'my heart sings and sings'[90], a rather muted song under the circumstances, one suspects.) March brought thaw and 'the worst floods for 150 years', visible from Aelfrida's windows but not, in spite of gloomy reports in *The Times* ("the situation … in Fenland is described as critical")[91], actually lapping at her bedroom door.

It was, in fact, during this terrible time – the weather in the first three months of 1947 was the worst for over a century; Father Lovell celebrated Mass in the oratory because Church Lane was blocked by 'drifts … like white dunes'; 'no post or milk or papers' arrived and groceries only occasionally[92] – that Aelfrida, 'never warm, always tired and with a pain somewhere, unable to take any brisk exercise to stir [her] blood or give [her] eyes a fresh picture on which to rest, sometimes too weary even to pray properly', feeling that God must have sent her to Lolworth 'to learn penitence, if nothing else' ('there is never a moment of rebellion', she added, 'but … there is *dreariness*')[93], and reduced to 'scribbling' her diary by 'dim candlelight'[94], sat down to write another book. She called it *Christian Old Age*.

Completing the revision of *The Glory of the West* in June 1946, Aelfrida felt she had now 'Said my Say … as well as I am able to deliver the message entrusted to me'.[95] (The elegiac tone of the later chapters may owe something to the expected-unexpected news of impending departure but there is no hint of the bitterness which colours contemporary diary entries. Nor had she said her final 'Say'.) Then life overtook her and although she noted how much she would like to start a new book immediately, it was not until October 1946 that she began a semi-fictional account of the SSC entitled *The Convent, its Aim and Life*. This, however, she abandoned, never to resume ('I hope I am wise in so doing', she noted without explanation) in favour of a 'short book' (the typed version runs to twenty-six pages and around 38,000 words) 'about Christian Old Age'[96], begun early in January 1947. The new book, a sequel in some measure to *The Glory of the West*, occupied her until 22 May ('now – what next?!' … I am trying to *listen* to

**Interior of Lolworth Church**

the Holy Spirit to see if He has work for me to do')[97], at which point Lolworth's Rogationtide procession complete with banner, crucifix, candles, holy water, incense, and acolytes borrowed from a Cambridge church (she was 'too lame to go with it further than the … head of the lane')[98] and 'golden pavements of buttercups and … white cascades of huge may trees' made her simultaneously cheerful and regretful: 'my soul … *tugged* to … fly away to heaven [but] why on a day when the earth was so supremely lovely … not in the bitter winter when life was so hard?!'[99]

For a book written in the depths of a ferocious winter by one who felt as emotionally '*crushed*' and 'shrivelled' by ill-health and the weather[100], *Christian Old Age,* displacement activity or occupational therapy though it undoubtedly was, is an amazingly cheerful, philosophical, and sensible book.[101] It was inspired by a single external event, namely the first of three longitudinal studies published by the Nuffield Foundation in 1946, 1958, and 1970 on the subject of *Old People.*[102]

Aelfrida's interest in 'Old People' dated back to her talk with Eardley Davidson on the problems of 'old age' with particular reference to the Oracle and possibly further, for housing schemes for the elderly described in *The Glory of the West* sound very like the 'Brilliant Idea' regarding property owned by Chiara shot down by Constantine early in their marriage. 'Deep in the Nuffield Report on Old Age' in January 1947, Aelfrida found it 'kind and sympathetic in tone' but limited in scope ('all it seems to aim at … is that the aged should be saved from acute physical discomfort, utter loneliness and unrelieved boredom and perhaps … be mildly useful') because the investigators were neither "setting out to deal with immortal souls" to be 'prepared for heaven' (they "did *just* mention chaplains and places of worship") nor valuing the elderly as potential and 'most precious …

centre[s] of prayer … worth treasuring'. So she set out to "add to their suggestions".[103]

Her own suggestions, as befits a book on *Christian* old age, are slanted more acutely towards topics of a religious nature than those discussed in *The Glory of the West* (e.g. the need to structure one's life by means of a "Scheme of Prayer covering every day of the week" at a time when physical activity "must be lessened")[104], though they also, as in her earlier book, contain practical advice on how best to conduct one's life as one gets older: the importance of keeping physically and, even more importantly, mentally active instead of dozing by a real or metaphorical fireside "with a little bit of soft music on the wireless [and] a copy of *The Times*"[105], of putting one's "temporal affairs in order"[106] in good time, and of maintaining friendships which might otherwise "grow mouldy in the damp and dark" and even be forgotten until an obituary in *The Times* recalls them to mind.[107] New and ancient prejudices also appear. The rising tide of "vulgarity" and "wickedness" embraces (*inter alia*, it is a long list) "the cigarette perpetually between the lips" and "American slang and the type of American magazine that is nothing but personalities, scandal and innuendo" as examples of the former. (Aelfrida clearly did not like the world into which she had emerged after a decade of seclusion but what is truly revealing is her comment a few pages later: "did we really mind vulgarity", she asks, "as long as it was confined to vulgar areas of towns or showed itself only on Bank Holidays? Now that it flaunts itself wherever we go we take offence".)[108] "Wickedness", on the other hand, presupposed moral turpitude: racing, gambling, "black-marketing", and "divorce courts", all evidence of "the devil … at work".[109] She also rants against (again *inter alia*) Communist Russia, "ornate … ritual" chiefly designed to satisfy "the personal taste of the congregation"[110], the post-war decline in personal religion ("the greatest disaster that could befall the human race would be the total loss of Christianity …*oremus, oremus*")[111] in a real hellfire and brimstone chapter entitled *Prayer,* and Spiritualism, including in the latter section a gibe at Sir Oliver Lodge[112] as evidence of a grudge maintained on Julius' behalf for nearly thirty years. Old enthusiasms reappear too, particularly Christian Unity to which she devotes a whole chapter; asking if "we old people" could devote our last years on earth to promotion of a cause so dear to *her* heart: "could I not imagine myself and my convictions integrated into a vaster whole without loss to myself or to [it]?" states this ecumenist *avant la lettre,* adding hastily that Unity must not be "man-made [or a] unity of expediency [but] God-inspired".

In *Christian Old Age* Aelfrida is once again both preacher and autobiographer: having passed her "sixtieth milestone", she sits down "as white flakes are falling fast" to write another volume encompassing homily and "*mémoires*".[113] Some memories are "very bitter": of "serious sins, even sins classed by theologians as *mortal*" (sins, that is to say, fatal to spiritual progress, involving a kind of spiritual 'death', and the source of all lesser venial sins, for reparation of which, mortal or venial, she must make herself a 'victim–soul': "if sin had been great, let reparation … exceed it")[114] or "petty infidelities": "faint self-complacency, small secret self-indulgences", the assumption that as a churchgoer and a good citizen she is automatically granted "entrée of the Celestial City"[115], this leading her to ask if she has been truly "*holy*" and to reply no, she has not, for "if we *feel* we have been holy, we cannot have been … no saint could possibly give himself 10/10 for virtue. Prigs conceivably might".[116] (A *mea culpa*, truly.) Some range from mild self-disgust ("who wants to be the kind of person … who [palms] himself off on society as a rather more admirable person than he is?"[117], a 'widow', say, rather than a divorcee) to the self-mockingly ironic: "old people who seem to be marvellously endowed with physical strength to perform their devotions and who were too frail to [perform] secular activities"[118] or "women [who] enjoy a milder and more equable spiritual climate than men". ("Saints", on the other hand, as she subtly hints she is, exist "in a climate of great extremes", "fiery fervour and self–suffering"[119] succeeding each other in quick succession.) Some are not so much memories or *meae culpae* as wishful thinking: the need in a world filled with "vulgarity" and "wickedness" and with the lesser but boring trials of "ration cards and [clothing] coupons [and] too few of all the 'consumer goods' one wants to buy", for "prayerful persons", men and women like herself who lead "prayerful lives" and who are "consciously in touch with God every hour of the day", to "dedicate themselves *seriously* to a life of prayer" so that "in the time of wrath [they] can be … a reconciliation". And who better to do this than a mature, leisured, trained (*sic*) person such as herself, "poor and ill and from an ordinary point of view useless" though she is?[120]

Ill she might be, but *poor*? True, this is how she liked to think of herself ('myself, old and shabby, in lower middle class surroundings' all, apart from her age, her own doing, even shabbiness, for when 'clothes rationing [came] to a sudden end' in 1949, it was 'Holy Poverty not lack of coupons' which had prevented the purchase of new and smarter garments)[121] and as one taking the high moral ground with regard to disposing of unsuitable investments or her legacy from Ancifera. (Alethea was now comparatively well off, for in addition to her doubled legacy and her allowance from the SSJE, she received the £120 per

annum rent of Wetenhall Cottage paid by Julius into his retained South African bank account and from that to hers; "the aged", noted her mother in *Christian Old Age*, "have considerable … purchasing power [and] wise and discriminating expenditure of money can accomplish much"[122], including, it seemed, financial retention of her remaining daughter's fealty.) But the high moral ground proved an uncomfortable perch ("it is hard, of course, to have formerly enjoyed a fine house, delicate food, the ministrations of loving servants and so on … and when one is old to live in a small way and even to suffer discomforts")[123] for one who had emerged from cloistered surroundings in which she had money to spare for bribes and donations, to a world in which dwindling rental income derived from crumbling properties provided meagre monies for a landlord who depended on them but who at the same time tended to be "less severe" on herself, to "clamber into a taxi when a walk would be the best thing" (a taxi, even for long distances, was her preferred alternative to the train and she would not have dreamed of taking a bus), and to spend more than formerly on a "long list of sundries"[124] and on 'small secret self-indulgences' such as bottles of eau de Cologne on her washstand. In 1947, for example, her total expenditure was £212-16-8d (she does not disclose her income but would not now have exceeded it), expenditure sanctioned only as a result of 'heart-searchings' occasioned by a bout of 'apparently-necessary-shopping-by-post' which made her wonder if by 'SSC tertiary standards' she surrounded herself 'with too many things for [her] comfort and convenience'. ('Of course', she assured herself, 'by ordinary worldly standards I spend too little' but God's 'righteous demands' that she live cheese-paringly must be obeyed.)[125] A guilty memory rose before her here which could not be "wholly exculpated" of herself as someone who had blithely spent money owed to the doctor on a holiday in the certainty that Chiara would settle her medical bills, nor was mystical "otherworldliness" now a valid excuse for having been "impractical and unbusinesslike"[126] with regard to boring necessities like income tax and college fees. On the other hand, referring to herself as one of the "gentlefolk … leading cramped lives in … mean lodgings" because their investments have been "rendered useless"[127] shows she had been unwise in entrusting 'stick-in-the-mud dear old Howard [Warren]' with her share of the money from the sale of Fordfield to the Sisters of Hope because investments made on his advice had provided poor returns, a particularly galling subject when she recalled (or the devil pointed out to her) that Eustace ('a wealthy man' whose wife had 'a fortune of her own') had 'pocketed' his legacy from Ancifera 'without offering her a share' ('Julius, of course, also retained his but his wife [has] no fortune')[128] and that stick-in-the-mud Howard had ensured Ancifera's servant's comfort by buying the Sunnyside Road house for her.[129] But with her pension, her remaining investments, her rents, and the undisclosed sum from the Sisters of Hope, she was not exactly hard up.

It did not help, of course, that much as she loathed and rejected 'covetous and worldly thoughts', the devil whispering in her ear that the fault was hers 'for having chosen Holy Poverty' and wasn't she a fool to have to have done so, reminded her that she *had* and *was*: 'yes, Devil', she wrote, defiantly employing a capital D (a sign of anger at her perceived folly perhaps), 'I *did* choose Holy Poverty and now, God helping me, I will rejoice in it'.[130]

Confusion of relative financial poverty and Holy Poverty led her to conflate 'doing without this or that' and '*fretting* because [she] could not have it' ('I hate this ugly room of mine with the paper peeling off the walls and my horrid old clothes' – though 'there *is* great joy in them', she reminded herself through gritted teeth, 'because they are part of a dedicated life'[131] and because in spite of distasteful outward trappings, she was 'rich in the gold of the spirit')[132] and the '*poverty of spirit*' recommended by her guardian angel and Bede Frost as a form of poverty chosen for its "essential worth" and because in practising it she was stewarding things of the spirit entrusted to her instead of lavishing things not of the spirit on herself, but relative to which "want and destitution … a state into which men are forced … or drift" was by no means a sine qua non.[133] She also regarded '*fretting*' over her lack of 'this and that' and being irked because unable to give 'handsome presents'[134] to Tymawr as manifestations of Holy Poverty, which they were not; they were manifestations of unspoken anger at earlier financial stupidity and wilful extravagance and of her having once again forced the square peg of her personality into the round hole of an unsuitable social and physical milieu. But it was not until 1948 that half a century of deliberate deprivation caused her to admit 'I don't *like* Holy Poverty'[135] and not until three years later still that the luxurious ascetic asked herself if she truly 'loved' Holy Poverty and provided one of her rare really truthful answers: she loved, she wrote, 'simplicity' and even 'moderate austerity' but loved neither 'real poverty' nor 'Holy Poverty … in the Franciscan sense' because she did not feel that either – but particularly the latter – were *au fond* her 'vocation'.[136]

When, therefore, she complained of Holy Poverty relative to her surroundings or to limitations placed on her life by (relative) lack of money (and, of course, by Mr Attlee's 'secular utopia' which denuded people like herself of their rightful inheritance in order to subsidise

the pursuits of the Vulgar and Wicked) and confessed to Father Lovell 'an imperfect acceptance of Holy Poverty'[137], the burden of both complaint and confession concerned herself and her attitude and inability to 'disentangle' the spiritual benefits of living a 'tertiary vocation' in yet another bower of 'Lady Poverty' from the heroic virtue needed to live such a life, be this life God's Will for her or her own wilful choice. Furthermore, the life she led contrasted strongly with the life she *should* now (and *could*, had she not been so obstinate) be leading of "cultured conversation" with '*very* Cambridgy people' on 'topics which rouse one's intelligence'[138] in her own 'fresh and clean and sunny' (and warm and well-lit) little house[139] with properly nourishing food instead of the poor fare provided at Lolworth. (In spite of stating that 'if there were more to eat … I should eat it with a thankful heart'[140], Aelfrida's *chosen* diet remained identical to that eaten at Tymawr; also worth noting here is that Alethea continued to send food parcels to her mother and that Julius, when abroad, sent chocolate and jam in quantity and cheese, rice, and condensed milk if permitted exports.) In Lolworth, by contrast, there was only 'Auntie Ivy' to pet her up and her relationship to a 'perfect College Master'[141] to add actual or implied lustre to an impoverished social life.

## Notes

1 GCPPT 1|1|41 2 July 1932.
2 GCPPT 1|1|64 4 June 1946.
3 ibid. 6 June 1946.
4 ibid. 6 and 11 June 1946.
5 ibid. 6 June 1946.
6 ibid. 26 June 1946.
7 GCPPT 1|1|40 6 March 1932. The Office of Deaconess in the Church of England had been revived in 1861. Deaconesses were 'ordained' by a bishop by laying-on of hands but were not endowed with holy orders. They therefore undertook no sanctuary duties nor were they subject to episcopal oversight. They were also free to resign at any time. The attraction of the position for Aelfrida is obvious.
8 The original editorial and the priest's response to it appear in *Theology* vol XXXII No 187 January 1936 pp 1–3 and vol XXIII No 188 February 1936 pp 66–69.
9 GCPPT 1|1|50 7 February and 30 April 1936.
10 Vidler, A. p 77.
11 GCPPT 1|1|64 11 July 1964.
12 ibid. 11 July 1964.
   Tillyard, Ae. *The Centaur* p 309 (GCPPT 2|21|1). Aelfrida's description of her hero's return to Cambridge after a sojourn in a monastery is taken almost verbatim from her diary.
13 GCPPT 1|1|49 21 August 1935.
   GCPPT 1|1|64 11 July 1964.
14 GCPPT 1|1|64 30 May 1946.
15 GCPPT 1|1|25 4 June 1921.
16 GCPPT 1|1|64 12 July 1946.
17 ibid. 14 July 1946.
18 ibid. 11 and 12 July 1946.

19   ibid. 14 and 15 July 1946.

20   ibid. 14 July 1946.

21   ibid. 15 and 24 July and 5 August 1946.

22   ibid. 12 July 1946.

23   ibid. 15 July 1946. 'Timothy' White was nicknamed after a contemporary chain of chemists' shops. As Terence (TH) White (1906–1964) he was the author of a sequence of novels on the life of King Arthur. In 1946 he settled on Alderney and it must have been on a visit from there to Cambridge that Aelfrida met him again. During his undergraduate years in Cambridge 1925–1929 (he read English and was known to both Eustace Tillyard and Tom Henn), White contracted TB and after treatment in a sanatorium, spent some months in Italy, returning to Cambridge in 1928. According to Tom Henn (quoted in Warner, S. p47), Terence White "went all Byronic" on receiving his diagnosis in 1927 ("the young poet about to die"; he was said to have only 6 months to live op. cit. p37), the point at which Agatha recorded her sympathy for one facing 'the reality of death'. White was also said to have conducted a flirtation with an older married woman while at Cambridge (op. cit. p41), a possible source for undergraduate 'Frederic Ellicott's' flirtation with married 'Anita Voyle' in Aelfrida's 1932 novel *The Approaching Storm*.

24   ibid. 23 July and 14 August 1946. Penicillin, hitherto reserved for use in hospitals and by the armed forces, became available to general practitioners on 1 June 1946; Aelfrida was therefore one of the earliest people to benefit from it.

25   ibid. 15 July and 5 August 1946.

26   ibid. 10 August 1946.

27   ibid. 18 July 1946.

28   ibid. 14 August 1946.

29   ibid. 18 July 1946.

30   ibid. 2 and 5 August 1946.

31   ibid. 10 August 1946.

32   ibid. 30 July 1946.

33   ibid. 23 July 1946.

34   ibid. 30 July 1946.

35   ibid. 2 August 1946.

36   ibid. 12 August 1946.

37   ibid. 30 July and 2 August 1946.

38   ibid. 18 July 1946.

39   GCPPT 1|1|35 28 May 1928.

40   GCPPT 1|1|64 18 July 1946.

41   ibid. 15 July 1946.

42   ibid. 17 August and 21 September 1946. Henry Richard Cobden Lovell was appointed rector of Lolworth in 1937, his first and only appointment as such, his curacy having lasted fifteen years in four different parishes. His third curacy (1929–1933) was at Whitchurch Canonicorum, the former home of Aelfrida's adored Archie Stent, his fourth was responsible for introducing him to the Franciscan monastery at Cerne Abbas to which he and his wife became attached as tertiaries. For further details of his clerical career see *Crockford's Clerical Directory* 1953–54.

43   ibid. 17 August and 21 September 1946.

44   ibid. 21 September 1946.

45   ibid. 12 September and 2 December 1946.

46   ibid. 27 November 1946.

47   GCPPT 1|1|64 15 January 1947.

48   ibid. 17 August 1946

49   ibid. 26 September 1946.

50   ibid. 17 August 1946. Until 1955 incumbents owned the freehold of their vicarage or rectory and paid all outgoings themselves; Father Lovell's stipend would have been insufficient to cover the maintenance of a large dilapidated house as well as household bills.

51   ibid. 12 and 26 September 1946.

52   ibid. 12 September 1946.

53   ibid. 12 July 1946.

54   ibid. 12 September 1946. The Society for the Maintenance of the Faith of which Lord Halifax (1839–1934), lay leader of the Anglo–Catholic Movement, had been a trustee, held seven advowsons in which the tenor of the liturgy was determined by the Society. For further details see Yelton, M. *Outposts of the Faith* pp58–59 and 67.

55   Leach, N. *Country Parishes* in *Theology* vol XXXVI No 192 June 1936 pp343–350. The article is a sequel to articles quoted earlier in this chapter.

56   GCPPT 1|1|64 28 August 1946.

57   ibid. 3 and 4 October 1946. In a later novel *Naomi da Costa* (pp162–166) Aelfrida has her heroine, "a young Jewish lady" and Orthodox to boot, betrayed to her guardian/brother (she has attended a Christian service in a church based on Lolworth's) by a maid whose father is the gardener of the priest who conducted the service.

58   ibid. 3 and 4 October 1946. The Mother's Union, founded in 1876, ruled in 1912 that divorcees could not be members.

59   ibid.

60   ibid. 9 and 14 December 1946.

61   ibid. 19 August 1946.

62   ibid. 6 September 1946.

63   ibid. 21 November 1946.

64   ibid. 21 August 1946.

65   ibid. 17 August 1946. For the history of All Saints, Lolworth, see http://www.honeyhill.org/llhi.html

66   ibid. 25 December 1946.

67   ibid. 18 November 1946.

68   ibid. 18 August 1946.

69   ibid. 17 August 1946.

70   ibid. 22 August 1946.

71   ibid. 21 August 1946.

72   ibid. 29 September 1946.

73   ibid. 30 August 1946.

74   ibid. 5 September 1946.

75   Tillyard, Ae. *Christian Old Age* p99 (GCPPT 2|17).

76   GCPPT 1|1|64 5 September 1946.

77   ibid. 17 August 1946.

78   ibid.

79   ibid. 20 September 1946.

80   ibid. 30 September 1946.

81   ibid. 16 October 1946.

82   ibid. 6 September 1946.

83   ibid. 24 August and 2 November 1946.

84   ibid. 8 September 1946.

85   ibid. 2 and 4 November 1946.

86   ibid. 6 December 1946.

87   GCPPT 1|1|64a. Letter from Father Cary to his "dear child" Aelfrida of 4 December 1946.

88   GCPPT 1|1|64 19 November 1946.
     GCPPT 1|1|66 16 October 1948

89   GCPP 1|1|64 6 January 1947.

90   ibid. 8 and 31 January and 19 and 24 February 1947 and 'Nature Notes' recorded in back of diary.

91   ibid. 20 March 1947.
     GCPPT 1|1|64a Captioned photograph of 'Floods near Ely' in *The Times* 18 March 1947. To a note inside the front cover of 1|1|64 of the telephone numbers of Wetenhall Cottage and Lolworth Post Office (the rectory had none) is added the quotation from Horace "*diffiugere nives, redeunt jam gramina campei*" paraphrased in Milton's *Lycidas* but spring 1947 was not as joyous as Horace's: crops frozen into the ground drowned in the melting snow and food shortages were rife. Bread, rationed since 21 July 1946, could be obtained in greater quantities only if Aelfrida relinquished her limited allocation of 'biscuits, dried fruit, etc.' (ibid. 30 June 1946) in exchange for it.

92  GCPPT 1|1|64 7 March 1947.

93  ibid. 12 March 1947.

94  ibid. 2 November 1946.

95  ibid. 7 June 1946.

96  ibid. 8 January 1947. The book was intended to describe the way in which two women's lives changed after visiting a convent with no thought at that point of associating themselves more closely with it. One of the women, as Tymawr oral history tells it, was Winifred Saville (later Sister Jeanne) who arrived with a friend on an informal visit but while taking tea neat the Campo Santo decided to join the SSC as a postulant. The other woman may have been based on Aelfrida herself.

97  GCPPT 1|1|65 22 and 15 May 1947.

98  ibid. 11 and 19 May 1947.

99  ibid. 12 May 1947.

100  GCPPT 1|1|64 22 February 1946.

101  Aelfrida kept a typed and a manuscript version of *Christian Old Age* (GCPPT 2|17). In spite of establishing her literary, social, and spiritual credentials on the title page as the 'Mrs Tillyard' (*sic*) who "has several successful books of a religious character to her credit" and "a sister of Dr Tillyard and Professor Tillyard. Sir Frank Tillyard, author of *The Worker and the State* is a … relation", the work remained unpublished. Aelfrida blamed this on current paper shortages but the book's old-fashioned tone probably militated against publication. Julius suggested *The Art of Growing Old* as a possible title when he wished his sister good luck with her '*Pro Senectute*' researches. (Letter from Julius Tillyard to Aelfrida of 2 September 1947. GCPPT 3|1|9a.)

102  The British Parliamentary Presentation of 1946 was an indication of the growing interest in medical circles of the specialised care of the elderly; it led to the founding of the (unfortunately named) British Geriatrics Society in 1947 with pioneer gerontologist Lord Amulree (1900–1983) as its first president. The Nuffield Foundation report was an aspect of this.

103  GCPPT 1|1|64 19 January 1947.
Tillyard, Ae. *Christian Old Age* pp 94–95.

104  Tillyard, Ae. *Christian Old Age* pp 93–94.

105  ibid. p12.

106  ibid. p112.

107  ibid. p117.

108  ibid. pp30–31 and 34.

109  ibid. pp5–6 and 30–32.

110  ibid. p40.

111  ibid. pp79–81.

112  ibid. pp43–46 and 101.

113  Tillyard, Ae. *Christian Old Age* pp4 and 51.

114  ibid. p5.

115  ibid. pp 5–6.

116  ibid. p26.

117  ibid. p110.

118  ibid. p48.

119  ibid. p50.

120  ibid. pp79–84 and 101.

121  GCPPT 1|1|64 17 December 1946.
GCPPT 1|1|66 15 March 1949.

122  Tillyard, Ae. *Christian Old Age* p35.

123  ibid. p75.

124  ibid. p114.

125  GCPPT 1|1|65 20 September 1947 and note on inside cover of same volume.

126  Tillyard, Ae. *Christian Old Age* pp112–113.

127  ibid. p54.

128  GCPPT 1|1|64 4 November 1944.

129  ibid. 5 August 1946. Assuming that Fordfield sold for more than the sum at which it was valued during negotiations with Dr Noble, Aelfrida's share of the proceeds may have been substantial by contemporary standards.

130  ibid. 4 November 1946.

131  GCPPT 1|1|65 13 February 1948.

132  GCPPT 1|1|64 4 November 1946.

133  GCPPT 1|1|46 18 September 1934.
Frost, B. *The Love of God* pp138–139.

134  GCPPT 1|1|64 4 November 1946.

135  GCPPT 1|1|65 13 February 1948.

136  GCPPT 1|1|69 'Birthday and Festival' (5 October) 1951.

137  GCPPT 1|1|46 24 December 1946.

138  Tillyard, Ae. *Christian Old Age* p54.
GCPPT 1|1|64 4 and 31 December 1946.

139  GCPPT 1|1|66 2 October 1948.

140  GCPPT 1|1|65 15 November 1947.

141  GCPPT 1|1|64 17 December 1946.

# Various People

Lolworth life was not, however, entirely devoid of comforts and Aelfrida's hopes for a 'dull vicarage' in which to live a prayerful secluded life were soon frustrated: 'Various People', she wrote, 'want to come and see me'.[1] 'Various', indeed: friends female, Little, clerical, supernatural, and some unseen for a dozen years: 'I seem', she noted, 'to talk to a good many people'.[2]

She did. Distant female relatives: Beatrice Zender Brown – Tom invariably in tow – whose 'American manner and *gush*' had not altered one iota[3]; Ruth Connolly née Warren home on leave looking 'hardly a day older than … when she was at Girton in spite of years in Madagascar and [a] husband and four children'[4]; Pattie Tillyard ('née Craske, Robin's widow', in case her biographer had forgotten), still 'the same independent and self-reliant Pattie, full of spirit, ready for anything, looking forward rather than back' – but also someone who asked Aelfrida no questions about herself and who seemed ill at ease with a cousin by marriage of whose recent past it was better not to speak[5]; Effie Stanley, 'cousin Percy's' sister, an 'ardent Anglo-Catholic'.[6] Old friends: Helen Megaw, now a 'physics don at Girton' with 'a car of her own' and once again – a preferable quality in Aelfrida's eyes in spite of references in her diary and in *Christian Old Age* to the benefits of free 'lifts' into Cambridge – a member of the St Columba's congregation[7]; Lilian Whitehouse, prone to 'blow in' in unsuitable clothes ('a "beach frock" … all blobs and scriggles') to provide 'conversation mainly this-worldly' and to amuse Aelfrida by stating 'that she hated pious females but just managed to stand me!!'[8]; Dorothea Conybeare, cycling over to share tea and ideas and to 'fit in'[9] with rectory life as godless Lilian did not. New friends such as missionary Laura Tillard who would have drowned herself in the rectory pond had she had to live there, someone who 'brought Alethea very close' because a former colleague at St Cuthbert's and who provided Aelfrida with information her daughter had not shared: 'convent life *as such*' suffocated Alethea, the Maritzburg convent had been 'too austere and … she never ought to have gone there', and that she loved her work in South Africa so much that she had no intention of living in England again.[10] Even a 'goup': Marjory Bates née Harrison 'all the way from London'[11] to visit a 'Straightener' who now, as

**Alethea Graham c 1948**

formerly, gently disengaged herself (the fact of Marjory knowing Aelfrida's current address shows that 'goup' and 'Straightener' continued to correspond) because 'Amrita's' nosiness concerning 'Straightener's' spiritual life was unabated. And a friend of whom Aelfrida had once written that she would 'never forget her' and that their 'solid woman friendship' was very important to her ('one must be honest about these things, not pretend one is more detached than one is')[12], Hilda Harrison.

Hilda's visit to Lolworth in June 1949 was much appreciated by Aelfrida on one level (Hilda was 'such a dear and *very* loving' towards her and 'intensely appreciative' of lunch at Wetenhall Cottage and afternoon tea at Jesus Lodge and of being shown Fordfield and driven through Cambridge *en fête* for an honorary degree day and for providing both intellectual stimulus and 'very interesting … ordinary conversation') but less so on another for Hilda, now living near Cheltenham as companion to two maiden ladies, had 'entirely severed' herself from Tymawr in spirit if not in fact and no longer chose to meet Aelfrida 'as Tertiary and Associate SSC'. Then too, Aelfrida suddenly saw Lolworth and the Lovells through an outsider's eyes, Lolworth as 'deadly dull', the church as 'nothing in particular', the rectory as 'ugly and inconvenient', and the Lovells as 'rather common'. The Lovells, in fact, seem to have found Hilda's stay rather a strain for although her behaviour towards them was 'most correct and gracious', Aelfrida hints that it was also condescending. Auntie Ivy too (who doubtless organised Hilda's bedroom and her separate sitting room where Aelfrida joined her for 'chats' and some meals; she and Hilda lunched *en famille*) seems to have resented the ladies' tendency to treat her like a servant and to act as if they owned the place.[13] In fact, ill-feeling engendered by Hilda's visit seems to have continued: from now on the cordial relationship between Aelfrida and the inhabitants of the rectory becomes more critical on her part (the Lovells revert from 'Brother' and 'Sister' to 'Father' and 'Mrs') and less amicable on theirs.

A woman with whom Aelfrida believed she had maintained another solid friendship, only to discover that particular friend disinclined to renew it, was Joan Cooper. Having written of 'dear "Dr Joan"' in 1945 that she and Aelfrida now met (so the latter liked to think) chiefly or even solely 'in *God*' (they had not met in person since 1937, Dr Cooper having refused to visit Oxford and failed to visit Tymawr in spite of promises to do so) and hence were 'much closer to each other than when we used to see each other often'[14], Aelfrida was aggrieved to discover that 'Dr Joan' had little wish to meet her 'either professionally or as a friend'.[15] Though Joan Cooper had other reasons for not making herself immediately available (a prolonged period of ill health culminating in spinal surgery; the 'breakdown' attributed by Aelfrida to overwork), Aelfrida's surprise at discovering that since her brusque dismissal of their former intimacy as 'aching tenderness'[16] on 'Dr Joan's' part and 'addiction' on her own, Dr Cooper was not open to meeting in or out of God, provides another demonstration of the 'addict's' insensitivity to others' feelings. In fact, it was not until almost two years after Aelfrida's arrival in Lolworth that she and 'Dr Joan' met again and then only because Aelfrida visited the latter's consulting rooms at 'Wytherton' as a private patient.

'She has white hair now and wears large rimless glasses', wrote Aelfrida of Joan Cooper, noting too that the latter seemed to have aged twenty years in a decade. (She also noted that 'the emotional temperature' between the two women was 'very much lower … better so'.[17] How 'Dr Joan' saw Aelfrida we do not know for there was, alas, no witness to their meeting but the latter implies that Joan Cooper was 'sorry' for her.) Bereft of a mother-figure, Aelfrida, it seems, had hoped that their relationship might be re-established if not on its former footing ('I must … not lean on her as I used …ah! Aelfrida! keep the guard of your heart!')[18], at least with 'everything spiritualised [and] the possessive element gone'[19] but discovered to her dismay that not even a professional relationship was possible because 'Dr Joan' could not have her as an NHS patient 'under the new Health Scheme' because Aelfrida was not resident in Cambridge.[20] This left Aelfrida with the meagre consolation that she herself had not *wanted* 'human consolation and so on and so forth'[21] and that 'Dr Joan's' departure from her life was a factor in ensuring this.

Some female visitors, though absent in the flesh, were with Aelfrida in spirit. At first desperately 'homesick for the convent', particularly for the convent 'as it was … in the wonderful days of *continuity* before the Mother … started sending me away'[22], she was also sufficiently insightful to note that it had done her good 'to come away from them' if only because at Tymawr she had been 'borne along on the stream of their spirituality' and fancied herself 'better than [she] was'. (In Lolworth, 'among "ordinary people" obviously better than myself, I think more soberly'.)[23] But though she confessed to feeling bereft without the Community's support in general and Mother Guenvrede's spiritual guidance in particular, she was comforted to discover that neither Mother nor Community had deserted her. Sisters Jeanne, Monica, and Sheila wrote regularly on festivals and on her birthday, albeit their letters were either homiletic (e.g. "don't you find in keeping outward silence the need of inwardness?" from Sister Jeanne, annotated by Aelfrida as 'a wee note … which expresses much of what I have been feeling')[24] or reactive to information imparted to them. What she craved, of course, was gossip of the kind imparted by Muriel Pont or Hilda Harrison e.g. that Mrs Donkin, now 'completely mad', had been admitted to the 'asylum' where she was to die in January 1947 (as an Associate, she was buried in the Tymawr Campo Santo) and that Mother Guenvrede's 'mental balance' had much improved as a result (Aelfrida, oblivious to the fact that her own departure also contributed, was convinced that '*no-one*' was telling her the truth)[25] and that the postulants for whose (ostensible) benefit she had been sent away were not staying, this latter item causing her to note that she had had 'a vehement impulse to … ask to be allowed back but [her] guardian angel checked it at once'. He also, it seems, gave a 'very decided *No*' to her suggestion that she 'go and be a hermit at Woodbine Cottage'.[26]

The informality of Mother Guenvrede's letters (e.g. that the latter's re-election as Mother in 1947 implied the Sisters' preference for "the evil they had … rather than [for] an unknown good"[27] or that Father Lovell who visited Tymawr in summer 1947 was 'a pathetic little man')[28] was in marked contrast to the icy formality with which she had greeted such 'Reuter-ish' remarks when made by Aelfrida; indeed, it seems that even when imparting spiritual advice (e.g. "I am sure you are being as good as you can" and wishing Aelfrida "her heart's desire if it is good for me to have it")[29], Mother Guenvrede was anxious to achieve the Hegelian synthesis with her life tertiary that Aelfrida as resident tertiary had hoped for: 'the dear Mother [and I]', she had once written prophetically and punningly, 'can't really continue at cross purposes in the bad sense [because] our Cross Purposes are good!'[30] But knowing intuitively that she would never be allowed to return to Tymawr ('not', she rationalised, 'that I wish to be at the convent, because God desires my presence here')[31], Aelfrida found comfort in the knowledge that though now unlikely to achieve her heart's desire to live and die there ('only *God*' remained and it seems for once that He was a poor substitute)[32], she was assured of the beloved Community's '*spiritual* … proximity'.[33]

Nor was she entirely devoid of the consolations of earthly masculine company at Lolworth, one manifestation being the reappearance in her life of Little Friends.

Frank Stokoe was, of course, the only Little Friend with whom Aelfrida had enjoyed an uninterrupted relationship in person or by letter (he was one of the very few men to whom she responded positively when they began their letters "my dearest Aelfrida")[34], not because he was no longer possessive but because he was the only man sufficiently tenacious to survive her attempts to dislodge him from her life. In spite of this, he did not rush to see her following her return to Cambridge and it was not until May 1947 that she met Fidelio coming up the lane: 'he is greyer', she noted, 'and has grown lame as I have but is otherwise just the same'. Meeting after thirteen years 'without a trace of awkwardness', Aelfrida was amused to find herself and Fidelio immediately 'in the same intellectual world where we used to meet before'[35], he, as usual, evincing no interest whatsoever in asking after 'Alethea or anyone' or putting to her any of the personal questions she put to him: 'we always meet', she once said, '*in vacuo*, … with no other people coming into the picture'.[36] Reflecting after he left – they had had a 'long chat' in the rectory drawing room – that their interview had been 'thoroughly satisfactory' and that

she had enjoyed it very much, Aelfrida added the startling comment 'and now, please God, may I never see him again so strongly is the current set to Silence and Solitude'. But knowing that Fidelio could be as insensitive to her feelings as she to his, she reminded herself of the need for 'patience, patience!'[37]

Fidelio being, as Aelfrida described him in her *Man of Gotham* poem, a man 'by nature solitary', he visited only once or twice a year thereafter and usually unannounced, but he visited notwithstanding his 'dearest Aelfrida's' lack of enthusiasm. (She herself was touched by the way in which he discussed *The Glory of the West* with her, not only because he had taken the trouble to read it thoroughly but also because he praised parts of it as being 'very beautiful indeed' and its author as 'a real artist'.)[38] A visit which took place in July 1949 shows how greatly Fidelio at least valued this 'communion of friends'[39], for he arrived requesting 'a little pleasant chat as relaxation' because 'stuck'[40] with the book for whose sake he had taken early retirement in 1945. (The book, described by Aelfrida as a refutation of 'Scientific Determinism' – the root of all modern evils, according to its author[41] – was never completed, in part, she suggests, because in spite of Fidelio's conviction that God had '*chosen* him to write this much-needed book'[42], as a linguist not a philosopher or a theologian by training he found it too difficult to relate knowledge in the form of scientific doctrines of evolution and ethics to the personal freedom of will assumed by Christianity in order to explain the presence of sin, and in part because he owned to 'a hard core of resistance to Orthodox Theology and Organised Religion'[43] and to fearing Christianity while at the same time believing in God and admiring Christ; in which latter respect, Aelfrida, we now discover, had offered 'long years of prayer and "*adoration réparatrice*" … for him'.)[44] The fact that Fidelio's soul (if not his presence) was 'very precious' to her, caused her to be 'not at all happy' about the physical welfare of a man she professed herself keen never to see again: Fidelio, she wrote in 1950, 'lives all alone in a furnished farmhouse for which he pays [out of] capital', a disaster should he live 'many years longer'. (Fidelio was then sixty-eight, like herself.) Still a recluse who 'dislikes almost everyone', his mind continued to be 'full of darkness and confusion' (chiefly, she thought, because he was not an enthusiastic Christian; she seems not to have noted the discrepancy between her own attacks of 'darkness and confusion' and her being an enthusiastic Christian) and his lifelong 'tendency to melancholia' still led to periods of 'black depression'. He was also physically unwell and so fatigued that he fell asleep after a lunchtime meeting he should have found stimulating because of the 'literary and artistic topics' discussed and the religious arguments which followed. He had, how-ever, been 'toying with a belief in Reincarnation' and said he '*must* go his own way to God', leaving Aelfrida to hope that even he would eventually attain 'the desired haven'.[45] This seemed unlikely given that Fidelio was consumed with remorse: "sometimes in the night when I can't sleep", he told her, "scenes from the past float up into consciousness and I begin to see that the life which I had thought a fairly good one has been full of horri-ble things". What these 'things' were he did not say or Aelfrida, as her hints of confidences given and her 'and so on and so on' suggests, did not transcribe, but though she tried to comfort him by saying "those things which I was proudest of are those of which I am most ashamed now", Fidelio remained uncomforted.[46]

Comberton, the village to the west of Cambridge in which Fidelio's 'furnished farmhouse' stood, also housed another of Aelfrida's friends. Juan Mascaró, would-be Little Friend, was now Supervisor in English at Cambridge University and had moved to Comberton 'to be near Fidelio'[47] to whom he was grateful for help and advice on arriving in England as a refugee. Following their 1937 meeting and desperate for silence and solitude at Tymawr, Aelfrida had commented 'I wish he wouldn't'[48] on reading the fulsome ending of a sub-sequent letter of thanks for having listened so patiently as he unburdened himself of pent-up emotions and experiences and prepared to disengage herself physically and emotionally from her *ami espirituel*; then too, and in spite of her recommendation that Juan ask for spiritual help from Dom Savinien Louismet, Juan had never become the monk she hoped he would, showing instead an unfortunate tendency to transform his 'hell … into heaven'[49] by falling in love with unsuitable girls. To her relief, one 'pretty little baggage … of common and not even respectable parentage' never became his wife[50] but to her surprise – and somewhat, it seems, to her dismay – Aelfrida received an 'absurd but touching' message from Juan ("tell her that I still have her in my heart" – this, she wrote, 'to a woman [in her sixties]!!!!')[51] passed on by Fidelio in the course of his first visit to Lolworth.

In spite of Lolworth being only four miles from Comberton, Juan seems to have made no move to meet Aelfrida again (nor she him) and the few remaining ref-erences to him in her diary are faintly disapproving: of 'a rather strange bit of news in the *Cambridge Independent Press*' informing her that "Juan Mascaró of Majorca is married to Miss Kathleen … Ellis of Comberton" (Kathleen Ellis, said Fidelio, was a teacher ten or twelve years younger than Juan and of "suitable disposition"), she wrote that Juan would be glad to take root *somewhere* at last[52], and news that 'Mrs Juan Mascaró … who is not

young' had had twins[53] was not greeted with the interest and enthusiasm usually expressed regarding the appear-ance on earth of little pieces of God Incarnate. Aelfrida, it seems, was insufficiently 'touched' by Juan's message to want to meet a man who disobeyed her wishes with regard to his spiritual life and who had transferred his affections from herself to his landlord's daughter.

Though plagued with what she half-humorously referred to as 'Echoes of the Past' which involved her in spite of herself in 'secular business … flowing against [her] craving for external and internal silence'[54], some echoes, it seems, were more welcome than others. A par-ticularly welcome echo began to reverberate in October 1950 at a point when (so she said) she received unhappy premonitions concerning the young son of a friend not Little except insofar as he was much younger than her-self: Anthony Wrightson.

Aelfrida had not contacted Anthony since discovering in 1938 that Elizabeth Wrightson disapproved of their correspondence (both Wrightsons and their children were listed in her Intercession Book as meriting special prayers) but in late 1950 concerns about young David Wrightson's health prompted her to write to Anthony to enquire. To her surprise and joy, Anthony replied in a long letter assuring her of David's recovery and provid-ing news of his own life ('head of his firm and enjoys the responsibility'; the tone of his letter, wrote Aelfrida, gave the impression of 'maturity and development') and of those whose lives had touched her own in happier days: John Wedgwood married, with his eldest son at Eton; Douglas Davidson, director of 'the finances of a large mining group', and so on.[55] He also asked her to write again (the man who 'even when most in love' always addressed her as 'Mrs Graham', now headed his letters "my dear Aelfrida")[56] but made no move to meet her. What Aelfrida does *not* tell us, though she hints broadly at it in a novel begun soon after hearing from Anthony whose hero, 'Clive Farwell', undergoes secret assign-ments while serving in the British Army of the Rhine, was that her wartime fears that Anthony was in great danger were not unfounded: Anthony, with his qualities of "patience, intelligence, loyalty and forbearance", had been a "diplomatic smuggler" under the auspices of the Ministry of Economic Warfare, instrumental in organis-ing and running a chain of staging posts across occupied Europe through which moved Swiss engineering prod-ucts vital to the British war effort.[57]

Not all echoes of the past were happy for there were 'more deaths to chronicle'[58] as an older generation passed on: Howard Warren, her 'stick-in-the-mud' exec-utor; Mr Goodman, the family solicitor who handled the early stages of her divorce; Louis de Glehn who played

Chouville to her Bélise in *Les Femmes Savantes*; Louisa Hoye, the old nurse who had known Aelfrida, Julius, and Eustace since childhood; Miss Butler of Girton who had 'graciously accepted all [her] Tymawr diaries for the college'.[59] Such deaths, though melancholy, did not touch her deeply; the deaths of Little Friends, however, 'brought the Past to Life'[60] in a disconcerting manner.

Among the first was that of prototype 'Little Friend' John Forbes Cameron. On 24 March 1952, Aelfrida, thinking of 'my old friend Cameron' and remembering 'the thrill I used to feel [at St Columba's] when he – head decorously averted – passed the [collection] plate to me', wondered why she should suddenly be 'calling him up out of the distant past'. (Her doing so was not as fortuitous as she suggests: Julius was in the process of renewing Cambridge friendships and had spoken to her of him.) Was it, she thought, her 'duty' to 'renew acquaintance' with a man unseen for twenty years next time she was in Cambridge? But she had left it, as her guardian angel pointed out, '*too late*'; there in *The Times* was Cameron's death "aged 78 after a long illness". The news brought her no 'personal grief' (she cut out and kept the obituary, nevertheless)[61] but a letter from Pattie Craske referring to Cameron's 'strong friendship' with Aelfrida caused the latter to mentally review 'the strange vicissitudes' of her relationship with a man who was not the 'solid silent young don' remembered by Pattie but 'anything but *solid*' where she herself was concerned, whose silence 'was punctuated by very emotional outbursts', and who, had he not married "Miss Elfrida Sturge, daughter of J E Sturge of Birmingham and Montserrat", might have allowed Aelfrida to style herself wife of the Master of Gonville and Caius College, Cambridge, for twenty years. 'Well, it doesn't matter now', wrote that jilted lady, comforted by the arrival of 'the most gloriously handsome and courteous Commanding Officer of the Oakington aerodrome' to apologise for the disturbance to a prayerful person complaining that his 'jet-planes' interrupted her meditations.[62] But her poem *Parallel Lines* 'dedicated to a mathematical friend' had accurately described her relationship with Cameron as "Twin lines that bravely fare through chilly space / Near, yet untouching" and its last line bade him "Goodbye. I'll meet you at Infinity".[63]

Another was that of Hubert Henderson of whom she heard only indirectly through her brothers. 'Professor Sir Hubert Henderson!', 'plain and clear-headed, the business-like economist'[64], had been appointed Warden of All Souls, Oxford and was no longer a young swain 'eager to talk and to admire' and prone to liking her 'exceedingly'[65] but "an argumentative, parsimonious Scot, cautious, sceptical [and] unheroic".[66] Hubert was not to enjoy his academic honour for long. In July 1951

Aelfrida reported his admittance to 'an Oxford nursing home with heart-trouble' ('nothing', she added, 'lays you low like Success!')[67], in January 1952 his resignation 'because he is ill'[68], and a month later, his death at sixty-one. Reading Hubert's obituary in *The Times* (she did not preserve it), she studied the portrait of a man remembered as 'a sunny eager undergraduate with an intellectual forehead' but who had become 'grim and burdened as if the cares of Economics had oppressed him'. (As they probably had, Henderson having been a member of the Government's Economics Advisory Council between 1929 and 1959.) Worse still, 'Economics' had banished spirituality.[69]

But although Aelfrida noted that she was 'sorry' to hear of Hubert's decline and death and signed off with an '*Oremus*' after a one-line eulogy ('he was happy in his family life and … just in all his dealings')[70], her sorrow seems conventional and rather forced. (Eustace, it seems, grieved more for the deaths of university contemporaries and friends than she did for younger men who had provided an 'Indian Summer' of love.) Were Little Friends who had been instrumental (as Hubert had) in dissipating dark clouds of postnatal depression and in raising the morale of a woman bruised by Constantine's callous behaviour now no more than 'episodes' recalled without overmuch nostalgia or gratitude? Or had so much transpired since then that they were of little importance relative to her Lolworth present?

News of a would-be husband reached Aelfrida in April 1952: 'Willie Searle has cancer of the lungs'.[71] Willie, like many men of his age, took up smoking as a glamorous and sophisticated pastime endorsed by celebrities and royalty (it was even advertised as promoting good health) or promoted as a means of suppressing hunger and maintaining alertness in the trenches of the Great War, and had continued to smoke thereafter; in 1952, however, he entered the realm of statistics, for it was men like him who first alerted physiologist/epidemiologist Richard Doll to the 1950s surge in cases of lung cancer in middle-aged men and its relationship to an adult lifetime of cigarette consumption.[72] (The best known 'statistic' of the 1950s was probably King George VI whose death early in February 1952 was greeted by Aelfrida with excitement – 'to think I have lived in six reigns now!'– and a degree of literary pride: had she not predicted, as Julius reminded her, 'a Queen Elizabeth at the end of *The Approaching Storm*'?)[73] But Willie, it seems, was not to be allowed to learn his true diagnosis and in reply to a platitudinous letter reminding him that 'he had once said that "the great thing is to *laugh* a great deal"', assured her that he was "recovering from pneumonia".[74] He also asked her to write again.

Unlike Hubert Henderson, Tommy Altounyan, and John Layard (a minor member of the coterie), Willie and Aelfrida had not lost touch completely and the coincidence of his birthday and her wedding anniversary on 19 January served to remind her of the man she nearly married. Willie, of course, kept in touch with Tillyard family happenings through Eustace; he also, though rarely, wrote directly to Aelfrida at times of crisis (Chiara's recovery from pneumonia in February 1932, for example) or at Christmas, the tone of the letters being always 'friendly'.[75] Aelfrida, for her part, seems to have stopped writing to Willie on a regular basis on becoming a probationary tertiary at Tymawr (he was relegated to remembrance 'only … in [her] prayers'[76] but was not the subject of reparative adoration because he was the wronged party in their relationship) and their only contact between then and 1952 had been on a matter of business concerning Aelfrida's loan of money to a farmer threatened with foreclosure to whom she believed Willie 'as a lawyer interested in agriculture'[77] would give sensible advice. 1952, however, seemed to be the start of a 'gentler [and] tenderer phase' of their relationship ('I think he is very fond of me and Eustace', she wrote) though she wondered how long it would be before 'poor Willie' discovered 'that he has not long to live'.[78] But as poor Willie was to discover, lung cancer sufferers take an unconscionable time a-dying.

Returning to 'the world' in July 1946 Aelfrida had discovered to her delight (and dismay) that she had retained her instinct to try and touch (and her ability to awaken) 'the admiration of every man I meet'.[79] She also discovered that Albert Erlande had been mistaken in saying that the only cure for a woman like her was to grow old – she *had* grown old but her instinct (and her ability), though rusty from lack of practice, remained as vigorous as ever – as witness the warning concerning 'unattached' Sisters received soon after her arrival in Lolworth. The warning – actually, as Aelfrida realised, a veiled reprimand – struck home: she had taken, she wrote, 'too much pleasure' in engaging the cleric who made it in conversation, had not thought it possible that a woman in her early sixties could take any interest in the opposite sex, and was 'aghast' that her nature was so 'corrupt' ('thank God for the confessional!'), but her reaction was wholly out of proportion: even had she behaved in as Bélisian a fashion as she intimated, 'good sense and good manners' would have kept her from doing anything 'outrageous'.[80] (In truth, her own and the cleric's behaviour was 'correct' and 'possibly even edifying'; the fact that he, described by Aelfrida as 'full of contradictory impulses and desires', was homosexual and imported a former altar boy into the rectory adds piquancy to her

protestations.) But her having behaved like this towards the first unrelated and unattached male encountered since leaving Tymawr made her recoil in horror at this 'unmasking of the root of sin' and it was a soberly penitential Aelfrida who decided to sin no more.[81] But clerics being in the majority among the few men she met and Aelfrida's vows being more honoured in the breach than the observance, it was inevitable that problems would sooner or later ensue.

In the meantime, she enjoyed the company of male visitors, be they Franciscan lay brothers, fellow tertiaries, or priests, because not only were they not women but also because they were suitably 'ascetic and visionary' or were enchanted to discover that 'the Master of Jesus is my brother'[82], or provided the intellectual conversation she craved, or were a respectable lay reader and eminent physicist who had known her for fifty years, namely Dr Searle FRS, with whom she enjoyed a fireside chat before receiving his blessing and a kiss. ('I think it was an early-Christian kiss – I certainly hope so – for I shouldn't at all approve of kissing my elderly gentlemen-friends however much I respect them … but still!!'; she returned his salutation.)[83] On another occasion, however, she reacted with exaggerated horror, in part, it seems, because Dr Searle kissed her in front of the Zender Browns, Mrs Lovell, and Archdeacon Kirkpatrick of Ely and she did not wish them to think that 'English rectories are places where silly old gentlemen kiss silly old ladies', but chiefly because, spiritually speaking, she was not sufficiently humble or quiet to prevent that kind of thing from happening. People with whom she discussed the incident either could not see her problem or told her that she was not responsible for the 'unwarranted … action of an eccentric' but Aelfrida, determined to repent 'being the kind of person I am', decided that four weeks of 'St Ignatius' Spiritual Exercises' would provide 'the strongest spiritual medicine' for her lamentable condition.[84]

With Canon Weekes, however, it was rather different. George Weekes, until 1945 Master of Sidney Sussex and known to Aelfrida as Alethea's spiritual director and as the conductor of Constantine's burial service, was now a widower, and besides being 'older and more saintly' than other clerical acquaintances, was good company insofar as his 'lovely manners and cultivated English'[85] were in marked contrast to Father Lovell's uncouthness and common accent. Like other Cambridge divines, Canon Weekes stood in for Father Lovell during the latter's frequent absences; meeting him again in the spring of 1947, Aelfrida found his visits theologically satisfactory and personally enjoyable. She also asked his opinion of books recently written by her and of work in progress and was pleased when the former appealed to him and the latter provided with suitable epigraphs. She also, however, regarded Canon Weekes in another light: 'the devil', she wrote, knowing that the canon was both lonely and strongly attracted to her, 'suggested that if [she] liked [she] could … evoke a proposal of marriage' ('of companionship only …of course') which would restore her to the 'nice position' she had had in Cambridge before she forfeited it.

That Aelfrida considered remarriage, even one of 'companionship only', seems strange but perhaps as a recently-revealed divorcée she felt she had rendered herself vulnerable once again to the kind of snubs administered by the parents of her daughters' schoolmates and by the wives and daughters of the Elders of St Columba's congregation. A companionate marriage, however, would allow her to remain chaste at the same time as she became the wife of a Cambridge cleric and emeritus academic living in a substantial house in Lensfield Road not far, as it happened, from that of former admirer William Bowen. And with status, comfort, and Cambridge restored, what could she not accomplish? But no; giving the devil 'a metaphorical box on the ear'[86], she settled for (comparative) poverty, lowly status, and unblemished chastity in Lolworth.

Of her Triple Vows, therefore, only Obedience remained – but obedience to whom? Aelfrida, as we know and as may have provided another reason for her decision not to evoke marital emotions in Dr Weekes' breast, was terrified of men, lay or clerical, who wanted to possess the innermost core of her personality. (Father Cary's failure to achieve this was, she later rationalised, 'the ultimate cause of his deserting me'[87]: *sic*.) But having now no spiritual director, she set out to find one and, somewhat to her surprise, found herself not only consulting him on spiritual exercises to be carried out in Lent or Advent, on the use of a discipline, and on books written or read, but carrying out his instructions also. Indeed, she was so pleased to find one that she wrote to Father Cary early in 1947 to inform him of his and Father Northcott's successor. (The cleric in question was not, she wrote on hearing of Father Cary's sudden death on St Lucian's Day 1950, as great a saint or mystic as the spiritual director she now appreciated 'more than I could when I was at Oxford'[88] but was nevertheless perfectly adequate.) Lucius Cary's reply was guarded: "it is so long since I saw you that I hesitate to attempt any opinion [but it seems that] you have passed through Father Northcott's hands and now have an Episcopal *corregidor* …"[89]

Edward Wynn, appointed Bishop of Ely in 1944, had had a distinguished theological, academic, pastoral, and wartime career[90], and it had been to him that Aelfrida applied for help in June 1946 in the hope that the bishop could find a suitably discouraged incumbent for her to prayerfully assist, and he, as Edward Ely (his official title) who intimated that he would like to meet her on her return to Cambridge.

Aelfrida's earlier dealings with Bishops of Ely had had precisely the required result (her discovery that even innocent parties in divorce cases were forbidden to marry in church had provided her escape clause with regard to Willie Searle) and later dealings too seemed about to achieve the same; indeed, her 'capacity for eliciting men's admiration'[91] was exercised so effectively that at their first meeting at Wetenhall Cottage, sixty-two-year-old Aelfrida stage-managed (as she thought) Edward Wynn into her 'magic net' so efficiently that she seemed to refute her statement that "it [was] for the young to seek romance"[92], not ladies (or gentlemen) of her own generation.

First impressions were good. 'The bishop', she diarised on 15 July 1946 of 'my appointment with the Bishop of Ely', was 'tall and broad with fine ecclesiastical features and warm dark colouring. His eyes are wonderfully kind and have a twinkle in them'. (Later she noted that he was 'immensely tall and dignified, not to say formidable', and that he appeared to be both 'self-disciplined' and 'very stern with himself'.) Either way, she felt so 'perfectly at ease with him'[93] that she was able to report their conversation at length and verbatim. Their interview began with social niceties and with the bishop extending his apologies for being five minutes late:

Aelfrida: "I have no engagements and don't in the least mind".

Bishop: "What! No engagements!"

Aelfrida: "No, nothing to do all day except to wait until you are ready to see me".

Welcoming her to the diocese, the bishop calls her 'an answer to prayer': since the departure of the religious community from their Hillside convent in Chesterton Road twenty years ago (Aelfrida smilingly corrects his dating but does not discuss her intimate knowledge of the Community of the Holy Family) he has felt the want of 'people who were devoted to prayer' but worries if he is not "too *geographical*" in his ideas: "ought I to be content with prayers offered outside the diocese? What do you think?"

Aelfrida: (this is the sort of conversation she enjoys) "There is the Light which is diffused everywhere and there is the intensification of that Light. One hopes that where there is prayer there may also be an intensification of Light".

Bishop: (realises they speak the same language) "Exactly".

Expressing a hope that Aelfrida will be 'the forerunner of other souls who would come and pray in his diocese', the Bishop then discusses the Lovells and Lolworth's spiritual 'deadness'. Finally he asks the question Aelfrida has been waiting for: "who is your spiritual director?"

Aelfrida: "Father Cary was my spiritual father. (*Sic*). At Tymawr Father Northcott had been helpful but the Reverend Mother herself had directed me".

Bishop: "What are you going to do now?"

Aelfrida explains that Father Lovell has agreed to confess her and she trusts that "the Holy Spirit would speak to me through him".

Bishop: "That is right but I doubt if Father Lovell is knowledgeable on things that you will need to know". ('I think', Aelfrida interpolates, 'he meant things to do with the Religious Life'.) "I wish I knew who to recommend".

Aelfrida: (with arabesque coyness; one can almost hear a pretty please) "would *you* direct me? I should not trouble you much". (As, of course, a prayerful person with an 'attraction towards silence' would not).

The Bishop does not answer her request immediately but suggests that he visit her once she is established in Lolworth: "*May* I?"

Aelfrida: "Surely you have the *right* to come – no permission on my part is needed".

'Punctually at the end of half an hour', she continues, 'I rose. The Bishop said "I should like to give you my blessing". So I knelt at once'. ('I love being blessed'.) Then after a genial (and, on Aelfrida's part, a flirtatious) farewell (the bishop was a bachelor five years younger than herself), her 'episcopal *corregidor*' departed in his chauffeured car and Aelfrida betook herself to the nearby Botanic Garden to 'ponder and consider'[94] the course their relationship should take.

To this superb demonstration of piety and spiritual capacity the Bishop could hardly fail to respond, inviting himself to tea in Lolworth on 18 October in a 'very gracious letter'. (He did not make a special journey but was on his way to an appointment in Cambridge.) The news put Aelfrida in a flutter: unless she was 'commanded to come down to the drawing room', she would take tea alone and see the Bishop only for confession because she did not want 'to meet [her] spiritual director socially' and

because she did not want to divert his attention 'from the rectory folk, *dear* people'.[95] And perhaps because a prayerful person with an *attrait* towards silence should not be seen partaking in family life.

On St Luke's Day 1946 'the Bishop came to Lolworth'. At 3.15pm Edward Ely in 'purple silk cassock, surplice and stole' and Aelfrida in tertiary veil and pectoral cross processed across the ragged lawn, through the wicket gate, and along the 'green glory' of Church Lane whose 'guard-of-honour trees' shone with the same 'unearthly light and beauty' which enveloped Tymawr. In the church, Aelfrida produced her 'routine confession' (it consisted of 'one difficulty: "myself" [and] one question, Silence, on which I needed advice') and the bishop responded by enquiring about the exact *nature* of her attraction to Silence ('awe in the Presence of God', according to a penitent who on her own admission was 'naturally talkative and sociable') and expressing concern that 'attachment to what *had* been God's Will in the past *might* prevent [her] from discovering His Will in the future'. Then after absolution and a brief interval for private prayer, she in her pew by the radiator, he at the altar steps, *corregidor* and penitent processed back to tea, hers solitary, his with the Lovells. An hour later, however, 'the Bishop wished to speak to me. Would I like him to come up to my room? Indeed I wouldn't!' (Was it the coldness and shabbiness of her bedroom or the hint of impropriety which worried her most?) So down she came and she and the Bishop chatted over the drawing room fire 'as if we had been friends all our lives'.[96]

Reflecting on the occasion, Aelfrida came to an important conclusion: the Bishop, she decided, had been given to her (to a reader of her diary it seems she was not so much *given* him as helped herself *to* him) as spiritual director 'not only [so] that he might guide me' but also so that she might 'if God pleases' open her 'own "treasury" … for him to draw on'.[97] A 'most benign letter … from "Edward our bishop"' reassured her on the latter score ('I do want him to feel at ease with me and to be able to be perfectly frank about anything and everything'; in spiritual terms, however, she felt closer to Father Lovell) though she worried lest its tentative tone betrayed a fear of saying the wrong thing to one as spiritually advanced as herself or indicated that he found 'pious ladies' like herself 'touchy'.[98]

The Bishop may have been tentative for another reason. In the course of their first meeting Aelfrida had suggested the creation of 'a home for aged priests [and] tertiaries and other devout ladies' (three 'aged clergymen' to '3 or 4 devout ladies' was the suggested ratio) in one of the diocese's 'large vicarages' (re-named 'St Etheldreda's House of Prayer') but when pressed to assume responsibility ("'would you –?", looking at me keenly') activated an escape-clause ('I was best under obedience')[99] and referred in future to her 'Centre' or 'House' of Prayer as 'the Bishop's'. In fact, Aelfrida was already planning a possible abode for herself should life in Lolworth become intolerable[100] (it was winter 1946/47, after all) but in spite of her decision to put herself 'at his disposal without reserve'[101] regarding an institution which might 'come into being as-it-were spontaneously'[102] (i.e. without her having to exert herself), the Bishop seemed oddly disinclined to involve himself other than prayerfully (he pleaded pressure of work, 'problems arising out of Finance, divorce, and a movement to restrict the baptism of infants, and so on')[103] and the scheme was dropped. (It was to reappear in a novel.) A brisk letter from Mother Guenvrede put a final stop to Aelfrida's latest 'Brilliant Idea': "don't encourage Dr Wynn to *do* anything, squash it in fact … it takes time to learn to *live* a life – as you ought to realise yourself – and [a] premature start only fails and causes *talk*".[104]

Though Aelfrida and her spiritual director met rarely, they corresponded on a regular basis. Initially Aelfrida kept his letters with a view to publication but finding them 'dull and scrappy' and 'not *remarkable* as letters of direction', burnt them. (There was also another reason: 'his letters to me are very *private* [and] of no interest to the general public' – and besides, she wanted to leave 'everything in order … in case of [her] sudden death'[105] – which begs the question: what *was* there in these 'very *private*' letters that she did not wish a future biographer to know?) Her lengthy diary accounts of their meetings, however, demonstrate both how Aelfrida used her spiritual director and her worries concerning the evolving relationship between Edward Wynn and herself, her preoccupation being shown by her occasionally and inadvertently replacing Father Lovell's name with his.

Confession to the Bishop (he in purple cassock, both in Lolworth church) in May 1947 shows Aelfrida in an interesting light. She began by confessing – as if a day trip to Cambridge which included a brief visit to Hope House, lunch at Wetenhall Cottage with 'dear, sweet' Mina, Constance and Walter, and a visit from Canon Weekes[106] constituted a venial, if not a mortal sin – 'a reversion to some worldly standards … liking to know the "right people" and being pleased at [her] ability to join in intellectual conversation'. ('It must be detestable', she wrote, 'to be a confessor … while souls wash their dirty linen in one's presence'; this begs another question: how much of her sometimes very dirty 'linen' did she 'wash' in the Bishop's presence? Or was it as a 'pious lady' that she preferred to be seen and worked hard at being

seen?) She then enquired about her 'continuing attraction to Silence' and asked the Bishop if she should 'resist' it. But on the Bishop asking if she had ever heard 'an inward voice' calling her back to 'the world' and showing her a 'place or work' waiting for her or had heard or still heard an inward voice 'calling her to more Silence', she lied twice, answering '*no, never*' to the first (how, then, to explain her departure from Tymawr, a departure in which the 'tug of the world' played as important a part as Mother Guenvrede's 'push' from within?) and to the second that she sought nothing but the will of God, 'more precious to [her] than either speech or silence'. To her diary, however, she admitted that 'something from the very depths of [her] heart' (or, rather, 'head', crossed out but a revealing Freudian slip nevertheless) cried out "yes, yes! [you] never had enough Silence at the convent and [you] never have enough now".

Temporising (he could not immediately "give a ruling on a question of such importance"), the Bishop advised that as vocation to Silence was so rare, Aelfrida was justified in not *seeking* company but, conversely, should not *deny* herself to "those who wish to see you". (Father Cary's advice a decade earlier.) Aelfrida then lied again, assuring the Bishop that what he said 'agreed exactly' with both her Rule and her practice (Mother Guenvrede's and Fidelio's views on the subject might have differed) and stating that although 'stricter silence might be possible later', she was satisfied with the degree of solitude and silence she now possessed. She omitted, however, to inform the Bishop that 'there [were] reasons too, of course' for her not wishing to retreat into 'stricter silence' at present (reasons over and above the 'physical austerities which normally accompanied a vocation to Silence')[107], reasons which may be guessed even as they remained undisclosed: the necessity of frequent visits to Cambridge to alleviate the material and social deprivation of life in Lolworth; a need to maintain regular contact with Julius; the likelihood of Alethea returning to England on leave in the near future; her '*natural*' self's desire to escape the stultifying self-imposed boredom inherent in claustration in a single room with only God and an oilstove for company[108]; the fact that her 'vocation to Silence' had sent her 'mad'. Next day she thought of an escape clause ('not presumptuously desiring more [silence] before God gives the signal') and wrote hastily to the Bishop to inform him that because 'various people' wanted to come and see her, '*more* Silence' (the mere thought of which filled her with anticipatory joy, joy the more joyful because the Bishop himself had provided her with an escape clause; perhaps he intuited that in spite of protestations to the contrary, she neither wanted nor needed more) would be placed 'in abeyance'.

**Bishop Wynn**

In earnest of good intent, she enclosed the typescript of *The Fruits of Silence* with her letter.[109]

In July 1947 Aelfrida rewarded herself for 'ten and a half happy months of Lolworth Rule-keeping' with three weeks' holiday in Cambridge, four days of which were spent 'in [her] old night nursery' in 'dear haven of peace' Hope House 'waited on' by the Sisters, the remainder in Wetenhall Cottage, now a 'Little Germany!!' filled by Mina with compatriot visitors, helpers, displaced persons, and former prisoners of war.[110] Visited in 'Little Germany' by Bishop Wynn, Aelfrida was pleased to find his 'natural fastidiousness' responding to 'cultured surroundings' and dismayed by the way in which cultured surroundings brought out 'his almost-worldly suavity and exquisite manners'. Was Wynn, she wondered as she experienced 'a sudden pang of loneliness', too worldly a prelate to be her spiritual director? Or was it disappointment at his handing back her latest manuscript with the tactful murmur that 'it would be an impertinence … to make any comment' when what she expected was fulsome praise? Or a pang of jealousy at his courtesy to Mina when she joined them for coffee prior to their chat *à deux*? Or because the Bishop referred to her use of a discipline (she had 'owned up' by letter, telling him that she – now – used it as Mother Guenvrede 'prescribed' i.e. seven strokes a day on her left thigh but not on Sundays, saints' days, or church festivals), something inappropriate in Wetenhall Cottage's pretty drawing room with its portrait of 'Little Katie' over the fireplace?[111]

On 27 November the Bishop visited her again, this time in Lolworth. Aelfrida owned to feeling 'troubled' prior to this meeting because the Bishop had warned her to be '*very careful*' over use of her discipline ('of course I *am*', she assures us) and because she was 'due to tell him about other "useful saints"' ('Saint Rose and Saint Bruno', in case we had forgotten), and in part because she had read an authoritative and 'steely-cold' letter from Edward Ely in the *Church Times* objecting to a statement made therein and had realised that despite 'the exquisite manners … unstudied humility and episcopal wisdom' displayed towards her as one directed, as one directed she came under his spiritual authority and might expect to be similarly castigated if she transgressed.[112] There was also the matter of Edward Wynn having transgressed the bounds of spiritual directorship by using her as a confidante with regard to both personal and diocesan anxieties and of she herself opening her 'treasury' in order to act as a spiritual support system to one limited in acceptable sources of female comfort – in which respect, 'a detestable little devil' kept suggesting that the Bishop's frequent visits were due to his being in the early stages of falling in love. Cursing the devil – and herself 'for being an aged Bélise' – Aelfrida 'prayed against idiotic thoughts' and prepared to meet her director.[113]

What transpired might have warned a man more experienced at dealing with the personal problems of soldiers and male Cambridge undergraduates than with the convolutions of female personality disorders that in Aelfrida he had met someone not entirely normal in religious or emotional terms and to whom shortly before his arrival Christ 'suddenly stood beside [her] *almost* visible … and said "today I will come to thee through thy spiritual father"'. Knowing that 'just one part of his time was for me' and the remainder for the Lovells, Aelfrida declined confession (she had only 'general unsatisfactoriness' to report and was '*very* glad not to … take him down to the *arctic* church') and after displaying her 'treasures' (her diurnal, pectoral crucifix, and tertiary's scapular and veils, carefully packed in a basket), requesting (and being refused) extra use of 'Saint Guenvrede' (also displayed) 'in case of special need', telling him the 'full story' of Saints 'Rose' and 'Bruno' (she was commended for having disposed of them), and receiving his blessing 'on [her] knees, body and soul', there to receive 'the most awe-inspiring … sense of the Presence of God', informed the Bishop that 'Our Lord had said He would come to me today through him'. To which the Bishop, obviously taken aback, replied in 'a tone of great emotion' and succinctly "thank you".[114]

He had had a narrow escape, for had it not been for her having to vacate the room in favour of Father Lovell, Aelfrida might have given herself up '*entirely*' ('much better psychologically') to the 'inrush of the [Holy] Spirit'. (It is amusing to speculate what might have happened had she not '[clung] to normal consciousness' or kept in touch 'with [her] ordinary self'.)[115] She was, however, anxious that Bishop Wynn be aware of "Episcopal Gifts" bestowed on him by her vision and herself and duly wrote to inform him of both vision and gifts. Judging by his muted response (he was "most grateful" to be told, would like to hear more, and would "think carefully" about the matter), the Bishop *was* warned but perhaps insufficiently for one already too 'interested' in her.[116]

Within a year, however, Aelfrida was as 'interested' in Edward Wynn as he (supposedly) in her. But rather than expose her true feelings for him openly and possibly in an effort to persuade herself that what she felt was admiration for his spiritual rather than his personal and physical qualities, she points her biographer to a particular chapter in a particular book (*The Voice of a Priest*)[117] in which Edward Wynn is described (not, it should be noted, as himself, but in the person of Jesus Christ) and her own sentiments expressed in terms of the charm of His/his personality being "magnetic", of His/his speech being irresistible because of His/his "strong sweet voice" imbued with "persuasive power", and of hearts being drawn to Him/him "with an attraction in which strong love [is] mingled with reverential awe". Furthermore, Wynn's position as Bishop is described as entailing both a "great dignity" ("as he stands at the altar he is clothed in the majesty of … Christ himself") and a "crushing burden" akin to Christ's "heavy burden of the cross" because in joining "the ranks of the episcopacy" Wynn, as his priestly clothing signifies, is both following in Christ's footsteps and personifying His life as preacher, teacher, leader, and pastor.[118] Dwelling further on the theme inspired by *The Voice of a Priest,* Aelfrida also reveals more than perhaps she intended about herself and her relationship with the Bishop; indeed, much can be deduced from a statement made at this juncture that 'alas and alas!!', the 'ape and the peacock' continued to flourish in the 'jungle' that was her own 'human' nature.[119] But which characteristic of ape or peacock (i.e. of her baser or higher natures) can we deduce that she particularly exhibited (or thought she exhibited) in relation to Edward Ely the bishop or to Edward Wynn the man?

In 'simian' terms it was her deliberately provocative demeanour at the time of their first meeting (the abbreviated version of their conversation given in this chapter provides only a glimpse of the sexualised intensity of Aelfrida's behaviour towards someone whose height and voice must have reminded her vividly of Anthony Wrightson or Albert Erlande) which recalls her habit of idealising a man (i.e. surrounding him with a 'shapeless flame'), only to regard him as depraved when he responds to her obvious interest in him and of regarding her own behaviour towards him as sinful or even 'beastly' insofar as normal human impulses remind her too forcibly of the animal aspects of her nature. Like the (male) peacock, however, she also needs to show off her spiritual credentials by bestowing spiritual 'treasures' upon him, by demonstrating her perfection as a female confidante (a 'mate', as it were, in a companionate 'marriage') to whom he can turn for advice knowing that she will not betray his confidence (except to her diary and her biographer) and that advice proffered will be sensible and appropriate because of her experience of the circles in which he moves and of ways in which he thinks as a cleric. But although such 'avian' or 'apelike' behaviour appears essentially harmless at in the context of Aelfrida's latest male relationship because she is keenly aware of its 'Bélisian' aspects and of how ridiculous she, a woman in her sixties, would appear pursuing another bachelor younger than herself, the natures of the animal and bird she singles out speak volumes: the ape wheedling and needy on its Lolworth branch, the peacock strutting proudly and possessively before its 'mate' at Wetenhall Cottage.

It was, however, as an *ancilla Domini* that Aelfrida's most peacock-like tendency manifested itself: her regarding Bishop Wynn less as the only spiritual director towards whom she behaved on correctly and more as someone at her spiritual back and call. The tendency was not, of course, a new one – she had treated Lucius Cary in exactly the same manner – but with regard to Bishop Wynn it took the curious form of accepting and following his advice while making it appear to a biographer as if he were the subordinate and she the superior. Her attitude may have arisen because idiosyncratic extrapolation of Edward Leen's themes persuaded her that an aspect of the episcopal role was to act as a servant of the servants of God (a '*servus servorum Dei*')[120], she being a 'handmade' of the Lord and Wynn her 'servant' and from expectation that even bishops should defer to her as Fordfield servants deferred to her as daughter of the house. The Bishop, however, was to prove that although in terms of humility before God, he was indeed her 'servant', as a man in a position of authority, he was not be trifled with: in the course of their sole meeting in 1949, Aelfrida, preparing 'to interview' Edward Ely on mistress/servant terms, found herself 'a little surprised' when on admitting that she 'had not a single spiritual problem or difficulty to lay before him' (a statement which hardly tallied with her subsequent admission that she had been nearly three years in Lolworth and had 'nothing obvious', spiritually speaking, to show for it) and noting that if she were thinking of leaving Lolworth, would his Lordship like her to consult him first, her 'servant' spoke authoritatively: "*most certainly* I should".[121]

In 1950 Aelfrida and the Bishop met twice, once at Lolworth, once in Cambridge, he being reluctant to visit Lolworth too often because he already visited it "far more than any other parish in the diocese" but assuring Aelfrida that he was always happy to receive her letters: 'God forgive me! What have I done that the Lord Bishop of Ely should be so attentive?' wrote *ancilla Domini* without irony. (Perhaps the Bishop was trying to distance himself from a woman about whom he may have been warned by Hubert Northcott, a friend since Great War days[122]; it is also obvious that his behaviour towards her was impeccable, pastor, director, or friend predominating as occasion demanded.) He also assured her that he had read her current writings "with great profit" ('I gasp when a Bishop makes a remark like that to me!', though she also seems to have thought his being '*humble* enough' to have profited by her remarks showed what a well-trained *servus* he was)[123] and arranged a visit for 5 May. The visit was brief but so 'wonderful' that its description filled five diary pages and culminated in a vision which began that night and continued 'with *superficial* interruptions only' for two days in the course of which 'many things which had been dimly seen or altogether missed' were made plain.[124]

The vision, initiated by the sudden appearance in her room of 'Our Lord as He will come in glory', continued in the form of a 'shewing' in church during which Aelfrida 'saw a temptation ... one of the greatest and subtlest' she had ever faced and had it not been for a 'detestable book' she had recently read and for Dr Searle's (supposedly) 'early-Christian kiss' the previous month (this was not the kiss to which she reacted in horror; that came after her 'shewing' and can now be seen as her reaction to it), she might, she wrote, have 'walked into [it] with [her] eyes shut'.[125]

It was the book, however, rather than the kiss, a series of letters written by Cardinal Vaughan to Lady Herbert of Lee[126] and compared by them to the correspondence between François de Sales and Jeanne de Chantal but described by a 'cruel Anglican reviewer' as a "spiritual flirtation" and by Aelfrida as 'vivid documents

of the power of human deception', which (so she said) opened her eyes to the iniquities (as she saw it) of her conduct vis-à-vis Edward Wynn, for it demonstrated (so she thought) how 'the relationship of a spiritual director to his charming penitent [became] less and less spiritual while remaining perfectly *decorous*' and how 'the character of the Cardinal and presumably of the lady suffered in consequence'. The discovery sent her into a tizzy: 'the last thing I ever expected to be at my age was to be [a] temptation to a bishop or anyone else ... [but he enjoys] confiding his experiences to me [and is happy] being my guardian and protector ... [and] there is nothing yet but the *shadow* of a taint of something natural, just where the harmless shades off into harmful, in our relationship but – on my knees, just before Consecration – I saw a choice before me ...', a choice made harder and bitterer because it was not only she who was a temptation to Edward Ely the Bishop but also Edward Wynn the man who was a temptation to her.[127] Of course, she continued, 'I greatly admire and am much attracted by Dr Wynn (I am too responsive and emotional) [because] ... he feels the pleasure of being appreciated and understood and ... has the familiar instinct to protect and dominate me' and (best of all) 'because he has the charm of the celibate', the last remark quickly qualified on re-reading: 'when I wrote of the "charm of the celibate" I did *not* mean physical charm ... I could at no age or in any circumstances imaginable, I think, have fallen in love with Dr Wynn'. But her 'I think' is revealing, that and her protesting speciously ('his being a bishop places [that] utterly out of the question') and too much. So to punish herself for firing-up Donne's 'shapeless flame' round yet another man and indulging in 'a thrillingly interesting human relationship carried on [in] the guise of a spiritual relationship', as Father Lovell elevated the consecrated Host she plumped for 'loneliness and the Way of the Cross', flung herself wholly 'upon God's mercy' – and blamed the 'diabolically clever' devil for having engineered the whole affair.[128] She also informed the Bishop of her decision in one of her many letters to him.

The Bishop, whose 'Episcopal Wisdom' must have been sorely tested by the revelation that he and Aelfrida had been conducting a 'spiritual flirtation', initially replied only with a blessing but on Aelfrida informing him that she would be in Cambridge during the summer, wrote suggesting that he visit her at Wetenhall Cottage 'if I want him to'.[129] To one who had recently settled for 'loneliness', her 'Way of the Cross' should have been clear but 12 August 1950 (the day after Fidelio came to lunch and asked her if she ever thought about her past, a day on which he had also made it clear that Julius' presence at the meal was de trop because he wanted Aelfrida to himself) saw Aelfrida *sans* her other two admirers meeting Edward Wynn once more.

Remembering, perhaps, her thoughts of the previous day on the subject of her 'capacity for enticing men's admiration', Aelfrida determined that 'the interview should be as much as possible a director-penitent one'. But discovering, to her unspoken delight, that 'Dr Wynn was in an overwhelmingly friendly mood', was pleased at being able to talk more freely than at Lolworth, and was waxing confidential while lounging on her sofa with a post-prandial cup of coffee, she recalled 'an absurd poem [she] had once read on the advantages of having a "cultivated female friend"' and wondered if she were not the first woman to understand Edward Wynn's 'carefree seriousness [and] entire lack of self-sufficiency'. (This, she thought, would account for his being so at home and at ease in her company.) She reciprocated his interest in her latest literary effort (her first novel for many years included a bishop modelled on Wynn himself) by assuring him (by implication) that although she felt increasingly drawn to Silence, Silence 'would [not] take [her] away from him' and that on his forthcoming visit to America, people would be as pleased to see him as she had been that day. No wonder, then, that human emotions clogged spiritual channels between *corregidor* and penitent when Aelfrida felt the Bishop's hand on her head during his parting blessing.[130]

Mulling things over prior to the Bishop's absence abroad, Aelfrida decided she much preferred her spiritual director 'vested in cope and mitre … or in his episcopal dress talking to me of spiritual things' to having him 'lounging on my sofa … in a clerical lounge suit with purple "dickey" … being as charming as a gentleman of his age can be'. Reminding herself, therefore, that 'the director-penitent-relationship [did] not include All That Sort of Thing', she wrote to the Bishop to inform him (by implication) of this (he had requested that she not write to him while he was abroad; one senses he was as deluged with letters as Lucius Cary) and that this being so, it was preferable to meet him formally in the impersonal surroundings of Lolworth rectory than informally in the pink-curtained drawing room of Wetenhall Cottage. 'All I want', she assured herself, 'is to be alone with God'.[131] And for over a year, she was.

She was not, of course, entirely solitary, for visiting to and fro between Lolworth and Cambridge continued unabated. So too did visits from 'various people' independent of time and place.

The day before she left Tymawr, Aelfrida speculated on whether or not 'those mysterious perfumes which … reappear from time to time'[132] would accompany her to Lolworth. They did. A month after her arrival, the perfumes assailed her, localising in her room as 'a definite sense of Our Lady's Presence', together with a message that she would teach Aelfrida 'purity'. ('Would that she might!')[133] Was it, she wondered, merely the scent of the *gloire de Dijon* rose outside her window? Informing a clerical visitor ('the first person I have told and I hope the last'; she never told Bishop Wynn, however, this being 'the kind of happening' she preferred to conceal from him), he too owned to having smelled it, describing it as a scent of 'ripe pineapples or something' pervading the house. Acting on his advice (such phenomena, he said, should be "taken in a common sense way" and dismissed from one's mind after accepting them with humility and gratitude; a 'wise' move, she noted), Aelfrida listed the perfume as one of the 'funny things' which 'happened' to her and made no further comment[134], but subsequent olfactory experiences by Mina in 1947 ('a smell "like fresh incense all about"', a not unlikely smell, given that there was an oratory in the house)[135] and by herself on several occasions but especially vividly in the church in March 1949 at a time when there were no flowers in bloom or on the altar, a sharp frost outside, no one wearing perfume in the vicinity, and shortly after she had said an Ave Maria, she persuaded herself that neither she nor Mina nor the cleric had smelt incense but the Blessed Virgin in the form of 'an exquisite perfume, fresh and invigorating as flowers from Paradise'.[136]

While it is possible that the Virgin's reappearance in Aelfrida's life echoed current controversies regarding the likelihood of Christ's mother being assumed 'in spirit *and body*'[137] into heaven after death (a subject which also exercised 'Presbyterian' Placida's mind), it is worth noting that by 1949 Aelfrida was sufficiently desperate to invite the Virgin into her life and to invoke her help 'to encourage [her] in [her] Silence'[138], Silence being harder to achieve in a country rectory than in an isolated Community. It may also be relevant to Aelfrida's desire for 'purity' that the Virgin's perfumy presence disappeared at the same time as Bishop Wynn departed on his extended tour of America.

A visitation in September 1951, however, was not invoked for encouragement: Thérèse of Lisieux, arriving on a mission to Mary Lovell, employed Aelfrida only as an intermediary.[139] Mary, now seventeen and as horse-mad as ever, had become emotionally entangled with a well-known jockey and although Aelfrida in her role of 'consul's wife'[140] (*sic*) proffered practical advice to Mary's parents with regard to moral welfare officers and application of legal sanctions, the imminence of Mary's eighteenth birthday and the girl's refusal to listen to reason (the jockey was older and married) required supernatural intervention. Aelfrida was not entirely surprised to receive a visit from St Thérèse – the Lovells had a special devotion to her and her portrait and a statuette adorned Father Lovell's oratory – but was taken aback when the saint appeared to her looking '*determined* and very *businesslike*' ('St Thérèse may have been a "Little Flower" but she had a *will* of tempered steel') and in her eyes 'a gleam of amusement … as if she meant [to say] "here I stay until you are absolutely convinced"'. Aelfrida *was* convinced ('if I had imagined [her] I should have made her speak in French' and clothed her in '*samite*', not in a dress 'of a blue like the sky at night' like her own tertiary veil; she also attributed a subsequent exacerbation of tinnitus to the shock of the visitation) and Thérèse vanished, leaving behind her 'a spiritual freshness and vigour' which persisted for hours.[141] Other, however, than intimating to Mary that St Thérèse had her in her special keeping (faced with legal sanctions, the jockey ended the affair), Aelfrida did not inform Father and Mrs Lovell of the saint's visit though she later submitted it to Bishop Wynn 'for judgement'. His reaction was that although it was 'a *good* experience', Aelfrida should "reserve judgement as to its validity"[142], an interesting comment with regard to her state of mind at the time and to his six months' absence incommunicado having clarified his view of his penitent's mental and spiritual competence in several respects. This she did, for she had begun to worry lest St Thérèse's visitation suggest that like St Anthony in Charles Kingsley's *The Hermits* (her current reading), she too might be considered 'quite mad' if she reported further events of this nature.

Contemporaneously, however, with reporting St Thérèse's visit to the Bishop in March 1952, Aelfrida experienced the first of a series of auditions lasting about a year in total. Lying awake one night she '*heard* a soft voice' say 'in exquisitely modulated tones … "this is an angel speaking"'. Aelfrida, so she said, '*thought*' an answer ("I am listening") and identified the voice as that of St Raphael of whom she thought it 'rather absurd for an angel to speak as if he were *telephoning*!!' (At Lolworth Aelfrida used the telephone as a medium of communication to a greater extent than before.) Conveying 'extreme urgency', the angel bade her "Love God" (Aelfrida, with an eye to an escape-clause, replied that she *tried* but 'being a poor thing', might fail), whereupon she was regaled with 'a most marvellous melody, not of human speech or song, of angels uttering the command *Love God!'* But although she usually experienced olfactory and visual experiences as comforting and 'real', on this occasion she worried lest her new audition be 'a delusion of the devil' (as, of course, some experiences had been) or a production of her own 'unconscious mind'[143] (or, one might suggest, a physiological manifestation of worsening tinnitus), rather than a genuine message from

God mediated through one of His agents. Concerned, however, lest recounting this particular experience to the Bishop underline an impression of her being 'quite mad', she said nothing to him (or anyone else) about it then or later, leaving it to her biographer to judge.

Against each relevant date in her diary it was Aelfrida's habit to note friends' and relatives' birthdays (but never Constantine's), dates of death (chiefly Chiara's, rarely the Oracle's), and her own wedding anniversary and other anniversaries deemed worthy of remembrance; Agatha who, had she lived, would be nearly 'middle aged'[144], was almost invariably remembered as to birthday and 'heavenly' birthday as if she were an early Christian martyr persecuted for her faith instead of an unhappy girl who threw herself under a train to escape her mother. (Her 'heavenly' birthday veered between 22 and 24 February according to the spiritual or other busyness of her mother's life but her earthly birthday was accurately recorded; other dates too reminded Aelfrida of Agatha's purgatorial experiences prior to death by suicide: 'could I have looked forward', she wrote on what would have been her and Constantine's forty-first wedding anniversary, 'and seen myself as a Poor Old Thing without home or husband and known all that was to befall Constantine and Agatha, I should have been in despair'.)[145] So much did Agatha occupy her mother's thoughts that her 'heavenly' birthday was often accompanied by vivid dreams, so vivid, in fact, that Aelfrida wondered if Agatha had not been 'astral travelling'[146] (a phrase unused since Aleister Crowley days) and taken her mother with her. But having seen her mother to Tymawr, Agatha made no further appearances until 1948 when, a few days prior to a 'heavenly' birthday celebrated on 22 February, Aelfrida dreamed vividly that her dead daughter, looking 'wonderful, radiant and youthful', was beside her, not in Lolworth as might have been expected of a place both had visited twenty years earlier, but at Fordfield. She transcribes the conversation thus:

Aelfrida:    "*Ought* you to be here? Do you know that you are dead?"
Agatha:    (smiling a wise and faintly mischievous smile) "Oh yes, I am allowed to be here. I do know that I am 'dead'".
Aelfrida:    "May I talk to you?"
Agatha:    "You may, but you mustn't touch me".

But on Aelfrida making an involuntary movement towards her, Agatha vanished, leaving her mother to wonder if her dead daughter was really near her or whether their closeness was only 'in Christ'.[147]

It was, perhaps, with Agatha's recent appearance in mind that Aelfrida paid a spring-time visit to Histon

Road Cemetery, her first visit for over ten years. She found it 'cheerful-looking' with 'perky … tulips' in flower (her parents' funerals, like those of Constantine and Agatha, had taken place in autumn or winter) but though 'the burials of Agatha's white coffin and Constantine's urn were unforgettable', failed to associate it with 'departed dear ones': 'I meet my dear ones *in God,* not there'.[148] Two years later, however, she met Agatha again though not in person. Holidaying at Wetenhall Cottage in July 1950, she found her heart aching 'unbearably' because of an action on Julius' part best described as insensitive but probably regarded by him in quite another light: on 21 July he brought down from the attic 'old diaries, note-books and pictures' belonging to Agatha and Alethea, together with a volume of Agatha's *Record Book*. Aelfrida permitted very limited browsing because 'only diaries of the *very* young are legitimately read by their elders'[149] (the girls' adolescent volumes portrayed Julius in an unflattering light) but was again distressed when Julius, 'because he loves me greatly', gave her as a Christmas present an album containing 'life-like pictures' (i.e. pho-tographs) among which were many of Agatha, with or without Alethea: 'perhaps', wrote Aelfrida almost in tears, 'perhaps when – or if – I am very old the *temps perdu* will have lost its poignancy but now a mere snapshot brings it all to life again [and] the joy and the pain have lost nothing of their intensity'.[150] It may be, however, that the visit to the cemetery and confrontation with material evidence of her dead daughter brought emo-tional healing in their train. Agatha's 1948 visit was her last; henceforth her mother experienced 'no feeling' that Agatha was near her even on real or 'heavenly' birthdays. Yet hoping that she and Agatha would meet again after her own death, she wished her daughter not adieu, but '*à bientôt*' ('perhaps!') and reminded her, in the phrase inscribed on her tombstone, to call to her mother in the hour of the latter's death.[151]

Aelfrida and her elder daughter had not, of course, parted friends, the former making little secret of the fact that she resented Alethea's re-appearance in her life and the latter none of the fact that she despised her mother and could hardly wait to put distance between them. Whether Aelfrida believed that she met Alethea 'in Christ' during the latter's twelve-year absence in South Africa is unclear but pride in her daughter's 'mission' at St Cuthbert's is obvious, particularly insofar as Alethea's mission activities supposedly reflected her mother's pre-cepts. In *Messages*, for example, she suggests that the proper way for an 'unattached' missionary to behave (the version Aelfrida now gave of Alethea's career was that having "private means", she had decided "not to offer [her] services to any missionary society but to go out

independently")[152] is not to tell people their religion is wrong but to build on the best of what is there in the (unspoken) hope of converting them to one's own[153], or, if unsuccessful, to help them achieve a general rais-ing of moral and spiritual standards; elsewhere she states that "missions" which force Christianity on unready or unwilling believers are a mistake.[154] They are also reflected in her belief that if she could not be (as she once hoped) the mother of a saint disguised as a nun, she could at least bask in the reflected glory of one who, having entered her novitiate, had decided that her call "was probably to the mission field rather than to the Religious Life".[155] (*Sic*). Her pride was not, however, reserved for her diary; not only did she lecture to Lolworth Mothers' Union on Alethea's life in South Africa as an 'unattached' mis-sionary, but soon after her arrival she gave the Lovells 'an illustrated talk on Alethea and her work' and provided them with 'black "prayer children"' similar to her own 'prayer child' Tembani with whom she exchanged let-ters.[156] That her pride (if not her version of events) was justified, is supported by an unexpected source: Julius, visiting South Africa in 1947, wrote of his once-derided niece that Alethea was "so happy and sure of her path, so competent and yet modest and unspoilt" that Aelfrida had every right to be proud of her.[157]

Mother Guenvrede's letter of 6 October 1947 wish-ing Aelfrida her heart's desire on her birthday (but only if it was good for her to have it) was followed next day by 'great news' from 'precious Alethea': she had arranged a passage home at last and would arrive in England soon after Easter 1948.[158]

Aelfrida greeted the news with mixed feelings. On the one hand, Alethea's decision to spend much of her leave at Malling or in Oxford near Father O'Brien and the SSJE worried her so much lest Alethea had '*still* not accepted God's NO' but continued to hanker after the 'Religious Life' and because of the deleterious effect of enclosure on her daughter's 'health [and] reason' that, forgetting Alethea now had 'private means' of her own, she decided to discontinue Alethea's allowance should the latter try to enter the Religious Life for the third time in the hope that, *sans dot*, dowerless Alethea would be prevented from making what her mother (a con-noisseur of such things) regarded as a wrong move. (A 'very sweet letter' from Malling from her "OSB Mother" Magdalen Mary regarding '"our" own daughter's return' failed to alleviate her fears, though a later letter asking for details of her own circumstances because "as I have no hopes of seeing you it is important that … I know HOW YOU ARE", proved that both her Mothers-in-Christ took continuing interest in her physical and spiritual welfare.)[159] On the other hand, she might not live to greet her daughter, God in His wisdom ensuring that what she had offered a decade earlier on achieving her ambition of becoming an SSC tertiary i.e. never to see Alethea again, would come to pass.[160] Something to Aelfrida's disappointment, He did not.

Torn between a desire to love Alethea 'with detachment' and with 'ordinary mother-love' (she saw no irony in her use of the word 'ordinary' in relation to her version of 'mother-love'), Aelfrida plumped for what she regarded as her daughter's 'right': the latter. Her reasons are interesting: there was 'nothing in a tertiary's vocation to forbid … ordinary mother-love', a lesson perhaps learnt from Mrs Lovell; to prioritise her own wish and need for 'detachment' would be a manifestation of 'Higher Selfishness … (worse even than the Higher Twaddle!)', a change of heart in one who had supposedly abandoned 'human affections'; although, given the choice, she might have chosen (*sic*) never to see her remaining daughter again, if God decided to restore Alethea to her ('I assume – she isn't here yet'), Alethea 'deserved' all the joy her mother could provide.[161]

As the date of Alethea's arrival drew closer and meeting seemed inevitable, diary entries demonstrate both tensions felt and ambiguities inherent in Aelfrida's relationship with her daughter. Vivid visions of telling significance: 'Our Lord before me' on a still dark night – by inference a John of the Cross *noche oscura* – 'His breast afire, His heart literally *fornax ardens caritas*'[162] as if to remind her that here her allegiance lay; a tendency to dwell on her 'unstable, vain and foolish nature' as this affected her relationships with people and with God[163]; creation of 'sin' out of 'a *glorious* day in Cambridge' encompassing lunch at Jesus Lodge, tea at Wetenhall Cottage, and 'a brief interlude at ex-Fordfield' to thank the Sisters for a birthday present of 'a basket of superb grapes'[164] persuading her of her intrinsically and unremittingly 'evil nature'; recrudescence of stigmatic pain on Christ calling her once again by name 'Placida of the Holy Passion', a reminder that she must purge herself 'of *self-importance in* all its forms' prior to Alethea's arrival ('I am sure this diary must be full of self-importance if only I could see it!')[165]; a decision not to undertake activities 'contrary to [her] vocation to Silence' on which Alethea would pour scorn because she would see them for what they were, namely 'silly ideas … pretending to be "guidance"' such as offering to give 'a little spiritual help at Girton' during Lent, a notion inspired by the Bishop having told her of his wish to appoint 'some kind of woman spiritual adviser' for that college and Newnham[166]; unusual interest in signs and portents such as visitations from a white owl, inhabitant of Lolworth church tower, announcing deaths in the village (not, it seems, her own) or an

'unpredicted comet', visible from the hemisphere from which Alethea would shortly set sail, suggestive of the imminence of a *Dies Irae*.[167]

News that Alethea's ship was due to dock at Southampton on Good Friday, the holiest day of Placida's religious year, set Aelfrida's nerves jangling for another reason and may have contributed to her decision not to meet Alethea but have her daughter come to her in Lolworth. (Another reason – physical infirmity – had also applied to Alethea's departure for South Africa.) The news, in fact, quite spoilt her second Lolworth Lent, 'many distractions' (chiefly letters from en route Alethea marked "*à bientôt* – isn't it lovely!") and the consequent difficulty in 'settling down' to 'Silence of a poor quality' causing Aelfrida to regard herself for once as a 'poor Lent-keeper'.[168] A 'Family Council' held to discuss 'Alethea's visits and arrangements' from which Alethea's mother was excluded added to her distress and might have provided 'ingredients for a Family Quarrel' had she not reflected that 'cutting remarks to all and sundry were not, perhaps, the best policy under the circumstances' and that advice proffered to Alethea by Phyllis and Mina that 'conditions in England [had] changed' since her departure was to be taken as possessing depths of meaning into which it was best not to enquire too closely.[169] Dispatching a final airmail to Alethea before she sailed to assure her that 'mother-love' *was* awaiting her in England ('she has had a long period of discipline and … has learned much from it [and] deserves green pastures and still waters now')[170], Aelfrida gave way to a burst of genuine emotion: 'this is a hard cold world and mothers cannot ensure the happiness of their children … and the pain of one's dear ones is far harder to bear than one's own [and] now I cannot see for tears but I do trust her to Him'.[171]

On the night of 27/28 November 1939 Aelfrida had dreamed vividly and, as it later transpired, prophetically, that Alethea returned 'all warm and glowing with life' to reply "yes, really" to her mother's question "is it really you?", only to disappear as Aelfrida put her arms round her.[172] On 3 April 1948 mother and daughter were physically reunited, Alethea 'altered surprisingly little, except that her hair is rather grey' and still dressed 'elegantly though quietly'; she had also retained her 'pretty ways and lovely manners' and looked 'brown and strong and there [was] a sense of *peace* and fundamental joy about her'.[173] (Joan Cooper's 1934 prediction that Alethea would not be 'cured' until separated from her mother separated had, it seems, come true, but Julius' contemporary command that Aelfrida not "treat Alethea as a patient" because the latter's health had been "largely restored" and because "too much fuss" would distress her[174], speaks volumes.) How Alethea saw her mother we do not know (many people were in a position to report so she was probably not as ignorant of Aelfrida's appearance and states of mind and health as perhaps the latter would have wished) but from references in the latter's diary and other writings we may guess: hair silver-white, rather deaf (she does not hear the arrival of visitors and hears names wrongly), very lame (Alethea immediately buys her a walking stick on which she leans heavily), and somewhat underweight (Aelfrida probably attributed her thinness to something other than ascetic diet; a novel written a year later has two sisters comment on a third unseen for some time that she is "rather thin" and that, England being still subject to food rationing, her weekly ration of cheese is "ludicrously small")[175], but otherwise in dress and appearance similar to the mother last seen at St Benedict's in 1936.

Aelfrida's low-key description of their meeting says nothing of the two women's emotions but that both exhibited strain can be gauged by Alethea's complaints of fatigue, by her going out for frequent walks (she had a separate bedroom and sitting room at the rectory, she and her mother meeting mostly at meals), by her staying in Lolworth for only two weeks initially and for much shorter periods thereafter, and by Aelfrida suffering from insomnia and migraine and feeling 'relieved' when her daughter was absent. (She was particularly relieved when Alethea's first visit was over, though both women admitted the visit had been more satisfactory than either had dared hope.) What they discussed in 'long talks about all sorts of things' Aelfrida does not divulge in except insofar as Alethea admitted to 'rather dreading' the thought of returning to England to find her mother still playing the part of a 'pious lady' at Tymawr, to which Aelfrida replied that Tymawr was her spiritual home and that she had felt more at home there 'than ever at Fordfield'. (To her diary she confided that she 'wasn't just a pious lady living there [but] a member of the Community' and that Alethea would never understand her sense of "belongingness".)[176] Alethea also urged her mother to 'be more sociable [and] to visit the village etc., etc.' because '*conversation*' was an art in which Aelfrida excelled. ('What an irony!!' commented one impatient to return – 'thank God' – to Solitude and Silence, there to confine herself as far as possible to 'pure contemplation'; Alethea, she wrote, 'seems to want to edge me back to "the world"'.)[177] It seems, however, that discussion of 'Things in General' predominated over 'Things that Matter' because the latter were still a little too 'vital' to be dwelt on safely[178] and because it was best that Aelfrida's 'nearest and dearest' female relative '*not* know' too much about her mother[179]; indeed, it seems that Aelfrida was more

than content that her and her daughter's love for each other remained 'wholly "in God"' and that neither she nor Alethea exhibited 'possessiveness'[180] by intruding on each other's spiritual, emotional, or intellectual privacy.

Something noted by Aelfrida with 'deep thankfulness'[181] was the change in Alethea's attitude to life from one of introspection, over-scrupulousness, and lack of a sense of proportion and humour to one which showed that she was now emotionally well and happy[182], 'full of God's own peace', 'intellectually … mature'[183], and enriched instead of impoverished by experience. It was, however, Julius, not his sister, who discerned the reason for this; Alethea, he wrote, had "found [a] niche where she is valued and can use many of her gifts".[184]

Among the 'vast numbers of friends and acquaintances' visited by Alethea during her furlough (significantly, perhaps, she was 'obliging but not eager' to visit her father's, sister's, and grandparents' grave in Histon Road Cemetery so Aelfrida went alone on the occasion described earlier), some were some encountered for the first time, notably the SSC Community at Tymawr. Alethea's original plans had emphatically *not* included a trip to Monmouthshire but a request that she visit the convent to collect books belonging to her but left behind by Aelfrida on her departure two years earlier and, it may be, curiosity as to exactly what her mother had been up to during her nine-year sojourn, changed her mind. Her arrival on 12 July 1948 caused sentimentalising on Aelfrida's part for 12 July was also 'precious Agatha's' birthday and this, together with Alethea's presence 'at [her] beloved convent' on such a significant date, made her hope that not only had their respective guardian angels arranged matters in this way but also that Agatha's spirit might be present at Tymawr in order that emotional wounds inflicted by the sisters on each other at Fordfield and Wetenhall Cottage and resulting in one's death and the other's 'unfulfilled' desire for the religious life[185] (a nice rationalisation, given that it was her *own* behaviour which had driven them away and apart) might be healed.

Hilda Harrison, present at Tymawr during Alethea's visit, wrote praising her soft voice and gentle manner and saying of her that "here [was] holiness walking in the world". ('Good!' noted Aelfrida on reading this.)[186] Mother Guenvrede noted that Alethea 'impressed the Community very favourably' and that she personally found her (in marked contrast, one suspects, to her mother) "quiet, sensible and sure of things".[187] (Alethea, so Aelfrida said, was 'not specially impressed' by Mother Guenvrede but enjoyed 'pleasant talks' with Sisters Sheila and Monica.)[188] Returning briefly to Lolworth, Alethea brought with her Aelfrida's 'Tertiary's cross', the plain black wooden cross sent to her in Oxford by Mother Magdalen Mary of Malling and taken by Aelfrida to Tymawr but inexplicably abandoned on departure. Its arrival prompted a vision of Christ standing under it to remind Aelfrida 'in wordless speech' that He had not sent her to Lolworth to make conversation but to manifest His Silence.[189]

Summing up her impressions of Alethea's visit to England, Aelfrida wrote 'I have enjoyed her society to the full. She is so *vigorous* in mind and body and so sweet and thoughtful and *Christian* that any … mother would be proud to have such a daughter'. But her panegyric had a sting in its tail: between the words 'any' and 'mother' she inserted (and emphasised) the weasel word '*reasonable*'.[190] This was not, of course, the first time she employed it in relation to Alethea – of her elder daughter's decision to enter Malling her mother had written that no 'reasonable' Christian could doubt that Alethea had a vocation (subsequent events, of course, proved both women wrong) and it is interesting to speculate exactly what she meant: that she herself was 'reasonable' insofar as she was able to exercise sound judgement in the matter of Alethea's character or was 'reasonable' insofar as she was showing moderation and lack of bias in her opinion? Or was she implying disagreement with a decision with which any other Christian might concur but with which she herself could not because Alethea's decision to devote herself as a single woman to conventual or missionary life put paid to her own hopes of grandchildren as incarnations of Godhead? If so, what we have here may be a coded signal of disapproval of the path her daughter's life has taken and possibly even of jealousy that Alethea, unlike herself, is universally respected and beloved.

Alethea left England on 4 November 1948. On 1 November Aelfrida accompanied her to Cambridge station where Alethea, having found her last days in England 'rather a strain', behaved as '[bravely] and splendidly as possible' and Aelfrida found herself 'hardly … sad' because God was 'upholding [her] as He did when [she] left Tymawr' and because after tea with Veronica at Jesus Lodge she was going to hurtle back (by taxi) to 'beloved Silence and Solitude'[191] in Lolworth.

## Notes

1  GCPPT 1|1|65 18 April 1947.
2  GCPPT 1|1|66 2 July 1949.
3  GCPPT 1|1|65 26 May 1947.
4  ibid. 18 June 1947.
5  GCPPT 1|1|69 5 July 1951.
6  GCPPT 1|1|66 13 October 1948.
7  GCPPT 1|1|65 27 April 1947.
8  GCPPT 1|1|64 18 November 1946.
    GCPPT 1|1|66 24 March and 2 July 1949.
9  GCPPT 1|1|65 21 August 1947.
    GCPPT 1|1|66 12 July 1949.
10  GCPPT 1|1|64 19 November 1946.
    GCPPT 1|1|65 23 August 1947.
    GCPPT 1|1|66 16 October 1948.
11  GCPPT 1|1|65 15 July 1947.
12  GCPPT 1|1|61 28 September 1943 and 28 March 1944.
13  GCPPT 1|1|66 Aelfrida's account of Hilda Harrison's visit is taken from diary entries written between 11 and 17 June 1949.
14  GCPPT 1|1|63 26 April 1945.
15  GCPPT 1|1|65 24 April 1945.
16  GCPPT 1|1|46 13 December 1934.
17  GCPPT 1|1|65 21 April 1948.
    GCPPT 1|1|70 22 May 1953.
18  GCPPT 1|1|53 22 and 23 May 1937.
19  ibid. 3 July 1937.
20  GCPPT 1|1|65 11 May 1948. The National Health Service, funded by national insurance contributions from employed people and providing treatment free at the point of service (dental and prescription charges were introduced later as a response to unexpected demand), was founded on 5 July 1948. Aelfrida, with private health insurance and an innate distrust of anything associated with the Labour Government's 'secular Utopia', makes no mention of this important event in her diary but was happy to use the service when it suited her.
21  GCPPT 1|1|67 23 April 1950.
22  GCPPT 1|1|64 2 November 1946.
23  GCPPT 1|1|65 2 May 1947.
24  GCPPT 1|1|66a Letter from Sister Jeanne SSC to 'dear Sister [Placida]' of 12 December 1948.
    GCPPT 1|1|66 20 December 1948.
25  GCPPT 1|1|64 6 December 1946 and 23 January and 12 March 1947.
26  GCPPT 1|1|64 6 December 1946.
    GCPPT 1|1|65 26 December 1947.
27  GCPPT 1|1|65 4 June 1947.
28  ibid. 4 August 1947.
29  ibid. 4 August and 6 October 1947.
30  GCPPT 1|1|53 6 July 1937.
31  GCPPT 1|1|65 5 June 1947. 5 June is the Feast of Corpus Christi, a particularly significant day for Sister Placida of the Holy Passion and the Society of the Sacred Cross; Aelfrida continued to note such days in her diary but largely reverted to calendar dates after leaving Tymawr.
32  ibid. 6 October 1947.
33  ibid. 30 April 1942. Author's emphasis.
34  GCPPT 1|1|27 26 December 1923.
35  GCPPT 1|1|65 9 May 1947.
36  GCPPT 1|1|45 19 December 1933.
37  GCPPT 1|1|65 9 May 1947.
38  GCPPT 1|1|66 3 June 1948.
39  GCPPT 1|1|63 21 December 1945.
40  GCPPT 1|1|66 15 July 1949.
41  GCPPT 1|1|64 24 December 1946.
42  GCPPT 1|1|66 18 February 1949.
43  GCPPT 1|1|65 10 July 1947.
    GCPPT 1|1|66 15 July 1949
    Stokoe's interest in 'Scientific Determinism' forms the basis for an otherwise inexplicable polemic in Aelfrida's *Christian Old Age* (pp 43–46) in which she defines it as an historic process of predetermination which will continue relentlessly until "the final doom", "no efforts on the part of the human race [nor] prayers to any heavenly spectators of [this] cosmic tragedy" being of any avail. (Though she wondered how anyone "infected with ideas such as these" could bring themselves to "go to church and worship God", Aelfrida consoled herself with the thought that "the man-in-the-street" was not intellectual enough for

"the baleful words … scientific determinism … to disturb him very much".) Harder to combat, she thought, was the contemporary belief "that Christianity [had] been tried and failed": "the greatest disaster that could befall the human race would be the loss of Christianity".

44 GCPPT 1|1|67 17 May 1950.

45 GCPPT 1|1|68 11 August 1950.
GCPPT 1|1|69 20 June 1951.

46 GCPPT 1|1|68 12 August 1950.

47 GCPPT 1|1|69 25 March 1951.

48 GCPPT 1|1|52 23 February 1937.

49 GCPPT 1|1|53 9 April 1937.

50 GCPPT 1|1|45 20 December 1933.

51 GCPPT 1|1|65 9 May 1947.

52 GCPPT1|1|69 25 and 27 March and 9 October 1951.

53 ibid. 22 November 1951.

54 ibid. 23 October 1951.

55 GCPPT 1|1|67 5 October 1950. Aelfrida's 'premonition' with regard to David Wrightson coincided with his father's birthday (3 October) and her own (the date of the entry) and from this and what follows we may deduce she was not as ignorant of Anthony's life as she professed to be.

56 GCPPT 1|1|69 23 October 1951.

57 For details of Anthony Wrightson's 1940–44 career with the MEW, see Lomax, J. pp131–132.

58 GCPPT 1|1|67 5 May 1950.

59 ibid.

60 GCPPT 1|1|69 27 March 1952.

61 ibid. 24 March 1952 and GCPPT 1|1|69a.

62 ibid. 27 March 1952.

63 Tillyard, Ae. *Parallel Lines. The Cambridge Magazine* vol V No 14 19 February 1916 p 313.

64 GCPPT 1|1|69 12 June 1951.

65 GCPPT 1|1|19 31 May and 4 July 1913.

66 Skidelsky, R. Vol.2 p 137.

67 GCPPT 1|1|69 17 July 1952.

68 ibid. 17 January 1952.

69 ibid 25 February 1952. For details of Hubert Henderson's later career, see the *ODNB* vol 26 pp 318–320.

70 GCPPT 1|1|69 17 July 1951 and 25 February 1952.

71 ibid. 17 April 1952.

72 In 1950 British men had the highest rate of lung cancer in the world; having established the correlation to his satisfaction, Sir Richard Doll (1912–2005) stopped smoking forthwith and lived to 83.

73 GCPPT 1|1|69 6 February 1952.
Tillyard, Ae. *The Approaching Storm* pp 286–287 describes a herald arriving by aeroplane to announce what in *Concrete* will prove to be a false dawn by reading a proclamation "in the name of Her Most Gracious Majesty Queen Elizabeth the Second" to an isolated group of survivors of a war and its aftermath which has reduced London to ruins and England to subsistence living and anarchy. Rereading her novel in 1948, Aelfrida found her prescience 'uncanny [because] in 1932 when I wrote [it] no one thought of Princess Elizabeth as heiress apparent' (GCPPT 1|1|66 13 December 1948).

74 GCPPT 1|1|69 25 April 1952.

75 GCPPT 1|1|52 28 December 1936.

76 GCPPT 1|1|56 19 January 1938.

77 ibid. 11 February 1939. The farmer was one of two (related) people to whom Aelfrida unwisely extended loans while at St Benedict's.

78 GCPPT 1|1|69 11 May 1952.

79 GCPPT 1|1|32 7 March 1926.

80 GCPPT 1|1|64 29 and 30 August 1946.

81 ibid. 29 and 30 August and 2 September 1946.

82 GCPPT 1|1|66 18 August and 2 September 1949.

83 GCPPT 1|1|67 24 April 1950.

84 GCPPT 1|1|69 23 and 31 July and 2 August 1951.

85 GCPPT 1|1|66 9 August 1948 and 11 July 1949.

86 ibid. 9 August 1948.

87 GCPPT 1|1|57 30 May 1940.

88 GCPPT 1|1|67 10 January and 8 May 1950. St Lucian's Day is 8 January.

89 GCPPT 1|1|65a Letter from Father Cary to Aelfrida of 5 July [1947].

90 For details of the life of Harold Edward Wynn (1889–1956) see *Who Was Who* Vol. 5.

91 GCPPT 1|1|68 12 August 1950.

92 Tillyard, Ae. *The Fruits of Silence* pp 3–5 (GCPPT 2|18).

93 GCPPT 1|1|64 15 July and 29 October 1946.

94 ibid. 15 July 1946.

95 GCPPT 1|1|64 26 September 1946.
GCPPT 1|1|65 8 May 1947.

96 GCPPT 1|1|64 29 October 1946.

97 ibid. 8 November 1946.

98 ibid. 4 December 1946 and 8 January 1947.

99 ibid. 15 July and 29 October 1946.

100 ibid. 20 March 1947.

101 ibid. 27 January 1947.

102 GCPPT 1|1| 65 8 May 1947.

103 ibid. 27 November 1947.

104 GCPPT 1|1|64 17 January 1947.

105 GCPPT 1|1|66 3 January and 3 May 1949.

106 GCPPT 1|1|65 30 April 1947.

107 ibid. 8 May 1947.

108 ibid. 30 November 1947.

109 GCPPT 1|1|65 8 and 9 May 1947.

110 ibid 1 and 5 July 1947.

111 ibid. 24 July 1947.

112 ibid. 24 July and 9 and 27 November 1947.

113 ibid. 27 November 1947.

114 ibid.

115 ibid. 30 November 1947.

116 ibid. 27 November 1947 and 26 and 28 February 1948.

117 Leen, E. Pt 2 pp 124–134 'The Episcopacy', a sermon preached in Dublin in September 1925.

118 ibid. Aelfrida first read *The Voice of a Priest* on 23 July 1948 (GCPPT1|1|66).

119 GCPPT 1|1|66 23 July 1948.

120 ibid. 19 and 21 October 1948. A *servus servorum Dei* was St Gregory's preferred description of himself as a Roman patrician who became successively monk, papal ambassador, and pope.

121 ibid. 24 and 25 July 1949. Aelfrida's 'surprise' at the 'note of authority' in the Bishop's voice was added as a postscript to her diary entry of 25 July.

122 GCPPT 1|1|67 9 and 14 February 1950.

123 ibid. 19 March 1950.

124 ibid. 5 and 7 May 1950. Aelfrida was so excited at the prospect of the Bishop's visit that she misdated her entry for 4 May ('his Lordship the Bishop is coming to see me!') as 5 May.

125 ibid.

126 Herbert Vaughan (1832–1903), of an old Roman Catholic family, was consecrated Archbishop of Westminster in 1892 and cardinal in 1893. (All his sisters entered convents and five of his brothers took holy orders, a fact which may have influenced Aelfrida's intense desire that Alethea marry in order to provide her mother with priestly and nunning grandchildren). The *Letters of Herbert, Cardinal Vaughan to Lady Herbert of Lea 1867–1903* were published in 1942; their tone is sometimes arch but the cardinal proffers sensible advice. His comments on Lady Herbert's spiritual adventures are, however, rather guarded. Lady Herbert became a Catholic in 1866.

127  GCPPT 1|1|67 7 May 1950.

128  ibid. 7 and 8 May 1950.

129  GCPPT 1|1|68 2 August 1950.

130  ibid. 12 August 1950.

131  GCPPT 1|1|67 2 September 1950.

132  GCPPT 1|1|64 9 July 1946.

133  ibid. 29 and 30 August 1946.

134  GCPPT 1|1|64 24 and 25 August 1946.
     GCPPT 1|1|66 11 March and 4 May 1949.

135  GCPPT 1|1|65 10 September 1947.

136  GCPPT 1|1|66 11 March 1949. Worth noting in this connection is that not only had Aelfrida never been taught (or asked for instruction in) the proper use of a rosary but also that she seems to have deliberately avoided using it in a 'Marian' manner. This may be because she preferred to emphasise its *Christocentric* nature as an aid to reflection and supplication, employing it as a device to assist what she described as her own 'special' rosaries e.g. of the Passion (GCPPT 1|1|65 28 September 1947) and regarding the telling of it as a spiritual exercise designed to promote interaction with aspects of Deity e.g. the Holy Spirit inviting her 'to see something of the world as He sees it' (GCPPT 1|1|67 22 March 1950).

137  GCPPT 1|1|67 3 November 1950 (Author's emphasis). The Assumption was proclaimed an article of faith by Pope Pius XII in 1950.

138  GCPPT 1|1|66 2 and 11 March 1949.

139  Carmelite nun Thérèse of Lisieux (1873–1897) was one of five sisters all of whom entered the religious life; her mother (another possible exemplar to Aelfrida) had aspired to it but, lacking a vocation, dedicated her children to God's service instead.

140  GCPPT 1|1|69 15 August 1951.

141  GCPPT 1|1|56 25 January 1939.
     GCPPT 1|1|69 20 September 1951.

142  GCPPT 1|1|69 15 March 1952.

143  ibid. 9 March 1952. Chapter 2 (pp 37–39) of Charles Kingsley's *The Hermits* emphasises St Anthony's struggles against the devil; her reference to it also demonstrates that this was not Aelfrida's first reading of the book for she used Kingsley's description of Anthony as "Christianly brought up" (p33) to describe her own upbringing when specially anxious to persuade herself or her interlocutor that this was the case.

144  ibid. 12 July 1951.

145  GCPPT 1|1|65 19 January 1948.

146  GCPPT 1|1|62 9 December 1944.

147  GCPPT 1|1|65 22 February 1948.

148  ibid. 30 April 1948.

149  GCPPT 1|1|68 22 July 1950. A poem transcribed by Aelfrida in GCPPT 2|13 entitled *Introducing Modern Poetry* reads more like one of Agatha's than one of her mother's and may have been among the notebooks discovered by Julius in the Wetenhall Cottage attic. Some lines are particularly relevant in the present context: "There was a time / When men sturdily chose between their Heaven or Hell / Till someone remembered / That there was Somewhere Else / A Shadow Land / So our words are shades, / Lingering on in dim and formless thoughts / Where shadows stand and shiver by the Styx…"

150  GCPPT 1|1|69 26 December 1950.

151  ibid. 23 February and 12 July 1951 and 23 February 1952.

152  Tillyard, Ae. *Just Alice* pp 287–288 (GCPPT 2|19).

153  Tillyard, Ae. *Messages* pp 21–27.

154  GCPPT 1|1|32 23 August 1926.

155  Tillyard, Ae. *Just Alice* pp 287–288.

156  GCPPT 1|1|64 9 September 1946.
     GCPPT 1|1|65 10 September 1947. A poem, *Nkosagana's Song,* subtitled 'to be sung by small black children, with actions' ('Nkosangana' was Alethea's name at St Cuthbert's), though undated, was probably written in Lolworth about this time (GCPPT 2|13).

157  GCPPT 3|1|9a Letters from Julius Tillyard to Aelfrida ("dearest Tit") of 23 April and 6 July 1947.

158  GCPPT 1|1|65 7 October 1947.

159  GCPPT 1|1|65 9 November 1947.
     GCPPT 1|1|69a Letter from Mother Magdalen Mary OSB to Aelfrida of 21 June 1951.

160  GCPPT 1|1|65 7 October 1947.

161  ibid. 20 January 1948.

162  ibid. 25 October 1947.

163  ibid. 'Eve of All Saints' (31 October) 1947.

164  ibid. 9 October 1947. Aelfrida's *glorious* day in Cambridge is chiefly notable for her first visit to the (Old) Library at Jesus College. In a poem entitled *The First Day of Full Term October 1947* included in her diary entry for 9 October, she describes the college garden and chapel and Eustace, "The Master, favoured sojourner", arriving hotfoot from 'welcoming freshmen' to escort her up "broad and smiling stairs" through a "private door" to where "light falls on wooden bookshelves, still and tall". "This is the library", he says, ushering her into – her biographer's life.

165  ibid. 26 January 1948.

166  ibid 27 and 30 November and 3 December 1947.

167  ibid. 26 November and 11 December 1947.

168  ibid. 13 and 17 March 1948.

169  ibid. 24 February 1948.

170  ibid. 10 October 1947.

171  ibid. 25 February 1948.

172  GCPPT 1|1|57 28 November 1939.

173  GCPPT 1|1|65 3 April 1948.

174  GCPPT 3|1|9a Letter from Julius Tillyard to Aelfrida of 19 February 1948.

175  Tillyard, Ae. *Just Alice* pp 312–313 (GCPPT 2|19). Statistics inscribed inside the front cover of GCPPT 1|1|65 give Aelfrida's April 1948 weight as marginally over eight stone with chest, waist, and hip measurements in proportion. This places her body mass index on the lowest appropriate percentile.

176  ibid. 5 April 1948.

177  GCPPT 1|1|65 21 April 1948.
     GCPPT 1|1|66 14 September 1948.

178  GCPPT 1|1|18 20 May 1911.

179  GCPPT 1|1|65 5 April 1948.

180  ibid. 3 April 1948.

181  ibid.

182  ibid. 18 June 1948.

183  GCPPT 1|1|66 13 and 24 August and 8 October 1948.

184  GCPPT 3|1|9a Letter from Julius Tillyard to Aelfrida of 3 August 1947.

185  GCPPT 1|1|66 11 and 12 July 1948.

186  ibid. 18 July 1948.

187  ibid. 7 August 1948.

188  ibid. 13 August 1948.

189  ibid. 21 October 1948.

190  ibid. 4 July 1948. Worth remembering in this connection that Aelfrida had once complained of Alethea's bodily and mental 'vigour' relative to her own and Agatha's; her repeated use of the word here may denote an epithet rather than a compliment.

191  ibid. 30 October and 1 November 1948.

# Beloved Silence and Solitude

Alethea departed for South Africa – Aelfrida read the *Itinerarium* for her as the boat train for Southampton left London – and her mother returned to Lolworth, ostensibly to 'beloved Silence and Solitude' but actually to visit a villager with whom she had struck up a pious friendship. In doing so she might have been obeying Alethea's instructions to be 'more sociable [and] … visit the village' even if this involved being '[edged] back into "the world"' or it might have been a ploy disguising a 'longing for Silence' which it was 'best that Alethea not see'[1]; it was neither. Having agreed with Father Lovell that relationships with Lolworth villagers be confined to prayers for their spiritual welfare, to brief salutations, and, if absolutely unavoidable, to short visits not involving the taking of refreshments, soon after Alethea's departure Aelfrida admitted to him that she was helping 'some of the women here in their prayer life'.[2] (To her relief, he approved but interference in other prayer-related matters would prove contentious; what she did not confess was that she was already steeped in village gossip to an extent Lovell might have found disconcerting and was prepared to meddle if intervention by a Consul-General's 'wife' seemed called for.) The woman whose prayer life Aelfrida had engaged herself to help (it seems there was only one) seems to have been chosen because of the similarity of their circumstances: Mrs Lee had been deserted by her husband for another woman and, crippled with rheumatoid arthritis, had had to move in with her daughter.

Besides being an excellent source of local gossip (Auntie Ivy was another), Mrs Lee was very pious. Aware that she herself had already gone 'beyond grace' in trying to 'give *active* help to Dr Wynn in his (*sic*) schemes for a house of prayer' and should in future confine herself 'as far as possible' to 'pure contemplation'[3], it seems that saintly Mrs Lee's 'undoubted spiritual gifts'[4] proved irresistible to one who dreamed of setting up 'a little prayer circle' in Lolworth in which selected women could discuss such enthralling topics as 'Intercession, Petition, Thanksgiving, Penitence, Self-oblation, and Adoration'.[5] The 'prayer-circle' failed to materialise – Aelfrida left practical arrangements to bedridden Mrs Lee and village apathy did the rest – but her sympathetic interest in an ill, isolated, and unhappy woman gained her further entrée into village society.

**Lolworth Rectory c1948**

Alethea's injunctions apart, Aelfrida had been encouraged to diminish the amount of time spent in silence in favour of interpersonal relationships by two spiritual advisers, Father Cary advising her to keep in touch with people 'at all times', cleverly phrasing his advice in terms of *their* 'need' of her not hers of them, and Bishop Wynn informing her that it pleased him to hear of her receiving people's confidences and of her trying to help their 'spiritual difficulties'.[6] Their advice chimed well with Aelfrida's ability to draw people out while revealing little or nothing about herself and allowed her an escape-clause: though her desire to live a contemplative life mindful only 'of spiritual things'[7] must never be subordinated to the secular delights of village life, helping people solve their spiritual difficulties was both permissible and laudable.

On the other hand, a higher authority than spiritual directors had warned her before leaving Tymawr that she was 'taking too much pleasure' in the contemplative life *as such* and was 'irresistibly drawing away from the common lot of simple people'[8] as a result. The 'common lot' was not, of course, something to which Aelfrida aspired except sentimentally or in a very abstract manner but guardian angels must be obeyed, so to the 'simple people' of Lolworth she turned, attending funerals, requiem masses, baptisms, and confirmations and entering into village social life provided events were suitable for one of superior social status and advancing years. She also paid visits to selected villagers (Emily Ansell of the extended Ansell clan, 'a dear old thing, all of a flutter to have a "real lady" call on her'[9], was socially acceptable, but a 'nice old hag' with an illegitimate grandchild in tow[10] was not), distributed produce to 'various cottages'[11], persuaded people 'not expected to bring anything' to contribute to the Harvest Festival[12], interceded ('I do hate Tiffs and Huffs!!')[13] in a long-standing dispute between three brothers and their wives, some of whom were good churchgoers and all of whom were intransigent, and tried to act as peacemaker in a quarrel between Father Lovell and a parishioner with 'a very real grievance'[14] regarding his behaviour towards her; she was also well informed about the marital problems of the village schoolmistress. In truth, Lolworthians were so fascinating that she recounted village life in detail in lengthy diary entries and vivid pen portraits (the churchwarden, for example, whose 'sense of ritual would grace St Alban's, Holborn')[15], voices and dialect were caught exactly (visions and 'shewings' diminish in quantity and intensity as a result), and she wrote of wishing she had more time to write about Lolworth because her life was 'interwoven' with that of the village 'in spite of [her] aloofness'.[16]

Visiting opened other doors too. Arriving somewhat reluctantly at the cottage of an elderly couple (the husband was said to suffer 'senile dementia as "Mrs D" had'), Aelfrida found herself regaled with a 'a perfect stream of reminiscences' of local and Cambridge history[17] – and realised 'how much History [she had] ignored and passed by' during her life because too preoccupied with '[her] self and [her] love affairs and other affairs' to listen to what 'voiceless stories' had to say.[18] Realisation pulled her up short: wherever she had lived, be this Cambridge, Lausanne, Florence, Odessa, Boston, Emden, Paris, Oxford, or Monmouthshire, had been regarded by her not as an interesting place in its own right but as stages on which the current act or scene of her private theatricals could be played out. (The same was true, of course, of people met there, her interest in them being not for who or what they were but because they provided sounding boards for the psychodrama she currently enacted, and of life lived in what she once called 'other people's houses', 'houses' useful only because such real or metaphorical abodes provided a readymade set on which she moved as actor and stage manager.) But it was not until ejection from a place where permanency seemed possible forced her to continue the restless and rootless existence her nature created (and in spite of protestations, craved) that Aelfrida became aware that 'History' *mattered*. When, therefore, Lolworth Parish Council asked her to write an article for the *Cambridge Independent Press* in aid of the church's 1951 Appeal Fund, she did so willingly, including in it both ancient and modern history ("a lady missionary home from South Africa" finding a fragment of Roman glass in a local field) and a plea to contributors to "remember little Lolworth in your prayers".[19]

Tensions between Aelfrida's expressed desire to 'keep aloof' and not allow herself to know 'each and all' of the villagers[20] and to achieve ever-closer communion with God (with, it should be noted, the spiritual assistance of 'worshippers at Lolworth'[21]; her having been a member of the Tymawr Community seems to have engendered a need for community support in one whose aim hitherto had been to be solitary or a solitary) and worries that if she acted the part of parish visitor to encourage people to attend church regardless of Father Lovell's 'personal unpopularity', she might do more harm than good (she restricted herself to establishing 'in secret' a Guild of St Ethelburga with crippled Mrs Lee as its only other member but widened her spiritual horizons by ordaining that the Guild pray for the entire diocese), were compounded by remembrance of having previously turned her devotion 'into active rather than contemplative channels' with marked lack of success.[22] Then too, her guardian angel seemed to be 'definitely barring the way to any active work in the parish', reproaching her with failing to heed admonitions regarding over-much interest in 'secular business' and that she was in danger of becoming ('for kindness' sake') a '*busybody*', reproaches underlined by a vision during a 'special Rosary of the Passion' of the crucified Christ dropping 'a few drops of deep crimson blood … straight into [her] heart'.[23] A year later, however, she noted that she 'had hope' (a significant phrase at this period of her life) that God would 'loosen [her] attraction' to Silence and permit her the 'pleasant duty' of talking to people; to her chagrin, she discovered that God had no intention of doing so, intensifying it instead 'to an almost unbearable degree' and accompanying it with stigmatic pain. At this point her guardian angel intervened again, explaining that her intense attraction to Silence was an aspect of 'the fellowship of Our Lord's sufferings' and that for Aelfrida to feel torn between an attraction to Silence and the 'pleasant duty … of talking' was an 'infinitely precious' sign of further initiation. Furthermore, the pain of '*longing* for Silence' was to be accepted and such 'snatches' of Silence as she was granted 'infinitely prized'.[24]

But whether because of Alethea's advice or because so many Cambridge friends made the trip to Lolworth to see her or gratification arising from the villagers' overtures of friendship to a newcomer, Aelfrida rebelled. Stating firmly that 'intercourse with … dear people … is very precious too'[25], she plunged enthusiastically into an 'external life almost too rich and varied and full of interest'[26], noting of it that 'snatches' of Silence and Solitude notwithstanding, she seemed to talk 'to a good many people'.[27]

As always, she had an excuse for behaving as she did: her life had become interwoven with that of the village 'largely … because of the children'. The children were primarily Mary and Clare Lovell but the village children too, taking smiles for 'advances', opened gates and posted letters for the lame lady leaning on her stick, showed her their toys, pets, and grazed knees, and offered to show her owls' nests to which she was unable to hobble.[28] She responded to inclusion in the 'normal joys'[29] of childhood with great happiness (as physical pain increased and the children reached adolescence, she became more censorious, noting of their noise and habits that she 'didn't *like* them'[30]; for now, she found them 'charming' chiefly because when she made 'suggestions', they obeyed her instantly)[31], arranging with a local farmer to have the long grass on the village green cut so that they could play on it without losing balls and toys, visiting the 'sweet and responsive' classes in the village school to admire drawings and copybooks or to deliver a copy of *Messages* and to give a talk ('alas for Silence') on 'Ancient Lolworth' illustrated by two 'Stone Age flint knives' (from Tymawr 'prehistory', not Lolworth's) and Alethea's Roman glass.[32] She also kept an Easter Monday 'in holiday mood by founding the Lolworth Junior Archaeology Society' (rules and constitution drafted by herself: she was 'enjoying the fun as much as any of them') whose firm financial footing she ensured by soliciting generous contributions from two eminent visitors to its first exhibition (exhibits were 'Prehistoric, Roman, Mediaeval and Bogus', 'bogus' being a gas bracket masquerading as a Saxon crown), opened by Aelfrida in her best clothes and 'Grand Manner': the Master of Jesus College and Emeritus Professor Julius Tillyard.[33]

These cheerful passages in Aelfrida's diaries make sad reading when we realise what a success her life might have been had circumstances been otherwise. Had she become a school teacher – a career which, judging by her experiences at Cambridge's County Schools and at St Columba's Sunday School, would have been immensely successful – she might have enjoyed a happy and fulfilled life. As the kind of inspirational pedagogue remembered by generations of children, a plea of dedication to her work and contemporary expectations that schoolmarms remain unmarried would have saved herself and others much anguish and permitted the physical and spiritual virginity she regarded as essential to her life as a mystic. Retirement after a lifetime of service to education would have been sweetened by visits from former pupils eager to tell her of their successes or, if unsuccessful, to avail themselves of constructive counsel and ready sympathy. Sadder still is that Aelfrida herself realised this, writing of a character in her last novel that he was "at his most lovable with children, telling them stories, inventing little plays for them to act, singing songs in several languages to [his own] accompaniment, showing them how to make all kinds of little objects and … organising a schoolroom exhibition of handicrafts" but that because he was also a "madman" subject to a "mysterious sense of compulsion" that God had other plans for him, he was unable to lead the life he would have chosen.[34]

A career Aelfrida *had* chosen but had long abandoned except in an epistolary capacity was that of 'Straightener'. In Lolworth, however, she seized the opportunity of 'straightening' two younger men.

Her first 'case' involved a young man whose problems were just the sort she loved to treat: in October 1948 she heard that Michael, son of James Stark, Julius' friend from Tonbridge School, had been committed to the Royal Bethlehem Hospital for 'psychological treatment'. His symptoms seemed chiefly of a depressive nature (he had, she noted on meeting him, a gloomy expression 'like a comic artist's idea of a tragic poet'), so after taking counsel from a Cambridge Franciscan as to the correctness of her advice (she was now aware of the dangers of 'soul-doctoring' without adequate – or any – training), she suggested that Michael take up wood carving and live in a small 'not-too-austere' Community following his discharge from hospital. Her advice proved acceptable (Michael was already a Franciscan tertiary; Christ himself had been a carpenter) and a sheltered religious community suitable for a young man who subsequently thanked his 'special friend'[35] for her help.

Her second 'case' ended inconclusively and with an addition to the dozen people for whom she still made reparative adoration. (On learning this, Bishop Wynn asked what she meant by 'reparation' and was she intending further physical austerities? Aelfrida assured him she no longer had the physical strength to submit to these but made reparation through acceptance of bodily pain and 'little snubs and humiliations' and that God regarded this as 'enough'. "*Quite* enough", replied Edward Ely sternly.)[36] Walter Roberts was a Cambridge graduate, a poet, and a wartime conscientious objector living with his wife in artistic squalor ('I declined tea', shuddered Aelfrida) in Clare Cottages near the rectory. Hearing that a fellow-author lived in Lolworth, Roberts extended urgent invitations to Aelfrida to 'talk the language', poetically speaking, with him; he also poured his marital problems into her sympathetic ears to such extent that Aelfrida was forced to warn herself not to 'yearn over [him] too much'.[37] Walter's problems and eventual divorce occupy several entries in Aelfrida's diaries of 1947 and 1948; as a (recently exposed) divorcee herself, she sympathised with a man deserted by his wife and 'divorced but not disgraced' and, 'being [her]self a penitent' for the same reason, preached 'wholehearted repentance and honesty towards God' to one embittered by experience. She also felt sorry for a man 'terribly lonely on the human side' (as she herself continued to be, though because of her 'agonised craving for more Silence and Solitude', could not admit it even to herself) whom 'heaps of priests and people' had tried to help with little success[38] (as they had herself) but something made her draw back: not only did Roberts encourage her spiritual pretensions ('he … flatters me about being spiritually advanced [and] to that kind of flattery … it is so hard to close one's ears *entirely*', an anxiety underlined by a disembodied voice informing her that she did not even come up to her own standards of goodness and asking "what, then, of God's?") but he was also 'very *carnal*'.[39] (Father Lovell termed him 'the poet of lust and lunacy'.)[40] This, and Walter presenting her with copies of poems intended for inclusion in his next anthology[41], reminded her uncomfortably of another 'Cambridge poet': '[he] gets his poems from the region where I got mine when I was in touch with Aleister Crowley'[42] (a possible explanation for writing only comic and religious verse and verses for children after publication of *The Garden and the Fire* in 1916) and in spite of Roberts assuring her that he wasn't as wicked as he seemed (Aelfrida's response was "perhaps I am not as good as I look")[43], she struck him off her list of 'patients' and added him to her list of those requiring reparation. She also noted that Roberts 'alarmed and repelled' her because 'the devil hovered near him'.[44]

Although Aelfrida's activities as 'Straightener' and parish visitor impinged on Silence and Solitude, she contrived her life so that the greater part of everyday was spent therein (it was lack of '*continuity*' she missed most) in spite of 'spirit language' gibes from her guardian angel (couched in remarkably Constantinan tones) that it was 'absurd' (or 'ludicrous' or 'preposterous') to want more silence when she made such poor use of what she had.[45] (His gibe was made two days after Fidelio's first visit.) Reminding herself that her prime desire was to

be nothing but a soul at prayer enjoying 'long hours of silence' unbroken save for 'holy purposes' and enhanced by '*much* solitude', she consoled herself that 'patience, patience, Placida'[46] would undoubtedly see her through the interruptions, much as she enjoyed them.

Calling herself 'Placida' is interesting because of the length of time (over a year) it took 'to disentangle the tertiary's vocation from that of the Sister', to see clearly that God's Will for her at Lolworth differed remarkably little from His Will at Tymawr, and to realise that 'to go out *entirely* from [herself] – to enter *wholly* into [Him] and to be completely possessed by Him' was the 'order of the day' in Cambridgeshire too.[47] Change of residence and lifestyle had been disconcertingly sudden nevertheless, and Aelfrida found re-orientation difficult in spite of consoling herself that it had been engineered by God, not herself (a nice rationalisation), and by reassurances from Father Lovell that he and his household believed that God had sent her to Lolworth and that her presence in house and church was a blessing.[48] Her guardian angel too insisted that there was to be no repining or 'hankering after convent precincts' ('or Saint Rose or Saint Bruno or anything else') though he obligingly promised that 'all kinds of delights and pains and surprises and sensations' would continue to occur in the 'outer courts' of her soul.[49] In spite of this, it took continual reminders that 'an ordinary Low Mass' in a village church came 'just as close to Heaven' in terms of being 'precious and celestial' as High Mass at Tymawr and a vision of the Holy Trinity concentrating its love on her 'wee wee speck of a self' to persuade her that because God had given her so much already, it ill-behoved her to complain of ill-treatment now.[50]

A book described as 'very distressing'[51] when first read in late 1949 (an all-too-appropriate Christmas present, maybe) suggests achievement of insight by other means too. Monica Baldwin's *I Leap over the Wall* is an account of a Carmelite nun's return to the world in 1941 after twenty-eight years' enclosure and judging by the number of pages devoted to it in Aelfrida's diary, its final pages made uncomfortable reading for one who had also failed to ensure that the life she had chosen was an "ought" ("the Will of God for you"), not merely an '*attrait*', and who had also found herself wrecked on "rocks ahead" as a result; who had also found the petty quarrels of women living in 'enclosure' unendurable (it seems that in convents the opening and closing of windows constituted a major bone of contention); who had also suffered a loss of vocation a decade or so after 'profession'; and whose own 'leap' had also been carefully engineered. (And who in 1949 was beginning to wonder if *Lolworth* was the right place for her.) Baldwin's excoriating list of faults with regard to "la Vocation Religieuse" also mirrors Aelfrida's experience: her wanting to be a nun because it "gave her prestige" in the eyes of others, they regarding her with "uncomfortable awe"; her persuading everyone (including herself) that she had "received a Call which must be instantly obeyed"; her private dread that because she "wanted" to be a nun *ipso facto* God must have chosen her; her not wanting to make "great sacrifices" ("the sacrifice of renouncing [her] longing to enter the convent" *not* being one of them) in order to achieve a perfect splendour "too wonderful to be realised" in any other way; her desire to escape from shouldering her share of "dreaded and disliked" family responsibilities. Dissection of her reasons for failure was equally apposite: inability to see her own "faults and tendencies"; "arrogance" in contemptuously ignoring temporal advice in favour of presuming that only God could tell her if she was behaving rightly or wrongly; the "selfishness" on which her religious life was built; forcing herself to live a life which went "savagely against the grain" in a place for which she was not intended, this resulting in spoilage of "that particular bit of the picture" and in defeat of "the whole purpose in life for which one was made".[52]

In fact, Aelfrida had been practising self-criticism since arriving in Lolworth, albeit less flamboyantly than before. Quoting an unnamed work by FW Faber, she noted (too late; hers, labelled as such, were in Girton College's keeping) his admonition that no one should keep a 'spiritual' journal unless ordered to by their spiritual director because "self-love" would be apparent on every page, and that if she chanced to reread hers (she never did), the amount of 'self-love' therein would make her feel 'sick with disgust'. ('And yet', she added, 'I feel the journal[s] should be kept and carefully kept. Surely God is glorified in mine even if I am shown up!')[53] A month later, on, appropriately, Holy Cross Day, the singing of a particular hymn reminded her of an evening many years ago (an event previously unrecorded) when she had chosen Watt's "When I survey the wondrous Cross" at family prayers and Chiara had objected, informing her daughter that the latter did *not* sacrifice "the vain things that charmed her most". ('I was silent', Aelfrida recalled, because 'she was right'.) Was she not still liable, she asked herself in 1947, to imagine 'that one is ready to give more than one does'[54], of particular relevance being a tendency to include in 'the "self-naughting" of the mystic' a 'side glance at Self, to admire it growing feebler'[55]? 'Mystic', however, was now a term she was chary of using. She does not say why, but could it be because she now realised that many of her spiritual experiences were inspired by or mediated through mental disorder or because, as she now admits, she was able to 'suggest'

herself into visions ('seeing' Jerusalem on Palm Sunday 1950 through Christ's eyes 'as he saw it from the back of the favoured ass'[56], for example), an admission with interesting implications for other, seemingly 'spontaneous', manifestations.

In June 1950 she also did some serious thinking on the subject of angels and devils 'according to [her] own experience'. Her conclusions are interesting: apropos angels, she noted that the majority of visions in which they appeared provided 'valuable spiritual experiences' but were 'worthless as giving *objective facts*'. (The criticism did not, of course, apply to her guardian angel whose advice was invariably objective and practical though not now invariably acted upon.) As for devils, she could not 'remember having any *vivid* apprehension of one'[57], a startling statement to which one can only, given revelations of diabolic intervention in previous volumes of her diary, append a surprised '*sic*', a '*sic*' all the more surprised because earlier that year she had experienced the devil 'pouring venomous thoughts' over her with regard to Father Lovell, had announced that the devil had fastened on Lolworth rectory and that she intended to ward off further attacks by practising 'pure contemplation' with all her might[58], and had noted that the devil had 'interfered' with her thrice: 'once at Oxford to keep [her] away from Tymawr' and twice at Tymawr ('as written in my diary, now at Girton') in the hopes of frightening her away 'in order that he might attack the Community', he altering his tactics from 'terrorism' to 'blandishments' as occasion demanded.[59]

Interesting as these revelations are for what they reveal of Aelfrida's ability to write and rewrite her diaries to suit herself, of even greater interest is a comparison between her current thoughts on the place of Silence and Solitude in her spiritual life and the books she read while making them.

Many pages of Aelfrida's Lolworth diaries are filled with records of Lenten and Advent withdrawals into Silence and Solitude, silence by no means as carefully kept as it should have been ('I do hope to … avoid any *consecutive* conversation except if a visitor comes to see me')[60] or 'full of distractions' because of 'almost insoluble problems' posed by the purchase of new soft furnishings for Wetenhall Cottage[61] or by the impossibility of wrapping herself up 'in pious or pietistic silence' when Mina was 'slipping into melancholia' again[62], solitude entered into (in spite of protestations that it constituted an '*attraction*', not a strain)[63] less and less enthusiastically because she was 'conscious of reluctance' to submit to the spiritual discomfort entailed in being undiluted Placida of the Holy Passion for forty days and forty nights. In this respect if no other, she also hoped each festival was her last 'on earth'[64] and in spite of remarks from perspicacious Auntie Ivy ("the six weeks will soon slip away", "do you want us all to wish you a miserable Lent?")[65] was delighted if Julius visited and 'we just talked and talked', a point not lost on Father Lovell who enquired sarcastically if she didn't need 'more relaxation'.[66] She was also careful to obtain Bishop Wynn's or her guardian angel's approval before embarking on withdrawal, possibly in the unspoken hope that either or both would forbid it. Accompanying visions, though vivid, were happily less wracking than before: a recurrent one of an 'invisible ray' or a 'ray of light' shooting from the Tabernacle containing the Blessed Sacrament to pierce her heart or accompanying Christ's voice as He called her by name, on both occasions on the eve of Passion Sunday [67]; at Mass 'the Holy Spirit in the likeness of a Dove' perceived by 'spiritual sight' hovering above her head ('I tried to transfer the vision to [Father Lovell] or Auntie Ivy ... but it persisted')[68]; '*My Lord [opening] His Heart and [bidding] me come in* [to] share His Agony in Gethsemane' ('I did my best ... through four decades of the rosary')[69]; 'angels and archangels in clouds of glory up into highest heaven', their appearance at this calmer period of her life making her wonder 'why I am getting these visions now!', 'now' being Maundy Thursday not, alas, her 'heavenly birthday'.[70] But it is from diary entries detailing her current reading that we learn more of the way her thoughts tended.

As *The Screwtape Letters* or *I Leap over the Wall* show, Aelfrida now read modern as well as less recent theology; she also cites Geoffrey Curtis' 1947 biography of twentieth century solitary William of Glasshampton.[71] She found Father Curtis' book difficult not because she disagreed with the route taken in life by his subject but because it stirred up 'the longing for more silence and solitude'[72] in one who was still 'too much attached to Tymawr as a place of residence' and in spite of discouragements, 'vehemently longing to be a hermit there'.[73] (And who noted of an opportunity for making a retreat at Lolworth during the Lovells' absence that she would have loved to have done so 'but as kind friends asked to come, [she] thought it was wise to fit them in when the Lovells were away', 'actively painful' though it was to be deprived of silence and solitude[74]; in fact, she paid one visit during the fortnight and received nine.) Even more revealingly, though she disliked William as a person because he had remained in the 'stage of excessive preoccupation with the state of [his] soul and with God's gifts' which she herself believed she had left behind, experiencing in exchange 'wonderful, *wonderful* ... awestruck abandonment' to God and the 'joy [and] darkness [and] always, always peace' which resulted therefrom, Aelfrida

identified with the lack of sympathetic recognition his eremetical calling received ('strange that none of the wise priests or Religious whom he knew *saw* what his vocation was') and drew parallels between her own '*call*' to be a tertiary and his to be a hermit-monk. She also noted with reference to life at Lolworth and thereafter (an increasingly likely prospect) that because she too had been 'strengthened by the coenobitic life' (William lived with the Cowley Fathers for some months), she was now able 'to go out and engage the devil in single combat'[75] whenever or wherever he manifested himself.

February and March 1951 found Aelfrida deep in Thomas Merton's autobiography *Elected Silence* and in his history of the Trappist Order and description of life in a modern Cistercian monastery of strict observance, *The Waters of Silence*.[76] As with William of Glasshampton, she found Merton's personality uncongenial and disagreed with much of what he wrote; indeed, she went so far as to describe him as a 'detestable young man' who, if brought to Fordfield by Hubert Henderson when a fellow of Clare, she would not have invited again because he was 'cheap and vulgar', agreed with Eustace that Merton's books were 'religious journalism', and compared Merton's life and ideals unfavourably to her younger brother's.[77] (Of the last chapter of *The Waters of Silence* in which Merton details the rigorously austere daily routine of a modern Cistercian monastery, she noted, conveniently forgetting a certain period in her own life, that she had 'always' wondered whether '*extreme asceticism*' was God's Will 'even as a means', a point neatly illustrated by Father Lovell 'grimly overdoing his Lent' at the time of writing.)[78] She did, however, feel sympathy for what Eustace called Merton's inability to maintain silence '*in his mind*'[79], a disability equated by Aelfrida with her own and, like hers, dealt with by lowering its emotional and spiritual 'temperature' through the therapeutic medium of compendious cathartic writings.

She had, however, another reason for calling Merton 'detestable': he revealed too much of herself to herself. By pointing us in her diary to the last chapter of *The Waters of Silence*, '*Paradisus Claustralis*', she allows us to discover exactly what made her 'detestable' in God's and, more recently, in her own eyes: that possessiveness of any kind implies ownership of possessions (possessions include people); that if you "own" something your will is attached to its possession for possession's sake (possessions in this context include yourself, owned "with an unshakeable attachment", an uncomfortable reminder to Aelfrida that her 'dearest idol' was still herself); that "even the holiest of things" (prayer, fasting, penances, the liturgy, contemplation) can become "possessions" if you love them as things you "own" or if you act possessively towards them; that because "we are what we love", possessiveness of this kind becomes an end in itself and a point of diminishing returns; that if you love the wrong things (or love the right things in the wrong way) you will become "a living caricature of what [you] are meant to be". Worse still, in view of Aelfrida's recent discovery of lack of vocation to Holy Poverty, were Merton's views on the need for total renunciation of body and will "in order that God can assume command of them", for how could she profess 'awestruck abandonment' to God and yet deny herself Holy Poverty? (And hate it because she could not bring herself to practise it or pretend that Poverty meant "just material things" and play at doing without them?) And had she not been so guilty of unwillingness to subscribe to the teachings and trainings of coenobitic life at Tymawr that she became a crank "seeking refuge in a skein of peculiarities" (living in "private corners", upsetting the Community by allowing "movements of [the] interior life" to appear as "eccentric devotional practices"), someone who implied that she was the only one at Tymawr "who [knew] anything about the spiritual life" and refused to ally herself "with all the others … united in the same love of God" as a result? Had she not said in effect "I am a solitary, living in community [but] my interior life is my own and I will live as one, inside myself"? Had she not had to "jump over the wall and run away" when she realised that she had utterly failed to love her companions "in God and for His sake" but had practised an impersonal and fruitless 'charity' which she mistook for *caritas*? And did all this mean she would *never* be able to drink the waters of silence and peace, Christ's "fountain of water springing up into life everlasting"?[80]

The final chapter of *Elected Silence* is even more discomfiting because it bears on events in Aelfrida's life which sentenced her to life lived in denial of 'human consolations' and to 'extreme asceticism' in Oxford. Speaking (in italics) to Merton, Christ promises him what he desires ("I will lead you into solitude … And your solitude will bear immense fruit in the souls of men you will never see on earth") but warns him that solitude (like any other "possession") has a dark side because of what it suggests forsaking and being forsaken, rejection and reduction and being reduced, and being "left alone" in a "desert" of one's own making because one is following a teacher not of this earth into a place not of this earth either. Achievement is also painful because the seeker after solitude will find that the world is "armed against him" and that everything in it sears and burns as he detaches himself from it; he will also find that love and all "created" joys (such joys include talents and even the "pleasures of prayer") become sickening. Finally, says

Christ, when "you have been praised a little and loved a little I will take away all your gifts and all your love and all your praise and in that day you shall begin to possess the solitude you have so long desired".[81] Threats so terrible that Aelfrida was moved – though not immediately – to amend her life more than she had already done (prior to reading Merton and remembering the damage done to her own daughters by her desire to possess them, she condemned Mina's 'possessiveness' of Constance)[82] and, as if by putting them in literary form she could remind herself of them more securely, to include many points made (and some actions carried out) by 'detestable young' Merton in a novel written contemporaneously with reading his books.

Other books read or reread (she does not always reveal previous familiarity) also provide insights into later and present views. Of Rendel Harris' *The Guiding Hand of God* of 1905, for example, she asked if 'his detachment was ever complete'?[83], Harris' paragraph on celibacy being less "a special or a superior order"[84] than a *divisive* element between those who practise it and the community to which they belong having perhaps reminded her of his rejection of her mother and made uncomfortable reading for Chiara's daughter with regard to her own marriage, and 'is anyone's?', noting ruefully that although she herself was sometimes '*amazed*' at her capacity for detachment ('nothing and no-one lives or matters for me except … in God'), she sometimes found herself 'not really as detached as [she] thought [she] was'.[85] A hint, perhaps, of her feelings for Edward Wynn though she also admitted to loving Julius and Alethea more than merely 'in God'.

Not content with criticising Rendel Harris, she also wrote critically of herself in relation to what she read so uncritically forty years earlier. Rereading Evelyn Underhill's 'big book *Mysticism*' reminded her of how, reading it for the first time (an occasion un-noted in her diary), she herself was then devoid of either "knowledge [or] good judgement" (rereading *Christian Old Age* had reminded her how little spiritual progress she had made since writing it in spite of decades of "Christian experience" and illumination) and had set out regardless along a 'mystic way' 'altogether strange' to her in the belief that because mystics were her 'spiritual kith and kin', she hardly needed an introduction before engaging with family. (Judging by a list of books read during Lent 1949, she may have Underhill's *Mystics of the Church* in mind here.) Or before turning to God as Father and Holy Spirit or betrothing herself to God as Son.[86]

Rereading Savinien Louismet's three books on Mysticism[87] 'which in the far-off days of our acquaintance seemed like travel-tales of a country … far off and which now tell of familiar places in the journeyings of the soul', reminded her less of the disastrous consequences of obeying Louismet's advice to seek reconciliation with Constantine and more of mistakes made in the spiritual sphere, particularly with regard to 'attaching too much importance to *wonderful* things'. (Coincidentally or not, on the same day that she reread Louismet she recorded the Virgin appearing to her once again in the form of an olfactory sensation of 'flowers from Paradise'.)[88] Wonderful things, wrote Louismet in terms of "visions and revelations", *may* be divinely inspired, especially if they are purely "intellectual" (i.e. have no perceptual element) and occur in "the most secret part of the soul" to which the devil (*pace* RH Benson) cannot penetrate, but they may also be inspired by the devil disguised as an "angel of light", the phrase used by Aelfrida in connection with her 'Brilliant Idea' to offer herself to Dr Noble as an auxiliary 'soul-doctor' at Fordfield. They may also, however, be manifestations of "sensible" (i.e. inferior, sensory) fervour at best or, at worst, "delusions".[89]

To one whose 'visions and revelations' were rarely 'intellectual' but whose acquaintance with the devil was intimate and who in the latter stages of her stay at Tymawr had begun to accept that it was she herself who was mentally disturbed rather than those on whom she projected her disturbance, Louismet's words must have had worrying implications: were her visions, 'shewings' and sensory manifestations merely symptoms (as she herself sometimes suspected) of mental disorder instead of the God-given glories she believed them to be? Was her mystic fervour not passion or zeal for God but a manifestation of her mental 'temperature' being too high, mental hyperpyrexia being yet another manifestation of mental disorder? Was her guardian angel a false 'angel of light' i.e. another means (or as Father Cary put it, a change of tactics) by which the devil controlled the actions of one who had once considered herself so spiritually advanced as to be beyond his reach? Then again, as Louismet points out in *The Mystical Life,* a life spent "alone with God alone" implied more than merely exercising the practice of the presence of God "so much ... recommended by modern writers on spirituality", something Aelfrida in her keenness to follow a spiritual life of her own had conveniently forgotten; it also implied not practising "untruths" in God's Presence (God being omnipresent and omniscient made this difficult), namely that she was a 'widow', never scattered her powers on "passing impressions", and practised "unshakeable humility".[90] Or again, as he points out in *Mysticism True and False,* one of the "two great functions of the mystical life" (the other was "Divine Contemplation") was "Saintly Action"[91], praised by Aelfrida when it was performed by someone

else ("St Theresa sweeping the corridors of the convent" or, as she now realised, by Mother Guenvrede cocking hay and milking cows) but only grudgingly performed (or carefully avoided; there had been rather too much 'saintly action' at Tymawr for one who fought against its imposition by 'Authority' but who now recognised that it encompassed a degree of willingness and spontaneity only just beginning to be apparent at Lolworth in visits to villagers and the school and in refusal to deny herself to melancholic Mina in Lent) by one who recalled with dismay that she herself had written stringently of "ecstasies and raptures" that they were of no value in the Christian life if they resulted in "mere dreaming".[92] On the other hand, "a life hid with Christ in God" by one determined to free herself from "inordinate affection" and other spiritual uncleanlinesses (not *necessarily* those listed by St Paul)[93] might be preferable to one of action; as contemporary diary entries show and as her reading (or, surely, rereading, for the parallels between Susan's and Aelfrida's lives are so close that the latter's must have been modelled on the former's) of Bishop Alfred Lee's memoir of Susan Allibone *A Life Hid with Christ in God*[94] demonstrated, Aelfrida continued to incline towards the 'green pastures and ... still waters' of life in seclusion[95] even when (reluctantly) obeying Alethea's and Bishop Wynn's advice to engage herself with 'the world' in general and Lolworth in particular.

Turning over these conundrums and contradictions in her mind as she completed *Christian Old Age* in May 1947 (and for some time thereafter, cogitations lasting throughout the remainder of the 1940s and into the 1950s), Aelfrida asked herself 'what next?'[96] Although one senses that it was not solely about books that she enquired, what transpired was part two of *The Fruits of Silence*, a promised sequel provisionally entitled – like the first volume's last chapter – *Our Lord's Own Silence* and said to be 'in preparation' in 1944[97] but postponed *sine die* pending the completion of *The Glory of the West* and its companion volume on Christian old age. Beginning part two in August 1947 (Bishop Wynn had read and approved *The Fruits of Silence* in manuscript three months earlier and had encouraged her to continue her 'meditations' on the theme of Silence)[98] but realising that the second book would be harder to write than the first, she decided to spend a week meditating on each chapter before putting pen to paper. ('The ... meditation', she wrote, 'will be more valuable than any account of it' though what she really needed was '*just one year* of *complete Silence*' on which to ponder her subject, a year and a totality symbolically and literally banished almost as soon as wished for by her first meeting with Fidelio for a decade.) It seems too that she approached her newest book with markedly less enthusiasm than before: she was ill and dispirited after the dreadful winter of 1946/47, had recently read Faber's strictures on the self-love 'entwined' with 'spiritual' diaries, had endured (and enjoyed) 'distractions from Cambridge'[99], and had decided that her theme was 'far too lofty' for her. She therefore put the manuscript aside for nearly two years, not 'tackling' it again until May 1949[100] and taking nine months to write what is essentially a booklet. She forwarded it to her 'spiritual father' Dr Wynn on 21 February 1950 shortly after their agreement that Lolworth had had 'more than its fair share of attention' from him (for 'Lolworth' read 'Aelfrida', as her subsequent comment 'God forgive me! What have I done that the Lord Bishop of Ely should be so attentive?' implies) and that 'it might be bad for [Lolworth] if this were to continue'.[101] She also decided that it should be sold at less than cost price 'as an offering to God'[102] and to acknowledge authorship, and in earnest of both decisions, to send fifty copies as Christmas cards.[103]

Her apparently impractical decision not to profit from *The Silence of God* (the booklet's final title) was not as improvident as it seems; true, the booklet was privately published but two signs mandated her extravagant gesture: Tymawr 'thriving' so not requiring more financial help than her annual £5 offering, and one of her Napier Street tenants asking to buy the freehold for £500. Two publishers' refusal of her manuscript (they pleaded 'paper shortage')[104], Julius' recent expenditure of £50 on three hundred copies of a volume of light verse entitled *A Ballad of Wimbledon* (described by his sister as 'very Cambridgey and *very* Duduesque … many very erudite, one all in Latin' with hints of the same 'cloud of bitterness or cynicism' apparent in poems written in Ruhleben), and an unspoken desire to emulate 'Uncle Sir Frank Tillyard' who had just published his *History of British Unemployment*'[105] at eighty-four, may also have influenced her decision.

*The Silence of God* was not, however, published in isolation. Copying out and revising its prequel in September 1946 two months after leaving Tymawr, Aelfrida decided that 'the question of publication'[106] could be settled later. Having already started work on what would become *The Silence of God*, she asked herself early in March 1947 if it was not also her 'duty' to publish 'the little meditations [she] wrote at Tymawr' while enjoying 'the maximum of "retreat"' because they were infused with the 'spirit of the Community'.[107] Discovering from the British Publishing Company, a Gloucester firm who, noting her address, headed their letters 'the Rev ACW Tillyard', that three hundred copies would cost £49, she closed the deal on her Napier Street cottage (she does not say what she did with the sum remaining – over £400 – after

the publication of both books) and by late March 1949 had corrected and returned proofs of her Tymawr 'booklet'. (She was in a hurry to do so because convinced she would not live to see its publication[108] nor, being in the process of reading *The Guiding Hand of God*, was she convinced that she was as 'detached' from it as she ought to be.) Fifty copies of *The Fruits of Silence*, covered in 'stout Cambridge blue paper'[109], duly arrived on 1 April 1949, followed shortly by the bill (paid 'at once'[110], for Aelfrida was a reformed woman when it came to settling accounts; besides, she now had no-one else to settle them for her) and, to her surprise, sold well.

*The Silence of God* was published in November 1950 and included a list of religious books by 'Aelfrida Tillyard'; it was, she said, 'much appreciated'. Appreciation, however, was 'rather a blow' to one trying to be humble and abandoned to the Will of God[111] and who suddenly realised that the contrast between God's Silence and her own was 'simply shattering'[112] and that this was why she had not written (or God had not inspired her to write) a '*much better* book' than *The Fruits of Silence*.[113] She also professed to have been 'baffled' while writing *The Silence of God*, not only because the contrast between God's Silence and her own was so marked but also because 'what I have written is *my* talk not my Lord's Silence'[114]; what, however, she omits to note – something very obvious as one reads it – is that though ostensibly an account of Christ's life and of the significance of His being silent at salient points in it, *The Silence of God* is autobiography.

In two other autobiographical works (*The Young Milliner* and *Just Alice,* the latter begun while completing *The Silence of God*) Aelfrida depicts herself in the guise of a band of sisters (Alcott's 'little women', as it were), each of whom represents a different aspect of herself. In *The Silence of God*, however, she draws parallels between two women and two men and between incidents in their respective lives and her own.

The first woman with whom Aelfrida equates herself is Eve. Eve/Aelfrida lives in the prelapsarian Eden of Fordford, "the fairest quarter of the world", in the midst of an "unfallen, spiritual" family. The family's innocent happiness arouses the jealousy of a 'bad' angel who slithers stealthily into Eden in the form of a snake. "Speaking as angels do", he rouses Eve/Aelfrida's curiosity and leads her to assert her will over God's, to desire knowledge of good and evil, and to claim the right to decide what is good and what evil "without reference to the Almighty". The bad angel is, of course, Lucifer/Constantine who insinuated himself into Fordfield during Aelfrida's absence in Florence (it was to Lucifer that Aelfrida only half-jokingly compared Constantine during her epistolary quarrel with Irene Michaelides) and it is Lucifer/

Constantine whom Aelfrida now describes as a "rebel" against God who, keen to "exalt himself above measure" and to be "lord of what is beneath him" (Lucifer is the angel-creator of Earth among the Stars) rather than "aspire humbly to what is above him", begins by denying God (and by jeering at Aelfrida for believing in Him), goes on to withdraw his homage from Him, and ends by being conscious only of himself and his own brilliance and by exerting pressure over "something that was his own", in Constantine's case, his wife. Worse still, so powerful is Lucifer/Constantine's "ownership" that he becomes not "Lucifer the Light-Bearer" (Constantine, we should remember, once appeared to Aelfrida and her parents as positively effulgent) but God's adversary, "Satan, Prince of the Powers of Darkness" and so powerfully does Satan call Eve/Aelfrida to follow him "by way of self-esteem" that she quits Paradise (via, as the *Cambridge Independent Press* put it, 'The Marriage of Miss Tillyard') to follow her "animal instincts"[115] in a not-Eden world.

At this point Aelfrida becomes a part of "sin-stained humanity" wandering the world "left to its own devices" and to "grossness" and "blindness". The Holy Spirit, however, acting as a "silent guide and companion", urges "sin-stained" mankind/Aelfrida to aspire to and reflect on God, gives a focus to its/her "groping search" for Him with the help of God-created Nature, provides "a sense of *vocation*" which calls it/her to "bold speech and bolder action" and to "solitude and prayer", and finally transforms its/her "feeble internal voice of conscience" into an ability to offer itself/herself "wholly for God's purposes".[116] Sin-stained humanity/Aelfrida now transmutes into Mary ("an heiress with a dowry of devotion" with kinsfolk as "spiritually fitted" for it as the "sires and dames" whose "godward vision" is described in *Heredity*)[117], a "Maiden" (as Aelfrida was not but being of 'virgin-mind' compensated for that omission) "prepared to receive so great a gift", i.e. tidings of the birth of a wonderful child to her. The tidings are transmitted by the angel Gabriel; receiving them, Aelfrida/Mary describes herself as the handmaid of the Lord (is *this* the phrase Constantine heard her cry out as she felt – so she believed – the Spirit of the Lord enter her womb in Odessa?) and prepares to receive "both pain and joy". As Aelfrida did in bearing *her* child, a child who, had it not been a girl, would have been her "God as well as her son" and his/His name Immanuel.[118]

Aelfrida's equation of herself with Mary now gains further nuances. (In view of her dominant personality, it is amusing to find her writing of the Virgin "had you or I met her we might have felt some sweetness like a perfume, emanating from her ... yet hardly noticed that she was there".)[119] Mary's husband Joseph believed pregnant Mary to have been "unchaste" and wished to repudiate her with the minimum of scandal; Mary "took refuge in Silence", intimating that had she tried to explain, "who would have believed her story?"[120] The only gospel to describe events surrounding the Annunciation is Luke's, but Luke, significantly, has Mary, far from taking refuge in silence, vocal in acceptance of a miraculous event she sees no reason to conceal. Aelfrida, on the other hand, frequently took refuge in silence as a means of dealing with Constantine's fulminations against her (to him) inexplicable behaviour and beliefs and was vocal only in her diary (and that to a limited extent, given that Constantine might read it) and in contemporary poetry and prose. Can it be that she is hinting here that Constantine suspected her of extramarital un-chastity (and this at a time when she was propounding marital chastity to him) and that she, confronted, took refuge in silence as the only possible (and the most infuriating) response to hurtful and unjust accusations, Constantine being disinclined to believe her and possibly, like Joseph, inclined to put her away privily? Or is her contextually irrelevant reference to Joseph's suspicions of Mary and Mary's silence no more than an introduction to her principal theme: the Silence of God?

Aelfrida's next move is to liken herself to John the Baptist, "a man whom Silence enlightened" and whom she describes as going into the desert to fast and pray because uncertain of his vocation. In the desert he "sought counsel of no teachers" but listened "to the instruction of the Holy Spirit in his own heart"[121] as she herself had done in 'deserts' of her own making. Her reason for making this particular comparison is twofold: she wishes to underline similarities between John and herself (both were messengers, both seers, both witnesses to 'the Light', both ascetic, and both preachers of repentance for sins committed) and she uses his baptism of Christ to enable her to draw further parallels between Christ and herself, the most important being that she, like Him, became aware after baptism that she too was destined to be (albeit on a minor scale) "both a Messiah and the destined Redeemer of the world".[122]

Aelfrida had long ago set out to imitate Christ as Thomas à Kempis recommended and had, on her terms, succeeded to a considerable extent. What we now discover, however, is the *degree* to which she engineered her life not only to conform with Christ's but also to ensure that events happened in a manner which would enable her to 'imitate' Christ so closely that she could believe herself to be both His human doppelgänger and a reincarnation of that member of the "perfect Unity" of the Trinity most intimately related to her because, like her, an embodiment of "Godhead".[123] Like Christ, she lived her life immediately following her earliest vision of Him in self-imposed 'silence' (adolescent attempts to reveal it and herself to family and friends seem to have been met with incomprehension and may have reinforced silence because demonstrating the inadvisability of premature disclosure of her future role, as she saw it, of preacher and saviour), breaking it only after her stigmatic Vision of May 1913 inspired publication of *The Making of a Mystic* and the first appearance of 'Catharine Sutherland', the 'Straightener' and 'soul-doctor' whose redeeming and messianic guidance of 'Audrey Talbot' set the latter's feet on the right path. (Do 'Catharine's' initials – CS – stand for Christ the Saviour?) Like Christ she then went out into the world preaching, teaching, behaving 'miraculously', even (so she thought) healing the spiritually sick and reviving the near-dead. Like Christ, she was tempted, but being only an imperfect imitation, fell – only to try to redeem herself by means of "the noblest … sacrifice … that can be procured", namely herself as imitator of Christ's own "Sacrifice" of Himself for mankind as an "unimaginably holy … victim".[124] Like Christ, she willingly and intentionally drew down "calumny" upon herself, making herself "to be sin" both for His sake and because of her longing to suffer with her Saviour in order that "unregenerate humanity", chiefly in the form of those who calumniated her but widened in scope as circumstances demanded, might be inspired to repent.[125] Like the calumniated Christ, she refused to say anything in her own defence (grovelling letters presumably did not count but her tactic of never losing her temper 'like everyone else' and of refusing to answer accusations of infidelity or religious aberration by remaining silent speaks volumes in this context), preferring instead to extend "a living Silence, full of prayer to God" over her accusers and to plead that they be forgiven because they knew not what they did in calumniating an imitator of Christ.[126] Like Christ, she was (metaphorically) "condemned, scourged, mocked [and] crucified" but faced her persecutors "with love and pity", not reproach; they, though struck by her calmness and silence in the face of physical injury or "bitter insults", did not realise that they had in her "no enemy"[127] but an imitator of One who nineteen hundred years earlier had unresistingly endured what she now underwent and who, like herself, goaded His accusers with the weapon of silence into behaving as they did in order that His Father's will might be fulfilled. (Christ, of course, did not keep a diary or write poems or *romans à clef* or homiletic books as a means of narrating His story and revealing His wounds in order that "listening souls might marvel and believe"[128] but Aelfrida did, possibly in the hope that a later biographer-gospeller

might make her story manifest to "listening souls" in such a way as to show that notions seemingly bizarre or explicable only in terms of personality disorder might be seen for what they were or for what Aelfrida hoped they were: imitation of Christ.) That this is more than supposition can be deduced from the fact that only after this lengthy preamble does Aelfrida refer to the subject of her title: in a chapter entitled 'The Blessed Sacrament' and filled with synonyms for silence ("stillness", "quiet", and so on), she begs God to fill her heart and mind with His Silence and to become "tabernacled in [her] soul". But the place to which she prays to be led to acquire Silence is one to which she knows she will never return: "the place that I love best … the chapel of a Religious House".[129] Nor will she ever, living, achieve the perfect splendid Silence for which she strains ('Lord, give me Thy Silence – I need it, I long for it') but which she can never attain because it is not hers but God's and because her own 'silence' is 'hardly silence at all'[130] because largely noisy 'talk' about herself.

*The Silence of God* is Aelfrida's last overtly religious and homiletic book. (Her last three completed works are novels and her last but uncompleted work a series of very short stories; all, however, are homiletic to some extent and all include implicit religious themes.) She does not say why but possible reasons are: *The Silence of God* is the apogee of all she wishes to say on religious themes in general and on her '*attrait*' to Silence in particular; writing it, she realises that she was never and never will be a great contemplative because she has no aptitude for *inner* silence and that no-one as vocal in print as herself (and Thomas Merton, also prone to preach what he did not practise) could be considered one; that writing out her past as a means of coming to terms with it will be more profitable, therapeutically speaking, if she spends less time dwelling on how far she has fallen short of perfect 'imitation of Christ' and more on discerning what caused her to fall short by studying her own 'Prehistory' so that she may remedy the defect and move on to another and more spiritually profitable stage of her life, unclear though she is as yet what that stage will be. (Ambiguous feelings regarding the correctness or incorrectness of interaction with the Lolworth villagers in terms of an '*attrait*' to Silence and Solitude provide a clue.) It may be too that she has begun to follow advice: Canon Weekes' letter thanking her for his copy of *The Fruits of Silence* quoted Thomas à Kempis on the importance of allowing God to be the only speaker, other persons, including those who set themselves up to teach, remaining silent[131], and Aelfrida may have understood his suggested epigraph for what it was intended to be: a hint.

Savinien Louismet, re-read contemporaneously with composition of *The Silence of God*, approached the subject of teachers on Mysticism from a different angle, limiting "authentic mystical writers" to seven men and women who in his opinion had truly enjoyed "the soul-experience of mystical Theology" and describing everyone else as "unmystical even when … they … write about genuine Mysticism" because their writings are the "outcome of mere human effort and mere external study of the subject matter" and because they tend to "stray into blind alleys … or into by-paths that lose themselves in a tangled wilderness of metaphysical nonsense"[132]; though his views on 'unmystical' writers were ignored by arrogant Aelfrida in the first flush of her enthusiasm for Mysticism, perhaps as an older and wiser mystic she found them uncomfortably true. Then too, Father Cary (whose death post-dated Aelfrida's 'booklets' on the subject of Silence) dismissed her latest efforts by implication in an article in the Cowley *Evangelist*, not written, he emphasised, "for persons who believe themselves to be called to some highly individualistic life of devotion". Aelfrida, sensing a reproof, 'wondered' if he was 'disapproving' of '[her] Silence', this prompting her to ask Cary if he had 'come across' *The Fruits of Silence* (as he probably had, given that she asked her publishers to send a copy to Cowley) by 'an Anglican Tertiary'. Cary had not nor would ever, he said, read anything issued over that particular pen-name; Aelfrida liked to think his objections were due to her using the adjective 'Anglican' (as opposed to 'Anglo-Catholic') but it is more likely that Cary, learning from the booklet's style and from references made in it that it was by the same 'Penitent' who pseudonymously slated his abilities as spiritual director in 1937 (a slating 'Penitent' herself would have gladly altered 'slightly' – *sic* – that same year)[133], refused to acknowledge its author. And possibly also because he had, ineffectually, advised 'Penitent' that writing books constituted a leakage of spiritual energy and a breach of spiritual silence, a reproof 'Anglican Tertiary' may have recalled ten years later and, following publication of *two* 'breaches' of Silence, acted upon.

Aelfrida's writings on Silence are also interesting for what they omit of lessening enthusiasm on her part for a life spent as exclusively as possible silent and alone. As early as 1948, diary entries eulogising her 'wonderfully conventual life' in Lolworth ('my Communions, Mass, Evensong, my Office, spiritual reading, meditations, private prayer, visits to the Blessed Sacrament') and the 'precious, precious Silence' accompanying her daily schedule, hint that 'human contacts' were increasingly important to her and that protestations to Father Lovell that she '*dreaded*' temptations inherent in longer or shorter visits

to Cambridge ('the world') were made more to impress him than to convince herself. (Or to forbid herself to go; the visit under discussion was actually to Hope House i.e. 'convent precincts'.)[134] Then too, requests to Bishop Wynn that he 'guide [her] about Silence' were accompanied by statements concerning her 'dual attraction' to Silence and to her 'fellow beings'[135] and enthusiastic descriptions of annual holidays at Wetenhall Cottage suggest increasing ennui with a 'vocation' less called-to than wilfully chosen; indeed, it may be said that in Lolworth Aelfrida downgraded Silence and Solitude from necessities of spiritual existence to therapeutic opportunities of recharging her emotional batteries between bouts of socialising and of assuaging the guilt which puritanically accompanied her pleasures. (She also regarded such holidays as well-earned periods of rest and recreation – Retreats, almost – after ten or eleven months 'Rule'.) There were, too, practical problems in living alone and silent in 'private corners' in a household which saw no reason to rearrange its routines to conform to the religious peculiarities of a paying guest, sympathetic to these though the head of household might be; indeed, she was sometimes driven to leave Lolworth during visits by the Lovells' extended families because she found their presence unconducive to either silence or solitude (and their 'cheap lower-middle-class' personalities grating) and when driven by summer heat from her south-facing room to sit in the rectory garden ('an outer court of the church … even in its neglect')[136], found her 'wonderful conventual life' disturbed by Clare Lovell's noisy games and by sounds of village life, both of which, though she complained about them, continued unreformed.

Life was no quieter or solitude more available – she was, she noted, less quiet and less alone – at Wetenhall Cottage. But although she frequently wished herself back in Lolworth, diminution was compensated for by being able, when not alone and silent in the 'overwhelmingly lovely' garden where she had strolled with Constantine 'across the bit of lawn where [Wetenhall Cottage] was yet to be and … love presented no problems and no fears'[137] or in whichever bedroom she was allocated (usually PRAISE; Mina occupied SERENITY and Julius JOY, inappropriate habitations, one would think, for a cyclothymic personality and a chronic depressive), to enjoy the company and conversation of 'people of [her] own kind'. (The phrase is Alethea's, she having given her mother a pep talk 'on the desirability of more conversation' with people of her 'own kind' before departing for South Africa.)[138] In fact, she enjoyed this kind of social interaction so much that protestations regarding the preciousness of silence and solitude ring increasingly hollow and the presence of her extended family becomes increasingly enjoyable because 'my "natural self" loves it'.[139]

It certainly did. Years of denying or deforming her 'natural self' so that it conformed to or was overridden by the 'unnatural' self she professed to prefer (perhaps the punitive element inherent in such an unnatural preference appealed to her) and of persuading herself that silence and solitude 'ought' to be her portion were suddenly placed in proper perspective and given proper balance, Aelfrida now believing that although inescapably back in the world, she was now able to balance socialising and seclusion 'extremely well'.[140] She also began to persuade herself that aspects of life in 'the world', particularly when they involved people of her 'own kind', ought not to be ignored or avoided because they bore important implications for her spiritual development.

Social life centred chiefly on Wetenhall Cottage and chiefly involved people of her own or her parents' generation, for after so long absence Aelfrida found herself out of touch with contemporary Cambridge life. Eustace and Phyllis, both entering their sixties, were, of course, in the thick of it (neither, to her chagrin, allowed her even a glimpse of the state of their souls), the former 'greatly enjoying his existence as Master of a College'[141], the latter tolerating her position as Master's wife. But apart from occasional invitations to Jesus Lodge for 'coffee and a pleasant chat' or visits paid by Master and Master's wife to Wetenhall Cottage during which the company enjoyed 'excellent Intellectual Conversation' (unravelling 'obscure passages' in Milton's 'Latin disputations' occupied one such session; no wonder Aelfrida came to regard silence as absence of 'chatter')[142], attendance at Angela's graduation ceremony (described in detail by her observant aunt with a view to 'copy'), inspection of Eustace's college portrait 'in Holbein style' ('in dim light the picture is impressive, in bright light the colouring is crude')[143], and reports of Eustace's and Phyllis' inclusion in the 'Select Few' attending royal visits to the university ('I like Eustace to grace all these occasions!)[144], Aelfrida's younger brother and his wife largely excluded her from their lives. As did, it seems, their children, for their aunt's actual or virtual absence for a decade from the lives of Stephen, Veronica, and Angela destroyed their former intimacy. (There was, too, the mystery of Agatha's suicide for which they were never told the reason.) Stephen, of course, was unlikely to appreciate an aunt who had made known her views of his pacifist principles by sending him the autobiography of German anti-Nazi activist/pastor Hans Ehrenburg; Angela, a 'fine wholesome girl'[145] in her early twenties but never as close to her aunt as Veronica, was now working in Belgrade, and Veronica herself was rather a disappointment to an aunt

whose talks about God seemed to have done 'no apparent good'[146] and who on her sole visit to Tymawr had, though she attended chapel, admitted to ignorance of 'Scripture' and not made the 'Godward move' attendance might have inspired.[147]

Constance and Walter had seen their aunt during the war and had even more contact with her following her return to Cambridge; neither, however, though 'dear, dear children of God'[148], demonstrated as much interest in religion as their aunt would have liked. Walter, now a Cambridge undergraduate, met with Aelfrida's approval but she was critical of Constance who, having happily abandoned nursing in favour of music, seemed constitutionally incapable of passing examinations, a failure attributed by her aunt to her 'reckless enthusiasm' for extracurricular activities and to a tendency to become 'too emotional'[149] if thwarted or pressured. To Mina, however, she became even closer than at Tymawr and in Cardiff, particularly during Julius' absences abroad to teach or to research 'Byz. Mus.' (Aelfrida's belief that he, now in his late sixties and an 'old man' by her reckoning, would not travel much more[150], was unfounded.) Wetenhall Cottage under Mina's supervision she found 'full of human joys', writing in her sister-in-law's Visitors Book of "golden days of undeserved delight" (Aelfrida's joys had to be 'undeserved', of course, because God was still trying to place 'spiritual enclosure' around her in order to prevent undue enjoyment of 'human consolations'), a line of her own composing which she left Mina to imagine was 'a quotation from one of the lesser Victorian poets!!' She was also delighted to discover that the inscription "The Lord be with You" over the front door had not been taken down[151] and to know that in her absence Julius and Mina used her little house (Aelfrida never forgot that it was *her* house, especially when she found Mina disposing of Graham wedding presents and 'valued possessions of Chiara's' stored on tops of cupboards for over a decade)[152] to dispense 'gracious hospitality to All and Sundry'.[153]

Gracious hospitality encompassed Wetenhall Cottage's first and last wedding, that of Constance to John Hibbs, an enterprising young man interested in transport systems, on 8 July 1950. In fact, July 1950 saw *three* Tillyard weddings ('it seems as if Chiara and the Oracle as well as Agatha and other dear ones are being allowed to look down from Paradise and see the weddings … perhaps so arranged by guardian angels for the convenience of Paradise-dwellers as being less distracting when so placed!')[154]: Constance's to John, held in Cambridge with the reception at Wetenhall Cottage (Aunt Aelfrida's diary chronicled the event in sentimental or censorious detail), Walter's to 'his Danish girl'[155], Bodil Egholm, in Copenhagen, and Stephen's to Angela's best friend Margot Watson[156] in Bury St Edmunds. Aelfrida considered Copenhagen too distant for a lame elderly lady to contemplate and was insufficiently fond of Stephen to have herself driven to Bury St Edmunds but presented all three couples with cheques for £10. She also, though reminded by a recent Easter message ("*For ye are dead…*", 'underlined' for her by her guardian angel), that she was not nearly as dead as she ought to be[157], stated firmly that when in Cambridge she *had* to turn her attention 'outwards rather than Godwards', duress, judging by her enthusiasm for 'five memorable weeks at Wetenhall Cottage'[158], less vile than she would have us believe and accompanied by a lively 'deadness' to spiritual matters unparalleled since her days as a 'Universal Aunt'. It was therefore fortunate (but also rather bewildering) that God was both drawing her towards 'an intenser solitude' and 'wanting' her in Cambridge, a town she enjoyed 'immensely', not least because of 'many happy Dudu days'[159] spent there.

Though diary references to Julius remained both loving and abundant, 'dear Dudu' had been absent from Cambridge and England for the greater part of his sister's first three years in Lolworth and it was not until December 1949 that he and she were properly reunited and not until her extended stay at Wetenhall Cottage in July and August 1950 that they spent more than a few hours alone together.

Julius' departure from Cambridge less than a year after his sister's return seems odd given that brother and sister now lived in closer proximity than for a decade and that each was welcome in the other's residence, but his acceptance in October 1946 of the post of lecturer in Classics at Rhodes University, Grahamstown, South Africa ('he and Alethea will meet!!!' wrote his sister excitedly)[160] within three months of Aelfrida's departure from Tymawr betokened discontent: 'Julius is not happy enough at Cambridge to stay there'.[161]

Julius' discontent was not, as he made abundantly clear, with his sister, but with life in a household from whose '(legitimate) noise and rush and unrest' he was unable to escape, given the constraints of life in a 'cottage'. There was, however, more to Julius' discontent than this: his recent retirement 'from a college and University'[162] which had failed to recognise his attainments in the field of Byzantine Musicology − not, it must be said, a Cardiff specialism and based on research conducted independently of his professorship − had left him depressed and disillusioned, and Phyllis' advice on hearing of his proposed move to Wetenhall Cottage that 'there was no place' for him in Cambridge academia now had presciently 'foredoomed' him to be 'ill-at-ease'[163] in surroundings where he knew no-one except former university contemporaries and childhood friends and where his 'attainments' went unrecognised because it was in Oxford that Byzantine Musicology now had its home and in Oxford (and elsewhere) that the name most closely associated in the 1940s with 'Byz.Mus.' was that of Julius' collaborator, Egon Wellesz.

Though sad at the prospect of parting from Julius after six months' reunion and at a time when she herself felt particularly rootless, Aelfrida was reminded by a recurrence of 'the pain of our Lord's wounds' and by a nudge from her guardian angel that since returning to Cambridge she had allowed herself to become too 'attached' to her brother ('after Alethea, he is the person I love best on earth'; Veronica and Joan Cooper were now unplaced in her affections), that whenever she '*attached*' herself to anyone ('i.e. when I love that person … *not* "in Christ"') they were invariably taken from her, and that because she was too weak to renounce such 'attachments' herself, 'God in his mercy' took them. (Albeit temporarily in this instance, for Julius' post in South Africa was of limited tenure.) But the shock she received on New Year's Eve 1946 was more profound than guilt that a 'spiritual' heart whose permanent position was 'at the foot of the Cross' had failed to put sufficient (silent) enclosure round her 'natural' self to prevent it indulging in 'human consolations' derived from Julius' presence or to silence a sneaking thought that Julius might make better use of his 'materials for happiness'[164] were his adored sister not at Wetenhall Cottage so often or he keeping her company in Lolworth. Sitting alone with Julius beside the drawing room fire at Wetenhall Cottage prior to the commencement of festivities ushering in the New Year, Aelfrida heard her brother say urgently "I want you to come to South Africa. Say you will. I will look after you. We will have a small house … and a black servant to wait on us. I don't mean ever to come back to England".[165]

## Notes

1  GCPPT 1|1|65 21 April 1948.
    GCPPT 1|1|66 14 September 1948.
2  GCPPT 1|1|66 13 December 1948.
3  GCPPT 1|1|65 21 April 1948.
4  GCPPT 1|1|66 28 September 1948.
    GCPPT 1|1|69 20 November 1951.
5  GCPPT 1|1|66 28 September and 4 November 1948.
6  ibid. 20 December 1949.
7  GCPPT 1|1|67 2 October 1950.
8  GCPPT 1|1|64 18 August 1946. Aelfrida, so she says, received the warning during Lent 1946 but does not refer to it in the relevant volume of her diary.
9  ibid. 28 August 1946.
10  GCPPT 1|1|65 24 September 1947.

11 GCPPT 1|1|64 30 August 1946.

12 GCPPT 1|1|65 1 October 1947.

13 GCPPT 1|1|67 30 August 1950.

14 GCPPT 1|1|69 15 April 1951.

15 GCPPT 1|1|64 2 September 1946.

16 GCPPT 1|1|66 18 July 1949.

17 GCPPT 1|1|67 14 September 1950.

18 GCPPT 1|1|64 29 September 1946.

19 The article, entitled *The Legends of Lolworth* appeared under the by-line 'Watchman' in the *CIP* of 13 July 1951; diary references (GCPPT 1|1|69 9 April 1951) confirm Aelfrida's authorship.

20 GCPPT 1|1|64 19 August 1946.

21 ibid. 21 November 1946.

22 GCPPT 1|1|65 28 September 1947.
GCPPT 1|1|66 23 June 1948.

23 GCPPT 1|1|65 28 September and 1 October 1947.

24 GCPPT 1|1|66 21 August 1948.

25 ibid.

26 GCPPT 1|1|67 8 April 1950.

27 GCPPT 1|1|66 2 July 1949.

28 ibid. 18 July 1949.

29 GCPPT 1|1|61 21 March 1943.

30 GCPPT 1|1|69 20 July 1951.

31 GCPPT 1|1|66 18 July 1949.

32 ibid. 19 July and 5 October 1949.

33 GCPPT 1|1|69 14 and 18 April 1952. The rules and constitution of the LJAS were drafted by Aelfrida on the last page of her Visitors Book; the Society's four members were Clare Lovell, the village schoolmistress's twin son and daughter, and a village boy.

34 Tillyard, Ae. *Naomi da Costa, Prophetess* pp 233, 239 and 243–244. (GCPPT 2|22.)

35 GCPPT 1|1|66 24 October, 23 November and 4 and 7 December 1948.
GCPPT 1|1|69 18 December 1951.

36 GCPPT 1|1|66 1948 21 October 1948.

37 GCPPT 1|1|64 9 March 1947.
GCPPT 1|1|65 'Ascension Day' (entry written between 14 and 18 May) 1947.

38 GCPPT 1|1|66 22 and 31 July 1948.

39 ibid. 30 and 31 July 1948.

40 GCPPT 1|1|72 24 August 1955.

41 Walter Roberts' anthology *The Banquet* was published in 1949. It contains poems as autobiographical as Aelfrida's but whose graphic descriptions of modern life (of his experiences as a conscientious objector during the war, Roberts wrote "He must find 'useful work' / or else assist the bloody surgeon's knife / by … carting buckets of cut adenoids". *Letter to Wren* p23) were unlikely to appeal to one whose poetic preferences were more refined.

42 GCPPT 1|1|66 2 October 1948.

43 ibid. 7 June 1949.

44 GCPPT 1|1|73 24 August 1955.

45 GCPPT 1|1|65 11 May 1947.
GCPPT 1|1|66 31 July 1948.

46 GCPPT 1|1|65 9 May and 25 July 1947.

47 ibid. 10 August 1947.

48 GCPPT 1|1|64 24 December 1946.

49 GCPPT 1|1|65 10 August 1947.

50 ibid. 12 and 15 September 1947.

51 GCPPT 1|1|66 25 December 1949.

52 Baldwin, M. pp293–297.

53 GCPPT 1|1|65 27 July 1947. Frederick William Faber (1814–1863) hymn writer, preacher, and theologian, converted from Calvinism to Roman Catholicism and founded a religious community in Birmingham, later incorporated in London's Brompton Oratory.

54 GCPPT 1|1|65 14 September 1947.

55 GCPPT 1|1|66 24 December 1949.

56 GCPPT 1|1|67 27 March 1950.

57 GCPPT 1|1|67 24 June 1950.

58 ibid. 4 and 12 January 1950.

59 ibid. 5 May 1950. Aelfrida dated two entries 5 May but by context this entry bears the correct date.

60 GCPPT 1|1|65 11 February 1948.

61 GCPPT 1|1|67 6 April 1950.

62 GCPPT 1|1|66 6 March 1949.

63 GCPPT 1|1|65 11 February 1948.

64 GCPPT 1|1|66 1 March 1949.

65 GCPPT 1|1|66 2 March 1949.
GCPPT 1|1|67 22 February 1950.

66 GCPPT 1|1|66 22 December 1948.

67 GCPPT 1|1|65 23 March 1947.
GCPPT 1|1|66 3 April 1949.

68 GCPPT 1|1|65 18 February 1947.

69 GCPPT 1|1|67 19 March 1950.

70 ibid. 6 April 1950.

71 There are numerous coincidences between William of Glasshampton's life and Aelfrida's, in part because the lives of men he met also crossed hers (Bishop Creighton, RM Benson, Lucius Cary, even William Collins, Bishop of Gibraltar), more because not only did he actually succeed in becoming a hermit in a hermitage created from the ruined stables of a burnt-out house not far from Tymawr but also because he too was a diarist, a writer, a 'straightener', and an enthusiastic letter writer and had once lived a 'semi-hermit life' in Oxford, albeit without the 'preoccupations about arrangements, finance, future plans etc.' suffered by Aelfrida at St Benedict's. (GCPPT 1|1|65 10 June 1947.) For further details see Curtis' somewhat hagiographic and irritatingly undated account of William's life *William of Glasshampton: Friar, Monk, Solitary. 1862–1937.*

72 GCPPT 1|1|65 8 June 1947.

73 ibid. 14 September 1947.

74 GCPPT 1|1|69 24 June 1951.

75 GCPPT 1|1|65 10 June 1947.

76 For details of the life of Thomas Merton (1915–1968) later Frater Louis OCR, see *Elected Silence,* first published in 1949, and *The Waters of Silence* of 1950.

77 GCPPT 1|1|69 13 September 1951. Aelfrida uses the conditional tense here; Henderson and Merton were not contemporaries at Cambridge.

78 ibid. 18 February and 15 March 1951.

79 ibid. 13 September 1951.

80 Merton, T. *The Waters of Silence* ch 13 pp 267–284.

81 Merton, T. *Elected Silence* pp 374–375.

82 GCPPT 1|1|65 18 December 1947.

83 GCPPT 1|1|66 11 March 1949.

84 Harris, R. p13. It is possible that Aelfrida derived her notion of standing beneath the Cross in order to partake of Christ's view of the world or so as to be shown God in one direction and the Evil One and his legions in the other from a vivid description on pp 2–3 of Harris' book. Her views on Christian Unity may also derive in part from this source.

85 GCPPT 1|1|66 11 March 1949.

86 GCPPT 1|1|67 13, 14 and 22 September 1949.

87 The three books of Louismet's to which Aelfrida refers were *The Mystical Knowledge of God, The Mystical Life* and *Mysticism True or False.* She read all three books when researching *Spiritual Exercises.*

88 GCPPT 1|1|66 11 March 1949.

89 Louismet, S. *The Mystical Knowledge of God* pp 32–35.

90 Louismet, S. *The Mystical Life* pp127–128.

91 Louismet, S. *Mysticism, True and False* pp 143–145.

92 Tillyard, Ae. *Spiritual Exercises* p 211.

93 GCPPT 1|1|66 5 October 1949.

94 Susan Allibone (1813–1854) was an American woman whose life was happy (other than demonstrating abnormal dependence on her mother) until a sermon on the wages of sin heard when she was sixteen convinced her she was a sinner and resulted in a lifelong religious fixation. Chronic ill-health later allowed her a great measure of withdrawal from the world, to greet every new symptom joyfully as a harbinger of imminent release by death, and to revel in a series of exemplary 'deathbeds' before enjoying a prolonged and saintly final one. She also kept a diary, wrote (and received) numerous letters and was an avid student of Psalm 119. For further details see *A Life with Christ in God* (1856) a hagiograpic biography chiefly compiled from Allibone's letters and diary with additional material from essays written by her admirers, among whom was her biographer, Alfred Lee.

95 GCPPT 1|1|66 24 July 1949.

96 GCPPT 1|1|65 22 May 1947.

97 Tillyard, Ae. *The Fruits of Silence* p4 (GCPPT 2|18).

98 GCPPT 1|1|65 9 May and 24 July 1947.

99 ibid. 9 May and 4 August 1947.

100 GCPPT 1|1|66 3 May 1949.

101 GCPPT 1|1|67 10,14 and 21 February 1950.

102 ibid. 2 October 1950.

103 GCPPT 1|1|69 1 December 1950.

104 GCPPT 1|1|66 10 March 1949.

105 ibid. 30 May 1949. At least one poem in GCPPT 2|13 is credited to Julius, others are almost certainly by him, one bears a note in Aelfrida's writing "attributed by me to *Julius* and by Julius to *me*!!"

106 GCPPT 1|1|62 9 December 1944.

107 GCPPT 1|1|64 2 September 1946.
GCPPT 11|66 10 March 1949.

108 GCPPT 1|1|66 20 March 1949.

109 ibid. 1 April 1949.

110 ibid. 10 April 1949.

111 GCPPT 1|1|69 10 January 1951.

112 GCPPT 1|1|66 19 May 1949.

113 ibid. 1 April 1949.

114 ibid. 19 May 1949.

115 Tillyard, Ae. *The Silence of God* pp 4–8 (GCPPT 2|20). *The Silence of God* is not without precedent, being closely based on Book 8 of E Schuré's *L'Evolution Divine* but without its references to occult lore.

116 ibid. pp 9–13.

117 ibid. p 13 (*Heredity* appears in *The Garden and the Fire* p54).

118 ibid. pp 18–22.

119 ibid. p 21.

120 ibid. p 20.

121 ibid. p 25.

122 ibid. pp 26–27. For descriptions of John the Baptist, see *Mark* 1:2–6 and *John* 1: 6 and 23.

123 ibid. p 1.

124 ibid. p 14.

125 ibid. pp 26–27.

126 ibid. p 37. Aelfrida's strategy, particularly with regard to Constantine but also with regard to other calumniators such as Anatolia and Phyllis, is described in a later diary entry. (GCPPT 1|1|75 19 March 1959).

127 ibid. pp 40–42.

128 ibid. p 43.

129 ibid. pp 52–53.

130 GCPPT 1|1|66 19 May 1949.

131 GCPPT 1|1|66a. Letter from Canon Weekes to Aelfrida of 8 April 1949.

132 Louismet, S. *The Mystical Life* pp xix–xx. Louismet's seven "authentic Mystical Writers" are Thomas Aquinas, François de Sales, Jan van Ruysbroek, Henry Suso, Catherine of Siena, Angela of Foligno and Teresa of Avila; all are named or quoted by Aelfrida at some point in her writings on religious subjects.

133 GCPPT 1|1|53 7 April 1937.
GCPPT 1|1|66 13 May 1949.

134 GCPPT 1|1|65 28 June 1948.

135 GCPPT 1|1|66 26 September 1948.

136 GCPPT 1|1|65 28 June 1947.

137 GCPPT 1|1|66 15 May 1948.

138 ibid. 30 October 1948.

139 GCPPT 1|1|65 9 July 1947.

140 GCPPT 1|1|66 16 July 1948.

141 ibid. 19 May 1949.

142 GCPPT 1|1|69 2 and 8 September and 15 November 1951.

143 ibid. 4 August 1951. The portrait is by Eric Kennington RA.

144 GCPPT 1|1|65 25 June 1947.
GCPPT 1|1|66 9 June 1948.

145 GCPPT 1|1|65 10 July 1947.

146 GCPPT 1|1|69 12 May 1951.

147 GCPPT 1|1|63 1 September 1945.
GCPPT 1|1|65 10 April 1947.

148 GCPPT 1|1|65 19 July 1947.

149 GCPPT 1|1|66 29 September 1948 and 1 January 1949.

150 GCPPT 1|1|67 2 May 1950.

151 GCPPT 1|1|66 30 September 1948 and 14 January 1949.

152 ibid. 30 July 1949.

153 GCPPT 1|1|72 28 April 1955.

154 GCPPT 1|1|67 6 July 1950.

155 GCPPT 1|1|66 26 July 1948.

156 ibid. 23 October 1949. The angel was quoting *Colossians* 3:3 (KJV): "for ye are dead and your life is hid with Christ in God".

157 GCPPT 1|1|67 9 April 1950.

158 ibid. 16 August 1950.

159 ibid. 11 July 1950.

160 GCPPT 1|1|64 28 October 1946.

161 ibid. 2 November 1946.

162 ibid. 17 December 1946.

163 GCPPT 1|1|65 24 February 1948.

164 GCPPT 1|1|66 14 January 1949.
GCPPT 1|1|67 4 February 1950.

165 GCPPT 1|1|64 31 January 1946.

# Dear Dudu

'I was', wrote Aelfrida of Julius' proposal, 'both touched and distressed'. 'Touched' because he was a man and a brother so desperate for a last chance of happiness that he was prepared to relinquish wife, home, children, and 'Byz. Mus.' in order to have his beloved sister to himself for the remainder of their respective lives. But for whom was she 'distressed'? Mina? Walter and Constance? Julius? Herself? She does not say. But nor did she give Julius a straight answer; instead, she temporised, warning him she might not be admitted to South Africa as a 'settler' because, presumably, of her age and state of health. Then she and Julius paid a call on Dr and Mrs Keynes (he, ninety-three and 'a rather pathetic old man', she, eighty-eight and '*years* younger in every way') and otherwise pretended to be part of the Tillyard 'family reunited' and 'altogether happy' until it was time to return to Lolworth, at which point she 'forgot' 'it might be goodbye for ever' when she kissed her brother before climbing into her taxi. But if one asks: how *could* Aelfrida 'forget', the answer is in her diary: 'in making the decision to go to South Africa or to stay here', she wrote, 'I *must not* say to myself "do I wish – ? do I like – ? etc., etc." but only enquire one thing "what is God's Will?"'[1]

Furthermore, and although touched and distressed by Julius' proposal, she was not surprised by it and this made it easy to 'forget' she might never see him again; indeed, she had already steeled herself to accept the inevitable. In May 1944 Julius had visited her at Tymawr and during 'the best of all the Dear-Dudu-Days!' asked if he went to South Africa when he retired, would she go with him? She temporised on that occasion too, saying that if ever sent away from Tymawr, she would follow her pillar of fire and cloud whether it led to South Africa or not. (Julius, she wrote, 'quite understood'.)[2] In June 1946, however, with sending away imminent, Julius tried again, suggesting 'that he and [she] should sail away to South Africa together!' At that point Placida had greater matters to concern her than her brother's happiness ('too much "clamour of selfhood"', the devil having succeeded in 'dislodging' her from Tymawr because she 'stood between him and the Mother when he wanted to attack her', and so on), though she also noted that she would not *dream* of encouraging Julius' unfortunate enterprise and that Julius had 'family responsibilities'.[3] (Worth noting here

**Alethea Graham at St Cuthbert's, South Africa**

is that it was *Aelfrida* who suggested in 1938 that Julius emigrate to the country he inexplicably loved after he retired and *Julius* who said it was impossible because Mina would not leave 'her people'.)[4] Julius' proposal of December 1946 was therefore his third and Aelfrida was already adamant that her pillar of fire and cloud would not leave England. And besides, she was in the earliest and most exciting stages of a relationship with another man – Edward Wynn – for '*drab*' though she might be in appearance, she was living disproof of her adolescent fear that 'men won't admire me for ever'.[5]

Insisting 'more insistently than ever' that Aelfrida join him in South Africa (a letter written within months of his arrival suggested she 'try' the life there)[6], Julius sailed on 26 February 1947. (Aelfrida recited the *Itinerarium* for him in Latin *and* English to make doubly sure of a safe journey and a flurry of letters described as '*gracieusetés*!!'[7]

from him to her and her to him accompanied his departure.) Aelfrida's '"natural" feelings' allowed her to express 'sadness' at his departure (she had used Alethea's impending leave, planned for 1948, and God having not yet fully revealed His Will to her as further escape clauses) and might even have tipped the balance (they abhorred the 'ghastly weather' of January 1947, 'such shortage of coal that … domestic heating [was] curtailed', that publication of broadsheet newspapers like *The Times* was temporarily banned, and that Lolworth church at 7am was even colder than her room)[8] but her guardian angel's urgings to relinquish '*all sense of proprietorship*' over herself, to be 'wholly God's', and to 'never, *never* forget'[9] that she was, won the day. She did not join Julius in South Africa and Julius eventually returned to England.

Nowhere in her diary, however, does Aelfrida explicitly state that it was *God's* Will that she *stay*. But had it been God's Will that she go, would she have gone? Or *was* it God's Will that she go and she deliberately failed to record it? We do not know, but further elucidation of her relationship with her elder brother may provide a clue. Had she gone, she and Julius could have been whoever they wanted to be to the world and whatever they wanted to each other: the 'Julius and Aelfrida Tillyard' of an Edwardian postcard kept by Aelfrida for forty years (and sent to Julius to welcome him to Wetenhall Cottage) which included in its view of a Cambridge street the back view of an unidentified couple as they strolled along together[10] speaks volumes of a possible South African relationship.

Julius and Aelfrida had enjoyed an emotionally-intense relationship amounting to co-dependency since childhood.[11] (Both intensity and relationship were recognised by Aelfrida as early as 1900, the year in which she wrote of her brother during a temporary separation that Julius 'never need dread that we shall cease to be to each other what we have always been'.)[12] Julius, it seems, languished without his sister and showed signs of jealousy when she exhibited serious interest in another man ('how Julius loves having me to himself!'[13]; flirtations were dismissed for what they were and because they supported her bruised ego), and nearly married a woman who said of and to his sister "we are very much alike, there is an affinity between our souls"[14] (Aelfrida, so she said, agreed with Nadja's remark) and who in later life and like Aelfrida, suffered a disorder which rendered her 'wild and haggard and emaciated' and looking as if she bore 'all the sorrows of the world' on her shoulders.[15]

In this latter respect, Julius' offer to 'look after' Aelfrida in South Africa has interesting implications: assuming she *was* incarcerated at Tymawr instead of being sent wild, haggard, and emaciated to a mental hospital, was she

discharged in 1946 because Julius, retired and living in Aelfrida's house, would be able to look after her? And was Julius' departure for South Africa less an attempt to escape 'family responsibilities' than a wish to look after his sister by removing her to a country whose novelty and benign climate might alleviate her physical *and her mental* ills? The contention is supported by a passage in a novel post-dating Julius' offer which may also represent something noted only in abbreviated paraphrase in her diary: can it be that Julius actually said to his sister on New Year's Eve 1946 "it is nothing whether I am happy or not … if I could stand between you and all that hurts [you] … Even from the wounds you give yourself I would protect you and all my heart's devotion should heal you"? But although the character addressed is moved by this expression of "human love at its purest, noblest and best" and although the love expressed is "infinitely desirable" to its recipient, the offer is refused, goodbyes are said, and, for the recipient at least, "a clear path lies ahead".[16] As Aelfrida's did – but not south or by sea.

Aelfrida herself wrote lovingly and revealingly of "the brother-sister relationship" in *The Glory of the West,* and what she wrote makes interesting reading in view of what transpired in Cambridge within a year of its revision. In a section entitled "The Ideal Sister", she describes the relationship "as interesting and as delicate and almost as romantically satisfying as the relationship of lovers" and notes that "some men" would be very happy if they had a sister rather than a wife as their "helpmeet" and that the sister/helpmeet in such a relationship would find herself a "far more complete and satisfactory person" than if she had a "career" of her own. (There would also be less friction than in a husband and wife relationship because brother and sister "would have practised mutual forbearance in the nursery" and their sharing and prizing of "early memories" would add sweetness to their love.) Even better would be if widower brother and widowed sister "picked up the threads of childhood" later in life at a point where both could "respect the period when each belonged to someone else" and return to each other's society "matured and sweetened by happiness and pain" to find "in the brother/sister relationship an unexpected harmony and romance".[17]

Aelfrida's prescience – if prescience it was, not a statement of intent – is even more interesting when we find her and Julius reverting after their respective returns to Cambridge to the 'Tit' and 'Dudu' relationship conducted at Fordfield half a century earlier; indeed, of the hero of the novel quoted above she notes that, returning to Cambridge at the start of his third academic year (as she herself had returned in her 'third age') to re-encounter a father from whom he had been separated since childhood and whose description, barring his blindness, is that of Julius (now very much the elderly Oracle's son in appearance), he had also "walked back into his childhood". Even more significantly, she notes that as "a child in his father's house"[18] once again, 'Clive' "need not exert himself to say or do anything in particular – it was enough that he was there" enjoying "the unselfconscious security of a child" in the company of "someone who never hurt him or exercised any pressure on him or exacted anything that he was reluctant to give".[19]

Julius, of course, was the one person in Aelfrida's life who knew (almost or absolutely) everything about her, who accepted her uncritically for *what she was* rather than what she might or ought to have been, and who was probably the only person she completely trusted. He alone also offered her *absolutely unconditional* love, the highest expression of the *caritas* which Aelfrida herself fought long and hard to achieve, and in practising it praised her and listened to her and never snubbed or belittled her, his only reward being the 'happifying' consolation of fulfilled emotional longing for the only person he really loved. He, in return, was the only person his sister was able to love unconditionally with a love described to Alethea as "a kind of quiet lying-open-to each other which has no need of understanding by the *conscious* mind".[20]

Why, therefore, did she not go to South Africa with him? Possibly she felt no need, quiet 'lying-open-to-each other' transcending time and space, but her use of the word 'unfortunate' to describe Julius' invitation suggests that there was more to her refusal than any spoken or written excuse. Earlier statements regarding her relationship to the man whose love for her and hers for him positively or negatively affected all aspects of her life support this contention: 'Do I love him only "in God"? I don't know', written of one of his visits to Tymawr[21] and, a year later, that the love between herself and Julius was becoming 'spiritualised'[22] *at last*. Returning to Cambridge in 1946 she may have expected to find the relationship of 'Sister Placida' with 'Brother Julius' more beautiful than before because it *was* "more ... spiritualised" (she even compared herself and Julius to sibling saints Benedict and Scholastica)[23] and was dismayed to find Julius as possessive as ever and possibly more so now that he and she could spend more time together. (Though possibly not as much as Julius anticipated or wanted: a letter sent by him to Aelfrida at Christmas 1952 notes that it saddens him to think that "of all the time through which we live, so little should be spent in each other's company".)[24] Aelfrida, of course, knew the dangers of possessive love and had no wish to find herself the object of it; indeed, her refusing to even '*dream*' of emigrating to South Africa

with her brother may relate to the pressure exerted on her soul by his '*very* possessive love'[25] and her fearing to surrender to it as she had absolutely surrendered to Constantine's. Or even half-surrender: "there are", she wrote in *The Centaur,* "disadvantages in being married" because a wife or husband "creeps inside your heart, puts [their] hand in the latch of your secret shrine [and] desires to go in and occupy the place which belongs by right to GOD".[26]

Aelfrida was now God's; there would be no surrender, absolute or partial, to Julius. So she spurned his offer.

Departure for South Africa of one of the three people who had '*really*' needed her[27] (of the three, Agatha was dead, and Veronica's relationship with her aunt was no longer as intimate as her aunt had believed it to be) nevertheless left Aelfrida bereft. Whenever Julius was more or less absent from her life (1904-1909, 1912-1915, 1919-1937), she turned to other men for support and consolation (John Forbes Cameron, Constantine Michaelides, Aleister Crowley, Albert Erlande, Willie Searle, and Anthony Wrightson); in 1947 she turned to yet another: Edward Wynn, a man far more 'detached' and much less possessive than Julius but, like him, a man who made no sexual demands on her and who, though he did not offer absolutely unconditional love, acted towards her in the same supportive manner and made her feel less bereft than she might have been. (The person to whom she turned immediately after Julius' departure was Joan Cooper, a woman who had once loved her with 'a kind of aching tenderness' but who now made it clear that she neither loved nor needed Aelfrida any more.)[28] Julius, however, was utterly miserable without the sister who had spurned the offer which culminated a lifetime of unconditional love, she noting that the man who was once 'wild to get to South Africa' seemed 'adrift' there because when bereft of Fordfield and Chiara he had looked to his sister and Wetenhall Cottage to take their place 'and it could not be' and bereft now of both sister and Cottage, it would never be.[29] But someone did take Aelfrida's place, at least in part: her daughter. In late April 1947, "one of the happiest days of [his] life"[30], Julius and Alethea met at Grahamstown (a subsequent photograph of uncle and niece walking along a South African beach is 'Julius and Aelfrida Tillyard' to the life) and Alethea's unselfish 'happifying' of her disconsolate (and formerly appallingly rude) uncle persuaded a man 'very discontented'[31] with his new life to remain for the agreed duration of his professorial position. But no longer.

'Mentioning *depression*'[32] in letters home during Alethea's extended stay in England in 1948 (Aelfrida's notion of therapy was that he join the Church of England), Julius returned, albeit for only two months, in

December 1948. ('Thrills ... Julius is here!' wrote his jubilant sister while making it clear that she intended to hear and say as little as possible about his future plans; Mina, she reported, was 'on the whole' glad to see her husband again.)[33] A visit from Julius' 'own dear self' on 21 December delighted her on three counts: they 'met as if we had only parted yesterday', no mention was made of her accompanying him back to South Africa, and because Julius appeared to have achieved a 'spiritual quickening' akin to her own.[34] By January 1949, however, Julius was 'restless [and] counting the days until he can sail away', but although Aelfrida noted the anguish in his eyes when he said goodbye 'as if he had a premonition that we should never see each other again'[35], she was so busy battling with Father Lovell over the latter's introduction of 'papist' practices into his services and so excited by publication of *The Fruits of Silence* and by Frank Stokoe's belief that God had '*chosen*' him to refute Scientific Determinism, that she put Julius quickly out of her mind and forgot the fourteenth anniversary of 'sweet Agatha's death' as well.[36]

Julius' absence in South Africa nevertheless affected his sister in one important way. (It also affected his wife, for Mina announced that an attack of 'the dumps' was imminent, in fact, a return of 'melancholia' so severe that medical intervention and much family support was required to see her through it, and although Aelfrida ascribed this to Mina being 'full of pique ... that Julius can go off quite cheerfully ... without her'[37], realisation on moving to Wetenhall Cottage that there were three people in her marriage may have been a contributing factor.) On 11 September 1949 she began 'a novel of the spirit', her first novel since *The Approaching Storm* of 1932. She called it *Just Alice*.[38]

Deciding in 1936 that though she had twelve novels in her head 'all word-perfect', she did not 'care a fig' for all or any of them and that she intended never to write 'even fiction with a moral' again because she now looked '*directly* to the glory of God'[39], a reading in 1943 of Dorothy Sayers' *The Mind of the Maker* seems to have reminded Aelfrida that she too remained very much 'the novelist': she still told herself 'night stories', new tales 'flashed up' into her mind and claimed her attention, and she often revisited abandoned or completed but unpublished works (*Aaron Lord, Communist* was a particular favourite), feeling as she did so 'like a mother looking down on a child asleep' or, more macabrely, as if she were 'lifting up a grave cloth from a dead face'.[40] Her reasons for returning to novel-writing in 1949 remain unstated though it is possible that cathartic release experienced on putting pen to paper at Tymawr reminded her of 'the pure joy' experienced when earlier novels flowed 'alive and eager' through her pen and that she required a similar release of tension following Julius' departure for South Africa and turned to (novel) writing as the best means of achieving it. Then too, days spent talking with Julius at Tymawr and since his and her return to Cambridge seem to have re-awakened childhood memories of an era now so far in the past that it and they could be safely consigned to paper, the coincidence of certain events in September 1949 providing the final impetus.

In August 1949 Mina and Constance departed for South Africa to visit Julius; during their absence (the trio returned together in December), Wetenhall Cottage was offered to the Sisters of Hope for the use of convalescent patients. Following re-arrangement of furniture and rooms and the installation of a nun-housekeeper, it proved 'admirably adapted' for the purpose: 'no doctors drawing up in their cars, no tradesmen call [and] no-one is very ill or dies as happens at Hope House itself'. It was therefore with much pleasure and a desire to escape a multitude of Mrs Lovell's relatives that Aelfrida accepted a 'pressing invitation' from Reverend Mother Mary Michael to spend a week there gratis early in September, finding herself somewhat to her chagrin ('did I hear my guardian angel smile?!!' she asked herself) with bed and washstand in the converted drawing room (a male patient occupied SERENITY) remembering 'gayer days' in a cottage full of 'past joys and the presence of dear ones'.[41] During her stay she had a long chat with her favourite cousin, uncle Frank Tillyard's married daughter Kathleen Perfect (the ladies rejoiced in having 'Tillyardness' in common; they had little else and rarely met) and remembered Chiara's birthday on 10 September; she also had a lengthy talk with one of the nuns in the course of which Sister Marie informed Sister Placida that the latter's vocation was to 'save souls'[42] (and how better to 'save souls' than by writing 'fiction with a moral'?) and that there would be 'a high place in heaven' for her if she did, the latter 'quite a new idea' for Aelfrida. Later the same day she had a 'shewing' during which she became aware of the Hope House Community on consecutively different levels ranging from basic 'efficiency, cleanliness [and] good cooking', through 'first rate nursing' and 'Christian *caritas*' shown to patients, to the presence in former Fordfield of the Blessed Sacrament and the 'sacred mystery of the Mass', to the 'All-powerful work of the Holy Spirit bringing the Will of God to pass'.[43] Or in her case, bringing the Will of God to pass by means of a novel 'of the spirit'.

Within ten days of starting, Aelfrida had written three chapters. (They were typed for her by Walter Roberts, currently resident at the rectory because his cottage had burnt down.) Within a month and 'working less than an hour a day' she had written 35,000 words and a week later a further 10,000. (Evidence of concentrated effort is found, *inter alia,* in uncorrected confusion of details of different characters.*)* On 13 November she noted that she was working 'really hard' and that the novel was already 'far too long'; on 24 November, she finished the first draft.[44] Further work took place following Julius' final return to England in December 1949 (their reminiscing at length on their childhood on 16 May 1950 suggests that corrections and emendations may have resulted), the second and final draft being completed on 23 June 1950 with the hopeful comment that its author '*wanted*' the novel 'to let Eternity shine through'.[45]

Sadly, it did not. Lilian Whitehouse thought it 'dull'; Angela Tillyard 'hadn't even *noticed* that *Just Alice* was a religious novel!'[46]; literary agents declined it because "public taste has changed very considerably, especially since … the last war"[47], and publishers deemed it interesting for 'older readers' only and turned it down. Aelfrida was unsurprised (against the flood of what the *Church Times* called unwholesome 'American novels', she had '*no chance*')[48] but cared enough for it because of the messages it contained to keep it among literary effects to be consigned to Girton College. She also – and unusually – allowed Alethea, her chief critic, to read it, stating that she did not want Alethea's "Literary Judgement" or approval (if any) but for her "to know some of the things that went on in my head while you were away".[49]

Alethea did not read the novel immediately and it was not until February 1954 that her mother recorded her daughter's 'Literary Judgement'. (It was all she received.) *Just Alice*, wrote Alethea perceptively, was both a polemic (a *roman-à-thèse*) and a 'Miltonic attempt at justifying God's ways to men'. (It was also improbable, its author being 'too arbitrary' in her characters and too prone to rely on 'sudden calamities' to forward the plot; Aelfrida found the latter criticisms 'absurd' but noted that had she been the novel's reader instead of its writer, she might have agreed. Nor did she note her debt to Albert Erlande's *romans à péripéties* of the 1920s and 30s.) Her account of Alethea's response also, it seems, paraphrases her own reply: noting that *Just Alice* existed as a 'night-story' for years before being consigned to paper, she explains how she began to write it. Musing 'one night, in bed, at Lolworth Rectory' on a particular street in Cambridge and on 'some of [Chiara's] old tales about the townees who lived there', she suddenly found herself 'watching the Marsden family and hearing a don's wife tell a friend that they were "in Cambridge but not of it"', then in the midst of a host of characters who 'lived and moved and acted spontaneously' with whom she sometimes had

'differences of opinion' regarding to the paths their lives would take and over whom she found herself 'watching and listening', loving one, liking another, distrusting a third, and finding a fourth 'selfish'.[50]

*Roman-à-thèse* the novel may be; *roman-à-clef* it certainly is, and as usual with Aelfrida's novels, provides a 'very true picture of the period'.[51] The period in this instance encompasses her own life from early October 1894 (i.e. about the time she began to keep a diary) to the 1950s with their pessimistic questions as to where "atom bombs [will] fall when they … begin to drop".[52] It is also the source of material quoted earlier regarding Frida's brief stay at the Perse School for Girls and of her social insecurity as a 'townee' in a town where "town did not count at all" in the "small and exclusive"[53] academic circles to which she later pretended she belonged ("I was born in a University town … my father and brothers, uncles and cousins were scholars and I lived in surroundings where intellectual gifts were supremely valued"[54], a true statement but not the whole truth), insecurity disguised by the distant manner assumed towards 'common' people lest they discover her 'trade' background. It is also crammed with references to people and events which have already thronged her diary: to a kingfisher, her 'Assurance of Beauty', "like a streak of blue fire"[55]; to the years "when Folk Dancing was all the rage in Cambridge"[56]; to an ex-naval man "engaged in chasing slave-dhows between Zanzibar and the mainland"[57]; to lying awake in Cambridge on a still night listening to "the guns in Flanders" or to "a great … Zeppelin" hovering overhead[58]; to two young girls "lying prone on the grass, gazing at a large tortoise"[59]; to a woman being "professionally forbidden by her doctor from attending an inquest"; to how nice it would be to have a "Dr Joan" in the family[60]; to a house as a prime example of "mid-Victorian bad taste" and to another "gay with … bright chintzes … and bowls and vases of flowers in great profusion"[61]; to a man whose mother "was a Graham of Montrose"[62]; to African natives living in "picturesque beehive huts with their own … church and weaving school" on a veldt "where it is all dark and the devils *swarm*"[63]; to "the reporters of the *Cambridge Independent Press*"[64]; to "autographs of … friends and relations adorning the pages of [a] Visitor's Book"[65]; to "séances where Eusapia Palladino produced most astonishing manifestations".[66]

*Just Alice*, begun as she completed *The Silence of God*, is also an enormously 'vocal' novel insofar as in it she discourses less 'silently' than before on matters concerning which she now feels herself able to enlarge (or to disclose) and which her diaries to date have readied us to receive. She does not, however, provide us with 'astonishing manifestations'; they come later.

The four 'Marsden' sisters are, as expected, aspects of herself which she loves, likes, distrusts, or abhors. When we and she first meet them, they form a close-knit quartet whose only brother has recently died in a tragic accident. (Aelfrida's description of the death-room where the boy lies on a makeshift catafalque under an embroidered pall surrounded by candles and white chrysanthemums, his head turned to one side so that the bruise made by the blow which killed him is concealed and "on his face a strange look of peace"[67] must be an elided account of Conrad's deathbed and of the chapel at Hillside where she 'prayed and prayed' beside Agatha's white coffin.) Then their lives diverge; only much later are they reunited.

The sister whom Aelfrida 'likes' is 'Diana' whose "clear brain [and] scientific mind" wins her a scholarship to Newnham whence she graduates with a first class degree. (Like Alethea and Chiara, she also has "glorious copper-coloured hair and ... indescribable feminine charm".)[68] She marries an ecologist and emigrates to the United States, returning to England after the Second World War. She is also a novelist, her first novel, *England's Best,* having one of her sisters as its heroine. The sister regarded by Aelfrida as 'selfish' is 'Barbara', "fragile-looking" as a little girl but "self-assured, even slightly dictatorial" as a woman.[69] Educated in Lausanne, 'Barbara' becomes an excellent linguist and a teacher enthused by the latest ideas on "*pédagogie*". She marries the widower head of the school she attended ("she ... married the school and ... never pretended to be in love")[70] and uses her children as 'copy' for articles on child education.

The sister whom Aelfrida 'distrusts' is 'Madeleine'.[71] Dark haired, with "clear-cut features, [a] brilliant complexion and eyes shining with intelligence", 'Madeleine' compels attention and likes "being noticed". She also lives "by emotion and not by reason", usually succeeds "in getting her own way in most things whenever she wanted to" (attempts by others "to make her bend to [their] will [send] her into hysterics"), relies on others to "save her from herself and her rash impulses", experiences "premonitions", keeps a diary into which she pastes relevant pieces of paper, and is adored by a group of young men known as "The Smitten".[72] Acting on impulse, she marries an Australian, a charming rotter ("rather a great man, good at all sorts of things ... but he didn't believe in ... there being any difference between right and wrong")[73] who rejects her when he discovers her affair with his best friend. The friend also rejects her and she returns penniless to England where she lies to her family[74], telling them that she is divorced when she is in fact widowed (her husband committed suicide shortly

after she left him) or that she is widowed in order to conceal the divorce she pretends to have had (she also hints at an abortion; was Aelfrida's 1918 'miscarriage' natural or contrived? A baby, as her alter ego notes, "would have been very inconvenient")[75], dresses "jauntily" in a style too youthful for her, dyes her hair, wears cosmetics and too much jewellery[76], and "takes drugs"[77], ostensibly to alleviate headaches but actually because she is an addict. Small wonder then, that the 'Marsdens' decide "Madeleine had disgraced the family"; 'Barbara' threatens to disown her and a relative by marriage "*won't* have" her in her house.[78] 'Madeleine' is cured by being handed over to a masterful lady in black "accustomed to exercise authority" who lives in a charming but isolated house in Norfolk and by being threatened with certification as mental patient if she misbehaves.[79] Recovered and penitent, she meets and marries a good man to whom she may or may not have revealed her past and with whom she emigrates to South Africa. She returns only briefly to England after the Second World War to own up to the lies she has told and lived.

The sister whom Aelfrida 'loves' is the 'Alice' of her title and the heroine of *England's Best*. 'Alice', brown haired with a "singularly serene and happy face", is not an intellectual; she is also a rather passive person to whom life happens. (Some members of her family regard her as "a *treasure*", others call her "goody goody" or believe she suffers from "repressions and neuroses" amenable to psychoanalysis.)[80] She has no ambitions nor can she "bring herself to do any war work" during the Great War though she sends parcels to prisoners of war in Germany[81]; eventually she drifts into an "idyllic" marriage with 'Will Harvey', heir to one of two Cambridge department stores of which the 'Marsdens' own the other. 'Will' is a perfect husband until 'Alice' suffers a near-fatal haemorrhage following the birth of twins and decides that she and 'Will' must live "more like brother and sister" than husband and wife, at which point 'Will' is tempted by other women.[82] The twins, with their marked togetherness, eventually become missionaries in Zanzibar, only to die six months later of yellow fever[83], leaving 'Alice' too depressed even "to reason or think". ('Barbara' believes she is suffering chiefly from "*nerves*".)[84] 'Will' dies too. After the Second World War, widowed 'Alice' gives the family home to a "Society for the Welfare of the Aged", becoming both warden of the new establishment and prime mover in the amalgamation of her former home with the house next door (already bequeathed to "a society for aged clergy and people")[85] in order to create a "House of Prayer" with its own chapel (consecrated by the Bishop of Ely)[86] in the garden.

There are, however, two further twists to 'Alice's' story. The first is discovered at the point at which the reader realises that 'Alice' is both the heroine *and* the narrator of the story, the only 'Marsden' sister, that is to say, who can write on one page of someone that "I missed most of what she said"[87] and on another of a particular summer of which "Alice only remembers one special day"[88], a disconcerting discovery revealed near the novel's end. The other twist is to be found in a life convergent on Alice's own.

Aged fourteen, 'Alice' "wanted to be good and tried to be good but somehow never succeeded in being as good as she might have been". Great longings "for the things of God"[89] rise in her heart, longings she tries to assuage by Bible study, by the study of Comparative Religion[90], and by becoming a Sunday School teacher. Aged fifteen, she meets a priest, 'Oswald Goodman'. He is "tall [and] strikingly handsome", has a soft, musical, rather sad voice, is both ascetic and commanding in manner, and when he prays it is "as if Jesus were [present] too". He also prefers to be called simply "Father".[91] When 'Alice' is nearly sixteen 'Father Goodman' proposes marriage, saying that although she is currently too young they will come together "in God's good time" and that until then he and she will lead "parallel lives of worship and service". Provided "with a lover and an aim in life", Alice wonders how she can become worthy of "the semi-celestial being who had honoured her with his attentions" and why she, a very ordinary person, has been accorded privileges through her dealings with her semi-celestial fiancé. (She cannot possibly possess any "rights".)[92] She also becomes very religious, reading books recommended by her lover (*The Imitation of Christ, The Dark Night of the Soul*) and keeping a copy of Holman Hunt's picture *The Soul's Awakening* in her room. 'Oswald', however, discovers a "religious vocation" and enters Cowley as a postulant; 'Alice', saddened by the termination of their "Understanding" but having always considered marriage to 'Oswald' as a "remote and … incredible" proposition (she is also relieved that there will be no more "interviews" with a lover who has the disconcerting habit of cutting them short by walking away and who has already warned her that their engagement must be conducted entirely circumspectly: "a glance, a wave of the hand [will] mean *everything*")[93], marries 'Will' and follows another path entirely.

'Alice' and 'Father Goodman' meet again when the latter, broken in health and spirit by missionary endeavours in South Africa, is brought back to Cambridge to live in the men's part of her House of Prayer of whose chapel (consecrated on the Eve of Corpus Christi) he becomes chaplain. On the day 'Alice' is reunited with her sisters, 'Goodman' is found dead in front of the altar lying on "a bit of Turkey carpet which had been chopped up into three and put together again end to end" and in the same position as the dying or dead Christ 'seen' by Aelfrida prone on the greensward below her Tymawr window.[94] And Christ, of course, He is.

Reading through the 120,000 words of her first draft in November 1949, Aelfrida realised that the novel's '*moral*' was that 'God could bring Alice by way of an ordinary life and [Oswald Goodman] by an *unusual* life to the same heights of spiritual achievement'.[95] She therefore shortened the book and underlined the moral more clearly (*and* forgot her Christ-figure's name, leaving a blank in her diary record) before passing the typescript round family and friends for their edification. No-one was edified; how could they be? Without recourse to her diary, her allusions (e.g. the importance of Houses of Prayer to the novel's author; ironically, she only ever created one on paper) are meaningless and the mass of detail burdening the text, though deeply significant to her biographer, obscures the meaning of her allegorical autobiography and obstructs the narrative flow of her real biography. Even sympathetic Julius, hearing his sister read *Just Alice* aloud in August 1950, was critical of its being 'a religious novel' (an oxymoron of which he disapproved) and 'contemptuous' of 'unashamedly pious' passages: 'Father Oswald's' mawkish death, he said firmly, 'must be cut out'. 'Yet another lesson in detachment'[96], wrote his sister sadly, for Julius, like everyone else (except perhaps Veronica who engaged her aunt in an 'interesting talk on Autobiographies, especially religious ones')[97] had completely missed her point.

Family incomprehension was a good thing given that Aelfrida's latest 'Autobiography' may conceal an important event under a veneer of fiction, an event hinted at in *The Silence of God* and described at length with regard to 'Madeleine'. To try to elucidate the truth we must return to summer 1911 and to the point at which the Grahams part company, Constantine to return to Emden on 23 June after a brief leave during which he has visited Eric Silvanus in London, Aelfrida to prolong her holiday at Fordfield. Her young daughters are with her, as is her father; Chiara and Julius depart for Russia on 30 June and Eustace, newly graduated with first class honours in Classics, has already left for the British School at Athens where he is to spend the greater part of the next two years. On 6 July Aelfrida receives a 'strange letter' from Eric which makes its recipient wonder 'not that he wrote it', but that he *sent* it.[98] On 10 July she begins a long diary entry 'now I want to tell you about Eric', going on to confide that '[as] you know' (we do not know because none of what follows had been recorded before) she had

25

### EPPING FOREST.

In thee life's moments, blended into song,
Have made thee like an instrument to stand,
Played by the year's fantastic eager hand,
With harmonies that to men's moods belong.
Thy springtime stir doth ape a city's throng,
Where chaffering voices, in some dealer's band,
Stamp the one murmur with coarse money's
    brand.
Thy summer's sound, like lovers, lingers long,
Whose speech is silence of a starlit night.
The red of autumn, staining leaf and tree
With glamour of a sinful world is bright,
With sin that fearless flaunts it to the end.
Stainless thy song, when winter's touch doth
    bend
The wind-swept branches echoing of the sea.

*Cambridge.*

*Epping Forest (To Malise 1910)*

made up her mind on first meeting Eric in 1903 that he and she 'would be friends and very intimate'. After which, she says, she 'bided [her] time' until Eric wrote a 'strange letter' containing 'a sudden outpouring of himself'. (Aelfrida is deliberately ambiguous here: the 'strange letter' is not necessarily the letter recently received and the 'sudden outpouring' occurs 'one July night' but not necessarily in July 1911.) She answers his question as to why *she* does not write to *him* by telling him 'because if I let you see how fond I am of you, you might think I were in love with you – and because in any dealings between a man and a woman there is always someone ready to imply … that love comes in somewhere'. Eric answers 'very outspokenly' (on the back of the sketch of Eric inserted – not stuck – into the volume of her diary covering this period is the poem in which the poet declares he will kill himself if the person he loves loves someone else) but in spite or because of this, she invites him to Fordfield for the weekend. On the Sunday she and Eric cycle out to a 'little wood made out of sunlight and beech boughs … near the Roman Road'. Eric produces the copy of *To Malise* she has sent him and speaks some praise of her 'which brought blushes to [her] cheeks'; he

then gazes 'long long into [her] eyes as though a look were a touch'. They return to Fordfield where she reads him some recent poetry and shows him pictures of himself stuck into earlier volumes of her diaries. Of his departure she writes 'I never saw a man sorrier to go'.[99]

At this point we too must revert to poetry. The first poem printed in the *Early Sonnets* section of *To Malise* is *Epping Forest*. Unlike any other piece of Aelfrida's poetry to date, *Epping Forest* is neither dated nor dateable by context except insofar as it must have been written prior to 1910, the anthology's year of publication. (It is, however, by-lined as having been written in Cambridge.) As usual with Aelfrida's poems it can be read on two levels: as a straightforward description of the well-known forest east of London (never visited, as far as we know, by her adolescent or adult self) or as a metaphorical description of a man of whom Aelfrida is fond and with whom she associates "lovers", the "glamour of a sinful world", and a "sin" that "fearless flaunts" itself.[100]

'Epping Forest' may, of course, have been the Tillyards' nickname for the 'little wood', then a very small forest indeed, but the coincidence of the first letter of 'Eric' and 'Epping' and of his surname with Silvanus, the Latin god of forests, suggests otherwise. So too does Aelfrida's remark shortly after meeting Eric for the first time that although 'beautiful and loveable and intelligent', he was also ('between ourselves') 'a bit of a rotter'[101] – but a rotter, it seems, with whom she wished to be both friendly and 'intimate'. Perhaps she was. Recorded instances of Eric's behaviour (writing to her in 1906 to say he loved her very much, his being the only person who looked unhappy at her wedding – though one cannot imagine that Julius looked too joyful either) suggest greater intimacy than she disclosed and Eric's intention of joining herself and her husband in Odessa a manifestation that there were already three in the Grahams' marriage and that it was only Constantine's intervention which prevented it from becoming a *ménage à trois*. Furthermore, Aelfrida wrote *two* poems entitled *Triolet*. The first, composed at Fordfield on 1 May 1911 a few weeks prior to Eric's visit, has written in pencil after the title 'Thirty! (Twenty-seven)', Eric's age and her own, and intimates that although her mouth "is growing old" it "would be bold / To eyes that always spoke the truth".[102] The second, written in Cambridge on 10 July 1911 and re-titled *To a King's Man* on publication in *Cambridge Poets* two years later, has Eric's initials (EMS) beside the original title but legibly crossed out.[103] (The next but one poem to this second *Triolet* has been cut out; was it the third of a trilogy and did she send any or all of its constituent poems to Eric himself?) Can it therefore be that Eric and Aelfrida's tryst was not their first and that what happened in the 'little wood' was the culmination of and not the opening move in their relationship?

That this is possible is shown by a poem, *Thought and Speech,* written in Emden on 19 February 1911 and dedicated 'To EMS' on publication in *The Garden and the Fire* in the section entitled 'poems about all sorts of things' and an anthology dedicated to 'Cambridge poets' of whom 'EMS' was one. In it Aelfrida begs 'EMS' not to remind her of troubling thoughts she tries to repress ("let them dree / Their silent weird in inmost soul of me") but is not wholly successful at repressing (they remain "asleep" but not "unslain"); at the same time, however, she assures him that she enjoys his letters ("gems of the sea" carried in "bright-sailed skiffs of speech") for the solace they bring to one pining for the 'little friend' whom she hopes to meet again "soon", forbidden fruit though he be.[104] How much Constantine knew of the correspondence we cannot tell; possibly nothing, possibly he, acting 'blind Greek', knew of it but turned a blind eye, complicity allowing him enjoyment of epistolary (or more than epistolary) 'little friendships' himself. As Aelfrida noted, *both* Grahams had 'little friends' while in Emden; she does not name hers and only hints at Constantine's.

So: what *did* happen in the beechwood? Arriving at Fordfield in July 1911, Eric behaves towards Aelfrida 'as though all barriers save one were down'. ('Though isn't that one barrier everything?' she asks, troubled by Eric's ardour.) The following day, they retire to the beechwood, a more secluded place then than now. There Eric explains a curious passage in his recent letter 'about going to extremes' by saying that what he meant was that (and here Aelfrida quotes Eric directly) "if I did lose my – I mean if I became very demonstrative, you were not to think that I imagined you were in love with me". His incoherent protestations leave Aelfrida (so she says) 'a little mystified' though she later confides to her diary that, judging by Eric's behaviour, he seemed 'very *much* in love' with her.[105] So what *did* happen? Oblique references in poems written after the event ("I see the limbs of love arise", "I have had my happiness, now take yours", and so on)[106] suggest that Eric *did* become 'very demonstrative', that Aelfrida responded, and that Eric lost his head or his control or both. Hence Aelfrida's extreme guilt when little Agatha fell desperately ill with gastroenteritis the following month ("Let even my conscience sore accusing be", "sin and loneliness" being her crime and its excuse)[107]; hence too her vow that she "would look no more into men's eyes / And watching, see them with desire grow dim"[108] *and* her keenness to achieve sexual congress with Constantine soon after her return to Emden lest Eric being 'very demonstrative'

had resulted in impregnation, a baby, in this case, being 'inconvenient' indeed.

"Adultery", wrote Aelfrida many years later, "is an ugly word even when it describes an extramarital union resulting from congenial temperaments" because "extramarital unions from whatever motives are apt to lead to the divorce courts".[109] But why, given her 'puritanism', did Aelfrida (as it seems) commit adultery? Her most likely motive was revenge for Constantine's relationship with Hilda Sollas, a woman about whom his wife had recently written and published – in the same volume of verse as intimations of her relationship with Eric Silvanus – two poems for which Constantine made her apologise to their subject. And what better revenge could she take than that of seducing her husband's best friend and best man (and how ironic that Constantine suspected his *mother* of seducing Eric!) and by letting him discover this 'accidentally' by leaving her diary or the notebook containing her poems lying around or, given her enjoyment of 'scenes' and compulsion to communicate, by informing him directly? It is also possible that Constantine's accusations (he could hardly remain 'blind' at this point) and Aelfrida's admission of guilt were described on the pages cut out of her diary in March 1912 on Constantine's instructions. But what happened to the pages? Did she destroy them – or did Constantine keep them in order to maintain a hold over her which would allow him to behave as he pleased while threatening to expose the adulterous behaviour of his pious and puritanical wife if she objected? Or did he retain them as evidence pending a contemplated divorce? This would explain much: Aelfrida condoning her husband's 'extra-marital unions'; her failure to claim alimony, failure being Constantine's condition for concealing her guilt and for consenting to act as guilty party in their divorce; her parents' horror – and subsequent flight to Hunstanton – when Constantine disclosed the matter to Alfred Tillyard and referred to what might be disclosed in public court, and their subsequent inflexible, indeed, almost paranoidally severe behaviour towards their errant daughter until such time as divorce allowed her to appear the innocent party; Anatolia's appalling behaviour in Emden. Furthermore, Aelfrida's pregnancy so soon after Constantine's discovery of her 'extramarital union' must have been more than merely 'inconvenient': whose 'brat', one wonders, did he accuse her of 'spawning'? (Eric, though neither he nor the Grahams could have known at the time, could not have been the father of the coming child though careful calculation of dates is needed to establish this.) Knowing his wife to have been 'unchaste', Constantine may have wished, like Joseph, to repudiate her privily but for reasons of his own (her pregnancy, his career, his daughters' reputations) did not, deciding instead to overlook her daring to look "into some strange man's eyes"[110] because of what she might reveal about himself if he did not. Possibly Aelfrida 'took refuge', like Mary, 'in silence', the least likely action to incriminate her further. Or possibly she, confronted with what Constantine believed was evidence of adultery, took refuge in silence as a manifestation of feelings deeply hurt by an unjust accusation, for 'who would have believed her story' that she and Eric did no more than turn the pages of *To Malise* and gaze deeply into each other's eyes in a Cambridgeshire beechwood one hot July day?

Evidence to support either contention must be treated with caution because provided by Aelfrida herself. First is her diary account of what transpired following Eric's visit to Cambridge: in an effort to explain Eric's behaviour (and possibly her own flustered appearance) Aelfrida ingenuously asked her father if it wasn't 'odd' that Eric had taken a sudden fancy to her. The Oracle, not yet physically and not then or ever metaphorically blind regarding his daughter, replied that suddenness had nothing to do with it, that Eric had been in love with her for a long time, and that Aelfrida's protestations that it was *Constantine* to whom Eric wished to be near were moonshine. To her diary she pretended innocence, asking herself if Eric had really been fond of her for a long time and thought she knew it when she did not; she also noted that after the events of the preceding day there seemed 'no reasonable doubt' that this *was* so but that if the Oracle not drawn her attention to it, she would have persuaded herself that Eric was just 'different from other people', not 'very *much* in love' with her. She also asked 'what's to be done … *now*?' and 'what will Constantine say?' before deciding to do nothing, other than 'manage not to see Eric very often'.[111]

Her *faux naïf* account may have been written for Constantine's delectation (her asking what he would say shows that she intended either to tell him or let him discover that *something* had transpired between herself and Eric, even if not exactly *what*); a version written long after Constantine's death provides further ambiguities. The eponymous heroine of Aelfrida's last novel, *Naomi da Costa,* written in 1954, finds herself in a copse on a hillside overlooking Cambridge[112] whither she has been driven by one 'Marcus Hare'. The weather is very hot, a conflagration is raging in the town, and 'Naomi' is unsure whether the oppressive heat is due to the fire or to an approaching storm. Suddenly 'Marcus' turns to her, telling her that he has something to say to her and that even if "all Cambridge burns" he is going to say it: "Will you marry me? … I cannot go on as I am. For God's sake have pity on me". As he holds his out arms to enfold her,

'Naomi' is seized with panic and runs away, vowing to "put all thought of [him] out of her mind". Days later she is told that 'Marcus Hare' has committed suicide (in fact, he has died of a disease affecting heart and brain) and realises with relief that no one will learn that she and he have been alone together in a hillside copse outside Cambridge or "what passed between them there".[113]

So what did 'pass between' Eric and Aelfrida? The latter's reference in *Naomi da Costa* to heat and conflagration may be merely symbolic but her state of mind while writing (and reliving?) the scene may be gauged from slips of the pen and from her leaving (unusual) gaps in her text as if temporarily lost for words. Her naming her third child Agneta (a name with fiery associations) also suggests that running away and putting her (actual or would-be) lover out of her mind was not what happened in fact. (Nor, of course, did Eric commit suicide though he certainly suffered a disease of the heart and brain with regard to Aelfrida.) Can we therefore assume that in Eric and Aelfrida's relationship there was no smoke without fire, that *all* barriers between them came down, and that they did indeed come together ('marry') in the 'little wood made out of sunlight and beech boughs'? (Eric himself later wrote to his '*chère amie*' that it was 'passing sweet' to be loved and that he would never let the 'new-forged chain' between them dwindle even by 'gossamer thickness'; Aelfrida noted apropos his visit that she missed him and had 'liked having him' and to pacify her husband if he read these incriminating words, she then asked what *was* Eric talking about when he talked of 'love' and noted that 'fond' of Eric as she was, *she* loved 'no man but Constantine' himself.) And can it be that Eric for all 'his own peculiar sweetness'[114], did behave like a 'rotter', making love to his best friend's wife and writing poems to her[115], poems which Aelfrida did not keep because in them Eric described or hinted at the 'sin' she had committed with Constantine's best friend and best man?

13 June 1911 saw Aelfrida return early from Hessle whither she had accompanied her husband. Constantine returned on 19 June 'rather Anatolianized' and on 22 June he and Aelfrida had a lengthy argument about 'the place of self-realisation in Christianity' which left both parties 'pretty well tired out'.[116] On 23 June Constantine departed for Emden leaving his wife inclined (as always) to turn to other men when her husband was unkind to her. The man she had in mind – indeed, may already have arranged to meet – was Eric Silvanus, a man with whom (like 'Madeleine's' husband's best friend, 'Hugo Rossi', also a poet) she is already 'intimate' because her husband, like 'Madeleine's' husband 'Horace Redpath', behaves unkindly towards her. 'Madeleine' and 'Hugo Rossi'

have an affair[117] after which, rejected by her husband, she lives with 'Rossi' until he too rejects her – as Eric was to reject Aelfrida by becoming engaged to another woman shortly after the 'beechwood' episode and by 'dropping' both Grahams once Aelfrida's pregnancy became known. 'Madeleine' returns to England, Aelfrida in late September to Emden where she urgently ensures physical intimacy with Constantine: the couple have been sexually estranged for five months (Constantine is so anxious 'not to have another child' that he refuses sexual intercourse with a wife who refuses to use contraception and feels an overwhelming urge for another baby; they perforce slept 'near'[118] each other in Hessle but though Aelfrida is coy about whether or not sexual congress took place, she cannot have been pregnant when she met Eric) and she may need to account for the possible arrival of an 'inconvenient' baby. She duly becomes pregnant but shortly before recording her certainty, records a major row with her husband of which she tells us only that there are certain matters about which 'one does not say anything even to one's diary'.[119] Can the row have happened as a result of her informing her husband or of Constantine discovering that Eric is his wife's 'paramour', a word which may have been used by Constantine then and is certainly adopted by Aelfrida with regard to another woman's liaison with a man not her husband? The names of the men in 'Madeleine's' life suggest as much: 'Madeleine', a 'fallen woman' or 'magdalene' (as the contemporary expression was), takes the 'red path' of adultery and is declared to be a 'scarlet' (*rosso*) woman by her family; Roman poet Horace included wistful intimations of past loves in his poetry; French poet Victor Hugo was notorious for keeping a mistress.

In late April 1912 Aelfrida returns to Fordfield to await the birth of Agneta; in the meantime, she records her ill-health and pregnancy in some detail but does not say when the baby is due. During her pregnancy two events occur which may have some bearing on what has happened on the interim: in November 1911 she defends Constantine against Irene's accusations of 'base' behaviour towards Karl Hillern's 'pretty *révoltée* sister Rose during his last visit to Hessle[120], a quid pro quo, perhaps, for Constantine's decision not to put her away 'privily', and in January 1912 she records in the course of arguments with Constantine and Anatolia regarding the impropriety of the former renewing his relationship with 'Juanita', that her mother–in–law had been doing everything in her power to separate her son and his children from Aelfrida's 'blighting influence' since the August of the previous year, a month, that is to say, after a possible confession by Aelfrida to Anatolia's son that something has transpired between herself and Eric.) On

3 May 1912 Aelfrida leaves Emden for Fordfield; she and Constantine are reunited a fortnight later – as also are Constantine and Hilda Sollas. On 28 May 1912 the Grahams are visited by Eric and his fiancée. Maude Taylor (about whom Aelfrida is derisory) intimates that she is 'jealous' of Aelfrida's 'intimacy' with Eric, and something happens between Eric and Constantine: the relationship between the two men suddenly cools, they never meet again, and exchange only formal civilities when Eric marries. Aelfrida goes into labour, Agneta is born dead, and Constantine departs for Panama where, if the evidence of letters discovered by his wife in 1918 is to be believed, he begins or continues to be serially unfaithful to a woman he knows or believes has been faithless to him. Eric, however, after initially distancing himself from his 'paramour', sends her poems from the front during the Great War, together with a photograph of himself in uniform; she destroys the former but preserves the latter. He also updates her as to his life and whereabouts thereafter, though it is not until the late 1930s that their correspondence finally ceases after Eric presses for another meeting and Aelfrida, racked with guilt over the death of the daughter at whose toddler sickbed she made her vow and by the physical effects of reparative adoration carried to extremes for sins among which she may number breaking the seventh commandment, refuses, entering Tymawr where she prays for purity and for purification of the sinful nature which will continue to haunt her even when 'far from the miring of the world's uncleanliness'.[121]

This lengthy divergence into possible events in Aelfrida's distant past is not irrelevance. First, the two novels may constitute admission to Julius that in having an affair with Eric Silvanus, she had been as unfaithful to an adored and adoring brother as to an unloved and unloving husband, a 'sin' all the greater in Julius' eyes and her own because of the deep spiritual and emotional bond between brother and sister. Second, Julius' absence in South Africa (an absence not then guaranteed temporary) may have been seen by his sister as an opportunity to distance herself from a man whose seemingly 'unspiritualised' devotion has become rather frightening by disclosing her betrayal of his love with a man by whom she was attracted but with whom she was not in love and to whom she was 'married' but not married. Third, Aelfrida's disclosure in *Just Alice* of errant behaviour may have contributed to Julius' distaste for a novel portraying his betrayal by a woman he idolised and her ambivalent attitude to matters sacred and sexual.

'Cast aside like an old shoe' when by Rhodes University declined to renew his contract, Julius returned to England 'tired and nervy'[122] in December 1949

(Aelfrida said she loved 'being with Dear Dudu again – and he rested in "togetherness" too'; 'sanctified' 'togetherness', she hoped, not 'wrong')[123], only to depart again almost immediately in pursuit of 'Byz. Mus.' Receiving a gratifying measure of recognition in Greece, he returned 'more serene' in April 1950, a state of mind attributed by his sister to God but more likely due to renewal of intimate relations with her in a house always hers but now '*his*' home' too.[124] And it was in '*his*' home and hers that Julius and Aelfrida spent a short but significant holiday together in the summer of 1950 following the weddings of Walter, Constance, and Stephen. Alone at Wetenhall Cottage (Mina, having seen her children married, went to Lahr to regale the Kaufmanns with the details, and Walter and Bodil and Constance and John were on their respective honeymoons), brother and sister settled down to domestic chores (Julius), domestic comfort (Aelfrida), socialising (both; Bishop Wynn excepted, their visitors represented past lives reaching back to Julius' boyhood at St Faith's School and Aelfrida's adolescent visits to Newnham College), and to reminiscences and discovery.

Remembrance was easy, for Julius' memory was excellent and he and Aelfrida supplemented each other's recall of childhood events.[125] On 21 July he brought down from the attic 'old diaries, notebooks and pictures' and brother and sister browsed through as much of their content as she allowed; significantly, perhaps, she refused him access to her own diaries, replacing the volumes with the typescript of *Just Alice*.[126] Two weeks later, however, she relented sufficiently to read aloud 'bits out of [her] earlier diaries'. ('I wonder a little at the topics I selected for inclusion', she noted, adding that Julius seemed to enjoy even the 'sillier' bits.)[127] The visit during which Frank Stokoe asked her if she ever thought about her past may have stimulated other recollections, some darker than those she was prepared to divulge to Julius, some prompting further diary readings. (Julius, she noted, was both 'devoted and complaisant' and seemed satisfied with her offerings of entertainment and solace.) She herself found the readings bitter-sweet, and although delighted by Julius' delight ('he *glowed*' on discovering that her account of his First Class degree was written in red ink[128] and that she had written so much about him, something at which diary-reading sessions thirty years earlier had only hinted)[129], was not altogether sorry when diaries and memories were consigned to the attic again.

While revelling in the 'perfectly exquisite drawing room' of Wetenhall Cottage, in 'making existence tolerable for Julius' (and not think it 'wrong' to do so)[130], and in mutual – and as we shall see, therapeutic – ruminations on 'Old Times', Aelfrida discovered that even before her marriage in 1907 and certainly since there were gaps in her knowledge of her elder brother's life and that their 'togetherness' was not as absolute as she thought. A week after substitution of *Just Alice* for diaries and notebooks she did not wish Julius to see, Julius reciprocated with a reading (or, rather, a translation; the original was in Latin) of one act of what was 'meant to be a melodrama'. The story '*shocked*' his sister so profoundly (it described a psychoanalyst arranging a tryst with his mistress in Paris and his 'lady-secretary' making 'tentative love' to a patient suffering from 'melancholia') that she refused to hear the rest of it, feeling she could neither express her feelings ('that is "the world" from which I shrink') nor expatiate on what particularly 'haunted' her ; she also wondered *why* Julius' mind 'ran on such things'.[131] And it may have been as a result of discovering that Julius' mind did indeed run on such things that she listed in the back of the current volume of her diary every trip abroad made by him between 1897 (the visit to Berneval of which his sister noted that she had 'always adored' her elder brother and asked why their parents separated them)[132] and 1950 (Copenhagen, for Walter's wedding); she did not, however, invariably note with whom he went or, more pertinently, when he travelled alone.[133]

Aelfrida, of course, knew perfectly well *why* Julius had travelled abroad so often – research into Byzantine Musicology involved visits to institutions sacred and secular – but her recent attempt to comfort a wife piqued by her husband's departure to South Africa without her with the information that Julius had always had 'a roving disposition' and 'used to go off alone on his travels … long before he knew her'[134], was both disingenuous (Mina must have guessed the reason for this particular departure) and hurtful to one who had been the cause of his first visit in 1919. In her next novel, however, Aelfrida essays a possible rationale for Julius' behaviour (the novel's hero enjoys going off somewhere "in search of adventure")[135] and describes the behaviour abroad of two young Cambridge dons whose "capacity for living in a world of their own" surprises someone who has recently uncovered evidence of it: though they travel together, one spends weeks "poring over original documents" in ancient libraries, the other, "after a cursory look round [wanders] off to the countryside … to learn the language in the quickest and most pleasant way from its young girls". Significantly, however, he "never got into mischief" though he went "as far as a young man can go who is resolved not to go any further"[136], a statement which makes one wonder how much of Aelfrida's "reconstruction" of Julius' 'roving' life (for Julius is both young dons) is "imaginative"[137] and how much true.

Julius himself seems to have made another discovery during the momentous weeks when brother and sister were alone together, a discovery made as a result of Aelfrida's substitution of *Just Alice* for her diaries. Rereading diary entries made on and immediately after the dreadful day in July 1919 when she and her father received letters from Constantine demanding a divorce, we discover that their immediate response was a mutual decision not to tell Chiara or Julius. This seems odd, given that divorce would be impossible to conceal from close family members; in fact, Chiara, returning from a short holiday, was duly told, but the news was concealed from Julius on the grounds that his 'nerves', never strong, might be shattered by disclosure. Given that in 1906 he had had to be talked into accepting Constantine as his sister's husband, this seems possible; far more probable in 1919 was the possibility that Julius might break down on discovering that the sister he idolised was not an abused Griselda but a 'scarlet woman'. In collusion with Chiara and the Oracle (the news of her daughter's adultery did not, as Aelfrida feared, 'kill' her mother, though it probably opened her eyes to other reasons for the imperfection of her daughter's 'perfect' marriage), Aelfrida decided not to disclose her affair with Eric to Julius. (Or to anyone else.) Hence it was not until Julius encountered 'Madeleine' in 1950 when *Just Alice* was read to him as literary confession that the truth was revealed, he in turn revealing aspects of *his* life hitherto unsuspected by his sister.

Mutual revelations of unsuspected private lives were cathartic. Julius' 'testiness' vanished and as he approached his seventieth birthday on 18 November 1951 he seemed more 'at peace with himself and the world' than she had ever known him to be.[138] Aelfrida too, if the tone of diary entries is anything to go by, seemed as if her perspective of and attitude to life had altered for the better: 'God', she wrote, 'has given me pardon and peace so that I can serve Him with a quiet mind'.[139]

Another factor contributing to her unwontedly quiet mind may be discerned in a second 'religious' novel begun, judging by hints in diary entries, shortly after her return to Lolworth in mid–August 1950 after the 'five memorable weeks' in Cambridge during which 'Old Times' conspired to turn her '*attention*' other than 'Godwards'[140] and to give 'a little thought to [her] own self'.[141] The novel was 'half-finished' by January 1951, 'all planned and *nearly* all written' by early March[142], completed *and* revised four months later[143], and read in part to Julius by 1 September the same year. (He had helped to research the Cambridge background for it; Aelfrida wondered what he would make of the story.)[144] In November 1951 she noted that 'the "catharsis" of writing [it] was good for [her]'.[145]

*The Centaur*, ostensibly the biography of a 'disillusioned post-war Major'[146], begins with a bang: "a fortnight before he was due to go up to Cambridge, Clive Farwell decided that he would commit suicide".[147] (Almost literally with a bang, for 'Clive' intends to shoot himself – but does not.) It then follows its hero through a series of picaresque adventures during his university career and ends with him deciding that "it was incredible that he should ever have wanted to take his own life" and (subject to the Abbot's permission) to become a monk at "St Bruno's Monastery" in Scotland.[148] The novel is, in fact and as usual, Autobiography with a capital A; every nuance can be referenced (to do so would require a book longer than *The Centaur* itself) and in the course of it Aelfrida opens a series of windows through which she looks back at her life to date. Some open onto forlorn landscapes: the events surrounding Conrad's death, for example, described here as having happened to traumatised refugee child 'Mara'[149], Chiara's distraught behaviour being depicted as that of 'Roma', 'Clive's' self-elected guardian.[150] Others open on events barely mentioned in contemporary diaries (the quarantine imposed on the Grahams when they suffered from 'smallpox' in Odessa, for example; only now can Aelfrida bring herself to write an excerpt from the 'Russian novel' everyone expected her to write following her return but unwritten then because she was too traumatised by married life to contemplate it) but important now because they frame episodes in 'Clive's' story. Others still provide another version of significant events in Aelfrida's spiritual life such as her Damascene experience while cycling home from lessons, described here as having happened to a dissolute miner (a significant occupation, given that Aelfrida is delving into her past) who, seeing a vision of "an angel with a fiery sword", is "struck to the heart" by a "subliminal uprush" of emotion and becomes a changed man[151], or suggest possible reasons for her behaving as she does when agonised by events she herself has promoted: 'Clive's' desire for silence and solitude, for example, has arisen because "people *hurt*; cruel people hurt on *purpose*, normal people hurt from clumsiness and stupidity [and] nice kind people [are] often the worst offenders because they [attempt] to penetrate too far and [hence] hurt … most acutely".[152] And others open onto scenes at which Aelfrida hardly dares look because they are so perilous or, having opened them, closes them again so quickly that what we see of what she sees is certainly incomplete and possibly inaccurate. No wonder, as she wrote ostensibly of the 'much news' disclosed in the '*many*' letters received while writing *The Centaur*, she seemed 'in touch with so many lives'.[153] She *was*. They were her own.

Although it is obvious from reading *The Centaur* that 'Clive's' path in life (and his arrival at a monastery which he hopes will be his '*Paradisus claustralis*') owes much to

Thomas Merton's biography (*Elected Silence* was one of the books read by Aelfrida during its composition), perhaps more influential is a work to which she refers only indirectly: Marcel Proust's *A la Recherche du Temps Perdu*, published between 1913 and 1927. Proust's imaginatively reconstructed account of his childhood and later life involves the sudden reawakening of vivid memories by a particular sensory stimulus: the taste of a small sweet cake called a *madeleine*. In Aelfrida's case, reawakening of repressed memories is a gradual process and it begins at a time and in a place where she has been confined for her own safety and where for the first time in her life she has the means and will to contemplate her past. She does not do this alone: she has an assistant, a man who has known her all her life, who himself has an excellent memory of 'Old Times', who is both able and willing to take her back and back with him into a distant past from which she has always shrunk because she cannot bear to recall the traumatic events which occurred there. He is also the only man she willingly entrusts with restoration of her mental equilibrium.

Julius begins his unconditionally loving task at Tymawr, walking and talking with his sister in the course of 'DearDududays' which leave her so physically and emotionally exhausted that she has to retire to bed to recover. He completes his task following his return from South Africa during a holiday spent in almost uninterrupted discourse with her and from which he emerges at peace with himself and the world and she returns to Lolworth with a quiet mind because pardoned for behaviour over which she had no control. (It may be too, that knowing how therapeutic it is for his sister to write things down, it is at Julius' suggestion that Aelfrida commits her discoveries to paper in the form of a novel in which 'Clive' is advised by 'Marcella'[154], a mature older woman who befriends him in Cambridge, to "sit with a blank sheet of paper in front of you and write down whatever comes into your head", knowing that what he writes – he is practising "automatic writing" – will "bypass [his] conscious self and go through [his] hand [onto] the paper" and that it does not matter if he "gets [only] *bits* of things" because she will later fit them "into other 'bits'"[155]; writing her latest novel, Aelfrida is writing so fast that her writing is virtually 'automatic', her thoughts, as always, seem dictated instead of consciously formulated, and only later does she – and her biographer – try to elucidate cross-correspondences she has made.) Pursuit of her lost past will last the rest of her life, not just the duration of her latest novel, and will culminate in a sequence of 'memory pictures', each provoked by a particular '*madeleine*', but beginning in 1950 with a "tale

of darknesses" almost too long to be told[156], she progresses to more explicit evocations as she discovers the reasons for both hints and confusions and writes her way through them. (*The Glory of the West* and *Christian Old Age*, conversely, may be regarded as attempts to persuade herself that her '*temps perdus*' were as golden as she liked to think they were and not, as the alternative meaning of the word '*perdu*' suggests – a meaning of which Aelfrida was aware – a period in her life when events ruined and spoilt her for ever.) Not until then (and perhaps not even then) will she, like 'Clive', understand what "*was* the matter with [her] personality" and why she "cannot manage [her] life better" and discover that the fault lies not in herself but in "circumstances [and] cruel fate".[157]

Aelfrida, of course, has Julius to guide her through elucidation of the fateful circumstances which shaped her life and personality but her biographer does not, so she provides a guide in the shape of the invigilator of an examination taken by 'Clive' at the end of his second Cambridge year. The invigilator, a man with "strange compelling eyes"[158], takes pity on a candidate so overwrought at the prospect of his final paper that he has to leave the room; offering a supportive arm, he escorts 'Clive' back to the examination hall, throws open some windows, and tells him "look up at me from time to time. I'll hold a thought for you [and] see you through". Thereafter whenever 'Clive' feels inspiration fail, he gazes into the invigilator's eyes "and in those eyes he seemed to see and from those eyes he took the answer … he was needing". And not only do answers to the examination questions become "luminously clear", but 'Clive' also realises that faint ticks have been placed against certain questions as if to indicate those he ought to attempt[159] – at which point we realise that Aelfrida's manuscript is starred with small asterisks, that she is invigilating our reading of it, that she is holding for us the thoughts we ought to be having in relation to it and is pointing out passages whose particular significance we should realise and pursue.[160] (The 'invigilator' episode itself is one of these.) Furthermore, as our 'invigilator' she tries to ensure that we provide the right answers, answers, that is to say, which are correct in terms of the windows she has opened for us.

Attending a séance in a house bequeathed to its present owner by 'Roma' herself, 'Clive' asks 'Marcella Cusack' if 'Roma', a "rather remarkable woman", has left "things behind for [him] to find and investigate?" And, he also asks, "how do [I] test the atmosphere? … Do I sniff?" Immediately, a word comes into his mind: "*spooks!*"[161] What 'spooks', therefore, has 'rather remarkable' Aelfrida left behind for us to investigate, bearing in mind that as she herself states in *The Centaur*, "strict censorship" has been exercised over "autobiographical remarks" made by its author?[162] And how do we sniff out what one of her spiritual mentors called mute messages concealed in things[163], things (*choses*) in this instance being words? The answer, as always, is that we must intuit, guess, and pick up and enlarge upon the smallest 'things' indicated by our helpful 'invigilator' as she throws open one window after another on the 'spooks' in her life.

Our first 'bit' of 'things' appears in a poem published in the *Cambridge Review* of January 1951 and saved by Aelfrida in the contemporary volume of her diary. Entitled *The Quest* and by-lined 'Traveller', the poem's theme and imagery must have been regarded by the author of *The Centaur* as relevant to work in progress, given that its reader is commanded to travel through scenery increasingly "magic" (a "singing tree" and "four-fold flaming swords" figure in it), through fire, water, and a mirror, to pass wild animals, and to undergo trials of courage until he reaches his goal[164], actions which, metaphorically speaking, we must perform as we track our 'invigilator' (with her help) through the pages of *The Centaur*.

Her (and our) first steps "back and back into a distant past"[165] take her in the guise of 'disillusioned' 'Major Farwell' to "Gockett Farm" where he finds himself "settled or stranded … miles from the nearest village [and] from Monmouth … with nothing to do but read and go for walks". Near "Gockett Farm" is "St Saviour's Convent" whose chapel bell 'Clive' hears as he explores "ancient quarries, … ruins that had once been manor houses, … dame-schools, inns, Roman camps, [and] on the hill-tops … shrines where Prehistoric Man had worshipped and in the fields … [and] traces of stone rings". To certain "ancient stones" 'Clive' feels strongly attracted, stones "not really set out for … inspection [but] muddled … up in a fascinating array of puzzles", stones which take him "back and back into the dim era of Primitive Man" and assert that "the Old Gods are not dead, they are but biding their time", stones among which he believes "he must have passed his psychological childhood". He therefore tries to "think himself back into his primitive past", not only so as to be able to return to his "ancient home" but also because in doing so he will find "a revelation of what it was that his present day … nature lacked".[166] Listening to the "wordless call of the stones" and "drawn to turn aside" to one "assemblage" after another, he seeks shelter from a thunderstorm in a "pit fortress". Climbing in, he falls, only to find himself, temporarily disabled by a bruised knee, "lying on runic stones" in a gloomy hollow peopled by "hostile denizens", menacing "ape-men" whose antics round an "altar of sacrifice" provoke "memories of a previous existence"

and "fragmentary pictures of age-old happenings" which took place "in a previous incarnation"; as in a nightmare he finds himself utterly helpless: "bound and gagged [and] no longer master of himself". Cursing himself for a "lunatic and a coward", he effects his escape from the "beastly … haunted pit" by climbing the branches of a huge sycamore which overhangs it. Emerging "into clear sunny air and freedom", he hears the sound of St Saviour's bell and knows he is safe.[167]

A powerful allegory requiring little explanation. More significant, however, in the terms of the 'psychological childhood' Aelfrida is working through, is realisation that the 'Prehistory' her hero uncovers is her own and that the thrills obtained from 'Monmouth stones' are those gained by dawning comprehension of 'queer things' lying in the 'cellars' of her mind discovered while thinking out 'questions and problems' on solitary walks. (Or on longer walks with Julius with whose help she sniffs out 'psychic scents' before tracking them to their lair.) Elucidation will be painful, for 'Little Frida' was so traumatised by events surrounding Conrad's death that she repressed them for years and it is only when she finds herself in 1950 at Wetenhall Cottage in "an atmosphere of security, warm human affection and intimacy such as [she] had never known"[168] that adult Aelfrida prepares to confront Conrad, the 'baby brother … ripe for heaven so young'[169], whose "cruel Fate" set in train the "circumstances" which blighted his sister's existence thereafter; Conrad the spectral figure who could truly say of her (as now-dead 'Roma' says of 'Clive' in a message received in séance) that she is "mine for ever and ever".[170] Or as Conrad's sister noted in her latest novel, 'one *doesn't* leave any of one's life behind – it is all stored up somewhere'.[171]

To be encouraged to attempt auto-analysis in the state of mental disequilibrium from which she suffered prior to entering Tymawr was extremely dangerous; conversely, Aelfrida might never have achieved a measure of equilibrium had she not begun to resolve mental conflicts inflicted by her parents' behaviour at the time of Conrad's death. But with her psyche "ingrained" with "scars of ancient hate and cruelty"[172], how could she have behaved otherwise, given that she so was engulfed in miserably 'assimilated and built in' memories[173] that she had become (like Mrs Donkin) 'her own gaoler and her own prison'[174], lodged behind barred gates she could not open without assistance. But with Julius' help, she did.

And what "evil legacies" and "suppressed complexes … [and] neuroses and phobias"[175] she uncovered when searching for the '*solution*' to the 'enigma of her personality, and what 'strange vast places'[176] her mind traversed (places from which neither silence nor solitude could protect her; indeed, they may have exaggerated their dangers, hence Alethea's insistence, following her visit to Tymawr, that her mother re-engage with the world) while she came to terms with how damaged she was and why and discovered that her 'deepest and most fundamental weakness' stemmed from the vast quantity of mental 'lumber'[177] cramming the 'attic' of her mind. Little wonder, then, that she found 'Prehistory' 'very weird' and 'didn't like it a bit'[178], that in exploring it she likened her head to "an empty skull inside which [her] thoughts were driven round and round by a burning wind like souls in a Dantesque hell" and was "on the verge of another and much worse breakdown"[179] as a result, and that she realised more very dark moments must be endured until 'dearDududays' lifted her from the "horrible pit" into which she had fallen, set her on sound ground once again, and ordered her goings.[180] (Aelfrida, of course, attributed her recovery to divine intervention; only at Wetenhall Cottage, it seems, did she realise and admit the invaluable role played by 'dear Dudu' in restoring her to a semblance of normality.) And no wonder she became distraught when Mother Guenvrede put a temporary stop to the walks she used for 'thinking out various questions and problems'[181] ('I went up to the woods', she wrote apropos *The Glory of the West*, 'and sat on a prehistoric stone musing on death … I think writing two chapters on death had helped me')[182] and to calm the "inner turbulence"[183] generated as she investigated her '*temps perdu*'.

Wartime clearances of the forested hills around Tymawr which exposed more and more 'Prehistory' to an exploring tertiary and extensive and refulgent skyscapes to Placida as she sat writing in the West Room came to symbolise the illumination cast on Aelfrida's personal 'prehistory' in the course of analytic ruminations. But always before embarking on explorations of Monmouthshire 'Prehistory', she took care to leave a 'sketch map'[184] in her room: if she got lost, someone would be able to find her. (Being Aelfrida, she departed wildly from her proposed course; she also took great risks when careering round the hills in pursuit of 'psychic scents' and was fortunate to sustain only scratches, bruises, and a sprained ankle.) In her books, however, she left literary sketch maps to ensure that perceptive readers would be able to 'find' her even when she seemed most mentally astray and although she decided against 'writing down what my past life looks like from the point of view of Tymawr'[185], it was only from the vantage point provided by Tymawr that she was able to do so (with Julius' help) in the pages of what might be called her 'psychological' as opposed to her 'spiritual' diaries, in the pages, that is to say, of every novel she wrote after 1946 and in those of *The Centaur* in particular.

Like 'Major Farwell', Aelfrida enjoyed "writing reports".[186] Suggesting to Alethea in March 1943 that she occupy her mind with 'a serious study of the History and Ethnology of South Africa' instead of brooding on her latest failure to become a nun, Aelfrida commented that she had done '*that*' a week or two before[187], '*that*' (and the substance of her 'reports') being not the history and ethnology of another continent but of the 'country' which housed her own 'prehistory' and the tortured family relationships that lumbered it. Of this '*that*' she made serious study, hoping that in doing so she would cease brooding on her failures as a person and dispel illusions concerning the nature of the 'sacrificial altars' and 'pit-fortresses' which monumentally marred her life. And it was this 'serious study' as much as anything else which prompted her to take back the 'great treasure' of manuscript paper bestowed on Hilda Harrison early in 1941 with the advice that Hilda write her 'spiritual autobiography' as a means of 'unfussing' herself, of ridding herself of 'suppressed complexes', and of preventing herself from 'harping back' to 'dark clouds of the past'. But the truthfulness of the 'autobiography'[188] (her word) Aelfrida consigned to paper in order to do the same, is a matter for conjecture.

One of the most difficult events for a biographer to 'unfuss' is that involving her visit to Ventnor in November/December 1912. Having let slip to Dr Bowen that she was contemplating suicide, she was, it seems, removed urgently from Fordfield and sent to the Isle of Wight to recover her equilibrium in 'one of the best resorts in England … for invalids'. She stayed, so she said, at a house called 'St David's', met there or elsewhere a 'Mrs St George' of whom prior to departure she had had 'second sight' with regard to her appearance and to gifts given and received, and discussed theology so intensively and interminably with a 'Father Berry' that she had to desist lest she develop 'brain fever' from too much 'religious truth'.[189] This may be so – and composition of three poems by-lined 'Ventnor' of 15 and 17 November and 1 December 1912 (*Treasure of Earth and Treasure of Heaven, Truce,* and *Mass – and a Kensit Row* respectively) suggests that she may have visited Ventnor for part of the time. But sending a suicidal woman to a place with easy opportunities for death by drowning does not seem a sensible move on the part of Dr Bowen or her family, and given that there are no references to a 'St David's' or to a 'Mrs St George' in contemporary Ventnor directories and that Aelfrida's name does not appear in the lists of arrivals published in local newspapers, did she actually visit Ventnor? And if not, where or what *was* 'Ventnor'?

Forty-two years later Aelfrida provides corroborative evidence – of a kind. Meeting a 'Miss Diamond' in

Oxford, she recalled the '*pensionnat*' for foreign girls in Ventnor owned by that lady, that the *pensionnat* stood near a church where 'a violently Anglo-Catholic Father Smith' preached 'a grim sermon on Hell' and where on another Sunday 'there was [a] Kensit Row about which [she] wrote a poem', and that while at Ventnor she herself stayed in the same house as a 'Father and Mrs Berry'.[190] According to *Crockford's Clerical Directory* for 1912, a Father Benjamin Smith *was* priest in charge of an Anglo-Catholic church in Ventnor in 1912 (St Alban's, Godshill) and it is possible that a 'Kensit Row' erupted here in November/December 1912 which went unrecorded in local newspapers, but no 'Miss Diamond' is recorded as living in Ventnor at that time nor any *pensionnat* listed, and nor was 'Father Berry' a resident but a High Church curate who, accompanied his wife and young child, had been sent to Ventnor for a 'rest'. Then too, Aelfrida is deliberately vague about her stay: she has introductions (her Tillyard aunts know Ventnor well and 'Aunt Laura' has lived there; indeed, it is possible that Aelfrida stayed with the woman she later described as being the only person who ever understood her, this being why she expended so much attention on her courtesy aunt when Miss Smith retired to Cambridge) but does not make use of them; she writes a description of Ventnor which could have been taken from a guidebook; she makes the 'mistake' of leaving her diary behind and has to write a retrospective account of her visit, and admits on her return that 'things seem to have twisted and changed and altered' as 'the varying shimmer of days and weeks [passed] over them'.[191] But the prominence given to a lengthy, detailed, and asterisked passage in *The Centaur* suggests that leaving her diary behind may have been deliberate and that the 'shimmer' she casts over things conceals them from prying eyes.

Leaving the examination room in which the invigilator with 'strange compelling eyes' has helped him complete his examination paper, 'Clive' heads to "the high footbridge that spans the river between Chesterton and Midsummer Common" (in fact, Jesus Green) from which he intends to throw himself into Jesus Lock in the hope that the "fire" which blazes in his head will be quenched as he drowns. He is rescued in the nick of time by 'Christopher Ransford', an undergraduate friend and a committed Christian, who wheels him back to college on his bicycle. For the next three days 'Clive' lies in a darkened room refusing to eat or answer questions and begging 'to be left alone'. (He is never left alone.) On the fourth day, 'Christopher' drives him to his family home where his doctor father will oversee 'Clive's' care. On arrival, 'Clive' is greeted by a "tall aristocratic lady" waiting under the portico attached to an elegant 18th

century house. (The lady is reminiscent in appearance to 'Mrs St George', an Anglo-Irish gentry widow, and to the matron at 'Foxhurst' in *Vision Triumphant*; the house, too, is similar to the one in which 'Noel Ashurst' was a patient.) He is escorted to a room with barred windows, his cry of "is this a madhouse?" being hushed by the explanation that his room was formerly the children's nursery. As "apathetic as ever" and with "attempts to cheer him up" serving to depress him further, he is visited by a 'Dr Biggart' whom he suspects is a psychiatrist. On 'Dr Biggart' questioning him about his early childhood, 'Clive' declares that his memory is "very poor" and turns the tables on his interlocutor by asking if *he* did not have a "normal childhood", if *he* sleeps poorly and dreams much, why *he* is perpetually "in such a state of nervous tension", and why *he* does not "take advice" and go as a voluntary patient to a mental hospital. Being able to summon up enough courage "to cheek the great psychiatrist" encourages 'Clive' ("he was, he told himself, still good for something") and this and revulsion against "being fussed over … for weeks and weeks … by the virtuous and well meaning" sets him "almost imperceptibly" on the road to recovery.[192]

What, then, does this disclose of Aelfrida? Can it be that she tried to put into effect the poetic threat uttered on 28 October 1912 that on the next stormy night she intends to die? Can it be that, suffering great "anguish of mind", she headed for Jesus Lock, a deep lock from which it would be difficult to escape especially if, like 'Frauke' in *Marrying a Stranger,* she weighted herself with stones, "[crept] quietly up to the parapet … and [leapt] into the water"? Or was prevented from leaping and brought home by one of her brothers? Can it be that a 'mind-doctor' tried to readjust her "to normal life in the place where [she] had lived out … [her] abnormal [girl] hood" but her refusal to co-operate saw her driven to "a … Home … for … girls … a little queer in the head"[193]? Can it also be that her parents, desperate to hush up the unfortunate affair, attributed it to the lingering (physical) effects of Agneta's stillbirth ("let us explain this madness of yours as kindly as we can")[194], informing family and friends that their daughter had gone to Ventnor (a place she may have visited after leaving the 'Home') and that she would return "as soon as she [was] strong enough"[195]? And if Aelfrida later regaled Agatha with details of the event (as 'Roma' did 'Clive' with regard to episodes in her life better kept to herself), her impulse to seek suicidal Agatha's body in Jesus Lock is understandable indeed.

Wherever Aelfrida was sent ("I suppose", says the abbot of 'St Bruno's monastery' to 'Clive' apropos an experimental farm with which the latter was deeply though briefly involved, "[it] was a mental hospital and you were temporarily quite mad")[196] – and hints in later novels and poetry suggest that she was indeed subjected to enforced therapeutic incarceration in the south of England – the Bournemouth/Brockenhurst area in Hampshire is a possibility[197], given that 'Noel Ashton' was hospitalised in that area in *Vision Triumphant*, a novel describing what may have happened to its author herself, that hints concerning the topography of the area appear in *The Centaur*, and that in the poem *A Guide to Modern Verse* which appeared in January 1913 in *The Cambridge Magazine*, she refers ironically to an "awfully jolly" little town in "Hants" i.e. Hampshire[198] – the experience seems to have left her determined never to place herself again in a position where she might be labelled a "madman" or threatened with being "locked up". (Or actually deprived of liberty.) Liberty, however, would mean leading either an introverted life of "controlled and guided lunacy"[199] in secluded surroundings of her own choosing because this would allow her to maintain a semblance of sanity when confronting 'the world' and the 'pressures' it imposed (her attempt to live a hermit-like existence of 'controlled and guided lunacy' at St Benedict's resulted in scurvy and in confinement in a different kind of institution) or a more public life, the antithesis of that she wished to lead, in which she would be forced to pretend interest and even take part in "the cultural and athletic life"[200] of wherever she lived to prove that people had no reason to believe her lunatic. (Either life was preferable to incarceration.) The experience, however, left her fascinated by and distrustful of 'New Psychology'. ('Do psychologists', she wrote, 'really understand or are they only experimenting?')[201] Fascinated insofar as she subsequently set herself up as one of the "practitioners" of whom she envisaged a whole "Harley Street" of clerical and lay members "equipped with up-to-date psychological knowledge" (which, given her possible encounter with 'New Psychology' and subsequent reading around the subject, she may have believed she had), called herself a 'soul-doctor' and emphasised the "necessity of 'going back and digging'"[202] in her patients' pasts before 'straightening' could occur, distrustful insofar as she extended her distaste for psychological intervention in her own life over similar interventions in her daughters' lives, describing therapies they separately underwent as certainly ineffectual and probably harmful.

Well might Aelfrida wonder what Julius would make of *The Centaur*, for although her disquisition on 'Clive's' (and her own) 'prehistory' would hardly surprise him, her comments concerning himself in the guise of dons 'Penrose' and 'Postlethwaite'[203] (and disclosure that 'Penrose' is 'Clive's' *father*) might cause him a frisson of anxiety. On the other hand, having Julius figure in the

book suggests that his represented presence was essential to her theme and that *The Centaur* may be a tribute to the brother who had spent a decade rescuing her from herself. Clues can be found in the book's title and in the name of the 'great psychiatrist' who visited 'Clive'.

A lengthy and pivotal episode in the novel describes the birth and raising of twin hybrid foals, one a female centaur, the other a human-faced horse, on an experimental farm (formerly a private house, before that a priory) run by one of 'Clive's' Cambridge friends. The episode, inspired by Aelfrida's distaste for eugenic practices of any kind, including contraception, is a disguised polemic against artificial insemination, and though interesting because it echoes many episodes in her life, a farrago of pseudo-scientific nonsense, unmatched, as a publisher's reader noted, by 'sufficient literary restraint'.[204] On Eustace also describing the 'centaur episode' as 'irrelevant and *impossible*', Aelfrida extirpated it and recast the novel as *Rich Man's Choice*[205]; she nevertheless retained her original version and ensured its safekeeping by issuing instructions for its deposition in Girton College. The reason for retention becomes clear when we realise that the 'centaur' of her original title must be a specific centaur: Chiron, tutor of numerous Ancient Greek heroes in knowledge and skills appropriate to their future life and in the case of one particular hero, Jason the Argonaut, privy to details of his birth and childhood of which Jason himself was ignorant.[206]

A centaur, as Aelfrida, daughter and sister of classicists, would know, was a therianthropic creature, half-human, half-horse, inhabiting the borderland between the human and animal worlds and possessing good and bad qualities of both. Julius, half studious don ('Penrose'), half enjoyer of the "strength and pleasure of unconscious animality"[207] ('Postlethwaite') is a perfect hybrid, a fact to which Aelfrida slyly draws our attention by having 'Clive' particularly notice a picture, Piero di Cosimo's *Battle of the Lapiths and Centaurs*.[208] Chiron, however, was also the wisest and most just of all the centaurs and, even more aptly, a famous musicologist; furthermore, it was he, as venerably bearded as Julius himself in 1951, who greeted Dante and arranged his onward guidance as the poet and Virgil penetrated deeper and deeper into the circles of Hell on his journey towards enlightened self-knowledge: "necessity beings him here, not sport or jest", says Virgil of his charge.[209] Aelfrida's use of centaurian imagery, characters, and title is therefore essential to the tribute paid in the novel to her brother and the key to deciphering aspects of it.

The name of the psychiatrist ('Biggart') whose probing questions are parried by 'Clive' sounds eminently probable when applied to Julius, a man currently playing the part of 'great psychiatrist' to his sister and without whose intervention in her chaotic life she might not now be free to write her current and most cathartic novel. (Aelfrida also painted a sympathetic portrayal of Julius as 'Andrew Keith' in *The Way We Grow Up*, a novel considered by Julius/Andrew to be her best.) An old name for compassion is 'greatheart', literally, 'big heart'; in Bunyan's *Pilgrim's Progress*, a book known by Aelfrida from childhood, we find a 'Mr Greatheart' (himself the servant of an 'interpreter') who conducts 'Christian's' widow 'Christiana' (a woman who wonders "whether her unbecoming behaviour towards her husband was not one cause that she never saw him more") on her path to the Celestial City. En route, 'Greatheart' protects 'Christiana' from 'Giant Grim' and his lions, ogres whose carnage has for a long time prevented travellers from passing that way[210]; parting from her at "the House called Beautiful", he goes on to kill 'Giant Despair' whose 'Doubting Castle' he demolishes. 'Christiana' herself eventually reaches the land of Beulah where she meets old friends 'Mr Standfast', 'Mr Honest', and 'Mr Valiant-for-Truth' (also attributes of Julius in the present context) and is in turn greeted by a messenger whose token is "an arrow with a point sharpened with love" who tells her that she will shortly reach her goal. She does so, leaving behind "desponds and slavish fears" entertained since she first became a pilgrim.[211] As an extended metaphor for Julius' loving and courageous guidance of his desponding and despairing sister at Tymawr and Wetenhall Cottage, this cannot be bettered or her application of 'greatheart' to her fraternal 'straightener' surpassed, and although the 'great psychiatrist' did not wholly achieve his aim of restoring his sister's mental equilibrium, of her gratitude for his attempt there can be no doubt.

After these disclosures – and in the interests of brevity only the most startling have been included – can Aelfrida have anything more to reveal? And in revealing it does she tell or hint at the truth or conceal and reveal simultaneously? The first disclosure concerns Albert Erlande; the second Alfred Tillyard; the third, a cross.

As a small boy, 'Clive' lives in Cambridge with his academic father and much younger and very pretty mother 'Maman'. A French painter, 'Auguste Martin' is engaged to produce a life size portrait of "*Maman serious*", entitled *The Golden Butterfly* after her favourite brooch, and a smaller one of "*Maman laughing*", the former to be retained by '*Maman's*' doting husband, the latter to be exhibited in Paris. The second picture interests 'Clive' most: at first sight it seems to portray "a vine-clad trellis with a golden butterfly alighting on a white flower" but on closer examination shows his mother's face with her dark curls as bunches of grapes and her white fingers

**Julius and Mina Tillyard at Wetenhall Cottage**

forming the petals of the flower.[212] Frightened by the portrait's ambiguities, 'Clive' regards the artist as a "devil" and as someone of whom he is rightly distrustful because of what he senses of unnatural intimacy between artist and sitter. Anxious to ensure the observant child's silence, 'Auguste Martin' gives him "six exquisitely modelled [toy] cuirassiers"; 'Clive', however, rejects them by pushing them to the back of a cupboard, then by wrapping them in cloth and concealing them in a hole at the base of one of the wych-elms lining the avenue leading to his home. "Gone for ever", he thinks happily.[213] 'Auguste Martin' departs for Paris; '*Maman*' leaves her husband and, with 'Clive', joins the artist as his mistress. The relationship deteriorates and 'Clive' and '*Maman*' return to England. Within hours of their arrival '*Maman*' disappears, never to return, leaving small 'Clive' sobbing uncontrollably and so distraught that he cannot remember his surname. He is taken to an orphanage whence he is adopted by 'Roma Farwell' whose surname he takes.

Apart from obvious references to events surrounding Conrad's death and to things not being what they seem,

Aelfrida also appears to hint at connections between 'Auguste Martin' and Albert Erlande and at a continuing relationship between herself and him. To decipher these we must return to 'Clive' and to his relationship with 'Marcella Cusak'. Visiting 'Marcella' one day, adult 'Clive' feels a "thrill of horror" on perceiving a life-sized portrait of 'Roma' painted by 'Auguste Martin', the artist whose "loathed name" is forever associated with his ruined childhood[214]; on a subsequent visit he learns that 'Marcella' is about to marry an elderly admirer, 'Louis Cuzac, Marquis de Perros-Cuzac', who calls her "lovely lady" and who, overcoming her initial reluctance, has persuaded her to meet him again with the words "give me a date. We must get to know one another better". 'Marcella', persuaded, decides that renewing acquaintance with 'Louis Cuzac' is "the right thing to do" because "God *does* speak to us through events and men"; she later marries him, becoming ("or so I *think*!", she laughingly remarks) 'La Marquise de Perros-Cuzac'.[215]

With these echoes of Albert Erlande in mind (books inscribed "*charmante femme*", flirtations in Perros Guirec in 1926), can it be that what Aelfrida describes here is a later meeting with the man from whose 'loathed name' she once recoiled in 'horror, *horror*'? As usual, she conceals as much as she reveals (everyone, 'Clive' informs 'Marcella', "puts mats over the holes in their carpets and turns the vases round so that no one sees the cracks. We are all frauds")[216], and in few places in her diary does she conceal more than when describing the only possible occasion on which she could have met Erlande again. But from what she hints, one may surmise that she did.

On 4 September 1930, four years after she and Erlande met at Perros Guirec and during which time Erlande had referred to Aelfrida in six or more novels, the latter crossed to France where she spent six days 'alone' at Puys, a small north coast resort, before meeting 'considerate … adaptable [and] tactful' Alethea (then working for *La Semaine à Paris*) in Dieppe on 10 September for a brief but '*perfect*' reunion before returning to England on or about the 16th. In Puys, she stayed in a small *pension* or, rather, in an annexe to the *pension* overlooking a green lane and a farm 'charming and animated to watch' even if prone to emit 'rural noises'. While there she 'made friends with one or two other visitors in the *pension*' (she does not, she adds, have time tell us about them, nor, rather oddly, did she take her diary on what was 'an otherwise perfect holiday', an action she later regretted when she discovered she had 'so much to say' that she feared she would 'never *never* get it all down'; she did not, at least, not in her diary), in particular 'a sad and lonely person' (recorded as female) in the throes of a divorce

(by July 1930 the Erlandes were living apart, divorcing later) and concerning whom Aelfrida wondered if her guardian angel had sent her to Puys 'to save … from despair'.[217] Following her return to England, she wrote feelingly of 'the excitement and the delight of personal relationships', of how she loved 'people', and of how 'passionately interesting' she found them even when they hurt her[218]; she also thought much of her 'lovely' and 'lonely' (i.e. without dependents) stay at Puys, listened to music on the radio while sitting pensively in the dark, and worked on *O Passionate World* (begun July 1930) in an extended episode of which 'Carola', holidaying with her daughter in Brittany, becomes romantically embroiled with a younger man (as Aelfrida was then embroiled with Anthony Wrightson) and engages in question and answer sessions on sex and marriage with an older one. (It would have been flattering for a woman of forty-six to find herself pursued by *two* ardent suitors, a younger man in absentia and an older one in person; 'Carola's' two men are uncle and nephew, surnamed Branthwaite, a name whose initial syllable is identical to Erlande's actual one: Brandenburg.) This being so, Aelfrida's description of her days at Puys as 'needed' and hoping that they were 'enough'[219] gains added interest, for given that she had just spent several weeks alone (save for the servants who in the context of solitude did not count) enjoying the 'perfect peace of Fordfield' (Chiara was in America and Agatha and Alethea abroad), she could hardly have 'needed' a holiday. Or was she revenging herself on Willie Searle, the '*perverte*' who married someone else on 1 May, by renewing acquaintance with a man with whom she had enjoyed a sexually-charged relationship while her abortive '*affaire*' with Searle himself was on-going?

And for what did she hope six days were 'enough'? Can it be that she had arranged to meet Erlande and worried lest so short a time prevent re-establishment of their former intimacy? Can it be she 'needed' to see Erlande again because he had hurt her deeply by his literary revelations of her soul-baring revelations and because she wished to discover and discuss his motives for doing so? Or was it because, emotionally aroused by Anthony's increasingly demonstrative love for her (he had kissed her for the first time the day before she left England), she felt impelled to turn from a man whose love she could never fully reciprocate to a man whose love she could now reciprocate because he had hurt her? And can this be why she had no compunction in leaving for France within hours of Chiara's return from America so unwell that she retired immediately to bed attended by Julius, Ancifera, and Joan Cooper, her coming tryst with Erlande providing ample reason for callous behaviour towards the sick and widowed mother whom she had sworn to cherish: 'I feel a brute going off to France. Still, Julius is here'.[220]

So: what happened in Puys? Did Aelfrida meet Erlande and even 'marry' (i.e. have sexual congress with) him either because she wanted to or because she believed it was 'the right thing to do', God, that is to say, speaking to her 'through events and men'? Did Erlande ask her to marry him following his impending divorce in order to achieve the few years' happiness envisaged at Perros-Guirec but she refused, pleading that a woman whose former husband was still alive (as Constantine then was) "must not ever consider remarriage"[221]? Or did something go very wrong, for Aelfrida has 'Auguste Martin' die a lingering death from "general paralysis of the insane" (tertiary syphilis) and 'Clive' exult on hearing of it "as primitive man might have exulted over an enemy who would strike no more blows"[222], a dreadful literary revenge on a man who by her own account had fallen in love with her and by whom she had been sexually aroused? (In fact, Albert Erlande died from the delayed effects of war wounds.) Can it be that Aelfrida, a woman for whom "marriage … was inseparably connected with unhappiness" (or as she originally put it but legibly crossed out: "intercourse … was inseparably connected with adultery")[223] and who regarded remarriage as legitimised adultery, found herself confronted in Puys with the possibility of renewed sexual intimacy with an estranged but still married man with whom she had hoped for nothing more than a 'marriage' of literary minds and, recoiling in horror, revenged herself by having his fictional counterpart die horribly of a sexually-transmitted disease?

This is, of course, conjecture, and it may be that as the title of Erlande's 1933 novel *Un Festin de Vautours* has it, we are vultures picking over the skeletal remains of an affair which exists only in our imagination. But corroborative evidence exists insofar as Erlande's novel (itself written in 1931, the year following his possible meeting with Aelfrida) describes a woman with an insatiable but involuntary penchant for ruining other people's lives; it also exists in the diary of 'considerate and tactful' Alethea. Given that Alethea was then in the early stages of the breakdown which was to terminate her position at *La Semaine à Paris*, that dateable diary entries are absent during the period of her Dieppe holiday, and that such evidence as she provides is incoherent and sketchy, one should not, perhaps, rely on it too much, but given too that she wrote of the mother she met in Dieppe that not only did Aelfrida shock her with her critical and entrenched views on 'religion, character-judging and even emotion', but also that 'with a rather disgusted air'

she had burdened her daughter with her views on 'what she calls sex', a subject which appeared to preoccupy her, Alethea may corroborate what we envision may have happened. (She also notes that for a woman as attractive to men and as conscience-stricken as Aelfrida, puritanism and 'sensuality' were always at war.)[224] But given that Aelfrida revelled in 'scenes', the 'excitement and delight' of re-engaging with a man for whom 'nothing [mattered] except sex', who had informed her at Grandcamp that she was 'made for love', and whose caresses she admitted to having 'thoroughly enjoyed', may have titillated rather than disgusted her, her conscience re-awakening only after her return to England, as subsequent diary references to having failed piteously in 'detachment' and revelled in 'human consolation' show.[225]

Other references too suggest that a sexual relationship of some kind ('so it *seems*') took place between Aelfrida and Albert Erlande somewhere in northern France in early autumn 1930. For one thing, although she expressed (muted) remorse for her failures, Aelfrida also indulged in cheerful cogitations in which love for God and for 'people as individuals' suddenly seemed compatible, referred to the onset of a 'certain serene indifference to the way God chooses to make use of one', and on her forty-seventh birthday three weeks later decided she looked no older than thirty-seven and felt stronger and more vivacious and much happier too[226], something which suggests that her lightness of mood in late September and early October owed as much to Albert Erlande as to her first (and only) solo holiday. For another, the names of the attached houses in which 'Alice' creates her 'House of Prayer' are 'Yvetot' and 'La Rochelle', meaningless names in the context of the novel until we discover that at Yvetot in 1592 Henry of Navarre (then a Protestant) defeated the troops of the Catholic League and that La Rochelle was the last Protestant stronghold in France, surrendering to the forces of France's Catholic king in 1628 after a heroic siege. Can the names be clues left by our 'invigilator' to indicate that although Aelfrida (a Protestant of distant Huguenot descent) parried nominal Catholic Albert Erlande's advances in Grandcamp, she submitted to them in Perros-Guirec or Puys or both? (And with what enjoyment must 'invigilator' have invented this hint to a future biographer!) And do they also suggest that Aelfrida's conscience did not trouble her as sorely then as it did four or five years later at a time when deaths and desertion could be seen as punishment for sins committed in France in 1925, 1926, and 1930? And could it have been Erlande's death on 10 May 1934 as much as Constantine's on 28 January which sent her headlong to oblation at Malling, to reparative adoration in Oxford, and to silence and solitude at Tymawr?

Of further relevance here are veiled references in Aelfrida's own literary productions to Albert Erlande's. These may, of course, be no more than devices demonstrating to a future biographer that she has indeed read them but the references' benign nature (those relating to 'Auguste Martin' always excepted; indeed, her unsympathetic depiction of him in *The Centaur* could be revenge for literary slights, for both *Edmée Combres* and *Un Festin de Vautours* figure a woman much like herself who destroys a once-happy family for her own perverted satisfaction) may also demonstrate her continuing affection for a man who overcame her sexual reticences sufficiently to enable her to relate to him as woman to man, not merely as author to author: the appearance of a 'golden butterfly' in *The Centaur* echoes Erlande's '*vipère dorée*'; the fact that the last chapter of Aelfrida's 1929 novel *The Way We Grow Up* parallels Erlande's 1927 novella *Ils Jouaient de la Vie* when 'Roy' is informed by 'Honoria' that he has been 'playing' at life hitherto and must now face the consequences. (Aelfrida's comments – of the several changes of title undergone by the book, she lists four and says she 'forget[s] what else besides', and on publication says 'it does not seem mine'[227] – suggest that a 'forgotten' title may have been too reminiscent of Erlande's and that the novel was not 'hers' because she had plagiarised Erlande as well as Charles Kingsley.) Furthermore, her use of the unusual word *bouffée* to describe the gust of scent emanating from the Virgin Mary at Tymawr may be an echo of the gusts of perfume (*bouffées de parfum*) emanating from secret gardens (*jardins cachés;* also a euphemism for extra-marital sex) recalled from happier days of walks in the countryside by 'Denise', unhappy sister of the 'Edmée Combres' who, grey haired, middle-aged, and in poor health, and who wears glasses only for reading, has invaded 'Denise's' life like a malignant tumour[228], and the thunderstorm which drives 'Clive' into the 'pit-fortress' and causes the earth to quiver "under a gigantic thunderbolt"[229] (a '*trajet de la foudre*'), and that the name of the brood mare ('Palmyra') which gives birth to the hybrid foals in *The Centaur* being also that of wet-nurse 'Palmira Perott' in Erlande's 1924 novel *A L'ordre de Dieu* (a book referred to by Aelfrida in her May 1926 lecture to the Sophists as one of his greatest), collectively suggestive veiled references to a literary mentor.

And, it may be, Erlande reciprocated; *Ils Jouaient de la Vie* paraphrases the threat made by Constantine to Aelfrida in 1913 (*je suis / il est capable de te / se tuer*) and has 'Gilberte' possess as many '*sigisbées*' (i.e. *cicisbeos*) as a married woman as Aelfrida had 'Little Friends'. It may even be that some kind of literary dialogue continued for four years: shortly before his death, judging by the valedictory tone of his introduction and by the narrator's comment that he is writing in bed, Erlande wrote his last novella, *Faby de Blanc Vêtue*. Published posthumously in 1935[230], it tells the story of an idyllic summer spent in intercommunicating rooms in a rural inn by artist 'Alain Hubert' and his model and mistress 'Fabienne Sergeant'. (The story ends sadly: 'Alain' achieves fame through his portrait-studies of 'Fabienne' and leaves her to move in and marry into social circles closed to one of 'Faby's' lowly status as artist's model and former prostitute; heartbroken, she commits suicide.) 'Alain' has much of Erlande about him; 'Faby' has nothing of Aelfrida except by implication, but the inn at which they stay is close to a farm whose animals delight a girl whose experience of life is wholly urban. 'Faby' also possesses the knack of attracting animals and birds; 'Alain' sketches them and other objects to which observant 'Faby' draws his attention, captioning his pictures with her charming verbal descriptions and telling her that in uniting words and pictures he is attempting to lay bare (*disséquer*) her soul.[231] (We might also note Erlande's hinting at Aelfrida's Four Points of the Compass meditation in the name of the inn, *L'Auberge de Quatre Points Cardinaux*, where the lovers stayed.) Perhaps Aelfrida responded, though too late for Erlande to know: in *The Centaur* we find 'Zenobia', the centauress born to 'Palmyra', startlingly like 'Faby' with her very white skin, flaxen mane, and ability to call birds and animals to her; we also find 'Clive Farwell' whiling away his wartime army service by making "sketches of things that interested [him] – birds on the wing, insects ... leaves, roots, shells"[232] and later offering to write captions for photographs taken by 'Marcella' on a cruise on which he – chastely – accompanies her. Hence too, perhaps, Aelfrida's recall when writing the first of her postwar sequence of 'Autobiographies' "of a friend ... rather forgotten recently", a friend in need of succour, a friend who may also be the "certain French writer, a noted libertine" who announced "in mixed company" that mothers were as worthy of veneration as any sacred object[233], and her description in *Just Alice* and *The Centaur* of a suite of rooms used as a place of concealment for a present or former adulteress, as it might be the *dependence* of *Les Grottes* where Aelfrida and Albert Erlande may have met for the last time.

Returning to 'Clive' and to the 'exquisitely modelled' French soldiers concealed in the wych-elm and believed by him to be 'gone for ever', we may now ask: is it possible that Aelfrida concealed Albert Erlande's books thus and if so which did she conceal, when did she conceal them, and had they indeed 'gone for ever'? Aelfrida knew each and every tree in Brooklands Avenue intimately – she had walked the road at a child's pace as a child and with her own children, had mentally labelled each tree with a letter of the Jewish alphabet as she recited Psalm 119 on slow recuperative walks following Agneta's stillbirth, and had trudged it at an old man's pace on dragging walks with her blind father, and would have had plenty of time to discern a hiding place safer by far than cupboards at Fordfield. As to which of Erlande's books she concealed, those sent by him to her to prepare for her lecture to the Sophists, though dedicated "*A Madame Graham, charmante femme*", contained nothing of 'Madame Graham' herself and did not therefore require concealment, but those written during or after their 1925/26 relationship did – and where more appropriate than a deep hole in a tree already noted to be a suitable receptacle for something one might wish to hide? (Six or more volumes would pose no problem, French novels being published in flexible paperback format.) Aelfrida makes no comment as to *when* she concealed them (nor, of course, does she mention receiving them) but perhaps did so serially as each novel was bought (or sent by Erlande with affectionate dedications therein: *son vieil ami*, for example, a dedication made to another woman, or something more affectionate still) in order to conceal incriminating evidence of an 'adulterous' relationship. (Or of plagiarism.) But trees, as 'Clive' himself notes, "go rotten in the middle and have to be cut down"[234] and the Brooklands Avenue elms, planted around 1850, were in a parlous state by 1937, at which time fifty were felled; by 1950 only ninety-two remained and these were felled as they decayed until all were gone. Assuming that Erlande's books were *not* in one of the fifty trees felled in 1937, one can imagine Aelfrida's horror on returning to Cambridge in 1946 to find 'her' tree in danger of destruction and her hiding place of being revealed. (She had, of course, buried saints 'Rose' and 'Bruno' under a Monmouthshire gorse bush, an episode, which may have suggested 'Clive's' interment of his French grenadiers, but in another episode, obviously a parable, we find 'Marcella', now the 'Marquise de Perros-Cuzac', sending 'Clive' twelve gourd seeds; he gives three to a 'Mrs Grey' who loses them, three to 'Zenobia' who plants them but they grow small and sickly; six he keeps for himself and they flourish.[235] Can it be that the lost and failed seeds represent earlier volumes sent by Erlande to 'Madame Graham', volumes passed on by her and subsequently mislaid or to Agatha – whom 'Zenobia' resembles in many ways other than physical appearance – whose own nascent literary aspirations they failed to inspire? 'Clive's' seeds, like Aelfrida's own works inspired by Albert Erlande's, survive and bear fruit.) It being essential to remove incriminating evidence, Aelfrida, like adult 'Clive' with his grenadiers, retrieved her "damp and earthy"[236] parcel from the tree and disposed of its

contents. But how or to whom? Perhaps she destroyed them. Perhaps, as with Aleister Crowley's letters, she gave them for safekeeping to a trusted man whose opportune (or pre-arranged?) arrival at Fordfield had allowed her to decamp to France in September 1930 and to whom as a 'perfect brother'[237] she may have confided her secret. Or, given that by the time of their retrieval she had become very lame, she may have had to enlist the help of and provide an explanation to a man living in the precincts of "his only real home"[238] with the decimated avenue of elms beyond its gate.

Or – and this is what makes Aelfrida's references so tantalising and so difficult to deduce – are we looking through a window opened for us by the author of *The Centaur*, only to see a view quite other than that intended by 'invigilator'? Can it be that 'Auguste Martin' is not Albert Erlande but Aleister Crowley, an artist/writer who gave her a number of books she was forced to conceal, a man whose proper name (Alexander) bears 'august' (*auguste*) connotations because it reminds us of Alexander the Great, whose surname has avian connotations (crow[ley]/martin), who caught syphilis from one of the 'townee' girls whose sexual favours he enjoyed as a Cambridge undergraduate, and who like 'Auguste Martin', diverted '*Maman's*' attention from her offspring in *Paris*? Or is all this no more than the product of the overheated imagination of a biographer determined to 'see' what exists only in their imagination?

The second disclosure made by Aelfrida in *The Centaur* seems utterly improbable but is the easiest to prove true. At the beginning of his third academic year 'Clive' returns to Cambridge. Disorientated by thick fog, he abandons his car and finds himself in front of a house he seems dimly to recall. Knocking on the door, he is shown into a study where, sitting amid "sombre bookcases" in "flickering firelight", he sees a frail, elderly, blind, white haired, bearded man. A scene of mutual recognition ensues: the man is 'Dr Penrose', once an intrepid researcher, always the father whom 'Clive' has not seen since his mother ran away to France as 'Auguste Martin's' mistress. Having "walked back into his childhood", 'Clive' moves into his father's house and hyphenates his true surname with 'Roma's'; he also switches from Natural Science to History in honour of 'Dr Penrose's' status as distinguished emeritus historian and in order to help his blind father complete his *magnum opus*.[239] 'Clive's' subsequent academic success as an historian is attributed to his father's coaching and, following the latter's death, he is thought worthy of preparing his father's 'great work' for publication.

Though proud of her father's intellectual achievements with regard to *A History of University Reform*,

Aelfrida was dismissive of his books on religious themes, *The Manuscripts of God*, completed mid-1915, and *Stones of Stumbling*, begun immediately afterwards. Whether this was because of Alfred Tillyard's rabidly anti-Catholic views (both books, though ostensibly evolutionary histories of Christian belief, are actually anti-Catholic polemics, Roman Catholicism being a religion which he, like 'Dr Drummond', a Presbyterian don in *The Centaur*, may have described to his daughter as the subordination of man's "God-given intellect" to temporal authority, i.e. to the Pope[240], an action which divests him of responsibility and "turns him into a machine")[241] or whether it was his distrust of "the inward and private logic" of Mysticism, described by him as a "rat-hole for superstition in distress" sought as a consequence of excess of emotion and found after making judgements based on insecure foundations[242], she does not say. Both criticisms would have hurt, the latter criticism most.

Aelfrida, though she would have denied it, was as good a 'hater' as her father. What better way, therefore, to revenge herself on a man who had prevented publication of two of her novels because they dealt with (supposedly) immoral subjects and had denigrated her religious enthusiasms because they caused her to act (to his way of thinking) irrationally, than by rewriting parts of *his* books to conform to *her* way of thinking? An opportunity arose when the ending of the Great War allowed Alfred Tillyard to have his second and third books published at last, *The Manuscripts of God* in 1919, *Stones of Stumbling* in 1921. Being now completely blind, his once "exquisitely clear" handwriting having deteriorated into "a tangle of warring lines, impossible to decipher"[243], and his references in need of checking for inaccuracies, Alfred Tillyard, it seems, accepted the offer made by a daughter forced by circumstances to exist as "a child in [her] father's house"[244] to oversee his manuscripts for publication. Deciphering, checking, and editing Aelfrida duly did – and to such effect that not only was she able to imitate her father's style ("this could pass for Prof Penrose's own", says a don to 'Clive'; for someone who imitated Jane Austen to perfection, her father's style would not present a problem) and "rifle the treasures of [her] father's intellect"[245], but she was also able to insert passages written by herself into his text. (As 'Nicole', daughter of man of letters 'Antoine Loré', also admits in her account of her accidental fratricide in Erlande's *Un Festin de Vautours*.) So cleverly did she do this that passages relating to Mysticism in both books could be attributed to Alfred Tillyard did one not know his views on Mysticism and evince surprise at his inclusion of references to and sympathetic regard for it, notably his description of Mysticism as a means of achieving

"personal and conscious perfection" in this world and of being "vouchsafed ... the beatific vision" in the next.[246]

But how could he not have discovered his daughter's deception? Had he lost interest in completed works, as authors notoriously do, with little likelihood of the published volumes being read aloud to him? If so – and Alfred Tillyard remained capable of remembering what he had written even if he could not read it – Aelfrida was fortunate, for had her father discovered her corruption of his intellectual copyright she might have found herself and her daughters cast out of Fordfield. Or perhaps a chance remark or a review read to him by an unsuspecting reader revealed her duplicity and he used the discovery to bend her to his will by threatening disclosure if her conduct in other spheres of life transgressed rules he himself had set. If so (and even if not, for though Aelfrida could hardly ask her father's opinion on her submission of her thoughts as his own, she may have suffered pangs of conscience at her dishonesty), she completed her revenge following her father's death. In October 1929 she gave copies of his two theological books to institutions and individuals to whom his views on religion would appear old-fashioned or incomprehensible and ensured those reading what passed for *his* books would subconsciously absorb *her* teachings on Mysticism: *The Manuscripts of God* describes Mysticism as an "inward" or "personal" experience of "the kingdom of heaven always with us", a kingdom unascertainable by formal definition or "abstract reasoning" but achievable by means of an "inward and private logic ... of the heart ... which each must have for himself and which no man can have for another", and *Stones of Stumbling* as "the immediate communication of man and his Maker" without intercessory assistance (*sine uno intermedio*) and notes the existence of "a realm of mysticism in the midst of everyday life ... something incomprehensible and inexplicable and manifestly divine". Readers wishing to know more were also directed to *The Making of a Mystic* and *Vision Triumphant* as listed – and the list was surely composed by Aelfrida herself – in the endpapers of *The Manuscripts of God,* a list which also includes books by Alfred, Julius, and Frank Tillyard as if to show that Aelfrida was as qualified to write on *her* subject as they on theirs.[247]

The most macabre event in *The Centaur* happens at the point at which 'Clive' decides to perform reparative adoration for sins committed by his mother and 'Auguste Martin'. Realising that "something ... must be done" to mark the event and to remind himself that he performs it not as a man "virtuous in his life", but as a penitent sinner, and that in performing it he makes the power of Christ's paradigmatic sacrifice available to his erring mother and her lover, he decides to "brand" himself: locking himself in the bathroom for fear of interruption, he bares his chest and with a penknife incises a cross two inches high and one wide over his heart. (Or, rather, a phrase legibly crossed out, "where he assumed his heart was".) The wound bleeds profusely and "some time [elapses] before a pack of cotton wool was not soaked through". To make sure of achieving a good scar (the incised cross is also to "keep him from forgetting" to perform as a 'victim soul' should), he resolves to rub salt into the wound twice a day for a week.[248]

Did Aelfrida likewise carve a cross on her chest and if so, when and where did she commit self-cicatrisation? Circumstantial evidence provided in *The Centaur* suggests she did (her anatomical knowledge was sketchy and 'Clive's' surprise at the amount of blood rings true) but as to when we may only guess. But she had myriad reasons and myriad opportunities and numerous anguished diary entries, particularly those made at 'borderland' times of year or stages of her life, can be interpreted as veiled descriptions of the action and its precipitating cause: in February 1921, for example, at a time when she acknowledges herself 'very unhappy' with domestic life at Fordfield, her own health ('more rheumatic aches and pains than [she] could conveniently bear'), and her impending divorce (Constantine has furnished 'more evidence of misconduct', though whether hers or his she does not say)[249], she has a vision of her guardian angel slashing a cross on her chest and, lifting out her heart, asking her to inspect the wound.[250]

But whence came the idea of acting as she did? Three possible inspirations spring to mind. The first is found in Dante's *Divine Comedy*. Soon after entering Purgatory, Dante and Virgil encounter the 'Late Repenter' and in a canto full of references to penitence, pardoning and purgation of guilt, intercessory prayer, and Psalm 51 (the *Miserere*), hear stories of those who led godless lives but repented at the point of death; among these is a man who, in sore plight and desperate pain, made a (physical, not a signed) cross upon his breast and was deemed worthy of entering Heaven.[251] The second is found in *Richard Raynal: Solitary*: 'Richard' wears a depiction of the five wounds of Christ fastened with thorns to the breast of his hermit's smock as an aid to recollection and as a reminder of the "wounded heart" (*cor vulneratum*) of the "true lover of Jesus Christ" and of Christ's self-sacrifice. (Following an incident during which 'Richard' is mocked and reviled, he receives on his head a wound reminiscent of Christ's head lacerated by the crown of thorns[252]; given that Aelfrida suffered 'eczema' of the scalp at Tymawr, might this be attributable to her secretly wearing a similar crown with the comment that she wanted 'Our Lord Himself' to add 'of the Holy

Passion' to her name and that she 'longed' for 'the fellowship of His Suffering' and did not *mind* if it hurt?)[253] A self-inflicted pectoral cross and subsequent salting of the wound might therefore be another manifestation of Aelfrida's predisposition to self-cicatrisation when emotionally or spiritually stressed, of stigmatisation artefactually enhanced to increase its impact and its value in keeping her 'recollected' or, if it occurred after her Malling oblation, a representation of the Calvary cross of the Benedictine insignia. Or, of course, of her role as 'victim-soul'.

The third stems from 1913. Early in his Cambridge career, 'Clive Farwell' becomes interested in and practises "Buddhist meditations". (He also experiences ecstatic moments during which he becomes "as God, knowing all truth", has visions in which the Christ-figure on an ebony crucifix comes alive as "Christ glorified and risen", and undergoes supernatural visitations, all of which make him "[wonder] vaguely if he was a mystic".)[254] At first he finds the meditations beneficial: his mind becomes quieter and more focussed, something which has a positive effect on his academic work and enables him to become "more of a master inside his own head"; subsequently, however, he experiences an "undefined feeling" that an "unknown agency" is working in his mind, an agency not altogether "wholesome" because of the "queer latent power" it emits. He decides not to submit and abandons meditation altogether.[255] The passage is, of course, a disguised description of the early days of Aelfrida's spiritual direction by Aleister Crowley, a man whom she initially believed to be "extending the frontiers of knowledge" but later, like 'Clive' when he confronts and kills a sinister black spider[256], regarded as a symbolic arachnid to be obliterated from her life as expeditiously as possible. And it is to Crowley we must turn for another possible explanation.

In a "Special Supplement" to the first volume and number of *The Equinox*, Crowley (as "John St John") records the "Magical Retirement" of a "Frater O∴M∴" During his 'Retirement', 'Frater OM' adopts for meditation the position of "the Hanged Man in the Tarot Cards"[257] (a liminal figure suspended between earth and sky), deprives himself of food ("a species of intoxicant, hence a fruitful source of error")[258] in order to subdue his physical self, and in order to further affirm "Mastery of Body", incises a "Cross of Blood upon [his] breast by means of a Magick Knife".[259] Can it be that with Crowley's description of a 'Magical Retirement' in mind, Aelfrida entered St Benedict's (in the 'Frater's' case, "an inaccessible lamaserie in Tibet")[260] where during a 'spiritual' retirement she levitated (i.e. imagined herself suspended between earth and sky), subjected herself to near-starvation in an effort to become 'clean', and locked herself in her bathroom to bare her breast and incise a cross in the region of her heart? But when? In November 1934, ill in bed soon after retiring to her Oxford 'Lamaserie' and 'too feverish to distinguish dream from reality', she notes that not even the pain in her joints or recurrent uterine bleeding can prevent her glancing at 'the crucifix from Malling so near [her] bed' in order to keep herself 'recollected' and that she is now feeding on Christ 'in [her] heart' and serving Him '*hiddenly* as He wanted'[261] – and is perhaps inspired to carve on her chest a symbol which will keep her 'recollected'. A symbol which bleeds profusely because she is currently ingesting large quantities of aspirin to counteract her pain and because she is already scorbutic and prone to bleed profusely and lengthily as a result. And if a doctor should notice the scar, she can say that it was the result of a surgical operation – which, in a sense, it was.

Soon after 'Clive's' reunion with his father, 'Dr Penrose' dies. 'Clive', distraught at losing a parent unknown for so long, locks his emotions "down into the deepest dungeon of his unconscious mind"[262] and prepares to carry on. But finding himself gripped again by his former "vehement longing for … merciful … oblivion" and prey to "suicidal impulses" ("what was the use of going on?", "which was the easiest way out": death by drowning or by throwing himself from a cliff or a window?)[263] but afraid that if he admits to them or a suicide attempt fails he will again be confined "behind bars and bolts" because, as the devil reminds him, he is "mad … quite mad"[264], he returns to the peaceful surroundings of 'St Saviour's Convent'. Arriving at 'Gockett Farm', he finds it transformed into a vulgar guesthouse and flees to Scotland. Mentally distraught and suffering a recurrence of wartime malaria, he realises that cowardice has prevented him from confronting a vital fact: he does not belong to the world of men and women and Cambridge society but "to God".[265] Caught on a bare mountainside in a storm, he half stumbles, half falls to shelter in "St Bruno's Monastery" where he is allowed to stay for a few days in the guest house, to use the library, and to attend all the services except the Night Office. Presently he begins "to wake up to the nature of the life around him, the strong secret rhythm of a household planned entirely for the praise of God … a living organism whose heart was in the chapel", and "to perceive things that are clear to the spirit but dark to the mind and in that perception to find extreme delight".[266]

He asks to enter as a postulant, receiving from the abbot the advice put earlier in Mother Guenvrede's mouth at the time of Aelfrida's request to be a resident tertiary at Tymawr. But before sending him back to

Cambridge for a period of instruction prior to reception into the Catholic Church, the abbot asks six very odd questions:

– "I suppose you have no illegitimate children?" to which 'Clive' responds indignantly "Heavens no!"
– is he "entangled" with any woman?
– has he had more than one mistress?
– has he ever broken off an engagement?
– has he ever been in love with a married woman?
– has any girl refused him?[267]

If we substitute 'Aelfrida' for 'Clive' and the feminine for the masculine, we find the Abbot's questions pertinent indeed. Aelfrida has *not* borne an illegitimate child; she *has* been 'entangled' with a woman; she *has*, it seems, been the mistress of more than one man; she *has* been in love with a married man; a man *has* refused her. And, as we now realise, in *Just Alice* and *The Centaur* (and earlier in *Marrying a Stranger* and *O Passionate World*) she has answered all the abbot's questions. Or has she?

The opening pages of *The Centaur* have 'Clive Farwell' writing the autobiography intended as a suicide note to be discovered after his death. Only after completing it does he realise that he has written *three* accounts: "the autobiography he would have liked to produce" which would assure him of lasting fame; "the autobiography he thought he had written", a revealing picture of his good qualities; and "what he actually had written, the pitiable record of a stupid frightened child".[268] A revealing comment; perhaps the most revealing Aelfrida ever wrote. But do all or any of 'Clive's' 'autobiographies' provide an accurate record of what transpired at various stages of Aelfrida's life?

Much does; "the exhilaration of a problem solved", the "fascination of bringing dead epochs to life as one studies History", and the delight experienced in "a clue followed up and a link forged"[269] cannot be underestimated when reconstructing her life. But Aelfrida has both the "true historian's gift of *imaginative* reconstruction" and the autobiographer's desire to exercise "strict censorship … over autobiographical remarks"[270]; she is also 'a moralist first and an "artist" afterwards', novels written 'to the glory of God' being constructed to that end (e.g. to the end of 'Clive' 'at last understanding what he was meant to do')[271], not to that of absolute veracity. Hence though we, like 'Clive', may believe we have been brought face to face with "the realities of the situation"[272], we may be mistaken because, as she herself feared when composing *The Centaur*, we are "too wrapped up" in a tale "where everything keeps changing and dissolving … and the story is glimpses and flashes and squibs"[273] to ascertain what is true and what is not. Or, as 'Clive' replies to the abbot's questions, questions whose answers are probably or actually 'yes', the answer to *all* of them is '*no*'.

An unforeseen consequence of Aelfrida's 'interesting talk' with Veronica on the subject of 'Autobiographies, especially religious ones' was that Veronica's father felt impelled to borrow the manuscript. (Perhaps the Master of Jesus needed to know if he was as pilloried in *The Centaur* as was his wife in *The Way We Grow Up*.) His subsequent objections were not, however, to the episode in which 'Christopher Ranstead' rescues 'Clive' from suicide by drowning, an episode which suggests that Eustace may have rescued his sister from a suicide attempt (he certainly rescued her from post-natal depression by introducing her to fellow undergraduates soon to become Little Friends) but to the (seemingly) irrelevant and (certainly) '*impossible*' 'centaur episode'. How much Eustace actually knew of his sister's life is open to question (perhaps more than she suspected, given that he abstracted the manuscript from Wetenhall Cottage without asking her permission and to her manifest alarm); how much was revealed to him during his reading of *The Centaur* we also do not know. (Perhaps he discussed it with Julius; under the circumstances it is difficult to believe that he did not. Perhaps Julius alerted him to events in their sister's life of which both were unaware prior to *The Centaur*.) What we *do* know is that Aelfrida took Eustace's criticisms to heart. Finding *The Centaur*, like *Just Alice* (a novel she 'preferred' to *The Centaur* because of the greater 'stability' of 'Alice's' environment[274], but is 'Alice Marsden's' story any more or less full of "half-grasped meanings, intricate and deep"[275] than 'Clive's'?), rejected by publishers because the 'centaur section' might 'offend' their readers and because 'much of the religious argument, though … leading up to the right conclusion', might 'shock' those unconvinced by her idiosyncratic views, Aelfrida '[got] an opinion out of her guardian angel'[276] and recast *The Centaur* as *Rich Man's Choice*. (She even began to plan a sequel which would 'follow [her hero] into his monastery' but believing this to be 'pure self-indulgence', never wrote it.)[277] By mid-January 1952 the 'new ex-*Centaur*' was 'developing magnificently' but the 'poor lookout'[278] envisaged for other post-Tymawr books sent to commercial publishing houses also affected *Rich Man's Choice* and it, like *The Centaur*, was eventually consigned unpublished to Girton College.

A comparison of the two versions is instructive for what it tells us of the change in Aelfrida's literary vision: the 'ape–men' incident is abbreviated and less dramatic ('Clive' is ejected, not detained, by the sinister creatures; the sacrificial altar is replaced by a pool of limpid water cupped in a rock); a single reference to the devil is replaced by extended passages on the role in 'Clive's'

life of a personage named only periphrastically, an interesting addition given the devil's prominent position in Aelfrida's recent and, as we shall see, future life; the 'Dr Penrose' episode remains but with greater emphasis on 'Clive' *suggesting* to his blind father that he read his work to him and undertake the updating of references as and if required; the 'Jesus Lock', 'Invigilator', and 'incised cross' episodes remain virtually unchanged. The 'centaur episode' is, however, replaced by a diatribe ostensibly promoting eugenic practices but actually condemning them and by a description of a "New Democracy", possibly Soviet Russia-controlled, condemned also.[279] The alterations, of course, greatly alter the narrative in terms of what is significant for its author but what remains or is substituted is significant in its own way; more importantly, however, a comparison of the two versions demonstrates that by the time she has completed *Rich Man's* Choice, Aelfrida is infinitely richer in self-knowledge. And given the cathartic experience she has recently undergone, she also possesses more freedom of choice regarding the way she behaves because she possesses sufficient insight to enable her to understand why she behaves as she does. This will not, unfortunately, prevent her behaving badly at Lolworth and thereafter because childhood damage to her psyche is so profound that she cannot help but act in preconditioned ways when presented with a particular circumstance or personality, but an important change has been wrought in her attitude to life: though she still tries to absolve herself of responsibility by placing the blame for her mistakes on others' shoulders, she no longer feels compelled to pick over the dead bones of her past.

An unexpected and, in the circumstances, uncanny echo of the childhood event which marred her life is preserved with the typescript of *Rich Man's Choice*. On the reverse of the sheet of brown paper in which Aelfrida (always a hoarder) wrapped the volume before sending it on fruitless journeys to publishers is written in faded black ink and an unsteady hand the name by which she was known as a child: FRIDA.

## Notes

1   GCPPT 1|1|64 28 and 31 December 1946.
2   GCPPT 1|1|62 22 May 1944.
3   GCPPT 1|1|64 17 June 1946.
4   GCPPT 1|1|56 20 October 1938.
5   GCPPT 1|1|09 Undated entry written on last page of volume following entry dated 20 November 1902.
6   GCPPT 1|1|64 12 and 22 February 1947.
    GCPPT 3|1|9a Letter from Julius Tillyard to Aelfrida ('dearest Tit') of 18 July (1947).
7   GCPPT 1|1|64 26 February 1947.
8   ibid. 19 and 22 February 1947.
9   ibid. 12 February 1947.

10 ibid. 1|1|64 28 June 1946.

11 Julius' perception of the relationship is perhaps expressed in Byron's poem *Stanzas to Augusta* of 12 April 1816, a poem written immediately prior to the poet's departure from England not knowing whether he and his beloved half-sister would ever meet again or their "ties of baf-fled love" remain unbroken.

12 GCPPT 1|1|6 1 November 1900.

13 GCPPT 1|1|41 3 April 1932.

14 GCPPT 1|1|46 26 August 1934.

15 GCPPT 1|1|37 7 June 1930.

16 Tillyard, Ae. *The Centaur* pp 328–329 (GCPPT 2|21|1).

17 Tillyard, Ae. *The Glory of the West* p 258 (GCPPT 2|16|1 Pt2).

18 Tillyard, Ae. *The Centaur* pp 247 and 229–235.

19 ibid. pp 248–259. "He need not … was there" is crossed out in the manuscript but remains legible.

20 GCPPGA1.4 Letter from Aelfrida to Alethea Graham of 12 July 1953.

21 GCPPT 1|1|56 2 October 1938.

22 GCPPT 1|1|57 22 September 1939.

23 Tillyard, Ae. *The Glory of the West* p 258. Saint Benedict was devoted to a sister whose enthusiasm for the religious life was as great as his own and allowed himself an annual meeting with her, she travelling from her nearby nunnery to Monte Cassino for the purpose. Scholastica predeceased Benedict, dying shortly after their last meeting; brother and sister shared a tomb.

24 GCPPT 1|1|70a. Letter from Julius Tillyard (then in Lahr) to Aelfrida dated "4th Sunday in Adv[ent] 1952". The letter is marked in Aelfrida's writing "*keep*".

25 GCPPT 1|1|64 17 June 1946.

26 Tillyard, Ae. *The Centaur* p 296. The word GOD is printed as Aelfrida wrote it, i.e. in capital letters.

27 GCPPT 1|1|46 13 December 1934.

28 GCPPT 1|1|46 13 December 1934.
   GCPPT 1|1|65 24 April 1947.

29 GCPPT 1|1|65 31 December 1947.

30 ibid. 21 April 1947.

31 ibid. 31 December 1947 and 24 January 1948.

32 GCPPT 1|1|66 10 June 1948.

33 ibid. 29 and 31 May and 18 December 1948.

34 ibid. 15 November and 21 December 1948.

35 ibid. 26 January 1949.

36 ibid. 1, 18 and 22 February 1949.

37 ibid. 24 February and 24 March 1949.

38 ibid. 11 September 1949. The Girton College archive contains three copies of *Just Alice* (GCPPT 2|19), two typed versions by-lined 'Mrs Graham, Wetenhall Cottage, 15 Brooklands Avenue, Cambridge', and one by-lined 'Mrs Graham' with the address of Lolworth Rectory, the latter being a carbon copy with several unsequentially numbered and/or added pages, corrections, and emendations; this version is quoted here.

39 GCPPT 1|1|51 30 July 1936.
   GCPPT 1|1|52 26 December 1936.

40 GCPPT 1|1|61 7 February 1943. Sayers' book, published in 1941, supposes an analogy between the creativity of a novelist or playwright and the notion of the Trinity as a triple force incorporating Idea, Energy, and Power. Aelfrida was critical of the book's content, noting that it was 'supposed to be … about the Trinity' but in practice said more about Sayers herself.

41 GCPPT 1|1|66 3 September 1949.

42 ibid. 8, 9 and 10 September 1949.

43 ibid. 9 September 1949.

44 ibid. 18 September, 8 and 15 October and 13 and 24 November 1949.

45 GCPPT 1|1|67 24 June 1950.

46 GCPPT 1|1|69 18 April and 17 May 1951.

47 Letter from The Authors' Alliance to 'Mrs Graham' of 5 September

1955 enclosed with GCPPT 2|19.

48 GCPPT 1|1|67 15 and 23 September 1950.

49 GCPPGA1.4 Letter from Aelfrida to Alethea Graham of 12 July 1953.

50 GCPPT 1|1|71 10 February 1954. The house in which the 'Marsden' family lived was a real house whose leaseholder was Aelfrida's 'Dear Grandpapa' Henry Joseph Wetenhall. It was to this house that dying Henry Joseph feared he and his wife might have to refugee, he in death-bed delirium thinking he had lost all his money and Fordfield with it.

51 GCPPT 1|1|69 17 May 1951.

52 Tillyard, Ae. *Just Alice* p324.

53 Raverat, G. p47.

54 Tillyard, Ae. *The Closer Walk with God* p 61.

55 ibid. p 4.

56 ibid. p 277.

57 ibid. p 278.

58 ibid. pp 284 and 286.

59 ibid. p 295.

60 ibid. pp 235 and 277.

61 ibid. pp 237 and 260.

62 ibid. p 273.

63 ibid. pp 38 and 321.

64 ibid. p 42.

65 ibid. p 70.

66 ibid. p 131.

67 ibid. pp 38–39.

68 ibid. pp 12, 14 and 20. Among the list of books read by Aelfrida at Lolworth only two are secular: the letters of Octavia Hill (1838–1912), reformer and pioneer social worker, and a biography of suffragette Emmeline Pankhurst (1858–1928) by her daughter Sylvia (GCPPT 1|1|64a). Echoes of the lives of these strong independent women are evident in 'Diana'.

69 ibid. pp 2 and 312.

70 ibid. pp 282–283.

71 The character of 'Madeleine' owes much to that of Madeleine Sémer, the 'convert and mystic' who was to have been included by Aelfrida as an example of a 'penitent' in her unwritten book on 'Saintliness'; reading Félix Klein's 1927 biography *Madeleine Sémer convert and mystic. 1874–1921,* Aelfrida commented that many of Sémer's experiences were 'much like' her own (GCPPT 1|1|57 14 March 1938).

72 Tillyard, Ae. *Just Alice* pp 1,5,16,23,26,126 and 252.

73 ibid. pp 184 and 239.

74 ibid. p 274.

75 ibid. p238.

76 ibid. p 236. In this respect at least 'Madeleine' is an interesting amalgam of Lilian Whitehouse and Aelfrida's disreputable relative Luna Eady.

77 ibid. p 245.

78 ibid. pp 244 and 271.

79 ibid. pp 260–264.

80 ibid. pp 2, 26, 59 and 296.

81 ibid. p 286.

82 ibid. pp 253–256 and 265.

83 ibid. pp 289–319. Their death is one of the 'sudden calamities … not true to life' criticised by Alethea.

84 ibid. p 296. There is something of Phyllis Tillyard in 'Barbara', though Phyllis' earlier acerbity regarding her sister-in-law was tempered by her having been 'so sweet' when she visited Aelfrida shortly after the 'shewing' which inspired her to begin *Just Alice* (GCPPT 1|1|66 9 September 1949).

85 ibid. pp 285 and 305. Aelfrida's inspiration for her dual 'House of Prayer' may derive in part from a never-realised SSC scheme to found a male Community in Michaelgarth to complement the female Community at Tymawr, in part from a Community (the Servants of the Will of God) established in Sussex in 1938 by the Rev RCS Gofton–Salmond and intended by him as a 'double monastery' of male and female

brethren following 'a simple 'Rule on Benedictine lines' (GCPPT 1|1|72 17 July 1955). Aelfrida described him as 'tall and striking looking … [with] the face of a visionary and ecstatic' and seeming, with his piercing eyes, 'large loose-lipped mouth' and dramatic clothing of skull cap and cloak, both 'little mad' (GCPPT 1|1|59 5 and 8 February 1942) and disconcertingly like Aleister Crowley. Father Gofton-Salmond visited Tymawr chiefly in order to train up a Lady Carmichael, then resident behind the grille, as head of the female side of his Community; Aelfrida feared that the Father's 'guileless' acolyte was being manipulated by her spiritual director for his own ends but forbore to comment (GCPPT 1|1|59 5 and 8 February 1942). Lady Carmichael is not mentioned in Peter Anson's *The Call of the Cloister* in which Father Gofton-Salmond's Community is discussed.

86  Wynn expressed concern at finding himself in *Just Alice* (Aelfrida's fictional bishop has "something wonderfully buoyant about him" in spite of his face being "rather sad … in repose") but was reassured after having her read the relevant pages to him: his expression, she noted, changed from 'faint apprehension' to 'extreme interest and grave approval'. (GCPPT 1|1|68 14 August 1950 and *Just Alice* p 192).

87  Tillyard, Ae. *Just Alice* p 313.

88  ibid. p 109

89  ibid. pp65–66.

90  The Max Müller to whom Aelfrida refers in *Just Alice* is the famous philologist (1923–1900), one of whose books she read while researching *Spiritual Exercises*. It is possible that she read others: Müller's fifty-volume translation of *Sacred Books* of the East was published between 1879 and 1910 and it may have been his translations of the *Vedas* that Mrs Venn encouraged her to read. Adolescent Frida seems to have sought out and read the *Koran* herself (GCPPT 2|25|2(4).)

91  ibid. pp 90–93.

92  ibid. pp 145–150 and 166.

93  ibid. pp 149, 163 and 166–167.

94  ibid. p 326.

95  GCPPT 1|1|71 10 February 1954.

96  GCPPT 1|1|68 10 August 1950.

97  GCPPT 1|1|69 20 June 1951.

98  GCPPT 1|1|18 6 July 1911.

99  GCPPT 1|1|13 14 June 1906.
    GCPPT 1|1|18 10 July 1911.

100 Tillyard, Ae. *To Malise* p 25.

101 GCPPT 1|1|13 22 August 1905.

102 GCPPT 2|5. The poem was never published.

103 ibid. and *Cambridge Poets 1900–1913* p 193.

104 *Thought and Speech* is the first poem in the section entitled 'oems about all sorts of things' in *The Garden and the Fire* (p 43).

105 GCPPT 1|1|18 10 and 11 July 1911.

106 GCPPT 2|5 The first quotation is from *Triolet ('To a King's Man)*, the second from an unpublished poem.

107 ibid. *To Agatha when she was ill*.

108 ibid. The poem written on 9 September 1911 in Cambridge is disguised as *The Vow of Olga Stanislovna* appears in *The Garden and the Fire* on the same page as *Thought and Speech* (p43).

109 Tillyard, Ae. *The Glory of the West* p 311 (GCPPT 2|16|1 Pt 2).

110 The quotation is taken from *The Difference*, Aelfrida's poem on the subject of infidelity in *Cambridge Poets 1900–13* pp 196–197.

111 GCPPT 1|1|18 11 July 1911.

112 Aelfrida's description of the 'copse' applies equally well to the beech-wood or to the wooded area on Madingley Hill to the northeast of Cambridge where the incident is supposed to have taken place.

113 Tillyard, Ae. *Naomi da Costa* p 260 (GCPPT 2|22).

114 GCPPT 1|1|18 11 July 1911.

115 *Cambridge Poets* contains one poem by Eric Silvanus. *Evening on the Downs,* ostensibly about "green Sussex", may contain references to his

and Aelfrida's tryst on a sunlit slope and to delight in knowing that "nothing ever shall estrange" their love; its allusions to the sea may echo the maritime metaphors of her own *Thought and Speech*. The date of composition of Eric's poem is unknown but must pre-date 1913.

116 GCPPT 1|1|18 21, 24, and 30 June 1911.

117 Worth noting here is that Madeleine Sémer, mystic, visionary, ascetic, and spiritual espouser of Christ, also had an affair as a result of which she lost "home, place and fortune" and had "a divorce pronounced against her" (Klein, F. pp 1–9).

118 GCPPT 1|1|18 3 and 13 June 1911.

119 ibid. 6 October 1911.

120 ibid. 11 November 1911.

121 GCPPT 1|1|61 30 July 1943.

122 GCPPT 1|1|66 19 October 1949.

123 GCPPT 1|1|67 18 January 1950.

124 ibid. 16 May and 4 October 1950.

125 GCPPT 1|1|68 16 May and 26 July 1950.

126 ibid. 22 July 1950.

127 ibid. 10 August 1950.

128 ibid. 15 August 1950.

129 GCPPT 1|1|23 23 September 1918.

130 GCPPT 1|1|68 12 and 28 July 1950.

131 ibid. 28 and 30 July 1950.

132 GCPPT 1|1|3 16 August [1897] .

133 For Aelfrida's list of Julius' travels, see GCPPT 1|1|68. Between 1904 and 1950 (with the exception of the war years) Julius travelled abroad at least once a year.

134 GCPPT 1|1|66 24 February 1949.

135 Tillyard, Ae. *The Centaur* p296.

136 ibid. p 258.

137 ibid. p 252.

138 GCPPT 1|1|69 7 and 18 November 1951.

139 GCPPT 1|1|67 31 October 1951.

140 ibid. 16 August 1950.

141 ibid. 2 September 1950.

142 GCPPT 1|1|69 10 January and 11 March 1951.

143 ibid. 20 July 1951.

144 ibid. 4 August and 1 September 1951.

145 ibid. 1 November 1951.

146 ibid. 20 July 1951.

147 Tillyard, Ae. *The Centaur* p1.

148 ibid. p 324. Worth noting here with regard to Monsignor Ronald Knox, a convert to Catholicism in 1916 is that two priests greatly influenced his decision: Father John Talbot (c.f. 'Audrey Talbot') of the Brompton Oratory and the abbot of a Scottish monastery at Fort Augustus. For further details, see Waugh, E. *Two Lives*.

149 In Buddhist mythology, 'Mara' is the name given to the spirit of evil, enemy of the Buddha. In other cultures the name is associated with bitterness or with malignant female demons whose pleasure it is destroy or mar men's lives – as Aelfrida herself believed she did when she noted her propensity to kill or mar or lose everything or everyone she valued.

150 'Roma Farwell's' love (*amor*) for 'Clive', is, like her name, a reversal of what love should be: she is not only possessive ("I'm going to keep you") but she also uses the young boy as her confidant, telling him "things [he] had no business to hear … the whole of her life story … repeated … again and again"; she also forces him to share a bedroom with her, rejects him violently when he refuses her requests, and weeps over him remorsefully when she realises what she has done. Eventually "out of her mind [and] living in a world of her own" where she makes "preposterous suggestions" which "can't be allowed", she is sent by her friend and companion 'Dr Joan Coldham' to a mental hospital, returning "almost herself but not quite". No further reference is made to the episode but 'Clive' never trusts her again.

(*The Centaur* pp 49 and 96). Insofar as 'Roma' also sees herself as a "Dictatrix Mundi", her behaviour towards 'Clive' mirrors Aelfrida's behaviour towards Agatha and Alethea.

151 Tillyard, Ae. *The Centaur* p158.

152 ibid. p 4.

153 GCPPT 1|1|69 10 January 1951.

154 In view of the possible influence of Marcel Proust's literary ideas on Aelfrida's work, it is interesting to note that the latter employs the name 'Marcella' twice, once as 'Marcella Cusac' in *The Centaur* and once as 'Marcella', wife of 'Adrian', in *The Glory of the West*. In both instances 'Marcella' is involved in investigations of a mediumistic nature in which forces and voices from the past or the supernatural are evoked with shattering results.

155 Tillyard, Ae. *The Centaur* p149. The reference is to Margaret Verrall and the 'cross-correspondences' engaged in by herself and other female members of the SPR.

156 Tillyard, Ae. *The Fruits of Silence* p17 (GCPPT 2|18).

157 Tillyard, Ae. *The Centaur* p 294.

158 ibid. p 160.

159 ibid. p 161.

160 In the volume of her diary (GCPPT 1|1|4) read by Aelfrida to Julius in July 1950, an extra sheet of paper has been inserted at the end on which are listed (in Aelfrida's handwriting) a series of dates, beginning with 9 September 1897 and ending with 25 December 1899. Checking the dated entries, we find a cross against each – and discover that each entry save one is particularly relevant to that period of her life. The only inexplicable entry ('Books') may be a pointer to a biographer that it is in her books that the 'truth' may be found or, given that the entry occurs at Christmas, to the fact that Aelfrida has received books of great significance to her.

161 Tillyard, Ae. *The Centaur* p137.

162 ibid. p 247.

163 Charles, P. p111.

164 *The Cambridge Review* vol XXII no.1754 20 January 1951 p 256. 'Traveller', Aelfrida informs us in 1955, was the pen name of one Peter Green. Coincidentally, the same volume of the *Review* also contains a short note (p125) by Professor HJW Tillyard on a scheme of cursive (phonetic) shorthand used by him during 50 years of "note-taking" on 'Byz Mus'.

165 The line quoted is taken from Aelfrida's poem *The First Day of Full Term* (GCPPT 1|1|65 9 October 1947).

166 Tillyard, Ae. *The Centaur* pp 6,9,15, 18 and 24.

167 ibid. pp 16–18 and 24–25.

168 ibid. p 10.

169 GCPPT 1|1|57 12 December 1939.

170 Tillyard, Ae. *The Centaur* pp 142–149.

171 GCPPT 1|1|67 8 April 1950.

172 GCPPT 1|1|74 1 June 1957.

173 GCPPT 1|1|53 8 June 1937.

174 GCPPT 1|1|61 21 March 1943.

175 Tillyard, Ae. *The Glory of the West* pp 61and 127 (GCPPT 2|16|3). GCPPT 1|1|61 20 April 1943.

176 GCPPT 1|1|52 19 and 29 November 1936.

177 GCPPT 1|1|55 21 July 1938.

178 GCPPT 1|1|61 26 February 1944.

179 Tillyard, Ae. *The Centaur* p239. Aelfrida's Dantean reference is to Canto III: 28–30 of the *Divine Comedy 1: Hell*.

180 The reference is to *The Book of Common Prayer* 40:1.

181 GCPPT 1|1|58 20 July 1940.

182 GCPPT 1|1|63 5 and 11 July 1945.

183 Tillyard, Ae. *The Centaur* p 8.

184 GCPPT 1|1|61 26 February 1944.

185 GCPPT 1|1|56 31 October 1938.

186 Tillyard, Ae. *The Centaur* p208. The sentence quoted is asterisked.

187 GCPPT 1|1|61 13 March 1943.

188 GCPPT 1|1|58 26 February 1941.

189 GCPPT 1|1|18 15 and 19 December 1912 (retrospective account).

190 GCPPT 1|1|71 10 May 1954.

191 GCPPT 1|1|18 15 December 1912.

192 Tillyard, Ae. *The Centaur* pp163–173.

193 ibid. pp 105–106.

194 Tillyard, Ae. *Marrying a Stranger* pp 223–225 (GCPPT 2|6).

195 Tillyard, Ae. *The Centaur* pp105–106.

196 ibid. p 304.

197 In *Alethea's Dream,* for example (*Bammie's Book* p 7), Alethea/Aelfrida dreams of birds visiting her as she lies asleep in a place where "Behind my bed the forest lies / Before me is the sea", a description truer of Hampshire and the New Forest than of Ventnor. In spite of later diary and novel references to the Maudesley Hospital in London, Aelfrida cannot have been a patient there in 1912 (the hospital was opened only in 1923); St Andrew's in Northampton, founded in 1838 for the treatment of "private and pauper lunatics" but by 1876 a lunatic asylum for the "middle and upper classes", is a possibility but records do not show her as a patient. (Fulbourn Asylum near Cambridge would not then have been worthy of consideration.) A search is complicated by the fact that possible institutions are legally obliged to keep records of patients for only 20 years; to free up storage space, most destroy them once 20 years have elapsed.

198 *The Cambridge Magazine* vol II no 9 18 January 1913 pp 218–219.

199 Tillyard, Ae, *The Centaur* p131.

200 ibid. p 304.

201 GCPPT 1|1|69 25 August 1951.

202 Tillyard, Ae. *Can I be a Mystic* pp 31 and 170–171.

203 Tillyard, Ae. *The Centaur* p258.

204 GCPPT 1|1|69 10 November 1951.

205 ibid. 7 and 27 December 1951.

206 Guerber, H. pp 189 and 278.

207 Tillyard, Ae. *The Centaur* p18.

208 ibid. p174. Even more relevant to the 'centaur' section of Aelfrida's book is that Piero di Cosimo's picture *The Forest Fire* includes a pair of deer of which the male has a human face. The picture hangs in the Ashmolean Museum, Oxford, where Aelfrida could have seen it during her time at St Benedict's.

209 Dante *Divine Comedy: Hell* Canto XII 55–99 and note by D L Sayers p 147.

210 Bunyan, J. Part 2 pp 182, 224–225 and 229.

211 ibid. pp 310–316.

212 The second portrait may owe something to R H Benson's story *The Green Robe* (included in *The Light Invisible* p 6) in which the protagonist, then roughly the same age as little 'Clive', sees a face "awash with a veritable confusion of emotive mysticism" (*sic*) look out from a wall. Also worthy of note is that the small girl (France Bocion) of whom Aelfrida grew fond in Lausanne was related to local proto-Impressionist painter François Bocion (1828–1890) whose pictures Aelfrida may have seen, and that one of his pictures (*The Bird Catchers*) depicts a man peering through a leafy aperture in a hide he has constructed to conceal himself from his prey.

213 Tillyard, Ae. *The Centaur* pp 33–41.

214 ibid. pp 95 and 126.

215 ibid. pp 169 and 173.

216 ibid, p 126. 'Clive's' statement is crossed out in Aelfrida's manuscript but remains legible.

217 GCPPT 1|1|38 16 September 1930 (retrospective account).

218 ibid. 27 September 1930.

219 ibid. 24 September 1930.

220 GCPPT 1|1|38 3 September 1930.

221 Tillyard, Ae. *O Passionate World* p 324.

222  Tillyard, Ae. *The Centaur* p320.

223  ibid.

224  GCPPG A1.1 Entry written between 17 and 24 September 1930. The probable conversation between Aelfrida (as 'Carola') and Alethea (as 'Vera') is reproduced at length in *O Passionate World* pp 304–309.

225  GCPPT 1|1|31 23 and 27 August 1925.
GCPPT 1|1|38 27 September 1930.

226  GCPPT 1|1|38 27 September and October 1930.

227  GCPPT 1|1|36 23 January and 8 October 1929.
Erlande, A. *Ils Jouaient de la Vie* p 5.

228  Erlande, A. *Edmée Combres* pp 34 and 127.

229  Tillyard, Ae. *The Centaur* p 24.

230  Erlande, A. *Faby de Blanc Vêtue*. The novella appeared in three successive numbers (884–886) of volume CCLIX of the *Mercure de France* (15 April, 1 May, and 15 May 1935).

231  Erlande, E. op cit. No 885 p555.

232  Tillyard, Ae. *The Centaur* p 5.

233  Tillyard, Ae. *The Glory of the West* GCPPT 1|16|1 pt 1, p 44, pt 2, p 245. Tucked inside the definitive typescript of this work (GCPPT 2|16|2) is a list of textual comments, one of which notes re chapter 14 p 2 "the French author – how relevant?" (The list is in Frank Stokoe's writing and probably refers to the 'supervision' conducted with Aelfrida 'as if I had been an undergraduate and he my supervisor' in Lolworth on 3 June 1948). If what Aelfrida hints is true, the reference was 'relevant' indeed.

234  Tillyard, Ae. *The Centaur* p 271.

235  ibid. p 214. The lines quoted are asterisked.

236  ibid. p 229.

237  GCPPT 1|1|38 29 September 1930.

238  Tillyard Ae. *The Centaur* p 229.

239  ibid. pp 229–246. Aelfrida may have been inspired here by Archie Venn who continued his father's magisterial *Alumni Cantabrigensis*, a work in progress in 1950/51.

240  ibid.p 312.

241  Tillyard, AI. *Stones of* Stumbling p 111.

242  Tillyard, AI. *The Manuscripts of God* pp 212–216.

243  Tillyard, Ae. *The Centaur* p257.

244  ibid. p 247.

245  ibid. p 263. The passage relating to the literary relationship between the Penroses *père et fils* is asterisked.

246  Tillyard, AI. *The Manuscripts of God* p123.

247  Tillyard, AI. *The Manuscripts of God* pp212–216, chapter entitled 'The Venture of Faith'.
Tillyard, AI. *Stones of Stumbling* p 92, chapter entitled 'Rome's greatest convert' i.e. Newman.

248  Tillyard, Ae. *The Centaur* p 321. The episode is asterisked at the end of the passage. The word initially used by Aelfrida to describe the event is 'sacrifice', appropriately an echo of Christ's 'sacrifice'. She later replaces it with 'immuration', presumably to imply that in branding himself 'Clive' is now irrevocably 'walled into' his vow.

249  GCPPT 1|1|25 12, 13, and 16 February 1921.

250  ibid. 19 February 1921.

251  Dante *The Divine Comedy; Purgatory* Canto V lines 23, 55, 70–72, 126–129. A reading of Psalm 51 will show how apposite Aelfrida would have found it.

252  Benson, R H. *Richard Raynal: Solitary* pp 48, 60 and 78.

253  GCPPT 1|1|53 23 and 24 March 1937.

254  Tillyard, Ae. *The Centaur* pp 3, 191, 265 and 279. Two of the passages are asterisked.

255  ibid. pp 82–97. The whole passage is asterisked.

256  ibid. pp 82 and 110. Both passages are asterisked and sentences on p 82 are further emphasised by marginal marks.

257  Crowley, A. *The Equinox* vol I no. 1 March 1909 *The Record of the Magical Retirement of G H Frater O∴M∴. (Special Supplement* p 14).

258  ibid. pp 30 and 79.

259  ibid. pp 10,16 and 32.

260  ibid. p 3.

261  GCPPT 1|1|56 20 September and 4 November 1934.

262  Tillyard, Ae. *The Centaur* p286.

263  ibid. pp 155, 178, and 298.

264  ibid. p 240.

265  ibid. p 296. The whole passage from which this phrase is quoted is asterisked.

266  ibid. p 302.

267  ibid. p 307. There is an asterisk at the end of this paragraph.

268  ibid. p 58.

269  Tillyard, Ae. *The Glory of the West* pp 44 and 56 (GCPPT 2|61|1 Pt 1).

270  Tillyard, Ae. *The Centaur* pp 247 and 252 (Author's emphasis). Worth noting is that as 'Clive', Aelfrida informs us that all the references in 'Dr Penrose's' book had been correct so far and that it was therefore "a waste of time to go on checking them" (ibid. p 316); a count of Aelfrida's asterisked passages, however, reveals that there are two more to go.

271  GCPPT 1|1|69 11 March and 10 October 1951.

272  Tillyard, Ae. *The Centaur* p 247.

273  GCPPT 1|1|69 20 July 1951. A squib is both a small explosive firework and a lampoon or satirical composition.

274  Tillyard, Ae. *The Centaur* p 307.
GCPPT 1|1|69 20 July 1951.

275  The quotation is from Frances Cornford's poem, *The Certain Knot of Peace,* reproduced in *Cambridge Poets 1900–1913* and used by Aelfrida as title and epigraph in *O Passionate World*; interestingly in view of what we have recently discovered, Aelfrida notes that she is feeling after "half-grasped meanings intricate and deep" during the months intervening between the completion of *Just Alice* and the commencement of *The Centaur.*

276  ibid. 10 November 1951.

277  ibid. 23 September and 27 December 1951.

278  ibid. 10 January and 20 March 1952.

279  In what may be an example of tit-for-tat plagiarism, this section of *Rich Man's Choice* (GCPPT 2|21|2) appears to owe much to Aldous Huxley's *Brave New World* (1932), a work noted earlier to owe much to *Concrete* (published in 1930), most notably in its use of the term "Big Brother" though there are other similarities. A diary entry of 14 August 1937 (GCPPT 1|1|54) discloses that Huxley knew of Aelfrida as a writer, her informant being the wife of Professor Mottram, the nutritionist who persuaded her that self-induced scurvy was not a divinely-mandated adjunct to reparative adoration. Aelfrida herself nowhere states she has read *Brave New World* (she could have gained an idea of its contents from contemporary reviews and friends and family could have commented on similarities between her book and Huxley's) but her failure to mention Huxley's possible plagiarism may stem from reluctance to lay herself open to similar charges with regard to May Sinclair, RH Benson, HG Wells, Charles Kingsley, et al. In all events, her opinion of Huxley was not high; in *The Way We Grow Up* (p45) she lists him disparagingly among "people considered by Cambridge to be important".

# Lolworth Rule-keeping

For one used to keeping a Rule since oblation was proposed by the Lady Abbess of Malling in 1934, its maintenance, reinforced by nine years at Tymawr, was second nature to a prayerful person resident in Lolworth. Maintenance in its harshest form had, however, been relinquished for some time and it was with relief that Aelfrida relaxed it further as infirmity increased in the post-war years. But one who regarded the epithet *'Dictatrix Mundi'* as a courtesy title found it distasteful to depend on others instead of exercising power over them and to be relegated to the wings of life when centre stage was her rightful position.

As lyrical diary descriptions attest, Lolworth in spring and summer was delightful but Lolworth in winter a trial to one whose physical and mental health were abnormally sensitive to changing proportions of daylight and darkness, to fluctuations in temperature, and to the taste-fulness or otherwise of her immediate surroundings, and the rigours of winter life in damp, chilly, ill-lit Lolworth Rectory became onerous to one who now regarded Tymawr austerities as luxuries to be pined for. Then too, much of Aelfrida's Lolworth diary is devoted to the miseries of 'various minor ailments', chiefly colds and sinus infections but also 'vile tummy upsets'[1] due to inadequate sanitation indoors and an open sewage pit outside, or by the side effects of medication taken to combat them, or migrainous symptoms induced by the pressures of living among people with whom, barring religion, she had nothing in common. Furthermore, a woman who had hitherto controlled her own health for better or worse, now found herself dictated to by ill-health. And unless seriously ill (a mere cold no longer counted) 'days in bed which one took without remorse [at] Fordfield'[2] were unthinkable, especially if 'dear Auntie Ivy' (who, said Aelfrida, 'loved' looking after her)[3] was away and Aelfrida left to explore 'feebleness and helplessness'[4] uncosseted. To one who had formerly exploited ill-health and other people's services for her own ends, such neglect was salutary.

It was not, however, a 'minor ailment' which chiefly afflicted Aelfrida now and which dissuaded her from begging Christ that she might enter deeper still into the 'Fellowship of His suffering'; it was osteoarthritis, a degenerative condition chiefly affecting the

**Father and Mrs Lovell**

weight-bearing joints of the lower limbs which usually develops as part of the normal aging process but may be potentiated by obesity (not a predisposing factor in this case) or by the sufferer having led a physically active life – as Aelfrida had done until protective cartilage in her knee wore away and bone impinged directly on bone. Indeed, and typically, her pain became increasingly severe and movement increasingly difficult until she was more crippled by a localised problem in her knee than by generalised rheumatoid arthritis.

Her history of rheumatoid arthritis delayed diagnosis, a doctor seen in Cambridge a year after her return from Tymawr attributing her present pain to 'starchy post-war food', to the recent severe winter, and to 'old age'.[5] (She was fortunate in one respect: although rheumatoid arthritis of thirty years' standing gave rise to disseminated discomfort exacerbated according to season or state of mind, her hands were comparatively unaffected and she was able to write firmly and legibly to the end of her life.) Eustace and Julius suggested spa treatment, a suggestion 'blocked' by their sister's guardian angel who wished her to remain at Lolworth keeping her Rule[6]; he relented sufficiently, however, to prompt her to ask the Hope House nuns if one of them was a 'trained masseuse' and on discovering that one was, to allow her to be admitted for a short course of massage during which she meditated while being treated (unless it tickled, in which case 'goodbye for a minute to holy thoughts!!') and enjoyed a brief respite from 'Lolworth Rule-keeping'.[7] (She was also gratified to hear from a Cambridge ophthalmologist that she still possessed 'airman's sight' for distance[8], an entirely appropriate diagnosis given her propensity to prefer visions of the next world to close focus on the present.) Massage being ineffectual therapy for osteoarthritis, Aelfrida was soon lamenting that although her lameness was '*supposed*' to be better, it was not, and that within a few months she was 'more lame than ever'[9] and her pain much worse, so much worse, in fact, that she warned Mrs Lovell in March 1948 in the course of a talk about 'Alethea and Arrangements' that her own stay at the Rectory might be curtailed if she became so incapacitated that she 'needed much help'. (Mrs Lovell's response was that she would 'never' turn Aelfrida out but other 'arrangements' conspired to bring about her departure.)[10] Alethea's arrival on furlough resulted not only in purchase of a walking stick but also in a private referral to Dr Joan Cooper who declined a 'medical verdict'[11] until an X-ray was performed. Diagnostic imaging finally provided a diagnosis two years and three months after the onset of Aelfrida's symptoms: 'severe osteoarthritis'.[12]

On 'Dr Joan's' recommendation she underwent a short course of the 'deep-ray treatment … sometimes used for cancer', radiotherapy being the treatment of choice for any unwanted bodily swelling, benign or malignant, until its deleterious side-effects became apparent. By this time Aelfrida was so 'very weary of constant pain' that she would have undergone anything that promised 'longed-for relief', so weary indeed that should she, she wrote, be given the chance of choosing pain in order to become 'a more fitting instrument of God's purpose', she would still '*choose*' but would be glad that the choice did not lie with *her*.[13]

Her course of radiotherapy lasted from May to September 1948. Though she enjoyed the opportunity of being a 'Perfect Patient', taking an intelligent interest in X-ray plates showing evidence of 'the damage done by disease to [her] bones', distributing largesse in the form of sweets and copies of her books to the nurses and doctors, and even discerning a mystical '*power*, force, energy rushing like a great river into [her]' while receiving 'deep-ray treatment', Aelfrida's first experience of a public hospital was unhappy. 'To be one of many – to be asked if I were receiving the old age pension – to be kept waiting and waiting' infuriated one hitherto accustomed to private medicine[14], as also did the treatment, for although she was warned that 'longed-for relief' might take weeks to appear, radiotherapy proved as ineffectual as massage for a condition for which there was then *no* effective treatment.

The onset of referred pain in her right hip and of neuritis in her right arm as a result of leaning heavily on her stick, together with the chief side-effect of her treatment, fatigue, brought Aelfrida metaphorically to her knees. Wishing she had 'more *courage*', she even contemplated leaving Lolworth and her 'austere life' there (and her daily Communion; treatment rendered her so tired that she sometimes forewent the short walk to church, receiving the Reserved Sacrament from Father Lovell in the oratory instead) and going to Wetenhall Cottage to '*rest*' even if this meant turning out Julius and Mina and offering it rent free to the Hope House Sisters 'if they would look after me till I die'. In the event she did not, in part because unable to decide if her thought was 'a *good* one' or a 'wicked temptation from the devil' to draw her away from her 'work' in Lolworth or 'a simple human longing for my own house and for kind people to care for me when I can no longer wait on myself', but also because she did not want to appear 'unsettled and restless' to those to whom she had announced the settling of her pillar of fire and cloud over Lolworth, because a vision at Vespers on the Eve of Corpus Christi of 'the whole company of Heaven' uniting to pass down to her the sacrament of 'my Lord's Body and Blood' pure and untransubstantiated[15] persuaded her that Lolworth was where she ought to receive it transubstantiatedly, and because Bishop Wynn to whom she confided her health problems, counselled 'patience'. (He also, a year later, countermanded the advice of members of her family that she move into Hope House on a permanent basis by saying that it was neither 'wise nor right' for her to 'live … in a Roman Catholic convent'[16], something with which Aelfrida concurred for continued proselytising by some of the senior nuns made her uneasy; with the best of theological intentions, he therefore condemned her to exile from Cambridge and to life in a home in which she was often unhappy.) Her radiotherapist's assurance that he could keep her going 'for many years yet' also failed to cheer a sufferer who, though happy to undergo some of her Purgatory in the here and now and to hope that worsening pain 'may help with *"adoration réparative"* too', was increasingly prone to shudder with dismay at the prospect of what she might have to endure before God called her home.[17] (In 1949 she hoped happily but incorrectly for her 'last Lent on earth'.)[18] There were, too, nights rendered sleepless by pain ('I *never* ask God to make it less [though] my natural self hates it')[19], increasing disability (the high chancel step became a formidable obstacle), and falls which left her 'shaken' but cognizant that Christ too fell under the weight of His cross.[20] Mrs Lovell's presence as housekeeper-companion during the five days spent minus family at Wetenhall Cottage at the time of Walter's Copenhagen wedding in July 1950 demonstrates just how incapacitated Aelfrida had become within four years of the onset of symptoms.

The unnerving feeling that she would soon be unable to dictate the terms of her own world, a feeling underlined by Alethea's gentle but determined intention of leading her own life, not the life her mother intended for her, was exacerbated by realisation that, persuade herself how she might to the contrary, the Christian faith to which she held was at best impotent in the post-war world and at worst a spent force. Although her most immediate worries were to do with the iniquities (as she saw them) of Britain's 'secular utopia' run by 'little Trades Union [nips]' spouting 'party parrot-talk' whose bullying imposition of 'a tyranny of Nationalisation, rationing and restrictions' was bearable only because imposed 'on all classes alike … for the good of all', Aelfrida's chief 'Distraction' was of a more global nature: the Kremlin's refusal of 'all friendship with countries outside the Russian sphere of influence in order that they may ultimately dominate the world, establish Communism and oust God'.[21]

Chiding herself 'silly mind, look away from self, look to God!', she suffered 'pains of sorrow for what the world is enduring'[22] of a severity rarely experienced in the haven of Tymawr when personal sorrow and salvation were of paramount importance. (And if even doughty Florence Keynes waxed despairing over the state of the world at morning coffee – in a nice bit of social distinction, Aelfrida's former housekeeper was invited to 'elevenses' which, unlike morning coffee, took place in the kitchen – what hope was there?)[23] Communism was her chief bogey ('*only* Satan could have planned this, … here in quiet Lolworth …one can hardly even *imagine* such wickedness') because controlling and repressive regimes represented the 'Authority' against which she had always rebelled and because Communism, were it to be imposed in England, implied loss of freedom to worship as she wished: would it ever come to pass, she wondered, that she herself might be tortured and 'brain-washed' for

bearing 'Christian witness'[24], a truly terrifying prospect to one to whom the pain of osteoarthritis reminded her of agonies she might have to endure. (One of 'Clive's' reasons for carving a cross on his chest is that the sight of it under torture will prevent him abjuring his faith.) 'Serene and happy letters from Tymawr' consoled her; a visit to the church to read 'Masses in Time of War and for Peace'[25] did not.

Russia's acquisition of the atomic bomb in 1949 and international testing of the hydrogen bomb in 1950 promoted with further gloom: 'is mankind *really* about to encompass its own destruction?' The contrast between diary entries chronicling amusing university events ('Cambridge … nobly living up to her best traditions') and those fearing that Lent 1950 might indeed be her last because nuclear science threatened the 'end of all *things*' is striking[26], but it is obvious from both diary and contemporary novels that she, like many people, believed that a *Dies Irae* was imminent, after which "land, air and water would be so contaminated that no food could be gathered from them" and "existent matter" annihilated, leaving only "spiritual bodies" behind.[27] In spite, therefore, of deciding that it was 'wisest not to dwell on these things' or to 'talk about them' (or to try to persuade herself – without much success, for this was another occasion on which Aelfrida's uncritical faith wavered – that if a nuclear winter was God's 'purpose' for her, it must be good)[28], she continued to worry lest mankind did not '*deserve*' to survive and even to fear that the king's intention of opening the Festival of Britain on (shock and horror) *Ascension Day* might precipitate Armageddon: 'will the Russians drop an atom bomb on London?' Something to the disappointment of the author of that prescient novel *The Approaching Storm* (reread in 1948 to refresh her memory before lending it to Edward Wynn with the comment that the 'storm' seemed about to break)[29], 'no Russian bombs fell'[30], but contemporary comments on world affairs in *The Times* echoed her conviction 'that combative nations can find a *casus belli* if they so desire'.[31] And the many diary entries devoted to the Korean War of 1950-53 ('we aren't a Christian country … why should God spare us if after the terrible warning of two wars we have not turned to Him? … I should be glad to see *some* (sic) of my dear ones *safely* dead in view of what may be coming upon us')[32] bear witness that they could and had.

Morbid thoughts concerning her own and the world's future did not, however, prevent remarkable tenacity of life in the face of imminent oblivion. Though morbidity extended even to the next generation (Walter and Bodil's coming baby and Lucy Verey's eleventh grandchild were greeted with the cry 'what a world to come to!' and 'poor wee' Prince Charles with the hope that a Russian invasion would not render him 'a king without a throne'and that he would 'grow up to see England happier and holier than she is now')[33], her guardian angel's advice not to '*fuss* about this or that trouble in the world' as her imagination seized on it, magnified its horrors, and applied them to her own life, and reminder her that her 'business' on earth was to heal a godless world by suffering on its behalf[34], seems to have calmed her mind. But more relevant, perhaps, than calmness of mind to hopes of continuing existence, was re-appearance in her life of the man she may have had in mind when she asked pardon at confession on 31 October 1950 (the thirteenth anniversary of her admission as a tertiary) for sins committed against the spirit of her 'threefold promises'.[35] She does not say which promise chiefly exercised her but the second seems particularly pertinent given that pasted in the back of the current volume of her diary is a cut-out picture of a white-haired man in clerical dress labelled 'Dr Wynn'.

Having, as she thought, discouraged Edward Wynn's attentions, Aelfrida was distressed to discover that the Holy Spirit did not seem to fill her heart as much as hitherto ('there are leaks somewhere!') and that although at times she still required His supernatural assistance, her heart did not always remain 'full of His gracious presence' when she did not.[36] The reason is not hard to find: Aelfrida was no longer *dictatrix* of her own heart but had fallen in love with Edward Wynn. And he, she hoped and believed, with her.

A visit to Lolworth in May 1951 seemed to demonstrate the truth of this when, after discussing 'a little theology' and his extended visit to America, Wynn informed Aelfrida that he had neglected her scandalously and that he would like to see her more often and, on Aelfrida begging him to see the Lovells before he left because it 'made things difficult' for her if he did not, called her "poor darling!", a term of endearment she 'did not quite like'.[37] Although this suggests no more than a spiritual director's spontaneous compassion for an unwell woman living with difficult Father Lovell in an isolated and dilapidated rectory or dismay that episcopal busyness had prevented his paying closer spiritual attention to someone who had asked him to direct her, there was, she wrote and believed, more to their interview than that: on Aelfrida asking that he devote plenty of time to the Lovells, Edward Wynn replied in a tone which left her in no doubt of his feelings for her: "I came here to see *you*. If you were not here, I should not come".

Wynn's declaration threw her into a state of emotional confusion, a state all the more confusing because *she* had made the first move at Wetenhall Cottage five years earlier. Could it be, she wondered, that Edward Wynn the man wanted to see her more than Edward Ely the spiritual director seen 'as and when [she] needed him' (it is noticeable that she followed Edward Ely's direction more than she did Bede Frost's, Lucius Cary's, or Hubert Northcott's) and that it was she herself *as herself* who was 'too much a reason for his visiting Lolworth'? As a one directed, however, she must not have Wynn 'as an "h.c."' (i.e. a 'human consolation') in the way that she was 'allowed' (*sic*) Alethea and Julius because 'channels of grace' between them would become clogged by 'human friendship' and her Rule diminished thereby. (The following day was a 'Dear Dudu day' and 'everything was as it should be', peacefully free, that is to say, from pangs of late love for a man not her brother and of possessive love from the man who was.) But in 'definitely rejecting the bishop's offer of *human* friendship' in favour of a 'mere' director-directed relationship, was she acting rightly or wrongly?[38] (She left the question unanswered.) Even worse for someone who herself determined the form a relationship would take, was that 'in this case it [was] he': in offering friendship ('eminently "correct"', though it was) beyond director-directed boundaries, Edward Wynn was exercising authority over her and it was this more than anything which made her hesitate to accept it.[39]

There was, however, another man in her life towards whom *Dictatrix Mundi* experienced such ambivalent feelings that earlier intimations of being unlikely 'to be called on to leave [Lolworth] *soon*'[40] now transformed themselves into a conviction that she could no longer stay.

Aelfrida's dislike of Father Lovell developed soon after her arrival in Lolworth, for apart from his 'common accent and bad manners', his being 'half-educated', his preference for the 'cheap shoddy world of the Light Programme and the *Daily Sketch*'[41] over 'Cambridgy' conversation and *The Times,* and his being 'an aloof papa'[42] towards his daughters, she found herself increasingly irritated by his conduct as a priest. Being a woman who knew how to exploit others' weaknesses, she set out to undermine his private and public authority.

In documents intended for third parties, she expressed praise and compassion. In *Christian Old Age* (an ironic title in view of what follows) she describes a clergyman who after years of labour in a slum parish, moves to a country vicarage where the congregation, already small, dwindles steadily in spite of his fulfilling his duties "with unfailing zeal", where "the choir [has] melted away and there [are] hardly any children in the Sunday School", where nobody "except one old lady comes to Holy Communion and [where] the devil … mocks him, crying out that God has rejected his life-offering"[43], and in a diary paraphrase of what seems like a letter sent to Bishop Wynn notes how '*privileged*' little Lolworth is to have a rector 'so full of intense burning devotion who arranges beautiful services to the glory of God'.[44] Privately, however, she criticised his 'injudicious' sermons (e.g. 'on Hell [when] there were none of the "ungodly" ... to hear him')[45] and admonitory parish letters 'calling his flock to notice the signs that the day of judgement is at hand'.[46] (She did it not, it seems, consider that some people might find her own 'deeply-earnest' remarks 'repellent'[47] or note the similarity between Father Lovell's spiritual pessimism and her own.) Over matters on which Father Lovell felt strongly and which she knew to be none of '*my* business' such as the baptism of the baby of an unmarried mother, she entered into discussions with Bishop Wynn and even offered her services as godmother for the ceremony[48], while in revenge for the Lovells' dilatoriness in dealing with overflowing cesspit 'effluent', she informed the Bishop that Father Lovell had adopted 'a more Romanising form' of Mass at home and in church. She was, however, careful not to challenge Father Lovell directly or to make a formal complaint against him, pleading that 'a mere lodger [was] helpless' and that she had no wish to upset her landlord by criticising him to his face. Bishop Wynn, to his credit and while agreeing that "papalists" were a divisive influence in the Church of England, rebuked her ("remember you are at Lolworth to pray and not to deal with ecclesiatical politics!!") and Aelfrida, as was her wont, grovelled in reply[49], but these and other examples of meddling and of betrayals of confidence were hardly conducive to maintenance of good relationships between 'lodger' and Lovells, Mrs Lovell naturally siding with her husband whenever trouble arose. As it frequently did and often with Bishop Wynn as its focus.

To have one's diocesan bishop paying frequent visits to one's parish would have been disconcerting to a less sensitive priest than Father Lovell and though these visits could be passed off as those of a spiritual director visiting his advisee, Aelfrida's breaches of 'ecclesiastical etiquette' (she also arranged for the Bishop to visit crippled Mrs Lee without informing Father Lovell first; a self-justifying and self-congratulatory account of the visit fills several pages of her diary)[50] must have seemed more like collusion between conspirators than spiritual direction. Her informing nervous Mrs Lovell that she liked the Bishop 'to find *everything all right*' when he visited (with the implication that she herself found matters not at all 'all right' and had told the Bishop so) and worried Father Lovell on an occasion when the Bishop 'had no talk with him' that she herself had had a 'good interview', must have seemed to both Lovells like a spy reporting to his controller. (Or a Reuters' agent to head office.) And, given the penetrating timbre of Aelfrida's voice and that increasing deafness may have caused her to raise it further, it may be that her asking her Bishop–director's 'reasoned opinion' of Mrs Lovell's 'sulks' and of an episode of malicious behaviour towards herself by Mary Lovell and hinting that the intensity of Father Lovell's fervour was attracting diabolic attention was overheard by Lovell himself, he shooting her 'such a look' when informed of the quality but not the content of her most recent interview.[51]

The devil's audacity in launching an attack on Father Lovell in a rectory visited by a bishop and inhabited by a prayerful tertiary impressed Aelfrida tremendously even as she realised the immensity of the task lying before her: that of 'foiling' the devil by her prayers and protecting his victim by her presence in Lolworth.[52] Furthermore, a recent statement by the Bishop concerning his own 'apprehensions of evil' seemed significant, given that during their interview he had told Aelfrida she had no need to "say anything to [him] about Father Lovell" because (she assumed) he already understood her concern that it was the devil who was to blame for the tensions in the household. It was therefore unfortunate that Aelfrida regarded the Bishop's statement as a suggestion that she herself once more 'join battle with the evil one'[53], that she remained insufficiently insightful to realise that it was her disordered mind, not a supernatural source of evil, which caused the inhabitants of the rectory to behave in the manner she believed they did, and that she found it easy to persuade herself that Father Lovell, like others who failed to share her inflexible views on morality and religion, was diabolically possessed. (In Lolworth, as earlier, Aelfrida never attributed Mina's mental disorder to diabolic possession; Mina's tendency to confide 'disappointments and fears and bitterness' to her saw to that.)[54] Recalling her guardian angel's recent reminder of Lucius Cary's call to her to help him battle the powers of evil[55], she sallied forth to combat. But in Father Lovell she met her match, for being a something of a dictator himself, he recognised her tactics for what they were and traded blow for blow.

Aelfrida's hatred of 'Authority' in any forms fuelled her animosity. Father Lovell, it seems, regarded Lolworth as his fiefdom (there was no squire) and arrogated to himself village matters beyond his remit as rector, another source of the dislike expressed by his parishioners ('Does *anyone* ... dare to stand up to him?' Aelfrida wondered.)[56] He also held old-fashioned views of himself as paterfamilias and expected the four females resident at the rectory to conform to his wishes in everything, and the presence in his house of a 'pious female' with a strong anti-authoritarian streak was bound to result in clash of personalities on several levels: as her confessor, as her parish priest, and as head of household.

As Aelfrida's confessor, Father Lovell was in a position of power with regard to his penitent and her living under the same roof as her confessor far from ideal. Not only was she privy to household secrets of which Lovell himself might have preferred her to remain ignorant (both Mrs Lovell and Auntie Ivy confided them to her) but he himself was not above using the confessional to chide her for trespasses committed but unconfessed: revelling in 'private communion with God' when she was supposed to be praying for the parish and for 'a tormented world'[57] and interfering in parish matters when she was supposed to have 'come [to Lolworth] to pray'. After one particular 'little breeze', confessor gave penitent 'a nice little homily on detachment' during a confession he insisted she attend (she had hoped to postpone it until he 'calmed down') and she admitted to having been annoyed with unspecified 'people'.[58]

As Aelfrida's parish priest Father Lovell found her presence at daily Mass comforting and supportive, particularly as she was there voluntarily, not under the compulsion exerted over members of his family, but his petty tyranny with regard to attendance at other services galled her when he failed to regard increasing infirmity as a legitimate excuse for non-attendance. Insistence that Aelfrida swell his humiliatingly small congregation (it seems he had no conception that people in a farming community might have more pressing concerns at 7am and 6pm than Mass and Evensong but the fact that Sunday attendances were small, festival attendances variable, and the turnout for a village funeral tremendous must have reminded him of his unpopularity) in spite of 'doctor's orders'[59] to the contrary, was met by blank refusal to attend on hers: she was 'too exhausted even to think of' Evensong (it was the 'hybrid muddle' form of service preferred by Lovell to 'proper prayer book Evening Prayer' which provided the real reason for refusal and if the 'proper' form was used by a visiting preacher, she attended) [60]; her rheumatic pains were 'aggravated by walking, kneeling, and sitting up straight in a hard pew' (not something which troubled her in Hope House chapel, perhaps because there were chairs, not pews)[61]; for 'the aged' to go out in chilly and foggy November weather 'would have been foolish in the extreme'.[62] From Father Lovell's point of view, however, it must have been galling to see a lady too exhausted to attend Evensong skipping off to Cambridge (in all weathers) to visit her family, too lame to walk to or kneel in church walking (slowly, admittedly, and with a stick) around Lolworth on 'dear Dudu days' or sitting with the bishop for an hour at a time or kneeling

by him to confess and receive absolution, and though too 'aged' to attend special Lenten devotions, happily breaking 'continuity of silence' to receive visitors.[63] He therefore matched what he regarded as hypocritical excuses with snide remarks ("baby come for nice ta-ta?" when Aelfrida graced Sunday tea but not Evensong)[64], icy comments ('he *had* thought her Advent Rule would include Sunday Evensong')[65], and hectoring demands for participation beginning 'I say'.[66]

Aelfrida had not been spoken to like this for many years and bitterly resented it. Arguments ended in her walking off in a huff or retreating into icy silence but to her diary she confided that a parish priest's rudeness to a lady such as herself was a breach of '*manners*' (he spoke 'as a farmer might speak to a ploughboy'; she muted her comments when informing the Bishop, but emphasied that it was Lovell's behaviour, not her own, which was at fault), that had she been '*under obedience* to Father Lovell' she would have made greater attempts to attend (*sic*), that too-frequent attendance would be adding a burden to a Rule which was 'already as heavy as I can bear', and that she had no intention of being 'bullied' as Father Lovell bullied his womenfolk'.[67] That, of course, was the crux of the problem.

Having escaped Mother Guenvrede's domineering jurisdiction in July 1946 only to find herself under the same roof as a man reminiscent of her late father and also, it now seems, of her former husband, must have come as a shock to one who prided herself on being a good judge of people. (And whose 'Prehistory' was in the process of being consigned to paper.) Finding that emotional battles with a living and a dead Mother and mother seemed to have replicated themselves in the form of battles with a living and a dead Father and father and between a dead and divorced husband and a living one not her own, Aelfrida proceeded to fight them in a manner similar to that employed earlier in relation to Constantine and the Oracle. Unable in this instance to separate Father Lovell from his daughters as she had done to her own daughters' father, she revenged herself through them in other ways. Towards Clare, the younger and, like Agatha, the more biddable, she acted the part of "dear Grannie"[68] and noted that she felt '*very* tenderly towards her'[69] but was carping and censorious towards traits and behaviour attributable to paternal neglect. Towards Mary, older and less biddable and whose behaviour (like Alethea's) often echoed her father's, she became positively vindictive, cancelling holiday lessons (she used the Direct Method in the hope of awakening the unacademic girl's interest in French) if Mary was taken to 'enemy territory' (i.e. Newmarket Races) to which as father, priest, and tertiary, Lovell should have forbidden entry and informing the Bishop in the guise of 'asking for counsel' of what a bad example Father Lovell set his parishioners in allowing his daughter to participate in activities associated with the 'wicked world' of betting, drink, and 'lust'.[70] Normal adolescent rebellion – reading detective stories in preference to going to church – was attributed to the 'new and alluring world' promoted by 'sex-instruction'[71] at school and went unreported, but Mary's dalliance with the jockey was transmitted to Ely as an example of her father's (and by extension the Church of England's) lax behaviour with regard to what Aelfrida termed '*morality*'.[72]

Mary's departure to her first job after leaving school in 1951 diverted Aelfrida's attention to Mary's Oracle-like father, but even before that her inability to 're-write' Father Lovell's life in the way that she had re-written her father's books aggravated her to such an extent that she felt forced to unburden herself in letters to the Bishop. No domestic detail went unreported, from 'the extent of his early morning devotions' for which Lovell rose at 4.30am (what Aelfrida objected to was because his 'making a huge clatter in his immense thick boots' so early in the morning woke her up; his exaggerated asceticism was of less account)[73] to the asthma whose onset in November 1949 caused major rows because Father Lovell's behaviour when ill reminded her of the Oracle, the man towards whom she had had to act in 'subjugation'[74] between her divorce and his death.

Father Lovell's asthmatic cough was caused, according to his uncharitable lodger, by 'stupidity' in not taking better care of himself and by ignoring his doctor's advice when unwell or, her preferred diagnosis, by 'over-strained nerves'. (Her own 'arthritis pain' was due 'to the wisdom of God'.)[75] His new habit of shouting out in his sleep disturbed Mrs Lovell so much that in December 1949 he moved from the marital bedroom at the other end of the house to the room next to Aelfrida's. (His shouting out, said Mrs Lovell, was due to his dreaming about Aelfrida who, while noting that those who studied dreams might deduce something from that, failed to note what her own Bélisian conclusion, namely that Lovell's dreams indicated that he had become so besotted with his lodger that his wife had become jealous of her husband's 'unfaithfulness of the mind', said of herself.)[76] Wondering if she ought to 'make a protest' but worried that if she did, 'the Lolworth limpet' might be ejected from the rectory, Aelfrida decided that a soul dead to everything but God should not mind being kept awake by Lovell's 'bronchial cough' even though his head was now 'only a foot from [her own]'.[77] By 1 January 1950, however, worn out by wakefulness ('the night of a person with arthritis' was disturbed by 'constant pain' in any case),

unable to obtain sleep by tried and tested means (meditation, a 'night story'), and too tired during the day to revise *Just Alice*, she overrode her guardian angel's advice ('*No* and no and NO' was his response to her suggesting a protest) and ventured 'a mild plea'[78] (by letter) to Mrs Lovell that her husband return to the marital bedroom.

But if Aelfrida thought what she termed an 'episode' would 'lead to deeper understanding between [herself] and [her] fellow tertiaries'[79], she was wrong. 1950 began with rows between Father Lovell and Aelfrida and between Mrs Lovell and Aelfrida, attributed by the latter to the devil having poured 'venomous thoughts' over her.[80] They also caused the rectory atmosphere to become as 'glacial' as the outside world, Aelfrida to be moved back to her former dark, damp, and draughty room so that Father Lovell could inhabit (fortunately only briefly) the warmer, drier, and sunnier one she had occupied for two years, and mild Mrs Lovell to reveal 'deeper hostility' towards her paying guest than that guest anticipated by informing her that Mrs Graham 'took too much' upon herself regarding the lives of those at the Rectory and that the current 'episode' was the last straw.

Aelfrida behaved as she always behaved in the face of opposition which might result in being sent away (or in the devil, '*determined* to make mischief', trying to force her away from 'where God means me to be') offering (by letter) 'very humble apologies' and excusing herself by saying that she had been 'led astray by the sweetness of human affections … towards others, especially children'. Privately, however, she noted that too-close association with the 'joys and sorrows of the household' and '*gracieusetés*' extended to it might be interpreted as '*Interference*', a marvellous euphemism for deliberate power-play and lack of charity. Realising, too, the ignominy of being 'put on the doorstep' less than four years after having been asked to leave a previous establishment (the 'episode', said her guardian angel, had been a '*test*' and '*whatever happened*' she must make no further protests or comments), it took all her social graces as a 'consul's wife' to thaw the chilliness pervading the rectory. She also reminded herself that she was a 'channel for our Lord's Silence' and was 'to pray and *only* … pray'[81], though silence/Silence was broken by a 'very guarded' letter to the Bishop (her second in six weeks on the same topic) in which she hinted that an enforced holiday for or the anointing by Dr Wynn of unwell, rigorist, 'Romanising', and 'mentally unfaithful' Father Lovell was required. Only in the privacy of her diary did she admit 'fundamentally *the fault is mine*' and that she had been a 'busybody'.[82]

Though Aelfrida disliked Father Lovell's (and the Oracle's and Constantine's) male desire 'to dominate the female', she also bore him (as also them) grudging respect for his good qualities, in Lovell's case his being a man of religious convictions and spiritual ardour similar to her own.[83] A 'strange interview' which occurred shortly after the onset of his ill-health demonstrates both the truth of this and how far Aelfrida herself had advanced from the tortured 'victim-soul' of Oxford days.

Late on 13 December 1949 she and Lovell met by accident in the rectory's gloomy kitchen, she clutching an electric torch (courtesy of Alethea), he a candle. On Lovell informing her that his doctor had forbidden early morning fasts on health grounds (gastric pain had suggested that Lovell was also suffering from an ulcer or worse but investigations proved negative) and that he was much distressed about this, Aelfrida, so she said, spoke to him like a Mother Superior 'for his body and soul's good' and 'out of [her] experience at Tymawr' reminded him what constituted 'the *essentials* and the *non-essentials* in the Religious Life'. A lengthy, productive, and friendly discussion followed, after which Lovell not only thanked her for her advice but also (but only after dispensation from Bishop Wynn) acted upon it and Aelfrida remembered that the Bishop '*likes* me to hear people's confidences and try and help them in their spiritual difficulties'.[84] (She does not say if she subsequently betrayed Lovell's confidences to the Bishop in her letter to him written early the next month but hints concerning leave of absence and anointing suggest she did.) Reviewing the interview the following day, she discovered another similarity between herself and her confessor: Lovell, she thought, was trying to live the life of a religious instead of that of a tertiary and was practising 'a too difficult Rule' and endangering his health and inconveniencing other people as a result. Noting that she too ought to be on her guard not to overstep the mark in either respect and 'claim or fancy' (or even act as if) she was leading the Religious Life, she noted with gratitude and relief how '*very* light' her present (and even Father Lovell's) Rule was compared to the 'daily, hourly Obedience rendered by monks or nuns in Communities'.[85] But in an addendum written later the same day she noted that although she and Father Lovell both cared 'for the same things in the same way', that God had led them both 'by the same inward ways', and that, as with Mother Guenvrede, she felt herself to be in 'spiritual harmony' with him even when at secular or ritualist cross-purposes, confronted with him outside the realm of the supernatural, she found him as little 'congenial' as 'the Mother SSC'.[86] So having encountered Father Lovell at a very low ebb spiritually, emotionally, and physically and realised that in giving her his confidence he had put himself in her power, Aelfrida proceeded to show her contempt, first, by her 'protest' of 29 December, then by abusing her privileged position

in his household. And it is a measure of both Lovells' spiritual stature that they remained on speaking terms with her even after that.

Though 'Alice Marsden' of *Just Alice* is depicted as the tranquil contemplative personality Aelfrida would have liked to have been or have people think she was, someone, that is to say, whose inner life of '*deep down* inward peace'[87] was reflected in the equanimity with which she faced and overcame pressures placed on her soul by distressing life-events, 'Clive Farwell' of *The Centaur* is angry with himself and with life. It was the Lovells' misfortune that Aelfrida found herself invaded by the 'Clive' aspect of her personality when composition and revision of *The Centaur* coincided with the onset of village trouble affecting Father Lovell on a personal and a priestly level.

A decision made after the December 1949 'episode' to follow Father Cary's advice (his remembrancing death occurred while the 'episode' reverberated round the rectory) 'not to get tangled up with people' ('do I?' she asked herself, knowing that she did and 'shall I?!', indicating by her exclamation mark that it was her vocation as *dictatrix*)[88] found Aelfrida resolving when trouble brewed in 1950 to 'keep pretty aloof' from the Lovells' affairs. (Given earlier contretemps, neither God nor the Bishop would 'blame' her for doing so.)[89] But given too that several people swirling in the currents of ill-feeling and gossip which ebbed and flowed around Father Lovell, the village school mistress, and a village family living next door to the rectory confided in Aelfrida, and that she, resident in the rectory but not regarded in the same 'exceedingly bitter' light[90] as its head of household (to complicate matters further, nor were Mrs Lovell and Auntie Ivy), was involuntarily placed in the difficult position of not being seen to take sides even with those whose cause she regarded as just, she found herself willy nilly at the centre of the tempest of "personalities, scandal and innuendo"[91] which enveloped rectory, schoolhouse, cottage, and village in the spring and summer of 1951.

Lengthy, detailed, and colourful diary entries show that Aelfrida was not only conversant with details of the many-stranded squabble (failed attempts to shut her eyes and ears 'to what is going on around [her]' were excused by it being impossible to do so)[92] but also that she was prone to invent others. At the same time she was anxious that the Lovells not suspect her of blabbing to the Bishop during the visit paid by him on 21 May 1951. (His calling her 'poor darling' on that occasion seems to have turned her mind to herself rather than to tale-bearing.) Early 1952, however, found her so exasperated by the unrest pervading rectory and village as accusation and counter-accusation were exchanged and alliances formed and

Aelfrida's pew, Lolworth Church

broke that neither her guardian angel's 'exquisitely mod-ulated' admonitions to "Love God"[93] (and avoid tittle tattle) nor lessons learnt at Tymawr regarding her need to strive for '*Holy Reserve* towards others' and to demon-strate *caritas* towards their 'faults and frailties'[94] nor more recent apprehension of God teaching 'humility and ten-derness towards our neighbours'[95] prevented an explo-sion of pent-up bitterness and wrath.

Having persuaded herself that there was 'no bar-rier to informing [the Bishop] on what is ... common knowledge in the village'[96], she unburdened her mind of tensions ostensibly but not actually arising as a result of stringent 'Lolworth Rule-keeping' by 'enlightening' him (as she put it) in an interview which was as much an 'ordeal' (and as 'cathartic') as writing *The Centaur* and its revision *Rich Man's Choice,* now in process of rejec-tion by London publishers. Seating the Bishop in an upright chair ('I felt I could not place *him* in an armchair when he was *in loco confessoris*') and herself in an arm-chair (she was soon to kneel in order that the Bishop should 'understand at once that [she] meant to speak as a penitent in the confessional') and knowing that she had only thirty minutes in which to tell her tale, she omit-ted all mention of the current state of her spirituality and only briefly submitted her vision of September 1951 of St Thérèse of Lisieux to episcopal scrutiny ("a *good* experience", he replied, "but I should reserve judgement as to its validity") before asking his permission ("I am entirely at your disposal", said rather coldly) to launch into a detailed dissection of 'the situation at Lolworth' as she saw it. The story, centred on Father Lovell's real or imagined misdemeanours with regard to his family and parishioners, was a sorry one however sympathetically or pseudo-sympathetically told, for it involved (she admit-ted that much of what she revealed was 'hearsay'), actual or 'mental' infidelity (the woman in question was not, in

this instance, herself), marital breakdown leading to legal separation, mental illness threatened or actual, physical violence, paternal indifference, bullying or domineering behaviour, and sins (or what Aelfrida called sins) of omis-sion or commission.

The resemblance between recent events in Lolworth and distant events in her own life was not, it seems, evi-dent to Aelfrida herself but it was in effect her own story which she poured out to Bishop Wynn in the rectory drawing room. This, and the fact that her story bore a remarkable similarity in tone and even (in part) in con-tent to Sister Placida's diatribe to Father Northcott against Mother Guenvrede in 1943 alerts us to the fact that whereas in 1943 it was her dead mother who was the real object of Aelfrida's outburst, in 1952 it was her dead father and dead husband and her daughters' dead father whom she castigated in the guise of Father Lovell. Then having unburdened herself of bitterness pent up for more years than six in Lolworth, she asked the Bishop if she had done right to 'enlighten him' and requested and received his blessing.

The Bishop's "*entirely* right" as transcribed by Aelfrida leaves its meaning ambiguous. In saying that she saw by his response that she had 'taken him with [her]', did she mean that the Bishop believed she was correct to inform him of Father Lovell's supposed transgressions or does she mean that he thought her 'entirely right' to unbur-den herself of (real or imaginary) worries to her priestly 'soul-doctor' in the safety of the confessional? Either way, she was wise to act the part of penitent, for having learnt by bitter experience at Tymawr that accusations made outside the confessional to Father Northcott were liable to be discussed with Mother Guenvrede and rebound on herself to her own detriment, she made sure in Lolworth that she was in a place of privilege because the Bishop could not betray her confidences without breaking the seal of the confessional. (This also protected Father Lovell, a fact which Aelfrida may or may not have consid-ered before choosing the confessional mode to reveal all, though her assuring the Bishop at the conclusion of their interview that she was '*very* happy' in Lolworth and that the Lovells were '*dear* people' and 'endlessly kind' to her suggests tactics aforethought. Conversely, it is hard to see why Aelfrida chose confessional mode if she wished the Bishop to intervene.)[97] Edward Ely's brief (and pre-arranged) meeting with Father Lovell between the end of his interview with his penitent and the start of the Children's Service which took place shortly afterwards must have tested his episcopal powers of diplomacy and self-control to the utmost.

Five days passed without a diary entry, that being the time it took Aelfrida to recover from her 'ordeal' and to realise the ethical enormity of what she had done. (A quoted definition of Ethics inscribed on the inside cover of the current volume of her diary is followed by two exclamation marks as if to emphasise departure from the principles of honourable conduct she affected to uphold and her noting the 'very subdued'[98] atmosphere in the rectory since the Bishop's visit suggests that Father Lovell, discovered outside the drawing room door at the end of the interview, may have eavesdropped and that her voice was pitched somewhat above the intended 'whisper'; she herself expressed ignorance as to the reason for it.) She began by ostensibly repenting 'most earnestly for any lack of charity I may have shown' (note that she does not say 'the' lack of charity or 'have' rather than 'may have' shown), went on to eulogise Father Lovell's conduct in Holy Week as being that of 'one of those contemplatives whose love of God expresses itself most naturally in ritual' (there were no sneers about his common accent and 'romanising' tendencies) and concluded by praising the manner in which his 'womenfolk' supported him in throughout the most draining rituals of the Church's year.[99] She then wrote a lengthy letter to Bishop Wynn in which she attempted to excuse her behaviour ('I had spoken as in the Presence of God the Judge … [because] I felt I *ought* to tell the Bishop how things had been'), warned of 'the possibility of having to do the same again', expressed regret, not for her actions – her only hint of apology occurred during the interview and was more in terms of regret that she had to 'burden' the Bishop with the weight now transferred from her shoulders to his than in terms of sorrow for her behaviour regarding Father Lovell – but for the deleterious effect of the '*bitter* … half hour of tale bearing' on her own deeply wounded soul, described her relief at discovering an escape clause ('the anguish I had experienced during that unhappy half hour was Our Lord in me grieving over the frailty of *good* people'), and hinted that because of what had transpired on 15 March and since, she 'felt [she] must now go away' to 'a Religious House where *everything* is done to the glory of God' (as it manifestly was not in Lolworth), then to 'another (*sic*) dilapidated parsonage in the diocese [to] be as contented (*sic*) there as I have been here'.[100] To which end she wrote immediately to Mother Guenvrede and Alethea informing them of her plans.

Having rendered her position at Lolworth untenable (a reason for leaving unshared with anyone save God, the Bishop, and her biographer), Aelfrida was relieved to discover shareable reasons for removing herself. (Or as she might have preferred to express it using words put into her mouth five years earlier by Father Cary,

circumstances indicated that "the Holy Spirit [was] calling for change".)[101] Fortunately for her, two eminently plausible reasons presented themselves.

The first concerned the rectory itself. The condition of Aelfrida's former and once again her present room had deteriorated to such an extent during her two years' sojourn in the room next door that, though bearable in summer (unless it rained, in which case she recorded 'water streaming down [the] … wall and falling … from three places in the ceiling')[102], it had become barely habitable in winter, her body feeling as if it were 'dying in bits' because of the inhospitable conditions in which she lived. (She also wished she were more 'heroic' and could pay less attention to corpse-like fingers and a 'spinal cord made of ice' but continued to inhabit a room 'not really fit for anyone to live in' as a mortification and because 'for the sake of solitude and quiet'[103], hypothermia was a small price to pay.) A year later, 'aching in all [her] bones' from cold and damp as she crouched over *The Centaur* while water dripped through the ceiling onto or into a waterproof sheet, basins, and 'wonderfully *slummy*' 'clouts', she was nearly driven to listen to Julius' and Mina's urgings and take refuge at Wetenhall Cottage; 'Orders from on High' transmitted via her guardian angel persuaded her to stay. (She also feared interruptions to her train of literary thought if she moved to a house more accessible to friends and relations.)[104] Yet even as she noted her sadness if she had to leave Lolworth, events ensured that should she stay, the rectory would no longer be her home.

In December 1950 the Ely diocese decided to dispose of a house deemed by Aelfrida unfit for human habitation 'even if thousands were spent on it'[105] and to transform smaller Rectory Cottage next door into the rectory. (The family living in Rectory Cottage naturally objected to being ejected in order to house a rector with whom they were at loggerheads, this fuelling the flames of the village quarrel.) The move concerned Aelfrida greatly, for although an extension to Rectory Cottage would enable her to continue to live in Lolworth, the fact that her new room would be smaller than her present one and her life lived in even closer proximity to the Lovells, made her decision to 'look out for another home' easier.[106]

But where to go? Dorothea Conybeare's suggestion of an almshouse in Radwinter in Essex seemed 'a chance for the unwise tertiary to go and be a hermit' but was dismissed with the thought that it would be indeed unwise for one who was 'alas! … too old' and suffering from 'the increasing difficulties and limitations' of physical disability to accept (and besides, Radwinter was not in Bishop Wynn's diocese), so 'another room in another dilapidated parsonage' seemed the only possible solution. (As she told her former architect 'Hugh' Hughes when he visited Lolworth at the request of a potential purchaser and failed to recognise his Wetenhall Cottage client in 'such poor surroundings' until she identified herself.)[107] First, however, she must find a 'Religious House' in which to recoup spiritual energies depleted by Lolworth squabbles.

An SSC newsletter of 1951 suggested the exact spot: "a place of quiet and retreat for our associates and friends in the South of England", Compton Durville Manor in Somerset, recently acquired by the SSC as 'a Priory' or, more accurately, as a 'daughter house' to which Tymawr Sisters were seconded in turn.[108] On first hearing of the existence of Compton Durville, Aelfrida had pondered *'should [one] ask to go too?'*[109] (she also entertained the forlorn hope that Tymawr's post-war 'building programme' would include a 'hermit's room – I must not say "cell" for it would contain deck chair and h.w.b!')[110] but deterred by her guardian angel's objection to her 'toying with the idea', decided to await further 'orders from on High'.[111]

'Soft gales of spring' blowing in March 1952 reminded her of her wish to be wafted towards 'the new SSC Home at Compton Durville … Priory' (the 'very subdued air about the household' at Lolworth following the Bishop's recent visit may have contributed to her wish to be 'blown' away from Lolworth)[112] so believing that there would be no harm in reminding 'on High' of her wish to overwinter in a house 'where *everything* is done for the glory of God' ('as I hoped to find here', an aside omitted from a paraphrasing letter to the Bishop) 'and to be with [her] Sisters-in-Christ as a tertiary ought to be from time to time'[113], she wrote to Sister Jeanne, then in charge at the 'daughter house', to ask for refuge.

But having informed the Lovells of her decision not to move to Rectory Cottage (a decision welcomed by Mrs Lovell with hints that sorry as she was to lose Aelfrida's financial contribution –'a bleak beginning to the new regime at the new rectory', wrote the latter snidely[114] – she was not overly sorry to see her go) and they and the Bishop of her intention of overwintering, if not at Tymawr itself, at least in 'spiritual proximity' to the 'beloved Community' of which she continued to feel herself an 'outpost'[115] and received what seemed to be the expected message from 'on High' (watching before the altar of repose on Maundy Thursday 1952 she experienced the same electric thrill of 'a continuous life [passing] between [her] soul and the tabernacle' as in RH Benson's description of the nun at Malling)[116], Aelfrida found herself less an 'outpost' than an outcast. Compton Durville, wrote Mother Guenvrede, was totally unsuited for the aged in winter (there was, it seems, no mention of Aelfrida overwintering at the mother-house but even she must have realised that a Community from whom

she had received so much 'and given so little in return'[117] was unlikely to welcome her back; to add insult to injury, Compton Durville's first visitor was elderly Miss Lowe of the Tymawr 'Library') and the rectory, said Mrs Lovell, was sold, the purchaser pressing for completion in July instead of October.

Of the two disappointments, the latter was the most inconvenient. Thwarted of her usual summer holiday at Wetenhall Cottage ('family plans this summer' revolved round 'Babies', not herself)[118], Aelfrida had counted on 'a quiet summer in Lolworth' but was now obliged to move in a hurry. ('The Lovells' … behaviour over the new rectory has been marked by the most complete selfishness and disregard of anyone else', a complaint whose irony was lost on a woman on whom collateral descendents spontaneously bestow the adjective 'selfish'.) She was also forced to perform the emotionally-draining task of putting out for salvage some of the mass of family papers carried round with her and stored during her stay in Lolworth in trunks and boxes in the Parish Room[119], it being while sorting out these relics that she discovered the rough draft of Agatha's suicide note and realised that the latter's death was considered and premeditated, not impulsive or a symptom of 'cerebral anaemia'. 'I had better not try and say how I felt', she wrote.

Mother Guenvrede's refusal to have aged and infirm Aelfrida at Compton Durville was justified. In January 1952 she was laid low by a chest infection: 'I think I really *was* as ill as I felt, gasping for breath, utterly exhausted, mind confused' ('my soul wasn't confused', she added) and though perhaps not as near death as she hoped ('I was quite ready … all my affairs in order, etc. etc. and would gladly meet the call'; there is no mention of her receiving antibiotics nor does her firm writing waver), she was ill enough to spend a week in bed cared for by 'the dear folks here' and even to agree with the local doctor that she had 'done [her] share' of early rising for Mass and must certainly relinquish it in winter, a 'bitter verdict' but one to be obeyed because no 'Orders from on High' countermanded it. (Mass in the oratory and 'spiritual' Communions constitued 'starvation diet!!' and made her 'spiritually indolent'.)[120] This brush with death, however, reminded her that perhaps not all her affairs were as orderly as she thought; early in February 1952 she wrote to Mother Guenvrede informing her that she was troubled by the possibility of her discipline being found among her effects when she died. The Mother's reply was wise: "the time comes when our activities are suspended and God takes us in hand and gives us our penances – the sort of things He sees we need and *not* what we would choose … Send me back Saint Guenvrede". Tears came into Aelfrida's eyes: 'St Guenvrede has taught me much and is very precious [but] I know the Mother is right'. 'Saint Guenvrede' was dispatched to Mother Guenvrede by registered post[121] but Aelfrida's request to Bishop Wynn that she be allowed to revert to a leather belt 'as an "ersatz" discipline' met with a more ambiguous response: she ought to follow her own conscience. But as the belt's tongue was ineffectual and the buckle inflicted too much pain, 'conscience – or guardian angel [said] NO!'[122]

On 1 May 1952 Aelfrida caught German measles from Clare Lovell. After nine days in bed feeling 'sub-human' from the 'very heavy attack' (she was tended by the 'Lovell womenfolk' and attended by 'charming Dr Dansie' but was not so ill she could not criticise Walter Tillyard's Latin announcement of the birth of Julius' first grandchild: 'wouldn't *est mihi filius* have been more elegant [than] *filium habeo*?')[123], she emerged to make a new will[124] and on the night of 10/11 May to dream 'a very odd dream … about the almost forgotten Aleister Crowley! Julius and I were in Paris and walked into a room where some men who looked like English undergraduates were performing Ceremonial Magic. We were handed wands tipped with wild arums and invited to take part. One of the men said to me "Aleister Crowley is dead but his spirit directs us". This made me very angry and Julius and I came out … then I woke up and began thinking of former days and how foolish I was to think Aleister Crowley was a safe guide. My longing for direct knowledge of God was certainly a good one but I ought at the outset to have felt the distrust of byways and short cuts which only came to me later. I went to sleep again and dreamed that the same young man reappeared … when he saw me he at once claimed me as a fellow-magician … I most vehemently disclaimed any connection with magic and woke myself up. So may my unconscious mind be cleansed from a taint which has perhaps persisted all this time, and may Jesus my Lord and Saviour claim every corner of my being'.[125]

Crowley's death from advanced heart and lung disease on 1 December 1947 passed unrecorded in Aelfrida's diary, deliberately so, it seems, given that sensational headlines appeared in newspapers favoured by the Lovells. (November 1947 diary references to the appearance in Lolworth of supposed harbingers of death[126] are too early unless we accept that Aelfrida was as prescient as she would have us believe.) More interesting, however, is her reference to persistent 'taint': can it be that remembering how 'disinterested, devoted [and] sincere' though Aleister Crowley might be but also that as a man who had (so he said) talked with God, he was a lamentably great hater and could be extremely 'bitter and revengeful' if he chose[127], she noted how similar their

personalities had been and remained and wondered if her dead 'Guru's' personality had posthumously 'tainted' her own and if it was this 'taint' (akin in its spiritually degenerative effects to the physical 'taints' of syphilis) which prompted her to act towards Father Lovell as she did? On the other hand, her denunciation of 'former days' is interesting because it demonstrates another shift in her ambiguous attitude towards her 'Guru'. (She had once defended Crowley to an editor of *The Sufi Quarterly* who had called him 'a very bad man' by stating that she owed Crowley 'a vast debt of gratitude' because he was the first to explain 'Mysticism' to her and to set her feet 'on the right path'[128]; later she regarded him as a "bad angel" disguised "on purpose to delude [her]"[129] and later still as not so much a 'false prophet' as a man as earnest in his endeavour to direct men's souls as she in hers and worthy of inclusion, at her guardian angel's behest, in her 1944 Lenten 'portion of labour'.)[130] Not only did it happen soon after her tirade against Father Lovell but it also suggests another reason for leaving Lolworth: Lovell, like Crowley, was among the many men who pressured her soul when exercising authority over her and further surrender was out of the question.

Having opened Edward Ely's eyes to an aspect of her personality which she might have concealed had it not been overridden by an episode of mental disequilibrium, Aelfrida seems to have decided that distancing herself physically from her spiritual director might encourage him to overlook what she now trivialised as a silly 'fuss' on her part regarding the faintly ridiculous '*affaire Lovelle*'. She seems too to have wanted to distance herself spiritually from Edward Wynn to punish herself for succumbing to the 'human consolations' he offered and to ensure that only 'spiritual' friendship would subsist between them in the future, monitored by 'Prudence, Piety and Discretion'.[131] The same seems to have been the case with regard to Julius, for although his sister allowed herself to rest in 'togetherness' with her beloved brother, it seems she now believed that 'togetherness' could never be as sanctioned or 'sanctified'[132] as she wanted and needed it to be and that not being with 'dear Dudu' so much might 'spiritualise' their relationship with the help of the same monitresses. Towards Frank Stokoe, however, with whom her relationship had been chiefly 'spiritual', she behaved with blatant unkindness: on the same day as she recorded her guardian angel 'trying to say something to me about friends … growing old and getting ill', she received 'a pathetic pencil-letter' from Fidelio, currently a patient in Addenbrooke's Hospital in Cambridge, saying he had been there a month 'slowly recovering from a heart attack'. She did not visit, excusing herself by noting that she 'could not grasp' the import of the angel's message with regard to him, but it was not incomprehension which prevented her: the day before she received Fidelio's message she jubilantly records 'a Wetenhall Cottage day!'[133] and four days later that Julius had visited Fidelio in hospital three times. It seems, therefore, that a forty-year friendship with her most faithful Little Friend, a man with whom she had sworn a 'compact of friendship' to be broken only by death, was not something she wished to pursue.

But although she closed some episodes, Aelfrida was more affected than she realised by the disappearance from her life of men whose presence in it had been important to her. Their departures were underscored by the roar of 'engines of death' from Oakington Aerodrome[134] (a contemporary slogan called it "the sound of freedom") reminding her that others besides Frank Stokoe had ridden or might be riding on to die: Julius, fit for his age but older than herself, Eustace in whom the first intimations of the arteriosclerotic disease which was to kill him were now appearing, and Willie Searle whose birthday on her wedding anniversary brought other deaths to mind, particularly that of Agatha, on whose death she no longer ruminated though the anguish of the February night when she and Eustace set out on their 'tragic search'[135] was never forgotten.

Other 'episodes' continued unclosed but it is obvious from Aelfrida's comment that she would not bother herself overmuch with once-beloved relatives if she met them for the first time now[136] (an attitude described as one of 'loving laissez-faire and non-interference'; others noted that she discouraged interaction by acting in a formal and reserved manner)[137] and from her decision to become nothing but a soul at prayer, that closing-in on herself was less an indication of a request to God to 'live Thou in me' in order to fill her with Himself[138] and more of deep world-weariness in a woman crippled with pain, unable to sustain even a milder Rule, despairing of the world and no longer capable of dictating to it. Only her comment that though 'in theory' she was 'content to be nothing', when it came to practising self-naughting 'oh dear! oh dear!!'[139], showed she had no intention of disengaging from life just yet: failing grandchildren of her own, there was Constance wanting her first baby to be born at Wetenhall Cottage ('I *should* be pleased', noted Aunt Aelfrida)[140] and little John Tillyard ('John *Christian* Tillyard', his great aunt emphasised) soon to be joined by the first girl of the new generation, Stephen and Margot's daughter Bridget Ruth, to whose mother Aelfrida sent a 'record book' for Margot to record the doings and sayings of her 'nice baby'. And although she noted even as she blessed young John that he, like Bridget Ruth, was 'the first [of] a new generation which

I shall never see grow up'[141], there was something to look forward: Alethea due home again on furlough in 1953. But an Alethea for whom Lolworth was no longer the 'right place', ostensibly because there was no room for her at the new rectory[142] but actually, it may be, because of what perspicacious Alethea might uncover of her mother leaving the old one.

Forces other than human also conspired to waft Aelfrida away from Lolworth. 'Orders from on High' about moving on her 'pillar of fire and cloud' became a three-line whip as God intensified His Presence and 'as it were' began to 'isolate' her from her present surroundings.[143] Matters of real estate also suggested that it was time to go because they constituted 'preoccupations' from which she wanted to escape[144]: Fordfield sold to the Sisters of Hope (the proceeds were divided between Julius, Eustace, and Aelfrida according to the terms of Chiara's will but the price left undisclosed by the sibling whose life interest in the house ended with its sale), its 'north part, kitchen, backstairs, etc.' being 'sliced off' in order that extension and modernisation could take place, and although Aelfrida waxed joyful over 'the ceremony at ex-Fordfield' when 'the foundation-stone of the new building was laid' and hoped that God would 'continue to bless Hope House'[145], the despondent tone of other diary entries suggests that loss of and alterations to the 'First House' were regretted by Julius and herself. But it was the impending compulsory purchase by Cambridge City Council of her Staffordshire Street cottages (a curious contemporary reference to 'a kind of touch of our Lord's dereliction' probably refers to her own soul rather than to her own dereliction of duty as a landlord but the fact that the cottages were condemned as unfit for human habitation speaks volumes)[146] and of an adjoining area of land leased to a local builder whose rents formed her major source of income which particularly exercised Aelfrida in 1952 (and would continue to do so for some years) as the prospect of involuntary 'Holy Poverty' appeared before her. (In fact she did very well out of the deal and could have lived more comfortably from the proceeds than she did had not residual asceticism and a desire to keep her daughter financially dependent on her decreed that she save the money instead.) But what else could she do under the circumstances except recall and obey Bishop O'Ferrall's Tymawr advice to '*pray and not worry*'.[147]

A major worry remained: where was she to live? Bishop Wynn, 'at his *most* understanding' and 'on the lookout for a suitable parsonage-home'[148], found one; on 20 May she received a letter from the wife of the vicar of 'Southea, Parson Drove (Wisbech 7 miles, Cambridge 42)' saying that she 'would like a tertiary in her house' and offering, subject to mutual approval, to take her. 'It looks', wrote Aelfrida, imminently homeless if she did not accept, 'as if this were my guardian angel's choice for me – so I have definitely asked to go'.[149] Julius, she added, would 'greatly prefer to have me [less than] 42 miles away' but God's Will overrode fraternal feelings.[150]

Father and Mrs Dunkin[151] visited Lolworth on 14 June to inspect their prospective tenant. Noting that Leslie Dunkin was tall and 'rather plain with fuzzy hair' but 'full of energy and enthusiasm' (and that it would be 'hard to start again with another confessor'), Aelfrida homed in on 'small and plump and pretty' Mrs Dunkin's weak point: her family had been 'in trade', a taint endowing her with 'a slight inferiority complex'. Fuzzy hair, trade, and the thought of four young children in the house notwithstanding, she arranged a reconnaisance visit to her new abode on 'the top floor of the vicarage'[152] up two flights of stairs; in fact, in the vicarage attic.

A taxi ride 'through the fenland' to Parson Drove was one of the highlights of this rather sad period of her life and she revelled in the wide skies and sense of space beloved by East Anglians and noted with approval how much more prosperous the countryside appeared than in the days of her youth. Arriving at Parson Drove, she found it to consist of little more than 'a pleasant avenue with houses standing back in gardens', a garage, a post office, and a *very* Victorian' church, built in 1872. The vicarage, however, a sturdy building of dark red brick and 'the kind of house [she] was expected to admire in [her] childhood and never did!', was not dilapidated but comfortable and well-equipped, and her 'top story' suite of 'a small dainty room looking east … and a kitchenette at the far end of the … spacious sunny landing' an improvement on truly dilapidated Lolworth. (And at £2-6/- a week something of a bargain.) So she 'gladly agreed to come', arranging her arrival for 9 July 1952.[153] Her guardian angel had the last word: '*not so*', he decreed on hearing of Aelfrida's decision to call her new quarters 'St Bruno', 'it shall be called Gethsemane'.[154]

The short time intervening between first intimations of departure and departure itself seemed to rush past. ('Easter! Ascension Day! Pentecost! … I say to myself my *last* [this] at Lolworth, my *last* [that] and [realise] that worship in the beloved little church brings me as much joy as … in the beloved chapel at Tymawr'.)[155] Sensing too, that it was a time of reparation, Aelfrida set out to re-establish good relations with the Lovells, with Mrs Lovell (restored to 'Sister Lilian') for practical reasons (she had agreed to make room for Aelfrida if 'Gethsemane' proved too agonisingly ungardenlike) and with Father Lovell, now noted to fulfil his 'priestly function' to perfection

and to have existed in 'deep spiritual harmony' with his sole churchgoer[156], for spiritual ones. At her final confession she apologised for 'much self-will', wished she had been 'humbler and quieter', and testified to his 'patience, kindness, understanding and helpful remarks'; 'on the human side', however, she continued to find him 'exasperating'[157], particularly when vacillating behaviour over leaving the rectory caused its buyer to pull out which meant she could have enjoyed a 'quiet summer' there after all. Lovell too seized the opportunity to apologise ('he is at his best … in the confessional', noted his penitent without irony) for his irritability and fault-finding ('a little discipline is good for me', she noted apropos this remark), to beg her to continue her prayers for his parish – and to remind her firmly that Deity who brought her to Lolworth was now calling her 'elsewhere'.[158]

At Mass the day before leaving for 'elsewhere', Aelfrida offered her six years at Lolworth to God. (He accepted, but not before warning her that she must now '*accept more from Him*', a warning that she chose to ignore until its full import became clearer.) She also said goodbye to 'sweet village and dear people', to 'dear village children', to the 'dear ugly room' with its 'tasteless furniture … damp spotted walls [and] many discomforts' where she had 'communed with God and learned more of Him and His ways', to the garden 'looking as if it were going back to jungle', to the 'beloved winding lane sanctified as the approach to the church', and to the church itself 'where … ancient prayers, like angels gather round'.[159] And a smudge on the paper suggests that the Lolworth Rule-keeper wept as she wrote.

## Notes

1 GCPPT 1|1|65 14 January 1948.
2 GCPPT 1|1|67 11 March 1950.
3 GCPPT 1|1|65 14 January 1948.
4 GCPPT 1|1|67 11 March 1950.
5 GCPPT 1|1|65 2 July 1947.
6 ibid. 16 April 1947.
7 ibid. 30 April and 1 and 5 July 1947.
8 ibid. 17 July 1947.
9 ibid. 21 July 1947 and 11 February 1948.
10 ibid. 30 March 1948.
11 ibid. 21 April 1948.
12 ibid. 7 May 1948.
13 ibid. 7 and 11 May 1948.
14 GCPPT 1|1|66 'Eve of Pentecost' (15 May) 1948. The National Health Service came into being on 5 July 1948 in the midst of Aelfrida's course of treatment; she makes no mention of this momentous event at the time, nor does she note if her sudden change in status as a patient meant that she paid for some of her treatment but not the rest.
15 ibid. 25 May and 'Eve of Corpus Christi' (26, 27 or 28 May) 1948.
16 ibid. 15 October 1949. Julius, Mina, and Alethea were not among family members who encouraged Aelfrida to gift Wetenhall Cottage to Hope House in order to be able to live there herself under the nuns' care, the former, it may be, because they would have to relinquish their

home and the latter because the greater part of her income derived from rental money paid by Julius into her account.

17  ibid. 16 June and 2 December 1948.
18  ibid. 1 March 1949.
19  ibid. 7 April 1949.
20  ibid.
21  GCPPT 1|1|66 7 April 1949.
    GCPPT 1|1|67 25 February 1950.
    GCPPT 1|1|69 21 October 1951.
22  GCPPT 1|1|66 7 April 1949.
23  ibid. 22 and 25 September 1948.
24  GCPPT 1|1|66 16 July 1949.
    GCPPT 1|1|67 22 June ('July' in error) 1950.
25  GCPPT 1|1|67 22 June ('July' in error) and 29 June 1950.
26  ibid. 24 February 1950.
27  Tillyard, Ae. *Naomi da Costa* p 248 (GCPPT 2|22).
28  GCPPT 1|1|67 24 February 1950.
29  GCPPT 1|1|66 13 December 1948.
30  GCPPT 1|1|69 2 and 4 May 1951.
31  GCPPT 1|1|65 4 January 1948.
32  GCPPT 1|1|67 22 August 1950.
    GCPPT 1|1|69 19 January 1951.
33  GCPPT 1|1|66 15 November and 15 December 1948.
    GCPPT 1|1|69 17 October 1951.
34  GCPPT 1|163 14 June 1946.
35  GCPPT 1|1|69 27 March 1951.
36  ibid. 13 May 1951.
37  ibid. 21 May 1951.
38  ibid. 21, 22 and 23 May 1951.
39  ibid. 18 December 1951.
40  GCPPT 1|1|66 21 October 1948.
41  GCPPT 1|1|67 7 January 1950.
    GCPPT 1|1|69 25 October 1951.
    GCPPT 1|1|70 19 May 1952.
42  GCPPT 1|1|65 24 January 1948.
43  Tillyard, Ae. *Christian Old Age* p 71 (GCPPT 2|17).
44  GCPPT 1|1|67 'Good Friday' (7 April) 1950.
45  GCPPT 1|1|65 21 December 1947.
46  ibid. 22 March 1948.
47  ibid. 21 December 1947.
48  ibid. 16 December 1947.
49  GCPPT 1|1|66 18 and 21 January and 1 February 1948.
50  ibid. 16, 19 and 21 October 1948.
51  GCPPT 1|1|67 5 May 1950.
52  ibid. 27 March and 5 May 1950.
53  ibid. 5 May 1950.
54  GCPPT 1|1|66 17 November 1948.
55  ibid. 5 March 1952.
56  ibid. 17 November 1948.
57  ibid. 2 October 1948.
58  ibid. 17 and 18 November 1948.
59  GCPPT 1|1|65 14 January 1948.
60  GCPPT 1|1|66 25 October 1948.
    GCPPT 1|1|67 24 April 1950.
61  GCPPT 1|1|66 4 May 1949.
62  ibid. 29 November 1948.
63  ibid. 24 March 1949.
64  GCPPT 1|1|65 14 January 1948.
65  GCPPT 1|1|66 28 November 1948.
66  ibid. 4 May 1949.
67  ibid. 29 November 1948 and 4 May 1949.
68  Tillyard, Ae. *Christian Old Age* p 77.
69  GCPPT 1|1|66 18 August 1949.
70  ibid. 23 April and 2 June 1949.
71  ibid. 'Good Friday' (15 April) 1949.
72  GCPPT 1|1|66 2 June 1949.
    GCPPT 1|1|67 24 April 1950.
73  GCPPT 1|1|66 29 June and 25 November 1949.
74  GCPPT 1|1|61 28 March 1943.
75  GCPPT 1|1|66 29 December 1949.
    GCPPT 1|1|67 17 January 1950.
76  GCPPT 1|1|66 7 December 1949.
    GCPPT 1|1|67 4 and 7 January 1950.
77  GCPPT 1|1|66 15 November and 29 December 1949.
    GCPPT 1|1|67 4 January 1950.
78  ibid. 29 December 1949 and 1 January 1950.
79  ibid. 1 January 1950.
80  GCPPT 1|1|67 3 and 4 January 1950.
81  ibid. 5 and 6 January 1950.
82  ibid. 5 and 7 January 1950.
83  ibid. 7 January 1950.
84  GCPPT 1|1|66 14 and 20 December 1949.
85  ibid. 14 December 1949 and 1 January 1950.
86  GCPPT 1|1|66 14 December 1949 (addendum).
    GCPPT 1|1|67 14 January 1950.
87  GCPPT 1|1|67 12 January 1950.
88  ibid. 13 January 1950.
89  GCPPT 1|1|69 17 September 1951.
90  ibid. 30 April 1951.
91  Tillyard, Ae. *Christian Old Age* p 30.
92  GCPPT 1|1|69 2 August 1951.
93  ibid. 9 March 1952.
94  GCPPT 1|1|64 16 June and 9 July 1946.
95  GCPPT 1|1|69 11 March 1952.
96  ibid. 9 March 1952.
97  ibid. 15 March 1952.
98  ibid. 20 March 1952.
99  ibid. 8 April 1952.
100  ibid. 15 March and 12 April 1952.
101  GCPPT 1|1|65a. Letter from Father Cary to Aelfrida of 5 July 1947.
102  GCPPT 1|1|67 3 July 1950.
103  ibid. 26 and 27 January 1950.
104  GCPPT 1|1|69 10 and 14 January 1951.
105  ibid. 5 March 1952.
106  ibid. 24 May 1952.
107  GCPPT 1|1|70 'Rogation Sunday ' (18 May) 1952.
108  GCPPT 1|1|69 9 November 1952. As 'daughter house', Compton Durville was used to house the post-war influx of candidates for the religious life; it was relinquished after only a few years when declining numbers and enlargement of the conventual area at Tymawr allowed all members of the Community to be housed on the same site (Sister Veronica Ann SSC, personal communication November 2008).
    GCPPT 1|1|69a SSC Newsletter dated "All Saints 1951".
109  GCPPT 1|1|69 9 November 1951.
110  GCPPT 1|1|61 'St Benedict's Day' (11 July) 1943.
111  GCPPT 1|1|69 9 November 1951.
112  ibid. 20 and 22 March 1952.
113  ibid. 'Palm Sunday' (6 March) 1952.
114  GCPPT 1|1|70 9 June 1952.
115  GCPPT 1|1|65 'Eve of Holy Cross' (2 May) 1947.
    GCPPT 1|1|69 15 August 1951.
116  GCPPT 1|1|69 'Maundy Thursday' (10 April) 1952.
117  ibid. 'Eve of All Saints' (31 October) 1951.
118  GCPPT 1|1|70 9 June 1952.
119  GCPPT 1|1|69 13 May 1952.
120  ibid. 10, 17, 19 and 23 January 1952.
121  ibid. 31 January and 4 February 1952.
122  ibid. 'Shrove Tuesday' (26 February) 1952.

123 ibid. 1 and 6 May 1952.

124 GCPPT 1|1|70 27 May 1952. Her will stated that Eustace Tillyard and Ernest Crundwell ('Bayard') as her surviving executors were to receive £10 each and her brothers, Mina (but not Phyllis), Girton College, and Malling £50 apiece. A fifth of the residue was to pass to the SSC and four fifths to Alethea.

125 GCPPT 1|1|69 11 May 1952.

126 GCPPT 1|1|65 26 November 1947.

127 GCPPT 1|1|19 1 December 1913.

128 GCPPT 1|1|38 15 November 1930.

129 Tillyard, Ae. *Christian Old Age* p 93.

130 GCPPT 1|1|61 25 February 1944.

131 GCPPT 1|1|70 30 June 1952.

132 GCPPT 1|1|67 18 January 1950.

133 GCPPT 1|1|70 25, 26 and 30 June 1952.

134 GCPPT 1|1|69 5 March and 'Palm Sunday' (6 March) 1952. Aelfrida may have suffered from 'recruitment' (distortion of sound perception as a result of cochlear damage probably caused by excessive use of aspirin) and from hyperacusis (pathological exaggeration of heard sounds), in which case jet noise would have been intolerable.

135 ibid. 23 February 1952.

136 GCPPT 1|1|65 6 September 1947.

137 GCPPT 1|1|69 17 February 1952.
John Hibbs personal communication 18 November 2008.

138 GCPPT 1|1|69 5 March 1952.

139 GCPPT 1|1|67 17 October 1950.

140 GCPPT 1|1|69 6 February 1952.

141 GCPPT 1|1|69 6 May 1952.
GCPPT 1|1|70 20 June and 2 July 1952.

142 GCPPT 1|1|69 8 April 1952.

143 GCPPT 1|1|70 8 July 1952.

144 GCPPT 1|1|69 29 January and 'Ash Wednesday' (27 February) 1952.

145 GCPPT 1|1|67 18 January and 19 May 1950. The 'new building', including a proper chapel, officially opened in 1952; there is no record of Aelfrida being invited to attend the ceremony though a contemporary reference to how dearly she would have loved 'three Fordfield days in bed with Ellen … waiting on me' (GCPPT 1|1|70 13 December 1952) suggests that she may have been invited but decided not to attend. There is no mention of any Tillyard attending the ceremony in the *Cambridge Daily News* report of the event (19 May 1950) but the Bishop of Northampton's reported comment that "good [had] come out of evil" (he was referring to the Sisters of Hope having had to evacuate their London quarters during the war) is appropriate given the house's history.

146 GCPPT 1|1|69 15 November 1951.
GCPPT 1|1|70 20 May 1952.

147 GCPPT 1|1|69 'Ash Wednesday' (27 February) 1952. For a graphic description of the Staffordshire Street area of Cambridge see Petty, M. *Grim days of dirt, damp and decay* (*CN* 5 October 2009).

148 ibid. 1 May 1952.

149 GCPPT 1|1|70 20 and 30 May 1952.

150 ibid. 4 June 1952.

151 The Rev Walter Leslie Jonathan Dunkin had been ordained during the war and after two curacies (one in Cambridge), appointed to Parson Drove in 1949. For further details see Yelton, M. *Outposts of the Faith* pp199–201.

152 ibid. 4, 9 and 14 June 1952.

153 ibid. 20 June 1952.

154 ibid. 'The Visitation' (2 July) 1952. Aelfrida's choice of name may have been influenced by Thomas Merton's "Cistercian Abbey of the poor men who labour in Gethsemane" (*Elected Silence* p 268) where he lived for some time as a hermit in a hut in the abbey grounds, but more likely derives from her vision of the prone wounded Christ in Tymawr garden ('our garden is Gethsemane' GCPPT 1|1|62 2 January 1945) or from a wartime 'shewing' in which God 'called' her into the garden of Gethsemane and informed her that there she was to share both Christ's taking on himself 'the unfelt remorse of the sinful' and His grief for their unfelt shame (GCPPT 1|1|59 18 April 1941) or, given the increased pain she now suffered, from a later Lenten experience during which Christ opened His heart to her bidding her enter and share His agony in Gethsemane (GCPPT 1|1|67 19 March 1950).

155 ibid. 1 June 1952.

156 ibid. 11 June 1952.

157 ibid. 11 June and 1 July 1952.

158 ibid. 1 July 1952.

159 ibid. 8 July 1952.

# Penance in the Fens

In September 1900 Aelfrida (as Frida) recorded in her diary that she and Julius, aged sixteen and eighteen respectively, had remained at Fordfield to entertain a school friend of Julius' from 'Tydd St Giles, wherever that may be' while 'Mayor and Mayoress and Mandeville' (i.e. Eustace, a boy of eleven) lunched with 'some worthy farmers at some benighted hole in the fens'.[1] In 1952, aged sixty-eight, she discovered its exact location: seven miles as the crow flies from Parson Drove and situated (like Parson Drove) and as Alethea put it in a letter to the mother who had just informed her of the new resting place of her pillar of fire and cloud, in 'incredibly fenny uncharted country'[2] a long way from family, friends, and Cambridgy conversation.

Though hardly a 'benighted hole' or 'uncharted', Parson Drove was certainly 'fenny', a small village straggling along both sides of a minor road with equally small hamlets as its nearest neighbours ('drove' provides a clue to the rural nature of surroundings in which the driving of sheep and cattle to market generated much of the traffic) and a much more 'remote country village in the fens'[3] than Lolworth. Quite why Aelfrida (or her guardian angel) accepted Parson Drove is a mystery: perhaps the remoteness of her 'attic room' from the rest of the Dunkin family reminded her of the 'nest high up'[4] at Fordfield where she had enjoyed peace and the stars away from the strife below; perhaps the village's isolation enticed one whose inclinations towards eremetic life were constantly interrupted by incursions of 'the world'; perhaps it seemed a good idea at this point in her life to "serve [her] title" at "some dead-end sort of place in the fens" as a "sort of jack-of-all-trades to the vicar"[5] and as a preliminary to a life in which *caritas* would play a more prominent part than hitherto. Perhaps, having made herself unwelcome at Lolworth and rendered herself homeless by 'yielding' Wetenhall Cottage to Julius 'till his death'[6] (he and Mina were now settled permanently in Cambridge and had sold their Cardiff house), she had nowhere else to go and had perforce to agree with her elder brother (and with Mina, as 'serene and happy' as Mrs Lovell at the prospect of having her husband to herself undistracted by Aelfrida's presence) that she was 'wise to go to Parson Drove and settle down there quietly'.[7] Whatever her reason, at 'fenny' Parson Drove she

**Parson Drove Church and vicarage, showing attic window**

duly arrived on 9 July 1952 accompanied by a 'huge' Pickford's van in which was stowed (it took an hour to pack) 'blankets, sheets and towels', a ten gallon drum of paraffin for her stove (designated the 'Virtuous Woman' because of its ruby glow)[8], her deckchair, a writing table, a dustpan and brush (she was amazed by the 'mechanisation' of the vicarage household: 'the most beautiful … washing machine which the ex-laundry director gazed at with deep interest' and a vacuum cleaner, the first she had seen)[9], two 'sacred pictures', a 'little table Dear gave me when I was 12', several 'drawing room (Fordfield) cane-seated chairs'[10], personal effects, and quantities of family and other papers including manuscripts written since the war. There were also many books, her own (of which she possessed several copies of some; furthermore, not all her 'Cambridge books' were bestowed on Tymawr and she had acquired more since), so many, in fact, that on 1 October and to Mrs Dunkin's alarm and dismay, a second Pickford's van brought 'ex-Fordfield's best bookcase (with cupboards in the middle)' which proved too large to fit into her room and had to remain on the landing and 'dear Grandpapa's … very majestic dressing cupboard' (a Saratoga trunk, judging from her description) used henceforth as wardrobe, chest of drawers, dressing table, and general store.[11] In fact, after leaving Lolworth and deciding that she required more creature comforts, Aelfrida dragged round with her an ever-increasing train of possessions (her own and some of Alethea's), irrelevant items of which (a pair of secateurs, for example) were discarded only with reluctance.

Subdued by increasing infirmity, Aelfrida may have intended to 'settle down … quietly'. Her general behaviour was certainly less inflammatory than at Lolworth (a village in which the devil seems to have remained, for other than passing mentions, he did not materialise in Parson Drove) and having all meals in her room save Sunday lunch (her midday meal was carried up by Audrey, the 'day girl', but breakfast, tea, and supper she made for – and washed up after – herself) meant less intrusion on the Dunkins than on the Lovells. The Dunkin children not yet being adolescents, she also behaved in 'dear grannie' fashion towards Jane, Jonathan, Mary, and toddler and 'young Tartar' Michael and even took Willie, the family dog, on 'pleasant stroll[s] towards Church End – which we shall never reach!', controlling him with her stick if the canine 'bandit' misbehaved.[12] But a statement written immediately prior to arrival ('I always feel *maternal* toward the people I am with') might, given her proclivities as a mother, have warned the Dunkins had they read it, of its implications for themselves.

Being younger and more resilient than the Lovells (and possibly having been warned of Aelfrida's tendency to dominate and disrupt any household in which she lived), the Dunkins proved unexpectedly resistant to maternalism. In spite of Aelfrida's efforts to pull rank by making it known she was 'a consul's widow'[13] and, when that tactic failed, by trying to ally herself with Irene Dunkin by emphasising her 'Barratt forebears and their china shop' while 'keeping Eustace etc. etc. well out of sight!'[14], Mrs Dunkin, inferiority complex notwithstanding, was not to be dictated to: if Aelfrida had friends to tea (she entertained only seven visitors during her stay, two of whom were Eustace and Phyllis and two friends of Alethea who doubtless reported back on her mother's new surroundings; neither Julius

nor Mina made the lengthy trek from Cambridge), she was to boil her own kettle and refrain from introducing them into family areas of the house.

Father Dunkin too (he was her confessor and she often his only congregation) proved resistant to being bullied and although she did not hesitate to reprimand him and to compare him unfavourably to Father Lovell to his face if he forgot confession or overslept and was late for 7.30 Communion ('a visit from the Bishop would do him all the good in the world!')[15], his attitude towards her, though sometimes justifiably apologetic, was never submissive; indeed, he made it clear from the start that he was 'a little on his guard against [her] religious or ritualistic pretensions or demands'[16] and was prepared to treat her like a 'Sunday School child' (something she rather resented given the 'relative ages of priest and penitent … and their experience too') if a lecture on the danger inherent in the contemplative life 'of attaching undue importance to trivialities'[17] was required. He also tended to 'harangue' her at confession, intimated that he found her confessions superficial (Aelfrida obligingly discovered some faults – liking to be the centre of attention and thought 'charming, clever and well-informed' and being 'too much interested in other people and their affairs and sometimes thinking I could arrange their lives much better for them'[18] – but remembering Father Northcott's advice that she confine confession to sins 'actually committed' and her own notion that people like herself '*do* most desperately need confession'[19], said no more) and expected her to submit her Lenten Rule to him for approval. (It included *Self-examination*, specifically avoidance of 'self-importance' in any form and ensuring that she not overlook 'other people's virtues'; *Fasting*, specifically 'fewer letters and … as few remarks about myself in each one', an interesting insight into the volume and content of her correspondence; *Almsgiving*, of which she noted 'the less said about this the better!' without further explanation, and *Reading*, specifically Lucius Cary's *Called of God*[20]; she omitted, however, what was of supreme importance to her, '[her] Lord's special *invitation … to enter more fully into His Silence*[21], her intimate relationship with Deity being no concern of 'Father Leslie'.) He also asked her to add 'some acts of what he calls "service"'[22] to her Rule; being 'jack-of-all-trades to the Vicar' did not apparently or automatically include these. But he visited her in clerical garb in her attic 'as if I had been any other sick parishioner' when she was unwell (they had a 'grand theological talk' which cheered that particular parishioner immensely)[23] to bless the room and to bring her Communion (at the Bishop's suggestion, Aelfrida suspected), so in spite of 'Father Leslie's' unfortunate tendency to be 'pally and matey' towards his parishioners (and with a cigarette in his mouth too!)[24] and to redecorate his house 'naked except for shorts and sandals'[25] (she was so shocked by the sight that she retreated upstairs without collecting her letters), she had perforce to agree with the Bishop that the Dunkins were 'very loveable'[26] and to admit to her diary that she was 'well content' at Parson Drove and that she numbered the Dunkins among her friends.[27]

She had another friend too: 'Captain the Reverend Mr Eager' (*sic.*)[28] Alwyn Eagar RN (retd) occupied two rooms in the vicarage directly below Aelfrida's and had he not been 'a brave Christian gentleman' with whom it was a 'privilege' to be friends[29], she might have lodged objections: not only did he possess a wireless and a television, but he was also a typist. Having discovered, however, that what he typed was Braille material for the blind, she refrained from complaining and, as lonely in her way as dignified widowed Captain Eagar in his, allowed herself to entertain the kind of friendship she craved with a man 'intensely chivalrous' in appreciating that she shrank from over-demonstrative 'human affection'[30] but happy to return the 'delicate attentions' (chiefly hot water bottles) with which he plied her when she was unwell[31] and to enter into interesting discussions (the Captain was compiling an Anglo–Spanish dictionary of naval terms but on Aelfrida asking him for a translation of 'splice the mainbrace', replied gravely but with a twinkle that 'Spanish sailors are not served with rum!')[32] without intruding into Silence and Solitude at inconvenient moments ('we are great friends, Father Eagar and I – silently so!'[33]) or probing into her 'religious or ritualistic pretensions' at any time.

Other aspects of Parson Drove were less appealing and if Aelfrida hoped to 'take up the *vie dévote* without interruption' there[34], devout her life may have been but uninterrupted it was not. Her 'attic cell', though very 'sweet' and with views through trees to the horizon, also had a 'grave and unusual view of the churchyard' ('no pun intended – I mean solemn!'[35]; Parson Drove diaries demonstrate a sense of humour not always apparent in earlier volumes) and of the 'hideous' church whose 'tinny' bell rang at the level of her window across the narrow lane separating church from vicarage.[36] Then again, because her room was situated over the front door, all 'arrivals and departures [were] audible'[37], the more so as the household owned two cars and made no attempt to regulate early or late arrivals or departures to suit its attic lodger. (And the telephone rang incessantly.) Being directly beneath the roof, the room suffered the 'full force'[38] of rain or wind and though Parson Drove was unaffected by the 'flood stretching far inland'[39] following the storm surge which devastated England's east coast

on 31 January 1953, the northerly gale which drove it disturbed Aelfrida's sleep and meditations.

So too did village youth. The Parish Hall was situated beyond the vicarage garden, youth club dances ended after midnight, and 'indecent remarks from boys to girls' wafted up from the lane beneath her window. ('A hell of a row', she called it, strong language indeed for her.) But with the consequences of Lolworth meddling vivid in her mind, she refrained from complaining 'about Saturday dances and against Church worldliness in general' ('suggestions' to Father Dunkin fell on deaf ears or resulted in contra-suggestions at confession that she not interfere) because although Dunkin was 'young and misguided' in his efforts to tame the local youth, he was 'a dear all the same'.[40]

Then too, there was the matter of a supposedly 'prayerful person' not making too much noise in terms of 'bright ideas' sadly irrelevant in the post war world of 'the heavy … plain … small, swarthy … earthbound-looking … relics of Primitive Britons that have survived in these remote fens' i.e. the 'Parson Drovers'. (Isolated in Tymawr and with only Walter of her immediate family in the armed forces, Aelfrida had no idea of the toll taken on ordinary people by the war and, with particular relevance to the 'Parson Drovers' whose men folk she described as 'grim', on East Anglian regiments.) She even refrained from writing 'books'[41], composing nothing in her 'attic cell' save letters and reminiscences. But having no duties 'while everyone else [was] desperately busy'[42] reminded her that God as well as Leslie Dunkin expected acts of 'service' from her, so demanding of herself what He would have her do, she settled on a twofold 'spiritual task': 'to praise God' and 'to *keep quiet* in order that I may be a channel of His grace … to Parson Drove'. She had also been too 'self-centred' i.e. had complained too loudly and too long with regard to 'trivialities', these having bulked so large in her mind as to cause her to forget that her pillar of fire and cloud had led her to 'fenny … country' as a *tertiary SSC* in order that Sister Placida might 'put the vicarage in touch with [her] Community', Tymawr's spirituality being what was needed to counteract 'Church Worldliness' and a tertiary the 'favoured channel' through which it and God's grace were to flow.[43]

But if God wanted 'tertiary SSC' to 'stay *here* and pray', Aelfrida had other plans. Forced by ill health to cancel a visit to Jesus (College, not Christ) arranged for 2 September 'though … it would have been a first class thrill to stay in a college lodge'[44], wrote the tertiary who had refused to do so because a Master's Lodge was a most 'unsuitable' place for such a person (some brief visits and life in Lolworth seem to have changed her mind), she compensated for the grave error committed when she moved away from 'Cambridge conversation and how much else besides'[45] to 'a dreary village where there is no-one to know and very little to do'[46] by spending the night of her sixty-ninth birthday on 5 October 1952 at 'the Master's Lodge, Jesus College, Cambridge'. Back in Parson Drove, she wrote nostalgically of the 'indescribable delight' induced by walks in the Fellows' and Lodge gardens, of the 'perfect taste' demonstrated by Phyllis' arrangement of the Lodge interior – and of her new-found ability to taste Cambridge academic 'joys and predilections without losing touch with Tymawr and all … it stands for'.[47]

One thing, however, put a 'stop on [her] mind' with regard to Cambridge life. This was neither nostalgia ('walking down Kings Parade … I felt as if the breeze might blow away 50 years and leave me 18 again. On the whole I am glad it didn't!') nor the elegiac note engendered by a 'coffee and reminiscences' birthday party at Wetenhall Cottage ('perhaps my last party!') for old friends (former schoolmates of Eustace and herself, one of the Coxes from Florence days, and one of the 'children we played with', now Deaconess Creighton) nor because inspection of the 'palatial new building' with its 'new elegant little chapel' to which Fordfield had been 'successfully joined' reminded her that the house was no longer hers. It was because the house which bore her mother's maiden name and which had been her 'last hostage to fortune' ('my one hope of getting properly looked after in my old age lay in my [offering] Wetenhall Cottage to Hope House as a convalescent home in return for nursing') was now *Julius'* home and with regard to care in 'old age' she must put her trust in God.[48]

Other matters too rendered her elegiac. Although she wrote cheerfully of acquaintances (Florence Keynes, for example, 'still young at 92 … dressed like a queen in velvets and satins and jewels'[49], still, judging by her letters, intensely engaged with the world and adamant in her refusal to brood over death of a son of whom Aelfrida wrote caustically that 'Maynard … hardened [into] one of the most conceited men I ever met [but] I suppose I may still pray for him')[50], she was beset by a need to weep over 'the snow that lies at the heart of mortal things'[51] and by a sadness engendered as much by the frequent tolling of 'the Passing Bell'[52] outside her window (at least sixteen funerals were held in the first nine months of her stay at Parson Drove; she prayed 'rather vague prayers' for them all)[53] as by more deaths of people known to her.

Though Willie Searle did not die yet (he was, wrote the woman who might have been his wife to the woman who married him, putting up the 'bravest of fights', must have known he was dying but kept up the 'pretence that

he is getting well', and should be told that his illness was mortal)[54] another man did: Frank Stokoe, on 2 November 1952 at Heacham, Norfolk, less than thirty miles from the friend to whom he had written four days earlier of the nursing home in which he found himself: "My dear Aelfrida, this is as good a place as might be for the endurance of a long convalescence. The charming house, the romantic garden, bring balm to the impatient mind and heart and there is much real kindness and good will about me". After describing his future plans (he was due to relinquish his rented 'Manor of Comberton Green' in March 1953 so would need to sort papers and books early in the new year; he would then "fly out to Aleppo on a long visit to the Altounyans" or settle somewhere else in rural Cambridgeshire), he admitted to feeling "rather jaded" by the effort of writing letters but assured her that an "afternoon nap" would help before signing off "much love from Fidelio".[55] Two days later Aelfrida, reading *The Times,* learnt that their 'compact of friendship' was broken at last.

'I have by me', she wrote, 'a letter from Fidelio of 28 October', adding that on receipt of it she had said to herself 'he will never leave the convalescent home'. (Fidelio's letter had spoken of "one or two slight setbacks lately" and "renewed cardiac discomfort".) She also noted her gladness (no publisher would have taken his book and 'the disappointment would have broken his heart') and her pleasure at how illness had 'softened' him ('his letters have been full of the kindness and charm of nurses, friends, etc. etc.')[56] and wrote him a loving epitaph: 'he had great courage, *personal* humility if intellectual pride, and a lovely awareness of Beauty in delicate shades and tones'.[57] But the woman whose diary recorded so many instances of Fidelio's support for a divorcee whom he, unlike other acquaintances, never ostracised, had not had herself driven from Parson Drove to Heacham (her description of Fidelio's letters in the plural suggests she knew he was there) and had left 'the man of Gotham whom nature intended to be lonely' to die among strangers more loving than herself "beside the sea" where he had always hoped to hear "the call at last".[58]

Relieved of the pressure of Fidelio's soul on hers (she noted in her diary that apart from Juan Mascarò, 'no-one will care very much')[59], Aelfrida had no notion that she might miss the man she would portray in a novel as 'Marcus Hare' the "Great Beauty-Mystic"[60], to whom she had once dedicated one of her 'poems about death'[61], and whose death from a heart attack she had predicted as happening to 'Alan George' in *O Passionate World.* But she did, particularly as his death followed so closely on and took place in the same year as those of 'Hubert Henderson and [her] old friend [John Forbes]

Cameron'.[62] But perhaps what she felt for him was not "disinterested affection"[63] but real 'human affection' and it was because of this she greeted with relief and gratitude and undisguised joy the unexpected reappearance of another man in her life: her 'old friend the Anteater'.[64]

Aelfrida had not met James Barkway since the August day in 1914 when she recorded that her former admirer had become 'grave and parsonic instead of grave and aesthetic' and still bent his head 'as if his big nose weighed him down'[65], but diary entries show she followed his ecclesiastical career with interest ('just been made Bishop of Bedford'; 'now Bishop of St Andrews', and so on.)[66] A letter from Bishop (emeritus) Barkway arrived on 30 July 1952.

Keen that he too not die 'without [her] having written to pick up the threads' (it was only through a chance meeting with an acquaintance of Aelfrida's that James Barkway received news of her), Aelfrida ("*My dear Aelfrida*", she noted amusedly; they had '*never* called each other by our Christian names' before) hastened to reply. Barkway having recalled "innumerable happy memories" (e.g. his escorting her to the belvedere at the top of the tower of Westminster College, an eyrie she had already visited in the company of other young men though she did not tell him so then or now), she responded with a few of her own e.g. her offer of 'Platonic Friendship' on the 'first Monday of Full Term 1905'; she also told him something of her 'spiritual pilgrimage' (e.g. that it was reading a book and hearing a sermon which had 'opened to [her] the possibility of direct personal knowledge of God') but as she neared Tymawr, switched to news of her brothers instead on the grounds that a bishop, even a retired one, would know what she meant without it being spelled out.[67] He did, saying that he wished he had known she was seeking God (an indication of how well twenty-two-year-old Aelfrida concealed her quest beneath a veneer of frivolity and flirtation) and assuring her that she was now more spiritually alive than he. ('For humility give me a bishop! He and Dr Wynn are a pair'.) He also expressed a wish to meet, concerning which Aelfrida wrote guardedly 'Do *I* want to see him?' before deciding that though it was touching to have an old friend want to see her again, she would leave it to God to arrange a meeting 'if He [saw] fit'[68]; in the meantime, it was important to keep in touch with the man who had looked at her 'sentimentally'[69] during their last meeting. It therefore seemed entirely appropriate that while she was replying to James Barkway's most recent letter, an 'awestruck' announcement by 'day-girl' Audrey of an ecclesiastical visitor ("the *Bishop*") caused her to rise to her feet exclaiming that she was just writing to *another* bishop.[70]

In spite of having confided to Bishop Wynn in August 1952 that a visit would do remiss Father Dunkin 'all the good in the world' (she issued a reminder the following month), her spiritual director had seemed curiously reluctant to check on the present welfare, spiritual or otherwise, of one he directed. Pleas of minor illness and of 'arrears of work'[71] were undoubtedly genuine (Wynn's devotion to pastoral duties was exemplary and his health suffering in consequence) but the Bishop's reluctance to encounter Aelfrida may have been for other reasons too: his archdeacon had been Eustace's boyhood friend and reacquaintance in Lolworth with Eustace's sister may have prompted warnings from archdeacon to bishop that that lady's behaviour tended to religious eccentricity, and correspondence between Edward Wynn and Hubert Northcott regarding the former's introduction to the latter's forthcoming book *The Venture of Prayer* may have included among reminiscences of Great War meetings as army chaplain and soldier-monk, warnings of Placida's behaviour at Tymawr towards those in religious authority over her, behaviour witnessed by Edward Ely himself on the occasion of his and her last meeting in Lolworth and a warning he would do well to heed.

He relented, however, in November 1952, visiting (chaperoned by his chaplain) straight from 'Convocation [and] wearing his episcopal garments'. (One hopes the lumpen 'Parson Drovers' were suitably impressed.) Following tea with the Dunkins and a private talk with 'Father Leslie', the Bishop mounted to Aelfrida's 'attic-cell', blessing it before enquiring after her comfort and signing her Visitors Book '+ Edward Ely Nov 14 1952'. (His being asked to do so was, he said, an honour, but unknown to him this was not the first of his signatures to grace it: cut out from one of the letters destroyed by Aelfrida in May 1949 was his signature, his firmly underlined name – 'Edward Ely' not 'Edward Wynn' for he was writing as spiritual director to one whom he addressed as 'my dear daughter' – being stuck into the book as a teenager might save a pop star's autograph.) With memories of their last meeting in mind, Aelfrida was pleased to find the bishop 'happy and at ease' (his talk with Father Dunkin may have reassured him on several scores) though this also served to remind her that offers of 'a friendship, intellectual, spiritual and very human' were 'almost impossible to refuse' and that she must accept only 'the intellectual and spiritual part' and maintain '"a holy reserve" about the rest'.[72] She also refrained from telling him the name of her room though on a subsequent visit confided that 'the room he had blessed ... was called Gethsemane' and noted – in her diary – the anomaly of 'the sort of person' she was 'living in comfort and beauty in a room bearing such a name!'[73] She did, however, inform him of guardian-angel-given 'mantras', describing them as 'short prayers'.

Three months passed before the Bishop's next visit (why, Aelfrida wondered, did Edward Ely 'bother' about her; was it God's will or 'did he perhaps see that [she] was in some grave spiritual danger on leaving the cloister for "the world" and needed his shielding?')[74], his arriving early for a Confirmation Service at Parson Drove so as to see her beforehand having to be explained away to '*just a little sore*' Father Dunkin that it was 'as a Religious', not as a bishop, that Dr Wynn had offered (*sic*) to be her spiritual director and that it was as director and directed, not as bishop and tale-bearing accuser, that they met.

The bishop's visit passed off well, for Aelfrida managed to divert his attention from herself by enquiring sympathetically about his health (he was, he said, exhausted) and the diocesan difficulties to which she attributed his look of 'spiritual suffering'. (It was, Edward Ely replied, only her prayers for him that were keeping him going.)[75] But a 'very bad dream indeed', repeated three times, of some kind of threat ('calumny and hatred', she mistakenly thought) hanging over 'Dr Wynn'[76] and the passing bell having been rung three times during their recent interview worried her intensely, so much so that she not only made him the object of her Lenten prayers (the Bishop professed himself "most grateful and encouraged" by her spiritual efforts on his behalf) but also spent four days in 'deep spiritual combat' with a 'particular small but highly intelligent devil' who had been instructed to tempt her. Into what she does not say ('details too long to write') but given that the incident was recorded in juxtaposition to further concerns for the Bishop's health, it is possible that an offer of 'human friendship' (or even of companionate marriage) to Edward Wynn was involved.

The guardian-angel-assisted victory was Aelfrida's and it seems that subsequent letters from her to Bishop Wynn dealt only with spiritual matters. (A rare episode of 'universal' – now 'cosmic' – consciousness, during which she became aware of how 'collective sin' burdened the world[77], maybe significant in this context, especially as she regaled the Bishop with it.) But when Audrey's awestruck announcement alerted her to his third visit to Parson Drove (a visit made specifically to see her) and she rose to her feet to see him striding along the landing looking 'superbly well, full of physical, intellectual and spiritual vigour' (and in the presence of so great a mystic, 'humble and diffident' too), she was so relieved at the change in his manner and appearance that had she been fifty years younger and had not arthritis and 'prudence, piety and discretion' forbidden spontaneous gestures of this kind, she might have done more than merely spring up from her chair exclaiming "I'm just

writing to another bishop" and flung herself into his arms instead. And perhaps prudence, piety, and discretion inhibited Edward Wynn too, for on leaving he said '*very gravely*, as if this meeting might well be our last, "you must forgive me for having seen so little of you … I have seen you all too seldom"' before going away 'sadly with his head down'.

There was, however, more, to their meeting than this, for Edward Wynn's thoughts had recently run much on '*Death*' (his elder brother had sustained a stroke which was soon to prove fatal) and he qualified future plans by remembering that he might not live to carry them out, sentiments whose gloom cannot have been alleviated by a 'curiously relevant' book (Jeremy Taylor's *Holy Living and Holy Dying* 'with pictures calling attention to skulls and so on') presented to him by Aelfrida. What she did not, however, disclose to Edward Wynn was that she did not '*mind*' if she never saw him again, in this instance less because he put pressure on her soul and more because their relationship was perfect *as it stood*: the Bishop, she wrote, now kept his 'human … and his spiritual affection' for her in such perfect balance and under such perfect control that she could 'safely' (*sic*: an interesting word given that immediately after their previous meeting she had declared that the only place where she felt 'really safe' was 'at the foot of the Cross') and 'fully' respond.[78]

The Bishop's gloom may have been attributable to another cause too: Aelfrida was preparing to leave his diocese and Taylor's 'curiously relevant' book was a farewell present.

Although removal to Parson Drove may have seemed to an outsider like a mistake (Florence Keynes, perhaps with insight – had rumours of '*l'affaire Lovelle*' penetrated beyond Lolworth? – or perhaps more appositely than she knew, described it as Aelfrida's 'penance in the fens'[79]; other friends would have preferred her in Cambridge 'rather than in the wilds of the fens' and went so far as to declare Cambridge her 'rightful place' and somewhere she 'ought to be')[80], for Aelfrida herself it provided a tranquil interlude for reading and reflection during which, Cambridge property dealings excepted, she rested emotionally and spiritually suspended "twixt strife and strife and never-ending … voices of passion and of will".[81] Further proof of the therapeutic effects of life in an 'attic-cell' in an isolated fenland village from whose inhabitants she deliberately secluded herself, a place where pressures on her soul were deliberately reduced to a level where she barely felt them, and where 'Authority' loomed no larger than Leslie Dunkin, a man who dealt with her firmly but mildly, is to be found in migrainous symptoms appearing only in response to upsetting news and in her recording only one vision (a glorious one of Christ Himself 'in the glory of his Transfiguration … offering [her] His Precious Blood'[82] as 'Father Leslie' put the chalice to her lips at Communion), both instances suggesting that tension-causing or -relieving experiences of this nature were unneeded. True, she suffered one episode of dark 'cosmic consciousness' and three 'very bad' dreams quite different from her 'stock nightmares' of lost children or of returning to Fordfield or Tymawr and 'finding … no place'[83] for herself, but these were explicable in terms of world events (the death of Stalin, for example, for whose soul she prayed while wishing him 'much suffering in Purgatory' and rejoicing that there was now 'much less danger of a Russian bomb being dropped on Westminster Abbey' at the coronation of Elizabeth II)[84] or worries concerning the health of Edward Wynn. Prompted, it may be, by a cup of tea in a Cambridge café situated across the road from 'Constantine's rooms in King's'[85], she also had a vivid dream of her former husband as she last saw him in Lyons with the 'barrier of misunderstanding' (an appropriate metaphor for a railway station) between them, and Mildred, her 'rival', standing next to him staring at her 'as one might stare at an animal believed to be extinct', a dream which brought home to her that she '*had* broken the last cord that held him to [her]' by divorcing him.[86] But all were accepted philosophically for what they revealed of past or present history and instead of being used as promoters of morbid introspections, were discarded after deposition in her diary. She even dealt calmly with the onset of what she called 'The Voices'.

Her earliest diarised account of her 'Voices' occurred on 11 October 1952 soon after her stay at Jesus Lodge and her 'coffee and reminiscences' party at Wetenhall Cottage. She describes her experience as a 'dream audition' similar to others recently experienced 'on waking from sleep' and during which she felt and heard her 'blessed dead' near her talking in low tones and although able to catch only a word or two of what they said, one – 'who might have been Oracle' – seemed to be passing on information to the others.[87] Given that during her stay at Jesus Lodge, she had slept in an 'ex-Fordfield' bed, that 8 October was the twenty-third anniversary of the Oracle's death, and that she had been so 'strangely conscious' of her dead mother (now dead nearly twenty years) on the latter's birthday on 10 September that she was convinced that Chiara was hovering at Wetenhall Cottage to welcome herself or Julius 'into the next life'[88], it is tempting to equate these 'dream auditions' with visions and 'shewings' associated with current events or religious festivals: their tone, however, was sad and pragmatic instead of elevated and spiritual and their subject not Deity, but herself.

On 10 October the 'Voice … who might be Oracle' imparted to the other presences the news that Aelfrida was "*slowly* withering away" (a description with which she agreed, noting that she was even thinner than before; vital statistics recorded in this volume of her diary refute with her statement), they in turn enquiring when she would die. The answer being "when she is 77", Aelfrida noted the fact 'to see whether it will come true'[89], marking the entry with a marginal cross as a reminder to her biographer to check its veracity. (A streaming cold caught not long after rereading Fidelio's last poem caused her to wonder if somebody or something had hinted to her on her arrival at Parson Drove that she would not stay long, though whether the feeling implied impending death 'or a decision to go elsewhere' had remained unclear; her 'dream audition' of 10 October suggested the former.) A further 'audition' recorded on 13 December suggested that departure rather than death was more likely (that she had recently recited the *Itinerarium* for Eustace and Julius when the brothers departed separately abroad may be relevant here) for on 'the Voices' asking each other when "the widow from Cambridge" was coming to join them, they mutually agreed "not yet" because she had still much to learn (the 'widow' agreed) and that Christ Himself would teach her.[90]

The 'odd Voices' persisted during the winter of 1952/3, Aelfrida recording that they came at rare intervals, talked sense, and spoke in quiet, clear, urgent 'audible words' 'sometimes in unison, sometimes led by an unnamed spokesman', and were occasionally associated with current events such as the Oracle's birthday (an event unrecorded for many years) or a sensory stimulus: waking from a 'little doze in [her] chair' during one of the frequent village funerals, she heard them say "they will come for you sooner or later … the angels are near you … and will come and bear you to Jesus". They also began to issue commands ("Love Jesus in Mary"; "model yourself on Jesus and give yourself in bondage to Christ") with which she concurred in thought: 'I will'; 'that is what I try to do'. She also began a dialogue with them, they through their spokesman asking "Why do you take to yourself teachers when the Holy Ghost Himself is teaching you?", she replying "because He speaks to me through teachers".[91]

Her reaction to 'the Voices' is interesting. She does not attribute them, as she might have done at Tymawr, to silent solitude or diabolic intervention nor does she regard them as symptoms of mental imbalance or worry when they inform her that "the end of all things is at hand". Noting in passing that they might be her 'unconscious mind speaking', she prefers to think of them as the voices of 'waiting souls in paradise' (i.e. of her 'beloved dead', beloved now because unloved in life) with whom she is suddenly and mediumistically in touch. She is also comforted by the fact that, hearing them, 'Heaven has never seemed so near' and that they have provided her with a *terminus ad quem* to a lengthy and often burdensome life: they have predicted that she will die within the decade and 'there can't be a great distance to go'. She does not, however, congratulate herself on being 'in touch with the saints in Paradise' or indulge in lengthy spiritual speculations on the provenance of messages given by her unseen interlocutors but decides instead that none of this '*matters*' because 'only God's Will matters'[92] and never discloses her 'Voices' to anyone but her diary and her biographer. But it was neither 'the Voices' nor life in 'the wilds of the fens' which drove Aelfrida from Parson Drove and her decision 'to go elsewhere' was involuntary; it was the dramatic decline in her health in January 1953.

The months following her arrival at Parson Drove saw her health plateau. True, she continued to suffer her usual ailments (a minor stomach upset cured by 'starvation and sleep'; a 'slight chill to the kidneys', and so on)[93] but apart from occasional colds and her osteoarthritic knee, she remained well; indeed, she expressed greater concern for illnesses suffered by Eustace, Phyllis, Julius, and Edward Wynn than for her own. The onset of winter in 1952 worsened her lameness (she needed Father Dunkin's assistance if she knelt too long at confession and was forced to lean on the altar rail when taking Communion) and a febrile illness suffered in late December 1952 caused her to record early in January 1953 that rapidly worsening 'arthritis' of some kind had attacked both legs from hip to ankle and that she would soon be unable to mount the stairs to her 'attic-cell'. Asking herself that if she left Parson Drove 'what next?'[94], bereft by her own doing of Wetenhall Cottage, reluctant to enter Hope House for reasons to do with Catholicism and 'Authority', and convinced that it was better in old age *not* to 'stay amid the scenes and memories of past days' but to 'go away to another place and be accepted as old … by people who do not remember one's former energy'[95] (or, of course, one's problematical past), she recorded an unwelcome answer: to 'bustle' herself off to an institution where she could be "looked after by … professional attendants" before her 'seen or unseen … pillar of fire and cloud' led her 'Home at last'.[96]

The 'Home' or home into which Aelfrida proposed to 'bustle' herself was neither Heaven nor another "mouldy old mansion in the fens"[97] far from civilisation, but St John's Home in Oxford, an institution first visited by her in November 1935 in support of a fund-raising sale of work. In the course of her visit she inspected the chapel,

finding it 'very pure and spiritual … a blend of consecrated womanhood and of suffering'[98] and pleasing on both counts to one whose life at St Benedict's was, as far as she could endure it, an amalgam of both. The Home also met with her approval because Richard Meux Benson SSJE had been instrumental in its foundation, since when the Home had remained closely associated with the Cowley Fathers in nearby Marston Street, and because it was a designated sanctuary for infirm elderly ladies in more or less straightened circumstances.

Aelfrida, of course, had always trusted in God to organise her future but now saw no reason for not making contingency plans herself. In 1941, therefore, and following a bout of dramatized illness at Tymawr, she noted that although she '*clung*' to the hope of burial in the Campo Santo, Mother Guenvrede's threats of ejection should ill-health render her unfit for life in Community had encouraged her to subscribe £1 a year to St John's Home and to request that she be put on their waiting list even though the possibility of her 'wanting to be an inmate [was] *extremely* remote'.[99]

Ejection from Tymawr in 1946 in no way altered her decision; indeed, having somewhere in default of anywhere else to which she could 'go and be an invalid'[100] if the need arose (a need which increasing lameness made increasingly *less* remote) encouraged her to continue her subscription in spite of also paying for private health insurance as a result of her first brush with the bureaucracy and lengthy waiting times of the National Health Service. Quite what stimulated the Sister Superior of St John's Home to offer Mrs Graham 'a nice room at 4 gns a week' early in December 1952 cannot be ascertained but the coincidence of a visit from Eustace and Phyllis to Parson Drove on 11 September and her stay at Jesus College a few weeks later suggests collusion between Master and Sister. Aelfrida's response at that point was 'Not Yet'[101], but worsening 'arthritis' later the same month and another letter from Sister Superior encouraging her to accept the next vacancy made her change her mind, subject, of course, to consultation with Julius, Bishop Wynn, and Deity. (There was also the matter of her 'natural self' not relishing the prospect of banishment to 'a Home for the Aged', a worry only partly assuaged by the thought that there might be no vacancy for '*ages*'.)[102] Deity's decision ('go') was quickly received, as was the Bishop's approval on hearing of it. (Aelfrida refused to burden him with 'emotions and suchlike feminine impedimenta' associated with departure; Edward Wynn replied decorously that her leaving Parson Drove would be "a great sorrow and loss" – to the parish.) Julius and Mina stated that Oxford appeared less remote and difficult of access than Parson Drove.[103] Alethea 'favoured' St John's Home too (a favour influenced, it may be, by information received from Lilian Whitehouse who had visited Aelfrida's 'attic-cell'), so with her 'better self' recalling the Home's 'exquisite chapel' and rejoicing in the 'humiliations' it would be forced to endure in 'a Home for the Aged'[104], Aelfrida informed Father Dunkin of her decision (he 'fully approved' on the grounds that *two* 'delicate old people'– Captain Eagar was also unwell – was too much for his wife), gave notice of her intention to quit (she intended to remain at Parson Drove over Easter, possibly till July), and proceeded to worry less over her future than about furniture and books by which she and Alethea 'set store'.[105]

In March 1943 Aelfrida had written of Alethea's work at St Cuthbert's that 'besides being useful in itself', it was also 'a preparation for something more'.[106] (What that 'something' was she does not relate but given that Alethea had recently separated herself from the Maritzburg convent, we may assume it did not include the Religious Life.) In May 1950, however, she recorded that Alethea's future in South Africa might be compromised by 'anti-white' risings[107] and that 'something more' might perforce include life elsewhere. A 'rather … agitated letter' received from Alethea in August 1952 informing her mother that the 'native sisterhood' who ran the girls' hostel while Alethea was at Maritzburg wished to re-install themselves there on a permanent basis (a demonstration, Aelfrida thought, 'of the rising desire of the natives to get rid of the Whites')[108] was followed by another two months later announcing her dismissal as part of a policy of enlarging the responsibilities of native sisterhoods; a third, received the following month, described the handover of 'her' hostel to the 'African Sisters'.[109]

Feeling it wiser not to profess indignation or express sympathy to a daughter who was not, after all, a member of a recognised missionary society and whose arrival at St Cuthbert's had been more the consequence of a flight from England and her mother than a desire to pursue a missionary vocation, Aelfrida replied comfortingly that homeless Alethea had three homes in England (Parson Drove, Wetenhall Cottage, and Jesus Lodge) to all of which she would be welcomed during her next furlough, a period of leave running from late March to late November 1953 with return to South Africa intended at the end of it even though Alethea had now no job to which to return.

Matters became even more complicated at this point by Aelfrida's decision to leave Parson Drove and by Alethea herself being hospitalised with what was first diagnosed as 'enteritis' but subsequently as amoebic dysentery, a serious relapsing condition with a tendency to cause gastrointestinal ulceration. Aelfrida then suggested

to Eustace that she and her daughter 'caretake' Jesus Lodge for a month while he and Phyllis were abroad and Alethea recovered sufficiently ('*Deo gratias*') to write 'brave and spirited letters' home.[110] At this point Aelfrida remembered Agatha on her 'Heavenly Birthday' and hoped she was still enjoying 'heavenly delights' uninterrupted by anything other than maternal love[111] but '*wondered*' on the same day as she dreamed one of her 'stock nightmares' of 'children lost', 'how Alethea and Lent went together'.[112] They did not: Alethea arrived in England on 21 March 1953 (ironically, St Cuthbert's Day) 'poor … [with] no job, no status [and] abominably treated', to stay with the friends in which she was luckily (as her mother congratulated herself) 'rich' and to be showered by them with the 'human affection' so singularly deficient in a woman who professed herself '*dying*' to meet her absent (and convalescent) daughter after a five year gap[113] but would not disturb her Lenten retreat to do so. It was therefore not until 8 April when Lent was safely over (Alethea arrived in Cambridge on Good Friday; Aelfrida spent the day on a fasting diet of left-over breakfast porridge and in silence in 'Gethsemane' apart from attendance at church where she poured her devotions into 'authorised traditional channels')[114] that mother and daughter met at '*The Master's Lodge, Jesus College*' and not until two days later still that Aelfrida recorded their meeting.

What forty-four-old Alethea thought of this example of power-play parading as piety we do not know, but that she found a month's proximity to her mother a strain is evident from hints let fall by Aelfrida: Alethea, she wrote, did not come home (as her mother had hoped) 'serene and at peace with all the world'[115] but 'rather strained and emotional' and, in spite of Aelfrida's probings, reluctant to disclose anything about her 'after-holiday plans'.[116] (Judging by a recent passport photograph she also appeared older than her years, intensely sad, and, with her circular horn-rimmed glasses, every inch her father's daughter.) She also seemed determined to spend as little time with her mother as possible. In public she maintained her composure and her 'gentle and welcoming' approach to visitors but beneath her 'wonderfully mature and beautiful'[117] demeanour and the efficiency with which she ran the Lodge and arranged driving lessons and a busy social life, Alethea, with perhaps no 'plans' to make, was deeply unsettled – as witness a 'strange little lapse' when the news arrived on 20 May that there was a room available at St John's Home whenever Aelfrida wished to avail herself of it (she accepted at once, paying a retainer to ensure the reservation of yet another 'attic-cell'; the room was on the second floor), crying out that there was now 'not even the semblance of a home to come back to' and that because her mother neither loved nor wanted her, it would have been better to have stayed in South Africa. 'Lost in a fog of her own unhappiness', Alethea still seemed 'sad and subdued' the following day but rather than attribute her daughter's unhappiness to its true cause (herself), Aelfrida preferred to believe her upset by 'worries and uncertainties' concerning her future or the subject of 'mischief' made by the devil.[118] But her comment 'solitude heals the wounds in my soul'[119] when Alethea departed on a brief visit to relatives suggests that emotional 'wounds' had been inflicted by daughter on mother and that Aelfrida infinitely preferred 'precious and beloved' Alethea's company 'in God' instead of in person.

But rather than dwell on old and new hurts, Aelfrida threw herself into Cambridge social life, expressing, in spite of fatigue and a desire for 'Silence and Solitude!', 'gratitude in great abundance for the company of dear people'.[120]

A comparison of Aelfrida's diary (she had to check her engagement diary daily to find out who she was to see and where and when) and Alethea's pocket diary for 1953 (all we have of her voice for this period save a few neutral letters written home from travels in Europe) demonstrates how busy she was. In Alethea's company and in the course of days 'almost too full – but full of joy', she met Julius and Mina, he 'rather glum' at having to share his sister with his niece, the Zender Browns (loquacious as ever), 'Aunt Helen' (not Helen Michaelides, but a friend of Alethea's), 'good and faithful' Lilian Whitehouse, Ruth Connolly 'home from Madagascar' and looking for a house in Cambridge, Angela Tillyard ('very independent … may she find a good husband – and in the Christian faith'), Helen Megaw 'grown livelier and more talkative', white-haired Dorothea Conybeare for a chat about 'Old Times', John and Constance Hibbs 'happy in spite of impecuniosity', Canon Weekes (no longer regarded with an eye to matrimony, companionate or otherwise), and 'Dr Joan'[121], to name a few.

'Old Times' recurred in ways unforeseen by two elderly ladies chatting at Jesus Lodge. On 28 April, for example, a letter from '*my* Reverend Mother' announced her retirement after thirty years 'mothering' the SSC and stated that it was a good idea to step down now "in case decay and mildew set in". (She also noted that should she seek re-election and be elected, she might become a Tennysonian "good custom" corrupting the world.)[122] Aelfrida accepted the news calmly, for having once had a Pentecostal vision of 'tiny flames on Sister Sheila's head'[123], she knew that it was only a matter of time before Sheila O'Ferrall succeeded Winifred Donkin as Mother Superior. What she did not anticipate but something she

took calmly, was that having substituted Obedience for 'Authority', Sister Guenvrede relinquished her role of Tertiary Placida's spiritual adviser and Mother Sheila Mary never took it up, contenting herself with sending newsletters and formal letters of thanks for annual monetary gifts.

Another rejection (more dogmatically phrased) also took place during Aelfrida's stay in Cambridge and although she describes the invitation leading up to it as the climax of her social life at Jesus Lodge, she emerged rather chastened from it.

On 1 January 1953 Aelfrida reveals that besides Roy Harrod's 1951 life of Maynard Keynes ('several men rolled into one'[124] she noted of the latter though how much she knew or guessed of aspects of Keynes' life undisclosed in a biography supervised by Keynes' mother is open to question), she was also engrossed in *Period Piece,* the recently published childhood memoirs of Charles Darwin's granddaughter and her own childhood contemporary Gwen Raverat.[125] Aelfrida had first met 'Gwen Darwin' when both were in their teens; there is no contemporary diary record of her having done so but from her tart comment in 1953 that Gwen had had a 'bold figure' (i.e. was plump) and wore glasses and a 'sullen expression' at parties, it is obvious that slim, popular, vivacious Frida Tillyard had little time for her. She therefore never guessed what a 'young rebel' Gwen was (Gwen, besides being 'gown' not 'town', moved in more socially elevated circles than Aelfrida, the latter knowing her through Silvia Myers, not on her own account) but given that Frida herself was sunk in religiosity, Gwen's lack of religious belief and tendency to find her chief joy in 'artistic sensations'[126] would not have endeared her to priggish Frida even had a Darwin condescended to know the daughter of the proprietor of a local newspaper, Cambridge graduate though he be.

On 19 May 1953, however, and Gwen having expressed a wish to meet a fellow Cambridge author, Aelfrida visited her at her home, The Old Granary in Silver Street, 'a rather "arty" house [with] the most fascinating view over Coe Fen'. Gwen, she wrote, 'is still … plain and fat and bespectacled but (*sic*) she greeted me most warmly'. (Gwen, she also noted, was partially paralysed, having suffered a stroke the previous year.) A 'grand talk' ensued, Gwen admitting she had 'always *longed* to join Mrs Verrall's class' and had envied Aelfrida as a result and Aelfrida trying to persuade Gwen that one as frail and helpless as herself ought to listen to 'Our Lord knocking, knocking at her soul's door'. Gwen, however, 'sheered off' from talk of religion[127] (she was, however, happy to meet again at Jesus Lodge, Alethea unhooking Olive Mudie Cooke's pictures from the walls for her to examine more closely), something which so depressed Aelfrida (Gwen was 'missing all the best things in life', life without religion being like living in a world without sky) that she added Gwen to 'the list of those for whom I offer *adoration réparatrice*'[128] and lent her a copy of one of her own novels to see if she could effect conversion-by-*Concrete*. The book, however, was returned accompanied by a 'vehement, almost abusive' letter wilfully misinterpreted by its recipient as showing on the grounds of a single piece of evidence in *Period Piece* that Gwen herself was an 'undeveloped mystic' and unhappy in her agnosticism.[129] Given that in her letter Gwen contrasted the validity of her own interpretation of religion with Aelfrida's, vehemence was to be expected: "I wish all you godly people weren't so maddeningly self-righteous and superior and certain. You feel quite sure you are right − so do I; but I AM QUITE SURE I am wrong, SO ARE YOU wrong, only you don't think so".[130]

Whether Aelfrida kept Gwen's letter as a pride's purge, as a reminder of the unwitting impression she herself made on people, as the expression of Gwen's envy of 'townee' Frida Tillyard, or to provide a frisson for a biographer, we do not know but *that* she kept it says much for her courage in doing so. (Her guardian angel, so she said, helped her compose an answer; she does not impart its content, but God, it seems, was mentioned.) But on hearing of Gwen's suicide by aspirin overdose in 1957, she wrote sadly (and probably correctly) that she had 'no intuition'[131] that her prayers had helped Gwen at all.

On 29 May 1953 Aelfrida recorded that she and Julius were now 'keeping house very happily together' at Wetenhall Cottage, Alethea (looking very chic and '*ever so much better than when she came*') and Mina having departed for Paris two days earlier.[132] (While in Paris Alethea renewed acquaintance with Madame Erlande who sent her love to Aelfrida and enquired fondly about her; the meeting went unrecorded in Aelfrida's diary but Alethea's reminder of a man who once said of and to her that she needed to be crucified may have inspired the 'Voices' to murmur confusedly that "she must be martyred as Christ was … she is ready [and] willing … shall it be here in Cambridge? No".)[133] For two weeks brother and sister revelled in each other's company: Julius 'demanded' diary readings (he had no reason to 'demand', a recently-installed loft ladder having made access to his sister's and nieces' diaries and other private papers stored in the cottage's attic an easier proposition, but it may be deduced from his choice of readings − in this instance the years following Aelfrida's return from Florence and of her formal engagement to Constantine − that he was eager to have her fill gaps in her diary record in her own words or to compare what she read

or wrote with what she omitted or with what he himself knew or did not know of her life; given Aelfrida's earlier propensity for leaving poems and diaries where Constantine could read them, perhaps she did not mind if Julius pried) and in return read her his own letters describing his first visit to Lahr and earliest impressions of sixteen-year-old Wilhelmina Kaufmann.[134] They also held family prayers together and on Coronation Day Julius cooked 'an unusually elaborate lunch' while Aelfrida, listening to the wireless, was 'in the Abbey in imagination and spirit', there being room for 'another soul at prayer' among the assembled dignitaries.[135] Aelfrida herself visited Hope House and was invited by the new and rather 'Alarming' (capital A) Mother Superior to stay as a guest for a week whenever she wished[136] and was visited by the 'dear Lovells' ('well and cheerful and *most* friendly'), by Mr Church with news of former Fordfield employees and full of questions about Parson Drove, and by Dr Strachan, former minister of St Columba's, who remembered Julius and Aelfrida as adolescents and who, waxing sentimental over "your father and mother … and the old days", was assured by Aelfrida who even after writing *The Centaur* maintained the fiction of her 'perfect' family, that her and Julius' memories were 'happy'.[137]

So many 'people, people, people!' Her interest in 'each and all' gave her such a bad conscience that she wrote to Bishop Wynn asking how to reconcile interest with vocation and how to synthesise the dichotomy between God intensifying her 'intense longing' to be alone and circumstances which made Solitude (and Silence) impossible. The Bishop's reply was thought-provoking: perhaps God, he wrote, now wished to lead her to a "spiritual silence" in which, while "properly taking part in conversation", she could be "interiorly silent in unison with Him". Aelfrida seized on the episcopal suggestion with great joy (she seems to have forgotten that the Bishop's message was one Mother Guenvrede had tried but failed to instil at Tymawr), deciding that her newest 'vocation' was to imitate Christ in yet another way, namely by remaining alone with her Heavenly Father at the same time as she took pleasure 'in the society of friends'.[138] And as one about to be 'relegated to an institution'[139], Aelfrida was about to practise what he preached.

Mina's return from Paris on 12 June (Alethea travelled on to Rome and Switzerland, returning to England in mid-July to embark on another round of visits to family and friends and to Malling, to take her driving test, to indulge in operas and plays, to undertake a four day retreat, and to visit her dressmaker and dentist prior to her return to South Africa) saw Julius restore his sister's diaries to the attic lest his wife 'should be hurt by our wanting to read them aloud' and postpone his and

Aelfrida's 'true brother and sister relationship' until the next opportunity. (Both statements are interesting for what they hint at of new jealousies and old passions; Julius and Aelfrida had no 'specially intimate conversations'[140] during their fortnight together for all, it seems, had been spoken earlier.) Hoping that God would bless and keep her dear ones whether or not they remained at Wetenhall Cottage or she herself 'ever came again', Aelfrida returned on 16 June to her 'well-blessed attic'[141] in Parson Drove to begin packing.

News received soon after her return of the sudden death of Canon Weekes presaged endings in more ways than one. Reading over her 1918 diary to Julius, Aelfrida had discovered inside it the letter written in 1902 by her nineteen-year-old self for perusal when she was forty. Now sixty-nine, she must have found it poignant reading: "Love to your husband – if you have one! – and to the chicks – if there are any … are your dear ones now dead? … fame without love – is that your fate? … perhaps you shake your head and say I had caught a glimpse of the future … thine for auld lang syne, Aelfrida CW Tillyard. PS. you needn't answer this letter. I am a ghost of your dead past".[142] And her 'dead past' was what Aelfrida describes in a poem ostensibly on the subject of the "rabble hordes of dirty paper" littering the streets of a town once a "picture of permanence" but now challenged by change with regard to three colleges of significance to her ("King's [has] leapt across the river and set up incongruous rooms across the Backs [and] were Girton and Jesus separately inspired to build in pink or did they meet … on Midsummer Common and agree that pink [was] becoming?")[143] but actually describing detritus representative of her parents', husband's, daughters', and her own discarded lives there: "Paper from the Gutter-Press, / College papers in a mess, / Envelopes for me and you, / Bits of bills and billet-doux. / Sad spoilt papers from exams, / Sticky tops of luscious jams …"[144]

Nothing persuaded her to stay: 'friendly letters … and friendly little talks on the telephone make me see how easily I could pick up old friendships and make new, supposing I had the money and strength to settle in Cambridge again … and yet I thank God that it is closed to me. A harder, lonelier and poorer life, more detached and other-worldly is surely [His] Will for me. All these dear people *are* in their right places – and so I am for these few weeks, but *I could not stay here* – the more I love it all, the more clearly I hear God's NO'.[145]

'Looking through belongings' prior to a move to an abode 'hardly bigger than a grave' (it was just under ten feet square), Aelfrida tried 'not to dislike preparations for flight' or to be 'sad at the prospect of institution-life'[146] – and failed. (She also discovered that 'being at the Lodge

… *did* make difficulties for me and give rise to inward struggles' and that 'looking through old letters [of] Alethea's … and poems of Agatha's … *is* upsetting'.)[147] And 'very weary with many aches and pains'[148], she was saddened to discover that apart from Captain Eagar (invited to her room, he signed her Visitors Book and received *The Bedside Bunyan* as a parting present, his farewell 'sweet things' reminding her of 'Mr Consul-General Smith's when he bade me goodbye at Odessa'), no one at Parson Drove seemed sad to see her go, the Dunkins' attitude being one of 'rather casual benevolence just tinged with pity' and the 'village folk' (now 'dear people' because 'wonderfully courteous' to a frail old lady) she hardly knew because having learnt the consequences of meddling in village politics at Lolworth, she had kept aloof – and besides, being 'simple-minded', they were no match for the Cambridge intelligentsia with whom she had lately mixed.[149] A final blow: though 'unspeakably glad' that 'Reverend Mother Sheila Mary SSC' wished her to be known as 'Sister Placida' at St John's Home subject to the Sister Superior's agreement, 'the All Saints Sisters do not allow tertiaries to be called "Sister" – only themselves'.[150]

On 8 July 1953 Aelfrida recorded the first (and last) anniversary of her stay in Parson Drove: 'physically the months spent here have been most uncomfortable – but would they have been less so elsewhere[?] … The time … has been full of interest – have I had a dull moment? Hardly, I think! … I have loved the holy atmosphere of the dear room [where] I have read books and prayed many prayers and thought and waited upon God … And now when the pillar of fire and cloud moves on I shall be ready to follow'.[151] On 13 July, Agatha's forty-third birthday had she lived, she received her usual 'special love' letter from Alethea (such a 'big load' that Aelfrida proposed to leave the unpacking of it till Oxford) whose help with moving she now regretted having rejected and to whom she sent a letter whose content suggests that whoever and whatever had failed her, her capacity for self-deception and for re-inventing the past had not. Realising early on, she wrote, that Alethea had an independent nature, she had decided (subject to the proviso that Alethea "wanted to go in the right direction") that the best thing to do was allow her daughter her freedom. Mothers, of course (fathers, even), had the advantage over their children of greater life experience and of having known their offspring since birth whereas – and here one can imagine Aelfrida taking a deep breath before she began her next sentence – daughters are at a disadvantage if they want to understand their parents because they can never know them so well and Alethea would do well to remember that although misunderstandings happened and mattered, in the last resort and even if some things could not be got clear until after a parent's death, while he or she was still alive it was better for all concerned if that parent was loved rather than "understood". Signing off "all the love in the world, Mother", it only remained to pack her diary with the promise 'next entry (if any) at St John's Home'.[152]

## Notes

1 GCPPT 1|1|5 2 September 1900.
2 GCPPT 3|1 Letter from Alethea Graham to Aelfrida of 6 July 1952.
3 GCPPT 1|1|64 4 April 1946.
4 GCPPT 1|1|43 2 January 1933.
5 Tillyard, Ae *Naomi da Costa* pp 168 and 269 (GCPPT 2|22).
6 GCPPT 1|1|70 30 August 1952.
7 ibid. 25 June 1952.
8 ibid. The name derives from *Proverbs* 31:10 "who can find a virtuous woman? For her price is far above rubies". (KJV).
9 ibid. 21 July 1952.
10 ibid. 20 December 1952 and 9 January 1953.
11 ibid. 1 October 1952.
12 ibid. 30 August and 10 November 1952.
13 ibid. 12 July 1952.
14 ibid. 12 August 1952.
15 ibid. 2 August 1952.
16 ibid. 17 July 1952.
17 ibid. 30 July 1952.
18 ibid. 24 December 1952.
19 ibid.
20 GCPPT 1|1|70a includes Aelfrida's 'Schedule for Lent 1953'.
21 GCPPT 1|1|70 12 February 1953. Aelfrida also sent a copy of her Lenten Rule to Bishop Wynn but does not disclose if this included her 'special *invitation*'.
22 ibid. 'Ash Wednesday' (18 February) 1953.
23 ibid. 24 August 1952.
24 ibid. 26 July 1952.
25 ibid. 12 August 1952.
26 ibid. 5 August 1952.
27 ibid. 16 September 1952.
28 The Rev Capt A Eveleigh Eagar was in his early sixties, his naval career having lasted from 1908 to 1933. He retired as rector of Coleorton, Leics, in 1951 and moved into Parson Drove vicarage where he assisted with church and parish duties.
29 GCPPT 1|1|71 28 June 1953.
   GCPPT 1|1|72 30 July 1954.
30 GCPPT 1|1|72 30 July 1954.
31 GCPPT 1|1|70 2 February 1953.
32 ibid. 7 September 1952.
33 ibid. 20 December 1952.
34 ibid. 6 October 1952.
35 ibid. 9 January 1953.
36 ibid. 10 and 11 July 1952.
37 ibid. 21 July 1952.
38 ibid. 7 November 1953.
39 ibid. 2 February 1953.
40 ibid. 26 July and 30 October 1952.
41 ibid. 26 July, 24 August and 10 November 1952 and 30 March 1953.
42 ibid. 24 December 1953.
43 ibid. 28 July and 24 August 1952.
44 ibid. 25 August 1952.

45 ibid. 5 October 1952.
46 ibid. 21 November 1952.
47 ibid. 5 October 1952.
48 ibid. 30 August, 3, 10, 21, and 24 September and 1 October 1952.
49 ibid. 9 May 1953. GCPPT 3|4 contains several letters from Florence Keynes to Aelfrida 1944–1954.
50 ibid. 1 January 1953.
51 ibid. 19 January 1953.
52 ibid. 30 March 1953.
53 ibid. 31 October 1952.
54 ibid. 19 and 27 January 1953.
55 GCPPT 1|1|70a Letter from Frank Stokoe to Aelfrida of 28 October 1952 annotated by her 'he died there on Nov 2'.
56 GCPPT 1|1|70 4 November 1952.
   GCPPT 1|1|70a Letter from Frank Stokoe to Aelfrida of 28 October 1952.
57 GCPPT 1|1|70 4 November 1952.
58 Stokoe, FW. *Three Songs to Fidelio* (*Cambridge Poets 1900–1913* p181).
59 GCPPT 1|1|70 4 November 1952.
60 Tillyard, Ae. *Naomi da Costa* p 112(GCPPT 2|22). GCPPT 1|1|70a contains a poem by Frank Stokoe entitled *The Moment of Beauty*. Of this Aelfrida commented on 4 November 1952 that although Fidelio's '*spirit*' saw God, his *mind* resolutely cried 'No! No! No!'; thirty years earlier almost to the day (GCPPT 1|1|26 5 November 1922) she noted that the 'something' of which Fidelio received 'strange alluring glimpses' was Deity disguised as Beauty.
61 Tillyard, Ae. *The White Horse Inn* (dedicated 'to FWS') from *The Garden and the Fire* (p 38).
62 GCPPT 1|1|70 10 November 1952.
63 Tillyard, Ae. *The Glory of the West* pp 44–45 (GCPPT 2|16|3).
64 GCPPT 1|1|48 20 June 1935.
65 GCPPT 1|1|20 7 August 1914.
66 GCPPT 1|1|48 20 June 1935.
   GCPPT 1|1|64 21 November 1946. James Barkway was Bishop of Bedford 1935–1938 and thereafter Bishop of St Andrews, Dunkeld and Dunblane.
67 GCPPT 1|1|70 30 July and 13 October 1953. The sermon was *Taste and See*, given at St Columba's by Dr Dykes of the London Presbytery, the book William James' *The Varieties of Religious Experience*.
68 GCPPT 1|1|70 13 October. 1953.
69 GCPPT 1|1|20 7 August 1914.
70 GCPPT 1|1|71 7 July 1953.
71 GCPPT 1|1|70 5 August 1952.
72 ibid. 16 November 1952.
73 ibid. 19 March 1953.
74 ibid. 'Lent I' (22 or 23 February) 1953.
75 ibid. 25 February 1953.
76 ibid. 2 March 1953.
77 ibid. 5 and 17 March 1953.
78 GCPPT 1|1|70 27 February 1953.
   GCPPT 1|1|71 7 July 1953. Jeremy Taylor's *Holy Living and Holy Dying* is an amalgamation of two books of Christian devotion. The first, published in 1650, concerns the art of living well according to the Christian ethic, the second, published in 1651 and more relevant to Aelfrida's life (especially her cancer scares), the art of dying well as an exemplar to others.
79 GCPPT 3|4 Letter from Florence Keynes to Aelfrida of 1 October 1953.
80 GCPPT 1|1|70 5 and 9 May 1953.
81 Tillyard, Ae. *Goodbye*, written at Fordfield 9 September 1911 (GCPPT 2|5).
82 GCPPT 1|1|70 21 February 1953.
83 ibid. 2 March 1953.
84 ibid. 5 March 1953.

85   ibid. 24 September 1952.
86   ibid. 15 December 1952.
87   ibid. 11 October 1952.
88   ibid. 10 September 1952.
89   ibid. 11 October 1952.
90   ibid. 13 December 1952.
91   ibid. 11 March and 1 April 1953.
92   ibid. 13 December 1952, 11 March and 2 April 1953. Worth noting in connection with Aelfrida's 'Voices' and her reaction to them is that American Quaker and missioner John Woolman (1720–1772) also heard voices announcing, *inter alia*, "John Woolman is dead"; Aelfrida describes aspects of his life in *Spiritual Exercises* (p11).
93   ibid. 24 August 1952 and 2 February 1953.
94   ibid. 29 December 1952 and 7 January 1953.
95   GCPPT 1|1|25 23 June 1921.
96   GCPPT 1|1|70.
     Tillyard, Ae. *The Glory of the West* p21 (GCPPT 2|16|3).
97   Tillyard, Ae. *Just Alice* p 286 (GCPPT 2|19).
98   GCPPT 1|1|50 21 November 1935. The chapel at St John's, designed by ecclesiastical architect Ninian Comper (1864–1960), was completed in 1907. It was divided by a traceried screen into two parts, one for the Home's patients ('the suffering') the other, including the altar, for the All Saints Sisters ('the consecrated womanhood') who ran it. For a detailed history of St John's Home see Mayhew, P. *All Saints: Birth and Growth of a Community* 1987.
99   GCPPT 1|1|58 6 February 1941.
100  GCPPT 1|1|60 8 June 1942.
101  GCPPT 1|1|70 6 December 1952.
102  ibid. 7 and 9 January 1953.
103  ibid. 9 and 22 January 1953.
104  ibid. 7 January 1953.
105  ibid. 9 February 1953.
106  GCPPT 1|1|61 26 March 1943.
107  GCPPT 1|1|67 24 May 1950.
108  GCPPT 1|1|70 5 August 1952.
     GCPPT 3|1 Letter from Alethea Graham to Aelfrida of 12 October 1952.
110  GCPPT 1|1|70 21 November 1952, 7 January and 'Ash Wednesday' (18 February) 1953.
111  ibid. 'Lent I' (22 or 23 February) 1953.
112  ibid. 2 March 1953.
113  ibid. 19 and 24 March 1953.
114  ibid. 'Good Friday' (3 April) 1953.
115  ibid. 19 March 1953.
116  ibid. 10 and 24 April 1953.
117  ibid. 22 August 1952 and 25 May 1953.
118  ibid. 24 April, 20 May and (by context) 25 May 1953.
119  ibid. 24 April 1953.
120  ibid. 21 April 1953.

121  ibid. 14, 18, 21, and 24 April and 3 and 22 May 1953.
122  ibid. 28 April 1953.
     GCPPT 1|1|70a SSC Newsletter of 3 May 1953. The quotation is taken from Tennyson's *Idylls of the King (The Passing of Arthur)*; it and Mother Guenvrede's farewell message received marginal emphasis in Aelfrida's copy.
123  GCPPT 1|1|65 'Eve of Holy Cross' (2 May) 1947.
124  GCPPT 1|1|70 1 January 1953.
125  *Period Piece* (1952), the description of the Edwardian Cambridge childhood of notable woodcut artist Gwen Raverat (née Darwin 1885–1957) is illustrated, as Aelfrida noted (GCPPT 1|1|70 1 January 1953), with Gwen's own 'slightly malicious' pictures.
126  GCPPT 1|1|70 1 January and 19 May 1953.
127  ibid. 19 May 1953.
128  GCPPT 1|1|73 14 February 1957.
129  GCPPT 1|1|71 18 August 1953.
130  GCPPT 3|3 Letter from Gwen Raverat to Aelfrida of 7 July 1953.
131  GCPPT 1|1|73 14 February 1957.
132  GCPPT 1|1|70 27 and 29 May ('27' in error) 1957.
133  GCPPT 1|1|70 3 May 1953.
134  GCPPT 1|1|70 21 September 1952, and 29 ('27' in error) May 1953.
135  ibid. 'Coronation Day' (2 June) 1953. An 'unusually elaborate' lunch at Wetenhall Cottage was indeed unusual; John Hibbs (personal communication 27 November 2008) described meals there as 'sparing'.
136  ibid. 7 June 1953.
137  ibid. 'Coronation Day' (2 June ) and 11 June 1953.
138  ibid. 21 April and 29 ('27' in error) May 1953.
139  ibid. 7 June 1953.
140  ibid. 14 June 1953.
141  GCPPT 1|1|70 15 June 1953.
     GCPPT 1|1|71 17 June 1953.
142  GCPPT 1|1|71a Letter from 'Frida' to Aelfrida of 12 October 1902.
143  Tillyard, Ae. *Naomi da Costa* p 198 GCPPT 2|22.
144  GCPPT 2|13 *Cambridge Litter,* written in Oxford 23 October 1953. The other end of the notebook in which the poems (of which *Cambridge Litter* is the penultimate) are transcribed seems to have once contained the first few pages of *The Centaur,* a work in which Aelfrida also scans her past.
145  GCPPT 1|1|70 5 May 1953.
146  GCPPT 1|1|71 20 and 28 June 1953.
147  ibid. 20 June 1953.
148  ibid. 5 July 1953.
149  GCPPT 1|1|70 30 March 1953.
     GCPPT 1|1|71 28 June 1953.
150  GCPPT 1|1|71 5 and 15 July 1953.
151  ibid. 8 July 1953.
152  GCPPT 1|1|71 13 July 1953.
     GCPPG A1.4 Letter from Aelfrida to Alethea Graham of 12 July 1953.

# Relegated to an Institution

'The next entry *is*!'[1] Kissing her hand to the Dunkins, Aelfrida set off by taxi for her "change of habitat"[2] and 'yet another fresh start'.[3] Driving across summery England, she and her guardian angel played an imaginary game, sprinkling highways, lanes, fields, and houses with blessings as water carts remembered from childhood days sprinkled roads to lay the dust.

A 'perfect day for a drive' it may have been, but an apprehensive lady in her seventieth year was whistling in the dark to enliven spirits sagging under the weight of realisation that her decision to relegate herself to an institution and the means by which she had consciously prevented herself from deciding otherwise had also deprived her of an escape clause. Hence although she professed herself 'thrilled' at remembering Oxford so well that she was able to direct her driver 'all along the High to Magdalen Bridge' ('after that he had to ask'), her first impression of the 'Institution' to which she had relegated herself was 'gloomy in the extreme!'[4]

St John's Home, as contemporary photographs show, was built to resemble an Oxford college or the Cowley St John headquarters of the SSJE nearby (Bishop Wynn, familiar with the latter, likened the Home to an Oxford Movement Clergy House)[5] but although it stood in spacious grounds, its forbidding exterior and the high stone wall surrounding it seem to have suggested to the lady clambering stiffly from her taxi not the '*gracieusetés*' of quad or cloister but the yard of Oxford Prison. Once inside, the Home's 'brick walls and long bleak corridors' and the 'terribly institutional' dining room full of 'ugly old women talking about their ailments' impressed her equally unfavourably. ('God give me grace to bear it if he wants me here!'.) Her room, when reached, was 'like an almshouse room' with its penthouse ceiling, gas fire, uncoordinated colour scheme, and dowdy furniture, and was approached along a narrow passage ('the Green Corridor') whose sloping roof and shared facilities promised the inconveniences of the servants' quarters at Fordfield without benefit of privacy. Deciding that 'Suffering Peace' was the 'spirit of this place', Aelfrida renamed her room ('officially *St Columba*') GETHSEMANE and decided, with her guardian angel's encouragement, 'to be good and not indulge in self-pity'.[6]

St John's Home, Oxford c1953

Self-pity came easily: the sound of her neighbour's wireless and of 'slummy noises' of 'dogs, children, cars, … etc. etc.' rising from the 'conglomeration of lower middle class houses … as ugly and dreary as can be' whose 'wilderness' of slated roofs pressed closely on the Home's walls[7]; the forty-nine steps (there was a lift but Aelfrida chose not to use it) and 'immense' length of corridor to dining room and chapel[8]; institutional food (of boiled potatoes, parsnips, and bread and butter pudding she commented 'well, well, well!!!') instead of individually-prepared baked eggs and stewed fruit, and 'the meat eaters … get theirs first'.[9] (Aelfrida now included fish in her 'vegetarian' diet and was probably better nourished than for many years.) She must also attend the dining room for breakfast and the mid-day meal (trays were provided only for those too unwell to attend) and a ward for afternoon tea (she immediately arranged to take tea and supper in her room but had to provide her own food if she did so) and submit personal effects (her bed, and 'the few other things I need here') for inspection by different Sisters representing different departments (her oil stoves were confiscated) 'and the Handy Man is on holiday, so *Pazienza* and *Mañana* and so on and so forth'.[10] Then too, her room was very hot in summer ('no wonder most people take soporifics … I may be driven to it') and cold in winter ('31° [F] close to the head of my bed'[11] — the home was centrally heated but Aelfrida turned it off at night; she did not, however, complain of cold during the day except in chapel which was icy); no nun super-vised the Green Corridor, only a 'person' in the form of an 'upstairs Servant-Dragon'[12] whose prying eyes and vacuum cleaner caused Aelfrida to mark her diary 'private' and to ban mechanical devices from her room (her comment on returning from a holiday that the room looked much brighter is revealing, the Home having seized the opportunity to spring-clean it) and what with this and an 'ungracious reception' on arrival, 'there was more to put up with' than she cared to say.[13]

She was also aggrieved at not being greeted in person by Sister Superior Elizabeth Noel[14] and by that lady subsequently demanding completion of a form listing personal details and her next of kin[15]. And, she discovered, there had been a change in the Home's policy. Whereas those receiving free care or paying only token amounts ("Patients") had been housed in wards of five or six beds with privacy provided by curtains drawn between them but fee-paying "Ladies" maintained their single rooms even when needing nursing care, "Ladies" requiring "extra nursing" were now moved at the Nursing Sister's discretion to one of the two wards (St Anne's or St Vincent's) for as long as their condition required, a policy which meant the new occupant of GETHSEMANE would remain there only if capable of independent existence. Should her health deteriorate, the matter of where she resided would be decided by the Sisters, not herself.[16]

GETHSEMANE's demerits notwithstanding (there was little she could do about the Home's rules though attempts to subvert them began on arrival), Aelfrida had no intention of leaving it then or later; she also rejected a larger and better-furnished room along the corridor because it was heated by electricity for which she would have to pay extra. ('Orders from On High' were to stay put and not spend more money on herself than was strictly necessary[17]; to Eustace, who 'looked round [her] room with great disfavour'[18], she pretended to be waiting for a better one to become vacant.) Nor, for all its demerits, had she any intention of leaving St John's Home, for having experienced the care extended by religious nursing orders in the convent of the Little Sisters of Mary in Fiesole and at Hope House, religious establishments where she could enjoy the privacy of her own room or the company of congenial people as and when she wished, could be 'petted up' when unwell, and would be fed nourishing food off dainty china, why return to the rigours of hermitages or convents or dilapidated or isolated clergy houses? And it was probably for these reasons too (even if not phrased in the same words) that everyone, including her guardian angel and Edward Wynn (the former so '*delighted*' she was in a place of safety at last that he kept '*purring*' round her; the latter more restrainedly

'glad')[19], was adamant that having relegated herself to an institution, she stay there.

If Bishop Wynn was 'glad' she was 'happy' at St John's Home, Aelfrida herself was exuberant, writing after only four days' stay that she was happier than she had been since she left Tymawr and that she could hardly believe she had felt such 'repugnance' on moving in.[20]

Her room, though 'tiny', had a lovely prospect through its triple-casemented window of Iffley church and of distant wooded hills, and the Home's four acre garden with its orchard, flower beds, and Campo Santo enticed her out to stroll and sit.[21] (She also took short daily walks outside the Home but though Fairacres and Cowley St John were nearby, did not visit the former and the latter only once.) Determined not to let her brain 'rust', she was delighted to discover that the Home had a library containing works on theology and associated topics; from contemporary diary entries we can also see that the mind of a lady bent on 'Exploration and Discovery' since childhood ranged beyond its usual fields to include human ecology, contemporary politics, and even astronomy, extra-galactic nebulae whose radio waves had taken '*a hundred million years to reach the earth!*' being humorously described as bringing 'rather stale news'.[22]

The dining room, designed by Ninian Comper, proved an unexpected source of delight: as a 'Lady', Aelfrida found herself seated among the Home's 'intellectual and social *élite*!!'[23] at one of the tables elevated on a dais above the throng of 'Patients'. ('Ladies' also had more elegant crockery and starched table napkins.) She also enjoyed Mass and Holy Communion every morning and Vespers sometimes, particularly as the chapel was little frequented by the Home's inmates and the Sisters convened beyond the rood screen; in fact, so much did she value private intimacy with God there that, though unable to see priest or altar, she sometimes sat in the Lady Chapel 'some way off the rest of the congregation'.[24] And not only did the Sisters sing Plainsong 'exquisitely'[25] but they, by the nature of their vocation and to a greater extent than Fathers Lovell and Dunkin by the nature of theirs (and their masculinity) were on Aelfrida's spiritual wavelength and spoke the same spiritual language as herself, so much so, in fact, that she soon understood that at St John's Home she was to lead a contemplative life 'as far as circumstances allow' and with the help of her All Saints 'Sisters-in-Christ' learn how to live 'according to the spirit of the house': 'just now', she wrote, 'the Unseen and Eternal are [as] luminously clear to me as they used to be at Tymawr and in their Light I see this place'.[26]

She also began to cultivate friendships with individual nuns: 'friendly and unaffected' Elizabeth Noel, elderly Naomi and Madeleine Mary, the former with thirty years' experience of South Africa, the latter keen to hear details of the life of a resident tertiary at Tymawr, and Sister Catherine, head of nursing and about to take her final vows, of whom some of the ladies expressed themselves afraid (one spoke of her 'cruelty') and Aelfrida herself wrote that she needed to be 'less dictatorial' and hoped never to be in a position where Sister Catherine could exercise her 'drastic methods with the helpless' upon her. She added, however, that although Sister Catherine was 'most authoritative' as a nurse, she supported Aelfrida's wish to fulfil her 'tertiary vocation' at the Home.[27]

This Aelfrida did, wearing the lighter of her two veils to services and her heavier one on festivals. (She expressed surprise that the Sisters knew she was a tertiary but given that she had hoped to be known as Sister Placida and wore her veil to chapel, her surprise is odd; her statement that she 'must be more careful' in future and would beg her guardian angel's protection[28] is also strange but given Alethea's statement that the All Saints Sisters resented '"the laity" wanting any of the spiritual privileges which they [considered] their exclusive right'[29], critical comments may have been made.) She also maintained silence on Fridays, recited her office (in Latin) from her Benedictine diurnal, and generally, she hoped and trusted, performed God's Will by 'living in the Spirit of the beloved Community' (Tymawr) entered as a tertiary fifteen eventful years earlier but which she had been 'obliged' to leave, and by maintaining the rhythm of 'Holy Communion, day Hours, rosary, meals, a little conversation, reading, odd jobs, sleep [and] prayer'[30] which had patterned her life for so long.

Divinely-mandated experiences continued at St John's Home, though not as floridly as earlier ones. For one thing, Aelfrida was now older and calmer and more accepting of whatever God might offer ('I had', she wrote on All Souls Day 1953, 'visions of angels one day last week … [but] I do not [now] attach any objective importance to that kind of vision, however beautiful')[31]; for another, having noting that she 'nearly went off into an ecstasy at Vespers' on Christmas Eve but would not 'let go' for fear of making herself 'conspicuous'[32], she had no wish to be labelled 'mad'. Yet experiences undergone were vivid enough: at Communion one morning, a 'blaze of spiritual light not as I have previously perceived it around the Reserved Sacrament or the celebrant but as *within myself*'[33]; again in chapel (her eyes being for once wide open) a vision seen as if through and above Comper's "loveliest … modern Gothic" roof [34] of 'Our Lord … enthroned … in glory … surrounded by His Saints', the saints then (and most appropriately given the title of the order to which the chapel belonged, though Aelfrida's comment that 'perhaps many saints are to be found in

this very place' may be taken to refer more to audience than to enactors) descending singing to the roodscreen before they flashed out of sight.[35] Her most dramatic experience, however, took place in GETHSEMANE while reciting Terce sitting in her deckchair 'with [her] feet up as usual': a sudden sensation of 'being' the Virgin Mary 'lying on her deathbed', a sensation not of illness or apprehension but of 'a perfect loving self-abandonment to the Will of God' in a state of 'marvellous peace', after which 'her-my personality-soul-spiritual-body slowly and with full consciousness passed through her-my physical body [and] without pause or transition entered the state which we call Heaven'.[36] Encouraged by Bishop Wynn ("accept it as an experience vouchsafed", though he added "beyond that I dare not go")[37], Aelfrida took her experience calmly – as she also did when 'The Voices' spoke to her on Ascension Day 1954 (a chorus enquiring "will she come and join us soon?", a solo voice answering "yes, He will bring her soon"), asking of them, supposing they were 'authentic', what 'soon' meant ('have the dead any sense of Time? Have angels?') and noting that whether 'soon' came sooner or later, she was both prepared for and unafraid of death.[38]

Another pleasing discovery was the presence of a Cowley Father as the Home's confessor. The Father in post on her arrival was one known to her from St Benedict's and from his having conducted the SSC's annual Retreat in November 1940. Meeting him again, Aelfrida was amused to find that his method of using 'Our Lord's words and ideas as *portals* through which our soul may pass' reminded her of Father Cary's and overjoyed to discover that he had been Lucius Cary's pupil and had inherited both Father Cary's spiritual mantle and his material biretta. (He also proffered much the same counsel at confession e.g. that the only remedy for self-centeredness was God-consciousness.)[39] That said, it seems on their first meeting at St John's Home that neither remembered the other.

Aelfrida's forgetfulness may have been due to her disordered mental state in 1940 but elderly Father Pridham's amnesia regarding a penitent unmet for thirteen years was understandable. He nevertheless made her 'extra welcome … for the sake of the beloved Community' known to both and on hearing her reply to his statement "I should like to hear a little more about you, Mrs Graham" (Mrs Graham duly described coming to Oxford at the instigation of the Lady Abbess of Malling and placing herself 'under the care of Father Cary' who proceeded to teach her 'as if I were a stupid child … which was exactly what I needed'), welcomed her back for Father Cary's sake also.[40] (Worth noting here is that Father Pridham's request for information may not have been wholly innocuous: he may have been alerted to Mrs Graham's religious foibles, personality disorder, and personal history by Father O'Brien SSJE, still Alethea's spiritual director and regularly consulted by her about problems posed by her mother, and whose personal knowledge of Mrs Graham dated back nearly twenty years.) Father Pridham, however, like his successors as confessor and possibly for the reason suggested, dealt gently with Aelfrida during regular confessions, advising her not to search too anxiously for '*sins*' but to give thanks instead for '*mercies*', to meditate on the Holy Trinity rather than on Christ's Passion[41], to regard relegation to an institution as "the beginning of the Communion of Saints", not a penance to be endured ('may we indeed find it so', commented his penitent tartly)[42], and to replace her usual macabre Lenten contemplation of Christ's agonies and wounds with lines from Charles Wesley's hymn *Love Divine*.[43] (Bishop Wynn forbade her to borrow a discipline from Tymawr and enjoined the woman spiritually compelled to crucify herself at all times and particularly during Lent to offer her pain instead, this being, as Aelfrida put it, 'a suitable *via crucis* for an old lady of 70'. Wynn's way of the cross the 'old lady' duly followed, finding 'wonderful spiritual encouragement' from it; Father Pridham preferred her to praise God – and said so.)[44] Furthermore, Father Pridham took confessions of consciousness of '*sinfulness*' lightly (as so often now, Aelfrida had no actual sins to confess and remembering Father Dunkin's strictures on there being no need to confess 'faults', did not mention them), exacting no greater penance than recitation of the General Thanksgiving[45]; his lightness of spiritual touch did not, however, prevent her from watching briefly before the Lenten altar of repose or from receiving as she knelt a vision of Christ standing in front of her with arms outstretched as on the Cross, asking her if she accepted spiritual crucifixion and her replying "yea, Lord, even as thou wilt".[46]

As part of her Lenten Rule Aelfrida now fasted only on Good Friday. ('Fasting' meant avoidance of dining room meals; she sustained herself throughout lengthy chapel services on 'bread – and things and biscuits'.)[47] She also maintained silence that day and on other Fridays and Sundays and as much as possible on other days. (Breakfast was a silent meal in any case, the Sisters extending their Greater Silence over the Home's inmates too.) She was encouraged in this by attendance at a Quiet Day conducted in the Home in December 1953 during which Father Triffitt expatiated on Silence as a form of adoration. His words inspired Aelfrida to ask God what should be her special portion of labour for Him at St John's, a request to which God replied enigmatically "gather up the fragments". On her enquiring 'fragments of *what*?',

her guardian angel explained that God's 'fragments' were the '*Fragments of Silence*' with which Christ fed everyone on earth and that his role as an angel was to see that nothing of this treasure was lost or wasted. ('Fragments' in this context imply not mere leftover bits and pieces but offerings; God was commanding Aelfrida to tithe her own and others' silences to Him as token of submission to His Silence.) Noting afterwards that a 'quiet day' in the Home was imperfectly kept but also how could it be, given the infirmity of some of its inmates[48], Aelfrida set about collecting as many 'Fragments of Silence' as she could. She began by writing to Sister Elizabeth Noel to suggest that silence be maintained at all meals on Fridays during Lent, only to receive a rebuff and a reprimand: for seventy-six' years, silence had been kept only at breakfast and there was no reason to alter the custom now and "unsociable people should go to their rooms and keep Silence there and not inflict penalties on others".

Aelfrida's reaction, at first amused ('whew!!'), then questioning ('is the fault mine?'), then apprehensive ('I must lie low in future!')[49], is indicative not only of her ingrained tendency to arrange others' lives to conform to her own but also that entrenched patterns of behaviour were already reasserting themselves and would render her last years more miserable than they need have been: she did not, as we shall see, 'lie low' and far from this episode being the first evidence of intransigence in the face of a new 'Authority', it was only the most recent in a series begun soon after her arrival. (It was, however, the first in which she tried to bring about changes in the running of the Home.) That problems posed by dislike of 'Authority' were about to render her life as difficult at St John's Home as elsewhere was obvious to everyone but herself; what she failed to anticipate was that being now (as Sister Superior put it) 'old and poorly'[50], she was more vulnerable to retribution and increasingly devoid of the physical, mental, and emotional energies needed to counteract it.

Lacking photographs of Aelfrida at this period of her life, it is invaluable to have her provide us with a written portrait which not only describes her physical appearance but also describes character traits promising approaching storms in comparison with which Sister Elizabeth Noel's Ash Wednesday reprimand was an April shower. 'I had', she wrote in August 1953, 'the opportunity (which has not been mine for many years) of seeing, thanks to a fortuitous arrangement of mirrors … the profile of an old lady who must be myself! I stared at her with some interest! She has rather a fine head with thick fluffy white hair that waves a little over the ears. Her profile is clear-cut, nose somewhat sharper than it used to be, chin a trifle more prominent … she carries her head well up with an air of serene assurance' ('which might be mistaken for haughtiness', she added in parenthesis, little thinking that she would soon be condemned by Sisters with 'an excessive love of *power*' for prideful behaviour of which she declared herself ignorant even while admitting that 'humility was indicated')[51] 'as if she were well equipped to deal with circumstances and people. She looks intelligent and eager [and] as she is taller than almost everybody here [is] somewhat conspicuous … I do not altogether admire the old lady – she ought to look humbler, indeed … some people think her formidable'[52] (John Hibbs, for example, noted "a certain sense of superiority … characteristic of the Tillyards" and that it was not easy to enter into conversation with her because, holding very definite views, she discouraged debate)[53] '[but] her life here may well add softening to her features. She looks gentler full face … with a welcome ready when needed' ("reserved but friendly in a polite and slightly formal way", said John Hibbs) 'especially when I catch a glimpse of her thinking about holy things in forgetfulness of herself'.[54] (A clear-sighted night nurse thought her behaviour with regard to 'holy things' false and pretentious, telling Mrs Graham that she attended chapel only to 'appear devout', paraded her piety by entering shortly before Holy Communion instead of, as other 'Ladies' did, a few minutes earlier to enjoy an interval of prayerful reflection, and would not behave as badly as she did were her religion 'genuine'. Did Aelfrida sail conspicuously into chapel to remind the congregation that she too was a Sister, Sister Placida of the Holy Passion and on relevant days deliberately wear full tertiary regalia to chapel in order to proclaim herself 'Sister Placida for all to see'? Aelfrida accepted the nurse's criticism as evidence that in receiving it uncomplainingly she shared 'in an infinitesimal degree'[55] in the mocking of Christ but failed to ask herself if there was any truth in it or to worry that how she appeared to others did not accord with her notion of herself.) But it was not only Aelfrida's height which rendered her 'somewhat conspicuous' at St John's Home and the fault lay not with her but with the devil: 'you would think [he] would hardly bother to haunt a place like this but he hopes to lead souls from regrets and self-pity' 'to discontent [and] active rebellion'.[56]

Diabolic haunting apart, others visited her too. Miss Randle, Aelfrida's much-maligned tenant at St Benedict's in whose favour and at two Mothers Superiors' command Mrs Graham relinquished the house, bearing a rose from a bush given by Phyllis Tillyard twenty years before and still flourishing in St Benedict's 'Trappist garden'. (Aelfrida later revisited her 'bower of Lady Poverty' but did not linger or explore it for, remembering 'how lonely [she] was and how sore and tormented in affections and soul', she 'did not wish the old days back again'; hearing shortly afterwards of the rigours imposed on herself by a friend of Alethea's, she described as 'very unwise' a life so reminiscent of her own 'in [her] very early days at Oxford' with regard to 'lack of fresh milk and fruit and far too much vehement and tempestuous private prayer'.)[57] Hilda Harrison with news of Tymawr, though apart from recent gossip Aelfrida was almost as well-informed as she, for letters, newsletters, and photographs of 'the convent as it is now … with the pie crust crenellations removed and a new storey [of cells] there instead'[58] arrived regularly. Dorothy Smith, unseen for eighteen years, 'met as if we had not been separated by time and distance' but still, as fifty years ago, unable to agree on religion and adamantly unable to believe in God.[59] And in spite of Aelfrida's analysis of Dorothy's problem ('*your … father* … stood for religion in your mind and when you lost your love for him you lost your faith too', a statement as true of Alfred and Aelfrida Tillyard as of Henry and Dorothy Smith, for *both* women, as Aelfrida finally admits, 'hated' their fathers and suffered 'paroxysms of impotent rage … which seemed to scorch them up' when living under the same roof as them), still resistant to Christian grace being channelled into her soul by one who continued to pray for those who had lost or never gained it.[60] Another Dorothy, Dorothea Conybeare, still devoutly religious, accompanied by her brother James, now eighty-two and Provost Emeritus of Southwell (and, alas, married) with whom as a 'strikingly handsome' and forget-me-not-blue-eyed archbishop's domestic chaplain Frida Tillyard had tried to flirt (and been rebuffed) and of whom (prompted by her guardian angel) she now asked blessing.[61] And two more ecclesiasts keen to see her again: Edward Ely looking forward to her next visit to Cambridge, James Barkway proposing to visit her in Oxford, both men making Aelfrida feel 'like Alice through the looking glass – having …tried to move away from bishops I [find] myself meeting them'.[62]

Another man too insisted on meeting her in spite of her decision to move away from Cambridge because Cambridge was where he lived: her brother Julius. Julius' first visit to St John's Home took place on 23 September 1953. Aelfrida records him as being 'in excellent form' (he and his collaborators in 'Byz. Mus.' were working on another volume of *Monumenta Byzantina* and chants interpreted by them were used in Greek Orthodox services in the United States), as exhibiting 'his most genial mood' when taking tea with 'everyone' i.e. the 'Ladies', and as saying feelingly that he had spent a '*wonderful*' day which he would remember as long as he lived.[63] But although she described the visit as 'a lovely Deardududay' and seemed genuinely pleased to see (and show off) her elder brother, she evinced irritation regarding the timing of another: 14 June 1954 being Trinity Sunday, she would prefer to spend it in 'silent contemplation of the central mystery of our religion'[64] than entertain a brother prepared to undertake a round rail trip of four hours and 160 miles at the age of seventy-three in order to keep in touch. Though she later admonished herself for complaining ('I *must* accept gratefully the blessings God sends me and not be … "choosy"!!')[65] for two visits in nine months could not be said to put unbearable pressure on her soul, it seems that Julius too had become an 'episode' in her life. Her reasons are implied rather than explicit. Perhaps, like Joan Cooper, Julius had provided so much 'copy' that he was now, metaphorically speaking, 'written out' of her life; perhaps she had been emotionally overwhelmed by discoveries made or elicited with regard to himself and their fraternal relationship and recoiled in alarm. Perhaps – a significant perhaps, given what might have gone before – her relationship with Julius (as with Edward Wynn with whom she makes direct comparison, noting that she had felt the same with him as when 'with Julius … at Wetenhall Cottage') was now 'perfect' because Julius was now able to keep his human and his spiritual affection for her in 'perfect balance' and under 'perfect control' (and to impose similar perfection on his sister so she could 'safely and fully respond' to him) and that because to continue it risked spoiling its perfection, it was better to 'let it Rest in Peace'[66] by separating herself from him.

She had, however, no wish to be forgotten. Hurt that no-one at St John's Home saluted her '70th birthday – and … Festival' on 5 October 1953[67] (she had informed no-one of this important milestone so could hardly complain), Aelfrida was highly gratified at the number of presents and cards received from friends and family and had no objection to news of them: John and Constance Hibbs 'radiantly … happy' though her aunt blamed the latter's 'restless scrambling life' and lack of 'servants to wait on her' for her frequent miscarriages[68] and did not approve of John's interest in the practicalities of public transport; Walter teaching in Shrewsbury; Stephen disillusioned with teaching and soon to abandon it for librarianship; Veronica pursuing her academic career in the United States and Angela now working in England, but neither young woman, to their aunt's regret, searching for God and both preferring an independent life to marriage, something regretted without insight by an aunt whose independent nature had contributed in great measure to the failure of her own. Perhaps the most exciting event was a visit made to 'Uncle Sir Frank Tillyard' in London, a town unvisited by her since, passing through on her way from Malling to Cambridge, she

had met Anthony Wrightson accidentally-on-purpose and her first view of the bomb-sites to which parts of it had been reduced during the war. Frank Tillyard was now 'a fine old gentleman' of eighty-eight with something of his elder brother about him; a recent widower, he lived with his son-in-law and elder daughter Kathleen Perfect, M.B. B.Chir., the latter still Aelfrida's favourite cousin in spite of the twelve years' difference in their ages. The occasion of their meeting was the twenty first birthday of Kathleen's daughter Margaret, bridesmaid at John Hibbs' and Constance's wedding, more recently an Oxford undergraduate, but of greater excitement to her elderly relative was Aelfrida's first meeting for many years with May Page, now aged and bent but once the "Miss May Cliff FRCO, Mus.Bac. of Durham University" who in 1907 accompanied the hymns and regaled the congregation with Handel, Beethoven, and Bach at the 'Marriage of Miss Tillyard'.[69] Alethea, on her way to Wetenhall Cottage to stay with Julius while Mina fussed over pregnant Constance in Suffolk, escorted her mother from Oxford to Highgate but left her to return alone, so tired she 'couldn't even *think!*'[70]

Following her return to England from her European tour, Alethea resumed her peripatetic life. Between 5 and 10 August 1953 she visited Aelfrida on several occasions though it was not until her own forty-fifth birthday that she informed her mother of her new South African responsibilities: manager of a girls' hostel on another mission, salary £10 a month. Further visits to St John's Home took place in October (Alethea's engagement diary record does not tally with Aelfrida's diary record but she visited at least thrice) with a final visit planned for early November. On her penultimate visit, however, Alethea 'looked a bad yellowish colour' but on questioning said she was 'all right'.[71] On All Souls' Day (2 November) Aelfrida noted that it was unlikely she herself would 'ever … be more ready for death' and prayed for her 'beloved dead'; ten days later she also noted that although enjoying spiritual 'green pastures and still waters', her guardian angel had warned her that these were given 'in preparation for some trial or sorrow'.[72] On 9 November Alethea, having recently passed the medical examination required prior to her return to South Africa, arrived at Wetenhall Cottage 'looking rather poorly' and, complaining of mild indigestion, went early to bed. Coming upstairs sometime later, Mina heard 'a groan and a thud' from Alethea's room. Opening the door, she found her niece unconscious on the floor 'with a pool of blood around her'.[73]

In spite of her mother's doom-laden prognostications (recorded retrospectively, we should remember) regarding readiness for death and trials and sorrows to come

St John's Home, Oxford, showing Ninian Comper Chapel

and of Joan Cooper's warning that Alethea would have to undergo 'a long, long convalescence even if all goes well' (i.e. assuming she survived)[74], Alethea did not join Aelfrida's 'beloved dead'. From hints in Aelfrida's diary, it seems she was treated conservatively (she was too weak to undergo surgery) with 'complete supine bed rest' and blood transfusion. (Contemporary treatments also included antacids by mouth and an intra-gastric infusion of milk but Aelfrida is infuriatingly vague on details.) Once past the critical stage, a diagnostic X-ray was performed[75], after which her doctors provided a reason for Miss Graham's sudden, profuse, bloody vomiting: 'severe haematomesis (*sic*: actually 'haematemesis') due to acute peptic ulcer', a well-known complication of infection by *Entamoeba histolytica*.[76]

Alethea remained in Addenbrooke's Hospital for two weeks before moving to Hope House for three weeks' convalescent care. She then spent a month at Jesus Lodge with Eustace and Phyllis and on 20 February 1954 went to 'Uncle Sir Frank's' under Kathleen Perfect's supervision. Hence it was not until five months after her collapse that she and Aelfrida met in Oxford on 14 March, the latter recording her joy that God had given Alethea back to her and that her daughter looked 'as if she had been through deep waters' since they last met.[77]

The reason for Aelfrida's vagueness concerning her daughter's illness, vagueness all the more noticeable when contrasted with the interest she took in and detailed account she gave of Agatha's near-fatal mastoid infection, is simple: she remained in Oxford, and in spite of being offered a lift to Cambridge, refused to go, saying that Alethea was better without her (she had the grace to add that she would visit '*if [Alethea] asks me to*') and that she preferred to wait 'for God's Will to unfold itself'.[78] (To which heartless statement one can only apply her

condemnation of Sister Superior to herself –'they say here that she has no heart' – and comment concerning the ladies of St John's Home –'dear me, how odd some of [them] are!'[79] – to describe her appalling conduct towards the daughter addressed in letters as 'precious and beloved Alethea' and assured of 'all the love in the world'.) But why did she not rush to the bedside of her desperately ill and possibly dying daughter? Because she was 'born callous'? Because she was too 'old and poorly'? Because Advent was imminent and she wished to maintain a forty-day retreat as at Tymawr? Because she and Alethea had parted on bad terms, as evidenced by her stating that she would (only) visit Alethea in hospital if the latter asked her? (Alethea, it seems, did not ask.) Because she was annoyed with Alethea for other reasons? Or because Alethea was now an 'episode' in her life?

All are possible, some probable. Aelfrida, though not 'born' callous, had been rendered callous by childhood events but was, prior to Alethea's illness, endeavouring to compensate for this by ingratiating herself with 'the Ladies' at St John's Home. 'Old and poorly' she was but not so old or so poorly as to be unable to enjoy a visit to London or lengthy holidays in Cambridge. A wish not to interrupt Advent 1953 is plausible (Aelfrida had been prepared to interrupt a Lolworth Lent for Mina's sake but not, it seems, an Oxford Advent for a sick daughter's) even if incredible. Perhaps Alethea had criticised her mother during their spat at Jesus Lodge and her words rankled and annoyance with Alethea for other reasons seems likely as comparisons between Alethea and other single female members of Aelfrida's extended family would make plain: they with their flats, careers, and regular incomes, Alethea, 'so brilliant, so good' but 'with so many apparently empty shells of discarded works behind her'. (And unmarried and childless to boot, a fact attributed by her mother to 'old repressions dating back to the time when her father was getting tired of us'[80]; had she not read Alethea's adolescent diaries stored at Wetenhall Cottage and discovered the truth?) And an 'episode' Alethea surely was, as witness her mother's chagrin at discovering that Alethea's return to South Africa was to be postponed for 'at least three months'[81] then, it seemed, *sine die,* for even had Alethea's 'haematomesis' not intervened, administrative changes at Holy Cross Mission jeopardised her intended job. In May 1954, however, Alethea was still so anaemic that strenuous work in a hot climate was considered inadvisable for the foreseeable future, but Aelfrida, wilfully ignoring the debility induced by severe acute haemorrhage, preferred to regard her convalescent daughter's 'languid and passive'[82] behaviour as indicative of psychosomatic, not physical, ill health. Alethea, she wrote, was sulking because her 'self-offerings' at Malling and Maritzburg had been 'refused by God' and her 'magnificent work at St Cuthbert's' voided of 'His seal of approval' and 'too much piety [and] too much sympathy' would 'make an invalid of her' and she ought to go and live in Switzerland where there was 'more commonsense to the acre that anywhere else'.[83]

As family's and friends' reactions to her non-appearance in Cambridge must have demonstrated and her own references to thinking especially of *Agatha* at this time show, Aelfrida may have become aware that she, the consummate stage-manager and actress, had missed her cue with regard to staging a dramatic scene at Alethea's bedside during which a 'widowed' mother could have mourned the imminent or actual passing of her sole remaining daughter. But how better, given her missed opportunity, to play the part of heroic martyr-mother relegated to an institution and too old and poorly to leave it, than by letter? ('Sheaves of letters' received at Christmas seem to have been of sympathy as much as of seasonal greetings.) 'Extra letter-writing necessitated by Alethea's illness'[84] caused writer's cramp; relief at not having to take responsibility for Alethea's convalescent care was outweighed by irritation at being unable to provide her correspondents with an exact diagnosis or pious platitudes on her daughter's demise, and it was not until 5 December with Alethea's diagnosis finally made that hers mother was able, cramp and Advent retreat notwithstanding, to 'tackle letters in good earnest' and to put an impressive (and misspelt) name to her daughter's illness.

But why behave so unfeelingly? First, Alethea may have returned to England unemployed and penurious but as her welcome from friends and relations showed, she returned beloved; second, she had trumped her mother's ace once again by suffering a dramatic and unforeseen illness in the course of which she behaved (as even Aelfrida had to admit) with sweetness of nature and gratitude for care given. (Aelfrida, by contrast, was merely undergoing the gradual worsening of a chronic medical condition glorified as a '*via crucis*'.) Hence although Aelfrida, so she said, loved having Alethea 'close at hand' once more[85], evidence provided by diary entries written during the months of Alethea's convalescence suggests that Aelfrida was jealous of her daughter's popularity and annoyed that no one, not even Julius or Edward Wynn, had tried to persuade her to stay in Cambridge once she announced her intention of relegating herself to an institution in Oxford.

Unable to show displeasure openly, Aelfrida revenged herself in two ways: by reminding Alethea that one of the latter's criticisms of *Just Alice* (read while convalescing at Jesus Lodge), namely that the plot's 'sudden calamities' were not 'true to life', was unjustified because one had just happened to 'a woman of forty-five, highly intelligent, devout [and] physically robust', i.e. Alethea herself, and that had it not been for 'timely help', the haemorrhage might have proved fatal[86], and by acting as if the serious illness which had altered the course of Alethea's life had never happened and by concentrating on the minutiae of life at St John's Home instead.

Incredible as it may seem, Aelfrida told no-one at the Home save Sister Elizabeth Noel of Alethea's illness; odder still, and even as she records details of her daughter's desperate condition, she wrote at greater length and with greater emotion about trivialities: a Sale of Work held at the Home ('great fun, everyone excited!')[87]; visits from friends in spite of it being Advent ('Florence Fisher dropped in to see me')[88]; visions in chapel; a 'pert and common little nurse … of the less-loved Ward Sister type'[89] to replace Sister Catherine while the latter took her final vows; extreme busyness in sending off Christmas presents before making her Advent retreat and in receiving 'sheaves of cards and letters' by every post during it[90]; the Home's 'festive' and 'magnificently organised' Christmas dinner[91]; goups, male and female, (by correspondence, and described at greater length than Alethea's illness) who seemed as prone as herself 'to take credit for holy desires, good counsels and just words'[92] and to express dissatisfaction with religious affiliations and practices. But Alethea was revenged: was it entirely without malice aforethought that she disturbed her mother's Lenten retreat of 1954 by paying her first post-illness visit to Oxford in the second week of that solemn period, a visit the retreatant could hardly forbid without being thought more 'callous' than she had already shown herself to be?

Lent over (Aelfrida herself felt particularly 'at home in … Holy Week')[93], Easter Monday was celebrated by the arrival of letters from Julius, Lillian Whitehouse, and 'paternal' Edward Ely and by the trip to London described earlier. (Aelfrida was humbled by the warmth of a welcome 'which I have done nothing to deserve'.)[94] Then news arrived of temporary light work for the woman whose position as head of the St Cuthbert's girls' hostel had been abolished 'without consulting the hostel's mistress'[95]; on 3 June 1954 Aelfrida announced 'with deepest gratitude to God'[96] that Alethea had accepted the post of general secretary of the Cowley, Wantage and All Saints Association (CWAS), a missionary endeavour based in London but soon to move to a small house in Marston Street opposite the SSJE headquarters. But even while accepting post and salary, Alethea was making other plans: her return passage to South Africa was booked for mid-December 1954. She never returned; ill-health and the Cowley Fathers kept her in England and moving with her job to Oxford (she occupied a small flat above the CWAS offices) and being Aelfrida's formal next of kin bound her willy-nilly to her mother for the foreseeable future. But living and working within quarter of a mile of St John's Home in no way improved the relationship between mother and daughter or narrowed the spiritual and emotional distance which had long existed – and now, it seems, had widened – between the two. A reason is not hard to find.

While convalescing in Cambridge, Alethea visited her father's old college. Sitting on a sunny bench amid snow and icicles, she watched skaters gliding along the frozen Cam and, it seems, thought long and hard about her relationship with her mother. A week later Aelfrida recorded Alethea's critique of *Just Alice* and hinted that it contained both literary and personal criticism: the 'odd little scene' made by Alethea while staying with her mother at Jesus Lodge in 1953 (attributed by Aelfrida then and now to 'mostly "nerves"' and to Alethea not having 'quite readjusted her child's conception of [her mother] to the right one for middle-aged daughter and aged mother') had, in fact, revealed something Aelfrida (so she said) 'wanted to know', namely that what she had dismissed as 'a ludicrous idea', i.e. the Archbishop of Capetown's description of herself as '*Dictatrix Mundi*', was a statement whose accuracy had 'haunted' Alethea since it was reported to her.[97]

That it had taken ten years for Alethea to pluck up sufficient courage to confront or to become sufficiently desperate to break away from her maternal *dictatrix* is unsurprising given her mother's 'too dominant … personality' ('not domineering', she added charitably, even as she told Aelfrida "when you come on the scene everything begins to revolve round you")[98] and her own gentler one, but Alethea, already tempered by the fires of adversity, had had her eyes opened by the Archbishop's statement and opened further by her mother's behaviour towards her since her return to England. Refusing to meet a daughter unseen for five years until Lent was over. Forcing her to camp in other people's houses when she could have stayed at Parson Drove. The dreadful letter written on 12 July 1953 in which Aelfrida describes her idea of how the relationship between middle-aged daughter and aged mother *ought* to be conducted by the former and states that the relationship existing between herself and Julius was exclusive and all-important and that what she felt for him was not extended to her daughter. Indifference to Alethea's recent 'calamity' which so closely paralleled her behaviour at the time of Agatha's 1931 illness that Alethea, convalescing in the very house in which she had been banished with bromides to her bedroom to recover from a breakdown

ascribed by her mother to 'nerves', must have realised at last that the mother who described her daughter as 'precious and beloved' and signed her letters 'all the love in the world' was an unloving prevaricator who had not loved her since 'Weta' became a schoolgirl at the Perse and who, while pretending to have seen the error of her ways with regard to management of her daughter's life, continued to exert – or try to exert – control over it by concealing dictatorship under a veneer of sickly sentiment and financial generosity.

From now on, Alethea never put herself in a position where her mother could exert power over her. Her small salary and rent from Wetenhall Cottage (described casuistically by Aelfrida as the 'allowance' she gave her daughter) provided a measure of financial independence and for the first time in her life she had her own home to which Aelfrida was admitted only by invitation and not oftener than once a week. Holidays (including Christmas) and many weekends were spent away from Oxford with Julius and Mina at Wetenhall Cottage, with Eustace and Phyllis at Jesus Lodge, or with her surrogate family, the Perfects and 'Uncle Sir Frank', in London.

Aelfrida took rejection calmly; she had, after all, two men in love with her, men with whom she enjoyed the kind of platonic relationship she preferred and was busily forging another *vita nuova* at St John's Home. She was, however, somewhat put out by Alethea's physical proximity, noting that her joy at hearing of the Marston Street office/flat was 'unselfish' (with the implication that selfishly she would have preferred Alethea to live and work in London) and of the latter's move to Oxford that 'naturally' she was pleased but spiritually she was not.[99] Ambivalence was less because she might have to make 'practical demands' on her daughter (she says nothing of emotional ones) or to love her otherwise than 'only in God'[100] (a fact of which she continually reminds herself in the early days of Alethea's Oxford sojourn) and more because Alethea's presence might cramp her mother's spiritual style, in particular her pretensions to life as an SSC tertiary (of which Alethea was always critical) or invite invidious comparisons between one lady's demonstrated *caritas* and the other's selfishness. Hence although she publically included herself in factors which attracted Alethea to Oxford (the others were 'the proximity of the Cowley Fathers' and 'the prospect of a … little flat') and which caused her to exhibit better 'health and spirits' than her mother had seen 'since Girton days'[101], it seems that mother and daughter now met less 'in God' and more in terms of guarded neutrality in which social proprieties were maintained but nothing else.

Protestations to the contrary notwithstanding, what Aelfrida now felt for her daughter was chiefly jealousy because, as Father Dalby, Father O'Brien's successor as Superior of the SSJE, pointed out, everyone who visited Alethea's Marston Street Office came away pleased with their reception. She was also torn between a desire to bask in her daughter's reflected glory ("Miss Graham … is a really good Christian") as the mother of a saint whose goodness was indubitably inherited ("you can say all the nice things you like about my daughter")[102] and disdain for a middle-aged menopausal spinster living in a 'poky little flat'[103] with borrowed or donated furniture in a working-class area of Oxford, earning a pittance, and a 'cloth moth' to boot: the Cowley Fathers, wrote her mother, held 'rather too large a place' in the life (and affections) of a woman of forty-seven who attended the Fathers' church daily and who turned to Father O'Brien for emotional support as well as spiritual direction. (Aelfrida attended Mass at Cowley St John only once during her new life in Oxford, sitting ostentatiously in her old place in the front row while Alethea and three ladies from the Home whom Aelfrida had persuaded to accompany her sat further back; during the service she felt herself 'slipping into an ecstasy' – 'it seemed as if I must leap clear of the body and unite myself to the Triune God' – but 'fear of being immobilised and making [herself] conspicuous' made her stop herself just in time.)[104] And it was in this light that Aelfrida now beheld her daughter, noting the contrast between the 'beautiful, vivid, adventurous' girl of Girton days ('"conquering Alethea", they called her') and the sad-eyed 'Miss Graham' who *seemed* not to regret the past but given that during their conversations Alethea refused to sigh 'a single sigh' over her former life, how could a mother tell?[105]

There was also, of course, the matter of her daughter's health, for although Aelfrida tended to dismiss the severity of Alethea's chronic amoebiasis (she never tried to divert attention to her own poor health; indeed, in the interest of remaining independent for as long as possible, she tended to play it down), the fact that Alethea was admitted to the Acland Nursing Home in July 1956 for 'nursing and tests' necessitated by a recrudescence of what Aelfrida downgraded to 'gastroenteritis' shows that, though tranquil in spirit, Miss Graham was far from well in body. (Aelfrida did not visit, being then on holiday in Cambridge and more preoccupied with past and present masculinity – 'radiant' Edward Ely, 'dear Dudu' with whom she enjoyed a weekend's tête-à-tête, and Aleister Crowley whose 1952 biography by John Symonds, *The Great Beast,* was a present from Julius[106] – than with a daughter who required further rest and recuperation before returning to work.) Less than two years later Alethea suffered a second haemorrhage ('a slight return of her peptic ulcer trouble') and was hospitalised for over

two weeks. This time Aelfrida was forced to visit – she was in Oxford and Sister Superior knew of the emergency – which she reluctantly did ('16|- for the taxi' upset her more than the sight of her 'languid and sleepy' daughter); indeed, she fretted more about the cost of hospitalisation (Alethea had private health insurance so there was no reason to worry on that score), that her sole visit to the nursing home made her appear less caring than the Cowley Fathers who visited daily and en masse, and that if Alethea predeceased her she would reach heaven before her mother.

Once assured of Alethea's recovery, Aelfrida waxed both tetchy at having the tenor of her life interrupted yet again ('all parties concerned [must] take it in a Christian spirit. God give me strength to do my part')[107] and relieved: as Alethea would not be coming to tea for a while she could write up her diary, compose a short essay on the subject of her own mother, and enjoy a 'DearDuduDay' during which Julius could enlighten her about a 'form of insanity' (homosexuality) reported in *The Times*. (Luckily, the 'Archbishops [were] tackling the subject' so she could dismiss the 'lunacy' of 'adult consenting males' from her mind[108] – as she also did Alethea for several diary pages.) On 22 January 1958, a brief visit to her recovering daughter (Alethea was staying with a friend pending convalescence in Bournemouth) produced the insensitive comment that Alethea looked as 'if 3½ weeks at the Acland at 20gns a week … had tried her nerves'[109]; had Aelfrida really no conception of Alethea's anguish at being unable to return to South Africa lest she die of haemorrhage on an isolated mission? (She herself preferred to believe that it was her own and Alethea's respective guardian angels who had arranged for *both* women to 'come and live in Oxford!')[110] Lent 1958 coincided with Alethea's return to work; Aelfrida added 'a few minor privations to [her] too-easy Rule' but did not consider that a visit to her daughter counted as one of these or that it need interrupt her almost 'Tymawrsome' silence. She relented sufficiently, however, to meet Alethea later in her 'retreat' – only to receive the unwelcome tidings that Alethea's life henceforth and on medical advice would be 'restricted'[111] and that she must prioritise her own welfare, not her mother's. Given that Aelfrida's own health was now in decline, Alethea's news should have filled her with foreboding; she continued, however, to behave as if her daughter's health and welfare were of less importance or concern to her than those of her friends and brothers, Alethea's well-being rarely, if ever, figuring in diary entries thereafter.

But this is to anticipate. Alethea's return to England and Aelfrida's annual visits to 'ex-Fordfield', to Wetenhall

Cottage, and to Cambridge friends known since the 1880s ('the train, puffing importantly, took me back into … my childhood')[112] seem to have stimulated the mind of an authoress to efforts of positively Proustian recall and the imagination of a 'Poor Old Lady in a Home'[113] to range widely in time and space (from long before she was born to the 1950s and from Cambridge to Haifa) in spite of relegation to an institution. 1954 therefore saw Aelfrida embark not only on a lengthy novel (*Naomi da Costa*) but also on a series of short essays generically entitled *Memory Pictures*.

Although it was probably no coincidence that Aelfrida's first formal reference to *Memory Pictures* (she wrote over forty in all and more than one version of some) occurred on 1 April 1954, a week after the visit to 'Uncle Sir Frank' during which he and she discussed 'Old Times', the idea of writing "family reminiscences"[114] or a 'Family Chronicle'[115] in the form of 'memory pictures' was largely inspired by Bishop Barkway. Discovering in 1953 that she was about to relegate herself to an institution, the 'Anteater' introduced her (or rather re-introduced her, for she had first come across 'a little paper published for a society of pious invalids' while convalescing at St Raphael's Home in Torquay in January 1936 and had met its editor during one of Father Cary's retreats at St Thomas' Convent)[116] to the Society of Watchers and Workers, founded in 1879 for "the better recognition of bodily infirmity as a power of witness for Christ" and as a vehicle by means of which "invalids may use their leisure for the work of the Church and the service of others"; more importantly for an inveterate writer, the Society published a magazine (*The Watchword*) to which members, when not engaged "prayer and intercession", were invited to contribute.[117] Feeling at that point in her life that her options were narrowing rather than expanding, Aelfrida accepted Bishop Barkway's suggestion that a 'little bit of work'[118] might be forthcoming and having received Bishop Wynn's approval, contacted the SWW shortly after arriving in Oxford.

Aelfrida, of course, can be said to have written 'memory pictures' since she began writing though it was only after the appearance of *The Glory of the West* that reminiscences started to pour forth in an unstoppable stream. Her return to Cambridge in 1946 saw the stream become a flood, and even before James Barkway's timely suggestion of *The Watchword* she had begun to compose essays entitled *Concerning the Beloved Dead* (1948) and *Memories of Cambridge* (1952) intended, according to a 'Brilliant Idea' put forward in *The Glory of the West*, to form part of a "best-selling line" of books brought out by "a Publishing House entirely devoted to books for and by the Aged" ('aged' meant "authors … over 60"), full

of "ripe wisdom [and] mellowed humour" and even of "Romance from … mature vintages".[119]

Her earliest published essay for the SWW, appropriately entitled *Blessings, the First Blessing,* appeared in *The Watchword* of December 1953. Though this suggests composition soon after arrival at St John's Home, it was probably written earlier: a version entitled *The Earliest Memory of All* seems to have been intended for inclusion in *Memories of Cambridge* of the preceding year.[120] Her initial relationship with the Society was not, unfortunately, cordial, it having been informed by Bishop Barkway that Aelfrida would act as a 'Watch-Sister' i.e. 'as a sort of prayer NCO to watch over about a dozen members'.[121] On arrival in Oxford, however, she discovered that being a Watch-Sister involved 'three times the amount of work I said I could do' and '*too much* organisation and intercession, papers and correspondence', so pleading writer's cramp and that *her* 'work' was prayer, she refused the position[122], but writer's cramp and prayer-work notwithstanding, contributed to the Society's magazine instead. Her essays, short, sentimental, and pious, were exactly right for 'a magazine circle of people'[123] of roughly her own age and approximate bodily infirmity, and both they and their author were welcomed by local organisers on visits to a woman they had imagined to be 'just' a 'Poor Old Lady in a Home'[124] but discovered was a published author with seemingly total recall and an ability to pen *Memory Pictures* of immediacy and interest. Better still (SWW organisers were female – and overbearing) was a visit in July 1954 from her introducer himself, her 'old friend Bishop Barkway', 'better looking than he was fifty years … ago' (she made no comment regarding the nose which provided his nickname) and 'most warmly delighted' ('*emotioné*' in fact, more so than she) at renewing their friendship on what both agreed was 'happy occasion'.[125]

*Memory Pictures* need not be described in detail here, because apart from Catharine Tillyard's *Record* and Julius' scanty reminiscences we have no available data on Aelfrida's childhood other than material provided by herself in the 'pictures' and so are forced to base a description of her early years on her own later (and undoubtedly fictionalised) account: once she began her diary, however, we have an abundance and this, together with *Memory Pictures,* provides us with an unusually complete autobiographical record of her life. Her diary, of course, was often written at white heat and chiefly at the time when events took place: *Memory Pictures*, on the other hand, were composed when looking back over what she had once (and inaccurately) described as 'the arid desert of the years'[126]; furthermore, she did not look with the innocent eyes of childhood or the unsparing gaze of adolescence but with the emotional astigmatism of later life, blurring or sharpening her focus according to the emotional charge of events she wished to portray. Some 'pictures' were not intended for publication, an anguished and involuntary stay on a ward at St John's Home being written for Eustace's eyes only[127]; some were composed as a means of calming her mind when battles with Sister Superior reached such a pitch that her mental equilibrium became unbalanced[128]; others, such as those in which Constantine appears either as himself or as 'Vadius'[129], were intended to be read only by those privy to her marriage and divorce. But as with her diary and her poetry or prose, *Memory Pictures* (where dateable) can be read as a series of Proustian '*madeleines*' in which a particular event provokes a corresponding 'picture': 'General Feebleness' engendered by her visit to London on 23 March 1954 which necessitated a day in bed 'sweetly fussed over by dear ladies' reminded her of being 'petted up' during days in bed at Fordfield and on 1 April 1954 she 'spent [the] afternoon writing a "memory picture" about Ellen for *The Watchword* and made [herself] cry'[130]; Julius' account of a visit to Paris in late October or early November 1954 during which he met Zelle for the first time for many years inspired a *Memory Picture* of "perfect darling" 'Zelle *au coeur d'or*'[131]; correspondence early in 1955 with the Rev Whigham Price concerning the lives of Margaret Gibson and Agnes Lewis resulted in 'pages of reminiscence' about the 'Learned Twins' ('the joy of artistic creation has not diminished'), some of which was included in a monograph presented to the Presbyterian Historical Society entitled *The Ladies of Castlebrae*.[132]

*Memory Pictures* have something in common with Aelfrida's diary and writings in another way. First, and in contrast to Julius who informed his sister that he could discern 'no plan or purpose' in History[133], Aelfrida believed that 'History' in general and her personal 'history' in particular were preordained as to plan *and* purpose by God, His plan for her and His purpose in providing it being revealed only gradually and frequently mistaken by her as to their manifestations. (In what way, for example, could Conrad's death be termed part of God's plan and purpose for Conrad's elder sister except insofar as any act of God was 'ipso facto good'[134] and must be realised to be even by one so stupid that she failed to recognise its 'goodness' until she had worked through the emotional consequences of that terrible event with the help of Conrad's elder brother? The published version of Conrad's death appeared in March 1954 shortly after one of Julius' visits.)[135] But if her life as preordained could be said to provide an example of Rendel Harris' 'guiding hand of God', what did this also say of its having been preordained by childhood trauma, be that trauma part

and parcel of God's plan or not? Can it be that Aelfrida wrote her 'memory pictures' as and when she did as an explanation and that they were written at a time when it was convenient for her to 'venture to explain'[136] Deity's plan and purpose for her as *ex post facto* justification for behaving as she had and did, and this to an audience (her family in general and Alethea in particular, readers of *The Watchword* merely providing a timely reason for writing her '*mémoires*') critical of her selfishness and seemingly phoney piety?

Furthermore, with regard to Aelfrida's belief that her (preordained) life constituted a spiritual 'pilgrimage', we may ask: did she set out to write a personalised version of her 'family chronicle' as a means of demonstrating that, raised (as she liked to think and to have others believe) in a 'Christian' family, she was continuing along the "Godward" path laid down for her by "the living prayer of sires and dames long dead"[137], a path whose glory was shed prospectively over herself and her daughters and by collateral association over her nephews and nieces and their children too? Or were *Memory Pictures* the retrospective account necessary to complete her picture of her life as a pilgrimage from youthful folly (sinfulness, even) via reparative adoration to mature contemplation of the purifying goodness of God, a life which (like Dante's, a simile never far from her mind at this time) included an idealised dead love, impolitic decisions with regard to conduct and belief, and exile from a beloved natal town? Or was her decision to pen a series of episodes in which she recreates figures from her past 'near though unseen'[138] a means of providing herself (and, with luck, other people) with greater insight into the problems which (Deity-purposed or not) had beset her life and into the motives of the people who caused them? And how better to do this than by concealing the bitter pill of her problematic past (had she described what she *truly* felt and thought, 'memory pictures' might have been so rancorous as to have been un-publishable – and unpardonable – but this would not have accorded with the picture she wished to present of herself as a saintly old lady) in the form of (seemingly) innocuous short stories?

A 'comedy' in the classic sense constitutes a particular dramatic genre whose ending is happy (or at least bitter-sweet) even if events which lead up to it are not. Hence, perhaps, Aelfrida's later desire to present her life less as a tragedy than as a 'comedy' tending to a happier conclusion than she once dared hope and as 'divine' in the Dantean sense of being devoted to God and lived in imitation of His Son. (Though not as 'godly' in practice as she liked to think.) Though old, ill, relegated, and bereft and impatiently awaiting the point at which her 'heavenly birthday' would bring down the curtain on a life joyful, pathetic, farcical, or tragic by turns, she therefore composed her 'Memory Pictures' to conform to the divinely comedic version she wished to present to the world. In order to do this it was, of course, necessary to reconstruct 'Prehistory' to make it conform both to the comedic genre and to the sanitised and idealised version she maintained in public and private. (And in the case of 'pictures' written specifically for *The Watchword*, to render it suitable for consumption by invalids: beef tea, as she herself might have said, rather than roast beef.) Hence when her guardian angel held up the 'magic mirror' in which 'this and that scene' of her past were reflected[139] (a phrase from a diary entry written on hearing the news of Sir James' and Lady Frazer's deaths in 1941 though it took another fifteen years for a '*mémoire*' on them to appear following the arrival at St John's Home of a biographer to whom Aelfrida made 'Frazer and the Strawberry-eater [come] very much alive')[140], she deliberately tuned her powers of recall to 'fast or slow', selected as her topic 'what [was] most exquisite and loved'[141], and placed the object of her scrutiny in a setting retrospectively appropriate to its re-appearance. A particularly telling example deals with the death of "my little brother – Conrad Francis", the key and certainly the most traumatic episode in Aelfrida's life.

Of the two extant versions of this episode[142], the published version is briefer and more sentimentalised and includes not only a description of the vision seen after the still birth of Agneta in 1912 ("once, years later, I saw Conrad again … radiant with ageless eternity") in order to emphasise (as she wrote of another *Memory Picture*) the significance of (her version of) the story 'for after life and experience'[143], but also a notable difference from the version intended for family reading with regard to the way in which puzzled Frida comes to terms with Conrad's disappearance: the *Watchword* version has Chiara read her Charles Kingsley's description of 'Little Ellie's' death from *The Water Babies* so that Frida may gently learn from a familiar book what has befallen Conrad (a significant misremembering, given that 'Ellie' does not, in fact, die but is temporarily removed from 'Tom's' life, only to reappear later) but the *Memories of Cambridge* version has a Fordfield servant inform her brusquely that Conrad had "gone to Jesus".

Lastly, and as usual with Aelfrida, it was necessary for her to show herself in the best possible light even if that meant blackening or distorting the characters of people with whom she currently or formerly interacted, or omitting data from or giving slanted versions of recorded events. Writing for *The Watchword* she could not indulge in character assassination to the same – or any – extent, but comparisons of diary, family chronicle,

and *Watchword* versions of the same 'picture' reveal how much she manipulated the truth to suit her audience. She also preserved the various versions for a future biographer; can it be that she, usually so eager to subvert the truth, is now and even as she marvels at her temerity in allowing a fuller record of her life "to come down to posterity"[144], anxious to reveal the extent to which she subverts it to suit her ends? A striking example of this occurs in the three extant versions of the death in 1920 of 'our dear little Ellen' from breast cancer.[145]

Ellen Ison, the housemaid engaged by Dear and inherited by Chiara, became "a dear friend" to the Tillyards in the course of her thirty-year sojourn at Fordfield.[146] In June 1916 she developed a breast lump, subsequently diagnosed as cancer. She refused surgery lest knowledge of her illness upset her mother. Knowing Ellen's diagnosis (and likely prognosis, given her refusal of surgical intervention), Aelfrida suffered no 'remorse'[147] at taking days in bed and having Ellen carry trays of food up several flights of stairs to one less ill than herself. In October 1919 the Tillyards fled to Hunstanton pending Aelfrida's divorce; on 7 May 1920 Aelfrida paid a brief visit to Fordfield but made no mention of Ellen, left behind to look after the Tillyards' tenants, though from comments made ten days later ('our dear little Ellen is … dying of cancer')[148] we can deduce that far from Ellen having been, as Aelfrida put it in her *Watchword* essay, 'overworked' by the tenants[149], was suffering from advanced disease and had already left Fordfield to die in her home village near Cambridge under her mother's care. The Tillyards returned to Fordfield in June 1920, Chiara expressing much sorrow at having lost someone regarded as more than a mere servant, and Aelfrida, who had just endured nine months' servantless existence in Hunstanton, extreme irritation at finding herself deprived of Ellen's services[150], the latter's terminal illness being in her eyes less a family tragedy than a domestic inconvenience. (Her comment that 'one *cannot* have sad thoughts in connection with Ellen'[151] may be read as resignation to God's Will, as a pious expression of 'light shining in darkness' as Ellen prepares for an exemplary deathbed, or as a belief that Ellen's death would provide a merciful release from suffering, but should be read with this in mind.) Keen, however, to present herself in a better light, Aelfrida recorded in *Concerning the Beloved Dead* that she cycled to Quy to visit Ellen "several times"; in fact, as her diary reveals, she visited once (a second visit, accompanied by her daughters, was to Ellen's grave), it being Chiara, aged seventy, who made the ten mile round trip several times. It is unsurprising, therefore, that only one visit (called "the last")[152] remained in Aelfrida's memory to be described in similar terms and with similar sentimentality (a substitute for real emotion, as she must have known) in both *The Watchword* and *Concerning the Beloved Dead* (not *that* beloved; her diary states bluntly 'dear Ellen is dead' and adds conventional platitudes)[153], because she remembered Ellen chiefly in terms of convenience or inconvenience. Thirty years later Ellen was resurrected as 'copy' over which (perhaps her conscience pricked her) Aelfrida wept as she wrote.

Aelfrida's earliest '*mémoire*' for *The Watchword* was published in December 1953 and seems to have inspired its author to attempt another novel. Early in February 1954 and 'at long last' she sat down to inscribe her 'Jewish "night story"': *Naomi da Costa, Prophetess*.[154] By mid-July *Naomi* was 'flowing grandly' from her pen[155] and by mid-August she had written enough to read it to Julius during a month's visit to the 'Deardududland' of Wetenhall Cottage. (There was now no need to worry about excluding Mina from fraternal tête-à-têtes; henceforth Aelfrida's visits to Cambridge took place by arrangement during Mina's visits to family in England or abroad, though whether this was due to an altruistic desire on Mina's part to allow elderly Julius and Aelfrida private time together or a wish to escape relegation to third place in her own home went unstated.) Undiscouraged by Julius not being 'as much interested in Jews'[156] as herself and by her narrative seeming to have gain a meaning of its own whose message she hoped 'may be made clear to me as I go on'[157], Aelfrida persisted with it throughout the autumn. In mid-November she noted that she had completed it with difficulty because devoid of 'the strength to make it as good as it ought to be'[158] (words may have flowed grandly from her pen but composition fatigued her to 'the point of exhaustion')[159] but hoped 'to improve it on revision'.[160] A 'very strong impulse' to begin revision in mid-January 1955 by recasting the whole novel save the last chapter in diary form was unsupported by the physical strength needed to begin it. (At pre-Christmas Communion she had had to apologise to God 'for being such a poor thing' but was rewarded with a brief 'taste of the life hereafter' unsusceptible, alas, to description: she was incubating influenza, 'fortunately a mild type', and it was not until the day before the 'strong impulse' seized her that she felt 'almost [her] usual rather shaky self' again.)[161] Possessing insufficient strength to continue with *Memory Pictures* and revise *Naomi*, she opted for the former. It is unlikely, therefore, that *Naomi* was ever submitted for publication (a September 1955 rejection slip from her literary agents shows that she continued to submit *Just Alice*, rejected by Hutchinson five years earlier) but given the important revelations made concerning her heroine's vocation as a 'prophetess' and the esteem in which Aelfrida held

her literary productions undeterred by mediocre reviews or by rejection, it is probable that had she been able to revise her text, submission might have followed.

Throughout the early years of her stay at St John's Home Aelfrida continued to tell herself 'night stories'; in spite of increasing physical disability she remained intellectually active and pain-induced insomnia unalleviated by barbiturate sleeping tablets was enlivened by tales such as that of a man 'not highly sexed at all' who 'in quite a natural way couldn't help marrying four good women one after the other', only to discover with the fourth that he was 'thoroughly self-centred!' (Given that the protagonists of Aelfrida's 'night stories' were invariably herself, it is amusing to ask: to whom she was 'married' four times? Constantine Graham, Eric Silvanus, and Albert Erlande physically, Christ mystically perhaps? Also worth noting is the appearance in *Naomi da Costa* of an aged aunt, "a gentle white-haired white-cheeked old lady, simply dressed in grey", whose chequered matrimonial career encompassed "*four* husbands", of none of whom she could remember "anything", not even their names, except that she "had suffered in their loss"; conversely she remembered "stories of her childhood … as if it were yesterday".)[162] Even more interesting in view of Aelfrida's joy in authorship, tendency to autobiography in everything she wrote, and penchant for 'night stories', are comments in contemporary and slightly later volumes of her diary with regard to 'authorship' and *romans à clef*. Concerning the first she quotes similarities between herself and John Buchan, noting the latter's propensity for telling himself stories in which a character or two and a series of incidents worked themselves into a narrative independently of conscious invention, the stories seemed told *to* him rather than invented *by* him and his characters real people, and that she too watched and heard her characters behave and not until their story had told itself to her did she transcribe it at speed. (In practice, she seems to have retained a greater degree of control over her stories than Buchan over his for, as she wrote apropos abandoned novels – or, one might say, 'episodes' in her life – 'sometimes I have to close down a story because the characters wouldn't behave as they ought', beginning afresh with 'another set of men and women' after sweeping the stage bare of the first.)[163] Concerning 'her own autobiography in a different form' (Aelfrida's description of Monica Baldwin's new 'novel', *The Called and the Chosen*), Aelfrida omitted all mention of its plot in favour of drawing parallels between Baldwin and herself as novelists: as isolated individuals 'indulging in daydreams and fantasies' who identified themselves with their fictional characters, as pre-eminently diarists who feel 'the need to record' so strongly that neither can

> I can tell you one thing, though. When my guardian angel gives an order, he always provides the means for carrying it out. My own schemes fall through at least nine times out of ten, but the plans of my guardian angel are invariably successful. I will give you a couple of instances. I had been studying Mysticism and the Psychology of Religion in a desultory way for some time, when, in 1915, my guardian angel commanded me to give some lectures on Spiritual Exercises. I firmly replied that the thing was impossible. No one would give me a lecture-room, no one would come and listen to me, I knew next to nothing of the subject, and so on. However, my guardian angel said I had better go and see Professor C. S. Myers, then professor of Psychology at Cambridge. I did so. He received me as though his mind had been prepared beforehand to be specially courteous to me. He put a room at my disposal, and gave me every encouragement. I did my best with the lectures. I suppose it was my guardian angel who sent the audience. Anyhow, the course was a complete success. I repeated it afterwards, and finally published the lectures in book-form. And it was this book, *Spiritual Exercises*, which put me in touch, dear Stranger, with you.

*Can I Be a Mystic?* p 82–3: a guardian angel

refrain from leaving 'some imprint on her private pages', and as '*artist[s]*' who find dissection of their '*own* personality' the most interesting subject of all.[164] Or because, we might say, they are so locked into the circle of self as to be unable to break free.

Though never recast wholly in diary form (pages describing 'Naomi's' death make this technically impossible), N*aomi da Costa* is largely narrated by its eponymous heroine, an impersonal narrator taking up the story as circumstances require. The significance of diarised chapters is underlined by 'Naomi' in her opening paragraph when she informs us that she is "beginning this journal not for my own praise or pleasure but that it may give my future biographer the true facts".[165] (How many of the 'facts' provided by 'Naomi' are 'true' is questionable but some, we may guess, are as near the truth as Aelfrida ever comes e.g. that her poetry, like 'Naomi's', "sings its way into her mind" in the form of dictated words which she hastens to inscribe before they fade[166]; that she has "no liking for responsibility" and that only a sense of duty prevents her from deserting family members dependent on her[167]; that it may have been her father's decree,

not her mother's, that she marry because he was "furious" at having wasted money "sending her to Italy"[168], her mother concurring because she could think of no other way to 'normalise' her daughter; that her guardian/brother-in-law's anger on discovering that Naomi, a Jewess, has "taken part in the most solemn rite of the Christian Church"[169] i.e. Holy Communion, may echo Constantine's towards his wife when he discovers that Aelfrida has attended – as she herself implies[170] – one of Aleister Crowley's 'magick' ceremonies in Paris, Crowley himself appearing during Holy Communion in the guise of a "pathetically small and feeble baby bat" [171] whose seemingly broken wings cause 'Naomi' to wonder if it is "venomous" or "merely quaint"; 'Naomi's' realisation on seeing 'Solomon's' "grey and cold and hard" look when he discovers what she has done that she does well to ask herself "what *had* she done? *what* had she done? … And what made her do it?")[172] Not only this, but 'Naomi' also finds it necessary to ask "what really [matters] to [a] future biographer?", to omit "trivialities" which tend to creep in to her account, and to keep her "record" meticulously up to date.[173]

*Naomi da Costa* tells the story of the arrival in England in 1952 of an Orthodox Jewess from South Africa, Naomi being the last of an extended family – she has six sisters[174] – to come to live there. The novel covers four years of Naomi's life and includes details of her studies in Hebrew and Arabic at Girton College, descriptions of the Gentile friends she makes at Cambridge, her interaction (not always amicable) with members of her family and of Cambridge's Anglo-Jewish community, her relationships with men, and her death when a boat carrying herself and Jewish settlers to Palestine blows up in sight of her and their Promised Land. But synopsis reveals little, for the novel is dense with allusions to Aelfrida's own past: to her childhood (stamp collecting; "gods and goddesses")[175]; to her adolescence (a mystic experience while crossing a bridge over the Cam)[176]; to her young womanhood (a college ball; "propinquity" as the necessary basis for marriage)[177]; to the grinding years at Fordfield during which she was forced to relinquish "any hopes of life or happiness of [her] own"[178]; to her being "not indifferent to men" but desirous of "life alone" to follow her vocation.[179] It also refers to her present life, notably her habit of hanging an ENGAGED notice on her door at St John's Home "to signify that she … did not wish to be disturbed".[180]

There remain, however, several questions which require answers: why a *Jewish* 'night-story'? Why a Jewish 'night-story' begun 'at long last'? And what is the novel's 'message'? To answer one is to answer all but to answer all is only to hint at some of Aelfrida's preoccupations – and to discover others for the first time because only now and in a *roman-à-clef* does she describe them.

Aelfrida's interest in the Jews and Judaism was long-standing but it was not until 1938 that accounts in *The Times* of 'Jewish persecutions and of how nobly and gently they have borne their troubles' and the Holy Spirit 'underlining' references in the Old Testament for her '*directed*' her thoughts in a more focussed fashion on God's 'Chosen People'. She also began to identify with the Jews as a race similar in many ways to her vision of herself as someone with allotted 'work' as yet unfinished[181] (in this particular instance, meek acceptance of suffering in order that her example might 'assist the healing of … so-called Christian nations [who] have forsaken God'), who underwent 'long sustained consciousness of God's overwhelming claims', and whose time was spent repeating 'old, old prayers' and practising 'an overt piety'.[182] (Interestingly, she saw no contradiction between two other statements made on this subject: that she thought 'we Christians' concentrated 'too much on ourselves' and that she felt impelled to 'pray and pray' that the 'Jewish racial unconscious' would eventually allow the Jews to convert to Christianity.)[183] In another act of identification she noted that "chosen of the Lord" and therefore "the most highly favoured of all nations" though the Jews might be, they (like herself) "had occasionally been stiff necked and rebellious" and, unheeding of warnings, "had brought [troubles] upon themselves".[184] In part because of this and in part because she believed that a 'Jewish novel' might provide 'a bulwark against anti-Semitism', Aelfrida, it seems, began to conceive of herself as a writer (a 'great' writer too, possibly even a 'Jewish' writer because of her empathy with the race) who would describe the '*significance*' of the Jewish nation as God's 'Chosen People'[185], 'chosen' because only to them did God confide "the fundamental Secret of the Unknown – Monotheism".[186]

Concentrating (as usual) too much on her own self and on herself as a Christian mystic bent on successive 'new lives' in her personal quest for God, Aelfrida failed to write her novel in time to avert the Holocaust and it was not until early 1953 when the prospect of 'a new persecution' of Jews 'in Soviet-ruled countries' seemed likely that she prepared to write the 'Jewish novel' which might cause the world to 'remember and protect'[187] them by way of "bold speech and bolder action".[188] (Aelfrida's voice was not the only one hoping to make itself heard; there was also tremendous press and radio coverage of Jewish matters and strongly divided opinions expressed. Perhaps she was moved by what she heard and read, perhaps she also believed that she stood a better chance of publication if she wrote a novel on a hot and a contentious topic.) But seeing herself as someone desirous of (temporarily) putting aside her vocation "to solitude and prayer" in the interest of "offering … [her] dowry of devotion … wholly for God's purposes"[189] in the hope of averting Jewish persecution, was one thing; quite another was to proclaim herself Jewish by spiritual adoption and as one of God's 'chosen people' too. But chosen as or for what?

What Aelfrida as 'Naomi da Costa' now chooses to reveal is that God chose her for a specific purpose: "I Naomi da Costa am a prophetess".[190] And a 'prophetess', we now discover, Aelfrida has believed herself to have been since adolescence. It is not, however, until she novelises her life as 'Naomi's' that she describes her journey as a woman desirous of conveying a divine message and of teaching and interpreting the will of Deity:

In her mid-teens Naomi learns from a South African professor that she is to be a "prophetess"[191] whose life must henceforth be a "life alone"[192] dedicated "to her people in the land of her fathers".[193] At first 'Naomi' can hardly believe that she, a sixteen-year-old girl, will become a "prophetess"; indeed, she hears a "*voice*" remind her that she is not yet a prophetess but will become one when she has "grown up"[194] spiritually and physically. By the time she arrives in Cambridge, Naomi is already experiencing visions (of herself in Jerusalem or fleeing from a mob or in a gas chamber) but is constrained from speaking out by her youth and because "a living presence which she dare not repel" bids her be silent. (It is not a sinister presence; a great feeling of peace emanates from it.)[195] She also begins to experience a "mysterious sense of compulsion" and as if God were "reserving some high destiny for her"[196] and decides to brook no interference in her need to "follow [His] call when it comes".[197] (Worth noting here is that Aelfrida had recently read the letter from her younger self in which the latter asks if she had proved worthy of her 'high calling'.) Naomi's decision naturally precludes marriage; although she sets "no store on virginity as such" nor believes God to be "more honoured by chastity than by marriage"[198], she does not envisage her future "in terms of life with someone else" as "Naomi, sweetheart, wife and mother" but as "Naomi the prophetess"[199] living a dedicated life apart. (As a child, Naomi had believed the Archangel Gabriel to be Christ's father, he having conferred pregnancy on Mary "by a mere word", and she too "longed to conceive a baby" without the need for coition, the resulting "wonder-child" growing up to be "the greatest of all prophets". Learning later that "this could not be", she "[took] upon herself the prophethood"[200] instead.) Life intervenes. Naomi's sister Sarah dies in childbirth and the former is forced by her brother-in-law Solomon to leave Girton and to relinquish "all thoughts of being a prophetess" and all hopes "of life or happiness of [her] own" in order that she may devote herself to his children and run his house. Asking herself "why has [God] allowed all these things to happen and put a kind of wall without a door round [her]?" but feeling that she *"can't* give up the idea of being a prophetess", Naomi settles down to wait and to regard her virtual imprisonment at Saville Court as a time of "preparation" for her future career. A fortunate change in circumstances and determination that "no-one *shall* interfere" with her compulsion to pursue her vocation restore her freedom and she is able to return to Girton and to resume "thoughts of being a prophetess".[201]

And with that revealing (and rather frightening) résumé of *Naomi da Costa, Prophetess* we return to 1953 or, rather, to "October 6 1952", the date given by 'Naomi' to the first proper entry (what has preceded it is essentially prologue) in a diarised autobiography which is to provide her biographer with true "facts". Checking with Aelfrida's diary for that date, we discover – a blank, or rather, a record of the kind of "trivialities" 'Naomi' hoped to omit: an increase in rent for her Parson Drove attic. The day prior to this, however, was her sixty-ninth birthday; can it be that Aelfrida, then staying, rather appropriately, at *Jesus* College, was inspired to enlarge upon her life as a self-styled 'prophetess' with part two of her 'Great Work' incomplete (she has not yet communicated God to man as fully as she would like) as soon as circumstances allow and before it is too late?

But a prophet, as the man whose life she had assiduously imitated since first meeting Him in a mandorla of light knew only too well, "is not without honour save in his own country and his own house". And as Aelfrida discovered to her cost, lecturing and teaching in the 'synagogue' of Cambridge University resulted only in literal and metaphorical dismissal ("whence hath this man this wisdom and these mighty works?"[202] as derogatory Nazarenes said of Christ the carpenter's son or as "offended" family members and academic Presbyterians may have said of Frida Tillyard) so she, like 'Naomi', turned to writing, only to discover that "mighty works" of pietistic literature were subject to "unbelief"[203] and failed to sell or even to be published. Admission of failure came hard to a "prophetess" who believed her audience rather than herself to be at fault, but as a reference in *Naomi da Costa* to Browning's poem *The Last Ride Together*[204] shows, only late in life did she admit that she

herself might have been wrong and that no-one save a few 'goupy' (and mistaken) reviewers described her books as "masterpiece[s] … of definite inspirational value" and prophesied that they would become "widely known".[205]

Worse even than loss of 'honour' from those living in her spiritual 'country' (of another character in *Naomi da Costa*, appropriately named 'Theodora', it is said that she is "one of those dreadful women who have a mission from on high to set everyone to rights [and] want to influence everyone for good")[206] and criticism from inhabitants of her family 'house', was that 'prophetic' behaviour may have become so bizarre at some point in her young womanhood (she hints in *Naomi da Costa* at "trances" from which she recovered exhausted and amnesic, at screaming fits, and at speaking in tongues; she also hints that one episode occurred in Fordfield garden and was witnessed by the gardener who called her parents and they a doctor who arranged a stay in a private "sanatorium")[207] that she was diagnosed as temporarily insane. She also hints that as a result of further manifestations of mental instability, she was formally certified non compos mentis, deprived of her papers and her money (but allowed to continue her 'researches' into her 'family'), incarcerated in "an old monastic building" on the border between one country and another, and only when deemed "apparently quite normal", allowed to leave – and that to all of this she lodged "no objection". But given that her behaviour as a 'prophetess' was so singular that it overrode her doctor's opinion that "marriage could … hardly … do [her] any harm" and might even render her "more normal"[208], what does this say of Aelfrida's 'prophetic powers', of the veracity of her 'prophetic' utterances, and of her credibility in the eyes of a future biographer to whom she will reveal the 'facts'?

It is not, however, only as a 'prophetess' that Aelfrida feels herself bewilderingly different from other people, much as this contributes to her sense of 'otherness'; it is because since the time of Conrad's death and her being banished from home without explanation, she has felt herself to be an *outsider*, a 'Stranger within the Gates'[209] or a member of a 'lost' tribe unable to assimilate herself into any 'community' in whose company she finds herself. Hence, one might say, her affinity with a race which, though 'chosen', are often regarded as alien to the communities in whose midst they dwell. (Not until quite late in life did Aelfrida realise that the Old Testament was a history of the Jewish people and that Christ was a Jew, not an Aryan, a fact underlined in *Naomi da Costa* when 'Naomi' reads the New Testament for the first time.)[210] Furthermore, the Jew whose life she imitates is by the nature of His vocation an outsider, and it is because of this as much as because she feels that as a 'prophetess' she must constrain herself from entering fully into other's lives but must remain a detached "New Girl"[211] befriended by none and little known by anyone, that she not only believes herself to *be* an outsider but is compelled to behave *as* an outsider even to the extent of ghettoising herself by leading, as Mother Guenvrede put it, 'quite a different life' to everyone else or by leading a life so 'out of tune' with the norm that her lifestyle and behaviour '[spoil] the harmony'[212] of whichever community she is in. And 'out of tune' behaviour ensures further rejection.

Aelfrida's compulsion to repeat the paradigmatic 'outsider' event in her life has other implications too. She emphasises her 'outsider' status by wearing clothes whose style or symbolism single her out from other women and by adopting habits (vegetarianism, abstinence from alcohol) which single her out on social occasions. ('Naomi's insistence on kosher food at Girton and on keeping a Saturday Sabbath single her out in the same way.) She sometimes behaves in an eccentric manner, this leading people to believe there is something 'uncanny' about her (an uncanniness which her distant demeanour and disconcertingly penetrating gaze do nothing to dispel) and that she is not bound by the same conventions as themselves. She also appears to identify with the 'wandering Jew' of mediaeval legend who, unlike Christ who deliberately led a nomadic life as a wandering teacher and preacher (as, of course, Aelfrida did in imitating Him, cutting herself off from her family in favour of what in medieval times was called "*peregrinatio*" and undergoing as a result the 'white martyrdom' of 'detachment' of a literal and very painful kind during which she followed a pillar of fire and cloud to promised lands, lands which never quite fulfil their promise when she reached them so that she felt compelled to seek another), is condemned to wander the earth because he treated Christ with contempt when the latter was led to crucifixion. Twice in her life by her own account Aelfrida herself treated Christ with contempt, once by reneging on her promise of Holy Virginity, once by rejecting her 'Vision' in favour of leading a life of 'Christianity without the Cross'; hence even when offered the opportunity of settled existence in her own house, she declined it because it did not accord with her vision of herself (or her need to envision herself) as a wanderer and an 'outsider'. Lastly, she behaves like a 'bad goat', a 'bad goat' being, so Mother Guenvrede said, an animal who wilfully wanders off to eat what it should not in places it should not go. But accurate as this description is of aspects of Aelfrida's behaviour, it does not adequately describe her need to *see* herself as a 'bad goat' and to continually drive herself out into a series of 'wildernesses' as the Old Testament Jews drove out into the desert a scapegoat metaphorically laden with the community's sins, there to nearly die while practising reparative adoration in respect of sins committed by members of her personal 'community'. (*And by herself.*) Her need to see herself as a 'bad goat' and to 'draw down calumny'[213] upon herself in her own mind or by behaving in such a way as to invite it from others, also explains her affinity with a nation who, as tradition had it, laid itself open to persecution because it (by Roman proxy) 'killed' Christ. And if, as Dom Bede Frost noted, "not to be persecuted [was] an indication of weakness"[214] and a disinclination to be persecuted indicative of a wish to pander to self rather than love God (and imitate His Son), then persecuted Aelfrida would be.

But why a 'Jewish' novel written 'at long last'? Because only now did Aelfrida realise how much she had in common with the Jewish people? This is possible for it was only when she saw 'heart-rending' pictures of Belsen concentration/extermination camp in *The Times* at the close of the Second World War that her views, partisan since Allenby's bloodless entry into Jerusalem in December 1917 (at which point she 'laid aside all carping about the rights and wrongs of the war and rejoiced unfeignedly that … the Jews will return to their promised land', though she was also pleased that 'the holy places [were] once more in Christian hands' and believed the general's pacific approach was due more to his being one "who follows the Inward Light"[215] than to political expediency), crystallised into one of positive support for and lengthy diary declamations on the state now called '*Israel*' which had 'once more come into being' with 'aged Zionist'[216] Chaim Weitzmann as president. (Aelfrida was no Arabist but her description of the United Nations Organisation as a 'not *Christian* … council manipulating mankind' in sending '100,000 Jews into Palestine' shows appreciation of rights and wrongs committed on both sides.)[217] It may also be that feeling herself complicit in the '*dire*' sin committed by nations which had 'closed' themselves to the Jews and left them 'at the mercy of Hitler'[218], *Naomi da Costa* was written as an act of reparation, or that, inspired by the discovery in 1949 of the Dead Sea Scrolls 'significantly now when the Jews are back in Palestine', she decided that the world '*needed*' a novel underlining the significance of their return and decided to provide one.[219] Or perhaps she had 'at last' accumulated sufficient material to write a 'Jewish' novel based on recent historical events: as contemporary diary entries show, she was reading round her subject in 1952–54 as actively as she had done around Buddhism, Sufism, Islam, and other faiths (and Judaism, though less intensively) when researching *Spiritual Exercises* thirty years earlier.[220] And given Aelfrida's interest in people, perhaps the most compelling reason lies in her relationships with individual Jews.

At first sight, 'Naomi's' undergraduate life at Girton appears to have been inspired by Girtonian Alethea's return to England; in fact, the novel contains obvious references to Alethea ('Naomi' suffers an intellectual and emotional breakdown in her first year of study and has her "probably psychosomatic" headaches and laryngitis treated by "a nice little lady doctor")[221] but is cleverly updated by details taken from Angela Tillyard's more recent stay of 1945–48. It is, however, to three Jewish girls that 'Naomi' owes much of her life and character: Olga Liebowitz, for practical details of problems encountered by an Orthodox Jew in a Cambridge college ("Kosher food will be provided", says 'Naomi's' letter of acceptance but as she herself notes, "this *kosher* business is rather a mistake. It complicates life so much [and makes] us conspicuous and impossible to live with")[222]; Ruth Schechter, who with her 'extraordinary gifts and great love of her race might have been a second Esther' pleading the cause of the people for whom she 'promised to do great things by writing novels which explain Jew to Gentile' but who failed to become 'the prophetess … she had felt herself called to be' by becoming 'an adulteress and a Communist' instead[223]; and the Tymawr novice with 'curvature of the spine'.[224]

It was, of course, Ruth Schechter who first drew "little English Frida into the sacred company of the Hebrews"[225] (a slight exaggeration: she was not 'drawn into' the 'sacred company of the Hebrews' but remained a committed Christian sympathetic to specific members of the Jewish race and religion who not infrequently expressed anti–Semitic sentiments) during the period of Solomon Schechter's stay in Cambridge from 1890 to 1902. But following the Schechters' departure for New York and more particularly following Ruth's marriage to the 'brilliant young Jew'[226] to whom she had considered herself engaged since age twelve, the two women's correspondence lapsed and it was not until 1919 when Julius and Mina were forced to move temporarily to South Africa when Oliver Lodge refused to allow Julius' appointment at Birmingham University, that Ruth, now Mrs Alexander, wife of the Mayor of Cape Town and mother of three children, reappeared in Aelfrida's life. Some years later, Ruth met and eloped with (and after divorcing her first husband, married and moved to England with) a young Irish Communist described by censorious Aelfrida as the 'paramour' with whom Ruth now lived in 'legitimised adultery' and because of whom she added Ruth (at her guardian angel's suggestion) to her list of those for whom she made reparative adoration. In 1937 Ruth's erstwhile 'paramour' was

appointed 'Professor of Greek at Swansea', she and her second husband staying a week in Cardiff with Julius and Mina while Professor Farrington gave a course of lectures there. Aelfrida, ensconced at Tymawr, refused to meet 'complete sceptic' (i.e. Communist) Ruth[227] (her later 'memory picture' of Ruth provides a wholly different version)[228] and the childhood friends never met again: Ruth was injured in bombing raid on Swansea in 1942 and died shortly afterwards aged fifty-five.

But while Ruth's death and Aelfrida's 'childhood memories of her'[229] might have played a part in the composition of the latter's 'Jewish' novel (several examples of Ruth's behaviour appear as 'Naomi's' e.g. her singing Hebrew psalms to a "tense and awestruck"[230] Gentile audience of Cambridge contemporaries), it may have been more than memories which stimulated her to write it. Perhaps in writing a novel 'which should explain Jew to Gentile', Aelfrida hoped to don the mantle of 'the prophetess of her people' (or more correctly, of Ruth's people) that Ruth had once thought to assume in the hopes of finding herself hailed as 'a second Esther'; possibly as a failed 'prophetess' she felt sympathy for Ruth as another such; possibly she wished to make an *amende honorable* to the memory of a friend towards whom as a "tiresome little girl" who defaced loaned books and read aloud extracts from Frida's purloined diary "to the assembled ladies on her mother's At Home day"[231] she bore a longstanding grudge – and how better to make amends than by depicting Ruth in a favourable light in a 'Jewish' novel? Or perhaps recalling her own 'paramour' episode with Eric Silvanus, she realised that she herself was in no position to cast stones and tried to amend her snubbing statements and behaviour by basing 'Naomi' in part on Ruth, 'Naomi', who, though imperfect with regard to relationships with other people and in her interest in creeds akin to but not her own, nevertheless becomes a Zionist, composes inspirational Zionist poetry[232], and dies as a result of an act of enemy aggression.

The young novice for whose spinal curvature Aelfrida expressed concern had arrived at Tymawr as an aspirant in July 1945. Aelfrida's interest in the girl stemmed, however, from something other than the latter's supposed physical symptoms and their resemblance to Agatha's: the aspirant whose admittance as a postulant in September 1945, clothing as a novice in March 1946, and final vows in April 1954 were carefully noted in Aelfrida's diary, was an English Jew. Having 'prayed so often that God would send [the SSC] a Jewess', Placida deemed herself '*awestruck*' to discover that her prayer had been granted when 'dear Jewess Anne … [the] Hebrew maid'[233] followed a convert and the religious life closely and affectionately. Sister Gabriel Anne ('Jewess Anne's' name in religion) and Aelfrida continued to correspond after the latter departed Tymawr in July 1946, two letters of hers being kept by Aelfrida to show that Sister Gabriel was not only 'penetrating deeper into the SSC vocation' and praying Aelfrida along with her[234] (in contrast to Alethea, who had 'longed so much for the Habit' but to whom it had been denied[235] and who now seemed reluctant to pray her mother along in any way) but was also consuming herself "in a life of prayer for the Gentile church" at the same time as she remembered her afflicted people and kept her Jewish flame alight.[236] But Aelfrida's spiritual affinity with and literary inspiration by 'Jewess Anne' also owes something to parallels between their lives: both underwent a change in religious affinity and were literally or metaphorically cast off by their respective families because of this, and both manifested a vocational curving away from the straight path of Judaism or Protestantism in order to follow "the slow, halting, poignant wondrous Way of the Cross"[237] of Anglo-Catholicism.

Two men too are germane to discussions of Aelfrida's 'Jewish novel'. The first was her 'old friend and suitor' (there is no record of his supposed wooing) Norman de Mattos Bentwich, recalled from visits with Ruth Schechter to the synagogue above the Barretts' china shop and from 'awfully tiring' efforts to be 'brilliant … and handsome' on social occasions at which he was present.[238] Although it was not until after completing *Naomi da Costa* that Aelfrida, searching the Home's library for background material for her 'memory picture' of the Schechters, discovered 'a grand picture of English Jewry'[239] in one of Bentwich's books, it is possible – likely, even, given her up-to-date knowledge of the subject – that she had already read, without acknowledgment, books by Bentwich, a prolific writer on modern Jewish history and ideals, and that the book on which (with her guardian angel's assistance) she alighted was already familiar to her. Furthermore, to be able to align herself in a 'Jewish' novel with an eminent Jewish author like Norman Bentwich would appeal to one regarding herself as Jewish by proxy. The second was Agatha's surgeon, Alfred Walford, unidentified by Aelfrida (and others) as a Jew until Nazi persecutions impelled him to proclaim his birthright[240], a deed which led Aelfrida to admire him even more and which may have inspired her to proclaim herself 'Jewish-by-sympathy'.

> Naomi returns to Cambridge after a year's absence at Saville Court to begin her final year of study and is introduced to a distant cousin, Raphael de Costa. Raphael, a postgraduate student about thirty years old, possesses both "intellectual and physical strength" and is, with his glowing eyes, lovely voice, and Jewish looks, "the most beautiful human being [Naomi] has ever seen or was ever to see", so beautiful, in fact, that she envisages him as illuminated from within and as radiating a light that is wholly spiritual.[241] Raphael and Naomi immediately discover a "mysterious connection" between themselves and decide to act towards each other as brother and sister.[242] Naomi, however, feels so strongly drawn to Raphael (he casts an "entirely sympathetic gaze" on her account of her life and hopes, revels in every word she speaks, and shares every emotion she expresses) that she is prepared to merge her life and her "prophetic vocation" with his even to the extent of marrying him and bearing his children.[243] Raphael warns her off by informing her that he is a "madman" who, though apparently "quite normal", inhabits a liminal world somewhere between the natural and the supernatural.[244] Naomi consults a Jewish psychiatrist, Jay Lazarus, who informs her that Raphael is *not* clinically "mad" ("we are all a bit queer, you know") but a "*mystic*" and an "ecstatic" who experiences "raptures" and whose "interests lie outside this world", and that though marriage might make him "more normal", Jay advises against it[245]; Naomi therefore settles for a brother and sister relationship. As ardent Zionists, Naomi and Raphael decide to leave England for Israel. They embark on the *Pandora*, a "mystery ship" which changes flag, name, and skipper as its cargo requires[246], but as they and the Jewish refugee passengers who accompany them enter Haifa harbour behind which glows "a golden cloud bank like the battlements of the heavenly Jerusalem", the ship explodes and Naomi and Raphael disappear beneath the swirling water.[247]

That this is something more than Aelfrida's literary adaptation of contemporary events in order to add immediacy and verisimilitude to an improbable and over-written story (the last chapter of *Naomi da Costa* derives from reports in *The Times* of 'strong military measures' taken by the British authorities against what they regarded as 'refugee Jews' 'illegal' entry into Palestine' and the 'terribly unwise' actions taken by the Jews as a consequence of this[248], and from accounts of the Jewish immigrant ship *Exodus*[249] whose arrival in Haifa harbour on 18 July 1947 symbolised to the world, if not the British authorities, the Jews' post-war determination to establish a homeland in what would become the state of Israel on 14 May 1948) can be deduced from 'Naomi's' conversations with 'Raphael' prior to departure for Haifa. Before they proceed with their arrangements, 'Raphael' suggests to 'Naomi' that his "sweet sister" ask her guardian angel (as he will ask his) if they should go, adding that if both angels "say *go* … we will go". On 'Naomi' enquiring of 'Raphael' if he 'sees' angels and what they are like, he replies that they are made of fire and 'speak' by "impressing thoughts on [your] mind".[250] At this point, hints provided by Aelfrida earlier in the novel (e.g. that 'Raphael's' interests "lie outside this world"; that he "lives" among "angels and archangels"; that he knows Jesus "better than anyone else in the world" and that Jesus is a "Messiah of the Spirit whose command he always obeys"; that he appears "like a messenger from a higher sphere, a being more angel than man" who condescends to visit and comfort his 'sister')[251] coalesce with descriptions of 'Raphael's' manner and appearance and we realise that Raphael, the angel in the apocryphal *Book of Tobit* who guides and protects Tobias in his quest for a remedy for his father's blindness and, on their return, drives out the demon which haunts Tobias' future wife, is also 'Naomi's' 'brother'.

The significance for Aelfrida of an angel who guides and guards is obvious, but his presence in her last novel accrues further meaning which she divulges to us four years after completing it that the name of her own guardian angel is 'Raphael'. She does so in a diary entry concerned *inter alia* with the tendency of senior nuns at Hope House to persuade her to convert to Roman Catholicism, noting in a brief postscript that because she has received no '"intimations" from St Raphael'[252] that this was a step she ought to take, she will not take it.

Three questions immediately present themselves, two answerable, one not. As to why Aelfrida chose St Raphael as her guardian angel (and how typical of her to choose an *archangel*!) we may guess that both the meaning of his name ('God hath healed') and the fact of his being invoked in prayers for travellers as a presence who will "preserve and defend them from every evil assault … visible and invisible … and [keep] them in peace and health'[253] were important to her as a peregrinating personality subject to 'evil assaults' of a demonic nature. (Tobias himself was saved by St Raphael from live burial, as Aelfrida herself was saved from 'live burial' in the 'pit' of a mental asylum by being sent to Tymawr with Julius as her guardian and guide.) Describing St Raphael as he appeared to her at Mass one Sunday, she notes 'he was like St Michael whom I saw in Tymawr chapel one Michaelmas Eve, about 8 feet high [with] wings outstretched [that] shone with celestial light [but] I could not look at his face for its brightness' – her physical eyes were shut – 'he gave me Holy Communion in both kinds [and] was gone. Alethea to tea in the aft[er]noon]'.[254] But why does she not name him until 1958? Perhaps a bout of illness during which she required medical intervention and nursing care day and night

(she diagnosed it as 'TB or cancer of the lungs'[255], the latter preferable because non-infectious and tending to a quicker 'heavenly birthday'; the doctor diagnosed a chest infection and cured her with penicillin) prompted her to disclose it lest death prevent her. As to whether her guardian angel's name was always 'Raphael' or whether 'Raphael' was the name given to him by Aelfrida after *Naomi da Costa,* we cannot tell, though in keeping with revelations made there, probably the former.

But why '*Naomi*' da Costa? Possibly after Sister Naomi at St John's Home or Norman Bentwich's sister Naomi, a younger Cambridge contemporary of her own, but the *Book of Ruth* suggests a more likely source: Naomi is the widow of an émigré Bethlehemite whose two sons have also died. Feeling that "the hand of the Lord [has] gone out against her", Naomi, accompanied by Ruth, one of her daughters-in-law (the other elects to remain in Moab, her native country), returns to Bethlehem where she begs her neighbours to "call me not Naomi, call me Mara: for the Almighty hath dealt bitterly with me … I went out full and he hath brought me home again empty".[256] Though too old to think of another husband, Naomi is comforted when Ruth, a childless widow, marries Naomi's kinsman Boaz and bears a child who will restore Naomi's happiness and nourish her old age. Parallels between biblical Naomi's and Aelfrida's own life are striking, particularly those concerning Naomi's real and Aelfrida's self-styled widowhood, Aelfrida's 'desertion' by Agatha following Constantine's death abroad, and her own eventual return to Oxford with a second daughter (de facto, not in-law) who then cleaves to another man. (Perhaps Father O'Brien, certainly Deity.) Bearing in mind too, Aelfrida's equation of her books with surrogate babies, how easily *Naomi da Costa* replaces the child menopausal spinster Alethea is unlikely to bear, her mother (like biblical Naomi with Ruth's child) laying the novel she is in process of writing in her bosom and nurturing it there.

And there is more. The layers within layers of meaning within *Naomi da Costa* (layers only hinted at here) show that Aelfrida, though in her seventies, still possesses what Sister Jeanne described as a "richly stored mind".[257] (And an inventive mind too.) Frail though she is and though she has described her own death in the final pages of her final novel (the swirling waters into which 'Naomi' and 'Raphael' fall have been "turned all sorts of colours"[258], prosaically, because the *Pandora* was carrying vats of dye which ruptured in the explosion, symbolically because the sheeny iridescence into which 'Naomi' and 'Raphael' fall represents the rainbow colours of the waters of death and the golden cloudbank beyond Haifa their rebirth 'after no long tarrying' in Purgatory[259] into a new life), she still has "a long long way to go"[260] before she, like 'Naomi da Costa' in her white dress and with the emblem of her faith about her neck, emerges from the waters of death to enter the heavenly Jerusalem. In witness whereof and although she scores a line and writes "The End" as she completes her text, she adds the date (19 November 1954) and a reminder to herself (and possibly also to her biographer) "*To be revised, of course*". But even as she does, she starts another hare: as a witness of 'Naomi's' and 'Raphael's' fall into the sea remarks, "they called each other brother and sister but of course they'd have married each other ultimately"[261] — and we realise, first , that it may be to Julius that Aelfrida refers when she has 'Raphael' repeat to his 'sister' 'Naomi' the vow of biblical Ruth to biblical Naomi[262]; second, that as St Teresa of Avila (herself from a *converso* Jewish family) wrote of "divine marriage" (a preliminary state to "spiritual betrothal" and not to be confused with it), such 'marriage' is between "two people ... whose lives are so entwined nothing could ever separate them"[263]; third, that there may be more to Julius' and Aelfrida's relationship than she openly disclosed. As the impersonal narrator of parts of *Naomi da Costa* notes, "though she did not know it, Naomi was … ready physically and emotionally for marriage with Raphael da Costa"[264], the man she calls 'brother'.

## Notes

1  GCPPT 1|1|71  15 July 1953.
2  GCPPT 3|4 Letter from Florence Keynes to Aelfrida of 1 October 1953.
3  GCPPT 1|1|71  25 July 1953.
4  ibid. 15 July 1953.
5  ibid. 20 August 1953.
6  ibid. 15 and 16 July 1953.  It is impossible to ascertain which room Aelfrida inhabited but it may be deduced from her description of the view from its window.
7  ibid. 15 and 23 July 1953.
8  ibid. 1 August 1953.
9  ibid. 26 January and 20 February 1954.
10  ibid. 5 August 1953. Aelfrida's last recorded poem, written on 5 March 1958, is entitled *The "Handy" or "Maintenance" Man* (GCPPT 2|13).
11  ibid. 3 February and 12 May 1954.
12  ibid. 15 July and 5 August 1953.
13  GCPPT 1|1|72  17 July 1955.
14  Sister Elizabeth Noel was Sister Superior of St John's Home from 1944–1954 and 1963–1968.
15  GCPPT 1|1|71  13 November 1953. Aelfrida's personal details were copied into the Home's *Register of Admissions*. Besides her own name and date of birth and marital status ('widow') they comprise 'husband's name: Constantine Graham', 'husband's profession: 'Consular Service', 'number of children: 2', and her brothers as 'nearest relatives'. Alethea, being then of no fixed abode, had her address added later as formal next of kin.
16  GCPPT 1|1|75a. Letter from Sister Superior Winifred Marcian dated 'Nativity of the BVM [8 September 1958]'. Aelfrida, temporarily absent

from Oxford, corresponded with Sister Winifred (Sister Elizabeth's successor) between 18 August and 11 September 1958; this letter (marked 'keep') is the only one to survive.
17  GCPPT 1|1|71  23 August 1953.
18  ibid. 9 January 1954.
19  ibid. 25 July 1953 and 11 February 1954.
20  ibid. 19 July 1953 and 11 February 1954.
21  ibid. 23 July 1953.
22  ibid. 5 September 1953.
23  GCPPG A1.4|2 Letter from Aelfrida to Alethea Graham of 29 December 1958.
24  GCPPT 1|1|71 'Christmas Day' (25 December) 1953.
25  ibid. 16 July 1953.
26  ibid. 19 July 1953.
27  ibid. 23 July 5 October and 1 and 12 December 1953. Sister Catherine, born in 1909 and professed in 1951, was noted to be an excellent nurse but with "a seeming lack of joy about her" attributable, perhaps, to an unhappy childhood (Mayhew, P. pp 210–221).
28  ibid. 17 October 1953.
29  ibid. 'Shrove Tuesday' (2 March) 1954.
30  ibid. 19 July, 10 October and 12 December 1953.
31  ibid. 'All Souls' (2 November) 1953.
32  ibid. 'Christmas Day' (25 December) 1953.
33  ibid. 6 August 1953.
34  Mayhew, P. p 211 quoting John Betjeman.
35  GCPPT 1|1|71  25 July and 1 December 1953.
36  ibid. 15 August 1953.
37  ibid. 19 October 1953.
38  ibid. 'Ascension Day' (27 May) 1954.
39  GCPPT 1|1|58  18 November 1940.
40  GCPPT 1|1|71  25 July 1953.
41  ibid. 5 September 1953.
42  ibid. 18 December 1953.
43  ibid. 27 February 1954.
44  ibid. 11 and 16 February 1954.
45  ibid. 28 October 1953 and 'Palm Sunday' (10 April) 1954.
46  ibid. 'Maundy Thursday' (14 April) 1954.
47  ibid. 'Good Friday' (15 April) 1954.
48  ibid. 8 December 1953. "Gather up the fragments that are left, that nothing is lost" (*John* 6:12 KJV) is Christ's exhortation to the disciples at the feeding of the five thousand.
49  ibid. 'Ash Wednesday' (3 March) 1954.
50  ibid. 1 October 1953.
51  GCPPT 1|1|75  18 September 1958
52  GCPPT 1|1|71  1 August 1953.
53  John Hibbs personal communication 18 November 2008.
54  GCPPT 1|1|71  1 August 1953.
55  GCPPT 1|1|72 'Ash Wednesday' (23 February) 1955. GCPPT 1|1|75  19 March 1959.
56  GCPPT 1|1|71  31 July 1953.
57  GCPPT 1|1|71  15 August 1955. GCPPT 1|1|72  3 May and 30 August 1955.
58  GCPPT 1|1|71  7 September and 5 October 1953 and 2 June 1954.
59  ibid. 'Eve of St Michael and All Angels' (28 September) 1953.
60  ibid. 29 December 1953.
61  ibid. 20 and 21 December 1953.
62  ibid. 21 June 1954.
63  ibid. 23 September 1953.
64  ibid. 23 September 1953 and 4 June 1954.
65  ibid. 14 June 1954.
66  ibid. 7 July 1953.
67  ibid. 5 October 1953.
68  ibid. 25 August and 23 September 1953.
69  *CIP* 25 January 1907.

70 GCPPT 1|1|72 30 March 1954.

71 ibid. 26 October 1953. Aelfrida did not note her concern at the time; the quotation is from an updated marginal note added later.

72 ibid. 'All Souls' (2 January) and 11 November 1953.

73 ibid. 11 November 1953.

74 ibid. 21 November 1953.

75 ibid. 11, 17 and 23 November 1953.

76 ibid. 11 November and 5 December 1953. Intestinal infection with *Entamoeba histolytica* causes amoebic dysentery and increases the risk of peptic ulceration and acute or chronic gastrointestinal bleeding.

77 ibid. 14 March 1954.

78 ibid. 11 November 1954.

79 ibid. 13 November and 12 December 1953.

80 GCPPT 1|1|72 'Christmas Eve' (24 December) 1953.

81 ibid. 17 November 1953.

82 ibid. 29 December 1953.

83 ibid. 12 and 14 May 1954.

84 ibid. 21 November 1953.

85 ibid. 16 February 1954.

86 ibid. 10 February 1954.

87 ibid. 26 November 1953.

88 ibid. 28 November 1953.

89 ibid. 1 December 1953.

90 ibid. 18 December 1953.

91 ibid. 'Christmas Day' (25 December) 1953.

92 ibid. 29 January 1954.

93 ibid. 'Easter [Sunday]' (17 April) and 'Easter Monday' (18 April) 1954.

94 ibid. 23 March 1954.

95 GCPPT 1|1|74 8 May 1957.

96 GCPPT 1|1|71 3 June 1954.

97 GCPPT 1|1|61 26 March 1933.
GCPPT 1|1|71 10 February 1954.

98 GCPPT 1|1|73 8 April 1955.

99 ibid. 23 October and 22 November 1955.

100 ibid. 6 June 1956.

101 ibid. 8 January 1956.

102 ibid. 26 April 1956.

103 ibid. 8 January 1956.

104 GCPPT 1|1|73 8 January 1957.
GCPPT 1|1|74 'Ascension Day' (30 May) 1957.

105 GCPPT 1|1|72 8 October 1955.

106 GCPPT 1|1|73 6 and 10 July 1956.

107 GCPPT 1|1|74 9 and 11 January 1958.

108 ibid. 19 January 1958. The report to which Aelfrida obliquely refers was that of the Departmental Committee on Homosexual Offences and Prostitution under its chairman John Wolfenden. The Wolfenden Report, as it was known, appeared in September 1957 and recommended, *inter alia*, that homosexual behaviour between consenting adults in private be no longer considered a crime.

109 ibid. 4 February 1958.

110 GCPPT 1|1|73 14 February 1957.

111 GCPPT 1|1|74 19, 22 and 25 February 1958.

112 GCPPT 1|1|73 16 June 1956.

113 GCPPT 1|1|74 13 October 1957.

114 GCPPT 3|4 Letter from Florence Keynes to Aelfrida of 1 October 1953.

115 Julius Tillyard's 'Notes for a Family Chronicle' are preserved in GCPPT 1|1|72a and although undated must have been written sometime between July 1954 and October 1955.

116 GCPPT 1|1|50 25 May 1936.

117 Details of the *Society of Workers and Watchers* are taken from copies of *The Watchword* preserved in Aelfrida's papers in the Girton College Archive (GCPPT 2|23).

118 GCPPT 1|1|71 7 July 1953.

119 Tillyard, Ae. *The Glory of the West* p 339 (GCPPT 2|16|1 Pt2).

120 GCPPT 2|24|1 *Blessings. The First Blessing* and *The Earliest Memory of All*.

121 GCPPT 1|1|71 7 July 1953. The SWW was divided into a series of 'Watches', each bearing the name of a saint and having a chaplain and a Watch-Sister attached to it (Oswald Barkway, Bishop Barkway's eldest son, was chaplain of St Luke's Watch). Aelfrida does not state to which 'Watch' she was attached but we may deduce from a scrap of paper enclosed in *Memory Pictures* that it was St Christopher's, the Watch supporting the University Mission to Central Africa.

122 GCPPT 1|1|71 29 October and 21 November 1953.

123 GCPPT 1|1|44 21 June 1933.

124 GCPPT 1|1|74 GCPPT 1|1|74 13 October 1957 and 15 July 1958.

125 GCPPT 1|1|72 7 July 1954. The Bishop's visit occurred on 6 July, as witness his dated signature 'Lumsden Barkway, Bp.' in Aelfrida's Visitors Book.

126 GCPPT 1|1|11 30 June 1904.

127 GCPPT 1|1|75 29 October 1958. This particular *Memory Picture* was not preserved with the others.

128 GCPPT 1|1|73 8 April 1956.

129 GCPPT 2|25|3|1(2) and GCPPT 2|27|2 (4)

130 GCPPT 1|1|71 30 March and 1 April 1954.
GCPPT 2|23 *The Watchword* June 1954.

131 GCPPT 1|1|72 8 December 1954.
GCPPT 1|1|73 15 March 1956.
GCPPT 2|23 *The Watchword* December 1954.

132 GCPPT 1|1|72 17 February 1955.
GCPPT 1|1|73a Letter from Rev A Whigham Price of 16 February 1955 thanking Aelfrida for "one of the most helpful documents that has come my way". Whigham Price's monograph was presented to the PHS in October 1964.
GCPPT 2|25|2 *Mrs Lewis and Mrs Gibson: The Learned Twins.*

133 GCPPT 1|1|71 24 February 1954.

134 ibid. 10 February 1954.

135 GCPPT 2|23 *The Watchword* March 1954.

136 GCPPT 1|1|71 10 February 1954.

137 Tillyard, Ae. *Heredity* in *The Garden and the Fire* (p54), section entitled 'borderland poems'.

138 GCPPT 1|1|72 19 January 1955.

139 GCPPT 1|1|59 11 May 1941.

140 GCPPT 1|1|73 9 and 31 August 1956.
GCPPT 2|25|2 *The Strawberry Eater.*

141 GCPPT 1|1|36 5 June 1929.

142 GCPPT 2|23|2 (5).
GCPPT 2|23 *The Watchword* March 1954.

143 GCPPT 1|1|73 1 May 1956.

144 Tillyard, Ae. *The Silence of God* p34 (GCPPT 2|20).

145 There are three versions of Ellen Ison's death: GCPPT 1|1|25 (entries made between 17 May and 25 August 1920), GCPPT 2|27|1(11), and GCPPT 2|23 *The Watchword* June 1954.

146 GCPPT 2|23 in *The Watchword* June 1954.

147 GCPPT 1|1|67 11 March 1950.

148 GCPPT 1|1|25 17 May 1920.

149 GCPPT 2|23 *The Watchword* June 1954.

150 GCPPT 1|1|25 14 June 1920.

151 ibid. 15 July 1920.

152 GCPPT 2|27|1 (11).

153 GCPPT 1|1|25 25 August 1920.

154 GCPPT 1|1|71 4 February 1954.

155 GCPPT 1|1|72 13 July 1954.

156 ibid. 12 August 1954.

157 ibid. 14 September 1954.

158 ibid. 10 November 1954.

159  ibid. 12 August 1954.

160  ibid. 10 November 1954.

161  GCPPT 1|1|72  22 December 1953 and 7 and 13 January 1954.

162  ibid. 12 September 1955.
     Tillyard, Ae. *Naomi da Costa* (pp 39–43).

163  GCPPT 1|1|72  12 September 1955. John Buchan (1875–1940) was a politician, a diplomat, and a prolific author; his autobiography *Memory Hold the Door* (an appropriate title with regard to Aelfrida's own '*mémoires*') was published in 1940. It is possible that Aelfrida adopted certain literary devices from Buchan for whose books there was a vogue in the first half of the 20th century, for he, like Albert Erlande, made dramatic use of sudden, unforeseen, and coincidental reversals of fortune; her penchant for introducing traits and attributes as her plot demands without previously developing or (even hinting at) them in the character concerned owes more to Buchan. Like Buchan too, she writes grippingly and vividly of people or places with which she is familiar and unconvincingly of those with which she is not. Comparing Aelfrida's diary version of what Buchan said with the passage in *Memory Hold-the-Door* (pp 195–196) she ostensibly quotes, it is interesting to note that the latter also describes his characters as "puppets" with whom he sometimes 'plays' and states that he wrote chiefly to please himself and that even if his books remained unread he would have felt "amply repaid" by the act of creating and writing. "Puppets" is, of course, an apt description of those whom Aelfrida tried to manipulate be they characters in a book or people in real life and her sentiments with regard to the emotional rewards of creating and writing also echo Buchan's.

164  GCPPT 1|1|74  29 August 1957. *The Called and the Chosen*, ostensibly the diary account of the life in a French enclosed order of a Sister Ursula Auberon, was published in 1957, the same year as Aelfrida's critique of its author.

165  Tillyard, Ae. *Naomi da Costa* p 1.

166  ibid. p 234.

167  ibid. p 174.

168  ibid. pp 3 and 129.

169  ibid. p 166.

170  In *Evening-Silence – A Shaded Lamp,* written at Le Vésinet on 28 November 1913 (*The Garden and the Fire* pp 64–65) ,she asks "How shall my wandering wishes dare | To find your house …"

171  Tillyard, Ae. *Naomi da Costa* pp 121–126.

172  Tillyard, Ae. *Naomi da Costa* pp 117–125 and 174.

173  ibid. p 15.

174  'Naomi's' sisters (Susan, Rachel, Rebecca, Esther, Ruth and Deborah) have two things in common; they are all Old Testament characters and their lives or personalities reflect Aelfrida's in some way. (Two of them, Esther and Ruth, also give their names to biographical books of the Bible.) Sarah removes herself "out of her country and from [her] kindred and [her] father's house" to a place shown her by God, pretends at one point to be her husband's sister, and deals "hardly" with a servant (*Genesis* 12 1 and 13, 16:6); Rachel is "well favoured", has a husband who labours several years before able to marry her and, thinking her children dead, makes "lamentation and bitter weeping" and refuses to be comforted (*Genesis* 28:17, *Jeremiah* 31:15); Rebecca, leaving home to marry, is assured by her family that in their hearts she is always "our sister" (*Genesis* 24:60); Esther, who has "neither father nor mother", marries the Persian king as a Jewess incognito and by bravely revealing herself, is able to plead the cause of her calumnied people so effectively that they achieve "joy and honour" (*Esther* 2:7 and 8:16); Deborah is a married "prophetess" and judge (*Judges* 4:4).

175  Tillyard, Ae. *Naomi da Costa* pp 134 and 136.

176  ibid. p 96.

177  ibid. pp 136 and 147–149.

178  ibid. p 175.

179  ibid. p 209.

180  ibid. p 107.

181  GCPPT 1|1|55  8 and 14 August 1938.

182  GCPPT 1|1|69  27 March 1952.

183  GCPPT 1|1|69  30 March 1952.
     GCPPT 1|1|55  21 August 1938. The original version of a Good Friday prayer with which Aelfrida must have been both familiar and aware of the significance of its repetition on that particular day, begs God to illuminate the Jews so that in acknowledging Christ they are delivered from spiritual darkness.

184  Tillyard, Ae. *Just Alice* pp 275–276 (GCPPT 2|19).

185  GCPPT 1|1|61  12 March 1943.

186  Tillyard, Ae. *The Silence of God* p13 (GCPPT 2|20).

187  GCPPT 1|1|70  19 January 1953.

188  Tillyard, Ae. *The Silence of God* pp 9–10.

189  ibid p 13.

190  Tillyard, Ae. *Naomi da Costa* p 1.

191  ibid. p 8.

192  ibid. p 209.

193  ibid. p 143.

194  ibid. p 16.

195  ibid. pp 25–26.

196  ibid. p 239.

197  ibid. p 225.

198  ibid. p 229.

199  ibid. p 209.

200  ibid. p 118.

201  ibid. pp 175–177.

202  *Matthew* 13:54–57 (KJV).

203  ibid.

204  As usual Aelfrida misquotes, substituting "ride, ride, ride, forever ride" (*Naomi da Costa* p 139) for Browning's "ride, ride together, forever ride" and it is probably to Browning's reference to "heaven … fair and strong" in the last verse of the poem that she wishes to draw our attention; in this context, however, Browning's first verse is more relevant: "since now at length my fate I know / Since nothing all my love avails / Since all my life seemed meant for, fails …"

205  Tillyard, Ae. *Naomi da Costa* p 235.

206  ibid. p 99.

207  ibid. pp 243–244.

208  ibid. p 247.

209  GCPPT 1|1|52  24 November 1936.

210  Tillyard, Ae. *Naomi da Costa* pp 219–223.

211  GCPPT 2|24|2(15).

212  GCPPT 1|1|40  16 and 25 October 1932.
     GCPPT 1|1|54  2 February 1938.
     GCPPT 1|1|61  20 November 1943.

213  Tillyard. Ae. *The Silence of God*. pp 26–27.

214  Frost, B. *The Love of God* p 197.

215  GCPPT 1|1|22  14 December 1917.
     GCPPT 1|1|22a contains a newspaper cutting describing the event. Tillyard, Ae. *Can I be a Mystic?* p 92.

216  GCPPT 1|1|66  17 May 1948 and 17 February 1949.

217  GCPPT 1|1|63  1 and 4 May 1946. As her diary shows (GCPPT 1|1|62  February 1945) Aelfrida tried to be impartial by reading Lawrence Browne's book *The Prospect of Islam*.

218  ibid. 29 August 1949.

219  GCPPT 1|1|66  11 August 1949.
     GCPPT 1|1|66a contains a newspaper cutting describing the discovery.

220  In 1952, for example, Aelfrida was reading a Jewish prayer book lent to her by Alethea and copying out articles of the Jewish faith (GCPPT 1|1|69  27 and 30 March 1952) and may even have bought a second-hand edition of *The Jewish Encyclopaedia* to assist her research (*Naomi da Costa* p 111); a year later she read *The Pillar of Fire,*

published in 1951, the autobiography of German Jew Karl Stern who 'after many vicissitudes [found] "more than all" in Christ' by becoming a Catholic (GCPPT 1|1|70 15 March 1953) and while working on *Naomi da Costa* read and refers to (p241) the current volume of the yearbook *Contemporary Jewry* in which, in 'one ghastly chapter' she discovered the methods used by Hitler to exterminate six million Jews ('and these were God's chosen people!' she exclaims in horror), 'methods which only Satan himself could have suggested' (GCPPT 1|1|72 14 September 1954). Worth noting too is that in 1944 she held a novena for Jews with 'much to endure' and (like herself) called to 'the fellowship of the Messiah's suffering' and used Jewish meditations during the 'silent minute' of remembrance announced by the striking of Big Ben which preceded the 9pm news on the radio.

221 Tillyard, Ae. *Naomi da Costa* pp 60–62.

222 ibid. pp 8 and 27.

223 GCPPT 1|1|52 17 March 1937.
GCPPT 1|1|55 14 August 1932.
GCPPT 1|1|59 13 March 1942.

224 GCPPT 1|1|64 21 June 1946.

225 GCPPT 2|26|3 *The Schechters,* Aelfrida's *mémoire* of Ruth Schechter was written shortly after *Naomi da Costa* was begun.

226 GCPPT 1|1|59 13 March 1942.

227 ibid.

228 GCPPT 2|26|3 *The Schechters.* Aelfrida, so she says, invited Ruth to visit Tymawr but Ruth "refused to come" on the grounds that "she had very clear and sweet memories of Frida Tillyard which she did not wish disturbed".

229 GCPPT 1|1|59 13 March 1942.

230 Tillyard, Ae. *Naomi da Costa* p 93.

231 GCPPT 2|26|3 *The Schechters.*

232 Tillyard, Ae. *Naomi da Costa* pp 30 and 234.

233 GCPPT1|1|63 22 July and 8 and 14 September 1945 and 26 March 1946.

234 GCPPT 1|1|74 26 December 1957.
GCPPT 1|1|75a Letter from 'Gabriel Anne SSC' to 'Sister Placida' of 'Trinity XXV' 1958; the letter is referred to by its recipient on 11 March 1959 (GCPPT 1|1|75).

235 GCPPT 1|1|63 26 March 1949.

236 GCPPT 1|1|74a Letter from 'Gabriel SSC' to 'Sister Placida' of 'Advent III' 1957. *The Schechters* was written in October 1957 and it may be that it is to a copy sent her by Aelfrida that Sister Gabriel Anne refers.

237 GCPPT 1|1|75a Letter from 'Gabriel SSC' to 'Sister Placida' of 'Trinity XXV' 1958.

238 GCPPT 1|1|13 12 July 1906.
GCPPT 1|1|74 4 October 1957

239 GCPPT 1|1|74 4 October 1957. That Aelfrida intended to write a 'memory picture' of Norman Bentwich is shown by a reference at the end of *The Schechters* to her next 'picture' as retailing "the story of a faithful Jew" in relation to the rebirth of Israel, but of her 'picture' only a sheet of paper headed *Norman Bentwich* survives (GCPPT 2|26|3).

240 GCPPT 1|1|64 24 July 1946.

241 Tillyard, Ae. *Naomi da Costa.* pp 205 and 215.

242 ibid. pp 229, 233 and 234.

243 ibid. pp 229 and 261.

244 ibid. pp 243–244.

245 ibid. pp 231 and 247.

246 ibid. p 261.

247 ibid. pp 261 and 267.

248 GCPPT 1|1|64 12 August 1946.

249 The eponymous novel by Leon Uris (1924–2003) describing the event was published in 1958 so cannot have been plagiarised by Aelfrida nor can Uris have known of *Naomi da Costa* for it was never published.

250 Tillyard, Ae. *Naomi da Costa* p 249.

251 ibid. pp 222–223 and 247.

252 GCPPT1|1|75 30 August 1958. Of the "holy angels" numbered by Raphael in *The Book of Tobit* (12:15) the names of four – Raphael himself, Uriel, Gabriel, and Michael – are the most generally agreed on; Aelfrida's choice of Raphael is obvious but Uriel ('my light is God') whose mission is to answer questions, Gabriel ('man of God'), herald of good things and charged with administering comfort to mankind, and Michael ('who is like God?') who wars against Satan and his forces and who has the Israelite nation as his special charge, seem appropriate in various ways.

253 SSC *Prayers for Travellers.*

254 GCPPT 1|1|74 3 March 1958.

255 GCPPT 1|1|75 29 July 1958.

256 *The Book of Ruth* 1:20 and 21. (KJV).

257 GCPPT 1|1|74a. Letter from 'Jeanne SSC' to 'my dear Sister Placida' of 22 June 1958.

258 Tillyard, Ae. *Naomi da Costa* p 268.

259 GCPPT 1|1|58 2 November 1940. Knowing Aelfrida's propensity for plagiarism it is amusing to note the similarity between her description and that given by Susanna Venn in *Some Married Fellows* (vol 2 p295) in which a character expires as a result of a chemical explosion in "a glorious mass of coloured flames". A comparison with Venn's elevated (visionary, almost) style in describing the incident is also interesting.

260 Tillyard, A. *Naomi da Costa* p 269.

261 ibid.

262 Ruth's declaration to Naomi appears in *The Book of Ruth* 1: 16–17.

263 Teresa of Avila. *The Interior Castle* pp 269–270.

264 Tillyard, Ae. *Naomi da Costa.* p 229.

# The Way We Grow Old

The former title of *The Way We Grow Up, The Way We Grow Old,* though appropriate insofar as immature personalities matured, was inappropriate insofar as the novel ended while its characters were still young, but as the title of a chapter dealing with aspects of Aelfrida's life from age sixty-nine to within a year or two of her death and with the period of which she had wondered 'whether I shall ever be an old woman living alone and whether I shall have the grace to bear it'[1], it is apt. (She leaves unclear whether age or solitude are the 'it' to which she refers.) But the sketch she prospectively draws of herself as an old lady sitting alone 'with her memories in the firelight'[2] or the poetic portrait she paints in *Old Age. A Mood Picture* of her aged self crouched over "flames as cold as firelight in a dream" watching "the years march past to die" as she muses on Time's slowness and on how "weary is the lifelong road to death"[3], though a seemingly accurate picture of one crouched in a deck chair by a gas fire in an attic room bearing the melancholy name GETHSEMANE, emerging only for meals, Mass, and confession or to venture away from Oxford once a year, and rarely visiting or visited (unless in spirit) by those limned in 'memory pictures', is inaccurate. Diary entries and her Visitors Book show that from July 1953 until almost the end of her life, Aelfrida's life was more sociable than her Cambridge years as a 'Universal Aunt'.

Noting shortly after arrival that such ladies – or, rather, 'Ladies'; two years later there were still 'residents whom I hardly know'[4], not because the Home was so large that she could not hope to know them all but because some were not 'ladies' and not 'known' socially – as she had already met were very kind to her and that several had Cambridge connections, she also noted her reciprocal interest in 'Inmate-patients'. Exploring 'as delicately as may be their varied personalities', she bought a notebook in which to inscribe names and 'information about each one' as she garnered it.[5] To her diary she confided 'pages about the ladies here'[6] (more than about Alethea or, with one exception, anyone else), describing their kindnesses when she was unwell and their confidences about the Home, their own lives, and each other's. A year later (she thought it 'strange' that it should have been one of the happiest years of her life but failed to note that happiness flowed in great measure 'from the

---

51

OLD AGE. A MOOD-PICTURE.

"The fire burns low. How chill the embers
    seem !
The flames are cold as firelight in a dream,
Woven of wind as phantom fires at sea.
I think the evening falls.   The nights drag long
And echo through the days ; beat out a song
From which my shuffling senses may not flee.
I cannot flee my thoughts, nor bid them go.
Some day I shall be old, but Time is slow,
And weary is the lifelong road to Death.
God set Death's city on a far-off hill,
Its golden portals made of human ill
And, for its keys, doth still demand our breath.
I have been young.   But, when the sun is high,
I only see the years march past to die.
But now the night sets free the prisoned past.
Did some one speak ?—Mother !—I'll say my
    prayer—
I thought I heard—No ! there was no one there.
The silence speaks.   When all are dead at last
How full of voices will these regions be,
And all speech meet as waves are fused at sea.
Death once seemed night, but now I see it day.
Daybreak or rest !   Answer to all its cries
Or all-blest nothing, for the soul that dies.
Dawn !  Dawn !  How night-time lingers on her
    way ! "

*Brookline, Mass., May 23rd, 1908.*

F

*Old Age. A Mood Picture* (*To Malise* 1910)

kindness and goodwill of *many* new friends')[7] she noted that if she detailed everything, she could fill the current volume of her diary 'in a week'[8] with accounts of 'little events and contacts with Dear People'.[9] The same 'dear people' wrote 'most animated'[10] letters to her during her absences and provided 'a real homecoming'[11] of kisses and greetings and interest in what she had been doing when she returned; they also made much of her when she attended the Home's garden fetes, bring and buy sales and ("I really have always loved parties")[12] Easter and Christmas festivities. And it was at Christmas 1956 that she wrote that not only had she enjoyed 'the *best* Advent' ever because of its being 'the most lived in the supernatural', but also that in coming to St John's Home, an institution in which she had not expected to find 'human consolations', she had discovered 'reservoirs of sweetness' and 'treasur[ies] of goodwill'.[13]

So instead of decrying 'human consolations', she sought them out and instead of shunning society for Silence and Solitude, she socialised. (A comment that she rarely enjoyed 'more than an hour's talking' a day and this chiefly at mealtimes must not be taken literally, for many pages of volumes written at St John's Home are packed with details of 'happenings too long to relate' and with descriptions of 'pleasant and happifying' interactions with 'dear people here', none of which could have lasted only the duration of an 'extra word or two a day'; an entry recording her having been 'almost *too* sociable' provides a more accurate account.)[14] Calls formal and informal made around the Home occupied several hours; in return she extended invitations to individual 'Ladies' to take morning coffee or afternoon tea, the latter an occasion for which her 'loquacious and responsive visitors' (she had not lost the knack of drawing people out) dressed formally and during which she herself acted the part of gracious hostess, being 'as charming as I know how' over fruit and cake. Shorter calls were no more than droppings-in: to proffer remedies to the unwell, to borrow or return a book, to read a 'Memory Picture' aloud, or to extend a friendly welcome to newcomers perceived to be as 'lonely and *émotionée*'[15] as she herself had been.

The 'Ladies' of St John's Home with whom Aelfrida deigned to mingle were, she decided, 'real gentlefolk … typically English "old school"'[16]: 'the perfect colonel's widow, dignified, devout, *genuine*'[17]; a former nun forced to leave her community when it disbanded after the Reverend Mother's death; a retired Church Missionary Society doctor with whom she discussed the Baha'i faith; a water-colourist whose commissions included 'gardens of the great'[18]; a former private secretary to author/cleric RH Benson. (The daughter of a Church of England vicar whose belief that Reservation of the Sacrament in the Home's chapel was 'little short of idolatry'[19] provided amusing 'copy' for one of her vignettes.) On a slightly lower but still acceptable social level were teachers (of particular interest was a one described by Aelfrida as brilliant but erratic and as a psychic who recognised herself as another such, something which reminded her of 'the danger of evil spirits creeping into mediums' … minds'[20] as, it seems, they had into hers), missionaries, nurses, and moral welfare workers. With all 'Ladies' she enjoyed 'really interesting and varied talk' almost 'Cambridge' in intellectuality and rarely enjoyed by her, except in Cambridge, since leaving Cambridge for Oxford in 1934, and ranging from 'literary and religious

matters' to semantics and 'Scientific Determinism'; its 'really interesting' element, however, stemmed from Home gossip about which Aelfrida was extremely well informed ('the only thing which [makes] gossip palatable is an intimate knowledge of the people or persons concerned')[21] even as she professed not to want to hear it. It therefore seemed appropriate to waken on her seventy-first birthday to the sound of 'the Voices' singing the hymn "How bright these glorious spirits shine" (their last visit, as it happened, and to a tune she failed to recognise), words expressive of sentiments appropriate to one who now hoped to be filled 'with praise of God and love of [her] neighbour'.[22]

Within months of arriving on the Green Corridor, therefore, Aelfrida had established another niche for herself. She had formed a friendship with her next door neighbour Juliana Clark, a lady a year or two older than herself and acquainted with Cambridge though not so intimately as to be aware of Mrs Graham's unfortunate past, and the ENGAGED sign on her door prevented unwanted visitors and encouraged her neighbours to turn their wirelesses down (all possessed one except save herself though she was not above listening to someone else's) and to lower their voices as they walked past lest they disturb her prayers and writing. She had also accustomed the 'Ladies' to the quirks of her Rule: silent Fridays, dry bread only for breakfast on Ash Wednesday ('it reminded me of the spiritual savour [of] my fast-meals at St Benedict's, Osney Lane')[23], no calls paid or received during Lent and Advent (she paid 'pre-Lent calls' to particular friends, 'cut out visitors and Sunday chats' during Advent, and began socialising again on Easter Monday and Christmas Day)[24], and an unusual holiday: a fortnight's stay at the Society of the Holy and Undivided Trinity[25] convent instead of a summer vacation. 'I shall not be going to Cambridge this year', noted miffed Aelfrida in 1955, Mina having filled Wetenhall Cottage with language pupils, '[though] it *was* part of the bargain that if I let them have the house for £120 I should be able to have a holiday there'. Deciding that 'there must on no account be Family Rows among the Tillyards!'[26], she decamped to South Leigh instead, to spend half her stay in formal retreat '*silent through and through*' and interrupted only by a vision of angels placing and lighting 'spiritual candles to burn to the glory of God' in 'my Lord's wounds burning … in my hands and feet'.[27]

The experience was not recounted to the 'warm-hearted ladies' who greeted her on her return (they remained unconvinced that Aelfrida's kind of holiday would suit *them*)[28], she having now she no desire to share such experiences with anyone (not even her confessor) save her diary and future biographer, a wise precaution because some 'ladies' were known to be rather 'odd'[29] (one had heard the walls shouting 'Mrs Graham') and if their behaviour became too 'odd', they were removed to 'the "confused minds" department' of the local geriatric hospital 'with no assurance of return'.[30] In fact, she was reluctant to talk about herself at all and beyond imparting 'the kind of information about where I have lived etc. to which everyone is welcome', seems to have played down her 'consular' connections so effectively in a milieu where such matters could be checked by 'dear ladies' with access to pertinent information that some 'ladies' found her difficult to 'place' socially. (Luckily, they soon found room for her among 'nice people'.)[31] To others she remained a mystery: an 'astonishingly inquisitive … spinster of means and leisure' who had visited Tymawr twice and had actually sat in chapel behind Sister Placida had difficulty in identifying 'loquacious Mrs Graham' with a silent resident tertiary and was provided with no help at all in reconciling the two by the woman who was both, but a new resident who had visited Tymawr and recalled the name 'Sister Placida' but could not connect her with 'Mrs Graham' of St John's Home was befriended, and a lady who radiated 'spiritual understanding' but had no connection with the SSC was allowed to read two of her homiletic books in order to come to know her 'that way' – but only 'that way'.[32]

Loquacious Mrs Graham was not, however, universally popular: an attempt to impose silence on the dinner table following the death of the Home's oldest inmate was countered by a spirited discussion on winter hats[33] and a perceptive lady (disparaged as 'poor Miss Camp') whose views resembled those of the Archbishop of Capetown with respect to Tillyards, declared that Aelfrida 'terrified'[34] her (though not why), something which may explain the falling-away of former 'dear ladies' as her stay progressed.

Her next move with regard to her St John's 'niche', a niche described in terms of having her 'physical and intellectual needs … met' and of having made 'many new friends'[35], was to progress from 'a kind of Cambridge afterglow of sociability'[36] to acting as the Home's 'Little Providence'. In order, however, to win the hearts and minds of those to whose company she had relegated herself, she had not only to abandon hopes of living as alone and silent as she wished but also to embark on a deliberate campaign to win them over, for only in this way could she ensure the best possible niche for one whose pillar of fire and cloud had finally stopped moving and whose increasing frailty might lead to reliance on others for support.

She therefore visited the sick (sick people, she noted, 'cling to me and like to have me near')[37] until her own ill health rendered her unable to continue. She was also supportive to those near or fearing death – having been 'very near death more than once'[38] herself, she was qualified to speak on the subject – and to those whose confusional states caused them to wander around or even out of the Home, guiding them to a place of safety before alerting a nurse to their whereabouts and (as with Mrs Donkin at Tymawr) trying to substitute 'happy associations for unhappy ones'[39] in order to calm their distressed confusion. (Attempted suicides were not unknown at the Home.) She successfully renewed an interest in life in institutionalised 'Inmate-Patients' liable to stare vacantly when un-stimulated but sparked into 'lively and responsive'[40] animation when given one-to-one attention. Solitary old ladies were provided with 'strong medicine'[41], sweetened by a hug and a kiss, in the form of a lecture on the perils of self-imposed isolation (she knew whereof she spoke) and told to visit her at any time if they felt overwhelmed by loneliness; unpopular ladies like the Home's 'rather weepy … sympathy-addict'[42] were invited to tea and 'straightened' with pious exhortation as only Aelfrida knew how. (Worth noting in passing is that she regarded herself as '*loving*' people as a 'reflection of Our Lord in me, loving them' at the same time as Alethea lay in 'ex-Fordfield' unvisited by a mother too busy loving other people to visit a daughter who had recently endured a 'severe haematomesis'.) And to those whose natal language was not English, she spoke or read Italian and German, writing of one that on hearing her native tongue again she lifted her head 'as a dog might do when it heard its master speak after a long absence'[43] and of others (e.g. foreign helpers in the Home whom she assisted with translations and essays set by their language schools) that she revelled in 'the joy of doing kindnesses'.[44]

She also acted as peacemaker, quelling noisy arguments with the command "whatever you have to say … say it quietly"[45], salting her comments with humour (concerning a 'first class fuss' which erupted in the Home 'over a naughty book that had got into the library!!' she compared the affair to 'a TS Eliot play in his latest style'[46] – *The Confidential Clerk,* perhaps, given her role at St John's Home, though *The Elder Statesman* seems equally appropriate), refusing to take sides when petty annoyances of life lived in proximity to those '[one] wouldn't have *chosen* as friends'[47] caused even 'Ladies' to lose their tempers ('who's been saying what to whom!?'[48] she noted with wry amusement), mediating by means of the written and spoken word and by suggesting practical remedies when 'tale-bearing, tiffs and huffs' (or 'the devil stirring up strife')[49] broke out into open warfare and 'the battle of the Green Corridor'[50] (a regular occurrence) raged. And with monies accruing from staged compulsory purchases of inherited Cambridge properties and from the sale of inherited shares in recently dissolved companies, she played Lady Bountiful to Juliana Clark (now nicknamed 'Princess Juliana' with reference to the mysterious 'Mlle J' of *Modern Mystics* and *Spiritual Exercises*) whom she treated to 'sumptuous'[51] teas, and to other 'Ladies', providing taxis to polling stations, to church, and even to places beyond Oxford. It also seems she did not stint herself, for we hear no more of shabby clothes and from diary hints may deduce that train journeys between Oxford and Cambridge were made in First Class carriages, ostensibly because this freed a seat in third class for someone poorer than herself.

She also gave three talks to a local Methodist Women's Meeting organised by Juliana Clark's niece. The first, in May 1956, was on the significance (an expurgated version, one suspects) of early memories 'for after life and experience' (by 'after life' Aelfrida presumably meant later life), the talk being illustrated by quotations from two *Memory Pictures*, probably *The First Blessing* in which she equates the Aurora Borealis seen by her as a small child with flashes of fire from the flaming sword wielded by the angel guarding Paradise after the expulsion of Adam and Eve, and *Conrad Francis*, the "angel child" called home by God when she and Julius were "not quite five and ... not quite seven respectively".[52] (During the lecture she sudden perceived 'Our Lord ... *really* present ... in our midst', '"saw" on [her own] head the fire of Pentecost', spoke with eloquence as never before, and realised from the 'awestruck faces' of her audience that they had listened to 'something unique'.)[53] Given that Aelfrida's relationship with Deity was no longer spiritually overwhelming and full of dread (and that visionary experiences diminished as she settled into her new 'niche') the second, of 21 May 1957 and entitled *Belonging to God,* was an altogether quieter occasion for lecturer and audience. The third, on the Devil, will be described later.

This sudden "shifting of [her] emotional centre" to encompass "an increase of tenderness for [her] fellow-creatures"[54] echoes an increase demonstrated in adolescence but derided by her father as pose ('Little Providence'), derision the more surprising given that practical piety in the form of 'good works' was an important aspect of his religion, but given too that much of Aelfrida's life was, as she admitted in Florence, 'emotional pose' or involved a tendency to 'play' at being religious, possibly a perspicacious comment. (Being 'Little Providence' at Tymawr had been discouraged by Mother Guenvrede for reasons known only to herself and at Lolworth was misinterpreted as interference.) Why it should happen at a point in her life when age and infirmity might have encouraged withdrawal from

society and increased her antipathy towards those for whose intellectual, moral, and physical frailties she felt little sympathy, she does not say. It is also unexpected given that self-centredness, one of Aelfrida's dominant traits, tends to increase rather than decrease with age and infirmity (as she herself noted, it was 'sad ... that one's love of comfort, one's silly little vanities and [one's] pathetic cravings ... should still be so strong')[55] and that at a point when an elderly infirm lady might decide to pass her time 'hid with Christ in God' instead of, as formerly, trying to impress others with her piety or edify them by her example (though both undoubtedly continued to play an important part in her 'tenderness') or 'straighten' them into the strait-jacket of her own mystical religiosity, she suddenly began to demonstrate *caritas* in terms of the spoken word and helpful gesture.

There were, however, problems inherent in interacting with and bestowing *caritas* on the inhabitants of the Home over which Aelfrida – and in terms of solitude and silence, 'absurdly' – 'spread quasi-maternal wings'.[56] For one thing, such behaviour directly contravened Father Cary's advice *'not to get tangled up with people'*.[57] His advice had been given with specific reference to Alethea, but because Aelfrida had had to bestow 'full independence' on her daughter to the extent of not daring to ask if the latter underwent the same experiences 'transparent of eternity' as she walked walks undertaken by her mother 'in the days of [her] residence at St Benedict's'[58], she now felt compelled to spread her wings over others instead, giving as her excuse 'they seem to need help'.[59] (This begs the question: who benefited most from Aelfrida's demonstrations of *caritas*, herself or 'Inmate-Patients'? Both, perhaps.) For another – and quite how 'expected-unexpected' this was, Aelfrida does not say – aspects of her behaviour attracted attention in what she described as an unwelcome manner. Juliana Clark's murmur apropos Aelfrida being served after the 'meat-eaters' at meals (the latter said 'airily' she did not mind) that when she (Juliana) read the words "clothed in humility" she thought of Aelfrida because the latter was 'so humble', elicited from 'humble' Mrs Graham a diarised hint that she was flattered at being compared to Dante's Beatrice *"benignamente d'umiltà vestita"* and the comment that, far from being clothed in humility, she was far removed from 'true humility' and that even when she fought against her 'greatest temptation', namely her instinctive desire to think well of herself, the victory was 'only partial and never more than temporary'.[60] Worse, however, was another 'Inmate-Patient's' statement that she had never met anyone who lived 'as close to God', a statement refuted by Aelfrida as 'normal Christian behaviour'[61], albeit with a diary rider that none of her qualities – she lists 'cleverness, charm, [and] power of affection' – was worth anything unless sanctified by Deity and that in this respect Deity should continue to remind her 'of all [she] had better not remember!!!'[62] (A reminder to herself that she *must* become '*wholly sanctified*' because this and only this was 'the way to perfect peace' included an escape clause: complete 'sanctification' was impossible because it depended on '*adequate* repentance' and hers 'so far' had 'never been *adequate*. Alethea has been to a Missionary Garden Party at Lambeth Palace'.)[63] So to a lady who demanded "*why* aren't you a saint?", she could only reply 'vaguely and feebly'[64], for no-one knew as well as she why not: because she revelled in 'admiration and affection' extended by 'dear people' at St John's Home[65] (whether dear because they extended it or intrinsically dear, she does not say); because given that she lived in God and God (she believed) in her, 'why, why, *why* [was she] not a better woman?'[66] (Gloomy meditations on her profound dissatisfaction with her disgraceful lack of goodness follow, together with a description of the Bishop of Ely as a *true* saint, though gloom may owe more to her thoughts wandering off to 'sad things' as the result of a recent bout of 'gastric flu'[67] than to actual dissatisfaction with her spiritual state, for a rapid resumption of interest in matters other than her own soul follows immediately.) Third, because her greatest fault was still 'to have *self* as a point of reference when it ought to be God'; as an afterthought she adds that she was 'often in danger of spiritual pride'[68] as well. Fourth, because William Gladstone's phrase "a Good Woman in the worst sense of the word!!!"[69] quoted by herself with reference to someone else fitted – as she doubtless realised – her own case exactly.

Having discussed *how* Aelfrida demonstrated *caritas* to the 'Inmate-Patients' of St John's Home we now need to ask *why*. As already noted and as she herself partly realised, she had both spiritual and emotional reasons for behaving as she did. In a revealing diary entry made in August 1941 with reference to visitors to Tymawr, she wrote that she felt obliged to 'widen the circle of [her] love' because, lacking children and grandchildren on whom to lavish 'maternal affection', she instinctively assumed the role of 'Little Providence' towards available substitutes. The role involved writing little notes and giving little presents to the well and offering 'remedies ... flowers, [and] delicacies etc. etc.' to the unwell though as one dedicated to Silence and Solitude she should have simply commended them to God or attempts to 'enlighten' individuals in terms of her own beliefs when she should have allowed them to make spiritual discoveries for themselves, and continued to be played even when she realised that it drew unnecessary attention to herself, was a way of capturing affection she 'ought not to have' either

because she did not desire it or because it pandered to selfish emotional needs and in terms of her Rule was 'contrary to the spirit of [her] vocation'. Nor could she excuse her behaviour by saying it was '*really* necessary'[70]: Sister Monica was available to medicate and to nurse the sick, flowers from the convent garden could be picked by anyone, Mother Guenvrede provided spiritual counsel, and affection should be reserved for God. So too at St John's Home where 'everything necessary was already provided'[71]: medical and nursing care, a pleasant garden, and spiritual comfort and counsel. When, therefore, we ask in her own words 'why, why, *why*' she felt impelled to demonstrate *caritas* at St John's Home, we discover (eventually, because her diary hints at other possible reasons, all of which have some bearing on her *real* reason) a reason improbable in the context of her present life but obvious when discussed in terms of her life as whole.

Her first possible reason stems from a wish to engage in what Savinien Louismet called "Saintly Action".[72] 'Saintly Action', as extrapolated by Aelfrida from his text, is activity undertaken by "Christian Mystics" who "have come down from the heights of spiritual communion" (in Louismet's words, "Divine Contemplation") "to preach the good news that human and divine can meet, ... to tend the sick, to care for the poor and to engage in the simplest and humblest of everyday tasks".[73] As examples of 'Christian Mystics' who demonstrated 'Saintly Action', she names Stephen Grellet, practitioner of Quakerly 'good works', Teresa of Avila, practical Mother Superior as well as ecstatic mystic, and Francis de Sales whose *Introduction à la Vie Dévote* (so much to be preferred in French) suggested that the *vie dévote* should include watching over the poor, visiting the sick – not an exercise lightly undertaken in days when infectious diseases were rife and modes of infection poorly understood – and caring for one's own family, and that it was not so much cleanliness which was next to godliness, as charity.

Aelfrida's discovery of 'Saintly Action' was not a new one. Not only had she read the writings and studied the lives of the mystics she quotes (perhaps even more relevant in the present context is that she obviously identified with St Francis de Sales' widowed disciple Jeanne de Chantal, a lady initially devoted to raising her children but whose later vocation and that of the Order of the Visitation founded by her on Salesian principles was to create an organisation under the auspices of which she herself and other women whose health, age, or circumstances made life in religion unsuitable could perform works of charity) but more recent writers on the subject also. Rendel Harris, for example, regarded God's "Guiding Hand" as both mediating and mediated in everyday life by those who have hitherto held themselves spiritually aloof, they having realised that in terms of a loved and loving Deity "all live in the same street … within arm's length and heart-reach"[74], and Evelyn Underhill reminded mystics that there was an "abundance of practical work" for them to do in the world, work "which [was] the direct outcome of their mystical experience" and through which and with the help of God-inspired "holy creative energy", they would "mend where they find things broken [and] make where [they] find the need", actualising within the trivialities of "the world of time and space" and its meanness and squalor, "mercy, order, beauty [and] significance".[75] Furthermore Harris's and Underhill's exemplars include (besides Grellet and St Teresa) St Francis of Assisi, St Catherine of Siena, Florence Nightingale, and Octavia Hill, and both emphasise in different ways that Mysticism can – indeed *should* – be an inclusive as well as an exclusive activity, Harris in terms of mystics possessing "a birthright of guidance" as men and women elected by God to be both directly guided and sent out into the world by Him to guide others as living pillars of fire and cloud[76], Underhill in terms of a mystic being required to become "a living, ardent tool" in God's hand through the workings of which He becomes manifest as a "concrete expression" of "Transcendent Love".[77] And Aelfrida herself had stated that "ecstasies and raptures which end in mere dreaming" were "of no value in the Christian life"[78] as it *should* be lived, i.e. with ministry and ministration taking priority over aloneness with the Alone even in a life inspirited by mystic communion with Deity. But knowing her tendency to ape the lifestyle of admired mystics as if by doing so she might inherit something of their charisma (mimesis, she failed to realise, does not automatically confer charisma on the mimetic), one may justifiably ask, is she not also doing the same here?

Given, however, the length of time taken to put 'Saintly Action' into practice, we must next ask why it had taken her so long? Had she not been urged to practise it by Bishop Wynn and Father Dunkin in terms of 'acts of service' to others and even by contemplative Lucius Cary who had reminded her before she left Tymawr that important in "true religion" was "execution of Christ's second commandment" to love one's neighbour as oneself in an "essentially social"[79] manner? Indeed, as she herself noted in *Christian Old Age* (seen in this light, a manifesto of what she hoped to practice when circumstances were favourable), "we cannot worship God … without benefiting our neighbour" by means of an expansion of "good will" over one's "fellow men", expansion made easier by the fact that in old age "our interest in ourselves is dying down".[80] Or so she liked to think.

Possibly she did not do so until 1954 because it only became obvious to her then that having hitherto been or posed as a mystic given to "lonely raptures" and dedicated to "solitude and contemplation", she should now cease to "stand aloof" from her fellow-men lest she be regarded as "a mystic who had never reached maturity" because instead of passing through all the recognised stages of the mystic life (sudden or gradual awakening to God, purification by privation, enlightened vision, and so on), she had failed to achieve the last and most important stage: a desire to "serve humanity". And who, because of this, would remain "a child of God who had failed to grow up".[81] And only she, well-versed in the 'New Psychology' she affected to abhor, could say how true her comment was of herself, a child fixated in childhood by a single traumatic event and unable to move on until enabled to do so by another such 'child', similarly fixated but more insightful, namely Julius. And how better to disguise her explanation or express it in religious terms than by making it appear to apply to all mystics, not solely to herself as a 'child' who had only now begun to 'grow up'.

Perhaps she now had 'more' (i.e. sufficient) 'Christian experience'[82] and felt herself better equipped than hitherto for 'saintly action'; perhaps she had reached the point on her 'mystic way' at which she felt better equipped, psychologically speaking, to re-engage with a world from which she fled. Perhaps at St John's Home she was under no compulsion to engage herself with 'the world' unless she wished (or was at liberty to engage with only a small, sympathetic, and socially-acceptable part of it) and that it was this freedom to take up 'practical religious or philanthropic work' of a rewarding nature which allowed her to do so, work, moreover, which did not involve domestic chores which made her 'weary and heartsick' when forced to perform them, which was not 'spendthrift of [her] poor store of energy', and which could be accomplished with a clear conscience because both her daughters were now 'settled'.[83] (Though perhaps not quite as anticipated, one being in a white coffin in a Cambridge cemetery, the other in a 'poky' flat in Oxford.) Work, in fact, in which she could serve God in service to her fellow men in the manner prescribed for 'Audrey Talbot', 'Noel Ashton', and 'Silvia Barrington'.

Her second reason can be read as the development of ideas mooted when planning *The Glory of the West* ten years earlier: of 'Old Age as an antechamber to Heaven'[84] and as the means of fulfilling a cherished hope to found a 'House of Prayer' whose elderly inmates would not only maintain a personal "Scheme of Prayer" but would also provide an example to others through the "Godward orientation of [their] daily existence".[85] And where better to found a 'House of Prayer' than in a home for elderly ladies (God's waiting room, in fact) whose inmates, instead of worrying about "their … physical welfare and future", could contemplate "things-as-they-are-in-themselves" in "grave and decorous surroundings" in which they would lead "an ordered Godward life", expansion "of understanding and sympathy" being their aim and enrichment of the community's collective spiritual treasury the result. (Collective enrichment, it should be noted, also allowed for, indeed positively encouraged, private "mystical experience".)[86] And as if this were not enough, the powerhouse of spiritual energy that the St John's Home House of Prayer would be would also provide ghostly social services for the spiritually needy of Oxford and environs.

Mindful of advice from Sister Marie de St Pierre at Hope House that her vocation as Sister Placida was to 'save souls'[87], Mrs Graham of St John's Home was unsurprised when her guardian angel informed her that her prime 'task' with regard to the House of Prayer she hoped to establish there was to counteract the devil's desire (though 'you would think the devil would hardly bother to haunt a place like this', he was certainly present despite the Home's 'high average of goodness and piety') 'to lead souls from regrets and self-pity to discontent [and] active rebellion'. Creating communal 'togetherness' from what was 'too much *a collection of individuals*' in order that the Home might become 'a superb offering of praise to God and a broad channel of His grace to humanity'[88] would help encompass this. As would task number two: 'to find opportunities here of helping souls to prepare for death' in order to expand the limited scope, as Aelfrida saw it, of the 1947 Nuffield Report with regard to the preparation of souls of the elderly for Heaven, though it seems that it was only on extant 'very good Christians and church-women'[89] that she expended much effort; to those who were neither she extended general but no less valuable comfort of a less spiritual kind.

But in spite of visions of spiritual light 'flashing out in all directions' from within herself[90], of general prayerful activity ('oremus, *oremus*, OREMUS') and specific intercessory prayers prayed for each resident in turn (prayed 'for convenience … as they are [placed] in the dining room')[91], of a belief that '*here*, among us derelict females the spirit of devotion deepens'[92], and of assuring herself that St John's Home was now 'less of a collection of ill-assorted pious ladies' and 'more of a community'[93], diary evidence shows that Aelfrida's designs on the Home existed more in her imagination than in fact and for two reasons. First, because in spite of being a self-proclaimed 'prayerful person'[94], she took no part in the Home's collective prayer life other than

attendance at chapel, refusing to attend its Prayer Guild on the grounds that while anyone was welcome to her 'opinions … on Prayer', she could not and would not discuss 'the secret commerce of [her] soul with the Triune Lord'.[95] (Prayer, she wrote, is a "private matter … the most personal, intimate private thing of all".)[96] Second, was that flushed with enthusiasm for her latest 'Brilliant Idea', she went about things the wrong way, trying in the guise of God's 'fellow-worker' to impose on a heterogeneous collection of '*derelict females*'[97] (she included herself in the description) what Evelyn Underhill called "the austere conditions of the workshop"[98] with reference to silence and without properly considering that meal-time conversation formed an important part of lonely old ladies' days. She was therefore met with rebuffs and was henceforth obliged to confine herself to "the free-lance activities of the … well-meaning amateur"[99] and to relationships with like-minded ladies unlikely to rebuff her. Nor, it seems, did she extend her community-enhancing activities to the inmates of St Anne's and St Vincent's wards where the bedridden, the very old, and the mildly confused might have welcomed a well-meaning visitor, however 'amateur'; possibly such 'Inmate-Patients' were too 'derelict' to comprehend her vision of what the Home might be or too much her social inferiors to be worthy of inclusion in it, possibly the nursing nuns forbade such visits. But who can say that the efforts of a 'well-meaning amateur' were not exactly what was needed at an institution like St John's Home or that Aelfrida, 'amateur' though she might be, might not have done good work there in terms of what one of her models described as an aspect of oblation (i.e. "serv[ing], reliev[ing] and cordially help[ing] the afflicted") and as a reflection in daily life of God's "most holy gift of charity".[100]

Her third reason seems to have been in hope of fulfilling a long-felt wish. Thirty years earlier she had recorded that she hoped to become a 'pious and welcoming' old lady 'diffusing a kind of pale evening sunlight'[101] over the world; now, at last, she was becoming "a lantern for the Light – my Lord's radiance showing through … my dimmed panes'.[102] As 'lantern', her light was to manifest itself insofar as its radiance illuminated her as a 'prayerful person' living 'as nearly as may be solely for God's glory'[103] and in terms of Brother Lawrence's Practice of the Presence of God and of Christ's revelation that good works performed "unto the least of [His] brethren" were carried out "unto [Him]".[104] So Aelfrida assiduously 'fed' the 'hungry', 'watered' the 'thirsty', welcomed strangers, visited the sick, 'clothed' the 'naked' ("*caritas*" as practised by "the aged Christian" ought to be "evoked by need rather than by charm")[105], and extended "Christian affection [and] … goodwill"[106] over those unhappily imprisoned in 'memories of Better Days'.[107]

Her fourth and fifth reasons were less altruistic: in these, the "last years of [her] existence", she needed "space for quietness and thought"[108] but was also afraid of what might happen if "space" overwhelmed her, for even as she continued to enjoy the 'everlasting "Flight of the alone to the Alone"'[109] in an 'attic-cell' protected by an ENGAGED notice on the door, she feared to find herself shut up once again in an emotional "prison house" or lost in a "desert of her own making".[110] Although her nine years at Tymawr had created (or had allowed her to create) the 'hush' she now experienced as continually present in her soul[111] and a 'warming' sense of Christ's presence as something no longer heavy and intimidating (a 'pressure' on her soul, in fact) but as so 'familiar and human' that it was as if He and she were 'at home in Nazareth'[112] (or as if she and Julius were tête-à-tête at Wetenhall Cottage), Aelfrida realised that *maintenance* of inner peace and certainty depended on her being willing to step out of herself in order to encompass '*God* [as] the point of reference, not self'[113], to accept affection extended to her by others, and to reciprocally practise benevolent behaviour towards others. Then too, and although she recognised that what she loved best at St John's Home (besides its chapel) was less 'the kindness and goodwill of *many* new friends' than a new-found ability to make her soul '*a pool of contemplation*' reflecting the Most High, she also recognised the necessity for her psychic health of there being 'an inflow and outflow of grace … for, and active love of, other people' lest the 'pool' grow as 'stagnant'[114] as it had done as a result of intensified claustration at Tymawr. By 'stagnant' she did not mean spiritually stagnant in the sense of becoming full of the accidic "weariness or distress of heart" to which those leading cloistered or eremetic lives were said to be particularly prone, or that she wilfully allowed a "morbid sombreness" to settle on her which might, if unchecked, become a Burtonian 'melancholy-madness'[115]; indeed, she protests vehemently (perhaps too vehemently, given that other symptoms of the condition fit well with her behaviour at Tymawr: maintaining a poor and scornful opinion of her 'Sisters-in-Christ' and stating that there was no "refreshment for [her] soul" to be got from them, complaining that all seemed "harsh and untoward" in the Spartan surroundings of the convent itself, vocalising her discontent and projecting it onto others, etc.)[116] that spiritual sloth ('an incipient mental illness to be treated accordingly')[117] is not and never has been something from which she has suffered. She meant, rather, "morbid … imaginings"[118] which beset her when deprived (of her own volition) of human contact. Fear of stagnation of this

latter kind was particularly relevant to one who found herself in the same town and in an institution bearing a saint's name and attached to a convent as twenty years ago when her mental equilibrium had become spectacularly disequilibriated and in similarly semi-conventual surroundings as ten years before when devotion to Silence and Solitude had both unhinged her and impeded her recovery; to this was added the fear that without an "antidote to melancholy" at hand in the form of "small private kindnesses"[119] to her neighbours, she might indeed find herself consigned without hope of escape to the 'wandering minds' department of Cowley Road geriatric hospital. Hence her post-Tymawr ambition to live, if not in a convent, at least in an institution where she could enjoy 'much solitude but no loneliness at all'[120] and be by herself "in order to forget [herself]"[121] but not so solitary that she needed protection from herself when memories of her past life, genuinely forgotten or consciously or unconsciously repressed, reappeared in consciousness in all their clarity as memories do in old age even though what happened yesterday cannot be recalled.

Fear of madness was not, it seems, the only fear which beset Aelfrida at St John's Home; increasing nearness of the age at which her 'Voices' had predicted she would die and the recent composition of novels in which so much of her past life was revealed for the first time appears to have concentrated her mind on the salvation of a soul increasingly regarded by its possessor as less worthy of salvation than she had hitherto liked to think. This is not to suggest that earlier Presbyterianism or her Wetenhall ancestors' Particular Baptist beliefs had caused her to regard herself as a soul predestined by God for salvation but, rather, that an earlier certainty that Tillyards were predestined for heaven by virtue of 'Tillyardness' had been undermined by uncertainty as to whether she herself was destined for a Dantean hell of physical and mental torment (of which her life had provided a foretaste) because of the selfish and uncaring life she had led: "*Have I been holy?* there can be but one answer and that is 'no'".[122] (The 1954 appearance at St John's Home of a lady met over forty years earlier at Ventnor who had lived 'near the church where a violently Anglo-Catholic Father … preached [a] grim sermon on Hell'[123] seems to have provided a Proustian *madeleine* in this respect). Hence, it seems, aging Aelfrida's wish to be 'good' as much for her own sake as for Christ's and her need to reassure herself that she *had* kept God's commandments, particularly the first ("no other Gods before me") and what she listed as the second: 'genuinely' (as she put it) loving her neighbour as herself.[124] (As always with Aelfrida there were escape clauses, the first being 'if I place no selfish obstacle in the way', the obstacle being, of course, that 'dearest idol' herself, the second, that only God's intervention with regard to loving her neighbour kept her obedience 'genuine'.) Even so, hinted or actual doubts crept in, though less, it must be said, with regard to honouring her parents, keeping the Sabbath holy ('Sunday teas' at Fordfield when 'aunting' for her daughters presumably did not count), killing, committing adultery, and bearing false witness, than with regard to covetousness: covetousness not of 'other people's things or happiness or success' but of 'affection and admiration'[125], covetousness which led to "faulty … affection" (including unwise love or to deficient love if admiration was not forthcoming) and to a need to atone for this particular broken commandment "while there is time".[126]

But if, as she also noted, "old age [was] given for repentance"[127], her hope on leaving Tymawr that she would be able to 'live in the world as a penitent'[128] did not, it seems, achieve even approximate fulfilment until she relegated herself to St John's Home. The delay seems strange given that with regard to two sins (neglecting or misusing the gift noted by Lucius Cary within a short time of first making her acquaintance, namely her ability to make it easy for people to open themselves to her[129] and her "hardening her heart to human affections" so that she ceased "to love her neighbour at all")[130], she had realised as early as 1935 that such behaviour was selfish and uncharitable and that with regard to fear she had (also in 1935) devoted a whole chapter in *The Closer Walk with God* to the subject, noting therein that though she numbered herself among "technically good" people, there was enough evil in her heart "to make easy the downward path to Hell", defined here as "the state of those who are lost forever".[131] So why delay? Agatha's suicide occurred in February 1935 but was directly linked to Constantine's death the previous year, his death setting in train the complex mental and emotional breakdown first manifest when staying with Ancifera in Ealing but ultimately to endure for twenty years. Hence it was not until twenty years later (a period whose length underlines the severity of her breakdown) that Aelfrida was able to face up to and come to terms with negative aspects of her personality and to realise that negative emotions formerly attributed to disappointment at falling short of her 'high calling' were manifestations of wounded pride, of destruction of her belief that she was a virtuous woman, and of underlying pathology.

The depth and extent of her fear can be gauged from her being careful to distinguish between fear which she designates "holy" (e.g. that experienced at Tymawr during the 'the bread miracle') and that experienced by a sinner (such as herself) naked "beneath the terrible eye of the Almighty" and doomed to the "logical necessity"

of the hell of those who are lost for ever.[132] Her fear, it seems, was less because venial sins (such as hers chiefly were) often had uncharitable outcomes, though in the context of her new life at St John's Home this was increasingly relevant, and more because, as Bede Frost emphasised in the copy of his book on mental prayer given with a dedication to 'Aelfrida Graham' in 1933/34, to sin them not only impeded spiritual progress but also opened the way to mortal sins, to loss of God's grace, and to spiritual 'death'.

As described in *The Art of Mental Prayer*, sins deemed 'mortal' do not seem deadly at first sight but when one considers their implications, reasons for Aelfrida's fear become clear; in fact, Frost's descriptions so accurately encompass her adult behaviour that we could almost believe the treatise to have been written for and about her did not incompatibility of dating preclude this. (*The Art of Mental Prayer* was published in 1932, a year prior to Aelfrida's first meeting with Dom Bede and her presentation to him of a lengthy list of 'sins'.) Describing mortal sins in terms of pride, avarice, luxury, anger, and gluttony and positing envy and sloth as two aspects of a single sin (he omitted lust), Bede Frost's words must have reverberated in the mind of an aging woman who had begun to realise that life would be more pleasant if she interacted with others and that if she was nice to them they would be nice to her in return. The prideful, he writes, are tempted to teach rather than to learn and to complain that their spiritual directors do not understand them; they also play down their sins in order that the same directors will think well of them, make much show of their piety, indulge in immoderate grief for their faults, think of themselves as saints, and are boastful even when exhibiting humility. The avaricious spend more time musing about their stock of spiritual 'goods' than doing their duty. The luxurious take "vain joy" in being seen to do good works and derive too much sensual sweetness from Holy Communion and from ascetic practices. The angry are "a burden to themselves and … intolerant to other people", making themselves "guardians of virtue" while blaming others with "unquiet zeal". The gluttonous practise "immoderate penances", act unreasonably without rule or advice, find spiritual consolation in books read uncritically, and discard their spiritual directors whose advice does not accord with their own wishes. The envious and slothful deprecate goodness in others and 'Authority' in all forms, even God's.[133] And with sins like these on her conscience and given that "to God all hearts [are] open and from Him no secrets are hid"[134], what else could Aelfrida feel but fear.

Her sudden adoption of *caritas* at St John's Home can be therefore be seen as reparative adoration of a very practical kind and as a kind eminently suitable to "old age"[135], a time of life particularly suited to repentance for past sins because it allows a longer and wider view of behaviour not deemed sinful when enacted but now realised to have been so. And, of course, reparative behaviour of an altruistic and charitable nature is reinforced by positive feedback received from those on whom it is expended, making reparative adoration a truly pleasing instead of a perversely pleasurable activity.

But for a woman who thirty years after Albert Erlande's perspicacious comment still needed to be crucified, reparative adoration still required her to be a 'victim-soul'. And how better for a frail elderly lady to become a 'victim-soul' than by doing something she did not wish to do? As early as March 1955, therefore, the 'lantern' through whose dimmed panes shone what she hoped was the 'Light of [her] Lord's radiance' wrote feelingly of experiencing 'a very real conflict between [her] vehement desire for Silence and Solitude' and the 'claims' made on her by those over whom she extended *caritas* at St John's Home. Reproved for this by her guardian angel (she was, he said, 'shirking part of the fellowship of [her] Lord's sufferings' and claims made on her were nothing compared to the 'incredibly exacting' ones made on *Him*), Aelfrida decided to suffer 'in His strength'[136], 'purring over' sick and lonely ladies being yet another manifestation of willing and lasting acceptance of "whatever pain God lays upon us".[137] Suffering, however, was sweetened by visions: of Christ emerging 'spiritually' from the tabernacle 'with arms outstretched as on the cross' to ask if she accepted His Cross ("Yea Lord, even as Thou wilt", was her reported reply as she watched before the altar of repose, the vision having occurred in chapel in Lent) or of 'our Lord in Gethsemane with … drops of blood falling from his brow to the ground'[138] as she said Prime in her private GETHSEMANE. A later dream of Christ 'coming to be crucified again' and of her determination (thwarted, significantly, by 'people' providing 'all sorts of reasons why she should refrain') to 'claim a place akin to that of the dying thief' or, failing that, to place her right hand over Christ's left 'so that the nail should pass through [her] hand too'[139] and an audition on Holy Cross Day 1957 of Christ calling her by name as she renewed her profession as a tertiary to remind Placida that 'if He sends the Cross, He will give His strength with it' and that if she fell under its weight 'so did He'[140], provided even more emphatic confirmation that reparative adoration in the form of *caritas* was right for her now.

She did not fall; in fact, she revelled in being once again 'part of "the fellowship of His sufferings"', in '*not shirk[ing]* … duties … of charity', and in offering God

the reparative adoration 'He [desired] of [her]'. (To add to her enjoyment, she gave herself up – as far as possible, given that *caritas* took up so much time – 'to contemplation and to pondering God's ways'[141] and to recapitulation of 'many marvellous experiences of rapture and ecstasy and the burning pain of His wounds in [her] hand', experiences chiefly from her time 'at St Benedict's, Osney Lane and Tymawr' but revisited now as 'purified … from horrid stains of … self-esteem and stupidity'.)[142] Reinforcement of her decision was received via 'angel-talk' from St Raphael, he reassuring her that 'loving … "people" with yearning tenderness' implied not only loving them as herself – knowing Aelfrida as we do, with a 'big love' it would seem – but also that her love for 'people' imitated Christ's for mankind[143], and via a chapel address on a Quiet Day on the subject of 'people being brought to love God by the road of loving their neighbours'.[144] Or, as Aelfrida put it, 'I am being very sociable as seems my duty … and my pleasure too!'[145]

A new-found ability to enjoy Christianity with and without the Cross simultaneously ("*Christi Crux mea Lux*", albeit with the proviso that one could temporarily "forget the Cross" or "pursue a way that [leads] round and past it") in the course of what seemed more and more a truly *Christian* old age, cheered Aelfrida immensely as she neared the time appointed for her to 'step through the Dark Gate' to join 'the whole company of heaven'. But – and for Aelfrida there must always be a but – was she bound directly for that 'company' or would she be consigned to Purgatory first? If the latter, would it be possible to regard (and be grateful for) the here-and-now 'purgatory' of self-imposed *caritas* as a portion or even as the whole of that heaven-postponing condition and 'pain [and] *privations*' suffered by the contemplative *manqué* as 'privileges' because, having suffered them, death would hold no further terrors and because, 'purified by [the] purgatorial fires' of St John's Home, she would be 'ready for the immediate Presence of God'?[146]

This glimpse of Aelfrida as a 'Good Woman' still so centred on self as to want to pre-empt God's design for her (there is no hint in her Oxonian 'purgatory' that God's Will might not accord with what she willed for herself) suggests a further fear: that in being forced like Piccarda Donati "back into the world against her will" by Chiara and the Oracle in an effort to normalise her through marriage and having thereby broken the vow made in her teens to live as a secular virgin consecrate, she, like Piccarda, would be penalised after death for *allowing* it to be broken by relegation to a lesser paradise than the one she hoped to attain, relegation which might be overcome if she were able to "compensate with such good deeds" on earth that she would not weigh short in heaven.[147]

And another: if she did not now amend her way of life to include the virtue deemed by St Paul the greatest of all, namely charity[148], would she find herself unable to rise above the 'Celestial Paradox': unless she loved God and Him alone, He would deny Himself to her but unless she loved her neighbour as herself she would "never attain to the fullness of the Beatific Vision"[149]? Or was all this merely an attempt to spiritually rationalise a very human decision?

It was, it seems, in the hope of attaining the 'perfect splendour' of the Beatific Vision, a splendour only hinted at to date, that Aelfrida transformed her life at St John's Home from personalised theophany to one of salvation through service. (The theme, an important one in Alfred Tillyard's *Manuscripts of God,* was probably not one inserted by his daughter for Aelfrida was not then bent on service to others unless under compulsion.) And how better to attain it than by practising *caritas* (St Paul's other listed qualities – faith and hope – she had in abundance) and in doing so proving that at long last she followed Omar Khayyám's way of love as the road to finding God instead of adopting Thomas à Kempis' disdain for 'human affections', expending all her love on God, and behaving callously towards others? Hence it was not only a desire to be remembered as something more than a sounding brass or tinkling cymbal who, though she spoke and wrote with the help of the tongues of men and of angels, possessed the gift of prophecy, and was able to move metaphorical mountains if the mood took her, was nothing but a 'cypher' because she did not actively practice charity; it was also the wholly selfish fear that if she did not do so, the Beatific Vision would be denied her because, however laudable and sacrificial her religious life had been, a life lived without charity was nullity in God's eyes.

Charity, alas, did not extend towards the Home's Sister Superior. Aelfrida's relationship with Sister Elizabeth Noel, though occasionally problematical, was generally amicable. (Besides attempting to impose silence at meals on Lenten Fridays, she was guilty of meddling in matters which did not concern her e.g. the dismissal of domestic staff, and instead of speaking to Sister Elizabeth Noel about the rudeness of the 'person' who 'supervised' the Green Corridor, wrote the 'person' a critical letter when she herself was safely ensconced at Wetenhall Cottage, only to find herself threatened with removal to the Blue Corridor one floor down, a threat which brought her to heel immediately.)[150] Her determination to 'lie low' lest she be asked to leave yet another establishment meant that Elizabeth Noel's less agreeable characteristics (Aelfrida was irritated by her facetiousness and her tendency to be either arbitrary or dithering and thought her heartless

insofar as she seemed to value her borrowed Pekinese more than her actual patients) were therefore criticised only on paper. Her initial reaction to news received in September 1954 of Elizabeth Noel's departure to head another of the Community's homes was 'YES!' but her subsequent discovery that the new Sister Superior was to be a '*very* strict' Sister newly promoted from a third home was greeted with the prayerful ejaculation '*oremus!*'[151] and her arrival in October 1954 with '*oremus, oremus!*', with worries that Sister Winifred Marcian might 'impose burdensome rules and withdraw cherished privileges', and with gloomy pronouncements concerning the All Saints Sisterhood's 'lack of human sympathy and spiritual enthusiasm'.[152]

First impressions were favourable: Sister Winifred was 'very "recollected" … a real Religious [who] brings the sense of God's Presence with her'; she also listened sympathetically to recitals of Alethea's work in South Africa and of Placida's life as resident tertiary at Tymawr. Having, she hoped, established her own and her daughter's credentials to the new Sister Superior's satisfaction (albeit without mentioning Alethea 'having tried her vocation anywhere'), Aelfrida expressed a hope that everyone 'would like St Winifred Marcian as much as I do!'[153]

Within two months of Sister Winifred's arrival, however, Sister Superior proved not 'as acceptable as she was at first'. 'Seething with discontent', Aelfrida proceeded to list the ways in which she found her unacceptable: complaints (signed and dated) were to be lodged in a Complaints Book 'for everyone to see'; residents' personal laundry was outsourced to 'a rather low class establishment nearby' (the former director of the Cambridge Steam Laundry enjoyed 'an interesting little talk' with the staff but complained of their starching); National Health Service cards were to be held centrally rather than individually and sick residents were to be attended by the Home's doctors, not their own; residents (herself?) found themselves 'in disgrace for little kind services' to the sick; visitors were to report on arrival and residents to notify their presence in or absence from the Home; changes were announced impersonally by means of a bewildering 'multiplicity of curt little notices posted up in the hall'. Worst of all was that rituals surrounding patients' deaths and funeral services were abolished.[154] She also expressed concern about Sister Elizabeth's dislike of the presence in St John's Home of 'the mother of the CWAS secretary'[155] because the said mother might 'leak' information derogatory to Home and Superior and that her dislike might affect the pleasantness or duration of the secretary's mother's stay.

In fairness to Aelfrida, it is important to note that others besides herself were unhappy (several 'Ladies' and members of staff left of their own volition; it also seems that nurses and domestics were subject to 'a policy of elimination') and to Sister Winifred Marcian, that she had taken over a Home slackly run, in financial difficulties, subject to constantly updated legislation concerning the safety of its fabric, inmates, and staff (legislation, moreover, on which under the terms of the Nursing Homes Registration Act of 1927 its survival depended), and inhabited by physically and mentally infirm ladies, only one of whom was under fifty (and she virtually bed-bound) and the majority over seventy, living in antiquated accommodation. A less anti-authoritarian person than Aelfrida would have realised that measures dictated by commonsense or current legislation would have to be implemented quickly and thoroughly if the Home was to remain open (her complaint that Sister Winifred trusted no-one and that 'everything has to go through her hands'[156] demonstrates her lack of insight), but instead of seeing them for what they were – sensible arrangements for her own and her fellow-patients' health and safety – she chose to regard them as restrictions deliberately imposed on her freedom of action and to disregard Sister Winifred Marcian's 'many excellent qualities'[157] in favour of a campaign of civil disobedience carried out by herself or by others with herself as agent provocateur, a campaign of which she said nothing to anyone and a poor example of a life lived (as she decided it should be three months after Sister Winifred's arrival) 'solely for God's glory'.[158] But – and even a life lived solely for God's glory contained an escape clause: 'as nearly as may be' – with regard to Sister Winifred Marcian 'nearly' was a long way from near or near enough.

Her campaign was organised along the same lines as that conducted at Tymawr, differing in detail only because of her changed circumstances. Instances are numerous: in April 1955 she arranged to sublet her room while on holiday and expressed surprise at being forbidden to do so[159]; in January 1956 she persisted in cleaning her room herself when suffering from an 'influenza cold' accompanied by vomiting ('the work will be done for you', insisted Sister Winifred who regarded what Aelfrida described as 'trying to spare the staff trouble' as engendering more trouble), looked after herself so maladroitly that she was forced to report sick – only to earn the unjust rebuke '[you] will never get well here, [you do] nothing but lie and think about [yourself]' and the just one that she had entered St John's Home to be 'looked after' and that she must allow the nurses to 'order [her] existence for [her]' if unable to do so herself. (To underline Sister Winifred's point, it was shortly after this that Aelfrida fell heavily in the dining room for the second time.) 'Coming and going' without informing anyone

earned the rebuke that she was 'treating the Home like a lodging house'. (Her – unspoken – response was '*could* I have guessed!' and 'fortunately the whole of one's life is *not* yet covered'.)[160] She also postponed payment of fees when relations between herself and Sister Winifred were bad, acted in a 'non-cooperative manner' when asked to join the 'Ladies' for tea on St Vincent's ward (attendance was a means of checking on their welfare), and ensured, as Sister Winifred informed her in exasperated tones at an interview arranged to try to sort matters out, that "there had never been a single improvement made for the benefit of patients without [her] writing and criticising it".[161] (During earlier negotiations Aelfrida had burst into tears of protest, a gesture she now recognised as foolish, but the passage in *Naomi da Costa* in which one character says to another "I wish you wouldn't cry. It doesn't do to be aggrieved if you can't arrange the whole world suit your idea of what is right"[162] suggests that strategic tearfulness relative to Superiors was not a new tactic and that the words paraphrased Mother Guenvrede's rebuke of May 1942 to a tertiary whose noisy sobbing had disrupted Community worship and hymn practice. She had also written so many letters of protest that Sister Winifred no longer bothered to read them. Only later and after playing off one of the doctors against Sister Winifred and receiving temporary demotion from 'the gentry' on the dining room dais to a table where she sat among retired domestic servants, did she admit to her diary – though not to Sister Winifred – that the latter had made many 'material improvements'[163] since her arrival.) And in a manner paralleling her behaviour towards Mother Guenvrede (she does not openly equate Winifred Donkin with Winifred Marcian but it is obvious that she saw resemblances in more than name between them), she sought to undermine Sister Winifred's authority by trying to persuade mentally-compromised patients on the Green Corridor to go elsewhere (she also queried their medical treatment and diagnosis in order to have them removed because they disturbed her peace) and by compiling a list of Sister Superior's supposed iniquities which 'set forth clearly' clashes with that lady and actions taken by her against an 'innocent' woman whose 'scapegoat' she was (the list also included Sister Winifred's attempts to 'shunt', that is to say oust, her from the Home) in order to present Alethea with an accusing letter.[164] To Cowley Fathers visiting the Home as confessor or because their mothers lived there, she hinted that Sister Superior's attitude created 'difficulties' for patients other than herself and that 'the rule of Sr Winifred Marcia[n] is not … a happy one'. ('Alas and alas! *Oremus*'.)[165] She even hoped to 'drum up an enquiry'[166] (its members were to include the Home's committee of management, its chaplain, and the Order's Reverend Mother, based in Birmingham) as the best and most public means of revenging herself on someone whose authority she resented.

Though Aelfrida's battles with Sister Winifred bear the stamp of and are described by her in much the same terms as those fought with Mother Guenvrede, they were more bitter because God had not 'called' her to St John's Home to have her 'whole time arranged by Authority'[167] in order to learn obedience and humility. (At Easter 1957 God reminded her that she was not 'humble enough' and that she was 'very far from' following the example of His Son's 'great humility', this causing her to remark sadly that she must 'go on trying'.[168] Her actions with regard to Sister Winifred could therefore be regarded as further attempts to achieve humility through humiliation were it not for the sadistic glee she took in besting Winifred Marcian in public and private.) Beginning with a comparatively mild and gently humorous description of Sister Winifred as a 'benevolent despot' whose benevolence was insufficient to 'sweeten the despotism'[169], within a short time she noted bitterly that Sister Winifred's 'tyranny' was growing worse, that she ran the Home with 'military' discipline[170], and that her '*reign*' was one of '*terror*'.[171] It was then a small step to stating that the devil was as 'active' at St John's Home as the cause of Sister Winifred's malevolent behaviour ('she was', recorded Aelfrida after a particularly vicious spat, 'a terrifying sight [as she] screamed ... and shouted at me ... in her Religious Habit') as he had been at Tymawr when he gained 'partial possession' of Mother Guenvrede's mind and to deciding to once more take up the 'task' inherited from (even, perhaps, assigned to her by) Father Cary of 'defying'[172] the devil.

Having learnt her lesson at Tymawr and not wishing to be ignominiously 'shunted' from the Home, Aelfrida confined her activities to 'quietness, humility [and] gaiety where possible' and delegated overt 'grumbling and discontent' to other 'Inmate-Patients'[173]; in fact, she was unwontedly silent on the subject of diabolical possession (she did, however, hint to Alethea that Sister Winifred might be suffering 'the beginning of mental trouble')[174], confining her activities to recitation of a novena for the afflicted nun and to fomenting rebellion by proxy.

There was, however, more to the matter than Aelfrida's tendency to "see the pathological in any mode of expression different from [her] own".[175] For one thing, the period of her most acute fear of the devil gaining possession of Sister Winifred's mind was preceded by prescription of ephedrine nasal drops for the 'influenza cold' which precipitated the latter's diatribe concerning Aelfrida's supposed hypochondria and unwarranted

independence and it may be that these again contributed to 'evidence' generated in her mind by the devil. For another, as even she herself realised, 'things' held against Sister Winifred might be 'nothing but malicious gossip'[176] emanating from inmates of the Home disgruntled at the contrast between Sister Elizabeth Noel's lax management and Sister Winifred Marcian's stringent but safer regime. Third and most likely, was that Sister Winifred's 'diabolic' possession was another manifestation of Aelfrida's disordered personality reacting negatively to 'Authority', so that when she recalled Cary's words on the 'tremendous reality' of the devil as man's 'ghostly foe'[177] she was, as she dimly realised, describing the demon within herself of whose 'reality' she had received ample proof since news of Constantine's fatal illness provided the '*madeleine*' which opened the dark gate beyond which lay, repressed for nearly fifty years, memories of hellish events surrounding Conrad's illness and death.

With Julius' help, Aelfrida was now more aware that when she believed someone other than herself to be possessed by the devil, it was in fact her own demons projected onto that person which roused her dramatic and panic-stricken response. Furthermore, realisation in Oxford that the devil was of the same 'fabric' as her guardian angel and the 'normal' and godly aspect of her own personality, may explain her decision to commit her thoughts solely to her diary. She also refraining from discussing the presence of the 'devil' in Sister Winifred with anyone (not even with Bishop Wynn as her spiritual director) lest others besides herself and her brother become aware of the Manichean qualities of a mind in which forces of light and darkness battled for supremacy and of her need of self-chastising behaviour to exorcise the darker aspects of her nature and lest they compel her to undergo psychotherapy or treat her remarks as manifestations of a mind so disordered that the 'disordered minds' ward at Cowley Hospital was the only place for her. Indeed, in *Rich Man's Choice*, 'Clive Farwell', locked through no fault of his own in a dark cellar, is visited by a "Discarnate Personality" who threatens him with "madness" if 'Clive', known to have been in a "queer state" earlier in his life, does not agree to his demands: non-compliance will result in him becoming "more and more peculiar until one day a nice doctor will take [him] ... in his car to a house with bolts and bars" where, locked into delusions, he "will die".[178]

It was, we can now see, the interweaving of the 'bright' and 'dark' aspects of her personality in one 'fabric' which allowed Aelfrida to be both charitable and revengeful simultaneously. (It also made her instinctively empathetic to disordered personalities like Frank and Ruth Stokoe and Nadja Laptchinski whose own 'darknesses' were manifest for longer or shorter periods and dismiss-ive of Frank and Nadja when their disordered personali-ties too accurately imaged her own.) It may also explain the (contextually incongruous) inclusion of the devil in her books and lectures, this being the only way open to her of conveying certain truths about herself – in which context it is worth noting that in September 1957 she gave an 'address on the Devil' to the 'Methodist Women', an address delivered because she 'thought a warning against his activities was needed'.[179] It may be too that the 'morbid curiosity'[180] demonstrated by a Cambridge audience when she lectured on 'The Devil' was both 'morbid' *and* 'curious' because in the course of the lec-ture she voluntarily or involuntarily made startling dis-closures about 'diabolic' aspects of her own mind, disclo-sures heard by Chiara as a member of the audience and as a mother who knew that her daughter was not and, it now seemed, never would be, 'normal'.

There is, however, one further aspect of Aelfrida's conviction of the devil's 'reality' to consider here. On the night of 21 October 1957, the devil, she confided, made an 'indescribable' (and as it happened, his final – or his last recorded) attack on her. Confused and fright-ened and feeling for once 'anything but combative', she begged her guardian angel to protect her; this he did, placing his 'spiritual wings' around her to such effect that 'Satan receded'.[181]

Her description of the event is interesting for several reasons. First, it is the second of only two occasions on which she gives the devil a name. (Her first reference to 'Satan' appeared a few days earlier in connection with the launch by the Russians of a 'foolish satellite' regarded by Aelfrida as indicative of the imminence of 'Wrath to Come'.)[182] Second, for the first time she does not take direct action herself to combat his attack but calls on St Raphael, vanquisher of demons, to do so on her behalf which, given that the devil never returned, he effec-tively did. (Worth noting in this respect is that in January 1957 Sister Winifred Marcian developed a throat infec-tion which compromised her airway to such an extent that she underwent emergency surgery to enable her to breathe; she was not well enough to return to work until nine days after Aelfrida's dream, the latter having in the meantime received 'Orders From on High' that she was to 'love [Sister Superior] as myself'.[183] No further bat-tles ensued.) Third, while rationalising the devil's attack in terms of Father Cary's reference to seasoned spiritual warriors having to 'do battle with the powers of evil', she did not, in this instance, do battle at all but called on St Raphael to protect her, possibly because she now realised that signing the Cross was ineffectual against the tremendous reality of attacks emanating from a place

within herself beyond the boundaries of '*normal* con-sciousness'.[184] Fourth, because her descriptions of the devil have changed over time.

First encountered as an entity whose perceptiveness and ability to deliver just the advice she wants to hear or whose most disconcerting tendency is to 'attack' her by shaking or tipping her bed or to appear as a menac-ing figure wreathed in clouds of evil-smelling smoke, the devil has now become an abstract figure: 'Satan' or the 'Devil'. A possible explanation is that whereas he for-merly appeared in the benevolent or despotic guise of her father, in daylight "the wisest [and] … the most reason-able of men"[185] but in darkness a hirsute 'ape-man' who, wreathed in clouds of smoke emitted by pastilles burnt to fumigate a nursery where two small boys demonstrate the dread symptoms of diphtheria, shakes his young daughter awake, tips her out of bed, and forcibly removes her to a place – as he thinks – of safety (Aelfrida's panic on smelling sulphurous fumigating smoke or finding her room roiling with fumes from a malfunctioning boiler must relate to this frightening experience too), now she knows him for what he really is: not as an entity made, as her 'old friend' Gian Falco put it in a book aptly subtitled 'The Role of the Devil in Divine and Human Affairs', "in the image and likeness" of her father but as a symbol of "the evil and the torment"[186] existing within herself since that terrible night in 1888.

Knowing that her life since then had been coloured by what today would be called post-traumatic stress dis-order – Aelfrida would have called it 'neurasthenia' or 'shell shock' in relation to Willie Searle and may even have noticed the similarity between symptoms of that condition (irrational behaviour, restlessness, excitability, suicidal or other morbid thoughts, unwarranted suspi-cions, a sense of alienation and consequent withdrawal from society, disinclination to follow advice, visual and auditory hallucinations, obsession with self, disturbance of sexuality, tendency to self-medicate, insomnia, repres-sion of unhappy memories interspersed with flashbacks, increased likelihood of relationship breakdown) and her own character traits (another reason not to marry him) – did not, of course, prevent her from behaving badly to yet another authority figure. Indeed, being unable to obey the diktats 'submit' and 'obey' in relation to Sister Winifred, she came close to being 'shunted' on more than one occasion and only Alethea's timely interventions reprieved her. Furthermore, not content with appealing to Alethea to save her (as St Raphael had done when she was faced with 'Satan'), she also traded on Alethea's offi-cial position as secretary of CWAS and unofficial posi-tion as protégée of Father O'Brien and the SSJE when engagements between 'benevolent despot' and '*dictatrix mundi*' threatened to end with the former '*determined*'[187] to eject the latter from the Home.

In spite of absolute determination *not* to be sent away (she was, she assured Sister Winifred, '*exceedingly* happy' at St John's Home and when the latter suggested that Aelfrida join Alethea in Marston Street, replied that she did not believe in 'an old mother being a burden on a daughter earning her own living'; in her diary, however, she noted the importance of giving Sister Winifred no 'reasonable excuse' to eject her and on her guardian angel reminding her that God was offering opportunities for 'Holy Obedience', that she should '*grasp*' them)[188], Sister Winifred Marcian's arrival saw Aelfrida's behaviour verge on the impossible. Confronted, she (as usual) apologised for being 'rude', invoked the irrefutable escape clause that God 'meant' her to be and stay at St John's Home ('of course, I don't mean to *go!*'), meekly accepted a scolding (in her diary she noted her refusal to be 'completely squashed'), affected innocence when confronted by Alethea with having caused 'difficulties', and promised to be 'humbler and less conspicuous' (and to 'accept more humiliations [even] as Christ accepted them') once Sister Superior and Alethea had met and the latter informed that if Aelfrida could not learn to 'trust' her more and to behave less disruptively, Sister Winifred saw no reason to '*keep*' her. At this climactic point Aelfrida decided to 'take up [her] writing again'[189] (she had completed one batch of '*mémoires*' and had not, it seems, intended to write more), it being better to achieve catharsis-by-*Memory Pictures* than by provoking Sister Winifred Marcian.

Following yet another episode, Aelfrida appealed to the Home's doctor and chaplain as well. Informing the latter that she was acting on 'Orders From On High' (she omitted to tell him that she, inheritor of 'Father Cary's strange legacy', was preparing to pass beyond 'the usual confines of thought and prayer' in order to fight the devil for Sister Winifred's soul), she added that she was 'not fighting against Sister Superior but on her behalf against the "rulers of the darkness of this world"'. (His suggestion that he talk the matter over with Father O'Brien shows he was accurately informed regarding the vagaries of Mrs Graham's mind and may have warned Aelfrida that she would do better to remain, like her guardian angel in this instance, 'silent'.) Apropos the doctor she quickly realised that complaints that Sister Superior's actions were damaging her health played into the latter's hands: 'she *knows* that a threat to move me into a ward *permanently* would dislodge me'.[190] Privy, perhaps, to evidence other than that presented to her by her mother, Alethea, accompanied this time by Aelfrida, met Sister Winifred and one of the nursing sisters to thrash the matter out. On this sole occasion she took her mother's

part in public and in private, advising the latter that Sister Winifred was a 'bully' who liked to inspire fear in the Home's residents and was angry when Aelfrida stood up to her. She also warned her that as Sister Superior, Winifred Marcian possessed the right 'of ejecting any resident without giving a reason'.[191]

As a result of Alethea's (and possibly others') intervention, both ladies kept the peace. Aelfrida herself attributed the change in Sister Winifred's behaviour to Alethea's 'haughty and disapproving'[192] demeanour at the meeting but there may have been another reason for improvement in her own behaviour vis-à-vis the supposedly 'despotic ways' of an authoritarian 'tyrant'[193] above and beyond Alethea's intervention and 'Orders From on High' that Aelfrida love Winifred Marcian as herself: in *The Glory of the West*, written when she was about to be ejected from Tymawr, Aelfrida noted apropos her notion of residential "Colleges for the Aged" (she was thinking of Oxford and Cambridge colleges but her own 'colleges' developed from 'Houses of Prayer' accommodating both sexes) that a member of a 'College' who had figured "thrice in a quarrel, whether as accuser or accused … be asked to leave [in order] to keep the peace". "Some people", she added revealingly, "have the knack of being the injured party and even when the fault is on the other side, bring an atmosphere of tiffs and huffs with them. A college is not the place for them (but alas! what is?) They had better go".[194] So aware of how many 'tiffs and huffs' in which she herself had recently figured, she held her peace at last.

There may, of course, be other reasons for Aelfrida's old age being anything but Christian and for the Sisters at St John's Home finding her statement that "the chief characteristic of Christian old age" was "serenity"[195] somewhat ironic in view of the disruption she caused. (Ironic too, under the circumstances, is her conviction that although she continued to suffer from pride and self-importance 'in various forms', God had at last bestowed on her His 'free gift' of 'the peace for which [she] longed'.)[196] Perhaps in relegating herself to an institution where learned dependency was expected, she reverted to "the same little faults which prevented us from being good in the nursery … obstinacy, inquisitiveness, love of showing off" and, significantly in view of what we know of her nursery years, a "craving for affection" "shockingly unmortified after all these years".[197] Perhaps – like her blind father under similar circumstances – she exhibited her worst personality traits to selected victims, particularly those whom she believed she could bully with impunity or whose authority she resented. Or was she so bored with life in an institution that, unable to exhibit "the old person's most suitable and necessary virtue, Patience" ("patience with ourselves, with other people and with the … maddeningly slow work of God's Providence" i.e. the delayed arrival of her 'heavenly birthday') and tired of trying "[her] own patience"[198], she tried that of the Sisters by inspiring 'scenes' of the kind enjoyed since adolescence and even – who knows – provoked participants in the battles of the Green Corridor to further warfare while pretending to act as peacemaker? ('In unregenerate man', she noted, 'there is a *love of strife for its own sake*. Peace of any kind would be insufferably *dull*'; she also noted, however, that she did not believe in 'the "*cherchez la femme*" view of history'[199], a statement with which the All Saints Sisters might have disagreed, not in this instance having far to look.) Or, given that she was making trouble within two months of her arrival at St John's Home, was she naughty out of sheer perversity, employing "voices of passion and of will" (it is obvious from the tone of contemporary diary entries that the 'fear' of Sister Winifred she expressed to her daughter was phony and that Aelfrida was both spoiling for and thoroughly enjoyed a fight and found Sister Winifred Marcian a worthier foe than Sister Elizabeth Noel) as a counterpoise to long hours spent being good in silence and in "power-imbued … loneliness"[200] behind a door marked ENGAGED, the monotony of self-confinement within claustrophobically-small GETHSEMANE by the demands of the Day Hours regularly recited as part of her Rule when her 'natural' self demanded company and conversation being too much to bear without an outlet? (No-one who has not experienced the rigid structuring of the religious life by the demands of the *opus Dei* can conceive of the lack of spontaneity of a life led in the same manner or of the fortitude required to live it.) Or were such scenes provoked as an astringent antidote and a holiday from being good with regard to *caritas* cloyingly dispensed to fellow 'Inmate-Patients'?

There are, however, more pathetic reasons than these. Early in 1956 Aelfrida's body 'start[ed] to grumble again" and although she did not feel an immediate need "to make final preparation for the next world"[201], by the end of the year it was apparent that she would soon require more nursing input into her care because less able to look after herself, the reason, of course, for relegating herself to St John's Home in the first place but suggestive now of further and frightening loss of independence; worse still, increasing physical weakness and the onset of new symptoms rendered her less able to practice her Rule and to partake in chapel services. Hence an old age formerly foreseen as an era of "growing graciousness and … maturity and a capacity for attention" and as a time in which to thank God for "increasing knowledge of him" came to be regarded as something "to be looked on with

fear and hate" and as likely to see her numbered among "invalids and cranks". [202]

A revealing passage in *The Silence of God* concerning the biblical account of the Agony in the Garden speaks volumes of her state of mind. (Aelfrida, so she says, "marvelled that Christ was prepared to "allow the record … to come down to posterity", but surely Christ's plea "Father if it be possible, let this cup pass from me" indicates that at this point in His life He was a desperate and frightened man and did not care who knew it.) Her asking of what was "God Incarnate afraid" in Gethsemane: physical pain? Humiliation? "Disappointment with those from whom He had expected better things"? "The sorrow His death would cause"? "Of His being the occasion of mortal sin"? "Of failure of His earthly ministry"? "Of death itself"? suggests that she too was afraid of them. But two worse fears remained: "fear of the Power of Darkness" (of Satan, that is to say, manifesting himself to and through her, for what else might trances, 'shewings', visions, auditions, olfactions, 'Voices', miracles, levitations, stigmatisations, and an ability to capture men in her 'magic net' be, but evidence of demonic possession?) and, given that she already counted herself among the mentally "distorted", "fear of being deprived of conscious communing with God".[203] For an ill old lady agonising in GETHSEMANE over the knowledge that there had been several occasions in her life when 'someone has thought me MAD'[204], there could be nothing worse than the thought that madness would deprive her of the ability to pray and that, unable to commune rationally with God, she would fail to recognise – or even to see – the Beatific Vision at the hour of her death.

## Notes

1 GCPPT 1|1|28 14 October 1924.
2 ibid.
3 *Old Age. A Mood-Picture* was written in Brookline, Mass. on 23 May 1908 and published in *To Malise* (p 51) two years later. At the time of writing Aelfrida was twenty-four and pregnant with her first child; the longing for death expressed in the sonnet seems at variance with what should have been a happy time in her life and only with the benefit of hindsight do we realise how appropriate it was: trapped in marriage and motherhood, she can never be a dedicate virgin again.
4 GCPPT 1|1|73 'Christmas Day' (25 December) 1956.
5 GCPPT 1|1|71 16 and 19 July 1953.
6 ibid. 29 December 1953.
7 GCPPT 1|1|72 17 July and 2 August 1954.
8 ibid. 21 July 1954.
9 GCPPT 1|1|74 6 January 1958.
10 GCPPT 1|1|72 24 August 1955.
11 ibid. 8 July 1955.
12 GCPPG A1 4|2 Letter from Aelfrida to Alethea Graham of 12 December 1958.
13 GCPPT 1|1|73 'Christmas Day' (25 December) 1956.

14  GCPPT 1|1|71 7 September and 'Easter [Sunday]' (17 April) 1953.
    GCPPT 1|1|72 13 January and 1 March 1955.
15  GCPPT 1|1|73 27 and 29 January 1957.
    GCPPT 1|1|74 'All Souls' (2 November) 1957.
16  GCPPT 1|1|73 9 June 1956.
17  ibid. 12 April 1956.
18  ibid. 10, 12 and 19 October 1953.
19  GCPPT1|1|72 5 and 24 April 1955.
20  GCPPT 1|1|75 4 March 1959.
    GCPPT 1|1|5 17 July 1900.
21  GCPPT 1|1|73 14 November 1956 and 2 January 1957.
    GCPPT 1|1|74 2 July 1958.
22  GCPPT 1|1|72 'St Placidus and his Companions' (5 October) 1954.
23  GCPPT 1|1|71 5 March 1954.
24  GCPPT 1|1|71 28 November 1593.
    GCPPT 1|1|72 21 February 1955.
25  The SHUT was an Anglican Sisterhood established in Oxford in the
    middle of the nineteenth century and closely associated with the SSJE.
    Aelfrida had visited their convent in Woodstock Road while prospect-
    ing in Oxford for somewhere to live while under Father Cary's men-
    torship but eventually settled on the Community of St Thomas the
    Martyr. The SHUT moved to South Leigh in 1946. For further details
    of the SHUT and other religious establishments known to Aelfrida see
    Anson, P. *The Call of the Cloister*. Aelfrida first read Anson's book shortly
    after returning from South Leigh (GCPPT 1|1|72 17 July 1955).
26  GCPPT 1|1|72 16 August 1955.
27  ibid. 25 and 30 June 1955.
28  ibid. 8 July 1955.
29  GCPPT 1|1|71 12 December 1953.
30  GCPPT 1|1|73 20 January 1956.
    GCPPT 1|1|74 29 August 1957.
31  GCPPT 1|1|74 21 August and 16 September 1957.
32  GCPPT 1|1|72 21 July 1954.
    GCPPT 1|1|74 16 September 1957.
33  GCPPT 1|1|71 21 October 1953.
34  GCPPT 1|1|73 25 December 1956.
35  GCPPT 1|1|72 1 January 1955.
36  GCPPT 1|1|74 31 July 1957.
37  GCPPT 1|1|74 22 November 1957.
38  GCPPT 1|1|71 10 August 1953.
39  GCPPT 1|1|74 7 August 1957.
40  ibid. 19 September 1957.
41  GCPPT 1|1|72 13 June 1955.
42  GCPPT 1|1|74 14 November 1957.
43  GCPPT 1|1|71 8 September and 1 December 1953.
44  ibid. 'Holy Cross Day' (14 September) 1953 and 9 June 1954.
45  ibid. 12 June 1954.
46  ibid. 'Shrove Tuesday' (2 March) 1954.
47  ibid. 18 December 1953.
48  GCPPT 1|1|72 28 March 1955.
49  ibid. 16 August and 14 December 1955.
50  GCPPT 1|1|73 30 August 1956.
51  GCPPT 1|1|71 26 November 1953.
52  GCPPT 2|23|1 *The Watchword* December 1953.
    GCPPT 2|23|1 *The Watchword* March 1954.
53  GCPPT1|1|73 1 May 1956. Aelfrida's talk took place shortly before
    Whitsun.
54  James, W. p 274. The quotation is from his chapter on 'saintliness'.
55  GCPPT 1|1|26 12 November 1921.
56  GCPPT 1|1|72 21 June 1955.
57  GCPPT 1|1|71 2 September 1953.
58  GCPPT 1|1|73 3 May 1956.
59  GCPPT 1|1|71 2 September 1953.
60  ibid. 26 January and 9 June 1954.
61  GCPPT 1|1|72 13 June 1955.
62  GCPPT 1|1|73 14 June 1956.
63  GCPPT 1|1|72 19 July 1954.
64  GCPPT 1|1|71 29 September 1953.
65  GCPPT 1|1|72 17 July 1954.
66  ibid. 31 May 1955.
67  ibid. 15 and 29 May 1955.
68  GCPPT 1|1|73 10 and 21 October 1955.
69  ibid. 26 July 1956.
70  GCPPT 1|1|59 30 August 1941.
71  GCPPT 1|1|71 10 August 1953.
72  Louismet, S. *Mysticism – True and False* pp 143–145. Extracts from the
    pages quoted here appear (with attribution) in the final paragraph of
    Aelfrida's *Spiritual Exercises*.
73  Tillyard, Ae. *Spiritual Exercises* p 211.
74  Harris, R. pp 48–50.
75  Underhill, E. *Practical Mysticism* pp 184–186.
76  Harris, R. p 20. Significantly, perhaps, in the context of *Naomi da
    Costa,* Harris couches his example in terms of the Jewish religion.
77  Underhill, E. *Practical Mysticism* p182.
78  Tillyard, Ae. *Spiritual Exercises* p 211.
79  GCPPT 1|1|62a. Letter from Father Cary to Aelfrida of 29 July
    1944.
80  Tillyard, Ae. *Christian Old Age* pp11 and 82 (GCPPT 2|17).
81  Tillyard, Ae. *A Little Road-Book for Mystics* pp 133–134.
82  GCPPT 1|1|73 23 October 1955
83  GCPPT 1|1|30 9 April 1925.
84  GCPPT 1|1|62 9 December 1944.
85  Tillyard, Ae. *Christian Old Age* pp 86 and 93.
86  Tillyard, Ae. *The Glory of the West* pp 213–215 (GCPPT 12|16|3).
87  GCPPT 1|1|66 9 September 1949.
88  GCPPT 1|1|71 31 July 1953.
89  ibid. 10 August 1953.
90  ibid. 6 August 1953.
91  GCPPT 1|1|71 31 July 1953.
    GCPPT 1|1|74 22 February 1958.
92  GCPPT 1|1|71 'Passion Sunday' (4 April) 1954.
93  GCPPG. A1 4|2 Letter from Aelfrida to Alethea Graham of 29
    December 1958.
94  Tillyard, Ae. *Christian Old Age* p 79.
95  GCPPT 1|1|73 24 February 1956.
96  Tillyard, Ae. *Christian Old Age* p 82.
97  GCPPT 1|1|71 4 April 1954.
98  Underhill, E. *The Spiritual Life* pp 43–45. *The Spiritual Life* was one of
    the new books reviewed by Aelfrida for *Theology* in 1937, reviews to
    which Father Cary objected in terms of her 'spiritual' silence.
99  ibid.
100 De Sales, F. *Treatise on the Love of God* pp 31 and 100–103.
101 GCPPT 1|1|34 16 December 1926.
102 GCPPT 1|1|72 26 March 1955.
103 GCPPT 1|1|72 1 January 1955.
    Tillyard, Ae. *Christian Old Age* p 79.
104 *Matthew* 25: 35, 36, and 40 (KJV).
105 Tillyard, Ae. *Christian Old Age* p 76.
106 ibid. pp 11 and 76.
107 GCPPT 1|1|74 4 November 1957.
108 Tillyard, Ae. *The Glory of the West* pp 1–3 (GCPPT 2|16|3).
109 ibid. p 179.
110 ibid. pp 191–194 (GCPPT 2|16|1 Pt 1).
111 GCPPT 1|1|73 'Christmas Eve' (24 December) 1955.
112 GCPPT 1|1|74 21 May 1957. The sentiment quoted was made by
    Aelfrida in the context of her lecture *Belonging to God*.
113 GCPPT 1|1|73 'Christmas Eve' (24 December) 1955.
114 GCPPT 1|1|72 2 August 1954.

115 Paget, F. Introductory essay *Concerning Discipline* pp 8–9 and 11 quoting Cassian's definition of *accidie*.

116 ibid. pp 8–9 and 13.

117 GCPPT 1|1|71 12 June 1954. Aelfrida agreed with Bishop Paget's book apart from the essay commented on in this diary entry.

118 Tillyard, Ae. *The Glory of the West* pp 174–175 (GCPPT 2|16|3).

119 Tillyard, Ae. *Christian Old Age* pp 52–53.

120 GCPPT 1|1|65 4 September 1947.

121 Tillyard. Ae. *Naomi da Costa* p207 (GCPPT 2|22).

122 Tillyard, Ae. *Christian Old Age* p 26.

123 GCPPT 1|1|71 10 May 1954.

124 GCPPT 1|1|73 'Christmas Eve' (24 December) 1955. The second commandment as listed in *Exodus* 20: 4 concerns the making of graven images; Aelfrida's second is taken from later interpretations of Mosaic Law (e.g. *Leviticus* 19:18) as quoted by Christ in *Matthew* 19:19.

125 GCPPT 1|1|73 'Christmas Eve' (24 December) 1955.
GCPPT 1|1|74 19 September 1957.

126 Tillyard, Ae. *Christian Old Age* p 118.

127 GCPPT 1|1|68 12 August 1950.

128 GCPPT 1|1|64 17 June 1946.

129 GCPPT 1|1|49 19 October 1935.

130 Tillyard, Ae. *The Closer Walk with God* pp 152–153.

131 ibid. p 129.

132 ibid. pp 122–131.

133 Frost, B. *The Art of Mental Prayer* pp 247–254.

134 Tillyard, Ae. *The Closer Walk with God* p 123.

135 GCPPT 1|1|68 12 August 1950.

136 GCPPT 1|1|72 26 and 27 March 1955.

137 Tillyard, Ae. *Christian Old Age* p 126.

138 GCPPT 1|1|71 'Maundy Thursday' (14 April) 1954.
GCPPT 1|1|72 7 September 1954.

139 GCPPT 1|1|73 27 January 1957.

140 GCPPT 1|1|74 4 May 1957.

141 GCPPT 1|1|73 10 October 1955 and 31 December 1956.
GCPPT 1|1|74 29 August 1957.

142 GCPPT 1|1|72 16 April 1955.

143 GCPPT 1|1|71 20 August 1953.

144 GCPPT 1|1|75 19 March 1959.

145 GCPPT 1|1|74 25 June 1958.

146 GCPPT 1|1|74 9 February and 28 April 1958.

147 Dante *The Divine Comedy: Paradise* 3: 115–116 and 4:136–139.

148 *Corinthians* I 13:13. (KJV).

149 Tillyard, Ae. *The Fruits of Silence* pp 31–36 (GCPPT 2|18).

150 GCPPT 1|1|72 9 and 14 September 1954.

151 ibid. 22 September 1954.

152 ibid. 19 October 1954.

153 ibid. 10 November 1954.

154 GCPPT 1|1|72 30 October and 14 December 1954 and 2 August 1955.
GCPPT 1|1|73 20 and 28 January and 1, 4 and 28 March 1956.

155 GCPPT 1|1|73 20 January 1956.

156 ibid.

157 GCPPT 1|1|72 1 April 1955.

158 ibid. 1 January 1955.

159 ibid. 26 April 1955.

160 GCPPT 1|1|73 20 and 21 January 1956.

161 ibid. 7 April 1956.

162 Tillyard, Ae. *Naomi da Costa* p 143.

163 GCPPT 1|1|73 17 October 1956.

164 ibid. 7 February and 7 April 1956. Aelfrida's list is preserved in GCPPT 1|1|73a; the diary entries from which it was compiled may be elucidated from her numbering the relevant pages of contemporary volumes of her diary (1|1|72 and 1|1|73) and marking relevant episodes in pencil e.g. on p 95 of 1|1|72 she described Sister Winifred as a 'despot' and on p 32 as 'full of wrath and determination' and marked the words accordingly.

165 GCPPT 1|1|73 7 February and 17 March 1956.

166 ibid. 17 October 1956.

167 GCPPT 1|158 20 July 1940.

168 GCPPT 1|1|74 'Easter [Day]' (21 April) 1957.

169 GCPPT 1|1|73 2 December 1955.

170 ibid. 1 March 1956.

171 ibid. 20 October 1956.

172 GCPPT 1|1|72 14 December 1954.
GCPPT 1|1|73 22 January 1956.

173 GCPPT 1|1|73 22 January 1956.

174 GCPPT 1|1|73 20 and 22 January and 10 February 1956.

175 Buchan, J. p 40.

176 GCPPT 1|1|73 31 January 1956.

177 GCPPT 1|1|52 13 November 1936.

178 Tillyard, Ae. *Rich Man's Choice* pp 266–269 (GCPPT 2|21|2 Pt 1) and pp 296–297 (2|21|3 Pt 2).

179 GCPPT 1|1|74 21 and 29 September 1957. The address, appropriately in the present context, was the last Aelfrida ever delivered and its preparation occasioned the bestowal of a capital D on the devil.

180 GCPPT 1|1|74 29 September 1957.

181 ibid. 23 October 1957.

182 ibid. 12 October 1957. The satellite to which Aelfrida refers was Sputnik I, launched by the Russians on 4 October 1957, ostensibly as a contribution to an International Geophysical Year but possibly also with a view to loading future man-made objects orbiting the earth with nuclear warheads, hence her reference to a '*Dies Irae*'.

183 GCPPT 1|1|73 23 January 1957.
GCPPT 1|1|74 30 October 1957.

184 GCPPT 1|1|74 23 October 1957 (Author's emphasis).

185 GCPPT 2|25|3. (11).

186 Papini, G. p143.

187 GCPPT 1|1|73 1 February 1956.

188 ibid. 20 and 21 January 1956.

189 ibid. 26 March and 8 April 1956.

190 ibid. 14, 15, and 26 October and 1 November 1956.

191 ibid. 20 and 21 October 1956.

192 ibid. 21 October 1956.

193 ibid. 17 and 21 October 1956.

194 Tillyard, Ae. *The Glory of the West* pp 201 and 208 (GCPPT 2|16|3).

195 Tillyard, Ae. *Christian Old Age* p120.

196 GCPPT 1|1|70 'Lent I' (22 or 23 February) 1953.

197 Tillyard, Ae. *Christian Old Age* pp 63–64.

198 ibid. pp 123–124.

199 GCPPT 1|1|73 12 April 1956.

200 Tillyard, Ae. Poem entitled *Goodbye* written at Fordfield as a farewell to Eric Silvanus on 9 September 1911 (GCPPT 2|5).

201 Tillyard, Ae. *Christian Old Age* p 107.

202 Tillyard Ae. *The Closer Walk with God* pp 33–34 (GCPPT 2|16|3).

203 Tillyard, Ae. *The Silence of God* p 34 (GCPPT 2|20).

204 GCPPT 1|1|74 2 December 1957.

# Via Crucis

Though increasingly handicapped by age and infirmity, Aelfrida maintained a lively interest in life beyond St John's Home. Towards some aspects her view remained locally and internationally gloomy ('the Grand National, the Boat Race [and] various spicy crime cases *seem* to draw people's attention away from God … oh! for an outpouring of the Holy Spirit on England'[1]; 'the Americans have detonated a hydrogen bomb … above some Pacific island [and] scientists hint darkly at evil effects as yet unknown')[2] but towards others (the excavation of a Mycenaean palace at Pylos in Greece[3]; discoveries of 'galaxies and solar systems, new worlds maybe in the making … beyond anything the human imagination can grasp')[4] she evinced excitement at a future which appeared less 'like the End of All Things'[5] than tending to revelations. Some aspects were incomprehensible (what, for example, was a 'flatlet'?) and while she could conceive of Veronica flying to the United States, for Julius – her contemporary – to fly to Malta in search of 'Byz. Mus.' seemed almost inconceivable. And, rather ironically, an aspect of a past 'long and so successfully ignored!' returned to haunt her: apropos John Hibbs' association with the 'Corona Transport Co.' of Sudbury, Suffolk, she reminded John's father-in-law that she and Julius were related once more to 'the great world of commerce'[6] from which, as Tillyards, they had successfully disassociated themselves.

Letters and annual visits to Cambridge kept her up to date with family affairs but it is clear that just as she had voluntarily cut herself off from her immediate family twenty years earlier on her departure for Oxford, twenty years later it (with the exception of Julius and Mina) was voluntarily or involuntarily cutting itself off from her as careers and the emergence of another generation took priority over an aging relative regarded by few with affection and by some of whom she was barely known. (By March 1957 Walter and Constance had two boys apiece and Stephen two girls; remembering Chiara's negative reaction to her own birth, Aelfrida gave each girl 'babe' a special welcome.) The press, as befitted a newspaper proprietor's daughter, remained important to her. A letter (*Dress Reforms for Sisters*) criticising "the wearing of complicated and burdensome clothes" irrespective of the weather and noting that "some of the unhealthier

**The Way of the Cross**

part of traditional dress [should] be modified, even discarded" by those of a "Religious Vocation" appeared in the *Church Times* of May 1955 to demonstrate that the pseudonymous '*Tertiary*' who had herself "spent nearly fourteen years in convent precincts"[7] and who twenty years earlier had noted that nuns' clothing was 'the last word in inconvenience and discomfort' was ahead of her time, though not until the Second Vatican Council of 1965 was her suggestion adopted. The Births, Marriages, and Deaths columns of *The Times* (particularly the Deaths) kept her in touch, for many of her acquaintances were – so it seemed – about to feature there. Dorothea Conybeare, 'paralysed' following a fall, called Aelfrida to her bedside 'to bid an implicit goodbye' and to assure herself that the latter was 'not leading too ascetic a life' at St John's Home but, following a pious letter 'more or less dictated' by St Raphael, left hospital able to walk, to compose godly poems, and to outlive her former school friend, but the 'astonishingly versatile Dr Thomas of the University Library', now an elderly gentleman resident in Hope House following a stroke, remembered her perfectly before predeceasing her: 'one of the most learned and humble men' was her eulogy.[8] The Zender Browns, both 'rather pathetic' now, he over eighty and forgetful 'but [with] goodwill unaltered' (we discover he was a professor from a caption in Alethea's photograph album; Aelfrida fails to mention it), she 'full of courage and determination' but 'if only she wouldn't sport a "mare's tail" coiffure, brilliant blue ... glasses and an *outré* blue and white dress ...')[9], faded from sight on their departure for California in 1954. Florence Keynes, intending 'to live to be a hundred' but dying in her ninety-eighth year in 1958 to a typical Aelfrida obituary: 'she was a great lady ... I wish I knew she was a Christian'.[10]

Correspondence from a living Little Friend concerning the literary remains of a dead one engaged Aelfrida in the summer of 1955: 'at last', she wrote, 'a letter from Tommy (Dr Ernest Altounyan)'. Tommy, sixty-five and 'thoroughly worked out as head and chief surgeon at the Altounyan Hospital in Aleppo' but jubilant at hearing from his "dear, dearer, dearest Aelfrida", was Frank Stokoe's literary executor and in this capacity had been entrusted with editing and publishing Fidelio's '*journal intime*'. Aelfrida's ostensible reason for replying to 'Tommy's' letter was to discover his progress to date but given Stokoe's death and his statement shortly before then that he had to sort out and dispose of books and papers prior to leaving Comberton, that death prevented him from doing so, and that Fidelio, as Taqui Altounyan's description of his study demonstrated, was a hoarder ("the mantelpiece was solid with letters, the ones at the back yellow, the ink faded and hardly readable")[11], circumstances may have suggested that Fidelio's comments about herself and letters from Aleister Crowley entrusted to him for safekeeping might appear. It seems, however, that neither Tommy nor Taqui's husband Robert Stephens, foreign correspondent of *The Observer*, considered the journal suitable for publication; Aelfrida, aware of Fidelio's sexual proclivities, herself considered it 'more suited for psychologists than the general public' and after having vainly suggested Juan Mascaró or Geoffrey Keynes as editors, the former because 'he knew FWS intimately', the latter because he was a doctor, resigned herself to having done 'all that Fidelio's ghost could possibly require of [her]'.[12]

Revenants of a younger generation also appeared in Aelfrida's life in the 1950s and were welcomed as much for who they were as to what they represented of youth and hope. On 24 July 1954 she was visited by her 'Barnardo child' (elsewhere she calls her '[her] dear Barnardo niece'), Heather Connon, aged twelve. Aelfrida had sponsored Heather since 1942 but only now do we hear that the child had suffered 'inhuman treatment'[13] as a baby before being taken into care; indeed, it seems that their Oxford rendezvous was the first time the two had met. (It was to Heather that Aelfrida gave one of the 'holy pictures' kept by her for many years, namely the copy of Andrea del Sarto's *Madonna delle Arpie* bought in Florence in 1904 and described by her then as 'the most beautiful picture in the world' and in 1958 as an object it 'cost [her] something to relinquish'[14]; the copy she sent to Constantine in 1904 may have had less pleasant associations, given that in Greek mythology a harpy is depicted as a malign monster with a woman's head and body and the wings and claws of a bird of prey and sometimes as a 'snatcher' of souls grasping a small symbolic person in her claws.) A child of more privilege, Annette Barron, Aelfrida's American goddaughter and the first child and only girl born at Wetenhall Cottage, wrote to Aelfrida in 1949 to tell her godmother 'all about herself'; seven years later, aged twenty, she enclosed a photograph of her 'sophisticated looking' self, vivid proof that the 'largest, fattest most staring baby' who visited septicaemic Aelfrida in the Brunswick Nursing Home in 1935 wearing a cap adapted from her godmother's 'great grandmother's nightcap'[15] had become a personable young lady.

Aelfrida's new tendency to greet each new year as if 'it may be *Ave atque Vale* – who knows'[16] found her bidding hail and farewell to others instead. Autumn 1953 found her 'talking ... telepathically about the old days in Cambridge' to Percy Stanley, but Percy, in the process of reading Florence Keynes' memoir *Gathering up the Threads* before copying out relevant pages for his former inamorata's perusal, died aged eighty on 16 October. Aelfrida's obituary was chastened: 'I was a graceless young thing in the days when he would make love to me but [now] I appreciate how he sang and worked and taught to the glory of God'.[17] Another admirer, 'poor old Owsie', the Welborn Owston Smith once described as a 'goggle-eyed friend of Agnes Slack' who fifty years later gave it to her 'hot and strong' regarding her treatment of men in general and himself in particular but of whom we do not hear much in her flirting days, died in April 1954: he and she had not corresponded for many years but he had been on her Friday '*adoration réparative*' list so she had 'thought of him once week'.[18] (What ex-missionary 'Owsie' had done to warrant inclusion, she does not say; perhaps his tendency to grope her teenage daughters qualified him?) On 16 December 1954 she was visited during the night by a 'disembodied soul passing through [her] room' who intimated that it was her 'old but eccentric friend Dr GFC Searle' on a 'friendly visit' (he failed to greet her with an 'early Christian kiss' on this occasion) and that he was "dead [and] going on"; she was therefore unsurprised to read in *The Times* of 17 December the obituary of a man who had died the previous day. (It is interesting to speculate how many of Aelfrida's premonitions with regard to the dead and dying were due to her being 'a visionary!'[19] and how much to news imbibed from other sources, for only rarely does she provide diary evidence of events as they happen: Dr Searle's visit went undescribed until after she read his obituary and her telepathic conversation with Percy Stanley took place 'some weeks'[20] before his death.) Mr Church the gardener (we never learn his first name) died in his sleep at ninety plus in spring 1955; Aelfrida arranged for flowers to be sent from the gardens he loved at Fordfield and Wetenhall Cottage but her eulogy bore a sting: 'he was a *good* man, good husband, father, friend, servant [though] his ideas on religion were very dim'. But, she added in mitigation, 'I am sure God deals gently with such'.[21]

Deaths of men who had loved her in their various ways as cousin, admirer, lecturer, and employee were followed by that of a woman unmet between 1913 and 1955 but corresponded with during the intervening decades: Charlotte Greene of Boston, USA. Charlotte, it seems, was a member of the Anglo-American coterie living in Le Vésinet when Constantine and Aelfrida inhabited the Villa *La Cigogne* though Charlotte's name appears only in Aelfrida's Visitors Book. (Her signature appears between those of two of Constantine's lady friends, Déla Bernet and Ethel Ponselle.) On 8 February 1955 Charlotte, on a visit to Europe, arrived at St John's Home where Aelfrida, 'very glad to see her', showed her the book bearing 'the names of Bostonians, some of them [Charlotte's] friends'.[22] A moving encounter for both old ladies but doomed never to be repeated: Charlotte died in December. But as testimony of Aelfrida's tenacity as a correspondent – and how interesting it would be to know what version of her life she gave to a woman she thought never to see again – her epistolary relationship with Mrs Greene can hardly be bettered.

1956, however, was the year in which Aelfrida bade '*vale*' to many people of whom she was or had been fond, so many, in fact, that this in itself might have provided sufficient cause for her distorted view of and her venomous behaviour towards Sister Winifred Marcian. (With her usual lack of insight she placed the blame squarely on Sister Winifred's shoulders: 'she is *not in charity with me*'.)[23]

The first to die was Lilian Whitehouse, once Aelfrida's sole 'lady-admirer', now a firm friend and one of the few people privy to Alethea's inclinations to suicide following her final departure from Malling. Aelfrida learnt the news from *The Times*, writing sadly in February 1956 that Lilian's 'vitality and zest for life' ought to have allowed her to outlive 'by many years' a woman three years younger than herself. (Their final meeting, judging by Aelfrida's diary and Visitors Book, took place on 21 August 1955.) Aelfrida and Lilian had known each other for over fifty years, Lilian's arrival in Brooklands Avenue attracting Aelfrida's attention not only because Lilian wore vividly coloured clothes ('russet brown and red with brown shoes – very daring in those days') but also because Lilian dared be openly something Aelfrida only dared be surreptitiously – 'a bit of a rebel' – although, she added, Lilian pretended 'to be more of a rebel than she was … to try and shock me' and though ostensibly irreligious, 'was deeply religious at heart'.[24] She may also have envied Lilian's teaching career, for although she derided Lilian's French accent, and noted snidely following Dr Whitehouse's death in 1916 that Lilian would have to 'turn out and earn her own living'[25], we learn from accounts of Lilian's career[26] that she was already doing so and was respected for what she did. Furthermore, gibes by Aelfrida concerning Lilian's over-familiarity with undergraduates did not come well from one whose Little Friendships were a flourishing phenomenon and whose relationship with Anthony Wrightson went further than any of Lilian's cheery flirtations.

In March 1956 'an envelope with [a] wide black border and a French stamp' enclosed sad news: 'dear Zelle … was dead', Zelle, 'perfect darling'[27] Marie Aubriet, appointed nursery governess in 1889 to teach Dudu and Frida French by the directest possible method beings someone with whom adult Julius and Aelfrida kept in loving touch throughout their adult lives. Later the same month ('so many deaths recently') came sad news of Edmund Whittaker 'who became world famous', dead at eighty-two (Aelfrida's description of him as 'an old friend … whom we knew in Presbyterian days' disguises the fact that Sir Edmund – as he became – had been part of 'Chiara's little plan'[28] to 'normalise' her daughter by marrying her to a fellow of Trinity College ten years Frida's senior) and of Effie Stanley, her death leaving only a single member of the bohemian family of which one sibling had adored fifteen-year-old Frida and another married a German girl whose cousin became Aelfrida's sister-in-law.

Willie Searle died at sixty-seven in April 1956. On receiving the news Aelfrida wrote a 'very brief note of sympathy' to Tess and hoped of her own nearly-husband that 'he RIP'. She also described his illness as 'long', which it was (her diary charts his slow decline in brief entries written in 1953, 1954, and 1955 whose tone ranges from sympathetic – 'poor Willie grows gradually weaker' – to mildly exasperated – 'instead of lying in his grave as everyone expected [he] is back … home') and 'mysterious' which it was not, except possibly to Willie himself, for Tess remained adamant that he not be told the truth. She provided the man who had kept faith with her since 1912 with a typical epitaph: hearing from Tess that Willie had become a Catholic, she dismissed him (she was bored with hearing the last of him) with the words: 'well, as long as [he enters] the Heavenly City we will not quarrel with the gate'.[29] She then added Mrs and the late Mr Searle to her Friday list, though what they done to require reparation she does not say.

On holiday at Wetenhall Cottage in July 1956, Aelfrida met Joan Cooper, very much alive and 'very up to date with permed hair and a flowery dress' who on leaving announced she had enjoyed "conversation at a different level" ('different from what?!!' asked her former patient amusedly, recalling perhaps, 'Dr Joan's' fears that Aelfrida might, had she succeeded in 'setting [her] cap', as the expression went, at Joseph Cooper, have become her stepmother)[30], but tidings of other people (men, that is to say; 'the womenfolk', she wrote later while noting how many of Julius' and Eustace's contemporaries predeceased them, 'live longer')[31] were less cheerful. Reading (or rather *not* reading: 'I looked at the pictures, gave [a] glance here and there and decided it wasn't fit for a lady') John Symonds' biography, she noted that Aleister Crowley 'died alone in a boarding house in Hastings, a miserable man' and hoped that 'Scientific Illuminism' died with him[32]. (Or *did* she merely 'glance'? Her description of Leo Myers' *The Root and Flower* as 'even more unwholesome' than Rose Macaulay's *The Towers of Trebizond* suggests a full reading of both, for how else glean the information that 'whoever you are and whatever you believe, your instincts, especially sex, dominate you' and why else decide to add Rose and Leo to her 'Friday list for *adoration réparative*', a list already adorned by Crowley himself)?[33] It was, however, while musing on Aleister Crowley's end that she received a disembodied prod from another man and suddenly 'came up against the *certainty* that he was dead'. And here, she adds, clipping it out, 'is his obituary notice from *The Times*'[34]: Gian Falco, dead in Florence on 9 July at the age of seventy-five.

Aelfrida and Gian Falco, now referred to as Giovanni Papini but with his pen name appended as a biographical aide-memoire, had corresponded at lengthening intervals for over fifty years. ('I have been neglectful', she admitted on receiving his prod; his aligning himself with Mussolini's fascist government may have contributed though she nowhere notes her disapproval and indeed wrote glowingly in *Christian Old Age* – albeit without mentioning his name – of there being "in Florence more than forty years ago a group of brilliant young men, philosophers, painters, poets, psychologists, who loved the Future and loathed the Past".)[35] She criticised her old friend's *Times* obituary (it described him as a "hagiologist and satirist") as '*not* very understanding'[36] of him but given that it also described Papini as possessing "a perverse twist in his nature which set [him] at enmity with his fellows and prevented his winning the affection for which he craved, thus permanently warping him", noted his "brilliant gift of invective", itself "in no small measure a weapon of defence [for] fending off the world from his inmost heart", and argued that he was frequently "more feared than loved" and that what made him interesting was "his spiritual odyssey in search of that crumb of certainty without which he … could not exist and the absence of which was the cause of most of his restless discontent"[37], it may be that in it Aelfrida saw too much of herself. But perhaps it was because of the similarity of their souls that she kept in touch with Papini throughout their respective marriages and credal conversions, two world wars, and his support for a political regime she abhorred.

To only two of the recent dead does Aelfrida refer again; one was Papini. In April 1957 she received an unexpected communication directed to 'ex-Fordfield' from Viola Papini, one of Papini's two daughters, in which Viola stated that once assured that Aelfrida was still alive, Viola would send her 'a Very Important Letter'. Intrigued, Aelfrida responded in Italian and by return. A week later, Viola informed her that while preparing a biography of her 'illustrious father', she had found '*all* the letters [Aelfrida] ever wrote him' among his papers. (They dealt 'chiefly', noted Aelfrida, with literary and philosophical subjects, 'chiefly' being an interesting word in this context given that on at least one occasion the tone of the correspondence had become flirtatious.) Had Aelfrida, asked Viola, kept Papini's letters to her and if so could she send her a selection with a view to publication? Aelfrida, so she said, had kept none (she had, but only one and that possibly inadvertently, slipped between the pages of her diary – where it remained) and proof of Papini's devotion left her cold: 'I … admired his brilliance', she wrote, 'but I never took him seriously as a thinker though just to please him I used to call him *caro maestro* [and] I didn't care for him personally'.[38] But if so, why lecture on him in Cambridge, why translate his books, why devote most of her *Independent Review* article of 1906 to a eulogy of a young man she regarded as the intellectual leader of the literary *Movimento Fiorentino*, and why recall so fondly the short time she spent in his company as one of 'adventure [and] quick glowing contacts with people and … ideas'?[39]

Added to the *Via Crucis* deemed 'suitable' for an elderly lady such as herself, the deaths in such quick succession of an old friend, a beloved governess, a distant relative, a former suitor, and an academic whose 'quick glowing contacts' with her sparked a lifetime's correspondence, must have seemed to exemplify and extend the 'privileges one does not usually appreciate' of 'pain, weariness, limitations and so and so forth'[40], 'privileges' sweetened only by their having been recommended by Bishop Wynn as appropriate Lenten replacements for a discipline reluctantly returned to Tymawr. And it was to the Bishop to whom Aelfrida turned for consolation in the course of her 1956 summer holiday in Cambridge. Meeting him on 7 July and, for once, in Ely, she was delighted to discover that not only did he '*wholeheartedly*' approve of her addressing the Methodist Women's meetings in Oxford and attending 'RC Mass' at Hope House, for these, he said, were human manifestations of the Holy Spirit's '*unifying* grace' (he also advised her to 'maintain a critical attitude' towards spiritual events like the 'Pentecostal' one experienced during her first lecture to the Methodist Women while assuring her that he believed it to be 'perfectly genuine' – on her terms) but also that 'he was *radiant*' (there was 'no other word for it') and showed in every 'permissible' (*sic*) way his delight at seeing her again.[41] Aelfrida, for her part, was delighted to see Edward Wynn recovered from a 'breakdown' suffered early in July 1954 which three months later found him still "suffering from much depression and disquiet" and requesting her prayers to assist his recovery.[42] (*The Times* had reported that he had been "ordered three months complete rest", on reading which Aelfrida persuaded herself that – 'alas! and alas!' – Wynn had not heeded her warnings regarding 'overwork', a diagnosis the Bishop appeared to confirm in a letter from the London Hospital saying he was "completely tired out".)[43] Recording her worry that the Bishop sounded so 'very gloomy' that she wondered if she might '*never*' hear from him again'[44], Aelfrida (who had, of course, encountered him at Parson Drove in the meantime) was gratified to see her friend and spiritual director after so long, to be granted an extended interview at Church House, to hear Edward Ely insist that he descend with her to her waiting taxi, and to overhear his *sotto voce* comment that for "such a precious person" he could do no less.[45] A month and a week later Edward Wynn was dead.

He died slowly; Aelfrida, back in Oxford, charted his decline from bulletins issued by *The Times*. (On the same day as her mother's meeting with him, Alethea suffered her second attack of 'gastroenteritis' and was admitted to the Acland Nursing Home for 'nursing and tests'[46]; Aelfrida gave redecoration of her room at St John's Home as a reason for not returning to Oxford and mother and daughter did not meet again until 22 July.) The first, issued on 26 July 1956, announced the Bishop's admission to Addenbrooke's Hospital on 23 July, the second his diagnosis: "coronal (*sic*) thrombosis"; both answered Aelfrida's diarised query 'I wonder how serious this is?' by stating that Wynn's condition gave "rise to anxiety".[47] (As it would, this being the Bishop's *second* 'coronal thrombosis', his first, disguised as fatigue, having occurred two years earlier to the month.) Daily bulletins interspersed with diary entries show how unwell he was ("still seriously ill", on 4 August; "condition unchanged", on 8 August; "still very weak", on 10 August) and Aelfrida's reaction: 'have I allowed him to be a "human consolation" beyond the limits imposed by God on me as a tertiary?'; 'I am surprised … how much his illness *hurts* me' (God refused her offer to bear '*some*' of Edward Wynn's pain or to exchange her life for his); 'it is not that I fear to be bereft of him – I have my guardian angel to guide me and … a confessor. I should mind very little if I were told that I should never see him again'; '[at our last meeting] he made over to me an as-yet-unexplored spiritual inheritance which will last me all my days'; 'what if he were to live after all!' (She also enquired of St Raphael if she should send Wynn a last message, but on his replying "no, leave him to God", wrote '*Fiat*. Miss Virginia Fitch to coffee'.) The bulletin of 11 August stated that Wynn's condition was "causing grave anxiety"; noting 'that looks as if the Angel of Death were by his bedside', Aelfrida read prayers for the Commendation of the Soul after Vespers. That night, waking after a horrible dream of being summoned to Wynn's bedside but being prevented by 'obstacles' from reaching it, she found her room '*full of his presence*'. On Sunday 12 August at 9.30am as she prayed for him in the Home's chapel, Edward Wynn died aged sixty-seven. 'Long ago', Aelfrida remembered, her guardian angel had warned her that if she '*leaned*' on any human consolation it would be taken from her; 'has it not been?' she asked herself now.[48] Then her heart broke.

Although Aelfrida's health had been far from robust prior to 12 August, diary entries chiefly record worsening arthritic pain and minor ailments magnified (as usual) into major episodes. She had virtually ceased complaining of 'heart attacks' and complained of 'cramp in the heart' only if particularly upset by the evil machinations (as she saw them) of Sisters Superior and their acolytes. Within a month of Edward Wynn's death, however, she showed signs of serious cardiac disease and within two had been seen on several occasions by two of the Home's trio of doctors and had spent four days on St Anne's ward because too ill to be nursed in her room. (That she was as ill as diary entries imply – her hand-writing deteriorates and she makes shorter entries – is obvious, but so too is her indomitable or incorrigible spirit: too ill to attend Mass and having to take confession in her room, she worms out from and records personal details of the nurse caring for her and proffers spiritual guidance in return.) Her tendency to misdiagnose her illnesses and to record only what she wishes to reveal makes accurate diagnosis difficult but from entries made in September/October 1956 we may deduce that, for once, she did not overplay her symptoms and that she rapidly became very ill indeed – virtually a cardiac cripple – with what seems to have been atrial fibrillation and congestive cardiac failure for which she was prescribed digoxin. Other prescribed medications were for 'high blood pressure and heart' and for shortness of breath, worse at night but overall so severe that she could no longer lie flat and sometimes wondered 'if [her] last hour had come'. Her symptoms she variously describes as 'a real Oxford cough'[49] due to 'congestion of the lungs'[50], loss of weight reducing her to 'an absolute skeleton', and, after a check by one of the doctors on 'the health records of [her] parents and collaterals' and an enquiry as to whether she herself had ever suffered rheumatic fever, as a 'strained' and 'weakened' heart which would probably 'last out a bit longer' provided she survived the coming winter.[51] It seems, however, that the emotional shock induced by meeting Edward Wynn again after a three-year separation, by his illness and death occurring so soon afterwards, and by her conviction that *his* death was the wages of *her* sin, was enough to 'break' a heart already weakened by cardiovascular disease.

Stress cardiomyopathy induced by Wynn's death had non-medical consequences too. Not the least of these and one which may have contributed to the others was Aelfrida's decision, 'bruised and wounded' though she was[52], to conceal her grief from everyone and confide in no-one, not Alethea who, unaware of the strength of her mother's feelings for Edward Wynn and of her illness (Aelfrida refused to have her told) was absent from Oxford during this time and given her mother's unfeeling behaviour towards herself might not have returned even if informed, and not the Home's confessor. To him she confided only her need to be as prepared as possible should her 'heavenly birthday' arrive sooner than expected, her 'lively faith' in Christ, and the continuing conflict between her 'need for solitude and silence' and the charitable clarity with which she regarded the

'value and beauty of [the] souls [of] the dear people here' and how much (though not why) it '*mattered*'[53] to her that 'dear people' be made to feel loved and understood. Father Hill, unaware of her distress, took her disguised plea for sympathy at face value.

Dismissive remarks notwithstanding, Aelfrida never regarded Edward Wynn as an 'episode' in her life. In spite of 'Bélisian' behaviour towards him, as witness her tendency to exaggerate his pleasantly civil reaction to something she said or did into over-reaction on his part to her physical, intellectual, or spiritual charms, and emotional silliness with regard to a relationship regarded as sinful because involving a member of the opposite sex or because it reminded her of the 'beastly' side of her nature, Aelfrida, it seems, loved Edward Wynn more deeply, perhaps, than any other man. More, perhaps, even than Julius, for Wynn offered escape from preoccupation with herself and her family, a chance of congenial companionship ("ripe wisdom, mellowed humour") with a 'Christian gentleman' in which intellectual and spiritual compatibility might 'marry' and create 'a large family of splendid children'[54], 'children of the brain', that is to say, in the form of books written together. And perhaps a modicum of "romance from [a] mature [vintage]".[55] But because to admit to emotions and emotional needs inappropriate to a tertiary or to a 'recuperated' virgin sworn to bodily and emotional chastity and even more inappropriate to a 'detached' mystic craving spiritual union with Deity at the expense of 'human affections' might be taken as a sign of spiritual weakness and censured or ridiculed as a result, and because even at this late stage in her life she was too proud to admit to having indulged in '*human consolations*', she suffered in silence – and ensured that others suffered too as a result of her intransigence.

The consequences of Edward Wynn's death to a woman who had once regarded (with hindsight, how ironically) their relationship as so 'perfect' that it should be allowed to rest in peace and he and she never to meet again, were manifest in her subsequent behaviour, the first manipulative, the second endlessly introspective. They also indicate that Aelfrida once again 'crashed', though less because being active for God and more because one of the 'sudden catastrophes'[56] criticised by Alethea as improbable had struck down both herself and the man she loved and had, as collateral damage, broken her heart.

Manipulative behaviour – she played off doctors against nurses, nurses against Sisters, Sisters against doctors – was the main reason for her finding herself temporarily in a ward, for how else could the Home deal with a patient suffering real and imaginary illnesses ('jaundice' being one of the latter) and refusing to take prescribed medication ('I am renouncing potions'[57], she wrote, 'in favour of letting nature take its course' – which nature, as we shall see, obligingly did) or differentiate 'fussification' from pathology (she had been well enough to go by taxi to Marston Street to visit Alethea but had telephoned the doctor to say she had a 'mortal illness')[58] without keeping her under closer supervision than GETHSEMANE afforded? Family too were subject to manipulation: if, she wrote, 'I should prove to be [dying] I … would go to Wetenhall Cottage and thence to Hope House – to facilitate funeral arrangements and to save Alethea the pain of seeing me on my deathbed', but plans submitted to Alethea and Julius in the event of her survival, namely the addition of a 'swallow's nest' onto the Hope House side of Wetenhall Cottage (always given as her permanent address, St John's Home being merely a temporary residence) in which she could live as a 'semi-hermit'[59], were vehemently objected to by Alethea on her own and her uncle's account. It therefore seemed likely that should she ever become 'unfit to resume ordinary existence'[60], Aelfrida's *via crucis* would lead inexorably back to the ward, a place tolerable for a short time by one as ill as she then was ('it is quite a different life, as different as a trip abroad – and things one doesn't like can be accepted as native customs … I thought I played my part as The Patient very well')[61] but intolerable as long-term accommodation because of its noise, lack of privacy, and regimented regime. (It was at this point that the interview between Sister Superior, nursing Sister Una Mary, Alethea, and Aelfrida took place after which Aelfrida begged Alethea to inform her of 'any faults … which may make me at all "difficult"' and promptly informed the Home's chaplain that 'the "rulers of the darkness of this world"'[62] were attacking Sister Winifred Marcian.) But how much trouble could have been avoided – and constructive sympathy extended – had pride not caused her to keep silent with regard to the event which precipitated this particular episode of physical and emotional disequilibrium.

'Older and more experienced than ever I was', as Aelfrida recorded of her seventy-third birthday on 5 October while 'opening letters and parcels … and saying [her] Office and … dear Ladies popping in and coughing filled the morning'[63], she was nevertheless not so ill as to be unable to fill pages of her diary with emotive and emotional dissections of her relationship with Edward Wynn. (Tucked inside it she preserved letters from his secretary describing his last days and funeral, and two obituaries, that from the *Church Times* describing Wynn's "warm and winning" personality, his ability to invite "confiding friendships", and how as man and bishop he was "approachable, beloved and trusted", that

from *The Times* ending "he was content to be a holy and humble man of God", a description annotated by Aelfrida 'very good indeed!')[64] 'I have not', she wrote, 'shed any tears for the Bishop and don't mean to but I am beginning … to realise how I long and shall continue to long for his warm handclasp, the sound of his voice and for the joy he felt in my presence as I in his'. Noting her appreciation of 'a guide who was both Bishop and Religious' and the great honour she felt 'when the Bishop decided (*sic*) that he would look after me spiritually', she also noted (a rationalisation, it seems) that she had been 'pretty stand-offish' during the first years of their director/directed relationship because she 'did not feel at home' with Edward Ely the public figure (Edward Wynn the man won her confidence: "with loving patience", his *Church Times* obituary noted, "he penetrated granite defences of reserve and inhibition") and, with more justification, that his visits made her position 'in Rectory and Vicarage extremely difficult'. (Father Lovell was 'angry' and Father Dunkin 'furious', but given that the Bishop described the former as one of his 'rather "difficult"' clergy and the latter as '*stupid* sometimes', it is possible that she maliciously revealed his opinions to them.) In self-defence, she noted that she was 'over 60 and no-one could imagine the Bishop was in love', if only because of his preference for keeping 'his inmost shrine inviolate for his own Lord'. ('To change the subject', she continues without a break, 'the 'Battle of the Green Corridor – a battle of wills between obstinate women – … has been raging all this time … How sad it is! Ladies – and Christians!!')[65] She also compared Edward Wynn to Lucius Cary, describing both as 'saints' and noting that the latter lived 'more in the supernatural than on earth' and that the former 'could have served God in any capacity, however difficult'.[66]

References to Lucius Cary are interesting because they shed further light on a previous Oxford relationship with an earlier mentor. The passage of twenty years had altered her view of the relationship and of the part she played in it; she also reveals aspects of it to which she had not made us privy before Edward Ely's death reminded her of them. 'I went to Father Cary', she writes, 'because the Lady Abbess sent me [because] she thought … I needed the help of a pure Contemplative. Had I known that Father Cary had the reputation of being the greatest … in the Church of England … I would never have gone near him because I instinctively avoid celebrities … When I attended his retreat at St Ursula's, Chiswick, [I believed him to be] just one of the Cowley Fathers. I understood next to nothing of his addresses but I did perceive that he had what I desperately needed [so] … I established myself in Oxford and presented myself at his confessional as if he had never seen or heard of me before … After the retreat he [wrote] to the Lady Abbess that he could do nothing for me as I did not understand how to use a director … [but] he took me in hand and began to teach me not only what I had to learn but [also] what I had to *un*learn, [though] Contemplation, of course, cannot be taught'. She also admits that she 'may' have dreamed of establishing with Father Cary 'some such relationship as existed between St Francis de Sales and Sainte Jeanne Chantal'[67] ("I wish", wrote Father O'Brien acerbically to Alethea in April 1936, "your mother would not form fantastic ideas about Father Cary – it will not help her")[68], an unlikely relationship given that Lucius Cary advocated contemplative withdrawal *from* the world and Francis de Sales' advice to 'Philothea' was to engage charitably *with* the world. (It was, in fact, Edward Wynn's gentle practical advice which resembled de Sales'.) She then admits to another reason for allowing 'God in His wisdom' to call her to Tymawr: Cary, she says, showed no inclination to adopt her as his Jeanne de Chantal and made it plain that he cared only 'for Fairacres and his nuns'. However, she adds, Father Cary 'was not pleased to lose a pupil who was just beginning to do him credit' and she herself did not feel as if she was deserting him because it seemed that in joining the SSC, she would draw nearer to him spiritually. This may be so, but the truth of the matter, as she finally admits, was that 'all I [really] needed to do was to calm down … [but] circumstances were anything but calm. [And] I longed for God too vehemently'.[69]

Wynn's death caused her to experience two visions. The first, incongruous and rather sinister but unsurprising given her tendency to suffer experiences of this kind when stressed, occurred while she was sitting in her deckchair, rosary in hand, and created in her mind a 'universal consciousness [of] *evil*' followed by a picture of Christ's tomb with a 'fringe of … darkness hinging over [it] like a great curved wave about to break'. (Was this, she wondered, because she had 'not yet assimilated [her] grief at the Bishop's death'.)[70] The second was of Christ lifting her up on His Cross to let her look out with Him 'over Time', a vision '*of very great* importance'[71] because it may have showed her not only her 'heavenly birthday' but also those with whom death would reunite her. Borrowing a book to which the Bishop had written an introduction brought some but scarcely adequate comfort to one desperately trying to follow his instructions to "try and welcome … pain"[72] because it represented Christ's suffering. The book, Hubert Northcott's *The Venture of Prayer* of 1951 (Aelfrida had known of its publication but had not read it prior to 1956), contained two passages of great relevance to her, one by Northcott

describing the spiritual life (and, as she must have realised, temporal life too) as a spiral way or staircase from which, as one climbs it, "one sees at each turn the same view … [but] from a higher standpoint" and meets "similar experiences but each time in an intenser form and a wider context"[73], the other by 'Edward Ely' himself stating that though prayer is essentially individual, "the prayerful activities of individual persons must be preserved from eccentricity".[74] 'Here is the book', Aelfrida wrote on the day she received the gentle reminder from beyond the grave which she hoped would show her 'the way' (the way she had come, she implies, but surely also the way she was to follow as advised by *two* spiritual mentors in one volume), adding as one whose 'heart and soul [ached] with pain' that she would not only 'offer it to the Lord' but would not let 'any shadow' of her sorrow 'depress anyone here'. And besides, how annoyed the Bishop would be if she 'moped'.

A single consolation (other than religion) presented itself in the form of the sole 'human' consolation she had left – 'Brother Julius' – and it was to him to whom she turned, or rather, having temporarily deserted him for Edward Wynn, returned.

Aelfrida, of course, had not literally deserted Julius – restricting herself to isolated visits to Cambridge may indicate increasing infirmity as much as arrangements made regarding annual holidays – but it is possible that opening a 'love-letter' from him ("Dearest Tit, this is to remind you of how much I love you …") on Christmas Day 1956, a day spent by Julius with his wife, family, and Alethea at Wetenhall Cottage, reminded her of "two long lives, side by side, in which we have never misunderstood each other" and that their brother/sister relationship *was* indeed 'perfect' in spite of both being 'very imperfect human beings'.[75] (Or, as she may have expressed it to Albert Erlande who paraphrased her in a novella describing a man and a woman who loved each other as children and believed they would never be separated, only to find themselves separated by circumstances and meeting again when it was too late for shared happiness, they were children whose lives were blighted by the same inauspicious star.)[76] Nor were her comments concerning him anything but loving. Each 'DearDuduDay' was now more welcome than the last, Aelfrida recording how much she enjoyed Julius' 'real *Cambridge* conversation' and much she loved him and was comforted by his being physically healthy and mentally alert in old age.[77] She was also, she noted, 'touched and humbled' by her brother's 'great love'[78] for her, a love expressed in everything he said and did, especially in his distress on saying goodbye, be this after snatched moments in Oxford (he did not always come exclusively to see his sister; some visits were paid during 'Byz. Mus.' conferences) or after lengthier holidays at Wetenhall Cottage where brother and sister trysted like lovers in Mina's absence and where Julius' face bore a 'tragic look' as he stood at the gate to watch his sister's taxi drive away because he 'hated to say good-bye' and because in one's seventies goodbyes 'may be final'. Aelfrida too found farewells increasingly 'poignant' even as she returned 'gladly' to the 'little room which I have dared to call GETHSEMANE'.[79]

She continued, however, to make revealing comments concerning her relationship with and feelings for her brother. The first was made at a point in 1955 when one of Julius' weekly letters expressed loneliness and isolation (Mina's emotional equilibrium had been disturbed by an extended stay in Lahr the previous year during which she had had to deal with a breakdown in her brother's mental health and Julius feared she might insist on both Tillyards moving to Germany permanently) and ended with expressions of gratitude at there being always a home for him "in a dear sister's heart". ('Meaning mine', Aelfrida added somewhat unnecessarily.) But although Julius was 'a dear! And inexpressibly precious', she would not be sorry to hear of his sudden death because he had 'such a capacity for suffering'. (Mina's behaviour oscillated unpredictably between a 'floodtide of activity' and 'melancholia' and both phases distressed Julius greatly; Aelfrida, for her part, feared suicidal impulses or even 'disappearance' by other means in a man who believed each person's life was his own 'to prolong or end it as he thinks fit'.)[80] The second, made later the same year when Mina's cyclothymic behaviour occasioned a temporary separation between Julius and herself, prompted Aelfrida to describe their subsequent reunion as 'a disappointment for *me*'.[81] Can it be that she hoped the separation would be permanent and that she would be able to move back into Wetenhall Cottage as chatelaine (Julius, of course, would look after her as he had once hoped to do in South Africa; even in his seventies he continued to 'saw logs and garden vigorously', to entertain visitors, and to 'tackle most of the washing up')[82], there to enjoy a "sister-brother relationship" which would make him "twice as happy" because "he had [his] sister as a helpmeet" and herself a "more complete and satisfactory person" because of the "harmony and romance" with which a sister-brother relationship was endowed?[83]

But even if thwarted of this particular 'glory of the west', Aelfrida's emotional Way of the Cross came to some kind of conclusion: in November 1956, Julius, still 'a Traveldudu', albeit on a smaller scale than hitherto, visited his sister at St John's Home. Aware, perhaps, how much she had supported him throughout 1955 (the year of his own *via crucis*) and perhaps more aware than

she guessed that 'Tit' *was* moping over death of a man she had once loved or professed to love or loved in her own strange way, Julius sat down to talk about – Nadja Laptchinski. His object in doing so may not have been as odd as it seems, for in the quiet safety of GETHSEMANE and to a brother she trusted, Aelfrida began to talk about Edward Wynn, and though in neither case did she or Julius 'come near the heart' of their respective relationships ('better so!')[84], perhaps she achieved closure of a kind by confiding in a man with whom she enjoyed a relationship akin to that which, had she not been such an 'imperfect' human being, she might have enjoyed with the man she still called 'the Bishop'.

## Notes

1  GCPPT 1|1|71 'Passion Sunday' (1 April) 1954.
2  GCPPT 1|1|73 22 May 1956. The 'hydrogen bomb' was exploded over Bikini Atoll on 1 March 1954.
3  GCPPT 1|1|72 25 September 1955.
4  ibid. 2 August 1955.
5  GCPPT 1|1|71 'Passion Sunday' (1 April) 1954.
6  GCPPT 1|1|73 28 January and 7 and 10 February 1956.
7  GCPPT 1|1|46 16 February 1935.
   GCPPT 1|1|72 8 May 1955.
   GCPPT 1|1|72a Undated cutting from the *Church Times,* by context May 1955.
8  GCPPT 1|1|73 21 June 1956.
   GCPPT 1|1|74 15 February 1958.
9  GCPPT 1|1|73 28 June 1956. The 'pony tail' hairstyle of the 1950s was more usually worn by young girls, hence Aelfrida's jibe.
10 GCPPT 1|1|73 16 July 1956.
   GCPPT 1|1|74 15 February 1958.
11 GCPPT 1|1|70a Letter from Frank Stokoe to Aelfrida of 28 October 1952. Altounyan, T. p183.
12 GCPPT 1|1|72 24 and 30 August 1955.
   GCPPT 1|1|74 14 August 1957. Tommy Altounyan, like Anthony Wrightson, had had an exciting war. (His second, for as a doctor he had been wounded by shell splinters during the Great War while loading wounded into his ambulance, his back being badly scarred thereafter). Ostensibly examining Syrian villages' water supplies for evidence of malaria-bearing mosquitoes, Tommy was actually engaged in gathering military intelligence for the British. For further details see Altounyan, T. pp 14 and 194.
13 GCPPT 1|1|72 25 July 1954.
   GCPPT 1|1|75 31 December 1958. Heather Connon's dated entry appears in Aelfrida's Visitors Book on the occasion of her first visit.
14 GCPPT 1|1|20 2 November 1904.
   GCPPT 1|1|75 31 December 1958. A copy of del Sarto's *Madonna delle Arpie* appears at a climactic moment in *The Way We Grow Up* (p265).
15 GCPPT 1|1|53 22 May 1937.
   GCPPT 1|1|66 9 December 1949.
   GCPPT 1|1|73 14 January 1956.
16 GCPPT 1|1|72 1 January 1955.
17 GCPPT 1|1|71 19 October 1953.
18 GCPPT 1|1|14 23 October 1906.
   GCPPT 1|1|71 'Maundy Thursday' (14 April) 1954.
19 GCPPT 1|1|72 23 April 1955.
20 GCPPT 1|1|71 19 October 1953.

21  GCPPT 1|1|72 16 April 1955.

22  GCPPT 1|1|72 9 February 1955.

23  GCPPT 1|1|73 24 March 1956.

24  GCPPT 1|1|72 21 August 1955.
GCPPT 1|1|73 21 February 1956. Lilian Whitehouse is the woman described in *The Glory of the West* (GCPPT 2|16|1 Pt 2 p 246) as "a strikingly handsome and romantic lady" who as an elderly spinster regretted she would never now "look upon the face of her own child". Only at the end of Lilian's life does Aelfrida disclose that the friend of whom she wrote so mockingly was a Girton graduate.

25  GCPPT 1|1|21 14 March and 20 April 1916.

26  The *Girton College Register* has Lilian graduating in 1902 with a degree in modern languages. She thereafter attended anthropological lectures given by Dr Haddon and herself lectured on the subject in 1914–1915 in the wartime absence of a Reader in Anthropology. She then taught French and German at various schools between 1918 and 1922 (from 1929 she was also a schools examiner) and from 1922 until retirement was Teaching Supervisor in German at several Cambridge colleges.

27  GCPPT 2|23|1 *The Watchword* December 1954.
GCPPT 1|1|73 15 March 1956.

28  GCPPT 1|1|6 22 March 1901.
GCPPT 1|1|61 23 November 1951.
GCPPT 1|1|73 28 March 1956. Edmund Whittaker (1873–1956) mathematician, astronomer, and historian of science had an illustrious post-Cambridge career culminating in the award of the Copley medal by the Royal Society in 1954.

29  GCPPT 1|1|71 23 April and 'Palm Sunday' (10 April) 1954.
GCPPT 1|1|73 21 January and 1 May 1956.

30  GCPPT 1|1|62 10 and 23 August 1944.
GCPPT 1|1|73 10 July 1956.

31  GCPPT 1|1|74 20 March 1958.

32  GCPPT 1|1|73 10 July 1956.

33  GCPPT 1|1|74 9 August 1957.

34  GCPPT 1|1|73 10 July 1956.

35  Tillyard, Ae. *Christian Old Age* pp 15–16 (GCPPT 2|17).

36  GCPPT 1|1|73 10 July 1956.

37  GCPPT 1|1|73a Obituary of Giovanni Papini, cut from *The Times* of 10 July 1956.

38  GCPPT 1|1|74 1 and 8 April 1957. Viola Papini was a writer and her father's ideological disciple and the proposed book was intended as homage to him.

39  GCPPT 1|1|38 2 August 1930.

40  GCPPT 1|1|71 11 February 1954.

41  GCPPT 1|1|73 6 July 1956.

42  GCPPT 1|1|72a. Letter from Edward Ely to his 'dear daughter' of 21 October 1954.

43  GCPPT 1|1|72 7 and 10 July 1954

44  GCPPT 1|1|72 24 October 1954.

45  GCPPT 1|1|73 6 July 1956.

46  ibid.

47  GCPPT 1|1|73 26 July and 1 August 1956.

48  ibid. 26 July and 4,9,11 and 13 August 1956.

49  ibid. 10 September 1956.

50  ibid.13 September 1956.

51  ibid. 17, 21, 24 and 26 September and 3 and 11 October 1956.

52  ibid. 8 September 1956.

53  ibid. 8 and 23 September 1956.

54  GCPPT 1|1|58 26 February 1941.

55  Tillyard, Ae. *The Glory of the West* p 339 (GCPPT 2|16|1 Pt 1).

56  GCPPT 1|1|71 10 February 1954.

57  GCPPT 1|1|73 25 September and 6 October 1956.

58  ibid. 6 October 1956.

59  ibid. 6 and 11 October 1956.

60  ibid. 8 October 1956.

61  ibid. 11 and 12 October 1956.

62  ibid. 26 October 1956.

63  ibid. 6 October 1956

64  Letters and obituaries appear in GCPPT 1|1|73a.

65  GCPPT 1|1|73 14 and 15 August 1956.

66  ibid. 15 August 1956.

67  ibid.

68  GCPPG A1 4|1(1) Letter from Father O'Brien to Alethea Graham of 16 April 1936.

69  GCPPT 1|1|73 14 August 1956.

70  ibid. 1 September 1956.

71  ibid. 13 September 1956.

72  ibid. 14 August 1956.

73  Northcott, H. p 289. As a reference in *The Making of a Mystic* shows, Aelfrida was familiar with Evelyn Underhill's 1912 book *The Spiral Way* (written as 'John Cordelier') in which Underhill lists and expounds the fifteen "Mysteries of the Soul's Ascent", five of which deal with events in Christ's life immediately preceding His crucifixion, using the same metaphor. Aelfrida may also, as a diary entry of 1 September 1956 (GCPPT 1|1|73) suggests, have used it as an aid to meditation when saying her rosary in her idiosyncratic way.

74  Northcott, H. Unpaginated preface by Edward Wynn.

75  GCPPT 1|1|73a 27 December 1956.
GCPPT 1|1|73a Undated letter from Julius Tillyard to Aelfrida, superscribed by him "please keep and read on Christmas Day", and by Aelfrida 'Julius' Christmas letter to me [so] stuck up that I had tear it to get it open'. Beside Julius' 'love letter', GCPPT 1|1|73a contains Papini's and Wynn's obituaries, Aelfrida's pencilled list of Sister Winifred Marcian's 'wickednesses' and a specimen of their chilly correspondence, and a cutting from *The Times* of 1 November 1955 noting the impossibility of even such a "gallant officer" as Peter Townsend being unable to marry Princess Margaret because his having a "divorced wife … still living" would suggest that many people could not "in conscience" regard the relationship as being a true marriage.

76  Erlande, A. *Ils Jouaient de la Vie* p 87.

77  GCPPT 1|1|73 18 November 1955 and 11 April and 16 November 1956.

78  GCPPT 1|1|72 11 July 1955.

79  ibid. 7 and 9 September and 8 December 1954 and 11 July 1955.

80  ibid. 'Eve of the Epiphany' (5 January) and 9 June 1955.

81  ibid. 13 June 1955.

82  GCPPT 1|1|73 18 November 1955.

83  Tillyard, Ae. *The Glory of the West* p 285 (GCPPT 2|16|1 Pt.2).

84  86 GCPPT 1|1|73 16 November 1956.

# Relegated to a Ward

Closure maybe, but only of a kind. Passion Sunday 1957 found Aelfrida in the throes of 'the most poignant fortnight of the year' and of making Lenten vows to give herself 'completely to God': 'I will live in Him and He in me'. To 'not wish [she] were at Tymawr'. To not pester her guardian angel for explanations. To not bother 'overmuch' about her faults. To 'not be sorry that Dr Wynn is dead'.[1] But poignant diary entries made to within a year of her own death show how sorry she was, a memory of Wynn's last Easter letter, written on Good Friday 1956, reminding her he was now in Paradise and her own thoughts 'very far from being all for God'[2] as a result and a vision of Christ calling her '*Placida of the Holy Passion*' on Holy Cross Day that if Christ wanted her to bear a burden of grief, He would also lend His strength to bear it.[3] And a feeling that Wynn was very close to her, a feeling she might almost have persuaded herself (and us) was wholly unsentimental and 'entirely bracing' were it not for a hint two days later that though she had 'never shed a tear' for 'Dr Wynn', overwhelmed now 'by waves of longing … for his warm hand-clasp, for the look in his eyes, for the tone of his voice when he said "it rests me to talk to you"', she was perhaps weeping as she wrote, so keen was the pain of her loss and the struggle to be 'wholly reasonable'[4] about their relationship. (Things were no better a year later, Aelfrida noting on the second anniversary of Wynn's death that she missed him 'acutely'[5] and a year later still, with no reference to him in the meantime, that she repeated the All Saints collect daily for him[6], possibly as a memorandum that she herself should follow the example of 'saint' Edward Wynn "in all virtuous godly living".)[7] A final vow made during the 'poignant fortnight' of 1957 was 'not [to] ask for this and that boon for my dear ones'[8] but letters bringing 'mostly news of sickness'[9] caused her to break it.

In February 1957 Aelfrida had heard that 'both dear brothers' were to undergo surgery in April, routine surgery but immediately associated by their sister with 'suppose both were to die?' Telling herself 'not to indulge in morbid suppositions', she indulged: 'of course, if I were to choose the outcome … I should choose that Eustace … should live on to write more books … after his retirement and go on being happy [but] Julius – I don't know. These last few years have been rich in … spiritual progress

The Hope Nursing Home, formerly Fordfield

but he is 75 and fears invalidism. Would death under the anaesthetic … not be preferable?'[10] In the event, Julius underwent surgery as planned but postoperative complications meant further and more serious surgery and for two days it seemed as if he might join Edward Wynn in Paradise. (Another reason for Aelfrida's thoughts being 'very far from … all for God'.) Fortunately for brother and sister, it was 'God [who] chooses not I!'[11], His choice being that Julius survive to write his sister 'a very Duduesque letter'[12] from Wetenhall Cottage later that month. But the Julius who survived was a diminished man, reduced at times to basket-making under the old medlar tree he and she climbed as 'children in the garden' and to complaining that time dragged as never before when bad weather confined him to the house.

Eustace too was diminished, his operation being postponed when he developed bacterial endocarditis in March 1957 as a result of contracting what Aelfrida wrongly called a 'virus' but correctly noted that it affected the valves of the heart. Hearing from Julius that Eustace was 'so ill' until penicillin effected improvement, she recalled how she had written to 'Swab' following Edward Wynn's death from cardiac disease to warn him not to 'overwork' but had not been reassured by his reply: "My last two years as Master [will] be … the busiest [but] that will make retirement sweeter".[13] Eustace's health remained compromised and it was with anxiety that Aelfrida noted the following year that 'news from Jesus Lodge [was] not good'. (His wife's 'obstinate stiff neck'[14] was obviously indicative of Phyllis Tillyard's unbending attitude towards herself.) A visit to Cambridge in June 1958 reassured her as to both brothers' survival and illness, it seemed, brought herself and them closer, for 'when the three of us were [alone] together, the old Fordfield spirit and "togetherness" flamed as if a banked fire had been stirred'.[15] But just as her own health was failing rapidly, it seemed others might fail her when she needed them most: Alethea (already unreliable, given her own health problems) as her legal next of kin; Julius – who saw nothing wrong in self-slaughter, whom she now knew had attempted suicide twice, and who increasingly found the responsibility of caring for a mentally-unstable wife too much to bear – as a confidant; Eustace as a man with such 'a strong sense of duty'[16] towards his sister that he had only recently ceased to provide ad hoc financial assistance and practical advice on her property holdings, but now, approaching seventy and 'troubled with heart trouble' ('can one be surprised?')[17], absolving himself of responsibility.[18] Of the three, it was Eustace's defection which hit hardest: though pleased by her younger brother's 'double success as Master and writer', she was sure success had removed him 'far from Julius and me' and that it was this rather than ill health which caused him to state that he did not want to be 'bothered' by her affairs any longer.[19] She was wrong: Eustace, conscientious, but tired and unwell, was no longer able to cope with the demands of a sister whose life had been almost as much a burden to him as to herself or practise damage-limitation exercises when she 'crashed'.

Compassion fatigue from those on whom she relied for support moved Aelfrida to rewrite her will. 'Bayard' Crundwell, an executor unseen for over twenty years, and Eustace as the other, received £10 – and a £50 bequest, the same as Mina, the Home ('towards the exp[enses] of the chapel'), and Girton College, the latter with a promise

of diaries to come. The SSC was bequeathed £500, Julius £200 and a life interest in his sister's 'personal effects and residue' should he survive, as sometimes seemed likely, Alethea. (The life interest was subsequently removed from Aelfrida's draft leaving the future of Wetenhall Cottage uncertain.) Alethea was to inherit everything else and 'failing her … my nephews and nieces'.

Intimations of mortality and the deaths of two childhood friends in 1957 (Silvia Blennerhasset née Myers, the 'most beautiful and most gifted of Mrs Verrall's class'[20]; Archie Venn, 'a dull lad … but … hardworking once he found a subject … that interested him and he never gave himself any airs [as] Provost of Queens')[21] caused Aelfrida to turn to ghostly comfort as the fires of her own life burned lower, and it was on her dead daughter, husband, and mother that she dwelt as 'dear ones … near though unseen'.[22]

Near and unseen, maybe, but not un-subjected to anamnesic reconstruction of the truth. Of Agatha, especially remembered on the anniversaries of her suicide when her mother lay 'awake for an hour or two during the night … [to] think of [her]'[23] and sometimes on her birthday ('I am glad she is not [middle aged] but only something in timeless eternity'), Aelfrida wrote perceptively that 'perhaps' she *had* 'loved [Agatha] too vehemently … and taken too much from her in return' but that her relationship with her daughter 'had *seemed* … perfect … then'.[24] Yet with wilful forgetfulness – she admitted to never losing 'the pain [she] felt at all [Agatha] suffered' or unfeeling 'the pathos of [her] last heroic message' "how can I ever leave you and who will look after you when I am gone?" a particularly poignant message now[25] – she also wrote that it was 'strange' that Agatha had shown 'no signs of irrationality' (*sic*) except 'only once when she found that her room at Wetenhall Cottage was called JOY [and] cried bitterly and would not tell me why' (a sign less of Agatha's 'irrationality' than her mother's deliberate obtuseness and insensitivity, surely) and of how Agatha's 'heroism' (*sic*) had not allowed her to tell her mother of 'the state of her mental health'.[26] (She had not needed to; diary evidence is damning.) Unable even now to face the truth, Aelfrida retreated into piety, asking the 'sweetest and most beloved' daughter whose death had removed a hindrance to the perfecting of her own soul if Agatha watched Alethea 'growing in grace' (Alethea herself had been the subject of a snide comment four days earlier: of her elder daughter, then on retreat at Malling, Aelfrida noted that the latter had 'refreshed herself spiritually at the dear Abbey … I assume'), if Agatha would be glad when her mother and sister joined her in 'timeless Eternity', and if she was helping 'Fuvver' too'.[27] Agatha's reply, if any, went unrecorded.

Of 'Fuvver', Aelfrida wrote chiefly on wedding anniversaries. Her views of Constantine's character appear to have mellowed since a disguised diatribe in *The Silence of God* portrayed him as a being who, like Lucifer, preferred "to be lord of what [was] beneath him rather than to aspire humbly to what [was] above him" (or rather, to his wife's version of what was above him or to aspire by the means his wife preferred), a being who, wishing to "exalt himself above measure", withdrew his attention and his homage from his Lord" (and from his wife) in order "to look at his handiwork and himself", to glory in "his own brilliance" and "self-esteem", and to cast off the wife towards whom he no longer displayed "pride of ownership"[28] because she had become a "prim child-ridden spouse"[29] who preferred God's and her daughters' company to his own. In *Naomi da Costa*, on the other hand, begun in 1954 within days of Aelfrida having prayerfully hoped on her forty-seventh wedding anniversary that Constantine was 'progressing spiritually'[30], she lauded him as a golden youth, "handsome, brave, intelligent, apt with all manly learning... intent on some ideal, moving as the gods and goddesses of old to music unheard by the crowd" but doomed, alas, "to disappear into oblivion leaving behind [only] a slender volume of verse".[31] A year later she studied him as someone who continued to puzzle her because the Consular Service seemed such a strange career choice for one so 'glorious and splendid', it being 'more in keeping' if, after tasting it but finding it wanting, he had 'thrown [it] over … in favour of authorship'. (Or 'gone on the stage', though whether this was Constantine's ambition or Aelfrida's belief that a man who once acted the part of Vadius was an actor *manqué,* she does not say.) But inevitably in a man with Anatolia for a mother, 'commonplace worldliness … attracted him' and he abandoned 'all-wise and all-loving God' (and given his wife's interpretation of Deity, who can blame him?) in favour of 'food and drink, display [and] "pleasure"'. But 'if only', she wails, 'I could have kept him unspotted from the world!'[32]

The conditional tense is ironic: had Aelfrida tried more gently and less intransigently, perhaps she *might* have 'kept' him, unspotted or not. Or had one who trembled at the thought of marriage deliberately distanced herself emotionally and physically from Constantine by wilfully misconstruing François de Sales' precepts on temperate sexual behaviour *within* marriage as exclusion of sexual activities *from* marriage[33], only to revenge herself on her husband for his natural response by committing adultery with his best friend and continue to behave in such a way as to engineer a divorce which would leave her as 'virginal' as before? (Hence, perhaps, her indignation with perceptive Florence Boyle when that lady accused

her of 'neglecting' her husband, her need to describe her divorce as a 'crash', and her loss as being 'sadder … than by death'[34] because of the part played by herself in bringing it about.) But in January 1957 on what would have been, had she 'kept' Constantine, her fiftieth wedding anniversary (writing to Lucy to announce the birth of Stephen and Margot's latest daughter, Stella, Aelfrida did not remind her that half a century earlier Lucy had been one of her bridesmaids), she finally abandoned the reason nurtured in public since Constantine's death – that he had been an innocent child for whom the wiles of the world had proved too strong – for the truth: 'the marriage was not wrecked because of differences in race or upbringing or outlook but because Constantine wished to *possess all of me* and "all myself was never mine to give"'.[35]

In which case, why submit? Can it be that the picture she presents in *The Silence of God* of Lucifer/Constantine worming his way into Eden/Fordfield is the version she wishes us to believe but that the truth of the matter lay in the Oracle and Chiara taking advantage of their daughter's absence in Florence to *entice* Constantine in on the grounds that here at last was a young man prepared to marry their daughter (and she, apparently, him), his unsuitability relative to the dons who were their first choice but who seemed understandably reluctant to propose marriage to one as odd as Miss Tillyard, they would disregard provided he married and 'normalised' her? And can it be that Aelfrida, informed of this by Constantine (or more likely by Anatolia who, uncovering the Tillyards' subterfuge, refused to attend her son's wedding when he ignored her "letter of solemn warning")[36], deliberately 'wrecked' what was essentially an arranged marriage in order to avenge herself on her parents? In support of this contention one may note that the bower in which 'Will Harvey' proposes to 'Alice' in *Just Alice* contains a snake and a scattering of apple pips, symbols, perhaps, of the deception practised upon their daughter by Chiara and the Oracle and of the depths of her despair when she discovered how they had deceived her into abandoning enabling spiritual and bodily virginity and of assuming an absolutely disabling emotional and physical surrender, the Edenic reference symbolising her knowledge of the evil perpetrated once again by her parents in the guise of doing good by sending her away yet again from the blighted Eden that was Fordfield. And perhaps too the geomancy to which a biographer must revert in an attempt to elicit the truth of and patterns in Aelfrida's life from a seemingly random scattering of 'pips' of information.

Further revelations, spoken and unspoken, appear during a visit by Aelfrida to Julius in June 1957. (Mina was in Germany; Aelfrida was housed in SERENITY and Julius 'content indeed'[37] at his sister sleeping in the room which was now his wife's but had once been her own; the Freudian implications of the situation are amusing and immense.) At Julius' request, Aelfrida again read passages from her diaries, some concerning the 'very emotional time'[38] surrounding her first meeting with Anatolia, some describing the Grahams' stay in Boston prior to moving to Arlington Heights, some of 1918 but omitting 'sad entries about Constantine and puzzling letters from Lyons'.[39] 'Puzzling letters' were not the only omissions; among entries omitted was one describing the potent occasion when Aelfrida, praying in St Botolph's, received a vision of a drop of Christ's blood falling on her heart from the Rood, another, even more significant because contemporary entries are so vague that it is often difficult to discern their meaning, that she *and Constantine* were 'seriously considering' joining the Roman Catholic Church because it might be there that 'the Eastern Church and the Scottish might meet', a statement which adds dimensionality to Constantine's antipathy to 'Roman claims'[40] and to making Aelfrida swear on the Bible to renounce them.

And there is more, for Aelfrida reveals yet another facet of the relationship between her brother, her former husband, and herself. (It is obvious to us if not to her that passages which Julius 'made' her read chiefly concerned his sister's relationship with another man.) Noting that the best photograph ever taken of Constantine was snapped by Julius some time prior to her marriage, she also noted that the picture was now 'so faded that it had almost gone' and that Julius seemed 'rather pleased than otherwise'[41], as indeed he would be at another disappearance of a rival for his sister's love. (Of four photographs known to have been taken by Julius of or including Constantine, all are so faded as to have become almost indecipherable. The first is the image described by Aelfrida, two are of Constantine and Aelfrida – and Charles Stewart Smith, another rival – in Odessa in 1907, the fourth of Constantine, Aelfrida, Chiara, and Willie Searle – yet another rival – at Fordfield in 1912. A strange coincidence but unsurprising when we recall that Julius developed his own films.) But both sad and ironic is that among the final entries in Aelfrida's diaries there are several friendly reflections about Constantine but only two brief and business-like references to Julius.

Of Chiara, Aelfrida wrote lovingly, briefly in her diary but at more length in recollections of childhood. (It is, perhaps, a symptom of her damaged personality that recollections of her mother – and father, for the Oracle also merited a *Memory Picture* – refer to ideal or idealised personalities: "the most charming woman I have ever met"; "one of the wisest men I ever met".)[42] References to Chiara appear on her birthday, 10 September ('I feel no anxiety about *her*, she is surely in Paradise', wrote Aelfrida on a day when her own death seemed imminent, nocturnal coughing having left her wondering if her own 'last hour had come'[43] and if so, whither she was bound) or on the anniversary of her 'heavenly birthday' on 17 December. On one such anniversary, Aelfrida thanks God 'for a good mother'[44]; on another she notes that as she gets older she appreciates Chiara more and more.[45] For which particular maternal qualities she now appreciates her mother, she does not say but given that the later entry appears at the time of the sudden decline in her health, her temporary removal to St Anne's ward, and Sister Una Mary's accusations of 'fussification', it may be her mother allowing her so many days in bed at Fordfield and arranging for her to be cared for there by Ellen Ison that Chiara's daughter chiefly remembered.

There are, however, other strands connecting Chiara and her daughter, each adding to the poignancy of Aelfrida's last years: not only did she herself die within two days of the thirty-seventh anniversary of Chiara's death but like her mother she undoubtedly hastened her demise by refusing to take the same medication as that prescribed by 'Dr Joan' for Chiara, namely digitalis.

Aelfrida's attitude towards medication at this point in her life is interesting because of her changed attitude towards self- or doctor-prescribed medication since being advised by Bishop Wynn not to take aspirin or barbiturates. Even if 'all [her] skeleton seemed on fire [and her] … hip gave savage jabs' and when officially prescribed two aspirin at night[46], she refused to take it saying she 'hated' to do so; of barbiturates we hear no more, so she may have refused sleeping tablets as well. And interesting too because of what she tells us – or omits to tell us or only hints at – of reasons for her decision.

Foremost was a desire not to have arthritic pain or cardiac symptoms alleviated because, as she confessed to appropriately-named Father Shrive, the Home's chaplain in 1957, 'sickness had brought [her] into closer touch with God'. (And possibly with Edward Wynn, given that he and she both had sickly hearts.) Father Shrive agreed, telling her that his having been grievously wounded as a cavalry officer during the Great War was 'a positive spiritual asset'. His comment, however, may have persuaded her to replace medical intervention with '[God's] strength' when further problems arose and when aware that her action might create further 'trials'[47] if illnesses from which she severally and inter-connectedly suffered recurred or relapsed.

Reference to 'trials' in one prone to perceive herself as a 'victim-soul' may also be significant: if, as she believed, St John's Home was her earthy Purgatory, how better to enhance its purgatorial aspects by means of unassuaged or self-inflicted symptomatology if by such means she could ensure Paradise quickly thereafter? She was supported from beyond the grave in this unfortunate belief by Edward Wynn, he reminding her in his preface to Hubert Northcott's book that "we do not go on pilgrimages in luxury liners"[48], and this and Evelyn Underhill's earlier advice that "the road to a Yea lies through a Nay"[49], must have seemed persuasive advice to one whose mind was so set on salvation-by-victimisation that she denied herself the 'sunny' side of *any* road even as she noted de Sales' view that God did not forbid pleasanter paths provided they led to Him in the end. Then too, what Evelyn Underhill called "the vision of God in His own light"[50] and Aelfrida the Beatific Vision would shine more brightly when contrasted with the darkness of unalleviated pain and the awfulness of drowning in the secretions of her congested lungs. And perhaps refusal of drugs represented a half-formulated wish to shorten her life in the hope of finding herself 'near [her] Heavenly Birthday … at last'.[51]

Less elevated reasons for Aelfrida's ambivalent attitude to medication are hinted at too. 'Musing on beliefs' one day and on the necessity in a spiritual context of having to accept the unproven or impossible (reports of 'flying saucers' stimulated this train of thought), she recalled her 'half crazy … imagination'[52] of wartime days and may have seen some connection between this and over-enthusiastic self-administration of drugs (ephedrine being a case in point) and decided that it was preferable to suffer discomfort and insomnia than be sent to Cowley Road Hospital if medication of any kind resulted in mental derangement. Or, perhaps she preferred self-prescribed treatments, for having previously practised self-prescription on many other aspects of her life, it would be easy to persuade herself that she knew best how to look after herself (experience should have, but unfortunately did not, remind her that she did not) and to revert to self-help doctrines popular in her youth. Perhaps it was the unpleasant side-effects of prescribed drugs which made her decide not to take them, digitalis causing her to feel sick[53] (a common, not a specific side-effect), others giving her 'fiendish nightmares'[54], others still diarrhoea, a symptom guaranteed to disturb spiritual exercises and embarrassing when living in proximity to others.

Her ambivalent attitude was also consistently inconsistent: either she refused to take certain drugs or all drugs or she took some of them some of the time. This drove Sister Catherine to justified distraction, for a patient who refused all drugs all the time would have been easier to deal with than one who took some sometimes. It was

also unfortunate that the Home's drug-dispensing policy operated in Aelfrida's favour: 'Ladies' not currently housed on a ward were dispensed a day's medication in the morning in the expectation that they would take it as directed, this allowing her to take or omit doses as she wished, to surreptitiously dispose of anything she did not wish to take, and to lie about having taken it. But she also demanded drugs inappropriate to current problems (she became agitated when Sister Catherine ignored her 'suggestion of penicillin'[55] for what Aelfrida called 'bronchitis' but was actually worsening cardiac failure) and in spite of insisting that she was 'getting on very well by the *vis medicatrix naturae*'[56], was happy to receive penicillin injections when the healing power of nature failed to relieve her symptoms as if penicillin was somehow a more 'natural' drug than other 'filthy medicines'[57] she took (or not) as the mood took her. Matters became even more fraught when she was 'relegated to a ward'[58] where drugs were dispensed by the Sisters at regular intervals and where she found herself 'in disgrace'[59] for refusing medication or for appealing to the prescribing doctor over Sister Catherine's head. (She informed the latter that she was not afraid of death, had suffered irregular heartbeats for years due to what Dr Bull in an appropriate double entendre diagnosed as 'excitability', and that if she had not been 'bothered with drugs' would doubtless have recovered sooner.)[60] Sister Superior, invoked by distracted Sister Catherine, announced that the Home 'could not be responsible for a patient who refused to take her medicine' and that if Aelfrida needed 'extra nursing' because of this she would have to go elsewhere. Her accusation was countered by Aelfrida stating that she '*was* taking' her medicine but her (diarised) admission that while on the ward she concealed drugs she did not wish to take[61] and that her hoard had been discovered by the nurses who moved her personal effects from her bedside locker back to her room, did nothing to disabuse Sister Winifred Marcian of Mrs Graham's deceitfulness and unreliability.

Of interest too in are changes in Aelfrida's approach to doctors: not only do they reflect the gamut of behaviour evinced towards everyone she met or to whom she was related but they also demonstrate clearly how she altered her attitude to suit. Towards doctors it varied from one of (self-styled) 'Perfect Patient' to one encapsulated in the term "heart-sink patient"[62], a patient, that is to say, whose attitude to illness and to their doctor makes diagnosis and treatment difficult, if not impossible, for they appear to have no wish to be restored to health but complain if they are not, are demanding of the doctor's time, energy, and medical skills, are manipulative because they play off doctor against doctor, and are adept at seizing on weaker but not necessarily less qualified persons as more likely to provide what they want. The negative response engendered in those who meet a 'heart-sink' patient in a medical context exactly mirrors that of people met outside it, their disillusion, exasperation, and anger causing the patient to continually seek new therapeutic relationships as others fail them and to express dissatisfaction with and loss of confidence in the medical profession as a whole on the grounds that no-one is able to 'cure' them or even alleviate their symptoms. As, of course, they cannot, because seeing only a challenging person before them, they fail to probe for reasons for such behaviour. Hence they misunderstand or ignore the 'stupid frightened child' within, a 'child' whose behaviour towards them is cause and manifestation of their need to challenge.

Towards some doctors (Joan Cooper in particular, but Charles du Bouchet and William Bowen to some extent, all of whom fell in love with her as a result) Aelfrida acted clingingly, emotional neediness exhibiting itself in hinted or partial confidences and in a constant need for reassurance and affection. Towards others, chiefly male consultant surgeons (Robin Canney, Alfred Walford, William Gilliatt, Ronald Macbeth) but also the three general practitioners in attendance on her at St John's Home, she assumed the role of one whose personal qualities, social standing, and medical knowledge entitled her to treatment as an equal. Others (Dorothy Hare, Dorothy Smith, and Mary Frazer in Oxford, the general practitioners who attended her at Tymawr) she tried to control by persuading them that her own (erroneous) diagnoses were correct or by rejecting their treatment as inefficacious or by assuring them that she knew best what was best for her. (Only to Marie Feyler did she willingly reveal herself – and Marie, it may be, betrayed her trust by passing on to Alfred and Catharine Tillyard information given in confidence, a fact which may have caused Aelfrida to mistrust doctors thereafter and to decide never to open herself to them again.) But although as a 'heart-sink' patient, she exhibited behaviour typical of the genre, at St John's Home she also added elements specific to herself: deliberately withholding important information, thus laying herself open to receive sub-optimal care, and accepting and even enjoying a degree of discomfort or pain concerning which another 'heart-sink' patient would complain bitterly and demand alleviation, behaviour symptomatic of her dysfunctional personality. (It cannot be attributed to physical causes such as confusional states due to low circulating levels of oxygen in her blood, because her diary and other contemporary writings are absolutely lucid and because it reflects earlier episodes arising because she did not feel in control of circumstances and of herself.) Her doctors and attendants, lacking evidence provided in her diary and other writings, saw her only as a cantankerous old lady.

A perfect example of Aelfrida's behaviour and her doctors' (and nurses') response occurred early in 1958 when sudden deterioration in sight in her right eye brought an NHS ophthalmic surgeon from the Radcliffe Infirmary to the Home to ascertain the cause. (Both eyes had been deemed 'quite healthy, *Deo gratias!*'[63] by her Cambridge ophthalmologist the previous year, a lady consulted privately in order to avoid what Aelfrida considered inferior service provided by the NHS.) Aelfrida initially refused to participate in his domiciliary visit and was only persuaded to do so when told she had a 'rare and thrilling'[64] complaint, a ruse quickly rumbled. In high dudgeon she betook herself to Cambridge and to Hope House 'where I could get proper nursing'[65] (a remark later attributed to her Oxford general practitioner) where she consulted a private general practitioner (retained, it seems, purely in order to obtain second opinions), and her private ophthalmologist and wrote an extremely rude letter to the Oxford medical practice accusing them of lying to her because their initial diagnosis had been over-ridden by the Radcliffe surgeon: 'I remarked', she wrote, 'that I was born and bred in Cambridge where *respect for truth* is considered the basis of all knowledge'[66], a rich remark from one who lied and omitted and if she told the truth, usually told it slant, and whose deteriorating health was in part attributable to deceit. Matters became further confused when she played off Hope House against St John's Home, insisting that the former had taken her in out of pity and that her guardian angel had 'arranged [it]'[67] but behaving in conciliatory fashion (she 'earnestly hoped to return' because no single Cambridge nursing home fulfilled her essential requirements: a chapel, a lift, and a night nurse) when St John's was reluctant to take her back.

At this point even her family lost patience with her (she had suggested as an alternative to House or Home that she move into Wetenhall Cottage 'to live a hermit's life, more or less, in FIDELITY' with a helper, funded by herself 'to lighten Mina's burden', housed in PRAISE), but following a 'magnificent sermon' (by letter, not preserved) from Alethea[68] whose own resolve had been strengthened by advice from Father O'Brien ("My dear Daughter, do not make too much of this trouble with your Mother. It may do no harm if you cannot fully respond … [and] might only lead to further demands if you did")[69] and by snubbing from everyone else, she settled down again in GETHSEMANE to await the next act in the medical drama playing itself out at St John's. Once back in Oxford, however, she accused the Home of destroying her sight by insisting on bright lighting (her notion that bright light damaged her eye is interesting, given that those with impaired vision generally prefer a well-lit environment; can it be that realising, as with scorbutic nyctalopia, that deterioration in her vision was chiefly due to her own stupid behaviour, she tried to exonerate herself by attributing blame elsewhere?) She also became angry with Sister Catherine when the latter (correctly) told her that her belief was 'pure illusion'[70] and hinted that it was Aelfrida's obstinacy with regard to the respective merits or demerits of *vis medicatrix naturae* and prescribed medication which brought about what for a writer was perhaps the most tragic consequence of choosing the former: sudden loss of sight in her right eye and a degree of deterioration in her left.

There was, as always with Aelfrida, more to the story than this. In late February 1957 she had postponed a visit from Julius on the grounds that she was 'feeling *very* unwell' with what she described as a sensation of pressure in her head; three bouts of 'violent nose-bleeding' relieved her symptoms but left her feeling very 'limp'.[71] Further lengthy and profuse epistaxes involving 'great clots of blood through nose and mouth' occurred in early March, to be described as '*undated invitations* such as Oracle had the year before he died'. (They were due, as she knew, having suffered from it for years, to 'hardening of the arteries'[72], an inherited condition worsened by refusing medication.) In part, perhaps, because such 'invitations' supported her belief on starting another volume of her diary that there would be no time to complete it because God would 'summon [her] home'.[73] (He did not, the new volume was the penultimate not the ultimate), she continued to refuse treatment, exhibiting instead her usual *belle indifférence* ('why fret?') as to whether she lived or died for God was with her and her 'heavenly birthday' – so she thought – imminent ('what more can I ask?')[74] and assuring her doctors that her symptoms were those of 'old age ailments'[75] which did not require medical intervention.

Perhaps not, but following a chest infection in December 1957 she noted in January 1958 in straggly writing quite unlike her usual firm hand that 'something [had] gone seriously wrong with [her] right eye', that a period of visual disturbance had ended in her 'whole field of vision [being] blacked out by a thick curtain', that although by the following day limited vision was returning, to all intents she was now blind in that eye, and that, given that the sight in her left eye was 'already a bit dim', she was faced with the possibility of 'total blindness'.[76]

Further but flickering sight returned within a few days and by early February she could see well enough to greet the first snowdrops in the Home's garden. But

on Christ asking her if, given a choice, she would choose 'sight or blindness', her answering instantly 'whichever would be most to His glory' and His acceptance of her answer brought the truth home to her: 'I was *appalled* lest I should have chosen blindness'. (Her subsequent prayer that if blindness, she should have 'the eyes of [her] spirit'[77] opened was answered in a visually and spiritually appropriate manner: on Good Friday 1958 in chapel, Christ calling her by name 'so clearly that [she] was quite startled' and bound her heart to His 'by a ray of light'; He also created an inexplicable 'white ray' between herself and Sister Superior but a 'new note of *gentleness*' in Sister Winifred Marcian's voice suggests that it represented either a guiding torch or an emanation of sympathy from former foe to virtually blind patient.)[78] Lack of improvement in what was diagnosed by her (Oxford) general practitioner as glaucoma (i.e. raised fluid pressure within the eyeball) occasioned the visit (rather appropriately, on the Oracle's birthday) by the 'senior surgeon' from the Radcliffe Infirmary who correctly diagnosed 'thrombosis of a small blood vessel'[79] behind the eye and held out little hope of improvement. Deciding therefore that an absolutely or 'almost sightless' right eye was God's Will[80], Aelfrida was delighted to discover early in May that God did not wish her to choose between sight or blindness but between blindness and partial vision: already able to discern colours clearly with her left eye (she described a repainted lavatory on the Green Corridor as 'flesh pink … Ninon de Lenclos'[81] after the famous courtesan), she soon reported return of 'airman's sight' in that eye and proved it by spotting plovers and a hare during her next train journey to Cambridge. Letters from Tymawr also brought comfort, Sister Gabriel writing that she hoped Placida found "joy in suffering" but that such joy was a bitter-sweet "will o' the wisp", and Sister Jeanne more practically that Aelfrida must be thankful for a "richly stored mind" and that she herself was pleased when improving vision allowed Placida to read and write[82] again.

Returning sight was fortunate given that Aelfrida's Cambridge ophthalmologist confirmed her Oxford diagnosis and noted that subsequent intraocular haemorrhage had irretrievably damaged her right eye. In fact, Aelfrida herself reported that a little '*muddy*'[83] sight *was* returning (a cry two months later that she could not see the lines on diary pages seems to refer only to her right eye and because it occurred on an anniversary of the death of Edward Wynn whom she still missed 'acutely'[84], might indicate that they were blurred by tears) but from the fact that she continued to write lengthy diary entries (her writing deteriorates only when she is very ill and occasional repetitions and misspellings are no more frequent than one might expect of a lady in her seventies) and numerous letters, to compose further *Memory Pictures,* to proof-read, to find her way around the Home unaided, and to read books, suggests that she could see reasonably well in one eye at least. Fortunately too, her 'richly stored' mind remained cogent, perhaps too cogent in some respects, for on reading Ronald Knox's 1958 translation of Thérèse de Lisieux's confessional autobiography, she discovered from his explanatory preface that the original version of *L'Histoire d'une Ame* of 1895/96, a book she had read and taken at face value forty years earlier, had been so much retouched prior to publication by the Carmelite nuns at Lisieux that the truth was 'almost undiscernible'. But although she found this '*disturbing*' (it was not the nuns' duplicity which disturbed her but her own uncritical reading of a book which was '*not the genuine confession of little Thérèse de L'Enfant Jésus*'), she consoled herself that Knox's disclosures would strip a too-credulous believer of the 'last vestiges of spiritual self-importance'.[85]

She also – and it is this rather than her uncritical approach which makes one pity her now – pleads with a future biographer not to judge her too harshly: just as in middle age 'spiritual self-importance' had allowed her to imagine herself a saint in the making, so in 1918 she had imagined a saint out of a disturbed Normandy adolescent, and since adolescence had herself kept a diary in which events are so much 'retouched' that the truth (that respected Cambridge commodity) is 'almost undiscoverable'. But now so old and ill that she collapses from the exertion of going to the toilet ('I am helpless!', she cries, 'I am so tired, so tired ... I could die of sheer exhaustion'), she is less able to dissemble or to care if readers of her diaries take them 'at face value[86] or uncover dissimulation as they probe deeper.

But note the exclamation mark. The fight has not gone out of Aelfrida yet and if she was to lose an adversary when Sister Winifred Marcian left in January 1959, she was soon to gain another in the shape of Sister Winifred's successor, namely Sister Catherine, towards whom as Sister Superior she exhibited no trace of *caritas* or of the "virtuous and godly living" of the All Saints Day collect she repeated daily for Edward Wynn but gloried instead in 'unsquashable'[87] behaviour even when forcibly relegated to a ward when another health crisis laid her low.

There were, however, consolations other (and better) than that of Sister Winifred Marcian's departure. The consolation of religion was now so much a fact of life that her 'lively faith' illuminated her way when so many former blessings could not or no longer did and attendance at chapel (in a wheelchair if necessary) and regular confession in her room or in the sacristy as her heath

waxed and waned because 'I want to be as ready as I can if the summons should come'[88] provided waymarks on her path towards the 'Dark Gate'. But hints of the 'old Eve' remain. Her supposed inability to recall at confession anything she had done wrong since her previous confession and propensity to confess only what she considered acceptable to the chaplain, suggests that one who prided herself on her powers of recall remained anxious to conceal aspects of her life and personality from successive Cowley Fathers. The flirtatious pleasure taken in intellectual jousts with chaplains whose university backgrounds rendered them worthy opponents (she elicited more personal details from them than they from her) demonstrated less a need to absolve herself from sins committed or fret about misdemeanours spotlighted 'as God's Light penetrates our souls'[89] than a wicked sense of humour and continued enjoyment of 'Cambridgy' conversations: on asking Father Rose (Selwyn College 1908, Captain Rose 1914-1918, later a missionary in Costa Rica) 'whether in Heaven we should *know* all that we had wanted to know ... in this life?' and receiving 'the Cambridge answer' that 'in Heaven we shall know only God and ... that will suffice', she flashed back 'what is the Oxford answer?' and on Father Rose having no notion, bade him consult his fellow Fathers at Cowley St John concerning 'the *intellectual* joys of Heaven'[90] she herself was keen to enjoy. She does not say if he reported back.

She found consolation in other visits too though these, judging by diary and Visitors Book, were fewer than before. Her persistent 'goup' 'Amrita' in a dress 'all over huge ox-eyed daisies' as if to demonstrate that compared 'with what she was at Girton with mind all on the alert ... *she [now] suffers from intellectual stagnation*'[91], the latter *not* one of 'Straightener's' myriad complaints and italics showing that professed *caritas* was poor prophylaxis against a waspish tongue. Muriel Pont, formerly Tertiary Teresa 'with no capacity for Obedience', now a stout middle-aged lady exhibiting 'any amount of enthusiasm' for collecting statistics for Mass Observation and Gallup Polls and bearing a bouquet of spring flowers to remind one confined to a largely indoor life that at Tymawr and '*there and there only*' she could step in a moment from 'the mysterious warmth of the Sacramental Presence on the altar into the Presence diffused over hill and vale, sky and streams'.[92] Hilda Harrison 'to spend the afternoon with Ter. Sr. Placida as we might have done at Tymawr', still living 'a good "church-life" and private life' and the 'only person who could ask [her] straight out "How is it with your soul?"' and be told 'there [is] a *great calm*'.[93] Kathleen Perfect with news of 'Uncle Sir Frank' and of her daughter Margaret, now married to writer/journalist Christopher Driver.

A writer herself, Aelfrida also found consolation in ensuring the safety of further volumes of her diaries. Early September 1958 with her "expectation of life … not now very good", she wrote at Eustace's suggestion to the Mistress of Girton to remind Miss Cartwright that Girton already possessed her 'spiritual diaries' and to ask if the college would like preceding and following volumes and copies or originals of published and unpublished works: five novels under Hutchinson's imprint, three unpublished novels "mostly of Cambridge", "various religious works published by different firms", "some not very good verse", and *Memory Pictures,* those pertaining to the Verralls, the Frazers, and parties at Trinity Lodge being of particular relevance. As an added enticement she reminded Miss Cartwright of her £50 bequest and that there was "a good deal of variety" (an understatement) in the diaries' content.[94] On 11 October she received the 'surprising' reply that Miss Cartwright and librarian Miss McMorran 'want not only all my old diaries … but *all* my books, published and unpublished!!!'[95] A 'sharp attack of bronchitis and [cardiac] asthma'[96] intervened, but later that month she was assured that Julius, helped by John and Constance Hibbs, had brought down her diaries from Wetenhall Cottage's attic 'and carted them off to Girton'[97] where, wrote Miss McMorran, they were sprinkled with insecticide before being locked in a trunk, their contents to remain unread "until sufficient time elapses as you wish". ("I am sure", Miss McMorran added presciently, "that the diaries will be of interest to some future reader".)[98] Further correspondence and much sorting of books in Oxford and Cambridge ensued. Aelfrida was currently too ill to do more than worry about missing volumes ('I gave away copies to the whole family and kept one for myself – where *can* they be?')[99] but in February 1959 noted with relief that Girton now possessed copies of several of her published works (the college would later amass almost everything save "notebooks of the various lectures which I had the hardihood to give", Julius deeming these too "bulky"[100] to include; considering the amount of donated material, his reticence is odd but perhaps content, not bulk, deterred him) and that in spite of a 'most charming letter of thanks [from] Miss McMorran', gratitude was due more from herself than from Girton because 'what have I ever done for the college but send my two brilliant daughters there?'[101]

The relief of knowing that much literary *matériel* and all diaries except two volumes currently in Oxford were in safe keeping was tremendous. (Further searches at Wetenhall Cottage uncovered "the children's verses of [Girton's] two Carlisle scholars"[102] and there was promise of more as Julius probed deeper.) But what Aelfrida deliberately or unwittingly fails to enlarge upon is the part played by Eustace (and possibly by Julius also) in the removal of so much inflammatory material to a place where, as she stipulated in 1946, "it should remain *unread* until personal interest in [it] is entirely passed away".[103]

As Aelfrida's imposed-on younger brother, literary victim, and executor, Eustace's views on the value to posterity of the "psychological, historical, religious … literary [and] personal"[104] disclosures made by his sister in diaries and literary productions may not have coincided with hers. Can it therefore be that his 1958 suggestion that she approach Girton with a view to deposition of material valued (by her) for its content was occasioned less by a belief that the material was of intrinsic merit than by a desire to bury disquieting disclosures as soon, as deep, and for as long as possible in the hope that the literary remains of a non-Girtonian might be of little interest to future Girtonians or to a researcher into college history? Or did he think that Julius might be moved to biography after his sister's death? (Julius, conversely, may have agreed to removal from circulation of diaries and other material divulging so much of his own life; alternatively he may have valued them highly and helped to engineer placement in order that Eustace as Aelfrida's executor could not engineer destruction.) By March 1958, however, almost everything of importance was in safe keeping at Girton, there to remain unexamined for "twenty-five years after [Aelfrida's] death or until after Alethea's death, whichever is the later".[105]

But perhaps Aelfrida's greatest earthly consolation as a frail purblind old lady was – to us – the most unexpected: 'the neatest little grey wireless set'[106] lent by a friend of Alethea's and dubbed 'a great blessing' and with the name of 'Griselda' in recognition of the patience her new acquisition helped to provide as she awaited 'the final call'.[107] And just possibly as a reminder to a future biographer that in mediaeval legend Griselda was regarded as prototypical of a Christian waiting sweetly and patiently to be united with Christ after a life of trial and sorrow.

Given Aelfrida's enjoyment of music and of *'celestial'* singing[108] transmitted during broadcast concerts and church services at Wetenhall Cottage, lack of a 'wireless' at St John's Home seems inexplicable. Refusal of Eustace's offer of a set was not, however, because other 'Ladies' might want to 'listen in' and disturb her concentration by doing crosswords or sewing as they listened, for only she on the Green Corridor lacked one, or because she wished to appear holier or more intellectual than they, or because an ascetic lifestyle, an 'amazing attraction to penance', and a continuing need to torture herself 'in all the traditional ways' save that of neglecting personal cleanliness in order to demonstrate 'love of our

Lord'[109] forbade the luxury of 'listening in' to music and services for which she craved emotionally and spiritually; it was for quite other reasons. The first was that although 'people are happiest with a definite *pattern* to their days', listeners to the wireless tended either to superimpose the pattern set by the British Broadcasting Corporation on their own pattern or, particularly if older and retired, to make their life conform to the BBC's alien 'rhythm', and to neither of these was Aelfrida prepared to conform: *her* pattern and rhythm conformed to 'the Tymawr pattern' of the canonical hours which gave her day its spiritual dimension. The second, that she did not want to fill her life with programmes not of her own devising: a 'wireless programme' would be a 'real distraction' to someone who wished to 'fill [her] life [only] with God' and who after saying Compline 'by heart in Latin' in the evening, enveloped herself in the 'Greater Silence' kept as part of her Rule and by the All Saints Sisters. Third, her mind produced 'too many irrelevant thoughts'[110] of its own accord and might be stimulated to produce more if subjected to disembodied voices describing doom-laden topics such as the launching by 'those wicked Russians' of 'a satellite … careering at unimaginable speed with a dog inside it … to show the world that they can do more devilish things still'.[111] Lastly, childhood warnings by Bosie concerning the perils of theatre-going made her worry lest the wireless be on when she died and she, 'listening in', die utterly unprepared for the Eternity into which she wanted to step 'straight out of Time'.[112] But perhaps it was because so little time remained to her that she accepted 'Griselda' now.

But Time had not yet finished with her nor she with Time, and what seemed at times an eternity of ill-health stretched before her. During her 1957 summer holiday at Wetenhall Cottage she had been able to walk from her ophthalmologist's consulting room in Newnham to her opticians in Market Square[113] (her exercise tolerance inexplicably improved in Cambridge; she took a taxi for the much shorter journey from St John's Home to Alethea's flat) but a self-diagnosed 'touch of Asian flu' confined her to bed for her seventy-fourth 'Festival-Birthday'. (She received 'not one' card from Eustace or his family' but 'a splendid batch from Tymawr' and an 'invisible parcel [of] Heavenly Joy'[114] from St Raphael compensated for their neglect.) Her diagnosis was unusually correct; on 20 November she reported that she, along with several 'Inmate-Patients' and a percentage of the world's population including Archie's sister Jessie Stent, whose death – or, rather, 'liberation' – from a life of 'muted songs [and] pastel shades' so unlike her own Aelfrida reported on 7 December[115], had been touched by the pandemic. And by more than a 'slight touch':

'wheezings, whistlings and mewings in [her] chest and tubes and accompanying gasping and heart flapping about'[116] rendered her 'far too ill to want [visits from] even my nearest and dearest'.[117] She concealed her symptoms lest she be removed to a ward but was eventually 'dragged' by angry Sister Catherine to St Anne's. She remained there for three weeks.

That Sister Catherine was entirely justified in removing her (and of accusing her of lying about her illness) is indicated by evidence provided by Aelfrida's diary. Not only does her writing deteriorate almost to illegibility but the incoherence of some entries shows that what she herself blamed on being 'disturbed' by 'waves of horror' emanating from a local and a far-off disaster (the Lewisham 'train accident', an earthquake in Mongolia) was in fact an influenza-induced confusional state in an elderly lady with a pre-existing medical condition, 'the real trouble … [being] not the … cough but … weakness of [her] heart'.[118]

The shock of finding herself involuntarily relegated to a ward brought her suddenly but temporarily to her senses. On hearing Sister Catherine describe her as '*mad*', she noted clearly and coherently that 'as this isn't the first time someone has thought me MAD, I know that the correct procedure is to attempt no defence and make no comment but to behave as conventionally as possible'; on arriving on the ward she therefore said 'good evening' and made other perfectly coherent remarks in order to prove that she was not. Then her diary entry tips over again into incoherence as rooted in reality as some of her visions: 'Oh dear! strange feeling of oppression – great earthquakes and rebelloons (*sic*), plots, horrible now (*sic*) weapons etc. etc., and crime rampant'.[119]

Aelfrida's second visit to St Anne's ward enabled recovery but reduced her to 'almost frantic' desperation; indeed, as she informed Alethea, she was 'rapidly becoming mentally unbalanced' as a result of the 'incessant noise'[120] of vacuum cleaners, of 'maddening jazz' from a patient's radio (it is amusing to think that the 'jazz' may have been rock and roll and that had she lived a little longer, Aelfrida would have experienced the 'Swinging Sixties') and of the 'laments' of the sick. Then too, 'religion on the ward seem[ed] sadly in abeyance' (Holy Communion was not brought to her bedside) and when unable to sleep, she could not put on her light and read but had to endure 'long periods of waiting'.[121] Worse even than this was her inability to perform an Advent retreat and discovery that a ward Christmas, though enlivened by 'an authentic ghost story' (very early on Christmas Eve, she beheld the room revert to its original use as the Home's chapel and watched its decoration by three ghostly nuns bearing box, holly, yew, and stars before the 'shadowy figures' vanished and she herself 'had a drink of Ribena and went to sleep again')[122], consisted of 'the King's College carol service roared out by the wireless and visitors up to 20 at a time tramping round'.[123] (Aelfrida herself had no visitors: Alethea spent Christmas at Jesus Lodge as planned.) Having recovered in spite of 'joyfully declining' all drugs and having to 'adapt to life' in St Anne's (a diary entry suggests some truth in Sister Catherine's accusation that she behaved as if "*she was the only lady in the ward*")[124], Aelfrida was restored to GETHSEMANE soon after Christmas (her bed was urgently needed for another patient), there to declare herself 'happy beyond words to return to peace and privacy' (and, incidentally, '*very* grateful for all the care, the discipline and the unusual view of life … enjoyed in the ward'), to confine herself to the increasingly uncertain benefits of 'the *vis medicatrix naturae*'[125], and to ponder at Epiphany the joys of 'mystical experience' as 'the most private and personal thing possible'.[126] But a short and grimly prayerful diary entry on New Year's Day 1958 said it all: 'strengthen me, dear Lord … to give Thee all that thou dost ask. Enable me … to receive all that Thou art minded to bestow'.[127]

Hoping that when her postponed 'heavenly birthday' arrived, a three-week stay in St Anne's ward might be considered the equivalent of purification by purgatorial fires and that she might now consider herself 'ready for the immediate presence of God'[128], Aelfrida dragged herself back to health. (On Julius enquiring as to what she did all day, she replied 'everything slowly, for one thing!')[129] A 'restful and happy' holiday in Hope House and at Wetenhall Cottage in May/June 1958 aided recovery but a feverish cold caught in late July set her back. (A chest X-ray demonstrated that there was 'nothing serious' in her lungs: 'was I a little disappointed?' she asked herself rhetorically, 'heaven seems so near [but] I suppose I am not ready yet'[130]. Not being quite ready to die yet, she postponed the event by accepting penicillin injections.) Early in August she once again booked herself into Hope House. Alethea escorted her there, unpacked for her, and departed, leaving her mother, to the latter's chagrin, alone in Cambridge: Julius was in Copenhagen, Mina with John and Constance in Suffolk, and Eustace, visiting briefly to review the situation ('I think he, more than the [others] sees how ill I have been and how exhausted I still am')[131] and to declare her Alethea's responsibility, departed shortly thereafter with Phyllis for Norway.

Unwell though she had undoubtedly been, Aelfrida's behaviour in Hope House was not that of a mortally sick woman. A subsequent comment that she seemed to be living her life 'backwards'[132], written with reference to visitors from past lives, is equally if not more relevant now, for in the 'ex-Fordfield part' of extended Hope House she found herself 'in the room where I was born and where I gave birth to Agatha (is she watching me – no, I hope better employed!) and where the vision of … the angel of death was vouchsafed to me'.[133] There was, however, no visit from the grey presence seen at the time of Agneta's stillbirth, so in the 'haven of peace' which was not St Anne's ward she recovered sufficiently to teach English to a visiting French nun. (Special emphasis: medical terminology.)[134] But on enquiring of her Cambridge general practitioner if she would '*ever* get back [her] strength and be able … to live [her] semi-independent life at St John's Home', she received a shock: her strength would never return and 'there was no chance … of [her] being able to go on as before'.[135]

Discussion of '*possible* alternatives' ensued; all were abandoned save that of ignominious return to St John's. (In spite of Sister Norbert's insistence that Aelfrida "come and spend the last years" at Hope House, the latter remained adamant that she would not do so, chiefly because the Reverend Mother and her deputy continued to press for conversion to Roman Catholicism and hence to '*submission* to Rome' but also because she was dismayed by the irreligious levity displayed at a Sister's Silver Jubilee party and by the inconvenience occasioned to herself by the celebrations.)[136] So to GETHSEMANE she returned on 30 August after a fortnight's stay at Wetenhall Cottage failed to prove to her own or to returned Julius' and Mina's satisfaction that all she needed to get 'quite well' and to lead 'a more normal life'[137] was German cuisine and the presence of a loving brother.

Back in Oxford, Aelfrida was faced with the consequences of insistence on *vis medicatrix naturae*, with her tendency to play off her medical attendants against one another ('I get equally scolded whether I obey or disobey whatever doctor is attending me!')[138], and with implacable nursing Sisters informing her of changes in her routine which might enable her to remain on the Green Corridor a little longer and of the absolute certainty of her being relegated permanently to St Anne's if her condition deteriorated again. ('Not if I know it!' was her sotto voce comment.)[139] Her seventy-fifth birthday on 5 October 1958 found her 'several years older and less strong' than the preceding one but content (for the moment) 'to do God's Will as it is shown me day by day' and to be where He wanted her to be.[140] But vitriolic diary comments regarding Sister Catherine's 'excessive love of *power*' and her tendency to ignore a patient determined to be as inconspicuous as possible lest she be summarily relegated[141] suggest both ladies were biding their time in their own way.

Neither had long to wait. Following yet another 'sharp attack'[142] of bronchitis and cardiac asthma, Aelfrida noted in a barely legible hand that the nurses were 'slowly piloting [her] through [her] illness', that she had not felt so ill since her attack of 'smallpox' in Odessa, and that she might have gone 'gladly … Home' had not Sister Catherine nursed her with 'a kind of … rather alarming tenderness' and postponed her 'heavenly birthday' yet again.[143] That she was indeed very ill is shown by the paucity of diary entries between 11 and 28 October, by the Home's doctors being 'very solemn' about her, by Alethea visiting on a daily basis, and by a Cowley Father arriving to hear a confession which might have been (and was treated by Aelfrida as) her last: 'coughing so much [she] could hardly get it out', she repented her sins, negligences, and ignorance and  put 'no trust at all in any of [her] merits but [only] of [her] 'crucified Saviour'. She was then faced with impossible alternatives: a move to another Oxford nursing home which had single rooms (it was full) or to Hope House (she was 'too ill to get there') or relegation to St Anne's: 'I can't'.[144] On 26 October 1958 she was moved willy-nilly with her bed and 'nearly all [her] belongings', not to St Anne's ward but to a 'quaint little annexe' nearby. She named it 'St Raphael's'.[145]

'St Raphael's' was a lofty arched room with tall windows and would have been 'considerably larger if laid on its side!'; it lacked a door but a screen ensured 'semi-privacy'. Nor was it as quiet as GETHSEMANE for it had the Home's front door on one side and its dispensary on the other and the 'huge lift' nearby reminded her of the easy descent 'from earth to Pluto's kingdom' as it rumbled past her bed. Surrounded by a jumble of possessions including her deckchair and 'dear Grandpapa's' Saratoga trunk, she dared not ask if she were in St Raphael's for good, but consultations between Eustace (he came to Oxford in a very bad mood, to settle matters once for all), Alethea, the doctor, and the Home and a statement from Aelfrida herself (she was feeling much better and enjoying the 'scene') that she was happy in her 'quaint little annexe', was well looked after, and was 'prepared to put up with anything in reason' so long as she was not 'relegated to the ward'[146] decided things: St Raphael's was hers from now on. And who could gainsay her, given that it was 'God's Will for [her]'[147] to be and remain there and that, as she once intimated to Frank Stokoe, she had every intention 'of ending [her] days in a sort of simple hermitage (not too uncomfortable!) all alone'.[148]

God's Will or not, implications of loss of independence, deferring of 'the longed-for call'[149] to pass through the Dark Gates (it would be difficult to self-neglect under closer supervision), and increased proximity to Sister Catherine upset Aelfrida greatly as pathetic references to offering her move and illness for 'stateless persons still in concentration camps' and for 'those suffering from … oppression'[150] show. She was also upset by 'another threat of blindness' ('I have only eyesight to read part of my Office and writing … is bad for me'; lengthy diary entries continued nevertheless)[151] and by Sister Catherine behaving towards her as she herself had once behaved towards others 'just like a cat playing with a mouse', at one moment looking after her tenderly, at another teasing her sadistically that 'a padded room' or the Cowley Road geriatric hospital would provide more suitable accommodation, and at yet another flying into a rage over 'the merest trifle or … nothing at all' and scolding Aelfrida in a 'virulent tone' for snivelling.[152] Attempts to keep her patient submissive included continued threats to move her into the ward (it is obvious from the latter's diary that she was a difficult and demanding patient and that although Sister Catherine behaved very badly, much can be excused her), a place where newly-ambulant Aelfrida had no wish to be: it contained ladies a generation older than herself, some of whom were 'not *compos mentis*'. Other 'inmate-patients' reminded her too vividly of herself as she now was, being verbally belligerent and, if well enough to get out of bed, seen by her 'painfully edging [their] way'[153] along the Home's corridors.

Much to her surprise and despite 'a silly balloon' hung by her bed, Aelfrida enjoyed Christmas 1958 immensely. Though forced to join other 'Old Dears' for Christmas dinner ('aged heads … crowned with paper hats [are] a sad sight'), she compensated for having enjoyed herself by praying for 'those … *who have no earthly hope*'. She tried (and failed) to avoid the Home's Christmas party (she later informed Sister Catherine that from the spiritual point of view it had been good for her to 'mix with those residents who have no home but St John's'; "we aren't keeping you, darling", Sister Catherine riposted) but judging by her diary account and a letter to Alethea she enjoyed that too.[154] Reminding herself that she had always loved parties even 'though I prefer Silence and Solitude' and slanting the truth somewhat ("Sister [Catherine] specially wanted me there"), she had no compunction ("responsibility", that is to say, because she had been made to go) "about breaking the letter of [her] Rule" by attending. Restored to her place on the dais among the Home's "intellectual and social elite!!" and with old friends coming up to greet her, she 'enjoyed some really intellectual conversation' until faintness overtook her and she was 'firmly escorted' back to her room by Sister Catherine. Safe in her new 'niche', she proclaimed that St John's Home could now claim more of her 'affection and loyalty' and that she must enlarge her heart and love it more in return albeit 'without detracting from love of Tymawr and Hope House'.[155] And 'so closes', wrote the lady who had barely survived it, 'this varied and interesting year'.[156]

1959 began with 'peaceful and uneventful days'[157] for which Aelfrida (and, no doubt, everyone else) was grateful, but hints that she missed the Home's garden (snow-light 'adversely' affected her eyes), that only limited times of day yielded 'a certain amount of quiet', that she was grateful for anything that broke 'the monotony of life here', and that though 'great friends' with the Home's chaplain, she lacked a spiritual director[158], suggest she was not altogether resigned to her lot. But a statement that though she rarely had 'definite religious experiences' now, she took comfort in musing on and communing with God 'most of the day', together with her last recorded vision on 29 January of being 'suddenly caught up' into the 'unimaginable Life, Power, Glory, Radiance [and] timeless Beauty … of the Holy Trinity'[159] suggests she was not without spiritual comforts and that loss of independence had compensations.

Yet just as her vision was '*not* altogether joyful' because although now 'in love and charity with all men', 'patches' (*sic*) of '*unlove*' constituted a 'spiritual obstacle' to salvation (diary entries describing Sister Catherine as her 'chief spiritual obstacle' support her contention)[160], so neither were musings on 'the joy of seeing [her] dear ones again' and on their being able 'to rejoice in God's Presence together' free from pain; in fact, they took on a revealingly acrid tone. Much as she wanted 'to see [her] dear ones again and to know that they rejoiced in God's Presence together', the fact that she also wanted 'those who have technically wronged me … Constantine, Anatolia, the woman who gave evidence at the divorce, other women, perhaps more than I know … to be there too' suggests that though all, even Anatolia, were 'precious in [her] Saviour's sight', Aelfrida herself required assurance that years of victimised soulfulness had not been in vain. Or was it to assure herself that the life to which she subjected herself on their behalf had been worthwhile insofar as it allowed those who had 'technically' wronged her (an interesting word in this context, given that stricter interpretation of *their* 'wrong' behaviour might place *her* in an uncomfortable position) to join with her at last in 'worship in its fullness'? Or was she impelled by curiosity: seeing Constantine's 'other women' en masse, she could discover how many there had been or if any had been figments of her overheated imagination? Or had she suddenly experienced solidarity with 'the women mentioned' because they too had

been 'muddled about right and wrong or led astray by lust and possessive affection'? ("I am … an adulterer", cries 'Frederic Ellicott', Aelfrida's masculine alter ego in *The Approaching Storm,* though his supposed 'adultery' is no more than fornication: 'Nita Voyle', like Aelfrida in 1911, is married but he himself, like Eric Silvanus at a critical point in Aelfrida's life, is not.) And who was she, she wrote, that she 'should cast the first stone?'[161]

Knowing she would be unable to spend Lent 1959 in as much 'Silence and Solitude' as previous Lents and saddened by her inability 'to make a nice tidy Lent Rule' 'as the pious love to do' (an unusual touch of self-mockery) or attend ceremonies specific to the forty days, Aelfrida, bidden by her guardian angel, made her '*special intention*' for '*the dying*'. (Her intention may have owed less to St Raphael than to an experience undergone two weeks earlier: awakened one night by noises overhead, she wandered into the hall to investigate, only to be confronted by 'a corpse under a sheet'.)[162] Premonition that her next attack of 'bronchitis' *would* bring about her 'so longed-for … heavenly birthday'[163] seemed about to be fulfilled when she recorded on 23 February a 'tiresome but not serious return' of illness[164] and next day that she was 'drifting into another bad attack' whose symptoms included shortness of breath, pains in her bones and at the back of her head, visual deterioration, and difficulty in swallowing. No-one, however, 'seemed to be alive' to the severity of her condition and Sister Catherine, intending (as perhaps Aelfrida with hopes that she was 'near [her] Heavenly Birthday … at last' being counterbalanced by a desire to stop letting nature take its course and take penicillin instead, was not) to let nature take its course, 'took no notice'. By 5pm that day, however, even Sister Catherine agreed that Aelfrida was indeed 'very ill' and arranged for a Cowley Father and the doctor (in that order) to attend her; she also summoned Alethea from 'Uncle Sir Frank's' where she was staying and administered unspecified medicines to 'keep … here' a patient she could not guarantee would live through the night.[165]

Sister Catherine's medicinal and the Cowley Father's ghostly remedies were efficacious. In writing which veered from wobbly to firm as her condition fluctuated Aelfrida recorded jubilantly 'here I still am'. She also appended an account of what might have been Unction *in extremis*: Father Campbell having arrived within thirty minutes, a 'wee altar' was brought in and with Sister Sacristan and Sister Catherine standing by, she was anointed on her forehead. Anointing over, she was asked if she would like to receive Holy Communion and on her replying she would be 'very glad' to do so, the Blessed Sacrament, announced by the ringing of the sacring bell, was brought to her bedside and administered.

Communion over, she asked to have her light put out and lay 'revelling in … peace for St Raphael to come for me'.[166] But, as she put it, 'not so'. At 11pm one of the Home's doctors arrived and 'with injections, capsules, tablets and what not drew [her] back'. Later still, Alethea arrived 'looking very sweet'. (Aelfrida did not record their conversation.) The following morning the doctor deemed her 'much better', so much better, in fact, that within a few days she was able to write to Julius, to Lucy Verey, to Kathleen Perfect, and to Tymawr announcing that she was indeed 'still … here' and within a week to reply to their 'very precious' responses with 'reassuring postcards'.[167]

Though sorry 'not to slip quietly across the dark waves' into whatever future awaited her, Aelfrida seems to have been doubly pleased that she did not. First, she had been able to provide a detailed record for a future biographer of an experience not given to many to record and to record it with regard to what she considered correct protocol ('after the service Father Campbell shook me warmly by the hand which seemed a little odd'; she also wondered why she had been anointed only on her forehead), to Sister Catherine having actually hugged and kissed her, and to St Raphael having witnessed the scene. Second, that although St Raphael's attempt to take her away was thwarted by Dr Neil, the sudden deterioration in her health might have precluded the edifying deathbed scene she hoped to stage but which it might be 'more convenient' (*sic*) to stage 'later on' with more people present and a speech prepared.[168] And from the tone of her diary entry one can deduce that, ill as she was, she had immensely enjoyed her deathbed *manqué*.

'Here' indeed she was but her hold was tenuous – and grumpy. Recurrent attacks of 'cramp in [her] heart' affected her so badly that attendance at chapel, even in a wheel chair, rendered her 'wretchedly ill and dizzy' and on one occasion required a pain-killing injection which made her feel as if her personality was being 'filched' from her.[169] The 'state of virtuous equanimity' engendered by 'the beautiful service of Unction' was not easily maintained for other reasons too. During an 'unusual' address in chapel she heard Sister Catherine speak through the mouth of a Cowley Father when he reminded his congregation that they were at St John's Home to have their physical needs met, that as 'Inmate-Patients' they should '*pray* for one another and NOT … criticise' (Aelfrida, said Sister Catherine, 'disorganised' the household with her demands and made herself ill with fretting over her present inability to take Communion fasting, a matter over which and in spite of clerical reassurance, she was particularly exercised; she also argued over trivial matters and letters of complaint still flowed from her pen), and

that they should enjoy chapel and the 'spiritual privileges' bestowed on them by the nuns' presence there.[170] Then too, 'distaste for the life here and the routine of invalidism'[171] irked one to whom the routine of a Rule had rarely seemed irksome nor days in bed anything but benisons and not all the consoling lessons and addresses she heard (the Shulamite's son revived by Elijah, the raising of Lazarus by Christ, 'people being brought to love God by the road of loving their neighbours') could persuade her that having been 'so near to the golden gates and … turned back'[172] was less a 'convenience' than another cross to bear. Furthermore, nobody who really mattered (where was Julius?) visited her, and Alethea whose life was 'pack[ed] too full'[173] to allow her to dance attendance on her mother, departed Oxford once assured she was 'supposed to be so much better' and, following her return to Marston Street, continued to visit her mother only on Sundays and only for tea.

Trying 'to be good'[174] despite of tribulations, Aelfrida passed Lent 1959 'earnestly [praying] for the dying', further reminding Tommy Altounyan – now living in his wife's old home in the Lake District – of his 'executor's task of preparing … Stokoe's *Journal* for publication'[175], enjoying 'lively talks' (gossip) with Juliana Clark, winding up her financial affairs (e.g. selling the Cambridge Steam Laundry to another company), revelling in news from Tymawr ('how the beloved community prospers!')[176], and listening to 'Griselda', a 'great blessing' in Holy Week though the coincidence of teatime and Evensong transmitted from York Minster made her feel 'mildly irreverent'. ('But if Evensong is at 4 and so is tea, what is one to do? Would a saint have gone without tea?'; not being a saint, she compromised: nine tenths of her attention to the service, one tenth to tea.) On Good Friday 1959 she heard 'an eloquent Welshman' preach on 'the Last Hour upon the Cross' and 'some of the words struck [her] to the heart': 'he cried that *glory* should be given to God alone and accused us professing Christians of desiring glory for ourselves … A ray from the Cross struck me deep down … I do long to be thought well of by those whose opinion I prize [but] there is that horrid form of pride wound round the roots of my character like worms round roots of primulas! I can't disentangle them but only pray the Holy Spirit to do it for me. Perhaps my guardian angel will say something sharp and help me too'.[177]

Volume and diary end here.

## Notes

1   GCPPT 1|1|74 'Passion Sunday' (7 April) 1957.
2   ibid. 'Holy Saturday' (20 April) 1957.
3   ibid. 4 May 1957
4   ibid. 12 August 1957.

5 GCPPT 1|1|75 13 August 1958.
6 ibid. All Saints' (1 November) 1958.
7 *The Book of Common Prayer: Collect for All Saints Day.*
8 GCPPT 1|1|74 'Passion Sunday' (7 April) 1957.
9 ibid. 8 April 1958.
10 GCPPT 1|1|73 18 and 21 February 1957.
11 ibid. 21 February 1957.
12 GCPPT 1|1|74 29 April 1957.
13 ibid. 11, 13, and 20 March 1957.
14 ibid. 8 April 1958.
15 ibid. 19 June 1958.
16 ibid. 15 March 1958.
17 GCPPT 1|1|75 29 January 1959.
18 ibid. 18 August 1958.
19 ibid. 'All Saints' (1 November) 1958.
20 ibid. 5 July 1957.
21 ibid. 20 March 1958.
22 GCPPT 1|1|72 19 January 1954.
23 ibid. 'Ash Wednesday' (23 February) 1955.
24 ibid. 13 July 1954.
25 GCPPT 1|1|72 29 May 1955.
   GCPPT 1|1|74 12 July 1958.
26 GCPPT 1|1|74 12 July 1958.
   GCPPT 1|1|75 23 February 1959.
27 GCPPT 1|1|74 8 and 12 July 1958.
28 Tillyard, Ae. *The Silence of God* p 4 (GCPPT 2|20).
29 Tillyard, Ae. *The Stones of Belgium* (*The Garden and the Fire* p4) a poem written in Cambridge on 13 March 1915.
30 GCPPT 1|1|71 19 January 1954.
31 Tillyard, Ae. *Naomi da Costa* p 134 (GCPPT 2|22).
32 GCPPT 1|1|72 19 January and 'Ascension Day' (19 May) 1955.
33 De Sales' precepts appear in part 3 Ch 12 (On the need for chastity) of his *Introduction to a Devout Life.*
34 GCPPT 2|27|2(4).
35 GCPPT 1|1|73 19 January 1957.
36 Tillyard, HJW. *The Letters of ACW Tillyard* (MTC). Letter from Aelfrida to Julius Tillyard of 28 March 1905.
37 GCPPT 1|1|74 24 June 1957.
38 ibid. 5 July 1937.
39 ibid. 24 July 1937.
40 ibid. 5 July 1957.
41 ibid. 'Holy Cross Day' (14 September) 1957.
42 GCPPT 2|23 *The Watchword* June 1958 and GCPPT 2|27|2(2).
   GCPPT 2|23 *The Watchword* June 1957.
   A note at the back of GCPPT 1|1|72 suggests that Aelfrida was collecting material for the portrait of her mother in 1954/55 but a diary entry of 19 January 1958 (GCPPT 1|1|74) hints that the date of composition of *Little Katie; Letter to my own Mother* is of earlier date, possibly 1948.
43 GCPPT 1|1|73 10 September 1956.
44 ibid. 17 December 1955.
45 ibid. 18 December 1955.
46 GCPPT 1|1|74 30 August 1957.
47 ibid. 30 August and 6 September 1957.
48 Northcott, H. Unpaginated preface by 'Edward Ely'.
49 Underhill, E. *Practical Mysticism* p183.
50 ibid. p 180.
51 GCPPT 1|1|75 'St Matthias' (24 February) 1959.
52 GCPPT 1|1|72 7 January 1955.
53 GCPPT 1|1|73 11 October 1956.
54 GCPPT 1|1|74 3 April 1958.
55 GCPPT 1|1|75 3 'St Matthias' (24 February) 1959.
56 GCPPT 1|1|74 31 December 1957.
57 GCPPT 1|1|75 9 August 1958.

58 GCPPT 1|1|73 4 March 1956.
59 ibid. 17 December 1957.
60 ibid. 22 December 1957.
61 GCPPT 1|1|75 30 July 1958.
62 For the origin of the term 'heart-sink patient' see O'Dowd, T. *Five years of Heart-Sink patients in General Practice* BMJ vol 212 August 20–27 1988 pp518–30. I am also indebted to Lalanda, M. *The Challenging Patient* (MPS UK Casebook vol 17 no. 2 May 2009 pp 12–14) for assistance in structuring the content of this paragraph and what follows.
63 GCPPT 1|1|74 18 July 1957.
64 ibid. 29 March 1958.
65 GCPPT 1|1|75 28 October 1958.
66 GCPPT 1|1|74 4 July 1958.
67 GCPPT 1|1|75 9 August 1958.
68 ibid. 18 August 1958.
69 GCPPG. Al. 4. Undated letter from Father O'Brien SSJE to Alethea Graham, noted by her as received on 28 August 1958.
70 GCPPT 1|1|74 4 July 1958.
   GCPPT 1|1|75 29 October 1958.
71 GCPPT 1|1|73 25 February 1957.
72 GCPPT 1|1|73 25 February 1957.
   GCPPT 1|1|74 8, 9, and 11 March 1958.
73 GCPPT 1|1|73 25 February 1957.
74 GCPPT 1|1|74 16 June 1957.
75 ibid. 21 June 1957.
76 ibid. 22 January 1958.
77 ibid. 2 February 1958.
78 ibid. 'Good Friday' (4 April) and 'Easter Sunday' (6 April) 1958.
79 ibid 'Maundy Thursday' (3 April) 1958.
80 ibid. 7 May 1958.
81 ibid. 20 April 1958.
82 GCPPT 1|1|75a Letter from Sister Gabriel Anne SSC to Aelfrida of 'Trinity XXV' 1958, referred to by its recipient on 11 March 1959 (GCPPT 1|1|75).
   GCPPT 1|1|74a. Letter from Sister Jeanne SSC to 'my dear Sister Placida' of 22 June 1958.
83 GCPPT 1|1|74 19 June 1958.
84 GCPPT 1|1|75 13 August 1958.
85 ibid. 25 July and 5 August 1958. Knox's *Autobiography of a Saint* was undertaken at the request of the Lisieux convent following the death in 1951 of its then Superior, Mother Agnes, Thérèse's elder sister, whose version of her dead sister's '*historie*' was published as Thérèse's own.
86 ibid. 5 August 1958.
87 ibid. 'Advent IV' (20 December) 1958.
88 GCPPT 1|1|73 23 September 1956.
89 GCPPT 1|1|75 9 August 1950.
90 ibid. 16 November 1958.
91 GCPPT 1|1|74 18 July 1958.
92 GCPPT 1|1|72 30 August 1955.
   GCPPT 1|1|74 11 March 1958. Mass Observation involved the study and recording of ordinary peoples' views, Gallup Polls the assessment of public opinion through the questioning of selected representative examples.
93 GCPPT 1|1|75 11 October 1958.
94 GCAC 4|6|3|3 Letter from Aelfrida Graham to Miss ML Cartwright of 2 September 1958. Mary Lucy Cartwright, FRS, a distinguished mathematician, was Mistress of Girton from 1949–1968.
95 GCPPT 1|1|75 11 October 1958.
96 ibid. 16 October 1958.
97 ibid. 21 October 1958.
98 GCAC 4|6|3|3 Letter from Miss H. McMorran to Aelfrida of 26 October 1958.

99   GCPPT 1|1|75 3 November 1958. Aelfrida's possession of large numbers of her own books may be explained by her publishers' decision to dispose of remaining copies of unremunerative volumes by selling them off cheaply (the alternative was to pulp them), albeit not without first informing the author that they could buy up as many copies as they wished. The option did not, of course, apply to self-published books which remained the property and responsibility of the author.

100   GCAC 4|6|3 Letter from Aelfrida Graham to Miss H. McMorran of 5 November 1958.

101   GCPPT 1|1|75 '5 February' (the entry is misdated; it was made on either 6 or 7 February) 1959.

102   GCAC 4|6|3 Letter from Aelfrida Graham to Miss H. McMorran of 3 March 1959.

103   GCAC 4|6|3|3 Letter from Aelfrida Graham to Miss KT Butler of 13 June 1946.

104   ibid.

105   GCAC 4|6|3|3 Letter from Aelfrida Graham to Miss KT Butler of 6 March 1946. There are interesting echoes here of an 1871 novel *The Miller's Daughter* by Grantchester resident Samuel Widnall (distant relative by marriage of Aelfrida herself), a novel so similar in its local references, historical accuracy, use of Cambridgeshire place names as names of characters, convoluted plot in which abductions, deaths or near-deaths by drowning, and supernatural characters and events occur, and in its archaic language to Aelfrida's *Haste to the Wedding* and *The Young Milliner* that it is probable she knew of it. Widnall has his heroine 'Alice Vert' end her account of her life ("a kind of diary") by locking it "in a nice little iron box ... where it will be quite safe" from anyone who is not "meant to see it" (op. cit. pp 6–7 and 176). She then conceals box and diary among the roots of an ash tree (a tree with magical and mystical connotations whose roots were said to reach down to the deepest pits of hell but whose crown reached heaven) where they remain for 400 years until their whereabouts is revealed to a chance passer-by by a fairy. The diary is transcribed by an anonymous editor and is said to throw light "on many things ... which have hitherto been [veiled] in obscurity" (op. cit. Preface).

106   GCPPT 1|1|75 14 March 1959.

107   ibid. 18 and 27 March ('Good Friday') 1959.

108   GCPPT 1|1|74 21 July 1957.

109   GCPPT 1|1|63 28 July 1945.

110   GCPPT 1|1|75 2 August 1958.

111   GCPPT 1|1|74 4 November 1957. The dog to which Aelfrida refers was Laika, the first animal to orbit the earth (and the first space casualty) on 3 November 1957.

112   GCPPT 1|1|75 2 August 1958.

113   GCPPT 1|1|74 18 July 1957.

114   ibid. 4 and 5 October 1957. The so-called 'Asian Flu' pandemic of 1957 originated in China and spread worldwide in the form of highly infectious avian influenza. Several inmates of St John's Home died of it.

115   ibid. 7 December 1957.

116   ibid. 20 November 1957.

117   ibid. 2 December 1957.

118   ibid. 5, 7 and 11 December 1957. The Lewisham railway disaster occurred on 4 December 1957; nearly 100 people were killed when two trains collided in South London.

119   ibid. 5 December 1957.

120   GCPPT 1|1|74 22 December 1957.
      GCPPT 1|1|75 29 October 1958.

121   GCPPT 1|1|74 11 December 1957.

122   ibid. 'Christmas Eve' (24 December) 1957. Aelfrida's waking dream, like so many of her visions, was influenced by current events: the Home's lay helpers had just decorated the ward for Christmas.

123   GCPPT 1|1|75 'Advent Sunday' (30 November) 1958.

124   GCPPT 1|1|74 13 and 22 December 1957.

125   ibid. 27 and 31 December 1957.

126   ibid. 'The Epiphany' (6 January) 1958.

127   ibid. 1 January 1958.

128   ibid. 28 April 1958.

129   ibid. 10 May 1958.

130   GCPPT 1|1|75 30 July 1958.

131   ibid. 9 August 1958.

132   ibid. 11 October 1958.

133   ibid. 9 August 1958.

134   ibid. 10 and 13 August 1958.

135   ibid. 15 August 1958.

136   ibid. 15, 19, and 21 August 1958.

137   ibid. 16 and 30 August 1958.

138   ibid. 18 August 1958.

139   ibid. 30 August 1958.

140   ibid. 'St Placid's Day' (5 October) 1958.

141   ibid. 12 and 18 September 1958.

142   ibid. 16 October 1958.

143   ibid. 'St Luke's Day' (18 October) and 21 October 1958.

144   ibid. 16 October and 'St Luke's Day' 1958.

145   ibid. 26 or 27 October 1958 (date illegible). The annexe to which Aelfrida refers may have formed the vestry to the Home's pre-Comper chapel; the name she gave it may derive from that of her own guardian angel or from Sister Gabriel Anne's particular "friends", St Raphael and St Anne, to whose care she recommended Aelfrida (GCPPT 1|1|75a Letter from Sister Gabriel Anne SSC to Sister Placida of 'Trinity XXV' 1958).

146   ibid. 26 or 27 October 1958 (date illegible).

147   ibid. 29 October and 'All Saints' (1 November) 1958.

148   GCPPT 1|1|23 31 July1918.

149   GCPPT 1|1| 75 29 October 1958.

150   ibid. 3 November 1958.

151   ibid. 7 November 1958.

152   ibid. 'Advent IV' (20 December) and 24 December 1958.

153   ibid. 25 and 31 January 1959.

154   ibid. 'St Stephen's Day' (26 December), 27 and 30 December 1958.

155   ibid. 30 December 1958.
      GCPPG A1 4|2 Letter from Aelfrida to 'P[recious] and B[eautiful]' Alethea Graham of 29 December 1958.

156   GCPPT 1|1|75 31 December 1958.

157   ibid. 23 January 1959.

158   ibid. 8, 10 and 23 January and 18 February 1959.

159   ibid. 30 January 1959.

160   ibid.

161   GCPPT 1|1|75 23 February and 'St Matthias' (24 February) 1959. Tillyard, Ae. *The Approaching Storm* p148.

162   GCPPT 1|1|75 31 January and 'Ash Wednesday' (11 February) 1959.

163   ibid. 7 November 1958.

164   ibid. 23 February 1958.

165   ibid. 'St Matthias' (24 February) 1959.

166   ibid. 25 February 1959.

167   ibid. 25, 27 and 28 February and 4 March 1959.

168   ibid. 25 February 1959.

169   ibid. 28 February and 19 and 20 March 1959.

170   ibid. 4, 7, 12 and 23 March 1959.

171   ibid. 10 March 1959.

172   ibid. 10, 13, and 19 March 1959.

173   ibid. 14 and 23 March 1959.

174   ibid. 10 and 13 March 1959.

175   ibid. 14 March 1959.

176   ibid. 20 March 1959.

177   ibid. 'Good Friday' (27 March ) 1959.

# In Hora Mortis Meae

Her diary ended here but Aelfrida herself did not. Like William of Glasshampton who also rallied after receiving Unction, albeit for only a few weeks, she has some months to live. We do not know why her diary ends so abruptly; the last page is blank but she usually left one or two pages unwritten in order to insert photographs, cuttings, and nature notes and it may be that a subsequent volume was given to or taken by a member of her family after her death and privately preserved or privily destroyed. Though it is difficult to solve the mystery of its sudden cessation – as she herself wrote of Christ's Resurrection and Ascension, "we cannot understand the manner of Thy withdrawal from our sight" – that withdrawal of her diary voice "was both actual and symbolic" and *deliberate* may be inferred from what we know of the workings of her mind to date. Hence although her "comings and goings" from the time of her resurrection-by-Unction until the day she was "taken up into Heaven" are "mysterious"[1], it is possible to recreate something of what she did and of why she acted as she did.

The first and seemingly most obvious reason for her sudden silence is suggested by a statement made four years earlier: 'lack of physical strength makes me lay down my pen'.[2] It is also possible to deduce from the 'horrid headache at the back of my head' which made her feel 'as if I were *falling* or, rather, my bed going down and down', from intermittent 'poor eyesight', and from her heart 'making itself felt'[3], that recrudescence of previous symptoms or the onset of new ones rendered her so 'confined in the prison of [her] own discomforts that nothing else mattered': "as an invalid", she once wrote, "I am more than normally prone to be self-regarding".[4] (Religion mattered, but perhaps she felt no further inclination to share her thoughts because she had 'Said my Say' even if 'not as well as it *ought* to be said but as well as I am able to deliver the message entrusted to me'[5] and because "much [remained] of necessity unuttered, audible to the ears of God only".)[6] Perhaps she suffered the dreaded 'humiliation of helplessness'[7] because suddenly dependent on 'the care of others for [her] physical needs'[8] and found little or no consolation in Father Cary's warning that, travelling 'the final stage of [her] soul's pilgrimage', she would plumb profound 'depths of

**Lucy Verey née Longstaffe in old age**

humility'[9], depths which could be regarded as a kind of 'self-naughting' by one less ill but which to one rendered so helpless that her personal belongings (including her very private diary) had been intruded upon by the strangers who carried them down to St Raphael's might render "this world well-nigh intolerable"[10] and further diary writing an impossibility.

Or perhaps not, as two pieces of evidence show. On 25 August 1959 Aelfrida wrote a longish letter to Alethea thanking her for an enjoyable Sunday tea and noting that even if she was not Alethea's mother she would "find her conversation interesting and stimulating and think … what a dear you are".[11] (Tribulations had not transformed her into a "dear sweet gentle old lady"[12]; a sting in the letter's tail informs Alethea that a Beethoven concert is beginning on the radio and that Alethea's mother must give *him* her undivided attention.) The same letter provides evidence of mental capacity: her writing is firm and legible and her thoughts cogent and she refers both to current affairs and to family members to whom she circulates letters of interest received by herself. Furthermore, a reference to her health insurance company having paid a recent Hope House bill suggests that a visit to Cambridge sometime between March and early August 1959 encompassed an extended stay at 'ex-Fordfield'. (If she stayed only a few days, the Sisters did not charge her.) Whether she stayed at Hope House while recuperating from another health crisis or because increasing immobility rendered a stay at Wetenhall Cottage impractical cannot be ascertained, but from this and from mention of an unnamed dentist's bill (Dorothy Smith had retired), we can deduce that she was well enough to travel around Oxford and across England.

We may also deduce that, her mind being as always 'a crowded seedbed of new books'[13], she continued to write articles for *The Watchword*. Of her three 'Theodore and Amanda' articles, diary evidence suggests that the first (*Theodore and Amanda Meet Again*) was written in September 1958[14] though the article itself was not published until September 1959, the second (*Theodore Gives Advice to Amanda*) refers to incidents which took place in spring 1958, the last time Aelfrida was well enough to go outside 'since I don't know when' (she was overjoyed at finding the Home's garden 'a symphony of white and emerald')[15] so was probably written prior to removal to St Raphael's in late October 1958. The third (*Theodore Visits Amanda Again*) is darker in tone than the others and refers to 'Amanda' having suffered a bad attack of illness the previous autumn (as Aelfrida herself had done in autumn 1958), to her listening to voices in the hall (as Aelfrida did after moving to St Raphael's), and to 'Theodore' receiving an urgent call to hear a dying man's confession as Father Campbell had done for her apparently dying self on 14 February 1959, all of which suggests that the article was written some time after the latter date given that Aelfrida was barely convalescent in March and was unlikely to have written even a homiletic article during Lent. The fact that both *Theodore Gives Advice to Amanda* and *Theodore Visits Amanda Again* exist in proof copy also suggests that their author was well enough to read and correct them, and that Aelfrida signed the September 1959 copy of *The Watchword* with her usual firm signature that physical and mental dexterity remained to her.

A second reason for silence may lie in her statement that 'the beautiful service of Unction' had left her so completely in God's hands with regard to going sooner to Him or to staying a little longer on earth[16] that, agreeing with Francis de Sales that she had 'no tomorrow save God's Providence'[17] (and, given that the Russians now possessed intercontinental nuclear missiles, that she 'ought not to worry about anything' because England's and her own 'last days must be drawing near')[18], she decided to employ her remaining time on earth as a period of gestation for her next – and surely imminent – *vita nuova* and although silent in diary terms, did much thinking on that same Providence. Conversely, and the negative evidence of a mute diary supports this, perhaps she had finally achieved suspension of the inner monologue which she felt impelled to consign it to paper as the only means of quietening her seething brain, so that what appears to us only as 'fragments' of silence[19] (Mother Guenvrede, we may remember, described her resident tertiary's silence as 'noisy')[20] is Aelfrida's final and most successful attempt to imitate Christ's Silence at important points in His life.

Achievement of inner silence suggests further reasons for diary silence. Perhaps aware that "not many years of life … remain to this Thy child"[21], she finally obeys Father Cary by curtailing leakages of spiritual energy (or, rather, by confining leakages to letters and to very short articles) and in conserving what remains of her spiritual energies (more than a quantum, one suspects) and becomes, as Bishop Wynn suggested, 'intentionally silent' in union with God.[22] Perhaps, though circumstances seem to militate against it, she now becomes more than ever before 'nothing but a soul at prayer' and '*a hermit*' because prayerful soulfulness in the hermitage–cell of St Raphael's 'will bring [her] Home at last'.[23] Perhaps having received Unction, she is now as good as dead and, being like the crucified but resurrected Christ no longer of this world, leads a life 'hid with Christ in God' and, being 'dead', finds that 'the *need to record*' is not 'dying down' but 'dead' too.[24] Perhaps having at last achieved "not merely abstention from speech but … [that] hush of the soul before the infinite majesty and holiness of the Most High"[25] which is not merely peace of mind but, given the 'noise' with which her unbalanced mind has been filled, an absence of sound more precious than sound because it is what she would like her mind's 'reality' to be: silent.[26] Perhaps, listening in silence to 'celestial music' on 'Griselda', she finds herself in a 'borderland' place full of such glorious perceptions and apperceptions that physical blindness and deafness become irrelevant and she revels in ineffably beautiful visual and auditory experiences, enjoys them without fear of being thought 'mad', and has no desire to record them because they transcend words. And if some of these experiences owe more to Sister Catherine's administration of opiates than to Deity – 'it was like coming round after an anaesthetic'[27], wrote Aelfrida on awakening from one episode – who can blame a frail old lady for deriving spiritual comfort from this source too.

There may, of course, be other reasons unspoken and un-hinted at. Perhaps, remembering the 'Voices' prediction that she would die at seventy-seven, she saw no need to begin a volume which she might not live to complete. Perhaps she feared to die while penning a comment so scurrilous that Heaven would be denied her. Perhaps re-reading entries written in delirium she did not wish to chronicle an entry into a state where she became what she most feared to become – "distracted or mad" – or the onset of a vegetable condition "without senses or memory"[28]. Perhaps she wished to enter further into the fellowship of Christ's suffering by abandoning the only earthly outlet for her churning thoughts. Perhaps she came to regard her diary as just another 'episode' in her life – and closed the book. Perhaps she chose to end it on a day of particular significance to the Society of the Sacred Cross of which she was a life tertiary and to herself as Placida of the Holy Passion, signs and signifiers of her vocation, the particular day of a particular week on which she felt 'more at home' and '*happiest*'[29] than on any other because it brought her closest to Him whose life she had to tried to imitate, the day celebrated by Frédéric Amiel in the penultimate entry of his *journal intime*: "tomorrow is Good Friday, the festival of pain. I know what it is to spend days of anguish and nights of pain; let me bear my cross humbly … My duty is to satisfy the claims of the present and to have everything in order. Let me try to end well, seeing that to undertake and even to continue are closed to me … I have no more future".[30]

1959, however, was by no means a silent year for other reasons too, for just as we receive messages from supposedly silent Aelfrida, so we also receive them from people who had played their part in her life.

Aelfrida's schoolmate and bridesmaid Helen Salter (née Verrall) died in April 1959 at the Crown House in Newport in Essex, the house in which Aelfrida had once seen ghosts dressed à la Nell Gwynne and received a plea for help from Frederic Myer's spirit. Helen and Aelfrida had long lost contact – possibly the former's continuing association with the SPR deterred one who had put her mediumistic days behind her – but their correspondence had been resumed following the death of Silvia Blennerhasset née Myers in 1957. No further reference to Helen appears in Aelfrida's diary, however, Helen having perhaps no desire to renew friendship with one who used 'virtuous' as a term of disparagement.

Eustace's seventieth birthday occurred in May 1959.

('He is an old man now … and knows it', wrote his sister following a visit from him in January 1959 during which earlier animosities seem to have been forgotten and she noted how much she loved and admired him.) Wistful at the prospect of retirement because 'the Mastership … has meant so much to him' and already regretting that he would no longer meet 'the succession of interesting visitors' to the college to which he had devoted his academic career'[31], Eustace nevertheless looked forward to his and Phyllis' new house on 'a plot of land in Millington Road … down what looks like a country lane and next door to an old gravel pit'.[32] The house, designed by Wetenhall Cottage's architect 'Hugh' Hughes in contemporary idiom, had not met with Aelfrida's approval when she visited it soon after completion in July 1957, for although it was 'astonishingly laboursaving' and had 'more built-in cupboards etc. etc.' than she could conceive of, its interior was 'glaring and monotonous' because 'everything [was] white paint'. But if, as we surmise, she visited Cambridge in summer 1959 she may have overcome her distaste sufficiently to visit for 'cosy tea and talk'.[33]

As Visitors Book entries show[34], Aelfrida was visited in a single week in September 1959 by two women towards whom she had always entertained warm feelings. The first was Veronica Tillyard, since September 1958 Mrs Subramanian Sankaran, who brought her husband of a year to Oxford to visit his aunt by marriage. Aelfrida had suspected that there might be a man in Veronica's life who had vowed that 'he can't live without her!'[35] but as sniping diary entries show, was 'deeply hurt' when Veronica left it to her father to break the news of his daughter's 'civil marriage' (another black mark) to an 'Indian Brahmin' mathematician. The shock of the news made Veronica's aunt 'quite giddy in the head' (she would not have been surprised, she wrote, 'at *Angela* marrying a foreigner because she … likes foreign lands and ways') but she recovered sufficiently to make favourable comparisons between her favourite niece's husband and her own 'holy Brahmin friend' Surendra Nath Maitra of *Spiritual Exercises* days and to write to Veronica to welcome Subramanian into the family.[36] But what would one not give for a diary account of the Sankarans' visit to St John's Home on 1 September 1959.

And of a visit made by Lucy Verey six days later. Lucy's signature is the last in Aelfrida's Visitors Book; the first, in a bold hand, is that of Charles Stewart Smith "HBM Consul for Odessa, Retired Lieutenant RN". (It is nice to think that the book's first and last entries contain the names of a man and a woman who loved her.) Lucy and Aelfrida had not met since January 1935 when the former arrived in Osney Lane to enquire about the details of the latter's latest 'indisposition'[37] (i.e. her latest cancer scare, soon to be dismissed by William Gilliatt as a nonsense but actually a symptom of scurvy) and perhaps to shudder, like her daughter Elizabeth who accompanied her, at the impoverished surroundings and austere conditions in which her friend had deliberately chosen to live, but the ladies had continued to correspond on birthdays and at Christmas (Lucy, it seems, sent Aelfrida 'writing paper, as usual'[38], an appropriate present for a prolific letter writer) or when events in their lives were of more than passing interest, and in 1956 Aelfrida had composed loving *Memory Pictures* of her 'dearest and best friend': *Littlehampton and Lucy* and *Staying with Lucy*.[39]

The reasons for Lucy and Aelfrida not having met for nearly a quarter of a century can only be guessed at. A world war and Aelfrida's successive moves may provide two, as may Lucy's busyness with children and grandchildren but it seems that not even Aelfrida's return to Oxford in 1953, a town less than thirty miles from the Vereys' country home, persuaded Lucy to make the visit she promised that year until six more had passed. There is no hint in Aelfrida's diaries of an estrangement – indeed, she wrote of her "best and oldest friend" that their friendship had endured for over half a century "without a misunderstanding or a coolness"[40] – but perhaps Lucy had lost patience with the vagaries of her friend's behaviour or Hal, becoming aware of aspects of Aelfrida's chequered past, suggested that his wife maintain contact only by letter. Or had Aelfrida, as with Joan Cooper, preached 'detachment' and thereby hurt Lucy's feelings and in the name of religion alienated a woman whose own religion was 'so unassuming that it [seemed] merely like super-good manners'[41]?

Whatever the reason, the two elderly ladies (both were seventy-five) met again on 7 September 1959 just over a mile from where they had last said goodbye. Their lives since their respective marriages in 1907 could hardly have been more different: Lucy's, though not without its trials, settled, 'gracious and dignified', wealthy, beloved, and 'full of quiet strength'[42], Aelfrida's full of trials, unsettled, sometimes disreputable, wilfully impoverished, and frequently unloved. Both, though similar in appearance in youth, being tall and slim with Lucy more elegant in dress and manner and Aelfrida more striking in appearance, could hardly have been more different in 1959, Lucy more reserved but recognisably the same person in feature and dress, Aelfrida purblind, desperately lame, and, it may be, showing physical stigmata of advanced cardiac disease, but still when 'excited' (as now), the same brilliant conversationalist able to extract more details of her friend's life than Lucy of hers. But let us hope that the 'odd pair of friends' as Agatha once described them, Lucy

'genuine and faithful through and through', Aelfrida frequently not, 'talked and talked as we used to, with no sense of strangeness though we meet so seldom'.[43]

Echoes of another odd friendship also resonate during the silent months of 1959, that of 'Sarasvati' (a name of which she later wrote disingenuously that it 'lasted for a while')[44] with the man whose small precise signature appears in her Visitors Book between those of 'modern mystic' Caroline Dalmas and Anatolia (Lila) Michaelides: Aleister Crowley.

In 1959 there was published as one of several books written for children by the same author a story entitled *Elfrida and the Pig*. The coincidence of Aelfrida's name with that of the child-heroine of the story might warrant no more than a smile were it not that the story was written by John Symonds and that John Symonds was Aleister Crowley's literary executor.

Symonds and Crowley first met in Hastings in 1946, the year before the latter's death. (A description of their meeting forms part of the last chapter of *The Great Beast*, the first of Symonds' biographies of Aelfrida's erstwhile 'Guru'; perhaps she noted as she read it how closely Symonds' description of 'Old Crow' parallels what we know of herself at this time: "I [felt]", he wrote, "that there was something a little strange about Crowley … he could be considered an ordinary old man … and yet there was a quality of remoteness about him that made him different. I can best describe this quality by saying that it suggested that he cared very little for the usual preoccupations of mankind".)[45] Symonds also knew of Aelfrida: in *The Magic of Aleister Crowley*, published in 1958, he notes that Crowley discussed with him his *Paris Working* dream of 1914 in which Frater Perdurabo explained to "a woman friend who appears in the dream" that he had "reduced all the objects which appeared in [it] to the yoni and lingam" and that he could actually "destroy" one of the objects "by perceiving that it is only the yoni in disguise", his explanation being received with "expressed wonder and dismay" by the woman friend herself, "A★★★★ T★★★★"[46] (*sic.*) It seems too, judging by *Elfrida and the Pig*, by corroborative evidence provided by Aelfrida's diary, and by 'memory pictures' describing her childhood, that Symonds knew something of Aelfrida's life (especially her childhood) as confided to Crowley and that Crowley, recipient of revealing letters from 'AeT Sarasvati', must have been the person to divulge details of it to Symonds. And Symonds' title with its Aelfrida/Elfrida conjunction suggests that he may have had 'A★★★★ T★★★★' in mind when he wrote his story:

Elfrida Spooner, nicknamed "the Clever Child", is an only child living with her parents in a house by a lake.

Her cleverness is evinced by her being able to "do sums as long as your arm, read Latin", and write letters full of very long words to "important people", but her parents, hoping to make her "cleverer" still, force her to lead a solitary life of study and even forbid her girlish toys, particularly "*dolls*". [47]

Aelfrida, a clever child living in a house and a town whose names have watery connotations, left the Perse School for Girls and prior to joining Mrs Verrall's class, 'read a great deal on [her] own [and ] taught [herself] a good deal of Greek and Italian and so on'. [48] (She was not, of course, an only child, but with Julius at school and Eustace still in the nursery, must have felt like a singleton; her parents' negative reaction to her departure from the Perse may have contributed too.) Joining Mrs Verrall's class, she studied "Classics all the morning and Mathematics all the afternoon", other subjects being "crammed in"[49] as time and space permitted. (And in later life she wrote very long letters not all of which, like 'Elfrida's' to the Station Master, were read right through by their recipients.) She was not forbidden to play – diaries and '*Memory Pictures*' are crammed with descriptions of games played with Julius, Conrad, and Eustace – but, as we suddenly realise, her childish pursuits are all boyish: she only once mentions a doll and then only to deny sacrificing it during a game of 'Gods and Goddesses'. Whether this was because boyish pursuits were inevitable given that she had no sisters or whether her mother, described in fictional form as "an early feminist", forbade dolls, we cannot tell but adolescent longing for a baby may suggest budding maternal instincts frustrated by circumstances or embargo. (The Oracle, similarly fictionalised, appears as an "eminent theologian"[50] but was neither.)

> Elfrida, though lacking human friends of her own age, is great friends with the huge Pig who lives next door and whose girth increases as Elfrida becomes thinner because, at table with her parents, she conceals unwanted food in her handkerchief to feed it to him later.

Aelfrida suffered what she later described as "loss of appetite"[51] when forced to attend school (Symonds' account of 'Elfrida's' technique of concealing and disposing of food is an accurate description of one employed by those with eating disorders) and practised ascetic self-starvation as an adolescent; she also, as we know from diary entries penned during her involvement with Crowley, sent him presents: poems, dress ornaments, and a gold necklace. [52]

> On a night illuminated by a full moon, Elfrida, "so clever that she couldn't sleep" because "all the things she'd learned" were whirling round in her head, hears the Pig grunt in the lane beneath her room; looking out the window, she sees him rush past with three dolls on his back. ("One of them was a teddy bear", Pig later informs her when she taxes him with what she has seen.) Plagued by curiosity, she begs the Pig to take her to wherever he goes and he, reluctantly at first, agrees.

This description of Aelfrida's whirling mind as she wrestles with postnatal depression and makes her first contact with Aleister Crowley (self-styled 'Great Beast') seems as accurate as Symonds could make it: he had seen copies of letters written by Crowley to 'A★★★★ T★★★★', would have known of his initial reluctance to take Aelfrida with him as he conducted men and women into the esoterics of Ceremonial Magic.

> The following night, the Pig takes Elfrida on his back to a lonely house whose owner is known to her as "Mr Manypenny … a peculiar sort of person [who] wears a black cloak … and was followed wherever he went by a little black dog". Elfrida explores the house, finding it full of objects collected by Manypenny and of dolls being trained by him to go out into the world to work as he bids. She also meets Mr Manypenny himself who suggests that she return in daylight. The Pig escorts her home. She says nothing to her parents of her nocturnal adventure then or later.

The mysterious 'Mr Manypenny' is harder to identify in the context of Aelfrida's brief relationship with Aleister Crowley but given that she (as 'Elfrida') visits him again, that he recognises her as the little girl who is not allowed toys (he gives her a doll he has rejected as not having achieved the required standard of training, a doll which her father, contrary to her mother's wishes, allows her to keep), and that he takes great interest in which books she reads ("Latin, geography and arithmetic", no "story books [but] only Hi-story books … all true of course"), he may be presumed to be the Devil (a personality well known to Aelfrida) with a black dog 'familiar'. The story ends with 'Elfrida', the Pig, and 'Mr Manypenny' going fishing with rods belonging to the latter (we are not told what they catch; souls, perhaps) and with the 'Clever Child' teaching her doll Latin. (Mr Manypenny's name for the doll is 'Penelope', a name whose classical connotations, suggestive of promises perpetually postponed by guileful excuses[53], provides a perfect synonym for Christianity's hints of a perfect splendour to be enjoyed only in the hereafter.) This "change of work [is] as good as play" to a lonely little girl who thereafter "[goes] on educating [herself]" by "[attending] lectures, soak[ing]

**Aleister Crowley in old age**

up new subjects and collect[ing] information as other people collect stamps or butterflies"[54] – and who, as 'Aelfrida Tillyard', composes *Spiritual Exercises* and other books in which she alternately praises and disparages the 'Great Beast' – though not by name. *Elfrida and the Pig* may therefore provide valuable insight into a period of Aelfrida's life predating her diaries and of which, other than *Memory Pictures* written late in life as bowdlerised versions of events, we have very little information.

There is, however, another possible connection with Aleister Crowley and his biographer which warrants exploration at this point; on two occasions in Aelfrida's life she records a disembodied voice calling her by name as "Mrs Graham". The first occurred at Tymawr on 22 June 1938, she noting that the voice had been both distant and unrecognised, the second at St John's Home in December 1953 when she stated that one of the 'Ladies' 'who believes that ghosts attack her sometimes' (this seems unlikely, given that Mrs Beloe was a graduate and a former missionary and that there is no further reference to her apparent quirk) had heard the walls shouting "Mrs Graham". (Aelfrida herself, so she said, 'heard nothing'.)[55] The events, separated as they are in time, place, and circumstance, might be no more than auditory hallucinations were it not for Mrs Graham's reaction to both.

Two weeks after the first occasion (i.e. on 7 July 1938) Aelfrida's guardian angel suggested that she inform Mother Guenvrede about her 'meditations with Aleister Crowley'.[56] (It seems she disobeyed him: revealing that she had been his disciple might have had more damning consequences than exposure as a divorcee.) The year in which she heard her name called and cogitated for two weeks on whether she should tell Mother Guenvrede of her relationship with an earlier spiritual director, was also that in which Aleister Crowley, aged sixty and in poor health and desperate financial straits (he had dissipated his inheritance and in May 1923 had had to flee Sicily when Mussolini outlawed secret societies of the kind he was suspected of conducting; in the event, he did not return to England until 1929[57], embarked on the "frenzied schedule of publishing" which was to dominate the rest of his life as he tried to raise funds by steering the unpublished backlog of his written works into the public domain. Can it be that, "looking back after forty years of study"[58], he decided to contact Aelfrida (she had after all, received several letters from him which, together with hers to him, had once been intended for publication) but she, a novice-tertiary working out her period of probation, refused to 'recognise' (i.e. acknowledge the existence of) this voice from her past even though she recognised (i.e. identified) its owner? And could this be why she decided on 1 January 1939 that Crowley should be 'prayed for' and added him to her list of those for whom she offered reparative adoration? And could it have been in recognition of his present plight and his earlier help in setting her feet on the 'mystic way' which had led her to Tymawr that she deemed him prayer-worthy?

The second occasion is harder to explain but given what we know of Aelfrida's propensity for telling the truth aslant, an explanation can be essayed: already familiar with Symonds' name as author of *The Great Beast*, she is horrified to receive a letter from him early in December 1953 requesting details of 'A★★★★ T★★★★'s' relationship with Aleister Crowley so that he can enlarge upon it in later editions or in future works. Her horror at being approached by a ghost from a past which pious Mrs Graham does not want to revive in the present and from whose return she had considered herself safe, is so extreme (she seems to have had little desire to be known at St John's Home as 'clever lady' author 'Aelfrida Tillyard' but she was known to have – indeed, boasted of having – brothers by the name of Tillyard and it would have been easy for someone with access to relevant information to associate Mrs Aelfrida Graham with the 'Aelfrida Tillyard' who had been a 'disciple' of Aleister

Crowley and to whom as 'ACWG', her present initials, and as 'Aelfrida Tillyard, Cambridge' he had dedicated poems) that on hearing, as it were, the walls shouting "Mrs Graham" (as Mrs Beloe might have heard someone bearing a letter from Symonds to Aelfrida call along the echoing corridors of the Home), she decides to 'hear nothing' of Symonds and to turn a metaphorically deaf ear to his request. In which case, could it be that Symonds, known to be an "intellectually aggressive"[59] man, composed *Elfrida and the Pig* as revenge for 'A★★★★ T★★★★'s' failure to cooperate?

St Placid's Day, 5 October 1959, was Aelfrida's seventy-sixth birthday. Sometime in late autumn 1959 the woman who in a moment of deep depression had declared she wanted nothing more than 'to go to bed and – metaphorically – turn [her] face to the wall'[60] turned her face to the wall and willed herself to die.[61] Perhaps she had no wish to endure the physical discomforts of another year of life before fulfilling 'the Voices' prediction of death at seventy-seven. Perhaps, despite an earlier belief that 'the capacity for suffering becomes lessened' as one grows older and that she 'would rather suffer than not feel at all' (without the contrast with misery, happiness would remain a concept only), she now agreed with her teenage self that both notions were 'nonsense'.[62] Perhaps she dreaded extreme old age 'infinitely more than death'[63] and decided to die '*long* before I am 82'.[64] Perhaps, 'impatient of the trammels of life'[65] and 'ready, even eager to go'[66], the woman who had always had 'a vivid sense' that death was waiting for her and a 'curious feeling of *waiting*' for that which waited for her[67] and who had once confided to her diary that she often thought about death, liked the idea of it, and was not afraid of it[68], and who, as 'Catharine Sutherland', advocated suicide as a means of bringing oneself more speedily to God, realised that "her body [was] only a transient affair holding her momentarily a prisoner" and willed it to "let go its grip" and allow her to return to the Spirit who made her.[69] Perhaps, couched in her 'ante-chamber of Heaven'[70], the longed-for 'poor little place just as I meant it to be … my bare room [with] my crucifix'[71] but liable to be moved to a ward at Sister Catherine's whim, she decided to die 'in a room alone [and] apart', ministered to in peace and privacy 'with *prayers* around [her]'.[72] Perhaps, worried about money but knowing that there was 'enough in Barclay's to pay [her] fees till past the turn of the year'[73], she decided to live no longer lest the All Saints Sisters *for the Poor* appropriate all her 'small fortune'.[74] (Or was it merely misplaced asceticism that made her decide 'not to spend a penny of [her] capital on [her]self'[75] when for little more expense she could spend her last days with the loving Sisters of Hope in the house – and possibly

even the room – where she was born?) Perhaps knowing that members of her family increasingly regarded her as a demanding nuisance (and that Eustace, her dependable younger brother/executor, had been hospitalised again in November 1959)[76], she decided in a rare act of altruism to reduce *her* pressure on *their* souls as quickly as possible. And being a *dictatrix* even to herself, succeeded.

We do not know the time or manner of her death but from her many descriptions of how she wanted or intended to die, we may choose our favourite. Perhaps she '*slowly* [withered] away' as her 'Voices' predicted, hearing 'the blessed dead [talking] in low tones'[77] around her, her soul attached to her dying body only by a 'misty navel-cord'.[78] Perhaps she remained conscious to the end with the "inward gazing look" on her face common in the dying and once seen by her on a reproduction "of the death mask of St Teresa of Avila".[79] Or was she forced to "exchange goodbye[s] in the most absurd way" with Alethea and others and like her old suitor Willie Searle, make several 'last appearances'[80] before the end? If so, was she able to practise Jeremy Taylor's 'Holy Dying', convening an edifying deathbed during which she demonstrated to those gathered about her "the radiant patience of some old woman dying on a pauper's bed [but] illuminated from within by the light of the Presence of God" and told them of how "the night-watches were very precious [to her] because God came and visited her then?"[81] And if so, who was there at her bedside to be edified?

Or did she doze away her life "with a little bit of soft music on the radio"[82] and *The Times* unread beside her, the music perhaps the "heavenly lovely Beethoven"[83] associated with Constantine ('Beethoven and undergarments … I mended his drawers while he played to me')[84] and the radio no longer the "confession of weakness"[85] 'Clive Farwell' held it to be but a source of comfort? Or did some kind Sister, nurse, or doctor hasten her end and ease her passing, not gainsaying the Angel of Death but doing "all they [could]"[86] to assist him? And did she allow them to do so, remembering in spite of anathemas against euthanasia (and divorce and contraception and 'road-hogging' and betting and many other things) that she had once said to an adored doctor "when I want to die … I shan't call you in. I shall have another doctor" and that 'Dr Joan' had replied with great gravity and sweetness "when you want to die in comfort … come to me"?[87] Or did she, remembering Chiara's death, decide even *in extremis* not to 'allow anyone to endanger their peace of mind by so helping [her]'[88] and to commit auto-euthanasia lest they be tempted to do so?

We must hope, however, that she did not die in her sleep. Writing apropos the death of Lilian Whitehouse's mother in 1931, Aelfrida noted it 'would be pity to die like that' because, sleeping, one would be unable 'to enter into death in full consciousness [meditating] on the words "in His will is our peace"' and because in dying thus she would miss the greatest experience of her life: that of "entering the heart of God's peace" and discovering that it was "not stagnant [but] generat[ing] waves of spiritual activity which are flowing over me now ..."[89]

As December 1959 advanced Aelfrida approached her "final winter beyond which there is no spring".[90] Let us hope that goodbyes (if any) were "said very quietly – as perhaps they always should be"[91], that when she received and answered her 'summons from God'[92] there were '*prayers* round [her]'[93] prayed as she herself prayed daily (in Latin and, once, for Gwen Raverat) 'for those "*positos in agonia et hodie morituros*"'[94] and that someone recited the 'journey prayers'[95] of the *Itinerarium* as "every image faded from [her], every symbol and memory died ... and the Grail was drunk and colours passed into whiteness and sounds into the silence of life"[96] and she drifted back as she had always done to the house of her birth: "past St Botolph's Church ... the water and the trees of Brookside, the Botanic Gardens, ... the gate ... which guards the Avenue ... left open for the night, ... [the] darkness under the wych-elms, the curve of the road with a dim gas lamp at long intervals – and then we turn in at the gate with 'Fordfield' on either post and we are home".[97]

Aelfrida Catharine Wetenhall and her avatars Frida, Tit, Miss Tillyard, Bélise, Mrs Constantine Graham, Mother, Sarasvati, Straightener, Placida of the Holy Passion, and *Dictatrix Mundi* received her 'summons from God' (always, for her 'the ultimate solution and triumph' and 'the prize')[98] on 15 December 1959 within two days of the twenty-seventh anniversary of her mother's 'heavenly birthday' on 17 December 1932, a mother who might be 'waiting to welcome [her] ... into the next life'.[99] She died in her seventy-seventh year: 'the Voices' prediction, carefully recorded in her diary and marked with a cross to show its significance, did not therefore *quite* 'come true'[100] – but then nor did Dr Hunt's, he at Tymawr having foretold the likely cause of her death (hypertension and ischaemic heart disease) but wrongly predicted that she would live 'to be seventy-eight or so'.[101] (But Aelfrida had never had much confidence in his diagnostic capabilities.) We cannot tell if, being psychic (in which case, how could she not know it?), she knew the date of her death and knowing the 'End [was] so near', was able 'to plan accordingly'[102] and to arrange to die in Advent, for Christians a time when they contemplate their own last days even as they prepare for Christ's nativity and for Aelfrida herself a 'point of sight' akin to Christmas and Good Friday whence she might

catch a glimpse of the 'Beatific Vision whither [she] would fain go quickly'.[103]

Many things we may hope for her when she received 'at long last – the clear call to step through the dark gateway and up the golden stairs'. That freed from the trammels of material existence and mental disequilibrium, God did 'not keep [her] waiting'.[104] That, dying, she experienced more than 'calm eagerness for the Beatific Vision'[105] or received only "hints" of the "perfect splendour" which Fidelio once called "earthly Joy" or a "Moment of Beauty"[106] and Aelfrida herself (quoting the Curé d'Ars) the ability to '*see God*'[107] but that as the mystic recipient of so many visionary experiences, she came not merely as close to seeing the Beatific Vision as she had done on the day of Agneta's birth and death ('a vision of "God's Throne"'[108] was all that was vouchsafed her then) or came close only to experience the strongest feeling of which she was capable, that of 'longing for the Beatific Vision'[109], but that she actually *saw* it. And afterwards '*could* desire nothing else'[110] and in an "astonishing display of inner grace transformed into glory [in] a world of more than matter and mind"[111], 'perceived God'.[112]

Aelfrida, of course, had been 'on the brink of revelation'[113] many times; indeed, it seems she once achieved "a rapture [that] is as timeless as it is intense" of the "infinitely Holy Presence of God" illuminated by "the white light of the undivided Trinity"[114] manifesting Himself in and to her. Because such experiences constituted one of her 'fruits' of Silence, it is appropriate that the occasion on which she came closest to the vision supposedly achieved only at the point of death was one in which 'everything was very quiet' and she not only '*perceived* God' with her spiritual eyes but was also able to describe for us something of what she may have 'seen' as she entered into death: '[God's] glory was Life and Power, Life which makes our earth-life seem semi-conscious by comparison and Power which ... *annihilated* evil ... The Glory was *alive* with adoring *angels* and *creatures* ... and *souls, their* life fused with and expressing God's Life and yet remaining distinct from Him and from each other ... It was the most wonderful vision, a kind of completion of all previous visions, *given* by the Holy Trinity'.[115] But let us hope she failed to act as she feared she might when face to face with 'revelation': 'I shouldn't believe it if I *did* get it'.[116]

Let us hope too that she was not disappointed with Heaven. Like Charles Foucault, she had once conceived of Heaven as a "great city whose dazzling outer wall [sat] atop a high mountain"[117], a "City of God" whose "towers and pinnacles" she was permitted to glimpse during long 'night watches' as an ill and useless encumbrance.[118] Or, more amusingly, as a place in which to her surprise and relief there was 'nothing definitely *pious*' ('anything less like … Sabbaths having no end could not possibly be imagined!') or, more fruitfully, as a 'new world' to which she would open her eyes after leaping into the waters of death (a 'new element' in themselves), a place of 'material but … infinitely finer matter and of indescribable beauty' in which 'hills and valleys and verdure and flowers … untainted by man [stretched] away and beneath [her] far wider powers of vision', lit by a 'peculiarly exquisite … spiritual … *light*', a place which 'had been there all the time only [she] had been too gross to see it' or too preoccupied with seeing what she did not want to see or too tortured 'by horrible intrusive sounds' to hear the '*silence*' there or too emotionally entangled with other people to appreciate the '*solitude*' there or too oppressed by the 'cramped sense of living behind invisible prison bars' to be able to think as clearly and as powerfully as she could there.[119] But perhaps a later, more spiritualised, and still only 'half-formulated' picture of Heaven (or, rather, of her place there) was the one she preferred: Heaven as a state of mind in which she was '*allowed* to adore' and where 'without … distractions or moods or taint of sin or grief for the world's wickedness and sorrow', she could 'pour out [herself] before [God] in an endless offering of love'.[120] And let us hope that, amid the "dazzling flashes of ecstasy" which illuminated "profound apprehension of the Triune God", Aelfrida also achieved the "deeper peace"[121] she sought, the '*peace*, the peace that strikes the balance between joy and suffering', and that '*there in that peace*' and in the splendour of 'perfect equilibrium', her God, pouring '*caritas*, compassion, pure love'[122] over her, allowed her to abide.

Finally let us hope that when she achieved the state 'which we call Heaven' that it was not only in the form she most wished to find – a state of 'marvellous peace' entered in 'perfect loving self-abandonment to the Will of God'[123] – but also that God willed she met there the two people she hoped to meet again after death, people she had grievously wronged during her life and theirs and on whom, because of this, the 'curse of Graeme', had fallen most heavily: Constantine Graham, né Michaelides, and the daughter, who, among her names, bore two of her mother's: Aelfrida Catharine Agatha Graham.

Was it with Constantine in mind that Aelfrida wrote of the heavenly joy "of seeing our beloved [dead] free from the almost inevitable faults of the earth, ambition, pride, self-regard"?[124] But her mental picture of a former husband unseen for forty years cannot have been wholly reassuring for she admitted to a 'haunting fear' that in spite of hours spent in reparative adoration on his behalf, Constantine might have obdurately chosen 'to remain outside the closed door'[125] and to a belief that although

Constantine's "taint of sin" might not have been as great as she imagined, it might have "left some small blemish"[126] on the character of one she professed to love so much. In spite of this she continued to hope his 'purgation' was complete and to 'feel sure that God [held] him fast' and that character defects notwithstanding and even if not quite as ready as herself 'for the Beatific Vision', he would be there to greet her on her arrival in Heaven[127] because he had progressed enough so as to 'have reached the same point' as herself when they met again.[128] (And rather curiously, given that most of the statements quoted above were written on or about anniversaries of her wedding day, to note that she would rejoice 'if Anatolia and the other Mrs Graham were there too'.)[129] And if she took comfort in having once received 'a kind of vision of the future' in which she put her hand in Constantine's and said "Look" and that, looking together, they saw God[130], who can refuse her this crumb, improbable though it may be? But let us remember that the woman who once told us 'someday I may write an article on *Michaelides as I knew him*' was a writer of fiction who told the truth aslant even to her diary and herself and that her next sentence was a question – 'do you grasp the humiliation of such a thought?' – which implied that 'humiliation' sprang less from being paid to write it than from having to reveal that the 'Michaelides' she 'knew' in 1904 was no more than an 'episode' on her path to God.[131]

There remains Agatha, the dead daughter she had in mind when she described the delight of finding predeceased children in Heaven in a condition "better than all the best you ever wished for them, more loveable, more intelligent, more holy" and Heaven itself as a place where those meeting them would be able to offer "affection [so] unpossessive" that they need never again "hold back the stream of [their] love lest it do … pain" or weigh like an intolerable burden on those on whom they poured it out.[132] (Of her mature love for Constantine, Aelfrida wrote 'I have no sense of possession unless it is that I have always loved him … with a spiritual as well as a this-world love. Perhaps the fading-away of a sense of possession … is part of the "mystical death"'. But note the insertion of an ambiguous 'I think' between 'him' and 'with' and wonder if the phrase refers to the quality of her love for Constantine or, given that she had once regarded him as "an inconvenient obstacle on [her] Heavenly Path"[133], to its existence.) Addressing 'beloved Agatha, sweet Temu' on one of the anniversaries of the latter's 'Heavenly Birthday', Aelfrida asked of her daughter if she was enjoying 'heavenly delights', adding that if she was, her mother did not intend to interrupt them and hoped her love might be interwoven with them'[134]; on another, she begged 'sweet Temu' to pray for her and added she felt sure Agatha was waiting for her, though five years were to pass before her desire not to keep her daughter waiting was fulfilled.[135] Believing too that Agatha had been granted the privilege 'of helping certain newly-arrived souls into the Light'[136] (her own 'privilege', or, rather, 'task', was 'to be a Straightener', though humbler now than heretofore, she admitted to such depths of ignorance that she would be forced 'to learn and learn at the same time')[137], did she see her dead daughter, nearer now to her mother's heart and soul 'than ever on earth', turn to her 'with her tenderest [and] most understanding smile'[138] and, as bidden, call to her mother in the hour of her death in words inlaid in bronze on the oaken cross which marked her grave: *in hora mortis meae, voca me*?[139]

Let us hope she did.

# Notes

1 Tillyard, Ae. *The Silence of God* p48 (GCPPT 2|20).
2 GCPPT 1|1|72 17 February 1955.
3 GCPPT 1|1|75 7 January, 'Ash Wednesday' (11 February) and 18 March 1959.
4 Tillyard Ae. *The Night Watches* pp 5–8.
5 GCPPT 1|1|64 7 June 1946.
6 Tillyard, Ae. *Christian Old Age* p 82 (GCPPT 2|17).
7 GCPPT 1|1|63 15 November 1945.
8 GCPPT 1|1|34 5 May 1927.
9 GCPPT 1|1|47 23 March 1935.
10 Tillyard, Ae. *The Silence of God* p 48.
11 GCPPG. A1 4|2 Letter from Aelfrida to Alethea Graham of 25 August 1959.
12 *Gleanings: Extracts from Mother Guenvrede's Writings* p22. The letter, written sometime in 1958, is among those written to SSC Oblates and Associates that year.
13 GCPPT 1|1|64 7 June 1946.
14 GCPPT 1|1|75 28 September 1958.
15 GCPPT 1|1|74 20 April and 12 May 1958.
16 GCPPT 1|1|75 4 March 1959.
17 GCPPT 1|1|73 31 December 1955.
18 ibid. 5 November 1956.
19 GCPPT 1|1|71 8 December 1953.
20 GCPPT 1|1|63 15 April 1954.
21 Tillyard, Ae. *The Fruits of Silence* pp 24–27 (GCPPT 2|18).
22 GCPPT 1|1|70 27 May 1953.
23 ibid. 'Corpus Christi' (12 or 13 June) 1952.
24 GCPPT 1|1|73 10 October 1955.
25 Tillyard, Ae. *Christian Old Age* p 86.
26 GCPPT 1|1|70a contains quotations taken by Aelfrida from Simone Weil's *Attente de Dieu*, published in 1950 and it is on one of these (silence as "*plus réele que les sons*") that I have based my suggestion. *Attente de Dieu* is an assemblage of essays and articles written in 1942 and collated for publication following Weil's death aged 34 from heart failure due to self-inflicted privations; Aelfrida, reading them sometime between 18 May 1952 and 14 June 1953, the first and last dates in the contemporary volume of her diary, stated that Weil exhibited 'signs of mental trouble' while writing them. There are notable similarities between Weil's short life (1909–1943) and Aelfrida's longer one.
27 GCPPT 1|1|75 28 February 1959.
28 Tillyard, Ae. *The Making of a Mystic* pp 39–40, quoting Augustine Baker.
29 GCPPT 1|1|71 'Good Friday' (15 April) and 'Easter [Sunday]' (17 April) 1954.
   GCPPT 1|1|54 17 April 1938.
30 Amiel, F. Journal entry for 15 April 1881.
31 GCPPT 1|1|75 10 January 1959.
32 GCPPT 1|1|72 11 July 1955.
   GCPPT 1|1|74 18 July 1957.
33 GCPPT 1|1|74 18 July 1957.
34 Aelfrida's Visitors Book, a wedding present from Jessie Stent, can be found at GCPPT 1/1b.
35 GCPPT 1|1|73 26 November 1956.
36 GCPPT 1|1|75 25 and 28 September 1958. Eustace Tillyard's 'truly astonishing' letter of 23 September 1958 giving fuller details of what he called the "domestic surprise!" engendered by Veronica's wedding was pasted by Aelfrida into this volume of her diary following the entry for 25 September 1958.
37 GCPPT 1|1|46 3 January 1935.
38 GCPPT 1|1|75 5 October 1958.
39 *Littlehampton and Lucy* (GCPPT 2|25|2) describes Lucy's and Aelfrida's first meeting, *Staying with Lucy* (GCPPT 2|26|2(5)) Aelfrida's annual childhood visits to the Longstaffe family.
40 Tillyard, Ae. *The Glory of the West* p251 (GCPPT 2|61|1 pt 2).
41 GCPPT 1|1|42 29 September 1932.
42 GCPPT 1|1|46 3 January 1935.
43 GCPPT 1|1|42 29 September 1932.
44 GCPPT 1|1|53 14 March 1937.
45 Symonds, J. *The Great Beast* p 397. The chapter from which the quotation is taken is entitled 'Magical Retirement', a not inapt description of this period of Aelfrida's own life at this time.
46 Symonds, J. *The Magic of Aleister Crowley* p 126. In *The Great Beast* (p176) Symonds is less specific, noting that Crowley failed to give "a clear account of [his] wonderful dream" and omitting all mention of a "woman friend" or of her (disguised) name.
47 Symonds, J. *Elfrida and the Pig* from which all otherwise unreferenced quotations are taken.
48 GCPPT 1|1|57 8 March 1940.
49 Tillyard, Ae. *The Centaur* p259 (GCPPT 2|21|1).
50 ibid.
51 GCPPT 2|24|1 *Little Frida leaves School*.
52 It is conceivable that the necklace 'offered' by Aelfrida to Aleister Crowley (GCPPT 1|1|9 3 July 1913) in return for three letters and an unspecified 'present' was the 'Panamanian gold necklace' brought or sent back by Constantine in 1913 and later bestowed by Aelfrida on her baby god-daughter Annette Barron (GCPPT 1|1|51 21 August 1935), in which case Constantine must have retrieved it from Crowley during their meeting at the British Consulate.
53 Homer's *Odyssey* describes how Odysseus' wife Penelope, plagued throughout his twenty year absence by importunate suitors, fended them off by promising to marry one of them when she had completed a weaving task, a task she failed to complete prior to Odysseus' return because each night she unpicked her work of the previous day.
54 Tillyard, Ae. *The Centaur* pp 259–260.
55 GCPPT 1|1|55 22 June 1938.
   GCPPT 1|1|71 12 December 1953.
56 GCPPT 1|1|55 7 July 1938.
57 Kaczynski, R. pp 312–313 and 350 (2002).
58 ibid. pp 410–411.
59 *Daily Telegraph* obituary of John Symonds of 11 November 2006.
60 GCPPT 1|1|20 1 March 1918.
61 Angela Yaffey (personal communication 5 May 2008) quoting Alethea Graham.
62 GCPPT 1|1|5 28 August 1900.
63 GCPPT 1|1|30 22 July 1925.

64 GCPPT 1|1|32 21 April 1926.

65 GCPPT 1|1|46 23 February 1935.

66 GCPPT 1|1|22 24 January 1918.

67 GCPPT 1|1|27 3 March and 1 July 1923.

68 GCPPT 1|1|13 17 October 1905.

69 Tillyard, Ae. *Naomi da Costa* p 96. (GCPPT 2|22).

70 GCPPT 1|1|72 16 August 1955.

71 GCPPT 1|1|46 7 August 1934.

72 GCPPT 1|1|72 30 July 1955.
   GCPPT 1|1|74 20 December 1957.

73 GCPPG A1 4|2 Letter from Aelfrida to Alethea Graham of 25 August 1959.

74 GCPPT 1|1|74 20 February 1954.

75 GCPPT 1|1|73 12 December 1956.

76 GCPPT 3|4 Letter from Patience Wardle (née Tillyard) to Julius Tillyard of 6 March 1960.

77 GCPPT 1|1|70 11 October 1952.

78 GCPPT 1|1|75 31 January 1959.

79 Tillyard, Ae. *The Glory of the West* p15 (GCPPT 2|16|3).

80 GCPPT 1|1|74 6 September 1957.

81 GCPPT 2|23 *The Watchword* September 1956.

82 Tillyard, Ae. *Christian Old Age* p 12.

83 GCPPG A1 4|2 Letter from Aelfrida to Alethea Graham of 25 August 1959.

84 GCPPT 1|1|13 12 February 1906.

85 Tillyard, Ae. *Rich Man's Choice* p 228 (GCPPT 2|21|2 Pt 1).

86 Tillyard, Ae. *The Closer Walk with God* p 173.

87 GCPPT 1|1|42 21 October 1932.

88 GCPPT 1|1|45 21 April 1934.

89 GCPPT 1|1|40 18 August 1931.

90 Tillyard, Ae. *Christian Old Age* p 120. Aelfrida is quoting Horace's *Diffugere nives* epode here.

91 GCPPT 2|23 *The Watchword* June 1956.

92 GCPPT 1|1|28 23 October 1924.

93 GCPPT 1|1|74 20 December 1957.

94 GCPPT 1|1|73 14 February 1957.

95 GCPPT 1|1|72 9 September 1955.

96 Benson, R H. *Initiation* p 396.

97 GCPPT 2|25|3 (2).

98 GCPPT 1|1|18 January 1913.
   GCPPT 1|1|28 23 October 1924.

99 GCPPT 1|1|70 10 September 1952.

100 ibid. 11 October 1952.

101 GCPPT 1|1|62 27 September 1944.

102 GCPPT 1|1|67 27 February 1950.

103 GCPPT 1|1|48 'Ascension Day' (30 May) 1935.

104 GCPPT 1|1|57 22 June 1940.

105 GCPPT 1|1|75 10 March 1959.

106 Stokoe, F. *Ode to Earthly Joy* (*Cambridge Poets 1900–1913* p 187) and *Moments of Beauty* (GCPPT 1|1|70a), the latter a poem of which Aelfrida later wrote that God '*did* send [Stokoe] one foretaste of eternal joy – and into that joy he has … entered … by the Beauty-gate'. (GCPPT 1|1|70 November 1952).

107 Tillyard, Ae. *The Closer Walk with God* p 166.

108 GCPPT 1|1|75 9 August 1958.

109 GCPPT 1|1|73 25 October 1955.

110 GCPPT 1|1|38 29 September 1930.

111 Benson, R H. *The Dawn of All* p 223.

112 GCPPT 1|1|73 'Advent Sunday' (2 December) 1956.

113 GCPPT 1|1|40 18 August 1931.

114 Tillyard, Ae. *The Fruits of Silence* pp 36–37.

115 GCPPT 1|1|73 'Advent Sunday' (2 December) 1956. As her diary entry shows ('yesterday something wonderful happened'), Aelfrida received her 'completion of all previous visions' on the previous day, 1 December 1956.

116 GCPPT 1|1|40 18 August 1931.

117 Fleming, F. p 280, quoting Charles Foucault.

118 Tillyard, Ae. *The Night Watches* p 5–8.

119 GCPPT 1|1|27 22 August 1923. This 'wonderfully vivid dream of life after death' was recorded by Aelfrida at '4.30am in bed', her guardian angel having just ordered her 'to go downstairs [and] get pen and ink and write', which she did 'though sleepy and protesting'. Her description is very similar to Amiel's description of Nature, quoted in William James' *Varieties of Religious Experience* p395.

120 GCPPT 1|1|58 23 November 1940.

121 Tillyard, Ae. *Christian Old Age* p 111.

122 GCPPT 1|1|46 10 February 1935.

123 GCPPT 1|1|71 5 August 1953.

124 Tillyard, Ae. *Christian Old Age* p108.

125 GCPPT 1|1|67 27 January 1950.

126 Tillyard, Ae. *Christian Old Age* p 108.

127 GCPPT 1|1|63 19 January 1946.
   GCPPT 1|1|67 27 January 1950.
   GCPPT 1|1|70 19 January 1953.

128 GCPPT 1|1|71 19 January 1954.

129 GCPPT 1|1|63 19 January 1946.

130 GCPPT 1|1|73 20 January 1956.

131 GCPPT 1|1|11 15 May 1904.

132 Tillyard, Ae. *Christian Old Age* p 108.

133 Tillyard, Ae. *Marrying a Stranger* p 247 (GCPPT 2|6).

134 GCPPT 1|1|70 'Lent I' (22 or 23 February) 1950.

135 GCPPT 1|1|71 20 February 1954.

136 GCPPT 1|1|73 18 February 1957.

137 GCPPT 1|1|27 22 August 1923.

138 ibid.

139 Tillyard, Ae. *The Glory of the West* p 358 (GCPPT 2|16|1 Pt 2). The phrase, underlined in red in the typescript of *The Glory of the West*, also forms the epigraph to *The Closer Walk with God,* a book written in the period between Constantine's and Agatha's deaths. It is taken from a Catholic invocation, the *Anima Christi*, which runs in part "From the malignant enemy, defend me. In the hour of my death, call to me. And bid me come to Thee".

# Epitaphic

On 18 December 1959 what remained of Aelfrida was incinerated at Oxford Crematorium. As befitted one who made splendid use of the postal service, her ashes were sent by registered post to Cambridge, the town of which she had written that she 'couldn't live away from'. There, with "no more moves ahead", the "well-to-do lady" who had said goodbye to the "big house and obsequious servants" and to the "small house and … one faithful maid" joined her ancestors in the "God's acre in which home-come souls are Blest". (This particular 'acre' was courtesy of landscape designer John Claudius Loudon; her maternal grandfather and great-grandfather had been shareholders in the company which established it in Histon Road in 1843.) And in the same town as and within two miles of Fordfield, having in the meantime said goodbye to the "little cottage and the rough daily woman" and to the "single room in a Home" in the university town jokingly referred to as "The Other Place".[1] Or did she? True, her name is inscribed on the family vault prefixed 'and of' because 'sacred to the memory of' begins the inscription dedicated to the collateral ancestor commemorated above her but in keeping with the life of this unknowable woman, there is no record in the cemetery's Burial Register of her interment.

As *dictatrix*, Aelfrida had already made her funeral wishes clear: deciding against confinement in "a narrow earthen bed"[2] and with the approval of '*my* Reverend Mother' (Guenvrede) and '*my* Bishop' (Edward Ely), in March 1954 she subscribed to '"life" i.e. Death' membership of the Cremation Society. ('My body', she added, 'could be cremated in Oxford and ashes taken to … Cambridge with very little trouble or expense'.)[3] Having pleased her executors by her thrift and foresight and arranged her affairs so as to give them 'the least possible trouble', she also commanded 'the ordinary Burial Service either at the Oxford Crematorium or at Cambridge when my ashes were placed in the family vault beside my husband's and the family coffins'[4], that the same hymns be sung as at the 'Marriage of Miss Tillyard', and that those attending the crematorium take lunch at an Oxford hotel, an occasion 'at which [Alethea] need not be present etc., etc.'[5] (Was Alethea's absence permitted because "of the sorrow [her mother's] death would cause"[6] or because

**Aelfrida Graham tombstone, Histon Road Cemetery**

"at some funerals the mourners weep not too much but too little?")[7] What she 'hoped for', however, was 'a requiem here and at Tymawr'.[8]

Her hopes of a requiem mass in the chapel at St John's Home were slim, the bier 'flanked by six tall candles and covered by a princely pall' used when the Home's 'Inmate-Patients' came to pay their last respects to a fellow-inmate in Sister Elizabeth Noel's day being abolished by a successor with 'no sense of ritual'.[9] It also seems (there is no record in the SSC's Book of Acts of one having taken place) she was not granted a 'beautiful requiem' at Tymawr at which the Community were to 'give each other a kiss of peace all round'.[10] But what of her wish that 'a small portion of [her ashes] … be sent to the convent and placed, with ceremony or without, at the foot of the Cross in the Campo Santo'[11], a wish agreed to by Mother Guenvrede in 1950 and transmitted by Aelfrida to Eustace shortly thereafter? There is no record in the Community's Book of Acts that it was granted but a Sister who had known Alethea in South Africa recalled her paying a visit to Tymawr sometime after the former arrived there in 1956 so perhaps Alethea brought the 'small portion' with her and, passing through the gate marked 'MORS JANUA VITAE', sprinkled it beneath the sycamore whereon hung the 'Figure on the Tree' 'as near the foot of the Cross as possible'[12] (the spot on which Aelfrida's 'spiritual heart'[13] was already laid), thereby allowing this remnant of her remains to 'see

Tymawr … [her] own spiritual home … again'[14] and 'to lie uncoffined in the ground' before passing 'into plant and flower and tree and back to earth again'[15] in a *Paradisus Claustralis* whose peace was broken only by bird-song and the west wind soughing in the branches. Then, it seems, Aelfrida was consigned, deliberately by some (Eustace for example, excluded her from his memoirs in what, given his classical background, looks like an act of *damnatio memoriae* in which all memory of the deceased is erased by destroying every scrap of evidence of them ever having lived; on the other hand, Julius received only two lines), unintentionally by others, to oblivion and apart from sparse family memories of a "background figure"[16] whose life was a closed book because she never spoke of it, or of a selfish aunt who wrote boring novels and who was invariably found reclining in a deckchair with her rug-wrapped feet on a stool and a supercilious expression on her face, or of an eccentric great-aunt who sent great-nephews and nieces toy balls made from the silver foil which wrapped the little cheeses she ate at her solitary tea, was virtually forgotten.

Among those who remembered her, not all memories were negative. People who did not know her well described her as "a very great lady"[17] or as someone who behaved so delightfully that she became "a person whose memory will not fade" (Aelfrida did not intend it to fade, her last letter to this particular person being written sometime in late autumn 1959)[18], and though letters of condolence are often more concerned with the feelings of the bereaved than with truth about the deceased, the writers' feelings seem genuine. A more revealing letter, however, was written by a Cowley Father to Alethea the day after her mother's death: "my sympathy on your present change, for that is what it is, not a loss".[19]

Aelfrida suspected what might happen. Passing St Botolph's Church in Cambridge a few days before Christmas 1924 she composed her epitaph:

'FORGET, if you will
Aelfrida Catharine Wetenhall Graham
But
REMEMBER GOD'.[20]

She also surmised (correctly) that her books would never admit her 'into any paradise of novelists, poets or divines' chiefly (and again correctly) because for her authorship 'was self-expression …not originality'[21] (a hint, perhaps, at her propensity to plagiarism), that the "articles [she] had written and lectures [she] had given" would be disregarded, and that memories of "the patients she had cured" as a 'soul-doctor' would disappear once her theories and treatments "die[d] out".[22] But although, like Thomas à Kempis, she believed that after death "men will forget you sooner than you think"[23], she also hoped such memories as people had of her as she "slip[ped] out of this world" would be "pleasant"[24] and worried lest her 'removal' from their lives "let in light and air as if [she] had been a dark tree growing close up against the windows of [the] souls [of her] nearest and dearest".[25] Or, what was worse, that she would not be utterly forgotten so much as actively rejected as someone of whom there was "evil thought of and evil spoken of"[26] after the manner of Psalm 109 (the 'cursing psalm') whose sentiments were all too appropriate now.

But this is not quite 'The Ending of the Way' and although a half-century was to pass before it was possible to 'pick up the threads, … gather up the fragments [and add] a few more years to the fabric'[27] of her life, it was possible to catch glimpses of her in unexpected places: in cardboard boxes in Berkshire and Norfolk, in sparse but intriguing references on the internet, and in inscriptions by, to, or referring to her in books garnered from miscellaneous sources.

"Some hostesses", wrote Aelfrida, "place in their visitors' rooms a little reminder LEAVE NOTHING BEHIND YOU EXCEPT A … MEMORY … [but] it is not easy to depart … without forgetting a toothbrush or a handkerchief or an old letter".[28] In her own case and though memories faded, a few metaphorical toothbrushes and handkerchiefs remained: records of her birth and early childhood, her daughters' diaries and record books, photograph albums, documents pertaining to people and events referred to in her diaries or in her writings or both, *Military and Civil Journals* and childhood magazines. There were also references to her in a study of women's utopian fiction which contrasts the "socialised dystopia" of 21st century England with the "Christian utopia (called Cambridge)"[29] depicted in the earlier and later pages of *Concrete*, and in a science fiction novel which describes her as a "psychosynchronic" (*sic*) character worthy of inclusion among other "touchstones of Friends' tradition" (William Penn, John Woolman) who quotes the writings of her earthly namesake in support of statements made by her avatar on a distant planet.[30] In 2009 she appears as an Anglo-Catholic who provides "an unusual window into church life in the early 1950s" during her time in Lolworth and Parson Drove.[31] (Conversely, a work of 1936 regards her view of the Mystic Way as thoroughly conventional because so imbued with the contemporary notion that "the different ways described by … mystics themselves [are] … in all essentials the same for all mystics" that she "feels justified in producing a map of the way".)[32] In 2008 and 2010 and appropriately for someone who read it assiduously, she appears in the *Church Times* as one who "in the shadow of Zeppelins in 1917" wrote disparagingly of repressive "orthodoxies" and of "upholders of Authority" which threaten penalties for disbelief in their particular religious system or tradition without realising that all 'orthodoxies' are essentially authoritarian (the writer was not, it seems, privy to the reason for Aelfrida's dislike of 'Authority') and as an "aspiring mystic [who] never … felt loved enough".[33] (A perspicacious remark indeed.) She also figured in the memoirs of an art historian/curator who renewed acquaintance with Aleister Crowley in March 1947 shortly before the latter's death and in the course of a discussion on Occultism received apropos "recent examples of the stigmata", a garbled (or misremembered) account of "one of his pupils, Elfrida Tyrell (*sic*) who, growing alarmed by his teaching because it was not sufficiently Christian, was told to go away using the meditations prescribed for her, to concentrate upon the crucifix" but who shortly afterwards "implored him to go and see her and he found that she had stigmata on her hands. They do not seem to have been actual wounds because he described them as 'rosy'".[34] One of her poems (*The Irish Poet*) was read aloud without knowing its place in and significance for her life and serendipitously in a building whose proximity to Hillside and Castlebrae rendered the setting appropriate, at a Cambridge literary festival held on 4 February 2006 entitled *Cambridge Poets: Lost Generation*, and three, together with brief biographies accurate as far as they went, appeared in two anthologies of women's poetry or poetry by men and women written during the Great War, poetry noted by the writer of the first book's preface to have been penned by women who had had "to learn to survive survival" (as Frida/Aelfrida had had to do in other contexts) and by that of the second as consisting of a "loose adaptation", of "gentle whimsy", and of "representative remnants of a destroyed civilisation"[35] without knowing how well the description applied to Aelfrida's life and family.

Of 'old letters' there were a few, written by, to, or about Aelfrida as she progressed from childhood to old age. Most have been quoted in appropriate contexts but two sets require further explanation.

At some point in his life but probably after his sister's death, Julius compiled a compendium of correspondence covering Aelfrida's life from childhood holidays with Lucy Longstaffe until her divorce from Constantine Graham, together with revealing introduction and explanatory notes. What moved him to do so is unknown ("husbands and wives … ought not to write about each other … but brothers and sisters are fair game"[36] was one of his accompanying remarks) unless he planned a biography but his words augment information provided by Aelfrida herself and provide an explanation of or a different view

of matters recorded or unrecorded by her but of relevance to an understanding of her life.

As do another group of letters which entered the public domain at an unspecified point during the four years immediately preceding Aelfrida's death. Their contents could not be compared with her account of her relationship with their writer until the embargo placed on examination of her literary remains was lifted by Girton College forty-five years after Alethea's April 1960 deposition of further books and manuscripts, of notebooks containing what at first sight seems to be merely childhood reminiscences, and of the final volume(s) of her mother's diaries, but when the embargo was lifted on 1 May 2005 fascinating correspondences could be made. The letters, eight in all[37], were written by Aleister Crowley between late June and mid-September 1913 to an acolyte variously addressed as 'Sarasvati', 'Soror Sarasvati', 'my dear sister', and 'Mrs Graham' and cover the period which began soon after Aelfrida noted excitedly that she had discovered a 'genius' for inclusion in her projected *Cambridge Poets 1900–1913* and ended a month before her first meeting with Crowley himself. It was, of course, the originals of these letters which Aelfrida gave to Frank Stokoe for safekeeping in July 1918 and never referred to again unless obliquely in terms of her 'Mrs Graham' experiences in Oxford and Monmouthshire, her anxieties regarding the disposal of Fidelio's estate, or in *Can I be a Mystic?* where she provides a disguised transcription of how 'Stranger' (no stranger, but Aelfrida herself) ultimately finds God without 'Author's' (i.e. Aleister Crowley's) help because (as she wrote, ostensibly of Erle Lunn who deserted her for Meredith Starr, 'a sort of minor Aleister Crowley'), he [was] not 'helping [her] enough'. (She later attributed deficiencies in Crowley's assistance to a fundamental omission from his doctrines, namely his utter lack of desire to follow 'the Way of the Cross', further rationalising her desertion of him by describing Crowley as a man 'afraid of the Cross' and prone to turn to false prophets 'who tell [him] it is not necessary'.)[38] She may also have worried that renewed interest in Aleister Crowley in the post-war era – she did not live long enough to experience his reinvention as an "irresistible … fantasy of the counterculture"[39] of the 1960s – might bring her own name into view. (And how she would have hated to discover herself linked with him in the 2010 edition of a book whose title underlines his enduring presence in her life: Richard Kaczynski's *Perdurabo*.) But reading shorthand or typed versions of Crowley's extant letters to her in conjunction with diary references to letters written to and received from him, we can go some way towards reconstructing the missing half of the correspondence: Aelfrida's letters to Crowley do not appear to have survived.

Some letters are purely business-like, dealing with how Crowley wishes his poems to appear in *Cambridge Poets* and outlining future meetings with Aelfrida in Paris; he also points out that it will be easier to discuss matters in person than by letter. Others list books he has sent her, suggest particular passages or articles she ought to read, and mention poems (e.g. *The Tyler*) dedicated to her by him. (Or by her to him e.g. *The Unofficial Biography*; she also appears to have sent him 'catechisms' of herself as 'Sarasvati' and of himself as 'AC'.) Others still stress that Aelfrida need not join the A∴A∴ ("there are certain definite forms of initiation but I don't know that it would be particularly useful to you at present"), the usefulness of maintaining "a definite continuous record" of her meditations and psychic experiences, and the importance of wearing the "Robe" he has sent her only when "doing [her] meditation" as a means of making "a complete distinction between … ordinary life and the work".[40] (At this point that Aelfrida's cryptic references to presents and robes become clear: contemporary photographs of Crowley provide some idea of what her own 'Robe' must have looked like and a passage in *Concrete* in which 'Eleuthera' dons a white "coverlet" as the "correct costume" for reading a forbidden book – *The Book of Common Prayer* – and for performing a "strange ritual"[41] assumes a significance it previously lacked.) Further letters offer advice regarding the importance of privacy when meditating and refer to records she sends him of yogic positions she adopts, of mantras she employs as aids to meditation, of 'pictures' she 'sees' while meditating, of 'trances' she sometimes enters, and of the occasional psychic 'explosions' she experiences as a result of practising spiritual exercises; they also contain warnings that as "an invalid", she ought not to "practise when unwell"[42] and that she should take regular breaks from practices she finds physically tiring and emotionally and spiritually overwhelming, especially as some of their accompanying sensations invoke physical manifestations. One, quoted by Aelfrida at some length ("I am really quite innocent of pulling your leg")[43], contains both an apology for upsetting her in his previous letter (apparently that of 1 September, described by Frank Stokoe as having been written under the influence of drink but in fact no more than a typical Crowley letter pointing out Aelfrida's credulity with regard to some of the paradoxes enshrined in his statements) and a warning: although Aelfrida Graham is a private person, "Aelfrida Tillyard is a public character"[44] to whom privacy need not be accorded. (Aelfrida, it seems, was concerned that as a vice-consul's wife her name not be associated with

a man about whom she already knew that 'odd legends' circulated.) Another answers her question "what is the Great Work?" by informing her that in terms of the oaths sworn by different grades of participants in the A∴A∴ up to the level of an Adeptus Minor it is "to obtain a scientific knowledge of the nature and powers of my own being", "to obtain control of the foundations of my own being", "to obtain control of the vacillations of my own being", "to obtain control of the aspirations and repulsions of my own being", and "to attain to the knowledge and conversation of the Holy Guardian Angel".[45] Finally, he psychoanalyses her.

Crowley's analysis of Aelfrida's personality is accurate and prophetic, given that he has not yet met her: "I think you will find more difficulty in controlling [your] mind than you suppose"; "your innate tendency … to mysticism has to be combated" (had she described it as hereditary?); "you asked where I think you will get to ultimately … the answer is 'same as everybody else'"[46]; "your mental activity is one of your worst features"[47]; "it is evident that you have a natural tendency to get into trances without very much difficulty. I would like to bet you … get Samadhi or its equivalent in the course of three months' work or less. Your great danger will … be to accept the results of … Samadhi as truth [because] you will presumably attain the vision of Christ or rather of what you call Christ and this will be an experience of unutterable bliss and glory"; "I am … afraid that your success will be so speedy that you will get a totally false idea of everything"; "your temptation is not to do too little meditation but to do too much"[48]; "you have the emotional side so well developed that I am anxious [that] you … cultivate an icily critical attitude … your mind [takes] on shapes too readily".[49] Finally and stingingly: "I can't deny that you are a Christian. All that I can say is that every other Christian would deny it".[50]

Not only do Crowley's replies confirm that Aelfrida was practising physical and mental exercises prescribed by him, informing him of 'true dreams' in which he appeared and transcribing 'visionary' dreams e.g. "a picture of cathedrals"[51], and describing the amusing incident of her abduction of Ernest Heffer's copy of Crowley's *Collected Works*, but they also reveal (as her diary does not) that she confided intimate details of her relationship with her husband. Indeed, as early as or possibly before 27 June, Aelfrida, it seems, had asked Crowley's views on "physical love", for his letter of 7 July assures her that "the most prolonged study of your excellent husband" would afford him "no information whatever on the point in dispute", states that "physical love is quite independent of the body … it is all brains", and contains a refusal to be drawn further.[52]

He nevertheless offered a piece of advice which, had Aelfrida followed it as a *chela* ought, would have made a biographer's task easier: "you should never mind anyone knowing every detail of your life". Aelfrida, however, never "set [herself] against secrecy"[53], for secrecy as a means of keeping control of her own and other peoples' lives was essential to her emotional well-being; she also ensured that it would be impossible to lift the veil of secrecy cast by her over herself and her relationships with others until long after she died. This makes her advice regarding the making of wills rather risible, given that although her legal will, published in synopsis in *The Times* of 4 May 1960 was clearly couched (at which point we discover that "Mrs Aelfrida Catharine Wetenhall Graham of Cambridge, widow of Constantine Graham, left £16,354 gross"[54], a considerable sum in 1959), the literary legacy she left was "full of ambiguities" as "wills drawn up by private individuals" are prone to be, was "conditional" ("but let … the conditions be reasonable"), was not "easily accessible" until her embargo was lifted, and has been discovered by those working on it to be "not always a blessing" ("think of the effects that your bequests are likely to have before you include them") because of the emotional intensity of its contents: her legacy, as Aelfrida seems to have suspected, "cannot leave any legatees unaffected and may subtly disturb many a character".[55] And certainly she had no need to bequeath £50 to the Girton College "Authorities" towards the publication of "certain portions of [her] diaries [as] the Mistress will, if it considered desirable" in order to "stimulate research and arouse interest"[56]; the content ensures both.

Having emphasised that Christians should save their executors the trouble of dealing with "unwanted commodities" ("cupboards and wardrobes and desks … crammed to overflowing" with "so many miscellaneous objects" that executors might be tempted to exclaim "burn the lot" – and do so), she herself "dispose[d] of [her] own rubbish" before departing "to a better world" by donating it to Girton College. The college, tempted though it might have been to 'burn the lot' (Aelfrida was not a Girtonian and had no claim to fame as a writer), acted responsibly as her legatee and after what she had warned would be "months and months of burdensome labour"[57], opened her conserved and catalogued literary remains ('perhaps one doesn't leave any of one's life behind – it is all stored up somewhere')[58] to the world.

As befitted one whose trajectory through life left chaos in its wake, a moment of panic occurred in 1960, the year in which Alethea unemotionally informed the college of her mother's death[59] and arranged for deposition of remaining *matériel*. (The military term is intentional, given the explosive nature of new and existing

deposits.) The two suitcases containing diaries and papers deposited in 1958/59 were in a cupboard under the library stairs but the four registered parcels containing volumes of 'spiritual diaries' retailing Aelfrida's life at St Benedict's and Tymawr had disappeared. They were eventually discovered ("Hooray!") "in a cupboard in the Stock Room Office"[60] and reunited with the rest of the 'Mrs Graham papers' in the college's archive where they remained pending expiration of the embargo. Forty-nine years later, the 'papers' entered the public domain and the question Aelfrida's 1946 question, namely "how long should diaries be kept before they become, so to speak, *anybody's* ?"[61] was answered at last.

The ship on which 'Naomi' and 'Ralph' da Costa sail to Israel in Aelfrida's final novel is described as "a Mystery Ship" which changes flag, name, and skipper between ports in order to provide safe passage for the "profitable contraband" of which its cargo consists. On what proves to be its final voyage, however, it does not change its name but keeps the one under which it sailed from England: *Pandora*.[62]

And what a Pandora's box the 'Mrs Graham papers' proves to be as those who examine its contents uncover the melancholy story of a child whose life was ruined by her parents' clumsy attempt to save it and who spent her life unable to free herself from the bonds of a family rendered hopelessly dysfunctional by the death of the child on whose account his sister's future happiness was sacrificed. (A sister, too who, in a paragraph immediately preceding the 'Pandora' chapter in the last of the novels in which she explores her childhood pain and hints at the reasons for it, prays in the character of 'Marcus Hare', a man who dies suddenly of a diseased heart, that if God deem him unworthy of entering His presence, He at least allow him the hope of "one glimpse of Thy glory before Thou dost cast me off for ever".)[63] And 'Pandora' in this context is not only someone who opens the 'box' containing Aelfrida's life; she is also Aelfrida herself, the 'mystery ship' which changes her name and captain as she sails on her course, whose contraband 'cargo' is 'profitable' because it consists of her spiritual life as a mystic, and whose 'sinking' in sight of the Promised Land foretells her own death.

More, however, remains to be said of the 'Mrs Graham papers' and the seventy-five volumes of diaries, the letters, the cuttings, the photographs, and the published and unpublished poetry, novels, and homiletic books which comprise them. Are we to regard them merely as safety valves through which Aelfrida compulsively vented pressures on her soul which had become intolerable? Or as the *mea culpa* of one who learnt the hard way the significance of early memories 'for after life and experience' and who was so damaged by them that she could not help inflicting damage on others? Or as a personal narrative of her spiritual pilgrimage from 'awakened' adolescence to 'Christian' old age, a narrative written by one who, like Aleister Crowley, admitted that he often wrote "to see if anyone were foolish enough to take him seriously" ("several have done so", he warns his own – and Aelfrida's – biographer) or which, though as much a 'spiritual autobiography'[64] as John Henry Newman's *Apologia pro vita sua*, might be accused, as Charles Kingsley accused Newman, of untruthfulness because, though absolutely rational on *her* terms (as Aelfrida once noted of Crowley, he genuinely believed his own message; he was also, she noted, 'not moral' and 'a little mad')[65] and accepted as such by those unaware of the reason why someone who appears quite sane when writing of matters mystical or spiritual but operates elsewhere as a personality distorted by enduring unease about whom, did one not know this, a different biography might be written?

Or, though she herself wrote in another context 'I have so little to forgive; so much I can't forget'[66], as a form of revenge by one who tried to forget but could never forgive that she, the "little child" whose laughter echoed in "the magic countryside of dreams" of Fordfield and its garden, had become a crying child since the moment she was "driven out of Paradise" with her capacity for "earthly joy"[67] destroyed and her laughter overcast by "shadowed murk" and by "cries and strivings"? This being so, are Aelfrida's literary remains the continuation of her mother's *Record of the being, doing and saying* of her children insofar as they record in dreadful detail the later lives of Catharine Tillyard's older children and the way in which events surrounding Conrad's death were so mismanaged by Catharine and her husband that both children were emotionally scarred for life? And if Aelfrida, preserving her papers as munitions in the war she had unconsciously waged against her parents since 1888, wished to preserve what were essentially dispatches from the front, how better to do so than by locking them in the ammunition box unwittingly provided by an archive? Or did she so desperately wish to leave her past behind (having once completed a work, Aelfrida, so she says, lost interest in it; her telling Miss McMorran that she had always been "hopelessly lazy" about submitting her work to publishers is a lie but her subsequent remark that she always had "another more absorbing book on hand"[68] rings true insofar as once completed, a work joined other closed 'compartments' and became another 'episode' in her life) that she left it physically behind at every opportunity, recalling and recording it later in a protectively fictionalised version or as an idealised version in which everyone behaved well and 'Christianly' to each other and no one lost their temper with a frightened child, a version whose very idealisation shows how damaged she was. Julius, with more insight and perhaps better able to forgive – though certainly not to forget – noted that "children, whether they glorify or disparage their parents usually turn out a caricature"[69]; his sister glorified *and* disparaged and bequeathed her representation to posterity.

Or did 'Mrs Graham' ensure the preservation of her 'papers' because she craved immortality? (And to this end provided a legacy to pay for eventual publication of 'certain portions' of her diaries?) The theme of the lecture given by Goldsworthy Lowes Dickinson in Boston in April 1909 and attended by both Grahams was *Is Immortality desirable?* Not until nearly fifty years later, however, when EM Forster's biography of Dickinson provided a *madeleine* does Aelfrida disclose it, adding that Dickinson 'did decide, on … balance, that Immortality might be desirable'.[70] (She fails to note that Dickinson also stated that Immortality is desirable only if we are granted continuity of experience and an opportunity for developing our better impulses after death.)[71] So, it seems, did she. Noting in October 1958 apropos the college's request that she send her entire *oeuvre*, not just her diaries, she wrote wistfully 'I thought of Lord Dunsany's sketch *Fame Comes Late*'[72] before arranging that all available 'papers' were taken urgently to Girton to ensure a chance of it. (In *Fame Comes Late*, a poet who has dreamed of fame as a Greek goddess with a golden trumpet is eventually visited by her in the form of a "tired and a little pathetic" old woman of whom he later says as he resigns himself to lack of that for which he is still eager, "Fame cannot be now what she was when we were young".)[73] But having embargoed her 'papers' until publication of 'certain portions' could do (as she thought) no harm, Aelfrida must have realised that fame would perforce come late, perhaps even later than she envisaged.

But which 'portions' did she hope would be submitted to public scrutiny? (And how interesting that she left the final choice to the Mistress of Girton and an unknown biographer.) 'Spiritual diaries' certainly, but what of the others? (Without some knowledge of her life, an impoverished account would appear.) Material sufficient to furnish a hagiographic biography (or even 'autohagiographic' as the ironic subtitle of Crowley's posthumously published confessions proclaims) in which she would appear as a Susan Allibone or as a Mathilde Bertrand, the latter the 'Lucie-Christine' whose *Spiritual Journal* was read by Aelfrida at Parson Drove with the comment that the mystic 'graces' bestowed on this simple family woman appeared 'quite genuine and perfectly intelligible' though

Mathilde's description of them was 'a trifle monotonous' (a monotony which applies equally to Aelfrida's own writings on the subject – and if Bertrand herself is 'a little deficient in personal interest in other people [and] … insensitive to their charm and not particularly quick to see their virtues'[74], so too was she), or even ('much retouched', for otherwise biography might appear less as an inspirational description of a spiritual journey than a chapter in a textbook of psychopathology) as a Thérèse of Lisieux, one of the three women who, like herself, had enjoyed 'an astonishing number of spiritual privileges'[75]? (Or as a Madeleine Lesueur, redeemed from sin by God's grace and personal amendment?) And was it to this end that she rewrote her childhood to make herself appear as a visionary mystic from toddler days, perfuming mundane activities and experiences with an odour of sanctity guaranteed to demonstrate her 'saintliness' even then? (And including in her account encounters with the devil, a recognised stage on the path to sainthood modelled on Christ's paradigmatic encounters with Satan.) Or did she hope for an account of herself as someone whose entire *oeuvre* was such an intimate extension of her diaries and of herself as a personality worth immortalising that a biographer could not fail to seize on it, thereby ensuring that her life outlived herself it even though she would be 'shown up' in an account of it?[76]

Or as 'shown up' as she intended to be? Her diary (in which we might expect to find the truth) is filled with deliberate omissions and elisions, veiled references, prevarications, seeming irrelevancies, palimpsests, sub-texts, glosses, and cross-correspondences, the latter in particular creating a suspicion that Aelfrida expects her biographer to imitate Margaret Verrall in an effort to discern correspondences (correspondences which may exist only in her biographer's mind) and that it is only when we turn to her poetry, novels, and homiletic books that we find ourselves approaching something like the truth. But not the whole truth or nothing but the truth, for here too Aelfrida created and recreated her life as she peregrinated on paper along the "long long scroll" of published and unpublished works, reminiscences, and anthologies in which is recorded "everything" she had "thought"[77] but in which and 'as usual' she transformed words into the '*dress* of [her] thoughts'[78], concealing herself as a shaman might with a 'robe' whose spangles, furs, feathers, beads, shells, bones, bells, and dazzling colours both hide the wearer and reveal the personality assumed with the donning of the costume. Or she wrote like a Sufi mystic in "a picturesque language all [her] own" of allusion and metaphor so that what she writes may be taken at face value or 'read' for its symbolic sense[79] – or both. Or perhaps when she wrote in November

1900 that she wanted to be like 'the Melancolia', she was already setting herself up to be seen as if she were Durer's *Melancolia*: a mysterious, mournful figure seated in the midst of abstrusely symbolic objects and coded messages impossible to interpret without a key.

Difficulties of interpretation also arise because the multifarious strands of her life as a "synthesis of different elements" or as an "inharmonious crowd" of personalities she "boldly calls *herself* " ("a child, pleased with new clothes [and] pretty sights; … a mother, with all her varied cares and preoccupations; … a business woman; a poet … living for beauty to whom the earth is half a dream; a woman of the world, who enjoys social success and a good position; a sick–nurse … ; a seeker after God, who feels that nothing matters in this world or the next but … knowledge of her Lord")[80] need to be separated out before we can see of what each consists and how each intertwines with others, a task made more difficult because of the screen of smoke and mirrors she erects between herself and us. A screen whose smoke she consumes so consummately that it seems never to have existed and whose mirrors, on examination, reflect only ourselves and what we wish to find.

Quiller Couch, delivering his inaugural lecture on 29 January 1913 as Arthur Verrall's successor as Cambridge's Professor of English Literature, quoted Ernest Renan, French historian, philologist, and scholar of religion with whose family Constantine spent childhood holidays at Perros Guirec; Renan, he proclaimed, said that truth was composed of shades of meaning: "*La verité consiste dans les nuances*".[81] To capture such shades of meaning in Aelfrida's literary remains is difficult: supporting evidence may be sparse or lacking; it is sometimes only by reference to books we know she read that we can make sense of her current thoughts or see why the course of her spiritual life tended in a particular way; vital evidence (e.g. her vision of Christ in a mandorla of light; her appearance in Erlande's novels) is omitted altogether from her diaries or is preserved in an insignificant notebook easy to overlook when dealing with a mass of *matériel*. And all too often a researcher's attempts to decipher mute messages concealed in the matter of her text (*le signe muet caché dans les choses*)[82] must rely on serendipitous guesswork, on an awareness of inconsistencies and of the need never to take statements at face value, on intuition, or even on a (literary or imaginary) tap on the shoulder administered at unexpected times or in incongruous places by one who, though she stated firmly that she had no intention of "trying to communicate from the Beyond"[83], frequently succeeds in doing so.

Hence although Aelfrida's 'physical body turned to dust' in the incinerator of Oxford Crematorium, those who look for her 'remains' do not find, as she once wrote of the dead and ascended Virgin Mary, 'nothing'[84], and although what we find (or what she allows us to find; reading her 'papers', one becomes aware of conundrums deliberately set and of edges deliberately unravelled to see if one can solve them or catch up the dropped stitch) may not be her life exactly as lived (one cannot say of Aelfrida as she once said of Jessie Stent that 'I can read her like a book now that I know the language')[85], it will be a life subject to the principle central to forensic science that 'every contact leaves traces'. (And how infuriating for a biographer tracking her elusive subject to discover – too late – that she had met – too early – contacts who might have provided valuable insights had they been still alive or in command of their mental faculties: Joan Cooper, Ronald Macbeth, Alfred Walford, and Helen McMorran.) And what traces they are: not only did Aelfrida record everything in some shape or form somewhere and at some point, because she never knew at the time of writing if it was important or not, but she also destroyed much of importance because "our privacy and what we do with it is …important"[86] or in order to present us with a picture of her life which accorded with her belief that history in general and hers in particular 'should be rewritten to show the development of God's plan'.[87] "Authors", she also noted, "have the right to do as they like".[88]

Tracking Aelfrida is also akin to archaeology insofar as one must probe for what lies beneath the stratum from which one currently excavates, artefact by artefact, relics of 'prehistory' in the hope of arriving at something approximating the truth. (An example appears in her 1958 description of Constantine as "a scholar of King's … who took a first in History"[89], information true only insofar as it was in the first part of his tripos that Constantine 'took a first'; his gaining a 2:1 in the second part is recorded in her diary and omitted from her account.) And, we may ask, by what right do we probe deeper than she intends us to go, for just as one must exercise discretion in revealing aspects of lives, other than her own, recorded in her diary and respect the reticences of those who choose to withhold pertinent material, so too one should not perhaps excavate to bedrock, however tempted one is to do so.

And yet – is this not what Aelfrida herself wanted? Why else preserve so much evidence and, as at Tymawr when setting out on one of her explorations, leave 'sketch maps' of the routes she intends to take in case we get lost on the way to the 'very weird'[90] places in which we find ourselves as we track her? And more than sketch maps: as one who discovered 'the lure of research' and in pursuit of knowledge compared herself to 'a bloodhound on a trail'[91], Aelfrida, it seems, enjoys "the ardour of the chase"

as much as any biographer and joins in "the delight of a clue followed up and a link forged … the exhilaration of a problem solved [and] the fascination of bringing dead epochs to light".[92] (Why else leave so many conundrums and riddles for us to solve? "Finding out", says 'Clive Farwell', "is the fun, not [just] knowing".)[93] And when she tires of mind-games, she 'forgets' (who *was* 'Mlle J'?) or retreats into silence. Perhaps her legacy is best described by what Albert Erlande has 'Coelius' say in *La Vipère Doré*: "those exercise books you see on the first shelf of that closed bookcase are collections of interesting incidents. What treasure trove for the inquisitive who come after us".[94]

But for the inquisitive there "remain so many questions to ask!"; indeed, in asking them one feels justified in saying like Aelfrida herself "if I were to sit down and try to answer them … one by one I should produce something like a sheaf of answers for an examination paper".[95] And even as one nears what may or not be the end of one's exploring one realises – as did Aelfrida as she neared the end of her life – that with her 'there will always be ragged edges and unwritten books'.[96] Then, to one's surprise, one finds Aelfrida on one's side: "you and I", she informs her biographer, "will work together [to] weave this book as one might weave a carpet. If a thread seems to have slipped out of my fingers, I shall know it is safe in yours and that it will be woven in again by and by [and] the finished product shall serve either as a fireside rug or [as] a magic carpet or as a prayer-mat – each Reader may have it as he will".[97]

The passage quoted at the end of the preceding paragraph, to a biographer one of the most significant in *The Glory of the West,* is crossed out in Aelfrida's typescript: did she consider it unworthy of publication or, private to the last, was she unwilling for the 'Reader' she addresses to create what might be a pattern quite different from her own though woven on the loom bearing her own warp and woof? But for a biographer asking, like Aelfrida herself, 'am I ready to go now?' the answer is also hers: 'perhaps as ready as I shall ever be'.[98] Or perhaps 'but no', for ragged edges and slipped threads remain to be caught or bound up and though her diary ends abruptly and dramatically – the curtain falls, the footlights go out, and we prepare (as we think) to leave the 'theatre' on whose 'stage' so many 'scenes' have been played out – Aelfrida has not yet taken her curtain call.

Our first question involves the 'papers' deposited at Girton: how or in what light should we read them? Should they be read as the record of the life of an utterly selfish woman who remains to the end 'the centre of her own universe, the hub … round which everything revolves for her benefit' but who at the same time is

> Buddhism, perhaps more than any other religion, has been changed and elaborated away from the simplicity of its early days. In Ceylon and other regions where the Hinayana " vehicle " is employed, it has grown, on the whole, more arid and pessimistic. Nirvana, the consolation of the faithful, is there, perhaps, even conceived as ceasing to be, and Not-Being as the final reality of the universe.[1] Among the Mahayanists, however, we find a rich flowering of cults, romantic deifications of aspects of Buddha both male and female, and also an exalted mysticism in which a universal god is worshipped under the appellation of Boundless Light, and the sayings of Gotama are understood in their spiritual sense.

*Spiritual Exercises*, chapter on Buddhist Meditations p 66

sufficiently insightful to realise that not caring what people think of her is 'tragic' and to hope that in setting out her life as she has done, she has 'maligned' herself? (And to note that parts of her account are, intentionally or unintentionally, 'very funny'.)[99] Or as "children of [the] brain" of a consummately clever writer whose diaries, texted 'messages' and spiritual 'exercise books' live on after her death to enable a future biographer to trace the spiral way of a life at which they look from different viewpoints as they ascend or descend its windings, their soul "fructified or deadened" by what is revealed at each turn? Or as descriptions of the "germs of corruption that festered in the brain of a [woman] long dead?" Or as traces of the "perfume of self-offering rising like incense from the heart of a nun of whom the world has never heard?" Or as "legacies of the spirit – ... the ideals we lived by, the thoughts we had of God, the ardour of our soul's inner life ... the most powerful [legacy] that man or woman has to leave!"? All perhaps, for "all ... have germinated and brought forth fruit".[100]

Our second question concerns the Aelfrida (or, rather, Sister Placida of the Holy Passion) of the 'prayer mat'. (Aelfrida/Sarasvati of the 'magic carpet' has been discussed already but worth noting here is the interest generated by the lifting of the embargo regarding her relationship with Aleister Crowley and Ceremonial Magic. Students of 'Crowley and Crowleyism' should, however, bear her warning in mind: of a certain point in her life when mentally unhinged as a result of recent traumatic life-events, she states – and her statement itself may or may not be true – that like Goldsworthy Lowes Dickinson, she 'toyed' with 'esoteric Buddhism, Hinduism ... and so on' but never penetrated so deeply that her enthusiasm developed further than that of a mere "undergraduate".)[101] The 'prayer-mat' aspect of Aelfrida's life stems, of course, from a statement made in her first published book on the subject: "I myself [as I] ... confess quite

frankly am a mystic", and it is as one who found the "world of spiritual experience more real than the material world", who regarded God as "the most *real*"[102], and who hoped for and, it seems, arrived at spiritual union with Him, that we must now consider her.

The "awakening of transcendental consciousness", wrote Evelyn Underhill in 1910 with reference to Starbuck's *Psychology of Religion* of 1901, is, psychologically speaking, "an intense form of the phenomenon of 'conversion'", conversion being an "unselfing" process whereby an individual emerges from his or her self-centred world into the world of "mystical consciousness" irrespective of whether or not he or she was "bred up in piety" i.e. is or is not "already 'religious', sometimes deeply and earnestly so". Conversion may be a process of "gradual and increasing lucidity" or may involve a sudden "opening of the soul's eye" which brings about such "an utter change in [the individual's] world" that "every department of [their] life" is crucially affected by it and they become (in the Christian context of which she writes) both convinced of the nearness *of* God and overwhelmed with feelings of love *for* God.[103] Aelfrida, of course, follows the latter pattern exactly, her vision at age fifteen seeming to single her out as an individual deemed worthy by God of receiving "particular messages or spiritual experiences" ("visions, auditions and the like") directly from Him and by whose means she became aware of a "reality" which had been there all the time but to which she had not been privy because in spite of being 'well and Christianly' brought up, God had not deemed her spiritually ready to receive it. (Or because she herself was impoverished by an innate human "poverty of apprehension" with regard to Deity till then.) Hence it was only after undergoing certain preparatory experiences that she became "capable of hearing God speak"[104], her new capability reinforcing a conviction that she had joined "God's adepts".[105] (That she was not altogether happy at being chosen by God in this way because of what His choice prescribed and proscribed for her is shown by an anguished speech put into the mouth of 'Cassandra Fazakerley': "have I not been dedicated without my consent and before I was of age to comprehend what sacrifice ... was involved? Must I indeed be a vestal?")[106] And as one of God's chosen 'adepts' she naturally wished to enlarge on her experience for the benefit of others, and though it was difficult to communicate experiences of a spiritual nature to those who had never undergone them, she possessed the inestimable advantage of having herself undergone the experiences she described.

A desire to communicate her experiences in vernacular (as opposed to formal 'theological') English grounds her in the tradition of women's spirituality (and of the stories heard and enacted in Fordfield nursery) in which emphasis is placed on the affective and experiential instead of the impartial and intellectual. It also seems she modelled her lifestyle at different times and as circumstances demanded or allowed on women who lived taught in this manner: on Evelyn Underhill, a married woman who withdrew at intervals to commune with God but who communicated her communings through books, poetry, letters, and retreats; on anchoress Julian of Norwich who dispensed spiritual advice from her cell while exploring and expounding her spiritual experiences in *Revelations of Divine Love*; and on that of a mediaeval 'beguine', a pious woman (possibly a widow) living prayerfully, chastely, and charitably in a self-sufficient community of like-minded women under the guidance of a 'mistress' (*magistra*) and a priestly spiritual director – but who, because she refused to submit to (papal) authority and because she might admit to experiences of a supernatural nature, laid herself open to accusations of madness and even of heresy.[107] But how unfortunate for Aelfrida that personality disorder ensured that instead of becoming a respected Underhill or Julian, she found herself regarded as silly, selfish, uncanny, beguinish in its unfavoured aspect, or 'MAD'.

If, as it seems, Aelfrida modelled her life on women like these (positive role-models, in the main) can we be sure she did not also model her life in another and more negative sense? The late nineteenth and early twentieth centuries saw revived interest in the lives of Western European mystics in general and it is obvious that she read widely both from the mystics' own writings and from commentaries on them. She also, at a slightly later date – ostensibly so as to be able to refute those who regarded religion as a manifestation of deep-seated natural urges thwarted in expression – read extensively on the psychology of religion. She was also familiar with the novels of RH Benson in which the lives of men and women who undergo intense supernatural experiences are described in dramatic literary form, She was also a plagiarist.

Can it be that she, a disturbed, suggestible, and manipulative personality with a known tendency to model herself on whichever 'guru' currently attracted her attention, deliberately set out to model her life on her readings less as a means of imitating Christ than with the aim of making it more interesting to herself and, more importantly, to other people, there is little point in leading an interesting life as a self-styled mystic if no-one knows about it? This would explain both her compulsive need to lecture, to write, and to record and to preserve records of her productions in order that attention would be paid to her even after her death and to attract attention to

herself when alive by acting in a manner which would ensure being noticed. (Can it also be that having been thought 'MAD', she played up to her diagnosis because 'madness' drew people's attention to her? No wonder she enjoyed making 'scenes'.) And did she also delay the start of her campaign of self-aggrandising publicity (she did not 'come out' as a mystic until fifteen years after coming to the conclusion that she was 'something of a mystic') until she had sufficiently perfected her role so as to appear word and action perfect in scenes played out on paper or enacted in real life? (Even here she may have had a role-model. Gladys Sanderson was a Cambridge cab-driver's daughter befriended by Ruth Schechter but passed on by her to Aelfrida when the Schechters left for America. Gladys and Aelfrida met only once – "the meeting was not a success", noted the latter – but corresponded for several years in the course of which Aelfrida married and travelled the world and Gladys trained as a teacher. Gladys, to Aelfrida's relief – she hoped that "devout ladies" would provide greater support to a woman she herself regarded as "just a dull little teacher" – became a Catholic, then, following visions of Christ and the Virgin Mary, a nun. Aelfrida, "*enormously* impressed" that Gladys, dull little teacher or not, was also "a saint to whom God accorded visions", was overjoyed to hear that "postulant Gladys" was happy in the "religious life" and even happier when as "Novice Valentine", Gladys looked set to become a "saintly young nun who would doubtless be favoured with more visions". But not having heard from 'Valentine' for four years and having in the meantime dedicated a poem to her, Aelfrida wrote to 'Valentine's' Mother Superior for news. The Mother's reply shocked and surprised her: "no such person … had ever entered the Community". Was the convent, Aelfrida wondered, a mental hospital?[108] As an example of a supposed 'mystic' who not only invented a new life for herself but also fooled someone whose spiritual agenda was akin to her own, 'Valentine's' story can hardly be bettered – though even here one should note inconsistencies in Aelfrida's account and that the Gladys/Valentine episode may be no more than a warning to a too-credulous reader not to believe what is actually a cautionary tale.) There is, too, the matter of Aelfrida's later reworking of childhood experiences into events of 'mystic' significance and of her omission from early diaries which could be (and on occasion, were) read by others of descriptions of 'mystic' experiences (her seminal adolescent experience appears fourteen years later in a collection of 'mystic' experiences described by people she designates 'modern' mystics), ostensibly because they were too sacred to record in a secular context but possibly because at the time of writing she had not yet invented them. (Or as she herself hints at the time of her 1904 'vision' of her mature self with mature Constantine and their putative son and daughter, she actually *had* invented them, something which would have been easy for one as versed as herself in *devotio moderna* with its propensity to *think oneself into* situations such as the Crucifixion or the Nativity or in 'acting out' stories like Noah's Ark during wet Sundays at Fordfield in "the early days before Conrad left us"[109] or, later, as an accomplished practitioner of Ignatian visualis-ations while engaged in spiritual exercises: the society of devils, for example, or one's own deathbed and funeral.) Or did she embellish everyday occurrences into 'visions' for dramatic effect? With the help of a vivid imagination, a moisture-bedewed male acquaintance illuminated by the glow of a carbide bicycle lamp on a foggy evening might easily become Christ in a mandorla of light and his polite greeting a salutation by Christ Himself.

And how is it that diaries contemporary with and later than her acquaintance with Aleister Crowley become suddenly full of 'visions'? Had she adopted his advice to record every spiritual experience, however fleeting or seemingly unimportant, as a record of her spiritual pro-gress and because its significance might become appar-ent later, or was it only now that she recorded them as evidence that her claim to '*see God*' was true? (A claim, one should remember, made by one who on her own admission 'played with religion' and whose religious feelings might be no more than 'emotional pose'.) Or was she making them up in order to impress her 'Guru' with spurious 'magick' credentials? And can it therefore be that the tensions she described as arising from her simultaneously inhabiting the spiritual and the mate-rial world arose less from 'mystic' propensities and more from the strain of sustaining through calumny and dis-belief the alternative life she had created for herself, a life now discovered to be so far from what her 'natural self' demanded of 'natural affections' and 'human con-solations' that she wondered if she had the strength to sustain it? Or from the strain of sustaining it in view of its damaging effects on those nearest and dearest to her? Or from realisation that she could not suddenly abandon it without revealing herself to be a duplicitous fantasist?

To further support her supposed life as a mystic it was important for Aelfrida to emphasise that she had "just *naively* undergone spiritual experiences"[110] and that such experiences appeared "strange and startling" to her. But if such experiences, whenever (and if ever) undergone, were so "strange and startling" to a girl who underwent them 'naively', why did she not record them at the time? Or did she record them, only to destroy during one of her periodic holocausts? If so, why destroy records which provided vital evidence for her claim to be a mystic? Was

it because the record might show that her mystic experi-ences were not in fact her own but were adapted to suit her circumstances from accounts written by those whom Henri Delacroix described in his eponymous book (described by Underhill in her bibliography to *Mysticism* as 'indispensable' reading for a student of the subject) as "*grands mystiques chrétiens*": Madame Guyon, whose com-pendious writings were, so she said, dictated to her by God Himself; Teresa of Avila, with her ecstasies and levi-tations; Henri Suso, with his extreme mortifications. And by other male and female mystics whose works linguisti-cally-accomplished Aelfrida could have read in the orig-inal? (Worth remembering here is that it was Julius, him-self in the throes of a crisis of belief, who first introduced her to William James' *Varieties of Religious Experience* with its lengthy chapter on Mysticism and who thereafter stated that the book 'fostered' his sister's pre-existing ten-dency to what he described as 'mysticism' but to which a psychologist might apply the term 'personality disorder'; that Aelfrida herself described James' book as having first 'opened' to her the 'possibility' of direct personal expe-rience of God; and that in *A Little Road-Book for Mystics* – a significant title in the present context – she describes books portraying "the exact qualities that make a state of mind deserve the epithet 'mystical'" in which the reader would find "raptures and fervours ... ticketed like speci-mens in a museum", books which she not only tried to imitate in her intended work on 'modern mystics' but which also caused her to become "self-conscious" with regard to her own spiritual life.)[111] Furthermore, when to her account she adds the strangeness and the unexpected arrival of experiences which "aroused [her] interest in the whole question of mysticism", she adds this without realising that, having noted that it was because of "*med-itations*"[112] which she found "strange and startling" that she began to write her account, she has already created discrepancies in that account: if, as she would have us believe, her first mystic experience took place when she was fifteen (i.e. sometime between October 1898 and October 1899) or possibly even earlier, given that on the day of Emma Wetenhall's death, 30 November 1897, her fourteen-year-old granddaughter, passing the church of Our Lady and the English Martyrs on her way home from a German lesson at 'Dear's' old school, received a (contemporaneously unrecorded) vision of "grey clouds parting" to disclose a brilliant shaft of light "which touched and rested on Fordfield" and up which a dove ('Dear's' soul) flew "following the light up and up until ... clouds closed over it"[113] (or was this another embel-lishment, this time of a meteorological phenomenon?), the events occurred over a decade before she began to meditate under Aleister Crowley's instruction. And if, as we know, she had already enjoyed discussions of matters mystical with Julius and Robin/Robert Tillyard, was engrossed by the writings of Thomas à Kempis and Omar Khayyám and, fired by her 'new' enthusiasm for Mysticism, went into Florentine churches to pray, how is it that it was not until after Aleister Crowley instructed her in meditation techniques in 1913 that she 'came out' as a mystic four years later? Was this solely because she could no longer keep silent – or was it because she had not yet honed her technique (as some mediums were notoriously wont to do) or 'meditated' sufficiently on 'psychic' phenomena before embarking on them and was chary of disclosing them until she had?

A further point made by Evelyn Underhill regarding mystic "conversion" and emergence of "mystical consciousness" is that both involve and result in "disturbance of the equilibrium of the self" and that both may occur as a result of or as the sequel to "a long period of restlessness, uncertainty and mental stress".[114] Unlike Starbuck, who based his statements on evidence provided by his juvenile subjects, childless Underhill fails to make an obvious connection: one of the most unsettling and prolonged periods of mental restlessness, uncertainty, and stress undergone by human beings is adolescence.

Writing of a woman known to her from St Benedict's days and as much her alter ego as Nadja Laptchinski, Aelfrida noted that Florence Fisher was 'a strange creature, full of moods, sometimes terribly gloomy, sometimes gay and joking, sometimes reserved and almost standoffish [or] ready to confide the most intimate of secrets' and that though Florence was full of 'lofty ideals and unusual spirituality', she had 'very little idea of how to manage herself'.[115] As a description of adolescents in general and of adolescent Frida in particular, this description can hardly be bettered and it is perhaps to Aelfrida's adolescence that we should turn once again as the spiral way of biography rounds another bend and we gain yet another glimpse of her complex personality.

Aelfrida's menarche occurred at thirteen. Her requests for physiological information were dismissed as unseemly and she never then or thereafter speaks directly of menstruation, except to hint that she suffered a good deal of menstrual discomfort. A year or so later she sustained facial injuries in the bicycle accident to which she also makes no further reference. (It is from Julius we glean details of her many sessions of restorative dentistry.) In October 1897 she noted the removal of 'two and a half teeth' and, significantly in this context, that she enjoyed her first experience of nitrous oxide anaesthesia: 'the gas was so nice … I could not feel anything but I could hear [what] they said … I didn't seem to go to sleep at all'.[116] Even more significantly, perhaps, was that within

a few days of experiencing the borderland state of light anaesthesia, she entered Fordfield to find that another death had occurred in her absence, that of her maternal grandmother. 'Dear's' death was not unexpected – she had been unconscious for three days and poorly before that – but it seems to have prompted memories so unhappy that Aelfrida entered an almost fugue-like state ('it does not seem to be me that is writing. I seem like a person in a story')[117] from which she emerged with difficulty because burdened by Catharine Tillyard's somewhat histrionic grief, because she had no-one to whom to confide her feelings (Julius, home for the funeral, had returned to Tonbridge School), and because 'Dear' was buried with gloomy Victorian ceremony in the same vault as Conrad.

Another event too, may have contributed to what might have been dismissed by her parents as no more than an unusually stormy or stressful adolescence, an event unrecorded in the volume of Aelfrida's diary covering the year of her life (October 1898–October 1899) during which her emotional equilibrium seems to have become spectacularly disequilibrated. It was not consigned to paper until 1932 and then only in fictionalised form but Aelfrida's fictional descriptions of events often reveal the truth of what really happened.

Towards the end of *The Approaching Storm*, a young couple, 'Jacinth' and 'Leopold', say goodbye to their wedding guests and to "what they know" and prepare to depart for "what they don't know"; their departure, however, is as symbolic as the Grahams', for they are only "going upstairs" to consummate their marriage.[118] The episode, however, has a prequel:

Leopold, aged seventeen, and Jacinth, aged fifteen, believe they are brother and sister. (They are disabused of the belief before they marry.) One evening, adolescent Leopold enters Jacinth's room to find her wearing a diaphanous white garment through which the lines of her developing body show clearly. He embraces her, kissing her on the lips and feeling for her lovingly with his body. A look of fear overspreads Jacinth's face; she runs from him, wraps the coverlet of the bed closely around her, and shaking with terror, plies him with anguished questions ("Why do you touch me like that? … What have you done to yourself") and in response to his attempts to calm her (he and she, he tells her, are one and the same person; he won't hurt her; what he wishes to do is what people are *for*), cries that he is suddenly "different", that she hates him "different", and she wishes she could turn back the clock to a yesterday in which Leopold was not "different" but someone she trusted.[119]

Reading this, what can one say – except to note the frequent lengthy gaps between entries in Aelfrida's diary for her fifteenth year and her excuse for leaving them: 'a lot of things have happened – I only wish I could give you an account of them'.[120] By 1950/51, the period in her life when she and Julius seem to have reached deeper understanding of each other's motivations and behaviour, perhaps she does – and we realise that her description of a suite of rooms in which alter egos 'Madeleine' and '*Maman*' are respectively though temporarily imprisoned may not represent those of the *dépendence* in which she may or may not have met Albert Erlande in 1930 but the attic floor of Fordfield with its suite of rooms occupied by the maids, by Eustace, by Julius (we are never told where the two boys slept when they out-grew the nursery but neither are recorded as occupying one of the bedrooms on the first floor), and by herself. And if what we learn of 'Jacinth' and 'Leopold' is correct, it is hardly surprising that as a "sequel [to] and the result of a long period of … mental stress"[121] begun at menarche and encompassing the emotional upheavals which beset her until she left for Switzerland, Aelfrida felt the need to embark on a life in which she could recreate the wonderfully comforting feeling of 'something warm …being put all around [her]'[122] experienced as she went under gas, and if this new life was not spontaneously forthcoming, a need to create it for herself on the basis of something with which she was already familiar: the Christian religion, with Deity replacing Julius as guide, comforter, and creator of stability in a world whose firm boundaries had become deliquescent borderlands once again. Or perhaps what we 'see' through the 'window' opened for us by our 'interpreter' is Constantine's attempt to consummate 'the Marriage of Miss Tillyard' and nothing to do with Julius at all.

Consolations of religion failed her too. The Nonconformist Christianity in which she was brought up disliked displays of religious emotion to the point that (as a sad little girl might experience it) the individual was segregated from Godhead (*séparé du divin*) by regulated means of communication with Him.[123] Furthermore, although Aelfrida herself declared that the "religion preached in the Presbyterian Church" was as much "mystical" as it was "intellectual"[124], Presbyterianism failed to provide an unhappy child with 'something warm' into which to snuggle and in the hope of achieving an "intimate and lovely … consciousness" of a divinely comforting Presence, she read her "daily portion of Scripture"[125] and recited her prayers alone. On the other hand, Baptists, of whom Alfred Tillyard had been one before seceding to Presbyterianism, laid great stress on "religious experience", candidates for adult (or at least adolescent) baptism and hence for full church membership (a privileged and exclusive group) being expected to have passed through a process of "conversion" in which "startling religious experiences" were commonplace before allowing themselves to be put forward. What better way, therefore, for a young girl who admitted that she had "fallen terribly short of what was expected"[126] both domestically and in terms of lack of emotion in the days following 'Dear's' death ('I have been trying so hard to be a help to Mama but somehow I don't manage it … I do try … to be good … but I am still lazy and horrid; I don't seem to be any use to anybody')[127] than to invent a life in which 'conversion' took place, 'startling religious experiences' were commonplace, and nympholeptic frenzies occurred? (And which had in its background Charcot's Salpêtrière demonstrations of hysterical women patients, some of whom publically underwent and were photographed undergoing experiences very similar to Aelfrida's own, then and later, and Pierre Janet's descriptions of patients such as Madeleine Le Bon whose religious beliefs and the physiological manifestations thereof parallel Aelfrida's to an uncanny extent.) A life which she (mistakenly) believed would entitle her to respect from her immediate and extended family (a privileged and exclusive group in her eyes, if no-one else's), because she, a mere girl, had been chosen by God as the representative in her generation of its 'mystical' heredity and as a sign of this had felt God's arms (but no-one else's: Chiara, freed from the burden of home nursing, had thrown herself into 'good works' and Julius was no longer 'trusted') put 'all around' her while hearing His voice speak directly to her in dream-like states which were neither sleep nor dream but somehow 'real'.

Alfred Tillyard may have sensed something of his daughter's distress and sought a remedy: within a month of Emma's death, he talked to her 'as if [she] were grown up'. Only one of the several matters they discussed was confided to her diary (others were deliberately suppressed) but it was an important one: 'he has been encouraging me to write'.[128] Christmas festivities intervened ('Dear's' death did not prevent the younger Tillyards from enjoying themselves; perhaps they did not miss her) and it was not until a week of 1898 had elapsed that Aelfrida recorded that she 'quite made up [her] mind to write a book' and had worked out the plot and 'some of the principal scenes'.[129] Given that she had already tried her hand at writing but had not to date written anything 'seriously'[130], it would have been easy for an intelligent girl in her fifteenth year to turn her life into a book, then, as she became more confident, to turn the book back into her life, creating an autobiography by turns factual, fictional, and veridical (or at least true *for her*), the plot of which was more or less contingent on reality insofar as it coincided with what Aelfrida deemed 'real' at the time of writing. A work, moreover, whose gnomon, like that of the 'open stone book on a pillar'[131] which sun-dialled the garden of Rupert Brooke's Grantchester vicarage, was the pages themselves, their curled corners casting a moving shadow on her happy hours but also – as a sundial, however bookish, could not – on some very dark hours as well.

In order to experience 'copy' essential for her new 'literary' life and inspired by reading about the abstinent lives of medieval mystics, adolescent Aelfrida embarked on two ascetic practices: "fasting [and] physical fatigue". The former was difficult to achieve but diminution of intake and judicious disposal of food helped and she hints that she managed so well that she not only became very thin but also (and temporarily) "arrested her physical growth". To "keep awake when she would like to sleep" was easier insofar as sleep deprivation could be undertaken in private, but both practices, especially if engaged in as "training … for the will" and combined with general "indifference to bodily comfort" and with concentration of her mind on notions promulgated by her readings (e.g. the spiritual benefits of suffering pain gladly), must have predisposed her – to her undoubted joy, for what better 'copy' could she find than this? – to entering a "certain state of extreme lucidity" which, given the religious nature of her studies, would be favourable to the development of what could be described as "mystic states of consciousness".[132] The state itself would also be conducive to 'visionary' experiences, contingent on reality but transcendent of it: of Christ (as frequently depicted) showing her His wounds or of herself mourning beside the body of a dead man, a scene familiar from stories of the Crucifixion, Deposition, and Entombment of Christ, experiences susceptible to subsequent 'crucifictional' transformation.

Guided by Aleister Crowley, Aelfrida was able to achieve 'mystic states of consciousness' without recourse to fasting and sleep deprivation. Spiritual exercises of all kinds nevertheless continued to be assisted by practices such these (and possibly by the taking of drugs discovered to promote them), particularly at times when she became mentally disequilibrated in response to traumatic events to which she had or imagined she had contributed, or when she embarked, often in response to such events, on a new chapter of fictionalised autobiography (an activity she found both stimulating *and* exhausting) or emerged from a period of intense sustained literary creativity catharsised because of what she uncovered during it of herself and of the psychopathological forces which moved her to behave as she did. Furthermore,

'The open stone book on a pillar', The Old Vicarage, Grantchester

and as she herself noted (though only to deny that it was so), "certain religious practices" undertaken on a regular basis (inclusive of fasting and sleep deprivation) can be seen as "forms of auto-hypnosis" in the course of which "the ordinary channels of sense-impression are closed in order that the 'subject' may be more accessible to certain suggestions from the 'operator'", the operator in this context being herself. And having come very close to admitting that 'autohypnosis' did indeed play an important part in her life, she also hints (she frames her statement as a question) that the reality of events she described owed much to an "image-making power" in her mind (always a powerful force in her case but with its power enhanced by training) which made it easy to translate "impressions" into "light, spoken words, … angels and the like" and even to believe that God (her omnipresent and omnipotent 'Operator') could cause to appear in her mind not a "picture or an illusion" but "some presentation of religious truth or … some message from [Himself]" directly transmitted to a recep-tive 'subject' singled out by Him to receive messages and to undergo religious experiences.[133] ("Push imagination to the point of vision", said Aleister Crowley, "and the trick is done".)[134] Alethea too, with personal knowledge of the way her mother's mind worked (e.g. her tendency to uncritical enthusiasms and capacity for histrionics), noted her propensity to undergo 'metaphysical' experi-ences[135] aptly described by Henri Delacroix as "*hallucina-tions psychiques*" manifesting themselves in consciousness as exteriorised "*constructions*".[136]

Though aware of the mental consequences of prac-tices or exercises undergone in order to create 'copy', Aelfrida could not have known – evidence only became available after her death – that those she practised in pursuit of it give rise to physiological changes in the body: brain scans, for example, show increased activ-ity in one area in the course of prayerful or meditative activity and in another in the course of what the sub-ject describes as religious experiences with a seemingly sensory component: visions, auditions, olfactions, and so on. Furthermore, such exercises and practices, if practised assiduously, endow the practitioner with the ability to manipulate his or her body chemistry in such a way that inhibition or disinhibition of certain enzymes results in powerful states of mind in which 'Deity' may be 'seen', diabolic or malevolent presences encountered, 'univer-sal consciousness' of a gladsome or sorrowful nature experienced, "supreme … spiritual joy"[137] entered into, "locutions" carried on with "discarnate" spirits[138], and apparently "magical" powers possessed, these for Aelfrida (already noted to have something of the shaman about her) including an ability "to foresee events" and a talent for "healing and … thought-reading".[139] And, one might add, an ability to levitate, to make contact with the dead, and to have miracles happen before her eyes.

Having now tracked Aelfrida from (as she might have put it in one of the pious similes which drove Constantine distracted) Genesis to Exodus via some appropriately titled books of Old and New Testaments (Judges, Kings, Chronicles, Psalms, Ecclesiastes, Lamentations, Gospels, Epistles, Acts, and Revelation spring to mind), we must now ask: was she, as she her-self believed, a mystic or was she, as others believed, 'MAD'? (But if truly 'MAD', not so 'mad' as to be unable to ensure that her 'papers' were safely preserved until those who called her 'MAD' were dead.) The 'papers' themselves provide ambiguous evidence. On the one hand, we have sufficient material to support the contention that she was, as she said of Thérèse de Lisieux, 'a humanly loving little girl [who] gave herself up wholeheartedly into the hands of God' and who

eventually achieved 'sanctification'[140], albeit not until after having been un-spared in the making. (And here one can visualise Aelfrida's anxiety lest a biographer base premises on false evidence – on evidence, that is to say, falsified by Aelfrida herself but also, as might happen when she herself was no longer available to 'correct' it, on evidence only contingent on reality – or empha-sise, depending on their capacity for religious belief, one or other aspect of her character, making her appear either as a devout Christian living a life dedicated to God in personal relationship with Him or as a 'sacred monster' sanctified by her piety but rendered directly susceptible to God's vengeance because of monstrously inhuman behaviour towards those to whom she owed a duty of care.) And being a humanly loving little girl who found God in this way or, as she would have pre-ferred to put it, was found by God in this way, she also found a Dantean *vita nuova* or as Henri Delacroix put it, "*une nouvelle forme de vie*", a new *kind* of life, of which she herself was unconsciously creator and inventor[141] and in which she found herself in such intimate com-munion with Deity that she seemed subsumed in Him. A life too, which was so 'real' that it possessed a logic all its own and was lived in a state of intense religious absorption ("*un état théopathic*")[142] but which because of its intensity and its bizarre manifestations appeared to those who did not share it as *théomanie*: religious mad-ness.

But had she never found (or been found by) God how much the worse for her, her lively faith being often all she had to cling to during mental upheavals made worse by that very faith. And had she never entered an '*état théopathic*', how much the worse for her biographer, for the diary and literary record she might have kept – and given her literary bent, almost certainly would have kept – would have been poorer. Not poorer, perhaps, because merely the record of an English gentlewoman's eventful life or because imitating the anodyne books an English gentlewoman might write, for Aelfrida was incapable of writing other than vividly and grippingly and would have made any account of her life, however quotidian, enthralling, but poorer because it would not be the riv-eting and revealing account of the spiritual struggles of a seared soul we study today.

Or was Aelfrida no more than the product of a trau-matic childhood, a woman whose disordered mind sought refuge from being 'powerlessly submerged in [her] own terrible emotions'[143] (a definition of hell, written on the day of her marital rape) by turning for help to a super-natural figure described to children as one who provides comfort and shelter: Christ as embedded in the culture in which she had been 'Christianly' brought up? In which case, was her 'mysticism' no more than "an operation of the law of reaction from stress"[144] (we have already noted exacerbation of 'mystic' manifestations at times of stress, symptoms greatly reduced following Julius' interventions at Tymawr and later), a reaction which itself caused her to become so intensely theomanic that she neglected her physical health? (But was it solely theomania which caused those who might have supported her when she was sunk in a psychopathological 'dark night' of the mind to regard her behaviour as odd or was it because her general behaviour was so idiosyncratic that people absented themselves from her for their own protection, that which we regard as unkindness being in fact self-preservation?) But was it only personality disorder which so disequilibrated her that untrammelled pursuit of the Mystic (or any kind of 'mystic') Way became difficult to maintain, first, because refusal to submit to 'Authority' prevented wholehearted submission even to the will of the Deity in whom she sought refuge, second, because even when living as an anchoress-hermit, emotional neediness and her need to control the lives of others (one and the same thing, though she never realised it) rendered her incapable of letting go of 'the world' from which she fled, and third, because she was too intrinsically disequilibrated ever to succeed as a contemplative: self-isolated in silence and solitude, she exhibited the florid symptoms of a mind unable to cope with either except by becoming even more disequilibrated? (The 'fruits of Silence', as she herself realised too late, were not always good to eat or nourishing when eaten, and Silence and Solitude disabling rather than enabling qualities for a woman who *needed* the presence of people around her, 'pressured' though her soul might be because of this, to keep her in touch with reality.) Or was it something else?

Later in life and following Julius' therapeutic intervention, it seems Aelfrida herself recognised the correlation between the 'mystic' and the disordered side of her personality and decided to play down the former (her bold statement of 1917 "I myself, as I had better confess quite frankly, am a mystic"[145] had been modified by 1945 into admission that "'mystical' is a word that I fight shy of, personally')[146]; indeed, it is possible to 'read' much of her post–Tymawr literary output as an attempt to rebut accusations of 'madness' levelled at her at each stage of her life lest she be thought 'MAD' again. (Knowing that James Stark's son was institutionalised in spite of her attempt to 'straighten' him may have discouraged her from revealing her own contemporary 'mad' activities e.g. her 'Voices'.) Or can it be that she, an intelligent woman versed in the 'New Psychology', realised early in her declared life as a 'mystic' that seemingly God-given experiences were psychopathological and only when her

mind was more than usually disequilibrated sought to amplify her 'mystic' credentials by revealing her experiences to others? Or, it may be, revealed them in the hope that they might be recognised for what they were – expressions of a mind drowning in a 'seething cauldron' of poorly-repressed memories sporadically and horribly illuminated by flashbacks – in the hope that someone might respond to her (all-too-well-disguised) cry for help, only to find that the mind-set of those alienated by her disordered behaviour, by her association with 'Crowley and Crowleyism', and by unChristian behaviour ill-suited to one whose pious pretensions (evidenced most notably by her post-1917 tendency to recount her "mystical experiences too freely"; she later describes one who does this as acting under the influence of "bad angels" acting on purpose to "delude" him) should have promoted a more 'Christianly' attitude towards others, was such that they came to regard her entire personality as "suspect"[147] and were blind to the reason for it being so. Or can it be that not content with exaggerating symptoms of 'madness' in order to make herself 'interesting', she used her (sometimes very real) 'madness' as a means of escape (the mental equivalent of a day in bed, perhaps) when the pressures of quotidian life became too pressing or in order to achieve a desired end, maintenance or 'recuperation' of a state of Holy Virginity being a case in point, for who would want to marry or remain married to a 'holy virgin' who was 'MAD'?

Further questions arise, all equally difficult to answer, when one asks if Aelfrida would have become a mystic had she not suffered a personality disorder i.e. was disorder the cause and 'mysticism' the effect. Did she receive her 'mystical' messages "according to the mode of the recipient"[148] and had her 'mode' not been what it was, would she have received quite different ones? Can one, to coin a word, regard her as 'mysterical' i.e. as both 'mystic' *and* 'MAD', because she lived on the borderland between sanity and insanity and between a heaven and hell where heaven was a "vision of fulfilled desire", hell, "a shadow of a soul on fire"?[149] And how do we explain *The Making of a Mystic* in whose preface Aelfrida first declares herself a mystic, a book which proffers sane advice to 'Audrey Talbot' regarding the manner in which one should conduct oneself as a mystic and derive spiritual and emotional benefit from one's exercises and experiences if one is to maintain one's physical and mental health at the same time? (Advice Aelfrida herself received from Aleister Crowley four years earlier but which she signally failed to follow, even to the point of placing herself in danger of death. And a book of which she might have written, as she wrote of Aleister Crowley's *Book of Lies,* that though it contained some 'profound sayings'[150], it was written in a language she did not 'know' i.e. had not 'learnt' even though she had written it herself or had decided not to 'recognise' because she had no intention of following his/her sensible advice herself.) And how do we reconcile the religious thinker who could write sanely and insight-fully that "a creed looks far more formidable than it is. It appears at first sight as definite as a geometrical proposi-tion so that we forget that it can be no more than the best possible expression of the inexpressible when it deals with super-sensual truths"[151] or the 'Straightener' of whom a 'goup' wrote that she had been "most kind, most helpful and most understanding [and] ... did much to clear away a lot of prejudice and mental rubbish"[152] with the woman who ranted of demonic possession, declared herself one of God's chosen warriors in the fight against Satan, and pronounced herself a 'prophetess'? And where do we place her admission of artefactual enhancement of what she described as 'stigmata'? Does her admission falsify evi-dence she provides of her capacity for mystic communion with Deity or of a mystic's compulsion to imitate Christ by cicatrising herself in imitation of Him or do we regard it as merely another manifestation of disturbed personality? Or both? Perhaps our only answer (if it is an answer) lies in a comment made by Aelfrida herself in connection with a volume sent to her by Alethea sometime in 1952/53; throughout Simone Weil's 'unhappy book' *Attente de Dieu,* there were, she noted, 'signs of mental trouble'; but, she added, Weil was a 'genuine mystic'.[153]

## Notes

1  Tillyard, Ae. *Homesickness* (*To Malise* p 5).
   Tillyard, Ae. *Christian Old Age* p 60 (GCPPT 2|17).
   GCPPG A1 4|2 Letter from Aelfrida to Alethea Graham of 29 December.
2  French, M. *From Town to Gown* (Friends of Histon Road Cemetery Newsletter No 12 Spring 2011).
   GCPPT 1|1|62 18 December 1944. The quotation is taken from a hymn inscribed in Aelfrida's diary and probably composed by herself.
3  GCPPT 1|1|71 10 March 1954.
4  ibid. 20 March 1954.
5  GCPPT 1|1|75 28 February 1959.
6  Tillyard, Ae. *The Silence of God* p 34 (GCPPT 2|20).
7  Tillyard, Ae. *The Glory of the West* p 356 (GCPPT 2|16|1 pt 2).
8  GCPPT 1|1|71 20 March 1954.
9  GCPPT 1|1|72 2 August 1955.
10 GCPPT 1|1|63 16 May 1946.
11 GCPPT 1|1|67 4 February 1950.
12 ibid. 12 February 1950.
13 ibid. 4 February 1950.
14 GCPPT 1|1|66 25 May 1949.
   GCPPT 1|1|69 20 March 1951.
15 GCPPT 1|1|52 21 June 1937.
16 John Hibbs. Personal communication 18 November 2008.
17 GCPPG A1.4|1(4). Undated letter from Josephine Phelps to Alethea Graham expressing her "deepest sympathy" for Alethea's "great loss".

Miss Phelps was the lady with whom Alethea convalesced after her second gastro-intestinal bleed, Aelfrida meeting her at her Iffley Road home when she visited her daughter (GCPPT 1|1|74 2 February 1958).
18 GCPPT 3|5 Letter from Patience Wardle (née Tillyard) to Julius Tillyard of 6 March 1960. Patience was one of the daughters of Robin and Pattie Tillyard; her 1933 memory of Fordfield in a "half-packed up state" and of seeing the foundations of Wetenhall Cottage is corroborated by a contemporary photograph which shows her standing with Aelfrida and Agatha on a part-built brick wall with scaffolding behind them.
19 GCPPG A1.4|1(5) Letter from Father Slade SSJE to Alethea Graham of 16 December 1959.
20 GCPPT 1|1|30 22 December 1924.
21 GCPPT 1|1|61 8 April 1943.
22 Tillyard, Ae. *Naomi da Costa* p 196 (GCPPT 2|22).
23 A Kempis, T. p57. Chapter entitled "Meditation on Death".
24 Tillyard, Ae. *Christian Old Age* p 112.
25 Tillyard, Ae. *The Glory of the West* p 187. (GCPPT 2|16|3).
26 Tillyard, Ae. *The Making of a Mystic* pp 39–40. The passage quoted is by Augustine Baker and appears in a letter from 'Catharine Sutherland' to 'Audrey Talbot' in which 'Catharine' also describes the 'Points of the Compass' meditation and quotes a Sufi poet and Frances Ridley Havergal.
   *Psalm* 109 v 13, 14 and 25 (KJV).
27 GCPPT 1|1|70 30 July 1953.
   GCPPT 1|1|71 8 December 1953.
   Tillyard, Ae. *The Glory of the West* p 259 (GCPPT 2|16|1 Pt 2.)
28 Tillyard, Ae. *Christian Old Age* p 112.
29 Albinski, N. pp 80 and 87.
30 Slonczewski, N. pp 90–92. The passage quoted ("The spark of spiritual apprehension [half dormant in the heart of the isolated believer] is kindled into flame by contact with the gathered fire of many souls together") is taken from *Spiritual Exercises* p 160.
31 Yelton, M. *Outposts of the Faith* pp199–201.
32 Hort, G. pp 151–152.
33 Parke, S. *Physician Heal Thyself* (*Church Times* 11 April 2008, quoting *The Making of a Mystic* p 49) and *The Making of Aelfrida* (*Church Times* 5 March 2010).
34 Laver, J. pp 226–231.
35 Two poems (*Invitation au Festin* and *A letter from Ealing Broadway Station*) appear in *Scars upon my Heart* (pp113 and 114) compiled C. Reilly, preface J. Kazantzis. Although the book's compiler has both poems appear in *The Garden and the Fire,* published in 1916, *Invitation au Festin* actually appears in *Verses for Alethea* (pp 14–15) published in 1920. The poems (and the error of attribution) together with *A letter from Ealing Broadway Station*, also appear in M. Copp's *Cambridge Poets of the Great War* (pp 29, 33 and 57 for quoted comments). The error is perpetuated in *War Girls*, a Crimson Cats audiobook (2011).
36 Tillyard, HJW. Introduction to *The Letters of ACW Tillyard* (MTC).
37 The letters, now in the Warburg Institute, London, were transcribed by Gerald Yorke from an imperfectly transcribed shorthand version. They were sent in 1955 to Karl Germer (1885–1962) of the OTO for safekeeping and at some unrecorded date thereafter passed into the Warburg Institute Yorke Collection. Folder NS 12 a–b; letters quoted in endnotes 39, 41–43 and 45–53 are sourced here.
38 GCPPT 1|1|54 18and 26 November 1937.
39 Sutin, L. p 3. And later; tracking Aelfrida in Lausanne in December 2006, the author discovered graffiti which included an amus-ingly inaccurate version of Crowley's Law of Thelema: "THOU (*sic*) WHAT YOU WILL SHALL BE THE WHOLE OF THE LAW".
40 Letter from Aleister Crowley to 'Sarasvati' of 13 July [1913]. William Northam, a London robemaker, provided robes for all grades of the

A including "adepts and aspirants", fitted according to grade "for all elemental operations [and] for the performance of all general invocations", at a cost of £5–£7. Northam's advertisement appears in *The Equinox* vol 1 no.6 September 1911.

41  Tillyard, Ae. *Concrete* pp102–112.

42  Undated letter from Aleister Crowley to 'Mrs Graham' [1913].

43  Letter from Aleister Crowley to 'Mrs Graham' of 11 September [1913].

44  ibid.

45  Undated letter from Aleister Crowley to 'Mrs Graham'.

46  Letter from Aleister Crowley to 'Sarasvati' of 27 June [1913]

47  Letter from Aleister Crowley to 'Soror Sarasvati' of 27 June [1913] possibly misdated.

48  Undated letter from Aleister Crowley to 'Mrs Graham'.

49  Letter from Aleister Crowley to 'My Dear Sister' of 8 September [1913].

50  Letter from Aleister Crowley to 'Sarasvati' of 1 September [1913]

51  Undated letter from Aleister Crowley to 'Mrs Graham'. Aelfrida's dream "on the subject of cathedral building" is described in *The Closer Walk with God* pp45–46.

52  Letters from Aleister Crowley to 'Sarasvati' of 27 June [19113] and to 'Mrs Graham' of 7 July [1913].

53  Undated letter from Aleister Crowley to 'My dear Sister'.

54  Aelfrida's will, published in *The Times* of 14 May 1960 and detailed in a letter of 24 October 1960 from her solicitors to the college bursar, is preserved at Girton College (File HR 41/16).

55  Tillyard, Ae. *The Glory of the West* pp 331–333 (GCPPT 2|16|1 Pt 2).

56  ibid. p 341 and GC File HR 41|16.

57  Tillyard, Ae. *Christian Old Age* pp 116–117.

58  GCPPT 1|1|67 8 April 1950.

59  GCAC 4|6|3|3 Letter from Alethea Graham to Helen McMorran of 8 April 1960.

60  GC File HR 41|16 Note by Helen McMorran appended to the 'Mrs Graham papers' on 2 November 1960.

61  GCAC 4|6|3|3 Letter from Aelfrida to Miss K Butler of 13 June 1946.

62  Tillyard, Ae. *Naomi da Costa* p 261. The 'Pandora' of Greek myth after whom Aelfrida's ship is named was a woman (the first woman) created by the gods who each in turn endow her with a special attribute: beauty, gentleness of disposition, and so on. She is entrusted by Mercury with a huge box, securely fastened, which he promises to call for shortly. Unable to contain her curiosity – voices from inside the box implore her to free the speakers from their gloomy prison – Pandora unties the cord which binds the box and raises the lid. Unfortunately for Pandora and for humanity, the box has been filled by Jupiter with all the diseases, sorrows, vices, and crimes from which they have so far been free and these in the form of winged evil spirits immediately afflict Pandora and her fellow-mortals. Closing the box, Pandora, now plagued by pain and misery, hears a further voice entreat its freedom; she opens the box and Hope, concealed by Jupiter among the evil spirits in an act of compassion, emerges on her mission to heal the ills inflicted by her fellow prisoners (Guerber, H. pp 17–21).

63  Tillyard, Ae. *Naomi da Costa* p 260.

64  GCPPT 1|1|58 'Ash Wednesday' (26 February) 1941.

65  GCPPT 1|1|54 18 and 26 November 1937.

66  GCPPT 1|1|71 14 September 1953. The phrase is taken from James Elroy Flecker's poem *The Ballad of Camden Town*, included in *Cambridge Poets 1900–1913* pp 75–76.

67  Tillyard, Ae. *Myself* (*Cambridge Poets, 1900–1913* p 189).
     Stokoe, F. *Ode to Earthly Joy* (ibid. pp 187–188).

68  GCAC 4|6|3|3 Letter from Aelfrida to Helen McMorran of 5 November 1958.

69  Tillyard, HJW. Introduction to *The Letters of ACW Tillyard* (MTC).

70  GCPPT 1|1|69 1 August 1951

71  Forster, E M. p 120.

72  GCPPT 1|1|75 11 October 1958. Edward Dunsany (1878–1957) was an Irish peer, poet, novelist, and playwright. The elevated tone of his writings may have inspired Aelfrida's extended poem *Kingdoms* (*The Garden and the Fire* pp 17–20) and the 1924 publication of his fantasy novel *The King of Elfland's Daughter* elements of *Haste to the Wedding*; pieces by Dunsany also appeared in the first two numbers of Crowley's *The Equinox*. *Fame comes late*, a play, was first broadcast in 1933.

73  Amory, M. p 236.

74  GCPPT 1|1|70 24 March 1953. Mathilde Bertrand (1844–1908) was a Frenchwoman who, brought up in the Christian tradition, achieved sudden spiritual intimacy with God and thereafter underwent numerous mystical experiences; these she disclosed to no-one but recorded them in a spiritual journal published after her death as the *Journal de Lucie-Christine* (Paris 1912) and (in translation) in London in 1915.

75  GCPPT 1|1|71 25 July 1953.

76  GCPPT 1|1|65 27 July 1947.

77  Tillyard, Ae. *The Glory of the West* pp 1–6 (GCPPT 1|16|1 Pt 1).

78  GCPPT 1|1|14 3 October 1906.

79  Tillyard, Ae. *Spiritual Exercises* p 151.

80  Tillyard, Ae. *A Little Road-Book for Mystics* p 131.

81  Quiller Couch, A. *Cambridge Lectures* p 1.

82  Charles, Père. *La Prière de Toutes les Heures* No 11 p 111.

83  Tillyard, Ae. *The Glory of the West* pp 1–6 (GCPPT 2|16|1 Pt 1).

84  GCPPT 1|1|71 15 August 1953.

85  GCPPT 1|1|13 29 August 1906.

86  Tillyard, Ae. *Christian Old Age* p 82.

87  GCPPT 1|1|61 31 July 1943.

88  Tillyard, Ae. *Naomi da Costa* p 119.

89  GCAC 4|6|3|3 Letter from Aelfrida to Helen McMorran of 5 November 1958.

90  GCPPT 1|1|61 26 February 1944.

91  GCPPT 1|1|19 30 May 1914.

92  Tillyard, Ae. *The Glory of the West* pp 44 and 56. (GCPPT 2|16|1 Pt 1).

93  Tillyard, Ae. *Rich Man's Choice* p 220 (GCPPT 2|21|2 Pt 1).

94  Erlande, A. *La Vipère Dorée* p120. "*Les cahiers que vous voyez là*", he says, "*au premier rang de cette bibilothèque fermée sont des recueils d'anecdotes. Quels documents pour les curieux de plus tard*".

95  Tillyard, Ae. *The Glory of the West* pp 402–414 (GCPPT 2|16|1 Pt 1).

96  GCPPT 1|1|74 7 December 1957.

97  Tillyard, Ae. *The Glory of the West* pp 402–414 (GCPPT 2|16|1 Pt 1).

98  GCPPT 1|1|74 7 December 1957.

99  GCPPT 1|1|70 1 January 1953.

100 Tillyard, Ae. *The Glory of the West* p 353 (GCPPT 2|16|1 Pt 2).

101 GCPPT 1|1|73 3 November 1956.

102 Tillyard, Ae. *The Making of a Mystic* pp v and 35.

103 Underhill, E, *Mysticism* pp 176–179.

104 Tillyard, Ae. *The Making of a Mystic* p 55.

105 Benson, R H. *Richard Raynal. Solitary* p136.

106 Tillyard, Ae. *Haste to the Wedding* p72.

107 King, U. pp88–91.

108 Burman, E. pp103–104.
     GCPPT 2|26|3 *The Schechters*. Gladys Sanderson's visionary experiences are related at some length in *Spiritual Exercises* pp 185–187. The poem dedicated to 'Valentine' (*The Church of our Lady and the English Martyrs*) written in Cambridge on 'Easter Day 1913' appears in *The Garden and the Fire* (p66) in the section entitled 'borderland poems'.

109 GCPPT 2|25|2 *A Wet Sunday at Fordfield*.

110 Tillyard, Ae. *Spiritual Exercises* p 154. (Author's emphasis).

111 Tillyard, Ae. *A Little Road-Book for Mystics* p 76. As a result of reading William James, Aelfrida could be said to have put each of his 'varieties of religious experience' into practice in turn: the "Reality

of the Unseen", the "Divided Self", "Conversion", "Saintliness", "Mysticism", and so on. Conversely, James' descriptions of characteristics pertaining to "religious persons" fit (or could have been made to fit by) Aelfrida herself: that "the religious are often neurotic" but that the significance of their individual neuroses must be tested by its "fruits", not its origins; that there is a "prevalence of the psychopathic temperament in religious biography"; that the "Sick Soul" relieves its symptoms in "supranormal religion" and may effect its own "Mind-Cure" by such means; that "religious persons have often ... professed to see the truth in a special manner ... known as mysticism"; that Mysticism's association with "the Anaesthetic Revelation[s]" induced by anaesthetic agents and other drugs should be borne in mind. James, W. pp xxxvii–xlii, 378, and 386–394.

112 Tillyard, Ae *Spiritual Exercises* p 154. (Author's emphasis).

113 GCPPT 2|23 *The Watch Word* June 1955.

114 Underhill, E. *Mysticism* pp 176–179.

115 GCPPT 1|1|70 14 May 1953.

116 GCPPT 1|1|4 30 October 1897. Aelfrida's enjoyment of anaesthesia was unusual at a time when patients commonly dreaded the unpleasant side effects of anaesthetic agents then in use. Following the publication in 1902 of William James' *Varieties of Religious Experience*, however, realisation that such agents could "stimulate the mystical consciousness in an extraordinary degree" (p387) may have enhanced her enjoyment; certainly she never expressed fear of either agents or effects and on at least one occasion 'broke away into the halls of infinity' where she 'had adventures now, alas, forgotten' (GCPPT 1|1|20 16 March 1915).

117 GCPPT 1|1|4 1 December 1897.

118 Tillyard, Ae. *The Approaching Storm* p280. The names 'Jacinth' and 'Leopold' are not without significance. 'Leopold' ('bold for the people') may remind us of Julius' supportive role in his sister's life; 'Jacinth' has deeper shades of meaning, 'jacinth' being synonymous with 'hyacinth' and Hyacinth in Greek mythology a beautiful youth beloved by Apollo who, as a consequence of Zephyr's jealousy, accidentally kills him.

119 ibid. pp 268–272.

120 GCPPT 1|1|4 4 April 1889.

121 Underhill, E. *Mysticism* pp 176–179.

122 GCPPT 1|1|4 30 October 1897.

123 Delacroix, H. Preface pp i–xix.

124 Tillyard, Ae. *Spiritual Exercises* p vii.

125 ibid. pp 159–160 and 280.

126 ibid.

127 GCPPT 1|1|4 8 September 1897.

128 ibid. 21 December 1897.

129 ibid. 6 January 1898.

130 ibid. 21 December 1897.

131 GCPPT 1|1|20 19 June 1915.

132 Tillyard, Ae. *Spiritual Exercises* pp 11–13.

133 Tillyard, Ae. *The Making of a Mystic* p 55.

134 Laver, J. pp 226–231, quoting Aleister Crowley.

135 GCPPG A.1|1 31 March 1928.

136 Delacroix, H. p 114.

137 Tillyard, Ae. *Spiritual Exercises* p 147.

138 ibid. p 184.

139 ibid. p 146.

140 GCPPT 1|1|75 5 August 1958.

141 Delacroix, H. pp i–xix.

142 ibid.

143 GCPPT 1|1|20 5 October 1914.

144 Underhill, E. *Mysticism* pp 382–385.

145 Tillyard, Ae. *The Making of a Mystic* p v.

146 GCPPT 1|1|63 27 December 1945.

147 Tillyard, Ae. *Christian Old Age* p 93. (GCPPT 2|17). Aelfrida's first version has one who "prates of" his mystical experiences too freely; she seems to have substituted a word with less loaded connotations.

148 Hort, G. p 154, Greta Hort was a Girton contemporary of Agatha Graham; it is interesting to speculate if some of Agatha's 'unorthodox' views on religion of that time stemmed from discussions of Mysticism in general and as practised by her mother in particular with a research fellow qualified by studies of mediaeval philosophy and theology to open Agatha's eyes to oddities inherent in Aelfrida's mystical religiosity.

149 Khayyám, O. Quatrain 72.

150 GCPPT 1|1|19 13 September 1913.

151 GCPPT 3|1|6c includes an undated note from Aelfrida to Mother Guenvrede (by context written shortly after May 1942) on the reverse of which appears part of a corrected page in Aelfrida's writing on which the quoted lines appear.

152 GCPPT 3|1|6a Letter from Alethea Graham to Aelfrida of 26 December 1940 written around an undated letter from an Elizabeth Shirley of Buffalo, NY, USA to Alethea herself.

153 GCPPT 1|1|70a. Undated note.

# Ragged edges and unwritten books

A story – a ghost story – is told about Hunstanton Hall, ancestral home of the Le Strange family in Old Hunstanton, the Norfolk fishing village which gave its name to New Hunstanton, the resort familiar to Aelfrida from childhood and adult holidays and from her extended visit during the preliminary stages of her divorce. The ghost, known as the 'Grey Lady', is said to haunt the Hall seeking the missing piece of a precious Persian carpet cut up by the charitable wife of a descendent for distribution among the villagers as hearthrugs, only to see the accusing face of Armine le Strange glaring at her from a window when she returned home. To pacify the revenant, Emmeline le Strange reclaimed the pieces of carpet, restoring them to the box in which the original carpet had been stored. One piece, however, was never found – and Armine haunts the rooms and corridors of the Hall to the present day.[1]

Aelfrida knew of the Hall (her mother paid visits there) and had probably heard of the Grey Lady: indeed, in *Just Alice*, 'Alice' takes 'Madeleine' to stay in the dower house of a hall modelled on Hunstanton Hall while the latter is cured of her drug addiction, and an extended episode in *The Centaur* has 'Clive Farwell' live in a house which resembles Hunstanton Hall with its ancient undercroft and Elizabethan and later additions. (His housekeeper's name is 'Mrs Grey'.) Hence Aelfrida's inclusion of a hearthrug among the 'carpets' a biographer might weave from her 'papers' makes sense in the context of a place and a story with which she was familiar and insofar as it refers a 'dear and gentle Reader' forwards to domestic aspects of her life – places in which she lived, people she knew – instead of back to magic carpets and prayer mats. (A prayer mat, we should remember, created from a cut-up *Middle Eastern* carpet.) No 'carpet' of which Aelfrida had a hand in the weaving will ever be complete (several 'ragged edges' remain) but information can be garnered from her 'papers' and from other sources which, pieced together, adds something to her patchwork account of places and people interwoven with the fabric of her life.

Cambridge begins and ends the story. Cambridge from which she could not bear to live away for long, which she loved 'with an inexplicable love made up of many strands', where she was born and to which her

Joan Cooper in old age

ashes drifted back when her star "flickered into a final darkness". A Cambridge, perhaps, which existed only as 'an archetype in some Platonic heaven … never realised here' but which would endure as a "Platonic Idea" even after "there are no men left to grasp the immortal concepts Truth and Beauty". (And "Goodness", inserted as an afterthought.) A Cambridge which would present "a picture of permanence"[2] long after her death, permanence extended even to street names (Wetenhall Road, Tillyard Way) and to St Columba's Church with its memorials to 'dear Scotties' and to the Learned Twins and still recognisably the place where adolescent Frida conducted her Sunday School classes of 'cherubs' and 'hooligans' in its parish rooms and where the disastrous 'Marriage of Miss Tillyard' took place.

Lausanne still contains the apartment block on the Avenue des Alpes where Frida lived under the chaperonage of Mlle Dumur, though its environs are vastly changed today. The apartment itself was described in detail by its erstwhile lodger fifty years later in *Just Alice* as the place to which the 'Marsden' family decamp for a family holiday and to which 'Will Harvey' follows them in order to propose to 'Alice'. ('Alice', unlike Aelfrida, had a pearl engagement ring but it seems that although 'Will', like Constantine, regarded it as a "goal to set [his] hopes upon", Alice/Aelfrida regarded it as a "glowing gaud" which "[made] of [her] a harlot"[3] even after she achieved the marital chastity into which 'Alice' drifted but she imposed.) Lausanne was also the place from which 'Barbara' returned "self-assured, even slightly dictatorial", wearing a coat and skirt of "rough chocolate brown wool"[4] ('an error of taste ACWT 1904') bought to please Hans Peter, the young engineer whose proposal Frida first accepted (on terms) then, following her mother's warning that 'one spends with one's husband not only days but nights'[5], rejected when safe in Cambridge again. And the little alpine resorts (Finhaut and others) where the Tillyards sojourned when they joined Aelfrida in Switzerland are recognisable as she knew them, as are the Alpine railways she rode and Hans Peter engineered.

Florence, where Signorina Tillyard tasted 'the extreme sourness of the Florentine grape' at the point when uncouth members of 'Young Italy' made improper suggestions (she kept a hatpin under her pillow to ward off improper advances) and where she began her 'half-intellectual, half-humorous correspondence' with Giovanni Papini, still throngs with tourists who, like her, dismiss cultural monuments with a brusque 'seen 'em' but is no longer malarial. (Two of the "brilliant young men who loved the future and loathed the past"[6] survived both 'Gian Falco' and herself: her 'old acquaintance Prezzolini' whose book on the rise of Fascism she described as demonstrating 'a dulling of early enthusiasms'[7], and Roberto Assagioli, sixteen-year-old "young futurist"[8] when she knew him, later the founder of 'psychosynthetic' or 'transpersonal' psychology with its motto 'Know Thyself' and a man whose interest in Judaism and Jewish Mysticism was more informed than her own.)[9] But the Fiesole convent of the Little Sisters of Mary with its garden statues of Mary cradling the Child Jesus and Jesus cradling a lost sheep[10] has been converted to secular use.

Of the places visited by 'absolutely surrendered' Mrs Constantine Graham, Odessa is now a commercial and cultural centre of an independent Ukraine. But still behind the cultivated façade it presents to visitors lie derelict tenements inhabited by a disaffected underclass, descendants, perhaps, of the Soyuzniks who haunted its streets in 1907 and added their horror to the 'devils' haunting Aelfrida's dreams, "beings of incredible malignity waiting to take up their abode in the bodies of such human beings as, through wickedness or sloth, [had] left open a crack in the door of their personalities".[11] (As she, her childhood burden of guilt made heavier by abandonment of 'Holy Virginity', persuaded herself she had done without realising that the 'devils' swarmed only in the catacombs of her unhappy mind.) Arcadia, the quiet seaside town where infatuated Charles Stewart Smith took his vice-consul's wife, is now a smart resort with expensive cafes and restaurants and beachside night clubs and "is surely … not for solitude seekers"[12] or those seeking to exchange quiet confidences. Boston, ostentatious and overheated by Aelfrida's puritanical standards, still houses the apartment block off Beacon Street she called 'little Gehenna'; Arlington Heights, however, as Aelfrida discovered in 1959 from a Cowley Father who had ministered there to 'a Home for naughty girls' ('in our time it was [the Ring] sanatorium')[13] was by then – and today is even more so – a suburban area dense with detached houses from which the widely-separated white frame houses of 1909 have all but disappeared. Emden, as she discovered from German prisoners of war scrumping apples in Lolworth, had eighty per cent of its houses and nearly all its historic buildings destroyed by an allied bombing raid on 6 September 1944; by 1962, however, the town within 'the Wall' where she walked with little 'Weta' and toddler 'Agata' had been reconstructed into a semblance of the town she knew. Paris too retains many respects of the town she preferred not to visit and Le Vésinet its 'town in a garden' appearance but the villa where Aelfrida and Constantine entertained Aleister Crowley and Aelfrida an 'airy tribe' of angels, demons, and sprites, became a restaurant.

Of Aelfrida's 'spiritual' homes only two remain. Since 1969 Miss Wrightson's retreat house at Leiston has been run by the Pro Corda Trust as a national school for young chamber music players, this according well with Aelfrida's conviction that Constantine would come to see God "arrayed in sound" in some "rainbow-harmony of notes divine".[14] (The 'blind Greek' did indeed list music as one of his interests in *Who's Who* but golf, tennis, riding, and walking preceded it.) St Mary's returned to Malling from Fownhope in 1945 though Aelfrida might not approve of even more modern additions to the convent buildings. (Would she approve of extracts from her diary being preserved in the convent's archives because providing valuable evidence for what was expected of an oblate in the 1930s?) She never achieved her ambition of being buried at Malling ('one day my body will lie there ... a distant light towards which I may walk') but nor, of course, did Constantine – his ex-wife saw to that – there being for different reasons 'no place for [either] within the enclosure'[15]; perhaps, as at Tymawr, what was important to her was the 'thing symbolised, not physical fact'.[16] Mother Magdalen Mary OSB, whose heart attack shortly after breaking the news of Agatha's suicide to postulant Alethea rendered her, if not a 'dying woman'[17], certainly an invalid one for years thereafter, was, it seems, 'quite rejuvenated by retirement from her high office'[18] in 1951 after twenty-three years' tenure; as 'dear Abbess Emerita', she survived both the "dearest Aelfrida" who "used to write me pages and pages on [her] spiritual states and ways" ("one comes through those in time just as you have", she reassured her)[19] and a former oblate ten years younger than herself, dying on 7 July 1966. But it was Aelfrida who wrote her epitaph: describing her as her "Saint of the Contemplative Life", she continues "[she is] a Religious who seems to come straight from the Presence of God [who] helps me, not by scolding me or lecturing me or arguing with me but by loving me in God and for God".[20]

St Thomas' Convent, apart from a brick archway opening onto the churchyard of St Thomas the Martyr next door, has disappeared. The convent closed in 1958 (Aelfrida, resident in Oxford, did not note its demise but had already provided a detailed account of its surroundings in *The Glory of the West*)[21] and it and the row of houses fronting Osney Lane of which St Benedict's was one, were pulled down and a Post Office depot built on the site, an appropriate replacement for the 'poor little place' whose occupant made such good use of the postal services that Father Cary suggested that curbing her correspondence would prevent leakage of spiritual energy. The SSJE (no longer the 'Cowley' Fathers) are now based in London. (A theological college occupies its Marston Street premises.) Fairacres remains a spiritual and intellectual powerhouse. Eileen Kermack, widowed shortly after the war, moved to South Africa to act as housekeeper for SSJE missions there; hearing from Alethea that Eileen sported lipstick and nylon stockings and exhibited an exuberance unknown in Oxford, Aelfrida found it hard to reconcile her memories of quiet, elegant, piously-veiled 'Philothea' with descriptions of the woman she had become.

Tymawr abides, the spot "beloved over all" by Aelfrida and Sister Jeanne[22], surrounded by 'incomparable countryside [of] hill and vale, sky and streams ... [and] of misty distances' whose 'dream-like beauty' meant so much to a woman who 'longed so much to see [her] spiritual home once more' before she died that she composed letters

in her mind asking when (not if) she could return to imbibe the 'sense of something spiritual' with which it was imbued. (And for which she longed more than she had ever longed for the sea[23], a phenomenon as restless and as profoundly impenetrable as herself.) And lest we are tempted to accuse her of bias because at Tymawr she found herself "under a roof [and] at rest" on "a pastoral forehead of Wales"[24] or because, like Philip Toynbee, she sought refuge there after a period of severe depression and discovered how much she too needed "the united *endorsement* of the Sisters for [their] peculiar faith"[25], even a 'dry, hopeless [and] sterile intellectual'[26] like Bertrand Russell was moved to write of the countryside of his birth that "the God who made this country was an artist; he moulded those hills so that their lines run down into the valleys quite magically and trimmed them with tufted woods so that not an acre grates".[27]

Aelfrida's descriptions of Tymawr apply today, for the storey added to the original house early in the 1950s and the angled wing added later the same decade do not detract from – in fact, may be said to positively enhance – its appearance. Oak and beech trees still shade the garden (white 'Sister Castanea' is a smaller version of herself – and pink) and the sycamore bearing 'the Figure on the Tree' still shades the Campo Santo and its MORS JANUA VITAE gate. The view from Aelfrida's West Room down the long border is essentially unaltered and a statue of the Virgin still graces the 'Lady Garden'. Even today, predominant sounds are natural ones and in house and chapel elected silence reigns, a silence which "hums like a powerful ... engine".[28] The convent now contains a refectory for guests ('I suppose', wrote Aelfrida in 1944, 'tertiaries, associates and ... friends ... will continue to come and perhaps others who impart their own atmosphere will be tolerated for a time'[29]; they do, and are more than merely 'tolerated' by a Community which follows the story of Sister Placida's stay with the same compassion it extended to their difficult visitor between 1936 and 1946), her fears that the SSC as a 'struggling' wartime Community might not survive[30] being unfounded given that '*Laus Deo* ... so powerful is the spiritual influence there'.[31] The library houses more books but is not otherwise much altered from the room she and other members of 'the Library' knew. The 'rather austere' chapel remains but is now "very full"[32] of the oak pews which replaced the chairs and prie-dieux of earlier days; discovering from an SSC newsletter that in 1957 the chapel's original altar had been replaced by 'a stone altar cut by masons from the garden', she declared herself 'not altogether happy' at the Community spending its money (*her* donations!) in this way: 'and anyhow frontals and super-frontals entirely hid the old one'. ('But I love them dearly all the same', she added.)[33] Michaelgarth, willed to the SSC by Father James Amos after his death in May 1958 following "a quiet failure of strength" (his wife predeceased him; he himself retired as chaplain in 1950), is now a retreat house with its own library. Woodbine Cottage was sold to a local farmer after the war and from him passed into private ownership where it remains; its present occupant cares for injured animals before releasing them into the wild, though probably does not whistle "Jerusalem, my happy home" to them as she does.

Mother Guenvrede's decision to retire in 1953 after having "mothered" the SSC for thirty years "in case decay and mildew set in"[34] was prophetic. Reports reaching Aelfrida thereafter noted the gradual decline of one 'who seems in the best of health and spirits'[35] to one now 'quite the little old woman'[36] who kept going "only with an effort".[37] (But a little old woman who made sure visitors knew she was "Mother Foundress of this convent".)[38] Aelfrida's comments on the 'Mother Foundress' were not always charitable nor in keeping with her reminder to herself to notice 'other people's virtues'[39] (she never, for example, altered her earlier view that although Mother Guenvrede had built up the Community, her intransigent behaviour suggested she was also bent on pulling it down)[40] but nor were her predictions accurate: foretelling in 1938 that the 'hardening of the arteries causing heart strain'[41] from which she believed Mother Guenvrede was suffering would see the latter inhabiting 'eternal habitations' by 1944, she failed to remind herself of the failure of her prediction six years later and would have been surprised to learn that a woman three years younger than herself survived her by eight. On 1 March 1964 Sister Guenvrede suffered what seems to have been a small stroke, her subsequent "clouding of the mind" causing herself "great humiliation" and her fellow-Sisters great problems as she became more and more confused; she died on 8 September 1967, her death preceding Father Northcott's by a week. Her ashes were interred in the convent chapel in an unmarked vault below the mural tabernacle which now houses the Blessed Sacrament.[42] Tributes show how much Aelfrida's view of her differed from those of others and, inadvertently, how much her character differed from that of her resident tertiary, for no one could possibly say of the latter that she possessed "an extraordinary competence" for welcoming and caring for "the ... family ... and the friends which God gave her" or the knack of inspiring others to "team-work" or describe her as one who had "a sense of great stillness about her" or whose "insight, understanding, common sense and gift of humour helped so many on their way". (Unless, of course, they were 'goups' – or male.) But of

both it may be said that they were directed by "spiritual vision and power".[43]

Of Sisters known to Aelfrida, most survived her. Sister Monica, noted by Sister Jeanne in 1958 to be 'frail but ... happy'[44], died in 1965, Sister Hilda and Mother Sheila Mary (the latter 'very mature, very thoughtful, very dignified and *quite* sure of her vocation')[45] in 1989. Sister Jeanne, 'a born contemplative ... absorbed in God'[46], died on 27 August 2004 in the seventy-first year of her profession, her friendship with Sister Placida still vivid in her mind the preceding year. Sister Gabriel Anne, Aelfrida's 'dear little Jewess'[47], died in 2010 as Mother Serafima, an Orthodox nun. Hilda Harrison survived both Aelfrida and breast cancer to die as a very old lady in 1983; her name or initials (HWH) appear in several books preserved at Tymawr.

And it is in books that we chiefly discover Aelfrida/Placida as we track her at Tymawr, the place most redolent of her presence today. None of the books she wrote are preserved there, not even her 'silly novels'. Books deemed unsuitable by Mother Guenvrede had already been removed and were probably taken away by the 'clever lady who writes books' on her enforced departure in 1946; 'silly novels' left behind were likely discarded by Mother Guenvrede once Aelfrida left the premises. Knowing, however, that every contact leaves a trace and that Aelfrida donated two wheelbarrow loads of her 'Cambridge books' to the SSC, many hours can be spent in the Tymawr and Michaelgarth libraries looking for volumes which might have belonged to her, volumes, it may be, for which she had no further use because they represented past stages of her 'mystic way' or which she discarded because in them can be discovered the sources of some of her novels and of her more extreme religious practices, or which she wished to leave in a place of safety for a future biographer to weave into their 'carpet'. And to feel, like their subject, that 'the sight of all those books in dull binding and ... small print' caused the same naughty thought to enter their mind, namely 'that there was enough of the goody-goody present to turn anyone atheist'.[48]

Of two volumes we may be sure: the copy of Mother Magdalen Mary's 'booklet on the contemplative life'[49] sent to Aelfrida in 1934 and inscribed by the latter 'Aelfrida Placida. St Benedict's. Oxford', and Bede Frost's *The Art of Mental Prayer*, dedicated to 'Aelfrida Graham' with his blessing. But knowing Aelfrida's habit of removing dust jackets from her books and replacing them with a wallpaper wrapper, we may deduce that the English translation of François de Sales' *Treatise on the Love of God* was hers (it bears what looks like her writing, on the cover, albeit distorted by the paper's embossing) and from marks left by adhesive tape in this and Bede Frost's book that books commented on by her (e.g. Saudreau's *Degrees of the Spiritual Life,* a 1926 edition of the *Ancren Riwle,* Dix's *The Shape of the Liturgy*) belonged to her as well. Other volumes (novels by RH Benson, biographies of Sundar Singh) may be presumed to be hers, as may a copy of Bede Frost's *The Mystery of Mary* bearing a Cambridge booksellers tag and Lucius Cary's *Hortus Inclusus.* Or again, the technique used in cutting from *The Works of Meister Eckhart* (of which the only two marked passages "we have got to make a habit of not seeking out or taking what is ours in anything at all but finding and seizing God in everything" and "attacks of restlessness are solely due to the personal will"[50] sum up Aelfrida's stay; the ink used and the manner of marking is also similar to hers) a section of the page on which one might find a personalised inscription is remarkably like that in Tymawr's copy of Julius Tillyard's *Greek Literature,* published in 1914, in which he might conceivably have written a solemn Latin dedication to his 'dearest Tit'.

None of Aelfrida's immediate family save Julius left traces at Tymawr: his *Greek Literature* and his *Plays of Roswitha*, both perhaps volumes left behind by his sister. But ghostly literary reminders exist of two people who visited her in spirit. The trunk and suitcase forwarded from Oxford to Tymawr in October 1939 were more than merely evidence of Aelfrida's tendency to leave deposits of possessions behind her as she disburdened herself of 'episodes' of her life; they also contained 'books with Precious Temu's writing in' and books belonging to Alethea whom at that point in her life her mother feared (or hoped) she would 'probably never see again'.[51]

Alethea, as we know, visited Tymawr in 1948 at Sister Sheila's request to collect relict books. Four remained uncollected, possibly intentionally, for all were reminders of particularly unhappy periods of her life: Ibsen's *Plays* including *The Doll's House* with its story of a woman's bid for freedom, two volumes of Swinburne's poetry, and a book on Marlowe's poetry and drama, all inscribed with her name and various dates in 1926 and reminders, it may be, less of her 'newfound passion for literature'[52] than of unrequited love for Tom Henn, and a translation from the French of *The High History of the Holy Grail*, inscribed with her name and as having been bought in Bath in 1932, possibly while returning from a visit to Cardiff in April but certainly around the time of her last meeting with Raffaelo Piccoli, of her becoming 'by way of being an Anglo-Catholic'[53], and shortly before her embarkation on what was to become – with conventual intermissions – a life of social service.

The most poignant book of all, however, was Agatha's Horace 'with her dear name in', forwarded by Julius to Aelfrida when unseasonably warm weather in January 1938 reminded the latter of the Roman poet's description of pastures appearing from beneath the melting snow and of Milton's adaptation of the seventh *Epode* quoted by Agatha in her suicide note before seeking death and a new life 'through so dark a gateway'.[54] The book, in keeping with Agatha's wish to live on the hills above the Wye, remained in the West Room until recently; like the oaken cross which marked her grave, it is now missing.

Lolworth, somewhat enlarged, remains much as before – and how pleased Aelfrida would be to discover that the village's History Society, meeting in the former schoolroom, took a lively interest in her life – though not even those who must have known her as children remember her now. The Rectory, 'deteriorating so rapidly' in 1952 as to be unfit for human habitation 'even if thousands were spent on it'[55], had thousands spent on it by subsequent owners and now stands regenerated, renamed, and trimly stuccoed, in a manicured garden whose (resited) pond is no longer evil-smelling and from which the parish room has been removed. Although the house never became a home for retired missionaries or a 'college for training ordinands with a rural bias' (*sic*), it retains the atmosphere of 'generation-old prayer' she found so precious and remains '*not* wholly secular'.[56] (But the oratory is now a bathroom.) The bedrooms in which she received Thérèse de Lisieux, heard her 'Voices', and dreamed of Aleister Crowley's acolytes are much as she knew them (and warmer and drier) as is the drawing room where she 'interviewed' the Bishop. (Edward Wynn, the "sincere, manly, practical and sensible Christian teacher"[57] concerning whom she was perhaps not wholly wrong in thinking that he loved her – or was he merely practising *caritas*? – is commemorated by a plaque in the north aisle of Ely Cathedral, a plaque whose modesty – it bears little more than his name, dates of birth and death and of his episcopate and a quotation extolling his "faithful and true heart" – is in marked contrast to the elaborate and effusive monuments of his predecessors.) The church, no warmer than before and retaining its exceptionally high chancel step, the radiator behind which Aelfrida knelt shivering and saw visions, the 'American' organ, and the polychromatic plaques representing the Way of the Cross to which she also objected, still stands at the end of Church Lane but shares its priest with another parish. (Gravestones commemorating people described in her diary stand in the churchyard.) Father Lovell's worsening asthma forced him to relinquish his incumbency in late 1957 to exist on a disability pension thereafter; in July 1957 he and his wife met Aelfrida for the last time, he dejected because believing that he had been 'a failure' as Lolworth's parish priest, his wife 'brave and splendid' as usual.[58] Retirement suited him: he died at seventy-seven in July 1970 to tombstone praise: "Well done thou good and faithful servant"; Lilian Lovell died aged ninety in October 1994. ("Her price was far above rubies", graced hers.) Clare and Mary Lovell and Auntie Ivy married and moved away. 'Fenny' Parson Drove still consists of 'a pleasant avenue of houses standing back in gardens'[59], its church visible across the lane and through intervening trees from what was Aelfrida's attic window high above the former '*very* Victorian' vicarage's front door.

St John's Home remains much as Aelfrida knew it down to the narrow Green Corridor along which 'battles' echoed, to its pretty garden, and to the Register listing Aelfrida Catharine Wetenhall Graham's admission on 15 July 1953; residents now include some Cowley Fathers. It is not now possible to identify GETHSEMANE but its position and appearance may be deduced from a visit to a similar room and from the view from its window. St Anne's ward is now the conventual refectory, 'St Raphael' has reverted to lobby. Sisters Elizabeth Noel and Winifred Marcian both returned to St John's Home; like Aelfrida, both died there. Sister Catherine carried out her tasks as Superior "with vision and efficiency" but remained "sometimes frightening even to those who knew and loved her"[60] (Eustace, wrote Aelfrida in November 1958, 'thinks it is childish of me to mind ... Sister Catherine's odd ways [so] ... I will try and not be terrified or bewildered')[61]; she died in 1984.

Following Aelfrida's ashes back to Cambridge to see if her 'picture of permanence' holds true of every place she knew we find that it does – and does not. Discussing with Joan Cooper 'the subject of Fordfield as a nursing home', Aelfrida expressed a hope that should it become a nursing home, her action might 'do nothing to damage [the] dear Evelyn!'.[62] But it did, though indirectly and not immediately. Both nursing homes weathered the war years 1939–1945 but responded to the arrival of the National Health Service in 1948 in different ways. The Hope built the extension noted by Aelfrida (she was more excited by its inclusion of a dedicated chapel than by the fact that it now possessed a more modern operating theatre than that created by the Fordhams in 1933 in former Fordfield's West Room), then expanded its already enlarged ward areas in 1964/65.[63] (The work involved much more than the 'little pulling about and building on'[64] that Aelfrida envisaged with regard to 'Fordfield Above'.) The Evelyn, with its Twenties operating theatre and refusal to recognise the effect on private medicine of a service free at the point of use, dwindled into a "just about viable" institution until it embarked on a "master plan of improvement" in the 1970s.[65] The rival nursing homes gradually became less competitive (they preferred to think of themselves as complementary), the Evelyn Hospital (as it now was) specialising in surgery and oncology, the Hope concentrating on 'special provision for the needs of the aged'[66], its mission statement paraphrases Aelfrida's hope that it be 'a haven of rest for old people, chronic invalids and the like'.[67]

Fordfield, in a sense unanticipated by Aelfrida, therefore remains both the nucleus of a much larger institution and the kind of 'retreat-house blessed with the glory of the sacramental presence'[68] she hoped it might become. But enough of Henry Joseph Wetenhall's house exists to enable a visitor to recognise his and his daughter's initials entwined in stained glass panels bordered by hops and his own over a doorway and '1869' surrounded by curlicues on a stone plaque to remind us of the departure (in his own eyes at least) of *arriviste* 'Henry J Wetenhall of Fordfield, Cambridge' (as his tombstone proudly proclaims) from 'trade'; rooms known to and used by Aelfrida are also recognisable, though PEACE, already altered by the Fordhams, has undergone further changes since. The garden, too, though diminished in size, bears traces of lawns, trees, shrubbery, and the Italianate 'panel garden', the latter now graced by a statue of the Virgin. (Presbyterian Alfred Tillyard, distrusting a religion which "[made] a man, and still more a woman, mistake sentiment for piety"[69] and a church he described as a "collection of wilful heretics"[70], must be spinning in his grave at the thought a Catholic organisation inhabiting his former home.) The 'gardens-at-the-back' along whose high-hedged paths Miss Tillyard strolled 'with how many men whose names I can now hardly recall'[71] are no more, they and 'Mount Olympus' reverting in the 1950s to Botanic Garden use.

Of members of Aelfrida's immediate and extended family it has been possible to acquire sufficient information to allow us to learn what happened to them after her death, to flesh out the sometimes inadequate and often biased picture she provided of them, and even in one instance to complete an 'unwritten' episode: "the silence speaks. When all are dead at last / How full of voices will those regions be".[72]

Of the two remaining Tillyard siblings, Eustace died first. Aelfrida had hoped that her younger brother would live long after retirement 'to write more books and inhabit [his] new house'[73] but his sudden death on 24 May 1962 left little time for either. Julius described him as "the most successful and best known of us three"[74] (Aelfrida, visited shortly after her arrival at St John's Home by the local vicar, commented grumpily when he, a Cambridge graduate, failed to recognise her maiden name, 'so much for the fame of this family')[75], Tom Henn as "a brilliant teacher ... with a love of all great literature which he invariably managed to communicate"[76], and his college obituary (quoting *The Times*) "as a man ... at once frank and reserved, simple and subtle [with a] capacity for good companionship and true friendship" and, on its own account, "the leading Miltonist of the day".[77] His sister's accounts of his teaching style and scholarship had been more measured ('his manner is only fair for he hesitates and looks worried [but] what he said was excellent'[78]; of his 'great work on MILTON', she noted that it was 'very scholarly but a little lacking in *vitality*')[79] but of his personality she wrote warmly, describing him as 'sweet natured', without equal 'for *breadth of sympathy and balance of judgement*', and (at sixty-six) as 'maturing wonderfully as he grows older'.[80] (Concerning Phyllis, who died in 1971, she was less charitable. Was this because she was tacitly jealous of Phyllis' 'comradeship' with Eustace[81] before marriage and contribution to his successful career thereafter[82] or because a woman of whom her first impression was that she was 'gentle and malleable', i.e. could be bullied, turned out 'so different'[83], i.e. could not? She also played down Phyllis' war service with the Red Cross and First Aid Nursing Yeomanry in France and Salonika as her 'VAD days'[84] but the outstanding record of the 'FANYs' between 1914 and 1918 shows that Phyllis demonstrated more than merely 'pluck'.)[85] Julius continued to write on 'Byz. Mus.' until two years prior to his death (Julius, wrote Florence Keynes in 1954, "must know more about Byzantine Music than anyone else in the world")[86] and was accorded credit by the other two "scholars who, each working on [their] own lines, learned to read the cypher of the old Byzantine neumes [which] the Eastern Church had forgotten"[87] but following a tribute published shortly after his death describing him as the "Patriarch of Byzantine Studies", his fame declined at the expense of that of Egon Wellesz, a better publicist and an established musician.[88]

Writing on Julius' seventy-first birthday in November 1952 and having seen his face filled with 'the first gleams of Heaven'[89] shortly before his seventieth, Aelfrida wrongly predicted that her elder brother '[had] not many years to live'.[90] She was, correct, however, when she noted that 'the eldest do not always die first'[91], for Julius lived until 2 January 1968. He did not die at Wetenhall Cottage. His prophecy that 'Mina will want to be near Constance' wherever Constance lived ('isn't it a pity to hang on to other people's lives?'[92] was Aelfrida's response, she having leant by experience that it was) came true in 1966/67 when the decision was taken for Julius and Mina, aged seventy-five and sixty-nine respectively, to move to Saffron Walden where John and Constance Hibbs now lived. Henry Julius Wetenhall Tillyard therefore abandoned the property bought a century earlier by

the grandfather whose name and initials he partly bore in favour of a house shared with his adopted daughter and her family. Aelfrida's prayer that God spare Julius 'pain and helplessness at the end'[93] seems to have been answered; absolved of responsibility now that his wife's future care was assured, Julius relinquished the life he had never particularly valued and was buried in the same plot as his beloved sister. (Given that there is no record in the Burial Register of Histon Road Cemetery of the deposition of Aelfrida's ashes, can it be that Julius kept those not sprinkled elsewhere so that they might be interred with his own remains in a *connubium* or marriage-in-death never achieved in life?) Following his death, Mina settled down happily with her Hibbs grandchildren until her own death on 22 September 1976.

Wetenhall Cottage's freehold passed to the Sisters of Hope. (An overmantel mirror from 'ex-Fordfield' was given to Girton College by Alethea in 1967; the carved head surmounting its elaborately gilded and stuccoed frame reminds us why Aelfrida felt the Fordfield furniture watching her and did her 'Flirting' in the garden.) Aelfrida's belief that the cottage as 'a *Christian* house' should pass to 'the most Christian'[94] among contenders for ownership became fact. Thereafter The Cottage, as the Sisters called it (street directories labelled it '15 Brooklands Avenue') housed visitors unqualified for admission to the conventual wing erected in 1964/65 on the site of Fordfield Cottage and its ancillary buildings. In 1989 the Sisters moved into a smaller custom-built convent in the grounds of Wetenhall Cottage then, as numbers dwindled, into Wetenhall Cottage itself. Serendipitously, therefore, Wetenhall Cottage achieved two of Aelfrida's hopes for it, the first, written in 1955 regarding its use while Julius and Mina were on an extended visit to Germany ('the *Sisters* are sleeping at Wetenhall Cottage', its absentee owner expressing herself 'so pleased'[95] at the thought of her house being put to conventual use, even if temporarily), the second, that the Cottage, still haunted in her mind by 'sadness as well as love'[96], should continue to possess 'its own soul, part of the Fordfield soul [but] humbler and gentler'. And perhaps her ghost 'circumambulate[s] the cottage at nightfall' as she, living, might have done had not increasing physical frailty rendered her 'so exhausted and swimmy in the head'[97] that she could not have succeeded even had she tried?

'Uncle Sir Frank' Tillyard, eighteen years older than his niece, survived both herself and her gloomy prognostications ('I think the summons must come to him soon', written in 1949)[98] and wishes ('I hope God will call him home as soon as possible', written on the occasion of his wife's death in 1952)[99] to die on 10 July 1961 three years short of his centenary. Aelfrida had never found him particularly congenial but was prepared to concede that he was 'good through and through'.[100] (His elder daughter, Kathleen Perfect, the cousin with whom Aelfrida shared feelings of 'Tillyardness', died in 1989.) Pattie Tillyard, entomologist Robert/Robin Tillyard's widow, had been a teacher and suffragist until her marriage and emigration to Australia in 1909; she died in 1971 after a life of social service there and in New Zealand. Antipodean accounts describe her as "a striking figure on her old fashioned Cambridge bicycle".[101] Ruth Connolly née Warren, moved with her family to a part of Cambridge rarely visited by Aelfrida, Chesterton being an *ultima Thule* so far beyond the Tillyard pale as not to be 'known') and became a pillar of local Nonconformism.

Then, an unwritten episode: Anatolia. Following her brief correspondence with Anatolia's grandson Michael Hillerns in 1942, Aelfrida may have persuaded herself that she had 'found' her mother-in-law again ('my heart sings and sings – and all the angels of the elect sing too')[102] but from 1944 comments concerning the Allies' landing near Antibes and her foiled desire to teach Anatolia what '*caritas* is'[103] by offering practical and financial help, we may deduce otherwise. (Nor, of course, do we know if her hope of meeting Anatolia 'glorified in Heaven' was fulfilled.) In 1953, however, a chance contact with a former pupil of Julius' allowed her to 'find' Helen Michaelides, now married and living in Michigan. To Helen, 'my sister-in-law … who gives lessons in French'[104], last seen in Arlington Heights half a century ago, Aelfrida duly wrote ('dear guardian angel, make friends with hers and see that she sends me the … answer I long for!')[105], noting that although it had been beneficial for her own daughters that the Michaelides 'dropped us after the divorce' (*sic*), she herself had continued to '*love* Constantine's people' ('it is Our Lord in me, loving them') and to 'long to renew friendship with them'.[106] She says no more but we may deduce that Helen replied from a passage in *Naomi da Costa* describing the death from "pleurisy and pneumonia" of a 'Mrs Buckingham', step grandmother to 'Raphael da Costa', who is Anatolia to the life. ("A volume of short stories about the Greek islands by Argyris Ephthaliotes"[107] figures in the same novel.) In fact, as we learn from Anatolia's death certificate, issued in Antibes on 18 December 1944 as of Elizabeth Graham (French death certificates bear a married woman's maiden name), she died at the Hillerns' *Villa Arcadia* on 16 December 1944 (her own villa, *La Farandole*, with its classical Greek detailing, still stands nearby), joining her late husband ('CC Michaelides' on his tombstone) in Antibes' *Cimetière de Rabac*.

Aelfrida's diary silence on the subject is odd given her keenness to demonstrate *caritas* and to place herself firmly on the high moral ground vis-à-vis her former mother-in-law; the answer may lie in the sentence which concludes her description of 'Mrs Buckingham': "fortunately she is now in her grave".[108] Can it be that Helen Michaelides not only provided the information she requested but also berated her over her behaviour towards Constantine: her flirtations with Little Friends, her possible liaison with Eric Silvanus; her domestic incompetence; her refusal to allow his daughters to visit their paternal grandparents; possibly even Aelfrida's sexually-charged behaviour towards herself while engaged to her brother – and if Helen informed her mother of this, how much more ammunition it would have given a woman already incensed by the entrapment by the Tillyards of her son, the only remotely presentable young man willing to marry their far from 'normal' daughter? Hence, perhaps, Aelfrida's decision to destroy Helen's letter without informing her diary and biographer of its contents and to omit further mention of *any* of Constantine's 'people' from her diary until shortly before her death.

When Alethea left the Maritzburg convent in 1942 her mother asked anxiously 'what will become of her if I die?'[109] What follows tells what did.

Aelfrida's prediction that her 'removal' would 'let in light and air' to the souls of her nearest and dearest seems to have come true in the case of her surviving daughter who, following a Cowley Father's advice to regard her mother's death less as a loss and more as "a call to adjust to new ways"[110], did so with such confidence and equanimity that she fulfilled another of Aelfrida's predictions: 'Alethea will soon rejoice in having a mother in heaven'.[111] She also became comparatively well-off, for Aelfrida's parsimony with regard to herself (with the exception of her 'Universal Aunt' period or, more correctly, when universally 'aunting' for Agatha and Alethea) ensured that Alethea's later years were spent in enjoyment of an inherited 'small fortune'.[112]

Monies inherited after deduction of bequests allowed Alethea to buy a car (one of the newly-invented Minis), a cottage in the village of Old Headington on the outskirts of Oxford, and, once settled in a 'stable home' of her own (a real home, not the 'semblance' endured since her mother relinquished Wetenhall Cottage and rendered both women effectively homeless) in which she enjoyed 'living alone in a university town'[113], two Burmese cats: Benson and Bingley. There she remained, a tall, spare, elegant, warm, but slightly detached person, much loved by her immediate and extended family, a woman whose "talent for languages [and] love of all fine arts … made her delightful company – though for life she preferred her own".[114]

Indeed she did. Sworn to perpetual virginity, Alethea never married and in earnest of her vow to the Deity whose 'bride' she had once been and always in a sense remained, gave the thirty yards of handmade silk sent to her at her baptism to Malling to be transformed into a set of vestments. Settling for wistfulness instead of fulfilment insofar as she never reached the spiritual heights 'she once sought to scale' as a professed nun, she opted instead for 'humility, simplicity [and] wholehearted devotion to Our Lord'[115], to enjoy "deeper intimacies with God"[116], to practise a "recondite but profound Anglo-Catholicism"[117], and to become if not the mystic her mother believed she would never be[118] (and that Alethea herself feared she would never be, writing of a mother and sister "dove-tailed into each other" that singly and together Agatha and Aelfrida had a gift that would never be bestowed on her: "they understand God. God, face to face")[119], at least a deeply religious woman living almost as ascetic a life as her mother and undergoing some near-identical spiritual experiences.

In one important respect, however, Alethea's spiritual life differed from her mother's. Giving the lie to Aelfrida's belief that her elder daughter was not 'pious enough or sufficiently interested in putting the world to rights'[120] and that 'the idea of dedicating herself and her life to God and her fellow men' had never entered Alethea's head[121] (and with her mother's idiosyncratic manner of practising what she preached as a dreadful and overpoweringly present example, what else could Alethea have done?), Alethea set out to lead a life of exemplary and unforced *caritas*. (Perhaps like her mother and maternal grandmother, she disguised insecurities and a sense of never being able to satisfy her own and other people's expectations by subduing her emotional and intellectual – but not spiritual – needs in favour of seeking fulfilment in looking after those committed in various ways to her care.)[122] Though distantly caring during Aelfrida's stay at St John's Home (if unable to visit, she prevailed on a nurse friend to check on her mother's welfare), it seems doubtful that she 'took energy … from her very sorrow … to do her work, showing her love for [her dead mother] by her noble carriage and strength'[123] for, being Alethea, she would have done it anyway, and it is obvious that she found living near Aelfrida a great strain and was glad when her burden was lifted. But Aelfrida's 1942 prediction that Alethea 'surely has a "mixed" vocation for she seems to make prayer and activity the [warp] and woof of the day's fabric'[124] came true after her mother's death when Alethea undertook private coaching in French ('[she] gets on admirably with the younger generation')[125], conducted oral examinations and marked examination papers in French and Italian for the Oxford Local Examination Board, and tutored prisoners in Oxford Prison. She also wrote for periodicals and journals and was responsible for translations included in the Phaidon *Encyclopaedia of Impressionism*, published in 1978. As she always said, "don't worry about me. When I want a job I'll find one".[126]

Another of Aelfrida's prophesies – that Alethea (unlike Agatha who was so good that she could easily die young like her uncle Conrad) *needed* 'to live longer – much longer'[127] in order to fulfil her potential – also came true, for Alethea survived her mother by over twenty years. God did not, unfortunately, answer her mother's prayer that when He took her, He would grant Alethea a 'sudden death'[128] or fulfil her hope that He would call her elder daughter home 'by some easier way than He called Agatha'[129] i.e. that she be killed in a road accident rather than endure 'some more horrible death later'[130]: Alethea died a lingering death from upper abdominal cancer in an Oxford hospice on 17 June 1980. She did not join the rest of her family in the Cambridge vault: her ashes were scattered beyond the daffodil beds at Oxford Crematorium. In her will she left £100 to the Cowley Fathers. (Her diaries were not, as she had once hoped, interred with her by those 'finding [them] after I am dead'[131] but, preserved by her family, were united with her mother's and sisters' diaries and literary remains in Girton College archive in April 2009 and at intervals thereafter as more material was uncovered.) Two years prior to her own death, Aelfrida wrote Alethea's epitaph: 'she is sound and wholesome in "natural" and spiritual beauty. She never parades her intelligence and is gay and simple and greatly beloved'.[132]

The coincidences between Aelfrida's life and the lives of those 'splendid young people'[133] her nephews and nieces are several and striking: all became fluent in languages other than their own; most became teachers by design or default; all save one married foreigners; one divorced. Of her great-nephews and nieces, of whom several were unborn at the time of her death (it was surely with them as well as those already born in mind that their great-aunt wrote in 1955 'perhaps [they] will be in the fashion and all live to be centenarians!' Or, she added gloomily, 'the end of the world may have come')[134], one became a writer of biographies of considerably greater merit than Aelfrida's of Agnes Slack. And at a gathering which included three generations of Aelfrida's collateral descendants it was possible to discern an elderly Chiara, a middle-aged Eustace, an adolescent Alethea, a childish Agatha, and two adult Aelfridas, a genetic frisson not often accorded a biographer.

Of Aelfrida's few surviving original or marginal Little Friends (Little Friends' children also pursued

**The Hope Nursing Home, formerly Fordfield, 2003**

careers amusingly relevant to a woman who had dealt so kindly with their fathers, becoming an economist, a diplomat, a Cambridge physician, and an author), Tommy Altounyan's promise to 'make a start' on preparing Fidelio's *journal intime* for publication[135] seems to have been broken: 'Dr Altounyan', though Aelfrida's junior by six years, survived her by only three, dying in 1962. John Layard, Aelfrida's junior by eight years, died at eighty-three in the place to which she herself had feared to be consigned, Cowley Road geriatric hospital; following treatment by and collaboration with Carl Jung (numbered among Aelfrida's 'New Psychologists') in the 1930s, Layard married and, after re-engaging briefly with anthropology, became a Jungian analyst with post-war practices in London and Oxford.[136] (There is no evidence that he and Aelfrida met in Oxford, but what interesting conversations might have ensued if they had.) Tom Henn also died in 1974; a brigadier during the Second World War, he was later Professor of English at Cambridge and a well-known literary critic specialising in Anglo-Irish literature.[137] (His brother William 'Billy' Henn, the blue-eyed 'Irish Poet' became, prosaically, Chief Constable of Gloucestershire.)[138] Aelfrida's 'old friend the Anteater', later Bishop Barkway, died in 1968; perhaps, as she suspected, if she had been 'a bit more sober in [her] demeonour'[139] (*sic*) he might have proposed to her for he had been much in love with her until supplanted (as he thought) by John Forbes Cameron.

Of younger friends, two survived her. Anthony Wrightson, once deemed 'Oh! So delicate!' by the woman to whom he briefly restored her lost youth and her faith in herself as a woman ('what I have had no one can take away while I have life and memory')[140] that only 'Swedish gym and psychotherapy' would cure his 'nervousness' and by her mother as '*far* too delicate to marry and have children', confounded both ladies' predictions

during his lifetime and the latter's belief that 'he won't live very long'[141]: like Tom Henn and John Layard he died in 1974. Juan Mascaró, philosopher, linguist, and 'mystical young man from the Balearic Isles'[142], died in Comberton in his ninetieth year in 1987; a poem provides an excellent summary of his own life and that of his '*amie espiritual*': "Traveller, your footsteps / Are the path, and nothing else; / Traveller, there is no path. / You make the path as you walk".[143]

Not only nuns survived one whose life they touched with greater or lesser significance. Lucy Verey, Aelfrida's "best and oldest friend"[144] to whom she paid tribute in her diary, in a novel (in *O Passionate World*, Lucy is 'Daphne', 'Carola's' loving and supportive friend; 'Daphne's' husband 'Geoffrey' is Hal Verey), and in *The Glory of the West*, survived Aelfrida by nine years, dying in 1968, the same year as her husband of over sixty years. (Hearing in Odessa of Lucy's marriage, Aelfrida had hoped that Lucy and 'her "Hal" … [would] be very happy together'.)[145] Aelfrida's comments regarding Lucy are never bitchy and rarely less than glowing and it is nice to think that in the course of her troubled life she had a female friend who remained 'true and loyal' to her and towards whom she felt bound to be faithful: 'I could never put anyone else in Lucy's place'.[146]

Hilda Sollas, the 'Italian student of marine biology' who turned a gleaming blue-grey gaze "so full of love" on Constantine but a wounding "slate and silver"[147] glare on his wife, died unmarried at ninety-three in 1970. If Aelfrida's relationship with Eric Silvanus was revenge for Constantine's with his Christian Scientist 'Minerva of the grey eyes' who knew not "pain … nor hateful lust / Nor motherhood"[148], much evidence may be deduced to support the surmise.

Knowing that Aelfrida composed *Minerva of the Grey Eyes* on 25 January 1909 and remembering acidic comments made by her in 1910 regarding the furore which accompanied Constantine's discovery in *To Malise* of poems referring to his Newnhamite 'little friend', it is instructive to turn to diary entries made shortly before and after the date of the couplet's composition. On 20 January Aelfrida notes that although baby Alethea 'has never been naughty', she herself has been 'stupid'.[149] On 15 February she notes of Gian Falco's marriage that 'he has not even the spirit left to be proud of his defeat' and replies to his letter with the phrase 'I understand'.[150] Five days later she admits that her mind is both 'much enduring' and – to her disgust – preoccupied with 'subjects' other than those occasioned by on-going 'Servant Questions'.[151] Early in March, having hinted that perhaps she expected too much of Constantine as a new father ('ought I to feel sad when he wheels the baby-carriage?')

and that she herself has been so absorbed in 'tending'[152] Alethea that she has neglected him, she is galvanised into action[153]: she starts weaning Alethea, greets Constantine on his daily return from Boston by dressing the dinner table and wearing a pretty frock, and begins to pay local and distant calls again. Can it be that at Christmastide 1908 Aelfrida taxed Constantine with or uncovered evidence of infidelity with Hilda Sollas ("*I know the Truth*") and that she composed *Minerva of the Grey Eyes* as a sequel to her earlier 'Sollas' poem and as a warning to Constantine and Hilda that she was aware of their (real or supposed) liaison? And if an aspect of her 'stupid' behaviour was to tax Constantine with her discovery and discover that, as in so many other aspects of her life, *her* 'Truth' was not *the* truth, or that what she uncovered and pretended was untrue *was* 'the Truth', how singularly appropriate to find her admitting in 1910 that publication of two poems about Hilda Sollas had been the action of a 'mild … fool' and that she would have done better to remain silent. But what better revenge could she take if revenge was appropriate[154] than to include a poem about Epping/Eric Forest/Silvanus (who appears in *Marrying a Stranger* under the ironic or accurate name of 'Victor' and who, though Aelfrida omits to say so, predeceased her, dying in Sussex in 1958) in the same volume as her 'Hilda Sollas' poems?

Of the physicians and surgeons who treated Aelfrida during her lifetime of real and imagined illnesses, two fell in love with her: William Bowen and Joan Cooper. Both survived her, the former dying in 1963, the latter as a very old lady over thirty years later. (She had hoped to see the year 2000 for then she, born in 1892, would then have lived in three centuries.) Joan Cooper's long life was predicted by Alethea in the 'Medical Number' of the *MCJ* of February 1932 in which she joked of the "gentle-eyed doctor named Joan" that there seemed to be a link between "rufo-capilliarity and longevity". She was correct: that red-haired lady did indeed "have the longest expectation of life"[155]; only sixteen years older than Alethea, Joan Cooper survived her by nearly twenty years, dying on 1 February 1999 at the age of a hundred and six.

We do not know the date of Aelfrida's last meeting with the woman with regard to whom she once castigated herself 'for … not loving Sarah-Joan in a perfectly balanced manner' but hoped that it might be possible in the future to love her 'for her own sake and not for my own gratification'.[156] They certainly met in 1957, Aelfrida recording in July that Joan Cooper was shortly to retire from anaesthesiology and that she herself, knowing Dr Cooper's interest in 'Old Age'[157], had suggested that 'Dr Joan' turn to a study of gerontology, but her

diary does not refer to a further meeting during her visits to Cambridge in 1958 and by the time of her probable visit in 1959 she no longer kept it. ('Such a sweet letter from Joan Cooper'[158] received in January 1959 shows the two ladies continued to correspond.) 'Dr Joan', however, had already developed an interest in 'Old Age'; in 1948 she was a founder of what Aelfrida, visiting dead Lilian Whitehouse's elder sister Enid there in 1957, described as 'a charming Home for old ladies [in] an old-fashioned, spacious, and extremely comfortable house … standing in a big garden on the Trumpington Road'.[159] It was also to this house, Meadowcroft, that Joan Cooper, one of the elderly people of the professional classes for whom the Home was designed, retired in 1983, residing there until news of the Home's impending closure hastened her death. To spare the undertakers the weight of her body and coffin, she arranged to be cremated prior to her funeral service, appearing at that ceremony as ashes in an urn.[160] The secret of her real name died with her.

Aelfrida's eulogy (and, now, epitaph) of 'Sarah-Joan' had been published sixty years earlier. Just as Mother Magdalen Mary OSB was her "saint of the Contemplative Life", so Joan Cooper was her "dear saint of the Active Life", and of her 'saint' she painted a portrait by means of "an enumeration of [her] qualities": "tireless devotion to duty; never-failing sympathy and help; … affection given where mere professional benevolence would … have been enough; an affection very restrained and unemotional showing itself above all in deeds; … a zest for life; … a fundamental humility and diffidence, a little difficult perhaps, to discern behind the brave exterior". And apart from her "zest for life", how unlike her eulogist's. Two things, however, doctor and patient shared: both deserted the religion of their birth, Joan Cooper for the Society of Friends, Aelfrida for Anglo-Catholicism, and both placed "direct reliance on God and on His strength".[161]

Helen Megaw had been a faithful friend to both Alethea and Aelfrida since the latter universally aunted so many gifted or notorious Cambridge students (besides Helen's, signatures in her Visitors Book include spy/defector Donald Maclean, nuclear physicists Frank Oppenheimer and Peter Kapitsa, artist Julian Trevelyan, and actor Michael Redgrave, Trevelyan giving his – eminently plausible – address as 'Mont Parnasse', Redgrave implausibly as 'Kamschatka') and was enormously supportive in the dark days following Agatha's suicide and Alethea's post-Malling breakdown. She and Alethea continued to correspond thereafter but, judging by the tone of the latter's rare postcards, met infrequently or not at all while Aelfrida was still alive.[162] Helen died at ninety-five in 2002, leaving a lasting and unusual memorial: in recognition of the value of her work in X-ray crystallography to their own endeavours, the Glaciological Society named an Antarctic island after her. It lies, appropriately, off the coast of Graham Land.

A visit to Histon Road Cemetery undertaken on 15 December 2009, the fiftieth anniversary of Aelfrida's death, proved both cheering and encouraging because it marked the beginning of the end of a biographical journey begun light-heartedly and unsuspectingly six years earlier, and sombre and sobering because of what had been learnt (more, possibly, than ought to have discovered) of Aelfrida herself and of the dysfunctional family to which she belonged. (As with other Victorian cemeteries, the class system operates here too; the Barrett/Wetenhall tomb borders a path close to where a mortuary chapel once stood at the crossroads of two. An earlier Wetenhall grave occupies an inferior position near the perimeter.) The ensemble of central and subsidiary monuments within the low granite kerb which demarcates the boundary of the plot reveals nothing of the complex inter-relationships of those whose lives they commemorate but unwittingly echoes the relationship of a particular person to those with whom he or she shares the cluster of incised or inlaid memorials.

The inscription on the east side of the central urn-capped monument proudly proclaims self-made man and 'dear grandpapa', HENRY J. WETENHALL *of Fordfield, Cambridge* born 21 March 1816, died 20 August 1882. Below his name appears that of EMMA his wife ('Dear', to Aelfrida) born 15 March 1820, died 30 November 1897. Below Henry and Emma are commemorated Aelfrida's parents, ALFRED ISAAC TILLYARD, born 1852, died 1929, and CATHARINE SARAH his wife, daughter of HENRY and EMMA WETENHALL, born 1852 died 1932. The monument's west side bears the name of Emma Wetenhall's mother CATHARINE MARY BARRETT (née Castle) who died on Christmas Day 25 December 1845 aged sixty-three and whose (ungiven) date of birth takes us back into the eighteenth century. Below Catharine Mary we find EUSTACE MANDEVILLE WETENHALL TILLYARD son of ALFRED AND CATHARINE TILLYARD; after his grandiloquent string of names comes his title: Master of Jesus College 1945–1959. Eustace's lengthy inscription (it includes his dates of birth and death, 19 May 1889 and 24 May 1962) forces that of his wife PHYLLIS BEATRICE TILLYARD (14 November 1887 to 28 September 1971) onto another but attached plaque. On the north side of the monument, below the inscription commemorating his maternal great-grandfather ('GEORGE BARRETT, died 19 December 1855 aged 73, a man we discover to have been a decade younger than his wife) is the memorial to HENRY JULIUS WETENHALL TILLYARD

(18 November 1881 to 2 January 1968) but the space left beneath his name for that of his wife is empty; Wilhelmina Kaufmann is commemorated by a small separate stone tablet nearby which says simply MINA TILLYARD 22 August 1887–22 September 1976. The south side of the monument commemorates GEORGE son of GEORGE and CATHARINE MARY BARRETT, 'Dear's' brother who died at thirty-four on 25 November 1847 and, below him, his great-niece AELFRIDA CATHARINE WETENHALL GRAHAM daughter of ALFRED and CATHARINE TILLYARD. Born 5 October 1883, died 15 December 1959.

But what of Constantine and Agatha? We know his ashes and her body were buried in the vault and that Aelfrida had an oak cross erected in their memory; we also know the words of the bronze inscription it bore. Nothing now remains. There is, however, an empty space in front of the main memorial (the empty area in front of Aelfrida's inscription presumably conceals access to the vault) and it may have been there that the memorial to AELFRIDA CATHARINE AGATHA GRAHAM, born 12 July 1910, died 23 February 1935, and to her father CONSTANTINE GRAHAM (MICHAELIDES), was to be found. And what of AGNETA GRAHAM, Agatha's sister and the 'brat' her father accused her mother of 'spawning'? "Child of Graham" (as the cemetery's Burial Register has it) was buried in an unmarked grave in the SE quarter of the cemetery on 29 May 1912 among 1500 stillborn babies or infants who died before their first birthday.

And Conrad Francis, what of him? Conrad's separate memorial stands a short distance from Julius' inscription. (Mina's tablet lies closer to Conrad's memorial than to her husband's.) A small truncated stone pyramid tapering on two sides into miniature acroteria, it once bore a stone cross too large in scale for its base and too portentous in its symbolism for the little boy it commemorated. The memorial has been vandalised; the pyramid with its near-illegible inscription remains intact (only the words 'sleep' and 'Conrad' can be deciphered; it once read "here sleeps our darling Conrad") but the cross which stretched its "cold grey arms"[163] to guard his rest lies in pieces, propped against the plaque bearing his elder brother's name.

"We are all gravestones now", wrote Conrad's sister a quarter of a century after his death but, addressing the stones themselves, she promised that though presently recumbent and inanimate, they would eventually "ARISE AGAIN" to evoke the dead into "some semblance of life"[164] as those they commemorate in Histon Road cemetery have been evoked in the pages of this book. It is, therefore, to one of those 'gravestones' to whom we must now turn, though that particular 'stone' is not Aelfrida but Conrad, Conrad who, though physically dead, continued as an undead 'spook' to blight the lives of his surviving siblings. (Being born later, Eustace escaped but although the 'good harvest' healed some of Catharine Tillyard's wounds, reverberations haunted him too.) But one particular way in which he blighted them remains to be discussed.

'Roy Hadstock', hero of *The Way We Grow Up*, decides to write a novel after leaving university. The novel will not be (as one might say of Aelfrida's diaries and literary remains) a "painstaking ... treatise on child-psychology" as his friends jokingly suggest but, following "a good look at life", the story of a Suffolk Nonconformist minister's family "engaged in the most gorgeous fight against the most adverse circumstances".[165] In search of 'copy', 'Roy' embeds himself in the family and prepares to keep "a very full and indiscreet journal of everything he saw" until the projected novel's plot "should suddenly emerge from the mobile chaos of his mind".[166] One of the first items he sees in the room allotted to him is a "large embroidered MIZPAH"[167] strategically sited over the chimneypiece – and it is just such a *Mizpah* which will lead us back and back into Aelfrida's past.

In Old Testament terms, *Mizpah* is the name given to a pillar of stones. The pillar may be used practically as a watchtower, boundary marker, or beacon, or symbolically as a 'heap of witness' to a particular event e.g. the establishment of a covenant between two or more people.[168] In the context of Histon Road Cemetery, Conrad's "small marble monument" whose inscription "cut ... quite clear and sharp" commemorates a three-year-old boy whose mother might be "too sad to go on living unless, of course, she had other children"[169], becomes just such a 'heap'. Aelfrida's 'memory picture' describing her dead younger brother (it is headed like a tombstone "Conrad Francis. Born 6 October 1885. Died 24 June 1888")[170], may also be 'read' as a literary 'heap of witness' which will lead us 'back and back' into her 'psychological childhood', a curious expression implying, perhaps, not her childhood as a whole but a 'psychological' moment of it, namely Conrad's death. A moment at which enclosures concealing a secret, ruins which have once been camps or shrines, red-berried trees, ancient quarries, and haunted or 'runic' stones play an important part.

To reread Aelfrida's account in *The Centaur* of the "ancient stones" among which 'Clive Farwell' wanders "back and back" into a dim era of his "primitive past" is to discover that it is not, perhaps, a Monmouthshire hillside she has in mind but a 'City of the Dead' nearer home: Cambridge's Histon Road Cemetery as seen through the eyes of a child taken to visit her little brother's *Mizpah*

installed above one of the largest brick vaults dug there (a 'vasty hall of death', indeed) in a cemetery whose marble crosses and erect or recumbent tombstones seem almost alive and the dead they represent 'evoked' to strange semblance of life. A cemetery, full of hollies and yews, situated on a hill above Victorian Cambridge on ground scarred by clay and gravel pits, demarcated by Norman and Cromwellian earthworks, and bearing an iron works and a mill and the ruins of Cambridge Castle or 'House of Defence', now in part a prison. A cemetery not far from the northern walls of Roman *Camboritum* whose boundaries appear on contemporary maps and whose ancient inhabitants (as early Ordnance Survey maps note) are interred in 'stone coffins ... poteries (*sic*) etc.' along roads traversed by 'Little Frida' herself. A cemetery among whose "ancient stones ... not really set out for ... inspection [but] muddled up in a fascinating array of puzzles", Frida wanders among her Barrett, Wetenhall, and Warren ancestors, absorbing from their monuments "memories of ... previous existence[s]" and "fragmentary pictures of age-old happenings" and feeling "drawn to turn aside [to one] assemblage after another" as she listens to "the wordless call of the stones". (Not quite wordless: in *Spiritual Exercises*, Aelfrida quotes the verse of a hymn inscribed on the Wetenhall tombstone elsewhere in the cemetery.)[171] Returning to her parents at the family grave-plot, she finds a "shrine" tended by "primitive men" at which she too is expected to worship and senses beneath it the "pit fortress" ('I had forgotten', she wrote apropos 'Aunt Laura's', 'that graves were so deep') in which Conrad's tiny coffin lies together with those of certain "Old Gods" (at that point in time, two George Barretts, Catharine Mary Barrett, and Henry Joseph Wetenhall) who, as the stones themselves assert, "are not dead, they are but biding their time".[172]

The revised version of the novel from which these sentences are taken reduces the part played by 'ancient stones' in 'Clive Farwell's' life but introduces another element at greater length. 'Clive', accidentally locked in a cellar (formerly a crypt; the building was once a religious foundation) on the "experimental farm" on which he has been working (a possible euphemism for the 'madhouse' to which the abbot suspects he had been temporarily consigned), is visited by a "Discarnate Personality" (as *Rich Man's Choice* makes clear, a periphrastic appellation given to the devil) who tells him that he is preparing a throne for him as an aspect of a "new world order". In the same breath he reminds 'Clive' that if he accepts the throne he will be imprisoned on it and unable to leave. To demonstrate his power – and the power that 'Clive' too will wield should he accept – the 'Discarnate Personality' summons up hellish "legions" trained by himself from "prehistoric times" to perform "whatever their leader willed" in a "display of power" made "in supreme scorn of human confusion" and from which "no man's prayer [can] turn them". The 'legions' duly arrive, "dark armies … cold, soundless, invisible … in perfect accord … up from the depths"[173] – and we realise that one of the 'old gods' who bides his time and the 'Discarnate Personality' whose power over 'Clive' is diabolic *but escapable* ('Clive' refuses his offer and frees himself from the cellar) are one and the same, namely Conrad. Conrad, the 'spook' which periodically seizes upon his sister and (as with a shaman) inhabits her and speaks and acts through her as a representative of the 'dark armies' which dwell in the depths of her personality. Conrad, the 'spook' who inhabits not one but *three* 'borderlands': his 'pit-fortress' below ground, his 'shrine' above ground at the central crossroads of the place of 'stones' where he is interred, and, as a 'discarnate personality' subtly and silently sabotaging Aelfrida's "present-day … nature"[174], his sister's mind. Conrad, the 'spook' from whom his sister struggles to 'detach' herself, crying 'no human affections' when what she really means is 'no inhuman effection'. And how that sister must have wished that she, like the anonymous Lolworth labourer quoted in *Christian Old Age,* believed that what came after death was "six feet of earth and nothing else".[175]

The 'Clive' of *The Centaur*, though briefly imprisoned in a "pit-fortress" at whose centre stands a pyramidal "altar of sacrifice" on which – as he suddenly remembers – he had found himself a prisoner "bound and gagged" in a "previous incarnation", escapes from "the beastly haunted pit" into "clean sunny air and freedom"[176]; the 'Clive' of *Rich Man's Choice* refuses the 'Discarnate Personality's' offer and ingeniously escapes from the crypt-cellar in which he had been briefly confined; Aelfrida, alas, and even with Julius' help, did neither (though she believed she had), for childhood experiences at the time of Conrad's death had left her "no longer master"[177] of herself and in the 'mobile chaos' of the crypt-cellar of a traumatic childhood experience she remained. And not even the 'scarlet thread' of religion which provided a life-line in times of spiritual turmoil provided sufficient 'clue' to lead her from the mental labyrinth in which lurked her fraternal 'spook'.

Aelfrida's use of the term 'psychological' to describe her childhood may, however, have connotations over and above those already noted, 'psychological' in another sense implying that a ground on which a particular person orders one or more aspects of their life (or a ground by which they feel it to be ordered) may exist only as a 'psychical' reality with little basis in fact. Conrad's death cannot, of course, be regarded as 'psychological' in this sense – it was, as his tombstone and an entry in the family

Bible would attest to a questing child, a fact, not an 'event' imagined by a highly intelligent little girl with a vivid imagination – but what she *may* have imagined, a notion which other peoples' reactions may have unwittingly (or, horrible thought, intentionally) corroborated was that Conrad died *because she had wished him dead.*

Was *this* the sin which adult Aelfrida could never bring herself to confess when she repeated ad nauseam to her current confessor a long list of sins major and minor guaranteed to scapegoat her in her own and her confessor's eyes? Was *this* the sin which little Frida believed she had committed, which lurked beneath the amorphous burden of guilt under which she laboured ("did you kill it, or did you only think you did?" Jacinth/Aelfrida asks Frederic Ellicott/Aelfrida of the "very small slight [boy], certainly not of school age" whom he has run over, a question unanswered until Julius embarked on his 'talking cure' but "I am a murderer", cries Aelfrida/Frederic Ellicott a few pages later)[178], and of which as an adolescent she felt the weight so acutely that she crouched weeping on the floor of the night nursery floor where Conrad died? Jealous of being supplanted in her mother's affections by a child so different in looks, character, and sex to herself and to whose living (*and posthumous*) perfection she could never live up, she had wished him dead – *and in that nursery he died.*

This dramatic fulfilment of her wish must have caused little Frida to experience both an enormous sense of power – she had wished Conrad dead *and he had died* – and enormous guilt: Conrad had been her mother's favourite child and the effect of his death on Catharine Tillyard had devastating consequences for herself and for her surviving children. As a mere child, however, Frida could not have foreseen the devastation the (coincidental) fulfilment of her wish would cause and it would be only years later and only after lengthy talks with Julius that Aelfrida came to terms with its consequences for herself and her brother. Prior to this, however, she wished the same wish with regard to members of her family as they stood literally or metaphorically in the way of whichever 'vocation' (holy virgin, mystic, 'recuperated' widow, oblate, tertiary, anchoress, prophetess) she currently pursued, but it was when the fatal illness and death of a man whose name (*Constantine*) began with the same syllable as that of the brother she had 'wished' dead (and had she not also wished Constantine dead, Constantine who, like Conrad, she professed to love even while actually hating him?) forcibly reminded her of a deeply repressed wish that she 'crashed' so catastrophically and for so long. Julius who, being older and present, remembered more of the actual circumstances surrounding Conrad's fatal illness and death, had then to try to extirpate both the scar left on his sister's mind by the events of June 1888 and that left by the events' sequel of 1933/34, a sequel which triggered the flashbacks which bedevilled her life thereafter.

But *why* should little Frida wish Conrad dead? Most children after all, exhibit jealousy of an – as they see it – supplanting sibling but do not go so far as to wish him or her dead. The answer may lie in Catharine Tillyard's reaction to her first two children: Julius, a sickly grizzly baby, now a moody and perpetually unwell little boy, and Aelfrida, a girl whose nine months' gestation was deemed wasted effort, now a headstrong toddler, both children dark-haired and heavy-featured like her respected but unloved husband; Conrad, by contrast, resembled her own family and was blond, beautiful, and angelically well-behaved and Catharine made no secret of her preference for him. (It is, of course, natural for a parent to prefer one child to another but Catharine Tillyard's preference seems to have been extreme and unconcealed.) Hence it would be natural for Frida to wish Conrad 'discarnate' by imagining, possibly in the course of 'solemn games, rituals and practices' played out by Poseidon/Dudu and Athene/Frida on their kitchen-garden Olympus, that as 'Athene' she could put a mortal curse on Conrad, a curse she later believed had been fulfilled. And here, perhaps, we should recall adult Aelfrida's literary obsession with children who die young of pneumonia or because run over by a car or run down by a horse – and remember with horror that one of her own children died after being hit by a train but only after having tried earlier that same day to fling herself under a London bus, an irony indeed if our 'Conrad' story is true.

Writing her 'Gods and Goddesses' memory picture seventy years later, Aelfrida describes 'Olympus' in detail down to the broken crockery with which it was decorated but has conveniently "forgotten" the "rituals" enacted there. Perhaps like 'Clive Farwell', she locked the curse "down, down into the deepest dungeon of [her] unconscious mind" and 'forgot' it. (She also notes that she was said to have 'sacrificed' a doll there – the only doll she ever mentions – only to swiftly deny that she did so.[179] Perhaps it represented Conrad.) Conrad dies. Julius is consumed with survivor's guilt for which he tries to atone by being particularly nice to the "babe" he has been sure God will send to "take Conrad's place": he takes Eustace's side in sibling squabbles and invites the boy to tea "in Dudu's rooms" at college "as an easy way of showing [his] affection".[180] Aelfrida reacts by 'forgetting', though references throughout her later life to *The Water Babies* and to malevolent 'Mrs Bedonebyasyoudid', a lady who metes out appropriate punishments, suggest that she is not as 'forgetful' as she pretends to be or likes

to think she is and that rather than assuage her 'guilt' by being kind to Conrad's successor, she expresses contempt for him, treats him like a servant, and bullies him. (As she would have treated Conrad, had she dared.) But not for sixty years is she able to come to terms with the 'jealousy and hatred' which made her act as she did and to understand that it was not she (with or without Julius' collusion) but the diphtheria bacillus which killed Conrad, to experience 'peace and pardon', to gain peace of mind, and to appreciate Eustace and the role he has played in her life.

In the meantime, Julius works through his guilt by demonstrating excessive devotion to the mother whose favourite child he survived and by throwing himself into the absorbing study of Byzantine Musicology. Aelfrida, lacking Julius' emotional and intellectual resources, reacts according to patterns set by her Nonconformist childhood, moving from a vague "conviction" or "sense" of sin[181] to a conviction that having behaved as she did, God would not deny her "such pain as may be [hers] by right", to "joyful acceptance … of all the pain He sends" (and if He does not, she creates it by "ardently [desiring] to share the suffering of Christ" and by enacting 'scenes' in which 'pain' is created), to the practice of "ascetic discipline[s]" by means of which a guilty person "may have his sense of sin increased"[182], and even to a conviction that "spiritual exercises" should not be undertaken in the mystic hope "of rising to heights of contemplation or of experiencing ecstasies" but in hope of a purely "practical" result[183], namely that the granting by God of ecstasies, visions, auditions, olfactions, and the stigmata to a sinner such as herself will enhance her guilt by making her feel unworthy of receiving them and force her to expiate her sin by continually punishing herself for a crime committed only in her mind.

Her life therefore involves something more than the gender-specific "model of suffering" supposedly prevalent in "women's spirituality" (men, it seems, prefer "models of action"[184] – as Julius did) or "the spontaneous practising of asceticism". ("Protestant Christianity", she herself notes, tends "against mortification"[185] but Catholicism taught her that it had a moral and spiritual value.) If so, was her asceticism a form of "deliberate self-torture" undertaken in an attempt to propitiate a "primitive deity who is feared [and] obeyed"[186] or an attempt to conceal her 'sin' from "the terrible eye of the Almighty … [the] gigantic lidless eye … of God which followed Cain whenever he tried to hide his guilt"[187], an eye given material form in her haunted childhood by a "horrible picture of a vast eye in the heavens which watched Cain wherever he went"[188]? And to make matters worse for the girl who sat weeping on the floor of the night nursery where Conrad died when puberty rendered consciousness of her "sinful nature ... agonisingly acute", "strange and overwhelming representations" hung on walls (which walls, she could not later 'remember' though she describes the pictures in detail) to remind her of the fates of transgressors like herself: *Belshazzar's Feast* where "terror stricken revellers stared at a Hand inscribing a threatening message on a wall", *Sodom and Gomorrah* "tottering in ruins", *The Golden Image* with King Nebuchadnezzar, on all fours like a beast, "being punished by Jehovah", and *The Deluge* "with waves and falling rocks, lightning and darkness blotting out mankind".[189] "Perhaps for me", she cries, "God keeps no promised land".[190]

In a brief chapter on fear in *The Closer Walk with God* Aelfrida answers the question "What place ... can fear have in the spiritual life?" by assuring us that what she means by 'fear' is ostensibly the "Holy Fear" felt during her Tymawr 'bread miracle' but actually (and using denial as a device to make her point) by hinting to us that what she has felt since 1888 is "the terror of the hunted animal, the mad impulse for flight at all cost ... the fear of helpless man before [an] avenging God". *And* that she feels it because her sins (or rather, one particular sin) "cry out for vengeance". The sin which cries out loudest for vengeance is, she tells us, "the sin of Cain", Cain who murdered his brother Abel as she 'murdered' hers, Conrad/Abel the "Sinless One".[191]

Old Testament Jehovah makes clear His preference for Abel. Cain kills Abel because he is jealous. Discovering Cain's sin, God cries out in horror "What hast thou done?"[192] Can it be that Catharine Tillyard, overhearing a childish remark or having Frida's jealousy and hatred of Conrad revealed in a childish tantrum or disclosed by Hubbard the gardener who, overhearing a childish 'sacrifice' as he works behind a concealing hedge in the kitchen garden, considers it his duty as a 'very pious' man[193] to inform Catharine Tillyard of the dreadful thing her daughter has said or done, discovers that Frida has wished Conrad dead and cries out "you killed that child" when Frida returns from Harston before weeping copiously over her in guilty anguish when she sees the enormity of her accusation reflected in the horror-stricken expression on the small girl's face? Is *this* the scene which adult Aelfrida reproduces in *The Centaur* when describing the relationship between 'Roma' and 'Clive'? (And replays with Constantine at the time of Agneta's death?) And can it be that when dead Conrad appears in the vision seen by Aelfrida on the day of Agneta's stillbirth, his arrival is not the comforting occasion into which she subsequently and sentimentally 'embroiders' it but a flashback in which the malevolent 'spook' which haunts

her life returns to haunt what was almost her deathbed and is certainly that of his baby niece? (The tomb of the third person in the vision – Eliza Gregory née Wetenhall – is so close to that in which Conrad and 'Dear' lie that one can almost touch it.) And can it be that Aelfrida, knowing that God heard Abel's blood cry out "from the ground", cursed Cain by concealing His face from him, ensured that Cain is driven out from home and family to become a "fugitive and vagabond", and set a "mark" on him as a sign that, so great is his sin, he is not to be killed by man because reserved for God's vengeance alone, 'sees' on *herself* the mark of Cain, feels her conscience pursue her "as the unsleeping eye of God pursued Cain in his "blood-guiltiness"[194], and spends the rest of her life re-enacting Cain's part? And as if to underline God's message and compound her guilt, her parents, like Adam and Eve, replace 'murdered' Conrad/Abel with Seth 'the appointed one'/Eustace the 'good harvest'.

No wonder, therefore, that Aelfrida's brief chapter on 'fear' is resonant with fear of "secret sins" lying deep down in one's personality, sins arising from grievances "nourished and brooded over" and from the "revengeful animosity" of one who cannot forgive an injury, sins which create a burden of "restless misery" in the mind of the sinner but which are repressed because too horrible to remember. Fear too that "there is more than enough evil in [her heart] to make easy the downward path to Hell".[195] And with this in mind, how pregnant are utterances chosen at random from her books and diaries:
- "All my life I killed and marred and lost".[196]
- 'For what sin have I, like Moses, been brought in sight of the Promised Land and not allowed to go in?'[197]
- 'God is angry with me – I have committed the unpardonable sin and lost the light by my own fault'.[198]
- "[I am] a lost and helpless sinner dependent for salvation on the sacrifice of Jesus".[199]
- 'To repent of the *whole world's sins* with my own as part of them ... I stand at the foot of the Cross and adore the one Perfect Sacrifice for sin'.[200]
- "If I am ever to come to Our Lord, I cannot pass Calvary by".[201]

Utterances made at times of great personal distress or on occasions associated with behaviour of an actually or possibly sinful nature or on a day associated in the Christian calendar with repentance or when a specific and more recent death was much in her mind, as if every sin and every death was a reminder of a sinful childish wish and its factual or factitious fulfilment.

Hence, too, some of Aelfrida's otherwise inexplicable obsessions. That she was only safe or safest at the foot of the Cross, as if the crucified Christ could protect her from Jehovah's wrath. That she had to (i.e. needed to) be 'crucified' for the 'sin' she had committed , a 'sin' compulsively and symbolically enacted later in life with regard to her parents (whose deaths she assisted), to Eustace and Constantine (both of whom she wished had been killed in the Great War), to Agatha (by neglect), to Alethea (by pushing her towards a country where life expectancy was short in the hope of never seeing her again) and towards anyone else by whom her 'soul' felt 'pressured'. That she must be always humiliated by 'Authority' even to the extent of regarding herself as a scapegoat bearing the sins of the 'whole world' as well as her own. (An end she not only sought but having been scapegoated, '[didn't] mind a bit'.)[202] That even in the absence of an accuser or a victimiser (and with what inevitability, given her perverted religiosity, did she cast those who led the life of a religious in that role), she felt compelled to seek enforcement of 'blood-guiltiness' in auto-martyrisation, casting herself in the role of 'victim-soul' in imitation of "Jesus-Victim" as if by doing so she could escape her earthly Purgatory. That, unable to commit suicide because bearing the 'mark of Cain' which rendered her subject to God's vengeance only, she must seek oblivion by insidious means: by willing herself to develop a fatal disease, by slow starvation, by refusing life-saving medication, by undertaking risky pursuits, by being prepared to put herself forward for slaughter ('I remember the leaping up of the spirit when … German invasion was imminent')[203], by turning her face to the wall and willing herself to die. And, as evidence of this, pointing a future biographer towards a book, *La prière de toutes les heures*[204], which would answer the question to *why* God appeared to behave towards her so vengefully (killing those she loved, ruining her health) and provide the reason for His doing so and for His preventing her death (even to extent of protecting her against herself) until He deemed her guilt sufficiently purged and allowed her to die: "he that shall endure unto the end, the same shall be saved".[205]

Hence her tendency to court ostracism by indulging in outrageous behaviour guaranteed to make her an 'outsider' in the eyes of others or to seem a 'heretic'[206] by adopting a moralistic or a religious stance guaranteed to alienate her from her family or social group, or to compulsively confess sins – but never the worst sin of which she convicted herself (unless possibly to Albert Erlande, who then 'embroidered' it into a novel)[207], though she came close to it at Malling when she admitted her part in the death of the mother who, in overtly preferring Conrad to herself, had set in train the events leading to Conrad's sister's 'sin', a 'sin' committed because, however much little Frida might protest that she 'didn't mind' Conrad being preferred to herself, she did. Hence too,

her tendency, noted by successive spiritual directors, to confess only venial sins – 'faults' – as if she could not bring herself to confess an imagined sin (the mortal sin of fratricide) more heinous than the real sin of 'murdering' her dying mother and to believe that in committing it she had not only turned away from God but had also allowed the devil to control her life – which, in a sense he did, the devil in this instance being Conrad and the hell from which he came, her own mind. Hence, therefore, her need to pretend that 'sins' entirely hers were actually attributable to what her 'old friend Papini' called "demonic inspiration" as if by doing so she could absolve herself of the particular 'sin' which had darkened her life since childhood and her inability to recognise that diabolic possession attributed to others was a projection of the "evil and torment"[208] within herself. Hence also, her belief that she was not only 'born callous' but was also stricken by an "absolute incapacity to love", an "absolute privation"[209] imposed on her because of a prideful childish conviction that, goddess-like, she held the power of life and death in her hand – and Conrad died. Hence, finally, her conviction that she might at the last receive more than a hint of God's 'perfect splendour' and might "enter into the Kingdom of God [even]through the dark portal of sin"[210] provided she made herself a 'victim-soul' by the ardent practice of reparative adoration.

Towards the end of the brief chapter on 'fear' which so oddly punctuates *The Closer Walk with God* (it is preceded by an equally brief one on 'sorrow' in which Aelfrida, again in the guise of denying it, provides herself with three excuses for behaving as she did: "I did this action because I [was] wrongly brought up … [and] because of … the exigencies of my situation" or had "inherited this tendency from my ancestors" or because "of the pressure of society upon me")[211], she pleads with her reader for forgiveness: "if wicked men", she writes, "understood the meaning of their actions, they would stay their hands" – but how could such a maturity of vision be expected of a child not yet "fully aware of the significance of sin"? But having sinned, how can this child-sinner "be saved from the consequences of their own actions"?[212] (She provides no answer to either question; she only suggests that someone pray Christ's own petition "*Father forgive them for they know what they do*".)[213] And how better to create forgiveness for a child who knew not what she did when she wished her little brother dead than by staging her own 'Day of Judgement' (and at the same time proving to herself that she had been 'a fool'[214] for believing for almost her entire life that she herself was responsible for killing him) than to "cause all the events of her earthly life" to pass before us in the form of 'papers' carefully preserved so that we will be able to read them after she is dead? 'Papers' which are both an 'Autobiography' and an exposition of her "wounds". 'Papers' by means of which those who followed – as they once thought – virtually trackless footprints or reached out for a hand too disembodied to be grasped are now able to hear a voice whose silence was formerly complete, to feel a tap on their shoulder, and to hear (if they listen hard enough) what she is really saying – and possibly "marvel" at and "believe"[215] (but not suspend all credulity concerning) a story she cannot bear to tell directly but can only hope that a stranger will in due course lay bare. 'Papers' which form "the confession of a dying man who feared death exceedingly because of a grievous sin" (a reason, perhaps, for clinging to life so tenaciously when suicide would have released her?) but who near or at the point of death was able to make his confession and so "died penitent"[216], death being here and indeed the 'ultimate solution and triumph'.[217] And who by deposition of her 'papers' in an archive was able to hold the gates "a moment ere they close" and by her 'confession' gain an 'epitaphic' opportunity to "say farewell to life"[218] on her own terms?

'Clive Farwell', reading over the pages of his confession–autobiography shortly before what he hopes will be his death, realises that he has written not one but three books. "The autobiography he would have liked to provide, the exquisite memorial of a life … which would have gained him a niche in the Hall of Fame". "The autobiography he thought he *had* written – not flawlessly beautiful but … deeply moving [because] it revealed to the world those qualities on which he prided himself most: uniqueness, dignity, insight, courage, charm, self-control and the pathos that clings to the noble soul pierced by the arrows of unfriendly Fate". And what he had actually written: "the pitiable record of a stupid frightened child".[219] And if that and all the other confessions made in Aelfrida's 'Estimable Autobiography' and 'pitiable record' are true, what can we do but remember as we stand in front of the *Mizpah* which is Conrad's tombstone (a stone even more *mizpah*-like today because shorn of the cross which once surmounted it) that it was in her aptly-named novel *The Way We Grow Up* that Conrad's sister noted the presence of a 'MIZPAH' in its hero's bedroom and described a small child's death, and feel for her, a 'stupid frightened' child–woman trapped in the "tumultuous privacy of storm"[220] which ensured that her life would be the tragedy she anticipated[221], anything other than an immense pity?

## Notes

1   Arnott, K. pp 15–16.
2   GCPPT 1|1|74 26 November 1957.
    Tillyard, Ae. *Naomi da Costa* p 198 (GCPPT 2|22).
3   Tillyard, Ae. *Gems (The Garden and the Fire)* pp 58–59, written at Le Vésinet on 30 April 1914.
4   Tillyard, Ae. *Just Alice* p 312 (GCPPT 2|19).
5   GCPPT 1|1|8 16 and 17 September 1901.
6   Tillyard, Ae. *Christian Old Age* pp 16–17 (GCPPT 2|17).
7   GCPPT 1|1|63 1 May 1956. Aelfrida might have waxed less than enthusiastic about his later appearance too; the mystic idealist reaching for the stars metamorphosed in later life into a short, tubby, balding, married man. Prezzolini died in his hundredth year in 1982.
8   Tillyard, Ae. *Christian Old Age* pp 15–16.
9   http://www.aap-psychosynthesis.org/assogioli.htm
    http://www.willparfitt.com/assag.html
    Roberto Assagioli died in 1974.
10  Tillyard, Ae. *Messages* p 67.
11  Tillyard, Ae. *The Approaching Storm* p 193. Although Odessa was besieged by the Axis armies between 8 August and 16 October 1941, departure of its Red Army defenders on 14 October meant that massive destruction of the kind suffered at Stalingrad did not occur; occupied by the Romanians, the city preserved its lively cosmopolitan air until liberated by the Russians in April 1944. Aelfrida, writing of it that same year described it as "the ruin that was once Odessa" (GCPPT 1|1|61 24 April 1944) but may have been speaking metaphorically.
12  http:ukraine-tours.com/information/city/odessa/sights.htm
13  GCPPT 1|1|75 8 January 1959.
14  Tillyard, Ae. *The way we see*, written in Arlington Heights on 30 July 1908, published in *To Malise* (p 17).
15  GCPPT 1|1|44 19 October 1933.
    GCPPT 1|1|48 14 July 1935.
16  GCPPT 1|1|44 1 October 1933.
17  GCPPT 1|1|69 1 June 1951.
18  GCPPT 1|1|74 8 July 1958.
19  GCPPT 1|1|74a Undated letter from Magdalen Mary OSB to Aelfrida referred to by the latter on 26 July 1957 (GCPPT 1|1|74).
20  Tillyard, Ae. *The Closer Walk with God* p 101 (GCPPT 2|2).
21  Tillyard, Ae. *The Glory of the West* pp201–202 (GCPPT 2|16|3).
22  GCPPT 1|1|74a Letter from 'Jeanne SSC' to 'Sister Placida' of 22 June 1958.
23  GCPPT 1|1|71 3 May 1954.
    GCPPT 1|1|72 'Holy Saturday' (9 April) 1955.
    GCPPT 1|1|73 'Holy Cross' (3 May) and 16 May 1956.
    GCPPT 1|1|74 11 March 1958.
24  Hopkins, G. M. *Wreck of the Deutschland* pt 2 verse 24. Hopkins was reading theology at St Beuno's College in North Wales when he wrote these lines in 1874/75.
25  Toynbee, P. p204. Writer Philip Toynbee (1916–1981) underwent an existential crisis in the 1970s, recording it and his recovery in two volumes of diarised memoirs.
26  GCPPT 1|1|22 16 June 1917.
27  Probert, Y. quoting an 1897 letter from Bertrand Russell (born in 1872 at Cleddon Shoots, less than three miles from Tymawr) to Ellen Terry.
28  Tymawr Library Pam. Box 225–279. Pamphlet 230. p 33.
29  GCPPT 1|1|61 23 January 1944.
30  GCPPT 1|1|63 3 May 1945.
31  GCPPT 1|1|73 12 September 1956.
32  GCPPT 1|1|74a Letter from 'Jeanne SSC' to 'Sister Placida' of 22 June 1958.
33  GCPPT 1|1|74 31 July and 27 August 1957.
34  GCPPT 1|1|70a SSC Newsletter of Holy Cross Day (3 May) 1953.
35  GCPPT 1|1|72 13 August 1955.

36 GCPPT 1|1|74 1 June 1957.
37 GCPPT 1|1|74a Letter from 'Jeanne SSC' to 'Sister Placida' of 22 June 1958.
38 GCPPT 1|1|73 22 January 1956.
39 GCPPT 1|1|70a *Schedule for Lent 1953*.
40 GCPPT 1|1|60 22 August 1942.
41 GCPPT 1|1|54 27 January 1938.
42 O'Ferrall, R. *Early Memories of Tymawr*.
43 O'Ferrall, R. ed. *Mother Guenvrede, Foundress SSC*.
44 GCPPT 1|1|74a Letter from 'Jeanne SSC' to 'Sister Placida' of 22 June 1958.
45 GCPPT 1|1|56 4 May 1939.
46 GCPPT 1|1|55 22 June 1938.
   GCPPT 1|1|57 10 March 1940.
47 GCPPT 1|1|71 26 April 1954.
48 GCPPT 1|1|74 4 October 1957.
49 GCPPT 1|1|46 28 December 1934.
50 Eckhart, Meister. Vol 2. pp 32–33.
51 GCPPT 1|1|57 15 October 1939.
52 GCPPT 3|2 *Agatha's Record Book* 1 January 1925.
53 GCPPT 1|1|41 24 May 1932.
54 GCPPT 1|1|54 26 January 1938. A usual, Aelfrida misquotes the passage.
55 GCPPT 1|1|69 5 March 1952.
56 ibid. 1 June 1952.
57 Knox Little, W. Introduction to the 1902 edition to François de Sales' *Treatise on the Love of God* (thought to be Aelfrida's copy; the dedication page is cut out) in Tymawr library.
58 GCPPT 1|1|74 7 June and 10 July 1957.
59 GCPPT 1|1|70 20 June 1952.
60 Mayhew, P. pp 210–211.
61 GCPPT 1|1|75 'All Saints' (2 November) 1958.
62 GCPPT 1|1|43 20 and 21 March 1933.
63 Mann, S. *The Hope Nursing Home* pp 8–9.
64 GCPPT 1|1|43 2 January 1933.
65 Mann, S. *A Wonderful Thing for Cambridge* pp 109 and 119.
66 GCPPT 1|1|60 16 December 1942.
67 GCPPT 1|1|43 21 March 1933.
68 GCPPT 1|1|40 7 November 1931.
   GCPPT 1|1|61 28 February 1943.
69 Tillyard, Ae. *Spiritual Exercises* p 158.
70 Tillyard, Ae. *The Making of a Mystic* p 4.
71 GCPPT 1|1|22 22 July 1918.
72 Tillyard, Ae. *Old Age. A Mood Picture* ('To Malise' p 51). The poem was written in Brookline, Mass. on 23 May 1908.
73 GCPPT 1|1|73 21 February 1957.
74 Tillyard, HJW. Introduction to *The Letters of ACW Tillyard* (MTC).
75 GCPPT 1|1|71 19 July 1953.
76 Henn, T. p 95.
77 JC CS Report 1962 pp 31–33.
78 GCPPT 1|1|36 15 February 1929.
79 GCPPT 1|1|37 25 April 1930.
80 GCPPT 1|1|72 20 August 1955.
81 GCPPT 1|1|37 21 February 1919.
82 For a résumé of the life of Phyllis Tillyard (née Mudie-Cooke) see the *Girton Review* 1972 pp 24–25.
83 GCPPT 1|1|71 29 and 30 June 1953.
84 GCPPT 1|1|44 4 May 1933.
85 GCPPT 1|1|21 7 June 1916.
86 GCPPT 3|4. Letter from Florence Keynes to Aelfrida of 20 September 1954.
87 Tillyard, Ae. *Christian Old Age* p 67.
88 Velimirovic, M. *HJW Tillyard Patriarch of Byzantine Studies* (*The Musical Quarterly* Vol LIV 3 July 1968 p345, listed in Benser, C. Bibliography). Like the third of Aelfrida's scholars – Dr Høeg of Copenhagen – Julius is mentioned only briefly in Wellesz's *History of Byzantine Musicology*; his leaving England for South Africa immediately after both world wars and in 1935 at times when research into 'Byz. Mus.' was having to pick up threads broken by events or was at its height, may have been a contributing factor.
89 GCPPT 1|1|69 7 November 1951.
90 GCPPT 1|1|70 18 November 1952.
91 GCPPT 1|1|35 5 November 1928.
92 GCPPT 1|1|70 5 June 1953.
93 GCPPT 1|1|73 18 November 1955.
94 GCPPT 1|1|75 7 November 1958.
95 GCPPT 1|1|72 7 January 1955.
96 GCPPT 1|1|58 28 August 1940.
97 GCPPT 1|1|75 10 August 1958.
98 GCPPT 1|1|66 September 1949.
99 GCPPT 1|1|70 12 August 1952.
100 GCPPT 1|1|25 30 December 1920.
101 http:||www.adb.online.anu.edu.au/biogs/A120257b.htm
102 GCPPT 1|1|60 11 June 1942.
103 GCPPT 1|1|62 21 August 1944.
104 GCPPT 1|1|71 12 August and 'Holy Cross Day' (14 September) 1953.
105 ibid. 19 September 1953.
106 ibid. 'Holy Cross Day' (14 September) 1953.
107 Tillyard, Ae. *Naomi da Costa* pp 247 and 264. From details given here and in Aelfrida's diaries we discover that the Michaelides married young but separated after quarrelling violently when Constantine was a baby, leaving him in the care of a paternal relative. The young couple were reconciled (when their daughter Irene was a toddler Anatolia left her husband again; she lived in the United States for three months before her parents restored her to her husband) but it seems that Anatolia "used to regale [Constantine] with tales of ... parental scenes and violence" as a means of securing his affections to herself. Aelfrida herself once said of Anatolia 'I do not think I have ever told you of [her] history but even on her own showing it is odd' (GCPPT 1|1|16 16 September 1908). Indeed it was: at one point in their stormy married life Argyris had his wife shadowed by detectives and forged her name to pay their fees; at another, returning from India where the family had been living to Switzerland, a country to which Anatolia and the children had earlier removed themselves, he was obliged to turn 'all sorts of odd people out of the house' before he moved back in (GCPPT 1|1|24 12 July 1919).
108 Tillyard, Ae. *Naomi da Costa* p 247.
109 GCPPT 1|1|60 14 December 1942.
110 GCPPG A1.4(5). Letter from Father Slade SSJE to Alethea Graham of 16 December 1959.
111 GCPPT 1|1|63 16 May 1946.
112 GCPPT 1|1|74 20 February 1954.
113 GCPPT 1|1|70 27 (by context) May and 7 June 1953.
   GCPPT 1|1|75 22 July 1958.
114 *Springtime in Girton* (MTC, extract), an article by Christopher Driver quoting Alethea's Girton diaries (including her love for Raffaelo Piccoli) which appeared in *The Charleston Magazine* in 1992. Journalist/writer Christopher Driver (1932–1997) was the husband of Kathleen Perfect's daughter Margaret; his and Margaret's courtship and marriage are chronicled in the later volumes of Aelfrida's diaries.
115 GCPPT 1|1|74 22 April 1958.
116 GCPPG A1.4(5). Letter from Father Slade SSJE to Alethea Graham of 16 December 1959.

117 Driver, C. Introduction to *Springtime in Girton* (MTC).

118 GCPPT 1|1|30 30 March 1925.

119 GCPPG A1.1 4 October 1928.

120 GCPPT 1|1|33 16 July 1926.

121 GCPPT 1|1|28 23 August 1924.

122 For an interesting discussion of "compulsive care-giving" as a distortion of normal affection, see Bowlby, J. *The Making and Breaking of Affectional Bonds* pp 164–166.

123 GCPPT 1|1|27 22 August 1923.

124 GCPPT 1|1|59 22 February 1942.

125 GCPPT 1|1|75 17 February 1959.

126 Driver, C. Introduction to *Springtime in Girton* (MTC).

127 GCPPT 1|1|39 10 March 1931.

128 GCPPT 1|1|56 17 January 1939.

129 GCPPT 1|1|66 11 July 1948.

130 GCPPT 1|1|73 5 January 1956.

131 GCPPG. A1.1 Summary written after diary entry for 13 September 1922.

132 GCPPT 1|1|74 24 December 1957.

133 GCPPT 1|1|72 8 March 1955.

134 GCPPT 1|1|72 24 January 1955.

135 GCPPT 1|1|74 14 August 1957.

136 For a detailed account of John Layard's later life, see *ODNB* Vol. 32 pp 919–920.

137 For further details of Thomas Rice Henn's life, see *Who Was Who* Vol. 7.

138 Henn, T. p 22. A comparison of Aelfrida's poem and one of William Henn's (*The Reefs of Aran*, published in *The Cambridge Magazine* vol III No 23 23 May 1914 p 633) shows how accurately she mimicked his style in the poem she dedicated to him.

139 GCPPT 1|1|9 10 October 1902.
GCPPT 1|1|48 20 June 1935.

140 GCPPT 1|1|42 6 November 1932.

141 GCPPT 1|1|36 23 May 1929.

142 GCPPG A1.1 1 March 1926.

143 The poem was read at the funeral of Juan's wife Kathleen, née Ellis (1912–2004) and may be a translation of one by Antonio Machado (1875–1939). For further details of Kathleen and Juan Mascaró, see www.williamradice.com/Notes/Mrs_Kathleen_Mascaro.htm

144 Tillyard, Ae. *The Glory of the West* p 251 (GCPPT 2|16|1 Pt 2).

145 GCPPT 1|1|15 8 June 1907. Lt Col Henry Verey DSO died on 23 November 1968.

146 GCPPT 1|1|18 14 July 1911 and 31 August 1912.

147 Tillyard, Ae. *About an Italian Student of Marine Biology* written at 'Fordfield, Cambridge' on 3 August 1910 and later published in *To Malise* (p 79).

148 Tillyard, Ae. *Minerva of the Grey Eyes* written at Arlington Heights on 25 January 1909. (*To Malise* p 69).

149 GCPPT 1|1|17 20 January 1909.

150 ibid. 15 February 1909.

151 ibid. 20 February 1909.

152 ibid. 22 February 1909.

153 ibid. 2 March 1909.

154 Although the couplet as it stands appears to be no more than a brief pen-portrait of a spinster Christian Scientist and of a tenet she held, namely that men are reflections of God's Life, Love, and Truth, it is more likely evidence of Aelfrida's revengeful nature and love of mind-games: the Roman (i.e. 'Italian') goddess Minerva represented in the couplet's first line and a half included wisdom among her attributes and so could be said to know 'the Truth' but the Greek goddess (usually described as 'grey-eyed') with whom Minerva was often identified was Athena, also wise but particularly in the arts of war; the persona adopted by little Frida in games of 'Gods and Goddesses' is Athena, a goddess often represented wearing a helmet and breastplate and carrying a spear and shield. The couplet's last half-line may be read as Athena/Aelfrida's warning to Minerva/Hilda that she *did* know 'the truth' – and would be revenged.

155 GCPPT 2|2a *MCJ Medical Number,* by context February 1932.

156 GCPPT 1|1|45 12 and 17 March 1934

157 GCPPT 1|1|74 13 July 1957.

158 GCPPT 1|1|75 29 January 1959.

159 GCPPT 1|1|74 5 July 1957.

160 For details of Joan Cooper's life and death see http://www.pubmedcentral.nih.ger/articlerender.fgci and Nathan, S. *Doctors die after losing campaign* (*CIP* 20 February 1999). The other doctor to whom the article refers was Joan Cooper's practice partner, Margaret Reed, Aelfrida's alternative general practitioner; Dr Reed also lived at Meadowcroft, predeceasing Dr Cooper by a few days.

161 Tillyard, Ae. *The Closer Walk with God* pp 101–102.

162 Helen Megaw left her papers to Girton College. They include references to Christmas cards or presents sent to Alethea and Aelfrida and two postcards to Helen from Alethea Graham written in 1957, one of 8 December noting that Aelfrida is a "bit under the weather after flu" (GCPP Megaw 1|2|1), a description in marked contrast to her mother's description of the same illness.

163 In *The Stones of Belgium,* written in Cambridge on 13 March 1915, Aelfrida describes a "a gravestone cross" on the grave in which a young wife sleeps "her baby by her side". Catharine Tillyard did not, of course, die when Conrad did but Aelfrida correctly hints that in emotional terms, her mother 'died' at the same moment as her most beloved child. The poem appears in *The Garden and the Fire* (pp 4–5).

164 Tillyard, Ae. *The Stones of Belgium.*

165 Tillyard, Ae. *Marrying a Stranger* p249.
Tillyard, Ae. *The Way We Grow Up* pp 15 and 18.

166 ibid. p 40.

167 ibid.

168 For an example of a *Mizpah* see *Genesis* 30: 44–49 (KJV).

169 Tillyard, Ae. *Concrete* p 191.

170 Tillyard, Ae. *Spiritual Exercises* 2|25|2(5).

171 Tillyard, Ae. *Spiritual Exercises* p 151. Eliza Wetenhall's tombstone also commemorates her unmarried daughter Mary.

172 GCPPT 1|1|37 22 January 1930.
Tillyard, Ae. *The Centaur* pp 6, 9, 15–18 and 24–25 (GCPPT 2|21|1).

173 Tillyard, Ae. *Rich Man's Choice* pp 266–269. (GCPPT 2|21|2).

174 Tillyard, Ae. *The Centaur* p 24 (GCPPT 2|21|1).

175 Tillyard, Ae. *Christian Old Age* p 121 (GCPPT 2|17).

176 Tillyard, Ae. *The Centaur* pp 16–18. (GCPPT 2|21|1).

177 ibid. p 18.

178 Tillyard, Ae. *The Approaching Storm* pp 133, 143, 146 and 148.

179 GCPPT 2|26|4 (9).
Tillyard, Ae. *The Centaur* p 286 (GCPPT 1|21|1).

180 Tillyard, HJW. Introduction to *The Letters of A C W Tillyard* (MTC).

181 Tillyard, Ae. *Spiritual Exercises* pp vii and 159–160.

182 Tillyard, Ae. *The Making of a Mystic* p 35.

183 Tillyard, Ae. *Spiritual Exercises* p 155.

184 King, U. pp 88–91.

185 Tillyard, Ae. *Spiritual Exercises* p 11.

186 Underhill, E. *The Mystic Way* p 40.

187 Tillyard, Ae. *The Closer Walk with God* p 123.
Tillyard, Ae *The Way We Grow Up.* p 236.

188 GCPPT 2|26|4| (9). It is possible, given that she was familiar with John Martin's works (or with mezzotint reproductions thereof) that the 'vast eye' recalled by adult Aelfrida appears in *The Death of Abel.* This mezzotint formed part of Martin's *Illustrations of the Bible* series of 1831 (it may even have illustrated 'Dear's' bible or a family bible) and contains, significantly in the present context, not only a 'vast eye from the heavens' whose rays illuminate guilty Cain as he flees but also a pair of *mizpah*-like structures marking the gate of Paradise from

which Adam and Eve have been expelled. Dead Abel, weeping Eve, and praying Adam (he prays with hands clasped on bent knee, as Aelfrida did at Tymawr) appear prominently in the foreground posed on a flat-topped rock reminiscent of the 'altar of sacrifice' on which 'Clive Farwell' finds himself imprisoned in *The Centaur*.

189  ibid.

190  Tillyard, Ae. *The Magician's Birthday* (*The Garden and the Fire* pp 60–62).

191  Tillyard, Ae. *The Closer Walk with God* pp 123 and 130.

192  *Genesis* 4:10 (KJV).

193  GCPPT 1│1│10 7 October 1903.

194  Tillyard, Ae. *The Approaching Storm* p 144.

195  Tillyard, Ae. *The Closer Walk with God* pp 128–129.

196  GCPPT 2│5 *To Agatha when she was ill*. Written at Fordfield 20 August 1911.

197  GCPPT 1│1│46 28 December 1934.

198  GCPPT 1│2.

199  Tillyard, Ae. *The Fruits of Silence* pp8–9 (GCPPT 2/18).

200  GCPPT 1│1│72 'Ash Wednesday' (23 February) 1955.

201  Tillyard, Ae. *The Closer Walk with God* p171.

202  GCPPT 1│1│73 17 October 1956.

203  ibid. 16 May 1956.

204  Charles, P. pp ix and 114–115.

205  *Matthew* 24:13 (KJV).

206  GCPPT 1│1│74 21 June 1957. Aelfrida was staying at Hope House ('ex-Fordfield') when she made this statement.

207  *A L'ordre de Dieu*, a novel published by Albert Erlande in 1928, describes both the protracted deathbed of a young child and its

mother's hysterical response to its illness and death and the guilt by association experienced by a woman emotionally involved with the child's father at the time of its death.

208  Papini. G. p 143.

209  ibid. pp 44–45.

210  ibid. pp 7–9.

211  Tillyard, Ae. *The Closer Walk with God*. p 113.

212  ibid. p 130.

213  *Luke* 23: 34 (KJV).

214  GCPPT 1│1│73 12 June 1956.

215  Tillyard, Ae. *The Silence of God* p 43 (GCPPT 2│20).

216  GCPPT 2│24│2 *Theodore Visits Amanda Again*.

217  GCPPT 1│1│18 7 January 1913.

218  Stokoe, F. *Epitaphic* (*Cambridge Poets 1914–1920* p 178).

219  Tillyard, Ae. *The Centaur* p 5. (GCPPT 2│21│1).

220  The phrase is taken from Ralph Waldo Emerson's poem *The Snowstorm*.

221  According to the Aristotelian canon laid down in the 4th century BC, a tragedy focusses on a heroic figure with whom audiences can identify because he/she is as flawed as themselves in personality and in the decisions he/she makes. As the tragedy unfolds, spectators experience both fear and pity and in a shared and safely theatrical context are able to purge themselves of their own negative feelings and experience a cleansing relief (catharsis) as a result. At the close of the tragedy, bodies of the slain (convention has them die offstage) are brought onto the stage in order that the spectators witness the consequences of the heroic figure's actions and learn a lesson from them. This completes and perfects their catharsis.

# Bibliography: Aelfrida Tillyard

**c1890–1891**
*The Illustrated Monthly* (MTC)
*Blue and Green* (MTC)
*The Monthly Pets* (MTC)

**1900–1907**
*The Military and Civil Journal* (GCPPT 2/2a)

**1901–1902**
*Cambridge Independent Press* (women's column, bylined 'Pertilote') 2 and 9 August 1901; 15 and 22 August 1902

**1906**
*Le Livre des Jeux* Blackie & Co London
*The Florentine Movement The Independent Review* Vol 9 No 31 April–June 1906 pp71–79

**1908–1910**
Composes poetry (GCPPT 2/2) some to be included in *To Malise* (1910)

**1910**
*The Baptist Times* (women's column, bylined 'Eleuthera') 8 July 1910
*To Malise* W. Heffer & Sons Cambridge

**1910–1913**
Composes poetry (GCPPT 2/5) some to be included in *Cambridge Poets 1900–1913* (1913)

**1913**
Notebook (GCPPT 1/3) containing notes for unpublished book on 'modern mystics'
Notebook (GCPPT 1/4) containing booklist and Jewish prayers
*The Lily-Billy Book* (GCPPT 2/3a)
*A Guide to Modern Verse* (bylined 'Elfred Kendal') *The Cambridge Magazine* Vol II No9 18 January 1913 pp218–219
*Cambridge Poets 1900–1913* An Anthology W. Heffer & Sons Cambridge

**1914**
*The Puff by Parody* (bylined 'AT') *The Granta* Vol XXVII No605 24 January 1914 pp143–144
*Mrs Graham Explains The Cambridge Magazine* Vol III No11 24 January 1914 p 284
*Marrying a Stranger* (GCPPT 2/6)

**1915**
*Bammie's Book* W.Heffer & Sons Cambridge

**1916**
*Parallel Lives The Cambridge Magazine* Vol V No14 19 February 1916 p313
*Economy for Men The Cambridge Magazine* Vol V No17 11 March 1916 p358
*Letters to Lucy The Cambridge Magazine* Vol VI No2 21 October 1916 p45
ibid    Vol VI No3 28 October 1916 p71
ibid    Vol VI No4 4 November 1916 p94
ibid    Vol VI No5 11 November 1916 p119
ibid    Vol VI No6 18 November 1916 p147
ibid    Vol VI No7 25 November 1916 p175
ibid    Vol VI No8 2 December 1916 p203
*The Garden and the Fire* W. Heffer & Sons Cambridge

**1917**
*The Making of a Mystic* W. Heffer & Sons Cambridge

**c1918–1919**
Notes for talk given at the New Cherry Hinton Free Church (GCPPT 1/2)
Notes for/synopsis of *A Little Road-Book for Mystics* (1922) (GCPPT 1/2)

**1919**
*Vision Triumphant* James Clarke & Co London

**1920**
*Verses for Alethea* W. Heffer & Sons Cambridge (also GCPPT 2/8a)

**1922**
*A Little Road-Book for Mystics* Faith Press London (2nd edition 1931 Student Christian Movement Press London)

**1924**
*Messages* Faith Press London

**1926**
*Agnes E. Slack* W. Heffer & Sons Cambridge

**1927**
*Spiritual Exercises* SPCK London

**1929**
*The Young Milliner* Hutchinson & Co London
*The Way We Grow Up* Hutchinson & Co London

**1930**
*Can I Be a Mystic?* Rider & Co London
*Concrete* Hutchinson & Co London
*O Passionate World* (GCPPT 2/11)

**1931**
*Haste to the Wedding* Hutchinson & Co London

**1932**
*Military and Civil Journal (Medical Number)* February 1932 (GCPPT 2/2a)
*The Approaching Storm* Hutchinson & Co London

**1935**
*The Closer Walk with God* SPCK London

**1936**
Poems 1936–1958 (GCPPT 2/13)

**1937**
*The Way of Praise* SPCK London
*The Spiritual Director* (bylined 'A penitent') *Theology* Vol XXXIV No202 April 1937 pp228–233

**1938**
*The Night Watches* Faith Press London

**1944**
*The Glory of the West* (GCPPT 2/16/1–3)

**1947**
*Christian Old Age* (GCPPT 2/17)

**1948–1959**
*Memory Pictures* (GCPPT 2/23–2/27 and *The Watchword*)

**1949**
*The Fruits of Silence* British Publishing Co Gloucester

**1950**
*Just Alice* (GCPPT 2/19)
*The Silence of God* British Publishing Co Gloucester

**1951**
*The Centaur* (GCPPT 2/21/1)

**1952**
*Rich Man's Choice* (GCPPT 2/21/2)

**1954**
*Naomi da Costa* (GCPPT 2/22)

# General Bibliography

– Adler, K. et al. *Americans in Paris* National Gallery Co Ltd London 2006.

A Kempis, T. *The Imitation of Christ* (trans. & intro. L. Sherley-Price) Penguin London 1952.

Albinski, N. *Women's Utopias in British & American Fiction* Routledge London 1988.

Alighieri, D. *The Divine Comedy* (*Hell* trans. D. Sayers; *Purgatory & Paradise* trans. M. Musa) Penguin London 1986.

Alighieri, D. *La Vita Nuova* Penguin London 2004.

Altounyan, E. *Ornament of Honour* Cambridge University Press 1937.

Altounyan, T. *In Aleppo Once* J. Murray London 1969.

Amiel, F. *Journal Intime* (trans. & intro. M. Ward) MacMillan London 1898.

Amory, M. *Biography of Lord Dunsany* Collins London 1972.

*An Anthology of Cambridge Women's Verse* (compiled M. Thomas) Hogarth Living Poets No 20 Hogarth Press London 1931.

Annan, N. *The Dons* HarperCollins London 2000.

Anson, P. *The Call of the Cloister* SPCK London 1955.

Anstruther, I. *Oscar Browning* John Murray London 1893.

Arnott, K. *Hunstanton* Borough Council of King's Lynn & West Norfolk 2000.

Atkins, A. *The Royal Albert* CRABS Cambridge 2002.

Auden, W. *The English Auden 1927–1939* (ed. E. Mendelson) Faber & Faber London 1977.

Baker, A. *Holy Wisdom or Directions for the Prayer of Contemplation* (ed. Abbot Sweeney OSB) Burns & Oates London 1911.

Baker, A. *Confessions* (ed. & intro. J. McCann) Burns, Oates & Washbourne London 1922.

Balwin, M. *I Leap Over The Wall* H. Hamilton 1949.

*Baptist Times, The.*

Baranski, Z. & West, R. *Cambridge Companion to Modern Italian Culture* CUP 2001.

Barrow, J. et al. *Lives of the English Saints* S. Freemantle London 1901.

Bazin, R. *Charles de Foucault, Hermit & Explorer* (trans. P. Keelan) Burns, Oates & Washbourne London 1923.

Beauman, N. *A Very Great Profession* Virago London 1983.

Beerbohm, M. *Zuleika Dobson* Limited Editions Club Baltimore 1960.

Benedict of Nursia *The Rule of St Benedict* (preface & trans. Abbot Parry OSB, commentary & intro. E. de Waal) Gracewing Leominster 2003.

Benser, C. *Egon Wellesz 1895–1974* P. Lang New York 1985.

Benson, E. F. *The Babe BA* Heinemann London 1911.

Benson, R. H. *A Book of the Love of Jesus* I. Pitman & Sons London 1909.

Benson, R. H. *The Dawn of All* Tauschnitz Leipzig 1911.

Benson, R. H. *Confessions of a Convert* Fisher Press Kent 1991.

Benson, R. H. *Initiation* Hutchinson London 1914.

Benson, R. H. *The Light Invisible* Ibister London 1903.

Benson, R. H. *Loneliness* Hutchinson London 1914.

Benson, R. H. *Lord of the World* Dodd, Mead & Co New York 1958.

Benson, R. H. *The Necromancers* Hutchinson London 1909.

Benson, R. H. *Richard Raynal. Solitary* Pitman & Sons London 1906.

Benson, R. M. *Instructions on the Religious Life* Cherwell Press Oxford 1930.

Benson, R. M. *The Religious Vocation* Mowbray London 1939.

*Bible, The.* (KJV).

Birks, E. *Papworth Hospital & Village Settlement* Papworth Hospital Cambs. 1999.

Bishop-Culpeper, N. *Mrs Salter: the Crown House Medium* Newport News No 23 June 1985 pp53–54.

Blum, D. *The Ghost Hunters* Century London 2007.

Boll, T. *Miss May Sinclair: Novelist* Fairleigh Dickinson University Press New Jersey 1973.

Bondanella, J. & P. (ed) *Cassel History of Italian Literature* Cassell London 1996.

*Book of Common Prayer, The.*

Booth, M. *A Magick Life* Coronet Books London 2000.

Bostridge, M. *Florence Nightingale* Viking/Penguin London 2008.

Bowlby, J. *Loss, Sadness & Deprivation* (*Attachment & Loss* Vol 3) Pimlico London 1998.

Bowlby, J. *The Making & Breaking of Affectional Bonds* Routledge London 2006.

Breed, G. *Particular Baptists in Victorian England* Baptist Historical Society Dunstable 2003.

*British National Formulary* BMJ Publishing Group London September 2005.

Brock, M. & Curthoys, M. *The History of the University of Oxford* Clarendon Press Oxford 2000.

Brooke, R. *Poetical Works* (ed. G. Keynes) Faber & Faber London 1960.

Buchan, J. *Memory-Hold-the-Door* Hodder & Stoughton London 1941.

Buckle, E. *Especially* Longmans,Green & Co London 1913.

Bunyan, J. *The Pilgrim's Progress* Nelson & Sons London (undated).

Burman, E. *The Inquisition* Sutton Publishing England 2004.

Butler, A. *The Lives of the Fathers, Martyrs & Other Principal Saints* Virtue & Co London 5 vols.

Butler, S. *Erewhon* (ed. P. Mudford) Penguin London 1985.

Calder, A. *The People's War 1939–1945* Cape London 1969.

Calder-Marshall, A. *The Magic of my Youth* Hart-Davis London 1951.

Calladine, C. *Fen Court* Peterhouse Annual Record 2002/3 pp77–94 Cambridge.

*Cambridge Independent Press.*

*Cambridge Magazine, The.*

*Cambridge News/ Daily News/ Evening News.*

*Cambridge Poets 1914–1920* (compiled E. Davidson) Heffer & Son Cambridge 1920.

*Cambridge Review, The.*

Carpenter, S. *"Nobody Cares"* Theology Vol XXX11 No 187 January 1936 pp1–3.

Carter, T. *Spiritual Instructions. The Holy Eucharist* Masters & Co London 1881.

Carter, T. *Spiritual Instructions. The Religious Life* Masters & Co London 1898.

Cary, L. *Called of God* Mowbray London 1937.

Cary, L. *Hortus Inclusus* Dux House London (undated).

Chainey, G. *A Literary History of Cambridge* CUP 1995.

Charles, P. *La Prière de Toutes les Heures* Giraudon Paris 1925/26.

Chittick, W. *Sufism* OneWorld Oxford 2003.

Chitty, S. *The Beast & the Monk* Hodder & Stoughton London 1974.

*Church Times, The.*

Coleridge, E. (ed.) *The Works of Lord Byron* J. Murray London 1900.

Coleridge, M. *Collected Poems* (ed. & intro. T. Whistler) Hart–Davis London 1954.

Converse, F. *The House of Prayer* Dent London 1908.

Conybeare, E. *Highways & Byways in Cambridge & Ely* MacMillan London 1923.

Copp, M. *Cambridge Poets of the Great War* Fairleigh Dickinson University Press 2001.

Corbin, H. *Creative Imagination in the Sufism of Ibn Arabi* (trans. R. Manheim) Routledge & Kegan Paul London 1969.

Creighton, M. *Counsel for the Young* (ed. L. Creighton) Longmans, Green & Co London 1905.

*Crockford's Clerical Directory.*

Crowley, A. *Collected Works* SPRT Boleskine 1903–1907 (3 vols).

Crowley, A. *The Confessions: An Autohagiography* (ed. J. Symonds & K. Grant) Routledge & Kegan Paul London 1969–1979.

Crowley, A. *The Dangers of Mysticism* The Equinox Vol 1 No 6 September 1911 pp153–158.

Crowley, A. *The Disciples* The Equinox Vol 1 No 10 October 1913 pp91–92.

Crowley, A. *The Magical Record of the Beast 666* (ed. J. Symonds & K. Grant) Duckworth London 1972.

Crowley, A. *Olla* OTO London 1946.

Crowley, A. *Oracles* SPRT Boleskine 1905

Crowley, A. *The Paris Working* Vol V No 4 March 1981 pp170–228 Thelema Publishing Co Nashville 1981.

Crowley, A. *777 Revisited* Neptune Press London 1955.

Crowley, A. *The Wizard Way* The Equinox Vol 1 No 1 March 1909 pp37–46.

Curtis, G. *William of Glasshampton* SPCK London 1947.

*Daily Telegraph, The.*

David, Sister Mary OSB (ed.) *Living Stones* (privately printed) 2005.

Delacroix, H. *Les Grands Mystiques Chrétiens* Alcan Paris 1938.

De Quincey, T. *The Confessions of an English Opium Eater* MacMillan London 1901.

De Sales, F. *Introduction à la Vie Dévote* (intro. H Bordeaux) Nelson Paris 1947.

De Sales, F. *Treatise on the Love of God* (intro. W. Knox Little) Methuen London 1902.

*Dictionnaire de Biographie Française* Letouzy & Ané Paris 1982.

Dix, G. *The Shape of the Liturgy* Dacre Press London 1943.

Dix, K. *Strict & Particular* Baptist Historical Society Dunstable 2001.

Dix, M. *Harriet Starr Cannon* Longmans, Green & Co New York 1896.

Donkin, W. (Mother Guinvrede SSC) *Gleanings* (privately published) 1974.

Eckhart, Meister. *The Works of Meister Eckhart* (trans. C. Evans) Watkins London 1931.

*Encyclopaedia Britannica* (Eleventh Edition) CUP 1910.

*Equinox, The* (ed. A. Crowley).

Erlande, A. *A L'Ordre de Dieu* La Nouvelle Revue Critique Paris 1928.

Erlande, A. *Coup-de-Pif* (preface F. de Paemelaere) Collection "La Joie de nos Enfants" Paris 1928.

Erlande, A. *Dongiovanninesca* Mercure de France Vol CCIX No 735 1 February 1926 pp549–576.

Erlande, A. *Edmée Combres* Librairie de France (Les Cahiers d'Occident No7) Paris 1927.

Erlande, A. *Faby de Blanc Vêtue* Mercure de France Paris Vol CCL1X No 884 15 April 1935 pp317–347; No 885 1 May 1935 pp539–567; No 886 15 May 1935 pp95–123).

Erlande, A. *Ils Jouaient de la Vie* Ferenczi & fils Paris 1927.

Erlande, A. *Si Belle en ce Miroir* Ferenczi & fils Paris 1929.

Erlande, A. *Le Trajet de la Foudre* Fayard & Cie (Les Oeuvres Libres No LXXII pp199–306) Paris 1927.

Erlande, A. *Un Festin de Vautours* Flammarion Paris 1933.

Erlande, A. *La Vipère Dorée* Editions Cosmopolites Paris 1927.

Faber, F. *The Blessed Sacrament* Richardson & Co London.

Falcetta, A. *James Rendel Harris* Phoenix Press Sheffield 2006.

Ferrier, S. *Marriage* Methuen London 1902. 2 vols.

Flanagan, M.-B. *A Good Man Has Passed This Way* (privately printed) 1992.

Fleming, F. *The Sword & the Cross* Faber & Faber London 2003.

Forshaw, C. *One Hundred of the Best Poems on the European War* Elliot Stock London 1916.

Forster, E. *Goldsworthy Lowes Dickinson* Arnold London 1934.

Fox, C. *South Wales & Monmouthshire* HMSO London No 4 1955.

Frassetto, M. *Heretic Lives* Profile Books London 2007.

French, M. *From Town to Gown 1843–1977* Friends of Histon Road Cemetery Newsletter No 12 Spring 2011.

Frost, B. *The Art of Mental Prayer* P. Allen London 1932.

Frost, B. *The Love of God* Hodder & Stoughton London 1938.

Frost, B. *The Mystery of Mary* Mowbray London 1938.

Fry, M. *Reflections on being an Oblate, Tertiary, Companion or Associate* Anglican Religious Communities Year Book 1999.

Geddes, J. *Bipolar Disorder-Services Need To Catch Up* BMJ Vol 332 7 January 2006 pp32-33.

Gibbs, P. *Out of the Ruins* Hutchinson London 1930.

Giloteaux, P. *Victim Souls* (trans. L. Bond) Burns, Oates & Washbourne London 1927.

*Girton College Register* Vol 1 1869–1946; Vol 2 1944–1969 CUP 1948 & 1991.

*Girton Review.*

Goulburn, E. *Thoughts on Personal Religion* Rivingstone London 1871.

*Granta, The.*

Guerber, H. *The Myths of Greece & Rome* Harrap London 1907.

Guy, J. et al. *Chola. Sacred Bronzes of Southern India* Royal Academy Publications London 2006.

Harris, E. & J. ed. *Field Guide to the Wild Flowers of Britain* Readers Digest London 1981.

Harris, R. *The Guiding Hand of God* National Council of Evangelical Free Churches London 1905.

Harrison, J. *In Memoriam–Mrs AW Verrall* Newnham College Letter 1916 Supplement VII to Part LXXIV pp376–385.

Havergal, M. *Memorials of Frances Ridley Havergal* Nisbet London 1882.

Heimann, M. *Catholic Devotion in Victorian England* Clarendon Press Oxford 1995.

Henn, T. *Five Arches* C. Smythe Gerrards Cross 1980.

Henn, T. *Selected Poems 1958* (privately printed) 1958.

Hirsch, P. & McBeth, M. *Teacher Training at Cambridge* Woburn Press Portland Oregon 2004.

Hochschild, A. *Bury the Chains* MacMillan London 2005.

Hort, G. *Sense & Thought* Allen & Unwin London 1936.

Houghton, G. & P. *Well Regulated Minds & Improper Moments* (privately published) Cambridge 2000.

Hughes, M. *A London Girl of the Eighties* Oxford University Press London 1936.

Huxley, A. *Brave New World* Flamingo London 1994.

Huxley, A. *Island* Flamingo London 1994.

James, W. *The Varieties of Religious Experience* Penguin London 1985.

Jebb, E. *Cambridge. A Brief Study in Social Questions* MacMillan & Bowes Cambridge 1906.

*Jesus College C.S. Report 1962.*

John of the Cross *Selected Writings* Paulist Press New York 1987.

Julian of Norwich *Revelations of Divine Love* (trans. E. Spearing, ed. A. Spearing) Penguin London 1998.

Kaczynski, R. *Perdurabo* New Falcon Publications Tempe Arizona (2002), North Atlantic Books Berkeley California 2010.

Katz, D. *The Occult Tradition* Cape London 2005.

Keynes, F. *Gathering Up the Threads* Heffer & Son Cambridge 1950.

Keynes, M. *A House by the River* Darwin College Cambridge.

Khayyám, O. *Rubáiyát* (trans. E. Fitzgerald, ed. T. Briggs) Phoenix Press London 2009.

King, U. *Christian Mystics* Routledge London 2004.

*King's College Annual Report* 17 November 1934 Cambridge.

Kingsley, C. *The Hermits* MacMillan London 1869.

Kingsley, C. *The Water Babies* Gollancz London 1983.

Kingsley, C. *Yeast* MacMillan London 1881.

Klein, F. *The Diary of a French Army Chaplain* (trans. M. Capes) A. Melrose London 1915.

Klein, F. *Madeleine Sémer. Convert & Mystic* (trans. F. Stearns) Burns, Oates & Washbourne London 1927.

Knox, R. *St Columba's Church Cambridge 1879–1979* (privately printed) 1979.

*Koran, The.* OUP 1983.

Lalanda, M. *The Challenging Patient* MPS UK Casebook Vol 17 No 2 May 2009 pp12–14 London.

Landre, J. *Les Idylles de Pont-aux-Muses* Fayard & Cie Paris (Les Oeuvres Libres No 72) pp147–198 1927.

Lane Fox, R. *Pagans & Christians* Penguin London 2006.

Laver, J. *Museum Piece* A. Deutsch London 1963.

Law, W. *A Serious Call to the Devout & Holy Life* Sovereign Grace Publishers Lafayette Indiana 2001.

Lee, A. *A Life Hid With Christ In God* Lippincott & Co Philadelphia 1856.

Leen, E. *The Holy Ghost & His Work in Souls* Sheed & Ward London 1937.

Leen, E. *The Voice of a Priest* Sheed & Ward London 1947.

Lehmann, R. *The Ballad & The Source* (intro. J. Watts) Virago London 1982.

Lewis, C. *The Screwtape Letters* G. Bles London 1946.

Lind, F. *My Occult Casebook* Rider & Co London 1953.

Lomax, J. *The Diplomatic Smuggler* A. Barker London 1965.

Louismet, S. *The Mystical Knowledge of God* Burns & Oates London 1917.

Louismet, S. *The Mystical Life* Burns & Oates London 1918.

Louismet, S. *Mysticism, True & False* Burns & Oates 1919.

Maeterlinck, M. *La Vie des Abeilles* OUP 1922.

Magdalen Mary, Mother OSB. *The Religious Life: Contemplative & Enclosed* St Mary's Abbey Malling 1934.

Mann, S. *The Hope Nursing Home* (privately printed) 2003.

Mann, S. *A Wonderful Thing for Cambridge* Granta Editions Cambridge 2005.

Martin, G. *Hughes Hall 1885–2010* Third Millennium London 2011.

Mayhew, P. *All Saints: Birth & Growth of a Community* Society of All Saints Oxford 1987.

McDowall, S. *Evolution & the Need for Atonement* CUP 1914.

Meacham, S. *The Church in the Victorian City* Victorian Studies (Symposium on the Victorian city No1) Vol XI No 3 March 1968 pp359–378 Indiana University Quarterly Journal of Humanities, Arts & Sciences.

Meredith, G. *Modern Love* The Penguin Book of Modern Verse pp385–386 Penguin London 1956.

Merton, T. *Elected Silence* Hollis & Carter London 1950.

Merton, T. *The Waters of Silence* Hollis & Carter London 1950.

Michaelides, C. (Argyris Ephtaliotes) *Tales from the Isles of Greece* (trans. W. Rouse) Dent London 1897.

Miller, M. *Letchworth. The First Garden City* Phillimore Chichester 2002.

Mir, G. ed. *Correspondencia de Juan Mascaró 1930–1986* Editorial Moll Mallorca 1998 2 vols.

Mitchell, S. *A History of the Perse School* Oleander Press Cambridge 1976.

Molière (J-B Poquelin). *Les Femmes Savantes* (intro. H. Gaston Hall) OUP 1986.

Monro, H. ed. *Poetry & Drama* Vol 1 June/July 1913 The Poetry Bookshop London 1913.

Mullett, M. *The Catholic Reformation* Routledge London 1999.

Mulley, C. *The Woman Who Saved the Children* OneWorld Oxford 2009.

Murray, N. *Aldous Huxley. An English Intellectual* Abacus Editions England 2002.

Murry, JM. *God. The Science of Metabiology* Cape London 1929.

Nathan, S. *Doctors die after losing campaign* CDN 20 February 1999.

Nicholson, V. *Singled Out* Viking London 2007.

Northcott, H. *The Venture of Prayer* (intro. Edward Ely) SPCK London 1951.

O'Dowd, T. *Five Years of Heartsink Patients in General Practice* BMJ Vol 292 (6647) August 20–27 1988 pp528–530 London.

O' Ferrall, R. *Early Memories of Tymawr* (privately printed) 1969.

O'Ferrall, R. ed. *Mother Guenvrede, Foundress SSC* (privately printed) undated.

*Occult Review, The* Vol LI No 5 May 1930 pp2900-2299; Vol LI No 6 June 1930 pp 405 & 412.

Orwell, G. *1984* Penguin London 1989.

*Oxford Book of Mystical Verse, The.* (ed. D. Nicholson & A. Lee) Clarendon Press Oxford 1916.

*Oxford Dictionary of National Biography, The.* OUP 2004.

*Oxford Times, The.*

Paget, F. *The Spirit of Discipline* Longmans, Green & Co London 1891.

Papini, G. *The Devil. Notes for a future diabology* (trans. A Foulke) Eyre & Spottiswood London 1955.

Parke, S. *The Making of Aelfrida* Church Times 5 March 2010.

Parke, S. *Physician, heal thyself* Church Times 11 April 2008.

Parker, A (Mrs). *Sadhu Sundar Singh* Christian Literature Society for India London 1918.

Pattenden, P. *On the Game* Peterhouse Annual Records 2005/6 pp103–122 Cambridge.

Peacey, E. *Saint Birgitta of Sweden* Washbourne & Bogan London 1933.

Petty, M. *Grim Days of dirt, damp & decay* CN 5 October 2009.

Piggott, S. *Ancient Europe* Edinburgh University Press 1973.

Probert, Y. *Parish of Penalt* (privately printed) 1958.

*Quest, The.*

Quiller-Couch, A. *The Commerce of Thought* (Cambridge Lectures) Dent London 1948.

Quiller-Couch, A. *On the Art of Writing* The Cambridge Magazine Vol III No 13 15 February 1913 p319.

Ransome, A. *Swallows & Amazons* J. Cape London 1953.

Raverat, G. *Period Piece* Faber & Faber London 2002.

*Register of Nursing Homes 1928–1947* Cambridgeshire Archives Cambridge.

Reilly, C. ed. *Scars Upon My Heart* Virago London 1981.

Renan, E. *The Apostles* (trans. W. Hutchinson) Watts London 1905.

Richards, P. *All in the Mind* Cambridge Alumni Magazine No 44 Lent Term 2005.

Roberts, W. *The Banquet* Staples Press London 1949.

Russell, M. (E. von Arnim) *Fräulein Schmit & Mr Anstruther* Smith, Elder & Co London 1907.

Russell, M. (E. von Arnim) *The Pastor's Wife* Smith, Elder & Co London 1914.

Salisbury-Woods, R. *Cambridge Doctor* J. Hale London 1962.

Salvin, P. & Cressy, S. *The Life of Father Augustine Baker 1574–1641* Burns, Oates & Washbourne London 1933.

Sassoon, S. *Selected Poems* Heinemann London 1925.

Saudreau, A. *The Degrees of the Spiritual Life* (trans. B. Camm) R & T Washbourne London 1907 (2 vols).

Schultz, B. *Henry Sidgwick. Eye of the Universe* CUP 2004.

Schuré, E. *L'Evolution Divine* Perrin & Cie Paris 1912.

Sinclair, M. *A Defense of Idealism* MacMillan London 1917.

Skidelsky, R. *John Maynard Keynes* Macmillan London 1992 (3 vols).

Slonczewski, J. *Still Forms on Foxfield* Ballantine Books New York 1980.

Smith, P. *An Introduction to the Baha'i Faith* CUP 2008.

Soskice, J. *Sisters of Sinai* Chatto & Windus London 2009.

Stephen, C. *Quaker Strongholds* E. Hicks London 1891.

Stern, K. *The Pillar of Fire* M. Joseph London 1951.

Stevens, R. et al *Linton, the story of a market town* (privately printed) 1992.

Stopes, M. *Married Love* Putnam London 1950.

Streeter, B. & Appasamy, A. *The Sadhu* Macmillan London 1921.

Sutin, L. *Do What Thou Wilt* St Martin's Press New York 2000.

Symonds, J. *Elfrida & the Pig* Franklin Watts New York 1959.

Symonds, J. *The Great Beast* MacDonald London 1971.

Symonds, J. *The Magic of Aleister Crowley* F. Muller London 1958.

Symonds, R. *Far Above Rubies* Gracewing Books Herefordshire 1993.

Teresa of Avila *The Interior Castle* Rider (Ebury Press) London 2003.

Teresa of Avila *The Life of St Teresa of Avila by Herself* (trans. & intro. M. Cohen) Penguin London 1957.

Tillyard, A.I. *A History of University Reform* W. Heffer Cambridge 1913.

Tillyard, A.I. *Manuscripts of God* Heffer & Sons Cambridge 1919.

Tillyard, A.I. *Stones of Stumbling* Heffer & Sons Cambridge 1919.

Tillyard, E.M.W. *The Muse Unchained* Bowes & Bowes London 1958.

Tillyard, H.J.W. *Byzantine Music & Hymnography* Faith Press London 1923.

Tillyard, H.J.W. *The Plays of Roswitha* Faith Press London 1923.

Toynbee, P. *End of a Journey 1971–1981* Bloomsbury London 1988.

Trevelyan, J. *Indigo Days* MacGibbon & Kee London 1957.

Turner, F. *John Henry Newman* Yale University Press 2002.

Underhill, E. *Light of Christ* Longmans London 1945.

Underhill, E. *Mysticism* OneWorld Oxford 2002.

Underhill, E. *The Mystic Way* Ariel Press Atlanta 1992.

Underhill, E. *The Mystics of the Church* J.Clark London 1925.

Underhill, E. *Practical Mysticism* Ariel Press Ohio 1986.

Underhill, E. (John Cordelier) *The Spiral Way* J.Watkins London 1922.

Underhill, E. *The Spiritual Life* Hodder & Stoughton London 1996.

Vaughan, H. *Letters of Herbert, Cardinal Vaughan, to Lady Herbert of Lea 1867–1903* (ed. S. Leslie) Burns, Oates London 1942.

Velimirovic, M. *HJW Tillyard, Patriarch of Byzantine Studies* The Musical Quarterly July 1968.

Venn, J & A. *Alumni Cantabrigiensis* CUP 1954.

Venn, S. *Marriage* Methuen London 1902 2 vols.

Venn, S. *Some Married Fellows* R. Bentley & Son London 1893 2 vols.

Vidler, A. *God's Judgement on Europe* Longmans, Green & Co London 1940.

Waddell, H. *The Desert Fathers* Constable London 1987.

Warner, S. *T.H. White. A Biography* J. Cape London 1967.

*Watchword, The.* Journal of The Society of Workers & Watchers Guild Wykeham Press Winchester.

Waugh, E. *Two Lives* Continuum Press London 2001.

Wedgwood, C. *The Last of the Radicals* Cape London 1951.

Wellesz, E. *A History of Byzantine Music & Hymnography* Clarendon Press Oxford 1943.

Wells, H. *When The Sleeper Wakes* Dent/Everyman 1994.

Whigham-Price, A. *The Ladies of Castlebrae* Presbyterian History Society of England London 1964.

Whitehead, J. *Parish of St Thomas the Martyr, Oxford* (privately printed) 2003.

*Who Was Who* A&C Black London 1967.

Widnall, S. *The Miller's Daughter* (privately printed) Grantchester 1871.

Wilson, F. *Rebel Daughter of a Country House* Allen & Unwin London 1967.

Wogan-Browne, J. *Saints' Lives & Women's Literary Culture c1150–1300* OUP 2001.

Wood, A. *The Origins of the Russian Revolution* Routledge London 1993.

Yelton, M. *Anglican Papalism* Canterbury Press Norwich 2008.

Yelton, M. *Outposts of the Faith* Canterbury Press Norwich 2009.

# Index